The Grants Register 2023

The Grants Register 2023

The Complete Guide to Postgraduate Funding Worldwide

Forty-First Edition

Palgrave Macmillan
Macmillan Publishers Ltd.

ISBN 978-1-349-96052-1   ISBN 978-1-349-96053-8 (eBook)
https://doi.org/10.1057/978-1-349-96053-8

The Palgrave imprint is published by Springer Nature.
The registered company is Macmillan Publishers Ltd. London.

Preface

The forty-first edition of *The Grants Register* provides a detailed, accurate and comprehensive survey of awards intended for students at or above the postgraduate level, or those who require further professional or advanced vocational training.

Student numbers around the world continue to grow rapidly, and overseas study is now the first choice for many of these students. *The Grants Register* provides comprehensive, up-to-date information about the availability of, and eligibility for, non-refundable postgraduate and professional awards worldwide.

We remain grateful to the institutions which have supplied information for inclusion in this edition, and would also like to thank the International Association of Universities for continued permission to use their subject index within our Subject and Eligibility Guide to Awards.

The Grants Register database is updated continually in order to ensure that the information provided is the most current available. **Therefore, if your details have changed or you would like to be included for the first time, please contact the Senior Editor, at the address below.** If you wish to obtain further information relating to specific application procedures, please contact the relevant grant-awarding institution, rather than the publisher.

The Grants Register
Palgrave Macmillan
Springer Nature Campus
4 Crinan St
London
N1 9XW
United Kingdom
Tel: 144 (0)207 843 4634
Fax: 144 (0)207 843 4650
Email: Grants.Register@spi-global.com

Ruth Lefèvre
Senior Editor

How to Use *The Grants Register*

For ease of use, *The Grants Register 2023* is divided into four sections:

- The Grants Register
- Subject and Eligibility Guide to Awards
- Index of Awards
- Index of Awarding Organisations

The Grants Register

Information in this section is supplied directly by the awarding organisations. Entries are arranged alphabetically by name of organisation, and awards are listed alphabetically within the awarding organisation. This section includes details on subject area, eligibility, purpose, type, numbers offered, frequency, value, length of study, study establishment, country of study, and application procedure. Full contact details appear with each awarding organisation and also appended to individual awards where additional addresses are given.

A

AACR - American Association for Cancer Research

615 Chestnut St., 17th Floor, Philadelphia, PA 19106-4404, United States of America.

Tel: (1) 215 440 9300
Email: aacr@aacr.org
Website: www.aacr.org/

From the simple beginning of a few scientists gathering to share information to the multifaceted organization that exists today, the growth of the AACR reflects the increasing complexity of our understanding of over 200 diseases we now know as cancer.

AACR Cancer Disparities Research Fellowships

Purpose: The AACR Cancer Disparities Research Fellowships represent an effort to encourage and support postdoctoral or clinical research fellows to conduct cancer disparities research and to establish a successful career path in this field. The research proposed for funding may be basic, translational, clinical, or epidemiological in nature and must have direct applicability and relevance to cancer disparities.
Eligibility: Applicants must have a doctoral degree (PhD, MD, MD/PhD, or equivalent) in a related field and not currently be a candidate for a further doctoral degree. At the start of the grant term on July 1, 2023, applicants must hold a mentored research position with the title of postdoctoral fellow, clinical research fellow, or the equivalent; have completed their most recent doctoral degree within the past five years (i.e., degree cannot have been conferred before July 1, 2018); and work under the auspices of a mentor at an academic, medical, or research institution anywhere in the world. Applicants with a medical degree must have completed their most recent doctoral degree or medical residency - whichever date is later - within the past five years. If eligibility is based on a future position, the position must be confirmed at the time of application and cannot be contingent upon receiving this grant. Investigators may submit only one application for the AACR Cancer Disparities Research Fellowships but may concurrently apply for other AACR grants. However, applicants are expected to accept the first grant they are awarded. Individuals may accept and hold only one AACR grant at a time. Employees or subcontractors of a U.S. government entity or for-profit private industry are not eligible. Postdoctoral or clinical research fellows conducting research in a U.S. government laboratory (e.g., NIH, CDC, FDA, etc.), are not eligible. Any individual who currently holds an active AACR grant may not apply. Past grantees may apply if they complied with all progress and financial report requirements. Investigators currently or previously holding the rank of instructor, adjunct professor, assistant professor, research assistant professor, the equivalent or higher are not eligible. Qualified researchers are invited to apply for an AACR Career Development Award.
Level of Study: Doctorate
Type: Grant
Value: US$120,000
Length of Study: 2 Years
Frequency: Annual
Country of Study: Any country
Application Procedure: The AACR requires applicants to submit an online application, using the ProposalCentral website at proposalcentral.com/.
Closing Date: 7 January

For further information contact:

Email: grants@aacr.org

© Springer Nature Limited 2022
Palgrave Macmillan (ed.), *The Grants Register 2023*,
https://doi.org/10.1057/978-1-349-96053-8

1

Subject and Eligibility Guide to Awards

Awards can be located through the Subject and Eligibility Guide to Awards. This section allows the user to find an award within a specific subject area. *The Grants Register* uses a list of subjects endorsed by the International Association of Universities (IAU), the information centre on higher education, located at UNESCO, Paris. It is further subdivided into eligibility by nationality. Thereafter, awards are listed alphabetically within their designated category, along with a page reference where full details of the award can be found.

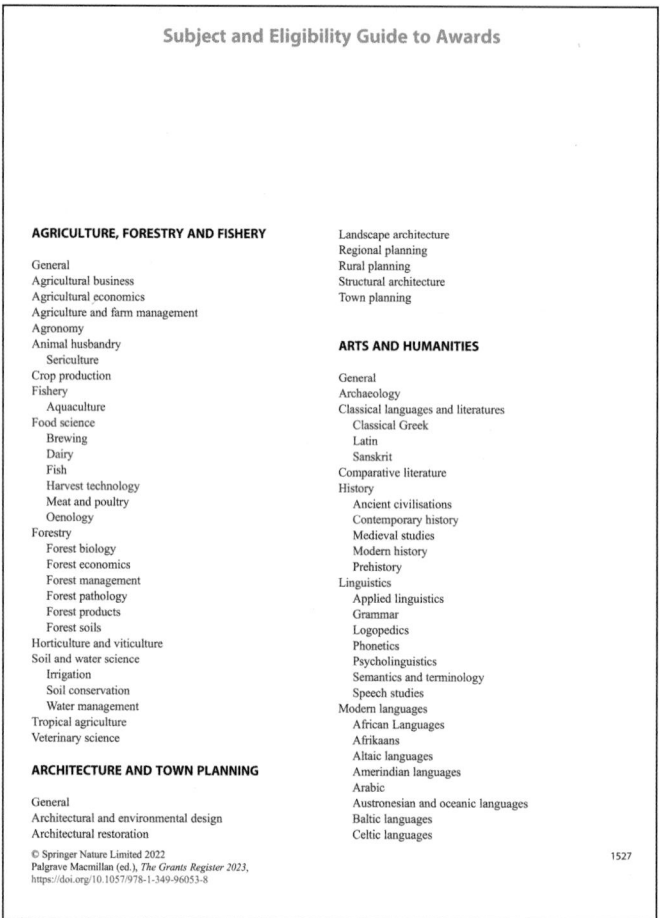

Subject and Eligibility Guide to Awards

AGRICULTURE, FORESTRY AND FISHERY

General
Agricultural business
Agricultural economics
Agriculture and farm management
Agronomy
Animal husbandry
   Sericulture
Crop production
Fishery
   Aquaculture
Food science
   Brewing
   Dairy
   Fish
   Harvest technology
   Meat and poultry
   Oenology
Forestry
   Forest biology
   Forest economics
   Forest management
   Forest pathology
   Forest products
   Forest soils
Horticulture and viticulture
Soil and water science
   Irrigation
   Soil conservation
   Water management
Tropical agriculture
Veterinary science

ARCHITECTURE AND TOWN PLANNING

General
Architectural and environmental design
Architectural restoration

Landscape architecture
Regional planning
Rural planning
Structural architecture
Town planning

ARTS AND HUMANITIES

General
Archaeology
Classical languages and literatures
   Classical Greek
   Latin
   Sanskrit
Comparative literature
History
   Ancient civilisations
   Contemporary history
   Medieval studies
   Modern history
   Prehistory
Linguistics
   Applied linguistics
   Grammar
   Logopedics
   Phonetics
   Psycholinguistics
   Semantics and terminology
   Speech studies
Modern languages
   African Languages
   Afrikaans
   Altaic languages
   Amerindian languages
   Arabic
   Austronesian and oceanic languages
   Baltic languages
   Celtic languages

© Springer Nature Limited 2022
Palgrave Macmillan (ed.), *The Grants Register 2023*,
https://doi.org/10.1057/978-1-349-96053-8

1527

Index of Awards

All awards are indexed alphabetically with a page reference.

Index of Awarding Organisations

A complete list of all awarding organisations, with country name and page reference.

List of Contents

A

AACR - American Association for Cancer Research

615 Chestnut St., 17th Floor, Philadelphia, PA 19106-4404, United States of America.

Tel: (1) 215 440 9300
Email: aacr@aacr.org
Website: www.aacr.org/

From the simple beginning of a few scientists gathering to share information to the multifaceted organization that exists today, the growth of the AACR reflects the increasing complexity of our understanding of over 200 diseases we now know as cancer.

AACR Cancer Disparities Research Fellowships

Purpose: The AACR Cancer Disparities Research Fellowships represent an effort to encourage and support postdoctoral or clinical research fellows to conduct cancer disparities research and to establish a successful career path in this field. The research proposed for funding may be basic, translational, clinical, or epidemiological in nature and must have direct applicability and relevance to cancer disparities.

Eligibility: Applicants must have a doctoral degree (PhD, MD, MD/PhD, or equivalent) in a related field and not currently be a candidate for a further doctoral degree. At the start of the grant term on July 1, 2023, applicants must hold a mentored research position with the title of postdoctoral fellow, clinical research fellow, or the equivalent; have completed their most recent doctoral degree within the past five years (i.e., degree cannot have been conferred before July 1, 2018); and work under the auspices of a mentor at an academic, medical, or research institution anywhere in the world. Applicants with a medical degree must have completed their most recent doctoral degree or medical residency - whichever date is later - within the past five years. If eligibility is based on a future position, the position must be confirmed at the time of application and cannot be contingent upon receiving this grant. Investigators may submit only one application for the AACR Cancer Disparities Research Fellowships but may concurrently apply for other AACR grants. However, applicants are expected to accept the first grant they are awarded. Individuals may accept and hold only one AACR grant at a time. Employees or subcontractors of a U.S. government entity or for-profit private industry are not eligible. Postdoctoral or clinical research fellows conducting research in a U.S. government laboratory (e.g., NIH, CDC, FDA, etc.), are not eligible. Any individual who currently holds an active AACR grant may not apply. Past grantees may apply if they complied with all progress and financial report requirements. Investigators currently or previously holding the rank of instructor, adjunct professor, assistant professor, research assistant professor, the equivalent or higher are not eligible. Qualified researchers are invited to apply for an AACR Career Development Award.

Level of Study: Doctorate
Type: Grant
Value: US$120,000
Length of Study: 2 Years
Frequency: Annual
Country of Study: Any country
Application Procedure: The AACR requires applicants to submit an online application, using the ProposalCentral website at proposalcentral.com/.
Closing Date: 7 January

For further information contact:

Email: grants@aacr.org

© Springer Nature Limited 2022
Palgrave Macmillan (ed.), *The Grants Register 2023*,
https://doi.org/10.1057/978-1-349-96053-8

AACR Clinical Oncology Research (CORE) Training Fellowships

Purpose: The AACR Clinical Oncology Research (CORE) Training Fellowships Program is designed to provide an effective industry-academic clinical practicum with a unique training opportunity to develop academic clinicians in drug development.

Eligibility: Applicants must 1. have a medical degree (including MD, DO, or MD/PhD), and not currently be a candidate for a further doctoral degree. 2. have enrolled in an accredited hematology/oncology or radiation oncology fellowship program at an academic, medical, or research institution within the United States. 3. not be employees or subcontractors of a U.S. government entity or for-profit private industry or be clinical fellows applying from a U.S. government laboratory (e.g., NIH, CDC, FDA, etc.).

Level of Study: Doctorate

Type: Fellowship

Value: Each fellowship provides US$100,000

Length of Study: 12 months

Country of Study: Any country

Application Procedure: 1. Applications will be accepted on a rolling basis via submission to grants@aacr.org. 2. Submitted applications will be reviewed quarterly by an AACR Scientific Review Committee 3. Selected fellows will be notified following this review. 4. The start of the grant term is flexible and will be negotiated based on the notification date.

Closing Date: 28 February

Additional Information: Please note that applications will be accepted after the above application deadline, but may be reviewed during a later quarterly review period. mail to: grants@aacr.org

For further information contact:

Email: grants@aacr.org

AACR NextGen Grants for Transformative Cancer Research

Purpose: The AACR NextGen Grants for Transformative Cancer Research represent a funding initiative to stimulate highly innovative research from young investigators. This grant mechanism is intended to promote and support creative, paradigm-shifting cancer research that may not be funded through conventional channels. It is expected that these grants will catalyze significant scientific discoveries and help talented young investigators gain scientific independence. The grants provide US$450,000 over three years for expenses related to the research project, which may include salary and benefits of the grant recipient, postdoctoral or clinical research fellows, graduate students (including tuition costs), and research assistants, research/laboratory supplies, equipment, travel applicable to the research project, publication charges for manuscripts that pertain directly to the funded project, other research expenses, and indirect costs.

Eligibility: Applicants must have a doctoral degree (PhD, MD, MD/PhD, or equivalent) in a related field and not currently be a candidate for a further doctoral degree. At the start of the grant term on Nov. 1, 2023, applicants must hold a tenure-eligible appointment (or equivalent, if institution does not follow a tenure system) at the rank of assistant professor (appointments such as research assistant professor, adjunct assistant professor, assistant professor research track, visiting professor, or instructor are not eligible; applicants that have progressed to associate professor appointments are also not eligible.); have held a tenure-eligible assistant professor appointment for less than three years (appointed on or after Nov. 1, 2020); and work at an academic, medical, or research institution anywhere in the world. If eligibility is based on a future position, the position must be confirmed at the time of submission, and CANNOT be contingent upon receiving this grant.

Level of Study: Masters

Type: Fellowship

Value: US$450,000

Length of Study: 3 years

Frequency: Annual

Country of Study: United States of America

Application Procedure: The AACR requires applicants to complete an online Letter of Intent submission website at proposalcentral.com. Program Guidelines and Competitive Letter of Intent Instructions are available for download.

Closing Date: 11 January

Additional Information: proposalcentral.com/

For further information contact:

Email: grants@aacr.org

AACR-Bayer Stimulating Therapeutic Advances through Research Training (START) Grants

Purpose: Dramatic advances made in recent years towards precision medicine initiatives, biomarker and novel target identification, and high-throughput examination of genomic data, have resulted in a trove of valuable data that can inform the development of new therapeutics to combat cancer. However, to effectively harness this wealth of information and advance the discovery and development of new therapies for cancer patients, enhanced collaboration between academia and industry will be needed. The AACR-Bayer Stimulating

Therapeutic Advances through Research Training (START) Grants represent an exciting and novel initiative to encourage and support such collaboration. These grants, which will provide support to postdoctoral or clinical research fellows, combines research experiences in both an academic and industry setting, following a research timeline that will be of greatest benefit to the proposed work. The training provided through this grants program will be invaluable to young investigators, by allowing fellows to attain a comprehensive research experience that will make them highly desirable to potential employers in either academic research or the pharmaceutical industry. Likewise, academic research centers and industry will benefit from the introduction of such dual-trained individuals into the field. Each fellowship provides a three-year grant of US$225,000 to support the salary and benefits of the fellow while working on a mentored cancer research project. Proposals focused on clinical research are highly encouraged. Applicants must plan to spend one year on site at a Bayer facility. One of a number of Bayer's locations are possible, at the discretion of Bayer. The year at Bayer will be determined on a case-by-case basis, and will be at a time agreed upon by the fellow, the academic supervisor, the Bayer mentor, and Bayer.

Eligibility: Applicants must have a doctoral degree (PhD, MD, MD/PhD, or equivalent) in a related field and not currently be a candidate for a further doctoral degree. At the start of the grant term on Nov. 1, applicants must hold a tenure-eligible appointment (or equivalent, if institution does not follow a tenure system) at the rank of assistant professor (appointments such as research assistant professor, adjunct assistant professor, assistant professor research track, visiting professor, or instructor are not eligible; applicants that have progressed to associate professor appointments are also not eligible.); have held a tenure-eligible assistant professor appointment for less than three years (appointed on or after Nov. 1, 2020); and work at an academic, medical, or research institution anywhere in the world. If eligibility is based on a future position, the position must be confirmed at the time of submission, and CANNOT be contingent upon receiving this grant. If the future position is at a different institution than the applicant's current institution, the applicant must contact AACR's Scientific Review and Grants Administration Department (AACR's SRGA) at grants@aacr.org before submitting their Letter of Intent for information on additional verification materials/signatures that may be required. There are no citizenship or geographic requirements. However, by submitting a Letter of Intent for this grant, an applicant applying from an institution located in a country in which they are not a citizen or a permanent resident assures that their visa status will provide sufficient time to complete the project and grant term at the institution from which they applied.

Level of Study: Masters

Type: Fellowship

Value: US$225,000

Length of Study: 3 years

Frequency: Annual

Country of Study: United States of America

Application Procedure: The AACR requires applicants to submit an online application website at proposalcentral.com/. Program Guidelines and Application Instructions are available for download.

Closing Date: 10 January

Additional Information: proposalcentral.com/

AACR-Novocure Career Development Awards For Tumor Treating Fields Research

Purpose: The research proposed for funding should be basic or translational in nature, promoting the transition of in vitro work into in vivo systems. Likewise, proposals focused on 1) translational approaches, promoting the transition of in vitro work into in vivo systems, 2) combination therapies involving TTFields, or 3) bringing treatments involving TTFields to the clinic, are strongly encouraged.

Eligibility: Applicants must have a doctoral degree (PhD, MD, MD/PhD, or equivalent) in a related field and not currently be a candidate for a further doctoral degree. Applications are invited from researchers affiliated with departments of institutions* that do not hold an active AACR-Novocure grant (*Please see Program Guidelines and Application Instructions for a list of departments of institutions that currently hold an active AACR-Novocure grant). Institutions may submit multiple applications for the AACR-Novocure Career Development Awards for Tumor Treating Fields Research and the AACR-Novocure Tumor Treating Fields Research Grants for multiple applicants. However, no more than one applicant will be awarded from the same department of an institution. At the start of the grant term on July 1, 2023, applicants must hold a faculty position with the title of assistant professor, instructor, research assistant professor, or the equivalent; have completed their most recent doctoral degree within the past 11 years (i.e., degree cannot have been conferred before July 1, 2012); have independent laboratory space as confirmed by their institution; and work at an academic, medical, or research institution anywhere in the world. Investigators may submit only one application for the AACR-Novocure Career Development Awards for Tumor Treating Fields Research but may concurrently apply for other AACR grants. However, applicants are expected to accept the first grant they are awarded. Individuals may accept and hold only one AACR grant at a time. Employees or subcontractors of a U.S. government entity or for-profit private industry are not eligible. Employees or subcontractors of a U.S. government entity or for-profit private industry may serve as Collaborators, but no grant funds may be directed towards these individuals. Investigators who are currently, or have been, a Principal Investigator on a substantial independent research award (e.g., an NIH R01 award, DP2 award, DP5 award, MIRA award, or the equivalent) are not eligible. Qualified investigators are invited to apply for AACR grants for independent investigators. Postdoctoral or clinical research fellows or the equivalent who are working under the auspices of a scientific mentor are not eligible to apply. Qualified fellows are invited to apply for an AACR Fellowship. Any individual who currently holds an active AACR grant may not apply. Past AACR grantees may apply if they complied with all progress and financial report requirements.

Level of Study: Doctorate

Type: Award

Value: US$225,000

Length of Study: 3 Years

Frequency: Annual

Country of Study: Any country

Application Procedure: The AACR requires applicants to submit an online application, using the ProposalCentral website at proposalcentral.com.

Closing Date: 7 February

Additional Information: All applicants with questions about eligibility should contact the AACR's Scientific Review and Grants Administration at mailto: grants@aacr.org before submitting an application.

For further information contact:

Email: membership@aacr.org

AACR-Novocure Tumor Treating Fields Research Grants

Purpose: The research proposed for funding should be basic or translational in nature, promoting the transition of in vitro work into in vivo systems. Proposals focused on 1) translational approaches, promoting the transition of in vitro work into in vivo systems, 2) combination therapies involving TTFields, or 3) bringing treatments involving TTFields to the clinic, are strongly encouraged.

Eligibility: Applicants must have a doctoral degree (PhD, MD, MD/PhD, or equivalent) in a related field and not currently be a candidate for a further doctoral degree. Applications are invited from researchers affiliated with departments of institutions* that do not hold an active AACR-Novocure grant (*Please see Table 1 found within the Program Guidelines and Application Instructions for a list of departments of institutions that currently hold an active AACR-Novocure grant). Institutions may submit multiple applications for the AACR-Novocure Career Development Awards for Tumor Treating Fields Research and the AACR-Novocure Tumor Treating Fields Research Grants for multiple applicants. However, no more than one applicant will be awarded from the same department of an institution. Investigators may submit only one application for the AACR-Novocure Tumor Treating Fields Research Grants but may concurrently apply for other AACR grants. However, applicants are expected to accept the first grant they are awarded. Individuals may accept and hold only one AACR grant at a time. Employees or subcontractors of a U.S. government entity or for-profit private industry are not eligible. Employees or subcontractors of a U.S. government entity or for-profit private industry may serve as Collaborators, but no grant funds may be directed towards these individuals. Any individual who currently holds an active AACR grant may not apply. Past AACR grantees may apply if they complied with all progress and financial report requirements. Postdoctoral or clinical research fellows or the equivalent who are working under the auspices of a scientific mentor are not eligible to apply. Qualified fellows are invited to apply for an AACR Fellowship. Members of the Scientific Review Committee are not eligible to apply for an AACR-Novocure Tumor Treating Fields Research Grant.

Level of Study: Doctorate

Type: Grant

Value: US$250,000

Length of Study: two years

Country of Study: Any country

Application Procedure: The AACR requires applicants to submit an online application, using the ProposalCentral website at proposalcentral.com.

Closing Date: 1 July

For further information contact:

Email: grants@aacr.org

Lustgarten Foundation-AACR Career Development Award for Pancreatic Cancer Research, in Honor of John Robert Lewis

Purpose: This award represents a joint effort to encourage and support early career scientists engaged in pancreatic cancer research relevant to the goals and mission of the Lustgarten Foundation. The proposed project may be basic, translational, clinical, or epidemiological in nature and must have direct applicability and relevance to the understanding, detection, diagnosis, or treatment of pancreatic cancer.

Eligibility: Applicants must belong to racial or ethnic group(s) that has(have) been shown to be underrepresented in the cancer related sciences workforce. For U.S. applicants, these groups include Blacks or African Americans, Hispanics or Latinos, American Indians or Alaska Natives, Native Hawaiians and other Pacific Islanders. It is recognized that for both

U.S. and international applicants, underrepresentation can vary from setting to setting and individuals from racial or ethnic groups not listed above may also be eligible to apply for this program.
Value: US$300,000
Length of Study: 3 Years
Country of Study: Any country
Application Procedure: The AACR requires applicants to submit an online application, using the ProposalCentral website at proposalcentral.com. Program Guidelines and Application Instructions are available for download. Please read all guidelines and instructions carefully before submitting an application.
Closing Date: 18 October

Lustgarten Foundation-AACR Career Development Award for Pancreatic Cancer Research, in honor of Ruth Bader Ginsburg

Purpose: This Award represents a joint effort to support the career advancement of a female scientist engaged in pancreatic cancer research relevant to the goals and mission of the Lustgarten Foundation. The proposed project may be basic, translational, clinical, or epidemiological in nature and must have direct applicability and relevance to the understanding, detection, diagnosis, or treatment of pancreatic cancer.
Eligibility: Applicants must be female investigators with a doctoral degree (PhD, MD, MD/PhD, or equivalent) in a related field and not currently be a candidate for a further doctoral degree
Level of Study: Doctorate
Value: US$300,000
Country of Study: Any country
Application Procedure: The AACR requires applicants to submit an online application, using the ProposalCentral website at proposalcentral.com. Program Guidelines and Application Instructions are available for download. Please read all guidelines and instructions carefully before submitting an application.
Closing Date: 11 February

The Bosarge Family Foundation-Waun Ki Hong Scholar Award for Regenerative Cancer Medicine

Purpose: The Bosarge Family Foundation-Waun Ki Hong Scholar Award for Regenerative Cancer Medicine represents a joint effort to encourage and support postdoctoral or clinical research fellows to conduct highly novel and provocative research in the field of regenerative cancer medicine and to establish a successful career path in this field. The research proposed for funding may be translational, clinical, or epidemiological in nature and must have direct applicability and relevance to enhancing the physiology or function of cancer survivors using regenerative medicine techniques.
Eligibility: Applicants must have a doctoral degree (including PhD, MD, MD/PhD, or equivalent) in a related field and not currently be a candidate for a further doctoral degree.
Level of Study: Postdoctorate
Country of Study: Any country
Application Procedure: The AACR requires applicants to submit an online application, using the ProposalCentral website at proposalcentral.com. Program Guidelines and Application Instructions are available for download. Please read all guidelines and instructions carefully before submitting an application.

Aarhus University

Nordre Ringgade 1, DK-8000 Aarhus C, Denmark.

Tel: (45) 8715 0000, (45) 30 31478610
Website: www.au.dk

Established in 1928, Aarhus University has since developed into a major Danish university with a strong international reputation across the entire research spectrum.

Aarhus University Scholarships

Purpose: Aarhus University Scholarships are available for highly qualified non-European Union/EEA/Swiss applicants to pursue 2-year master's degree programmes
Value: A monthly scholarship for a maximum of 1 year and 11 months
Country of Study: Denmark
Application Procedure: All applications for Master's degree programmes at Aarhus University must be submitted online through the digital application portal
Closing Date: 15 March
Additional Information: The scholarships are awarded on the basis of the following criteria: 1. Students may apply for any English-taught Master's degree programme at Aarhus University. 2. The scholarships generally include a full tuition waiver and generally, but not always, including a monthly scholarship for a maximum of 1 year and 11 months for the duration of the degree programme. 3. The general admission requirements and application procedures and deadlines at Aarhus University apply. Prior to applying for admission, applicants are kindly asked to make themselves acquainted with the specific admission requirements for the Master's

degree programmes they wish to apply for international.au.
dk/education/admissions/exchange/studying-at-aarhus-uni
versity/scholarships/

For further information contact:

Email: ELKLIT@ps.au.dk

Aaron Siskind Foundation

C/o School of Visual Arts, MFA Photography, 209 East 23rd
Street, New York, NY 10010, United States of America.

Tel: (1) 212 592 2363
Email: info@aaronsiskind.org
Website: www.aaronsiskind.org

The Foundation works to preserve and protect Aaron
Siskind's artistic legacy, and foster knowledge of and appreciation of his art.

Individual Photographer

Purpose: To stimulate excellence and the promise of future
achievement in the photographic field
Eligibility: Applicants must be at least 21 years of age.
Students enrolled in a college degree program are not eligible
to apply. Please note students who will graduate before the
application deadline are eligible to apply. Previous IPF recip-
ients are not currently being considered for new awards.
Level of Study: Postgraduate
Type: Fellowship or Grant
Value: US$15,000 each
Frequency: Annual
Country of Study: Any country
Application Procedure: Applications must be submitted
through the Slideroom application portal at www.slideroom.com
Closing Date: 18 May
Funding: Private
Additional Information: aaronsiskind.org/grant.html

Abbey Harris Mural Fund

43 Carson Road, London SE21 8HT, United Kingdom.

Tel: (44) 20 8761 7980
Email: contact@abbey.org.uk
Website: www.abbey.org.uk
Contact: Ms Jane Reid, Administrator

The Abbey Harris Mural Fund supports the creation of murals
in public places in the United Kingdom.

Abbey Harris Mural Fund

Purpose: The fund supports the production of murals in
public places throughout the United Kingdom
Eligibility: A mural is understood to mean site-specific works
on walls, including vinyl, relief, sculpture sculptural work and
projections/light works as well as painting. Permanent and
temporary artworks are eligible.
Level of Study: Unrestricted
Type: Grant
Value: Up to £3,000
Frequency: Annual
Country of Study: United Kingdom
Application Procedure: Application Materials: 1. A letter
explaining the project 2. Plans and sketches/drawings for the
proposed work 3. Images of your/the 4. proposed artist's work
5. Images of the place where it is to be placed 5. A fully
budgeted funding request
Funding: Private
Contributor: The EA Abbey Memorial Trust Fund for Mural
Painting in Great Britain and The E Vincent Harris Fund for
Mural Decoration

For further information contact:

Email: contact@abbey.org.uk

Abdul Aziz Al Ghurair Foundation For Education

Website: alghurairfoundation.org/

Abdul Aziz Al Ghurair Refugee Education Fund, a new initiative
to benefit refugee youth in Jordan, Lebanon and Arab children
affected by wars and disasters residing in the United Arab Emirates. The 100M AED initiative will run for 3 years and will
support the education of a minimum of 5000 children and youth.

The Abdul Aziz Al Ghurair Refugee Education Fund

Purpose: The Abdul Aziz Al Ghurair Refugee Education
Fund invites proposals for programs that explore and identify
new solutions to long-standing challenges in refugee education that can improve impact at scale. The Abdul Aziz Al
Ghurair Refugee Education Fund aims to equip young refugees with a pathway to sustainable livelihoods

Eligibility: 1. Organisations must have experience in at least one successful program with refugees (Syrian and/or Palestinian). 2. be able to demonstrate proof of concept and potential for scale; be a non-profit organisation; be registered in either Jordan and/or Lebanon or have programmes or partners based there. Other eligibility terms for this fundings are listed below. Able to demonstrate proof of concept, that the program or pilot has had significant impact and has potential to be scaled to benefit larger number of refugee youth in Jordan and/or Lebanon. 1. Be a non-profit organization, including educational institutions. The Fund will consider forprofit companies on an exceptional basis and with clear rationale. 2. Be a registered organization in either Jordan and/or Lebanon where the activities would take place or have programs or partners based in either Lebanon and/or Jordan
Level of Study: Foundation programme, Professional development
Type: Funding support
Frequency: Annual
Country of Study: Jordan
Application Procedure: Application form details are entitled on the below link. Kindly check the following files. www.alghurairfoundation.org/sites/default/files/The%20Abdul%20Aziz%20Al%20Ghurair%20Refugee%20Education%20Fund%20Grant%20Guidelines%20February%202019.pdf
Closing Date: 19 March
Funding: Private
Additional Information: www.alghurairfoundation.org/en/content/abdul-aziz-al-ghurair-refugee-education-fund-call-proposals-0

For further information contact:

Abdulla Al Ghurair Foundation for Education, P.O.Box 6999, Dubai, United Arab Emirates.

Email: info@alghurairfoundation.org

Abdus Salam International Centre for Theoretical Physics (ICTP)

Strada Costiera 11, I-34151 Trieste, Italy.

Tel: (39) 40 224 0111
Email: pio@ictp.it
Website: www.ictp.it

The Abdus Salam International Centre for Theoretical Physics (ICTP) is an institution for research and high-level training in physics and mathematics, mainly for scientists from developing countries. It also maintains a network of associate members and federated institutes.

Abdus Salam ICTP Fellowships

Purpose: To enable qualified applicants to pursue research in the fields of condensed matter physics, mathematics and high-energy physics
Eligibility: Open to qualified applicants of any nationality who have a PhD in physics or mathematics
Level of Study: Postdoctorate
Type: Fellowship
Value: Monthly stipend and round-trip expenses where applicable, and allowances according to the length of the visit
Length of Study: Up to 1 year
Frequency: Dependent on funds available
Study Establishment: ICTP
Country of Study: Italy
Application Procedure: Applicants must visit the ICTP website
Closing Date: 31 January
Funding: Government
Contributor: The Italian government, IAEA and UNESCO

For further information contact:

Email: calligar@ictp.it

Abell Foundation

Suite 2300, 111 S. Calvert Street, Baltimore, MD 21202-6174, United States of America.

Tel: (1) 410 547 1300
Website: www.abell.org/

The Abell Foundation, formerly known as The A.S. Abell Company Foundation, was established on December 31, 1953 by Harry C. Black, philanthropist and then chairman of the board of the A.S. Abell Company, the former publisher of The Baltimore Sun. Upon the sale of the A.S. Abell Company in 1986, the resources of the Foundation increased significantly. The Abell Foundation is the largest private foundation serving only Maryland. The Foundation has acted as an agent of change by supporting innovative, results-oriented efforts to ameliorate the systemic social, economic, and environmental challenges encountered by those living in concentrated poverty. With a unique focus on Baltimore City, Abell provides grant funding to enterprising non-profits as well as research to better inform civic conversation. It also invests in new businesses and technologies that have the potential to benefit society and build Baltimore's workforce. Since its establishment, the Abell Foundation has contributed more than US$339,000,000 to the community.

Abell Foundation - For Small Grant Requests

Purpose: The Abell Foundation is dedicated to the enhancement of the quality of life in Maryland, with a focus on Baltimore City. The Foundation is committed to improving the lives of underserved populations by supporting innovative, results-oriented efforts to solve systemic social, economic, and environmental problems.
Eligibility: The Foundation funds nonprofit organizations located and active in Maryland. Our focus is on Baltimore City, with more than 95% of our grants being awarded to organizations in the Baltimore metropolitan area.
Level of Study: Masters/PhD Degree
Type: Grant
Value: Up to US$10,000 or less
Country of Study: United States of America
Closing Date: 15 October
Additional Information: www.abell.org/applying-funding

For further information contact:

Robert C. Embry, Jr., President, Abell Foundation, 111 South Calvert Street, Suite 2300, Baltimore, MD 21202, United States of America.

Email: abell@abell.org

Abell Foundation - Grant Requests Greater than US$10,000

Purpose: The Abell Foundation is dedicated to the enhancement of the quality of life in Maryland, with a focus on Baltimore City. The Foundation is committed to improving the lives of underserved populations by supporting innovative, results-oriented efforts to solve systemic social, economic, and environmental problems.
Eligibility: The Foundation accepts requests for programs serving disadvantaged communities, with a particular focus on Baltimore City. Nonprofit organizations must be designated by the IRS as 501c3 and 509a organizations.
Level of Study: Masters/PhD Degree
Type: Grant
Value: US$10,000
Frequency: Annual
Country of Study: United States of America

Application Procedure: The Foundation requests that applications for new grants in excess of US$10,000 are initiated by providing a letter of inquiry. A letter of inquiry should include: 1. Description of the project; 2. Amount requested; 3. Total budget: 4. Population served.
Closing Date: 15 October
Additional Information: www.abell.org/applying-funding

For further information contact:

Robert C. Embry, Jr., President, Abell Foundation, 111 South Calvert Street, Suite 2300, Baltimore, MD 21202, United States of America.

Email: abell@abell.org

Abilene Christian University

College of Business Administration, MBA Program Graduate School Office, PO Box 29140, Abilene, TX 79699, United States of America.

Website: www.acu.edu/

Abilene Christian University is a hub of rigorous academic excellence and devoted community. Through residential and online undergraduate and graduate programs, we equip students for lives of service leadership, empowering them through exceptional teaching that unlocks the power of their curiosity and prepares them to create the solutions that will address the opportunities of today and tomorrow.

Abilene Christian University National Merit Finalist or Semifinalist Scholarship

Purpose: This award is for U.S high school students who are named National Merit Finalist and list ACU as their first choice school. The student must plan to attend ACU as a freshman.
Eligibility: To be eligible for this award, 1. National Merit Finalists and Semifinalist are required to list ACU as first choice with the National Merit Corporation. 2. Recipients must also participate in the Honors College by completing four honors courses within your first year. Students must complete an Honors College application as soon as he/she is awarded a scholarship
Level of Study: Postgraduate
Type: Scholarship

Value: wards cover the cost of full-tuition (valued at approximately US$37,800 for the current academic year), plus an additional US$2,000 per year. The total dollars awarded for this scholarship is US$119,400
Frequency: Annual
Country of Study: Any country
Application Procedure: To apply, students must apply for admission to Abilene Christian University (ACU) and provide their National Merit Certificate to the admissions office. For further information, check the below link. www.acu.edu/parents.html
No. of awards offered: 3
Closing Date: 1 February
Funding: Private
Additional Information: No application is required. Provide a copy of your National Merit Certificate to your Admissions Counselor to claim this award. www.unigo.com/scholarships/all/abilene-christian-university-national-merit-finalist-or-semifinalist-scholarship/1002888

For further information contact:

1600 Campus Ct, Abilene, TX 79601, United States of America.

Tel: (1) 800 460 6228
Email: info@admissions.acu.edu

Abilene Christian University Valedictorian/ Salutatorian Scholarship

Purpose: This award is for U.S high school students who graduated either Valedictorian or Salutatorian status and plan to attend Abilene Christian University
Eligibility: all eligible students will be awarded
Level of Study: Postgraduate
Type: Scholarship
Value: Covered tuition plus an additional US$1,000. The total dollars awarded for this scholarship is US$116,400
Frequency: Annual
Country of Study: Any country
No. of awards offered: 3
Closing Date: 1 February
Funding: Private
Additional Information: Abilene Christian University offers a variety of levels of academic scholarships to incoming first-time freshmen (students entering ACU with fewer than 12 hours, excluding dual credit, AP and IB) based on academic achievements, class rank, and standardized test scores at the time of admission. Interested students should contact ACU for additional information or visit the college website.

www.unigo.com/scholarships/all/abilene-christian-university-valedictoriansalutatorian-scholarship-/1002884

For further information contact:

Hunter Welcome Center, Rm 140 ACU Box 29000, Abilene, TX 79699-9000, United States of America.

Tel: (1) 800 460 6228; 325 674 2650
Email: info@admissions.acu.edu

Society for Immunotherapy of Cancer Scholarship

Purpose: The School of Information Technology and Computing awards scholarships in varying amounts to a select number of incoming freshmen and transfer students each year
Eligibility: Scholarship applicants must declare a major in Computer Science, Computer Science/Math Teaching or Digital Entertainment Technology (DET)
Level of Study: Graduate
Type: Scholarship
Frequency: Annual
Country of Study: Any country
Application Procedure: Application has to be processed through physical mailing address. apply.acu.edu/register/?id=3f5eee06-eddd-41c3-9d36-2dffb4f8400b
Funding: Private

For further information contact:

Email: info@admissions.acu.edu

Abraham Lincoln High School

Website: www.alhs.nyc/

Abraham Lincoln High School Alumni Association

Purpose: The purpose of the ALHS Alumni Association Scholarship Program is to make available scholarships to Lincoln High School students who are graduating and going onto college or continuing education
Eligibility: 1. ALHS Alumni will award scholarships. 2. ALHS graduating seniors seeking to further his/her education by obtaining a higher degree such as AA, BA, BS, or Certificated from a Trade, Vocational School or Military Academy. 3. Applications shall be completed by the applicant together with the official transcript, recommendation

(s) by faculty/staff member(s), school activities records and a personal statement by the applicant of his/her goals. 4. Applicants will be evaluated and judged on the following factors. a. Their scholastic record. b. Their activity and other evidence of leadership and character. c. Recommendations of faculty and/or staff. d. A personal statement by applicant of his/her goals must be attached together with official transcripts, school activities records and personal statement by the applicant. 5. Results of the competition will be announced in April. Judging will be done by the ALHS Alumni Association Scholarship Committee. The committee looks forward to honoring the recipients in person at the Annual Wall of Fame/Scholarship Dinner. If the recipient is unable to attend the Scholarship Dinner a family member should attend to accept the scholarship on their behalf

Level of Study: Postgraduate
Type: Funding support
Frequency: Annual
Country of Study: Any country
Closing Date: 20 April
Funding: Private
Additional Information: www.sfusd.edu/school/abraham-lincoln-high-school/alumni/alumni-association

For further information contact:

2162 24th Avenue, San Francisco, CA 94116, United States of America.

Tel: (1) 415 759 2700
Email: scholarships@lincolnalumni.com

Academia Resource Management (ARM)

535 East 4500 South, Suite D-120, Salt Lake City, UT 84107, United States of America.

Tel: (1) 801 273 8911
Email: info@armanagement.org
Website: www.awu.org

Academia Resource Management (ARM) is committed to the advancement of scientific knowledge and enrichment of the academic experience. Its mission is to identify and facilitate mutually beneficial research and training endeavours among academic institutions, government agencies and private industry.

Academia Resource Management Postgraduate Fellowship

Purpose: To fund postgraduate research and technology at co-operating facilities
Level of Study: Postgraduate
Type: Fellowship
Value: Varies
Frequency: Annual
Country of Study: United States of America
Application Procedure: Applicants need to submit their application form, transcripts and reference letters
Funding: Foundation
Contributor: Academia Resource Management

Academy of Marketing Science Foundation

Academy of Marketing Science, c/o Louisiana Tech University, P.O. Box 3072, Ruston, LA 71272, United States of America.

Email: ams@latech.edu
Website: www.ams-web.org

Under the direction of Dr Harold W Berkman, the Academy of Marketing Science may be considered a full service scholarly professional organisation. The AMS established the Academy of Marketing Science Foundation to provide awards to marketing students, primarily at the graduate level. It is also the intention of the Foundation to provide awards for both the advancement of the teaching of marketing and for research in marketing.

Mary Kay Doctoral Dissertation Award

Purpose: Sponsored by Mary Kay, Inc. and the Academy of Marketing Science, doctoral candidates in marketing who have completed their dissertation during January 1–December 31 of the calendar year prior to the AMS Annual Conference to which they wish to submit are eligible for the AMS Mary Kay Doctoral Dissertation Award. A completed dissertation is defined as one successfully defended during the calendar year prior to the year in which the AMS Annual Conference of submission takes place.
Eligibility: doctoral candidates in marketing who have defended their dissertation proposal eligible for the AMS Mary Kay Doctoral Dissertation Proposal Award.

Level of Study: Doctorate
Value: the winner will receive US$600 and a one-year membership in the Academy of Marketing Science. Two runners up will receive US$500 each.
Frequency: Annual
Country of Study: Any country
Application Procedure: To be considered, please submit an electronic version of a dissertation abstract that is no longer than 15 double-spaced pages (including appendices, tables, figures, and references).
Closing Date: 5 January
Additional Information: Before the AMS Annual Conference in Coral Gables, Florida three finalists will be chosen for each award based on the blind reviewer feedback. The winners for each award will be chosen from these three finalists at the AMS annual conference based on the quality of their dissertation research and their presentation at AMS. Finalists MUST attend and register for the AMS Annual Conference in order to be considered as the winner or a runner-up for either award. Candidates may not be considered for both the proposal and dissertation awards during the same year. Doctoral students from programs at any recognized university, college of higher learning, business school or management school worldwide are eligible for the AMS Mary Kay Doctoral Dissertation or Proposal Competition. cdn.ymaws.com/www.ams-web.org/resource/resmgr/2020_ac/2020_dissert_invtn.pdf

For further information contact:

Email: raj2@iastate.edu, saini@uta.edu

Academy of Medical Sciences

41 Portland Place, London W1B 1QH, United Kingdom.

Email: newton-advanced@acmedsci.ac.uk
Website: www.acmedsci.ac.uk

Finding the brightest and best, celebrating their achievements and harnessing their expertise for the benefit of wider society is central to our role as a National Academy.

Daniel Turnberg Travel Fellowships

Purpose: The scheme was established by the Academy in partnership with Lord and Lady Turnberg, in memory of their late son Daniel Turnberg, a doctor and researcher with a keen interest in fostering links between the UK and the Middle East. The aim of the scheme is to encourage researchers to experience an alternative research environment, to learn new techniques and develop ideas for future collaborations. The Travel Fellowships are aimed primarily at early- and mid-career scientists, particularly those just embarking on a career in research.

Eligibility: These Travel Fellowships provide an opportunity for biomedical researchers from the Middle East to visit a research institution of their choice in the UK, and for those from the UK to visit a research institution of their choice in the Middle East. They are open to medical and biomedical graduates who can show a commitment to a career in research. Applicants will typically, but not necessarily, be at postdoctoral level. Your research may be in any field within biomedical research, but the funding may only be used to support studies that are relevant to human health. Your proposal must be a discrete research project, it cannot be used as additional funding for another project or help pay for conference or PhD travel. While there can be a training element to the project it must not be wholly training. The countries included in the scheme are the UK, Israel, Egypt, Jordan, Lebanon and the Palestinian Territories. Applicants must either be based in the UK and plan to work in one of the other countries, or intend to come to a UK institution from one of the other countries.

Level of Study: Research
Type: Fellowship
Value: Funding is provided to an upper limit of £4,000 per fellowship (up to £750 of which can be used to cover the cost of airfares)
Length of Study: Four weeks or three months
Frequency: Annual
Country of Study: United Kingdom
Application Procedure: Applications will need to be submitted online using the Academy's electronic Grants and Awards management system Flexi-Grant®. Please download the guidance notes from the web page to assist you in your application. If you have any queries after referring to the guidance notes. For further details, contact turnberg.fellowships@acmedsci.ac.uk
Closing Date: 1 March
Funding: Private
Additional Information: Use the below link for scholarship application. acmedsci.ac.uk/grants-and-schemes/grant-schemes/daniel-turnberg-travel-fellowship

For further information contact:

The Academy of Medical Sciences, 41 Portland Place, London W1B 1QH, United Kingdom.

Email: turnberg.fellowships@acmedsci.ac.uk

Global Challenges Research Fund Networking Grants

Purpose: These grants provide opportunities for researchers, drawn from a wide spectrum of disciplines and backgrounds. It helps to develop new collaborations and improve interactions between United Kingdom researchers and those in developing countries

Eligibility: The GCRF Networking Grants will be delivered as part of the Joint Academies Resilient Futures programme. Your application will be reviewed by Fellows across all of the partnership Academies and experts from developing or Low and Middle Income Countries (LMICs), and you will not need to attend an interview

Level of Study: Research

Type: Grant

Value: Awards provide up to £25,000 over a year

Frequency: Annual

Country of Study: Any country

Application Procedure: Applications are invited from researchers affiliated to institutions in DAC-listed countries in collaboration with researchers within eligible United Kingdom higher education institutions (HEIs). You will need to apply for the programme using the Academy's online grant management system Flexi-Grant. Grants cannot be used to pay for salary costs or to employ research assistants, PhD students or postdoctoral staff

Closing Date: 31 March

Funding: Private

Additional Information: acmedsci.ac.uk/grants-and-schemes/grant-schemes/gcrf-networking-grants

For further information contact:

Tel: (44) 203 1413 221
Email: gcrfnetworking@acmedsci.ac.uk

Newton Advanced Fellowships

Purpose: Mid-career postdoctoral career-development fellowship. Available for overseas researchers from specific countries in collaboration with a researcher at a United Kingdom institution

Eligibility: To be eligible to apply the Applicant must 1. have a PhD or equivalent research experience. 2. hold a contract in an eligible university or research institute (in the partner countries), which must span the duration of the project. 3. have no more than 15 years (18 years for researchers from China) postdoctoral experience.

Level of Study: Postdoctorate

Type: Fellowship

Value: Up to £37,000 each year

Length of Study: 3 years

Frequency: Annual

Country of Study: United Kingdom

Application Procedure: Applications can only be submitted online using the Royal Society's electronic Grant. Application and Processing (e-GAP) system. Please download Newton Advanced Fellowship Scheme notes for guidance on applying. To find out more information about the application process and to apply please follow the link royalsociety.org/grants/schemes/newton-advanced-fellowships

Closing Date: 10 March

Funding: Government

Contributor: The Academy of Medical Sciences, in partnership with the Royal Society and the British Academy

Additional Information: We are working to include additional countries in future calls royalsociety.org/grants-schemes-awards/grants/newton-advanced-fellowships/

For further information contact:

Tel: (44) 20 7451 2666

Newton International Fellowships

Purpose: Early-career postdoctoral fellowship opportunity for overseas (non-United Kingdom) researchers to spend 2 years, full-time researching at a United Kingdom institution

Eligibility: To be eligible to apply the Applicant must 1. have a PhD or be in the final stage of their PhD provided that it will be completed (including viva) before the start date of the fellowship. 2. have no more than 7 years (4 years for researchers from India) active full-time postdoctoral experience at the time of application, including industry experience, honorary positions and visiting researcher positions. Career breaks must be clearly detailed and explained in the application. 3. not hold a UK citizenship and be based at an eligible institution in one of the partner countries. Each round is open to researcher from specific Newton partner countries. Please check the scheme notes and the top of the page to see which countries are eligible for the current round. Please see Page 4 of the scheme notes for country specific eligibility.

Level of Study: Postdoctorate

Type: Fellowship

Value: Up to £32,000 each year

Length of Study: 2 years

Frequency: Annual

Country of Study: Any country

Application Procedure: Applications can only be submitted online using the Royal Society's electronic Grant Application and Processing (e-GAP) system. Please download Newton Advanced Fellowship Scheme notes for guidance on applying. To find out more information about the application

process and to apply please follow the link royalsociety.org/grants/schemes/newton-advanced-fellowships
Closing Date: 26 March
Funding: Government
Additional Information: royalsociety.org/grants-schemes-awards/grants/newton-international/

For further information contact:

Tel: (44) 20 7451 2666

Academy of Sciences of the Czech Republic

UNESCO-ROSTE Course Institute of Microbiology Videnská 1083, CS-142 20 Prague, Czech Republic.

Tel: (420) 2 4752 379
Email: nerud@biomed.cas.cz
Website: www.biomed.cas.cz
Contact: Mr F Nerud, Director of Course

The Institute of Microbiology is one of the major biological institutes of the Academy of Sciences. Main areas of research at the Institute include biogenesis and biotechnology of natural compounds, cell and molecular microbiology, ecology, immunology, gnotobiology and autotrophic micro-organisms.

United Nations Educational, Scientific and Cultural Organization-ROSTE Long-term Postgraduate Training Course

Purpose: To enable young scientists to obtain a more profound education and prepare for a research career
Eligibility: Open to young scientists from European countries and a limited number of students from other regions who hold an MSc, PhD or equivalent degree, and who have two-three years of practical experience in their field. Candidates should be no more than 35 years of age and should possess a good knowledge of English
Level of Study: Postgraduate
Type: Grant
Value: CZK 5,000 plus accommodation
Length of Study: 11 months
Frequency: Annual
Study Establishment: Insitute of Microbiology of the Academy of Sciences of the Czech Republic
Country of Study: Czech Republic
Application Procedure: Applicants must write for details

No. of awards offered: 12
Closing Date: 31 March
Funding: Government
Contributor: The Academy of Sciences of the Czech Republic
No. of awards given last year: 6
No. of applicants last year: 12
Additional Information: The course is given in co-operation with the Czech Commission for UNESCO and sponsored by the Academy of Sciences of the Czech Republic royalsociety.org/grants-schemes-awards/grants/newton-international/

Acadia University

Room 214 Horton Hall, 18 University Avenue, Wolfville, NS B4P 2R6, Canada.

Tel: (1) 902 585 1914
Email: theresa.starratt@acadiau.ca
Website: www.acadiau.ca
Contact: Ms Theresa Starratt, Graduate Studies Officer-Research and Graduate Studies

Acadia University is an institution that is committed to providing a liberal education based on the highest standards. The University houses a scholarly community that aims to ensure a broadening life experience for students, faculty and staff.

Acadia Graduate Scholarship / Acadia Graduate Teaching Assistantships

Purpose: To financially support students
Eligibility: Open to registered full-time graduate students at Acadia University. In order to be eligible for an award, students must have a GPA of not less than 3.0 in their major field in each of their last 2 years of undergraduate study
Level of Study: Postgraduate
Type: Award
Value: Canadian Dollars. Value can vary
Length of Study: 1–2 years
Frequency: Annual
Study Establishment: The Division of Research and Graduate Studies at Acadia University
Country of Study: Canada
Application Procedure: Applicants must write for details. In almost all cases, to be automatically considered for funding, applicants need to apply by 1 February of each year
Funding: Private
Additional Information: Recipients of an Acadia Graduate Teaching Assistantship should expect to undertake certain

duties during the academic year (up to 10 hours per week and a maximum of 120 hours per semester) as a condition of tenure gradstudies.acadiau.ca/tl_files/sites/gradstudies/docs/University%20Support.pdf

Action Cancer

1 Marlborough Park, Belfast, Co Antrim, BT9 6XS, Northern Ireland, United Kingdom.

Tel: (44) 28 9080 3363
Email: info@actioncancer.org
Website: www.actioncancer.org
Contact: Caroline Hughes, Research and Evaluation Officer

Action Cancer is a Northern Ireland cancer charity that relies entirely on voluntary donations. Founded in 1973, it offers awareness and health promotion, free early-detection clinics for men and women concerned about cancer and a support service for cancer patients and their families. Action Cancer also provides funding for research at local universities.

Action Cancer Project Grant

Purpose: To help researchers in Northern Ireland carry out significant cancer-related projects by contributing to salaries, the purchase of materials and equipments and to other appropriate costs
Eligibility: Researchers must be working in Northern Ireland
Level of Study: Postdoctorate
Type: Project grant
Value: Up to £45,000 per year for up to 3 years
Length of Study: 3 years
Frequency: Every 2 years
Country of Study: United Kingdom
Application Procedure: Awards are advertised in the local press in March. Applicants must submit a form, based on which a decision is taken by the Action Cancer Scientific and Research Committee, which also takes advice from external reviewers
Closing Date: May
Funding: Private
Contributor: Voluntary donations

For further information contact:

Email: grants@solvingkidscancer.org

Action Medical Research

Vincent House, North Parade, West Sussex, Horsham RH12 2DP, United Kingdom.

Tel: (44) 14 0321 0406
Email: applications@action.org.uk
Website: www.action.org.uk

Action Medical Research is dedicated to preventing and treating disease and disability by funding vital medical research in United Kingdom-based hospitals and universities. The remit focuses on child health with an emphasis on clinical research or research at the clinical/basic interface. Research applications are judged by rigorous peer review.

Action Medical Research Project Grants

Subjects: A broad spectrum of research with the objective of preventing and treating disease and disability and alleviating physical disability. The remit focuses on child health to include problems affecting pregnancy, childbirth, babies, children and adolescents.
Purpose: Supports research which focuses on child health to include problems affecting pregnancy, childbirth, babies, children and young people. Emphasis is on clinical research or research at the interface between clinical and basic science
Eligibility: Open to researchers based in the United Kingdom. Grants are not awarded to other charities or for higher education
Level of Study: Unrestricted
Type: Project grant
Value: £200,000. to £250,000
Length of Study: Up to 3 years, assessed annually
Frequency: Dependent on funds available
Study Establishment: Hospitals, universities and recognised research establishments in the United Kingdom
Country of Study: United Kingdom
Application Procedure: Applicants must submit a one-page outline of the project before an application form can be issued. Full details and outline proposals are available on the website
No. of awards offered: Varies
Closing Date: March
Funding: Individuals, Private, Trusts
Contributor: Voluntary income
No. of awards given last year: 42
No. of applicants last year: 83

Action Medical Research Training Fellowship

Subjects: A broad spectrum of research with the objective of preventing and treating disease and disability and alleviating physical disability. The remit focuses on child health to include problems affecting pregnancy, childbirth, babies, children and adolescents.
Purpose: To support training in research techniques and methodology applied to subjects relevant to the aims of the charity.
Eligibility: Open to researchers based in the United Kingdom. Grants are not awarded to other charities or for higher education.
Level of Study: Medical graduates,clinicians,bioengineers, research nurses,physiotherapists and allied health professionals
Type: Research fellowship
Value: £240,000-£250,000
Length of Study: three year
Frequency: Dependent on funds available
Study Establishment: Hospitals, universities and recognised research establishments in the UK
Country of Study: United Kingdom
Application Procedure: Applicants must submit an outline of the project and may then be invited to submit a full application. Full details are available on the website.
No. of awards offered: Typically 2 or 3 annually
Closing Date: 25 November
Contributor: Voluntary income
No. of awards given last year: 9
No. of applicants last year: 26
Additional Information: Please contact us on (1) 403 327407 if you have not received an acknowledgement email within 7 days to confirm the application has been received

For further information contact:

Tel: (1) 403 327407

Adelphi University

1 South Avenue, PO BOX 701, Garden City, NY 11530-0701, United States of America.

Tel: (1) 516 877 3412/3080
Email: ucinfo@adelphi.edu
Website: www.adelphi.edu/

Adelphi University is the oldest institution of higher education for liberal arts and sciences on Long Island.

Adelphi University Full-Time Transfer Merit Award

Purpose: Adelphi University has made a substantial commitment to make the cost of attending the University more affordable through its institutional scholarship and grant programs
Eligibility: Eligible students will receive a letter of notification from the Scholarship Committee. After filing the FAFSA, a financial assistance summary detailing all financial aid will be mailed to the student
Type: Award
Value: Up to US$11,000 depending upon the individual's academic profile
Frequency: Annual
Country of Study: Any country
Application Procedure: A student must first file an admissions application and is encouraged to file the FAFSA as soon as possible after 1 January, but no later than 15 February to ensure maximum eligibility for other sources of financial aid
Additional Information: financial-aid.adelphi.edu/files/2018/02/2018-2019-Transfer-Scholarship-for-Full-Time-Study.pdf

For further information contact:

Tel: (1) 516 877 3080
Email: admissions@adelphi.edu

Advance Africa

Baxter International Foundation Grants

Purpose: The Baxter International Foundation offers grants to NGOs working to provide accessibility and affordability of healthcare services to disadvantaged communities around the world
Eligibility: NGOs need to understand Foundation priorities, besides following the application procedures carefully while submitting the proposal. Although proposals are accepted round the year, there are quarterly deadlines
Level of Study: Graduate
Type: Grant
Frequency: Annual
Country of Study: Any country
Application Procedure: Submit the proposal via communication with the address below
Funding: Private
Additional Information: www.advance-africa.com/Baxter-International-Foundation-Grants.html

For further information contact:

The Baxter International Foundation, One Baxter Parkway - DF2-2E, Deerfield, IL 60015, United States of America.

Tel: (1) 847 948 4605
Email: baxtersupport@cybergrants.com, fdninfo@baxter. com

Maypole Fund Grants for Women

Purpose: Grants from the Maypole Fund have contributed to a wide range of activities
Eligibility: 1. Young women's groups/individuals. 2. Activities or projects not yet started. 3. Women who do not have access to other sources of funding or whose projects find it difficult to attract funding from elsewhere. 4. Imaginative/ creative activities. 5. Individual and small women's groups over larger established women's groups
Level of Study: Postgraduate
Type: Funding support
Value: £750
Frequency: Annual
Country of Study: Any country
Application Procedure: Interested applicants can download the application forms via given website. The Maypole Fund is seeking applications from women only for projects and activities for any of the following 1. Anti-militarism. 2. Action against the arms trade. 3. Action against nuclear weapons and weapons systems. Creating a culture of peace and non-violence and the prevention of conflict and war
Closing Date: 30 June
Funding: Private
Additional Information: www.maypolefund.org/the-grant/

Rudolf Steiner Foundation Seed Fund

Purpose: It helps in Providing Small Grants to Organizations. The Rudolf Steiner Foundation (RSF) is inviting applicants for its Seed Fund to provide small grants to organizations that offer innovative solutions to challenges in the areas of social finance, food and agriculture, education and the arts, or ecological stewardship
Eligibility: 1. Alignment with RSF's mission and focus areas. 2. Non-profit status The RSF Seed Fund accepts proposals from organizations that are any of the following 501(c)(3) tax-exempt per the IRS Fiscally sponsored with 501(c)(3) tax-exempt status per the IRS. 3. Schools or universities. 4. Non-governmental entities, Indian tribes or tribal non-profit organizations, and territorial, tribal, or unit of local government entities

Level of Study: Postgraduate
Type: Award
Value: US$500 - US$3,500
Frequency: Annual
Country of Study: United States of America
Application Procedure: Apply online. 1. Interested applicants can apply online via given website. 2. Eligible Country United States. For more information and grant application details, see; application details, see; RSF Seed Fund - Providing Small Grants to Organizations
Closing Date: 13 March
Funding: Private
Additional Information: www.instrumentl.com/grants/ rudolf-steiner-foundation-seed-fund-grant-programme

For further information contact:

1002 O'Reilly Avenue, San Francisco, CA 94129, United States of America.

Tel: (1) 415 561 3900

African Forest Forum (AFF)

The African Forest Forum, United Nations Avenue, P.O. Box 30677-00100, Nairobi, KE, Kenya.

Tel: (254) 207 224 000
Email: exec.sec@afforum.org
Website: www.afforum.org/

The African Forest Forum is an association of individuals with a commitment to the sustainable management, wise use and conservation of Africa's forest and tree resources for the socio-economic well-being of its peoples and for the stability and improvement of its environment.

African Forest Forum (AFF) Research Fellowships

Purpose: The African Forest Forum (AFF) is a pan-African non-governmental organization with its headquarters in Nairobi, Kenya. It is an association of individuals who share the quest for and commitment to the sustainable management, use and conservation of the forest and tree resources of Africa for the socio-economic wellbeing of its people and for the stability and improvement of its environment
Eligibility: Applicants must meet the general eligibility criteria as well as the specific eligibility criteria. Applications that do not meet eligibility criteria will not receive further

evaluation. Should have a Master's or Bachelor's degree plus two or more years of professional experience related to forestry, natural resource management, development studies, climate change and environmental studies. Please refer to the website for more information
Level of Study: Postdoctorate, Postgraduate
Value: Each fellow will receive up to AF$10,000 for research and AF$2,000 to cover cost of travel, subsistence, and accommodation while in the field including supervision
Country of Study: Kenya
Application Procedure: Check website for more details
Closing Date: 31 May
Funding: Trusts

African Mathematics Millennium Scientific Initiative

School of Mathematics, University of Nairobi, PO Box 30197, Nairobi, GPO 00100, Kenya.

Tel: (254) 20 445 0934
Email: ammsi@uonbi.ac.ke
Website: www.ammsi.org
Contact: Professor Wandera Ogana, AMMSI Programme Director

The African Mathematics Millennium Science Initiative (AMMSI) is a distributed network of mathematics research, training and promotion throughout sub-Saharan Africa. It has five regional offices located in Botswana, Cameroon, Kenya, Nigeria and Senegal. It is a project established by the Millennium Science Initiative (MSI), administered by the Science Initiative Group (SIG). The primary goal of the MSI is to create and nurture world-class science and scientific talent in the developing world by strengthening S&T capacity through integrated programmes of research and training, planned and driven by local scientists in the field of mathematics.

Research/Visiting Scientist Fellowships

Purpose: The Scientific and Technological Research Council of Turkey (TÜBITAK) grants fellowships for international scientists/researchers who would like to give workshops/conferences/lectures, or conduct R&D activities in Turkey in the fields of Natural Sciences, Engineering and Technological Sciences, Medical Sciences, Agricultural Sciences, Social Sciences and Humanities. The program aims to promote Turkey's scientific and technological collaboration with countries of the prospective fellows

Eligibility: Candidates should undertake research and postgraduate teaching in mathematics at any university in sub-Saharan Africa, should be a staff member at a university and hold at least a Master's degree, and should obtain an official invitation from the host institution
Level of Study: Postgraduate
Type: Fellowships
Value: A monthly stipend of up to US$3,500 for Visiting Scientists on Sabbatical Leave
Length of Study: 1–12 months
Application Procedure: Application forms should be filled and submitted online. In exceptional circumstances, hard copy application forms may be obtained from the nearest AMMSI Regional Coordinator whose contact details can be found in the website
Closing Date: 15 September
Additional Information: e-bideb.tubitak.gov.tr

For further information contact:

Tel: (254) 20 235 8569/20 445 0934
Fax: (254) 20 445 0934
Email: progoffice@ammsi.org

African Wildlife Foundation (AWF)

PO Box 48177, Nairobi, Kenya.

Tel: (254) 2 710 367
Email: awfnrb@awfke.org
Website: www.awf.org

The African Wildlife Foundation (AWF) has been working with the people of Africa to protect their environment since 1961. Most of AWF's staff are based in Africa, working with park managers and communities to safeguard wildlife and wilderness areas. AWF helps African nations design long-term strategies for conserving their magnificent natural treasures for all the world to enjoy.

African Institute for Mathematical Sciences Postdoctoral Fellowship in Data Science

Purpose: African Institute for Mathematical Sciences (AIMS) is a pan-African network of centers of excellence for Postgraduate education, research and outreach in mathematical sciences
Eligibility: Applicants should be SADC member state, and applicant should be proficient in English language with good

communication skills. A relevant doctorate of high standing and developing research capability which will lead to good publications. Candidates should have a ability to tutor post-graduate students successfully work as part of an interdisciplinary team

Level of Study: Graduate
Type: Fellowship
Value: R200–R240,000 per annul, tax-free, subject to qualification and experience. Other benefits include the provision of a laptop, coverage of all cost associated with the use of HPC resource
Frequency: Annual
Country of Study: Any country
Closing Date: February
Funding: Private
Additional Information: scholarship-fellowship.com/aims-postdoctoral-fellowship/

For further information contact:

Email: joan@aims.ac.za

After School Africa

Tel: (1) 877 725 7721
Email: info@aftercollege.com
Website: www.aftercollege.com

AfterCollege STEM Inclusion Scholarship

Purpose: We not only help students find jobs & internships, but also offer scholarships to help fund their education. After-College has awarded more than US$1,600,000 in scholarships and student activities through our program to date.
Eligibility: 1. Open to currently enrolled students working toward a degree in a field of Science, Technology, Engineering or Mathematics from a group underrepresented in their field of study. Underrepresented groups may be defined by gender, race, ethnic background, disability, sexual orientation, age, socio-economic status, nationality and other non-visible differences. 2. Minimum 3.0 GPA
Level of Study: Graduate
Type: Scholarship
Value: US$500
Frequency: Annual
Country of Study: Any country
Application Procedure: When logged-in to the website, a pop-up will prompt you to either create or update your After-College profile, which serves as your scholarship application. Complete your profile step-by-step in the pop-up window. You

can edit your profile as much as you'd like until the deadline. The scholarship committee will review applicants' profiles to determine the scholarship recipient. 1. Edit Your Personal Details This is where you'll enter your personal statement, which is the main criteria used to determine the scholarship recipient. We look for a succinct but impactful, resume-style personal statement that describes your goals and the value that you bring in an academic and/or professional context (200 words or less). You also have the option to upload an introductory video 2. Edit Your Education, your school, major, graduation date and GPA. 3. Edit Your Work Experience Not all students are expected to have relevant work experience yet, but part-time jobs, internships and volunteer positions can help demonstrate your character, skills and strengths. 4. Edit Your Honors, Awards, And Scholarships Showcase what you've already accomplished. 5. Edit Your Skills And Languages Enter your Hard Skills (specific skills, like expertise in specific programs, typing speed, special certifications or licenses), Soft Skills (general skills, like communication, networking or time management) and any languages you speak. 6. Hit "Apply Now" to check out your profile to make sure you're happy with it. Feel free to go the extra mile by uploading a picture or linking to samples of your work or projects.
Closing Date: 31 March
Funding: Private
Additional Information: More details on making a great After College Profile: blog.aftercollege.com/what-can-an-aftercollege-profile-do-for-me/

For further information contact:

After College 98 Battery Street, Suite 502 San Francisco, CA 94111, United States of America.

Email: scholarships@aftercollege.com

HKBU Fully Funded International Postgraduate Scholarship

Subjects: Master of Accountancy, MSc in Applied Accounting and Finance, MSc in Applied Economics, MSc in Business Management, MSc in Corporate Governance and Compliance.
Purpose: The International Postgraduate Scholarship (IPS) scheme at the HKBU School of Business is a global initiative designed to nurture business leaders, bringing together highly talented and intellectually-motivated students from around the world to one of our selected taught postgraduate programmes. Although these young achievers come from diverse backgrounds, they have all demonstrated leadership potential and have a common interest in making a difference in the world.

Eligibility: Scholarships are available to students from all around the world.
Level of Study: Postgraduate
Type: Scholarship
Value: Full tuition fee waiver and allowance (HK$100,000 = ~US$12,800)
Application Procedure: 1. Submit your application online to one of the 5 masters programmes listed above. Competition increases as the year progress, so we recommend starting your application early. 2. No individual application for the IPS is required.
Closing Date: May
Additional Information: www.afterschoolafrica.com/32703/hkbu-fully-funded-international-postgraduate-scholarship-ips-scheme/

Zhengzhou University President Scholarships

Purpose: The scholarship aims to sponsor international postgraduate students to pursue their degree, especially the doctor degree, in Zhengzhou University
Eligibility: 1. Non-Chinese citizen, physically healthy, without a criminal record; 2. Abide by the laws and regulations of the People's Republic of China as well as regulations of ZZU; 3. Good learning attitude and with a solid academic foundation and intellectual potential to become a highly specialized researcher or expert. 4. Applicants must not be a registered PhD student in Chinese universities at the time of application. 5. Requirements for applicant's degree and age: Applicants for doctoral program should have an excellent academic record in a master program or higher degree or equivalent degree, and aged less than 40 years old; 6. Requirements for applicant's language competence: a. Applicants for doctoral programs in Chinese should be HSK 5 scored 210; b. Applicants for doctoral programs in English should be IELTS 6.5 or higher if they are from non-English speaking countries.
Level of Study: Postgraduate
Type: Scholarship
Value: Tuition: Full tuition, Accommodation: CNY 1000/month, Stipend: CNY 3,500/month
Length of Study: 4 academic years
Frequency: Annual
Country of Study: China
Application Procedure: Applicants must fill in Application Form and submit the following supporting documents: 1. CV and Passport (should be valid for at least one year). 2. Original or notarized copies of degree certificates and complete transcripts of both undergraduate and postgraduate studies (applicants should additionally submit study certificate or employment certificate issued by the applicants' schools if the applicants are students or employed). Documents in neither Chinese nor English must be attached with a notarized Chinese or English translations; 3. The statement of research interest and research proposal. In general, a statement of research interest should include your reasons for undertaking work at ZZU, while a research proposal should include the background, the objectives and the methodology or approach you propose to take in studying the subject matter. The minimum word limit for the proposal is 2000. Proper referencing is needed in the preparation of research proposals. Applicants are strongly suggested to contact their potential supervisor to discuss the research proposal before submission. The result of the plagiarism check will be taken into consideration when the Department, Faculty and Graduate School review the application. The application may be deemed unsuccessful if plagiarized materials are identified; 4. Two recommendation letters from professors who know the applicant well, and the letter should have their contact email and phone number; 5. Official score report of HSK, TOEFL, IELTS or other language proficiency tests; 6. Physical examination record. Foreigner Physical Examination Form with blood test reports in Chinese or English. These reports must have been issued within the last six months; 7. Original or notarized copies of no criminal certificate; 8. Other documents, e.g. list of publications, documentary evidence of academic awards and professional qualifications, and summary of relevant experience.
Closing Date: 15 June
Funding: Private
Additional Information: www.buddy4study.com/scholarship/zhengzhou-university-president-scholarship

For further information contact:

No.100 Science Avenue, 450001, Zhengzhou, Henan Province, China.

Tel: (86) 371 67780102
Email: zhaochun@zzu.edu.cn

Agency for Science, Technology and Research (A*STAR)

1 Fusionopolis Way, 20-10 Connexis North Tower, 138632, Singapore.

Tel: (65) 6826 6111
Email: contact@a-star.edu.sg
Website: www.a-star.edu.sg/astar

A*STAR comprises of the Biomedical Research Council (BMRC), the Science and Engineering Research Council (SERC), Exploit Technologies Private Ltd (ETPL), the

A*STAR Graduate Academy (AGA) and the Corporate Planning and Administration Division (CPAD). Both BMRC and SERC promote, support and oversee the public sector R&D research activities in Singapore.

A*Star Graduate Scholarship

Purpose: A fully funded overseas post-doctoral programme, the AGS Post-Doctoral Fellowship is opened only to A*STAR Graduate Scholarship (AGS) awardees. With this fellowship, scholars may conduct post-doctoral research at a leading overseas laboratory of their choice for up to two years.
Eligibility: Applicants must: 1. Singaporeans and other nationals are welcome to apply 2. Non-Singaporeans must have completed a degree in a Singapore autonomous university 3. Satisfy criteria for and seek admission to PhD or EngD programme in an autonomous university 4. Have obtained at least a 2nd Upper Class Honours Degree or equivalent in relevant disciplines 5. Have strong interest in a research career The eligibility criteria are not exhaustive. A*STAR may include additional selection criteria based on prevailing scholarship policies. These policies may be amended from time to time without notice.
Level of Study: Postgraduate
Type: Scholarship
Value: Full tuition fees; Monthly sustenance allowance, inclusive of CPF contribution (where applicable)
Length of Study: 12 months
Frequency: Every 2 years
Country of Study: Any country
Application Procedure: As AGS (PDF) awardees are required to serve in an A*STAR Research Institute after their post-doctoral training, AGS (PDF) applicants should identify the relevant Research Institute in which they will work during their service commitment period, and engage the Research Institute Executive Director and prospective supervisor prior to their AGS (PDF) application.
Closing Date: 1 August
Funding: Private
Additional Information: www.a-star.edu.sg/Scholarships/for-post-doctoral-studies/a-star-graduate-scholarship-(post-doc)

For further information contact:

Email: tellusmore@hq.a-star.edu.sg

Singapore International Graduate Award (SINGA)

Purpose: The Singapore International Graduate Award (SINGA) is a collaboration between the Agency for Science, Technology & Research (A*STAR), the Nanyang Technological University (NTU) and the National University of Singapore (NUS). PhD training will be carried out in English at chosen lab at A*STAR Research Institutes, NTU or NUS
Eligibility: 1. Open for application to all international graduates with a passion for research and excellent academic results 2. Good skills in written and spoken English 3. Good reports from academic referees 4. The above eligibility criteria are not exhaustive. A*STAR may include additional selection criteria based on prevailing scholarship policies. These policies may be amended from time to time without notice.
Type: Award
Value: The award provides support for up to 4 years of PhD studies including a monthly stipend of S$2,000, which will be increased to S$2,500 after the passing of the Qualifying Examination. One-time airfare grant of up to S$1,500*. One-time settling-in allowance of S$1,000
Country of Study: Singapore
Application Procedure: 1. Browse PhD Research Projects Go to Research Areas to browse the projects you are interested in. 2. Documents required: prepare the following documents in advance before applying. Note: Do NOT mail any hard copy documents to SINGA Office. All necessary documents are to be submitted online. a. Valid Passport b. A recent passport-sized photo (in .jpeg or .png format) 3. Transcripts & Reports. ALL transcripts need to be in English translation
Closing Date: January
Additional Information: Only shortlisted candidates will be notified within 12 weeks from the application closing date.

For further information contact:

Email: singa_enquiries@hq.a-star.edu.sg

Agilent Technology and American Association of Critical Care Nurses

3000 Minuteman Road MS210, Andover, MA 01810, United States of America.

Tel: (1) 978 659 4748
Contact: Ms Joan Hodges, Learning Products Manager

Agilent Technology Critical Care Nursing Research Grant

Purpose: To support research in critical care nursing. Preferred topics will address information technology requirements of patient management in critical care

Eligibility: AACN members may apply (current registered nurse members only). Research must be undertaken in the United States of America
Level of Study: Postgraduate
Type: Other
Value: US$37,000
Length of Study: 1 year
Frequency: Annual
Study Establishment: Hospital
Country of Study: United States of America
Application Procedure: Applicants must write to the Agilent Technology address for applications
No. of awards offered: 22
No. of awards given last year: 1
No. of applicants last year: 22
Additional Information: Questions about suitability of research topics should be addressed to the AACN Research Department www.a-star.edu.sg/Scholarships/For-Graduate-Studies/Singapore-International-Graduate-Award-SINGA

For further information contact:

Tel: (1) 800 394 5995
Email: research@aacn.org

Agricultural History Society

MSU History Department, PO Box H, Mississippi State, MS 39762, United States of America.

Tel: (1) 501 569 8782/662 268 2247
Email: CSTROM@Rollins.edu
Website: www.aghistorysociety.org
Contact: Claire Strom, Editor, Agricultural History

The Agricultural History Society recognizes the roles of agriculture and agri-business in shaping the political, economic, social and historical profiles of different countries worldwide. Since 1927, the Society's publication, Agricultural History, has been the international journal for the field and publishes innovative research on agricultural and rural history.

Agriculture Awareness Grants

Purpose: Metro Vancouver supports agriculture awareness by providing funding grants to community organizations to educate the public about local food and agricultural production. Grants are open to non-profit organizations that meet the eligibility criteria

Eligibility: The activity contributes to the following desirable outcomes that support regional policy objectives, where a high score is awarded when the agriculture awareness activity aligns with two or more of the regional policy objectives. 1. Educates residents about local food production; 2. Enhances food literacy and skills in schools; 3. Communicates how food choices support the local economy; 4. Supports the next generation of food producers; and Involves community gatherings that educate residents about local food.
Level of Study: Postgraduate
Type: Grant
Value: The grant request is in the range of US$500 to US$6,000. A higher score will be awarded if the Metro Vancouver cash contribution is greater than 20% of the total cash budget, so that new or smaller projects that may have a greater financial need are prioritized
Frequency: Annual
Country of Study: Any country
No. of awards offered: 12
Closing Date: 2 March
Funding: Private
No. of awards given last year: 12
No. of applicants last year: 113
Additional Information: www.metrovancouver.org/services/regional-planning/agriculture/awareness-grants/Pages/default.aspx

For further information contact:

GrantsAlert, P.O. Box 706, Newton, Catawba, NC 28658, United States of America.

Email: maitca@maine.gov

Henry A Wallace Award

Purpose: Presented to the author of the best book on any aspect of agricultural history outside the United States. The book must be based on substantial primary research and should represent new scholarly interpretation or reinterpretation of agricultural history scholarship
Level of Study: Unrestricted
Type: Award
Value: US$500
Frequency: Annual
Country of Study: Any country
Application Procedure: Applicants must send four copies of the book to the editor. Books may be nominated by their authors, the publisher, a member of the award committee, or a member of the society
Closing Date: 31 December
No. of awards given last year: 1

Additional Information: Available upon request to the Society www.metrovancouver.org/services/regional-planning/agriculture/awareness-grants/Pages/default.aspx

For further information contact:

Email: mikegaul@iastate.edu

Air Force Office of Scientific Research (AFOSR)

AFOSR/PIE, 4015 Wilson Boulevard Room 713, Arlington, VA 22203-1954, United States of America.

Tel: (1) 703 696 7319
Email: info@afosr.af.mil
Website: www.afosr.af.mil
Contact: Dr Koto White, Chief External Programmes & Resources Interface

The Air Force Office of Scientific Research's (AFOSR) mission is to sponsor and sustain basic research, transfer and transition research results and support Air Force goals of control and maximum utilisation of air and space.

United States Air Force Academy/National Research Council Summer Faculty Research Program (SFFP)

Purpose: To provide research opportunities for qualified faculty members of United States colleges and universities at Air Force research facilities within the continental United States
Eligibility: 1. Applicants to the U.S. Air Force Research Lab Summer Faculty Fellowship Program must be citizens of the United States. Dual U.S. Citizens may apply with an exception to those applying to Directed Energy (RD) and Space Vehicles (RV) Directorate programs. Those applying to RD and RV must be U.S. Citizens only. 2. Applicants must currently hold a full-time appointment at a U.S. accredited baccalaureate-granting college, university, or technical institution. 3. Applicants must have a Ph.D in science, mathematics, or Air Force-relevant engineering disciplines. 4. Applicants' research interests must be in line with the interests and needs of the various Air Force Research Facilities. These include the nine Air Force Research Laboratory Directorates, Air Force Test Center, the United States Air Force Academy, and the Air Force Institute of Technology. Click here to learn more about the areas of interest to the

various Air Force Research Facilities as well as to learn more about the areas of interest to the various Air Force Research Facilities and for contact information for each facility. 4. Selected fellows are expected to conduct research at an Air Force Research Laboratory Directorate, Air Force Test Center, the U.S. Air Force Academy, or the Air Force Institute of Technology, not at their home institution or any other site. 6. All appointments are subject to the participant's successful security investigation and approved access to unclassified government information systems.
Level of Study: Professional development
Value: Assistant professors receive US$1,250, associate professors receive US$1,450, and full professors receive US$1,650 per week
Length of Study: 8–12 weeks
Frequency: Annual
Study Establishment: An Air Force facility
Country of Study: United States of America
Application Procedure: Applicants must contact the National Research Council on (1) 202 334 2760
Closing Date: 1 November
Funding: Government
Additional Information: Please see the website www.national-academies.org/rap

Air-Conditioning, Heating, and Refrigeration Institute

Air-Conditioning, Heating, and Refrigeration Institute MSc Scholarship

Purpose: The AHRI MSc Scholarship, sponsored by University College London (UCL), is a singular award for the United Kingdom academic year. The scholarship is administered via AHRI and is for applicants whose academic background and interests are aligned with the programmes of research at AHRI
Eligibility: 1. Must be permanently based in South Africa at the time of application. 2. Must hold a valid passport at the time of application. 3. Must have an Honours degree equivalent to a Bachelor (Honours) degree with Second Class Division 1 Honours or 70% in an appropriate subject. 4. The successful applicant must be in London to start their chosen course in September
Level of Study: Postdoctorate
Type: Scholarship
Frequency: Annual
Country of Study: Any country
Closing Date: 29 March
Funding: Foundation

For further information contact:

Nelson R. Mandela School of Medicine, 3rd Floor, K-RITH Tower Building, 719 Umbilo Road, Durban 4001, South Africa.

Tel: (27) 31 260 4991
Email: info@ahri.org

Alberta Innovates Health Solutions

Suite 1500, Bell Tower, 10104-103 Avenue, Edmonton, AB T5J 4A7, Canada.

Tel: (1) 780 423 5727
Email: pamela.valentine@albertainnovates.ca
Website: www.albertainnovates.ca
Contact: Dr Pamela Valentine, Interim Vice-President

Alberta Innovates Health Solutions supports a community of researchers who generate knowledge that improves the health and quality of life of Albertans and people throughout the world. The long-term commitment is to fund basic patient and health research based on international standards of excellence and carried out by new and established investigators and researchers in training.

Alberta Heritage Foundation for Medical Research Part-Time Studentship

Purpose: To enable full-time degree students to continue research training on a part-time basis
Eligibility: Candidates must normally have been accepted into, or be currently engaged in, a full-time graduate program at an Alberta-based university in a health-related discipline leading to a Master's or doctoral degree
Level of Study: Doctorate, Graduate
Type: Studentship
Value: Pro-rated on full-time studentship stipend and dependent on the amount of time spent in research
Length of Study: 3 years, maximum
Frequency: Annual
Study Establishment: A university in Alberta
Country of Study: Canada
Application Procedure: Applicants must complete an application form
No. of awards offered: 1
Closing Date: 1 October

Funding: Government
No. of awards given last year: 1
No. of applicants last year: 1

For further information contact:

Email: grants.health@albertainnovates.ca

Alberta Innovates - Health Solutions Postgraduate Fellowships

Purpose: To provide opportunities for individuals to pursue postgraduate health-related research at an Alberta University
Eligibility: Open to candidates with a PhD, MD, DDS, DVM or DPharm degree. Normally, support will not be provided beyond 5 years after receipt of the PhD degree, or beyond 8 years after receipt of the MD, DDS, DVM or DPharm degrees
Level of Study: Postdoctorate
Type: Fellowship
Value: C$50,000 per year research training stipend and a career development allowance (C$5,000 annually) for a maximum of 36 months.
Length of Study: 1 year, with a possibility of renewal for a maximum of 3 years of support
Frequency: Annual
Study Establishment: Usually at a university in Alberta
Country of Study: Canada
Application Procedure: Applicants must complete an application form. Candidates must submit, in full, the original application to the AIHS office by the deadline
No. of awards offered: 156
Closing Date: 1 October
Funding: Government
No. of awards given last year: 39
No. of applicants last year: 156
Additional Information: Please contact at grants.health@albertainnovates.ca albertainnovates.ca/programs/postgraduate-fellowships-in-health-innovation/

For further information contact:

Email: Kathy.Morrison@albertainnovates.ca

Graduate Studentships

Purpose: To provide opportunities for support for individuals undertaking health-related research areas in pursuit of a Master's or PhD.
Eligibility: Applicants must be currently enrolled in a graduate program at an Alberta University undertaking

health-related research training leading to thesis-based graduate degree

Level of Study: Doctorate, Graduate

Type: Studentship

Value: C$30,000 stipend and a research and career development allowance of C$2,000 per year for up to 4 years (maximum of 2 years support towards a Master)

Length of Study: 1 year with the possibility of renewal for a maximum of 5 years of support; 2 years maximum at the masters level

Frequency: Annual

Study Establishment: A university in Alberta

Country of Study: Canada

Application Procedure: Candidates must submit, in full, the original application to the AIHS offices by the deadlines

No. of awards offered: 200

Closing Date: 1 April

Funding: Government

No. of awards given last year: 49

No. of applicants last year: 200

Additional Information: Please contact at grants.health@albertainnovates.ca www.trophoblast.cam.ac.uk/opportunities/studentships

For further information contact:

Email: health@albertainnovates.ca

Alex's Lemonade Stand Foundation

Alex's Lemonade Stand Foundation for Childhood Cancer, 333 E. Lancaster Ave, #414, Wynnewood, PA 19096, United States of America.

Tel: (1) 866 333 1213

Website: www.alexslemonade.org

POST Program Grants

Subjects: Pediatric Oncology

Purpose: The Pediatric Oncology Student Training (POST) Program is designed for undergraduate, graduate and medical students who have an interest in pediatric oncology research and would like to experience the field first hand. Students train with a pediatric oncology research mentor. Students may join a research project underway in a mentor's lab or begin an original investigation with the mentor.

Eligibility: The following eligibility criteria apply: 1. Mentors must be ALSF grantees (past or present, including those who have previously mentored POST students), Advisory Board, or Review Board members. 2. Mentors must be active in the field of pediatric oncology research. 3. The Mentor's Institution must be in the U.S. or Canada. The Mentor/Mentee do not need to be U.S.citizens. 4. Mentor/Student pairs must be identified prior to submitting an application. 5. Mentor must commit to training the student by submitting a commitment letter with the application, and during the Program period, plan training activities and provide guidance. 6. Student must currently be enrolled in an undergraduate, graduate, or medical degree-granting program. 7. Student must be able to dedicate at least eight full consecutive weeks to the program, typically between May 1 and August 31. The dates may vary depending on the student's scheduled school break.

Type: Grant

Value: Max US$5,000

Country of Study: Any country

Application Procedure: All sections described below should be combined into one PDF (max 20 MB) and uploaded to the ALSF online application form (see Application Submission Instructions www.alexslemonade.org/sites/default/files/images/alsf1/2022_post_program_guidelines_final.pdf#page=6&zoom=100,68,509).

No. of awards offered: Approximately 1/3

Closing Date: 21 February

Additional Information: www.alexslemonade.org/grants/program-areas/early-career-research-programs

For further information contact:

Tel: (1) 267 228 4530

Email: G.Dyer@AlexsLemonade.org

RUNX1 Early Career Investigator Grants

Subjects: Leukemia

Purpose: The RUNX1 Early Career Investigator grant is a 3-year award designed to fund research in strategies leading to the development of therapies to prevent the transition from pre-leukemia to leukemia for patients with RUNX1-FPD. Collaboration and data sharing are a priority for this research program. The RUNX1 Research Program and ALSF host an annual scientific meeting that brings together grant recipients and other scientists. Grant recipients are expected to present their progress as part of the annual review.

Eligibility: Applicants must have an M.D., PhD or dual M.D., PhD (D.O., MBBS or equivalent) and be within 5 years of their first faculty appointment as an Assistant Professor or equivalent. Associate and Full Professors are ineligible. If still at the Instructor level, the applicant must have a commitment from the Department Chief at the time of grant submission for an Assistant Professor position within one year of receiving the award. A minimum of 75% of the applicant's time during the award period must be allocated as protected time for all research activities. This percentage of time includes both activities on this grant and the applicant's other research responsibilities. Applicants may have research grants from other funding sources during the award period, but there must be clear documentation of mechanisms to avoid scientific and budgetary overlap. Applicants must have research experience working in and a deep understanding of normal or malignant hematopoiesis and/or immunology. Applicant institutions may be based in the U.S. or outside of the U.S. Applicants need not be United States citizens. Funds must be granted to non-profit institutions or organizations. One resubmission of a previously unfunded application is allowed. Use the Resubmission section of the application to respond to the prior RRP/ALSF critique of the proposal. The response will be scored in the review process in addition to the criteria used for new applications. Resubmissions compete with new applicants for funding.

Type: Grant
Value: US$180,000 over 3 years (maximum US$60,000 per year may be requested).
Length of Study: 3 years
Country of Study: Any country
Application Procedure: See website for further details.
Closing Date: 20 December
Additional Information: www.alexslemonade.org/grants/program-areas/early-career-research-programs

For further information contact:

Email: Grants@AlexsLemonade.org

Alfred L and Constance C Wolf Aviation Fund

The Alfred L. & Constance C. Wolf Aviation Fund, 2060 State Highway 595, Gavilan Community, Lindrith, NM 87029, United States of America.

Tel: (1) 505 362 8232
Email: mail@wolf-aviation.org
Website: www.wolf-aviation.org

The Wolf Aviation Fund was established in the wills of Alfred L. and Constance C. Wolf. The Wolf Foundation hopes to help people and projects that benefit general aviation by identifying talented, worthy individuals - often working in collaboration with others - and worthwhile projects and providing them support.

Wolf Aviation Fund Grants Program

Purpose: To promote and support the advancement of personal air transportation by seeking and funding the most promising individuals and worthy projects which advance the field of general aviation
Level of Study: Postgraduate
Type: Grant
Value: Grants range in size from a few hundred dollars to a maximum of five thousand dollars
Frequency: Annual
Country of Study: Any country
Application Procedure: For more details please visit the website
Closing Date: 15 December
Additional Information: In preparing proposals, the foundation strongly encourages applicants to browse the Resources section and learn how to find out what kinds of grants might be available from any source and to learn in general how to properly prepare grant requests www.alexslemonade.org/grants/program-areas/early-career-research-programs

Alfred Toepfer Foundation

Georgsplatz 10, D-20099 Hamburg, Germany.

Tel: (49) 4033 402 10
Email: meyer@toepfer-stiftung.de
Website: www.toepfer-fvs.de
Contact: Assistant to the CEO

Alfred Toepfer Natural Heritage Scholarships

Purpose: To provide scholarships for doctoral candidates from the humanities and the social sciences who are in the final stages of research on European issues
Eligibility: The Alfred Toepfer Natural Heritage Scholarship is a great opportunity for young professionals who have chosen to develop a career to our natural and cultural heritage. The winners of the Scholarship will have the chance to improve their skills and learn from other professionals, by carrying out study visits in European Protected Areas. The call is open to all young professionals working in topics related to Protected Areas in Europe. Conditions to apply 1. candidates must be under 35 2. have a European nationality 3. be employed by a Protected Area or nature conservation organisation or be employed by an organisation that develops its work in a Protected Area Applications for study visits to prepare master or doctoral thesis will not be considered.

Level of Study: Doctorate
Type: Scholarship
Value: €3,000
Length of Study: Up to 1 year
Frequency: Annual
Country of Study: Germany
Application Procedure: Applications have to be submitted online. 1. Online application form– that includes your Curriculum vitae, your motivation letter, the proposed programme of your study visit, and contact details of protected areas you want to visit. 2. Proof of employment
Closing Date: 3 May
Contributor: Alfred Toepfer Foundation
Additional Information: Available on www.toepfer-fvs.de

For further information contact:

Email: ericke@toepfer-fvs.de

Max Brauer Award

Purpose: To honour personalities and institutions in the City of Hamburg for their services to the city's cultural, scientific, or intellectual life and for extraordinary impulses for the preservation of its architecture and architectural monuments, its city and landscape and renewal of the city, as well as its tradition and its customs
Type: Award
Value: €20,000
Frequency: Annual
Country of Study: Any country
Contributor: Alfred Toepfer Foundation in association with European school
Additional Information: The selection of the Preisträgerin and/or the winner is decided by the Kuratorium Max Brauer award www.youthop.com/scholarships/alfred-toepfer-natural-heritage-scholarships-2019

For further information contact:

Tel: (49) 4033 402 16
Email: luthe@toepfer-fvs.de

Alzheimer's Association

225 N. Michigan Ave. Floor 17, Chicago, IL 60601, United States of America.

Website: www.alz.org

Alzheimer's Association Clinician Scientist Fellowship (AACSF) Program

Subjects: Clinical fields that include patient contact (e.g., neurology, psychiatry, geriatrics, psychology)
Purpose: The Alzheimer's Association recognizes the need to support the training of clinician scientists in Alzheimer's and all other dementia. For the purpose of this program, a clinician scientist is defined as an individual already trained, licensed and practicing in a clinical field that includes patient contact (e.g., neurology, psychiatry, geriatrics, psychology) or patient-related diagnostic studies (e.g., neuropathology and radiology). Applicants who hold an M.D. or D.O. degree or applicants with a PhD who have licensure for clinical practice are eligible.
Eligibility: Applicants must be clinicians (postdoctoral fellows through assistant professors; or equivalent positions) interested in an academic career who have 1. Full-time positions at an recognized non-academic institution and 2. Less than 10 years of research experience after receipt of their terminal degree and 3. Licensure for clinical practice.
Level of Study: Postdoctorate
Type: Fellowship
Value: Each AACSF award is limited to US$175,000. A total of US$155,000 will be awarded for costs related to the proposed research for up to three years (minimum two years) for direct and indirect costs. Requests in any given year may not exceed US$60,000 (direct and indirect costs). Indirect costs are capped at 10% (rent for laboratory/office space is expected to be covered by indirect costs paid to the institution). This is inclusive of indirect costs for the implementing institution as well as any to subcontracts. The Principal Investigator must commit up to an average of two protected days per week (40%) effort toward their research efforts during each funding year. The remaining funds, US$10,000 to the applicant and US$10,000 to the primary mentor, will be awarded upon successful completion of the three years (minimum two years). These additional funds are to be applied to sustaining ongoing research in the Alzheimer's field and will be awarded through the applicant's and mentor's institutions. Successful completion of the program includes "but is not limited to" reaching all of the demonstrable benchmarks listed. A total of US$5,000 over a three-year period (two-year minimum) may be requested for travel purposes and is not to exceed US$3,000 in one given year. A portion must be allocated to support registration and travel to the annual Alzheimer's Association International Conference® (AAIC®), as AAIC attendance is a condition of the award. If you request the full US$5,000 for two years of travel and are requesting a three-year award, you will not be able to request travel funds for one of those years.
Length of Study: Two to three years
Country of Study: Any country

Application Procedure: See website for further details.
Closing Date: 19 November
Funding: Private
Additional Information: See Website: www.alz.org/research/for_researchers/grants/types-of-grants/aacf

For further information contact:

Email: grantsapp@alz.org

Alzheimer's Association Clinician Scientist Fellowship to Promote Diversity (AACSF-D)

Subjects: Alzheimer's and all dementia research
Purpose: The Alzheimer's Association Clinician Scientist Fellowship to Promote Diversity is up to three years (minimum two years) and is intended to support exceptional clinician scientists who are currently underrepresented at academic institutions in clinical research training in Alzheimer's and all dementias. Applicants who hold an M.D. or D.O. degree or applicants with a PhD who have licensure for clinical practice are eligible.
Eligibility: Applicants must be clinicians (postdoctoral fellows through assistant professors; or equivalent positions) interested in an academic career who have A 1. Full-time positions at an recognized non- academic institution and 2. Less than 10 years of research experience after receipt of their terminal degree and 3. Licensure for clinical practice.
Level of Study: Postdoctorate
Type: Fellowship
Value: Each Alzheimer's Association Clinician Scientist Fellowship to Promote Diversity is limited to US$175,000. A total of US$155,000 will be awarded for costs related to the proposed research for up to three years (minimum two years) for direct and indirect costs. Requests in any given year may not exceed US$60,000 (direct and indirect costs). Indirect costs are capped at 10% (rent for laboratory/office space is expected to be covered by indirect costs paid to the institution). This is inclusive of indirect costs for the implementing institution as well as any to subcontracts. The Principal Investigator (PI) must commit up to an average of two protected days per week (40%) effort toward their research efforts during each funding year. The remaining funds, US$10,000 to the applicant and US$10,000 to the primary mentor, will be awarded upon successful completion of the three-year program (minimum two years). These additional funds are to be applied to sustaining ongoing research in the Alzheimer's field and will be awarded through the applicant's and mentor's institutions. Successful completion of the program includes, but is not limited to, reaching all of the demonstrable benchmarks listed. A total of US$5,000 over a three-year period (minimum two years) may be requested for travel purposes and is not to exceed US$3,000 in any given year. A portion must be allocated to support registration and travel to the annual Alzheimer's Association International Conference® (AAIC®), as AAIC attendance is a condition of the award.
Length of Study: Three years
Country of Study: Any country
Application Procedure: See website for further details.
Closing Date: 19 November
Funding: Private
Additional Information: See Website: www.alz.org/research/for_researchers/grants/types-of-grants/alzheimer_s_association_clinician_scientist_fellow

For further information contact:

Email: grantsapp@alz.org

Alzheimer's Association Research Fellowship (AARF)

Purpose: The Alzheimer's Association Research Fellowship award is intended to support exceptional researchers who are engaged in their post-graduate work
Eligibility: Applications will be accepted from postdoctoral fellows (or an equivalent level position) with full-time positions at their respective academic institution and less than 10 years of research experience after receipt of their terminal degree.
Level of Study: Postdoctorate
Type: Fellowship
Value: Each Fellowship award is limited to US$175,000
Length of Study: Up to three years
Country of Study: Any country
Closing Date: 19 November
Additional Information: For any inquiries or additional information, please contact a member of the Alzheimer's Association Grants staff at grantsapp@alz.org.

For further information contact:

Email: grantsapp@alz.org

Alzheimer's Association Research Fellowship to Promote Diversity (AARF-D)

Subjects: Alzheimer's and all dementia research
Purpose: The Alzheimer's Association Research Fellowship to Promote Diversity (AARF-D) award is intended to support exceptional scientists from underrepresented groups who are working in Alzheimer's or all other dementias research and who are engaged in their post-graduate work (i.e. postdoctoral

fellows) and before their first independent faculty positions (i.e. Assistant Professor) and working in diverse areas of research, including basic, translational, clinical, functional and social-behavioral research. Investigators doing clinically-focused research without clinical practice are encouraged to apply to this AARF-D program.

Eligibility: Applications will be accepted from postdoctoral fellows (or an equivalent level position) with full-time positions at their respective academic institution and less than 10 years of research experience after receipt of their terminal degree.

Level of Study: Postdoctorate

Type: Fellowship

Value: Each AARF-D award is limited to US$175,000

Length of Study: Three years

Country of Study: Any country

Application Procedure: See website for further details.

Closing Date: 19 November

Funding: Private

Additional Information: For any inquires or additional information, please contact a member of the Alzheimer's Association Grants staff at grantsapp@alz.org. www.alz.org/research/for_researchers/grants/types-of-grants/alzheimers_association_research_fellowship_to_pro

For further information contact:

Email: grantsapp@alz.org

Alzheimer's Association Research Grant (AARG)

Subjects: Alzheimer's and all dementia research

Purpose: The Alzheimer's Association Research Grant (AARG) award aims to fund early-career investigators who are less than 15 years past their doctoral degree or post-residency (M.D. or D.O.). The purpose of this program is to provide newly independent investigators with funding that will allow them to develop preliminary or pilot data, to test procedures and to develop hypotheses. The intent is to support early-career development that will lay the groundwork for future research grant applications to federal or other funding entities, like the National Institutes of Health, including future proposals to the Alzheimer's Association.

Eligibility: Applicants must be an Assistant Professors or above at their respective academic institution and less than 15 years past their doctoral degree or post-residency (M.D. or D.O.). 1. The 15-year period applies to the date of submission of the grant application. Adjustments for career interruptions can be made for events such as family leave, military service, and major illness or injury. It is the responsibility of the applicant to point out and document such interruptions within their application. 2. Applications will be accepted from postdoctoral fellows and other junior faculty members (for example

Instructor, Research Associate Scientist, Lecturer etc.) who can provide a letter of employment verification indicating they will have a fulltime faculty position of an Assistant Professor or above prior to notification of funding (August 31, 2021) should the proposal be in funding range and funded. 1. The letter of employment must be uploaded with the application and dated within three months from application submission date, printed on the hiring institution letterhead, signed by an authorized institutional official (i.e. Grants and Contracts officer) and must indicate that the position will be activated by the grant award date. If the anticipated position is not activated by the award date for any reason, any offer of funding will be withdrawn. There will be no exceptions. 2. In the event your application is funded, you will be required to provide an official letter on organizational letterhead, signed by an institutional signing official, stating you have a full-time faculty position of an Assistant Professor and above. 3. If the applicant's institution does not have an Assistant Professor position, the letter of employment should include sufficient information to allow the Alzheimer's Association staff to evaluate the eligibility of the applicant.

Level of Study: Doctorate, Masters Degree

Type: Research grant

Value: Each AARG total award is limited to US$150,000 (direct and indirect costs) for up to three years (minimum two years). Requests in any given year may not exceed US$60,000 (direct and indirect costs). Indirect costs are capped at 10% (rent for laboratory/office space is expected to be covered by indirect costs paid to the institution). This is inclusive of indirect costs for the implementing institution as well as any to subcontracts.

Length of Study: Two to three years

Country of Study: Any country

Application Procedure: See website for further details.

Closing Date: 19 November

Funding: Private

Additional Information: For any inquires or additional information, please contact a member of the Alzheimer's Association Grants staff at grantsapp@alz.org. www.alz.org/research/for_researchers/grants/types-of-grants/aarg

For further information contact:

Email: grantsapp@alz.org

Alzheimer's Association Research Grant - New to the Field (AARG-NTF)

Subjects: Alzheimer's and all dementia research

Purpose: The Alzheimer's Association Research Grant – New to the Field award aims to fund investigators who are new to Alzheimer's and all other dementia field of research.

The purpose of this program is to provide independent investigators with unique expertise and apply their knowledge to Alzheimer's and all dementias. This program aims to provide these investigators with funding to establish a research path in Alzheimer's and all dementias, to develop preliminary or pilot data, to test procedures and to develop hypotheses. Individuals who are new to the field of neuroscience or neurodegeneration (Alzheimer's, Parkinson's, Lewy body dementia, etc.) will be considered for this program. The intent is to support research that will lay the groundwork for future research grant applications to federal or other funding entities, like the National Institutes of Health, including future proposals to the Alzheimer's Association. The Alzheimer's Association recognizes the need to increase the number of scientists from underrepresented groups in the research enterprise.

Eligibility: Applicants must be an Assistant Professors or above at their respective academic institution and who are new to the field of neuroscience or neurodegeneration (Alzheimer's, Parkinson's, Lewy body dementia, etc.). If the applicant's institution does not have an Assistant Professor position, the letter of employment should include sufficient information to allow the Alzheimer's Association staff to evaluate the eligibility of the applicant. Applicants must contact the Alzheimer's Association at grantsapp@alz.org to receive an exception prior to submitting an LOI. Please include your full CV, which must include full publication and funding record (biosketches are not accepted).

Level of Study: Postdoctorate
Type: Research grant
Value: Each AARG-NTF award total is limited to US$150,000 (direct and indirect costs) for up to three years (minimum two years = US$120,000). Requests may not exceed US$60,000 in any given year (direct and indirect costs). Indirect costs are capped at 10% of total direct costs and is inclusive of indirect costs for the implementing institution as well as to any subcontracts.
Length of Study: Two to three years
Country of Study: Any country
Application Procedure: See website for further details.
Closing Date: 19 November
Funding: Private
Additional Information: See website: www.alz.org/research/for_researchers/grants/types-of-grants/aarg-ntf

For further information contact:

Email: grantsapp@alz.org

Alzheimer's Association Research Grant to Promote Diversity (AARG-D)

Subjects: Alzheimer's and all dementia research

Purpose: The Alzheimer's Association Research Grant to Promote Diversity award is up to three years (minimum two years) to increase the number of scientists from underrepresented groups at academic institutions in Alzheimer's or all other dementias research. The objective of this award is to increase the number of highly trained investigators from diverse backgrounds whose basic, clinical and social/behavioral research interests are grounded in the advanced methods and experimental approaches needed to solve problems related to Alzheimer's and all dementias in general and in health disparities populations. The Alzheimer's Association recognizes the need to increase the number of scientists from underrepresented groups participating in biomedical and behavioral research. The Association anticipates that by providing these research opportunities, the number of scientists from underrepresented groups entering and remaining in biomedical research careers in Alzheimer's and all other dementia will increase.

Eligibility: Applicants must be an Assistant Professors or above at their respective academic institution and less than 15 years past their doctoral degree or post-residency (M.D. or D.O.). 1. The 15-year period applies to the date of submission of the grant application. Adjustments for career interruptions can be made for events such as family leave, military service, and major illness or injury. It is the responsibility of the applicant to point out and document such interruptions within their application. 2. Applications will be accepted from postdoctoral fellows and other junior faculty members (for example Instructor, Research Associate Scientist, Lecturer etc.) who can provide a letter of employment verification indicating they will have a full-time faculty position of an Assistant Professor or above prior to notification of funding (August 31, 2021) should the proposal be in funding range and funded. 1. The letter of employment must be uploaded with the application and dated within three months from application submission date, printed on the hiring institution letterhead, signed by an authorized institutional official (i.e. Grants and Contracts officer) and must indicate that the position will be activated by the grant award date. If the anticipated position is not activated by the award date for any reason, any offer of funding will be withdrawn. There will be no exceptions. 2. In the event your application is funded, you will be required to provide an official letter on organizational letterhead, signed by an institutional signing official, stating you have a full-time faculty position of an Assistant Professor and above. 3. If the applicant's institution does not have an Assistant Professor position, the letter of employment should include sufficient information to allow the Alzheimer's Association staff to evaluate the eligibility of the applicant.

Level of Study: Postdoctorate
Type: Research grant
Value: Each AARG-D award total is limited to US$150,000 (direct and indirect costs) for up to three years (minimum two

years = US$120,000). Requests may not exceed US$60,000 in any given year (direct and indirect costs). Indirect costs are capped at 10% of total direct costs and is inclusive of indirect costs for the implementing institution as well as to any subcontracts.

Length of Study: Two to three years
Country of Study: Any country
Application Procedure: See website for further details.
Closing Date: 19 November
Funding: Private

For further information contact:

Email: grantsapp@alz.org

Alzheimer's Association Research Grant to Promote Diversity - New to the Field (AARG-D-NTF)

Subjects: Alzheimer's and all dementia research
Purpose: The Alzheimer's Association Research Grant to Promote Diversity- New to the Field award is up to three years (minimum two years) to increase the number of scientists from underrepresented groups at academic institutions in Alzheimer's and all other dementia research. The AARG-D-NTF aims to fund investigators that are new to Alzheimer's and all dementia field of research. Individuals who are new to the field of neuroscience or neurodegeneration (Alzheimer's, Parkinson's, Lewy body dementia, etc.) will be considered for this program. The goal of the New to the Field program is to provide an opportunity for investigators with expertise outside neurodegenerative research to apply their expertise to advance and accelerate Alzheimer's and all other dementia research. Competitive applications to this program emphasize how the specific expertise/approach will advance research
Eligibility: Applicants must be an Assistant Professors or above at their respective academic institution and who are new to the field of neuroscience or neurodegeneration (Alzheimer's, Parkinson's, Lewy body dementia, etc.). 1. If the applicant's institution does not have an Assistant Professor position, the letter of employment should include sufficient information to allow the Alzheimer's Association staff to evaluate the eligibility of the applicant. 2. Applicants must contact the Alzheimer's Association at grantsapp@alz.org to receive an exception prior to submitting an LOI. Please include your full CV, which must include full publication and funding record (biosketches are not accepted).
Level of Study: Postdoctorate
Type: Research grant
Value: Each AARG-D-NTF award total is limited to US$150,000 (direct and indirect costs) for up to three years (minimum two years = US$120,000). Requests may not

exceed US$60,000 in any given year (direct and indirect costs). Indirect costs are capped at 10% of total direct costs and is inclusive of indirect costs for the implementing institution as well as to any subcontracts.
Length of Study: Two to three years
Country of Study: Any country
Application Procedure: See website for further details.
Closing Date: 19 November
Funding: Private

For further information contact:

Email: grantsapp@alz.org

New Connections: Increasing Diversity

Subjects: Alzheimer's Research
Purpose: The fellowship is intended to support exceptional researchers who are engaged in their post-graduate work (i.e. postdoctoral fellows) and before they have their first independent faculty positions (i.e. Assistant Professor) and working in diverse areas of research, including basic, translational, clinical, functional and social-behavioral research.
Eligibility: Individuals applying to the AARF program will be accepted from postdoctoral fellows with full-time positions at their respective institution who have less than 10 years of research experience after receipt of their terminal degree. Individuals who have a position of an Assistant Professorship or above are not eligible. Applications from currently funded investigators who are delinquent in submitting required reports and other deliverables on active grants. Investigators that have previous Alzheimer's Association awards closed as 'Incomplete' are not eligible to apply without exception. This policy will be strictly adhered to with no exceptions.
Type: Fellowship
Value: Max. US$175,000. A total of US$155,000 will be awarded for costs related to the proposed research for up to three years (minimum two years) for direct and indirect costs. Requests in any given year may not exceed US$60,000 (direct and indirect costs). Indirect costs are capped at 10% (rent for laboratory/office space is expected to be covered by indirect costs paid to the institution). This is inclusive of indirect costs for the implementing institution as well as any to subcontracts. The Principal Investigator must commit to a 50% effort toward the proposed project each funding year. The remaining funds, US$10,000 to the applicant and US$10,000 to the primary mentor, will be awarded upon successful completion of the three years (minimum two years). These additional funds are to be applied to sustaining ongoing research in the Alzheimer's field and will be awarded through the applicant's and mentor's institutions. Successful completion of the program includes, but is not limited to, reaching all of the

demonstrable benchmarks listed. A total of US$5,000 over a three-year period may be requested for travel purposes and is not to exceed US$3,000 in any given year. A portion must be allocated to support registration and travel to the annual Alzheimer's Association International Conference® (AAIC®), as AAIC attendance is a condition of the award. If you request the full US$5,000 for two years of travel and are requesting a three-year award, you will not be able to request travel funds for one of those years.

Length of Study: Two to three years
Country of Study: Any country
Application Procedure: See website for further details.
Closing Date: 19 November
Additional Information: For individuals who are at non-academic institutions, please contact the Alzheimer's Association at grantsapp@alz.org, to verify your eligibility. www.alz.org/research/for_researchers/grants/types-of-grants

Part the Cloud Translational (PTC) Research for Alzheimer's Disease Program

Purpose: This new grant mechanism aims to fill the gap in Alzheimer's disease drug development by providing support for early phase studies of potential Alzheimer's therapeutics; this can include validation of biological markers of disease progression in the context of evaluating a potential therapy.
Eligibility: Both non-profit and small for-profit agencies are eligible. Open to International Applicants. Small for-profit agencies must submit documentation of net assets and annual earnings during the letter of intent process as a part of the review process. Not-for-profit organizations must submit documentation verifying status during the letter of intent process.
Level of Study: Research
Type: Research
Value: US$750,000
Length of Study: two or three years
Frequency: Annual
Country of Study: Any country
Application Procedure: The full grant application consists of the following: 1. Problem Statement – 1 page. 2. Work Plan – 5 pages. 3. Available Resources & Budget Justification – 2 pages. 4. Plan for Data Sharing -1 page. 5. Recruitment Plan - 1 page, If applicable. 6. Reference and Citations – 1 page. 7. Resubmissions – FOR resubmissions only – 1 page. 8. Therapeutic Rationale – 1 page. 9. Gannt Chart – 1 page (Optional). 10. Biosketch (PI/Co-PI) – 5 pages max for each.; Applications will be reviewed with special attention to: 1. Significance of the question being studied & rationale of the target being pursued. 2. Applicant information. 3. Quality of the proposed trial design. 4. Quality and adequacy of available resources and budget. 5. Impact-Risk.
Closing Date: 15 November

Additional Information: Applications will be accepted from organizations conducting studies around the world. Researchers with full-time staff or faculty appointments are encouraged to apply. Applications from post- doctoral candidates will not be accepted. For questions as to whether an investigator or organization is eligible, please contact the Alzheimer's Association at grantsapp@alz.org.

For further information contact:

Email: grantsapp@alz.org

The Zenith Fellows Award Program (Zenith)

Purpose: The Alzheimer's Association was founded in 1980 by a small group of family members caring for loved ones with Alzheimer's disease. These individuals united in disappointment with the quality of information available to them and in dissatisfaction with the lack of medical and social awareness of this devastating condition.
Eligibility: Only established independent investigators are eligible as evidenced by: 1. Academic appointment. 2. Major, peer-reviewed, external multi-year grant support on which the applicant is the principal investigator (PI). 3. Independent laboratory operation. 4. Quality and independence of publication record.; Only applicants who have already contributed significantly to the field of Alzheimer's and all other dementia research and/or have the clear likelihood of making significant contributions will be seriously considered. The Alzheimer's Association recognizes the need to increase the number of scientists from underrepresented groups in the research enterprise. Researchers from these groups are encouraged to apply. The Alzheimer's Association recognizes the need to increase the number of scientists from underrepresented groups in the research enterprise, including women scientists. Researchers from these groups are encouraged to apply. In general, scientists and clinicians from public, private, domestic and foreign research laboratories, medical centers, hospitals and universities are eligible to apply. State and federal government-appropriated laboratories in the U.S. and abroad and for-profit organizations are prohibited from serving as the applicant institution. However, state and federal government scientists can participate as collaborating scientists with research teams from other eligible applicant institutions.
Level of Study: Doctorate, Masters Degree
Type: Award
Value: Each award is limited to US$450,000 total funding
Length of Study: three years
Frequency: Annual
Country of Study: Any country

Application Procedure: See Website: www.alz.org/research/
for_researchers/grants/types-of-grants/the_zenith_fellows_
award_program_(zenith)
Closing Date: 25 March

For further information contact:

Email: grantsapp@alz.org.

Alzheimer's Australia

1 Frewin Place, Scullin, ACT 2614, Australia.

Tel: (61) 2 6254 4233
Email: secretariat@alzheimers.org.au
Website: www.fightdementia.org.au
Contact: Dr Mary Gray, Manager AADRF

Alzheimer's Australia Dementia Research Foundation (AADRF) was established as the research arm of Alzheimer's Australia to provide funds and disseminate into Alzheimer's disease and other forms of dementia. AADRF provides annual research grants and a key priority is to support emerging researchers and to encourage the next generation of dementia researchers.

Association of American Railroads Janssen Cilag Dementia Research Grant

Purpose: To support research into Alzheimer's disease and other types of dementia
Eligibility: Open to citizens of Australia or permanent residents
Level of Study: Postgraduate, Research
Type: Scholarship
Value: Maximum AU$20,000
Length of Study: 1 year
Frequency: Annual
Country of Study: Australia
Application Procedure: Check website for further details
Closing Date: 4 June
Contributor: Janssen Cilag Pty Ltd

For further information contact:

Alzheimer's Australia Research Ltd, PO Box 4019, Scullin, ACT 2614, Australia.

 Email: aar@alzheimers.org.au

Association of American Railroads Rosemary Foundation Travel Project Grant-Dementia Research

Purpose: For undertaking research that is not fully available in Australia and is relevant to the advancement of understanding dementia
Eligibility: Open to citizens of Australia or permanent residents who have a degree in a discipline relevant to the field of dementia and be associated with an institute of higher learning
Level of Study: Postgraduate, Research
Type: Scholarship
Value: AU$10,000
Length of Study: 6 weeks to 3 months
Frequency: Annual
Application Procedure: Check website for further details
Closing Date: 4 June
Additional Information: The applicant must undertake to return to a position in Australia for at least 1 year after the completion of the travel www.alz.org/research/for_researchers/grants/types-of-grants

For further information contact:

Email: aar@alzheimers.org.au

Hunter Postgraduate Scholarship

Purpose: This scholarship is to encourage and support students to pursue postgraduate study at Victoria University of Wellington. The scholarship will be awarded as a fees contribution to the top ranked applicant across all disciplines who applied but does not receive a Victoria Master's by Thesis Scholarship.
Eligibility: All applicants who have applied and submitted an application for the Victoria Master's by Thesis Scholarship will be considered.
Level of Study: Masters Research; Postgraduate
Type: Scholarship
Value: Up to US$5,000 towards fees
Length of Study: 1 year
Frequency: Annual
Application Procedure: Check website for further details. Applications will be open from 1 September
Closing Date: 1 October
Additional Information: www.wgtn.ac.nz/scholarships/current/hunter-postgraduate-scholarship

For further information contact:

Tel: (64) 463 5557
Email: scholarships-office@vuw.ac.nz; pg-research@vuw.ac.nz; summer-research@vuw.ac.nz

Rosemary Foundation Travel Grant

Purpose: To enable an Australian researcher to travel overseas in order to learn new techniques and/or network with international dementia research teams

Eligibility: Open to citizens of Australia or permanent residents and New Zealand citizens residing permanently in Australia

Level of Study: Doctorate, Postdoctorate, Postgraduate, Research

Type: Grant

Value: AU$15,000

Length of Study: 1 month

Country of Study: Any country

Application Procedure: Please check the website for details

No. of awards offered: 5

Closing Date: April

Funding: Foundation

Contributor: The Rosemary Foundation for Memory Support Inc

No. of awards given last year: 1

No. of applicants last year: 5

For further information contact:

Email: Admin@RosaMary.org

Alzheimer's Drug Discovery Foundation (ADDF)

57 W 57th Street, Suit 904, New York, NY 10019, United States of America.

Tel: (1) 212 901 8000
Email: nthakker@alzdiscovery.org
Website: www.alzdiscovery.org
Contact: Mr Niyati Thakker, Grants Associate

The ADDF is an affiliated public charity of the Institute for the Study of Aging (ISOA), a private foundation founded by the Estè Lauder family in 1998.

Alzheimers Drug Discovery Foundation Grants Program

Purpose: This program supports studies advancing lead molecules to clinical candidate selection or building preclinical evidence in relevant animal models for repurposed/repositioned drugs.

Eligibility: Funding is open to researchers and clinicians worldwide

Level of Study: Unrestricted

Type: Grant

Value: US$150,000-US$600,000

Length of Study: one year

Frequency: Dependent on funds available

Study Establishment: A non-profit public foundation

Country of Study: Any country

Application Procedure: Candidates must submit a letter of intent through our online submission system at www.alzdiscovery.org

Funding: Foundation, Government, Individuals, Private

No. of awards given last year: 29

Additional Information: In addition to funding research activities, the foundation sponsors and/or co-sponsors conferences, scientific and medical workshops to advance knowledge on issues related to Alzheimer's disease and cognitive vitality mcgill.ca/research/files/research/listserv_addf_program_to_accelerate_clinical_trials_march2019.docx.pdf

For further information contact:

Katarina Stojkovic, Grants Officer.

Tel: (1) 514 398 5184

America–Israel Cultural Foundation (AICF)

1140 Broadway, Suite #304, New York, NY 10001, United States of America.

Tel: (1) 212 557 1600
Email: info@aicf.co.il
Website: www.aicf.org
Contact: Mr David Homan, Executive Director

The America–Israel Cultural Foundation (AICF) has been promoting and supporting the arts in Israel for over 60 years. Through its Sharett Scholarship Program, the AICF grants hundreds of study scholarships each year to Israeli students of the arts, music, dance, visual arts, film, television and theatre, mainly for studies in Israel. The AICF also provides short-term fellowships to artists and art teachers and financially supports various projects in art schools, workshops, master classes, etc.

AICF Sharett Scholarship Program

Purpose: To respond to Israel's ever-evolving artistic life and the needs of her artists and institutions
Eligibility: Open to Israeli citizens only
Level of Study: Unrestricted
Type: Scholarship
Value: US$750–2,000
Length of Study: Varies
Frequency: Annual
Country of Study: Any country
Application Procedure: Applicants must complete and submit an application form with recommendations and pre-required repertoire. Application forms are available from 1 February of each year
No. of awards offered: 2300
Closing Date: February
Funding: Private
Contributor: America—Israel Cultural Foundation
No. of awards given last year: 1110
No. of applicants last year: 2300
Additional Information: The programme is revised on an annual basis. For more detailed information, please contact the Foundation after 1 February aicf.org/

America-Norway Heritage Fund

Norwegian Information Service in the US, 825 Third Avenue 38th Floor, New York, NY 10022-7584, United States of America.

Tel:　　　(1) 212 421 7333
Email:　　norcons@interport.net
Website:　www.norway.org
Contact:　Grants Management Officer

Norwegian Emigration Fund

Purpose: To award scholarships to Americans for advanced or specialised studies in Norway of subjects dealing with emigration history and relations between the United States and Norway
Eligibility: Open to citizens and residents of the United States. The fund may also give grants to institutions in the United States whose activities are primarily centred on the subjects mentioned
Level of Study: Graduate, Professional development
Type: Grant
Value: The individual grants last year were between NOK 5,000 and NOK 20,000
Country of Study: Norway
Application Procedure: Applicants must send applications to Nordmanns-Forbundet in envelopes that are clearly marked with 'Emigration Fund'
Closing Date: 15 February
Additional Information: Please see the website www.folkehogskole.no/undersider/engminnefond.html

For further information contact:

Nordmanns-Forbundet, Råhusgtgata 23 B, N-0158056, Norway.

Tel:　　　(47) 2 335 7170
Fax:　　　(47) 2 335 7175
Email:　　norseman@online.no

American Academy of Child and Adolescent Psychiatry

AACAP Pilot Research Award for Attention Disorders

Subjects: Child and adolescent mental health
Purpose: To support young investigators at a critical stage, encouraging a future career in child and adolescent psychiatry research.
Eligibility: Candidates must be board eligible/certified in child and adolescent psychiatry, or enrolled in a child psychiatry residency or fellowship program. Candidates must have a faculty appointment in an accredited medical school or be in a fully accredited child and adolescent psychiatry clinical research or training program. At the time of application, candidates may not have more than two years of experience following graduation from residency/fellowship training. Candidates must not have any previous significant, individual research funding in the field of child and adolescent mental health. These include the following NIMH/NIH funding (Small Grants, R-01) or similar foundation or industry research funding. Candidates who have received or are currently receiving "T32" funding support are eligible to apply. Candidates must either be AACAP members or have a membership application pending (not paid by the award)
Type: Award
Value: US$15,000
Country of Study: Any country
Application Procedure: Application Guidelines: Application Form: A proposal, no more than seven pages (single spaced, no less than 12 pt. font and 1" margins), including four pages of research strategy, a one-page detailed project timeline, one-page budget and justification, and one page

addressing the inclusion or exclusion of women and minorities. (References may exceed the page limit). 1. The research strategy should include the following sections: significance and specific aims; hypotheses; background and rationale; and a research plan (including data analysis plan). Research may be pre-clinical, epidemiological, or clinical. 2. The detailed project timeline should list tentative dates of all procedures for the proposed research project. These include but are not limited to: data collection processes; analysis of results; and final report writing. 3. The budget should contain sufficient detail so that each item can be separately judged. Computer related items (e.g., personal computers, printers, modems, etc.) are extremely unlikely to receive budget approval. No salary support for the principal investigator will be provided. No indirect costs for the institution will be provided. Typical budget items may include but are not limited to: subject honoraria and travel expenses; instrumentation costs; assay and lab test costs; and/or payment to research assistants. 4. If women or minorities will not be included, detailed justification of the rationale for their exclusion is mandatory. Such exclusion may lower enthusiasm for the proposal. A letter of support from section chief or department chair. A letter of support from the proposed mentor. Candidate's current curriculum vitae. Mentor's curriculum vitae. Letter detailing any current research funding (role on project, title, type of project, and source of funds).(Human and Animal Subjects must be verified at time of award and do not need to be included with the application.)
No. of awards offered: more than two years
Closing Date: 1 April
Additional Information: www.aacap.org/aacap/Awards/Resident_and_ECP_Awards/AACAP_Pilot_Research_Award_for_Attention_Disorders.aspx

For further information contact:

Tel: (1) 202 966 7300
Email: research@aacap.org

AACAP Pilot Research Award for Early Career Faculty and Child and Adolescent Psychiatry Fellows

Subjects: Child and adolescent mental health
Purpose: To award general psychiatry residents who have an interest in beginning a career in child and adolescent mental health research.
Eligibility: Candidates must be enrolled in a general psychiatry residency. Candidates must not have any previous significant, individual research funding in the field of child and adolescent mental health. These include the following NIMH/NIH funding (Small Grants, R-01) or similar foundation or industry research funding. Candidates who have received or are currently receiving "T32" funding support are eligible to apply. Candidates must either be AACAP members or have a membership application pending (not paid by the award) and agree to submit a poster presentation on his or her research for AACAP's 68th Annual Meeting in Atlanta, Georgia, October 25-30, 2021.
Type: Award
Value: US$15,000
Frequency: Annual
Country of Study: Any country
Application Procedure: Application Guidelines: Application Form: A proposal, no more than seven pages (single spaced, no less than 12 pt. font and 1" margins), including four pages of research strategy, a one-page detailed project timeline, one-page budget and justification, and one page addressing the inclusion or exclusion of women and minorities. (References may exceed the page limit). 1. The research strategy should include the following sections: significance and specific aims; hypotheses; background and rationale; and a research plan (including data analysis plan). Research may be pre-clinical, epidemiological, or clinical. 2. The detailed project timeline should list tentative dates of all procedures for the proposed research project. These include but are not limited to: data collection processes; analysis of results; and final report writing. 3. The budget should contain sufficient detail so that each item can be separately judged. Computer related items (e.g., personal computers, printers, modems, etc.) are extremely unlikely to receive budget approval. No salary support for the principal investigator will be provided. No indirect costs for the institution will be provided. Typical budget items may include but are not limited to: subject honoraria and travel expenses; instrumentation costs; assay and lab test costs; and/or payment to research assistants. 4. If women or minorities will not be included, detailed justification of the rationale for their exclusion is mandatory. Such exclusion may lower enthusiasm for the proposal. A letter of support from section chief or department chair. A letter of support from the proposed mentor. Candidate's current curriculum vitae. Mentor's curriculum vitae. Letter detailing any current research funding (role on project, title, type of project, and source of funds). (Human and Animal Subjects must be verified at time of award and do not need to be included with the application.)
No. of awards offered: Up to two
Closing Date: 1 April
Additional Information: www.aacap.org/AACAP/Awards/Resident_and_ECP_Awards/Pilot_Research_Award_Early_Career_Faculty_and_Child_and_Adolescent_Psychiatry_Fellows.aspx

For further information contact:

Tel: (1) 202 966 7300
Email: research@aacap.org

AACAP Pilot Research Award for Learning Disabilities

Subjects: Child and adolescent mental health

Purpose: To support child and adolescent psychiatry fellows and junior faculty who have an interest in beginning a career in child and adolescent mental health research.

Eligibility: Candidates must be board eligible/certified in child and adolescent psychiatry, or enrolled in a child psychiatry residency or fellowship program. Candidates must have a faculty appointment in an accredited medical school or be in a fully accredited child and adolescent psychiatry clinical research or training program. At the time of application, candidates may not have more than two years of experience following graduation from residency/fellowship training. Candidates must not have any previous significant, individual research funding in the field of child and adolescent mental health. These include the following NIMH/NIH Funding (Small Grants, R-01) or similar foundation or industry research funding. Candidates who have received or are currently receiving "T32" funding support are eligible to apply. Candidates must either be AACAP members or have a membership application pending (not paid by the award)

Type: Award

Value: US$15,000

Country of Study: Any country

Application Procedure: Application Guidelines: Application Form: A proposal, no more than seven pages (single spaced, no less than 12 pt. font and 1" margins), including four pages of research strategy, a one-page detailed project timeline, one-page budget and justification, and one page addressing the inclusion or exclusion of women and minorities. (References may exceed the page limit). 1. The research strategy should include the following sections: significance and specific aims; hypotheses; background and rationale; and a research plan (including data analysis plan). Research may be pre-clinical, epidemiological, or clinical. 2. The detailed project timeline should list tentative dates of all procedures for the proposed research project. These include but are not limited to: data collection processes; analysis of results; and final report writing. 3. The budget should contain sufficient detail so that each item can be separately judged. Computer related items (e.g., personal computers, printers, modems, etc.) are extremely unlikely to receive budget approval. No salary support for the principal investigator will be provided. No indirect costs for the institution will be provided. Typical budget items may include but are not limited to: subject honoraria and travel expenses; instrumentation costs; assay and lab test costs; and/or payment to research assistants. 4. If women or minorities will not be included, detailed justification of the rationale for their exclusion is mandatory. Such exclusion may lower enthusiasm for the proposal. A letter of support from section chief or department chair. A letter of support from the proposed mentor. Candidate's current curriculum vitae. Mentor's curriculum vitae. Letter detailing any current research funding (role on project, title, type of project, and source of funds). (Human and Animal Subjects must be verified at time of award and do not need to be included with the application.)

No. of awards offered: Up to two

Closing Date: 1 April

Additional Information: www.aacap.org/aacap/Awards/Resident_and_ECP_Awards/AACAP_Pilot_Research_Award_for_Attention_Disorders.aspx

For further information contact:

Tel: (1) 202 966 7300

Email: research@aacap.org

Pilot Research Award for General Psychiatry Residents

Subjects: Child and adolescent mental health

Purpose: To award general psychiatry residents who have an interest in beginning a career in child and adolescent mental health research.

Eligibility: Candidates must be enrolled in a general psychiatry residency. Candidates must not have any previous significant, individual research funding in the field of child and adolescent mental health. These include the following NIMH/NIH funding (Small Grants, R-01) or similar foundation or industry research funding. Candidates who have received or are currently receiving "T32" funding support are eligible to apply. Candidates must either be AACAP members or have a membership application pending (not paid by the award)

Type: Award

Value: US$15,000

Country of Study: Any country

Application Procedure: Application Guidelines: Application Form: A proposal, no more than seven pages (single spaced, no less than 12 pt. font and 1" margins), including four pages of research strategy, a one-page detailed project timeline, one-page budget and justification, and one page addressing the inclusion or exclusion of women and minorities. (References may exceed the page limit). 1. The research strategy should include the following sections: significance and specific aims; hypotheses; background and rationale; and a research plan (including data analysis plan). Research may be pre-clinical, epidemiological, or clinical. 2. The detailed project timeline should list tentative dates of all procedures for the proposed research project. These include but are not limited to: data collection processes; analysis of results; and final report writing. 3. The budget should contain sufficient detail so that each item can be separately judged. Computer related items (e.g., personal computers, printers, modems, etc.) are extremely unlikely to receive budget approval. No salary support for the principal investigator will be provided. No indirect costs for the institution will be provided. Typical budget items may include but are not limited to: subject honoraria and travel expenses; instrumentation costs; assay and lab test costs; and/or payment to research assistants. 4. If women or minorities will not be included, detailed justification of the rationale for their exclusion is mandatory. Such exclusion may lower enthusiasm for the proposal. A letter of support from section chief or department chair. A letter of support from the proposed mentor. Candidate's current curriculum vitae. Mentor's curriculum vitae. Letter detailing any current research funding (role on project, title, type of project, and source of funds). (Human and Animal Subjects must be verified at time of award and do not need to be included with the application.)

No. of awards offered: Up to two
Closing Date: 1 April
Additional Information: www.aacap.org/aacap/Awards/Resident_and_ECP_Awards/AACAP_Pilot_Research_Award_for_Attention_Disorders.aspx

For further information contact:

Tel:　　(1) 202 966 7300
Email:　research@aacap.org

The AACAP Rieger Psychodynamic Psychotherapy Award

Type: Prize
Value: US$4,500 prize
Country of Study: Any country
Closing Date: 3 May

For further information contact:

Email:　clinical@aacap.org

American Academy of Neurology (AAN)

IAC Foreign Scholarship Award Subcommittee, 1080 Montreal Avenue, St Paul, MN 55116, United States of America.

Tel:　　(1) 612 695 1940
Email:　kjames@aan.com
Website:　www.aan.com
Contact:　Ms Kathleen James

A. B. Baker Award for Lifetime Achievement in Neurologic Education

Purpose: To provide funding for training in neuropharmacology
Eligibility: Nominee should exhibit lifetime career achievements in the field of neurologic education, with an emphasis on national accomplishments. Nominee should exhibit leadership, creativity, and scholarship. Nominee's neurological education activities should include significant current or past work in the AAN. Nominations should be inclusive in regards to gender and under-represented groups. Posthumous nominations will not be accepted
Level of Study: Postgraduate
Type: Other
Value: The Award will consist of a minimum commitment of two years
Frequency: Annual
Country of Study: Any country
Closing Date: 31 December
Funding: Private
Additional Information: tools.aan.com/science/awards/?fuseaction=home.info&id=99

For further information contact:

Tel:　　(1) 612 623 8115
Fax:　　(1) 612 623 3504
Email:　lpersaud@aan.com

American Academy of Pediatrics (AAP)

Division of Member Sections, 141 Northwest Point Boulevard, Elk Grove Village, IL 60007, United States of America.

Tel:　　(1) 847 952 4926
Email:　membership@aap.org
Website:　www.aap.org

The American Academy of Pediatrics (AAP) is an organisation of 55,000 primary care paediatricians, paediatric medical subspecialists and paediatric surgical specialists dedicated to the health, safety and well being of infants, children, adolescents and young adults.

Advocacy Training Grants

Purpose: CPTI supports 4 pediatric faculty-resident pairs annually to attend the AAP Legislative Conference in

Washington, DC. Following the conference, the faculty-resident pairs are required to implement an educational project in collaboration with their AAP chapter to strengthen the advocacy skills of their trainees.

Value: Up to US$1,000

Country of Study: Any country

Closing Date: March

Additional Information: www.aap.org/en-us/advocacy-and-policy/aap-health-initiatives/CPTI/Pages/Grants.aspx

American Academy of Pediatrics Resident Research Grants

Purpose: To enhance the development of research skills among physicians in paediatric training. Pediatric residents have an opportunity to initiate and completeprojects related to their professional interests through the AAP Resident Research Grant program

Eligibility: Open to paediatric residents in a training programme and have a definite commitment for another year of residency in a programme accredited by the Residency Review Committee for Paediatrics. Applicants must be United States or Canadian citizens or permanent residents. International medical graduates are eligible

Type: Research grant

Value: Up to US$2,000

Length of Study: Up to 2 years

Frequency: Annual

Country of Study: Any country

Application Procedure: Applications are sent automatically to AAP Residents and programme directors every year. Non members should write for details

Additional Information: research.weill.cornell.edu/funding/open-submission-grants/resident-research-grant-american-academy-pediatrics

American Alpine Club (AAC)

710 Tenth Street, Suite 100, Golden, CO 80401, United States of America.

Tel: (1) 303 384 0110
Email: info@americanalpineclub.org
Website: americanalpineclub.org
Contact: Janet Miller, Grants Administrator

The American Alpine Club (AAC) is a national non-profit organization that has represented mountaineers and rock climbers for almost a century. AAC has been the only national climbers' organization devoted to the exploration and scientific study of high mountain elevations and polar regions of the world, and the promotion and dissemination of knowledge about the mountains and mountaineering through its meetings, publications and libraries. It is also dedicated to the conservation and preservation of mountain regions and other climbing areas and the representation of the interests and concerns of the American climbing community.

American Alpine Club Research Grants

Purpose: to see focal areas that will be prioritized.

Eligibility: Must be a graduate student or a postgraduate student. Must attend a university or a four-year college. Must not be attending high school currently. Both full-time and part-time students

Level of Study: Postgraduate

Type: Research grant

Value: US$1,500

Frequency: Annual

Country of Study: Any country

Application Procedure: Applicants must call or write for application forms, which are also available from the website

Closing Date: 17 January

Funding: Private

Contributor: The Arthur K. Gilkey Memorial Research Fund, the R.L. Putnam Research Fund, and the Bedayn Research Fund

Additional Information: A report must be submitted upon completion of the project www.petersons.com/scholarship/american-alpine-club-research-grants-111_189245.aspx

For further information contact:

710 10th St, Suite 100, Golden, CO 80401, United States of America.

Email: grants@americanalpineclub.org

Research Grants

Purpose: The American Alpine Club (AAC) Research Grants have supported scientific endeavors in mountains and crags around the world. We fund projects that enrich our understanding of the ecosystems and landscapes that are a part of the climbing experience, contribute vital knowledge to the management of climbing environments, and improve the health and sustainability of the climbing community.

Type: Research grant

Value: US$500 to US$1,500

Frequency: Annual

Country of Study: Any country

Closing Date: 17 January

Rocky Talkie Search and Rescue Award

Purpose: Rocky Talkie will be giving a total of US$25,000 to four SAR teams who responded to 2021 incidents in exceptional and inspirational ways. The goal of this award is to give back to teams for their invaluable service to our community and raise awareness of the rescues that regularly occur outside the public eye (many of which are performed by volunteers!).

Eligibility: Any Search and Rescue team that is registered in the United States or Canada as a non-profit.

Type: Award

Value: US$25,000; The first place winner will receive US$10,000, the second place winner will receive US$7,000, the third place winner will receive US$5,000 and the fourth place winner will receive US$3,000.

Country of Study: Any country

Closing Date: 31 January

Funding: Individuals

American Association for Cancer Research (AACR)

615 Chestnut Street, 17th Floor, Philadelphia, PA 19106-4404, United States of America.

Tel: (1) 215 440 9300
Email: aacr@aacr.org
Website: www.aacr.org
Contact: Ms Sheri Ozard, Program Co-ordinator

The American Association for Cancer Research (AACR) is a scientific society of over 17,000 laboratory and clinical cancer researchers. It was founded in 1907 to facilitate communication and dissemination of knowledge among scientists and others dedicated to the cancer problem, and to foster research in cancer and related biomedical sciences. It is also dedicated to encouraging the presentation and discussion of new and important observations in the field, fostering public education, science education and training, and advancing the understanding of cancer aetiology, prevention, diagnosis and treatment throughout the world.

American Association for Cancer Research Anna D. Barker Basic Cancer Research Fellowship

Purpose: The AACR Anna D. Barker Basic Cancer Research Fellowship encourages and supports postdoctoral or clinical research fellows to establish a successful career path in cancer research. The research proposed for funding may be in any area of basic cancer research

Eligibility: Applicants must have a doctoral degree (including PhD, MD, DO, DC, ND, DDS, DVM, ScD, DNS, PharmD, or equivalent) in a related field and not currently be a candidate for a further doctoral degree. applicants must 1. Hold a mentored research position with the title of postdoctoral fellow, clinical research fellow, or the equivalent. i. If eligibility is based on a future position, the position must be confirmed at the time of application and CANNOT be contingent upon receiving this grant. ii. If the future position is at a different institution than the applicant's current institution, the applicant must contact AACR's Scientific Review and Grants Administration Department (AACR's SRGA) at 28T grants@aacr.org 28T before submitting their application for information on additional verification materials/signatures that may be required. 2. Have completed their most recent doctoral degree within the past three years (i.e., degree cannot have been conferred before 1 July; the formal date of receipt of doctoral degree is the date the degree was conferred, as indicated on their diploma and/or transcript). i. Applicants with a medical degree must have completed their most recent doctoral degree or medical residency - whichever date is later - within the past three years. 3. Work under the auspices of a mentor at an academic, medical, or research institution anywhere in the world (There are no citizenship or geographic requirements. However, by submitting a Letter of Intent for this grant, an applicant applying from an institution located in a country in which they are not a citizen or a permanent resident assures that the visa status will provide sufficient time to complete the project and grant term at the institution from which they applied)

Level of Study: Postdoctorate

Type: Fellowship or Grant

Value: US$110,000

Length of Study: 2 years

Frequency: Dependent on funds available

Country of Study: Any country

Application Procedure: Please visit funding page for details at www.aacr.org/FUNDING/PAGES/DEFAULT.ASPX

Closing Date: 28 January

Funding: Foundation, Private

Contributor: AACR

No. of awards given last year: 2

Additional Information: memento.epfl.ch/event/aacr-anna-d-barker-basic-cancer-research-fellowshi/

For further information contact:

Email: grants@aacr.org

American Association for Cancer Research Career Development Awards

Purpose: To support cancer research by junior faculty

Eligibility: Applicants must have a doctoral degree (including PhD, MD, DO, DC, ND, DDS, DVM, ScD, DNS, PharmD, or equivalent doctoral degree, or a combined clinical and research doctoral degree) in a related field and not currently be a candidate for a further doctoral or professional degree

Level of Study: Postdoctorate, Research

Type: Award

Value: US$50,000 per year

Length of Study: 2 years

Frequency: Annual

Study Establishment: Universities or research institutions

Country of Study: Any country

Application Procedure: Candidates must be nominated by a member of AACR and must be an AACR member or apply for membership by the time the application is submitted. Associate members may not be nominators. The online application is available at the AACR website. Please see the website for further details regarding eligibility at www.aacr.org/Uploads/DocumentRepository/Grants/2012_FCC_CDA_PG.rev.pdf

No. of awards offered: 75

Closing Date: 1 February

Funding: Private

Contributor: The Cancer Research and Prevention Foundation, the Susan G Komen Breast Cancer Foundation, Genentech Inc., the Pancreatic Cancer Action Network

No. of awards given last year: 6

No. of applicants last year: 75

Additional Information: www.aacr.org/Funding/Pages/Funding-Detail.aspx?ItemID=30

For further information contact:

Tel: (1) 215 446 7191
Fax: (1) 215 440 9372
Email: grants@aacr.org

American Association for Cancer Research Gertrude B. Elion Cancer Research Award

Purpose: The AACR Gertrude B. Elion Cancer Research Award represents a joint effort to encourage and support tenure-eligible junior faculty

Eligibility: Applicants must have a doctoral degree (including PhD, MD, DO, DC, ND, DDS, DVM, ScD, DNS, PharmD, or equivalent) in a related field and not currently be a candidate for a further doctoral degree. At the start of the grant term on 1 July, applicants must 1. Hold a tenure-eligible appointment (or equivalent, if institution does not follow a tenure system) at the rank of assistant professor (Appointments such as research assistant professor, adjunct assistant professor, assistant professor research track, visiting professor, or instructor are not eligible. Applicants cannot be tenured or under consideration for a tenured academic position at the time of the application. Applicants that have progressed to associate professor appointments are also not eligible). i. If eligibility is based on a future position, the position must be confirmed at the time of application, and CANNOT be contingent upon receiving this grant. ii. If the future position is at a different institution than the applicant's current institution, the applicant must contact AACR's Scientific Review and Grants Administration Department (AACR's SRGA) at grants@aacr.org before submitting their application for information on additional verification materials/signatures that may be required. 2. Have completed their most recent doctoral degree within the past 11 years (i.e., degree cannot have been conferred before 1 July; the formal date of receipt of doctoral degree is the date the degree was conferred, as indicated on their diploma and/or transcript). i. Applicants with a medical degree must have completed their most recent doctoral degree or medical residency (or equivalent) - whichever date is later - within the past 11 years. 3. Work at an academic, medical, or research institution anywhere in the world. (There are no citizenship or geographic requirements. However, by submitting an application for this grant, an applicant applying from an institution located in a country in which they are not a citizen or a permanent resident assures that the visa status will provide sufficient time to complete the project and grant term at the institution from which they applied)

Level of Study: Postdoctorate, Research

Type: Grant

Value: US$75,000

Length of Study: 1 year

Frequency: Annual

Study Establishment: Universities or research institutions

Country of Study: Any country

Funding: Private

Contributor: GlaxoSmithKline

No. of awards given last year: 1

Additional Information: www.aacr.org/Funding/Pages/Funding-Detail.aspx?ItemID=7

For further information contact:

Email: grants@aacr.org

American Association for Cancer Research NextGen Grants for Transformative Cancer Research

Purpose: The AACR NextGen Grants for Transformative Cancer Research represent the AACR's flagship funding initiative to stimulate highly innovative research from young investigators. This grant mechanism is intended to promote and support creative, paradigm-shifting cancer research that may not be funded through conventional channels. It is expected that these grants will catalyze significant scientific discoveries and help talented young investigators gain scientific independence

Eligibility: Applicants must have a doctoral degree (including PhD, MD, DO, DC, ND, DDS, DVM, ScD, DNS, PharmD, or equivalent) in a related field and not currently be a candidate for a further doctoral degree. At the start of the grant term on 1 July, applicants must 1. Hold a tenure-eligible appointment (or equivalent, if institution does not follow a tenure system) at the rank of assistant professor (appointments such as research assistant professor, adjunct assistant professor, assistant professor research track, visiting professor, or instructor are not eligible. Applicants that have progressed to associate professor appointments are also not eligible). i. If eligibility is based on a future position, the position must be confirmed at the time of submission, and CANNOT be contingent upon receiving this grant. ii. If the future position is at a different institution than the applicant's current institution, the applicant must contact AACR's Scientific Review and Grants Administration. Department (AACR's SRGA) at grants@aacr.org before submitting their Letter of Intent for information on additional verification materials/signatures that may be required. 2. Have held a tenure-eligible assistant professor appointment for no more than three years (i.e., cannot have held a tenure-eligible appointment prior to 1 July). 3. Work at an academic, medical, or research institution anywhere in the world (there are no citizenship or geographic requirements. However, by submitting a Letter of Intent for this grant, an applicant applying from an institution located in a country in which they are not a citizen or a permanent resident assures that their visa status will provide sufficient time to complete the project and grant term at the institution from which they applied)

Level of Study: Postdoctorate
Type: Grant
Value: US$450,000
Length of Study: 3 years
Frequency: Dependent on funds available
Country of Study: Any country
Application Procedure: Please visit our funding page for details www.aacr.org/FUNDING/PAGES/DEFAULT.ASPX

Closing Date: 11 January
Funding: Foundation, Private
Contributor: AACR
No. of awards given last year: 2
Additional Information: researchfunding.duke.edu/aacr-nextgen-grants-transformative-cancer-research

For further information contact:

Email: grants@aacr.org

American Association for Cancer Research-AstraZeneca Stimulating Therapeutic Advancements through Research Training (START) Grants

Purpose: Dramatic advances made in recent years towards precision medicine initiatives, biomarker and novel target identification, and high-throughput examination of genomic data, have resulted in a trove of valuable data that can inform the development of new therapeutics to combat cancer. However, to effectively harness this wealth of information and advance the discovery and development of new therapies for cancer patients, enhanced collaboration between academia and industry will be needed. The AACR-AstraZeneca Stimulating Therapeutic Advancements through Research Training (START) Grants represent an exciting new initiative to encourage and support such collaboration. This novel model, which will provide support to postdoctoral or clinical research fellows, combines research experiences in both an academic and industry setting, following a research timeline that will be of greatest benefit to the proposed work. The training provided through this grant program will be invaluable to young investigators, by allowing fellows to attain a comprehensive research experience that will make them highly desirable to potential employers in either academic research or the pharmaceutical industry. Likewise, academic research centers and industry will benefit from the introduction of such dual-trained individuals into the field

Eligibility: Applicants must have a doctoral degree (including PhD, MD, DO, DC, ND, DDS, DVM, ScD, DNS, PharmD, or equivalent) in a related field and not currently be a candidate for a further doctoral degree. At the start of the grant term on 1 July, applicants must 1. Hold a full-time, mentored research position with the title of postdoctoral fellow, clinical research fellow, or the equivalent; this position must have been held for at least one, but not more than three, years. i. If eligibility is based on a future position, the position must be confirmed at the time of application, and CANNOT be contingent upon receiving this grant. ii. If the future position is at a different institution than the applicant's current institution, the applicant must contact AACR's Scientific Review and Grants Administration Department (AACR's SRGA) at grants@aacr.org before submitting their application forinformation on additional verification materials/signatures that may be required. 2. Have completed their most recent doctoral degree within the past one to three years (i.e., degree cannot have been conferred before 1 July; the formal date of receipt ofdoctoral degree is the date the degree was conferred, as indicated on their diploma and/ortranscript). i. Applicants with a medical degree must have completed their most recent doctoraldegree or medical residency - whichever date is later - within the past three years. 3. Work under the auspices of a mentor at an academic, medical, or research institution in the United States of America (there are no citizenship requirements. However, by submitting an application for this grant, the applicant who is not a United States citizen or a permanent resident assures that the visa status will provide sufficient time to complete the project and grant term)

Level of Study: Postdoctorate
Type: Fellowship or Grant
Value: US$225,000
Length of Study: 3 years
Frequency: Dependent on funds available
Country of Study: United States of America
Application Procedure: Please visit funding page for details at www.aacr.org/FUNDING/PAGES/DEFAULT.ASPX
Closing Date: 6 October
Funding: Private
Contributor: AstraZeneca
No. of awards given last year: 2
Additional Information: www.aacr.org/Funding/Pages/Funding-Detail.aspx?ItemID=73

For further information contact:

Email: grants@aacr.org

QuadW Foundation-AACR Fellowship for Clinical/Translational Sarcoma Research

Purpose: The QuadW Foundation-AACR Fellowship for Clinical/Translational Sarcoma Research represents a joint effort to encourage and support a postdoctoral or clinical research fellow to conduct translational or clinical sarcoma research and to establish a successful career path in this field
Eligibility: Applicants must have a doctoral degree (including PhD, MD, DO, DC, ND, DDS, DVM, ScD, DNS, PharmD, or equivalent) in a related field and not currently be a candidate for a further doctoral degree. At the start of the grant term on 1 July, applicants must 1. Hold

a mentored research position with the title of postdoctoral fellow, clinical research fellow, or the equivalent. i. If eligibility is based on a future position, the position must be confirmed at the time of application and CANNOT be contingent upon receiving this grant. ii. If the future position is at a different institution than the applicant's current institution, the applicant must contact AACR's Scientific Review and Grants Administration Department (AACR's SRGA) at grants@aacr.org before submitting their application for information on additional verification materials/signatures that may be required. 2. Have completed their most recent doctoral degree within the past five years (i.e., degree cannot have been conferred before 1 July; the formal date of receipt of doctoral degree is the date the degree was conferred, as indicated on your diploma and/or transcript). i. Applicants with a medical degree must have completed their most recent doctoral degree or medical residency - whichever date is later - within the past five years. 3. Work under the auspices of a mentor at an academic, medical, or research institution anywhere in the world. (There are no citizenship or geographic requirements. However, by submitting an application for this grant, an applicant applying from an institution located in a country in which they are not a citizen or a permanent resident assures that the visa status will provide sufficient time to complete the project and grant term at the institution from which they applied)

Level of Study: Postdoctorate
Type: Fellowship or Grant
Value: US$55,000
Length of Study: 1 year
Frequency: Dependent on funds available
Country of Study: Any country
Application Procedure: Please visit our funding page for details www.aacr.org/FUNDING/PAGES/DEFAULT.ASPX
Funding: Foundation, Private
Contributor: QuadW Foundation
No. of awards given last year: 1
Additional Information: www.aacr.org/Funding/Pages/Funding-Detail.aspx?ItemID=12

For further information contact:

Email: grants@aacr.org

American Association for the History of Nursing (AAHN)

PO Box 7, Mullica Hill, NJ 08062, United States of America.

Tel: (1) 609 693 7250
Email: aahn@aahn.org

Website: www.aahn.org
Contact: Executive Secretary

The American Association for the History of Nursing (AAHN) is a professional organization open to everyone interested in the history of nursing. Originally founded in 1978 as a historical methodology group, the association was briefly named the International History of Nursing Society

H 31 Pre-Doctoral Grant

Purpose: This grant is designed to encourage and support graduate training and historical research at the Masters and research Doctoral levels
Eligibility: 1. Proposals will focus on a significant question in the history of nursing. 2. The student will be enrolled in an accredited masters program or doctoral program. 3. The student will be a member of AAHN. 4. The research advisor will be doctorally prepared with scholarly activity in the field of nursing history and prior experience in guidance of research training
Level of Study: Doctorate
Type: Award/Grant
Value: US$2,000
Frequency: Annual
Country of Study: Any country
Application Procedure: Application Form 1. Title Page. 2. Narrative (four [4] double-spaced pages, maximum). Include the following 1. Central thesis or questions of the study. 2. Explanation of your approach to the study, identifying pertinent secondary sources and primary sources critical to the project. 3. Any additional relevant facilities and resources. 4. Significance of the study. Attachments 1. Applicant's curriculum vitae, including education and any research publications and presentations relevant to the proposed project. 2. Letter of support from advisor. 3. Budget Outline and itemize the budget detailing the ways you will use the award and briefly justify each item. For example travel, purchase of equipment, copying. A copy of the proposal should be sent by email to grants@aahn.org
Closing Date: 15 April
Funding: Private
Additional Information: www.aahn.org/research-grants

H-15 Grant

Purpose: The H-15 Grant is awarded to faculty members or independent researchers for proposals outlining a historical research study.
Eligibility: Only AAHN members are eligible to apply for these grants

Level of Study: Doctorate
Type: Grant
Value: US$3,000
Frequency: Annual
Country of Study: Any country
Application Procedure: A copy of the proposal should be sent by email to grants@aahn.org. Only word or pdf documents will be accepted. The application should not exceed 6 pages double-spaced, excluding references, curriculum vitae and writing sample. The outline below specifies the information which should be included in your application. The form and length of your application should be adapted to the research that you propose to do.
Closing Date: 15 April
Funding: Private
Additional Information: www.aahn.org/research-grants

For further information contact:

Email: grants@aahn.org

H-21 Grant

Purpose: The Eleanor Crowder Bjoring Research (H-21) Grant is awarded to senior scholars (faculty members or independent researchers) for proposals outlining a new historical research study
Eligibility: 1. Proposals for a new historical research study in the history of nursing. 2. The scholar will be a faculty member or independent researcher who holds a research doctorate. 3. The scholar will be the author of a published book in the field of history based on original research
Level of Study: Doctorate
Type: Award/Grant
Value: US$3,000
Frequency: Annual
Country of Study: Any country
Application Procedure: A copy of the proposal should be sent by email to grants@aahn.org. Only word or pdf documents will be accepted. The application should not exceed 6 pages double-spaced, excluding references, curriculum vitae and writing sample. The outline below specifies the information which should be included in your application. The form and length of your application should be adapted to the research that you propose to do
Closing Date: 15 April
Funding: Private
Additional Information: www.aahn.org/research-grants

For further information contact:

Email: grants@aahn.org

American Association for Women Radiologists (AAWR)

1891 Preston White Drive, Reston, VA 20191, United States of America.

Tel:	(1) 713 965 0566
Email:	admin@aawr.org
Website:	www.aawr.org

The Association was founded in 1981 to provide a forum for issues unique to women in radiology, radiation oncology and related professions; sponsor programs that promote opportunities for women; and facilitate networking among members and other professionals.

Alice Ettinger Distinguished Achievement Award

Purpose: The Alice Ettinger Distinguished Achievement Award recognizes the lifetime achievement and lasting contribution to radiology/radiation oncology and to the American Association for Women in Radiology. Candidates must be long-term members of the AAWR and must have distinguished careers as mentors, teachers, and leaders in radiology/radiation oncology, and public service
Eligibility: Open to AAWR members only
Level of Study: Unrestricted
Type: Award
Value: Plaque
Frequency: Annual
Country of Study: Any country
Application Procedure: Candidates must submit a current curriculum vitae and letters of support
Closing Date: 31 August
Contributor: Membership dues
Additional Information: www.aawr.org/AAWR-Awards#42621451-alice-ettinger-distinguished-achievement-award

Lucy Frank Squire Distinguished Resident Award in Diagnostic Radiology

Purpose: The Lucy Frank Squire Distinguished Resident Award in Diagnostic Radiology recognizes outstanding contributions in clinical care and scholarship. The nominees must be members of the AAWR and must be in residency training at the time of the award. Only one nomination per residency program is allowed. Nominees will be evaluated on the basis of outstanding contributions in clinical care, teaching, research, or public service
Eligibility: Open to candidates in the field of diagnostic radiology who are members of the AAWR as of 1 January of the year of the award
Level of Study: Unrestricted
Type: Award
Value: Plaque
Frequency: Annual
Country of Study: Any country
Application Procedure: To apply, the following information must be submitted in addition to completing the on-line application 1. Nominating Letter from Program Director OR other supporting faculty member, which should include a notation regarding what year the candidate will be in residency at the time of the award ceremony. 2. A copy of the candidate's curriculum vitae.
Closing Date: 31 August
Contributor: Membership dues
Additional Information: Nominees will be evaluated on the basis of outstanding contributions in clinical care, teaching, research, or public service www.aawr.org/AAWR-Awards#42621452-lucy-frank-squire-distinguished-resident-award-in-diagnostic-radiology

For further information contact:

Email: info@aawr.org

American Association of Critical-Care Nurses (AACN)

101 Columbia, Aliso Viejo, CA 92656-4109, United States of America.

Tel:	(1) 800 899 2226
Email:	info@aacn.org
Website:	www.aacn.org
Contact:	Research Department

The American Association of Critical-Care Nurses (AACN) is the world's largest nursing speciality organization with approx. 68,000 members worldwide. The AACN is committed to providing the highest quality resources to maximize nurses' contributions to caring and improving the healthcare of critically ill patients and their families.

AACN Impact Research Grant

Purpose: The AACN Impact Research Grants are funded and supported by AACN. We encourage experienced clinicians and researchers to propose projects that support inquiry and systematic research that generates new knowledge. The grants are designed to ensure a vital source of clinically relevant research for creating the evidence-based resources that influence high acuity critical care nursing practice.

Eligibility: 1. Principal investigators must be AACN members, and must hold an earned master's degree or have completed candidacy requirements in a BSN-to-PhD or DNP program. 2. Investigators will be expected to present completed studies at the National Teaching Institute & Critical Care Exposition. 3. When you are ready to present your results, please contact AACN staff (do not submit through the NTI abstract process).

Level of Study: Research
Type: Grant
Value: US$50,000
Length of Study: 2 years
Frequency: Annual
Country of Study: Any country
No. of awards offered: 3

For further information contact:

Email:　research@aacn.org

AACN-Sigma Theta Tau Critical Care Grant

Purpose: This grant supports experienced nurses in conducting clearly articulated research studies.

Eligibility: 1. Principal investigator must be a member of either AACN or Sigma Theta Tau International. 2. At a minimum the principal investigator must hold an earned master's degree or have completed candidacy requirements in a BSN-to-PhD or DNP program.

Type: Award
Value: Up to US$10,000
Frequency: Annual
Country of Study: Any country
No. of awards offered: 1
Additional Information: Please review eligibility, application instructions and requirements after receiving an award. www.aawr.org/AAWR-Awards#42621452-lucy-frank-squire-distinguished-resident-award-in-diagnostic-radiology

For further information contact:

Email:　research@aacn.org

Agilent Technologies - AACN Critical-Care Nursing Research Grant

Purpose: To fund research for study conducted by a critical care nurse

Eligibility: Principal investigators must be nurses holding current AACN membership. Investigators who have received funding from the AACN are ineligible to receive additional funding during the lifetime of their original award. They may apply for a new award when their original award obligations have been met

Level of Study: Research
Type: Grant
Value: US$35,000, providing US$33,000 for the research study and US$2,000 for travel expenses associated with presentations of the study findings
Country of Study: Any country
Application Procedure: Applicants must submit a completed application form and supporting materials. Details and forms are available directly from the organisation or from the website
Closing Date: 1 September
Contributor: Hewlett-Packard, Inc

American Nurses Foundation Research Grant Program

Purpose: To encourage the research career development of nurses
Eligibility: Principal investigators must be nurses holding current AACN membership. Investigators who have received funding from the AACN are ineligible to receive additional funding during the lifetime of their original award. They may apply for a new award when their original award obligations have been met
Level of Study: Research
Type: Research grant
Value: Up to US$5,000 is awarded by the American Nurses Foundation
Application Procedure: Applicants must obtain information and application forms from the American Nurses Foundation, and should see the website for further details
Closing Date: 1 May
Contributor: The AACN
Additional Information: www.petersons.com/scholarship/american-nurses-foundationnursing-research-grants-111_179095.aspx

For further information contact:

The American Nurses Foundation, 600 Maryland Avenue SW, Suite 100W, Washington, DC 20024, United States of America.

Tel:　(1) 202 651 7298
Email:　anf@ana.org

American Association of Family and Consumer Sciences (AAFCS)

400 N. Columbus Street, Suite 202, Alexandria, VA 22314-2752, United States of America.

Tel: (1) 703 706 4600
Email: cislamd@aafcs.org
Website: www.aafcs.org
Contact: Ms Amy Campbell, Grants Management Officer

Founded in 1909 as the American Home Economics Association, the American Association of Family and Consumer Sciences (AAFCS) is an organisation of members dedicated to improving the quality of individual and family life through programs that educate, influence public policy, disseminate information and publish research findings. Representing nearly 16,000 professionals in the family and consumer sciences, AAFCS members include elementary, secondary and post secondary educators and administrators, co-operative extension agents and other professionals in government, business and non-profit sectors.

American Association of Family and Consumer Sciences National Fellowships in Family and Consumer Sciences

Purpose: To support a student pursuing study in family and consumer sciences at the graduate level
Eligibility: Applicants must be current members of the AAFCS
Level of Study: Doctorate, Graduate, Postgraduate
Type: Fellowship
Value: US$3,000–5,000
Frequency: Annual
Country of Study: United States of America
Application Procedure: Applicants must apply using official AAFCS application forms. Seven copies of the completed application must be submitted. All requests for fellowship application materials must be accompanied by a fee of US$25 (non refundable)
Closing Date: 31 December
Additional Information: awards@aafcs.org higherlogic download.s3.amazonaws.com/AAFCS/1c95de14-d78f-40b8-a6ef-a1fb628c68fe/UploadedImages/awards/DSA_Nomination_Guidelines_2019_2020.pdf

American Association of Family and Consumer Sciences New Achievers Award

Purpose: The programme was developed to recognise emerging professionals who have exhibited the potential for making significant contributions in or through family and consumer sciences
Eligibility: Any living family and consumer sciences professional who is 35 years of age or younger or who has a least three years service in the field, but no more than eight years of service to the field, and is an active member of AAFCS is eligible for consideration by a nominating group
Type: Award
Value: A desk plaque and commemorative pin
Frequency: Annual
Country of Study: Any country
Application Procedure: One nomination will be accepted from each nominating group. Eligible nominating groups include the AAFCS affiliates, sections and divisions, the Higher Education Unit, and the Past President Unit
Additional Information: www.aafcs.org/resources/recognition/fellowships

For further information contact:

Email: awards@aafcs.org

Ethel L. Parker International Fellowship Fund

Purpose: To be awarded to no more than one (1) FCS graduate student from the U.S. who participates in international study or an international graduate student who studies family and consumer sciences in the U.S.
Level of Study: Postgraduate
Value: Funding includes a US$5,000 fellowship and up to US$2,500 of support for one year of AAFCS membership, International Federation of Home Economics (IFHE) Registration, AAFCS Annual Conference & IFHE travel. (reimbursable upon event participation and receipt submission).
Additional Information: www.aafcs.org/resources/recognition/fellowships

For further information contact:

Email: awards@aafcs.org

Helen Strow International Fellowship Fund

Purpose: To be awarded to no more than one (1) international student who is working to complete a graduate degree in family and consumer sciences in the United States.
Level of Study: Postgraduate
Value: Funding includes a US$5,000 fellowship and up to US$2,500 of support for one year of AAFCS membership, International Federation of Home Economics (IFHE)

Registration, AAFCS Annual Conference & IFHE travel. (reimbursable upon event participation and receipt submission).

Additional Information: www.aafcs.org/resources/recognition/fellowships

For further information contact:

Email: awards@aafcs.org

Jewell L. Taylor National Graduate Fellowship

Purpose: The Taylor Fellowship was established through a generous bequest from Jewell L. Taylor, a dedicated family and consumer sciences professional for more than 50 years.
Eligibility: See website: higherlogicdownload.s3.amazonaws.com/AAFCS/1c95de14-d78f-40b8-a6ef-a1fb628c68fe/UploadedImages/2022_Graduate_Fellowship_Guidelines_1.pdf
Level of Study: Postgraduate
Type: Fellowship
Value: US$5,000
Length of Study: 1 year
Frequency: Annual
Country of Study: United States of America
No. of awards offered: 5
Closing Date: 14 March
Funding: Private

For further information contact:

Email: awards@aafcs.org

Margaret E. Terrell National Graduate Fellowship

Purpose: The Terrell Fellowship is supported by a gift from the AAFCS Washington Affiliate, as well as contributions from Margaret Terrell and University of Washington Dietetics alumni. Margaret E. Terrell was recognized for expertise in food service systems management.
Eligibility: See Website: higherlogicdownload.s3.amazonaws.com/AAFCS/1c95de14-d78f-40b8-a6ef-a1fb628c68fe/UploadedImages/2022_Graduate_Fellowship_Guidelines_1.pdf
Type: Fellowship
Value: US$5,000
Length of Study: 1 year
Frequency: Annual
Country of Study: Any country
No. of awards offered: 1
Closing Date: 14 March

For further information contact:

Email: awards@aafcs.org

Ruth O Brian Project Grant

Eligibility: Open to suitably qualified individuals of any nationality
Level of Study: Graduate, Postgraduate
Type: Project grant
Value: Up to US$5,000
Country of Study: Any country
Application Procedure: Applicants must write for details
Closing Date: 14 January

For further information contact:

Email: robrien@gc.cuny.edu

American Association of Law Libraries (AALL)

105 W. Adams Street, Suite 3300, Chicago, IL 60603, United States of America.

Tel: (1) 312 939 4764
Email: scholarships@aall.org
Website: www.aallnet.org

The American Association of Law Libraries (AALL) was founded in 1906 to promote and enhance the value of law libraries to legal and public communities, to foster the profession of law librarianship and to provide leadership in the field of legal information. Today, the AALL represents law librarians and related professionals who are affiliated with a wide range of institutions including law firms, law schools, corporate legal departments and courts, and local, state and federal government agencies.

AALL Research Fund: An Endowment Established by Lexisnexis

Purpose: The grant will fund one or more projects of value to those professions that create, disseminate, or use legal and law-related information. The AALL Research Grant program aims to stimulate a diverse range of scholarship in any format.
Eligibility: 1. Applicants should have experience with research projects, and an understanding of the creation, dissemination and/or use of legal and law-related information. Applicants may be individuals or partnerships. 2. Preference

will be given to members of AALL, working individually or in partnership with others. 3. Applicant(s) must provide a resume and statement of their qualifications for carrying out this project. AALL reserves the right to request additional supporting documents. 4. Applicant(s) currently working on an AALL Research Grant of any type is not eligible to apply for another research grant until the previously awarded grant is judged complete. 5. Participation in this AALL research project shall not be denied to any applicant or abridged on account of race, color, religion, gender, age, national origin, disability or sexual orientation.

Level of Study: Research

Type: Grant

Value: US$5,000.00

Frequency: Twice a year

Country of Study: Any country

Application Procedure: 1. Download and submit the Research Grant Application along with all the required documentation. 2. Applicants must follow instructions on the application form. 3. Grant recipients will submit their final report and project results by the scheduled date. AALL retains a right of first refusal for publication or other use of project results. If the project results are not accepted for publication in an AALL publication or the Association declines to make some other use of the results, the grant recipient may publish or distribute the research results in another manner. In that case, recognition of AALL support must be included with the research results. Ownership rights to the project results, including copyright or other intellectual property rights, are subject to negotiation between the grant recipient and AALL. 4. For further information, contact AALL Director of Content Strategy Megan Mall.

No. of awards offered: One or more grants

Closing Date: 1 December

Funding: Private

American Association of Law Libraries James F Connolly LexisNexis Academic and Library Solutions Scholarship

Eligibility: Awarded to library school graduates with law library experience who are presently attending an accredited law school with the intention of pursuing a career as a law librarian. Preference will be given to individuals who have demonstrated an interest in government documents

Level of Study: Graduate

Type: Scholarship

Value: Up to US$3,000 for tuition and school-related expenses

Frequency: Annual

Study Establishment: ABA-accredited Law Schools

Country of Study: Any country

Application Procedure: Applicants must write for details or download an application form from the website

Closing Date: 1 April

Additional Information: www.encyclopedia.com/education/news-and-education-magazines/american-association-law-libraries#E

For further information contact:

53 West Jackson Boulevard, Suite 940, Chicago, IL 60604, United States of America.

Email: scholarships@csulb.edu

American Association of Law Libraries LexisNexis/John R Johnson Memorial Scholarship Endowment

Purpose: Candidates who apply for any AALL Educational Scholarships, all categories, become automatically eligible to receive this award. No separate application necessary. Scholarship amount and the number of Scholarships granted varies. This endowed scholarship was established by LexisNexis in honor of John R. Johnson, who served as the director of the law library segment at LexisNexis. The scholarship is awarded annually to individuals seeking a degree from an accredited library or law school, and who intend to have a career in legal information, or to a library school graduate seeking an advanced degree in a related field.

Eligibility: Candidates who apply for AALL educational scholarships, types I–IV, become automatically eligible to receive the LexisNexis/John R Johnson Memorial Scholarship

Level of Study: Graduate

Type: Scholarship

Value: US$500 - US$2,500

Frequency: Annual

Study Establishment: ALA-accredited library schools or ABA-Accredited Law Schools

Country of Study: Any country

Application Procedure: Applicants must write for details or download an application form from the website

No. of awards offered: 1

Closing Date: 1 April

Additional Information: www.lifelaunchr.com/scholarship/lexisnexis-john-r-johnson-memorial-scholarship-endowment/

For further information contact:

Chair, Scholarships Committee, 105 West Adams Street, Suite 3300, Chicago, IL 60603, United States of America.

Email: scholarships@aall.org

American Association of Law Libraries Scholarship (Type II)

Purpose: Candidates should apply for more than one scholarship when appropriate

Eligibility: Open to library school graduates working towards a degree in an accredited law school who have no more than 36 semester credit hours remaining before qualifying for the law degree, who have law library experience and who have the intention of pursuing a career as a law librarian. Preference is given to members of the AALL

Level of Study: Graduate

Value: Up to US$2,000 for tuition and school-related expenses

Frequency: Annual

Study Establishment: ABA-accredited law schools

Country of Study: Any country

Application Procedure: Applicants must write for details or download an application form from the website

Closing Date: 1 April

American Association of Neurological Surgeons (AANS)

5550 Meadowbrook Drive, Rolling Meadows, IL 60008-3852, United States of America.

Tel: (1) 847 378 0500
Email: info@aans.org
Website: www.aans.org
Contact: Julie Qattrocchi, Development Coordinator

Founded in 1931 as the Harvey Cushing Society, the American Association of Neurological Surgeons (AANS) is a scientific and educational association with more than 6,500 members worldwide. The AANS is dedicated to advancing the specialty of neurological surgery in order to provide the highest quality of neurosurgical care to the public. All active members of the AANS are certified by the American Board of Neurological Surgery, The Royal College of Physicians and Surgeons (Neurosurgery) of Canada or the Mexican Council of Neurological Surgery, AC. Neurological surgery is the medical specialty concerned with the prevention, diagnosis, treatment and rehabilitation of disorders that affect the entire nervous system including the spinal column, spinal cord, brain and peripheral nerves.

AANS International Visiting Surgeon Fellowship

Purpose: The AANS is committed to increasing its involvement in international neurosurgery, with particular interest in furthering educational opportunities in countries with limited access. One meaningful offering is the AANS International Visiting Surgeon Fellowship. The AANS funds two observational fellowships per fiscal year to provide meaningful educational experiences in North America to international neurosurgeons who will practice and/or teach neurosurgery in their home countries.

Eligibility: The applicant must be a neurosurgeon or neurosurgeon-in-training from a World Bank designated country. He/she should be on staff at a local hospital (and preferably medical school) involved in neurosurgical patient care and neurosurgical education.

Value: US$2,000/month stipend for up to three months (US$6,000 maximum)

Country of Study: Any country

Closing Date: 15 July

For further information contact:

AANS International Visiting Surgeon Fellowship, American Association of Neurological Surgeons (AANS), 5550 Meadowbrook Drive, Rolling Meadows, IL 60008-3852, United States of America.

Fax: (1) 847 378 0600
Email: kyoshikawa@aans.org

Neurosurgery Research and Education Foundation Research Fellowship

Purpose: To provide training for neurosurgeons who are preparing for academic careers as clinician investigators

Eligibility: Open to MDs who have been accepted into, or who are in, an approved residency training programme in neurological surgery in North America

Level of Study: Postdoctorate

Type: Fellowship

Value: US$40,000 for a 1-year fellowship

Length of Study: 1–2 years

Frequency: Annual

Application Procedure: Applicants must send a completed application, sponsor statement, programme director comments and letters of recommendation. Responses to questions 1–9, a curriculum vitae and photographic images must also be submitted. Applications are available at the website www.aans.org

No. of awards offered: 25

Closing Date: 31 October

Funding: Private

Contributor: Corporations and membership

No. of awards given last year: 5

No. of applicants last year: 25

Additional Information: Notification of awards will be made by 28 February. After notification of the award, the applicant must indicate acceptance, in writing, no later than 1 April. If unwilling to accept the award by that date, funds will be awarded to the first runner-up. A report of findings and accounting of funds will be expected at the halfway point and upon completion of the fellowship. Normally, no more than one award per year will be made to any one institution. Individuals who accept a grant from another source, NIH or private, for the same research project will become ineligible for the award. A budget must be prepared by the applicant and the sponsor indicating how the grant funds will be expended. It is the policy of the NREF to fund only direct costs involved with the research awards. This means no fringe benefits, publication costs or travel expenses. The signature representing the applicant's institution's financial officer on page four should be that of their chief financial officer or grants and contracts manager. The award will be made payable to the institution and disbursed by it according to its institutional policy research.weill.cornell.edu/funding/open-submission-grants/research-fellowship-neurosurgery-research-and-education-foundation

For further information contact:

Email: nref@aans.org

William P Van Wagenen Fellowship

Purpose: The Van Wagenen Fellowship was designed to give freedom in scientific development without the restrictive limitations usually imposed by many research grants and fellowships. The AANS offers the Van Wagenen Fellowship program to neurosurgical residents interested in studying scientific development abroad. The fellowship is open to all senior neurological residents (PGY5, PGY6 & PGY7) in approved North American neurosurgery residency programs and whose intent is to pursue an academic career in neurological surgery.
Eligibility: Applicants must be neurosurgeons, no more than two years from having completed their neurosurgical residency training, and/or clinical fellowship, who are full-time faculty in North American teaching institutions.
Level of Study: Postdoctorate
Type: Award
Value: US$120,000
Length of Study: 1 year
Frequency: Annual
Country of Study: Country of study must be different than the country of residence
Application Procedure: Complete an application for each subspecialty for which funding is requested. However, based

on an evaluation of proposals from recent awardees, here are factors to consider when applying 1. Is the research plan detailed and comprehensive? Is the training environment supportive? Does the institution offer strong mentorship? 2. Does the institution offer the recipient a unique opportunity to learn new techniques? 3. Does the proposal align with the overall goals and objectives of the fellowship? 3. NOTE Including these elements should not be interpreted as a guarantee of an award.
Closing Date: 1 October
Funding: Private
Contributor: Corporations and membership

For further information contact:

5550 Meadowbrook Industrial Ct., Rolling Meadows, IL 60008, United States of America.

Email: grants@nref.org; lcoleman@nref.org

American Association of University Women (AAUW)

American Association of University Women (AAUW) American Fellowships

Subjects: Business
Purpose: AAUW American Fellowships support women scholars who are pursuing full-time study to complete dissertations, conducting postdoctoral research full time, or preparing research for publication for eight consecutive weeks
Eligibility: 1. American Fellowships are not open to previous recipients of any AAUW national fellowship or grant (not including branch or local awards or Community Action Grants). 2. Members of the AAUW Board of Directors, committees, panels, task forces and staff, including current interns, are not eligible to apply for AAUW's fellowships and grants. A person holding a current award is eligible for election or appointment to boards, committees, panels, and task forces. 3. American Fellowship candidates must be U.S. citizens or permanent residents. 4. American Fellowships are open to scholars who identify as women in all fields of study at an accredited institution of higher education or research. AAUW will make final decisions about what constitutes eligible institutions. 5. American Postdoctoral Research Leave Fellowship applicants must hold a doctorate classified as a research degree (e.g., Ph.D., Ed.D., D.B.A., D.M.) or an M.F.A at the time of application. 6. Tenured professors are not eligible. 7. Applicants may not apply for another AAUW national fellowship or grant in the same year.
Level of Study: Postdoctorate

Type: Fellowship
Value: US$6,000–US$30,000
Length of Study: One year
Country of Study: United States of America
Closing Date: 1 November

For further information contact:

Email: aauw@applyists.com

American Association of University Women (AAUW) Career Development Grants

Subjects: Business
Purpose: Career Development Grants provide funding to women who hold a bachelor's degree and are preparing to advance or change careers or re-enter the workforce in education, health and medical sciences, or social sciences. Primary consideration is given to women of color and women pursuing their first advanced degree or credentials in non-traditional fields.
Eligibility: Career Development Grants are open to individuals who identify as women and 1. are U.S. citizens or permanent residents. 2. hold an earned (not honorary) bachelor's degree. 3. received their bachelor's degree on or before June 30, 2013. 4. do not hold an earned (not honorary) graduate or professional degree. 5. plan to enroll or are enrolled in courses/activities that are required for professional employment or advancement, and 6. plan to enroll or are enrolled in one of the following program types a. Bachelor's or associate degree program that is different from the field of study of the previously earned bachelor's degree. b. Master's degree program. c. Certification program. d. Technical school. 6. Plan to enroll or are enrolled in one of the following fields of study a. Education. b. Health and Medical Sciences. c. Social Sciences. All courses of study must occur at a regionally accredited two- or four-year college or university in the United States or at a technical school that is fully licensed and/or accredited by the U.S. Department of Education. Applicants must reside within the United States during the grant period. Distance or online learning programs will be funded only if they are conducted through an accredited institution appearing on the U.S. Department of Education's list of approved online/distance learning programs. Final decisions about what constitutes distance learning under these grants will be made by AAUW. Applicants are required to indicate their matriculation status within the application. While applicants are not required to already be enrolled or accepted into their preferred institution of study in order to apply, preference is given to those who are able to demonstrate strong commitment or intent in following the proposed plan of study. Awardees must be able to show proof of admission when submitting their acceptance materials.
Type: Grant
Value: US$2,000–US$12,000
Country of Study: United States of America
Closing Date: 15 November
Additional Information: The grants apply only to coursework; not for dissertation research or writing. www.aauw.org

For further information contact:

Email: aauw@applyists.com

American Association of University Women (AAUW) International Fellowships

Subjects: Business
Purpose: When AAUW International Fellows pursue education in the United States, their commitment to empowering women and girls in their home countries doesn't end — and neither does their need for financial support.
Eligibility: See website: www.aauw.org/resources/programs/fellowships-grants/current-opportunities/international/
Type: Fellowship
Value: The Masters/First Professional Fellowship award is US$18,000 and the Doctoral Fellowship is US$20,000.
Length of Study: One year
Country of Study: United States of America
Closing Date: 15 November
Additional Information: www.aauw.org

For further information contact:

Email: aauw@applyists.com

American Association of University Women Educational Foundation

1111 16 Street North West, Washington, DC 20036, United States of America.

Tel: (1) 202 785 7700
Email: fellowships@aauw.org
Website: www.aauw.org
Contact: Gloria Blackwell, Director of Fellowship

The AAUW Educational Foundation is composed of three corporations. These are the Association, a 150,000 member organization with more than 1,500 branches nationwide that lobbies and advocates for education and equity; the AAUW Educational Foundation, which funds pioneering research on girls and education, community action projects, and fellowships and grants for outstanding women around the globe; and the AAUW Legal Advocacy Fund, which provides funds and a support system for women seeking judicial redress for sexual discrimination in higher education.

American Association of University Women Career Development Grants

Purpose: To support women who hold a bachelor's degree and are preparing to advance their careers, change careers, or re-enter the work force
Eligibility: Primary consideration is given to women of color and women pursuing their first advanced degree or credentials in nontraditional fields
Level of Study: Graduate, Postgraduate
Type: Grant
Value: US$2,000–12,000 (Funds are available for tuition, fees, books, supplies, local transportation, and dependent care.)
Length of Study: 1 year
Frequency: Annual
Closing Date: 15 December
No. of awards given last year: 47
Additional Information: Materials sent to the Washington, DC office will be disqualified and will not be reviewed www.unigo.com/scholarships/all/aauw-career-development-grant/4362

For further information contact:

ACT, Inc., 101 ACT Dr., Iowa City, IA 52243, United States of America.

Tel: (1) 319 337 1716 ext. 60
Email: aauw@act.org

American Association of University Women Case Support Travel Grants

Purpose: To enable Legal Advocacy Fund-supported plaintiffs, their lawyers, and related experts to speak at state meetings or conventions about LAF-supported cases, sex discrimination issues in the workplace and higher education, and the work of LAF
Eligibility: Please see website for conditions
Level of Study: Postgraduate, Research
Type: Grant
Value: The grant covers the speaker's travel, lodging, and meal expenses

Frequency: Annual
Application Procedure: Apply online
Closing Date: 15 October
Additional Information: Please note that materials sent to the Washington, DC office will be disqualified and will not be reviewed www.aauw.org/act/laf/travelgrant.cfm

For further information contact:

Fax: (1) 202 463 7169
Email: laf@aauw.org

American Association of University Women Community Action Grants

Purpose: To provide seed money to individual women, local community-based non-profit organizations, AAUW branches and AAUW state organizations for innovative programmes or non-degree research projects that engage girls in mathematics, science and technology
Eligibility: Applicants must be women who are citizens or permanent residents of the United States of America. Special consideration will be given to AAUW members and AAUW branch and state applicants who seek partners for collaborative projects. Collaborators can include local schools or school districts, businesses and other community-based organizations. 2-year grants are restricted to projects focused on girls' achievement in mathematics, science or technology. Projects must involve community and school collaboration. The fund supports planning and coalition-building activities during the 1st year and implementation and evaluation the following year
Type: Grant
Value: US$2,000–7,000 (1-year grant); US$5,000–10,000 (2-year grant)
Length of Study: 1 or 2 years
Frequency: Annual
Application Procedure: Applicants must write for an application form, which is also available from the website
Closing Date: 15 January
Additional Information: Please note that materials sent to the Washington, DC office will be disqualified and will not be reviewed. Two types of grant are available: 1-year grants are for short-term projects. Topic areas are unrestricted but should have a clearly defined educational activity; 2-year grants are for longer term programmes and are restricted to projects focused on K-12 girls achievement in mathematics, science and/or technology. Funds support planning activities and coalition-building during the 1st year and implementation and evaluation the following year www.aauw.org/what-we-do/educational-funding-and-awards/community-action-grants/

For further information contact:

Tel: (1) 319 337 1716 ext. 60
Email: aauw@act.org

American Association of University Women Eleanor Roosevelt Fund Award

Purpose: To remove barriers to women's and girls' partici-pation in education; to promote the value of diversity and cross-cultural communication; and to develop greater under-standing of the ways women learn, think, work, and play
Eligibility: To be eligible for the award, projects or activities must take place within the United States and recipients or organizational representatives must reside in the United States at the time the award is given. AAUA programs are not eligible for this award
Level of Study: Professional development
Type: Award
Value: US$5,000 plus travel expenses to attend the AAUW National Convention
Frequency: Every 2 years
Application Procedure: Please see the website for details
Closing Date: 1 August
Funding: Individuals, Private
No. of awards given last year: 1
Additional Information: www.aauw.org/resource/eleanor-roosevelt-fund-award-nominate/

For further information contact:

Tel: (1) 202 728 3300

American Association of University Women International Fellowships

Purpose: To support full-time study or research to women who are not United States citizen or permanent residents
Eligibility: Have citizenship in a country other than the U.S. or possession of a nonimmigrant visa if residing in the U.S. Women who are currently, or expect to be during the fellowship year, a U.S. citizen, U.S. permanent resident, or dual citizen with the U.S. and another country are not eligible. Hold an academic degree (earned in the U.S. or abroad) equivalent to a U.S. bachelor's degree completed by the application deadline. Intend to devote herself full-time to the proposed academic plan during the fellowship year. Intend to return to her home country to pursue a professional career. Be proficient in English. Unless the applicant can verify that her native language is English (written statement required), that she received her secondary diploma or undergraduate degree from an English-speaking institution (transcript required), or that she will have completed one semester of full-time study in her discipline at an English-speaking college or university between November 2017 and November 2019 (transcript required), she must upload a recent ETS TOEFL* (Test of English as a Foreign Language) score (no older than November 2017). Institutional TOEFL scores and other English proficiency test scores (such as IELTS) will not be accepted. Minimum score acceptable 550 for Paper-Based Test (TOEFL PBT); 79 for Internet-Based Test (TOEFL iBT); 60 for Revised TOEFL Paper-Delivered Test.. Master's/first professional degree and doctoral applicants must have applied by 15 November, to an accredited institution of study for the period of the fellowship year and must indicate the name of the institution in the International Fellowship application.
Level of Study: Doctorate, MBA, Postdoctorate, Postgradu-ate, Professional development
Type: Fellowship
Value: US$18,000 (Master's/First Professional Degree Fel-lowship); US$20,000 (Doctoral Fellowship); US$30,000 (Postdoctoral Fellowship)
Length of Study: 1 year
Frequency: Annual
Study Establishment: Any accredited institution
Country of Study: United States of America
Application Procedure: Applicants must complete an appli-cation for each year applying. Applications must be obtained from the customer service centre or the AAUW website between 1 August and 15 December. Three letters of recommendation, transcripts and a minimum score of 550 on the Test of English as a Foreign Language (213 computer-based) are also required. Order for brochure at www.act.org/aauw/brochurerequest.html
No. of awards offered: 1194
Closing Date: 1 December
Funding: Foundation
No. of awards given last year: 36
No. of applicants last year: 1194
Additional Information: Please note that materials sent to the Washington, DC office will be disqualified and will not be reviewed www.scholars4dev.com/1877/aauw-international-fellowships-in-usa-for-women/

For further information contact:

Tel: (1) 319 337 1716 ext. 60
Email: aauw@act.org

American Association of University Women Selected Professions Fellowships

Purpose: To support women who intend to pursue a full-time course of study at accredited institutions during the fellowship year in one of the designated degree programs where women's participation has been low

Eligibility: Women candidates who intend to pursue a full-time course of study at accredited United States institutions during the fellowship year in one of the designated degree programs where women's participation traditionally has been low (see list below). Applicants must be United States citizens or permanent residents. Please check the website for further details of eligibility

Level of Study: Doctorate, Postdoctorate, Postgraduate

Type: Fellowships

Value: US$5,000–18,000

Length of Study: 1 year

Frequency: Annual

Study Establishment: Any accredited institution

Application Procedure: Check website for details

Closing Date: 10 January

Additional Information: Materials sent to the Washington, DC office will be disqualified and will not be reviewed www.aauw.org/what-we-do/educational-funding-and-awards/selected-professions-fellowships/

For further information contact:

C/O ACT, Inc., P.O. Box 4030, Iowa City, IA 52243 4030, United States of America.

Tel: (1) 319 337 1716 ext. 60
Email: aauw@act.org

American Australian Association (AAA)

50 Broadway, Suite 2003, New York, NY 10004, United States of America.

Tel: (1) 212 338 6860
Email: information@aaanyc.org
Website: www.americanaustralian.org
Contact: Diane Sinclair, Director of Education

The American Australian Association (AAA), founded in 1948, is the largest non-profit organization in the United States devoted to relations between the United States, Australia and New Zealand, with operations throughout the tri-state and the New England regions. Its goal is to encourage stronger ties across the Pacific, particularly in the private sector.

AAA Graduate Education Scholarships

Purpose: The AAA Graduate Education Scholarships support American and Australian individuals undertaking or planning to undertake full-time Graduate level study (Masters, PhD or Postdoctoral Research) at an accredited

institution in the country of the other, for a minimum of one year. The scholarships outlined below will provide support of up to US$40,000 to those in the specialty fields of Science, Technology, Engineering, Mathematics, Health, Medicine and Sustainability. Scholarship funds may be used toward travel, living, tuition and other associated educational costs.

Eligibility: 1. All AUS to USA applicants must be an Australian citizen or permanent resident (dual citizens or USA permanent residents are not eligible); 2. Applicants must have a formal letter of offer into the accredited institution, program or course, in the country of the other, at the time of application; 3. Applicants must be conducting research or studying within the fields supported; 4. Applicants must be studying at Graduate-level or above (Masters, PhD or Postdoctoral Research); 5. Applicants may already have commenced their studies in the USA, but must have at least one-year of full-time study left at the time of application.

Level of Study: Postdoctorate

Type: Scholarship

Value: US$40,000

Length of Study: 1 year

Application Procedure: 1. High-resolution headshot & in-action study field shot (min 1MB, 300 DPI); 2. Video presentation (max 1 minute – introducing yourself & your planned research/study abroad); 3. Passport biographic page from Australia or USA; 4. Offer or acceptance letter from your host university or research supervisor, confirming your placement; 5. Academic transcripts for Graduate and/or Undergraduate study; 6. Resume (please reduce to 1-page); 7. Detailed budget outlining expenses and income throughout the year of supported study – please download and use the Graduate Education Scholarships Budget Template as a guide. This is available to download in the application portal; 8. Three referees to list in the Letter of Recommendation section. Please note after listing, referees will be automatically contacted to complete a recommendation within the online submission form. This is not viewable to the applicant.

Closing Date: 15 October

Additional Information: www.americanaustralian.org/scholarships/education-fund/specialty-field-scholarships/

For further information contact:

50 Broadway Suite 2003, New York, NY 10004, United States of America.

Email: scholarships@aaanyc.org

Sir Keith Murdoch Fellowships

Purpose: To facilitate intellectual interchange between Australia and the United States and create a channel for ongoing collaborative research

Level of Study: Graduate, Postdoctorate
Type: Fellowships
Value: Up to US$320,000
Frequency: Annual
Study Establishment: Harvard Medical, John Hopkins, MIT, Stanford Business School and Cold Spring Harbor Laboratory
Country of Study: United States of America
Closing Date: 31 October
Contributor: American Australian Association
Additional Information: ecms.adelaide.edu.au/faculty-intranet/news/list/2019/11/19/sir-keith-murdoch-fellowship-award-winner

For further information contact:

Email: jhelum.bagchi@aaanyc.org

American Cancer Society (ACS)

1599 Clifton Road North East, Atlanta, GA 30329-4251, United States of America.

Email: fellows@uicc.org
Website: fellows.uicc.org
Contact: Ms Brita Baker, Head of Fellowships Department

The American Cancer Society (ACS) is the largest non government fund holder of cancer research in the United States. ACS has devoted more than US$2 billion to cancer research.

American Cancer Society International Fellowships for Beginning Investigators

Purpose: To foster a bi-directional flow of knowledge, experience, expertise, and innovation to and from the United States of America. To enable beginning investigators and clinicians, who are in the early stages of their careers, to carry out basic or clinical research projects and to develop, acquire and apply advanced research procedures and techniques
Eligibility: 1. Be a beginning investigator or clinician in the early stages of their independent investigator career and possessing a terminal, advanced degree. 2. Applicants must be in the early phases of their career and no longer under research mentoring. 3. Hold an academic university or hospital position with an explicit commitment to return to the home institute 4. Conduct the research project at not-for-profit institutions. 5. Fellowships cannot be granted to candidates who

are already physically present at the proposed host institute whilst their applications are under consideration.
Level of Study: Postdoctorate
Type: Fellowship
Value: US$50,000 each for travel and stipend
Length of Study: 1 year
Frequency: Annual
Country of Study: United States of America
Application Procedure: Applicants must obtain an application form from the Fellowships department
No. of awards offered: 6-8 per year
Closing Date: 1 November
Additional Information: No allowances are made for accompanying dependants www.caca.org.cn/system/2015/07/03/011227242.shtml

For further information contact:

International Union Against Cancer, 3 rue Conseil-Général, CH-1205 Genève, Switzerland.

Tel: (1) 22 809 1840
Fax: (1) 22 809 1081
Email: fellows@uicc.ch

American Chemical Society (ACS)

1155 16th Street, NW, Washington, DC 20036-4801, United States of America.

Tel: (1) 614 447 3776
Email: service@acs.org

The American Chemical Society is a self-governed individual membership organization that consists of more than 160,000 members at all degree levels and in all fields of chemistry. The organization provides a broad range of opportunities for peer interaction and career development, regardless of professional or scientific interests. The program and activities conducted by ACS today are the products of a tradition of excellence in meeting member needs that dates from the Society's founding in 1876.

Alfred Burger Award in Medicinal Chemistry

Purpose: To recognize outstanding contributions to research in medicinal chemistry.
Eligibility: The award will be granted for outstanding contributions in the field of medicinal chemistry regardless of race, gender, age, religion, ethnicity, nationality, sexual orientation,

gender expression, gender identity, presence of disabilities and educational background
Level of Study: Postgraduate
Type: Award
Value: The award consists of US$5,000 and a certificate. Up to US$2,500 for travel expenses to the meeting at which the award will be presented will be reimbursed
Frequency: Annual
Country of Study: Any country
Application Procedure: A completed nomination form available on the website www.chemistry.org
Closing Date: 1 November
Contributor: Glaxo Smith Kline
Additional Information: www.acs.org/content/acs/en/funding-and-awards/awards/national/bytopic/alfred-burger-award-in-medicinal-chemistry.html

For further information contact:

American Chemical Society, 1155 16th Street NW, Washington, DC 20036-4801, United States of America.

Tel: (1) 202 872 4575
Fax: (1) 202 776 8008
Email: awards@acs.org

American Chemical Society Ahmed Zewail Award in Ultrafast Science and Technology

Purpose: To recognize outstanding and creative contributions to fundamental discoveries or inventions in ultrafast science and technology
Eligibility: The award will be for outstanding and creative contributions by a nominee to fundamental discoveries or inventions in ultrafast science and technology in the areas of physics, chemistry, biology, or related fields. Please see the website for further details regarding eligibility
Level of Study: Postgraduate
Type: Award
Value: The award will consist of US$5,000 and a certificate. Up to US$2,500 for travel expenses to the meeting at which the award will be presented will be reimbursed
Frequency: Annual
Country of Study: Any country
Application Procedure: See website for details
Closing Date: 1 November
Funding: Trusts
Contributor: Ahmed Zewail Endowment Fund
Additional Information: www.acs.org/content/acs/en/funding-and-awards/awards/national/bytopic/the-ahmed-zewail-award-in-ultrafast-science-and-technology.html

For further information contact:

Tel: (1) 202 872 4575
Fax: (1) 202 776 8008
Email: awards@acs.org

American Chemical Society Award for Creative Advances in Environmental Science and Technology

Purpose: To encourage creativity in research and technology or methods of analysis to provide a scientific basis for informed environmental control decision-making processes, or to provide practical technologies that will reduce health risk factors.
Eligibility: The award will be granted regardless of race, gender, age, religion, ethnicity, nationality, sexual orientation, gender expression, gender identity, presence of disabilities, and educational background.
Level of Study: Postgraduate
Type: Award
Value: The award consists of US$5,000 and a certificate. Up to US$2,500 for travel expenses to the meeting at which the award will be presented will be reimbursed
Frequency: Annual
Country of Study: Any country
Application Procedure: See the website for more details
Closing Date: 1 November
Contributor: ACS Division of Environmental Chemistry
Additional Information: Air Products and Chemicals, Inc www.acs.org/content/acs/en/funding-and-awards/awards/national/bytopic/acs-award-for-creative-advances-in-environmental-science-and-technology.html

For further information contact:

Tel: (1) 202 872 4575
Fax: (1) 202 776 8008
Email: awards@acs.org

American Chemical Society Award for Creative Research and Applications of Iodine Chemistry

Purpose: To support, promote, and motivate global research of iodine chemistry and develop its use and knowledge through applications.
Eligibility: A nominee must have performed outstanding and creative research related to iodine chemistry or its applications. Applications of iodine chemistry may include but are not limited to its uses in medicine, catalysis, food, and photography. The award will be granted regardless of

race, gender, age, religion, ethnicity, nationality, sexual orientation, gender expression, gender identity, presence of disabilities, and educational background.

Level of Study: Postgraduate

Type: Award

Value: The award consists of US$10,000 and a certificate. Up to US$1,000 for travel expenses to the meeting at which the award will be presented will be reimbursed. The award is presented biennially in odd-numbered years

Application Procedure: A completed nomination form and curriculum vitae must be sent

Closing Date: 1 November

Contributor: Sociedad Quimica y Minera de chile S.A. (SQM S.A.)

Additional Information: www.acs.org/content/acs/en/funding-and-awards/awards/national/bytopic/acs-award-for-creative-research-and-applications-of-iodine-chemistry.html

For further information contact:

Tel: (1) 202 872 4575
Fax: (1) 202 776 8008
Email: awards@acs.org

American Chemical Society Award for Creative Work in Synthetic Organic Chemistry

Purpose: To recognize and encourage creative work in synthetic organic chemistry

Eligibility: A nominee must have accomplished outstanding creative work in synthetic organic chemistry that has been published. Please see website for further details regarding eligibility

Level of Study: Postgraduate

Type: Award

Value: The award consists of US$5,000 and a certificate. Up to US$1,000 for travel expenses to the meeting at which the award will be presented will be reimbursed

Frequency: Annual

Application Procedure: See the website for more details

Closing Date: 1 November

Contributor: The Aldrich Chemical Company, Inc

Additional Information: www.acs.org/content/acs/en/funding-and-awards/awards/national/bytopic/acs-award-for-creative-work-in-synthetic-organic-chemistry.html

For further information contact:

Tel: (1) 202 872 4575
Fax: (1) 202 776 8008
Email: awards@acs.org

American Chemical Society Award for Encouraging Disadvantaged Students into Careers in the Chemical Sciences

Purpose: To recognize significant accomplishments by individuals in stimulating students, underrepresented in the profession, to elect careers in the chemical sciences and engineering

Eligibility: Nominees for the award may come from any professional setting academia, industry, government or other independent facility. Please see the website for further details regarding eligibility

Level of Study: Postgraduate

Type: Award

Value: The award consists of US$5,000 and a certificate. A grant of US$10,000 will be made to an academic institution, designated by the recipient, to strengthen its activities in meeting the objectives of the award. Up to US$1,500 for travel expenses to the meeting at which the award will be presented will be reimbursed

Frequency: Annual

Country of Study: United States of America

Application Procedure: Completed nomination and optional support forms must be submitted to the awards office

Closing Date: 1 November

Contributor: The Camille and Henry Dreyfus Foundation, Inc

Additional Information: www.acs.org/content/acs/en/funding-and-awards/awards/national/bytopic/acs-award-for-encouraging-disadvantaged-students-into-careers-in-the-chemical-sciences.html

For further information contact:

Tel: (1) 202 872 4575
Fax: (1) 202 776 8008
Email: awards@acs.org

American Chemical Society Award for Encouraging Women into Careers in the Chemical Sciences

Purpose: To recognize significant accomplishments by individuals who have stimulated or fostered the interest of women in chemistry, promoting their professional developments as chemists or chemical engineers.

Eligibility: Open to candidates of all nationalities. Nominees for the award may come from any professional setting academia, industry, government, or other independent facility

Level of Study: Professional development

Type: Award

Value: The award consists of US$5,000 and a certificate. A grant of US$10,000 will be made to an academic institution, designated by the recipient, to strengthen its activities in meeting the objectives of the award. Up to US$1,500 for travel expenses to the meeting at which the award will be presented will be reimbursed

Frequency: Annual

Application Procedure: For more details visit the website

Closing Date: 1 November

Contributor: The Camille and Henry Dreyfus Foundation, Inc

Additional Information: www.acs.org/content/acs/en/funding-and-awards/awards/national/bytopic/acs-award-for-encouraging-women-into-careers-in-the-chemical-sciences.html

For further information contact:

Tel: (1) 202 872 4575
Fax: (1) 202 776 8008
Email: awards@acs.org

American Chemical Society Award in Chromatography

Purpose: To recognize outstanding contributions to the fields of chromatography

Eligibility: A nominee must have made an outstanding contribution to the fields of chromatography with particular consideration given to developments of new methods. Please see the website for further details regarding eligibility

Level of Study: Postgraduate

Type: Award

Value: The award consists of US$5,000 and a certificate. Up to US$2,500 for travel expenses to the meeting at which the award will be presented will be reimbursed

Frequency: Annual

Country of Study: Any country

Application Procedure: See the website for more details

Closing Date: 1 November

Contributor: MilliporeSigma

Additional Information: www.acs.org/content/acs/en/funding-and-awards/awards/national/bytopic/acs-award-in-chromatography.html

For further information contact:

The Awards Office, American Chemical Society, 1155 16th Street NW, Washington, DC 20036-4801, United States of America.

Tel: (1) 202 872 4575
Fax: (1) 202 776 8008
Email: awards@acs.org

American Chemical Society Award in Colloid Chemistry

Purpose: To recognize and encourage outstanding scientific contributions to colloid chemistry

Eligibility: The nominee must have made outstanding scientific contributions to colloid chemistry. The award will be granted regardless of race, gender, age, religion, ethnicity, nationality, sexual orientation, gender expression, gender identity, presence of disabilities, and educational background

Level of Study: Postgraduate

Type: Award

Value: The award consists of US$5,000 and a certificate. Up to US$2,500 for travel expenses to the meeting at which the award will be presented will be reimbursed

Frequency: Annual

Country of Study: Any country

Closing Date: 1 November

Contributor: Colgate-Palmolive Company

Additional Information: www.acs.org/content/acs/en/funding-and-awards/awards/national/bytopic/acs-award-in-colloid-chemistry.html

For further information contact:

Tel: (1) 202 872 4575
Fax: (1) 202 776 8008
Email: awards@acs.org

American Chemical Society National Awards

Purpose: The ACS National Awards program is designed to encourage the advancement of chemistry in all its branches, to support research in chemical science and industry, and to promote the careers of chemists

Eligibility: 1. Nominators are not required to be members of the Society. 2. A nomination can only have one nominator and the recommendation letter is written by this person. 3. Any individual, except a member of the award selection committee or an ACS Board member during their terms of service on the Board, may submit one nomination and/or one support letter for each award. However, selection committee members may submit other nominations or support letters for awards in which they are not serving as a judge.

Level of Study: Postgraduate

Type: Grant

Length of Study: 2 years

Frequency: Annual

Country of Study: Any country

Application Procedure: See website for details

Closing Date: July

Additional Information: Inquiries concerning awards should be directed to the office of the National Awards office awards@acs.org www.acs.org/content/acs/en/funding-and-awards/awards/national.html

For further information contact:

Email: awards@acs.org

American Chemical Society Priestley Medal

Purpose: To recognize distinguished services to chemistry
Eligibility: The award will be granted regardless of race, gender, age, religion, ethnicity, nationality, sexual orientation, gender expression, gender identity, presence of disabilities, and educational background. The medal may be awarded not only to members of the Society, but also to non-members and to representatives of any nation. Members of the ACS Board of Directors are ineligible to receive this award.
Level of Study: Doctorate
Type: Award
Value: Gold medallion + up to US$2,500 expenses
Frequency: Annual
Country of Study: Any country
Application Procedure: Applicants must send their nominations to the ACS Board of Directors
Closing Date: 1 November
Funding: Trusts
Contributor: The American Chemical Society
Additional Information: www.acs.org/content/acs/en/funding-and-awards/awards/national/bytopic/priestley-medal.html

For further information contact:

Tel: (1) 202 872 4575
Fax: (1) 202 776 8008
Email: awards@acs.org

American Chemical Society Roger Adams Award in Organic Chemistry

Purpose: To recognize and encourage outstanding contributions to research in organic chemistry
Eligibility: The award will be granted regardless of race, gender, age, religion, ethnicity, nationality, sexual orientation, gender expression, gender identity, presence of disabilities and educational background
Type: Award

Value: The award consists of a medallion and a replica, a certificate and US$25,000
Application Procedure: A completed nomination form must be sent as an email attachment. See the website www.chemistry.org
Closing Date: 1 November
Contributor: Organic Reactions, Inc. and Organic Synthesis, Inc
Additional Information: www.acs.org/content/acs/en/funding-and-awards/awards/national/bytopic/roger-adams-award-in-organic-chemistry.html

For further information contact:

Tel: (1) 202 872 4575
Fax: (1) 202 776 8008
Email: awards@acs.org

American Chemical Society Stanley C. Israel Regional Award for Advancing Diversity in the Chemical Sciences

Purpose: To recognize individuals who have advanced diversity in the chemical sciences and significantly stimulated or fostered activities that promote inclusiveness within the region
Eligibility: Nominees may come from academia, industry, government, or independent entities, and may also be organizations, including ACS Local Sections and Divisions. The nominee must have created and fostered ongoing programs or activities that result in increased numbers of persons from diverse and underrepresented minority groups, persons with disabilities, or women who participate in the chemical enterprise
Level of Study: Postgraduate
Type: Award
Value: The award consists of a medal and a US$1,000 grant to support and further the activities for which the award was made. The award also will include funding to cover the recipient's travel expenses to the ACS regional meeting at which the award will be presented
Frequency: Annual
Application Procedure: See website for details
Closing Date: 1 August
Contributor: ACS Committee on Minority Affairs
Additional Information: First deadline is for Middle Atlantic (MARM), Central (CERM), and Northwest (NORM) and second deadline is for Midwest (MWRM), Northeast (NERM), Southeastern (SERMACS), Southwest (SWRM), and Rocky Mountain (RMRM) www.acs.org/content/acs/en/funding-and-awards/awards/other/diversity/stan-israel-award.html

For further information contact:

Fax: (1) 202 776 8003
Email: Diversity@acs.org

Arthur C. Cope Scholar Awards

Purpose: To recognize outstanding achievement in the field of organic chemistry
Eligibility: Ten Arthur C. Cope Scholars will be named annually in three categories two who have less than ten years of experience since their terminal degree will receive the Arthur C. Cope Early Career Scholars Award; four who have 10 to 25 years of experience since their terminal degree will receive the Arthur C. Cope Mid Career Scholars Award; and four who have 25 plus years of experience since their terminal degree will receive the Arthur C. Cope Late Career Scholars Award. No individual may receive a second Arthur C. Cope Scholar Award. Recipients of an Arthur C. Cope Award are ineligible to be named an Arthur C. Cope Scholar. The award will be granted regardless of race, gender, religion, ethnicity, nationality, sexual orientation, gender expression, gender identity, presence of disabilities, and educational background.
Level of Study: Postgraduate
Type: Award
Value: The award consists of US$5,000, a certificate, and a US$40,000 unrestricted research grant to be assigned by the recipient to any university or nonprofit institution. Up to US$2,500 for travel expenses to the fall national meeting will be reimbursed
Frequency: Annual
Application Procedure: See the website
Closing Date: 1 November
Contributor: The Arthur C. Cope Fund
Additional Information: www.acs.org/content/acs/en/funding-and-awards/awards/national/bytopic/arthur-cope-scholar-award.html

For further information contact:

Tel: (1) 202 872 4575
Fax: (1) 202 776 8008
Email: awards@acs.org

Award in Chemical Instrumentation

Purpose: Conceptualization and development of unique instrumentation that has made a significant impact on the field. Demonstration of innovative use of instrumentation in chemical measurement. Stimulation of other researchers to use instrumentation in chemical measurement. Authorship of research papers or books that have had an influential role in the use of chemical instrumentation
Eligibility: Eligibility is not restricted to members of the Division of Analytical Chemistry. Nominees for the J. Calvin Giddings Award for Excellence in Education must, however, must have demonstrated excellence in teaching through at least five years at the time the award is presented
Level of Study: Postgraduate
Type: Grant
Frequency: Annual
Country of Study: Any country
Application Procedure: Apply online
Funding: Trusts
Additional Information: www.acs.org/content/acs/en/funding-and-awards/awards/national/bytopic/arthur-cope-scholar-award.html

For further information contact:

Email: miquela@sciencemanagers.com

Award in Spectrochemical Analysis

Purpose: Development of novel and important instrumentation. Elucidation of fundamental events or processes important to the field. Authorship of important research papers and/or books that have had an influential role in the development of the field. role in the use of chemical instrumentation
Eligibility: 1. Eligibility is not restricted to members of the Division of Analytical Chemistry. Nominees for the J. Calvin Giddings Award for Excellence in Education must, however, must have demonstrated excellence in teaching through at least five years at the time the award is presented. 2. Contributions by a candidate that have been recognized by a prior Divisional or ACS national award generally will not be considered by the jury for a Divisional award, especially if an award has been received within the past three years and within a similar area. This does not apply to the Award for Distinguished Service. Previous award winners for the divisional awards are listed below. The jury shall receive from its chairperson a list for each nominee of any such prior awards, their dates, and their citations. 3. Any candidate previously nominated for an award who was not chosen as the awardee will be considered for up to three additional years without further action by the nominator being required.
Level of Study: Postgraduate
Type: Award
Value: US$2,500
Length of Study: 1 year
Frequency: Annual
Country of Study: Any country
Application Procedure: Apply online

Funding: Trusts
Additional Information: www.acs.org/content/acs/en/funding-and-awards/awards/division/analytical/anyl-award-in-spectrochemical-analysis.html

For further information contact:

Email: miquela@sciencemanagers.com

Ernest Guenther Award in the Chemistry of Natural Products

Purpose: To recognize and encourage outstanding achievements in analysis, structure elucidation and chemical synthesis of natural products
Eligibility: A nominee must have accomplished outstanding work in the analysis, structure elucidation, and chemical synthesis of natural products. Special consideration will be given to the independence of thought and originality. The award will be granted regardless of race, gender, age, religion, ethnicity, nationality, sexual orientation, gender expression, gender identity, presence of disabilities, and educational background.
Type: Grant
Value: US$6,000, a medallion and a certificate. Up to US$2,500 for travel expenses to the meeting at which the award will be presented will be reimbursed
Frequency: Annual
Country of Study: Any country
Application Procedure: A completed nomination form and optional support forms must be mailed to awards@acs.org
Closing Date: 1 November
Contributor: Givaudan
No. of awards given last year: 1
Additional Information: www.acs.org/content/acs/en/funding-and-awards/awards/national/bytopic/ernest-guenther-award-in-the-chemistry-of-natural-products.html

For further information contact:

Tel: (1) 202 872 4575
Fax: (1) 202 776 8008
Email: awards@acs.org

F. Albert Cotton Award in Synthetic Inorganic Chemistry

Purpose: To recognize distinguished work in synthetic inorganic chemistry
Eligibility: The award recognizes outstanding synthetic accomplishment in the field of inorganic chemistry. The award will be granted regardless of race, gender, age, religion, ethnicity, nationality, sexual orientation, gender expression, gender identity, presence of disabilities and educational background
Level of Study: Postgraduate
Type: Award
Value: US$5,000 and a certificate. Up to US$2,500 for travel expenses to the meeting at which the award will be presented will be reimbursed
Frequency: Annual
Country of Study: Any country
Application Procedure: A completed application form to be submitted as an email attachment to awards@acs.org
Closing Date: 1 November
Funding: Private
Contributor: F. Albert Cotton Endowment Fund
No. of awards given last year: 1

For further information contact:

Tel: (1) 202 872 4575
Fax: (1) 202 776 8008
Email: awards@acs.org

Frederic Stanley Kipping Award in Silicon Chemistry

Purpose: To recognize distinguished contributions to the field of silicon chemistry
Eligibility: A nominee must have made distinguished contributions in the field of silicon chemistry during the 10 years preceding the current nomination. The measure of this achievement should focus primarily on the nominee's significant publications in the field of silicon chemistry, silicon-based material sciences or the related field of organometallic chemistry particularly embracing the elements of Group IV. The award will be granted regardless of race, gender, age, religion, ethnicity, nationality, sexual orientation, gender expression, gender identity, presence of disabilities, and educational background.
Level of Study: Postgraduate
Type: Award
Value: US$5,000 and a certificate. Up to US$2,500 for travel expenses will be reimbursed to the spring national meeting at which the award will be presented and to the United States based Silicon Symposium to deliver an award address
Country of Study: Any country
Application Procedure: A completed nomination form to be mailed to awards@acs.org
Closing Date: 1 November
Funding: Corporation
Contributor: Dow Corning Corporation

Additional Information: www.acs.org/content/acs/en/funding-and-awards/awards/national/bytopic/frederic-stanley-kipping-award-in-silicon-chemistry.html

For further information contact:

Tel: (1) 202 872 4575
Fax: (1) 202 776 8008
Email: awards@acs.org

Glenn T. Seaborg Award for Nuclear Chemistry

Purpose: To recognize and encourage research in nuclear and radiochemistry or their applications
Eligibility: A nominee must have made outstanding contributions to nuclear or radiochemistry or to their applications. The award will be granted regardless of race, gender, age, religion, ethnicity, nationality, sexual orientation, gender expression, gender identity, presence of disabilities, and educational background.
Level of Study: Postgraduate
Type: Award
Value: US$5,000 and a certificate. Up to US$2,500 for expenses to the meeting at which the award will be presented will be reimbursed
Frequency: Annual
Country of Study: Any country
Closing Date: 1 November
Contributor: ACS Division of Nuclear Chemistry and Technology
No. of awards given last year: 1
Additional Information: www.acs.org/content/acs/en/funding-and-awards/awards/national/bytopic/glenn-t-seaborg-award-for-nuclear-chemistry.html

For further information contact:

Tel: (1) 202 8721 4575
Fax: (1) 202 776 8008
Email: awards@acs.org

Ipatieff Prize

Purpose: To recognize outstanding chemical experimental work in the field of catalysis
Eligibility: A nominee must not have passed his or her 40th birthday on April 30 of the year in which the award is presented, and will have done outstanding chemical experimental work in the field of catalysis or high pressure. If experimental investigations in these fields have been abandoned to such a degree that no outstanding results have been achieved, then the award may be given for highly meritorious work in a closely allied field of chemistry. Special weight will be given to independence of thought and originality. The award may be made for investigations carried out in any country and without consideration of nationality. Preference will be given to American chemists. The award will be granted regardless of race, gender, religion, ethnicity, nationality, sexual orientation, gender expression, gender identity, presence of disabilities, and educational background.
Level of Study: Postgraduate
Type: Prize
Value: Approximately US$5,000
Frequency: Every 3 years
Country of Study: Any country
Closing Date: 1 November
Contributor: Ipatieff Trust Fund
Additional Information: Preference will be given to American chemists www.acs.org/content/acs/en/funding-and-awards/awards/national/bytopic/ipatieff-prize.html

For further information contact:

Tel: (1) 202 872 4575
Email: awards@acs.org

Irving Langmuir Award in Chemical Physics

Purpose: To encourage research in chemistry and physics
Eligibility: This award is made to one person who has made an outstanding contribution in the field of chemical physics or physical chemistry within the ten years prior to the award. The award is granted without restriction. Nominations will be considered for two review cycles provided the nominator re-certifies the nomination before the next deadline.
Level of Study: Postgraduate
Type: Award
Value: US$75,000 for full Professor and scholars of equivalent accomplishment. US$50,000 for Associate Professor and equivalent. US$40,000 for Assistant Professor and equivalent
Frequency: Every 2 years
Country of Study: United States of America
Closing Date: 1 June
Funding: Foundation
Contributor: GE Global Research and The American Chemical Society Division of Physical Chemistry
Additional Information: www.aps.org/programs/honors/prizes/langmuir.cfm

For further information contact:

Tel: (1) 202 872 4575
Email: awards@acs.org

James Bryant Conant Award in High School Chemistry Teaching

Purpose: To recognize outstanding teachers of high school chemistry in the United States

Eligibility: The nominee must be actively engaged in the teaching of chemistry in a high school (grades 9-12). The nomination should clearly demonstrate as many of the following attributes of the nominee as possible: 1. Quality of teaching (unusually effective methods of presentation should be emphasized) 2. Ability to challenge and inspire students 3. Extracurricular work in chemistry including science fairs, science clubs, and activities that stimulate the interest of young people in chemistry and related sciences 4. Willingness to keep up-to-date in the field, as evidenced by pursuit of a higher degree in chemistry, enrollment in refresher courses and summer institutions, regular attendance at scientific meetings, and other means of self-improvement

Level of Study: Postgraduate

Type: Award

Value: US$5,000 and a certificate. Up to US$2,500 for travel expenses to the meeting at which the award will be presented will be reimbursed

Frequency: Annual

Country of Study: United States of America

Closing Date: 1 November

Contributor: The Thermo Fisher Scientific, Inc

No. of awards given last year: 1

Additional Information: A certificate will also be provided to the recipient's institution for display www.acs.org/content/acs/en/funding-and-awards/awards/national/bytopic/james-bryant-conant-award-in-high-school-chemistry-teaching.html

For further information contact:

Tel: (1) 202 872 4575
Fax: (1) 202 776 8008
Email: awards@acs.org

Peter Debye Award in Physical Chemistry

Purpose: To encourage and reward outstanding research in physical chemistry

Eligibility: A nominee must have accomplished outstanding research of a theoretical or experimental nature in the field of physical chemistry. Because much of the impact of research depends upon the extension of the work by others, some consideration should be given to the nominee's success as a mentor and colleague. The award will be granted regardless of race, gender, age, religion, ethnicity, nationality, sexual orientation, gender expression, gender identity, presence of disabilities, and educational background.

Level of Study: Postgraduate

Type: Award

Value: US$5,000 and a certificate. Up to US$2,500 for travel expenses to the meeting at which the award will be presented will be reimbursed

Frequency: Annual

Country of Study: Any country

Application Procedure: A completed nominations form to be sent as an email attachment to awards@acs.org

Closing Date: 1 November

Contributor: E.I. du Pont de Nemours and Company

No. of awards given last year: 1

Additional Information: www.acs.org/content/acs/en/funding-and-awards/awards/national/bytopic/peter-debye-award-in-physical-chemistry.html

For further information contact:

Tel: (1) 202 872 4575
Fax: (1) 202 776 8008
Email: awards@acs.org

Pfizer Graduate Travel Awards in Analytical Chemistry

Purpose: To provide funds for students to travel to an ACS National meeting and present the results of their research

Eligibility: Open to candidates who are United States citizens and permanent residents

Level of Study: Postgraduate

Type: Award

Value: US$1,000

Frequency: Annual

Study Establishment: Open to candidates who are United States citizens and permanent residents

Application Procedure: A completed application form, which may be downloaded from the website, must be sent

Closing Date: 21 October

Contributor: The Division of Analytical Chemistry of the ACS

Additional Information: www.acs.org/content/acs/en/funding-and-awards/awards/division/analytical/anyl-pfizer-graduate-travel-awards-in-analytical-chemistry.html

For further information contact:

Department of Chemistry, The College of Wooster, Wooster, OH 44691, United States of America.

Tel: (1) 202 872 4575
Email: awards@acs.org

American College of Chest Physicians

CHEST Foundation Grants

Subjects: Lung health
Purpose: The CHEST Foundation, the American College of Chest Physician's charitable foundation, champions lung health by supporting clinical research, community service, and patient education. Through CHEST Foundation-supported programs, CHEST's 20,000+ members engage in advancing the lung health of millions of patients in local communities around the world.
Eligibility: No restrictions on eligibility
Type: Grant
Value: Varies
Frequency: Annual
Country of Study: Any country
Application Procedure: Visit website for details
Closing Date: 6 April

American Congress on Surveying and Mapping (ACSM)

6, Montgomery Village Avenue, Suite 403, Gaithersburg, MD 20879, United States of America.

Tel: (1) 240 632 9716 ext. 109
Email: ilse.genovese@acsm.net
Website: www.acsm.net

The ACSM is a nonprofit association dedicated to serving the public interest and advancing the profession of surveying and mapping.

American College of Sports Medicine Fellows Scholarship

Purpose: The purpose of fellowship is to recognize commendable service to ACSM; to encourage continued service to the College in a leadership role with ongoing dedication; also, to recognize distinguished achievement in sports medicine and related disciplines.
Eligibility: Open to students with a junior or higher degree and enrolled in four-year degree programs in surveying or in closely related programs such as geomatics or surveying engineering
Level of Study: Graduate, Postgraduate
Type: Scholarship

Value: US$2,000
Length of Study: 4 years
Frequency: Annual
Country of Study: Any country
Application Procedure: Applicants must submit a completed application form along with proof of membership in ACSM, a complete statement indicating educational objectives, future plans of study or research, professional activities and financial need, three letters of recommendation and a complete original official transcript
Closing Date: 1 August
Funding: Corporation

American Council of Learned Societies (ACLS)

633 3rd Avenue, 8th Floor between 40th & 41st Streets, New York, NY 10017-6795, United States of America.

Tel: (1) 212 697 1505
Email: sfisher@acls.org
Website: www.acls.org

The American Council of Learned Societies (ACLS) is a private non-profit federation of 68 national scholarly organizations. The mission of the ACLS, as set forth in its Constitution is the advancement of humanistic studies in all fields of learning in the humanities and the social sciences and the maintenance and strengthening of relations among the national societies devoted to such studies.

ACLS Emerging Voices Fellowships

Purpose: The American Council of Learned Societies is pleased to announce the third competition of the Emerging Voices Fellowship which allows recent PhDs in the humanities and interpretive social sciences to take up two-year positions at select institutions in ACLS's Research University Consortium for the 2022-23 and 2023-24 academic years.
Eligibility: Applicants must have received their PhD in the humanities or humanistic social sciences from a US institution
Type: Fellowship
Value: US$65,000 plus health insurance, a one-time relocation allowance of US$3,000, and US$3,500
Length of Study: 2 year
Frequency: Annual
Country of Study: Any country

Application Procedure: Once nominated, applications must be submitted online and must include 1. A completed brief application form including demographic information 2. A CV (1-2 pages) 3. A single-spaced, three-page (max) personal statement (in place of a cover letter) responding to specific prompts. Nominees should log into the online application portal for information about the writing prompts and document upload. 4. Dissertation abstract (no more than one full page, single-spaced) 5. A letter of recommendation submitted by a faculty adviser or the departmental director of graduate studies, identifying the nominees' potential suitability for particular departments, programs, and/or initiatives. Letters must be submitted through the ACLS application portal (nominees will be prompted to request this letter from recommenders using our system).

No. of awards offered: 45
Closing Date: 12 January

For further information contact:

Email: EVFapplications@acls.org

American Council of Learned Societies Humanities Program in Belarus, Russia and Ukraine

Purpose: To sustain individuals doing exemplary work, so as to assure continued future leadership in the humanities
Eligibility: Applicants should be involved in studies related to performing arts, ethnographic and cultural studies, gender studies, philosophy or religious studies. ACLS organizes annual regional meetings for advisers and grant recipients
Level of Study: Research
Type: Grant
Value: Varies
Frequency: Annual
Country of Study: Any country
Application Procedure: Application forms can be obtained by writing to hp@acls.org
Closing Date: 18 November
Funding: Foundation
Additional Information: In 2007, with the help of the Carnegie Corporation of New York and the American Council of Learned Societies, the International Association for the Humanities (IAH) was founded as an independent association of humanities scholars primarily in Belarus, Russia and Ukraine to help represent the post-Soviet region in the international scholarly community. IAH organizes a competition for short-term grants in the humanities. For further details and current competition application form, see the IAH website www.acls.org/Past-Programs/ACLS-Humanities-Program-in-Belarus-Russia-and-Ukraine

For further information contact:

Email: hp@acls.org

American Council of Learned Societies/New York Public Library (NYPL) Fellowships

Purpose: To explore the rich and diverse collections of the NYPL Humanities and Social Sciences Library
Eligibility: US citizen or permanent resident. have a PhD that was conferred at least two years before the application deadline. (An established scholar who can demonstrate the equivalent of a PhD in publications and professional experience may also qualify.). have had a lapse of at least two years between the last "supported research leave" and September 1. Please see FAQ about the definition of supported research leaves and how the timing of such leaves affects eligibility.
Level of Study: Postdoctorate
Type: Fellowship
Value: Up to US$50,000 for full professor and equivalent, US$40,000 for associate professor and equivalent and US$30,000 for assistant professor and equivalent
Length of Study: 6–12 months
Application Procedure: Applications must be made to the ACLS Fellowship Program. Note that applications must also be made to the competition for residential fellowships administered separately by the NYPL Center for Scholars and Writers
Additional Information: More information about the NYPL is available at www.nypl.org www.acls.org/Competitions-and-Deadlines/ACLS-Fellowships

For further information contact:

Center for Scholars & Writers, The New York Public Library Humanities & Social Sciences Library, Fifth Avenue & 42nd Street, New York, NY 10001, United States of America.

Email: csw@nypl.org

Andrew W. Mellon Foundation/ACLS Early Career Fellowships Program Dissertation Completion Fellowships

Purpose: To assist graduates in the last year of their PhD dissertation writing
Eligibility: Open to a PhD candidate in a humanities or social science department in an American University. Applicant should not be in the degree programme for more than 6 years and the successful candidates cannot hold this fellowship after the 7th year
Level of Study: Doctorate

Type: Fellowships
Value: Stipend US$35,000, plus funds for research costs of up to US$3,000 and for university fees of up toUS$5,000
Length of Study: 1 year
Frequency: Annual
Country of Study: United States of America
Application Procedure: Applicants can apply online (ofa. acls.org)
Closing Date: 9 November
Contributor: The Andrew W. Mellon Foundation
Additional Information: www.acls.org/programs/dcf/

For further information contact:

Email: grants@acls.org

American Council on Rural Special Education (ACRES)

West Virginia University, 509 Allen Hall, PO Box 6122, Morgantown, WV 26506-6122, United States of America.

Tel: (1) 304 293 3450
Email: acres-sped@mail.wvu.edu
Website: acres-sped.org
Contact: David Forbush, Headquarters Co-ordinator

Alliance for Clinical Research Excellence and Safety Teacher Scholarship Award

Purpose: To give a rural teacher an opportunity to pursue education and training not otherwise affordable within his or her district
Eligibility: To be eligible for an ACRES teacher scholarship award, an individual must be currently or recently employed by a rural school district as a certified teacher in regular or special education; working with students with disabilities or with regular education students and "retooling" for work in a special education setting; pursuing a goal of increasing skills in special education or "retooling" from a regular education to a special education career; and a citizen of the United States
Level of Study: Graduate
Type: Scholarship
Value: Up to US$1,000
Length of Study: 1 year
Frequency: Annual
Country of Study: United States of America
Application Procedure: Applications must consist of a completed application form; an essay describing the

opportunities and challenges of rural special education, the reason why funds are needed for the training, the plans for using the scholarship award for further education or training, and how the information gained from the education or training will be shared with other educators in rural schools; and two letters of recommendation from persons in a position to judge capabilities as a rural special educator; at least one reference must be from an individual actively involved in rural special education
Closing Date: 15 February
Funding: Private
Additional Information: The award will be announced at the March ACRES conference www.acenet.edu/Programs-Services/Pages/Professional-Learning/ACE-Fellows-Program.aspx

For further information contact:

Tel: (1) 304 293 4384

American Diabetes Association (ADA)

1701 North Beauregard Street, Alexandria, VA 22311, United States of America.

Tel: (1) 703 549 1500, ext. 2362
Email: grantquestions@diabetes.org
Website: professional.diabetes.org/grants

The American Diabetes Association (ADA) is the nation's leading non-profit health organization providing diabetes research information and advocacy. The mission of the organization is to prevent and cure diabetes, and to improve the lives of all people affected by diabetes. To fulfil this mission, the ADA funds research, publishes scientific findings and provides information and other services to people with diabetes, their families, healthcare professionals and the public.

Lions Clubs International Foundation Clinical Research Grant Program

Purpose: To support clinical or applied research
Eligibility: Open to holders of an MD or PhD degree, or, in the case of other health professions, an appropriate health or science related degree. The applicant must hold a faculty level appointment or its equivalent at a research institution. The programme is intended for any investigator with or without NIH or other significant support

Level of Study: Postdoctorate

Type: Research grant

Value: Up to US$100,000 per year. The grants carry no commitment for overhead costs or tuition. The funds may be used for equipment, supplies, salary support or a combination of the three. The funds may not be used for the principal investigator

Length of Study: 3 years

Frequency: Annual

Country of Study: Any country

Closing Date: 1 July

Additional Information: This programme is part of the Lions Sightfirst Diabetic Retinopathy Research Program, funded by the Lions Club International Foundation temp. lionsclubs.org/EN/pdfs/lcif/lcif109.pdf

For further information contact:

300 W. 22nd Street, Oak Brook, IL 60523-8842, United States of America.

Tel: (1) 630 203 3819
Fax: (1)630 571 5735
Email: lcif@lionsclubs.org

Lions Clubs International Foundation Equipment Grant Program

Purpose: To enable investigators to purchase equipment in order to conduct clinical research projects

Eligibility: Open to holders of an MD or PhD degree, or, in the case of other health professions, an appropriate health- or science-related degree. The applicant must hold a faculty-level appointment at a research institution

Level of Study: Research

Type: Grant

Value: US$25,000 for the purchase of equipment. One payment is made in July

Frequency: Annual

Country of Study: Any country

Application Procedure: Applicants must submit a detailed justification of the need to purchase the equipment and an explanation of its intended use. All applications must be submitted online via the website

Closing Date: 15 January

Additional Information: This programme is part of the Lions Sightfirst Diabetic Retinopathy Research Program, funded by the Lions Club International Foundation temp. lionsclubs.org/EN/pdfs/lcif/lcif109.pdf

For further information contact:

Email: lcif@lionsclubs.org

Lions Clubs International Foundation Training Grant Program

Purpose: To enable foreign investigators to visit American research institutions and receive training in clinical research and the implementation of public health programmes, eg. screening or epidemiology. The programme also aims to enable United States of America investigators to visit foreign institutions, particularly institutions in developing countries, to conduct training programmes in clinical research and implement public health programmes

Eligibility: Open to citizens of the United States of America who have an MD or a PhD degree, or, in the case of other health professions, an appropriate health- or science-related degree, and hold a faculty-level appointment at a United States of America research institution. The programme is also open to citizens of other countries who have an MD or a PhD degree

Level of Study: Research

Value: Up to US$40,000 per year

Length of Study: 2 years

Frequency: Annual

Study Establishment: An approved institution

Country of Study: Any country

Application Procedure: All applications must be submitted online via the website

Closing Date: 15 January

Additional Information: This programme is part of the Lions Sightfirst Diabetic Retinopathy Research Program, funded by the Lions Club International Foundation temp. lionsclubs.org/EN/pdfs/lcif/lcif109.pdf

For further information contact:

Email: LCIFHumanitarianPrograms@lionsclubs.org

Pathway to Stop Diabetes Diabetes Initiator Award

Purpose: This two-phased award is designed to support the transition of scientists from mentored training to independent research faculty.

Eligibility: Eligible applicants must currently be in research training positions (post-doctoral fellow, research fellowship) and have no more than seven years of research training following terminal doctoral degree. Applicants cannot concurrently hold an NIH K99/R00 grant. Candidates must be identified through institutional nomination; applications will be accepted only from individuals with the appropriate institution support.

Level of Study: Postdoctoral

Type: Award

Value: Up to US$100,000/year in Phase 1, Up to US$325,000/year in Phase 2
Length of Study: Up to 7 years
Frequency: Annual
Country of Study: United States of America
Closing Date: 1 July
Additional Information: professional.diabetes.org/meetings/pathway-stop-diabetes%C2%AE

American Federation for Aging Research (AFAR)

55 West 39th Street, 16th Floor, New York, NY 10018, United States of America.

Tel: (1) 212 703 9977
Email: grants@afar.org
Website: www.afar.org
Contact: Director, Grant Programs

The American Federation for Aging Research (AFAR) is a leading non-profit organization supporting biomedical aging research. Since its founding in 1981, AFAR has provided approximately US$124 million to more than 2,600 new investigators and students conducting cutting-edge biomedical research on the aging process and age-related diseases. The important work AFAR supports leads to a better understanding of the aging process and to improvements in the health of all Americans as they age.

American Federation for Aging Research Research Grants for Junior Faculty

Purpose: To help junior faculty to carry out research that will serve as the basis for longer term research efforts
Eligibility: The Glenn Foundation for Medical Research and AFAR Grants for Junior Faculty do not provide support for 1. Postdoctoral fellows in the laboratory of a senior investigator 2. Investigators who have received major extramural funding for research in any area (such as an NIH R01, DP5, R35 or NSF Research or equivalent grant) prior to and including the start date of this award (applicants may hold K or R21 funding) 3. Senior faculty, i.e. at the rank of Associate Professor level or higher 4. Former Glenn and AFAR Grants for Junior Faculty recipients 5. Federal employees 6. Applicants for the 2021 Glenn Foundation for Medical Research Breakthroughs in Gerontology (BIG) award 7. Applicants who are conducting research at a for-profit institution, or at an

institution outside of the United States 8. Alzheimer's Disease and/or related dementias research
Level of Study: Postdoctorate, Research
Type: Research grant
Value: Up to US$125,000 each
Length of Study: 1–2 years
Frequency: Annual
Country of Study: United States of America
Application Procedure: Please refer to the LOI instructions. Incomplete applications cannot be considered. All Letters of Intent must be uploaded here; Institutional Commitment forms must be submitted via email to afarapplication@afar.org. The Letters of Intent will be reviewed by a committee. Applicants will be notified by late-February, and a subset of applicants will be invited to submit a full application by early April.
No. of awards offered: 10
Closing Date: 15 December
Funding: Foundation, Private
Contributor: AFAR
No. of applicants last year: 10
Additional Information: Exceptions to the ten year rule may be requested for unusual circumstances by emailing an NIH-style biosketch to AFAR at grants@afar.org research.weill.cornell.edu/funding/open-submission-grants/afar-research-grants-junior-faculty-american-federation-aging

For further information contact:

Email: afarapplication@afar.org

American Federation for Aging Research/Pfizer Research Grants in Metabolic Control and Late Life Diseases

Purpose: To address specific areas of research that focus on the aging process and age related diseases
Eligibility: Applicants must be MD, DO, PhD, or combined degree students in good standing at a not-for-profit institution in the United States, such as universities, medical schools, hospitals, or non-government agencies. If accepted, applicants will be asked to submit a Proof of Enrollment form confirming their enrollment at a U.S. institution. Applicants who also receive NIH, NSF or DOD stipend support are eligible to receive the AFAR Scholarship, but may not hold another award or participate in another scholarship program concurrently with the Kalman/AFAR Scholarship. The research project must be carried out under the supervision of a faculty mentor.
Level of Study: Research
Type: Grant
Value: US$60,000

Length of Study: 1–2 years
Frequency: Annual
Country of Study: United States of America
Application Procedure: Please refer to the Kalman/AFAR Scholarships Instruction Sheet and Application for complete application procedures. Applications should be submitted through the online application form, available here. Incomplete applications cannot be considered.
Closing Date: 14 December
Funding: Private
Contributor: Pfizer Pharmaceuticals, Inc
Additional Information: Projects may involve basic, clinical or epidemiological research research.weill.cornell.edu/funding/open-submission-grants/afar-research-grants-junior-faculty-american-federation-aging

Diana Jacobs Kalman/AFAR Scholarships for Research in the Biology of Aging

Purpose: An opportunity to conduct a three-to-six-month research project focused on biomedical research in aging.
Eligibility: Applicants must: 1. Have completed at least two years of an MD, DO, PhD, or combined degree program by the start date of the award. 2. Be in good standing at a not-for-profit institution in the United States, such as universities, medical schools, hospitals, or non-government agencies. If accepted, applicants will be asked to submit a Proof of Enrollment form confirming their enrollment at a U.S. institution. 3. Not hold another award or participate in another scholarship program concurrently with the Kalman/AFAR Scholarship, however those who also receive NIH, NSF or DOD stipend support are eligible to receive the Kalman/AFAR Scholarship. 4. Carry out the project under the supervision of a faculty mentor(s).
Level of Study: Three to six month research project
Type: Scholarships
Value: Each scholarship is US$5,000
Length of Study: 3-6 months
Frequency: Annual
Country of Study: Any country
Application Procedure: The full application in pdf form with instructions on all required parts is available afar.org/docs/Kalman_AFAR_Scholarship_WuFoo.pdf
Closing Date: 14 April
Contributor: The Kalman/AFAR Student Scholarships are supported by Diana Jacobs Kalman, an endowment from the former American Foundation for Aging Research, the Nicole Girard Charitable Fund of the Jewish Communal Fund, and individual contribution
Additional Information: www.afar.org/research/funding/afar-scholarships/

For further information contact:

Email: scholarship@afar.org

Glenn Foundation for Medical Research Postdoctoral Fellowships in Aging Research

Purpose: he Glenn Foundation for Medical Research, in partnership with the American Federation for Aging Research (AFAR), created the Glenn Foundation for Medical Research Postdoctoral Fellowships in Aging Research to encourage and further the careers of postdoctoral fellows who are conducting research in the basic biology of aging, as well as translating advances in basic research from the laboratory to the clinic
Eligibility: 1. The applicant must be a postdoctoral fellow (MD and/or PhD degree or equivalent) at the start date of the award (July). 2. The proposed research must be conducted at a qualified not-for-profit setting in the United States. 3. Individuals who are employees in the NIH Intramural program are not eligible. 4. Postdoctoral fellows in laboratories that receive support as part of a Paul F. Glenn Center for Biology of Aging Research are not eligible to apply. 5. Applicants who will have received more than 5 years of postdoctoral training at the time of the start of the award must provide a justification for the additional training period. Because of COVID pandemic related challenges, eligibility has been extended to allow one additional year of training - 6 years total - for the 2022 award cycle. 6. Fellows may not hold any concurrent funding for the same research project.
Country of Study: Any country
Application Procedure: The following criteria are used to determine the merit of an application: 1. Qualifications of the applicant 2. Quality of the proposed research (*see note below) 3. Proposed career development plan, and training opportunities for the applicant 4. Excellence of the research environment Likelihood that the applicant will pursue a career in aging research 5. Mentor's strength and qualifications to guide the applicant's research and career planning; * We recognize that most applicants' postdoctoral projects will be multi-year projects. As such, the applicant should describe the overall project but indicate the scope of the work that is being proposed for the year to be funded by a Fellowship if awarded.
Closing Date: 25 January

Glenn/American Federation for Aging Research Scholarships for Research in the Biology of Aging

Purpose: To attract potential scientists to aging research and provide students with the opportunity to conduct a research project
Eligibility: Open to students completing MD or PhD degrees

Level of Study: Doctorate, Research
Type: Scholarship
Value: US$6,000
Length of Study: 3 months
Frequency: Annual
Country of Study: Any country
Application Procedure: Applicants should submit one original and four copies of the application and of all supporting materials, including academic transcripts from all institutions attended, Graduate Record Examination and/or MCAT scores, and a biographical sketch and endorsing letter of the designated mentor. In addition, one letter of reference is also required
Closing Date: 26 February
Funding: Private
Contributor: The Glenn Foundation for Medical Research
Additional Information: www.afar.org/research/funding/afar-scholarships/

For further information contact:

Email: info@afar.org

Merck/American Federation for Aging Research Junior Investigator Award in Geriatric Clinical Pharmacology

Purpose: To help develop a cadre of physicians with a command of the emerging field of geriatric clinical pharmacology
Eligibility: Open to candidates who are board certified or eligible in a primary specialty having completed postdoctoral or fellowship training
Level of Study: Research
Type: Award
Value: US$60,000
Length of Study: 2 years
Frequency: Annual
Country of Study: Any country
Application Procedure: Applications must be submitted by an institution on behalf of the candidate. See the AFAR website for details
Funding: Foundation
Contributor: Merck Company Foundation
Additional Information: www.unmc.edu/media/intmed/geriatrics/pdf/2004%20AFAR%20AWARD%20PROGRAMS.pdf

Royal Photographic Society/American Federation for Aging Research Medical Student Geriatric Scholars Program

Purpose: To encourage medical students, particularly budding researchers, to consider a career in academic geriatrics

Eligibility: Applicants must be citizens of the United States of America or permanent residents and have completed at least 1 year of medical school by the start date of the award
Level of Study: Doctorate
Type: Scholarship
Value: US$4,000
Length of Study: 8 weeks
Frequency: Annual
Country of Study: United States of America
Application Procedure: Applicants must complete and return the application by the annual deadline. Applications are available from the website
Closing Date: 6 February
Funding: Private
Contributor: Anonymous donor
Additional Information: www.unmc.edu/media/intmed/geriatrics/pdf/2004%20AFAR%20AWARD%20PROGRAMS.pdf

For further information contact:

Email: info@afar.org

The Paul Beeson Career Development Awards in Aging Research for the Island of Ireland

Purpose: To encourage and assist the development of future leaders in the field of aging, deepen the commitment of research institutions to academic research in aging, and to expand medical research on aging
Level of Study: Research
Type: Award
Value: US$225,000
Length of Study: 5 years
Country of Study: Ireland
Application Procedure: All candidates must submit applications endorsed by the Dean of School of Medicine (or equivalent). Scholars will be required to submit a brief annual narrative report on the progress of their research and career plans
No. of awards offered: 10
Closing Date: 21 October
Funding: Private
Additional Information: www.unmc.edu/media/intmed/geriatrics/pdf/2004%20AFAR%20AWARD%20PROGRAMS.pdf

For further information contact:

Email: NIAtraining@nih.gov

American Foundation for Suicide Prevention (AFSP)

120 Wall Street, 29th Floor, New York, NY 10005, United States of America.

Tel:	(1) 212 363 3500
Email:	grantsmanager@afsp.org
Website:	www.afsp.org
Contact:	Carl Niedzielski, Grants Manager

The American Foundation for Suicide Prevention (AFSP) is the only national non-profit organization exclusively dedicated to understanding and preventing suicide through research and education, and to reaching out to people with mood disorders and those affected by suicide.

American Foundation for Suicide Prevention Distinguished Investigator Awards

Purpose: Awarded to investigators at the level of associate professor or higher with a proven history of research in the area of suicide
Level of Study: Research
Type: Grant
Value: Up to US$125,000 over 2 years
Length of Study: 2 years
Frequency: Annual
Country of Study: Worldwide
Application Procedure: Application information at afsp.org/grants.
No. of awards offered: 14
Closing Date: 15 November
Funding: Private
No. of applicants last year: 14
Additional Information: Decisions regarding awards are made in May and funding begins in October afsp.org/our-work/research/grant-information/

Blue Sky Focus Grant

Purpose: Under this mechanism AFSP supports an innovative, impactful high risk/high reward study in an area of suicide research that will achieve significant goals. This mechanism is intended for studies that, by their very nature, are clearly beyond the financial scope of our Innovation Grants.
Eligibility: Investigators from all academic disciplines are eligible to apply, and both basic science and applied research projects will be considered, provided that the proposed study has an essential focus on suicide or suicide prevention. Grant applications are not accepted from for-profit organizations, or from federal or state government agencies. Applications from the Veterans Administration are eligible
Level of Study: Research
Type: Research grant
Value: They are awarded in the amount of US$500,000 per year for a maximum of three years
Length of Study: 3 years
Frequency: Annual
Country of Study: Any country
Application Procedure: Applicants must submit a Letter of Intent by email to JHarkavyFriedman@afsp.org
No. of awards offered: 4
Closing Date: 6 December
Funding: Private
No. of awards given last year: 1
No. of applicants last year: 4
Additional Information: afsp.org/our-work/research/grant-information/the-focus-grants/

Distinguished Investigator Grant

Purpose: We welcome innovative studies relevant to understanding and preventing suicide. Applications are open to biological, psychological, and sociological approaches, and we encourage multidisciplinary research. These are investigator initiated grants
Eligibility: Investigators from all academic disciplines are eligible to apply, and both basic science and applied research projects will be considered, provided that the proposed study has an essential focus on suicide or suicide prevention. Grant applications are not accepted from for-profit organizations, or from federal or state government agencies. Applications from the Veterans Administration are eligible
Level of Study: Research
Type: Grant
Value: Up to US$125,000 over 2 Years
Length of Study: 2 years
Frequency: Annual
Country of Study: Any country
Application Procedure: Applicants are instructed to apply afsp.org/our-work/research/apply-for-a-grant/
No. of awards offered: 9
Closing Date: 14 November
Funding: Private
No. of awards given last year: 3
No. of applicants last year: 9
Additional Information: afsp.org/our-work/research/grant-information/

Linked Standard Research Grant

Purpose: We welcome innovative studies relevant to understanding and preventing suicide. Applications are open to biological, psychological, and sociological approaches, and we encourage multidisciplinary research. These are investigator initiated grants

Eligibility: Investigators from all academic disciplines are eligible to apply, and both basic science and applied research projects will be considered, provided that the proposed study has an essential focus on suicide or suicide prevention. Grant applications are not accepted from for-profit organizations, or from federal or state government agencies. Applications from the Veterans Administration are eligible

Level of Study: Research

Type: Grant

Value: Up to US$450,000

Length of Study: 2 years

Frequency: Annual

Country of Study: Any country

Application Procedure: Applicants must submit a Letter of Intent by email to JHarkavyFriedman@afsp.org

No. of awards offered: 13

Closing Date: 15 September

Funding: Private

No. of awards given last year: 2

No. of applicants last year: 13

Additional Information: afsp.org/our-work/research/grant-information/

Pilot Innovation Grants

Purpose: We welcome innovative studies relevant to understanding and preventing suicide. Applications are open to biological, psychological, and sociological approaches, and we encourage multidisciplinary research. These are investigator initiated grants

Eligibility: Investigators from all academic disciplines are eligible to apply, and both basic science and applied research projects will be considered, provided that the proposed study has an essential focus on suicide or suicide prevention. Grant applications are not accepted from for-profit organizations, or from federal or state government agencies. Applications from the Veterans Administration are eligible

Level of Study: Research

Type: Grant

Value: Up to US$30,000

Length of Study: 2 years

Frequency: Annual

Application Procedure: Applicants are instructed to apply afsp.org/our-work/research/apply-for-a-grant/

Closing Date: 14 November

Funding: Private

No. of awards given last year: 3

No. of applicants last year: 32

Additional Information: www.thepsf.org/research/grants-program/pilot-research-grants

Postdoctoral Fellowship

Purpose: We welcome innovative studies relevant to understanding and preventing suicide. Applications are open to biological, psychological, and sociological approaches, and we encourage multidisciplinary research. These are investigator initiated grants

Eligibility: Investigators from all academic disciplines are eligible to apply, and both basic science and applied research projects will be considered, provided that the proposed study has an essential focus on suicide or suicide prevention. New grantees must begin their studies within 6 months of the approved start date. Failure to begin the study within this time frame may result in withdrawal of the grant award

Level of Study: Postdoctorate, Research

Type: Grant

Value: Up to US$112,000 over 2 years

Length of Study: 2 years

Frequency: Annual

Country of Study: Any country

Application Procedure: Applicants are instructed to apply afsp.org/our-work/research/apply-for-a-grant/

No. of awards offered: 9

Closing Date: 14 November

Funding: Private

No. of awards given last year: 1

No. of applicants last year: 9

Additional Information: afsp.org/our-work/research/grant-information/

Reaching 20% by 2025

Purpose: Focus grants are targeted, innovative and potentially high impact studies that seek to inform and even transform suicide prevention efforts

Eligibility: Investigators from all academic disciplines are eligible to apply, and both basic science and applied research projects will be considered, provided that the proposed study has an essential focus on suicide or suicide prevention. Grant applications are not accepted from for-profit organizations, or from federal or state government agencies. Applications from the Veterans Administration are eligible

Level of Study: Research

Type: Grant

Value: They are awarded in the amount of US$500,000 per year for a maximum of three years
Length of Study: 3 years
Frequency: Annual
Country of Study: Any country
Application Procedure: Applicants must submit a Letter of Intent by email to JHarkavyFriedman@afsp.org
Closing Date: 6 December
Funding: Private
Additional Information: cpb-us-e1.wpmucdn.com/blogs. gwu.edu/dist/e/969/files/2018/07/AFSP_2018_Focus_ Grants_Flyer-14f56ys.pdf

Short-Term Risk Focus Grant

Purpose: The Focus grant for short-term risk is open to innovative, potentially high-yield proposals that focus on short-term risk for suicide.
Eligibility: Investigators from all academic disciplines are eligible to apply, and both basic science and applied research projects will be considered, provided that the proposed study has an essential focus on suicide or suicide prevention. Grant applications are not accepted from for-profit organizations, or from federal or state government agencies. Applications from the Veterans Administration are eligible
Level of Study: Research
Type: Grant
Value: Up to US$500,000 per year
Length of Study: 3 years
Frequency: Annual
Country of Study: Any country
Application Procedure: Applicants must submit a Letter of Intent by email to JHarkavyFriedman@afsp.org
No. of awards offered: 1
Closing Date: 7 December
Funding: Private
No. of awards given last year: 1
No. of applicants last year: 1

For further information contact:

Jill M. Harkavy-Friedman, PhD Vice President of Research

Tel: (1) 212 363 3500 ext. 2039
Email: JHarkavyFriedman@afsp.org

Standard Research Grant

Purpose: We welcome innovative studies relevant to understanding and preventing suicide. Applications are open to biological, psychological, and sociological approaches, and we encourage multidisciplinary research. These are investigator initiated grants
Eligibility: Investigators from all academic disciplines are eligible to apply, and both basic science and applied research projects will be considered, provided that the proposed study has an essential focus on suicide or suicide prevention. Grant applications are not accepted from for-profit organizations, or from federal or state government agencies. Applications from the Veterans Administration are eligible
Level of Study: Research
Type: Grant
Value: Up to US$100,000 over 2 Years
Length of Study: 2 years
Frequency: Annual
Country of Study: Any country
Application Procedure: Applicants are instructed to apply afsp.org/our-work/research/apply-for-a-grant/
No. of awards offered: 70
Closing Date: 14 November
Funding: Private
No. of awards given last year: 10
No. of applicants last year: 70
Additional Information: afsp.org/our-work/research/grant-information/

American Foundation for Urologic Disease, Inc. (AFUD)

Research Program Division, 300 West Pratt Street Suite 401, Baltimore, MD 21202 2463, United States of America.

Tel: (1) 410 689 3990
Website: www.auanet.org/
Contact: Grants Management Officer

The mission of the American Foundation for Urologic Disease (AFUD) is the prevention and cure of urologic diseases through the expansion of medical research and the education of the public and health care professionals concerning urologic diseases.

National Institute of Diabetes and Digestive and Kidney Diseases (NIDDK)/AFUD Intramural Urology Research Training Program

Purpose: Provides an opportunity for selected individuals to complete a research project under the direction of a Senior Investigator in the Intramural Programme of NIDDK

Eligibility: Open to physicians who have recently completed a urology residency. Applicants must have less than five years postdoctoral experience (clinical residency training is not counted as postdoctoral research)

Level of Study: Postdoctorate

Type: Fellowship

Value: US$45,000–52,000 per year depending on experience

Length of Study: 2 years, possible extension for a further year

Study Establishment: Participating NIDDK laboratories

Country of Study: United States of America

Application Procedure: Applicants must submit a cover letter, curriculum vitae and three letters of recommendation. Further information available from NIDDK or the American Foundation for Urologic Disease

Additional Information: Further information available on request afsp.org/our-work/research/grant-information/

For further information contact:

Division of Kidney, Urology & Hematology, National Institute of Diabetes, Digestive & Kidney Diseases, Natcher Building Room 6AS13D, Bethesda, MD 20892-6600, United States of America.

Tel: (1) 301 594 7717
Fax: (1) 301 480 3510
Email: nybergl@ep.niddk.nih.gov

American Geophysical Union (AGU)

2000 Florida Avenue, N.W, Washington, DC 20009, United States of America.

Tel: (1) 202 462 6900
Email: service@agu.org
Website: www.agu.org
Contact: Director, Outreach and Research Support

The American Geophysical Union (AGU) is an international scientific society with more than 45,000 members, primarily research scientists, dedicated to advancing the understanding of Earth and space and making the results of the AGU's research available to the public.

Fred. L. Scarf Award

Purpose: The Fred L. Scarf Award is given annually to one honoree in recognition of an outstanding dissertation that contributes directly to solar-planetary science. The award is presented at the AGU Fall Meeting and awardees are invited to deliver a talk on their dissertation topic at the meeting.

Eligibility: Open to all candidates with a PhD (or equivalent) degree

Level of Study: Doctorate

Type: Award

Value: US$1,000, a complimentary ticket for the SPA dinner, and a certificate

Frequency: Annual

Country of Study: Any country

Application Procedure: Nominations to be sent to outreach administrator at AGU

Closing Date: 1 April

Funding: Private

Contributor: The Space Physics and Aeronomy section of AGU

Additional Information: Awardee will have the opportunity to deliver an invited paper on the dissertation topic at appropriate SPA session at the upcoming AGU Fall Meeting www.agu.org/Honor-and-Recognize/Honors/Section-Awards/Scarf-Award

For further information contact:

2000 Florida Ave. NW, Washington, DC 20009, United States of America.

Email: leadership@agu.org

Mineral and Rock Physics Graduate Research Award

Purpose: The Mineral and Rock Physics Graduate Research Award is presented annually to one or more promising young scientists and recognizes outstanding contributions to the field of mineral and rock physics achieved during the honoree's PhD research. The nominee should be engaged in experimental or theoretical studies on Earth and planetary materials with the purpose of unravelling the physics and chemistry behind their origin and physical properties.

Eligibility: Open to students who have completed their PhD.

Level of Study: Doctorate

Type: Award

Value: US$500, a certificate and Announcement in Eos. Recognition at the AGU Fall Meeting during the award presentation year

Frequency: Annual

Country of Study: Any country

Application Procedure: A letter of nomination along with a curriculum vitae, two supporting letters and 3 reprints or preprints of the nominee's work should be sent

Closing Date: 1 April

Contributor: Mineral and Rock Physics community at AGU

No. of awards given last year: 2

Additional Information: www.agu.org/Honor-and-Recognize/Honors/Section-Awards/MRP-Graduate-Research-Award

For further information contact:

Department of Geology and Environmental Geoscience, Northern Illinois University, Davis Hall 312, Normal Road, DeKalb, IL 60115, United States of America.

Email: hwatson@niu.edu

American Gynecological Club

2331 Rock Spring Rd., Forest Hill, MD 21050, United States of America.

Tel: (1) 443 640 1079
Email: info@americangynclub.org
Website: americangynclub.org/

American Gynecological Club / Gynaecological Visiting Society Fellowship

Purpose: Through generous funding from the American Gynecological Club and the Gynaecological Visiting Society of Great Britain, the RCOG can offer up to £1,200 to an individual to visit and gain knowledge from a specific centre offering new techniques of clinical management within O&G

Eligibility: This award is open to Trainees in the UK and Republic of Ireland and their equivalents in the US in alternating years.

Level of Study: Postdoctorate

Type: Fellowship

Value: £1,200

Length of Study: 1 year

Frequency: Annual

Country of Study: Any country

Closing Date: 1 September

Funding: Foundation

Additional Information: www.rcog.org.uk/en/careers-training/awards-grants-prizes/american-gynecological-clubgynaecological-visiting-society-fellowship/

For further information contact:

10 –18 Union Street, London SE1 1SZ, United Kingdom.

Email: awards@rcog.org.uk

American Head and Neck Society (AHNS)

11300 W. Olympic Boulevard, Suite 600, Los Angeles, CA 90064, United States of America.

Tel: (1) 310 437 0559
Email: admin@ahns.info
Website: www.headandneckcancer.org
Contact: Joyce Hasper, Research Grants Enquiries

The purpose of the American Head and Neck Society (AHNS) is to promote and advance the knowledge of prevention, diagnosis, treatment and rehabilitation of neoplasms and other diseases of the head and neck.

AHNS Endocrine Surgery Section Eisai Research Grant Policies

Purpose: The purpose of this award is to support basic, translational, or clinical research projects that further the mission of the Endocrine Section of the American Head and Neck Society. Projects should be specifically related to the prevention, diagnosis, treatment, outcomes, or pathophysiology of endocrine diseases of the head and neck.

Eligibility: Candidates for this award should reside in the U.S. or Canada and be AHNS members in good standing. They may be medical students focusing in otolaryngology, otolaryngology residents, PhDs or faculty members in otolaryngology departments. Preference will be given to early-stage investigators (10 years or less from a terminal degree or fellowship training) or more experienced researchers pursuing a new line of inquiry for which pilot data are needed. Previous AHNS or AAO-HNS Foundation research grant recipients are eligible to compete for this grant. However, candidates who have successfully obtained funding from a private or federal funding agency for the same research are ineligible. Candidates who have applied for support of the same research from other funding sources, and who are notified of an award from both another agency and from AHNS must choose only one of the awards.

Level of Study: Research

Type: Grant

Value: US$10,000 maximum

Length of Study: One year, non-renewable

Frequency: Annual

Country of Study: Any country

Closing Date: 18 January

Funding: Private

For further information contact:

Email: monia@ahns.info

AHNS Endocrine Surgery Section Stryker Research Grant Policies

Purpose: The purpose of this award is to support basic, translational, or clinical research projects that further the mission of the Endocrine Section of the American Head and Neck Society. Projects should be specifically related to the prevention, diagnosis, treatment, outcomes, or pathophysiology of endocrine diseases of the head and neck.

Eligibility: Candidates for this award should reside in the U.S. or Canada and be AHNS members in good standing. They may be medical students focusing in otolaryngology, otolaryngology residents, PhDs or faculty members in otolaryngology departments. Preference will be given to early-stage investigators (10 years or less from a terminal degree or fellowship training) or more experienced researchers pursuing a new line of inquiry for which pilot data are needed. Previous AHNS or AAO-HNS Foundation research grant recipients are eligible to compete for this grant. However, candidates who have successfully obtained funding from a private or federal funding agency for the same research are ineligible. Candidates who have applied for support of the same research from other funding sources, and who are notified of an award from both another agency and from AHNS must choose only one of the awards.

Level of Study: Research

Type: Grant

Value: US$10,000 maximum

Length of Study: One year, non-renewable

Frequency: Annual

Country of Study: Any country

Closing Date: 18 January

Additional Information: Applications submitted by ineligible PIs will NOT be reviewed by the CORE Study Section.

For further information contact:

Email: monia@ahns.info

American Academy of Otolaryngology - Head and Neck Surgery Translational Innovator Award

Purpose: The purpose of this award is to support contemporary basic or clinical research focused on neoplastic disease by full time academic head and neck surgeons; to promote novel translational research preferably with biomarker ideas

Eligibility: Candidates for this award must be 1. Otolaryngologist—Head and Neck surgeons, who are active members of the AAO-HNS. OR Surgeons who are in head and neck fellowships, or have completed a head and neck surgery fellowship and are active or candidate members of the AHNS. PLEASE NOTE Medical oncologists and radiation oncologists are not eligible to apply for this award. 2. Citizens of the United States, noncitizen nationals, or have been lawfully admitted for permanent residency at the time of application. 3. Full-time academic surgeons in faculty positions at the rank of instructor or assistant professor. 4. Hold a Doctor of Medicine (MD) degree or equivalent (DO, MBBS) from an accredited institution. 5. Have demonstrated the capacity or potential for a highly productive independent research career with an emphasis in head and neck surgical oncology

Level of Study: Graduate

Type: Award

Value: US$80,000 maximum (US$40,000 per year)

Length of Study: 24 months

Frequency: Annual

Country of Study: Any country

Closing Date: 17 December

Funding: Private

For further information contact:

AHNS, 11300 W. Olympic Blvd, Suite 600, Los Angeles, CA 90064, United States of America.

Email: betty@ahns.info

American Head and Neck Society Endocrine Research Grant

Purpose: Open to medical students focusing in otolaryngology, otolaryngology residents, PhDs or faculty members in otolaryngology departments

Level of Study: Graduate

Type: Research grant

Value: Up to US$10,000 are available per year

Frequency: Annual

Country of Study: Any country

Closing Date: 15 March

Funding: Private

Additional Information: www.ahns.info/ahns-endocrine-research-grants/

For further information contact:

Email: betty@ahns.info

American Head and Neck Society Pilot Research Grant

Purpose: To support students who wish to try a pilot project in head- and neck-related research
Eligibility: Open to residents and fellows in the junior faculty
Level of Study: Doctorate, Postgraduate
Type: Award
Value: US$10,000
Length of Study: 12 months, non-renewable
Frequency: Annual
Study Establishment: A university in the United States of America
Country of Study: United States of America
Closing Date: 18 January
Funding: Private

For further information contact:

Email: betty@ahns.info

American Head and Neck Society Surgeon Scientist Career Development Award (with AAOHNS)

Purpose: To support research in the pathogenesis, pathophysiology, diagnosis, prevention or treatment of head and neck neoplastic disease
Eligibility: Open to surgeons beginning a clinician-scientist career
Level of Study: Postdoctorate
Type: Award
Value: US$35,000 per year (non-renewable)
Length of Study: 2 years
Frequency: Annual
Study Establishment: A university in the United States of America
Country of Study: United States of America
Application Procedure: The grants are reviewed through the Academy CORE (combined otolaryngologic research evaluation) process
Closing Date: 16 January
Funding: Private
Additional Information: Applicants are requested to submit their LOI early to gain advanced access to the full application. Forms are available through American Academy of Otolaryngology CORE www.entnet.org/sites/default/files/uploads/PracticeManagement/Research/_files/2019_ahns_aaohnsf_translational_innovator_award_final.pdf

For further information contact:

Email: pcsupport@altum.com

American Head and Neck Society Young Investigator Award (with AAOHNS)

Purpose: The purpose of this award is to support a collaborative AHNS/AAO-HNSF research project by fostering the development of contemporary basic or clinical research skills focused on neoplastic disease of the head and neck among new full-time academic head and neck surgeons. The award is intended as a preliminary step in clinical investigator career development and is expected to facilitate the recipient's preparation of a more comprehensive individualized research plan suitable for submission to the National Institutes of Health or comparable funding agency.
Eligibility: Applicants for this award must: 1. Be either an Otolaryngologist—Head and Neck surgeon, who are active members of the AAO-HNS. OR: Surgeons who are in head and neck fellowships or have completed a head and neck surgery fellowship and are active or candidate members of the AHNS. PLEASE NOTE: Medical oncologists and radiation oncologists are not eligible to apply for this award. 2. Be citizens of the United States, noncitizen nations, or have been lawfully admitted for permanent residency at the time of application. 3. Have with demonstrated potential for excellence in research and teaching and serious commitment to an academic research career in head and neck surgery. 4. Be sponsored by the Chair of his/her Division or Department and by an official representative of the institution which would administer the Award and in whose name the application is formally submitted. 5. Are members or candidate members of the American Academy of Otolaryngology-Head and Neck Surgery and the American Head and Neck Society.
Level of Study: Doctorate
Type: Award
Value: US$40,000 maximum (US$20,000 per year)
Length of Study: Up to 2 years
Frequency: Annual
Study Establishment: A university in the United States of America
Country of Study: United States of America
Application Procedure: The grants are reviewed through the Academy CORE (combined otolaryngologic research evaluation) process
Closing Date: 18 January
Funding: Private

For further information contact:

Email: monia@ahns.info

American Head and Neck Society-American Cyronics Society Career Development Award

Purpose: To facilitate research in connection with career development
Eligibility: Applicants must be a member or candidate member of ACS and AHNS. Applicants must be within 5 years of completion of training, and be full-time faculty member
Level of Study: Postgraduate
Type: Award
Value: US$40,000 per year (non-renewable)
Length of Study: 2 years
Frequency: Annual
Study Establishment: A university in the United States of America
Country of Study: United States of America
Funding: Private
Additional Information: Please check website for more details www.entnet.org/sites/default/files/uploads/PracticeManagement/Resources/_files/2020_ahns_aaohnsf_ynginv_foa.pdf

For further information contact:

Email: COREGrants@entnet.org; betty@ahns.info

American Hearing Research Foundation - AHRF

275 N. York Street, Suite 201, Elmhurst, IL 60126, United States of America.

Tel: (1) 630 617 5079
Email: info@american-hearing.org
Website: www.american-hearing.org/

At the American Hearing Research Foundation (AHRF), we recognize the boundless potential of new ideas. That's why we focus our resources on providing seed grants for novel research to better understand and overcome hearing and balance disorders of the inner ear, funding five to ten research projects each year, with an average grant of US$20,000. We also work hard to educate the public about these life-altering conditions, which are inextricably linked to people's quality of life and their ability to meet the challenges of day-to-day living. Tracing our roots back to the first-ever successful operation to restore hearing, AHRF has been making new discoveries possible for more than 60 years. Founded in 1956 by Dr. George E. Shaumbaugh, Jr., our mission is to better understand why we lose hearing and balance functions and to learn all that we can about how to preserve and restore them.

AHRF Discovery Grants

Purpose: Each year AHRF typically funds six to ten Discovery Grants for studies that investigate various aspects of hearing and balance disorders related to the inner ear. Applicants may request up to US$50,000 for one year of research. Grants are paid in one lump sum in January in the year after the application deadline. Priority is given to investigators early in their careers who need seed funds to generate results and data that can be used to support applications for larger grants (i.e., NIH grants) in the future.
Eligibility: Applicants must hold an MD, PhD, AuD, or equivalent degree(s) and be associated with a university or hospital in the United States.
Level of Study: Masters
Value: Up to US$50,000
Length of Study: 1 year
Frequency: Annual
Country of Study: United States of America
Application Procedure: Please write your application using this checklist. Please follow these guidelines carefully Title Page (first page of proposal), Title of research project, Principal investigator name(s), Credentials, Institution name, USPS mailing address, Telephone number, Email address, Financial officer contact information, Description, Brief 2-page summary of the project, Include performance site and key personnel of project. Table of Contents, Include all first-level headings with page numbers. Detailed Budget Provide a one-year budget that includes salary for support staff (students, post-doctorate fellows, etc.), equipment and supplies. Salaries plus fringe benefits may not be more than 80% of your total direct costs. Do not include salaries for principal investigator(s), travel or conference attendance expenses, educational costs, or indirect costs (overhead). AHRF does not fund these costs. The budget should include the total amount requested. Biographical Sketch, Include contact information (USPS mailing address, telephone, email, etc.) with each investigator's biographical sketch page. List all publications (maximum of two pages), current funding, pending funding, and requested funding. Indicate what you will do if you receive overlapping funding. Letters of support from colleagues are welcome, but not required. Include any letters of support within your proposal document whenever possible. Main Body, Include specific aims of the project (body no longer than 10-15 pages at 12-point type, standard margins); background and significance; methods; and what type of subjects (human or animal), if applicable. Progress Report (For Renewal Projects Only), Indicate if you are requesting that your proposal be renewed for additional funding, which is considered on a case-by-case basis. Saving your proposal as a PDF Save your proposal as a PDF, naming it as follows "Yourlastname_Yourfirstname" If the PDF file is 5 MG or smaller, you can submit it via the online portal. If your PDF is

larger than 5 MB, please email the PDF and application form data to Info@American-Hearing.org.

Closing Date: 15 August

Additional Information: www.american-hearing.org/research-grants/grant-process/

Bernard & Lottie Drazin Memorial Grants

Purpose: AHRF offers up to five US$1,000 awards to otolaryngology residents to support research projects during their residency.

Eligibility: Applicants must be otolaryngology residents associated with these specific institutions: 1. Northwestern University 2. Loyola University Chicago 3. University of Illinois 4. University of Chicago 5. Rosalind Franklin University of Medicine and Science 6. Rush University 7. - Washington University, St. Louis, MO 8. University of Miami, FL 9. Baylor College of Medicine, Houston, TX

Level of Study: Masters

Type: Award

Value: US$1,000

Frequency: Annual

Country of Study: United States of America

Application Procedure: See website: www.american-hearing.org/research-grants/grant-process/

No. of awards offered: 5

Closing Date: 15 August

Additional Information: www.american-hearing.org/research-grants/grant-process/

Causes of Sudden Hearing Loss Grant

Purpose: This one-year grant will be offered in 2021. It will be paid in one lump sum in January. About the Grant AHRF is matching an individual donor's contribution to provide up to US$40,000 in funding for a one-year project. This donor was affected by sudden hearing loss, in two instances 38 years apart. The donor would like to spur investigation in the field. Grant funds may only be used for direct costs, including salaries of technical and supporting staff, equipment related to the research, and supplies. Note that the cost for salaries plus fringe benefits cannot be more than 80% of the direct costs. Funding may not be used for the salary of the principal investigator, travel, conference attendance, educational costs, or indirect costs.

Eligibility: Applicants must hold an MD, PhD, AuD, or equivalent degree(s) and be associated with a university or hospital in the United States.

Level of Study: Masters

Value: US$40,000

Length of Study: 1 year

Frequency: Annual

Country of Study: United States of America

Application Procedure: Please write your application using this checklist. Please follow these guidelines carefully Title Page (first page of proposal), Title of research project, Principal investigator name(s), Credentials, Institution name, USPS mailing address, Telephone number, Email address, Financial officer contact information, Description, Brief 2-page summary of the project, Include performance site and key personnel of project. Table of Contents, Include all first-level headings with page numbers. Detailed Budget Provide a one-year budget that includes salary for support staff (students, post-doctorate fellows, etc.), equipment and supplies. Salaries plus fringe benefits may not be more than 80% of your total direct costs. Do not include salaries for principal investigator(s), travel or conference attendance expenses, educational costs, or indirect costs (overhead). AHRF does not fund these costs. The budget should include the total amount requested. Biographical Sketch, Include contact information (USPS mailing address, telephone, email, etc.) with each investigator's biographical sketch page. List all publications (maximum of two pages), current funding, pending funding, and requested funding. Indicate what you will do if you receive overlapping funding. Letters of support from colleagues are welcome, but not required. Include any letters of support within your proposal document whenever possible. Main Body, Include specific aims of the project (body no longer than 10-15 pages at 12-point type, standard margins); background and significance; methods; and what type of subjects (human or animal), if applicable. Progress Report (For Renewal Projects Only), Indicate if you are requesting that your proposal be renewed for additional funding, which is considered on a case-by-case basis. Saving your proposal as a PDF Save your proposal as a PDF, naming it as follows "Yourlastname_Yourfirstname" If the PDF file is 5 MG or smaller, you can submit it via the online portal. If your PDF is larger than 5 MB, please email the PDF and application form data to Info@American-Hearing.org.

Closing Date: 13 August

Additional Information: www.american-hearing.org/research-grants/grant-process/

Meniere's Disease Grant

Purpose: AHRF occasionally awards grants specifically related to the study of Meniere's disease. The amount can range from US$20,000 to US$25,000. Meniere's research grants are paid in one lump sum in January in the year after the application deadline. These grants are supported through the fundraising efforts of run because and subsidized by AHRF. Grant funds may only be used for direct costs, including salaries of technical and supporting staff, equipment related to the research, and supplies. Note that the cost for salaries plus fringe benefits cannot be more than 80% of the direct costs. Funding may not be used for the salary of the principal investigator, travel, conference attendance, educational costs, or indirect costs.

Eligibility: Applicants must hold an MD, PhD, AuD, or equivalent degree(s) and be associated with a university or hospital in the United States.

Level of Study: Masters

Value: US$20,000 - US$25,000

Frequency: Annual

Country of Study: United States of America

Application Procedure: Please write your application using this checklist. Please follow these guidelines carefully Title Page (first page of proposal), Title of research project, Principal investigator name(s), Credentials, Institution name, USPS mailing address, Telephone number, Email address, Financial officer contact information, Description, Brief 2-page summary of the project, Include performance site and key personnel of project. Table of Contents, Include all first-level headings with page numbers. Detailed Budget, Provide a one-year budget that includes salary for support staff (students, post-doctorate fellows, etc.), equipment and supplies. Salaries plus fringe benefits may not be more than 80% of your total direct costs. Do not include salaries for principal investigator(s), travel or conference attendance expenses, educational costs, or indirect costs (overhead). AHRF does not fund these costs. The budget should include the total amount requested. Biographical Sketch, Include contact information (USPS mailing address, telephone, email, etc.) with each investigator's biographical sketch page. List all publications (maximum of two pages), current funding, pending funding, and requested funding. Indicate what you will do if you receive overlapping funding. Letters of support from colleagues are welcome, but not required. Include any letters of support within your proposal document whenever possible. Main Body, Include specific aims of the project (body no longer than 10-15 pages at 12-point type, standard margins); background and significance; methods; and what type of subjects (human or animal), if applicable. Progress Report (For Renewal Projects Only), Indicate if you are requesting that your proposal be renewed for additional funding, which is considered on a case-by-case basis., Saving your proposal as a PDF Save your proposal as a PDF, naming it as follows "Yourlastname_Yourfirstname" If the PDF file is 5 MG or smaller, you can submit it via the online portal. If your PDF is larger than 5 MB, please email the PDF and application form data to Info@American-Hearing.org.

Closing Date: 13 August

Additional Information: www.american-hearing.org/grant/menieres-disease-grant/#:~:text=About%20the%20Grant%3A,year%20after%20the%20application%20deadline

American Heart Association (AHA)

AHA Postdoctoral Fellowship

Subjects: AHA awards are open to the array of academic and health professionals. This includes but is not limited to all academic disciplines (biology, chemistry, mathematics, technology, physics, etc.) and all health-related professions (physicians, nurses, nurse practitioners, pharmacists, dentists, physical and occupational therapists, statisticians, nutritionists, etc.). Clinical, translational, population, and basic scientists are encouraged to apply.

Purpose: To enhance the integrated research and clinical training of postdoctoral applicants who are not yet independent. The applicant must be embedded in an appropriate research group with the mentorship, support, and relevant scientific guidance of a research sponsor. Recognizing the unique challenges that clinicians, in particular, experience in balancing research and clinical activity, this award mechanism aims to be as flexible as possible to enable applicants to develop academic careers in research alongside fulfilling clinical service commitments.

Eligibility: At the time of award activation, the applicant must hold a post-baccalaureate PhD degree or equivalent, or a doctoral-level clinical degree, such as M.D., D.O., D.V.M., Pharm.D., D.D.S., Dr.Ph, PhD in nursing, public health, or other clinical health science., or equivalent clinical health science doctoral student who seeks research training with a sponsor prior to embarking upon a research career. At the time of award activation, the awardee may not be pursuing a doctoral degree. At the time of award activation, the applicant may have no more than five years of research training or experience since obtaining a post-baccalaureate doctoral-level degree (excluding clinical training). The awardee will be expected to devote at least 80 % of full-time work either to research or to activities pursuant to independent research (instead of administrative, clinical duties that are not an integral part of the research training program, or teaching responsibilities). This award is not intended for individuals of faculty rank.

Type: Fellowship

Value: Not to exceed US$77,858 per period and US$155,716 total

Length of Study: One or two years

Frequency: Annual

Country of Study: Any country

Additional Information: The following designations are also eligible to apply: Pending permanent resident (any resident who has an approved I-765 form and has submitted an I-485 application with the United States Citizenship and

Immigration Services). E-3 Visa - specialty occupation worker, F1 Visa - student, H1-B Visa - temporary worker in a specialty occupation, J-1 Visa - exchange visitor, O-1 Visa - temporary worker with extraordinary abilities in the sciences, TN Visa - North American Free Trade Agreement (NAFTA) professional, G-4 Visa - family member of employee of international organizations, DACA - Deferred Action for Childhood Arrivals status requires additional AHA approval to apply. Send an email to apply@heart.org with an explanation of your status and a statement of support from your sponsor. professional.heart.org/professional/ResearchProgr ams/ApplicationInformation/UCM_443314_Postdoctoral-Fellowship.jsp

For further information contact:

Email: apply@heart.org

American Indian Science and Engineering Society

1630 30th Street Suite 301, Boulder, CO 80301-1014, United States of America.

Tel: (1) 303 939 0023
Email: ascholar@spot.colorado.edu
Contact: Ms Sonya Todacheene

Naval Sea Systems Command (NAVSEA) and Strategic Systems Programs Scholarship

Purpose: This scholarship is open to United States college freshmen who are American Indian, Alaskan Native, or Native Hawaiian and enrolled at a minority-serving institution (as designated by the United States Department of Education) that is ABET-accredited
Eligibility: Must be a US Citizen
Level of Study: Graduate
Type: Scholarship
Value: US$10,000
Frequency: Annual
Country of Study: Any country
Application Procedure: Apply online
No. of awards offered: 1
Closing Date: 20 September
Funding: Foundation
Additional Information: www.smartscholar.com/scholar ship/naval-sea-systems-command-navsea-and-strategic-systems-programs-scholarship/

For further information contact:

203 N. La Salle St. Suite 1675, Chicago, IL 60601, United States of America.

Tel: (1) 505 7651052
Email: scholarships@swe.org

American Institute for Economic Research (AIER)

250 Division St, PO Box 1000, Great Barrington, MA 01230, United States of America.

Tel: (1) 888 528 1216
Email: info@aier.org
Website: www.aier.org

The American Institute for Economic Research (AIER), founded in 1933, is an independent scientific educational organization. The Institute conducts scientific enquiry into general economics with a focus on monetary issues. Attention is also given to business cycle analysis and forecasting as well as monetary economics.

American Institute for Economic Research Summer Fellowship

Purpose: To further the development of economic scientists
Eligibility: Open to graduating seniors who are entering doctoral programmes in economics, or those enrolled in doctoral programmes in economics for no longer than 2 years. The programme is not designed for those enrolling into business school
Level of Study: Postgraduate
Type: Fellowship
Value: US$500 weekly stipend plus room and full board
Length of Study: 8 weeks
Frequency: Annual
Study Establishment: AIER
Country of Study: United States of America
Application Procedure: A current resume; a writing sample; a statement explaining why you would like to be a student fellow at AIER and whether you qualify to reside on campus; an official transcript directly from your school or university; two letters of recommendation from teachers, college professors, or employers should be sent either by electronic or United States mail to the American Institute for Economic

Research. Please state "Summer Fellowship Practicum" in the subject line

No. of awards offered: 47

Closing Date: 23 March

Funding: Private

No. of awards given last year: 17

No. of applicants last year: 47

Additional Information: AIER does not sponsor visa applications for foreign nationals. However, foreign nationals are welcome to apply if they are enrolled in a United States degree granting institution, have CPT or OPT, or have employment authorization in the United States drexel.edu/fellowships/search/fellowships/American_Institute_for_Economic_Research/

For further information contact:

Summer Fellowship Program Coordinator, American Institute for Economic Research, PO Box 1000, 250 Division St, Great Barrington, MA 01230, United States of America.

Fax: (1) 413 528 0103

Email: internships@aier.org

American Institute for Sri Lankan Studies (AISLS)

155 Pine Street, Belmont, MA 02478, United States of America.

Email: rogersjohnd@aol.com

Website: www.aisls.org

Contact: John Rogers

The American Institute for Sri Lankan Studies (AISLS) was established in 1995, to foster excellence in American research and teaching on Sri Lanka, and to promote the exchange of scholars and scholarly information between the United States and Sri Lanka. The Institute serves as the professional association for United States-based scholars and other professionals who are interested in Sri Lanka.

Dissertation Planning Grants

Purpose: AISLS dissertation planning grants are designed to enable graduate students intending to do doctoral research in Sri Lanka to make a pre-dissertation visit to Sri Lanka to investigate the feasibility of their topic, to sharpen their research design, or to make other practical arrangements for future research.

Eligibility: Applicants who are enrolled at a US university need not be American citizens. US citizens enrolled at a foreign university are also eligible. Some funds designated for this program can only be used for awards for US citizens.

Level of Study: Graduate

Type: Grant

Value: 1. A per diem of US$560/week, for a period up to eight weeks. 2. Reimbursement for roundtrip airfare between the United States and Colombo, for an amount up to US$2,000. All travel for US citizens must be consistent with the Fly America Act. 3. Reimbursement for any visa fees paid to the Sri Lankan government.

Length of Study: Six and eight weeks

Frequency: Annual

Country of Study: Any country

Application Procedure: Application Contents: The completed application should contain the following items: 1. A one-page cover sheet giving name, mailing address, telephone, email address, citizenship, major field of study, institutional affiliation, foreign languages (including proficiency), length of proposed stay in Sri Lanka, tentative dates of project, project title, and a brief project description. 2. A curriculum vitae, not to exceed two pages, which should include the name and email address of the applicant's dissertation supervisor. 3. A copy of the applicant's graduate transcript. An unofficial copy is acceptable. 4. A project narrative, not to exceed two single-spaced pages. This is the most important part of the application. It should cover the following topics: a. a summary of the proposed dissertation project, or, if the purpose of the planning grant is to define a dissertation project, a summary of the more general questions the applicant hopes to address in his or her dissertation b. a description of what the applicant intends to do during the grant period c. the applicant's competence to carry out his or her proposed project, including language training 5. A one-page project bibliography, including a selected list of publications by other scholars or primary sources that have been or will be used in the project 6. A confidential letter of recommendation from the applicant's dissertation supervisor. This letter should cover the applicant's academic record and be specific about the applicant's progress to date within the graduate program concerned. This letter should be sent by email directly to John Rogers.;Application Format: 1. Pages should have one-inch margins on all sides. 2. Type size should be 10 points or larger. 3. Applications should be sent in a single Word or PDF file, collated in the order given above (cover sheet, c.v., graduate transcript, project description, bibliography). If it is not possible to integrate the transcript into the application, it is acceptable to submit it as a separate file.

Closing Date: 1 December

For further information contact:

Email: rogersjohnd@aol.com

Fellowship Program

Purpose: AISLS fellowships support two to six months of research in Sri Lanka by US citizens who already hold a PhD or the equivalent at the time they begin their fellowship tenure.

Eligibility: 1. Applicants must hold US citizenship. 2. Applicants must hold a PhD or equivalent academic degree or show that they will hold such a degree before taking up the fellowship. Scholars at all ranks are eligible. Members of the AISLS Board of Directors are not eligible. Please see the AISLS policy on board membership and fellowships. 3. No individual may be awarded AISLS fellowships for more than seven months over any three consecutive fellowship competitions. 4. Applicants must plan to spend at least two months in Sri Lanka and complete the fellowship (including travel back to the United States) before December 31, 2023. The time in Sri Lanka supported by the fellowship need not be continuous (e.g., it might be divided between the summers of 2022 and 2023), but only one round trip airfare will be reimbursed.

Level of Study: Postdoctorate

Type: Fellowship

Value: A per diem of US$3,700/month, for a period of two to six months. Reimbursement for round trip airfare between the United States and Colombo, for an amount up to US$2,000. Travel must comply with the Fly America Act. Details will be provided to successful applicants.

Length of Study: 2 to 6 months

Frequency: Annual

Country of Study: Any country

Application Procedure: Questions to be addressed by the project. The approach to be taken. work done to date. work to be accomplished during the fellowship period. The applicant's competence to carry out the project. how the project addresses the criteria of the competition. a statement of other support received or being sought for the project

Closing Date: 1 December

Funding: Government

Contributor: Bureau of Economic and Cultural Affairs, United States State Department

No. of awards given last year: 2

Additional Information: www.aisls.org/grants/aisls-fellowship-program/

American Institute of Bangladesh Studies (AIBS)

B 488 Medical Sciences Center, 1300 University Ave, Madison, WI 53706, United States of America.

Tel: (1) 608 265 1471

Email: info@aibs.net

Website: www.aibs.net

Contact: Laura Hammond, Administrative Program Manager

The American Institute of Bangladesh Studies (AIBS) is a consortium of United States universities and colleges involved in research on Bangladesh. It strives to improve the scholarly understanding of Bangladesh culture and society in the United States and to promote educational exchange between the two countries.

AIBS Bangladeshi Graduate Student Fellowship

Purpose: The American Institute of Bangladesh Studies is pleased to announce research fellowships for Bangladeshi graduate students studying in the U.S. The fellowships are intended to help PhD and Masters students meet expenses related to scholarly research and creative endeavors in Bangladesh.

Eligibility: 1. Bangladeshi citizen 2. Currently enrolled PhD, MA, MS, or MFA students at a U.S. based institution 3. Research projects must be from one of the following disciplines: a. Humanities and Sciences b. Social Sciences c. Education and Public Health d. Music and Fine Arts e. Social Policies and Management f. Other relevant fields and interdisciplinary studies 4. At the time of the application, graduate students should be in the later stages of their programs. 5. Applicants who have applied before and have not received an award may apply again.

Level of Study: Graduate

Type: Fellowship

Value: US$3,000

Frequency: Annual

Country of Study: Any country

Closing Date: 1 February

Funding: Private

AIBS Professional Development Fellowships for Bangladeshi Scholars

Purpose: The American Institute of Bangladesh Studies is pleased to announce Professional Development Fellowship for Bangladeshi scholars working at one of the AIBS partner universities in Bangladesh. As visiting fellows, selected Bangladeshi scholars will work with U.S. faculty members at their host universities to develop research agenda, utilize library facilities, and receive hands-on training on academic writing and publication.

Eligibility: 1. Be a Bangladeshi citizen 2. Currently employed at one of the AIBS partner universities in

Bangladesh. For a full list of Bangladeshi partner universities, please see here: aibs.net/about/member-institutions/. 3. A letter of invitation from a faculty member at the U.S. institution the scholar will be visiting. 4. Applicants who have applied before and have not received an award may apply again.

Level of Study: Graduate

Type: Scholarship

Value: US$4,000-US$8,000

Length of Study: Six weeks

Frequency: Annual

Country of Study: Any country

Application Procedure: The following documents will be needed to successfully complete the application: 1. An online application form with basic biographical details and outlines of the goals and outcomes for the visit, the way that the funds will be used, and the visit timeline (500 words max) 2. A recent CV 3. A letter of invitation from a faculty member at the institution you will be visiting. The letter should outline if there are any additional resources on campus to support the scholar during their visit and outline plans for a public facing event while the scholar is in residents (a community-based seminar, a public talk, a zoom seminar, etc.) that will showcase the researcher's work and/or the collaborations emerging from the visit.

Closing Date: 1 February

American Institute of Bangladesh Studies Junior Fellowship

Purpose: To improve the scholarly understanding of Bangladesh culture and society in the United States

Eligibility: Open to an individual member of AIBS; currently in the ABD phase of your PhD program; is in the data collection and writing stage of the dissertation, and must be United States citizen

Level of Study: Research

Type: Fellowship

Value: Fellowships will be equivalent to 1,150 Tk per month, plus economy Round-Trip Air Transportation (up to 2,500 Tk) via the most direct route

Length of Study: 2–12 months

Frequency: Annual

Country of Study: Bangladesh

Application Procedure: Applicants can access our online application form at www.aibs.net

Closing Date: 15 September

Funding: Government

Contributor: United States Department of State Bureau of Educational and Cultural Affairs through the Council of American Overseas Research Centers

Additional Information: Please check AIBS website www. aibs.net www.aibs.net/fellowship/junior

American Institute of Bangladesh Studies Pre-Dissertation Fellowships

Purpose: The American Institute of Bangladesh Studies offers short-term grants to graduate students pursuing studies of Bangladesh funded by the United States Department of State Bureau of Educational and Cultural Affairs through the Council of American Overseas Research Centers

Eligibility: All applicants must be enrolled/employed at a United States academic institution and a United States citizen. Open to an individual member of AIBS and must have completed at least 1 year of graduate study in a recognized PhD granting institution and enrolled in a graduate program but not yet at the dissertation research or writing stage

Level of Study: Research

Type: Fellowship

Value: The award is for 3,000 Tk plus economy round trip transportation (up to 2,500 Tk) via the most direct route

Frequency: Annual

Country of Study: Bangladesh

Application Procedure: Applicants can access the online application at www.aibs.net

No. of awards offered: Varies

Closing Date: 15 September

Funding: Government

Contributor: United States Department of State Bureau of Educational and Cultural Affairs through the council of American Overseas Research Centres

No. of awards given last year: Varies

No. of applicants last year: Varies

Additional Information: Please check ABIS website (www. aibs.net) www.aibs.net/fellowship/pre-dissertation

American Institute of Bangladesh Studies Senior Fellowship

Purpose: To improve the scholarly understanding of Bangladesh culture and society in the United States

Eligibility: Enrolled/employed/affiliated with a US or non-US academic institution (independent scholars are also welcome to apply). US Citizens. be an individual member of AIBS (click here for membership information). have a well-developed research agenda relevant to Bangladesh

Level of Study: Doctorate, Postdoctorate, Predoctorate, Research

Type: Fellowship

Value: 1,400 Tk per month plus research and dependent

Length of Study: 2–12 months

Frequency: Annual

Country of Study: Bangladesh

Application Procedure: Applicants can access our online application form at www.aibs.net

No. of awards offered: Varies
Closing Date: 1 March
Funding: Government
Contributor: United States department of State Bureau of Educational and Cultural Affairs through the council of American overseas research centres
No. of awards given last year: Varies
No. of applicants last year: Varies
Additional Information: Please check AIBS website for additional information (www.aibs.net) www.aibs.net/fellowship/senior

For further information contact:

Email: sudiptaroy.aibs@gmail.com

American Institute of Bangladesh Studies Travel Grants

Purpose: AIBS can provide funding for conference travel for the presentation of papers or organization of panels that include topics relevant to Bangladesh Studies at scholarly conferences
Eligibility: Must be a United States citizen travelling within the United States
Level of Study: Graduate
Type: Travel grant
Value: Up to 600 Tk for travel to conferences within the United States. International travel grants have been suspended until further notice due to budgetary constraints
Frequency: Annual
Country of Study: Bangladesh
Application Procedure: Please fill out online application at www.aibs.net
Funding: Government
Additional Information: Please check the AIBS website for more information www.aibs.net/node/179

American Institute of Certified Public Accountants (AICPA)

1211 Avenue of the Americas, New York, NY 10036-8775, United States of America.

Tel: (1) 212 596 6200
Email: service@aicpa.org
Website: www.aicpa.org

The American Institute of Certified Public Accountants (AICPA) is a national, professional organization for all Certified Public Accountants. Its mission is to provide members with the resources, information and leadership that enable them to provide valuable services in the highest professional manner to benefit the public as well as employers and clients. In fulfilling its mission, the AICPA works with state CPA organizations and gives priority to those areas where public reliance on CPA skills is most significant.

American Institute of Certified Public Accountants Fellowship for Minority Doctoral students

Purpose: To encourage practising CPAs to consider a career change to academe
Eligibility: 1. Applied to an AACSB, ACBSP or IACBE accredited, full-time Ph.D. program and awaiting word on acceptance; b) been accepted into an accredited, full-time Ph.D. program; or c) already matriculated in an accredited, full-time Ph.D. program and pursuing appropriate coursework. (Fellowships will be awarded to only those who are admitted and attend traditional, residential, full-time doctoral programs in accounting at universities accredited by the AACSB, ACBSP and IACBE. Part-time or on-line Ph.D.; full-time, part-time or online DBA; and full-time, part-time or online executive doctoral programs will not be considered for funding. Earned a Master's degree or completed at least 3 years of full-time experience in the accounting profession 2. Minority student of Black or African American; Hispanic or Latino; Native American or Alaska Native; Native Hawaiian or Pacific Islander ethnicity 3. Attend school on a full-time basis and plan to remain enrolled full-time until attainment of Ph.D. degree 4. Agree not to work full-time in a paid position or accept responsibility for teaching more than one course per semester as a teaching assistant, or dedicate more than one quarter of your time as a research assistant 5. CPA or plan to pursue CPA licensure6. U.S. citizen or permanent resident (green card holder)
Level of Study: Doctorate
Type: Fellowship
Value: US$12,000
Length of Study: A maximum of 3 years
Frequency: Annual
Study Establishment: A college or university whose business administration programs are accredited by the AACSB - the International Association for Management Education
Country of Study: United States of America
Application Procedure: 1. A completed application form. 2. An official academic transcript from each institution from which you have received a degree. 3. Confidential references from two individuals. 4. Visit ThisWayToCPA.com for more application requirements
Closing Date: 30 May

Additional Information: usascholarships.com/aicpa-fellowship-for-minority-doctoral-students/

For further information contact:

Email: academics@aicpa.org

American Library Association (ALA)

50 E. Huron Street, Chicago, IL 60611, United States of America.

Tel: (1) 800 545 2433 ext. 4274
Email: ala@ala.org
Website: www.ala.org
Contact: Ms Melissa Jacobsen, Manager, Prof. Dev

Each year the American Library Association (ALA) and its member units sponsor awards to honour distinguished service and foster professional growth.

American Library Association Carroll Preston Baber Research Grant

Purpose: To encourage innovative research that could lead to an improvement in library services to any specified group or groups of people. The project should aim to answer a question that is of vital importance to the library community and the researchers should plan to provide documentation of the results of their work
Eligibility: Any ALA member may apply. The Jury would welcome projects that involve both a practicing librarian and a researcher
Level of Study: Unrestricted
Type: Research grant
Value: Up to US$3,000
Length of Study: Up to 18 months
Frequency: Annual
Country of Study: Any country
Application Procedure: Applicants must submit an application including a research proposal
No. of awards offered: 5
Closing Date: 12 February
Funding: Private
Contributor: Eric R Baber
No. of awards given last year: 1
No. of applicants last year: 5
Additional Information: The project should aim to answer a question that is of vital importance to the library community

and the researchers should plan to provide documentation of the results of their work. The jury would welcome proposals that involve innovative uses of technology and proposals that involve co-operation between libraries and other agencies, or between librarians and persons in other disciplines www.ala.org/aboutala/offices/ors/orsawards/baberresearchgrant/babercarroll

For further information contact:

Tel: (1) 312 280 4273
Email: krosa@ala.org

American Library Association John Phillip Immroth Memorial Award

Purpose: The John Phillip Immroth Memorial Award, presented annually, honors notable contributions to intellectual freedom and demonstrations of personal courage in defense of freedom of expression.
Eligibility: Open to intellectual freedom fighters. Individuals, a group of individuals or an organization are eligible for the award
Level of Study: Unrestricted
Type: Award
Value: US$500 plus a citation
Frequency: Annual
Country of Study: Any country
Application Procedure: Applicants must submit a detailed statement explaining why the nominator believes that the nominee should receive the award. Nominations should be submitted to IFRT Staff Liaison at the ALA
Closing Date: 1 December
Funding: Private
Contributor: Intellectual Freedom Round Table (IFRT) of the American Library Association
Additional Information: www.ala.org/rt/ifrt/john-phillip-immroth-memorial-award

For further information contact:

American Library Association, Office for Intellectual Freedom, 50 East Huron Street, Chicago, IL 60611, United States of America.

Tel: (1) 312 280 4226
Fax: (1) 312 280 4227
Email: oif@ala.org

American Library Association Loleta D. Fyan Grant

Purpose: To facilitate the development and improvement of public libraries and the services they provide

Eligibility: Applicants can include but are not limited to local, regional or state libraries, associations or organizations including units of the ALA, library schools or individuals
Level of Study: Unrestricted
Type: Research grant
Value: Up to US$5,000
Frequency: Annual
Country of Study: Any country
Application Procedure: Applicants must submit an application form in addition to a proposal and budget to the ALA Staff Liaison. Please do not fax or mail
No. of awards offered: 10
Closing Date: 21 December
Funding: Private
No. of awards given last year: 1
No. of applicants last year: 10
Additional Information: The project must result in the development and improvement of public libraries and the services they provide, have the potential for broader impact and application beyond meeting a specific local need, should be designed to effect changes in public library services that are innovative and responsive to the future and should be capable of completion within one year www.ala.org/aboutala/offices/ors/orsawards/fyanloletad/fyanloletad

For further information contact:

American Library Association, 225 N Michigan Ave, Suite 1300, Chicago, IL 60611, United States of America.

Tel: (1) 312 280 3217
Email: cbourdon@ala.org

American Library Association Miriam L Hornback Scholarship

Purpose: To assist an individual pursuing a Master's degree
Eligibility: Open to ALA or library support staff who are pursuing a Master's degree in library science and who are citizens of the United States of America or Canada
Level of Study: Postgraduate
Type: Scholarship
Value: US$3,000
Frequency: Annual
Country of Study: Any country
Application Procedure: Applicants must write for details
Closing Date: 1 March
No. of awards given last year: 2
Additional Information: www.ala.org/awardsgrants/miriam-l-hornback-scholarship

For further information contact:

Email: klredd@ala.org

American Library Association Shirley Olofson Memorial Awards

Purpose: To allow individuals to attend ALA conferences
Eligibility: Open to members of the ALA who are also current or potential members of the New Members Round Table. Applicants should not have attended any more than five conferences
Level of Study: Unrestricted
Type: Award
Value: US$1,000
Frequency: Annual
Country of Study: Any country
Application Procedure: Applicants must write for details. Fill out the application online
Closing Date: 10 December
Contributor: The New Members Round Table (NMRT) and the Shirley Olofson Memorial Award Committee
Additional Information: www.ala.org/awardsgrants/shirley-olofson-memorial-award

American Library Association W. David Rozkuszka Scholarship

Purpose: To provide financial assistance to an individual who is currently working with government documents in a library
Eligibility: Open to applicants currently completing a Master's programme in library science
Level of Study: Postgraduate
Type: Scholarship
Value: US$3,000
Frequency: Annual
Country of Study: Any country
Application Procedure: Applicants must write for details
Closing Date: 31 December
Additional Information: www.ala.org/awardsgrants/w-david-rozkuszka-scholarship

For further information contact:

Tel: (1) 541 992 5461
Email: asevetson@hotmail.com

American Library Association YALSA/Baker and Taylor Conference Grant

Purpose: To allow young adult librarians who work directly with young adults in either a public library or a school library to attend the Annual Conference of the ALA

Eligibility: 1. The degree of need for additional materials for young adults. 2. The degree of the current collection's use and the specificity of examples used. 3. The soundness of the rationale for the selection of materials. The quality of the description of the benefits this grant will bring to young adults.

Level of Study: Professional development

Type: Grant

Value: US$1,000 each

Frequency: Annual

Country of Study: Any country

Application Procedure: Applicants must submit applications to the Young Adult Library Services Association, ALA, by email to Nichole Gilbert at ngilbert@ala.org

No. of awards offered: 2

Closing Date: 1 December

Additional Information: www.ala.org/yalsa/awardsandgrants/bwi

For further information contact:

50 E. Huron St., Chicago, IL 60611, United States of America.

Tel: (1) 800 545 2433
Email: YALSA@ala.org

Dixie Electric Membership Corporation New Leaders Travel Grant

Purpose: To enhance professional development and improve the expertise of public librarians new to the field by making possible their attendance at major PLA professional development activities

Eligibility: Open to qualified public librarians, MLS, PLA member

Level of Study: Professional development

Type: Travel grant

Value: Plaque and travel grant of up to US$1,500 per awardee

Frequency: Annual

Country of Study: Any country

Application Procedure: Visit website www.pla.org

Closing Date: 1 December

Funding: Corporation

No. of awards given last year: 4

Additional Information: www.ala.org/awardsgrants/awards/48/apply

For further information contact:

Email: jkloeppel@ala.org

Spectrum Initiative Scholarship Program

Purpose: To encourage admission to an ALA recognized Master's degree programme by the four largest underrepresented minority groups

Eligibility: 1. be a citizen or permanent resident of the U.S. or Canada. 2. identify as American Indian/Alaska Native, Asian, Black/African American, Hispanic/Latino, Middle Eastern/North African, and/or Native Hawaiian/Other Pacific Islander. 3. be enrolled in an accredited program and begin no later than September 1st or Fall Semester. have full or part-time status.

Level of Study: Postgraduate

Type: Scholarship

Value: US$5,000

Frequency: Annual

Country of Study: United States of America or Canada

Application Procedure: Applicants must request details via fax or visit the website

Closing Date: 1 March

Additional Information: Applications accepted from mid-October to 1 March each year www.ala.org/advocacy/spectrum/apply

For further information contact:

Tel: (1) 800 545 2433 ext 5048
Email: spectrum@ala.org

American Lung Association

1301 Pennsylvania Ave., NW, Suite 800, Washington, DC 20004, United States of America.

Tel: (1) 202 785 3355
Email: info@lungusa.org
Website: www.lungusa.org
Contact: Ms Evita Mendoza

The American Lung Association is the oldest voluntary health organization in the United States, with a National Office and constituent and affiliate associations around the country. Founded in 1904 to fight tuberculosis, the American Lung Association today fights lung disease in all its forms, with special emphasis on asthma, tobacco control and environmental health.

Lung Health (LH) Research Dissertation Grants

Purpose: To provide financial assistance for Doctoral research training for dissertation research on issues relevant to lung disease

Eligibility: Open to citizens or permanent residents of the United States
Level of Study: Doctorate
Type: Research grant
Value: US$21,000 per year
Length of Study: 1–2 years
Frequency: Annual
Country of Study: United States of America
Closing Date: 20 October
Funding: Corporation, Foundation, Government
Contributor: American Lung Association
Additional Information: Up to US$16,000 of the award may be used for a student stipend. Funds may not be used for tuition. The award will terminate at the time the awardee is granted a doctoral degree action.lung.org/site/DocServer/2016_LH_LUNG_HEALTH_RESEARCH_DISSERTA TION_GRANT_Program_.pdf?docID=36206

For further information contact:

Research and Program Services, American Lung Association, 14 Wall Street, 8th Floor, New York, NY 10006, United States of America.

American Mathematical Society

201 Charles Street, Providence, RI 02904-2294, United States of America.

Tel: (1) 401 455 4000
Website: www.ams.org

The AMS, founded in 1888 to further the interests of mathematical research and scholarship, serves the national and international community through its publications, meetings, advocacy and other programs, which promote mathematical research, its communication and uses, encourage and promote the transmission of mathematical understanding and skills, support mathematical education at all levels, advance the status of the profession of mathematics, encouraging and facilitating full participation of all individuals, foster an awareness and appreciation of mathematics and its connections to other disciplines and everyday life.

American Meteorological Society Centennial Fellowships in Mathematics

Purpose: To help mathematicians in their careers in research

Eligibility: The primary selection criterion for the Centennial Fellowship is the excellence of the candidate's research. Preference will be given to candidates who have not had extensive fellowship support in the past. Recipients may not hold the Centennial Fellowship concurrently with other major research award such as a Sloan fellowship, NSF Postdoctoral fellowship, or career award. Under normal circumstances, the fellowship cannot be deferred. The students of North America can apply for these scholarships. For detailed information, visit website
Level of Study: Research
Type: Fellowship
Value: The stipend for fellowships awarded was US$89,000, with an additional expense allowance of US$8,900
Country of Study: Any country
Application Procedure: The mode of applying is by post
Closing Date: 1 December
Additional Information: Scholarship can be taken at North America   www.ams.org/prizes-awards/paview.cgi?parent_id=11

For further information contact:

Professional Programs Department, American Mathematical Society, 201 Charles Street, Providence, RI 02904-2213, United States of America.

Tel: (1) 401 455 4096
Email: development@ams.org

AMS Congressional Fellowship

Purpose: The American Mathematical Society (AMS), in conjunction with the American Association for the Advancement of Science (AAAS), sponsors this fellowship. It includes an orientation on congressional and executive branch operations, and a year-long seminar series on issues involving science, technology and public policy. The AMS Congressional Fellow spends a year working on the staff of either a member of Congress or a congressional committee, working in legislative and policy areas requiring scientific and technical input.
Eligibility: Applications are invited from individuals in the mathematical sciences. Applicants must have a Ph.D. or an equivalent doctoral-level degree by the application deadline of February 1. Applicants must be U.S. citizens.
Level of Study: Graduate, Undergraduate
Type: Fellowship
Value: US$93,013
Frequency: Annual
Country of Study: Any country

Application Procedure: To apply, submit a 2-3 page statement expressing interest and qualifications for the AMS Congressional Fellowship, as well as a current curriculum vitae. Candidates should also have three letters of recommendation sent to the AMS by the February 1 deadline
Closing Date: 1 February

AMS-AAAS Mass Media Fellowship

Purpose: The American Mathematical Society (AMS) sponsors a Mass Media Fellow each summer through the Mass Media Science & Engineering Fellowship program organized by the American Association for the Advancement of Science (AAAS). This program is designed to improve public understanding of science and technology by placing advanced science, mathematics and engineering students in newsrooms nationwide.
Level of Study: Graduate
Type: Fellowship
Value: US$8,000
Frequency: Annual
Country of Study: Any country
Application Procedure: Applicants must be a) enrolled as students (upper level undergraduate or graduate); b) be a postdoctoral trainee; or c) apply within one year of the completion of a) or b). Applicants must be in the life, physical, health, engineering, computer or social sciences or mathematics and related fields with outstanding written and oral communication skills and a strong interest in learning about the media. In its 45-year history, the program has supported over 700 fellows
Closing Date: 1 January

MS Catalyzing Advocacy in Science and Engineering (CASE) Workshop

Eligibility: Students must be enrolled full-time in a graduate degree program in the mathematical sciences at an institution located in the United States. Students from foreign countries are eligible if studying here in the United States.
Level of Study: Graduate
Type: Fellowship
Value: Up to US$1600
Frequency: Annual
Country of Study: Any country
Application Procedure: Please submit a one-page resume, a brief statement of interest (maximum 500 words), and the contact information for two references. References are not required to submit letters but should be asked for their permission to list their contact information.
Closing Date: 30 January

American Meteorological Society (AMS)

45 Beacon Street, Boston, MA 02108-3693, United States of America.

Tel: (1) 617 227 2425
Email: amsinfo@ametsoc.org
Website: www.ametsoc.org

The American Meteorological Society (AMS) promotes the development and dissemination of information and education on the atmospheric and related oceanic and hydrologic sciences and the advancement of their professional applications. Founded in 1919, AMS has a membership of more than 11,000 professionals, professors, students and weather enthusiasts.

American Meteorological Society Graduate Fellowships

Purpose: The AMS Fellowship Program is a source of unique opportunities for outstanding students looking to pursue graduate education in the atmospheric or related sciences. To date, 368 students have been designated as AMS fellowship recipients. The program helps these first-year graduate students to be educated about unique challenges facing the world so that they may better tackle real-world issues after graduation. Fellowships come with several benefits that include financial support, the opportunity to be special guests at the AMS Annual Meeting with exclusive events therein, and ongoing academic and career support from AMS.
Eligibility: To be eligible to apply for a fellowship, a student must be. . . 1. Entering their first year of graduate school in the fall of 2022 2. Pursuing a degree in the atmospheric or related sciences at a US accredited institution. 3. Have a minimum grade point average of 3.0 on a 4.0-point scale. 4. U.S. citizens or hold permanent resident status. No age restriction exists.
Level of Study: Graduate
Type: Fellowship
Value: vary
Length of Study: 9 months
Frequency: Annual
Country of Study: United States of America
Application Procedure: Prospective candidates from the fields of atmospheric sciences, chemistry, computer sciences, engineering, environmental sciences, hydrology, mathematics, oceanography, and physics are encouraged to apply. A candidate must complete all sections of the application and upload all required supporting documents. With the

completed application should be three written references, relevant official transcripts.

Closing Date: 1 January

Funding: Corporation, Foundation, Government

Contributor: Industry leaders and government agencies

For further information contact:

Tel: (1) 617 227 2426 ext. 3907

Email: dfernandez@ametsoc.org

American Museum of Natural History (AMNH)

Central Park West, 79th Street, New York, NY 10024-5192, United States of America.

Tel: (1) 212 769 5100

Email: yna@amnh.org

Website: www.amnh.org

Contact: Ms Maria Dixon, Office of Grants & Fellowships

For 125 years, the American Museum of Natural History (AMNH) has been one of the world's pre-eminent science and research institutions, renowned for its collections and exhibitions that illuminate millions of years of the Earth's evolution.

American Museum of Natural History Collection Study Grants

Purpose: Collection Study Grants provide financial assistance to enable pre-doctoral and recent postdoctoral investigators to study the scientific collections at the American Museum of Natural History. These collections represent the fields in the divisions of Anthropology, Invertebrate Zoology, Physical Sciences, Paleontology, and Vertebrate Zoology. The visit must be arranged through and sponsored by an American Museum of Natural History curator. Projects of four days or longer are encouraged.

Eligibility: Open to predoctoral and recent postdoctoral investigators. The award is not available to investigators residing within daily commuting distance of the Museum

Level of Study: Postdoctorate, Predoctorate

Type: Grant

Value: Up to US$1,500 to support travel and subsistence while visiting the Museum

Frequency: Twice a year

Study Establishment: The Museum

Country of Study: United States of America

Application Procedure: Applicants must contact the appropriate Museum department to discuss the feasibility of the project and obtain written approval from the Chairman. A special application form is required and should be requested by name from the Office of Grants and Fellowships. A final report is also required. Application forms can be obtained from the website

Closing Date: May

Additional Information: Mammalogy, herpetology and ichthyology have one deadline date of 1 November. All other departments can submit 1 May and 1 November. Ornithology applications can be submitted two months prior to the visit and has no deadline date www.instrumentl.com/grants/amnh-collection-study-grants

For further information contact:

Email: careers@amnh.org

American Nuclear Society (ANS)

555 North Kensington Avenue, La Grange Park, IL 60526, United States of America.

Tel: (1) 708 352 6611

Email: outreach@ans.org

Website: www.ans.org

The American Nuclear Society (ANS) is a non-profit, international, scientific and educational organization. It was established by a group of individuals who recognized the need to unify the professional activities within the diverse fields of nuclear science and technology.

American Nuclear Society Mishima Award

Purpose: The Mishima Award recognizes outstanding contributions of an individual in research and development work on nuclear fuel and materials.

Level of Study: Postgraduate

Type: Award

Value: An engraved plaque and a monetary award

Frequency: Annual

Country of Study: Any country

Application Procedure: Nominations must include the completed nomination form accompanied by the following supporting documents: 1. A letter of recommendation from the nominator. 2. A narrative summary of about 500 words,

including accomplishments, period of activity, and significance of achievements. The significance and implications of the nominee's contribution to research and development work on nuclear fuel and materials should be included in the statement. 3. A list of relevant publications and patents (if applicable) 4. A brief chronological resume 5. Letters of support recommended but not required (no more than five)
Closing Date: 1 March
Additional Information: www.ans.org/honors/awards/award-mishima/

For further information contact:

Honors and Awards, American Nuclear Society, 555 N. Kensington Avenue, La Grange Park, IL 60526-5535, United States of America.

Email: honors@ans.org

American Nuclear Society Utility Achievement Award

Purpose: To recognize professional excellence and leadership
Eligibility: Open to members of ANS
Level of Study: Postgraduate
Type: Award
Value: An engraved plaque that is presented in August each year in conjunction with the ANS
Frequency: Annual
Country of Study: Any country
Application Procedure: Nominations must be sent before the deadline
Closing Date: 1 March
Additional Information: www.ans.org/honors/awards/award-utilachieve/

For further information contact:

Email: meetings@ans.org

Ely M. Gelbard Graduate Scholarship

Level of Study: Graduate, Postgraduate
Type: Scholarship
Value: US$3,500/each
Frequency: Annual
Country of Study: Any country
Application Procedure: A selection committee will be established by the Mathematics and Computation Division
No. of awards offered: 1
Closing Date: 1 February

Funding: Individuals, Private
Contributor: Mathematics and Computation Division (MCD)
Additional Information: For further information, check the below link. www.ans.org/honors/scholarships/gelbard/

For further information contact:

American Nuclear Society, 555 North Kensington Avenue, La Grange Park, IL 60526, United States of America.

Tel: (1) 800 323 3044
Email: nuclear@illinois.edu

Henry DeWolf Smyth Nuclear Statesman Award

Purpose: To recognize outstanding and statesmanlike contributions to many aspects of nuclear energy activities
Eligibility: Nominations for candidates for the award are selected by the American Nuclear Society and the Nuclear Energy Institute.
Level of Study: Postgraduate
Type: Award
Value: An engraved medal
Country of Study: Any country
Application Procedure: Nominations must include the completed nomination form accompanied by the following supporting documents 1. A letter of recommendation 2. A narrative summary of about 1,000 words, including accomplishments, period of activity, and significance of achievements 3. A list of publications (if applicable) or other relevant literature or evidence 4. A brief chronological resume 5. Letters of support recommended but not required (no more than five)
Closing Date: 1 March
Contributor: ANS and Nuclear Energy Institute
Additional Information: www.ans.org/honors/awards/award-smyth/

For further information contact:

Email: honors@ans.org

John R. Lamarsh Scholarship

Eligibility: United States and non-United States applicants must be ANS student members enrolled in and attending an accredited institution in the United States. Academic accomplishments must be confirmed by transcript
Level of Study: Graduate
Type: Award
Value: US$2,000
Frequency: Annual

Study Establishment: An accredited institution
Country of Study: United States of America
Application Procedure: Applications are available online at www.ans.org/honors/scholarships
No. of awards offered: 1
Closing Date: 1 February
No. of awards given last year: 1
Additional Information: www.ans.org/honors/scholarships/lamarsh/

Landis Public Communication and Education Award

Purpose: To award outstanding efforts in furthering public education
Eligibility: Open to both members and non-members of ANS
Level of Study: Postgraduate
Type: Award
Value: US$1,000 and an engraved plaque
Frequency: Annual
Country of Study: Any country
Application Procedure: Eight sets of the completed application form and supporting documents must be sent
Closing Date: 1 August
Contributor: The Landis Public Communication and Education Award
Additional Information: www.ans.org/honors/awards/award-pubcomm/

For further information contact:

Email: honors@ans.org

Landis Young Member Engineering Achievement Award

Purpose: To recognize outstanding achievement in the field of engineering
Eligibility: Open to candidates who are members of ANS below the age of 40 years
Level of Study: Postgraduate
Type: Award
Value: An engraved plaque and US$2,000
Frequency: Annual
Country of Study: Any country
Application Procedure: Nominations must include the completed nomination form accompanied by the following supporting documents: 1. A letter of recommendation 2. A narrative summary of about 1,000 words, including accomplishments, period of activity, and significance of achievements 3. A list of publications 4. A brief chronological resume

5. Letters of support (support letters recommended but not required, no more than five)
Closing Date: 1 March
Additional Information: www.ans.org/honors/awards/award-yngmbreng/

For further information contact:

Email: honors@ans.org

Mark Mills Award

Purpose: To recognise the important contributions of the late Mark Mills to the field. Established in 1958, it is awarded to the author who submits the best original technical paper
Eligibility: To be eligible for the award, the student must have been registered in a graduate degree program in a recognized institution of higher learning for one (1) year prior to the award, and his faculty advisor must make a certification of this fact on the nomination form. Thus, this competition is open to a graduate student completing the work on which his paper is based from a minimum of 4 months prior to the award to a maximum of 16 months prior to the award. A thesis is not acceptable. Multiple nominees by a nominator, nomination of past recipients of the award, and multiple-year nominations of the same paper are prohibited.
Level of Study: Graduate
Type: Award
Value: An engraved plaque and US$500
Frequency: Annual
Country of Study: Any country
Application Procedure: Applicants must be nominated by the student faculty adviser. Multiple nominees by one nominator, nomination of past recipients of the award, and multiple year nominations of the same paper are prohibited. Forms are available from the ANS headquarters
Closing Date: 1 August
Additional Information: www.ans.org/honors/awards/award-mills/

For further information contact:

Honors and Awards, American Nuclear Society, 555 N. Kensington Avenue, La Grange Park, IL 60526-5535, United States of America.

Email: honors@ans.org

Mary Jane Oestmann Professional Women

Purpose: The Mary Jane Oestmann Professional Women's Achievement Award recognizes the outstanding personal dedication and technical achievement by a woman for work she has performed in the fields of nuclear science, engineering, research or education. This award is made to recognize outstanding achievements by women who might not have the tenure or visibility to be considered for other awards of the Society.

Eligibility: Open to female candidates who need not be members of ANS but should be affiliated with the nuclear community in some manner

Level of Study: Graduate

Type: Award

Value: US$1,000

Frequency: Annual

Country of Study: Any country

Application Procedure: Nominations must include the completed nomination form accompanied by the following supporting documents 1. A letter of recommendation from the nominator 2. A narrative summary of about 1,000 words, including accomplishments, period of activity, and significance of achievements 3. A list of publications (if applicable) 4. A brief chronological resume 5. Letters of support (support letters recommended but not required; no more than five)

Closing Date: 1 August

Additional Information: www.ans.org/honors/award-oestmann/

For further information contact:

Email: honors@ans.org

Operations and Power Division Scholarship Award

Purpose: The OPD Scholarship is intended for an undergraduate or graduate student

Eligibility: United States and non-United States applicants must be ANS student members enrolled in and attending an accredited institution in the United States. Academic accomplishments must be confirmed by transcript. The OPD Scholarship is intended for an undergraduate or graduate student. Applicants must be enrolled in a course of study leading to a degree in nuclear science or engineering at an accredited institution in the United States; must have completed a minimum of two complete academic years in a four-year nuclear science or engineering program; must be United States citizens or possess a permanent resident visa; must have intentions of working in the nuclear power industry

Value: US$2,500

Frequency: Annual

Study Establishment: An accredited institution

Country of Study: United States of America

Application Procedure: Applicants 1. must be enrolled in a course of study leading to a degree in nuclear science or engineering at an accredited institution in the United States. 2. must have completed a minimum of two complete academic years in a four-year nuclear science or engineering program. 3. must be U.S. citizens or possess a permanent resident visa. 4. Academic accomplishments must be substantiated by transcript.

Closing Date: 1 February

For further information contact:

Email: honors@ans.org

Samuel Glasstone Award

Purpose: The Samuel Glasstone Award recognizes outstanding ANS Student Sections. The award consists of a certificate and a monetary award (up to US$1,200 distributed amongst the recipients). It is presented after the ANS Annual Meeting.

Level of Study: Postgraduate

Type: Award

Value: US$1,200 divided amongst winning student sections

Frequency: Annual

Country of Study: Any country

Closing Date: 1 May

Funding: Private

Additional Information: www.ans.org/honors/awards/award-glasstone/

For further information contact:

Honors and Awards, American Nuclear Society 555 N. Kensington Avenue La Grange Park, IL 60526-5535, United States of America.

Email: ssc@ans.org; honors@ans.org

Verne R Dapp Memorial Scholarship

Purpose: Applicant must be a U.S. citizen or permanent resident enrolled in a course of study relating to a degree in nuclear science and technology. Applicant must be sponsored by an ANS local section, division, student branch, committee member or organization member.

Eligibility: Open to citizens of the United States of America or holders of a permanent resident visa who are full-time graduate students enrolled in a programme leading to an advanced degree

Level of Study: Graduate

Type: Scholarship

Value: US$3,000

Frequency: Varies
Study Establishment: An accredited institution
Country of Study: United States of America
Application Procedure: Applicants must submit a request for an application form that includes the name of the university the candidate will be attending, the year the candidate will be in during the Autumn of the award, the major course of study and a stamped addressed envelope. Completed applications must include a grade transcript and three confidential reference forms. Candidates must be sponsored by an ANS section, division, student branch, committee, member or organization member. Applications are available online at www.ans.org/honors/scholarships
Closing Date: 1 February
Additional Information: www.collegexpress.com/scholarships/verne-r-dapp-memorial-scholarship/544/

For further information contact:

Fax: (1) 708 352 0499
Email: outreach@ans.org

American Numismatic Society (ANS)

75 Varick Street, floor 11, New York, NY 10013, United States of America.

Tel: (1) 212 571 4470
Email: wartenberg@numismatics.org
Website: www.numismatics.org
Contact: Dr Ute Wartenberg Kagan, Executive Director

The mission of the American Numismatic Society (ANS) is to be the preeminent national institution advancing the study and appreciation of coins, medals and related objects of all cultures as historical and artistic documents. It aims to do this by maintaining the foremost numismatic collection and library, supporting scholarly research and publications, and sponsoring educational and interpretative programmes for diverse audiences.

Grants for ANS Summer Seminar in Numismatics

Purpose: To provide a selected number of graduate students with a deeper understanding of the contribution that this subject makes to other fields
Eligibility: Open to applicants who have had at least one year's graduate study at a university in the United States of America or Canada and who are students of classical studies, history, near eastern studies or other humanistic fields

Level of Study: Postgraduate
Type: Grant
Value: US$4,000
Length of Study: 9 weeks during the Summer
Frequency: Annual
Study Establishment: Museum of the American Numismatic Society
Country of Study: United States of America
Application Procedure: Applicants must write well in advance for details of the application process
No. of awards offered: 21
Closing Date: 31 July
Funding: Private
No. of awards given last year: 12
No. of applicants last year: 21
Additional Information: One or two students from overseas are usually accepted to the seminar but will not receive a grant numismatics.org/seminar/

For further information contact:

Email: community.matters@dia.govt.nz

American Orchid Society

Fairchild Tropical Botanic Garden, 10901 Old Cutler Road, Coral Gables, FL 33156, United States of America.

Tel: (1) 305 740 2010
Email: theaos@aos.org
Website: www.aos.org
Contact: Ms Pamela S Giust, Awards Registrar

Grants for Orchid Research

Purpose: The following details the new application procedure for the submission of research proposals to the American Orchid Society. As of spring 2017, the former combined Research and Conservation Committee has been split into two discrete committees. The guidelines here apply for the Research Committee only.
Eligibility: Any orchid researcher with some form of institutional affiliation appointment at college, university, museum, herbarium, or botanical garden as research staff or research associate or similar; membership in an orchid society including AOS is not sufficient or required. If you are unsure, please contact the Chair of the Research Committee. All nationalities, all places of residence.
Level of Study: Postgraduate
Type: Grant

Value: US$920–12,000
Length of Study: Up to 3 years
Frequency: Annual
Country of Study: Any country
Application Procedure: 1. Language is English (US, UK, AU are accepted). 2. Proposal narrative of no more than five pages, 12 point font, single spaced, 1″/2.5 cm margins, including all illustrations and references. 3. Identify explicitly the organization that has agreed to administer a potential award on budget sheet. 4. CV with information relevant to proposal, usually one page should suffice. 5. Budget including justification of generally one page. Use budget template (DOCX, 92 KB). 6. Letter of recommendation/support. Degree-seeking students include a one-page letter or recommendation by advisor. Third-party commitments must be confirmed by third party with brief statement. One to two sentences should generally suffice. 7. All application material is submitted in a single pdf no larger than 3 MB. The file name is last name of principal investigator AOSRC year SmithAOSRC2018.pdf
Closing Date: 1 March
Additional Information: www.aos.org/about-us/orchid-research.aspx

For further information contact:

Tel: (1) 561 404 2000

American Ornithologists' Union (AOU)

MRC-116 National Museum of Natural History Smithsonian Institution, Washington, DC 20560-0116, United States of America.

Tel: (1) 202 357 2051
Email: aou@nmnh.si.edu
Website: www.aou.org
Contact: Secretary

The American Ornithologists' Union (AOU) is the oldest and largest organisation in the New World devoted to the scientific study of birds. The organisation's primary function is the publication and dissemination of ornithology research results.

Marcia Brady Tucker Travel Award

Purpose: To assist student AOU members planning to give a paper to attend the annual meeting

Eligibility: Open to students in a relevant discipline. Applicants must be student members of the organisation and planning to present a paper or poster at the annual meeting
Level of Study: Unrestricted
Type: Travel grant
Value: Travel expenses. Maximum expense of US$1,000 will be given
Length of Study: US$500-US$1,000
Frequency: Annual
Country of Study: Any country
Application Procedure: Applicants must submit eight copies of an expanded abstract of the presentation or poster they plan to present at the meeting, a curriculum vitae and anticipated transportation costs to the Student Awards Committee
No. of awards offered: 5-20
Closing Date: 6 November
Funding: Private
Additional Information: www.collegexpress.com/scholarships/marcia-brady-tucker-travel-award/14154/

For further information contact:

American Ornithologists' Union, Archbold Biological Station, P.O. Box 2057, Lake Placid, FL 33862, United States of America.

American Otological Society (AOS)

3096 Riverdale Road, The Villages, FL 32162, United States of America.

Tel: (1) 352 751 0932
Email: segossard@aol.com
Website: www.americanotologicalsociety.org
Contact: Ms Shirley Gossard, Administrator

The AOS is a society focused upon 'aural' medicine. The society's mission is to advance and promote medical and surgical otology, encouraging research in the related disciplines.

American Otological Society Research Training Fellowships

Purpose: To support research
Eligibility: Open to physicians, residents and medical students in the United States of America and Canada
Level of Study: Postgraduate
Type: Fellowship

Value: Up to US$40,000 depending on position and institutional norms (US$35,000 for stipend, US$5,000 for supplies)
Length of Study: 1–2 years
Frequency: Annual
Country of Study: United States of America or Canada
No. of awards offered: 1
Closing Date: 31 January
Contributor: American Otological Society, Inc
No. of awards given last year: 1
No. of applicants last year: 1
Additional Information: The organization requires institutional documentation that facilities and faculty are appropriate for the requested research www.americanotologicalsociety.org/research-grants

For further information contact:

American Otological Society, Inc, American Otological Society Research Foundation, 5830 1st St N, St Petersburg, FL 33703, United States of America.

Tel: (1) 410 955 7381
Fax: (1) 410 955 0035
Email: jcarey@jhmi.edu

American Parkinson Disease Association

135 Parkinson Avenue, Staten Island, NY 10305, United States of America.

Email: apda@apdaparkinson.org

Dr. George C. Cotzias Memorial Fellowship

Subjects: Parkinson's Disease
Purpose: George C. Cotzias, MD was a pathfinder in the pharmacologic exploration of brain functions and in the treatment of Parkinson's disease with levodopa. His work stimulated much of the current interest and research on neurological movement disorders. The American Parkinson Disease Association has established the Cotzias fellowship, in honor of his memory, to stimulate neurologists to follow his leadership. The goal of the Cotzias fellowship is to assist promising young neurologists in establishing careers in research, teaching and clinical services relevant to the problems, causes, prevention, diagnosis and treatment of Parkinson's disease and related neurological movement disorders.
Eligibility: The applicant must be a physician who is licensed to practice medicine in the US and who is completing, or has

completed, training in a clinical discipline concerned with disorders of the nervous system (i.e. adult neurology, child neurology, neurosurgery, neuropathology). The applicant should be an instructor or assistant professor and demonstrate a clear commitment to the goal described above. There should also be evidence that the sponsoring institution will provide the environment and support needed for career development. The applicant should be no more than 10 years beyond completion of his/her clinical training at the time of submission and must be sponsored by a non-profit institution in the US or its territories. Applicants with questions about their eligibility should contact the APDA in advance of submitting an application.
Level of Study: Junior Faculty
Type: Fellowship
Value: US$100,000 per year
Length of Study: Three years
Country of Study: Any country
Application Procedure: Description of the proposed research plan should not exceed six (6) pages and should consist of background, specific aims, research design, and a statement of significance for Parkinson disease research. The applicant's NIH biosketch as well as two letters of reference, one from the applicant's direct sponsor and one from a professional person with personal knowledge of the applicant's academic past and ability, should be included. An optional third letter can be submitted as well. The applicant should list all current and pending support, including sponsoring agency, amount and dates for awards. The application should indicate how other sponsored research complements or supplements the present proposal. The six page limit only applies to the length of the proposal, not the entire application.
Closing Date: 3 November

Research Grants

Subjects: MD, MD/PhD, or PhD
Purpose: Research grants are intended and available for junior investigators to pursue research in Parkinson's disease.
Eligibility: All research scientists in the field of Parkinson's research can apply, including scientists from outside the US. The selection committee will more favorably consider researchers who are new to the field of Parkinson's disease.
Level of Study: Junior Faculty
Type: Grant
Value: Up to US$75,000
Length of Study: One year
Country of Study: Any country
Application Procedure: Complete application form. Upload as one PDF document. Description of the research proposal should not exceed three (3) pages and should consist of background, specific aims, research design, and a statement

of significance for Parkinson disease research. The applicant's NIH biosketch should be included. The applicant should list all current and pending support, including sponsoring agency, amount and dates for awards. The application should indicate how other sponsored research complements or supplements the present proposal. The three page limit only applies to the length of the proposal, not the entire application. After the submit button is clicked, applicants can print the complete application.

Closing Date: 3 November

Additional Information: Funding is not to be used for: Indirect costs; Institutional overhead; Salary for the principal investigator higher than US$50,000; Travel expenses; Publication costs higher than US$1,000; Equipment costs higher than US$8,000. www.apdaparkinson.org/research/research-opportunities/grants/

American Philosophical Association (APA)

University of Delaware, 31 Amstel Avenue, Newark, DE 19716, United States of America.

Tel:	(1) 212 366 5260
Email:	anna@amc.net
Website:	www.apa.udel.edu/apa
Contact:	Dr Anna Smith, Manager of Grantmaking Programs

The American Philosophical Association (APA) was founded in 1900 to promote the exchange of ideas among philosophers, to encourage creative and scholarly activity in philosophy, to facilitate the professional work and teaching of philosophers and to represent philosophy as a discipline.

Frank Chapman Sharp Memorial Prize

Purpose: This prize is awarded to the best unpublished essay or monograph on the philosophy of war and peace submitted for the competition.

Eligibility: Authors must be members of the APA. Undergraduate entrants must be philosophy majors (or something close); graduate students must be enrolled in, or on leave from, a graduate program in philosophy. Manuscripts should be between 7,500 and 75,000 words (between 30 and 300 double-spaced typed pages)

Level of Study: Postgraduate

Type: Prize

Value: US$1,500

Country of Study: Any country

Application Procedure: Applicants must write for details or visit the website

No. of awards offered: 8

Closing Date: 10 March

Funding: Private

Additional Information: www.apaonline.org/page/sharp

For further information contact:

University of Delaware, 31 Amstel Avenue, Newark, DE 19716, United States of America.

Tel:	(1) 302 831 1112
Fax:	(1) 302 831 8690
Email:	prizes@apaonline.org

American Philosophical Society

APS Administrative Offices & APS Museum, 104 South Fifth Street, Philadelphia, PA 19106, United States of America.

Tel: (1) 215 440 3400

Phillips Fund for Native American Research

Subjects: Native American studies

Purpose: The Phillips Fund of the American Philosophical Society provides grants for research in Native American linguistics, ethnohistory, and the history of studies of Native Americans, in the continental United States and Canada. Grants are not made for projects in archaeology, ethnography, psycholinguistics, or for the preparation of pedagogical materials. The committee distinguishes ethnohistory from contemporary ethnography as the study of cultures and culture change through time. The grants are intended for such costs as travel, tapes, films, and consultants' fees but not for the purchase of books or permanent equipment or to pay income tax on the award.

Eligibility: The committee prefers to support the work of younger scholars who have received the doctorate. Applications are also accepted from graduate students for research on master's theses or doctoral dissertations. Applicants conducting research with Indigenous communities should provide information on appropriate contacts and the current state of consultation or arrangements made with those communities on any issues of research approval and ethical access that pertain to the proposed research. Details of preparations and plans will be requested within the application. The committee sometimes approves two awards to the same person within a five-year period.

Level of Study: Junior Faculty

Value: Approximately US$3,000

Length of Study: One year

Country of Study: United States of America

Application Procedure: Apply online.

Closing Date: 1 March

Additional Information: www.amphilsoc.org/grants/phillips-fund-native-american-research

For further information contact:

Tel: (1) 215 440 3418
Email: bcarpenter@amphilsoc.org

American Physiological Society (APS)

9650 Rockville Pike, Bethesda, MD 20814-3991, United States of America.

Tel: (1) 301 634 7164
Email: webmaster@the-aps.org
Website: www.the-aps.org
Contact: Ms Linda Jean Dresser, Executive Assistant

The American Physiological Society (APS) is a non-profit scientific society devoted to fostering education, scientific research and the dissemination of information in the physiological sciences. The Society strives to play a role in the progress of science and the advancement of knowledge.

American Physiological Society Minority Travel Fellowship Awards

Purpose: To increase the participation of predoctoral and postdoctoral minority students in the physiological sciences

Eligibility: Open to advanced predoctoral and postdoctoral students. Students in the APS Porter Physiology Development programme are also eligible. Minority faculty members at MBRS and MARC eligible institutions may also submit applications

Level of Study: Postdoctorate, Predoctorate

Type: Travel grant

Value: US$1,800

Length of Study: The duration of the conference or meeting

Country of Study: United States of America

Application Procedure: Applicants must contact the Education Office of the APS for further details

No. of awards offered: 31

Contributor: NIDDK and NIGMS

No. of applicants last year: 70

Additional Information: www.the-aps.org/professional-development/awards/trainees/martin-frank-diversity-travel-awards?SSO=Y

For further information contact:

Brooke Bruthers, Senior Program Manager, Minority Programs, American Physiological Society, 9650 Rockville Pike, Bethesda, MD 20814, United States of America.

Tel: (1) 301 634 7226
Fax: (1) 301 634 7098
Email: education@the-aps.org

American Psychological Association Minority Fellowship Program (APA/MFP)

Minority Fellowships Program (MFP), 750 First Street, N.E., Washington, DC 20002-4242, United States of America.

Tel: (1) 800 374 2721, 202 336 5500
Email: mfp@apa.org
Website: www.apa.org/pi/mfp
Contact: Administrative Assistant

The American Psychological Association's (APA) Minority Fellowship Program (MFP) is an innovative, comprehensive and coordinated training and career development program that promotes psychological and behavioural outcomes of ethnic minority communities. MFP is committed to increasing the number of ethnic minority professionals in the field and enhancing our understanding of the life experiences of ethnic minority communities.

Dissertation Research Grants

Purpose: The purpose of the APA Science Directorate's Dissertation Research Award program is to assist science-oriented doctoral students of psychology with research costs.

Eligibility: 1. Funding preference is given to projects that addresses the ONS Research Priorities and/or the ONS Research Agenda. 2. Membership in ONS is not required for eligibility

Type: Grants, work-study (not just grants)

Value: Up to US$5,000 each

Country of Study: Any country
Closing Date: 1 September
Additional Information: www.apa.org/about/awards/scidir-dissertre

---

American Psychological Foundation (APF)

Esther Katz Rosen Fund Grants

Subjects: Child psychology
Purpose: The Ester Katz Rosen Fund was established in 1974 by a generous bequest intended to support activities related to the advancement and application of knowledge about gifted children. Rosen Fund grants Enable and enhance development of identified gifted and talented children and adolescents. Encourage promising psychologists to continue innovative research and programs in this area.
Eligibility: Applicants must Be affiliated with a school or education institution. Hold a doctoral degree from, or be a graduate student at, an accredited university for research proposals. Graduate students and early career psychologists (10 years or less postdoctoral) are encouraged to apply. APF also supports pilot projects that, if successful, would be strong candidates for support from major federal and foundation funding agencies, and 'demonstration projects' that promise to generalize broadly to other geographical areas and/or to other settings. Teaching time releases are not supported from the Rosen Fund.
Type: Grant
Value: Grant amounts range from US$1,000 to US$50,000.
Country of Study: United States of America
Application Procedure: Apply online.
Closing Date: 1 March
Additional Information: www.apa.org/apf/funding/rosen?tab=3

F.J. McGuigan Early Career Investigator Research Grant on Understanding the Human Mind

Subjects: Psychology
Purpose: The award aims to support research that aims to address any aspect of mental function (e.g., cognition, affect, motivation) and seeks to understand the mind from both a behavioral and neural perspective.
Eligibility: The applicant must Have demonstrated commitment to stated program goals. Be a psychologist or in a related field with a doctoral degree from an accredited university. Be no more than 10 years postdoctoral.
Level of Study: Junior Faculty
Type: Research grant
Value: US$15,000

Length of Study: Two years
Frequency: Every 2 years
Country of Study: United States of America
Application Procedure: Apply online
Closing Date: 1 March
Additional Information: www.apa.org/apf/funding/mcguigan-grant-human-mind?tab=3

John and Polly Sparks Early Career Grant for Psychologists Investigating Serious Emotional Disturbance (SED)

Subjects: Children's psychology
Purpose: The John and Polly Sparks Early Career Grant supports early career psychologists conducting research in the area of early intervention and treatment for serious emotional disturbance in children. The John and Polly Sparks Foundation partnered with APF to empower early career psychologists to produce scientifically-based research and programs that could provide models for broad-based applications across the country.
Eligibility: Be an early career psychologist (no more than 10 years postdoctoral with a degree from an accredited university).
Level of Study: Junior Faculty
Type: Grant
Value: Three grants of up to US$20,000 and one grant of up to US$19,000.
Country of Study: Any country
Application Procedure: Apply online.
No. of awards offered: Four
Closing Date: 15 March
Additional Information: www.apa.org/apf/funding/sparks-early-career

---

American Public Power Association (APPA)

2551 Crystal Drive, Suite 1000, Arlington, VA 22202, United States of America.

Tel: (1) 202 467 2942
Email: DEED@PublicPower.org
Website: www.PublicPower.org/DEED
Contact: Ms Michele Suddleson, DEED Program Manager

The American Public Power Association (APPA), based in Washington, D.C., is the service organization for the nation's more than 2,000 community-owned electric utilities. Collectively, these utilities serve more than 47 million Americans. Its purpose is to advance the public policy interests of its members and their consumers, and provide member services to ensure adequate, reliable electricity at a reasonable price with the proper protection of the environment.

The American Research Institute in Turkey's (ARIT) aim is to support U.S based scholarly research in all fields of the humanities and social sciences in Turkey through administering fellowship programmes at the doctoral and postdoctoral level and through maintaining research centres in Ankara and Istanbul.

Demonstration of Energy & Efficiency Developments (DEED) - Technical Design Project

Purpose: Technical Design Projects support students working on a technical project of interest to electric utilities, especially engineering students working on their senior design or a capstone project

Eligibility: This scholarship targets full-time college juniors and seniors, and graduate students attending a college/university or vocational school in the United States Students must be majoring in a field that could lead to a career in the public power industry. Applicants must obtain a DEED member utility to sponsor their application. An official transcript must be received by the application deadline

Level of Study: Doctorate, Graduate

Type: Scholarship

Value: US$5,000 plus up to US$3,000 in travel funds to share project results at APPA's Engineering & Operations Technical Conference

Frequency: Annual

Country of Study: United States of America

Application Procedure: If you wish to apply for a scholarship please DEED@publicpower.org

Closing Date: 15 October

Funding: Private

For further information contact:

2451 Crystal Drive Suite 1000, Arlington, VA 22202, United States of America.

Tel: (1) 202 467 2960
Email: DEED@publcipower.org

American Research Institute in Turkey (ARIT)

University of Pennsylvania Museum, 3260 South Street, Philadelphia, PA 19104-6324, United States of America.

Email: leinwand@sas.upenn.edu
Website: ccat.sas.upenn.edu/ARIT
Contact: Nancy Leinwand, Executive Director

BIAA – ANAMED Joint Fellowship in Heritage Studies

Purpose: The BIAA and ANAMED joint fellowship will support research in heritage studies, concerned with the understanding, promotion, and/or preservation of the historical and archaeological material culture of Turkey and the Black Sea region with particular reference to specific sites, monuments, or regions. Successful applicants should have an MA or PhD qualification in museology, heritage management, conservation, or a related specialization, or have appropriate and comparable professional experience in these fields.

Eligibility: 1. A monthly stipend calculated by Koç University each year to cover most local expenses not covered by the fellowship. 2. Accommodation at ANAMED's residential facility in the center of Beyoglu, Istanbul. 3. ANAMED provides fellows five meals per week. These include two in-house dinners a week during the academic year (excepting national and university holidays) and a meal card for three meals a week at rates set by Koç University. 4. One lowest-possible cost, economy class, round-trip airfare will be reimbursed upon the beginning of the fellowship based on a region of origin. 5. Expenses may include books, research materials, research-related travel expenses within Turkey, and/or travel expenses for the presentation of papers at academic conferences during the period of the fellow's appointment. 6. Currently available health insurance plans cover general in-patient and limited outpatient treatments, including medicines and advanced diagnostic methods.

Level of Study: Fellowship

Country of Study: Any country

Application Procedure: All applicants should complete the ONLINE APPLICATION FORM.

Closing Date: 15 December

Additional Information: anamed.ku.edu.tr/en/fellowships/joint-fellowships/biaa-anamed-joint-fellowship-in-heritage-studies/

For further information contact:

Email: anamedapplication@ku.edu.tr

Fellowships for Intensive Advanced Turkish Language Study in Istanbul, Turkey

Purpose: To provide full travel and fellowship to students and scholars for participation in the summer program in advanced Turkish language at Bogazici University in Istanbul
Eligibility: 1. Be a citizen, national, or permanent resident of the United States. 2. Be currently enrolled in an undergraduate or graduate level academic program, or be faculty. 3. Have a minimum B average in current program of study. 4. Perform at the high-intermediate level on a proficiency-based admissions examination
Level of Study: Graduate, Postdoctorate, Postgraduate, Predoctorate
Type: Fellowship
Value: Fellowship includes round-trip airfare to Istanbul, application and tuition fees, and a maintenance stipend
Length of Study: 8 weeks
Frequency: Annual
Study Establishment: Bogazici University
Country of Study: Turkey
Application Procedure: Application forms and procedure are available at the ARIT website ccat.sas.upenn.edu/ARIT
No. of awards offered: 65
Closing Date: 3 February
Funding: Government
Contributor: United States Department of Education, Fulbright-Hays Group Projects Abroad Programme
No. of awards given last year: 17
No. of applicants last year: 65
Additional Information: ccat.sas.upenn.edu/ARIT/ARITSummerLanguageProgram.html

For further information contact:

Tel: (1) 212 359 4913
Fax: (1) 212 265 7131
Email: aritfellowship@georgtown.edu

National Endowment for the Humanities American Research Institute in Turkey-National Endowment for the Humanities Fellowships for Research in Turkey

Purpose: To support research on ancient, medieval or modern times
Eligibility: Open to scholars who have completed their formal training by the application deadline and plan to carry out research in Turkey may apply. They may be United States citizens or 3-year residents of the United States. Please consult ARIT headquarters on questions of eligibility. Advanced scholars also may apply for ARIT Fellowships in the Humanities and Social Sciences

Level of Study: Postdoctorate, Postgraduate, Professional development, Research
Type: Fellowship
Value: 16,800–50,400 lira
Length of Study: 4–12 months
Frequency: Annual
Study Establishment: Either of ARIT's two research establishments in Ankara or Istanbul
Country of Study: Turkey
Application Procedure: Applicants must submit an application form, project statement and references
No. of awards offered: 16
Closing Date: 1 November
Funding: Government
Contributor: National Endowment for the Humanities (NEH)
No. of awards given last year: 3
No. of applicants last year: 16
Additional Information: The hostel, research and study facilities are available at ARIT's branch centers in Istanbul and Ankara ccat.sas.upenn.edu/ARIT/NEHFellowships.html

For further information contact:

Tel: (1) 215 898 3474
Fax: (1) 215 898 0657
Email: aritoffice@gmail.com

American School of Classical Studies at Athens (ASCSA)

6-8 Charlton Street, Princeton, NJ 08540-5232, United States of America.

Tel: (1) 609 683 0800
Email: ascsa@ascsa.org
Website: www.ascsa.edu.gr
Contact: Ms Mary E Darlington, Executive Associate

The ASCSA supports and encourages the teaching of the archaeology, art, history, language and literature of Greece from early times to the present.

American School of Classical Studies at Athens Advanced Fellowships

Subjects: Archaeology, History, Classics, Medieval Studies, Literature, Classical Philology
Purpose: Several fellowships for the full academic year at the School are available to students who plan to stay on or return

to the School to pursue independent research, usually for their PhD dissertation. Advanced Fellowships fields awarded by the School include one each in art and architecture of antiquity, history of architecture, Mycenaean archaeology or Athenian architecture and/or archaeology, and the study of pottery; and three unrestricted as to field.

Eligibility: Applicants must have completed the Regular Program or one academic year (Sept. – May) as a Student Associate Member.

Level of Study: Doctorate, Graduate

Type: Fellowship

Value: US$11,500 stipend plus fees, room and partial board (The Kress Fellowship is US$15,000 plus room and partial board.)

Length of Study: 1 academic year

Frequency: Annual

Study Establishment: American School of Classical Studies at Athens (ASCSA)

Country of Study: Greece

Application Procedure: Applicants must complete online applications. For guidelines and application visit www.ascsa.edu.gr.

No. of awards offered: 5

Closing Date: 15 February

No. of awards given last year: 5

No. of applicants last year: 18

Additional Information: The fellowships include: the Edward Capps, the Doreen C Spitzer and the Eugene Vanderpool Fellowships (subject unrestricted); the Samuel H. Kress Fellowships in art and architecture in antiquity; the Gorham P Stevens Fellowship in the history of architecture; and the Homer A and Dorothy B Thompson Fellowship in the study of pottery. Ione Mylonas Shear in Mycenaean Archaeology or Athenian architecture. www.ascsa.edu.gr/fellowships-and-grants/graduate-and-postdoctoral

American School of Classical Studies at Athens Fellowships

Eligibility: Open to graduate and well-qualified undergraduate students preparing for an advanced degree in Classical Studies or a related field. Applicants must be enrolled in a North American Institution

Level of Study: Graduate, Predoctorate

Type: Fellowship

Value: US$11,500 stipend plus fees, room and partial board

Length of Study: 1 academic year

Frequency: Annual

Study Establishment: ASCSA

Country of Study: Greece

Application Procedure: Submit online application form for "Associate Membership with Fellowship", curriculum vitae, a detailed description of the project to be pursued in Greece

(250-word abstract and a statement up to three pages, single spaced). Arrange for three letters of recommendation. Student applicants are required to submit scans of official academic transcripts as part of the online application.

No. of awards offered: 21

Closing Date: 15 January

Funding: Private

No. of awards given last year: 12

No. of applicants last year: 21

Additional Information: www.ascsa.edu.gr/fellowships-and-grants/postdoctoral-and-senior-scholars

For further information contact:

54 Souidias Street, GR-106 76 Athens, Greece.

Tel:	(30) 213 000 2400
Fax:	(30) 210 725 0584
Email:	Ascsa_info@ascsa.edu.gr

American School of Classical Studies at Athens Research Fellowship in Environmental Studies

Purpose: To support research on studies from archaeological contexts in Greece

Eligibility: Doctoral candidates working on their dissertation and postdoctoral scholars with well-defined projects that can be completed during the academic year of the fellowship

Level of Study: Doctorate, Graduate, Postdoctorate, Postgraduate, Predoctorate

Type: Fellowship

Value: US$15,500–27,000 stipend depending on seniority and experience

Length of Study: 1 academic year

Frequency: Annual

Study Establishment: The Malcolm H Wiener Research Laboratory for Archaeological Science, ASCSA

Country of Study: Greece

Application Procedure: Applicants must complete online applications. For guidelines and application visit www.ascsa.edu.gr

No. of awards offered: 8

Closing Date: 15 January

Funding: Private

No. of awards given last year: 1

No. of applicants last year: 8

American School of Classical Studies at Athens Research Fellowship in Faunal Studies

Purpose: To study faunal remains from archaeological contexts in Greece

Eligibility: Doctoral candidates working on their dissertation and postdoctoral scholars with well-defined projects that can be completed during the academic year of the fellowship. There is no citizenship requirement

Level of Study: Doctorate, Graduate, Postdoctorate, Postgraduate, Predoctorate

Type: Fellowship

Value: US$15,500–27,000 stipend depending on seniority and experience

Length of Study: 1 academic year

Frequency: Annual

Study Establishment: The Malcolm H Wiener Research Laboratory for Archaeological Science, ASCSA

Country of Study: Greece

Application Procedure: Applicants must complete online applications. For guidelines and application visit www.ascsa.edu.gr

No. of awards offered: 8

Closing Date: 15 January

Funding: Private

No. of awards given last year: 1

No. of applicants last year: 8

American School of Classical Studies at Athens Research Fellowship in Geoarchaeology

Purpose: To support research on a geoarchaeological topic in Greece

Eligibility: Doctoral candidates working on their dissertation and postdoctoral scholars with well-defined projects that can be completed during the academic year of the fellowship. There is no citizenship requirement

Level of Study: Doctorate, Graduate, Postdoctorate, Postgraduate, Predoctorate

Type: Fellowship

Value: US$15,500–27,000 stipend depending on seniority and experience

Length of Study: 1 academic year

Frequency: Annual

Study Establishment: The Malcolm H Wiener Research Laboratory for Archaeological Science, ASCSA

Country of Study: Greece

Application Procedure: Applicants must complete online applications. For guidelines and application visit www.ascsa.edu.gr

No. of awards offered: 8

Closing Date: 15 January

Funding: Private

No. of awards given last year: 1

No. of applicants last year: 8

American School of Classical Studies at Athens Summer Sessions

Purpose: The two 6-week sessions are designed for those who wish to become acquainted with Greece and its antiquities, and to improve their understanding of the relationship between the monuments, landscape, and climate of the country and its history, literature and culture

Eligibility: Enrolment is open to graduate and advanced undergraduate students and to high school and college instructors of classics and related subjects

Level of Study: Graduate, Postdoctorate, Postgraduate, Professional development

Type: Scholarship

Length of Study: 6 weeks

Frequency: Annual

Study Establishment: ASCSA

Country of Study: Greece

Application Procedure: Submit the application form online by January 15. Applicants for School scholarships must review the program material on the website to learn about the requirements. High school teachers and college professors should be prepared to attach a copy of their curriculum vitae (saved as doc, docx, or pdf) to the application form. Student applicants are required to submit scans of undergraduate and graduate transcripts (unofficial are acceptable) in legible pdf format as part of the online application. Please be sure to name the file "LastnameTranscripts.pdf" (e.g. SmithTranscripts.pdf) Applicants arrange for two letters of recommendation to be submitted online by their recommenders. After you submit your online application, your recommenders will automatically be sent instructions about how to upload their recommendation. Recommendations are due January 10.

No. of awards offered: 83

Closing Date: March

Funding: Private

Additional Information: www.ascsa.edu.gr/programs/summer-session

For further information contact:

Email: ssapplication@ascsa.org

Archaeological Institute of America (AIA) Anna C. and Oliver C. Colburn Fellowships

Purpose: To support studies undertaken at the ASCSA for no more than a year.

Eligibility: Applicants must be citizens or permanent residents of the United States or Canada. To be eligible, applicants must have been AIA (Graduate or Professional level) in

good standing for at least two consecutive years (or one year for graduate students) by the application deadline. Applicants must be at the pre-doctoral stage or have received a Ph.D within five years of application. Each applicant must apply concurrently to the ASCSA for associate membership and to the AIA. An applicant may not be a member of the ASCSA during the year of application.
Type: Fellowship
Value: US$5,500
Country of Study: Any country
Closing Date: 15 January

For further information contact:

Email: fellowships@archaeological.org

Cotsen Traveling Fellowship

Purpose: The Gennadius Library offers the Cotsen Traveling Fellowship, a short-term grant awarded each year to scholars and graduate students pursuing research topics that require the use of the Gennadeion collections
Eligibility: 1. Senior scholars and graduate students of any nationality. 2. School fees are waived for a maximum of two months
Level of Study: Postgraduate
Type: Fellowship
Value: US$2,000
Frequency: Annual
Country of Study: Any country
Application Procedure: 1. Submit "Associate Membership with Fellowship" application online. 2. The application should include a curriculum vitae, a letter (up to 750 words) describing the project and its relation to the Gennadius Library collections, proposed dates, a brief budget (not more than one page), and two letters of recommendation
Closing Date: 15 January
Funding: Private
Additional Information: www.ascsa.edu.gr/fellowships-and-grants/postdoctoral-and-senior-scholars

For further information contact:

ASCSA, 54 Souidias Street, GR-106 76 Athens, Greece.

Email: application@ascsa.org

Cotsen Traveling Fellowship for Research in Greece

Subjects: Archaeology, History, Classics, Medieval Studies.

Purpose: Short term travel award for senior scholars and graduate students for projects and research at the Gennadius Library.
Eligibility: Senior scholars (PhD holders) and graduate students of any nationality.
Level of Study: Doctorate, Graduate, Postdoctorate, Postgraduate
Type: Fellowship
Value: Stipend of €2,000 and School fees waived
Length of Study: At least 1 month in residence.
Frequency: Annual
Study Establishment: The Gennadius Library, American School of Classical Studies at Athens (ASCSA)
Country of Study: Greece
Application Procedure: Applicants must complete online applications. For guidelines and application visit www.ascsa.edu.gr.
No. of awards offered: 1
Closing Date: 15 January
Funding: Private
No. of awards given last year: 1
No. of applicants last year: 12
Additional Information: Programs Administrator, Alicia Dissinger www.ascsa.edu.gr/programs/summer-session

Council of American Overseas Research Centers Multi Country Research Fellowships

Subjects: Graduate students/scholars in ancient studies, archaeology, classical studies, anthropology, Byzantine, post-Byzantine, Ottoman studies and modern Greek.
Purpose: The Multi-Country Research Fellowship supports advanced regional or trans-regional research in the humanities, social sciences, or allied natural sciences for U.S. doctoral candidates, and postdoctoral scholars. Preference will be given to candidates examining comparative and/or cross-regional research.
Eligibility: Applicants must be U.S. citizens; Fellowship awards will not exceed US$11,000; Funding is not available for research conducted in the U.S.; Group projects are admissible and will be evaluated as a single application. Groups should submit one 1. application for the group project and Curriculum Vitae for each member of the group. Two 2. letters of recommendation are required for the group. If awarded, a single grant of US$11,000 will be issued to the group; It is not required that you be affiliated with a U.S. academic institution to apply. As long as you are a PhD candidate at an accredited university, or have already earned your PhD, you are eligible for the fellowships; PhD candidates must be ABD (all but dissertation) by May; If you have held a Multi-

Country Fellowship in the past, you must wait 3 years before you are eligible to apply again.

Level of Study: Doctorate, Graduate, Postdoctorate, Postgraduate

Type: Fellowship

Value: Up to US$11,000 each will be given

Length of Study: 90 day minimum

Frequency: Annual

Study Establishment: American School of Classical Studies at Athens (ASCSA)

Country of Study: Greece

Application Procedure: Consult CAORC website for application and deadline www.caorc.org.

No. of awards offered: 8

Closing Date: 23 January

No. of awards given last year: 1

No. of applicants last year: 1

Fowler-Merle Smith Summer Scholarship for Teachers

Subjects: Archaeology, History, Classics, Medieval Studies

Purpose: To attend the ASCSA Summer Session or Summer Seminars

Eligibility: The Fowler Merle-Smith scholarships are for high school teachers. The scholarships are designed for teachers who wish to become acquainted with Greece and its major monuments, and to improve their understanding of the country's landscape, history, literature, and culture from antiquity to the present.

Level of Study: Teachers

Type: Scholarship

Value: All Fees and US$2,000 to offset the cost of international travel.

Length of Study: 6 weeks (Session) or 18 days (Seminar)

Frequency: Annual

Study Establishment: American School of Classical Studies at Athens (ASCSA)

Country of Study: Greece

Application Procedure: Applicants will be considered for this scholarship when they apply for the Summer Session and/or Summer Seminars. No additional forms are required. For guidelines and application visit www.ascsa.edu.gr.

No. of awards offered: 6

Closing Date: 15 January

No. of awards given last year: 7

No. of applicants last year: 10

Harry Bikakis Fellowship

Subjects: Archaeology, History, Ancient Law, Classics.

Purpose: To support research on ancient Greek law Greek graduate students working on excavations conducted by or affiliated with the ASCSA.

Eligibility: North American or Greek graduate students researching ancient Greek law or Greek graduate students working on a School excavation.

Level of Study: Doctorate, Graduate

Type: Fellowship

Value: A stipend of €1,875 and all School fees are waived.

Length of Study: Short-term

Frequency: Annual

Study Establishment: American School of Classical Studies at Athens (ASCSA)

Country of Study: Greece

Application Procedure: Applicants must complete online applications. For guidelines and application visit www.ascsa.edu.gr.

No. of awards offered: 1

Closing Date: 15 January

Funding: Private

No. of awards given last year: 1

No. of applicants last year: 2

Jacob Hirsch Fellowship

Subjects: Archaeology

Purpose: Students who hold U.S. or Israeli citizenship, and who are PhD candidates writing their dissertations in archaeology, and early-career scholars (PhD earned within the last five years) completing a project, such as the revision of a dissertation for publication, which requires a lengthy residence in Greece.

Eligibility: U.S. or Israeli citizens who are either Ph.D. candidates writing their dissertations in archaeology, or early-career scholars (Ph.D. earned within the last five years) completing a project that requires a lengthy residence in Greece.

Level of Study: Doctorate, Graduate, Postdoctorate, Postgraduate

Type: Fellowship

Value: Stipend of US$11,500 plus room, board and waiver of School fees.

Length of Study: Academic year

Frequency: Annual

Study Establishment: American School of Classical Studies at Athens (ASCSA)

Country of Study: Greece

Application Procedure: Submit online application form for "Associate Membership with Fellowship", curriculum vitae, and a detailed description of the project to be pursued in Greece (250-word abstract and a statement up to three pages, single spaced). Arrange for three letters of

recommendation. Student applicants are required to submit scans of official academic transcripts as part of the online application.
No. of awards offered: 1
Closing Date: 15 January
Funding: Private
No. of awards given last year: 1
No. of applicants last year: 6

Kress Publications Fellowships

Subjects: Archaeology, History, Classics, Medieval Studies.
Purpose: Postdoctoral scholars working on assigned material from excavations at Ancient Corinth, the Athenian Agora, Lerna, and affiliated projects of the ASCSA to support research for publication of the excavated material.
Eligibility: Postdoctoral scholars working on assigned material from excavations at Ancient Corinth, the Athenian Agora, Lerna, and affiliated projects of the ASCSA to support research for publication of the excavated material.
Level of Study: Postdoctorate
Type: Fellowship
Value: Three months up to US$100,000; Nine months up to US$30,000
Length of Study: Minimum of three, maximum of nine months
Frequency: Annual
Study Establishment: American School of Classical Studies at Athens (ASCSA)
Country of Study: Greece
Application Procedure: Applicants must complete online applications. For guidelines and application visit www.ascsa.edu.gr.
No. of awards offered: Up to 3
Closing Date: 16 January
No. of awards given last year: 2
No. of applicants last year: 5

Malcolm H. Wiener Laboratory for Archaeological Science Senior Fellowship

Purpose: To conduct research at the Malcolm H. Wiener Laboratory for Archaeological Science pertaining to the ancient Greek world and adjacent areas through the application of interdisciplinary methods in the archaeological sciences. Laboratory facilities are especially well-equipped to support the study of human skeletal biology, archaeobiological remains (faunal and botanical), environmental studies, and geoarchaeology (particularly studies in human-landscape interactions and the study of site formation processes)

Eligibility: Open to recent PhDs (at least 5 years) previous to application. Research projects utilizing other archaeological scientific approaches are also eligible for consideration, depending on the; strength of the questions asked and the suitability of the plan for access to other equipment or resources available elsewhere in Greece
Level of Study: Postdoctorate
Type: Fellowship
Value: Stipend of US$15,000 (5-month term); stipend of US$30,000 (10-month term)
Length of Study: 5–10 months with the next term beginning early September. It is expected that the applicant will maintain a physical presence at the Wiener Laboratory during the academic year (1 September to 1 June)
Frequency: Annual
Country of Study: Greece
Application Procedure: Applicants must complete online application. For guidelines and application, visit www.asca.edu.gr/index.php/wiener-laboratory/senior-instructions
Closing Date: 15 January
Funding: Private
Additional Information: www.ascsa.edu.gr/research/wiener-laboratory/fellowships-and-research-associate-appointments/research-associate-appointment

For further information contact:

54 Souidias Street, GR-106 76 Athens, Greece.

Tel: (30) 213 000 2400
Fax: (30) 210 725 0584
Email: ascsa_info@ascsa.edu.gr

Malcolm H. Wiener Laboratory Postdoctoral Fellowship

Purpose: To conduct research at the Malcolm H. Wiener Laboratory for Archaeological Science at the American School of Classical Studies at Athens that addresses substantive problems pertaining to the ancient Greek world and adjacent areas through the application of interdisciplinary methods in the archaeological sciences. Laboratory facilities are especially well equipped to support the study of human skeletal biology, archaeobiological remains (faunal and botanical), environmental studies, and geoarchaeology (particularly studies in human-landscape interactions and the study of site formation processes). Research projects utilizing other archaeological scientific approaches are also eligible for consideration, depending on the strength of the questions asked and the suitability of the plan for access to other equipment or resources available elsewhere in Greece

Eligibility: The Post-Doctoral Fellowship is limited to individuals who have received their PhD within the last seven (7) years. Individuals who have received prior support as Pre-Doctoral Fellows must wait four (4) years before applying for a Post-Doctoral Fellowship. Former Research Associates must wait two (2) years before applying for a Post-Doctoral Fellowship.

Level of Study: Postdoctorate

Type: Fellowship

Value: US$35,000 per year

Length of Study: 3 years

Frequency: Every 3 years

Study Establishment: Malcom H. Wiener Laboratory for Archaeological Science at the American School of Classical Studies at Athens (ASCSA)

Country of Study: Greece

Application Procedure: Submit cover sheet naming the applicant, current research interests, and title and brief summary of the proposed research project. Objectives, Significance and Background Briefly describe the project's major goals and their impact on the state of the field and how the proposed work relates to the present state of knowledge and discuss the progress made on this research to date by the applicant. Research Description. Present a brief technical description of research plan for the overall research and a detailed presentation of what is to be accomplished during the tenure of the Research Associate appointment. Timeframe. A plan of how the research questions will be addressed throughout the proposed duration of the Research Associate appointment. Applicants should discuss how the tenure of this appointment will advance on-going research and include a plan of publication/dissemination of the results. Results of prior Wiener Laboratory Research. If the applicant has received Wiener Laboratory funding in the past, information on the prior award and its impact is required (half a page double spaced Times Roman 12pt).

No. of awards offered: 8

Closing Date: 15 January

No. of awards given last year: 1

No. of applicants last year: 8

Additional Information: www.ascsa.edu.gr/fellowships-and-grants/postdoctoral-and-senior-scholars

For further information contact:

Email: TKarkanas@ascsa.edu.gr

Malcom H. Wiener Laboratory for Archaeological Science Research Associate Appointments

Purpose: To conduct short-term focused research at the Malcolm H. Wiener Laboratory for Archaeological Science

of the American School of Classical Studies at Athens as part of a program of research that addresses substantive problems pertaining to the ancient Greek world and adjacent areas through the application of interdisciplinary methods in the archaeological sciences. Laboratory facilities are especially well equipped to support the study of human skeletal biology, archaeobiological remains (faunal and botanical), environmental studies, and geoarchaeology (particularly studies in human-landscape interactions and the study of site formation processes). Research projects utilizing other archaeological scientific approaches are also eligible for consideration, depending on the strength of the questions asked and the suitability of the plan for access to other equipment or resources available elsewhere in Greece

Eligibility: Individuals actively enrolled in a graduate program and individuals with a Masters or Doctorate in a relevant discipline. Applicants are welcome from any college or university worldwide. Independent scholars are also welcome to apply

Level of Study: Doctorate, Graduate, Postdoctorate, Postgraduate

Type: One fellowship

Value: Up to €7,000

Length of Study: Variable up to nine (9) months

Frequency: Annual

Study Establishment: ASCSA

Country of Study: Greece

Application Procedure: Link to Research Associate application instructions at www.ascsa.edu.gr/index.php/wiener-laboratory/research-associate-appointment

No. of awards offered: 14

Closing Date: 15 January

Funding: Private

Contributor: ASCSA

No. of awards given last year: 1

No. of applicants last year: 14

Additional Information: www.ascsa.edu.gr/fellowships-and-grants/postdoctoral-and-senior-scholars

For further information contact:

54 Souidias Street, GR-106 76 Athens, Greece.

Tel: (30) 213 000 2400
Fax: (30) 210 725 0584
Email: application@ascsa.org

National Endowment for the Humanities (NEH) Fellowships

Subjects: Archaeology, History, Classics, Medieval Studies.

Purpose: Postdoctoral Scholars and Professionals in the Humanities

Eligibility: Postdoctoral scholars and professionals in all fields relevant to the mission of the ASCSA who are US citizens, or foreign nationals who have lived in the US for the three years immediately preceding the application deadline. Applicants must already hold their PhD or have completed all requirements, except for the actual conferral of the degree, by the application deadline.

Level of Study: Postdoctorate

Type: Fellowship

Value: Montly stipend of US$4,200 from a total pool of US$75,600 per year

Length of Study: 4, 5, or 9-month duration

Frequency: Annual

Study Establishment: American School of Classical Studies at Athens (ASCSA)

Country of Study: Greece

Application Procedure: Applicants must complete online applications. For guidelines and application visit www.ascsa.edu.gr.

No. of awards offered: Two to Four

Closing Date: 31 October

No. of awards given last year: 4

No. of applicants last year: 9

Open Scholarship for Summer Sessions

Purpose: To attend ASCSA Summer Session

Level of Study: Postgraduate, Predoctorate, Professional development

Type: Scholarship

Value: US$5,000

Length of Study: 6 weeks

Study Establishment: American School of Classical Studies at Athens (ASCSA)

Country of Study: Greece

Application Procedure: Applicants must complete online application. For guidelines and application visit www.ascsa.edu.gr

No. of awards offered: 65

Closing Date: 15 January

No. of awards given last year: 5

No. of applicants last year: 65

For further information contact:

Email: ssapplication@ascsa.org

Open Scholarship for the Summer Session and Summer Seminars

Subjects: Archaeology, History, Classics, Medieval Studies

Purpose: To attend the ASCSA Summer Session or Summer Seminars

Eligibility: Catered towards graduate students enrolled in programs that focus on Greek and/or Latin languages and literature, ancient history, ancient philosophy or Classical art and archaeology. Funding is restricted to graduate students, who at the time of application, are enrolled at Cooperating Institutions of the American School of Classical Studies at Athens.

Level of Study: Graduate, Postdoctorate, Postgraduate, Predoctorate

Type: Scholarship

Value: All Fees

Length of Study: 6 weeks (Session) or 18 days (Seminar)

Frequency: Annual

Study Establishment: American School of Classical Studies at Athens (ASCSA)

Country of Study: Greece

Application Procedure: Applicants will be considered for this scholarship when they apply for the Summer Session and/or Summer Seminars. No additional forms are required. For guidelines and application visit www.ascsa.edu.gr.

No. of awards offered: 10

Closing Date: 10 January

Funding: Private

No. of awards given last year: 6

No. of applicants last year: 89

Regular Member Fellowships

Subjects: Archaeology, History, Classics, Medieval Studies, Literature, Classical Philology

Purpose: Students preparing for an advanced degree in classical and ancient Mediterranean studies, post-classical Greek studies, or a related field. Well-qualified students with a B.A. will be considered for admission and fellowships, although preference is given to those who have completed at least one year of graduate study.

Eligibility: Open to students at colleges or universities in the U.S. or Canada who have completed a B.A. but not a PhD, and who are preparing for an advanced degree in classical or ancient Mediterranean studies, or a related field.

Level of Study: Doctorate, Graduate

Type: Fellowship

Value: US$11,500 stipend plus fees, room and partial board

Length of Study: 1 academic year

Frequency: Annual

Study Establishment: American School of Classical Studies at Athens (ASCSA)

Country of Study: Greece

Application Procedure: Applicants must complete online applications. For guidelines and application visit www.ascsa.edu.gr.

No. of awards offered: 12
Closing Date: 15 January
Funding: Private
No. of awards given last year: 12
No. of applicants last year: 27

Samuel H Kress Joint Athens-Jerusalem Fellowship

Purpose: To enable students to conduct research in Greece and Israel in the same academic year and to promote better understanding of interrelationships between the cultures, languages, literature and history of the Aegean and the Near East
Eligibility: Advanced graduate students in classical studies, ancient Mediterranean studies, post-classical Greek studies, or related fields who have a specific project that requires extended residence in Greece.
Level of Study: Doctorate, Postgraduate, Predoctorate
Type: Fellowship
Value: US$15,000
Length of Study: 1 academic year
Frequency: Annual
Study Establishment: The ASCSA and the W F Albright Institute of Archaeological Research in Jerusalem
Application Procedure: Submit an online application. The application will include the following: 1. An up-to-date curriculum vitae; 2. A project statement of no more than three single-spaced pages in length. A bibliography of not more than one page may be submitted along with the project statement (the bibliography does not count towards the length of the project statement); 3. A list of other fellowships, if any, applied for with dates of notification of these awards; 4. A letter of reference from your dissertation advisor on the feasibility of your work. Applicants who are not at the School during the current academic year should also obtain a second letter of reference, in addition to the advisor's letter, from a scholar who can evaluate your academic progress since leaving the School.
No. of awards offered: 5
Closing Date: 15 February
Funding: Private
No. of awards given last year: 1
No. of applicants last year: 5

For further information contact:

Albright Institute Department of Religious Studies, John Carroll University, 20,700 North Park Boulevard, University Heights, OH 44118, United States of America.

Tel: (1) 216 397 4705
Fax: (1) 216 397 4478
Email: spencer@jcu.edu

The William Sanders Scarborough Fellowships

Purpose: This fellowship is intended to honor and remember Professor William Sanders Scarborough and to help foster diversity in the fields of Classical and Hellenic Studies and the Humanities more broadly by supporting students and teachers from underrepresented groups in their study and research at the American School of Classical Studies at Athens.
Eligibility: Graduate students, faculty members (K-12 and all levels of post-secondary education), and independent scholars residing in the United States or Canada, regardless of citizenship, whose geographic origin, diverse experiences, and socio-economic background are underrepresented at the School (including persons from the Black, Indigenous, and Persons of Color communities), and whose studies, research, or teaching would benefit from residency at the School. Fellowship recipients need not be specialists in the field of Classical Studies. The School welcomes applicants from faculty of K-12 schools and from students or faculty from public and private universities, colleges, and community colleges; and encourages applications from Historically Black Colleges and Universities.
Level of Study: Graduate
Type: Fellowship
Length of Study: Up to three months
Frequency: Annual
Country of Study: Greece
Application Procedure: Submit an online application here ascsa.submittable.com/submit/171376/william-sanders-scarborough-fellowship by the deadline. 1. A complete application will include: 2. A 2-page, single-spaced, statement indicating your eligibility, describing the proposed use of the fellowship including any formal program at the School you plan to apply for, the proposed timeframe for your work at the School, and your project or research goals (as applicable). 3. A curriculum vitae. 4. A copy of current transcripts for student applicants (scans of official transcripts are acceptable). 5. Arrange for two letters of recommendation. Once an online application is submitted, recommenders will be sent an automated email with instructions about how to submit their letters of recommendation. Recommenders will be asked to upload their letters via the online application system, Submittable. It is also acceptable for recommenders to submit letters directly to this email address: application@ascsa.org.
Closing Date: 15 January

For further information contact:

Email: application@ascsa.org

W.D.E. Coulson & Toni M. Cross Aegean Exchange Program

Purpose: W.D.E. Coulson and Toni M. Cross Aegean Exchange Program for Greek Ph.D. level graduate students and senior scholars in any field of the humanities and social sciences from prehistoric to modern times to conduct research in Turkey

Eligibility: Greek nationals, including staff of the Ministry of Culture and Sport, doctoral candidates and faculty members of Greek institutions of higher education.

Level of Study: Doctorate

Value: Stipend of US$250 per week plus up to US$500 for travel expenses

Country of Study: Any country

Application Procedure: Submit "Associate Membership with Fellowship" application online. The application includes a curriculum vitae, statement of the project to be pursued during the period of grant (up to three pages, single-spaced in length), two letters of reference from scholars in the field commenting on the value and feasibility of the project.

No. of awards offered: Four to eight awards

Closing Date: 15 March

Contributor: American Research Institute in Turkey (ARIT)

Wiener Laboratory Predoctoral Fellowship

Purpose: To conduct research at the Malcolm H. Wiener Laboratory for Archaeological Science at the American School of Classical Studies at Athens that addresses substantive problems pertaining to the ancient Greek world and adjacent areas through the application of interdisciplinary methods in the archaeological sciences. Laboratory facilities are especially well equipped to support the study of human skeletal biology, archaeobiological remains (faunal and botanical), environmental studies, and geoarchaeology (particularly studies in human-landscape interactions and the study of site formation processes). Research projects utilizing other archaeological scientific approaches are also eligible for consideration, depending on the strength of the questions asked and the suitability of the plan for access to other equipment or resources available elsewhere in Greece.

Eligibility: The Post-Doctoral Fellowship is limited to individuals who have received their PhD within the last seven (7) years. Individuals who have received prior support as Pre-Doctoral Fellows must wait four (4) years before applying for a Post-Doctoral Fellowship. Former Research Associates must wait two (2) years before applying for a Post-Doctoral Fellowship.

Level of Study: Predoctorate

Type: Fellowship

Value: Stipend of US$20,000 for 12 months

Length of Study: 2 academic years

Study Establishment: Malcolm H. Wiener Laboratory for Archaeological Science at the American School of Classical Studies

Country of Study: Greece

Application Procedure: Applicants must complete online application. For guidelines and application visit www.ascsa.edu.gr

Closing Date: 16 January

Additional Information: www.ascsa.edu.gr/fellowships-and-grants/postdoctoral-and-senior-scholars

For further information contact:

54 Souidias Street, GR-106 76 Athens, Greece.

Tel:	(30) 213 000 2400
Fax:	(30) 210 725 0584
Email:	application@ascsa.org

Wiener Laboratory Research Associate Appointment

Subjects: To conduct short-term, focused research at the Malcolm H. Wiener Laboratory for Archaeological Science of the American School of Classical Studies at Athens as part of a program of research that addresses substantive problems pertaining to the ancient Greek world, or adjacent areas, through the application of interdisciplinary methods in the archaeological sciences. Wiener Laboratory facilities are especially well equipped to support the study of human skeletal biology, archaeobiological remains (faunal and botanical), environmental studies, and geoarchaeology (particularly studies in human-landscape interactions and the study of site formation processes).

Purpose: To support research on studies from archaeology related to the ancient Greek world.

Eligibility: Individuals actively enrolled in a graduate program and individuals with a Masters or Doctorate in a relevant discipline. Applicants are welcome from any college or university worldwide. Independent scholars are also welcome to apply. Former Research Associates must wait two (2) years before applying for a Post- or pre- Doctoral Fellowship. Exceptions to these basic eligibility requirements will be granted only in extraordinary cases.

Level of Study: Doctorate, Graduate, Postdoctorate, Postgraduate

Value: Variable

Length of Study: Up to nine months

Frequency: Annual
Study Establishment: The Malcolm H. Wiener Research Laboratory for Archaeological Science, ASCSA
Country of Study: Greece
Application Procedure: Applicants must complete online applications. For guidelines and application visit www. ascsa.edu.gr.
No. of awards offered: 1
Closing Date: 15 January
Funding: Private
No. of awards given last year: 1
No. of applicants last year: 12

American Schools of Oriental Research (ASOR)

656 Beacon Street, 5th Floor, Boston, MA 02215-2010, United States of America.

Tel: (1) 617 353 6570
Email: asor@bu.edu
Website: www.asor.org
Contact: Britta Abeln, Office Coordinator

The American Schools of Oriental Research's (ASOR) mission is to initiate, encourage and support research into, and public understanding of the people and cultures of the near East from the earliest times by fostering original research, archaeological excavations and explorations, by encouraging scholarship in the basic languages, cultural histories and traditions of the near Eastern world.

Albright Institute of Archaeological Research (AIAR) Annual Professorship

Purpose: To support studies in Near Eastern archaeology, geography, history and biblical studies
Eligibility: Open to qualified applicants of any nationality. Citizens of the United States of America are eligible for the entire award. Non-United States of America citizens may apply but, by United States of America law, are only eligible for non-governmental funds
Level of Study: Postdoctorate
Type: Professorship
Value: A stipend of 30,000 new shekels. This consists of 14,200 new shekels plus 15,800 new shekels for room and half board for appointee and spouse at the Institute. The entire award is available via USIA for an appointee who is an citizen of the United States of America. Non-governmental funds for

non United States of America citizens total 15,000 new shekels
Length of Study: 10 months
Frequency: Annual
Study Establishment: The W F Albright Institute of Archaeological Research (AIAR) in Jerusalem
Country of Study: Israel
Application Procedure: Applicants must write for details
No. of awards offered: 5
Closing Date: 15 October
No. of awards given last year: 1
No. of applicants last year: 5
Additional Information: The professorship period should be continuous, without frequent trips outside the country. Residence at the Institute is required www.ascsa.edu.gr/ fellowships-and-grants/postdoctoral-and-senior-scholars

For further information contact:

Email: spencer@jcu.edu

American Schools of Oriental Research Mesopotamian Fellowship

Purpose: To financially support field research in ancient Mesopotamian civilization carried out in Middle East
Eligibility: Open to applicants affiliated with an institution that is a corporate member of ASOR or who have an individual membership. See website for further details
Level of Study: Research
Type: Fellowship
Value: Amount of US$7,500 for one three-to-six month period of research
Length of Study: 3–12 months
Frequency: Annual
Application Procedure: Applicants need to submit cover sheet (with contact information, ASOR membership information, title of project, and brief abstract) and a short proposal. Applicants currently in graduate degree programs should provide three recommendations
Closing Date: 1 November
Additional Information: This fellowship is primarily intended to support field/research projects on ancient Mesopotamian civilization carried out in the Middle East, but other research projects such as museum or archival research related to Mesopotamian studies may also be considered www.asor. org/fellowships/mesopotamian-fellowship/

For further information contact:

209 Commerce Street, Alexandria, VA 22314, United States of America.

Tel: (1) 703 789 9229
Email: programs@asor.org

American Schools of Oriental Research
W.F. Albright Institute of Archaeological Research/
National Endowment of the Humanities
Fellowships

Purpose: To financially support scholars holding a PhD or equivalent degree with a research project
Eligibility: Open to citizens of the United States or alien residents residing in the United States for the last 3 years. Please see the website for further details regarding eligibility
Level of Study: Doctorate
Type: Fellowships
Value: US$58,800 available for up to three awards from 4 to 6 months. The award is US$4,200 per month. Room and half-board at the Institute is US$1,200 per month and the remainder is stipend.
Length of Study: 4–12 months
Frequency: Annual
Country of Study: United States of America
Application Procedure: A completed application form must be sent
No. of awards offered: 3
Closing Date: 1 October
Contributor: National Endowment of the Humanities
Additional Information: Residence at the Institute in Jerusalem is preferred aiar.org/home/fellowships/available-fellowships/#associatefellowships

For further information contact:

Albright Fellowship Committee, Department of Art and Art History, Providence College, Providence, RI 02918, United States of America.

Tel: (1) 401 865 1789
Fax: (1) 401 865 2410
Email: jbranham@providence.edu

Andrew W Mellon Foundation Fellowships

Purpose: To support Eastern European scholars
Eligibility: Open to Bulgarian, Czech, Hungarian, Polish, Romanian and Slovak scholars who have obtained a doctorate by the time the fellowship is awarded. Candidates should not be permanently resident outside the six countries concerned
Level of Study: Postdoctorate
Type: Fellowship
Value: IS$34,500 in total
Length of Study: 3 months

Frequency: Annual
Study Establishment: AIAR, Jerusalem
Country of Study: Israel
Application Procedure: Applicants must write for details
No. of awards offered: 15
Closing Date: 2 April
No. of awards given last year: 3
No. of applicants last year: 15
Additional Information: Fellows are expected to reside at the AIAR if room is available. The 3-month periods are 1 September – 30 November, 1 December – 29 February and 1 March – 31 May. The research period should be continuous without frequent trips outside the country aiar.org/home/fellowships/available-fellowships/#associatefellowships

For further information contact:

Email: spencer@jcu.edu

Council of American Overseas Research Centers (CAORC) Fellowships for Advanced Multi-Country Research

Purpose: The Council of American Overseas Research Centers Multi-Country Research Fellowship Program supports advanced regional or trans-regional research in the humanities, social sciences, or allied natural sciences for U.S. doctoral candidates and scholars who have already earned their PhD. Preference will be given to candidates examining comparative and/or cross-regional research. Scholars must carry out research for a minimum of 90 days in two or more countries outside the United States, at least one of which hosts a participating American overseas research center. Approximately eight awards of up to US$11,000 each will be given each year.
Eligibility: Be a U.S. citizen. Proof of citizenship (photocopy of passport) must be shown upon award notification. have a PhD or be a doctoral candidate who has completed all PhD requirements with the exception of the dissertation. Be engaged in the study of and research in the humanities, social sciences, and allied natural sciences. seek to conduct research of regional or trans-regional significance in two or more countries outside the United States, one of which must host a participating American overseas research center (ORC).
Level of Study: Doctorate
Type: Fellowship
Value: US$11,000
Frequency: Annual
Study Establishment: The W F Albright Institute of Archaeological Research in Jerusalem
Application Procedure: Applicants must write for details
Closing Date: 25 January

Additional Information: Preference will be given to candidates examining comparative or cross-regional questions requiring research in two or more countries www.caorc.org/multi-fellowship-guidelines

For further information contact:

Council of American Overseas Research Centers (CAORC), PO Box 37012, MRC 178, Washington, DC 20013, United States of America.

Email: fellowships@caorc.org

Samuel H Kress Joint Athens-Jerusalem Fellowship

Purpose: To support a joint fellowship for research
Eligibility: Open to predoctoral students who are United States citizens, or North American citizens studying at United States universities
Level of Study: Predoctorate
Type: Fellowship
Value: US$15,000. The stipend is US$7,600 and the remainder covers room and board at the two institutions
Length of Study: 10 months comprised of 5 months in Athens and 5 months in Jerusalem
Frequency: Annual
Study Establishment: The American School of Classical Studies in Athens and the W F Albright Institute of Archaeological Research in Jerusalem
Application Procedure: Applicants must write for details and an application form
No. of awards offered: 4
Closing Date: 15 February
No. of awards given last year: 1
No. of applicants last year: 4
Additional Information: Residence at the Albright Institute is required. The research period should be continuous without frequent trips outside Greece and Israel orcfellowships.fluidreview.com/res/p/orcfellowshipscaorc/

For further information contact:

Email: spencer@jcu.edu

W. F. Albright Institute of Archaeological Research/National Endowment for the Humanities Fellowship

Eligibility: Open to scholars in Near Eastern studies holding a PhD, who are citizens of the United States of America or alien residents residing in the country for the last 3 years. Research projects must have a clear humanities focus

Level of Study: Postdoctorate
Type: Fellowship
Value: IS$40,000 for 1 year. A total of IS$60,000 is to be available for 1.5 awards
Length of Study: 4 months–1 year
Frequency: Annual
Study Establishment: The W F Albright Institute of Archaeological Research in Jerusalem
Country of Study: Israel
Application Procedure: Applicants must write for details
No. of awards offered: 8
Closing Date: 17 October
Funding: Government
No. of awards given last year: 2
No. of applicants last year: 8
Additional Information: The research period should be continuous, without frequent trips outside the country. Residence at the Institute is preferred orcfellowships.fluidreview.com/res/p/orcfellowshipscaorc/

For further information contact:

Department of Religious Studies, John Carroll University, 20,700 North Park Boulevard, University Heights, OH 44118, United States of America.

Email: spencer@jcu.edu

American Society for Engineering Education (ASEE)

1818 North Street NW, Suite 600, Washington, DC 20036 2479, United States of America.

Tel: (1) 202 331 3525
Email: projects@asee.org
Website: www.asee.org
Contact: Mr Michael More, Projects Department

The American Society for Engineering Education (ASEE) is committed to furthering education in engineering and engineering technology by promoting excellence in instruction, research, public service and practice, exercising worldwide leadership, fostering the technological education of society and providing quality products and services to members.

American Society for Engineering Education Air Force Summer Faculty Fellowship Program

Purpose: To enhance the research interests and capabilities of faculty and also to elevate the awareness in the United States academic community of Air Force research

Eligibility: Open to citizens or permanent residents of the United States and must hold a full-time appointment at a college or university located in the United States, preferably with a minimum of 2 years experience
Level of Study: Postgraduate, Research
Type: Fellowship
Value: A weekly stipend of up to US$1,650
Length of Study: 1 year
Frequency: Annual
Country of Study: United States of America

American Society for Engineering Education Helen T Carr Fellowship Program

Purpose: To increase the number of engineering professors for the historically Black engineering colleges by providing financial aid for doctoral study in engineering
Eligibility: Open to African American faculty members, graduate students and other African Americans who have completed at least the equivalent of 1 academic year of full-time engineering graduate study. Candidates must be sponsored by the Dean of one of the historically Black engineering colleges at which they later intend to teach
Level of Study: Doctorate
Value: Up to US$10,000
Length of Study: 1 year, renewable as funding allows
Frequency: Annual
Country of Study: United States of America
Application Procedure: Applicants must first submit a letter to the Dean of a historically Black engineering college asking to be sponsored. Transcripts of undergraduate and graduate course credits and at least three references testifying to intellectual capacity and educational attainments, which give promise of satisfactory performance in advanced study, must then be submitted to the ASEE. A covering letter from the sponsoring Dean is required, and a single copy of each of these documents is to be sent to the committee through its secretary at ASEE headquarters
No. of awards offered: Varies
Closing Date: 15 January
Funding: Commercial, Government, Private
Contributor: The Allied-Signal Foundation, the AMOCO Foundation, AT&T-Bell Laboratories, EI Dupont De Numours & Co., the Exxon Education Foundation, the General Electric Foundation, the IBM Corporation, the Mobil Oil Corporation, NASA, RCA and the Union Carbide
Additional Information: www.collegescholarships.com/scholarships/detail/86377

For further information contact:

Email: a.hicks@asee.org

National Defense Science and Engineering Graduate Fellowship Program
Purpose: To increase the number of United States citizens and nationals trained in science and engineering disciplines of military importance

Eligibility: Must be a United States citizen or national. Applicants must be at or near beginning of graduate studies in one of the above-named fields. Applicants must be either enrolled in their final year of undergraduate studies or have completed no more than the equivalent of 2 year's of full-time graduate study in the field in which they are applying. Exceptional circumstances may qualify other applicants as being at the early stages of their graduate studies
Level of Study: Doctorate
Type: Fellowship
Value: US$34,000 annual stipend. Full tuition and required fees. Medical insurance coverage offered through the institution, up to a total value of US$1,000 per year
Length of Study: 3 years
Frequency: Annual
Country of Study: United States of America
Application Procedure: Apply online at www.asee.org/ndseg
No. of awards offered: 2000
Closing Date: 18 December
Funding: Government
Contributor: United States Department of Defense
No. of awards given last year: 200
No. of applicants last year: 2000
Additional Information: ndseg.asee.org/about_ndseg

For further information contact:

Email: ndseg@asee.org

Naval Research Laboratory Post Doctoral Fellowship Program

Purpose: To increase the involvement of creative and highly trained scientists to scientific and technical areas of interest and relevance to the United States Navy
Eligibility: 1. Citizenship Opportunities at NRL are open to citizens of the United States and to legal permanent residents. 2. Permanent Resident Status-All permanent residents applying to the NRL program must have their green card at the time of application. 3. Dual Citizenship If offered an award, those who hold another citizenship in addition to that of the United States must provide the following to NRL's Personnel Security Office before beginning tenure 1. A statement expressing the willingness to renounce their non-US citizenship 2. Acknowledgement of the willingness to surrender or relinquish their foreign passport if needed or required. 4. Security Clearance It is anticipated that the basic research

undertaken by the participants will usually be unclassified, in which case the participants will only need to be processed for a Facility Access Determination (FAD) if their sponsor verifies their need to work outside normal duty hours. For some laboratories, a DoD security clearance at "Secret" level may be required to gain access to research facilities, in which case participation in the program is contingent upon the participants obtaining the proper clearance. Security clearance and access requirements vary from laboratory to laboratory. Please check with the laboratory program coordinator. 5. Education and Experience Before appointment, participants must present evidence of having received the Ph.D., Sc.D., or other earned research doctoral degree recognized in U.S. academic circles as equivalent to the Ph.D. within five years of the date of application, or must present acceptable evidence of having completed all formal academic requirements for one of these degrees. 6. Prior Fellowships A person who has received a prior postdoctoral fellowship at a navy laboratory under any program may not be eligible to participate in the NRL Postdoctoral Fellowship Program at the same laboratory. A person who has prior afficiation with NRL may not be eligible to participate in the program. 7. Equal Opportunity In accordance with Federal statutes and regulations and Navy policies, no person on the grounds of race, color, age, sex, national origin or disability shall be excluded from participation in, denied the benefits of, or be subject to discrimination under, any program or activity receiving financial assistance from the U.S. Navy.

Level of Study: Doctorate, Postdoctorate
Type: Fellowship
Value: Up to a maximum of US$83,398
Length of Study: one year, and are renewable for a second and third year
Frequency: Annual
Study Establishment: Naval Research Laboratory
Country of Study: United States of America
Application Procedure: To apply to the fellowship program, go here nrl.asee.org/apply
Funding: Government
Contributor: United States Navy
Additional Information: nrl.asee.org/about

For further information contact:

Email: postdocs@asee.org

Office of Naval Research Summer Faculty Research Program

Purpose: Summer Faculty Research Program. The Summer Faculty Research Program provides science and engineering faculty members from institutions of higher education the

opportunity to participate in research of mutual interest to the faculty member and peers at U.S. Navy laboratories for a 10-week period.

Eligibility: United States citizen or permanent resident, must hold teaching or research appointment at United States college or university
Level of Study: Postdoctorate
Type: Fellowship
Value: US$1,400–1,900 (US$1,400 per week at the Summer Faculty Fellow level, US$1,650 per week at the Senior Summer Faculty Fellow level, and US$1,900 per week at the Distinguished Summer Faculty Fellow level)
Length of Study: 10 weeks
Frequency: Annual
Country of Study: United States of America
Application Procedure: Apply online at www.asee.org/summer
No. of awards offered: 544
Closing Date: 15 March
Funding: Government
No. of awards given last year: 73
No. of applicants last year: 544
Additional Information: There are three levels of appointment: Summer Faculty Fellow, Senior Summer Faculty Fellow, and Distinguished Summer Faculty Fellow. Each fellow will be reimbursed for expenses incurred on an optional pre-program visit to the sponsoring laboratory and one round-trip encompassing travel to the sponsoring laboratory at the beginning of the program and travel back to their home residence at the end of the program www.onr.navy.mil/en/Education-Outreach/faculty/summer-faculty-research-program

For further information contact:

Email: anthony.c.smith1@navy.mil

American Society for Microbiology (ASM)

1752 N Street North West, Washington, DC 20036-2904, United States of America.

Tel: (1) 202 737 3600
Email: awards@asmusa.org
Website: www.asm.org/awards
Contact: Ms Leah Gibbons, Program Assistant

The American Society for Microbiology (ASM) is the oldest and largest single life science membership organization in the world. With 43,000 members throughout the world. The ASM represents all disciplines of microbiological specialization including microbiology education. The ASM's mission is to promote research and research training in the microbiological sciences and to assist communication between scientists, policymakers and the public to improve health, the environment and economic well-being.

American Society for Microbiology Microbe Minority Travel Awards

Purpose: The ASM Undergraduate Research Fellowship provides students an opportunity to conduct research and attend ASM Microbe to present their research results. Faculty have an opportunity to mentor students and receive stipend and travel support for their students to conduct research. It generally awards a limited number of travel awards to supports recipients and traval to ASM Microbe

Eligibility: To qualify for consideration the applicant must be 1. A current ASM member at the time of ASM Microbe. 2. From one of the targeted groups. a. Faculty from a Minority Serving Institution (MSI), such as Historically Black Colleges and Universities (HBCU), Hispanic Serving Institutions (HSI), and Tribal Colleges and Universities (TCU). b. Faculty from community colleges. c. URM Faculty regardless of institutional type. d. URM Postdoctoral Scholars. e. URM Graduate Students 3. A U.S. citizen. 4. Positioned to have access to students from URM groups pursuing areas related to the microbiological sciences. 5. Experienced in training and mentoring minority students (URM postdoctoral fellows can be selected in this category because of their potential to serve as role models and mentors for URMs training at their institutions). 6. Committed to research in microbiology and related sciences, diversity and volunteer services.

Level of Study: Graduate
Type: Award
Value: US$1,000
Frequency: Annual
Country of Study: United States of America, Canada or Mexico
Application Procedure: The program requires a joint application from the student and the faculty research mentor, both parts must be completed by the deadline. The student's portion of the application includes 1. ASM member number. 2. Letter of recommendation. 3. Personal statement
Closing Date: 19 January
Funding: Private

For further information contact:

Email: services@asm.org

American Society for Photogrammetry & Remote Sensing (ASPRS)

The Imaging and Geospatial Information Society 5410 Grosvenor Lane, Suite 210, Bethesda, MD 20814-2160, United States of America.

Tel:	(1) 301 493 0290
Email:	asprs@asprs.org
Website:	www.asprs.org

The American Society for Photogrammetry and Remote Sensing (ASPRS) was founded in 1934. It is a scientific association serving over 7,000 professional members around the world whose mission is to advance knowledge and improve understanding of mapping sciences to promote the responsible applications of photogrammetry, remote sensing, geographic information systems and supporting technologies.

American Society for Photogrammetry and Remote Sensing Robert N. Colwell Memorial Fellowship

Purpose: The purpose of the award is to encourage and commend college/university graduate students or postdoctoral researchers who display exceptional interest, desire, ability, and aptitude in the field of remote sensing or other related geospatial information technologies and who have a special interest in developing practical uses of these technologies. For graduate students (masters or Ph.D. level) currently enrolled or intending to enroll in a college or university in the United States or Canada, or a recently graduated (within three years of graduation) post-doctoral researcher, who is pursuing a program of study aimed at starting a professional career where expertise is required in remote sensing or other related geospatial information technologies.

Eligibility: Must be a postgraduate student. Must attend a university. Citizenship requirements USA or Canada. Must not be attending high school currently. Must study full-time. Restricted to students studying Engineering/Technology, Geography. Must be affiliated with American Society for Photogrammetry and Remote Sensin

Level of Study: Doctorate, Postgraduate
Type: Fellowship
Value: US$7,000
Frequency: Annual
Country of Study: United States of America or Canada
Application Procedure: Applicants must include a listing of courses, transcripts, listing of internship, 3 letters of

recommendation and statement of purpose along with a completed application form
Closing Date: 15 November
Contributor: ASPRS Foundation

For further information contact:

Jesse Winch, Scholarship Administrator.

Email: scholarships@asprs.org

American Society for Quality (ASQ)

600 North Plankinton Avenue, Milwaukee, WI 53203, United States of America.

Tel: (1) 414 272 8575
Email: help@asq.org
Website: www.asq.org

The American Society for Quality (ASQ) is the world's leading authority on quality. With more than 100,000 individual and organizational members, this professional association advances learning, quality improvement and knowledge exchange to improve business results and to create better workplaces and communities worldwide.

Ellis R. Ott Scholarship for Applied Statistics and Quality Management

Purpose: To encourage students to pursue a career in a field related to statistics and/or quality management
Eligibility: Open to candidates who are planning to enroll or are enrolled in a Master's degree or; higher level programme in the United States or Canada
Level of Study: Doctorate, Graduate, Postgraduate
Type: Scholarships
Value: US$7500
Length of Study: 1 year
Frequency: Annual
Country of Study: United States of America
Application Procedure: Applicants can download the application form from the website. The completed application form along with curriculum vitae, academic transcripts and two letters of recommendation are to be submitted
No. of awards offered: 6
Closing Date: 1 April
Funding: Foundation

Additional Information: studyabroad.shiksha.com/scholarships/ellis-r-ott-scholarship-for-applied-statistics-and-quality-management

For further information contact:

55 Buckskin Path, Plymouth, MA 02360, United States of America.

Tel: (1) 774 413 5268
Email: lynne.hare@comcast.net

American Society of Colon and Rectal Surgeons

2549 Waukegan Road, #210, Bannockburn, IL 60015, United States of America.

Tel: (1) 847 607 6410
Email: ascrs@fascrs.org

Anastomotic Leak Grant, Special Limited Project Grant

Purpose: To provide investigators the opportunity to pursue research interest, specifically germane to the incidence and severity of anastomotic leaks as relevant to the field of colon and rectal surgery. It is anticipated that successful research projects, initially funded through The Research Foundation of the ASCRS granting mechanism, will ultimately secure funding from other national funding agencies.
Eligibility: 1. Proposed research must be investigator-initiated, hypothesis-driven 2. Proposed research must be conducted within the United States or Canada 3. ASCRS members must be co-principal investigators or principal investigators 4. Applicant submitting a proposal to this funding opportunity may not submit the same application to any other funding body at the same time 5. Prior to submitting your application, any proposed research that includes human or animal studies must have approval from the institutions appropriate review board
Value: US$67,500
Length of Study: 1 year
Country of Study: Any country
Application Procedure: Research project applications to the Research Foundation of the ASCRS are made on Public Health Service grant application form PHS 398. The PHS grant application process has had a long history of satisfactory operation. By using PHS 398, the process of renewal or extension to subsequent Research Foundation or NIH

funding, if applicable, will be facilitated. The Research Committee of the Research Foundation will make every effort to perform a comprehensive review of your application in an expeditious manner. This review may require assignment of appropriate expertise from the scientific community outside of the colon and rectal surgical field.

Closing Date: 1 March

For further information contact:

Email: rf@fascrs.org

Career Development Award

Subjects: The pathophysiology or management of diseases of the colon, rectum, anus or small bowel.

Purpose: To provide young surgeons with the support necessary for the initiation and development of an academic career in colorectal surgery. The CDA focuses on career development and mentorship of the individual rather than solely on the research proposal. The award is intended for the academic investigator demonstrating significant creativity in research relevant to the pathophysiology or management of diseases of the colon, rectum, anus or small bowel.

Eligibility: Must be Within 5 years of first full-time faculty appointment in the United States or Canadian government, public or private not-for-profit medical institution. United States or Canadian citizen having completed an approved colorectal surgery training program; if foreign national, then must have valid working visa at time of application for colorectal department/institution where work is proposed. ASCRS members only. Grant can support up to 10% of the of the NIH Cap salary. Applications should also include a letter of support from the department of surgery chair confirming at least 25% non-clinical time will be committed to the applicant. Applicant must not currently have or have previously received a career development award from another external funding source. If the applicant receives the Career Development Award from the Research Foundation of the ASCRS and is subsequently awarded another career development award from another external funding source with overlapping funding period, the applicant must return the residual funds to the Research Foundation of the ASCRS, or decline the funding from another source. The exception is a career development award from the NIH K-series award or funding from the applicants own institution.

Type: Award
Value: US$75,000 per year
Length of Study: Two years
Frequency: Annual
Country of Study: United States of America or Canada
Application Procedure: Apply online

Closing Date: 1 July
Additional Information: fascrs.org/my-ascrs/research-foundation/grants-awards#CDG

For further information contact:

Email: rf@fascrs.org

General Surgery Resident Research Initiation Grant

Subjects: Diseases of the colon, rectum and anus.

Purpose: To attract General Surgery Residents or recent graduates of such programs into the field of colon and rectal surgery by providing opportunities to engage in clinical or laboratory-based research focused on diseases of the colon, rectum and anus.

Eligibility: 1. Must be General Surgical Residents or recent (within 2 years) Graduates of a US or Canadian approved General Surgery Training Program. 2. Applicant must have designated time for research and no clinical responsibility. 3. Preference is given to applicants with research or clinical career goals in the field of Colon & Rectal Surgery and whose research Mentor or Co-Investigator is a Fellow of ASCRS.

Type: Grant
Value: US$20,000
Length of Study: One year
Frequency: Annual
Country of Study: United States of America or Canada
Application Procedure: Research project applications to the Research Foundation of ASCRS are made on Public Health Service grant application form PHS 398. The PHS grant application process has had a long history of satisfactory operation. By using PHS 398, the process of renewal or extension to subsequent Research Foundation or NIH funding, if applicable, will be facilitated. The Research Committee of the Research Foundation will make every effort to perform a comprehensive review of your application in an expeditious manner. This review may require assignment of appropriate expertise from the scientific community outside of the colon and rectal surgical field.

Closing Date: 15 August
Additional Information: fascrs.org/my-ascrs/research-foundation/grants-awards#International%20Fellowship

International Fellowship Grant

Subjects: Colon, rectum and anus diseases
Purpose: To provide support to research programs that are focused on diseases of the colon, rectum and anus that will ultimately impact how we treat these patients. This grant will

focus on providing support to clinical investigators in the United States or Canada who would like to participate in research outside the United States or Canada, including US investigator engagement in global health research projects focused in colorectal surgery.

Eligibility: Must be ASCRS members only. ASCRS member must be co-principal investigator or principal investigator. The applicant must be pursuing a career in colorectal surgery. For Citizens of USA or Canada The applicant must be currently enlisted in or a graduate of an accredited residency program in either general or colon and rectal surgery or be a recent graduate of a program approved by the Research Foundation. The applicant must be sponsored by a colon and rectal program director or ASCRS Fellow. For foreigners traveling to USA or Canada The applicant must be sponsored by a clinician investigator who is an ASCRS member and board certified by the ABCRS with a research program.

Type: Grant

Value: US$12,500

Length of Study: One year

Frequency: Annual

Country of Study: United States of America or Canada

Application Procedure: Apply online

Closing Date: 15 August

Additional Information: fascrs.org/my-ascrs/research-foundation/grants-awards#International%20Fellowship

Limited Project Grant (LPG)

Subjects: Colon and rectal surgery

Purpose: To provide investigators the opportunity to pursue research interest, specifically germane to the field of colon and rectal surgery. It is anticipated that successful research projects, initially funded through the Research Foundation's LPG mechanism, will ultimately secure funding from other national funding agencies.

Eligibility: The proposed research must be investigator-initiated, hypothesis-driven. The proposed research must be conducted within the United States or Canada. ASCRS members must be co-principal investigators or principal investigators. Prior to submitting your application, any proposed research that includes human or animal studies must have approval from the institutions appropriate review board.

Type: Grant

Value: Up to US$25,000

Length of Study: One year

Frequency: Annual

Country of Study: United States of America or Canada

Application Procedure: Research project applications to the Research Foundation of ASCRS are made on Public Health Service grant application form PHS 398. The PHS grant application process has had a long history of satisfactory

operation. By using PHS 398, the process of renewal or extension to subsequent Research Foundation or NIH funding, if applicable, will be facilitated. The Research Committee of the Research Foundation will make every effort to perform a comprehensive review of your application in an expeditious manner. This review may require assignment of appropriate expertise from the scientific community outside of the colon and rectal surgical field.

Closing Date: 15 March

Additional Information: fascrs.org/my-ascrs/research-foundation/grants-awards#International%20Fellowship

Medical Student Research Initiation Grant

Subjects: Diseases of the colon, rectum and anus.

Purpose: To provide opportunities for Medical Students to participate in clinical or laboratory-based research focused on diseases of the colon, rectum and anus.

Eligibility: Must be a Medical Student in a US or Canadian Medical School. Applicant must have designated time for research and no competing clinical responsibility. Preference is given to individuals who will pursue or who are considering pursuit of a career in Colon and Rectal Surgery and whose project has a mentor or co-investigator who is a Fellow or Member of the American Society of Colon and Rectal Surgeons.

Type: Grant

Value: US$4,000 per year

Length of Study: 2-3 months

Frequency: Annual

Country of Study: United States of America or Canada

Application Procedure: Research project applications to the Research Foundation of ASCRS are made on Public Health Service grant application form PHS 398. The PHS grant application process has had a long history of satisfactory operation. By using PHS 398, the process of renewal or extension to subsequent Research Foundation or NIH funding, if applicable, will be facilitated. The Research Committee of the Research Foundation will make every effort to perform a comprehensive review of your application in an expeditious manner. This review may require assignment of appropriate expertise from the scientific community outside of the colon and rectal surgical field.

Closing Date: 15 March

Additional Information: fascrs.org/my-ascrs/research-foundation/grants-awards#International%20Fellowship

Research in Robotic Surgical Technology Grant

Subjects: Robotic surgical technology in the field of colon and rectal surgery

Purpose: The Research in Robotic Surgical Technology Grant provides an investigator the opportunity to pursue research interests, specifically germane to robotic surgical technology in the field of colon and rectal surgery. Innovative projects are encouraged. The Research Committee is particularly interested in fostering collaborative research. Proposals which include two or more institutions may be eligible for additional funding. This grant is supported by Intuitive Surgical Inc.

Eligibility: 1. Proposed research must be investigator-initiated, hypothesis-driven. 2. Proposed research must be conducted within the United States or Canada. 3. ASCRS members must be co-principal investigators or principal investigators. 4. Applicant submitting a proposal to this funding opportunity may not submit the same application to any other funding body at the same time. 5. Prior to submitting your application, any proposed research that includes human or animal studies must have approval from the institutions appropriate review board.

Type: Grant

Value: US$50,000 for one year, or collaborative proposals may be funded up to US$100,000 for one year.

Frequency: Annual

Country of Study: United States of America or Canada

Application Procedure: Research project applications to the Research Foundation of the ASCRS are made on Public Health Service grant application form PHS 398. The PHS grant application process has had a long history of satisfactory operation. By using PHS 398, the process of renewal or extension to subsequent Research Foundation or NIH funding, if applicable, will be facilitated. The Research Committee of the Research Foundation will make every effort to perform a comprehensive review of your application in an expeditious manner. This review may require assignment of appropriate expertise from the scientific community outside of the colon and rectal surgical field.

Closing Date: 15 August

Additional Information: fascrs.org/my-ascrs/research-foundation/grants-awards#International%20Fellowship

Training in Research Methodology Grant

Subjects: Research methodology

Purpose: This award provides an opportunity for a graduating CRS resident to attend training that will enhance their career. They may attend one of the following courses the Career Development Course, Fundamentals of Surgical Research Course or the Early Career Development Course offered by the Association for Academic Surgery (AAS) or the American College of Surgeons (ACS) Health Services Research Methods Course.

Eligibility: 1. Must be a graduating Colon and Rectal Surgeon resident or first year faculty with demonstrated interest in pursuing academic career in colon and rectal surgery. 2. Applicant must be a Member or a Candidate member of ASCRS in good standing.

Type: Award

Value: Up to US$3,000 to be used for coach air travel, hotel accommodations, meals and registration for one of the following courses AAS Fall Career Development Course, or AAS Fall Fundamentals of Surgical Research Course o ACS Health Services Research Methods Course

Length of Study: The length of one of three available courses

Frequency: Annual

Country of Study: Any country

Application Procedure: The Young Researchers Committee will review and score the applications and then submit their recommendation to the Research Committee for approval.

Closing Date: 15 March

Additional Information: fascrs.org/my-ascrs/research-foundation/grants-awards#International%20Fellowship

American Society of Composers, Authors and Publishers Foundation

One Lincoln Plaza, New York, NY 10023-7142, United States of America.

Tel:	(1) 212 621 6219
Email:	info@ascapfoundation.com
Website:	www.ascapfoundation.org
Contact:	Michael Spudic

The American Society of Composers, Authors and Publishers (ASCAP) is a membership association of over 260,000 composers, songwriters, lyricists and music publishers. It is dedicated to nurturing the music talent of tomorrow, preserving the legacy of the past and sustaining the creative incentive for today's creators through a variety of educational, professional and humanitarian programmes and activities which serve the entire music community. ASCAP's function is to protect the rights of its members by licensing and paying royalties for the public performances of their copyrighted works.

American Society of Composers, Authors and Publishers Foundation Morton Gould Young Composer Awards

Purpose: To encourage talented young composers by providing recognition, appreciation and monetary awards

Eligibility: To be eligible for participation in the Awards, an entrant must be, at the time of entry, (a) at least 13 years of age; and (b) a U.S. citizen, permanent resident or enrolled student with a valid and current U.S. student visa (each, an "Entrant")

Level of Study: Unrestricted

Type: Award

Frequency: Annual

Country of Study: Any country

Application Procedure: Applicants must complete an application form and other materials. For more information write to organization

Closing Date: 1 February

Funding: Foundation, Private

Contributor: The ASCAP Foundation's Jack and Amy Norworth Memorial Fund, the Leo Kaplan Fund and the Frank & Lydia Bergen Foundation

No. of awards given last year: 39

Additional Information: Each year the top award winner receives an additional cash prize, The ASCAP Foundation Leo Kaplan Award www.ascapfoundation.org/ ascapfoundation/programs/awards/young-composer-awards

For further information contact:

The ASCAP Foundation/Morton Gould Young Composer Awards, 250 West 57th Street, New York, NY 10107, United States of America.

Tel: (1) 212 621 6329
Email: concertmusic@ascap.com

American Society of Hematology

ASH Scholar Award

Subjects: Hematology research

Purpose: Since 1985, the ASH Scholar Award has helped ease the difficult transition between completion of training and establishment of an independent career by providing partial salary or other support during that critical period required for completion of training and achievement of status as an independent investigator.

Eligibility: Applicants must meet the following criteria in order to qualify Be a citizen of the United States or Canada. Both of which may now conduct work outside of the U.S. and Canada; Hold a visa or permanent resident status in the United States or Canada and plan to conduct his/her research within the U.S. or Canada (Individuals outside of the U.S. or Canada should consider the Global Research Award); Be an ASH member in good standing at the time of the letter of intent deadline and plan to maintain membership for the duration of the award term; Have confirmation from the applicant's institution that at least 75 % of the applicant's full-time professional effort is devoted to research. If you have successfully competed for a substantial award (e.g. NIH R01 or equivalent grant) as the PI or co-PI before the application (not LOI) deadline, you are no longer eligible for the Scholar Award.

Type: Award

Value: Fellow Scholar Award provides up to US$100,000 over a two- to three-year period in equal quarterly payments over the award term. Fellow to Faculty Scholar Award provides up to US$125,000 over a two- to three-year period in equal quarterly payments over the award term. Junior Faculty Scholar Award provides up to US$150,000 over a two- to three-year period in equal quarterly payments over the award term.

Length of Study: Two to three years depending on the award

Country of Study: Any country

Application Procedure: The Scholar Award letter of intent (LOI) and the supporting documents outlined below must be submitted through the ASH online awards system. The LOI is mandatory and will be reviewed for eligibility to submit a full proposal. In addition to the letter of intent, the applicant must submit the following Abstract of proposed project (350 words maximum). Applicant's NIH Biographical Sketch. Fellow to Faculty applicants will need to submit the Supplemental Budget Form. Please see the instruction in the online award system.

Closing Date: 1 May

Additional Information: www.hematology.org/awards/ career-enhancement-and-training/scholar-award/ apply#eligibility

---

American Society of Interior Designers (ASID) Educational Foundation, Inc.

608 Massachusetts Avenue North East, Washington, DC 20002, United States of America.

Tel: (1) 202 546 3480
Email: education@asid.org
Website: www.asidfoundation.org
Contact: Education Department

The American Society of Interior Designers (ASID) Educational Foundation represents the interests of more than 30,500 members including interior design practitioners, students and industry and retail partners. ASID's mission is to be the definitive resource for professional education and knowledge sharing, advocacy of interior designers' right to practice and expansion of interior design markets.

The ASID Educational Foundation/Irene Winifred Eno Grant

Country of Study: Any country
Additional Information: www.asid.org/press-releases/asid-announces-2019-asid-foundation-scholarship-and-grant-recipients

For further information contact:

Email: schung@asid.org

American Society of Mechanical Engineers (ASME International)

Two Park Avenue, New York, NY 10016-5990, United States of America.

Tel: (1) 800 843 2763
Email: CustomerCare@asme.org
Website: www.asme.org/education/enged/aid
Contact: Theresa Oluwanifise, Coordinator Educational Operations

Founded in 1880 as the American Society of Mechanical Engineers (ASME International), today ASME International is a non-profit educational and technical organization serving a worldwide membership.

Elisabeth M and Winchell M Parsons Scholarship

Purpose: To assist ASME student members working towards a doctoral degree
Eligibility: Must be a U.S. citizen. Must be enrolled full time. Must be working toward a doctoral degree in engineering. Must major in mechanical engineering. This award is for U.S. students.
Level of Study: Doctorate
Type: Award
Value: US$3,000
Frequency: Annual
Country of Study: United States of America
Application Procedure: Application forms are available from the website
No. of awards offered: 2
Closing Date: 3 March

No. of awards given last year: 3
No. of applicants last year: 5
Additional Information: www.unigo.com/scholarships/by-major/engineering-scholarships/elisabeth-m-and-winchell-m-parsons-scholarship/1003462

For further information contact:

2 Park Ave., New York, NY 10016, United States of America.

Tel: (1) 212 591 8131; 212 591 7143
Email: LefeverB@asme.org

Marjorie Roy Rothermel Scholarship

Purpose: To assist students working towards a Master's degree
Eligibility: Selection is based on academic performance, character, need and ASME participation. Applicants must be citizens of the United States of America and must be enrolled in a United States school in an ABET-accredited mechanical engineering department. No student may receive more than one auxiliary scholarship or loan in the same academic year
Level of Study: Graduate
Type: Scholarship
Value: US$3,000
Frequency: Annual
Country of Study: United States of America
Application Procedure: Application forms are available from the website
Closing Date: 3 March
Additional Information: www.unigo.com/scholarships/by-major/engineering-scholarships/marjorie-roy-rothermel-scholarship/1003463

For further information contact:

2 Park Ave., New York, NY 10016, United States of America.

Tel: (1) 212 591 8131; 212 591 7143
Email: LefeverB@asme.org

American Society of Nephrology (ASN)

1510 H Street, NW, Suite 800, Washington, DC 20005, United States of America.

Tel: (1) 202 640 4660
Email: email@asn-online.org
Website: www.asn-online.org
Contact: Grants Co-ordinator

The American Society of Nephrology (ASN) was founded in 1967 as a non-profit corporation to enhance and assist the study and practice of nephrology, to provide a forum for the promulgation of research and to meet the professional and continuing education needs of its members.

Carl W Gottschalk Research Scholar Grant

Purpose: To provide funding for young faculty to foster evolution to an independent research career and a successful application a National Institutes of Health (NIH) R01 grant or equivalent

Eligibility: Applicants must an active member of the ASN and hold an MD or PhD or equivalent degree. At the time of submission the applicant's membership must be current and their dues paid. Appointment to full-time faculty must be conformed in writing by the department chair

Level of Study: Postdoctorate, Postgraduate

Type: Grant

Value: US$100,000

Length of Study: 2 years

Frequency: Annual

Country of Study: United States of America

Application Procedure: Online application

Closing Date: 28 January

Funding: Foundation

Contributor: ASN Foundation for Kidney Research

For further information contact:

Email: grants@asn-online.org

American University in Cairo (AUC)

PO Box 2511, 113 Kasr EI Aini Street, Cairo 11511, Egypt.

Tel: (20) 2 2794 2964
Email: ocm@aucegypt.edu
Website: www.aucegypt.edu/Pages/default.aspx
Contact: Mrs Sawsan Mardini, Director of Graduate
                Students Services

The American University in Cairo (AUC) provides quality higher and continuing education for students from Egypt and the surrounding region. The University is an independent, non-profit, apolitical, non-sectarian and equal opportunity institution. English is the primary language of instruction. The University is accredited in the United States of America by the Commission of Higher Education of the Middle States Association of Colleges and Schools.

African Graduate Fellowships

Purpose: The African Graduate fellowship is a competitive fellowship program for bright, highly motivated African students interested in pursuing a master degree at AUC. Each year, fellowships are offered to nationals of African countries (not including Egyptians) for full-time study (nine credits or as required by the program) in any of the graduate programs offered at the AUC.

Eligibility: 1. Non-Egyptian African nationals 2. Open to all disciplines of graduate studies 3. For new graduate degree-seeking students; full admission to one of the graduate programs in AUC, satisfying AUC graduate full admissions requirements 4. Submit an international TOEFL iBT exam score or academic IELTS exam score as per the cut-off scores for AUC graduate admissions 5. For continuing students; to retain the fellowship, the recipient must maintain a GPA of 3.2 6. Financial need

Level of Study: Graduate

Type: Fellowship

Value: A waiver of tuition fee; student services and activities fees; a monthly stipend of LE 600 for 10 months

Length of Study: Two academic years

Frequency: Annual

Country of Study: Any country except India

Application Procedure: There are two steps which need to be followed to process the application. To Apply Step 1 Check how to apply and submit the online application Step 2 Submit the online fellowship application Application link is mentioned below

Closing Date: 15 January

For further information contact:

Email: gradserv@aucegypt.edu

American University of Beirut

American University of Beirut, 3 Dag Hammarskjold Plaza, 8th Floor, New York, NY 10017-2303, United States of America.

Tel: (1) 212 583 7600
Website: www.aub.edu.lb/main/about/Pages/index.aspx

AUB currently offers more than 120 programs leading to the bachelor's, master's, MD, and PhD degrees. The language of instruction is English (except for courses in the Arabic Department and other language courses).

American University of Beirut Mediterranean Scholarships

Purpose: To strengthen capacity in implementation research on the neglected tropical diseases as well as malaria and tuberculosis. The American University of Beirut (AUB) is delighted to offer a number of scholarships for students from low- and middle-income countries

Eligibility: To be eligible, all candidates are expected to have good academic record in undergraduate education (and graduate education where relevant) in any discipline (health sciences, social sciences, nutrition, medicine, nursing, pharmacy, dentistry sciences or related discipline) and hold a bachelor's degree from AUB, or an equivalent degree from another recognized institution. Please note, all candidates must be a national of and resident in a low- or middle-income country of the Eastern Mediterranean region

Level of Study: Postgraduate

Value: The scholarships cover travel, tuition and living expenses for the duration of the program. English language training at AUB prior to enrolment is also covered for some students who need it

Country of Study: Any country

Application Procedure: The application should be made through the online system at graduateadmissions.aub.edu.lb/

Closing Date: 1 April

Funding: Trusts

Additional Information: Place of Study – American University of Beirut (AUB), Lebanon scholarship-positions.com/american-university-of-beirut-aub-mediterranean-scholarships/2015/06/26/

For further information contact:

Email: GPHP@aub.edu.lb

American Urological Association

Research Scholar Awards

Subjects: Urology

Purpose: The AUA offers a portfolio of mentored research training awards to recruit outstanding young investigators into urologic research and foster their career success.

Eligibility: Must be either clinical and postdoctoral fellows who are no more than five years beyond completing a doctorate or residency, or early career investigators who are in the first five years after beginning a faculty position

Type: Award

Value: US$40,000 per year

Length of Study: One and two years

Frequency: Annual

Country of Study: Any country

Application Procedure: Apply online

Additional Information: www.auanet.org/research/research-funding/aua-funding/research-scholar-awards

American Water Works Association (AWWA)

6666 West Quincy Avenue, Denver, CO 80235, United States of America.

Tel: (1) 303 794 7711
Email: lmoody@awwa.org
Website: www.awwa.org
Contact: Administrative Assistant

The American Water Works Association (AWWA) is an international non-profit scientific and educational society dedicated to the improvement of drinking water quality and supply. The Association has more than 57,000 members who represent the full spectrum of the drinking water community, e.g. treatment plant operators and managers, scientists, environmentalists, manufacturers, academics, regulators and others who have a genuine interest in water supply and public health.

American Water Works Association Abel Wolman Fellowship

Purpose: To encourage and support promising students from countries with AWWA sections to pursue advanced training and research

Eligibility: Open to candidates who anticipate completing the requirements for their PhD degree within 2 years of the award. Applicants must be citizens of a country that has an AWWA section, i.e. the United States of America, Canada or Mexico. Applicants will be considered without regard to colour, gender, race, creed or country of origin

Level of Study: Doctorate

Type: Fellowship

Value: US$30,000

Length of Study: Initially 1 year, renewable for 1 further year on submission of evidence of satisfactory progress and approval by a review committee

Frequency: Annual

Country of Study: United States of America, Canada or Mexico

Application Procedure: Applicants must submit an official application form, official transcripts of all university education, official copies of Graduate Record Examination scores, three letters of recommendation, a proposed curriculum of study and brief plans of dissertation research study

No. of awards offered: 17

Closing Date: 15 January

Funding: Private

Additional Information: www.awwa.org/Membership-Volunteering/Students-Young-Professionals/AWWA-Scholarships

For further information contact:

Tel: (1) 303 347 6201
Email: swheeler@awwa.org

American Woman's Society of Certified Public Accountants

AWSCPA Administrative Offices, 136 South Keowee Street, Dayton, OH 45402, United States of America.

Tel: (1) 937 222 1872
Email: info@awscpa.org
Website: www.awscpa.org

The American Woman's Society of CPA provides annual scholarships to women working towards an accounting degree as well as to those working towards their Certified Public Accountant License.

Call for Nominations for Urdang Medal and Kremers Award

Purpose: The George Urdang Medal is awarded for an original and scholarly publication, or series of publications, pertaining primarily to historical or historico-social aspects of pharmacy. The Medal may also be awarded for popular works intended to achieve more widespread appreciation for, and better understanding of, pharmacy and its past among members of the pharmaceutical profession, allied professions, or the public. The Urdang Medal was established in 1952 in honor of Professor George Urdang, one of AIHP's founders and a renowned scholar of the history of pharmacy

Eligibility: 1. The Urdang Medal is awarded without restriction as to citizenship of the author or place of publication. Evaluation is based on competence of research and skill of interpretation and presentation. 2. The nominee's age, total number of publications or previous honors is not given primary consideration

Level of Study: Professional development

Type: Award

Frequency: Annual

Country of Study: Any country

Application Procedure: In order to apply for the nominations for this award, kindly access the below link for the application form and procedures to be followed. networks.h-net.org/node/9782/discussions/3798798/call-nominations-2019-urdang-medal-and-kremers-award

Closing Date: 30 April

Funding: Private

Additional Information: networks.h-net.org/node/73374/announcements/3735293/call-nominations-2019-urdang-medal-and-kremers-award

For further information contact:

H-Net: Humanities & Social Sciences Online Old Horticulture, 141H 506 East Circle Drive, East Lansing, MI 48824, United States of America.

Tel: (1) 517 432 5134
Email: aihp@aihp.org

American-Scandinavian Foundation (ASF)

58 Park Avenue at 38th Street, New York, NY 10016, United States of America.

Tel: (1) 212 779 3587
Email: grants@amscan.org
Website: www.amscan.org
Contact: Director of Fellowships and Grants

The ASF is a publicity supported, non-profit organization that promotes international understanding through educational and cultural exchange between the United States and the Nordic countries.

Awards for American Universities and Colleges to host Norwegian lecturers

Purpose: The American-Scandinavian Foundation (ASF) invites United States colleges and universities to apply for funding to host a visiting lecturer from Norway. The awards are for appointments of one semester, and should fall within an academic year

Eligibility: Terms of Award; 1. US$20,000 teaching/research stipend. 2. 5,000 travel stipend for lecture appearances outside home institution. Lectureships should be in the area of contemporary studies with an emphasis on one of five areas 1. Public Policy. 2. Conflict Resolution. 3. Environmental Studies. 4. Multiculturalism. 5. Healthcare. Conditions of Award; 1. The lecturer must be a Norwegian citizen, and a scholar or expert in a field appropriate to the host department or program. 2. The ASF encourages consideration of the practitioner as well as the academic as a lectureship candidate. Responsibilities of the Host Institution; 1. The institution is responsible for selecting the lecturer it wishes to host. The ASF cannot assist in establishing contacts. 2. All pre-appointment communication with the lecturer, and arrangements for teaching, public presentations and housing during the lectureship appointment are the responsibility of the host institution. The host institution would be expected to provide support complementing the US$20,000 stipend. Additional support may be in the form of 1. Subsidized faculty housing. 2. International Travel and insurance expenses. 3. Office and computer use. 4. Additional stipend support. Responsibilities of the Lecturer; 1. The selected lecturer is expected to teach one course (undergraduate or graduate level) and perform modest public activities (lectures, etc.) for which s/he will receive US$20,000. 2. The selected lecturer is expected to accept invitations to visit other academic institutions or conferences (including the NorTANA conference, the Swedish Teachers' conference, and the SASS conference) for which s/he will have US$5,000 available in travel funds

Level of Study: Unrestricted
Type: Lectureship/Prize
Value: US$25,000
Length of Study: One semester
Frequency: Annual
Country of Study: United States of America
Application Procedure: Complete online application - www. amscan.org/fellowships-grants/visiting-lectureships/
Closing Date: 15 February
Funding: Private
No. of awards given last year: 1
Additional Information: www.amscan.org/fellowships-grants/visiting-lectureships/

Grants for Public Projects

Purpose: Through its public project grants, ASF funds a wide variety of programs that bring American and Scandinavian culture, art and thought to public audiences. The American-Scandinavian Foundation promotes the cultures of the Nordic countries in the United States and American culture in the Nordic countries by encouraging programs that will enhance public appreciation of culture, art, and thought

Eligibility: Must be a non-profit organization and the project must be open to the public. ASF's funding priority has traditionally been to underwrite public programming and defined events. Awards are given to non-profit organizations only. Proof of an organization's non-profit status (as a 501(c)(3) in the United States or equivalent in Scandinavia) is required. ASF does NOT support 1. Capital expenses. 2. Institutional overhead and other administrative fees. 3. Underwriting book, periodical or website publication. 4. Production of commercial CDs or cassettes. 5. Conference participation or conference registration for individuals. However, general conference expenses such as costs for special invitees/speakers can be supported. 6. Participation in studio residencies other than those with which ASF already has an ongoing affiliation. 7. Retroactive funding. Projects cannot begin before the decision announcement date. 8. The maximum award amount is US$5,000; however, average grants range between US$1,000 to US$2,000. ASF will only accept one application per organization per competition cycle and will grant only one award per organization per fiscal year in any one grant category

Level of Study: Unrestricted
Type: Project grant
Value: Up to US$5,000
Length of Study: varies
Frequency: Twice a year
Country of Study: Scandinavian countries
Application Procedure: Complete online application - www. amscan.org/fellowships-and-grants/public-project-proposal-guidelines/
Closing Date: 15 February
Funding: Private
Additional Information: www.amscan.org/fellowships-grants/grants-for-organizations/

Translation Competition

Purpose: ASF Translation Competition is an international competition for literary translations into English from any Nordic language and genre. Our annual competition recognizes outstanding translations of Scandinavian literature authored by a Scandinavian writer born after 1900

Eligibility: 1. The prizes are for outstanding English translations of poetry, fiction, drama or literary prose originally written in a Nordic language. 2. If prose, manuscripts must be no longer than 50 pages; if poetry, 25 (Do not exceed these limits). Manuscripts must be typed and double-spaced with numbered pages. 3. Translations must be from the writing of one author, although not necessarily from a single work. Please include a one-paragraph description about the author. 4. An entry must consist of One copy of the translation, including a title page and a table of contents for the proposed book of which the manuscript submitted is a part. One copy of the work(s) in the original language; please send the relevant pages. A CV containing all contact information, including email address, for the translator; and; A letter or other document signed by the author, the author's agent or the author's estate granting permission for the translation to be entered in this competition and published in Scandinavian Review. 5. Translator's names may not appear on any page of their manuscripts, including the title page. 6. The translation submitted in the competition may not have been previously published in the English language by the submission deadline. (If the translation being submitted to this competition is also under consideration by a publisher, you must inform us of the expected publication date.); 7. Translators may submit one entry only and may not submit the same entry in more than two competitions. 8. The Translation Prize cannot be won more than three times by the same translator

Level of Study: Unrestricted
Type: Translation prize
Value: US$2,000–US$2,500
Frequency: Annual
Country of Study: Any country
Application Procedure: Complete online application - www.amscan.org/fellowships-grants/translation-competition/
Closing Date: 1 September
Funding: Private
No. of awards given last year: 2
Additional Information: amscan.secure-platform.com/a/page/translation2020

Analytics India

University of Sydney: Data Science Scholarships

Purpose: The University of Sydney, one of Australia's premier universities is offering scholarships for international students for intake to high performing candidates
Eligibility: 1. Applicants must be a graduate of a quantitative degree program. A quantitative program includes Data Science, Computer Science, Mathematics, Statistics, Engineering, Physics, Economics and more. 2. Applicants must have achieved a minimum distinction average (equivalent to 75 at the University of Sydney) in their UG studies
Level of Study: Postgraduate
Type: Scholarship
Value: AU$6,000
Frequency: Annual
Study Establishment: University of Sydney
Country of Study: Australia
Closing Date: 30 April
Funding: Private
Additional Information: analyticsindiamag.com/8-scholarships-top-universities-data-science-2019/

For further information contact:

Email: info@analyticsindiamag.com

Anglo-Austrian Music Society

158 Rosendale Road, London SE21 8LG, United Kingdom.

Tel: (44) 20 8761 0444
Email: info@aams.org.uk
Website: www.aams.org.uk
Contact: Jane Avery, Secretary

The Anglo-Austrian Music Society promotes lectures and concerts and is closely associated with its parent organization, the Anglo-Austrian Society, which was founded in 1944 to promote friendship and understanding between the people of the United Kingdom and Austria through personal contacts, educational programmes and cultural exchanges. AAMS awards the Richard Tauber prize for singers.

Wigmore Hall/Independent Opera International Song Competition

Purpose: Wigmore Hall is responsible for the biennial International Song Competition
Eligibility: The Competition attracts singers and pianists of the highest calibre aged 33 or under, keen to pursue performing careers at the highest level
Level of Study: Graduate, Postgraduate, Undergraduate
Type: Competition
Value: It provides valuable opportunities for feedback from Jury members drawn from vocal artists of global stature; provides opportunities for participants to meet their peers from other countries and to exchange ideas on performance, technique and repertoire; and provides a vital public platform

from which young singers and pianists can break into the world of professional performance at the highest level

Frequency: Every 2 years

Country of Study: Any country

Application Procedure: Application form and recording (MP3 or WAV files only) of prescribed repertoire plus application fee

No. of awards offered: 150 plus

Closing Date: 9 September

Funding: Private

Contributor: Independent Opera

No. of awards given last year: 6

No. of applicants last year: 150 plus

Additional Information: Please check at www.wigmore-hall.org.uk/song-competition   wigmore-hall.org.uk/song-competition/wigmore-hall-independent-opera-international-song-competition

For further information contact:

Wigmore Hall/Independent Opera International Song Competition, Wigmore Hall, 36 Wigmore Street, Marylebone, London W1U 2BP, United Kingdom.

Tel: (44) 20 7258 8244
Email: songcompetition@wigmore-hall.org.uk

Anglo-Danish Society

43 Maresfield Gardens, London NW3 5TF, United Kingdom.

Tel: (44) 1728 638 345
Email: scholarships@anglo-danishsociety.org.uk
Website: www.anglo-danishsociety.org.uk
Contact: Mrs Margit Staehr, Administrator

The Anglo-Danish Society exists to promote closer understanding between the United Kingdom and Denmark by arranging lectures, outings, social gatherings and other events of interest for its members and their guests. The society administers scholarship funds which help Danish students visit the United Kingdom or British students visit Denmark, for the purpose of advanced or postgraduate studies.

Denmark Liberation Scholarships

Purpose: To promote Anglo Danish relations

Eligibility: Open to graduates of British nationality only

Level of Study: Doctorate, Postdoctorate, Postgraduate, Professional development

Type: Scholarship

Value: One major award of DKK 9,000 and others at DKK 6,000 each

Length of Study: A minimum of 6 months

Frequency: Annual

Study Establishment: A Danish university or other approved institution

Country of Study: Denmark

Application Procedure: Applicants must complete an application form, available from the Secretary between 1 October and 31 December. Applicants should include a stamped addressed envelope or international reply coupons

No. of awards offered: 12

Closing Date: 30 June

Funding: Private

No. of awards given last year: 4

No. of applicants last year: 12

Additional Information: www.anglo-danishsociety.org.uk/scholarships

For further information contact:

Email: scholars@anglo-danishsociety.org.uk

Ove Arup Foundation Award

Purpose: Ove Arup Foundation and the Foundation's commitment to support and publicise any publication made as a result of the scholarship. For this reason, candidates who can demonstrate that their research is likely to result in publication will be favoured.

Eligibility: Open to graduates of British nationality only

Level of Study: Postdoctorate

Type: Scholarship

Value: £2,500

Country of Study: Any country

Additional Information: www.anglo-danishsociety.org.uk/scholarships

For further information contact:

Email: scholars@anglo-danishsociety.org.uk

The ACE Foundation Scholarship

Purpose: The Anglo-Danish Society administers a special scholarship, together with the ACE Foundation.

Eligibility: Open to graduates of British nationality only

Level of Study: Postdoctorate
Type: Scholarship
Value: £2,500
Closing Date: 30 June
Additional Information: www.anglo-danishsociety.org.uk/scholarships

For further information contact:

Email: scholars@anglo-danishsociety.org.uk

William Charnley Anglo-Danish Scholarship

Subjects: MPhil, MASt or LLM course
Purpose: As the award is for a British University postgraduate place, applicants should normally be Danish postgraduate students. However, British students who have taken their first degree or other postgraduate course in a Danish University will also be considered. Full details should be included in the Application.
Eligibility: Open to graduates of British nationality only
Level of Study: Postdoctorate
Type: Scholarship
Value: £2,500
Country of Study: Any country
Closing Date: 30 June
Additional Information: www.anglo-danishsociety.org.uk/scholarships

For further information contact:

Email: scholars@anglo-danishsociety.org.uk

Anglo-Norse Society

Norwegian Embassy 25, Belgrave Square, London SW1X 8QD, United Kingdom.

Tel: (44) 208 452 4843
Email: Secretariat@anglo-norse.org.uk
Website: www.anglo-norse.org.uk/

The Anglo-Norse Society in London is a registered charity for the purpose of promoting better understanding between Britain and Norway through learning about each other's country and way of life.

The Anglo-Norse Dame Gillian Brown Postgraduate Scholarship

Purpose: To help towards the cost for a British student of undertaking 1 year of postgraduate study in Norway in the field of the humanities or social sciences.
Eligibility: Any person holding a British passport and normally resident in the United Kingdom
Level of Study: Postgraduate
Type: Scholarship
Value: £2,000
Length of Study: Up to a year
Frequency: Annual
Study Establishment: University or equivalent, dependent on the nature of the research
Country of Study: Norway
Application Procedure: Applicants should download the application form from the Scholarship and Grants page of the Anglo-Norse website www.anglo-norse.org.uk, and when completed, return it to one of the addresses at the bottom of the form with a letter of acceptance from the institution at which they hope to study.
No. of awards offered: 1
Closing Date: 31 March
Contributor: A bequest from Dame Gillian Brown and interest on capital built up by the Society
No. of awards given last year: 1
No. of applicants last year: 2
Additional Information: The Anglo-Norse Society also offers grants normally of up to £500 each for research or travel relating to Norway. Deadline for applications 31 March and 30 September. See Scholarship and Grants page of www.anglo-norse.org.uk for more information.

For further information contact:

The Anglo-Norse Society c/oThe Royal Norwegian Embassy, 25 Belgrave Square, London SW1X 8QD, United Kingdom.

Email: scholarships@anglo-norse.org.uk

Appraisal Institute Education Trust

200 W. Madison, Suite 1500, Chicago, IL 60606, United States of America.

Tel: (1) 312 335 4133
Email: educationtrust@appraisalinstitute.org
Website: www.aiedtrust.org

The Appraisal Institute is an international membership association of professional real estate appraisers, with more than 21,000 members and 99 chapters throughout the United States of America, Canada and abroad. Its mission is to support and advance its members as the choice for real estate solutions and uphold professional credentials, standards of professional practice and ethics consistent with the public good.

Appraisal Institute Education Trust Minorities and Women Education Scholarship

Purpose: The Minority and Women Educational Scholarship is geared towards college students working towards a degree in real estate appraisal or a related field. The scholarship is to help offset the cost of tuition

Eligibility: Applicant must be a member of a racial, ethnic or gender group underrepresented in the appraisal profession and full- or part-time student enroled-in real estate related courses at a degree-granting college/university or junior college/university. Individuals must have proof a cumulative grade point average of no less than 2.5 on 4.0 scale and have demonstrated financial need. Scholarship award must be used in the same calendar year as awarded by the committee

Level of Study: Graduate, Postgraduate

Type: Scholarship

Value: US$1,000 per person

Frequency: Annual

Country of Study: United States of America

Application Procedure: An official student transcript for all college work completed to date. A 500-word written essay stating why applicant should be awarded the scholarship. Two letters of recommendation from previous employers and/or college professors. An attestation that the scholarship will be applied toward tuition/books expense as stated in the application. Optional Applicants are asked to include a head and shoulders photograph as scholarship recipients may be profiled in Appraisal Institute newsletter/news releases

Closing Date: 15 April

Funding: Private

Additional Information: Applicants must visit the website www.aiedtrust.org www.appraisalinstitute.org/education/education-resources/scholarships/

For further information contact:

Email: aierf@appraisalinstitute.org

Arc of the United States

1825 K Street, NW, Suite 1200, Washington, DC 20006, United States of America.

Tel: (1) 800 433 5255
Email: info@thearc.org
Website: www.thearc.org

The Arc of the United States advocates for the rights and full participation of all children and adults with intellectual and developmental disabilities. Together with our network of members and affiliation chapters, we improve systems of supports and services, connect families, inspire communities and influence public policy.

Arc of the United States Research Grant

Purpose: To support research leading towards prevention, amelioration or cure of mental retardation

Eligibility: Open to United States nationals only

Level of Study: Unrestricted

Type: Research grant

Value: Various amounts up to US$25,000

Length of Study: 1 year, with the option of extension

Frequency: Annual

Country of Study: United States of America

Application Procedure: Applicants must submit project authorisation form, budget form, project summary, maximum of 15 double-spaced pages for narrative, and letters of support

No. of awards offered: 25

Closing Date: 1 April

Funding: Private

No. of awards given last year: 1

No. of applicants last year: 25

Additional Information: www.arc.gov/funding/GrantsandFunding.asp

For further information contact:

Department of Research & Program Services, The Arc PO Box 1047, Arlington, Texas 76004, United States of America.

Tel: (1) 817 261 6003
Email: mwehmeye@metronet.com

Archaeological Institute of America

The University of Calgary, 2500 University Drive North West, ES-1040, Calgary, AB T2N 1N4, Canada.

Anna C. & Oliver C. Colburn Fellowships

Purpose: To support studies undertaken at the American School of Classical Studies at Athens, Greece for no more than a year.
Eligibility: For members of the AIA at the time of application and until the end of the fellowship term. Applicant must be a citizen or permanent resident of the United States or Canada, must be at the pre-doctoral stage or have recently received a PhD (within five years of the date of the application).
Level of Study: Graduate
Type: Fellowship
Value: US$5,500 each
Length of Study: 1 year
Country of Study: United States of America or Canada
Application Procedure: Apply online www.archaeological. org/programs/professionals/grants-awards/applications/aia-fellowships/
No. of awards offered: 2 Awards
Closing Date: 15 January
Funding: Foundation
Additional Information: www.archaeological.org/programs/professionals/grants-awards/

For further information contact:

Email: fellowships@archaeological.org

Archaeology of Portugal Fellowship

Purpose: For archaeological research in Portugal, including the Autonomous Regions of the Azores and Madeira
Eligibility: Open to scholars of all nations.
Level of Study: Graduate
Type: Fellowship
Value: Varies; typical awards range from US$2,000 to US$8,000 (US$7,500 is the current maximum)
Length of Study: 1 year
Frequency: Annual
Country of Study: United States of America or Canada
Application Procedure: Apply online www.archaeological. org/programs/professionals/grants-awards/applications/aia-fellowships/
No. of awards offered: 1 Award
Closing Date: 1 November

Funding: Foundation
Additional Information: www.archaeological.org/programs/professionals/grants-awards/

For further information contact:

Email: fellowships@archaeological.org

C. Brian Rose AIA/DAI Exchange Fellowships

Purpose: The Archaeological Institute of America is pleased to announce a Fellowship for archaeologists employed by the Deutsches Archäologisches Institut (DAI), or project collaborators who have temporary contracts with the DAI. The purpose of the Fellowship is to encourage and support scholarship of the highest quality on various aspects of archaeology, and to promote contact between North American archaeologists and DAI scholars.
Eligibility: Applicants who are archaeologists must have a PhD degree; architects must have their diploma. Both must demonstrate professional competence in archaeology in their applications. Project collaborators must show proof of a long-time participation with a current DAI project by providing a letter of recommendation from a DAI project supervisor.
Level of Study: Postgraduate
Type: Fellowship
Frequency: Annual
Country of Study: Any country
Application Procedure: 1. completed online application form. 2. a curriculum vitae, including a list of publications. 3. two references (please note that these are due by the November 1st application deadline). 4. a brief description of DAI project they are involved in, and the nature of their participation. 5. a letter of recommendation from a DAI project supervisor (also due by November 1st)
Closing Date: 1 November
Additional Information: www.archaeological.org/grant/aia-dai-exchange-fellowship-us/

For further information contact:

Tel: (1) 857 305 9360
Email: fellowships@archaeological.org

Harrietand Leon Pomerance Fellowship

Purpose: To support an individual project of a scholarly nature, related to Aegean Bronze Age Archaeology
Eligibility: For members of the AIA at the time of application and until the end of the fellowship term. Applicant must be a citizen or permanent resident of the United States or Canada,

must be at the pre-doctoral stage or have recently received a PhD (within five years of the date of the application).
Level of Study: Graduate
Type: Fellowship
Value: US$5,000
Length of Study: 1 year
Frequency: Annual
Country of Study: United States of America or Canada
Application Procedure: Apply online www.archaeological. org/programs/professionals/grants-awards/applications/aia-fellowships/
No. of awards offered: 1 Award
Closing Date: 1 November
Funding: Foundation

For further information contact:

Email: fellowships@archaeological.org

John R. Coleman Traveling Fellowship

Purpose: The Coleman Fellowship is to be used for travel and study in Italy, the western Mediterranean, or North Africa, between July 1 of the award year and the following June 30
Eligibility: Applicants must be engaged in dissertation research in a U.S. graduate program; applicants must have been AIA members in good standing for at least one year by the application deadline
Level of Study: Graduate
Type: Fellowship
Value: US$10,000
Length of Study: 1 year
Frequency: Annual
Country of Study: Any country
Application Procedure: Apply online www.archaeological. org/programs/professionals/grants-awards/applications/aia-fellowships/
No. of awards offered: 1
Closing Date: 1 November
Funding: Foundation
No. of awards given last year: 2021
Additional Information: www.archaeological.org/programs/professionals/grants-awards/

For further information contact:

Email: fellowships@archaeological.org

Olivia James Traveling Fellowship

Purpose: For archaeological travel and research in Greece (the modern state), Cyprus, the Aegean Islands, Sicily,

southern Italy (Campania, Molise, Apulia, Basilicata, and Calabria), Asia Minor (Turkey) or Mesopotamia (that is, the territory between the Tigris and Euphrates rivers, that is modern Iraq and parts of northern Syria and eastern Turkey).
Eligibility: For members of the AIA (see website). Applicant must be a citizen of the United States, must be at the pre-doctoral stage or have recently received a PhD (within five years of the date of the application).
Level of Study: Graduate
Type: Fellowship
Value: US$24,000
Length of Study: 1 year
Frequency: Annual
Country of Study: United States of America
Application Procedure: Apply online www.archaeological. org/programs/professionals/grants-awards/applications/aia-fellowships/
No. of awards offered: 1 Award
Closing Date: 1 November
Funding: Foundation
No. of awards given last year: 2020
Additional Information: www.archaeological.org/programs/professionals/grants-awards/

For further information contact:

Email: fellowships@archaeological.org

The Archaeology Of Portugal Fellowship

Subjects: Archaeologists and archaeology
Purpose: The fellowship can be used to support research and study related to the archaeology of Portugal, including the Autonomous Regions of the Azores and Madeira. This includes, but is not limited to, excavations, research projects, colloquia, symposia, publications, and travel for research or to academic meetings for the purpose of presenting papers on the archaeology of Portugal. Funds may not be used for institutional overhead, institutional administrative recovery costs, or institutional indirect costs.
Eligibility: To be eligible, applicants from Portugal who already hold Ph.D.'s must have been AIA members in good standing for at least one year by the time of application; Portuguese graduate students must become AIA student members in order to apply for the fellowship. Portuguese graduate students wishing to study in the United States must be enrolled in or have been accepted to an accredited US university or college, and must provide evidence that they have been authorized to travel to and study in the US. Portuguese nationals seeking funds for research or study in the US must provide a detailed plan of their project that includes the institutions and organizations with which

they will be affiliated while in the US. All Portuguese applicants must provide proof of Portuguese citizenship. Applicants from the U.S. or countries other than Portugal must have been AIA members in good standing for at least two years (one year if still graduate students).

Level of Study: Graduate, Postgraduate
Type: Fellowship
Value: Varies; typical awards range from US$2,000 to US$8,000 (US$7,500 is the current maximum)
Frequency: Annual
Country of Study: Any country
Application Procedure: AIA Fellowship Coordinator
Closing Date: 1 November

For further information contact:

Email: fellowships@archaeological.org

Arctic Institute of North America (AINA)

2500 University Drive North West, ES-1040, Calgary, AB T2N 1N4, Canada.

Tel: (1) 403 220 7515
Email: arctic@ucalgary.ca
Website: www.arctic.ucalgary.ca
Contact: Executive Director

Created in 1945, the Arctic Institute of North America (AINA) is a non-profit membership organization and a multidisciplinary research institute for the University of Calgary.

Arctic Institute of North America Grants-in-Aid

Purpose: To support young investigators and provide funding to augment their research
Eligibility: Enrolled in or affiliated with a scientist working at a U.S. or Canadian academic institution.
Level of Study: Postgraduate
Type: Grant
Value: Up to C$1,000 which can be used for travel, supplies, equipment and services but not salary or wages
Length of Study: Varies
Frequency: Annual
Country of Study: United States of America
Application Procedure: Applicants must submit proposals which must not exceed four double spaced pages. A title,

introduction, objectives, methodology, anticipated results, period of performance and proposed use of the AINA award should be clearly stated. The total estimated budget for the project should be provided on a separate page and should clearly identify other anticipated and committed sources and amounts of funding
Closing Date: 7 February
Additional Information: A report to the committee will be required within one year following the award. Any report or publication resulting from the investigation should include acknowledgement of the AINA Grant-in-Aid programme. One copy of all publications should be sent to ASTIS at the AINA Calgary office for inclusion in the ASTIS database and AINA library arctic.ucalgary.ca/webform/aina-grant-aid-application

For further information contact:

Arctic Institute of North America Attn: AINA Grant-in-Aid University of Calgary, 2500 University Drive N.W., ES-1040, Calgary, Alberta T2N 1N4, Canada.

Email: arctic@ucalgary.ca

Jim Bourque Scholarship

Purpose: This scholarship honours the legacy of the late Hon. James W. Bourque, PC. Born in Wandering River, Alberta, Bourque was of Cree and Métis background. At the age of 18 he was elected president of an association of hunters and trappers in Fort Chipewyan before working as a park warden in Wood Buffalo National Park from 1955 to 1963. He served as president of the Métis Association of the Northwest Territories from 1980 to 1982, was deputy minister of renewable resources for the government of the Northwest Territories from 1982 to 1991 and chairman of the Northwest Territories' Commission for Constitutional Development.
Eligibility: To be eligible you must be 1. Enrolled in postsecondary training in Education, Environmental Studies, Traditional Knowledge or Telecommunications; and 2. a Canadian Aboriginal student.
Type: Award
Value: C$1000
Frequency: Annual
Country of Study: Any country
Application Procedure: To apply, please submit the following information via the online Scholarship Application or by email. 1. Cover letter (please include an email address where we can contact you); 2. a description of your intended program of study and the reasons you chose the program, in 500 words or less; 3. transcripts (most recent from

college/university or high school); 4. a signed letter of recommendation from a community leader (e.g., Town or Band Council, Chamber of Commerce, Metis Local, etc.); 5. a statement of financial need which indicates funding already received or expected; 6. proof of enrollment in, or application to, a post-secondary institution; and 7. proof of Canadian Aboriginal descent.

No. of awards offered: 1
Closing Date: 9 July

For further information contact:

2500 University Drive N.W., ES-1040, Calgary, AB T2N 1N4, Canada.

Email: arctic@ucalgary.ca

The H.M. Ali Family Educational Award

Eligibility: If you meet the eligibility requirements, we welcome your application for The H.M. Ali Family Educational Award 1. A student (graduate or undergraduate); 2. Enrolled in any Faculty at the University of Calgary; and 3. The focus of your education and research is on northern and arctic sustainable development
Level of Study: Graduate, Undergraduate
Type: Award
Value: C$500
Frequency: Annual
Country of Study: Any country
Application Procedure: 1. Cover letter (please include an email address where we can contact you) 2. Brief description of the proposed research, or relevant educational opportunity, (2 - 3 pages), including a clear hypothesis, relevance, title and statement of the purpose of the research, the area and type of study, the methodology and plan for evaluation of findings. Any collaborative relationship or work should be briefly identified; 3. One reference letter; 4. Complete curriculum vitae; 5. Official transcripts (transcripts issued to students are acceptable); and 6. A list of current sources and amounts of research funding, including scholarships, grants and bursaries.
No. of awards offered: 1
Closing Date: 31 January

For further information contact:

2500 University Drive N.W., ES-1040, Calgary, Alberta T2N 1N4, Canada.

Email: arctic@ucalgary.ca

The Jennifer Robinson Memorial Scholarship

Eligibility: 1. A graduate student; 2. Enrolled at a Canadian university; and 3. Study Northern biology (northern is defined as locations that lie north of the southern limit of the discontinuous permafrost zone)
Level of Study: Graduate
Type: Scholarship
Value: C$5,000
Frequency: Annual
Country of Study: Any country
Application Procedure: 1. Cover Letter (please include an email address where we can contact you) 2. Brief description of the proposed research (2 to 3 pages), including a clear hypothesis, relevance, title and statement of the purpose of the research, the area and type of study, the methodology and plan for evaluation of findings. Any collaborative relationship or work should be briefly identified; 3. Three reference letters; 4. Complete curriculum vitae; 5. Official transcripts (transcripts issued to students are acceptable); and 6. A list of current sources and amounts of research funding, including scholarships, grants and bursaries.
No. of awards offered: 1
Closing Date: 21 January

For further information contact:

Email: arctic@ucalgary.ca

The Lorraine Allison Memorial Scholarship

Subjects: Science or social science
Eligibility: 1. A graduate student; 2. Enrolled at a Canadian University; 3. Enrolled in a program of study related to northern issues (northern is defined as locations that lie north of the southern limit of the discontinuous permafrost zone). 4. Candidates in biological science fields will be preferred, but social science topics will also be considered. 5. Scholars from Yukon, the Northwest Territories and Nunavut are encouraged to apply.
Level of Study: Graduate
Type: Scholarship
Value: C$3,000
Frequency: Annual
Country of Study: Any country
Application Procedure: 1. Cover Letter (please include an email address where we can contact you) 2. Brief description of the proposed research (2 to 3 pages), including a clear hypothesis, relevance, title and statement of the purpose of the research, the area and type of study, the methodology and plan for evaluation of findings. Any collaborative relationship or work should be briefly identified; 3. Three reference letters;

4. Complete curriculum vitae; 5. Official transcripts (transcripts issued to students are acceptable); and 6. A list of current sources and amounts of research funding, including scholarships, grants and bursaries.

No. of awards offered: 1

Closing Date: 21 January

For further information contact:

Email: arctic@ucalgary.ca

Aristotle University of Thessaloniki

University Campus, GR-541 24 Thessaloniki, Greece.

Tel: (30) 2310 99 4168, 99 6771
Email: dps@auth.gr
Website: www.auth.gr/services/admin/studies_
              department.en.php3
Contact: Studies Department

Summer Intensive Course in modern Greek Language Scholarship

Subjects: 4/weeks, 20h/week intensive summer course of modern Greek language classes, plus cultural program Each year mid August to mid September 3 levels (beginners, intermediate, advance) following the common European framework of reference for languages.

Purpose: Diffusion of Greek language & culture

Eligibility: Nationals of any country; priority given to students of Greek (language, history, art, etc.)

Level of Study: Unrestricted

Type: Studentship

Value: Tuition fee waiver (€324)

Length of Study: 4 weeks

Frequency: Annual

Study Establishment: Aristotle University of Thessaloniki, School of Modern Greek Language

Country of Study: Greece

Application Procedure: Application form and supporting documents to be sent to the Aristotle University Department of Studies by 28th February

No. of awards offered: Varies, decided each year by the Senate

Closing Date: 28 February

Funding: Government

No. of awards given last year: 18

No. of applicants last year: 54

For further information contact:

Aristotle University of Thessaloniki, Department of Studies, University Campus, GR-541 24 Thessaloniki Hellas, Greece.

Arizona Community Foundation

George F. Wellik Scholarship

Purpose: George F. Wellik Scholarship was established to provide a college education for worthy and needy students from Wickenburg, Arizona.

Eligibility: High school student graduating from the greater Wickenburg area. Based on financial need and/or academic potential. Attending any 2 or 4 year, private or public college/ university or vocational/trade school in the U.S. Open to any field of study. Minimum of 2.5 GPA.

Level of Study: Graduate

Type: Scholarship

Value: US$5,000

Frequency: Annual

Country of Study: United States of America

Application Procedure: Applications for the George F. Wellik Scholarship are available on the Arizona Community Foundation website. To apply, the applicant must register with the foundation. In addition to a completed application, the applicant must also submit the following two letters of recommendation, one from his/her guidance counselor and one from a high school academic teacher, attesting to his/her academic strengths and determination to succeed at the university; a high school transcript through the seventh semester; a 500- to 700-word essay addressing the topic listed on the application; typed personal statements; verification of SAT and/or ACT test scores; and a Free Application for Federal Student Aid form (FAFSA). The FAFSA is available online at www.fafsa.ed.gov

Closing Date: 8 April

Funding: Foundation

Additional Information: azfoundation.academicworks.com/ opportunities/4168

For further information contact:

2201 E. Camelback Road, Suite 202, Phoenix, AZ 85016, United States of America.

Tel: (1) 800 222 8221
Email: scholarships@swe.org

Arizona State University College of Business

PO Box 874906, Tempe, AZ 85287-4906, United States of America.

Tel: (1) 602 965 3332
Email: asu.mba@asu.edu
Website: www.cob.asu.edu/mba
Contact: MBA Admissions Officer

Madbury Road Design Success Award Scholarship

Purpose: Madbury Road is offering a US$1,000 scholarship in support designers and architects of the future
Eligibility: This is an award that is only available for students currently enrolled at a university or college
Level of Study: Professional development
Type: Scholarship
Value: US$1,000
Frequency: Annual
Country of Study: Any country
Application Procedure: Your full name, telephone number and mailing address. The name of the college or university that you currently attend or will be attending. Proof that you have, either been accepted, or are currently attending the college or university that you specified. The area that you study.
Closing Date: 31 March
Funding: Private
Additional Information: www.madburyroad.com/scholarship/

For further information contact:

Email: scholarship@madburyroad.com

The Ship Smart Annual Scholarship

Purpose: Ship Smart leads the industry in moving small amounts of high value goods and small shipments of household goods, electronics and artwork
Eligibility: Applicants must be current, full-time or part-time students of an accredited, non-accredited institute, truck driving school or other logistics program. They must have a minimum cumulative GPA of 3.0 to become eligible. There is no age requirement.
Level of Study: Graduate

Type: Scholarship
Frequency: Annual
Country of Study: United States of America
Application Procedure: To apply for the scholarship write a 1,000 word original essay or article, that may not have been posted anywhere on the internet, about an article related to our website. Some topics could be anything related to 1. Shipping Furniture. 2. Small Moves. 3. Shipping Antiques. 4. Shipping Artwork. 5. Shipping Electronics. 6. Packing and Shipping
Closing Date: 12 April
Funding: Private
Additional Information: www.shipsmart.com/info/shipsmart-scholarship

For further information contact:

Email: scholarships@shipsmart.com

Armenian International Women's Association

65 Main Street, #3A, Watertown, MA 02472, United States of America.

Tel: (1) 617 926 0171

Armenian International Women

Purpose: AIWA annually awards scholarships in honor of Ethel Jaffarian Duffett, Agnes Missirian, Lucy Kasparian Aharonian
Eligibility: 1. Female of Armenian Descent. 2. Financial Need. 3. Full-Time Student. 4. Accredited University/College. 5. Junior, Senior, or Graduate Student. 6. 3.2 Minimum GPA. 7. Certified Copy of University/College Transcripts. 8. Two Letters of Recommendation, one from an academic instructor/advisor, one from a community representative. 9. Small (Passport Size) Photograph
Level of Study: Graduate
Type: Scholarship
Frequency: Annual
Country of Study: Any country
Closing Date: 17 April
Funding: Private
Additional Information: aiwainternational.org/scholarships-internships/

For further information contact:

Armenian International Women's Association, Inc., 65 Main St., #3A, Watertown, MA 02472, United States of America.

Email: scholarships@aiwainternational.org

Arthritis Research United Kingdom

Copeman House, St Mary's Court, St Mary's Gate, Chesterfield S41 7TD, United Kingdom.

Tel: (44) 12 4655 8033
Email: info@arc.org.uk
Website: www.arc.org.uk
Contact: Mr Michael Patnick, Head of Research & Education Funding

The Arthritis Research Campaign (arc) is the fourth largest medical research charity in the United Kingdom, and the only charity in the country dedicated to finding the cause of and cure for arthritis, relying entirely upon voluntary donations to sustain its wide-ranging research and educational programmes.

Clinical Research Fellowships

Purpose: Aim to provide an opportunity for training in clinical and/or laboratory research techniques in a project that demonstrates clear relevance to the aims of Arthritis Research United Kingdom in a centre of excellence in the United Kingdom
Eligibility: Open to medical graduates (including orthopaedic surgeons), usually during speciality training, who are expected to register for a higher degree, usually a PhD.
Level of Study: Doctorate, Professional development, Research
Type: Fellowship
Value: Salaries will be according to age and experience on the appropriate clinical salary scale. Applications may also be made for reasonable running costs although tuition fees will not generally be provided
Length of Study: 3 years
Frequency: Annual
Study Establishment: A university, hospital or recognized research institute
Country of Study: United Kingdom
Application Procedure: Applications for funding are available via an online system accessible from the website

No. of awards offered: 17
Closing Date: January
Funding: Private
Contributor: Voluntary charitable contributions
No. of awards given last year: 2
No. of applicants last year: 17

For further information contact:

Email: cdftdr@who.int

Artist Trust

1835, 12th Ave, Seattle, WA 98122, United States of America.

Tel: (1) 2 064 678 734
Email: info@artisttrust.org
Website: www.artisttrust.org
Contact: Zach Frimmel, Programs Assistant

Artist Trust is a non-profit organization whose sole mission is to support and encourage individual artists working in all disciplines in order to enhance community life throughout Washington state.

Arts Innovator Award

Purpose: Funding for this award is generously donated by the Dale and Leslie Chihuly Foundation. Dale recalls receiving grants that supported experimentation early in his career, adding credibility, opening doors, and enabling new connections for him as an artist. Today Dale remembers the importance of this support, and he and Leslie would like to help artists in a similar way.
Eligibility: 1. 18 years of age or older by application deadline; 2. Washington State residents at the time of both application and payment (payment will be made in June); 3. Generative artists (those who are the originators of works of art) with a minimum of five years in professional art practice
Level of Study: Unrestricted
Type: Award
Value: US$25,000
Frequency: Annual
Country of Study: Any country
No. of awards offered: 2
Closing Date: 21 March

Fellowship Awards

Subjects: Literary, Media, Multidisciplinary, Performing, Visual

Purpose: Artist Trust Fellowship Awards are merit-based awards of US$10,000 to practicing professional artists of exceptional talent and ability residing in Washington State. These unrestricted awards are open to artists of all disciplines and are given annually to 8+ artists of in recognition of artistic excellence and dedication to their practice.

Eligibility: 1. 18 years of age or older; 2. Washington State residents at the time of application and payment; 3. Individual artists (or artist teams): those who are the originators of works of art.

Type: Award

Value: US$10,000

Country of Study: Any country

No. of awards offered: 8

Closing Date: 9 November

Grants for Artist Projects (GAP)

Purpose: GAP Awards support the development of new ideas and are intended to be a catalyst for the work of artists at critical points in their practice.

Eligibility: The 2021 GAP Awards are open to artists residing in Washington State working in all disciplines. APPLICANTS MUST BE 1. 18 years of age or older; 2. Washington State residents at the time of both application and payment (payment will be made in December.); 3. Generative artists those who are the originators of works of art, OR artist teams with documented history of creating and presenting work as a team for at least three consecutive years.

Level of Study: Unrestricted

Type: Grant

Value: Up to US$1,500

Frequency: Annual

Country of Study: United States of America

Application Procedure: Apply hear artisttrust.submittable.com/submit

No. of awards offered: 65

Closing Date: 7 September

Funding: Commercial, Corporation, Foundation, Government, Individuals, Private

No. of awards given last year: 58

No. of applicants last year: 698

Additional Information: philanthropynewsdigest.org/rfps/rfp10846-artist-trust-accepting-nominations-for-twining-humber-award-for-lifetime-artistic-achievement

For further information contact:

1835 12th Avenue, Seattle, WA 98122-2437, United States of America.

Tel: (1) 206 467 8734
Fax: (1) 206 467 9633
Email: heatherjoy@srtisttrust.org

Irving and Yvonne Twining Humber Award for Lifetime Artistic Achievement

Purpose: To reward a female visual artist over the age of 60 from Washington State

Eligibility: Artists must be nominated. Nominees must be female, over the age of 60, a Washington State resident and a visual artist who has been practicing for 25 years or more

Level of Study: Postgraduate, Unrestricted

Type: Award

Value: US$10,000

Frequency: Annual

Country of Study: Any country

Application Procedure: Nomination forms are available by mail or online

No. of awards offered: Approx. 50

Closing Date: 23 March

Funding: Commercial, Corporation, Foundation, Government, Individuals, Private

Contributor: Mrs Twining Humber

No. of awards given last year: 1

No. of applicants last year: Approx. 50

Additional Information: www.artscouncil.ie/Funds/Artist-in-the-community-scheme/

SOLA Awards

Subjects: Visual

Purpose: The SOLA (Support Old Lady Artists) Awards are three unrestricted awards of US$3,000 given annually to Washington State female-identified visual artists, age 60 or over, who have dedicated 25 years or more to creating art. The awards were created by artist Ginny Ruffner.

Eligibility: The 2021 SOLA (Support Old Lady Artists) Awards is open to female-identified visual artists living in Washington State, age 60 or over, who have dedicated 25 years or more to creating art.; APPLICANTS MUST BE:1. A female-identified visual artist; 60 years of age or older by June 20, 2022; 2. Washington State residents at the time of application and payment; 3. A practicing artist who has dedicated 25 years or more to creating art.

Type: Award

Value: US$3,000
Frequency: Annual
Country of Study: Any country
No. of awards offered: 3
Closing Date: 20 June

Twining Humber Award

Subjects: Visual
Purpose: The award is made possible by a generous gift from the painter Yvonne Twining Humber (1907-2004), who established the Irving and Yvonne Twining Humber Fund for Artistic Excellence to support the grant through Artist Trust in recognition of female-identified artists who oftentimes must interrupt or postpone art-making in order to answer the demands of family life. The award recognizes artistic excellence, professional accomplishment, and longstanding dedication to the visual arts.
Eligibility: The 202 Twining Humber Award is open to female-identified visual artists living in Washington State, age 60 or over, who have dedicated 25 years or more to creating art.; APPLICANTS MUST BE: 1. A female-identified visual artist; 60 years of age or older by June 20, 2022; 2. Washington State residents at the time of application and payment; 3. A practicing artist who has dedicated 25 years or more to creating art.
Type: Award
Value: US$10,000
Frequency: Annual
Country of Study: Any country
No. of awards offered: 1
Closing Date: 20 June

Arts Council of Ireland

70 Merrion Square, Dublin 2, Ireland.

Tel: (353) 1 661 1840
Email: info@artscouncil.ie
Website: www.artscouncil.ie
Contact: Ms Tara Byrne, Artists' Support Executive

The Arts Council, the development agency for the arts in Ireland, exists to promote and support the arts. Its core

Arts Council of Ireland Artist-in-the-Community Scheme

Purpose: To enable artists and community groups to work together on projects

Eligibility: Open to artists of Irish birth or residence and community groups. The artist must have evidence of having produced a body of work of recognised quality and significance, or in the case of individuals with less experience, demonstrable potential. They need to be able to show evidence of artistic developmental needs, evidence of financial need, including availability of other funding and a likelihood that an award will reach the desired effect. Applicants must be practising artists or arts workers but need not necessarily earn income from their arts practice. They must identify themselves and be recognised by their peers as practising artists
Level of Study: Professional development
Type: Grant
Length of Study: Varies
Country of Study: Ireland
Application Procedure: Applicants must contact CAFE for application information. Applications will be considered not eligible and returned if the eligibility criteria is not met, if all the support material specified is not included, if funding is requested for activities that have already occurred or will be completed before the closing date and also if the application or supporting documentation is late
Closing Date: 30 March
Contributor: CAFE

For further information contact:

70 Merrion Square S, Saint Peter's, Dublin 2, D02 NY52, Ireland.

Tel: (353) 1 473 66 00
Email: support@create-ireland.ie

Arts Council of Ireland Frameworks Animation Scheme

Purpose: To add to the range and scope of Irish animation and encourage new and established animation, which makes use of the medium and is primarily aimed at an adult audience
Eligibility: The artist must be an Irish national or permanent resident and have evidence of having produced a body of work of recognised quality and significance, or in the case of individuals with less experience, demonstrable potential. They need to be able to show evidence of artistic developmental needs, evidence of financial need, including availability of other funding and a likelihood that an award will reach the desired effect. Applicants must be practising artists or arts workers but need not necessarily earn income from their arts practice. They must identify themselves and be recognised by their peers as practising artists

Value: Approx. €25,000–32,000 to fund up to six animated shorts

Country of Study: Ireland

Application Procedure: Applicants must send completed applications to Bord Scannán na hÉireann. Applications will be considered not eligible and returned if the eligibility criteria is not met, if all the support material specified is not included, if funding is requested for activities that have already occurred or will be completed before the closing date and also if the application or supporting documentation is late

Contributor: The scheme is co-funded by RTÉ, Bord Scannán na hÉireann and The Arts Council

For further information contact:

70 Merrion Square S, Saint Peter's, Dublin 2, D02 NY52, Ireland.

Tel: (353) 9 156 1398
Fax: (353) 9 156 1405
Email: info@filmboard.ie

Arts Council of Wales

Museum Place, Cardiff CF10 3NX, United Kingdom.

Tel: (44) 29 2037 6500
Email: info@artswales.org.uk
Website: www.artswales.org.uk
Contact: Angela Blackburn

The Arts Council of Wales is the national organization with specific responsibility for the funding and development of the arts in Wales. Most of its funds come from the National Assembly for Wales, but it also distributes National Lottery funds to the arts in Wales.

Artists at Work

Purpose: To support businesses and artists to benefit from sharing their workplaces

Eligibility: Available for businesses that are interested in exploring the potential of creative collaboration and hosting an artist in residence and for artists keen to develop their practice through working in industry

Type: Grant

Value: Up to £6,000

Country of Study: Wales

For further information contact:

11-12 Mount Stuart Square, Cardiff CF10 5EE, United Kingdom.

Tel: (44) 29 2048 9543
Email: info@cywaithcymru.org

Arts Council of Wales Artform Development Scheme

Purpose: To support new talent and ideas in a range of activities eg. platforms of work in process or exploratory productions in mixed art-forms

Type: Grant

Value: £2,000–10,000

Country of Study: Wales

Application Procedure: Applicants must submit a completed application. These can be submitted at any time but early notice is needed for major projects. Applicants must contact Performing Arts at the Artform Development Division in Cardiff

Closing Date: March

For further information contact:

Email: acw@wilsonarts.com

Arts Council of Wales Awards for Career Development of Individual Visual Artists and Craftspeople

Purpose: Financial assistance for travel, research, the acquisition of new skills and collaboration which extends professional horizons

Eligibility: For individual professional visual artists and craftspeople at all stages of career development and whose work shows originality and excellence. For those who live and work in Wales for at least nine months of the year

Level of Study: Professional development

Type: Grant

Country of Study: Wales

Application Procedure: Applicants must contact Visual Arts and Craft, Artform Development Division, Cardiff office

Additional Information: Smaller awards of up to £500 are also available to emerging visual artists to help establish a studio, research contacts and potential markets www.artscouncil.ie/Funds/Artist-in-the-community-scheme/

For further information contact:

Email: acw@wilsonarts.com

Arts Council of Wales Awards for Individual Visual Artists and Craftspeople

Purpose: To assist with research and developing skills to undertake a specific project or in developing new work in particular by releasing them from their normal commitments
Eligibility: For visual artists and individual craftspeople permanently living in Wales
Level of Study: Professional development
Type: Bursary
Frequency: Twice a year
Country of Study: Wales
Application Procedure: Applicants must contact Visual Arts and Craft, Artform Development Division, Cardiff office

For further information contact:

Email: acw@wilsonarts.com

Arts Council of Wales Barclays Stage Partners

Purpose: To enable the production and tour of a new theatrical production in Wales
Type: Grant
Value: Up to £53,000
Country of Study: Wales
Application Procedure: Applicants must contact the Arts Council for guidelines
Funding: Commercial

For further information contact:

Email: acw@wilsonarts.com

Arts Council of Wales Community Touring Night Out

Purpose: To support community-based organizations throughout Wales with access to suitable premises, who wish to promote occasional professional performing arts events for their locality
Eligibility: Eligibility for promoters of events is restricted to community organizations within Wales. Schools and colleges may participate if offering a service to the wider community that is beyond this normal educational role. Eligibility for performers governed by this ability to provide a professional service at an affordable price regardless of nationality and location
Type: Fees to performers
Value: Variable
Country of Study: Wales

Application Procedure: Applications may be submitted at any time to the Community Touring unit in Cardiff and must come from the local promoters of the event. The single-page application form is obtainable from the unit by post or may be found on the website at www.nightout.org.uk
No. of awards offered: 206
Contributor: 51% from National Assembly of Wales, 49% box office supported by local authority guarantees
No. of awards given last year: 392
No. of applicants last year: 206
Additional Information: Community-based organizations dedicated to the arts who wish to plan more than five events in a year or more than 6 months ahead should seek advice from their local ACW office or the Community Touring Manager. This scheme assists community organizations by making professional performances available at a fraction of their real price. It covers all aspects of the performing arts www.artscouncil.ie/Funds/Artist-in-the-community-scheme/

For further information contact:

Community Touring Manager, Community Touring Unit, Arts Council of Wales, Museum Place, Cardiff, CF1 3NX, Wales, United Kingdom.

Email: acw@wilsonarts.com

Arts Council of Wales Music Projects Grants

Purpose: To help with either CD production of works by Welsh composers or books and journals concerned with Welsh music
Type: Grant
Country of Study: Any country
Application Procedure: Applications are invited from publishers and recording companies and should be sent to Performing Arts, Artform Development Division, Cardiff office

For further information contact:

Email: acw@wilsonarts.com

Arts Council of Wales Performing Arts Projects

Purpose: To enable production by professional artists based in Wales working with a presenting organisation
Eligibility: Partnerships are a particular feature of this scheme and the involvement of a venue or presenter is essential. Applications may come from groups of artists, arts organisations or presenters

Type: Grant
Value: Grants range from £5,000–40,000. Quality, innovation and potential to enrich programming for the public will be priorities
Country of Study: Any country
Application Procedure: Applications should be sent to Performing Arts, Artform Development Division in Cardiff
Closing Date: 1 February
Additional Information: Venue commissions of artists may be one form of application www.artscouncil.ie/Funds/Artist-in-the-community-scheme/

For further information contact:

Email: acw@wilsonarts.com

Arts Council of Wales Pilot Training Grants Scheme

Purpose: Provides grants to arts organisations and owner managers in Wales for members of staff to attend or deliver training in IT, finance, marketing, management and other vocational skills
Level of Study: Professional development
Type: Grant
Value: The maximum grant awarded will be £5,000 and the scheme will provide a maximum of 45% of the total cost of attending or delivering training
Country of Study: Wales
Application Procedure: Applications must be submitted to Access Development Division, Cardiff Office
Additional Information: Training supported by this scheme must be completed and a monitoring report form submitted to ACW www.artscouncil.ie/Funds/Artist-in-the-community-scheme/

For further information contact:

Email: acw@wilsonarts.com

Community Dance Wales Grants

Purpose: To promote professional interest in community dance in Wales
Level of Study: Professional development
Type: Grant
Value: £25,342
Frequency: Annual
Country of Study: United Kingdom
Funding: Government

For further information contact:

Tel: (44) 1495 224425
Fax: (44) 1495 226457
Email: roonem@caerphilly.gov.uk

Cultural Enterprise Service Grant

Purpose: To provide financial assistance in the purchase of equipment, software and consultancy
Level of Study: Professional development
Type: Grant
Value: £10,000
Frequency: Annual
Country of Study: United Kingdom
Application Procedure: See the website
Funding: Government
Contributor: The Arts Council of Wales

For further information contact:

Tel: (44) 29 2034 3205
Fax: (44) 29 2034 5436
Email: stephan@cultural-enterprise.com

Good Ideas-Artist Led Projects

Purpose: To fulfil the needs of artists by providing funding for projects that develop their artistic practice and to help alleviate the associated administration
Eligibility: Open to artists who have project initiatives that involve community collaboration and that demonstrate innovative thinking and artistic practice
Type: Grant
Value: £6,000

For further information contact:

Email: info@cywaithcymru.org

International Opportunities Funding

Purpose: To encourage professional arts practitioners and presenters
Type: Funding support

For further information contact:

Wales Arts International, 28 Park place, Cardiff CF10 3Qe, United Kingdom.

Tel: (44) 29 20393037
Fax: (44) 29 20398779
Email: Nikki.Morgan@wai.org.uk

Vital Knowledge-Artists' Mentoring Scheme

Purpose: To encourage new applicants to gain experience and mentoring in all aspects of residency work
Eligibility: Open to candidates who would benefit from working alongside an artist in residence on one of the Cywaith Cymru
Type: Grant

For further information contact:

Tel: (44) 29 2048 9543
Email: info@cywaithcymru.org

Wales One World Film Festival Grant

Purpose: To present audiences with the best in world cinema through the Festival
Level of Study: Professional development
Type: Grant
Value: £24,936
Length of Study: 2 years
Frequency: Annual
Country of Study: United Kingdom
Application Procedure: See the website
Funding: Government
Contributor: The Media Agency for Wales and the Arts Council of Wales

For further information contact:

Tel: (44) 1239 615066
Fax: (44) 1239 615066
Email: sa3657@eclipse.co.uk

Welsh Independent Dance Grant

Purpose: To develop a successful dance sector in Wales
Level of Study: Professional development
Type: Grant
Length of Study: £71,296
Frequency: Annual
Country of Study: United Kingdom
Application Procedure: See the website
Funding: Government
Contributor: The Arts Council of Wales

Additional Information: www.culturenet.hr/default.aspx?id=35969

For further information contact:

Tel: (44) 29 2038 7314
Fax: (44) 29 2038 7314
Email: welshindance@btconnect.com

Arts International

251 Park Avenue South, 5th Floor, New York, NY 10010-7302, United States of America.

Tel: (1) 212 674 9744
Email: info@artsinternational.org
Website: www.artsinternational.org
Contact: Mr Adam Bernstein, Director, Advised Funds & Regranting Programs

Arts International is an independent, non-profit, contemporary arts organization dedicated to global, cultural interchange. It carries out its work through developing global networks and partnerships, information services and grantmaking opportunities.

Croatian Arts and Cultural Exchange Croatia

Purpose: FACE Croatia is designed to encourage tax deductible (for United States tax payers) donor advised contributions from private and public sources including individuals, private foundations, corporations and public sector donors. FACE Croatia maintains an active database of information on Croatian artists, arts and culture
Eligibility: FACE Croatia has two funding categories Croatian Arts and Culture Projects, and United States/Croatian Cultural Exchange. 1. Croatian Arts and Culture Projects Grants. Any Croatian organization that qualifies as a charity under Croatian law is eligible (museums, galleries, theaters, etc.). 2. Croatian based non-governmental organizations (NGO's) engaged in arts and culture activity in Croatia are eligible to apply. 3. The program is open to any arts discipline and/or cultural activity. 4. Individual artists may not make direct application to the program and must be sponsored by an eligible organization
Level of Study: Unrestricted
Type: Arts discipline or cultural activity
Value: Variable
Length of Study: Variable

Study Establishment: As approved. Typically museum, art gallery, theatre
Country of Study: United States of America and Croatia
Application Procedure: Proposals must include a narrative and budget, an organizational narrative and budget, evidence of non-profit status, and three letters of recommendation from professionals in the field
Funding: Private
Contributor: Heathcote Art Foundation

For further information contact:

CEC ArtsLink, 291 Broadway, 14th Floor, New York, NY 10007, United States of America.

Email: al@cecartslink.org

Arts NSW

Level 5, 323 Castlereagh Street, Sydney, NSW 2000, Australia.

Tel: (61) 1800 358 594
Email: arts.funding@arts.nsw.gov.au
Website: www.arts.nsw.gov.au

Arts NSW is part of the NSW Department of the Arts, Sport and Recreation. Arts NSW advises the Minister for the Arts on all aspects of the arts and cultural activity. Arts NSW works closely with the state's 8 major cultural institutions, providing policy advice to Government on their operations. The institutions manage significant cultural heritage collections and provide services and programmes throughout the state and beyond.

Asialink Residency Program

Purpose: To promote cultural understanding, information exchange and artistic endeavour between Australia and Asian countries
Eligibility: Open to Australian citizens or permanent residents who have at least 3 years professional experience in their field
Level of Study: Unrestricted
Type: Grant
Value: A travel grant of US$6,000–US$12,000 is provided to each resident to assist with residency-related expenses including airfares, accommodation, language lessons, living expenses, materials and production costs. The amount awarded is reflective of the residency period
Length of Study: 3 months
Application Procedure: Check website for further details
Closing Date: 1 March
Contributor: Arts NSW, in association with the Asialink Centre
Additional Information: adb.anu.edu.au/biography/landa-david-paul-paul-14142

For further information contact:

Arts Program, The Asialink Centre, The University of Melbourne, Sidney Myer Asia Centre, Parkville, VIC 3010, Australia.

Tel: (61) 3 8344 4800
Fax: (61) 3 9347 1768
Email: arts@asialink.unimelb.edu.au

David Paul Landa Memorial Scholarships for Pianists

Eligibility: Open to the Australian citizens currently residing in New South Wales or holding residence visas who have been residents of New South Wales for two consecutive years
Level of Study: Unrestricted
Type: Scholarship
Value: AU$25,000
Frequency: Every 2 years
Application Procedure: Applicants must forward the completed application form (and one copy of it), two copies of all written supporting material, single copies of other supporting material, the completed EFT authorization form and, if applicable, two copies of the completed RCTI to Program Support

For further information contact:

David Paul Landa Memorial Scholarship for Pianists, Musica Viva Australia, PO Box 1687, Strawberry Hills, NSW 2012, Australia.

Tel: (61) 2 8394 6666
Fax: (61) 2 9698 3878
Email: musicaviva@mva.org.au

New South Wales Indigenous History Fellowship

Purpose: To assist a person living in New South Wales to research and produce a work on a subject of historical interest relating to New South Wales from an Indigenous point of view

Eligibility: Open to the candidates who may be independent historians, or historians working in conjunction with indigenous communities
Level of Study: Unrestricted
Type: Fellowship
Value: AU$20,000
Length of Study: 2 years
Frequency: Every 2 years
Application Procedure: Applicants must submit form with details of the proposal and their qualifications and experience details. Check website for further details
Closing Date: May
Additional Information: The fellowship will be administered by the History Council of New South Wales www.sl.nsw.gov.au/about-library/awards/nsw-premiers-history-awards/nsw-premiers-history-awards-nomination-form-and

For further information contact:

History Council of New South Wales Inc., PO Box R1737, Royal Exchange, NSW 1225, Australia.

Tel: (61) 2 9252 8715
Fax: (61) 2 9252 8716
Email: scholarship@sl.nsw.gov.au

New South Wales Premier's History Awards

Purpose: To establish values and standards in historical research and publication and promote the excellence in the interpretation of history
Eligibility: Open only to the citizens of Australia
Level of Study: Unrestricted
Type: Award
Value: Total prize money is US$75,000.
Frequency: Annual
Country of Study: Any country
Application Procedure: Check website for further details
Closing Date: 8 April
Additional Information: Nominees may enter a published book or ebook in only one of the following categories: Australian History Prize; General History Prize; New South Wales Community and Regional History Prize; Young People's History Prize. Nominees may enter a non-print media work such as a film, television, or radio program, a DVD or website in one or both of the following categories (if appropriate): Young People's History Prize; Multimedia History Prize. (Note: If entering into both categories, only one nomination form needs to be completed.) All works must have been first published, produced, performed or made publicly available between 1 April and 31 March www.sl.nsw.gov.au/about-library/awards/nsw-premiers-history-awards/nsw-premiers-history-awards-nomination-form-and

For further information contact:

Corner of Macquarie Street and Shakespeare Place, Sydney, NSW 2000, Australia.

Tel: (61) 2 9273 1605 or (61) 2 9273 1582
Email: awards@sl.nsw.gov.au

Philip Parsons Young Playwright's Award

Purpose: To honor a playwright living in NSW for an original and compelling theatrical voice
Eligibility: Writers must be under 35 years of age, based in NSW, and have had a play produced between 1 June and 31 May either in Australia or abroad. Shortlisted writers will be asked to submit a treatment of up to five pages for a proposed new work
Level of Study: Unrestricted
Type: Scholarship
Value: AU$12,500
Frequency: Annual
Country of Study: Any country
Application Procedure: Check website for further details
Closing Date: October
Additional Information: Please check website for more details   belvoir.com.au/media-release/philip-parsons-fellowship-emerging-playwrights/

For further information contact:

18 & 25 Belvoir, St Surry Hills, NSW 2010, Australia.

Tel: (61) 2 8396 6242; 407 163 921
Email: elly@belvoir.com.au

Western Sydney Artists

Purpose: To support the creative development of new work or professional development by Western Sydney artists
Eligibility: Open to professional artists working in music or literature who are the residents of, or whose practice is located primarily in, Western Sydney
Level of Study: Unrestricted
Type: Fellowship
Value: AU$5,000–25,000
Country of Study: Any country
Application Procedure: Check website for further details
Closing Date: 14 September
Additional Information: www.aaronsiskind.org/grant.html

For further information contact:

Email: mail@create.nsw.gov.au

Artwork Archive

Aaron Siskind Foundation - Individual Photographer's Fellowship

Purpose: The Aaron Siskind Foundation is offering a limited number of Individual Photographer's Fellowship grants of up to US$15,000 each, for artists working in photography and photo-based art

Eligibility: Work must be based on the idea of still-based photography, but can include digital imagery, installations, documentary projects, and photo-generated print media. Doctoral candidates considered on a case-by-case basis. 1. Applicants must be at least 21 years of age. Students enrolled in a college degree program are not eligible to apply. 2. Previous IPF recipients are not currently being considered for new awards

Level of Study: Postgraduate

Type: Fellowship

Value: Up to US$10,000 each

Frequency: Annual

Country of Study: Any country

Closing Date: 31 May

Funding: Private

Additional Information: en.ashinaga.org/apply/aai/

For further information contact:

Aaron Siskind Foundation, c/o School of Visual Arts, MFA Photo Dept. 209 East 23rd Street, New York, NY 10010, United States of America.

Email: grant@aaronsiskind.org

Ashinaga

Ashinaga Scholarships

Purpose: Ashinaga is sponsoring scholarships to bereaved undergraduate Africans to Study in Japan, United States of America and the United Kingdom, Applicants are able to participate in the two Ashinaga preparatory programs before attending university

Eligibility: 1. Applicants should have a citizenship in any one of the countries listed below and pursued high school are eligible. 2. Applicants who have lost one or both parents (can submit an official document proving). 3. Applicants are able to participate in the two Ashinaga preparatory programs before attending university. 4. Students are willing to contribute to society in Africa after graduating from university and have no dependents who could interfere with academic progress and be in good condition of health and capable of studying abroad

Level of Study: Graduate

Type: Scholarship

Frequency: Annual

Country of Study: Any country

Application Procedure: 1. Have lost one or both parents. 2. Have completed secondary school and passed national secondary school examination (technical and vocational degrees not accepted) within the last two years. 3. Were born after 1st September. 4. Have an outstanding academic performance at high school and were amongst the top students in their class. 5. Be committed to returning home, or to Sub-Saharan Africa, and contribute to society in Sub-Saharan Africa after graduating from university.

Closing Date: August

Funding: Private

Additional Information: Citizens of the following Sub-Saharan African countries: a). English speaking: Uganda, Rwanda, Kenya, Ethiopia, Tanzania, Ghana, Namibia, Zimbabwe, Zambia, Malawi, Sudan, Botswana, South Africa, Lesotho, Swaziland, Mauritius, Somalia, Nigeria, The Gambia, Cape Verde, Mozambique, Guinea Bissau, Angola. b). French-speaking: Côte d'Ivoire, Senegal, Benin, Burundi, Gabon, Mali, Burkina Faso, Mauritania, DR Congo, Republic of Congo, Djibouti, Cameroon, Togo, Madagascar, Comoros   www.arts.ac.uk/study-at-ual/fees-and-funding/scholarships-search/ashley-family-foundation-scholarship

For further information contact:

1-6-8 Hirakawa-cho, Chiyoda-Ku, Tokyo, 102-8639, Japan.

Email: admissions.en@ashinaga.org

Ashley Family Foundation

6 Trull Farm Buildings, Trull, Tetbury GL8 8SQ, United Kingdom.

Tel: (44) 3030 401 005

Email: info@ashleyfamilyfoundation.org.uk

Website: www.ashleyfamilyfoundation.org.uk

Contact: The Administrator

The Ashley Family Foundation (formerly The Laura Ashley Foundation) is a United Kingdom registered charity, founded by Sir Bernard Ashley and his wife Laura Ashley following the success of the Laura Ashley brand.

Ashley Family Foundation MA Photography Scholarship

Eligibility: To be eligible for the opportunity a candidate must be Ordinarily resident in the UK and considered Home status. Accepted on the Full-Time MA Photography course at London College of Communication, commencing January 2015. A graduate, having already gained a first or 2:1 in a Bachelors Degree from a Higher Education institution, or a HE accredited Further Education institution.

Level of Study: MBA
Type: Scholarship
Value: £12,000
Frequency: Annual
Study Establishment: London College of Communication
Country of Study: United Kingdom
Application Procedure: 1. How to Apply Applications should be submitted by post. In addition to the application form you will need to send the following supplementary material 2. A CD/ DVD portfolio of your work formatted into 1 PDF document which includes a title page with 3. your name and course title followed by 10-15 images of recent work. 4. An explanatory statement about the projects of no more than 300 words. 5. A study proposal of no more than 300 words indicating the intended practice project and accompanying research
Closing Date: 31 September
Contributor: The Ashley Family Foundation
Additional Information: scholarship-positions.com/ashley-family-foundation-masters-scholarships-uk-2019/2013/08/14/

For further information contact:

Scholarships & Bursaries, SFS University of the Arts London, 272 High Holborn, Holborn, London WC1V 7EY, United Kingdom.

Tel: (44) 20 7514 8080
Email: funding@arts.ac.uk

Asian Cultural Council (ACC)

6 West 48th Street, 12th floor, New York, NY 10036-1802, United States of America.

Tel: (1) 2 524 5032, 2 524 5033/5024
Email: acc@accny.org
Website: www.asianculturalcouncil.org
Contact: Miho Walsh, Executive Director

The Asian Cultural Council (ACC) is a foundation that supports cultural exchange in the visual and performing arts between the United States and the countries of Asia. The emphasis of the ACC's programme is on providing individual fellowships to artists, scholars and specialists from Asia undertaking research, study and creative work in the United States. Grants are also made to United States citizens pursuing similar work in Asia.

Asian Cultural Council Humanities Fellowship Program

Purpose: To assist American scholars, graduate students and specialists in the humanities to undertake research, training and study in Asia
Eligibility: 1. All nationalities. Meeting AIT's English Proficiency Requirement (i.e. IELTS-Academic or AIT EET score of 5.0 or above for Master and 5.5 for Doctoral program). 3. Having four-year Bachelor's degree from a recognized university. 4. Having a master's degree from recognized university for PhD applicants and should have a Cumulative GPA of 3.50 in their Master's degree and 2.75 in their undergraduate program from top universities.
Level of Study: Graduate, Postdoctorate, Postgraduate, Predoctorate, Professional development, Research, Unrestricted
Type: Fellowship or Grant
Value: Varies
Length of Study: 1–9 months
Frequency: Annual
Country of Study: United States of America or other countries if appropriate
Application Procedure: Applicants should send a brief description of the activity for which assistance is being sought to the Council
No. of awards offered: 49 (Humanities Program only)
Closing Date: 10 June
Funding: Foundation, Government, Individuals, Private
Contributor: The JDR 3rd Fund and the Andrew W. Mellon Foundation
No. of awards given last year: 11 (Humanities Program only)
No. of applicants last year: 49 (Humanities Program only)
Additional Information: The programme also supports American and Asian scholars participating in international conferences, exhibitions, visiting professorships and similar projects. Please see the website for further details www.asianculturalcouncil.org.hk/en/app/information_and_deadline

For further information contact:

AIT Admissions Office.

Email: admissions@ait.ac.th

Graduate Scholarship

Subjects: Archaeology, Architecture, Art History, Arts Administration, Arts Criticism, Conservation, Crafts, Curation, Dance, Ethnomusicology, Film/Video/Photography, Literature, Museum Studies, Music, Theater, Visual Art
Level of Study: Graduate
Type: Scholarship
Length of Study: One year
Frequency: Annual
Country of Study: Any country
Closing Date: 1 March
Funding: Individuals

Associated General Contractors of America (AGC)

2300 Wilson Boulevard, Suite 300, Arlington, VA 22201, United States of America.

Tel: (1) 548 3118, 800 242 1767
Email: info@agc.org
Website: www.agc.org

The Associated General Contractors of America (AGC), the voice of the construction industry, is an organization of qualified construction contractors and industry-related companies dedicated to skill, integrity and responsibility. Operating in partnership with its chapters, the association provides a full range of services satisfying the needs and concerns of its members, thereby improving the quality of construction and protecting the public interest.

Associated General Contractors of America The Saul Horowitz, Jr. Memorial Graduate Award

Purpose: To provide financial assistance to students who wish to pursue higher studies
Eligibility: Open to applicants enroled or planning to enroll, in a Master's or Doctoral level construction or civil engineering programme as a full-time student

Level of Study: Doctorate, Postgraduate
Type: Scholarship
Value: US$7,500. Paid in 2 installments of US$3,750
Length of Study: Up to 5 years
Frequency: Annual
Country of Study: United States of America
Application Procedure: Applications will only be accepted online. Apply online at scholarship.agc.org. Applicants must send an email to foundation@agc.org
Closing Date: 1 November

Association for Canadian Studies in the United States

1317 F Street NW Suite 920, Washington, DC 20004-1151, United States of America.

Tel: (1) 202 393 2580
Email: info@acsus.org
Website: www.acsus.org
Contact: Publication Award Committee

Distinguished Dissertation Award

Purpose: To recognize the best dissertation successfully defended in the two years prior to the Biennial conference that deals substantially or wholly with some aspect of Canada or Canadian Studies
Eligibility: Doctoral dissertations written at Universities in the United States within the two years before the Biennial conference at which the award will be made
Level of Study: Doctorate
Type: Cash prize
Value: US$500 and expenses to attend the Biennial conference
Frequency: Every 2 years
Country of Study: United States of America
Application Procedure: The nomination must be accompanied by two letters of support, one from the student's dissertation advisor and one from a second referee. The advisor and referee need not be members of ACSUS. Supporting Materials. Each nomination should be accompanied by a copy of the dissertation, a dissertation abstract not to exceed 500 words (typed, double-spaced), and a one-page resume of the nominee. The successful nominee's dissertation should represent original work that makes a significant contribution to the nominee's discipline and to the study of Canada. The dissertation must contain at least 50% content on Canada; the topic may, however, be comparative in nature. The

dissertation will be judged on substantive and methodological quality, originality of thought, and clarity

No. of awards offered: 2
Closing Date: 1 August
Funding: Individuals
Contributor: Membership dues and royalties coming to the Association for Canadian Studies in the United States
No. of applicants last year: 2
Additional Information: www.acsus.org/programs/ distinguished-dissertation-award

For further information contact:

Email: info@acsus.org

Donner Medal in Canadian Studies

Purpose: The Donner Medal in Canadian Studies is presented biennially by The Association for Canadian Studies in the United States (ACSUS) for distinguished achievement, scholarship and program innovation in the area of Canadian Studies in the United States

Eligibility: The recipient is selected by a committee of members of the Association after nominations have been publicly solicited. Nominees can include a person in any field who has made a significant contribution to Canadian studies in the United States during a reasonable period of residence in the United States, even if no longer a resident. Current officers of ACSUS are ineligible for consideration. The primary criterion for selection is contribution to Canadian studies in the United States. The recipient shall have been active in and made contributions in at least one of the following categories teaching, scholarship, administration, public affairs

Level of Study: Doctorate
Type: Honorific
Frequency: Every 2 years
Country of Study: United States of America
No. of awards offered: 1
Closing Date: 1 March
Funding: Foundation, Government, Individuals
Contributor: Individual membership dues and royalties from publications; some government grants; Donner Foundation
No. of awards given last year: 1
No. of applicants last year: 1
Additional Information: www.acsus.org/programs/donner-medal

For further information contact:

Tel: (1) 716 645 8440
Fax: (1) 716 645 2166
Email: info@acsus.org

Association for Spina Bifida and Hydrocephalus (ASBAH)

ASBAH House, 42 Park Road, Peterborough, Cambridgeshire PE1 2UQ, United Kingdom.

Tel: (44) 1733 555 988, 0845 450 7755
Email: info@asbah.org
Website: www.mencap.org.uk
Contact: Rylance

The Association for Spina Bifida and Hydrocephalus (ASBAH) is a voluntary organization that works for people with spina bifida and hydrocephalus. The charity lobbies for improvements in legislation and provides advisory and support services to clients and their families or carers, in addition to supplying information to professionals and sponsoring medical, social and educational research.

Association for Spina Bifida and Hydrocephalus Research Grant

Purpose: To support research in an area directly related to spina bifida and/or hydrocephalus, and to explore ways of improving the quality of life for people with these conditions through medical, scientific, educational and social research

Eligibility: Applicants must be resident in the United Kingdom
Level of Study: Postgraduate
Value: Varies
Length of Study: Varies
Frequency: Dependent on funds available
Study Establishment: Varies
Country of Study: United Kingdom
Application Procedure: Applicants must make an initial enquiry to the Chief Executive. If the proposed research is considered to be interesting, the applicant will be asked to complete an application form. Applications must be submitted on time to the committees, which meet in February and September to October
No. of awards offered: 1
Closing Date: 1 August
Funding: Individuals, Private, Trusts
Contributor: Charitable donations
No. of awards given last year: 1
No. of applicants last year: 1
Additional Information: Award subjects: biology and life sciences; economics; medicine and surgery; social sciences; teacher training and education; theology and religious studies www.acsus.org/programs/donner-medal

Association of American Geographers (AAG)

1710 16th Street NW, Washington, DC 20009-3198, United States of America.

Tel: (1) 202 234 1450
Email: cmannozzi@aag.org
Website: www.aag.org
Contact: Dr Patricia Solis, Director of Outreach and Strategic Initiatives

The Association of American Geographers (AAG) is a non-profit organization founded in 1904 to advance professional studies in geography and to encourage the application of geographic research in business, education and government. The AAG was amalgamated with the American Society of Professional Geographers (ASPG).

Association of American Geographers NSF International Geographical Union Conference Travel Grants

Purpose: To provide Travel Grants to the IGU conference
Eligibility: All scientists employed by United States agencies, firms and academic institutions may apply for support. All grantees must be citizens or hold permanent residency in the United States of America, be registered for the main international congress or main regional conference even if their presentations are scheduled for a symposium or study group, and travel via a United States carrier in accordance with United States government regulations
Level of Study: Professional development
Type: Grant
Value: US$1,250 each to junior scholars, including graduate students and US$1,000 each to senior scholars
Frequency: Annual
Country of Study: As applicable
Application Procedure: Applications must be submitted digitally using the online application form provided in website
Closing Date: 31 May
Contributor: National Science Foundation
Additional Information: Please see the website for further details www.aag.org/cs/grantsawards/igutravel

For further information contact:

Email: psolis@aag.org

Visiting Geographical Scientist Program

Purpose: To stimulate interest in geography
Eligibility: To qualify for the program, at least one-half of the institutions hosting a visiting scientist during the academic year must have active chapters of Gamma Theta Upsilon (an active chapter is one that has reported initiates in the past 2 years)
Level of Study: Professional development
Type: Grant
Value: US$100 per institutional visit to each visiting scientist and will reimburse the visitor up to US$600 for travel costs to and from the area of the institutions visited
Frequency: Annual
Study Establishment: Institution with an active chapter of Gamma Theta Upsilon
Country of Study: United States of America
Application Procedure: Applicants must write to Oscar Laron, VGSP Coordinator, at the main organization address at olarson@aag.org
Closing Date: 31 December
Contributor: Gamma Theta Upsilon (GTU), the International Geographical Honor Society

For further information contact:

Email: olarson@aag.org

Association of Anaesthetists of Great Britain and Ireland

9 Bedford Square, London WC1B 3RA, United Kingdom.

Tel: (44) 20 7631 1650
Email: 100567.3364@compuserve.com
Website: www.ncl.ac.uk/2nanaes/aagbi.html
Contact: Honorary Secretary

The Association of Anaesthetists of Great Britain and Ireland encourages its members to participate in research to increase knowledge, to improve standards of anaesthesia and to enhance the standing of the speciality. It also aims to enable members to travel to centres of excellence throughout the world to increase their expertise in clinical work, teaching or research so that there may be benefit to members, trainees and patients at home.

Baxter Travelling Fellowships, Research Grants, Travel Grants

Eligibility: Open to members in any category of the Association
Level of Study: Unrestricted
Value: Up to £2,500 (Baxter Travelling Fellowship), up to £5,000 (Research Grants), up to £500 (Travel Grants)
Length of Study: Unspecified duration
Application Procedure: Application form is required
Additional Information: There are also special Travel Grants to Third World Countries. Travel Grants are not awarded for attendance at a meeting of a learned society, but may be considered for extensions of such a journey. They may be given for study or for assistance in undertaking an approved teaching tour. Recipients of Travel Fellowships are expected to prepare a report www.aag.org/vgsp

For further information contact:

Email: Education_Grants@baxter.com

Association of Clinical Pathologists

189 Dyke Road, East Sussex, Hove BN3 1TL, United Kingdom.

Tel: (44) 1273 775 700
Email: info@pathologists.org.uk
Website: www.pathologists.org.uk
Contact: Administrative Assistant

The Association of Clinical Pathologists promotes the practice of clinical pathology by running postgraduate education courses and national scientific meetings and has a membership of 2,000 worldwide.

Student Research Fund

Purpose: To encourage undergraduates to undertake some research within laboratory medicine, to raise the profile of laboratory medicine within the minds of undergraduates and to aid in recruitment of young graduates
Level of Study: Graduate
Type: Scholarship
Value: Up to £150 per week for a maximum of six weeks (Funding of a small project), £5,000 maximum (Financial sponsorship to help support living expenses during their extra undergraduate year), up to £1,000 (Funding for the cost of consumables). See the website for details
Frequency: Annual
Country of Study: Any country
Application Procedure: Applicants should complete the relevant application form, including a brief statement of not more than 400 words outlining their interest in laboratory medicine, and include a full curriculum vitae. Applications should include details of the work to be undertaken as part of the project or during the BSc and be supported in writing by the project supervisor, or by the Head of Department in which the student will be placed
No. of awards offered: 5
Closing Date: 12 April
Contributor: Association of Clinical Pathologists
No. of awards given last year: 3
No. of applicants last year: 5
Additional Information: Please return completed form by post to ACP Postgraduate Education Secretary, and also by email to mailto: rachel@pathologists.org.uk

For further information contact:

Email: rachel@pathologists.org.uk

Association of Flight Attendants

501 3rd Street NW, Washington, DC 20001, United States of America.

Association of Flight Attendants Annual Scholarship

Purpose: This award is for United States high school seniors who are dependents of an Association of Flight Attendants member. Students must rank in the top 15% of their class, and must have or expect to have excellent SAT and ACT scores
Eligibility: 1. Must be a graduating high school senior at time of application. 2. Must be a United States citizen. 3. Must be ranked in the top 15% of his/her high school class. 4. Must be the dependent of an Association of Flight Attendants member. 5. Must have, or expect to have, excellent SAT or ACT scores. 6. This award is for United States students
Level of Study: Graduate
Type: Scholarship
Value: US$5,000
Frequency: Annual
Country of Study: United States of America
Application Procedure: Apply online cdn.afacwa.org/docs/afa/afa-scholarship-application.pdf

Closing Date: 10 April
Funding: Foundation

For further information contact:

Email: scholarships@swe.org

Association of Management Development Institutions in South Asia (AMDISA)

Post Office Gachibowli, Hyderabad, Telangana 500 046, India.

Tel: (91) 40 64545226, 40 64543774
Email: amdisa@amdisa.org
Website: www.amdisa.org
Contact: Executive Director

Association of Management Development Institutions in South Asia (AMDISA) was established in 1988, with the initiative of leading management development institutions in the SAARC region. It is the only association that networks management development centres across 8 nations and promotes partnership between business schools, business leaders and policy administrators for enhancing the quality and effectiveness of management education in South Asia.

Association of Management Development Institutions in South Asia Doctoral Fellowships

Purpose: To contribute to the development of South Asian academic perspectives, networks and communities in management and related areas
Eligibility: Open to citizens of any South Asian Commonwealth member country who are registered PhD scholars in a recognized university and are not more than 40 years of age
Level of Study: Doctorate
Type: Fellowship
Value: £1,500–4,500
Country of Study: Commonwealth countries
Application Procedure: Applications must have the applicant's name and contact co-ordinates, proof of registration as PhD scholar, curriculum vitae with list of publications and confidential recommendation letters
Closing Date: 31 December

For further information contact:

Email: arifwaqif@amdisa.org

Association of Management Development Institutions in South Asia Postdoctoral Fellowship

Purpose: To provide financial and academic-institutional assistance to PhD scholars and younger academics
Eligibility: Open to citizens of South Asian Commonwealth member country, not older than 50 years, who hold a PhD degree in management or related disciplines and are employed as a full-time teacher/researcher
Level of Study: Postdoctorate
Type: Fellowship
Value: £1,500–4,500
Frequency: Annual
Application Procedure: The application must contain proof of registration as PhD scholar, a curriculum vitae with list of publications
Closing Date: 30 April

For further information contact:

Email: arifwaqif@amdisa.org

Association of perioperative Registered Nurses Foundation

2170 South Parker Road, Suite 300, Denver, CO 80231, United States of America.

Tel: (1) 800 755 2676
Email: ibendzsa@aorn.org
Website: www.aorn.org
Contact: Ms Ingrid Bendzsa, Executive assistant

The AORN Foundation is a charitable and educational foundation created in 1992 by the Association of Perioperative Registered Nurses. Its mission is to secure resources and administer assets that provide support for the aim of preparing a new generation of surgical nurses.

Association of perioperative Registered Nurses Scholarship Program

Purpose: The AORN Foundation supports your professional goals and helps you maintain evidence-based knowledge and competencies. We have awarded scholarships to more than 3,000 nurses working to earn a degree, achieve advanced certification, and complete continuing nurse education
Eligibility: Applicant must have been a member of AORN for 1 year and have a current licence to practice nursing

Level of Study: Doctorate
Type: Scholarship
Frequency: Annual
Study Establishment: Suitable accredited institution
Country of Study: United States of America
Application Procedure: Applicants must check the detailed guidelines on the website or obtain a copy from the Foundation's offices
Closing Date: 15 June
Additional Information: www.aorn.org/aorn-foundation/foundation-scholarships

For further information contact:

Email: foundation@aorn.org

Association of Surgeons of Great Britain and Ireland

Association of Surgeons of Great Britain and Ireland, 35-43 Lincoln's Inn Fields, London WC2A 3PE, United Kingdom.

Tel: (44) 20 7973 0300
Email: admin@asgbi.org.uk
Website: www.asgbi.org.uk

The founding objectives of the Association of Surgeons of Great Britain and Ireland, in 1920, were the advancement of the science and art of surgery and the promotion of friendship among surgeons. As other surgical specialities developed, the Association came to represent general surgery, encompassing breast, colorectal, endocrine, laparoscopic, transplant, upper gastrointestinal and vascular surgery.

Moynihan Travelling Fellowship

Purpose: To enable specialist registrars or consultants to broaden their education, and to present and discuss their contribution to British or Irish surgery overseas
Eligibility: Open to either specialist registrars approaching the end of their higher surgical training or consultants in general surgery within 5 years of appointment after the closing date for applications. Candidates must be nationals of and residents of the United Kingdom or the Republic of Ireland, but need not be Fellows or affiliate Fellows of the Association. They may be engaged in general surgery or a sub-speciality thereof
Level of Study: Postdoctorate
Type: Fellowship
Value: £5,000

Frequency: Annual
Country of Study: Any country
Application Procedure: Applicants must submit 12 copies of an application, which must include a full curriculum vitae giving details of past and present appointments and publications, a detailed account of the proposed programme of travel, costs involved and the object to be achieved. Applications must be addressed to the Honorary Secretary at the Association of Surgeons. For further details contact Bhavnita Borkhatria at bhavnita@asgbi.org.uk
No. of awards offered: 6
Closing Date: 28 September
Funding: Private
Contributor: Charitable association funds
No. of awards given last year: 1
No. of applicants last year: 6
Additional Information: Shortlisted candidates will be interviewed by the Scientific Committee of the Association, which will pay particular attention to the originality, scope and feasibility of the proposed itinerary. The successful candidate will be expected to act as an ambassador for British and Irish surgery and should therefore be fully acquainted with the aims and objectives of the Association of Surgeons and its role in surgery. After the completion of the fellowship, the successful candidate will be asked to address the Association at its annual general meeting and to provide a written report for inclusion in the Executive Newsletter. A critical appraisal of the centres visited should form the basis of the report. Please see the website for further details www.asgbi.org.uk/en/awards_fellowships/moynihan_travelling_fellowship.cfm

For further information contact:

Email: bhavnita@asgbi.org.uk

Association of Universities and Colleges of Canada (AUCC)

1710-350 Albert Street, Ottawa, ON K1R 1B1, Canada.

Tel: (1) 613 563 1236
Email: info@aucc.ca
Website: www.aucc.ca
Contact: Mr Paul Davidson, President and CEO

The AUCC is a non-profit, non-governmental association that represents Canadian universities at home and abroad. The Association's mandate is to foster and promote the interests of higher education in the firm belief that strong universities are vital to the prosperity and wellbeing of Canada.

Department of National Defence Postdoctoral Fellowships in Military History

Eligibility: Open to Canadian citizens or permanent residents who hold or will hold, prior to closing date of competition, a PhD degree or equivalent level of knowledge or experience in the field considered adequate by the Selection Committee
Level of Study: Postgraduate
Type: One fellowship
Value: C$24,000. Research expenses of up to C$1,500 may also be considered
Frequency: Annual
Study Establishment: for 1 year
Closing Date: 1 February
Additional Information: Fellows may not concurrently hold any other awards whose cumulative value exceeds two thirds of the value of the fellowship accepted under this program. Upon completion of the fellowship, a manuscript resulting from research done should be submitted to AUCC www.asgbi.org.uk/awards/moynihan-travelling-fellowship

For further information contact:

Fax: (1) 613 563 9745
Email: awards@aucc.ca

Aston University

Aston University, Aston Triangle, Birmingham B4 7ET, United Kingdom.

Tel: (44) 121 204 3000
Email: a.levey@aston.ac.uk
Website: www.aston.ac.uk
Contact: Alison Levey, Academic Registrar

Aston University is a long-established research – Centre for Executive Development (CED) university. It is known for its world-class teaching quality, strong links to industry, government & commerce, and its friendly and safe campus environment. Aston University is consistently featured in the top 30 universities in the country.

Aston Dean

Purpose: To encourage students to pursue a PhD programme on a full-time basis
Eligibility: Scholarships are open to Home/European Union and Overseas applicants

Level of Study: Doctorate
Type: Scholarship
Value: £17,000 stipend and full fee waives
Length of Study: 3 years
Frequency: Annual
Country of Study: Any country
Application Procedure: Complete the online application form for entry to the programme www.aston.ac.uk/study/postgraduate/apply/
Closing Date: August
No. of awards given last year: 7

Computer Science Scholarship

Purpose: UK/EU students applying to study the Aston Masters MSc Computer Science.
Eligibility: 1. UK/EU citizen. 2. You must meet the entry requirements for MSc Computer Science. 3. Minimum three years' work experience.
Level of Study: Postgraduate
Type: Scholarship
Value: £2,500
Application Procedure: There is no need to submit a scholarship application as you will be assessed for the scholarship when you applly for the course. You must complete the work experience section of the course application form for us to be able to assess your eligiblity.
Additional Information: www.aston.ac.uk/scholarships/stem-scholarship

Ferguson Scholarships

Purpose: The School of Life & Health Sciences is offering 9 scholarships of £15,000 to students from Africa and South America
Eligibility: 1. Hold a conditional or unconditional offer for one of the above courses 2. Be a national from an African or South American country 3. Hold a 21 degree or equivalent in a relevant subject for the course you are applying for 4. Be a self-funded student 5. Provide a strong personal statement when submitting your course application.
Level of Study: Postgraduate (MSc)
Type: Scholarship
Value: £10,500
Frequency: As available
Study Establishment: Aston University
Country of Study: United Kingdom
Application Procedure: If you wish to be considered for one of these scholarships and you meet the above eligibility criteria you will need to 1. Submit an application for your chosen course via our online application form before the

scholarship deadline (please see below). 2. Following this, you will be required to register your interest for the scholarship

Closing Date: 30 April
Funding: Trusts
Contributor: Allan and Nesta Ferguson Charitable Trust
Additional Information: www.aston.ac.uk/study/postgraduate/taught-programmes/life-health-sciences/fees-financial-support/ferguson-scholarships

For further information contact:

Email: b.koner@aston.ac.uk

Global Excellence Scholarship

Purpose: Aston University welcomes students from over 120 different countries every year to study with us. Located in the centre of Birmingham, the UK's second largest city with one of Europe's youngest populations, Aston University is a dynamic centre of learning in a dynamic city. We are committed to offering the highest quality of teaching, based on cutting-edge research, and aim to give our students the skills and knowledge they need to make a success of their future career. In order to support the best students to study at Aston University we are delighted to offer the Global Excellence Scholarship.
Eligibility: 1. You must hold a conditional or unconditional offer for one of the above courses 2. Be a national from India or an African country 3. Hold a 2:1 degree or equivalent in a relevant subject for the course you are applying for 4. Provide a strong personal statement when submitting your course application 5. Be a self-funded student
Level of Study: Graduate, Postgraduate
Type: Scholarship
Value: £10,500
Frequency: As available
Study Establishment: Aston University
Country of Study: United Kingdom
Application Procedure: 1. Submit an application for your chosen course via our online application form at the bottom of this page before the scholarship deadline (please see below). 2. Next, register your interest for the scholarship by filling in the online form below. 3. Applications for this scholarship close 30th April 2022.
No. of awards offered: 7
Closing Date: 30 April
Funding: International office

For further information contact:

Email: b.koner@aston.ac.uk

Master of Business Administration Global Ambassador Scholarship

Purpose: Aston University has a proud network of Global Ambassadors, made up of international students who share their story and experience of studying at Aston with others around the world. Global Ambassadors represent Aston University in many different ways, such as attending events and Open Days, making videos and posting on social media, and speaking to people about what life is like as an international student at Aston.
Eligibility: MBA Global Ambassador Scholarship recipients will be awarded on merit to well-qualified applicants applying to study the MBA programme starting in January
Level of Study: MBA
Type: Scholarship
Value: £3,000
Length of Study: 1 year
Frequency: As available
Study Establishment: Aston Business School
Country of Study: United Kingdom
Closing Date: 31 March
Funding: International office
Contributor: Aston University
Additional Information: www.aston.ac.uk/scholarships

For further information contact:

Aston Business School, Aston University, Aston St, Birmingham B4 7ET, United Kingdom.

Email: ask@aston.ac.uk

Postgraduate Scholarships (ABS)

Purpose: To assist students with tuition fees
Eligibility: There are different eligibility criteria for each MSc scholarship. Please check website for complete and clear information
Level of Study: MBA, Postgraduate
Value: £1,000–5,000
Frequency: Annual
Study Establishment: Aston University
Country of Study: United Kingdom
Application Procedure: In order to be eligible to apply for a scholarship, candidates must hold an offer of a place. Notification of awards will be made at the end of July
Funding: International office
Additional Information: There are many MSc scholarships as well as Aston award scholarships www.aston.ac.uk/scholarships

For further information contact:

Email: apply@aston.ac.uk

School of Languages & Social Studies PhD Bursaries

Purpose: Financial support for PhD study
Level of Study: Doctorate
Value: Combination of fees only and fees plus maintenance offered
Length of Study: 3 years, full-time
Frequency: Annual
Study Establishment: Aston University
Country of Study: United Kingdom
Application Procedure: Please visit www.aston.ac.uk/study/postgraduate/apply/
No. of awards offered: 9
Closing Date: 29 February
No. of awards given last year: 4
No. of applicants last year: 9
Additional Information: Open to all nationals of any country; however, the bursaries only cover the HOME/European Union fees rate. Therefore those classified as overseas must pay the difference between the HOME and overseas fees rates www.aston.ac.uk/scholarships

For further information contact:

Email: apply@aston.ac.uk

School of Life and Health Sciences Postgraduate Masters Scholarships – Commonwealth Shared Scholarship Scheme

Purpose: These scholarships are for students from developing Commonwealth countries who would not otherwise be able to study in the United Kingdom
Eligibility: Applicants must hold an offer for MSc in molecular toxicology or MSc in psychology of health and illness; must hold an undergraduate Bachelor's degree at either First/Upper Second class or equivalent (work experience cannot be accepted as an alternative); must be a national of an eligible Commonwealth country and permanently living in that country; must have the minimum English language requirement for the programme as no funding will be given for pre-sessional language programmes; must not have studied for 1 year or more in a developed country previously; must not be employed by a national government or an organisation owned or part-owned by the government (parastatal organisation) – higher education institutions are exempted from this restriction
Level of Study: Postgraduate
Type: Scholarship

Value: These are fully funded scholarships and include living stipend
Frequency: Annual
Study Establishment: Aston University
Country of Study: Any country
Application Procedure: Application form is available on the website
No. of awards offered: 16
Closing Date: 18 December
No. of awards given last year: 2
No. of applicants last year: 16
Additional Information: cscuk.dfid.gov.uk/apply/shared-scholarships/

For further information contact:

Commonwealth Scholarship Commission in the UK, Woburn House 20-24 Tavistock Square, London WC1H 9HF, United Kingdom.

Tel: (44) 207 380 6700
Email: c.m.hoban@aston.ac.uk

Vice-Chancellor's International Scholarship

Purpose: We are committed to offering the highest quality of teaching, based on cutting-edge research, and we aim to give our students the skills and knowledge they need to achieve career success.
Eligibility: International students from any country outside of the European Union can apply. This scholarship is available for applicants applying to all foundation, undergraduate and postgraduate programmes (except the MBChB in Medicine)
Level of Study: Postgraduate
Type: One scholarship
Value: £8,000
Frequency: As available
Study Establishment: Aston University
Country of Study: United Kingdom
Funding: International office

For further information contact:

Email: ask@aston.ac.uk

Ataxia United Kingdom

Lincoln House, Kennington Park, 1-3 Brixton Road, London SW9 6DE, United Kingdom.

Tel: (44) 20 7582 1444
Email: research@ataxia.org.uk

Website: www.ataxia.org.uk
Contact: Mrs Julie Greenfield, Research Projects Manager

Ataxia United Kingdom is the leading charity in the United Kingdom working with and for people with ataxia. It will support research projects and related activities in order to enhance scientific understanding of ataxia, develop and evaluate therapeutic and supportive strategies and encourage wider involvement with ataxia research.

Ataxia United Kingdom PhD Studentship

Purpose: To further research into causes of and treatments for progressive ataxias
Eligibility: Proposals are accepted from academic institutions, private sector research companies and suitably qualified individuals. There are no restrictions on age, nationality or residency
Level of Study: Postgraduate
Type: Studentship
Value: £5,000
Length of Study: Varies
Frequency: Annual, if funds are available
Country of Study: Any country
Application Procedure: Applicants must complete an application form available from Ataxia United Kingdom Research Projects Manager at research@ataxia.org.uk
No. of awards offered: 3
Closing Date: 1 June
Funding: Commercial, Individuals, Private, Trusts
No. of applicants last year: 3
Additional Information: There are a number of priority areas of research and these can be obtained from the Research Projects Manager www.ataxia.org.uk/News/apply-for-funding

Ataxia United Kingdom Research Grant

Purpose: To further research into causes of and treatments for progressive ataxias
Eligibility: Proposals are accepted from academic institutions, private sector research companies and suitably qualified individuals. There are no restrictions on age, nationality or residency
Level of Study: Unrestricted
Type: Project grant
Value: Varies
Length of Study: Varies
Frequency: Dependent on funds available
Country of Study: Any country

Application Procedure: Applicants must complete an application form available from Ataxia's Research Projects Manager at research@ataxia.org.uk
No. of awards offered: 16
Funding: Commercial, Individuals, Private, Trusts
No. of awards given last year: 1
No. of applicants last year: 16
Additional Information: There are a number of priority areas of research and these can be obtained from the Research Projects Manager www.ataxia.org.uk/News/apply-for-funding

Ataxia United Kingdom Travel Grant

Purpose: To enable researchers to present their ataxia research at national and international conferences
Eligibility: Proposals are accepted from academic institutions, private sector research companies and suitably qualified individuals. There are no restrictions on age, nationality or residency, although preference will be given to events which could potentially benefit patients and researchers in the United Kingdom or Europe
Level of Study: Unrestricted
Type: Travel grant
Value: Dependent on the conference
Length of Study: Varies
Frequency: Dependent on funds available
Country of Study: Any country
Application Procedure: Applicants must complete an application form available from Ataxia's Research Projects Manager at research@ataxia.org.uk
Funding: Commercial, Individuals, Private, Trusts
Additional Information: There are a number of priority areas of research and these can be obtained from the Research Projects Manager www.ataxia.org.uk/News/apply-for-funding

Athens State University

300 North Beaty Street, Athens, AL 35611, United States of America.

Website: www.athens.edu
Contact: Ms Helen Marks, Secretary, Financial Aid

Athens State University Phi Theta Kappa Transfer Scholarship

Purpose: This scholarship is in the form of a tuition waiver only and will not pay in combination with any other ASU institutional scholarship

Eligibility: 1. Must be a new entering student with a minimum of 36 transfer credit hours and plan to enroll immediately in Athens State University in Alabama after completion of coursework at the two-year college level. 2. Students must not have more than six hours of coursework attempted at ASU by the end of the spring term of application year
Level of Study: Graduate
Type: Scholarship
Frequency: Annual
Country of Study: United States of America
Application Procedure: 1. Applications are available online at the Athens State University (ASU) website. 2. The student must submit a complete ASU application form, official transcripts from all prior colleges, two letters of recommendation from faculty members at transfer institutions, a letter verifying membership in Phi Theta Kappa from an adviser at transfer institution, and an essay outlining why the student feels he/she is deserving of the scholarship. 3. The student must submit his/her application to Student Financial Services before 4.30 p.m. EST by the deadline date
Closing Date: 31 March
Funding: Private
Additional Information: www.unigo.com/scholarships/by-state/alabama-scholarships/athens-state-university-phi-theta-kappa-transfer-scholarship/1000707

For further information contact:

Email: sarah.mcabee@athens.edu

Auckland Medical Research Foundation

89 Grafton Road, Grafton, Auckland 1010, New Zealand.

Tel: (64) 9 307 2886
Contact: Secretary

Auckland Medical Research Foundation Travel Grant

Purpose: To allow staff engaged in or associated with research projects to travel for a specific purpose
Eligibility: Open normally, but not exclusively, to staff associated with the Auckland Area Health Board, the School of Medicine in the University of Auckland, or to recipients of other grants from the Foundation. There are no requirements as to age, sex or citizenship
Level of Study: Postgraduate

Type: Varies
Value: Varies
Study Establishment: as approved
Country of Study: Any country
Additional Information: www.medicalresearch.org.nz/how-to-apply

For further information contact:

Email: amrf@medicalresearch.org.nz

Auckland University of Technology University of Technology

55 Wellesley Street, Auckland 1010, New Zealand.

Contact: Auckland University of Technology

Auckland University of Technology (AUT) is a university in New Zealand. It has five faculties across three campuses in Auckland: City, North, and South campuses, and an additional three specialist locations: AUT Millennium, Warkworth Radio Astronomical Observatory and AUT Centre for Refugee Education.

Access & Rural Women New Zealand Scholarship

Purpose: This is a scholarship for a health worker who wishes to further his/her studies in the health and/or disability fields, with a particular focus on the provision of services to the rural sector
Type: Scholarship
Value: NZ$3,000
Length of Study: 1 year
Country of Study: Any country
Application Procedure: For application procedure, please visit website www.aut.ac.nz/study/fees-and-scholarships/scholarships-and-awards-at-aut/scholarships-database/detailpage?detailCode=802935&sessionID=27587614&sourceIP=&X_FORWARDED_FOR=
Closing Date: 1 July
Additional Information: For guidelines, application forms and more information about this award contact: Rural Women New Zealand, PO Box 12-021 Wellington, New Zealand; Email: enquiries@ruralwomen.org.nz www.aut.ac.nz/study/fees-and-scholarships/scholarships-and-awards-at-aut/scholarships-database/alphapage?letter=A&sessionID=34556024&sourceIP=&X_FORWARDED_FOR=

For further information contact:

Email: enquiries@ruralwomen.org.nz

Auckland University of Technology and Cyclone Computers Laptop and Tablet Scholarship

Purpose: The primary objectives of this award are to enhance the student learning experience and to increase study options for undergraduate and postgraduate students through the laptop scholarship programme
Type: Scholarship
Value: HP Elitebook or HP Elite X2 1,012 G2or AUT Optn A Macbook (A&D only)or devices of similar specification
Country of Study: Any country
Closing Date: 1 July
Additional Information: For guidelines, application forms and more information about this award contact: Auckland University of Technology, Phone: (64) 9 921 9837, Email: scholars@aut.ac.nz www.aut.ac.nz/study/fees-and-scholarships/scholarships-and-awards-at-aut/scholarships-database/detailpage?detailCode=501009&sessionID=285 45165&sourceIP=&X_FORWARDED_FOR=

For further information contact:

Email: scholars@aut.ac.nz

Auckland University of Technology Master of Human Rights Scholarship

Purpose: The purpose of this scholarship is to encourage and stimulate full-time students into the Master Human Rights, AUT will offer two AUT Master of Human Rights Scholarships to applicants wishing to enroll full-time into this Masters programme
Eligibility: IELTS (Academic) 6.5 overall with all bands 6.0 or higher; or equivalent
Type: Scholarship
Length of Study: 1 year full-time
Frequency: Annual
Country of Study: Any country
Closing Date: 13 July
Additional Information: www.aut.ac.nz/study/study-options/social-sciences-and-public-policy/courses/master-of-human-rights

For further information contact:

Tel: (64) 9 921 9999
Email: contact@studyspy.ac.nz

Auckland University of Technology Post Graduate Scholarships

Purpose: Auckland University of Technology offers AUT Postgraduate Scholarships - Equity (Maori and Pacific) to Maori and Pacific students for postgraduate study at AUT. UT Postgraduate Scholarship (coursework) is available to full-time students undertaking study at Level 8 or above (New Zealand Qualifications Framework) who have demonstrated the potential to achieve highly
Eligibility: Applicants must complete the online application available through the AUT Scholarships Database www.aut.ac.nz/scholarships. Applications will be open from 5 April
Level of Study: Postgraduate
Type: Scholarship
Value: Domestic full fees for 120pts
Length of Study: The scholarship is normally awarded for 12 months of full time study only
Frequency: Annual
Country of Study: New Zealand
Application Procedure: Application is through the AUT online scholarship portal accessed from the link above. Applications will open in October of the year preceding study for Semester 1 study or May for study in Semester 2. The following documentation must be received on or before the closing date. A one-page personal statement outlining the applicant's academic goals and career aspirations stating why they believe they merit the scholarship and provide an outline of their Maori or Pacific cultural involvement. The personal statement should also attach an outline of recent leadership positions or responsibilities held within the University or community. A copy of the applicant's transcript will be added to the application by the Scholarships Office once grades have been finalized
Closing Date: 15 June
Additional Information: For guidelines, application forms and more information about this award contact: Auckland University of Technology; Phone: (64) 9 921 9837; Email: scholars@aut.ac.nz www.auckland.ac.nz/en/study/scholarships-and-awards/scholarship-types/postgraduate-scholarships.html

For further information contact:

Email: stefania.patrone@aut.ac.nz

Auckland University of Technology Vice Chancellor Doctoral Scholarship

Purpose: Auckland University of Technology (AUT) awards scholarships to high achieving candidates applying to an approved doctoral programme at AUT

Type: Scholarship
Value: Tuition fees (at the domestic rate) plus the compulsory student services fee; and an annual stipend of NZ$25,000 per annum
Length of Study: The scholarship is tenable for up to 3 years
Country of Study: New Zealand
Application Procedure: Applicants must meet the normal admission criteria for the doctoral programme. www.aut.ac.nz/study-at-aut/entry-requirements/postgraduate-and-graduate-admission-requirements
Closing Date: 15 January
Additional Information: www.aut.ac.nz/study/fees-and-scholarships/scholarships-and-awards-at-aut/scholarships-database/detailpage?detailCode=803262&sessionID=28550450&sourceIP=&X_FORWARDED_FOR=

For further information contact:

Tel: (64) 9 921 9837
Email: scholars@aut.ac.nz

AUT Doctoral Scholarships

Purpose: Auckland University of Technology (AUT) awards scholarships to high achieving candidates applying to an approved doctoral programme at AUT. AUT offers AUT Doctoral Scholarships in order to attract highly achieving doctoral research students to AUT and to encourage and stimulate doctoral studies in areas that enhance the University's research capability.
Eligibility: Applicants must meet English language proficiency requirements as stated in the Academic Calendar at the time of application. Applicants must meet the normal admission criteria for the doctoral programme. Recipients of this scholarship will have excellent academic record, strong academic references and have demonstrated the potential for high quality research.
Type: Scholarship
Value: NZ$25,000
Length of Study: 2 year
Country of Study: New Zealand
Application Procedure: In order for the application to be submitted applicants must complete all sections and request the required support statements. Incomplete applications will not be forwarded to the selection panel. The following documents or statements will need to be uploaded and submitted with the AUT Doctoral Scholarship On-line Application Form. Academic transcript(s) for any previous tertiary study that was completed at a university other than AUT. A brief C.V. (maximum three pages).
No. of awards offered: Various
Closing Date: 1 November

Additional Information: www.studyinnewzealand.govt.nz/how-to-apply/scholarship/details?scholarshipid=128068&institutionid=142314

Awarua Trust Scholarship

Purpose: To provide financial support to people in their pursuit of excellence
Value: Up to NZ$2,000 (or more by approval)
Length of Study: One year
Country of Study: Any country
Closing Date: 30 June
Contributor: The Awarua Trust
Additional Information: For guidelines, application forms and more information about this award contact: Gavin Haddon, (CA) trustee, The Awarua Trust, PO Box 388, Email: info@awaruatrust.org.nz www.awaruatrust.org.nz/page/scholarship-applications/

For further information contact:

Email: info@awaruatrust.org.nz

Betty Loughhead Soroptimist Scholarship Trust

Purpose: This scholarship provides financial support to women over the age of 25 who are studying to gain a further qualification to advance a careers in business, the professions, the arts
Value: NZ$3,000–NZ$5,000 (per award)
Country of Study: Any country
Application Procedure: Please ensure you provide 6 clean collated (stapled) copies (one for each trustee) of your application and references. Emailed applications cannot be accepted (and will not be considered).
Closing Date: 30 August
Additional Information: For guidelines, application forms and more information about this award contact: Hayley Denoual, Secretary, The Betty Loughhead Soroptimist Scholarship Trust, BLSST Secretary Sarnia, 52 Raukawa Street Strathmore Park, New Zealand; Phone: 04 388 2115; Email: retary@blsst.co.nz www.blsst.co.nz/

For further information contact:

BLSST Secretary Sarnia, 52 Raukawa Street Strathmore Park, New Zealand.

Email: secretary@blsst.co.nz

Business, Economics & Law Postgraduate Academic Excellence Scholarship

Purpose: The purpose of the Business, Economics and Law Postgraduate Academic Excellence Scholarship is to encourage students with an excellent academic record to undertake postgraduate research in the Faculty of Business and Law

Eligibility: Applicants for this scholarship must complete an AUT Application for Enrolment (AFE) for the Bachelor of Business (Honours), the Master of Laws, the Master of Business or the Master of Philosophy

Type: Scholarship

Value: Tuition fees (up to 120 pts) and student levies

Frequency: Annual

Country of Study: New Zealand

Application Procedure: Application for this scholarship is via our AUT online scholarship application portal

No. of awards offered: 2

Closing Date: 1 June

Additional Information: For guidelines, application forms and more information about this award contact: Auckland University of Technology; Phone: (64) 9 921 9837; Email: scholars@aut.ac.nz scholarshipdb.net/scholarships-in-New-Zealand/Business-Economics-Law-Postgraduate-Academic-Excellence-Scholarship-Auckland-University-Of-Technology=C7FaW0Jq6BGUVQAlkGUTnw.html

For further information contact:

Tel: (64) 9 921 9837
Email: scholars@aut.ac.nz

Colab PhD/MPhil Fees Scholarship

Purpose: Colab is the collaboratory for Design and Creative Technologies at the Auckland University of Technology (AUT), New Zealand. Our aim is to encourage researchers, students and stakeholders to imagine, construct, articulate and navigate rapidly changing social, economic, technological and career environments. To support innovative interdisciplinary research that reflects Colab's future focused aspirations in such areas as gaming, entrepreneurship, smart materials, wearable tech, making and digital civics Colab will offer fees scholarships for the doctoral programme and domestic equivalent fees Scholarships for the MPhil ptogramme

Type: Scholarship

Value: Full fees-PHD Domestic equivalent fees - MPhil

Length of Study: Up to 3 years for a PhD programme but will be reviewed annually

Country of Study: New Zealand

Closing Date: 14 December

Additional Information: For guidelines, application forms and more information about this award contact: Auckland University of Technology, Phone: (64) 9 921 9837, Email: scholars@aut.ac.nz studyspy.ac.nz/scholarships/10389/colab-phd-mphil-fees-scholarship

For further information contact:

Email: scholars@aut.ac.nz

Discrete Cosine Transform Mâori and Pacific Mature Student Doctoral Scholarship

Purpose: This scholarship is intended to provide support for Doctoral study completion, to Mâori and Pacific Island students who choose to undertake Doctoral studies later in life and who are making good progress towards PhD studies

Eligibility: All students nominated for this scholarship must be 1. Of Maori and/or Pacific Island descent, and be NZ Citizens or permanent residents (Note Pacific Island descent relates to one of the following Pacific countries, Cook Islands, Fiji, Kiribati, Nauru, Niue) Nominated by their PhD supervisor. Able to present a solid case for the scholarship to be awarded to them

Type: Scholarship

Value: An annual NZ$25,000 stipend, tuition fees

Length of Study: 2 years

Country of Study: New Zealand

Closing Date: 1 December

Additional Information: For guidelines, application forms and more information about this award contact: Auckland University of Technology, Phone: (64) 9 921 9837, Email: scholars@aut.ac.nz www.academicgates.com/job/detail/9d956ecd-e996-423f-b4af-e1348d5a15bb

For further information contact:

Email: scholars@aut.ac.nz

Doctoral Fee Scholarships (Art & Design)

Purpose: The Doctoral Fee Scholarship (Art & Design) is offered to PhD candidates to nurture and support the research culture of the School of Art & Design

Value: Tuition fee and learner services levy

Length of Study: Up to three years

Country of Study: Any country

Application Procedure: For application procedure, please visit website www.aut.ac.nz/study/fees-and-scholarships/scholarships-and-awards-at-aut/scholarships-database/detail page?detailCode=501191&sessionID=27587614&sourceIP=&X_FORWARDED_FOR=

No. of awards offered: Varies
Closing Date: 1 November
Additional Information: For guidelines, application forms and more information about this award contact: Auckland University of Technology; Phone: (64) 9 921 9837; Email: scholars@aut.ac.nz scholarshipdb.net/scholarships-in-New-Zealand/Aut-Doctoral-Scholarships-School-Of-Art-And-Design-Fees-Auckland-University-Of-Technology=RTdvIe6n6RGUWgAlkGUTnw.html

For further information contact:

Tel: (64) 9 921 9837
Email: scholars@aut.ac.nz

Fulbright New Zealand General Graduate Awards

Purpose: Fulbright New Zealand General Graduate Awards are for promising New Zealand graduate students to undertake postgraduate study or research at United States institutions in any field
Eligibility: To be eligible, you must: 1. have achieved 480 points, which must include a completed undergraduate degree. Fulbright New Zealand will also accept applications from candidates who were granted direct entry into the second year of a degree programme, therefore completing a 480-point degree with 360 points. 2. In exceptional circumstances, Fulbright New Zealand may consider the application of a student with a 360-point degree provided they have both: a. the strong support of their tertiary institution (from a Dean or member of senior management); and b.a conditional offer from a US institution; 3. not yet hold a doctoral degree; 4. plan to undertake full-time postgraduate study or research at a US institution for a period of at least six months; and 5. meet the citizenship requirements for this award.
Type: Award
Value: US$40,000
Length of Study: 6-12 months
Frequency: Annual
Country of Study: Any country
Application Procedure: For online application, please visit website apply.embark.com/student/fulbright/international/20/
No. of awards offered: 8
Closing Date: 1 August
Additional Information: For guidelines, application forms and more information about this award contact: Shauna Mendez, Programme Manager, Fulbright New Zealand, PO Box 3465, Level 8, 120 Featherston Street, 6140 Wellington, New Zealand; Phone: (64) 4 494 1500; Email: shauna@fulbright.org.nz www.aut.ac.nz/study/fees-and-scholarships/scholarships-and-awards-at-aut/scholarships-

database/detailpage?detailCode=100207&sessionID=34546231&sourceIP=&X_FORWARDED_FOR=

For further information contact:

Email: magnolia@fulbright.org.nz

Kate Edger Educational Charitable Trust - Expenses / Class Materials Awards

Purpose: The main purpose of these awards is to assist women, who are studying undergraduate or post graduate degree or diploma courses which incur high materials' expenditure, with payment of essential costs
Type: Grant
Value: NZ$300–NZ$1,000 each
Length of Study: Each Expenses/Class Materials
Frequency: Annual
Country of Study: New Zealand
Application Procedure: Application forms for these awards are available from www.academicdresshire.co.nz/Academic+Awards+Available/Postgraduate+Awards.html
Closing Date: 16 March
Additional Information: For guidelines, application forms and more information about this award contact: Kate Edger Educational Charitable Trust, Private Bag 93208 Parnell, Email: enquiries@kateedgertrust.org.nz www.aut.ac.nz/study/fees-and-scholarships/scholarships-and-awards-at-aut/scholarships-database/detailpage?detailCode=500559&sessionID=34546231&sourceIP=&X_FORWARDED_FOR=

For further information contact:

Kate Edger Educational Charitable Trust, Private Bag 93208, Parnell, New Zealand.

Tel: (64) 9 358 1044
Email: awards@kateedgertrust.org.nz

Master of Arts Scholarship in Applied Language Studies or Professional Language Studies

Purpose: The purpose of this scholarship is to encourage and support postgraduate study in the area of Language Teaching or Applied Language Study AUT's language and culture programmes focus on language in its widest sense
Eligibility: Applicants must 1. Be new students enrolling full-time into the Master of Professional Language Studies (Language Teaching) or the Master of Arts in Applied Language Studies. Applicants who have not applied for admission to the master's programme should commence this

process as well. Information about these programmes is available from www.aut.ac.nz/study-at-aut/study-areas/language-culture/postgraduate-study/. 2. Have demonstrated academic excellence in past tertiary study
Type: Scholarship
Value: NZ$8,000 towards fees
Length of Study: One year of full-time study only
Country of Study: New Zealand
Application Procedure: Information about these programmes is available from www.aut.ac.nz/study-at-aut/study-areas/language-culture/postgraduate-study/
Closing Date: September
Additional Information: For guidelines, application forms and more information about this award contact: Auckland University of Technology, Phone: +64 9 921 9837 www.aut.ac.nz/study/study-options/language-and-culture

For further information contact:

Auckland University of Technology, 55 Wellesley Street East, Auckland CBD, Auckland 1010, New Zealand.

Tel: (64) 9 921 9837
Email: scholars@aut.ac.nz

Master of Cultural & Creative Practice Scholarships (Art & Design)

Purpose: The Master of Cultural & Creative Practice (MCCP) is a one and a half year (full-time) taught degree aimed at developing expertise in cultural expression. Mixing live projects with coursework you can tailor your journey, choose to specialise or develop your existing skills and experience in a diverse array of subjects, for example; Arts Management, Cultural Production, Curatorial Practices, the Interarts, Interactive and Mixed Reality, Heritage Promotion and Cultural and Creative Production. Implementing creative strategies, whilst continuing to develop expertise related to your chosen field, you will contribute to a vibrant creative community critiquing notions of leadership and entrepreneurship in the cultural and creative sector. Considerate of cultural and ethical issues and their implications when working across cultural, social, and historical contexts you will be thoughtful and respectful in your research and production. Creative thinking will empower your decision-making and inform your professional encounters.
Type: Scholarship
Value: Tuition fees and learner services levy for the MCCP programme of study
Length of Study: The tenure of this scholarship is for up to three semesters of full-time study in the Master of Cultural & Creative Practice programme of study (180 points)

Country of Study: New Zealand
Application Procedure: For details, please visit website www.aut.ac.nz/study/fees-and-scholarships/scholarships-and-awards-at-aut/scholarships-database/detailpage?detailCode=501192&sessionID=27587614&sourceIP=&X_FORWARDED_FOR=
Closing Date: 1 June
Additional Information: For guidelines, application forms and more information about this award contact: Auckland University of Technology; Phone: (64) 9 921 9837; Email: scholars@aut.ac.nz www.aut.ac.nz/study/fees-and-scholarships/scholarships-and-awards-at-aut/scholarships-database/detailpage?detailCode=501192&sessionID=275876 14&sourceIP=&X_FORWARDED_FOR=

For further information contact:

Tel: (64) 800 288 864
Email: pgartdes@aut.ac.nz

Master of Professional Language Studies (Language Teaching) Scholarships

Purpose: The purpose of this scholarship is to encourage and support postgraduate study in the area of language teaching. The scholarship is open to domestic students only
Type: Scholarship
Value: Full fees and student levies up to 120 points of study
Length of Study: 1 year full-time / part-time available
Country of Study: Any country
Application Procedure: Applications are available from www.aut.ac.nz/study-at-aut/study-areas/language-culture/postgraduate-study/master-of-professional-language-studies—language-teaching
Closing Date: 13 July
Additional Information: www.aut.ac.nz/study/study-options/language-and-culture/courses/master-of-professional-language-studies-language-teaching

For further information contact:

Email: cdsouza@aut.ac.nz

Ministry of Primary Industries/National Institute of Water and Atmospheric Research Masters Scholarships in Quantitative Fisheries Science

Purpose: To attract high performing New Zealand students into quantitative marine science; to encourage postgraduate students to contribute to priority research areas identified by the New Zealand Government; to train students at the postgraduate level by sharing and using the combined expertise of university academics, MPI and practising NIWA scientists; and to facilitate the professional development of postgraduate students by exposure to an applied commercial research environment

Eligibility: 1. Applicants need to be New Zealand citizens or permanent residents. 2. Study must be undertaken within New Zealand (with the possibility of some course work being undertaken through an Australian university). 3. You must be eligible to undertake an MSc at any New Zealand university. 4. You must undertake full-time study. 5. A suitable university supervisor and NIWA or Fisheries New Zealand technical advisor must be agreed prior to stage 2 of the application (organising a potential University supervisor is desirable but not necessary for stage 1). 6. There are no age restrictions. 7. Study must commence within 6 months of receiving this scholarship. 8. You may hold other scholarships but these must be disclosed to Fisheries New Zealand. Students are encouraged to apply for additional scholarships that cover the payment of fees.

Value: US$20,000

Length of Study: 2 years

Country of Study: Any country

Application Procedure: Application has to be processed using the link www.victoria.ac.nz/study/student-finance/scholarships

Closing Date: 7 December

Additional Information: niwa.co.nz/education-and-training/scholarships

For further information contact:

Email: science.officer@mpi.govt.nz

Peace and Disarmament Education Trust (PADET)

Purpose: The purpose of PADET is to advance education and promote international peace, arms control and disarmament. PADET funds not-for-profit projects and scholarship topics that support these objectives

Type: Scholarship

Value: Scholarships are awarded in two categories, depending on the individual's circumstances Up to NZ$14,000 for a full year's work is available for a Master's research thesis scholarship; up to NZ$21,000, plus up to NZ$5,000 for tuition fees, per year for up to three years is available for a PhD doctoral thesis scholarship

Length of Study: One year for a master

Country of Study: Any country

Closing Date: 29 July

For further information contact:

Trust Advisor, Dept of Internal Affairs, PO Box 805, Wellington 6140, New Zealand.

Tel: (64) 800 824 824
Email: community.matters@dia.govt.nz

Resource Management Law Association of New Zealand Masters Scholarship

Subjects: Masters Scholarship

Purpose: To encourage graduate students studying law, planning, engineering, geography, science, landscape architecture, urban planning and resource management, to focus their research theses or dissertations on topics related to the application of resource management in New Zealand

Eligibility: The scholarship is open to any graduate student in a University (New Zealand or Overseas) registered for a Masters (including an undergraduate Honours degree involving advanced levels of research and study at Masters degree level).

Level of Study: Masters

Type: Scholarship

Value: NZ$5,000 per year

Length of Study: one year only

Country of Study: Any country

Application Procedure: To apply for an RMLA scholarship, simply download the RMLA Scholarship Application and post it to RMLA so it arrives before before 01 September. Selection will be based on relevance of the proposed thesis or dissertation topic to advancing excellence in resource management policy and process; and Resource management processes which are legally sound, effective and efficient and which produce high quality environmental outcomes

No. of awards offered: 3

Closing Date: 1 September

Additional Information: For guidelines, application forms and more information about this award contact: Karol Helmink, Executive Officer, Resource Management Law Association, RMLA Scholarship Selection Committee, RMLA, PO Box 89187, Torbay, Auckland 0742, New Zealand www.rmla.org.nz/scholarships

For further information contact:

RMLA, PO Box 89187, Torbay, Auckland 0742, New Zealand.

Tel: (64) 272723960
Email: Karol.helmink@rmla.org.nz

The AUT Queen Elizabeth II Diamond Jubilee Doctoral Scholarship

Purpose: To develop an internationally aware, skilled future leader and establish enduring education and professional linkages. The Queen Elizabeth II Diamond Jubilee AUT Doctoral Scholarship marks the 60th anniversary of the accession of Her Majesty The Queen to the throne and will be awarded annually
Type: Scholarship
Value: NZ$25,000 annual stipend tuition fees and student services levies
Length of Study: One each year
Country of Study: New Zealand
No. of awards offered: One each year
Closing Date: 1 November
Additional Information: For guidelines, application forms and more information about this award contact: Auckland University of Technology, Phone: (64) 9 921 9837, Email: scholars@aut.ac.nz www.aut.ac.nz/study/fees-and-scholarships/scholarships-and-awards-at-aut/scholarships-database/detailpage?detailCode=500675&amp

For further information contact:

Auckland University of Technology, 55 Wellesley St E, Auckland 1010, New Zealand.

Tel: (64) 9 921 9837
Email: scholars@aut.ac.nz

The Capstone Editing Conference Travel Grant for Postgraduate Research Students

Purpose: The purpose of attending the conference should be to assist with the student's research or professional development. The student does not necessarily have to be presenting a paper or poster at the conference to be eligible to apply for the grant, though it is preferred
Eligibility: For eligibility, please visit website www.aut.ac.nz/study/fees-and-scholarships/scholarships-and-awards-at-aut/scholarships-database/detailpage?detailCode=804076&sessionID=27587614&sourceIP=&X_FORWARDED_FOR=
Type: Grant
Value: Up to AU$3,000
Country of Study: Any country
No. of awards offered: 1
Closing Date: 20 May

For further information contact:

Lisa Lines, Director and Head Editor, Capstone Editing, Tower A Level 5/7 London Circuit, Canberra, ACT 2601, Australia.

Tel: (61) 1800 224 468
Email: lisa.lines@capstoneediting.com.au

The Capstone Editing Early Career Academic Research Grant for Women

Purpose: In offering this grant, Capstone Editing acknowledges the greater difficulties faced by female academics in developing and continuing their careers and seeks to ameliorate this situation with practical, financial support
Eligibility: You must be a woman. You must be employed as an academic staff member in a position that involves research at an Australian or New Zealand university (i.e. staff in teaching-only positions are not eligible). You may be employed on a continuing or fixed-term basis. (Casual staff are not eligible.) - You may be employed part time or full time. You must be an early career academic. This is defined as someone who has graduated from their PhD within the past six years or who has begun continuing or fixed-term employment in an academic position for the first time within the past two years. - The research project must be one intended to lead to publication. This is defined as a research project for which one of the expected outcomes is publication of a peer-reviewed journal article, book chapter or book. It is recognised that academic research is incredibly varied and that some research will result clearly and quickly in a publication while other research might not lead to a publication for some time. Part of the purpose of this grant is to assist women to overcome barriers to their career progression, and publication is crucial to this. That is why one of the goals of the research project should be publication. You can specify in your application the type of publication you are aiming for and how it is related to your research project. - Previous recipients of this grant may not apply again. - Previous unsuccessful applicants may reapply every year if they wish. - You cannot apply if you are an employee or contractor of Capstone Editing (or a family member of an employee or contractor).
Value: Up to NZ$5,000
Country of Study: New Zealand
No. of awards offered: 1
Closing Date: 7 June

For further information contact:

Lisa Lines, Director and Head Editor, Capstone Editing, Tower A Level 5/7 London Circuit, Canberra, ACT 2601, Australia.

Tel: (61) 1800 224 468
Email: lisa.lines@capstoneediting.com.au

Toloa Scholarships for Pacific STEM Scholars

Purpose: These scholarships are designed to motivate, celebrate and inspire Pacific people to study STEM courses and enter a career in STEM
Type: Scholarship
Value: NZ$10,000 per academic year
Length of Study: Three years
Country of Study: New Zealand
Application Procedure: For application, visit website www.mpp.govt.nz/toloa-application-form-2018/
No. of awards offered: 50
Closing Date: 23 October
Additional Information: For guidelines, application forms and more information about this award contact: Ofania Ikiua, Ministry for Pacific Peoples, PO Box 833, - New Zealand, Phone: (64) 4 473 4493, Email: contact@mpp.govt.nz www.aut.ac.nz/study/fees-and-scholarships/scholarships-and-awards-at-aut/scholarships-database/detailpage?detailCode=803894&sessionID=33762433&sourceIP=&X_FORWARDED_FOR=

For further information contact:

Ofania Ikiua, Ministry for Pacific Peoples, PO Box 833, New Zealand.

Tel: (64) 4 473 4493
Email: contact@mpp.govt.nz

Zonta Club of South Auckland Area Study Award

Purpose: To assist in women's education
Value: Up to NZ$5,000
Country of Study: Any country
Application Procedure: For further information and an application form see the website www.zontasouthauckland.org.nz
No. of awards offered: 1
Closing Date: 16 August
Additional Information: www.aut.ac.nz/study/fees-and-scholarships/scholarships-and-awards-at-aut/scholarships-database/detailpage?detailCode=800997&sessionID=26786870&sourceIP=&X_FORWARDED_FOR=

For further information contact:

Tel: (64) 9 299 8759
Email: bev.pointon@gmail.com

Zonta International Amelia Earhart Fellowships

Purpose: The Amelia Earhart Fellowship is awarded annually to women pursuing PhD/doctoral degrees in aerospace-related sciences and aerospace-related engineering
Type: Fellowship
Value: NZ$10,000
Length of Study: 1 year
Country of Study: New Zealand
Application Procedure: For application form, please visit website www.aut.ac.nz/study/fees-and-scholarships/scholarships-and-awards-at-aut/scholarships-database/detailpage?detailCode=100341&sessionID=26783186&sourceIP=&X_FORWARDED_FOR=
Closing Date: 15 November
Additional Information: For guidelines, application forms and more information about this award contact: Zonta International Foundation, 1211 West 22nd Street Suite 900 Oak Brook, United States, Phone: (1) 630-928-1400, Email: programs@zonta.org www.aut.ac.nz/study/fees-and-scholarships/scholarships-and-awards-at-aut/scholarships-database/detailpage?detailCode=100341&sessionID=32593825&sourceIP=&X_FORWARDED_FOR=

For further information contact:

Email: zifoundation@zonta.org

Australia Council for the Arts

372 Elizabeth Street, PO Box 788, Strawberry Hills, Surry Hills, NSW 2012, Australia.

Tel: (61) 2 9215 9000
Email: mail@australiacouncil.gov.au
Website: www.australiacouncil.gov.au

The Australia Council for the Arts is the Australian Government's arts funding and advisory body. Each year, the council delivers more than AU$160 million in funding for arts organisations and individual artists across the country. Individuals, groups and organisations can apply to the Australia Council for funding. Individuals must be Australian citizens or have permanent resident status in Australia. All amounts are in Australian dollars.

Aboriginal and Torres Strait Islander Arts Fellowship

Purpose: These grants provide financial support for two years to Aboriginal and Torres Strait Islander artists to enable them to undertake a major creative project or program in their artform

Eligibility: Open to practicing Aboriginal and Torres Strait Islander artists who are able to demonstrate at least 10 years experience as a practicing professional artist

Level of Study: Postgraduate

Type: Fellowship

Value: AU$100,000 up to two years for dance, emerging artforms and experimental practices

Length of Study: 2 years

Frequency: Annual

Country of Study: Australia

Application Procedure: Apply online. For further details mail to atsia@australiacouncil.gov.au

Closing Date: 19 November

Funding: Government

Additional Information: www.australiacouncil.gov.au/ aboriginal-and-torres-strait-islander-arts/

For further information contact:

Level 5, 60 Union St, PO Box 576, Pyrmont, NSW 2009, Australia.

Email: enquiries@australiacouncil.gov.au

Aboriginal and Torres Strait Islander Arts Key Organisations Triennial

Purpose: To support a limited number of Aboriginal and Torres Strait Islander arts organisations to advance Aboriginal and Torres Strait Islander arts in Australia

Eligibility: Open to Aboriginal and Torres Strait Islander arts organisations only and must be outstanding organisations with a substantial record of achievement in their field

Frequency: Annual

Country of Study: Any country

Application Procedure: Application forms should include evidence of eligibility and the required support materials. Check website for further details

Closing Date: 15 July

For further information contact:

Email: stephanie.lord@sa.gov.au

Aboriginal and Torres Strait Islander Arts Presentation and Promotion

Purpose: Presentation and Promotion grants support projects that promote Aboriginal and Torres Strait Islander artists and their work regionally, nationally and internationally through

publications, recordings, performances, exhibitions and international export

Eligibility: Open to Aboriginal and Torres Strait Islander artists and community organisations and Aboriginal and Torres Strait Islander and non-indigenous arts organisations (including publishers)

Type: Grant

Value: Up to a maximum of AU$10,000 for CD/DVD recording projects involving writing, recording, production, manufacture, distribution and promotion

Frequency: Annual

Country of Study: Any country

Application Procedure: Apply online. Please mail to atsia@australiacouncil.gov.au

Closing Date: 18 November

Additional Information: Overseas applicants for international projects must provide written evidence of co-funding from the host country or organisation. All applicants are encouraged to seek further funding support for the project from other sources www.australiacouncil.gov.au/aboriginal-and-torres-strait-islander-arts/

For further information contact:

Email: vichealth@vichealth.vic.gov.au

Aboriginal and Torres Strait Islander Arts Program

Purpose: To provide support towards the cost of an organisation wishing to employ an Aboriginal and Torres Strait Islander artworker or artist to organise, develop and initiate a programme or arts activities in their community or region

Eligibility: Open to Aboriginal and Torres Strait Islander arts organisations only

Length of Study: 1 year

Frequency: Annual

Country of Study: Any country

Application Procedure: Applications should include evidence of eligibility and required support materials. Check website for further details

Closing Date: 15 July

For further information contact:

Email: stephanie.lord@sa.gov.au

Aboriginal and Torres Strait Islander Arts Skills and Arts Development

Purpose: These grants support Aboriginal and Torres Strait Islander artists, groups, organisations and accredited non-Indigenous organisations to develop their ideas and skills

such as mentorship programs, arts workshops, professional development programs, conferences, seminars or planning and development programs
Eligibility: Applicants should be Aboriginal and Torres Strait Islander individuals, organisations or groups
Type: Grant
Value: Varies
Country of Study: Any country
Application Procedure: Apply online
Closing Date: 19 November
Additional Information: Applicants are encouraged to seek funding from a number of sources. Please mail to mailto: atsia@australiacouncil.gov.au

For further information contact:

Email: stephanie.lord@sa.gov.au

Aboriginal and Torres Strait Islander New Work Grant

Purpose: This grant supports the creative development, production and presentation of new work. Aboriginal and Torres Strait Islander individual artists and arts and cultural workers, groups and arts and cultural organisations can apply for projects across all art forms
Eligibility: Open to Aboriginal and Torres Strait Islander artists who demonstrate artistic merit and innovation
Level of Study: Professional development
Type: Grant
Value: Up to AU$25 000
Length of Study: Up to 12 months
Frequency: Annual
Country of Study: Australia
Application Procedure: Apply online. For further information mail to atsia@australiacouncil.gov.au
Closing Date: February
Funding: Government
Additional Information: All applicants are encouraged to seek further funding support for the project from other sources mailto: atsia@australiacouncil.gov.au

For further information contact:

Email: atsia@australiacouncil.gov.au

Community Cultural Development Category A

Purpose: To develop significant project ideas and/or extension of effective partnerships that enable future projects to take place

Eligibility: Open to individuals, groups and organisations and who have discussed their proposal with Community Partnerships staff
Type: Grant
Value: Up to AU$5,000 per grant
Frequency: Annual
Country of Study: Any country
Application Procedure: Applications should include required support materials. Check website for further details
Closing Date: 1 November

Community Cultural Development Category B

Purpose: To support off community arts and culture projects which may have a public outcome and must involve a range of partners
Eligibility: Open to individuals, groups and organisations
Type: Grant
Value: Up to AU$20,000
Frequency: Annual
Country of Study: Any country
Application Procedure: Applications should include required support materials. Check website for further details
Closing Date: 1 July

Community Cultural Development Category C

Purpose: To support one-off community arts and culture projects which have a public outcome and involve cross-sectoral partners
Eligibility: Open to individuals, groups and organisations who meet the general eligibility requirements
Value: AU$20,000–35,000
Frequency: Annual
Country of Study: Any country
Application Procedure: Applications should include required support materials. Check website for further details
Closing Date: 1 July

Community Cultural Development Presentation and Promotion

Purpose: To support project that promote the value of community cultural development practice. This includes projects that create opportunities for practitioners to explore new ways of presenting the outcomes of existing best-practice models to new audiences
Eligibility: Open to individuals and organisations who meet the general eligibility requirements
Type: Grant

Frequency: Annual
Country of Study: Any country
Application Procedure: Applications should include required support materials. Check website for further details
Closing Date: 1 August

For further information contact:

Email: arts.office@nt.gov.au

Community Partnerships - Projects

Purpose: These grants provide funding for individuals, groups and organisations to develop and implement community arts and cultural development projects with a range of partners. These projects may or may not have a public outcome. Consideration of an evaluation strategy is recommended
Eligibility: Open to individuals, groups and organisations
Type: Grant
Value: Up to AU$20,000
Length of Study: Varies
Frequency: Annual
Application Procedure: Apply online
Closing Date: 5 September
Additional Information: Please mail to mailto: cp@australiacouncil.gov.au

For further information contact:

Tel: (61) 2 9215 9034
Email: cp@australiacouncil.gov.au

Dance New Work Creative Development

Purpose: To support the creation of new dance works
Eligibility: Open to individuals, groups, and organisations who meet the general eligibility requirements
Level of Study: Professional development
Type: Grant
Value: Varies
Length of Study: Varies
Application Procedure: Applications should include required support materials. Apply online. Check website for further details or contact Program Officer
Closing Date: 10 February
Additional Information: These are Projects Creative Development and Projects Presentation mailto: cp@australiacouncil.gov.au

For further information contact:

Tel: (61) 2 9215 9179
Email: e.johnson@australiacouncil.gov.au

Dance New Work Presentation

Purpose: To support public performance of a new work and any stages leading up to the production
Eligibility: Open to individuals who meet the general eligibility requirements. This can include final stage creative development and presentation/s and remounts of dance works. Applicants must provide information about presentation partner/s or presentation arrangements. Arrangements can include self presentation
Value: Varies
Application Procedure: Applications should include required support materials. Apply online. Check website for further details and contact Program Officer
Closing Date: 15 August

For further information contact:

Tel: (61) 2 9215 9179
Email: e.johnson@australiacouncil.gov.au

Festivals Australia

Purpose: These grants support regional, remote and community festivals to present quality arts projects which have not been presented before, and would not be possible without financial support
Eligibility: In order to apply you must be, or must apply through, a registered legal entity (with an ABN) or an incorporated organisation, which is able to produce an annual audited financial statement. Check website for complete details
Type: Grant
Application Procedure: Apply online
Closing Date: 29 August
Additional Information: Please mail to mailto: artsdevelopment@australiacouncil.gov.au

For further information contact:

Tel: (61) 2 9215 9176
Email: T.Kita@australiacouncil.gov.au

International Market Development Program

Purpose: International Pathways aims to assist with strategic international artistic and market development activities for Australian music and musicians
Eligibility: Applicants must have a commercially available CD, and touring experience
Level of Study: Professional development
Type: Grant

Value: AU$2,500–20,000
Length of Study: A maximum of 3 years
Frequency: Annual
Country of Study: Australia
Application Procedure: Contact the department
Funding: Government

For further information contact:

Tel: (61) 2 9215 9115
Email: music@ozco.gov.au

Literature Program

Purpose: These grants provide funding to established Australian organisations that support Australia's literary infrastructure
Eligibility: Open to Australian organisations which meet the eligibility requirements and provide the necessary support materials
Value: Covers production, program and/or operational costs
Length of Study: 1 year
Frequency: Annual
Application Procedure: Apply Online. Check website for further details. Applicant must provide evidence of his eligibility and all required support material by the application closing date.

For further information contact:

Tel: (61) 2 9215 9057
Email: l.byrne@australiacouncil.gov.au

Music Presentation and Promotion

Purpose: To support one-off projects that present, publish, distribute and/or market quality music of any style within Australia
Eligibility: Open to individuals, performing groups/ensembles/bands and organisations which meet the eligibility requirements and provide the necessary support materials
Value: Up to AU$30,000 and associated expenses
Length of Study: Varies
Application Procedure: Application form should include the required supporting materials. Apply online. Check website for further details. For further details contact the Program Officer
Closing Date: 12 November

For further information contact:

Tel: (61) 2 9215 9108
Email: p.keogh@australiacouncil.gov.au

Music Program

Purpose: Supports organisations with a track record of achievement in presentation, service delivery, skills development or other relevant areas
Eligibility: Open to organisations which meet the eligibility requirements and provide the necessary support materials
Value: Up to AU$50,000
Length of Study: 1 year
Frequency: Annual

For further information contact:

Tel: (61) 2 9215 9301
Email: m.collett@australiacouncil.gov.au

Music Skills and Development

Purpose: To support skills development for professional artists and arts workers
Eligibility: Open to individuals and organisations which meet the eligibility requirements and provide the necessary support materials
Type: Grant
Value: Up to AU$10,000
Frequency: Every 2 years
Application Procedure: Apply online
Closing Date: 25 March
Additional Information: There are two subcategories: individuals and groups (established and emerging), and organisations (legally constituted). Please mail to mailto: music@australiacouncil.gov.au

For further information contact:

Tel: (61) 2 9215 9108
Email: p.keogh@australiacouncil.gov.au

OZCO Community Cultural Development Fellowship

Purpose: To enhance the capacity of artists and artsworkers to provide leadership in the field
Eligibility: Applicants should have a solid record of achievement in community arts and culture, including community cultural development
Level of Study: Postgraduate, Professional development
Type: Fellowship
Value: AU$40,000
Length of Study: 2 years
Frequency: Annual
Country of Study: Australia
Application Procedure: Contact the department

Closing Date: 15 April
Funding: Government

For further information contact:

Tel: (61) 2 9215 9029
Email: ccd@ozco.gov.au

OZCO Community Culture Development Grant Residency

Purpose: To afford an artist or arts worker the opportunity to take time out of project-based work and focus on professional development, reflection or individual arts practice
Eligibility: Artists applying require a driver's licence
Level of Study: Professional development
Type: Grant
Value: AU$14,000 and an AU$1,000 materials allowance
Frequency: Annual
Study Establishment: Hastings Council and Camden Haven Community College Inc
Country of Study: Australia
Application Procedure: Contact the department
Closing Date: 1 August
Funding: Government

For further information contact:

Tel: (61) 2 9215 9034
Email: m.martin@ozco.gov.au

OZCO Dance Fellowship

Purpose: This grant is designed to support an established dance artist to undertake creative or professional development
Eligibility: This category is only open to individuals who are practising artists or arts workers. Applicant must meet the general eligibility requirements
Level of Study: Postdoctorate, Professional development
Type: Fellowship
Value: AU$50,000 per year
Length of Study: 2 years
Frequency: Annual
Country of Study: Australia
Application Procedure: Applicants are encouraged to apply online for this category
Closing Date: 31 July
Funding: Government
Additional Information: Please contact to mailto: dance@australiacouncil.gov.au

For further information contact:

Tel: (61) 2 9215 9164
Email: a.burnett@australiacouncil.gov.au

OZCO Dance Grant Initiative: Take Your Partner

Purpose: To support young and emerging dance artists and art workers to forge a new relationship or build on an existing one through a specific project
Level of Study: Professional development
Type: Grant
Value: AU$15,000
Frequency: Annual
Country of Study: Australia
Application Procedure: Contact the department
Closing Date: June
Funding: Government

For further information contact:

Tel: (61) 2 9215 9179
Email: s.woo@ozco.gov.au

OZCO Literature Fellowships

Purpose: To support excellence in Australian literature
Eligibility: Applications will only be accepted from individuals who have had a minimum of major works published or performed and have achieved substantial critical recognition
Level of Study: Postgraduate, Professional development
Type: Fellowship
Value: AU$100,000 over two years (paid in three instalments)
Length of Study: 2 years
Frequency: Annual
Country of Study: Australia
Application Procedure: Applicants are encouraged to apply online for this category. Duly filled application along with relevant supporting material, curriculum vitae, and one copy of two published books or performed plays in the genre of the project should be provided. For further details contact the Program Manager
Closing Date: 15 May
Funding: Government

For further information contact:

Tel: (61) 2 9215 9057
Email: literature@ozco.gov.au

OZCO Literature Grants Initiative: Write in Your Face

Purpose: To support young writers using language in innovative ways
Eligibility: Applicant must be aged 30 years or under
Level of Study: Professional development
Type: Grant
Value: Up to AU$5,000
Frequency: Annual
Country of Study: Australia
Application Procedure: Contact the department. Apply online
Closing Date: 9 December

For further information contact:

Tel: (61) 29215 9058
Email: j.jones@ozco.gov.au

OZCO Music Fellowship

Purpose: These two-year fellowship support outstanding, established music artists to produce new work and/or undertake professional development
Eligibility: This category is open to individuals who meet the general eligibility requirements. Fellowship recipients may not apply for a Project Fellowship where the start date of the Project Fellowship is less than five years after the end date of their Fellowship
Level of Study: Postdoctorate, Professional development
Type: Fellowship
Value: AU$100,000 (AU$50,000 per year for two years)
Length of Study: 2 years
Frequency: Annual
Country of Study: Australia
Application Procedure: Applicants are encouraged to apply online for this category
Closing Date: 31 July
Funding: Government
Additional Information: Fellowship recipients may apply for funding from other categories during the term of the Fellowship, with the exception of the project Fellowships initiative. Fellowships are granted only once in an artist's lifetime mailto: dance@australiacouncil.gov.au

For further information contact:

Tel: (61) 2 9215 9115
Email: music@australiacouncil.gov.au

OZCO Music Project Fellowship

Purpose: These grants support mid-career and established artists to develop significant creative and/or developmental projects over a period of up to 12 months
Eligibility: Music artists working in music theatre and indigenous music artists are particularly encouraged to apply
Level of Study: Postgraduate, Professional development
Type: Fellowship
Value: AU$30,000
Length of Study: 1 year
Frequency: Annual
Country of Study: Australia
Application Procedure: Apply online
Closing Date: 31 July
Funding: Government
Additional Information: Please mail to mailto: music@australiacouncil.gov.au

For further information contact:

Tel: (61) 2 9215 9108
Email: music@ozco.gov.au

OZCO New Media Residency

Purpose: To support hybrid and new media study abroad
Level of Study: Postdoctorate, Postgraduate
Type: Fellowship
Length of Study: 1 year
Frequency: Annual
Study Establishment: Banff Centre for the Arts
Country of Study: Canada
Application Procedure: Apply online
Closing Date: 1 November
Funding: Government

For further information contact:

Email: nma@ozco.gov.au

OZCO Theatre Fellowship

Purpose: To financially support an individuals professional development
Eligibility: It is for artists with a record of outstanding achievement. Applicant must meet the general eligibility requirements and any specific eligibility requirements provided for this grant. In addition, applicant must be able to demonstrate at least 10 years' professional theatre experience
Level of Study: Postgraduate, Professional development
Type: Fellowship

Value: AU$45,000 per year over two years
Length of Study: 2 years
Frequency: Annual
Country of Study: Australia
Application Procedure: It is strongly recommended that you discuss your application with staff before applying. Applicants are encouraged to apply online for this category. Duly filled application along with relevant supporting material should be sent. For further details contact the Program Manager
Closing Date: 5 November
Funding: Government

For further information contact:

Tel: (61) 2 9215 9040
Email: theatre@ozco.gov.au

OZCO Visual Arts Fellowship

Purpose: To provide financial support to visual artists, crafts-people and specialist visual arts and craft writers of outstanding achievement to enable them to create new work and further develop their practice
Eligibility: This category is open to individual artists. Applications will be selected that best demonstrate outstanding professional achievement; the artistic merit of the activities proposed for the fellowship period
Level of Study: Postgraduate
Type: Fellowship
Value: AU$120,000 over two years (in three instalments)
Length of Study: Up to 2 years
Frequency: Annual
Country of Study: Australia
Application Procedure: Applicants are encouraged to apply online for this category. Duly filled application along with relevant supporting material should be sent. For further details contact the Program Manager
Closing Date: 16 April
Funding: Government
Additional Information: Fellowships are granted only once in an artist's lifetime mailto: music@australiacouncil.gov.au

For further information contact:

Tel: (61) 2 9215 9020
Email: vac@ozco.gov.au

Playing Australia: Regional Performing Arts Touring Fund

Purpose: These grants assist the touring of professionally produced performing arts across Australia, including regional and remote areas, where there is a demonstrated public demand and tours are otherwise not commercially viable
Eligibility: We accept applications from individuals and organisations.
Type: Grant
Value: Varies
Country of Study: Any country
Application Procedure: Apply online
Closing Date: 1 June
Additional Information: Please mail to mailto: artsdevelopment@australiacouncil.gov.au

For further information contact:

Tel: (61) 2 9215 9176
Email: enquiries@australiacouncil.gov.au

Projects – Creative Development

Purpose: These grants provide support for the research and creative development of new dance works
Eligibility: To be eligible, you must meet the general eligibility requirements and the specific eligibility requirements given below. This category is open to individuals, groups and organisations. Dance Key Organisations are not eligible to apply to this category
Type: Grant
Application Procedure: Apply online
Closing Date: 16 August
Additional Information: Please mail to mailto: dance@australiacouncil.gov.au

For further information contact:

Tel: (61) 2 9215 9179
Email: k.morcombe@australiacouncil.gov.au

Projects – Presentation

Purpose: The purpose of this grant is to provide support for dance works with a presentation outcome. This can include final stage creative development and presentation/s and remounts of dance works
Eligibility: To be eligible, you must meet the general eligibility requirements and the specific eligibility requirements given at the website. This category is open to individuals, groups and organisations. Key Organisations are not eligible to apply to this category
Type: Grant
Value: Up to AU$50,000
Application Procedure: Apply online
Closing Date: 15 August

Additional Information: Please mail to mailto: dance@australiacouncil.gov.au

For further information contact:

Tel: (61) 2 9215 9179
Email: k.morcombe@australiacouncil.gov.au

The Dreaming Award

Purpose: The Dreaming Award was established in 2012 to support an inspirational young First Nations artist aged 18-30 years to create a major body of work through mentoring and partnerships. The mentor/partner will be another established professional artist or partner nominated by the artist who will guide and mentor the applicant to assist in the development of work. This award will be presented at the 2021 First Nations Arts Awards.

Eligibility: 1. Open to First Nations Australian artists living here or overseas. 2. Age open to 18-30. 3. Disciplines include dance, literature, poetry, visual arts, theatre, community arts and music. 4. You cannot apply for activities that have already commenced.

Type: Award
Value: AU$20,000
Country of Study: Any country
Application Procedure: To apply log in here to our Application Management System (AMS) if you have an account. You can create an account if you do not already have one. 1. Select 'Apply for a Grant' from the left panel menu. 2. From the list of opportunities select 'Apply for the Dreaming Award'. 3. Complete the fields and select answers with dropdown menus. 4. Upload any necessary support material. 5. Select 'Save' once complete. 6. If you are not ready to submit your application you can return to it through 'Your Draft Applications' in the left panel menu at a later date. 7. Otherwise select 'Submit'.

Closing Date: 7 December
Additional Information: Please mail to atsia@australiacouncil.gov.au www.australiacouncil.gov.au/funding/funding-index/the-dreaming-award/

For further information contact:

Tel: (61) 2 9215 9040
Email: j.gillis@australiacouncil.gov.au

The Red Ochre Award

Purpose: The Aboriginal and the Torres Strait Islander Arts Board established The Red Ochre Award in 1993 to pay tribute to an Aboriginal or Torres Strait Islander artist who, throughout their lifetime, has made outstanding contributions to the recognition of Aboriginal and Torres Strait Islander arts, both nationally and internationally

Eligibility: Nominations will be accepted from arts and community organisations and individuals. Nominations may only be made for living artists and individuals cannot nominate themselves. This award is not project based and, therefore is not given to assist any particular project, program or intended activity

Type: Award
Value: AU$50,000
Country of Study: Any country
Application Procedure: To apply log in here to our Application Management System (AMS) if you have an account. You can create an account if you do not already have one. 1. Select 'Apply for a Grant' from the left panel menu. 2. From the list of opportunities select 'Apply for the Red Ochre Award'. 3. Complete the fields and select answers with dropdown menus. 4. Upload any necessary support material. 5. Select 'Save' once complete. 6. If you are not ready to submit your application you can return to it through 'Your Draft Applications' in the left panel menu at a later date. 7. Otherwise select 'Submit'.

Closing Date: 7 December
Additional Information: Please mail to atsia@australiacouncil.gov.au www.australiacouncil.gov.au/funding/travel-rights-and-translation-funds-for-literature-faqs/the-red-ochre-award-lifetime-achievement/

For further information contact:

Tel: (61) 2 9215 9040
Email: j.gillis@australiacouncil.gov.au

Visions of Australia: Regional Exhibition Touring Fund

Purpose: Visions of Australia supports the development and touring of major public exhibitions of Australian cultural material throughout Australia, particularly into regional and remote areas

Eligibility: To be eligible, you must meet the general eligibility requirements and the specific eligibility requirements given at the website. This category is open to organisations only

Type: Funding support
Value: No maximum grant amount
Application Procedure: You are encouraged to apply online for this grant. To begin an online application, use the 'Apply online' button (www.australiacouncil.gov.au/grants/2013/visions-of-australia)
Closing Date: October

Additional Information: Please mail to artsdevelopmen t@australiacouncil.gov.au   www.arts.gov.au/funding-and-support/visions-australia

For further information contact:

The Program Officer, Visions of Australia, Department of Communications and the Arts, GPO Box 2154, Canberra, ACT 2601, Australia.

Tel: (61) 800 590 577
Email: visions@arts.gov.au

Visual Arts New Work

Purpose: To support the creation of new work by emerging and established craftspeople, designers, new media artists, visual artists, and arts writers
Eligibility: Open to individuals and groups that meet the eligibility requirements and provide the necessary support materials
Value: AU$10,000 for emerging and AU$20,000 for established craftpeople, designers, new media artists, visual artists and arts writers
Frequency: Annual
Application Procedure: Applications should include the required support materials. Apply online. Check website for further details. For further details contact the Program Officer
Closing Date: 16 April
Contributor: National Association for the Visual Arts (NAVA)

For further information contact:

Tel: (61) 2 9215 9020
Email: s.saxon@australiacouncil.gov.au

Visual Arts Presentation and Promotion

Purpose: To assist arts organisations to present and promote contemporary Australian craft, design, new media art and visual arts, to audiences in Australia and overseas
Eligibility: Open to organisations that meet the eligibility requirements and provide the necessary support materials
Frequency: Annual
Application Procedure: Applications should include the required support materials and apply online
Closing Date: 20 August

For further information contact:

Tel: (61) 2 9215 9131
Email: v.lloyd@australiacouncil.gov.au

Visual Arts Skills and Arts Development

Purpose: To enable professional development opportunities for craftspeople, designers, media artists, visual artists, arts writers and curators
Eligibility: Open to individuals and groups which meet the eligibility requirements and provide the necessary support materials
Type: Grant
Value: Supports artists to undertake professional development activities in Australia or overseas. AU$10,000 for Barcelona, Helsinki, Liverpool, London, New York, Paris, Rome or Tokyo; AU$25,000 for New York; AU$35,000 for Berlin residencies
Length of Study: More than 1 year (General). 3-month residency in Barcelona, Helsinki, Liverpool, London, New York, Paris, Rome or Tokyo; 6-month residency in New York; 12-month residency in Berlin
Frequency: Annual
Application Procedure: Apply online
Closing Date: 20 August
Additional Information: Please mail to mailto: visualart s@australiacouncil.gov.au

For further information contact:

Tel: (61) 2 9215 9336
Email: r.petersen@australiacouncil.gov.au

Australian Academy of Science

PO Box 783, Canberra, ACT 2601, Australia.

Tel: (61) 2 6247 3966
Email: io@science.org.au
Website: www.science.org.au/internat
Contact: International Programmes Officer

The Australian Academy of Science is an independent, non-profit organisation with a membership of 300 Fellows elected for making distinguished contributions in the area of natural sciences and their applications. The objectives of the Academy are to promote science and science education through a range of activities.

Max Day Environmental Science Fellowship Award

Purpose: The Australian Academy of Science is inviting applications Max Day Environmental Science Fellowship

Award. These fellowships are available to assist early stage PhD students or early career researchers with their research

Eligibility: 1. Applicants must be Australian citizens or permanent residents at the time of application. 2. be accepted to undertake a PhD (or equivalent research doctorate), have completed their confirmation and be enrolled in their first or second year of research (at the time of the award closing date). have held a PhD (or equivalent) for no more than 5 years at the time of the award closing date*

Type: Research

Value: The Max Day Environmental Science Fellowship Award is an annual award of up to AU$20,000 per awardee to assist early stage PhD students or early career researchers with their research. It provides funding support toward the costs of travel, courses or research expenses. Grants are GST exclusive

Study Establishment: Applicants must demonstrate a multi-disciplinary approach to their research work and conduct their research in one or more of the biological sciences relating to one or more of the following disciplines Conservation of Australia's flora and fauna, Ecologically sustainable resource use, Environmental protection and Ecosystem services (either provisioning services, or habitat and supporting services)

Country of Study: Australia

Application Procedure: 1. A proposal summarising your chosen area of study/research and why the Max Day Fellowship will be of particular benefit to you. Please refer to the selection criteria section above for information outlining how the proposals are assessed. Maximum of two pages using size 12 font. 2. Itemised budget detailing eligible expenses with brief justification for each item, the names and details of funding already received (funding body, amount). Maximum of one page using size 12 font. The applicant must show they have been recognised by one or more research institutions, such as their host institution, by the provision of some level of direct financial contribution towards their project (excluding salaries). 3. Brief CV including qualifications, summary of any professional/research experience and publications/presentations. A full publications list is not required. Maximum of three pages using size 12 font. 4. PhD students require a letter of reference from their supervisor confirming and commenting on their existing research. Maximum of one page using size 12 font. 5. Post-doctoral researchers must attach two referee reports to the application. The reports should be addressed to the Awards Committee and should indicate the referee's knowledge of the applicant's proposed Max Day Fellowship activities, and the potential benefits of these activities to the researcher and/or the research field. Maximum of one page using size 12 font per report.

Closing Date: 1 June

Additional Information: For more details please visit the website scholarship-positions.com/max-day-environmental-science-fellowship-award-australia/2018/02/22/ www.science.org.au/supporting-science/awards-and-opportunities/max-day-environmental-science-fellowship-award

For further information contact:

Email: awards@science.org.au

Prostate Cancer Research Centre - NSW

Purpose: The objectives of the grant are 1. to safeguard a prostate cancer biobank and databank through providing support for infrastructure and its maintenance for a period of up to six months. 2. establish a sustainability plan for future funding for the Australian Prostate Cancer Research Centre – NSW, Garvan Institute of Medical Research

Eligibility: The Australian Prostate Cancer Research Centre (APCRC) – NSW is the eligible organisation to apply for this Grant Opportunity

Level of Study: Postgraduate, Research

Type: Grant

Frequency: Annual

Country of Study: Any country

Closing Date: 21 January

Funding: Government

Additional Information: www.cancer.nsw.gov.au/data-research/grants/grant-opportunities

For further information contact:

Email: Grant.ATM@health.gov.au

Australian Academy of the Humanities (AAH)

3 Liversidge Street Acton, Canberra, ACT 2601, Australia.

Tel: (61) 2 6125 9860
Email: enquiries@humanities.org.au
Website: www.humanities.org.au
Contact: Administration Officer

The Australian Academy of the Humanities (AAH) was established under Royal Charter in 1969 for the advancement of the scholarship, interest in and understanding of the humanities. Humanities disciplines include, but are not limited to, history, classics, English, European languages and cultures, Asian studies, philosophy, the arts, linguistics, prehistory and archaeology and cultural and communications studies.

Australian Academy of the Humanities Visiting Scholar Programmes

Purpose: To encourage scholarly contact with scholars from both Russia/the former USSR and Indonesia/South—East Asia and to assist scholars from those countries to obtain access to research materials held in Australia
Eligibility: Applicants must be identified as being appropriate representatives at Australia-based conferences
Level of Study: Doctorate, Postdoctorate
Type: Award
Value: AU$7,000 (for 2 scholars from Russia and the Former USSR) and AU$4,000 (for 2 scholars from Indonesia and South—East Asia)
Frequency: Annual
Country of Study: Australia
Application Procedure: Applicant (Australian host scholar) must send the Secretariat a brief explanation of the reason for the visit, a copy of the visiting scholar's curriculum vitae and a list of their most significant publications (in English), a provisional itinerary listing speaking engagements, potential contact with Australian scholars and research institutions to be visited and a provisional budget for the expenditure of the funds
No. of awards offered: 7
Closing Date: 31 July
Funding: Government
No. of awards given last year: 2
No. of applicants last year: 7
Additional Information: Eligible to nationals of: Russia and SE Asia www.humanities.org.au/opportunities/

For further information contact:

Tel: (61) 2 6125 8950
Email: grants@humanities.org.au

The British Special Joint Project Funding Scheme

Eligibility: The principal applicant on the Australian side should be normally a resident of Australia. Other scholars associated with the project will normally be expected to be of postdoctoral status
Level of Study: Postdoctorate
Type: Award
Value: Up to £8,000 (if 1 award is given) or up to £4,000 per project (if 2 awards are given)
Length of Study: Up to 1 year
Frequency: Annual
Country of Study: United Kingdom and Australia
Application Procedure: Applicants from both sides must submit applications to the appropriate Academy. Australian

scholars should apply through either the AAH or ASSA, depending on the nature of their project. Australian partners should consult the AAH or ASSA for application procedures. Equivalent information must be included on all application forms. All applications for Academy grants are considered in the light of referees comments
No. of awards offered: 22
No. of awards given last year: 2
No. of applicants last year: 22
Additional Information: www.humanities.org.au/opportunities/

For further information contact:

Tel: (61) 2 6125 8950
Email: grants@humanities.org.au

Australian Bio Security-CRC (AB-CRC)

Building 76 Molecular Biosciences The University of Queensland, St Lucia, QLD 4072, Australia.

Tel: (61) 3346 8866
Email: corinna.lange@abcrc.org.au
Website: www.abcrc.org.au
Contact: Mrs Corinna Lange, Communications Manager

The mission of the ABCRC is to protect Australia's public health, livestock, wildlife and economic resources through research and education that strengthens the national capability to detect, diagnose, identify, monitor, assess, predict and to respond to emerging infectious disease threats.

AB-CRC Honours Scholarships

Purpose: To encourage students of high academic ability to take the first step in their career path as a researcher. To build research capacity in high priority areas related to biosecurity
Eligibility: Scholarships will be awarded preferentially to Australian residents and students from the Asia-Pacific region
Level of Study: Postgraduate
Type: Scholarship
Value: AU$5,000 per year (full-time) or AU$2,500 per year (part-time)
Length of Study: 1 or 2 years for a part-time scholarship
Frequency: Annual
Study Establishment: AB-CRC participating university
Country of Study: Australia

Application Procedure: Contact the scholarships Administrator officer

Closing Date: 31 October

For further information contact:

Tel: (61) 8 9266 1634
Email: debra.gendle@abcrc.org.au

AB-CRC Professional Development Scholarships

Purpose: To enhance linkages with research projects of relevance to the AB-CRC. To expand our capability to support the training of specialists. To provide students with access to the AB-CRC network and enhanced learning opportunities

Eligibility: PhD students enroled at AB-CRC partner organizations

Level of Study: Professional development

Type: Scholarship

Value: AU$2,000 per year

Length of Study: Varies

Frequency: Annual

Study Establishment: AB-CRC participating university

Country of Study: Australia

Application Procedure: Students must submit a Professional Development Plan. Contact the Scholarships Administration officer

Closing Date: 16 November

Additional Information: Candidates will be required to sign a confidentially agreement. Funding awarded in a Professional Development Scholarship will be on a sliding scale depending upon the student's enrolment date www.humanities.org.au/opportunities/

For further information contact:

Email: debra.gendle@abcrc.org.uk

The John Mulvaney Fellowship

Purpose: The Academy launched The John Mulvaney Fellowship in 2019. This award honours the outstanding contribution to Humanities scholarship, the Academy and the cultural life of the nation of one of our longest serving Fellows and former Academy Secretary John Mulvaney AO CMG FBA FSA FRAI FAHA.

Eligibility: 1. Applicants must be Aboriginal and/or Torres Strait Islander people. 2. The Fellowship is open to early career researchers (ECRs) and PhD students currently enrolled in an Australian institution. 3. Applicants must be Citizens or Permanent Residents of the Commonwealth of Australia, whose principal place of residence is Australia.

4. Applicants must be working in the Humanities, defined as those discipline areas by which the Academy is structured – Archaeology; Asian Studies; Classical Studies; English; European Languages and Cultures; History; Linguistics; Philosophy and the History of Ideas; Religion; Cultural and Communication Studies; and The Arts. Applicants working on projects in Indigenous Studies; Digital Humanities; and Environmental Humanities will also be eligible to apply. 5. Interdisciplinary work is encouraged, provided that it includes a substantial proportion of work in the Humanities. 6. Applications will be accepted from independent scholars holding a PhD as well as those working in institutional settings. 7. Early Career Researcher applicants must be in the early stages of their careers, which will be determined, inter alia, by how recently a PhD was conferred. In normal circumstances it should have been conferred no more than five years prior to the closing date for applications. 8. Recipients of a Humanities Travelling Fellowship offered by this Academy are ineligible. 9. Applicants must submit a complete application in order to be assessed for eligibility. 10. The decision of the Awards Committee upon the eligibility of an application is final.

Level of Study: Postgraduate

Type: Fellowship

Value: AU$4,000

Study Establishment: AB-CRC participating university

Country of Study: Australia

Application Procedure: 1. Rigour and significance of the research. 2. Likely impact within a specialist field. 3. Potential to engage and/or benefit the wider community. 4. Relevance of the project to their career development and be able to show evidence of this through either traditional or non-traditional research outputs.

Closing Date: 5 June

Additional Information: www.humanities.org.au/opportunities/mulvaney/

Australian Catholic University (ACU)

Brisbane Campus (McAuley at Banyo), PO Box 456, Virginia, QLD 4014, Australia.

Tel: (61) 2 9739 2305, 7 3623 7100
Email: studentcentre@mcauley.acu.edu.au
Website: www.acu.edu.au

Australian Catholic University (ACU) is a public university funded by the Australian Government and is open to students and staff of all beliefs. It has established a reputation for quality and innovative teaching and specialist tertiary education in health, education, business and informatics, arts, social sciences and theology.

Adolescent Health and Performance Scholarship

Purpose: To attract a highly motivated postgraduate student who is interested in serially tracking the musculoskeletal health and performance of elite adolescent female athletes
Eligibility: Open to citizens or permanent residents of Australia between the ages of 22 and 30 to study in Australia. The candidate must have achieved First Class Honours or equivalent and have studied at or be currently studying at Australian Catholic University
Level of Study: Graduate
Type: Scholarship
Value: AU$25,627 per year
Length of Study: 3 years
Study Establishment: Australian Catholic University
Country of Study: Australia
Application Procedure: Candidates must apply directly to the Australian Catholic University
Additional Information: It is required that the study starts no earlier than 15 September and no later than 15 October www. humanities.org.au/opportunities/mulvaney/

For further information contact:

Email: robina.bamforth@acu.edu.au

Co-op Bookshop Scholarship

Purpose: The Co-op Bookshop Scholarship has been established to assist high achieving students with financial costs associated with attending university.
Eligibility: Applicants must be Australian citizens or permanent residents; be undergraduate students; be enrolled in Faculty of Law and Business or Faculty of Theology and Philosophy; and be in the first year of their course.
Type: Scholarship
Value: The scholarship is valued at AU$2,500, paid in one lump sum.
Length of Study: 1 year
Frequency: Annual
Country of Study: Any country
Application Procedure: Scholarship Website www.acu.edu.au/382374
Closing Date: March
Additional Information: www.australianuniversities.com.au/scholarships/guide/7886-co-op-bookshop-scholarship.html

For further information contact:

Student Centre, ACU, Locked Bag 4115, Fitzroy, VIC 3065, Australia.

Tel: (61) 399 533 062
Email: studentcentre@patrick.acu.edu.au

Council of Catholic School Parents (NSW) Indigenous Postgraduate Scholarship (IES)

Purpose: The Council of Catholic School Parents (CCSP) is the peak body representing the interests of Catholic school parents in NSW/ACT and is the largest non-government school parent body in NSW.
Eligibility: Applications are open to current ACU students who meet all the following criteria: 1. Citizenship: domestic 2. Faculty: Education and Arts 3. Course: any ACU Education degree 4. Campus: North Sydney, Strathfield or Blacktown 5. Year level: final year in 2023 6. Study load: full-time
Type: Scholarship
Value: The scholarship is valued at AU$2,500, to be paid in one lump sum
Frequency: Annual
Study Establishment: Strathfield campus
Country of Study: Australia
Application Procedure: Applicants will be required to provide the following as part of the application: 1. A written statement of approximately 500 words outlining: a. your passion and strategies for engaging parents in their child's learning journey b. why you have chosen to undertake your degree and what do you hope to achieve with it in the future. 2. (If relevant) evidence of your regional, rural or remote NSW address as classified by the Rural, Remote and Metropolitan Area (RRMA) 3. (If relevant) evidence that you attended a Catholic high school.
Closing Date: 6 March
Contributor: Council of Catholic School Parents (NSW)

For further information contact:

Email: futurestudents@acu.edu.au

International Postgraduate Research Scholarships (IPRS)

Purpose: To financially assist student to undertake full time postgraduate study who are otherwise unable to take up studies due to personal reasons (excluding employment)
Eligibility: The Commonwealth Scholarship Guidelines (Research) 2017 set the basis for the conditions of award

and outline the basic eligibility requirements for this scholarship. The ANU has established an RTP Policy & Procedure which outlines the standards, processes and conditions for this scholarship. These documents are available from the reference document section of this page.

Level of Study: Research
Type: Scholarship
Value: Full tuition fees (as approved by Common wealth Govt)
Length of Study: 2–3 years
Frequency: Annual
Study Establishment: Australian Catholic University (ACU)
Country of Study: Australia
Application Procedure: No application is required specifically for this scholarship as all eligible candidates will be considered.
Closing Date: 31 October

For further information contact:

Graduate Research Office

Tel: (61) 6125 5777
Email: gro@anu.edu.au

Pratt Foundation Bursary (IES)

Purpose: To make available a bursary to a suitably qualified Aboriginal and Torres Strait Islander student undertaking postgraduate study at ACU
Eligibility: 1. Citizenship Australian Citizens. 2. Target group Aboriginal and Torres Strait Islander. 3. Faculty any. 4. Course any ACU postgraduate degree. 5. Campus any. 6. Year level any
Level of Study: Graduate
Type: Bursary
Value: AU$2,500
Frequency: Annual
Study Establishment: Australian Catholic University (ACU)
Country of Study: Australia
Application Procedure: Candidates can obtain further information from Weemala Indigenous Unit, Brisbane campus. Online applications only
No. of awards offered: 1
Closing Date: 18 March
Funding: Foundation
Contributor: The Pratt Foundation
Additional Information: acu.fluidreview.com/p/a/110245/

For further information contact:

Email: futurestudents@acu.edu.au

Victorian International Research Scholarships

Purpose: The Victorian International Research Scholarship (VIRS) is offered in partnership between the Victorian Government and Victorian Universities. The Scholarship supports high-calibre international PhD scholars to undertake research in Victoria
Eligibility: Open to an international student; who accepted into a doctoral programme at ACU; intend to complete the majority of work related to the doctorate in Victoria; not have completed a degree equivalent to an Australian doctorate; willingness to act as an ambassador for the (VIRS) program
Level of Study: Doctorate
Type: Scholarship
Value: AU$90,000 over 3 years
Length of Study: Successful applicants will receive a scholarship of AU$90,000 for the duration of their PhD.
Frequency: Every 3 years
Country of Study: Any country
Application Procedure: Applicants must be a citizen of a country other than Australia
Additional Information: For further information, visit Study Melbourne, or email your application (MS Word document, 2.8 MB) to mailto: VIC.cand@acu.edu.au

Australian Centre for Blood Diseases (ACBD)

6th Floor, Burnet Tower, 89 Commercial Road, Melbourne, VIC 3004, Australia.

Tel: (61) 3 990 30122
Email: acbd@med.monash.edu.au
Website: www.acbd.monash.org

The Australian Centre for Blood Diseases (ACBD) brings together the skills and facilities of separate yet complementary organizations to enhance understanding of blood and its diseases. Its aim is to provide excellence in the diagnosis and treatment of blood conditions as well as play a leading role in the advancement of knowledge in this increasingly important area of medicine.

Firkin PhD Scholarship

Purpose: To undertake a PhD programme at the ACBD or affiliated institutes comprising AMREP
Eligibility: Open to students interested in pursuing doctorate studies in cardiovascular disciplines, and who have the appropriate graduate qualifications

Level of Study: Graduate
Type: Scholarships
Value: AU$22,500 per year
Length of Study: 3 years
Frequency: Annual
Country of Study: Any country
Application Procedure: For further information, please contact Dr Robert Medcalf
Additional Information: www.monash.edu/medicine/ccs/blood-disease/education/firkin

For further information contact:

Australian Centre for Blood Diseases, Monash University, 6th Floor, Burnet Building, AMREP, Commercial Road, Melbourne, Victoria 3004, Australia.

Email: Robert.Medcalf@med.monash.edu.au

Australian Department of Science

PO Box 65, Belconnen, ACT 2616, Australia.

Contact: Grants & Fellowships Branch

Disability, Mental Health and Carers: National Disability Conference Initiative

Purpose: The Australian Government is inviting applications in an open process to apply to deliver services under the Disability, Mental Health and Carer National Disability Conference Initiative in
Eligibility: To be eligible, applicants to the National Disability Conference Initiative (NDCI) must be one of the following entity types 1. Indigenous Corporation. 2. Company. 3. Incorporated Association. 4. Cooperative. Applications from consortia are acceptable, as long as you have a lead applicant who is solely accountable to the Commonwealth for the delivery of grant activities
Level of Study: Graduate
Type: Grant
Value: A maximum of AU$10,000 (GST exclusive) per conference is available for this grant opportunity
Frequency: Annual
Country of Study: Any country
Application Procedure: For further information on this grants, visit the website. www.communitygrants.gov.au/grants/disability-mental-health-and-carers-conference
Closing Date: 7 January
Funding: Government

For further information contact:

Tel: (61) 800 020 283
Email: support@communitygrants.gov.au

Australian Federation of University Women (AFUW)

School of Education, University of Ballarat, PO Box 663, Ballarat, VIC 3353, Australia.

Tel: (61) 9557 2556
Email: AFGW.Fellowships@gmail.com
Website: www.afuw.org.au
Contact: Dr Jacqueline Wilson, AFUW Vic Membership Secretary

Australian Federation of University Women (AFUW) Victoria was formed in 1922 as part of the international network of women Graduates for the benefit of women and society. AFUW Victoria is a member association of AFUW and serves a number of benefits both at personal and societal level in providing women with opportunities.

Australian Federation of University Women - Western Australian -Foundation Bursary

Eligibility: Candidate should be women and must be a graduate members of the Australian Federation of University Women
Level of Study: Postdoctorate
Type: Bursary
Value: AU$2,500
Frequency: Annual
Country of Study: Any country
Funding: Private

For further information contact:

Bursary Office, AFUW (WA), Inc., PO Box 48, Nedlands, WT 6009, Australia.

Email: afuwwa@afuw.org.au

Study in Australia - Northern Territory Scholarships

Purpose: This scholarship is provided to talented students from all over the world to study in Australia's Northern

Territory. The scholarships recognize student's academic merit, leadership and community engagement

Eligibility: Applicants must 1. have a demonstrated record of academic excellence, community engagement and leadership. 2. meet the Northern Territory education provider's academic and English entry requirement. 3. have applied and obtained an offer of admission to a Northern Territory education provider for study in the Northern Territory. i. Alana Kaye College. ii. Australian Careers College. iii. BCA National Training Group. iv. Charles Darwin University. v. Darwin High School. vi. International College of Advanced Education. vii. International House Darwin. viii. Navitas English Darwin. ix. Navitas Professional. x. The Essington International School Darwin. 4. reside in the Northern Territory. 5. not already be studying in the Northern Territory, or with a Northern Territory education provider. 6. not hold any other scholarship

Level of Study: Graduate

Type: Scholarship

Value: The scholarships are worth school (AU$10 000), English language (AU$5,000), vocational education and training (AU$7,500), Professional Year Program (AU$2,500) and higher education

Frequency: Annual

Country of Study: Australia

Application Procedure: For the complete information on the application methods, use the below link. studynt.nt.gov.au/file/923

Closing Date: 31 May

Funding: Private

Women's Leadership and Development Program (WLDP) - Women's Economic Security Grant Guidelines

Purpose: The grant opportunity is to provide funding for one-off or small-scale projects that contribute towards achieving Women's Economic Security on a national scale within Australia

Eligibility: 1. A Company incorporated in Australia. 2. A Company incorporated by guarantee. 3. An Incorporated trustee on behalf of a trust. 4. A Publicly funded research organisation as defined in the Glossary. 5. An Aboriginal and/or Torres Strait Islander Corporation registered under the Corporations

Level of Study: Foundation programme

Type: Grant

Frequency: Annual

Country of Study: Any country

Closing Date: 25 January

Funding: Foundation

For further information contact:

Tel: (61) 2 6271 6074
Email: WLDP17-18@pmc.gov.au

Australian Government Research Training Scholarships

Australian Biological Resources Study (ABRS) National Taxonomy Research Grant Program

Purpose: The Australian Biological Resources Study (ABRS) provides research grants to Postdoctoral Fellows and established researchers to undertake research relevant to the taxonomy and systematics of the Australian biota

Eligibility: 1. All Research grants have a co-funding requirement. That is, applicants must have obtained a commitment for the applicable amount of co-funding for their application to be considered. 2. The ABRS will place no restrictions on the source of this contribution, but applicants will need to be aware of the rules of other granting agencies, which may limit how funds contributed by them may be used

Level of Study: Doctorate, Postdoctorate

Type: Research grant

Value: Research Grants of AU$10,000, AU$35,000, AU$70,000 or AU$90,000 per annum (excluding GST) are available, as well as a AU$90,000 per annum (excluding GST) Postdoctoral Fellowship grant

Frequency: Every 3 years

Country of Study: Any country

Closing Date: 22 November

Funding: Private

Additional Information: There are some funding agreement being meant for this funding scheme. All grant recipients who receive funding from the ABRS under the current and upcoming round, are subject to the terms and conditions set out in the ABRS Grant Funding Agreement. The Department of the Environment and Energy has developed standard funding agreements for grants. Applicants who are successful in receiving funding under the ABRS NTRGP are subject to the conditions set out in the following funding agreement templates. For further information towards the template, kindly visit our website. www.environment.gov.au/science/abrs/grants/research-grants www.communitygrants.gov.au/grants/national-taxonomy-research-grant-program

For further information contact:

Department of the Environment and Energy GPO, Business and Grants Manager Australian Biological Resources Study

Department of the Environment and Energy, Box 787, Canberra, ACT 2601, Australia.

Email: abrs.grants@environment.gov.au

Australian Security Intelligence Organisation Scheme

Purpose: It provides legal financial assistance for a person summoned by the Australian Security Intelligence Organisation (ASIO) to appear before a prescribed authority for questioning
Eligibility: At a minimum, you must be a non-tax-exempt company, Australian University, Cooperative Research Centre (CRC) or Publicly Funded Research Agency (PRFA) have ownership, access to, or the beneficial use of any intellectual property necessary to carry out the projects under the JSF Program be able to match the value of funding dollar for dollar (co-contribution required) not be one of the companies engaged on the development of the Joint Strike Fighter (JSF)
Level of Study: Graduate
Type: Other
Value: complete value of the award is AU$3,316,000.00
Frequency: Annual
Country of Study: Any country
Closing Date: 7 September
Funding: Government
Additional Information: www.ag.gov.au/LegalSystem/ Legalaidprogrammes/ Commonwealthlegalfinancialassistance/Pages/Australian-Security-Intelligence-Organisation-scheme.aspx

For further information contact:

Tel: (61) 2 6141 4770
Email: finass@ag.gov.au

Expensive Commonwealth Criminal Cases Fund (ECCCF)

Purpose: The Australian Government is inviting legal aid commissions to apply for reimbursement under the Expensive Commonwealth Criminal Cases Fund. This program, open to legal aid commissions, ensures that legal aid commissions have sufficient resources to provide a legal defence for people charged with serious Commonwealth criminal offences who cannot afford private legal representation
Eligibility: 1. Only legal aid commissions can apply for reimbursement under the ECCCF. 2. A legal aid commission is a statutory body established pursuant to legislation in the relevant state or territory to provide legal aid services

Level of Study: Graduate
Type: Funding support
Frequency: Annual
Country of Study: Any country
Closing Date: 28 November
Funding: Private
Additional Information: www.communitygrants.gov.au/ grants/ecccf-2019-20

For further information contact:

Tel: (61) 800 020 283
Email: support@communitygrants.gov.au

National Disability Insurance Scheme Jobs and Market Fund Round 1

Purpose: The National Disability Insurance Scheme (NDIS) is a significant social and economic policy reform representing one of the largest job creation opportunities in Australia. Achieving choice and control for participants requires a well-functioning market of NDIS providers, from which empowered NDIS participants are able to choose quality services that meet their needs
Eligibility: To be eligible you must be one of the following entity types 1. Indigenous Corporation. 2. Company. 3. Local Government. 4. Cooperative. 5. Incorporated Association. 6. Sole Trader. 7. Statutory Entity. 8. Partnership. 9. Trustee on behalf of a Trust
Level of Study: Graduate
Type: Scholarships
Frequency: Annual
Country of Study: Any country
Closing Date: 17 January
Funding: Government
Additional Information: This grant round is being administered by the Community Grants Hub, on behalf of the Department of Social Services www.communitygrants.gov.au/ grants/ndis-jobs-and-market-fund-round-1

For further information contact:

Email: support@communitygrants.gov.au

Volunteer Grants

Purpose: The Volunteer Grants program aims to support the efforts of Australia's Volunteers. They provide small amounts of money that organisations can use to help their volunteers. The grants form part of the Government's work to support the volunteers who help disadvantaged Australian communities

and encourage inclusion of vulnerable people in community life
Eligibility: Eligible applicants must be Australian not-for-profit organisations or community groups; whose volunteers' work supports families and/or communities in Australia
Level of Study: Graduate
Type: Grants and studentships
Value: £5,000
Frequency: Annual
Country of Study: United Kingdom
Closing Date: 6 April
Funding: Private
Additional Information: www.communitygrants.gov.au/grants/volunteer-grants-activity-2019-20

For further information contact:

Tel: (61) 800 020 283
Email: support@communitygrants.gov.au

Australian Institute of Aboriginal and Torres Strait Islander Studies (AIATSIS)

GPO Box 553, Canberra, ACT 2601, Australia.

Tel: (61) 2 6246 1157
Email: grants@aiatsis.gov.au
Website: www.aiatsis.gov.au
Contact: Mr Peter Veth, Research Administration Team

The Australian Institute of Aboriginal and Torres Strait Islander Studies (AIATSIS) is a federally funded organization devoted to Aboriginal and Torres Strait Islander research. Its principal function is to promote Australian Aboriginal and Torres Strait Islander studies. A staff of 90, directed by the Principal, engages in a range of services through the Research Programme, the Research Grants Programme, the archives and production team and the library.

Australian Institute of Aboriginal and Torres Strait Islander Studies Conference Call for papers

Purpose: To promote research into Aboriginal and Torres Strait Islander studies. AIATSIS welcomes a variety of presentation and workshop formats (ranging from 30 mins to 1.5 hours) including
Eligibility: Open to nationals of any country
Level of Study: Unrestricted
Type: Grant

Value: No pre-determined value
Length of Study: Up to 1 year
Frequency: Annual
Country of Study: Australia
Application Procedure: Applicants must complete an application form, available from the website
No. of awards offered: 101
Closing Date: 27 May
Funding: Government
Contributor: The Australian Federal Government
No. of awards given last year: 31
No. of applicants last year: 101
Additional Information: Permission to conduct research projects must be obtained from the appropriate Aboriginal or Torres Strait Island community or organization aiatsis.gov.au/news-and-events/events/national-native-title-conference-2020

For further information contact:

Twin Towns Conference & Function Centre, 2 Wharf St, Tweed Heads, New Wales South 2485, Australia.

Email: research@aiatsis.gov.au

Australian Institute of Nuclear Science and Engineering (AINSE)

Private Mail Bag 1, Menai, NSW 2234, Australia.

Tel: (61) 2 9717 3376
Email: ainse@ansto.gov.au
Website: www.ansto.gov.au
Contact: Dr Dennis Mather, Scientific Secretary

Established in 1958, the Australian Institute of Nuclear Science and Engineering (AINSE) is a consortium of Australian universities and the University of Auckland

Australian Institute of Nuclear Science and Engineering Awards

Purpose: Postgraduate Research Awards (PGRAs) are offered by AINSE Limited (the Australian Institute of Nuclear Science and Engineering) for suitably qualified persons wishing to undertake studies in AINSE's fields of interest for a higher degree at an AINSE member university
Eligibility: Open to member organizations of AINSE that are undertaking projects in an appropriate field

Level of Study: Unrestricted
Type: Grant
Value: Supplement stipend of AU$7,500 per annum and a generous travel and accommodation allowance to enable students to work at ANSTO facilities
Length of Study: 1 year
Frequency: Annual
Study Establishment: Lucas Heights Science and Technology Centre
Country of Study: Australia
Application Procedure: Applicants must contact the Scientific Secretary, AINSE or Research Office at member universities
No. of awards offered: 232
Closing Date: 15 April
Funding: Government
No. of awards given last year: 179
No. of applicants last year: 232

For further information contact:

AINSE Ltd, Locked Bag 2001, Kirrawee DC, NSW 2232, Australia.

Tel: (61) 2 9717 3436
Email: ainse@ainse.edu.au

Early Career Researcher Grant (ECRG)

Purpose: The grant can be spent on travel, accommodation, consumables and carer requirements, subject to AINSE discretion.
Eligibility: Eligible applicants must be in their first five years (full-time equivalent) of employment in a postdoctoral Early Career Research position at an AINSE Member Institution. Allowances are made for career breaks when assessing the five-year FTE eligibility requirement. The postdoctoral research work must be undertaken in collaboration with ANSTO.
Level of Study: Postgraduate
Type: Grant
Value: AU$10,000
Frequency: Annual
Country of Study: Any country
Application Procedure: To apply for the ECRG, you must have established a connection with an appropriate ANSTO collaborator on the instrument(s) you will be using for your research, and plan to commence work at an ANSTO facility under an approved proposal within the period 1st October 2022 – 31st December 2023. The application form linked below must then be completed and submitted, along with all required attachments, to enquiries@ainse.edu.au prior to the deadline.
Closing Date: 31 July

For further information contact:

Email: enquiries@ainse.edu.au

Honours Scholarship

Purpose: The AINSE Honours Scholarship consists of an AU$5,000 payment given to students undertaking an honours project involving the use of nuclear techniques, materials or by using prior AINSE-sponsored research data.
Eligibility: Eligible students will be enrolled in an honours degree OR a Masters by coursework+thesis degree at an AINSE Member University for some period between 1st January 2023 and 31st March 2024. The student's research project must involve the use of ANSTO facilities, or the analysis of data previously collected from ANSTO facilities, in collaboration with an ANSTO staff member.
Type: Scholarship
Value: AU$5,000
Frequency: Annual
Country of Study: Any country
Application Procedure: To apply for the Honours Scholarship, contact your AINSE Councillor and complete the application form using our online application portal linked below. First-time users should press the "Request PIN" button to receive login details to the portal within 24 hours. Once logged in, navigate to "Start New Application" and select "Honours Scholarship 2023" as the Application Type. Complete applications, including all supporting documentation, must be submitted and received prior to the deadline.
Closing Date: 15 March

For further information contact:

Email: enquiries@ainse.edu.au

Postgraduate Research Award (PGRA)

Subjects: Archaeology, Geosciences and Environmental Sciences, Biotechnology and Biomedical Sciences, Materials Science and Engineering
Purpose: The Award also provides travel and accommodation support for students to present at conferences, undertake field work or travel to ANSTO facilities.
Eligibility: Eligible students will be enrolled in an postgraduate research degree at an AINSE Member University and receiving an RTP scholarship or equivalent. The research project must require the use of ANSTO's facilities and expertise.
Level of Study: Postgraduate

Type: Award
Value: AU$8,250
Frequency: Annual
Country of Study: Any country
Application Procedure: To apply for the PGRA Scholarship, contact your AINSE Councillor and establish a connection with an appropriate ANSTO co-supervisor on the instrument you will be using for your research. You must complete the application form using our online application portal prior to the application deadline.
Closing Date: 15 April

For further information contact:

Email: enquiries@ainse.edu.au

Residential Student Scholarship (RSS)

Purpose: The Residential Student Scholarship (RSS) is for students who will need to stay at ANSTO
Eligibility: Eligible students will be enrolled in an post-graduate research degree at an AINSE Member University and receiving an RTP scholarship or equivalent. The research project must require the use of ANSTO's facilities and expertise for an minimum of 6 months per year on average.
Level of Study: Postgraduate
Type: Scholarship
Value: The RSS comprises an AU$8,250 stipend (newly-increased as of 1 July 2021) and up to AU$5,000 travel support per annum.
Length of Study: 6 months
Frequency: Annual
Country of Study: Any country
Application Procedure: To apply for the RSS Scholarship, contact your AINSE Councillor and establish a connection with an appropriate ANSTO co-supervisor on the instrument you will be using for your research. You must complete the application form using our online application portal prior to the application deadline.
Closing Date: 15 April

Australian National University (ANU)

Fees and Scholarships Office, Building X-005, Canberra, ACT 2601, Australia.

Tel: (61) 2 6125 5111
Email: research.scholarships@anu.edu.au
Website: www.anu.edu.au

The Australian National University (ANU) was founded by the Australian Government in 1946 as Australia's only completely research-orientated university. It comprises of seven colleges and many research schools.

A&A Masters Higher Degree Research Award

Subjects: Visual Art; Design; Art History and Art Theory
Purpose: The A&A Masters award is to assist students who are enrolled full-time in the final year of a Higher Degree by Research program, offered by the School of Art in the ANU College of Arts and Social Sciences, who have demonstrated a high capacity for achievement in his or her chosen field of Arts practice.
Eligibility: The applicant must be enrolled full-time in the final year of a Higher Degree by Research program of study at the ANU School of Art, ANU College of Arts and Social Sciences.
Level of Study: Masters Degree
Type: Award
Value: A one off payment award valued at AU$1,000.00
Length of Study: 1 year
Frequency: Annual
Country of Study: Any country
Application Procedure: The application form will be posted on the SoA HDR Wattle site. For more information on this and opening and closing dates please contact graduateadmin.soa@anu.edu.au
No. of awards offered: 1

For further information contact:

Email: graduateadmin.soa@anu.edu.au

Australian National University Doctoral Fellowships

Purpose: To help Doctoral students pursue research and dissertation writing
Eligibility: Open to candidates who have obtained their graduate degree from a university located in the United States
Level of Study: Doctorate
Type: Fellowships
Value: AU$1,600 per month, one round-trip economy class airfare and some funding for research
Length of Study: 3–9 months
Frequency: Annual
Study Establishment: Australian National University
Country of Study: Australia
Application Procedure: Applicants can download the application form from the website. The completed application form can be sent by post or electronically
Closing Date: 30 January

Additional Information: Fellows accompanied by their family and staying for 6 months or more at the ANU will be entitled to family support of up to AU$5,000, depending on the number of family members and other circumstances www.anu.edu.au/study/scholarships

For further information contact:

Email: hr.rspas@anu.edu.au

Australian National University Excellence Scholarship Program

Purpose: To study full-time in postgraduate program at the Australian National University
Value: AU$5,000 in the first 12 months of study at ANU followed by 10% discount of tuition fees for years of study thereafter
Country of Study: Australia
Closing Date: 30 May
Additional Information: www.anu.edu.au/study/scholarships

For further information contact:

Email: coursework.scholarships@anu.edu.au

Australian National University-Study Canberra India Scholarship for Postgraduate and Undergraduates in Australia

Purpose: The objective of the award is to provide support for living costs to successful applicants who have achieved at an excellent level in their final years of schooling or university studies
Eligibility: Indian citizens are eligible to apply for this scholarship programme. Applicants whose first language is not English are usually required to provide evidence of proficiency in English at the higher level required by the University
Type: Postgraduate scholarships
Value: The Scholarship will be valued at AU$10,000. The first instalment of AU$2,500 will be paid to the student upon them enrolling in the first semester of their chosen undergraduate or postgraduate coursework program. The remaining funds will be paid after the census date of the first semester that the student is enrolled
Study Establishment: Scholarships are awarded in any of the subjects offered by the university
Country of Study: Australia
Application Procedure: The mode of application is online
Closing Date: 15 January

Additional Information: For more details please visit the website scholarship-positions.com/anu-study-canberra-india-scholarship-postgraduate-undergraduates-australia/2017/12/18/ www.anu.edu.au/study/scholarships

For further information contact:

Email: international.recruitment@anu.edu.au

College of Engineering and Computer Science: College Postgraduate International Award

Eligibility: The Scholarships are offered on the basis of offer of a place in the Master Degree by Coursework programs offered by the College of Engineering and Computer Science and other criteria as set out from time to time by the Program Authority. Eligible students will be automatically considered for the Scholarship on academic merit. The Scholarship is offered on the condition that the recipient is admitted to and continues to pursue a full-time postgraduate program of study at this University and in a program offered by the College of Engineering and Computer Science
Type: Award
Value: Stipend is AU$5,000, payable in two equal instalments of AU$2,500 at the beginning of each semester for one year. Scholars are required to meet all costs associated with their studies including travel, accommodation, books and incidental expenses. The scholar is responsible for paying International Tuition fees for the duration of the program
Frequency: Annual
Additional Information: A scholar may not hold concurrently another scholarship awarded by the University or another University College. A scholar must obtain permission from the College Coursework Scholarships Committee to hold any other scholarship or award concurrently with a College of Engineering and Computer Science Postgraduate Scholarship www.anu.edu.au/study/scholarships

For further information contact:

Tel: (61) 2 6125 0677
Email: student.services@cecs.anu.edu.au

College of Engineering and Computer Science: College Postgraduate International Honours Award

Type: Award
Value: Stipend is AU$5,000, payable in two equal instalments of AU$2,500 at the beginning of each semester for one year

Frequency: Annual

Additional Information: The Scholarships are offered on the basis of offer of a place in the Master Degree by Coursework programs offered by the College of Engineering and Computer Science and other criteria as set out from time to time by the Program Authority www.anu.edu.au/study/scholarships

For further information contact:

Associate Dean (Education), ANU College of Engineering and Computer Science, Australia.

Tel: (61) 2 6125 0677
Email: student.services@cecs.anu.edu.au

Full Tuition International Relations Scholarships

Eligibility: Scholarships are available for all students. There is no restriction or nationality criteria
Value: This scholarship will pay full tuition fees
Length of Study: Up to 4 full time semesters (24 months)
Country of Study: Australia
Closing Date: 31 October

For further information contact:

Email: info@InternationalRelationsEDU.org

National Security College Entry Scholarship for Aboriginal and Torres Strait Islander Students

Eligibility: The Scholarship shall be available to an applicant who is of Australian Aboriginal and/or Torres Strait Islander descent; has completed a Bachelors degree; has been offered admission to the Graduate Certificate in National Security Policy or Master of National Security Policy; is not the recipient of a College sponsored place
Type: Scholarship
Value: The Scholarship covers the full domestic tuition fee for up to 24 units of College core courses. The Scholarship does not cover any necessary admissions and deposit fees, the payment of reading and study materials, living expenses, accommodation or any other costs associated with studying
Country of Study: Any country
Application Procedure: Please print and complete application form, available on the website
Closing Date: 15 December
Additional Information: The Scholarship is available in the first two semesters of study only. Please write to mailto: national.security.college@anu.edu.au

For further information contact:

Email: Crawford.degrees@anu.edu.au

Research School of Accounting India Merit Scholarships

Eligibility: Students from India are eligible to apply
Value: The award will cover 50% of the awardees ANU International Student Fees per semester, for the standard full time duration of the degree in which the student is enrolled in
Country of Study: Australia
Application Procedure: Applications are called for with a closing date as set by the ANU CBE Scholarships Office. The application is submitted on the prescribed electronic form and supporting documentation forwarded to CBE by email
Closing Date: 18 May
Additional Information: Please visit scholarship-positions.com/research-school-of-accounting-india-merit-scholarships-australia/2018/03/31/ mailto: national.security.college@anu.edu.au

For further information contact:

Email: scholarships.cbe@anu.edu.au

Tim and Margaret Bourke PhD Scholarships

Subjects: Pure (Theoretical) Mathematics
Purpose: To support an ANU PhD student working in the area of pure (theoretical) mathematics, the advancement of women in the field of mathematics, and the teaching of mathematics at the Australian National University
Eligibility: A domestic or international student. Enrolled or enrolling full-time in a program of study for the degree of Doctor of Philosophy at the Australian National University
Type: Scholarship
Value: AU$5,000 per annum
Country of Study: Australia
No. of awards offered: 1
Closing Date: 31 March
Additional Information: For further details, please visit www.scholarshipsupdates.com/australian-national-university-tim-and-margaret-bourke-phd-scholarships-2018/ www.anu.edu.au/study/scholarships/find-a-scholarship/tim-and-margaret-bourke-phd-scholarship

For further information contact:

Kate Liesinger, MSI Administrative Officer John Dedman Building 27, Canberra, ACT 2601, Australia.

Tel: (61) 2 6125 0723
Email: msi.hdr.sa@anu.edu.au

Yuill Scholarship

Subjects: Law
Purpose: The Yuill Scholarship has been established by the University to provide funding to support participation in the International Court of Justice (ICJ) Judicial Fellows Programme. The purpose of the scholarship is to defray the living expenses of the successful applicant while undertaking the traineeship. The ANU College of Law currently offers one scholarship a year in accordance with the program dates of the Court.
Eligibility: The scholarship applicant must be 1. a final year student in a Bachelor of Laws program in the ANU College of Law 2. a final year student in a Juris Doctor program in the ANU College of Law 3. enrolled in a Master of Laws program in the ANU College of Law 4.a recent graduate of the Bachelor of Laws, Juris Doctor or Master of Laws program from the ANU College of Law. The Bachelor of Laws program may be undertaken as a single or a combined degree
Type: Scholarship
Value: AU$25,000
Frequency: Annual
Country of Study: Any country
Closing Date: 15 January
Additional Information: The scholarship will apply for the duration of the traineeship (9 months in total). Application process and criteria is set out in the Conditions of Award. Applications can be sent electronically or in hard copy. Electronic applications can be sent to karen.heuer@anu.edu.au law.anu.edu.au/yuill-scholarship-application

For further information contact:

Email: scholarships.law@anu.edu.au

Australian Research Council (ARC)

Level 2, 11 Lancaster Place, Canberra Airport, Canberra, ACT 2609, Australia.

Tel: (61) 2 6287 6600
Email: ncgp@arc.gov.au
Website: www.arc.gov.au
Contact: Dr Laura Dan, Chief Program Officer

The Australian Research Council (ARC) is a statutory authority within the Australian Government's Innovation, Industry, Science and Research portfolio. The ARC advises the Government on research matters, manages the National Competitive Grants Program, a significant component of Australia's investment in research and development, and has responsibility for the Excellence in Research for Australia initiative.

Australia-India Strategic Research Fund (AISRF)

Purpose: The aim of Australia- India Strategic Research Fund is to 1. increase the uptake of leading science and technology by supporting collaboration between Australian and Indian researchers in strategically focused, leading-edge scientific research and technology projects. 2. strengthen strategic alliances between Australian and Indian researchers
Eligibility: To be eligible you must 1. have an Australian Business Number (ABN) and be one of the following entities. 2. a company, incorporated in Australia. 3. an incorporated not for profit organisation. We can only accept applications that have a primary Indian partner that has submitted, or is in the process of submitting, a corresponding application to India's Department of Science and Technology (DST) or the Department of Biotechnology (DBT)
Level of Study: Graduate
Type: Funding support
Frequency: Annual
Country of Study: Any country
Closing Date: 23 January
Funding: Government

For further information contact:

Email: enquiries@industry.gov.au

Australian Sports Commission (ASC)

Australian Sports Commission, Leverrier Street, Bruce, ACT 2617, Australia.

Email: recruitment@ausport.gov.au
Website: www.ausport.gov.au

The Australian Sports Commission (ASC) is responsible for implementing the Australian Government's national sports policy, which is based on a sports philosophy of excellence and participation. It promotes an effective national sports system that offers improved participation in quality sports activities by all Australians and helps the talented and motivated to reach their potential excellence in sports performance. Its work is guided by the Australian Government's national sports policy, Building Australian Communities through Sport (BACTS).

Biomechanics Postgraduate Scholarship (General Sports)

Purpose: To provide an opportunity for graduates with degrees with a major emphasis in biomechanics to have experience in the application of biomechanics to enhance elite sports performance
Eligibility: Applicants must have tertiary qualification in science, human movement, mathematics or a related area, should have an interest and/or understanding of research principles and some knowledge of biomechanical systems and equipment
Level of Study: Graduate
Type: Scholarship
Value: AU$21,434 per year
Length of Study: 48 weeks
Application Procedure: Applicants must submit a covering letter, a statement of experience and curriculum vitae along with the application form
Closing Date: 29 September

For further information contact:

Tel: (61) 2 6214 1659

Indigenous Sporting Excellence Scholarships

Purpose: To give indigenous sportspeople the opportunity to improve their sporting performance at an elite level
Eligibility: Applicants must be over 12 years of age, representing their state in national competition or Australia internationally within sport or the school sport system, a coach with level 1 or level 2 accreditation, a sports trainer with level 1 accreditation, a sports official with accreditation, competing in a sport that is recognized by the Australian Sports Commission
Type: Scholarship
Value: AU$500
Country of Study: Any country
Application Procedure: Check website for further details
Closing Date: 31 May
Additional Information: Athletes, coaches, sports trainers and officials who receive this scholarship are also eligible to apply for the Elite Indigenous Travel and Accommodation Assistance Program if they are selected for a state representative team attending national championships or an Australian

team competing internationally law.anu.edu.au/yuill-scholarship-application

For further information contact:

Email: school.sport.victoria@edumail.vic.gov.au

Performance Analysis Scholarship

Purpose: To provide performance analysis services to AIS sport programmes through coaches as directed and as required work on projects relating to enhancement of knowledge and coach education
Eligibility: Applicants must have a tertiary qualification in computer science, software engineering, information technology, human movement or a related area and an interest and/or understanding of research principles
Type: Scholarship
Value: AU$21,434 per year
Length of Study: 48 weeks
Application Procedure: Applicants must write a covering letter referencing the position title, prepare a thorough (but concise) statement that focuses on the relevant experience, curriculum vitae that summarize the qualifications including contact details for two referees and can be submitted by email
Closing Date: 29 September

For further information contact:

Tel: (61) 2 6214 1659

PhD Scholarship Programs

Eligibility: Open to candidates who are keen to have a scholar carrying out innovative research specific to their needs
Level of Study: Doctorate
Type: Scholarship
Value: AU$21,000 per year, with a further AU$3,000 per year set aside to cover routine expenses
Country of Study: Australia
Application Procedure: For application details, please visit the website, www.ausport.gov.au/jobs/index.asp
Funding: Government
Contributor: Australian Institute of Sports Medicine
Additional Information: Interested applicants need to visit the site regularly to watch for vacancies law.anu.edu.au/yuill-scholarship-application

For further information contact:

Email: john.williamsr@ausport.gov.au

Postgraduate Scholarship Program–Physiology (Quality Control)

Purpose: To provide opportunity for a graduate whose primary role will be to assist in the area of quality control under the direction of the laboratory manager
Eligibility: Applicants must have a tertiary qualification in science or a related area, an interest and/or understanding of research principles and an experience in an administrative role and good computing skills
Level of Study: Graduate
Type: Scholarship
Value: AU$21,434 per year
Length of Study: 54 weeks
Application Procedure: Applicants must submit a covering letter, a statement of experience and curriculum vitae along with the application form
Closing Date: 29 September
Contributor: Australian Sports Commission
Additional Information: Terms and conditions are subject to change. Always confirm details with scholarship provider before applying. law.anu.edu.au/yuill-scholarship-application

For further information contact:

Tel: (61) 2 6214 1564

Postgraduate Scholarship–Biomechanics (Swimming)

Purpose: To provide the opportunity for graduates of degrees with major emphasis in biomechanics and to have experience in the application of biomechanics to enhance elite sports performance
Eligibility: Applicants must have a degree in biomechanics or human movement sciences, an interest and/or understanding of research principles, experience in biomechanics services and knowledge of and experience in a competitive swimming environment
Level of Study: Graduate
Type: Scholarship
Value: AU$21,434 per year
Length of Study: 48 weeks
Application Procedure: Applicants must submit a covering letter, a statement of experience and curriculum vitae along with the application form
Closing Date: 29 September

For further information contact:

PO Box 176, Belconnen, ACT 2616, Australia.

Tel: (61) 2 6214 1732

Postgraduate Scholarship–Physiology (Biochemistry/Haematology)

Purpose: To provide an opportunity for a graduate whose primary role will be to assist in the area of biochemistry and haematology under the direction of the biochemistry/haematology manager
Eligibility: Applicants must have a degree in medical laboratory science or biological sciences and an interest and/or understanding of research principles, good computer skills
Level of Study: Postgraduate
Type: Scholarship
Value: AU$21,434 per year
Length of Study: 50 weeks
Application Procedure: Applicants must write a covering letter referencing the position title, prepare a thorough (but concise) statement that focuses on the relevant experience, curriculum vitae that summarize the qualifications including contact details for two referees and can be submitted by email
Closing Date: 29 September

For further information contact:

PO Box 176, Belconnen, ACT 2616, Australia.

Tel: (61) 2 6214 1111
Fax: (61) 2 6251 2680, 2 6214 1836

Sport Leadership Grants for Women Program

Purpose: To provide women with an opportunity to undertake sport leadership training
Eligibility: Applicants must be indigenous women, women in disability sport, women from culturally and linguistically diverse backgrounds and women in general sport leadership
Type: Grant
Value: Up to AU$5,000 for individuals and up to AU$10,000 for incorporated organizations
Application Procedure: Check website for further details
Closing Date: 29 April
Funding: Government

Additional Information: www.sportaus.gov.au/grants_and_funding/women_leaders_in_sport

For further information contact:

Tel: (61) 2 6214 7994
Email: leadershipgrants@ausport.gov.au

Sports Medicine Fellowship Program

Eligibility: Open to Australasian College of Sports Physicians (ACSP) trainees
Level of Study: Postgraduate
Frequency: Annual
Study Establishment: Australian Institute of Sports Science
Country of Study: Australia
Application Procedure: For application details, please visit the website, www.ausport.gov.au/jobs/sssmpostgrad.asp
Funding: Government

For further information contact:

Tel: (61) 2 6214 1578
Email: jill.flanagan@ausport.gov.au

Sports Physiology Postgraduate Scholarship–Fatigue and Recovery

Purpose: To offer an Honours graduate in science or a related field the opportunity to complete a scholarship in physiology (fatigue and recovery)
Eligibility: Applicants must have an Honours Degree in science or a related area, basic skills in conducting routine physiological testing procedures, good computing skills, outstanding organizational skills and a high level of initiative
Level of Study: Graduate
Type: Scholarship
Value: AU$19,890 per year
Length of Study: 1 year
Application Procedure: Applicants must submit a covering letter, a statement of experience and curriculum vitae along with the application form
Closing Date: 6 April

For further information contact:

PO Box 176, Belconnen, ACT 2616, Australia.

Tel: (61) 2 6214 1111
Fax: (61) 2 6251 2680, 2 6214 1836
Email: Recruitment@ausport.gov.au

Austrian Academy of Sciences

Institute of Limnology, Mondseestrasse 9, A-5310 Mondsee, Austria.

Tel: (43) 623 240 79
Email: ipgl.mondsee@oeaw.ac.at
Website: www.ipgl.at
Contact: Mr Regina Brandstätter, IPGL Officer

The Institute of Limnology of the Austrian Academy of Sciences performs ecological research on inland waters. The overall research goal is to understand the structure, function and dynamics of freshwater ecosystems. Although the Institute primarily conducts basic research, aspects of applied research are also considered. The Institute at Mondsee, located close to Salzburg, was established in 1981 and has a staff of 26, including 13 scientists. Currently, the Institute's main fields of research are tropic interactions and food-web structures in lakes.

Austrian Academy of Sciences, 4-months Trimester at Egerton University, Kenya

Purpose: Postgraduate training of water experts of African countries Ethiopia, Uganda, Kenya, Burundi, Tansania, Rwanda, Cape Verde, Burkina Faso, Senegal
Eligibility: Principal requirement for admission is a BSc degree or equivalent qualification in a relevant subject from a recognized university (e.g. BSc in botany, zoology, chemistry, agriculture, environmental science, aquaculture and fisheries, water resource management, environmental economics or engineering, etc.). Priority countries Eastern Africa Ethiopia, Uganda, Kenya, Burundi, Tanzania, Rwanda, Western Africa Cape Verde, Burkina Faso, Senegal. Southern Africa Mozambique
Type: Fellowship
Value: €450 monthly, to cover food, personal needs plus free tuition, health insurance, study material, equipment for lab work, field work and travelling expenses
Length of Study: 4 months
Frequency: Annual
Study Establishment: Egerton University, Kenya
Country of Study: Kenya
Application Procedure: Application forms are provided by Egerton University and IPGL Office within the Institute for Limnology of the Austrian Academy of Sciences
No. of awards offered: 2 qualified

Closing Date: 30 November
Contributor: The Austrian Development Cooperation
No. of awards given last year: 2
No. of applicants last year: 2 qualified
Additional Information: No provisions are made for dependants. Country of study is Kenya. www.sportaus.gov.au/grants_and_funding/women_leaders_in_sport

For further information contact:

Egerton University, PO Box 536, Egerton 20115, Kenya.

Email:　info@egerton.ac.ke

Austrian Academy of Sciences, MSc Course in Limnology and Wetland Ecosystems

Purpose: To understand the structure and functioning of aquatic and wetland ecosystems for the conservation of biodiversity and sustainable management of natural resources. To acquire skills for interacting with stakeholders, managers and policy makers in the development of best practices
Eligibility: Open to candidates from developing countries who are maximum 35 years of age, have a good working knowledge of English and have an academic degree in science, agriculture or veterinary medicine from a university or any other recognized Institute of Higher Education. Applicants should have 3 years practical experience in at least one special subject in their field of professional training. All applications are considered on their individual merits
Level of Study: Postgraduate
Type: Scholarship
Value: US$1,350 paid monthly to cover food, lodging and personal needs plus free tuition, health insurance, study material and equipment for laboratory work, field work and travelling expenses
Length of Study: 18 months
Frequency: Annual
Study Establishment: Institute for Limnology, Mondsee; Institute UNESCO-IHE, Delft, The Netherlands; Egerton University, Kenya; Czech Academy of Sciences, Trebon, Czech Republic; Austrian Universities and Federal Institutes in Austria
Application Procedure: Applicants must obtain application forms from the website. Filled application forms can be sent to Institute for Limnology of the Austrian Academy of Sciences
No. of awards offered: 90
Closing Date: January

Funding: Government
Contributor: The Austrian Development Co-operation
No. of awards given last year: 4
No. of applicants last year: 90
Additional Information: No provisions are made for dependants. It is strongly advised that dependants do not accompany fellows due to frequent moves during the course. Fellows must also provide their own transportation to and from Austria. www.sportaus.gov.au/grants_and_funding/women_leaders_in_sport

For further information contact:

Institute of Limnology, Dr. Ignaz Seipel-Platz 2, A-1010 Vienna, Austria.

Tel:　(43) 6232 4079
Fax:　(43) 6232 3578

Austrian Academy of Sciences, Short Course—Tropical Limnology

Purpose: To assist students studying the special characteristics of tropical river and lake ecosystems, its interactions with activities, processes in the watershed and relevant ecosystem services
Eligibility: Open to candidates from East African countries who have a good working knowledge of English and have an academic degree either in science, agriculture or veterinary medicine from a university or other recognised Institute of Higher Education. Applicants should have practical experience within at least one special subject in their field of professional training
Level of Study: Postgraduate
Type: Scholarship
Value: US$21 paid per day including accommodation, full board and US$2,500 d.s.a. plus free tuition, health insurance, study material and equipment for laboratory work, field work and travelling expenses
Length of Study: 3 weeks
Frequency: Annual
Study Establishment: Egerton University, Kenya, Sagana Fish Farm, Kenya
Application Procedure: Application forms are also available from the website
No. of awards offered: 75
Closing Date: 30 July
Funding: Government
Contributor: The Austrian Development Co-operation
No. of awards given last year: 10
No. of applicants last year: 75

Additional Information: No provisions are made for dependants. It is strongly advised that dependants do not accompany Fellows due to frequent moves during the course. Fellows must also arrange their own transportation to and from Kenya. www.sportaus.gov.au/grants_and_funding/women_leaders_in_sport

For further information contact:

Dept. of Zoology, Egerton University, PO Box 536, Egerton 20115, Kenya.

Email: mathookoj@yahoo.com

Austrian Exchange Service

Agency for International Co-operation in Education & Research Bureau for Academic Mobility Alserstrasse 4/1/15/7, A-1090 Vienna, Austria.

Tel: (43) 142 772 8188
Email: bamo@oead.ac.at
Website: www.oead.ac.at
Contact: Dr Lydia Skarits, Head of Office

Austrian Academic Exchange Service Unilateral Scholarship Programs

Purpose: To enable postgraduates from developing countries to undertake professional training
Eligibility: Applicants must be postgraduates of natural scientific, technical, social and economic studies or medical doctors wishing to conduct professional training in Austria
Level of Study: Postgraduate, Professional development
Type: Scholarship
Value: Monthly scholarship payment, plus a possible additional payment for housing, as well as cover for accident and health insurance. After four months a start payment is granted. Under certain conditions there is the possibility of the coverage of travel costs
Country of Study: Austria
Application Procedure: Applicants can obtain information from the website or contact the Austrian Exchange Service

For further information contact:

Tel: (43) 142 772 8180
Fax: (43) 142 772 8195
Email: vbs@oead.ac.at

Austrian Federal Ministry for Science and Research

Embassy of Austria, 12 Talbot Street, Forrest, ACT 2603, Australia.

Tel: (61) 2 6295 1533
Contact: Grants Management Officer

Australian Prostate Centre - Victoria

Purpose: The purpose of the grant is to support prostate cancer research through the safeguarding of rare tissue and bioinformatics assets at the Australian Prostate Centre (Victoria)
Eligibility: The Australian Prostate Centre Victoria is the eligible organisation to apply for this Grant Opportunity
Level of Study: Research
Type: Grant
Value: AU$600,000.00
Frequency: Annual
Country of Study: Australia
Closing Date: 21 January
Funding: Government

For further information contact:

Email: grant.atm@health.gov.au

Austro-American Association of Boston

Austro-American Association of Boston, Inc. c/o Traude Schieber-Acker, President 67 Bridle Path, Sudbury, MA 01776, United States of America.

Tel: (1) 978 579 2191
Email: thansen@wellesley.edu
Website: www.austria-boston.org/

Membership of the Austro-American Association of Boston is open toany individual interested in any aspect of Austrian history, economy, culture, politics and tourism. The association conducts meetings and get togethers focusing on events and experiences related to Austria.

A-AA Austrian Studies Scholarship Award

Purpose: Project areas may include history, literature, art, architecture, folk customs, music and contemporary life
Eligibility: All undergraduate and graduate students at New England colleges and Universities are eligible to apply
Level of Study: Graduate
Type: Award
Value: US$1,500
Application Procedure: There is no application form. Applicants should submit the following information a detailed project proposal, including the reason for selecting it; curriculum vitae; and two confidential letters of support from faculty members who know the applicant well and can comment on the feasibility of the project
Closing Date: 23 March
Additional Information: Please feel free to email any or submissions or inquiries to the co-chair of the scholarship committee, Dr Johann Nittmann at Johann. Nittmann@cavium.com www.austria-boston.org/scholar.asp

For further information contact:

Department of German, Wellesley College, 106 Central St, Wellesley, MA 02481, United States of America.

Tel: (1) 781 283 2255
Email: scholarship@austria-boston.org

Austro-American Association of Boston Stipend

Purpose: To promote the understanding and dissemination of Austrian culture
Eligibility: Junior faculty members and students enroled in a college in New England
Level of Study: Unrestricted
Type: Stipendiary
Value: US$3,000
Study Establishment: Any in New England
Country of Study: United States of America
Application Procedure: Applicants must submit a detailed description of the project including the reasons for selecting it, a curriculum vitae and two letters of recommendation from faculty members who know the applicant well and can comment on the feasibility of the project
No. of awards offered: 1
Closing Date: 23 March
Funding: Private
Contributor: Association members
No. of applicants last year: 1

Additional Information: The award is limited to individuals living or studying in New England. Projects funded in the past have included the preparation of musical or dramatic performances, the facilitation of appropriate publications and research trips to Austria. Culture is defined to include the humanities and the arts. The recipient may be asked to present the results of the project at an event of the Austro-American Association. The award may not be used to pay tuition fees at a college or university in New England www.austria-boston.org/scholar.asp

For further information contact:

Wellesley College, 106 Central St, Wellesley, MA 02481, United States of America.

Email: scholarship@austria-boston.org

Autism Speaks

1 East 33rd Street, 4th Floor, New York, NY 10016, United States of America.

Tel: (1) 646 385 8500
Email: autismspeaks@charitydynamics.com
Website: www.autismspeaks.org

Postdoctoral Fellowship

Subjects: Autism research
Purpose: Autism Speaks is dedicated to promoting solutions, across the spectrum and throughout the life span, for the needs of individuals with autism and their families. We do this through advocacy and support; increasing understanding and acceptance of autism spectrum disorder; and advancing research into causes and better interventions for autism spectrum disorder and related conditions. The goal of our postdoctoral fellowships is to support well-qualified postdoctoral scientists pursuing training in autism.
Eligibility: The program is open to applicants from public or private institutions doing preclinical or clinical research.
Type: Fellowship
Value: Each fellowship includes both a competitive stipend and an US$11,000 annual allowance intended to cover professional conference travel, research costs and supplies, and/or fringe benefits. Indirect costs are not allowed. Stipend amounts based on years of experience since PhD can be found below, with the year 7 level being the maximum. The latest start year is 5 years.

Length of Study: Two years

Country of Study: Any country

Application Procedure: All proposals must be submitted online via Autism Speaks Science Grants System. Through its various user-friendly features, applicants and institutional officials can monitor the status of their applications and grants. System access instructions can be found in the RFAs. Electronic submissions are mandatory. No paper or e-mailed applications will be accepted.

Closing Date: 19 January

Additional Information: For queries contact research@autismspeaks.org. www.autismspeaks.org/scientific-research-grants-how-apply

B

Bath Spa University

Newton Park, Newton St Loe, Bath BA2 9BN, United Kingdom.

Tel: (44) 122 587 5875
Email: international@bathspa.ac.uk
Website: www.bathspa.ac.uk/

Bath Spa University is where creative minds meet. We teach and research across art, sciences, education, social science, and business. The University employs outstanding creative professionals who support its aim to be a leading educational institution in creativity, culture and enterprise.

Educations.com scholarship (Study a Master's in Europe)

Purpose: At educations.com, we believe that students who study abroad become the next generation of globally-minded leaders – and we want more of you to do it!
Eligibility: You must have applied (or will apply) to a university or graduate school within Europe (see the FAQs below for an official list of European countries). You must have applied (or will apply) for a Master's-level degree starting the Fall 2022 semester. The degree program must be studied either within Europe or online via distance learning from a European institute. You must meet the entry requirements for the university or graduate school, including: Holding a valid undergraduate (Bachelor's) degree Meeting language requirements for the program You must hold or be eligible to apply for a relevant study visa (if applicable). You must be studying abroad in a country that you are not a citizen of or currently reside in (unless currently studying abroad).
Level of Study: Postgraduate

Type: Scholarship
Value: Up to €5000
Country of Study: Any country
No. of awards offered: 1
Closing Date: 16 May
Additional Information: www.educations.com/scholarships/study-a-masters-in-europe-15211

International Partner Scholarship

Purpose: Bath Spa University's International Partner Scholarships celebrate our strong partnerships with leading universities across the world
Eligibility: Open to postgraduate taught Master's applicants from Bath Spa University partner institutions. Applications are welcome from international students who have completed undergraduate or postgraduate education at a partner institution; achieved high academic results; can demonstrate experience in university, community and society activities; can show future aspirations to become involved in university life at Bath Spa University; plus show ideas on how Bath Spa University can work with its partner institutions towards promoting global citizenship.
Type: Scholarship
Value: £3,000
Frequency: Annual
Application Procedure: Applications are made through the international scholarship application form. Applicants must hold an offer of admission for a Bath Spa University postgraduate taught degree programme that is full-time and taught on-campus, be a graduate of a Bath Spa University partner institution, and complete the International Scholarship Application Form
Additional Information: For further information, please check at www.bathspa.ac.uk/international-students/scholarships/international-partner-scholarship

© Springer Nature Limited 2022
Palgrave Macmillan (ed.), *The Grants Register 2023*,
https://doi.org/10.1057/978-1-349-96053-8

International Recruitment Office Scholarship

Purpose: Bath Spa University is pleased to be able to offer funding opportunities for high achieving students from outside the UK who are entering undergraduate or postgraduate studies with us.

Eligibility: Applications are open for candidates who are entering three-year undergraduate or one-year postgraduate programmes at Bath Spa University

Type: Scholarship

Value: £5,000 of first year of fees

Frequency: Annual

Country of Study: Any country

Application Procedure: 1. Please complete all the details, including your name, contact details, student number and qualifications. Applications with missing details will be automatically rejected. 2. If you're awaiting your final results, you're still able to apply. Please state 'pending results' in the qualification section. You must submit your results when they're available. 3. The scholarship essay question is very important. To answer this question you should include details that cover all the criteria (a) Academic achievement / results (b) Involvement in activities at your previous university, community work and your contribution to society (c) Charity / volunteer work you've done (d) Information on your future aspirations (e) Examples on how you'll contribute to the social and economic development of your country. 4. You should also give examples on how you intend to become involved in university life at Bath Spa. To be eligible to apply for the scholarship, you must be an applicant and have accepted your offer.

No. of awards offered: 1

Closing Date: 6 June

Invertimos en el talento de los Colombianos (ICETEX) Artistas Jovenes Scholarships

Purpose: ICETEX's Artistas Jovenes Talentos programme is a unique programme that supports young Colombian artists and designers, filmmakers, performers and musicians, writers and poets. As the leading United Kingdom university for partner of ICETEX, and the top United Kingdom creative university, the ICETEX Artistas Jovenes Talentos is a perfect fit for applicants to Bath Spa University's programmes across art, design, film, writing, music and performance

Eligibility: Applications are open for candidates who meet the requirements of ICETEX application process. Full details of eligibility are available on the ICETEX website

Level of Study: Graduate, Postgraduate

Type: Scholarship

Country of Study: Any country

Application Procedure: (i) Eligible candidates must first have an offer of admission for the chosen programme, If you meet the entry criteria for the chosen course you will be sent a conditional offer of admission by email. You must meet all the academic conditions of offer, including submission of certificates and transcripts, translated copies, English Language requirement, passport copy, references. (ii) Once you have received an offer letter to the chosen programme of study you then complete the ICETEX Artistas Jovenes Talentos process

Additional Information: Bath Spa University can provide individual help and advice on your application and has a dedicated office in Colombia www.bathspa.ac.uk/international-students/scholarships/international-partner-scholarship

For further information contact:

Bath Spa University, Newton Park, Newton St Loe, Bath BA2 9BN, United Kingdom.

Tel: (44) 1 300 3710

Email: BSUColombia@bathspa.ac.uk

Invertimos en el Talento de los Colombianos (ICETEX) Scholarships

Purpose: The University of Salford is pleased to work with ICETEX to offer funding opportunities for Colombian students to study in the United Kingdom

Eligibility: Applications are open for candidates who meet the requirements of ICETEX application process. Full details of eligibility are available on the ICETEX website at

Type: Scholarship

Value: 50% tuition fee

Frequency: Annual

Country of Study: Any country

Application Procedure: Applicants must apply for the programme of study and then the scholarship via ICETEX. Applicants must also submit a completed Bath Spa University International Scholarship Application form and include the ICETEX reference number. Further application details are given in the website

Closing Date: 10 May

Funding: Private

Additional Information: Applications will be reviewed on submission of the relevant documentation to ICETEX and the Bath Spa University Application Form. The applications are reviewed within two weeks after the deadline by the University Committee. For further information, refer the website link below.   beta.salford.ac.uk/international/icetex-scholarships-colombia

Latin America – Creative and Culture Scholarships

Purpose: Bath Spa University is the UK's leading university for creativity, culture and enterprise. To celebrate this excellence, and to support Bath Spa University's work in Latin America, the Creativity and Culture Scholarships - Latin America are open to eligible applicants for our most creative programs.

Eligibility: Applicants must be nationals from Latin America who have applied for and hold an offer for any of the eligible programs, have high academic results and can demonstrate a commitment to creativity, culture and enterprise in Latin America.

Level of Study: Graduate, Postgraduate

Type: Scholarship

Value: £5,000 off tuition fees for your first year of study

Country of Study: Any country

Application Procedure: Once you've received an offer letter to your chosen programme of study, please submit the International Scholarships application form, or see our advice on How to apply for an International Scholarship.

No. of awards offered: 2

Closing Date: 5 June

Additional Information: www.bathspa.ac.uk/students/ student-finance/scholarships-and-bursaries/scholarships-latin-america/

For further information contact:

Tel: (44) 1225 875875
Fax: (44) 1225 875444

Master's Compare Postgraduate Scholarship

Purpose: which provides an exciting opportunity to help you continue your postgraduate studies and start a Masters course. The funding can be used alongside the Postgraduate Loans scheme which is now available for home students to study at universities across the United Kingdom.

Eligibility: You must register to receive the MastersCompare email newsletter You must have received an unconditional offer of a place on a part-time or full-time postgraduate programme You must be studying at a UK institution

Level of Study: Postgraduate

Type: Scholarship

Value: £5,000

Country of Study: Any country

Closing Date: 26 August

Additional Information: www.masterscompare.co.uk/ PGscholarship/

Postgraduate Overseas Scholarship

Eligibility: Open to applicants who have met the required entry qualification and been offered a place (conditional or unconditional) on a postgraduate taught Masters' programme. It is awarded on the basis of academic merit

Type: Scholarship

Value: £1,000

Application Procedure: Eligibility for the Overseas Scholarship is judged on the basis of the application to the chosen programme of study. There is no need to submit a separate application form. If you are selected for a Postgraduate Overseas Scholarship you will receive a confirmation letter at the time of your offer of admission

For further information contact:

Tel: (44) 1225 875 777

Regional Office Scholarship - India

Purpose: Bath Spa University works with a number of regional offices to support its work across the world. A number of scholarships are available to support applicants from India.

Eligibility: 1. Postgraduate students require 70% in their degree. 2. Undergraduate students require 70% overall in their 12th grade (for example, A-Levels).

Level of Study: Postgraduate, Undergraduate

Type: Scholarship

Value: £2,000 off tuition fees for first year of study (five available) £1,000 off tuition fees (for the first 20 students who apply to study).

Frequency: Annual

Country of Study: Any country

No. of awards offered: 20

Closing Date: 5 June

Additional Information: To be eligible to apply for the scholarship, you must be an applicant and have accepted your offer. www.bathspa.ac.uk/students/student-finance/ scholarships-and-bursaries/regional-office-scholarship-india/

Regional Office Scholarships - China

Purpose: Bath Spa University works with a number of regional offices to support its work across the world. A number of scholarships are available to support applicants from China.

Eligibility: To be eligible to apply for the scholarship, you must be an applicant and have accepted your offer.

Type: Scholarship

Value: £3,000 off tuition fees for the first year of study (three available) £2,000 off tuition fees for the first year of study

(four available) £1,000 off tuition fees for the first year of study (eight available).
Length of Study: 1 year
Country of Study: Any country
No. of awards offered: 8
Closing Date: 5 June

The Enterprise Showcase Fund

Purpose: The Bath Spa University Enterprise Showcase Fund was created in response to the expenses incurred by many of our students, particularly those in creative practice fields, when they put on their end of course exhibitions, performances and events; whether here at the University or at industry showcases.
Type: Fellowship
Value: Individuals may apply for up to £300 and groups of students may apply for a maximum of £1000.
Country of Study: Any country
Closing Date: 21 February

For further information contact:

Email: daro@bathspa.ac.uk.

The Gane Trust Travel Award

Purpose: The Gane Trust is a charity based in Bristol whose aim is to support people engaged in any aspect of craft, design, and the arts. The Trust was created in memory of Crofton Gane the pioneering furniture designer (1877 - 1967).
Eligibility: The Award is open to students in the second year of their undergraduate studies at Bath School of Art, Film and Media and Bath School of Design.
Type: Award
Value: £1,000
Country of Study: Any country
No. of awards offered: 2
Closing Date: 21 February
Additional Information: www.bathspa.ac.uk/students/student-finance/scholarships-and-bursaries/the-gane-travel-award/

For further information contact:

Email: daro@bathspa.ac.uk.

USA Transfer Scholarship

Purpose: Bath Spa University is pleased to offer the USA Transfer Scholarships for international students who have completed the first two years of their undergraduate degrees in a USA Community College and are wishing to transfer to Bath Spa to complete their degree course here with us.
Type: Scholarship
Value: £1,000 off tuition fees
Study Establishment: Applications are open for candidates who are entering year two of an undergraduate programme at Bath Spa University starting in September.
Country of Study: Any country
No. of awards offered: 3
Closing Date: 5 June
Additional Information: To be eligible to apply for the scholarship, you must be www.bathspa.ac.uk/students/student-finance/scholarships-and-bursaries/usa-transfer-scholarship/an applicant and have accepted your offer.

Vice Chancellor's International Scholarship

Purpose: The Bath Spa University Vice Chancellor's International Scholarship celebrates our commitment to internationalization and excellence in creativity, culture and enterprise
Eligibility: Applications are welcome from international students who have achieved high academic results and can demonstrate a commitment to creativity, culture and enterprise
Level of Study: Graduate, Postgraduate
Type: Scholarship
Value: £5,000
Application Procedure: Applicants must hold an offer of admission for a Bath Spa University postgraduate taught Master's degree programme that is full-time and taught on-campus, and complete the International Scholarship Application Form. Please complete all the details, including your name, contact details, student number and qualifications. Applications with missing details will be automatically rejected
Closing Date: 30 June
Additional Information: Please check details at www.bathspa.ac.uk/international-students/scholarships/vice-chancellors-international-scholarship

For further information contact:

Tel: (44) 1225 875 777

Bayer AG

Werk Leverkusen, D-51368 Leverkusen, Germany.

Tel: (49) 214 3026672
Email: gisela.dambach.gd@bayer-ag.de
Website: www.aspirin.com
Contact: Gisela Dambach, International Aspirin Award

Bayer Foundation Scholarships

Purpose: Bayer Foundation supports students aspiring to study in Germany with five fellowship programmes in biology, medical science, agricultural science, non-academic professions, and chemistry

Eligibility: The project to be supported must be innovative and international. 1. Scholarships are granted to students and young professionals (up to 2 years after graduation) German student wishing to realize a study or research project abroad or Foreign students pursuing a project in Germany. 2. An innovative project plan. All applicants should have a high level of commitment, dedication and an innovative project plan. Scholarships are granted to students and young professionals (up to two years after graduation) from Germany wishing to realize a study or research project abroad or to foreign students/young professionals pursuing a project in Germany

Level of Study: Graduate

Type: Research grant

Value: Approximately €6,400 per year up to 2 years after graduation

Frequency: Annual

Country of Study: Any country

Application Procedure: The Bayer Science & Education Foundation supports students and young professionals that would like to study or work outside of their home country with the Bayer Foundation Fellowship Program, which consists of five scholarships. All applicants should have a high level of commitment, dedication and an innovative project plan. Scholarships are granted to students and young professionals (up to two years after graduation) from Germany wishing to realize a study or research project abroad or to foreign students/young professionals pursuing a project in Germany

Closing Date: 18 July

Funding: Private

For further information contact:

Email: info@global-opportunities.net

Bayreuth International Graduate School of African Studies (BIGSAS)

University of Bayreuth, D-95440 Bayreuth, Germany.

Tel: (49) 921 55 5101
Email: bigsas@uni-bayreuth.de
Contact: BIGSAS

The University of Bayreuth is a hub of international and interdisciplinary research. African Studies have been a priority at the University of Bayreuth since its foundation in 1975. The Bayreuth International Graduate School of African Studies (BIGSAS) brings together African and European academic networks and fosters partnership.

Bayreuth International Graduate School of African Studies Sandwich Scholarship Programme

Eligibility: Applicants must have a very good Master's Degree in one of the disciplines represented at the Graduate School. Applications may be sent in German, English or French; the working language of BIGSAS is English

Level of Study: Doctorate

Type: Programme grant

Value: €1,200 monthly

Length of Study: 3 years

Frequency: Annual

Study Establishment: The Bayreuth International Graduate School of African Studies

Country of Study: Germany

Application Procedure: For more information on your online application please refer to www.bigsas.uni-bayreuth. de/en/phd_programme/application/index.html

Closing Date: 28 February

Contributor: German Research Foundation of the Excellence Initiative of the German Federal and State Governments

Additional Information: scholarship-fellowship.com/bigsas-sandwich-scholarship/

For further information contact:

Email: bigsas-application@uni-bayreuth.de

Beinecke Scholarship Program

Box 125, Fogelsville, PA 18051-0125, United States of America.

Tel: (1) 610 395 5560
Email: BeineckeScholarship@earthlink.net
Website: www.beineckescholarship.org
Contact: Dr Thomas L. Parkinson, Program director

The Beinecke Scholarship Program, established in 1970, seeks to encourage and enable highly motivated students to take the fullest advantage of graduate opportunities available to them and be courageous in the selection of graduate study programmes.

Beinecke Scholarship

Subjects: arts, humanities and social sciences
Purpose: Established by the Board of Directors of The Sperry and Hutchinson Company, the Beinecke Scholarship Program awards substantial scholarships to students to support their graduate education in the arts, humanities and social sciences at any accredited institution.
Eligibility: junior at the time of application
Level of Study: Postgraduate
Type: Scholarship
Value: US$34,000
Length of Study: 5 years
Study Establishment: Any accredited university
Country of Study: Any country
Application Procedure: Request and submit a completed application form a curriculum vitae, a personal statement of 1,000 words and three letters of recommendation from faculty members
No. of awards offered: 20
Closing Date: 9 February
Funding: Corporation
Contributor: The Sperry and Hutchinson Company
Additional Information: www.nyu.edu/academics/awards-and-highlights/global-awards/scholarships/beinecke-scholarship-program.html

For further information contact:

Email: globalawards@nyu.edu
Website: fdnweb.org/beinecke/

Beit Trust (Zimbabwe, Zambia and Malawi)

PO Box CH 76, Chisipite, Harare, Zimbabwe.

Tel: (263) 4 496132
Email: beitrust@africaonline.co.zw
Website: www.beittrust.org.uk

Beit Trust Postgraduate Scholarships

Purpose: To support postgraduate study or research
Eligibility: Open to persons under 30 years of age or 35 years for medical doctors, who are university graduates domiciled in Zambia, Zimbabwe or Malawi. Applicants must be nationals of those countries
Level of Study: Postgraduate
Type: Scholarship

Value: Fees and costs of tuition and related academic expenses are paid by the Trust direct to the universities. Payment of a personal allowance, index linked in accordance with guidance from an independent authority covering maintenance support. Other allowances are paid for arrival, a laptop and printing of a thesis, and return home. Economy Class air passages are provided by the Trust for the initial journey to the place of study, and for the return at the end of the course
Frequency: Annual
Study Establishment: Approved universities and other institutions in South Africa, Britain and Ireland
Country of Study: Any country
Application Procedure: Applicants must complete an application form
Closing Date: 11 February
Funding: Private
Additional Information: Zambian applicants should contact the BEIT Trust United Kingdom office. Zimbabwe and Malawi applicants should contact the Zimbabwe office beittrust.org.uk/beit-trust-scholarships

For further information contact:

The BEIT Trust, BEIT House, Grove Road, Woking, Surrey GU21 5JB, United Kingdom.

Tel: (44) 1483 772 575
Fax: (44) 1483 725 833
Email: scholarships@beittrust.org.uk

Belgian American Educational Foundation (B.A.E.F.)

195 Church Street, NH 06510, United States of America.

Email: Emile.Boulpaep@Yale.edu
Website: www.baef.us
Contact: Belgian American Educational Foundation, Inc

Belgian American Educational Foundation (B.A.E.F.)

Purpose: For fellowships for advanced study or research
Eligibility: Applicants must be citizens or permanent residents of the United States. Knowledge of Dutch, or French, or German is optional
Type: Fellowship
Value: US$27,000 for Master
Length of Study: 1 year

Frequency: Annual
Country of Study: Any country
Application Procedure: Application forms can be downloaded from the B.A.E.F. website at www.baef.us
Closing Date: 31 October
Additional Information: For additional information contact the Foundation at the above address or email: Emile. Boulpaep@Yale.eduwww.baef.be/documents/fellowships-for-belgian-citizens/initial-master-degree-in-the-usa1.xml? lang=en

For further information contact:

Email: mail@baef.be

Fellowships for study of research in Belgium

Purpose: Fellowships for advanced study or research during the academic year, at a Belgian university or institution of higher learning. The fellowships provide outright non-renewable grants carrying a stipend of US$28,000 for Master's or PhD students US$32,000 for Post-doctoral Fellows
Eligibility: Applicants must be citizens or permanent residents of the United States. Applicants must 1. Either at the time of application be registered in a PhD or equivalent degree program in the United States. 2. Or while holding the BAEF fellowship register in a graduate program (Master's or PhD) in Belgium. 3. Or hold a Master's, PhD, or equivalent degree. Post-doctoral applicants should by 1 July have no more than 2 years since obtaining their PhD degree
Level of Study: Doctorate, Graduate, MBA, Postdoctorate, Postgraduate, Postgraduate (MSc), Predoctorate, Professional development, Research
Value: US$28,000 for Master's or PhD students, US$32,000 for Post-doctoral Fellows
Length of Study: 12 months in Belgium. If the Fellow chooses to remain less than the full 12 months in Belgium, the stipend will be prorated accordingly. The minimum fellowship period is 6 months
Frequency: Annual
Country of Study: Belgium
Application Procedure: Applicants must be citizens or permanent residents of the United States Applicants must either at the time of application be registered in a PhD or equivalent degree program in the United States, or while holding the BAEF Fellowship register in a graduate program (Master's or PhD) in Belgium, or hold a Master's, PhD, or equivalent degree. Post-doctoral applicants should by July 1, have no more than 2 years since obtaining their PhD degree.
No. of awards offered: 40
Closing Date: 1 July
Funding: Foundation

Contributor: Foundation Endowment
No. of awards given last year: 10
No. of applicants last year: 40
Additional Information: Application forms can be downloaded from the B.A.E.F. website at: www.baef.us. www. baef.be/documents/fellowships-for-us-citizens/study-res-fellow.-for-us-citizen-.xml?lang=en

For further information contact:

Belgian American Educational Foundation, Inc., 195 Church Street, New Haven, CT 06510, United States of America.

Email: emile.boulpaep@yale.edu

Belgian Flemish University, VLIR-UOS

Website: www.vliruos.be/6323.aspx

VLIR-UOS Training and Masters Scholarships

Purpose: VLIR-UOS awards scholarships to students from 31 eligible countries in Africa, Asia and Latin-America, to follow an English-taught training or master programme at a Flemish university or university college in Belgium
Eligibility: You can only apply for a scholarship if you meet the following requisites 1. Nationality and Country of Residence, A candidate should be a national and resident of one of the 31 countries of the VLIR-UOS country list for scholarships (not necessarily the same country) at the time of application. 2. Age. The maximum age for a Master programme candidate is 35 years for an initial masters and 40 years for an advanced masters. The candidate cannot succeed this age on January 1 of the intake year. 3. Professional background and experience, Priority is given to candidates who are employed in academic institutions, research institutes, governments, the social economy or NGOs, or who aim at a career in one of these sectors. However, master candidates employed in the profit sector or newly graduated candidates without any work experience can be eligible for the scholarship as well, depending on their motivation and profile. The training candidate should have relevant professional experience and a support letter confirming (re)integration in a professional context where the acquired knowledge and skills will be immediately applicable.
Level of Study: Postgraduate
Type: Scholarship
Value: VLIR-UOS only provides full scholarships for the total duration of the training or Master, The scholarships cover cover tuition fees, travel, insurance and living expenses (board and lodging).

Length of Study: 12/24 months
Frequency: Annual
Country of Study: Belgium
Application Procedure: Via the university's website, you will have to apply for both admission to the programme as well as for the scholarship itself. When you apply for the programme, be sure to mention whether you wish to apply for a scholarship. The deadline varies and are determined by the programme but most deadlines are around 1 February or 1 March for Masters Programmes. The call of applications for training programmes will open at various times and can be monitored at this link. It is important to visit the official website and the websites of the specific Training or Master's Programme you have chosen for detailed information on how to apply for this scholarship.
No. of awards offered: 10
Closing Date: 1 February
Contributor: Flemish university
Additional Information: For more information, please visit official scholarship website: www.vliruos.be/6323.aspx www.scholars4dev.com/2257/vlir-uos-masters-scholarships-for-developing-countries/

For further information contact:

Email: scholarships@vliruos.be

Belgian Technical Cooperation agency (BTC), Ghent University

BTC - Belgian Development Agency, Rue Haute, 147, B-1000 Brussels, Belgium.

Tel: (32) 2 505 37 00
Website: www.belspo.be/belspo/index_nl.stm

The Belgian Technical Cooperation agency (BTC) is the administrator and coordinator for scholarships awarded by the Belgian Directorate-General for Development Cooperation (DGDC). The BTC itself does not award grants. The BTC's Scholarship Unit implements the scholarship files, welcomes the students and provides them with guidance for the duration of their academic training and stay in Belgium.

Belgian Technical Cooperation Scholarships

Purpose: The Belgian Technical Cooperation agency (BTC) is the administrator and coordinator for scholarships awarded by the Belgian Directorate-General for Development

Cooperation (DGDC). The BTC itself does not award grants. The BTC's Scholarship Unit implements the scholarship files, welcomes the students and provides them with guidance for the duration of their academic training and stay in Belgium.
Eligibility: Candidates from one of the BTC partner countries
Level of Study: Postgraduate
Type: Scholarship
Value: The scholarships are awarded primarily to finance third– cycle (postgraduate) courses.
Length of Study: 1 or 2 academic years
Country of Study: Belgium
Application Procedure: Candidates interested in a scholarship should send their application form directly to the Attaché for Development Cooperation or to the Embassy of Belgium in the partner country
Contributor: Belgian Directorate-General
Additional Information: www.ugent.be/en/research/funding/devcoop/btc.htm

For further information contact:

Email: development.cooperation@vub.ac.be

Berkeley Graduate Division

Conference Travel Grants

Purpose: Academic master's and all doctoral students may apply for funding to attend professional conferences or to participate in professional development activities
Eligibility: 1. Be registered for the term in which they are planning to attend the conference, which also includes payment of fees/tuitions. Note students on filing fee are not eligible. 2. Be in good academic standing. 3. Be presenting a paper or poster at the conference.
Level of Study: Postgraduate
Type: Fellowship
Value: (up to US$600 within California, US$900 elsewhere in North America, including Canada and Mexico, and US$1,500 outside of North America)
Frequency: Annual
Country of Study: Any country
Closing Date: 1 May
Additional Information: grad.berkeley.edu/financial/fellowships/

For further information contact:

318 Sproul Hall, Barrow Lane, Berkeley, CA 94704, United States of America.

Tel: (1) 510 642 0672

Robert E. Thunen Memorial Scholarships

Subjects: fields of lighting (such as architectural, commercial, residential, airport, navigational, theatrical or television, agricultural, vision and so forth)

Purpose: These scholarships are for students who wish to study any and all fields of lighting (such as architectural, commercial, residential, airport, navigational, theatrical or television, agricultural, and vision)

Eligibility: They arrange for at least three letters of recommendation, at least one of which shall be from someone involved with lighting professionally or academically. The Thunen Scholars for each year will be announced in mid-May of each year

Level of Study: Graduate

Type: Scholarship

Value: US$2,500

Frequency: Annual

Country of Study: Any country

Application Procedure: Applications and letters of recommendation should be submitted before 1 April of each year

Closing Date: 1 April

Funding: Private

Additional Information: grad.berkeley.edu/news/funding/robert-thunen-memorial-scholarships/

For further information contact:

Mary-Jane Lawless Thunen Scholarship Committee, IES San Francisco Section, 1201 Park Ave Ste 100, Emeryville, CA 94608, United States of America.

Tel: (510) 655 1200 ext 214
Fax: (510) 655 1344
Email: mlaw@silvermanlight.com

Berlin Graduate School Muslim Cultures and Societies

Altensteinstrasse 48, D-14195 Berlin, Germany.

Tel: (49) 30 838 53417
Email: office@bgsmcs.fu-berlin.de
Website: www.fu-berlin.de/en/

Zentrum Moderner Orient and Berlin Graduate School of Muslim Cultures and Societies Visiting Research Fellowship

Purpose: We are interested in attracting outstanding researchers who are engaged in research projects that are relevant to the respective research profiles at ZMO and BGSMCS

Eligibility: The call is open for senior researchers and recent postdocs in the humanities and the social sciences. Applications by candidates from Africa, Asia and the Middle East are particularly encouraged

Level of Study: Postgraduate

Value: Successful applicants will receive a monthly stipend (€2,500, covering all expenses including travel and accommodation), and a period of stay that should normally last up to 3 months

Country of Study: Germany

Closing Date: 15 September

Funding: Trusts

Additional Information: mideast.unc.edu/zmo-bgsmc/

Berlin Mathematical School

TU Berlin, Sekr. MA 2-2, Strasse des 17. Juni 136, D-10623 Berlin, Germany.

Tel: (49) 30 314 78611
Email: office@math-berlin.de
Contact: Berlin Mathematical School

The Berlin Mathematical School (BMS) is a joint graduate school of the mathematics departments of the three major Berlin universities, TU Berlin, FU Berlin, and HU Berlin. BMS invites excellent mathematics students from Berlin, Germany, Europe and all over the world to join BMS – and to make good use of the ample opportunities offered by the rich and diverse mathematics teaching and research environment.

Dirichlet International Postdoctoral Fellowship at Berlin Mathematical School in Germany

Purpose: In 2012 the Berlin Mathematical School (BMS) implemented its Dirichlet Postdoctoral Fellowship Program. This program, advertised widely across the broad range of mathematical fields represented in Berlin, contributed to making the BMS even more visible internationally, and attracted outstanding applications from all around the world. This was evidenced by the many letters of recommendation from very prominent and international mathematicians.

Eligibility: International applicants are eligible to apply for this fellowship. For more details, please check the website

Type: Postdoctoral fellowship

Value: The competitive full-year salary includes health insurance

Frequency: Annual

Study Establishment: Fellowship is awarded to young mathematicians who want to pursue their own research in one of the eight research fields of mathematics offered by the Berlin Mathematical School

Country of Study: Germany

Application Procedure: Applications will be accepted via our online portal probably from 1 October to 1 December

Closing Date: 1 December

Additional Information: For more details, please browse the below website. scholarship-positions.com/dirichlet-international-postdoctoral-fellowship-berlin-mathematical-school-germany www.math-berlin.de/bms-faculty/dirichlet-postdoctoral-program

For further information contact:

Email: postdoc@math-berlin.de

Beta Phi Mu Headquarters

PO Box 42139, Philadelphia, PA 19101, United States of America.

Tel: (1) 267 361 5018
Email: headquarters@betaphimu.org
Website: www.betaphimu.org
Contact: Isabel Gray, Program Director

Beta Phi Mu is a library and information studies honor society, founded in 1948, with over 35,000 graduates of the ALA-initiated accredited professional programmes. Beta Phi Mu was founded at the University of Illinois

American Library Association Beta Phi Mu Award

Purpose: An award of achievement to a library school faculty member or to an individual for distinguished service to education for librarianship.

Eligibility: Library school faculty member or individual

Type: Award

Frequency: Annual

Country of Study: Any country

Application Procedure: Guidelines and application available on the American Library Association website www.ala.org/awardsgrants/awards/43/apply

Closing Date: 1 February

Contributor: Beta Phi Mu International Library Science Honorary Society

Additional Information: www.ala.org/awardsgrants/beta-phi-mu-award

For further information contact:

American Library Association, 50 East Huron Street, Chicago, IL 60611-2795, United States of America.

Tel: (1) 312 944 6780
Fax: (1) 312 440 9374
Email: cmalden@ala.org

Eugene Garfield Doctoral Dissertation Fellowship

Subjects: Information Science, Information Studies, Informatics, or a related field

Purpose: Up to six of these fellowships are awarded each year to Library and Information Science doctoral students who are working on their dissertations.

Eligibility: To be eligible, candidates must be enrolled in a doctoral-level research program at an institution with ALA, CILIP, or other Beta Phi Mu Executive Board approved accreditation

Type: Fellowship

Value: US$3,000

Frequency: Annual

Country of Study: Any country

Application Procedure: 1. Current Vita. 2. Met your program's requirements for advancement to candidacy. 3. Abstract of dissertation (300 word limit). 4. Letter from Dean or Director indicating dissertation topic has been approved. 5. Applicant's candidacy has been advanced. All requirements for degree except writing and defense of dissertation have been completed. 6. Three letters of recommendation. 7. Personal statement from applicant not to exceed 500 words relating to post-dissertation plans.

No. of awards offered: 6

Closing Date: 15 March

Additional Information: NOTE: All required documents must be submitted online www.betaphimu.org/garfield.html

Frank B. Sessa Scholarships for Continuing Professional Education of Beta Phi Mu Members

Purpose: Sessa Scholarships are intended to support Beta Phi Mu members in pursuing continuing professional education in LIS, archival studies, or other approved information-related studies.

Level of Study: Doctorate, Masters Degree

Type: Scholarship

Value: US$150 each

Frequency: Annual
Country of Study: Any country
Application Procedure: 1. Must be a Beta Phi Mu member 2. Must use the funds for approved professional development within one year of receiving the award 3. Must send a brief report of the funded educational experience to Beta Phi Mu Headquarters within three months of its completion 4. Must not have received a Sessa scholarship within the last five years 5. Must agree to and follow all requirements set out in the Sessa Scholarship Guidelines
No. of awards offered: 10
Closing Date: 31 August
Funding: Private
Contributor: Library Juice Academy
Additional Information: Please do not register for the lottery more than once in a calendar year; multiple submissions will result in disqualification. If you register prior to the March drawing but do not win, you are still enrolled in the lottery for the September drawing. www.betaphimu.org/sessa.html

For further information contact:

Email: headquarters@betaphimu.org

Bibliographical Society of America (BSA)

PO Box 1537, Lenox Hill Station, New York, NY 10021, United States of America.

Tel: (1) 212 452 2710
Email: bsa@bibsocamer.org
Website: www.bibsocamer.org, https://bibsocamer.org/ awards/new-scholars-program/2022-new-scholars/
Contact: Ms Michele Randall, Executive Director

The Bibliographical Society of America (BSA) invites applications for its annual short-term fellowships, which supports bibliographical inquiry as well as research in the history of the book trades and in publishing history.

Bibliographical Society of America - Harry Ransom Center Pforzheimer Fellowship in Bibliography

Purpose: Supports the bibliographical study of early modern books and manuscripts, 1455-1700, held in the Ransom Center's Pforzheimer Library and in related collections of early printed books and manuscripts, including the Pforzheimer Gutenberg Bible

Eligibility: Due to Covid-19, the regular awards cycle has been temporarily suspended. It is hoped to resume the application process in 2022 for the 2023-2024 academic year.
With the exception of The BSA-Harry Ransom Center Pforzheimer Fellowship in Bibliography, eligibility is limited to:
1. US Citizens and Residents
2. Citizens of other nations without US residency who wish to conduct research outside of the United States only
The BSA-Harry Ransom Center Pforzheimer Fellowship is open to non-US residents who wish to conduct research at the Harry Ransom Center, which will sponsor their visas and assist with the visa application process
Level of Study: Unrestricted
Type: Fellowship
Value: US$3,000
Frequency: Annual
Country of Study: Any country
Application Procedure: Applications should include the following components Applicant's curriculum vitae, project proposal of no more than 1,000 words, project budget, project timeline, Two letters of recommendation submitted via Kaleidoscope. The committee will not accept letters of recommendation by any other means.
Closing Date: 1 November
Funding: Private
Contributor: BSA-Harry Ransom Center Pforzheimer
Additional Information: www.hrc.utexas.edu/research/fellowships/bsa/
bibsocamer.org/awards/fellowships/

For further information contact:

Email: bsafellowships@bibsocamer.org

Justin G. Schiller Prize

Purpose: The Schiller Prize for Bibliographical Work on pre-twentieth century children's books is intended to encourage scholarship in the bibliography of historical children's books
Eligibility: Works put into nomination, which must be in English, may concentrate on any children's book printed before the year 1901 in any country or any language. Submissions should involve research into bibliography and printing history broadly conceived and should focus on the physical book as historical evidence for studying topics such as the history of book production, publication, distribution, collecting, or reading. Studies of the printing, publishing, and allied trades, as these relate to children's books, are also welcome. Eligible scholarship may take the form of

a published book or article, a master's thesis or doctoral dissertation that has been defended and approved, or research results distributed in another manner, such as on a website or a CD-ROM. Eligible scholarship must have been published, approved, or posted between 1 January and 1 October. Nominations, with copies of the monographs or links to articles and websites, must be completed by 15 November

Level of Study: Unrestricted

Type: Prize

Value: US$3,000

Frequency: Every 3 years

Study Establishment: pre-twentieth century children's books

Country of Study: Any country

Application Procedure: Applications must contain the following items a letter of intent addressed to the "Schiller Prize Committee," a one-page curriculum vitae, any documentation regarding the approval of a thesis or a dissertation or confirming the date of a publication, if required. A hard copy of a published monograph or essay placed into nomination is encouraged, but a PDF is acceptable. If a copy is not submitted, a complete citation of the work must be included with the application. Authors of web-based or online resources should provide the URL for the full-text or submit a PDF. Web-based resources require free access to the website and instructions regarding its use, along with a statement regarding plans for maintaining ongoing access

Closing Date: 15 November

Funding: Individuals

Contributor: Endowed by Justin G. Schiller

Additional Information: Please also send an additional applications to this email - aimmel@Princeton.EDU bibsocamer.org/awards/justin-g-shiller-prize/

For further information contact:

Department of Rare Books and Special Collections, Princeton University Library, 1 Washington Road, Princeton, NJ 08544-2098, United States of America.

Tel: (1) 609 258 1470
Email: aimmel@Princeton.EDU

St. Louis Mercantile Library Prize

Purpose: Encourage scholarship in the bibliography of American history and literature

Eligibility: Submissions for the Mercantile Library Prize should concentrate on some aspect of American history and culture in territories that now comprise the United States, or on literature by American authors, or literature intended for publication in territories that now comprise the United States. They should involve research in bibliography and printing history broadly conceived and focus on the book (the physical object) as historical evidence for studying topics such as the history of book production, publication, distribution, collecting, or reading. Studies of the printing, publishing, and allied trades, as these relate to American history and literature, are also welcome. Submissions may take the form of a published book or article, a master's thesis or doctoral dissertation defended and approved, or research results distributed in another manner, such as the website or CD-ROM. Submissions must have been published or, if a dissertation or thesis, approved the year of the deadline or in the three previous calendar years. If a publication has an incorrect nominal date disqualifying it for submission but an actual date of publication within the prize period, it may be nominated with a letter by the publisher or editor testifying to the actual date of publication. Unpublished dissertations and theses must be accompanied by a letter from the director attesting their approval. Scholars are eligible to apply for the Prize without regard to membership in the Bibliographical Society of America or any other society, and without regard to citizenship or academic affiliation, degree, or rank. The Prize will be awarded to the author of a particular work of scholarship without regard to the author's prolonged or repeated contributions to the field. Applications are encouraged from young or junior scholars who have not as yet published extensively. Applicants may nominate themselves or be nominated by others

Level of Study: Doctorate

Type: Prize

Value: US$2,000

Frequency: Every 3 years

Study Establishment: Bibliography of American History and Literature

Country of Study: United States of America

Application Procedure: Please send the following as separate PDF or Word (.doc or .docx) files to mercantile.prize@bibsocamer.org

Closing Date: 1 November

Funding: Private

Contributor: St. Louis Mercantile Library at the University of Missouri, St. Louis

Additional Information: If for any reason the cost of securing review copies is prohibitive to submitting a nomination, please contact Erin Schreiner, BSA Executive Director, by email at bsa@bibsocamer.orgbibsocamer.org/awards/st-louis-mercantile-library-prize/

For further information contact:

Email: mercantile.prize@bibsocamer.org

The Bibliographical Society of America Short-term Fellowships

Purpose: These fellowships support bibliographical research that focuses on the physical aspects of books or manuscripts as historical evidence. Books and manuscripts in any field and of any period are eligible for consideration. Projects may include studying the history of book or manuscript production, publication, distribution, collecting, or reading. Projects to establish a text are also eligible.

Eligibility: 1. US Citizens and Residents
2. Citizens of other nations without US residency who wish to conduct research outside of the United States only

Level of Study: Unrestricted

Type: Fellowship

Value: US$3,000

Frequency: Varies

Study Establishment: Bibliographical research that focuses on the physical aspects of books or manuscripts as historical evidence

Country of Study: Any country

Application Procedure: Applications should include the following components Applicant's curriculum vitae. Project proposal of no more than 1,000 words, Project budget, Project timeline, Two letters of recommendation submitted via Kaleidoscope. The committee will not accept letters of recommendation by any other means.

Closing Date: 1 November

Funding: Foundation

Contributor: The BSA

Additional Information: For more information, please contact Hope Mayo, Chair of the Fellowship Committee at bsafellowships@bibsocamer.org. bibsocamer.org/awards/fellowships/

For further information contact:

Email: bsafellowships@bibsocamer.org

The Bibliographical Society of America-Rare Book School Fellowship

Purpose: The BSA-Rare Book School Fellowship funds tuition for one course for one first-year attendee each year at the University of Virginia's Rare Book School

Eligibility: 1. US Citizens and Residents
2. Citizens of other nations without US residency who wish to conduct research outside of the United States only

Level of Study: Unrestricted

Type: Fellowship

Value: Tuition for 1 course and US$500 toward travel

Length of Study: 1 year

Frequency: Annual

Country of Study: United States of America

Application Procedure: Applications should include the following components Applicant's curriculum vitae, Project proposal of no more than 1,000 words, Project budget, Project timeline, Two letters of recommendation submitted via Kaleidoscope. The committee will not accept letters of recommendation by any other means.

Closing Date: 1 November

Funding: Private

Contributor: Rare Book School University of Virgina

Additional Information: Candidates should consult the Rare Book School website and apply as there as directed. bibsocamer.org/awards/st-louis-mercantile-library-prize/

For further information contact:

Email: bsafellowships@bibsocamer.org

The Bibliographical Society of America - American Society for Eighteenth-Century Studies Fellowship for Bibliographical Studies in the Eighteenth Century

Purpose: Recipients must be a member of the American Society for Eighteenth-Century Studies at the time of the award

Eligibility: 1. US Citizens and Residents
2. Citizens of other nations without US residency who wish to conduct research outside of the United States only

Type: Fellowship

Value: US$3,000

Frequency: Annual

Country of Study: Any country

Application Procedure: Applications should include the following components Applicant's curriculum vitae, Project proposal of no more than 1,000 words, Project budget, Project timeline, Two letters of recommendation submitted via Kaleidoscope. The committee will not accept letters of recommendation by any other means.

Closing Date: 1 November

Contributor: American Society for Eighteenth-Century Studies

Additional Information: For more information, please contact Hope Mayo, Chair of the Fellowship Committee at bsafellowships@bibsocamer.org. bibsocamer.org/awards/fellowships/

For further information contact:

Email: bsafellowships@bibsocamer.org

The Bibliographical Society of America - Pine Tree Foundation Fellowship in Culinary Bibliography

Purpose: Supports the bibliographical study of printed and manuscript cookbooks (once commonly known as receipt books); medical recipe books that also contain culinary recipes; other types of books, manuscript, and printed material that include a substantial body of culinary recipes; treatises on and studies of gastronomy; or memoirs, diary accounts, or descriptions of food and cooking. Projects may cover any period or country
Eligibility: 1. US Citizens and Residents
2. Citizens of other nations without US residency who wish to conduct research outside of the United States only
Level of Study: Unrestricted
Type: Fellowship
Value: US$3,000
Frequency: Annual
Country of Study: Any country
Application Procedure: Applications should include the following components Applicant's curriculum vitae, Project proposal of no more than 1,000 words, Project budget, Project timeline, Two letters of recommendation submitted via Kaleidoscope. The committee will not accept letters of recommendation by any other means.
Closing Date: 1 November
Funding: Foundation
Contributor: BSA-Pine Tree Foundation
Additional Information: Links to the new Fellowship Application form will be available by 1 August. The application package and two supporting letters of recommendation must be received by 1 November. We regret that we cannot consider late or incomplete applications. Applicants are advised to request recommendation letters well in advance. For more information, please contact Hope Mayo, Chair of the Fellowship Committee at bsafellowships@bibsocamer.org bibsocamer.org/awards/fellowships/

For further information contact:

Email: bsafellowships@bibsocamer.org

The Bibliographical Society of America - Pine Tree Foundation Fellowship in Hispanic Bibliography

Purpose: Supports the bibliographical study of printed and manuscript items 1) in the Spanish language produced during any period and in any country; or 2) in any language provided they were produced in Spain, or in its overseas dominions during the time of Spanish sovereignty; or 3) the bibliographical study of book and manuscript collections in Spain, or in its overseas dominions during the time of Spanish sovereignty; or 4) the bibliographical study of Spanish-language book and manuscript collections during any period and in any country
Eligibility: 1. US Citizens and Residents
2. Citizens of other nations without US residency who wish to conduct research outside of the United States only
Level of Study: Unrestricted
Type: Fellowship
Value: US$3,000
Frequency: Annual
Country of Study: Any country
Application Procedure: Applications should include the following components Applicant's curriculum vitae, Project proposal of no more than 1,000 words, Project budget, Project timeline, Two letters of recommendation submitted via Kaleidoscope. The committee will not accept letters of recommendation by any other means.
Closing Date: 1 November
Funding: Foundation
Contributor: BSA- Pine Tree Foundation
Additional Information: Links to the new Fellowship Application form will be available by 1 August. The application package and two supporting letters of recommendation must be received by 1 November. We regret that we cannot consider late or incomplete applications. Applicants are advised to request recommendation letters well in advance. For more information, please contact Hope Mayo, Chair of the Fellowship Committee at bsafellowships@bibsocamer.org bibsocamer.org/awards/fellowships/

For further information contact:

Email: bsafellowships@bibsocamer.org

The Bibliographical Society of America - St. Louis Mercantile Library Fellowship

Purpose: Supports research in North American bibliography, including studies in the North American book trade, production and distribution of North American Books, North American book illustration and design, North American collecting and connoisseurship, and North American bibliographical history in general. Non-traditional and innovative projects will be especially welcome and encouraged
Eligibility: 1. US Citizens and Residents
2. Citizens of other nations without US residency who wish to conduct research outside of the United States only
Level of Study: Unrestricted
Type: Fellowship
Value: US$3,000

Frequency: Annual
Country of Study: Any country
Application Procedure: Applications should include the following components Applicant's curriculum vitae, Project proposal of no more than 1,000 words, Project budget, Project timeline, Two letters of recommendation submitted via Kaleidoscope. The committee will not accept letters of recommendation by any other means.
Closing Date: 1 November
Funding: Private
Contributor: St. Louis Mercantile Library
Additional Information: Links to the new Fellowship Application form will be available by 1 August. The application package and two supporting letters of recommendation must be received by 1 November. We regret that we cannot consider late or incomplete applications. Applicants are advised to request recommendation letters well in advance. For more information, please contact Hope Mayo, Chair of the Fellowship Committee at bsafellowships@bibsocamer.org bibsocamer.org/awards/fellowships/

For further information contact:

Email: bsafellowships@bibsocamer.org

The Charles J. Tanenbaum Fellowship in Cartographical Bibliography

Purpose: Supports projects dealing with all aspects of the history, presentation, printing, design, distribution and reception of cartographical documents from Renaissance times to the present, with a special emphasis on eighteenth-century cartography
Eligibility: 1. US Citizens and Residents
2. Citizens of other nations without US residency who wish to conduct research outside of the United States only
Level of Study: Unrestricted
Type: Fellowship
Value: US$3,000
Frequency: Annual
Country of Study: Any country
Application Procedure: Applications should include the following components Applicant's curriculum vitae, Project proposal of no more than 1,000 words, Project budget, Project timeline, Two letters of recommendation submitted via Kaleidoscope. The committee will not accept letters of recommendation by any other means.
Closing Date: 1 November
Funding: Foundation
Contributor: Pine Tree Foundation of New York

Additional Information: Links to the new Fellowship Application form will be available by 1 August. The application package and two supporting letters of recommendation must be received by 1 November. We regret that we cannot consider late or incomplete applications. Applicants are advised to request recommendation letters well in advance. For more information, please contact Hope Mayo, Chair of the Fellowship Committee at bsafellowships@bibsocamer.org bibsocamer.org/awards/fellowships/

For further information contact:

Email: bsafellowships@bibsocamer.org

The Fredson Bowers Award

Purpose: Major grant funded jointly with the Bibliographical Society of the UK
Eligibility: 1. US Citizens and Residents
2. Citizens of other nations without US residency who wish to conduct research outside of the United States only
Level of Study: Unrestricted
Type: Bursary
Value: £1,500
Frequency: Annual
Country of Study: United Kingdom or United States of America
Application Procedure: Applications for the Pantzer Fellowship and for major grants (including the Pantzer Scholarship) must be submitted, on the appropriate form (with no additional documentation). Two referees familiar with the applicant's work should be asked to email references to the Secretary to the Fellowships and Bursaries Sub-committee
Closing Date: 6 January
Funding: Private
Contributor: Bibliographical Society of America and Bibliographical Society of the United Kingdom
Additional Information: United Kingdom entries should follow application instructions located at this website www. bibsoc.org.uk/fellowships/application-procedurebibsocamer. org/awards/fellowships/

For further information contact:

Email: acrd2002@aol.com

The Katharine F. Pantzer Senior Fellowship in the British Book Trades

Purpose: To support the mission of the Society to foster the study of books and other textual artifacts in traditional and emerging formats, and in keeping with the value which the Society places on the field of bibliography as a critical interpretative framework for understanding such artifacts, the BSA funds a number of fellowships designed to promote bibliographical inquiry and research.

Eligibility: Supports research by a senior scholar engaged in bibliographical inquiry into the history of the book trades and publishing history in Britain during the hand-press period, as well as studies of authorship, reading and collecting based on the examination of British books published in that period, with a special emphasis on descriptive bibliography

Type: Fellowship

Value: US$6,000

Frequency: Varies

Study Establishment: Bibliographical research of the British Book Trades

Country of Study: Any country

Application Procedure: Applications are due 1 November of each year. Applications should include the following components Application form; project proposal of no more than 1,000 words; Applicant's curriculum vitae; two signed letters of recommendation on official letterhead submitted independently by referees. The two letters of recommendation must be signed and submitted independently by referees (in PDF or MS Word format) via the BSA Fellowship recommendation submission form. No other documentation will be considered by the committee. - Please visit the website to download the form. The fellowship committee will match proposed projects to suitable fellowships, and the awards will be announced at the annual meeting of the Society in January of each year. All fellowships require a project report within one year of receipt of the award, and copies of any publications resulting from the project are to be sent to the BSA. Links to the new Fellowship Application form will be available by 1 August. The application package and two supporting letters of recommendation must be received by 1 November. We regret that we cannot consider late or incomplete applications. Applicants are advised to request recommendation letters well in advance. For more information, please contact Hope Mayo, Chair of the Fellowship Committee at bsafellowships@ bibsocamer.org

Closing Date: 1 November

Funding: Individuals

Contributor: Katherine Panzer

Additional Information: Links to the new Fellowship Application form will be available by 1 August. The application package and two supporting letters of recommendation must be received by 1 November. We regret that we cannot consider late or incomplete applications. Applicants are advised to request recommendation letters well in advance. For more information, please contact Hope Mayo, Chair of the Fellowship Committee at bsafellowships@bibsocamer.org bibsocamer.org/awards/fellowships/

The Katharine Pantzer Junior Fellowship in the British Book Trades

Purpose: Supports bibliographical inquiry into the history of the book trades and publishing history in Britain during the hand-press period, as well as studies of authorship, reading and collecting based on the examination of British books published in that period, with a special emphasis on descriptive bibliography

Eligibility: Supports bibliographical inquiry into the history of the book trades and publishing history in Britain during the hand-press period, as well as studies of authorship, reading and collecting based on the examination of British books published in that period, with a special emphasis on descriptive bibliography

Level of Study: Unrestricted

Type: Fellowship

Value: US$3,000

Frequency: Annual

Country of Study: Any country

Application Procedure: Applications are due 1 November of each year. Applications should include the following components Application form; projectproposal of no more than 1,000 words; Applicant's curriculum vitae; two signed letters of recommendation on official letterhead submitted independently by referees. The two letters of recommendation must be signed and submitted independently by referees (in PDF or MS Word format) via the BSA Fellowship recommendation submission form. No other documentation will be considered by the committee. Please visit the website to download the form. The fellowship committee will match proposed projects to suitable fellowships, and the awards will be announced at the annual meeting of the Society in January of each year. All fellowships require a project report within one year of receipt of the award, and copies of any publications resulting from the project are to be sent to the BSA. Links to the new Fellowship Application form will be available by 1 August. The application package and two supporting letters of recommendation must be received by 1 November. We regret that we cannot consider late or incomplete applications. Applicants are advised to request recommendation letters well in advance. For more information, please contact Hope Mayo, Chair of the Fellowship Committee at bsafellowships@ bibsocamer.org

Closing Date: 1 November

Funding: Individuals

Contributor: Katherine Panzer

Additional Information: Links to the new Fellowship Application form will be available by 1 August. The application package and two supporting letters of recommendation must be received by 1 November. We regret that we cannot consider late or incomplete applications. Applicants are advised to request recommendation letters well in advance.

For more information, please contact Hope Mayo, Chair of the Fellowship Committee at bsafellowships@bibsocamer.org bibsocamer.org/awards/fellowships/

The Reese Fellowship for American Bibliography and the History of the Book in the Americas

Purpose: The fellowship may be awarded to any scholar, whether academic or independent, whose project explores the history of print culture in the Western Hemisphere
Eligibility: The fellowship may be awarded to any scholar, whether academic or independent, whose project explores the history of print culture in the Western Hemisphere
Level of Study: Unrestricted
Type: Fellowship
Value: US$3,000
Frequency: Annual
Country of Study: Any country
Application Procedure: Applications are due 1 November of each year. Applications should include the following components Application form Project proposal of no more than 1,000 words Applicant's curriculum vitae Two signed letters of recommendation on official letterhead submitted independently by referees. The two letters of recommendation must be signed and submitted independently by referees (in PDF or MS Word format) via the BSA Fellowship recommendation submission form. No other documentation will be considered by the committee. The fellowship committee will match proposed projects to suitable fellowships, and the awards will be announced at the annual meeting of the Society in January of each year. All fellowships require a project report within one year of receipt of the award, and copies of any publications resulting from the project are to be sent to the BSA. Links to the new Fellowship Application form will be available by 1 August. The application package and two supporting letters of recommendation must be received by 1 November. We regret that we cannot consider late or incomplete applications. Applicants are advised to request recommendation letters well in advance. For more information, please contact Hope Mayo, Chair of the Fellowship Committee at bsafellowships@bibsocamer.org
Closing Date: 7 February
Funding: Corporation
Contributor: William Reese Company
Additional Information: Links to the new Fellowship Application form will be available by 01 August. The application package and two supporting letters of recommendation must be received by 1 November. We regret that we cannot consider late or incomplete applications. Applicants are advised to request recommendation letters well in advance. For more information, please contact Hope Mayo, Chair of the Fellowship Committee at bsafellowships@bibsocamer.org bibsocamer.org/awards/fellowships/

Bielefeld University

Bielefeld Graduate School in History and Sociology, Postfach 10 01 31, D-33501 Bielefeld, Germany.

Tel: (49) 521 106 6526
Email: bghs@uni-bielefeld.de
Website: www.uni-bielefeld.de/bghs

Bielefeld Graduate School in History and Sociology Start-up Doctoral Scholarships

Purpose: The Bielefeld Graduate School in History and Sociology is inviting applications for six scholarships for international prospective doctoral researchers starting in 1 April
Eligibility: Applicants should hold a Master's degree or equivalent in sociology, history, political science, social anthropology or gender studies; applications from related disciplines are welcome. The university strongly encourages women to apply. Graduates from abroad who wish to pursue a doctoral degree in history, sociology, anthropology or political science may apply for a start-up scholarship. We welcome applications from predoctoral researchers. Applicants should speak either German or English fluently
Level of Study: Doctorate, Postgraduate
Type: Scholarship
Value: A stipend of €1,200 per month. This amount will be supplemented by an allowance for children if applicable. Upon application, travel costs can also be covered by the Graduate School
Length of Study: 4 months
Frequency: Annual
Study Establishment: University of Bielefeld
Country of Study: Germany
Application Procedure: Applications should be submitted online (www.uni-bielefeld.de/(en)/bghs/bewerbung/startup/start-up.html)
Closing Date: 31 July
Contributor: University of Bielefeld
Additional Information: www.uni-bielefeld.de/(en)/bghs/neu/Ausschreibungen/startup_scholarships.html

Bielefeld Science Award

Purpose: As a remembrance to Bielefeld's grand sociologist Niklas Luhmann Bielefeld Science Award has been awarded every two years by Sparkasse Bielefeld Foundation in close cooperation with Bielefeld University and the City of Bielefeld since 2004.
Type: Award
Value: 25,000 Euro

Country of Study: Any country
Closing Date: 24 November

Bilkent University

Faculty of Business Administration, MBA Programme, Office of the Dean, TR-06800 Ankara, Turkey.

Tel: (90) 312 290 1596
Email: fba@bilkent.edu.tr
Website: www.bilkent.edu.tr
Contact: MBA Admissions Officer

Bilkent University is a non-profit research university. Courses are conducted in English. The University has more than 11,000 students and an international teaching staff of 1,000.

Bilkent Industrial Engineering Fellowship

Level of Study: Doctorate

For further information contact:

Bilkent University Department of Industrial Engineering, Main Campus Engineering Building Floor 3, Bilkent, TR-06800 Ankara, Turkey.

Tel: (90) 312 290 1262
Fax: (90) 312 266 4054
Email: barbaros@bilkent.edu.tr

Bilkent International Relations Fellowship

Purpose: To develop skills in international political analysis
Eligibility: Candidates are selected on the basis of past academic achievement and references
Level of Study: Doctorate
Type: Fellowship
Value: A monthly stipend and a tuition waiver
Frequency: Annual
Study Establishment: Bilkent University
Country of Study: Turkey
Application Procedure: Contact the Department of International Relations

For further information contact:

Tel: (90) 312 266 4195
Fax: (90) 312 266 4326
Email: ir@bilkent.edu.tr

Bilkent Mathematics Fellowship

Eligibility: Preference is given to research proposals focused on non-linear differential equations and general relativity
Level of Study: Doctorate, Postdoctorate
Type: Fellowship
Value: A monthly stipend and a tuition fee waiver
Frequency: Annual
Study Establishment: Bilkent University
Country of Study: Turkey
Application Procedure: Contact the department

For further information contact:

Tel: (90) 312 266 4377
Fax: (90) 312 266 4579
Email: kocatepe@fen.bilkent.edu.tr

Bilkent MIAPP Fellowship

Purpose: To fund International and European affairs and executives who, understand and can deal with the increasing complex problems of a rapidly changing world
Level of Study: Doctorate, Postdoctorate
Type: Fellowship
Value: A monthly stipend and a tuition fee waiver
Length of Study: 2 year
Frequency: Annual
Study Establishment: Bilkent University
Country of Study: Turkey
Application Procedure: Contact the Department
Additional Information: w3.bilkent.edu.tr/bilkent/gradstudents/master-of-international-affairs-and-public-policy/

For further information contact:

Tel: (90) 312 2901 249
Fax: (90) 312 266 4960
Email: muge@bilkent.edu.tr

Bilkent Political Science Fellowship

Purpose: To provide a sophisticated conceptual framework and the analytical skills to specialize in a particular aspect of Turkish or comparative politics
Eligibility: Applicants are required to have an MA degree in Political Science, Public Administrator or International Relations
Level of Study: Doctorate
Type: Fellowship
Value: A monthly stipend and a tuition fee waiver
Frequency: Annual

Study Establishment: Bilkent University
Country of Study: Turkey
Application Procedure: Contact the department

For further information contact:

Tel: (90) 312 290 1931
Fax: (90) 312 290 2792
Email: cindoglu@bilkent.edu.tr

Bilkent Turkish Literature Fellowship

Purpose: To enhance the standards of Turkish literary studies and universalize the field
Eligibility: Candidates will be required to take written and/or oral exams to prove their competence in Turkish, Ottoman and English
Level of Study: Doctorate
Type: Fellowship
Value: A monthly stipend and a tuition fee waiver
Length of Study: 3 years
Frequency: Annual
Study Establishment: Bilkent University
Country of Study: Turkey
Application Procedure: Contact the department

For further information contact:

Tel: (90) 312 290 2711
Fax: (90) 312 266 4059
Email: turkedeb@bilkent.edu.tr

Biola University

The Financial Aid Office, 13800 Biola Avenue, La Mirada, CA 90639, United States of America.

Tel: (1) 562 903 4742
Email: finaid@biola.edu
Website: www.biola.edu
Contact: Financial Aid Officer

Church Matching Scholarship

Purpose: Biola-funded match to church sponsorship
Eligibility: Students must meet the following eligibility requirements Student must be enrolled at least half-time, Student must be enrolled in a traditional degree program. Student must demonstrate financial need based on FAFSA information. Student must receive financial sponsorship from a church. Special programs are not eligible.
Level of Study: Graduate
Type: Scholarship
Value: Up to US$1,300 per year
Length of Study: 1 year
Frequency: Annual
Country of Study: Any country
Application Procedure: Completed FAFSA (Biola listed), Complete the Church Matching Scholarship application, Church sponsorship check should be written out to Biola University and attached to the Church Matching Scholarship Application
Closing Date: 2 March
Funding: Private
Additional Information: This scholarship is not renewable. Student must reapply annually based on financial need and additional church sponsorship www.biola.edu/financial-aid/scholarships-and-aid/undergrad/biola-scholarships

For further information contact:

13800 Biola Ave. La Mirada, CA 90639, United States of America.

Tel: (1) 562 903 6000
Email: business@biola.edu

Biomedical Engineering Society (BMES)

Career Development Awards

Subjects: Biomedical Engineering
Purpose: BMES is committed to inclusive excellence in building pathways to biomedical engineering careers and developing a diverse, technically and globally competent biomedical workforce. To that end, BMES has an award category to support travel to the BMES Annual Meeting for Graduate Students, Postdoctoral Fellows, and Early Career Professionals from underrepresented populations in biomedical engineering and/or involved in research and training focused on health disparities and minority health.
Eligibility: Applicant must be A Graduate Student, Postdoctoral Fellow, or Early Career Professional at a critical transition or re-entry point in their career from an underrepresented population that includes racial and ethnic minorities and/or involved in research or training focused on health disparities or minority health. Early Career Professional is defined as a junior professional, junior faculty, and young investigators who received a degree in biomedical engineering or a related

science within three (3) years of the date of application. Groups identified as underrepresented in science and engineering include; Women, African Americans, Alaskan Natives, Hispanics, American Indians/Native Americans, and Pacific Islanders (Guam, Hawaii and American Samoa). A BMES Member in good standing who has not received BMES funding to attend the 2023 BMES Annual Meeting through any other BMES source.

Type: Award

Value: The award recipients will receive a complimentary registration to attend the meeting and a stipend in the amount of US$599 to assist with travel expenses to and from the meeting.

Country of Study: Any country

Additional Information: www.bmes.org/content.asp?admin=Y&contentid=594

For further information contact:

Email: CareerDevelopmentAwards@bmes.org

Diversity Lecture Award

Subjects: Biomedical Engineering

Purpose: The BMES Diversity Award honors an individual, project, organization, or institution for outstanding contributions to improving gender and racial diversity in biomedical engineering. The award is given for a broad range of activities, including research, education, and service improving diversity in the biomedical engineering industry and/or academia. The award seeks to recognize lifetime achievements as well as innovative and/or high impact activities.

Eligibility: The nominee must be an individual, project, or organization/institution demonstrating outstanding contributions to improving gender and racial diversity in biomedical engineering. The nominee is not required to be a BMES member. The award recipient (individual or representative of the project or organization/institution) is expected to accept the award in person and deliver a 20-minute lecture at the Annual Meeting. The recipient is expected to publish an article regarding aspects of the works recognized by the award in the Annals of Biomedical Engineering.

Type: Award

Value: This award consists of a US$5,000 check, a crystal plaque, and a complimentary registration for the BMES Annual Meeting

Frequency: Annual

Country of Study: Any country

Application Procedure: The application, including CV and Nomination Summary on letterhead (not to exceed 3 pages), must be submitted by May 15.

Additional Information: www.bmes.org/content.asp?admin=Y&contentid=593

For further information contact:

Email: membership@bmes.org

Robert A. Pritzker Distinguished Lecture Award

Subjects: Biomedical Engineering

Purpose: This prestigious award is given each year to recognize an individual's outstanding achievements and leadership in the science and practice of biomedical engineering.

Eligibility: The award recipient may have achieved excellence in biomedical engineering by contributions within the setting of the university, industry, or government. The awardee's contributions are not required to precede the award date by any specific period of time. Applicants must be a member of BMES in good standing.

Type: Award

Value: This recipient receives complimentary registration for the Annual Meeting, a crystal plaque, an honorarium of US$12,000 and travel expenses up to US$1,250.

Frequency: Annual

Country of Study: Any country

Application Procedure: Please complete the application form along with a letter describing the nominee's service to biomedical engineering, the nominee's Curriculum Vitae, and letter(s) of support (not to exceed 5 letters).

Closing Date: 15 May

Additional Information: www.bmes.org/content.asp?admin=Y&contentid=597

Shu Chien Achievement Award

Purpose: This Award is bestowed upon an individual who has demonstrated meritorious contributions to the field of cellular and molecular bioengineering. These contributions will include groundbreaking scientific advances in the field of cell and molecular bioengineering, the development of programs to support this emerging field, and the mentoring and training of the next generation of scientists working in our field.

Type: Award

Value: This award will consist of a plaque, complimentary registration for the CMBE annual conference, and an honorarium of US$1,000.

Frequency: Annual

Country of Study: Any country

Biotechnology and Biological Sciences Research Council (BBSRC)

Polaris House, North Star Avenue, Swindon, Wiltshire SN2 1UH, United Kingdom.

Tel: (44) 1793 413 200
Email: postdoc.fellowships@bbsrc.ac.uk
Website: www.bbsrc.ac.uk

BBSRC is the United Kingdom's principal funder of basic and strategic biological research. It is a non-departmental public body, one of the seven Research Councils supported through the Science and Innovation Group of the Department for Innovation, Universities and Skills (DIUS). It supports research and research training in universities and research centres throughout the United Kingdom, including BBSRC-sponsored institutes, and promotes knowledge transfer from research to applications in business, industry and policy, and public engagement in the biosciences. It funds research in some exciting areas including genomics, stem cell biology, and bionanotechnology.

David Phillips Fellowships

Purpose: The David Phillips Fellowship (DPF) provides support for researchers wishing to establish their first independent research group
Eligibility: DPF applicants are not eligible to apply to any additional BBSRC fellowship competitions or to the UK Research and Innovation Future Leaders Fellowship call in the same calendar year. Please see the Fellowship Handbook for further details on eligibility criteria.
Level of Study: Postdoctorate
Type: Fellowship
Value: value of up to £1 million (80% fEC)
Length of Study: 5 years
Application Procedure: Applicants should have considered their training needs (as detailed in the Career Development Plan), and the research environment should be supportive and the best place for the applicant to carry out their research project and advance their career.
Closing Date: 12 May
Additional Information: Fellowships are awarded under full economic costing (fEC). Further queries, please contact Postgraduate Training and Research Career Development Branch. Important: applicants should ensure proposals are submitted to their host institution's Je-S submitter/approval pool well in advance (a minimum of 5 working days) of the published deadline bbsrc.ukri.org/funding/filter/david-phillips/

For further information contact:
Email: postdoc.fellowships@bbsrc.ukri.org

Institute Career Path Fellowships

Eligibility: Open to candidates who have a minimum of 3 years and no more than 10 years of active postdoctoral research experience
Level of Study: Doctorate, Postdoctorate

For further information contact:
Email: fiona.tomley@bbsrc.ac.uk

Institute Development Fellowships

Purpose: To enable BBSRC scientists to spend a period of collaborative work at another research organization and to provide a mechanism for the influx of new ideas and new skills in strategically important areas to enhance the quality of science in BBSRC sponsored institutes
Eligibility: Open to all BBSRC scientists at Band 5 and above on an open-ended contract, who have worked for a minimum of 5 years in their current or similar post
Level of Study: Research
Type: Fellowships
Value: To cover the costs associated with the proposed research development activities
Length of Study: 6–12 months
Application Procedure: All applications must be submitted online
Closing Date: 14 November
Additional Information: Further queries, please contact Postgraduate Training and Research Career Development Branch bbsrc.ukri.org/funding/filter/david-phillips/

Professorial Fellowships

Purpose: To support world-class scientists with a proven track record of developing new and innovative directions of research and who have the potential to use a fellowship to open up dramatic and novel lines of work
Eligibility: Open to scientists who are already recognized at an international level as outstanding researchers with exceptional research and interpretative achievements
Type: Fellowships
Value: Grant to cover the costs of the research programme
Length of Study: 5 years
Application Procedure: Check website for further details
Closing Date: 14 November

Additional Information: Further queries, please contact Postgraduate Training and Research Career Development Branch bbsrc.ukri.org/funding/filter/david-phillips/

Research Development Fellowships

Purpose: To support scientists wishing to undertake new directions in their research. Applicants seeking to develop interdisciplinary dimensions by integrating new techniques or methodologies into their research are particularly encouraged
Eligibility: Open to scientists who are full-time members of academic staff of a United Kingdom university who have worked for a minimum of 5 years in their current or similar post
Type: Fellowship
Value: To cover the costs associated with the proposed research development activities
Length of Study: 1–3 years
Application Procedure: Applications must be submitted online
Closing Date: 14 November
Additional Information: Further queries, please contact Postgraduate Training and Research Career Development Branch bbsrc.ukri.org/funding/filter/david-phillips/

Birkbeck, University of London

Malet Street, Bloomsbury WC1E 7HX, United Kingdom. Birkbeck, University of London, is a public research university located in Bloomsbury, London, United Kingdom, and a constituent college of the federal University of London

Birkbeck International Merit Scholarships

Eligibility: Birkbeck is offering a number of merit scholarships to suitably qualified students from Japan, Russia, South Korea, Turkey, Latin America, South-East Asia (ASEAN) and Taiwan. Accepted International Student by the University; Excellent Academic and Leadership Achievements
Type: Scholarship
Value: Scholarship amount £2,500–£5,000
Country of Study: United Kingdom
Application Procedure: 1. Initially, you will have to apply to Birkbeck, University of London. 2. Once you have received an offer from Birkbeck, you must email them an essay of no more than 500 words. The essay should detail why you are the ideal candidate to receive the International Merit Scholarship. Recipients will be chosen based on a combination of academic merit and financial need

Closing Date: 1 June
Additional Information: scholarship-positions.com/fully-funded-birkbeck-postgraduate-scholarships-international-students-uk/2017/11/15/

For further information contact:
Email: international-office@bbk.ac.uk

Bonnart Trust Master's Studentships

Subjects: The Bonnart Trust looks to support students who 1. have an excellent academic record 2. intend to study part time 3. are working in an organisation where the issues that concern the Bonnart Trust are a significant focus of activity, or who aspire to work in such an organisation 4. demonstrate how undertaking a Master's course will enhance their effectiveness in their work 5. show an understanding of the importance that research can play in their field, and a desire to increase that understanding 6. show enthusiasm for contributing to the wider network of Bonnart Trust scholars.
Purpose: The Bonnart Trust offers two studentships each year to support part-time Master's students whose work involves them in the major themes of concern to the Trust 1. social cohesion 2. conflict resolution 3. racial, ethnic and religious justice. The studentships are only available for those studying relevant MA/MSc programmes
Country of Study: Any country
Application Procedure: 1. To apply for the studentship, you must have been offered a place on one of the eligible MA/MSc programmes (see above) in the School of SSHP by 31 May in the year of application. 2. Complete the Bonnart Trust Master's Studentship application form and email the completed form, together with a two-page CV, to the School of SSHP. Please ensure you rename your files to include your surname at the beginning of the file name.
Closing Date: 14 June
Contributor: Bonnart Trust

Bonnart Trust PhD Scholarship

Purpose: The scholarship will be awarded to an outstanding candidate whose research topic explores a theme concerned with either 'diversity and belonging' or 'minorities and social justice'
Eligibility: 1. You should usually have an upper second-class undergraduate honours degree, or equivalent, and a Master's degree, or equivalent. 2. You will need to be an outstanding candidate whose research topic explores a theme concerned with either diversity and belonging or minorities and social justice. (a)Diversity and belonging research topics include,

but are not limited to subjective and attitudinal dimensions of intolerance, the ways in which racial, religious, linguistic and other minorities challenge societies and cultures to think of themselves in new ways, the extent to which minorities identify with and seek to integrate within mainstream society. (b) Minorities and social justice concerned with the social outcomes experienced by minorities. Research topics include, but are not limited to the entitlements and social trajectory of minorities, how these vary across place and time, the concept of social justice as applied to minorities, including minority language speakers. 3. We encourage applications from candidates who are able to draw connections between their doctoral research and contemporary concerns and practical outcomes beyond the university. 4. We will only consider current Birkbeck students who are already enrolled on an MPhil/PhD degree within the School of Social Sciences, History and Philosophy or School of Law under exceptional circumstances.

Type: Scholarship and award

Value: The scholarship will cover tuition fees at the home fee rate (£4,500 in 2021-22) and a stipend (£17,609 per year for 2021-22) for up to three years. In addition, the Trust provides funding of up to £1,000 per scholar

Length of Study: 3 years

Frequency: Every 3 years

Country of Study: Any country

Application Procedure: For further information, check the following website. www.bbk.ac.uk/sshp/research/funding-for-research-students

No. of awards offered: 1

Closing Date: 31 January

Funding: Trusts

Additional Information: If you have any questions about the Bonnart Trust PhD Scholarhip, please contact: sshp-studentships@bbk.ac.uk
www.bbk.ac.uk/student-services/financial-support/phd-funding/bonnart-trust-scholarship

For further information contact:

School of Social Sciences, History and Philosophy, Birkbeck University of London, 26 Russell Square, London WC1B 5DT, United Kingdom.

Email: sshp-studentships@bbk.ac.uk

School of Arts Master's Bursaries and Studentships

Purpose: We are delighted to be able to offer up to twenty bursaries to Masters students coming into the School of Arts, Birkbeck. Please see details of each available award and

application deadlines below. All applications should be made using the right application form which must be completed in addition to a College application.

Eligibility: Applicants should have an outstanding academic record and show excellent promise.

Level of Study: Postgraduate

Value: Up to £20,000

Length of Study: 12/24 months

Country of Study: Any country

Closing Date: 9 September

Additional Information: www.bbk.ac.uk/arts/research/research-bursaries-studentships-funding/arts-ma-bursaries

Blakemore Foundation

1201 3rd Avenue, Suite 4900, Seattle, WA 98101-3099, United States of America.

Tel: (1) 206 359 8778
Email: blakemorefoundation@gmail.com
Website: www.blakemorefoundation.org
Contact: Eugene H. Lee, Trustee

Blakemore Freeman Fellowships for Advanced Asian Language Study

Purpose: To permit American citizens or permanent residents of the United States to raise their language skills in Chinese, Japanese, Korean, Thai, Vietnamese, Indonesian, Khmer or Burmese to professional working proficiency

Eligibility: Pursuing a professional, business, technical or academic career that involves the regular use of Chinese, Japanese, Korean, Thai, Vietnamese, Indonesian, Khmer or Burmese. 1. By the start of the grant, have (at minimum) a college undergraduate degree. 2. Be at or near an advanced level in the language. By the start of the grant, applicants must have completed (at minimum) the equivalent of the third year of languages classes at the college level, either through classes taken in the United States or through a combination of study at the college level in the United States and intensive language study abroad programs. 3. Be able to devote oneself exclusively to full-time intensive language study during the term of the grant; grants are not made for part-time study or research. 4. Be a citizen or permanent resident of the United States of America

Type: A variable number of grants

Value: Full tuition at approved language schools in East & SE Asia plus stipend for travel, study & living expenses

Length of Study: 9–10 months

Frequency: Annual

Study Establishment: See website for list of approved language programs

Application Procedure: To apply for a Blakemore Freeman Fellowship the applicant must complete an application form on our application portal at blakemorefoundation.communityforce.com

No. of awards offered: 139

Closing Date: 30 December

Funding: Foundation, Trusts

Contributor: Blakemore Foundation; The Freeman Foundation

No. of awards given last year: 14

No. of applicants last year: 139

Additional Information: Email address above is incorrect: The new email for the Foundation is contactus@blakemore foundation.orgeinaudi.cornell.edu/opportunity/blakemore-fou ndation-blakemore-freeman-fellowships-advanced-asian-lang uage-study

Bond University

School of Business, c/o International Office, Gold Coast, QLD 4229, Australia.

Tel: (61) 7 5595 1706
Email: international@bond.edu.au
Contact: MBA Admissions Officer

Bond University United Kingdom Excellence Scholarship in Australia

Purpose: Bond University is now accepting applications from citizens of the United Kingdom for the United Kingdom Excellence Scholarship. Bond University aims to help identify future leaders and realize their full potential by providing access to an exceptional educational experience

Eligibility: To be considered applicants must High achieving citizens of the United Kingdom who are currently residing outside of Australia are encouraged to apply; Applicants must have received an offer to study at Bond prior to applying. People studying in English as part of packaged offers at the Bond University College are still eligible to apply; Keep excellent academic qualifications; Students have already received a proposal from Bond University to start a bachelor or postgraduate degree; Examples of high academic achievement may include students with high achieving A Level or IB results; High achieving academic students applying for the undergraduate study who are not currently completing an Australian High School equivalent in the United Kingdom are also eligible to apply

Level of Study: Postgraduate

Type: Scholarship

Value: 25% tuition remission

Frequency: Annual

Country of Study: Australia, the United Kingdom, Europe or the United States of America

Application Procedure: To apply, students must complete the Bond University Online Application Form to receive their program offer before applying for this scholarship. 1. Once an offer has been received, students must download and complete the United Kingdom Excellence Scholarship Application Form through the given link Application Form. 2. Applicants must submit their complete application to international@bond.edu.au

Closing Date: 21 February

Funding: Private

Contributor: Bond University

Additional Information: Applications close on 24 May for students commencing in September semester bond.edu.au/intl/scholarship/uk-excellence-scholarship

For further information contact:

14 University Drive, Robina, QLD 4226, Australia.

Hancock Prospecting Swimming Excellence Scholarship

Purpose: The Hancock Prospecting Swimming Excellence Scholarship is among the most prestigious scholarships available in Australia, targeted to provide an opportunity for a series of high performance swimming scholars to compete at an elite level, while gaining an outstanding education

Eligibility: Available to all Australian students applying for a single undergraduate degree, postgraduate degree or diploma at Bond University (excluding the Bond Medical Program, Doctor of Physiotherapy, Master of Psychology (Clinical) and Master of Professional Psychology). Australian students eligible to represent Australian Swimming. Meet the Academic requirements for selected program. Currently swimming at a very elite level. Strong leadership skills and community involvement. Recipients will be chosen in conjunction with Swimming Australia.

Type: Scholarship

Value: US$21,000

Length of Study: 3 Years

Country of Study: Any country

Closing Date: 31 October

Additional Information: bond.edu.au/intl/scholarship/hancock-prospecting-swimming-excellence-scholarship

International Leadership Scholarship

Purpose: Bond University offers undergraduate and postgraduate students who have outstanding leadership experience and community involvement with a partial-fee tuition remission scholarship. International Leadership Scholarships are awarded on the basis of academic excellence and evidence of outstanding leadership and community achievements.

Eligibility: Have submitted the Bond University Online Application Form to apply for chosen program. The following programs are not eligible for consideration for scholarships – Master of Psychology (Clinical), Master of Professional Psychology, Study Abroad and Exchange Programs, the Bond Medical Program and Doctor of Physiotherapy. Have achieved a minimum of ATAR 84.00 or IB Diploma 30 (or equivalent) for undergraduate applicants, or achieved commendable results from undergraduate studies for postgraduate applicants*Be a citizen of one of the countries listed at the top of this page, or be an international student currently residing in Australia (any nationality). Evidence of your leadership, initiative, and service to your school/university and/or community. Please use the Supporting Statement Template (PDF) to present this evidence and submit this along with your completed scholarship application form. Complete and submit a scholarship application form by the scholarship application closing date relevant to chosen starting semester. See further details on the scholarship application process in the How to Apply section below. Not have already commenced undergraduate or postgraduate studies at Bond University. Those studying English at Bond University College as part of a packaged Offer are still eligible to apply

Type: Scholarship
Value: US$10,000 tuition remission
Country of Study: Any country
Closing Date: 13 February
Additional Information: bond.edu.au/intl/scholarship/international-leadership-scholarship

International Stand Out Scholarship

Subjects: Actuarial Science, Architecture and Built Environment, Business and Commerce, Communication and Creative Media, Health Sciences, Hotel and Tourism, International Relations and Humanities, Law, Social Sciences, Psychology and Counselling, Sport

Purpose: Bond University offers 'stand out' students who are applying to study at an undergraduate or postgraduate level, with tuition remission scholarships.

Eligibility: Have submitted the Bond University Online Application Form to apply for chosen program. The following programs are not eligible for consideration for scholarships – Master of Psychology (Clinical), Master of Professional

Psychology, Study Abroad and Exchange Programs, the Bond Medical Program and Doctor of Physiotherapy.Have achieved a minimum academic result of ATAR 89.00 or IB Diploma 32 (or equivalent) for undergraduate applicants or achieved 'stand out' academic results from undergraduate studies for postgraduate applicants.Be a citizen of one of the countries listed at the top of this page, or be an international student currently residing in Australia (any nationality). Complete and submit a scholarship application form by the scholarship application closing date relevant to chosen starting semester. See further details on the scholarship application process in the How to Apply section below.Not have already commenced undergraduate or postgraduate studies at Bond University. Those studying English at Bond University College as part of a packaged Offer are still eligible to apply.

Type: Scholarship
Value: Up to 25% tuition remission
Country of Study: Any country
Closing Date: 13 February
Additional Information: bond.edu.au/intl/scholarship/international-stand-out-scholarship

John Eales Rugby Excellence Scholarship

Purpose: The goal of the scholarship is to prepare the individual for life beyond rugby with an internationally recognised degree in the discipline of the student's choice, which is enhanced by the global networks, industry connections, and work experience opportunities for which Bond University is renowned.

Eligibility: Australian resident eligible to represent Australian Rugby. Meet the Academic requirements for selected program. Experience playing rugby at a high level. Strong leadership skills and community involvement.

Type: Scholarship
Value: US$20,000
Frequency: Annual
Country of Study: Any country
Closing Date: 5 September
Additional Information: bond.edu.au/intl/scholarship/john-eales-rugby-excellence-scholarship

Transformer Scholarship

Purpose: The Transformer is a co-curricular program offering at Bond designed to enable students to innovatively tackle real-world problems that matter. It is a program that attracts motivated, self-directed individuals who want to work in collaborative, interdisciplinary teams on challenging projects that typically span multiple semesters.

Eligibility: Strong leadership skills, community involvement and demonstrated potential to affect change; Extensive involvement in extracurricular activities; and Applicants must also meet the entry requirements for their chosen program of study.

Level of Study: Masters Degree

Type: Scholarship

Value: Up to 50% tuition remission

Frequency: Annual

Country of Study: Any country

No. of awards offered: 2

Closing Date: 5 September

Additional Information: bond.edu.au/intl/scholarship/transformer-scholarship

Boren Awards

Boren Scholarship

Purpose: Boren Scholars represent a vital pool of highly motivated individuals who wish to work in the federal national security arena. In exchange for funding, Boren Scholars commit to working in the federal government for at least one year after graduation

Eligibility: 1. A United States citizen at the time of application. 2. A high school graduate, or have earned a GED. 3. Matriculated in an undergraduate degree program located within the United States accredited by an accrediting body recognized by the United States Department of Education. Boren Scholars must remain matriculated in their undergraduate programs for the duration of the scholarship and may not graduate until the scholarship is complete. 4. Applying to a study abroad program that meets home institution standards in a country outside of Western Europe, Canada, Australia, or New Zealand. Boren Scholarships are not for study in the United States

Level of Study: Graduate

Type: Scholarship

Value: Up to US$20,000 for 25-52 weeks (preferred), US$10,000 for 12-24 weeks, US$8,000 for 8-11 weeks (STEM majors only)

Frequency: Annual

Country of Study: United States of America

Closing Date: 2 February

Funding: Private

Additional Information: www.borenawards.org/

For further information contact:

1400 K Street, NW 7TH floor, Washington, DC 20005, United States of America.

Tel: (1) 800 618 6737

Email: boren@iie.org

Botswana Insurance Holdings Limited Trust

PO Box 336, Gaborone, BW Botswana.

Tel: (267) 3707400

Email: webmaster@bihl.co.bw

Website: www.bihl.co.bw/

BIHL Group is a leading financial services group, originally established in 1975. BIHL has been listed on the Botswana Stock Exchange and is the holding company for three subsidiaries and holds a stake in two associate companies.

Botswana Insurance Holdings Limited Trust Thomas Tlou Scholarship for Master Programme

Purpose: The BIHL Trust Thomas Tlou Scholarship aims to benefit talented young Batswana with aspirations to pursue postgraduate studies in any discipline aimed at contributing to Botswana's socio-economic development

Eligibility: The scholarship is open to all citizens of Botswana who wish to pursue a master's programme in any discipline at a local reputable and recognized institution of higher learning on Botswana. The intended recipients must be aged between 18–35

Level of Study: Postgraduate

Type: Scholarship

Value: The Trust will spend a total of P 450,000

Country of Study: Any country

Application Procedure: Citizens of Botswana can apply for this scholarship

Closing Date: 30 June

For further information contact:

BIHL Group, Plot 66458, Block A, 3rd Floor, Fairgrounds Office Park, Gaborone, Botswana.

Fax: (267) 3973705

Email: tkeepetsoe@bihl.co.bw

Bournemouth University

Fern Barrow, Poole, Dorset BH12 5BB, United Kingdom.

Tel: (44) 1202 524111

Email: enquiries@bournemouth.ac.uk

Website: www.bournemouth.ac.uk
Contact: Ms Karen Ward, Research Administrator

If you choose BU, you'll be learning from top academics in a community of academic excellence, with excellent industry links, accredited courses and placement opportunities, preparing you for professional practice. With a range of scholarships available, there's never been a better time to take charge of your own future with BU.

Bournemouth University Dean

Eligibility: You will need to have a minimum of an upper second-class honours degree (2i). You cannot be in receipt of any other BU scholarship
Type: Scholarship
Frequency: Annual
Study Establishment: Bournemouth University
Country of Study: Any country
Application Procedure: Apply via online application form available on the BU website
Closing Date: 31 May
Contributor: Bournemouth University

Bournemouth University Dean's Scholarship – The Media School

Eligibility: You will need to have a minimum of an upper second-class honours degree (2i), or overseas equivalent
Level of Study: Graduate, Postgraduate
Value: 50% tuition fee reduction
Country of Study: Any country
Closing Date: 31 July

Bournemouth University Music Scholarships

Subjects: Music
Purpose: The scholarship supports young people with academic ability, leadership potential and a commitment to their community to achieve their full academic and leadership potential
Eligibility: 1. Any applicant for a full-time undergraduate or postgraduate course at BU. 2. You must be able to demonstrate that you are a talented musician or vocalist, and that you have been involved in ensemble activity.
Type: Scholarship
Value: £600
Frequency: Annual

Study Establishment: Bournemouth University
Country of Study: United Kingdom
Application Procedure: Apply via online form available on the BU website. As part of your application, you will need to source two references. Referees can include your Director of Music, music teacher, instrumental/vocal coach, ensemble conductor etc, or any other person qualified to write about your musical abilities. They need to complete and submit the online reference form. Scholarships will be awarded for the first year of study and may be continued for subsequent years of study providing you continue to meet the criteria
Closing Date: 31 August
Contributor: Bournemouth University
Additional Information: www.bournemouth.ac.uk/study/undergraduate/fees-funding/scholarships/ukeu-student-scholarships/bu-music-scholarships

For further information contact:

Tel: (44) 1202 961916

Bournemouth University Vice-Chancellor's Scholarship – Most Promising Postgraduate Applicant

Eligibility: Any United Kingdom or European Union student who has completed an undergraduate degree at BU and who is applying for postgraduate study at BU
Level of Study: Graduate, Postgraduate
Country of Study: Any country

Reham al-Farra International Scholarship in Journalism

Purpose: The Reham Al-Farra Memorial Journalism Fellowship is a unique opportunity for young journalists from developing countries and countries with economies in transition to cover the United Nations
Eligibility: The Reham al-Farra International Scholarship in Journalism is offered to an international applicant for MA Multimedia Journalism. You must be classed as an overseas student for fees purposes. You cannot be in receipt of any other BU scholarships
Type: Scholarship
Value: £3,000
Frequency: Annual
Study Establishment: Bournemouth University
Country of Study: Any country
Application Procedure: Apply via online form available on the BU website
Closing Date: 31 May

Contributor: Bournemouth University
Additional Information: www.european-funding-guide.eu/ scholarship/11272-reham-al-farra-international-scholarship- journalism

The Business School Dean's Scholarship

Eligibility: You must be an applicant for a full-time taught Master's degree delivered by The Business School. Applicants will be considered based upon 1. Academic achievement. 2. Work or voluntary experience relevant to the programme for which they have applied. 3. Any additional skills, experience or extra-curricular activities that will add value and indicate that they will make a significant contribution to the cohort on the programme or the Business School
Level of Study: Graduate, Postgraduate
Type: Scholarship
Value: Up to £12,500
Frequency: Annual
Country of Study: Any country
Application Procedure: In order to apply for the scholarship, the following steps needs to be followed. To secure the scholarship award applicants must confirm acceptance of the award by the date stated on the scholarship offer email. Failure to confirm acceptance of the scholarship by this date may result in the applicant's right to the scholarship being removed and the scholarship being awarded to another applicant
Closing Date: 31 May
Additional Information: www.european-funding-guide.eu/ scholarship/11270-business-school-dean%E2%80%99s-mba- scholarship

Bradford Chamber of Commerce and Industry

Devere House, Vicar Lane, Little Germany, Bradford, York-shire BD1 5AH, United Kingdom.

Tel: (44) 1274 772 777
Email: info@bradfordchamber.co.uk
Website: www.bradfordchamber.co.uk
Contact: Julie Snook, Financial Controller

The Bradford Chamber of Commerce and Industry represents member companies in the Bradford and district area. It works with local partners to develop the economic health of the district and has a major voice within the British Chamber of Commerce movement in order to promote the needs of local business on a national basis.

John Speak Trust Scholarships

Purpose: To promote British trade abroad by assisting people in perfecting their basic knowledge of a foreign language
Eligibility: Open to British nationals intending to follow a career connected with the export trade in the United Kingdom. Applicants must be over 18 years of age with a sound, basic knowledge of at least one language
Level of Study: Professional development
Type: Scholarship
Value: Contribution towards living expenses and an amount towards the cost of travel
Length of Study: Between 3 months and 1 full academic year abroad depending on the circumstances and each candidate
Frequency: Annual
Study Establishment: A recognized college or university
Country of Study: Any country
Application Procedure: Applicants must complete an application form and undertake an interview.
No. of awards offered: 10
Closing Date: 28 February
Funding: Private
Additional Information: www.postgraduatefunding.com/ award-3084

Brain Research Institute

Florey Institute of Neuroscience and Mental Health, Melbourne Brain Centre - Austin campus, 245 Burgundy Street, Heidelberg, VIC 3084, Australia.

Tel: (61) 3 9035 7000
Email: BRI@brain.org.au
Website: www.brain.org.au/

The Brain Research Institute (BRI) was established at Austin Health, Melbourne, Australia in 1996. It supports collaboration between specialities in order to develop a better understanding of how a healthy or diseased brain functions. It is an affiliated institution of The University of Melbourne

Brain Research Institute PhD Scholarships

Purpose: To encourage competitive research in understanding the structure and function of the human brain

Eligibility: Open to candidates who have obtained Honours 1 or equivalent, or Honours 2a or equivalent

Level of Study: Doctorate

Type: Scholarship

Value: Varies

Length of Study: 3 years

Frequency: Annual

Country of Study: Australia

Application Procedure: Applicants must send a curriculum vitae, academic transcripts, expression of interest for area of research and details of two academic referees

For further information contact:

Email: scholarships@brain.org.au

Brandeis University

415 South Street, Waltham, MA 02453, United States of America.

Tel: (1) 781 736 2000
Email: helleradmissions@brandeis.edu
Website: www.brandeis.edu/

Sidney Topol Fellowship in Nonviolence Practice

Purpose: Practice honors the work of peace advocate, philanthropist, and entrepreneur, Sidney Topol, through the establishment of a full tuition scholarship to the Master's Degree program in Coexistence and Conflict (COEX) at the Heller School for Social Policy and Management at Brandeis University. This fellowship does not cover airfare, fees, health insurance, or housing. The Master's Degree in Coexistence and Conflict at Brandeis University trains students to recognize, understand and begin to heal the ethnic, religious and cultural fault lines that endanger our world. Through an approach that is equal parts theoretical and practical, graduate students investigate the root causes of violent conflict and they uncover effective means to prevent conflicts and to promote peaceful coexistence After a full year in residence at the Heller School, students take their knowledge into the field, working with a conflict prevention organization. They graduate with a firm grasp of the delicate role that peace professionals play in bringing antagonistic parties together and the leadership expertise to help communities build shared societies.

Eligibility: Applicants for the Sidney Topol Fellowship in Nonviolence Practice must prove that their community benefited from their personal commitment to nonviolent principles through prior volunteer or work projects and they must commit to returning to their community within the next 2 years after graduation from the COEX program, to establish projects in nonviolence.

Level of Study: Postgraduate

Value: Full tuition scholarship. This fellowship does not cover airfare, fees, health insurance, or housing

Application Procedure: In addition to submitting a complete application to the Coexistence and Conflict program, fellowship applicants must submit the following materials; A personal essay which outlines their prior work in nonviolence, and their proposed work, and how completing the MA in Coexistence and Conflict will help them be successful in these endeavors; An interview either by phone or in person may be required. The deadline for applications for the fellowship is 15 April 2023. It is important to visit the official website (link found below) for detailed information on how to apply for this scholarship apply.heller.brandeis.edu/register/TopolFellowshipsinNonviolence

Closing Date: 15 April

Additional Information: apply.heller.brandeis.edu/register/TopolFellowshipsinNonviolence

---

BrightFocus Foundation

22512 Gateway Center Drive, Clarksburg, MD 20871, United States of America.

Tel: (1) 800 437 2423
Email: info@brightfocus.org
Website: www.brightfocus.org/
Contact: Dr Kara Summers, Grants Coordinator

BrightFocus Foundation (formerly American Health Assistance Foundation [AHAF]) is a non-profit charitable organization that funds research and public education on age related and degenerative diseases including: Alzheimer's disease, macular degeneration, glaucoma.

American Health Assistance Foundation Macular Degeneration Research

Purpose: To enable basic research on the causes of, or the treatment for, macular degeneration

Eligibility: The principal investigator must hold a tenure track or tenured position and the rank of assistant professor or higher

Level of Study: Research

Type: Grant

Value: maximum US$60,000 per year, payable over 2 years (total value US$120,000)
Length of Study: 2 year
Frequency: Annual
Study Establishment: Non-profit institutions and organizations
Country of Study: Any country
Application Procedure: Applicants must complete an application form. The current application form should be requested for each year or can be downloaded from the website
No. of awards offered: 81
Closing Date: July
Funding: Private
No. of awards given last year: 16
No. of applicants last year: 81
Additional Information: www.brightfocus.org/grants/request-proposal-fy20-macular-degeneration-research-program

For further information contact:

Email: researchgrants@brightfocus.org

British & Foreign School Society

Maybrook House, Godstone Road, Caterham, Surrey CR3 6RE, United Kingdom.

Tel: (44) 1883 331 177
Website: www.bfss.org.uk
Contact: Mr J Kidd ACIB, Director

Global Professorships

Purpose: This programme aims to demonstrate and further enhance the UK's commitment to international research partnerships and collaboration as well as strengthen the UK's research capacity and capability in the humanities and the social sciences.
Eligibility: Applications must be submitted online using the British Academy's grants application system, Flexi-Grant. Be a world-class internationally-recognised mid-career to senior researchers who are currently employed outside the United Kingdom, on a permanent contract (which may be part-time or full-time) or, if temporary, would normally be on a contract that will not end during the course of the grant unless expressly agreed with the Academy prior to the application being submitted that such an application would be considered eligible, in any field of the humanities or the social sciences. Hold a doctoral degree (or have equivalent research experience). Be available to take up an unpaid leave of absence,

a long-term secondment or employment at an eligible United Kingdom host institution. Eligible institutions include but are not limited to the British International Research Institutes
Level of Study: Graduate, Postgraduate, Professional development, Research, Unrestricted
Type: Position (Employment)
Value: Up to £187,500 per annum, and up to £750,000 over four years
Length of Study: For a period of 4 years
Frequency: Every 3 years
Country of Study: United Kingdom
Application Procedure: 1. Applications must be submitted online using the British Academy's grants application system, Flexi-Grant. 2. Application, reference, supporting statement and UK host institution application approval deadline 17.00 (UK time) on Wednesday 19 February.
Closing Date: 19 February
Funding: Government
Additional Information: All eligible proposals submitted in response to this funding call will be assessed by relevant British Academy peer reviewers and then considered by a final selection panel https://www.thebritishacademy.ac.uk/funding/global-professorships/

For further information contact:

Tel: (44) 20 7969 5220
Email: internationalgrants@thebritishacademy.ac.uk

The British & Foreign School Society

Purpose: We support charitable organisations that work to improve access to education or the quality of education for children and young people in remote or impoverished areas both in the UK and internationally. We do not have a particular geographic preference or focus.
Eligibility: 1. Organisations applying for funding should have UK charitable status or, in the case of schools, colleges, universities and Churches, "exempt charity" status. We do not fund non-UK based organisations, Community Interest Companies (CICs) or individuals. 2. Organisations should have continuous UK accounts for at least three years. 3. BFSS will only fund one project per charity at a time. If you are running a project with our funding, you cannot apply for a new grant until you have submitted your final project report. 4. BFSS focuses support on small to medium sized organisations who do not have ready access to much larger funding sources. We therefore do not usually fund charities with an average annual income above £2.5 million or below £5,000, except in exceptional circumstances. These restrictions do not apply to UK based schools, colleges and other educational establishments. 5. Organisations should be directly involved in the provision

of charitable services. We do not fund organisations whose primary purpose is fundraising. 6. We encourage close partnerships with local organisations. However, the applicant organisation must be willing to take full responsibility for the management, delivery, finances and integrity of the project.

Application Procedure: Applications from charitable organisations which meet the grant criteria are initially reviewed by the BFSS Grants Manager, and may then be submitted to the Grants Committee, which normally meets three times a year.

Additional Information: bfss.org.uk/grants/

For further information contact:

7-14 Great Dover St, London SE1 4YR, United Kingdom.

Tel: (44) 20 7922 7814
Email: grants@bfss.org.uk

British Academy

10-11 Carlton House Terrace, London SW1Y 5AH, United Kingdom.

Tel: (44) 20 7969 5200
Email: chiefexec@britac.ac.uk
Website: www.britac.ac.uk
Contact: Dr Ken Emond, Head of Research Awards

The British Academy is the premier national learned society in the United Kingdom devoted to the promotion of advanced research and scholarship in the humanities and social sciences.

Browning Fund Grants

Purpose: To promote historical studies in the field of British history in the early modern period with particular reference to the 17th century
Eligibility: Applicants must be of postdoctoral status and ordinarily resident in the United Kingdom
Level of Study: Postdoctorate
Type: Research grant
Value: Up to £10,000
Length of Study: Up to 2 years
Frequency: Annual
Country of Study: Any country

Application Procedure: Application must be made to the BA/Leverhulme Small Research Grants Scheme via the BA's online e-GAP system at egap.britac.ac.uk
No. of awards offered: Part of a larger scheme
Funding: Private
No. of awards given last year: 1
No. of applicants last year: Part of a larger scheme
Additional Information: www.britac.ac.uk

For further information contact:

Email: bfi@brownfoundation.org

Early Childhood Development Funding

Purpose: This programme is intended as the foundation for a wider research programme in subsequent years and thus aims to support a new generation of interlinked research and policy intervention that focuses on what works at scale in different contexts whilst building, and working with, local capacity to deliver effective research and change
Eligibility: 1. The Early Childhood Development Programme is open to researchers based at United Kingdom and overseas institutions. The main applicant must be based at a university or research institute and be of postdoctoral or above equivalent status. 2. The applicant must either be in a permanent position at the institution or have a fixed-term position for the duration of the award
Level of Study: Graduate
Type: Funding support
Frequency: Varies
Country of Study: Any country
Closing Date: 21 June
Funding: Private

For further information contact:

10-11 Carlton House Terrace, London SW1Y 5AH, United Kingdom.

Email: ECD@britac.ac.uk

Honor Frost Foundation Grants

Purpose: To provide support for research maritime archaeology and maritime cultural heritage
Level of Study: Postdoctorate
Type: Research grant
Value: Up to £10,000
Length of Study: Up to 2 years
Frequency: Annual

Application Procedure: Applications must be submitted via e-GAP2, the Academy's electronic grant application system, by applying for a BA/Leverhulme Small Research Grant

No. of awards offered: Part of a larger scheme

Funding: Private

Contributor: Honor Frost Foundation

No. of awards given last year: 2

No. of applicants last year: Part of a larger scheme

Additional Information: www.thebritishacademy.ac.uk/funding/honor-frost-foundation

For further information contact:

Email: rebeccagould@honorfrostfoundation.org

Newton International Fellowships

Purpose: The Newton International Fellowships aim to attract the most promising early career postdoctoral researchers from overseas in the fields of natural sciences, physical sciences, medical sciences, social sciences and the humanities. The Newton International Fellowships enable researchers to work for two years at a UK institution with the aim of fostering long-term international collaborations.

Eligibility: The applicant must 1. Have a PhD, or applicants in the final stages of their PhD will be accepted provided that the PhD will be completed (including viva) before the start date of the Fellowship. Confirmation of award of the PhD will be required before any Fellowship award is confirmed 2. Applicants should have no more than 7 years of active full time postdoctoral experience at the time of application (discounting career breaks, but including teaching experience and/or time spent in industry) 3. Be working outside the UK 4. Not hold UK citizenship 5. Be competent in oral and written English 6. Have a clearly defined and mutually-beneficial research proposal agreed with a UK host researcher.

Level of Study: Postdoctorate

Value: £24,000 per annum

Length of Study: Up to 2 years

Country of Study: Any country

Closing Date: 1 October

Additional Information: www.thebritishacademy.ac.uk/funding/newton-international-fellowships/

For further information contact:

Tel: (44) 207 969 5217

Email: overseas@thebritishacademy.ac.uk

Newton Mobility Grants

Purpose: Newton Mobility Grants provide support for international researchers based in a country covered by the Newton Fund to establish and develop collaboration with UK researchers around a specific jointly defined research project.

Eligibility: Both a UK-based applicant and an overseas-based applicant are required for this scheme. Both applicants must have a PhD or equivalent research experience and hold a permanent or fixed-term contract in an eligible university or research institute, which must span the duration of the project. Collaborations should focus on a single jointly defined research project involving (or lead by) the two applicants.

Level of Study: Research

Type: Grant

Value: maximum of £10,000

Length of Study: 1 year

Frequency: Annual

Country of Study: United Kingdom

Application Procedure: Applications must be submitted online using the British Academy's online grants management system, Flexi-Grant. For the assessment criteria please see the detailed scheme notes.

Closing Date: 5 September

Funding: Private

Contributor: Newton Fund

Additional Information: www.thebritishacademy.ac.uk/funding/newton-mobility-grants

For further information contact:

10-11 Carlton House Terrace, London SW1Y 5AH, United Kingdom.

Tel: (44) 207 969 5217

Email: newtonfund@thebritishacademy.ac.uk

British Association for American Studies (BAAS)

American Studies, School of Humanities, Keele University, Staffordshire ST5 5BG, United Kingdom.

Tel: (44) 1782 732000

Email: jo.gill@baas.ac.uk

Website: www.baas.ac.uk

Contact: Dr Sue Currell, BAAS Chair

The British Association for American Studies (BAAS), established in 1955, promotes research and teaching in all aspects of American studies. The Association organizes annual conferences and specialist regional meetings for students, teachers and researchers. The publications produced are The Journal of American Studies with Cambridge University Press, BAAS Paperbacks with Edinburgh University Press and British Records Relating to America in Microform with Microform Publishing.

British Association for American Studies Postgraduate and Early Career Short-Term Travel Awards

Purpose: To foster talent among the American Studies community in the United Kingdom. Fund travel to the United States of America for short-term research projects
Eligibility: Open to residents in the United Kingdom. Preference is given to young postgraduates and to members of BAAS. Successful candidates are required to provide a brief report of their research trip for publication in American Studies in Britain, and they are requested to acknowledge the assistance of BAAS in any other publication that results from research carried out during the tenure of the award
Level of Study: Doctorate, Postdoctorate, Postgraduate, Professional development
Type: Award
Value: £1,000
Frequency: Annual
Country of Study: United Kingdom or Australia
Application Procedure: Applicants must complete an application form
No. of awards offered: Classified
Closing Date: 10 December
Funding: Foundation
Contributor: American Embassy
No. of awards given last year: 6
No. of applicants last year: Classified
Additional Information: Successful candidates must write a report and acknowledge BAAS assistance in any related publication. Please contact at awards@baas.ac.uk www.baas.ac.uk/baas-postgraduate-short-term-travel-awards-2009/

For further information contact:

Email: awards@baas.ac.uk

British Association for Canadian Studies (BACS)

UCL Institute of the Americas 51 Gordon Square, London WC1H 0PN, United Kingdom.

Tel: (44) 20 3108 9711
Email: bacs@canadian-studies.org

Website: www.canadian-studies.net
Contact: Dr Tony McCulloch, President

In response to the growing academic interest in Canada, the British Association for Canadian Studies (BACS) was established in 1975. Its aim is to foster teaching and research on Canada and Canadian issues by locating study resources in Britain, facilitating travel and exchange schemes for professorial staff and ensuring that the expertise of Canadian scholars who visit the United Kingdom is put to effective use. Principal activities include the publication of The British Journal of Canadian Studies and the BACS Newsletter, and the organization of the Association's annual multidisciplinary conference, which attracts scholars from Canada and Europe as well as from the United Kingdom.

Ontario Bicentennial Award

Purpose: To fund travel to Ontario to research topics concerned with that province in history or political science
Eligibility: Graduate students will normally only be considered in the final stages of their doctoral research, priority will be given to BACS members
Level of Study: Doctorate
Type: Travel grant
Value: C$500 approximately
Length of Study: Short visit
Frequency: Dependent on funds available
Study Establishment: University or library
Country of Study: Canada
Application Procedure: Application form, plus supporting letter, curriculum vitae, and the names of two referees must be submitted
No. of awards offered: 2
Closing Date: 1 May
No. of awards given last year: 1
No. of applicants last year: 2
Additional Information: Administered by BACS on behalf of the Foundation for Canadian Studies in the United Kingdom www.baas.ac.uk/baas-postgraduate-short-term-travel-awards-2009/

British Association for Japanese Studies

c/o Mrs Lynn Baird, BAJS Secretariat, University of Essex, Wivenhoe Park, Colchester, Essex CO4 3SQ, United Kingdom.

Tel: (44) 7580 178 960
Email: bajs@bajs.org.uk
Website: www.bajs.org.uk

The Association was formed in 1974, with the 'aim to encourage Japanese studies in the United Kingdom, in particular by stimulating teaching and research'. With this in mind, the Association's first Conference was convened in Cambridge at Easter 1975, and since then the BAJS Conference has been an annual event.

British Association for Japanese Studies Postgraduate Studentships

Eligibility: The studentships are open to postgraduate or prospective postgraduate students of all nationalities. Applicants must have been accepted onto a full-time or part-time course at a United Kingdom university at the time application. Their dissertation (or proposed dissertation) must be in the field of Japanese studies. For PhD students in particular, it will normally be expected that they will be using Japanese language materials in their research. They must use the award either to contribute towards their fees, maintenance, or extended fieldwork. Applicants must be a member of BAJS at the time of application

Type: Studentship

Value: Up to 5 individual scholarships of £4,000 will be granted for use in given academic year. No awards of less than £4,000 will be made

Country of Study: United Kingdom

Application Procedure: Application for BAJS Postgraduate Studentships is via the online application form. For detailed information, please visit www.bajs.org.uk/funding/bajs_studentship/

Closing Date: 15 May

Additional Information: Applicants will not be eligible to receive an award if they accept full scholarships from the AHRC, ESRC, or any other funding body (United Kingdom or overseas). Successful applicants will be expected to acknowledge the support of BAJS in their dissertations, presentations, and any subsequent publications; they will also be expected to submit a 500-word report on how they used the studentship to BAJS council by the end of November. Unsuccessful applicants will be considered for the BAJS Toshiba International Foundation studentship, provided they are eligible worldscholarshipforum.com/bajs-postgraduate-studentships-international-students-uk-2017/

For further information contact:

Email: h.spurling@southampton.ac.uk

British Association of Plastic Reconstructive and Aesthetic Surgeons (BAPRAS)

The Royal College of Surgeons, 35-43 Lincoln's Inn Fields, London WC2A 3PE, United Kingdom.

Tel: (44) 20 7831 5161
Email: secretariat@bapras.org.uk
Website: www.bapras.org.uk
Contact: Ms Angela Rausch, Administrator

Founded in 1946 as British Association of Plastic Surgeons. The objective of the association is to relieve sickness and to protect and preserve public health by the promotion and development of Plastic Surgery. A name change to British Association of Plastic Reconstructive and Aesthetic Surgeons (BAPRAS).

BAPRAS Pump Priming Fund for Clinical Trials

Purpose: The BAPRAS Research Committee administers the BAPRAS Pump Priming Fund for Clinical Trials.

Eligibility: The lead applicant must be a consultant plastic surgeon working in the United Kingdom. All plastic surgeons on the application must be members of BAPRAS at the time of applying.

Value: £20,000 each year

Country of Study: Any country

Closing Date: 31 October

British Association of Plastic Reconstructive and Aesthetic Surgeons European Travelling Scholarships

Purpose: To enable Specialist Registrars from United Kingdom to visit any plastic surgical centre in Europe

Eligibility: Specialist Registrars (4–6) enrolled on a recognised training programme with the Specialist Advisory Committee in plastic surgery are eligible to apply. Preference will be given to trainees travelling abroad without other financial awards and those applying for funding prior travel. Candidates seeking funds to travel abroad in paid jobs are less preferred

Type: Scholarship

Value: £1,000.00 each

Frequency: Annual

Study Establishment: Plastic Surgery Units
Country of Study: European Union
Application Procedure: Applicants should complete an application form, submit a proposed itinerary that should be detailed and give costs and the reasons for particular visits and a curriculum vitae (maximum length of two pages) to the Chairman of the Education and Research Sub-Committee, BAPRAS
No. of awards offered: 2
Closing Date: 7 January
No. of awards given last year: 1
No. of applicants last year: 1

For further information contact:

Email: bursaries@bapras.org.uk

Fellowship Travelling Bursary

Purpose: This award is designed for BAPRAS members who are specialist registrars (years 4-8) enrolled on a recognised training programme with the Specialist Advisory Committee in Plastic Surgery and consultant plastic surgeons of not more than three years' standing
Eligibility: OPEN ONLY TO MEMBERS OF BAPRAS
Type: Fellowship
Value: A total amount of £25,000 is available annually Maximum value of one award is £5,000.
Frequency: Annual
Country of Study: Any country
Application Procedure: 1. Proposed itinerary – This should be detailed and should give costs and the reason why you consider that these particular visits would be of value. 2. Curriculum vitae – Maximum length two pages. 3. You will be able to 'copy-and-paste' these into the form. Incomplete applications will not be considered.
Closing Date: 7 January
Additional Information: Recipients of awards will be required to write a report for publication on the BAPRAS website   worldscholarshipforum.com/bajs-postgraduate-studentships-international-students-uk-2017/

For further information contact:

Email: bursaries@bapras.org.uk

Paton Masser Memorial Fund

Value: Up to the value of £5,000.00
Frequency: Annual
Country of Study: Any country

Application Procedure: 1. All applicants should convince the assessors that the proposed project is viable, completable and subsequently publishable. 2. Applications are to include well-written introduction and method sections 3. Further CVs or project descriptions should not be submitted 4. Relevant reference should be included 5. Section D must not be longer than one side of single spaced A4 (font size no smaller than 10 points), but it must be convincing 6. When planning costs, please ensure that add on costs are included to salaries (NI contributions and superannuation). You are strongly advised to discuss this with the proposed employing organisation (Trust/University). The cost of consumables, postage, telephones, etc., should also be covered. Subsequent applications for additional funding to cover shortfalls will not usually be entertained 7. Applicants are strongly advised to seek statistical advice. Power studies should be presented, if appropriate, and the proposed statistical methods should be described 8. Please ensure that Ethical Committee approval has been obtained for the proposed project before submitting this application for consideration. Applications without proof of Ethical Committee approval will not be considered. If the applicant does not consider that Ethical Committee approval is required for the project, this should be clearly stated and explained. However, the Committee reserve the right to challenge this viewpoint.
Closing Date: 31 October
Additional Information: Applicants should not apply for different prizes with the same or similar projects. In such cases, only the application for the larger prize will be considered. worldscholarshipforum.com/bajs-postgraduate-studentships-international-students-uk-2017/

For further information contact:

Email: bursaries@bapras.org.uk

Travelling Bursaries for Presentation at Overseas Meetings

Purpose: To cover the expenses for overseas travel by a consultant or trainee to present papers at international meetings
Eligibility: Applicants must submit an application form to the Chairman of the Education and Research Sub-Committee, BAPRAS
Type: Travel award
Value: £600.00
Frequency: Annual
Study Establishment: Various
Country of Study: Any country
Application Procedure: Applicants must submit application form, abstract of paper to be presented and letter of acceptance to BAPRAS secretariat

No. of awards offered: 4
Closing Date: 7 January
Contributor: BAPRAS
Additional Information: www.bapras.org.uk/professionals/
training-and-education/prizes-grants-and-fellowships/travelling-
bursaries-for-presentations-overseas

For further information contact:

Email: bursaries@bapras.org.uk

British Broadcasting Corporation Writersroom

1st Floor, Grafton House, 379-381 Euston Road, London NW1 3AU, United Kingdom.

Email: writersroom@bbc.co.uk
Website: www.bbc.co.uk/writersroom/opportunity

BBC Writersroom identifies and champions new writing talent and diversity across BBC Drama, Entertainment and Children's programmes. Writersroom is constantly on the lookout for writers of any age and experience who show real potential for the BBC. It invests in new writing projects nationwide and builds creative partnerships, including work with theatres, writer's organizations and film agencies across the country.

Alfred Bradley Bursary Award

Purpose: The aim of the Award is to encourage new radio drama writing in the North of United Kingdom
Eligibility: Open to people who live in the North of United Kingdom and who have not had a previous network radio drama commission
Level of Study: Professional development
Type: Bursary
Value: Up to £5,000, writing bursary and the chance of a Radio 4 drama commission to Northern writers new to radio, and a 12 month mentorship with a Radio Drama producer
Frequency: Every 2 years
Country of Study: United Kingdom
Application Procedure: Applicants must send completed afternoon play scripts for consideration. Details published on www.bbc.co.uk/writersroom
Closing Date: 9 November
Funding: Corporation, Private
Contributor: BBC
Additional Information: There is a change of focus for each award, e.g. previous years have targeted comedy, drama,

verse drama, etc. www.bapras.org.uk/professionals/training-
and-education/prizes-grants-and-fellowships/travelling-bursaries-
for-presentations-overseas

For further information contact:

Email: admin@nawe.co.uk

British Council

Bridgewater House, 58 Whitworth Street, Manchester M1 6BB, United Kingdom.

Tel: (44) 161 957 7755
Email: general.enquiries@britishcouncil.org
Website: www.britishcouncil.org

The British Council is the United Kingdom's public diplomacy and cultural organization working in more than 100 countries, in arts, education, governance and science. The British Council promotes the diversity and creativity of British society and culture. The Foreign and Commonwealth Office provides The British Council with the core grant-in-aid.

Commonwealth Scholarships

Purpose: For students from the developed Commonwealth to study in the United Kingdom
Level of Study: Doctorate
Type: Scholarship
Value: Student visas for the United Kingdom will be arranged gratis by the British Council
Application Procedure: See British Council website
Closing Date: 22 February
Funding: Government

For further information contact:

Department of Higher Education, External Scholarship Division, ES.4 Section, West Block-1, Wing-6, 2nd Floor, R.K. Puram, New Delhi, 110066, India.

Tel: (91) 11 26172491/26172492
Email: delhi.scholarship@in.britishcouncil.org

GREAT Scholarships India

Subjects: Faculty of Medicine, MA Fashion Marketing and Branding, MA English Literary Studies, MSc Electrochemistry and Battery Technologies.

Purpose: GREAT Scholarships offers 60 scholarships from UK universities, across a variety of subjects for students from India

Eligibility: To be eligible for a scholarship, you must 1. be a citizen of India. 2. have an undergraduate degree that will enable you to enter a postgraduate (taught) programme in a UK university. 3. be motivated and academically able to follow a UK postgraduate course 4. active in the field with work experience or proven interest in the subject area. 5. meet the English language requirement of the UK university.

Level of Study: Postgraduate

Type: Scholarship

Value: £10,000

Length of Study: 1 year

Frequency: Annual

Country of Study: United Kingdom

Application Procedure: 1. Filter the universities listed by India on the find a scholarship page and click on university page to access detailed information about the scholarships on offer. 2. Apply for individual scholarships following the instructions given on each universities scholarship webpages. 3. The deadline to apply for a GREAT Scholarship varies according to each institution. For details on individual institutions deadlines please see the institutions page. 4. Successful scholars will be informed by individual universities on the result of their applications. 5. Scholarship funding will be issued to successful scholars by individual universities after registration

Closing Date: 31 May

Contributor: The University of Southampton, UK government's GREAT Britain campaign and the British Council.

Additional Information: www.southampton.ac.uk/courses/funding/scholarships-awards/great-scholarship-india.page

For further information contact:

University of Southampton, University Road, Southampton SO17 1BJ, United Kingdom.

Tel: (44) 23 8059 5000
Fax: (44) 23 8059 3131

Marshall Scholarships

Purpose: To finance young Americans of high ability to study for a degree in the United Kingdom

Eligibility: Open only to United States citizens who (at the time they take up their Scholarship) hold a first degree from an accredited four-year college or university in the United States with a minimum GPA of 3.7. To qualify for awards tenable from October 2022, candidates must have graduated from their undergraduate college or university after April 2019.

Type: Scholarship

Value: University fees, cost of living expenses, annual book grant, thesis grant, research and daily travel grants, fares to and from the United States and, where applicable, a contribution towards the support of a dependent spouse

Frequency: Annual

Country of Study: United Kingdom

No. of awards offered: 50

Closing Date: October

Contributor: British Council

Additional Information: www.marshallscholarship.org/apply/criteria-and-who-is-eligible

For further information contact:

11766 Wilshire Boulevard, Suite 1200, Los Angeles, CA 90025-6538, United States of America.

Email: apps@marshallscholarship.org

The Goa Education Trust (GET) Scholarships

Purpose: To provide opportunities for dynamic young men and women of Goan origin who have demonstrated academic excellence and extra-curricular achievements to study or train in the United Kingdom

Eligibility: Open to Indian nationals, domiciled and resident in Goa or born of Goan parents, who are not more than 30 years of age at the time of applying for the scholarship and have an excellent academic track record. Candidates must have confirmed admission for any technical/vocational/academic course of study in the United Kingdom for up to 1 year

Level of Study: Postgraduate

Type: Scholarship

Value: Scholarships will fund young Indians to pursue a Masters in the United Kingdom and will cover part or full tuition fees not exceeding £15,000

Length of Study: 1 year

Frequency: Annual

Country of Study: United Kingdom

Application Procedure: A completed application form must be sent by post

Closing Date: 10 May

Additional Information: studyabroad.shiksha.com/scholarships/goa-education-trust-scholarships

For further information contact:

British Council Division, British Deputy High Commission, 901, 9th Floor, Tower1, One Indiabulls Centre, 841, Senapati Bapat Marg, Elphinstone Road (West), Mumbai, 400 013, India.

Tel: (91) 22 67486748
Email: mumbai.enquiry@in.britishcouncil.org

British Dental Association

64 Wimpole Street, London W1G 8YS, United Kingdom.

Tel: (44) 20 7935 0875
Email: enquiries@bda.org
Website: www.bda.org
Contact: Miss Sarah Leithead, Marketing Executive

The British Dental Association (BDA) is the national professional association for dentists. With over 20,000 members, the Association strives to enhance the science, art and ethics of dentistry, improve the nation's oral health and promote the interests of its members.

British Dental Association/Dentsply Student Support Fund

Purpose: To give financial assistance to students who are in severe financial hardship. Only open to 4th- and 5th-year BDS students or postgraduates
Eligibility: Open to BDA members only. All applicants must be registered students at a United Kingdom Dental School
Level of Study: Graduate, Postgraduate
Type: Scholarship/Hardship fund
Value: Varies
Frequency: Annual
Country of Study: United Kingdom
Application Procedure: Applicants must complete and submit application forms, accompanied by an academic reference or supporting letter. Application forms can be found in the student section of the BDA website
No. of awards offered: 30
Closing Date: 1 July
Funding: Commercial
Contributor: Dentsply United Kingdom Ltd
No. of awards given last year: 7
No. of applicants last year: 30
Additional Information: For BDS/Dental Students only studyabroad.shiksha.com/scholarships/goa-education-trust-scholarships

For further information contact:

Email: SSF@contacts.bham.ac.uk

British Dietetic Association

The British Dietetic Association, 5th floor, Charles House, 148/9 Great Charles Street Queensway, Birmingham B3 3HT, United Kingdom.

Tel: (44) 1 2120 0802
Email: info@bda.uk.com
Website: www.bda.uk.com
Contact: Mr Nula Marnell, Assistant to the Chief Executive

The British Dietetic Association (BDA) is the professional body for dietitians in the United Kingdom and provides grants for research into human nutrition and dietetic practice that advances the profession.

Pace Award

Purpose: For the development or implementation of a nutrition education programme for staff addressing the problem of undernutrition
Eligibility: Applicants should be full members of the BDA and resident in the United Kingdom or Eire
Level of Study: Research
Type: Grant
Value: £500 to fund the development of the project and £300 worth of pace learning units for staff to use
Country of Study: Any country
Application Procedure: To apply, dietitians are to submit an outline of the proposed education programme that includes which staff is targeted, subject area and level of the programme, which format will be taken, how the learner will be assessed, what effect it will have on nutritional care and how it will raise the profile of nutrition in your organization, potential benefits to employers and estimated cost of development and implementation. Four copies of the application are to be submitted
Closing Date: 28 January
Funding: Commercial
Additional Information: Applications should not exceed 1,000 words studyabroad.shiksha.com/scholarships/goa-education-trust-scholarships

For further information contact:

Email: financial.aid@ohio.edu

British Ecological Society (BES)

Charles Darwin House, 12 Roger Street, London WC1N 2JU, United Kingdom.

Tel: (44) 20 7685 2500
Email: grants@britishecologicalsociety.org
Website: www.britishecologicalsociety.org

As a learned society and registered charity, the British Ecological Society (BES) is an independent organization receiving little outside funding. The aims of the Society are to promote the science of ecology through research, publications and conferences and to use the findings of such research to educate the public and to influence policy decisions that involve ecological matters. The BES is an active and thriving organization with something to offer anyone with an interest in ecology. Academic journals, teaching resources, meetings for scientists and policy makers, career advice and grants for ecologists are just a few of the societies areas of activity.

Outreach Grant

Purpose: We define ecology as the scientific study of the distribution, abundance and dynamics of organisms, their interactions with other organisms and their physical environment. Applications should promote and engage the public with the science of ecology. Grants will not be awarded for purely nature conservation purposes or any activity that does not promote the science of ecology.
Eligibility: Awards are open to individuals and organisations to organise ecological public engagement events. This includes, but is not limited to, our members, researchers, schools, museums, libraries and community groups. Your proposal must be aimed at a non-academic audience and all projects must provide a clear demonstration of direct interaction with them. They should also show evidence of links to the research community at UK, regional and international levels, where appropriate.
Type: Project grant
Value: The maximum award is £2,000
Frequency: Annual
Country of Study: Any country
Application Procedure: Applicants must complete an online application form through the BES website at www.britisheco logicalsociety.org/grants-awards/outreach-grants
Closing Date: 18 March
Contributor: British Ecological Society

Additional Information: www.britishecologicalsociety.org/ funding/outreach-grants/

For further information contact:
Email: outreach@physoc.org

Research Grants

Purpose: These grants support scientific ecological research where there are limited alternative sources of funding.
Eligibility: 1. These grants are given to individuals, not organisations. 2. Only current BES members may apply. 3. Applicants cannot use a Research Grant to fund a component of a larger, already funded study. We understand that there may be additional contributors to the project, but our contribution must make up the majority of the project funding, or form a recognisable and distinct component which would otherwise not take place. 4. Funding is not available for work that will form part of a degree/masters/ PhD/fellowship. Those with fellowships and PhDs that only cover their salary, are eligible to apply. 5. Applications to take part in an expedition will not be considered (e.g. Operation Wallacea). We shall, though, consider applications for a stand-alone research project which take place during an expedition. 6. Applicants are responsible for obtaining all relevant permits and permissions required to undertake the proposed work. 7. Projects can take place anywhere in the world. Applications for projects based outside the UK should demonstrate liaison with collaborating organisations, local environmental agencies, NGOs and/or communities within the country the project is taking place. 8. This grant will not fund attendance to a conference. 9. This grant will not fund publication costs. 10. We will not award more than one grant to any one applicant in any one year, and no more than three grants in any five year period. 11. Failure to submit a satisfactory report at the end of a grant will mean the grantee is ineligible to apply for further grants.
Value: Up to £5,000
Country of Study: Any country
Application Procedure: 1. When applications open, register/ log into our online grants system, complete your contact details, and navigate to 'Your Applications'. 2. We aim to notify all applicants within two months of the grant deadline. Shortlisted Large Research Grants applicants will be notified via email with details of how to apply to Part B. 3. Applicants are only able to submit one grant application per round, across all grant schemes. 4. All projects should start within 6 months of the grant award date. Small Research Grants should run for a maximum of 12 months and Large Research may run for a maximum of 24 months. Any projects running for longer

than this should be clearly outlined and justified in the submitted application. 5. It is a condition of all of our grant schemes that applicants submit a report within three months of the end date of your award. Reports will be submitted via our online grants system.

Closing Date: 18 March
Additional Information: www.britishecologicalsociety.org/funding/research-grants/

For further information contact:

Email: siri@britishecologicalsociety.org

Training & Travel Grants

Purpose: These grants help PhD students and postgraduate research assistants to meet the costs of specialist field training courses and to network and publicise their research by presenting their work at workshops and conferences.
Eligibility: 1. be a BES member. 2. have at least a B.Sc. or equivalent degree. 3. be a PhD student, postgraduate research assistant (within 3 years of completing relevant degree) or equivalent (Postdoc researchers are therefore not eligible to apply). 4. work or study at a university or research institution (including field centres, NGOs, museums, etc.) that provide research facilities. 5. work in scientific areas within our remit (the science of ecology) and of relevance to the training course or meeting they are applying to attend. 6. give a presentation if attending a meeting. 7. no retrospective claims for funding will be considered. 8. no applicant may receive more than two Training & Travel Grants in any five year period. There must be at least three years between grants.
Value: Up to £1,000
Country of Study: Any country
Closing Date: 18 March
Additional Information: www.britishecologicalsociety.org/funding/training-travel-grants/

For further information contact:

Email: siri@britishecologicalsociety.org

British Federation of Women Graduates (BFWG)

4 Mandeville Courtyard, 142 Battersea Park Road, London SW11 4NB, United Kingdom.

Tel: (44) 20 7498 8037
Email: awards@bfwg.org.uk
Website: www.bfwg.org.uk

The British Federation of Women Graduates (BFWG) provides opportunities to women in education and public life. BFWG works as part of an international organization to improve the lives of women and girls, fosters local, national and international friendship and offers scholarships for third year doctorate research.

American Association of University Women/ International Federation of University Women International Fellowships

Purpose: To assist study or research that demonstrates a continued interest in the advancement of women
Eligibility: Open to female members of the British Federation of Women Graduates (BFWG) or another national federation or association (NFA) of the International Federation of University Women (IFUW), who are not United States citizens, with acceptance by an institution in America at which the applicant proposes to undertake her work
Level of Study: Graduate, Postdoctorate, Postgraduate, Predoctorate, Research
Type: Fellowships
Value: Master's/first professional degree US$18,000; Doctoral US$20,000; Postdoctoral US$30,000. These fellowships do not cover travel costs
Length of Study: 1 year
Frequency: Annual
Study Establishment: An Institute of Higher Education
Country of Study: United States of America
Application Procedure: Application material can be downloaded from AAUW's website
Closing Date: 15 November
Funding: Private
Contributor: AAUW members
Additional Information: A list of NFA's can be found on IFUW's website www.ifuw.org

For further information contact:

AAUW Educational Foundation, International Fellowships, PO Box 4030, Iowa City, IA 52243-4030, United States of America.

Email: aauw@act.org

British Federation of Women Graduates Scholarships

Purpose: The British Federation of Women Graduates (BFWG) Scholarships support between six and ten female doctoral students in their third year of study. Awards are made on a basis of academic excellence.

Eligibility: Academic excellence as evidenced by a proven ability to carry out independent research is the chief criterion. Open to female students, regardless of nationality, whose studies take place in Great Britain. Research students should be entering into their final year of formal study towards a PhD degree. Taught Master's degrees do not count as research, although MPhil research students would need to be upgraded to a PhD during the close of the competition or thereabouts
Level of Study: Doctorate, Predoctorate, Research
Type: Scholarship
Value: £1,000–£6,000
Length of Study: Student must be in her third year (or part time equivalent) at the time of giving out the awards (October each year)
Frequency: Annual
Study Establishment: A university or institution of university status in Britain
Country of Study: Great Britain
Application Procedure: Application materials can be downloaded from BFWG's website or www.bfwg.org.uk
No. of awards offered: 6-10
Closing Date: 4 March
Funding: Private
Contributor: BFWG members
Additional Information: Recipients must submit a written report within 6 months of being awarded their PhD bfwg.org.uk/bfwg2/how-to-apply-for-a-bfwg-academic-award/

For further information contact:

Email: awardsqueries@bfwg.org.uk

French Association of University Women (AFFDU) Grants

Purpose: To assist those at doctoral or postdoctoral levels whose studies or research take place in France
Eligibility: Open to female members of the British Federation of Women Graduates (BFWG) or another national federation or association (NFA) of the International Federation of University Women (IFUW), who know the language of the country in which they plan to study
Level of Study: Doctorate, Postdoctorate, Postgraduate, Research
Type: Grant
Value: €1,000–1,500, should preferably cover a study or research project involving travelling to or outside of France
Length of Study: Up to 12 months
Frequency: Annual
Study Establishment: An Institute of Higher Education
Country of Study: France

Application Procedure: Applicants should be undergraduate or postgraduate students, should have applied for admission to the University for a full-time scheme and have satisfied the entry requirements
Closing Date: 30 April
Funding: Private
Contributor: AFFDU members
Additional Information: A list of NFA's can be found on IFUW's website (www.ifuw.org) www.european-funding-guide.eu/scholarship/6992-affdu-grants-archaelogy-history-literature-physics-chemistry

For further information contact:

AFFDU, Reid Hall, 4 rue de Chevreuse, F-75006 Paris, France.

Email: affdu@club-internet.fr

French Association of University Women (AFFDU) Monique Fouet Grant

Purpose: To support a women postgraduate studying Political Science
Eligibility: Open to female members of the British Federation of Women Graduates (BFWG) or another National Federation of Association (NFA) of the International Federation of University Women (IFUW), who wish to undertake research on the AFFDU project site in Nabasdju Civol. Candidates must speak French
Level of Study: Postgraduate, Research
Type: Grant
Value: From €1,000–1,500. The award does not cover travel costs
Length of Study: Up to 1 year
Frequency: Annual
Study Establishment: A university or institution of university status
Country of Study: Any country
Application Procedure: Application materials can be downloaded from AFFDU's website or obtained via email
Closing Date: 30 March
Funding: Private
Contributor: AFFDU members
Additional Information: A list of NFA's can be found on IFUW's website www.ifuw.org

For further information contact:

AFFDU, Reid Hall, 4 rue de Chevreuse, F-75006 Paris, France.

Email: affdu@club-internet.fr

NKA Ellen Gleditsch Scholarship

Purpose: To assist independent research or advanced studies by women at the post-graduate or doctoral level

Eligibility: Open to female members of the British Federation of Women Graduates (BFWG) or another national federation or association (NFA) of the International Federation of University Women (IFUW) with acceptance by a Norwegian institution at which the applicant proposes to undertake her work and proof of adequate health insurance

Level of Study: Doctorate, Postgraduate, Research

Type: Scholarship

Value: NOK 40,000. The scholarship does not cover travel costs

Length of Study: 3–4 months

Frequency: Every 3 years

Study Establishment: A university or institution of university status

Country of Study: Norway

Application Procedure: Applicants studying in Great Britain must apply through BFWG. Application material and membership details can be downloaded from their website or for paper copies write to BFWG, 4 Mandeville Courtyard, 142 Battersea Park Road, London SW11 4NB, United Kingdom enclosing a C5 self-addressed stamped envelope

Closing Date: 1 September

Funding: Private

Contributor: NKA members

Additional Information: If studying outside Great Britain, candidates should check the list of NFAs on IFUW's website www.ifuw.org

For further information contact:

EGS, PO Box 251, N-5000 Bergen, Norway.

Email: elisabeth.haavet@hi.uib.no

British Heart Foundation (BHF)

14 Fitzhardinge Street, London W1H 6DH, United Kingdom.

Tel: (44) 20 7935 0185
Email: internet@bhf.org.uk
Website: www.bhf.org.uk
Contact: Ms Valerie Mason, Research Funds Manager

The British Heart Foundation (BHF) exists to encourage research into the causes, diagnosis, prevention and advances of cardiovascular disease, to inform doctors throughout the country of advances in the diagnosis, cure and treatment of heart diseases, and to improve facilities for the treatment of heart patients where the National Health Service is unable to help.

British Heart Foundation-Daphne Jackson Fellowships

Purpose: To provide an opportunity for basic scientists to return to cardiovascular research at an established research institution in the United Kingdom after a career break of two years or more

Eligibility: Your eligibility and suitability are initially assessed using the information submitted to us in the CV and personal statement forms. If you do fit our eligibility criteria, one of our Fellowship Advisors will arrange an informal telephone interview with you to talk through your CV, your career break, your desire to retrain, your field of interest and assess your future employment prospects

Type: Fellowship

Length of Study: Up to three years

Frequency: Annual

Country of Study: Any country

Application Procedure: 1. Applicants will need to approach and agree a plan of work with a potential academic sponsor as part of the application process. We are particularly interested in supporting applicants working in interdisciplinary research, but applicants working in single disciplines will be considered equally. 2. The Elizabeth Blackwell Institute will half-sponsor the Fellowship and the remaining funding will be secured by the Daphne Jackson Trust from an additional sponsor

Closing Date: 18 February

Additional Information: The fellowship will be part-time for a fixed term of up to three years daphnejackson.org/wp-content/uploads/2019/07/British-Heart-Foundation-Daphne-Jackson-Fellowship-2019.pdf

For further information contact:

The Daphne Jackson Trust, Department of Physics, University of Surrey, Guildford, Surrey GU2 7XH, United Kingdom.

Email: djmft@surrey.ac.uk

Career Re-entry Research Fellowships

Purpose: To provide an opportunity to re-establish a career in cardiovascular science in an established research institution in the United Kingdom, after a break of more than one year

Eligibility: 1. Successful post-doc returning after a career break of one or more years. 2. The candidate must have the support of a named senior investigator who will guarantee access to space and resources and provide scientific guidance for the duration of their fellowship. This individual should be named on the application form as a 'Supervisor' and provide an appropriate letter of support as part of the application. 3. The fellowship may be taken up on a part-time employment basis, where appropriate, following discussion and agreement with us and the employing institution. For more information read about our Flexible working policies

Level of Study: Postdoctorate researcher

Type: Fellowship

Value: £500 per year

Length of Study: Up to 1 year full-time or up to 3 years part-time

Frequency: Varies

Country of Study: United Kingdom

Application Procedure: Application link for the grants are as follows gms.bhf.org.uk/Pages/Default.aspx?ReturnUrl=%252f_layouts%252fAuthenticate.aspx%253fSource%253d%252f&Source=%252f

Additional Information: For further information, visit the website www.bhf.org.uk

www.bhf.org.uk/for-professionals/information-for-researchers/what-we-fund/career-re-entry-research-fellowship

For further information contact:

British Heart Foundation, Lyndon Place, 2096 Coventry Road, Sheldon, Birmingham B26 3YU, United Kingdom.

Tel: (44) 20 7554 0442

Email: gmsqueries@bhf.org.uk

Clinical Research Leave Fellowships

Purpose: To provide an opportunity for talented NHS staff to undertake dedicated PAs in research in a recognised United Kingdom centre of excellence in cardiovascular medicine

Eligibility: Awards may include 1. Reimbursement of reasonable costs to cover relinquished PAs. 2. Research consumables directly attributable to the project

Level of Study: Graduate

Type: Fellowship

Value: £500 per year

Length of Study: Up to 1 year full-time or up to 3 years part-time

Frequency: Annual

Country of Study: Any country

Application Procedure: Candidates may be interviewed and a decision on this will be reached by the Fellowships Committee (four meetings a year) after it has considered external peer review reports

Funding: Private

Additional Information: www.bhf.org.uk/for-professionals/information-for-researchers/what-we-fund/clinical-research-leave-fellowship

For further information contact:

180, Hampstead Road, London NW1 7AW, United Kingdom.

Tel: (44) 20 7554 0442

Email: gmsqueries@bhf.org.uk

Clinical Study Grants

Purpose: To provide an opportunity for talented NHS staff to undertake dedicated PAs in research in a recognised United Kingdom centre of excellence in cardiovascular medicine

Eligibility: 1. The principal investigator will be a senior researcher working in an established research institution in the United Kingdom. She/he must have a strong track record of grant support, usually from us, and an internationally recognised research profile. 2. Any multicentre interventional clinical trial, while remaining under the scientific control of the principal investigator, should usually be managed by a United Kingdom CRC-registered Clinical Trials Unit (CTU) and should usually include a member of the CTU as a co-applicant or principal investigator unless there are clearly justified reasons for not doing so

Level of Study: Graduate

Type: Fellowship or Grant

Value: £350,000

Length of Study: Usually up to 5 years, with regular progress reports, initially annual reports

Frequency: Every 5 years

Country of Study: Any country

Application Procedure: Once a preliminary application is approved you should submit a full application 1. Read the information in How to apply. 2. Read about the SoECAT form. 3. Also read Costing a clinical study. Excess treatment costs. Costing a clinical research imaging scan. Clinical Trials Units. Clinical Study Guidelines. Patient and public involvement. 4. Log onto the online application form. Application has to be completed through online procedurals

Closing Date: 12 January

Funding: Private

Additional Information: www.bhf.org.uk/for-professionals/information-for-researchers/what-we-fund/clinical-study

For further information contact:

180 Hampstead Road, London NW1 7AW, United Kingdom.

Tel: (44) 20 7554 0442
Email: gmsqueries@bhf.org.uk

Immediate Postdoctoral Basic Science Research Fellowships

Purpose: To provide an opportunity for the most promising newly qualified postdoctoral researchers to make an early start in developing their independent cardiovascular research careers in an established institution in the United Kingdom
Eligibility: Candidates should be in the final year of their PhD studies or have no more than two years of postdoctoral research experience from the date of the PhD viva. Candidates must be able to show, by publications or otherwise, evidence of exceptional research ability. The fellowship should not be held in the institution where the PhD was carried out. Residency requirements do not apply
Level of Study: Postgraduate
Type: Fellowship
Value: Travel funding of up to £500 per year & Housing contribution up to £3,000
Length of Study: 1.5 years
Country of Study: Any country
Application Procedure: The online application form must be completed by the applicant
Funding: Private
Additional Information: www.bhf.org.uk/for-professionals/information-for-researchers/what-we-fund/immediate-postdoctoral-basic-science-research-fellowship

For further information contact:

Tel: (44) 20 7554 0442
Email: gmsqueries@bhf.org.uk

Intermediate Clinical Research Fellowships

Purpose: To provide a career opportunity in an established research institution in the United Kingdom for individuals with an established research record who intend to become leaders in academic medical research
Eligibility: Successful PhD (or MD) plus NTN and at least two years completed specialist training, but usually no more than two years after CCT. NTN will be exchanged for NTN (A) on appointment, and the individual may progress to consultant level during the fellowship
Level of Study: Graduate
Type: Fellowships, operating grants
Value: Travel funding of up to £500 per year & Housing contribution up to £3,000
Length of Study: 5 years duration

Frequency: Annual
Country of Study: Any country
Application Procedure: 1. Read the information in How to apply. 2. Read our commitment to Improving Support for Clinical Academics. If you are applying for funding for a clinical study, also read 1. Costing a clinical study. 2. Costing a clinical research imaging scan. 3. Clinical Trials Units. 4. Clinical Study Guidelines. 5. Log onto the online application form. Complete all the sections of the online application form following the instructions in the GMS User Guide. The online application must be completed by the applicant. Short-listed candidates may be interviewed
Funding: Government
Additional Information: www.bhf.org.uk/for-professionals/information-for-researchers/what-we-fund/intermediate-clinical-research-fellowships

For further information contact:

Research Funds Department, British Heart Foundation Greater London House, 180 Hampstead Road, London NW1 7AW, United Kingdom.

Tel: (44) 20 7554 0442
Email: gmsqueries@bhf.org.uk

New Horizon Grants

Purpose: To encourage scientists from outside traditional cardiovascular biology to engage in cardiovascular research and bring novel expertise to the field, and to develop new technologies, models or methodologies
Eligibility: 1. The principal investigator will be a senior researcher working in an established research institution in the United Kingdom. He/she must have a strong track record of project grant support and an internationally recognised research profile. 2. The principal investigator or co-applicant(s) should include researcher(s) with a strong track record of relevant cardiovascular research. 3. The principal investigator or co-applicant(s) should include researcher(s) from outside traditional cardiovascular biology, who do not have extensive existing collaborations with cardiovascular researchers
Level of Study: Graduate
Type: Grant
Value: Up to £300,000 and up to three years & Travel funding of up to £2,000 per year
Frequency: Every 3 years
Country of Study: Any country
Application Procedure: Kindly check the website for further information. www.bhf.org.uk/for-professionals/information-for-researchers/what-we-fund/new-horizon-grants
Funding: Private

Additional Information: You will be asked to attach a single PDF document to your online application form containing the following information: 1. For resubmissions, include an unedited copy of the original feedback followed by a detailed response, limited to 3 sides of A4, explaining how the revised application has changed from the original submission. 2. Abstract of the proposed investigation in 200 words or less. 3. Background to the project and pilot data. 4. Original hypothesis. 5. Experimental details and design of proposed investigation. 6. Power calculations. 7. Expected value of results. 8. List of references relevant to the proposed project www.bhf.org.uk/for-professionals/information-for-researchers/what-we-fund/new-horizon-grants

For further information contact:

180 Hampstead Road, London NW1 7AW, United Kingdom.

Tel: (44) 20 7554 0442
Email: gmsqueries@bhf.org.uk

Non-Clinical PhD Studentships

Purpose: To allow talented students to complete a PhD in cardiovascular science in an established research institution in the United Kingdom
Eligibility: The application must be made by an established investigator who will be the supervisor and may be for a named or unnamed student. The primary supervisor must devote a minimum of 10% of their time to supervising the student and a second supervisor should also be included. Extra scrutiny will be given to applications from institutions in receipt of a BHF Research Excellence award or from supervisors named on a BHF 4 year PhD Scheme. These applications will require additional justification and should be for named students only. The BHF does not provide 'top-up' funding for existing PhD studentships supported by other grant giving organisations, which are incompletely funded
Level of Study: Graduate, Postgraduate
Type: Studentship and scholarship
Value: £10,000 per year
Frequency: Every 3 years
Country of Study: Any country
Application Procedure: Apply through online mode post registration on the below link. gms.bhf.org.uk/Pages/Default.aspx?ReturnUrl=%252f_layouts%252fAuthenticate.aspx%253fSource%253d%252f&Source=%252f
Funding: Private
Additional Information: www.bhf.org.uk/for-professionals/information-for-researchers/what-we-fund/phd-studentships

For further information contact:

Tel: (44) 20 7554 0442
Email: gmsqueries@bhf.org.uk

Research Training Fellowships for Nurses and Allied Health Professionals

Purpose: To provide a foundation in research training in an established research institution in the United Kingdom for nurses and allied health professionals, leading to the award of a PhD.
Eligibility: The named student should usually hold a good quality Masters degree or equivalent. 1. Students who have started a PhD (or equivalent) may be eligible to apply for a Research Training Fellowship, but the application must be received within 6 months of having registered for their PhD In these circumstances, the proposed start date for the Research Training Fellowship should also be no more than 12 months (or full-time equivalent) from the date of registration for the degree. 2. If the fellowship is taken up on a full-time research basis, we recognise that part of the time (ideally no more than 20% though sometimes more if it can be argued that the research directly involves their patients) may be spent on patient care. 3. The fellowship may be taken up on a part-time employment basis, where appropriate, following discussion and agreement with us and the employing institution. For more information, read about our Flexible working policies
Level of Study: Postgraduate
Type: Fellowship
Value: £10,000 per year, Travel funding of up to £500 per year
Length of Study: 5 years
Country of Study: Any country
Application Procedure: Check through the website link. www.bhf.org.uk/for-professionals/information-for-researchers/what-we-fund/research-training-fellowships-for-nurses-and-allied-health-professionals
Closing Date: 20 April
Funding: Foundation
Additional Information: www.bhf.org.uk/for-professionals/information-for-researchers/what-we-fund/research-training-fellowships-for-nurses-and-allied-health-professionals

For further information contact:

Email: research@bhf.org.uk

Travel Fellowships

Purpose: To enable a postdoctoral researcher to undertake a visit to a distinguished laboratory abroad, either for a short period of up to six months to acquire specialist knowledge or expertise, or for a longer period to carry out a research project that can not be done in United Kingdom

Eligibility: Usually more than three years postdoctoral experience, but applicants with less postdoctoral experience are also eligible to apply. Applicant must hold a post in the United Kingdom and a guaranteed post to return to after the fellowship

Level of Study: Postdoctorate

Type: Fellowship

Frequency: Annual

Country of Study: Any country

Application Procedure: 1. Read the information in How to apply. 2. Log onto the online application form. 3. Complete all the sections of the online application form following the instructions in the GMS User Guide. 4. Ensure the named Supervisor in the application form is your United Kingdom Supervisor

Funding: Private

Additional Information: www.bhf.org.uk/for-professionals/information-for-researchers/what-we-fund/travel-fellowships

For further information contact:

Email: research@bhf.org.uk

British Institute at Ankara (BIAA)

10 Carlton House Terrace, London SW1Y 5AH, United Kingdom.

Tel: (44) 20 7969 5204
Email: biaa@britac.ac.uk
Website: www.biaa.ac.uk
Contact: Claire McCafferty, London Administrator

BIAA aims to support, promote, facilitate, and publish British research focused on Turkey and the Black Sea littoral in all academic disciplines within the arts, humanities, and social sciences and to maintain a centre of excellence in Ankara focused on the archaeology and related subjects of Turkey.

British Institute at Ankara Research Scholarship

Purpose: To conduct their own research at doctoral level

Eligibility: Open to candidates who hold a Master's degree and have a demonstrable connection to United Kingdom academia

Level of Study: Postgraduate, Research

Type: Research scholarship

Value: £800 per month and the cost of one return flight between the United Kingdom and Turkey

Length of Study: 9 months

Frequency: Annual

Country of Study: Turkey

Application Procedure: Deadline for applications is mid-September. Check website for further details

Closing Date: September

For further information contact:

British Institute at Ankara, Çankaya, Atatürk Blv No:154, TR-06690 Çankaya/Ankara, Turkey.

Fax: (44) 20 7969 5401

Martin Harrison Memorial Fellowship

Purpose: To assist junior Turkish archaeologists, who are not able to take advantage of travelling, working in any area of the archaeology of Anatolia from Prehistory to the Ottoman period, to visit the United Kingdom, especially Oxford, in connection with their research work

Eligibility: Open to Turkish citizens residing in Turkey who have completed at least 2 years of postgraduate research and at most held a doctorate for 5 years, working in any area of the archaeology of Anatolia (from the Prehistoric to the Ottoman period)

Level of Study: Doctorate, Postgraduate, Research

Type: Short-term fellowship

Value: £1,500 and travel expenses from and to Turkey

Length of Study: 6–13 weeks

Frequency: Annual

Study Establishment: University of Oxford

Country of Study: United Kingdom

Application Procedure: Completed applications, including a curriculum vitae, should be sent to the Turkey address

Closing Date: 31 March

Funding: Foundation

Contributor: Martin Harrison Fund for living expenses and British Institute at Ankara (BlAA) for travel

Additional Information: The selection will be made on the basis of the applicant's academic record, coherent research proposal, ability to benefit from libraries and scholars in Oxford, and a working knowledge of spoken and written English biaa.ac.uk/opportunities/item/name/martin-harrison-memorial-fund-fellowship

For further information contact:

The British Institute at Ankara, 24 Tahran Caddesi, Kavaklidere, TR-06700 Ankara, Turkey.

Tel:	(90) 312 427 5487
Fax:	(90) 312 428 0159
Email:	ggirdivan@biaatr.org

British Institute in Eastern Africa

British Institute in Eastern Africa, Laikipia Road, Kileleshwa, Nairobi, PO Box 30710-00100 GPO, Kenya.

Tel:	(254) 20 815 5186
Email:	office@biea.ac.uk
Website:	www.biea.ac.uk
Contact:	Dr David Anderson, Director

The British Institute in Eastern Africa (BIEA) exists to promote research in the humanities and social sciences. BIEA is based in Nairobi, but supports work across Eastern Africa, and is one of the schools and institutes supported by the British Academy.

British Institute in Eastern Africa Minor Grants

Purpose: To assist with the costs of research projects in Eastern Africa
Eligibility: Open to applicants from United Kingdom and Eastern Africa
Level of Study: Postgraduate
Type: Grant
Value: Up to £1,000
Study Establishment: The British Institute in Eastern Africa
Application Procedure: Application forms can be downloaded from the BIEA website
No. of awards offered: 45
Closing Date: 31 January
Funding: Government
Contributor: British Academy
No. of awards given last year: 22
No. of applicants last year: 45
Additional Information: Applicants must contact the Director for further information on relevant topics likely to receive support. Those awarded grants will be required to keep the Institute regularly informed of the progress of their research, to provide a preliminary statement of accounts within 18 months of the award dates and to provide the Institute with copies of all relevant publications. They are encouraged to discuss with the Director the possibility of publishing their results in the Institute's journal, Azania. Results for the Minor Grants Award may be expected within 2 months of either 30 May or 30 November. Those awarded grants are required to become members of the BIEA www.biea.ac.uk/

For further information contact:

Email:	pjlane@insightkenya.com

British Medical Association (BMA)

BMA Research Grants, BMA House, Tavistock Square, London WC1H 9JP, United Kingdom.

Tel:	(44) 20 7383 6341
Email:	info.sciencegrants@bma.org.uk
Website:	www.bma.org.uk

The BMA is a voluntary professional association with over two-thirds of practising United Kingdom doctors in membership and an independent trade union dedicated to protecting individual members and the collective interests of doctors.

Helen H Lawson Research Grant

Purpose: To promote research into novel technologies and IT to assist in patient care, primary care or public health
Eligibility: Open to registered medical practitioners in the United Kingdom who are BMA members
Level of Study: Research
Type: Research grant
Value: £65,000
Length of Study: 3 years
Frequency: Annual
Country of Study: United Kingdom
Application Procedure: Applicants must complete an online application form. Applications that do not comply with all of the above terms and conditions will be rejected without exception
Closing Date: 4 March
Funding: Trusts
Additional Information: Please check at bma.org.uk/developing-your-career/portfolio-career/research-grants/research-grants-details/research-grants-roscoe www.bmafoundationmr.org.uk/media/a3ucevmt/helen-h-lawson-2022.pdf

For further information contact:

Corporate Development Directorate, British Medical Association, Tavistock Square, London WC1H 9JP, United Kingdom.

Email:	researchgrants@bma.org.uk

Josephine Lansdell Research Grant

Purpose: To assist and support research into the field of heart diseases
Eligibility: Open to registered medical practitioners in the United Kingdom who are BMA members
Level of Study: Research
Type: Research grant
Value: £65,000
Length of Study: 3 years
Frequency: Annual
Country of Study: Any country
Application Procedure: Applicants must complete an online application form. Applicants are required to upload (PDF format) two references during the online application process. Please note each reference MUST bear the electronic (scanned) signature of the referee. For joint applications, each applicant requires two referees (these can be the same for both applicants)
Closing Date: 4 March
Funding: Trusts
Additional Information: Please check at bma.org.uk/developing-your-career/portfolio-career/research-grants/research-grants-details/research-grants-lansdell www.bmafoundationmr.org.uk/media/iezokzog/josephine-lansdell-2022.pdf

For further information contact:

Corporate Development Directorate, British Medical Association, Tavistock Square, London WC1H 9JP, United Kingdom.

Email: researchgrants@bma.org.uk

Vera Down Research Grant

Purpose: To assist and support research
Eligibility: Open to registered medical practitioners in the United Kingdom who are BMA members
Level of Study: Research
Type: Research grant
Value: £65,000
Length of Study: 3 years
Frequency: Annual
Country of Study: United Kingdom
Application Procedure: Applicants must complete an online application form
Closing Date: 4 March
Funding: Trusts
Additional Information: Please check at bma.org.uk/developing-your-career/portfolio-career/research-grants/research-grants-details/research-grants-down www.bmafoundationmr.org.uk/media/14hpgl3c/vera-down-2022.pdf

For further information contact:

Corporate and Member Development Directorate, British Medical Association, Tavistock Square, London WC1H 9JP, United Kingdom.

Tel: (44) 20 7383 6341
Email: researchgrants@bma.org.uk

British School at Athens

BMA Research Grants, 52 Souedias Street, GR-10676 Athens, Greece.

Tel: (30) 211 102 2800
Email: admin@bsa.ac.uk
Website: www.bsa.gla.ac.uk
Contact: Dr Chryssanthi Papadopoulou, Assistant
             Director

The British School at Athens promotes research into the archaeology, architecture, art, history, language, literature, religion and topography of Greece in ancient, medieval and modern times. It consists of the Library, Fitch Laboratory for Archaeological Science, Archive, Museum, hostel and a second base at Knossos for research and fieldwork.

Early Career Fellowship

Purpose: The Fellowship is non-stipendiary, but accommodation and airfare are provided, either to Athens or Knossos
Type: Fellowship
Length of Study: 3 Months
Country of Study: Any country
Application Procedure: Applications should be sent by e-mail to The School Administrator, school.administrator@bsa.ac.uk
Closing Date: 13 May

For further information contact:

Email: school.administrator@bsa.ac.uk

Hector and Elizabeth Catling Bursary

Purpose: To assist travel, maintenance costs and for the purchase of scientific equipments. Its aim is to encourage excellence in archaeological drawing, including the preparation of finished drawings for publication

Eligibility: Open to researchers of British, Irish or Commonwealth nationality

Level of Study: Doctorate, Postdoctorate, Postgraduate, Research

Type: Bursary

Value: £500 per bursary to assist with travel and maintenance costs incurred in fieldwork, to pay for the use of scientific or other specialized equipment in or outside the laboratory in Greece or elsewhere and to buy necessary supplies

Frequency: Annual

Study Establishment: The British School at Athens

Country of Study: Any country

Application Procedure: 1. Applicants must submit a curriculum vitae and state concisely the nature of the intended work, a breakdown of budget, the amount requested from the Fund and how this will be spent. 2. Applications should include two sealed letters of reference. Bursary holders must submit a short report to the Committee upon completion of the project

Closing Date: 15 May

Funding: Private

Additional Information: The bursary is not intended for publication costs, and cannot be awarded to an excavation or field survey team www.bsa.ac.uk/awards/research-awards/the-hector-and-elizabeth-catling-bursary/

For further information contact:

Email: assistant.director@bsa.ac.uk

School Teacher Fellowship

Purpose: The School Teacher Fellowship at the British School at Athens is offered each year to enable a teacher to pursue a project in Greece designed to enhance their teaching (for example by researching a course, preparing teaching materials, visiting sites or using the Library)

Type: Fellowship

Value: Up to £300

Frequency: Annual

Country of Study: Any country

Application Procedure: Applicants should submit the following by e-mail to the School Administrator, Mrs Tania Gerousi (school.administrator@bsa.ac.uk) 1. a Curriculum Vitae 2. a short proposal (1,000 words maximum) 3. a reference letter from the applicant's Head Teacher or Head of Department, as appropriate.

Closing Date: 31 January

For further information contact:

Email: school.administrator@bsa.ac.uk

The Elizabeth Catling Memorial Fund for Archaeological Draughtsmanship

Purpose: To encourage excellence in archaeological drawing, including the preparation of finished drawings for publication. It is hoped that awards will help individuals to improve their standards of draughtsmanship and also enable the preparation of a larger number of drawings, of higher quality, than might otherwise have been possible

Eligibility: Individual applicants must show that drawings are an essential part of their research. Furthermore, although not a precondition, it is hoped that they may be draughtsmen themselves. Applications from project directors, who may also apply during the course of a field campaign, are limited to unexpected expenses that are not provided for in the project's budget, such as extra maintenance costs to enable a draughtsman to draw unforeseen material and finds

Level of Study: Predoctorate

Type: Funding support

Value: £500

Frequency: Annual

Country of Study: Any country

Application Procedure: Candidates should submit letters of application to the School's London office by post in four copies or by email. Letters should not be longer than two pages and should include a statement of the purposes of the application and a budget and timetable for the proposed work, together with the name and address of a referee whom the awarding panel(s) may consult. Applications may be made for but are not limited to, grants towards the maintenance costs of longer stays at museums and other study centres so as to achieve work that would not otherwise have been attempted. Recipients of awards must have been admitted as Students of the School for the appropriate Session before receiving their grants, and must submit a short report on the use of the grant to the London office

Closing Date: 13 May

Additional Information: The Fund does not support printing expenses, or site drawings such as plans and sections, or computer graphics www.bsa.ac.uk/awards/research-awards/the-elizabeth-catling-memorial-fund-for-archaeological-draughtmanship/

For further information contact:

British School at Athens, Senate House, Malet Street, London WC1E 7HU, United Kingdom.

Email: bsa@sas.ac.uk

The Hector and Elizabeth Catling Doctoral Award

Level of Study: Postgraduate

Type: Award

Value: 1. One return flight to Greece 2. One month's membership of the British School at Athens, granting full access to all BSA facilities and a museum pass for free access to archaeological sites and museums in Greece. 3. Ten days of accommodation in the BSA hostel. (The stay in Greece can be extended at the candidate's own expense)
Country of Study: Any country
Closing Date: 25 February

For further information contact:

Email: assistant.director@bsa.ac.uk

The John Morrison Memorial Fund for Hellenic Maritime Studies

Purpose: To further research into all branches of Hellenic maritime studies of any period
Type: Funding support
Value: £500
Frequency: Annual
Country of Study: Any country
Application Procedure: Candidates should submit letters of application to the School's London office by post in four copies or by email. Letters should not be longer than two pages and should include a statement of the purposes of the application and a budget and timetable for the proposed work, together with the name and address of a referee whom the awarding panel(s) may consult. Applications may be made for but are not limited to, grants towards the maintenance costs of longer stays at museums and other study centres so as to achieve work that would not otherwise have been attempted. Recipients of awards must have been admitted as Students of the School for the appropriate Session before receiving their grants, and must submit a short report on the use of the grant to the London office
Closing Date: 30 April
Additional Information: Grants may also be available from the Fund for buying maritime books and journals for the School's Library www.bsa.ac.uk/awards/research-awards/the-john-morrison-memorial-fund-for-hellenic-maritime-studies/

For further information contact:

British School at Athens, Senate House, Malet Street, London WC1E 7HU, United Kingdom.

Email: assistant.director@bsa.ac.uk

The Knossos Research Fund

Level of Study: Postgraduate
Country of Study: Any country
Application Procedure: Please send an application not exceeding two pages (using font of size 11 and margins of 1.5 cm minimum), under the following headings to the School Administrator (school.administrator@bsa.ac.uk) 1. Name (s) and address(es) of applicant(s) 2. Title of project 3. Description of project (maximum 500 words) 4. Budget (outline of total expenditure) 5. Sum applied for from the Knossos Research Fund, and for what specific purpose 6. Relevant grants (already received/pending) for this or related work 7. Plans for publication.; Successful applicants must submit a short report (maximum 2 pages, using font size 11 and margins of 1.5 cm minimum) by the end of the following October.
Closing Date: 31 December

For further information contact:

Email: school.administrator@bsa.ac.uk

The Macmillan-Rodewald Studentship

Level of Study: Postdoctorate, Postgraduate
Type: Fellowship
Country of Study: Any country
Application Procedure: Applicants should submit a CV and research proposal (maximum 1,000 words) which includes a brief statement of the research question or questions, an outline of the overall research programme in its scholarly context, a timetable for completion, and the benefits for the research of residence in Greece based at the School. Two references will be required. Applications are automatically considered for both the 'Macmillan-Rodewald' and the 'Richard Bradford McConnell Studentship'. Applicants should ask referees to write directly to the School Administrator by the deadline. Applicants should be prepared to attend an interview in London in May/June.
No. of awards offered: 2
Closing Date: 13 May

The Richard Bradford McConnell Fund for Landscape Studies

Purpose: To assist research in the interaction of place and people in Greece and Cyprus at any period(s)
Type: Funding support

Value: £400
Frequency: Annual
Country of Study: Any country
Application Procedure: Candidates should submit letters of application to the School's London office by post in four copies or by email. Letters should not be longer than two pages and should include a statement of the purposes of the application and a budget and timetable for the proposed work, together with the name and address of a referee whom the awarding panel(s) may consult. Applications may be made for but are not limited to, grants towards the maintenance costs of longer stays at museums and other study centres so as to achieve work that would not otherwise have been attempted. Recipients of awards must have been admitted as Students of the School for the appropriate Session before receiving their grants, and must submit a short report on the use of the grant to the London office
Closing Date: 13 May
Contributor: Richard Bradford Trust
Additional Information: www.bsa.ac.uk/awards/research-awards/the-richard-bradford-mcconnell-fund-for-landscape-studies/

For further information contact:

British School at Athens, Senate House, Malet Street, London WC1E 7HU, United Kingdom.

Email: school.administrator@bsa.ac.uk

The Vronwy Hankey Memorial Fund for Aegean Studies

Purpose: The Vronwy Hankey Memorial Fund for Aegean Studies was funded by gifts to the School's Appeal in memory of Vronwy Hankey and her husband Henry
Type: Funding support
Value: £1000
Country of Study: Any country
Closing Date: 13 May

For further information contact:

Email: school.administrator@bsa.ac.uk

To support research in the prehistory of the Aegean and its connections with the East Mediterranean

Purpose: To support research in the prehistory of the Aegean and its connections with the East Mediterranean

Eligibility: Preference may be given to younger Students
Type: Funding support
Value: One return flight to Greece • One month's membership of the British School at Athens, granting full access to all BSA facilities and a museum pass for free access to archaeological sites and museums in Greece. • Ten days of accommodation in the BSA hostel.
Country of Study: Any country
Application Procedure: Candidates should submit letters of application to the School's London office by post in four copies or by email. Letters should not be longer than two pages and should include a statement of the purposes of the application and a budget and timetable for the proposed work, together with the name and address of a referee whom the awarding panel(s) may consult. Applications may be made for but are not limited to, grants towards the maintenance costs of longer stays at museums and other study centres so as to achieve work that would not otherwise have been attempted. Recipients of awards must have been admitted as Students of the School for the appropriate Session before receiving their grants, and must submit a short report on the use of the grant to the London office
Closing Date: 25 January
Additional Information: Check website for more details www.bsa.ac.uk/awards/#:~:text=Award%20holders,-Marcella%20Giobbe%20(University&text=Visiting%20Fellowships%20at%20the%20British,accommodation%20and%20airfare%20are%20provided

For further information contact:

British School at Athens, Senate House, Malet Street, London WC1E 7HU, United Kingdom.

Email: bsa@sas.ac.uk

Visiting Fellowships

Purpose: Visiting Fellowships at the British School at Athens are offered for 2-3 months for research in any branch of the arts or social sciences related to Greece. The Fellowship is non-stipendiary, but accommodation and airfare are provided
Eligibility: The Fellow is required to submit a report covering their research and their time at the School to the School's Council
Level of Study: Postgraduate
Type: Fellowship
Length of Study: 2-3 Months
Frequency: Annual
Country of Study: Any country

Application Procedure: The School Administrator, school. administrator@bsa.ac.uk
Closing Date: 13 May
Funding: Private
Additional Information: www.bsa.ac.uk/awards/fellow ships/visiting-fellowship/

For further information contact:

The British School at Athens, 52 Souedias Street, GR-10676 Athens, Greece.

Fax: (30) 211 102 2803
Email: school.administrator@bsa.ac.uk

British School at Rome (BSR)

The BSR at the British Academy, 10 Carlton House Terrace, London SW1Y 5AH, United Kingdom.

Tel: (44) 20 7969 5202
Email: bsr@britac.ac.uk
Website: www.bsr.ac.uk
Contact: Natalie Arrowsmith, Communications Manager

The British School at Rome (BSR) is an interdisciplinary research centre for the humanities, visual arts and architecture. Each year, the School offers a range of awards in its principal fields of interest. These interests are further promoted by lectures, conferences, publications, exhibitions, archaeological research and an excellent reference library.

Abbey Scholarship in Painting

Purpose: To give exceptionally promising early career painters the opportunity to work in Rome
Eligibility: offers one early-career artist a full academic year (October to June) at the British School at Rome
Level of Study: Doctorate, Graduate, Postdoctorate, Postgraduate
Type: Scholarship
Value: £1,000.
Length of Study: 9 months
Frequency: Annual
Study Establishment: The British School at Rome
Country of Study: Italy
Closing Date: 23 January
Funding: Private
Contributor: The Abbey Council

Additional Information: Check website for more details abbey.org.uk/

For further information contact:

Abbey Awards, 1 St Lukes Court, 136 Falcon Road, London SW11 2LP, United Kingdom.

Email: contact@abbey.org.uk

Giles Worsley Travel Fellowship

Purpose: To enable an architect or architectural historian to spend 3 months in Rome studying an architectural topic of his choice
Eligibility: Open to those who are of British nationality or who have been living and studying in Britain for at least the last 3 years
Level of Study: Postdoctorate, Postgraduate, Professional development
Type: Fellowship
Value: Approx.€700 per month plus full board and lodging at the British School at Rome
Length of Study: 3 months
Frequency: Annual
Study Establishment: The British School at Rome
Country of Study: Italy
Application Procedure: Applicants must submit a curriculum vitae, a statement indicating the subject of their proposal and arrange for two references to be sent
Closing Date: February
Funding: Private
No. of awards given last year: 1
Additional Information: www.bsr.ac.uk/awards/ architecture-awards-ii#giles

Paul Mellon Centre Rome Fellowship

Purpose: To assist research on grand tour subjects or on Anglo-Italian cultural and artistic relations
Eligibility: Open to established scholars in the United Kingdom, United States or elsewhere. Applicants should be fluent in Italian
Level of Study: Doctorate, Graduate, Postdoctorate, Postgraduate, Professional development, Research
Type: Fellowship
Value: For applicants employed by an organisation, institution, or university there will also be an honorarium of £3,000 and up to £8,000 towards replacement staff costs, if required. For independent scholars there will be an honorarium of £7,000.
Length of Study: 3 months

Frequency: Annual
Study Establishment: The British School at Rome
Country of Study: Italy
Application Procedure: Applicants must contact the Paul Mellon Centre for Studies in British Art for details
Closing Date: 31 January
Funding: Private
Contributor: The Paul Mellon Centre for Studies in British Art
Additional Information: www.paul-mellon-centre.ac.uk/fellowships-and-grants/rome-fellowship

For further information contact:

The Paul Mellon Centre for Studies in British Art, 16 Bedford Square, London WC1B 3JA, United Kingdom.

Email: grants@paul-mellon-centre.ac.uk

British Society for Antimicrobial Chemotherapy

British Society for Antimicrobial Chemotherapy, Griffin House, 53 Regent Place, Birmingham B1 3NJ, United Kingdom.

Tel: (44) 121 236 1988
Website: www.bsac.org.uk
Contact: Ms Tracey Guise, Executive Director

BSAC is an inter-professional organization with 40 years of experience and achievement in antibiotic education, research and leadership. It is dedicated to saving lives through appropriate use and development of antibiotics now and in the future.

British Society for Antimicrobial Chemotherapy Overseas Scholarship

Purpose: Overseas Scholarships are to enable workers from other countries the opportunity to work in United Kingdom Departments for up to 6 months
Level of Study: Postgraduate, Professional development
Type: Scholarship
Value: £1,000 per calendar month for up to 6 months. The host institution will receive a consumables grant of £200 per calendar month for the duration of the scholarship. The Society will reimburse the cost of return air fares and travel via the most economical route. Candidates will be asked to seek approval of travel costs in advance

Length of Study: 6 months
Frequency: Annual
Country of Study: United Kingdom
Application Procedure: Successful applicants are required to submit a 500-word written report to the Secretary of the Grants Committee on completion of their project, and to forward details of any publications arising from the work undertaken. Applications for Overseas Scholarships should be made to the Society's HQ using the form provided on the BSAC website
Closing Date: 1 December
Funding: Foundation
Additional Information: Excludes applicants from United Kingdom www.bsac.org.uk/funding/overseas-scholarship/

For further information contact:

Email: tguise@bsac.org.uk

British Society for Middle Eastern Studies

Institute for Middle Eastern & Islamic Studies, Durham University, Al-Qasimi Building, Elvet Hill Road, Durham DH1 3TU, United Kingdom.

Tel: (44) 191 33 45179
Email: a.l.haysey@durham.ac.uk
Website: www.brismes.ac.uk/

Master's Scholarship

Purpose: BRISMES offers an annual Master's scholarship for taught Master's study at a United Kingdom institution. The Master's programme can be in any discipline but should include a majority component specifically relating to the Middle East
Eligibility: Preference will be given to candidates resident in the European Union, and to institutions who are members of BRISMES
Level of Study: Doctorate
Type: Scholarship
Value: £1,200
Frequency: Annual
Country of Study: United Kingdom
Application Procedure: Applications should be forwarded by the Director of the Master's programme concerned, to the BRISMES Administrative Office, and should include a supporting statement from the course Director not exceeding 500 words; the programme syllabus; a statement by the

candidate not exceeding 500 words; the candidate's curriculum vitae and transcript of previous academic results; two academic references. Applications should be sent to Institute for Middle Eastern & Islamic Studies

Closing Date: 31 March

Funding: Foundation

Additional Information: Please check website for more details www.birmingham.ac.uk/postgraduate/funding/BRISMES-Scholarships.aspx

For further information contact:

Email: a.l.haysey@dur.ac.uk

The Abdullah Al-Mubarak Al-Sabah Foundation BRISMES Scholarships

Purpose: The purpose of the scholarships is to encourage more people to pursue postgraduate studies in disciplines related to the Middle East in British universities

Eligibility: To qualify you must be a paid-up member of BRISMES (student membership suffices) but the time you apply

Level of Study: Postgraduate

Type: Scholarship

Value: £2,000

Length of Study: 1 academic year

Frequency: Annual

Country of Study: United Kingdom

Application Procedure: To qualify applicants must fulfil the following conditions 1. be registered at any UK university, 2. be a paid-up student member of BRISMES at the time of application, 3. submit an application of 600 - 1000 words, by E-mail to the BRISMES research committee This should include a sketch of the overall research topic, and a description of the purpose for which the grant would be used, 4. obtain a brief supporting statement from their supervisor

Funding: Foundation

Additional Information: www.brismes.ac.uk/student-area/the-abdullah-mubarak-brismes-scholarshp

For further information contact:

Email: a.l.haysey@dur.ac.uk

British Veterinary Association

7 Mansfield Street, London W1G 9NQ, United Kingdom.

Tel: (44) 20 7636 6541
Email: bvahq@bva.co.uk
Website: www.bva.co.uk

The British Veterinary Association's chief interests are the standards of animal health and veterinary surgeons' working practices. The organization's main functions are the development of policy in areas affecting the profession, protecting and promoting the profession in matters propounded by government and other external bodies and the provision of services to members.

Harry Steele-Bodger Memorial Travelling Scholarship

Subjects: Veterinary science and agriculture.

Purpose: The BVA overseas travel grant scheme gives students the chance to gain experience in the prevention and control of exotic and emerging animal diseases, as well as helping them to develop beneficial life skills such as communication, adaptability and open-mindedness.

Eligibility: Open to graduates of veterinary schools in the UK or the Republic of Ireland who have been qualified for not more than 3 years, and to penultimate or final-year students at those schools.

Level of Study: Graduate, Postdoctorate, Postgraduate

Type: Scholarship

Value: £1000

Frequency: Annual

Study Establishment: A veterinary or agricultural research institute or some other course of study approved by the governing committee

Country of Study: United Kingdom

Application Procedure: Applications can be submitted online www.bva.co.uk/Membership-and-benefits/Students/Travel-grants-for-students/

Closing Date: 10 June

Funding: Private

Additional Information: www.bva.co.uk/membership/bva-student-membership/travel-grants-for-vet-students/

For further information contact:

Tel: (44) 20 7908 6340
Email: helenac@bva.co.uk

Broadcast Education Association

613 Kane Street, Mount Pleasant, MI 48858, United States of America.

Tel: (1) 989 773 9370
Email: orlik1pb@cmich.edu
Website: www.beaweb.org
Contact: Dr Peter Orlik, Scholarship Chair

Abe Voron Award

Subjects: Radio Industry
Purpose: Study for a career in radio at a BEA-member institution
Eligibility: 1. Must be a graduate student, 2. Must attend a university or a four-year college, 3. Must not be attending high school currently, 4. Must study full-time, 5. Restricted to students studying TV/Radio Broadcasting
Level of Study: Graduate, Undergraduate
Type: Scholarship
Value: US$3,000
Length of Study: One full academic year
Frequency: Annual
Country of Study: Any country
Application Procedure: The application MUST be typed to be considered. Keep an additional copy for your files. Remember to date and sign the form on the last page. Applications not typed and signed will be disqualified. Each copy of the application MUST be collated and securely stapled. The application asks for personal and academic data and transcripts, media and other experience, a written statement of goals, and supportive statements from two references, at least one of which must be an electronic media faculty member
No. of awards offered: 3
Closing Date: 16 October
Funding: Private
Contributor: Abe Voron Committee
Additional Information: www.petersons.com/scholarship/abe-voron-award-111_219381.aspx

For further information contact:

613 Kane St, Mt. Pleasant, MI 48858, United States of America.

John Bayliss Award

Purpose: Study toward a career in Radio at a Broadcast Education Association member institution.
Eligibility: 1. Must be a graduate student, 2. Must attend a university or a four-year college, 3. Must not be attending high school currently 4. Must study full-time, 5. Restricted to students studying TV/Radio Broadcasting
Level of Study: Graduate
Type: Scholarship
Value: US$3,500
Length of Study: Full-time for one academic year
Frequency: Annual
Country of Study: Any country

Application Procedure: The application MUST be typed to be considered. Keep an additional copy for your files. Remember to date and sign the form on the last page. Applications not typed and signed will be disqualified. Each copy of the application MUST be collated and securely stapled. The application asks for personal and academic data and transcripts, media and other experience, a written statement of goals, and supportive statements from two references, at least one of which must be an electronic media faculty member
No. of awards offered: 1
Closing Date: 15 October
Funding: Private
Contributor: John Bayliss Foundation
Additional Information: www.petersons.com/scholarship/john-bayliss-award-111_219383.aspx

For further information contact:

613 Kane St, Mt. Pleasant, MI 48858, United States of America.

Library of American Broadcasting Foundation Award

Purpose: Support for a graduate student focusing on the study of broadcast history
Eligibility: graduate student focusing on broadcast history
Level of Study: Graduate
Type: Scholarship
Value: US$5,000
Length of Study: One full academic year
Frequency: Annual
Country of Study: Any country
Application Procedure: see and fill out application found on BEA website www.beaweb.org
No. of awards offered: 5
Closing Date: 15 October
Funding: Foundation
Contributor: Library of American Broadcasting Foundation
No. of awards given last year: 1
No. of applicants last year: 5
Additional Information: www.beaweb.org/wp/?page_id=2431

Vincent T. Wasilewski Award

Purpose: For graduate study of electronic media at a BEA member institution
Eligibility: Any full-time graduate student at a BEA member institution

Level of Study: Graduate
Type: Scholarship
Value: US$4,000
Length of Study: One academic year
Frequency: Annual
Country of Study: Any country
Application Procedure: See and complete application found at BEA website www.beaweb.org
No. of awards offered: 1
Closing Date: 15 October
Funding: Private
Contributor: Patrick Communications
No. of awards given last year: 1
No. of applicants last year: 20
Additional Information: www.unigo.com/scholarships/by-major/advertising-scholarships/vincent-t-wasilewski-award/1004552

Brunel University London

Kingston Lane, Uxbridge, Middlesex UB8 3PH, United Kingdom.

Tel: (44) 1895 274000
Email: admissions@brunel.ac.uk
Website: www.brunel.ac.uk
Contact: Professor Adrian Woods, Dean of the Graduate School

Brunel University London is a public research university based in the Uxbridge area of London, England. It was founded in 1966 and named after the Victorian engineer Isambard Kingdom Brunel.

British Council Scholarship for Women in STEM Terms and Conditions

Subjects: Science, technology, engineering and mathematics
Purpose: Brunel is proud to support the British Council Scholarship for Women in STEM. We are offering eight fully funded scholarships for female students from the South Asia region (eligible countries only) as part of the British Council Scholarship for Women in STEM.
Eligibility: See Website
Level of Study: Postgraduate
Type: Scholarship
Value: The Scholarship is fully funded and covers Tuition fees, Monthly stipend, Travel costs, Visa, Health coverage fees, Child allowance

Country of Study: Any country
Application Procedure: Applicants should apply for their chosen programme (see eligible programmes below) in the usual way, via UCAS or via the Brunel online application portal.
No. of awards offered: 5
Closing Date: 9 March
Additional Information: www.brunel.ac.uk/scholarships/page?id=be6c2d16-396a-4cbe-8103-0961a870b657

For further information contact:

Email: scholarships@brunel.ac.uk

Brunel Family Discount Terms and Conditions

Eligibility: See Website
Level of Study: Postgraduate
Type: Scholarship
Value: 10% off the tuition fees for every year
Country of Study: Any country
Closing Date: 31 August

For further information contact:

Email: scholarships@brunel.ac.uk

Brunel Santander International Scholarship

Purpose: Brunel University London is pleased to offer a prestigious package of scholarships for International students. The Brunel Santander International Scholarship is for self-funded students.
Eligibility: 1. The candidate must for reasons related to fees, classified in the category "overseas" and financed from own resources (unfunded). 2. Applicants who are unsure of the status of their fees should note that Brunel uses the information provided in their application form to evaluate the fee status according to the rules established by the UK Government. 3. Applicants must have the opportunity to study in a post-graduate program or postdoctoral research program in September and must complete the corresponding fellowship application within the required timeframe. 4. Candidates must have accepted their course offer before the scholarship deadline.
Level of Study: Postgraduate
Type: Scholarship
Value: £3,000
Length of Study: 1 year
Frequency: Annual
Country of Study: Any country

Application Procedure: To apply for a Brunel Santander International Scholarship, candidates must fill out the application form, which requires a personal declaration within the prescribed deadlines. Supported Documents As part of the application, the applicant must provide a personal statement.

Closing Date: 30 April

Funding: International office

Additional Information: worldscholarshipforum.com/brunel-santander-international-scholarship/

For further information contact:

Email: scholarships@brunel.ac.uk

International Excellence Scholarship

Purpose: Brunel University London is pleased to offer a prestigious package of scholarships for International students. The scholarship scheme is for fully self-funded students only and is based on overall academic merit and professional experience. We will award scholarships to applicants who most closely meet or exceed the criteria for the award.

Level of Study: Postgraduate

Type: Scholarship

Value: £6,000 as a tuition fee

Length of Study: 3 years

Frequency: Annual

Country of Study: Any country

No. of awards offered: 60

Closing Date: 20 November

For further information contact:

Email: scholarships@brunel.ac.uk

Postgraduate Care Leaver Bursary Terms and Conditions

Eligibility: See website

Level of Study: Postgraduate

Type: Scholarship

Value: £5,000

Frequency: Annual

Country of Study: Any country

Application Procedure: To be considered applicants must complete an application form, which requires a supporting statement of 250 words explaining why they would be a suitable recipient of the Bursary. The applicant must submit evidence of Care Leaver status, as defined below, in the application form.

No. of awards offered: 1

Closing Date: 31 August

Additional Information: www.brunel.ac.uk/scholarships/page?id=f634a0dd-a3c0-4e8a-9215-d504a182dcb0

For further information contact:

Email: Karen.Western@Brunel.ac.uk.

Budapest International Music Competition

Philharmonia Budapest, Alkotmany u.31 1/2, H-1054 Budapest, Hungary.

Tel: (36) 1 266 1459, 302 4961

Email: liszkay.maria@hu.inter.net

Contact: Ms Maria Liszkay, Secretary

The Budapest Music Competition has been held since 1933. Competitions in different categories alternate annually.

International Carl Flesch Violin Competition

Purpose: To promote European violinists

Eligibility: Competitors should possess at least 2 years of musical study in Europe and should be born on or after 1 January, 1980

Type: Competition

Value: HUF 4,000 net (first prize), HUF 3,000 net (second prize) and HUF 2,000 net (third prize)

Country of Study: Hungary

Application Procedure: Application forms should contain brief curriculum vitae, certificate of musical qualification, letter of recommendation from a prominent musical personality, two recent photographs and a copy receipt about the transfer of the entry fee. For competitors outside Europe, a certificate of their European studies is required

Closing Date: 1 February

Funding: Private

Contributor: Philharmonia Budapest Concert Agency and Ms. Fejes Music Foundation

Additional Information: Special prizes will be offered to the winners worldscholarshipforum.com/brunel-santander-international-scholarship/

For further information contact:

Fax: (36) 1 302 4962

Bupa Foundation

Bupa House, 15-19 Bloomsbury Way, London WC1A 2BA, United Kingdom.

Tel: (44) 20 7656 2591
Email: Bupafoundation@Bupa.com
Website: www.bupafoundation.co.uk
Contact: Lee Saunders, Registrar

The Bupa Foundation is an independent medical research charity that funds medical research to prevent, relieve and cure sickness and ill health.

Bupa Foundation Annual Specialist Grant

Eligibility: The competition is open to those based in the United Kingdom, Australia, Denmark, Hong Kong, New Zealand, Saudi Arabia, Spain and Thailand. Entries must be compliant with the local health and safety legislation if applicable. The Foundation will seek peer reviews from the home country of each shortlisted entry. Researchers and health professionals working for public or private organisations may apply for Bupa Foundation specialist grants for United Kingdom-based projects.

For further information contact:

Tel: (36) 20 7656 2591
Email: bupafoundation@bupa.com

Bupa Foundation Medical Research Grant for Health at Work

Purpose: To support research into the feasibility and potential value of workplace conditions for health promotion and active management of employee health

Eligibility: Open to health professionals and health researchers
Level of Study: Doctorate, Postdoctorate, Postgraduate, Research
Value: Restricted by project need only
Length of Study: A maximum of 3 years
Country of Study: United Kingdom
Application Procedure: For all queries contact Lee Saunders, the Foundation's Registrar
Funding: Foundation

For further information contact:

Email: bupafoundation@bupa.com

Bupa Foundation Medical Research Grant for Information and Communication

Purpose: To support research designed to enhance partnership between health professionals and public/patients
Eligibility: Open to health professional and health researchers
Level of Study: Doctorate, Postdoctorate, Postgraduate, Research
Value: Restricted by project needs only
Length of Study: Maximum of 3 years
Country of Study: United Kingdom
Application Procedure: For all queries contact Lee Saunders, the Foundation's Registrar
Funding: Foundation

For further information contact:

Email: bupafoundation@bupa.com

C

Camargo Foundation

1, Avenue Jermini, F-13260 Cassis, France.

Tel: (33) 4 4201 1311
Email: apply@camargofoundation.org
Website: www.camargofoundation.org
Contact: Cynthia A. Gehrig, President

The Camargo Foundation is a residential center offering programming in the humanities and the arts.

The Camargo Core Program

Purpose: The Camargo Foundation, located in Cassis, France, and founded by artist and philanthropist Jerome Hill, is a residential center offering programming in the Arts and Humanities. It offers time and space in a contemplative environment to think, create, and connect. The Foundation encourages the visionary work of artists, scholars, and thinkers in the Arts and Humanities. The Camargo Core Program is the historical and flagship program of the Camargo Foundation. Each year an international call is launched through which 18 fellows (9 artists and 9 scholars/thinkers) are selected. The Camargo Core Program offers time and space in a contemplative environment to think, create, and connect. By supporting groundbreaking research and experimentation, it contributes to the visionary work of artists, scholars and thinkers in the Arts and Humanities. By encouraging multidisciplinary and interdisciplinary approaches, it intends to foster connections between research and creation

Eligibility: The Camargo Foundation prizes diversity and welcomes applicants from all countries and nationalities, representing a broad range of creative thought and practice. Three main categories are available, and several subcategories for artists' applications. 1. Scholars should be connected to the Arts and Humanities working on French and Francophone cultures, or cross-cultural studies that engage the cultures and influences of the Mediterranean region. To be eligible for a fellowship in the "Scholars" category, applicants are expected either to hold a PhD and a record of post-doctoral scholarship, or, to be PhD candidates completing the final stages of research for, or writing of, their dissertation. 2. Thinkers include accomplished professionals and practitioners in cultural and creative fields (such as curators, journalists, critics, urban planners, independent scholars, etc.) who are professionally engaged in critical thought. We are interested in work attuned to the theoretical arena, the arts, and society. 3. Artists in all disciplines should be the primary creators of a new work/project and should have a track record of publications, performances, exhibitions, credits, awards, and/or grants. We are interested in artists who have a fully developed, mature artistic voice. Applicants may include artists who are engaged in critical thought and research-oriented projects. When applying, artists will have to choose among the following subcategories Visual Artists / Choreographers, Theater Directors, and Performance Artists / Writers and Playwrights / Film, Video and Digital Artists / Composers and Sound Artists / Multidisciplinary Artists.

Level of Study: Doctorate, Foundation programme, Postdoctorate, Postgraduate, Professional development, Research

Type: Residential fellowships

Value: A stipend of €250 per week is available, as is funding for basic transportation to and from Cassis for the Fellow for the residency. In the case of air travel, basic coach class booked far in advance is covered

Frequency: Annual

Country of Study: France

Application Procedure: The call for applications for the Camargo Core Program for the upcoming years will be open in summer years. More information will be available on www.camargofoundation.org

Closing Date: 1 October

© Springer Nature Limited 2022
Palgrave Macmillan (ed.), *The Grants Register 2023*,
https://doi.org/10.1057/978-1-349-96053-8

Funding: Foundation, Government, Individuals, Private, Trusts

Additional Information: More information is available on camargofoundation.org/programs/camargo-core-program/

The Cultural Diaspora

Purpose: The Camargo Foundation offers Fellows an isolated retreat for the soul, nurtured by the natural beauty of it grounds and surrounding environment, to escape and create.

Eligibility: 1. The program welcomes applications from Black text-based theater artists from the African Diaspora, including but not limited to: Africa, the Americas, the Caribbean, and Europe. 2. Eligible applicants have an interest in the African Diaspora and Afro-Atlantic culture as an influence on and factor in their craft, work, and thinking. 3. Eligible applicants are established or mid-career artists who assume primary responsibility for creating the texts of theatrical productions and/or performance. This program recognizes that practice is increasingly interdisciplinary (including performances that embrace a combination of live theater/dance/film, for example), can include both spoken and musical work, and can assume different scales and forms (from solo performances to storytelling to large-scale theatrical spectacle). This program is designed for artists who play a primary or exclusive role in creating the text component of live theatrical or performance work where spoken language is a critical and primary component, whatever the scale and form. Text creators, of course, may play additional roles, such as directing, designing, and/or performing without compromising their eligibility. Actors, choreographers, designers, directors, etc. who have not been a primary creator of texts, however, are not eligible to apply. 4. Eligible applicants have had at least three different texts/performances fully produced at reputable venues for public audiences. 5. Students enrolled in undergraduate or graduate degree programs at the time of application are not eligible to apply. 6. Work developed during the residency may be in any language. In the interests of Camargo's interdisciplinary, multicultural community, eligible applicants are able to communicate well in English. A basic knowledge of French is useful, but not required. 7. Playwrights who participated in the 2018 edition of the program are not eligible to apply.

Type: Grant

Value: Each of the eight participants will receive plane fare, local transport to and from the home airport and Camargo, and both a per diem allowance of US$1,250 and a grant of US$1,000 (making a total of US$2,250 per artist) to participate.

Frequency: Annual

Country of Study: France

Application Procedure: Applications should be submitted via Submittable and can be accessed at: camargofoundation. submittable.com/submit

Closing Date: 22 August

Additional Information: camargofoundation.org/programs/cultural-diaspora-program/

Canada Council for the Arts

150 Elgin St., PO Box 1047, Ottawa, ON K1P 5V8, Canada.

Tel: (1) 800 263 5588
Email: info@canadacouncil.ca
Website: www.canadacouncil.ca
Contact: Martin, Program Officer

The Canada Council for the Arts is a national agency that provides grants and services to professional Canadian artists and art organizations in dance, media arts, music, theatre, writing and publishing, inter-arts and the visual arts.

Canada-Japan Literary Awards

Eligibility: Author and translator eligibility: Authors and translators must be Canadian citizens or have permanent resident status, as defined by Immigration, Refugees and Citizenship Canada. They do not need to be living in Canada. Eligibility of books: Nominated books must have been published professionally, between 1 May 2021 and 30 April 2023, to be eligible for the 2023 awards competition. An eligible book may be nominated to either the English-language component or the French-language component, but not to both.

Type: Award

Value: C$10,000 each

Frequency: Annual

Country of Study: Any country

No. of awards offered: 2

Closing Date: 1 October

Additional Information: canadacouncil.ca/funding/prizes/canada-japan-literary-awards

For further information contact:

Email: canadajapan-prizes@canadacouncil.ca

CBC Literary Prizes

Eligibility: The competition is open to amateur and professional Canadian writers.
Type: Prize
Frequency: Annual
Country of Study: Canada
Application Procedure: Apply to the CBC Literary Prizes program.
No. of awards offered: 6
Closing Date: 28 February
Additional Information: canadacouncil.ca/funding/prizes/cbc-literary-prizes

For further information contact:

Email: prizes@canadacouncil.ca

Duke and Duchess of York Prize in Photography

Eligibility: This award is the only Canada Council prize dedicated to photography.
Type: Prize
Value: C$8,000
Frequency: Annual
Country of Study: Canada
Application Procedure: You do not apply for this prize. Applicants to some grant programs are eligible and will be considered for prizes.
Additional Information: canadacouncil.ca/funding/prizes/duke-and-duchess-of-york-prize-in-photography

For further information contact:

Email: prizes@canadacouncil.ca

Eckhardt-Gramatté National Music Competition

Eligibility: 1. This year's competition is open to pianists born after January 1, 1987 and before January 1, 2004. 2. Competitors must be either Canadian citizens or permanent residents. Previous first-place winners of the E-Gré Competition are not eligible to compete in subsequent E-Gré Competitions. 3. Winners should be able to inspire and communicate effectively with their audience and should be ready to launch or further a professional performing career. 4. The competition's mission is to promote excellence in the performance of Canadian and new contemporary music. 5. For all rounds, competitors should consider an innovative, balanced and effective program that best reflects their musical strengths in concert.

Performances should reflect the competitor's imagination, intellectual and emotional understanding of musical works in addition to technical virtuosity.
Type: Prize
Value: First prize: C$8,000, a Canadian tour and a three-week residency at the Casalmaggiore International Music Festival in Italy. Second prize: C$3,000 Third prize: C$2,000
Country of Study: Canada
Closing Date: 30 December
Additional Information: canadacouncil.ca/funding/prizes/eckhardt-gramatte-national-music-competition

For further information contact:

Email: prizes@canadacouncil.ca

Governor General's Literary Awards

Eligibility: The Canada Council may contact the publisher for supplementary information to determine eligibility.
Type: Award
Value: C$1,000 to C$25,000
Frequency: Annual
Country of Study: Canada
Closing Date: 15 March
Additional Information: canadacouncil.ca/funding/prizes/governor-generals-literary-awards

For further information contact:

Email: ggbooks@canadacouncil.ca

Governor General's Performing Arts Awards

Type: Award
Value: Up to C$25,000
Frequency: Annual
Country of Study: Canada
No. of awards offered: 6
Closing Date: 9 December
Additional Information: canadacouncil.ca/funding/prizes/governor-generals-performing-arts-awards

J.B.C. Watkins Award: Architecture

Eligibility: To be eligible, you must be: 1. an architecture graduate of a Canadian university, postsecondary art institution or training school 2. a Canadian citizen or permanent resident, as defined by Immigration, Refugees and

Citizenship Canada 3. pursuing graduate studies in a country other than Canada. You do not need to be living in Canada when you apply. You cannot apply to this award for a program of graduate studies that has already been completed before the program deadline.
Type: Prize
Value: C$5,000
Country of Study: Canada
Closing Date: 1 October
Additional Information: canadacouncil.ca/funding/prizes/jbc-watkins-award-architecture

For further information contact:

Email: architecture-prizes@canadacouncil.ca

Jacqueline Lemieux Prize

Subjects: The Jacqueline Lemieux Prize recognizes the work of an established dance professional who has made an outstanding contribution to dance in Canada.
Type: Prize
Value: C$6,000
Country of Study: Canada
Application Procedure: You do not apply for this prize. Applicants to some grant programs are eligible and will be considered for prizes.
Additional Information: canadacouncil.ca/funding/prizes/jacqueline-lemieux-prize

For further information contact:

Email: prizes@canadacouncil.ca

Jean A. Chalmers Fund for the Crafts

Eligibility: Fine crafts professionals can apply to the Research and Policy Development Assistance component only. This includes: 1. contemporary fine craft artists 2. independent curators or critics. You must meet the following criteria: 1. have specialized training in the artistic field (not necessarily in academic institutions) 2. be recognized as a professional by your peers (artists working in the same artistic tradition) 3. be a Canadian citizen or permanent resident of Canada, as defined by Immigration, Refugees and Citizenship You do not need to be living in Canada when you apply.
Type: Prize
Value: C$5,000 to C$7,000
Frequency: Annual
Country of Study: Canada

Application Procedure: canadacouncil.ca/priorities/ongoing-priorities/equity/application-assistance
Closing Date: 1 March
Additional Information: canadacouncil.ca/funding/prizes/jean-a-chalmers-fund-for-the-crafts

For further information contact:

Email: chalmers-prizes@canadacouncil.ca

Joan Yvonne Lowndes Award

Type: Award
Value: C$3,500
Frequency: Annual
Country of Study: Canada
Additional Information: canadacouncil.ca/funding/prizes/joan-lowndes-award

For further information contact:

Email: prizes@canadacouncil.ca

John G. Diefenbaker Award

Purpose: The John G. Diefenbaker Award is funded by an endowment given to the Canada Council for the Arts by the Government of Canada. The endowment, announced by Prime Minister Brian Mulroney during his visit to Germany in the spring of 1991, honours the memory of former Prime Minister John G. Diefenbaker. The award is given annually, and it enables a distinguished German scholar to do research in Canada, which may include brief periods in the United States. The spirit of the award is to encourage exchange between scholarly communities in Canada and Germany
Eligibility: Candidates may not apply for this award they must be nominated by a department within a host university or research institute in Canada. This award is open to German scholars who have demonstrated outstanding ability, especially through a substantial publication record over several years. The award is offered in support of research in any of the disciplines of the social sciences and humanities. Candidates must be German citizens with a contractual or working relationship with an academic institution in Germany. They must have a sound working knowledge of at least one of Canada's two official languages
Type: Award
Value: Up to C$95,000
Country of Study: Any country
Application Procedure: Check website for more details
Closing Date: 1 November
Additional Information: Not available in internet

For further information contact:

Tel: (1) 613 566 4414
Email: prizes@canadacouncil.ca

John Hirsch Prizes

Eligibility: This is a prize for emerging theatre directors. There is no age restriction for this prize. Individuals with no more than 10 years of experience as a professional theatre director can apply. The 10-year period is calculated from the application deadline date. Your application should demonstrate a history of professional theatre direction. You must also be a Canadian citizen or have permanent resident status, as defined by Immigration, Refugees and Citizenship Canada. You do not need to be living in Canada. You must also meet the Canada Council's definition of a professional artist, which is an artist who: 1. has specialized training in the field (not necessarily in academic institutions) 2. is recognized as such by peers (artists working in the same artistic tradition) 3. is committed to devoting more time to artistic activity, if possible financially 4. has a history of public presentation.
Type: Prize
Value: C$6,000 each
Frequency: Annual
Country of Study: Canada
No. of awards offered: 2
Closing Date: 1 October
Additional Information: canadacouncil.ca/funding/prizes/john-hirsch-prize

For further information contact:

Email: johnhirsch-prizes@canadacouncil.ca

John Hobday Awards in Arts Management

Purpose: Established through a donation of C$1,000,000 from The Samuel and Saidye Bronfman Family Foundation to the Canada Council for the Arts, the awards recognize outstanding established and mid-career arts managers in Canadian professional arts organizations. Arts managers from any artistic discipline supported by the Canada Council may apply for the awards, which are intended for professional development, mentoring and related purposes
Eligibility: 1. be currently employed by a Canadian professional arts organization. Your mentor must also be currently employed by a Canadian professional arts organization (if applicable). 2. have a minimum of 10 years of professional activities (but not necessarily in consecutive years) 3. have significant expertise in arts management in one or more of the fields of practice funded by the Canada Council

(multidisciplinary activities, circus arts, dance, deaf and disability arts, digital arts, traditional Indigenous arts/culture, inter-arts, literature, media arts, music and sound, theatre and visual arts) 4. be a Canadian citizen or have permanent resident status, as defined by Immigration, Refugees and Citizenship Canada. You do not need to be living in Canada when you apply.
Level of Study: Postgraduate
Type: Award
Value: C$10,000 each
Frequency: Annual
Country of Study: Canada
No. of awards offered: 2
Closing Date: 1 March
Additional Information: canadacouncil.ca/funding/prizes/john-hobday-awards-in-arts-management

For further information contact:

Tel: (1) 613 566 4414
Email: johnhobday-prizes@canadacouncil.ca

Killam Research Fellowships

Purpose: The Canada Council is committed to equity and inclusion, and encourages applications and nominations from culturally diverse, deaf, disability and official language minority artists, groups and organizations. The Canada Council recognizes and affirms the Aboriginal and treaty rights of the Indigenous peoples of this land and encourages applications and nominations from First Nations, Inuit and Métis individuals, groups, and organizations in all its programs. Measures are in place in all programs to support these commitments.
Eligibility: Note that meeting the eligibility criteria allows candidates to be nominated for a Killam Prize. It does not, however, guarantee that they will receive a prize. The Canada Council retains the right to interpret the contents of the nomination guidelines and form. Eligible candidates Scholars may not apply for the Killam Prizes; they must be nominated by an expert in their field. Killam Prizes are intended for active (not retired) Canadian scholars who have made a substantial and distinguished contribution, over a significant period, to scholarly research. A Killam Prize is not intended as an "end of service" reward, as recognition for one great accomplishment, or in expectation of future distinguished contributions. Only Canadian citizens are eligible, and the prizes are awarded only to living candidates. The candidate does not need to be living in Canada when she or he is nominated.
Level of Study: Postgraduate
Type: Fellowship
Value: C$100,000 each

Length of Study: 2 years
Frequency: Annual
Country of Study: Any country
Application Procedure: There are no hard copy application forms applicants must submit their requests through the Canada Council's online application system at killam. canadacouncil.ca
No. of awards offered: 5
Closing Date: 30 June
Funding: Private
Contributor: Killam Trust
Additional Information: The competition for the Killam Research Fellowship is suspended while the Canada Council for the Arts is reviewing its suite of prizes. More information will soon be available. killamprogram.canadacouncil.ca/ research-fellowships

For further information contact:

Email: Killam@canadacouncil.ca

Musical Instrument Bank

Purpose: Every 3 years, talented Canadian classical musicians compete for the chance to borrow legendary instruments from the Canada Council's Musical Instrument Bank (MIB). The competition is intense and is decided by a jury of professional musicians and peers. Musicians who win the competition are often invited to perform with their instruments on some of the world's most celebrated stages. The MIB includes over 20 magnificent instruments worth a total of over C$41,000,000. These violins, cellos and bows, created by such master craftsmen as Stradivari, Gagliano and Pressenda, have been donated or lent to the MIB since it was created in 1985
Eligibility: For eligibility criteria, the application form and further information on this competition, see the Canada Council's Musical Instrument Bank Guidelines and the Musical Instrument Bank website.
Level of Study: Doctorate
Value: A three-year loan of a rare instrument from the Canada Council's Musical Instrument Bank.
Length of Study: 3 years
Country of Study: Canada
Closing Date: 1 April
Additional Information: canadacouncil.ca/funding/prizes/ musical-instrument-bank

For further information contact:

Tel: (1) 403 244 3074
Email: instrumentbank@canadacouncil.ca

Prix de Rome in Architecture - Emerging Practitioners

Purpose: The Canada Council for the Arts Prix de Rome in Architecture for Emerging Practitioners is awarded to a recent graduate of a Canadian school of architecture who demonstrates exceptional potential in contemporary architectural design
Eligibility: 1. be a Canadian citizen or have permanent resident status, as defined by Immigration, Refugees and Citizenship Canada. 2. have received a professional Bachelor or Master degree from a Canadian school of architecture that is certified by the Canadian Architectural Certification Board within 14 months prior to the deadline for submitting applications 3. be recommended by the director of the school of architecture that issued the degree.
Level of Study: Postdoctorate
Type: Award
Value: C$34,000
Country of Study: Canada
Application Procedure: canadacouncil.ca/funding/prizes/ prix-de-rome-in-architecture-for-emerging-practitioners
Closing Date: 1 October
Additional Information: canadacouncil.ca/funding/prizes/ prix-de-rome-in-architecture-for-emerging-practitioners

For further information contact:

Email: architecture-prizes@canadacouncil.ca

The Coburn Award

Purpose: The award is intended to cover travel expenses, tuition and accommodation for the year.
Eligibility: This program is open to all students studying in the Faculty of Arts & Science at the University of Toronto, but Victoria College students will get first priority. Students must be studying in the fields of the humanities or the fine arts. Recipients will be selected on the basis of academic or artistic excellence and their ability to benefit from study abroad. 1. have at least a B+ average (GPA 3.30+) 2. be prepared to share with other students the benefits of their experience abroad when they return home 3. be entering the third or fourth year of their undergraduate program be registered through the Centre for International Experience Students must: 3a. meet the admission requirements at Tel-Aviv University or at the Hebrew University of Jerusalem 3b. register at one of these two institutions for the academic year. 3c. be capable of studying in Hebrew or register for the English program offered at either University.

Level of Study: Postdoctorate
Type: Award
Value: C$20,000 each
Frequency: Annual
Country of Study: Canada
Application Procedure: awards.vicu.utoronto.ca/secure/apps/auth/studyabroad.aspx
No. of awards offered: 2
Closing Date: 1 March
No. of applicants last year: 2
Additional Information: www.vic.utoronto.ca/current-students/finances/the-coburn-award/ Canada and Israel

For further information contact:

Email: vic.awards@utoronto.ca

Canadian Association of Broadcasters (CAB)

770-45 O'Connor St., Ottawa, ON K1P 1A4, Canada.

Tel: (1) 613 233 4035
Email: cab@cab-acr.ca
Website: www.cab-acr.ca
Contact: Vanessa Dawson, Special Events and Projects Co-ordinator

The Canadian Association of Broadcasters (CAB) is the collective voice of Canada's private radio and television stations and speciality services. The CAB develops industry-wide strategic plans, works to improve the financial health of the industry, and promotes private broadcasting's role as Canada's leading programmer and local service provider.

Canada Council for the Arts Molson Prizes

Purpose: The Canada Council is committed to equity and inclusion, and encourages applications and nominations from culturally diverse, deaf, disability and official language minority artists, groups and organizations.
Eligibility: These prizes are for individuals. Candidates must: 1. be Canadian citizens or permanent residents of Canada, as defined by Immigration, Refugees and Citizenship Canada. They do not need to be residing in Canada. 2. have made a substantial and distinguished contribution over a significant period. 3. still be active and productive in their career.
Type: Prize

Value: C$50,000 each
Country of Study: Canada
No. of awards offered: 2
Closing Date: 1 October
Additional Information: canadacouncil.ca/funding/prizes/molson-prizes

For further information contact:

Email: molson-prizes@canadacouncil.ca

Horatio Alger Association Canadian Scholarships

Purpose: Horatio Alger Association Canadian Scholarships are funded through the generosity of the Association's Members
Eligibility: 1. Be graduating high school (or be in the final year of CEGEP). 2. Exhibit a strong commitment to pursue and complete a bachelor's degree program at an accredited university 3. Demonstrate critical financial need (C$65,000 or less annual net income per family is required) 4. Be involved in co-curricular and community service activities 5. Display integrity and perseverance in overcoming adversity 6. Maintain a minimum grade percentage of 65. 7. Attend high school (or CEGEP) and reside in Canada 8. Be Canadian citizens
Level of Study: Graduate
Type: Scholarship
Value: C$10,000
Frequency: Annual
Country of Study: Canada
No. of awards offered: 160
Closing Date: 15 March
Funding: Private
Additional Information: horatioalger.ca/en/scholarships/about-our-scholarships-programs/provincial-programs/

For further information contact:

Email: scholarships@horatioalger.org

Joseph S. Stauffer Prizes

Type: Prize
Value: C$5,000
Frequency: Annual
Country of Study: Canada
No. of awards offered: 3
Additional Information: canadacouncil.ca/funding/prizes/joseph-s-stauffer-prizes

For further information contact:

Email: prizes@canadacouncil.ca

Jules Léger Prize for New Chamber Music

Purpose: The Jules Léger Prize for New Chamber Music encourages Canadian professional composers to create avant-garde chamber music and to foster its performance by Canadian ensembles.
Eligibility: To be eligible for this prize, you must: 1. be a professional artist 2. maintain a professional music and sound practice as defined by the Canada Council 3. have maintained a professional artistic practice for a minimum of 2 years 4. have at least 1 professional public performance for which you were paid an artist's fee 5. be committed to your own artistic vision, retain creative control and are committed to the creation and/or promotion of original work 6. be dedicated to the ongoing development of your artistic practice actively seek to maximize the audience for your work, regardless of commercial appeal 7. be a Canadian citizen or have permanent resident status, as defined by Immigration, Refugees and Citizenship Canada. You do not need to be living in Canada when you apply.
Type: Prize
Value: C$7,500
Frequency: Annual
Country of Study: Canada
Closing Date: 1 June
Additional Information: canadacouncil.ca/funding/prizes/jules-leger-prize-for-new-chamber-music

For further information contact:

Email: juleslegerprizes@canadacouncil.ca

Prix de Rome in Architecture - Professional

Purpose: The Professional Prix de Rome in Architecture is awarded to a young practitioner of architecture or an architectural firm that has completed their first built works and has demonstrated exceptional artistic potential.
Eligibility: To apply for this prize as an individual, you must be a Canadian citizen or have permanent resident status, as defined byimmigration, Refugees and Citizenship Canada. You do not need to be living in Canada when you apply. Architects and architectural firms specializing in architecture, landscape architecture and/or urban design can submit their candidature. You must also meet one of the following definitions: To be eligible as an architect, you must: 1. have maintained a professional practice for a minimum of 2 years

2. have completed a professional body of work 3. have published or have presented at least 1 work in a public setting.
Type: Prize
Value: C$50,000
Frequency: Annual
Country of Study: Canada
Closing Date: 1 October
Additional Information: canadacouncil.ca/funding/prizes/professional-prix-de-rome-in-architecture

For further information contact:

Email: architecture-prizes@canadacouncil.ca

Ronald J. Thom Award for Early Design Achievement

Eligibility: Architects, architectural professionals and architectural firms specializing in architecture, landscape architecture and/or urban design can apply. To apply for this award as an individual, you must be a Canadian citizen or have permanent resident status, as defined by Immigration, Refugees and Citizenship Canada. You do not need to be living in Canada when you apply. You must also meet one of the following definitions: 1. To be eligible as an architect, you must: 2. have maintained a professional practice for a minimum of 2 years. 3 .have completed a professional body of work have published or have presented at least 1 work in a public setting.
Type: Prize
Value: C$10,000
Frequency: Annual
Country of Study: Canada
Closing Date: 1 October
Additional Information: canadacouncil.ca/funding/prizes/ronald-j-thom-award-for-early-design-achievement

For further information contact:

Email: architecture-prizes@canadacouncil.ca

Virginia Parker Prize

Eligibility: To be eligible, you must: 1. be a classical singer, instrumentalist or conductor 2. be a recipient of at least 2 Canada Council grants and/or Canada Council prizes for professional musicians as an individual 3. have conducted or performed as a soloist or chamber musician internationally 4. be under the age of 32 as of January 1st of the deadline year. For the 2023 competition, you must be born after January 1, 1991 5. be a Canadian citizen or have permanent resident status, as defined by Immigration, Refugees and Citizenship Canada; you do not need to be living in Canada when you apply. 6. not have previously received the Virginia Parker Prize.

Type: Prize
Value: C$25,000
Frequency: Annual
Country of Study: Canada
Closing Date: 30 April
Additional Information: canadacouncil.ca/funding/prizes/virginia-parker-prize

For further information contact:

Email: virginiaparker-prizes@canadacouncil.ca

Walter Carsen Prize for Excellence in the Performing Arts

Eligibility: This prize recognizes individual achievement or artistic partnerships. An artistic partnership may include up to 3 individuals who have developed a singular artistic practice. Each artist must meet the eligibility requirements below. Nominees must: 1. be a professional artist in the performing arts 2. be actively involved in the performing arts in Canada or have spent the majority of their artistic career in Canada 3. have created, as creative and/or interpretive artists, an outstanding and a distinguished body of work in any music forms or genres over a significant period 4. have work that has been recognized for its artistic excellence at national and international levels 5. be Canadian citizens or permanent residents of Canada as defined by Immigration, Refugees and Citizenship Canada. They do not need to be living in Canada when their nomination is submitted.

Type: Prize
Value: C$50,000
Country of Study: Canada
Closing Date: 30 April
Additional Information: canadacouncil.ca/funding/prizes/walter-carsen-prize-for-excellence-in-the-performing-arts

For further information contact:

Email: waltercarsen-prizes@canadacouncil.ca

Canadian Blood Services (CBS)

1800 Alta Vista Drive, Ottawa, ON K1G 4J5, Canada.

Tel: (1) 613 739 2300
Email: onematch@blood.ca
Website: www.bloodservices.ca

Canadian Blood Services (CBS) is a non-profit, charitable organization whose sole mission is to manage the blood system for Canadians. CBS collects approx. 900,000 units of blood annually and processes it into components and products that are administered to thousands of patients each year.

Canadian Blood Services Graduate Fellowship Program

Purpose: To attract and support young investigators to initiate or continue training in the field of blood or blood products research

Eligibility: 1. Applicants must not hold another competitive stipend award at the same time as the Canadian Blood Services Graduate Fellowship. 2. Applicants must be engaged in full-time training in research in a graduate program at a Canadian university leading to a Ph.D. or combined health professional Ph.D. program. While priority will be given to applicants enrolled in a PhD Program, applications from applicants enrolled in an MSc Program will be considered, if, at the applicant's institution, it is not possible to register directly in the PhD stream. Applicants registered solely for a Master's degree will not be considered. 3. The program is open to both Canadians and citizens of other countries. 4. Applicants must be enrolled in a training program that includes actual involvement in research and not only courses in research methods. 5. Applicants' proposed research must be relevant to one or more of the research priorities described in Section I of these Guidelines. 6. The proposed primary academic supervisor must be prepared to host the successful applicant in their laboratory for the duration of the training (2-4 years).

Level of Study: Graduate, Postdoctorate
Type: Fellowship
Value: C$25,000 per annum with an additional travel allowance of C$4,000 per year
Length of Study: 4 years
Country of Study: Canada
Application Procedure: Candidates are required to submit a completed application form (GFP-01) that is available either from the website, from or the main address
No. of awards offered: 15
Closing Date: 23 September
Funding: Government
No. of applicants last year: 15
Additional Information: Please check at www.blood.ca/en/research/our-research-activities/our-research-funding-opportunities/canadian-blood-services-graduate-fellowship-program Guidelines: www.blood.ca/sites/default/files/CBS%20GFP_Guidelines%202021.pdf

For further information contact:

Program Assistant, R&D, Canadian Blood Services, 1800 Alta Vista Drive, Ottawa, ON K1G 4J5, Canada.

Tel: (1) 613 739 2564
Email: centreforinnovation@blood.ca

Canadian Breast Cancer Research Alliance (CBCRA)

375 University Avenue, 6th Floor, Toronto, ON M5G 2JS, Canada.

Tel: (1) 416 596 6598
Email: pmacgregor@cbcra.ca
Website: www.breast.cancer.ca
Contact: Dr Pascale Macgregor, Research Program
               Director

Established in 1993, the Canadian Breast Cancer Research Alliance (CBCRA) is Canada's primary funder of breast cancer study. As a unique partnership of groups from the public, private and non-profit sectors, CBCRA is committed to reducing the incidence of breast cancer, increasing survival and enhancing the lives of those affected by the disease.

Canadian Federation of University Women Bourse Georgette Lemoyne

Purpose: Award is for graduate study in any field at a Canadian university. The candidate must be studying in French and write the Statement of Intent essay (Section I) of the application in French
Eligibility: 1. Must be a graduate student 2. Must attend a university 3. Citizenship requirements Canada 4. Restricted to female students 5. Must not be attending high school currently 6. Both full-time and part-time students 7. Restricted to residents of Alberta, British Columbia, Manitoba, New Brunswick, Newfoundland, Nova Scotia, Northwest Territories, Ontario, Prince Edward Island, Quebec, Saskatchewan, Yukon 8. Restricted to students studying in Alberta, British Columbia, Manitoba, New Brunswick, Newfoundland, Nova Scotia, Northwest Territories, Ontario, Prince Edward Island, Quebec, Saskatchewan, Yukon 9. Restricted to Canadian
Value: C$5,000
Country of Study: Any country
Closing Date: 1 November
No. of awards given last year: 1

Additional Information: cfuwcharitabletrust.ca/cfuw-bourse-georgette-lemoyne-award-2019-2020/

For further information contact:

331 Cooper Street, Suite 502, Ottawa, ON K2P 0G5, Canada.

Tel: (1) 613 234 8252
Email: fellowships@cfuw.org

Canadian Bureau for International Education (CBIE)

220 Laurier West, Suite 1550, Ottawa, ON K1P 5Z9, Canada.

Tel: (1) 613 237 4820
Email: scholarships-bourses@cbie.ca
Website: www.cbie.ca

The Canadian Bureau for International Education (CBIE) is a national non-profit association comprising educational institutions, organizations and individuals dedicated to internal education and intercultural training. CBIE's mission is to promote the free movement of learners and trainees across national borders.

Canada-Asia-Pacific Awards

Purpose: To assist scholars in higher education institutions in Asia Pacific Region to undertake short-term research
Eligibility: Open to students from the Asia-Pacific region
Level of Study: Postgraduate
Type: Award
Value: C$5,000 and C$10,000
Frequency: Annual
Country of Study: Canada
Application Procedure: A completed application form must be submitted
No. of awards offered: 2
Closing Date: 30 September
Funding: Government
Additional Information: scholarshippositions.blogspot.com/2010/09/canada-asia-pacific-award-capa.html

For further information contact:

Email: charles.labrecque@asiapacific.ca

Canada-Brazil Awards - Joint Research Projects

Purpose: The Canada-Brazil Awards – Joint Research Projects support exchanges of research teams collaborating on bilateral research projects. The projects must engage in collaborative research in mutually beneficial areas of research that is of benefit to both Canada and Brazil.

Eligibility: This competition is open to research teams from Canadian and Brazilian universities. The coordination of the project will be the responsibility of both the Canadian and Brazilian Project Leads and the teams will consist of PhD students from both institutions. Canadian and Brazilian Project Members Must be citizens or permanent residents of the country of their institution; Must be doctoral students - Master's students and post-doctoral researchers will not be considered; Must be enrolled full-time at a post-secondary institution in their country of origin and paying the tuition fees required by that institution for the full duration of the exchange; Must be proficient in the language of instruction at the Canadian institution (English or French). Students already participating in an exchange program in Canada or in Brazil are not eligible

Level of Study: Research

Type: Award

Value: A) C$7,200 for the Canadian Project where Members will travel for a research exchange for a minimum period of four months; or B) C$9,700 for the Canadian Project where Members will travel for a research exchange for a minimum of five to six months; or C) C$2,700 for the Canadian Project where the Lead will travel for a faculty visit for a minimum period of seven days.

Length of Study: 2 years

Country of Study: Canada

Closing Date: 26 November

Funding: Government

Contributor: Government of Canada, Foreign Affairs, Trade and Development Canada (DFATD)

Additional Information: www.educanada.ca/scholarships-bourses/can/institutions/brazil-cbjp-brezil.aspx?lang=eng

For further information contact:

Email: admin-scholarships-bourses@cbie.ca

Canada-CARICOM Faculty Leadership Program

Purpose: The Canada-CARICOM Faculty Leadership Program provides faculty or international liaison officers/managers from post-secondary institutions located in the CARICOM member and associate member states with short-term exchange opportunities for professional development, graduate study or research at Canadian post-secondary institutions.

Eligibility: 1. citizens of one of the CARICOM member and associate member states: 1a. Anguilla, Antigua and Barbuda, Bahamas, Barbados, Belize, Bermuda, British Virgin Islands, Cayman Islands, Dominica, Grenada, Guyana, Haiti, Jamaica, Montserrat, Saint Kitts and Nevis, Saint Lucia, Saint Vincent and the Grenadines, Suriname, Trinidad and Tobago, and Turks and Caicos; and 2. employed full-time as faculty or international liaison officers/managers at a post-secondary institution in the eligible countries/territories at the time of application and for the entire duration of their stay in Canada.

Value: CAD 3,200 for faculty members for two to three weeks of course work or research as part of their professional development; CAD 3,200 for international directors, managers or administrators for two to three weeks of course work or practicum in the area of internationalization or student mobility as part of their professional development; or CAD 11,100 for faculty members for five to six months of study or research at the graduate level. CAD 500 per scholarship recipient to assist with administrative costs once the scholarship recipient arrives in Canada.

Country of Study: Canada

Closing Date: 22 March

Contributor: Global Affairs Canada the Department of Foreign Affairs, Trade and Development (DFATD)

Additional Information: www.educanada.ca/scholarships-bourses/can/institutions/flpp-pplpe.aspx?lang=eng

Canada-CARICOM Leadership Scholarships Program

Purpose: The Canada-CARICOM Leadership Scholarships are facilitated through institutional collaborations and student exchange agreements between Canadian institutions and institutions in the CARICOM

Eligibility: Canadian institutions will disburse scholarship funds to the scholarship recipient to contribute to the following costs 1. visa and/or study/work permit fees 2. airfare, for the scholarship recipient only, to Canada by the most direct and economical route and return airfare upon completion of the scholarship 3. health insurance 4. living expenses, such as accommodation, utilities and food 5. ground transportation expenses, including a public transportation pass and 6. books and supplies required for the recipient's study or research, excluding computers and other equipment.

Value: C$7,200 for college, C$9,700 for graduate students, C$14,700 for undergraduate and college

Length of Study: 4 month, 5 or 6 months, 8 months of study or research

Country of Study: Any country

Application Procedure: The Canadian institution must apply on behalf of the candidate(s) by submitting the online application form and uploading all supporting documents prior to the deadline. The following documents must be uploaded and attached to the online application form in one of the following formats .pdf, .jpg, .doc, .docx, .txt or .gif. Each document must be smaller than 5 MB in order for the application to upload successfully.

Closing Date: 17 April

Contributor: Canadian institutions

Additional Information: oyaop.com/opportunity/scholarships-and-fellowships/canada-caricom-leadership-scholarships-program/

Canada-Chile Leadership Exchange Scholarship

Purpose: The Canada-Chile Leadership Exchange Scholarship program provides students and researchers from Chile with short-term exchange opportunities for study or research, in Canada, at the college, undergraduate and graduate levels

Eligibility: 1. Must be citizens of Chile. Must be enrolled full-time at a post-secondary institution in Chile and paying any tuition fees regulated by that institution for the full duration of the exchange. 2. People from Canadian institution can apply for this scholarship

Value: C$7,200 for college, undergraduate or graduate students (Master)

Country of Study: Any country

Application Procedure: Selected candidates are encouraged to ensure that they fulfill the requirements of the Canadian institution including academic requirements and language proficiency; submit their visa application as early as possible and follow the procedures of Immigration, Refugees and Citizenship Canada as outlined by the Canadian institution (generally a study permit is required for course work and a work permit is required for research); initiate the process for the transfer of credits to their home institution as soon as their Canadian courses have been identified; and contact alumni of the program through their home institution for advice and a local perspective on the scholarship experience

Closing Date: 21 March

Additional Information: ustpaul.ca/upload-files/researchservices/documents/scholarships/Work_Study/Roxana_Scholarships/Canada-Chile_Leadership_Exchange_Scholarship.pdf

Canada-China Scholars

Eligibility: 1. be Canadian citizens; 2. be either: 2a. a full-time teaching or research sta ff at a post-secondary or research institution in Canada; 2b. a student enrolled in either a college, undergraduate or graduate program at Designated Learning Institution (DLI) in Canada; or 2c.a mid-career professional from a Canadian government, media or cultural organization, or a national education association, who has a graduate (Master's or doctoral) degree and has had managerial, policy development or decision making responsibilities within this organization for at least three years; 3. have achieved the required level of written and spoken Chinese by the host institution in China, if applicable; 4. undertake studies in an approved subject area in a Chinese institution; 5. not be seeking a degree in China; 6. be under 45 years of age if applying under the "General Scholar" category of the China Scholarship Council (CSC); and 7. be under 50 years of age if applying under the "Senior Scholar" category of the CSC.

Level of Study: Doctorate, Graduate, Postdoctorate

Type: Scholarship

Value: 3,000 Yuan for Master's students/general scholars 3,500 Yuan for Doctoral students/senior scholars.

Frequency: Annual

Country of Study: China

Closing Date: 20 January

Additional Information: www.educanada.ca/scholarships-bourses/can/ccsep-peucc.aspx?lang=eng

Canadian Prime Minister's Awards for Publishing (CPMA)

Purpose: To increase the amount of published material related to Canada available in Japanese

Eligibility: Open to Japanese publishers who are likely to increase the knowledge and understanding of contemporary Canada

Level of Study: Postgraduate

Type: Scholarship

Frequency: Annual

Country of Study: Any country

Application Procedure: Further information available on the website

Closing Date: 15 November

Funding: Government

For further information contact:

Academic Relations (CPMA), Public Affairs, Embassy of Canada, 7-3-38 Akasaka, Minato-Ku, Japan.

Tel: (81) 3 5412 6298
Fax: (81) 3 5412 6249
Email: tokyo.lib-bib@international.gc.ca

Emerging Leaders in the Americas Program (ELAP)

Purpose: The Emerging Leaders in the Americas Program (ELAP) scholarships provide students and researchers from Latin America and the Caribbean with short-term exchange opportunities for study or research, in Canada, at the college, undergraduate and graduate levels

Eligibility: Candidates who have obtained Canadian citizenship or who have applied for permanent residency in Canada are not eligible; candidates who have already participating in an exchange scholarship program funded by the Government of Canada are not eligible; candidates who have already enrolled in a degree or diploma program at a Canadian university or college are not eligible; and the candidates must be enrolled full-time at a post-secondary institution in an eligible country and paying any tuition fees regulated by that institution for the full duration of the exchange

Level of Study: Doctorate, Postgraduate

Type: Scholarship

Value: C$11,000

Length of Study: 4 months to 1 academic year (master's and PhD)/ 5 to 6 months of study of research

Country of Study: Canada

Application Procedure: If institutions experience difficulty filling out or submitting the form, they should send an email to admin-scholarships-bourses@cbie.ca

Closing Date: 22 March

Contributor: Government of Canada

Additional Information: www.educanada.ca/scholarships-bourses/can/institutions/elap-pfla.aspx?lang=eng

International Council for Canadian Studies Graduate Student Scholarships

Purpose: To provide access to crucial scholarly information and resources in Canada in support of a thesis/dissertation

Eligibility: Students in the social sciences or humanities who are in the process of preparing a graduate thesis or doctoral dissertation on Canada. (Master's/Ph.D. level)

Type: Scholarship

Value: C$4,000

Frequency: Annual

Study Establishment: Any accredited Canadian University

Country of Study: Canada

Application Procedure: A completed application form and all supporting materials should be submitted to the Canadian Studies Associations

No. of awards offered: 6

Closing Date: 24 November

Additional Information: www.iccs-ciec.ca/graduate-student-scholarships.php

For further information contact:

Tel: (1) 613 789 7834 ext. 242
Email: kknopf@uni-bremen.de

Organization of American States (OAS) Fellowships Programs

Purpose: To fund education of Canadian residents and nationals in other American nations

Eligibility: 1. be Canadian citizens or permanent residents in Canada; 2. have completed the prerequisite degree(s) for the proposed program of study at the time of submitting an application; 3. have an overall grade point average (GPA) that is above the minimum standard required by the host university; 4 be in good physical and mental health to complete the proposed program of study successfully; and 5. possess the linguistic competencies necessary to undertake the academic studies in the language of the institution in the country of study.

Level of Study: Doctorate, Graduate, MBA

Type: Fellowship

Value: US$10,000 per academic year, which includes a round-trip economy-class airfare ticket; tuition fees and mandatory expenses for the academic program, a fixed monthly allowance, medical insurance, and a fixed annual book allowance

Length of Study: 1–2 years

Frequency: Annual

Country of Study: Canada

Application Procedure: A completed application form must be submitted on time. Please refer website for more information

Closing Date: 22 June

Funding: Government

Additional Information: www.educanada.ca/scholarships-bourses/can/oas-oea.aspx?lang=eng

For further information contact:

Email: scholarships@oas.org

Canadian Cancer Society Research Institute (CCSRI)

Suite 300, 55 St. Clair Avenue W, Toronto, ON M4V 2Y7, Canada.

Tel: (1) 416 961 7223
Email: research@cancer.ca
Website: www.cancer.ca/research

The Canadian Cancer Society (CCS) is the largest non-government funder of cancer research in Canada. The CCS provides support for research and related programmes undertaken at Canadian universities, hospitals and other research institutions.

Union for International Cancer Control American Cancer Society International Fellowships for Beginning Investigators (ACSBI)

Purpose: To provide funding for research that fosters a bi-directional flow of knowledge, experience, expertise and innovation to and from the United States of America
Eligibility: Candidates should be in the early stages of their career. Applications that are geared to the development of cancer control measures in developing central and east European countries are particularly encouraged
Level of Study: Postdoctorate, Professional development, Research
Type: Research grant
Value: Approx. US$35,000
Length of Study: 1 year
Frequency: Annual
Country of Study: Any country
Application Procedure: Applicants must write for details or refer to the website
Closing Date: 1 October
Funding: Private
Contributor: American Cancer Society
Additional Information: Results are available in April of the following year. Further information is available on the website www.uicc.org/news/acsbi-fellowship-call-proposals-now-open-0

For further information contact:

UICC Fellowships Department 3 rue du Conseil-General, CH-1205 Geneva, Switzerland.

Tel: (41) 22 809 1811
Fax: (41) 22 809 1810
Email: fellows@uicc.ch

Union for International Cancer Control International Oncology Nursing Fellowships (IDNF)

Purpose: The NCIC financially supports the International Union Against Cancer (UICC) which administers a number of fellowships to qualified professionals

Eligibility: English speaking nurses who are actively engaged in the management of cancer patients and who come from the developing and East European countries
Level of Study: Professional development
Type: Fellowship
Value: US$2,800
Length of Study: 1–3 months
Frequency: Annual
Country of Study: Any country
Application Procedure: Applicants must request information
Closing Date: 1 November

For further information contact:

UICC Fellowships Department, 3 Rue de Conseil-Général, CH-1205 Geneva, Switzerland.

Tel: (41) 22 809 1811
Fax: (41) 22 809 1810
Email: fellows@uicc.org

Canadian Crafts Council

345 Lakeshore Road West, Oakville, ON L6K 1G3, Canada.

Tel: (1) 905 845 5357
Email: kingfish@spectranet.ca
Contact: Ms Jan Waldorf

Saidye Bronfman Award

Purpose: To recognise excellence in the crafts. The award is made to a craftsperson judged to be an outstanding practitioner in their field, shown by their output over a working life, and their current level of achievement
Eligibility: Open to Canadian citizens, or individuals who have had landed immigrant status for at least three years. The nominee must have made a significant contribution to the development of crafts in Canada over a significant period of time, usually more than ten years
Level of Study: Postgraduate
Type: Award
Value: C$25,000
Frequency: Annual
Country of Study: Any country
Application Procedure: Nominations are made through CCC member associations across Canada. Award recipients are selected by a committee of leading Canadian craftspersons, including the current President of the Canadian Crafts

Council, a past recipient of the Award, a nominee of the Bronfman Foundation, a gallery or museum director, and a member of the CCC Board. Members are selected to represent all major disciplines and geographic areas of Canada

No. of awards offered: 8
Closing Date: 1 June
Additional Information: canadacouncil.ca/funding/prizes/saidye-bronfman-award

For further information contact:

Tel: (1) 613 566 4414
Email: ggarts@canadacouncil.ca

Canadian Embassy (United States of America)

501 Pennsylvania Ave. N.W., Washington, DC 20001-2114, United States of America.

Tel: (1) 202 682 1740
Email: enqserv@dfait-maeci.gc.ca
Website: www.canadianembassy.org

Canadian Embassy (United States of America) Research Grant Program

Purpose: To assist individual scholars or a group of scholars in writing an article length manuscript of publishable quality and reporting their findings in scholarly publications

Eligibility: Open to full-time faculty members at accredited 4-year United States colleges and universities, as well as scholars at American research and policy planning institutes who undertake significant research projects concerning Canada, Canada and the United States, or Canada and North America. Recent PhD recipients who are citizens or permanent residents of the United States are also eligible to apply

Level of Study: Postgraduate
Type: Programme grant
Value: Up to US$15,000; applicants whose project focuses on the priority topics listed above and who can demonstrate matching funds from others sources may request funding up to US$20,000
Frequency: Annual
Study Establishment: An accredited 4-year college or university
Country of Study: United States of America
Application Procedure: Applicants must provide 6 copies of the following in this order the completed application form,

a concise proposal of 4–8 pages which will identify all members of the research team, if a team project, and specify each member's affiliation and role in the study, identify the key issues or the main theoretical problem, describe and justify the appropriate methodology, present a general schedule of research activities, indicate clearly both the nature and scope of the projects contribution to the advancement of Canadian Studies, include a detailed budget including all other funding sources and a description of anticipated expenditures. A curriculum vitae, and the names and addresses of two scholars from whom the applicants will solicit recommendations should also be included. Application forms are available on request

Closing Date: 1 November
Funding: Government
Additional Information: The Research Grant Program promotes research in the social sciences and humanities with a view to contributing to a better knowledge and understanding of Canada and its relationship with the United States or other countries of the world canadacouncil.ca/funding/prizes/saidye-bronfman-award

For further information contact:

Tel: (1) 202 682 7717
Email: daniel.abele@dfait-maeci.gc.ca

Canadian Embassy Faculty Enrichment Program

Purpose: To provide faculty members with the opportunity to develop or redevelop courses with substantial Canadian content that will be offered as part of their regular teaching load, or as a special offering to select audiences in continuing or distance education

Eligibility: Open to full-time, tenured or tenure track faculty members at accredited 4-year United States colleges and universities. Candidates should be able to demonstrate that they are already teaching, or will be authorized to teach, courses with substantial Canadian content (33% or more). Team teaching applications are welcome. Applicants are ineligible to receive the same grant in 2 consecutive years or to receive two individual category Canadian Studies grants in the same grant period

Type: Programme
Value: Funding up to US$6,000; applicants may request an additional US$5,000 specifically to support student travel to Canada
Frequency: Annual
Country of Study: United States of America
Application Procedure: Applicants must contact the organization for an application form
Closing Date: 1 December

Additional Information: The Embassy especially encourages the use of new Internet technology to enhance existing courses, including the creation of instructional websites, interactive technologies and distance learning links to Canadian Universities grants.humanities.ufl.edu/2018/03/19/canadian-embassy-faculty-enrichment-course-development-program/

For further information contact:

Tel: (1) 202 682 7717
Email: daniel.abele@dfait-maeci.gc.ca

Canadian Embassy Graduate Student Fellowship Program

Purpose: To assist graduate students in conducting part of their doctoral research in Canada to acquire a better knowledge and understanding of Canada or its relationship with the United States and other countries of the world
Eligibility: Open to full-time doctoral students at accredited 4-year colleges and universities in the United States or Canada whose dissertations are related in substantial part to the study of Canada, Canada and the United States or Canada and North America. Candidates must be citizens or permanent residents of the United States and should have completed all doctoral requirements except the dissertation when they apply for a grant
Level of Study: Graduate
Type: Fellowship
Value: Fellowships carrying stipends of up to US$850 per month for up to 9 months
Length of Study: 9 months
Frequency: Annual
Study Establishment: An accredited 4-year college or university
Application Procedure: Applicants must provide six copies of the following in the order listed the completed application form, a concise letter of three to four pages which will explain clearly the present status of the candidate's doctoral studies, describe the candidate's study plans in Canada, list Canadian contacts such as Scholars, research institutes, academic institutions or libraries, state clearly the exact number of months for which financial support is needed, provide a complete and detailed budget, indicate what other funding sources are available, give the names and addresses of two referees, one of which must be the dissertation advisor, contain the dissertation prospectus which must identify the key issues or the main theoretical problem, justify the methodology and indicate clearly the nature of the dissertation's contribution to the advancement of Canadian Studies. An unofficial transcript of grades, a curriculum vitae and proof of United States

citizenship or permanent residency must also be included. Application forms are available on request
Closing Date: October
Funding: Government
Additional Information: The Graduate Student Fellowship Program promotes research in the social sciences and humanities with a view to contributing to a better knowledge and understanding of Canada and its relationship with the United States or other countries of the world grants.humanities.ufl.edu/2018/03/19/canadian-embassy-faculty-enrichment-course-development-program/

For further information contact:

Tel: (1) 202 682 7727
Email: daniel.abele@dfait-maeci.gc.ca

Outreach Grant

Purpose: To encourage training and resource development
Eligibility: Open to all K-12 teacher who teach about Canada or Canada–United States relations
Level of Study: Professional development
Type: Grant
Value: Up to US$14,000
Frequency: Annual
Country of Study: United States of America
Application Procedure: Contact the academic relations officer
Closing Date: 30 June
Funding: Government
Contributor: Foreign Affairs Canada

For further information contact:

Email: outreach@physoc.org

Canadian Federation of University Women (CFUW)

331 Cooper Street, Suite 502, Ottawa, ON K2P 0G5, Canada.

Tel: (1) 613 234 8252
Email: cfuwfls@rogers.com
Website: www.cfuw.org
Contact: Betty A Dunlop, CFUW Fellowships Program Manager

CFUW is a non-partisan, voluntary, self-funded organization with over 100 CFUW Clubs, located in every province across

Canada. Since its founding in 1919, CFUW has been working to improve the status of women, and to promote human rights, public education, social justice, and peace.

CFUW 100th Anniversary Legacy Fellowship funded by the Charitable Trust

Purpose: To promote the education of girls and women.
Eligibility: The PhD thesis research/project must focus on advancing gender equality. It is not restricted to a specific field of studies. Some examples falling within our criteria 1. Thesis/project in the field of Law or International Law on access to justice for Aboriginal women. 2. Thesis/project in the field of International Development on an intersectional feminist approach to international cooperation. 3. Thesis/project in the field of Philosophy in Pharmacy on sex and gender bias in clinical research. 4. Thesis/project in the field of Computer Science focusing on exploring the gender bias in big data. 5. The PhD thesis/project must be well defined in terms of objectives, implementation, and expected results. 6. Applicants must have completed one calendar year of a doctoral program, at the time of application. 7. The Fellowship is tenable in Canada or abroad.
Level of Study: Doctorate
Type: Fellowship
Value: C$5,000
Length of Study: 1 year
Frequency: Throughout the year
Country of Study: Any country
Closing Date: 10 September
Funding: Trusts
Additional Information: fcfdu.smapply.io/

Dr. A. Vibert Douglas Fellowship

Purpose: The Fellowship is for a PhD thesis/project which focuses on advancing gender equality. The project must be led by women. The Fellowship is for a PhD thesis/project which focuses on advancing gender equality
Eligibility: If an applicant does not belong to an NFA of the GWI or to an organization that belongs to the IAW but meets the other criteria for the Fellowship they must make a C$10 donation that will be split between those two organizations
Level of Study: Postgraduate
Type: Fellowship
Value: C$8,000
Frequency: Annual
Country of Study: Any country
Application Procedure: Those who are interested in this fellowship will need to pay a C$60 application fee
Closing Date: 3 December

Funding: Private
Additional Information: For more information, visit fcfdu. fluidreview.com/
www.fcfdu.org/fellowshipsawards/dravibertdouglasfellowship. aspx

Canadian Foundation for the Study of Infant Deaths

Suite 308, 586 Eglinton Avenue East, Toronto, ON M4P 1P2, Canada.

Tel:	(1) 416 488 3260
Email:	sidsinfo@sidscanada.org
Website:	www.sidscanada.org
Contact:	Ravit Lasman, Executive Director

The Canadian Foundation for the Study of Infant Deaths is a federally incorporated charitable organization that was set up in 1973 to respond to the needs of families experiencing sudden and unexpected infant death. It is the only organization in Canada solely dedicated to finding the causes of Sudden Infant Death Syndrome, its effect on families and the education of the public.

Cypress-Fairbanks Independent School District/ CIHR Doctoral and Postdoctoral Research Awards

Type: Award
Country of Study: Any country

For further information contact:

The Canadian Institutes of Health Research, 440 Laurier Ave. 9th fl., Locator 4209A, Ottawa, ON K1A 0W9, Canada.

Tel:	(1) 613 954 1964
Fax:	(1) 613 941 1800
Email:	srobertson@cihr.ca

Canadian Institute for Advanced Legal Studies

PO Box 43538, Leaside Post Office, 1601 Bayview Avenue, Toronto, ON M4G 4G8, Canada.

Tel:	(1) 416 429 3292
Email:	info@canadian-institute.com

Website: www.canadian-institute.com
Contact: Mr Randall J. Hofley, Vice-President

The Canadian Institute for Advanced Legal Studies conducts legal seminars for judges and lawyers in Cambridge, United Kingdom and Strasbourg, France.

French Language Scholarship

Purpose: The Canadian Institute for Advanced Legal Studies' French Language Scholarship ordinarily covers the full amount of the tuition fees payable by the recipient to a French-language European university and includes an allowance to cover a portion of living expenses and reasonable travel expenses to and from the European university, subject to any other awards received by the successful candidate.

Eligibility: The purpose of the scholarship is to support advanced legal studies leading to a second-cycle or third-cycle diploma (the equivalent of a master's or doctoral degree from a Canadian university) at university outside Canada in a program of study that is conducted in French, or to allow for a one-year stay within the scope of a doctoral program jointly supervised with a French-language university outside Canada. The recipient must have earned a bachelor's or master's degree in law from a Canadian university within four years preceding the proposed year of studies. In order to receive the scholarship, the recipient must have been accepted by a university outside Canada into a graduate course of study in law conducted in French or must already be enrolled in and pursuing a jointly supervised doctoral program. Candidates need not have received confirmation of their acceptance at the time of their application or at the time the scholarship recipient is selected.

Level of Study: Postgraduate
Type: Scholarship
Value: US$20,000
Length of Study: 1 year
Frequency: Annual
Study Establishment: French Language European University
Country of Study: Europe, Germany
Application Procedure: Applications must include 1. Curriculum vitae; 2. A personal statement indicating why the applicant wishes to undertake graduate studies in law and why the applicant is suited to undertake such studies, as well as an undertaking that the proposed program study is conducted principally in the French language. 3. A copy of transcripts for undergraduate and graduate studies, for studies in law or for a Bar Admission Course, as applicable. 4. A maximum of

three letters of reference. 5. A statement of tuition fees and anticipated living and travel expenses
Closing Date: 31 December
Funding: Trusts
Contributor: Canadian Institute for Advanced Legal Studies
Additional Information: www.canadian-institute.com/english/FRscholarship-e.html

For further information contact:

Canadian Institute for Advanced Legal Studies, P.O.Box 43538, Leaside Post Office, 1601 Bayview Avenue, Toronto, ON M4G 4G8, Canada.

Fax: (1) 416 429 9805

The Right Honorable Paul Martin Sr. Scholarship

Purpose: The Canadian Institute for Advanced Legal Studies annually awards two scholarships for the LLM degree at the University of Cambridge, England. The Right Honourable Paul Martin Sr. Scholarships cover full tuition at the University of Cambridge, a monthly living allowance, the Immigration Health Surcharge, and one return airfare, subject to any other awards received by the successful candidate.

Eligibility: Candidates who have been awarded a law degree from a three or four-year program at a faculty of law in a Canadian university in the four years before the candidate will commence his or her studies at the University of Cambridge are eligible for these scholarships. An applicant must be accepted into the University of Cambridge and a Cambridge College for the LLM in order to receive this scholarship, although such acceptance need not be confirmed at the time of the application for the scholarship nor at the time that the Institute provides the candidate with notice that he or she has been selected to receive the scholarship.

Level of Study: Postgraduate
Type: Scholarship
Value: University tuition fee, Anual stipend, Immigration Health Surcharge
Length of Study: 1 year
Frequency: Annual
Study Establishment: The University of Cambridge
Country of Study: United Kingdom
Application Procedure: Applications must include curriculum vitae; a personal statement indicating why the applicant wishes to undertake graduate studies in law at the University of Cambridge and why the applicant is suited to undertake such studies; a copy of transcripts for undergraduate and graduate studies, for studies in law and for a Bar Admissions

Course, as applicable; and a maximum of three letters of references
No. of awards offered: 25
Closing Date: 31 December
Funding: Private
No. of awards given last year: 2
Additional Information: Please check at www.canadian-institute.com/english/index.html

For further information contact:

Canadian Institute for Advanced Legal Studies, P.O.Box 43538, Leaside Post Office, 1601 Bayview Avenue, Toronto, ON M4G 4G8, Canada.

Fax: (1) 416 429 9805

Canadian Institutes of Health Research

Canadian Institutes of Health Research, 160 Elgin Street, 9th Floor; Address Locator 4809A, Ottawa, ON K1A 0W9, Canada.
The Canadian Institutes of Health Research (CIHR) is Canada's federal funding agency for health research. Composed of 13 Institutes, we collaborate with partners and researchers to support the discoveries and innovations that improve our health and strengthen our health care system.

Banting Postdoctoral Fellowships

Purpose: 1. attract and retain top-tier postdoctoral talent, both nationally and internationally 2. develop their leadership potential 3. position them for success as research leaders of tomorrow
Eligibility: Open to Canadian citizen, permanent resident of Canada, foreign citizens
Level of Study: Postdoctorate
Type: Award
Value: C$70,000 per year (taxable)
Length of Study: 2 years
Country of Study: Canada
No. of awards offered: 70
Closing Date: February
Additional Information: For more details, visit website banting.fellowships-bourses.gc.ca/en/app-dem_guide.html

For further information contact:

Email: banting@cihr-irsc.gc.ca

Canadian Institutes of Health Research Gold Leaf Prizes

Eligibility: Open to Canadian citizen, permanent resident of Canada, foreign citizens
Type: Grant
Value: C$100,000
Length of Study: 2 years
Frequency: Every 2 years
Country of Study: Canada
Additional Information: cihr-irsc.gc.ca/e/27894.html

For further information contact:

Tel: (1) 613 954 1968
Email: support-soutien@cihr-irsc.gc.ca

Foundation Grant Program

Purpose: Foundation grants are designed to support research leaders at any career stage to build and conduct programmes of health research across CIHR's mandate
Eligibility: Open to Canadian citizen, permanent resident of Canada, foreign citizens
Type: Grant
Value: 1. Proportionate to the requirements of the research proposed; and, 2. Vary depending on the research field, research approach, and scope of program activities.
Length of Study: 7 years
Country of Study: Canada
Application Procedure: Please refer website www.cihr-irsc.gc.ca
Closing Date: 20 January
Additional Information: For more details, please visit the Contact Centre: support@cihr-irsc.gc.ca
cihr-irsc.gc.ca/e/49798.html

For further information contact:

Email: support-soutien@cihr-irsc.gc.ca

Project Grant Program

Purpose: Project grants are designed to support researchers at any career stage to build and conduct health-related research and knowledge translation projects across CIHR's mandate
Eligibility: The Project Grant program is open to researchers at any career stage to build and conduct health-related research and knowledge translation projects across CIHR's mandate.
Type: Grant
Country of Study: Canada

Application Procedure: Your research proposal must include all crucial information (including tables, charts, figures and photographs) that a reviewer will need to read in order to assess your application. Reviewers are under no obligation to read other supplementary application materials that you may attach.

Closing Date: 9 May

Additional Information: For more details, please contact the Contact Centre: support-soutien@cihr-irsc.gc.ca cihr-irsc.gc.ca/e/49051.html

For further information contact:

Fax: (1) 613 954 1968
Email: support-soutien@cihr-irsc.gc.ca

Vanier Canada Graduate Scholarships

Purpose: The Vanier Canada Graduate Scholarships (Vanier CGS) was created to attract and retain world-class doctoral students and to establish Canada as a global centre of excellence in research and higher learning. The scholarships are towards a doctoral degree (or combined MA/PhD or MD/PhD).

Eligibility: 1. be nominated by only one Canadian institution, which must have received a Vanier CGS quota 2. be pursuing your first doctoral degree (including joint undergraduate/graduate research program such as MD/PhD, DVM/PhD, JD/PhD - if it has a demonstrated and significant research component). Note that only the PhD portion of a combined degree is eligible for funding 3. intend to pursue, in the summer semester or the academic year following the announcement of results, full-time doctoral (or a joint graduate program such as MD/PhD, DVM/PhD, JD/PhD) studies and research at the nominating institution Note that only the PhD portion of a combined degree is eligible for funding 4. not have completed more than 20 months of doctoral studies as of May 1. 5. have achieved a first-class average, as determined by your institution, in each of the last two years of full-time study or equivalent. Candidates are encouraged to contact the institution for its definition of a first-class average and 6. must not hold, or have held, a doctoral-level scholarship or fellowship from CIHR, NSERC or SSHRC to undertake or complete a doctoral degree.

Level of Study: Doctorate
Type: Scholarship
Value: C$50,000 per year
Length of Study: 3 years
Frequency: Annual
Country of Study: Canada
No. of awards offered: 166
Closing Date: 2 November

Additional Information: vanier.gc.ca/en/nomination_process-processus_de_mise_en_candidature.html

For further information contact:

Email: vanier@cihr-irsc.gc.ca

Canadian Library Association (CLA)

1150 Morrison Drive, Suite 400, Ottawa, ON K2H 8S9, Canada.

Tel: (1) 613 232 9625
Email: info@cla.ca
Website: www.cla.ca
Contact: Valoree McKay, Executive Director

The Canadian Library Association works to maintain a tradition of commitment to excellence in library education and to advance continuing research in the field of library and information science.

Canadian Library Association Library Research and Development Grants

Purpose: To support members of the Canadian Library Association for theoretical and applied research in the related fields. To encourage and support research undertaken by practitionares in the field of library and information services. To promote research in the field of library and information services by and/or about Canadians

Eligibility: Open to personal members of the Canadian Library Association
Level of Study: Postgraduate
Type: Grant
Value: C$1,000
Frequency: Annual
Country of Study: Canada
Application Procedure: Applicants must submit grant applications via emails and MS word document in either French or English containing contact details, description of the research project, duration of the project, detailed assessment of costs and statement of other grants/awards received. Proposals should be submitted via email
Additional Information: cla.ca/cla-at-work/cla-library-research-and-development-grants/

For further information contact:

Tel: (1) 613 232 9625 ext 322
Fax: (1) 613 563 9895

Canadian National Institute for the Blind (CNIB)

1929 Bayview Avenue, East York, Toronto, ON M4G 0A1, Canada.

Tel: (1) 800 563 2642
Email: info@cnib.ca
Website: www.cnib.ca
Contact: Mr John M Rafferty, President and CEO

CNIB is a nationwide, community-based, registered charity committed to public education, research and the vision health of all Canadians. CNIB provides the services and support necessary to enjoy a good quality of life while living with vision loss. Founded in 1918, CNIB reaches out to communities across the country, offering access to rehabilitation training, innovative consumer products and peer support programs as well as one of the world's largest libraries for people with a print disability. CNIB supports research to advance knowledge in the field of vision health. Our research program funds projects that focus on ways to cure, treat and prevent eye disease, and improve the quality of life for people with vision loss.

Canadian National Institute for the Blind Baker Applied Research Fund

Purpose: To promote non-medical applied research that will enhance the life of the blind or visually impaired
Eligibility: Open to residents of Canada enrolled in graduate study in Canada, and includes a co-applicant who is either a supervisor or mentor with an academic appointment in Canada, or a supervisory position at a healthcare facility. Refer to the website for complete details
Level of Study: Research
Type: Award
Value: Up to C$40,000 plus travel and publications costs up to C$2,000
Length of Study: One year
Frequency: Annual
Country of Study: Canada
Closing Date: 15 January
Funding: Private
Additional Information: www.cnib.ca/en?region=on

For further information contact:

Tel: (1) 416 486 2500 ext. 7622
Fax: (1) 416 480 7059
Email: shampa.bose@cnib.ca

Canadian National Institute for the Blind Baker Fellowship Fund

Purpose: CNIB's Baker Fellowships are awarded annually for post-graduate training in ophthalmic subspecialties
Eligibility: Open to Canadians for research or study in Canada, or abroad if returning to practice in Canada, with priority given to university teaching
Level of Study: Postgraduate, Professional development, Research
Value: Up to C$40,000
Length of Study: 1–2 years
Frequency: Annual
Country of Study: Canada
Funding: Private
Additional Information: Scholarship applications for the 2023/24 school year will open spring 2023. Please check back then.

For further information contact:

Tel: (1) 416 486 2500 ext. 7622
Fax: (1) 416 480 7059
Email: shampa.bose@cnib.ca

Canadian National Institute for the Blind Baker New Researcher Fund

Purpose: To provide one-year grants to encourage new investigations that may lead to the prevention of vision loss. It is intended to benefit new investigators (within 5 years after an academic faculty appointment) by giving them experience and results which can assist them in further grant applications and pilot investigations
Eligibility: Applicants must be residents of Canada and research must be conducted primarily in Canada
Level of Study: Postdoctorate, Professional development, Research
Type: Award
Value: Up to C$40,000
Length of Study: 1 year
Frequency: Annual
Country of Study: Canada
Closing Date: 15 January
Funding: Private
Additional Information: Scholarship applications for the 2023/24 school year will open spring 2024. Please check back then.

For further information contact:

Tel: (1) 416 486 2500 ext. 7622
Fax: (1) 416 480 7059
Email: shampa.bose@cnib.ca

Canadian National Institute for the Blind Winston Gordon Award

Purpose: The award is presented to an individual or group who has made significant technological advances benefiting people with vision loss
Eligibility: The significant advances in, or application of, technology must have occurred within 10 years of nomination. The device or application must have a documented benefit to people who are blind or visually impaired. The award may be presented to an individual, group, or organization, including corporations and academic institutions
Type: Award
Value: The award consists of a cash prize of up to C$10,000
Country of Study: Any country
Application Procedure: To submit a nomination, please write a letter to the Winston Gordon Committee nominating the individual or group for its products or services, and explaining how the nominee meets or surpasses the eligibility criteria and matches the goals of the award
Closing Date: 16 January
Additional Information: cnib.ca/en/about-us/awards/winston-gordon-award-excellence-accessible-technology?region=gta

For further information contact:

Winston Gordon Award Committee, CNIB, 1929 Bayview Avenue, East York, ON M4G 3E8, Canada.

Fax: (1) 416 480 7000
Email: shampa.bose@cnib.ca

Chanchlani Global Vision Research Award

Purpose: The CNIB Chanchlani Global Vision Research Award was established in 2011 with the goal of encouraging world researchers in the area of vision science and vision rehabilitation. The award is consistent with the goals of CNIB (Canadian National Institute for the Blind) of conducting and funding world-class research to reduce the impact of sight loss in people's lives. The award will be given to vision scientists anywhere in the world who have made a major original contribution to the fields of vision science or vision rehabilitation.
Eligibility: Open to individual researchers from any part of the world whose work has substantially advanced the field of vision science or vision-loss rehabilitation. Self-nominations are permitted.
Level of Study: Research
Type: Award
Value: C$25,000
Frequency: Annual

Country of Study: Any country
Closing Date: 31 January
Funding: Individuals
Additional Information: cnib.ca/en/about-us/awards/chanchlani-global-vision-research-award?region=gta

For further information contact:

Email: cheryl-ann.ali@cnib.ca

CNIB Barbara Tuck MacPhee Award

Purpose: The CNIB Barbara Tuck MacPhee Award supports researchers in the field of macular degeneration.
Eligibility: This award is open to all researchers; however, applicants must be residents of Canada and research must be conducted primarily in Canada.
Level of Study: Research
Type: Award
Value: Up to C$25,000
Length of Study: 12 months
Frequency: Annual
Country of Study: Canada
Closing Date: 15 January
Additional Information: cnib.ca/en/about-us/awards/cnib-barbara-tuck-macphee-award?region=gta

For further information contact:

Cheryl-Ann Ali.

Tel: (1) 416 486 2500
Fax: (1) 416 480 7700
Email: cheryl-ann.ali@cnib.ca

Gretzky Scholarship Foundation for the Blind Youth of Canada

Purpose: To provide scholarships to eligible blind and visually impaired students planning to study at the post-secondary level
Eligibility: All applicants must be blind or visually impaired, a graduate from secondary school entering their first year of post-secondary education, and a Canadian citizen. Candidates must be blind or living with vision loss. A secondary school graduate entering their first year of post-secondary education. A Canadian citizen or have held landed immigrant status for one year prior to date of application. Academic excellence, service to the community, financial need, superior leadership
Type: Scholarship
Value: C$3,000–5,000 each
Frequency: Annual

Country of Study: Canada
Application Procedure: All documents requested in the application form must be included with your application. Please send application and documents to Kim Kohler
Closing Date: 31 May
No. of awards given last year: 23

For further information contact:

955256 Canning Rd, Paris, ON N3L 3E2, Canada.

Tel:	(1) 519 458 8665
Fax:	(1) 519 458 8609
Email:	Kim.Kohler@cnib.ca

Ross Purse Doctoral Fellowship

Purpose: To encourage and support theoretical and practical research and studies at the postgraduate or doctoral level in the field of vision loss in Canada
Eligibility: Applications will be considered from persons studying at a Canadian University or college, or at a foreign University, where a commitment to work in the field of vision loss in Canada for at least 2 years can be demonstrated
Level of Study: Doctorate, Postgraduate
Type: Fellowship
Value: Up to C$12,500 to be paid in three equal installments
Length of Study: 2 years
Frequency: Annual
Country of Study: Any country
Application Procedure: Please send completed applications to Research Coordinator
No. of awards offered: 1
Closing Date: 30 June
Funding: Private
Additional Information: www.cnib.ca/en/about-us/awards/ross-c-purse-doctoral-fellowship?region=gta

For further information contact:

CNIB, 1929 Bayview Avenue, East York, ON M4G 3E8, Canada.

Tel:	(1) 416 486 2500
Fax:	(1) 416 480 7000
Email:	cheryl-ann.ali@cnib.ca

The E. (Ben) & Mary Hochhausen Access Technology Research Award

Purpose: To encourage research in the field of access technology for people living with vision loss

Eligibility: Applications are accepted from any country in the world
Level of Study: Research
Type: Research award
Value: Up to C$10,000
Country of Study: International
Application Procedure: Please check at www.cnib.ca/en/research/funding/hochhausen/
Closing Date: 30 September
Funding: Private
No. of awards given last year: 1
Additional Information: www.cnib.ca/en/about-us/awards/ross-c-purse-doctoral-fellowship?region=gta

For further information contact:

Email:	shampa.bose@cnib.ca

Canadian Political Science Association

1 Stewart Street, Suite 205, University of Ottawa, Ottawa, ON K1N 6H7, Canada.

Tel:	(1) 613 562 1202
Email:	pip@csse.ca
Contact:	Grants Management Officer

The Canadian Political Science Association was founded in 1913 with the aim of encouraging and developing political science and its relationship with other disciplines. To this end the Association holds conferences, meetings and exhibitions, gives grants, scholarships and fellowships and publishes journals, newspapers, books and monographs relating to political science.

Canadian Parliamentary Internship Programme

Purpose: To give university graduates an opportunity to supplement their theoretical knowledge of Parliament with practical experience of the day to day work of the Members of Parliament and to provide back bench Members with highly qualified assistants
Eligibility: 1. Hold Canadian citizenship or permanent resident status. 2. Hold at least one university or college degree (a CEGEP diploma alone is insufficient). 3. Are available to work full-time from September 1, 2023 to June 30, 2024.
Level of Study: Postgraduate
Type: Scholarship
Value: C$27,000 for the ten month

Length of Study: 10 months
Frequency: Annual, if funds are available
Study Establishment: The Canadian Parliament
Country of Study: Canada
Application Procedure: Applicants must submit the original and four copies of the completed application form, transcripts, letters of reference (two academic, one employer), and C$10 administrative fee cheque
Closing Date: 31 January
Funding: Private
Contributor: The Social Sciences and Humanities Research council of Canada, Bank of Montreal, Canadian Airlines International, Canadian Bankers Association, Canadian Cable Television Association, The Canadian Life and Health Association, The Co-operators
Additional Information: Interns will be assigned specific responsibilities with Members of the House of Commons and will be required to attend seminars and prepare a paper analysing an aspect of parliamentary government in Canada www.cnib.ca/en/about-us/awards/ross-c-purse-doctoral-fellowship?region=gta

For further information contact:

The Parliamentary Internship Programme, Room 1200, La Promenade Building, 151 Sparks Street, House of Commons, Ottawa, ON K1P 5E3, Canada.

Tel: (1) 613 995 0764
Fax: (1) 613 995 5357
Email: alumni-anciens@pip-psp.org

Ontario Legislature Internship Programme

Purpose: To provide university graduates with the opportunity to supplement their theoretical knowledge of the Legislature and its processes with practical experience of the day to day work of the members, and to provide back bench members with highly qualified assistants
Eligibility: OLIP open to all candidates who, at the start of the internship 1. Hold Canadian citizenship or Permanent Residency; 2. Hold at least one university degree, from which you graduated in the last two years; 3. Are available to work full-time from September 2023 to June 2024.
Level of Study: Postgraduate
Type: Internship
Value: C$2,600+ monthly plus an additional C$1,000 paid upon completion
Length of Study: 10 months
Frequency: Dependent on funds available
Country of Study: Canada

Application Procedure: 1. A letter to the Academic Director explaining why you would like to be an intern. (600 words) 2. Curriculum Vitae 3. Transcript (Official or Unofficial) 4. Three Letters of Reference. We recommend two academic references and one other. Your referee will upload their letter to the online system, you will be asked to provide their email.
Closing Date: 31 January
Funding: Commercial, Government, Private
Additional Information: www.olipinterns.ca/apply-to-olip

For further information contact:

Department of Political Science, University of Waterloo, 200 University Ave W, Waterloo, ON N2L 3G1, Canada.

Tel: (1) 519 888 4567 ext. 5682
Fax: (1) 519 746 5622
Email: admin@olipinterns.ca

Canadian Society for Chemical Technology

Chemical Institute of Canada, 222 Queen Street, Suite 400, Ottawa, ON K1P 5V9, Canada.

Tel: (1) 613 232 6252 ext 223, (1) 888 542 2242
Email: awards@cheminst.ca
Website: www.cheminst.ca/about/cic/csct
Contact: Gale Thirlwall, Awards Manager

The Canadian Society for Chemical Technology is the national technical association of chemical and biochemical technicians and technologists with members across Canada who work in industry, government or academia. The purpose of the Society is the advancement of chemical technology, the maintenance and improvement of practitioners and educators and the continual evaluation of chemical technology in Canada. The Society hopes to maintain a dialogue with educators, government and industry, to assist in the technology content of the education process of technologists, to attract qualified people into the professions and the Society, to develop and maintain high standards and enhance the usefulness of chemical technology to both the industry and the public.

Canadian National Committee/IUPAC Travel Awards

Purpose: The purpose of these Awards is to help young Canadian scientists and engineers within 10 years of having gained their PhD who are currently working at a Canadian institution, present a paper at an IUPAC-sponsored conference outside of Canada.

Eligibility: A list of IUPAC-sponsored conferences for 2022 can be found on the IUPAC web-site (www.iupac.org/) and also in Chemistry International, the IUPAC magazine. Awards are made to attend the conference identified in the application, and no changes are allowed without written permission from the Chair

Level of Study: Postdoctorate

Type: Award

Value: Up to US$2,500, paid in arrears after travel-expense receipts and a 150-word report on the conference have been received by the Secretary

Country of Study: Any country

Application Procedure: 1. a short Curriculum Vitae, 2. two Letters of Reference, including one from someone not at the applicant's university, research institution or company. 3. a cover letter outlining the name and location of the conference, a copy or link to the conference circular and the reasons why this particular conference fits your research goals.

No. of awards offered: 3–4

Closing Date: 17 October

Funding: Private

Contributor: Gendron Fund and CNC/IUPAC company associates

No. of awards given last year: 4

Additional Information: www.cnc-iupac.ca/awards_e.html

For further information contact:

Steacie Institute for Molecular Sciences, NRC 100 Sussex Dr, Ottawa, ON K1A 0R6, Canada.

Tel: (1) 613 990 8326
Email: homin.shin@nrc-cnrc.gc.ca

Canadian Society for Chemistry (CSC)

222 Queen Street, Suite 400, Ottawa, ON KIP 5V9, Canada.

Tel: (1) 613 232 6252 ext 223
Email: awards@cheminst.ca
Website: www.cheminst.ca/about/cic/csc
Contact: Gale Thirlwall, Awards Manager

The Canadian Society for Chemistry (CSC), one of three constituent societies of The Chemical Institute of Canada, is the national scientific and educational society of chemists. The purpose of the CSC is to promote the practice and application of chemistry in Canada.

Award for Research Excellence in Materials Chemistry

Purpose: To recognize outstanding contribution to materials chemistry while working in Canada

Eligibility: Membership in the CIC is not a prerequisite for this award. 1. If the nominee has previously received awards by the CSC and/or CIC, the nominator has to differentiate the current achievements from those that have been previously recognized. 2. All nominations will remain in force for three years. Nominators are responsible for keeping the record of the nominee up to date and complete.

Level of Study: Research

Type: Fellowship

Value: Up to US$1,000 travel costs for award tour, framed scroll

Frequency: Annual

Country of Study: Any country

Application Procedure: Please check website for details

Closing Date: 2 July

Funding: Private

Additional Information: Please check at www.cheminst.ca/awards/csc-awards

www.cheminst.ca/wp-content/uploads/2019/04/Award20for20Research20Excellence20in20Materials20Chemistry20TofR.pdf

Canadian Space Agency

John H. Chapman 6767 Route de l'Aéroport Saint-Hubert, Quebec, J3Y 8Y9, Canada.

Tel: (1) 450 926 4800
Email: dave.kendall@space.gc.ca
Website: www.asc-csa.gc.ca
Contact: David Kendall, Director General, Space Science

The Canadian Space Agency (CSA) was established in 1989 by the Canadian Space Agency Act. The agency operates like a government department

Canadian Space Agency Supplements Postgraduate Scholarships

Purpose: To foster advanced studies in space science by offering a supplement to the regular National Science and Engineering Research Council (NSERC) postgraduate scholarships

Eligibility: Open to graduate and permanent resident and citizen of Canada engaged in Masters or Doctoral studies in the natural sciences or engineering, or intend to pursue such studies in the following year, is successful in obtaining a NSERC postgraduate scholarship (PGS) or a Canada graduate scholarships (CGS-Master's)

Level of Study: Postgraduate

Type: Scholarship

Value: C$7,500 per year for one year for masters students and up to two years for doctoral students

Length of Study: 2 years

Frequency: Annual

Country of Study: Canada

Application Procedure: Candidates should apply to the NSERC postgraduate scholarship or Canada graduate scholarship programs by completing Form 200. After reviewing the forms, notification of award will be sent to the selected applicants

Closing Date: 1 May

Funding: Government

Contributor: National Science and Engineering Research Council

Additional Information: A candidate who is in receipt of a scholarship from federal sources other than NSERC will not be eligible for this supplement. Please check at www.asc-csa. gc.ca/eng/resources/gc/research.asp#recipients-2

For further information contact:

Email: sc-gc.centre.expertise@asc-csa.gc.ca

Cancer Council N.S.W

153 Dowling Street, Woolloomooloo, NSW 2011, Australia.

Tel: (61) 2 9334 1900
Email: rong@nswcc.org.au
Website: www.cancercouncil.com.au

The Cancer Council NSW is one of the leading cancer charity organizations in New South Wales. Its mission is to defeat cancer and is working to build a cancer-smart community. In building a cancer-smart community, the Council undertakes high-quality research and is an advocate on cancer issues, providing information and services to the public and raising funds for cancer programmes

The Cancer Council NSW Research Project Grants

Purpose: To provide flexible support for cancer researchers
Eligibility: 1. Chief Investigator A (CIA) may hold no more than two concurrent Cancer Council NSW Project Grants.

2. At least one named and qualified consumer must be involved in the research proposal. For further guidance, please refer to the Consumer Review Guidelines. 3. Chief Investigators (CIA to CIJ) on any current Cancer Council NSW Program Grant (Program Grant) may not apply or hold a Cancer Council NSW Project Grant during the term of the Program Grant. Any Program Grant Chief Investigators named on a Cancer Council Project Grant application (CIA to CIJ) will make the Project Grant application ineligible. 4. Researchers not applying for NHMRC's Ideas Grant funding can still apply for Cancer Council NSW funding. 5. Applicants applying for funding from both NHMRC and Cancer Council NSW must adhere to both the NHMRC and Cancer Council NSW eligibility criteria and guidelines. For further information on the NHMRC's Ideas Grants - www.nhmrc.gov.au/funding/findfunding. 6. The list and sequence of all named chief investigators on the Cancer Council NSW application must be the same as that on the NHMRC Idea's Grant application. 7. Current funding recipients applying for new funding should note that Cancer Council NSW must have received all due Annual Progress Reports.

Level of Study: Unrestricted

Type: Project grant

Value: Up to AU$450,000

Length of Study: Up to 3 years

Frequency: Annual

Study Establishment: An approved institution in New South Wales

Country of Study: Australia

Application Procedure: Applicants must complete an application form, available on request or from the website. Applications are submitted through the researcher's institution to NHMRC. Applicants must also complete a supplementary question form and a consumer review form

Closing Date: 4 May

Funding: Private

Contributor: Community fund-raising

Additional Information: Further information is available from either the NHMRC Liaison Officer (National Cancer Research Grants Secretariat) or from Cancer Council NSW. Please check at www.cancercouncil.com.au/1221/research/research-funding-and-governance/funding-opportunities/new-grants/
www.cancercouncil.com.au/research/for-researchers/cancer-research-grants/project-grant-applications/

For further information contact:

NHMRC, GPO Box 9848, Canberra, ACT 2601, Australia.

Tel: (61) 3 9635 5028
Email: CancerCouncilGrants@cancervic.org.au

Cancer Council South Australia

202 Greenhill Road, Eastwood, SA 5063, Australia.

Tel: (61) 8291 4111
Email: cc@cancersa.org.au
Website: www.cancersa.org.au

The Cancer Council South Australia is a community-based charity independent of government control that has developed since 1928 with the support of South Australians. The Foundation's mission is to pursue the eradication of cancer through research and education on the prevention and early detection of cancer, thus enhancing the quality of life for people living with cancer.

PhD Scholarships

Purpose: To support cancer researchers in South Australia through the provision of research and senior research fellowships
Eligibility: Applicant must be a student judged to be the best applicant from University of Adelaide, Flinders University or University of South Australia, who is commencing PhD studies. The applicant must not be currently enroled in a PhD, must be eligible for the Research Training Scheme and must not have been previously enroled for a Research Degree. Students are eligible to apply for the scholarship if they are enroled in the Faculty or Division of Health Sciences at their institution and if their PhD topic is in an area of cancer research
Level of Study: Postgraduate
Type: Scholarship
Value: Equivalent to the value of the stipend for an APA award
Length of Study: 3 years
Frequency: Annual
Country of Study: Australia
Application Procedure: Applicants must contact the relevant Scholarships Offices of The University of Adelaide, University of South Australia and Flinders University for further information and closing dates

For further information contact:

Tel: (61) 8 8291 4297
Email: npolglase@cancersa.org.au

Cancer Immunotherapy

National Cancer Institute Immunotherapy Fellowship

Purpose: This fellowship provides opportunities to understand how to design, write and run clinical trials, how to treat patients, how manage toxicities, as well as opportunities to work with multiple experimental agents.
Eligibility: 1. Able to relocate to Bethesda, MD., for the duration of the fellowship 2. Trained in Medical Oncology, Hematology, Pediatric Oncology, Radiation Oncology, or Surgical Oncology 3. Interest in learning about immunotherapy 4. Preference is given to those with an academic interest 5. Open to U.S. and Non-U.S. trained physicians 6. If trained outside of North America, ECFMG certification is required
Level of Study: Research
Type: Fellowships
Value: It is based on applicable laws, regulations, and policies
Frequency: Annual
Country of Study: United States of America
Application Procedure: For further information, refer the below web link. www.sitcancer.org/funding/fellowships/2019/nci-immunotherapy-fellowship
Closing Date: 14 September
Funding: Private
Additional Information: www.sitcancer.org/funding/fellowships/2019/nci-immunotherapy-fellowship

For further information contact:

555 East Wells Street, Suite 1100, Milwaukee, WI 53202-2823, United States of America.

Email: education@sitcancer.org

SITC-Bristol Myers Squibb Postdoctoral Cancer Immunotherapy Translational Fellowship

Purpose: To support the development of the next generation of immunotherapy experts, this two -year award (24 months) aims to provide support for cancer immunotherapy by an individual who has an MD, PhD or combined MD/PhD degree and a vested interest in furthering the research and translation of cancer immunotherapy
Eligibility: 1. Current SITC member 2. Hold an MD, PhD or combined MD/PhD degree 3. Currently hold a position at an academic institution or government cancer center as a postdoctoral fellow, resident, research scientist or comparable position 4. Domestic and international applicant are eligible to apply 5. Be within postdoctoral or postgraduate

training, or no more than four years from completing such training 6. Commit 75 percent of workday to research supported by the fellowship

Level of Study: Doctorate

Type: Fellowship

Value: US$200,000 award

Length of Study: Two year

Frequency: Annual

Country of Study: Any country

Application Procedure: Applicants will submit a completed application form, applicant statement of purpose, mentor statement of support, letter of institutional support, mentor and applicant biosketches, research plan, description of facilities, and personal references (full details on application sample). Application submission will be open for five weeks.

Closing Date: 5 April

Additional Information: www.sitcancer.org/funding/fellow ships/2020/bms

SITC-Genentech Women in Cancer Immunotherapy Fellowship

Eligibility: 1. Current SITC member 2. Hold an MD, PhD or combined MD/PhD degree 3. Currently hold a position at a leading U.S. based academic cancer center as a postdoctoral fellow, resident, research scientist or comparable position 4. Be within postdoctoral or postgraduate training or no more than four years from completing such training 5. Commit 75 percent of workday to research supported by the fellowship

Level of Study: Postdoctorate

Type: Fellowship

Value: US$50,000

Frequency: Annual

Country of Study: Any country

Additional Information: www.sitcancer.org/funding/fellow ships/2020/sitc-genentech

SITC-Merck Cancer Immunotherapy Clinical Fellowship

Eligibility: 1. Current SITC member 2. Hold an MD or combined MD/PhD degree 3. Currently hold a position at a leading academic cancer center as a postdoctoral fellow, resident, research scientist or comparable position 4. Be within postdoctoral or postgraduate training, or no more than four years from completing such training 5. Commit 75 percent of workday to research supported by the fellowship.

Level of Study: Postdoctorate

Type: Fellowship

Value: US$100,000 award

Frequency: Annual

Country of Study: Any country

Closing Date: 5 April

Additional Information: www.sitcancer.org/funding/fellow ships/2020/merck

SITC-Nektar Therapeutics Equity and Inclusion in Cancer Immunotherapy Fellowship

Purpose: This one-year award aims to provide support to an individual who has an MD, PhD or combined MD/PhD degree and a vested interest in furthering the research and translation of cancer immunotherapy, as well as to encourage individuals from diverse backgrounds, including those from groups underrepresented in the biomedical and behavioural sciences, to pursue further studies or careers in research.

Eligibility: 1. Current SITC member 2. Hold an MD, PhD or combined MD/PhD degree 3. Currently hold a position at an academic institution or government cancer center as a postdoctoral fellow, resident, research scientist or comparable position 4. Domestic and international applicant are eligible to apply 5. Be within postdoctoral or postgraduate training, or no more than four years from completing such training 6. Commit 75 percent of workday to research supported by the fellowship 7 . In order to encourage diversity in the biomedical research field, applicant should self-identify ethnic minority status according to the NIH's guidance on inderrepresented Populations.

Level of Study: Postdoctorate

Type: Fellowship

Value: US$100,000

Frequency: Annual

Country of Study: Any country

Additional Information: www.sitcancer.org/funding/ fellowships

Society for Immunotherapy of Cancer - Amgen Cancer Immunotherapy in Hematologic Malignancies Fellowship Award

Purpose: This cancer immunotherapy fellowship award aims to provide support for an individual who has a vested interest in furthering the research and translation of immunotherapeutic approaches for treating patients with hematologic malignancies

Eligibility: Candidature must follow the below eligibility to obtain the fellowship award. 1. Current SITC member. 2. Hold an MD or combined MD/PhD degree. 3. Currently hold a position at a leading academic cancer center as a postdoctoral fellow, resident, research scientist or comparable position. 4. Be within postdoctoral or postgraduate training, or no more than four years from completing such training. 5. Commit 75% of workday to research supported by the fellowship

Level of Study: Professional development

Type: Award/Grant

Value: US$100,000

Length of Study: 1 year

Frequency: Annual

Country of Study: Any country

Application Procedure: The successful applicant will obtain the following benefits along with the award amount, omce they are eligible for the fellowship award. 1. Complimentary registration and travel for SITC's Annual Meeting. 2. Recognition during the Award Ceremony at SITC's Annual Meeting

Closing Date: 5 April

Funding: Private

Additional Information: www.sitcancer.org/funding/fellow ships/2019/amgen-immunotherapy-hematologic-malignancies

For further information contact:

Tel: (1) 414 271 2456
Email: development@sitcancer.org

Cancer Prevention and Research Institute of Texas - CPRIT

1701 North Congress Avenue, Suite 6-127, Austin, TX 78701, United States of America.

Tel: (1) 512 463 3190
Email: cprit@cprit.texas.gov
Website: www.cprit.state.tx.us/

Texas voters overwhelmingly approved a constitutional amendment in 2007 establishing the Cancer Prevention and Research Institute of Texas (CPRIT) and authorizing the state to issue US$3 billion in bonds to fund groundbreaking cancer research and prevention programs and services in Texas. CPRIT's goal is to expedite innovation in cancer research and product development, and to enhance access to evidence-based prevention programs throughout the state. Under the guidance of its governing body, the Oversight Committee, CPRIT accepts applications and awards grants for a wide variety of cancer-related research and for the delivery of cancer prevention programs and services by public and private entities located in Texas. All CPRIT-funded research will be conducted in state by Texas-based scientists and reflect CPRIT's mission to attract and expand the state's research capabilities and create high quality new jobs in Texas.

Individual Investigator Research Awards (IIRA)

Purpose: Supports applications for innovative research projects addressing critically important questions that will significantly advance knowledge of the causes, prevention, and/or treatment of cancer. Areas of interest include laboratory research, translational studies, and/or clinical investigations. Competitive renewal applications accepted.

Eligibility: The applicant must be a Texas-based institution of higher education or a component of a university system with appropriately accredited degree-granting training programs (if support is requested for training leading to a degree). 1. The Principal Investigator (PI) must have a doctoral degree, including MD, PhD, DDS, DMD, DrPH, DO, DVM, or equivalent, and must be a full-time resident of Texas during the time the research that is the subject of the grant is conducted. 2. An institution may submit only 1 new or renewal application under this RFA during this funding cycle. An exception will be made for institutions submitting applications for cancer prevention training; in this case, institutions may submit 1 prevention training program application and 1 additional application in another aspect of cancer research (new or renewal). 3. For the purposes of this RFA, an institution is defined as that component of a university system that has its own president. 4. There must be only 1 PI, but Co-PIs may direct individual components of the overall program described in the application. 5. An institution may apply for as many components of the training program as are appropriate for the institution. 6. An applicant is eligible to receive a grant award only if the applicant certifies that the applicant institution or organization, including the PI, any senior member or key personnel listed on the grant application, or any officer or director of the grant applicant's institution or organization (or any person related to 1 or more of these individuals within the second degree of consanguinity or affinity), has not made and will not make a contribution to CPRIT or to any foundation specifically created to benefit CPRIT. 7. An applicant is not eligible to receive a CPRIT grant award if the applicant PI, any senior member or key personnel listed on the grant application, or any officer or director of the grant applicant's organization or institution is related to a CPRIT Oversight Committee member. CPRIT RFA R-21.1-RTA Research Training Awards Page 10 of 24 (Rev 1/31/20) 8. The applicant must report whether the applicant institution or organization, the PI, or other individuals who contribute to the execution of the proposed project in a substantive, measurable way, whether or not those individuals are slated to receive salary or compensation under the grant award, are currently ineligible to receive federal grant funds or have had a grant terminated for cause within 5 years prior to the submission date of the grant application. 9. CPRIT grants will be awarded by contract to successful applicants. Certain contractual requirements are mandated by Texas law or by administrative rules. Although applicants need not demonstrate the ability to comply with these contractual requirements at the time the application is submitted, applicants should make themselves aware of these standards before submitting a grant application. Significant issues addressed by the CPRIT contract are listed in section 10 and section 11. All statutory provisions and relevant administrative rules can be found at www.cprit.state.tx.us.

Level of Study: Masters

Type: Scholarships

Value: Award Up to US$300,000 per year in total costs. Exceptions permitted if extremely well justified;

Length of Study: 3 years

Country of Study: United States of America

Application Procedure: Each application must be accompanied by a letter of institutional support from the president or provost indicating support and commitment to the training program. The letter could include, but is not limited to, information about laboratory space, shared laboratory facilities and equipment, funds for curriculum development, support for additional trainees in the program, and initiatives to support recruitment of underrepresented minorities. A maximum of 3 pages may be provided. Applications that are missing 1 or more of these components, exceed the specified page, word, or budget limits, or that do not meet the eligibility requirements listed above will be administratively rejected without review. Formatting guidelines for all submitted CPRIT applications are as follows 1. Language English. 2. Document Format PDF only. 3. Font Type/Size Arial (11 point), Calibri (11 point), or Times New Roman (12 point). 4. Line Spacing Single. 5. Page Size 8.5 x 11 inches. 6. Margins 0.75 inch, all directions. 7. Color and High-Resolution Images Images, graphs, figures, and other illustrations must be submitted as part of the appropriate submitted document. Applicants should include text to explain illustrations that may be difficult to interpret when printed in black and white. CPRIT RFA R-21.1-RTA Research Training Awards Page 17 of 24 (Rev 1/31/20) 8. Scanning Resolution Images and figures must be of lowest reasonable resolution that permits clarity and readability. Unnecessarily large files will NOT be accepted, especially those that include only text. 9. References Applicants should use a citation style that includes the full name of the article and that lists at least the first 3 authors. Official journal abbreviations may be used. An example is included below; however, other citation styles meeting these parameters are also acceptable as long as the journal information is stated. Include URLs of publications referenced in the application. Smith, P.T., Doe, J., White, J.M., et al (2006). Elaborating on

a novel mechanism for cancer progression. Journal of Cancer Research, 135 45-67. 10. Internet URLs Applicants are encouraged to provide the URLs of publications referenced in the application; however, applicants should not include URLs directing reviewers to websites containing additional information about the proposed research. 11. Headers and Footers These should not be used unless they are part of a provided template. Page numbers may be included in the footer (see following point). 12. Page Numbering Pages should be numbered at the bottom right corner of each page. 13. All attachments that require signatures must be filled out, printed, signed, scanned, and then uploaded in PDF format

Closing Date: 14 January

Additional Information: www.cprit.texas.gov/media/2441/rfa_r_221-iira.pdf

Individual Investigator Research Awards for Cancer in Children and Adolescents (IIRACCA)

Purpose: Supports applications for innovative research projects addressing questions that will advance knowledge of the causes, prevention, progression, detection, or treatment of cancer in children and adolescents. Laboratory, clinical, or population-based studies are all acceptable. CPRIT expects the outcome of the research to reduce the incidence, morbidity, or mortality from cancer in children and/or adolescents in the near or long term. Competitive renewal applications accepted.

Eligibility: The applicant must be a Texas-based institution of higher education or a component of a university system with appropriately accredited degree-granting training programs (if support is requested for training leading to a degree). 1. The Principal Investigator (PI) must have a doctoral degree, including MD, PhD, DDS, DMD, DrPH, DO, DVM, or equivalent, and must be a full-time resident of Texas during the time the research that is the subject of the grant is conducted. 2. An institution may submit only 1 new or renewal application under this RFA during this funding cycle. An exception will be made for institutions submitting applications for cancer prevention training; in this case, institutions may submit 1 prevention training program application and 1 additional application in another aspect of cancer research (new or renewal). 3. For the purposes of this RFA, an institution is defined as that component of a university system that has its own president. 4. There must be only 1 PI, but Co-PIs may direct individual components of the overall program described in the application. 5. An institution may apply for as many components of the training program as are appropriate for the institution. 6. An applicant is eligible to receive a grant award only if the applicant certifies that the applicant institution or organization, including the PI, any senior member or key personnel listed on the grant application, or any officer or director of the grant applicant's institution or organization (or any person related to 1 or more of these individuals within the second degree of consanguinity or affinity), has not made and will not make a contribution to CPRIT or to any foundation specifically created to benefit CPRIT. 7. An applicant is not eligible to receive a CPRIT grant award if the applicant PI, any senior member or key personnel listed on the grant application, or any officer or director of the grant applicant's organization or institution is related to a CPRIT Oversight Committee member. CPRIT RFA R-21.1-RTA Research Training Awards Page 10 of 24 (Rev 1/31/20) 8. The applicant must report whether the applicant institution or organization, the PI, or other individuals who contribute to the execution of the proposed project in a substantive, measurable way, whether or not those individuals are slated to receive salary or compensation under the grant award, are currently ineligible to receive federal grant funds or have had a grant terminated for cause within 5 years prior to the submission date of the grant application. 9. CPRIT grants will be awarded by contract to successful applicants. Certain contractual requirements are mandated by Texas law or by administrative rules. Although applicants need not demonstrate the ability to comply with these contractual requirements at the time the application is submitted, applicants should make themselves aware of these standards before submitting a grant application. Significant issues addressed by the CPRIT contract are listed in section 10 and section 11. All statutory provisions and relevant administrative rules can be found at www.cprit.state.tx.us.

Level of Study: Masters

Type: Scholarships

Value: Up to US$350,000 per year. Applicants that plan on conducting a clinical trial as part of the project may request up to US$500,000 in total costs. Exceptions permitted if extremely well justified.

Length of Study: 4 years+

Country of Study: United States of America

Application Procedure: Each application must be accompanied by a letter of institutional support from the president or provost indicating support and commitment to the training program. The letter could include, but is not limited to, information about laboratory space, shared laboratory facilities and equipment, funds for curriculum development, support for additional trainees in the program, and initiatives to support recruitment of underrepresented minorities. A maximum of 3 pages may be provided. Applications that are missing 1 or more of these components, exceed the specified page, word, or budget limits, or that do not meet the eligibility requirements listed above will be administratively rejected without review. Formatting guidelines for all submitted CPRIT applications are as follows 1. Language English. 2. Document Format PDF only. 3. Font Type/Size Arial (11 point), Calibri (11 point), or Times New Roman

(12 point). 4. Line Spacing Single. 5. Page Size 8.5 x 11 inches. 6. Margins 0.75 inch, all directions. 7. Color and High-Resolution Images Images, graphs, figures, and other illustrations must be submitted as part of the appropriate submitted document. Applicants should include text to explain illustrations that may be difficult to interpret when printed in black and white. CPRIT RFA R-21.1-RTA Research Training Awards Page 17 of 24 (Rev 1/31/20) 8. Scanning Resolution Images and figures must be of lowest reasonable resolution that permits clarity and readability. Unnecessarily large files will NOT be accepted, especially those that include only text. 9. References Applicants should use a citation style that includes the full name of the article and that lists at least the first 3 authors. Official journal abbreviations may be used. An example is included below; however, other citation styles meeting these parameters are also acceptable as long as the journal information is stated. Include URLs of publications referenced in the application. Smith, P.T., Doe, J., White, J.M., et al (2006). Elaborating on a novel mechanism for cancer progression. Journal of Cancer Research, 135 45-67. 10. Internet URLs Applicants are encouraged to provide the URLs of publications referenced in the application; however, applicants should not include URLs directing reviewers to websites containing additional information about the proposed research. 11. Headers and Footers These should not be used unless they are part of a provided template. Page numbers may be included in the footer (see following point). 12. Page Numbering Pages should be numbered at the bottom right corner of each page. 13. All attachments that require signatures must be filled out, printed, signed, scanned, and then uploaded in PDF format

Closing Date: 14 January

Additional Information: www.cprit.state.tx.us/media/2665/rfa-r-231-iiracca.pdf

Individual Investigator Research Awards for Clinical Translation (IIRACT)

Purpose: Supports applications which propose innovative clinical studies that are hypothesis driven and involve patients enrolled prospectively on a clinical trial or involve analyses of biospecimens from patients enrolled on a completed trial for which the outcomes are known. Areas of interest include clinical studies of new or repurposed drugs, hormonal therapies, immune therapies, surgery, radiation therapy, stem cell transplantation, combinations of interventions, or therapeutic devices.

Eligibility: The applicant must be a Texas-based institution of higher education or a component of a university system with appropriately accredited degree-granting training programs (if support is requested for training leading to a degree). 1. The Principal Investigator (PI) must have a doctoral degree, including MD, PhD, DDS, DMD, DrPH, DO, DVM, or equivalent, and must be a full-time resident of Texas during the time the research that is the subject of the grant is conducted. 2. An institution may submit only 1 new or renewal application under this RFA during this funding cycle. An exception will be made for institutions submitting applications for cancer prevention training; in this case, institutions may submit 1 prevention training program application and 1 additional application in another aspect of cancer research (new or renewal). 3. For the purposes of this RFA, an institution is defined as that component of a university system that has its own president. 4. There must be only 1 PI, but Co-PIs may direct individual components of the overall program described in the application. 5. An institution may apply for as many components of the training program as are appropriate for the institution. 6. An applicant is eligible to receive a grant award only if the applicant certifies that the applicant institution or organization, including the PI, any senior member or key personnel listed on the grant application, or any officer or director of the grant applicant's institution or organization (or any person related to 1 or more of these individuals within the second degree of consanguinity or affinity), has not made and will not make a contribution to CPRIT or to any foundation specifically created to benefit CPRIT. 7. An applicant is not eligible to receive a CPRIT grant award if the applicant PI, any senior member or key personnel listed on the grant application, or any officer or director of the grant applicant's organization or institution is related to a CPRIT Oversight Committee member. CPRIT RFA R-21.1-RTA Research Training Awards Page 10 of 24 (Rev 1/31/20) 8. The applicant must report whether the applicant institution or organization, the PI, or other individuals who contribute to the execution of the proposed project in a substantive, measurable way, whether or not those individuals are slated to receive salary or compensation under the grant award, are currently ineligible to receive federal grant funds or have had a grant terminated for cause within 5 years prior to the submission date of the grant application. 9. CPRIT grants will be awarded by contract to successful applicants. Certain contractual requirements are mandated by Texas law or by administrative rules. Although applicants need not demonstrate the ability to comply with these contractual requirements at the time the application is submitted, applicants should make themselves aware of these standards before submitting a grant application. Significant issues addressed by the CPRIT contract are listed in section 10 and section 11. All statutory provisions and relevant administrative rules can be found at www.cprit.state.tx.us.

Level of Study: Masters

Type: Scholarships

Value: Award Up to US$500,000 per year

Length of Study: 4 years

Country of Study: United States of America

Application Procedure: Each application must be accompanied by a letter of institutional support from the president or provost indicating support and commitment to the training program. The letter could include, but is not limited to, information about laboratory space, shared laboratory facilities and equipment, funds for curriculum development, support for additional trainees in the program, and initiatives to support recruitment of underrepresented minorities. A maximum of 3 pages may be provided. Applications that are missing 1 or more of these components, exceed the specified page, word, or budget limits, or that do not meet the eligibility requirements listed above will be administratively rejected without review. Formatting guidelines for all submitted CPRIT applications are as follows 1. Language English. 2. Document Format PDF only. 3. Font Type/Size Arial (11 point), Calibri (11 point), or Times New Roman (12 point). 4. Line Spacing Single. 5. Page Size 8.5 x 11 inches. 6. Margins 0.75 inch, all directions. 7. Color and High-Resolution Images Images, graphs, figures, and other illustrations must be submitted as part of the appropriate submitted document. Applicants should include text to explain illustrations that may be difficult to interpret when printed in black and white. CPRIT RFA R-21.1-RTA Research Training Awards Page 17 of 24 (Rev 1/31/20) 8. Scanning Resolution Images and figures must be of lowest reasonable resolution that permits clarity and readability. Unnecessarily large files will NOT be accepted, especially those that include only text. 9. References Applicants should use a citation style that includes the full name of the article and that lists at least the first 3 authors. Official journal abbreviations may be used. An example is included below; however, other citation styles meeting these parameters are also acceptable as long as the journal information is stated. Include URLs of publications referenced in the application. Smith, P.T., Doe, J., White, J. M., et al (2006). Elaborating on a novel mechanism for cancer progression. Journal of Cancer Research, 135 45-67. 10. Internet URLs Applicants are encouraged to provide the URLs of publications referenced in the application; however, applicants should not include URLs directing reviewers to websites containing additional information about the proposed research. 11. Headers and Footers These should not be used unless they are part of a provided template. Page numbers may be included in the footer (see following point). 12. Page Numbering Pages should be numbered at the bottom right corner of each page. 13. All attachments that require signatures must be filled out, printed, signed, scanned, and then uploaded in PDF format

Closing Date: 2 June

Additional Information: www.cprit.state.tx.us/funding-opportunities

Individual Investigator Research Awards for Computational Systems Biology of Cancer (IIRACSBC)

Purpose: Supports applications for innovative mathematical and/or computational research projects addressing questions that will advance current knowledge in the (a) mechanisms that tie altered gene expression and downstream molecular mechanisms to functional cancer phenotypes and/or (b) mechanisms that tie tumor morphology to functional cancer phenotypes, and/or (c) mechanisms that tie treatment sequence and combination to evolving functional cancer phenotypes (that emerge as a result of treatment selection). Broadly speaking, functional cancer phenotypes include migratory, proliferative, metabolic and resistant cancer cell phenotypes. Partnering of mathematical or computational scientists with cancer biologists or oncologists is highly recommended to form a truly interdisciplinary team that can both develop and validate models leading to a deeper integrated understanding of cancer progression and treatment.

Eligibility: The applicant must be a Texas-based institution of higher education or a component of a university system with appropriately accredited degree-granting training programs (if support is requested for training leading to a degree). 1. The Principal Investigator (PI) must have a doctoral degree, including MD, PhD, DDS, DMD, DrPH, DO, DVM, or equivalent, and must be a full-time resident of Texas during the time the research that is the subject of the grant is conducted. 2. An institution may submit only 1 new or renewal application under this RFA during this funding cycle. An exception will be made for institutions submitting applications for cancer prevention training; in this case, institutions may submit 1 prevention training program application and 1 additional application in another aspect of cancer research (new or renewal). 3. For the purposes of this RFA, an institution is defined as that component of a university system that has its own president. 4. There must be only 1 PI, but Co-PIs may direct individual components of the overall program described in the application. 5. An institution may apply for as many components of the training program as are appropriate for the institution. 6. An applicant is eligible to receive a grant award only if the applicant certifies that the applicant institution or organization, including the PI, any senior member or key personnel listed on the grant application, or any officer or director of the grant applicant's institution or organization (or any person related to 1 or more of these individuals within the second degree of consanguinity or affinity), has not made and will not make a contribution to CPRIT or to any foundation specifically created to benefit CPRIT. 7. An applicant is not eligible to receive a CPRIT grant award if the applicant PI, any senior member or key personnel listed on the grant application, or any officer or director of the grant applicant's organization or institution is related to a CPRIT Oversight Committee member. CPRIT RFA R-21.1-RTA Research Training Awards Page 10 of 24 (Rev 1/31/20) 8. The applicant must report whether the applicant institution or organization, the PI, or other individuals who contribute to the execution of the proposed project in a substantive, measurable way, whether or not those individuals are slated to receive salary or compensation under the grant award, are currently ineligible to receive federal grant funds or have had a grant terminated for cause within 5 years prior to the submission date of the grant application. 9. CPRIT grants will be awarded by contract to successful applicants. Certain contractual requirements are mandated by Texas law or by administrative rules. Although applicants need not demonstrate the ability to comply with these contractual requirements at the time the application is submitted, applicants should make themselves aware of these standards before submitting a grant application. Significant issues addressed by the CPRIT contract are listed in section 10 and section 11. All statutory provisions and relevant administrative rules can be found at www.cprit.state.tx.us.

Level of Study: Masters

Type: Scholarships

Value: Award Up to US$400,000 per year. Exceptions permitted if extremely well justified.

Length of Study: 4 years

Country of Study: United States of America

Application Procedure: Each application must be accompanied by a letter of institutional support from the president or provost indicating support and commitment to the training program. The letter could include, but is not limited to, information about laboratory space, shared laboratory facilities and equipment, funds for curriculum development, support for additional trainees in the program, and initiatives to support recruitment of underrepresented minorities. A maximum of 3 pages may be provided. Applications that are missing 1 or more of these components, exceed the specified page, word, or budget limits, or that do not meet the eligibility requirements listed above will be administratively rejected without review. Formatting guidelines for all submitted CPRIT applications are as follows 1. Language English. 2. Document Format PDF only. 3. Font Type/Size Arial (11 point), Calibri (11 point), or Times New Roman (12 point). 4. Line Spacing Single. 5. Page Size 8.5 x 11 inches. 6. Margins 0.75 inch, all directions. 7. Color and High-Resolution Images Images, graphs, figures, and other illustrations must be submitted as part of the appropriate submitted document. Applicants should include text to explain illustrations that may be difficult to interpret when printed in black and white. CPRIT RFA R-21.1-RTA Research Training Awards Page 17 of 24 (Rev 1/31/20) 8. Scanning Resolution Images and figures must be of lowest reasonable resolution that permits clarity and readability. Unnecessarily large files will NOT be accepted, especially those that include only text. 9. References Applicants should use a citation style that includes the full name of the article and that lists at least the first 3 authors. Official journal abbreviations may be used. An example is included below; however, other citation styles meeting these parameters are also acceptable as long as the journal information is stated. Include URLs of publications referenced in the application. Smith, P.T., Doe, J., White, J.M., et al (2006). Elaborating on a novel mechanism for cancer progression. Journal of Cancer Research, 135 45-67. 10. Internet URLs Applicants are encouraged to provide the URLs of publications referenced in the application; however, applicants should not include URLs directing reviewers to websites containing additional information about the proposed research. 11. Headers and Footers These should not be used unless they are part of a provided template. Page numbers may be included in the footer (see following point). 12. Page Numbering Pages should be numbered at the bottom right corner of each page. 13. All attachments that require signatures must be filled out, printed, signed, scanned, and then uploaded in PDF format

Closing Date: 8 June

Additional Information: www.cprit.state.tx.us/funding-opportunities

Individual Investigator Research Awards for Prevention and Early Detection (IIRAP)

Purpose: Supports applications for innovative research projects addressing questions that will advance knowledge of the causes, prevention, early-stage progression, and/or early detection of cancer. Research may be laboratory-, clinical-, or population- based, and may include behavioral/intervention, dissemination or health services/outcomes research to reduce cancer incidence or promote early detection. Competitive renewal applications accepted.

Eligibility: The applicant must be a Texas-based institution of higher education or a component of a university system with appropriately accredited degree-granting training programs (if support is requested for training leading to a degree). 1. The Principal Investigator (PI) must have a doctoral degree, including MD, PhD, DDS, DMD, DrPH, DO, DVM, or equivalent, and must be a full-time resident of Texas during the time the research that is the subject of the grant is conducted. 2. An institution may submit only 1 new or renewal application under this RFA during this funding cycle. An exception will be made for institutions submitting applications for cancer prevention training; in this case, institutions may submit 1 prevention training program application and 1 additional application in another aspect of cancer research (new or renewal). 3. For the purposes of this RFA, an institution is defined as that component of a university system that has its own president. 4. There must be only 1 PI, but Co-PIs may direct individual components of the overall program described in the application. 5. An institution may apply for as many components of the training program as are appropriate for the institution. 6. An applicant is eligible to receive a grant award only if the applicant certifies that the applicant institution or organization, including the PI, any senior member or key personnel listed on the grant application, or any officer or director of the grant applicant's

institution or organization (or any person related to 1 or more of these individuals within the second degree of consanguinity or affinity), has not made and will not make a contribution to CPRIT or to any foundation specifically created to benefit CPRIT. 7. An applicant is not eligible to receive a CPRIT grant award if the applicant PI, any senior member or key personnel listed on the grant application, or any officer or director of the grant applicant's organization or institution is related to a CPRIT Oversight Committee member. CPRIT RFA R-21.1-RTA Research Training Awards Page 10 of 24 (Rev 1/31/20) 8. The applicant must report whether the applicant institution or organization, the PI, or other individuals who contribute to the execution of the proposed project in a substantive, measurable way, whether or not those individuals are slated to receive salary or compensation under the grant award, are currently ineligible to receive federal grant funds or have had a grant terminated for cause within 5 years prior to the submission date of the grant application. 9. CPRIT grants will be awarded by contract to successful applicants. Certain contractual requirements are mandated by Texas law or by administrative rules. Although applicants need not demonstrate the ability to comply with these contractual requirements at the time the application is submitted, applicants should make themselves aware of these standards before submitting a grant application. Significant issues addressed by the CPRIT contract are listed in section 10 and section 11. All statutory provisions and relevant administrative rules can be found at www.cprit.state.tx.us.

Level of Study: Masters

Type: Scholarships

Value: Up to US$400,000 per year. Exceptions permitted if extremely well justified;

Length of Study: 5 years

Country of Study: United States of America

Application Procedure: Each application must be accompanied by a letter of institutional support from the president or provost indicating support and commitment to the training program. The letter could include, but is not limited to, information about laboratory space, shared laboratory facilities and equipment, funds for curriculum development, support for additional trainees in the program, and initiatives to support recruitment of underrepresented minorities. A maximum of 3 pages may be provided. Applications that are missing 1 or more of these components, exceed the specified page, word, or budget limits, or that do not meet the eligibility requirements listed above will be administratively rejected without review. Formatting guidelines for all submitted CPRIT applications are as follows 1. Language English. 2. Document Format PDF only. 3. Font Type/Size Arial (11 point), Calibri (11 point), or Times New Roman (12 point). 4. Line Spacing Single. 5. Page Size 8.5 x 11 inches. 6. Margins 0.75 inch, all directions. 7. Color and High-Resolution Images Images, graphs, figures, and other illustrations must be submitted as part of the appropriate submitted document. Applicants should include text to explain illustrations that may be difficult to interpret when printed in black and white. CPRIT RFA R-21.1-RTA Research Training Awards Page 17 of 24 (Rev 1/31/20) 8. Scanning Resolution Images and figures must be of lowest reasonable resolution that permits clarity and readability. Unnecessarily large files will NOT be accepted, especially those that include only text. 9. References Applicants should use a citation style that includes the full name of the article and that lists at least the first 3 authors. Official journal abbreviations may be used. An example is included below; however, other citation styles meeting these parameters are also acceptable as long as the journal information is stated. Include URLs of publications referenced in the application. Smith, P.T., Doe, J., White, J.M., et al (2006). Elaborating on a novel mechanism for cancer progression. Journal of Cancer Research, 135 45-67. 10. Internet URLs Applicants are encouraged to provide the URLs of publications referenced in the application; however, applicants should not include URLs directing reviewers to websites containing additional information about the proposed research. 11. Headers and Footers These should not be used unless they are part of a provided template. Page numbers may be included in the footer (see following point). 12. Page Numbering Pages should be numbered at the bottom right corner of each page. 13. All attachments that require signatures must be filled out, printed, signed, scanned, and then uploaded in PDF format

Closing Date: 8 June

Additional Information: cpritgrants.org/

Recruitment of Established Investigators

Eligibility: 1. The applicant must be a Texas-based entity. Any not-for-profit institution that conducts research is eligible to apply for funding under this award mechanism. A public or private company is not eligible for funding under this award mechanism. 2. Candidates must be nominated by the president, provost, vice president for research, or appropriate dean of a Texas-based public or private institution of higher education, including academic health institutions. The application must be submitted on behalf of a specific candidate. 3. A candidate may be nominated by only 1 institution. If more than 1 institution is interested in a given candidate, negotiations as to which institution will nominate him or her must be concluded before the nomination is made. 4. There is no limit to the number of applications that an institution may submit during a review cycle. 5. A candidate who has already accepted a position at the recruiting institution prior to the time that the Scientific Review Council reviews the candidate for a recruitment award is not eligible for a recruitment award, as an investment by CPRIT is obviously not necessary. No

award is final until approved by the Oversight Committee at a public review decision following the Review Council meeting. If a position is offered to the candidate during the period following the Scientific Review Council's review decision but prior to the Oversight Committee's final approval, the institution does so at its own risk. There is no guarantee that the recruitment award will be approved by the Oversight Committee. 6. The candidate must have a doctoral degree, including MD, PhD, DDS, DMD, DrPH, DO, DVM, or equivalent, and reside in Texas for the duration of the appointment. The candidate must devote at least 70% time to research activities. Candidates whose major responsibilities are clinical care, teaching, or administration are not eligible. 7. At the time of the application, the candidate should hold an appointment at the rank of professor (or equivalent) at an accredited academic institution, research institution, industry, government agency, or private foundation. The candidate must not reside in Texas at the time the application is submitted. 8. An applicant is eligible to receive a grant award only if the applicant certifies that the applicant institution or organization, including the nominator, any senior member or key personnel listed on the grant application, or any officer or director of the grant applicant's institution or organization (or any person related to 1 or more of these individuals within the second degree of consanguinity or affinity), has not made and will not make a contribution to CPRIT or to any foundation specifically created to benefit CPRIT. 9. An applicant is not eligible to receive a CPRIT grant award if the applicant nominator, any senior member or key personnel listed on the grant application, or any officer or director of the grant applicant's institution or organization is related to a CPRIT Oversight Committee member. 10. The applicant must report whether the applicant institution or organization, the nominator, or other individuals who contribute to the execution of the proposed project in a substantive, measurable way, whether or not the individuals will receive salary or compensation under the grant award, are currently ineligible to receive federal grant funds or have had a grant terminated for cause within 5 years prior to the submission date of the grant application meeting. However, in recognition of the timeline involved with recruiting highly soughtafter candidates who are often considering multiple offers, CPRIT's Academic Research program staff will notify the nominating institution of the Scientific Review Council's.

Level of Study: Faculty

Type: Award

Value: Up to US$6 million

Length of Study: 5 years

Frequency: Annual

Country of Study: United States of America

Closing Date: 20 June

Additional Information: www.cprit.state.tx.us/media/2539/rfa_r-221-rei.pdf

Research Training Awards (RTA)

Purpose: Supports applications for integrated institutional research training programs to support promising individuals who seek specialized training in the area of cancer research. Successful applicant institutions are expected to provide trainees with broad access to research opportunities across disciplinary lines and to maintain high standards for intellectual rigor and creativity.

Eligibility: The applicant must be a Texas-based institution of higher education or a component of a university system with appropriately accredited degree-granting training programs (if support is requested for training leading to a degree). 1. The Principal Investigator (PI) must have a doctoral degree, including MD, PhD, DDS, DMD, DrPH, DO, DVM, or equivalent, and must be a full-time resident of Texas during the time the research that is the subject of the grant is conducted. 2. An institution may submit only 1 new or renewal application under this RFA during this funding cycle. An exception will be made for institutions submitting applications forcancer prevention training; in this case, institutions may submit 1 prevention traininga program application and 1 additional application in another aspect of cancer research (new or renewal). 3. For the purposes of this RFA, an institution is defined as that component of a university system that has its own president. 4. There must be only 1 PI, but Co-PIs may direct individual components of the overall program described in the application. 5. An institution may apply for as many components of the training program as are appropriate for the institution. 6. An applicant is eligible to receive a grant award only if the applicant certifies that the applicant institution or organization, including the PI, any senior member or key personnel listed on the grant application, or any officer or director of the grant applicant's institution or organization (or any person related to 1 or more of these individuals within the second degree of consanguinity or affinity), has not made and will not make a contribution to CPRIT or to any foundation specifically created to benefit CPRIT. 7. An applicant is not eligible to receive a CPRIT grant award if the applicant PI, any senior member or key personnel listed on the grant application, or any officer or director of the grant applicant's organization or institution is related to a CPRIT Oversight Committee member. CPRIT RFA R-21.1-RTA Research Training Awards Page 10 of 24 (Rev 1/31/20) 8. The applicant must report whether the applicant institution or organization, the PI, or other individuals who contribute to the execution of the proposed project in a substantive, measurable way, whether or not those individuals are slated to receive salary or compensation under the grant award, are currently ineligible to receive federal grant funds or have had a grant terminated for cause within 5 years prior to the submission date of the grant application. 9. CPRIT grants will be awarded by contract to successful applicants. Certain contractual requirements are mandated by Texas law or by administrative rules. Although applicants need not demonstrate the ability to comply with these contractual requirements at the time the application is submitted, applicants should make themselves aware of these standards before submitting a grant application. Significant issues addressed by the CPRIT contract are listed in section 10 and section 11. All statutory provisions and relevant administrative rules can be found at www.cprit.state.tx.us.

Level of Study: Masters

Type: Scholarships

Value: Up to US$800,000 per year in total costs

Length of Study: 5 years

Country of Study: United States of America

Application Procedure: Each application must be accompanied by a letter of institutional support from the president or provost indicating support and commitment to the training program. The letter could include, but is not limited to, information about laboratory space, shared laboratory facilities and equipment, funds for curriculum development, support for additional trainees in the program, and initiatives to support recruitment of underrepresented minorities. A maximum of 3 pages may be provided. Applications that are missing 1 or more of these components, exceed the specified page, word, or budget limits, or that do not meet the eligibility requirements listed above will be administratively rejected without review. Formatting guidelines for all submitted CPRIT applications are as follows 1. Language English. 2. Document Format PDF only. 3. Font Type/Size Arial (11 point), Calibri (11 point), or Times New Roman (12 point). 4. Line Spacing Single. 5. Page Size 8.5 x 11 inches. 6. Margins 0.75 inch, all directions. 7. Color and High-Resolution Images Images, graphs, figures, and other illustrations must be submitted as part of the appropriate submitted document. Applicants should include text to explain illustrations that may be difficult to interpret when printed in black and white. CPRIT RFA R-21.1-RTA Research Training Awards Page 17 of 24 (Rev 1/31/20) 1. Scanning Resolution Images and figures must be of lowest reasonable resolution that permits clarity and readability. Unnecessarily large files will NOT be accepted, especially those that include only text. 2. References Applicants should use a citation style that includes the full name of the article and that lists at least the first 3 authors. Official journal abbreviations may be used. An example is included below; however, other citation styles meeting these parameters are also acceptable as long as the journal information is stated. Include URLs of publications referenced in the application. Smith, P.T., Doe, J., White, J.M., et al (2006). Elaborating on a novel mechanism for cancer progression. Journal of Cancer Research, 135 45-67. 3. Internet URLs Applicants are encouraged to provide the URLs of publications referenced in the application; however, applicants should not include URLs directing reviewers to websites containing additional information about the proposed research. 4. Headers and Footers These should not be used unless they are part of a provided template. Page numbers may be included in the footer (see following point). 5. Page Numbering Pages should be numbered at the bottom right corner of each page. 6. All attachments that require signatures must be filled out, printed, signed, scanned, and then uploaded in PDF format

Closing Date: 28 October

Additional Information: cpritgrants.org/

Texas Regional Excellence in Cancer Award

Eligibility: 1. Applicants must complete a preapplication process (see section 8.1).2. An institution may submit only 1 application under this RFA during this funding cycle. For purposes of this RFA, an institution is defined as that component of a university system that has a President. 3. An institution with an active TREC award from CRPIT is not eligible to respond to this RFA. 4. A university and a health science center that are components of the same university system and share a contiguous or near-contiguous campus are strongly encouraged to submit a single application that will leverage their combined assets to build a cancer research program to serve their region. 5. Academic health science centers with multiple campuses are eligible to participate in a single application under this RFA. 6. The Principal Investigator (PI) must be the director of the center and must have a doctoral degree, including MD, PhD, DDS, DMD, DrPH, DO, DVM, or equivalent, and must reside in Texas during the time the research that is the subject of the grant is conducted. The PI should hold a full-time faculty position, at the level of associate or full professor or the equivalent. Ideally, an institution will identify an established investigator with a record of peer-reviewed funding to lead the TREC. 7. This award must be directed by the PI. Multiple PIs are not permitted. 8. TREC PI, research project leaders, and core resource must be located on a TREC-eligible campus located 100 miles or greater from an existing NCI-designated cancer center. 9. Collaborations with Texas-based institutions to provide access to technology and counsel are permitted and can be supported with TREC funds through subcontracts. Texas institutions are eligible to hold subcontracts with multiple TREC grantees. 10. Collaborators may or may not reside in Texas; however, collaborators who do not reside in Texas are not eligible to receive CPRIT funds. Collaborators should have specific and well-defined roles. Subcontracting and collaborating organizations may include public, not-for-profit, and for-profit entities. Such entities may be located outside of the State of Texas, but non-Texas-based organizations are not eligible to receive CPRIT funds. In no event shall equipment purchased under this award leave the State of Texas.

Type: Award

Value: US$6,000,000

Length of Study: 5 years

Country of Study: Any country

Closing Date: 8 September

Additional Information: cpritgrants.org/Current_Funding_ Opportunities/index.cfm?prg=CPRITR&prg_fy=2023

Cancer Research Fund of the Damon Runyon-Walter Winchell Foundation

Fellowship Department, 131 East 36th Street, New York, NY 10016, United States of America.

Tel: (1) 212 532 3888

Email: drwwfellow@aol.com

Contact: Ms Clare M Cahill, Assistant to the Director

Cancer Research Fund of the Damon Runyon - Walter Winchell Foundation Research Fellowships for Physician Scientists

Purpose: To augment the training of a physician scientist who has demonstrated the motivation and potential to conduct original research under the supervision of a sponsor, thus, equipping the Fellow to become an independent investigator

Eligibility: Applicants must have completed at least one of the following degrees or its equivalent MD, PhD, DDS, DVM, and have completed their residencies or clinical fellowship training within three years prior to the Scientific Advisory Committee meeting at which their applications are to be considered

Level of Study: Postdoctorate

Type: Fellowship

Value: US$46,500 stipend for the first year, US$47,500 for the second year and US$49,000 for the third year. In addition, US$2,000 expenses is awarded annually

Length of Study: 3 years, renewable annually

Frequency: 3 times each year

Study Establishment: An approved institution under a sponsor

Application Procedure: Application form must be completed

No. of awards offered: 700

No. of awards given last year: 45

No. of applicants last year: 700

For further information contact:

Email: awards@damonrunyon.org

Damon Runyon Clinical Investigator Award

Purpose: The Damon Runyon Clinical Investigator Award supports early career physician-scientists conducting patient-oriented research. The goal of this innovative program is to increase the number of physicians capable of moving seamlessly between the laboratory and the patient's bedside in search of breakthrough treatments. Damon Runyon Clinical Investigators are eligible to apply for Continuation Grants in the final year of their award.

Eligibility: 1. The applicant must be a U.S. citizen or permanent legal resident. 2. The applicant must hold an independent assistant professor position or equivalent. 3. Each applicant must be nominated by their institution. Applications will only be accepted from institutions that have been invited to submit them by the Foundation (See list). Five (5) nominations per institution, including its affiliated schools, will be accepted. 4. The applicant must have received an MD, DO, or MD/PhD degree(s) from an accredited institution, completed their subspecialty training and be U.S. Board eligible. 5. The applicant must hold a valid, active U.S. medical license at the time of application. 6. The applicant must apply within the first five (5) years of their initial full faculty appointment (Cut-off date: July 1, 2017). Adjunct or acting positions are not eligible. 7. Candidates holding or awarded R01s (or R01-equivalent grants such as the DP2 and DP5) at the time of application are not eligible to apply. 8. The applicant must commit to spending 80% of their time conducting research. [In rare unique circumstances, the CIA Committee may consider an applicant with a very modest reduction of 80% protected time if their Department Chair can provide a compelling reason explaining why a waiver of the 80% requirement should be granted, what percentage of effort will be guaranteed, and what safeguards will be put in place to make sure the individual's research will not be compromised by their clinical/administrative activities.] 9. The applicant is required to apply in conjunction with a Mentor who is established in the field of clinical translational cancer research, cancer prevention and/or epidemiology and can provide the critical guidance needed during the period of the award. No more than two Damon Runyon Clinical Investigators will be funded to work with the same Mentor at any given time (including Co-Mentors). 10. Candidates may apply up to two times during this eligibility period. 1. Only one application will be accepted from a Mentor per review session (including Co-Mentors).

Level of Study: Postdoctorate

Type: Award

Value: The US$600,000 award will be for a period of three years. Funding in the amount of US$200,000 will be allocated to the awardee's institution each year for the support of the Clinical Investigaton

Length of Study: 3 years

Country of Study: United States of America

Closing Date: 1 February

Additional Information: www.damonrunyon.org/for-scientists/application-guidelines/clinical-investigator

For further information contact:

Email: awards@damonrunyon.org

Cancer Research Institute

681 Fifth Avenue, New York, NY 10022-2707, United States of America.

Email: info@cancerresearch.org
Website: www.cancerresearch.org
Contact: Grants Enquiries

Cancer Research Institute Irvington Postdoctoral Fellowship Program

Purpose: The CRI Irvington Postdoctoral Fellowship Program supports qualified young scientists at leading universities and research centers around the world who wish to receive training in fundamental immunology or cancer immunology

Eligibility: Applicants for the CRI Irvington Postdoctoral Fellowship Program must be working in areas directly related to immunology or cancer immunology. An eligible project must fall into the broad field of immunology with relevance to solving the cancer problem. Applicants must have a doctoral degree by the date of award activation and must conduct their proposed research under a sponsor who holds a formal appointment at the host institution. Applicants with 5 or more years of relevant postdoctoral experience are not eligible, with the exception of M.D. applicants, who should not include years of residency in this calculation. Only in exceptional circumstances will applicants who have already spent 3 or more years in a sponsor's laboratory by the start date of fellowship be considered for a fellowship award. The fellowship can be performed in the United States or abroad, but must take place at a non-profit institution. There are no citizenship restrictions. Only one fellow per sponsor may apply per application round, and faculty sponsors may not have more than three CRI-supported fellows at any time

Level of Study: Doctorate, Postdoctorate

Type: Fellowships

Value: US$55,000 for the first year, US$57,000 for the second year, and US$59,000 for the third year. In addition, an allowance of US$1,500 per year

Length of Study: 3 years
Frequency: Twice a year
Country of Study: Any country
Application Procedure: The application deadlines are April 1 and October 1; when those dates fall on the weekend, applications are due the following Monday. Applications are due by 5 p.m. Eastern Time on these dates. Applicants are notified of fellowship committee decisions within approximately 10–12 weeks of the application deadline. Fellowships can be activated three months after the application deadline but no later than one year following the deadline. Awards activate on the first of the month
Closing Date: 1 September
Funding: Individuals, Private
Additional Information: www.cancerresearch.org/scientists/fellowships-grants/post-doctoral-fellows

For further information contact:

29 Broadway, 4th fl, New York, NY 10006, United States of America.

Tel: (1) 212 688 7515
Email: grants@cancerresearch.org

Clinical and Laboratory Integration Program

Purpose: The Cancer Research Institute funds research aimed at furthering the development of immunological approaches to the diagnosis, treatment, and prevention of cancer. The Institute's mission is to bring effective immune system-based therapies to cancer patients sooner. To this end, CRI offers its Clinic and Laboratory Integration Program (CLIP) Grants to qualified scientists who are working to explore clinically relevant questions aimed at improving the effectiveness of cancer immunotherapies. The program supports pre-clinical and translational research that can be directly applied to optimizing cancer immunotherapy in the clinic
Eligibility: CLIP Grants provide funding for qualified scientists who are working to explore clinically relevant questions aimed at improving the effectiveness of cancer immunotherapies. The grant will support pre-clinical and translational research, which will provide information that can be directly applied to optimizing cancer immunotherapy in the clinic. Candidates for a CLIP Grant must hold a faculty appointment as a tenure-track assistant professor (or higher rank) at the time of award activation. If not, documentation from their institution must accompany the Letter of Intent indicating they will hold the position of assistant professor (or higher rank) by the time of award activation. CRI has no citizenship restrictions, and research supported by the award may be conducted at medical schools and research centers in the United States or abroad. Please note that CLIP Grants do not support research at for-profit institutions.
Type: Grant
Value: Up to US$100,000 per year
Length of Study: two years
Country of Study: Africa
Closing Date: 1 March
Additional Information: www.cancerresearch.org/scientists/fellowships-grants/translational-research-grants

For further information contact:

Email: grants@cancerresearch.org

Lloyd J. Old STAR Program

Purpose: The Lloyd J. Old STAR Program provides grants of US$1.25 million over 5 years to mid-career scientists. This long-term funding will not be tied to a specific research project, but rather will aim to provide a degree of flexibility and freedom for investigators to explore out-of-the-box and disruptive avenues of research. Candidates selected for this award are expected to be future "stars" in the field of cancer immunology Scientists Taking Risks
Eligibility: Candidates for the Lloyd J. Old STAR program must meet the following eligibility requirements 1. The applicant must have an M.D., Ph.D., or M.D./Ph.D. (or equivalent) 2. Applicants must belong to one of the following categories 1. Tenure-track assistant professor with a minimum of 3 years in this position 2. Tenure-track associate professor with a maximum of 3 years in this position
Level of Study: Research
Type: Grant
Value: Up to US$250,000 per year
Length of Study: 5 years
Frequency: Annual
Country of Study: Any country
Application Procedure: 1. Complete the Application Form (PDF) 2. Abstract A 300-word overview of the research questions, goals, and approaches of your lab. The content should be written in nontechnical English. 3. Research summary A summary (not to exceed 4 pages) of your ongoing and planned research, highlighting your past work and plans for the next 5 years. Tables, figures, and references may be attached as an appendix. 4. List five (5) publications of note Five peer-reviewed papers that cover your most important scientific contributions. For each publication, provide a citation followed by a 300 word or less summary of the publication's significance. Do not include copies of the publications with your application. 5. Curriculum vitae and bibliography (limit bibliography to past 5 years and relevant publications). 6. List of your current research support. Only

PDF documents will be accepted. All files must be uploaded individually in their respective sections on the online application form.

Closing Date: 15 January

Funding: Foundation, Individuals, Private

Additional Information: researchfunding.duke.edu/lloyd-j-old-star-program

Technology Impact Award

Purpose: The Cancer Research Institute Technology Impact Award provides seed funding of up to US$200,000 to be used over 12–24 months to address the gap between technology development and clinical application of cancer immunotherapies. These grants aim to encourage collaboration between technology developers and clinical cancer immunologists and to generate the proof-of-principle of a novel platform technology in bioinformatics, ex vivo or in silico modeling systems, immunological or tumor profiling instrumentation, methods, reagents and assays, or other relevant technologies that can enable clinician scientists to generate deeper insights into the mechanisms of action of effective or ineffective cancer immunotherapies

Eligibility: Applicants must hold a faculty appointment as a tenure-track assistant professor (or higher rank) at the time of award activation. The grant will be awarded to a scientist who describes an extraordinarily novel, yet practical research plan that is creative and technically sophisticated. Joint submissions from collaborators will also be considered. (The collaborators will share the award.) Each collaborator must meet the eligibility criteria

Level of Study: Research

Type: Grant

Value: Up to US$100,000 per year

Length of Study: Two years

Frequency: Annual

Country of Study: Any country

Application Procedure: 1. Abstract of research in non-technical English explaining the significance of the new technology platform and its impact on the field of cancer immunotherapy. Not to exceed 250 words. 2. An initial research concept (succinct description of the proposed research plan with specific aims and timelines, description of the how the proposed technology platform has the potential to transform the field of cancer immunotherapy), not to exceed 3 pages. 3. Brief description of your current research. Curriculum vitae and bibliography (limit bibliography to past 5 years or publications relevant to proposed research). 4. If applicable, curriculum vitae for all group members, as well as a description of each member's research focus. Only PDF documents will be accepted. All files must be uploaded individually in their respective sections on the online application form.

Closing Date: 15 November

Funding: Corporation, Foundation, Individuals, Private, Trusts

Additional Information: www.cancerresearch.org/scientists/fellowships-grants/technology-impact-award

For further information contact:

Email: grants@cancerresearch.org

Cancer Research United Kingdom

London Research Institute, PO Box 123, Lincoln's Inn Fields, London WC2A 3PX, United Kingdom.

Tel: (44) 20 7269 3609
Website: www.cancerresearch.org
Contact: Mrs Yvonne Harman, Graduate Programme Administrator

Cancer Research United Kingdom London Research Institute is part of CR-United Kingdom, which is a registered United Kingdom charity dedicated to saving lives through research into the causes, prevention, treatment and cure of cancer.

Cancer Research United Kingdom LRI Graduate Studentships

Purpose: To enable research training

Eligibility: Open to candidates who have normally been resident in the United Kingdom for more than 3 years and have obtained, or are about to obtain, a First or Upper Second Class (Honours) Degree in science. Applicants must also be aged 25 years or younger. Non-residents are not excluded from consideration

Level of Study: Doctorate

Type: Studentship

Value: Approx. United Kingdom £13,701–£14,821 per year, depending on location

Length of Study: 3 years

Frequency: Annual

Study Establishment: Cancer Research United Kingdom LRI laboratories

Country of Study: United Kingdom

Application Procedure: Applicants must refer to the advertisements that list procedure information.

For further information contact:

Email: eric.eve@hmc.ox.ac.uk

Cancer Research United Kingdom Manchester Institute

The University of Manchester, Wilmslow Road, Manchester M20 4BX, United Kingdom.

Tel: (44) 16 1446 3156
Email: enquiries@cruk.manchester.ac.uk
Website: www.cruk.manchester.ac.uk

The CRUK Manchester Institute is a leading cancer research institute within The University of Manchester

4-Year Studentship

Purpose: To support study towards a PhD.
Eligibility: We invite talented and motivated students or graduates to apply for our PhD programme. Applications are invited from graduates or final year undergraduates who have, or expect to obtain, a first or upper second class honours degree or equivalent from any recognised University worldwide. Previous laboratory research experience is not a requirement for acceptance to the PhD programme, however, such research experience in cancer will give a realistic insight into academic research. A Master's degree is not a condition for making a PhD application.
Level of Study: Doctorate, Postgraduate
Type: Studentship
Value: £19,000 as stipend per year, university fees and bench fees
Length of Study: 4 years
Frequency: Annual
Study Establishment: The University of Manchester
Country of Study: United Kingdom
Application Procedure: Please visit www.cruk.manchester.ac.uk
No. of awards offered: 4 to 8
Closing Date: 31 January
Funding: Private
Contributor: Cancer Research United Kingdom
No. of awards given last year: 5
Additional Information: www.cruk.manchester.ac.uk/Education/PhD-About-the-Programme

For further information contact:

Oglesby Building, 555 Wilmslow Rd, Manchester M20 4G, United Kingdom.

Email: pgt@cruk.manchester.ac.uk

Canon Collins Trust

22 The Ivories, 6 Northampton Street, London N1 2HY, United Kingdom.

Tel: (44) 20 7354 1462
Email: info@canoncollins.org.uk
Website: www.canoncollins.org.uk
Contact: Victoria Reed, Scholarships Officer

We believe that southern Africa's development depends on strong leadership in key fields. Our scholars are outstanding academics and professionals who are dedicated to the development of their countries. We seek to invest in those who share our commitment to social justice and who can demonstrate their intention to return to their home countries after their study.

Canon Collins Scholarship for Distance Learning Master of Laws (LLM)

Purpose: This scholarship allows the individual to study for the Postgraduate certificate, Post graduate diploma and Master of laws
Eligibility: 1. a national of, or have refugee status in, one of the following countries: Malawi, South Africa, Zambia, Zimbabwe 2. normally resident in one of these countries 3. in possession of the necessary qualifications required for admission to the programme 4. currently employed in full or part-time work; 5. able to commit a minimum of 10 hours to study per week.
Level of Study: Postgraduate
Type: Scholarship
Value: waiver full tuition and examination entry fees
Length of Study: 1 to 5 years
Frequency: Annual
Country of Study: United Kingdom
Application   Procedure: canoncollins.ams3.digitaloceanspaces.com/media/2021/04/22102935/university_of_london_guidelines_for_applicants_2021.pdf
No. of awards offered: 4
Closing Date: 16 April

Additional Information: scholarship-positions.com/canon-collins-scholarship-distance-learning-master-laws-llm-program-uk-2015/2015/05/13/

Canterbury Christ Church, University College, Graduate School

North Holmes Road, Canterbury CT1 1QU, United Kingdom.

Tel:	(44) 1227 767 700
Email:	research@cant.ac.uk
Website:	www.cant.ac.uk
Contact:	Miss Ashleigh Stuart, Research Secretary

Faculty PhD Scholarships

Purpose: Scholarships are available for doctoral projects which fall within the main research priorities of the University (healthcare and medicine; education; science and technology; creative and digital arts; business, the economy and policy) and within one of our four Faculties (Arts and Humanities, Education, Health and Wellbeing, Social and Applied Sciences).
Level of Study: Postgraduate
Type: Scholarship
Value: (a stipend of £13,000 p.a., tuition fee waiver for three years and an expense allowance of £500 p.a.).
Length of Study: 4 year
Country of Study: Any country
Additional Information: www.canterbury.ac.uk/study-here/postgraduate-research/funding-for-research-degrees.aspx

For further information contact:

Email: lynn.revell@canterbury.ac.uk

L.B. Wood Travelling Scholarship

Purpose: This scholarship is available to all graduates from any university in New Zealand, from any faculty providing that the application for the scholarship is made within three years from the date of graduation. The scholarship is offered as a supplement to some other postgraduate scholarships held for the purpose of study in Great Britain
Eligibility: 1. be graduates of or graduating from a New Zealand university 2. apply for the scholarship within three years from the date of their graduation 3. have applied for or been awarded another postgraduate scholarship.
Level of Study: Postgraduate

Type: Scholarship
Value: US$3,000 p.a.
Length of Study: 3 year
Frequency: Annual
Country of Study: Any country
Application Procedure: 1. Check your eligibility. 2. Read the Regulations 3. Applications must be done online. A link to the application website is available here universitiesnz.communityforce.com/
Closing Date: 1 April
Funding: Foundation
Additional Information: www.universitiesnz.ac.nz/sites/default/files/uni-nz/documents/scholarships/LB%20Wood%20Regulations.pdf

For further information contact:

Email: scholarships-cf@universitiesnz.ac.nz

Lawson Robinson Hawke's Bay A&P Scholarship

Purpose: The Lawson Robinson Hawke's Bay A & P Scholarship aims to recognise outstanding academic and leadership qualities in a student currently enrolled in a full time land based programme. Applicants should have a familial association with Hawke's Bay
Eligibility: New Zealand Citizen or Permanent Resident Students
Level of Study: Postgraduate
Type: Scholarship
Value: US$3,000
Length of Study: 1 year
Frequency: Varies
Country of Study: Any country
Application Procedure: Apply online
Closing Date: 28 February
Funding: Foundation
Additional Information: www.lawsonrobinson.co.nz/scholarship.html

For further information contact:

Email: awards@showgroundshb.co.nz

Canterbury Historical Association

History Department, University of Canterbury, Private Bag 4800, Christchurch 8140, New Zealand.

Tel:	(64) 3 364 2555
Email:	david.monger@canterbury.ac.nz

Website: www.hums.canterbury.ac.nz/hist/
Contact: Mrs Lynn McClelland, Director of Student
                Services and Communications

The Canterbury Historical Association (founded 1922, but in recess between 1940 and 1953) aims to foster public interest in all fields of history by holding meetings for the discussion of historical issues, and to promote historical research and writing through its administration of the J M Sherrard Award in New Zealand local and regional history.

Anne Reid Memorial Trust Scholarship

Purpose: The scholarship commemorates Anne Reid of Blenheim/Christchurch/Singapore/Auckland who studied and taught at the University of Canterbury and The National University of Singapore. The purpose of this scholarship is to assist a graduate student from either the University of Canterbury or the University of Auckland overseas in an environment that encourages the completion of a course or work in progress, or the undertaking of further training in a recognised institution

Eligibility: 1. The Scholarship will be known as the Anne Reid Memorial Trust Scholarship and will be awarded for postgraduate study in the fields of Art History, English Literature, or Music, or Fine Arts. 2. The Scholarship will normally be tenable for one year only, but in exceptional circumstances the Selection Committee may determine that the Scholarship will be tenable for up to two years, or permit a Scholarship holder to reapply for a further award in the following year. 3. The Scholarship is tenable by a student who is a New Zealand citizen. 4. The Selection Committee may determine to award more than one scholarship in any year. 5. To be eligible a candidate will be a graduate of the University of Canterbury or the University of Auckland, or enrolled in a postgraduate degree course at either of those Universities and studying Art History, English Literature, Music or Fine Arts. 6. Selection will be based on academic achievement based on grade point average as well as demonstrated artistic ability, proposed course of study and potential to contribute to society in their chosen field, and demonstrated financial need. Short-listed candidates may be required to attend an interview (see Notes I-II). 7. The value of the Scholarship will be determined by the Selection Committee, taking into account the case presented by the applicant. The maximum value is NZ$30,000 per annum and this may be used to cover the cost of fees in further approved courses, travel and living expenses while studying away from New Zealand. 8. The Scholarship will be awarded to PhD or Masters students who wish to undertake a period of postgraduate study or research or creative work in Art History, English Literature, Music or Fine Arts at a recognised institution overseas. 9. The shortlisting of applicants will be undertaken by a committee comprising the Head of the School of Humanities (or nominee), the Head of the School of Music (or nominee) and the Head of the Elam School of Fine Arts (or nominee). 10. The committee will seek to identify the best applicant from each subject area. 11. The Trustees of the Anne Reid Memorial Trust will appoint the Selection Committee which will comprise three trustees and one nominee of the Vice Chancellor of the University of Auckland and one nominee of the Vice Chancellor of the University of Canterbury. It will be chaired by one of the trustees who may exercise a casting vote to determine a matter. Except as specified in these Regulations the Selection Committee may regulate its own procedures. 12. The Scholarship will be awarded by the relevant University upon the recommendation of the Selection Committee. Payment will be made to the successful candidate upon receipt of evidence that all conditions relating to the award have been satisfied. 13. The Scholarship may be held concurrently with any other scholarship, award or grant as long as the regulations for that scholarship, award or grant permit and the University of Auckland Council, or the Dean of Postgraduate Research at the University of Canterbury, is informed and approves. It is the responsibility of the recipient to declare to the Scholarships Office all other scholarship, awards or grant funding received and for which the awardee receives payment while also in payment for this Scholarship. 14. The Trustees of the Fund may from time to time vary the conditions of the Scholarship awarded to a particular applicant upon the recommendation of the Vice Chancellor (or nominee) of the University of Auckland or the University of Canterbury provided there is no departure from the main purpose of the Scholarship. 15. Applications close with the Scholarships Office of relevant Universities on TBC.

Level of Study: Doctorate, Postdoctorate, Postgraduate
Type: Scholarship
Value: NZ$30,000
Length of Study: 1 year
Frequency: Annual
Country of Study: New Zealand
Application Procedure: Apply online
Funding: Trusts
Additional Information: www.auckland.ac.nz/en/study/scholarships-and-awards/find-a-scholarship/anne-reid-memorial-trust-scholarship-408-cai.html

For further information contact:

Email: scholarships-cf@universitiesnz.ac.nz

BayTrust Bruce Cronin Scholarship

Purpose: This scholarship has been established to recognise his service to the people of the Bay of Plenty
Eligibility: Applicants will be eligible if they were born in, or attended school in, or have whakapapa back to the area
Level of Study: Postgraduate
Type: Scholarship
Value: NZ$5,000
Length of Study: 1 year
Frequency: Annual
Country of Study: New Zealand
Application Procedure: Apply online universitiesnz. communityforce.com/
No. of awards offered: 2
Closing Date: 1 February
Funding: Foundation
Additional Information: www.universitiesnz.ac.nz/scholarships/baytrust-bruce-cronin-scholarship

For further information contact:

Level 1, 752 Cameron Road, Tauranga South, Tauranga 3112, New Zealand.

Tel: (64) 7 578 6546
Email: info@baytrust.org.nz

Canterbury Scholarship

Purpose: These scholarships, tenable for study towards the degree of Doctor of Philosophy at the University of Canterbury, were established to recognise students of the highest calibre undertaking PhD research at the university
Eligibility: To apply for a Canterbury Scholarship, please use the UC Doctoral Scholarship application form. The very top ranked domestic applicants who apply for the UC Doctoral Scholarship will be awarded one of the limited number of Canterbury Scholarships available. Domestic students who do not receive a Canterbury Scholarship will be automatically considered for the UC Doctoral Scholarship.
Level of Study: Postgraduate
Type: Scholarship
Value: NZ$21,000
Length of Study: 3 year
Frequency: Annual
Country of Study: New Zealand
Application Procedure: See website address in additional information.
Closing Date: 15 May
Funding: Trusts
Additional Information: scholarshipscanterbury. communityforce.com/Funds/Search.aspx

For further information contact:

Email: scholarships-cf@universitiesnz.ac.nz

Clifford Wallace Collins Memorial Trust Scholarship

Purpose: The trust fund was established in 1980 to provide an annual award to support graduates of the University of Canterbury undertaking a course of study in Librarianship at a New Zealand university, and to commemorate the contribution made to the University and its library by Clifford Wallace Collins (1909–1979). Applications, addressing the selection criteria, must be made by letter to the Information Studies Programme Director of Victoria University of Wellington by 15 April
Eligibility: The trust fund was established in 1980 to provide an annual award to support graduates of the University of Canterbury undertaking a course of study in Librarianship at a New Zealand university, and to commemorate the contribution made to the University and its library by Clifford Wallace Collins (1909–1979). Mr Collins was Librarian to Canterbury University College and the University of Canterbury from 1934 to 1971
Level of Study: Postgraduate
Type: Scholarship
Value: NZ$750
Length of Study: 1 year
Frequency: Annual
Country of Study: New Zealand
Application Procedure: Apply online
Closing Date: 15 April
Funding: Trusts
Additional Information: www.wgtn.ac.nz/scholarships/annual-prizes/prize-details?result_1736977_result_page=19

For further information contact:

Email: scholarships-cf@universitiesnz.ac.nz

Marian D'Eve Memorial Scholarship

Purpose: This scholarship supports students studying, researching, or developing, resources for early-childhood special-needs education at the University of Canterbury. The scholarship was established in 2009 in memory of Marian D'Eve, an early-childhood education specialist and author of a handbook for teachers
Eligibility: 1 Applicants must be studying, researching, or developing, in any discipline, aids for early childhood special-needs education. 2 Applicants must be enrolled full-time at the University.

Level of Study: Postgraduate
Type: Scholarship
Value: US$2,000
Length of Study: 1 year
Frequency: Annual
Country of Study: New Zealand
Application Procedure: Apply online
Closing Date: 31 March
Funding: Foundation
Additional Information: scholarshipscanterbury.commun ityforce.com/Funds/FundDetails.aspx?766C425A624C4C6 E30424B38424D707348786A724164383642666967 63456 A79335A347077324C51726F4C30545453 5265474878384 A57594F4B77445148436F

For further information contact:

Email: scholarships@canterbury.ac.nz

Roger Helm Scholarship in Pure Mathematics

Purpose: The scholarship supports students for study towards a research master's degree or a PhD degree in Pure Mathematics at the University of Canterbury. It was established in 2018 from a bequest by Roger Helm (1947–2015)
Eligibility: At the time of application, applicants must be enrolled in either a programme for a PhD degree in Pure Mathematics, or in Part II of a master's degree in Pure Mathematics. Applications are not accepted from candidates who already hold a research doctoral degree. Applications are not accepted from previous holders of the scholarship
Level of Study: Postgraduate
Type: Scholarship
Value: NZ$5,000
Length of Study: 1 year
Frequency: Annual
Country of Study: New Zealand
Application Procedure: Apply online
Closing Date: 15 March
Funding: Trusts
Additional Information: aseanop.com/roger-helm-scholarship-in-pure-mathematics/

For further information contact:

Email: scholarships-cf@universitiesnz.ac.nz

Susan Barnes Memorial Scholarship

Purpose: The scholarship supports students with a vision impairment in undertaking study at the University of Canterbury. It was established in 2016 by the Lighthouse Vision Trust
Eligibility: 1 Applicants must have a vision impairment of 6/18 or less with both eyes and best possible correction, or less than 20 degrees of vision. 2 By the closing date for applications, an applicant must have registered with the University's Equity & Disability Service as a student with a vision impairment. 3 Applicants must be citizens of Aotearoa New Zealand or holders of Aotearoa New Zealand residence class visas. 4 Applicants must be enrolled, full-time or part-time, at the University at either undergraduate or postgraduate level.
Level of Study: Postgraduate
Type: Scholarship
Value: NZ$10,000
Length of Study: 1 year
Frequency: Annual
Country of Study: New Zealand
Application Procedure: Apply online
Closing Date: 31 March
Funding: Foundation
Additional Information: www.canterbury.ac.nz/ scholarshipsforms/regulations/Lighthouse_Vision_Trust_ Scholarship_&_Susan_Barnes_Memorial_Scholarship.pdf

For further information contact:

Email: scholarships-cf@universitiesnz.ac.nz

The Auckland Medical Aid Trust Scholarship

Purpose: This scholarship was established in 2004 and is financed by the Auckland Medical Aid Trust to encourage research into social issues concerning being and becoming human, and provides funds for a doctoral candidate at a New Zealand university
Eligibility: An applicant will be registered as a candidate or will be in the process of registering; as a candidate for a doctoral degree at a New Zealand university. (No award will be made to a candidate who has not successfully completed; registration for a doctoral degree.)
Level of Study: Postdoctorate
Type: Scholarship
Value: NZ$25,000
Length of Study: 3 year
Frequency: Annual
Country of Study: New Zealand
No. of awards offered: 1
Closing Date: 1 October
Funding: Foundation
Additional Information: www.universitiesnz.ac.nz/scholar ships/auckland-medical-aid-trust-scholarship

For further information contact:

PO Box 11915, Wellington 6142, New Zealand.

Tel: (64) 4 381 8510
Email: jon.winnall@universitiesnz.ac.nz

Three Nations Conference Award

Purpose: This award assists Maori or Pasifika students, or students who are indigenous to states or territories of Australia, whose financial circumstances would otherwise preclude them from undertaking postgraduate study in the Department of Sociology and Anthropology at the University of Canterbury
Eligibility: Anthropology;Sociology
Level of Study: Doctorate, Postgraduate
Type: Scholarship
Value: US$1,000
Length of Study: 1 year
Frequency: Annual
Country of Study: New Zealand
Application Procedure: Apply online
No. of awards offered: 1
Closing Date: 31 March
Funding: Foundation
Additional Information: www.canterbury.ac.nz/ scholarshipsearch/ScholarshipDetails.aspx? ScholarshipID=6935.136

For further information contact:

Email: scholarships@canterbury.ac.nz

University of Canterbury Mathematics and Statistics Scholarship

Purpose: These scholarships recognise and support high-achieving 200-, 300-, and 400-level students majoring in Mathematics, Statistics, Computational and Applied Mathematical Sciences, Data Science, Applied Data Science or Financial Engineering. The scholarships will be awarded in three categories, with the value of each category (NZ$1,000, NZ$2,500, NZ$5,000) reflecting the recipients' levels of achievement. Up to 45 scholarships will be available annually
Eligibility: By 31 March in the year of application, applicants must be enrolled full-time at the University in at least 60 points of 200-, 300-, or 400-level taught courses (not including any thesis course) for an undergraduate or post-graduate programme in a. Applied Data Science;

b. Computational and Applied Mathematical Sciences; c. Data Science; d. Financial Engineering; e. Mathematics; or f. Statistics.
Level of Study: Postgraduate
Type: Scholarship
Value: NZ$5,000 (Category A awards) NZ$2,500 (Category B awards) NZ$1,000 (Category C awards)
Length of Study: 1 year
Frequency: Annual
Country of Study: Any country
Application Procedure: Apply online
Closing Date: 31 March
Funding: Foundation
Additional   Information: www.canterbury.ac.nz/ scholarshipsforms/regulations/UC_Mathematics_and_Statis tics_Scholarship.pdf

For further information contact:

Email: scholarships@canterbury.ac.nz

Cardiff University

Deri House, 2-4 Park Grove, Cardiff CF10 3PA, Wales, United Kingdom.

Tel: (44) 29 2087 0084
Email: graduate@cardiff.ac.uk
Website: www.cardiff.ac.uk/postgraduate

Cardiff University is recognized in independent government assessments as one of the UK's leading teaching and research universities. Founded by Royal Charter in 1883, the University today combines impressive modern facilities and a dynamic approach to teaching and research with its proud heritage of service and achievement. Having gained national and international standing, Cardiff University's vision is to be recognized as a world-class university and to achieve the associated benefits for its students, staff and all other stakeholders.

Cardiff Business School - ESRC Wales DTP Fully Funded General Studentships (Economics)

Eligibility: ESRC studentships are highly competitive. Wales DTP studentships are available to both home and international (including EU and EEA) students. All applicants will be eligible for a full award consisting of a maintenance stipend and payment of tuition fees at the UKRI rate. Applicants must satisfy studentship eligibility requirements. Successful international student applicants will receive a fully-funded Wales DTP studentship and will not be charged the fees difference between the UK and international rate.

Level of Study: Doctorate

Type: Studentship

Value: tuition fees as well as a maintenance grant currently £15,609 p.a.

Frequency: Annual

Country of Study: United Kingdom

Closing Date: 4 February

Additional Information: www.cardiff.ac.uk/study/postgraduate/funding/phd-studentships-and-projects

For further information contact:

Email: postgradmarketing@cardiff.ac.uk

Cardiff Business School Scholarships in Business and Management and Economics

Eligibility: 1. A specialist Master-level degree in Business, Management, Social Sciences or related subjects, from an internationally renowned University of comparable or higher standing than Cardiff Business School. 2. A minimum of 60% grades for a UK master's degree, or the equivalent grading for international degrees. 3. Evidence of previous research training, including attending research-focussed taught modules and submitting a research-based Master dissertation. 4. As part of your application process you will have to submit a research proposal demonstrating the intellectual ability to identify viable research questions and a potential to develop a valuable contribution to knowledge in your elected area. 5. Applicants whose first language is not English are normally expected to have reached a minimum IELTS score of 7.0 (writing scored 7.0, with no subscore less than 6.5). Copies of appropriate English language certificates must be supplied with your application.

Level of Study: Doctorate

Value: full fees and stipend (currently £15,609pa) and fees only.

Frequency: Annual

Country of Study: Any country

Closing Date: 1 April

Additional Information: www.cardiff.ac.uk/study/postgraduate/funding/phd-studentships-and-projects

For further information contact:

Email: carbs-researchoffice@cardiff.ac.uk

Cardiff India scholarships

Eligibility: 1. You must submit your application to the University by 17 July 2023. 2. You must pay your deposit by 31 July 2023 unless your deposit deadline is after this date, in which case, your deposit much be paid by your initial deposit deadline. Deposit deadline extensions past the 31 July 2023 will not be accepted for scholarship purposes. 3. You must accept your offer and meet all the offer conditions, including any English Language conditions as stated in your offer by 20 August 2023. 4. Applicants who do not meet the conditions of their offer will not be eligible for the scholarship, even if they are accepted into the University.

Level of Study: Postgraduate

Type: Scholarship

Value: £5,000

Frequency: Annual

Country of Study: United Kingdom

Closing Date: 17 July

Additional Information: www.cardiff.ac.uk/study/international/funding-and-fees/international-scholarships/india-scholarship-schemes

For further information contact:

Email: international@cardiff.ac.uk

Cardiff Institute of Tissue Engineering and Repair (CITER) – EPSRC Studentship

Purpose: To support study on the MSc in Tissue Engineering at CITER

Eligibility: Applicants must be graduates in a biomedical/veterinary or other science subject or an engineering or clinical discipline from medicine or dentistry. United Kingdom or European Union students who have been resident in the United Kingdom for at least 3 years can apply. Other European Union participants may receive a fees only award

Level of Study: Postgraduate

Type: Studentship

Value: Fees and stipend at the current EPSRC rate

Length of Study: 1 year

Country of Study: Any country

Application Procedure: Check website for further details

Closing Date: 30 June

For further information contact:

Tel: (44) 29 2087 0129

Email: HatchS@cardiff.ac.uk

Cardiff School of Chemistry – Master's Bursaries

Purpose: To support study for the MSc in Molecular Modelling
Eligibility: Applicants must possess a 22 Honours Degree or equivalent in chemistry or a related discipline (e.g. physics, engineering, pharmacy, biosciences)
Level of Study: Postgraduate
Type: Bursary
Value: Cost of tuition fees at the United Kingdom/European Union rate
Length of Study: 1 year
Country of Study: United Kingdom
Application Procedure: Applicants must submit an application including two references for postgraduate study. Application forms can be downloaded from the website
Closing Date: 31 August

For further information contact:

The Postgraduate Admissions Office, The Registry Cardiff University, 30-36 Newport Road, Cardiff CF10 3AT, United Kingdom.

Tel: (44) 29 2087 4950
Email: platts@cardifff.ac.uk

Cardiff School of Chemistry – MSc Studentships in Computing in the Physical Sciences

Purpose: To support study on a new MSc programme in Computing in the Physical Sciences
Eligibility: Applicants must be United Kingdom-resident European Union citizens. A minimum qualification of a 2ii degree or equivalent in a relevant scientific discipline is required
Level of Study: Postgraduate
Type: Studentship
Length of Study: 1 year
Country of Study: Any country
Application Procedure: Applicants must submit an application for postgraduate study along with two references
Closing Date: 31 August
Contributor: Schools of Computer Science and Mathematics

For further information contact:

Email: platts@cardiff.ac.uk

Cardiff School of City and Regional Planning – Master's Bursaries

Purpose: To support study on the MSc in Transport and Planning
Eligibility: Applicants must have been offered and will have accepted a place on the MSc in Transport and Planning and must then be nominated for an award by the School. They must have a relevant honours degree at 2i or higher and they must be United Kingdom/European Union students intending to practice in the United Kingdom
Level of Study: Postgraduate
Type: Bursary
Value: Full United Kingdom/European Union fees and a maintenance stipend of £1,000 (by The Rees Jeffreys Road Fund Bursary) and £5,000 (by The Brian Largs Bursary Fund)
Length of Study: 1 year
Country of Study: Any country
Application Procedure: Check website for further details
Closing Date: 30 June
Contributor: The Rees Jeffreys Road Fund Bursary, The Brian Largs Bursary Fund

For further information contact:

Tel: (44) 29 2087 5294
Email: Yewlett@cardiff.ac.uk

Cardiff School of Mathematics – PhD Studentships

Eligibility: Applicants should hold a first or upper second class Honours degree (or overseas equivalent) in a relevant subject area or have appropriate professional experience.
Level of Study: Postgraduate
Type: Studentship
Value: UK and EU students £9,700, Students from outside the EU £21,950
Length of Study: 1 year
Country of Study: United Kingdom
Application Procedure: Applicants must submit an application for postgraduate study which can be downloaded from the website
Closing Date: 30 April
Additional Information: www.cardiff.ac.uk/study/postgraduate/taught/courses/course/mathematics-msc

For further information contact:

Cardiff School of Mathematics, Senghennydd Rd, Cardiff CF24 4AG, United Kingdom.

Tel: (44) 29 2087 4813
Email: MScMaths@cardiff.ac.uk

Cardiff School of Medicine – PhD Studentships

Eligibility: Applicants must be United Kingdom/European Union students. They must possess a First or at least Upper Second Class Honours in a subject of relevance to the project (preferably biological science)
Level of Study: Postgraduate
Type: Studentship
Value: Fees support at the United Kingdom/European Union level along with a maintenance stipend at the Research Council level (£12,600)
Length of Study: PhD 3–4 years
Country of Study: Any country
Application Procedure: Applicants must send a covering letter and an up-to-date curriculum vitae, including a breakdown of Year 2/Year 3 university grades, along with references
Closing Date: 15 December
Contributor: School and Research Council Funds
Additional Information: www.cardiff.ac.uk/study/postgraduate/research/programmes/programme/medicine

For further information contact:

Institute of Medical Genetics, Cardiff University, Heath Park, 210 King George V Dr E, Cardiff CF14 4ER, United Kingdom.

Tel: (44) 29 2074 6716
Fax: (44) 29 2074 6551
Email: pgrmedic@cardiff.ac.uk

Cardiff School of Medicine – PhD Studentships (Department of Surgery)

Eligibility: Applicants must be United Kingdom/European Union students and must possess (or be expected to obtain) a First or at least Upper Second Class Honours in a subject of relevance to the project
Level of Study: Postgraduate
Type: Studentship
Value: Fees support at the United Kingdom/European Union level plus £12,600
Length of Study: 3 years
Country of Study: Any country
Application Procedure: Applicants must send a covering letter and an up-to-date curriculum vitae along with references
Closing Date: 30 June

For further information contact:

Department of Surgery, Cardiff School of Medicine, Cardiff University, Heath Park, Neuadd Meirionnydd, Cardiff CF14 4YS, United Kingdom.

Tel: (44) 29 2074 2895/2896
Fax: (44) 29 2076 1623
Email: JiangW@cardiff.ac.uk

Cardiff School of Music – PhD Studentships

Eligibility: Applicants must have a good Honours Degree in Music (or be expecting to obtain one in the present year) and a Master's Degree is desirable. They should be United Kingdom/European Union citizens or have been resident in the United Kingdom/European Union for at least 3 years prior to starting their PhD.
Level of Study: Postgraduate
Type: Studentship
Value: One full studentship covering United Kingdom/European Union tuition fees and a maintenance stipend at the AHRC level (£12,300) and another, United Kingdom/European Union fees-only studentship
Length of Study: 3 years
Application Procedure: Applicants must complete and submit an application for postgraduate study. Application forms can be downloaded from the website
Closing Date: 30 June
Additional Information: www.cardiff.ac.uk/music/courses/postgraduate-research/postgraduate-research-scholarships

For further information contact:

School of Music, Cardiff University, Corbett Road, Cardiff CF10 3EB, United Kingdom.

Tel: (44) 29 2087 4816
Fax: (44) 29 2087 4379
Email: musicschool@cardiff.ac.uk

Cardiff School of Optometry and Vision Sciences – PhD Studentship

Purpose: To adopt a completely new approach to understanding the relationship between retinal structure and visual function in AMD
Eligibility: Applicants must possess a United Kingdom higher education Degree at First or Upper Second Class Honours or equivalent in a relevant discipline (optometry would be most suitable)
Level of Study: Postgraduate

Type: Studentship
Value: £12,600
Length of Study: 3 years
Country of Study: Any country
Application Procedure: Applicants must complete and submit a standard Cardiff University application form along with a curriculum vitae and covering letter. Application forms can be downloaded from the website
Closing Date: 30 June
Additional Information: The studentship is available to United Kingdom, European Union and overseas students, but will only cover tuition fees at the European Union/United Kingdom level www.cardiff.ac.uk/music/courses/postgraduate-research/postgraduate-research-scholarships

For further information contact:

Email: BinnsAM@cardiff.ac.uk

Cardiff University Marshall Scholarship

Eligibility: To qualify for the 2023 one year Scholarships, candidates should: 1. be citizens of the United States of America (at the time they apply for a scholarship); 2. (by the time they take up their scholarship ie September 2023) hold their first undergraduate degree from an accredited four- year college or university in the United States; 3. have obtained a grade point average of not less than 3.7 on their undergraduate degree at the time of application (if the last grades the candidate received were Fall 2020 this GPA will be used). 4. have graduated from their first undergraduate college or university after April 2020. 5. not have studied for, or hold a degree or degree equivalent qualification from a British University or GCSE or A level qualifications undertaken in the UK.
Level of Study: Doctorate
Type: Scholarship
Value: £38,000 a year (a personal allowance to cover residence and cost of living expenses at the rate of £1,116 per month £1,369 for Scholars at Central London institutions); payment of tuition fees; fares to and fro m the United States; Claimable allowances totalling approximately £3,300.)
Frequency: Annual
Country of Study: Any country
Additional Information: www.cardiff.ac.uk/study/international/funding-and-fees/international-scholarships/cardiff-university-marshall-scholarship

For further information contact:

Email: prog.admin@marshallscholarship.org

Cardiff University MSc/Diploma in Housing Studentship

Purpose: To fund a postgraduate course in housing
Eligibility: Studentships are available to United Kingdom applicants with a First or Upper Second Class (Honours) Degree only
Level of Study: Postgraduate
Type: Studentship
Value: University fees and maintenance grant
Length of Study: 2 years
Frequency: Annual
Study Establishment: Cardiff University
Country of Study: United Kingdom
Application Procedure: Applicants must contact the School of City and Regional Planning
Closing Date: June

For further information contact:

Cardiff School of City and Regional Planning, Glamorgan Building, King Edward VII Avenue, Cardiff CF10 3WA, United Kingdom.

Tel: (44) 29 2087 6092
Email: cardpd@cardiff.ac.uk

Cardiff University PhD Music Studentship

Purpose: To fund doctoral study in music
Eligibility: Applicants should have a good Honours degree in Music, be a United Kingdom or European Union citizen or have been a resident for at least 3 years for reasons other than education
Level of Study: Doctorate
Type: Studentship
Value: Tuition fees and £1,200 for research expenses
Length of Study: 3 years
Frequency: Annual
Study Establishment: Cardiff University
Country of Study: United Kingdom
Application Procedure: Applicants must contact the School of Music. They will need to have received an offer of a place to study before they can apply for financial support
Closing Date: 7 March
Additional Information: www.cardiff.ac.uk/study/postgraduate/funding/phd-studentships-and-projects

For further information contact:

School of Music, 31 Corbett Road, Cardiff CF10 3EB, United Kingdom.

Tel: (44) 29 2087 4816
Fax: (44) 29 2087 4379
Email: musicschool@cardiff.ac.uk

Cardiff University PhD Social Sciences Studentship

Purpose: To fund PhD study in social sciences
Eligibility: Only United Kingdom and European Union students with a First or Upper Second Class (Honours) Degree can apply for a PhD studentship
Level of Study: Doctorate
Length of Study: 3–4 years
Frequency: Annual
Study Establishment: Cardiff University
Country of Study: United Kingdom
Application Procedure: Applicants must contact the School of Social Sciences. They will need to have received an offer of a place before they can apply for financial support
Closing Date: June
Additional Information: www.cardiff.ac.uk/study/postgraduate/research/programmes/programme/social-sciences

For further information contact:

School of Social Sciences, Glamorgan Building, King Edward VII Avenue, Cardiff CF10 3WT, United Kingdom.

Tel: (44) 29 2087 4972
Fax: (44) 29 2087 4436
Email: graduateoffice@cardiff.ac.uk

Cardiff University PhD Studentship in European Studies

Purpose: To support students working towards a thesis in European Studies
Eligibility: All students accepted by the School of European Studies to study for a postgraduate research degree are automatically considered
Level of Study: Doctorate
Type: Studentship
Value: Full tuition fee plus stipend
Frequency: Annual
Study Establishment: Cardiff University
Country of Study: Wales
Application Procedure: Applicants must check the application guidelines available on the postgraduate webpages
Closing Date: 30 June

For further information contact:

Email: business-phd@cardiff.ac.uk

Cardiff University School of Law and Politics - ESRC Wales DTP General Studentships - Empirical Studies in Law

Eligibility: Applicants should have a good Honours degree in Law (2:1 or equivalent) or overseas equivalent in a relevant subject. We will consider all individual applicants on their specific merits. If you do not have the standard qualifications for the course, you may still apply. Your application will be considered if you have the following; Masters' degree in Law (or equivalent) with an average mark of at least 65%. Applicants with appropriate professional experience. Those whose first language is not English must obtain a score of at least 7.0 in IELTS (with no less than 6.5 in the Writing element and no less than 5.5 in Listening, Speaking and Reading).
Level of Study: Doctorate
Type: Studentship
Value: Tuition fees as well as a maintenance grant (currently £15,609 for one year.
Frequency: Annual
Country of Study: Any country
Closing Date: 4 February
Additional Information: www.cardiff.ac.uk/study/postgraduate/funding/phd-studentships-and-projects

For further information contact:

Tel: (44) 02920 874 351
Email: awpol-pgr@cardiff.ac.uk

Cardiff University School of Law and Politics - ESRC-funded PhD Studentship in Politics and International Relations

Eligibility: Applicants should have a good Honours degree in Politics or International Relations (2:1 or equivalent) or overseas equivalent in a relevant subject. We will consider all individual applicants on their specific merits. If you do not have the standard qualifications for the course, you may still apply. Your application will be considered if you have the following; 1. Masters' degree in Politics or International Relations (or equivalent) with an average mark of at least 65%. 2. Applicants with appropriate professional experience. Those whose first language is not English must obtain a score of at least 7.0 in IELTS (with no less than 6.5 in the Writing element and no less than 5.5 in Listening, Speaking and Reading).
Level of Study: Doctorate
Type: Studentship
Value: Tuition fees as well as a maintenance grant (currently £15,609 per year
Frequency: Annual

Country of Study: Any country
Closing Date: 4 February
Additional Information: www.cardiff.ac.uk/study/postgraduate/funding/phd-studentships-and-projects

For further information contact:

Tel: (44) 02920 874 351
Email: lawpol-pgr@cardiff.ac.uk

Economic & Social Research Council (1+3) Sociology Studentship

Purpose: To fund postgraduate training
Eligibility: Applicants must have a First or Upper Second Class (Honours) Degree
Level of Study: Postgraduate
Type: Studentship
Length of Study: 1 year for MSc and 3 years for PhD
Frequency: Annual
Study Establishment: Cardiff University
Country of Study: United Kingdom
Application Procedure: Applicants must contact the School of Social Sciences
Closing Date: 15 October

Engineering and Physical Sciences Research Council Studentships for Biophotonics

Purpose: To support study on the new MSc in Biophotonics
Eligibility: Applicants must be excellent candidates. Funding is available to United Kingdom and European Union students only
Level of Study: Postgraduate
Type: Studentship
Value: Fully funded studentships include a maintenance stipend
Length of Study: 1 year
Country of Study: Any country
Application Procedure: Applicants can apply via the standard Cardiff University postgraduate application form, which can be downloaded from the website
Closing Date: 31 July
Contributor: Cardiff School of Biosciences and Cardiff School of Physics and Astronomy

For further information contact:

Tel: (44) 29 2087 0172
Email: mscbiophotonics@cardiff.ac.uk

Fully-Funded PhD Studentship in Sustainable Place-Making

Eligibility: Residency full awards (fees plus maintenance stipend) are open to United Kingdom nationals and European Union students without further restrictions. Academic criteria successful applicants are likely to have a very good first degree (a first or upper second class BA or BSc Honours or equivalent), and an appropriate Masters degree in a relevant subject (e.g. social sciences; environmental studies; sustainable development; environmental psychology; sociology of technology/environment; human geography), with an average mark of at least 65
Level of Study: Postgraduate, Research
Type: Studentship
Value: Full United Kingdom/European Union tuition fees, as well as a doctoral stipend matching United Kingdom Research Council National minimum (£13,863 per year for current year, updated each year)
Length of Study: 3 years
Country of Study: United Kingdom
Application Procedure: (1) Submit a complete application form for admission to doctoral study in the School of Social Sciences, submitted to the Academic Registry via the online admissions portal (www.cardiff.ac.uk/regis/general/applyonline/index.html)
Closing Date: 16 November
Additional Information: Cardiff University reserves the right to close applications early should sufficient applications be received www.cardiff.ac.uk/study/postgraduate/research/programmes/programme/social-sciences

For further information contact:

Tel: (44) 29 2087 0855
Email: parkinva@cardiff.ac.uk

Global Wales Postgraduate Scholarship

Eligibility: To be eligible for this scheme, candidates must meet the following criteria: 1. be a citizen of Vietnam, India, the USA or a country within the European Union 2. have submitted an application to study an eligible postgraduate programme at Cardiff University be classed as an overseas student for fee paying purposes. 3. Applicants must pay their course deposit by the deadline stated in their offer letter in order to be eligible for this scholarship.
Level of Study: Postgraduate
Type: Scholarship
Value: £10,000 each
Length of Study: 1 year

Frequency: Annual
Country of Study: United Kingdom
No. of awards offered: 24
Closing Date: March
Additional Information: www.cardiff.ac.uk/study/international/funding-and-fees/international-scholarships/global-wales-scholarship

GREAT Scholarships

Eligibility: 1. You must pay your deposit by the deadline stated in your original/first offer. If you are granted a deposit extension you must pay by your new deadline. This applies until 31 July - scholarships will not be awarded to applicants who make their deposit payment after 31 July 2023. 2. You must accept your offer and meet all the offer conditions, including any English Language conditions as stated in your offer by 16 September 2023.
Level of Study: Postgraduate
Type: Scholarship
Value: £10,000
Length of Study: 1 year
Frequency: Annual
Country of Study: United Kingdom
No. of awards offered: 3
Closing Date: 31 May
Additional Information: www.cardiff.ac.uk/study/international/funding-and-fees/international-scholarships/great-scholarships-2022

International Engineering MSc Studentship

Purpose: To fund postgraduate study in areas of engineering
Eligibility: First or Upper Second Class (Honours) Degree
Level of Study: Postgraduate
Type: Studentship
Value: £1,500
Length of Study: 1 year
Frequency: Annual
Study Establishment: Cardiff University
Country of Study: United Kingdom
Application Procedure: Applicants must contact the School of Engineering
Additional Information: There is no need to apply seperately for scholarships as eligible applicants will be considered on the basis of their application forms www.cardiff.ac.uk/study/postgraduate/research/programmes/programme/social-sciences

For further information contact:

Admission Office, Cardiff School of Engineering, Cardiff University, Cardiff CF24 0YZ, United Kingdom.

Tel: (44) 29 2087 4656
Email: engineering-pg@cardiff.ac.uk

Morgan E. Williams MRes Scholarship in Helminthology

Eligibility: English language proficiency is required. Applicants must have a undergraduate degree at level 22 (or higher) in a relevant biological, bio medical or bio-molecular science subject. For detailed information, please visit the website
Level of Study: Postgraduate
Type: Scholarship
Value: There is one scholarship offering a reduction of £2,500 off the tuition fees for MRes Biosciences
Country of Study: United Kingdom
Application Procedure: Applicants should submit a curriculum vitae and Covering Letter to Rachel Patterson, PatersonRJ@cardiff.ac.uk
Closing Date: 27 May
Contributor: Cardiff School of Bio sciences
Additional Information: Scholarship is offered for 1 year armacad.info/cardiff-university-school-of-biosciences-morgan-e-williams-mres-scholarship-in-helminthology-uk

For further information contact:

Email: BIOSI-MRes@cardiff.ac.uk

PhD Research Scholarships

Level of Study: Doctorate
Type: Scholarship
Value: tuition fee only scholarships
Length of Study: 3 years
Frequency: Annual
Country of Study: United Kingdom
Closing Date: 5 January
Additional Information: www.cardiff.ac.uk/study/international/funding-and-fees/international-scholarships/phd-research-scholarships

For further information contact:

Email: doctoral-academy@cardiff.ac.uk

PhD Studentship in Organisms and Environment at Cardiff University

Eligibility: Residency full awards (fees plus maintenance stipend) are open to United Kingdom nationals and European Union students who can satisfy United Kingdom residency requirements. To be eligible for the full award, European Union nationals must have been in the United Kingdom for at least 3 years prior to the start of the course for which they are seeking funding, including for the purposes of full-time education. European Union nationals who do not meet the above residency requirement are eligible for a fees only award, provided that they have been ordinarily resident in the European Union for at least 3 years prior to the start of their proposed programme of study. Academic criteria applicants for a studentship must have obtained, or be about to obtain, a 2.1 degree or higher in microbiology, ecology, biology or other relevant discipline. If you have a 2.2 degree, but have also obtained a Masters qualification, you are also eligible. If you do not have these qualifications but you have substantial relevant postgraduate experience please contact the department holding the studentship to find out if your relevant experience is sufficient
Level of Study: Doctorate, Postgraduate, Research
Type: Studentship
Value: This studentship consists of full United Kingdom/European Union tuition fees, as well as a Doctoral Stipend matching United Kingdom Research Council National Minimum
Length of Study: 3.5 years
Frequency: Annual
Country of Study: United Kingdom
Application Procedure: To apply, please email your curriculum vitae, 2 references and relevant academic qualifications along with a covering letter to Professor Lynne Boddy at BoddyL@cf.ac.uk
Closing Date: 30 November
Additional Information: Internal interviews will be conducted before the January 30th. Shortlisted candidates will then go on to an institutional interview which will take place between February 9th and 20th. Cardiff University reserves the right to close applications early should sufficient applications be received scholarship-positions.com/phd-studentship-in-organisms-and-environment-at-cardiff-university-in-uk-2015/2014/10/08/

For further information contact:

Email: BoddyL@cf.ac.uk

Postgraduate History and Archaeology Studentship

Purpose: To fund postgraduate training in history and archaeology
Eligibility: First or Upper Second Class (Honours) Degree. Those from the United Kingdom should apply for an award from the Arts and Humanities Research Board (AHRB)
Level of Study: Doctorate, Postgraduate
Type: Studentship
Value: Tuition fees and maintenance grant
Length of Study: 1 year for Masters, 3 years for PhD
Frequency: Annual
Study Establishment: Cardiff University
Country of Study: United Kingdom
Application Procedure: Applicants must submit an application form, which includes a research proposal and the names of two referees
Closing Date: 1 June

For further information contact:

Cardiff School of History and Archaeology, Humanities Building, Colum Drive, Cardiff CF10 3EU, United Kingdom.

Tel: (44) 29 2087 4258
Email: hisaroffice@cardiff.ac.uk

The Beacon Scholarship

Purpose: The scholarship is awarded to students from Kenya, Tanzania, and Uganda looking to study a 3–4 year undergraduate course (excluding medicine)
Eligibility: To be eligible for this scheme, candidates must be able to demonstrate 1. their normal residence is in Kenya, Tanzania or Uganda. 2. leadership capabilities i. academic excellence. ii. achievement in sport, music or drama. iii. social influence and communication. iv. citizenship. 3. a capacity to study independently overseas. 4. financial need for study, ie annual gross household income not exceeding £80k (US$100k). 5. that they are aged 18–21. 6. a commitment to return to their home country within one month of degree completion
Level of Study: Postgraduate
Type: Scholarship
Value: Tuition and maintenance fees
Length of Study: 3–4 year
Frequency: Annual
Country of Study: Any country
Closing Date: 17 July
Funding: Private

Additional Information: www.studyin-uk.in/profiles/univer
sity/cardiff/scholarships/523/

For further information contact:

The Beacon Scholarship Sandells House Cliftons Lane Reigate, Surrey RH2 9RA, United Kingdom.

Email: delhi@studyin-uk.com

Ursula Henriques Scholarships

Purpose: Scholarships are available for pursuing postgradu-
ate taught and postgraduate research programme
Eligibility: For eligibility details, please visit website http//
scholarship-positions.com/ursula-henriques-scholarships-uk-
eu-international-students/
Type: Scholarship
Value: Cardiff University received a gift of £100,000 from Professor Henriques (1,914–2,008), a former member of staff in the Department of History and Welsh History, University College Cardiff
Frequency: Annual
Country of Study: Any country
Application Procedure: The application form can be obtained by email. Completed forms should be returned elec-
tronically to the School Postgraduate Office
Closing Date: 18 May
Contributor: Cardiff University
Additional Information: For more details, please visit website www.cardiff.ac.uk/study/postgraduate/funding/
view/Ursula-Henriques-Scholarship
scholarship-positions.com/ursula-henriques-ma-phd-
scholarship-cardiff-university-uk/2018/04/23/

For further information contact:

Email: share-pg@cardiff.ac.uk

Vice-Chancellors China Scholarship Scheme

Eligibility: 1. be a Chinese national when your academic application is made and be classed an international fee paying student 2. have a bachelor's degree awarded or to be awarded by a Project 211, Project 985 or Double First Class Project University 3. have met the academic and English language requirement (IELTS/TOEFL) and have accepted an unconditional offer by the 16 September 2023 be self-financed (tuition fees are being paid by you or your parents) 4. pay

your deposit within two weeks of being informed that you are in receipt of an award.
Level of Study: Postgraduate
Type: Scholarship
Value: £5,000
Frequency: Annual
Country of Study: Any country
Application Procedure: www.cardiff.ac.uk/__data/assets/
pdf_file/0004/1744942/China-PG-Scholarship-Application-
2022.pdf
No. of awards offered: 33
Closing Date: 29 April
Additional Information: www.cardiff.ac.uk/study/interna
tional/funding-and-fees/international-scholarships/vice-
chancellors-china-scholarship-scheme

For further information contact:

Email: international@cardiff.ac.uk

Vice-Chancellors EU Scholarship

Eligibility: To be awarded a Vice-Chancellor's EU Scholar-
ship you must meet, or exceed, the conditions of your offer. Applicants initially awarded unconditional offers will auto-
matically be granted the scholarship, which will be in the form of a tuition fee discount.
Level of Study: Postgraduate
Type: Scholarship
Value: £5,000
Length of Study: 1 year
Frequency: Annual
Country of Study: United Kingdom
Closing Date: 17 July
Additional Information: www.cardiff.ac.uk/study/interna
tional/funding-and-fees/international-scholarships/vice-
chancellors-eu-scholarship

For further information contact:

Email: international@cardiff.ac.uk

Vice-Chancellors International Scholarship

Eligibility: International applicants from the following coun-
tries who apply before 17 July 2023 and are holding offers for selected postgraduate programmes will automatically be con-
sidered for the Vice-Chancellor's International Scholarship. If you are from one of the following countries/territories you will automatically be considered for a postgraduate award:

Azerbaijan, Bahrain, Barbados, Bosnia and Herzegovina, Canada, Cameroon, Chile, Colombia, Costa Rica, Egypt, Ghana, Hong Kong, India, Indonesia, Iran, Iraq, Jamaica, Japan, Kazakhstan, Korea, Kuwait, Malaysia, Nepal, Occupied Palestinian Territories Oman, Panama, Peru, The Philippines, Qatar, Russia, Saudi Arabia, Singapore, South Africa, Sri Lanka, Sudan, Taiwan, Tanzania, Thailand, Turkey, UAE, Uganda, USA, Vietnam

Level of Study: Postgraduate
Type: Scholarship
Value: £2,000 to £5,000
Length of Study: 1 year
Frequency: Annual
Country of Study: United Kingdom
Closing Date: 31 July
Additional Information: www.cardiff.ac.uk/study/international/funding-and-fees/international-scholarships/vc-international-scholarship

For further information contact:

Email: international@cardiff.ac.uk

Visiting scholars funding schemes

Subjects: Cardiff University is collaborating with the China Scholarships Council (CSC) to offer funding for research visits of up to 24 months by Chinese students registered for PhD research at top Chinese universities.
Eligibility: To qualify for an award, potential candidates must: 1. be a Chinese national (mainland China) pursuing MPhil/PhD research at a recognised top Chinese university 2. satisfy all entry requirements, including relevant English Language requirements 3. seek a formal invitation from a supervisor or Head of Academic School 4. obtain an invitation letter from the supervisor/Head of relevant Academic School 5 .be qualified and prepared to apply for a matching scholarship from the China Scholarship Council (CSC), if offered a tuition fee waiver from Cardiff University.
Level of Study: Predoctorate
Type: Award
Value: maintenance, travel and visa costs
Length of Study: 2 years
Frequency: Annual
Country of Study: United Kingdom
Application Procedure: Further information about this scheme can be found on the China Scholarship Council website: www.csc.edu.cn/search?k=scholarship
Additional Information: www.cardiff.ac.uk/study/international/funding-and-fees/international-scholarships/visiting-scholars

Carnegie Corporation of New York

437 Madison Avenue, Ne York, NY 10022, United States of America.

Tel: (1) 212 371 3200
Website: www.carnegie.org

Andrew Carnegie envisioned Carnegie Corporation as a foundation that would promote the advancement and diffusion of knowledge and understanding. In keeping with this mandate, our work incorporates an affirmation of our historic role as an education foundation but also honors Andrew Carnegie's passion for international peace and the health of our democracy.

Next Gen Fellowship Program for Sub-Saharan African Countries

Purpose: This fellowship is available for pursuing PhD research level
Eligibility: 1. be citizens of and reside in a sub-Saharan African country 2. hold a master's degree 3. be enrolled in a PhD program at an accredited university in Ghana, Kenya, Nigeria, South Africa, Tanzania, or Uganda have an approved dissertation research proposal. 4. The program seeks to promote diversity and encourages women to apply.
Level of Study: Doctorate
Type: Fellowship
Value: The doctoral dissertation research fellowship supports research costs of up to US$15,000 on a topic related to peace, security, and development. The doctoral dissertation proposal fellowship supports short-term research costs of up to US$3,000 to develop a doctoral dissertation proposal. The doctoral dissertation completion fellowship supports a one-year leave from teaching responsibilities and a stipend up to US$15,000 to permit the completion of a dissertation that advances research on peace, security, and development topics.
Length of Study: 6–12 months
Frequency: Annual
Country of Study: Africa
Application Procedure: The mode of applying is online. All applications must be submitted using the online application portal
No. of awards offered: 45
Closing Date: 1 February
Additional Information: www.afterschoolafrica.com/8444/next-gen-fellowship-program-for-sub-saharan-african/

For further information contact:

Email: nextgenafrica@ssrc.org

Carnegie Trust

Carnegie PhD Scholarships

Purpose: Candidates must have, or be on track to achieve, a first class Honours undergraduate degree from a Scottish institution of higher education

Eligibility: You are eligible to be nominated for this award by a Scottish university if: 1. you already hold, or are on track to graduate with a First Class Honours degree from one of the eligible host organisations in Scotland; 2. This undergraduate degree is in a subject related to the academic field of your proposed doctoral research; 3. you have been accepted on a doctoral programme at one of the eligible host organisations; 4. this doctoral programme will start in the coming academic year (2023–24). You are not eligible for nomination if: 1. Your undergraduate degree is not from an eligible host organisation in Scotland 2. You came to Scotland to study for a Postgraduate Masters but completed your undergraduate degree in a different country 3. Your First Class Honours Degree is in a discipline unrelated to the academic field of your PhD. 4. You have already started a PhD or will be starting before academic year 2023–24.

Level of Study: Graduate

Type: Scholarship

Value: £16,800 for academic year one and £3,000 for the whole tenure

Length of Study: 3 year

Frequency: Annual

Country of Study: Any country

No. of awards offered: 12–15 each year

Closing Date: 28 February

Funding: Foundation

Additional Information: www.carnegie-trust.org/award-schemes/carnegie-phd-scholarships/

For further information contact:

Andrew Carnegie House, Pittencrieff St, Dunfermline KY12 8AW, United Kingdom.

Tel: (44) 1383 724 990

Email: phd-scholarships@carnegie-trust.org

St Andrews Society of New York Scholarships

Purpose: The Carnegie Trust for the Universities of Scotland administers this scholarship programme for students in the United Kingdom who wish to apply for graduate study in the United States. Successful candidates are expected to be the highest caliber, both academically and in their wider personal interests

Eligibility: 1. Candidates must be Scottish by birth or descent, and have up-do-date knowledge of Scotland, Scottish current affairs and of the Scottish tradition generally. The Society expects its scholars to be good ambassadors for Scotland. 2. Candidates must also be: 2a. either graduates of a Scottish university, Glasgow School of Art, Royal Conservatoire of Scotland, or of Oxford or Cambridge, who have completed their first degree course (so as to be qualified to graduate) not earlier than 2022. 2b. Or students of a Scottish university, Glasgow School of Art, Royal Conservatoire of Scotland, or of Oxford or Cambridge, who expect to complete their first degree course (so as to be qualified to graduate) in 2023. 3. Preference is given to candidates who have no previous, or limited, experience of the United States and for whom a period of study in that country may provide a life-changing experience.

Level of Study: Postgraduate

Type: Scholarship

Value: US$35,000

Length of Study: 1 year

Frequency: Annual

Country of Study: Scotland

Application Procedure: Candidates apply directly to the university where they are studying in Scotland, Cambridge or Oxford. Under no circumstances should candidates apply directly to the trust.

No. of awards offered: 2 each year

Closing Date: 15 March

Funding: Private

Additional Information: www.carnegie-trust.org/award-schemes/st-andrews-society-of-new-york-scholarships/

For further information contact:

Andrew Carnegie House, Pittencrieff St, Dunfermline KY12 8AW, United Kingdom.

Tel: (44) 1383 724 990

Email: admin@carnegie-trust.org

Casino Mucho

Casinomucho Research Scholarship (CSR)

Purpose: This research scholarship provide an individual with a grant to shape up and change the face of online gambling industry within the next few years

Eligibility: 1. Full time student at college/university (preferred Marketing, Business or Communication courses). 2. No entry limit per contestant. 3. Casinomucho.com employees immediate families are not eligible. 4. 3,000–5,000 words essay on one of the given topic in Microsoft Word format with correct grammar, heading and punctuation. 5. The article must be plagiarism free

Level of Study: Postgraduate
Type: Scholarship
Value: £500
Frequency: Annual
Country of Study: United Kingdom
Application Procedure: 1. Students must submit their applications to scholarship [at] muchoent.com. 2. Applications should include full name, date of birth, name or degree course, essay in Word format
Closing Date: 31 March
Funding: Private
Additional Information: casinomucho.com/scholarship/

For further information contact:

Email: scholarship@muchoent.com

Catholic University of Louvain

1, Place de l'Université, Louvain-la-Neuve, B-1348, Belgium.

Tel: (32) 10 472 111
Website: www.uclouvain.be

Hoover Fellowships for International Scholars

Eligibility: Candidates must be scholars from outside Belgium, who hold a doctorate or possess equivalent qualifications and are active in the field of economic or social ethics broadly conceived. Candidates for a full fellowship must have no professional income from other sources in the period concerned. Proficiency in either English or French is required, and at least a passive knowledge in both is desirable
Type: Fellowship
Value: One full Hoover fellowship of €2,000 per month (plus social security contributions) for a duration of 3 months. Several honorary Hoover fellowships for a duration of 1 to 6 months with a contribution to housing and travelling costs of up to €500 per month
Frequency: Annual
Study Establishment: UCL

Country of Study: Belgium
Application Procedure: Applications must reach Thérèse Davio by email (therese.davio@uclouvain.be)
Closing Date: 28 February
Contributor: UCL
Additional Information: For more information, please visit www.uclouvain.be/398682.html
www.hoover.org/library-archives/about/fellowships

CEC Artslink

291 Broadway, 12th Floor, New York, NY 10022, United States of America.

Tel: (1) 212 643 1985
Email: info@cecartslink.org
Website: www.cecartslink.org

CEC Artslink is an international arts service organization. Our programmes encourage and support exchange of artists and cultural managers between the United States and Central Europe, Russia, and Eurasia. We believe that the arts are a society's most deliberate and complex means of communication.

ArtsLink Independent Projects

Purpose: To provide funding to artists and arts managers who propose to undertake projects in the United States in collaboration with a United States non-profit arts organization
Eligibility: Candidates must be citizens of, and reside in, an eligible countries Albania, Armenia, Azerbaijan, Belarus, Bosnia and Herzegovina, Bulgaria, Croatia, Czech Republic, Estonia, Georgia, Hungary, Kazakhstan, Kosovo, Kyrgyzstan, Latvia, Lithuania, Macedonia, Moldova, Mongolia, Montenegro, Poland, Romania, Russia, Serbia, Slovak Republic, Slovenia, Tajikistan, Turkmenistan, Ukraine and Uzbekistan. There are no age limitations. Arts managers must be affiliated with an organization in the non-commercial sector
Type: Fellowship
Value: US$5,000
Length of Study: 1 year
Frequency: Annual
Country of Study: United States of America
Application Procedure: Complete online application form
Closing Date: 3 December
No. of awards given last year: 5

Additional Information: Please check at www.cecartslink.org/grants/independent_projects/ www.transartists.org/air/cec-artslink

For further information contact:

CEC ArtsLink, 435 Hudson Street, 8th Floor, New York, NY 10014, United States of America.

Email: al@cecartslink.org

ArtsLink Projects

Purpose: To support United States artists, curators, presenters, and non-profit arts organizations undertaking projects in Eastern and Central Europe, Russia, Central Asia and the Caucasus

Eligibility: Open to citizens of eligible countries Albania, Armenia, Azerbaijan, Belarus, Bosnia and Herzegovina, Bulgaria, Croatia, Czech Republic, Estonia, Georgia, Hungary, Kazakhstan, Kosovo, Kyrgyzstan, Latvia, Lithuania, Macedonia, Moldova, Mongolia, Montenegro, Poland, Romania, Russia, Serbia, Slovak Republic, Slovenia, Tajikistan, Turkmenistan, Ukraine and Uzbekistan

Level of Study: Postgraduate

Type: Fellowship

Value: Up to US$10,000

Length of Study: 1 year

Frequency: Annual

Country of Study: Any country

Application Procedure: Complete online application form

Closing Date: 15 January

Funding: Private, Trusts

No. of awards given last year: 10

Additional Information: Please check at www.cecartslink.org/grants/artslink_projects/

ArtsLink Residencies

Purpose: To create opportunities for artists and communities across the United States to share artistic practices with artists and arts managers from abroad and engage in dialogue that advances understanding across cultures

Eligibility: Applicants must be the citizens of, and reside in, eligible countries Afghanistan, Albania, Armenia, Azerbaijan, Belarus, Bosnia and Herzegovina, Bulgaria, Croatia, Czech Republic, Estonia, Georgia, Hungary, Kazakhstan, Kosovo, Kyrgyzstan, Latvia, Lithuania, Macedonia, Moldova, Mongolia, Montenegro, Poland, Romania, Russia, Serbia, Slovak Republic, Slovenia, Tajikistan, Turkmenistan, Ukraine and Uzbekistan

Level of Study: Postgraduate

Type: Fellowship

Value: offer artists and arts managers/curators from eligible overseas countries a six-week residency at an established, non-profit arts organization in the US

Length of Study: 6 weeks

Frequency: Annual

Country of Study: United States of America

Application Procedure: 1. A completed ArtsLink International Fellowship online application form. 2. Answers to the following questions a. Describe the current issues in your work and explain how a residency in the United States will advance your professional development as an artist or arts manager. (300 words maximum) b. Please describe previous projects that have involved engagement or participation, and explain how you plan to engage with US artists and communities during your residency. (300 words maximum) c. Please list the most important types of activities and arts events you are hoping to take part in, keeping in mind that your residency may take place in any of the 50 states of the US. (300 words maximum) d. What prior experience or contact have you had with the United States (300 words maximum) e. Have you traveled outside your country of residence to pursue research or study If so, please indicate when and where you have traveled and in what capacity. (300 words maximum) g. How will you share your ArtsLink experience with your home community (300 words maximum) 3. The most recent CV or résumé (only one-page PDF file) that lists your professional accomplishments in reverse chronological order starting from the most recent one. Only one-page documents will be submitted for panel review. 4. A letter of recommendation (only one-page PDF file) from a colleague or supervisor that explains how a residency in the United States will benefit you professionally and why it is an important endeavor at this time in your career. If written in a language other than English, please include an English translation. This letter can be submitted to mtumenev@cecartslink.org separately from your application, but it must arrive within two weeks of the application deadline. No emails will be accepted unless approved by ArtsLink staff. Letters without signatures will also not be accepted. 5. If you are applying as an arts manager / curator submit a one-page PDF file with description of your organization in English. Include information about staff size and resources.

Closing Date: 15 October

Funding: Private, Trusts

Contributor: ArtsLink Residencies are funded through public and private sources including CEC ArtsLink, the National Endowment for the Arts, the Trust for Mutual Understanding, the Ohio Arts Council, the Kettering Fund and the Milton and Sally Avery Arts Foundation with additional support from the Polish Cultural Institute and the Romanian Cultural Institute

No. of awards given last year: 16

Additional Information: Please check at www.cecartslink.org/grants/artslink_residencies/

For further information contact:

291 Broadway, 14th Floor, New York, NY 10007, United States of America.

Fax: (1) 212 643 1996

Center for Creative Photography (CCP)

The University of Arizona, 1030 North Olive Road, Tucson, AZ 210103, United States of America.

Tel: (1) 520 621 7970
Email: info@ccp.library.arizona.edu
Website: www.creativephotography.org/

The Center for Creative Photography (CCP) is an archive and research centre located on the University of Arizona campus.

Center for Creative Photography Ansel Adams Research Fellowship

Purpose: To promote and support research on the Center's photograph, archive and library collections
Eligibility: Advanced scholars and researchers from any discipline are encouraged to apply. Pre-doctoral applicants must have completed coursework and preliminary examinations for the doctoral degree and must be engaged in dissertation research
Level of Study: Research
Type: Fellowship
Value: US$5,000
Length of Study: 2–4 weeks
Frequency: Annual
Country of Study: United States of America
Application Procedure: 1. Complete the application form. Please check back in Fall for new application form. 2. Include a 500-1,000 word statement detailing your research interests and project, and how they will be advanced by study of the Center's archives, library, and print collection 3. Attach a Curriculum Vitae of no more than four pages
Additional Information: Please check at ccp.arizona.edu/about/opportunities/ansel-adams-research-fellowship

For further information contact:

Center for Creative Photography, 1030 N. Olive Road, Tucson, AZ 85719, United States of America.

Tel: (1) 520 621 0050
Fax: (1) 520 621 9444
Email: peregoya@ccp.arizona.edu

Center for Defense Information (CDI)

1100 G Street NW, Suite 500, Washington, DC 20005-3806, United States of America.

Tel: (1) 202 347 1122
Email: info@cdi.org
Website: www.cdi.org
Contact: Joe Newman, Director of Communications

The Center for Defense Information (CDI) provides responsible, non-partisan research and analysis on the social, economic, environmental, political and military components of national and global security, and aims to educate the public and inform policy makers about these issues. The organization is staffed by retired senior government officials and knowledgeable researchers and is directed by Dr Bruce G Blair.

Center for Defense Information Internship

Purpose: To support the work of CDI's senior staff while gaining exposure to research, issues and communications related to national security and foreign policy
Eligibility: There are no eligibility restrictions. Paid internships are available for nationals of the United States and legal immigrants
Level of Study: Unrestricted
Type: Internship
Value: US$1,000 per month
Length of Study: 3–5 months
Study Establishment: CDI
Country of Study: Any country
Application Procedure: Applicants must submit a curriculum vitae, covering letter, brief writing sample, transcript and two letters of recommendation
No. of awards offered: 200
Closing Date: 15 October

Funding: Private
No. of awards given last year: 12
No. of applicants last year: 200

For further information contact:

Center for Defense Information, 1779 Massachusetts Avenue, N.W, Washington, DC 20036, United States of America.

Fax: (1) 202 462 4559
Email: internships@cdi.org

Central Queensland University

Building 5 Bruce Highway, Rockhampton, QLD 4702, Australia.

Tel: (61) 7 4930 9000
Email: research-enquiries@cqu.edu.au
Website: www.cqu.edu.au

The Central Queensland University (CQU) is committed to excellence in research and innovation with a particular emphasis on issues that affect the region. CQU achieves relevance in its research goals through linkages with industry, business, government and the community and through collaboration with national and international researchers and research networks. CQU provides a range of exciting and relevant research opportunities for Masters and PhD candidates and is committed to excellence and quality in the research training experience of its candidates.

CQUniCares Emergency Grant

Purpose: CQUniCares Emergency Grants provide financial assistance to low-income students who experience unexpected financial hardship as a result of an emergency or unforeseen situation, that has the potential to derail their studies. The purpose of the grant is to support these students in continuing their studies.
Eligibility: To be eligible to receive the CQUniCares Emergency Grant, an applicant must: 1. be in genuine need of urgent financial assistance as a result of unforeseen circumstances or an emergency situation that has the potential to significantly impact study progress* 1a. be enrolled and actively studying in either a CQUniversity Certificate (I-IV); Enabling/Pathway; Undergraduate or Postgraduate program

1b. have successfully completed at least one term of study at CQUniversity 1c. not be a cross-institutional student (your home institution is not CQUniversity) 1d. be an Australian or New Zealand citizen, permanent resident, or holder of a humanitarian visa with a permanent home address in Australia 1e. have not previously received a CQUniCares Emergency Grant in the last twelve months be able to demonstrate low personal/family income 2. Applicants will need to substantiate requests for financial assistance with copies of bills, invoices or where applicable letter of support from relevant individuals.
Type: Grant
Value: Considered on a case-by-case basis
Frequency: Annual
Country of Study: Any country
Closing Date: 13 December
Additional Information: www.cqu.edu.au/courses/future-students/scholarships/offerings/cqunicares-emergency-grant

CQUniversity Indigenous Australian Postgraduate Research Award

Eligibility: To be eligible for a CQUniversity Research Stipend Scholarship (Australian Indigenous), an applicant must 1. Be an Indigenous Australian citizen. Recipients would be required to provide verification of their community acceptance as an Australian Aboriginal and/or Torres Strait Islander. 2. Be undertaking, or approved for admission and enrolling in, a research higher degree program at CQUniversity. 3. If undertaking 1. A Research Masters, not hold a research Doctorate or a Research Masters or an equivalent research qualification; and 2. a Research Doctorate, not hold a Research Doctorate or an equivalent research qualification; and 3. must not be receiving income from another source to support the student's general living costs while undertaking the course of study if that income is greater than 75 per cent of the CQUniversity Research Stipend Scholarship (Australian Indigenous) stipend rate.
Level of Study: Postgraduate, Research
Type: Scholarship
Value: AU$35,000 per year
Length of Study: 2nd year
Frequency: Every 3 years
Study Establishment: Central Queensland University
Country of Study: Australia
Application Procedure: Applicants must be currently enrolled in, or approved for admission and commencing in 2020, in a research higher degree at CQUniversity. To apply for this Award please contact the School of Graduate Research team at sgr@cqu.edu.au to request a CQUniversity Research Stipend Scholarship (Australian Indigenous)

Application Form. Applicants will be notified of the outcome of their applications by email
Closing Date: 29 February
Funding: Government
Additional Information: Applicants will be required to provide a Community Referee Report to confirm their acceptance in the Indigenous Australian community. www.cqu.edu.au/courses-and-programs/scholarships/offerings/cquniversity-postgraduate-research-award-upra

For further information contact:

Office of Research, Building 351, Central Queensland University, Rockhampton, QLD 4702, Australia.

Tel: (61) 7 4923 2607
Fax: (61) 7 4923 2600

CQUniversity Womens Equal Opportunity Research Award

Purpose: To enable a woman to undertake full-time postgraduate research towards a PhD or Master's degree after having experienced a break in study
Eligibility: Open only to female candiates who are citizens or permanent residents of Australia and New Zealand
Level of Study: Doctorate, Postgraduate
Type: Research award
Value: AU$19,616 (maximum per year)
Frequency: Annual
Study Establishment: Central Queensland University
Country of Study: Australia
Application Procedure: Check website for further details
Closing Date: 31 October
Funding: Government
Additional Information: This scholarship is paid fortnightly for the period of 2 years (Masters) or 3 years (PhD). Open for applications from 1 July www.scholarshipcare.com/womens-equal-opportunity-postgraduate-research-award-upra-w/

CQUniversity/Industry Collaborative Grants Scheme

Purpose: To encourage active research collaboration between the university and eligible industry partners
Eligibility: Open for candidates who are full-time members of staff (either individuals or teams) and are able to demonstrate through their track record that they have the capability to successfully complete the proposed project
Type: Grant

Value: Up to AU$10,000 is tenable for 1 year, commencing 1 January and ending 31 December
Length of Study: 12 months
Study Establishment: Central Queensland University
Country of Study: Australia
Application Procedure: Applications must be submitted on the current application form, in the required format with the required number of copies. One original application, and one identical copy must be submitted in hard copy, and one copy must be submitted electronically, either as a word or pdf document
Closing Date: 11 August

For further information contact:

Bldg 351, Rockhampton (City) Campus, Rockhampton, QLD 4702, Australia.

Tel: (61) 4923 2601
Fax: (61) 4923 2600
Email: l.walker@cqu.edu.au

Destination Australia Scholarship (Master of Research)

Eligibility: To be eligible for a Destination Australia Scholarship (Master of Research) an applicant must: 1. be a new full-time internal international Master of Research applicant 2. be new to CQUniversity 3. be commencing in a Master of Research at CQUniversity Rockhampton North or Bundaberg Campus.
Level of Study: Postgraduate
Value: US$30,000 per year
Length of Study: 2 years
Country of Study: Any country
No. of awards offered: 2
Closing Date: 28 February
Funding: Government
Additional Information: www.cqu.edu.au/courses/future-students/scholarships/offerings/destination-australia-scholarship-master-of-research

HeART of the Basin Scholarship

Eligibility: To be eligible to receive the HeART of the Basin Scholarship, an applicant must meet the following criteria: 1. Be enrolled in an Honours, Masters by Research or PhD in a relevant field of research at CQUniversity. Relevant Research fields include: 1a. Agriculture 1b. Built Environment 1c. Economics 1d. Engineering 1e. Environmental Science 1f. Science 2. Be studying on campus in Rockhampton or through online study 3. Devote time during the length of the scholarship (12 months) to an agreed research topic relating to advancing waterway health and/or understanding and use of waterways in the Fitzroy Basin. 4. Be an Australian Citizen or Permanent Resident 5. Not be receiving another CQUniversity Scholarship of similar or higher value. 6. Please refer to the Fitzroy Partnership for River Health website for further details.

Level of Study: Postgraduate
Type: Scholarship
Value: AU$3,000
Length of Study: Once-off
Frequency: Annual
Country of Study: Any country
No. of awards offered: 1
Closing Date: 25 March

International Student Scholarship

Purpose: The International Student Scholarship is available to all new international undergraduate and postgraduate coursework students who meet the academic criteria at CQUniversity Australia. The Scholarship rewards successful applicants with up to the value of 20% of your tuition fees for the duration of their studies, subject to meeting terms and conditions.
Eligibility: 1. The International Student Scholarship is awarded, at the discretion of the University, to exceptional international students, undertaking on-campus, full-time degree study at CQUniversity Australia. 2. The International Student Scholarship is only available to students applying for undergraduate or postgraduate coursework. 3. The International Student Scholarship is only available for full degree courses (full bachelor or masters only). 4. The International Student Scholarship is only available to students new to CQUniversity Australia - it is not available to students who are currently studying at CQUniversity Australia. Students currently studying at CQUniversity and applying for Change of Course will also not be eligible for the International Student Scholarship. 5. The International Student Scholarship is not available in conjunction with any other CQUniversity Australia scholarship. 6. The International Student Scholarship is not available to any student who has been given entrance to CQUniversity Australia based on work experience. 7. The International Student Scholarship is not transferable to a third party or redeemable for cash. 8. The International Student Scholarship is calculated and applied on a per term basis.
Level of Study: Postgraduate
Type: Scholarship
Value: 25% for new students
Frequency: Annual

Country of Study: Australia
Closing Date: 31 December
Additional Information: www.cqu.edu.au/courses/future-students/scholarships/offerings/international-student-scholarship

International Student Scholarship – Regional

Eligibility: Successful completion of most recent studies prior to applying to CQUniversity Australia.
Type: Scholarship
Value: 25% for new students commencing from 2023 onwards
Length of Study: Duration of course
Country of Study: Any country
Closing Date: 31 December
Additional Information: www.cqu.edu.au/courses/future-students/scholarships/offerings/international-student-scholarship-regional

Master of Research Elevate Scholarship - CQUniversity and Surf Lifesaving Queensland

Eligibility: Citizen of any country. The successful applicant should be available to commence the project early 2024.
Level of Study: Postgraduate
Type: Scholarship
Value: US$30,000 stipend per year
Length of Study: 2 years
Frequency: Annual
Country of Study: Any country
No. of awards offered: 1
Closing Date: 31 January
Additional Information: www.cqu.edu.au/courses/future-students/scholarships/offerings/master-of-research-elevate-scholarship-cquniversity-and-surf-lifesaving-queensland

For further information contact:

Email: s.fien@cqu.edu.au

Merit Grants Scheme

Purpose: To provide opportunities for individuals or groups with well established or developing track records in research to initiate high quality research projects
Eligibility: Members of the full-time staff of the University with a proven research record 'relative to opportunity' are eligible to compete for Merit Research Grants. Candidates must not be absent for a period exceeding eight weeks during

the proposed period of grant. A researcher may be in receipt of only one Merit Grant at any one time
Type: Grant
Value: AU$10,000–30,000
Length of Study: 1 year
Study Establishment: Central Queensland University
Country of Study: Australia
Application Procedure: Applications must be submitted on the current application form, in the required format, and with the required number of copies
Additional Information: A researcher may be in receipt of only one Merit Grant at any one time

PhD Elevate Scholarship - CQUniversity and CRC for Developing Northern Australia Partnership - Climate Change (External)

Eligibility: Have completed a Bachelor's degree with honours or master's degree or be regarded by CQUniversity as having an equivalent level of attainment. The degree should be in the field of agricultural science, biological science, environmental science or equivalent, with significant studies in crop science related fields.
Level of Study: Doctorate
Type: Scholarship
Value: AU$30,000 stipend per year (total value of scholarship AU$112,500) Additional travel support will be provided for travel between Australia and USA
Length of Study: 3 years
Frequency: Annual
Country of Study: Australia
No. of awards offered: 1
Closing Date: 31 January
Additional Information: www.cqu.edu.au/courses/future-students/scholarships/offerings/phd-elevate-scholarship-cquniversity-and-crc-for-developing-northern-australia-partnership-climate-change

For further information contact:

Email: s.bhattarai@cqu.edu.au

PhD Elevate Scholarship - CQUniversity and Surf Lifesaving Queensland

Eligibility: The successful applicant should be available to commence the project early 2024
Level of Study: Doctorate
Type: Scholarship
Value: AU$30,000 stipend per year
Length of Study: 3 years

Frequency: Annual
Country of Study: Any country
No. of awards offered: 1
Closing Date: 31 January
Additional Information: www.cqu.edu.au/courses/future-students/scholarships/offerings/phd-elevate-scholarship-cquniversity-and-surf-lifesaving-queensland

PhD Elevate Scholarship – CQUniversity and FutureFeed Pty Ltd Partnership (External)

Eligibility: 1. A degree in biology, marine biology, environmental science or equivalent (honours or MSc); 2. An interest in applied science and ecosystem services; 3. Experience in designing and performing marine ecological fieldwork; 4. Experience in ecological statistical data analysis; 5. Experience working with marine flora and/or fauna; 6. Ability to work both independently and in a team; 7. Excellent communication skills, including the ability to engage with industry and stakeholders; 8. Scuba diving certification or willingness to get certification.
Level of Study: Doctorate
Type: Scholarship
Value: AU$30,000 stipend (AU$90,000 total), plus project/travel support
Length of Study: 3 years
Frequency: Annual
Country of Study: Australia
No. of awards offered: 1
Closing Date: 21 January
Additional Information: www.cqu.edu.au/courses/future-students/scholarships/offerings/phd-elevate-scholarship-cquniversity-and-futurefeed-pty-ltd-partnership

For further information contact:

Email: j.ferreiracosta@cqu.edu.au

PhD Elevate Scholarship – CQUniversity and FutureFeed Pty Ltd Partnership (External)

Eligibility: 1. A degree in biology, marine biology, environmental science or equivalent (honours or MSc); 2. An interest in applied science and ecosystem services; 3. Experience in designing and performing marine ecological fieldwork; 4. Experience in ecological statistical data analysis; 5. Experience working with marine flora and/or fauna; 6. Ability to work both independently and in a team; 7. Excellent communication skills, including the ability to engage with industry and stakeholders; 8. Scuba diving certification or willingness to get certification.

Level of Study: Doctorate
Type: Scholarship
Value: AU$30,000 stipend (AU$90,000 total), plus project/travel support
Length of Study: 3 years
Frequency: Annual
Country of Study: Australia
No. of awards offered: 1
Closing Date: 21 January
Additional Information: www.cqu.edu.au/courses/future-students/scholarships/offerings/phd-elevate-scholarship-cquniversity-and-futurefeed-pty-ltd-partnership

For further information contact:

Email: j.ferreiracosta@cqu.edu.au

Research Administration Assistants Postdoctoral Award

Purpose: To provide for the university's intellectual environment by facilitating mentoring, team building, and career development in areas of current or future research strength
Eligibility: The applicant must remain based on a Central Queensland University campus (excluding international campuses) for the duration of the award
Level of Study: Postdoctorate
Type: Award
Value: On-costs of 28% will be paid in addition to salary
Frequency: Annual
Study Establishment: Central Queensland University
Country of Study: Australia
Application Procedure: Applications must be submitted on the current application form, in the required format, and with the required number of copies
Funding: Government
Additional Information: Applicants may seek funding for 1, 2, or 3 years www.cqu.edu.au/courses/future-students/scholarships/offerings/international-student-scholarship

Research Training Program (RTP) Stipend Scholarship

Purpose: RTP Stipend Scholarships are funded by the Australian Government. They provide funding allocated to students to assist with their living costs while undertaking a research higher degree.
Eligibility: In accordance with the Commonwealth Scholarship Guidelines (Research) 2017, to be eligible for a RTP Scholarship a candidate must be a domestic candidate or an overseas candidate enrolled in an accredited RHD course of study at CQUniversity. To be eligible for an RTP Stipend a candidate must not be receiving income from another source to support the candidate's general living costs while undertaking their course of study if that income is greater than 75 per cent of the candidate's RTP Stipend rate. Income unrelated to the candidate's course of study or income received for the candidate's course of study but not for the purposes of supporting general living costs is not taken into account. To be eligible for a RTP Fees Offset a candidate must not be receiving an equivalent award of scholarship from the Commonwealth designed to offset RHD tuition fees.
Type: Scholarship
Value: AU$28,854 per annum
Length of Study: 3 years
Frequency: Annual
Country of Study: Australia
Application Procedure: There are no direct applications for RTP Scholarships. Please discuss your interest in an RHD Scholarship with your supervisory team. Prospective applicants will be invited by the School of Graduate Research to complete an application, based on the recommendation of the supervisory team. Applicants will be notified by email when the scholarships have been awarded.
No. of awards offered: 2
Closing Date: 31 December
Additional Information: www.cqu.edu.au/courses/future-students/scholarships/offerings/australian-postgraduate-award-apa-scholarship

Seed Grants Scheme

Purpose: To provide seed funding to encourage new research-trained staff to undertake a funded research project
Eligibility: Open to newly trained researchers, who are currently within the first 5 years of academic or other research-related performance allowing uninterrupted, stable research development following completion of their postgraduate research training
Level of Study: Research
Type: Grant
Value: Up to AU$10,000
Length of Study: 1 year
Study Establishment: Central Queensland University
Country of Study: Australia
Application Procedure: Applications must be submitted on the current application form, in the required format, and with the required number of copies
Closing Date: 11 August
Funding: Government

Centre de Recherches et d'Investigations Epidermiques et Sensorielles

20 rue Victor Noir, F-92200 Neuilly-sur-Seine, France.

Tel: (33) 146 434 900
Email: contact@ceries.com
Website: www.ceries.com

CERIES (Centre de Recherches et d'Investigations Epidermiques et Sensorielles or Centre for Epidermal and Sensory Research and Investigation) is the healthy skin research centre of Chanel.

Centre de Recherches et d'Investigations Epidermiques et Sensorielles Research Award

Purpose: To honour a scientific researcher for a fundamental or clinical research project in the field of healthy skin
Eligibility: There are no eligibility restrictions
Level of Study: Research
Value: €40,000
Length of Study: 1 year
Frequency: Annual
Country of Study: Any country
Application Procedure: Applicants must consult the website
No. of awards offered: 26
Closing Date: 1 June
Funding: Private
Contributor: Chanel
No. of awards given last year: 1
No. of applicants last year: 26
Additional Information: www.nature.com/naturecareers/events/event/8348

For further information contact:

Email: chanelrt.award@ruderfinnasia.com

Centre De Science Humaines (CSH)

2 Aurangzeb Road, New Delhi, 110011, India.

Tel: (91) 11 30410070
Email: direction@csh-delhi.com
Website: www.csh-delhi.com

The Centre de Sciences Humaines (CSH), created in 1989, is a research centre funded by the French Ministry of Foreign Affairs

Centre de Sciences Humaines Post-Doctoral Fellowship

Purpose: To question the status of India as an emerging power in the international scene
Eligibility: Open to candidates who hold a PhD in economics/economic geography/urban studies and are prefereable below 35 years of age
Level of Study: Postdoctorate
Type: Fellowship
Value: Indian Rupees 20,000–25,000 per month
Length of Study: 1 year
Frequency: Annual
Country of Study: India
Application Procedure: Applicants must send their curriculum vitae, 2 academic references letters, a synopsis of the PhD theses and a comprehensive research proposal
Closing Date: 31 January
Additional Information: calenda.org/203026

For further information contact:

Email: veronique.dupont@csh-delhi.com

Centre for Clinical Research Excellence

Centre for Clinical Research Excellence - Infection and Bioethics in Haematological Malignancies, Level 3, ICPMR, Westmead Hospital, Institute Road, Westmead, NSW 2145, Australia.

Tel: (61) 9845 6255
Email: cjordens@med.usyd.edu.au
Website: www.ccre-ibhm.org.au

The Centre for Clinical Research Excellence (CCRE) is multi-centre research collaboration with a special focus on bioethics, consisting of four research sites affiliated with the University of Sydney

Postgraduate Scholarships for Interdisciplinary Bioethics Research

Purpose: To develop surveillance methods and interventions to improve infection-related outcomes in malignant haematology and bone marrow transplantation, with inter-disciplinary bioethics research underpinning all major themes

Eligibility: Open to Australian citizens or permanent resident meeting the standard criteria for NHMRC scholarships, including full-time enrollment and status, as well as the criteria for admission to postgraduate study in the faculty of medicine or faculty of science at the University of Sydney

Level of Study: Graduate

Type: Scholarship

Country of Study: Australia

Application Procedure: Check website for further details

For further information contact:

Tel: (61) 434 07 07 88

Centre for Environment Planning and Technology University

Kasturbhai Lalbhai Campus, University Road, Vasant Vihar, Navrangpura, Ahmedabad, Gujarat 380009, India.

Contact: CEPT University

Centre for Environmental Planning and Technology University, formerly the Centre for Environmental Planning and Technology, is an academic institution located near university area in Ahmedabad, India offering postgraduate programmes in areas of the natural and developed environment of human society and related disciplines.

Full-Tuition Fees Waiver for MPhil/PhD Students

Purpose: Scholarships are available for pursuing MPhil/PhD programme

Eligibility: Students from India are eligible to apply

Type: Grant

Value: The university offers full tuition fees waiver to MPhil/PhD students for their entire term of registration in the program. The university also offers a scholarship (Rs. 36,700 per month-subject to change) for the first six months (mandatory) of the coursework against teaching assignments (15–20 hours/week) as allocated by the respective faculty

Country of Study: India

Application Procedure: Go to the Centre for Environmental Planning and Technology(CEPT) website Click on the 'Admissions' button (on the header menu) at the top of the page. This will open a page with all the programs offered at CEPT University. Click on the program you wish to apply. This will open the tab with 'About' 'FAQ' & 'How to Apply'. Click on the 'How to Apply' button and you will be redirected to a page containing eligibility criteria, program details and the link to the admissions portal. For further information, kindly check the following link. cept.ac.in/2/37/faculty-of-architecture/479/fees-scholarship

Closing Date: 30 April

Contributor: .

Additional Information: For detailed information, check with the below link. scholarship-positions.com/full-tuition-fees-waiver-mphil-phd-students-cept-university-india/2018/04/24/

For further information contact:

Harvard Square, Mifflin Pl, Cambridge, MA 02138, United States of America.

Centre for Groundwater Studies (CGS)

GPO, Box 2100, Adelaide, SA 5001, Australia.

Tel: (61) 8 8201 5632

Email: cgs@groundwater.com.au

Website: www.groundwater.com.au

Centre for Groundwater Studies (CGS) is an international leader in water and environmental research and education.

Chinese Government Scholarship Water and Environmental Research Scholarships

Purpose: To assist students with research projects in the specified areas

Eligibility: Open to Australian citizens and permanent residents who have a background in science, mathematics or engineering

Level of Study: Postgraduate

Type: Scholarship

Value: AU$22,231

Length of Study: 1 year

Frequency: Annual

Country of Study: Australia

Closing Date: September

Additional Information: For additional information see the website scholarship-positions.com/full-tuition-fees-waiver-mphil-phd-students-cept-university-india/2018/04/24/

For further information contact:

Email: impt@scholars4dev.com

Chandigarh University

NH-95 Chandigarh-Ludhiana Highway, Mohali, Punjab 140413, India.

Contact: Chandigarh University

A renowned university in India is offering scholarships for brilliant but less privileged students across the globe who have interest in studying in India.

Chandigarh University Scholarships in India

Purpose: Chandigarh University offers undergraduate and post-graduate and doctorate courses in various disciplines including Engineering, Management, Computing, Education, Animation and Multimedia, Tourism, Pharma Sciences, Biotechnology, Architecture, Commerce and Legal Studies
Eligibility: Students outside India, Nepal and Bhutan can apply for these scholarships. Not Required but all academic documents are to be sent to micheal.africa-at-cumail.in for eligibility checking. Not required but the applicant must be able to read, write and understand the English Language
Level of Study: Graduate, Postgraduate
Value: It is between 15% and 50% (maximum) for tuition fees only
Study Establishment: Scholarships are awarded to study the subjects offered by the university
Country of Study: India
Application Procedure: Interested students can contact Mr. Michael on micheal.africa@cumail.in
Closing Date: July
Additional Information: For more details please contact the website scholarship-positions.com/chandigarh-university-scholarships-india/
www.shiksha.com/university/cu-chandigarh-university-45668/scholarships

For further information contact:

Email: micheal.africa@cumail.in

Charles Babbage Institute (CBI)

211 Andersen Library, University of MN, 222 21st Avenue South, Minneapolis, MN 55455, United States of America.

Tel: (1) 612 624 5050
Email: cbi@umn.edu
Website: www.cbi.umn.edu

The Charles Babbage Institute (CBI) is a research centre dedicated to promoting the study of the history of computing, its impact on society and preserving relevant documentation. CBI fosters research and writing in the history of computing by providing fellowship support, archival resources and information to scholars, computer scientists and the general public.

Adelle and Erwin Tomash Fellowship in the History of Information Processing

Purpose: To advance the professional development of historians in the field
Eligibility: 1. Must be a graduate student or a postgraduate student 2. Must attend a university 3. Must not be attending high school currently 4. Must study full-time 5. Restricted to students studying Computer Science/Data Processing, Electrical Engineering/Electronics, Engineering/Technology, History, Humanities, Science, Technology, and Society
Level of Study: Doctorate
Type: Fellowship
Value: US$14,000
Length of Study: 1 year
Frequency: Annual
Country of Study: Any country
Application Procedure: 1. Recommendations or References 2. Other - Research proposal 3. Resume 4. Transcript
No. of awards offered: 1
Closing Date: 15 January
Funding: Private
Additional Information: Please check at www.cbi.umn.edu/research/tfellowship.html
www.petersons.com/scholarship/adelle-and-erwin-tomash-fellowship-in-the-history-of-information-processing-111_150883.aspx

For further information contact:

University of Minnesota, 211 Elmer Andersen Library, 222-21st Avenue, South, Minneapolis, MN 55455, United States of America.

Email: yostx003@umn.edu

Charles Darwin University

Charles Darwin University, 21 Kitchener Dr, Darwin City, NT 0800, Australia.

Tel: (61) 8 8946 6666
Website: www.cdu.edu.au/

Charles Darwin University is a new world university built on social justice, sustainability, creativity and collective effort.

CDU Vice-Chancellor's International High Achievers Scholarships

Purpose: Charles Darwin University (CDU) offers the Vice-Chancellor's International High Achievers Scholarships to international students who have a record of academic excellence and high achievement and who are seeking to commence an Undergraduate or Postgraduate coursework degree at CDU.
Eligibility: 1. Applicant must apply to commence study in S1 2023 2. Applicant must meet the University's academic and English language entry requirement for their chosen courseb 3. Applicant must have a minimum overall score of 95% in their highest completed qualification 4. Applicant must be an international student paying international student fees 5. Applicant must not hold another scholarship from an Australian or foreign sponsoring agency.
Level of Study: Bachelors/Masters Degree
Type: Scholarships
Value: 25% or 50% of the tuition fee. The tuition scholarships apply to the tuition fees for the full duration of the degree.
Frequency: Annual
Country of Study: Australia
Application Procedure: To apply, you must complete the scholarship application form and submit it together with your application for admission to a degree program at CDU
No. of awards offered: Limited
Closing Date: 31 January
Additional Information: www.cdu.edu.au/international/future-students/scholarships

Destination Australia Scholarships

Purpose: Destination Australia is an Australian Government initiative. The scholarships are aimed to provide financial support to Domestic and International students who choose to study in regional and rural Australia.
Level of Study: Doctorate
Type: Award

Frequency: Annual
Country of Study: Any country
No. of awards offered: US$7,500 in scholarship funding per semester
Closing Date: 3 March
Funding: Private

Menzies Global Leader Scholarship

Subjects: Menzies Education offers a limited number of Menzies Global Leader Scholarships to international students who have a record of academic excellence and high achievement. The scholarship is neither transferable for cash nor refundable and cannot be transferred to another person, semester, course or year.
Eligibility: 1. Applicant must apply to commence study in S1 2023 2. Applicants must meet the University's academic and English language entry requirements for their chosen course 3. Applicants must have a minimum overall score of 70% in their highest completed qualification 4. Applicant must be an international student on a student visa 5. Applicant must not hold another scholarship from an Australian or foreign sponsorship agency 6. Must take on a minimum of two units of study in a compulsory study period
Level of Study: Postgraduate
Type: Scholarship
Value: The scholarship covers 25% of the tuition fee for the first year of study (compulsory semesters only) and 10% in subsequent years.
Length of Study: 2 year
Frequency: Annual
Country of Study: Any country
Closing Date: 7 March
Additional Information: www.cdu.edu.au/international/how-apply/scholarships#applying-for-a-scholarship

Charles Darwin University (CDU)

Charles Darwin University Ellengowan Drive, Casuarina, NT 0811, Australia.

Tel: (61) 8 8946 6666
Email: scholarships@cdu.edu.au
Website: www.cdu.edu.au

The Charles Darwin University (CDU) offers programmes from certificate level to PhD, incorporating the full range of vocational education courses. CDU has a distinctive research profile, reflecting the priorities appropriate to its location. It is a participating member of several CRCs.

Nanyang Technological University MBA Programme

Length of Study: 1 year, 18 months or 4 years
Country of Study: Any country
Application Procedure: Applicants must submit, with their application form, three recent passport sized photographs, official copies of degrees and professional qualifications, two references in sealed envelopes, evidence of finance, TOEFL and IELTS scores (overseas applicants only)

For further information contact:

Tel: (61) 8 8946 6447
Fax: (61) 8 8946 6777
Email: busgrad@business.ntu.edu.au

Vocational Education and Training (VET) Distinction Scholarship

Purpose: CDU Global offers a limited number of VET Distinction Scholarships to international students who come from China PRC, Indonesia or the Philippines and have a record of academic excellence and high achievement.
Eligibility: 1. have a demonstrated record of academic excellence, community engagement and leadership 2. meet your NT education provider's academic and English entry requirements 3. have applied for and obtained an offer of admission to a NT education provider between 1 October 2023 and 30 June 2024 4. not be already studying or residing in the NT, or with a NT education provider 5. not hold any other scholarship 6. have submitted a completed scholarship application form to your NT education provider 7. not hold current Australian or New Zealand citizenship, or Australian permanent residency.
Level of Study: Postgraduate
Type: Scholarship
Value: AU$7500.
Length of Study: 1 year
Country of Study: Any country
Application Procedure: Download the form below to apply now! theterritory.com.au/system/files/uploads/2021/scholarship-application-form_0.pdf
Closing Date: 30 June
Additional Information: www.cdu.edu.au/international/how-apply/scholarships

Charles Sturt University (CSU)

Charles Sturt University, Boorooma Street, Locked Bag 588, Wagga Wagga, NSW 2678, Australia.

Tel: (61) 2 6338 6077
Email: inquiry@csu.edu.au
Website: www.csu.edu.au

CSU is one of the leading Australian universities for graduate employment and largest provider in distance education. Utilizing our expertise in distance education, CSU provides educational opportunities to students around the world. Around 36,000 students undertake their choice of study with CSU on one of our campuses, from home, their workplace or anywhere around the globe.

AHO Tertiary Accommodation Grants

Purpose: The grants will provide eligible Aboriginal students with assistance to source affordable accommodation options.
Eligibility: To be eligible for this grant you must be: able to provide evidence of Aboriginality; 2. enrolled as a full-time student in an approved course; 3. enrolled as an internal student 4. able to provide a brief statement outlining why you need a tertiary university accommodation grant (less than 600 words); 5. able to provide evidence of either: 6. being a social housing tenant or; in housing stress (for this program - housing stress is defined as expending more than 40% of weekly income on accommodation).
Type: Grant
Value: AU$5,000
Frequency: Annual
Country of Study: Any country
Closing Date: 16 February
Additional Information: study.csu.edu.au/get-support/scholarships/find-scholarship/equity/university-accommodation-grants#tab1

For further information contact:

Email: scholarships@csu.edu.au

Australian Postgraduate Awards

Purpose: To financially support postgraduate students of exceptional research promise in Master or Doctoral programs at Charles Sturt University

Eligibility: Awards will only be available to those who are Australian citizens and New Zealand citizens; have been granted permanent resident status by October 31st; have lived in Australia continuously for at least 12 months prior to October 31st; have completed at least 4 years of tertiary education studies at a high level of achievement; have obtained First Class Honours or equivalent results; will undertake a Master's (Honours) or Doctoral degree; are enroling as full-time students or, in exceptional circumstances, be granted approval by CSU for a part-time award; have had their enrolment into the proposed higher degree programme accepted by CSU

Level of Study: Postgraduate, Research
Type: Award
Value: AU$32,500 per year
Length of Study: 2–3 years
Frequency: Annual
Study Establishment: Charles Sturt University
Country of Study: Australia
Application Procedure: Applicants must submit an application form
Closing Date: 31 July
Funding: Government
Additional Information: Please check at www.csu.edu.au/research/support/research-students/my-hdr/getting-started/scholarship-opportunities/main-round

For further information contact:

Email: rgs@latrobe.edu.au

BCEF Future Regional Doctors Scholarship

Purpose: The Bush Children's Education Foundation wants to support the future generation of regional doctors by offering this scholarship to students from the regions studying medicine

Eligibility: Your home origin address has a Regional Rating of RA2-RA5, please check your Regional Rating prior to applying, (tick 2016 then search) Rurality Rating Check Demonstrated financial hardship by providing a Centrelink Income Statement or outline your financial need in the 'Additional Financial Information' free text box in application Applicant should be studying for a career that could be applied to a rural context. There would be an intention that upon graduation the graduate would work in a country area; Applicant should have a strong empathy with the bush community; Applicants are required to write a 250 word essay "Provide information on the remote/isolated area of NSW where you live and also indicate your empathy with the community". Preference may be given to applicants who were in receipt of the Federal Government's AIC Allowance

or the LAFHA (Living Away from Home) Allowance (supporting documentation to be provided).

Level of Study: Postdoctorate
Type: Scholarship
Value: AU$17500
Frequency: Annual
Country of Study: Any country
No. of awards offered: 300
Closing Date: 2 February
Additional Information: study.csu.edu.au/get-support/scholarships/find-scholarship/foundation/1st-year/bcef-future-regional-doctors-scholarship#tab2

For further information contact:

Email: advancement@csu.edu.au

Biology of Annual Ryegrass Scholarship

Purpose: To characterize annual ryegrass in Australian winter cropping areas
Eligibility: Open only for the citizens of Australia or permanent residents those who have a background in agriculture, biology, or plant science and achieved Honours 2a or equivalent
Level of Study: Graduate
Value: AU$24,616 (maximum per year) paid fortnightly for the period of 3 years
Country of Study: Australia

For further information contact:

Charles Sturt University, Wagga Wagga, Boorooma St, North Wagga Wagga, NSW 2650, Australia.

Tel: (61) 2 69 33 2862
Email: jpratley@csu.edu.au

Casella Family Brands PhD Scholarship

Eligibility: 1. PhD in Viticulture and Oenology CONDITIONS: 1. Must be a domestic student 2. Meet the requirements for entry to the Charles Sturt PhD program 3. Provide a copy of the research proposal 4. Outline your career goals and aspirations
Level of Study: Postdoctorate
Type: Scholarship
Value: AU$30,000
Frequency: Annual
Country of Study: Any country
No. of awards offered: 300
Closing Date: 2 February

Additional Information: study.csu.edu.au/get-support/schol arships/find-scholarship/foundation/continuing/casella-family-brands-phd-scholarship#tab2

For further information contact:

Email: advancement@csu.edu.au

Charles Sturt Accommodation Equity Scholarship

Purpose: The Charles Sturt Accommodation Scholarship is designed to assist commencing and continuing students who are residing in on-campus residences.

Eligibility: To be eligible for this scholarship you must be: 1. studying an undergraduate degree as an active student; 2. enrolled in a Charles Sturt University course as a Commonwealth supported student in a Commonwealth supported place. Full fee-paying students are not eligible; 3. enrolled as an internal student; 4. a commencing or continuing student. Continuing students must have a Grade Point Average (GPA) of 3.0 or higher (pass grade average); 5. an Australian citizen, a New Zealand citizen, a permanent Australian resident or a student with an Australian permanent visa; 6. in financial need: 6a. in receipt of an eligible means-tested Centrelink Benefit (refer guidelines); or 6b. must be able to demonstrate financial need; 7. residing continuously in on-campus accommodation full-time (29–40 weeks) in Albury, Bathurst, Dubbo, Orange, Port Macquarie or Wagga Wagga. For the year in which this scholarship is awarded. This Scholarship is not intended for students undertaking multiple or long term placements.

Value: AU$5,000 commencing, AU$3,000 continuing
Length of Study: 2 years
Frequency: Annual
Country of Study: Any country
Closing Date: 12 February
Additional Information: study.csu.edu.au/get-support/schol arships/find-scholarship/equity/accommodation#tab2

Charles Sturt University Postgraduate Research Studentships (CSUPRS)

Purpose: To support high quality research students in Masters or Doctoral programs at Charles Sturt University
Eligibility: Open to the candidates who hold or expect to hold, at least a Bachelor degree with upper second class honours or a qualification deemed equivalent from CSU
Level of Study: Graduate, Research
Type: Studentship

Value: US$22,500 stipend plus allowances
Frequency: Annual
Country of Study: Any country
Application Procedure: Scholarship application form can be downloaded from the website. Send in the filled application to the center with original referee report and five copies of their report
Closing Date: 30 October
Additional Information: Offers of scholarships cannot be made to candidates until their enrolment as Research Higher Degree students has been approved by the Board of Graduate Studies. Please check at www.csu.edu.au/research/support/research-students/my-hdr/getting-started/scholarship-opportunities/main-round
www.gooduniversitiesguide.com.au/scholarships/csu-post graduate-research-scholarship-csuprs/charles-sturt-univer sity/12142

For further information contact:

Postgraduate Scholarships, Center for Research & Graduate Training, Charles Sturt University, Locked Bag 588, Wagga Wagga, NSW 2678, Australia.

Tel: (61) 2 6933 4162
Email: pgscholars@csu.edu.au

CSU Foundation Persistence Scholarship

Eligibility: Postgraduate Any course studied on any campus full time, part time, on campus or online CONDITIONS: Applicants must demonstrate in their application how they have shown persistence in the face of adversity to undertake/complete their studies Demonstrated financial hardship by providing a Centrelink Income Statement or outline your financial need in the 'Additional Financial Information' free text box in application
Level of Study: Postgraduate
Type: Scholarship
Frequency: Annual
Country of Study: Australia
No. of awards offered: 300
Closing Date: 2 February
Additional Information: study.csu.edu.au/get-support/schol arships/find-scholarship/foundation/continuing/csu-persis tence-scholarship#tab2

For further information contact:

Email: advancement@csu.edu.au

CSU give - Research Scholarship

Eligibility: 1. A research based degree in any area CONDITIONS: Available to students studying either on campus or online 1. satisfactory progress - all University milestones must be satisfactorily met, including completion of six monthly progress reports. 2. HDR student is within approved Candidature Time. 3. regional community development 4. 500 words demonstrating that their Research has regional focus and how the funds would be expended.
Type: Scholarship
Value: AU$5000
Country of Study: Australia
Closing Date: 2 February
Additional Information: study.csu.edu.au/get-support/scholarships/find-scholarship/foundation/continuing/csu-give-student-research-scholarship#tab2

For further information contact:

Email: advancement@csu.edu.au

Elite Athlete Scholarship

Purpose: The Charles Sturt University Elite Athlete and Performer Scholarship will provide support to elite athletes or performers to meet their training or competition requirements.
Eligibility: To be eligible for this scholarship you must be: 1. studying an undergraduate or postgraduate degree as an active student; 2. enrolled in a Charles Sturt University course as a Commonwealth supported student in a Commonwealth supported place. Full fee-paying students are not eligible; 3. a commencing or continuing student. Continuing students must have a Grade Point Average (GPA) of 3.0 or higher (pass grade average); 4. an Australian citizen, a New Zealand citizen, a permanent Australian resident or a student with an Australian permanent visa; 5. able to demonstrate financial circumstances associated with sporting or performing representation costs; 6. able to demonstrate proven sporting or performing representation at state, national or international level in 2022 or 2023 7. a member of the Charles Sturt University Elite and pre-elite Athlete and Performer program.
Level of Study: Postgraduate
Type: Scholarship
Value: AU$2,500
Length of Study: 2 years
Frequency: Annual
Country of Study: Any country
Closing Date: 16 February

Additional Information: study.csu.edu.au/get-support/scholarships/find-scholarship/equity/elite-athlete-scholarship#tab2

For further information contact:

Email: scholarships@csu.edu.au

Emergency Equity Grant

Purpose: The Charles Sturt University Student Emergency Equity Grant provides assistance to students who are experiencing financial hardship. Grants are provided to help with the costs of accommodation, basic living costs, groceries, textbook and course material/equipment and transport costs.
Eligibility: 1. studying an undergraduate or postgraduate degree as an active student and have completed one semester of study or be enrolled after the census date of your first semester. 2. enrolled in a Charles Sturt University course as a Commonwealth supported student in a Commonwealth supported place. 3. full fee-paying students may be considered on a case by case basis. 4. continuing students must have a Grade Point Average (GPA) of 3.0 or higher (pass grade average). 5. an Australian citizen, a New Zealand citizen, a permanent Australian resident or a student with an Australian permanent visa. 6. able to demonstrate you are in financial need and your continued study might be placed in jeopardy without assistance.
Level of Study: Graduate, Postgraduate
Type: Grant
Value: AU$1,000
Frequency: Annual
Country of Study: Australia
Additional Information: study.csu.edu.au/get-support/scholarships/find-scholarship/equity/eeg#tab3

For further information contact:

Email: scholarships@csu.edu.au

Evidence-Based Approach to Improve Insulin Sensitivity in Horses, Using Dietary Ingredients

Eligibility: Open only for the citizens of Australia or permanent residents those who have achieved Honours 1 (Semester 1)
Level of Study: Graduate
Value: AU$19,231 (maximum per year) paid fortnightly for the period of 3 years and to be used for living expenses

Country of Study: Australia

For further information contact:

Charles Sturt University, Locked Bag 588, Wagga Wagga, NSW 2678, Australia.

Tel: (61) 2 6933 4242
Email: gnoble@csu.edu.au

First Nations Accommodation and Relocation Scholarship

Purpose: The First Nations Accommodation and Relocation Scholarship is to assist students with relocation and accommodation costs (removalists hire, bond payment, rent assistance).
Eligibility: To be eligible for this scholarship you must be: 1. a First Nations Australian citizen; 2. an active student studying in enabling, undergraduate, honours or postgraduate awards; 3. enrolled in a Charles Sturt course as a Commonwealth supported student in a Commonwealth supported place; 4. a commencing or continuing student. Continuing students must have a Grade Point Average (GPA) of 3.0 or higher (pass grade average); 5. enrolled as an internal or mixed mode student; 6. full time or part-time; 7. applicants must not be receiving or have received a payment from any other source for the same purpose of relocation or accommodation costs, including the Centrelink Relocation Scholarship or Centrelink Residential Cost Option. 8. in financial need: 8a. in receipt of an eligible means tested Centrelink Benefit or 8b. able to demonstrate financial hardship.
Type: Scholarship
Frequency: Annual
Country of Study: Any country
Closing Date: 16 February
Additional Information: study.csu.edu.au/get-support/scholarships/find-scholarship/equity/indigenous-accommodation-relocation#tab2

For further information contact:

Email: scholarships@csu.edu.au

First Nations Education Costs Scholarship

Purpose: The First Nations Education Costs Scholarship is to assist students with the cost of study (compulsory textbooks, study equipment and laptops).

Eligibility: To be eligible for this scholarship you must be: 1. a First Nations Australian citizen; 2. an active student studying in enabling, undergraduate, honours or postgraduate awards; 3. enrolled in a Charles Sturt course as a Commonwealth supported student in a Commonwealth supported place; 4. a commencing or continuing student. Continuing students must have a Grade Point Average (GPA) of 3.0 or higher (pass grade average); 5. full time or part time 6. applicants must not be in receipt of the Centrelink Student Start up Loan or have received a payment from any other source for the same purpose of education costs. 7. in financial need: 7a. in receipt of an eligible means tested Centrelink Benefit or 7b. able to demonstrate financial hardship
Type: Scholarship
Value: AU$3000+
Length of Study: 2 years
Frequency: Annual
Country of Study: Australia
Closing Date: 16 February
Additional Information: study.csu.edu.au/get-support/scholarships/find-scholarship/equity/indigenous-education-costs#tab2

Full-time scholarship (Australian Government's Research Training Program)

Eligibility: AGRTP scholarships are generally for full-time study towards higher degrees by research. These scholarships are highly competitive, and only applicants who meet the following eligibility criteria will be considered: 1. Commencing a Charles Sturt University HDR program, or currently enrolled. 2. Enrolling/enrolled as a full-time student. AGRTP scholarships will not be available to those who: 1. Are enrolled concurrently in any other program, unless it is essential to the success of the HDR, or exceptional circumstances exist and are approved. 2. Are receiving another Commonwealth-funded postgraduate research scholarship.
Level of Study: Postgraduate
Value: AU$28,854 per annum. Scholarship recipients may be eligible to receive a relocation allowance for the cost of relocating themselves, their spouse, and dependants to a Charles Sturt University campus, to a maximum of AU$5,000.
Length of Study: 4 to 3 years
Frequency: Annual
Country of Study: Any country
Closing Date: 30 April
Additional Information: research.csu.edu.au/study-with-us/scholarships/full-time-scholarship-agrtp

Honours Scholarship HECS Exempt Award

Purpose: A cash scholarship for meritorious students studying Honours courses, plus HECS-HELP exemption for successful Honours Scholarship recipients.

Eligibility: To be eligible for this scholarship you must be: 1. studying an Honours degree at Charles Sturt University as an active student 2. enrolled in a Charles Sturt University course as a Commonwealth supported student in a Commonwealth supported place. Full fee-paying students are not eligible 3. enrolled as a full-time or part-time student 4. Continuing students must have a Grade Point Average (GPA) of 5.0 of higher (pass grade average); 5. an Australian citizen, a New Zealand citizen, a permanent Australian resident or a student with an Australian permanent visa 6. able to demonstrate you have maintained a Grade Point Average (GPA) of 5.0 or above in your undergraduate or Honours course 7. must not have been in receipt of this scholarship previously; you can only receive this scholarship once during your enrolment at Charles Sturt University.

Type: Scholarship
Value: AU$4000
Length of Study: 1–2 years
Frequency: Annual
Country of Study: Australia
Closing Date: 16 February
Additional Information: study.csu.edu.au/get-support/scholarships/find-scholarship/equity/csuhs-scfea#tab1

International student support scholarship

Purpose: This scholarship recognises international students whose study plans have been impacted by COVID-19 border closures. The scholarship provides a 30% fee discount for the first two sessions of study

Eligibility: Awarded to eligible new commencing March 2024 international applicants studying in internal mode at Albury-Wodonga, Bathurst, Orange, Port Macquarie and Wagga Wagga.

Level of Study: Doctorate
Type: Scholarship
Value: 30% fee discount for first two sessions
Frequency: Twice a year
Country of Study: Any country
Closing Date: March
Additional Information: Applications are open for 2024 intake and until further advice. www.csu.edu.au/current-students/support-services/help-information/student-central

For further information contact:

Email: internationalclient@csu.edu.au

John Cassim Scholarship

Eligibility: 1. Doctor Veterinary Studies 2. Veterinary Resident at Charles Sturt University CONDITIONS: 1. Please provide a proposal for a research project you would like to undertake as part of your studies (this can be attached as a separate document) 2. Continuing students to have a GPA of 4.0 or above.

Level of Study: Postdoctorate
Type: Scholarship
Value: AU$3000
Frequency: Annual
Country of Study: Australia
Closing Date: 2 February
Additional Information: study.csu.edu.au/get-support/scholarships/find-scholarship/foundation/continuing/john-cassim-scholarship#tab2

For further information contact:

Email: advancement@csu.edu.au

Online Student Representative Committee Post-Graduate Scholarship

Eligibility: Any Postgraduate course with 75% online content (excluding single subject study) CONDITIONS: 1. Satisfactory Academic Performance. Continuing students to have a GPA of 4.0 or above. 2. Preference for a student experiencing financial hardship. Demonstrate financial hardship by providing a Centrelink Income Statement or outline your financial need in the 'Additional Financial Information' free text box in application. 3. Additional Question must be completed (max 200 words) and attached as a word document or pdf - What do you enjoy most about online study? How will this scholarship help you achieve your study goals? 4. Online or mixed-mode students completing at least 75% of units online and off campus.

Level of Study: Postgraduate
Value: AU$2000
Frequency: Annual
Country of Study: Australia
Closing Date: 2 February

Email: advancement@csu.edu.au

Postgraduate Equity Scholarship

Purpose: Assists students from Equity Groups to study at Charles Sturt University in a Postgraduate (coursework) course
Eligibility: To be eligible for this scholarship you must be: 1. studying a postgraduate degree as an active student; 2. enrolled in a Charles Sturt University course as a Commonwealth supported student, HECS-HELP or FEE-HELP. Full fee-paying students are not eligible; 3. enrolled as a full-time or part-time student; 4. a commencing or continuing student. Continuing students must have a Grade Point Average (GPA) of 3.0 or higher (pass grade average); 5. an Australian citizen, a New Zealand citizen, a permanent Australian resident or a student with an Australian permanent visa; 6. in financial need: 6a. in receipt of an eligible means-tested Centrelink Benefit (refer to guidelines) or 6b. able to demonstrate financial hardship.
Level of Study: Postgraduate
Type: Scholarship
Value: AU$2000
Length of Study: 2 years
Frequency: Annual
Country of Study: Australia
Closing Date: 16 February
Additional Information: study.csu.edu.au/get-support/scholarships/find-scholarship/equity/csupes#tab3

Residential School Equity Grant

Purpose: Provides financial assistance to students attending a compulsory residential school.
Eligibility: To be eligible for this grant you must be: 1. studying an undergraduate or postgraduate degree (this includes honours) as an active student 2. enrolled in a Charles Sturt University course as a Commonwealth supported student in a Commonwealth supported place. Full fee-paying students are not eligible 3. enrolled as an internal or online student 4. enrolled as a full time or part-time student 5. a commencing or continuing student. Continuing students must have a Grade Point Average (GPA) of 3.0 or higher (pass grade average) 6. an Australian citizen, a New Zealand citizen, a permanent Australian resident or a student with an Australian permanent visa 7. in financial need: 7a. in receipt of an eligible means-tested Centrelink Benefit (refer guidelines) or 7b. must be able to demonstrate financial hardship 8. enrolled in a compulsory residential school; 9. submitting an application prior to the completion date of the residential school period. Applications submitted after the residential school is completed with be ineligible.
Level of Study: Postgraduate
Value: Up to AU$1000
Frequency: Annual
Country of Study: Australia
Closing Date: 5 September
Additional Information: study.csu.edu.au/get-support/scholarships/find-scholarship/equity/rseg#tab3

Email: scholarships@csu.edu.au

Technology Equity Grant

Purpose: Provides financial assistance to eligible, undergraduate, Commonwealth supported students to purchase computer equipment.
Eligibility: To be eligible for this grant you must be: 1. studying an undergraduate degree as an active student in the 2023–24 session 2. enrolled in a Charles Sturt University course as a Commonwealth supported student in a Commonwealth Supported Place. Full fee paying students are not eligible. 3. a commencing or continuing student. Continuing students must have a Grade Point Average (GPA) of 3.0 or higher (pass grade average); 4. an Australian citizen, a New Zealand citizen, a permanent Australian resident or a student with an Australian permanent visa; 5. in financial need: 5a. in receipt of an eligible means tested Centrelink Benefit, or 5b. able to demonstrate financial hardship
Type: Scholarship
Value: Up to AU$1,000
Frequency: Annual
Country of Study: Australia
Closing Date: 16 February
Additional Information: study.csu.edu.au/get-support/scholarships/find-scholarship/equity/tech-eg#tab1

Charlie Trotter Culinary Education Foundation

40 E. Chicago Avenue, Suite 418, Chicago, IL 60611, United States of America.

Tel: (1) 312 600 9724
Email: info@charlietrotters.com
Website: www.charlietrotters.com/about/foundation.asp

Charlie Trotter's is regarded as one of the finest restaurants in the world, dedicated to excellence in the culinary arts. It has been instrumental in establishing new standards for fine dining. Its main goal is to educate and expose youth to the great culinary arts in as many ways as possible. The Charlie Trotter Culinary Education Foundation, a non-profit organization, has been established to promote culinary arts among youth. The foundation is involved in awarding scholarships to students who are seeking careers in the culinary arts and working with Chicago-area youth to promote the enthusiastic quest for education as well as an interest in the cooking and food.

Charlie Trotter's Culinary Education Foundation Culinary Study Scholarship

Eligibility: Open to an Illinois resident at the time of application
Level of Study: Professional development
Type: Scholarship
Value: US$5,000 cash scholarship for a pre-enroled student
Length of Study: 1 year
Frequency: Annual
Country of Study: United States of America
Application Procedure: Check website for further details
Closing Date: 1 March
Funding: Foundation, Private
Contributor: Charlie Trotter's

For further information contact:

The Culinary Trust Scholarship Program, P.O. Box 273, New York, NY 10013, United States of America.

Tel: (1) 646 224 6989
Email: cholarships@theculinarytrust.com

Chiang Ching Kuo Foundation for International Scholarly Exchange

13F, 65 Tun Hwa South Road, Section 2, 106-ROC, Taiwan, China.

Tel: (86) 2 2704 5333
Email: cckf@ms1.hinet.net
Website: www.cckf.org

The Chiang Ching Kuo Foundation for International Scholarly Exchange is a non-profit organization headquartered in Taipei, the capital of the Republic of China. The Foundation was established in 1989 in honour of the late President Chiang Ching kuo. The main objective of the Foundation is to promote the study of Chinese culture and society, broadly defined.

Chiang Ching Kuo Foundation Doctoral Fellowships

Purpose: To financially support Doctoral candidates while writing their dissertations
Eligibility: Applications for Doctoral Fellowships will be evaluated according to the following criteria: 1. The significance of the contribution that the proposed project will make to the advancement of research in the field of Chinese Studies. 2. The quality or potential quality of the applicant's work, including its originality in the field of Chinese Studies. 3. The quality of the approach, organization, and methodology of the proposed project. 4. The likelihood that the applicant can successfully complete the entire project during the grant period.
Level of Study: Doctorate
Type: Fellowships
Value: Up to US$20,000
Length of Study: 1 year
Frequency: Annual
Country of Study: Any country
Application Procedure: 1. Applications must be submitted to our online application database. E-mail and paper applications will not be accepted. Applications may be submitted every year from August 1 to October 15 (to start the application process, please click here). 2. Each application should include the following steps, which includes the on-line submission of the applicant's personal information, basic project data, and project abstract. In addition, you may only submit one PDF file. Please combine all relevant documents into a file no larger than 5 M
No. of awards offered: 104
Closing Date: 15 October
Funding: Commercial, Private
Additional Information: www.cckf.org/en/programs/american/doctoral-fellowships

For further information contact:

Email: maggielin@cckf.org.tw

Chiang Ching Kuo Foundation for International Scholarly Exchange Eminent Scholar Lectureship

Purpose: To sponsor eminent foreign scholars to come to Taiwan to take up lectureships or positions as visiting scholars

Eligibility: Open to eminent scholars invited by universities or academic institutions of Taiwan

Type: Lectureship/Prize

Length of Study: 1 year

Frequency: Annual

Study Establishment: Universities or academic institutions in Taiwan

Country of Study: Taiwan

Application Procedure: Applicants must use the application forms provided by the Foundation. The application must be sent by registered mail to the Secretariat. Electronic version of all application materials must be enclosed on diskette or sent as email attachment to cckf@ms1.hinet.net with heading 'Application Materials from (Name)' in the header of the message. Applications are accepted from June 1st

Closing Date: 15 October

Additional Information: Project directors who are currently receiving Foundation aid are ineligible to apply. Project directors may not submit more than one application

Chiang Ching Kuo Foundation for International Scholarly Exchange Publication Subsidies

Purpose: To assist in the final stages of publishing academic works

Eligibility: Open to scholars in the final stages of publishing academic works. Applications from scholars affiliated with institutions in Taiwan must involve cooperation with one or more scholars from other countries. Applicants for publication subsidies must be affiliated with a university or other academic institution

Level of Study: Research

Type: Grant

Frequency: Annual

Country of Study: Any country

Application Procedure: Applicants must use the application forms provided directly from the Foundation Secretariat. Three copies of the application and supporting documents must be submitted by registered mail to the Secretariat. In addition, electronic version of all application materials must be enclosed on diskette or sent as email attachment to cckf@ms1.hinet.net with heading 'Application Materials from (Name)' in the header of the message

Closing Date: 15 September

Additional Information: Please check the website for more details research.csu.edu.au/study-with-us/scholarships/full-time-scholarship-agrtp

For further information contact:

The Chiang Ching-kuo Foundation for International Scholarly Exchange, 8361 B Greensboro Dr. McLean, VA 22102, United States of America.

Email: maggielin@cckf.org.tw

Conference/Seminar/Workshop Grants

Type: Grant

Value: US$25,000

Frequency: Annual

Country of Study: Any country

Application Procedure: All applications must be submitted to our online application database. E-mail and paper applications will not be accepted

Closing Date: 15 January

Additional Information: www.cckf.org/en/programs/american/conference-seminar#:~:text=The%20Foundation's%20grants%20provide%20support,the%20humanities%20and%20social%20sciences.&text=The%20research%20grant%20must%20end,matching%20funds%20from%20other%20sources.

For further information contact:

Tel: (886) 2 2704 5333 ext.19

Email: maggielin@cckf.org.tw

Dissertation Fellowships for ROC Students Abroad

Eligibility: Doctoral candidates who are Republic of China (ROC) citizens and who are completing the last year of their Ph.D. research at an accredited university in New Zealand, Australia or Japan may apply for fellowships for the completion of dissertations in the humanities and social sciences. Applicants for ROC dissertation fellowships must be doing research on topics related to Chinese culture and society, the development of the Republic of China, or Taiwan Studies. Their dissertations should cover one of the following fields: literature, history, philosophy, linguistics, art, sociology, anthropology, psychology, political science, legal studies, economics, or media studies. Only students who have graduated from an accredited university or college in the Republic of China, and who do not have foreign permanent residence status or citizenship, are eligible to apply.

Level of Study: Postdoctorate

Type: Fellowship

Value: US$20,000

Frequency: Annual

Country of Study: Any country

Application Procedure: Applications must be submitted to our online application database. E-mail and paper applications will not be accepted. Applications may be submitted every year from August 1 to October 15 (to start the application process, please click here: application.cckf.org.tw/e-login.html).

Closing Date: 15 October

Additional Information: www.cckf.org/en/programs/apac/ADF

For further information contact:

Email: maggielin@cckf.org.tw

Doctoral Fellowships

Purpose: Supporting doctoral candidates for completing their dissertation in the last stage of their doctoral programs
Eligibility: 1. The significance of the contribution that the proposed project will make to the advancement of research in the field of Chinese Studies. 2. The quality or potential quality of the applicant's work, including its originality in the field of Chinese Studies. 3. The quality of the approach, organization, and methodology of the proposed project. 4. The likelihood that the applicant can successfully complete the entire project during the grant period.
Level of Study: Doctorate
Type: Fellowship
Value: US$20,000
Length of Study: 1 year
Frequency: Annual
Country of Study: Any country
Closing Date: 15 October
Funding: Foundation
Additional Information: www.cckf.org/en/programs/american/doctoral-fellowships

For further information contact:

Email: maggielin@cckf.org.tw

Junior Scholar Grants

Purpose: The Foundation provides grants for time off for research and writing to postdoctoral and assistant professors without tenure who are affiliated with an accredited American university and who have taught for no more than 6 years since receiving PhD degree
Eligibility: Junior Scholar Grants is only available for applicants who are affiliated with an American university
Type: Grant
Value: Up to US$30,000
Frequency: Annual
Country of Study: Any country
No. of awards offered: 80
Closing Date: 15 October
No. of awards given last year: 20
No. of applicants last year: 80

Lecture Series Grants

Eligibility: Full-time faculty at academic institutions may apply for Lecture Series Grants, Research Grants, Database Grants, Conference and Seminar Grants, and Publication Subsidies. Doctoral candidates who are non-ROC citizens and who are enrolled in an accredited university in this region may apply for Doctoral Fellowships. Doctoral candidates who are Republic of China (ROC) citizens and who are enrolled in an accredited university in this region may apply for Dissertation Fellowships for ROC Students Abroad. Junior scholars who are affiliated with an accredited university, who have received the Ph.D. degree within five years of the date of application, and who do not hold full-time salaried positions may apply for Postdoctoral Research Fellowships.
Type: Grant
Value: €25,000
Length of Study: 1 to 3 years
Frequency: Annual
Country of Study: Any country
Application Procedure: Applications must be submitted to our online application database. E-mail and paper applications will not be accepted. Applications may be submitted every year from August 1 (to start the application process, please click here: application.cckf.org.tw/e-login.html).
Closing Date: 15 October
Additional Information: www.cckf.org/en/programs/european/lecture

For further information contact:

Email: amberhl@cckf.org.tw

Publication Subsidies

Eligibility: Academic publishers or full-time faculty may apply for subsidies for the publication of scholarly works related to the goals of the Foundation. The publication may be in the form of a book or a monograph. Applications will be accepted for completed book manuscripts, but not for books in a series. Priority will be given to first book projects by junior scholars. Publication budgets should not exceed US$10,000. Publication Subsidy Grants may only be used to cover editing, indexing, and other relevant publication costs. Translation and research-related expenses may not be included. For periodicals and journals, the Foundation will support one year's worth of publication. The application for the publication of conference proceedings requires a completed, edited draft. Priority will be given to collaborative projects involving institutions in Taiwan. Projects on Taiwan Studies are especially encouraged.
Level of Study: Predoctorate
Value: US$10,000

Frequency: Annual
Country of Study: Any country
Closing Date: 15 January
Additional Information: www.cckf.org/en/programs/apac/publication

For further information contact:

Email: amberhl@cckf.org.tw

Research Grants

Eligibility: 1. The Foundation's grants provide support for research on Chinese Studies in the humanities and social sciences. 2. Funding is not provided for capital equipment (including computers and printers), building design, construction, or maintenance. 3. Funding is not available for university administrative costs including overhead or endowments. 4. The Foundation does not subsidize administrative expenses or the purchase of equipment. 5. Foundation funds can only be transferred to and managed by institutional accounts. Endorsement letter(s) from the applicant's institution must express the institution's willingness to comply with these procedures. 6. With the exception of Scholar Grants, the Foundation does not supply funding for the salaries for project directors or co-directors. 7. The Foundation does not fund library acquisitions. 8. An applicant who already has a two-year research grant is not eligible to apply for a CCK Grant for Scholars that would run concurrently with the research grant. The research grant must end before an applicant can apply for a CCK Grant for Scholars. 9. The Foundation encourages applications with matching funds from other sources.
Level of Study: Research
Type: Research grant
Value: 1. First month US$120 a day 2. Thereafter US$60 a day 3. Round trip costs from the East coast to East Asia are approximately US$1,500.
Length of Study: 2 years
Frequency: Annual
Country of Study: Any country
Application Procedure: Applications must be submitted to our online application database. E-mail and paper applications will not be accepted.
Closing Date: 15 October
Funding: Foundation
Additional Information: www.cckf.org/en/programs/american/research

For further information contact:

Email: maggielin@cckf.org.tw

Scholar Grants

Purpose: To help replace half of the salary of faculty on sabbatical, or for time off for research and writing
Eligibility: Tenure faculty, including full professors and associate professor, in the accredited universities in the United States, Canada, Mexico, and Central and Southern America are eligible to apply for scholar grants
Type: Grant
Value: US$20,000 or US$35,000
Frequency: Annual
Country of Study: Any country
Closing Date: 15 October
Additional Information: www.cckf.org/en/programs/american/scholar

For further information contact:

Email: maggielin@cckf.org.tw

Chicago Tribune

435 North Michigan Avenue, Chicago, IL 60611, United States of America.

Tel: (1) 312 222 3232
Email: jwoelffer@tribune.com
Website: www.chicagotribune.com

The Chicago Tribune is the Midwest's leading newspaper. The Chicago Tribune Literary Awards are part of a continued dedication to readers, writers and ideas.

Nelson Algren Awards

Purpose: To award writers of short fiction
Eligibility: Each entrant must be at least 18 years old and a legal resident of the contest area (above) as of the date of entry
Level of Study: Unrestricted
Type: Award
Value: one grand prize winner (US$3,500) and five finalists (US$750)
Frequency: Annual
Country of Study: Any country
Application Procedure: Visit algren.submittable.com (the "Contest Page"), complete an entry form with the following required information (a) name, (b) telephone number, (c) email address, (d) the title and word count of your

submission, and submit it along with your short story (a "Story") (together with the entry form referred as an "Entry") that otherwise meets all Submission Requirements below. Entries will not be accepted through any other method

Closing Date: 31 January

Funding: Corporation

Additional Information: Please contact to Chicago Tribune for latest updates. Please check at articles.chicagotribune.com/2013-11-26/news/chi-2013-nelson-algren-award-official-rules-20120906_1_grand-prize-enter-or-win-chicago-tribune-company-llc www.chicagotribune.com/entertainment/books/literary-awards/ct-algren-contest-announcement-2019-20181121-story.html#nt=standard-embed

For further information contact:

Chicago Tribune Nelson Algren Awards, 435 N. TT200, Michigan Avenue, Chicago, IL 60611, United States of America.

Email: printersrow@tribune.com

Chilean International Cooperation Agency

Chile: Nelson Mandela Scholarships

Purpose: The Chilean International Cooperation Agency (AGCI) is offering scholarships for accredited Spanish-taught Master's program at Chilean higher education institutions. The scholarships are offered to professionals who are citizens of South Africa, Mozambique and Angola

Eligibility: 1. Experience in the subjects they choose to pursue Master's studies in unconditional acceptance offer at a Chilean higher education institution. 2. 4-year university degree. 3. If employed already, you will need a letter of support, indicating that you will be released for the duration of your studies

Level of Study: Postgraduate

Type: Scholarship

Value: R$500

Length of Study: 4 year

Frequency: Annual

Country of Study: South Africa

Application Procedure: Apply online www.agci.gob.cl

Closing Date: 1 February

Funding: Foundation

For further information contact:

Email: becasmandela@gmail.com

China Scholarship Council

Level 13, Building A3 No.9 Chegongzhuang Avenue, 100044, Beijing, China.

Tel: (86) 660 93900
Email: webmaster@csc.edu.cn
Website: www.csc.edu.cn

The China Scholarship council (CSC) is a non-profit institution, which is affiliated with the ministry of education. The main objective of the CSC is to develop the educational, scientific and technological, and cultural exchanges and economic and trade cooperation between China and other countries.

K C Wong Postgraduate Scholarship Programme

Purpose: To support students who intend to study further at King's College London

Eligibility: Open to applicants who are citizens and permanent residents of People's Republic of china

Type: Scholarship

Value: Tuition fees at the international rate plus an annual stipend of £8,400

Length of Study: 3 years

Frequency: Annual

Study Establishment: King's College London

Country of Study: United Kingdom

Application Procedure: A completed application form, which is available online, must be sent

Closing Date: 1 February

Contributor: K C Wong Education Foundation

For further information contact:

Research & Graduate School Support Section, King's College London, London WC2R 2LS, United Kingdom.

Tel: (44) 20 7848 3376
Fax: (44) 20 7848 3328
Email: graduateschool@kcl.ac.uk

KC Wong Postdoctoral Fellowships

Eligibility: Applicant eligibility 1. be current residents of the People's Republic of China (PRC) 2. hold a PhD degree 3. be within 10 years of the award of a PhD degree 4. be scientists of post-doctoral level or equivalent status who are employed by a scientific or academic institution in the PRC, or who have confirmed employment with such institutions after the completion of their fellowships 5. agree to return to work in the PRC and contribute to the field of their studies/research, after completion of the fellowships 6. have a good command of spoken and written English (for work and visa requirements)

Level of Study: Postdoctorate

Type: Fellowship

Value: Fellowship to undertake research in the following faculties of King

Frequency: Annual

Country of Study: United Kingdom

No. of awards offered: 4

Closing Date: 31 January

Additional Information: documentcloud.adobe.com/link/review?uri=urn%3Aaaid%3Ascds%3AUS%3A9a09c36e-feb8-302c-8d95-3e5ecee52b0e#pageNum=1

For further information contact:

Email: globalengagement@kcl.ac.uk

Chinese American Medical Society (CAMS)

41 Elizabeth Street, Suite 600, New York, NY 10013, United States of America.

Tel: (1) 212 334 4760
Email: jlove@camsociety.org
Website: www.camsociety.org
Contact: Dr H H Wang, Executive Director

The Chinese American Medical Society (CAMS) is a non-profit, charitable, educational and scientific society that aims to promote the scientific association of medical professionals of Chinese descent. It also aims to advance medical knowledge and scientific research with emphasis on aspects unique to the Chinese and to promote the health status of Chinese Americans. The Society makes scholarships available to medical dental students and provides summer fellowships for students conducting research in health problems related to the Chinese

Chinese American Medical Society Scholarship Program

Purpose: In the early 1970's the Chinese American Medical Society went to considerable lengths to provide scholarships to outstanding medical students in need of financial assistance

Eligibility: 1. Must be a graduate student 2. Must attend a university 3. Must not be attending high school currently 4. Must study full-time 5. Restricted to students studying Health and Medical Sciences

Level of Study: Graduate, Postgraduate

Type: Programme grant

Value: US$5,000–US$20,000

Frequency: Annual

Country of Study: Any country

Application Procedure: The submission has to be made to the email address scholarship@camsociety.org Email is the preferred method of submission for applications. The committee asks that all applications and supporting materials be sent as a single PDF file and emailed to scholarship@camsociety.org

Closing Date: 31 March

Funding: Private

Additional Information: camsociety.org/scholarship-apply

For further information contact:

Scholarship Committee, 265 Canal Street, Suite 515, New York, NY 10013, United States of America.

Email: scholarship@camsociety.org

Chinook Regional Career Transitions for Youth

Room B310, 1701 - 5 Avenue South, Lethbridge, AB T1J 0W4, Canada.

Tel: (1) 403 328 3996
Email: mvennard@pallisersd.ab.ca
Website: www.careersteps.ca

The Chinook regional career transitions for youth aims to improve the school-to-work transitions for students, promoting lifelong learning and coordinating and implementing career development activities and programming for youth.

Robin Rousseau Memorial Mountain Achievement Scholarship

Purpose: To bring about awareness of ways to improve safety in the mountains

Eligibility: Applicants must be Alberta residents and active in the mountain community; and plan to study in any recognized Mountain Leadership and Safety program

Level of Study: Professional development

Type: Scholarship

Value: Course fee
Frequency: Annual
Country of Study: Any country
Application Procedure: A completed application form must be sent
Closing Date: 30 January
Additional Information: www.careersteps.ca/

For further information contact:

Alberta Scholarship Programs Box 28000 Stn Main, Edmonton, AB T5J 4R4, Canada.

Tel: (1) 780 427 8640
Fax: (1) 780 427 1288
Email: scholarships@gov.ab.ca

Toyota Earth Day Scholarship Program

Purpose: To encourage community service
Eligibility: Open to students who have achieved academic excellence and distinguished themselves in environmental community service and extracurricular and volunteer activities
Level of Study: Professional development
Type: Scholarship
Value: C$5,000
Frequency: Annual
Country of Study: Any country
Application Procedure: Application form available online
Closing Date: 15 February
Additional Information: opps.tigweb.org/5947

For further information contact:

Toyota Earth Day Scholarship Program, III Peter St., Suite 503, Toronto, ON M5V 2H1, Canada.

Email: scholarship@earthday.ca

Choirs Ontario

Choirs Ontario A-1422 Bayview Avenue, Toronto, ON M4G 3A7, Canada.

Tel: (1) 416 923 1144
Email: info@choirsontario.org
Website: www.choirsontario.org
Contact: Melva Graham

Choirs Ontario is an arts service organization dedicated to the promotion of choral activities and standards of excellence.

Established in 1971 as the Ontario Choral Federation, Choirs Ontario provides services to choirs, conductors, choristers, composers, administrators and educators as well as anyone who enjoys listening to the sound of choral music. Choirs Ontario operates with the financial assistance of the Ministry of Culture, the Ontario Arts Council, the Trillium Foundation, the Toronto Arts Council and numerous foundations, corporations and individual donors.

Ruth Watson Henderson Choral Composition Competition

Purpose: The competition exists to provide Canadian composers with an opportunity of contributing to Canada's rich choral tradition through the writing of original choral works.
Eligibility: Candidates must be Canadian citizens or landed immigrants who are permanent residents of Ontario. 1. The composition must be an original SATB work, 4-6 minutes, a cappella or piano accompaniment 2. A cappella submissions MUST include piano reduction. 3. Texts may be sacred or secular and can be in languages other than English/French. The text must be either original, known to be in public domain or be accompanied by a letter of permission from copyright owner. 4. All submissions must not have been previously commissioned, published or performed and must have been composed within the last two years. Arrangements of previously composed works are not acceptable. The composer shall retain the copyright of the work. 5. Previous competition finalists reapplying must submit a different piece.
Level of Study: Postgraduate
Type: Prize
Value: C$1,000
Country of Study: Canada
Application Procedure: Further information available on the website
Closing Date: 1 December
Funding: Private
Additional Information: choirsontario.org/event/ruth-watson-henderson-choral-composition-competition-deadline/

Citizens United in Research for Epilepsy (CURE)

Taking Flight Award

Subjects: Basic mechanisms of epilepsy; Acquired epilepsies; Pediatric epilepsies; SUDEP; Treatment-resistant epilepsies; and Sleep & epilepsy.

Purpose: The award seeks to promote the careers of young epilepsy investigators to allow them to develop a research focus independent of their mentor(s).

Eligibility: You must fall into one of the following categories to be eligible for the Taking Flight Award: 1. A senior post-doctoral fellow who has a minimum of 3 years postdoctoral experience 2. A clinical fellow who is a Neurology Resident in his/her Neurology training and considering Epilepsy Fellowships. 3. Newly appointed faculty within one year of having completed postdoctoral training International applicants are welcome; you do not have to be a US citizen or working in the US to apply for this award. All materials must be submitted in English.

Type: Award

Value: US$100,000

Length of Study: One year

Country of Study: Any country

Application Procedure: See website for further details.

Closing Date: 11 January

Additional Information: www.cureepilepsy.org/grants-program/#:~:text=The%20Taking%20Flight%20Award%20(1,of%20their%20mentor(s).

The CURE Epilepsy Award

Subjects: Basic mechanisms of epilepsy; Acquired epilepsies; Pediatric epilepsies; SUDEP; Treatment-resistant epilepsies; and Sleep & epilepsy.

Purpose: The award reflects CURE's continued focus on scientific advances that have the potential to truly transform the lives of those affected by epilepsy, with prevention and disease modification as critical goals

Eligibility: This award is available to both established and early career investigators*. Researchers who serve on CURE Epilepsy's Scientific Advisory Council are ineligible to apply for or sponsor a grant for the duration of their term. International applicants are welcome. All materials must be submitted in English.

Type: Award

Value: Requests may be made for up to a total of US$250,000 paid over 2 years. Funding requests may include salary support for the Principal Investigator (PI), co-PIs, technical staff, supplies, animal costs, publication fees and travel to an epilepsy-related conference if the PI is presenting his/her CURE-funded research. Limited equipment purchases that are required to complete goals will be considered. Indirect costs are not supported.

Length of Study: Two years

Country of Study: Any country

Application Procedure: See website for further details.

Closing Date: 11 January

Additional Information: www.cureepilepsy.org/get-involved/scholarships/

Clara Haskil Competition

Case Postale 234, 31 rue du Conseil, CH-1800 Vevey, Switzerland.

Tel: (41) 21 922 6704
Email: info@clara-haskil.ch
Website: www.regart.ch/clara-haskil
Contact: Mr Patrick Peikert, Director

The Clara Haskil Competition exists to recognize and help a young pianist whose approach to piano interpretation is of the same spirit that constantly inspired Clara Haskil, and that she illustrated so perfectly.

Clara Haskil International Piano Competition

Purpose: To recognize and financially help a young pianist

Eligibility: Open to pianists of any nationality and either sex who are no more than 27 years of age

Level of Study: Postgraduate

Type: Prize

Value: CHF 25,000

Frequency: Every 2 years

Country of Study: Any country

Application Procedure: Applicants must pay an entry fee of CHF 200

No. of awards offered: Approx. 150

Closing Date: 28 April

Funding: Corporation, International office, Trusts

Contributor: Fondation Nestlé pour l'Art

No. of awards given last year: 2

No. of applicants last year: Approx. 150

Additional Information: The competition is usually held during the last weeks of August or the beginning of September app.getacceptd.com/clarahaskil

For further information contact:

International Piano Competition, Concours Clara Haskil, CH-1800 Vevey, Switzerland.

Tel: (41) 21 922 67 04
Fax: (41) 21 922 67 34
Email: vevey@clara-haskil.ch

Clare Hall Cambridge

Clare Hall Research Fellowships in the Arts and Social Sciences

Purpose: Research Fellowships are primarily intended to provide opportunities for scholars at an early stage of their academic careers to establish and pursue their research in a supportive academic environment

Eligibility: 1. During their tenure, Research Fellows have no college teaching duties other than to pursue their research. They are however members of the College Governing Body and may serve on other College committees. 2. Successful candidates are expected to be graduate students who have recently completed or who are about to complete their PhD 3. There is no restriction on age, sex or previous standing, except that candidates may not already have held a Research Fellowship at a college of either the University of Oxford or the University of Cambridge, and some preference may be given to candidates who are at a fairly early stage of their research career. 4. Research Fellows are required to live in Cambridge during Full Term, but leave may be granted to work away if necessary. Small grants for research expenses may be made available on application to the Senior Tutor

Level of Study: Research

Type: Fellowship

Length of Study: 5 years

Frequency: Annual

Country of Study: Any country

Application Procedure: Applications must be made online using the following link app.casc.cam.ac.uk/fas_live/clh_arts.aspx

Closing Date: 23 January

Funding: Private

Additional Information: www.clarehall.cam.ac.uk/research-fellowships

For further information contact:

Clare Hall, Herschel Road, Cambridge CB3 9AL, United Kingdom.

Email: college.registrar@clarehall.cam.ac.uk

Claude Leon Foundation

P.O. Box 30538, Tokai 7966, South Africa.

Tel: (27) 21 787 0418
Email: postdocadmin@leonfoundation.co.za
Website: www.leonfoundation.co.za

The Claude Leon Foundation is a South African Charitable Trust. resulting from a Bequest by Claude Leon (1884-1972), A prominent Johannesburg businessman. CLF funds a postdoctoral fellowship programme, now in it's 18th Year - It's goal is the building of research capacity in the faculties of Science, Engineering and Medical Sciences at South African Universities via awards to both South African and foreign postdoctoral scientists.

Claude Leon Foundation Postdoctoral Fellowship

Purpose: To fund postdoctoral research

Eligibility: Open to South African and foreign nationals. Preference will be given to candidates who have received their doctoral degrees in the last 5 years, and to those who are currently underrepresented in South African tertiary institutions

Level of Study: Postdoctorate

Value: R235,000 PA for a 2-year fellowship plus travel grant up to a maximum of R45,000 to present a paper on poster at an international conference during the 2nd year of fellowship

Length of Study: 2 years on renewal after the first year

Frequency: Annual

Study Establishment: South African universities and some institutions.

Country of Study: South Africa

Application Procedure: Applications are not accepted directly from candidates. They must have been offered a postdoctoral position at a tertiary institution. The application should then be sent to the foundation by the institution not by the candidate

No. of awards offered: 400

Closing Date: 31 May

Contributor: The Claude Leon Foundation, South Africa

No. of awards given last year: 58

No. of applicants last year: 400

Additional Information: Applications should be sent to the foundation by the institution at which the candidate has secured a postdoctoral position, not by the candidate www.leonfoundation.co.za/postdoctoral.htm

For further information contact:

Email: billfrankel@kayacomm.com

Coimbra Group

Coimbra Group Scholarship Programme for Young Professors and Researchers from Latin American Universities

Purpose: This initiative, which offers grants to finance short-term research visits, aims at favouring mobility and academic exchange between both regions.

Eligibility: 1. To be a national of and currently resident in a Latin American country. Candidates already living and/or studying in Europe will not be considered. 2. To hold a university degree or equivalent. 3. To be linked as a professor or researcher to a Latin American University recognised as such by the authorities of the country. 4. To use the Coimbra Group Office electronic application process. Only one application per candidate will be accepted. 5. To submit online an Acceptance Letter/email from the tutor/partner with whom the work programme will be undertaken in the host institution. This document is mandatory. 6. To be born on or after 1 January 1983. 7. Previously selected candidates can apply for a second grant, but they will not be prioritised.

Level of Study: Graduate
Type: Scholarship
Frequency: Annual
Country of Study: Any country
Application Procedure: The online application is available until 15 April 2023 midnight (Brussels time) on the Coimbra Group website: (www.coimbra-group.eu/activities/scholarships).
Closing Date: 15 April
Funding: Private
No. of awards given last year: 32
No. of applicants last year: 251
Additional Information: www.coimbra-group.eu/scholarships/latin-america-la/

For further information contact:

Egmontstraat, 11, rue d'Egmont, B-1000 Brussels, Belgium.

Tel: (32) 2 513 83 32
Email: Moleiro@coimbra-group.eu

Coimbra Group Scholarship Programme for Young Researchers from the European Neighbourhood

Purpose: The main aim of this scholarship programme is to enable scholars to undertake research in which they are engaged in their home institution and to help them to establish academic and research contacts
Eligibility: Applicants must fulfil all the following criteria: 1. be born on or after 1 January 1988 2. be nationals of and current residents in one of the above-listed countries 3. be current academic staff members of a university or an equivalent higher education institution located in one of the above-listed countries 4. be of postdoctoral or equivalent status, although some institutions may offer opportunities to doctoral students.
Level of Study: Research
Type: Programme grant
Frequency: Annual

Country of Study: Any country
Application Procedure: Applicants will be able to fill in the on-line registration until 15 April 2023 midnight (Brussels time) on the Coimbra Group website: www.coimbra-group.eu/activities/scholarships.
No. of awards offered: 91
Closing Date: 15 April
Funding: Private
No. of awards given last year: 15
Additional Information: www.coimbra-group.eu/scholarships/european-neighbourhood/

For further information contact:

Email: quici@coimbra-group.eu

Coimbra Group Short Stay Scholarship Programme for Young Researchers

Purpose: It aims to increase cooperation amongst its members by enhancing special academic and cultural ties, and creating channels of information and exchange
Eligibility: Applicants should be: 1. born on or after 1 January 1978. 2. nationals of and current residents in a country in Sub-Saharan Africa. 3. current staff members of a university or an equivalent higher education institution in SubSaharan Africa. 4. preferably of doctoral/postdoctoral or equivalent status.
Level of Study: Research
Type: Scholarship
Frequency: Annual
Country of Study: Any country
Application Procedure: Online application form: www.coimbra-group.eu/activities/scholarships
Closing Date: 30 April
Funding: Private
No. of awards given last year: 172
Additional Information: www.coimbra-group.eu/wp-content/uploads/CALL-Africa-2019-brochure.pdf

For further information contact:

Email: office@coimbra-group.eu

Collegeville Institute for Ecumenical and Cultural Research

14027 Fruit Farm Road, Box 2000, Collegeville, MN 56321, United States of America.

Tel: (1) 320 363 3366
Email: staff@collegevilleinstitute.org
Website: www.collegevilleinstitute.org
Contact: Donald Ottenhoff, Executive Director

The Institute for Ecumenical and Cultural Research seeks to discern the meaning of Christian identity and unity in a religiously and culturally diverse nation and world and to communicate that meaning for the mission of the church and the renewal of human community. The Institute is committed to research, study, prayer, reflection and dialogue, in a place shaped by the Benedictine tradition of worship and work.

Bishop Thomas Hoyt Jr Fellowship

Purpose: To provide the Institute's residency fee to a North American person of colour writing a doctoral dissertation, in order to help the churches to increase the number of persons of colour working in ecumenical and cultural research
Eligibility: 1. Must be a graduate student. 2. Must attend a university3. Must not be attending high school currently 4. Both full-time and part-time students North American persons of color who are writing a doctoral dissertation and who apply to the Collegeville Institute's Resident Scholars Program or Short Term Residencies Program are also eligible to apply for the Hoyt Fellowship.
Level of Study: Postgraduate
Type: Fellowship
Value: US$2,500
Length of Study: 1 academic year
Frequency: Annual
Study Establishment: The Institute
Country of Study: United States of America
Application Procedure: Applicants must apply in the usual way to the Resident Scholars Programme (see separate listing). If invited by the admissions committee to be a Resident Scholar, the person will then be eligible for consideration for the Hoyt Fellowship
No. of awards offered: 1
Closing Date: 1 November
Funding: Private
No. of awards given last year: 1
No. of applicants last year: 1

For further information contact:

Tel: (1) 320 363 3367

Columbia College of Missouri

Columbia College of Missouri Boone County Endowed Award

Purpose: This award is for Missouri high school seniors who are residents of Boone County and planning to attend Columbia College
Eligibility: Must be a graduating high school senior. Must be a resident of Boone County, MO. 1. Must be a United States citizen or permanent resident. 2. Must demonstrate community service/volunteer work. 3. Must enroll as a full-time student. 4. Must have a cumulative grade point average of 3.1 or higher. 5. Must have an ACT score of 22 or higher or the equivalent SAT score
Level of Study: Graduate
Type: Award
Value: US$1,000
Frequency: Annual
Country of Study: United States of America
Application Procedure: The scholarship is made possible through the support of more than 200 area businesses. Recipients of the award will be chosen by committee in April and will be notified appropriately. Application details are available in the form of pdf. www.ccis.edu/offices/financialaid/booneendowed/boonecountyendowedscholarshipday.pdf
Closing Date: 31 March
Funding: Private
No. of awards given last year: 5
Additional Information: www.unigo.com/scholarships/all/columbia-college-of-missouri-boone-county-endowed-award/1070

For further information contact:

1001 Rogers St., Columbia, MO 65216, United States of America.

Tel: (1) 573 875 7506
Email: admissions@ccis.edu

Columbia GSAS

Foreign Language and Area Studies Fellowship

Purpose: Administered by the Title VI National Resource Centers at the University of Pennsylvania, the Foreign Language and Area Studies (FLAS) Fellowships program funding to Graduate and Undergraduate Students studying modern foreign languages and related area studies

Eligibility: The Summer Foreign Language and Area Studies (FLAS) Fellowship competition is open to undergraduates and graduate students who are US citizens, nationals, or permanent residents who are enrolled or accepted for enrollment in a full-time program (either domestic—at Columbia University or at another US institution—or overseas) that combines modern foreign-language training with international or area studies.

Level of Study: Postgraduate

Type: Fellowship

Value: Graduate students: tuition grant is US$18,000 and the stipend is US$15,000

Frequency: Annual

Country of Study: Any country

Application Procedure: You will need to create a free online Interfolio account and complete the application in that system. In addition to entering information into the account, you will need to upload 1. A personal statement regarding your planned use of the FLAS fellowship. This is a one-page, single-spaced, essay describing why this language study is essential to realizing your study and career goals. 2. Your curriculum vitae. 3. Unofficial higher education transcript(s) of your most recent academic work, whether at the University of Pennsylvania or another university or college, in digital format. Transcripts may be verified during the review process. 4. Two letters of recommendation (you will request them through the system). When you ask the faculty members for a recommendation, tell them that all letters of recommendation must specifically address how a FLAS would contribute to your current program of study or would be integrated with it

Closing Date: 11 February

Funding: Private

Additional Information: gsas.columbia.edu/student-guide/financing-your-education/flas-fellowship-summer

For further information contact:

Graduate School of Arts and Sciences, 107 Low Memorial Library, 535 West 116th Street, New York, NY 10027, United States of America.

Email: gsas-fellowships@columbia.edu

Graduate School of Arts and Sciences International Travel Fellowships

Purpose: Travel Fellowships provide funding for international travel (outside of the United States) that is necessary for the completion of the dissertation. Travel Fellowship funds may not be used for research in residence at Columbia

Eligibility: To be eligible to receive an International Travel Fellowship, students must: 1. Be a PhD student in an Arts and Sciences program 2. Have completed all requirements for the MPhil degree and passed the prospectus defense before May 31, 2023, 3. Be within their seventh year of study in 2023–24

Level of Study: Graduate

Type: Fellowships, operating grants

Frequency: Annual

Country of Study: Any country

Application Procedure: Applications must include the following items 1. Completed GSAS online application form. 2. An up-to-date GSAS transcript (official PDF transcript from the Registrar's office). Note The GSAS Fellowship application does not accept encrypted files for upload. Official Columbia transcript PDFs are encrypted; you may order a paper copy through SSOL or print the official transcript PDF you receive from Parchment, then scan and upload it. 3. A curriculum vitae (three pages maximum). 4. A statement of your language preparation for research abroad, specifying the language(s) needed to carry out your research and your proficiency in each (one page maximum). 5. A project proposal of no more than 1,500 words, which should include a justification of your need to travel and a specific discussion of your research plans during the fellowship period. Please do not submit a copy of the departmental dissertation prospectus. Proposals will be read by an inter-departmental faculty committee and should emphasize the potential of your research to make a contribution to the particular field and to scholarship in general. 6. A timetable for completion of research and writing (two pages maximum). Please be as specific as possible. Applicants can apply for only one of the following terms academic year (fall and spring). 7. Two letters of recommendation. GSAS prefers that recommenders submit their letters of recommendation electronically to expedite processing. 8. A budget proposal

Closing Date: 1 March

Funding: Private

Additional Information: The terms of the GSAS Travel Fellowship prohibit grantees from holding teaching assignments or any other position concurrently gsas.columbia.edu/student-guide/dissertation/gsas-international-travel-awards

For further information contact:

109 Low Memorial Library, MC 4306, 535 West 116th Street, New York, NY 10027, United States of America.

Email: fellowships@columbia.edu

GSAS Summer Language Fellowships for International Students

Eligibility: The GSAS Summer Language Fellowships for International Students supports international PhD students in

Arts and Sciences programs in the humanities and social sciences who need to study a less common foreign language during the summer. International students who are permanent residents are not eligible to apply for these funds. They may instead apply for the FLAS award.

Level of Study: Doctorate
Type: Fellowship
Value: US$3,000
Frequency: Annual
Country of Study: Any country
Closing Date: 1 March
Additional Information: gsas.columbia.edu/content/gsas-summer-language-fellowships-international-students

For further information contact:

Email: gsas-fellowships@columbia.edu

Columbia University

405 Low Library, MC 4335, 535 West 116th Street, New York, NY 10027, United States of America.

Tel: (1) 212 854 3830
Email: support@ei.columbia.edu
Website: www.earth.columbia.edu

The Earth Institute at Columbia University brings together talent from throughout the University to address complex issues facing the planet and its inhabitants, with particular focus on sustainable development and the needs of the world's poor.

Benjamin A. Gilman International Scholarship Program

Purpose: The U.S. Department of State's Benjamin A. Gilman International Scholarship is a grant program that enables students of limited financial means to study or intern abroad, thereby gaining skills critical to our national security and economic competitiveness.
Eligibility: 1. A citizen of the United States; 2. An undergraduate student in good standing at an accredited institution of higher education in the United States (including both two-year and four-year institutions); 3. Receiving a Federal Pell Grant during the time of application or provide proof that they will be receiving a Pell Grant during the term of their study abroad program or internship; 4. In the process of applying to, or accepted to, a credit-bearing study abroad or

internship program, or a virtual international program. Virtual programs and internships will be eligible until April 30, 2024. Proof of program acceptance is required prior to award disbursement; 5. Applying for credit-bearing study abroad programs in a country or area with an overall Travel Advisory Level 1 or 2, according to the U.S. Department of State's Travel Advisory System. However, certain locations within these countries or areas may be designated within the Travel Advisory as either "Do not travel to" (Level 4) or "Reconsider travel to" (Level 3) locations, as such; students will not be allowed to travel to these specific locations.
Level of Study: Postgraduate
Type: Scholarship
Value: Awards of up to US$5,000 for semester or academic year program
Frequency: Annual
Country of Study: Any country
No. of awards offered: 3000
Closing Date: 1 March
Funding: Private
Additional Information: urf.columbia.edu/fellowship/benjamin-gilman-international-scholarships

For further information contact:

202 Hamilton Hall, MC 2811, 1130 Amsterdam Ave, New York, NY 10027, United States of America.

Tel: (1) 212 853 2375
Fax: (1) 212 854 2797
Email: ugrad-urf@columbia.edu

Knight-Bagehot Fellowships in Economics and Business Journalism at Columbia University

Purpose: To improve the quality of economics and business journalism through instruction to mid career journalists.
Eligibility: Open to professional journalists globally;
Level of Study: Graduate, MBA, Postgraduate
Type: Fellowship
Value: An approximately US$60,000 stipend to cover living expenses, plus tuition for the full academic year at Columbia University
Length of Study: 1 academic year
Frequency: Annual
Study Establishment: School of Journalism, Columbia University
Country of Study: United States of America
Application Procedure: Applicants must submit a completed application form, two 1,000 word essays, three letters of reference, and five work samples. journalism.columbia.edu/kb

No. of awards offered: 10 Fellows each year
Closing Date: 31 January
Funding: Corporation, Foundation, Trusts
Contributor: Knight Foundation
No. of awards given last year: 10
No. of applicants last year: 100
Additional Information: journalism.columbia.edu/kb

For further information contact:

Graduate School of Journalism, Columbia University, 2950 Broadway, New York, NY 10027, United States of America.

Tel: (1) 212 854 2711
Fax: (1) 212 854 7837
Email: ann.grimes@columbia.edu

Marie Tharp Visiting Fellowships

Purpose: To provide an opportunity for women scientists to conduct research at one of the related departments within the Earth Institute
Eligibility: The competition is open to women scientists in the natural sciences and engineering. Faculty, staff and research scientists at Columbia University are not eligible to apply. Applicants must hold a Ph.D. Minorities and mid-career women are especially encouraged to apply. Applicants must be eligible to work in the U.S.
Level of Study: Doctorate, Research
Type: Fellowships
Value: US$30,000
Length of Study: 3 months
Frequency: Annual
Country of Study: United States of America
Application Procedure: Applicants must submit a 3-page proposal, a curriculum vitae, a proposed budget and complete contact information of 3 references
Closing Date: 16 January
Additional Information: All application materials may be submitted by mail or by email www.earth.columbia.edu/sitefiles/file/Research/Marie_Tharp_Information_Packet.pdf

For further information contact:

ADVANCE at The Earth Institute at Columbia University Lamont-Doherty Earth Observatory of Columbia University, 61 Rte 9W, Palisades, NY 10964, United States of America.

Email: kdutt@ldeo.columbia.edu

Commonwealth Eye Health Consortium

International Centre for Eye Health, London School of Hygiene & Tropical Medicine, Keppel Street, London WC1E 7HT, United Kingdom.

Tel: (44) 20 7636 8636
Email: press@lshtm.ac.uk
Contact: Commonwealth Eye Health Consortium

The Commonwealth Eye Health Consortium is a group of expert organizations working together to deliver a five-year programme of fellowships, research, and technology to strengthen eye health systems across the Commonwealth.

CEHC Masters Scholarships in Public Health for Eye Care

Purpose: The Masters in Public Health for Eye Care at the London School of Hygiene & Tropical Medicine is a well-established course that aims to train leaders in the prevention of blindness and to strengthen research and academic capacity for eye care programmes and training facilities, particularly in low- and middle-income countries
Eligibility: See the website. Entrance Requirement 1. Come from low or middle-income Commonwealth countries that are less represented in the alumni body of the MSc Public health for eye care. 2. Work in regions where there are severe constraints in human resources for eye health work in regions where there are no / limited training opportunities in PHEC / community eye health. 3. Demonstrate previous involvement/commitment to community eye health activities or VISION2020 programmes Present a clear career plan in public health for eye care, which they will realistically. 4. Be able to follow on completion of the MSc. 5. Have experience in public health for eye care based research and/or training in eye care. 6. Fulfill the United Kingdom Border Agency English Language Requirement by passing the LSHTM English language requirement by 11 May
Value: Several scholarships are awarded each year. Each scholarship covers the following All course feesTwo return flightsDissertation project fundLiving costsAccommodation with food at the International Students House in Central London. Find out more about the International Students House
Study Establishment: Scholarships are awarded to undertake MSc in Public Health for Eye Care

Country of Study: United Kingdom

Application Procedure: Apply to the London School of Hygiene & Tropical Medicine for a place on the course if you have applied and been accepted to the academic year you must request to "be reconsidered" for the academic year. Please contact the LSHTM Registry to be asked to "be reconsidered" Once you have received an offer from the London School of Hygiene & Tropical Medicine here CEHC; MSc Scholarships Application

Closing Date: 11 May

Additional Information: For more details please browse the website iceh.lshtm.ac.uk/commonwealth-eye-health-consortium-cehc-scholarships-2018-19-for-msc-public-health-for-eye-care/

For further information contact:

Email: Romulo.Fabunan@Lshtm.ac.uk

Commonwealth Fund

1 East 75th Street, New York, NY 10027, United States of America.

Tel: (1) 212 606 3800
Email: grants@cmwf.org
Website: www.cmwf.org

The Commonwealth Fund of New York is a philanthropic foundation established in 1918. The Fund supports independent research on health and social issues and makes grants to improve healthcare practice and policy.

Australian-American Health Policy Fellowship

Purpose: To enable Fellows to gain an in-depth understanding of the Australian health care system and policy process, recent reforms, and models for best practice, thus enhancing their ability to make innovative contributions to policymaking in the United States, to improve the theory and practice of health policy in Australia and the United States by stimulating the cross-fertilization of ideas and experience and to encourage ongoing health policy collaboration and exchange between Australia and the United States by creating a network of international health policy experts

Eligibility: Open to accomplished, mid-career health policy researchers and practitioners including academics,

physicians, decision makers in managed care and other private organizations, federal and state health officials and journalists

Level of Study: Research

Type: Fellowship

Value: For a full 10-month stay in Australia, the fellowship awards up to AU$87,000 which includes a living allowance, relocation expenses, research related travel and conferences, etc. There is also a family supplement available (e.g. up to AU$26,000 for a partner and two children). Round trip airfares to Australia are also covered

Length of Study: Up to 10 months

Frequency: Annual

Study Establishment: Suitable establishment in Australia

Country of Study: Australia

Application Procedure: Please go to www.commonwealthfund.org/grants-and-fellowships/fellowships/australian-american-health-policy-fellowship/application-form to know complete procedure to apply for this program

Closing Date: February

Funding: Government

Additional Information: In Australia: Director; International Strategies Branch Portfolio Strategies Division Department of Health and Ageing MDP 85, GPO Box 9848, Canberra ACT 2601, Australia; Tel: (61) 2 6289 4593; Fax: (61) 2 6289 7087. Australian-American Health Policy Fellowships is the successor of the Packer Policy Fellowship Program, which ran from 2003 to 2009. Email at packerpolicyfellowship@health.gov.au
www.commonwealthfund.org/publications/newsletter-article/australian-american-health-policy-fellowship-0

For further information contact:

Email: ro@cmwf.org

Harkness Fellowships in Health Care Policy

Purpose: To build a network of policy orientated health care researchers whose multinational experience and outlook stimulate innovative policies and practices in the United States and other industrialised countries

Eligibility: Open to Australian, British, and New Zealand citizens. Applicants must be at postgraduate level or have equivalent experience

Level of Study: Postgraduate

Type: Fellowship

Value: Up to US$75,000

Length of Study: 4 months–1 year

Frequency: Annual

Study Establishment: A host institution which is normally, but not exclusively, of an intellectual kind, such as a university graduate school, a research institute or a 'think tank'
Country of Study: United States of America
Application Procedure: Applicants must write for details
Closing Date: 30 June
Additional Information: 2023–24 Program Update: The 2023–24 Harkness Fellowship application will be open June 30 through November 1, 2022, for qualified individuals from France, Germany, the Netherlands, New Zealand, Norway, and the United Kingdom.* The application can be accessed here beginning June 30, 2022.

For further information contact:

Harkness Fellowship in Health Care, Associate Professor & Directo, Center for Health Economics Research & Evaluation, University of Sydney, Mallett Street Campus, 88 Mallett Street Level 6 Building F, Camperdown, NSW 2050, Australia.

Tel: (61) 2 9351 0900
Fax: (61) 2 9351 0930
Email: mf@cmwf.org

Harkness Fellowships in Healthcare Policy and Practice

Purpose: To encourage the professional development of promising healthcare policy researchers and practitioners who will contribute to innovation in healthcare policy and practice in the United States of America and their home countries
Eligibility: Open to individuals who have completed a Master's degree or PhD in health services or health policy research. Applicants must also have shown significant promise as a policy-orientated researcher or practitioner, e.g. physicians or health service managers, journalists and government officials, with a strong interest in policy issues. Candidates should also be at the research Fellow to senior lecturer level, if academically based; be in their late 20s to early 40s, and have been nominated by their department chair or the director of their institution
Level of Study: Postgraduate, Professional development, Research
Type: Fellowship
Value: Up to US$130,000 in support, with an additional family supplement (up to US$60,000 for a partner and two children up to age 18)
Length of Study: spend up to 12 months in the United States
Frequency: Annual

Study Establishment: An academic or other research policy institution
Country of Study: United States of America
Application Procedure: Applicants must complete a formal application available online at the website www.cmwf.org/fellowships
Funding: Private
Contributor: The Commonwealth Fund
Additional Information: www.commonwealthfund.org/fellowships/harkness-fellowships-health-care-policy-and-practice 2023–24 Program Update: The 2023–24 Harkness Fellowship application will be open June 30 through November 1, 2022, for qualified individuals from France, Germany, the Netherlands, New Zealand, Norway, and the United Kingdom.* The application can be accessed here beginning June 30, 2022.

For further information contact:

Email: mf@cmwf.org

The Commonwealth Fund Mongan Fellowship in Minority Health Policy

Purpose: To create physician-leaders who will pursue careers in minority health policy
Eligibility: 1. Physicians who have completed residency in the U.S., either BE/BC. Additional experience beyond residency, such as chief residency, is preferred. 2. Experience or interest in addressing and improving the health needs of minority, disadvantaged and vulnerable populations as well as in advancing system change in ways that improve the health for all populations, but with particular emphasis on vulnerable populations. 3. Strong evidence of leadership experience or potential, especially as related to community efforts, quality improvement, transformation of health care delivery systems, and/or health policy. 4. Intention to pursue a career in policy, public service, and/or academia. 5. U.S. citizenship or U.S. permanent residency.
Level of Study: Graduate, Postgraduate, Professional development, Research
Type: Fellowship
Value: US$60,000 stipend, full tuition, health insurance, books, travel, and related program expenses, including financial assistance for a practicum project
Length of Study: five one-year, degree-granting
Frequency: Annual
Study Establishment: Harvard Medical School
Country of Study: United States of America
Application Procedure: Applications available online at the website www.cmwf.org/fellowships
Closing Date: 1 December

Funding: Foundation
Additional Information: For more information, please visit:
mfdp.med.harvard.edu/cff/how-apply
www.commonwealthfund.org/fellowships/commonwealth-fund-fellowships-minority-health

For further information contact:

Minority Faculty Development Program, Harvard Medical School, 164 Longwood Avenue, 2nd Floor, West Court, Boston, MA 02115, United States of America.

Tel: (1) 617 432 2922
Fax: (1) 617 432 3834
Email: mfdp_cfhuf@hms.harvard.edu

Commonwealth Scholarship and Fellowship Plan

Commonwealth Scholarship Commission in the United Kingdom, c/o Association of Commonwealth Universities, John Foster House, 36 Gordon Square, London WC1H 0PF, United Kingdom.
The Plan was drawn up at the first Commonwealth Education Conference held in Oxford in 1959. It is a system of awards for men and women from all Commonwealth countries to study in countries other than their own. One of its guiding principles is that it be based on mutual co-operation

Commonwealth Shared Scholarship Scheme at United Kingdom Universities

Purpose: Commonwealth Shared Scholarships are for candidates from least developed and lower middle income Commonwealth countries, for full-time Master's study on selected courses, jointly supported by United Kingdom universities. The scholarships do not cover undergraduate courses, PhD study, or any pre-sessional English language teaching
Eligibility: 1. Be a citizen of or have been granted refugee status by an eligible Commonwealth country, or be a British Protected Person. 2. Be permanently resident in a developing Commonwealth country. 3. Be available to start your academic studies in the United Kingdom by the start of the United Kingdom academic year in September/October. 4. By October, hold a first degree of at least upper second class (21) standard, or a second class degree and a relevant postgraduate qualification (usually a Master's degree). 5. Not have studied or worked for one (academic) year or more in a developed country. 6. Be unable to afford to study in the United Kingdom without this scholarship

Level of Study: Postgraduate
Type: Scholarship
Value: £1,330
Length of Study: 1 year
Frequency: Annual
Country of Study: Any country
Application Procedure: Apply online
Closing Date: 14 March
Funding: Foundation
Additional Information: cscuk.fcdo.gov.uk/scholarships/commonwealth-shared-scholarships-2022/#:~:text=Enquiries-,Overview,partnership%20with%20select%20UK%20universities.&text=Intended%20beneficiaries%3A%20Commonwealth%20Shared%20Scholarships,courses%20at%20a%20UK%20university

For further information contact:

Woburn House, 20-24 Tavistock Square, London WC1H 9HF, United Kingdom.

Email: csc.safeguarding@cscuk.org.uk

Commonwealth Scholarship Commission in the United Kingdom

The Association of Commonwealth Universities, Woburn House, 20;24 Tavistock Square, London WC1H 9HF, United Kingdom.

Tel: (44) 20 7380 6700
Email: info@cscuk.org.uk
Website: www.dfid.gov.uk/cscuk
Contact: Ms Natasha Lokhun, Communications Officer

The Commonwealth Scholarship Commission (CSC) in the United Kingdom is responsible for managing Britain's contribution to the Commonwealth Scholarship and Fellowship Plan (CSFP). The CSC makes available seven types of award and supports around 700 awards in total annually.

Association of Commonwealth Universities Titular Fellowships

Purpose: To enable the universities of the commonwealth to develop the human resources of their institutions and countries through the interchanging of people, knowledge, skills and technologies. Not intended for degree courses, or for immediately postdoctoral programmes

Eligibility: Applicants must be on the staff of member universities under the ACU, the Commonwealth interuniversity organization or working in industry, commerce or public service in a Commonwealth country. Applicant must be within 28–50 years of age

Level of Study: Professional development

Type: Scholarship

Value: £5,000 for travel, board, insurance and fees where the approved programme includes a training programme

Length of Study: 6 months

Frequency: Annual

Study Establishment: ACU member university or in industry, commerce or public sector

Country of Study: Commonwealth countries

Application Procedure: Candidates must be nominated by executive heads of ACU member universities or by the chief executive officer of a Commonwealth interuniversity organization. Full application details on ACU website

No. of awards offered: 50

Closing Date: June

Contributor: ACU

No. of awards given last year: 8

No. of applicants last year: 50

Additional Information: www.vergemagazine.com/program-search/funding/the-association-of-commonwealth-universities-acu-titular-fellowships.html

For further information contact:

Email: acuawards@acu.ac.uk

Community Foundation for Calderdale

Office 158, Dean Clough, Halifax, Yorkshire HX3 5AX, United Kingdom.

Tel: (44) 1422 349 700
Email: enquiries@ccfound.co.uk
Website: www.ccfund.co.uk
Contact: Mr Mohammad Aslam, Director of the Board, Grants

W.D. Farr Endowment Fund Grants

Purpose: The Greeley Rotary W. D. Farr Endowment Fund at the Community Foundation Serving Greeley and Weld County welcomes applications and considers grant requests from US$500 to US$2,500 for the benefit of the youth of Greeley, Colorado. The W.D. Farr Endowment Fund supports programs in the Greeley area that enhance

Level of Study: Graduate

Type: Grant

Value: US$500 to US$2,500

Frequency: Annual

Country of Study: Any country

Application Procedure: Attachment Checklist requires following information to process further proposal. 1. Cover letter. 2. Project budget sheet. 3. Board of Directors list

Closing Date: 31 January

Funding: Private

Additional Information: weldcommunityfoundation.org/grant-programs/#:~:text=Farr%20Endowment%20Fund%20awards%20grants,or%20K%2D12%20education%20projects.&a,p;text=The%20W.D.

For further information contact:

2425 35th Avenue, Suite 201, Greeley, CO 80634, United States of America.

Email: info@cfsgwc.org

Concordia University

Sir George Williams Campus, 1455 De Maisonneuve Blvd. W., Montréal, QC H3G 1M8, Canada.

Tel: (1) 514 848 2424
Website: www.concordia.ca
Contact: Ms Patricia Verret, Graduate Awards Manager

Concordia University is the result of the 1974 merger between Sir George Williams University and Loyola College. The University incorporates superior teaching methods with an interdisciplinary approach to learning and is dedicated to offering the best possible scholarship to the student body and to promoting research beneficial to society

Bank of Montréal Pauline Varnier Fellowship

Purpose: To support graduate students to acquire higher degree in the fields of business and commerce

Eligibility: Open to women with 2 years of cumulative business experience who are entering full-time studies in the MBA program at the John Molson School of Business. Candidates must be Canadian citizens or permanent residents

Level of Study: MBA

Type: Fellowship

Value: C$10,000 per year

Length of Study: 2 years
Frequency: Annual
Study Establishment: Concordia University
Country of Study: Canada
Application Procedure: Applicants must submit a completed application form, three letters of recommendation and official transcripts of all university studies by the closing date
Closing Date: 1 February
Funding: Private
No. of awards given last year: 1
Additional Information: Academic merit is the prime consideration in the granting of the awards cscuk.dfid.gov.uk/apply/shared-scholarships/

For further information contact:

M.B.A. Program, Faculty of Commerce and Administration, Concordia University, 1455 Boulevard de Maisonneuve O, Montréal, QC H3G 1M8, Canada.

Tel:　　(1) 848 2424 ext 2717
Email:　gradprograms@jmsb.concordia.ca

Congressional Black Caucas Foundation

CBC Spouses Education Scholarship

Purpose: This opportunity awards scholarships to academically talented and highly motivated full-time African-American or Black students pursuing an undergraduate, graduate or doctoral degrees in a variety of fields.
Eligibility: Candidate Requirements 1. Be a U.S. citizen or legal permanent resident 2. Permanent residence or attend academic institution in a CBC Members district 3. Preparing to pursue or currently pursuing an undergraduate, graduate or doctoral degree full-time at an accredited college or university. Current high school seniors are also eligible to apply. 4. Have a minimum 2.5 GPA on 4.0 scale 5. Exhibit leadership and be active in community 6. Selected applicants will be qualified African-American or black students
Level of Study: Doctorate, Postgraduate
Type: Scholarship
Value: Varies
Frequency: Annual
Country of Study: United States of America
Closing Date: 30 April
Additional Information: cbcfinc.academicworks.com/opportunities/903

CBCF Congressional Summer Internship Program

Eligibility: You must use your full first and last name as your display name when creating your application account. 1. Interns must have at least a 2.5 GPA on a 4.0 scale 2. Interns must have full COVID vaccination, including COVID booster shot 3. Interns must have U.S. citizenship or a permit to work in the U.S. for the duration of the program (May 31, 2023 to July 29, 2023) 4. Interns must have availability to participate full-time upon acceptance 5. Interns cannot be enrolled in classes for the duration of the program (in some cases, the program can be used for credit with university approval) 6. Interns must currently be a rising college sophomore, junior, or senior, OR must have not graduated with a bachelor's degree more than a year from the internship program start date 7. Interns cannot yet have obtained an advanced degree 8. Interns cannot be actively enrolled in graduate studies 9. Interns must have general familiarity with the federal legislative process, the U.S. Congress, the Congressional Black Caucus and its members, and related policy 10. Interns must have superior analytical skills 11. Interns must have outstanding oral and written communication skills
Level of Study: Doctorate
Type: Internship
Value: Interns receive housing and a US$3,000 stipend
Frequency: Annual
Country of Study: United States of America
Closing Date: 31 March
Additional Information: cbcfinc.academicworks.com/opportunities/909

For further information contact:

Email:　internships@cbcfinc.org

CBCF Louis Stokes Health Scholars Program, sponsored by United Health Foundation

Purpose: This opportunity offers multi-year scholarships to increase the number of qualified, competitive African-American or Black students pursuing a degree in healthcare, to include, but not limited to internal medicine, family medicine and pediatrics.
Eligibility: Candidate Requirements 1. Be a U.S. citizen or legal permanent resident 2. Be pursuing an undergraduate, graduate or doctoral degree full-time at an accredited college or university. Current high school seniors are eligible to apply. 3. Pursuing a major that will lead to a career as a primary health care professional 4. Have a minimum 3.0 GPA on 4.0 scale 5. Exhibit leadership and be active in community

6. Selected applicants will be qualified African-American or black students
Level of Study: Doctorate, Postgraduate
Type: Scholarship
Value: US$8,000
Frequency: Annual
Country of Study: United States of America
Additional Information: cbcfinc.academicworks.com/opportunities/915

CBCF NREI Historically Black Colleges and Universities (HBCU) Scholarship

Purpose: The Congressional Black Caucus Foundation's National Racial Equity Initiative for Social Justice (NREI) HBCU Social Justice Scholarships were created to encourage and support the next generation of social justice leaders committed to dismantling systemic barriers and advancing equity, freedom, and justice for all, especially the Black community and racial minorities.
Eligibility: Candidate Requirements 1. Selected applicants will be qualified African-American or black students 2. Be a U.S. citizen/legal permanent resident 3. Attend an accredited HBCU 4. Have a GPA minimum of 3.0 on a 4.0 scale 5. Demonstrate a commitment to social justice 6. Exhibit leadership and be active in community
Level of Study: Doctorate, Postgraduate
Type: Scholarship
Value: Varies
Frequency: Annual
Country of Study: United States of America
Closing Date: 30 April
Additional Information: cbcfinc.academicworks.com/opportunities/921

Congressional Black Caucus Foundation Spouses Visual Arts Scholarship

Purpose: This award is for students with majors in the visual arts including, but not limited to, architecture, ceramics, drawing, fashion, graphic design, illustration, interior design, painting, photography, sketching, video production and other decorative arts
Eligibility: Candidate Requirements 1. Be a U.S. citizen or legal permanent resident 2. Be preparing to pursue, or currently pursuing, an undergraduate, graduate or doctoral degree full-time at an accredited college or university. Current high school seniors are also eligible to apply. 3. Be pursuing a career in the visual arts with an eligible major 4. Have a minimum 2.5 GPA on 4.0 scale

5. Exhibit leadership and be active in community
6. Selected applicants will be qualified African-American or black students
Level of Study: Postgraduate
Type: Scholarships
Value: US$3,000
Frequency: Annual
Country of Study: United States of America
Application Procedure: 1. The online application is available on the Congressional Black Caucus Foundations (CBC) website. During the online application process, the applicant must upload and/or complete the following forms. 2. A personal statement essay from the student (500–1,000 words) that addresses all four (4) of the topics listed on the application in one cohesive essay. 3. Two (2) letters of recommendation (Email addresses will be requested of each recommender for electronic submission of the letter. Hard copy letters will not be accepted.)
Funding: Private
Additional Information: Late applications and materials will not be accepted cbcfinc.academicworks.com/opportunities/905

For further information contact:

1720 Massachusetts Avenue NW, Washington, DC, 20036, United States of America.

Tel: (1) 202 263 2800
Email: scholarships@cbcfinc.org

Stephen Feinberg Scholars Scholarship Program

Purpose: The Stephen Feinberg Scholars Scholarship awards academically talented and highly motivated full-time African-American or Black scholars pursuing a graduate or doctoral degree in all discipline areas.
Eligibility: Candidate Requirements 1. Be a U.S. citizen or legal permanent resident 2. Preparing to pursue, or currently pursuing, a graduate or doctoral degree full-time at an accredited college or university. 3. Have a minimum 3.0 GPA on 4.0 scale 4. Exhibit leadership and be active in community 5. Selected applicants will be qualified African-American or black students
Level of Study: Doctorate, Postgraduate
Type: Scholarship
Frequency: Annual
Country of Study: United States of America
Closing Date: 30 April
Additional Information: cbcfinc.academicworks.com/opportunities/935

Conseil Européen Pour la Recherche Nucléaire European Organization for Nuclear Research

CH-1211, Geneva 23, Switzerland.

Tel: (41) 22 76 784 84
Email: recruitment.service@cern.ch
Website: www.cern.ch

CERN European Laboratory for Particle Physics is the world's leading laboratory in its field, that being the study of the smallest constituents of matter and of the forces that hold them together. The laboratory's tools are its particle accelerators and detectors, which are among the largest and most complex scientific instruments ever built

Conseil Européen Pour la Recherche Nucléaire Summer Student Programme

Purpose: To awaken the interest of undergraduates in CERN's activities by offering them hands-on experience during their long summer vacation
Eligibility: 1. You are a Bachelor or Master student (not PhD) in the Fields of Physics, Engineering, Computer Science or Mathematics. 2. Should have completed, at least Three Years of Full-Time Studies at University Level. 3. You have a good knowledge of English (However, IELTS or TOEFL is Not Required). 4. Candidates of all nationalities are welcome to apply for this Summer Student Programme.
Value: A 90 CHF Per Day Allowance to Cover the Cost of Accommodation & Meals for a single person and A Round Airfare Tickets Travel Allowance to & From Geneva.
Length of Study: 8 to 13 weeks
Study Establishment: CERN
Country of Study: Switzerland
Application Procedure: You need to apply online careers.cern/summer
Closing Date: 31 January
Additional Information: Please check at home.web.cern.ch/students-educators/summer-student-programme opportunitiescorners.info/cern-summer-student-program-2020/

For further information contact:

Email: jkrich@umich.edu

Conseil Européen Pour la Recherche Nucléaire-Japan Fellowship Programme

Purpose: To support young researchers who are interested in LHC data analysis and physics studies
Eligibility: Applicants should be nationals or permanent residents of Japan and have a doctorate for applicants in experimental or phenomenological physics and/or accelerator science. Candidates who are currently preparing a PhD are eligible to apply. However, they are expected to have obtained their PhD by the time they take up their appointment at CERN
Level of Study: Doctorate
Type: Fellowship
Value: Covers travel expense and insurance coverage
Length of Study: Up to 3 years
Frequency: Annual
Country of Study: Any country
Application Procedure: A completed electronic application form along with a curriculum vitae should be submitted
Contributor: CERN
Additional Information: Please check at jobs.web.cern.ch/job/10941

Marie Curie Fellowships for Early Stage Training at CERN

Purpose: To offer structured scientific and/or technological training and to encourage participants to take up long-term research careers
Eligibility: Open to researchers in the first 4 years of their research activity. Persons who have obtained a doctorate are ineligible
Type: Fellowship
Study Establishment: CERN
Country of Study: Any country
Application Procedure: Candidates should register and apply for the Marie Curie Fellowship programme using the CERN e-recruitment system
Contributor: European Comission

Conservation Leadership Programme

Conservation Leadership Programme, Birdlife International, Wellbrook Court, Girton Road, Cambridge CB3 0NA, United Kingdom.

Email: clp@birdlife.org
Website: www.conservationleadershipprogramme.org

Since 1985, the Conservation Leadership Programme has supported and encouraged international conservation projects that address global conservation priorities at a local level. This is achieved through a comprehensive system of advice, training and awards. The programme is managed through a partnership between BP, FFI, CI, WCS and Birdlife International.

Future Conservationist Awards

Purpose: To develop leadership capacity amongst emerging conservationists to address the most pressing conservation issues of our time
Eligibility: The project must address a globally recognized conservation priority, involve people, have host government approval, be run by teams of at least three people, be student-led, have over 50% students registered, last for less than 1 year and take place in Africa, Asia Pacific, Middle East, Eastern Europe, Latin America or the Caribbean
Level of Study: Doctorate, Graduate, Postgraduate
Type: Award
Value: Up to US$15,000
Length of Study: 3 to 12 months
Frequency: Annual
Application Procedure: Application forms are available from the website. Applications should be made electronically
No. of awards offered: 360
Funding: Private
Contributor: BP, BirdLife International, Conservation International, WildLife Conservation Society, and Fauna and Flora International
No. of awards given last year: 29
No. of applicants last year: 360
Additional Information: www.conservationleadershipprogramme.org/grants/grant-overview/future-conservationist-award/

Conservation Trust

National Geographic Society, 1145 17th Street NW, Washington, DC 20036-4688, United States of America.

Email: conservationtrust@ngs.org
Website: www.nationalgeographic.com/conservation

The objective of the Conservation Trust is to support conservation activities around the world as they fit within the mission of the National Geographic Society. The trust will fund projects that contribute significantly to the preservation and sustainable use of the Earth's biological, cultural, and historical resources.

National Geographic Conservation Trust Grant

Purpose: To support cutting programmes that contribute to the preservation and sustainable use of the Earth's resources
Eligibility: Applicants must provide a record of prior research or conservation action. Researchers planning work in foreign countries should include at least one local collaboration as part of their research teams. Grants recipients are excepted to provide the National Geographic Society with rights of first refusal for popular publication of their findings
Level of Study: Research
Type: Research grant
Value: US$15,000–20,000
Frequency: Annual
Country of Study: Any country
Application Procedure: Apply online at www.nationalgeographic.com/explorers/grants-programs/conservation-trust-application
Funding: Trusts
Contributor: National Geographic Society

For further information contact:

Conservation Trust, National Geographic Society, 1145 17th Street NW, Washington, DC 20036, United States of America.

Consortium for Advanced Research Training in Africa (CARTA)

Email: carta@aphrc.org
Website: www.cartafrica.org/

CARTA's mission is to promote the health and development of African populations through high-quality research on policy-relevant priority issues. The initiative will foster the emergence of vibrant and viable multidisciplinary research hubs of locally-trained internationally recognized scholars.

Consortium for Advanced Research Training in Africa PhD Fellowships

Purpose: CARTA offers an innovative model for doctoral training in sub-Saharan Africa to strengthen the capacity of participating institutions to conduct and lead internationally-competitive research

Eligibility: A Masters degree in a relevant field, Prior admission into a PhD program is not required for application but awards are contingent on such admission being obtained at one of the participating African universities, Male applicants must be under the age of 40 years and female applicants under the age 45 years

Level of Study: Postgraduate

Type: Fellowship

Value: Fellowships cover tuition fees, medical insurance and other university fees in special circumstances only

Length of Study: The fellowship runs for a maximum of 4 years

Country of Study: Africa

Funding: International office

Additional Information: Please check website for more details www.opportunitiesforafricans.com/carta-phd-fellowships-2019-2020/

For further information contact:

Email: carta_fellowship@aphrc.org

Consortium for Applied Research on International Migration

PO Box 616, NL-6200 MD Maastricht, Netherlands.

Email: secretariaat-carim@maaastrichtuniversity.nl

CARIM is one of the top institutes for translational cardiovascular research in Europe. It is among the world leaders in the fields of research into vascular and thrombotic disorders and atrial fibrillation as well as translational heart failure research. It has also made important international contributions to molecular imaging in the cardiovascular field.

Consortium for Applied Research on International Migration Postdoctoral Talent Fellowship

Purpose: Purpose is to provide recently promoted top CARIM talent a chance to gain experience abroad and return to CARIM to perform excellent research

Eligibility: For eligibility details, please visit the website

Level of Study: Postdoctoral

Type: Fellowship

Value: The fellowship amounts to €53,011 gross which is meant for a period of 12 months. Bench fees are not included

in this fellowship. The fellowship includes one return flight to the host institute (based on economy fare)

Country of Study: Any country

Application Procedure: There will be one call a year, and the deadline for the "CARIM - Postdoctoral Talent Fellowship" is the 13th of May, 00.00 hours. To apply for the "CARIM - Postdoctoral Talent Fellowship", the applicants from within (or connected to) CARIM are invited to submit an application (by mail) to the CARIM office (secretariaat-carim-at-maastrichtuniversity.nl)

Closing Date: 13 May

Additional Information: www.nationalmeritscholarships.com/carim-postdoctoral-talent-fellowship.html

For further information contact:

Email: secretariaat-carim@maastrichtuniversity.nl

Cooperative Research Centre for Water Quality and Treatment (CRCWQT)

Australia Water Quality Centre, Private Mail Bag 3, Salisbury, SA 5108, Australia.

Tel: (61) 8 8259 0326
Email: dennis.steffensen@sawater.com.au
Website: www.waterquality.crc.org.au
Contact: Professor Dennis Mulcahy, Training Leader

The Cooperative Research Centre for Water Quality and Treatment (CRCWQT) provides a national strategic research capacity for the Australian water industry and focuses on issues relating to water quality management and health risk reduction.

Cooperative Research Center for Water Quality and Treatment Young Water Scientist of the Year Scholarship

Purpose: To provide support to PhD students for research done within the Water Forum CRC

Eligibility: Open to candidates who are in the final year of their PhD.

Level of Study: Doctorate

Type: Scholarship

Value: AU$2,500

Length of Study: 1 year

Frequency: Annual

Country of Study: Australia

Closing Date: 28 February

For further information contact:

Email: detr@wmo.int

Copenhagen Business School

Solbjerg Plads 3, DK-2000 Frederiksberg, Denmark.

Tel: (45) 3815 3815
Email: cbs@cbs.dk
Website: www.cbs.dk

Copenhagen Business School PhD Scholarship on IT Management

Eligibility: To be considered, the candidate should have a basic training at the Masters level (similar to the 3 + 2 Bologna process). An educational background in the social sciences is necessary. The applicant must have successfully completed the Masters degree before commencing PhD at CBS. The applicants must be fluent in English
Level of Study: Doctorate, Research
Type: Scholarship
Value: The scholarships are fully salaried positions, according to the national Danish collective agreement. The scholarship includes the tuition fees, office space, travel grants, plus a salary, currently starting with per month approx. DKK 23,770 (approx. DKK 3,160) up to DKK 28,964 (approx. DKK 3,860) depending on seniority, plus a pension contribution totalling 17.1% of 85% of the base salary
Length of Study: 3 years
Country of Study: Denmark
Application Procedure: Application must be sent via the electronic recruitment system. The application must include a 5-page project description. This research proposal should contain a presentation of an original research question, a description of the initial theoretical framework and methodology, a presentation of the suggested empirical material as well as a work plan. In addition to the research proposal, the application must include copies of a Master's degree certificate or other certificates of a corresponding level, brief curriculum vitae, a list of papers and publications, and one copy of a selected written work (e.g. Master's thesis)
Closing Date: 28 February
Contributor: Copenhagen Business School
Additional Information: The scholarship requires the student to spend a minimum of 12 months of their PhD programme in a research institution in China. Countries of study are Denmark and China www.nationalmeritscholarships.com/carim-postdoctoral-talent-fellowship.html

For further information contact:

Email: dsi.msc@cbs.dk

PhD scholarships in Finance

Purpose: The three-year PhD program at CBS allows students to conduct research under the supervision of CBS faculty, supported by research training courses. The program is highly international, and students are expected to participate in international research conferences and to spend time abroad at another research institution as a visiting PhD student.
Eligibility: To be considered, the candidate should have a basic education at the Master's level (similar to the 3+2 Bologna process). The applicant must have successfully completed the Master's degree before commencing PhD at CBS, but we also welcome applications from individuals close to completion of the Master's degree. Generally, a completed MBA education does not fulfil this requirement. The applicants must be fluent in English. For admittance to the 4+4 PhD scheme, the candidate must have completed a bachelor's degree (or equivalent) and have passed subjects corresponding to 60 ECTS in a relevant master's program within the CBS' subject areas. Applicants who are not enrolled in a master's program at CBS will be assessed by the CBS Admissions Office. The successful applicant must have shown academic excellence with a record of top grades from previously completed programs. Priority will be given to candidates who have both a strong quantitative background and strong previous training in financial economics.
Level of Study: Doctorate
Type: Scholarship
Value: The scholarships are fully salaried positions, according to the national Danish collective agreement. The scholarship includes the tuition fees, office space, travel grants plus a salary, currently starting from app. DKK 32,400.00 (app. 4,354.00 €) per month up to app. DKK 39,170.00 (app. 5,265.00 €) per month including pension contributions, depending on seniority.
Length of Study: 4 years
Frequency: Annual
Country of Study: Denmark
Application Procedure: Fill in the online form with your personal data and upload the relevant documentation (see guide to required documentation below).
Closing Date: 21 February
Additional Information: www.cbs.dk/en/about-cbs/jobs-cbs/vacant-positions/phd-scholarships-in-finance

For further information contact:

Email: nso.fi@cbs.dk

Core

3 St Andrew's Place, London NW1 4LB, United Kingdom.

Tel: (44) 20 7486 0341
Email: info@corecharity.org.uk
Website: www.corecharity.org.uk
Contact: Alice Kington, Finance and Research Manager

Core Fellowships and Grants

Purpose: To provide funding for gastroenterological research
Eligibility: Open to applicants resident within the United Kingdom. Fellowship projects must contain an element of basic science training
Level of Study: Doctorate, Postdoctorate, Postgraduate, Research
Type: Fellowship or Grant
Value: £50,000 per year salary and £10,000 per year consumables (Research Fellowships); £50,000 total (Development Grants)
Length of Study: 1–3 years
Frequency: Dependent on funds available
Study Establishment: Recognized and established research centres
Country of Study: United Kingdom
Application Procedure: Applicants must complete an application form for consideration in a research competition. Details are available from the website
No. of awards offered: Varies
Funding: Commercial, Foundation, Individuals, Private, Trusts
Contributor: Charitable donations
No. of awards given last year: 4
No. of applicants last year: Varies
Additional Information: Conditions are advertised on the core website www.corecharity.org.uk
serb.gov.in/emr.php

For further information contact:

Email: IAS_applications@ceu.edu

Council of American Overseas Research Centers (CAORC)

PO Box 37012, MRC 178, Washington, DC20013-7012, United States of America.

Tel: (1) 202 633 1599
Email: fellowships@caorc.org
Website: www.caorc.org

Council of American Overseas Research Centers (CAORC) serve as a base for virtually every American scholar undertaking research in the host countries. The members have centres in many locations across the world.

CAORC-NEH Senior Research Fellowship

Purpose: The CAORC - National Endowment for the Humanities Senior Research Fellowship provides the opportunity for scholars to spend significant time in one country with an ORC as a research base.
Eligibility: 1. All applicants must hold a PhD. 2. Applicants who are US citizens are eligible to apply. 3. US citizens living outside of the US are eligible to apply. 4. Foreign nationals who have resided in the US for three years prior to the application deadline are eligible to apply. 5. Independent scholars are welcome to apply. It is not a requirement that applicants be affiliated with a US academic institution. 6. Funding is not available for research conducted in the US. 7. Minority scholars and scholars from Minority-Serving Institutions are especially encouraged to apply.
Level of Study: Postdoctorate
Type: Fellowship
Value: US$5,000 per month
Frequency: Annual
Country of Study: United States of America
Application Procedure: Applications can be accessed via orcfellowships.smapply.org/. You must sign up for an account to access the application. This will allow you to save and return to your application before submitting. Please save your login/password information for future applications.
Closing Date: 25 January
Additional Information: Applications can be accessed via orcfellowships.smapply.org/. You must sign up for an account to access the application. This will allow you to save and return to your application before submitting. Please save your login/password information for future applications.

Council of American Overseas Research Centers Andrew W. Mellon East-Central European Research Fellows

Purpose: To help scholars in the humanities and allied social sciences to carry out research at institutes of advanced study in other countries

Eligibility: Open to candidates who have obtained a PhD and are nationals of Bulgaria, Czech, Estonia, Hungary, Latvia, Lithuania, Poland, Romania or Slovakia
Level of Study: Research
Type: Fellowships
Value: Varies
Length of Study: Short-term residencies
Frequency: Annual
Country of Study: Any country
Additional Information: www.iwm.at/program/andrew-w-mellon-east-central-european-research-fellowship

For further information contact:

Email:	fellowships@iwm.at

Council of American Overseas Research Centers Multi-Country Research Fellowship Program for Advanced Multi-Country Research

Purpose: To advance higher learning and scholarly research and to conduct research of regional or trans-regional significance
Eligibility: Applicants must have obtained a PhD or be established postdoctoral scholars. The candidate should be a citizen of the United States. Preference will be given to Candidates examining comparative and/or cross-regional research
Level of Study: Doctorate, Postdoctorate, Research
Type: Fellowships
Value: Up to US$10,500
Frequency: Annual
Country of Study: Any country
Application Procedure: The application can be downloaded from the website. To obtain hard copy of the application, please contact CAORC
No. of awards offered: 120
Closing Date: 20 January
Contributor: United States State Department
No. of awards given last year: 9
No. of applicants last year: 120
Additional Information: Scholars must carry out research in at least one of the countries that host overseas research centres. Please check website for further information www.caorc.org/multi-fellowship-guidelines

Council of American Overseas Research Centers Neh Research Fellowships

Purpose: The National Endowment for the Humanities (NEH) Senior Research Fellowship supports advanced research in the humanities. Fellowship awards are for four consecutive months
Eligibility: 1. Applicants must be United States citizens or foreign nationals who have resided in the United States for three years prior to the application deadline. 2. Applicants must be postdoctoral scholars. 3. Funding is not available for research conducted in the United States. 4. It is not required that you be affiliated with a United States academic institution to apply
Level of Study: Graduate
Type: Fellowship
Value: US$4,200
Frequency: Annual
Country of Study: Any country
Closing Date: 24 January
Funding: Foundation
Additional Information: www.caorc.org/neh-fellowship-guidelines

Multi-Country Research Fellowship

Purpose: The Multi-Country Research Fellowship enables US scholars to carry out trans-regional and comparative research in countries across the network of Overseas Research Centers as well as other countries.
Eligibility: 1. Applicants must be US citizens. 2. Funding is not available for research conducted in the US. 3. Team projects are admissible and will be evaluated as a single application. Teams should submit one (1) application for the team project and a CV for each member. Note that all team members must fulfil the fellowship eligibility requirements. If awarded, a single grant of US$11,500 will be issued to the team. 4. Independent scholars are welcome to apply. 5. PhD candidates must be ABD (all but dissertation) by May 2022. If you have held a Multi-Country Fellowship in the past, you must wait three years before you are eligible to apply again. Minority scholars and scholars from Minority Serving Institutions are especially encouraged to apply.
Level of Study: Doctorate
Type: Fellowship
Value: US$11,500 each
Length of Study: 6 months
Frequency: Annual
Country of Study: United States of America
Application Procedure: Applications can be accessed via orcfellowships.smapply.org/. You must sign up for an account to access the application. This will allow you to save and return to your application before submitting. Please save your login/password information for future applications.
No. of awards offered: 9
Closing Date: 8 December
Additional Information: www.caorc.org/multi-fellowship-guidelines

Council of Independent Colleges

One Dupont Circle, N.W, Suite 320, Washington, DC 20036-1142, United States of America.

Tel: (1) 202 466 7230
Email: visitingfellows@cic.nche.edu
Website: www.cic.org/projects_services/visitingfellows.asp
Contact: Michelle Friedman, Program Manager

Woodrow Wilson Visiting Fellows

Purpose: To encourage the flow of ideas between the academic and non-academic sectors of society
Eligibility: The program is available to all four-year public and private, nonprofit colleges and universities in the United States as well as CIC International Member institutions. CIC member campuses participate at a discounted rate.
Level of Study: Postgraduate
Type: Fellowships
Value: STANDARD VISIT CIC Non-Member Price US$6,000, CIC Member Price US$5,500 ABBREVIATED VISIT CIC Non-Member Price US$4,900, CIC Member Price US$4,500
Length of Study: 1 year
Frequency: Annual
Country of Study: Any country
Application Procedure: If your campus is ready to start the process of hosting a Fellow, please complete this online form. The form should be completed by a campus-designated "campus coordinator" who will be CIC's point of contact throughout the planning and execution of the visit. Be prepared to provide a short list of preferred Fellows, preferred time to host a Fellow, preferred visit length, and a brief paragraph about the intended engagement of the Fellow on campus
Closing Date: 17 April
Funding: Private
Contributor: Lilly Endowment
Additional Information: www.cic.edu/member-services/woodrow-wilson-visiting-fellows

For further information contact:

Visiting Fellows Program, 5 Vaughn Drive, Suite 300, Princeton, NJ 08540-6313, United States of America.

Tel: (1) 609 452 7007 ext. 181
Email: sanford@woodrow.org

Council of Logistics Management

George A. Gecowets Graduate Scholarship Program

Subjects: Logistics; all programs leading to careers in logistics management
Purpose: To grant scholarships solely on merit - academic achievement, work experience, leadership, and career commitment - rather than financial need.
Eligibility: A student is eligible to apply for this scholarship if they are already enrolled in the first year of a Master's degree program leading to a career in Logistics related graduate program.
Type: Scholarship
Value: US$1,000
Country of Study: United States of America
Closing Date: 1 April
Additional Information: phdstudents.smeal.psu.edu/scholarship-fellowship-opportunities/external-awards/gecowets.html

Council of Supply Chain Management Professionals (CSCMP)

333 East Butterfield Road, Suite 140, Lombard, IL 60148, United States of America.

Tel: (1) 630 574 0985
Email: membership@cscmp.org
Website: www.cscmp.org
Contact: Kathleen Hedland, Director Education and Roundtable Services

The Council of Supply Chain Management Professionals (CSCMP) is a non-profit organization of business personnel who are interested in improving their logistics management skills. CSCMP works in co-operation with private industry and various organizations to further the understanding and development of the logistics concept. This is accomplished through a continuing programme of organized activities, research and meetings designed to develop the theory and understanding of the logistics process, promote the art and science of managing logistics systems, and foster professional dialogue and development within the profession.

Council of Supply Chain Management Professionals Distinguished Service Award

Purpose: To provide honor to an individual for achievement in supply chain management

Eligibility: All individuals who have made contributions to the field of supply chain management are eligible for the DSA. This includes practitioners with responsibilities in a functional area of supply chain management, consultants and educators-anyone who has made a significant contribution to the advancement of supply chain management. Please check at cscmp.org/career/awards/distinguished-service-award-process for more detailed information

Type: Award

Frequency: Annual

Country of Study: Any country

Application Procedure: Nominations must be accompanied by a fully completed nomination form and should be emailed to Sue Paulson

Closing Date: 16 March

Additional Information: cscmp.org/CSCMP/Awards/Distinguished_Service_Award.aspx

Council of Supply Chain Management Professionals Doctoral Dissertation Award

Purpose: To encourage research leading to advancement of the theory and practice to supply chain management

Eligibility: Open to all candidates whose doctoral dissertation demonstrates signified originality and contributes to the logistics knowledge base. See cscmp.org/downloads/public/education/awards/dda-guidelines.pdf for details

Level of Study: Postdoctorate

Type: Award

Value: US$5,000

Frequency: Annual

Country of Study: Any country

Closing Date: 15 May

Additional Information: cscmp.org/CSCMP/Awards/Doctoral_Dissertation_Award.aspx

For further information contact:

Email: kmcinerney@cscmp.org

Supply Chain Innovation Award

Purpose: CSCMP's Research Strategies Committee (RSC) and Supply Chain Brain established the Supply Chain Innovation Award in 2005 to highlight and recognize the top players in the supply chain industry when it comes to innovative programs, projects and collaboration

Eligibility: The submitting company must be a CSCMP member. In addition, each member of your team must be registered for the annual conference by 1 August. All travel, accommodations, and related expenses are the responsibilities of the finalist teams

Type: Scholarship

Frequency: Annual

Country of Study: Any country

Application Procedure: While the finalist teams present their case studies, the panel of judges evaluates the session as it happens live in front of the audience of conference attendees

Closing Date: 16 March

Contributor: CSCMP's Research Strategies Committee (RSC) and Supply Chain Brain

Additional Information: Please check complete guidelines at cscmp.org/CSCMP/Awards/Supply_Chain_Innovation_Award.aspx

For further information contact:

Tel: (1) 630 645 3454

Email: cscmpresearch@cscmp.org

Council on Foreign Relations (CFR)

The Harold Pratt House, 58 East 68th Street, New York, NY 10065, United States of America.

Tel: (1) 212 434 9400

Email: fellowships@cfr.org

Website: www.cfr.org

Contact: Janine Hill, Director, Fellowship Affairs and Studies

The Council on Foreign Relations (CFR) is dedicated to increasing America's understanding of the world and contributing ideas to United States foreign policy. The Council accomplishes this mainly by promoting constructive debates and discussions, clarifying world issues and publishing Foreign Affairs, the leading journal on global issues.

Council on Foreign Relations International Affairs Fellowship in Japan

Purpose: To cultivate the United State's understanding of Japan and to strengthen communication between emerging leaders of the two nations

Eligibility: 1. Applicants must be U.S. citizens. 2. Applicants must be mid-career professionals. 3. Applicants must have a strong record of professional achievement. 4. Applicants must have an interest in U.S.-Japan relations. 5. Applicants must hold at least a bachelor's degree. 6. Although the program is intended primarily for those without substantial prior experience in Japan, exceptions have been made when an applicant has demonstrated that the fellowship would add a significant new dimension to his or her career. 7. Knowledge of the Japanese language is not a requirement.

Level of Study: Professional development
Type: Fellowship
Value: monthly stipend of US$7,700 along with a US$5,000 travel grant
Length of Study: 3–12 months
Frequency: Annual
Country of Study: Japan
Application Procedure: Application is primarily by invitation, on the recommendation of individuals in academic, government and other institutions who have occasion to know candidates particularly well suited for the experience offered by this fellowship. Others who inquire directly and who meet preliminary requirements may also be invited to apply without formal nomination. Those invited to apply will be forwarded application materials
No. of awards offered: 6
Closing Date: 31 October
Funding: Private
Contributor: Hitachi Limited
No. of awards given last year: 3
No. of applicants last year: 6
Additional Information: The IAF in Japan program will not be accepting applications for the 2023–24 fellowship year. Interested applicants who meet the program's eligibility requirements may apply online for the 2023–24 fellowship between July 1 and October 31, 2023. www.cfr.org/fellowships/international-affairs-fellowship-japan

For further information contact:

Fellowship Affairs, Council on Foreign Relations, 58 East 68th Street, New York, NY 10065, United States of America.

Tel: (1) 212 434 9740
Fax: (1) 212 434 9870

Council on Library and Information Resources (CLIR)

1707 L Street, NW Suite 650, Washington, DC 20036, United States of America.

Tel: (1) 202 939 4750/4751
Email: abishop@clir.org
Website: www.clir.org
Contact: Alice Bishop, Senior Program Officer

CLIR is an independent, nonprofit organization that forges strategies to enhance research, teaching, and learning in collaboration with libraries, cultural institutions, and communities of higher learning.

Council on Library and Information Resources Postdoctoral Fellowship

Purpose: The CLIR Postdoctoral Fellowship Program offers recent PhD graduates the chance to develop research tools, resources, and services while exploring new career opportunities. CLIR Postdoctoral Fellows work on projects that forge and strengthen connections among library collections, educational technologies, and current research. Host institutions benefit from fellows' field-specific expertise by gaining insights into their collections' potential uses and users, scholarly information behaviors, and current teaching and learning practices
Eligibility: Applicants must have received a PhD in a discipline no more than five years before applying; if a PhD has not yet been received, all work toward the degree (including dissertation defense and final dissertation editing) must be completed before starting the fellowship. Applicants can be citizens of any country but MUST be legally permitted to work in the United States and/or Canada
Level of Study: Postdoctorate
Type: Postdoctoral fellowship
Value: Varies by host institution
Length of Study: 2 years
Frequency: Annual
Country of Study: Any country
Application Procedure: Complete an online application www.clir.org/fellowships/postdoc/applicants/
No. of awards offered: 115
Closing Date: 1 March
Funding: Foundation, Private
Contributor: Alfred P. Sloan Foundation, Andrew W. Mellon Foundation, individual host institutions
No. of awards given last year: 15
No. of applicants last year: 115
Additional Information: www.postdocs.ubc.ca/award/council-library-information-resources-postdoctoral-fellowship-program

Craig H. Neilsen Foundation

16830 Ventura Boulevard, Suite 352, Encino, CA 91436, United States of America.

Tel: (1) 818 925 1245
Website: chnfoundation.org/

Established by Craig H. Neilsen in 2002 as a private foundation, the Craig H. Neilsen Foundation is dedicated to supporting both programs and scientific research to improve the quality of life for those affected by and living with spinal cord injury

Community Support Grants

Purpose: Harnessing the power of collaboration to increase independence for all individuals living with SCI, the Creating Opportunity & Independence (CO&I) portfolio supports non profit organizations providing programs and services that are community-driven, empowering, and inclusive of all ages and backgrounds to enhance quality of life.

Eligibility: 1. The grantee must be a nonprofit organization or rehabilitation facility located in the United States or Canada with the capability to conduct grant-funded programs or activities. 2. Neilsen Foundation grants are not awarded to individuals, private foundations, or non-functionally integrated Type III supporting organizations. 3. The Applicant named in a grant application must have his/her organization's authorization to apply for a grant and is expected to be responsible for conduct of the grant activities. 4. Generally, an organization may only submit one CO&I application in each program cycle and may hold only one Neilsen Foundation CO&I Community Support Grant at a time. However, major academic or medical organizations (e.g., universities, large medical or healthcare systems) may submit concurrent applications provided that the proposed projects are distinct. 4a. Individuals cannot be the Applicant for more than one submission and cannot have a previously funded Community Support Grant active on the Full Grant Application due date. 5. If two or more people are directing a project, one must serve as the Applicant; the other(s) should be listed as collaborator (s). The Neilsen Foundation does not recognize co-Applicant leadership on its grants.

Type: Grant

Value: budgets must be from US$25,000–US$200,000. The budget for any year cannot exceed US$125,000.

Frequency: Annual

Country of Study: United States of America

Closing Date: 31 March

Additional Information: chnfoundation.org/programs/creating-opportunity-independence/

For further information contact:

Email: darrell@chnfoundation.org

Neilsen SCIRTS Postdoctoral Fellowship Grants

Purpose: The Spinal Cord Injury Research on the Translational Spectrum (SCIRTS) portfolio supports research to improve the understanding of traumatic spinal cord injury and develop new approaches to alleviate the dysfunction and complications that follow. The scope of this portfolio is broad, encompassing mechanistic, preclinical modeling, translational and/or clinical research. These two-year Postdoctoral Fellowships encourage early-career training and specialization in the field of spinal cord injury research.

Eligibility: 1. Applicants must have a doctoral degree or an equivalent terminal professional degree (e.g., PhD, MD, DVM). Non-fellowship applicants must demonstrate appropriate experience to serve as an independent Principal Investigator (PI). The Neilsen Foundation encourages submissions from eligible PIs who represent a wide range of disciplines; however, it is required that relevant SCI expertise is represented on the proposed research project team. 2. The grantee must be a nonprofit academic/research institution or rehabilitation facility located in the United States or Canada with the capability to conduct grant-funded research. 3. The Applicant is not required to be a citizen of the United States or Canada; however, the Applicant must be employed by an eligible grantee institution. 4. Neilsen Foundation grants are not awarded to individuals, private foundations or non-functionally integrated Type III supporting organizations. 5. The Applicant named in a grant application must be deemed eligible by his/her organization to apply for a grant, and is expected to be responsible for conduct of the research. Each application must include the appropriate endorsement of an institutional official who is responsible for the administration of grant funds (hereafter known as the "Grants Administrator"). 6. A PI may submit only one application in a given cycle in this portfolio (see CONCURRENT GRANTS section under PART 2, SECTION F., below). 7. The Neilsen Foundation does not allow Co-Principal Investigators on its research grants. If two or more investigators are working together on a research project, one must serve as the PI; the other(s) should be listed as collaborator(s). Collaborators and/or consultants do not need to be affiliated with the same institution as the PI; a subcontract may be used to support a domestic or international collaborator or consultant. 8. Multiple PIs from an institution may submit concurrent, independent applications in a given grant cycle. In such cases, each project must be distinct, with no-overlapping Aims. 9. The Neilsen Foundation discourages Postdoctoral Fellows and their mentor (s) from submitting concurrent applications with overlapping Aims to multiple funding categories within this portfolio. 10. It may not be necessary to provide preliminary data. Neilsen Foundation funding may be sought to allow the Applicant to obtain data to establish a line of research if the proposal provides strong rationale (e.g., support from the literature or use in an indication other than SCI) that justifies testing the hypotheses with the proposed experimental design. However, if feasibility issues add an unacceptable risk of failure, reviewers may note that preliminary data to address this risk should be provided.

Level of Study: Postdoctoral

Type: Fellowships

Value: US$75,000 for a maximum total cost of US$150,000.

Length of Study: Two-year

Frequency: Annual

Country of Study: United States of America

Closing Date: 10 June

Additional Information: chnfoundation.org/programs/spinal-cord-injury-research-on-the-translational-spectrum/

For further information contact:

Email: tracey@chnfoundation.org

SCIRTS Pilot Research Grants

Purpose: Supporting the wide array of research possibilities and opportunities, with the Spinal Cord Injury Research on the Translational Spectrum (SCIRTS) portfolio, we seek to improve the understanding of traumatic spinal cord injury and develop new approaches to alleviate the dysfunction and complications that follow.

Eligibility: 1. Applicants must be independent investigators, actively employed at the grantee institution at the time of FGA submission, and can be at any stage of their research career. 2. Junior investigators should demonstrate evidence of a strong research background that is relevant to the proposed study. As independence is an important component for investigators who are not in a tenure track position (e.g., Instructor, Research Assistant, etc.), a letter of support from the institution's Director or Department Chair is recommended at the LOI and FGA stage. The letter should indicate that the applicant is an independent investigator and that necessary space and equipment are available for this research. 3. Established investigators' proposals should demonstrate a new direction in SCI research that is considered "high risk" balanced by high potential impact. While new directions may be explored in both Pilot and Senior categories, in cases where preliminary evidence is being developed to show that new approach is worth pursuing, a Pilot grant is the appropriate category.

Level of Study: Postdoctorate

Type: Grant

Value: US$150,000 for a maximum total cost of US$300,000.

Frequency: Annual

Country of Study: United States of America

Closing Date: 10 June

Additional Information: chnfoundation.org/programs/spinal-cord-injury-research-on-the-translational-spectrum/

For further information contact:

Email: jacob@chnfoundation.org

SCIRTS Senior Research Grants

Purpose: Three-year Senior Research Grants encourage senior-level investigators to expand the scope of their work into new directions through targeted studies with high potential to move the field forward.

Eligibility: 1. This funding is for individuals who are senior, independent investigators (equivalent to Associate Professor or above), employed at the grantee institution, at the time of the FGA submission. 2. The grant category focuses on highly innovative projects by established PIs exploring new areas of SCI research or filling important gaps in the SCI field. The goal is not to substitute for federal funding, but to use Neilsen Foundation funds to encourage cutting-edge ideas and approaches that have great potential, despite some additional risk. The importance of the research goal should balance the risk due to the early stage of innovation. 3. Key criteria include the innovative nature of the proposed research, the likelihood that success will move the field forward, and a history of productivity and significant contributions by the investigator. Applicants should carefully consider their qualifications and the relevance of their Aims to the Neilsen Foundation before applying for a Senior Research Grant.

Level of Study: Postdoctorate

Type: Grant

Value: US$200,000 for a maximum total cost of US$600,000.

Length of Study: 3 year

Frequency: Annual

Country of Study: United States of America

Closing Date: 10 March

Additional Information: chnfoundation.org/programs/spinal-cord-injury-research-on-the-translational-spectrum/

For further information contact:

Email: tracey@chnfoundation.org

Craig H. Neilsen Foundation

Pilot Grants

Subjects: Aging, caregiving, employment, health behaviors and fitness, independent living, self-management and technology access.

Purpose: This funding is intended to support pilot studies that lay essential groundwork, allow the applicant to test the feasibility of novel methods and procedures and/or collect new data that can lead to or enhance larger-scale studies. Proposed pilot projects should indicate how they will establish a new investigational program or take on 'risk' balanced by high potential impact.

Eligibility: Applicants must have a doctoral degree or other equivalent terminal professional degree, be beyond the post-doctoral level at the time of the FGA submission, and demonstrate appropriate experience to serve as an independent PI. chnfoundation.org/wp-content/uploads/2022/01/PSR-2023-Application-Guide_FINAL-12.16.21.pdf

Type: Grant

Value: Funding for PSR Pilot grants is for up to two years, US$300,000 total costs

Length of Study: Two years

Country of Study: United States of America

Application Procedure: See website for further details.

Closing Date: 3 March

Additional Information: chnfoundation.org/psychosocial-research/ site not working

Postdoctoral Fellowships

Subjects: Spinal cord injury

Purpose: To encourage early-career mentored training to increase professional interest in the field and to encourage researchers from related health disciplines to undertake training in psychosocial research focused on spinal cord injury.

Eligibility: Fellows must have attained their doctoral degree or an equivalent terminal professional degree by the FGA submission deadline and have held that degree no longer than five years prior to the FGA submission deadline. For Fellows with an MD degree, the five-year period begins after completion of their residency program. Unique circumstances related to this criterion must be communicated to the Neilsen Foundation for approval prior to submission. chnfoundation.org/wp-content/uploads/2022/01/PSR-2023-Application-Guide_FINAL-12.16.21.pdf

Level of Study: Postdoctorate

Type: Fellowship

Value: US$100,000 for a maximum total cost of US$200,000.

Length of Study: Two years

Country of Study: United States of America

Application Procedure: See website for further details.

Closing Date: 3 March

Additional Information: chnfoundation.org/programs/psychosocial-research/

Studies and Demonstration Projects

Subjects: Spinal cord injury

Purpose: This funding is intended to support substantive studies that fill important gaps in the SCI field, that open

new areas of SCI psychosocial research, or that develop and evaluate interventions to address psychosocial issues after SCI. Submissions in this category should facilitate, expand or improve the translation of knowledge and/or the adoption of interventions and practices that will have a positive impact for those living with SCI. Based within a psychosocial framework, PSR Studies and Demonstration Projects can range from SCI epidemiological studies to interventions that will enhance clinical treatment, rehabilitation, habilitation and/or other related quality of life outcomes.

Eligibility: Applicants must be independent investigators, actively employed at the grantee institution at the time of FGA submission, and can be at any stage of their research career. o Criteria for funding junior investigators include evidence of a research background that is relevant to the proposed study and the mission of the Neilsen Foundation. To establish independence, Applicants who hold a non-tenure track position (Instructor, Research Assistant, etc.) may include, with their Biosketch, a letter of support from the institution's Director or Department Chair at the LOI and FGA stage. Such a letter should confirm the Applicant's position as independent and that all needed space and equipment are available to this PI.

Type: Grant

Value: Funding for PSR Studies and Demonstration Projects is for up to three years, US$400,000 total costs

Length of Study: Three years

Country of Study: Any country

Application Procedure: See website for further details.

Closing Date: 25 March

Additional Information: chnfoundation.org/psychosocial-research/ site not working

Cranfield University

School of Applied Sciences, Bedfordshire MK43 OAL, United Kingdom.

Tel: (44) 1234 754086
Email: info@cranfield.ac.uk
Website: www.cranfield.ac.uk/sas
Contact: Vicky Mason, Online Marketing Manager

The School of Applied Sciences is recognized globally for its multidisciplinary approach to teaching and research in the key areas of manufacturing, materials, and environmental science and technology. Our focus is on fundamental research and its application, together with teaching, to meet the needs of industry and society.

Cranfield Global Manufacturing Leadership Masters Scholarship

Type: Scholarship
Value: Tuition fee plus £1,000 cash
Country of Study: United Kingdom
Application Procedure: A number of Cranfield's full-time Manufacturing programme MSc courses are applicable to the Global Manufacturing Leadership (GML) Scholarships, please see the course list above. Applicants should submit a normal Cranfield application through the online application system. The online application forms part of the evaluation of academic achievement. Note the 6-digit online application number
Additional Information: www.cranfield.ac.uk/funding/funding-opportunities/cranfield-global-manufacturing-leadership-masters-scholarship

For further information contact:

College Road, Cranfield MK43 0AL, United Kingdom.

Tel: (44) 1234758181
Email: studentfunding@cranfield.ac.uk

Cranfield Merit Scholarship in Leadership and Management

Eligibility: Sub-Saharan African countries are eligible
Type: Scholarship
Value: £4,000 for tuition fees
Country of Study: United Kingdom
Application Procedure: For application details, send an email to studysom@cranfield.ac.uk
Closing Date: 25 May
Additional Information: worldscholarshipforum.com/20182019-cranfield-merit-scholarship-leadership-management-cranfield-university-uk/

For further information contact:

Email: studysom@cranfield.ac.uk

Cranfield Sub-Saharan Africa Merit Scholarship

Purpose: To commence full-time study in one of the eligible master courses for the current academic year
Type: Scholarship
Value: £4,000 for tuition fees
Frequency: Annual
Country of Study: Any country
Closing Date: 25 May

Additional Information: www.afterschoolafrica.com/25189/cranfield-sub-saharan-africa-merit-scholarship/

For further information contact:

Email: studysom@cranfield.ac.uk

The Diamond Education Grant

Purpose: Its purpose is to provide grants to assist women to update their skills after employment breaks or to acquire new skills to improve their opportunities for employment and promotion
Type: Small project grant
Value: Small grants towards tuition fees and other study costs
Frequency: Annual
Country of Study: Any country
Application Procedure: Apply online at the Diamond Education Grant website
Contributor: Soroptimist International
Additional Information: www.cranfield.ac.uk/funding/funding-opportunities/diamond-education-grant

For further information contact:

Soroptimist International Great Britain & Ireland (SIGBI) Ltd, 2nd Floor, Beckwith House, 1-3 Wellington Road North, Stockport SK4 1AF, United Kingdom.

Tel: (44) 1234 758181
Email: studentfunding@cranfield.ac.uk

The Lorch Foundation MSc Student Bursary

Purpose: To assist postgraduate study
Eligibility: Applicants should be United Kingdom citizens and possess a minimum 21 United Kingdom Honours degree in Engineering or Physical Sciences or related discipline, and have been offered a place on the 1-year full-time MSc in Water and Wastewater Engineering or Water and Wastewater Technology
Level of Study: Postgraduate
Type: Bursary
Value: £5,000 plus tuition fees
Length of Study: 1 year
Frequency: Annual
Study Establishment: Cranfield University, School of Applied Sciences
Country of Study: United Kingdom
Application Procedure: Applicants must apply directly to the university
Closing Date: 31 July
Funding: Foundation

Contributor: The Lorch Foundation
No. of awards given last year: 1
Additional Information: The bursary is provided by the Lorch Foundation, a charitable institution founded to support and promote education and research in the field of water purification and related sciences for the benefit of mankind. The successful applicant will undertake thesis research on processes of water purification and industrial effluent recycling as part of the MSc programme www.cranfield.ac.uk/funding/funding-opportunities/lorch-foundation-bursaries

For further information contact:

Tel: (44) 1234758181
Email: studentfunding@cranfield.ac.uk

Water MSc Scholarship for Students from Malawi and Vietnam

Purpose: The aim of the scholarship is to recruit students across all of our areas of academic specialisms with expertise in a wide range of disciplines to pursue MSc programme
Eligibility: The scholarship is open to students from Malawi and Vietnam
Value: The Cranfield Water Scholarship provides funding of £6,000 towards tuition fees
Country of Study: Any country
Closing Date: 25 May
Additional Information: scholarship-positions.com/cranfield-water-msc-scholarship-students-malawi-vietnam-uk/2018/03/15/

For further information contact:

Email: studywater@cranfield.ac.uk

Women as Cyber Leaders Scholarship

Purpose: For female students wishing to develop a career in Cyber
Type: Postgraduate scholarships
Value: £6,500 toward tuition fees
Country of Study: United Kingdom
Application Procedure: For eligibility and application details, please visit website www.cranfield.ac.uk/funding/funding-opportunities/women-as-cyber-leaders-scholarship
Closing Date: 30 June
Contributor: Cranfield Defence and Security
Additional Information: aseanop.com/women-cyber-leaders-scholarship-cranfield-university-uk/

For further information contact:

Email: cdsadmissionsoffice@cranfield.ac.uk

Crohn's and Colitis Foundation of America

386 Park Avenue South, 17th Floor, New York, NY 10016, United States of America.

Tel: (1) 800 932 2423
Email: info@ccfa.org
Website: www.ccfa.org/

Crohn's & Coltis Foundation Career Development Award

Purpose: Career Development Awards are mentored awards intended to facilitate the development of individuals with research potential to prepare for a career of independent basic research investigation in the area of inflammatory bowel disease (IBD).
Eligibility: Candidates should hold an MD, must have 5 years of experience (with 2 years of research relevant to IBD)
Level of Study: Postdoctorate, Research
Type: Fellowship
Value: US$90,000
Length of Study: 1 to 3 years
Frequency: Annual
Study Establishment: Approved research institute
Country of Study: United States of America
Application Procedure: See details at this link www.crohnscolitisfoundation.org/sites/default/files/2019-06/CDAGuidelines2019.pdf
Closing Date: 20 July
Funding: Corporation, Foundation, Individuals
Additional Information: www.crohnscolitisfoundation.org/research/grants-fellowships/career-development-awards

For further information contact:

Email: ogreen@crohnscolitisfoundation.org

Crohn's & Coltis Foundation Research Fellowship Awards

Purpose: Research Fellowship Awards are intended to support individuals in the post-doctoral
Eligibility: Individuals who are already well established in the field of IBD research are not considered eligible for this

award. Applicants should identify a senior investigator to serve as a mentor throughout the term of the award. At the time of application, applicants must be employed by an institution (public non-profit, private non-profit, or government) engaged in health care and/or health related research within the United States. Research is not restricted by citizenship; however, proof of legal work status is required. Applicants must hold an MD and/or PhD (or equivalent degree). Candidates holding MD degrees must have two years of experience after receiving their terminal degree - one year of which must be documented research experience relevant to IBD. Applicants holding PhDs must have at least one year of documented post-doctoral research relevant to IBD. MD applicants in excess of seven years and PhD applicants in excess of five years of receiving their terminal degree should explain how additional support in the post-doctoral phase would benefit their development beyond their current training.

Level of Study: Predoctorate, Research
Type: Fellowship/Scholarship
Value: Up to US$58,250 per year, also provide up to US$2,000 to be used for non-salary
Length of Study: 1 to 3 years
Frequency: Annual
Country of Study: Any country
Closing Date: 20 July
Funding: Corporation, Foundation, Individuals
Additional Information: www.crohnscolitisfoundation.org/research/grants-fellowships/research-fellowship-awards

For further information contact:

Email: ogreen@crohnscolitisfoundation.org

Crohn's & Coltis Foundation Senior Research Award

Purpose: To provide established researchers with funds to generate sufficient preliminary data to become competitive for funds from other sources such as the National Institutes of Health (NIH).
Eligibility: Applicant must hold an MD and/or PhD (or equivalent degree) and must be employed by an institution (public non-profit, private non-profit, or government) that is engaged in health care and/or health-related research. He/she must have attained independence from his/her mentor. Eligibility is not restricted by citizenship or geography.
Level of Study: Predoctorate, Research
Type: Research award
Value: Direct Costs: Up to US$105,300 per year. Indirect Costs: 10% of direct costs, or up to US$10,530
Length of Study: 1 to 3 years

Frequency: Annual
Study Establishment: Approved research institute
Country of Study: United States of America
Application Procedure: All completed applications must include one CD ROM or disk in PDF or word format, one master and four copies collected in order per check list. The complete application must be complied and saved as a single document
Closing Date: 20 July
Funding: Corporation, Foundation, Individuals
Additional Information: www.crohnscolitisfoundation.org/research/grants-fellowships/senior-research-awards

For further information contact:

Email: grant@crohnscolitisfoundation.org

Croucher Foundation

Suite 501, Nine Queen's Road Central, Hong Kong.

Tel: (852) 2 736 6337
Email: cfadmin@croucher.org.hk
Website: www.croucher.org.hk
Contact: Ms Elaine Sit, Administrative Officer

Founded to promote education, learning and research in the areas of natural sciences, technology and medicine, the Croucher Foundation operates a scholarship and fellowship scheme for individual applicants who are permanent residents of Hong Kong wishing to pursue doctoral or postdoctoral research overseas. The Foundation otherwise makes grants to institutions only.

Clinical Assistant Professorships

Purpose: The Scheme will provide the right candidate(s) with a solid platform for a long-term career with the medical faculties of the Chinese University of Hong Kong (CUHK) and the University of Hong Kong (HKU) by supporting an initial four-year appointment as Clinical Assistant Professor.
Eligibility: Applicants should possess a medical degree registrable with the Medical Council of Hong Kong and an interest in pursuing a career in academic medicine. Preference would be given to those candidates who have established a credible research record and/or have obtained, on top of a medical degree, a Doctor of Medicine (MD), Master of Surgery (MS) or Doctor of Philosophy (PhD) degree. The appointee is expected to undertake basic and applied clinical

research and teaching duties. He/she should demonstrate a strong commitment to, and evidence of, excellence in research and teaching to help reinforce and advance the strengths of the Faculty in the broad spectrum of medical and health sciences education. The appointee is expected to develop his/her research portfolio under close supervision of a mentor, and to conduct high-quality scholarly research. Direct communication with patients in Cantonese is required. The appointment(s) will be made in the two medical faculties of CUHK and HKU and the candidate(s) appointed will be mapped to the academic departments of the faculties as appropriate.

Level of Study: Postdoctorate
Type: Professorship
Frequency: Annual
Country of Study: Any country
Application Procedure: apply.croucher.org.hk/rounds/csu/2022-Q1/applying
Closing Date: 31 May
Additional Information: croucher.org.hk/funding/recognising-outstanding-hong-kong-scientists-mid-career/clinical-assistant-professorships

Croucher Foundation PhD Scholarships and Postdoctoral Fellowships

Purpose: Our goal is to identify and support a group of talented Hong Kong students and early-career researchers who, through a process of intensive education and exposure to prominent academics in their respective fields, will develop independent and critical abilities and form enduring collaborative partnerships, to enable them to become next generation of leaders of science, technology and medicine in Hong Kong. Eligibility under the following programmes is restricted to permanent Hong Kong residents
Eligibility: These are educational awards for graduates who obtained their doctoral degrees after September 2021. It is worth noting that these awards are not primarily meant as grants for enabling a university or institution to employ research personnel for research projects. Some Fellowships are also available for fully qualified medical doctors who wish to pursue research under a speciality. We will view your application more favourably if you are proposing to move to a new institution. Please note that we cannot consider applications who are already receiving full financial support from their proposed host institutions/supervisors.
Level of Study: Doctorate, Postdoctorate
Type: Scholarships and fellowships
Value: an annual maintenance allowance has been set to US$48,240 per annum. one economy class single air fare and a one-off arrival allowance of US$1,000
Length of Study: 1 to 3 years

Frequency: Annual
Country of Study: Any country
Closing Date: 15 November
Funding: Foundation
Additional Information: croucher.org.hk/funding/study_awards/postdoctoral_fellowships

For further information contact:

Croucher Foundation, Suite 501, Nine Queen's Road Central, Hong Kong.

Fax: (852) 2730 0742
Email: references@croucher.org.hk

Croucher Innovation Awards

Eligibility: The selected candidate is expected: 1. to have a strong, internationally competitive track record in research, relative to the stage of his/her career and research experience to date; 2. to have published significant intellectual contributions to research; 3. to have completed his/her doctorate with distinction less than six years ago; 4. to show evidence of achievement as an independent researcher in his/her chosen area; 5. to have been lead investigator on at least one significant research grant from a major funding body, or have been the recipient of an independent research fellowship before taking up his/her current post; 6. to have held competitive fellowships at the key career stages if he/she has clinical qualifications; 7. to have begun to establish a training record and to coach or mentor less experienced researchers.
Level of Study: Postdoctorate
Type: Award
Frequency: Annual
Country of Study: Any country
Application Procedure: To apply, please enter the online system here: apply.croucher.org.hk/rounds/cia/2022/applying
Closing Date: 31 July
Additional Information: croucher.org.hk/funding/recognising-outstanding-hong-kong-scientists-mid-career/croucher-innovation-awards

Croucher Science Communication Studentships

Purpose: These awards are intended for those engaged in full-time study leading to a Master's degree.
Eligibility: These awards are intended for those engaged in full-time study leading to a Master's degree. Applicants must have obtained at least Second Class Honours Division One in their first degree. Otherwise they must obtain substantively a higher degree by September 2023 to become eligible.

Students in their final year of first degree may also apply, but any offer of award will be conditional on their obtaining a suitable qualification upon their graduation by July 2023.

Level of Study: Postdoctorate

Type: Fellowship

Value: A Croucher Science Communication Studentship normally comprises the following: an annual maintenance allowance which is set at USD22,400; a one-way economy class air fare at both the beginning and end of tenure (if awards are tenable overseas); tuition fees; a one-off arrival allowance of USD1,000 to cover the costs of arriving in a new country during the first year of tenure (if awards are tenable overseas); an academic development allowance of up to USD2,000 to allow Croucher Studentship recipients to attend conferences, workshops or courses during the tenure of their awards; a medical insurance allowance of up to USD2,000 to cover medical insurance costs (if awards are tenable overseas); a family allowance of up to USD16,000 for the first child and up to USD6,800 for every additional child who resides with the scholar during the entire duration of the award; a commencement award of USD2,500 to be offered towards the completion of the Master's degree to contribute towards the cost of travel expenses for family members to attend their graduation ceremonies

Length of Study: 1 year

Frequency: Annual

Country of Study: Any country

Closing Date: 15 November

Additional Information: croucher.org.hk/funding/croucher-science-communication-studentships

For further information contact:

Tel: (852) 2730 0742
Email: references@croucher.org.hk

Croucher Senior Research Fellowships

Purpose: The main objective of this scheme is to provide opportunities for scientists aged mainly between 30 and 55 to be relieved of all teaching and administrative duties for a period of one year to do full-time research in Hong Kong.

Eligibility: 1. The selected fellow's employing institution will be reimbursed up to a certain limit for the actual salary costs of a younger academic (say up to 35 years of age) employed to take over the fellow's duties for the period of the fellowship; 2. The research during fellowship should normally be conducted at the applicant's own university but may be exceptionally done at another university in Hong Kong; fellows who wish to hold the fellowship outside Hong Kong must explicitly make a special case at the time of application, but even in the event of the award of the fellowship, the Foundation will not be responsible for any costs incurred as a result of the fellowship being held outside of Hong Kong; 3. Eligibility of these Senior Research Fellowships is usually restricted to holders of a full Hong Kong Permanent Identity Card issued by the Hong Kong SAR Government. This status of the applicant must be clearly declared on the application form at the time of application, and the Foundation reserves the right to request to see the ID Card if necessary. Exceptionally in cases where there are significant benefits for Hong Kong sciences, the Foundation may at its discretion consider applications from candidates who are not permanent Hong Kong residents.

Level of Study: Postdoctorate

Type: Fellowship

Length of Study: 1 year

Frequency: Annual

Country of Study: Any country

Application Procedure: To apply, please enter the online system here: apply.croucher.org.hk/rounds/srf/2022/applying

Closing Date: 31 May

Additional Information: croucher.org.hk/funding/recognising-outstanding-hong-kong-scientists-mid-career/croucher-senior-research-fellowships

Culinary Trust

PO Box 5485, Portland, OR 10013, United States of America.

Tel: (1) 97228 5485
Email: scholarships@theculinarytrust.org
Website: www.theculinarytrust.org/

The Culinary Trust has been the philanthropic partner to over 4,000 members of the International Association of Culinary Professionals (IACP) for over 20 years. The Trust solicits, manages and distributes funds for educational and charitable programmes related to the culinary industry in many areas.

L' Academie de Cuisine Culinary Arts Scholarship

Purpose: To financially prospective students prospective students for the Culinary Arts Program each year

Eligibility: Open to a student pre-enroled for the 12 months, Culinary Arts or Pastry Arts Certificate Program

Type: Scholarship

Value: US$5,000

Length of Study: 1 year

Country of Study: Any country

Application Procedure: Check the website for further details

Additional Information: Scholarship is valid for enrollment during July or October only

For further information contact:

Tel: (1) 646 224 6989

The Julia Child Endowment Fund Scholarship

Purpose: To support a career professional to conduct independent study and research in France, as it relates to French food, wine, history, culture and traditions. This programme also encourages, enables and assists aspiring students and career professionals to advance their knowledge of the culinary arts
Eligibility: Open to applicants who have 2 years of food service experience
Level of Study: Professional development
Type: Scholarship
Value: US$5,000
Frequency: Annual
Country of Study: France
Application Procedure: Applicants are required to include a three-page project proposal, an itemized budget detailing the use of this award, a tentative travel schedule with dates and locations, and provide a current curriculum vitae to qualify for this scholarship
Closing Date: 15 December
Funding: Trusts

For further information contact:

Email: foodwine@bu.edu

Zwilling, J.A. Henckels Culinary Arts Scholarship

Purpose: To provide financial assistance to students from designated states who are interested in pursuing a degree in the culinary arts
Eligibility: Open to any pre-enroled student, currently enroled student or career professional toward any culinary arts degree or certificate program at any nationally accredited culinary school
Level of Study: Postgraduate
Type: Scholarship
Value: US$5,000
Country of Study: Any country
Application Procedure: Check the website for further details
No. of awards offered: 1
Closing Date: 15 December
Contributor: Zwilling, J.A. Henckels Trust

Additional Information: www.collegescholarships.com/scholarships/detail/129381

Curtin University

Kent Street, Bentley, Perth, WA 6102, Australia.

Contact: Curtin University

Curtin University is an Australian public research university based in Bentley and Perth, Western Australia. The university is named after the 14th Prime Minister of Australia, John Curtin, and is the largest university in Western Australia, with over 58,000 students (as of 2016).

Association of Firearm and Tool Mark Examiners Scholarship

Purpose: The scholarships listed here are offered to Curtin students by external organisations and individuals (Scholarship Providers) that are not affiliated with Curtin University. Curtin University cannot vouch for the accuracy of the information provided by these scholarship providers. All enquiries should be directed to the relevant scholarship provider
Eligibility: 1. Applicants must be entering their third year or higher of a Bachelor's degree or enrolled in any year of an advanced degree (MS, PhD, MD or comparable) program for the academic school year beginning on or about the following September. Proof of enrollment status may be required. 2. The applicant must be enrolled as a half-time student or greater with the intent of seeking a career in Forensic Science and majoring in a natural, physical, or biological science. 3. Minimum grade point average of 3.0 on a 4.0 scale, or equivalent (76% or higher).
Level of Study: Doctorate, Postgraduate
Type: Scholarship
Value: US$2,000
Length of Study: 3 year
Frequency: Annual
Country of Study: United States of America
Closing Date: 1 April
Funding: International office
Additional Information: scholarship-positions.com/association-of-firearm-and-tool-mark-examiners-scholarship-for-international-students-in-australia/2019/03/12/

For further information contact:

Email: AFTEScholarship@gmail.com

Three-year Fully Funded PhD Scholarship in Public Health

Purpose: Curtin University is offering three-year fully-funded PhD scholarship in Public Health. The scholarship is awarded to conduct health services research that focuses on health systems and implementation science at the School of Public Health

Eligibility: International students can apply for these scholarships. If English is not your first language then you will need to show that your English language skills are at a high enough level to succeed in your studies

Value: The successful candidate will receive a stipend of AU$27,082 per annum

Study Establishment: Scholarship is awarded to conduct health services research that focuses on health systems and implementation science at the School of Public Health

Country of Study: Australia

Application Procedure: The mode of applying is online

Closing Date: 9 April

Additional Information: For more details please visit our website scholarship-positions.com/three-year-fully-funded-phd-scholarship-public-health-australia/2018/02/27/

For further information contact:

Email: lynda.bergey@curtin.edu.au

Curtin University of Technology

Office of Research and Development, GPO Box U1987, Perth, WA 6845, Australia.

Tel: (61) 8 9266 9266
Email: research_scholarships@curtin.edu.au
Website: www.curtin.edu.au/

Curtin University of Technology is a world class, internationally focused, culturally diverse institution. They foster tolerance and encourage the development of the individual. Their programmes centre around the provision of knowledge and skills to meet industry and workplace standards. A combination of first rate resources, staff and technology makes Curtin a forerunner in tertiary education both within Australia and internationally.

Aboriginal and Torres Strait Islander Scholarship Program

Eligibility: 1. Applicants must meet the following criteria to be eligible to apply through the Indigenous Scholarships Program: 2. Aboriginal or Torres Strait Islander descent 3. Other eligibility criteria will vary according to the scholarship. The Scholarships Team will assess you and match you to a potential scholarship if possible, then advise you regarding eligibility. Usually if you are successful in more than one scholarship, then you will be awarded the highest value scholarship. You may have the opportunity to select your preferred scholarship.

Level of Study: Postgraduate

Type: Scholarship

Value: There are many scholarships available in 2023 - some provide one-off payments, others provide support for the expected duration of the recipient

Frequency: Annual

Country of Study: Australia

Closing Date: 9 March

Additional Information: scholarships.curtin.edu.au/Scholarship/?id=5671

For further information contact:

Email: scholarships@curtin.edu.au

American Planning Association(I) - Innovation, Competition and Economic Performance

Purpose: To encourage students to undertake a Higher Degree by Research within the the Centre for Research in Applied Economics (CRAE)

Eligibility: Candidates must be Australian citizens or permanent residents or New Zealand citizens, should hold or are expected to hold a First Class Honours Degree or its equivalent and must meet Curtin University of Technology's requirements for admission to a PhD.

Level of Study: Graduate

Type: Competition

Value: AU$25,118 per year

Length of Study: 3 years with the possibility of an extension of up to 6 months

Country of Study: Any country

Application Procedure: Candidates must forward the completed application for admission to a higher degree by research to the Centre for Research into Applied Economics (CRAE)

For further information contact:

Tel: (61) 8 9266 2035
Email: H.Bloch@exchange.curtin.edu.au

Australian Biological Resources Study Postgraduate Scholarship

Purpose: To foster research training compatible with ABRS and national research priorities
Eligibility: Applicants must be Australian citizens or permanent residents, must hold a First or Upper Second Class Honours or equivalent degree in an appropriate discipline and be enroled as a full-time student in a PhD degree at an Australian institution
Level of Study: Graduate
Type: Scholarship
Value: AU$22,500
Country of Study: Australia
Application Procedure: Applicants must submit the application to ABRS through the host institution. The application form will then be submitted to the ABRS Advisory Committee for consideration and assessment using the selection criteria. The individual selected as most worthy of funding will be awarded the scholarship
Closing Date: 26 October
Additional Information: scholarships.adelaide.edu.au/ Scholarships/honours/faculty-of-sciences/australian-biological-resources-study-abrs-national

For further information contact:

Australian Biological Resources Study, GPO Box 787, Canberra, ACT 2601, Australia.

Tel: (61) 2 6250 9554
Fax: (61) 2 6250 9555
Email: abrs.grants@environment.gov.au

Civil and Structural Engineering PhD Scholarship

Eligibility: 1. Full time enrolment, for both domestic and international students 2. Minimum required: Bachelor degree (the first class honours or upper second class honours) in Civil Engineering, Structural Engineering or related fields. 3. The language requirement (IELTS: Overall 6.5, Speaking, Writing, Reading and Listening 6.0; or TOEFL, internet based Overall 79, Reading 13, Listening 13, Speaking 18 and Writing 21) is provided at study.curtin.edu.au/applying/english-language-requirements/accepted-english-proficiency-tests/.
Other general admission requirements and procedures can be checked at futurestudents.curtin.edu.au/research/apply/.
4. Applicants with Master degrees by research with technical publications and research experiences in structural dynamics and structural health monitoring, especially on computer vision, image processing, machine learning, deep learning, signal processing and data analysis techniques, are preferred.

Level of Study: Doctorate
Type: Scholarship
Value: AU$28,092 stipend per annum, based on full-time studies, up to a maximum of three and a half years.
Length of Study: 3.5 years
Frequency: Annual
Country of Study: Any country
No. of awards offered: 2
Closing Date: 31 December
Additional Information: scholarships.curtin.edu.au/Scholarship/?id=4080

For further information contact:

Email: junli@curtin.edu.au

Cultural Learnings: Strengthening Aboriginal children's wellbeing

Eligibility: 1. Demonstrated experience working with urban Western Australian Aboriginal community, particularly with children and Elders 2. Demonstrated knowledge, skills and experience of urban Western Australian Aboriginal cultural protocols, especially with regard to 3. cultural security, communication, obligations and kinship responsibilities 4. Genuine desire to journey with Aboriginal people in their pursuit of self-determination and social justice 5. English language IELTS level of 6.5.
Level of Study: Postgraduate
Type: Scholarship
Value: AU$28,106 p.a. pro rata for up to a maximum of 3.5 years.
Length of Study: 3+ years
Frequency: Annual
Country of Study: Australia
Closing Date: 3 March
Additional Information: scholarships.curtin.edu.au/Scholarship/?id=4900

For further information contact:

Email: CulturalLearnings@curtin.edu.au

Curtin Business School Doctoral Scholarship

Purpose: To enable doctoral (PhD, DBA) students to study at the Curtin Business School
Eligibility: Applicants must have completed at least 4 years of tertiary education studies at a high level of achievement and have First/Upper Second Class Honours or equivalent results. See scholarships.curtin.edu.au/scholarship.cfm?id=52 for more details

Level of Study: Postgraduate
Type: Scholarship
Value: US$25,000
Length of Study: Up to 3 years
Frequency: Annual
Country of Study: Any country
Application Procedure: Applicants can download the application form and obtain further information from the website
Closing Date: 31 December

For further information contact:

Tel: (61) 8 9266 4301
Email: GRS.CurrentStudents@curtin.edu.au

Curtin International Scholarships - Alumni and Family Scholarship

Eligibility: 1. International, fee-paying, non-sponsored students of any nationality except Australian 2. Students commencing studies at Curtin's Western Australia in 2023 3. Students commencing a full Curtin undergraduate or master by coursework program 4. Students who themselves or their siblings/parents/children are Curtin Alumni (must have completed a whole qualification) OR; their sibling, parent or child have a current enrolment in an academic program at Curtin's Western Australia campuses
Level of Study: Postgraduate
Type: Scholarship
Value: The scholarship provides 25% off first year tuition fee, up to a maximum of 200 credit points
Frequency: Annual
Country of Study: Any country
Closing Date: 15 October
Additional Information: scholarships.curtin.edu.au/Scholarship/?id=5618

For further information contact:

Email: study@curtin.edu.au

Curtin International Scholarships – Merit Scholarship

Eligibility: 1. International, fee-paying, non-sponsored students of any nationality except Australian 2. Students commencing studies at Curtin's Western Australia campuses for the first time in 2023 3. Students commencing a full Curtin undergraduate or master by coursework program
Level of Study: Postgraduate
Type: Scholarship

Value: This scholarship provides eligible students 25% off their first year tuition fee, up to a maximum of 200 credit points only.
Frequency: Annual
Country of Study: Australia
Closing Date: 15 October
Additional Information: scholarships.curtin.edu.au/Scholarship/?id=5614

For further information contact:

Email: study@curtin.edu.au

Curtin University Postgraduate Scholarship (CUPS)

Purpose: To assist with general living costs
Eligibility: Applicants must be Australian or New Zealand citizens or Australian permanent residents and must have completed 4 years of higher education studies at a high level of achievement and must hold, or are expected to obtain, First Class Honours or equivalent results; be enroled in or accepted to enrol in a Higher Degree by Research as a full-time student in the previous year in which the award is to be given
Level of Study: Graduate, Postgraduate
Type: Scholarship
Value: Varies, an annual living allowance of US$23,728 was given last year. This stipend is indexed annually and is tax-free unless taken on a part-time basis
Length of Study: 2 years for a Master by Research and 3 years, with a possible extension of up to 6 months, for a Doctoral degree
Country of Study: Any country
Application Procedure: Check website for further details
Closing Date: 31 October
Additional Information: www.australianuniversities.com.au/scholarships/guide/8014-curtin-university-postgraduate-scholarship-cups.html

For further information contact:

Tel: (61) 8 9266 4906
Fax: (61) 8 9266 3793

Destination Australia Scholarship - International Students

Eligibility: 1. International, full fee-paying, non-sponsored students 2. International students who are studying on a valid student VISA 3. Evidence of academic merit for the highest completed qualification 4. You must remain enrolled at the Kalgoorlie campus. 75% of your course needs to be completed at our Kalgoorlie Campus for courses with a duration of 2 years or less 5. Not available to students who are sponsored by a government entity or a corporate body 6. Can be revoked at the discretion of Curtin if the recipient already has a scholarship, sponsorship or fee offset for their mainstream course. 7. Enrolled full-time

Level of Study: Doctorate, Postgraduate
Type: Scholarship
Value: AU$15,000 per annum for the duration of your postgraduate degree. The scholarship will be paid as a cash stipend of AU$7,500 per semester.
Frequency: Annual
Country of Study: Australia
Closing Date: Applications accepted at any time
Additional Information: scholarships.curtin.edu.au/Scholarship/?id=4858

For further information contact:

Email: ci-enquiries@curtin.edu.au

Establishing the Source of Gas in Australia's Offshore Petroleum Basins Scholarship

Purpose: To develop an isotopic method to analyse gases in fluid inclusions and to establish the source of gas in Australia's offshore petroleum basins
Eligibility: Applicants must have First Class Honours or equivalent science degree, preferably in chemistry/geology/geochemistry. Interests in analytical organic chemistry, laboratory skills in trace analysis, wet chemical methods, GC/GCMS or GC-IRMS instrumentation and awareness of stable isotopic concepts is desirable
Level of Study: Postgraduate
Type: Scholarship
Value: At least US$20,000 per year
Country of Study: Any country
Application Procedure: Check website for further details
Closing Date: 31 December
Contributor: The Stable Isotope and Molecular Biogeochemistry Research Group, Geoscience Australia, GFZ

For further information contact:

Stable Isotope and Molecular Biogeochemistry Group, Centre for Applied Organic Geochemistry, Department of Applied Chemistry, Curtin University of Technology, GPO Box U1987, Perth, WA 6845, Australia.

Tel: (61) 8 9266 2474
Fax: (61) 8 9266 2300
Email: K.grice@curtin.edu.au

French-Australian Cotutelle

Purpose: To support the development of the double doctoral degree Cotutelle' between Australia and France
Eligibility: Applicants must be PhD students (of any nationality) enroled in a Cotutelle project between a French and an Australian university; should not have benefited from the French Embassy Cotutelle grant in previous years and should be registered with FEAST-France
Level of Study: Postgraduate
Type: Grant
Value: US$2,500
Country of Study: Any country
Application Procedure: Applicants must provide the French Embassy with the completed application form and a copy of the Cotutelle convention

For further information contact:

Email: Stephane.GRIVELET@diplomatie.gouv.fr

HDR Scholarship - Geotechnical Engineering PhD Scholarship

Purpose: The purpose of the fund is to provide an eco-friendly, sustainable, and innovative cementation treatment methods, including bio-cementation and geopolymerization, for improving the performance of mining by-product materials in mining infrastructure applications.
Eligibility: 1. Bachelor's degree (H1 or First-Class Honours) in Civil Engineering or related fields. 2. English language proficiency (refer to the English language requirements in Curtin University website). 3. Knowledge or master's degree in relevant research field including publications is desirable.
Value: AU$30,000 per annum, tax-free. The duration of the scholarship is three years. If the successful candidate is an international student, the scholarship will cover the tuition fees for the duration of the award.
Country of Study: Australia
Closing Date: 5 March
Additional Information: scholarships.curtin.edu.au/Scholarship/?id=5731

For further information contact:

Email: m.shahin@curtin.edu.au

HDR Scholarship in Structural Vibration Control

Eligibility: 1. Minimum requirement: Bachelor degree (first class honours or upper second class honours) in

Structural Engineering with strong background in Structural Dynamics. 2. Applicants with Master degrees with technical publications and research experiences in structural vibration control, earthquake engineering, and fluid dynamics are preferred. 3. Language requirement: IELTS, Overall 6.5, Speaking, Writing, Reading and Listening 6.0 or TOEFL, Overall 79, Reading, 13, Listening 13, Speaking 18, Writing 21. Details can be found via study.curtin.edu.au/applying/english-language-requirements/accepted-english-proficiency-tests/ 4. Full time enrolment for both domestic and international students.
Level of Study: Postgraduate
Type: Scholarship
Value: AU$28,092 per annum.
Frequency: Annual
Country of Study: Any country
No. of awards offered: 2
Closing Date: 30 December
Additional Information: scholarships.curtin.edu.au/Scholarship/?id=4935

For further information contact:

Email: Kaiming.bi@curtin.edu.au

Hunter Postgraduate Scholarship

Purpose: To support a PhD student undertaking research in an area relevant to understanding the causes of Alzheimer's disease
Eligibility: Candidates must be PhD students undertaking research in an area relevant to understanding the causes of Alzheimer's disease
Level of Study: Postgraduate
Type: Scholarship
Value: Up to NZ$5,000 towards fees subject to funds available
Length of Study: 1 years
Country of Study: Any country
Application Procedure: Check website for further details
Closing Date: 31 October
Additional Information: www.wgtn.ac.nz/scholarships/current/hunter-postgraduate-scholarship Victoria University of Wellington

For further information contact:

Tel: (61) 2 6254 7233
Email: aar@alzheimers.org.au

International Onshore Postgraduate Support Scholarship

Eligibility: 1. New students commencing a Curtin Master by coursework program of at least 1.5 years (300 credit points) in duration, between January and June 2024. 2. International, full fee-paying, non-sponsored students. 3. Onshore students who have studied at an institution or university in Australia
Level of Study: Postgraduate
Type: Scholarship
Value: a maximum of 20% off the 2024 first-year tuition fee up to a maximum of 200 credit points only.
Frequency: Annual
Country of Study: Australia
Closing Date: Applications accepted at any time
Additional Information: scholarships.curtin.edu.au/Scholarship/?id=5621

For further information contact:

Email: study@curtin.edu.au

Masters Scholarship in Scotland

Purpose: The Scottish International Scholarship Programme is targeted at graduates in science, technology and the creative industries, and aims to create lasting connections between Scotland and industry leaders and entrepreneurs across the world
Eligibility: Open to Australian citizens who are presently studing science and technology
Level of Study: Postgraduate
Value: The Scotland Scholarship covers the tuition fee, airfare and a stipend for a taught masters course of up to 12 months duration at any Scottish Institution
Length of Study: Varies
Frequency: Annual
Study Establishment: Any Scottish institution
Country of Study: Scotland
Application Procedure: For more information including application forms please visit www.gla.ac.uk/

For further information contact:

Email: scholarships@glasgow.ac

MPhil Scholarship – Reconnecting to Rivers: Urban Water & Water Sensitive Urban Design

Eligibility: The 'Reconnecting to Rivers' team is inviting applications for a Masters candidate; 1. Australian domestic applicants (Permanent Residents and Citizens) having an undergraduate (Bachelor's degree) in Engineering or 2. Built Environment or Science/ Chemistry field with First-Class Honours or 2nd upper Honours or equivalent. 3. Experience in urban water / WSUD is an advantage.

Level of Study: Postdoctorate
Type: Scholarship
Value: AU$28,597 PA
Length of Study: 2 years
Frequency: Annual
Country of Study: Australia
No. of awards offered: 1
Additional Information: scholarships.curtin.edu.au/Scholarship/?id=5638

For further information contact:

Email: P.Sarukkalige@curtin.edu.au

Postgraduate Merit Scholarship

Level of Study: Postgraduate
Type: Scholarship
Value: ash payment of AU$5,000 per annum paid as a stipend of AU$2,500 per semester. Payment will be pro-rata for part-time enrolment.
Length of Study: 4 years
Frequency: Annual
Country of Study: Australia
Closing Date: 28 January
Additional Information: scholarships.curtin.edu.au/Scholarship/?id=5657

For further information contact:

Email: scholarships@curtin.edu.au

Scots Australian Council Scholarships

Purpose: To develop lasting links between young Scots and Australians by offering outstanding graduates and young professionals the opportunity to study at a Scottish university
Eligibility: Applicants must be Australian citizens or Australian permanent residents or New Zealand citizens or on permanent Humanitarian Visa. They must be indigenous or Torres Strait Islander students or students with a disability or students from rural or regional areas or mature students or sole parents or current students or prospective students
Level of Study: Postgraduate
Type: Scholarship
Value: £12,000

Country of Study: Any country
Application Procedure: Check website for further details
Closing Date: 14 January
Contributor: Scottish universities, Scottish business and industry, British Foreign and Commonwealth Office

For further information contact:

The Scots Australian Council, 19 Dean Terrace, Stockbridge, Edinburgh EH4 1NL, United Kingdom.

Email: scholarships@scotsoz.org

Sediment and Asphaltite Transport by Canyon Upwelling - Top Up Scholarship

Purpose: To investigate the role of upwelling currents in transporting material across the continental slope of the Morum Sub-Basin, southern Australia using an integrated geological, oceanographic, and organic geochemical approach
Eligibility: Applicants must be Australian and New Zealand residents, First Class Honours or equivalent science degree holders, preferably in chemistry/geology/geochemistry. Interests in analytical organic chemistry, laboratory skills in trace analysis, wet chemical methods, GC/GCMS or GC-IRMS instrumentation; awareness of stable isotopic concepts is desirable
Level of Study: Graduate
Type: Scholarship
Value: See the organization website
Country of Study: Any country
Application Procedure: Applicants must forward their interests, curriculum vitae and names of two referees to Stable Isotope and Molecular Biogeochemistry Group, Centre for Applied Organic Geochemistry, Department of Applied Chemistry
Contributor: The Stable Isotope and Molecular Biogeochemistry Research Group, Adelaide University, a petroleum industry partner

Starter Support Scholarship

Purpose: Curtin University recognises that you may be impacted by the travel restrictions to Australia due to the Novel Coronavirus and offers you the Starter Support Scholarship to provide financial assistance to support you in those circumstances.
Eligibility: 1. Students travelling from outside of Australia to Perth, Western Australia, to study on campus with Curtin

University in the first half of 2024. 2. Students studying online with Curtin University, outside of Australia and remain/continue in that study mode in the first half of 2024. 3. Students commencing (or continuing) a Curtin undergraduate or postgraduate by coursework program at one of Curtin University's Western Australian campuses

Level of Study: Postgraduate
Type: Scholarship
Value: 1. Enrolled in 50 credit points AU$2,000 reduction. 2. Enrolled in 75 credit points AU$3,750 reduction. 3. Enrolled in 100 credit points AU$5,000 reduction.
Frequency: Annual
Country of Study: Australia
Closing Date: accepted at any time
Additional Information: scholarships.curtin.edu.au/Scholarship/?id=5620

For further information contact:

Email: study@curtin.edu.au

The applications of drugs in enhancing scaffold-associated healing in the middle ear

Purpose: The aim is to support and grow the ongoing collaboration between Curtin, Deakin and Ear Science and engage best students to grow their skills and capabilities and benefit everyone involved.
Eligibility: The eligibility is consistent with Curtin eligibility criteria and include: 1. Domestic and international 2. Full-time enrolment 3. Successful recipients must also not be in receipt of any other scholarship
Level of Study: Postgraduate
Type: Scholarship
Value: This scholarship provides a living stipend of AU$28,600 p.a. pro rata indexed, based on full-time studies
Length of Study: 3 years
Country of Study: Australia
Closing Date: 1 June
Additional Information: scholarships.curtin.edu.au/Scholarship/?id=5652

For further information contact:

Email: hani.al-salami@earscience.org.au

The applications of nanotechnology in prevention of chemotherapy-induced hearing impairment

Purpose: The aim is to support and grow the ongoing collaboration between Curtin and Ear Science and engage best students to grow their skills and capabilities and benefit everyone involved.
Level of Study: Postgraduate
Type: Scholarship
Value: AU$28,597 p.a. pro rata indexed, based on full-time studies
Length of Study: 3 years
Frequency: Annual
Country of Study: Australia
Closing Date: 1 June
Additional Information: scholarships.curtin.edu.au/Scholarship/?id=5651

For further information contact:

Email: hani.al-salami@earscience.org.au

The General Sir John Monash Awards

Purpose: To enable them to undertake postgraduate study abroad at the world's best universities, appropriate to their field of study
Eligibility: Applicants must be Australian citizens who have graduated from an Australian University with outstanding levels of academic achievement
Level of Study: Postgraduate Research
Type: Award
Value: AU$70,000 per annum
Length of Study: 3 years
Frequency: Annual
Country of Study: Any country
Application Procedure: 1. Be an Australian Citizen; 2. Have completed or be about to complete a full degree from an Australian university, and; 3. Be planning to undertake postgraduate study at an overseas university commencing in the calendar year following the year of application and selection; it is not necessary to have already been accepted to the institution at the time of applying.
No. of awards offered: Between 15 and 20
Closing Date: 10 July
Additional Information: scholarships.adelaide.edu.au/Scholarships/postgraduate-research/all-faculties/general-sir-john-monash-awards

For further information contact:

The General Sir John Monash Foundation, Level 1, Bennelong House, 9 Queen Street, Melbourne, VIC 3000, Australia.

Tel: (61) 613 9620 2428
Email: peter.binks@monashawards.org

Trimester 2 - Rob Riley MBA Memorial Scholarship

Purpose: The purpose of the Rob Riley Memorial MBA Scholarship is to honour the memory of Rob Riley by supporting and encouraging Indigenous students in business studies.

Eligibility: 1. Be an Indigenous Australian 2. Commencing their course in the trimester for which this scholarship is offered 3. Applied for admission into any of the courses below: 3a. Graduate Certificate in Business 3b. Graduate Diploma in Business 3c. Master of Business Administration 4. Be a domestic full fee paying student 5. Must not be in receipt of any other scholarship, fee discount or sponsorship

Level of Study: Postgraduate

Type: Scholarship

Value: support for the normal expected duration of your course (based on a full-time study load of 75 credits per trimester): Total cost of student tuition fees (excluding SSAF)

Frequency: Annual

Country of Study: Australia

Closing Date: 2 May

Additional Information: scholarships.curtin.edu.au/Scholarship/?id=5743

For further information contact:

Email: scholarships@curtin.edu.au

Water Corporation Scholarship in Biosolids Research

Purpose: To investigate the potential impacts to soil and plants following the agricultural land application of alum-dosed wastewater sludge

Eligibility: Applicants must be Australian Citizens, Australian permanent residents or must hold an Australian permanent Humanitarian Visa. They must hold a relevant degree from a recognized University in the preferred fields of Agriculture, Environmental Science or the equivalent and demonstrate a high level in their Honours project or equivalent

Level of Study: Graduate, Postgraduate

Type: Scholarship

Value: US$23,400 per year

Length of Study: 3 years for a doctoral program and 2 years for a masters program

Country of Study: Any country

Application Procedure: Check website for further details

Closing Date: 31 October

For further information contact:

Email: D.Pritchard@curtin.edu.au

Cystinosis Research Foundation

Postdoctoral Research Fellowships

Subjects: Cystinosis research

Purpose: The ultimate goal of the Cystinosis Research Foundation is to find better treatments and a cure for cystinosis. Research and fellowship applications must take into consideration the mission and goals of the foundation in order to be considered.

Eligibility: First priority will be given to 'named' postdoctoral trainees. However, investigators who are already studying cystinosis can apply for a fellowship position with the expectation of attracting a suitable postdoctoral fellow within a year. Pre-doctoral students, who are already studying cystinosis, will be considered if funding is available.

Type: Fellowship

Value: Max. US$75,000 per year

Length of Study: One to two years

Frequency: Annual

Country of Study: Any country

Application Procedure: Maximum length is six one-sided pages, single-spaced, using a standard 12-point font with 1-inch margins (2.54 cm) on all sides including figures, diagrams and drawings. Cover sheet, documentation, budget and budget justification and curriculum vitae (CV limit is 5 pages maximum or a bio sketch) are not included in the 6-page limit. Longer applications will not be evaluated.

Closing Date: April

Additional Information: Fellowship applications must provide a CV (maximum of 5 pages) of the proposed candidate and a statement outlining his/her career goals. Please discuss why this fellowship is important to the applicant. It should be clear who the fellow's mentor(s) will be. The mentor must provide a CV (maximum of 5 pages) or a bio sketch as well as a statement of the plan for training the fellow. www.cystinosisresearch.org/research/for-researchers/ The Fall 2022 Grant Proposal and Fellowship Applications are now closed. Applications will be available again in March 2023.

Research Proposals

Subjects: Cystinosis research

Purpose: The ultimate goal of the Cystinosis Research Foundation is to find better treatments and a cure for cystinosis. The Cystinosis Research Foundation is prepared to fund proposals to improve the immediate care of children and adults with cystinosis and to develop a new understanding and treatment of cystinosis in an effort to help these patients in the future.

Eligibility: No limitations to eligibility

Type: Research grant
Length of Study: One to two years
Frequency: Annual
Country of Study: Any country
Application Procedure: Maximum length is nine one-sided pages, single-spaced, using a standard 12-point font with 1-inch margins (2.54 cm) on all sides including figures, diagrams and drawings. Cover sheet, documentation, budget and budget justification and curriculum vitae (CV limit is 5 pages maximum or a bio sketch) are not included in the 9-page limit. Longer applications will not be evaluated.

Closing Date: 20 April

Additional Information: Applicants must submit the original completed application, nine (9) printed copies of each proposal and an electronic copy (PDF format if possible) www.cystinosisresearch.org/research/for-researchers/ The Fall 2022 Grant Proposal and Fellowship Applications are now closed. Applications will be available again in March 2023.

D

Daiwa Anglo-Japanese Foundation

Daiwa Foundation Japan House, 13-14 Cornwall Terrace, London NW1 4QP, United Kingdom.

Tel:	(44) 20 7486 4348
Email:	grants@dajf.org.uk
Website:	www.dajf.org.uk
Contact:	Grants & Scholarships Office

The Daiwa Anglo-Japanese Foundation is a UK charity, established in 1988 with a generous benefaction from Daiwa Securities Co Ltd. The Foundation's purpose is to support closer links between Britain and Japan.

Cambridge Trust Scholarships

Eligibility: It is tenable at any College within the University of Cambridge. Applicants must be Japanese nationals and must have been accepted onto a qualifying course at the University of Cambridge.

Level of Study: Masters Degree

Type: Scholarship

Value: tuition fee for any one-year Master's course, £35,000, as well as a stipend

Length of Study: 1 year

Country of Study: United Kingdom

Additional Information: dajf.org.uk/scholarships/cambridge-trust-scholarships

For further information contact:

Daiwa Foundation Japan House, 13/14 Cornwall Terrace (Outer Circle) London NW1 4QP, United Kingdom.

Daiwa Foundation Awards

Subjects: Daiwa Foundation Awards can cover projects in most academic, professional, arts, cultural and educational fields.

Purpose: Awards of £7,000–£15,000 are available for collaborative projects that enable British and Japanese partners to work together in the context of an institutional relationship. In order to fund as many applications as possible, an average of £7,000 to successful Award applications is normal. Funding rarely covers an application's budget in full, but is meant to be a "contribution" to the proposed project.

Eligibility: Daiwa Foundation Awards can cover projects in academic, professional, arts, cultural and educational fields. Awards seek to encourage the development and sustainability of UK-Japan partnerships between such organisations as museums and art galleries, theatres and performing arts groups, schools and universities, and grassroots and professional bodies.

Type: Award

Value: £7,000–£15,000

Frequency: Annual

Country of Study: United Kingdom

Application Procedure: Please read the online application notes (http://dajf.org.uk/wp-content/uploads/Online-Grant-Application-Notes.pdf), before beginning the application form: (www.dajf-applications.org.uk/form1/init.pl).

Closing Date: 31 March

Additional Information: All applicants are notified by letter from the Foundation. The decision of the Trustees is final and the Foundation is unable to discuss unsuccessful applications. dajf.org.uk/daiwa-foundation-small-grants-and-awards/daiwa-foundation-awards

© Springer Nature Limited 2022
Palgrave Macmillan (ed.), *The Grants Register 2023*,
https://doi.org/10.1057/978-1-349-96053-8

Daiwa Foundation Small Grants

Purpose: Grants of £2,000–£7,000 are available to individuals, societies, associations or other bodies in the United Kingdom or Japan to promote and support interaction between the two countries.
Eligibility: Daiwa Foundation Small Grants can cover all fields of activity, including educational and grassroots exchanges, research travel, the organisation of conferences, exhibitions, and other projects and events that fulfil this broad objective. New initiatives are especially encouraged.
Type: Grant
Value: £2,000–£7,000
Frequency: Annual
Country of Study: United Kingdom
Application Procedure: United Kingdom-based applicants can apply online. Applications from Japan should be posted to the Tokyo Office. Please apply using our online application form available at: www.dajf-applications.org.uk/form1/init.pl
Closing Date: 31 March
Additional Information: All applicants are notified by letter from the Foundation. The decision of the Trustees is final and the Foundation is unable to discuss unsuccessful applications. dajf.org.uk/daiwa-foundation-small-grants-and-awards/daiwa-foundation-small-grants.

For further information contact:

Daiwa Foundation Japan House, 13/14 Cornwall Terrace (Outer Circle), London NW14QP, United Kingdom.

Daiwa Scholarships

Purpose: The Daiwa Scholarship is a unique 19-month programme of language study, work placement and homestay in Japan, following a month of Japanese language tuition in the UK. Daiwa Scholarships offer young and talented UK citizens with strong leadership potential, the opportunity to acquire Japanese language skills, and to access expertise and knowledge relevant to their career goals.
Eligibility: Candidates for the Daiwa Scholarships must be 1. British citizens. 2. between 21 and 35 years of age by the time of departure. Candidates should be 1. graduates or due to graduate by the time of departure. 2. equipped with a strong degree in any subject or with a strong record of achievement in their field. 3. in possession of clear career objectives and a commitment to furthering United Kingdom-Japan links.
Type: Scholarships
Value: ¥260,000 per month
Length of Study: Japanese for 1 year; 1 month homestay 6 month work placement

Frequency: Annual
Country of Study: United Kingdom
Application Procedure: Apply Online
No. of awards offered: 8
Closing Date: December
No. of awards given last year: 8
No. of applicants: 263 for 2021 programme

For further information contact:

Email: scholarships@dajf.org.uk

Daiwa Scholarships in Japanese Studies

Subjects: Japan related studies
Purpose: To support postgraduate studies connected to Japan
Eligibility: UK nationals who have a degree in Japanese and have strong Japanese language ability
Level of Study: Doctorate, Postgraduate
Type: Postgraduate scholarships
Value: Living expenses will be payable at a rate of £1,200 per month for periods spent in the UK, and ¥260,000 per month for periods spent in Japan
Length of Study: length of MA or PhD
Frequency: Annual
Study Establishment: universities in Japan or the UK
Country of Study: United Kingdom
Application Procedure: Applications can be submitted online.
No. of awards offered: maximum of 6 a year
Closing Date: 27 January
Funding: Foundation
No. of awards given last year: 4
No. of applicants last year: 25
Additional Information: dajf.org.uk/scholarships/japanese-studies

For further information contact:

Email: scholarships@dajf.org.uk
Website: www.dajf.org.uk

Dalai Lama Foundation

Universitätstrasse 51, CH-8006 Zürich, Switzerland.

Tel: (41) 43 537 61 43
Email: gp-foundation@dalailama.com
Contact: Gaden Phodrang Foundation of the Dalai Lama

The Gaden Phodrang Foundation of the Dalai Lama was founded by His Holiness the 14th Dalai Lama and aims to promote basic human values, mutual understanding among religions, peace and non-violence and the protection of the environment. It helps to preserve the unique Tibetan culture and supports the Tibetan people, but also other people in need, regardless of nationality, religion and origin.

The Dalai Lama Foundation Graduate Scholarship Program

Subjects: The Dalai Lama Graduate Scholarships are highly competitive supplementary bursary awarded to outstanding Tibetan graduate students pursuing a full-time graduate degree in any reputable University in Europe/Australia/North Americas.
Purpose: The purpose of the scholarship program is to further the human capital development of Tibetan people by encouraging the pursuit of excellence among Tibetan students in a graduate field of study that has relevance and potential to contribute to the welfare of humanity and the Tibetan people in particular
Eligibility: 1. Applicants must have already been enrolled in or be accepted to a full-time graduate degree program at a university in Australia, Europe or the Americas 2. Applicants must show proof of Tibetan heritage and continuity of Dhanglang Chatrel (Green Book) contribution. 3. Applicants are solely and directly responsible for obtaining the necessary visas to attend the university of their choice. 4. Eligible candidates must be pursuing graduate studies, whether at the master's or PhD level, or at a professional school. 5. All graduate programs should be at least one year or multi-year, full-time courses, offered by reputable and accredited universities
Level of Study: Graduate
Type: Scholarship
Value: US$10,000
Frequency: Annual
Country of Study: United States of America
Application Procedure: The applications are evaluated by the independent Selection Committee of the Dalai Lama Graduate Scholarship program. Selected applicants will be contacted for a Skype or phone interview.
No. of awards offered: 10 to 18
Closing Date: March
Funding: Foundation
No. of applicants last year: 10 to 18

The Dalai Lama Trust Scholarship

Level of Study: Postgraduate
Type: Scholarship

Country of Study: Any country
No. of awards offered: 5
Closing Date: 15 September
Contributor: The Office of Gaden Phodrang.
Additional Information: dalailamatrust.org/scholarship_information/

David & Lucile Packard Foundation

343 Second Street, Los Altos, CA 94022, United States of America.

Tel: (1) 650 948 7658
Website: www.packard.org
Contact: The David and Lucile Packard Foundation

A family foundation guided by the enduring business philosophy and personal values of Lucile and David Packard.

Packard Fellowships for Science and Engineering

Subjects: Science; engineering
Purpose: In 1988, the Packard Foundation established the Packard Fellowships for Science and Engineering to allow the nation's most promising professors to pursue science and engineering research early in their careers with few funding restrictions and limited reporting requirements. The program arose out of David Packard's commitment to strengthening university-based science and engineering programs in recognition that the success of the Hewlett-Packard Company, which he cofounded, derived in large measure from the research and development in university laboratories.
Eligibility: Candidates must be faculty members in the first three years of their faculty careers.
Level of Study: Junior Faculty
Type: Fellowship
Value: US$875,000 over five years.
Length of Study: Five years
Frequency: Every 5 years
Country of Study: Any country
No. of awards offered: 20
Closing Date: 19 February
No. of applicants last year: 20
Additional Information: www.packard.org/what-we-fund/science/packard-fellowships-for-science-and-engineering/about-the-packard-fellowship-awards/

Davies Charitable Foundation

245 Alwington Place, Kingston, ON K7L 4P9, Canada.

Tel: (1) 613 546 4000
Email: daviesfoundation@cogeco.ca
Website: www.daviesfoundation.ca

The Davies Charitable Foundation is a registered, non-profit charitable organization founded in 1990 by Elaine and Michael Davies, former owner and publisher of the Kingston Whig-Standard. The purpose of the Davies Charitable Foundation is to support individuals and registered charitable organizations within the Kingston, Ontario region in the areas of the arts, education, health and sports. Since its inception, the Davies Charitable Foundation has supported more than 500 individuals and organizations and has donated over US$11 million to local charities.

The Davies Charitable Foundation Fellowship

Purpose: The purpose of the Davies Charitable Foundation is to support individuals and registered charitable organizations within the Kingston, Ontario region in the areas of the arts, education, health and sports
Eligibility: Applications will be accepted from eligible charitable organizations and individuals from the Kingston area. The Davies Charitable Foundation defines the Kingston area as encompassing the area encircled by Gananoque and the Thousand Islands to the east, Portland to the north and Picton to the west.
Type: Fellowship
Frequency: Annual
Country of Study: Canada
Application Procedure: Only online applications will be accepted.
No. of awards offered: Vary
Closing Date: 19 February
Contributor: Davies Charitable Foundation
No. of applicants last year: Vary
Additional Information: The available funding and number of awards will vary and will be made available with the announcement of the competition

For further information contact:

The Davies Charitable Foundation, 245, Alwington Place, Kingston, ON K7L 4P9, Canada.

The Winter 2022 Gift Competition

Subjects: Arts, education, sports and health
Purpose: The Davies Charitable Foundation has periodic competitions for charitable funding
Eligibility: The competitions will entertain applications from the arts, education, sports and health. Applications will be accepted from eligible charitable organizations and individuals from the Kingston area.
Type: Award
Value: C$25,000–C$100,000
Country of Study: Canada
Application Procedure: Only online applications will be accepted. The links to the online forms will be listed here when the competition opens.
No. of awards offered: 3
Closing Date: 31 January
Additional Information: www.daviesfoundation.ca/about-awards-and-grants

De Montfort University

The Gateway, Leicestershire, Leicester LE1 9BH, United Kingdom.

Tel: (44) 116 255 1551
Email: enquiry@dmu.ac.uk
Website: www.dmu.ac.uk

DMU offers the perfect combination of award-winning teaching, world-class facilities and a fantastic student experience. Over the next few years we are continuing our investment in the DMU campus to provide the modern, inspiring environment our students deserve.

De Montfort University Awards to Women for Final Year Doctoral Research

Purpose: To help women graduates with their living expenses (not fees) while registered for study or research at an approved institution of higher education in Great Britain
Eligibility: Open to students who are studying or intend to study in Great Britain at a postgraduate or postdoctoral level, there is no upper age limit to apply
Level of Study: Postdoctorate, Postgraduate
Type: Award/Grant
Value: Up to £2,500
Frequency: Annual
Country of Study: United Kingdom
Funding: Foundation

For further information contact:

BFWG Charitable Foundation, 28 Great James Street, London WC1N 3ES, United Kingdom.

Tel: (44) 20 7404 6447
Fax: (44) 20 7404 6505
Email: BFWG.Charity@btinternet.com

De Montfort University PhD Scholarships

Type: Scholarship
Value: £15,840
Length of Study: 3 years
Country of Study: Any country
Application Procedure: Initial applications must be submitted on: www.dmu.ac.uk/documents/doctoral-college/showcase/dmu-doctoral-college-phd-scholarships-2022-application-form.docx
Closing Date: 21 March
Additional Information: www.dmu.ac.uk/doctoral-college/study/scholarships.aspx

For further information contact:

Email: PGRscholarships@dmu.ac.uk

DMU Sport Scholarship

Subjects: Scholars must be on an undergraduate or postgraduate course at DMU* and compete in a sport that is part of the British Universities and Colleges Sport (BUCS) programme or included in the Commonwealth, Olympic or Paralympic Games programme.
Purpose: We support all our scholars to excel and reach their sporting potential, whilst allowing them to succeed in their academic studies.
Eligibility: 1. Students representing their sport internationally at an elite level 2. Students representing their sport internationally at a junior level and/or on a National Governing Body development pathway 3. Students consistently playing for a regional team and selected to represent their region in national competitions 4. Students at exceptional county/regional level, who are raising the level of their club.
Type: Scholarship
Value: Up to £4,000 and up to £2,000
Country of Study: Any country
No. of awards offered: 5
Closing Date: 28 August
Additional Information: www.dmu.ac.uk/study/fees-funding/sport-scholarship/eligibility-and-application.aspx

For further information contact:

De Montfort University The Gateway, Leicester LE1 9BH, United Kingdom.

Email: sport.scholarships@dmu.ac.uk

Executive MBA Scholarship

Subjects: Have a track record of academic excellence (such as 1st class honours, MSc/MA level qualification, PhD), or experiential equivalent. Be wholly or partly self-financing
Purpose: It is available to three outstanding professionals who have excelled in their career to date, who Leicester Castle Business School believes can make an exceptional contribution to the academic experience for the wider Executive MBA
Eligibility: It is desirable that successful candidates are also able to demonstrate one or more of the following experience in a managerial/leadership role, including in an overseas setting: Entrepreneurialism (and/or innovation). Experience of working in a complex environment and managing it through a period of change. An offer of admission must have been received in order to be eligible to apply for this scholarship. Only wholly or partly self-funded students are entitled to apply for this scholarship.
Level of Study: MBA
Type: Scholarship
Value: £5,000
Frequency: Annual
Country of Study: United Kingdom
Application Procedure: To apply for a scholarship, please send in your curriculum vitae and a 500-word statement covering the following points: How do you meet the criteria above and why you should be awarded the scholarship? How would you make a positive contribution to Leicester Castle Business School and the other students on your course during your studies? How would an Executive MBA gained at Leicester Castle Business School would benefit you in the future?
No. of awards offered: 3
Closing Date: 21 September
Funding: Private
Contributor: Leicester Castle Business School
No. of applicants last year: 3
Additional Information: Students awarded the scholarship will be notified in writing. The award of this scholarship is at the discretion of the selection panel. No cash alternatives will be offered and the scholarship cannot be transferred to another recipient or to another course. The scholarship amount will be granted in the form of a fee reduction. The scholarship will be forfeited if the student defers entry, withdraws his or her application or does not enrol. If a student is found to be in

breach of his or her commitments to the University, has in any way not acted in good faith, or not responded fully or accurately to a University request for information, the University is entitled to immediately suspend a scholarship. Any fee reduction is reversed and the student will become liable for the full amount of such reduction.

Global MBA International Scholarship Fund

Purpose: These are available to international students who have excelled academically and have an offer of admission for our full-time Global MBA programme. Award of this scholarship is through an application and selection process, where you will need to provide a statement of no more than 1000 words, demonstrating your commitment to the DMU values. The criteria for your statement is detailed below. Successful applicants will also have a 1st Class or 21 degree or international equivalent qualification at a Distinction or Merit.

Eligibility: Only full-time Leicester Castle Business School Global MBA applicants are eligible for this scholarship. Only fully self-funded students are entitled to apply for this scholarship.

Level of Study: MBA

Type: Scholarship

Value: £500

Frequency: Annual

Country of Study: United Kingdom

Application Procedure: To apply please send an email, with your statement attached, and ensure you include your name and contact details on the statement to pgbal@dmu.ac.uk. Please entitle the email 'Global MBA International Scholarship'. The 1000 word statement should cover the following areas Why you feel you should be awarded the scholarship. 1. How will an MBA at DMU help your development both personally and from a career perspective? 2. How you would make a positive contribution to Leicester Castle Business School both during and following your studies. 3. How a Leicester Castle Business School education would benefit you in the future.

No. of awards offered: 4

Closing Date: 31 July

Contributor: The Leicester Castle Business School

No. of applicants last year: 4

Additional Information: All applications must be made following the prescribed process, above. Applications received after the deadline will not be considered. Students awarded the scholarship will be notified in writing. The award of this scholarship is at the discretion of the selection panel and is subject to available funds. An offer of admission must have been received in order to be eligible to apply for this scholarship. The scholarship is valid only for entry into the 2023/2024 intake - scholarships cannot be deferred by the applicant. Applicants who have already completed a postgraduate course with DMU will not be eligible for the scholarship. Distance learning and part-time students are not eligible for this scholarship. No cash alternatives will be offered and the scholarship cannot be transferred to another recipient. The scholarship amount will be granted in the form of a fee reduction. De Montfort University (DMU) and Leicester Castle Business School (LCBS) reserve the right to revise, review or withdraw the scholarship up to the point of enrolment if the applied for course is no longer run. The student will be informed in advance of this decision at the earliest opportunity. Any changes will not be applied retrospectively.

For further information contact:

Email: pgbal@dmu.ac.uk

India GREAT Scholarship

Purpose: GREAT Scholarship awarded in partnership with the British Council to Indian students

Eligibility: 1. Applicants must be Indian passport holders and resident in India at the time of application. 2. Have an undergraduate degree that will enable you to gain entry onto a postgraduate programme at a UK university. 3. Meet the English language requirement of the UK Higher Education Institution. 4. Have an offer from one of the participating UK universities. 5. The course applied is starting in September 2023

Level of Study: Postgraduate

Type: Scholarship

Value: £4,000

Frequency: Annual

Country of Study: United Kingdom

Application Procedure: For application, please visit www.dmu.ac.uk/international/en/fees-and-scholarships/india-great-scholarship.aspx

Closing Date: 31 July

Additional Information: For more details, visit website www.dmu.ac.uk/international/en/fees-and-scholarships/international-scholarships.aspx
www.britishcouncil.in/study-uk/scholarships/great-scholarships

For further information contact:

Email: Greatedu.india@britishcouncil.org

International Postgraduate Taught Merit Scholarship

Subjects: Award of this scholarship is through an application and selection process, where you will need to provide a statement of no more than 1000 words demonstrating your commitment to the DMU values. The criteria for your statement is detailed below. Successful applicants will also have a 1st Class or 2:1 degree or international equivalent qualification at a Distinction or Merit.

Purpose: These are available to international students who have excelled academically and have an offer of admission for one of our Leicester Castle Business School postgraduate taught degree programmes (excluding the Global MBA, which has its own specific scholarship).

Eligibility: An offer of admission must have been received in order to be eligible to apply for this scholarship. Only full-time Leicester Castle Business School postgraduate taught applicants are eligible for this scholarship. Only fully self-funded students are entitled to apply for this scholarship.

Level of Study: Postgraduate

Type: Scholarship

Value: £2,500

Frequency: Annual

Country of Study: United Kingdom

Application Procedure: To apply please send an email, with your statement attached, and ensure you include your name and contact details on the statement to pgbal@dmu.ac.uk. Please entitle the email 'International Postgraduate Taught Merit Scholarship'. The 1000 word statement should cover the following points: Why you feel you should be awarded the scholarship. How will a postgraduate degree at DMU help your development from an academic and personal perspective as well as from a career point of view? How you would make a positive contribution to Leicester Castle Business School both during and following your studies. How a Leicester Castle Business School education would benefit you in the future.

No. of awards offered: 8

Closing Date: 31 July

Funding: Private

Contributor: The Leicester Castle Business School

No. of applicants last year: 8

Additional Information: Students awarded the scholarship will be notified in writing. The award of this scholarship is at the discretion of the selection panel and is subject to available funds. The scholarship is valid only for entry into the 2023/2024 intake - scholarships cannot be deferred by the applicant. No cash alternatives will be offered and the scholarship cannot be transferred to another recipient. The scholarship amount will be granted in the form of a fee reduction. By accepting this award, the student also accepts to participate in any university publicity or promotion as required. De Montfort University (DMU) and Leicester Castle Business School (LCBS) reserve the right to revise, review or withdraw the scholarship up to the point of enrolment if the applied for course is no longer run. The student will be informed in advance of this decision at the earliest opportunity. Any changes will not be applied retrospectively. www.britishcouncil.in/study-uk/scholarships/great-scholarships

For further information contact:

Email: pgbal@dmu.ac.uk

International Scholarship Award program

Eligibility: 1. Hold an offer of admission from DMU for a full-time or part-time, UG and PGT course starting September 2023 or January 2024. 2. To be assessed as an international fee payer. 3. To have paid a tuition fee pre-payment of a minimum of £4,000

Type: Scholarship

Value: £1,500

Length of Study: 1 year

Country of Study: Any country

Additional Information: www.dmu.ac.uk/international/en/fees-and-scholarships/dmu-international-scholarship/index.aspx

For further information contact:

De Montfort University The Gateway, Leicester LE1 9BH, United Kingdom.

Email: ask.international@dmu.ac.uk

Leicester Castle Business School Full Postgraduate Scholarship

Purpose: Leicester Castle Business School is pleased to announce a full-fee postgraduate scholarship offering for those wishing to study in September

Eligibility: This scholarship is only available to students domiciled within the eligible areas (the continent of Africa, Russia, Taiwan, Thailand, United States of America)

Level of Study: Postgraduate

Type: Scholarship

Value: Our Full Postgraduate Scholarships which will cover the total value of the course fee. The scholarship also includes an additional £5,000 which can be used towards assistance with accommodation and living costs

Length of Study: 1 year

Frequency: Annual

Country of Study: United Kingdom

Application Procedure: To apply, please complete the scholarship application web form

Closing Date: 31 July

Additional Information: For more details, please visit website lcbs.ac.uk/full-postgraduate-scholarships/

www.scholarshiproar.com/leicester-castle-business-school-postgraduate-scholarship/

For further information contact:

Email: enquiry@lcbs.ac.uk

Leicester Castle Business School MBA Scholarship

Purpose: It is available to Global MBA students who have excelled academically and have an offer of admission for our full-time Global MBA programme
Eligibility: For eligibility, please refer website
Type: Scholarship
Value: £2,500
Country of Study: United Kingdom
Application Procedure: To apply, please complete the scholarship application web form available at www.dmu.ac.uk/international/en/fees-and-scholarships/leicester-castle-business-school-scholarships.aspx?_ga=2.249885056.7275375
58.1523602564-1792966074.1523602564
Closing Date: 31 July
Contributor: Leicester Castle Business School
Additional Information: www.dmu.ac.uk/International/en/EU-fees-and-scholarships/EU-fees-and-scholarships.aspx

For further information contact:

Email: enquiry@lcbs.ac.uk

Lesbian, Gay, Bisexual and Transgender+Allies Scholarship

Purpose: This scholarship will allow prospective students to study in a welcoming and inclusive environment to inspire and enhance continued activism during and after study, promoting LGBTQ+ rights worldwide
Eligibility: Eligible recipients should be domiciled outside the United Kingdom and EU area and have an offer of admission for any one year post-graduate taught programme
Level of Study: Postgraduate
Type: Postgraduate scholarships
Value: The scholarships also include an additional £1,015 (excluding any taxes) per month for the duration of the course, to assist with accommodation and living costs
Length of Study: 1 year
Country of Study: United Kingdom
Closing Date: 3 August
Additional Information: For details, visit website www.dmu.ac.uk/documents/international-documents/2018-scholarships-and-discounts/global-lgbtqallies-scholarship-tcs-final-v3.pdf

For further information contact:

Email: campus@hrc.org

Square Mile International Scholarship

Purpose: One Square Mile International Scholarship will be awarded to a student who demonstrates significant experience in engaging with their local community and a willingness to contribute to the DMU Square Mile Project
Eligibility: For eligibility details, please visit website
Type: Scholarship
Value: Full tuition fees, a monthly bursary to cover living costs and one return flight to the United Kingdom
Frequency: Annual
Country of Study: United Kingdom
Application Procedure: To apply, please complete the scholarship application web form available at www.dmu.ac.uk/international/en/fees-and-scholarships/dmu-square-mile-international-scholarship.aspx
Closing Date: 29 June
Contributor: De Montfort University
Additional Information: scholarship-positions.com/dmu-square-mile-international-scholarship-uk/2016/06/14/

For further information contact:

Email: ask.international@dmu.ac.uk

Sustainability Scholarship

Purpose: The Sustainability Scholarship scheme aims to support high-calibre students to come to DMU and develop the skills they need to make a difference.
Level of Study: Postgraduate
Type: Scholarship
Value: £4,000
Frequency: Annual
Country of Study: Any country
Closing Date: 29 July
Additional Information: www.dmu.ac.uk/international/en/fees-and-scholarships/sustainability-scholarship/index.aspx

For further information contact:

Email: ask.international@dmu.ac.uk

Deakin University

221 Burwood Highway, Burwood, VIC 3125, Australia.

Tel: (61) 3 9244 6100

Email: enquire@deakin.edu.au
Website: www.deakin.edu

Deakin University is one of Australia's largest universities providing all the resources of a major university to more than 32,000 award students. The University's reputation for excellent teaching and innovative course delivery has been recognized through many awards over the past few years.

Deakin Scholarship for Excellence

Purpose: The scholarship is awarded for the normal full time duration of the course. Different study load rules apply to undergraduate and postgraduate students.
Eligibility: 1. an Australian citizen, New Zealand citizen, Australian permanent resident or holder of an Australian permanent humanitarian visa 2. commencing or currently enrolled in a bachelor or honours degree in a Commonwealth supported place (CSP), or postgraduate by coursework degree (CSP or full fee) 3. enrolled at Deakin University in Trimester 1 2023 4. bachelor and honours students enrolled full time unless there are exceptional circumstances preventing full time study, or postgraduate students enrolled in at least two credit points
Type: Scholarship
Value: AU$10,000 per year (AU$1250 per credit point) paid as cash or towards student contributions (tuition fees), or a combination of both.
Frequency: Annual
Country of Study: Australia
Application Procedure: You can apply for this scholarship directly to Deakin through our Application Portal. applicantportal.deakin.edu.au/connect/webconnect?_ga=2.39043043.1331903424.1644829948-1768384682.1644829948
Closing Date: 15 February
Additional Information: www.deakin.edu.au/study/fees-and-scholarships/scholarships/find-a-scholarship/deakin-scholarship-for-excellence

Deakin Student Support Scholarship

Purpose: A Deakin Student Support Scholarship offers financial support to students who display passion, perseverance and commitment to study, and experience financial or personal hardship.
Eligibility: 1. an Australian citizen, New Zealand citizen, Australian permanent resident or holder of an Australian permanent humanitarian visa 2. enrolled in an associate, bachelor or honours degree in a Commonwealth supported place (CSP) or a postgraduate by coursework degree (CSP or full fee) 3. enrolled at Deakin University in Trimester 1 2023 4. enrolled full time unless there are circumstances preventing full-time study 5. experiencing financial hardship, personal hardship or a long term medical condition.
Level of Study: Postgraduate
Type: Scholarship
Value: Up to US$10,000 per year
Frequency: Annual
Country of Study: Any country
Closing Date: 8 December
Additional Information: When applying directly to Deakin for this scholarship select the 'Deakin Funded Scholarships Program' option and, if eligible, your application will automatically be considered for the Vice-Chancellor's Academic Excellence Scholarship, Deakin Scholarship for Excellence and the Deakin Student Support Scholarship in the selection process. www.deakin.edu.au/study/fees-and-scholarships/scholarships/find-a-scholarship/deakin-student-support-scholarship

Deakin University Postgraduate Research Scholarship (DUPR)

Eligibility: 1. To be eligible for an RTP Stipend, RTP Fees Offset, RTP Allowance or DUPRS a student must be a domestic or international student enrolled in an HDR course of study at Deakin University 2. To be eligible for an RTP Fees Offset an applicant must not be receiving an equivalent award or scholarship from the Commonwealth designed to offset HDR fees. 3. To be eligible for an RTP or DUPRS Stipend a student must not be receiving income from another source to support that student's general living costs while undertaking their course of study if that income is greater than 75 per cent of that student's RTP or DUPRS Stipend rate. Income unrelated to the student's course of study or income received for the student's course of study but not for the purposes of supporting general living costs is not to be taken into account.
Level of Study: Postgraduate, Research
Type: Scholarship
Value: AU$28,900 per annum. A relocation allowance from AU$500 to AU$1,500
Length of Study: 3 to 4 years
Frequency: Annual
Country of Study: Australia
Additional Information: www.deakin.edu.au/study/fees-and-scholarships/scholarships/find-a-scholarship/rtp-and-duprs

Deakin University Postgraduate Research Scholarships (DUPRS)

Purpose: Deakin University, this Higher Degree by Research (HDR) scholarship offers multiple awards to both domestic as well as international students.

Eligibility: Applicants must meet Deakin's PhD entry requirements, be enrolling full-time and hold an Honours degree (First Class) or a Master's degree with a substantial research component in a related field. Applicants applying for Research Masters or Research Doctorate must not hold an equivalent research qualification

Level of Study: Postgraduate

Type: Scholarship

Value: A stipend of AU$26,682 per annum, a relocation allowance up to AU$1,500, tuition fee and overseas health coverage for international students for the duration of 4 years. Paid sick, maternity and parental leave are applicable

Length of Study: 3 years

Frequency: Annual

Country of Study: Australia

Application Procedure: 1. click Website www.deakin.edu. au/research/become-a-research-student/how-to-apply-research-degrees. 2. The candidates applying in the areas of Arts and Education, Business and Law, Science, Engineering and Built Environment, and Frontier Materials need to submit an Expression of Interest (EOI) prior to formal application. 3. Refer to the guidelines specified for the application. 4. Prepare all relevant documents and follow the steps as specified.

Closing Date: 31 October

Additional Information: Applications can be made throughout the year except for Arts and Education. Arts and Education applications must be submitted before 31st October. Please contact the Deakin Research Scholarships Office: research-scholarships@deakin.edu.au www.buddy4study. com/scholarship/deakin-university-postgraduate-research-scholarships-duprs

For further information contact:

Deakin Research HDR International Admissions Officer Deakin University, Building BC, 221 Burwood Highway, Burwood, VIC 3125, Australia.

Email: research-scholarships@deakin.edu.au

Marine Biotechnology PhD Studentship

Purpose: Candidates must carry out research that is relevant to marine biology. Projects on offer can be found on the list of available projects. Applicants are also invited to suggest their own projects; please visit our research pages for more information on our supervisors and their research areas.

Level of Study: Research

Type: Scholarship

Value: AU$25,000 per annum

Frequency: Annual

Country of Study: Australia

Closing Date: 7 January

Contributor: Jointly funded by Deakin University and Plant and Food Research, Nelson, NZ

Additional Information: Interested candidates please forward your CV and expression of interest to Professor Colin Barrow or Dr Susan Marshall www.zoo.cam.ac.uk/study/post graduate/phd-studentships-marine-biology

For further information contact:

Email: graduate@zoo.cam.ac.uk

Serendib Community Cultural Association Sri Lanka Bursary

Purpose: Deakin University is awarding SCCA Sri Lanka Undergraduate Bursary in the field of Arts and Communication. The scholarship will cover 20% of the student contributions (tuition fees)

Eligibility: Applicants must 1. be a prospective international student. 2. be a Sri Lankan citizen. 3. must meet eligibility criteria for their chosen Deakin degree. 4. have applied to study one of the following degrees i. A353 Bachelor of Creative Arts (Animation); ii. A352 Bachelor of Creative Arts (Photography); iii. A359 Bachelor of Creative Arts (Visual Art); iv. A356 Bachelor of Creative Arts (Drama); v. A355 Bachelor of Creative Arts (Visual Communications Design); vi. A351 Bachelor of Creative Arts (Film & Television); vii. A331 Bachelor of Communications (Journalism); viii. A325 Bachelor of Communications (Public Relations); ix. A333 Bachelor of Communications (Digital Media); x. A743 Master of Communication

Level of Study: Graduate

Type: Bursary

Value: 20% of the student contributions (tuition fees)

Frequency: Annual

Country of Study: Australia, the United Kingdom, Europe or the United States of America

Application Procedure: The bursaries will automatically be offered to eligible students and will be awarded on a first come, first served basis. Strict quotas apply

Closing Date: July

Funding: Private

Additional Information: www.chevening.org/scholarship/ sri-lanka/

For further information contact:

Deakin University, 221 Burwood Highway, Burwood, VIC 3125, Australia.

Email: deakin-int-scholarships@deakin.edu.au

Vice-Chancellor's Academic Excellence Scholarship

Eligibility: 1. an Australian citizen, New Zealand citizen, Australian permanent resident or holder of an Australian permanent humanitarian visa. 2. commencing at Deakin University in an undergraduate bachelor degree in Trimester 1 2022. 3. enrolled full time unless there are exceptional circumstances preventing full-time study. 4. enrolled in a Commonwealth supported place (CSP).
Type: Scholarship
Value: 100% of your student contribution (tuition fees). A cash payment of AU$5000 per year (AU$625 per credit point).
Frequency: Annual
Country of Study: Australia
Application Procedure: You can apply for this scholarship directly to Deakin through our Scholarship Application Portal: applicantportal.deakin.edu.au/connect/webconnect?_ ga=2.115670086.1556930932.1645975111-1768384682. 1644829948
Closing Date: 8 December
Additional Information: www.deakin.edu.au/study/fees-and-scholarships/scholarships/find-a-scholarship/vice-chan cellors-academic-excellence-scholarship

Defense Personnel Security Research Center

Tel: (1) 831 583 2800
Email: perserec@mail.mil

The Defense Personnel and Security Research Center (PERSEREC) is a Department of Defense entity dedicated to improving the effectiveness, efficiency, and fairness of DoD personnel suitability, security, and reliability systems. PERSEREC is part of the Office of People Analytics (OPA), which is a component of the Defense Human Resources

Activity (DHRA) under the Office of the Under Secretary of Defense (Personnel and Readiness).

Thesis, Dissertation and Institutional Research Awards

Subjects: The areas covered by this funding program include financial and credit, candidate screening and crime detection procedures, prescreening, background investigation, adjudication, continuing evaluation, employee assistance programs, security awareness, security education, and forensic psychophysiology.
Purpose: The purpose of the awards is to help fund research addressing issues pertinent to personnel security policy.
Eligibility: To be eligible for the thesis or dissertation award, applicants must be students enrolled in a graduate program at a university accredited by the Association of Colleges and Secondary Schools for their region and be sponsored by both their university and the chair of their thesis or dissertation committee. Candidates for a thesis award must also have satisfactorily completed at least 2/3 of the non-thesis credit hours required for graduation in their program. To receive a dissertation award candidates must be eligible to enter doctoral candidacy within six months from the date of their application. Prior to the dissertation award being granted, recipients must have completed all degree requirements except for the dissertation defense.
Level of Study: Research
Type: Award
Value: The maximum award for masters degree thesis awards is US$5,000/student. The maximum award for dissertation grants is US$15,000/student. The maximum award for institutional awards is US$30,000/project. The maximum awards for forensic psychophysiology are US$5,000, US$15,000 and US$150,000 respectively. Institutions are eligible to receive multiple awards.
Frequency: Annual
Country of Study: Any country
Closing Date: 15 July

Deloitte Foundation

30 Rockefeller Plaza, 41st floor, New York, NY 10112-0015, United States of America.

Tel: (1) 212 492 4000
Contact: New York - National Office

The Deloitte Foundation, a nonprofit organization founded in 1928, supports education initiatives benefiting high school students, undergraduate, graduate students and educators that help develop future diverse business leaders and promote excellence in teaching, research, and curriculum innovation

Doctoral Fellowship Program

Subjects: Accounting

Purpose: The Deloitte Foundation has awarded US$25,000 grants to 10 top accounting Ph.D. candidates across the U.S. through the Deloitte Foundations annual Doctoral Fellowship program.

Eligibility: Any graduate student enrolled in and successfully pursuing a doctoral program in accounting at an accredited U.S. university who has completed two or more semesters (or the equivalent) of that program is eligible to apply for a Deloitte Foundation Fellowship. Applicants should have plans to teach at a U.S. college or university upon graduation. At some time during their doctoral studies Fellows are expected to teach or to prepare themselves for their teaching careers by participating in elective programs designed to enhance their teaching skills.

Level of Study: Doctorate

Type: Fellowship

Value: US$25,000

Frequency: Annual

Country of Study: United States of America

No. of awards offered: 10

Closing Date: 8 February

Additional Information: Each year, more than 100 universities are invited to apply for the fellowship. A selection committee composed of four eminent accounting educators chose this year's recipients from 60 applicants nominated by accounting faculty of their school. More than 1,100 future educators have been awarded this fellowship since the program's inception in 1956. www.chevening.org/scholarship/sri-lanka/

For further information contact:

Public Relations Deloitte Services LP.

Tel: (1) 617 449 5071

Denmark-America Foundation

Otto Mønsteds Gade 5, DK-1165 Copenhagen, Denmark.

Tel: (45) 3532 4545
Email: daf-fulb@daf-fulb.dk
Website: www.wemakeithappen.dk
Contact: Ms Marie Monsted, Executive Director

Founded in 1914 as a private foundation with the purpose of promoting the cultural and practical cooperation between Denmark and the United States. Several of the founders of Danish industry were involved and the Royal House was early represented as a patron of the Foundation, which continues to this day.

Denmark-America Foundation Grants

Purpose: To further understanding between Denmark and the United States of America

Eligibility: Open to Danes and Danish-American citizens

Level of Study: Graduate, MBA, Postgraduate, Professional development, Research

Type: Grant

Value: Varies

Length of Study: 3–12 months

Frequency: Annual

Country of Study: Denmark

Application Procedure: Applicants must complete a special application form, available by contacting the secretariat

Funding: Foundation

Department of Biotechnology

6th-8th Floor, Block 2 CGO Complex, Lodhi Road, New Delhi, 110 003, India.

Tel: (91) 26717102
Website: www.dbtindia.gov.in
Contact: Department of Biotechnology

The remarkable march of India into the world of biosciences and technological advances began in 1986. That year, the then Prime Minister of the country, late Rajiv Gandhi accepted the vision that unless India created a separate Department for Biotechnology, within the Ministry of Science and Technology, Government of India the country would not progress to the desired extent.

Janaki Ammal-National Women Bioscientist Award

Purpose: The Department of Biotechnology instituted the National Women Bioscientist Award in the year 1999 to recognize the contributions of senior and young women scientists in the country who are working in the areas of Biology and Biotechnology

Eligibility: 1. Any citizen of India who is engaged in basic and applied research in the areas of Biosciences and Bio-technology in the country. The work (of last 5 years) for which nomination is made must have been carried out in Indian institutes and acknowledged in the publications. 2. The senior category award is for excellence in research (not for governance/management of Science) and there is no age limit. For the young category, the candidate should be below 45 years of age as on closing date of application submission.

Level of Study: Research

Type: Award

Value: The Award carries a cash prize of Rs 1.00 lakh with citation and a gold medal and Research Grant of Rs 5.00 lakhs per annum

Length of Study: 5 Years

Country of Study: India

Additional Information: dbtindia.gov.in/sites/default/files/JA-National%20Women%20Bioscience%20Award-Advertisement%20and%20application%20proforma%20%282021-22%29_0.pdf

For further information contact:

Email: sundeep@dbt.nic.in

National Bioscience Awards for Career Development (NBACD)

Subjects: Biotechnology, Agricultural, Medical and Environmental Sciences.

Purpose: The award aims to boost outstanding research in basic and applied biosciences.

Eligibility: Citizens of India are eligible to apply

Level of Study: Research

Type: Award

Value: cash prize of Rs 1 lakh, a citation and Rs 3 lakh/year as research grant.

Length of Study: 3 years

Frequency: Annual

Country of Study: India

Application Procedure: Online Application

No. of awards offered: Up to 10 Awards

Additional Information: www.nationalmeritscholarships.com/national-bioscience-awards-for-career-development.html

For further information contact:

Email: jagadish.dora@nic.in

S. Ramachandran-National Bioscience Award for Career Development

Purpose: The Department of Biotechnology (DBT) instituted the National Bioscience Award for Career Development in the year 1999 to recognize outstanding contributions of young scientists below 45 years of age who are engaged in basic and applied research in Biological Sciences including Biotechnology, Agricultural, Medical and Environmental Sciences.

Eligibility: 1. Any citizen of India who is engaged in basic and applied research in the areas of Biosciences and Biotechnology in the country. 2. He/she should have made outstanding contribution in the areas of Biosciences/Biotechnology during last 5 years and the work must have been carried out entirely in India. 3. He/she should be below the age of 45 years as on closing date of application submission.

Level of Study: Research

Type: Award

Value: Each Award carries a cash prize of Rs 2.00 lakh, a citation and a trophy along with research project grant of Rs 15.00 lakh (Rs 5.00 lakh/year).

Length of Study: 3 Years

Frequency: Annual

Country of Study: India

No. of awards offered: 10

Closing Date: 30 November

Additional Information: dbtindia.gov.in/sites/default/files/S.%20Ramachandran%20National%20Bioscience%20Award%20for%20Career%20Development%202021-22%20Advertisement%20and%20Nomination%20Proforma_0.pdf dbtindia.gov.in/schemes-programmes/building-capacities/awards/national-bioscience-awards-career-development

For further information contact:

Email: sundeep@dbt.nic.in

Tata Innovation Fellowship

Subjects: Biological sciences/biotechnology and commitment to find innovative solutions in healthcare, agriculture, environment, conservation of natural resources, livestock production manufacturing process etc.

Purpose: Applications are invited through advertisement each year and awardees are selected by Selection Committee constituted by the Department. The awardees receive a fellowship amount of Rs. 25,000/- per month in addition to regular salary and contingency grant of Rs. 6 lakhs per annum. The duration of the fellowship is initially for three years which can be extended further by another two years on a fresh appraisal.

Eligibility: 1. The applicant should possess a Ph.D degree in Life Sciences, Agriculture, Veterinary Science or a Master's degree in Medical. 2. Sciences, Engineering or an equivalent degree in Biotechnology/related areas. The applicant must have outstanding contribution and publication in the specific area. 3. The candidate must have a regular permanent position in a University/Institute/Organization and should be engaged in research and development. If he/she is availing any other fellowship, he/she will have to opt for only one of the fellowships. 4. The applicant should have spent at least 5 years in India before applying for the fellowship. 5. Open to Indian Nationals residing in India who are below the age of 55 years as on closing date of application submission. The fellowship is co-terminus with the superannuation of fellow in his/her organization.

Type: Fellowship

Value: Rs. 25,000 per month in addition to regular salary from the host institute. Each Fellow will receive a contingency grant of Rs. 6.00 lakh per annum for meeting the expenses in connection with the implementation of the research project under the fellowship.

Length of Study: 3 years and extendable by another 2 years based on fresh appraisal.

Frequency: Annual

Country of Study: India

No. of awards offered: 5

Additional Information: dbtindia.gov.in/schemes-programmes/building-capacities/awards/tata-innovation-fellowships

For further information contact:

Tel: (91) 11 24361035
Email: sundeep@dbt.nic.in

Department of Education Services

22 Hasler Road, Osborne Park, Perth, WA 6017, Australia.

Tel: (61) 8 9441 1900
Email: des@des.wa.gov.au
Website: www.des.wa.gov.au

The Department of Education Services provides policy advice to the Minister for Education and Training and supporting universities, non-government schools and international education providers and in some cases individual students and teachers through scholarship programmes in Western Australia.

Western Australian Government Japanese Studies Scholarships

Subjects: Japanese studies.

Purpose: To provide students with the opportunity to spend 1 year studying at a tertiary institution in Japan

Eligibility: Candidates must have Australian citizenship, or evidence that Australian citizenship status will be approved prior to departure for Japan; be a student of a higher education institution in Western Australia, or an institution of equivalent standing, and have completed at least 2 years of full-time study (or equivalent of part-time study) in an appropriate Japanese language course; or be a graduate from a university, having a reasonable command of the Japanese language and developed an interest in Japan through employment or further studies.

Level of Study: Postgraduate

Type: Scholarship

Value: The scholarship includes a return economy airfare, an initial payment of AU$3,000 for fees and other expenses and a monthly maintenance allowance of ¥200,000

Length of Study: 1 year

Frequency: Annual

Country of Study: Japan

No. of awards offered: Two

Closing Date: July

Funding: Government

Contributor: Government

Additional Information: www.jtsi.wa.gov.au/trade-with-wa/buying-from-wa/education/japanese-studies-scholarships

For further information contact:

Department of Jobs, Tourism, Science and Innovation.

Email: diana.phang@jtsi.wa.gov.au

Department of Foreign Affairs and Trade

R.G. Casey Building, John McEwen Crescent, Barton ACT 0221, Australia.

Tel: (61) 2 6261 1111
Website: www.dfat.gov.au/about-us/about-us

The department works to make Australia stronger, safer and more prosperous, to provide timely and responsive consular and passport services, and to ensure a secure Australian Government presence overseas.

Australia Awards Scholarships

Subjects: Australia Awards Scholarships, formerly known as Australian Development Scholarships (ADS), provide opportunities for people from developing countries, particularly those countries located in the Indo-Pacific region, to undertake full time undergraduate or postgraduate study at participating Australian universities and Technical and Further Education (TAFE) institutions.

Purpose: They aim to contribute to the development needs of Australia's partner countries in line with bilateral and regional agreements

Eligibility: The Australian Government Scholarship is open to students of Asia, Middle East, Africa and Pacific. The Australia Awards Scholarship is fully funded scholarship and is administered by the Department of Foreign Affairs and Trade. To be eligible to receive an Australia Awards Scholarship, applicants must 1. Be a minimum of 18 years of age on 1 February of the year of commencing the scholarship. 2. Be a citizen of a participating country (as listed on the Australia Awards website) and be residing in and applying for the scholarship from their country of citizenship. 3. Not be a citizen of Australia, hold permanent residency in Australia or be applying for a visa to live in Australia permanently. 4. Not be married to, engaged to, or a de facto of a person who holds, or is eligible to hold, Australian or New Zealand citizenship or permanent residency, at any time during the application, selection or mobilisation phases (note residents of Cook Islands, Niue and Tokelau with New Zealand citizenship are eligible but must apply for a Student visa [subclass 500])

Level of Study: Postgraduate

Type: Scholarship

Value: full tuition fees, return air travel, establishment allowance, Contribution to Living Expenses (CLE), etc

Frequency: Annual

Country of Study: Australia

Application Procedure: Check the open and close dates for your country, and select your country of citizenship/residency from the list of participating countries for specific information on eligibility, priority areas and how to apply. It is important to read the how to apply page and visit the country specific pages, and the official website (link found below) for detailed and updated information on how to apply for this scholarship. Official Scholarship Website www.dfat.gov.au/people-to-people/australia-awards/Pages/australia-awards-scholarships.aspx

Closing Date: 30 April

Funding: Private

Additional Information: www.scholars4dev.com/3253/australia-awards-scholarships/

For further information contact:

R.G. Casey Building John McEwen Crescent, Barton, ACT 0221, Australia.

Department of Innovation, Industry and Regional Development

GPO Box 4509, Melbourne, VIC 3001, Australia.

Tel: (61) 3 9651 9999
Email: innovation@diird.vic.gov.au
Website: www.diird.vic.gov.au

The Office of Science and Technology at the Department of Innovation, Industry and Regional Development, supports the ongoing development and advancement of a scientifically and technologically advanced Victoria.

Victoria Fellowships

Purpose: To offer support and encouragement to aspiring students to broaden their experience and develop networks. The fellowship also provides an opportunity for recipients to develop commercial ideas

Eligibility: Open to candidates who are either currently employed or enroled in post-graduate studies in Victoria in a field relating to science, engineering or technology and Australian citizens or hold permanent residence in Australia and a current resident of Victoria

Level of Study: Postgraduate, Professional development

Type: Fellowships

Value: AU$3,500

Length of Study: 1 year

Frequency: Annual

Country of Study: Australia

Application Procedure: A completed application form should be submitted

Closing Date: April

Funding: Government

Contributor: Government of Victoria

No. of awards given last year: 6

Additional Information: www.veski.org.au/vicfellow

For further information contact:

Tel: (61) 3 9864 0905/9655 1040
Email: vicprize.fellows@atse.org.au

Department of Science and Technology and Indo-United States Science and Technology Forum (IUSSTF)

Indo-United States Science and Technology Forum, Fulbright House, 12 Hailey Road, New Delhi, 110001, India.

Tel:	(91) 11 2691700
Website:	www.iusstf.org
Contact:	Dr Nishritha Bopana

The Indo-U.S. Science and Technology Forum (IUSSTF) established under an agreement between the Governments of India and the United States of America in March 2000, is an autonomous bilateral organization jointly funded by both the Governments that promotes Science, Technology, Engineering and Innovation through substantive interaction among government, academia and industry. The Department of Science & Technology, Governments of India and the U.S. Department of States are respective nodal departments.

Bhaskara Advanced Solar Energy (BASE) Fellowship Program

Purpose: The Department of Science and Technology, Government of India in partnership with Indo-US Science and Technology Forum (IUSSTF) invites applications from students who are pursuing or have completed their PhD in the field of Solar Energy for Bhaskara Advanced Solar Energy (BASE) Fellowship Program 2022. Through this fellowship programme, Indian students and scientists get an opportunity to gain exposure and access to world-class facilities in the leading US institutions and interact with their American peers. A monthly allowance, return air-fare and a contingency fund will be awarded to the selected fellows.

Eligibility: Indian citizens currently pursuing a PhD as full time scholars in the field of solar energy, in a public-funded R&D Laboratory/S&T institution (non-private)/recognized academic institute (University/College) in India

Type: Fellowship

Value: Monthly stipend, return air-fare, contingency allowance

Length of Study: Internship Minimum 3 months and up to 6 months; Fellowship Minimum 3 months and up to 1 year

Frequency: Annual

Country of Study: Any country

Application Procedure: 1. Register through the online application portal and make an account. 2. Verify account using the activation link sent on the email. 3. Login using the user id and password and fill in details in the application form. 4. Upload the supporting documents. 5. Submit the application form.

Closing Date: 31 January

Funding: Government

Additional Information: For programe information contact: Dr. Nishritha Bopana, energy.fellowship@indousstf.org www.buddy4study.com/scholarship/bhaskara-advanced-solar-energy-base-fellowship-program

For further information contact:

Dr. Nishritha Bopana, Indo-U.S. Science and Technology Forum, Fulbright House, 12, Hailey Road, New Delhi, 110001, India.

Tel:	(91) 11 42691700

Deutsche Forschungsgemeinschaft (DFG)

Kennedyallee 40, D-53175 Bonn, Germany.

Tel:	(49) 228 885 1
Email:	postmaster@dfg.de
Website:	www.dfg.de

The DFG is a central, self-governing research organization, which promotes research at universities and other publicity financial research institutions in Germany. The DFG serves all branches of science and the humanities by funding research projects and facilitating cooperation among researchers.

Albert Maucher Prize in Geoscience

Subjects: Geoscientific research

Purpose: The Albert Maucher Prize in Geoscience is awarded once every three years to early career researchers in recognition of outstanding research findings and original approaches. Researchers who already have a full professorship cannot be nominated. The award is given to early career geoscientists who have achieved outstanding research results "even using unconventional methods". In order to be considered for the prize, researchers must have initiated their own projects and carried them out independently

Level of Study: Research

Type: Prize

Value: €10,000

Length of Study: Varies
Frequency: Every 3 years
Country of Study: Germany
Application Procedure: Documents that provide detailed evidence of previous scientific achievements (such as doctoral dissertations, manuscripts and offprints) and of planned research should be submitted for review. CVs in tabular form, lists of publications, etc, should also be submitted.
No. of awards offered: 1 or 2
Funding: Foundation
Contributor: Munich geologist Albert Maucher
Additional Information: www.dfg.de/en/research_funding/programmes/prizes/maucher_prize/index.html

For further information contact:

Tel: (49) 228 885 2333
Email: Guido.Lueniger@dfg.de

Bernd Rendel Prize in Geoscience

Subjects: Geoscientists who have demonstrated great potential in their scientific career
Purpose: The prize is awarded to early career geoscientists who have graduated, but do not yet hold a doctorate, and who have demonstrated great potential in their scientific career. The award must be used for scientific purposes, e.g. enabling prizewinners to attend international conferences and congresses.
Eligibility: Open to early career geoscientists who have graduated, but do not yet hold a doctorate, and who have demonstrated great potential in their scientific career.
Level of Study: Graduate
Type: Prize
Value: €2,000
Frequency: Annual
Country of Study: Germany
Application Procedure: Nominations may be submitted either by the researchers themselves, or by any researcher or academic working in a closely related field. Detailed information of documents required Letter with max. 1-page justification. Curriculum vitae and brief description of work in progress and any planned work which places previous publications in context (DFG form 10.40). Diploma or master's thesis and any publications. Letter of endorsement. Statement on the proposed use of the prize money
No. of awards offered: 2
Closing Date: February
Funding: Foundation
Additional Information: www.dfg.de/en/research_funding/programmes/prizes/rendel_prize/index.html

For further information contact:

Tel: (49) 228 885 2825
Email: Ismene.Seeberg-elverfeldt@dfg.de

Communicator Award

Purpose: The award acknowledges a researcher's commitment to making their work and research area accessible to a wider audience in a particularly innovative, diverse and effective way and engaging in a dialogue between the research community and the public. Researchers who are particularly creative in their science communication, taking new, courageous paths and addressing their target groups in suitable and effective ways, now take centre stage.
Level of Study: Research
Type: Award
Value: €50,000
Frequency: Annual
Country of Study: Germany
Application Procedure: Proposals for candidates can be put forward by researchers who are capable of assessing both the communication effort and professional qualification of the nominee(s)
No. of awards offered: 1
Funding: Foundation
Contributor: Donors Association
Additional Information: www.dfg.de/en/research_funding/programmes/prizes/communicator_award/index.html

For further information contact:

Tel: (49) 0228 885 2443
Email: Jutta.Hoehn@dfg.de

Copernicus Award

Purpose: The award is conferred for outstanding contributions to German-Polish research cooperation.
Eligibility: Open to outstanding researchers in Germany and Poland who work at universities or research institutions
Level of Study: Research
Type: Award
Value: €200,000 (donated in equal shares)
Length of Study: 3 years
Frequency: Every 2 years
Country of Study: Germany
Application Procedure: A completed application form along with the required documents should be submitted. An appraisal (description of achievements with regard to German-Polish scientific cooperation). Curriculum vitae in tabular form. A list of up to ten joint research publications.

An additional independent letter of reference for each couple of scientists when the nomination is submitted by a third party, two independent letters of reference in case of self-nomination.

No. of awards offered: Varies

Funding: Foundation

Contributor: The Foundation for Polish Science and the DFG

Additional Information: www.dfg.de/en/research_funding/programmes/prizes/copernicus_award/index.html

For further information contact:

Tel: (49) 228 885 2802

Email: annina.lottermann@dfg.de

Deutsche Forschungsgemeinschaft Collaborative Research Centres

Purpose: To promote long-term co-operative research in universities and academic research

Eligibility: Universities (and institutions of equivalent status entitled to confer doctorates) in Germany; other research institutions which are to make essential contributions to the research programme can be integrated

Level of Study: Postdoctorate, Research

Type: Research grant

Value: Dependent on the requirements of the project

Length of Study: Up to 12 years

Study Establishment: Universities and academic institutions

Country of Study: Germany

Application Procedure: Applicants must write or visit the website for further information. Applications must be formally filed by the universities

Additional Information: A list of collaborative research centres is available in Germany only from the DFG www.dfg.de/en/research_funding/programmes/coordinated_programmes/collaborative_research_centres/

For further information contact:

Tel: (49) 228 885 2312

Email: petra.hammel@dfg.de

Deutsche Forschungsgemeinschaft Mercator Programme

Purpose: The DFG offers the Mercator Programme to enable Germany's research universities to invite highly qualified scientists and academics working abroad to complete a DFG-funded stay at their institutes

Eligibility: Open to foreign scientists whose individual research is of special interest to research and teaching in Germany

Level of Study: Postdoctorate

Type: Fellowship

Value: Dependent on the duration of the stay

Length of Study: 3 to 12 months

Frequency: Annual

Study Establishment: German universities

Country of Study: Germany

Application Procedure: A proposal must be submitted by the university intending to host the guest professor

Additional Information: www.dfg.de/en/research_funding/programmes/international_cooperation/mercator_fellows/

For further information contact:

Tel: (49) 228 885 2232

Email: cora.laforet@dfg.de

Deutsche Forschungsgemeinschaft Research Training Groups

Purpose: To promote high-quality graduate studies at the doctoral level through the participation of graduate students recruited through countrywide calls in research programmes

Eligibility: Open to highly qualified graduate and doctoral students of any nationality

Level of Study: Postgraduate, Predoctorate

Type: Grant

Length of Study: Up to 9 years

Frequency: Annual

Study Establishment: Any approved university

Country of Study: Germany

Application Procedure: Applications should be submitted in response to calls. For further information applicants must visit the website

Closing Date: 1 October

Additional Information: A list of graduate colleges presently funded is available (in Germany only) from the DFG www.dfg.de/en/research_funding/programmes/coordinated_programmes/research_training_groups/

For further information contact:

Tel: (49) 228 885 288

Email: sebastian.granderath@dfg.de

Emmy Noether Programme

Purpose: To give highly qualified researchers the opportunity to satisfy the prerequisites for appointment as a university professor by leading an independent junior research group and performing relevant teaching duties.

Eligibility: 1. Normally at least two years of postdoctoral experience 2. Substantial international research experience 3. Applicants from abroad are expected to continue their research careers in Germany after the funding comes to an end. 4. A written letter of intent must be attached to the proposal. 5. The ENP is not open to those who have already satisfied the requirements for a professorship, in particular those who have completed or are about to embark on the habilitation process, as the funding objective has already been achieved in these cases. 6. An individual is not eligible if they are in receipt of a type of funding similar to the ENP for an independent (junior) research group from a national research institution, programmes offered by the federal and state governments, or an international institution located in Germany.

Level of Study: Postdoctorate

Type: Project grant

Value: Standard Allowance-A total of €1,000 per funding year; Family Allowance-up to €6,000 per year

Length of Study: 6 years

Frequency: Annual

Study Establishment: Universities or research institutions

Country of Study: Any country

Application Procedure: Applicants must complete an application form. For further information applicants must write or visit the website

Closing Date: 30 June

Additional Information: www.dfg.de/en/research_funding/programmes/individual/emmy_noether/

For further information contact:

Tel: (49) 228 885 3008

Email: Verfahren-Nachwuchs@dfg.de

European Young Investigator Award

Purpose: To enable and encourage outstanding young researchers from all over the world, to work in an European environment for the benefit of the development of European science and the building up of the next generation of leading European researchers

Eligibility: 1. Applicants must be practising paediatricians who are ESPE members. 2. Candidates should be still in training or no more than 5 years in a Senior (PI) role.

Type: Prize

Value: Up to €1,250,000

Length of Study: 5 years

Country of Study: Any country

Application Procedure: Applicants should provide a completed application form, letters of recommendation and the letter of support from the host institution to the DFG

Closing Date: 30 November

Contributor: The European Union Research Organizations Heads of Research Councils (EuroHORCS)

Additional Information: www.eurospe.org/grants-awards/awards/young-investigator-award/

For further information contact:

Bioscientifica Starling House, 1600 Bristol Parkway North, Bristol BS34 8YU, United Kingdom.

Tel: (44) 1454 642246

Email: espe@eurospe.org

Excellence Initiative

Purpose: To promote top-level research and improve the quality of German universities and research institutions in general, thus making Germany a more attractive research location, and more internationally competitive and focussing attention on the outstanding achievements of German universities and the German scientific community

Eligibility: The precise conditions for receiving funding were defined in accordance with the criteria specified by the federal and state governments

Level of Study: Postgraduate

Type: Funding support

Length of Study: 5 years

Frequency: Annual

Country of Study: Any country

Contributor: German federal and state governments

Additional Information: The three funding lines of the initiative: graduate schools to promote young scientists, clusters of excellence to promote top-level research, institutional strategies to promote top-level university research. For more details log on to www.dfg.de/en/research_funding/programmes/excellence_initiative/

For further information contact:

Tel: (49) 228 885 2254

Email: internetredaktion@uni-konstanz.de

Gottfried Wilhelm Leibniz Prize

Purpose: The programme aims to improve the working conditions of outstanding scientists and academics, expand their research opportunities, relieve them of administrative tasks, and help them employ particularly qualified early career researchers

Eligibility: Open to outstanding scholars in German universities

Type: Prize

Value: €2.5 million is provided per award.

Frequency: Annual

Study Establishment: Any approved university or research institution

Country of Study: Germany

No. of awards offered: 10

Closing Date: 12 May

No. of applicants last year: 10

Additional Information: www.dfg.de/en/research_funding/ programmes/prizes/leibniz_prize/index.html

For further information contact:

Tel: (49) 228 885 2835
Email: Annette.Lessenich@dfg.de

Heinz Maier–Leibnitz Prize

Purpose: Since 1977 the prize is awarded by the DFG to early career researchers as a distinction for outstanding achievement. It is intended to assist in furthering their scientific careers. The prize is not to be seen simply as a distinction of the thesis alone. Rather, prizewinners will have already established an independent scientific career since having gained their doctorates.

Type: Prize

Value: €20,000

Frequency: Annual

Study Establishment: Any approved university or research institution

Country of Study: Germany

No. of awards offered: 10

No. of applicants last year: 10

Additional Information: www.dfg.de/en/funded_projects/ prizewinners/maier_leibnitz_prize/index.html

For further information contact:

Tel: (49) 228 885 2835
Email: Annette.Lessenich@dfg.de

Heisenberg Programme

Purpose: To promote outstanding young and highly qualified researchers

Eligibility: Open to high-calibre young scientists up to the age of 35 years who are German nationals or permanent residents of Germany

Level of Study: Postdoctorate

Type: Scholarship

Value: Varies

Length of Study: 5 years

Frequency: Annual

Study Establishment: Any approved university or research institution

Country of Study: Germany

Application Procedure: Applicants must submit a research proposal, a detailed curriculum vitae, copies of degree certificates, a copy of the thesis, a letter explaining the choice of host institution, a list of all previously published material and a letter outlining financial requirements in duplicate. For further information applicants must contact the DFG

Additional Information: www.dfg.de/en/research_funding/ programmes/individual/heisenberg/

For further information contact:

Tel: (49) 228 885 2398
Email: paul.heuermann@dfg.de

The Eugen and Ilse Seibold Prize

Purpose: With this prize, Japanese and German scientists will be awarded, whose work has contributed to a better understanding of the other country.

Eligibility: Open to outstanding young German or Japanese scholars

Type: Prize

Value: €15,000

Frequency: Every 2 years

Country of Study: Germany

No. of awards offered: 4

Additional Information: www.dfg.de/en/research_funding/ programmes/prizes/seibold_prize/index.html

For further information contact:

Tel: (49) 228 885 2786
Email: Ingrid.Kruessmann@dfg.de

The Von Kaven Awards

Purpose: The DFG presents the von Kaven Award to EU-based mathematicians for their outstanding scientific achievements. The prize is intended to help them in their mathematical research. Provided that no other suitable nominations are submitted, the von Kaven Award is given to the previous years best-performing mathematical researcher in the Heisenberg Programme.

Eligibility: Persons who meet the general eligibility criteria stipulated by the DFG within the individual grants programme

Level of Study: Postgraduate

Type: Award

Value: €10,000

Frequency: Annual

Country of Study: Germany

Application Procedure: Nominations for the von Kaven (Prize and) award may be made by the members of the mathematics review board, its previous chairs and other DFG committee members in the field of mathematics (such as senators and members of the senate committee working in the field of mathematics). It is not possible to apply directly for the von Kaven (Prize and) award

Closing Date: 31 January

Funding: Private

Additional Information: www.dfg.de/en/research_funding/programmes/prizes/von_kaven_award/index.html

For further information contact:

Tel: (49) 228 885 2567
Email: frank.kiefer@dfg.de

Ursula M. Händel Animal Welfare Prize

Purpose: The prize is awarded to scientists who make committed efforts to promote animal welfare in their research work. In particular, this includes the development of processes contributing, in accordance with the 3R principle, to the reduction, refinement and replacement of animal experimentation.

Eligibility: Open to scientists who aim at improving the welfare of animals through research

Level of Study: Postdoctorate

Type: Prize

Value: €80,000

Frequency: Annual

Country of Study: Germany

Application Procedure: A completed application form and required documents must be submitted Documents suitable for review and providing detailed information on previous and, if applicable, planned scientific work according to the 3R principle; curriculum vitae in table format; publication list

Funding: Foundation

Contributor: Mrs Ursula M. Handel

Additional Information: www.dfg.de/en/research_funding/programmes/prizes/haendel_prize/index.htmldex.html

For further information contact:

Tel: (49) 228 885 2362
Email: Sonja.Ihle@dfg.de

Deutscher Akademischer Austauschdienst

German Academic Exchange Service, 1 Southampton Place, London WCIA 2DA, United Kingdom.

Tel: (44) 20 7831 9511
Email: info@daad.org.uk
Website: www.daad.org.uk
Contact: Ms Judie Cole

Daad-Master Studies

Purpose: This scholarship programme offers you the opportunity to continue your academic education in Germany with a postgraduate course of study.

Eligibility: 1. Participation in a postgraduate programme after a first undergraduate course of study for the purpose of technical or scientific specialisation. 2. Specifically, the following is supported a postgraduate or Master's degree programme completed at a state or state-recognised university in Germany.

Level of Study: Postdoctorate

Type: Scholarships

Value: €850 a month

Length of Study: 2-year

Country of Study: Any country

Closing Date: 1 October

Additional Information: www.daad.de/deutschland/stipendium/datenbank/en/21148-scholarship-database/?detail=50026200

Research Internships in Science and Engineering (RISE)

Purpose: To offer research internships to students in science and engineering

Type: Grant

Value: €650 per month

Length of Study: 1.5 to 3 years

Frequency: Annual

Country of Study: Germany

Closing Date: December

Additional Information: Please visit www.daad.de/rise www.abroad.pitt.edu/RISE

For further information contact:

Email: a.olalde@pitt.edu

Deutsches Museum

Museumsinsel 1, D-80538 Munich, Germany.

Tel: (49) 89 217 91, 89 217 9433
Email: information@deutsches-museum.de
Website: www.deutsches-museum.de/en

Scholar-in-Residence Program

Purpose: The Fulbright Scholar-in-Residence (S-I-R) Program assists U.S. higher education institutions in expanding programs of academic exchange, by supporting non-U.S. scholars through grants for teaching at institutions that might not have a strong international component and/or serve minority audiences. Both the U.S. institution and the scholar grantee benefit from this experience.
Eligibility: 1. Minority Serving Institutions Asian American Native American Pacific Islander-Serving Institutions (AANAPISIs), American Indian and Alaskan Native-Serving Institutions (AIANSIs), Historically Black Colleges and Universities (HBCUs), Hispanic-Serving Institutions (HISs), Tribal Colleges and Universities (TCUs), and Predominately Black Institutions (PBIs). 2. Community Colleges. 3. Small Liberal Arts Colleges. 4. Rural Colleges and Universities.
Level of Study: Research
Type: Scholarship
Value: Predoctoral stipends €7,500 (6 months) or €15,000 (full year). Postdoctoral stipends €15,000 (6 months) or €30,000 (full year).
Country of Study: Germany
Application Procedure: Applicants should send their applications by post, including completed application form, curriculum vitae, project description (3–5 pages), two confidential references (can be sent directly by the referees)
Closing Date: 1 November
Contributor: Deutsches Museum
Additional Information: www.cies.org/program/fulbright-scholar-residence-program

For further information contact:

Email: Scholars@iie.org

Diabetes United Kingdom

Macleod House, 10 Parkway, London NW1 7AA, United Kingdom.

Tel: (44) 20 7424 1000
Email: victoria.king@diabetes.org.uk
Website: www.diabetes.org.uk
Contact: Dr Victoria King, Research Manager

Diabetes United Kingdom's overall aim is to help and care for both people with diabetes and those closest to them, to represent and campaign for their interests and to fund research into diabetes. Diabetes United Kingdom continues to encourage research into all areas of diabetes.

Endeavour Postgraduate Leadership Award

Purpose: The Endeavour Postgraduate Leadership Award provides financial support for international applicants to undertake a postgraduate qualification at a Masters or PhD level either by coursework or research in any field in Australia for up to 2 years for Masters and 4 years for PhD.
Eligibility: To participate in the ELP, individual applicants must 1. not be undertaking their Leadership Activity in a country where they hold citizenship/dual citizenship or permanent residency (International Individual Endeavour Leaders must undertake their activity in Australia and not hold citizenship/dual citizenship or be a permanent resident of Australia.). 2. be aged 18 years or over at the commencement of their Leadership Activity. 3. not be in receipt of any other Australian Government sponsored mobility, scholarship or fellowship benefits
Level of Study: Postgraduate
Type: Award
Length of Study: 2 years for a Masters and up to 4 years for a PhD
Frequency: Annual
Country of Study: Any country
Closing Date: November
Funding: Private
Additional Information: internationaleducation.gov.au/Endeavour%20program/Scholarships-and-Fellowships/Pages/default.aspx
www.scholars4dev.com/3710/endeavour-postgraduate-scholarship-awards/

For further information contact:

Email: endeavour@education.gov.au

Doctoral New Investigator (DNI) Grants

1155 Sixteenth Street, NW, Washington, DC 20036, United States of America.

Tel: (1) 800 333 9511
Email: service@acs.org

The Doctoral New Investigator grants program aims to promote the careers of young faculty by supporting research of high scientific caliber, and to enhance the career opportunities of their undergraduate/ graduate students, and postdoctoral associates through the research experience

Doctoral New Investigator (DNI) Grants

Subjects: Chemical science; Chemical engineering
Purpose: Grants provide start-up funding for scientists and engineers in the United States who are within the first three years of their first academic appointment at the level of Assistant Professor or the equivalent.
Eligibility: Applicants must be regularly-appointed faculty members at U.S. academic institutions who are within the first three years of their first academic appointment at the rank of Assistant Professor or the equivalent are eligible to apply. In addition, applicants must meet the following criteria The non-profit institution submitting the DNI proposal must certify that the individual listed as a principal investigator on the cover page qualifies as a principal investigator under the institution's policies. In view of the long-standing policy of The ACS Petroleum Research Fund to give priority to support of students (undergraduate, graduate, or postdoctoral), each principal investigator must be eligible to serve as the formal, official supervisor of graduate students in graduate degree programs. The terms of appointment of the principal investigator must promise reasonable continuity of service. The appointment should continue at least through the period of funding requested in the proposal.
Level of Study: Junior Faculty
Type: Grant
Value: US$110,000 over two years
Length of Study: Two years
Frequency: Annual
Country of Study: United States of America
Application Procedure: Online application www.acs.org/content/acs/en/funding-and-awards/grants/prf/programs/sf-proposal-submission-help.html
No. of awards offered: Approx. 75 each year
Closing Date: 11 March
No. of applicants last year: Approx. 75 each year

Additional Information: www.acs.org/content/acs/en/funding-and-awards/grants/prf/programs/dni.html

Dominican College of San Rafael

School of Business & International Studies Graduate Program in Pacific Basin Studies, 50 Acacia Avenue, San Rafael, CA 94912-9962, United States of America.

Tel: (1) 415 257 1359
Email: pbsad@dominican.edu
Contact: MBA Admissions Officer

Dominican College of San Rafael MBA in Strategic Leadership

Length of Study: 2 years
Country of Study: Any country
Application Procedure: All applicants must submit a completed application form, with official academic transcripts, a curriculum vitae, a statement of purpose (three-five pages), TOEFL score (if applicable), and a fee of US$40
Additional Information: www.gradschools.com/graduate-schools-in-united-states/california/dominican-university-california-san-rafael/mba-strategic-leadership-194144

For further information contact:

Division of Liberal & Professional Studies MBA in Strategic Leadership, 50 Acacia Avenue, CA 94901, United States of America.

Tel: (1) 415 485 3280
Fax: (1) 415 485 3293
Email: 87pathways@dominican.edu

Doris Duke Charitable Foundation (DDCF)

650 Fifth Avenue, 19th Floor, New York, NY 10019, United States of America.

Tel: (1) 212 974 7000
Email: webmaster@ddcf.org
Contact: DDCF Headquarters & Grant-making Programs

The mission of the Doris Duke Charitable Foundation is to improve the quality of people's lives through grants supporting the performing arts, environmental conservation, medical research and child well-being, and through preservation of the cultural and environmental legacy of Doris Duke's properties.

Physician Scientist Fellowship

Subjects: Physician science

Purpose: The Doris Duke Physician Scientist Fellowship program provides grants to physician scientists at the subspecialty fellowship level who are seeking to conduct additional years of research beyond their subspecialty requirement. The goal is to aid in the transition into a research faculty appointment.

Eligibility: To be eligible for this award, applicants must: 1. Have a clinical subspecialty fellowship with a completion date that falls between June 30, 2022, and July 1, 2024. 2. Have completed the majority of the clinical training portion of the fellowship by the award start date, July 1, 2023. If in the structure of your subspecialty fellowship program, clinical training happens after your research year(s), a request must be submitted to ask for an exemption to this eligibility criterion (see page 5). • Not have an appointment as a full-time faculty member including but not limited to Instructor or Assistant Professor as of the award start date. Please note this award is intended for fellows whose transition to a faculty position is not imminent. While full-time faculty are ineligible, grantees may transition to full-time faculty during the award period. Assistant Professors may be eligible for the Doris Duke Clinical Scientist Development Award. We realize that some fellowship programs give their fellows the title of "instructor," but it is not a fulltime faculty appointment. You may be eligible to apply if you have this type of instructor title so please apply for an exemption as indicated on page 5. 3. Be guaranteed a minimum overall research time protection of 75 percent of full-time professional effort by the applicant's institution if an award is made. This protection ensures that the applicant develops skills and knowledge necessary for a career in biomedical research. 4. Not be in a doctoral degree program at the time of the award. Applicants may be enrolled in a master's degree program at the start of the award, July 1, 2023. A description of the purpose and goals of obtaining the master's degree should be included in the proposal, if applicable (see the "Career Goals and Accomplishments" section on page 16). Time spent in a master's program cannot infringe on the 75 percent research effort required for this award. 5. Have received an MD, MD/PhD, DO, or foreign equivalent degree from an accredited institution. 6. Work at a US medical institution that is able to receive an award as an organization with tax exemption under 501(c)(3) Internal Revenue Code, as amended. Please see the information on page 3 and consult with your institutional grants office. 7. Be working at the institution through which they are applying as of the start date of the award, July 1, 2023.

Level of Study: Doctorate, Postdoctorate, Postgraduate

Type: Fellowship

Value: US$220,000 (US$100,000 for annual direct costs plus US$10,000 for indirect costs)

Length of Study: Two years

Frequency: Annual

Country of Study: Any country

Application Procedure: ddcf-portal.givingdata.com/campaign/psf

Closing Date: 7 January

Additional Information: www.ddcf.org/what-we-fund/medical-research/goals-and-strategies/encourage-and-develop-clinical-research-careers/physician-scientist-fellowship/

For further information contact:

Email: ddcf@aibs.org

Doshisha University

Karasuma-Higashi-iru Imadegawa-dori, Kamigyo-ku, Kyoto 602-8580, Japan.

Tel:	(81) 75 251 3257
Email:	ji-intad@mail.doshisha.ac.jp
Website:	www.doshisha.ac.jp
Contact:	International Center Office of International Students

Doshisha Elementary School was opened in April 2006, some 130 years after Doshisha was originally founded in 1875. This opening finally brought to fruition the dream of an integrated educational system "from kindergarten through to university," a strongly-held ambition of Doshisha's founder Joseph Hardy Neesima

Doshisha University Doctoral-Program Young Researcher Scholarship

Subjects: Theology Letters; Social Studies, Law, Economics, Commerce, Policy and Management, Culture and Information Science, Science and Engineering, Life and Medical Sciences, Health and Sports Science, Psychology and Global Studies

Purpose: To support young researchers who hold future promise and display a strong passion toward academic research.

Eligibility: Students with a passion for academic research who have received a recommendation from one of the graduate schools and match one of the following profiles 1. Students enroled in doctoral programs at the Graduate Schools of Theology Letters; Social Studies, Law, Economics, Commerce, Policy and Management, Culture and Information Science, Science and Engineering, Life and Medical Sciences, Health and Sports Science, Psychology and Global Studies, who are aiming to acquire a doctoral degree and are under 34 years of age at the time of admission. 2. Students enroled in an integrated program (master's and doctoral programs) (except the Graduate School of Brain Science) for a minimum of 2 years, who are aiming to acquire a doctoral degree and are under 32 years of age at the time of enrollment

Level of Study: Doctorate

Type: Scholarship

Value: Amount equivalent to annual school fees (including admission fees at the time of enrollment, tuition fee for educational support and lab/practical fees)

Length of Study: 1 year (renewable for up to the standard number of years required for graduation)

Frequency: Annual

Study Establishment: Doshisha University

Country of Study: Japan

Application Procedure: The scholarship is awarded on the basis of recommendations from the graduate schools and cannot be applied for individually

Doshisha University Graduate School Reduced Tuition Special Scholarships for Self-Funded International Students

Purpose: To enable international students to concentrate on their studies free from financial concerns

Eligibility: Those who satisfy one of the following qualifications are eligible 1. who have passed the entrance examination for international students and who hold a 'college student' visa prescribed in the, Emigration and Immigration Management and Refuge Recognition Law', at the time of enrollment. 2. who have passed the entrance examination for international students and who hold a 'Permanent Resident' visa etc. 3. who are enroled in Doshisha regardless of the type of admission (type of entrance examination) and who hold a 'College Student' visa

Level of Study: Doctorate, MBA, Postgraduate

Type: Scholarship

Value: Annual tuition fees

Length of Study: 2 years (renewable for up to the standard number of years required for graduation)

Frequency: Annual

Study Establishment: Doshisha University

Country of Study: Japan

Application Procedure: The Scholarship is awarded based on Doshisha's criteria without application

Doshisha University Graduate School Scholarship

Purpose: To provide for students enroled in master's or doctoral programs experiencing difficulty meeting educational costs required for them to continue their academic research activities

Eligibility: Graduate students (regular students). Please note Law School, Business School, and Graduate School of Brain Science students may not apply. Students who have been enrolled at school longer than the standard number of years for course completion (a leave of absence is not counted as) may not apply. Students selected to receive the following scholarships may not apply Doshisha University Doctoral-Program Young Researcher Scholarship, Japanese Government (MEXT) Scholarship, Doshisha University Graduate School Reduced Tuition Special Scholarship for Self-Funded International Students

Level of Study: Doctorate, Postgraduate

Type: Scholarship

Value: Half of the total annual tuition fee

Length of Study: 1 year

Frequency: Annual

Study Establishment: Doshisha University

Country of Study: Japan

Application Procedure: Eligible applicants are required to submit an application to the Section for Scholarship by specified date

No. of awards offered: To be made based on recommendations from each graduate school

No. of awards given last year: 16

Doshisha University Merit Scholarships for Self-Funded International Students

Eligibility: Applicants must be self-funded international students with a strong desire to enroll in the International Science and Technology Course and satisfy one of the following requirements: (1) Those who have passed the entrance examination for international students and hold a "College Student" visa. (2) Those who have passed the entrance examination for international students, and hold a certain visa such as "Permanent Resident", "Long-Term Resident", and "Dependent" visa. (3) Those who are enrolled in Doshisha University, regardless of type of entrance

examination and who hold a "College Student" visa. (*applicants' eligibility will be preliminarily screened.)
Type: Scholarship
Value: (1) Equivalent to full amount of Tuition (2) Equivalent to 50% of Tuition (3) Equivalent to 30% of Tuition
Length of Study: 2 years
Country of Study: Japan
Additional Information: istc.doshisha.ac.jp/en/tuition/scholarship.html

Doshisha University Reduced Tuition Scholarships for Self-Funded International Students

Purpose: To enable international students to concentrate on their studies free from financial concerns
Eligibility: Those who satisfy one of the following qualifications are eligible 1. who have passed the entrance examination for international students and who hold a 'College Student' visa prescribed in the 'Emigration and Immigration Management and Refuge Recognition Law', at the time of enrollment. 2. who have passed the entrance examination for international students and who hold a 'Permanent Resident' visa etc. 3. who are enroled in Doshisha regardless of the type of admission (type of entrance examination), and who hold a 'College Student' visa
Level of Study: Doctorate, MBA, Postgraduate
Type: Scholarship
Value: Equivalent to 50% of tuition, equivalent to 30% of tuition, to be made based on Doshisha's criteria
Length of Study: 2 years (renewable for up to the standard number of years required for graduation)
Frequency: Annual
Study Establishment: Doshisha University
Country of Study: Japan
Application Procedure: The scholarship is awarded based on Doshisha's criteria without application
Additional Information: Nationals of Japan are not eligible ois.doshisha.ac.jp/en/scholarships/reduced.html

Graduate School of Brain Science Special Scholarship

Eligibility: Open to doctorate students with academic excellence and depending on the candidate's contribution to the field. Those who have passed the entrance examination at the Graduate School of Brain Science and are under the age of 32 (for 3rd-year transfer students under the age of 34) at the time of enrollment
Type: Scholarship
Value: Full-time fee ¥8,850; Full-time fee ¥23,500

Length of Study: 1 year (renewable for up to 5 years (for transfer students, for up to 3 years))
Frequency: Annual
Study Establishment: Doshisha University
Country of Study: Japan
Application Procedure: As the initial registration procedure, eligible applicants are required to remit the registration fee and submit an application for the 'Graduate School of Brain Science Special Scholarship' by specified date
Additional Information: Additional Information: www.gla.ac.uk/postgraduate/taught/brainsciences/#depositsterms&conditions

For further information contact:

Email: mvls-brainsci@glasgow.ac.uk

Duke University

2127 Campus Drive, PO Box 90065, Durham, NC 27708, United States of America.

Tel: (1) 919 681 3257
Email: grm@duke.edu
Website: www.gradschool.duke.edu
Contact: Co-ordinator

The Duke University ideally has a small number of superior students working closely with esteemed scholars. It has approximately 2,200 graduate students enroled there, working with more than 1,000 graduate faculty members.

Bass Connections – Collaborative Project Expeditions

Level of Study: Faculty
Type: Grant
Value: a stipend of US$1,500
Frequency: Annual
Country of Study: United States of America
Application Procedure: Participating students are responsible for adhering to financial policies and restrictions (including restrictions on hours of work per week) set by grantors of any other fellowships or positions held during the funding period. Please note that some fellowships do not allow supplemental funding. Please see the Graduate School Supplementation Policy for more information. We also advise that students consult with their advisor and Director of Graduate Studies about how this opportunity

would fit in their academic and funding plans for the proposed period of work.

No. of awards offered: 2 to 4

Closing Date: 17 April

Additional Information: researchfunding.duke.edu/bass-connections-collaborative-project-expeditions-duke-internal-funding-duke-grad-students-only

Career Development Bridge Funding Program

Eligibility: Candidates must be either junior faculty within five (5) years of completing fellowship or a fellow within the Department of Medicine. Candidates must have competed unsuccessfully for a Career Development Award (as described previously e.g. NIH K08, K23, or equivalent) within the past year to be considered eligible for funding.

Level of Study: Faculty

Type: Award

Value: Up to US$85,000

Length of Study: 1 year and may be extended for an additional year at Chairs discretion.

Frequency: Annual

Country of Study: United States of America

Closing Date: 15 April

Additional Information: researchfunding.duke.edu/career-development-bridge-funding-program-duke-internal-funding-duke-faculty-only

Climate Data Expeditions: Climate + Health – Request for Proposals

Eligibility: The Principal Investigator (PI) must be at the regular rank Assistant Professor, Associate Professor, or Professor level, or have PI status per Duke's written policy. Both MD and non-MD faculty may be Principal Investigators. Team members must have PI status to register for a planning grant token (details on the registration page).

Level of Study: Faculty

Type: Grant

Value: US$250,000 to US$500,000 per year

Length of Study: 2 years

Frequency: Annual

Country of Study: United States of America

No. of awards offered: 5

Closing Date: 31 March

Additional Information: researchfunding.duke.edu/climate-data-expeditions-climate-health-request-proposals-duke-internal-funding-duke-faculty-only

Duke Aging Center – Busse Research Awards

Purpose: The purpose of these awards is to recognize the achievements of late junior to mid-career scientists and to encourage their continued contributions to aging research.

Eligibility: Candidates for these awards must be nominated (self nominations are not accepted) and two seconders are recommended. Nominations must be written in English. International nominees welcome.

Level of Study: Faculty

Type: Award

Value: US$10,000

Frequency: Annual

Country of Study: United States of America

Closing Date: 15 March

Additional Information: researchfunding.duke.edu/duke-aging-center-busse-research-awards

Duke Cancer Institute / Duke Microbiome Center Joint Partnership Pilot Award

Level of Study: Faculty

Type: Fellowship

Value: US$50,000

Length of Study: 1 year

Frequency: Annual

Country of Study: United States of America

Closing Date: 14 March

Additional Information: researchfunding.duke.edu/duke-cancer-institute-duke-microbiome-center-joint-partnership-pilot-award

Duke Microbiome Center Development Grants

Purpose: Microbial communities (microbiomes) are known to contribute significantly to human health and disease, regulate global biogeochemistry, and harbor much of our planet's genetic diversity. The Duke Microbiome Center (DMC) supports microbiome science at Duke University through pilot project funding.

Eligibility: To be eligible for consideration, the PI of the proposal must be a faculty member at Duke University currently affiliated with the DMC (see DMC faculty list here). Applications must include as co-investigators at least one additional faculty member at Duke, though they need not be currently affiliated with the DMC.

Level of Study: Faculty

Type: Grant

Value: US$50,000

Length of Study: 1 year

Frequency: Annual

Country of Study: United States of America

Closing Date: 30 April

Additional Information: researchfunding.duke.edu/duke-microbiome-center-development-grants-duke-internal-funding-duke-faculty-and-staff-only

Duke/NCCU Collaborative Translational Research Awards

Eligibility: Proposed projects must involve a lead investigator from Duke and a lead investigator from NCCU. Proposals are encouraged from new teams of investigators from different disciplines. Applicants at each institution must have principal investigator status per the specific institution's written policy.

Level of Study: Faculty

Type: Grant

Value: US$50,000 per award.

Frequency: Annual

Country of Study: United States of America

Closing Date: 5 April

Additional Information: researchfunding.duke.edu/dukenccu-collaborative-translational-research-awards-0

Frontier Research in Earth Sciences (FRES)

Purpose: The FRES program will support research in Earth systems from the core through the critical zone. The project may focus on all or part of the surface, continental lithospheric, and deeper Earth systems over the entire range of temporal and spatial scales. FRES projects should have a larger scientific scope and budget than those considered for funding by disciplinary programs in the Division of Earth Sciences (EAR). FRES projects may be interdisciplinary studies that do not fit well within EAR's disciplinary programs or cannot be routinely managed by sharing between disciplinary programs. Innovative proposals within a single disciplinary area with outcomes of potential broad relevance to Earth Science research are also encouraged. Investigations may employ any combination of field, laboratory, and computational studies with observational, theoretical, or experimental approaches. Projects should be focused on topics that meet the guidelines for research funded by the Division of Earth Sciences.

Eligibility: 1. Institutions of Higher Education (IHEs) - Two- and four-year IHEs (including community colleges) accredited in, and having a campus located in the US, acting on behalf of their faculty members. Special Instructions for International Branch Campuses of US IHEs: If the proposal includes funding to be provided to an international branch campus of a US institution of higher education (including

through use of subawards and consultant arrangements), the proposer must explain the benefit(s) to the project of performance at the international branch campus, and justify why the project activities cannot be performed at the US campus. 2. Non-profit, non-academic organizations: Independent museums, observatories, research labs, professional societies and similar organizations in the U.S. associated with educational or research activities.

Level of Study: Foundation programme

Type: Research grant

Value: US$3,000,000

Frequency: Annual

Country of Study: Any country

Application Procedure: Many of the projects will be collaborative research from multiple institutions. There is no upper or lower limit on award size, but investigators proposing projects with budgets of less than US$1,000,000 or more than US$3,000,000 are encouraged to contact a Program Officer before submitting a proposal

Closing Date: 2 February

Funding: Private

Additional Information: For-profit organizations: United States commercial organizations, especially small businesses with strong capabilities in scientific or engineering research or educationt researchfunding.duke.edu/frontier-research-earth-sciences-fres

For further information contact:

Email: mbenoit@nsf.gov

Josiah Charles Trent Memorial Foundation Endowment Fund

Level of Study: Faculty

Type: Grant

Value: average US$3,000, with a maximum of US$5,000

Length of Study: 1 year

Frequency: Twice a year

Country of Study: United States of America

Closing Date: 1 April

Additional Information: researchfunding.duke.edu/josiah-charles-trent-memorial-foundation-endowment-fund-grants-limited-duke-university-faculty-and

MEDx Colloquia

Eligibility: 1. Proposals must be jointly submitted by a faculty member in the Pratt School of Engineering AND a faculty member in the School of Medicine. 2. Proposals must include a clear statement of the objectives of the colloquium, anticipated deliverables and approximate budget.

Level of Study: Faculty

Type: Grant

Value: US$5,000

Frequency: Annual

Country of Study: United States of America

Closing Date: 7 March

Additional Information: researchfunding.duke.edu/medx-colloquia-duke-internal-funding-duke-faculty-only

MEDx Engineering, Environment, and Health 2022 Request for Proposals

Purpose: Duke MEDx's purpose is to foster collaborations between faculty members from the Duke School of Medicine and the Pratt School of Engineering. With this request for proposals, we seek to catalyze inter and trans-disciplinary, early-stage and translational research that increases insight into; measures; or addresses the effects of environmental exposures on health.

Eligibility: The project team must have at least two and up to three Primary Investigators. While there must be a PI with an appointment in Medicine and one with an appointment in Pratt, they should be joined by a faculty member from Nicholas, or one of the Medicine or Pratt PIs should have a joint appointment in Nicholas. PIs may be regular rank or non-regular rank. If the faculty member does not have and/or requires permission to dedicate time to the project or space to conduct the research, this must be obtained prior to submission. Additionally, we strongly encourage collaborations with extramural partners. For details on how to operationalize these collaborations, please contact us, as MEDx funds cannot be provided in the form of grant support for extramural collaborators.

Level of Study: Research

Type: Grant

Value: US$50,000

Length of Study: 1 year

Country of Study: United States of America

No. of awards offered: 3

Closing Date: 18 May

Additional Information: researchfunding.duke.edu/medx-engineering-environment-and-health-2022-request-proposals-duke-internal-funding-duke-faculty

Post-Doctoral Training in Genomic Medicine Research

Purpose: The Duke Center for Applied Genomics and Precision Medicine is pleased to announce a two-year post-doctoral training program in genomic medicine. This unique program will provide training in a fast-growing field marked by the advent of new technologies, increased use of clinical genomic medicine, and large-scale federally- and privately-funded research efforts. The Post-Doctoral Training Program in Genomic Medicine is supported by a Ruth L. Kirschstein Institutional National Research Service Award (T32).

Eligibility: 1. MDs who have completed clinical training in a non-genetics related discipline, such as internal medicine (with or without subspecialty training), pediatrics, surgery, etc., and are eligible for board certification in their discipline. 2. PhDs who have decided to focus their careers on clinical or translational research related to genomic medicine. 3. Post-doctoral trainees must have received, as of the beginning date of the appointment, a PhD, M.D., D.D.S., or comparable doctoral degree from an accredited domestic or foreign institution. Comparable doctoral degrees include, but are not limited to, the following D.M.D., D.C., D.O., D.V.M., O.D., D.P.M., Sc.D., Eng.D., Dr. P.H., D.N.Sc., D.P.T., Pharm.D., N.D. (Doctor of Naturopathy), D.S.W., Psy.D, as well as a doctoral degree in nursing research. Documentation by an authorized official of the degree-granting institution certifying that all degree requirements have been met prior to the beginning date of the training appointment is acceptable. Individuals in postgraduate clinical training, who wish to interrupt their studies for a year or more to engage in full-time research training before completing their formal training programs, are also eligible. Applicants must be a U.S. Citizen, noncitizen national, or have permanent resident status.

Level of Study: Graduate, Postdoctorate

Type: Fellowship

Study Establishment: Duke University

Country of Study: Any country

Closing Date: 1 April

Additional Information: researchfunding.duke.edu/post-doctoral-training-genomic-medicine-research

Research@Pickett Community Outreach and Engagement Voucher Program

Eligibility: Permanent, full-time, Duke faculty, including professional and non-tenure track; open to all levels of investigators, but early stage investigators are encouraged to apply. SOM PI eligibility requirements are located here: myresearchpath.duke.edu/procedure-requesting-eligibility-serve-p.... Non-faculty members must apply for PI eligibility for any externally funded project and receive approval from ORA.

Level of Study: Faculty

Type: Grant

Value: US$195,000

Frequency: Annual

Country of Study: United States of America
No. of awards offered: 4
Closing Date: 1 April
Additional Information: researchfunding.duke.edu/researchpickett-community-outreach-and-engagement-voucher-program

Ruth K. Broad Biomedical Research Foundation – Ellen Luken Student Awards

Eligibility: Eligibility: PhD or MD/PhD students who work in the field of neuroscience in basic science or clinical departments in the Duke School of Medicine. Students should be in their third year of study or beyond; all areas of neuroscience will be considered, with particular encouragement to students whose work has relevance to neurodegeneration and, specifically, Alzheimer's disease. Students applying for funding must specify the extracurricular opportunity they will pursue, however it is not necessary to have secured acceptance or admission prior to seeking an Ellen Luken Student Award. These awards may be approved conditionally with a commitment that the student will receive the funding upon final acceptance into the chosen opportunity.
Level of Study: Doctorate
Type: Grant
Value: US$1,500
Country of Study: United States of America
Closing Date: 1 April
Additional Information: mangalaskitchen.blogspot.in/2013/06/kothamalli-pudina-combo-biriyani.html

School of Medicine (SoM) Bridge Funding Program

Eligibility: 1. Candidates include SoM faculty members who were unsuccessful with a first submission of a competitive renewal of an independent investigator award (NIH R01 or equivalent) or a program project grant. 2. Applications that were unsuccessful but received a priority score will be most competitive, and the candidate must effectively address the concerns outlined in the summary statement. 3. Applications for bridge funding of an unsuccessful (A1) resubmission of a competitive renewal will be considered if: the applicant received a strong priority score, and 4. the applicant effectively describes how the summary statement will guide development of a new application. 5. Applications for bridge funding of an unsuccessful first submission of a new R01 proposal will be considered only if: 5a. the new proposal represents replacement funding for a previous R01-level, NIH-funded line of investigation that has run its course within the last 2 years, or 5b. the applicant has completed a K08,

K23, K12, or K0l grant or an equivalent NIH K grant intended for transition to independence and has received a priority score on the subsequent R0l submission. 6. An application will not be considered by the Committee if the expired grant to which it is linked has already received bridge funds. 7. Two separate applications by co-PIs on the same R01 will not reviewed.
Type: Grant
Value: Up to US$100,000 per lapsed R0l grant or up to US$200,000 per lapsed P0l grant
Country of Study: United States of America
Closing Date: 15 April
Additional Information: researchfunding.duke.edu/school-medicine-som-bridge-funding-program-duke-internal-funding-duke-faculty-only

Special Call for Proposals for Bass Connections Projects: Democracy and Governance in a Polarized World

Eligibility: 1. Proposals may be submitted by faculty, staff, graduate students, postdocs and trainees/fellows, but all projects must have at least one faculty team leader. 2. Individuals may propose more than one project but should not serve as a team leader on more than one project per year, unless those projects each have another committed co-leader who is a regular rank faculty member. Individuals may serve as a team contributor on more than one project. 3. Team leaders are expected to be regularly available (i.e., not on sabbatical away from Durham or extended leave) during the year in which the project would take place (2022-2023), and at least one team leader is expected to attend each team meeting. We recommend that faculty notify their department chairs of their intent to apply, in order to help with departmental planning. 4. Teams should provide opportunities for at least five students (both graduate and undergraduate) to participate. 5. Bass Connections teams are expected to meet at least weekly. During the academic year, students receive academic credit as the default mechanism (via a tutorial or independent study). Student compensation during the academic year is generally reserved for students in leadership roles on a team.
Level of Study: Faculty
Type: Grant
Value: US$5,000 and US$25,000.
Length of Study: 1 year
Frequency: Annual
Country of Study: United States of America
Closing Date: 21 March
Additional Information: researchfunding.duke.edu/special-call-proposals-bass-connections-projects-democracy-and-governance-polarized-world

Summer Research Fellowship

Eligibility: 1. Applicants must be in good academic standing. 2. Applicants must be completing their first or second academic year of study. 3. Applicants must be currently enrolled in a Ph.D. program that participates in the guaranteed Summer Research Fellowship program (see below). Generally this will exclude departments and programs that already offer 11 or 12 months of summer support(At this time, Ph.D. students in classical studies and in the Nicholas School of the Environment are not eligible for guaranteed summer research fellowships from The Graduate School. Ph.D. students in ecology and environmental policy, which are partially funded by the Nicholas School of the Environment, are eligible.)

Level of Study: Predoctorate
Type: Fellowship
Value: a summer stipend of US$8,250
Frequency: Annual
Country of Study: United States of America
Closing Date: 31 March
Additional Information: researchfunding.duke.edu/summer-research-fellowship-first-and-second-year-phd-students-duke-internal-funding-duke-grad

The Prof. Rahamimoff Travel Grants Program

Purpose: The Prof. Rahamimoff Travel Grants Program is open to PhD students doing research that requires facilities or expertise not available in their home countries. Each trip will be for a maximum length of 2 months

Eligibility: 1. Applicants must be U.S. or Israeli citizens. 2. Applicants must be conducting supervised research towards a PhD in an accredited higher education institution, or in a non-profit research institution (government or other, including hospitals). 3. The BSF will only accept applications that are in the scientific fields it supports. 4. Applicants must be 35 years old or younger.

Level of Study: Graduate, Postdoctorate
Type: Grant
Value: US$4,000
Frequency: Annual
Country of Study: Any country
Application Procedure: Applications will be evaluated by a special committee on the basis of their merit in light of the overall aim of the program, and the qualifications of the candidates. In particular, the significance of the trip to the candidate's research will be estimated. One of the criteria frequently used by the panel is the stage of the research program. Trips planned very early or very late in the research program are often not approved
Closing Date: 7 May

Funding: Private
Additional Information: www.instrumentl.com/grants/afbsf-travel-grant-programme

For further information contact:

Email: fundopps@duke.edu

Durham University

Stockton Road, Durham DH1 3LE, United Kingdom.

Tel: (44) 191 334 2000
Website: www.dur.ac.uk/
Contact: The Palatine Centre Durham University

A globally outstanding centre of teaching and research excellence, a collegiate community of extraordinary people, a unique and historic setting - Durham is a university like no other.

British Council Scholarships for Women in STEM

Eligibility: 1. Be a woman (cis-gendered or trans) or identify as non-binary; 2. Be a passport holder and permanent resident of one of the eligible countries - ~Bangladesh, India, Nepal, Pakistan, Sri Lanka; 3. Have submitted an academic application to study on one of the eligible Durham University postgraduate programmes, as listed above; 4. Have completed all components of an undergraduate degree that will enable you to gain entry onto a postgraduate programme at Durham University by the time you submit your application and be due to start your postgraduate programme in the UK during 2023; 5. Have not previously studied at degree level or higher in the UK or lived recently in the UK; 6. Meet the English Language requirements of your chosen Masters programme at Durham University; 7. Demonstrate your case for financial support; 8. Return to your country of citizenship for a minimum of two years after your scholarship award has ended

Type: Award
Value: Full payment of tuition fees, 12 months stipend, A return economy class flight, Visa application fee, Insurance, NHS surcharge, Other study related costs
Length of Study: 1 year
Country of Study: United Kingdom
No. of awards offered: 5
Closing Date: 18 March

Additional Information: www.durham.ac.uk/study/scholar ships/postgraduate-scholarships-2022-entry/british-council-scholarships-for-women-in-stem/

For further information contact:

Email: international.internal@durham.ac.uk

Chevening Scholarships

Eligibility: Applicants must be a citizen of a Chevening-eligible country, and intend to return there for a minimum of 2 years after your Chevening Award has finished. For specific eligibility criteria please refer to the Chevening webpage: www.chevening.org/news/applications-for-2020-2021-chevening-scholarships-open/
Level of Study: Postgraduate
Type: Scholarship
Value: tuition fees, a living allowance at a set rate (for one individual), an economy class return airfare to the UK, additional grants to cover essential expenditure
Length of Study: 1 year
Frequency: Annual
Country of Study: United Kingdom
No. of awards offered: 10
Closing Date: 2 November
Additional Information: www.durham.ac.uk/study/schol arships/postgraduate-scholarships-2022-entry/chevening-scholarships/

Chinese Scholarships Council

Eligibility: 1. Be citizens and permanent residents of the People's Republic of China at the time of application. Chinese students studying overseas may also be eligible for application subject to CSC policies 2. Hold an unconditional offer to study for a PhD degree at Durham commencing in October 2022, including English language requirements at the time of application to the CSC 3. Satisfy entry required as outlined by the CSC at the time of application 4. Successful candidates are required to return home upon completion of their studies.
Level of Study: Doctorate
Type: Scholarship
Value: Full payment of tuition fees, Annual allowance, Overseas student health cover, Return airfare, Visa application fees.
Length of Study: 4 years
Frequency: Annual
Country of Study: United Kingdom
No. of awards offered: 20
Closing Date: 30 April

Additional Information: www.durham.ac.uk/study/scholar ships/postgraduate-scholarships-2022-entry/chinese-scholar ships-council/

Commonwealth Masters Scholarships

Eligibility: 1. Be a citizen of or have been granted refugee status by an eligible Commonwealth country, or be a British Protected Person 2. Be permanently resident in an eligible Commonwealth country 3. Be available to start your academic studies in the UK by the start of the UK academic year in September 2023 4. By September 2023, hold a first degree of at least upper second class (2:1) honours standard, or a second class degree (2:2) and a relevant postgraduate qualification (usually a Master's degree). The CSC would not normally fund a second UK Master's degree. If you are applying for a second UK Master's degree, you will need to provide justification as to why you wish to undertake this study 5. Be unable to afford to study in the UK without this scholarship Have provided all supporting documentation in the required format
Type: Scholarship
Value: Approved airfare from your home country to the UK and return, Approved tuition fees, Stipend (living allowance) at the rate of £1,133 per month, or £1,390 per month, Warm clothing allowance, Thesis grant towards the cost of preparing a thesis or dissertation,
Length of Study: 1 year
Frequency: Annual
Country of Study: United Kingdom
Closing Date: 1 November
Additional Information: cscuk.fcdo.gov.uk/scholarships/commonwealth-masters-scholarships/

Commonwealth Scholarships for Developing Countries

Eligibility: Applicants must be a citizen of a developing Commonwealth country.
Level of Study: Doctorate, Postgraduate
Type: Scholarship
Frequency: Annual
Country of Study: United Kingdom
Closing Date: 1 November
Additional Information: www.durham.ac.uk/study/scholar ships/postgraduate-scholarships-2022-entry/commonwealth-scholarships-for-developing-countries/

Commonwealth Shared Scholarships - PGT

Eligibility: 1. Be a citizen of or be granted refugee status by an eligible Commonwealth country, or be a British Protected

Person 2. Be permanently or continually resident in an eligible Commonwealth country 3. By 1st August 2023, hold a first degree of at least upper second class (2:1) standard, or lower second class level plus a relevant postgraduate qualification usually a Masters degree 4. The CSC cannot assess work experience in lieu of this minimum academic qualification 5. Not have studied or worked for one (academic) year or more in a developed country 6. Be unable to afford to study in the UK without this scholarship

Level of Study: Postgraduate

Type: Scholarship

Value: Full payment of approved tuition fees Airfares to and from the UK (booked in line with CSC policy) Excess baggage allowance on return home, up to CSC rate A stipend of £1,133.00 per month Warm clothing allowance of £439.00 Tuberculosis test fees (where required by the UK) For scholars who are widowed, divorced, or a single parent: child allowance of £485 per month for the first child, and £120 per month for the second and third child

Length of Study: 1 year

Frequency: Annual

Country of Study: United Kingdom

No. of awards offered: 5

Closing Date: 20 December

Additional Information: www.durham.ac.uk/study/scholar ships/postgraduate-scholarships-2022-entry/commonwealth-shared-scholarships/

Commonwealth Split-Site Doctoral Scholarships

Eligibility: To apply for these scholarships, prospective Scholars must: 1. Be a citizen of or have been granted refugee status by an eligible Commonwealth country, or be a British Protected Person 2. Be permanently resident in an eligible Commonwealth country 3. Be registered for a PhD at a university in an eligible Commonwealth country by the time your scholarship starts (September 2023) 4. Ensure that an institutional or departmental link exists between your home university and your proposed UK university. This link must be greater than simply a collaboration between individuals – see section on 'Tenure and placement' for further details. Both supervisors must provide a supporting statement which provides further details of the link to ensure your application is eligible 5. Be available to start your academic studies in the UK in September 2023 6. By September 2023, hold a first degree of at least upper second class (2:1) honours standard, or a second-class degree and a relevant postgraduate qualification (usually a Master's degree) 7. Be unable to afford to study in the UK without this scholarship

Type: Scholarship

Value: Approved airfare from your home country to the UK and return, Approved tuition fees, Stipend (living allowance) at the rate of £1,133 per month, or £1,390 per month

Length of Study: 1 year

Country of Study: United Kingdom

Closing Date: 17 February

Additional Information: cscuk.fcdo.gov.uk/scholarships/commonwealth-split-site-scholarships-for-low-and-middle-income-countries/

Durham Palestine Educational Trust

Eligibility: Geographical Criteria: 1. Palestinian Occupied Territories. For specific scholarship eligibility criteria please refer to the Durham Palestine Educational Trust webpage: www.dur.ac.uk/durham.palestine/scholarships/

Type: Scholarship

Value: Full tuition fees covered by Durham University (excluding MBA programmes)

Length of Study: 1 year

Country of Study: United Kingdom

No. of awards offered: 2

Closing Date: 1 January

Additional Information: www.durham.ac.uk/study/scholar ships/postgraduate-scholarships-2022-entry/durham-palestine-educational-trust/

For further information contact:

Email: palestine.education@durham.ac.uk

Durham University Arts Management Group

Eligibility: 1. Read the Arts Management COVID-19 Guidance 2. If you receive support for an activity you must submit your final accounts and/or your report before an additional application can be considered 3. Due to funding restrictions, the Arts Management Group are unable to approve applications for consumable items 4. Funding will be provided for personal development rather than career or academic development 5. Retrospective applications will not normally be considered i.e. activities that are scheduled to take place before each terms outcome notification date

Level of Study: Postgraduate

Type: Scholarship

Frequency: Annual

Country of Study: United Kingdom

Closing Date: 2 May

Additional Information: www.durham.ac.uk/study/scholar ships/current-students/durham-university-arts-management-group/

Fulbright - Durham University Award

Eligibility: For specific eligibility criteria please refer to the Fulbright website for further information. Applicants must be US citizens resident anywhere except the United Kingdom and hold or expect to receive a Bachelors degree (or equivalent professional training or experience) in a relevant area before departure to the UK.
Type: Award
Value: Full payment of tuition fees £12,000 towards general maintenance costs (accommodation, travel, subsistence), Organisational memberships Invitation to European Fulbright Conferences, Networking Opportunities.
Length of Study: 1 year
Country of Study: United Kingdom
No. of awards offered: 2
Closing Date: 12 October
Additional Information: www.durham.ac.uk/study/scholarships/postgraduate-scholarships-2022-entry/fulbright-durham-university-award/

For further information contact:

Email: scholarships.advice@durham.ac.uk

Hatfield Lioness Scholarship

Purpose: The aim of the Hatfield Lioness Scholarship is to enable a female student from a developing country where access to tertiary education is limited to benefit from undertaking postgraduate study at the Durham University.
Eligibility: 1. Applicants must have applied for and been offered an unconditional place on their chosen master's programme by June 2023. 2. Applicants must not be in receipt of any other scholarship to fund their postgraduate studies. 3. Applicants must be female.
Level of Study: Postgraduate
Type: Scholarship
Value: Full payment of University tuition fees, Stipend for living expenses, One return economy air ticket from the home country to the UK, and the cost of return, travel between the UK airport and Durham City Fully funded, self-catered, mixed accommodation at Hatfield College 'Settling in allowance' on arrival Cost of UK visa and the UK Health surcharge
Frequency: Annual
Country of Study: United Kingdom
No. of awards offered: 1
Closing Date: 31 March
Additional Information: www.durham.ac.uk/colleges-and-student-experience/colleges/hatfield/college-life/hatfield-lioness-scholarship/

For further information contact:

Email: hatfield.trust@durham.ac.uk

Internships and Industry Fund for Computer Science

Purpose: The aim of the fund is to support students with some of the costs associated with completing an internship, placement or similar activity, both in the UK and internationally.
Eligibility: Be enrolled as an active student on a Computer Science or Natural Sciences programme AND have a household income of £42,875 or less, as assessed by Student Finance England (or equivalent) OR Be enrolled as an active student on a Computer Science or Natural Sciences programme AND be applying to support a Global Internship or similar opportunity.
Type: Scholarship
Value: £1,500
Country of Study: United Kingdom
No. of awards offered: 20 to 30
Closing Date: 24 June
Additional Information: www.durham.ac.uk/study/scholarships/current-students/internships-and-industry-fund-computer-science/

Marshall Scholarship

Eligibility: Open only to United States citizens who (at the time they take up their Scholarship) hold a first degree from an accredited four-year college or university in the United States with a minimum GPA of 3.7. To qualify for awards tenable from October 2023, candidates must have graduated from their undergraduate college or university after April 2020.
Level of Study: Postgraduate
Type: Scholarship
Value: University fees, cost of living expenses, annual book grant, thesis grant, research and daily travel grants, fares to and from the United States and, where applicable, a contribution towards the support of a dependent spouse.
Length of Study: 2 year
Frequency: Annual
Country of Study: United Kingdom
No. of awards offered: 50
Closing Date: September
Additional Information: www.marshallscholarship.org/the-scholarship

Master in Business Analytics Scholarships

Eligibility: 1. have an impressive academic record 2. have the potential to contribute and enrich all aspects of the Masters programme and the diverse academic and cultural profile of the Masters class. 3. can demonstrate involvement in volunteering and/or community support activity 4. can demonstrate how they have provided a supportive, inclusive environment and/or built a culture of belonging, by actively inviting the contribution and participation of all people. Examples can include projects, group work, events etc. 5. can tell us how, as a global citizen, they will create, share and use their knowledge to deliver equitable and sustainable futures around the world. 6. have the potential to become an outstanding future alumni ambassador and contribute positively back to the School, organisations and communities.

Level of Study: Postgraduate

Type: Scholarship

Value: Up to £8,000 off tuition fees

Frequency: Annual

Country of Study: United Kingdom

No. of awards offered: 12

Closing Date: October

Additional Information: www.durham.ac.uk/business/programmes/masters/scholarships/masters-business-analytics-scholarships/

Master of Energy Systems Management (MESM) Scholarships

Eligibility: 1. have an impressive academic record 2. have the potential to contribute to and enrich the diverse academic and cultural profile of the MESM class 3. can demonstrate significant involvement in volunteering and/or community support activity 4. can demonstrate how they have provided a supportive, inclusive environment and/or built a culture of belonging in their community, by actively inviting the contribution and participation of all people. Examples can include projects, group work, events etc. 5. can tell us how they will create, share, and use their knowledge to deliver equitable and sustainable futures around the world 6. can demonstrate commitment to addressing the major issues of climate change that confront the world 7. can show us how they have the potential to become an outstanding future alumni ambassador and contribute positively back to Durham University, its student organisations, and communities.

Level of Study: Postgraduate

Type: Scholarship

Value: £6,625 (25% off the tuition fees)

Frequency: Annual

Country of Study: United Kingdom

No. of awards offered: 8

Closing Date: October

Additional Information: www.durham.ac.uk/business/programmes/masters/scholarships/mesm-scholarships/

Masters Achievement Scholarships

Eligibility: 1. have studied their full undergraduate degree, or equivalent, at a UK based institution 2. have an impressive academic record have the potential to contribute and enrich all aspects of the Masters programme and the diverse academic and cultural profile of the Masters class 3. can demonstrate involvement in volunteering and/or community support activity 4. can demonstrate how they have provided a supportive, inclusive environment and/or built a culture of belonging, by actively inviting the contribution and participation of all people. Examples can include projects, group work, events etc. 5. can tell us how, as a global citizen, they will create, share and use their knowledge to deliver equitable and sustainable futures around the world. 6. have the potential to become an outstanding future alumni ambassador and contribute positively back to the School, organisations and communities.

Level of Study: Postgraduate

Type: Scholarship

Value: Up to £7,500 off tuition fees

Frequency: Annual

Country of Study: United Kingdom

Closing Date: October

Additional Information: www.durham.ac.uk/business/programmes/masters/scholarships/masters-achievement-scholarships/

Masters International Scholarships

Eligibility: 1. have studied their undergraduate degree, or equivalent, at an overseas institution (non-UK based) 2. have an impressive academic record 3. have the potential to contribute and enrich all aspects of the Masters programme and the diverse academic and cultural profile of the Masters class 4. can demonstrate involvement in volunteering and/or community support activity 5. can demonstrate how they have provided a supportive, inclusive environment and/or built a culture of belonging, by actively inviting the contribution and participation of all people. Examples can include projects, group work, events etc. 6. can tell us how, as a global citizen, they will create, share and use their knowledge to deliver equitable and sustainable futures around the world. 7. have the potential to become an outstanding future alumni ambassador and contribute positively back to the School, organisations and communities.

Level of Study: Postgraduate

Type: Scholarship

Value: Up to £7,500 off tuition fees

Frequency: Annual

Country of Study: United Kingdom

No. of awards offered: 40 plus

Closing Date: October
Additional Information: www.durham.ac.uk/business/programmes/masters/scholarships/masters-international-scholarships/

Queen's Transfer Fund

Eligibility: The University has agreed that special financial support for students will be made available to those who are suffering financial hardship in any of the three areas below: 1. Additional accommodation costs between Queen's Campus and Durham/Newcastle 2. Additional travel expenses incurred by having to travel to new study locations 3. Childcare/other costs specific to individual circumstances.
Type: Scholarship
Value: payment equivalent to the average additional cost of accommodation, financial support for travelling expenses based on appropriate transport links, , Childcare/Other: On a case by case basis, financial support may be forthcoming to students.
Country of Study: United Kingdom
Closing Date: 17 December
Additional Information: www.durham.ac.uk/study/scholarships/current-students/queens-transfer-fund/

For further information contact:

Email: funded.students@durham.ac.uk

Ruth First Scholarship

Eligibility: 1. Full payment of tuition fees 2. Stipend for living expenses - 12 monthly payments 3. One return air ticket from the home country to the UK and the cost of return travel between the UK airport and Durham City 4. Fully funded accommodation and meals at St Chad's College 5. 'Settling in allowance' on arrival 6. A contribution towards the cost of a UK visa and the UK Health surcharge
Level of Study: Postgraduate
Type: Scholarship
Value: Full payment of tuition fees, Stipend for living expenses - 12 monthly payments, One return air ticket from the home country to the UK and the cost of return travel between the UK airport and Durham City Fully funded accommodation and meals at St Chad's College 'Settling in allowance' on arrival A contribution towards the cost of a UK visa and the UK Health surcharge
Length of Study: 1 year
Frequency: Annual
Country of Study: United Kingdom
Closing Date: 24 March

Additional Information: www.durham.ac.uk/study/scholarships/postgraduate-scholarships-2022-entry/ruth-first-scholarship/

For further information contact:

Email: m.p.thompson@durham.ac.uk

Said Scholarship

Eligibility: For specific eligibility criteria please refer to the Said Foundation website for further information. Geographical Criteria: Applications are restricted to candidates who are: Lebanese, Jordanian, Palestinian (including Palestinians inside Israel), Syrian.
Level of Study: Postgraduate
Type: Scholarship
Value: full tuition fees full maintenance/living costs for the duration of your course an arrival allowance a thesis allowance visa fees IHS fees one economy return flight
Length of Study: 1 year
Frequency: Annual
Country of Study: United Kingdom
Closing Date: 29 October
Additional Information: www.durham.ac.uk/study/scholarships/postgraduate-scholarships-2022-entry/said-foundation-scholarships/

For further information contact:

Email: scholarships.advice@durham.ac.uk

Santander Scholarships

Eligibility: In order to be eligible for support, students will come from families who have a household income* level of £42,875 or below per annum and who are able to provide confirmation of their 2023/24 student loan entitlement together with appropriate evidence to support their request for financial support. If your income has not been assessed by the Student Loans Company you will need to provide evidence of your household income in the form of documents such as: 1. 3 months payslips 2. Latest annual tax summary document 3. An employment contract 4. Self-employed accounts *Your household income is that of your parent(s), in the household you were living in immediately prior to commencing studies. There are exceptions, which are a) if you are a postgraduate student, b) if you were aged 25, on the first day of the academic year support is being applied for, c) you have been married (even if now separated or divorced), d) you were financially self-supporting for at least three years prior to the commencement of your course, e) you have no living parents or that they cannot be traced/contacted. If any of these exceptions apply, then the household income is determined by your personal income.

Level of Study: Postgraduate
Type: Scholarship
Value: Up to a value of £1,900.00
Length of Study: 1 year
Frequency: Annual
Country of Study: United Kingdom
Closing Date: 31 March
Additional Information: www.durham.ac.uk/study/scholarships/undergraduate-scholarships-2022-entry/santander-scholarships/

Student Employability Fund

Eligibility: In order to be considered for this support, students will come from families who have a household income, as assessed by Student Finance England (or equivalent), of below £42,875 per annum.
Level of Study: Postgraduate
Type: Scholarship
Value: Up to £500
Frequency: Annual
Country of Study: United Kingdom
Closing Date: 18 March
Additional Information: www.durham.ac.uk/study/scholarships/current-students/north-east/

For further information contact:

Email: adelle.fairclough@durham.ac.uk

The Durham MBA (Full-time) Scholarships

Eligibility: 1. can demonstrate they bring outstanding experience, this will include a significant amount of postgraduate work experience in roles demonstrating a high level of managerial responsibility 2. have an impressive academic record – candidates with only the minimum of years work experience required must include extra-curricular activities in their application 3. have the potential to contribute to and enrich all aspects of the MBA programme, including the diverse academic and cultural profile of the MBA cohort 4. can demonstrate involvement in volunteering and/or community support activity 5. can demonstrate how they have provided a supportive, inclusive environment and/or built a culture of belonging, by actively inviting the contribution and participation of all people ie projects, group work, events etc. 6. can tell us, as a global citizen, how they will

create, share and use their knowledge to deliver equitable and sustainable futures around the world. 7. have the potential to become an outstanding future alumni ambassador and contribute positively back to the School, organisations and communities.

Level of Study: Postgraduate
Type: Scholarship
Value: Executive Dean's £17,500 (Up to 3) Executive Dean's - Women in Business £17,500 (Up to 5) Achievement Up to £15,000 (Up to 40)
Frequency: Annual
Country of Study: United Kingdom
No. of awards offered: 48
Closing Date: September
Additional Information: www.durham.ac.uk/business/programmes/mba/scholarships/the-durham-mba-full-time-scholarships/

The Durham MBA (Online) Scholarships

Eligibility: 1. can demonstrate they bring outstanding experience; this will include a significant amount of postgraduate work experience in roles demonstrating a high level of managerial responsibility. 2. have an impressive academic record - MBA candidates with only the minimum number of years work experience required must include extra-curricular activities in their application. 3. have the potential to contribute to and enrich all aspects of the MBA programme, including the diverse academic and cultural profile of the MBA cohort. 4. can demonstrate involvement in volunteering and/or community support activity. 5. can demonstrate how they have provided a supportive, inclusive environment and/or built a culture of belonging, by actively inviting the contribution and participation of all people ie projects, group work, events etc. 6. can tell us, as a global citizen, how they will create, share and use their knowledge to deliver equitable and sustainable futures around the world. 7. have the potential to become an outstanding future alumni ambassador and contribute positively back to the School, organisations and communities.

Level of Study: Postgraduate
Type: Scholarship
Value: Executive Dean's £13,000 (Up to 2) Executive Dean's - Women in Business £13,000 (Up to 4) Achievement £8,000 (Up to 17)
Frequency: Annual
Country of Study: United Kingdom
No. of awards offered: 23
Closing Date: 4 March
Additional Information: www.durham.ac.uk/business/programmes/mba/scholarships/the-durham-mba-online–blended-scholarships/

The Durham University Business School's Dean's Scholarship

Purpose: Durham University Business School Dean's Scholarship - awarded to an exceptional candidate who can demonstrate significant academic and extra-curricular achievements

Eligibility: Applicants will be considered based upon: Academic achievement, Work or voluntary experience relevant to the programme for which they have applied, Any additional skills, experience or extra-curricular activities that will add value and indicate that they will make a significant contribution to the cohort on the programme or the Business School. Open to applicants for MSc Programmes (excluding MSc Business Analytics)

Level of Study: Postgraduate

Type: Scholarship

Value: Up to £12,500

Frequency: Annual

Country of Study: Any country

Closing Date: 31 May

Funding: Private

Additional Information: scholarship-positions.com/durham-university-business-school-deans-scholarship-for-international-students-in-uk/2019/01/10/

For further information contact:

Durham University Business School, Mill Hill, Lane Durham DH1 3LB, United Kingdom.

Tel: (44) 191 334 5200
Email: research.admissions@durham.ac.uk

Dutch Ministry of Foreign Affairs

Bezuidenhoutseweg 67, The Hague, PO Box 20061, NL-2500 EB The Hague, the Netherlands.

Tel: (31) 70 3486486
Email: dsi-my@minbuza.nl
Website: www.minbuza.nl
Contact: The Ministry of Foreign Affairs

Dutch foreign policy is driven by the conviction that international cooperation brings peace and promotes security, prosperity, and justice. It is bound by the obligation to promote Dutch interests abroad as effectively and efficiently as possible. To do so, the Netherlands needs a worldwide network of embassies, consulates, and permanent representations to international organizations. The activities, composition, and size of each mission depend on its host country and region. Embassies and consulates-bilateral missions-concern themselves with relations between the Netherlands and other countries.

Netherlands Fellowship Programmes

Purpose: To support mid-career professionals nominated by their employers

Eligibility: Open to candidates who are employed by an organization other than a large industrial, commercial and/or multinational firm, must be nationals of one of the 57 selected countries (see 'Eligible countries'), must declare that they will return to their home country immediately after they complete the master programme, must have gained admission to a TU/e master course, which is on the NFP course list and have sufficient mastery of the English language. Priority is given to female candidates and to candidates coming from sub-Saharan Africa

Level of Study: Postgraduate

Type: Fellowships

Value: Full-cost scholarship (including international travel, monthly subsistence allowance, tuition fee, books, and health insurance)

Length of Study: 2 years

Frequency: Annual

Country of Study: Netherlands

Application Procedure: Applicants must apply for an NFP fellowship through the Netherlands embassy or consulate in their own country by completing an NFP Application Form and submitting it together with all the required documents and information to the embassy or consulate. Then the Embassy checks and sends the forms to the Nuffic checks. Nuffic decides how many fellowships will be available for each program and sends TU/e the list of NFP candidates

Closing Date: June

Funding: Government

Contributor: Dutch Ministry of Foreign Affairs

Additional Information: Eligible countries: Afghanistan, Albania, Armenia, Autonomous Palestinian Territories, Bangladesh, Benin, Bhutan, Bolivia, Bosnia–Hercegovina, Brazil, Burkina Faso, Cambodia, Cape Verde, China, Colombia, Costa Rica, Cuba, Ecuador, Egypt, El Salvador, Eritrea, Ethiopia, Georgia, Ghana, Guatemala, Guinea–Bissau, Honduras, India, Indonesia, Iran, Ivory Coast, Jordan, Kenya,

Macedonia, Mali, Moldova, Mongolia, Mozambique, Namibia, Nepal, Nicaragua, Nigeria, Pakistan, Peru, Philippines, Rwanda, Senegal, South Africa, Sri Lanka, Suriname, Tanzania, Thailand, Uganda, Vietnam, Yemen, Zambia, Zimbabwe. For a more detailed list of criteria, please check website www.scholars4dev.com/7672/netherlands-fellowship-program/

For further information contact:

Tel: (31) 40 247 4690
Fax: (31) 40 244 1692
Email: io@remove-this.tue.nl

E

Earthwatch Institute

1380 Soldiers Field Rd., Suite 2700, Boston, MA 02135, United States of America.

Tel: (1) 800 776 0188
Email: info@earthwatch.org
Website: earthwatch.org/

Since its founding in 1971, Earthwatch has been taking action to address global change through a time-tested model of citizen science and community engagement. By pairing citizen science volunteers from all sectors of society with researchers around the world, Earthwatch teams have helped to safeguard critical habitats, conserve biodiversity, and promote the sustainable use of natural resources.

Earthwatch Field Research Grants

Purpose: Earthwatch funds field-based scientific research that is rigorous, relevant, and impactful. Earthwatch-funded projects conduct research around the globe. All research must incorporate citizen-scientist participation in data collection. Citizen-scientist participants are recruited by Earthwatch. Requests for pre-proposals are distributed annually. Pre-proposals must be submitted by the PI. All PIs must have a PhD and an affiliation with a university, government agency, or science-focused NGO.
Eligibility: All proposals must be submitted by the Principal Investigator (PI). All PIs must have a PhD and an affiliation with a university, government agency, or NGO
Level of Study: Doctorate, Postdoctorate, Postgraduate, Research
Type: Grant
Value: US$20,000–80,000 annually

Length of Study: Successful proposals are funded for 3 years, subject to passing an annual performance review
Frequency: Annual
Study Establishment: Research sites
Country of Study: Any country
Application Procedure: Requests for proposals are distributed in the spring. Applicants must submit a pre-proposal for consideration. Please see the Earthwatch website (earthwatch.org) for more information
Closing Date: 31 December
Funding: Corporation, Foundation, Private
Contributor: Volunteers' contributions
Additional Information: For additional project requirements and information: earthwatch.org/research-funding www.archaeological.org/grant/field-research-grants/

École Normale Supérieure (ENS)

Tel: (33) 1 44 32 28 01
Email: ens-international@ens.fr
Website: www.ens.fr/admission/selection-internationale/?lang=en

École Normale Supérieure (ENS) allows the most promising international students, either in Science or in Arts & Humanities, to follow a three-year Masters Degree at the University.

École Normale Supérieure International Selection Scholarships

Level of Study: Postgraduate
Type: Scholarship

© Springer Nature Limited 2022
Palgrave Macmillan (ed.), *The Grants Register 2023*,
https://doi.org/10.1057/978-1-349-96053-8

Value: monthly grant of €1,000 for 3 years and accomodation facility provided
Length of Study: 3 years
Frequency: Annual
Country of Study: France
Application Procedure: You must fill and validate the initial application form which will be available at the official website when the application opens. Within 2 days, you will receive an email to activate an account on Dematec, an application platform where you must upload the required documents
Closing Date: 31 October
Contributor: Ècole Normale Supérieure in Paris, France
Additional Information: For more details, please visit official scholarship website: greatyop.com/ens-international-selection-scholarship/

For further information contact:

Email: ens-international@ens.fr

École Normale Supérieure de Lyon

15 parvis René Descartes, BP 7000, F-69342 Lyon Cedex 07, France.

Tel: (33) 4 37 37 60 00
Website: www.ens-lyon.fr/en/
Contact: ENS de Lyon

The École Normale Supérieure de Lyon is an elite French public institution that trains professors, researchers, senior civil servants as well as business and political leaders. Students choose their courses and split their time between training and research in sciences and humanities. Built on the tradition of the ENS de Fontenay-Saint-Cloud, founded in 1880, the ENS de Lyon also focuses on educational research. It is a symbol of French Republican meritocracy and it remains committed today to disseminating knowledge to the widest audience and to promoting equal opportunity.

Ampère & MILYON Excellence Scholarships for International Students

Purpose: The ENS de Lyon and its partners offer scholarships for excellent international students to enrol in its Masters programs in the Exact Sciences, the Arts, and Human and Social Sciences
Eligibility: Priority to students coming from abroad. Candidate for admission in Masters Year 1 provide proof that you

have obtained a Licence (equivalent to 180 ECTS European credits) or an equivalent diploma/level. Candidate for admission in Masters Year 2 provide proof that you have successfully reached Masters Year 1 level (equivalent to 240 ECTS European credits) or have attained an equivalent diploma/level
Level of Study: Graduate
Type: Scholarship
Value: €1,000 per month or in addition to another scholarship to reach a maximum of 1000 €/month (e.g. a bursary of the French Embassy in Chile)
Length of Study: 1–2 years
Frequency: Annual
Study Establishment: Masters program in Advanced Mathematics, Masters in Fundamental Computer Science
Country of Study: France
Application Procedure: Complete and submit the online application form.
Closing Date: 8 January
Funding: Government, Private
Additional Information: Please note : before beginning your application, read carefully all information and documents requested, and choose your Master's program www.ens-lyon.fr/en/studies/academic-programs/bachelor-masters/biosciences-and-modeling-complex-systems. www.ens-lyon.fr/en/studies/admissions/application-masters-degrees-scholarships

For further information contact:

Email: ampere.scholarship@ens-lyon.fr

Ampère Excellence Scholarships for International Students

Purpose: The Ampère Scholarships of Excellence offer scholarships for excellent international students with the opportunity to pursue one of the eligible Masters programs offered at ENS de Lyon
Eligibility: You must be a foreign national. Born after January, 1st 1997 (26 years maximum). Candidate for admission in Masters Year 1 provide proof that you have obtained a Licence (equivalent to 180 ECTS European credits) or an equivalent diploma/level. Candidate for admission in Masters Year 2 provide proof that you have successfully reached Masters Year 1 level (equivalent to 240 ECTS European credits) or have attained an equivalent diploma/level.
Level of Study: Masters Degree
Type: Scholarship
Value: 1,000€ a month during one or two academic years
Frequency: As available
Country of Study: France

Application Procedure: Complete and submit the online application form.

No. of awards offered: 20

Closing Date: 8 January

Additional Information: For more details, please visit official scholarship website: www.ens-lyon.fr/en/studies/admis sions/application-masters-degrees-scholarships

For further information contact:

Email: ampere.scholarship@ens-lyon.fr

École Normale Supérieure Paris-Saclay

61, avenue du Président Wilson, F-94235 Cachan Cedex, France.

Tel: (33) 1 47 40 20 00

Email: communication@ens-paris-saclay.fr

Website: ens-paris-saclay.fr/en

ENS Paris-Saclay is a training and research centre with an international and multidisciplinary outlook. It offers students an early immersive contact with research and mobilises the laboratories in their training in basic sciences, humanities and social sciences, and engineering sciences.

Monabiphot Masters Scholarships

Purpose: This masters course offers an original qualification in the highly innovative domain of molecular photonics for telecommunications and biology. Skills will be acquired at the strongly interdisciplinary level needed to master emerging technologies and to develop original concepts and applications aiming at novel technological breakthroughs in this domain

Eligibility: Both European Union students and Non-European Union students are eligible to apply

Level of Study: Postgraduate

Type: Scholarship

Value: Non-European Union students €23,500 per year, European Union students €16,000 per year, Additional scholarships for specific regions €47.000

Country of Study: France

Closing Date: 31 January

Additional Information: www.scholarshipsads.com/monabiphot-masters-scholarships-international-students-france-2017/

For further information contact:

LPQM ENS-Cachan, 61, Avenue du President Wilson, F-94235 Cachan Cedex, France.

Tel: (33) 1 47 40 55 60

Email: ledoux@lpqm.ens-cachan.fr

Ecole Polytechnique Federale de Lausanne

EPFL SB B2F-LAB, PH H1 446 (Bâtiment PH), Station 3, CH-1015 Lausanne, Switzerland.

Tel: (41) 21 693 11 11

Website: www.epfl.ch/en/

EPFL is Europe's most cosmopolitan technical university. It welcomes students, professors and collaborators of more than 120 nationalities. EPFL has both a Swiss and international vocation and focuses on three missions: teaching, research and innovation. EPFL collaborates with an important network of partners, including other universities and colleges, secondary schools and gymnasiums, industry and the economy, political circles and the general public, with the aim of having a real impact on society.

Excellence Fellowships

Purpose: EPFL offers a limited number of fellowships at the Master's level to students with outstanding academic records. Some of the fellowships are financed by EPFL directly and others through partnerships with foundations or companies.

Eligibility: Anyone applying to an EPFL master's program is eligible. EPFL grants a limited number of fellowships to the most deserving candidates based solely on their academic records.

Level of Study: Masters Degree

Type: Scholarships

Value: For external applicants, 1. CHF 8,000 per semester (CHF 32,000 for a 2-year degree - 120 credits or CHF 24,000 for a 1.5-year degree - 90 credits). 2. Reservation of an accommodation (student room in a student residence) and for internal applicants (after EPFL bachelor's degree), CHF 5,000 per year (CHF 10,000 for a master)

Country of Study: Switzerland

Application Procedure: For EXTERNAL applications Candidates should apply via the same online form than their application to a master's program by April 15 or December

15. Please note that it is necessary to tick a box indicating that the candidates profile should also be considered for an excellence fellowship. For INTERNAL applications (after EPFL bachelor's degree) Sections might contact students to ask if they want to submit an application for an excellence fellowship. Students can also submit an application to their section by April 30. The application should contain 1. a CV. 2. a motivation letter. 3. a transcript of all grades earned at EPFL. 4. a recommendation letter from the sections' director.

Closing Date: 15 April

Additional Information: If the master at EPFL is a second master's degree, candidates are not eligible for an excellence fellowship. www.epfl.ch/education/studies/en/financing-study/grants/excellence-fellowships/

For further information contact:

Email: e-fellowship@epfl.ch; student.services@epfl.ch

Economic History Association (EHA)

Economic History Association, Department of Economics, University of Wisconsin-La Crosse, 1725 State St., La Crosse, WI 54601, United States of America.

Tel: (1) 608 785 6863
Email: mhaupert@uwlax.edu
Website: eh.net/eha/
Contact: Michael Haupert, Executive Director

The Economic History Association was founded in 1940. Its purpose is to encourage and promote teaching, research, and publication on every phase of economic history, broadly defined, and to encourage and assist in the preservation and administration of the materials for research in economic history.

Alexander Gerschenkron Prize

Purpose: The Alexander Gerschenkron Prize is awarded for the best dissertation in the economic history of an area outside of the United States or Canada completed during the preceding year.

Eligibility: Those who received their Ph.D. between June 1, 2022 and May 30, 2023 are eligible and invited to submit their dissertation for consideration. All candidates for these prizes must be members of the Economic History Association. Dissertations submitted for consideration must be in English. Submission of a dissertation implies that candidates are prepared to attend the 2023 meetings. Presentation of a dissertation summary is required by all finalists.

Level of Study: Postdoctorate
Type: Prize
Frequency: Annual
Country of Study: Any country
Application Procedure: To be considered for this prize, completed dissertations must be submitted by email on or before May 15, 2023. Submissions of more than 5MB should prepare to send a download link rather than an attachment.
Closing Date: 15 May

For further information contact:

Email: cfohlin@emory.edu

Alice Hanson Jones Biennial Prize

Purpose: The Alice Hanson Jones Biennial Prize is awarded every other year for an Outstanding Book on North American Economic History.
Value: US$1,200
Frequency: Annual
Country of Study: Any country
Closing Date: 1 March

For further information contact:

Email: ferrie@northwestern.edu

Annual Meetings Travel and Hotel Subsidies

Purpose: Intended for disseminating preliminary results from graduate thesis work.
Eligibility: Who have presented a poster are eligible for the dissertation session in a subsequent year, but may present a poster session only once during their graduate career. If a student applies both for the dissertation session and to present a poster, and the student is accepted to be part of the dissertation session, a prior invitation to present a poster that year will be withdrawn. Participating in the poster session does not preclude submitting a paper and having it accepted for the regular program the following year. Applicants must be members of the Association.
Level of Study: Postdoctorate
Type: Travel grant
Value: 1. Up to US$500 for domestic flights or train fare, up to US$800 for international flights. 2. Complimentary hotel rooms for up to 3 nights. 3. 60 percent discount on the registration fee.
Country of Study: Any country

Application Procedure: Applicants will need to provide a 250 word abstract, a current CV, and request a letter of support from their dissertation advisor.
Closing Date: 20 May

For further information contact:

Email: taylor.jaworski@colorado.edu, jeremy.land@helsinki.fi, antoine.parent02@univ-paris8.fr

Arthur H Cole Grants-in-Aid

Purpose: The Committee on Research in Economic History awards Arthur H. Cole grants-in-aid to support research in economic history, regardless of time period or geographic area.
Eligibility: Applicants must be members of the Association and must hold the Ph.D. degree.
Type: Grant
Value: Up to US$5,000
Frequency: As available
Country of Study: Any country
Application Procedure: Apply online eh.net/eha/cole-grant-application/
Closing Date: 1 March
Additional Information: Membership enquiries should be addressed to the office of the Executive Director or the website eh.net/eha/grants-and-fellowships/

For further information contact:

Professor Carl Kitchen, Committee on Research in Economic History.

Email: antoine.parent02@univ-paris8.fr

Engerman-Goldin Prize

Purpose: The Engerman-Goldin Prize is awarded for creating, compiling, and sharing data and information with scholars. It is awarded in even number years (beginning in 2018) for contributions made in the previous six years.
Level of Study: Masters Degree
Type: Prize
Frequency: Annual
Country of Study: Any country
Closing Date: 28 February

For further information contact:

Email: jmoen@olemiss.edu

Gyorgy Ranki Biennial Prize

Purpose: The Gyorgy Ranki Biennial Prize is awarded every other year for an Outstanding Book on the Economic History of Europe
Eligibility: To be eligible, a book must be published in English and must, in whole or in substantial part, treat aspects of European economic history in any period from classical antiquity to the present. For purposes of this prize, Europe is understood to include European Russia as well as the British Isles. Books that compare European experience to that of other parts of the world, or that use historical information to examine present or anticipate future issues and trends, are also eligible as long as they pay significant attention to European economic history.
Type: Prize
Value: US$1,200
Frequency: Annual
Country of Study: Any country

For further information contact:

Email: gf63@nyu.edu

Jonathan Hughes Prize

Purpose: Jonathan Hughes Prize is awarded to recognize excellence in teaching economic history (both at the undergraduate and graduate level). Jonathan Hughes was an outstanding scholar and a committed and influential teacher of economic history.
Type: Prize
Value: US$1,200 cash award
Frequency: Annual
Country of Study: Any country
Closing Date: 1 April

For further information contact:

Northwestern University, Department of Economics, KGH 3479, 2211 Campus Drive, 3rd Floor, Evanston, IL 60208, United States of America.

Email: lcain@northwestern.edu

The Allan Nevins Prize in American Economic History

Purpose: The Allan Nevins Prize in American Economic History is awarded annually by the Economic History Association on behalf of Columbia University Press for the best dissertation in U.S. or Canadian economic history completed during the previous year.

Eligibility: Those who received their Ph.D. between June 1, 2022 and May 30, 2023 are eligible and invited to submit their dissertation for consideration. All candidates for these prizes must be members of the Economic History Association. Dissertations submitted for consideration must be in English. Submission of a dissertation implies that candidates are prepared to attend the 2023 meetings in La Crosse. Presentation of a dissertation summary is required by all finalists.

Level of Study: Postgraduate

Type: Prize

Frequency: Annual

Application Procedure: To be considered for this prize, completed dissertations must be submitted by email on or before May 15, 2023. Dissertations must include a page with the names of the dissertation committee members. The version of the dissertation submitted for consideration for the prize must be the same one that was submitted for the degree. It may not be a later version. Submissions of more than 5MB should prepare to send a download link rather than an attachment.

Closing Date: 15 May

For further information contact:

Email: joshua.lewis@umontreal.ca

The Lindert-Williamson Biennial Prize

Purpose: The Peter Lindert-Jeffrey Williamson Prize is awarded every other year for an Outstanding Book in Global, African, Asian, Australian, and/or South American Economic History

Type: Prize

Value: US$1,200

Frequency: Annual

Country of Study: Any country

Closing Date: 1 March

For further information contact:

Email: okazaki@e.u-tokyo.ac.jp

Edinburgh Napier University

Sighthill Campus, Sighthill Court, Edinburgh EH11 4BN, United Kingdom.

Tel: (44) 333 900 6040
Email: studentrecruitment@napier.ac.uk

Website: www.napier.ac.uk/
Contact: Edinburgh Napier University

Edinburgh Napier University is a public university in Edinburgh, Scotland. Napier Technical College, the predecessor of the university was founded in 1964, taking its name from Scottish mathematician John Napier.

African Scholarships

Purpose: The University has partial scholarships for self-funding students from Africa.

Eligibility: You must be 1. domiciled in Africa at the time of application. 2. self-funding your course. 3. meet the entry criteria for a bachelors or 1 year masters course in September 2023 or January 2024

Level of Study: Masters Degree

Type: Scholarship

Value: £2,000

Length of Study: 1 year

Country of Study: United Kingdom

Application Procedure: Scholarships are awarded automatically once you have paid your £3,500 deposit payment towards your tuition fees. The number of scholarships is limited and they are offered on a first-come, first-served basis.

Closing Date: September

For further information contact:

Buchi Chinwuba, Regional Recruitment Officer.

Tel: (44) 816 678 2704
Email: O.Chinwuba@napier.ac.uk

ASEAN Scholarship

Purpose: The University has partial scholarships for self-funding students from South East Asia.

Eligibility: In order to be eligible for this award, you must be: 1. domiciled in one of the following countries; Malaysia, Singapore, Thailand, Vietnam, Indonesia, Myanmar, Cambodia, Laos, Brunei and Philippines 2. be self-funding your course 3. holding an offer to study a full-time bachelors or masters course in January 2024 or September 2023 4. Please note, you are not eligible for this scholarship if you are studying a two-year Masters course

Level of Study: Postgraduate

Type: Scholarship

Length of Study: 12 months

Country of Study: United Kingdom

Application Procedure: The scholarships will be awarded on a first-come, first-served basis. You will be automatically considered for the scholarship and be advised of the scholarship amount you are eligible for if you meet the following selection criteria: 1. you hold an unconditional offer to study a full-time undergraduate or postgraduate course at Edinburgh Napier 2. you meet the eligibility criteria above 3. you have made your £3,500 deposit payment towards your fees.

Additional Information: If you have discounted tuition fees from a partner university, you are not eligible for this scholarship. www.napier.ac.uk/study-with-us/bursaries/asean-scholarship

For further information contact:

Subra Singaram.

Tel: (60) 12 579 0105

Brazil Scholarship

Purpose: The University has partial scholarships for self-funding students from Brazil.

Eligibility: 1. be living in Brazil at the time of application 2. be self-funding your course 3. be holding an unconditional offer to study a masters course in January 2024 or September 2023 4. have made your £3,500 deposit payment toward your fees

Level of Study: Postgraduate

Type: Scholarship

Value: £4,000

Country of Study: United Kingdom

Application Procedure: The scholarships will be awarded on a first-come, first-served basis when you meet the eligibility criteria.

Additional Information: If you have discounted tuition fees from a partner university, you are not eligible for this scholarship. You do not have to hold an unconditional offer and have paid the deposit in order to apply. www.napier.ac.uk/study-with-us/bursaries/brazil-scholarship

For further information contact:

Rua Dr. Cesário Mota Junior, 369, Conj 52, B-01221020 São Paulo, Brazil.

Tel: (55) 11 3957 0488
Email: s.patterson@napier.ac.uk

Colombia Scholarship

Purpose: The University has partial scholarships for self-funding students from Colombia.

Eligibility: You must 1. be living in Columbia at the time of application 2. be self-funding your course 3. be holding an unconditional offer to study a masters course in January 2024 or September 2023 4. have made your £3,500 deposit payment toward your fees

Level of Study: Postgraduate

Type: Scholarship

Value: £4,000

Country of Study: United Kingdom

Application Procedure: The scholarships will be awarded on a first-come, first-served basis when you meet the eligibility criteria.

Additional Information: If you have discounted tuition fees from a partner university, you are not eligible for this scholarship. You do not have to hold an unconditional offer and have paid the deposit in order to apply. www.napier.ac.uk/study-with-us/bursaries/colombia-scholarship

For further information contact:

Federica Giuntol.

Tel: (52) 55 8421 4929
Email: f.giuntoli@napier.ac.ukinfo@studyacrossthepond.com

Data Visualisation Design, Ambiguity & Decision Making in Megaprojects: EPSRC Studentship

Purpose: Professor Paolo Quattrone has successfully been allocated a studentship for this project in collaboration with Costain

Eligibility: 1. United Kingdom/European Union Countries. 2. Applicants must meet EPSRC eligibility criteria. 3. Please note that international students are not eligible for this funding

Level of Study: Postgraduate

Type: Studentship

Value: £22,159

Length of Study: 4 year

Frequency: Annual

Country of Study: Any country

Closing Date: 31 May

Funding: International office

For further information contact:

Email: phd@business-school.ed.ac.uk

European Union Postgraduate Scholarship

Purpose: The University has partial scholarships for self-funding students from the EU.

Eligibility: You must be 1. Domiciled and ordinarily resident in one of the following EU countries at the time of application Austria, Belgium, Bulgaria, Croatia, Cyprus, Czech Republic, Denmark, Estonia, Finland, France, Germany, Greece, Hungary, Italy, Latvia, Lithuania, Luxembourg, Malta, Netherlands, Poland, Portugal, Romania, Slovakia, Slovenia, Spain, Sweden
Level of Study: Postgraduate
Type: Scholarship
Value: £8,000
Country of Study: United Kingdom
Application Procedure: The number of scholarships is limited and they are offered on a first-come, first-served basis. 1. You meet the eligibility criteria detailed above. 2. You have made your £3,500 deposit payment towards your fees.
Closing Date: September

European Union Visiting Students Scholarship

Purpose: The University has partial scholarships for self-funding visiting students from the EU.
Eligibility: You must be 1. Domiciled in one of the following EU countries at the time of application Austria, Belgium, Bulgaria, Croatia, Cyprus, Czech Republic, Denmark, Estonia, Finland, France, Germany, Greece, Hungary, Italy, Latvia, Lithuania, Luxembourg, Malta, Netherlands, Poland, Portugal, Romania, Slovakia, Slovenia, Spain, Sweden.
Type: Scholarship
Value: £2,000
Length of Study: one or two trimesters
Country of Study: United Kingdom
Application Procedure: The number of scholarships is limited and they are offered on a first-come, first-served basis. You will be automatically considered for the scholarship if you meet the following selection criteria 1. You meet the eligibility criteria detailed above. 2. You have made your £3,500 deposit payment towards your fees.
Additional Information: You are not eligible for this award if: 1. You have discounted tuition fees from a partner university or are in receipt of another scholarship. 2. You are coming via a partnership agreement or a study abroad provider. www.napier.ac.uk/study-with-us/bursaries/european-union-visiting-students-scholarship

Gordon David Family Scholarship

Purpose: The Edinburgh Centre for Carbon Innovation (ECCI) is offering two scholarships for those undertaking research related to the work of ECCI
Eligibility: 1. An eligible MSc programme (see below). 2. PhD in a subject related to the work of the ECCI
Level of Study: Postgraduate

Type: Scholarship
Value: £8,000
Length of Study: 3 year
Frequency: Annual
Country of Study: Any country
Closing Date: 30 April
Funding: Foundation

For further information contact:

Email: phd@business-school.ed.ac.uk

GREAT India Scholarship

Purpose: Edinburgh Napier has partnered with the British Council to offer a scholarship for a Masters students from India.
Eligibility: You must be 1. Domiciled in India at the time of application. 2. self-funding your course. 3. meet the entry criteria for your masters course in September 2023
Level of Study: Masters Degree
Type: Scholarship
Value: £10,000
Country of Study: United Kingdom
Application Procedure: The scholarship will be awarded on the basis of academic merit. View our available courses and apply online.
Closing Date: 27 May

GREAT Pakistan Scholarship

Purpose: Edinburgh Napier has partnered with the British Council to offer a scholarship for a Masters students from Pakistan.
Eligibility: You must be 1. Domiciled in Pakistan at the time of application. 2. Self-funding your course. 3. meet the entry criteria for your chosen Masters course in September 2023
Level of Study: Masters Degree
Type: Scholarship
Value: £10,000
Country of Study: United Kingdom
Application Procedure: The scholarship will be awarded on the basis of academic merit. View our available courses and apply online.
Closing Date: 27 May

Ian Kay Scholarships

Purpose: The Ian Kay Scholarship Fund provides scholarships to help Chinese students to study at Edinburgh Napier

University, and to help students from Edinburgh Napier University to study in China.

Eligibility: The Ian Kay Scholarship Fund provides scholarships to help Chinese students to study at Edinburgh Napier University, and to help students from Edinburgh Napier University to study in China. You must have a firm offer (conditional or unconditional) from Edinburgh Napier University to study on a course related to 1. Finance. 2. Business Management. 3. International Business. You must be aged between 20 and 35 at the time of applying for your course.

Level of Study: Postgraduate

Type: Scholarship

Value: £10,000 to either a postgraduate or an undergraduate Chinese student for a course of study in Financial Services/Up to £5,000 for a Scottish student to study in China for one year.

Study Establishment: Financial Services (i.e. Business Management or International Affairs); Business Management; or International Business at Edinburgh Napier University

Country of Study: China

Application Procedure: An application form is available for download. For applicants from China wishing to study in Scotland, completed application forms, including photocopies of all relevant supporting documents, should be sent to china@napier.ac.uk

Closing Date: 30 April

Additional Information: Once a candidate has been selected for an award, the level of the Scholarship will be carefully judged bearing in mind the student's educational fees and living costs. The decision of the awarding committee is final. Applicants have no right of appeal. www.napier.ac.uk/study-with-us/bursaries/ian-kay-scholarships

For further information contact:

Email: findafund@napier.ac.uk.

Improving Project Delivery: ESRC Studentship

Purpose: Professor Paolo Quattrone has successfully been allocated a studentship for the project 'Improving Project Delivery' in collaboration with the Infrastructure and Project Authority

Eligibility: 1. United Kingdom/European Union Countries. 2. Applicants must meet ESRC eligibility criteria. 3. Please note that international students are not eligible for this funding

Level of Study: Postgraduate

Type: Studentship

Value: £14,777

Length of Study: 3 year

Frequency: Annual

Country of Study: Any country

Closing Date: 31 May

Funding: International office

For further information contact:

University of Edinburgh Business School, 29 Buccleuch Place, Edinburgh EH8 9JS, United Kingdom.

Tel: (44) 131 651 5337, (44) 131 651 5541

Email: paolo.quattrone@ed.ac.ukphd@business-school.ed.ac.uk

Institute for Particle and Nuclear Physics MSc Prize Scholarships

Subjects: We offer taught masters (MSc) programmes in Theoretical Physics and Mathematical Physics, and Particle & Nuclear Physics.

Eligibility: Applicants must have applied to study full-time on the MSc Particle and Nuclear Physics programme of study.

Level of Study: Postgraduate

Type: Scholarship

Value: £5,000

Length of Study: 1 year

Frequency: Annual

Country of Study: Any country

Application Procedure: The deadline for applying for this scholarship is 1 June, details on how to apply are found on the University's Scholarships and Student Funding pages.

No. of awards offered: 6

Closing Date: 1 June

For further information contact:

Email: msc.pnp@ph.ed.ac.uk

Jean Kennoway Howells Scholarship

Purpose: One scholarship available for taught masters programmes offered by the Reid School of Music

Eligibility: The scholarship will be awarded to students who have applied for admission on a full-time basis for a postgraduate taught Masters programme of study within the Reid School of Music commencing in the academic year. To be eligible, applicants must have received an offer to study by the scholarship deadline

Level of Study: Postgraduate

Type: Scholarship

Value: £15,000

Length of Study: 1 year

Frequency: Annual

Country of Study: Any country

Closing Date: 2 March

Funding: Foundation

For further information contact:

Email: ecapgtdegrees@ed.ac.uk

Lawrence Ho Scholarship

Purpose: Established in 2009, the Lawrence Ho Scholarship and Research Fund currently provides scholarships support for students from China and Hong Kong who wish to study at Edinburgh Napier University in Scotland.

Eligibility: You must be from Hong Kong or China and have a firm offer (conditional or unconditional) from Edinburgh Napier University to study on a postgraduate course. The value of the scholarship will be based on the following undergraduate degree levels 1. £1500, for applicants with a 2.2 UK honour degree, lower-second class Hong Kong honour degree or 75% from a Chinese Benke degree. 2. £3000, for applicants with a 2.1 or first class UK honour degree, upper-second class or higher Hong Kong honour degree, or 80%+ from a Chinese Benke degree.

Level of Study: Postgraduate

Type: Scholarship

Value: £1,500 to £3,000

Country of Study: United Kingdom

Application Procedure: The scholarships will be awarded on a first-come, first-served basis. You will be automatically considered for the scholarship and be advised of the scholarship amount you are eligible for if you meet the following selection criteria 1. You meet the eligibility criteria detailed above. 2. You have made your £3,500 deposit payment towards your fees.

Additional Information: www.napier.ac.uk/study-with-us/bursaries/lawrence-ho-scholarship

Mexico Scholarship

Purpose: The University has partial scholarships for self-funding students from Mexico.

Eligibility: You must 1. be living in Mexico at the time of application. 2. be self-funding your course. 3. be holding an unconditional offer to study a masters course in January 2024 or September 2023. 4. have made your £3,500 deposit payment toward your fees.

Level of Study: Postgraduate

Type: Scholarship

Value: £4,000

Country of Study: United Kingdom

Application Procedure: The scholarships will be awarded on a first-come, first-served basis when you meet the eligibility criteria. Apply by completing the scholarship application form available from our local representatives.

Additional Information: If you have discounted tuition fees from a partner university, you are not eligible for this scholarship. You do not have to hold an unconditional offer and have paid the deposit in order to apply. Please contact Senior International Officer for the Americas, Federica Giuntoli, if you have questions about our Mexico Scholarship. f.giuntoli@napier.ac.uk. la.studyacrossthepond.com/ www.napier.ac.uk/study-with-us/bursaries/mexico-scholarship

For further information contact:

Tel: (52) 55 8421 4929
Email: info@studyacrossthepond.com;
            s.patterson@napier.ac.uk

North American Postgraduate Scholarship

Purpose: The University has partial scholarships for self-funding students from North America.

Eligibility: Students who are from the USA and Canada who are self-funding their course are eligible for a merit-based one-time North American Postgraduate Scholarship

Level of Study: Postgraduate

Type: Scholarship

Value: £2,000

Country of Study: United Kingdom

Application Procedure: To apply for the scholarship, please email responses to the below to international@napier.ac.uk with your student ID and North American Scholarship in the subject. Please provide 1. a 250-word response to Why did you choose Edinburgh Napier University and your programme of study? 2. a 250-word personal statement describing your major achievements, whether they be academic or personal, and the difference it will make to your studies at Edinburgh Napier University.

Closing Date: 24 April

Additional Information: Please note, you are not eligible for this scholarship if you are studying a full-time course lasting longer than 12 months. www.napier.ac.uk/study-with-us/bursaries/north-american-postgraduate-scholarship

For further information contact:

Email: international@napier.ac.uk

Pakistan Scholarship

Purpose: The University has partial scholarships for self-funding students from Pakistan.

Eligibility: You must be 1. living in Pakistan at the time of application. 2. self-funding your course. 3. holding an offer to study a masters or PhD course. You must also achieve the following academic requirements in your most recent masters or bachelors course Masters or Bachelor degree at 70% or above.

Level of Study: Doctorate, Masters Degree

Type: Scholarship

Value: £2,000 to £3,000

Country of Study: United Kingdom

Application Procedure: The scholarships will be awarded on a first-come, first-served basis. You will be automatically considered for the scholarship and be advised of the scholarship amount you are eligible for if you meet the following selection criteria 1. You hold an unconditional offer to study on a full-time masters course at Edinburgh Napier. 2. You meet the eligibility criteria detailed above. 3. You have made your £3,500 deposit payment towards your fees.

Additional Information: Students studying full-time courses lasting longer than 12 months are not eligible for this award. If you have discounted tuition fees from a partner university, you are not eligible for this scholarship. www.napier.ac.uk/study-with-us/bursaries/pakistan-scholarship

For further information contact:

Email: international@napier.ac.uk

Scotland's Saltire Scholarship

Purpose: Edinburgh Napier has a number of scholarships for students from Canada, China, Hong Kong, India, Japan, Pakistan and the United States of America. Scotland's Saltire Scholarship is a programme of scholarships run by the Scottish Government, in partnership with Edinburgh Napier University.

Eligibility: You must 1. have a conditional or unconditional offer to study on an eligible course at Edinburgh Napier. 2. studying a full time masters-examples of subjects that can be studied can also be found in www.scotland.org/study/saltire-scholarships/what-can-i-study. 3. be a citizen of Canada, China, Hong Kong, India, Japan, Pakistan or the United States of America. 4. be able to demonstrate that you can meet the costs of living in Scotland and the remaining tuition fees. 5. not have previously studied for a full undergraduate degree in Scotland. 6. not have previously received a Saltire Scholarship. 7. meet the language requirements for the course. 8. Scholarships for 2023–24 Saltire programmes will continue to be available for online/distance learning.

Level of Study: Postgraduate

Type: Scholarship

Value: £8,000

Country of Study: United Kingdom

Application Procedure: Applicant must demonstrate 1. The aspiration to work and study in a global context and take a position of leadership in their chosen career. 2. A willingness and the necessary interpersonal and communication skills required to participate in the programme of activities that accompanies the scholarships. Apply here: www.scotland.org/study/saltire-scholarships

No. of awards offered: 50

Closing Date: 28 May

Funding: Government

Additional Information: For further information, or if you have any questions about the scheme contact Scotland's Saltire Scholarships www.scotland.org/more-info/contact-us

For further information contact:

Email: ScotlandsSaltireScholarships@gov.scot

South Asian Scholarships at Edinburgh Napier University

Purpose: The University has partial scholarships for self-funding students from India, Bangladesh, Nepal or Sri Lanka.

Eligibility: 1. Living in India, Bangladesh, Sri Lanka, Nepal at the time of application. 2. Self-funding your course. 3. Holding an offer to study a masters or PhD course.

Level of Study: Doctorate, Masters Degree

Type: Scholarship

Value: £2,000 to £3,000

Country of Study: United Kingdom

Application Procedure: The scholarships will be awarded on a first-come, first-served basis. You will be automatically considered for the scholarship and be advised of the scholarship amount you are eligible for if you meet the following selection criteria 1. You hold an unconditional offer to study on a full-time bachelors or masters course at Edinburgh Napier. 2. You meet the eligibility criteria detailed above. 3. You have made your £3,500 deposit payment towards your fees.

Additional Information: Students studying full-time courses lasting longer than 12 months or those who study MBA (Engineering Management), MBA (Strategic Project Management) and MBA (Leadership Practice) are not eligible for this award. If you have discounted tuition fees from a partner university, you are not eligible for this scholarship. www.napier.ac.uk/study-with-us/bursaries/south-asia-scholarship

For further information contact:

Tel: (44) 40 4240 8800

Email: india@napier.ac.uk or international@napier.ac.uk

Edith Cowan University

270 Joondalup Drive, Joondalup, WA 6027, Australia.

Tel: (61) 8 6304 0000
Email: enquiries@ecu.edu.au
Website: www.ecu.edu.au/
Contact: Edith Cowan University

Edith Cowan University (ECU) provides the ideal learning environment for people who want to reach their potential. Located in Western Australia, our industry-relevant teaching and research, supportive study environment and award-winning facilities enable ECU students to do more than just survive in this world. Established in 1991, ECU took the opportunity to reshape the way higher education is delivered in a distinctive and inspiring campus environment.

Brett Lockyer Scholarship

Purpose: To enable the further development of jazz clarinet studies at ECU and to develop those specialist skills in a currently enrolled jazz clarinet student at WAAPA
Eligibility: Open for students studying jazz clarinet within the jazz programme
Level of Study: Postgraduate
Type: Scholarship
Value: Up to AU$5,000
Application Procedure: Check website for further details.

For further information contact:

Tel: (61) 8 9370 6594
Email: j.hamilton@ecu.edu.au

Luke Pen Fund-Honours Scholarships

Purpose: To encourage young people to be involved in the gaining of scientific knowledge of river characteristics
Level of Study: Graduate
Type: Scholarship
Value: AU$50,000
Length of Study: 1 year
Frequency: Annual
Application Procedure: Check website address for further details
Closing Date: 31 March
Funding: Trusts
Contributor: Luke Pen Scholarship Trust

Additional Information: www.mediastatements.wa.gov.au/Pages/Gallop/2004/03/The-inaugural-Luke-Pen-Scholarship.aspx

For further information contact:

Department of Water, Drainage and Waterways Branch, PO Box K822, Perth, WA 6842, Australia.

Email: james.mackintosh@water.wa.gov.au

Merit International Postgraduate Scholarship

Purpose: The Edith Cowan University is inviting applications for Merit International Postgraduate Scholarship to study in Australia. This scholarship is available to students who can demonstrate high levels of academic achievement and English competency in their previous studies
Eligibility: 1. Your programme must commence at the University of Sheffield. 2. Distance learning courses are ineligible for a merit scholarship. 3. You must receive an offer for a course studied in full at the University of Sheffield. Masters programmes split between the University of Sheffield and a partner institution are not eligible to apply for a scholarship. 4. All Crossways courses and Erasmus Mundus courses are ineligible for a merit scholarship. 5. For tuition fee purposes you must be self-funded and required to pay the overseas tuition fee. 6. You must not be a sponsored student*. 7. For scholarship purposes all March programmes are considered as postgraduate taught programmes and are not eligible for undergraduate scholarships. 8. Anyone studying a Masters/integrated PhD programme is eligible for a merit scholarship in the Masters element of the programme only. 9.
Type: Postgraduate scholarships
Value: The scholarship offers a 10% reduction in your tuition fees for the duration of your course at ECU
Study Establishment: Scholarships are awarded to learn any of the courses offered by the university
Country of Study: Australia
Application Procedure: See the website
Closing Date: 4 May
Additional Information: For more details please visit the website scholarship-positions.com/merit-international-postgraduate-scholarship-edith-cowan-university-australia/2018/02/03/

For further information contact:

The University of Sheffield, Western Bank, Sheffield S10 2TN, United Kingdom.

Tel: (44) 114 222 2000

Postgraduate Petroleum Engineering Scholarship

Purpose: Petroleum Engineering has evolved into one of the well sought courses in universities. It is the field of engineering that deals with the exploration, extraction, and production of oil. It also increasingly deals with the production of natural gas.
Eligibility: 1. Be commencing study of a Graduate Diploma in Petroleum Engineering (J69); Master of Engineering (Petroleum Engineering specialization) (I59); or the Master of Technology (Petroleum Engineering) (J70). 2. Meet ECU's academic direct entry requirements for the course of your choice. 3. Not be in receipt of another scholarship or sponsorship. 4. Be an International student, not an Australian Citizen, Australian Permanent Resident, or New Zealand Citizen. 5. Intend to study a postgraduate degree. 6. Be studying at ECU Joondalup
Level of Study: Postgraduate
Type: Scholarship
Frequency: Annual
Country of Study: Any country
Closing Date: 31 July
Funding: International office
Additional Information: www.ecu.edu.au/scholarships/details/petroleum-engineering-scholarship-undergraduate-and-postgraduate.

For further information contact:

Email: international.parternships@ecu.edu.au

Education and Research Foundation for the Society of Nuclear Medicine (SNM)

14301 FNB Parkway, Suite 100, Omaha, NE 68154, United States of America.

Tel: (1) 402 507 5125
Email: theresa.pinkham@mierf.org
Website: www.mierf.org/

For over four decades ERF has supported the Society of Nuclear Medicine and Molecular Imaging (SNMMI) Grants, Awards and Scholarship program.

Society of Nuclear Medicine Pilot Research Grants in Nuclear Medicine/Molecular Imaging

Purpose: To support Master's or PhD students to start research in nuclear medicine

Eligibility: Open to basic and clinical scientists in early stages of their career.
Level of Study: Doctorate, Postgraduate
Type: Grant
Value: US$25,000
Frequency: Annual
Country of Study: United States of America
Application Procedure: Applicants must submit a completed application form along with abstract of project proposal and budget proposal
No. of awards offered: 2
Closing Date: 20 February

For further information contact:

Email: tpinkham@erfsnm.org

Education New Zealand (ENZ)

Level 5, Lambton House, 160 Lambton Quay, Wellington 6011, New Zealand.

Tel: (64) 4 472 0788
Email: info@enz.govt.nz
Website: enz.govt.nz/

ENZ is New Zealand's government agency for building international education. We promote New Zealand as a study destination and support the delivery of education services offshore.

Korea New Zealand Agricultural Cooperation Scholarships (KNZACS)

Purpose: To promote greater understanding between Korea and New Zealand, and strengthen the trade and economic relationship in veterinary or animal science or forestry sectors
Level of Study: Doctorate, Postgraduate
Type: Scholarship
Value: New Zealand University fees and associated student levies for duration of study and stipend of NZ$30,000 per year
Country of Study: New Zealand
Application Procedure: Please visit website to apply
No. of awards offered: 6
Funding: Government

For further information contact:

Email: christine.roberts@enz.govt.nz

NZ-GRADS New Zealand Global Research Alliance Doctoral Scholarship

Purpose: NZ-GRADS is a doctoral scholarship (PhD) scholarship offered to science students from developing countries to complete their PhD at a New Zealand university. The NZ-GRADS is a government-funded scholarship administered by Education New Zealand.

Eligibility: Criteria are non-negotiable 1. You must have an offer of place for a (direct-start) PhD programme at a New Zealand university (this may be conditional or non-conditional). 2. You must conduct your PhD study in New Zealand (not from a distance). 3. You cannot hold citizenship or permanent residency status in New Zealand or Australia. 4. You must be from a developing country www.imf.org/external/pubs/ft/weo/2018/02/weodata/groups.htm#oem. 5. Your PhD research topic must relate to greenhouse gas emissions from agricultural systems. 6. Your research may be hosted/facilitated by any New Zealand research organisation, however, your PhD programme must be organised through a New Zealand university.

Level of Study: Postgraduate
Type: Scholarship
Value: NZ$124,600 total value (1. New Zealand University annual tuition fees and associated student levies up to a total of NZ$10,000 per year. 2. An annual living stipend of NZ$28,000 per year (tax free). 3. Medical insurance cover up to NZ$700 per year. 4. Visa application costs to a maximum of NZ$1,000. 5. Return flights to New Zealand up to a maximum of NZ$6,000. 6. Book and thesis preparation allowance of up to NZ$1,500)
Length of Study: 3 years
Application Procedure: To complete the application, you will need to upload the following documents 1. Evidence of citizenship for every country for which you hold citizenship. 2. Evidence of an offer of place for a PhD programme from a New Zealand university. 3. Academic transcripts, grading scale and certificates of completion. 4. Curriculum Vitae. You will also need to provide the names and emails of two academic referees for your references.
No. of awards offered: 6
Closing Date: 1 June
Funding: Government
Additional Information: www.studyinnewzealand.govt.nz/how-to-apply/scholarship/details?scholarshipid=138518&institutionid=378394

Shirtcliffe Fellowship

Purpose: The purpose of the Shirtcliffe Fellowships is to assist students of outstanding ability and character who are graduates of a university in New Zealand, in the continuation of their studies in New Zealand or the Commonwealth.

Eligibility: Applicants must be 1. New Zealand citizens. 2. ordinarily resident in New Zealand. 3. New Zealand university graduates. 4. planning to register or be currently registered as a doctoral candidate at a university in New Zealand or other Commonwealth country.
Level of Study: Doctorate
Type: Fellowship
Value: NZ$5,000 per year
Length of Study: three years
Frequency: Annual
Country of Study: New Zealand
Application Procedure: The on-line application process will request and candidates must provide 1. proof of New Zealand citizenship. 2. a statement describing their doctoral research. 3. the names and contact information of two referees. 4. a statement giving an outline of non-academic/extracurricular activities. 5. a budget of anticipated costs. Apply online universitiesnz.communityforce.com/Login.aspx
Closing Date: 1 April
Funding: Private
Additional Information: www.universitiesnz.ac.nz/scholarships/shirtcliffe-fellowship

Education.govt.nz

Mātauranga House, Level 1, 33 Bowen Street, Wellington 6011, New Zealand.

Tel: (64) 4 463 8000
Email: enquiries.national@education.govt.nz
Website: www.education.govt.nz/

The Ministry of Education is the Government's lead advisor on the New Zealand education system, shaping direction for sector agencies and providers. We shape an education system that delivers equitable and excellent outcomes.

Ngarimu VC and 28th (Maori) Battalion Memorial Scholarships

Subjects: Ethnicity General
Purpose: These scholarships support high achieving tertiary students of Maori descent
Eligibility: 1. Applications for both scholarships will need to include a brief statement of up to 250 words, outlining the topic, the reasons for your interest in the subject area and your future expectations. 2. Preference will be given to applicants who are

able to demonstrate that their studies aim to improve the social, economic and cultural wellbeing of Maori or are on Maori issues. Eligible applicants can apply for both scholarships

Level of Study: Research

Type: Scholarship

Value: NZ$15,000 per year of full-time study

Length of Study: 2 years

Frequency: Annual

Country of Study: Any country

Application Procedure: All applicants will need to include 1. a form completed by a Kaumatua, Maori leader that certifies your whakapapa. 2. a form completed by someone who can endorse your academic achievement and suitability to study. 3. a Te Reo Maori statement that demonstrates your language capabilities. 4. a statement about the Nga Ahuatanga characteristics you possess that are similar to those identified as consistent with the 28th (Maori) Battalion soldiers

No. of awards offered: 7

Closing Date: February

Funding: Private

Additional Information: www.education.govt.nz/further-education/information-for-tertiary-students/scholarships/ngarimu-scholarships/

For further information contact:

Tel: (64) 800 165 225
Email: ngārimu.scholarship@education.govt.nz

Educational Testing Service (ETS)

660 Rosedale Road, Princeton, NJ 08541, United States of America.

Tel: (1) 609 921 9000
Website: www.ets.org/

The Educational Testing Service (ETS) an independent, non-profit organization devoted to educational research and assessment could expand opportunities for learners of all income and social status levels through more informed, objective methods for evaluation.

Educational Testing Service Harold Gulliksen Psychometric Fellowship Program

Purpose: The fellowship provides funding for promising graduate students in psychometrics, or a related field, who are conducting innovative, applied research.

Eligibility: At the time of application, candidates must be enrolled in a doctoral program, have completed all the coursework toward the doctorate, and be at the dissertation stage of their program. Dissertation topics in the areas of psychometrics, statistics, educational measurement or quantitative methods will be given priority. At the time of application, candidates will be asked to provide a statement describing any additional financial assistance such as assistantship or grant commitment that he/she will have during the fellowship period.

Level of Study: Predoctorate

Type: Fellowship

Value: US$20,000 (stipend), US$8,000 (tuition fees, and work-study program commitments), and a small grant to facilitate work on the fellow's research project

Frequency: As available

Country of Study: United States of America or other countries if appropriate

Application Procedure: Submit all application materials via email with PDF attachments. Two applications have to be submitted for this program. Preliminary application 1. Letter of interest describing the research that would be undertaken during the award year and how the research fits with ETS research efforts. 2. Statement describing any additional financial assistance, such as assistantship or grant commitment, that you would have during the fellowship period. 3. Nomination letter (either as an email or as an email with a PDF attachment) from an academic advisor in support of your interest in the fellowship award. 4. Current curriculum vitae and Final Application If your preliminary application is approved, you will be invited to submit the following materials 1. Detailed project description (approximately 15 double-spaced pages) of the research the individual will carry out at the host university, including the purpose, goals and methods of the research. 2. Graduate academic transcripts (unofficial copies are acceptable). 3. Evidence of scholarship (presentations, manuscripts, etc.)

Closing Date: 21 January

Funding: Private

Contributor: ETS

Additional Information: Kindly refer the website for further information.   www.ets.org/research/internship-fellowship/gulliksen/

For further information contact:

Email: internfellowships@ets.org

Educational Testing Service Postdoctoral Fellowships

Purpose: To provide research opportunities to individuals who hold a doctorate in education and related fields, and to increase the number of women and minority professionals conducting research in educational measurement and related fields

Eligibility: Open to applicants who have received their doctoral degree within the past 3 years. Selections will be based on the candidate's scholarship, the technical strength of the proposed topic of research, and the explicit objective of the research and its relationship to ETS research goals and priorities

Level of Study: Postdoctorate

Type: Fellowship

Value: The amount is US$50,000 for the 1-year period. In addition, limited relocation expenses consistent with the ETS guidelines will be reimbursed. Renewal for a second year by mutual consent

Length of Study: Up to 2 years, renewable after the first year by mutual agreement

Frequency: Annual

Country of Study: United States of America

Application Procedure: Refer the ETS website for further details. All application materials should be sent electronically as attachments

No. of awards offered: 15

Closing Date: 1 January

Funding: Private

Contributor: ETS

For further information contact:

Email: internfellowships@ets.org

Educational Testing Service Summer Internship Program in Research for Graduate Students

Purpose: To provide research opportunities to individuals enroled in a doctoral program and to increase the number of women and underrepresented minority professionals conducting research in educational and related fields

Eligibility: Current full-time enrollment in a relevant doctoral program Completion of at least 2 years of coursework toward the PhD or EdD. prior to the program start date

Level of Study: Predoctorate

Type: Internship

Value: US$6,000 salary; Transportation allowance for relocating to and from the Princeton area; Housing will be provided for interns commuting more than 50 miles

Length of Study: June to July (8 weeks)

Frequency: Annual

Country of Study: United States of America

Application Procedure: 1. Choose up to two research areas in which you are interested and provide written statements about your interest in the particular area(s) of research. 2. Attach a copy of your curriculum vitae (preferably as a PDF). 3. Attach a copy of your graduate transcripts (unofficial copies are acceptable). 4. Download the recommendation form and share it with your recommenders. Recommendations should come from your academic advisor and/or major professors who are familiar with your work. ETS will only accept two recommendation forms. Recommendations should be sent electronically to internfellowships@ets.org and must be received by February 1. If you would like to download the recommendation form for sending to your recommenders before submitting your application, the option to save your application information for later is available.

Closing Date: 1 February

Funding: Private

Contributor: ETS

Additional Information: Duration of Research Internship is eight weeks: 3 June–26 July www.ets.org/research/internship-fellowship/gulliksen/

For further information contact:

Email: internfellowships@ets.org

Educational Testing Service Summer Internships in Programme Direction

Purpose: To provide opportunities, especially for women and minority professionals, for a work and learning experience that will assist the participants in exploring career alternatives in the field of measurement and evaluation

Eligibility: Current full-time enrollment in a relevant doctoral program; Completion of at least two years of coursework toward the doctorate prior to the program start date

Level of Study: Doctorate, Postgraduate

Type: Internship

Value: Salary of US$6,000 with the transportation allowance and housing for interns who commute more than 50 miles

Length of Study: 8 weeks (3 June-26 July)

Study Establishment: ETS headquarters in Princeton

Country of Study: United States of America

Application Procedure: Application should include references and transcripts

Closing Date: 1 February

Additional Information: Applicants will be notified of selection decisions by 30 March www.ets.org/research/internship-fellowship/gulliksen/

Educational Testing Service Sylvia Taylor Johnson Minority Fellowship in Educational Measurement

Purpose: An award to a minority scholar who has received a doctorate degree within the past ten years. The fellow will conduct independent research under the mentorship of ETS researchers. The award is for a period of up to two years, renewable after the first year by mutual agreement. Applicant must have a commitment to education, particularly educational measurement.

Eligibility: Open to applicants who have received their doctoral degree within the past 10 years and who are citizens or permanent residents of the United States. Selections will be based on the applicant's record of accomplishment, and proposed topic of research. Applicants should have a commitment to education and an independent body of scholarship that signals the promise of continuing outstanding contributions to educational measurement

Level of Study: Postdoctorate

Type: Fellowship

Value: Salary is competitive. US$5,000 one-time relocation incentive for round-trip relocation expenses. In addition, limited relocation expenses, consistent with ETS guidelines, will be reimbursed

Length of Study: Up to 2 years, renewable after the first year by mutual agreement

Frequency: Annual

Country of Study: United States of America

Application Procedure: Refer the ETS website for further details. All application materials should be sent electronically as attachments

No. of awards offered: 15

Closing Date: 1 February

Funding: Private

Contributor: ETS

Additional Information: Through her research, extensive writings and service to the educational community as an educator, editor, counsellor, committee member and collaborator during her lifetime, Sylvia Taylor Johnson had a significant influence in educational measurement and assessment nationally. In honour of Dr Johnson's important contributions to the field of education, the ETS has established the Sylvia Taylor Johnson Minority Fellowship in educational measurement www.ets.org/research/internship-fellowship/gulliksen/

For further information contact:

Rosedale Road, MS-19T, Princeton, NJ 08541-0001, United States of America.

Tel: (1) 609 734 1806
Fax: (1) 609 734 5410
Email: internfellowships@ets.org

Postdoctoral Fellowship Program

Purpose: Individuals who have earned their doctoral degree within the last three years are invited to apply for a rewarding fellowship experience which combines working on cutting-edge ETS research projects and conducting independent research that is relevant to ETS's goals. The fellowship is carried out in the ETS offices in Princeton, N.J.

Eligibility: 1. Doctorate in a relevant discipline within the past three years. 2. Evidence of prior independent research

Level of Study: Postdoctorate

Type: Fellowship

Value: US$5,000 one-time relocation incentive for round-trip relocation expenses

Length of Study: Up to 2 years and it is renewable

Frequency: Annual

Country of Study: Any country

Application Procedure: Two applications have to be submitted. Preliminary Application complete the electronic preliminary application form. On the application form 1. Indicate your research area of interest. 2. Enter your statement of interest. 3. Enter an abstract about the independent research you propose to conduct while at ETS. 4. Attach a copy of your curriculum vitae. 5. Attach a copy of your graduate transcripts (student copy is acceptable). Final Application If your preliminary application is approved, you will be invited to submit the following materials 1. a detailed proposal (approximately five double-spaced pages) describing the research that will be carried out at ETS and how it relates to current ETS research. 2. samples of published research. 3. names and email addresses of three individuals who are familiar with your work, and who are willing to complete a recommendation form that will be sent to them electronically

Closing Date: 15 April

Funding: Private

For further information contact:

Email: internfellowships@ets.org

Eidgenössische Technische Hochschule Zurich

Patricia Heuberger-Meyer, HG E 68.1, Rämistrasse 101, CH-8092 Zürich, Switzerland.

Tel: (41) 44 632 11 11
Website: ethz.ch/en.html
Contact: ETH Zurich

Ever since it was founded under the name Polytechnikum back in 1855, ETH Zurich has been a national educational institution of international standing, attracting talent from all over the world.

The Engineering for Development (E4D) Doctoral Scholarship Programme

Purpose: The goal of the Engineering for Development (E4D) Programme is to promote research and education for the benefit of underprivileged people in low-income countries.

Eligibility: Only candidates with the support of an ETH professor are eligible to apply.

Level of Study: Doctorate

Type: Scholarship

Value: CHF 175,000

Frequency: As available

Country of Study: Switzerland

Application Procedure: Application Documentation comprises of Completed Concept Note Application Form (DOCX, 38 KB) (download from eth4d.ethz.ch/funding-opportunities/E4D-Scholarships/e4d-doctoral-scholarships.html) along with the following compulsory annexes 1. CV of the candidate. 2. Excellent MSc degree from a recognised university and grade transcripts. 3. Support letter of the supervising professor at ETH Zurich. 4. 2 reference letters from your field of research. 5. Relevant own publications or documentation of relevant activities relating to the project. 6. Bibliography. 7. Names and contacts of 5 independent external reviewers. Please read the Eligibility Criteria and Application Requirements (PDF, 186 KB) ethz.ch/content/dam/ethz/special-interest/dual/eth4d-dam/documents/ETH4D_Doctoral_Scholarship_Criteria_2021.pdf. Please submit your application in one single pdf to e4d@sl.ethz.ch.

Closing Date: 30 April

Funding: Foundation

Contributor: Sawiris Foundation for Social Development and Swiss Agency for Development and Cooperation

Additional Information: Applications submitted without the letter of support will not be considered. eth4d.ethz.ch/funding-opportunities/E4D-Scholarships/e4d-doctoral-scholarships.html

For further information contact:

Priya Mohanty, Clausiusstrasse 37, CH-8092 Zurich, Switzerland.

Email: e4d@sl.ethz.ch

Electoral Commission New Zealand

Level 6, Greenock House 39, The Terrace, PO Box 3220, Wellington 6140, New Zealand.

Tel: (64) 800 36 76 56
Email: enquiries@elections.govt.nz
Website: vote.nz/

Electoral Commission New Zealand responsible for running New Zealand's parliamentary elections and keeping the electoral rolls up to date. We're a Crown Entity which means we work independently from government. We administer the Electoral Act 1993 which provides the rules for parliamentary elections and the electoral roll.

Wallace Scholarships for Tertiary Student Research

Purpose: To encourage research work that will be useful in designing electoral education and information programmes and help raise public awareness of electoral issues

Eligibility: Scholarships are for research as part of a New Zealand university degree

Level of Study: Research

Type: Scholarships

Value: NZ$500–2,000

Length of Study: usually 1 year

Frequency: Annual

Country of Study: New Zealand

Application Procedure: Applicants must send a 1-page research proposal, letter of endorsement from an academic supervisor and contact details and enrollment qualifications

No. of awards offered: 6

Closing Date: 2 February

Funding: Government

Embassy of France in Australia

6 Perth Avenue, Yarralumla, Canberra, ACT 2600, Australia.

Tel: (61) 2 6216 0100
Email: education@ambafrance-au.org
Website: au.ambafrance.org

The Embassy of France in Australia supports the partnership between French and Australian Universities and offers grants and scholarships to help the students' mobility.

Language Assistantships in France and New Caledonia

Purpose: To enable graduates who intend to teach French in the future or beginning teachers of French to improve their language skills

Eligibility: 1. Candidates must be Australian citizens or permanent residents. 2. Candidates must be enrolled at an Australian university or be recently graduated at the time of application. Candidates must have completed at least two years of university studies. 3. Candidates must be between 20 and 35 years of age at the time of taking up their positions (from 11 March). 4. Candidates must have a minimum Level B1 in French. 5. Candidates should preferably be single, as the salary of an assistant is not adequate to support dependents. 6. At the time of their visa appointment, candidates will be required to submit a National Police Check dated no older than three months.
Level of Study: Graduate
Type: Assistantship
Value: Net monthly allowance €1,529.
Length of Study: 7 months
Frequency: Annual
Study Establishment: Any approved high school
Country of Study: Any country
Application Procedure: Application forms are available on the website of the French Embassy www.ambafrance-au.org
No. of awards offered: 120
Closing Date: November
Funding: Government
Additional Information: These awards are organized by the higher education office of the Embassy of France in Australia. Successful applicants will conduct English conversation classes with small groups of students for 12 hours per week au.ambafrance.org/Grants-and-Opportunities-6980#English-Language-Teaching-Assistants-Programs

Ministry of Foreign Affairs (France) International Teaching Fellowships

Purpose: To enable experienced teachers of French to spend time at a French primary school, a French college, or a French lycée
Eligibility: Open to Australian teachers of French employed by state education authorities
Level of Study: Professional development
Type: Fellowship
Length of Study: 1 year
Frequency: Annual
Study Establishment: A lycée, collège, primary school or Institut Universitaire de Formation de Maîtres (IUFM)
Country of Study: France
Application Procedure: Applicants must complete an application form, available from state departments of education and on the French Embassy website www.ambafrance-au.org

Closing Date: 30 April
Funding: Government
Additional Information: These awards are organized by the higher education office of the Embassy of France in Australia (BCF) au.ambafrance.org/Grants-and-Opportunities-6980#English-Language-Teaching-Assistants-Programs

For further information contact:

Email: candidatures.eiffel@campusfrance.org

Ministry of Foreign Affairs (France) Stage de la Réunion (One Month Scholarships)

Purpose: To enable school teachers of French to attend a course on the methodology specific to the teaching of French at primary or secondary level
Eligibility: Open to Australian teachers of French only
Level of Study: Professional development
Type: Scholarship
Value: All costs except travel costs between Australia and Réunion Island
Length of Study: 1 month
Frequency: Annual
Study Establishment: Cifept in Le Tampon
Country of Study: Other
Application Procedure: Applicants must write for details
Closing Date: 15 March
Funding: Government
Additional Information: These awards are organised by the Bureau de Co-opération pour le Francais of the Embassy of France in Australia (BCF) au.ambafrance.org/Grants-and-Opportunities-6980#English-Language-Teaching-Assistants-Programs

For further information contact:

Email: candidatures.eiffel@campusfrance.org

SAAFE Program

Purpose: The objective of the SAAFE program is to foster research collaborations between France and Australia in nuclear science and engineering in the field of human health, environment and nuclear fuel cycle.
Eligibility: 1. A PhD student currently enrolled in a French university or Australian AINSE-member university; OR. 2. Enrolled in a PhD in collaboration between French and Australian institutions; OR. 3. Hold a postdoctoral appointment at a French university or Australian AINSE-member university. In addition, eligible applicants must be carrying out a research project using nuclear science techniques that will stimulate research collaborations between

France and Australia in the areas of Human Health Research, Environmental Research, or Nuclear Fuel Cycle Research.

Level of Study: Doctorate, Postdoctorate

Type: Scholarship

Application Procedure: Download the SAAFE application form from www.ainse.edu.au/saafe/. Please review the guidelines within the form carefully. Completed application forms, along with all supporting documentation, must be received by enquiries@ainse.edu.au

Closing Date: 30 April

Contributor: Australian Institute of Nuclear Science and Engineering Inc.

Additional Information: More information, guidelines and conditions, as well as the application form are available on the AINSE website: www.ainse.edu.au/saafe/ au.ambafrance.org/Grants-and-Opportunities-6980#SAAFE-program-2020

For further information contact:

Email: enquiries@ainse.edu.au

Embassy of the United States in Kabul

Humphrey Fellowship Program, Public Affairs Section, United States Embassy, Kabul, Afghanistan.

Tel: (93) 700 10 8000
Website: af.usembassy.gov/embassy/kabul/

The mission of the U.S. Embassy in Kabul is to promote bilateral ties between the United States and Afghanistan. Embassy activities focus on strengthening democratic institutions, enhancing security and regional stability, fighting international terrorism, combating narcotics production and trafficking, and fostering expanded trade and investment. The U.S. Embassy's Public Affairs Section offers a wealth of information on all facets of life in the United States and also provides a forum for U.S.-Afghan cultural exchanges. The Information Resource Center (IRC) has extensive information on a variety of topics, including current and historical events and educational opportunities in the United States.

Ambassadors Fund for Cultural Preservation Small Grants Competition

Eligibility: 1. Full and complete Application for Federal Assistance (SF-424), including Budget Information for Non-Construction Programs (SF-424A), Assurances for Non-Construction Programs (SF-424B), Applicant Organizational Information Form, and, if applicable, Disclosure of Lobbying Activities (SF-LLL). 2. Project basics, including title, project dates, and AFCP focus area. 3. Project applicant information, including contact information, DUNS Number, and SAM registration status. 4. Project location. 5. Proof of official permission to undertake the project from the office, agency, or organization that either owns or is otherwise responsible for the preservation and protection of the site, object, or collection. 6. Project purpose that summarizes the project objectives and desired results. 7. Project activities description that presents the project tasks in chronological order (Note If the proposed project is part of a larger effort involving multiple projects supported by other entities, the plan must present the full scope of the preservation effort and the place of the proposed project within that larger effort). 8. Project time frame or schedule that lists the major project phases and milestones with target dates for achieving them (Note Applicants may propose project periods of up to 60 months [five years]). All submitted documents must be in English. 9. Project participant information, including resumes or CVs of the proposed project director and other primary project participants. For further information, refer website

Level of Study: Graduate

Type: Grant

Frequency: Annual

Country of Study: Any country

Application Procedure: The applicants will first be screened for technical eligibility based on the objectives, priorities, requirements, ineligible activities, and unallowable costs contained in this funding opportunity. The Embassy and its Washington office may deem applications ineligible if they do not fully adhere to the criteria stated

Closing Date: 28 November

Funding: Private

For further information contact:

United States Embassy New Delhi, Shantipath, Chanakyapuri, New Delhi, 110021, India.

Tel: (91) 11 2419 8000
Email: Nd_GrantApplications@state.gov

Hubert H. Humphrey Fellowship Program

Purpose: The Program provides a year of professional enrichment in the United States for experienced professionals from designated countries undergoing development or political transition. The Humphrey Program is a Fulbright exchange activity. Its primary funding is provided by the U.S. Congress through the Bureau of Educational and Cultural Affairs of the U.S. Department of State.

Eligibility: 1. An undergraduate (first university or Bachelor's) degree. A candidates must have completed a university degree program requiring at least four years of full-time study to qualify for participation in U.-S. graduate study programs. 2. Prospective Fellows should have a minimum of five years full-time professional experience in the relevant field and should be interested in the policy aspects of their field of specialization. 3. Limited or no prior experience in the United States. 4. Demonstrated leadership qualities. 5. Applicant should be a mid-career professionals in leadership positions who have demonstrated a commitment to public service and the potential for professional advancement. 6. English Language Ability TOEFL Score of 71 iBT or 6.0. – 7.0 IELTS is required but in the absence of TOEFL and IELTS at the time of submitting application, a certificate of formal English study should be provided.

Level of Study: Postdoctorate
Type: Fellowship
Length of Study: 10 month
Frequency: Annual
Country of Study: United States of America
Application Procedure: Please submit your complete application (af.usembassy.gov/wp-content/uploads/sites/268/Humphrey-2021-2022-Application-Form.pdf) to Kabul Humphrey Team (kabulhumphrey@state.gov)
Closing Date: 2 September
Funding: Government
Contributor: U.S. Congress through the Bureau of Educational and Cultural Affairs of the U.S. Department of State
Additional Information: af.usembassy.gov/humphrey-fellowship-program/?_ga=2.58160042.1290610849.161526 2936-1085123320.1615262936

For further information contact:

Kabul Humphrey Team, Afghanistan.

Email: kabulhumphrey@state.gov

Endeavour Research Fellowship

Canberra, ACT 2601 9880, Australia.

Email: endeavour@education.gov.au
Contact: Endeavour Research Fellowship

The Endeavour Scholarships and Fellowships are the Australian Government's competitive, merit-based scholarships and fellowships providing opportunities for Australians to undertake study, research or professional development overseas and for overseas citizens to do the same in Australia.

Endeavour Research Fellowship for International Applicants

Purpose: The Endeavour Scholarships and Fellowships aim to build Australia's reputation for excellence in the provision of education and research, support the internationalisation of the Australian higher education and research sectors and offer high-achieving individuals from overseas and Australia opportunities to increase their productivity and expertise in their field. The Endeavour Scholarships and Fellowships are the Australian Government's competitive, merit-based scholarships and fellowships providing opportunities for Australians to undertake study, research or professional development overseas and for overseas citizens to do the same in Australia.

Eligibility: Students from eligible countries can apply for the Endeavour Postgraduate Scholarship. List of Countries available in following link scholarship-positions.com/endeavour-research-fellowship-international-students-2014/2013/04/13/ You must 1. apply as an Individual Endeavour Leader or Applicant Institution. 2. submit your application by the closing date, answer all mandatory questions and attach all documents as specified in the application form. 3. not be undertaking their Leadership Activity in a country where they hold citizenship/dual citizenship or permanent residency. 4. be aged 18 years or over at the commencement of their Leadership Activity. 5. not be in receipt of any other Australian Government sponsored mobility, scholarship or fellowship benefits. 6. for Postgraduate or VET Leadership Activities, be undertaking an award course under the Australian Qualifications Framework at an Australian (Home or Host) organisation.

Level of Study: Doctorate, Masters Degree, Postdoctorate, Postgraduate
Type: Fellowship
Value: All recipients will receive travel allowance AU$3,000 (provision to pay up to AU$4,500 under special circumstances); establishment allowance AU$2,000 (fellowships) or AU$4,000 (scholarships); monthly stipend AU$3,000 (paid up to the maximum category duration on a pro-rata basis); health insurance for the full category duration (OSHC for international recipients); travel insurance (excluding during programme for international recipients); Endeavour scholarship recipients will also receive tuition fees paid up to the maximum study/research duration on

a pro-rata basis. Tuition includes student service and amenities fees

Length of Study: 4–6 months

Study Establishment: Fellowships are awarded in any field of study

Country of Study: Australia

Application Procedure: Applications must be submitted using the Endeavour Online application system. To apply you must 1. complete the online application form through EOL (for individual applicants) or ISEO (for applicant institutions) by the closing date. 2. provide all the information requested. 3. address all eligibility criteria and assessment criteria. 4. include all necessary attachments. Before applying, you must read and understand these Program Guidelines, the application form, the FAQs, the relevant Applicant Guide and the draft Award Agreement/Leadership Activity Schedule. These documents may be found at GrantConnect at www.grants.gov.au.

Closing Date: 15 November

Funding: Government

Additional Information: For more details please visit the website: scholarship-positions.com/endeavour-research-fellowship-international-students-2014/2013/04/13/

Engineering and Physical Sciences Research Council (EPSRC)

Polaris House, North Star Avenue, Wiltshire, Swindon SN2 1ET, United Kingdom.

Tel: (44) 17 93 444120
Email: grants@epsrc.ac.uk
Website: epsrc.ukri.org/

The Engineering and Physical Sciences Research Council (EPSRC) is the main funding body for engineering and physical sciences research in the UK. By investing in research and postgraduate training, we are building the knowledge and skills base needed to address the scientific and technological challenges facing the nation.

Daphne Jackson Fellowships

Purpose: Daphne Jackson Fellowships are unique. They offer researchers the opportunity to return to a research career after a break of two or more years for a family, health or caring reason. By combining a personlised retraining programme with

a challenging research project, held in a supportive UK university or research establishment, our Fellowships provide a vital opportunity for those looking to return to a research career.

Eligibility: The application process for a Daphne Jackson Fellowship is competitive. Individuals wishing to be considered for a Fellowship must meet the following criteria 1. A career break of at least two years' duration, taken for family, health or caring reasons. 2. A good first degree in a research subject. 3. A PhD, or at least three years research experience (academic or industrial) prior to the career break (with evidence of research impacts and outcomes). 4. UK residency status / right to remain in the UK indefinitely and based in the UK on application. 5. Good command of English (spoken and written). 6. Good computer skills. 7. Your application will be stronger if you also have post-doctoral experience and research impacts and outcomes.

Level of Study: Graduate, Postdoctorate, Research

Type: Fellowship

Value: A Daphne Jackson Fellowship covers the salary costs of the Fellow but it does not include the bench fees and consumables associated with a Fellowship.

Length of Study: 2 or 3 years

Frequency: As available

Country of Study: United Kingdom

Application Procedure: You can apply for a Daphne Jackson Fellowship in two ways 1. Submit an application for an advertised sponsored Fellowship where the field of research and/or the host institution may already be specified by the sponsor. The sponsor will then select their preferred candidate. You can view the opportunities currently available here daphnejackson.org/about-fellowships/current-opportunities/ Sponsored Fellowships are also advertised on university websites and on www.jobs.ac.uk/. 2. If you know the area of research you would like to return to and/or have identified a potential host institution and/or supervisors, you can apply for a Daphne Jackson Fellowship at any time. If your application is successful, the Trust will endeavour to find suitable sponsorship. Please contact us daphnejackson.org/contact/ to obtain further advice.

No. of awards offered: 25

Funding: Trusts

Contributor: The Daphne Jackson Trust

For further information contact:

Catherine Barber, Communications Manager, The Daphne Jackson Trust, Department of Physics, University of Surrey, Guildford, Surrey GU2 7XH, United Kingdom.

Tel: (44) 1483 689166
Email: c.barber@surrey.ac.uk; djmft@surrey.ac.uk

Engineering and Physical Sciences Research Council Standard Research Studentships

Purpose: To enable training in the methods of research

Eligibility: Non European Union nationals must be settled in the United Kingdom without being subject under immigration law to any restriction for the period to which they remain. European Union nationals may apply, provided their qualifications are equivalent to a British Upper Second Class (Honours) Degree. Support will be fees only unless migrant worker status has been established

Level of Study: Postgraduate

Type: Studentship

Value: £8,265 for students in London. £6,620 for students elsewhere (1,999–2,000 rates). Values are reviewed annually. In addition, other allowances are payable under certain conditions. Approved tuition fees are paid directly to the institution

Length of Study: Maximum 3 years

Frequency: Annual

Study Establishment: Higher education institution

Country of Study: Other

Application Procedure: Applicants must be nominated by departments of higher education institutes. Applications on behalf of students should be directed to the relevant address. Full information can be found on the web pages or from academic institutions

Closing Date: 12 July

Funding: Government

Royal Society EPSRC BBSRC and Rolls Royce PLC Industry Fellowships

Purpose: To enhance the communication on science and technology between those in industry and those in universities or similar institutions of higher education to the benefit of United Kingdom firms, higher education institutions and the individual scientist. The aim is to establish long-lasting personal and corporate linkages between the two sectors in the United Kingdom

Eligibility: Open to applicants of any nationality. Candidates should be at the mid-career level and have had significant achievement in their home organisations. Also a substantial career should be ahead of the candidate towards the end of the award, to build upon the contacts made during the fellowship. Candidates must hold a PhD or equivalent in their profession and a substantive post in a university or similar academic institution as a scientist, mathematician or engineer, or be employed as a scientist, mathematician or engineer in any industry, an industrial research organisation or a nationalised industry. Organisations partly or wholly supported by public funds may not act as the industrial partner for an award. Preference will be given to candidates showing evidence of previous contact with or interest in the other sector of employment

Level of Study: Postdoctorate

Type: Fellowship

Value: Payment of salary but not employers' National Insurance and pension contributions

Length of Study: Up to 2 years full–time. A part–time equivalent is available

Country of Study: Other

Application Procedure: Applicants must complete an application form available from the website. Details are available from the Royal Society Research Appointments Department

Closing Date: December

Funding: Commercial, Government, Private

Additional Information: The scheme provides opportunities for academic scientists, mathematicians and engineers to work in an industrial environment and undertake a project at any stage from fundamental science to industrial innovation, and for industrial scientists, mathematicians and engineers to undertake research or course development work in an institution of higher education daphnejackson.org/about-fellowships/

For further information contact:

The Royal Society, Research Appointments Department, 6 Carlton House Terrace, London SW1Y 5AR, United Kingdom.

Tel:	(44) 20 7451 2547
Fax:	(44) 20 7930 2170
Email:	e-gap@royalsoc.ac.uk

Engineers Canada

55 Metcalfe Street, Suite 300, Ottawa, ON K1P 6L5, Canada.

Tel:	(1) 613 232 2474
Email:	awards@engineerscanada.ca
Website:	engineerscanada.ca/

Engineers Canada upholds the honour, integrity, and interests of the engineering profession by supporting consistent high standards in the regulation of engineering, encouraging the growth of the profession in Canada, and inspiring public confidence.

Engineers Canada's National Scholarship Program

Purpose: To reward excellence in the Canadian engineering profession and support advanced studies and research
Eligibility: Open to citizens or permanent residents of Canada who are registered as professional engineers in good standing with a provincial/territorial engineering association/order
Level of Study: Doctorate, Graduate, MBA, Postgraduate, Research
Type: Scholarships
Value: Canadian C$70,000 in total
Frequency: Annual
Country of Study: Canada and abroad
Application Procedure: Applicants must contact Marc Bourgeois for further details
No. of awards offered: Approx. 50-55
Closing Date: 1 March
Contributor: TD Insurance Meloche-Monnex Insurance and Manulife Financial

For further information contact:

Tel: (1) 613 232 2474 ext. 238
Fax: (1) 613 230 5759
Email: marc.bourgeois@engineerscanada.ca

Engineers Canada-Manulife Scholarship

Purpose: The Manulife Scholarship program offers three scholarships to provide financial assistance to engineers returning to university for further study or research in an engineering field.
Eligibility: To be eligible for the scholarships program, candidates must be registered as an engineer (P.Eng./ing.) in good standing with one of the 12 regulators (engineerscanada.ca/regulatory-excellence/engineering-regulators) throughout the duration of their academic year. You are a Canadian citizen or a permanent resident of Canada. Candidates must be accepted or registered for a minimum of two full-time semesters.
Level of Study: Postgraduate
Type: Scholarship
Value: C$12,500 each
Frequency: Annual
Application Procedure: 1. You are encouraged to read the general information carefully, as only complete applications will be considered. 2. Applications can be submitted in either English or French and Engineers Canada will arrange for translation as required. 3. Submit only the required documents. 4. All questions must be clearly answered in the space provided on the webform. 5. Click the link to submit the webform engineerscanada.ca/awards-and-honours/scholarships/application
No. of awards offered: 3
Closing Date: 31 March
Additional Information: Applicants may only apply in one scholarship category per year. Selection of the scholarship recipients will be based only on the information provided on the application. No restrictions will be placed on scholarship recipients holding other grants or awards or receiving assistance or income from other sources. It should be noted that no individual is eligible to hold two scholarships from Engineers Canada within a competition year. Candidates must show how the degree undertaken fulfills the stated purpose of the scholarship. For more information: engineerscanada.ca/awards-and-honours/scholarships/engineers-canada-manulife-scholarship

English-Speaking Union (ESU)

Dartmouth House, 37 Charles Street, London W1J 5ED, United Kingdom.

Tel: (44) 20 7529 1550
Email: info@dartmouthhouse.co.uk
Website: www.esu.org/

The English-Speaking Union is a charity working to give young people the speaking and listening skills and the cross-cultural understanding they need to thrive Listen, Speak, Succeed.

English-Speaking Union Travelling Librarian Award

Purpose: To encourage United States and United Kingdom contacts in the library world and establish links between pairs of libraries
Eligibility: Open to professionally qualified United Kingdom and information professionals
Level of Study: Professional development
Type: Award
Value: Up to £3,000. Board and lodging and relevant flight costs
Length of Study: A minimum of 3 weeks
Frequency: Annual
Country of Study: United States of America
Application Procedure: Candidates must submit a curriculum vitae and a covering letter explaining why they are the ideal candidates for the award

No. of awards offered: 16
Closing Date: April
Funding: Commercial, Private
Contributor: The English-Speaking Union and The Chartered Institute of Library and Information Professionals
Additional Information: Candidates should contact the Librarian by telephone or email at library@esu.org
www.sla.intexta.co.uk/blg-travelling-librarian-award.php

For further information contact:

37 Charles Street, London W1J 5ED, United Kingdom.

Email: education@esu.org

Entente Cordiale Scholarships

c/o The British Library, 96 Euston Road, London NW1 2DB, United Kingdom.

Tel: (44) 207 412 5507
Email: info@francobritish.org
Website: francobritish.org/en/entente-cordiale/
Contact: Franco-British Council

The Entente Cordiale Scholarship Programme is a prestigious awards scheme that funds British postgraduate students who want to study in France. The Entente Cordiale Scholarships provide students with the opportunity to experience life on the other side of the channel and widen their horizons. The programme was founded in 1995 by President Jacques Chirac and Prime Minister John Major at a summit meeting. In December 2017, the Franco-British Council became the trustee of the Entente Cordiale Scholarship Trust.

Bourses Scholarships

Purpose: To allow individuals to study or carry out research in France
Eligibility: Open to British citizens
Level of Study: Postgraduate
Type: Scholarship
Value: £8,000 for students living in Paris and £7,500 for those studying outside Paris for the 1-year award, £3,000 for 3 months, £6,000 for 6 months
Length of Study: 3 months, 6 months, or 1-year
Frequency: Annual

Study Establishment: Approved universities or grande écoles
Country of Study: France
Application Procedure: Applicants must complete an application form, available from the website
No. of awards offered: 60
Closing Date: 15 March
Funding: Private
Contributor: Blue Circle (Lafarge), BP, Kingfisher PLC, EDF Energy, UBS, Xerox, Paul Minet, Sir Patrick Sheehy Schlumberger, Vodafone, Rolls Royce, Parthenon Trust
Additional Information: Scholarships are also awarded to French postgraduates to study in the United Kingdom. Interested parties should contact the British Council in Paris www.sla.intexta.co.uk/blg-travelling-librarian-award.php

For further information contact:

Email: scholarships-bourses@cbie.ca

Entomological Society of Canada (ESC)

503-386 Broadway, Winnipeg, MB R3C 3R6, Canada.

Tel: (1) 888 821 8387
Email: info@esc-sec.ca
Website: www.esc-sec.ca
Contact: Ryan Jones, Association Coordinator

Founded in Toronto on 16 April 1863, The Entomological Society of Canada was open to all students and lovers of Entomology. The Entomological Society of Canada will be the lead organization to promote, facilitate, communicate and advocate for research and education on insects and their relatives, mentor the development of younger entomologists, and showcase Canada's entomological expertise nationally and internationally.

John H. Borden Scholarship

Subjects: Integrated Pest Management (IPM) with an entomological emphasis
Purpose: In honour of Dr. John H. Borden, and his prestigious contributions in the field of forest pest ecology, the Entomological Society of Canada is offering one postgraduate award.

Eligibility: Applicant must be a full time postgraduate student at the time of application, studying IPM at a degree granting institution in Canada.
Level of Study: Postgraduate
Type: Scholarship
Value: C$1,000
Frequency: Annual
Country of Study: Canada
Application Procedure: Applications for Scholarships are to be submitted by email to the ESC Association Coordinator at info@esc-sec.ca. The application must contain the following documents in this order and be in a single pdf file 1. Cover page (1. Scholarship being applied for John H. Borden Scholarship in IPM. 2. our name and email address. 3. Email addresses of those providing letters of support.). 2. Curriculum vitae (6 pages maximum). 3. Scanned set of transcripts, either of originals, or copies certified as such by a graduate secretary/administrator or graduate supervisor, showing undergraduate and post graduate (if applicable) grades. Scan at low quality to reduce the size of the file as much as possible. Reduce size of pdf file as well. 4. A statement (1 page) of why you are studying entomology, or IPM for the Borden Scholarship. 5. A summary of your thesis research (1 page). 6. Arrange for letters of reference from your supervisor and one other person, which clearly indicate your academic abilities, communication skills, progress as a graduate student, and the novelty and scholastic contribution of your research to the field of entomology. For the John Borden Scholarship the letters should indicate the contribution of your work to IPM.
No. of awards offered: 1
Closing Date: 1 March
Additional Information: During the course of a single degree program, a student cannot receive the same scholarship more than once. esc-sec.ca/student/student-awards/#toggle-id-4

For further information contact:

ESC Association Coordinator.

Email: info@esc-sec.ca

Environmental Leadership Program

P.O. BOX 907, Greenbelt, MD 20768-0907, United States of America.

Email: info@elpnet.org
Website: elpnet.org/

The mission of the Environmental Leadership Program (ELP) is to support visionary, action-oriented, and diverse leadership for a just and sustainable future. ELP aims to catalyze change by providing emerging leaders with the support and guidance they need to launch new endeavors, achieve new successes, and rise to new leadership positions.

Environmental Leadership Fellowships

Purpose: To build the leadership capacity of the environmental field's most promising and emerging practitioners
Eligibility: Open to citizens of the United States only
Level of Study: Postgraduate
Type: Fellowship
Value: US$750 which includes room and board for the 3 overnight retreats, participation in 10 days of training and community building and access to our network of over 480 Senior Fellows
Length of Study: 2 years
Frequency: Annual
Country of Study: United States of America
Closing Date: 2 April

For further information contact:

Email: lori@elpnet.org

Environmental Protection Agency

PO Box 3000, Johnstown Castle Estate, Wexford, Y35 W821, Ireland.

Tel: (353) 53 916 0600
Email: info@epa.ie
Website: www.epa.ie/

The Environmental Protection Agency is at the front line of environmental protection and policing. We ensure that Ireland's environment is protected, and we monitor changes in environmental trends to detect early warning signs of neglect or deterioration. To protect and improve the environment as a valuable asset for the people of Ireland. To protect our people and the environment from harmful effects of radiation and pollution

Environmental Protection Agency-IRC Scholarship Scheme

Purpose: In partnership with the Irish Research Council, the Environmental Protection Agency (EPA) invites applications for an Environmental Protection Agency Postgraduate Scholarship, hereinafter referred to as an EPA Postgraduate Scholarship.

Eligibility: Under the EPA Co-funded Scholarships Scheme, funding is available for a small number of awards, as per the following 48-month PhDs (indicative budget of €96,000); Limited to new and innovative projects; Co-funded by an Irish host research institution on a 50/50 basis; EPA is to be consulted in the drafting of the proposed PhD scope, as well as in the selection process of the candidate (i.e. interview panel); All co-funded PhDs would have to adhere to the EPA's funding rules and reporting requirements

Level of Study: Postgraduate

Type: Scholarship

Value: a stipend of €16,000 per annum a contribution to fees, including non-European Union fees, up to a maximum of €5,750 per annum eligible direct research expenses of €2,250 per annum

Frequency: Annual

Country of Study: Any country

Application Procedure: All participants must create and submit their forms via the online system.

Funding: Private

For further information contact:

3 Shelbourne Buildings, Crampton Avenue, Ballsbridge, D04 C2Y6, Ireland.

Tel: (353) 1 231 5000
Email: info@research.ie

Escola Superior d'Administració i Direcció d'Empreses (ESADE)

Mateo Inurria, 25-27, E-28036 Madrid, Spain.

Tel: (34) 913 597 714
Email: esade.madrid@esade.edu
Website: www.esade.edu/en

Esade is a global institution structured as a Business School, a Law School, and an Executive Education area. Esade is a global academic institution known for the quality of its education, its international outlook, and its focus on holistic personal development. Esade has strong ties to the business world. Dating back to its founding in 1958, Esade's history has been marked by a global and innovative character.

Escola Superior d'Administració i Direcció d'Empreses (ESADE) MBA Scholarships

Purpose: To help outstanding candidates access the MBA programme, Esade awards several scholarships during the admissions process.

Eligibility: Depending on the scholarship enroled students (Fellowships plus Impact); Admitted students (Direct, Merit & Need-based Scholarships plus Excellence). Scholarships are awarded, restricted by merit achievement, geographical area, sector of activity and need based

Level of Study: MBA

Type: Scholarships

Value: Awards range from 10% to 50% of programme tuition fees, being the average award last intake 21% of tuition fees.

Length of Study: 12, 15, or 18 months

Frequency: Annual

Study Establishment: ESADE Business School

Country of Study: Spain

Application Procedure: Send all required documents for your admittance to Admission Department, complete your Scholarship Application Form (Annex 1), include supporting documents, send all required documents in PDF format to mba@esade.edu

Additional Information: www.esade.edu/mba/en/programmes/full-time-mba/fees-and-financing/full-time-mba-scholarships

For further information contact:

Avinguda d'Esplugues, 92-96, E-08034 Barcelona, Spain.

Email: esadecrm@esade.edu

ESMOD Berlin

Hessnatur Foundation Scholarship

Purpose: Hessnatur Foundation offering Scholarships for ESMOD Berlin students to provide financial assistance for pursuing Master's Program in Sustainability in Fashion, the Hessnatur foundation is a non-profit, independent foundation conducting research and development in the field of applied sustainability, the main objective of Hessnatur Foundation covers the following charitable fields of activity.

Eligibility: 1. Candidates applying for Hessnatur Foundation Scholarship, must have applied successfully and received acceptance to the M.A. Sustainability in Fashion at ESMOD Berlin. 2. Applicants must be able to afford other expenses which include living costs and course related material costs. 3. Applicants of Hessnatur Foundation Scholarship, must possess the visas and insurances that are required to study in Germany by the start date of the course. 4. Scholarship holders are required to agree to allow ESMOD Berlin and the Hessnatur Foundation to use their images/other media and their works for educational and promotional purposes

Level of Study: Masters Degree, Postgraduate

Type: Scholarship

Study Establishment: ESMOD Berlin

Country of Study: Germany

Application Procedure: Applications must be sent via email to j.hurley@esmod.de

Closing Date: March

Additional Information: scholarship-fellowship.com/hessnatur-foundation-scholarship/

Eta Sigma Phi

School of Arts and Humanities, Stockton University, 101 Vera King Farris Dr., Galloway, NJ 08205, United States of America.

Website: www.etasigmaphi.org/
Contact: Dr. Katherine Panagakos, Executive Secretary

Eta Sigma Phi had its beginning in 1914 when a group of students in the Department of Greek at the University of Chicago organized an undergraduate classical club to which honor students in Greek and Latin were elected to membership. This organization later united with a similar organization at Northwestern University and became Eta Sigma Phi. In 1924 the society became national, and chapters were organized at leading colleges and universities. Eta Sigma Phi is the national honorary collegiate society for students of Latin and/or Greek. Members are elected by local chapters which have been chartered by the society.

Eta Sigma Phi Summer Scholarships

Purpose: To enable one member of Eta Sigma Phi to attend the summer session of the American Academy in Rome, Italy, another to attend the summer session of the American School of Classical Studies in Athens, Greece and a third to attend a session of the Vergilian Society at Cumae, Italy

Eligibility: This scholarship open to members who have received a Bachelor's degree within the eight years prior to application (or shall have received it by June 1st of the current year) and who have not received a doctoral degree. For Scholarship to the American Academy in Rome, Six semester hours of credit may be earned and applied toward an advanced degree in Classics at most graduate schools, provided that arrangements have been made in advance with the graduate school. For The Vergilian Society at Cumae, members who will be rising juniors or seniors in the coming summer; preference will be given to such undergraduate students.

Level of Study: Postgraduate

Type: Scholarship

Value: Scholarship to the American Academy in Rome has a value of US$3,575, The Brent Malcolm Froberg Scholarship to the American School of Classical Studies at Athens has a value of up to US$3,300 (Eta Sigma Phi covers one-half of program fees and the American School remits the other half.) and The Theodore Bedrick Scholarship to the Vergilian Society at Cumae has a total value of up to US$2,900, including the remission of one-half the tuition fee by the Vergilian Society. Only tours in Italy are covered by this scholarship

Frequency: Annual

Study Establishment: The American Academy in Rome, The American School of Classical Studies at Athens, and the Virgilian Society at Cumae

Country of Study: Other

Application Procedure: Applicants must submit a transcript of undergraduate work, letters of recommendation, and a statement not to exceed 500 words to include purpose and reasons for desiring the scholarship. For scholarship application 32cw1q2flwho2fg8v42gqwuk-wpengine.netdna-ssl.com/wp-content/uploads/2017/10/SummerTravelScholarshipApplication.pdf. Send applications and letters of recommendation to postal address or by email mpranger@olemiss.edu

Closing Date: 15 February

Funding: Private

Additional Information: Note: In order to be valid membership must have been registered with the national office of Eta Sigma Phi by the application deadline. www.etasigmaphi.org/summer-2021-scholarship-deadlines/

For further information contact:

Dr. Molly Pasco-Pranger, Department of Classics, P.O. Box 1848, University of Mississippi, University, MS 38677, United States of America.

Tel: (1) 662 915 7097
Email: mpranger@olemiss.edu

Ethnic Minority Foundation

Boardman House, 64 Broadway, Stratford E15 1NT, United Kingdom.

Tel:	(44) 20 8432 0602
Email:	enquiries@emfoundation.org.uk
Website:	www.emfoundation.org.uk/

EMF is a national registered charity created in 1999; it is a social enterprise charity that uses surplus from its investment property income in London to fund its charitable activities. Our policy is to maintain reasonable salaries and overheads to maximise our capacity for public benefit.

Ethnic Minority Foundation Grants

Purpose: To provide long-term and short-term funding of minority ethnic voluntary and community organizations, and funding for other community needs such as education, health, women's and youth projects
Type: Grant

For further information contact:

Tel: (44) 208 432 0300, Free Phone: 800 652 0390
Fax: (44) 208 432 0319

Eugène Vinaver Memorial Trust

Email:	jane.taylor@durham.ac.uk or g.n. bromiley@durham.ac.uk
Website:	www.internationalarthuriansociety.com/vinaver
Contact:	Director, Professor Jane Taylor or Secretary, Dr Geoffrey Bromiley

The Vinaver Trust awards grants towards the publication costs of books on Arthurian topics. It was established in 1981, when the British Branch of the International Arthurian Society, at the urging of Eugène Vinaver, formerly professor of medieval French at Manchester University, and Cedric Pickford, professor of Medieval French at the University of Hull, found the British Branch had earned an astonishingly large sum in royalties from endorsing Arthurian plates for a Swiss ceramics firm, Atelier Arts. Grants extend to any scholarly publication on an Arthurian topic, in any of the languages endorsed by the International Arthurian Society, that is German, French and English; they have covered Arthurian topics of all sorts, literary, historical, artistic, cinematic.

Barron Bequest

Subjects: Any field of Arthurian studies
Purpose: The Eugène Vinaver Trust, in association with the British Branch of the International Arthurian Society and under the terms of the Barron Bequest, offers a number of annual awards for postgraduate research in any field of Arthurian Studies.
Eligibility: The awards are open to graduates of any university in the British Isles, including those of the Republic of Ireland.
Level of Study: Postgraduate
Type: Grant
Value: £1,250, are intended as a contribution to postgraduate fees.
Frequency: Annual
Study Establishment: Any university in United Kingdom or Ireland
Country of Study: United Kingdom, Republic of Ireland
Application Procedure: They may be held at any university in the British Isles, including those of the Republic of Ireland, except Owens College, University of Manchester. For application details, please download application document form www.internationalarthuriansociety.com/british-branch/view/awards and send the completed form as a paper copy to Professor Jane H M Taylor.
Closing Date: 30 April
Funding: Private
Contributor: The Eugène Vinaver Memorial Trust
Additional Information: www.internationalarthuriansociety.com/british-branch/view/awards

For further information contact:

Professor Jane H M Taylor, Garth Head, Penruddock, Penrith, Cumbria CA11 0QU, United Kingdom.

Email: jane.taylor@durham.ac.uk

European Association for the Study of Diabetes

Rheindorfer Weg 3, D-40591 Dusseldorf, Germany.

Tel:	(49) 211 758 469 0
Email:	secretariat@easd.org
Website:	www.easd.org/
Contact:	Dr. Monika Grüsser, Managing Director

The European Association for the Study of Diabetes e.V. (EASD) is a non-profit, medical scientific association. It was founded in 1965 and its headquarters is based in Duesseldorf, Germany. The aims of the Association are to encourage and support research in the field of diabetes, the rapid diffusion of acquired knowledge and to facilitate its application.

European Association for the Study of Diabetes-ADA Transatlantic Fellowships

Purpose: To encourage research into basic or clinical questions related to diabetes and its complications
Eligibility: Applicants should have completed their MD, PhD or equivalent within the previous 7 years and cannot be serving an internship or residency during the fellowship. European applicants must be EASD members and United States of America applicants should be ADA members
Level of Study: Research
Type: Fellowship
Value: US$50,000
Length of Study: 1 year
Frequency: Annual
Country of Study: United States of America
Application Procedure: Applications must be made on the forms provided. Two copies of the application forms should be submitted
Closing Date: 1 February
Contributor: EASD-Lilly Research Fund
Additional Information: Successful applicants will be notified of the award by 1 April. Funding begins on 1 July www.internationalarthuriansociety.com/british-branch/view/awards

European Calcified Tissue Society

Rue Washington 40, B-1050 Brussels, Belgium.

Tel: (32) 476 520 716
Email: ects@ectsoc.org; Roberta.mugnai@ectsoc.org
Website: www.ectsoc.org
Contact: Roberta Mugnai, Executive Director

The European Calcified Tissue Society is a volunteer-led, non-for-profit medical society and our members are basic and clinical researchers, allied health professionals who join forces to foster a multidisciplinary approach in the musculoskeletal field. ECTS can support your professional journey

and membership is open to anyone working in the field at whatever stage in the career and from anywhere in the world.

European Calcified Tissue Society/Servier Fellowship

Purpose: To encourage the research involving pathophysiology of osteoporosis, particularly the coupling and uncoupling processes between bone formation and bone resorption and all related matters
Eligibility: Open for ECTS members who qualified PhD/MD within the last 10 years. Applications to include details of a preclinical or clinical research project on the pathophysiology of osteoporosis, particularly the coupling and uncoupling processes between bone formation and bone resorption and all related matters
Level of Study: Research
Type: Fellowship
Value: €80,000
Length of Study: 2 years
Frequency: Every 2 years
Country of Study: Any country
Application Procedure: Applicants should fill an application form. For further details log on to www.ectsoc.org
No. of awards offered: 20
Closing Date: November
Funding: Commercial
Contributor: Servier
Additional Information: ectsoc.org/grants-awards-funding/grants/ectsservier-fellowship/

For further information contact:

Email: ects@ectsoc.org

European Committee for Treatment and Research in Multiple Sclerosis (ECTRIMS)

Reinacherstrasse 131, CH-4053 Basel, Switzerland.

Tel: (41) 61 686 77 79
Email: secretariat@ectrims.eu
Website: www.ectrims.eu/
Contact: ECTRIMS Secretariat

The European Committee for Treatment and Research in Multiple Sclerosis (ECTRIMS) is a non-profit organisation and an independent representative European-wide organisation devoted to MS. ECTRIMS works with researchers and clinicians of its member countries and with other organisations that share similar missions and objectives on a worldwide scale, creating networking and collaboration opportunities. The ultimate goal of ECTRIMS is to improve basic and clinical research and clinical outcomes in MS.

Allied Health Care Professionals

Subjects: psychologists, physiotherapists
Eligibility: 1. Citizens of any country are eligible to apply to this programme; however, the training must be undertaken in a European institution or clinic. 2. Candidates must have a professional qualification (with relevant degree) such as nursing, psychology, physiotherapy/ rehabilitation, etc. and, if appropriate, be licensed to practise in their home country. 3. It is anticipated that successful candidates will have either no prior MS experience or some prior, but not necessarily extensive, full- or part-time MS experience at their home institution; and that the candidate will return to their home institution after training or move on to an MS-related position at another institution, better prepared to excel in MS care, management and research and to better support people living with MS and the MS clinical care team. 4. In general, successful candidates will be 55 years of age or younger and will anticipate continuing in their MS careers upon completion of the training. 5. Candidates and their mentors must affirm that there will be no language barriers that will impede the training experience.
Type: Award
Value: €27,500
Length of Study: six-month programme
Frequency: Annual
Country of Study: Any country
Application Procedure: ECTRIMS MS Professional Training Fellowships for Nurses, Psychologists, Physiotherapists, and Related Allied Health Care Professionals will be awarded in a competitive review process conducted by members of the ECTRIMS Executive Committee and designated consultants. Applications will be evaluated based on the: 1. candidate's qualifications, including education, previous employment history, current employment responsibilities, self-stated goals of training, and an evaluation of the candidate's career plans 2. qualifications and characteristics of the proposed training mentor 3. qualifications and characteristics of the host institution 4. the nature of the proposed training plan and its plausibility 5. the quality of letters of endorsement from the proposed mentor and from the home institution and from professional references.
Closing Date: 1 December

For further information contact:

Email: fellowship@ectrims.eu

European Committee for Treatment and Research in Multiple Sclerosis-MAGNIMS Fellowship in Magnetic Resonance Imaging in MS

Purpose: The European MAGNIMS network (Magnetic Resonance Imaging in MS) and ECTRIMS jointly support research fellowships for young European researchers in the application of magnetic resonance studies to MS.
Eligibility: Applicants should be under 40 years and affiliated to an academic department, which can guarantee a continuation of his or her research.
Type: Fellowship
Value: €55,000
Length of Study: 1 year
Frequency: Annual
Country of Study: Any country
Application Procedure: The following documents are required 1. Letter of intention. 2. Applicant's curriculum vitae including her/his past experience, goals for training, future career plans and publications (not to exceed 5 pages). 3. Project description. 4. Letter of acceptance from and short description of the host institution. 5. Letter of support from the home institution. 6. Acceptance of the ECTRIMS-MAGNIMS payment rules including a certification from the host institution accepting the terms of the ECTRIMS fellowship and payments. The necessary form is available from the online application system; the applicant should forward this form to the host institution for completion. 7. Applicant's proof of sufficient English language knowledge to ensure no language barriers with their training location, and to hold presentations, write the final report and prepare a scientific article for an international journal.
No. of awards offered: 2
Closing Date: 1 December
No. of awards given last year: 2

For further information contact:

Prof. Christian Enzinger, Division of General Neurology, University Clinic of Neurology - Medical University of Graz, Graz, Austria.

Email: chris.enzinger@medunigraz.at

Postdoctoral Research Training

Purpose: ECTRIMS offers a postdoctoral research fellowship exchange programme for young neuroscientists to facilitate their conduct of and training in basic, clinical or applied research related to multiple sclerosis (MS).

Eligibility: 1. Scientists and physicians who hold or are candidates for an MD, PhD, ScD or equivalent professional degree are eligible. 2. Candidates must have received their advanced degree(s) prior to initiation of the fellowship. 3. At the time of application, fellows should have no more than one year of prior postdoctoral training at the same host institution/mentor. More senior candidates may have no more than five years total of postdoctoral experience beyond their final degree (PhD, MD, ScD or equivalent) at the time of application. 4. In general, successful applicants will be less than 40 years of age at the time of application; exceptions under special circumstances will be considered. 5. Citizens of any country are eligible to apply to this programme; however, postdoctoral research training must be undertaken in a European laboratory or clinic. 6. Candidates and their mentors must affirm that there will be no language barriers that will impede the training experience.

Type: Research grant
Value: €55,000
Frequency: Annual
Country of Study: Any country
Application Procedure: ECTRIMS Research Fellowships will be awarded in a competitive review process conducted by members of the ECTRIMS Research Fellowship Review Committee. Applications will be evaluated based on the: 1. candidate qualifications, educational history and evaluation of career plans 2. qualifications and characteristics of the proposed fellowship mentor and host institution 3. the proposed research plan, including assessment of the scientific quality, innovation, perceived feasibility, quality of letters of endorsement from the proposed mentor and from referees at the fellow's home institution, etc.

For further information contact:

Email: fellowship@ectrims.eu

European Crohn's and Colitis Organisation

Ungargasse 6/13, A-1030 Vienna, Austria.

Tel: (43) 1 710 2242 0
Email: ecco@ecco-ibd.eu
Website: www.ecco-ibd.eu/

The European Crohn's and Colitis Organisation (ECCO), founded in 2001 to improve the care of patients with inflammatory bowel disease (IBD) in Europe, is now the largest forum for specialists in IBD in the world. It is a non-profit association, which successfully expanded from an organisation comprising 14 Country Members to an association assembling 36 member states of the Council of Europe and facilitating collaborations beyond Europe's borders. In 2009, we introduced individual membership allowing anyone around the globe interested in IBD to both benefit from our programmes and services and to join us in our mission. The ECCO Office is headquartered in Vienna, Austria, providing day-to-day support to its members and committees, and securing the seamless planning and organisation of the annual ECCO Congress and educational events.

ECCO GRANT

Purpose: ECCO Grants are designed to support IBD Research within the country of affiliation. Typically, research for ECCO Grant projects is undertaken in the home institution of the applicant. Promote innovative scientific research in IBD in Europe. Promote innovative scientific research in IBD in Europe.
Eligibility: 1. Not be older than 40 years. 2. If older than 40 years, who are within 5 years of the date of completion of their GI training or PhD graduation (a certificate needs to be provided). 3. The applicant needs to be an ECCO Member at the time of application. 4. ECCO Grants are not limited to applicants from ECCO Member countries. Applicants from non-European countries have to clearly state the impact of the proposed project on the IBD Community. 5. If your institute holds a current ECCO Grant, then another application for this period is not possible. Therefore, an institute cannot apply for two ECCO Grants in consecutive years. 6. Applicants can apply for one ECCO Award category only per annual application round. 7. Recipients that have been awarded an ECCO Grant in the past cannot reapply. 8. Submit an original research project proposal using the ECCO Fellowships and Grants Online Submission Pages.
Level of Study: Postgraduate
Type: Grant
Value: €80,000
Length of Study: 1 year
Frequency: Annual
Country of Study: Any country
Application Procedure: Applications are to be submitted using the ECCO Fellowships and Grants Online Submission Pages cm.ecco-ibd.eu/cmPortal/Account/Login?ReturnUrl= %2FcmPortal%2FPortal%2FGEN00%2Fnormal.   Please refer www.ecco-ibd.eu/images/5_Science/5_2_Fellowships_Grants/2021/2022_MASTER_ECCO%20Grants%20Fact% 20Sheet_new.pdf.

No. of awards offered: 8
Closing Date: 1 August
Additional Information: www.ecco-ibd.eu/science/fellowships-and-grants.html

For further information contact:

Email: ecco@ecco-ibd.eu

ECCO Pioneer Award

Purpose: Promote visionary, innovative, and inter-disciplinary research projects in the field of IBD.
Eligibility: See Website.
Level of Study: Research
Type: Award
Value: € 300,000
Length of Study: 2 year
Frequency: Annual
Country of Study: Any country
No. of awards offered: 1
Closing Date: 1 August

For further information contact:

Email: ecco@ecco-ibd.eu

ECCO-AOCC Visiting Travel Grant

Purpose: Offering European and Asian investigators exchange visits to IBD Centres in Asia or Europe, respectively
Type: Grant
Value: €10,000
Length of Study: 3 months
Frequency: Annual
Country of Study: Any country
No. of awards offered: 2
Closing Date: 1 August

For further information contact:

Email: ecco@ecco-ibd.eu

European Crohn's and Colitis Organisation Fellowship

Purpose: The European Crohn's and Colitis Organisation (ECCO) offers Research Fellowships to encourage and support young individuals in their career and promote innovative scientific research in the area of Inflammatory Bowel Diseases (IBD) in Europe. ECCO Research Fellowships aim to enhance the opportunity for IBD Trainees to work in European centres other than their own. Promote innovative scientific research and knowledge exchange in IBD in Europe.

Eligibility: 1. Not be older than 40 years or still in training at the time of application. 2. Submit an original research project using the ECCO Fellowships and Grants Online Submission Pages. Incomplete applications will not be evaluated. 3. Provide a confirmation from the host institute stating that the applicant is accepted for a Fellowship, and will be under the supervision of a designated host. Both the host institute and the fellow are responsible for the successful outcome of the Fellowship. 4. At the time of the application as well as prior to the commencement of the Fellowship the candidate cannot be involved/work in any research project at the future host institute. 5. If your host institute holds a current ECCO Fellowship, then another application for this period is not possible. Therefore, an institute cannot apply for two ECCO Fellowships in consecutive years. 6. Both the applicant and the host supervisor need to be ECCO Members at the time of application. 7. ECCO Fellowships are not limited to applicants from ECCO Member countries. Applicants from non-European countries have to clearly state the impact of the proposed project on the IBD Community. 8. Fellowships aim to enhance the opportunity for IBD Trainees to work in European centres. Exceptional circumstances such as an applicant from an ECCO Member Country travelling to a non-member country will be considered, but such an application is likely to receive a lower priority than an applicant from a member/nonmember country visiting an ECCO Member Country. 9. Applicants can apply for one ECCO Award category only per annual application round. 10. Recipients who were awarded an ECCO Fellowship in the past cannot reapply.

Type: Fellowship
Value: €60,000
Length of Study: 1 year
Frequency: Annual
Country of Study: Any country
Application Procedure: All applicants should submit a proposal for the research project using the ECCO Fellowships and Grants Online Submission Pages. Please refer www.ecco-ibd.eu/images/5_Science/5_2_Fellowships_Grants/2021/2022_MASTER_ECCO_Fellowship_Fact_Sheet.pdf . Apply online cm.ecco-ibd.eu/cmPortal/Account/Login?ReturnUrl=%2FcmPortal%2FPortal%2FGEN00%2Fnormal

No. of awards offered: 2
Closing Date: 1 August
Additional Information: www.ecco-ibd.eu/science/fellowships-and-grants.html

For further information contact:

Email: ecco@ecco-ibd.eu

European Molecular Biology Organization (EMBO)

EMBO, Meyerhofstrasse 1, D-69117 Heidelberg, Germany.

Tel: (49) 622 188 910
Email: astrid.gall@embo.org; embo@embo.org
Website: www.embo.org/
Contact: Astrid Gall, Communications Officer and Writer

The European Molecular Biology Organization (EMBO) was established in 1964. EMBO stands for excellence in the life sciences. EMBO is an organization of more than 1800 leading researchers that promotes excellence in the life sciences in Europe and beyond. The major goals of the organization are to support talented researchers at all stages of their careers, stimulate the exchange of scientific information, and help build a research environment where scientists can achieve their best work.

European Molecular Biology Organisation Award for Communication in the Life Sciences

Purpose: To promote and reward public communication of the life sciences and their applications by practising scientists in Europe
Eligibility: Open to scientists working in active research in an area of life sciences at the time of nomination. Candidates must be working in Europe or Israel, and the criterion for consideration is excellence in public communication of science via any medium or activity
Type: Monetary award and medal
Value: €5,000 accompanied by a silver and gold medal inscribed with the winner's name
Frequency: Annual
Application Procedure: Applicants must apply using the forms available on the website
No. of awards offered: 27
Closing Date: 1 May
Contributor: EMBO

For further information contact:

EMBO, Meyerhofstrasse 1, Heidelberg, D-69117, Germany.

Tel: (49) 622 188 91119
Fax: (49) 622 188 91200

Long-Term Fellowship

Purpose: The EMBO Long-Term Fellowships are awarded for a period of up to two years and support post-doctoral research visits to laboratories throughout Europe and the world. International exchange is a key feature in the application process.
Eligibility: Applicants must hold a doctorate degree or equivalent at the start of the fellowship. Applicants who already hold a PhD degree at the time of application are eligible to apply only if they obtained their PhD degree during the two years prior to the date the application is complete. Applicants must have at least one first author publication accepted in or published in an international peer reviewed journal at the time of application. All applications must involve movement between countries (detailed information about mobility requirements is listed in guidelines).
Level of Study: Postgraduate
Type: Fellowships
Value: stipend & allowances over 2 years
Length of Study: 2 years
Frequency: Annual
Closing Date: 8 September

European Science Foundation (ESF)

1, quai Lezay-Marnésia - BP 90015, F-67080 Strasbourg, France.

Tel: (33) 3 88 76 71 00
Website: www.esf.org/

The European Science Foundation (ESF) is a non-governmental, internationally-oriented, non-profit association established in France in 1974. ESF is committed to promoting the highest quality science in Europe to drive progress in research and innovation. We partner with diverse institutions by leading successful projects, facilitating informed decision-making through a broad range of science support partnerships: Research Project Grant Evaluation, the coordination of European projects, funding programmes and the administration of scientific platforms.

European Science Foundation Response of the Earth System to Impact Processes (IMPACT) Mobility Grants

Purpose: To initiate longer term research projects, encourage scientific exchanges, promote international and multidisciplinary collaborations, and build strong ties between

European institutions working on impact processes and their influence on the geological and biological evolution of the earth

Eligibility: Open to young scientists, graduate students or postdoctoral researchers. Established researchers can apply but must document that they do not have access to any other form of funding for this particular project. There are no restrictions regarding citizenship but applicants must be working in a European laboratory and applying for a stay in another European country

Level of Study: Graduate, Postdoctorate

Country of Study: Other

Application Procedure: Applicants must submit their personal details, institutional affiliation, brief curriculum vitae, a short invitation letter from the prospective host, a few key-words summarising the research, proposed investigation (maximum two printed pages in font size 12 or 600–1,000 words), significance of the investigation, justification of the collaborative research, and a detailed budget. One copy of the complete application must be sent to ESF and one to Dr Christian Koeberl at the University of Vienna

Contributor: The European Science Foundation

Additional Information: archives.esf.org/coordinating-research/research-networking-programmes/life-earth-and-environmental-sciences-lee/completed-esf-research-net working-programmes-in-life-earth-and-environmental-sciences/response-of-the-earth-system-to-impact-processes-impact.html

For further information contact:

University of Vienna, Althanstrae 14, Vienna, A-1090, Austria.

Fax: (43) 131 336 7841
Email: christian.koeberl@univie.ac.at

European Society of Surgical Oncology (ESSO)

Clos Chapelle-aux-Champs, 30 - bte 1.30.30, BE-1200 Brussels, Belgium.

Tel: (32) 2 880 62 62
Email: carine.lecoq@essoweb.org; info@essoweb.org
Website: www.essoweb.org/
Contact: Carine Lecoq, Chief Operating Officer

The European Society of Surgical Oncology, ESSO, was established in 1981 to support it's members in advancing

the science and practice of surgical oncology for the benefit of cancer patients. ESSO's mission is to support its members in advancing the science and practice of surgical oncology for the benefit of cancer patients. The Society aims to achieve this through a range of activities related to education, research and leadership in multidisciplinary care.

European Society of Surgical Oncology Training Fellowships

Purpose: The ESSO Education Committee offers trainees in Surgical Oncology the possibility to visit a specialist centre outside of their own country, helping them to expand their experience and learn new techniques.

Eligibility: 1. Applicants must be a specialist, trainee or junior doctor with a declared intention of specialising in a sub-specialty of surgical oncology (breast, upper GI, hepatobiliary and pancreatic, colorectal, endocrine, head and neck, thoracic, skin cancer and melanoma, gynaecology, urology, sarcoma). 2. Applicants must be ESSO members in good standing. 3. Applicants must be younger than 40 years of age or be in a training grade. 4. Both European and non-European citizens can apply. European applicants may choose to visit European or non-European units, while non-European applicants must choose to visit a European centre.

Level of Study: Postdoctorate

Type: Fellowship

Value: €1.500 for Standard training fellowships and €6.000 for Major training fellowship

Length of Study: 1 to 3 months for Standard training fellowships and 4 to 12 months for Major training fellowship

Frequency: Annual

Country of Study: Any country

Application Procedure: Applications must be submitted online (in English only) and include the following information 1. A motivation letter describing the applicant's area of interest, research plan and reasons behind the visit. 2. A letter of support from their Head of Department. 3. A letter of invitation from the Head of the Department they wish to visit. 4. A proposal budget sheet estimating how the funds will be spent. 5. A CV including present and previous positions held (include dates from and to), relevant publications and presentations to learned societies. Applicants must submit all above documents in a single PDF document.

No. of awards offered: 9

Additional Information: Please note: Applications from non-members will not be considered. Previous Fellowship recipients will be ineligible to apply for a second award. www.essoweb.org/fellowships/training-fellowships/

For further information contact:

Adriana Pereira, Communications and Education Coordinator.

Tel: (32) 2 880 62 63
Email: adriana.pereira@essoweb.org; info@essoweb.org

European Space Agency

Email: education@esa.int
Website: www.esa.int/
Contact: ESA HQ

The European Space Agency (ESA) is Europe's gateway to space. Its mission is to shape the development of Europe's space capability and ensure that investment in space continues to deliver benefits to the citizens of Europe and the world.

European Space Agency's Postdoctoral Internal Research Fellowship Programme

Purpose: ESA's postdoctoral Research Fellowship programme aims to offer young scientists and engineers the possibility to carry out research for two years in a variety of disciplines related to space science, space applications or space technology.
Eligibility: You must 1. Have recently completed, or be close to completing a PhD in a relevant technical or scientific discipline. Preference will be given to applications submitted by candidates within five years of receiving their PhD. 2. Be a citizen from one of the ESA Member States and European Cooperating States (www.esa.int/About_Us/Corporate_news/Member_States_Cooperating_States), or from Latvia and Slovenia as Associated Member States and Canada as a Cooperating State.
Level of Study: Doctorate
Type: Postdoctoral fellowship
Value: 1. A monthly remuneration (basic net salary or take-home pay) which ranges from €3,000 to €3,800 per month depending on thelocation of the ESA Establishment. 2. Comprehensive health cover under ESA's social security scheme. 3. Comprehensive health cover under ESA's social security scheme
Length of Study: 2 years
Study Establishment: Space science, Space applications and technology
Country of Study: Any country

Application Procedure: To apply for ESA Research Fellowship opportunities 1. To see open Research Fellowships, look for those positions titled Internal Research Fellow among the ESA job opportunities. Candidates are selected on the basis of their application to a Research Fellowship. 2. To apply, you first have to register and create your candidate profile. Once you have applied, you will be able to track the status of your application. 3. In addition to your CV and your motivation letter, please add a proposal of up to five pages outlining your proposed research.
Additional Information: For more details please refer to the link www.esa.int/About_Us/Careers_at_ESA/Post_docs_Research_Fellowship

For further information contact:

Email: contact.human.resources@esa.int

European Synchrotron Radiation Facility (ESRF)

71, avenue des Martyrs, CS 40220, F-38043 Grenoble Cedex 9, France.

Tel: (33) 4 76 88 27 57
Website: www.esrf.eu/
Contact: Gary Admans, Scientific Editor ESRF
             Communication Group

In 1988, the ESRF made history as the world's first third-generation synchrotron light source. The ESRF also offers research opportunities for industrial research and development. The experimental techniques available allow for testing in real time and under real operating conditions. Major companies in the fields of pharmaceuticals, chemistry, catalysis, cosmetics, food, batteries, nanotechnologies, medicine and materials use the ESRF's non-destructive techniques to improve their products and processes.

European Synchrotron Radiation Facility Postdoctoral Fellowships

Purpose: The post doctorate programme of the ESRF aims to allow young scientists from the international scientific community to acquire knowledge on the use of synchrotron radiation by participating in the running of the beamlines and in their associated research programmes.

Eligibility: 1. PhD in physics, biophysics, or closely related science obtained less than 3 years ago. 2. A strong background in computer programing is desirable. 3. Ability to interact with multi-disciplinary staff and facility users. 4. Proficiency in English (working language at the ESRF)

Level of Study: Postdoctorate

Type: Fellowship

Value: 1. The annual gross salary is fixed at €40,910 for the first two years. This salary may be increased during the third year depending upon performance. 2. In addition to the salary, the ESRF will pay a monthly expatriation allowance to new staff recruited from outside France under certain conditions of residence. For staff members recruited from outside the Grenoble area the ESRF will pay upon arrival, in one instalment, an installation allowance to contribute to installation costs. 3. Benefits include private health insurance and a supplementary pension scheme. The total contributions (for social security, pensions, health insurance and unemployment) amount to about 23% of the total remuneration (salary and allowances).

Length of Study: 2 to 3 years

Frequency: As available

Country of Study: France

Application Procedure: Applicants must complete an application form, available on www.esrf.eu

Funding: International office

Additional Information: Salary and allowances (total remuneration) are subject both to French income tax and to contributions to the French Social Security and other compulsory schemes. For more informations: www.esrf.eu/Jobs/Conditions/PostDocs www.eurosciencejobs.com/job_display/194368/Postdoctoral_Fellow_for_the_Structural_Biology_Group_ESRF_European_Synchrotron_Radiation_Facility_Grenoble_France.

For further information contact:

Max Nanao, France.

Tel: (33) 4 76 88 40 87
Email: max.nanao@esrf.fr

European Synchrotron Radiation Facility Thesis Studentships

Subjects: Machine, Computing Services and the Experiments Division

Purpose: The ESRF supports research projects related to the use of synchrotron radiation (SR) or to synchrotron/storage ring technology. In general projects will be proposed by the ESRF.

Eligibility: Candidates must be eligible for a Ph.D. programme and have to register at a university (in one of the member or associated countries available in follwoing link www.esrf.eu/about/organisation/members-and-associates). Special conditions apply to the first year for students based at a UK university.

Level of Study: Doctorate

Type: Studentship

Value: The monthly gross salary will be within the range of €2,286 to €2,560 determined initially for a 2-year period and is revised for the third year. The total contribution (for social security, pensions, health insurance and unemployment) represents about 23% of the gross remuneration.

Length of Study: 2–3 years

Frequency: As available

Country of Study: France

Application Procedure: Application should contain 1. The project title, 2. a 500 word description of the project describing its scientific basis, promise and relevance to the ESRF, 3. the nature of the arrangement with the university, 4. the name of the supervisor at the university, 5. an estimate of the financial costs and time limit. Applicants must complete an application form, available on www.esrf.eu.

Funding: International office

Additional Information: Travel expenses are reimbursed at the beginning and at the end of the contract according to the ESRF regulations. Removal costs, however, will not be refunded. This remuneration is subject both to French income tax which depends on the individual's family situation and to contributions to the French social security and other compulsory schemes. www.esrf.eu/Jobs/Conditions/PhDStudents

For further information contact:

Evelyne JEAN-BAPTISTE, Human Resources Service, CS 40220, F-38043 Grenoble cedex 9, France.

Tel: (33) 4 76 88 20 19

European University Institute (EUI)

Badia Fiesolana, via dei Roccettini, 9, San Domenico di Fiesole (FI), I-50014, Italy.

Tel: (39) 55 4685 359 (Int. 2359)
Email: mathias.neukirchen@eui.eu
Website: www.eui.eu/
Contact: Dr. Mathias Neukirchen, Director

The European University Institute (EUI) is a unique international centre for doctorate and post-doctorate studies and research, situated in the Tuscan hills overlooking Florence. Since its founding in 1972 by the six original members of the then European Communities, the EUI has earned a reputation as a leading international academic institution with a European focus. The EUI offers one of the largest doctoral and postdoctoral programmes in the social sciences in Europe.

150 Fully Funded PhD Degree Scholarships for International Students

Subjects: Economics, History and Civilization, Law and Political and Social Sciences
Purpose: The European University Institute is pleased to offer four-year PhD Degree Scholarships in Economics, History and Civilization, Law, and Political and Social Sciences.
Eligibility: To qualify for national funding, you must meet the specific requirements set by the national funding authorities. These may include conditions with regard to your nationality, residence, degree and its time of award. For an overview of the specific funding conditions, eligibility criteria and application instructions, please visit the information page of each relevant funding authority. You must meet the minimum degree requirements set by the relevant funding authority for admission to the EUI Ph.-D. Programme. The expected level of English proficiency is level C1 of the Common European Framework of Reference (CEFR). Applicants are required to submit an English international language certificate to demonstrate their level.
Level of Study: Doctorate
Type: Scholarship
Value: Fully funded, 4-year Ph.D. programme (tuition fees, living expenses are covered)
Length of Study: 4 Year
Country of Study: Italy
Application Procedure: The application for admission to the EUI doctoral programme is automatically an application for national funding, with the following exceptions Greece, Portugal, Slovenia, Spain and the United Kingdom . If you apply for funding from one of these countries, your application to the EUI can ONLY be accepted if you separately file a mandatory separate application. Please refer www.eui.eu/ServicesAndAdmin/AcademicService/DoctoralProgramme
No. of awards offered: 150
Closing Date: 31 January
Additional Information: www.eui.eu/en/services/academic-service/doctoral-programme

For further information contact:

Tel: (39) 554685 373
Email: applyres@eui.eu

Doctor of Philosophy Scholarships in the Social Sciences

Purpose: Four-year fully-funded PhD programmes in History and the Social Sciences
Eligibility: To qualify for national funding, you must meet the specific requirements set by the national funding authorities. These may include conditions with regard to your nationality, residence, degree and its time of award. For an overview of the specific funding conditions, eligibility criteria and application instructions, please visit the information page of each relevant funding authority. You must meet the minimum degree requirements set by the relevant funding authority for admission to the EUI Ph.D. Programme. Please refer www.eui.eu/DepartmentsAndCentres/PoliticalAndSocialSciences/DoctoralProgramme
Level of Study: Doctorate
Type: Scholarship
Value: Fully funded, 4-year Ph.D. programme (tuition fees, living expenses are covered) leading to an internationally recognised Ph.D. degree
Length of Study: Four years
Frequency: Annual
Study Establishment: European University Institute
Country of Study: Italy
Application Procedure: You must submit your application and all required documents via the interactive online application. The application for admission to the EUI doctoral programme is automatically an application for national funding, with the following exceptions Greece, Portugal, Slovenia, Spain and the United Kingdom . If you apply for funding from one of these countries, your application to the EUI can ONLY be accepted if you separately file a mandatory separate application. For further information visit www.eui.eu/DepartmentsAndCentres/PoliticalAndSocialSciences/DoctoralProgramme
Closing Date: 31 January
Additional Information: www.eui.eu/ServicesAndAdmin/AcademicService/DoctoralProgramme. www.eui.eu/DepartmentsAndCentres/PoliticalAndSocialSciences/DoctoralProgramme

For further information contact:

Via della Badia dei Roccettini, 9, I-50014 Fiesole FI, Italy.

Tel: (39) 554685 373
Email: applyres@eui.eu

EuroTech Universities Alliance

Square de MeeÛs 23, 8th floor, B-1000 Brussels, Belgium.

Tel:	(32) 2 274 0532
Email:	tatiana.panteli@eurotech-universities.eu;
	info@eurotech-universities.eu
Website:	eurotech-universities.eu/
Contact:	Tatiana Panteli, Head of Brussels Office

The EuroTech Universities Alliance is a strategic partnership of leading European universities of science and technology committed to excellence in research and education, jointly developing solutions to the grand challenges of society. The members are: 1. Technical University of Denmark (DTU), 2. École polytechnique fédérale de Lausanne (EPFL), 3. École Polytechnique (L'X), 4. Technion - Israel Institute of Technology, 5. Eindhoven University of Technology (TU/e), 6. Technical University of Munich (TUM). By promoting in-depth collaboration across research and education, as well as nurturing innovation and entrepreneurship, the Alliance combines the complementary strengths of its partner universities to jointly achieve multi-scale initiatives of high impact to society and to industry. The Alliance also openly engages with all societal actors to raise awareness on the opportunities offered by science and technology.

Collaborative Offline & Online Platform for Research EuroTechPostdoc Fellowships for International Students at European Universities

Purpose: The EuroTechPostdoc Programme is a postdoctoral fellowship programme for young experienced researchers who have already demonstrated excellence and potential in their field of research

Eligibility: Applicants of all nationalities are eligible. Please refer the website for more details

Level of Study: Postdoctorate

Type: Postdoctoral fellowship

Value: The fellowship consists of a monthly salary for the postdoctoral researcher based on the salary scale of the host institution and is granted for a period of twenty-four (24) months maximum. Prolongation of the fellowship is not possible

Length of Study: Up to 24 months

Frequency: Annual, if funds are available

Study Establishment: Applicants may apply within one of the five focus research areas of the EuroTech Universities Alliance Health & Bio Engineering Smart & Urban Mobility

Data Science & Engineering High-Performance Computing Entrepreneurship & Innovation

Country of Study: Any country

Application Procedure: Please use the following templates for your application 1. Project proposal template. 2. CV and publications template. 3. Ethics self-assessment

Closing Date: 28 February

Funding: Government

Contributor: European Commission This project has received funding from the European Union's Horizon research and innovation programme under the Marie Sklodowska-Curie grant agreement No 754462

Additional Information: For more details, please browse the below website, www.scholarshipsads.com/80-coorp-eurotechpostdoc-fellowships-international-students-european-universities-2018/

For further information contact:

Arcisstrasse 21, D-80333 Munich, Germany.

Tel:	(49) 892 892 2813
Email:	postdoc@eurotech-universities.eu

EuroTechPostdoc

Purpose: The EuroTech Universities Alliance is a strategic partnership of leading universities of science and technology. The EuroTechPostdoc2 programme grants fellowships to excellent experienced researchers with the objective of providing them with exceptional research and career development opportunities thanks to the joint capacity and complementary training options offered at the six universities of the EuroTech Universities Alliance.

Eligibility: There are no restrictions concerning age, gender, religion, ethnicity, sexual orientation, political views, language or nationality of the applicants. Applicants should be Experienced Researchers, and fulfill the Mobility Rule. For details, see the Rules and Regulations on postdoc2.eurotech-universities.eu/

Level of Study: Postdoctorate

Type: A variable number of fellowships

Value: The fellowship consists of a monthly salary for the postdoctoral researcher (see details on our website) and a dedicated research budget (up to €8,000) and collaboration and travel budget (up to €6,000) related to the project.

Length of Study: 2 years

Country of Study: Other

Country of Study: Denmark, France, Germany, The Netherlands

Application Procedure: To be considered admissible, the application must be complete and submitted in the electronic submission system before the deadline of the call. For an application to be complete, it must contain the following elements 1. Research plan (maximum five (5) pages, following the template provided). 2. Prioritized CV - including career breaks and list of all publications of the applicant, following the template provided. 3. Completed and signed ethical issues form, following the template provided. 4. Scanned copy of PhD diploma or an official statement of the awarding university that the degree has been awarded, or official statement(s) proving the four years of fulltime equivalent research experience in English. Names of intended Host Supervisor and intended Co-host Supervisor. 5. Motivation letter on carrying out a cross-border collaborative project (maximum one (1) page

No. of awards offered: 35

Closing Date: February

Funding: Foundation

Contributor: European Commission and EuroTech universities

Additional Information: Please check our online presence: postdoc2.eurotech-universities.eu/

For further information contact:

Tel: (31) 40 247 4332

Email: postdoc2@eurotech-universities.eu

Evangelical Lutheran Church in America (ELCA)

8765 W Higgins Road, Chicago, IL 60631, United States of America.

Tel: (1) 773 380 2700

Website: www.elca.org/

The Evangelical Lutheran Church in America (ELCA) is one of the largest Christian denominations in the United States, with about 4 million members in nearly 10,000 congregations across the United States, Puerto Rico and the U.S. Virgin Islands. A merger of three Lutheran churches formed the ELCA in 1988. They were The American Lutheran Church, the Association of Evangelical Lutheran Churches and the Lutheran Church in America.

Evangelical Lutheran Church in America Educational Grant Program

Purpose: ELCA's Educational Grant Program (EGP) grants provides financial aids to Ph.D., Th.D., and Ed.D. candidates in heological study appropriate to seminary teaching.

Eligibility: Open to members of the Evangelical Lutheran Church in America who are enroled in an accredited graduate institution for study in a PhD, EdD, or ThD programme in a theological area appropriate to seminary teaching.

Level of Study: Doctorate

Type: Grant

Value: Grants for a total of four years of support. In addition, a fifth year of support may be awarded as a dissertation grant.

Frequency: Annual

Country of Study: United States of America

Application Procedure: Recipients may apply annually to renew their grants for a total of four years of support. Apply online at elca.fluxx.io/user_sessions/new

Closing Date: May

Funding: Private

Additional Information: www.elca.org/grants, elca.org/Resources/Grants#Applicants, download.elca.org/ELCA%20Resource%20Repository/ELCA_Grants_and_Scholarships_Description_List.pdf?_ga=2.62258730.767686752.16154406 50-1851674278.1615440650

Evonik Foundation

Evonik Industries AG, Rellinghauser Straße 1–11, D-45128 Essen, Germany.

Tel: (49) 201 177 3475

Email: info@evonik.com

Website: www.evonik-stiftung.de/de

Contact: Evonik Foundation

The Evonik Foundation is a nonprofit foundation based in Essen. The Evonik Foundation has a special place in Evonik's social commitment. Its motto is supporting people because it is people who shape the future. The Evonik Foundation pursues its goals through its own programs and projects and by making donations to support projects run by other organizations. The Evonik Foundation supports measures aimed, in particular, at upcoming scientists, and educational programs for socially disadvantaged children and young people.

Evonik Stiftung Scholarships

Purpose: Promoting talented young people is a top priority at the Evonik Foundation. The focus is on the Evonik Foundation scholarship for master's theses and doctorates.

Eligibility: Prerequisites for the award of a scholarship are 1. Your research project must be thematically aligned with our annual research focus or the area of Amino acid research match. 2. Your scientific research takes place in a renowned, chemical oriented working group at a German university or at a non-university research institution. 3. Your academic achievements to date are excellent. 4. The scientific training you are aiming for cannot be adequately financed by your own funds, grants from your parents or third parties.

Level of Study: Doctorate, Masters Degree

Type: Scholarship

Value: 1. Master theses six months, €250 to €600 per month. 2. Doctorates two years (option to extend for a maximum of one year), €1,400 per month. 3. In addition, applications can be made to acquire specialist literature and to attend scientific conferences.

Frequency: Annual

Country of Study: Germany

Application Procedure: Details on the application process can be found in the following file, which is available as a download (pdf only in German) corporate.evonik.com/Downloads/Evonik_Stiftung/Bewerbungsverfahren%20Stipendium%202021_.pdf

Closing Date: 15 February

For further information contact:

Andrea Wurow, Evonik Stiftung, Rellinghauser Straße 1-11, D-45128 Essen, Germany.

Email: info@evonik-stiftung.de

F

Fahs-Beck Fund for Research and Experimentation

909 Third Avenue, 22nd Floor, New York, NY 10022, United States of America.

Email: james.herbert1@asu.edu
Website: www.fahsbeckfund.org/

Doctoral Dissertation Grant Program (Fahs-Beck Scholars)

Subjects: Problems in the functioning or well being of children, adults, couples, families, or communities, or about interventions designed to prevent or alleviate such problems.
Purpose: To help support dissertation expenses of doctoral students in the United States and Canada whose studies have the potential for adding significantly to knowledge about problems in the functioning or well being of children, adults, couples, families, or communities, or about interventions designed to prevent or alleviate such problems.
Eligibility: To help support dissertation expenses of doctoral students in the United States and Canada whose studies have the potential for adding significantly to knowledge about the well-being of children, adults, couples, families, communities using interventions or preventive/interventions designed to prevent or alleviate behavioural, social, psychological health problems.
Type: Grant
Value: Up to US$7,000
Frequency: Twice a year
Country of Study: United States of America or Canada
Application Procedure: Apply online

Closing Date: 1 November
Additional Information: www.fahsbeckfund.org/grant_programs.html

Faculty/Post -Doctoral Grant Program (Fahs-Beck Fellows)

Purpose: To help support the research of faculty members or post-doctoral researchers in the United States and Canada. Areas of interest for funding are: studies to develop, refine, evaluate, or disseminate interventions and preventive/intervention to address social, psychological, behavioural or public health problems affecting children, adults, couples, families, and communities with outcomes that have the potential add to the knowledge base for services and program development.
Level of Study: Doctorate, Postdoctorate
Type: Grant
Value: US$25,000
Frequency: Twice a year
Country of Study: United States of America
Application Procedure: Faculty members of accredited colleges or universities in the United States or Canada are eligible to apply. The applicant organization must agree to accept administrative responsibility for the project and submit required financial forms and reports to the Fund. The principal investigator (PI) must have an earned doctorate in a relevant discipline. The PI must lead the research and be the principal author of the final report.
Closing Date: 1 April
Additional Information: www.fahsbeckfund.org/grant-programs/

Fanconi Anemia Research Fund, Inc.

360 E. 10th Avenue, Suite 201, Eugene, OR 97401, United States of America.

Tel: (1) 541 687 4658
Email: info@fanconi.org
Website: www.fanconi.org
Contact: Fanconi Anemia Research Fund

To support research into effective treatments and a cure for Fanconi anemia.

Fanconi Anemia Research Fund Award

Purpose: To support research into effective treatments and a cure for Fanconi anemia
Eligibility: Eligibility: 1. Established FA support organizations outside of the United States or; 2. Individuals wanting to create support 3. Organizations within countries outside of the United States (that do not currently have an established support organization) 4. Institutions such as hospitals or universities wanting to create support systems for individuals with FA.
Level of Study: Doctorate, Postdoctorate
Type: Award
Value: US$10,000
Length of Study: 1 years
Frequency: Annual
Country of Study: Any country
Application Procedure: Applicants must email to obtain information and application forms: www.fanconi.org/images/uploads/other/INTL_RFP_2022.pdf
No. of awards offered: 29
Closing Date: 6 May
Funding: Foundation
Additional Information: The Internal Revenue Service has confirmed that the Fund is not a private foundation for the purposes of tax-exempt donations but a public charitable organization under 501(c) 3 of the Internal Revenue Code www.fanconi.org/explore/international-fa-support-grants

For further information contact:

Email: grants@fanconi.org

Federation University Australia

Vice-Chancellor's Office, P.O. Box 663, University Drive, Mt Helen, VIC 3350, Australia.

Tel: (61) 5327 9000
Website: federation.edu.au
Contact: Sue Read

The University of Ballarat is Australia's only regional, multi-sector university acknowledged for its excellence in education, training, and research, committed to providing high quality services to students, the community, and the industry. It provides educational and training programs from apprenticeships, certificates and diplomas to post-graduate qualifications, masters, and doctorates by research. International students at the University come from over 25 different countries to participate in a diverse range of TAFE and higher education programmes. The University is proud of its track record in business innovation and entrepreneurship, research, consulting, and educational programs, and promoting new technology in products and services through scientific and industrial research.

2022 Foundation Scholarships - Continuing Scholarships

Eligibility: Eligibility: 1. Continuing students in 2023 2. Domestic and international students 3. Enrolled an undergraduate or postgraduate degree (excluding research degrees) 4. Can be studying at Mt Helen, Berwick, Gippsland, Wimmera or Online 5. Active and enrolled full-time for full year post census date 6. Must not be in their final semester of studying when applying.
Level of Study: Postgraduate
Type: Award
Value: AU$4,000.00
Frequency: Annual
Country of Study: Australia
No. of awards offered: 9
Closing Date: 4 March
Additional Information: federation.smapply.io/prog/foundation_scholarships_-_continuing_scholarships/

Aboriginal and Torres Strait Islander Staff Scholarship

Eligibility: Higher education undergraduate or postgraduate level studies, excluding PhD undertaken by a Federation University Aboriginal or Torres Strait Islander staff member, Aboriginal Education Centre staff member or general administration staff, TAFE teaching staff identified as Indigenous or Torres Strait Islander
Level of Study: Postgraduate
Type: Scholarship
Value: AU$2,000
Frequency: Annual
Country of Study: Australia

Application Procedure: Apply directly through our Scholarships and Grants portal. federation.smapply.io/prog/founda tion_scholarship_-_aboriginal_and_torres_strait_islander_ staff_scholarship
No. of awards offered: 1
Closing Date: 4 March
Additional Information: federation.edu.au/connect/founda tion/supporting-the-foundation/scholarships/foundation-scholarships/aboriginal-and-torres-strait-islander-staff-scholarship

AGL Jungurra Wunnik Scholarship

Eligibility: Higher Education domestic Aboriginal or Torres Strait Islander student undertaking studies in a STEAM course – Science, Technology, Engineering, the Arts or Mathematics at the Federation University Gippsland campus in the second or third year of their program.
Type: Scholarship
Value: AU$4,000
Frequency: Annual
Country of Study: Australia
Closing Date: 4 March
Additional Information: federation.edu.au/connect/founda tion/supporting-the-foundation/scholarships/foundation-scho larships/agl-scholarship

Alex Gusbeth Scholarship

Eligibility: Available for commencing or continuing Higher Education domestic, undergraduate (including honours) or postgraduate student studying in the field of science at the Gippsland campus.
Level of Study: Postgraduate
Type: Scholarship
Value: AU$5,000
Frequency: Annual
Country of Study: Australia
No. of awards offered: 2
Closing Date: 4 March
Additional Information: federation.edu.au/connect/founda tion/supporting-the-foundation/scholarships/foundation-scho larships/alex-gusbeth-scholarship

Australian Postgraduate Award

Purpose: To support postgraduate students undertaking research in either a Doctorate or Masters by Research program
Eligibility: Open to candidates who have a First Class (Honours) Degree or equivalent. The APA is open to candidates who have received a Masters by Research (for Doctorate applicants) and/or a Honours degree (First Class/ H1A) or equivalent
Level of Study: Doctorate, Postgraduate, Research
Type: Scholarship
Value: AU$26,288 per year, Indexed annually
Frequency: Annual
Study Establishment: The University of Ballarat
Country of Study: Australia
Application Procedure: Application forms and further information about the Scholarships process can be found at feder ation.edu.au/research/research-degrees/scholarships
No. of awards offered: 130
Closing Date: 3 December
Funding: Government
Additional Information: It is required that the successful applicant commence studies in the year the scholarship was awarded for. Studies should commence no earlier than 1 February, and no later than 31 August

For further information contact:

Tel: (61) 3 5327 9508
Fax: (61) 3 5327 9602
Email: HDResearch@ballarat.edu.au

Buninyong Community Bank Scholarship

Eligibility: Higher education domestic students enrolled in an undergraduate (including honours) studying in agricultural or environmental pursuits (Bachelor of Environmental and Conservation Science, Bachelor of Veterinary and Wildlife Science or Bachelor of Science with a major in Ecology and Environmental restoration) in the first year of their program at the Mt Helen Campus.
Level of Study: Postgraduate
Type: Scholarship
Value: AU$7,000
Frequency: Annual
Country of Study: Australia
Closing Date: 4 March
Additional Information: federation.edu.au/connect/founda tion/supporting-the-foundation/scholarships/foundation-scholarships/buninyong-community-bank-scholarship-tafe

Cameron Beyer Scholarship

Eligibility: Higher education domestic, CALD, migrant, refugee, international, undergraduate or postgraduate Federation University Ballarat campus student and online students.

Level of Study: Postgraduate
Type: Scholarship
Value: AU$7,000
Frequency: Annual
Country of Study: Australia
Closing Date: 4 March
Additional Information: federation.edu.au/connect/founda tion/supporting-the-foundation/scholarships/foundation-scholarships/council-scholarship

Care-leavers Scholarship (Continuing)

Eligibility: Higher education domestic undergraduate (including honours) or postgraduate student who has been in care, kinship care or a state ward for 12 months or more in the second or third year of their program.
Level of Study: Postgraduate
Type: Scholarship
Value: AU$4,000
Frequency: Annual
Country of Study: Australia
Closing Date: 4 March
Additional Information: federation.edu.au/connect/founda tion/supporting-the-foundation/scholarships/foundation-scholarships/care-leavers-scholarship-continuing

Care-leavers Scholarships (Commencing)

Eligibility: Higher education domestic undergraduate or postgraduate student who has been in care, kinship care or a state ward for 12 months or more.
Type: Scholarship
Value: AU$7,000
Frequency: Annual
Country of Study: Australia
Closing Date: 4 March
Additional Information: federation.edu.au/connect/founda tion/supporting-the-foundation/scholarships/foundation-scholarships/care-leavers-scholarship-commencing

Carol Lynette Grant (Prowse) Scholarship

Eligibility: Postgraduate Mt Helen Campus student.
Level of Study: Postgraduate
Type: Scholarship
Value: AU$7,000
Frequency: Annual
Country of Study: Australia
Closing Date: 4 March

Additional Information: federation.edu.au/connect/founda tion/supporting-the-foundation/scholarships/foundation-scho larships/carol-lynette-grant-prowse-scholarship

Council Scholarship

Eligibility: Higher education domestic, CALD, migrant, refugee, international, undergraduate or postgraduate Federation University campus students and online students.
Level of Study: Postgraduate
Type: Scholarship
Value: AU$7,000
Frequency: Annual
Country of Study: Australia
Closing Date: 4 March
Additional Information: federation.edu.au/connect/founda tion/supporting-the-foundation/scholarships/foundation-scho larships/council-scholarship2

Deadly Education Scholarships - Aboriginal and Torres Strait Islanders

Eligibility: Eligibility: 1. Domestic student 2. Be an Australian Aboriginal and/or Torres Strait Islander person 3. Provide either a Confirmation of Aboriginality or a statutory declaration. 4. Provide evidence of low socioeconomic status or financial hardship (documents such as Centrelink statement, payslips. Bank statements can be used if an explanation is provided in a personal statement) 5. Enrolled in an enabling course (FAST program) Undergraduate, Honours or Post-graduate course at Federation University.
Level of Study: Postgraduate
Type: Scholarship
Value: AU$2000 per semester(up to 8 payments)
Frequency: Annual
Country of Study: Australia
Closing Date: 31 March
Additional Information: federation.smapply.io/prog/ deadly_education_scholarships_-_aboriginal_and_torres_strait_islanders/

Destination Australia

Eligibility: To be eligible for a Destination Australia scholarship you must be: 1. Living in a regional area on an ongoing basis throughout your course 2. A new student at Federation University or commencing a new course at a higher level of study 3. Enrolled at a regional campus of Federation

University (Ballarat, Gippsland or Wimmera) 4. Enrolled in a course that is fully-delivered in face-to-face mode at a regional campus 5. Studying at a qualification level from Certificate 4 to PhD 6. In possession of a valid student visa (if an international student).

Level of Study: Postgraduate
Type: Award
Value: AU$15,000 per year
Frequency: Annual
Country of Study: Australia
Closing Date: 28 February
Additional Information: federation.smapply.io/prog/destination_australia/

Doctoral Research on Family Relationships

Purpose: To undertake doctoral research on family relationships
Eligibility: Open to Australian citizens or permanent residents who have achieved First Class (Honours) or equivalent
Level of Study: Postgraduate
Type: Scholarship
Value: AU$19,231
Length of Study: 3 years and 6 months
Frequency: Annual
Study Establishment: The University of Ballarat
Country of Study: Australia
Application Procedure: Check website for further details. Applications are open from 25 July
Closing Date: 30 November

For further information contact:

Tel: (61) 3 5327 9818
Email: j.mcdonald@ballarat.edu.au

Dunkeld Refugee and Asylum Seeker

Eligibility: Higher education or TAFE student undertaking studies at the Federation University mt Helen or Wimmera campus.
Level of Study: Postgraduate
Type: Scholarship
Value: AUS1,000
Frequency: Annual
Country of Study: Australia
Closing Date: 4 March
Additional Information: federation.edu.au/connect/foundation/supporting-the-foundation/scholarships/foundation-scholarships/dunkeld-refugee-and-asylum-seeker

Early Childhood Scholarships

Purpose: To pursue a rewarding career as an early childhood teacher.
Eligibility: Scholarships are available for people looking to become an early childhood teacher through study in a degree or postgraduate qualification. Educators wanting to upskill and take the next step to become degree-qualified are also eligible. To be eligible for this scholarship you must be 1. An Australian citizen; or New Zealand citizen; or an Australian permanent resident 2. A continuing or new commencing student in the area of Early Childhood Education
Level of Study: Postgraduate
Type: Scholarship
Value: US$25,000
Frequency: Annual
Country of Study: Any country
Application Procedure: See website www.education.vic.gov.au/ecscholarships
No. of awards offered: 400
Closing Date: 1 December

East Gippsland Water Scholarship

Eligibility: This scholarship is open to students who are undertaking civil engineering (preferred) or an engineering degree with a focus on chemical and environmental engineering at the Gippsland campus in their first, second or third year of their degree. Preference will be given to students who reside in the East Gippsland region, but is open to other Gippsland based students who will commit to being directly involved with East Gippsland Water.
Level of Study: Postgraduate
Type: Scholarship
Value: AU$5,000
Frequency: Annual
Country of Study: Australia
Closing Date: 4 March
Additional Information: federation.edu.au/connect/foundation/supporting-the-foundation/scholarships/foundation-scholarships/east-gippsland-water-scholarship

Elite Athlete Scholarship

Eligibility: Higher education domestic, undergraduate (including honours) or postgraduate FedUni campus students. Elite athletes must be recognised as an elite athlete by the AIS, State Institute or Academy of Sport, AFL Players' Association, Rugby Union Players' Association, Rugby League Professionals Association, Australian Professional Footballers'

Association or a national squad member from Australian Sports Commission funded sports.
Level of Study: Postgraduate
Type: Scholarship
Value: AU$7,000
Frequency: Annual
Country of Study: Australia
Closing Date: 4 March
Additional Information: federation.edu.au/connect/founda tion/supporting-the-foundation/scholarships/foundation-scho larships/elite-athlete-scholarship

Executive Dean's Postgraduate Scholarship

Purpose: These scholarships are designed to encourage and reward excellence in postgraduate academic performance by School of Health students.
Eligibility: Academic merit 1. Where equal GPAs are attained, individual grades will be considered to determine recipients. 2. Students must be enrolled in 75% load to be eligible.
Level of Study: Postgraduate
Value: AU$800.00
Country of Study: Any country
Application Procedure: Applications are not required as a selection panel will determine recipients based on GPA scores each semester.
No. of awards offered: 8

For further information contact:

Tel: (61) 3 5327 9340
Email: scholarships@federation.edu.au

Foundation Commencing Scholarships

Eligibility: Higher education domestic, CALD, migrant, refugee, international, undergraduate or postgraduate Federation University campus students and online students.
Level of Study: Postgraduate
Type: Scholarship
Value: AU$7,000
Frequency: Annual
Country of Study: Australia
Closing Date: 4 March
Additional Information: federation.edu.au/connect/founda tion/supporting-the-foundation/scholarships/foundation-scho larships/foundation-commencing-scholarships

Foundation Continuing Scholarships

Eligibility: Higher education domestic, CALD, migrant, refugee, international, undergraduate (including honours) or postgraduate Federation University campus students and online students in the second or third year of their program.
Level of Study: Postgraduate
Type: Scholarship
Value: AU$4,000
Frequency: Annual
Country of Study: Australia
Closing Date: 4 March
Additional Information: federation.edu.au/connect/founda tion/supporting-the-foundation/scholarships/foundation-scho larships/foundation-continuing-scholarships

Foundation HDR Scholarships

Eligibility: Domestic, CALD, migrant, refugee, or international Higher Degree by Research candidates enrolled at Federation University.
Level of Study: Research
Type: Scholarship
Value: AU$7,000
Frequency: Annual
Country of Study: Australia
Closing Date: 4 March
Additional Information: federation.edu.au/connect/founda tion/supporting-the-foundation/scholarships/foundation-scho larships/hdr-scholarship

Ian Alexander Gordon Scholarship

Eligibility: Higher education domestic undergraduate or postgraduate Mt Helen Campus student.
Level of Study: Postgraduate
Type: Scholarship
Value: AU$7,000
Frequency: Annual
Country of Study: Australia
Closing Date: 4 March
Additional Information: federation.edu.au/connect/founda tion/supporting-the-foundation/scholarships/foundation-scho larships/ian-alexander-gordon-scholarship

Ilona Takacs Scholarship

Eligibility: Higher education domestic, migrant or refugee female student in the first year of their program undertaking studies in Science, Mathematics or Physics at the Federation University Mt Helen campus
Level of Study: Postgraduate
Type: Scholarship
Value: AU$500
Frequency: Annual

Country of Study: Australia
Closing Date: 4 March
Additional Information: federation.edu.au/connect/founda tion/supporting-the-foundation/scholarships/foundation-scho larships/soroptimist-scholarship

International Excellence Scholarship

Purpose: The International Excellence scholarships commencing 2023 are equivalent to 16% of your tuition fees.
Eligibility: 1. A prospective international student. 2. Eligible to study in Australia with a student visa. 3. Not have accepted, or be in receipt of, any other FedUni scholarship or bursary, or any other reduced fee arrangements at the time of entry to the University (with the exception of Federation University Accommodation Scholarships). 4. Not be in receipt of credit transfers or exemptions. 5. Meet minimum academic English entry requirement and offered with no more than 10 weeks English pathway program (e.g. academic IELTS overall 5.5 with no band less than 5.5 for general programs). 6. Enrolling in an eligible program. 7. Enrolling in a program at a higher level than your existing qualification. 8. Studying full-time at a home campus of Federation University Australia. Home campuses are located in Ballarat, Gippsland and Berwick. These scholarships do not apply to students studying at a Federation University Partner Provider teaching location.
Type: Scholarship
Length of Study: The scholarship will apply for the normal duration of your program.
Frequency: Annual
Country of Study: Any country
Closing Date: 31 August

Isobella Foundation Scholarship

Eligibility: Higher education domestic undergraduate or postgraduate Mt Helen Campus student.
Level of Study: Postgraduate
Type: Scholarship
Value: AU$7,000
Frequency: Annual
Country of Study: Australia
Closing Date: 4 March
Additional Information: federation.edu.au/connect/founda tion/supporting-the-foundation/scholarships/foundation-scho larships/isobella-foundation-scholarship

James Stewart Bequest (Geology)

Eligibility: Higher Education domestic undergraduate or postgraduate student undertaking studies in Geology at the Mt Helen campus.

Level of Study: Postgraduate
Type: Scholarship
Value: AU$3,500
Frequency: Annual
Country of Study: Australia
Closing Date: 4 March
Additional Information: federation.edu.au/connect/founda tion/supporting-the-foundation/scholarships/foundation-scho larships/james-stewart-bequest-geology

Kiran Mazumdar-Shaw Scholarship

Eligibility: Higher education Indian student undertaking studies in the fields of science, technology, engineering or mathematics at the Mt Helen Campus.
Level of Study: Postgraduate
Type: Scholarship
Value: AU$7,000
Frequency: Annual
Country of Study: Australia
No. of awards offered: 1
Closing Date: 4 March
Additional Information: federation.edu.au/connect/founda tion/supporting-the-foundation/scholarships/foundation-scho larships/kiran-mazumdar-shaw-scholarship

Meredith Doig Scholarship

Eligibility: Higher education domestic female student undertaking studies in the fields of science, technology, engineering or mathematics at the Mt Helen Campus in the second or third year of their program.
Level of Study: Postgraduate
Type: Scholarship
Value: AU$4,000
Frequency: Annual
Country of Study: Australia
No. of awards offered: 1
Closing Date: 4 March
Additional Information: federation.edu.au/connect/founda tion/supporting-the-foundation/scholarships/foundation-scho larships/meredith-doig-scholarship

Narre Warren South Bendigo Bank Scholarship

Eligibility: Higher education domestic, undergraduate (including honours) or postgraduate students in the first year of their program at the Berwick Campus.
Level of Study: Postgraduate
Type: Scholarship
Value: AU$1,000

Frequency: Annual
Country of Study: Australia
Closing Date: 4 March
Additional Information: federation.edu.au/connect/founda
tion/supporting-the-foundation/scholarships/foundation-scho
larships/narre-warren-south-bendigo-bank-scholarship/narre-
warren-south-bendigo-bank-scholarship

Philip Chui East Asia Scholarship

Eligibility: Available for a Chinese National student under-
taking studies at the Berwick campus.
Level of Study: Postgraduate
Type: Scholarship
Value: AU$1,000
Frequency: Annual
Country of Study: Australia
Closing Date: 4 March
Additional Information: federation.edu.au/connect/founda
tion/supporting-the-foundation/scholarships/foundation-scho
larships/philip-chui-scholarship

Rural and Regional Enterprise Scholarships (RRES)

Eligibility: 1. You must be an Australian citizen, Australian
permanent resident, holder of a permanent humanitarian visa,
or a New Zealand citizen living in Australia. 2. Have commenced the first year of your Eligible Course of Study in
Semester 1, Semester 2 or Trimester 3 of 2023. 3. Your
permanent home address must be in a regional or remote
area as defined by the Australian Statistical Geography Standard (ASGS). 4. Applicants must not have relocated to
a major city more than 3 months prior to commencing their
chosen course of study.
Level of Study: Postgraduate
Type: Award
Value: Up to AU$18,000
Frequency: Annual
Country of Study: Australia
Application Procedure: Please note this is an external scholarship and you will need to apply directly through the Rural &
Regional Enterprise Scholarships website found here; www.
qtac.edu.au/rres-program
Closing Date: 1 December
Additional Information: federation.smapply.io/prog/
rural_and_regional_enterprise_scholarships_rres_-_external_
scholarship/

SG and JG Scholarship (MIT Melbourne)

Eligibility: Higher education domestic or international
female undergraduate (including honours) or postgraduate
student studying at the MIT Melbourne campus.

Level of Study: Postgraduate
Type: Scholarship
Value: AU$7,000
Frequency: Annual
Country of Study: Australia
Closing Date: 4 March
Additional Information: federation.edu.au/connect/founda
tion/supporting-the-foundation/scholarships/foundation-scho
larships/sg-and-jg-scholarship-mit-melbourne

SG and JG Scholarship (MIT Sydney)

Level of Study: Postgraduate
Type: Scholarship
Frequency: Annual
Study Establishment: AU$7,000
Country of Study: Australia
Application Procedure: Higher education domestic or inter-
national female undergraduate (including honours) or post-
graduate student studying at the MIT Sydney campus.
No. of awards offered: 1
Closing Date: 1 April
Additional Information: federation.edu.au/connect/founda
tion/supporting-the-foundation/scholarships/foundation-scho
larships/sg-and-jg-scholarship-mit-sydney

SG and JG Scholarships (Mt Helen)

Eligibility: Higher education domestic or international
female undergraduate (including honours) or postgraduate
student studying at the Mt Helen campus.
Level of Study: Postgraduate
Type: Scholarship
Study Establishment: AU$7,000
Country of Study: Australia
No. of awards offered: 1
Closing Date: 4 March
Additional Information: federation.edu.au/connect/founda
tion/supporting-the-foundation/scholarships/foundation-scho
larships/sg-and-jg-scholarship-mt-helen

Staff Scholarship - Continuing

Eligibility: Higher education domestic, CALD, migrant, ref-
ugee, international, undergraduate (including honours) or
postgraduate Federation University campus students and
online students in the second or third year of their program.
Level of Study: Postgraduate
Type: Scholarship
Value: AU$4,000
Frequency: Annual

Country of Study: Australia
No. of awards offered: 1
Closing Date: 4 March
Additional Information: federation.edu.au/connect/founda
tion/supporting-the-foundation/scholarships/foundation-scho
larships/staff-scholarship-continuing

Staff Scholarship - Domestic

Eligibility: Higher education domestic undergraduate or postgraduate Federation University campus students and online students.
Level of Study: Postgraduate
Type: Scholarship
Value: AU$7,000
Frequency: Annual
Country of Study: Australia
No. of awards offered: 1
Closing Date: 4 March
Additional Information: federation.edu.au/connect/founda
tion/supporting-the-foundation/scholarships/foundation-scho
larships/staff-scholarship

Staff Scholarship - International

Eligibility: Higher education migrant, refugee, international, undergraduate or postgraduate Federation University campus students and online students.
Level of Study: Postgraduate
Type: Scholarship
Frequency: Annual
Study Establishment: AU$7,000
Country of Study: Australia
No. of awards offered: 1
Closing Date: 4 March
Additional Information: federation.edu.au/connect/founda
tion/supporting-the-foundation/scholarships/foundation-scho
larships/staff-scholarship-international

Tohmae Pa Scholarships

Eligibility: Higher education or TAFE student undertaking studies at the Federation University Wimmera campus. Available for a Karen refugee or refugee living within the Nhill district.
Level of Study: Postgraduate
Type: Scholarship
Value: AU$1,000
Frequency: Annual
Country of Study: Australia
Closing Date: 4 March

Additional Information: federation.edu.au/connect/founda
tion/supporting-the-foundation/scholarships/foundation-scho
larships/tohmae-pa-scholarships

University of Ballarat Part Postgraduate Research Scholarship

Eligibility: Open to citizens of Australia or permanent residents who have achieved First Class (Honours) or equivalent
Level of Study: Doctorate, Postgraduate, Research
Type: Scholarship
Value: AU$22,500
Length of Study: 3 years (PhD and Professional Doctorate) and 1.5 years (Masters)
Frequency: Annual
Study Establishment: University of Ballarat
Country of Study: Australia
Application Procedure: Check website for further details. Applications are open from 3 January
Closing Date: 31 October
Funding: Commercial, Government
Additional Information: The study should start no earlier than 1 February www.fanconi.org/explore/international-fa-
support-grants

For further information contact:

Tel: (61) 3 5327 9508
Fax: (61) 3 5327 9602
Email: s.murphy@ballarat.edu.au

Vanne Trompf Scholarship

Eligibility: Higher education or TAFE student undertaking studies at the Federation University Mt Helen or Wimmera campus.
Level of Study: Postgraduate
Type: Scholarship
Value: AU$1,000
Frequency: Annual
Country of Study: Australia
No. of awards offered: 1
Closing Date: 4 March
Additional Information: federation.edu.au/current-students/
starting-at-federation/scholarships/find-a-scholarship/founda
tion/vanne-trompf-scholarship

Wai-man Woo Scholarship

Eligibility: Higher education international student undertaking Higher Education undergraduate (including honours) or postgraduate studies at the Federation University Mt Helen campus.

Level of Study: Postgraduate
Type: Scholarship
Value: AU$7,000
Frequency: Annual
Country of Study: Australia
No. of awards offered: 1
Closing Date: 4 March
Additional Information: federation.edu.au/connect/founda tion/supporting-the-foundation/scholarships/foundation-scho larships/wai-man-woo-scholarship

Wellington Shire Council Scholarship

Eligibility: Available for students who are undertaking Civil Engineering studies at the Gippsland campus. Applicants must live within the Wellington Shire.
Level of Study: Postgraduate
Type: Scholarship
Frequency: Annual
Study Establishment: AU$4,000
Country of Study: Australia
No. of awards offered: 1
Additional Information: federation.edu.au/connect/founda tion/supporting-the-foundation/scholarships/foundation-scho larships/wellington-shire-council-scholarship

Fellowship Program in Academic Medicine

National Medical Fellowship, Inc., 254 West 31st Street, New York, NY 10001, United States of America.

Contact: Awards Committee

Akhtarali H. Tobaccowala Fellowship

Purpose: The fellowship was established in the memory of Akhtarali H. Tobaccowala who was a 1952 graduate of the Booth school
Eligibility: The fellowship which offer tuition support is available for students of Booth's full-time MBA program
Level of Study: Postgraduate
Type: Scholarship
Value: Up to US$25,000 per annum
Frequency: Annual
Country of Study: Any country

Application Procedure: There is no formal application process
Funding: Private

For further information contact:

The Tobaccowala Foundation, 35. Printing House, Police Court Lane (Behind Handloom House) Fort, Mumbai, Maharashtra 400 001, India.

Tel: (91) 22 22640386
Email: tobaccowalafoundation@gmail.com

Therla Drake Postgraduate Scholarships

Purpose: The scholarship is for postgraduate classical performance overseas study and application should be made in the year for which the project is planned. While the terms of the bequest are that preference be given to a piano student, other applicants will be considered.
Eligibility: The applicant must be enrolling or have enrolled for postgraduate study at Te Kōkī New Zealand School of Music at Te Herenga Waka - Victoria University of Wellington, and remain in good academic standing.
Level of Study: Postgraduate
Type: Scholarship
Value: One at NZ$25,000 annually for full Master's scholarship plus fees, or two at NZ$9,000 each annually toward fees for postgraduate study.
Length of Study: 1 year
Frequency: Annual
Country of Study: Any country
Application Procedure: Applicants will complete the online application by the closing date. No late applications will be accepted. Applicants should provide the following supporting documentation 1. A letter outlining the project and its benefit to your career plans. 2. A detailed budget. 3. Copies of any communication with the host person(s) or organisation(s) overseas. 4. A supporting statement from the principal supervisor. In order to proceed with the application, kindly check the below link. www.victoria.ac.nz/study/student-finance/scholarships
No. of awards offered: 2
Closing Date: 15 November
Funding: Private
Additional Information: www.wgtn.ac.nz/scholarships/cur rent/therle-drake-postgraduate-scholarship

For further information contact:

Scholarships Office, Victoria University of Wellington, PO Box 600, Wellington, 6140, New Zealand.

Email: scholarships-office@vuw.ac.nz

Ferrari

Direzione e stablimento Abetone int. 4, I-41053 Maranello (MO), Italy.

Tel: (39) 536 949111
Email: carrerservice@mip.polimi.it
Website: www.ferrariworld.com

Born in 1947, Ferrari has always produced vehicles at its current site and has maintained its direction. It has progressively widened it range using visionary planning to both on a design level and on the quality of work produced.

Ferrari Innovation Team Project Scholarship

Purpose: To create members of a new and innovative team for the new and innovative cars of the future
Eligibility: Knowledge of ergonomics will be considered a plus
Level of Study: Postgraduate, Professional development
Type: Scholarship
Value: €25,000 and all accommodation and training
Length of Study: 1 year
Frequency: Annual
Study Establishment: Ferrari Spa
Country of Study: Italy
Closing Date: 25 May
Funding: Commercial
Contributor: Ferrari

For further information contact:

Email: cdozio@ferrari.it

Fight for Sight

18 Mansell Street, London E1 8AA, United Kingdom.

Website: www.fightforsight.org.uk

Fight for Sight

Purpose: Fight for Sight is one of the leading United Kingdom charities dedicated to funding pioneering research to prevent sight loss and treat eye disease

Eligibility: Young (under 40) ophthalmologists and scientists working in the field of ophthalmology in the United Kingdom - awarded recognition of the completion of a significant piece of research completed within 18 months prior to the closing date
Level of Study: Postgraduate
Type: Grant
Value: £5,000
Frequency: Annual
Country of Study: Any country
Closing Date: February
Funding: Foundation
Additional Information: www.eyedocs.co.uk/ophthalmology-research-awards/1079-fight-for-sight-award

For further information contact:

Email: training@rcophth.ac.uk

PhD Studentships

Purpose: Fight for Sights mission is to stop sight loss by funding the highest quality medical research. To help us achieve our goals we are committed to encouraging new and highly motivated graduates to take up and pursue a career in ophthalmic and vision research.
Eligibility: 1. Applications must be made by the potential PhD Supervisor(s). 2. Please note that Fight for Sight will only accept one PhD Studentship application from the same individual acting either as Supervisor or Co-Supervisor. 3. Supervisors must be affiliated with UK academic or medical institutions. 4. The student must be attached to a UK institution but the research can be undertaken in the UK and/or overseas. 5. Supervisor(s) must have a contract which extends beyond the termination date of the PhD Studentship. 6. The student appointed must not be medically or otherwise clinically qualified professionals. Clinically active individuals should consider the MRC/Fight for Sight Clinical Research Training Fellowships. 7. The scheme does not cover funding gaps for studentships already started. 8. The proposed project must aim to stop or reduce sight loss.
Level of Study: Postgraduate
Type: Studentship
Value: Up to £100,000
Length of Study: 3 years
Country of Study: Any country
Closing Date: 28 October
Additional Information: www.fightforsight.org.uk/apply-for-funding/funding-opportunities/phd-studentships/

For further information contact:

Email: grants@fightforsight.org.uk

Finnish National Agency for Education - EDUFI

Hakaniemenranta 6, P.O. Box 380, FI-00531 Helsinki, Finland.

Tel: (358) 29 533 1000
Website: www.oph.fi/

The Finnish National Agency for Education is the national development agency responsible for early childhood education and care, pre-primary, basic, general and vocational upper secondary education as well as for adult education and training. Higher education is the responsibility of the Ministry of Education and Culture.

EDUFI Fellowship

Purpose: The EDUFI Fellowships programme is open to young Doctoral level students and researchers from all countries and from all academic fields who wish to pursue their Doctorate (or Double Doctorate) at a Finnish university. Master's level studies or post-doctoral studies/research are not supported in the programme.
Eligibility: You can apply for the fellowship grant if 1. you work as a researcher or a teacher in a Finnish university department 2. you will be hosting the research fellow 3. you will commit to common objectives with the research fellow 4. you will offer facilities and equipment for the use of the research fellow 5. you will supervise the research. 6. You can apply for a fellowship for a non-Finnish post-graduate (post Master's degree) student or a young researcher that you will invite to Finland or who has been in Finland for a maximum of one year before applying for the fellowship. The EDUFI Fellowship is available to all foreign nationals and all fields of study.
Level of Study: Masters Degree
Type: Scholarships
Value: €1,500/month
Length of Study: 3 to12 months, visits 3 to 6 months
Frequency: Annual
Country of Study: Finland
Application Procedure: You can fill in the EDUFI Fellowship application form in Finnish, Swedish or English. The application form comes with instructions on how to fill it and a list of required annexes. Please post the signed form and annexes by e-mail to: Kirjaamo(at) oph.fi, and write "EDUFI Fellowship" in the subject line of the e-mail. www.oph.fi/sites/default/files/documents/edufi-fellowships_application_form_and_instructions_30092020.doc
Additional Information: www.oph.fi/en/development/edufi-fellowship

For further information contact:

Email: Kirjaamo@oph.fi

Flinders University

GPO, Box 2100, Adelaide, SA 5001, Australia.

Tel: (61) 8 8201 2916
Email: newsdesk@flinders.edu.au
Website: www.flinders.edu.au

Flinders University is an integral part of Australia's respected higher education system and makes an important economic and social contribution to South Australia and to the nation. Flinders has a high research profile and consistently ranks among Australia's top universities on a per capita basis for research. It emphasizes innovation and excellence in its educational programs and researches across a wide range of disciplines.

2022 Great Artesian Basin Lynn Brake Scholarship

Eligibility: This annual Scholarship Grant will support new or continuing Postgraduate students (PhD, Masters, Honours, Diploma or Graduate Certificate) to undertake new research within an Australian tertiary institution in a field related to the Great Artesian Basin including water resource management, hydrogeology and management of springs connected to the water resources of the Basin.
Level of Study: Doctorate, Postgraduate
Type: Scholarship
Value: AU$20,000
Frequency: Annual
Country of Study: Australia
Closing Date: 31 January
Additional Information: www.flinders.edu.au/scholarships-system/index.cfm/scholarships/display/aa1d692

For further information contact:

Email: gabsecretariat@agriculture.gov.au

Advanced Community Care Scholarship

Purpose: To undertake a research project within the Faculty of Health Sciences related to the practical clinical, organizational and financial implications of home-based alternatives to hospital care

Eligibility: Applicants must be Australian citizens or permanent residents of Australia and have completed at least 4 years of tertiary education studies at a high level of achievement and have an appropriate Honours 1 or high 2A (or equivalent) undergraduate degree. They must enroll as full-time students (part-time awards are available in certain circumstances)

Level of Study: Doctorate

Type: Scholarship

Value: AU$25,849 per year plus generous leave provisions and allowances.

Length of Study: 3 years

Frequency: Annual

Country of Study: Any country

Application Procedure: Applicants must obtain the application kits from the Higher Degree Administration and Scholarships Office or can download it from the scholarships website

Closing Date: 31 October

Contributor: Advanced Community Care Association

For further information contact:

Tel: (61) 8 8201 3115
Email: scholarships@flinders.edu.au

Austin Taylor Indigenous NT Medical Program Scholarship

Eligibility: Applicants must: 1. be of Australian Aboriginal or Torres Strait Islander descent; and 2. identify as an Australian Aboriginal or Torres Strait Islander; and 3. be accepted as an Australian Aboriginal or Torres Strait Islander by the community in which they live or have lived; and 4. be enrolled as a student in the Flinders University Northern Territory Medical Program.

Level of Study: Postgraduate

Type: Scholarship

Frequency: Annual

Study Establishment: AU$750 each year

Country of Study: Australia

Closing Date: 16 February

Additional Information: www.flinders.edu.au/scholarships-system/index.cfm/scholarships/display/a935ec

Australian Health Inequities Program Research Scholarship

Purpose: To address health inequities, understand the social determinants of health and analyze policy and program strategies that aim to reduce inequities

Eligibility: Applicants should be Australian citizens, permanent residents of Australia or New Zealand citizens and have completed at least four years of tertiary education studies at a high level of achievement and have an appropriate Honours 1 or high 2A (or equivalent) undergraduate degree. They should enroll as full-time students (a part-time award may be available in certain circumstances) and should commence a Doctorate by research

Level of Study: Postgraduate

Type: Scholarship

Value: AU$19,616 per year

Length of Study: 3 years

Frequency: Annual

Country of Study: Any country

Application Procedure: Applicants can obtain the application kits from the Higher Degree Administration and Scholarships Office or download it from Flinders University scholarships website

Closing Date: 31 October

For further information contact:

Department of Public Health.

Tel: (61) 8 8204 5983
Email: fran.baum@flinders.edu.au

Australian Health Inequities Program University Research Scholarship

Purpose: To address health inequities, to understand the social determinants of health and to analyze policy and program strategies that aim to reduce them

Eligibility: Applicants must be Australian citizens, permanent residents of Australia or New Zealand citizens and have completed at least 4 years of tertiary education studies at a high level of achievement and have an appropriate Honours 1 or high 2A (or equivalent) undergraduate degree. They should enroll as full–time students (a part–time award may be available in certain circumstances) and should commence a Doctorate by research

Level of Study: Postgraduate

Type: Scholarship

Value: AU$19,616 per year

Length of Study: 3 years

Country of Study: Any country

Application Procedure: Applicants can obtain the application kits from the Higher Degree Administration and Scholarships Office or download it from Flinders University scholarships website. It is essential to consult Prof. Baum or Dr. Newman before submitting an application

Closing Date: 31 October

For further information contact:

Department of Public Health.

Tel: (61) 8 8204 5983
Email: fran.baum@flinders.edu.au

Carson Northern Territory Medical Program Scholarship

Eligibility: Applicants must: 1. be enrolled in the second or third year of the Northern Territory Medical Program at Flinders University; and 2. be able to demonstrate consistent professional behaviour and a commitment to working on the Northern Territory.
Level of Study: Postgraduate
Type: Scholarship
Value: AU$5,000
Frequency: Annual
Country of Study: Australia
Closing Date: 16 February
Additional Information: www.flinders.edu.au/scholarships-system/index.cfm/scholarships/display/ac1ec54

Cheryl Ann Keatley Scholarship

Eligibility: Applicants must: 1. be Australian citizens or permanent residents of Australia; and 2. have applied for admission to, or be enrolled in, the Graduate Certificate in Primary Health Care (Aged Care) or the Graduate Diploma in Nursing (Aged Care) or the Master of Nursing (Aged Care) offered by Flinders University; and 3. be able to demonstrate financial hardship; and 4. be able to demonstrate active involvement in the delivery of care to the older person.
Level of Study: Postgraduate
Type: Scholarship
Value: AU$1,000
Frequency: Annual
Country of Study: Australia
Closing Date: 11 March
Additional Information: www.flinders.edu.au/scholarships-system/index.cfm/scholarships/display/a328ee

Choosing the Way Forward: Addressing the Post-Parental Housing Transition Needs with Intellectual Disability and Their Older Family Carers

Eligibility: To be eligible for the award of this scholarship a student must: 1. Be an Australian citizen; or New Zealand citizen; or have been granted permanent resident status; and 2. meet PhD admission requirements including: have an Australian Honours degree Class 1 or 2A or equivalent qualification (at least AQF Level 8), including a research component of at least 6 months' full-time study achieving Distinction (75%) OR including evidence of equivalent research experience, such as a substantial first-author refereed publication or track record as an investigator on a competitive grant; and 3. be available to commence as a full-time PhD student at Flinders University in semester 1, 2023.
Level of Study: Doctorate
Type: Scholarship
Value: a stipend valued at AU$28,592 (Year 1); AU$29,092 (Year 2); AU$29,592 (Year 3) tax free
Length of Study: 3 years
Frequency: Annual
Country of Study: Australia
Closing Date: 28 February
Additional Information: www.flinders.edu.au/scholarships-system/index.cfm/scholarships/display/a920562

For further information contact:

Email: ruth.walker@flinders.edu.au

College of Business Government and Law PhD Top-up

Eligibility: All scholarship applicants must be: 1. a full-time PhD student at the College of Business, Government and Law at Flinders University – that is a PhD student studying business, government, law or criminology; 2. newly enrolled students: that is students who will commence in 2023; a domestic student (Australian citizens or permanent residents of Australia), or New Zealand citizen, or an international student; 3. (for domestic students) in receipt of the Australian Research Training Program (RTP), the Flinders University Research Scholarship (FURS), or an equivalent scholarship; 4. (for international students) in receipt of the Australian Government Research Training Program (AGRTP), or an equivalent scholarship which includes an Overseas Student Health Cover (OSHC); 5. able to demonstrate academic merit and research potential.
Level of Study: Doctorate
Type: Scholarship
Value: AU$5,000
Length of Study: 3 years
Frequency: Annual
Country of Study: Australia
Closing Date: 31 January
Additional Information: www.flinders.edu.au/scholarships-system/index.cfm/scholarships/display/aa2e7a0

For further information contact:

Email: cbgl.research@flinders.edu.au

Community Bridging Services (CBS) Inc Scholarship

Eligibility: 1. be enrolled in a degree program at Flinders University; and 2. be registered and have an Access Plan with Disability Services.
Level of Study: Postgraduate
Type: Scholarship
Value: AU$3,000
Frequency: Annual
Country of Study: Australia
Closing Date: 11 March
Additional Information: www.flinders.edu.au/scholarships-system/index.cfm/scholarships/display/a91d736

Connellan Airways Trust Diabetes Management and Education Scholarship

Eligibility: 1. be an Australian citizen, permanent resident or permanent humanitarian visa holder; and 2. be enrolled in the Graduate Certificate in Primary Health Care (Diabetes Management and Education) at Flinders University; and 3. be working or residing in an ASGS Remoteness Areas RA4 remote or RA5 very remote area; 4. not be in receipt of another similar scholarship.
Level of Study: Postgraduate
Type: Scholarship
Value: AU$2,000
Frequency: Annual
Country of Study: Australia
No. of awards offered: 2
Closing Date: 11 March
Additional Information: www.flinders.edu.au/scholarships-system/index.cfm/scholarships/display/ad1e756

Diamond Jubilee Bursary

Purpose: It is helpful for women, who are Australian citizens or permanent residents, enrolled in a postgraduate Masters degree (by research or including a thesis) at a South Australian university
Eligibility: Applicants 1. Women students who are Australian citizens or permanent residents. 2. Must be studying at a South Australian University for a postgraduate award which is classified. 3. at Masters Degree level. This must be by research or include a thesis component. 4. Must have

completed at least six months full time equivalent of their masters program. 5. Must have a good undergraduate academic record. 6. Must not be in full time paid employment or on fully paid leave during the tenure of the Scholarship. 7. Must not have received a scholarship or award in the same category
Level of Study: Postgraduate
Type: Bursary
Value: AU$3,000
Length of Study: 1 year
Frequency: Annual
Country of Study: Australia
Application Procedure: Application forms can be downloaded from the AFUW-SA website listed below. 1. Your application must reach the Trust Fund's secretarial service by 29 March. 2. Scholarship Type postgraduate, academic merit, financial, commencing, continuing
Closing Date: 31 March
Funding: Private
Additional Information: Selection of winners is based primarily on academic merit, but also on the importance of the purpose for which the scholarship will be used to the progress or completion of the degree, on referees' report, on financial need as well as community activities and other interests www.afuwsa-trust.com.au/dj-scholarships/

For further information contact:

The AFUW-SA Inc. Trust Fund, 213 Greenhill Road, Eastwood, SA 5063, Australia.

Email: internationalapply@flinders.edu.au

Ember Venning Postgraduate Research Scholarship in Speech Pathology and Audiology

Eligibility: Applicants for the scholarship must: 1. be Australian citizens or permanent residents of Australia; and 2. have applied for admission to or be enrolled in a Higher Degree by Research to undertake or be undertaking research in the area of Speech Pathology or Audiology, preferably in relation to the Indigenous community.
Level of Study: Postgraduate
Type: Scholarship
Value: AU$4,000
Length of Study: 3 years
Frequency: Annual
Country of Study: Australia
Closing Date: 1 February
Additional Information: www.flinders.edu.au/scholarships-system/index.cfm/scholarships/display/9f4d2

Faculty of Science and Engineering Research Awards (FSERA)

Purpose: To enable students to pursue a Masters Degree by research or Doctorate by research in the Faculty of Science and Engineering

Eligibility: 1. To be eligible for consideration for the award of a Faculty of Science and Engineering Research Award, applicants must: 1. a. be an Australian citizen, or a New Zealand citizen or an Australian permanent resident at the closing date of applications; and b. have completed at least four years of tertiary education studies at a high level of achievement and have an appropriate first class Honours degree or an equivalent qualification; and c. be currently admitted, or be eligible for admission, to a Masters degree by research or Doctorate by research in the Faculty of Science and Engineering; and 2. normally intend to enrol as full-time students (part-time awards are available in certain, limited circumstances); and 3. A Faculty of Science and Engineering Research Award will not normally be awarded to an applicant a. is in receipt of an award which directly duplicates the purpose of the Faculty of Science and Engineering Research Award; b. is on paid study leave; 2.3. holds a fractional academic appointment; c. is seeking the award to undertake a second higher degree at the same level of a previously awarded degree.

Level of Study: Graduate, Postgraduate
Type: Research award
Value: AU$28,0926 per year
Length of Study: 2 years if masters or 3 years if PhD
Country of Study: Australia
Application Procedure: Applicants must apply directly to the university
Closing Date: 9 July
Additional Information: scholarship-positions.com/faculty-science-engineering-research-scholarships-fsera-flinders-university-australia/2017/05/26/

For further information contact:

Tel: (61) 8 8201 3115
Fax: (61) 8 8201 5175
Email: scholarships@flinders.edu.au

Flinders University and Defence Science: Defence Science Partnership Grant

Eligibility: To be eligible for the award of this scholarship, a student must: 1. Be an Australian citizen, or New Zealand citizen; or have been granted permanent resident status; and 2. meet ME admission requirements 3. be available to commence as a full-time ME student at Flinders University in semester 1, 2023.

Level of Study: Research
Type: Scholarship
Value: A stipend valued at AU$30,000 per annum tax-free The scholarship will be awarded for two years A Research Training Program Fee Offset Scholarship covers tuition fees for Australian Citizens, NZ Citizens and Permanent Residents. There is a possibility to convert ME to PHD research and extend the scholarship to three years
Length of Study: 2 years
Frequency: Annual
Country of Study: Australia
Application Procedure: Applications for admission to candidature are submitted electronically www.flinders.edu.au/study/apply/apply-research-degree/how-to-apply
Closing Date: 30 March
Additional Information: www.flinders.edu.au/scholarships-system/index.cfm/scholarships/display/ac1ff1e

For further information contact:

Email: Saeed.rehman@flinders.edu.au

Flinders University Research Scholarships (FURS)

Purpose: The purpose of the scholarship is to enable a suitably qualified graduate to carry out, under the supervision of a member of staff appointed by the College, a program of study leading to a Higher Degree by Research (HDR).

Eligibility: ELIGIBILITY: 1 To be eligible for the award of a Flinders University Research Scholarship, a student must: a. be an Australian citizen or a New Zealand citizen or an Australian permanent resident at the closing date for applications; or be an international student who has completed an honours degree or equivalent qualification at an Australian University no more than three years prior to the application closing date; and b. be enrolled, or be seeking to enrol, as a full-time student in a research higher degree at Flinders University; and c. have completed a Bachelors degree with Second Class (Division A) Honours or above, or an equivalent level of academic attainment. 2 A Flinders University Research Scholarship will not be awarded to a student who: a. is in receipt of an award which directly duplicates the purpose of the Flinders University Research Scholarship; b. is on paid study leave; c. holds a fractional academic appointment; d. holds a Research Doctorate or equivalent, or holds a Research Masters or equivalent and is seeking a FURS to undertake a Research Masters degree.

Level of Study: Postgraduate
Type: Scholarship
Value: Full-time AU$28,597 pa tax-free, Part-time AU$14,198 pa taxable. Relocation Allowance AU$1,485
Length of Study: 2 years for masters or 3 years for PhD
Frequency: Annual
Country of Study: Australia

Application Procedure: Applications are submitted via the student information system available via the Flinders University website: www.flinders.edu.au/study/apply/apply-researchdegree/how-to-apply

Closing Date: 31 March

Additional Information: www.australianuniversities.com.au/scholarships/guide/8495-flinders-university-research-scholarship-furs.html

For further information contact:

Tel: (61) 8 8201 3115
Fax: (61) 8 8201 5175
Email: scholarships@flinders.edu.au

FMC Foundation Pink Ribbon Ball Committee Breast Cancer Research Scholarship

Purpose: To undertake a breast cancer biomedical research project within the Faculty of Health Sciences

Eligibility: Applicants must be Australian citizens or permanent residents of Australia and have completed at least 4 years of tertiary education studies at a high level of achievement and have an appropriate Honours 1 or high 2A (or equivalent) undergraduate degree. They must enroll as full-time students (part-time awards are available in certain circumstances) and must commence a Doctorate by research

Level of Study: Postgraduate

Type: Scholarship

Value: AU$25,000 plus up to AU$2,000 per year for conference travel and consumables

Length of Study: 3 years

Frequency: Annual

Country of Study: Any country

Application Procedure: Applicants can obtain the application kits from the Higher Degree Administration and Scholarships Office and can download it from the scholarship website

Closing Date: 31 October

Contributor: Flinders Medical Centre Foundation

Additional Information: breastcancernow.org/get-involved/social-events/pink-ribbon-ball-london

For further information contact:

Tel: (61) 8 8204 4100
Email: johnno.oliver@flinders.edu.au

FMC Foundation Research Scholarship

Purpose: To undertake a health-related project within the Faculty of Health Sciences

Eligibility: Applicants should be Australian citizens or permanent residents of Australia and have completed at least 4 years

of tertiary education studies at a high level of achievement and have an appropriate Honours 1 or high 2A (or equivalent) undergraduate degree. They should enroll as full-time students (part-time awards are available in certain circumstances) and should commence a Doctorate by research

Level of Study: Postgraduate

Type: Scholarship

Value: AU$25,000 plus up to AU$2,000 per year for conference travel and consumables

Length of Study: 3 years

Frequency: Annual

Country of Study: Any country

Application Procedure: Applicants can obtain application kits from the Higher Degree Administration and Scholarships Office or download from the scholarships website

Closing Date: 31 October

Funding: Foundation

Contributor: FMC Foundation

Additional Information: www.flinders.edu.au/scholarships-system/index.cfm/scholarships/display/a0502

For further information contact:

Tel: (61) 8 8204 4100
Email: johnno.oliver@flinders.edu.au

Francis Regan Student Scholarship

Eligibility: Applicants for the scholarship must: 1. be enrolled in an Honours degree or Masters degree in Education, Humanities or Law at Flinders University; and 2. be undertaking a research or creative project in any area of social justice; and 3. be able to demonstrate a commitment to social justice through employment, study, or volunteer work, or in some other way and 4. not have previously held the Francis Regan Student Scholarship.

Level of Study: Postgraduate

Type: Scholarship

Value: AU$1,000

Frequency: Annual

Country of Study: Australia

Closing Date: 16 February

Additional Information: www.flinders.edu.au/scholarships-system/index.cfm/scholarships/display/b03037

Honours/Masters Scholarship for AI, User Interface or Robotics

Purpose: To enable students to undertake an Honours or Masters project in the Artificial Intelligence Laboratory in the School of Informatics and Engineering at Flinders University

Eligibility: Applicants must have Australian citizenship or permanent residence, plus distinction-level completion of the requirements of 3 years of undergraduate degree in cognitive science, computer science, mathematics, or engineering program
Level of Study: Graduate
Type: Scholarship
Value: AU$5,000
Country of Study: Any country
Application Procedure: Check website for further details
Closing Date: 15 November

For further information contact:

Email: David.Powers@flinders.edu.au

Indigenous Commonwealth Accommodation Scholarship

Eligibility: 1. be of Australian Aboriginal or Torres Strait Islander descent; and 2. identify as an Australian Aboriginal or Torres Strait Islander; and 3. be accepted as an Australian Aboriginal or Torres Strait Islander by the community in which they live or have lived; and 4. normally be enrolled full-time at Flinders University in an undergraduate or post-graduate course of study or the Foundation Studies program; and 5. have a permanent home address in Inner or Outer Regional, Remote or Very Remote Australia as defined by the Australian Standard Geographic Classification (ASGC); and 6. have relocated to undertake study as per section 2. 10.15 of the Commonwealth Scholarship Guidelines (Education) 2010; and 7. not be in receipt of a Relocation Scholarship (available to ABSTUDY and Youth Allowance recipients); and 8. not be in receipt of the ABSTUDY residential costs payment.
Level of Study: Postgraduate
Type: Scholarship
Value: AU$7,500
Length of Study: 2 years
Frequency: Annual
Country of Study: Australia
Closing Date: 4 February
Additional Information: www.flinders.edu.au/scholarships-system/index.cfm/scholarships/display/a02e8a

Indigenous Commonwealth Accomodation Top-up Scholarship

Eligibility: 1. be of Australian Aboriginal or Torres Strait Islander descent; and 2. identify as an Australian Aboriginal or Torres Strait Islander; and 3. be accepted as an Australian

Aboriginal or Torres Strait Islander by the community in which they live or have lived; and 4. normally be enrolled full-time at Flinders University in an undergraduate or post-graduate course of study or the Foundation Studies program; and 5. have a permanent home address in Inner or Outer Regional, Remote or Very Remote Australia as defined by the Australian Standard Geographic Classification (ASGC); and 6. have relocated to undertake study as per section 2. 10.15 of the Commonwealth Scholarship Guidelines (Education) 2010; and 7 . be living on-campus at Bedford Park in Flinders living; and 8. be able to demonstrate financial need; and 9. be in receipt of an ICAS.
Level of Study: Postgraduate
Type: Scholarship
Frequency: Annual
Study Establishment: AU$9,000 and AU$3,110
Country of Study: Australia
Closing Date: 4 February
Additional Information: www.flinders.edu.au/scholarships-system/index.cfm/scholarships/display/ad1ec30

Indigenous Commonwealth Education Costs Scholarship

Eligibility: 1. be of Australian Aboriginal or Torres Strait Islander descent; and 2. identify as an Australian Aboriginal or Torres Strait Islander; and 3. be accepted as an Australian Aboriginal or Torres Strait Islander by the community in which they live or have lived; and 4. normally be enrolled full-time at Flinders University in an undergraduate or postgraduate course of study or the Foundation Studies program; and 5. not be in receipt of a Student Start-up Scholarship or Student Start-up Loan (available to ABSTUDY, Austudy and Youth Allowance recipients); and 6. be able to demonstrate financial disadvantage or have a permanent home address in Inner or Outer Regional, Remote or Very Remote Australia as defined by the Australian Standard Geographic Classification (ASGC).
Level of Study: Postgraduate
Type: Scholarship
Value: AU$2,756
Frequency: Annual
Country of Study: Australia
Closing Date: 11 March
Additional Information: www.flinders.edu.au/scholarships-system/index.cfm/scholarships/display/a91d736

Investigation of the Human Intestinal Nervous System

Purpose: To support investigation of the human intestinal nervous system

Eligibility: Applicants must be Australian citizens or permanent residents of Australia and have completed at least 4 years of tertiary education studies at a high level of achievement and have an appropriate undergraduate medical degree. They should enroll as full-time students and commence a Doctorate by research
Level of Study: Graduate
Type: Scholarship
Value: AU$29,172
Length of Study: 3 years
Frequency: Annual
Country of Study: Any country
Application Procedure: Applicants can obtain application kits from the Higher Degree Administration and Scholarships Office or can download from the scholarships website
Closing Date: 31 October

For further information contact:

Tel: (61) 8 8204 4253
Email: david.wattchow@flinders.edu.au

Jacqui Thorburn and Family Bursary for Indigenous Archaeology and Cultural Heritage Management

Eligibility: 1. be of Australian Aboriginal or Torres Strait Islander descent; and 2. identify as an Australian Aboriginal or Torres Strait Islander; and 3. be accepted as an Australian Aboriginal or Torres Strait Islander by the community in which they live or have lived; and 4. be making satisfactory academic progress; and 5. normally be enrolled in an undergraduate or postgraduate coursework degree at Flinders University specialising in Indigenous Archaeology or Cultural Heritage Management.
Level of Study: Postgraduate
Type: Scholarship
Value: AU$2,000
Frequency: Annual
Country of Study: Australia
Closing Date: 11 March
Additional Information: www.flinders.edu.au/scholarships-system/index.cfm/scholarships/display/af1f400

Margaret Fay Fuller Scholarship: Margaret Fay Fuller PhD top up Scholarship

Eligibility: Applicants for the scholarship must: 1. be Australian citizens or permanent residents of South

Australia; and 2. be enrolled in their final year of a Higher Degree by Research at Flinders University and be undertaking research in any area of cancer research.
Level of Study: Postgraduate, Research
Type: Scholarship
Value: AU$5,000
Frequency: Annual
Country of Study: Australia
Application Procedure: Download the application form for this scholarship scheme.: www.flinders.edu.au/scholarships-system/Application%20Form%20MFuller%20H.pdf
No. of awards offered: 1
Closing Date: 20 April
Additional Information: www.flinders.edu.au/scholarships-system/index.cfm/scholarships/display/af20fa4

For further information contact:

Email: rhdscholarships@flinders.edu.au

May Mills Scholarship for Women

Purpose: The purpose of the scholarship is to encourage women who have experienced significant interruptions to their studies due to family responsibilities, to proceed to a research higher degree at Flinders University. The scholarship covers programs of study that will qualify women for admission to a research higher degree, such as honours, postgraduate coursework studies or bridging studies programs.
Eligibility: Applicants must be female citizens or permanent residents of Australia
Level of Study: Graduate, Postgraduate
Type: Scholarship
Value: Maximum AU$9,000 per year
Length of Study: 1 year
Frequency: Annual
Country of Study: Australia
Application Procedure: Applicants may consult the scholarship website
Closing Date: 31 January
Contributor: Flinders University
Additional Information: www.flinders.edu.au/scholarships-system/index.cfm/scholarships/display/9e595

For further information contact:

Tel: (61) 8 82013143
Fax: (61) 8 8201 5175
Email: scholarships@flinders.edu.au

Mediserve Northern Territory Diabetes Management and Education Scholarship

Eligibility: 1. be an Australian citizen, permanent resident or permanent humanitarian visa holder; and 2. be enrolled in the Graduate Certificate in Primary Health Care (Diabetes Management and Education) at Flinders University; and 3. have a permanent home address in the Northern Territory.
Level of Study: Postgraduate
Type: Scholarship
Value: AU$2,000
Frequency: Annual
Country of Study: Australia
Closing Date: 11 March
Additional Information: www.flinders.edu.au/scholarships-system/index.cfm/scholarships/display/ae1f4c2

Multi Scale Biomechanical Investigations of the Intervertebral Disc

Purpose: To undertake a challenging program of research that combines both analytical (finite element analysis) and experimental
Eligibility: Applicants must be Australian or international students who have completed at least 4 years of tertiary education studies at a high level of achievement and have an appropriate Honours 1 or high 2A (or equivalent) undergraduate degree in mechanical/biomedical/civil/chemical engineering or related fields
Level of Study: Postgraduate
Type: Scholarship
Value: AU$25,313
Length of Study: 3 years
Frequency: Annual
Country of Study: Any country
Application Procedure: Applicants can obtain the application kits from the Higher Degree Administration and Scholarships Office at Flinders University
Closing Date: 1 June

For further information contact:

Tel: (61) 8 8275 1751
Email: john.costi@rgh.sa.gov.au

National Health and Medical Research Council Centre of Clinical Eye Research: PhD Scholarships

Purpose: To conduct clinical research in the major blinding diseases – cataract, glaucoma, diabetic retinopathy and corneal disease

Eligibility: Applicants must be Australian citizens, permanent residents of Australia or New Zealand citizens and have completed at least 4 years of tertiary education studies at a high level of achievement and have an appropriate Honours 1 or high 2A (or equivalent) undergraduate degree
Level of Study: Postgraduate
Type: Scholarship
Value: A stipend of AU$20,007–29,172 plus AU$2,000 for conference travel and consumables
Length of Study: 3 years
Frequency: Annual
Country of Study: Any country
Application Procedure: Applicants can obtain the application kits from the Higher Degree Administration and Scholarships Office or can download it from the scholarships website
Closing Date: 31 October

For further information contact:

Tel: (61) 8 8204 4899
Email: Konrad.Pesudovs@flinders.edu.au

National Health and Medical Research Council Medical and Dental Postgraduate Research Scholarships

Purpose: To provide full-time research experience to medical or dental graduates registered to practice in Australia
Eligibility: Applicants must be medical or dental graduates registered to practice in Australia. Graduates from overseas who hold permanent resident status and are currently resident in Australia are eligible to apply
Level of Study: Graduate
Type: Scholarship
Value: AU$29,172 per year plus AU$2,250 per year towards the cost of consumables and travel to approved conferences
Length of Study: 3 years
Country of Study: Australia
Application Procedure: Applicants can obtain application forms, instruction booklets, referee report pro formae and various attachments to the instructions from the NHMRC website
Closing Date: 25 July

For further information contact:

Email: research@nhmrc.gov.au

National Health and Medical Research Council Public Health Postgraduate Scholarships

Purpose: To encourage graduates to obtain formal training in public health research

Eligibility: Applicants must be Australian citizens who have already completed a degree in an area applicable in public health research at the time of submission of the application or graduates in areas applicable to public health who are from overseas, have permanent resident status and are currently residing in Australia. All candidates must enroll for a higher degree requiring full-time research

Level of Study: Graduate

Type: Scholarship

Value: AU$19,616 (Australian postgraduate award), AU$25,313 (nursing and allied health professionals) and AU$29,172 (medical/dental)

Frequency: Annual

Country of Study: Australia

Application Procedure: Applicants must submit the application forms to the Higher Degree Administration and Scholarships Office and should include one additional copy for University records. Application forms, instruction booklets, referee report pro formae and various attachments to the instructions are available from the NHMRC website

Closing Date: June

For further information contact:

Tel: (61) 2 8627 1444

Email: research@nhmrc.gov.au

National Health and Medical Research Council: Primary Health Care Postgraduate Research Scholarships

Purpose: To encourage graduates to obtain formal training in primary health care related research, with an emphasis on rural communities

Eligibility: Applicants must be Australian citizens or have permanent resident status, who are medical, dental or health-related graduates currently registered to practice within Australia or who have already completed a degree (or equivalent) at the time of submission of the application

Level of Study: Graduate

Type: Scholarship

Value: AU$19,616 (Australian postgraduate award), AU$25,313 (nursing and allied health professionals) and AU$29,172 (medical/dental) per year

Country of Study: Australia

Application Procedure: Applications must be submitted to the Higher Degree Administration and Scholarships Office and should include one additional copy for University records. Application forms, instruction booklets, referee report pro formae and various attachments to the instructions are available from the NHMRC website

Closing Date: 25 July

For further information contact:

Email: research@nhmrc.gov.au

Northern Territory Territory Medical Program Aboriginal and Torres Strait Islander Bursary

Eligibility: 1. Be of Australian Aboriginal or Torres Strait Islander descent and be accepted as an Australian Aboriginal or Torres Strait Islander by the community in which he or she lives or has lived; and; 2. Be an Australian citizen; and 3. Be enrolled as a full-time student in the Flinders University Northern Territory Medical Program; and 4. Be able to demonstrate financial need.

Level of Study: Postgraduate

Type: Scholarship

Value: AU$20,000

Length of Study: 4 years

Frequency: Annual

Country of Study: Australia

Closing Date: 11 March

Additional Information: www.flinders.edu.au/scholarships-system/index.cfm/scholarships/display/b2330f

PhD Scholarship for Vascular and Metabolic Research

Purpose: To focus on the relationship between obesity, adipose tissue distribution, endothelial function and cardiovascular risk in humans using established techniques such as liver MRI and spectroscopy, pulse-wave analysis, and forearm occlusion plethysmography

Eligibility: Applicants should be Australian citizens or permanent residents of Australia and have completed at least 4 years of tertiary education studies at a high level of achievement and have an appropriate undergraduate medical degree

Level of Study: Postgraduate

Type: Scholarship

Value: AU$20,007 per year

Length of Study: Up to 3 years

Frequency: Annual

Study Establishment: Faculty of Health Sciences, Flinders University

Country of Study: Australia

Application Procedure: Applicants can obtain the application kits from the Higher Degree Administration and Scholarships Office or can download it from the scholarships website

Closing Date: 31 October

For further information contact:

Tel: (61) 8 8204 5202

Email: arduino.mangoni@flinders.edu.au

PhD Scholarship in Material Science and/or Civil Engineering

Eligibility: 1. Have a research background in Materials Science or Civil Engineering (being familiar with nanotechnology and characterisation). 1a. Be either a domestic candidate (an Australian or New Zealand citizen; or permanent resident), or international candidate. 1b. Support for the university tuition fees needs to be provided separately, as the scholarship is not provided to cover tuition fee expenses. 1c. Meet PhD admission requirements including: have an Australian Honours degree Class 1 or 2A or equivalent qualification (at least AQF Level 8) including a research component of at least 6 months' full-time study achieving Distinction (75%) OR including evidence of equivalent research experience, such as a substantial first-author refereed publication or track record as an investigator on a competitive grant. 1d. Be available to commence as a full-time PhD student at Flinders University in 2023.
Level of Study: Postgraduate
Type: Scholarship
Value: AU$28,854 per annum
Length of Study: 3 years
Frequency: Annual
Country of Study: Australia
Closing Date: 31 December
Additional Information: www.flinders.edu.au/scholarships-system/index.cfm/scholarships/display/b01f41a

Playford Trust: Playford Trust: PhD Scholarships

Purpose: Each year the Playford Trust offers two PhD scholarships for students planning to carry out research in its priority areas. The scholarships are intended to supplement an existing Australian Government Research Training Program Stipend Scholarship (RTPS) or similar institutional PhD stipend scholarship
Eligibility: Applicants must be: 1. ready to commence a PhD with The University of Adelaide, Flinders University or University of South Australia in the following priority areas for the Trust; 1a. agriculture and food production 1b. water, energy and climate change 1c. advanced manufacturing and new technologies 1d. health sciences and enabling technologies 1e. mining and resources development 2. primarily supported by an Australian Government Research Training Program Stipend Scholarship (RTPS) or similar institutional PhD stipend scholarship. A copy of the letter of confirmation is required by the Trust before the scholarship can be awarded 3. an Australian citizen or a holder of a permanent resident visa, and resident in South Australia 4. intending to spend a significant part of their career in South Australia or are likely to provide a benefit to the State 5. a high achiever, with an

excellent undergraduate academic record 6. of good character. Preference will be given to students who display leadership potential. 7. It is essential that the applicant's supervisor or an academic referee (e.g. dean of school/faculty, or lecturer) provides a supporting comment about the student's achievements, character and leadership potential.
Level of Study: Doctorate
Type: Scholarship
Value: AU$17,500
Length of Study: 3.5 years
Frequency: Annual
Country of Study: Australia
Application Procedure: For information on how to apply, please refer to: playfordtrust.com.au/scholarships-and-awards/
Closing Date: 22 January
Additional Information: www.flinders.edu.au/scholarships-system/index.cfm/scholarships/display/ac1ec3e

Professor Lowitja O'Donoghue Indigenous Student Postgraduate Research Scholarship

Purpose: To enable suitably qualified applicants to proceed to a full-time Masters by research or Doctorate by research
Eligibility: Applicants must be Australian citizen, must have achieved Honours 1 or equivalent or Honours 2a or equivalent and must be an Aboriginal or Torres Strait Islander
Level of Study: Graduate
Type: Scholarship
Value: AU$25,627
Length of Study: 2 years if Masters and 3 years if PhD
Frequency: Annual
Study Establishment: Flinders University
Country of Study: Australia
Application Procedure: Applicants must apply directly to the university
Closing Date: 31 October

For further information contact:

Tel: (61) 8 8201 3115
Fax: (61) 8 8201 5175
Email: scholarships@flinders.edu.au

Professor Michael Kidd AM Scholarship

Eligibility: Applicants must: 1. be of Australian Aboriginal or Torres Strait Islander descent; and 2. identify as an Australian Aboriginal or Torres Strait Islander; and 3. be accepted as an Australian Aboriginal or Torres Strait Islander by the community in which they live or have lived; and 4. normally reside in South Australia or the Northern Territory; and 5. be enrolled in a health professional course within the College of Medicine and Public Health or the College of Nursing and Health Sciences at Flinders University.

Level of Study: Postgraduate
Type: Scholarship
Value: AU$2000 each year
Frequency: Annual
Country of Study: Australia
Application Procedure: Applications should be submitted online through the Flinders University Student System by the specified closing date
Closing Date: 11 March
Additional Information: www.flinders.edu.au/scholarships-system/index.cfm/scholarships/display/a831f4

Professor Ross Kalucy Indigenous Well-Being Scholarship

Eligibility: Applicants must: 1. be of Australian Aboriginal or Torres Strait Islander descent; and 2. identify as an Australian Aboriginal or Torres Strait Islander; and 3. be accepted as an Australian Aboriginal or Torres Strait Islander by the community in which they live or have lived; and 4. normally reside in South Australia or the Northern Territory; and 5. be enrolled in a Flinders University course relevant to Indigenous mental health and or social and emotional well-being, including clinical, health promotion, public health, allied health or community related study.

Level of Study: Postgraduate
Type: Scholarship
Value: AU$750
Frequency: Annual
Country of Study: Australia
Closing Date: 11 March
Additional Information: www.flinders.edu.au/scholarships-system/index.cfm/scholarships/display/af3356

Radiology SA Scholarship

Eligibility: 1. be enrolled full-time in the Doctor of Medicine at Flinders University; and 2. be able to demonstrate financial need.

Level of Study: Postgraduate
Type: Scholarship
Value: AU$5,000
Length of Study: 1 year
Frequency: Annual
Country of Study: Australia
Closing Date: 11 March

Additional Information: www.flinders.edu.au/scholarships-system/index.cfm/scholarships/display/af25aaa

Reconciliation SA Aboriginal Education Leaders Fund Postgraduate Research Scholarship

Purpose: To foster leadership potential and skill development and to promote the vision of the Council for Aboriginal Reconciliation in South Australia
Eligibility: Applicants must have applied for admission to, or be enrolled in, a research higher degree on a full or part-time basis at Flinders University, University of Adelaide or University of South Australia and normally reside in South Australia and be of Australian Aboriginal or Torres Strait Islander descent and be identified and be accepted as an Australian Aboriginal or Torres Strait Islander by the community in which he or she lives or has lived
Level of Study: Graduate
Type: Scholarship
Value: AU$5,000
Frequency: Annual
Country of Study: Any country
Application Procedure: Applicants must contact the Yunggorendi First Nations Centre for Higher Education for further information and application forms
Closing Date: 31 January

For further information contact:

Email: shane.carr@flinders.edu.au

Repatriation General Hospital Department of Rehabilitation and Aged Care: Health Professionals Research Scholarship

Purpose: To undertake research in an area of rehabilitation (cerebral palsy, driving rehabilitation, hydrotherapy, multiple sclerosis rehabilitation, hip fracture recovery)
Eligibility: Applicants must normally be Australian citizens, permanent residents of Australia or New Zealand citizens, who hold a First Class or upper Second Class Honours Degree in an appropriate health-related discipline, or an equivalent qualification
Level of Study: Graduate
Type: Scholarship
Value: AU$25,000–29,172
Length of Study: 3 years
Frequency: Annual
Country of Study: Any country
Application Procedure: Applicants can obtain the application kits and further information from the scholarships web

site or from the Higher Degree Administration and Scholarships Office
Closing Date: 7 January

For further information contact:

Tel: (61) 8 8275 1103
Email: maria.crotty@rgh.sa.gov.au

Repatriation General Hospital Department of Rehabilitation and Aged Care: Medical Research Scholarship

Purpose: To join a world class research team and improve health care
Eligibility: Applicants must be medical graduates and normally Australian citizens, permanent residents of Australia or New Zealand citizens, who hold a First Class or upper Second Class Honours Degree in an appropriate health-related discipline, or an equivalent qualification
Level of Study: Graduate
Type: Scholarship
Value: AU$29,172
Length of Study: 3 years
Country of Study: Any country
Application Procedure: Applicants can obtain the application kits and further information from the scholarships web site or from the Higher Degree Administration and Scholarships Office
Closing Date: 31 October

For further information contact:

Tel: (61) 8 8275 1103
Email: maria.crotty@rgh.sa.gov.au

Repatriation General Hospital Department of Rehabilitation and Aged Care: Nursing Research Scholarship

Eligibility: Applicants must be nursing graduates and normally Australian citizens, permanent residents of Australia or New Zealand citizens, who hold a First Class or upper Second Class Honours Degree in an appropriate health-related discipline, or an equivalent qualification
Level of Study: Graduate
Type: Scholarship
Value: AU$25,000–29,172 per year
Length of Study: 3 years
Country of Study: New Zealand
Application Procedure: Applicants can obtain the application kits and further information from the scholarships web

site or from the Higher Degree Administration and Scholarships Office
Closing Date: 31 October

For further information contact:

Tel: (61) 8 8275 1103
Email: maria.crotty@rgh.sa.gov.au

Research Student Conference Travel Grants semester 2, 2023

Eligibility: Candidates for Research Student Conference Travel Grants must: 1. normally be enrolled in the University in the second year full-time equivalent of a Masters degree by research or in the third or fourth year full-time equivalent of a Doctorate by research; 2. be presenting a paper or poster at a conference; 3. have the unqualified support of his/her supervisor; 4. not be members of staff eligible for AOU travel funds; and 5. not have been in previous receipt of conference travel assistance funded by the University in their current candidature.
Level of Study: Postgraduate, Research
Type: Grant
Value: Assistance will normally be based on the equivalent cost of a return economy class or concession airfare to the location of the conference venue.
Frequency: Annual
Country of Study: Australia
Application Procedure: Applications should be submitted online through the Flinders University Student System: stuadmin.flinders.edu.au/student/
Closing Date: 7 April
Additional Information: www.flinders.edu.au/scholarships-system/index.cfm/scholarships/display/a443e

Rex Elliot Wegener Memorial Fund for Mesothelioma Research

Purpose: To support a PhD candidate who is researching in the area of Asbestos-related malignancies, namely Mesothelioma and lung cancer.
Eligibility: To be considered for the Rex Elliot Wegener PhD Scholarship, a student must: 1. meet PhD admission requirements including: have an Australian Honours degree Class 1 or 2A or equivalent qualification (at least AQF Level 8), including a research component of at least 6 months' full-time study achieving Distinction (75%) OR including evidence of equivalent research experience. 2. be intending to enrol Full time in a Higher Degree by Research at Flinders University. 3. be intending to undertake research in an area that is relevant to the areas specified above.

Level of Study: Doctorate
Type: Scholarship
Value: A stipend valued at AU$28,597pa (2021 rate) will be awarded and paid to the successful recipient over 3 years on a fortnightly basis; a Research Training Program Fee Offset Scholarship to cover tuition fees for Australian Citizens, NZ Citizens and Permanent Residents;
Length of Study: 3 years
Frequency: Annual
Country of Study: Australia
Application Procedure: Download the application form for this scholarship scheme: www.flinders.edu.au/scholarships-system/generic_Application%20Klebe%20.doc
Closing Date: 31 December
Additional Information: www.flinders.edu.au/scholarships-system/index.cfm/scholarships/display/a71d740

For further information contact:

Email: Sonja.klebe@sa.gov.au

South Australian Department of Health Research Award

Purpose: To undertake a research project relevant to the health of South Australians, the South Australian health system, or the health-related targets in South Australia's Strategic Plan
Eligibility: Applicants must have achieved Honours 1 or equivalent, or Honours 2a or equivalent. Only citizens of Australia or permanent residents can apply
Level of Study: Postgraduate
Type: Scholarship
Value: AU$19,231 per year
Length of Study: 3 years
Frequency: Annual
Country of Study: Australia
Application Procedure: Applicants must apply directly to the university
Closing Date: 31 October

For further information contact:

Tel: (61) 8 8201 3115
Fax: (61) 8 8201 5175
Email: scholarships@flinders.edu.au

The Jack Loader Top-Up Scholarship

Purpose: To encourage research into dementia, in particular Alzheimer's Disease, and related disorders and/or the consequences of these diseases
Eligibility: Applicants must be Australian citizens or permanent residents of Australia and be enrolled full time in

a research degree at one of the South Australian universities. Applicants should have received an Australian Postgraduate Award or equivalent University Scholarship
Level of Study: Graduate
Type: Scholarship
Value: AU$8,000
Length of Study: 12 months
Frequency: Annual
Country of Study: Any country
Application Procedure: Check website for further details
Closing Date: 31 October
Funding: Foundation
Contributor: The Rosemary Foundation for Memory Support Inc and Alzheimer's Australia South Australia

For further information contact:

Email: jmck1279@bigpond.net.au

The Nita Curtis Scholarship

Eligibility: Applicants must: 1. be Australian citizens or permanent residents of Australia; and 2. be undertaking one of the following programs offered by the Department of Disability Studies at the University: Honours; or Graduate Certificate in Disability Studies; or Master of Disability Studies; or Masters Degree by research; and 3. be undertaking a research project relevant to the Community Accommodation and Respite Agency (CARA) and its client population.
Level of Study: Postgraduate
Type: Scholarship
Value: AU$5,000 awarded annually
Frequency: Annual
Country of Study: Any country
Closing Date: 3 November
Additional Information: www.flinders.edu.au/scholarships-system/index.cfm/scholarships/display/a44fb

University Hall Dean's Scholarship

Eligibility: Applicants must be resident in University Hall and enrolled in a degree course at the Flinders University at the time of application. Only citizens of Australia or New Zealand living in Australia over 1 year can apply
Level of Study: Graduate
Type: Scholarship
Value: AU$2,000 per year
Length of Study: 1 year
Frequency: Annual
Country of Study: Australia
Application Procedure: Applicants must apply directly to the scholarship provider

For further information contact:

Tel: (61) 8 8201 3115
Fax: (61) 8 8201 5175
Email: scholarships@flinders.edu.au

University Hall Eurest Overseas Study Scholarship

Purpose: To enable full-time students residing in University Hall, who have demonstrated outstanding aptitude for research, to undertake a period of further study or research in approved universities or other institutions outside Australia
Eligibility: Applicants must have lived in University Hall for a period of not less than one academic year, have gained unqualified support for his/her supervisor for the proposed overseas visit, have gained approval from the overseas institution that he/she is acceptable for the proposed period of study and have demonstrated a suitable academic record in the previous academic year
Level of Study: Postgraduate
Type: Scholarship
Value: AU$2,500
Length of Study: 1 year
Frequency: Annual
Country of Study: Any country
Application Procedure: Applicants must contact the Higher Degree Administration and Scholarships Office and University Hall for application forms and further information
Closing Date: 20 October

For further information contact:

Email: flinders.housing@flinders.edu.au

Winifred E. Preedy Postgraduate Bursary

Purpose: The aim of this scholarship is to assist women to undertake and complete higher degrees in dentistry or an allied field, either via coursework or research.
Eligibility: The AFUW Winifred E Preedy Postgraduate Scholarship is available to: 1. Women who are enrolled at an Australian university and are Australian citizens or permanent residents; 2. Must be enrolled in a Master's Degree or a PhD in dentistry or a related field; 3. Must be past or present students in the Dental School at the University of Adelaide; 4. Must have completed at least one year of their postgraduate degree; 5. Must not be in full-time paid employment or on fully-paid leave during the tenure of the Scholarship; Must not have previously won the Winifred E. Preedy Postgraduate Scholarship.
Level of Study: Postgraduate
Type: Bursary

Value: AU$2,000
Length of Study: 1 year
Frequency: Annual
Country of Study: Australia
Closing Date: 9 April
Funding: Private
Additional Information: scholarships.adelaide.edu.au/ Scholarships/postgraduate-research/faculty-of-health-and-medical-sciences/australian-federation-of

For further information contact:

Email: bursaries@afuwsa-trust.com.au

Fogarty International Center

Fogarty International Center, National Institutes of Health, 31 Center Drive, MSC 2220, Bethesda, MD 20892-2220, United States of America.

Website: www.fic.nih.gov

The Fogarty International Center is dedicated to advancing the mission of the National Institutes of Health (NIH) by supporting and facilitating global health research conducted by U.S. and international investigators, building partnerships between health research institutions in the U.S. and abroad, and training the next generation of scientists to address global health needs.

African Association for Health Professions Education and Research

Purpose: The African Association for Health Professions Education and Research builds on the Medical Education Partnership Initiative (MEPI) and the Nursing Education Partnership Initiative (NEPI)
Eligibility: 1. Non-African partners may not be listed as Multiple Principal Investigators. 2. An international African consortium of committed institutions should submit an application together and form the basis for the founding network leadership. 3. Named participating institutions for the establishment of the Association must include at least one former MEPI awardee institution (programmatic, linked or pilot awards) and at least one former NEPI awardee institution; but are not limited to these institutions
Level of Study: Postgraduate
Type: Grant
Frequency: Annual

Country of Study: Any country
Closing Date: 28 March
Funding: Private
Additional Information: www.fic.nih.gov/Programs/Pages/african-association-health-professions.aspx (www.fic.nih.gov/Funding/Pages/Fogarty-Funding-Opps.aspx) Website Status: No plans to recompete at this time

For further information contact:

Tel: (61) 301 402 9591
Email: flora.katz@nih.gov

Chronic, Noncommunicable Diseases and Disorders Research Training (NCD-Lifespan)

Purpose: The Chronic, Noncommunicable Diseases and Disorders Across the Lifespan Fogarty International Research Training Award program supports collaborative research training between institutions in the United States and low-and middle-income countries (LMICs), defined by the World Bank classification system
Eligibility: 1. Applicants should carefully note which NIH Institutes, Centers and Offices are participating in this announcement and view their respective areas of research interest and requirements under "Specific Interests of the FOA Sponsors" 2. Notice of eligibility change for cancer-related D43 applications (NOT-TW-20-008), released September 11, 2020 3. Notice of change in country eligibility for Fogarty international training grants (NOT-TW-12-011) beginning with receipt dates after January 1, 2013 4. Applications from U.S. institutions must demonstrate collaborations with institutions in the low- and middle-income countries (LMICs), defined by the World Bank classification system, named in their application 5. Foreign applications will only be accepted from LMIC institutions 6. U.S. applicants must identify at least one scientist from each LMIC institution as the main foreign collaborator for that institution 7. View eligibility information in the Program Announcement.
Level of Study: Graduate
Type: Research grant
Frequency: Annual
Country of Study: Any country
Closing Date: 13 July
Funding: Private
Additional Information: www.fic.nih.gov/Programs/Pages/chronic-lifespan.aspx

For further information contact:

Division of International Training and Research, Fogarty International Center, National Institutes of Health, Building 31, Room B2C39, Bethesda, MD 20892-2220, United States of America.

Tel: (1) 301 496 1653
Fax: (1) 301 402 0779
Email: Kathleen.Michels@nih.gov

Ernst Mach Grant for Young Researchers

Purpose: 1. The Ernst Mach grant is named after the famous Austrian physicist. Student and young researchers from foreign universities are invited to apply for this grant to come to Austria for research. 2. It promote research cooperation
Eligibility: 1. Very good knowledge of English/German
Level of Study: Graduate
Type: Grant
Value: For graduates with PhD degree the value is €1,150
Frequency: Annual
Country of Study: Any country
Application Procedure: 1. Applicants who seek admission to an university in Austria have to contact the institution of their choice. 2. The selection process for all grants is competitive, i.e., there is no legal claim to a grant even if all the application requirements are fulfilled. 3. Short-term grants (1-3 months) have a priority in the period from January to June. When applying for a short-term grant therefore consideration should be given primarily for a period of January to June
Closing Date: 30 September
Funding: Private

For further information contact:

Tel: (61) 1 534 080

H3Africa Global Health Bioinformatics Research Training Program

Purpose: Through the Human Heredity and Health in Africa (H3Africa) Initiative, the Global Health Bioinformatics Research Training Program supports bioinformatics research training programs at low- and middle-income country (LMIC) institutions in Africa with significant genomics research capacity
Eligibility: H3Africa fosters genomic and epidemiological research in African scientific institutions
Level of Study: Postgraduate
Type: Programme grant
Frequency: Annual
Country of Study: Any country

Application Procedure: The training programs address the need for bioinformatics research expertise in the H3Africa Consortium, resulting in sustainable centers of bioinformatics research training relevant to global health research for the African continent
Funding: Private

For further information contact:

Tel: (1) 301 827 2227
Fax: (1) 301 402 0779
Email: laura.povlich@nih.gov

Fondation des Etats-Unis

15 Boulevard Jourdan, F-75014 Paris, France.

Tel: (33) 1 5380 6880
Email: administration@feusa.org
Website: www.feusa.org
Contact: Mr Sophie Uasset, Director

For the past 75 years the Fondation des Etats-Unis has been welcoming American and International Students during their studies in Paris.

Harriet Hale Woolley Scholarship

Purpose: To support the study of visual arts, music and psychiatry in Paris
Eligibility: Open to citizens of the United States of America, who are 21–30 years of age and have graduated with high academic standing from a United States college, university or professional school of recognized standing. Applicants should provide evidence of artistic or musical accomplishment. Applicants should have a good working knowledge of French, sufficient to enable the student to benefit from his or her study in France. Grants are for those studying painting, printmaking or sculpture and for instrumentalists, not for research in art history, musicology or composition, nor for students of dance or theatre. Successful candidates propose a unique and detailed project related to their study, which requires a 1-year residency in Paris
Level of Study: Doctorate, Graduate, Postgraduate, Predoctorate
Type: Scholarship
Value: €10,000/year and a reservation of a personal room at the FEU during the academic year (October-June)
Length of Study: 1 academic year

Frequency: Annual
Country of Study: France
Application Procedure: For a complete description of the scholarship including a list of general requirements, an application checklist and an application form, please visit www. feusa.org/harriet-hale-woolley-scholarship
Closing Date: 31 January
Funding: Private
Additional Information: www.fondationdesetatsunis.org/ hhw-scholarship/

For further information contact:

Fondation des Etats-Unis, 15 Boulevard Jourdan, F-75014 Paris, France.

Tel: (33) 1 53 80 68 82
Email: culture@feusa.org

Fondation Fyssen

194 Rue de Rivoli, F-75001 Paris, France.

Tel: (33) 1 42 97 53 16
Email: secretariat@fondation-fyssen.org
Website: www.fondation-fyssen.org
Contact: Mrs Nadia Ferchal, Director

The aim of the Fyssen Foundation is to encourage all forms of scientific enquiry into cognitive mechanisms, including thought and reasoning, that underlie animal and human behaviour, their biological and cultural bases and phylogenetic and ontogenetic development.

International Prize

Purpose: To encourage a scientist who has conducted distinguished research in the areas supported by the Foundation
Eligibility: Applicants are requested to visit the website
Type: Award
Value: €100 000
Frequency: Annual
Country of Study: Any country
Application Procedure: Candidates cannot apply directly but should be proposed by recognized scientists. Proposals for candidates should consist of (i) curriculum vitae, (ii) a list of publications, (iii) a summary (4 pages maximum) of the research. The proposal should be submitted in 14 copies to Secrétariat de la Fondation Fyssen

Closing Date: 6 November
Additional Information: www.fondationfyssen.fr/en/international-scientific-prize/international-prize-thematic/

Post-doctoral Study Grants

Purpose: These grants are awarded to French or foreign researchers, holders of a foreign Phd and who wish to achieve their project in a Laboratory in France; or either french or foreign researchers holders of a French Phd who wish to achieve their project in a Laboratory abroad (excluded co-tutorship country)
Eligibility: 1. Start its first post-doctoral fellowship with this financial support. 2. If the recipient has already reached its host lab, he should be settled for no more than 3 months maximum at the date of September 1st, 2023. 3. Be 35 year old maximum on the closing day of the call. 4. Be a holder of a Phd of less than two years on September 1st of the year of application, or achieve its viva thesis on December 31st of the year of application at the latest. The applicant should have achieved its PhD before starting the fellowship. 5. Regarding the host laboratories located in France: the recipient hosted within a framework of a fixed-term contract will have to make sure that a convention of co-financing can be signed between the Foundation and the laboratory to reach the level of the gross salary.
Level of Study: Doctorate
Type: Grant
Value: €40 000
Length of Study: 12months or 24 months
Frequency: Annual
Country of Study: France
Closing Date: 31 March
Additional Information: www.fondationfyssen.fr/en/study-grants/aim-award/

Fondation Jeunesse Internationale, Ecole Franchaise d'Extreme-Orient

Tel: (33) 1 53 70 18 60
Email: contrats.postdocs@efeo.net
Contact: Ms Evelise Bruneau

Short-Term EFEO Postdoctoral Contracts

Eligibility: 1. Fellowships are offered in the fields of the Humanities and Social Sciences (Anthropology, Literature and Art Studies, History, Geography, Philosophy, Political Science, Sociology, etc.) 2. Applicants must have obtained a PhD following a viva voce examination held in or after 2013. There is no age limit. 3. Successful applicants must hold a bank account in France. 4. Applicants should have a good command of the language(s) required to successfully complete the research project. 5. The postdoctoral fellowships cannot be combined with any other full-time salaried employment
Value: €1,500
Length of Study: 3 to 6 months
Country of Study: France
Application Procedure: Applications may be submitted in French or English. Applications should be in PDF format (one document only) entitled NAME Surname Candidature Post-docs EFEO
Closing Date: 14 October
Additional Information: For further information, please contact Ms. Evelise Bruneau (contrats.postdocs@efeo.net) www.efeo.fr/base.php?code=971

For further information contact:

Fax: (33) 1 53 70 18 60

Ford Foundation

320 East 43rd Street, New York, NY 10017, United States of America.

Tel: (1) 212 573 5000
Website: www.fordfoundation.org

The Ford Foundation was established on 15 January, 1936, with an initial gift of US$25,000 from Edsel Ford, whose father Henry, founded the Ford Motor Company. During its early years, the foundation operated in Michigan under the leadership of Ford family members. Since the founding charter stated that resources should be used 'for scientific, educational and charitable purposes, all for the public welfare,' the foundation made grants to many kinds of organizations.

Ford Foundation Predoctoral Fellowships for Research-Based PhD or ScD Programs in United States of America

Purpose: The fellowships are available for pursuing predoctoral level
Eligibility: Eligibility to apply for a predoctoral fellowship is limited to: 1. All U.S. citizens, U.S. nationals, and U.S. permanent residents (holders of a Permanent Resident

Card); individuals granted deferred action status under the Deferred Action for Childhood Arrivals Program; Indigenous individuals exercising rights associated with the Jay Treaty of 1794; individuals granted Temporary Protected Status; asylees; and refugees, regardless of race, national origin, religion, gender, age, disability, or sexual orientation; 2. Individuals with evidence of superior academic achievement (such as grade point average, class rank, honors, or other designations); 3. Individuals committed to a career in teaching and research at the college or university level in the U.S.; 4. Individuals enrolled in or planning to enroll in an eligible research-based (dissertation-required) program leading to a Ph.D. or Sc.D. degree at a non-proprietary (not for profit) U.S. institution of higher education no later than Fall 2023; 5. Individuals who as of the 2023 fall semester require a minimum of three years of study2 to complete their Ph.D. or Sc.D. degree; and 6. Individuals who have not earned a doctoral degree at any time, in any field.

Level of Study: Research
Type: Fellowship
Value: Annual stipend US$20,000. Award to the institution in lieu of tuition and fees US$2,000. Expenses paid to attend at least one Conference of Ford Fellows
Length of Study: 3 years
Country of Study: United States of America
Application Procedure: Follow the steps below to prepare and submit an application for a Ford Foundation Predoctoral Fellowship. Read through the following: Predoctoral Fellowship Fact Sheet Predoctoral Application Instructions; Familiarize yourself with Navigating the Online Application; Start an application here: nrc58.nas.edu/InfoFord20/Home/SignIn.aspx?c=FordApplicants
Closing Date: 16 September
Contributor: Ford Foundation
Additional Information: sites.nationalacademies.org/PGA/FordFellowships/PGA_166320

For further information contact:

Email: fordapplications@nas.edu

Foreign Affairs and International Trade Canada

Enquiries Service Foreign Affairs Canada, 125 Sussex Drive, Ottawa, ON K1A 0G2, Canada.

Tel: (1) 613 944 4000
Email: enqserv@dfait-maeci.gc.ca
Website: www.dfait-maeci.gc.ca

Foreign Affairs and International Trade Canada supports Canadians abroad, helps Canadian companies succeed in global markets, promotes Canada's culture and values and works to build a more peaceful and secure world.

Graduate Research Awards for Disarmament, Arms Control and Non-Proliferation

Purpose: To enhance Canadian graduate-level scholarship on disarmament, arms control and non-proliferation issues
Eligibility: The competition is open to Canadian citizens and Canadian permanent residents/landed immigrants currently enrolled in a graduate programme. Graduate students studying outside Canada are eligible to apply but please note that funding to cover the cost of successful applicants' travel to Ottawa for the event at Global Affairs Canada is limited to domestic travel within Canada (or the equivalent). In order to expand the community of Canadian scholars working on non-proliferation, arms control and disarmament (NACD) issues, employees of Global Affairs Canada, and previous recipients of a Graduate Research Award are not eligible.
Level of Study: Doctorate, Postgraduate
Value: awards of C$5,000 are available to Canadian Master's
Frequency: Annual
Country of Study: Canada
No. of awards offered: 4
Closing Date: 15 March
Funding: Government
No. of applicants last year: 4
Additional Information: www.grad.ubc.ca/awards/graduate-research-awards-disarmament-arms-control-non-proliferation

For further information contact:

Tel: (1)778 782 7779
Email: ehynes@thesimonsfoundation.ca

Forgarty International Center

Ecology and Evolution of Infectious Diseases Initiative (EEID)

Purpose: This joint National Institutes of Health (NIH) - National Science Foundation (NSF) initiative supports efforts to understand the underlying ecological and biological mechanisms that govern relationships between human-induced environmental changes and the emergence and transmission of infectious diseases
Eligibility: Check the website for further details.

Level of Study: Graduate
Type: Funding support
Frequency: Annual
Country of Study: Any country
Closing Date: 17 November
Funding: Private

For further information contact:

Fogarty International Center, National Institutes of Health, Building 31, B2C39, Bethesda, MD 20892-2220, United States of America.

Tel: (1) 301 496 1653
Fax: (1) 301 402 0779
Email: Christine.Jessup@nih.gov

Ford Foundation Dissertation Fellowship

Eligibility: Eligibility to apply for a dissertation fellowship is limited to: 1. All U.S. citizens, U.S. nationals, and U.S. permanent residents (holders of a Permanent Resident Card); individuals granted deferred action status under the Deferred Action for Childhood Arrivals Program; Indigenous individuals exercising rights associated with the Jay Treaty of 1794; individuals granted Temporary Protected Status; asylees; and refugees, regardless of race, national origin, religion, gender, age, disability, or sexual orientation; 2. Individuals with evidence of superior academic achievement (such as grade point average, class rank, honors, or other designations); 3. Individuals committed to a career in teaching and research at the college or university level in the U.S.; 4. Ph.D. or Sc.D. degree candidates studying in an eligible research-based discipline in a dissertation-required program at a non-proprietary (not for profit) U.S. institution of higher education who will complete the dissertation in a period of 9–12 months during the 2023–2024 academic year; 5. Individuals who, by December 9, 2022, have completed all departmental and institutional requirements for their degree, except for writing and defense of the dissertation; and 6. Individuals who have not earned a doctoral degree at any time, in any field.
Level of Study: Research
Type: Fellowship
Value: One-year stipend: US$28,000 An invitation to attend the Conference of Ford Fellows Access to Ford Fellow Regional Liaisons – a network of former Ford Fellows who have volunteered to provide mentoring and support to current Fellows – and access to other networking resource
Length of Study: 1 year
Frequency: Annual
Country of Study: United States of America

Application Procedure: sites.nationalacademies.org/PGA/FordFellowships/PGA_166318
No. of awards offered: 36
Closing Date: 9 December
Additional Information: sites.nationalacademies.org/PGA/FordFellowships/PGA_171939

For further information contact:

Email: FordApplications@nas.edu

PhD Fellowship

Purpose: The Boehringer Ingelheim Fonds (BIF) awards PhD fellowships to European citizens working in Europe or overseas and to non-European citizens pursuing their PhD projects in Europe.
Eligibility: The basic monthly stipend amounts to €1,650. In most countries, fellows are paid an additional flat rate of €150 per month to cover minor research-related costs (books, travel expenses, etc.). To adjust, e.g. for differences in living costs, country-related premiums may be added (in the United Kingdom, Austria, and the Netherlands currently €650, in the USA €1,175, in Switzerland €1,600, in Canada and Sweden €600, in Denmark and Belgium €700, and in Germany €200). Depending on the cost of living, most other countries are grouped into one of these categories. For example, an unmarried fellow working in Germany currently receives €2,000, in the USA €2,975, in the United Kingdom €2,450, and in Switzerland €3,400.
Level of Study: Postgraduate
Country of Study: Any country
Closing Date: 1 October
Additional Information: www.bifonds.de/fellowships-grants/phd-fellowships/who-can-apply-phd.html

Forum Transregional Studies

Wallotstrae 14, D-14193, Berlin, Germany.
The Forum Transregional Studies in Berlin is a research organization on the content internationalization of the humanities and social sciences.

Forum Transregional Studies Postdoctoral Fellowships for International Students

Purpose: By creating a space of dialogue for university and museum scholars from all regions, it aims to discuss the potentials and contours of a plural history of art

Eligibility: International students are eligible to apply for this fellowship. Applicants whose first language is not English are usually required to provide evidence of proficiency in English at the higher level required by the University

Type: Postdoctoral fellowship

Value: In particular cases, shorter fellowship terms may be considered. Postdoctoral fellows will receive a monthly stipend of €2,500 plus supplements depending on their personal situation. Organizational support regarding visas, insurances, housing, etc. will be provided. Successful applicants become fellows of the program Art Histories and Aesthetic Practices at the Forum Transregionale Studien and are expected to take up residence in Berlin

Country of Study: Germany

Application Procedure: PDF files 1. a curriculum vitae (in English). 2. a project description (no longer than five pages / in English). 3. a sample of scholarly work (about 20 pages of an article, conference paper, or dissertation chapter) names of two referees (including their e-mail addresses). The complete application should be submitted latest by 15 January and addressed to arthistories_application@trafo-berlin.de

Closing Date: 15 January

Additional Information: For more details please browse the link www.scholarshipsads.com/forum-transregional-studies-postdoctoral-fellowships-germany-2018-19/

For further information contact:

Email: arthistories_application@trafo-berlin.de

Foundation for Digestive Health and Nutrition

4930 Del Ray Avenue, Bethesda, MD 20814, United States of America.

Tel: (1) 301 222 4002
Email: awards@fdhn.org
Website: www.fdhn.org
Contact: Ms Wykenna S.C.Vailor, Research Awards Manager

The Foundation for Digestive Health and Nutrition is the foundation of the American Gastroenterological Association (AGA), the leading professional society representing gastroenterological and hepatologists worldwide. It is separately incorporated and governed by a distinguished board of AGA physicians and members of the lay public. The Foundation raises funds for research and public education in the prevention, diagnosis, treatment and cure of digestive diseases. Along with the AGA, it conducts public education initiatives related to digestive diseases. The Foundation also administers the disbursement of grants on the behalf of the AGA and other funders.

AGA Abstract Award for Health Disparities Research

Eligibility: 1. Applicants must be the first author of an abstract or the designated speaker of an oral presentation accepted by AGA for presentation at DDW. 2. Applicants must be: Graduate students, medical students or medical residents (residents up to postgraduate year three) at an institution in North America who have performed original research. Clinical or postdoctoral fellows with MD, PhD or equivalent degrees at institutions in North America (U.S., Canada and Mexico). 3. The research presented in the abstract must be related to health or health care disparities associated with a digestive disease or disorder. 4. All high school and undergraduate students are ineligible. 5. Students and fellows training outside North America (U.S., Canada and Mexico) are ineligible. 6. Applicants who are physician-scientists, female or from racial/ethnic groups underrepresented in biomedical research are strongly encouraged to apply.

Level of Study: Postdoctorate

Type: Research grant

Value: US$500

Frequency: Annual

Country of Study: United States of America

No. of awards offered: 4

Closing Date: 22 February

Additional Information: gastro.org/research-and-awards/apply-for-awards/award/aga-abstract-award-for-health-disparities-research/

AGA Fellow Abstract Award

Eligibility: 1. Applicants must be the first author of an abstract or the designated speaker of an oral presentation accepted by AGA for presentation at DDW. 2. Students and medical residents are ineligible for this award. 3. Fellows outside of North America are ineligible for this award. 4. Applicants must be clinical or postdoctoral fellows with MD, PhD or equivalent degrees at institutions in North America (U.S., Canada and Mexico). 5. Applicants must be active trainee members of AGA. Please visit the AGA membership page or call 301-654-2055 for membership information. 6. Applicants who are physician-scientists, female or from racial/ethnic groups underrepresented in biomedical research are strongly encouraged to apply.

Level of Study: Postdoctorate
Type: Award
Value: US$500–US$1,000
Frequency: Annual
Country of Study: United States of America
No. of awards offered: 14
Closing Date: 22 February
Additional Information: gastro.org/research-and-awards/apply-for-awards/award/aga-fellow-abstract-award/

AGA Student Abstract Award

Eligibility: 1. Applicants must be the first author of an abstract or the designated speaker of an oral presentation accepted by AGA for presentation at DDW. 2. Applicants must be graduate students, medical students or medical residents (residents up to postgraduate year three) at an institution in North America who have performed original research related to diseases, structure or function of the digestive system. 3. Postdoctoral fellows, technicians, visiting scientists and MD research fellows are not eligible for this award. 4. All high school and undergraduate students are ineligible. 5. Graduate students, medical students and medical residents training outside North America (U.S., Canada and Mexico) are ineligible. 6. Applicants who are physician-scientists, female or from racial/ethnic groups underrepresented in biomedical research are strongly encouraged to apply.
Level of Study: Postgraduate
Type: Award
Value: US$1,000
Frequency: Annual
Country of Study: United States of America
No. of awards offered: 14
Closing Date: 1 July

AGA-APFED Abstract Award in Eosinophilic GI Diseases

Eligibility: 1. Applicants must be the first author of an abstract or the designated speaker of an oral presentation accepted by AGA for presentation at DDW®. 2. Applicants must be graduate students, medical students, medical residents (residents up to postgraduate year three), or clinical or postdoctoral fellows at an institution in North America who have performed original research related to eosinophilic gastrointestinal diseases. 3. All high school and undergraduate students are ineligible. 4. Graduate students, medical students, medical residents and fellows training outside North America (U.S., Canada and Mexico) are ineligible. 5. Applicants who are physician-scientists, female or from racial/

ethnic groups underrepresented in biomedical research are strongly encouraged to apply.
Level of Study: Postdoctorate
Type: Award
Value: US$500
Frequency: Annual
Country of Study: United States of America
No. of awards offered: 3
Closing Date: 1 July
Additional Information: gastro.org/research-and-awards/apply-for-awards/award/aga-apfed-abstract-award-in-eosinophilic-gi-diseases/

AGA-Moti L. & Kamla Rustgi International Travel Awards

Eligibility: 1. Applicants must hold an MD and/or PhD degree or equivalent degree (e.g. MB, ChB, MBBS, DO). 2. Applicants must be 35 years of age or younger at the time of DDW. 3. Applicants must be fluent in English. 4. Applicants residing in North America are ineligible for this award. 5. Applicants must be the first author of an abstract or the designated speaker of an oral presentation accepted by AGA for presentation at DDW. 6. Applicants must be members of AGA. Please visit the AGA membership page or call 301-654-2055 for membership information. 7. Applicants who are physician-scientists, female or from racial/ethnic groups underrepresented in biomedical research are strongly encouraged to apply.
Level of Study: Postdoctorate
Type: Award
Value: US$750
Frequency: Annual
Country of Study: United States of America
Closing Date: 22 February
Additional Information: gastro.org/research-and-awards/apply-for-awards/award/aga-moti-l-kamla-rustgi-international-travel-awards/

American Gastroenterological Association - Elsevier Pilot Research Award

Purpose: To provide non-salary funds for new investigators to help them establish their research careers or to support pilot projects that represent new research directions for established investigators. The intent is to stimulate research in gastroenterology- or hepatology-related areas by permitting investigators to obtain new data that can ultimately provide the basis for subsequent grant applications of more substantial funding and duration

Eligibility: Applicants must possess an MD or PhD degree or equivalent and must hold faculty positions at accredited North American institutions. In addition, they must be AGA members at the time of application submission. Women and minorities are strongly encouraged to apply

Level of Study: Postdoctorate, Postgraduate, Predoctorate, Research

Type: Grant

Value: US$25,000

Length of Study: 1 year

Frequency: Annual

Country of Study: Any country

Application Procedure: Applications can be downloaded from the AGA Foundation website. The completed application, letters of support or commitment and other documents must be submitted as one PDF document, titled by the applicant's last name and first initial only. Hard copies are not permitted. For further information visit the AGA Foundation website

No. of awards offered: 22

Closing Date: 12 January

Funding: Private

Contributor: The AGA

For further information contact:

Tel: (1) 301 222 4012

American Gastroenterological Association Fellowship to Faculty Transition Awards

Purpose: To prepare physicians for independent research careers in digestive diseases

Eligibility: Applicants must be MDs or MD/PhDs currently in a gastroenterology-related fellowship, at a North American institution and committed to academic careers. They should have completed at least 2 years of research training at the start of this award. Women and minority investigators are strongly encouraged to apply. Applicants must be AGA Trainee Members or be sponsored by an AGA Member at the time of application

Level of Study: Postgraduate

Type: Award

Value: US$40,000 per year

Length of Study: 2 years

Frequency: Annual

Country of Study: Any country

Application Procedure: Applications can be downloaded from the AGA Foundation website. The completed application, letters of support or commitment and other documents must be submitted as one PDF document, titled by the applicant's last name and first initial only. Hard copies are not

permitted. For further information visit the AGA Foundation website

No. of awards offered: 8

Closing Date: 31 August

Funding: Private

Contributor: The AGA

For further information contact:

Tel: (1) 301 222 4012

American Gastroenterological Association R Robert and Sally D Funderburg Research Scholar Award in Gastric Cancer

Purpose: To support active, established investigators in the field of gastric biology who enhance the fundamental understanding of gastric cancer pathobiology in order to ultimately develop a cure for the disease

Eligibility: 1. Applicants must be established as an independent investigator in the field of gastric biology. a. MD applicants are considered "established" if seven or more years have elapsed following the completion of clinical training (GI fellowship or its equivalent) at the start date of this award (i.e., January 2024). b. PhD applicants are considered "established" if seven or more years have elapsed following the awarding of the PhD degree and the start date of this award (i.e., January 2024). 2. Applicants for this award must hold an MD, PhD and/or equivalent degree (e.g., MBBS, MBChB, DO). 3. Applicants must hold a full-time faculty or equivalent position at an institution in North America (United States, Canada and Mexico). 4. AGA membership is required at the time of application submission. Please visit AGA's membership page or call 301-654-2055 for membership information. 5. Applicants performing any type of research (basic, translational, clinical) relevant to gastric cancer are eligible to apply. 6. Applicants who are physician-scientists, female or from racial/ethnic groups underrepresented in biomedical research are strongly encouraged to apply. AGA Institute Governing Board members are not eligible to apply while they are actively serving on the governing board.

Level of Study: Postgraduate

Type: Award

Value: US$100,000

Length of Study: 2 years

Frequency: Annual

Country of Study: The United States of America, Canada or Mexico

Application Procedure: Applications can be downloaded from the AGA Foundation website. The completed application, letters of support or commitment and other documents must be submitted as one PDF document, titled by the applicant's last name and first initial only. Hard copies are not permitted. For further information visit the AGA Foundation website

No. of awards offered: 1

Closing Date: 21 July

Contributor: The AGA, the late R Robert and the late Sally D Funderburg

Additional Information: gastro.org/research-and-awards/apply-for-awards/award/aga-r-robert-sally-funderburg-research-award-in-gastric-cancer/

For further information contact:

Tel: (1) 301 222 4012
Email: awards@gastro.org

American Gastroenterological Association Research Scholar Awards

Purpose: To enable young investigators to develop independent and productive research careers in digestive diseases by ensuring that a major proportion of their time is protected for research

Eligibility: Candidates must hold an MD, PhD, or equivalent degree and a full-time faculty positions at North American universities or professional institutes at the time of commencement of the award. They must be members of the AGA at the time of application submission. The award is for young faculty, who have demonstrated unusual promise and have some record of accomplishment in research. Candidates must devote at least 70% of their efforts to gastrointestinal tract or liver-related research. Women, minorities and physician/scientist investigators are strongly encouraged to apply

Level of Study: Graduate

Type: Research grant

Value: US$100,000 per year. Travel, not to exceed US$1,500 per year.

Length of Study: 3 years

Frequency: Annual

Country of Study: United States of America

Application Procedure: Applications can be downloaded from the AGA Foundation website. The completed application, letters of support or commitment and other documents must be submitted as one PDF document, titled by the applicant's last name and first initial only. Hard copies are not permitted. For further information visit the AGA Foundation website

No. of awards offered: 4

Closing Date: 10 November

Funding: Private

Additional Information: www.gastro.org/research-and-awards/research-awards/apply-for-awards/award/aga-research-scholar-award-rsa

For further information contact:

Tel: (1) 301 222 4012
Email: awards@gastro.org

American Gastroenterological Association/ American Gastroenterological Association-Eli & Edythe Broad Student Research Fellowship(s)

Purpose: To stimulate interest in research careers in digestive diseases by providing salary support for research projects

Eligibility: Applicants must be students at accredited North American institutions, may not hold similar salary support awards from other agencies. Women and minority students are strongly encouraged to apply

Level of Study: Graduate, Postgraduate, Professional development

Type: Award

Value: US$2,500 to 3,000 per year

Length of Study: 10 weeks

Frequency: Annual

Country of Study: Any country

Application Procedure: Applications can be downloaded from the AGA Foundation website. The completed application, letters of support or commitment and other documents must be submitted as one PDF document, titled by the applicant's last name and first initial only. Hard copies are not permitted. For further information visit the AGA Foundation website

No. of awards offered: 48

Funding: Private

Contributor: The AGA

For further information contact:

Tel: (1) 301 222 4012

Foundation for Liberal and Management Education University

Gat No. 1270, Lavale, Off. Pune Bangalore Highway, Pune, Maharashtra 412115, India.

Contact: Foundation for Liberal and Management Education University

FLAME University is a private, coeducational and fully residential university, anchored in liberal education located in Pune city in the state of Maharashtra. Earlier it was known as FLAME – Foundation for Liberal and Management Education.

Foundation for Liberal and Management Education University Scholars Program

Purpose: The scholarship is designed to give students an opportunity to further their education at FLAME University
Eligibility: Students from India are eligible to apply
Type: Postgraduate scholarships
Value: FLAME University offers a range of scholarships that recognize the inherent excellence and distinctive attributes of students ensuring that FLAME attracts the brightest of minds. In addition, merit, need-based and special scholarships are provided with that may range from partial to full fee waivers
Study Establishment: Scholarships are awarded to study the students offered by the university
Country of Study: India
Application Procedure: To be considered for the scholarship, students need to email the supporting documents of achievements at admission-at-flame.edu.in. FLAME University's Scholarship Committee will evaluate your application and make the final decision
Additional Information: For more details please browse the website www.flame.edu.in/academics/flame-scholars-program

For further information contact:

Tel: (61) 800 209 4567
Email: enquiry@flame.edu.in

Foundation for Science and Disability, Inc.

1700 SW 23rd Dr, Gainesville, FL 32608, United States of America.

Tel: (1) 352 374 5774
Email: richard.mankin@ars.usda.gov
Website: stemd.org
Contact: Dr Richard Mankin, Chair, Student Grants

The Foundation for Science and Disability aims to promote the integration of scientists with disabilities into all activities of the scientific community and of society as a whole, and to promote the removal of barriers in order to enable students with disabilities to choose careers in science.

Foundation for Science and Disability Student Grant Fund

Subjects: Engineering, mathematics, medicine, natural sciences and computer science.
Purpose: To increase opportunities in science for graduate-level students who have disabilities.
Eligibility: Open to candidates from the USA.
Level of Study: Doctorate, Postgraduate
Type: Grant
Value: US$1,000
Length of Study: 1 year
Frequency: Annual
Country of Study: United States of America
Application Procedure: Applicants must submit a completed application form, copies of official college transcripts, a letter from the research or academic supervisor in support of the request and a second letter from another faculty member.
No. of awards offered: 1 to 3
Closing Date: 1 December
Funding: Private
No. of awards given last year: 1
No. of applicants last year: 8
Additional Information: The award may be used for an assistive device or instrument, or as financial support to work with a professor on an individual research project or for some other special need. www.stemd.org/

For further information contact:

Email: Richard.Mankin@USDA.GOV

Graduate Student Grant

Purpose: The Student Award Program of FSD helps to increase opportunities in science, engineering, mathematics, technology, and pre-medical/dental areas for graduate or professional students with disabilities. FSD has established a Science Graduate Student Grant Fund, which is available to fourth year undergraduates (who are disabled and have been accepted to a graduate or professional school in the sciences) and graduate science students who have a disability. Awards of US$1000 each are made to support research projects of qualified university students in any field of Mathematics, Science, Medicine, Technology, or Engineering

Eligibility: graduate students with a disability who have a research program in a science, technology, engineering or mathematics program

Level of Study: Doctorate, Graduate, Postgraduate (MSc)

Type: Award/Grant

Value: US$1,000

Length of Study: 1 year

Frequency: Annual

Country of Study: United States of America

Application Procedure: application form must be completed. Two letters of reference. Copy of passport or birth certificate

No. of awards offered: 11

Closing Date: 1 December

Funding: Foundation

Contributor: Foundation for Science and Disability

Foundation of the American College of Healthcare Executives

Suite 1700, One North Franklin Street, Chicago, IL 60606-4425, United States of America.

Tel:	(1) 312 424 9388
Email:	membershipl@ache.org
Website:	www.ache.org
Contact:	The Membership Marketing Representative

It is the mission of the Foundation of the American College of Healthcare Executives to be the professional membership society for healthcare executives; to meet its members' professional, educational and leadership needs; to promote high ethical standards and conduct; and to advance healthcare leadership and management excellence.

Albert W Dent Graduate Student Scholarship

Purpose: Albert W. Dent, the first African-American Fellow of ACHE. This scholarship is offered to provide financial aid to racially/ethnically students in healthcare management graduate programs to help offset tuition costs, student loans and expenses.

Eligibility: 1. You are a racially/ethnically diverse student enrolled full-time in a healthcare management graduate program - MHA, MPH, MBA in Healthcare Administration or similar. 2. You are entering your final year (fall/spring) of full-time study. 3. You expect to graduate or have graduated between Sept. 1, 2023 and Aug. 31, 2024. 1. If you have a residency as part of your program and the upcoming fall term will be your second year of study, you may apply for a scholarship. 2. If you have

already completed your classroom work and are in the residency part of your program, you are not eligible to apply. 3. Doctoral students are also not eligible to apply. 4. You are not required to be a Student Associate of the American College of Healthcare Executives. However, during the selection process, preference is given to applicants who are Student Associates of ACHE. 5. You can demonstrate financial need. 6. You are a U.S. citizen or lawful permanent resident; or a Canadian citizen.

Level of Study: Graduate

Type: Scholarship

Value: Each scholarship is worth US$5,000

Frequency: Annual

Country of Study: United States of America or Canada

Application Procedure: account.ache.org/eweb/?WebCode=HubbSSO&link=achedmacfp2022

No. of awards offered: 15

Closing Date: 31 March

Additional Information: www.ache.org/membership/student-resources/albert-w-dent-graduate-student-scholarship

Foster G McGaw Graduate Student Scholarship

Purpose: To help students better prepare themselves for a career in healthcare management

Eligibility: 1. You are a student enrolled full-time in a healthcare management graduate program - MHA, MPH, MBA in Healthcare Administration or similar. 2. You are entering your final year (fall/spring) of full-time study. 3. You expect to graduate between Sept. 1, 2023 and Aug. 31, 2024. 4. If you have a residency as part of your program and the upcoming fall term will be your second year of study, you may apply for a scholarship. 5. If you have already completed your classroom work and are in the residency part of your program, you are not eligible to apply. 6. If you currently hold a paid healthcare management position, you are not eligible to apply. 7. Doctoral students are also not eligible to apply. 8. You are not required to be a Student Associate of the American College of Healthcare Executives. However, during the selection process, preference is given to applicants who are Student Associates of ACHE. 9. You can demonstrate financial need. 10. You are a U.S. citizen or lawful permanent resident; or a Canadian citizen. You are not a previous recipient of this scholarship or the Albert W. Dent Graduate Student Scholarship.

Level of Study: Graduate

Type: Scholarship

Value: Each scholarship is worth US$5,000

Frequency: Annual

Country of Study: United States of America or Canada

Application Procedure: account.ache.org/eweb/?WebCode=HubbSSO&link=achedmacfp2022

No. of awards offered: 15

Closing Date: 31 March

Additional Information: www.ache.org/membership/student-resources/albert-w-dent-graduate-student-scholarship

For further information contact:

Email: contact@ache.org

Foundation Praemium Erasmianum

Jan van Goyenkade 5, NL-1075 HN Amsterdam, Netherlands.

Tel: (31) 20 676 0222
Email: spe@erasmusprijs.org
Website: www.erasmusprijs.org
Contact: Y C Goester, Secretary

The Foundation Praemium Erasmianum operates internationally in the fields of social studies and the arts and humanities, through the awarding of the Erasmus Prize and other activities.

Foundation Praemium Erasmianum Study Prize

Purpose: To honour young academics who have written an excellent thesis in the field of humanities or social sciences
Eligibility: Open to students of Dutch universities
Level of Study: Postdoctorate
Type: Money prize
Value: €3,000
Frequency: Annual
Country of Study: Any country
Application Procedure: Relevant faculties or universities nominate candidates, from which the Foundation selects five winners
No. of awards offered: 21
Closing Date: 15 July
Funding: Private

For further information contact:

Email: l.aalbers@erasmusprijs.org

Freie Universitat Berlin and Peking University

No.5 Yiheyuan Road Haidian District, 100871 Beijing, P.R.China.

Email: beate.rogler@fu-berlin.de
Website: www.fu-berlin.de
Contact: Freie Universitat Berlin and Peking University

Free University of Berlin and Peking University Joint Postdoctoral Fellowship

Purpose: Applications are invited for Freie Universitat Berlin and Peking University Joint Postdoctoral Fellowship Program awarded for the duration of 24 months, starting 1 November. The fellowship is open to highly qualified researchers of all nationalities who received their PhD no more than three years prior to the deadline for this call
Eligibility: Applicants of all nationalities are eligible to apply. Applicants whose first language is not English are usually required to provide evidence of proficiency in English at the higher level required by the University
Type: Postdoctoral fellowship
Value: During their stay in Berlin, the Joint Postdoctoral Fellows will receive a monthly stipend of €1,853 and a one-time relocation allowance of €2,000. They are eligible for a monthly child allowance if travelling to Berlin with dependent children. All Fellows will furthermore have access to the Researcher Development Program of the Dahlem Research School. During their stay at PKU, Joint Postdoctoral Fellows will receive a monthly stipend of RMB 15,000. They can receive an additional RMB 3,500 per month for self-organized accommodation or choose to live in a PKU postdoc flat. The Fellows are furthermore eligible to apply for travel funding. They will have access to China's Postdoctoral Funds or other national research funds upon registration at the Office of National Postdoctoral Affairs Management Committee
Study Establishment: Area Studies, Data Science & Mathematics, Each fellowship is awarded for 24 months, starting 1 November. It consists of two phases Phase 1 12 months of research at FUB (November to October) Phase 2 12 months of research at PKU The Fellowship applicants must identify and secure the endorsement of two tenured faculty members, one at each university, who will serve as hosts. They will conduct their research projects under the
Country of Study: Any country
Application Procedure: Please refer the website
Closing Date: 22 February
Additional Information: Please browse the website for more details   www.fu-berlin.de/en/sites/china/aktuelles/news/2017_11_FUB_PKU_Joint-Postdoc.html

For further information contact:

Email: judith.winkler@fu-berlin.de

French Ministry of Foreign Affairs

Website: www.campusfrance.org/en/eiffel

Eiffel Scholarships in France for International Students

Purpose: The Eiffel Excellence Scholarship Programme was established by the French Ministry of Foreign Affairs and International Development to enable French higher education establishments to attract top foreign students to enroll in their master's and PhD courses
Level of Study: Doctorate, Postgraduate
Type: Scholarship
Value: For masters level studies, the Eiffel scholarship includes a monthly allowance of €1,181 (a maintenance allowance of €1,031 and a monthly stipend of €150) and can be awarded for 1 to 3 years. For PhD level studies, the Eiffel scholarship includes a monthly allowance of €1,400 and is awarded for a maximum of 10 months
Length of Study: 1 to 3 years
Frequency: Annual
Study Establishment: French Universities and Academic Institutions
Country of Study: France
Application Procedure: Only applications submitted by French higher education institutions are accepted
Closing Date: 7 January
Contributor: French Ministry of Foreign Affairs and International Development
Additional Information: Please visit Official Scholarship Website: www.campusfrance.org/en/eiffel-scholarship-program-of-excellence

For further information contact:

Campus France - Programme Eiffel, 28 rue de la Grange-aux-Belles, F-75010 Paris, France.

Email: candidatures.eiffel@campusfrance.org

Friends of Israel Educational Foundation

Academic Study Group, POB 42763, London N2 0YJ, United Kingdom.

Tel: (44) 20 8444 0777
Email: info@foi-asg.org
Website: www.foi-asg.org
Contact: Mr John D A Levy

The Friends of Israel Educational Foundation and its sister operation, the Academic Study Group, aim to encourage a critical understanding of the achievements, hopes and problems of modern Israel, and to forge new collaborative working links between the United Kingdom and Israel.

Friends of Israel Educational Foundation Academic Study Bursary

Purpose: To provide funding for British academics planning to pay a first research or study visit to Israel
Eligibility: Open to research or teaching postgraduates. The Academic Study Group will only consider proposals from British academics who have already linked up with professional counterparts in Israel and agreed terms of reference for an initial visit
Level of Study: Postdoctorate
Type: Bursary
Value: £300 per person
Frequency: Annual
Country of Study: Israel
Application Procedure: Applicants must contact the organization. There is no application form
No. of awards offered: Approx. 50
Closing Date: 1 May
Funding: Private
Contributor: Trusts and individual donations

Fujitsu

1250 E. Arques Avenue, Sunnyvale, CA 94085-3470, United States of America.
Fujitsu is the Japanese global information and communication technology (ICT) company, offering a full range of technology products, solutions and services.

Fujitsu Scholarship Program for Asia-Pacific Region

Purpose: Applications are invited for Fujitsu Scholarship program open to applicants of United States of America and Asia pacific region. The scholarship provides full financial assistance for postgraduate education and cross-cultural management training in the Global Leaders for Innovation and Knowledge program at JAIMS, the Japan-America Institute of Management Science in Hawaii, United States of America
Eligibility: A minimum TOEFL score of 577/233/90 (paper/computer/Internet), TOEIC score of 750, or IELTS

(Academic) overall band test result of 6.5 or higher from a test taken within the last five years at the time of application
Type: Postgraduate scholarships
Value: See the website
Study Establishment: Scholarship is awarded for education and cross-cultural management training in the Global Leaders for Innovation and Knowledge program by Fujitsu-JAIMS Foundation
Country of Study: United States of America
Application Procedure: See the website
Closing Date: 7 March
Additional Information: For more details please visit the website scholarship-positions.com/fujitsu-scholarship-program-asia-pacific-region-usa/2013/12/07/

For further information contact:

Tel: (33) 81 0 44 754 3413
Email: Dina.Tiongson@au.fujitsu.com

Fulbright Commission (Argentina)

Viamonte 1653, 2 Piso, C1055 ABE, Buenos Aires, Argentina.

Tel: (54) 11 4814 3561
Email: info@fulbright.com.ar
Website: fulbright.edu.ar/en
Contact: Melina Ginszparg, Educational Advisor

The Fulbright Programme is an educational exchange programme that sponsors awards for individuals approved by the J William Fulbright Board. The programme's major aim is to promote international co-operation and contribute to the development of friendly, sympathetic and peaceful relations between the United States and other countries in the world.

Fulbright Commission (Argentina) Awards for United States Lecturers and Researchers

Purpose: To enable United States lecturers to teach at an Argentine university for one semester, and to enable United States researchers to conduct research at an Argentine institution for 3 months
Eligibility: Open to United States researchers and lecturers. Applicants must be proficient in spoken Spanish
Level of Study: Professional development

Value: Varies according to professional experience
Length of Study: 3 months
Frequency: Annual
Country of Study: Argentina
Closing Date: 31 July
Funding: Government
Contributor: The United States of America and the Argentine governments

For further information contact:

The Council for International Exchange of Scholars, 3001 Tilden Street, Washington, DC 20008-3009, United States of America.

Tel: (1) 202 686 4000
Email: info@ciesnet.cies.org

Fulbright Scholar-in-Residence

Purpose: To enable visiting scholars to teach in the United States about their home country or world region
Eligibility: Open to candidates with strong international interest and some experience in study abroad and exchange programmes
Level of Study: Professional development
Type: Grant
Value: Fulbright funding plus salary supplement and in-kind support from the host institution
Length of Study: 1 year
Frequency: Annual
Country of Study: Any country
Application Procedure: Candidates must submit a Fulbright visiting scholar application form and a brief project statement
Closing Date: March

For further information contact:

Tel: (33) 1 481 435 61/62
Email: sir@iie.org

Fulbright Foundation (United Kingdom)

Fulbright House, 62 Doughty Street, London WC1N 2LS, United Kingdom.

Tel: (44) 20 7404 6880
Contact: Grants Management Officer

American Studies (Lecturing Award)

Eligibility: 1. all U.S. citizens are eligible to apply, regardless of dual citizenship or residency. 2. faculty of all academic ranks with a Ph.D., appropriate teaching experience and relevant expertise. 3. English is sufficient. However, feasibility of conducting the project must be demonstrated in the project statement.
Level of Study: Faculty
Type: Award
Value: €4,000 per month. All grantees receive a travel and relocation allowance of €1,000
Length of Study: 4 months
Frequency: Annual
Country of Study: Any country
Closing Date: 15 September
Additional Information: awards.cies.org/content/american-studies-lecturing-award

British-American Chamber of Commerce Awards

Purpose: To fund postgraduate education between Britain and America
Eligibility: Open to graduates of any nationality
Level of Study: Postgraduate
Value: US$8,000
Frequency: Annual
Country of Study: United States of America
Application Procedure: Please write for details.

For further information contact:

Email: fulbrighttgc@irex.org

Fulbright Distinguished Chair in Science, Technology, and Innovation (CSIRO)

Eligibility: 1. A letter of invitation is required. 2. Open to senior academics at the level of Associate or Full Professor by the grant start date with a distinguished career in the proposed field. If you are not at the level of Associate or Full Professor at the time of application, but will be by grant start, please include information about your career progression and timeline in the personal section of your project statement.
Level of Study: Faculty
Type: Award
Value: A stipend of AU$9,166 (approximately AU$6,575) per month.
Length of Study: 6 months
Frequency: Annual
Country of Study: Australia

Closing Date: 15 September
Additional Information: awards.cies.org/content/fulbright-distinguished-chair-science-technology-and-innovation-csiro-4

For further information contact:

Email: ro@csiro.au

Fulbright Postdoctoral Scholarship in All Disciplines

Eligibility: Applicants should check the University website www.deakin.edu.au/research and identify which Faculty, Research Institute or Strategic Research Centre aligns with their area of research. They should then contact researchers with whom they would like to work. Institutes, Centres or Faculties will consider the alignment of the proposal and the candidate and will provide applicants with a Letter of Invitation if the application is supported.
Level of Study: Doctorate
Type: Scholarship
Length of Study: 3 to 10months
Frequency: Annual
Country of Study: Australia
Closing Date: 15 September
Additional Information: awards.cies.org/content/fulbright-postdoctoral-scholarship-all-disciplines-deakin-university-4

For further information contact:

Email: research_prizes_awards@deakin.edu.au

Fulbright Scholarship Program for Nigerians

Purpose: The Fulbright Scholarship program for Nigerians is offering Scholarships to students of Nigeria who are interested in pursuing two years doctoral studies in United States of America, in the fields of natural and social sciences, arts, and humanities
Eligibility: Applicants must be a resident of the state of Hawaii, USA, or a citizen of one of the following countries Australia, Cambodia, China, Hong Kong, India, Indonesia, Laos, Malaysia, Myanmar, New Zealand, the Philippines, Singapore, South Korea, Sri Lanka, Taiwan, Thailand, or Vietnam. Applicants who are residents of the State of Hawaii will be requested to prove Hawaii residency.
Level of Study: Doctorate
Type: Scholarship
Value: It includes all related expenses
Length of Study: 2 years
Frequency: Annual

Country of Study: United States of America

Application Procedure: 1. To apply for the Fulbright Scholarship for Nigerians the applicants must be citizens or nationals of Nigeria, or permanent residents holding a valid passport issued by the government of Nigeria. 2. The applicants must be doctoral students who conducted research in their home institution, applicants must be at least two years into their doctoral program in any discipline that was related to the subjects offered by the university

Closing Date: June

Funding: Private

Additional Information: Young and talented scholars of Nigeria are invited to apply for Fulbright Scholarship Program for Nigerians to pursue doctoral studies in United States of America scholarship-positions.com/fujitsu-scholarship-program-asia-pacific-region-usa/2013/12/07/

For further information contact:

Email: professionalexchange@state.gov

Fulbright-Freud Visiting Lecturer of Psychoanalysis

Eligibility: 1. all U.S. citizens are eligible to apply, regardless of dual citizenship or residency. 2. Fulbright-Freud scholars are expected to have a basic knowledge of German; English may be used as the language of instruction. 3. Open to associate and full professors. Several years of teaching/lecturing or professional experience in relevant fields of psychoanalysis.

Type: Scholarship

Value: €3,300 per month.

Length of Study: 4 months

Country of Study: Any country

Closing Date: 15 September

Additional Information: awards.cies.org/content/fulbright-freud-visiting-lecturer-psychoanalysis-2

For further information contact:

Email: fbrunner@fulbright.at

Fulbright United States Student Program

Fulbright-National Geographic Digital Storytelling Fellowship

Purpose: The Fulbright-National Geographic Storytelling Fellowship, a component of the Fulbright United States Student Program, provides opportunities for United States citizens to participate in an academic year of overseas travel

Eligibility: Applications will be accepted for Fulbright-National Geographic Storytelling Fellowships in any country to which there is an active Fulbright United States Student Program with the exception of China

Level of Study: Postgraduate, Professional development

Type: Fellowship

Frequency: Annual

Country of Study: Any country

Application Procedure: Candidates must have completed at least an undergraduate degree by the commencement of the Fulbright awa Candidates from all fields are encouraged to apply. All application materials, including academic transcripts and letters of recommendation must be submitted in the Embark Online Application and Recommendation System by 9 October at 5pm Eastern Time

Closing Date: 9 October

Funding: Private

For further information contact:

United States Student Programs Division, 809 United Nations Plaza, New York, NY 10017 3580, United States of America.

Email: FBstudent.natgeo@iie.org

Fund for Epilepsy

Ripponden Mill, Mill Fold, Ripponden, Halifax H6 4DH, United Kingdom.

Tel: (44) 1422 823508
Email: ffe@epilepsyfund.org.uk
Website: www.epilepsyfund.org.uk
Contact: The Administrator

Emergency Medicine Foundation Grants

Purpose: To aid various ethnic minority voluntary organizations

Type: Grant

Value: Dependent, for 1–3 years

Frequency: Dependent on funds available

Country of Study: Any country

Application Procedure: Please write in to EMF, grants officer

For further information contact:

Tel: (44) 208 432 0000 Free phone : (44) 8000 652 0390
Fax: (44) 208 432 0319
Email: enquiries@emf-cemvo.co.uk

The Sergievsky Award For Epilepsy Health Equity And Diversity

Eligibility: 1. Hol d a MD, DO, PhD, PharmD, doctorate of nursing, or, other professional degree within the appropriate track. 2. Have a job title of clinical fellow, research fellow, clinical instructor, or clinician investigator or assistant professor for clinicians, or equivalent levels of career for non-physicians in neuropsychology, psychology, pharmacology, nursing, or research. Applicants who are in training at the time of submission (e.g., clinical fellows or similar) must have a position offered as an incoming faculty member. Applicants with appointments at the level of Adjunct Professor or Associate Professor are not eligible, nor are research assistants, graduate or medical students, postdoctoral research fellows, medical residents, permanent government employees, or employees of private industry. 3. Self-identify as an under-represented minority in medicine (URM), with preference for Black or African American applicants in keeping with the intentions of the benefactor of this program. For this award, AES interprets URM as racial and ethnic populations that are underrepresented in the medical profession relative to their numbers in the general population. Please see NIH's definitions for Racial and Ethnic Categories here. 4. Have a defined research plan and access to institutional resources to conduct the proposed project. 5. Preference will be given to clinical research that addresses issues affecting medically under-served people with epilepsy or seizures or related aspects of health equity. 6. Be able to devote at least 50% of their professional effort to research. If reduced protected time is deemed necessary by an early career clinical faculty applicant, such requests will be considered on a case-by-case manner and on a competitive basis, provided that such requests do not compromise the training experience and research goals of the applicant's project. Early career clinical faculty applicants who request reduced effort for this award must include in their application a justification and elaborate on their plans to ensure that the research and training goals of the award will be met. 7. Have a qualified mentor or mentoring team with expertise relevant to the scientific goals of the application and who has a focus on career development. 8. Not be, or have previously been, the Principal Investigator on a multiyear research or career development or project grant, such as an NIH K08, K23, K99/R00, R01, or R03. However, individuals who received support through an institutional K award (e.g., K12) are eligible so long as the provided funds do not overlap. 9. Should not have previously received the Susan Spencer Fellowship or an AES Research and Training Fellowship for Clinicians.

Level of Study: Postdoctorate

Type: Award

Value: US$150,000

Country of Study: United States of America

Closing Date: 14 January

Additional Information: www.epilepsy.com/about-us/research-and-new-therapies/upcoming-grants

Fundacion Educativa Carlos M. Castaneda

1925 Brickell Ave, Miami, FL 33129, United States of America.

Tel: (1) 305 283 4963
Email: fecmc@me.com
Website: www.fecmc.org

We are a community-based organization focused on helping make the world around us a better, happier place. With the help of our tireless staff, we organize fundraisers, exciting community-building events, and in-depth training sessions for our volunteers.

Carlos M. Castaeda Journalism Scholarship

Purpose: This award is for Spanish speaking students who are pursuing a graduate degree in journalism. Applicants must have a grade point average of 3.0 or higher

Eligibility: 1. Must be a graduate student 2. Must attend a university 3. Minimum 3.0 GPA 4. Must be at least 20 years old 5. Must not be older than 35 years old 6. Must study full-time 7. Restricted to students studying Communications, Journalism, Photojournalism/Photography 8. Restricted by ethnic heritage Hispanic, Spanish

Level of Study: Graduate

Type: Scholarship

Value: US$7,000

Frequency: Annual

Country of Study: United States of America

Application Procedure: Applications and award information are available on the Carlos M. Castaeda Educational Foundation website at the address provided. In addition to the completed online application form, students must submit the following items Official transcripts of all academic work completed; Proof of acceptance in an accredited graduate program; Recent 1,040 documents or equivalent information describing the student and his/her parents' financial status; Recent curriculum vitae describing the applicant's work history and activities; Three letters of reference in separately sealed envelopes; A portfolio showcasing three recently written works that have been published in the Spanish language

Closing Date: 15 April

Funding: Foundation
No. of awards given last year: 1

For further information contact:

1925 Brickell Avenue D-1108, Miami, FL 33129, United States of America.

Funds for Women Graduates

57 Alma Road, Leeds LS6 2AH, United Kingdom.

Tel: (44) 113 2747988
Email: secretary@ffwg.org.uk
Website: www.ffwg.org.uk
Contact: Mrs Sally Dowell, Co. Secretary

FFWG is the registered Trading Name for the BFWG Charitable Foundation. FfWG seeks to promote the advancement of education and the promotion of higher education of women graduates by offering grants to help women graduates with their living costs while registered for study or research at institutions in Great Britain.

Emergency Grants

Subjects: Any subject
Purpose: The criteria for awarding Grants are the proven needs of the applicant and her academic calibre. Competition is very great so not all qualifying applicants will receive a Grant. Grants are offered on a needs basis therefore not all grants will be for the maximum sum quoted for the grant.
Eligibility: Please see website for details. www.ffwg.org.uk
Level of Study: Postgraduate
Type: Grant
Value: Up to £2,500
Length of Study: Any postgraduate course eligible
Frequency: Twice a year
Study Establishment: Any approved institution of higher education in Great Britain
Country of Study: England, Scotland and Wales
Application Procedure: Please see website for details. www.ffwg.org.uk
Closing Date: 4 October
Funding: Private
Contributor: Investment funds
Additional Information: www.ffwg.org.uk/grants-bursaries-fellowships/

For further information contact:

4 St Michaels Gate, Shrewsbury SY1 2HL, United Kingdom.

Email: grants@ffwg.org.uk

Emergency Grants for United Kingdom and International Women Graduates

Purpose: To allow a woman facing unexpected financial crises to continue in postgraduate study
Eligibility: Women graduates from Britain and overseas are eligible to apply. There is no upper age limit
Type: Grant
Value: These are one off payments to assist with the completion of an academic years work. No grant is likely to exceed £2,500. All grants are offered on a needs basis and therefore not all grants will be for £2,500
Frequency: Twice a year
Country of Study: United Kingdom
Application Procedure: The mode of applying is by post. An application form for an Emergency Grant may be obtained by email only from the Grants Administrator at grants@ffwg.org.uk
No. of awards offered: 170
Closing Date: 31 October
Additional Information: All grants are offered on a needs basis www.ffwg.org.uk/grants-bursaries-fellowships/

For further information contact:

Email: grants@ffwg.org.uk

FfWG Foundation Grants

Purpose: To financially assist female graduates registered for study or research at an approved Institute of Higher Education within Great Britain
Eligibility: Open to female graduates who are in their final year or writing-up year of a PhD There is no restriction on nationality or age. Any subject
Level of Study: Doctorate, Postdoctorate, Postgraduate
Type: Grant
Value: Foundation Grants are up to £4,000 and Emergency Grants are up to £1,500. (these values are being reviewed)
Length of Study: Courses that exceed 1 year in length
Frequency: Annual
Study Establishment: Approved Institutes of Higher Education
Country of Study: Great Britain
Application Procedure: Applicants must complete an application form and submit it with two references and a brief

summary of the thesis, if applicable. Requests for application forms must be made by email
No. of awards offered: 376
Closing Date: 31 May
Funding: Private
Contributor: Investment income
Additional Information: Closing dates are liable to change each year. Please refer to our website for details of the current year www.ffwg.org.uk/grants-bursaries-fellowships/

For further information contact:

Email: grants@ffwg.org.uk

Foundation Grants

Purpose: FfWG offers Foundation Grants to help women graduates with their living expenses (not fees) while registered for study or research at an approved institution of higher education in Great Britain. The criteria are the proven needs of the applicant and her academic calibre. Foundation Grants will only be given for the final year of a PhD or DPhil. The closing date for applications for current and upcoming year is 5 March and the grants are awarded in July for the following academic year. Request for applications must be made by 28 February
Eligibility: For your application to be considered you must meet all the eligibility conditions which may be found on the 'Am I Eligible' (www.ffwg.org.uk/am-i-eligible-.html) page of the site. In brief, to be eligible you must be a woman postgraduate studying in Great Britain at an approved higher education institution (typically a university) and entering the final year for completing your PhD (or equivalent) thesis. Applications may only be made for financial support with living costs (not for fees) where there is genuine financial need to complete the course of study.
Level of Study: Doctorate
Type: Grant
Value: Up to £6,000
Frequency: Annual
Study Establishment: Any recognised university
Country of Study: Any country
Application Procedure: please see website for details www.ffwg.org.uk
No. of awards offered: 309
Closing Date: 1 April
Funding: Private
Contributor: Investment income
Additional Information: Please contact www.ffwg.org.uk/grants-bursaries-fellowships/

For further information contact:

Sally Dowell, 57 Alma Road, Leeds LS6 2AH, United Kingdom.

International Fellowship

Purpose: The award is aimed at post first year PhD students studying at a British university but from any country. The topic is not stipulated but is usually deemed of merit if it falls within the aims and objectives of GWI and the British Federation of University Women.
Type: Fellowship
Value: £6,000
Frequency: Every 3 years
Country of Study: Any country
Closing Date: 15 December
Additional   Information: www.ffwg.org.uk/grants-bursaries-fellowships/

Theodora Bosanquet Bursary

Subjects: History or English Literature
Purpose: This Bursary is offered annually to women graduates whose research in History or English Literature requires a short residence in London in the summer. It provides accommodation in a hall of residence for up to 4 weeks between end of June and mid September. The closing date for applications is 31st October of the preceding year.
Eligibility: Please see website for details. www.ffwg.org.uk
Level of Study: Postgraduate
Type: Bursary
Value: Up to four weeks accommodation
Country of Study: England, Scotland and Wales
Application Procedure: Please see website for details. www.ffwg.org.uk
No. of awards offered: 2
Closing Date: 31 October
Funding: Private
Contributor: Investment funds
No. of awards given last year: 1
No. of applicants last year: 1
Additional Information: Please contact grants@ffwg.org.uk for further details www.advance-africa.com/Theodora-Bosanquet-Bursary.html

Fylde College

Email: fylde@lancaster.ac.uk

Alumni Loyalty Scholarship

Eligibility: 1. Undergraduate Awardees must achieve A*A*A at A level, or equivalent. 2. For Postgraduate Taught Awardees, please refer to the educational equivalences table. 3. Awardees for the MBA must achieve the equivalent of a UK 2.1 undergraduate degree. 4. The Lancaster Global Scholarship is available for eligible applicants to all full-time and part-time taught undergraduate and Postgraduate Taught degree-level programmes, offered fully on-campus at Lancaster University for October 2023 entry. 5. Applicants must be in receipt of either a conditional or an unconditional offer for a place at Lancaster University for October 2023 entry, which you have accepted (non-UCAS applications) or accepted firmly (UCAS applications). 6. The scholarship is only available to undergraduates students joining Part 1 of our degree programmes. 7. Fully funded applicants are not eligible for this scholarship. 8. Applicants applying from 1+3, 2+2 and pre-masters programmes offered by Lancaster University articulation partners, are not eligible for this scholarship. 9. Partially funded applicants for less than 50% of their fees would be eligible for this scholarship. 10. Awardees must be classed as Overseas or International fee-paying students for tuition fee purposes, for the duration of their studies. If you are awarded the scholarship and are subsequently reassessed as a 'Home' fee-payer, you will no longer be eligible for the scholarship.
Level of Study: Postgraduate
Type: Scholarship
Value: 20% fee reduction for 1st Class Hons degree holders 10% fee reduction for 2:1 Hons degree holders
Frequency: Annual
Country of Study: United Kingdom
Additional Information: www.lancaster.ac.uk/student-and-education-services/money/funding/alumni-loyalty-scholarship

Cartmel College Postgraduate Studentship

Eligibility: 1. Undergraduate Awardees must achieve A*A*A at A level, or equivalent. 2. For Postgraduate Taught Awardees, please refer to the educational equivalences table. 3. Awardees for the MBA must achieve the equivalent of a UK 2.1 undergraduate degree. 4. The Lancaster Global Scholarship is available for eligible applicants to all full-time and part-time taught undergraduate and postgraduate Taught degree-level programmes, offered fully on-campus at Lancaster University for October 2023 entry. 5. Applicants must be in receipt of either a conditional or an unconditional offer for a place at Lancaster University for October 2023 entry, which you have accepted (non-UCAS applications) or accepted firmly (UCAS applications). 6. The scholarship is only available to undergraduates students joining Part 1 of our degree programmes. 7. Fully funded applicants are not eligible for this scholarship. 8. Applicants applying from 1+3, 2+2 and pre-masters programmes offered by Lancaster University articulation partners, are not eligible for this scholarship. 9. Partially funded applicants for less than 50% of their fees would be eligible for this scholarship. 10. Awardees must be classed as Overseas or International fee-paying students for tuition fee purposes, for the duration of their studies. If you are awarded the scholarship and are subsequently reassessed as a 'Home' fee-payer, you will no longer be eligible for the scholarship.
Level of Study: Postgraduate
Type: Scholarship
Value: £1,000
Frequency: Annual
Country of Study: United Kingdom
No. of awards offered: 2
Closing Date: 1 June
Additional Information: www.lancaster.ac.uk/student-and-education-services/money/funding/cartmel-college-postgraduate-studentship

Churches Together in Britain and Ireland

Eligibility: 1. permanent resident of Britain, Ireland, EU or other developed countries; 2. students who begin their course without assured funding to meet the full costs involved (tuition, accommodation, living expenses etc); 3. students whose fees and living expenses have been covered by major award(s); 4. candidates who have not begun their studies and those who have already finished; 5. those studying outside Britain/Ireland or those requiring help for a field trip abroad; asylum seekers and refugees; 6. students undertaking courses in subjects related to arms manufacture or experimentation on live animals.
Type: Scholarship
Value: £1,000
Frequency: Annual
Country of Study: United Kingdom

County College Studentship

Eligibility: 1. Undergraduate Awardees must achieve A*A*A at A level, or equivalent. 2. For Postgraduate Taught Awardees, please refer to the educational equivalences table. 3. Awardees for the MBA must achieve the equivalent of a UK 2.1 undergraduate degree. 4. The Lancaster Global Scholarship is available for eligible applicants to all full-time and part-time taught undergraduate and Postgraduate Taught degree-level programmes, offered fully on-campus at Lancaster University for October 2023 entry. 5. Applicants must be in receipt of either a conditional or an unconditional offer for a place at Lancaster University for October 2023 entry, which you have accepted (non-UCAS applications) or accepted firmly (UCAS applications). 6. The scholarship is only available to undergraduates students joining Part 1 of our degree programmes. 7. Fully funded applicants are not eligible for this scholarship. 8. Applicants applying from 1+3, 2+2 and pre-masters programmes offered by Lancaster University articulation partners, are not eligible for this scholarship. 9. Partially funded applicants for less than 50% of their fees would be eligible for this scholarship. 10. Awardees must be classed as Overseas or International fee-paying students for tuition fee purposes, for the duration of their studies. If you are awarded the scholarship and are subsequently reassessed as a 'Home' fee-payer, you will no longer be eligible for the scholarship.

Level of Study: Postgraduate
Type: Scholarship
Value: £1,000
Frequency: Annual
Country of Study: United Kingdom
No. of awards offered: 2
Closing Date: 1 June
Additional Information: www.lancaster.ac.uk/student-and-education-services/money/funding/county-college-studentship

County College Travel Award

Eligibility: 1. Undergraduate Awardees must achieve A*A*A at A level, or equivalent. 2. For Postgraduate Taught Awardees, please refer to the educational equivalences table. 3. Awardees for the MBA must achieve the equivalent of a UK 2.1 undergraduate degree. 4. The Lancaster Global Scholarship is available for eligible applicants to all full-time and part-time taught undergraduate and Postgraduate Taught degree-level programmes, offered fully on-campus at Lancaster University for October 2023 entry. 5. Applicants must be in receipt of either a conditional or an unconditional offer for a place at Lancaster University for October 2023 entry, which you have accepted (non-UCAS applications) or accepted firmly (UCAS applications). 6. The scholarship is only available to undergraduates students joining Part 1 of our degree programmes. 7. Fully funded applicants are not eligible for this scholarship. 8. Applicants applying from 1+3, 2+2 and pre-masters programmes offered by Lancaster University articulation partners, are not eligible for this scholarship. 9. Partially funded applicants for less than 50% of their fees would be eligible for this scholarship. 10. Awardees must be classed as Overseas or International fee-paying students for tuition fee purposes, for the duration of their studies. If you are

awarded the scholarship and are subsequently reassessed as a 'Home' fee-payer, you will no longer be eligible for the scholarship.
Level of Study: Postgraduate
Type: Scholarship
Value: £150
Frequency: Annual
Country of Study: United Kingdom
Additional Information: www.lancaster.ac.uk/student-and-education-services/money/funding/county-college-travel-award

For further information contact:

Email: countywelfare@lancaster.ac.uk

FfWG - Foundation Grants for Women Graduates

Level of Study: Postgraduate
Type: Scholarship
Value: £4,000
Frequency: Annual
Country of Study: United Kingdom
Additional Information: www.lancaster.ac.uk/student-and-education-services/money/funding/ffwg—foundation-grants-for-women-graduates

For further information contact:

Email: jean.c@blueyonder.co.uk

Fylde College - Travel Award

Purpose: The scholarship is available to enable Fylde students to travel to 1. Conferences or training. 2. Dissertation locations where costs exceed that normally expected as part of the degree course. 3. Undertake voluntary work in vacation time
Eligibility: For further information, refer the official website link
Level of Study: Undergraduate and Postgraduate
Type: Travel award
Frequency: Annual
Country of Study: Any country
Application Procedure: Please ask in the Fylde College office for an application form or visit www.lancaster.ac.uk/fylde/welfare-and-support/financial-support/.
Funding: Private

For further information contact:

Tel: (44) 1524 65201

IT Support Fund

Level of Study: Postgraduate
Type: Scholarship
Value: £500
Frequency: Annual
Country of Study: United Kingdom
Closing Date: 1 June
Additional Information: www.lancaster.ac.uk/student-and-education-services/money/funding/it-support-fund

Lancaster Enabling Access Fund

Level of Study: Postgraduate
Type: Grant
Value: £50 and £500
Frequency: Annual
Country of Study: United Kingdom
Additional Information: www.lancaster.ac.uk/student-and-education-services/money/funding/lancaster-enabling-access-fund

Leverhulme Trade Charities Trust

Eligibility: Eligible students will be in financial need, resident in the UK and have a parent or spouse who is a Commercial Traveller, Pharmacist or Grocer. Applications are eligible if their parent or spouse retired within the last 10 years.
Type: Award
Value: Maximum of £5,000 p.a. for Postgraduate
Country of Study: United Kingdom
Closing Date: 15 October
Additional Information: www.lancaster.ac.uk/student-and-education-services/money/funding/leverhulme-trade-charities-trust

Lone Parents Child Care Grant

Level of Study: Postgraduate
Type: Grant
Value: £1,000
Frequency: Annual
Country of Study: United Kingdom
Closing Date: 1 June
Additional Information: www.lancaster.ac.uk/student-and-education-services/money/funding/lone-parents-child-care-grant

Robinson Scholarship

Level of Study: Postgraduate
Type: Grant
Value: £5,000
Frequency: Annual
Country of Study: United Kingdom
Closing Date: 1 May
Additional Information: www.lancaster.ac.uk/student-and-education-services/money/funding/robinson-scholarship

Snowdon Masters Scholarships

Eligibility: To be eligible for the Snowdon Scholarship applicants must meet the following criteria: 1. Applying for a master's programme at a UK institution. 2. The master's programme commences in the academic year 2023/24. 3. You experience one or more of the following impairments: 3a. Physical impairment b. Vision impairment/Blind c. Hearing impairment/Deaf. d. Specific Learning Difficulty e.g. Dyslexia, Dyspraxia. e. Learning or intellectual disability f. Neurodivergence.
Level of Study: Postgraduate
Type: Scholarship
Value: Up to £30.000
Frequency: Annual
Country of Study: United Kingdom
Application Procedure: The full eligibility and guidance criteria togther with details on how to apply can be found at:- www.disabilityinnovation.com/projects/snowdon-masters-scholarships?fbclid=IwAR0sAXTGxGT7alr4iUhE154QBKmW5sM-zXL4nXCBjcUMs3nFtys8j0G86LY
Closing Date: 1 April
Additional Information: www.lancaster.ac.uk/student-and-education-services/money/funding/snowdon-masters-scholarships

The Peel Trust Studentship

Level of Study: Postgraduate
Type: Studentship
Value: £2,500
Frequency: Annual
Country of Study: United Kingdom
No. of awards offered: 25
Closing Date: 28 May
Additional Information: www.lancaster.ac.uk/student-and-education-services/money/funding/the-peel-trust-studentship

G

Garden Club of America

14 East 60th Street 3rd Floor, New York, NY 10022, United States of America.

Tel: (1) 212 753 8287
Email: judygow@comcast.net
Website: www.gcamerica.org
Contact: Judy Gow, Vice Chairman

The Garden Club of America stimulates the knowledge and love of gardening, shares the advantages of association by means of educational meetings, conferences, correspondence and publications, and restores, improves and protects the quality of the environment through educational programmes and action in the fields of conservation and civic improvement.

Garden Club of America Summer Scholarship in Field Botany

Purpose: To support student's field studies and offer an opportunity to gain knowledge and experience beyond the regular course of study.
Eligibility: Open to undergraduate and master's degree students. Research must be conducted in the Western Hemisphere. Eligibility is open to U.S. Citizens and permanent residents who are enrolled in a U.S. - based institution.
Value: US$3000
Length of Study: 1 year
Country of Study: Any country
Closing Date: 1 February
Additional Information: www.gcamerica.org/scholarships/details/s/gca-summer-scholarship-in-field-botany

For further information contact:

The Garden Club of America, Attn: Scholarship Applications, 14 East 60th Street, New York, NY 10022-1006, United States of America.

Tel: (1) 212 753 8287
Email: scholarshipapplications@gcamerica.org

The Anne S. Chatham Fellowship

Purpose: To protect and preserve knowledge about the medicinal use of plants and thus prevent the disappearance of plants with therapeutic potential
Eligibility: Open to candidates who are currently enroled in PhD programmes or have obtained a PhD or a graduate degree
Level of Study: Doctorate, Postdoctorate
Type: Fellowship
Value: US$4,500
Frequency: Annual
Country of Study: Any country
Application Procedure: Applicants must submit an application letter, an abstract, a research proposal and a curriculum vitae
Closing Date: 31 January
Contributor: Garden Club of America
Additional Information: Contact Wendy Applequist for more information www.missouribotanicalgarden.org/plant-science/plant-science/william-l-brown-center/wlbc-resources/wlbc-awards/anne-s.-chatham-fellowship.aspx

For further information contact:

Missouri Botanical Garden, PO Box 299, St Louis, MO 63166, United States of America.

Tel: (1) 314 577 9503
Email: wendy.applequist@mobot.org

The Garden Club of America Fellowship in Tropical Botany

Purpose: To promote the preservation of tropical forests by enlarging the body of botanists with field experience.

Eligibility: Open to students who anticipate completing the requirements for a Ph.D. in Botany within two years. Applicants must already be Ph.D. candidates enrolled at a US university. Eligibility is open to U.S. Citizens and permanent residents who are enrolled in a U.S. - based institution.

Level of Study: Doctorate
Type: Fellowship
Value: US$5500
Length of Study: 2 years
Frequency: Annual
Country of Study: Any country
No. of awards offered: 2 or more
Closing Date: 15 January
Contributor: the Visiting Gardens Tropical Botany Scholarship Fund
Additional Information: www.gcamerica.org/scholarships/details/s/gca-awards-in-tropical-botany
www.vims.edu/ccrm/outreach/gca/index.php

The Zeller Summer Scholarship in Medicinal Botany

Purpose: To encourage US undergraduate students to expand their knowledge of medicinal botany by pursuing summer study in various projects, courses, and/or internship with supervision and structure.

Eligibility: Open to undergraduate students enrolled in an accredited US college or university for study or work during the summer following the freshman, sophomore, junior, or senior year. Open to U.S. Citizens and permanent residents who are enrolled in a U.S. - based institution.

Value: US$3000
Country of Study: Any country
Closing Date: 1 February
Additional Information: www.gcamerica.org/scholarships/details/s/zeller-summer-scholarship-in-medicinal-botany

For further information contact:

The Garden Club of America, attn: Scholarship Applications, 14 East 60th Street, New York, NY 10022-1006, United States of America.

Tel: (1) 212 753 8287
Email: scholarshipapplications@gcamerica.org

Gates Cambridge Trust

PO Box 252, Cambridge CB2 1TZ, United Kingdom.

Tel: (44) 1223 338 467
Email: info@gates.scholarships.cam.ac.uk
Website: www.gates.scholarships.cam.ac.uk
Contact: Board of Graduate Studies

Gates Cambridge Scholarship

Purpose: The Gates Cambridge Scholarship programme was established in October 2000 by a donation of US$210m from the Bill and Melinda Gates Foundation to the University of Cambridge; this is the largest ever single donation to a United Kingdom university. Scholarships are awarded to outstanding applicants from countries outside the United Kingdom to pursue a full-time postgraduate degree in any subject available at the University of Cambridge. The selection criteria are 1. outstanding intellectual ability. 2. leadership potential. 3. a commitment to improving the lives of others. 4. a good fit between the applicant's qualifications and aspirations and the postgraduate programme at Cambridge for which they are applying. While at Cambridge, Scholars pursue the full range of subjects available at the University and are spread across its departments and Colleges. The aim of the Gates Cambridge programme is to build a global network of future leaders committed to improving the lives of others

Eligibility: You can apply for a Gates Cambridge Scholarship if you are 1. a citizen of any country outside the United Kingdom. 2. applying to pursue one of the following full-time residential courses of study at the University of Cambridge. PhD (three year research-only degree). MSc or MLitt (two year research-only degree). One year postgraduate course (e.g. MPhil, LLM, MA, Diploma, MBA etc.). There is no age restriction for applications

Level of Study: Doctorate, MBA, Postgraduate, Postgraduate (MSc)
Type: Scholarship
Value: Tuition fees and maintenance allowance of £17,500
Length of Study: 12 months & PhD scholars the award is for up to 4 years
Frequency: Annual
Study Establishment: University of Cambridge
Country of Study: United Kingdom
Application Procedure: Complete relevant funding section of the University of Cambridge application form
Closing Date: 7 January
Funding: Foundation
Contributor: Bill and Melinda Gates Foundation
No. of awards given last year: 90

Additional Information: Candidates must apply for a place at the University of Cambridge and for funding at the same time, using the University of Cambridge application portal - there is no separate Gates Cambridge application form except for MBA and MFin applicants who should consult the Cambridge Judge Business School website www.gatescambridge.org/apply-overview

For further information contact:

The Warehouse, Ground Floor, 33 Bridge Street, Cambridge CB2 1UW, United Kingdom.

Fax: (44) 1223 577004
Email: info@gatescambridge.org

General Social Care Council

Goldings House, 2 Hay's Lane, London SE1 2HB, United Kingdom.

Tel: (44) 20 7397 5100
Email: info@bursaries.gscc.org.uk
Website: www.gscc.org.uk
Contact: Administrative Officer

The General Social Care Council is the first ever regulatory body for the social care profession in United Kingdom. It was set up to establish codes of conduct and practice for social care workers, a register of practicing professionals and to regulate and support social work, education and training. It takes forward some of the work of the Central Council for Education and Training in Social Work, which closed on September 28, 2001. Similar councils exist for Northern Ireland, Scotland and Wales.

Social Work Bursary

Purpose: To support those seeking the qualifications required for social work
Eligibility: Open to graduates, who have ordinarily been resident in United Kingdom studying on an approved full-time postgraduate course. Amongst other eligibility criteria, students must also meet certain residency criteria. Please refer to the application packs for full eligibility criterion
Level of Study: Postgraduate
Type: Bursary
Value: Non-income-assessed grant of £2,500–2,900 and a contribution towards practice learning opportunity related

expenses and tuition fees. It also includes a income-assessed maitenance grant and allowances to assist cost of living
Length of Study: 2 years
Frequency: Annual
Study Establishment: Accredited higher education institutions running a social work course approved by the General Social Care Council, the Scottish Social Services Council, the Care Council for Wales or the Northern Ireland Social Care Council
Country of Study: United Kingdom
Application Procedure: Application guide is available on the following link www.nhsbsa.nhs.uk/sites/default/files/2019-07/Your%20guide%20to%20Social%20Work%20Bursaries%202019-20%20%28V2%29%2007%202019.pdf
No. of awards offered: 2300
Closing Date: 1 February
Funding: Government
Contributor: The Department of Health
No. of awards given last year: 2100
No. of applicants last year: 2300
Additional Information: The bursary is a year-to-year funding arrangement. The bursary terms and conditions (including rates) may change from year-to-year www.gov.uk/social-work-bursaries

For further information contact:

NHS Business Services Authority, Sandyford House, Archbold Terrace, Newcastle Upon Tyne NE2 1DB, United Kingdom.

Tel: (44) 300 330 1343
Email: swb@ppa.nhs.uk

GeneTex

GeneTex Scholarship Program

Purpose: GeneTex believes in accelerating scientific advancement and the notion that the genesis of future discoveries begins with the support of young scientists today. The GeneTex Scholarship Program is intended for students that have declared a STEM major or are enrolled in a STEM graduate program
Eligibility: 1. Student in good standing and enrolled at an accredited college or university. 2. Declared STEM major. 3. Open to international students. 4. All accredited Universities are eligible.
Level of Study: Postgraduate
Type: Programme grant
Value: US$2,000

Frequency: Annual

Country of Study: Any country

Application Procedure: See the website. www.genetex.com/Article/Company?param1=Scholarship

Closing Date: 16 July

Funding: Private

Additional Information: www.genetex.com/Article/Company/Index/Scholarship

For further information contact:

2456 Alton Parkway, Irvine, CA 92606, United States of America.

Tel: (1) 949 553 1900

Email: scholarship@genetex.com

Geological Society of America (GSA)

3300 Penrose Place, PO Box 9140, Boulder, CO 80301-1806, United States of America.

Tel: (1) 303 357 1000

Email: awards@geosociety.org

Website: www.geosociety.org

Contact: Ms Program Manager, Grants, Awards and Recognition

Established in 1888, the GSA is a non-profit organization dedicated to the advancement of the science of geology. GSA membership is for the generalist and the specialist in the field of geology and offers something for everyone

Graduate Student Research Grants

Purpose: The primary role of the GSA research grants program is to provide partial support of master's and doctoral thesis research in the geological sciences for graduate students enrolled in universities in the United States, Canada, Mexico and Central America.

Eligibility: 1. Eligibility is restricted to GSA members. 2. Applicants must be currently enrolled in a North American or Central American university or college in an earth science graduate degree program (with a geologic component). Applicants do not need to be a U.S. Citizen or a U.S. Resident Alien. 3. The research focus can be any subject matter within the geological sciences, such as paleontology, karst, geochemistry, stratigraphy, geoscience education, petroleum geology, and more. 4. Students may receive

a total of two GSA graduate student grants in their entire academic career, regardless of what program currently enrolled in.

Type: Grant

Value: US$1,820.00

Country of Study: Any country

Closing Date: 2 February

Contributor: National Science Foundation under Grant no 1949901

Additional Information: www.geosociety.org/GSA/Education_Careers/Grants_Scholarships/Research_Grants/GSA/grants/gradgrants.aspx

For further information contact:

Geological Society of America, P.O. Box 9140 Boulder, CO 80301-9140, United States of America.

Tel: (1) 303 357 1025

Email: researchgrants@geosociety.org

J. Hoover Mackin Award

Purpose: The award is given annually to an outstanding PhD student, on the basis of a research proposal submitted to the GSA student research grant program

Eligibility: 1. Eligibility is restricted to GSA members. 2. Applicants must be currently enrolled in a North American or Central American university or college in an earth science graduate degree program (with a geologic component). 3. The research focus can be any subject matter within the geological sciences, such as paleontology, karst, geochemistry, stratigraphy, geoscience education, petroleum geology, and more. 4. Students may receive a total of two GSA graduate student grants in their entire academic career, regardless of what program currently enrolled in.

Level of Study: Postgraduate

Type: Award

Country of Study: Any country

Application Procedure: The s are Available at www.geosociety.org/gradgrants

Closing Date: 1 February

Additional Information: community.geosociety.org/qggdivision/awards/mackin

For further information contact:

Geological Society of America, P.O. Box 9140, Boulder, CO 80301-9140, United States of America.

Tel: (1) 303 357 1025

Email: researchgrants@geosociety.org

Marie Morisawa Award

Purpose: To support promising female MS and PhD graduate students pursuing a career in geomorphology

Eligibility: Female scientists in geomorphology currently enroled in a Masters or PhD program are encouraged to apply

Level of Study: Graduate, Research

Type: Fellowship

Value: US$1,000

Frequency: Annual

Country of Study: Any country

Application Procedure: The forms are available at www.geosociety.org/gradgrants

Closing Date: 1 February

No. of awards given last year: 1

Additional Information: Please check at rock.geosociety.org/qgg/M-H%20As.html community.geosociety.org/qggdivision/awards/morisawa

For further information contact:

Geological Society of America, P.O. Box 9140, Boulder, CO 80301-9140, United States of America.

Tel: (1) 303 357 1025
Email: researchgrants@geosociety.org

George A and Eliza Gardner Howard Foundation

Brown University, Box 1867, 42 Charlesfield Street, Providence, RI 02912, United States of America.

Tel: (1) 401 863 2640
Email: howard_foundation@brown.edu
Website: www.brown.edu/divisions/graduate_school/howard
Contact: Ms Susan M Clifford, Co-ordinator

The George A and Eliza Gardner Howard Foundation was established in 1952 by Nicea Howard in memory of her grandparents. Although Miss Howard had a special interest in the arts, her stated purpose was to aid the personal development of promising individuals at the crucial middle stages of their careers.

George A. and Eliza Gardner Howard Foundation

Purpose: Awards a limited number of fellowships each year for independent projects in selected fields, targeting its support specifically to early mid-career individuals, those who have achieved recognition for at least one major project. Our support is particularly intended to augment paid sabbatical leaves. In the case of independent artists or scholars, or those without paid leaves, we would expect that a Howard Fellowship would enable them to devote a substantial block of time to the proposed project. A total of eight fellowships of US$35,000 will be awarded in April 2023 for 2023–24 in the fields of Fiction, Poetry, and Playwriting and Theater Studies

Eligibility: In order to be eligible to apply for a Howard Fellowship, candidates should be able to answer "yes" to each of the following questions. If "no" is the correct answer to any of them, they are asked to explain on the application form what special circumstances might make them eligible anyway, given the requirements for a Howard Fellowship. Can your current professional status appropriately be viewed as "early mid-career" as understood by the Howard Foundation? Appropriate candidates for a Howard Fellowship should have completed their formal studies within the past five to fifteen years of the application date and should also have successfully completed at least one major project beyond degree requirements that would be sufficient for the awarding of tenure at a research institution or for achieving comparable peer recognition, e.g., through publication or exhibition. Candidates who are already nationally and internationally recognized leaders in their fields as reflected by their promotion to full professor or by comparable recognition in their fields of endeavor are not normally eligible for a Howard Fellowship. Would a Howard Fellowship provide you with time off from other responsibilities to work on your proposed project? Our support is particularly intended to augment paid sabbatical leaves. In the case of independent artists or scholars, or those without paid leaves, we would expect that a Howard Fellowship would enable them to devote a substantial block of time to the proposed project. Are you, regardless of your citizenship, currently living and working in the United States or United States of America Territories?; Does your proposed project fall within one of the fields established for this year's round of applications? Given the limits of our resources, we must adhere strictly to the fields announced each year for project proposals

Level of Study: Doctorate, Postdoctorate, Postgraduate, Postgraduate (MSc)

Type: Fellowships

Value: US$35,000

Frequency: Annual

Country of Study: United States of America

Application Procedure: Applications accepted through howardfoundation.smapply.org/

No. of awards offered: 9

Closing Date: 1 November

Funding: Foundation

No. of awards given last year: 9

No. of applicants last year: 100-300

Additional Information: www.brown.edu/howard-foundation/

For further information contact:

Brown University, Box 1867, 42 Charlesfield Street, Providence, RI 02912, United States of America.

Tel: (1) 401 863 2429
Fax: (1) 401 863 1339
Email: Howard_Foundation@brown.edu

Gerber Foundation

Novice Research Awards

Subjects: Pediatric research
Purpose: To provide funding for novice researchers studying pediatrics and related subjects
Eligibility: Organizations recognized as tax-exempt under Internal Revenue Code 501(c)(3) are eligible to apply for Foundation grants. Public governmental institutions such as universities are included in this definition. Organizations must also be determined not to be private foundations under Internal Revenue Code 509. No grants are made to individuals. With few exceptions, only organizations with principal operations in the United States and its territories are eligible for funding. Within the United States, there is no geographic limitation to the Foundation' grantmaking.
Type: Grant
Value: Max. US$20,000 in total
Frequency: Twice a year
Country of Study: Any country
Application Procedure: Apply online
Closing Date: 15 November
Additional Information: www.gerberfoundation.org/how-to-apply/

The Daniel Gerber Sr, Medallion Scholarship

Purpose: The Daniel Gerber, Sr. Medallion Scholarship is available to students graduating from select school districts in Newaygo County, Michigan. School districts include Fremont, Grant, Hesperia, Newaygo and White Cloud. GPA must be 3.71 or higher. Home schooled students within these districts are eligible.
Eligibility: 1. High school seniors graduating from Fremont HS, Grant HS, Hesperia HS, Newaygo HS, White Cloud HS, or Home School students in those areas. 2. GPA of 3.71 or above (use higher of weighted or unweighted) 3. Students planning to attend an accredited post-secondary program in the US leading to a baccalaureate or associate degree, or a vocational or technical training program leading to

a certificate. 4. Students planning to attend one of the federal military or maritime academies are not eligible. 5. Foreign exchange students are not eligible
Value: US$11,500 for post-secondary education. Scholarship may be used for tuition, books, or required course fees, tools or equipment
Country of Study: Any country
Closing Date: 28 February
Additional Information: www.gerberfoundation.org/wp-content/uploads/Medallion-Scholarship-Flyer.pdf

For further information contact:

The Gerber Foundation 231.924.3175 4747 W 48th Street, Suite 153 Fremont, MI 49412, United States of America.

The Gerber Foundation Merit Scholarship

Eligibility: 1. High school seniors graduating from select high schools in Newaygo, Muskegon, or Oceana County as indicated below: Newaygo: Fremont, Grant, Hesperia, Newaygo, White Cloud, or home-schooled students Muskegon: Holton, Muskegon, Ravenna Oceana: Hart, Pentwater, Shelby, Walkerville GPA of 2.0 - 3.70 (use higher of weighted or unweighted) Students planning to attend an accredited post-secondary program in the US leading to a baccalaureate or associate degree, or a vocational or technical training program leading to a certificate Students planning to attend one of the federal military or maritime academies are not eligible Foreign exchange students are not eligible
Value: US$2,800 for post-secondary education. Scholarship may be used for tuition, books, or required course fees, tools or equipment
Country of Study: Any country
Additional Information: www.gerberfoundation.org/wp-content/uploads/Merit-Scholarship-Flyer.pdf

For further information contact:

The Gerber Foundation 231.924.3175 4747 W 48th Street, Suite 153 Fremont, MI 49412, United States of America.

Email: tgf@gerberfoundation.org

German Academic Exchange Service (DAAD)

Dissertation Research Scholarship

Subjects: All
Purpose: Study scholarships are awarded to highly qualified graduate students to study in Germany or complete a post

graduate or Master's degree course and obtain a degree at a German university or institution

Eligibility: Research grants are awarded primarily to highly qualified doctoral candidates as well as Master's degree holders and post-doc researcher for research or a course of study and training at universities or other institutes in Germany.

Type: Research grant

Country of Study: Germany

Closing Date: 15 Novermber

Additional Information: Applicants should possess knowledge of the German language commensurate with the demands of their research project. The grant consists of a monthly maintenance allowance, international travel subsidy and health insurance www.daad.org

German Historical Institute

1607 New Hampshire Avenue North West, Washington DC 20009-2562, United States of America.

Tel: (1) 202 387 3355
Email: fellowships@ghi-dc.org
Website: www.ghi-dc.org
Contact: Bryan Hart

The German Historical Institute is an independent research institute dedicated to the promotion of historical research in the Federal Republic of Germany and the United States of America. The Institute supports and advises German and American historians and encourages co-operation between them. It is part of the foundation Deutsche Geisteswissenschaftliche Institute im Ausland (DGIA).

German Historical Institute Collaborative Research Program for Postdoctoral Scholars

Purpose: To support a research programme for postdoctoral scholars on the topic of continuity, change and globalization in postwar Germany and the United States of America

Eligibility: Open to German and United States of America postdoctoral students. Applications from women and minorities are especially encouraged

Level of Study: Postdoctorate

Type: Fellowship

Value: US$20,000–40,000, dependent on length of study

Length of Study: 6 months–1 year

Frequency: Dependent on funds available

Country of Study: United States of America

Application Procedure: Applicants must refer to the website for details

Funding: Government

Contributor: The National Endowment for Humanities

No. of awards given last year: 1

For further information contact:

Email: westermann@ghi-dc.org

GHI Fellowships at the Horner Library

Purpose: The fellowship will be awarded to PhD and M.A. students and advanced scholars without restrictions in research fields or geographical provenance.

Level of Study: Doctorate, Masters Degree

Type: Fellowship

Value: travel subsidy and an allowance of US$1,000 to US$3,500 depending on the length of the stay

Frequency: Annual

Country of Study: Any country

Application Procedure: To apply please send the following materials using the online application form or (as a single pdf). They should include 1. a project description of no more than 2,000 words, 2. curriculum vitae, 3. copies of academic degrees, 4. and one letter of reference (sent seperately to fellow ships@ghi-dc.org). Applicants may write in either English or German; we recommend that they use the language in which they are most proficient. Applicants will be notified about the outcome approximately two months after the deadline.

Closing Date: 1 March

For further information contact:

Email: hart@ghi-dc.org

Summer Seminar in Germany

Purpose: To introduce students to German handwriting of previous centuries by exposing them to a variety of German archives, familiarizing them with major research topics in German culture and history and encouraging the exchange of ideas among the next generation of United States of America scholars

Eligibility: Open to United States of America doctoral students. Applications from women and minorities are especially encouraged

Level of Study: Doctorate

Type: Scholarship

Value: All transportation and accommodations

Length of Study: 2 weeks

Frequency: Annual

Country of Study: Germany

Application Procedure: Applicants must refer to the website for details
Closing Date: 31 January
Funding: Government
No. of awards given last year: Varies
Additional Information: Questions may be directed to Elisabeth Engel at mailto: engel@ghi-dc.org

For further information contact:

Email: laurence.mcfalls@umontreal.ca

Transatlantic Doctoral Seminar in German History

Purpose: To bring together young scholars from Germany and the United States of America who are nearing completion of their doctoral degrees. It provides an opportunity to debate doctoral projects in a transatlantic setting
Eligibility: Open to doctoral students in German history at North American and European Universities. Applications from women and minorities are especially encouraged
Level of Study: Doctorate
Type: Scholarship
Value: Travel and accommodation
Length of Study: 4 days
Frequency: Annual
Country of Study: Germany
Application Procedure: Applicants must refer to the website for details
No. of awards offered: Varies
Closing Date: 15 January
Funding: Government
Contributor: German Historical Institute Washington Georgetown University
No. of awards given last year: 16
No. of applicants last year: Varies
Additional Information: Questions may be directed to Dr Richard F. Wetzell at mailto: r.wetzell@ghi-dc.org

For further information contact:

Email: mlist@ghi-dc.org

German Marshall Fund of the United States (GMF)

1744 R Street NW, Washington DC 20009, United States of America.

Tel: (1) 202 683 2650
Email: info@gmfus.org

Website: www.gmfus.org
Contact: Lea Rosenbohm, Administrative Assistant

The German Marshall Fund (GMF) of the United States is an American institution that stimulates the exchange of ideas and promotes co-operation between the United States and Europe in the spirit of the post war Marshall Plan. GMF was created in 1972 by a gift from Germany as a permanent memorial to Marshall Plan Aid.

German Marshall Fund Journalism Program

Purpose: To contribute to better reporting on transatlantic issues by both American and European journalist
Eligibility: Open to American and European journalists who have an outstanding record in reporting on foreign affairs
Level of Study: Postdoctorate, Professional development
Type: Fellowship
Value: US$2,000–25,000 and funds for travel
Frequency: Annual
Application Procedure: Applicants including a description of the proposed project, current curriculum vitae and samples of previous work must be sent
Funding: Foundation
Contributor: The German Marshall Fund

For further information contact:

Email: usoyez@gmfus.org

German Studies Association

Kalamazoo College, 1200 Academy Street, Kalamazoo, MI 49006-3295, United States of America.

Tel: (1) 269 267 7585
Email: director@thegsa.org
Website: www.thegsa.org
Contact: David E. Barclay, Executive Director

The German Studies Association (GSA) is a non-profit educational organization that promotes the research and study of Germany, Austria and Switzerland. The GSA Endowment Fund provides financial support to Association projects, the annual conference, and general operations.

Berlin Program Fellowship

Purpose: To support doctoral dissertation research as well as postdoctoral research leading to the completion of a monograph

Eligibility: Applicants for a dissertation fellowship must be full-time graduate students who have completed all coursework required for the PhD and must have achieved ABD status by the time the proposed research stay in Berlin begins. Also eligible are United States of America and Canadian PhDs who have received their doctorates within the past 2 calendar years

Level of Study: Doctorate, Postdoctorate

Type: Fellowship

Value: €1,100 per month for dissertation fellows, €1,400 per month for postdoctoral fellows

Length of Study: 10–12 months

Frequency: Annual

Study Establishment: Freie Universität Berlin

Country of Study: Germany

Application Procedure: Applicants must submit a single application packet consisting of completed application forms, a proposal, three letters of reference, language evaluation(s) and graduate school transcripts. Proposals should be no longer than 2,500 words or 10 pages, followed by a one- or two-page bibliography or bibliographic essay

Closing Date: 17 March

Contributor: Halle Foundation and the National Endowment for the Humanities

For further information contact:

Berlin Program for Advanced German and European Studies, Freie Universität Berlin, Garystrasse 45, D-14195 Berlin, Germany.

Tel: (49) 30 838 56671
Fax: (49) 30 838 56672
Email: bprogram@zedat.fu-berlin.de

Getty Foundation

1200 Getty Center Drive, Suite 800, Los Angeles, CA 90049-1685, United States of America.

Tel: (1) 310 440 7320
Email: researchgrants@getty.edu
Website: www.getty.edu/grants
Contact: Grants Administration

The J Paul Getty Trust is a privately operating foundation dedicated to the visual arts and the humanities. The Getty supports a wide range of projects that promote research in fields related to the history of art, the advancement of the understanding of art and the conservation of cultural heritage.

Conservation Guest Scholars

Purpose: The Conservation Guest Scholars Program provides an opportunity for professionals to pursue research on topics that bring new knowledge and fresh perspectives to the field of conservation.

Eligibility: Applications are welcome from researchers of all nationalities working in conservation, historic preservation, heritage science, and related fields. Applicants should have at least five years' experience and should have an established record of publications and other contributions to the field. Proposals for research that contributes to a PhD or other academic degree will not be considered.

Type: Grant

Value: Three-month residency: September to December, January to March, April to June: US$21,500 Six-month residency: September to March, January to June: US$43,000

Country of Study: Any country

Closing Date: 15 November

Additional Information: www.getty.edu/foundation/initia tives/residential/conservation_guest_scholars.html

For further information contact:

Email: gcischolars@getty.edu

Getty Pre- and Postdoctoral Fellowships and GRI-NEH Postdoctoral Fellowships

Purpose: Getty Predoctoral and Postdoctoral Fellowships are intended for emerging scholars to complete work on projects related to the Getty Research Institute's annual research theme or the African American Art History Initiative. Recipients may be in residence at the Getty Research Institute or Getty Villa, where they pursue research projects, complete their dissertations, or expand dissertation for publication.

Eligibility: Applications for Getty Pre- and Postdoctoral fellowships are welcome from scholars of all nationalities.

Level of Study: Postdoctorate

Type: Fellowship

Value: stipend of US$30,000 or stipend of US$35,000

Length of Study: 9 Months

Frequency: Annual

Country of Study: Any country

Closing Date: 1 October

Additional Information: www.getty.edu/foundation/initia tives/residential/getty_pre_postdoctoral_fellowships.html

For further information contact:

Tel: (1) 310 440 7374
Email: researchgrants@getty.edu

Getty Scholar Grants

Purpose: Getty Scholar Grants are for established scholars, or individuals who have attained distinction in their fields.
Eligibility: Applications are welcome from researchers of all nationalities who are working in the arts, humanities, or social sciences.
Type: Grant
Value: Three-month residency: September to December, January to April, April to June: US$21,500 Six-month residency: September to April, January to June: US$43,000 Nine-month residency: September to June: US$65,000
Country of Study: Any country
Closing Date: 1 October
Additional Information: www.getty.edu/foundation/initia tives/residential/getty_scholars.html

For further information contact:

Tel: (1) 310 440 7374
Email: researchgrants@getty.edu

Postdoctoral Fellowships in Conservation Science

Purpose: To provide recent PhDs in chemistry or the physical sciences with experience in the GCI's Museum Research Laboratory
Eligibility: Open to scientists of all nationalities who are interested in pursuing a career in conservation science and have received a PhD in chemistry/physical science and have excellent written and oral communication skills
Level of Study: Research
Type: Fellowship
Value: US$29,300 per year
Length of Study: 2 years
Country of Study: Any country
Application Procedure: Applicants must complete and submit an online application which includes completing an online information form, and uploading a Statement of Interest in Conservation Science, Doctoral Dissertation Abstract, Curriculum Vitae, Writing Sample, and Degree Confirmation Letter. Applicants are also required to submit two confidential letters of recommendation in support of the their application
Closing Date: November
Additional Information: The successful candidate will have a record of scientific accomplishment combined with a strong

interest in the visual arts www.getty.edu/conservation/publi cations_resources/newsletters/33_2/gcinews12.html

For further information contact:

Attn: Postdoctoral Fellowship in Conservation Science, The Getty Foundation, 1200 Getty Center Drive, Suite 800, Los Angeles, CA 90049, United States of America.

Tel: (1) 310 440 7374
Fax: (1) 310 440 7703

Ghent University

Ghent University, Campus Ufo, Rectorate, Sint-Pietersnieuwstraat 25, B-9000 Ghent, Belgium.

Tel: (32) 9 331 01 01
Email: info@ugent.be
Website: www.ugent.be/en/

The Government of Flanders awards scholarships to academically outstanding students for master programmes in Flanders and Brussels.

BOF postdoctoral fellowships

Type: Fellowship
Value: €4.000/ year.
Length of Study: 3 Years
Country of Study: Any country
Closing Date: 1 December
Additional Information: www.ugent.be/en/research/ funding/bof/postdoctoral

Master Mind Scholarships

Purpose: The Flemish Ministry of Education awards scholarships to outstanding students for Master programmes in Flanders and Brussels. The programme aims to promote Flanders and Brussels as a top study destination
Eligibility: 1. The applicant applies to take up a Master degree programme at a higher education institution in Flanders (hereafter 'Flemish host institution'). 2. The applicant should have a high standard of academic performance and/or potential. The student has a Grade Point Average of 3.5 out of 4.0 and has a good knowledge of the English language. 3. The student has to be accepted by the Host institution to be able to

receive the scholarship. Even if the Host institution's decision to accept the student is taken after the selection of the Master Mind Scholarships programme, this criterion applies. 4. All nationalities can apply. The previous degree obtained should be from a higher education institution located outside Flanders. 5. Students who are already enrolled in a Flemish higher education institution cannot apply. See the full eligibility criteria at the 2023–2024 Master Mind Scholarship Guidelines (link found below)

Level of Study: Masters Degree
Type: Scholarships
Value: Maximum scholarship of €8,200 per academic year
Frequency: Annual
Country of Study: Belgium
Application Procedure: Application procedure fully furnished at www.ugent.be/prospect/en/administration/application/application-degree
No. of awards offered: 30
Closing Date: 1 March
Additional Information: www.ugent.be/en/research/funding/devcoop/grants-scholarships/master-mind

Special Research Fund- Doctoral Scholarship

Type: Scholarship
Value: € 2.225 per month
Length of Study: 1+3 years
Country of Study: Any country
No. of awards offered: 50
Closing Date: 28 April
Contributor: United Nations University Institute on Comparative Regional Integration Studies, I-SITE Université Lille Nord-Europe, Ghent University Global Campus - South Korea
Additional Information: www.ugent.be/en/research/funding/bof/doc/docen.htm

For further information contact:

Email: BOF@UGent.be

Gilchrist Educational Trust (GET)

43 Fern Road, Storrington, Pulborough, West Sussex RH20 4LW, United Kingdom.

Tel: (44) 1903 746 723
Email: gilchrist.et@blueyonder.co.uk
Website: www.gilchristgrants.org.uk
Contact: Mrs J V Considine, Secretary

Gilchrist Educational Trust awards grants to: individuals who face unexpected financial difficulties, which may prevent completion of a degree or higher education course; organizations if it seems likely that a project for which funds to sought will fill an educational gap of an academic nature or make more widely available for a particular aspect of academic education or learning; British expeditions proposing to carry out research of a scientific nature abroad.

Gilchrist Fieldwork Award

Purpose: To fund a period of fieldwork by established scientists or academics
Eligibility: Open to teams wishing to undertake a field season of over 6 weeks in relation to one or more scientific objectives. Teams should consist of not more than 10 members, most of whom should be British and holding established positions in research departments at universities or similar establishments. The proposed research must be original and challenging, achievable within the timetable and preferably of benefit to the host country or region
Level of Study: Research
Type: Grant
Value: £15,000
Length of Study: At least 6 weeks
Frequency: Every 2 years
Country of Study: Any country
Application Procedure: Send proposal to Secretary
Closing Date: 22 February
Funding: Private
Additional Information: The award is competitive www.rgs.org/in-the-field/in-the-field-grants/research-grants/gilchrist-fieldwork-award/

For further information contact:

RGS, 1 Kensington Gore, South Kensington, London SW7 2AR, United Kingdom.

Email: grants@rgs.org

Glasgow Caledonian University

Cowcaddens Road, Glasgow G4 0BA, Scotland, United Kingdom.

Tel: (44) 1413 313 000
Contact: Ms Irene Urquhart, MBA Admissions Officer

Fulbright Awards

Purpose: The scholarships are offered by the US-UK Fulbright Commission, whose mission is to advance knowledge, promote civic engagement and develop compassionate leaders through education exchange between the peoples of the UK and US.

Eligibility: Open to students and faculty, the Fulbright Awards provide funding and support for postgraduate study or research in the United States.

Level of Study: Postgraduate

Type: Award

Value: Up to US$45,000

Country of Study: Any country

Closing Date: November

Additional Information: www.gcu.ac.uk/study/scholarships/travelscholarships/fulbrightawardprogramme/

Glasgow School for Business and Society Postgraduate EU scholarships for MSc International Fashion Marketing

Purpose: This scholarship scheme is for Postgraduate EU students studying MSc International Fashion Marketing as a new student in academic year 2023–24 who are classified as international students for fees purposes.

Eligibility: 1. These scholarships are restricted to EU applicants who are classified as international students for fees purposes. 2. Applicants must be ordinarily resident in an EU country. 3. Applicants must be entirely self-funded. 4. Applicants must be starting their first year of study on an postgraduate degree course at GCU in September 2023 5. Only one scholarship award can be made per student and the award will not be carried over if you defer studies to another academic year 6. Successful applicants should be available for promotional activities.

Level of Study: Postgraduate

Type: Scholarship

Value: £7,500

Frequency: Annual

Country of Study: Any country

Application Procedure: Apply online

Closing Date: 1 August

Glasgow School for Business and Society Scholarship

Purpose: Glasgow School for Business and Society (GSBS) are delighted to introduce new partially funded scholarships. For a wide range of our postgraduate full-time degrees we can offer support with the cost of tuition fees

Eligibility: You must meet the following criteria to be eligible to apply for the scholarship; 1. A permanent resident of Scotland for at least 3 years 2. An EU national or a student from England, Northern Ireland, Wales residing in your own country for 3 years prior to the start of the programme. The partial cost of tuition fees will be covered for eligible students who are successful in gaining an award on the specified programme for one academic year only. Funding is not available for part-time or distance learning versions of these programmes. Awards are non-transferable.

Level of Study: Postgraduate

Type: Scholarship

Value: £3,000 towards tuition fees.

Frequency: Annual

Country of Study: Any country

Application Procedure: Apply online

Closing Date: 7 January

GREAT Scholarships

Purpose: GREAT Scholarships are jointly funded by Glasgow Caledonian University with the UK government's GREAT Britain campaign and the British Council.

Eligibility: At GCU, the Scholarships will be awarded to nationals and residents of Egypt and Nepal who are accepted for admission on a full-time basis for an eligible one-year on campus postgraduate Masters programme of study.

Type: Scholarship

Value: £10,000

Length of Study: 1 year

Frequency: Annual

Country of Study: Any country

No. of awards offered: 3

Closing Date: 1 May

Contributor: UK government's GREAT Britain campaign and the British Council.

Additional Information: www.gcu.ac.uk/study/scholarships/postgraduate/greatscholarships2022-23/

For further information contact:

Tel: (44) 141 331 8770

Email: scholarships@gcu.ac.uk.

Magnusson Awards

Eligibility: GCU students in their second year and upwards and early career researchers

Type: Award

Value: £5,000

Country of Study: Any country

Closing Date: 14 February

Contributor: Sir Alex Ferguson and Santander

Master of Public Health Scholarship

Purpose: The scholarship associated with this programme offers full-time International students funding towards their tuition fees for the Masters

Eligibility: Any International fee paying student who has applied for the full time Master of Public Health programme at GCU Glasgow Campus

Length of Study: £4,500

Country of Study: Any country

Application Procedure: Apply online

Closing Date: 15 November

Additional Information: Scholarships will not be deferred to another academic session. www.rgs.org/in-the-field/in-the-field-grants/research-grants/gilchrist-fieldwork-award/

For further information contact:

Tel: (44) 141 331 8770

Email: scholarships@gcu.ac.uk

MSc International Fashion Marketing Scholarship

Purpose: This scholarship scheme is for postgraduate students studying MSc International Fashion Marketing as a new student in academic year 2023–24 who are classified as international students for fees purposes.

Eligibility: These scholarships are restricted to International and EU applicants who are classified as international students for fees purposes. Applicants must be ordinarily resident in an EU or International country. Applicants must be entirely self-funded. Applicants must be starting their first year of study on an postgraduate degree course at GCU in September 2023 Only one scholarship award can be made per student and the award will not be carried over if you defer studies to another academic year Successful applicants should be available for promotional activities.

Type: Scholarship

Value: £7,500

Country of Study: Any country

No. of awards offered: 5

Closing Date: 5 December

Additional Information: www.gcu.ac.uk/study/scholar ships/postgraduate/gsbseumscintfashionmarketing/

Postgraduate Ambassador Studentship

Purpose: Glasgow Caledonian is the University for the Common Good. Our mission is to make a positive difference to the communities we serve and this is at the heart of all we do, especially in our social innovation teaching and research.

Eligibility: 1. Must hold an offer of study with GCU before applying or the application will be rejected. 2. You must be able to cover your living costs in line with the UKVI requirements when applying for a Visa. 3. All awards are non-transferable to any other programme or academic session if you are awarded the scholarship. 4. Only applicants on a Full Time Taught Postgraduate Masters course are eligible to apply. 5. No late applications will be accepted. 6. Video Link must be submitted or application will be automatically be rejected.

Level of Study: Postgraduate

Type: Scholarship

Value: Full tuition fee Scholarship up to £15,000

Country of Study: Any country

Closing Date: 1 June

For further information contact:

Email: scholarships@gcu.ac.uk

Scotland's Saltire Scholarships

Purpose: These scholarships are supported and funded by the Scottish Government in partnership with Glasgow Caledonian University

Eligibility: Further information on the eligibility criteria and application process for the Scotland's Saltire Scholarships Scheme is available on the Study in Scotland website.

Level of Study: Doctorate

Value: £8,000 Tuition fee

Length of Study: one academic year

Frequency: Annual

Country of Study: Any country

Closing Date: 28 May

Funding: Private

For further information contact:

Email: scholarships@gcu.ac.uk

ScottishPower Masters Scholarships

Purpose: ScottishPower will provide scholarships for the academic year for postgraduate studies at universities in the United Kingdom

Eligibility: Students who are looking to study the following areas of knowledge 1. Electrical/Mechanical/Civil Engineering. 2. Renewable/Sustainable Energy. 3. Onshore/Offshore Renewable Engineering. 4. Environmental Sciences /Climate Change. 5. Global Energy Management

Level of Study: Postgraduate

Type: Scholarship

Value: £1,200 per month

Frequency: Annual

Country of Study: Any country

Application Procedure: ScottishPower are looking for each scholar to 1. Promote career opportunities available within the company. 2. Act as a STEM ambassador for the industry. 3. Introduce future scholarship applicants to the scheme

Closing Date: 29 March

Funding: Private

Additional Information: Kindly access the below link for processing the application. www.iberdrola.com/people-talent/international-scholarships-master-iberdrola/apply-scholarships-access www.scottishpower.com/pages/scottishpower_mas ters_scholarships.aspx

For further information contact:

Glasgow Caledonian University, Cowcaddens Road, Glasgow G4 0BA, Scotland, United Kingdom.

Email:　ukroenquiries@gcu.ac.uk

Goethe-Institut

Kundenmanagement, Goethestrasse 20, D-80336 München, Germany.

Tel:　　　　(49) 89 159 21200
Email:　　deutsch@goethe.de
Contact:　Goethe-Institut

The Goethe-Institut is a non-profit German cultural association operational worldwide with 159 institutes, promoting the study of the German language abroad and encouraging international cultural exchange and relations.

Goethe-Institut Postdoctoral Fellowship for International Students

Purpose: The aim of the fellowship is to support promising and exceptional scholar for one academic year and shall concentrate on the research for a comprehensive exhibition project on the global art historical developments of the Postcolonial era covering the period 1955–1980

Eligibility: International applicants are eligible to apply for the fellowship. Applicants must have a doctorate degree in art history, museum studies or related fields. Applicants must be fluent in English

Type: Postdoctoral fellowship

Value: An overall remuneration package of €30.000 for the entire year. This includes any health care and tax payments. Accommodation is the responsibility of the successful candidate. Haus der Kunst will provide supplementary support to the scholar for accommodation in the amount of €300 per month. Haus der Kunst will support the fellow in organizing administrational paperwork such as limited residency, work permit, etc. Fellow will be provided with work area and full access to the infrastructure of Haus der Kunst and facilities in Munich

Frequency: Annual

Study Establishment: Fellowship is awarded for scholars whose research focuses on global perspectives on modern and contemporary art in the second half of the 20th century and the 21st century

Country of Study: Any country

Application Procedure: Interested scholars are invited to send their application via email. The application should be in English and include a Curriculum Vitae, bibliography, reference letters and a cover letter explaining the motivation for the application

Closing Date: 14 January

For further information contact:

Email:　kredler@hausderkunst.de

Google Sydney

Google Headquarters, Google Inc., 1600 Amphitheatre Parkway, Mountain View, CA 94043, United States of America.

Tel:　　　　(1) 650 253 0000
Website:　www.google.com

Google is a public and profitable company focused on search services. Google operates web sites at many international domains. Google is widely recognized as the "world's best search engine" because it is fast, accurate and easy to use. The company also serves corporate clients, including advertisers, content publishers and site managers with cost–effective advertising and a wide range of revenue generating search services. Google's breakthrough technology and continued innovation serve the company's mission of "organizing the world's information and making it universally accessible and useful".

Lionel Murphy Endowment Postgraduate Scholarship

Purpose: A number of Australian and overseas postgraduate scholarships are awarded annually by the Lionel Murphy Foundation Endowment. These scholarships are known as the Lionel Murphy Endowment Postgraduate Scholarship. The number of scholarships awarded each year, and the method of payment, is recommended by the Advisory Committee.

Eligibility: This scholarship is applicable for candidates having the preference to study in any of the following areas. 1. The law and the legal system in a social context and their practical application; 2. Science and/or the law as a means of attaining social justice and human rights and as vehicles for change; 3. International law as a developing force for peace and as a means of achieving the rule of law in all nations. 4. Science as a tool for social benefit, particularly in meeting the needs of those most disadvantaged within society 5. Other disciplines, where the proposed nature and area of study are likely to promote the goals of social justice and benefit for the disadvantaged

Level of Study: Postgraduate

Type: Scholarship

Value: AU$40,000 each per annum

Length of Study: 1 year

Frequency: Annual

Country of Study: Australia

Application Procedure: Check the website online. lionelmurphy.law.anu.edu.au/postgraduate-scholarship

Closing Date: 30 November

Funding: Private

For further information contact:

Lionel Murphy Foundation Endowment, c/- Secretariat Coordinator, ANU College of Law, Australian National University, Canberra, ACT 2601, Australia.

Email: lionelmurphy.law@anu.edu.au

Government of the Punjab

The Punjab Educational Endowment Fund

Eligibility: 1. Valid PhD admission offer from one of the Top 50 (Subject Wise) Universities of the World (QS ranking) in preferred subject areas. 2. Not less than 60% marks throughout the academic career. 3. Declared monthly family income (including self, spouse and parents) is equal to or less than PKR. 20,000/. 4. Maximum age of 35 years at the time of submission of application. 5. Not availed any foreign scholarship in the past. 6. Must take up the scholarship in the year for which it is offered and the scholarship shall not be deferred to the next year. 7. All Pakistani nationals, both males and females are eligible to apply

Level of Study: Postgraduate

Type: Award

Frequency: Annual

Country of Study: Any country

Closing Date: 22 April

Funding: International office

Additional Information: www.peef.org.pk/update.html

Graduate Fellowships for Science, Technology, Engineering, and Mathematics Diversity

Graduate Fellowships for Science, Technology, Engineering, and Mathematics Diversity

Subjects: Astronomy, Chemistry, Computer Science, Geology, Materials Science, Mathematical Sciences, Physics, and their subdisciplines, and related engineering fields Chemical, Computer, Electrical, Environmental, Mechanical.

Purpose: GFSD's goal is to increase the number of American citizens with graduate degrees in STEM fields, emphasizing recruitment of a diverse applicant pool.

Eligibility: Any qualified U.S. citizen who has the ability to pursue graduate work at an GFSD univresity associate. Applicants at any stage of their graduate program may apply, as long as they will be available to accept two summers of paid internship. Those who already possess a doctoral degree are ineligible.

Type: Fellowship

Value: US$27,000 annually, of which US$20,000 is the fellow's expense allowance and US$7,000 is GFSD's fee to support its operations. The charge is subject to change at the discretion of the GFSD Board of Directors.

Length of Study: Initial support may be for two or three years, or for a full six years, depending on the employer-sponsor.

Frequency: Annual

Country of Study: United States of America

No. of awards offered: Varies yearly

Closing Date: December

Additional Information: Applicants must be accepted at a participating GFSD-member university or college and progress through a full-time study program leading to a graduate degree in the physical sciences or related engineering fields. Fellows must complete one or two summer internships, as the sponsoring employer requires. To continue in good standing, fellows must submit a transcript annually as well as any forms and information that GFSD requests. Fellows must perform satisfactorily in their summer internship and during the academic year. A fellow who switches his or her field of study to one not of interest to the sponsoring employer will likely have support terminated. stemfellowships.org/fellows/

Greek Ministry of National Education and Religious Affairs

Greek Ministry of Education and Religious Affairs, Cultural and Sport, Directorate of International Relations in Education, GR-15180 Maroussi, Greece.

Tel:	(30) 2103442469, 2103443129
Email:	des-a@minedu.gov.gr
Website:	www.minedu.gov.gr
Contact:	Directorate General of European and International Affairs

The Ministry's department of scholarships grants exclusively scholarships to students and PhD holders from developing countries through the OECD's D.A.C.

Scholarships for a Summer Seminar in Greek Language and Culture

Purpose: To allow nationals from the Balkans, Eastern Europe, Asia and Africa to study Greek language

Eligibility: Applicants must be nationals of Albania, Armenia, Azerbaijan, Bosnia & Herzegovina, China, Egypt, Ethiopia, FYROM, Georgia, India, Indonesia, Iran, Iraq, Jordan, Kazakhstan, Korea, Lebanon, Moldove, Montenegro, Mongolia, Pakistan, Palestine, Russia, Serbia, Sudan, Syria, Thailand, Tunisia, Turkey, Ukraine, or Uzbekistan. Applicants should be foreign students/foreign professors of, Greek languages, or even foreign students/foreign professors of different fields who wish to improve their level of Greek language

Type: Scholarship

Value: The scholarships covers accomodation, meals, tuition fees, small personal expenses, in case of an emergency medical care, visits to archaeological sites, museums, as well as instructive material

Frequency: Dependent on funds available

Country of Study: Greece

Funding: Government

For further information contact:

Email: foreigners@iky.gr

Scholarships Granted by the GR Government to Foreign Citizens

Purpose: To support candidates who wish to study or conduct research project in Greek Universities, or summer seminars of Greek language and culture, postgraduate studies

Eligibility: Applicants must be nationals of China, Belgium, Bulgary France, Germany, Serbia, Syria, Turkey. Applicants should have an excellent knowledge of Greek or French or English language. Applicant must be of foreign nationality of Estonia, Israel, Croatia, Cyprus, Luxembourg, Mexico, Norway, Netherlands, Hungary, Poland, Romania, Slovakia, Slovenia, Czech Republic, and Finland

Level of Study: Doctorate, Graduate, MBA, Postdoctorate, Postgraduate, Predoctorate, Research

Type: Scholarship

Value: €550 per month, €500 lump sum for establishment expenses, €150 for transport expenses, exemption from tuition fees (only in selected master's degree) plus all expenses for summer seminars except travel expenses

Length of Study: Varies

Frequency: Annual

Study Establishment: Greek public universities

Country of Study: Greece

Application Procedure: Check with Ministry of Education or Ministry of Foreign Affairs in Individual country. Applicants must apply through their home countries. Find out about deadlines of their own countries but also refer to the website

No. of awards offered: 60

Closing Date: 31 March

Funding: Government

Contributor: Greek Ministry of Education and Religious Affairs, Culture and Sport

No. of awards given last year: 40

No. of applicants last year: 60

Additional Information: Information about eligible countries, number of scholarships and the way to apply is renewed every year and candidates can find next year's decision by the end of December at www.minedu.gov.gr

For further information contact:

Directorate of Studies and Student's Welfare, Greece.

Tel:	(30) 2103443469, 2103443451
Email:	foitmer.yp@minedu.gov.gr

Griffith University

Griffith University, Nathan Campus, 170 Kessels Road, Nathan, QLD 4111, Australia.

Tel:	(61) 7 3735 3870
Email:	scholarships@griffith.edu.au
Website:	www.gu.edu.au

In the pursuit of excellence in teaching, research and community service, Griffith University is committed to innovation, bringing disciplines together, internationalization, equity and social justice and lifelong learning, for the enrichment of Queensland, Australia and the international community.

Griffith Remarkable Scholarship

Eligibility: 1. Be a citizen of a country other than Australia or New Zealand. 2. Have a minimum GPA in previous studies of 5.5 or above on a 7 point scale or equivalent. Check your suitability in the Minimum GPA criteria (PDF). 3. Have applied to study at Griffith by the scholarship application closing date. 4. Satisfy all academic and English language entry requirements for your chosen undergraduate or postgraduate coursework program. 5. Be a full-time student starting in Trimester 1, 2 or 3 2021.
Level of Study: Postgraduate
Value: 50% of tuition fees
Frequency: Annual
Country of Study: Any country
Closing Date: 6 August

International Student Academic Excellence Scholarship

Eligibility: 1. Be a citizen of a country other than Australia or New Zealand. 2. Have a minimum GPA in previous studies of 5.5 or above on a 7 point scale or equivalent. Check your suitability in the Minimum GPA criteria (PDF). 3. Satisfy all academic and English language entry requirements for your chosen undergraduate or postgraduate coursework program. 4. Be a full-time student starting in either Trimester 3 2020, or Trimester 1, 2 or 3 2021.
Level of Study: Postgraduate
Type: Scholarship
Value: 25% of tuition fees
Frequency: Annual
Country of Study: Any country

International Student Academic Merit Scholarship

Eligibility: 1. Be a citizen of a country other than Australia or New Zealand. 2. Have a minimum GPA in previous studies of 5.0 to 5.49 on a 7 point scale or equivalent. Check your suitability in the Minimum GPA criteria (PDF). 3. Satisfy all academic and English language entry requirements for your chosen undergraduate or postgraduate coursework program. 4. Be a full-time student starting in either Trimester 3 2020, or Trimester 1, 2 or 3 2021.
Level of Study: Postgraduate
Type: Scholarship
Value: 20% of tuition fees

Frequency: Annual
Country of Study: Any country

Master of Business Administration Programme

Length of Study: 1–3 years
Country of Study: Any country
Application Procedure: Applicants must complete an application form supplying Australian AU$50 fee, official transcripts, and TOEFL score

For further information contact:

Tel: (61) 7 3875 7111
Fax: (61) 7 3875 3900
Email: gsm_enquiry@gsm.gu.edu.au

PhD Scholarship in Water Resources Management in Remote Indigenous Communities

Purpose: To utilize smart meters and loggers to gauge the degree of water savings attributable to the execution of various water conservation strategies
Eligibility: Open only to the citizens of Australia or New Zealand or permanent residents who have achieved Honours 1 or equivalent, Honours 2a or equivalent, or Masters or equivalent
Level of Study: Graduate, Postgraduate
Type: Scholarship
Value: The scholarship has an annual tax-free stipend of AU$30,000–35,000 per year
Frequency: Annual
Study Establishment: Griffith University
Country of Study: Australia
Application Procedure: Applicants must apply directly to the scholarship provider. Check the website for further details
Closing Date: 23 October

For further information contact:

Tel: (61) 7 3735 6596
Email: M.Mitchell@griffith.edu.au

Gypsy Lore Society

5607 Greenleaf Road, Cheverly, MD 20785, United States of America.

Tel: (1) 301 341 1261
Email: headquarters@gypsyloresociety.org
Website: www.gypsyloresociety.org
Contact: Ms Sheila Salo, Treasurer

The Gypsy Lore Society, an international association of persons interested in Gypsy Studies, was formed in the United Kingdom in 1888. The Gypsy Lore Society, North American Chapter, was founded in 1977 in the United States of America and since 1989, has continued as the Gypsy Lore Society. The Society's goals include the promotion of the study of the Gypsy peoples and analogous itinerant or nomadic groups, dissemination of information aimed at increasing understanding of Gypsy culture in its diverse forms and establishment of closer contacts among Gypsy scholars.

Marian Madison Gypsy Lore Society Young Scholar's Prize

Purpose: To recognize outstanding work by young scholars in Romani (Gypsy) studies

Eligibility: Graduate students beyond the 1st year of study and PhD holders no more than 3 years beyond the degree. An unpublished paper not under consideration for publication is eligible for this award as well as self-contained scholarly articles of publishable quality that treat a relevant topic in an interesting and insightful way

Level of Study: Doctorate, Graduate, Postdoctorate
Type: Cash prize
Value: US$500
Study Establishment: Any
Country of Study: Any country
Application Procedure: Submission file format is rich text file (RTF, PDF, MS word compatible). Files bigger than 5 MB should be presented on CD to the postal address below. A cover sheet should be included with the title of the paper, the author's name, affiliation, mailing, email address, telephone and fax number, date of entrance into an appropriate program or of awarding of the PhD, and United States of America social security number, if the author has one. The applicant's name should appear on the cover sheet only
Closing Date: 15 January
Funding: Corporation
Contributor: Gypsy Lore Society
Additional Information: www.gypsyloresociety.org/gypsy-lore-society-young-scholars-prize

For further information contact:

Email: szahova@yahoo.com

H

Hague University of Applied Sciences

Johanna Westerdijkplein 75, NL-2521 EN Den Haag, the Netherlands.

Tel: (31) 70 445 88 88
Website: www.thehagueuniversity.com/

Let's change. You. Us. The world. That's our message at The Hague University of Applied Sciences (THUAS). We want to empower our students to change and improve the world they live in, but this can only happen if we work together – if we evolve and change. We constantly need to apply new perspectives and solutions to resolve present and future challenges. We'll find the answers more quickly if we're prepared to share and apply each other's insights, skills and methods.

Holland Scholarship

Purpose: Holland Scholarship financed by the Dutch Ministry of Education, Culture and Science and Dutch universities.
Eligibility: www.thehagueuniversity.com/study-choice/applications-finances-and-moving-here/finance/finance-your-study
Type: Scholarship
Value: €5,000
Country of Study: Any country
Closing Date: 1 June
Contributor: Dutch Ministry of Education, Culture and Science and Dutch universities
Additional Information: www.thehagueuniversity.com/study-choice/applications-finances-and-moving-here/finance/finance-your-study

For further information contact:

Fax: (31)70 445 88 25
Email: talentscholarship@hhs.nl

Susana Menendez Bright Future Scholarship

Purpose: 'Bright Future Scholarship' is a full scholarship opportunity for Dutch asylum status holders
Level of Study: Masters Degree
Value: full tuition fee
Country of Study: Any country
Application Procedure: Step 1. Apply for the Master's programme of your choice using the online application tool. Step 2. Write an essay (in English, 900 to 1100 words) outlining in what ways you intend to be an impactful innovator. What would you like to contribute to creating a better world with your degree? Please read our essay guidelines and further information on the assessment procedure below before you start writing. Step 3. Submit your essay by emailing it to masters-admission@hhs.nl. Please write 'BFS' in the subject line and state your student number in the essay. Step 4. If you are required to take a PPS-V test, we will provide you with more information.
Closing Date: 15 May

For further information contact:

Tel: (31) 70 445 8900
Email: masters-admission@hhs.nl

World Citizen Talent Scholarship for International Students

Purpose: Each year, a maximum of three (one-time) scholarships each worth €5,000 are available to prospective master's degree students. The University is seeking young, intelligent, talented and ambitious people who view themselves as citizens of the world.
Eligibility: You are eligible for a World Citizen Talent Scholarship if you 1. Come from outside The Netherlands and don't live in the Netherlands. 2. Are enrolling for the first time at

The Hague University of Applied Sciences. 3. Have never applied for this scholarship before. 4. Have been conditionally accepted as a student (also-called offer of student position) on or before 31 March for the upcoming academic year.

Level of Study: Masters Degree

Type: Scholarships

Value: €5,000

Frequency: Annual

Country of Study: the Netherlands

Application Procedure: To apply for the scholarship, you must first apply to the Master programme of your choice and write an essay following the essay guidelines. Submit your essay by completing the scholarship application form between 1 November–31 March. It is important to visit the official website to access the application form and for detailed information on how to apply for this scholarship.

No. of awards offered: 3

Closing Date: 31 March

Additional Information: www.thehagueuniversity.com/study-choice/masters-professional-courses/scholarships/world-citizen-talent-scholarship

For further information contact:

Email: masters-admission@hhs.nl

Harish-Chandra Research Institute

Chhatnag Road, Jhusi, Allahabad, Uttar Pradesh 211019, India.

Tel: (91) 532 256 9509

Contact: The Harish-Chandra Research Institute

The Institute started in 1975, on an endowment from the B.S. Mehta Trust, Calcutta. Indeed, until October, 2001, the Institute was named the Mehta Research Institute.

Postdoctoral Fellowships in Mathematics at Harish-Chandra Research Institute

Purpose: The Harish-Chandra Research Institute (HRI) welcomes applications to its active post-doctoral programme in mathematics. Post-doctoral fellows at HRI have the opportunity to work with the members of the mathematics group in diverse areas including Number Theory, Cryptography, Group Theory, Representation Theory, Harmonic Analysis, Algebraic Geometry and Differential Geometry.

Eligibility: Covering letter, Curriculum Vitae, List of publications, A list of referees, A research plan for the next two years, PhD degree/Provisional certificate, if available, Document showing prior PDF experience, if any.

Type: Postdoctoral fellowship

Length of Study: Three years

Country of Study: Any country

Closing Date: 28 February

Additional Information: www.hri.res.in/academics/mathematics/pdf-fellowships/

For further information contact:

Email: physvisit@hri.res.in

Postdoctoral Fellowships in Physics at Harish-Chandra Research Institute

Purpose: The aim of the fellowships is to support Indian students and provide opportunities to researchers working in Astrophysics, Condensed Matter Physics, High Energy Phenomenology, Quantum Information & Computing, and String Theory

Eligibility: Applicants from India are eligible to apply for the fellowship. Applicants must be researchers

Type: Postdoctoral fellowship

Value: HRI offers opportunities to researchers working in Astrophysics, Condensed matter physics, High energy phenomenology, Quantum information & computing, and String theory

Study Establishment: Fellowships are awarded in the field of Physics

Country of Study: India

Application Procedure: See the website

Closing Date: 30 June

Additional Information: For more details please visit the website at scholarship-positions.com/postdoctoral-fellowships-physics-harish-chandra-research-institute-india/2017/12/26/ www.hri.res.in/academics/physics/pdf-fellowships/

For further information contact:

Coordinator (Postdoctoral Programme, Physics), Harish-Chandra Research Institute, Chhatnag Road, Jhunsi, Prayagraj (Allahabad) 211 019, India.

Email: physvisit@hri.res.in

Harpo Foundation

Tel: (1) 757 735 4269

Website: www.harpofoundation.org/

The Harpo Foundation was established in 2006 by artist Ed Levine to support emerging and under recognized visual artists. Through grants and residency programs, the foundation seeks to stimulate creative inquiry and encourage new modes of making and thinking about art.

Harpo Foundation Grants for Visual Artists

Subjects: Visual Arts
Purpose: The award provides direct support to under-recognized artists
Eligibility: 1. Self-defined under-recognized visual artist 21 years or older 2. United States citizen 3. Students who are enrolled in an undergraduate/graduate program are not eligible. 4. Not a previous recipient of a direct artist grant from Harpo. 5. Artists who have been supported by an organizational grant from Harpo in the past are eligible to apply for a direct grant.
Level of Study: Professional development
Type: Grant
Value: Up to US$10,000
Length of Study: 10-months
Frequency: Annual
Country of Study: United States of America
Application Procedure: To apply, a US$15 application fee is required. Fees are applied to grant administration and program development. Applicants must use the foundation's online application system to submit the following 1. Artist resume 2. Artist statement (up to 200 words) 3. Work samples (up to 10)
Closing Date: 29 April
Funding: Foundation
Additional Information: www.harpofoundation.org/apply/grants-for-visual-artists/

For further information contact:

Email: mwest@harpofoundation.org

New Work Projects Grants

Purpose: New Work Projects Grants are made to Non-Profit Organizations in support of new work by under-recognized artist
Eligibility: For Eligibility Information visit www.harpofoundation.org/grants/new-work-project-grants/
Type: Grant
Value: US$10000
Length of Study: 10 Months
Country of Study: Any country
Closing Date: 22 April

Additional Information: www.harpofoundation.org/grants/new-work-project-grants/

Harry S Truman Library Institute

5151 Troost Ave., Suite 300, Kansas City, MO 64110, United States of America.

Tel:	(1) 816 400 1212
Email:	truman.reference@nara.gov
Website:	www.trumanlibrary.org

The Harry S Truman Library Institute is a non-profit partner of the Harry S Truman Library. The institute's purpose is to foster the Truman Library as a centre for research and as a provider of educational and public programmes.

Harry S Truman Library Institute Dissertation Year Fellowships

Purpose: Dissertation Year Fellowships are intended to encourage historical scholarship of the public career of Harry S. Truman or the Truman era.
Eligibility: 1. Must be a graduate student 2. Must attend a university 3. Must not be attending high school currently 4. Must study full-time
Level of Study: Graduate, Postgraduate
Type: Fellowship
Value: US$16,000
Length of Study: 1 year
Frequency: Annual
Country of Study: United States of America
Application Procedure: Application forms are available from the website
Closing Date: 1 February
Funding: Private
No. of awards given last year: 2
Additional Information: Recipients will not be required to come to the Truman Library but will be expected to furnish the Library with a copy of their dissertation www.trumanlibraryinstitute.org/research-grants/dissertation-year-fellowships/

For further information contact:

Truman Library Institute, 5151 Troost Avenue, Suite 300, Kansas City, MO 64110, United States of America.

Tel:	(1) 816 400 1216
Fax:	(1) 816 268 8299
Email:	Lisa.Sullivan@TrumanLibraryInstitute.org

Harry S Truman Library Institute Research Grant

Purpose: As part of our mission, Truman Library Institute grants are given for the purpose of supporting scholarship based on some aspect of the life and career of Harry S. Truman or of the public and foreign policy issues which were prominent during the Truman administration

Eligibility: 1. Must be a graduate student or a postgraduate student 2. Must attend a university or a four-year college 3. Must not be attending high school currently 4. Must study full-time 5. Restricted to students studying History, Political Science, Women's Studies

Level of Study: Research

Type: Research grant

Value: US$2,500 are awarded twice annually

Length of Study: 1-3 weeks

Frequency: Twice a year

Country of Study: Unrestricted

Application Procedure: Competitive proposals will evidence a clear understanding of the existing research in the field and how the proposed work adds significantly to that body of literature. Applicants are expected to demonstrate both an analytical and descriptive grasp of the project and its centrality to the Truman era. Application packages must include the following completed Research Grant application; curriculum vitae (3 pages, maximum); project description and justification (5 pages, maximum); a list of specific files the candidate expects to access at the Harry S. Truman Library and Museum; and two letters of reference from persons familiar with the applicant's scholarly work, including one from the project advisor, if candidate is a graduate or postdoctoral student. Letters must be received by the deadline and mailed or emailed directly to the Grants Administrator by the referring individual

No. of awards offered: 25

Closing Date: 1 April

Funding: Foundation

No. of awards given last year: 15

No. of applicants last year: 25

Additional Information: Please visit www.trumanlibraryinstitute.org/research-grants/research-grants/

For further information contact:

Truman Library Institute, 5151 Troost Avenue, Suite 300, Kansas City, MO 64110, United States of America.

Tel: (1) 816 400 1216
Fax: (1) 816 400 1213
Email: Lisa.Sullivan@TrumanLibraryInstitute.org

Harry S Truman Library Institute Scholar's Award

Eligibility: 1. Must be a postgraduate student 2. Must attend a university 3. Must not be attending high school currently 4. Must study full-time 5. Restricted to students studying History, Political Science, Women's Studies

Level of Study: Postdoctorate

Type: Award

Value: US$30,000

Application Procedure: Please check at trumanlibraryinstitute.org/research-grants/scholars-award

Closing Date: 15 December

Funding: Private

Additional Information: www.trumanlibraryinstitute.org/research-grants/scholars-award/

For further information contact:

Truman Library Institute, 5151 Troost Avenue, Suite 300, Kansas City, MO 64110, United States of America.

Tel: (1) 816 400 1216
Fax: (1) 816 400 1213
Email: Lisa.Sullivan@TrumanLibraryInstitute.org

HARRY S. TRUMAN BOOK AWARD

Purpose: The Harry S. Truman Book Award is presented biennially by the Truman Library Institute. Established in 1963, the Harry S. Truman Book Award recognizes the best book published within a two-year period dealing primarily and substantially with some aspect of the history of the United States between April 12, 1945 and January 20, 1953, or with the life or career of Harry S. Truman.

Type: Award

Country of Study: Any country

Closing Date: 20 January

Additional Information: www.trumanlibraryinstitute.org/research-grants/bookaward/

For further information contact:

Tel: (1) 816 400 1216
Email: Lisa.Sullivan@TrumanLibraryInstitute.org

Harvard Business School

Soldiers Field, Boston, MA 02163, United States of America.

Tel: (1) 617 495 6555
Email: executive_education@hbs.edu

Harvard University Master of Business Administration Scholarship in the United States of America

Subjects: Business Administration
Purpose: Harvard MBA has been taught at one of the most prestigious universities in the world as one of the world's leading management programs. Once every two years, the Boustany MBA Harvard Bursary is awarded for a two-year program at Harvard Business School.
Eligibility: Candidates need an excellent academic background and a significant commitment. Even if the bursary can be granted to candidates from any country, the candidates from Lebanese origins will receive priority. Only upon receipt of an admission offer under the Harvard MBA program can applicants apply for a scholarship. During their Internship, students are required to work on a project which relates to one of the objectives of the Foundation. Students may also be required to work during their Internship with one of our partners.
Type: Scholarship
Value: US$95,000 (US$47,500 per year) towards tuition fees
Length of Study: Two years
Frequency: Every 2 years
Study Establishment: Harvard University
Country of Study: United States of America
Application Procedure: Send your copy of your curriculum vitae to admissions@boustany-foundation.org with a photograph, GMAT scores, and acceptance letter from the University.

Harvard Travellers Club

PO Box 190, Canton, MA 02021, United States of America.

Tel: (1) 781 821 0400
Email: gpbdtes@shieldpdckdging.com
Website: www.travellersfund.org
Contact: George Bates

Harvard Travellers Club Permanent Fund

Subjects: Geography, Humanities & Social Science, Anthropology & Cultural Studies, Education Science, Health & Medicine.
Purpose: To support research involving travel from which results can be obtained of permanent scientific and educational value
Eligibility: 1. Must be an undergraduate student, a graduate student or a postgraduate student 2. Must attend a university or a four-year college 3. Must be at least 18 years old 4. Both full-time and part-time students
Level of Study: Doctorate, Graduate, Postdoctorate, Postgraduate, Predoctorate, Research, Unrestricted
Type: Grant
Value: $10,000
Frequency: Annual
Country of Study: Worldwide
Application Procedure: Please check website for all details
Closing Date: 28 February
Funding: Trusts
Contributor: Club membership contributions (no major contributor)
Additional Information: www.petersons.com/scholarship/harvard-travellers-club-permanent-fund-111_151392.aspx

For further information contact:

170 Hubbard St., Lenox, MA 01240, United States of America.

Email: Jackdeary@harvardtravellersclub.org

Health Canada

Applied Research & Analysis Directorate, Analysis & Connectivity Branch, 15th Floor, Jeanne Mance Building, Tunney's Pasture, Ottawa, ON K1A 1B4, Canada.

Tel: (1) 613 954 8549
Email: nhrdpinfo@isdicp3.hwc.ca
Website: www.hc-sc.gc.ca
Contact: Information & Resource Officer

The National Health Research and Development Programme (NHRDP) funds research with scientific merit to support the Federal Department of Health's mission and national health priorities, and researchers whose work will contribute to policy development and strategic planning. In general, the NHRDP funds research that relates to issues of concern to the federal government and to those that may be of concern to provincial and territorial health ministries pertaining to the health system and the promotion of population health.

MSc Fellowships and PhD Fellowships

Purpose: To provide support to highly qualified students who wish to undertake full-time research training leading to an MSc degree (or equivalent) or a PhD degree (or equivalent)

Eligibility: 1. Must be an undergraduate student, a graduate student or a postgraduate student 2. Must attend a university 3. Both full-time and part-time students

Level of Study: Postgraduate

Type: A variable number of fellowships

Value: $10,000

Frequency: Annual

Study Establishment: at universities or affiliated institutions

Country of Study: Canada

Closing Date: 28 February

Additional Information: Prior to application, candidates should obtain a copy of the Training Awards Guide. www.petersons.com/scholarship/harvard-travellers-club-permanent-fund-111_151392.aspx

For further information contact:

Extramural Research Programs Directorate, Health Programs & Services Branch, Health Canada, Ottawa, ON K1A 0S5, Canada.

Fax: (1) 613 954 7363

Health Research Board (HRB)

Research and Development for Health, 73 Lower Baggot Street, Dublin 2, Ireland.

Tel: (353) 1 234 5000
Email: hrb@hrb.ie
Website: www.hrb.ie
Contact: The Research Grants Manager

The Health Research Board (HRB) comprises 16 members appointed by the Minister of Health, with eight of the members being nominated on the co-joint nomination of the universities and colleges. The main functions of the HRB are to promote or commission health research, to promote and conduct epidemiological research as may be appropriate at national level, to promote or commission health services research, to liaise and co-operate with other research bodies in Ireland and overseas in the promotion of relevant research and to undertake such other cognate functions as the Minister may from time to time determine.

Primary Care Training and Enhancement - Physician Assistant Program

Purpose: The purpose of the PCTE - PA Program is to increase the number of primary care physician assistants

(PA), particularly in rural and underserved settings, and improve primary care training in order to strengthen access to and delivery of primary care services nationally

Eligibility: Eligible applicants must be academically affiliated PA training programs, accredited by the Accreditation Review Commission on Education for the Physician Assistant (ARC-PA). Domestic faith-based and community-based organizations, tribes and tribal organizations may apply for these funds, if otherwise eligible

Level of Study: Graduate

Type: Training award

Value: US$2,000,000 (estimated total program funding); Award ceiling US$300,000 per year.

Frequency: Annual

Country of Study: Any country

Application Procedure: Links to the full announcement and online application process are available through grants.gov. check the website appropriately

Closing Date: 14 January

Funding: Private

Additional Information: Preference will be given to applicants that: 1. Demonstrate a high rate for placing graduates in practice settings having the principal focus of serving residents of Medically Underserved Communities. 2. Demonstrate a significant increase in the rate of placing graduates in Medically Underserved Community settings over the preceding 2 years. www.ruralhealthinfo.org/funding/4519

For further information contact:

Tel: (1) 301 443 7271
Email: SCicale@hrsa.gov

Research Leaders Awards

Eligibility: All applications must involve a partnership with at least one health-related partner organization involved in the delivery of health and social care and/or health and social care policy. Applications should be aligned with the strategic plans of the nominating organizations, and should reflect national priorities and strategies in health and social care

Level of Study: Doctorate, Postdoctorate

Type: Award

Value: The awards will be for up to £1,000,000, for staff salaries and associated costs

Length of Study: A maximum of 5 years

Frequency: Annual

Country of Study: Ireland

Application Procedure: All applications must be made online using the HRB GEMS. To access the application form the nominating Higher Education Institution must provide the HRB with the contact details of their nominated Principal Investigator. The HRB will then invite the nominated candidate to initiate the application form

Closing Date: 31 March

Funding: Government

Additional Information: Please check at www.hrb.ie/ research-strategy-funding/grants-and-fellowships/hrb-grants-and-fellowships/grant/133

For further information contact:

Email:	ferrism@queensu.ca

Hearst Corporation

801 Texas Avenue, Houston, TX 77002, United States of America.

Email:	kenn.altine@chron.com

Website:	www.hearstfellowships.com

Hearst Corporation is one of the largest diversified communications companies.

Hearst Fellowships

Purpose: To help develop excellent reporters, editors, photographers, designers and graphic artists

Eligibility: Open to candidates who are graduates and have experience or background in journalism or related fields

Level of Study: Professional development

Type: Fellowships

Value: Varies

Length of Study: 2 years

Frequency: Annual

Country of Study: Any country

Application Procedure: The applicants must download the application form from the website. The completed application form along with other enclosures is to be sent to Hearst Fellowships

Closing Date: 18 Februray

Additional Information: hearstfellowships.com/

For further information contact:

Email:	fellowships@hearstnp.com

Heart and Stroke Foundation

Suite 1402, 222 Queen Street, Ottawa, ON K1P 5V9, Canada.

Tel:	(1) 613 569 4361

Email:	research@hsf.ca

Website:	www.heartandstroke.ca

The Heart and Stroke Foundation is involved in eliminating heart disease and stroke and reducing their impact through the advancement of research and its application, and advocacy for the promotion of healthy living. It is a federation of 10 provincial foundations, led and supported by a force of more than 140,000 volunteers.

Canada Doctoral Research Award

Purpose: To award highly qualified graduate students enrolled in a PhD program, undertaking full-time research training in the cardiovascular or cerebrovascular fields

Eligibility: Open to students enrolled in a PhD program and must be a full-time medical student

Level of Study: Doctorate, Research

Type: Research

Value: C$21,000

Country of Study: Canada

Application Procedure: Applicants must send the application form along with the transcript, essay references and a self-addressed stamped envelope

Closing Date: 1 November

For further information contact:

Research Department, Room 9A-27, Parklawn Building, 5600 Fishers Lane, Rockville, MD 20857, United States of America.

Tel:	(1) 613 569 4361 ext. 327

Fax:	(1) 613 569 3278

Email:	lhodgson@hsf.ca

Career Investigator Award

Purpose: To support established independent researchers who wish to make research their full-time career (Ontario applicants only)

Eligibility: Awards for individuals with an MD, PhD or equivalent degree working in the field of cardiovascular and/or cerebrovascular disease who wish to make their research a full-time career. Applicants must provide proof of national recognition

Level of Study: Postgraduate
Type: Scholarship
Value: Stipend C$81,500 per year, C$1,500 per year for travel, and minimum C$48,282 for scientific purpose
Application Procedure: Applicants must send the application form along with the transcript, essay references and a self-addressed stamped envelope and must provide proof of national recognition
Closing Date: 1 September
Contributor: Heart and Stroke Foundations of Ontario and British Columbia and the Yukon
Additional Information: For more details see website or contact the foundation. www.hrb.ie/fileadmin/2._Plugin_related_files/Funding_schemes/Research_Leader_Awards_2020_Guidance_Notes.pdf

Dr Andres Petrasovits Fellowship in Cardiovascular Health Policy Research

Eligibility: Please visit the website
Level of Study: Postgraduate
Type: Fellowship
Value: C$70,000
Length of Study: 3 years
Application Procedure: Please contact the foundation for application form

Grants-in-Aid of Research and Development

Purpose: To support researchers in projects of experimental nature in cardiovascular or cerebrovascular development
Eligibility: Open for full-time medical student
Level of Study: Postgraduate
Type: Grant
Value: Approx. C$33,000,000
Frequency: Every 3 years
Application Procedure: Applicants must send the application form along with the transcript, essay references and a self-addressed stamped envelope
Closing Date: 27 August
Additional Information: Please check website for more details. www.hrb.ie/fileadmin/2._Plugin_related_files/Funding_schemes/Research_Leader_Awards_2020_Guidance_Notes.pdf

Heart and Stroke Foundation of Canada Doctoral Research Award

Purpose: To support individuals enroled in a PhD program and undertaking full-time research training in the stroke field

Eligibility: Applicants must be Canadians studying abroad or in Canada or for foreign visitors to Canada. The fellowship is open to citizens of United States
Level of Study: Postgraduate
Type: Fellowship
Value: Varies
Country of Study: Canada
Application Procedure: Applicants must send the application form along with the transcript, essay references and a self-addressed stamped envelope
Closing Date: 1 November

For further information contact:

Heart and Stroke Foundation of Canada, 1037 Topsail Rd, Mount Pearl, NL A1N 5E9, Canada.

Tel: (1) 613 569 4361 ext. 268
Fax: (1) 613 569 3278
Email: anguyen@hsf.ca

Heart and Stroke Foundation of Canada New Investigator Research Scholarships

Eligibility: 1. Must be a graduate student or a postgraduate student 2. Must attend a university 3. Citizenship requirements Canada 4. Must not be attending high school currently 5. Must study full-time 6. Restricted to students studying Health and Medical Sciences
Level of Study: Postgraduate
Type: Scholarship
Value: Maximum C$30,000
Country of Study: Any country
Application Procedure: Applicants must send the application form along with the transcript, essay references and a self-addressed stamped envelope
Closing Date: 4 September
Additional Information: www.petersons.com/scholarship/heart-and-stroke-foundation-of-canada-new-investigator-111_151415.aspx

For further information contact:

1525 Carling Avenue, Suite 110, Ottawa, ON K1Z 8R9, Canada.

Tel: (1) 613 569 4361
Email: research@heartandstroke.ca

Heart and Stroke Foundation of Canada Nursing Research Fellowships

Eligibility: Applicants must possess a nursing degree. For master's degree candidates, the programmes must include a thesis or project requirement

Level of Study: Postgraduate
Type: Fellowship
Value: Minimum C$18,570
Country of Study: Canada
Application Procedure: Applicants must send the application form along with the transcript, essay references and a self-addressed stamped envelope
Closing Date: 4 September
Additional Information: Please check website for more details. www.petersons.com/scholarship/heart-and-stroke-foundation-of-canada-new-investigator-111_151415.aspx

For further information contact:

Research Department, 222 Queen Street, Suite 1402, Ottawa, ON K1P 5V9, Canada.

Tel: (1) 613 569 4361 ext. 327
Fax: (1) 613 569 3278
Email: lhodgson@hsf.ca

Heart and Stroke Foundation of Canada Research Fellowships

Eligibility: Applicants must possess a full-time degree for study towards an MSc or PhD.
Level of Study: Postgraduate
Type: Fellowship
Value: C$25,998 (minimum) and C$33,426 (maximum)
Country of Study: Canada
Application Procedure: Applicants must send the application form along with the transcript, essay references and a self-addressed stamped envelope
Closing Date: 1 November

Heart Research United Kingdom

Suite 12D, Joseph's Well, Leeds LS3 1AB, United Kingdom.

Tel: (44) 11 3234 7474
Email: mail@heartresearch.org.uk
Website: www.heartresearch.org.uk
Contact: Helen Wilson, Senior Research Officer

Heart Research United Kingdom funds pioneering medical research into the prevention, treatment and cure of heart disease. Heart Research United Kingdom is a visionary charity leading the way in funding ground-breaking, innovative medical research projects at the cutting edge of science into the prevention, treatment and cure of heart disease. There is a strong emphasis on clinical and surgical projects and young researchers. Heart Research United Kingdom encourages and supports original health lifestyle initiatives exploring novel ways of preventing heart disease in all sectors of the community.

Heart Research United Kingdom Translational Research Project Grants

Purpose: To support ground-breaking, innovative medical research into prevention, treatment and cure of heart disease and related conditions
Eligibility: Graduates or those holding a suitable professional qualification. Research must be carried out in the United Kingdom at a university, hospital or other recognized research institution
Level of Study: Research, Unrestricted
Type: Project grant
Value: £200,000
Length of Study: Up to 3 years
Frequency: Annual
Study Establishment: Centres of health and educational establishments
Country of Study: United Kingdom
Application Procedure: Information and application forms available at heartresearch.org.uk/grants/translational-research-project-trp-grants
No. of awards offered: 45
Closing Date: 1 June
Funding: Corporation, Foundation, Individuals, Private, Trusts
Contributor: Voluntary funding from supporters and grant-making trusts
Additional Information: Please note that the HRUK office is closed on Saturdays and Sundays and therefore deliveries cannot be accepted at the weekend. heartresearch.org.uk/trp-apply/

For further information contact:

Heart Research UK, Suite 12D, Joseph's Well, Leeds LS3 1AB, United Kingdom.

Email: research@heartresearch.org.uk

Novel and Emerging Technologies (NET) Grants

Purpose: This unique grant gives researchers the opportunity to apply for funding to develop a novel and emerging technology or a new application of an existing technology.
Eligibility: Research projects with the emphasis on (1) novel and emerging technologies and (2) their application into

cardiovascular disease prevention and/or treatment, which can be expected to benefit patients within a foreseeable timeframe, will be considered. Appropriate approaches include tissue and bioengineering, the development and evaluation of new diagnostic devices, bio imaging, nanotechnology, biomaterials, genomic, and proteomic approaches, computational biology and bioinformatics.
Type: Grant
Value: £250,000
Country of Study: Any country
Closing Date: 10 January
Additional Information: heartresearch.org.uk/net-grants/

For further information contact:

Tel: (44) 113 234 7474
Email: research@heartresearch.org.uk

PhD Studentship

Purpose: PHD studentships give exceptional students the opportunity to gain the knowledge, skills and expertise needed for a career as a research scientist. From 2021, Heart Research UK is introducing a new, dedicated PhD studentship scheme.
Type: Studentship
Value: £110,500 (outside London), £122,500 (within London)
Country of Study: Any country
Closing Date: 1 June
Additional Information: heartresearch.org.uk/wp-content/uploads/2021/04/PhD-Studentships-T-C-2021.pdf

For further information contact:

Tel: (44) 113 234 7474
Email: helenw@heartresearch.org.uk

Scotland Grant

Subjects:
Purpose: Heart Research UK is committed to supporting research at hospitals and universities across the United Kingdom, including Scotland. In 2018, we announced a new, regional grant for Scotland and we are pleased to offer this grant again in 2021.
Eligibility: This year, we are inviting applications again from researchers at institutions in Scotland for research projects into the prevention, treatment and cure of heart disease and related conditions.
Type: Grant
Value: £200,000

Country of Study: Any country
Closing Date: 1 June

For further information contact:

Tel: (44) 113 234 7474
Email: info@heartresearch.org.uk

Heinrich Boll Foundation

Heinrich-Böll-Stiftung e.V. Schumannstr. 8, D-10117 Berlin, Germany.

Tel: (49) 30 28 534 400
Email: studienwerk@boell.de
Website: www.boell.de/en

Fostering democracy and upholding human rights, taking action to prevent the destruction of the global ecosystem, advancing equality between women and men, securing peace through conflict prevention in crisis zones, and defending the freedom of individuals against excessive state and economic power – these are the objectives that drive the ideas and actions of the Heinrich Böll Foundation. We maintain close ties to the German Green Party (Alliance 90/The Greens) and as a think tank for green visions and projects, we are part of an international encompassing well over 100 partner projects in approximately 60 countries. The Heinrich Böll Foundation works independently and nurtures a spirit of intellectual openness. We maintain a worldwide network with currently 30 international offices. We co–operate closely with 16 state-level Böll Foundations in each of Germany's federal states, and we support talented, socio-politically engaged undergraduate and graduate students in Germany and abroad. We gladly follow Heinrich Böll's exhortation for citizens to get involved in politics, and we want to inspire others to do the same.

Heinrich Boll Scholarships in Germany for International Students

Purpose: The Heinrich Böll Foundation awards some scholarships to international students who gained their university entrance qualification from a school outside of Germany who wish to study a Masters or PhD Degree in Germany.
Eligibility: International Master students who earned their university entrance qualification outside Germany You may apply before commencing your Masters programme or at any time up to the end of the first semester of the Masters

programme. Proof of first professional qualification must be provided, International Doctoral students who earned the university entrance qualification outside Germany The applicant must have been accepted as a doctoral student by a state or state-recognised university in Germany. Proof of admission, as a rule in Germany, must be included with the application. By the application date, preliminary work must have been completed and a valid timetable for completion must be submitted. PhD subjects related to focal points of the Foundation's activities will be given priority.

Level of Study: Masters Studies/PhD Studies

Type: Scholarships

Value: Masters Studies Non-EU students €850 per month plus various individual allowances; tuition fees are in certain cases possible in Germany. EU students varies, max. €649 plus €300 book money per month; tuition fees not possible in Germany but possible to a limited extent in other countries. The scholarship is awarded for the regular period of study, may be extended by one semester. PhD Studies Non-EU students €1,200 per month plus €100 mobility allowance per month, plus various individual allowances; tuition fees are not possible. EU students €1,350 per month basic scholarship plus €100 per month research costs allowance; tuition fees are not possible in Germany but possible to a limited extent in other countries. The scholarship is awarded for two years as a rule, may be extended twice at most by half a year.

Frequency: Annual

Country of Study: Germany

Application Procedure: For details of application requirements and procedures, please consult information sheet A 1-1 ("scholarship application for undergraduate and graduate students", PDF) or A 2-1 ("scholarship application for doctoral studies"). The online application portal closes on 1 March at the latest. It is important to visit the official website (link found below) for details on how to apply for this scholarship.

Closing Date: 1 March

Additional Information: www.boell.de/en/foundation/application

Helen Hay Whitney Foundation

Postdoctoral Research Fellowship

Subjects: Biomedical sciences

Purpose: To attain its ultimate goal of increasing the number of imaginative, well-trained and dedicated medical scientists, the Foundation grants financial support of sufficient duration to help further the careers of young men and women engaged in biological or medical research.

Eligibility: Candidates who hold, or are in the final stages of obtaining a PhD, M.D., or equivalent degree and are seeking beginning postdoctoral training in basic biomedical research are eligible to apply for a fellowship. The Foundation accepts applications from candidates who have no more than one year of postdoctoral research experience at the time of the deadline for submitting the application (June 15), and who have received a PhD (or D.Phil. or equivalent) degree no more than two years before the deadline, or an M.D. degree no more than three years before the deadline. Fellowships may be awarded to US citizens planning to work in laboratories either in the US, Canada, or abroad and also to foreign citizens for research in laboratories in the US only. We expect that most applicants will reside in North America at the time of application. Foreign Students will need to obtain appropriate visa documentation, as required by US Immigration. Applications from established scientists or advanced fellows will not be considered. The fellowships are for early postdoctoral training only. Clinical house-staff training does not count as postdoctoral laboratory training. The Foundation will not ordinarily consider applicants who plan tenure of the fellowship in the laboratory in which they have already received extensive predoctoral or postdoctoral training. The aim of the fellowship is to broaden postdoctoral training and experience, and a significant change of venue is advisable. Since the number of available fellowships is limited, the Foundation does not make more than one award per year for training with a given supervisor. It also does not support more than two fellows per laboratory at one time.

Type: Fellowship

Value: Up to US$54,000 in the first year; US$57,000 in the second and US$60,000 in the third, plus a US$1,500 annual research allowance. There is a Dependent Child Allowance of US$1,500 per annum for each child. There is no allowance for a spouse.

Length of Study: Three years

Country of Study: Any country

Application Procedure: Applications are to be filled out and submitted online at www.hhwf.org.

Closing Date: 15 June

Additional Information: Apply online. hhwf.org/research-fellowship/

Research Fellowship

Subjects: biological or medical research

Purpose: Foundation grants financial support of sufficient duration to help further the careers of young men and women engaged in biological or medical research

Eligibility: Fellowships may be awarded to US citizens planning to work in laboratories either in the US, Canada, or abroad and also to foreign citizens for research in laboratories in the US only. We expect that most applicants will reside in North America at the time of application. Foreign Students will need to obtain appropriate visa documentation, as required by US Immigration.

Level of Study: Research
Type: Grant
Value: research allowance of US$1,500
Length of Study: 3 years
Frequency: Annual
Application Procedure: Applications are to be filled out and submitted online at www.hhwf.org
Closing Date: 15 June
Funding: Foundation
Additional Information: Late applications will not be considered hhwf.org/research-fellowship/

Hellenic Pasteur Institute

Vas Sofias Avenue 127, GR-11521 Athens, Greece.

Tel: (30) 1 647 8800
Website: www.pasteur.gr
Contact: Dr S Tzartos

W.D.E. Coulson & Toni M. Cross Aegean Exchange Program

Purpose: The purpose of these fellowships is to provide an opportunity for Greek scholars to meet with their Turkish colleagues, and to pursue research interests in the museum, archive, and library collections and at the sites and monuments of Turkey
Eligibility: Greek nationals, including staff of the Ministry of Culture and Sport; doctoral candidates and faculty members of Greek institutions of higher education.
Level of Study: Postdoctorate
Type: Fellowship
Value: Stipend of US$250 per week plus up to US$500 for travel expenses.
Length of Study: From two weeks to two months
Frequency: Annual
Country of Study: Any country
Application Procedure: 1. Stipend of US$250 is required. 2. Submit "Associate Membership with Fellowship" application online. 3. The application should include a curriculum vitae, statement of the project to be pursued during the period of grant (up to three pages, single-spaced in length), two letters of reference from scholars in the field commenting on the value and feasibility of the project
Closing Date: 15 March
Funding: Private
Contributor: U.S. Department of State Bureau of Educational and Cultural Affairs through the Council of American Overseas Research Centers

Additional Information: For more details about Application visit: www.ascsa.edu.gr/fellowships-and-grants. For more details visit: www.archaeological.org/grant/coulson-cross-aegean-fellowship/

For further information contact:

Email: application@ascsa.org

Help Musicians United Kingdom

POP Awards

Purpose: Help Musicians' postgraduate awards offer support to students who wish to complete their studies at the leading UK conservatoires and performing arts colleges
Level of Study: Postgraduate
Type: Award
Value: £40,000
Length of Study: 2 year
Frequency: Annual
Country of Study: Any country
Closing Date: 1 March

For further information contact:

Email: creative@helpmusicians.org.uk

Postgraduate Awards

Purpose: Help Musicians' postgraduate awards offer support to students who wish to complete their studies at the leading UK conservatoires and performing arts colleges.
Level of Study: Postgraduate
Type: Award
Value: Up to £5,000
Length of Study: Annual Awards
Frequency: Annual
Country of Study: United Kingdom
Application Procedure: Must have lived in United Kingdom for 3 consecutive years by Postgraduate start date. Applications made via online application form
Closing Date: 17 January
Funding: Private
Contributor: Help Musicians United Kingdom
Additional Information: www.helpmusicians.org.uk/creative-programme/current-opportunities/postgraduate-awards

For further information contact:

Tel: (44) 20 7239 9119
Email: creative@helpmusicians.org.uk

Sybil Tutton Awards

Purpose: Help Musicians launched the Sybil Tutton Opera Awards to help opera students with the costs of postgraduate study.

Eligibility: This year our awards are open to students who are hoping to start a postgraduate degree or move in to a second year of postgraduate

Level of Study: Postgraduate

Type: Award

Value: £1,000–5,000

Frequency: Annual

Country of Study: Any country

Application Procedure: Application is by nomination only from head of voice at the United Kingdom conservatoires and the National Opera Studio

Closing Date: 1 March

For further information contact:

Email: awards@helpmusicians.org.uk

Transmission Fund

Purpose: We want our support to make a real difference to you and your career, so you are free to specify opportunities relevant to your own circumstances and ambitions - whether it's a course or 1-on-1 time you need to hone your skills, we can help you to feel confident in making your next move

Eligibility: 1. Be aged over 18 2. Have been resident in the UK for at least 3 consecutive years 3. Help Musicians refers to the UK residency rules noting that you are eligible for our support 1. If you are a UK National living in the UK you automatically qualify 2. If you are a non-UK National, you have been living in the UK for at least 183 days and have the legal right to live in the UK 4. Already have an active career in music

Type: Funding support

Frequency: Annual

Country of Study: Any country

Closing Date: 12 April

Henry Moore Institute

The Headrow, Leeds LS1 3AH, United Kingdom.

Tel: (44) 113 246 7467
Email: kirstie@henry-moore.org
Website: www.henry-moore.org
Contact: Kirstie Gregory, Research Programme Assistant

The Henry Moore Institute is a world-recognized centre for the study of sculpture. The institute hosts exhibitions, conferences and lectures, as well as developing research to expand the understanding and scholarship of historical and contemporary sculpture.

Henry Moore Institute Research Fellowships

Purpose: To enable scholars to use the Institute's facilities, which include the sculpture collection, library, archive and slide library, to assist them in researching their particular field

Eligibility: There are no restrictions

Level of Study: Doctorate, Postdoctorate, Postgraduate, Research

Type: Fellowship

Value: Accommodation, travel and daily living expenses

Length of Study: 1 month

Frequency: Annual

Study Establishment: The Henry Moore Institute

Country of Study: United Kingdom

Application Procedure: Applicants must send a letter of application, a proposal (maximum 1,000 words) and a curriculum vitae. Visit the website

No. of awards offered: 80

Closing Date: 12 January

Funding: Foundation

Contributor: The Henry Moore Foundation

No. of awards given last year: 4

No. of applicants last year: 80

Additional Information: www.henry-moore.org/grants/grants-programme/research-fellowships

Henry Moore Institute Senior Fellowships

Purpose: Senior fellowships are intended to give established scholars (working on any aspect of sculpture) time and space to develop a research project free from their usual work commitments

Level of Study: Doctorate, Postdoctorate

Type: Fellowship

Value: Fellowships provide accommodation, travel expenses, and a per diem

Length of Study: 3–6 weeks

Frequency: Annual

Study Establishment: Henry Moore Institute

Country of Study: United Kingdom

Application Procedure: Full details are available from the website www.henry-moore.ac.uk

No. of awards offered: 15

Closing Date: 12 January

Funding: Foundation

Contributor: Henry Moore Foundation

No. of awards given last year: 1

No. of applicants last year: 15

Additional Information: Research fellowships are also available. The institute offers the possibility of presenting finished research in published form as a seminar or as a small exhibition www.henry-moore.org/grants/grants-programme/research-fellowships

Herb Society of America, Inc.

9019 Kirtland Chardon Road, Kirtland, OH 44094, United States of America.

Tel: (1) 440 256 0514
Email: herbs@herbsociety.org
Website: www.herbsociety.org
Contact: Ms Michelle Milks, Office Administrator

The aim of the Herb Society of America Inc. is to promote the knowledge, use and delight of herbs through educational programmes, research and sharing the experience of its members with the community.

Herb Society of America Research Grant

Purpose: This grant supports the research of the horticultural, scientific, and/or social use of herbs throughout history. Research must define an herb as historically useful for flavoring, medicine, economic, industrial, or cosmetic purposes and have the potential to significantly increase the knowledge of the field.
Eligibility: Open to persons with a proposed programme of scientific, academic or artistic investigation of herbal plants
Level of Study: Unrestricted
Type: Grant
Value: Up to US$10,000
Frequency: Annual
Country of Study: Any country
Application Procedure: Applicants must submit an application clearly defining all their research in 500 words or less and a proposed budget with specific budget items listed. Requests for funds will not be considered unless accompanied by five copies of the application form and proposal. The application must be submitted in electronic form via email to herbs@herbsociety.org
Closing Date: 31 January
Contributor: Members
Additional Information: Finalists will be interviewed. In order to complete the application, use the below link.

herbsocietyorg.presencehost.net/support/grants-scholarships/application-for-the-hsa-research-grant.html www.herbsociety.org/get-involved/grants-scholarships/grant-details.html

For further information contact:

Email: grants@herbsociety.org

Heriot-Watt University

Postgraduate Admissions Office, Edinburgh EH14 4AS, United Kingdom.

Tel: (44) 131 449 5111
Email: edu.liaison@hw.ac.uk
Website: www.hw.ac.uk
Contact: Fiona Watt, Wider Access Assistant

Heriot-Watt University, one of the oldest higher education institutions in the United Kingdom, is Scotland's most international university. Our six academic schools and two postgraduate institutes offer research opportunities and postgraduate taught programmes in science and engineering, business, languages and design. We disburse over £6M in fee and stipend scholarships annually.

Heriot-Watt Expo Award

Eligibility: This award is applicable for students who have received an unconditional offer letter or a conditional offer letter from the university.
Level of Study: MBA, Postgraduate, Undergraduate
Type: Award
Value: A discount of AED 8,000 and paying tuition fee
Frequency: Annual
Country of Study: Any country
Closing Date: 28 February
Additional Information: www.hw.ac.uk/dubai/study/fees/scholarships.htm

Mexican Scholarships

Purpose: Financial assistance for Mexican students in science, engineering and technology
Eligibility: Mexican citizens

Level of Study: Postgraduate
Type: Scholarship
Value: Tuition fees and living costs
Frequency: Annual
Study Establishment: Heriot-Watt University
Country of Study: Scotland
Application Procedure: Contact Bob Tuttle
Funding: Government
Contributor: Heriot-Watt and CONACYT (Mexican National Council for Science and Technology)

For further information contact:

Tel: (44) 131 451 3746
Email: b.tuttle@hw.ac.uk

Music Scholarships

Purpose: To support musicians in obtaining a postgraduate qualification whilst developing their musical skills
Eligibility: All instrumentalists and vocalists who have been accepted for a course. The following criteria are taken into consideration musical ability and potential, proof of exam results and membership of orchestras or choirs; a reference from your last vocal or instrumental teacher; in the case of the Archer Music Scholarships, a personal statement is also required; auditions will be held during Semester 1
Level of Study: Postgraduate, Research
Type: Scholarship
Value: free music tuition for talented singers and instrumentalists, up to a value of £400 per year and talented musician to receive music tuition up to a value of £500
Length of Study: 1 year
Frequency: Annual
Study Establishment: Heriot-Watt University
Country of Study: Scotland
Application Procedure: For an application form or more information please contact Steve King MBE, Director of Music
Additional Information: There will be a music scholar's concert in HWU in March each year at which all music scholars are all expected to participate. www.hw.ac.uk/news.htm

For further information contact:

Tel: (44) 131 451 3705
Email: s.king@hw.ac.uk

Overseas Research Students Awards Scheme (ORSAS)

Purpose: Assist international postgraduate research students with payment of tuition fees
Eligibility: Non-European Union research applicants
Level of Study: Research
Type: Scholarship
Length of Study: 3 years
Frequency: Annual
Study Establishment: Heriot-Watt University
Country of Study: Scotland
Application Procedure: Apply to School of Study
Closing Date: 30 November
Contributor: Heriot-Watt University
Additional Information: Successful applicants usually receive James Watt Scholarships for the remainder of their fees plus a maintenance contribution. www.hw.ac.uk/news.htm

For further information contact:

Email: pgadmissions@glasgow.ac.uk

Postgraduate Merit Award

Purpose: We aim to encourage well-qualified, ambitious students to study with us and we offer a wide variety of scholarships and bursaries to achieve this. Over £6 million worth of opportunities are available in fee and stipend scholarships, and more than 400 students benefit from this support.
Eligibility: 1. Domiciled in one of the countries listed above at the time of application and classified as an overseas student for fee purposes starting a full-time on-campus programme of study. 2. Self-funding your course. 3. Holding an offer to study a full-time postgraduate taught degree course starting in September 2023.
Level of Study: Postgraduate
Type: Scholarship
Value: £3000 & £1500.
Frequency: Annual
Country of Study: Any country
Application Procedure: You will be automatically considered for the scholarship if you meet the academic criteria.
No. of awards offered: Multiple
Closing Date: January
Additional Information: www.hw.ac.uk/study/scholarships/postgraduate-merit-award.htm

For further information contact:

EH14 4AS Edinburgh, Scotland, United Kingdom.

Vice Chancellor's Scholarship

Eligibility: These scholarships will be awarded based on a range of criteria including merit, sports, service to community and industry etc. and will only be applicable to applicants who are nominally resident in China.
Level of Study: Postgraduate, Undergraduate
Type: Scholarship
Value: Up to 50% of the tuition fee
Country of Study: Any country
No. of awards offered: 50
Closing Date: 1 September

Higher & Education South Africa

Africa: Mwalimu Julius Nyerere African Union Scholarship

Purpose: Mwalimu Julius Nyerere African Union Scholarship is intended to enable young Africans to study at reputable African universities with a binding agreement that scholarship beneficiaries will work in any African country for at least the same duration of the scholarship period after graduation. The scholarship aims to provide an opportunity to enhance knowledge, professional skills and capacity of refugees and displaced people, in order to streamline their integration to contribute towards sustainable development in Africa
Eligibility: 1. Applicants must be a citizen of an African Union Member State. 2. Must be a formally registered refugee/displaced person with a UNHCR registration number or be able to demonstrate confirmed refugee status in an African Union Member State. 3. Must be under the age of thirty five (35) years. 4. Must be a holder of a Bachelor's degree in the relevant field, at least at the level of Upper Second class Honours. The degree must be from a recognised university. 5. Must have demonstrated outstanding academic achievement as evidenced by academic transcripts, and academic awards if any. 6. Have proof of admission to undertake a full time Master's programme in a recognized university in an African Union Member State. 7. Be willing to commit to work in an African Union Member State on completion of studies for at least three (3) years
Level of Study: Postgraduate
Type: Scholarship
Value: Stipend to the value of R500 monthly to cover accommodation, meals, utilities, local transport and medication, Travel allowance once-off R250, R350 to assist with shipping and other terminal expenses, Computer allowance R1,000
Frequency: Annual

Country of Study: South Africa
Application Procedure: Apply online www.edu-au.org/scholarshipg
Closing Date: 30 April
Funding: Foundation

For further information contact:

Department of Human Resources, Science and Technology, African Union Commission, PO Box 3243, Addis Ababa, Ethiopia, Eastern Africa.

Tel: (251) 11 551 77 00
Fax: (251) 11 551 78 44
Email: internationalscholarships@dhet.gov.za

Africa: Next Einstein Forum (NEF) Fellows Programme

Purpose: The Next Einstein Forum (NEF) is an initiative of the African Institute for Mathematical Sciences (AIMS) in partnership with the Robert Bosch Stiftung. The NEF is a platform that connects science, society and policy in Africa and the rest of the world — with the goal to leverage science for human development globally. The Fellows Programme consists of Africa's most brilliant young scientists that the NEF showcases on the global stage. The Programme provides Fellows with the opportunity to present their research and draw upon the vast networks of NEF members and participants for support, connections and advice to advance their work
Eligibility: 1. Africans from around the world — including those who currently reside in the Diaspora. 2. Hold a passport from an African country. 3. Hold a PhD in a field of science, Technology, Engineering, Mathematics or the social sciences. 4. Have a demonstrated track record of research/findings that have global impact. 5. You are passionate about raising Africa's profile in STEM globally. 6. Able to clearly present their work to an audience in English or French
Level of Study: Postgraduate
Type: Fellowship
Frequency: Annual
Country of Study: South Africa
Closing Date: 27 January
Funding: Foundation
Additional Information: www.afterschoolafrica.com/17391/next-einstein-forum-fellowship/

For further information contact:

Email: info@nef.org

Austria: Erasmus+ Master in Research and Innovation in Higher Education (MARIHE) Programme

Purpose: The Master in Research and Innovation in Higher Education (MARIHE) is supported by the Erasmus+ Programme of the European Union (EU) under the action of an Erasmus Mundus Joint Master Degree (EMJMD)

Eligibility: 1. Must hold a first university degree, this should be at least a Bachelor degree issued by a university, quantified as three years of studies corresponding. 2. Show a strong motivation and interest. 3. Have sufficient knowledge of English for academic purposes

Level of Study: Postgraduate

Type: Grant

Frequency: Annual

Country of Study: South Africa

Application Procedure: Apply online www.marihe.eu/how-to-apply/application-process-and-timetable

Closing Date: 5 December

Funding: Private

For further information contact:

Email: marihe@donau-uni.ac.at

Azerbaijan: Non-Aligned Movement (NAM) Scholarship

Purpose: The Government of the Republic of Azerbaijan is offering scholarships for Bachelor's, Master's and Doctoral programmes to the citizens of Non-Aligned Movement (NAM) countries (including South Africa)

Eligibility: 1. Citizen of Non-Aligned Movement (NAM) countries (this includes South Africa) 2. For undergraduate programmes applicants must be younger than 25 years old 3. For Master's programmes applicants must be younger than 30 years old 4. For doctoral programmes applicants must be younger than 40 years old

Level of Study: Postgraduate

Type: Scholarship

Value: Value of AZN 800

Frequency: Annual

Country of Study: South Africa

Application Procedure: Apply www.internationalscholarships. dhet.gov.za/Application%20form.pdf

Closing Date: 8 February

Funding: Foundation

Additional Information: (NAM) Scholarship202021.html www.internationalscholarships.dhet.gov.za/AZERBAIJAN Non-AlignedMovement

For further information contact:

Tel: (994) 12 596 92 96

Email: scholars@mfa.gov.az

Brunei Darussalam: Government of Brunei Darussalam Scholarship

Purpose: The Brunei Darussalam Ministry of Foreign Affairs invites applications for the Government of Brunei Darussalam Scholarship. The scholarship is tenable at higher education institutions in Brunei Darussalam and provides applicants with an opportunity to pursue Diploma, Bachelor's and Master's degrees

Eligibility: 1. Applicant must be citizen of Pakistan/AJK 2. Must be between the ages of 18-25 for undergraduate programmes 3. Age should not exceed from 35 years for candidates who are applying for Postgraduate programmes. 4. Applicants having 3rd division in their academic career are eligible to apply but NOT in the terminal degree. 5. The applicant must have completed HSSC/Intermediate or equivalent for application to 04 year Bachelor Program. 6. The applicant must have completed 16 years education or (04 years) Bachelors/ equivalent Degree for application to Postgraduate Masters Program. 7. Certificates/Transcript/Degrees to be attached must be attested by the attesting authorities such as IBCC and HEC. Equivalence of O & A level is mandatory by IBCC. 8. The applicant must provide Health certificate with his application. 9. IELTS/TOEFL scores are required, where applicable.

Level of Study: Postgraduate

Type: Scholarship

Frequency: Annual

Country of Study: South Africa

Application Procedure: Apply online www.ubd.edu.bn/ admission/scholarships.html

No. of awards offered: Several

Closing Date: 15 February

Funding: Foundation

Additional Information: www.afterschoolafrica.com/ 11428/brunei-darussalam-government-scholarships/

For further information contact:

Assistant Director, Learning Opportunities Abroad (LOA), HRD Division, Higher Education Commission, Sector H-8, Islamabad, Pakistan.

Tel: (92) 51 111 119 432

Email: applyBDGS2020@mfa.gov.bn

China: Chinese Government Scholarship

Purpose: The Chinese Government is offering scholarships for South African students to study at Chinese institutions. The Department of Higher Education and Training is responsible for nominations

Eligibility: Listed below are the eligibility factors for the scholarship 1. South African citizens in good health (medical check will be required for successful applicants). 2. Strong academic record with a minimum 65% average in previous studies. 3. Demonstrated interest in China and commitment to the development of South Africa. 4. Applications in all fields of study except medicine will be considered. 5. Preference will be given to postgraduate applicants, previously disadvantaged applicants and applications in the following fields. The scholarship is offered for undergraduate (Bachelors) in the identified scarce skills, postgraduate (Masters or PhD) or non-degree Chinese language studies. Bachelor's degree scholarships are taught in Chinese and will only be awarded to applicants who already have the required level of Chinese proficiency (HSK 5 or above). Preference is given to applications for postgraduate studies

Level of Study: Postgraduate

Type: Scholarship

Frequency: Annual

Country of Study: South Africa

Application Procedure: Apply online www.campuschina. org/universities/index.html

Closing Date: 31 January

Funding: Foundation

Additional Information: fj.china-embassy.org/eng/zytz/ 202112/t20211211_10466950.htm

For further information contact:

Level 13, Building A3 No. 9 Chegongzhuang St, Dong Wu Yuan, Xicheng Qu, CN 100738 Beijing Shi, China.

Email: internationalscholarships@dhet.gov.za

China: One Belt One Road Scholarship

Purpose: Peking University Guanghua School of Management is offering One Belt One Road Scholarship to pursue an MBA programme at Peking University. The International MBA programme is a full-time (2 years) English-taught programme

Eligibility: 1. Applicants must hold a non-Chinese citizenship and be citizens from Belt and Road Initiative (BRI) countries. 2. Must hold a Bachelor's degree equivalent to a Bachelor's degree in China. 3. Must have two or more years of relevant full-time work experience. 4. Must obtain

a competitive score from the Guanghua MBA entrance exam. 5. Must have leadership quality

Level of Study: Postgraduate

Type: Scholarship

Value: Accommodation subsidy (RMB 4,000/person/month), Living allowance (RMB 3,000/person/month), edical insurance fee (RMB 800/person/year), Application fee of RMB 800 will be waived

Length of Study: 2 year

Frequency: Annual

Country of Study: South Africa

Application Procedure: Apply online applymba.pku.edu. cn/. The One Belt One Road Scholarship will not only provide the opportunity to study at Peking University which is one of the most prestigious universities in China, and is ranked #1 in China and #2 in the Asia-Pacific region by Times Higher Education World University Rankings, but also a chance to become an expert in China affairs and gain a solid foothold in the China market

Closing Date: 31 March

Funding: Private

For further information contact:

Tel: (86) 15010 656 075

Email: yul@gsm.pku.edu.cn

China: Renmin University Master of Contemporary Chinese Studies Scholarship

Purpose: The Silk Road School at the Renmin University of China (Suzhou) offers scholarships to foreign students who wish to pursue a Master of Contemporary Chinese studies at Renmin University of China (Suzhou)

Eligibility: 1. Be foreign citizens who have interest in Belt and Road Initiative (BRI) and Chinese culture. 2. Have the ability to speak, read and write English at an equivalent score of IELTS 6.5 or TOEFL 90

Level of Study: Postgraduate

Type: Scholarship

Frequency: Annual

Country of Study: South Africa

Application Procedure: Apply online www.rdcy.org/ displaynewsen.php?id=45928

Closing Date: 10 June

Funding: Foundation

Additional Information: www.internationalscholarships. dhet.gov.za/china%20-%20Copy.html

For further information contact:

Tel: (86) 10 6251 6305

Email: srsruc@ruc.edu.cn

Embassy of France in South Africa Master Scholarship Programme

Purpose: The Embassy of France invites students who wish to continue their tertiary education at Master level in France for the academic year September apply for its scholarship programme

Eligibility: 1. Citizenship of South Africa or Lesotho. 2. Bachelor's or Honour's graduate (depending on the academic year to enrol for), completed or to be completed by the time the student would depart for France. 3. Acceptance from three selected French institutions of the candidate's choice. Students should apply for admission to these universities concurrently to the bursary application (admission letters or at least correspondence with the institutions will be required for complete applications). 4. Maximum academic fees (administration and tuition fees combined) financed with a full scholarship €5,000. For academic fees higher than €5,000 co-financing options must be provided (personal savings and/or enterprise sponsorship). 5. Maximum academic fees (administration and tuition fees combined) financed with a full scholarship €5,000. For academic fees higher than €5,000 co-financing options must be provided (personal savings and/or enterprise sponsorship). 6. No knowledge of French language required, depending on the availability of study course in English. Courses relating to the French Language (i.e. translation, interpreting or French language teaching) must follow a different application process

Level of Study: Postgraduate

Type: Scholarship

Value: €5,000

Length of Study: 1 year

Frequency: Annual

Country of Study: Any country

Closing Date: 15 March

Funding: Foundation

For further information contact:

Email: audrey.delattre@diplomatie.gouv.fr

Embassy of France in South Africa PhD Grants

Purpose: The French Embassy scholarship programme offers grants to facilitate in the international academic and scientific mobility of South African and non-South African researchers to French Higher Education institutions. The programme offers the opportunity for doctoral students to integrate into French establishments for specified time periods in order to participate in collaborative research as part of their doctoral research project

Eligibility: 1. Registration for a PhD at a South African university. 2. A hosting agreement from the French institution. 3. Support letters from your South African supervisor and French co-supervisor, supporting the proposed research project. 4. Applications from all academic disciplines will be considered. 5. No knowledge of French language required, provided the student will be able to conduct research in English

Level of Study: Postgraduate

Type: Scholarship

Value: €1,065

Frequency: Annual

Country of Study: Any country

Funding: Foundation

For further information contact:

Tel: (27) 12 343 6563

Email: pretoria@campusfrance.org

France: French Embassy and Saint-Gobain Master Scholarship

Purpose: Saint-Gobain and the Embassy of France in South Africa are offering scholarships to South Africans and Basotho graduates to pursue a Master's degree in Business studies or Engineering at public French universities

Level of Study: Postgraduate

Type: Scholarship

Value: €767 and annual tuition fees (€3,770) at public universities

Frequency: Annual

Country of Study: Any country

Application Procedure: Apply online www.southafrica. campusfrance.org/page/campusfrance-south-africa-office

Closing Date: 30 March

Funding: Private

Additional Information: Contacts could be further established with the below link. www.southafrica. campusfrance.org/page/campusfrance-south-africa-office www.internationalscholarships.dhet.gov.za/FRANCEFrench EmbassyandSaint-GobainMasterScholarship20192020.html

For further information contact:

Email: pretoria.bourses@campusfrance.org

France: French Embassy Masters and PhD Scholarship Programme

Purpose: The Embassy of France is offering scholarships to postgraduate South Africans who wish to pursue Master's and Doctoral studies at French higher education institutions

Eligibility: 1. Be a citizen and resident of South Africa. 2. Apply for university admission at three French universities concurrent to the scholarship application (admission letters or at least correspondence with the institutions will be required). Applications to French public universities are recommended since they have French government subsidised fees. 3. French proficiency is not required, provided they are pursuing a study course in English and have the ability to conduct research in English. 4. Courses relating to French language studies (i.e. translation, interpreting or French language teaching) must follow a different application process by contacting Audrey Delattre

Level of Study: Postgraduate

Type: Scholarship

Frequency: Annual

Country of Study: South Africa

Application Procedure: Apply online www.southafrica. campusfrance.org/sites/locaux/files/PhD%20French%20 Embassy%20application%20form%202019.pdf

Closing Date: 15 March

Funding: Foundation

Additional Information: www.internationalscholarships. dhet.gov.za/France%204-%20Copy.html

For further information contact:

Email: pretoria@campusfrance.org

France: ISAE-SUPAERO Scholarship Programmes

Purpose: The ISAE-SUPAERO Institute offers a wide range of science and engineering degree programs with a number of scholarships offered through industry support and the SUPAERO Foundation for pursuing studies towards a Master of Science in Aerospace Engineering degree. These scholarships cover tuition and part of living expenses

Eligibility: Applicants who hold a Bachelor's degree or the equivalent in Mechanical Engineering, Mechatronics, Aerospace, Electronics, Electrical Systems, Telecommunications or a French licence in Science and Engineering

Level of Study: Postgraduate

Type: Scholarship

Value: Tuition fees R10,600, Living expenses R8,000 to R10,000

Frequency: Annual

Country of Study: South Africa

Application Procedure: Apply online www.isae-supaero.fr/ en/academics/master-s-degree-msc/admissions/

Funding: Foundation

Additional Information: www.isae-supaero.fr/en/aca demics/MSc/financing-144/financing/

For further information contact:

Tel: (33) 561 338 027

Email: philippe.galaup@isae-supaero.fr

Hungary: Stipendium Hungaricum for South Africa

Purpose: The Hungarian Government is offering 100 scholarships to South African students to study at participating public university in Hungary. All courses available for South Africans are taught in English

Eligibility: 1. Be a South African citizen in good health. 2. Have a strong academic record. 3. An interest in studying in Hungary and demonstrated commitment to the development of South Africa. 4. Meet the entry criteria for their selected programme in Hungary. 5. Meet the minimum academic requirement for entry into a similar programme at a South African university

Level of Study: Postgraduate

Type: Grant

Frequency: Annual

Country of Study: South Africa

Application Procedure: Apply online apply.stipendium hungaricum.hu/

Closing Date: 16 January

Funding: Foundation

Additional Information: www.internationalscholarships. dhet.gov.za/HUNGARY%20Stipendium%20Hungaricum% 20for%20South%20Africa.html

For further information contact:

Email: HungaryScholarshipApplications2019@dhet.gov.za

India: Export-Import Bank of India BRICS Economic Research Award

Purpose: : Stimulating advanced research on economics related topics of relevance to the member nations of BRICS.

Eligibility: Nationals of any of the five member nations of BRICS, who have been awarded a Doctorate or accepted for award of a Doctorate from any recognized nationally accredited University or academic institution globally, are eligible to receive the Award.

Level of Study: Postgraduate

Type: Award

Value: Rs. 1.5 million (approximately US$21,000)

Frequency: Annual

Country of Study: South Africa

Application Procedure: Apply online www.eximbankindia. in/awards

Closing Date: 31 March
Funding: Foundation
Additional Information: www.eximbankindia.in/Assets/pdf/award/EXIM%20Bank%20BRICS%20Economic%20Research%20Award%20-%20Guidelines%20English_07012022.pdf

For further information contact:

Tel: (91) 22 2217 2701
Email: rag@eximbankindia.in

Indonesia: Kemitraan Negara Berkembang (Developing Countries Partnership) Scholarship

Purpose: The Kemitraan Negara Berkembang (KNB) Scholarship was first introduced by the Ministry of Education and Culture to embrace higher education globalization by providing financial assistance (scholarship) to the selected Indonesian Universities, to recruit potential international students to acquire Master's degrees in those universities. The KNB Scholarship program has expanded and is now offered to potential students from developing countries to acquire Bachelor's or Master's degrees at the prestigious universities in Indonesia. The Indonesian Government is offering 140 Master's and five Bachelor's degrees scholarships. All programmes are delivered in Bahasa Indonesia
Eligibility: 1. Applicants must not be older than 35 years of age. 2. Applicants must hold a Bachelor degree (Master's degree holder is not eligible to apply). 3. Applicants must have a TOEFL (or other certified English Proficiency) score of 500. 4. Applicants must be between the ages of 18-35 for Undergraduate and Diploma programmes
Level of Study: Postgraduate
Type: Scholarship
Frequency: Annual
Country of Study: South Africa
Application Procedure: Apply online www.knb.ristekdikti.go.id
Closing Date: 30 April
Funding: Foundation
Additional Information: www.internationalscholarships.dhet.gov.za/INDONESIAKemitraanNegaraBerkembang(Developing%20Countries%20Partnership)Scholarship.html

For further information contact:

The Information and Socio-Cultural Section, The Embassy of the Republic of Indonesia, 949 Francis Baard Street, Arcardia 0083, South Africa.

Tel: (27) 12 342 3350
Email: info@indonesia-pretoria.org.za

Ireland: Kader Asmal Fellowship Programme

Purpose: The Embassy of Ireland in South Africa in partnership with the Department of Higher Education and Training and the Canon Collins Trust invites applications for scholarships for one-year Master's degree study in Ireland commencing in September
Eligibility: 1. Be a South African citizen. 2. Have achieved the necessary standard to be accepted onto a postgraduate course in an institute of higher education in Ireland. 3. Be seeking funding for a full-time postgraduate programme in one of the above listed subject areas. 4. Be able to take up fellowship in the academic year. 5. Not have already applied for a course at an institution in Ireland - if you have already been admitted to a university you are not eligible
Level of Study: Postgraduate
Type: Fellowships, operating grants
Frequency: Annual
Country of Study: South Africa
Application Procedure: Apply online www.canoncollins.org.uk/apply/scholarship/kader-asmal-fellowship
Closing Date: 31 August
Funding: Private
Additional Information: www.internationalscholarships.dhet.gov.za/IRELANDKaderAsmalFellowshipProgramme2020.html

For further information contact:

Email: Rose.Machobane@dfa.ie

Japan: MEXT Scholarships

Purpose: The Japanese Ministry of Education, Culture, Sports, Science, and Technology (MEXT) offers scholarships to foreign students who wish to study at Japanese universities under the Japanese Government Scholarship Program
Eligibility: see website www.za.emb-japan.go.jp/itpr_en/MEXT_Scholarship.html
Level of Study: Postgraduate
Type: Scholarship
Frequency: Annual
Country of Study: South Africa
Application Procedure: Applications must be couriered or be hand delivered and addressed to Cultural Section of the Embassy of Japan in South Africa 259 Baines Street, Groenkloof, Pretoria, 0181, South Africa
Closing Date: 8 June
Funding: Foundation

For further information contact:

Cultural Section of the Embassy of Japan in South Africa, 259 Baines Street, Groenkloof, Pretoria 0181, South Africa.

Email: ryan.keet@pr.mofa.go.jp

Jordan: Talal Abu-Ghazaleh University College for Innovation Scholarship

Purpose: Talal Abu-Ghazaleh University College for Innovation (TAGUCI) is offering a scholarship for a South African student who wishes to pursue a Master of Business Administration (MBA) degree at TAGUCI. Registration is now open for the semester
Eligibility: 1. Applicants must submit official Bachelor's degree transcripts and certificate, stamped by the Ministry of Higher Education and Scientific Research in Jordan. 2. English Language Equivalency exam mark of 65%. 3. Minimum of two years of work experience. 4. Written essay of up to 3,000 words. 5. Candidates must be prepared to fund any costs not covered by the scholarship
Level of Study: Postgraduate
Type: Scholarship
Frequency: Annual
Country of Study: Any country
Application Procedure: Apply online www.taguci.edu.jo/RegistrationForm.aspx
Closing Date: 28 February
Funding: Foundation

For further information contact:

Tel: (962) 65100 900
Email: info@taguci.edu.jo

Mauritius: Mauritius-Africa Scholarship Scheme

Purpose: As part of a commitment to promote capacity-building at high level across thecontinent, the Government of Mauritius is awarding scholarships to deserving students who are resident citizens of member states of the African Union or of African Commonwealth countries for full-time, on-campus undergraduate and postgraduate programmes tenable in public Higher Education Institutions (HEIs) in Mauritius
Eligibility: The Government of Mauritius is awarding scholarships to deserving students who are resident citizens of member states of the African Union or of African Commonwealth countries as per the following criteria 1. For undergraduate programmes, applicants should be above 18 years of age and should not have reached their 26th birthday by the closing date of application. 2. For Master's programmes, applicants should not have reached 35 years and, for PhD programmes, applicants should not have reached 40 years by the closing date of application. 3. Applicants must have already applied for a full-time on-campus programme (Diploma, Degree, Master's or PhD) at a public Higher Education Institution in Mauritius (listed in Section 8 in the Guidelines for Applicants).
Level of Study: Postgraduate
Type: Scholarship
Value: tuition fees and contribute to their living expenses during their studies in Mauritius
Frequency: Annual
Country of Study: South Africa
Closing Date: 7 March
Funding: Foundation
Additional Information: www.afterschoolafrica.com/54554/government-of-mauritius-africa-scholarships/

For further information contact:

Email: internationalscholarships@dhet.gov.za

New Zealand: Scholarships for International Tertiary Students and Commonwealth Scholarship

Purpose: The New Zealand Aid Programme offers scholarships to potential applicants from eligible African countries (including South Africa) who are motivated to make a difference at home. Applications are now open for studies
Level of Study: Postgraduate
Type: Scholarship
Frequency: Annual
Country of Study: Any country
Application Procedure: All applications for the New Zealand Scholarship for International Tertiary Students must be submitted online. Please see the below links for more details on the process All applications for the New Zealand Commonwealth Scholarship must be submitted on this application form. www.internationalscholarships.dhet.gov.za/
Closing Date: 31 March
Funding: Foundation
Additional Information: www.bursariesportal.co.za/bursary/new-zealand-scholarships-international-tertiary-students-and-commonwealth-scholarship-2021

For further information contact:

Email: commonwealthscholarship@dhet.gov.za

Romania: Romanian State Scholarships

Purpose: The Romanian Ministry of Foreign Affairs (MFA) and the Romanian Department of Public, Cultural and Scientific Diplomacy are offering 85 scholarship opportunities to foreign citizens, to study in Romania. This opportunity is open to students who wish to pursue studies in Bachelor's, Master's and PhD. Courses will be taught in Romanian language

Eligibility: 1. Applicants must be in good health and have a strong academic record. 2. Must present study papers issued by accredited / recognized educational institutions. 3. Applicants must not be older than 35 years of age for Bachelor's and Master's studies and 45 years respectively for Doctoral studies, by 31 December of the year in which they are nominated. 4. Candidates must be prepared to fund any costs not covered by the scholarship

Level of Study: Postgraduate

Type: Scholarship

Value: R85

Length of Study: 1 year

Frequency: Annual

Country of Study: South Africa

Application Procedure: www.mae.ro/en/node/10251

Closing Date: 15 March

Funding: Foundation

For further information contact:

Email: internationalscholarships@dhet.gov.za

Romanian State Scholarships

Purpose: The Romanian Ministry of Foreign Affairs (MFA) and the Romanian Department of Public, Cultural and Scientific Diplomacy are offering 85 scholarship opportunities to foreign citizens, to study in Romania. This opportunity is open to students who wish to pursue studies in Bachelor's, Master's and PhD.

Eligibility: 1. Applicants must be in good health and have a strong academic record. 2. Must present study papers issued by accredited/recognized educational institutions. 3. Applicants must not be older than 35 years of age for Bachelor's and Master's studies and 45 years respectively for Doctoral studies, by 31 December of the year in which they are nominated. 4. Candidates must be prepared to fund any costs not covered by the scholarship

Level of Study: Postgraduate

Type: Scholarship

Value: R85

Frequency: Annual

Country of Study: South Africa

Closing Date: 15 March

Funding: Foundation

For further information contact:

Email: internationalscholarships@dhet.gov.za

Russia: Scholarships for South Africans

Purpose: The Russian Government offers annual scholarships for South Africans to study at Russian institutions. The scholarship is offered for Bachelor's, Masters and PhD degrees. Most programmes are taught in the Russian language. Scholarship recipients are required to undertake a preparatory course related to their field of study (including language training) for one year before pursuing their degree studies. Only after passing the examinations of the college preparatory course can they start their degree studies

Eligibility: 1. South African citizens in good health (medical test are required for successful applicants). 2. Have a strong academic record. 3. Demonstrated interest in Russia and commitment to the development of South Africa. 4. Applications in all fields of study except medicine will be considered. 5. Preference will be given to postgraduate applicants, previously disadvantaged applicants and applicants in the following fields

Level of Study: Doctorate

Type: Scholarship

Value: US$400 and US$600 per month for living in Russia

Frequency: Annual

Country of Study: South Africa

Application Procedure: Apply online www.russia.study/en

Closing Date: 20 February

Funding: Foundation

Additional Information: website of the Ministry of Foreign Affairs of the Russian Federation russianembassyza.mid.ru/

For further information contact:

Email: south_africa@rs.gov.ru

Spain: Student and Staff Exchange between South Africa and Spain

Purpose: Alianza 4 Universidades (A4U) is a consortium of four Spanish public universities. The consortium is funded by the Erasmus+ Programme of the European Union to enable student and staff exchange between universities members of the A4U and six South African partner universities

Eligibility: 1. Applicants from South African partner universities and A4U universities. South African partner universities include University of Pretoria, University of the

Witwatersrand, Stellenbosch University, University of Cape Town, University of the Western Cape and University of the Free State. 2. A4U Universities participating universities are Universitat Autònoma de Barcelona, Universidad Autònoma de Madrid, Universidad Carlos III de Madrid and Universitat Pompeu Fabra in Barcelona
Level of Study: Postgraduate
Type: Grant
Frequency: Annual
Country of Study: South Africa
Application Procedure: Apply online alliance4universities.eu/en/mobility-scholarships/
Closing Date: December
Funding: Foundation
Additional Information: www.internationalscholarships.dhet.gov.za/SPAIN%20Student%20and%20staff%20exchange%20between%20South%20Africa%20and%20Spain.html

For further information contact:

Tel: (34) 935 422 079
Email: coordinacion@a-4u.eu

Sweden: Swedish Institute Scholarships for South Africa (SISSA)

Purpose: The Swedish Institute Scholarships for South Africa (SISSA) are being offered for South Africans to undertake Master's degrees at Swedish universities from September
Eligibility: 1. South African citizens in good health with a strong academic record. 2. Must have Bachelor's with Honours or equivalent, and should have performed well in his/her previous studies with minimum 65% average mark achieved. 3. Have applied for a Master's degree programme at a Swedish university on a full-time basis. 4. Intend to return to South Africa at the end of your studies. 5. Work and leadership experience is not a requirement but will be viewed favourably
Level of Study: Masters Degree
Type: Scholarship
Value: SEK 900
Frequency: Annual
Country of Study: South Africa
Application Procedure: Apply online si.se/en/apply/scholarships/swedish-institute-scholarships-for-south-africa/
Closing Date: 1 February
Funding: Foundation
Additional Information: si.se/en/apply/sissa-who-can-apply/#:~:text=The%20Swedish%20Institute's%20scholarships%20for,from%20the%202022%20autumn%20semester.

For further information contact:

Email: Internationalscholarships@dhet.gov.za

Switzerland: Swiss Government Excellence Scholarship for Foreign Students

Purpose: Through the Swiss Federal Commission for Scholarships for Foreign Students, the Swiss Government Grants foreign researchers, postgraduate scholarships at Swiss higher education institutions. The Swiss Government Excellence Scholarship are intended for highly motivated, competitive young researchers who have graduated from university. These scholarships will enable applicants to undertake research work in the fields in which the Swiss universities are particularly active.
Eligibility: 1. South African citizens. 2. Research fellowship applicants must have Master's degree or equivalent achieved and must be born after 31 December 1985. 3. PhD scholarship applicants must have a Master's degree or equivalent achieved and must be born after 31 December 1985. 4. Post-doctoral scholarship applicants must have a PhD degree achieved after 31 December 2016. 5. Applicants with admission letter from academic host institution. 6. Support letter from supervisor or academic host professor. 7. Research proposal including timeframe.
Level of Study: PhD, Post-doc and Research Fellow
Type: Scholarship
Value: CHF 1,920/month to CHF 3,500/month
Length of Study: 1 year-3 years
Frequency: Annual
Study Establishment: Swiss Confederation
Country of Study: Switzerland
Application Procedure: visit www.sbfi.admin.ch/scholarships_eng and click on South Africa. Request the application package at pre.vertretung@eda.admin.ch
Closing Date: 15 December
Funding: Foundation
Contributor: Swiss Confederation

For further information contact:

Tel: (27) 12 452 0660
Email: pre.vertretung@eda.admin.ch

Turkey: Türkiye Scholarships

Purpose: Türkiye Scholarships is a government-funded, competitive scholarship program, awarded to outstanding students to pursue full-time or short-term program at the top universities in Turkey. Applications will be open to applicants who wish to study at bachelor's, master's and doctoral levels.

Eligibility: 1. Applications for Türkiye Scholarships are open to citizens of all countries. 2. Applicants should not be older than 21 for Bachelor's, 30 for Master's and 35 for Doctoral studies. 3. For Undergraduate degree applications 70 %. 4. For Master's and Doctoral degree applications 75 %

Level of Study: Postgraduate

Type: Scholarship

Value: Bachelor TRY 800 per month; Masters TRY 1,100 per month; PhD TRY 1,600 per month

Length of Study: 1. Undergraduate 1 year Turkish Language course + 4-6 years (depending on the normal duration of the program) 2. Master's 1 year Turkish Language course + 2 years 3. PhD 1 year Turkish Language course + 4 years

Frequency: Annual

Country of Study: South Africa

Application Procedure: Apply online www.turkiyeburslari.gov.tr

Closing Date: 20 February

Funding: Foundation

Contributor: Participating Universities in Turkey

Additional Information: www.turkiyeburslari.gov.tr/announcements/turkiye-scholarships-2022-applications-19#:~:text=T%C3%BCrkiye%20Scholarships%20is%20a%20government,the%20top%20universities%20in%20Turkey.

For further information contact:

Email: info@turkiyeburslari.org

United Arab Emirates: Khalifa University Postgraduate Scholarships

Purpose: Khalifa University (KU) of Science and Technology is offering postgraduate scholarships to students who wish to pursue postgraduate studies in the field of Engineering Sciences in Abu Dhabi. Through these scholarships, the University aims to highlight the importance of investing in intellectual and human capital as well as its role in enhancing the performance of higher education system

Eligibility: Check website www.ku.ac.ae/admissions/graduate-admissions/

Level of Study: Masters Degree

Type: Scholarship

Value: R10,000

Length of Study: 2 Year

Frequency: Annual

Country of Study: South Africa

Application Procedure: Apply online admissions.kustar.ac.ae/pg/Account/Login

Closing Date: 14 February

Funding: Foundation

Additional Information: opportunitiescorners.info/khalifa-university-scholarship/

For further information contact:

Email: pgadmission@ku.ac.ae

United States: Fulbright Foreign Student Program

Purpose: The Fulbright Foreign Student Program enables graduate students, young professionals and artists from abroad to study and conduct research in the United States at U.S. universities or other academic institutions.

Eligibility: All Foreign Student Program applications are processed by bi-national Fulbright Commissions/Foundations or U.S. Embassies. Therefore, foreign students must apply through the Fulbright Commission/Foundation or U.S. Embassy in their home countries. Deadline varies per country but is around February to October annually.

Level of Study: Postgraduate

Type: Studentship

Value: living stipend of £15,144 per annum and all University and College fees.

Frequency: Annual

Country of Study: South Africa

Application Procedure: In order to apply for this scholarship, you could use the following link. apply.iie.org/ffsp2020

No. of awards offered: Approximately 4,000 foreign students receive Fulbright scholarships each year.

Closing Date: February

Funding: Private

Additional Information: For further, kindly contact the organisation using the below link. za.usembassy.gov/education-culture/educational-exchanges/fulbright-flagship-programs/foreign-student-program-frequently-asked-questions/ www.scholarshiproar.com/fulbright-scholarships-usa/

United States: Harvard South Africa Fellowship Program

Purpose: The HSAFP was initiated to provide educational enrichment for mid-career individuals in various occupations who have shown considerable skills and leadership in their chosen fields. Applications are invited for the Harvard South Africa Fellowship Program

Eligibility: 1. Fellows must be South African citizens. 2. Usually between 30 and 45 years of age. 3. Must not have just completed or not completed a Bachelor's degree, unless this degree has been pursued concurrently with or subsequent to experience in the workplace. 4. Applicants should determine well in advance whether if awarded a fellowship, they can be granted leave by their employers for Harvard's academic year

Level of Study: Postgraduate

Type: Fellowships, operating grants

Frequency: Annual

Country of Study: South Africa

Application Procedure: Apply onlline africa.harvard.edu/south-africa-fellowship-program

Closing Date: 4 April

Funding: Foundation

Additional Information: www.internationalscholarships.dhet.gov.za/UNITED%20STATES%20Harvard%20South%20Africa%20Fellowship%20Program%202020-2021.html

For further information contact:

Tel: (27) 877 010 715

Email: AfricaOffice@Harvard.edu

Hilda Martindale Educational Trust

Royal Holloway, University of London, Egham, Surrey TW20 0EX, United Kingdom.

Tel: (44) 17 8427 6158

Email: hildamartindaletrust@rhul.ac.uk

Contact: Miss Sarah Moffat, Administrator to the Trust

The Hilda Martindale Trust makes one-off awards to British women undertaking training or professional qualifications in areas in which women are underrepresented.

Hilda Martindale Trust Awards

Purpose: To assist with the costs of training or professional qualifications in areas in which women are under represented

Eligibility: 1. British women 2. taking an undergraduate or postgraduate course or training at a UK-based Higher Education Institution 3. following a profession/career in areas where women are underrepresented

Level of Study: Doctorate, Graduate, MBA, Postdoctorate, Postgraduate, Postgraduate (MSc), Predoctorate, Professional development, Undergraduate

Type: Grant

Value: Up to £3,000.

Length of Study: 1 year

Frequency: Annual

Study Establishment: Any establishment approved by the trustees

Country of Study: United Kingdom

Application Procedure: The application form and guidance for applicants are available from the website address below. In addition, requests for an application form can be made by email to Hildamartindaletrust@rhul.ac.uk

Closing Date: 9 February

Funding: Private

Contributor: Private trust

Additional Information: Further information can be obtained via email at hildamartindaletrust@rhul.ac.uk www.royalholloway.ac.uk/studying-here/fees-and-funding/undergraduate/scholarships-and-bursaries/scholarships/hilda-martindale-trust-awards/

For further information contact:

College Secretary's Office, RHUL, Egham, Surrey TW20 0EX, United Kingdom.

Email: HildaMartindaleTrust@royalholloway.ac.uk

Hong Kong Baptist University

AAB703, Level 7, Academic and Administration Building, Baptist University Road Campus, Kowloon Tong, Hong Kong.

Tel: (852) 3411 2188

Contact: Hong Kong Baptist University

Hong Kong Baptist University (HKBU) is a publicly funded tertiary institution with a Christian education heritage.

Fully Funded Master Scholarship at Hong Kong Baptist University

Purpose: The aim of the scholarship is to encourage the study of International Journalism

Eligibility: 1. Required Languages: English 2. Eligible Countries: All World Countries 3. A bachelors' degree from a recognized tertiary institution 4. Proof of English proficiency by IELTS or TOEFL 5. Shortlisted candidates may be invited for an online interview

Level of Study: Masters Degree

Value: Full tuition fee waiver, Allowance (HK$100,000 = ~US$12,800)

Country of Study: Any country

Application Procedure: The mode of applying is online

Closing Date: April

Additional Information: scholarshiproar.com/hong-kong-baptist-university-scholarship/#:~:text=Hong%20Kong%20Baptist%20University%20Scholarship%202022%2D2023%20is%20a%20fully,HK%24100%2C000%20%3D%20~US%2412%2C800.

For further information contact:

Email: busd-external@hkbu.edu.hk

Horowitz Foundation for Social Policy

106 Somerset St, 7th Floor, New Brunswick, NJ 08901, United States of America.

Tel: (1) 732 445 2280
Website: www.horowitz-foundation.org

The Horowitz Foundation for Social Policy was established to support the advancement of research and understanding in the social sciences including: psychology, anthropology, sociology, economics, and political science. The Foundation assists individual scholars at the early stages of their career who require small grants to complete their dissertations.

Irving Louis Horowitz Award

Purpose: Awarded to the project that best represents the goals of the Horowitz Foundation in a specific award year
Eligibility: Open to nationals of any country. Candidates may solicit support for final work on a dissertation, including travel funds
Level of Study: Doctorate
Type: Award
Value: US$12,500 (US$10,000 initially and an additional US$2,500 upon receipt of a final report on a copy of the research)
Length of Study: 1 year
Frequency: Annual
Country of Study: Any country
Application Procedure: Applicants are not required to be United States citizens or United States residents. Candidates may propose new projects, and they may also solicit support for research in progress, including final work on a dissertation, supplementing research in progress, or travel funds. Awards are only open to aspiring PhDs at the dissertation level whose project has received approval from their appropriate department head/university. Grants are normally made for 1 year on a non-renewable basis. Awards will be made to individuals, not institutions, and if processed through an institution, a waiver for overhead is requested. A copy of the product of the research is expected no later than 1 year after completion. Upon receipt an additional US$2,500 will be paid. Recipients are expected to acknowledge assistance provided by the Foundation in any publication resulting from their research. Awards are publicized in appropriate professional media and on the Foundation website
No. of awards offered: 300
Closing Date: 31 January
Funding: Private
No. of awards given last year: 15
No. of applicants last year: 300
Additional Information: The cover sheet in the application is most important, as it is the basis for the initial screening of prospects. www.horowitz-foundation.org/grant-info

For further information contact:

Email: wagner.events@nyu.edu

Refugee Study Awards

Purpose: The Refugee Study Awards are for women who are studying for a New Zealand tertiary qualification, and who have not been through the New Zealand school system. The awards are a one off grant to help with study and/or living expenses
Eligibility: To apply for the Refugee Study Awards you must meet all the following eligibility criteria The applicant is a woman, who 1. Is enrolled in a NZ approved tertiary qualification. 2. Is studying at diploma or degree level (NZQA level 5 or above). 3. Is a New Zealand citizen or holds a resident class visa, and lives in New Zealand. 4. Provides evidence of having arrived in New Zealand as a refugee - ID card or NZ Immigration Service refugee travel document. Has not previously received a NHWTHK Award
Level of Study: Graduate
Type: Award
Value: NZ$3,000
Frequency: Annual
Country of Study: Any country
Application Procedure: Please check the following website link for further details. www.newhorizonsforwomen.org.nz/awards/manawatu-charitable-trust-refugee/
No. of awards offered: 2
Closing Date: 15 April
Funding: Private

For further information contact:

New Horizons for Women Trust, PO Box 12498, Wellington, NZL 6144, New Zealand.

Email: enquiries@newhorizonsforwomen.org.nz

The Horowitz Foundation for Social Policy

Eligibility: Awards are open only to PhD candidates whose project has received approval from their appropriate department head/university. Preference is given to projects that address contemporary issues in the social sciences and issues of policy relevance. Applicants are not required to be citizens or residents of the United States. Awards are based solely on merit, not to ensure a representative base of recipients or disciplines

Level of Study: Doctorate

Type: Grants and fellowships

Value: NZ$7,500—NZ$5,000 initially and an additional NZ$2,500 upon completion of the project. Criteria for completion include approval of the dissertation, acceptance of an article based on the research by a peer-reviewed journal, or an invitation to write a book chapter based on the research. Additional awards are given in certain suspect areas. The best overall project (as determined by the trustees) receives an additional NZ$5,000

Frequency: Annual

Country of Study: Any country

Application Procedure: Applications must be submitted through our online system which can be found on our website www.horowitz-foundation.org

No. of awards offered: 700

Closing Date: 1 December

Funding: Private

No. of awards given last year: 20

No. of applicants last year: 700

Additional Information: All submitted applications, letters, and documents must be in English. Applications are open 1 July through 1 December. Applicants are encouraged to apply as early as possible. Submitted materials become the property of the Foundation and will not be returned. Applicants should not send originals or other materials that cannot be replaced sociol ogy.fas.harvard.edu/horowitz-foundation-social-policy-grant

Hosei University

17-1 Fujimi 2 chome, Chiyoda-ku, Tokyo, JP 102, Japan.

Tel: (81) 3 3264 9564
Email: ic@I.hosei.ac.jp
Website: www.hosei.ac.jp/ic
Contact: Ms Keiko Takahata, Executive Assistant

Master of Business Administration Programme

Application Procedure: Applicants must complete an application form supplying official transcripts, passport sized photograph, curriculum vitae and a statement of financial support

Closing Date: 30 November

For further information contact:

Business Adminstration, 2-17-1 Fujimi, Tokyo 102, Japan.

Tel: (81) 3 3264 9315
Fax: (81) 3 3238 9873
Email: ic@fujimi.hosei.ac.jp

Hospitality Maine

Hospitality Maine, 45, Melville St., Augusta, ME, 04330, United States of America.

Tel: (1) 207 623 2178
Website: www.hospitalitymaine.com

Hospitality Maine Scholarships

Purpose: This scholarship is available for Maine students who plan to pursue a career in culinary arts or hospitality. It is open to graduating high school students, as well as those already enrolled in a culinary or hospitality program.

Eligibility: 1. Must be a resident of Maine. 2. Must be a United States citizen or permanent resident. 3. Must be a high school senior or older to apply for this undergraduate award. 4. Must be planning to pursue a culinary arts or hospitality-oriented program.

Level of Study: Graduate

Type: Scholarship

Value: US$1,000 - US$2,000

Frequency: Annual

Country of Study: United States of America

Application Procedure: Applications are available on the Hospitality Maine website under Resources.

No. of awards offered: Multiple

Funding: Foundation

For further information contact:

Email: becky@hospitalitymaine.com
Website: www.hospitalitymaine.com

Howard Hughes Medical Institute (HHMI)

4000 Jones Bridge Road, Chevy Chase, MD 20815-6789, United States of America.

Tel: (1) 301 215 8500
Website: www.hhmi.org

HHMI is a science philanthropy whose mission is to advance biomedical research and science education for the benefit of humanity. We empower exceptional scientists and students to pursue fundamental questions about living systems.

Howard Hughes Medical Institute Gilliam Fellowships for Advanced Study

Purpose: The goal of the Gilliam Fellowships for Advanced Study program is to ensure the development of a diverse and highly trained workforce is available to assume leadership roles in science, including college and university faculty, who have the responsibility to teach the next generation of scientists

Eligibility: Adviser-student pairs from eligible disciplines must be nominated by the HHMI-designated institutional representative. Prospective fellows must be i) U.S. citizens, U.S. permanent residents, undocumented childhood arrivals, or undocumented individuals who have been granted temporary permission to stay in the US (DACA), and ii) be from populations excluded from science, or alumni of the HHMI EXROP and iii) be at the appropriate stage of their PhD training.

Type: Fellowship

Value: US$50,000 per year

Length of Study: Up to 3 years of their dissertation research, typically in years 3, 4, and 5 of their PhD studies

Frequency: Annual

Country of Study: United States of America

Closing Date: 10 December

Additional Information: www.hhmi.org/science-education/programs/gilliam-fellowships-advanced-study

For further information contact:

Email: Gilliam@hhmi.org

Postdoctoral Research Fellowships for Physicians

Purpose: To help increase the supply of well-trained physician-scientists, through fellowships for three years of training in fundamental research (basic biological processes or disease mechanisms)

Eligibility: Applicants must have gained their first degree within the last ten years, and must have had two years of postgraduate clinical training, and no more than two years of postdoctoral training in fundamental research

Level of Study: Postdoctorate

Type: Fellowship

Value: US$69,000–86,500 per year

Length of Study: 3 years

Frequency: Annual

Study Establishment: Academic or non-profit research institution

Country of Study: United States of America

Application Procedure: Application forms and instructions should be obtained from the address shown. Panels of scientists review applications, and the Institute makes the final selection

No. of awards offered: 255

Closing Date: December

No. of awards given last year: 30

No. of applicants last year: 255

Additional Information: Fellows must engage in full-time research. During the fellowship term, they may not be enrolled in a graduate degree program, nor hold a faculty appointment. The applicant is responsible for selecting a research mentor and making arrangements to work in that person's laboratory. www.hhmi.org/programs/gilliam-fellowships-for-advanced-study

For further information contact:

4000 Jones Bridge Road, Chevy Chase, MD 20815, United States of America.

Tel: (1) 301 215 8889
Fax: (1) 301 215 8888
Email: fellows@hq.hhmi.org

Humane Research Trust

The Humane Research Trust, Brook House, 29 Bramhall Lane South, Bramhall, Stockport, Greater Manchester SK7 2DN, United Kingdom.

Tel: (44) 161 439 8041
Website: www.humaneresearch.org.uk
Contact: Jane McAllister, Trust Administrator

The Humane Research Trust is a national charity, which funds a range of unique medical research programmes on human illness at hospitals and universities around the country. In keeping with the philosophy of the Trust, none of the research involves animals and much of it seeks to establish and develop pioneering techniques that will replace animal intensive experiments.

The Humane Research Trust Grant

Subjects: Humane Research

Purpose: To encourage scientific programmes where the use of animals is replaced by other methods

Eligibility: Open to established scientific workers engaged in productive research. Nationals of any country are considered but for the sake of overseeing, projects should be undertaken in a UK establishment.

Level of Study: Unrestricted

Type: Grant

Value: Full funding of a project

Length of Study: Varies

Frequency: Dependent on funds available

Country of Study: United Kingdom

Application Procedure: Applicants must complete an application form, available on the website www.humaneresearch.org.uk Please ensure you email all of the required documents, i.e. one fully complete application to info@humaneresearch.org.uk and post 10 hard copies to The Humane Research Trust.

No. of awards offered: Varies

Closing Date: 26 January

Funding: Private

Additional Information: The Humane Research Trust is a registered charity and donations are encouraged. www.humaneresearch.org.uk/apply-for-funding/

For further information contact:

The Humane Research Trust, 29 Bramhall Lane South, Bramhall, Stockport SK7 2DN, United Kingdom.

Email: info@humaneresearch.org.uk

Humboldt University of Berlin

Office for Promotion of Young Researchers in the Excellence Initiative, Berlin, D-10099, Germany.

Tel: (49) 30 2093 1795

Contact: Humboldt Graduate School

Humboldt Postdoc Scholarships

Purpose: To support young researchers in taking the next step in their academic career after acquiring their PhD.

Eligibility: Eligible to excellent researchers who either already hold a PhD from Humboldt-Universität or are about to complete their doctorate at Humboldt-Universität zu Berlin and who wish to conduct a postdoctoral research project. Half of the scholarships will be awarded to women

Type: Scholarship

Value: US$25,000 - US$105,000

Study Establishment: Humboldt-Universität

Country of Study: Germany

Application Procedure: Applications can be received only via an online application portal

No. of awards offered: 500

Closing Date: 31 December

Additional Information: scholarships.unimelb.edu.au/awards/humboldt-research-fellowships-for-postdoctoral-researchers

For further information contact:

Email: hgs-grants@hu-berlin.de

Imperial College of Science, Technology and Medicine

Exhibition Road, London SW7 2AZ, United Kingdom.

Tel: (44) 20 7594 8023
Email: r.a.clay@ic.ac.uk
Contact: Ms R A Clay, Scholarships co-ordinator registry

The Imperial College of Science, Technology and Medicine is a college of the University of London and provides university education at first degree and postgraduate level in the fields of science, engineering and medicine.

British Council Scholarships for Women in STEM

Purpose: The Scholarships have been created with the aim to help address the under-representation of women in STEM. Applicants will be required to demonstrate their financial need and how they would inspire future generations of women to pursue a career in STEM.

Eligibility: Be a passport holder and permanent resident of Brazil, Mexico, or Peru. Be available to commence your academic studies in the UK by the start of the UK academic year in September/October 2023. Have submitted an application to study at Imperial College London before your scholarship application can be considered and have received an offer to study for one of the eligible programmes by the time selection takes place to be considered for a Scholarship. It is expected that selection will take place shortly after the scholarship deadline. Have completed your undergraduate degree or have all components of an undergraduate degree that will enable you to gain entry onto a postgraduate programme at Imperial College London and meet the academic entry requirement for admissions before the start of the UK academic year in September/October 2023. Have not previously studied at degree level or higher in the UK or lived recently in the UK. Meet the English language requirement for your programme at Imperial College London. Applicants who are awarded this scholarship will be required to have met College English entry requirements (Pre-sessional English courses are not supported by this programme) by 29 July 2023. Demonstrate a case for financial need. Return to the country of your citizenship for a minimum of two years after your course/scholarship has finished. Demonstrate active in the field with work experience or with a proven interest in the programme area you are applying for. Demonstrate that you are willing to contribute in the future to capacity-building and socio-economic advancement through the benefits achieved after graduating from Imperial College London and returning your home country. Demonstrate in your application a plan and passion to engage other women and girls in STEM from your home country. Agree to maintain contact with the British Council and act as an ambassador for the UK and engage with activities as part of a British Council Scholarships for Women in STEM alumnus during and after your study in the UK. Any involvement in these activities during your study in the UK will take up no more than five hours per term.

Type: Scholarship

Value: scholarship covers full tuition fees, an annual stipend of up to £16,680, and a return economy-class flight from home country to UK

Country of Study: Any country

No. of awards offered: 5

Closing Date: 16 March

Contributor: British Council

Additional Information: www.imperial.ac.uk/study/pg/fees-and-funding/scholarships/international-scholarship-collaborations/british-council-scholarships-for-women-in-stem/

For further information contact:

Tel: (44) 20 7589 5111
Email: student.funding@imperial.ac.uk

© Springer Nature Limited 2022
Palgrave Macmillan (ed.), *The Grants Register 2023*,
https://doi.org/10.1057/978-1-349-96053-8

GREAT - Imperial College London Scholarship

Subjects: Science, Technology, Engineering, Medicine and Business subjects.

Purpose: In partnership with the British Council and the GREAT Britain Campaign, Imperial College London is offering 3 scholarships to students from Kenya, Nigeria and Thailand applying for postgraduate courses in Science, Technology, Engineering, Medicine and Business subjects.

Eligibility: All eligible applicants holding a valid passport of Kenya, Nigeria and Thailand will be invited to apply for a GREAT scholarship be a citizen of Kenya, Nigeria and Thailand have been classified as Overseas for fee status apply for a one-year full-time Master's course. have received an offer of admission to study for a one-year full-time Master's Course from the Faculty of Engineering, Faculty of Medicine, Faculty of Natural Sciences, Business School or Science Communication Unit by Monday, 14 March 2023. be available to commence your academic studies in the UK by the start of the UK academic year in September/October 2023

Level of Study: Postgraduate

Type: Scholarship

Value: £10,000

Country of Study: Any country

No. of awards offered: 3

Closing Date: 14 March

Additional Information: www.imperial.ac.uk/study/pg/fees-and-funding/scholarships/international-scholarship-collaborations/great—imperial-college-london-scholarship/

For further information contact:

Tel: (44) 20 7589 5111

President's PhD Scholarships

Purpose: The President's PhD Scholarships are an outstanding opportunity for potential PhD students. If you are a high performing undergraduate or Master's student and have a strong desire to undertake a PhD programme at a world-class research institution, you could be selected to receive full tuition fees and a generous stipend for a PhD place at Imperial College London.

Eligibility: Candidates must be in receipt of, or due to receive, a first-class UK degree or equivalent. Candidates with a standalone Master's qualification must have achieved a distinction or, where this has yet to have been achieved, be able to provide evidence of high performance that will lead to a distinction. They must also hold a first-class UK undergraduate degree or equivalent (integrated Masters that form part of an undergraduate degree, e.g. MEng, MSci, M.Math, are assessed by Admissions as an undergraduate qualification

when determining eligibility). Candidates with multiple standalone Master's qualifications must have achieved a distinction in the one most relevant to their PhD study. Applications are accepted from talented candidates from Imperial College London, the UK and worldwide. There are no restrictions on nationality, although some departments may be unable to support international candidates. Candidates with degrees from overseas institutions should check with the relevant Admissions team if their scores/grades are equivalent to the scholarship entry criteria. Prior to applying candidates must have made contact with a supervisor in an academic department at Imperial College London who has agreed to supervise their research project. Please note that supervisors are limited to supervise one scholar at any time. Please review the President's PhD Scholarships - Unavailable Supervisors page for more information. The scheme is only open to new PhD applications. Current registered Imperial PhD students are not eligible to be considered for a President's PhD Scholarship.

Type: Scholarship

Value: stipend of £21,800 per annum, tuition fees, consumables fund of £2,000 per annum for the first 3 years of study

Country of Study: Any country

No. of awards offered: 50

Closing Date: 11 March

Additional Information: www.imperial.ac.uk/study/pg/fees-and-funding/scholarships/presidents-phd-scholarships/

For further information contact:

Tel: (44) 20 7589 5111
Email: phdscholarshipscheme@imperial.ac.uk

Presidential Scholarships for students of Black heritage

Subjects: Business, Engineering, Medicine and Natural Sciences

Purpose: Our new Presidential Scholarships for students of Black heritage provide a package of financial and mentoring support for students applying for Master's study in autumn 2023.

Eligibility: Black – African Black – Caribbean Black – Other Mixed – White and Black African Mixed White and Black Caribbean Other Mixed background – including Black African, Black Caribbean or Other Black background

Type: Scholarship

Value: Home tuition fees up to £18,500, annual maintenance grant of £16,500, allowance of £1,500 for equipment, Mentoring support

Country of Study: Any country

Closing Date: 25 May

Additional Information: www.imperial.ac.uk/study/pg/fees-and-funding/scholarships/presidential-scholarships-black-students/

For further information contact:

Tel: (44) 20 7589 5111

Stephen and Anna Hui Fellowship

Purpose: To facilitate postgraduate study or research

Eligibility: Open to graduates with a First or Upper Second Class (Honours) Degree from universities in China including Hong Kong and Taiwan

Level of Study: Doctorate, Postgraduate

Type: Fellowship

Value: It provide financial support to meet the full cost of tuition fees and an annual stipend equal to the College minimum (£15,863)

Length of Study: 3 years

Study Establishment: Imperial College

Country of Study: United Kingdom

Application Procedure: Applicants must complete an application form and submit this with two references and a transcript or academic record

Closing Date: 31 January

Funding: Private

Contributor: Stephen and Anna Hui Fellowship Trust Fund

Additional Information: Further information is available on request   www.imperial.ac.uk/apex/apps/f?p=1007:201:0::NO:201:P201_AWARD_INSTANCE_ID,%20P201_FEE_STATUS_ELIGIBILITY_TY,%20P201_PROGRAM_TYPE:2049,%20OVERSEAS,%20PHD

For further information contact:

Email: j.picken@imperial.ac.uk

India Alliance

Early Career Fellowship

Purpose: The proposed research should fall within the India Alliance's remit which is to support biomedical research that is relevant to human and animal welfare. If you are unsure if your research programme falls within our remit

Eligibility: The Early Career Fellowship (ECF) competition is open for basic science/veterinary researchers with 1 to 4 years of Post PhD research experience. This means that you must be in the final year of your PhD studies or have no more than four years of postdoctoral research experience from the date of your PhD viva to the full application submission deadline in order to be eligible for the competition. Applicant must have 0-4 years Post PhD Applicant in the final year of their PhD are also eligible. In line with the scheme's mandate to foster independence, Early Career Fellows are strongly encouraged to carry out their Fellowship project in a laboratory that is not their thesis laboratory or thesis environment. If you have compelling reasons to continue in or return to your thesis laboratory/environment, please present these appropriately in the preliminary application and arrange for a letter from the Fellowship Supervisor commenting on this decision

Level of Study: Postgraduate

Type: Fellowship

Length of Study: 4 years

Frequency: Annual

Country of Study: Any country

Application Procedure: To complete a preliminary application use our online system, IASys. Refer to the IASys user guide for guidance on completing the application form and the submission process. Please ensure that the form is submitted by the published deadline. Your preliminary application is assessed and If successful, you will be invited to submit a full application. Your full application will be peer reviewed and considered by the appropriate Selection Committee and, if successful, you will be short-listed for interview. Short-listed candidates will be notified two weeks before the interview date. Applicants are not permitted to apply to multiple Fellowship schemes within the India Alliance in parallel. Only one application to one scheme will be entertained, at a time

Closing Date: August

Funding: Private

Additional Information: indiaalliance.org/applicants/fellowships-at-a-glance

For further information contact:

Email: info@indiaalliance.org

India Habitat Centre

Visual Arts Galley, Lodhi Road, New Delhi, 110003, India.

Tel: (91) 11 246 820 01/05
Email: info@indiahabitat.org
Website: www.indiahabitat.org

The India Habitat Centre was conceived to provide a physical environment that would serve as a catalyst for a synergetic relationship between individuals and institutions working in diverse habitat related areas and, therefore, maximize their total effectiveness.

India Habitat Centre Fellowship for Photography

Purpose: To promote photography as an art form
Eligibility: Open to Indian nationals who are between 21 and 40 years of age and who do not hold any other fellowship
Level of Study: Professional development
Type: Fellowship
Value: ₹120,000
Frequency: Annual
Country of Study: India
Application Procedure: Applicants must send a project summary, curriculum vitae and reference letters
Closing Date: 31 August
Additional Information: Entries with less/more than the required 12 images will be eliminated www.indiaalliance. org/fellowships-at-a-glance

For further information contact:

Email: alkapande@indiahabitat.org

Indian Council for Cultural Relations

Azad Bhavan, I.p. Estate, New Delhi, 110002, India.

Contact: Indian Council for Cultural Relations

The Indian Council for Cultural Relations (ICCR), is an autonomous organisation of the Government of India, involved in India's external cultural relations, through cultural exchange with other countries and their peoples. It was founded by Maulana Abul Kalam Azad, the first Education Minister of independent India.

Indian Council for Cultural Relations Indian High Commission Bangladesh Scholarship Scheme

Purpose: The aim of the scholarship is to support meritorious Bangladeshi nationals who want to undertake engineering, graduate, post-graduate and PhD / post-doctoral course
Eligibility: 1. Applicants from Bangladesh are eligible to apply for the scholarship. 2. Candidates who wish to get scholarships must be proficient in English and have at least 60% marks in the passed examination or 3 in GPA 5. 3. Candidates will have to take part in 30-minute English proficiency test, whose time and place will be announced
Level of Study: Graduate
Type: Scholarship
Value: The Indian government has so far given ICCR education to nearly 3,000 Bangladeshi nationals
Frequency: Annual
Study Establishment: Scholarship is awarded in the subjects offered by the university
Country of Study: India
Application Procedure: To apply online for interested students, you need to create your own private login ID and password. The applicants are requested to apply online through the instructions. The applicant should keep the following points during the application process Those BE / B Tech. Must apply for the course, in their school-college syllabus must include Physics, Mathematics and Chemistry. The applicant's age must be 18 in July. All students must stay in the hostel. Cannot be outside without family and health reasons. The last date for submission of online application is 20 January, 5.00 pm. Candidates will have to take part in 30-minute English proficiency test, whose time and place will be announced
Closing Date: 20 January
Additional Information: For more details please see the website   scholarship-positions.com/iccr-indian-high-commission-bangladesh-scholarship-scheme-india/2018/01/08/

For further information contact:

Email: admin@scholarship-positions.com

Indian Council of Medical Research

V. Ramalingaswami Bhawan, Ansari Nagar, P.O. Box No. 4911, New Delhi, 110029, India.

Tel: (91) 11 265 888 95 / 11 265 889 80 / 11 265 897 94
Email: icmrhqds@sansad.nic.in
Website: www.icmr.nic.in

The Indian Council of Medical Research (ICMR), New Delhi, the apex body in India for the formulation, coordination and promotion of biomedical research, is one of the oldest medical research bodies in the world.

Indian Council of Medical Research Centenary- Postdoctoral Fellowship

Purpose: The aim of the fellowships is to giving research opportunities to promising fresh PhD/ MD/MS holders

Eligibility: Indian applicants are eligible for these fellowships. Entrance Requirement Applicants must be PhDs/MD/MS

Type: Postdoctoral fellowship

Value: ICMR Postdoctoral Fellows will be paid a consolidated fellowship of ₹50,000/- per month plus house rent allowance (HRA), Non-Practicing Allowance (NPA) as admissible and a contingency grant of ₹3.0 lakhs per annum. 25% of the contingency grant can be used for travel including per diem expenses

Study Establishment: These fellowships are awarded in cutting edge areas of basic science, communicable and non-communicable diseases, and reproductive health including nutrition

Country of Study: India

Application Procedure: See the website

Closing Date: 31 December

Indian Education Department

Government of India, Ministry of Human Resource Department, Shastri Bhavan, New Delhi, 110001, India.

Tel: (91) 11 233 839 36
Email: webmaster.edu@nic.in
Website: www.education.nic.in

The origin of the Indian Education Department, Government of India, dates back to pre-independence days when for the first time a separate Department was created in 1910 to look after education. However, soon after India achieved its independence, a full fledged ministry of Education was established.

China Scholarships

Subjects: Chinese Language & Literature, Fine Arts (Painting & Sculpture), Botany, Environmental Science, Plant Breeding & Genetics, Political Science/International Relations, MBA, Sericulture and Agronomy.

Eligibility: Indian nationals, Below 40 Years. Qualification for Chinese Lang 2 - 3 year Cert/Dip in basic Chinese Language from recognized Institution/University. Bachelor degree in Fine Arts with 60% marks at Post Graduates level with work research experience of two years.

Level of Study: Graduate

Type: Scholarship

Value: Scholarship covers expenditure on board & lodging Tuition fees pocket expenses which is paid by Chinese Government, partly paid by Government of India at a supplementary stipend grant.

Length of Study: 1–4 Years

Country of Study: Any country

Application Procedure: Application, duly sponsored by the employers (if employed) furnishing particulars (as per notified format) may be submitted on plain paper, by the prescribed date.

No. of awards offered: 25

Closing Date: January

Contributor: Government of China in association with the government of India

Additional Information: www.education.gov.in/en/external-scholarships-china

For further information contact:

Email: scholarship@dreamgo.com

Erasmus Mundus Scholarship Programme

Purpose: For the benefit of Indian students

Eligibility: Open to Indian nationals who are graduates from recognized institutions or universities

Level of Study: Graduate

Type: Scholarships

Value: EUR 1,000 each month for living costs, Euroculture participation costs of EUR 9.000 (EU students) / 18.000 (non-EU students) including health insurance

Length of Study: 1-2 years duration depending on the subject areas of study

Country of Study: Any country

Application Procedure: Applicants must apply directly to the universities/consortium of universities constituted under the Erasmus Mundus Programme

No. of awards offered: 22 Grants are available per year

Closing Date: 15 January

Contributor: European Union (EU)

Additional Information: www.euroculturemaster.eu/how-to-apply/erasmus-mundus-scholarship-programme

For further information contact:

University of Groningen, Faculty of Arts, Oude Kijk in 't Jatstraat 26, NL-9712 EK Groningen, Netherlands.

Tel: (31) 50 363 9111
Email: eac-info@cec.eu.int

National Centre for Promotion of Employment for Disabled People (NCPEDP) Rajiv Gandhi Postgraduate Scholarship Scheme

Purpose: To enable disabled students with limited means to receive education or professional training at postgraduate and doctoral levels

Eligibility: Open to Indian nationals between 18 and 35 years of age. The scholarship may be awarded to students with the disabilities as recognized by N.C.P.E.D.P. The candidate should be either pursuing or should have gained admission to a full-time course in an Indian university established by law or in a recognized equivalent institution

Level of Study: Doctorate, Postgraduate

Type: Scholarship

Value: ₹1,200 per month

Frequency: Annual

Application Procedure: Applicants must apply to the National Centre for Promotion of Employment for Disabled People

Funding: Government

Additional Information: A scholarship will be provided for the entire duration of the approved course. Scholarship money will be released every 3 months. N.C.P.E.D.P. reserves the right to change the scheme and/or amend the rules without any notice. The income of the candidate or his parents/guardians should not exceed ₹5,000 per month. At the discretion of the awarding authority, a scholarship may also be awarded for a professional course of Indira Gandhi National Open University (IGNOU) or any other recognized Open University www.scholarships.net.in/1989.html

For further information contact:

National Centre for Promotion of Employment for Disabled People, A-77, South Extension, Part II, New Delhi, 110 049, India.

Tel: (91) 11 262 656 47/48
Email: education@ncpedp.org

Indian Institute of Management Ranchi

Post-Doctoral Fellowship

Purpose: The Post-Doctoral Fellowship in Management (PDFM) is designed keeping in view IIM Ranchi's goal to create a high quality research environment in the institute. Its objective is to support high quality research by scholars with a doctoral degree and an outstanding academic record

Eligibility: 1. Contingency Grant A contingency grant of ₹50,000 per annum will be provided to the post-doctoral research fellow for research purposes. 2. The IIM Ranchi would pay the expenses for a fellow to attend one conference abroad from an approved list of conferences if their joint paper with a resident faculty member is accepted for presentation at that conference. 3. Office space will be provided to post-doctoral research fellows along with a computer and printer. They will be issued special research library card, enabling them to borrow up to ten books from the library at a time. 4. A post-doctoral research fellow will be eligible for leave from the fellowship not exceeding 30 days in a year for each completed year of the fellowship. 5. The leave can be availed on a pro-rata basis for the duration (on a 6 months' basis) of the fellowship completed. The age limit for applicants for the Post-Doctoral Fellowship will be a maximum of 40 years (this limit may be relaxed by 5 years for women and reserved category)

Level of Study: Postgraduate

Type: Fellowship

Value: Contigency grants of ₹50,000 per annum will be provided

Length of Study: 2 years

Frequency: Annual

Country of Study: Any country

Application Procedure: 1. Selection will be based on demonstrated research skills and a fit with the research interests of resident faculty. Shortlisted candidates will be invited to campus to present their research before a final decision is made. 2. Past research I PhD thesis work demonstrating potential for scholarly work would facilitate the initial shortlist process. 3. The shortlisted candidates will be invited for on-campus presentation and interview. 4. The candidates selected for the PDFM will be attached to the given area and will be associated with a faculty member of the group who will essentially perform the role of a mentor and collaborator. 5. Selection will be based on demonstrated research skills and a fit with the research interests of resident faculty

Closing Date: 24 March

Funding: Private

Additional Information: iimranchi.ac.in/p/post-doctoral-fellowship-in-management

For further information contact:

Indian Institute of Management Ranchi, Suchana Bhawan, 5th Floor, Audrey House Campus, Meur's Road, Ranchi, Jharkhand 834 008, India.

Tel: (91) 65 1228 0113
Fax: (91) 651 2280940
Email: office.fpm@iimranchi.ac.in

Indian Institute of Management, Calcutta

Diamond Harbour Road, Joka, Kolkata, West Bengal 700104, India.

Contact: The Indian Institute of Management

Indian Institute of Management, Calcutta abbreviated as IIM Calcutta or IIM-C is a public business school located in Joka, Kolkata, India. It was the first Indian Institute of Management to be established.

Postdoctoral Research Fellowship (PDRF)

Purpose: These fellowships are available for researchers who want to contribute to the theory and practice of management
Eligibility: Citizens of India are eligible to apply. These positions are open for candidates with 0–2 years of experience after obtaining PhD degree
Level of Study: Doctorate
Type: Fellowship
Value: Each fellowship will carry a stipend of ₹40,000/p.m. consolidated, depending on the level of prior experience of the chosen candidate. In addition, a contingency grant of ₹50,000/- per annum will be provided
Length of Study: 2 years
Country of Study: India
Application Procedure: Fellowships are negotiable up to 3 years. Under exceptional circumstances, tenure may be extended to a maximum of 5 years
Closing Date: 5 March
Additional Information: www.nationalmeritscholarships.com/postdoctoral-research-fellowships-at-iim-calcutta.html

For further information contact:

Email: pgfunding@uct.ac.za

Indian Institute of Science Bangalore (IISc)

Bangalore, Karnataka 560012, India.

Tel: (91) 80 2360 0757
Email: regr@admin.iisc.ernet.in
Website: www.iisc.ernet.in
Contact: The Registrar

The Indian Institute of Science (IISc) was started in 1909 through the pioneering vision of J N Tata. Since then, it has grown into a premier institution of research and advanced instruction, with more than 2,000 active researchers working in almost all frontier areas of science and technology.

Indian Institute of Science Bangalore Kishore Vaigyanik Protsahan Yojana Fellowships

Purpose: To assist students in realizing their potential and to ensure that the best scientific talent is developed for research and growth in the country
Eligibility: Open to Indian citizens
Level of Study: Graduate, Postdoctorate, Postgraduate, Predoctorate, Research
Type: Fellowship
Value: ₹4,000–7,000 per month and contingency grants of ₹16,000–28,000
Frequency: Annual
Study Establishment: Indian Institute of Science, Bangalore
Country of Study: India
Application Procedure: Applicants can download the application form from the website
Closing Date: September
Additional Information: www.kvpy.iisc.ernet.in/main/index.htm

For further information contact:

Indian Institute of Science, CV Raman Rd, Bengaluru, Karnataka 560012, India.

Tel: (91) 80 2360 1008/80 2293 2976
Email: kvpy@admin.iisc.ernet.in

Indian Institute of Technology (IIT)

Department of Computer Science and Engineering, Kanpur, Uttar Pradesh 208016, India.

Tel: (91) 512 259 7338/7638
Email: pgadm@cse.iitk.ac.in
Website: www.cse.iitk.ac.in
Contact: Harish Karnick, Professor and Head

Indian Institute of Technology (IIT) imparts training to students to make them competent, motivated engineers and scientists. The Institute not only celebrates freedom of thought, cultivates vision and encourages growth, but also inculcates human values and concern for the environment and the society.

Infosys Fellowship for PhD Students

Purpose: To support those interested in pursuing the PhD programme in the Department of Computer Science and Engineering at IIT Kanpur

Eligibility: Open to deserving students who have a MTech/ME in any branch of engineering and who have secured admission into the PhD programme

Level of Study: Postgraduate

Type: Fellowship

Value: ₹225,000 and ₹250,000 per year. Out of this grant, ₹180,000 (₹15,000 per month) will paid as stipend, remaining money can be utilized by the fellow for purchase of books, journals, payment of tuition fee, and travel for domestic and international conference attendance

Length of Study: 3.5–4 years

Frequency: Annual

Study Establishment: IIT Kanpur

Country of Study: India

Application Procedure: The applicant must submit a separate application form to the Department of Computer Science and Engineering. Please check at www.cse.iitk.ac.in

Additional Information: www.cse.iitm.ac.in/awards_details.php?arg=Nw==

Indian Institute of Technology Kharagpur

IT Kharagpur Post Doctoral Fellowship

Purpose: IIT Kharagpur is giving an excellent platform for the students possessing PhD degree with an excellent academic record by offering them IIT Kharagpur Post Doctoral Fellowship. The main objective of this fellowship is to give an opportunity to deserving scholars to carry out their research in the field of science and technology

Eligibility: 1. Must hold PhD Degree with the outstanding academic record. 2. Must have published research paper / patents on his/her name. 3. Age limit of a candidate is 35 years. 4. The candidates who are belonging to AICTE / UGC recognized teaching institution or sponsored by DISR recognized industrial organization they will get age relaxation up to 45 years of age

Level of Study: Postdoctorate

Type: Fellowship

Value: ₹25,000

Frequency: Annual

Country of Study: India

Closing Date: 31 December

Funding: Foundation

Additional Information: www.iitkgp.ac.in/academics-post-doc-fellowships

For further information contact:

Assistant Registrar (PGS&R), Indian Institute of Technology, Kharagpur, West Bengal India.

Email: asregpgr@adm.iitkgp.ac.in

Indian Institute of Technology Ropar

Rupnagar, Punjab 140001, India.

Contact: Indian Institute of Technology Ropar

The Indian Institute of Technology Ropar (IIT Ropar) or IIT-RPR, is an engineering and technology higher education institute located in Rupnagar, Punjab, India. It is one of the eight newer Indian Institutes of Technology (IITs) established by the Ministry of Human Resource Development MHRD, Government of India under The Institutes of Technology (Amendment) Act.

Indian Institute of Technology Ropar Institute Postdoctoral Fellowship

Purpose: The aim of the fellowship is to support Indian students and provide a contingency grant of ₹1,00,000/- per annum to the Post-Doctoral Fellow for research purposes. The unspent amount can be carried over to the next financial year

Eligibility: PhD degree holders are eligible to apply within five years after completion of their PhD Candidates completed PhD supervised/co-supervised by faculty members from IIT Ropar can apply after 3 years of completion of their PhD.

Type: Fellowship

Value: Between ₹45,000–55,000/- consolidated

Length of Study: 3 years

Study Establishment: Fellowship is awarded in the subjects offered by the university

Country of Study: Any country

Application Procedure: The application has to be submitted to the Department/Center in which the candidate intends to join as a Post Doctoral Fellow. Applicants can apply through the post and submit the application form to the Department/ Center. Applicants can apply by rolling basis

Closing Date: 2 February

Additional Information: For more information please browse the website www.iitrpr.ac.in/institute-post-doctoral-fellowship

For further information contact:

Email: rmml@iitrpr.ac.in

Indian School of Business

Knowledge City, Sector 81, SAS Nagar, Mohali, Punjab 140 306, India.

Tel: (91) 172 459 0000
Contact: Indian School of Business

Indian School of Business is a private business school with campuses in Hyderabad, Telangana, India and Mohali, Punjab, India. The institute has various Management programs with the Post Graduate Program in Management as its flagship course.

Indian Health Service Health Professions Scholarship Program

Purpose: The student must apply annually to request continued scholarship support until he/she has earned his/her degree and is eligible to pursue post-graduate clinical training or begin his/her Indian health career

Eligibility: 1. All applicants must intend to serve Indian people as a health professional in their chosen specialties. 2. They must also be willing to sign an IHS Scholarship Program Contract when accepting the scholarship. 3. By signing, the student agrees to fulfill a minimum two-year service commitment in full-time clinical practice at an Indian health facility in his/her chosen health profession after completing his/her academic or post-graduate clinical training. 4. The student must apply annually to request continued scholarship support until he/she has earned his/her degree and is eligible to pursue post-graduate clinical training or begin his/her Indian health career

Level of Study: Postgraduate

Type: Scholarship

Value: US$1,500

Frequency: Annual

Country of Study: Any country

Application Procedure: The IHS Scholarship Program awards scholarships based on a 100-point ranking system divided among three categories academic performance, based on official transcripts (40 points); faculty/employer evaluations (30 points); and applicant essays (30 points)

Closing Date: 28 March

Funding: Private

Additional Information: www.unigo.com/scholarships/by-major/psychology-scholarships/ihs-health-professions-scholarship-program/1675

Indian School of Business Funded Tuition Waivers at Indian School of Business

Purpose: The Post Graduate Programme in Management (PGP) is designed for those who want to transform their careers by expanding their existing thought process and refining their goals and objectives

Eligibility: Citizens of all nationalities are eligible to apply. Students whose first language is not English must demonstrate proficiency in English by submitting satisfactory scores from the Test of English as a Foreign Language (TOEFL)

Type: Postgraduate scholarships

Value: These waivers vary in amount from ₹5 Lakh to full tuition fee and are disbursed either on merit or need-based criteria. These scholarships are awarded to candidates during admission or after enrolment, at the discretion of the AdCom or the corporate donor

Study Establishment: Scholarships are awarded in the field of Business

Country of Study: India

Application Procedure: These scholarships are awarded to candidates during admission or after enrolment, at the discretion of the AdCom or the corporate donor

Closing Date: 15 January

Additional Information: For more details please browse the website scholarship-positions.com/isb-funded-tuition-waivers-indian-school-business-india/2017/10/28/

For further information contact:

Email: admin@scholarship-positions.com

Indian Veterinary Research Institute

Izatnagar, Bareilly, Uttar Pradesh 243122, India.

Contact: The Indian Veterinary Research Institute

The Indian Veterinary Research Institute (IVRI) is located at Izatnagar, Bareilly in Uttar Pradesh state. It is India's premier advanced research facility in the field of veterinary medicine and allied branches.

Scholarships at Indian Veterinary Research Institute

Purpose: The Indian Veterinary Research Institute (IVRI) is offering scholarships for MVSc and PhD students. The duration of scholarship for MVSc course will be of two years and scholarship for the PhD course will be of three years

Eligibility: Students from India are eligible to apply. The candidates for admission to Master's programme must have Bachelor's Degree in Veterinary Science in the concerned discipline as specified by the Veterinary Council of India with a minimum of 60% marks in aggregate (55% for SC/ST or sponsored candidates) or equivalent CGPA

Type: Postgraduate scholarships

Value: The amount of the scholarship for Master's Degree programme is ₹7,560/- per month for 2 years with a contingent grant of ₹6,000/- per annum for two years and for Doctoral programme, it is ₹13,125/- per month for three years with a contingent grant of ₹10,000/- per annum for three years

Study Establishment: Scholarships are awarded to study the subjects offered by the university

Country of Study: India

Application Procedure: See the website

Additional Information: For more details please visit our website scholarship-positions.com/scholarships-indian-veterinary-research-institute/2017/11/18/

For further information contact:

Email: sao_unitone@ivri.res.in

Indira Gandhi Institute of Development Research

Film City Road, IGIDR, Nagri Niwara, Cooperative Housing Society, Goregaon East, Mumbai, Maharashtra 400065, India.

Contact: Indira Gandhi Institute of Development Research

Indira Gandhi Institute of Development Research (IGIDR) is an advanced research institute established and fully funded by the Reserve Bank of India for carrying out research on development issues from a multi-disciplinary point of view.

Indira Gandhi Institute of Development Research-International Development Research Centre Scholarships and Fellowships for Asian Countries Students

Purpose: The aims and objectives of the Institute are to promote and conduct research on developmental issues from a broad inter- disciplinary perspective (economic, technological, social, political and ecological)

Eligibility: Scholarship is open for citizens of the following Asian countries Afghanistan, Bangladesh, Bhutan, Cambodia, Indonesia, Malaysia, Maldives, Myanmar, Nepal, Philippines, Sri Lanka, Thailand and Vietnam

Type: Postdoctoral fellowship

Value: Selected scholar will be paid a scholarship of ₹100,000 per month, One round trip travel expense up to a maximum of ₹50,000, fixed medical coverage of ₹25,000, book grant of ₹50,000, research grant of ₹100,000, and conference travel support up to a maximum of ₹150,000

Study Establishment: Scholarships and fellowships are awarded in the field of labor market and industrial policy

Country of Study: India

Application Procedure: See the website

Closing Date: 30 April

Additional Information: For more details please browse the website scholarship-positions.com/igidr-idrc-scholarships-and-fellowships-asian-countries-students-2015/2014/12/27/ www.igidr.ac.in/igidr-idrc-scholarships-programs/

For further information contact:

Email: asianhub@igidr.ac.in

IndusInd Foundation

IndusInd Foundation Scholarship for Postgraduate Students

Purpose: The IndusInd Foundation has invited applications from meritorious students studying in a degree course under the IndusInd Foundation Scholarship

Eligibility: 1. The student must have passed class 12 board or equivalent exam from an approved board/university with minimum 80% marks. 2. The student must have taken admission to any of regular degree courses in Science, Arts, Commerce, Eng., Medical, Computer, Mgt. etc. in an approved college/institute to any recognized university in India. 3. The student's family financial income should justify the grant of scholarship

Level of Study: Postdoctorate

Type: Scholarship

Value: Amount of Scholarship will range from ₹600/- to ₹2,200/- Actual Rate to be decided by the Foundation in each case
Frequency: Annual
Country of Study: Any country
Closing Date: 15 January
Funding: Foundation
Additional Information: www.scholarshiplives.com/indusind-foundation-scholarship/

For further information contact:

The Trustee, IndusInd Foundation Hinduja House, 171, Dr Annie Besant Road, Worli, Mumbai, 400018, India.

Email: indusindfoundation@gmail.com

Innovation and Entrepreneurship Development Centre Bled School of Management

Prešernova cesta 33, SI-4260 Bled, Slovenia.

Tel: (386) 457 92 500
Email: info@iedc.si
Website: www.iedc.si

The school is a center of excellence in management development and a business meeting point, where leaders and potential leaders come to learn and reflect. We offer a unique environment for developing leadership and management potential of international business executives at every stage of their careers.

Innovation and Entrepreneurship Development Centre MBA Scholarship

Purpose: To finance an MBA programme for outstanding candidates from Moldova and Ukraine
Eligibility: Only outstanding candidates from Moldova and Ukraine will be considered
Level of Study: Professional development
Value: All tuition fees
Length of Study: 1 year
Frequency: Annual
Study Establishment: IEDC
Application Procedure: See website
Closing Date: 30 October

For further information contact:

Tel: (386) 457 92 506
Email: emba@iedc.si

Trimo MBA Scholarship

Purpose: To finance an outstanding candidate from Serbia
Eligibility: The candidate must be from Serbia
Level of Study: Professional development
Type: Scholarship
Value: All tuition fees and agreed costs
Length of Study: 1 year
Frequency: Annual
Study Establishment: IEDC
Application Procedure: See website
Closing Date: 1 December
Funding: Corporation
Contributor: Trimo d.d. Slovenia
Additional Information: The successful candidate will be offered a position at Trimo Inženjering d.o.o Serbia www.scholarshiplives.com/indusind-foundation-scholarship/

For further information contact:

Tel: (386) 457 92 506
Email: emba@iedc.si

Institut de Recherche Robert-Sauvé en Santé et en Sécurité du Travail (IRSST)

505, De Maisonneuve Ouest, Montréal, QC H3A 3C2, Canada.

Tel: (1) 514 288 1551
Email: grants@irsst.qc.ca
Website: www.irsst.qc.ca

Institut de Recherche Robert-Sauvé en Santé et en Sécurité du Travail (IRSST), established in Quebec since 1980, is a scientific research organization known for the quality of its work and the expertise of its personnel. The Institute is a private, non-profit agency.

Collaborative Research

Purpose: The Collaborative Research Grant Program covers work that may include studies, analyses, design or development carried out according to a scientific process and likely to contribute to the advancement of knowledge. This work is defined in collaboration with the IRSST and falls within the priority themes. Proposals for collaborative research studies are developed by researchers in collaboration with the research field leader, knowledge transfer advisor and research management advisor. First, the researchers are asked to send a brief summary of their proposed study, using the Summary page of the Letter of Intent form, to the research management advisor for the field concerned. This person coordinates the collaborative process. Once the process has been completed, the researcher may officially file his or her grant application by one of the periodically announced deadlines.

Eligibility: An applicant who files an application as a principal investigator must be a Canadian citizen or permanent resident of Canada, hold a doctorate or the equivalent, and hold a position as a professor or teacher in a Québec postsecondary educational or research establishment. The principal investigator is responsible for the intellectual direction of the proposed research, performs the administrative duties related to the grant, and acts as the contact person with the IRSST. Only one person may play this role.

Value: US$100,000 per year

Country of Study: Any country

Additional Information: www.irsst.qc.ca/en/grants/collaborative-research

For further information contact:

Email: subventions@irsst.qc.ca

Competitive Research

Purpose: The Competitive Research Grant Program is intended exclusively for researchers affiliated with Québec universities or research centres who take the initiative of submitting occupational health and safety research proposals that the IRSST is likely to consider relevant, even if in some cases such projects go beyond the official bounds of the Institute's stated research priorities

Eligibility: An applicant who files an application as a principal investigator must be a Canadian citizen or permanent resident of Canada, hold a doctorate or the equivalent, and hold a position as a professor or teacher in a Québec postsecondary educational or research establishment. The principal investigator is responsible for the intellectual direction of the proposed research, performs the administrative duties related to the grant, and acts as the contact person with the IRSST. Only one person may play this role.

Level of Study: doctorate

Value: US$100,000 IRSST + US$30,000

Additional Information: www.irsst.qc.ca/en/grants/competitive-research

For further information contact:

Email: subventions@irsst.qc.ca

Institut de Recherche Robert-Sauvé en Santé et en Sécurité du Travail Graduate Studies Scholarship and Postdoctoral Fellowship Program

Purpose: To support Master's and doctoral students who wish to acquire research training in the occupational health and safety field

Eligibility: Open to students who are registered full-time in a Master's or doctoral programme and have obtained a cumulative average of B+ for all of their undergraduate studies

Level of Study: Doctorate, Postgraduate

Type: Scholarship

Value: US$14,250 per year. In addition, a scholarship recipient whose training and research program is outside Canada is reimbursed for the amount exceeding the first US$750 in annual tuition fees; the cost of travelling to the training and research location, representing the cost of one round-trip economy airplane ticket or one round trip by car, for each year of the effective period of the scholarship (maximum of 2 years)

Length of Study: 2–3 years

Frequency: Annual

Closing Date: July

Contributor: The Commission des normes, de l'équité, de la santé et de la sécurité du travail provides most of the Institute's funding from the contributions it collects from the employers

Additional Information: Please check the website for further details www.irsst.qc.ca/en/grants/competitive-research

For further information contact:

Email: bourses@irsst.qc.ca

Institut Européen d'Administration des Affaires

Boulevard de Constance, F-77305 Fontainebleau Cedex, France.

Tel: (33) 1 60 72 40 00
Email: mba.europe@insead.edu
Website: www.insead.edu/mba
Contact: Ms Irina Schneider-Maunoury, Senior Manager, MBA Financing

INSEAD is widely recognized as one of the most influential business schools in the world. With its second campus in Asia to complement its established presence in Europe, INSEAD is setting the pace in globalizing the MBA. The 1-year intensive MBA programme is focused on international general management.

Institut Européen d'Administration des Affaires Goldman Sachs Scholarship for African Nationals

Purpose: The Goldman Sachs scholarships for African nationals at INSEAD is designed to give candidates from African countries access to a world-class MBA education. The scholarship winners will be allocated a Goldman Sachs mentor throughout the 10-month MBA programme

Eligibility: The scholarship is open to all candidates from African countries studying at INSEAD on the Full-time MBA Programme. Successful candidates must demonstrate their desire to work in Africa and explain why building business in Africa is important to them

Type: Scholarship

Value: Up to €15,000 per class

Frequency: Annual

Country of Study: Any country

Application Procedure: For further information, kindly refer the official link. www.insead.edu/

Closing Date: 20 April

Additional Information: Please check website for further information www.advance-africa.com/Goldman-Sachs-Scholarship-for-African-Nationals.html

Institut Européen d'Administration des Affaires Jewish Scholarship

Purpose: An INSEAD alumnus offers scholarships to Jewish students admitted to the INSEAD MBA Programme; a limited number of small awards are made each year. In keeping with the spirit and tradition behind this award, the winners are encouraged to give back by making their own donation to scholarships at INSEAD through the Alumni Fund within a few years after graduation

Eligibility: Jewish students who can justify difficulty in raising sufficient finances for their living expenses

Type: Scholarship

Value: Up to €5,000

Frequency: Annual

Country of Study: Any country

Closing Date: 13 February

Additional Information: Please check website for further information www.postgraduatefunding.com/award-230

Institut Européen d'Administration des Affaires MBA Programme

Value: €91,225

Length of Study: 10 months

Country of Study: Any country

Application Procedure: Applicants must complete an application form supplying a €110 fee, photograph, essay, two letters of recommendation, transcripts of grades, Graduate Management Admission Test score, TOEFL score and self addressed acknowledgment card

Closing Date: August

Additional Information: For more details, visit official scholarship website: mba.insead.edu/schlmgmt/dsp_schl_info.cfm?schlcode=AFR02

For further information contact:

MBA Admissions Office Boulevard de Constance, Boulevard de Constance, F-77300 Fontainebleau, France.

Tel:	(33) 1 60 72 42 73
Fax:	(33) 1 60 74 55 30
Email:	mba.info@insead.fr

Institut Européen d'Administration des Affaires Nelson Mandela Endowment Scholarships

Purpose: To honour the life and work of President Nelson Mandela of South Africa, the INSEAD MBA Class of 75 created the INSEAD Nelson Mandela Endowment Scholarships at their 30th Class Reunion to provide financial support for one or more African participants per year at INSEAD in perpetuity

Eligibility: To be eligible for the Nelson Mandela Endowed Scholarship, candidates must be a national of a sub-Saharan African country and have spent a substantial part of their lives and received part of their prior education in Africa. Preference will be given to candidates who require proven financial assistance

Level of Study: Postgraduate

Type: Scholarship

Value: Up to €20,000

Country of Study: Africa

Closing Date: 23 February

Funding: Government

Contributor: INSEAD

Additional Information: For more details, visit official scholarship website: sites.insead.edu/schlmgmt/dsp_schl_info.cfm?schlcode=AFR02&prog=1-mba

Institut Français d'Amérique

Department of History, CB# 3195, Chapel Hill, NC 27599-3195, United States of America.

Tel:	(1) 919 962 2115
Email:	IFA@unc.edu
Website:	institut.unc.edu/
Contact:	Professor Jay Smith

The mission of the Institut Français de Washington is to promote the American study of French culture, language, history and society, and to encourage the work of teachers, scholars and students in these fields. The Institute also sponsors events to foster public understanding of French-American relations. The IFW provides funds for fellowships, prizes, and conferences that serve this mission.

Edouard Morot-Sir Fellowship in French Studies

Eligibility: Open to those in the final stages of a PhD dissertation or who have held a PhD for no longer than 3 years before the application deadline
Level of Study: Doctorate, Postdoctorate
Type: Fellowship
Value: US$1,500
Length of Study: At least 1 month
Frequency: Annual
Country of Study: France
Application Procedure: Applicants must write a maximum of two pages describing the research project and planned trip and enclose a curriculum vitae. A letter of recommendation from the dissertation director is required and a letter from a specialist in the field for assistant professors
No. of awards offered: 2
Closing Date: 15 January
Funding: Foundation, Private
No. of awards given last year: 3
No. of applicants last year: 90
Additional Information: www.iefa.org/scholarships/140/Gilbert_Chinard_Fellowships_And_Edouard_Morot-sir_Fellowship_In_Literature

Gilbert Chinard Fellowships

Eligibility: Open to those in the final stages of a PhD dissertation or who have held a PhD for no longer than 3 years before the application deadline
Level of Study: Doctorate, Postdoctorate
Type: Fellowship
Value: US$1,500
Length of Study: At least 1 month
Frequency: Annual
Country of Study: France
Application Procedure: Applicants must write a maximum of two pages describing the research project and planned trip and enclose a curriculum vitae. A letter of recommendation from the dissertation director is also required for PhD candidates and a letter from a specialist in the field for assistant professors
No. of awards offered: 2
Closing Date: 15 January
Funding: Private
No. of awards given last year: 1
No. of applicants last year: 28
Additional Information: www.postgraduatefunding.com/award-2977

Harmon Chadbourn Rorison Fellowship

Eligibility: Open to those in the final stages of a PhD dissertation or who have held a PhD for no longer than 3 years before the application deadline
Level of Study: Doctorate, Postdoctorate, Postgraduate
Type: Fellowship
Value: US$1,500
Length of Study: At least 1 month
Frequency: Every 2 years
Country of Study: France
Application Procedure: Applicants must write a maximum of two pages describing the research project and planned trip and enclose a curriculum vitae. A letter of recommendation from the dissertation director is required for PhD candidates and a letter from a specialist in the field for assistant professors
No. of awards offered: 4
Closing Date: 15 January
Funding: Foundation, Private
No. of awards given last year: 1
No. of applicants last year: 27
Additional Information: www.eduinreview.com/scholarships/harmon-chadbourn-rorison-gilbert-chinard-fellowships-and-edouard-morot-sir-fellowship-in-literature-283686

Institute for Advanced Studies in the Humanities

The Institute for Advanced Studies in the Humanities, The University of Edinburgh, Hope Park Square, Edinburgh EH8 9NW, United Kingdom.

Tel:	(44) 131 650 4671
Email:	iash@ed.ac.uk
Contact:	The Secretary

The Institute for Advanced Studies in the Humanities was established in 1969 to promote interdisciplinary research in the arts, humanities and social sciences at the University of Edinburgh. It provides an international, interdisciplinary and autonomous space for discussion and debate.

Institute for Advanced Studies in the Humanities (The Institute for Advanced Studies in the Humanities)-SSPS (School of Social and Political Science) Research Fellowships

Purpose: The IASH-SSPS Research Fellowships are intended to encourage outstanding interdisciplinary research, international scholarly collaboration, and networking activities of visiting Research Fellows together with academics in the School of Social and Political Science (SSPS)

Eligibility: For eligibility criteria, please visit website

Type: Fellowship

Value: £1,300 and £3,900.

Country of Study: Any country

Application Procedure: Applications received after that date will not be considered. Successful candidates will be notified by email with a formal letter of confirmation to follow; please ensure that you supply a valid email address so that you can be contacted quickly after decisions are made.

Closing Date: 25 February

Contributor: The Institute for Advanced Studies in the Humanities

Additional Information: For more details, visit www.iash. ed.ac.uk/iash-ssps-research-fellowships

For further information contact:

The University of Edinburgh, Hope Park Square, Edinburgh EH8 9NW, United Kingdom.

Tel: (44) 131 650 4671

Visiting Scholars Programme

Purpose: The Visiting Scholars Programme aims to encourage exceptional scholars working in areas relevant to our research strengths to spend a period of time—from one or two weeks to several months—conducting research and collaborating with scholars within the Institute. IASH aims to select a mixture of early, mid, and senior career scholars.

Eligibility: Applicants would normally have at least a PhD (or equivalent professional experience, research, and

publications), and normally have an institutional affiliation to a University or to an equivalent research organisation. Students working to complete a research higher degree are not eligible to apply. International applicants are strongly encouraged. Visa documents, if required, are the responsibility of the applicant. The University of Queensland will provide a formal letter of invitation to successful applicants which may be used for visa purposes. While some financial support may be provided to some Visiting Scholars, all applicants will be responsible for their own financial costs during their stay in Brisbane

Level of Study: Postgraduate

Value: Up to US$2,500

Closing Date: 31 May

Additional Information: iash.uq.edu.au/fellowships-and-scholarships/visiting-scholars-programme

Institute for Advanced Studies on Science, Technology and Society (IAS-STS)

Kopernikusgasse 9, A-8010 Graz, Austria.

Tel: (43) 316 813909 34
Email: info@sts.tugraz.at
Website: www.sts.tugraz.at
Contact: Günter Getzinger, Acting Director

In 1999 the Inter University Research Centre for Technology, Work and Culture (IFZ) launched the IAS-STS in Graz, Austria. It promotes the interdisciplinary investigation of the links and interaction between science, technology and society as well as research on the development and implementation of socially and environmentally sound, sustainable technologies.

Institute for Advanced Studies on Science, Technology and Society Fellowship Programme

Purpose: To give the students the opportunity to explore issues

Eligibility: Applicants must hold an academic degree

Level of Study: Doctorate, Postdoctorate, Postgraduate, Research

Type: Fellowships

Value: €940 per month

Length of Study: Up to 9 months

Frequency: Annual

Study Establishment: IAS-STS

Country of Study: Austria

Application Procedure: Application forms can be download from the website
No. of awards offered: 50
Closing Date: 30 June
Funding: Government
Contributor: Styrian Government
No. of awards given last year: 5
No. of applicants last year: 50
Additional Information: www.tugraz.at/fileadmin/user_upload/tugrazExternal/2e4e46a4-d5bd-4ce0-8c2c-ea331b7e7175/IAS-STS_Fellowship_Programme_2021-2022.pdf

For further information contact:

Institute for Advanced Studies on Science, Technology and Society (IAS-STS), Attn. Günter Getzinger, Kopernikusgasse 9, A-8010 Graz, Austria.

Tel: (43) 316/813909
Email: office@sts.tugraz.at

Institute for Advanced Study (IAS) Technical University of Munich

Rudolf Diesel Industry Fellowship

Purpose: It is the Fellowship's purpose to enhance collaboration and knowledge-sharing between research units at TUM and company research laboratories. To increase international collaboration, TUM-IAS especially welcomes applications from companies from outside Germany
Eligibility: 1. a nomination letter including a description of the facilities provided for the Fellow by the TUM Host institute. 2. a CV including a list of publications. 3. a statement of purpose jointly signed by the candidate and the hosting professor, describing the content of the. 4. joint research, its innovative potential and the concrete implementation plans (budget), including any planned. 5. events to enhance the Institute's intellectual environment
Level of Study: Postgraduate
Type: Fellowship
Value: Up to €20,000
Frequency: Annual
Country of Study: Any country
Application Procedure: Please submit the following application documents 1. a nomination letter including a description of the facilities provided for the Fellow by the TUM Host institute. 2. a CV (no more than 5 pages) and a list of publications. 3. a statement of purpose jointly signed by the candidate and the hosting professor, describing the content of the joint research, its innovative potential

and the concrete implementation plans. This statement should also include. 4. a budget plan. 5. a time plan regarding the candidate's projected periods of stay at TUM. 6. an identification of possible additional (interdisciplinary) collaboration partners both within TUM-IAS and within TUM as well as a short explanation as to why this collaboration would be beneficial. 7. an outline for an international, ideally interdisciplinary workshop/colloquium, to be organized during the active Fellowship period. 8. a letter of nomination from the Dean of the hosting faculty or another member of the EHP or Board of Trustees
Closing Date: 1 February
Funding: Private
Additional Information: www.ias.tum.de/ias/news/news-single-view/article/call-for-applications-albrecht-struppler-anna-boyksen-hans-fischer-hans-fischer-senior-and-rudolf-diesel-industry-fellowships/

For further information contact:

Lichtenbergstrasse 2 a, D-85748 Garching, Germany.

Tel: (49) 89 289 10550
Email: info@ias.tum.de

Institute for Labour Market Policy Evaluation (IFAU)

Box 513, S751-20 Uppsala, Sweden.

Tel: (46) 184 717 070
Email: ifau@ifau.uu.se
Website: www.ifau.se

The Institute for Labour Market Policy Evaluation (IFAU) is a research institute under the Swedish Ministry of industry, employment and communications. IFAU's objective is to promote, support and carry out evaluations of the effects of labour market policies, studies of the functioning of the labour market and evaluations of the labour market effects of measures within the educational system.

Institute for Labour Market Policy Evaluation Post Doctoral Scholarship

Purpose: To evaluate measures motivated by labour market policy

Eligibility: Open to candidates who have recently obtained a PhD degree in economics or another social science and are EU nationals (not Sweden) or non-EU nationals if they have been resident in the EU (not Sweden) for more than 4 out of the last 5 years

Level of Study: Postdoctorate

Type: Scholarship

Value: €52,029 per year with a mobility allowance of €550 per month for single and €886 for researchers with a partner and/or children

Length of Study: 1 year

Frequency: Annual

Application Procedure: Applicants can download the application form from the website. The completed application form must be sent along with a curriculum vitae, names and addresses of 3 referees, a research paper (or link) and a research proposal (not more than 3 pages)

For further information contact:

Email: Cecilia.Andersson@ifau.uu.se

Institute for South ASIA Studies UC Berkeley

Berreman-Yamanaka Award for Himalayan Studies

Purpose: The Berreman-Yamanaka Fellowship for Himalayan Studies' provides for an annual award of up to US$1500 to UC Berkeley graduate students for research on topics related to Himalayan Studies across Bhutan, India, Nepal and Pakistan

Level of Study: Graduate

Type: Award

Value: US$1,500

Frequency: Annual

Country of Study: Any country

Application Procedure: In your application please include the following 1. A cover letter stating the need for travel. (750 words or less, PDF format) 2. A 2-page project proposal. Which should include the proposed date of travel, as well as all other sources of funding available in the given summer or given AY. (double-spaced) (PDF format) 3. A budget (only for research) (PDF format) 4. A CV (PDF format) 5. One letter of support from your advisor (PDF, sent by the recommenders directly)

Closing Date: 15 April

Funding: Foundation

Additional Information: southasia.berkeley.edu/himalayan-studies-award

For further information contact:

10 Stephens Hall (Rear Annex), University of California, Berkeley, Berkeley, CA 94720-2310, United States of America.

Tel: (1) 510 642 3608
Email: pkala@berkeley.edu

Bhattacharya Graduate Fellowship

Purpose: The Bhattacharya Graduate Fellowship will award UC Berkeley graduate students competitive grants for topics related to contemporary India

Level of Study: Graduate

Type: Fellowship

Value: US$1,000 for research travel to India (a total of two will be awarded) and US$500 for domestic conference travel for presentations (a total of four will be awarded).

Frequency: Annual

Country of Study: Any country

Closing Date: 15 April

Funding: Foundation

Additional Information: southasia.berkeley.edu/bhattacharaya-graduate-fellowship

For further information contact:

10 Stephens Hall (Rear Annex), University of California, Berkeley, Berkeley, CA 94720-2310, United States of America.

Tel: (1) 510 642 3608
Email: pkala@berkeley.edu

Bodha Pravaham Fellowship

Purpose: The Bodha Pravaham Undergraduate Fellowship for Tamil Studies, established with a generous contribution from Professor George Hart and Professor Kausalya Hart, both cornerstones of Tamil Studies at UC Berkeley, supports undergraduate students pursuing research projects focusing on Tamil studies

Level of Study: Graduate

Type: Fellowship

Value: US$900

Length of Study: 1 year

Frequency: Annual

Country of Study: Any country

Application Procedure: In your application for RESEARCH TRAVEL, please include the following 1. A cover letter stating the need for travel (750 words or less) 2. A 2-page

project proposal (double-spaced) (PDF format) 3. A budget (only for research) (PDF format) 4. A CV (PDF format) 5. One letter of support from your advisor (PDF, sent by the recommenders directly)
Closing Date: 15 April
Funding: Foundation
Additional Information: southasia.berkeley.edu/bodha-fund

For further information contact:

10 Stephens Hall (Rear Annex), University of California, Berkeley, Berkeley, CA 94720-2310, United States of America.

Tel: (1) 510 642 3608
Email: pkala@berkeley.edu

Hart Fellowship

Purpose: The Hart Fellowship for Tamil Studies, established with a generous contribution from Professor George Hart and Professor Kausalya Hart, both cornerstones of Tamil Studies at UC Berkeley, supports graduate students pursuing research projects focusing on Tamil studies
Level of Study: Graduate
Type: Fellowship
Value: US$2,000
Length of Study: 1 year
Frequency: Annual
Country of Study: Any country
Closing Date: 15 April
Funding: Foundation
Additional Information: southasia.berkeley.edu/hart-fund

For further information contact:

10 Stephens Hall (Rear Annex), University of California, Berkeley, Berkeley, CA 94720-2310, United States of America.

Tel: (1) 510 642 3608
Email: pkala@berkeley.edu

International Affairs Fellowship in India

Purpose: The Council on Foreign Relations International Affairs Fellowship (IAF) in India, sponsored by Bharti, seeks to strengthen mutual understanding and cooperation between rising generations of leaders and thinkers in the United States and India. The program provides for one to four mid-career United States professionals, who have had little or no substantial prior experience in India, the

opportunity to spend three to twelve months conducting research and working in India. Fellows are drawn from academia, business, government, journalism, NGOs, and think tanks. While in India, fellows develop a new professional network as well as gain fresh insights and perspectives into the country and the opportunities and challenges that confront the region. CFR will work with its network of contacts to assist selected fellows in finding suitable host organizations that best match the fellow's proposed work in India. Possible placements include but are not limited to the CFR's local partner, the Centre for Policy Research; the Institute for Defense Studies and Analyses; or the Centre for Insurance and Risk Management
Eligibility: 1. Applicants must be United States citizens. 2. Applicants must be mid-career professionals. 3. Applicants must possess a strong record of professional achievement. 4. Applicants must hold at least a bachelor's degree
Level of Study: Graduate
Type: Fellowship
Value: US$90,000
Length of Study: 1 year
Frequency: Annual
Country of Study: Any country
Closing Date: 28 February
Funding: Foundation

For further information contact:

Email: fellowships@cfr.org

International Studies Research Lab

Purpose: The Center for Global Studies at the University of Illinois, Urbana-Champaign, is pleased to announce funding to support the internationalization of community colleges nationwide. We invite applications from faculty, librarians, and administrators interested in expanding global studies curricula, instruction in less commonly taught languages, library collections, or international education programs at their home institutions. Projects for minority-serving institutions are particularly welcome. During their stay, Fellows can work one-on-one with international and area studies reference librarians and explore the unlimited print and online resources of the University of Illinois Library
Eligibility: Applicants must be faculty or administrators at 2-year community colleges or 4-year universities that offer associate degrees. The Center for Global Studies encourages applications particularly from minority-serving institutions. While fellowships that cover housing and parking will be reserved to applicants from outside of the Champaign-Urbana area, all participants will be eligible to receive research honoraria

Level of Study: Graduate
Type: Fellowship
Frequency: Annual
Country of Study: Any country
Application Procedure: Apply online forms.illinois.edu/sec/5427515
Closing Date: 30 July
Funding: Foundation
Additional Information: emails.illinois.edu/newsletter/147164.html

For further information contact:

Lynne Rudasill Global Studies Librarian, Center for Global Studies 306 International Studies Building, M/C 402 uiuc campus mail, IL 00001, United States of America.

Email: rudasill@illinois.edu

Maharaj Kaul Memorial Trust

Purpose: UC Berkeley graduate students are invited to apply for competitive grants of up to US$1000 for research travel to South Asia (a total of two will be awarded), and up to US$500 for conference travel (a total of two will be awarded) made available through a gift from the Maharaj Kaul Memorial Fund to the Institute for South Asia Studies
Level of Study: Graduate
Type: Grant
Value: US$1,000
Frequency: Annual
Country of Study: Any country
Application Procedure: In your application for RESEARCH TRAVEL, please include the following 1. A cover letter stating the need for travel (750 words or less) 2. A 2-page project proposal (double-spaced) (PDF format) 3. A budget (PDF format) 4. A CV (PDF format) 5. One letter of support from your advisor (PDF, sent by the recommenders directly) 6. Please note two awards of up to US$1000 will be given for Research Travel to South Asia
No. of awards offered: 2
Closing Date: 15 April
Funding: Foundation
Additional Information: southasia.berkeley.edu/maharaj-kaul-grants

For further information contact:

10 Stephens Hall (Rear Annex), University of California, Berkeley, Berkeley, CA 94720-2310, United States of America.

Tel: (1) 510 642 3608
Email: pkala@berkeley.edu

Outstanding Paper Prize

Purpose: The Subir and Malini Chowdhury Center for Bangladesh Studies welcomes submissions for the Outstanding Paper Prize in Bangladesh Studies. Submissions are welcome from any discipline, though preference will be given to papers in a social science field
Eligibility: 1. Full time UC Berkeley graduate students or undergraduates with upperclass standing. 2. Students must have been registered as a full time student at any accredited university. 3. Papers must be linked to a course for undergraduates, must be linked to a departmental thesis program
Level of Study: Graduate
Type: Grant
Value: US$500
Frequency: Annual
Country of Study: Any country
Application Procedure: 1. Only electronic submissions will be accepted. Please email all documents to chowdhury-center@berkeley.edu with subject heading "Submission for Outstanding Bangladesh Paper Prize" 2. All documents should be in PDF format. 3. Please email copies of 1) the paper, 2) the page with identifying information, and 3) the abstract attached as PDF fles. 4. Please send entries no later than 5pm on, April 15
Closing Date: 1 April
Funding: Foundation
Additional Information: chowdhurycenter.berkeley.edu/paper-prize

For further information contact:

The Subir & Malini Chowdhury Center Institute for South Asia Studies UC Berkeley, 10 Stephens Hall, Berkeley, CA 94720-2310, United States of America.

Tel: (1) 510 642 3608
Email: chowdhury-center@berkeley.edu

South Asia Program Junior Fellowship

Purpose: The one-year, full-time fellowship will provide individuals with a unique opportunity to expand their knowledge of security issues in the subcontinent, engage the South Asia policy community in Washington and the region, and experience working at a dynamic think tank that provides close interaction with senior staff and researchers
Eligibility: 1. A strong background in South Asian political, economic, or security issues; strategic studies; international relations theory; or economics. 2. Demonstrated analytical, research, and writing skills. 3. Ability to work independently and to collaborate with peers in a team environment.

4. Bachelor's degree. All applicants must be eligible to work in the United States for the full twelve months of the fellowship following graduation

Level of Study: Graduate

Type: Fellowship

Value: US$37,000

Length of Study: 1 year

Frequency: Annual

Country of Study: Any country

Closing Date: 21 February

Funding: Foundation

Additional Information: www.stimson.org/content/south-asia-program-junior-fellowship

For further information contact:

Email: southasiaadmin@stimson.org

Institute for Supply Management (ISM)

2055 E. Centennial Circle, Tempe, AZ 85285-2160, United States of America.

Tel:	(1) 480 752 6276
Email:	ssturzl@ism.ws
Website:	www.ism.ws
Contact:	Valerie Gryniewicz, Manager, Education

The Institute for Supply Management (ISM) is a non-profit association that provides national and international leadership in purchasing and supply management research and education. ISM provides more than 40,000 members with opportunities to expand their professional skills and knowledge.

Institute for Supply Management Professional Research Development Grant

Purpose: This program is designed to support assistants and young associate professor with terminal degree that are teaching in the field of a significant research track in supply management and associated areas. The goal is to help competitively selected faculty build a research and publication field and establish themselves in the profession (i.e. academic institutions, professional organisation, research fund granting bodies such as CAPS Research etc.). This would include CAPS research. Faculty selected will generally have 2 and 8 years of teaching and research experience

and have successful publication experiments beyond the doctoral degree

Eligibility: Open to assistant professors, associate professors or equivalent who have demonstrated exceptional academic productivity in research and teaching. Candidates are chosen from those who can help produce useful research that can be applied to the advancement of purchasing and supply management. Candidates must be full-time faculty members within or outside the United States of America and be present or past members of ISM committees, groups, forums or affiliated organizations. An assistant professor should have 3 or more years of post-degree experience. Previous awardees are ineligible

Level of Study: Postdoctorate

Type: Grant

Value: US$10,000

Frequency: Annual

Country of Study: United States of America

Application Procedure: (1) Letter of application explaining qualifications of the grant. (2) Research proposal of no more than five pages, including problem statement or hypothesis; research methodology, with data sources, collection and analysis; and value to the field of supply management. (3) Curriculum vitae, including works in progress

No. of awards offered: 5–10

Closing Date: 30 January

Funding: Private

Contributor: ISM

No. of awards given last year: 1

No. of applicants last year: 5–10

Additional Information: It is expected that the recipients will present the results of their research at an ISM forum, e.g. research symposium, ISM Annual International Purchasing Conference and/or an ISM publication such as The Journal of Supply Chain Management www.stimson.org/content/south-asia-program-junior-fellowship

For further information contact:

Robert A Kemp, PhD, CPM, Institute for Supply Management, P.O. Box 22160, Tempe, AZ 85285-2160, United States of America.

Email: kempr@mchsi.com

R. Gene Richter Scholarship Program

Purpose: The R. Gene and Nancy D. Richter Foundation and the R. Gene Richter Scholarship fund at ISM will provide a US$10,000 scholarship (US$5,000 for

December graduates) to individuals seeking education in supply management, supply chain management or procurement

Eligibility: 1. Enrolled full-time in an accredited supply chain management curriculum (supply management, purchasing or procurement) 2. Entering their senior year during the 2022-2023 academic year 3. Graduating in either December 2022 or Spring 2023 4. A citizen of the United States or Canada, or possess a valid green card 5. Available to attend the Institute for Supply Management® (ISM®) Annual International Conference. 6. Willing to sign a contract pledging that the monetary award will be used for educational expenses (this includes living expenses)

Value: US$10,000

Country of Study: Any country

Closing Date: 2 February

For further information contact:

Website: www.richterfoundation.org.

Institute of Advanced Legal Studies (IALS)

Institute of Advanced Legal Studies, Charles Clore House, 17 Russell Square, London WC1B 5DR, United Kingdom.

Tel: (44) 20 7862 5800
Email: ials.administrator@sas.ac.uk
Website: www.ials.sas.ac.uk
Contact: Margaret Wilson, Institute Manager

The Institute of Advanced Legal Studies (IALS) plays a national and international role in the promotion and facilitation of legal research. It possesses one of the leading research libraries in Europe and organizes a regular programme of conferences, seminars and lectures. It also offers postgraduate taught and research programmes and specialized training courses.

Institute of Advanced Legal Studies Visiting Fellowship in Law Librarianship

Purpose: To enable experienced law librarians, who are undertaking research in, appropriate fields, to relate their work to activities in which the Institutes own library is involved

Eligibility: Open to experienced law librarians from any country

Level of Study: Unrestricted

Type: Fellowship

Value: Fellowships can consist of or include a period working with Institute library staff or be a period of research based in a research carrel

Length of Study: Between 2 and 6 months

Frequency: Annual

Study Establishment: The IALS

Country of Study: United Kingdom

Application Procedure: Applicants must submit a full curriculum vitae, the names, addresses and telephone numbers of two referees and a brief statement of the research programme to be undertaken to the Administrative Secretary

No. of awards offered: 1

No. of awards given last year: 1

No. of applicants last year: 1

Additional Information: ials.sas.ac.uk/fellowships/institute-advanced-legal-studies-visiting-research-fellowship-programme/visiting/past

Institute of Advanced Legal Studies Visiting Fellowship in Legislative Studies

Purpose: To enable individuals in the field to undertake research

Eligibility: Open to established academics and practitioners from any country. This award is not available for postgraduate research

Level of Study: Unrestricted

Type: Fellowship

Value: Non-stipendary

Length of Study: A minimum of 3 months and a maximum of 1 year

Frequency: Annual

Study Establishment: The IALS

Country of Study: United Kingdom

Application Procedure: Applicants must submit a full curriculum vitae, the names, addresses and telephone numbers of two referees and a brief statement of the research programme to be undertaken

No. of awards offered: 1

Closing Date: 30 January

No. of applicants last year: 1

Additional Information: ials.sas.ac.uk/fellowships/institute-advanced-legal-studies-visiting-research-fellowship-programme

For further information contact:

Email: eliza.boudier@sas.ac.uk

Institute of Behavioural Science (IBS), University of Colorado at Boulder

Department of Geography & Institute of Behavioural Science Campus Box 487, Boulder, CO 80309-0487, United States of America.

Tel: (1) 303 492 1619
Email: johno@colorado.edu
Website: www.colorado.edu/IBS
Contact: Mr John O'Loughlin

The Institute of Behavioural Science (IBS) provides a setting for interdisciplinary research on problems of societal concern. By engaging faculty from all of the social and behavioural sciences at the University of Colorado at Boulder, the Institute encourages work that transcends disciplinary boundaries, that illuminates the complexity of social behaviour and social life, and that has important implications for social policy.

Master of Business Administration Programme

Length of Study: 1 year and 2 months
Application Procedure: Applicants must complete an application form supplying, TOEFL score, Graduate Management Admission Test score, plus personal and professional recommendations with career goals
Closing Date: 30 May

For further information contact:

Graduate School of Business Administration Campus, Box 419, Boulder, CO 80309-0030, United States of America.

Tel: (1) 303 492 1831
Fax: (1) 303 492 1727
Email: busgrad@colorado.edu

Institute of Biology

20 Queensberry Place, London SW7 2DZ, United Kingdom.

Tel: (44) 20 7581 8333
Email: info@iob.org
Website: www.iob.org
Contact: Ms Georgina Day, Education Officer

The Institute of Biology's mission is to promote biology and the biological sciences, to foster the public understanding of science, to enhance the status of the biology profession and to represent its members as a whole to government and other bodies worldwide. The Institute is the 'voice' of British biology.

Dax Copp Travelling Fellowship

Purpose: To support overseas travel in connection with biological study, teaching or research and to aid those who would otherwise not have this opportunity
Eligibility: Open to students in the biological sciences studying in the United Kingdom
Level of Study: Unrestricted
Type: Fellowship
Value: £500
Frequency: Annual
Application Procedure: Applicants must complete an application form, available from the Expeditions Grants Manager. Applicants are also required to produce a reasoned statement of the purpose to which the fellowship will be put, supported by three referees
No. of awards offered: 20
Closing Date: January
Funding: Private
Contributor: Membership
No. of awards given last year: 1
No. of applicants last year: 20
Additional Information: Applicants receiving a fellowship will be expected to provide the Institute with a report within six months of the fellowship ending ials.sas.ac.uk/fellow ships/institute-advanced-legal-studies-visiting-research-fellowship-programme

For further information contact:

Royal Geographical Society, 1 Kensington Gore, Kensington, London SW7 2DZ, United Kingdom.

Tel: (44) 20 7591 3073
Email: grants@rsg.org

Institute of Education

20 Bedford Way, London WC1H 0AL, United Kingdom.

Tel: (44) 20 7612 6000
Email: info@ioe.ac.uk

Website: www.ioe.ac.uk
Contact: Josie Charlton, Head of Marketing and
Development

Founded in 1902, the Institute of Education is a world-class centre of excellence for research, teacher training, higher degrees and consultancy in education and education-related areas of social science. Our pre-eminent scholars and talented students from all walks of life make up an intellectually rich and diverse learning community.

Nicholas Hans Comparative Education Scholarship

Purpose: To assist a well-qualified student to study for a PhD in comparative education at the Institute of Education
Eligibility: Candidates must be registered Institute students not normally resident in the United Kingdom
Level of Study: Doctorate
Type: Scholarship
Value: Full-time tuition fees
Length of Study: 3–7 years
Frequency: Annual
Study Establishment: Institute of Education
Country of Study: United Kingdom
Application Procedure: Candidates are required to submit an extended essay of 25,000–30,000 words, based upon their research or proposed research, that exemplifies, extends or develops by critique the concerns of Nicholas Hans in comparative education
Closing Date: 1 June
Funding: Trusts
Contributor: Trust fund based upon money left in the will of Nicholas Hans' widow

For further information contact:

Email: p.kelly@ioe.ac.uk

Institute of Electrical and Electronics Engineers History Center

Samuel C. Williams Library, 3rd floor, 1 Castle point on Hudson, Hoboken, NJ 07030, United States of America.

Tel: (1) 732 562 5450
Email: ieee-history@ieee.org

Website: www.ieee.org/about/history_center/fellowship.
html
Contact: Mr Robert Colburn, Research Co-ordinator

The mission of the IEEE History Center is to preserve, research and promote the history of information and electrical technologies.

Charles LeGeyt Fortescue Fellowship

Purpose: The Charles LeGeyt Fortescue Scholarship was established in 1939 as a memorial to Charles LeGeyt in recognition of his valuable contributions to the field of electrical engineering
Eligibility: 1. To be eligible, the student must be a permanent resident of the United States, have majored in the field of electrical engineering, and have received a bachelor's degree from an engineering college of recognized standing. 2. The scholarship will be awarded to a first-year full-time graduate student only. In the event the college is conducting a combined BS and MS degree program, the student in the penultimate year would be eligible for the award, which would apply in the final year of the program
Level of Study: Postgraduate
Type: Fellowship
Value: US$24,000
Length of Study: 1 year
Frequency: Every 2 years
Study Establishment: An engineering school of recognised standing
Country of Study: United States of America or Canada
Application Procedure: 1. Complete the entire application form. 2. Submit certified transcripts from all colleges/universities attended. 3. Provide letters of recommendation from three college/university professors who are familiar with your work. 4. The complete name, title, and address of the reference must be clearly noted on the letter. Letters of recommendation should address the following areas the applicant's ability to perform graduate work; originality and creativity; character; diligence and social responsibility; ability to lead; ability to communicate; where the reference would rank the applicant among students he/she has known in this field in recent years. 5. All application documentation must be received by the first Monday after 30 April each year
Closing Date: 3 May
Funding: Private

For further information contact:

445 Hoes Lane, Piscataway, NJ 08854, United States of America.

Institute of Electrical and Electronics Engineers Fellowship in the History of Electrical and Computing Technology

Purpose: To support graduate work in the history of electrical engineering
Eligibility: 1. Must be a graduate student or a postgraduate student 2. Must attend a university 3. Must not be attending high school currently 4. Must study full-time 5. Restricted to students studying Energy and Power Engineering, Engineering/Technology, Historic Preservation and Conservation, History, Science, Technology, and Society
Level of Study: Doctorate, Postdoctorate, Postgraduate
Type: Fellowship
Value: US$25,000 plus US$3,000 research budget
Length of Study: 1 year
Frequency: Annual
Study Establishment: A college or university of recognized standing
Country of Study: Any country
Application Procedure: Applicants must submit a completed application, transcripts, three letters of recommendation and a research proposal. Application materials can be downloaded from the website
Closing Date: 1 February
Funding: Corporation

Institute of European Studies

Tel: (32) 2 614 80 01

Ana Hatherly Graduate Student Research Grant

Purpose: Cátedra Ana Hatherly promotes the work of one of the most important and multifaceted Portuguese poets, Ana Hatherly. In this context Camões, Instituto da Cooperação e da Língua and the Center for Portuguese Studies are pleased to announce a competition for 1 research grant of US$1000,00 each for Graduate Students in all areas of research at UC, Berkeley. Preference will be given to applicants interested in publishing research papers about Ana Hatherly's poetry, cinematography, and painting
Eligibility: All research topics in the field of Portuguese Studies (broadly defined) qualify, but preference will be given to applicants intending to do research relating to Ana Hatherly's poetry, cinematography, and painting.
Level of Study: Postgraduate
Type: Grant
Value: US$1,000
Frequency: Annual

Country of Study: Any country
Application Procedure: Applicants must submit the following materials 1. A one-page application letter, including a 500-word (maximum) abstract of your research. 2. A short CV 3. One recommendation letter from a UC faculty member
Closing Date: 1 March
Funding: International office
Additional Information: For more information, please contact Duarte Pinheiro at mailto: dpinheiro@berkeley.edu

For further information contact:

Email: ies@berkeley.edu

Regents' Junior Faculty Fellowships

Purpose: It is a pleasure to bring to the attention of junior faculty members the Regents' Junior Faculty Fellowships for the summer
Eligibility: Eligibility is limited to academic year appointees in the ranks of Assistant Professor, Acting Assistant Professor, Acting Associate Professor, and, in the School of Law, Acting Professor
Level of Study: Postgraduate
Type: Fellowship
Value: US$7,500
Frequency: Annual
Country of Study: Any country
Closing Date: 8 April
Funding: International office
Additional Information: vpf.berkeley.edu/faculty-fellowships/regents-junior-faculty-fellowships

For further information contact:

Email: yasyavg@berkeley.edu

Institute of Fundamental Sciences, Massey University

Institute of Fundamental Sciences, Massey University, Private Bag 11 222, Palmerston North, 4442, New Zealand.

Tel: (64) 6 350 5799 ext. 2909
Email: r.mclachlan@massey.ac.nz
Website: www.massey.ac.nz
Contact: Professor Robert McLachlan

Massey University has over 40,000 students, of which 19,000 study on three campuses, with the remaining 21,000 studying by correspondence. The five colleges of business, education, science, humanities and social sciences and design, fine arts and music provide a comprehensive range of undergraduate and graduate degrees and diplomas all tailored to meeting national and international needs.

Massey Business School - PhD Scholarships

Purpose: The Massey Business School is seeking to strengthen its strategic research platforms

Eligibility: At a minimum, you must meet MU admission criteria GPA of 7.5 or higher (on a 9 point scale). This is above an average grade of A- (an MBA is not a direct pathway to a PhD). Applicants should have a conditional or unconditional offer of place in a doctoral programme at Massey University. Full-time and part-time candidates are eligible to apply

Level of Study: Doctorate

Type: Scholarship

Value: NZ$25,000 per annum for a maximum of 3 years

Length of Study: 3 years

Study Establishment: Institute of Fundamental Sciences, Massey University

Country of Study: New Zealand

Application Procedure: you need to submit your academic CV, academic transcripts, a one-page research proposal and other supporting documents to the appropriate person listed 1. School of Accountancy Dr Lin Mei Tan L.M.Tan@massey. ac.nz

Closing Date: 19 January

Additional Information: www.massey.ac.nz/massey/learn ing/colleges/college-of-sciences/about/fundamental-sciences/ phd-scholarships-and-jobs.cfm

For further information contact:

Tel: (64) 6 350 5701
Email: contact@massey.ac.nz

PhD Opportunity - Engineering

Eligibility: The successful candidate will likely have a background in physics or engineering and will provide evidence of well-developed mathematical skills and practical ability

Level of Study: Doctorate

Value: The project will be carried out with an industrial partner (Ravensdown) and a stipend is offered for a duration of 3 years

Length of Study: 3 years

Study Establishment: Institute of Fundamental Sciences, Massey University

Country of Study: New Zealand

Application Procedure: Applicants should provide their CV to Professor Clive Davies C.Davies@massey.ac.nz

Closing Date: 19 January

For further information contact:

Email: admissions@gcu.ac.uk

PhD Scholarship (Drug Research Team, SHORE & Whariki Research Centre)

Level of Study: Doctorate

Type: Scholarship

Value: NZ$25,000 per annum (tax free) plus tuition fees

Length of Study: 3 year

Frequency: Annual

Country of Study: New Zealand

Application Procedure: To apply please send a covering letter, curriculum vitae and 3 recent examples of your written work via email to Dr. Chris Wilkins. If you would like to discuss this opportunity further please contact Dr. Chris Wilkins (c.wilkins@massey.ac.nz)

Closing Date: 20 March

For further information contact:

Email: shore&whariki@massey.ac.nz

PhD Scholarship in Mathematics

Eligibility: Applicants should have or expect to receive a BSc (Hons) or MSc degree or equivalent in mathematics

Level of Study: Doctorate

Type: Scholarship

Value: The scholarship covers all tuition fees for international and domestic students and includes a tax-free stipend of NZ$25,000 per annum

Study Establishment: Institute of Fundamental Sciences, Massey University

Country of Study: New Zealand

Application Procedure: Applications including a CV, academic transcript and cover letter should be sent to Professor Robert McLachlan, Institute of Fundamental Sciences, Massey University, Palmerston North, New Zealand or by email to r.mclachlan@massey.ac.nz

Additional Information: See web site for further information dynamics.massey.ac.nz

For further information contact:

Email: jag.roberts@unsw.edu.au

School of Engineering and Advanced Technology Scholarships

Eligibility: To be eligible you must hold a recognized entrance qualification
Level of Study: Doctorate
Type: Scholarship
Value: NZ$25,000 a year for 3 years, to cover fees and living expenses
Length of Study: 3 years
Frequency: Annual
Study Establishment: Institute of Fundamental Sciences, Massey University
Country of Study: New Zealand
Application Procedure: Initial applications should be on the Massey University form. Please send the form to Michele Wagner (m.wagner@massey.ac.nz)
Closing Date: Novermber

For further information contact:

21 North Park Street, Madison, WI 53715, United States of America.

Email: info@dcs.wisc.edu

Institute of Museum and Library Services

Accelerating Promising Practices for Small Libraries

Purpose: The goal of this initiative is to support projects that strengthen the ability of small and/or rural libraries and archives to serve their communities and to build grantee capacity through participation in a community of practice.
Eligibility: See the Notice of Funding Opportunity for eligibility criteria for this program
Level of Study: Postgraduate
Type: Grant
Value: US$10,000–US$50,000
Frequency: Annual
Country of Study: Any country

Funding: Government, Private
Additional Information: If you have general questions, please contact mailto: imls-librarygrants@imls.gov

For further information contact:

Tel: (1) 202 653 4650
Email: clandrum@imls.gov

Inspire! Grants for Small Museums

Purpose: Inspire! Grants for Small Museums is a special initiative of the Museums for America program
Type: Grant
Value: $5,000–$50,000
Length of Study: Up to 2 years
Country of Study: Any country
Closing Date: 15 November

Native American Library Services: Enhancement Grants

Purpose: This program is designed to assist Native American tribes in improving core library services for their communities.
Eligibility: Federally recognized tribes are eligible to apply for funding under the Native American Library Services Enhancement Grant program. See the Notice of Funding Opportunity for eligibility criteria for this program
Level of Study: Postgraduate
Type: Award
Value: US$10,000 to US$150,000
Length of Study: 2 years
Frequency: Annual
Country of Study: Any country
Application Procedure: Digital Services projects feature activities dedicated to the establishment and refinement of digital services and programs related to infrastructure, platforms, and technology, in general
Closing Date: 1 April
Funding: Private
Additional Information: www.imls.gov/grants/available/native-american-library-services-enhancement-grants

For further information contact:

Anthony D. Smith, Associate Deputy Director.

Tel: (1) 202 653 4716, (1) 202 653 4715
Email: asmith@imls.gov, mcoudrelle@imls.gov

Institution of Engineering and Technology (IET)

Michael Faraday House, Six Hills Way,, Stevenage, Hertford-shire SG1 2AY, United Kingdom.

Tel:	(44) 1438 313 311
Email:	awards@theiet.org
Website:	www.theiet.org/awards
Contact:	J Tilley, Scholarships Coordinator

The IET is one of the world's largest engineering institutions with over 163,000 members in 127 countries. It is also the most interdisciplinary – to reflect the increasingly diverse nature of engineering in the 21st century. Energy, transport, manufacturing, information and communications, and the built environment: the IET covers them all.

Hudswell International Research Scholarship

Subjects: Electronic, Electrical and Systems Engineering
Purpose: To encourage excellence in engineering and technology research, with a preference for electrical, electronic or manufacturing engineering.
Eligibility: 1. You can apply for an award if you have a student loan, research grant, company bursary or similar, but you can't be a recipient of any other IET scholarship or bursary. 2. On the application form you'll need to include details of your referee. 3. The panel will consider you for all postgraduate awards where you meet the eligibility requirements. 4. If you're successful, you'll only be able to receive one IET Postgraduate Award during your PhD research.
Type: Scholarship
Value: £5,000.
Country of Study: Any country
No. of awards offered: 1
Closing Date: 7 April
Additional Information: www.birmingham.ac.uk/postgradu ate/funding/hudswell-international-research-scholarship-institution-of-engineering-and-technology.aspx

Institution of Engineering and Technology Postgraduate Scholarship for an Outstanding Researcher

Purpose: To help researchers share their knowledge throughout the global science, engineering and technology community, with the aim of improving people's lives around the world.
Eligibility: Applicants should be members of the IET and must have commenced their studies prior to applying for this scholarship
Level of Study: Doctorate, Postgraduate, Research
Type: Scholarship
Value: £10,000
Length of Study: 1 year
Frequency: Annual
Country of Study: Any country
Application Procedure: Applicants should complete the online application form at www.theiet.org/postgradawards
Closing Date: 8 April
Funding: Trusts
Additional Information: www.theiet.org/impact-society/awards-scholarships/iet-postgraduate-research-awards/#:~:text=IET%20Postgraduate%20Scholarship%20for%20an,people's%20lives%20around%20the%20world. www.bir mingham.ac.uk/postgraduate/funding/hudswell-international-research-scholarship-institution-of-engineering-and-technology.aspx

Institution of Engineering and Technology Travel Awards

Purpose: To assist IET members undertaking international travel to attend conferences, participate in international research visits or projects
Eligibility: 1. Have been a member for a minimum of one year up to the date of application 2. Are IET members i.e. Student, Member, Fellow and some Associate categories. Lapsed members are not eligible 3. Reside in any country, as long as the travel is international
Level of Study: Unrestricted
Type: Travel grant
Value: We can award grants of up to £1,500 - a maximum of 75% of the total cost of the visit would be funded by the IET.
Frequency: Annual
Country of Study: Any country
Application Procedure: 1. You can apply for a grant at any time during the year 2. The travel should take place at least one month after the closing date for applications 3. You can't submit an application after an event has taken place 4. You can make up to two applications within a twelve-month period 5. If you have already received an IET Travel Award, a year must have passed before you can apply again 6. Please click the 'Apply' button above 7. You will be asked to attach documentary evidence of the travel intention (e.g. invitation

from the conference organiser) and confirmation that a visa has been sought (if required) 8. You will be requested to provide details of how any difference between the cost of the visit and the IET award will be funded 9. You'll need to provide contact details of your referee and send a request for a reference during the application

Closing Date: 19 January

Funding: Trusts

Additional Information: If a successful applicant does not undertake the visit, or submit a report within 1 month of the visit, they must return the funding to the IET. Awards are available throughout the year for IET members who present a paper/poster at conferences around the world, or participate in international research visits or projects www.theiet.org/impact-society/awards-scholarships/travel-awards/

Leslie H. Paddle Scholarship

Purpose: To encourage excellence in engineering and technology research, with a preference for electrical, electronic or manufacturing engineering.

Eligibility: 1. You can apply for an award if you have a student loan, research grant, company bursary or similar, but you can't be a recipient of any other IET scholarship or bursary. 2. On the application form you'll need to include details of your referee. 3. The panel will consider you for all postgraduate awards where you meet the eligibility requirements. 4. If you're successful, you'll only be able to receive one IET Postgraduate Award during your PhD research.

Type: Scholarship

Value: £5,000

Country of Study: Any country

Closing Date: 7 April

Additional Information: www.theiet.org/impact-society/awards-scholarships/iet-postgraduate-research-awards/#:~:text=IET%20Postgraduate%20Scholarship%20for%20an, people's%20lives%20around%20the%20world. www.theiet.org/impact-society/awards-scholarships/travel-awards/

Institution of Mechanical Engineers (IMechE)

1 Birdcage Walk, Westminster, London SW1H 9JJ, United Kingdom.

Tel: (44) 20 7222 7899
Email: enquiries@imeche.org
Website: www.imeche.org
Contact: The Prizes and Awards Officer

The Institution of Mechanical Engineers (IMechE) was founded in 1847 by engineers. They formed an institution to promote the exchange of ideas and encourage individuals or groups in creating inventions that would be crucial to the development of the world as a whole. Now, over 150 years later, IMechE is one of the largest engineering institutions in the world, with over 88,000 members in 120 countries.

Astridge Postgraduate Research Scholarship

Eligibility: This award will be made annually to support a postgraduate conducting research or working in the field of aviation safety/airworthiness.

Level of Study: Doctorate

Type: Scholarship

Value: £6,500 per year

Country of Study: Any country

Closing Date: 1 August

James Clayton Lectures

Purpose: Awards are normally made for periods of not greater than one year to enable the recipients to obtain advanced training to supplement that previously obtained in mechanical engineering.

Eligibility: Applicants must have satisfied the academic requirements needed for professional registration at either IEng or CEng level; Applicants must 1. be currently resident in the UK 2. intend to commence their advanced training course in the next academic session. If you have already commenced you are not eligible to apply 3. have received an offer of a place on the advanced training course 4. be an Associate Member of the Institution, or higher grade, at the time of applying for a scholarship.

Level of Study: Postgraduate

Type: Grant

Value: Up to £5,000

Frequency: Annual

Country of Study: United Kingdom

Application Procedure: Applicants must write for details

Closing Date: 1 August

Funding: Private

Additional Information: www.imeche.org/careers-education/scholarships-and-awards/university-awards/postgraduate-awards/james-clayton-award

For further information contact:

Tel: (44) 1284 717887
Email: awards@imeche.org

Postgraduate Masters Scholarships

Purpose: The purpose of obtaining the academic requirements for professional registration as a Chartered Engineer (CEng)

Eligibility: The scholarships are open to students who 1. are currently resident in the United Kingdom, who will commence their IMechE accredited masters degree in the next academic session 2. have received an offer of a place at a university. 3. are expecting or have already gained a first class or 21 honours IMechE accredited degree 4. are undertaking instructional or research-based study programmes 5. are supported in their application by three referees 6. one who can vouch for your academic abilities (normally your Undergraduate Personal Tutor or Head of Department) 7. one who can confirm your suitability to embark on the postgraduate course you have chosen, and the likelihood of your success 8. one who can vouch for your character 9. referees should preferably be members of the Institution.

Level of Study: Postgraduate

Type: Scholarship

Value: Up to £6,500

Frequency: Annual

Country of Study: Any country

Closing Date: 1 August

For further information contact:

Tel: (44) 1284 717887

Email: awards@imeche.org

Spencer Wilks Postgraduate Masters Scholarships

Purpose: The Institution invests in the future of developing engineers.

Eligibility: The scholarships are open to students who 1. are currently resident in the United Kingdom, who will commence their IMechE accredited masters degree in the next academic session 2. have received an offer of a place at a university. 3. are expecting or have already gained a first class or 21 honours IMechE accredited degree 4. are undertaking instructional or research-based study programmes 5. are supported in their application by three referees 1. one who can vouch for your academic abilities (normally your Undergraduate Personal Tutor or Head of Department) 2. one who can confirm your suitability to embark on the postgraduate course you have chosen, and the likelihood of your success 3. one who can vouch for your character 4. referees should preferably be members of the Institution.

Level of Study: Masters Degree, Postgraduate

Type: Scholarship

Value: Up to £6,500

Country of Study: Any country

Closing Date: 1 August

For further information contact:

Tel: (44) 1284 717887

Email: awards@imeche.org

Spencer Wilks Scholarship/Fellowship

Purpose: To promote or encourage the study of automobile engineering

Level of Study: Postgraduate

Type: Scholarship

Value: £10,000

Frequency: Annual

Country of Study: Any country

Application Procedure: Applicants must write for details

Funding: Private

For further information contact:

Email: n.udovidchik03@imperial.ac.uk

Intel Corporation

2200 Mission College Blvd, Santa Clara, CA 95054-1549, United States of America.

Tel: (1) 408 765 8080

Email: scholarships@intel.com

Website: www.intel.com

Intel Corporation is committed to maintaining and enhancing the quality of life in the communities where the company has a major presence.

Intel Public Affairs Russia Grant

Purpose: To support further study programmes with educational and technological components in Russia

Eligibility: Each request will be evaluated on the basis of the services offered and the programme's impact on the community and the potential for Intel employee involvement

Type: Grant

Frequency: Annual

Country of Study: Russia

Application Procedure: Apply online or contact the office

Funding: Corporation

Contributor: Intel Corporation

For further information contact:

Tel: (7) 831 296 94 44

Email: paris@intel.com

International Airline Training Fund (IATF)

33, Route de I'Aeroport PO Box 416, Gineva-15 Airport, CH-1215 Geneva, Switzerland.

Tel: (41) 22 770 2525

Email: iatf@iata.org

Website: www.iata.org

Contact: IATF Co-ordinator

The International Airline Training Fund's (IATF) mission is to provide vocational training opportunities for staff of IATA member airlines based in countries with developing economies. It does so by providing scholarships and other training opportunities to enable worthy candidates to follow vocational training courses conducted by the IATA Aviation Training & Development Institute, the Aviation MBA at Concordia University, as well as several other courses.

International Airline Training Fund IATA Aviation Training and Development Institute (ATDI) Scholarships

Purpose: To enable staff of IATA member airlines based in countries with developing economies to follow short courses of specialist vocational training provided under the auspices of the IATA Aviation Training & Development Institute (ATDI)

Eligibility: Open to staff from IATA member airlines from countries with developing economies

Level of Study: Postgraduate

Type: Scholarship

Value: Please contact the organization

Country of Study: Switzerland, the United States of America or Singapore

Application Procedure: Applicants must channel applications through the human resources director of the IATA member airline which employs the applicant for an IATF-IATDI scholarship

Funding: Commercial, Private

Contributor: IATA member airlines and aviation industry suppliers

Additional Information: The scholarship committee meets quarterly to assess accumulated applications as of that date and to make awards. The ATDI seeks to offer skills training for managers, supervisors and other airline industry specialist staff who wish to add to their professional knowledge and ability. The range of courses taught is wide, with courses in heavy demand being repeated during the course of the year www.theiet.org/impact-society/awards-scholarships/iet-postgraduate-research-awards/

For further information contact:

Email: haroo@iata.org

International Arctic Research Center Fellowships for Cancer Research

150 cours Albert-Thomas, F-69372 Lyon Cedex 08, France.

Tel: (33) 472 73 84 48

Email: fel@iarc.fr

Contact: Research on Cancer

Postdoctoral Fellowships for Training in Cancer Research

Purpose: The IARC fellowships are intended for early career scientists wishing to complete their training in those aspects of cancer research related to the Agency's mission. Disciplines covered are epidemiology (all disciplines included), biostatistics, bioinformatics, and areas related to, mechanisms of carcinogenesis including molecular and cell biology, molecular genetics, epigenetics, and molecular pathology

Level of Study: Research

Type: Fellowship

Value: The annual stipend with dependent allowance is competitive compared with other international fellowship schemes. The cost of travel for the Fellow, and in certain circumstances for dependants, will be met, and health insurance covered

Length of Study: 2 years

Country of Study: France

Closing Date: 30 November

Additional Information: For more details, please visit www.iarc.fr

training.iarc.fr/education-and-training/

International Association for the Study of Obesity

Charles Darwin House, 12 Roger Street, London WCIN 2JU, United Kingdom.

Tel:	(44) 20 7685 2580
Email:	enquiries@iaso.org
Website:	www.iaso.org

The International Association for the Study of Obesity (IASO) aims to improve global health by promoting the understanding of obesity and weight-related diseases through scientific research and dialogue whilst encouraging the development of effective policies for their prevention and management. IASO is the leading global professional organization concerned with obesity, operating in over 50 countries around the world.

International Association for the Study of Obesity Per Björntorp Travelling Fellowship Award

Purpose: To provide travel grants to enable young researchers to attend the International Congress of Obesity

Eligibility: Applicants for this award must demonstrate their financial need for such support to attend the Congress. Applicants must be an IASO member. There is no age limit

Level of Study: Doctorate, Postdoctorate, Postgraduate, Predoctorate, Research

Type: Studentships and bursaries

Value: Up to US$2,000 of return economy flights, congress Registration and hotel accommodation at the International Congress of Obesity

Study Establishment: Any

Country of Study: Any country

Application Procedure: Download the application form from website

Additional Information: For further information about the IASO Travelling Fellowships Award please write to mailto: mailto: awards@iaso.org

For further information contact:

28 Portland Place, Marylebone London W1B 1LY, United Kingdom.

Tel:	(44) 20 7467 9610
Fax:	(44) 20 7636 9258
Email:	kate.baillie@iaso.org

International Business Machines Corporation

1 New Orchard Road, Armonk, New York, NY 10504-1722, United States of America.

Tel:	(1) 877 426 6006
Email:	ews@us.ibm.com
Website:	www.ibm.com

IBM stands today at the forefront of a worldwide industry that is revolutionizing the way in which enterprises, organizations and people operate and thrive. IBM strives to lead in the invention, development and manufacture of the industry's most advanced information technologies, including computer systems, software, storage systems, and microelectronics.

International Business Machines Herman Goldstine Postdoctoral Fellowship

Purpose: To provide scientists of outstanding ability an opportunity to advance their scholarship as resident department members at the Research Center

Eligibility: Open to candidates who have obtained a PhD or expect to receive a PhD before the fellowship commences in the second half of current year

Level of Study: Research

Type: Fellowship

Value: The stipend is expected to be at least US$150,000

Length of Study: 1 year

Frequency: Annual

Country of Study: United States of America

Application Procedure: Applicants can download the application form from the website. The completed application form, curriculum vitae and abstract of PhD dissertation must be sent

Closing Date: 20 January

Additional Information: Applications shall be accepted through email at goldpost@watson.ibm.comscholarship-positions.com/ibm-herman-goldstine-postdoctoral-fellowships-mathematical-sciences/2016/01/07/

International Business Machines PhD Fellowship Program

Purpose: To honour exceptional PhD students in an array of focus areas of interest to IBM and fundamental to innovation

Eligibility: Open to students nominated by a faculty member. They must be enroled full-time in a college or university PhD programme and they should have completed at least 1 year of study in their Doctoral programme at the time of their nomination

Level of Study: Doctorate
Type: Fellowships
Value: US$17,500
Length of Study: 3 years
Frequency: Annual
Country of Study: Any country
Application Procedure: All nominations for the IBM PhD Fellowship must be submitted by faculty electronically over the web on a standardized form. The nomination form will be available on the IBM PhD Fellowship nomination website from 19 September to 31 October
Closing Date: 31 October
Additional Information: Non-United States citizens who wish to participate in an internship in the United States must obtain work authorization under the specifics of their particular visa. For further information, see website at www.research.ibm.com/university/phdfellowship/#about

International Centre for Education in Islamic Finance (INCEIF)

Email: syarina@inceif.org
Contact: Noorsyarina Mohd Sapiai

Khazanah – INCEIF Scholarship

Eligibility: Information available on website www.inceif.org/khazanah-inceif-scholarship-programme/
Level of Study: Doctorate, Postgraduate
Value: All applicable tuition fees and monthly allowances for the duration of the course
Study Establishment: INCEIF
Country of Study: Malaysia
Application Procedure: Kindly contact Ms Noorsyarina Mohd Sapiai at syarina@inceif.org
Closing Date: 16 March
Additional Information: Eligible to nationals of Malaysia. All communications will be done via email. Therefore please ensure the email address given is correct and active afters chool.my/scholarship/khazanah-inceif-scholarship-programme-2017

International Centre for Genetic Engineering and Biotechnology (ICGEB)

AREA Science Park, Padriciano 99, I-34149 Trieste, Italy.

Tel: (39) 40 375 71
Email: fellowships@icgeb.org

Website: www.icgeb.org
Contact: Human Resources Unit

The International Centre for Genetic Engineering and Biotechnology (ICGEB) is an organization devoted to advanced research and training in molecular biology and biotechnology, with special regard to the needs of the developing world. The component host countries are Italy, India and South Africa. The full member states of ICGEB are Afghanistan, Algeria, Argentina, Bangladesh, Bhutan, Bosnia and Herzegovina, Brazil, Bulgaria, Burundi, Cameroon, Chile, China, Colombia, Costa Rica, Côte d'Ivoire, Croatia, Cuba, Ecuador, Egypt, Eritrea, FYR Macedonia, Hungary, Iran, Iraq, Jordan, Kenya, Kuwait, Kyrgyzstan, Liberia, Libya, Malaysia, Mauritius, Mexico, Montenegro, Morocco, Nigeria, Pakistan, Panama, Peru, Poland, Qatar, Romania, Russia, Saudi Arabia, Senegal, Serbia, Slovakia, Slovenia, Sri Lanka, Sudan, Syria, Tanzania, Trinidad and Tobago, Tunisia, Turkey, United Arab Emirates, Uruguay, Venezuela, and Vietnam.

ICGEB PhD and POSTDOC Fellowships, South Africa

Eligibility: 1. Applicants must be nationals of an ICGEB Member State. Nationals of India and South Africa, ICGEB Host Countries, are not eligible to apply for ICGEB Fellowships in their home country. 2. Degree requirements applicants for ICGEB Trieste should hold a BSc (Honours) degree; applicants for ICGEB Cape Town and New Delhi should hold an MSc degree. 3. Candidates must have a good working knowledge of the English language, supported by a proficiency certificate (TOEFL, Cambridge Certificate, or equivalent). Not required when scholastic education has been undertaken in English. 4. Candidates for Trieste, Italy must be below the age of 32 years at the time of application. There is no age limit for applications for ICGEB New Delhi and Cape Town
Level of Study: Postdoctorate, Postgraduate
Type: Fellowship
Value: Trieste (Italy): €2,000, New Delhi (India): US$1,590, Cape Town (South Africa): ZAR 18,750.
Length of Study: 3 years PhD course with the possibility of 1-year extension
Country of Study: Any country
Closing Date: 31 March

ICGEB PhD Fellowships

Eligibility: 1. Applicants must be nationals of an ICGEB Member State. Nationals of India and South Africa, ICGEB

Host Countries, are not eligible to apply for ICGEB Fellowships in their home country. 2. Degree requirements applicants for ICGEB Trieste should hold a BSc (Honours) degree; applicants for ICGEB Cape Town and New Delhi should hold an MSc degree. 3. Candidates must have a good working knowledge of the English language, supported by a proficiency certificate (TOEFL, Cambridge Certificate, or equivalent). Not required when scholastic education has been undertaken in English. 4. Candidates for Trieste, Italy must be below the age of 32 years at the time of application. There is no age limit for applications for ICGEB New Delhi and Cape Town.

Type: Fellowship

Value: Trieste (Italy): Euro 1,300, New Delhi (India): US$1,020, Cape Town (South Africa): ZAR 12,500.

Length of Study: 3 years PhD course with the possibility of 1-year extension

Country of Study: Any country

Closing Date: 31 March

ICGEB Postdoctoral Fellowships

Purpose: ICGEB offers competitive Postdoctoral Fellowships in the Life Sciences to highly motivated scientists wishing to pursue postdoctoral research in a world-class scientific environment. The Fellowships consist of a very competitive package including stipend, health insurance and additional benefits. The most successful fellows will also be eligible to apply for ICGEB Early Career Research Grants to support their own research programmes as young PIs upon return to an ICGEB Member State.

Type: Fellowship

Value: Trieste (Italy) €2,000, New Delhi (India) US$1,590, Cape Town (South Africa) R18,750

Length of Study: 2 years with the possibility of a 1-year extension.

Country of Study: Any country

Closing Date: 30 September

ICGEB Short-Term PhD Fellowships

Purpose: ICGEB offers Short-term fellowships for Pre-doctoral studies in ICGEB Component laboratories to fund ongoing collaborative research between scientists from ICGEB Member States and research groups at ICGEB laboratories in Trieste, Italy, New Delhi, India and Cape Town, South Africa, with the aim of facilitating access to the latest research techniques and to strengthen capacity building.

Eligibility: 1. Applicants must be nationals of an ICGEB Member State and may not apply for fellowships to be undertaken in their country of origin, unless working abroad at the time of application. 2. Degree requirements applicants for ICGEB Trieste and Cape Town should hold a BSc (Honours) degree; applicants for ICGEB New Delhi should hold a MSc degree. 3. Candidates must have a good working knowledge of the English language, supported by a proficiency certificate (TOEFL, Cambridge Certificate, or equivalent). Not required when scholastic education has been undertaken in English.

Level of Study: Pre-doctoral

Type: Fellowship

Value: Monthly stipend: Trieste (Italy): Euro 1,300, New Delhi (India): US$1,020, Cape Town (South Africa): ZAR 12,500.

Length of Study: 1–12 months

Country of Study: Any country

Closing Date: 31 March

Additional Information: www.icgeb.org/activities/fellow ship/short-term-phd-application/

ICGEB Short-Term Postdoctoral Fellowships

Purpose: In ICGEB Laboratories ICGEB offers Short-term fellowships for Postdoctoral studies in ICGEB Component laboratories to fund ongoing collaborative research between scientists from ICGEB Member States and research groups at ICGEB laboratories in Trieste, Italy, New Delhi, India and Cape Town, South Africa, with the aim of facilitating access to the latest research techniques and to strengthen capacity building.

Eligibility: 1. Applicants must be nationals of an ICGEB Member State and may not apply for fellowships to be undertaken in their country of origin, unless working abroad at the time of application. 2. Degree requirements applicants should hold a recent PhD in Life Sciences or have at least 3 years research experience. 3. Candidates must have a good working knowledge of the English language, supported by a proficiency certificate (TOEFL, Cambridge Certificate, or equivalent). Not required when scholastic education has been undertaken in English.

Type: Fellowship

Value: Monthly stipend: Trieste (Italy): Euro 2,000, New Delhi (India): US$1,590, Cape Town (South Africa): ZAR 18,750.

Length of Study: 1–6 months

Country of Study: Any country

Closing Date: 31 March

Additional Information: www.icgeb.org/activities/fellow ship/guidelines-and-application-form-arturo-falaschi-short-term-postdoc-fellowships/#:~:text=ICGEB%20offers%20 Short%2Dterm%20fellowships,the%20aim%20of%20facilitat ing%20access

ICGEB Smart Fellowships

Subjects: Applications are welcome in any area of the Life Sciences.

Purpose: The programme promotes the mobility of researchers between ICGEB Member States as a way of enhancing skill development, acquisition of specific hands-on training in technologies available in the receiving laboratory and increasing bilateral cooperation in science and technology, and should show clear evidence of strong collaboration between the two laboratories. Applicants should focus on the impact for the fellow's career, the benefit to the applicant's home laboratory and the suitability of the receiving laboratory.

Eligibility: The call is open to nationals of ICGEB Member States and provides fellowships to scientists in the early stage of their career wishing to spend between 3 and 9 months at a research institution in an ICGEB Member State other than their own. SMART Fellowships are intended to promote collaboration among researchers in ICGEB Member Countries. Mobility support to laboratories located in Italy, India and South Africa can be considered under exceptional circumstances and only if the research activity proposed is not covered by one of the ICGEB laboratories in Trieste, New Delhi or Cape Town. If the latter case applies, please see ICGEB Arturo Falaschi Short-term fellowships programme. There is no age limit. However, preference is given to young scientists at the beginning of their research career. Applicants should be either registered for a PhD or have obtained their PhD degree within the last 5 years and be actively working in a research Institution. Young scientists holding an MSc or equivalent can apply. SMART Fellowships support mobility between laboratories located in Member States. Awards are not intended to prolong visits begun under other auspices; to support participation in courses, workshops or symposia or as bridging fellowships between, or prior to, long term stays funded by ICGEB or other organizations.

Level of Study: Postgraduate
Type: Fellowship
Value: The stipend ranges from US$800 to 1,500 per month
Length of Study: minimum of 3 to a maximum of 9 months
Country of Study: Any country
Closing Date: 31 March

ICGEB-Elettra Sincrotrone Trieste International Fellowship Programme

Purpose: ICGEB and Elettra offer competitive Postdoc Fellowships in Life Sciences to highly motivated scientists wishing to pursue their studies in a world-class scientific environment.

Eligibility: 1. Applicants must be nationals of an ICGEB Member State and may not apply for fellowships to be undertaken in their country of origin, unless they have been working abroad for, at least, the last 3 years and at the time of application. 2. Degree requirements applicants should hold a recent PhD in Life Sciences or have at least 3 years research experience. 3. Preference is given to candidates below the age of 35.

Level of Study: Postgraduate
Type: Fellowship
Value: Trieste (Italy) €2,000, New Delhi (India) US$1,590, Cape Town (South Africa) R18,750
Length of Study: 2 years with the possibility of a 1-year extension
Country of Study: Any country
Closing Date: 31 March

International Center for Genetic Engineering and Biotechnology Arturo Falaschi PhD and Postdoctoral Fellowships for Member Countries

Purpose: Funding opportunities are made available through the Collaborative Research Programme (CRP) – ICGEB Research Grants, which is a dedicated source of funding aimed at financing projects addressing original scientific problems of particular relevance for the host country and of regional interest

Eligibility: Candidates must have a good working knowledge of the English language, supported by a proficiency certificate (TOEFL, Cambridge Certificate, or equivalent). Not required when scholastic education has been undertaken in English

Type: Fellowship
Value: See the website
Study Establishment: Fellowships are awarded in Life Sciences. The programme provides support for research projects in basic science, human healthcare, industrial and agricultural biotechnology and bioenergy
Country of Study: Any country
Application Procedure: The mode of application is online
Closing Date: 31 March
Additional Information: Please browse the website for more details scholarship-positions.com/icgeb-arturo-falaschi-phd-postdoctoral-fellowships-member-countries/2018/01/17/ www.icgeb.org/activities/fellowship/short-term-phd-application/

The Arturo Falaschi ICGEB Predoctoral Fellowships ICGEB Trieste International PhD Programme

Purpose: To enable promising young students to attend and complete the PhD programme at ICGEB Trieste in

Italy. The programme is validated by the Open University, United Kingdom, and the University of Nova Gorica, Slovenia

Eligibility: 1. Applicants must be nationals of an ICGEB Member State. Nationals of India and South Africa, ICGEB Host Countries, are not eligible to apply for ICGEB Fellowships in their home country. 2. Degree requirements applicants for ICGEB Trieste should hold a BSc (Honours) degree; applicants for ICGEB Cape Town and New Delhi should hold an MSc degree. 3. Candidates must have a good working knowledge of the English language, supported by a proficiency certificate (TOEFL, Cambridge Certificate, or equivalent). Not required when scholastic education has been undertaken in English. 4. Candidates for Trieste, Italy must be below the age of 32 years at the time of application (i.e. date of birth after 31/03/1988). There is no age limit for applications for ICGEB New Delhi and Cape Town.

Level of Study: Predoctorate

Type: Fellowship

Value: Trieste (Italy) €1,300, New Delhi (India) US$1,020, Cape Town (South Africa) R$12,500

Length of Study: 3 years PhD course with the possibility of 1-year extension

Frequency: Annual

Study Establishment: ICGEB laboratories in Trieste and Monterotondo (Rome)

Country of Study: Italy

Application Procedure: Applicants must refer to the website

Closing Date: 31 March

Additional Information: For more information on this programme please refer to the website www.icgeb.org/activities/fellowship/guidelines-and-application-form-arturo-falaschi-phd-fellowships/

For further information contact:

Email: admissions@cgebicgeb.res.in

WE-STAR Fellowships

Eligibility: 1. Applicants must be nationals of ICGEB Member States in the African Continent* 2. Applicants may not apply for fellowships to be undertaken in their country of origin unless working abroad at the time of application 3. Pre-docs having completed their university degree and enrolled in a PhD course, as well as postdoctoral researchers having completed their PhD or equivalent may apply. Tentatively, 5 – Pre-doc and 5 post-doc fellowships will be awarded. 4. No age limit applies, but preference will be given to candidates below the age of 45 5. Good working knowledge of English is mandatory

Value: Monthly stipend: Euro 1300 for PhD students and Euro 2000 for postdoctoral fellows, or equivalent.

Country of Study: Any country

Closing Date: 28 January

For further information contact:

Email: mobility@icgeb.org

International Centre for Theoretical Sciences

Survey No. 151, Shivakote, Hesaraghatta Hobli, Bengaluru, Karnataka 560 089, India.

Tel: (91) 80 6730 6000, 80 4653 6000
Email: info@icts.res.in
Contact: International Centre for Theoretical Sciences

International Centre for Theoretical Sciences (ICTS)contributes to research excellence in science in various ways. It has a high-quality faculty together with a large floating population comprising visitors, postdoctoral fellows and graduate students.

International Centre for Theoretical Sciences S. N. Bhatt Memorial Excellence Research Fellowship

Purpose: The aim of the fellowship is to give an opportunity to master's students of Science and Engineering to work with faculty and post-doctoral fellows of the Centre and to participate in research at the frontiers of knowledge

Eligibility: Undergraduate students of science, mathematics and engineering, who are in their third, fourth or fifth year of the program are eligible to apply. Exceptional undergraduates in their second year may also apply. Masters degree students and those who have completed their undergraduate are also welcome to apply.

Type: Research

Value: This program offers a unique opportunity masters students of Science and Engineering to work with faculty and postdoctoral fellows of the Centre and to participate in research at the frontiers of knowledge

Study Establishment: The fellowship is awarded in the field of Science and Engineering

Country of Study: India

Application Procedure: Interested candidates should apply online with their CV and relevant details. The applicants also need to arrange at least two recommendation letters. Applications will be normally reviewed in February and results will be declared around early March every year.

Closing Date: 31 January

Additional Information: please visit our website for more information   scholarship-positions.com/icts-s-n-bhatt-memorial-excellence-research-fellowship-india/2017/11/04/icts.res.in/academic/summer-research-program

For further information contact:

Survey No. 151, Shivakote, Hesaraghatta Hobli, Bengaluru, 560 089, India.

Tel: (91) 80 4653 6000
Email: summer.program@icts.res.in

International Dairy-Deli-Bakery Association

IDDBA, 636 Science Drive, PO Box 5528, Madison, WI 53711-1073, United States of America.

Tel: (1) 608 310 5000
Email: iddba@iddba.org
Website: www.iddba.org

Our mission is to expand our leadership role in promoting the growth and development of daily, deli, and bakery sales in the food industry. Our vision is to be the essential resource for relevant information and services that add value across all food channels for the dairy, deli and bakery categories.

International Dairy-Deli-Bakery Association Graduate Scholarships

Purpose: To support employees of IDDBA-member companies

Eligibility: Applicants must be a current full- or part-time employee of an IDDBA-member company with an academic background in a food-related field and have a 2.5 grade-point average on a 4.0 scale, or equivalent

Level of Study: Postgraduate

Type: Scholarship

Value: Up to $2,000 toward tuition

Length of Study: 1 year

Frequency: Annual

Country of Study: United States of America

Application Procedure: Contact the Education Information Specialist

Closing Date: 10 April

Funding: Foundation

Contributor: IDDBA

Additional Information: www.iddba.org/professional-resources/scholarships-grants/scholarship-for-growing-the-future

For further information contact:

Email: scholarships@iddba.org

International Education Specialist

World Citizen Talent Scholarship

Purpose: We are seeking intelligent, talented and ambitious people who view themselves as citizens of the world.

Eligibility: You are eligible to apply for the scholarship if you; 1. Come from outside The Netherlands and don't live in the Netherlands. 2. Are enrolling for the first time at The Hague University of Applied Sciences. 3. Have never applied for this scholarship before. 4. Have been conditionally accepted as a student (also-called offer of student position) on or before 31 March for the upcoming academic year

Level of Study: Masters Degree

Type: Scholarship

Value: €5,000

Frequency: Annual

Country of Study: Any country

Application Procedure: Applicants must submit the below documents to process further. 1. Outstanding Master's-level students can apply for these scholarships by submitting the application form including an essay of no more than 1,000 words, detailing their cultural background and contribution they wish to make to the university as global citizens. 2. Applications will be reviewed by an academic panel

Closing Date: 15 May

Funding: Private

Additional Information: www.thehagueuniversity.com/study-choice/masters-professional-courses/scholarships/world-citizen-talent-scholarship

For further information contact:

Email: master-scholarship@hhs.nl

International Federation of Library Associations and Institutions WLIC

Chartered Institute of Library and Information Professionals International Library and Information Group Alan Hopkinson Award

Purpose: The Chartered Institute of Library and Information Professionals (CILIP) and its International Library and Information Group (ILIG) invite applicants from Europe to attend the International Federation of Library Associations and Institutions (IFLA) conference in Athens
Eligibility: 1. Applicants are required to write a reflective report of not more than 4,000 words within six months of their visit, and a version for publication in Focus on International Library and Information Work, the ILIG journal. 2. Applicants should submit a formal proposal in English of up to 500 words (equivalent to 1–2 pages of A4 paper) detailing how the visit will support their professional development within the context of their career to date and using the headings of 'Visit objectives' 'Planned approach and content' 'Application of learning post-visit'
Level of Study: Postgraduate
Type: Award
Frequency: Annual
Country of Study: Any country
Closing Date: 31 March
Funding: Private
Additional Information: 2019.ifla.org/2019-alan-hopkinson-award-cilip/

For further information contact:

IFLA Headquarters IFLA, P.O. Box 95312, NL-2509 CH The Hague, Netherlands.

Email: ilig@cilip.org.uk

Dr. Shawky Salem Conference Grant

Purpose: The aim of the grant is to enable one expert in library and information sciences from the Arab Countries (AC) to attend the Annual IFLA Conference
Eligibility: 1. The grant is available to a librarian of Arab nationality, not exceeding 45 years. 2. Priority is given to applicants who are first-time attendees to the IFLA Congress. 3. The applicant should have at least 5 years of experience in LIS profession. 4. The applicant must have the approval of his / her organization to attend the IFLA WLIC
Level of Study: Graduate, Professional development
Type: Grant
Value: US$1,900

Frequency: Annual
Country of Study: Any country
Application Procedure: Application has to b eprocessed physically
Closing Date: 31 March
Funding: Private
Additional Information: www.ifla.org/funds-grants-awards/SSCG

For further information contact:

Email: grants@ifla.org

International Federation of Library Associations and Institutions Green Library Award

Purpose: To create awareness of libraries' social responsibility and leadership in environmental education. Libraries of all types are encouraged to participate. To support the worldwide Green Library movement, concerned with 1. environmentally sustainable buildings. 2. environmentally sustainable information resources and programming conservation of resources and energy
Eligibility: They also focus on related services, activities, events, literature and projects, demonstrating the social role and responsibility of libraries as leaders in environmental sustainability. 1. Any type of library with an outstanding Green Library project, initiative or idea may apply for the IFLA Green Library Award. The project, initiative or idea may be presented in various ways (e.g. essay, video, poster, article, set of slides). 2. Applications must be written in one of the seven IFLA languages. 3. Applicants may also submit an English translation if they prefer. 4. Film and Video materials in languages other than English must have English subtitles. 5. The presentation of the project, initiative or idea should be submitted to the ENSULIB award reviewing committee
Level of Study: Postgraduate
Type: Grant
Frequency: Annual
Country of Study: Any country
Application Procedure: The quality and relevance of the project, initiative or idea will be evaluated by the ENSULIB committee in terms of applicability to the goals and the scope of ENSULIB. ifla.org/ifla-green-library-award-2019/
Closing Date: 28 February
Funding: Private
Additional Information: www.ifla.org/news/ifla-green-library-award-2022-announcement/

For further information contact:

P.O. Box 95312, NL-2509 CH The Hague, Netherlands.

Email: petra.hauke@hu-berlin.de

International Federation of University Women (IFUW)

IFUW Headquarters, 10 rue de Lac, CH-1207 Geneva, Switzerland.

Tel: (41) 22 731 2380
Email: info@ifuw.org
Website: www.ifuw.org

The International Federation of University Women (IFUW) is a non-profit, non-governmental organization comprising graduate women working locally, nationally and internationally to advocate the improvement of the status of women and girls at the international level, by promoting lifelong education and enabling graduate women to use their expertise to effect change.

Canadian Federation of University Women/A. Vibert Douglas Fellowship

Value: US$8,000
Country of Study: Any country

For further information contact:

Email: fellowships@cfuw.org

Ida Smedley MacLean Fellowship

Purpose: To encourage advanced scholarship and original research relevant to IFUW's mission
Eligibility: Open to female applicants who are either members of one of IFUW's national federations or associations or, in the case of female graduates living in countries where there is not yet a national affiliate, independent members of IFUW, or other applicants who pay a filing fee. Applicants should have completed at least the first year of a doctoral programme
Level of Study: Doctorate
Type: Fellowship
Value: CHF 8,000
Length of Study: More than 8 months
Frequency: Dependent on funds available
Study Establishment: An approved Institute of Higher Education
Country of Study: Worldwide
Application Procedure: Applicants must apply through their respective federation or association. A list of IFUW national

federations and associations can be obtained from the IFUW website. IFUW independent members and others must apply directly to the IFUW headquarters in Geneva
Funding: Private
Contributor: British Federation of Women Graduates
No. of awards given last year: 1 of each fellowship
Additional Information: Please see the website for further details www.ifuw.org/what-we-do/grants-fellowships/international-awards/

The CFUW/A Vibert Douglas International Fellowship

Purpose: To encourage advanced scholarship and original research relevant to IFUW's mission
Eligibility: Open to female applicants who are either members of one of IFUW's national federations or associations or, in the case of female graduates living in countries where there is not yet a national affiliate, independent members of IFUW, or other applicants who pay a filing fee. Applicants should have completed at least the first year of a doctoral programme
Level of Study: Doctorate, Postdoctorate, Postgraduate
Type: Fellowship
Value: C$12,000
Length of Study: Requires 8–12 months' work in a country other than that in which the applicant was educated or habitually resides
Frequency: Dependent on funds available
Study Establishment: An approved Institute of Higher Education
Country of Study: Worldwide
Application Procedure: Applicants must apply through their respective federation or association. A list of IFUW national federations and associations can be obtained from the IFUW website. IFUW independent members and others must apply directly to the IFUW headquarters in Geneva
Funding: Private
Contributor: Canadian Federation of University Women
Additional Information: scwist.ca/cfuwa-vibert-douglas-fellowship/

International Furnishings and Design Association Education Foundation

Vercille Voss Scholarship

Purpose: The IFDA Illinois Chapter initiated the Vercille Voss Graduate Student Scholarship in memory of Vercille Voss, longtime chapter member and mentor to new members and students. The applicant must be enrolled as a part-time or full-time graduate student at an accredited university

Eligibility: 1. Must be a graduate student or a postgraduate student 2. Must attend a university or a four-year college 3. Both full-time and part-time students 4. Restricted to students studying Architecture, Interior Design, Industrial Design, Trade/Technical Specialties

Level of Study: Graduate

Type: Scholarship

Value: US$2,000

Frequency: Annual

Country of Study: Any country

Application Procedure: The IFDA Educational Foundation Board of Trustees will select the scholarship recipient based on the student's academic achievement, awards and accomplishments, future plans and goals, and letter of recommendation. All applicants must be graduate students and have completed four design courses in post-secondary education at the time of application and be majoring in Interior Design or a related field. For more information or to apply, please visit the scholarship provider's website

Closing Date: 31 March

Funding: Private

For further information contact:

112 Hidden Lake, Canton, GA 30114, United States of America.

Tel: (1) 770 378 7221
Email: ef.ifda@tapestries.org

International Human Frontier Science Program Organization (HFSP)

Bureaux Europe, 20 Place des Halles, F-67080 Strasbourg, France.

Tel: (33) 3 88 21 51 12
Email: info@hfsp.org
Website: www.hfsp.org
Contact: Mr Patrick Vincent, Director of Scientific Affairs and Communications

The International Human Frontier Science Program Organization (HFSP) promotes basic research into the complex mechanisms underlying the function of living organisms by supporting interdisciplinary and international collaboration. The programme only supports research that transcends national boundaries.

Career Development Award

Level of Study: 3 years

Value: US$231,000

Country of Study: Any country

Closing Date: 29 March

Additional Information: wellcome.org/grant-funding/schemes/career-development-awards

For further information contact:

Email: communications@hfsp.org

Cross-Disciplinary Fellowships

Purpose: Cross-Disciplinary Fellowships (CDF) are for applicants with a PhD from outside the life sciences (e.g. in physics, chemistry, mathematics, engineering or computer sciences), who have had limited exposure to biology during their previous training

Eligibility: See application guidelines www.hfsp.org/funding/postdoctoral-fellowships/guidelines

Level of Study: Postdoctorate

Type: Fellowship

Value: About US$180,000 over three years (depending on host country)

Length of Study: 3 years

Frequency: Annual

Country of Study: Africa

Application Procedure: Online

No. of awards offered: 54

Funding: Government

Contributor: Australia, Canada, European Commission, France, Germany, India, Italy, Korea, Japan, New Zealand, Norway, Singapore, Switzerland, United Kingdom and United States of America

No. of awards given last year: 12

No. of applicants last year: 54

Additional Information: www.hfsp.org/sites/default/files/Sciences/fellows/2020%20Fellowship%20application%20guidelines.pdf

For further information contact:

12 quai Saint Jean, F-67080 Strasbourg Cedex, France.

Long-Term Fellowships

Purpose: Long-Term Fellowships (LTF) are for applicants with a PhD in a biological discipline, who will broaden their expertise by proposing a project in the life sciences which is significantly different from their previous PhD or postdoctoral work. The HFSP fellowship program strongly supports frontier, potentially transformative ('out-of-the-box') proposals and encourages applications for high-risk projects. The projects should be interdisciplinary in nature and should challenge existing paradigms by using novel approaches and techniques. Scientifically, they should address an important problem or a barrier to progress in the field

Eligibility: See application guidelines www.hfsp.org/funding/postdoctoral-fellowships/guidelines

Level of Study: Postdoctorate

Type: Fellowship

Value: About US$180,000 over three years (depending on host country)

Length of Study: 3 years

Frequency: Annual

Country of Study: Any country

Application Procedure: Online

No. of awards offered: 534

Funding: Government

Contributor: Australia, Canada, European Commission, France, Germany, India, Italy, Korea, Japan, New Zealand, Norway, Singapore, Switzerland, United Kingdom and United States of America

No. of awards given last year: 79

No. of applicants last year: 534

Additional Information: www.hfsp.org/sites/default/files/Sciences/fellows/2020%20Fellowship%20application%20guidelines.pdf

Program Grants

Purpose: Research grants are provided for teams of scientists from different countries who wish to combine their expertise in innovative approaches to questions that could not be answered by individual laboratories. Emphasis is placed on novel collaborations that bring together scientists preferably from different disciplines (e.g. from chemistry, physics, computer science, engineering) to focus on problems in the life sciences. Note, HFSPO funds only basic research. Applied applications, including medical research typically funded by national medical research bodies, will be deemed ineligible. Program Grants are awarded to teams of independent researchers at any stage of their careers. The research team is expected to develop new lines of research through the collaboration. Up to US$450,000 per grant per year may be applied for. Applications including independent investigators early in their careers are encouraged

Eligibility: See application guidelines www.hfsp.org/sites/www.hfsp.org/files/webfm/Grants/LI%20Guidelines.pdf

Level of Study: Postdoctorate

Type: Grant

Value: For 2022 awards, a team of 2 investigators will receive USD 280,000, a team of 3 investigators will receive USD 380,000 and a team of 4 investigators or more will receive USD 480,000 per year

Length of Study: 3 years

Frequency: Annual

Country of Study: Any country

Application Procedure: See application guidelines www.hfsp.org/sites/www.hfsp.org/files/webfm/Grants/LI%20Guidelines.pdf

Closing Date: 24 March

Funding: Government

Contributor: Australia, Canada, European Commission, France, Germany, India, Italy, Japan, Republic of Korea, New Zealand, Norway, Singapore, Switzerland, United Kingdom, United States of America

Additional Information: www.hfsp.org/funding/hfsp-funding/research-grants

For further information contact:

12 quai Saint-Jean, F-67080 Strasbourg, France.

Tel: (33) 3 88 21 51 23

Email: grant@hfsp.org

Young Investigator Grant

Purpose: Research grants are provided for teams of scientists from different countries who wish to combine their expertise in innovative approaches to questions that could not be answered by individual laboratories. Emphasis is placed on novel collaborations that bring together scientists preferably from different disciplines (e.g. from chemistry, physics, computer science, engineering) to focus on problems in the life sciences. Note, HFSPO funds only basic research. Applied applications, including medical research typically funded by national medical research bodies, will be deemed ineligible. The research teams must be international. The principal applicant must be from one of the eligible countries. However, other participating scientists and laboratories may be situated anywhere in the world. Young Investigators' Grants are awarded to teams of researchers, all of whom are within the first five years after obtaining an independent laboratory (e.g. Assistant Professor, Lecturer or equivalent). Applications for Young Investigators' Grants will be reviewed in competition with each other independently of applications for Program Grants

Eligibility: See application guidelines www.hfsp.org/funding/postdoctoral-fellowships/guidelines

Level of Study: Postdoctorate

Type: Grant

Value: Teams will receive up to US$450,000 per year for the whole team depending on the size of the team
Length of Study: 3 years
Frequency: Annual
Country of Study: Any country
Application Procedure: See application guidelines www.hfsp.org/sites/www.hfsp.org/files/webfm/Grants/LI%20Guidelines.pdf
No. of awards offered: 158
Funding: Government
Contributor: Australia, Canada, European Commission, France, Germany, India, Italy, Japan, Korea, New Zealand, Norway, Singapore, Switzerland, United Kingdom, United States
No. of awards given last year: 8
No. of applicants last year: 158

For further information contact:

HFSPO, 12 quai Saint Jean, F-67080 Strasbourg, France.

International Institute for Management Development (IMD)

Chemin de Bellerive 23, PO Box 915, CH-1001 Lausanne, Switzerland.

Tel:	(41) 21 618 0298
Email:	mbainfo@imd.ch
Website:	www.imd.ch/mba
Contact:	Suzanne Laurent

The International Institute for Management Development (IMD), created by industry to serve industry, develops cutting-edge research and programmes that meet real world needs. Their clients include dozens of leading international companies and their experienced faculty incorporate new management practices into the small and exclusive MBA programme. With no nationality dominating, IMD is truly global, practical and relevant.

International Institute for Management Development MBA Merit Scholarships

Purpose: To financially support applicants who consistently demonstrate exceptional qualities
Eligibility: Candidates who have already completed the IMD MBA application and admission process

Level of Study: MBA
Type: Scholarship
Value: CHF 10,000 towards tuition
Length of Study: 1 year
Frequency: Annual
Study Establishment: IMD
Country of Study: Switzerland
Closing Date: 30 September
Funding: Private
No. of awards given last year: 4
Additional Information: www.imd.org/news/updates/imd-mba-scholarship-program-a-commitment-to-diversity-and-impact/

For further information contact:

Email: MBAfinance@imd.org

Stewart Hamilton Scholarship

Purpose: Financially support applicants who demonstrate an understanding of corporate governance and responsibility
Eligibility: Candidates who have already applied to the full-time IMD MBA program and who demonstrate financial need
Level of Study: MBA
Type: Scholarship
Value: CHF 15,000 payment each semester for the standard duration of the course
Length of Study: 1 year
Frequency: Annual
Study Establishment: IMD
Country of Study: Switzerland
Application Procedure: Applicants must complete and submit the IMD MBA application form for financial assistance and the MBA application form
No. of awards offered: 14
Closing Date: 10 March
Funding: Private
No. of awards given last year: 1
No. of applicants last year: 14
Additional Information: Scholarship essays or questions should be sent to mbafinance@imd.orgwww.imd.org/news/updates/the-imd-stewart-hamilton-scholarship-to-benefit-outstanding-women/

For further information contact:

P.O. Box 915, CH-1001 Lausanne, Switzerland.

Email: clientmarketdevelopmenteurope@imd.org

International Institute for Population Sciences (IIPS)

Govandi Station Road Deonar, Bombay, Maharashtra 400088, India.

Tel: (91) 22 2556 3254
Email: diriips@bom8.vsnl.net.in
Website: www.iipsindia.org
Contact: Professor T K Roy, Director

The International Institute for Population Sciences (IIPS) is one of the few institutes set up solely for the purpose of studying demography. The only institute of its kind in the world, it was declared a deemed university on 15 August. The IIPS offers academic courses in population sciences and takes major initiatives to strengthen reproductive health, research and training programmes.

International Institute for Population Sciences Diploma in Population Studies

Purpose: To train the recipient in obtaining basic knowledge in the field of population
Eligibility: Open to ESCAP and Pacific Region nationals who are already working in the fields of population and health. Applicants are required to be graduates
Level of Study: Professional development
Type: Fellowship
Value: Return air ticket plus Rs6,000 per student per year as course fee and Rs6,000 fellowship for students
Length of Study: 10 months
Frequency: Annual
Country of Study: India
Application Procedure: Applicants must make an application through UNFPA country directors or representatives in the applicant's own country
No. of awards offered: Unknown
Closing Date: 30 April
Funding: Private
Contributor: UNFPA
No. of awards given last year: 5
No. of applicants last year: Unknown
Additional Information: Further information on this programme is also available from the London School of Economics, on (44) 20 7405 7686 iipsindia.org/course/DPS%20Brochure.pdf

For further information contact:

International Institute for Population Sciences (Deemed University), Govandi Station Road, Mumbai, Maharashtra 400088, India.

Tel: (91) 55 620 62
Fax: (91) 22 556 3257

International Institute of Tropical Agriculture (IITA)

L W Lambourn & Co Ltd Carolyn House, 26 Dingwall Road, Croydon, Surrey CR9 3EE, United Kingdom.

Email: iita@cgnet.com
Website: www.cgiar.org/iita
Contact: Programme Leader

The International Institute of Tropical Agriculture (IITA) was founded in 1967 as an international agricultural research institute with a mandate for special food crops and with ecological and regional responsibilities to develop sustainable production systems in Africa.

International Institute of Tropical Agriculture Research Fellowships

Purpose: To enable African postgraduate degree candidates to conduct research at the Institute or one of its satellites
Eligibility: Candidates should be residents of Sub Saharan Africa and be registered for a postgraduate degree at a university in Africa or abroad (generally a faculty of agriculture). Preference will be given to candidates of IITA stations - Nigeria, Cameroon, Uganda, Benin and Cote d'Ivoire
Level of Study: Doctorate, Postgraduate
Type: Fellowship
Value: Up to US$12,000 per year, includes board and lodging, various allowances for personal and other expenses, travel to and from the Institute, medical accident insurance, and all research costs. It also includes one round trip ticket for the student's university supervisor to IITA for PhD students
Length of Study: MSc is 1 year, the PhD is 2–3 years
Frequency: Annual
Study Establishment: IITA
Country of Study: Other
Application Procedure: Application form must be completed and submitted with a research proposal of no more

than 10 pages and three letters of recommendation from the candidate's advisor at the university. Applications may be submitted by individuals. However it is preferred that all applications are made through the university. Candidate, advisor and university must accept a scientist from IITA as a supervisor of research while the Fellow is at IITA

No. of awards offered: 150
Closing Date: September
Funding: Government
Contributor: Donor agencies and the government
No. of awards given last year: 30
No. of applicants last year: 150
Additional Information: scholarshipstory.com/iita/

For further information contact:

Head Training & Information Services, Oyo Road, PMB 5320, Ibadan, Nigeria.

Tel: (234) 2 241 2626
Fax: (234) 2 241 2221
Email: iita@cgiar.org

International Mathematical Union (IMU)

International Mathematical Union, Office of the Secretariat, Zuse Institute Berlin, Takustrasse 7, D-14195 Berlin, Germany.

Email: secretary@mathunion.org
Website: www.mathunion.org
Contact: Martin Grötschel, Secretary

The International Mathematical Union (IMU) is an international, non-governmental and non-profit scientific organization, with the purpose of promoting international co-operation in mathematics. It belongs to the International Council of Scientific Unions (ICSU).

International Mathematical Union Visiting Mathematician Programme

Purpose: To provide partial travel support for extended research visits in an advanced mathematical centre
Eligibility: Open to active mathematicians at PhD level with strong research possibilities. The programme is mainly

intended for mathematicians working in a developing country to make an extended research visit to an advanced mathematical centre
Level of Study: Postdoctorate, Professional development
Type: Travel grant
Value: Up to 4,400 EUR (5,000 Dollars)
Length of Study: 1 month
Frequency: Annual, if funds are available
Study Establishment: An advanced mathematical research centre
Country of Study: Any country
Application Procedure: 1. hold at the time of application a PhD in Mathematics, 2. be based in a developing country at the time of application 3. hold a position in a university/ research institution 4. be in the early stages of their professional careers, more precisely the applicants should 4. 1) not yet be of full professorial rank but have a working contract in a university/ college 4. 2) be under 40 years of age at the day of the application deadline.
No. of awards offered: 30
Closing Date: 31 January
Additional Information: The host centre must commit itself to supporting local expenses www.mathunion.org/cdc/ grantsresearch-travel-grants/abel-visiting-scholar-program

For further information contact:

Mathematics Department Zuse Institute Berlin, D-14195 Berlin, Germany.

Tel: (49) 801 581 5275
Fax: (49) 801 581 4148
Email: clemens@math.utah.edu

International School of Crystallography, E Majorana Centre

Dip to Scienze Della Terra Geo Ambientoli, Piazza di Porta San Donato 1, I-40126 Bologna, Italy.

Tel: (39) 51 209 4912
Email: riva@geomin.unibo.it
Website: www.geomin.unibo.it
Contact: Professor L Riva Di Sanseverino

The International School of Crystallography is an international organizing committee that offers, once a year, short advanced courses of 9–11 days on frontier topics in crystallography, solid state chemistry, materials science, structure activity relationship, molecular biology and biophysics.

International School of Crystallography Grants

Purpose: To enable postgraduates to attend short high-level courses held at Erice once a year

Eligibility: Open to all who have scientific interests related to the topic chosen each year at a PhD or postdoctoral level. English language proficiency is mandatory

Level of Study: Doctorate, Postdoctorate, Postgraduate

Type: Grant

Value: Fees, board and lodging during the course

Length of Study: 8–12 days

Frequency: Annual

Study Establishment: E Majorana Centre, Erice, Sicily, Italy

Country of Study: Italy

Application Procedure: Young applicants must submit a letter of recommendation stating their financial needs, personal data and details of scientific interests. Further details can be found at www.crystalerice.org

No. of awards offered: 250

Closing Date: 31 May

Funding: Government

Contributor: NATO, the European Commission and the Italian National Research Council

For further information contact:

Department of Organic Chemistry, Via Francesco Marzolo, I-135122 PD Padova, Italy.

Tel:	(39) 49 827 5275
Fax:	(39) 49 827 5239
Email:	paola.spadon@unipd.it

International Society of Nephrology (ISN)

Avenue de Tervueren, 300, B-1150 Brussels, Belgium.

Tel:	(32) 2 743 1546
Email:	info@isn-online.org
Website:	www.nature.com/isn/about/index.html
Contact:	Professor John Feehally ISN Secretary General

The International Society of Nephrology (ISN) pursues the goal of worldwide advancement of education, science and patient care in nephrology. ISN achieves this through its journal Kidney International, organizing international congresses, symposia, specific programmes and fellowships. As a result, ISN helps to improve renal science and renal patient care worldwide, especially in emerging countries.

International Society of Nephrology Fellowship Awards

Purpose: To offer training opportunities to young nephrologists in emerging countries with the ultimate goal of improving the standards of nephrology practice in their home institutions upon their return

Eligibility: Open to young nephrologists from emerging countries, as defined by World Bank criteria. Applicants must have received sufficient training in internal medicine or other fields to pass all host country examinations that are necessary for the care of patients. Fellowships are primarily offered for clinical training in nephrology, but in some circumstances research training may be allowed, priority can be considered for training in epidemiology

Level of Study: Postdoctorate, Predoctorate

Type: Fellowship

Value: The stipends are subject to indexation based on-the-cost-of-living in their host country; the top and bottom level grants are respectively US$26,000 and US$20,000 for 12 months of training. If the host country is contributing funds then this is subtracted from the standard fund

Length of Study: Short-term fellowships are for 3–6 months and long-term fellowships are for 12 months. Extensions are possible

Frequency: Annual

Study Establishment: Any suitable university, scientific institution or hospital

Application Procedure: Applicants must complete an application form, which is subjected to the review of an international committee. Applicants must provide evidence of a guaranteed position in a medical institution upon return to their home country. The applicant must agree to return to their home country upon completion of the training; if not, the recipient will have to refund the ISN fellowship in full

Closing Date: Novermber

Funding: Foundation, Private

Contributor: Offered in collaboration with sister societies and industry, the American Society of Nephrology, the National Kidney Research Fund in the United Kingdom, Fresenius Medical care in Germany and the European renal Association

No. of awards given last year: 44

Additional Information: The selection procedure has three parts: data verification, where information provided by applicants is verified and evaluated through correspondence;

evaluation, where 7 members of the Committee, one from each Continent, score each application according to standard format; and finally, selection, which is largely based on the aforementioned scores but also considers the geographical balance, urgent needs in certain regions and the preference of certain sponsors www.mathunion.org/cdc/grantsresearch-travel-grants/abel-visiting-scholar-program

For further information contact:

ISN Global Headquarters Av., Tervueren 300, B-1150 Brussels, Belgium.

Email: an@associationhg.com

International Society of Nephrology Travel Grants

Purpose: To encourage young physicians and scientists to attend conferences, especially those from emerging countries. Travel grants are offered to facilitate attendance at the ISN International Congress and the ISN Forefronts Commission Conference

Eligibility: 1. ISN Travel Grants are reserved for ISN members in good standing. 2. ISN Travel Grants are reserved for the benefit of physicians and scientists from developing countries. 3. In some cases, only abstract presenters at the event are eligible for a Travel Grant (an accepted abstract is not a guarantee to obtain a grant). 4. Past ISN Fellows and selected participants in the Sister Renal Centers Program receive priority consideration for a Travel Grant to ensure their continued education.

Level of Study: Doctorate, Postdoctorate, Postgraduate, Research

Type: Travel grant

Value: The size of the grant is decided according to each conference and congress

Length of Study: Varies

Country of Study: Any country

Funding: Foundation, Private

Contributor: Offered in collaboration with sponsors of ISN

No. of awards given last year: 120

No. of applicants last year: 395

For further information contact:

Email: registrationswcn@theisn.org

International Society of Nephrology Visiting Scholars Program

Purpose: To improve the long-term quality of patient care, education and research in fields relevant to the kidney at the host institution, and enable senior physicians or scientists who are experts in nephrology and related disciplines to spend between 6 weeks and 3 months at an institution in the developing world

Eligibility: Applicants must focus primarily on hands-on activities that are the focus of this award, e.g. the establishment of a new clinical programme, research programme or laboratory technique. ISN visiting scholars should spend the duration of their study time at an institution in the developing world. Applicants must be experts in nephrology and related disciplines

Level of Study: Postdoctorate, Research

Type: Scholarship

Value: US$20,000, inclusive of travel and expenses, for 3 months or a pro rata amount for a shorter period of time

Length of Study: 6 weeks–3 months

Country of Study: Any country

Application Procedure: Applicants must send a description of the programme, its objectives, personal references and a letter of acceptance from the host institution to the ISN Secretary General. Applicants must be members of the ISN

No. of awards offered: 2

Closing Date: 1 May

Funding: Foundation, Private

No. of awards given last year: 2

No. of applicants last year: 2

For further information contact:

Cairo Kidney Centre, 3 Hussein El-Memar Street, Antikhana, PO Box 91, Bab El-Louk, Egypt.

Tel: (20) 2 579 0267
Email: isn@rusys.eg.net

International Union for Vacuum Science and Technology (IUVSTA)

84 Oldfield Drive, Vicars Cross, Chester CH3 5LW, United Kingdom.

Tel: (44) 1244 34 2675, 771 34 03525
Email: eisenmenger@ifp.tuwien.ac.at
Website: www.iuvsta.org
Contact: Dr Christoph Eisenmenger-Sittner, Secretary General

The International Union for Vacuum Science and Technology (IUVSTA) is a non-government organization whose member societies represent all vacuum scientists, engineers and technologists in their country.

Welch Scholarship

Purpose: To encourage promising scholars who wish to study vacuum science, techniques or their application in any field

Eligibility: Open to applicants of any nationality who hold the minimum of a Bachelor's degree, although preference is given to those holding a doctoral degree

Level of Study: Doctorate, Postdoctorate, Postgraduate

Type: Scholarship

Value: US$15,000. The scholarship money is paid in three installments – one of US$7,500 at the beginning, another of US$7,000, 6 months after he/she has started work, and a third of US$500 upon delivery of a final report after completion of work

Length of Study: 1 year

Frequency: Annual

Study Establishment: An appropriate laboratory

Country of Study: Any country

Application Procedure: Applicants must complete and submit an application form with a research proposal, a curriculum vitae and two letters of reference. More information and application forms can be obtained from the website

No. of awards offered: 6

Closing Date: 15 June

Funding: Private

Contributor: IUVSTA

For further information contact:

Canadian Photorics Fabrication Centre, Institute for Microstructural Sciences, National Research Council, 1200 Montreal Rd, Building M-50, Ottawa, ON K1A 0R6, Canada.

Email: welchaward@iuvsta.org

International Union of Biochemistry and Molecular Biology (IUBMB)

University of Calgary, Department of Biochemistry & Molecular Biology, 3330 Hospital Drive NW, HM G72B, Calgary, AB T2N 4N1, Canada.

Tel: (1) 403 220 3021
Email: walsh@ucalgary.ca
Website: www.iubmb.org
Contact: Professor Michael P Walsh, IUBMB General Secretary

IUBMB seeks to advance the international molecular life sciences community by: Promoting interactions across the diversity of endeavours in the molecular life sciences, creating networks that transcend barriers of ethnicity, culture, gender, and economic status, creating pathways for young scientists to fulfil their potential, providing evidence-based advice on public policy, promoting the values, standards, and ethics of science and the free and unhampered movement of scientists of all nations.

IUBMB Mid-Career Research Fellowships

Purpose: The Mid-Career Research Fellowships are designed to support junior biochemists and molecular biologists, from countries that are full or associate members of IUBMB who need to travel to other laboratories in the IUBMB region for the purpose of learning new state-of-the-art techniques or for other forms of scientific collaboration or advanced training.

Eligibility: The Fellowship will cover the cheapest airfare available and reasonable accommodation costs. The Fellowship will not cover insurance or research expenses at the host laboratory. Applicants are required to make a full declaration to IUBMB of all other support received in connection with the proposed visit. A Fellowship cannot be used to supplement scientific visits otherwise already fully covered from other sources. Fellowships will not be awarded to attend courses, symposia, meetings or congresses. Applicants must be residents of countries that are members of the IUBMB. Applicants should hold a faculty position and be actively involved in the training of PhD students. Retrospective applications to fund an already completed visit will not be considered. Travel should commence within three months of the award being made.

Level of Study: Research

Type: Fellowship

Value: US$5,000

Length of Study: 1–2 Months

Country of Study: Any country

Closing Date: 1 April

Additional Information: iubmb.org/about/standing-orders-and-statutes/standing-orders/iubmb-mid-career-research-fellowships/

IUBMB Tang Education Fellowships

Purpose: The IUBMB Tang Education Fellowships will provide opportunities for the development of both biochemistry and molecular biology educational programs and educators

Eligibility: increasing expertise and capability in biochemistry and molecular biology education supporting engaged educators promoting change/innovation in approaches to education improving student learning experiences, outcomes, and engagement with biochemistry and molecular biology building an evidence base on which to make future recommendations on biochemistry and molecular biology education supporting biochemistry and molecular biology education in developing countries.

Type: Fellowship
Value: US$4,000.
Length of Study: 2 Months
Country of Study: Any country
Closing Date: 1 April
Additional Information: iubmb.org/about/standing-orders-and-statutes/standing-orders/tang-education-fellowships/

IUBMB Travel Fellowships

Purpose: The IUBMB Travel Fellowships are designed to support biochemistry and molecular biology trainees (graduate students and postdoctoral fellows), from countries that are full or associate members of IUBMB to travel to and attend meetings in the IUBMB region. Applicants are required to present a poster or oral presentation in order to be considered for a fellowship award.
Level of Study: Postgraduate
Type: Fellowships
Frequency: Annual
Country of Study: Any country
Application Procedure: Applications will be sent and reviewed by Dr. Ilona Concha Grabinger
Closing Date: 1 April
Additional Information: Late applications will not be con sidered.iubmb.org/about/standing-orders-and-statutes/standing-orders/iubmb-travel-fellowships/

PROLAB Fellowships

Purpose: The long-term objective of this program is to foster cooperation between the Pan-American Association for Biochemistry and Molecular Biology (PABMB), the International Union of Biochemistry and Molecular Biology (IUBMB) and the American Society for Biochemistry and Molecular Biology (ASBMB) that would benefit their members, trainees and science.
Eligibility: A research proposal of no more than two pages, single-spaced, indicating clearly: the nature of the project and the type of experiments to be carried out the reason it is necessary to travel to a particular laboratory to conduct the experiments rather than to perform them in the applicant's own laboratory the rationale for the required time period requested A budget should be provided, indicating all other sources of support, whether awarded or applied for A short curriculum vitae of the applicant, including academic record

(for graduate students) and a list of publications. A letter of agreement from the Head of the hosting laboratory, stating that the institute will receive the applicant. A list of papers published by the hosting faculty member during the past five years and current grant support for the laboratory should be provided. This letter should also indicate whether the receiving institute will contribute toward the costs of the visit.
Type: Fellowship
Value: US$5,000
Length of Study: 1–6 months
Country of Study: Any country
Closing Date: 25 February
Additional Information: iubmb.org/activities/fellowship-programs/prolab-fellowships/

Wood-Whelan Research Fellowships

Purpose: To provide financial assistance to young biochemists and molecular biologists to carry out research and training in a laboratory other than their own
Eligibility: Open to applicants who are residents of countries that are members of IUBMB and students or young researchers less than 35 years old. Retroactive applications will not be considered
Level of Study: Graduate, Postdoctorate, Postgraduate, Research
Type: Fellowship
Value: Up to US$4,000. It covers travel and incidental costs, as well as living expenses
Length of Study: 1–4 months
Frequency: Annual
Country of Study: Any country
Application Procedure: Applicants must submit a completed application form along with details of the research proposal, budget, curriculum vitae with a list of publications and letters of recommendation following the guidelines which can be found at website. The original application should be sent by the applicant by email as PDF files
No. of awards offered: 32
Closing Date: 1 April
Contributor: The main sources of income for IUBMB are dues from adhering bodies (member societies) and revenue from publications
No. of awards given last year: 15
No. of applicants last year: 32
Additional Information: Travel should commence within 4 months of the award being made iubmb.org/guidelines-statutes/guidelines/wood-whelan-research-fellowships/

For further information contact:

Email: janet.macaulay@monash.edu

Iota Sigma Pi

Microelectronics Technology, Lord Corporation, 110 Lord Drive, Cary, NC 27511, United States of America.

Tel: (1) 919 468 5979
Email: sara.paisner@lord.com
Website: www.iotasigmapi.info
Contact: Sara Paisner, Senior Scientist

Iota Sigma Pi, founded in 1902, is a National Honor Society that serves to promote the advancement of women in chemistry by granting recognition to women who have demonstrated superior scholastic achievement and high professional competence by election into Iota Sigma Pi.

Agnes Fay Morgan Research Award

Purpose: To acknowledge research achievements in chemistry or biochemistry
Eligibility: Open to female applicants who are not more than 40 years of age
Level of Study: Postgraduate
Type: Award
Value: US$1,500
Frequency: Annual
Study Establishment: Any accredited institution
Country of Study: Any country
Application Procedure: The nomination dossier must be sent electronically (preferably as a pdf) to Dr Nancy Eddy Hopkins
Closing Date: 15 February
Contributor: Iota Sigma Pi
Additional Information: Please see the website for further details www.iotasigmapi.info/awards/professionalawards.html

For further information contact:

Tel: (1) 504 862 3162
Email: nhopkin@tulane.edu

Anna Louise Hoffman Award for Outstanding Achievement in Graduate Research

Purpose: To recognize outstanding achievement in chemical research
Eligibility: The candidate must be a full-time (as defined by the nominee's institution) woman graduate student who is a candidate for a graduate degree in an accredited institution. The research presented by the candidate must be original research which can be described by one of the main chemical divisions (e.g., analytical, biochemical, inorganic, organic, physical, and/or ancillary divisions of chemistry). The nominee may be, but need not be, a member of Iota Sigma Pi
Level of Study: Postgraduate
Type: Award
Value: US$500
Frequency: Annual
Study Establishment: Any accredited institution
Country of Study: Any country
Application Procedure: The complete dossier must be sent electronically as a single file (pdf format is recommended) to Professor Jill Nelson Granger
No. of awards offered: 1
Closing Date: 15 February
Contributor: Iota Sigma Pi
Additional Information: Please see the website for further details www.iotasigmapi.info/awards/studentawards.html#alh

For further information contact:

Department of Chemistry Sweet Briar College, Sweet Briar College, Department of Chemistry, Sweet Briar, VA 24595, United States of America.

Tel: (1) 434 381 6166
Email: granger@sbc.edu

Gladys Anderson Emerson Scholarship

Purpose: To award excellence in chemistry or biochemistry
Eligibility: Applicants must have attained junior status at an accredited college or university, be female and be nominated by a member of Iota Sigma Pi
Level of Study: Postgraduate
Type: Scholarship
Value: US$2,000 and a certificate
Frequency: Annual
Study Establishment: Any accredited institution
Country of Study: Any country
Application Procedure: The complete dossier must be sent electronically as a single file (pdf format is recommended) to Professor Jill Nelson Granger
No. of awards offered: 2
Closing Date: 15 February
Contributor: Iota Sigma Pi
Additional Information: Please see the website for further details www.iotasigmapi.info/awards/studentawards.html#gae

For further information contact:

University of North Dakota, Department of Chemistry, P.O. Box 9024, Grand Forks, ND 58202-9024, United States of America.

Iota Sigma Pi Centennial Award

Purpose: To award excellence in teaching chemistry, biochemistry or chemistry-related subjects

Eligibility: Holds a teaching position at an institution that does not have a graduate program in her department or holds a teaching position that is for teaching undergraduates >75% of her time at an institution that does have a graduate program in her department. The nominee may be, but need not be, a member of Iota Sigma Pi

Level of Study: Postgraduate

Type: Award

Value: US$500, a certificate and membership in Iota Sigma Pi with a waiver of dues for 1 year

Frequency: Annual

Application Procedure: One copy of the nomination dossier must be sent electronically (preferably as a pdf) to Dr Nancy Eddy Hopkins

Closing Date: 15 February

Contributor: Iota Sigma Pi

Additional Information: Please see the website for details www.iotasigmapi.info/awards/studentawards.html#gae

For further information contact:

Tel: (1) 504 862 3162
Email: nhopkin@tulane.edu

Iota Sigma Pi National Honorary Member Award

Purpose: To honour outstanding women chemists

Eligibility: Open to female candidate with exceptional achievements in chemistry. Applicants may or may not be members of Iota Sigma Pi

Type: Award

Value: US$1,500 a certificate and membership in Iota Sigma Pi with a lifetime waiver of dues

Length of Study: Every 3 years

Frequency: Every 3 years

Application Procedure: One copy of the nomination dossier must be sent electronically (preferably as a pdf) to Nancy Eddy Hopkins

Closing Date: 15 February

Additional Information: Please see the website for details www.iotasigmapi.info/awards/studentawards.html#gae

For further information contact:

Email: nhopkin@tulane.edu

National Honorary Member

Purpose: This is the highest honor that Iota Sigma Pi bestows on outstanding women chemists. This is a triennial award.

Type: Award

Value: $2000

Country of Study: Any country

Closing Date: 1 May

Additional Information: www.iotasigmapi.org/professional-awards

Violet Diller Professional Excellence Award

Purpose: To recognize significant accomplishments in academic, governmental or industrial chemistry

Eligibility: Open to female applicants who have contributed to the scientific community or society on a national level

Level of Study: Postgraduate

Type: Award

Value: US$1,000, a certificate and membership in Iota sigma Pi with a lifetime waiver of dues

Frequency: Every 3 years

Application Procedure: One copy of the nomination dossier must be sent electronically (preferably as a pdf) to Nancy Eddy Hopkins

Closing Date: 15 February

Contributor: Iota Sigma Pi

Additional Information: Please see the website for further details   www.iotasigmapi.info/awards/professionalawards. html

For further information contact:

Email: nhopkin@tulane.edu

Violet Diller Professional Excellence Award

Purpose: The award is for outstanding contribution to chemistry and allied fields by a woman. This is a triennial awardEach active chapter shall be entitled to make one nomination, but individual members or chemists or groups of chemists may make independent nominations, if properly documented.

Eligibility: Each active chapter shall be entitled to make one nomination, but individual members or chemists or groups of chemists may make independent nominations, if properly documented.

Type: Award
Value: $1500
Country of Study: Any country
Closing Date: 1 May
Additional Information: www.iotasigmapi.org/professional-awards

Iowa State University

Iowa State University, Ames, IA 50011, United States of America.

Tel: (1) 515 2944111
Email: online@iastate.edu
Website: www.iastate.edu
Contact: Dr James R Bloedell, Dean

Iowa State University of Science and Technology is a public band-grant institution serving the people of Iowa, the nation and the world.

American Institute of Certified Public Accountants/Robert Half Student Scholarship Award

Purpose: AICPA and Robert Half offer the AICPA/Robert Half Student Scholarship Award to provide financial assistance to outstanding accounting students who demonstrate potential to become leaders in the CPA profession
Eligibility: Not eligible to students who have already gained their CPA
Level of Study: Postgraduate
Type: Scholarship
Value: US$3,000–US$10,000
Length of Study: 1 year
Frequency: Annual
Study Establishment: Iowa State University
Country of Study: United States of America
Application Procedure: When available, publication and application details for this award can be found at ThisWayToCPA.com
No. of awards offered: 25
Closing Date: 1 March
Funding: Private
Contributor: AICPA
Additional Information: www.aicpa.org/interestareas/accountingeducation/resources/aicpaaccountemps.html

For further information contact:

AICPA/Accountemps Student Scholarship Program, AICPA-Team 331, 1211 Avenue of the Americas, New York, NY 10036-8775, United States of America.

Email: scholarships@aicpa.org

Iowa State University of Science and Technology

Institute of Social and Behavior Research, 2625 N Loop Drive Suite 500, Ames, IA 50010, United States of America.

Email: rconger@iastate.edu
Website: www.iastate.edu
Contact: Mr Rand D Conger

Acute Generalized Exanthematous Pustulosis Fellowship

Purpose: The primary goals of the ISU AGEP program are to (a) increase the number of underrepresented students obtaining graduate degrees in science, technology, engineering and mathematics (STEM)
Eligibility: You must meet the following requirements 1. Member of an underrepresented ethnic group (African American, American Indian, Hispanic, Alaska Natives, and Native Hawaiian or Pacific Islander). 2. Admitted into a STEM (science, technology, engineering, mathematics) field. 3. United States citizenship (permanent residents are ineligible). 4. Enrolled as a first semester PhD student with a fall entry date
Level of Study: Graduate
Type: Fellowship
Value: The annual stipend is US$27,500
Frequency: Annual
Country of Study: Any country
Application Procedure: 1. The fellowship is for five (5) years from the term of entry. 2. Changing to another program of study may terminate the fellowship
Funding: Private

For further information contact:

1137 Pearson Hall 505 Morrill Rd, Ames, IA 50011, United States of America.

Email: grad_college@iastate.edu

Irish Research Council

First Floor, Brooklawn House, Crampton Avenue (off Shelbourne Road), Ballsbridge, Dublin 4, Ireland.

Tel: (353) 1 231 5000
Email: info@research.ie
Website: www.research.ie

The Irish Research Council was formally launched by the Minister for Research and Innovation, Seán Sherlock TD, on 29 March. A sub-board of the Higher Education Authority, the Council was established through a merger of the Irish Research Council for Humanities and Social Sciences (IRCHSS) and the Irish Research Council for Science, Engineering and Technology (IRCSET).

Employment-Based Postgraduate Programme

Subjects: All disciplines
Purpose: Employment-based co-funded scholarships
Level of Study: Doctorate, Postgraduate
Type: Scholarship
Value: €24,000–€96,000
Length of Study: One to four years
Frequency: Annual
Country of Study: Republic of Ireland
Application Procedure: Online system
Closing Date: 20 February
Contributor: Employment Partner
Additional Information: www.research.ie

Enterprise Partnership Scheme

Subjects: All disciplines
Purpose: Enterprise co-funded scholarships & fellowships
Level of Study: Doctorate, Postdoctorate, Postgraduate
Type: Fellowship/Scholarship
Value: €24,000–€96,000
Length of Study: One to four years
Frequency: Annual
Country of Study: Republic of Ireland
Application Procedure: Online system
Closing Date: 17 September
Contributor: Enterprise Partner
Additional Information: www.research.ie

For further information contact:

Tel: (353) 1 231 5009
Fax: (353) 1 231 5009

Government of Ireland Postgraduate Scholarship Programme

Subjects: AHSS, STEM
Purpose: The programme provides outstanding students with the opportunity to direct their own research at the early-career stage, working with a supervisor, in their chosen area of interest.
Eligibility: Must have a first class or upper second-class honours bachelor's, or the equivalent, degree - Must be eligible to register for a Research Masters or PhD in a Higher Education Institution in Ireland. While the majority of scholarships will be awarded to applicants from the EFTA/EEA* member states a proportion of scholarships will also be made to exceptional applicants from non-EFTA/EEA countries. For more information see Terms and Conditions Document for eligibility criteria available on research.ie/funding/. *The European Free Trade Area (EFTA) and the European Economic Area (EEA)
Level of Study: Doctorate, Postgraduate
Type: Scholarship
Value: €24,000 per annum
Length of Study: One to four years
Frequency: Annual
Country of Study: Ireland
Application Procedure: Online application system
No. of awards offered: 200
Funding: Government
Additional Information: research.ie/funding/goipg/

Ulysses

Purpose: The aim of the Ulysses scheme is to foster new collaborations between Ireland and France-based researchers by providing seed funding for reciprocal travel visits over the course of 16 months.
Type: Award
Value: €2,500
Length of Study: 16 Months
Country of Study: Any country
Closing Date: 27 January
Contributor: EirGrid, Réseau de Transport d'Électricité, Health Research Board, Sustainable Energy Authority of Ireland, ADEME
Additional Information: research.ie/funding/ulysses/?f=postgraduate

For further information contact:

3 Shelbourne Buildings, Crampton Avenue, Ballsbridge, D04 C2Y6, Ireland.

Tel: (353) 1 231 5000
Fax: (353) 1 231 5009
Email: info@research.ie

Islamic Cooperation Organization (OIC)

Islamic Cooperation Organization International Internship Program

Purpose: OIC Intern gives the opportunity for professional experience to young people through work ethic and teamwork experience
Eligibility: The international students who pursue their study in Turkey, and meet the following criteria will be eligible for OIC Intern International Internship Program 1. International bachelor students who are at 3rd or 4th grade 2. Pursuing post graduate degree 3. Knowledge of Turkish or English at least at the level of B1 4. Additionally, Knowledge of Arabic or French at least at the level of B1 5. Willing to improve themselves and are open to career opportunities 6. Under 30 years old
Level of Study: Postgraduate
Type: Programme grant
Frequency: Annual
Country of Study: Any country
Closing Date: 24 March
Funding: Private
Additional Information: oyaop.com/opportunity/intern ships/islamic-cooperation-organization-oic-internship-program/

For further information contact:

P.O.Box 178, Jeddah, 21411, Saudi Arabia.

Tel: (966) 12 6515222
Email: info@opportunitiesforafricans.com

IT University of Copenhagen

Rued Langgaards Vej 7, DK-2300 Copenhagen S, Denmark.

Tel: (45) 7218 5000
Email: itu@itu.dk
Website: en.itu.dk/

The IT University of Copenhagen (ITU) was established in 1999 and is Denmark's leading university focusing on IT research and education. We deliver state-of-the-art teaching and research within computer science, business IT and digital design. Our ambition is to create and share knowledge that is profound and leads to ground-breaking information technology and services for the benefit of humanity. The university collaborates closely with industry, the public sector and international researchers and is characterized by a strong entrepreneurial spirit among students as well as researchers. ITU's modern campus in central Copenhagen is designed by the world-renowned Danish architect Henning Larsen.

IT University of Copenhagen State Scholarships

Purpose: The IT University of Copenhagen offers state scholarships to three or four exceptionally talented MSc applicants (full-degree students) from outside EU and EEA every year.
Eligibility: To be eligible for the scholarship, you must be admitted to a MSc Programme at IT University of Copenhagen. The scholarships will be offered to the applicants who achieve the best scores according to the criteria in the admission rules.
Level of Study: Masters Degree
Type: Scholarships
Value: Free tuition and partly covering of living expenses.
Frequency: Annual
Country of Study: Denmark
Application Procedure: Applicants cannot apply for the scholarships. The IT University considers all admitted MSc students for the scholarships and informs the students chosen for the scholarships in their letter of admission. Therefore, you must apply for admissions to be considered for the scholarship. Deadline for admissions is 1 April for September entry and 1 October for February entry. It is important to visit the official website (link found below) for detailed information on how to apply for this scholarshipOfficial Scholarship Website en.itu.dk/Programmes/MSc-Programmes/Applying-to-a-MSc-Programme
No. of awards offered: 3–4
Closing Date: 1 March
Contributor: IT University of Copenhagen in Denmark
Additional Information: www.scholars4dev.com/10752/it-university-of-copenhagen-state-scholarships/#:~:text=The% 20IT%20University%20of%20Copenhagen,EU%20and% 20EEA%20every%20year.&text=Scholarship%20value% 2Finclusions%3A,partly%20covering%20of%20living%20 expenses.

J

James Cook University

1 James Cook Dr, Douglas, QLD 4811, Australia.

Tel: (61) 7 4781 5255
Email: enquiries@jcu.edu.au
Website: www.jcu.edu.au/

JCU is a world-class university ranked in the top two per cent of tertiary institutions in the world. JCU develops graduates who have the knowledge, skills and experience to succeed and thrive in a global workforce.

Arrow Energy-JCU Go Further Indigenous Tertiary Scholarships

Eligibility: 1. Identify as Aboriginal and/or Torres Strait Islander; 2. Are Australian citizens or Australian permanent residents; 3. Are enrolled at James Cook University; 4. Are studying a bachelor of coursework masters in Engineering, Geology, Ecology, IT/Data, Business or Communications; 5. Are on track to complete their degree in 2024.
Level of Study: Postgraduate
Type: Scholarship
Value: AU$10,000 for full time students AU$5,000 for part time students
Frequency: Annual
Country of Study: Australia
Closing Date: 28 February
Additional Information: www.jcu.edu.au/scholarships/search/arrow-energy-jcu-go-further-indigenous-tertiary-scholarships

AIMS@JCU Scholarship

Purpose: The scholarships are provided to assist with the general living costs of the candidate.

Eligibility: Both domestic and international applicants
Level of Study: Postgraduate, Research
Type: Scholarship
Value: US$28,854 pa in 2022 (living allowance paid fortnightly) + US$5,000 pa as living allowance or project expenses
Length of Study: 3.5 years
Frequency: Annual
Country of Study: Any country
Application Procedure: www.jcu.edu.au/__data/assets/pdf_file/0007/273670/2020-Scholarship-Scoring-Procedure-310519.pdf
Closing Date: 30 September
Additional Information: aims.jcu.edu.au/phd-scholarships/

For further information contact:

Email: grsapplications@jcu.edu.au

AMA Queensland Foundation Medical Scholarships

Eligibility: 1. Be an Australian citizen, New Zealand citizen or Australian permanent visa holder; 2. Have commenced the MBBS program at a Queensland university; 3. Have a GPA of 4.0 or above; 4. Demonstrate financial disadvantage (refer to application form found at www.amaqfoundation.com.au/page/AMA_Queensland_Foundation_Medical_Scholarships); 5. Demonstrate evidence of personal effort to address his/her financial need i.e has the applicant applied for Centrelink assistance via start-up or relocation grant? Has the applicant considered other scholarship options? Does the applicant's family have the financial capacity to offer support? 6. Be enrolled as a full-time student. In exceptional circumstances, a scholarship may be provided to a part-time student (e.g. taking into account requirements to undertake employment to maintain financial solvency, the impact of disability and/or significant care responsibilities, etc.)

© Springer Nature Limited 2022
Palgrave Macmillan (ed.), *The Grants Register 2023*,
https://doi.org/10.1057/978-1-349-96053-8

7. Provide a suitable referee who may support the request for financial assistance.

Level of Study: Doctorate
Type: Scholarship
Value: AU$10,000 paid in two equal instalments
Frequency: Annual
Country of Study: Australia
No. of awards offered: 2
Closing Date: 28 February
Additional Information: www.jcu.edu.au/scholarships/browse-scholarships/non-jcu-scholarships

For further information contact:

Email: amaqfoundation@amaq.com.au

Australian Banana Growers' Council Mort Johnston Scholarship

Eligibility: The Australian Banana Growers' Council Mort Johnston Scholarship is open for you to apply if you: 1. Are enrolled in an undergraduate or postgraduate degree with links to the banana industry. This could include, but is not limited to: science, technology, engineering, environmental studies, conservation, agriculture, marketing, law, economics or business; 2. Are in your final year of your undergraduate degree, are undertaking an honours year or are a Masters or PhD student.

Level of Study: Postgraduate
Type: Scholarship
Value: AU$5,000 for full time students, AU$2,500 for part time students. Plus at least 2 weeks paid work experience.
Length of Study: 1 year
Frequency: Annual
Country of Study: Australia
Closing Date: 30 April
Additional Information: www.jcu.edu.au/scholarships/search/australian-banana-growers-council-mort-johnston-scholarship

Australian Orthopaedic Association Joint University Scholarship

Eligibility: If all the below statements describe you and your current situation, you can apply for this scholarship: 1. I am an Australian citizen, New Zealand citizen or Australian permanent visa holder; 2. I am currently enrolled in Bachelor of Medicine, Bachelor of Surgery year 5 and will be enrolled in year 6 in 2023; 3. I have been approved to undertake an Elective Term in the medical program in which I am enrolled;

and 4. I have maintained a course GPA of 5.0 or above at the time of application.

Level of Study: Masters Degree
Type: Scholarship
Value: AU$4,000
Length of Study: 1 year
Frequency: Annual
Country of Study: Australia
Closing Date: 31 March
Additional Information: www.jcu.edu.au/scholarships/search/australian-orthopaedic-association-joint-university-scholarship

Burralga Yumba Bursary

Eligibility: 1. are enrolled full time (minimum of 9 credit points); and 2. are enrolled at the Townsville, Bebegu Yumba Campus, Douglas 3. have a home address which is greater than 40km from the JCU Townsville, Bebegu Yumba Campus, Douglas 4. have applied to live at the JCU Halls of Residence for the full academic year

Type: Bursary
Value: AU$1,000
Frequency: Annual
Country of Study: Australia
Closing Date: 22 February
Additional Information: www.jcu.edu.au/scholarships/search/burralga-yumba-bursary

Elizabeth Pearse Music Scholarship

Level of Study: Doctorate, Postgraduate
Value: AU$8,000
Length of Study: 1 year
Frequency: Annual
Country of Study: Australia
Application Procedure: The Elizabeth Pearse Music Scholarship will be open to competition among applicants who: 1. Are domestic students, i.e. Australian citizens, New Zealand citizens and holders of a permanent visa; and 2. Are or intend to enrol full time in PhD, or Master of Philosophy with Music as their specialist area of study
No. of awards offered: 1
Closing Date: 31 January
Additional Information: www.jcu.edu.au/scholarships/search/elizabeth-pearse-music-scholarship

For further information contact:

Email: scholarships@jcu.edu.au

ER Walker Bequest Bursary

Eligibility: The ER Walker Bequest Scholarship shall be open to competition among applicants who: 1. are admitted to an honours or postgraduate degree at James Cook University; and 2. are undertaking research on stinging jellyfishes (Class Cubozoa).
Level of Study: Postgraduate, Research
Type: Bursary
Value: AU$2,500
Length of Study: 1 year
Frequency: Annual
Country of Study: Australia
No. of awards offered: 2
Closing Date: 15 August
Additional Information: www.jcu.edu.au/scholarships/search/er-walker-bequest-bursary

Indigenous Education Costs Scholarship

Purpose: The Indigenous Education Costs Scholarship has been established to support Academic achievement of Indigenous students at James Cook University.
Eligibility: The Indigenous Education Costs Scholarship is open for you to apply if you:1. Identify as Aboriginal or Torres Strait Islander in descent; and 2. Are a enrolled or intend to enrol full-time; and 3. Have a minimum GPA of 4.0 if not a commencing student.
Level of Study: Postgraduate
Type: Scholarship
Value: AU$5,000
Length of Study: 4 years
Frequency: Annual
Country of Study: Australia
No. of awards offered: 4
Closing Date: 4 March
Additional Information: www.jcu.edu.au/scholarships/search/indigenous-education-costs-scholarship

Indigenous Research Training Program Scholarship (RTPSI)

Purpose: The scholarships are provided to assist with the general living costs of the candidate.
Eligibility: Applicants who identify as Australian Indigenous and/or Torres Strait Islander
Level of Study: Postgraduate, Research
Type: Scholarship
Value: AU$45,076 pa in 2022 (living allowance paid fortnightly) + AU$10,000 one off for project expenses.

Length of Study: 3.5 years
Frequency: Annual
Country of Study: Any country
Application Procedure: https://www.jcu.edu.au/graduate-research-school/hdr-candidates/postgraduate-research-scholarships
Closing Date: 30 September

For further information contact:

Email: grsapplications@jcu.edu.au

Indigenous Student On-Campus Accommodation Scholarship

Eligibility: The Indigenous Student On-Campus Accommodation Scholarships are open for you to apply if you: 1. Identify as an Australian Aboriginal or Torres Strait Islander; and 2. Are enrolled, or will be enrolled by semester one, as a full time student at the Townsville, Bebegu Yumba Campus, Douglas; and 3. Have applied, or intend to apply, to live on-campus, in university-owned accommodation, for the full academic year. E.g. Burralga Yumba, George Roberts Hall and Rotary International House.
Type: Scholarship
Value: Up to AU$15,000 per year
Length of Study: Minimum duration of degree
Frequency: Annual
Country of Study: Australia
Additional Information: www.jcu.edu.au/scholarships/search/burralga-yumba-indigenous-student-accommodation-scholarship

International Excellence Scholarship

Eligibility: Scholarship eligibility is automatically assessed during the JCU admissions process. There is not application required for this scholarship. Eligible candidates will receive an offer for their program of study and the International Excellence Scholarship concurrently.
Level of Study: Postgraduate
Type: Scholarship
Value: 25% off tuition fee
Frequency: Annual
Country of Study: Australia
Additional Information: www.jcu.edu.au/scholarships/search/international-excellence-scholarship

International Master of Engineering (Professional) Scholarship

Eligibility: The International Master of Engineering (Professional) Scholarship is for eligible students enrolling in the Master of Engineering (Professional) program. Australia Awards students and SACM students and all other government scholarships/sponsorships covering full tuition fees, international students transferring from joint programs, and study abroad and exchange students are not eligible.
Level of Study: Postgraduate
Type: Scholarship
Value: 15% off tuition fee
Length of Study: 2 years
Frequency: Annual
Country of Study: Any country
Additional Information: www.jcu.edu.au/scholarships/search/international-master-of-engineering-scholarship

International Merit Stipend

Eligibility: The International Merit Stipend is for eligible students from Asia, Africa, Papua New Guinea and the Middle East.
Level of Study: Postgraduate
Type: Stipendiary
Value: AU$350 per fortnight
Frequency: Annual
Country of Study: Australia
Additional Information: www.jcu.edu.au/scholarships/search/international-merit-stipend

International Research Training Program Scholarship (IRTPS)

Purpose: The scholarships are provided to assist with the general living costs of the candidate.
Eligibility: Both domestic (RTPS) and international (IRTPS) applicants
Level of Study: Postgraduate, Research
Type: Scholarship
Value: AU$28,854 pa in 2022 (living allowance paid fortnightly) + Overseas Health Cover
Length of Study: 3.5 years
Frequency: Annual
Country of Study: Any country
Application Procedure: www.jcu.edu.au/__data/assets/pdf_file/0007/273670/2020-Scholarship-Scoring-Procedure-310519.pdf
Closing Date: 30 September

Additional Information: scholarship-positions.com/international-research-training-program-scholarships-at-james-cook-university-australia/2021/07/17/

For further information contact:

Email: grsapplications@jcu.edu.au

James Cook University Postgraduate Research Scholarship

Purpose: To encourage full-time postgraduate research leading to a Master's or PhD degree
Eligibility: Open to any student who has attained at least an Upper Second Class (Honours) Bachelor's Degree
Level of Study: Postgraduate
Type: Scholarship
Value: AU$28,854 pa in 2022 (living allowance paid fortnightly)
Length of Study: 3.5 years
Frequency: Annual
Study Establishment: James Cook University
Country of Study: Australia
Application Procedure: Details of how to apply can be found here www.jcu.edu.au/graduate-research-school/candidates/prospective-students/how-to-apply
Additional Information: For further details visit the website www.jcu.edu.au/grs/scholarships/JCUDEV_014879.html www.jcu.edu.au/graduate-research-school/candidates/postgraduate-research-scholarships

For further information contact:

Fax: (61) 7 4781 6204
Email: grsapplications@jcu.edu.au

John and Janice King Bursary

Eligibility: The John and Janice King Bursary shall be open to competition among candidates who: 1. are Papua New Guinean citizens and holders of a student visa; and 2. are enrolled as a full-time student within the Division of Tropical Health & Medicine for an Award of the University.
Level of Study: Postgraduate
Value: AU$3,000
Length of Study: 1 year
Frequency: Annual
Country of Study: Australia
Closing Date: 24 March
Additional Information: www.jcu.edu.au/scholarships/search/john-and-janice-king-bursary

John Grey Hall of Residence Scholarship

Purpose: This scholarship is designed to support students overcoming financial hardship, drought, disability or other circumstances which would significantly impact their capacity to fully engage in tertiary studies. This scholarship is funded by JCU.

Eligibility: The John Grey Hall of Residence Scholarship shall be open to competition among candidates who: 1. Are or will be enrolled as a full time student at JCU Cairns campus; 2. have a home address that is greater than 40km from JCU Cairns campus; 3. have applied to live at John Grey Hall in a standard room starting for the full academic year.

Level of Study: Postgraduate
Type: Scholarship
Value: AU$3,780
Frequency: Annual
Country of Study: Australia
No. of awards offered: 10
Additional Information: www.jcu.edu.au/scholarships/search/john-grey-hall-of-residence-scholarship

Joyce and George Vaughan Bequest Scholarship

Eligibility: 1. are domestic students, ie Australian citizens, New Zealand citizens and holders of a permanent visa; 2. are currently enrolled in a MSc (Research) or a PhD in the area of Marine Biology; and 3. priority to be given to Australian Aboriginal or Torres Strait Islanders from Thursday Island or the Torres Strait Islands.(A certified copy of your birth certificate, passport or permanent visa must be attached)

Level of Study: Postgraduate
Type: Scholarship
Value: AU$16,000
Length of Study: 2
Frequency: Annual
Country of Study: Australia
Additional Information: www.jcu.edu.au/scholarships/search/joyce-and-george-vaughan-bequest-scholarship

Master of Business Administration Programme

Type: Award
Length of Study: 1 year
Country of Study: Any country
Application Procedure: Applicants must complete an application form supplying transcripts, a curriculum vitae, a one page essay, and referee reports
Closing Date: 15 June

Additional Information: www.jcu.edu.au/graduate-research-school/hdr-candidates/postgraduate-research-scholarships

For further information contact:

Faculty of Arts Commerce & Economics MBA Programme Office of International Affairs.

Tel: (61) 7 7814 407
Fax: (61) 7 7815 988
Email: InternationalAffairs@jcu.edu.aau

Richard Brookdale Scholarship

Eligibility: The Richard Brookdale Scholarship shall be open to competition among nominees who:1. have been accepted into the Bachelor of Arts (Honours) or Masters at JCU's Cairns campus; 2. are undertaking an honours or masters topic in Australian Indigenous archaeology; and 3. are enrolled in a minimum of 6 credit points per teaching period.

Level of Study: Postgraduate
Type: Scholarship
Value: AU$2,500
Length of Study: 1 year
Frequency: Annual
Country of Study: Australia
Closing Date: 31 January
Additional Information: www.jcu.edu.au/scholarships/search/richard-brookdale-scholarship

Robert Logan Memorial Bursary

Eligibility: The Robert Logan Memorial Bursary shall be open to competition among candidates who: 1. Any full time or part time Honours or postgraduate students in the discipline of Biochemistry at James Cook University; and 2. not previously received this bursary during their current course of study.

Level of Study: Postgraduate
Type: Scholarship
Value: AU$14,000
Frequency: Annual
Country of Study: Australia
Additional Information: www.jcu.edu.au/scholarships/search/robert-logan-memorial-bursary

RSL Queensland Scholarships

Level of Study: Postgraduate
Type: Scholarship

Value: AU$4,000
Length of Study: 3 years
Frequency: Annual
Country of Study: Australia
Closing Date: 30 April
Additional Information: rslqld.org/find-help/ex-defence-scholarships

For further information contact:

Email: partnerships@rslqld.org

Samuel & Eileen Gluyas Fellowship

Eligibility: If all the below statements describe you and your current situation, you can apply for this scholarship: 1. I am an Australian citizen, New Zealand citizen or Australian permanent visa holder; 2. I am a graduate in the field of veterinary science, rural science, animal science, biomedical science or agriculture; and 3. I am or will be a Masters or Doctorate student, conducting research in relation to diseases of cattle, breeding of cattle, or general cattle husbandry.
Level of Study: Doctorate, Postgraduate
Type: Fellowship
Frequency: Annual
Study Establishment: The value of a Postgraduate Stipend, plus AU$4,000 shall be made available to assist with expenses relating to a Fellow's research.
Country of Study: Australia
Contributor: 2 to 3 years
Additional Information: www.jcu.edu.au/scholarships/search/samuel-and-eileen-gluyas-fellowship

Shirley Gilliver Memorial Fund Grant

Purpose: The Fund was established to promote the study of social welfare policy and problems of rural North Queensland.
Eligibility: If all the below statements describe you and your current situation, you can apply for this scholarship: 1. I am an Australian citizen or Australian permanent resident; 2. I am or will be enrolled full-time in: 2a. a Masters of Social Work; 2b. a Masters of Social Work (PQ) 2c. a Masters of Social Policy; or 2d. a Doctorate undertaking research in rural communities. 3. I am or will be undertaking social work field education or research in rural or remote communities.
Level of Study: Masters Degree, Research
Type: Grant
Value: Varies
Length of Study: 1 year

Frequency: Annual
Country of Study: Australia
Additional Information: www.jcu.edu.au/scholarships/search/shirley-gilliver-memorial-fund-grant

Sustainable Tourism CRC – Climate Change PhD Scholarship

Eligibility: Open to the candidates who have achieved Honours 1 or equivalent
Level of Study: Postgraduate, Research
Study Establishment: 3 years
Country of Study: Any country
Application Procedure: AU$19,930 per year
No. of awards given last year: James Cook University

For further information contact:

STCRC Education Program, Sustainable Tourism CRC.

Tel: (61) 7 5552 9063
Email: Jane@crctourism.com.au

Tom and Dorothy Cook Scholarships in Public Health and Tropical Medicine

Purpose: These scholarships are offered to higher degree research students to undertake a Master of Philosophy or Doctor of Philosophy in the field of public health, laboratory and clinical investigation of population health in Tropical Northern Australia.
Eligibility: 1. Are commencing or considering a MPhil or PhD at JCU; and 2. Have a research project related to the Tropical Public Health field in the Mackay region; and 3. An element of the research program includes the Mackay and central Queensland region: and 4. Meet the JCU's admission requirements for MPhil or PhD degree. 5. Students identifying as Aboriginal or Torres Strait Islander in descent are highly encouraged to apply.
Level of Study: Doctorate, Postgraduate
Type: Scholarship
Value: AU$30,000 per year plus AU$5,000 project expenses
Length of Study: 3.5 years PhD /2 years MPhil
Frequency: Annual
Country of Study: Australia
No. of awards offered: 2
Closing Date: 23 May
Additional Information: www.jcu.edu.au/scholarships/search/tom-and-dorothy-cook-scholarships-in-tropical-health

William Thomas Williams Postgraduate Scholarship

Eligibility: The William Thomas Williams Postgraduate studies scholarship shall be open to competition among candidates who: 1. Are Australian citizens, Australian permanent resident or international students; 2. Are or intend to enrol full time in PhD, or Master of Philosophy with Creative Arts as their specialist area of study. the Bachelor of Creative Arts and Media in Music, Sound and Moving Image.

Level of Study: Doctorate, Postgraduate
Type: Scholarship
Value: AU$20,000 per year
Length of Study: 2 years for Masters or up to 3 years for PhD
Frequency: Annual
Country of Study: Australia
Closing Date: 31 January
Additional Information: www.jcu.edu.au/scholarships/search/william-thomas-williams-bursary

James S. McDonnell Foundation

JSMF Opportunity Awards

Eligibility: Priority will be given to applicants requesting funds: 1. to support collaboration or to obtain training that allows new theories and new tools to alter the conduct of ongoing research. 2. to provide a researcher with supported time while acquiring the new skills and knowledge to alter future research design. 3. to pilot or test novel experimental approaches and to allow laboratories primarily using artificial laboratory constrained tasks to explore behavioral studies with more natural free flowing behaviors. 4. to refine and extend the temporal dimension of data acquisition allowing for more dynamic assessments of how behavior unfolds over time. 5. to diversify and expand study populations. 6. In order to be eligible for funding, it is expected that projects would commence before the end of 2023.

Type: Award
Value: US$250,000
Length of Study: 2 to 4 years
Frequency: Annual
Country of Study: Any country
Closing Date: 1 April
Additional Information: www.jsmf.org/apply/opportunity/

For further information contact:

Email: info@jsmf.org

Postdoctoral Fellowship Awards

Subjects: Brain sciences
Purpose: The program supports scholarship and research directed toward the discovery and refinement of theoretical and mathematical tools contributing to the continued development of the study of complex, adaptive, nonlinear systems. The program's emphasis is on the development and application of the theory and tools used in the study of complex research questions and not on particular fields of research per se. JSMF is also interested in projects attempting to apply complex systems approaches to coherently articulated questions where such approaches are not yet standard but could open up new paths to progress. The JSMF Fellowship is designed to provide students with opportunities to pursue postdoctoral training that might not be otherwise readily available. The Fellowships are intended to allow students to seek postdoctoral research opportunities aligned with the student's interest and desire to obtain additional skills and experience that will further their pursuit of careers in complex systems science.
Eligibility: The JSMF Fellowship is a unique opportunity for students with an interest in and an aptitude for complexity science who are in the final stages of completing their PhD and looking to make a significant change in direction for their first postdoctoral fellowship (field of study, model organism, theory vs experimental, etc.) that will either be difficult or impossible without an external source of funding.
Type: Fellowship
Value: US$200,000
Length of Study: Two to three years
Frequency: Annual
Country of Study: Any country
Application Procedure: Complete applications must be uploaded to the JSMF website.
Closing Date: 11 June
Additional Information: www.jsmf.org/apply/fellowship/

Japan Society for the Promotion of Science (JSPS)

5-3-1 Kojimachi, Chiyoda-ku, Tokyo, 102-0083, Japan.

Tel: (81) 3263 9094
Email: gaitoku@jsps.go.jp
Website: www.jsps.go.jp

The Japan Society for the Promotion of Science (JSPS) is an independent administrative institution, established for the purpose of contributing to the advancement of science in all fields of the natural and social sciences and the humanities. The JSPS plays a pivotal role in the administration of a wide spectrum of Japan's scientific and academic programmes.

Japan Society for the Promotion of Science Postdoctoral Fellowships for North American and European Researchers (Short-term)

Purpose: To assist promising and highly qualified young foreign researchers wishing to conduct research in Japan

Eligibility: Be a citizen or permanent resident of an eligible country (the US, Canada, EU countries, Switzerland, Norway, and Russia). Candidates must have obtained their doctoral degree at a university outside Japan within 6 years of the date the fellowship goes into effect, or must be currently enroled in a doctoral course at a university outside Japan and scheduled to receive their PhD within 2 years

Level of Study: Postdoctorate, Predoctorate

Type: Fellowship

Value: Round-trip air ticket, monthly maintenance allowance of ¥362,000 for PhD holder and ¥200,000 for non-PhD holder, settling-in allowance of ¥200,000 and overseas travel insurance, research support allowance

Length of Study: 1 year but a minimum of 1 month

Frequency: Annual

Study Establishment: Universities and research institutions

Country of Study: Japan

Application Procedure: Applicants must write for details. Application must be submitted to JSPS by the host researcher in Japan

Funding: Government

Additional Information: Please see the website for further details www.jsps.go.jp/english/e-fellow/postdoctoral.html

For further information contact:

Email: agneta.granlund@stint.se

Research Fellowships for Young Researchers

Purpose: Awarded to excellent young researchers, these fellowships offer the fellows an opportunity to focus on a freely chosen research topic based on their own innovative ideas. Ultimately, the program works to foster and secure excellent researchers.

Eligibility: 1. Be a citizen of a country that has diplomatic relations with Japan. 2. Candidates must have obtained their doctoral degree within six years of the date the fellowship goes into effect. 3. Universities and inter-university research institutes. 4. MEXT-affiliated institutions engaged in

research. 5. Colleges of technology. 6. Institutions designated by the Minister of MEXT.

Level of Study: Postdoctorate

Type: Fellowship

Value: Up to ¥1.5 million/year

Length of Study: 3 years

Frequency: Annual

Country of Study: Any country

Additional Information: www.jsps.go.jp/english/e-pd/index.html

For further information contact:

5-3-1 Kojimachi, Chiyoda-ku, Tokyo, 102-0083, Japan.

Tel: (81) 3 3263 3444

Japanese American Citizens League (JACL)

National Headquarters, 1765 Sutter Street, San Francisco, CA 94115, United States of America.

Tel: (1) 415 345 1075, 415 921 5225
Email: ncwnp@jacl.org
Website: www.jacl.org
Contact: Scholarships Officer

The Japanese American Citizens League (JACL) was founded in 1929 to fight discrimination against people of Japanese ancestry. It is the largest and one of the oldest Asian American organizations in the USA. The JACL has over 24,500 members in 112 chapters located in 25 states, Washington, DC, and Japan. The organization operates within a structure of eight district councils, with headquarters in San Francisco, CA.

Mike M. Masaoka Congressional Fellowship

Purpose: To financially support and develop leaders for public service

Eligibility: Candidates must be U.S. citizens who are graduating college seniors or students in graduate or professional programs and a member of the JACL. Preference will be given to those who have demonstrated a commitment to Asian American issues, particularly those affecting the Japanese American community. Communication skills, especially in writing, are important

Level of Study: Postgraduate, Professional development

Type: Fellowship
Value: US$2,200 to US$2,500 a month
Length of Study: 1 year
Frequency: Annual
Country of Study: United States of America
Application Procedure: Applicants must send a completed application form and a letter of reference to the JACL national headquarters
Closing Date: May
Funding: Foundation
Additional Information: Preference will be given to those who have demonstrated a commitment to Asian American issues, particularly those affecting the Japanese American community. Please see the website for further details at www.jacl.org/now-accepting-applications-for-mike-m-masaoka-congressional-fellowship/ jacl.org/about/jobs-at-jacl/mike-m-masaoka-congressional-fellowship/

For further information contact:

Japanese American Citizens League Headquarters, Mike M. Masaoka Fellowship, 1850 M Street NW, Suite 1100, Washington, DC 20036, United States of America.

Email: policy@jacl.org

Norman Y. Mineta Fellowship

Purpose: To focus on public policy advocacy as well as programs of safety awareness in the Asian Pacific American (APA) community
Eligibility: Open to the members of the JACL with 4-year degree from an accredited college or university having excellent writing, analytical, and computer skills
Level of Study: Postgraduate
Type: Fellowship
Value: US$2,500 a month
Length of Study: 12 months
Country of Study: Any country
Application Procedure: Interested applicants should submit a curriculum vitae, a sample of writing, and names and contact information for two references to the Washington, DC office of the JACL at policy@jacl.org with 'Mineta Fellowship' in the subject line
Closing Date: 18 May
Contributor: State Farm Insurance
Additional Information: Candidates must have ability to take directions and follow through with assignments, must work well with others, and have good interpersonal skills. Please see the website for further details www.jacl.org/internships-and-fellowships/

For further information contact:

JACL, 1828 L Street, NW Suite 802, Washington, DC 20036, United States of America.

Tel: (1) 202 223 1240
Fax: (1) 202 296 8082
Email: dc@jacl.org

Jiamusi University

Heilongjiang Provincial Government Scholarships

Purpose: The Jiamusi is the provincial key construction university with high level in Heilongjiang province, which is also a comprehensive university with a wide range of categories and medical specialties
Eligibility: For a Bachelors's degree, the candidate should have a high school degree with good marks/percentages. Also for a master's degree, you need to have a bachelor's degree with excellent grades. Similarly for PhD applicant needs a masters degree as well as an excellent percentage.
Level of Study: Doctorate, Postgraduate
Type: Scholarship
Value: Doctoral Degree Student's Scholarship-¥50,000 per year; Master's Degree Student's Scholarship-¥40,000 per year
Frequency: Annual
Country of Study: Any country
Application Procedure: A. The Application Requirements of Scholarship 1. Applicants under the age of 25 applying for the Bachelor's Degree with scholarship must have the high school diploma with excellent grades. 2. Applicants under the age of 35 applying for the Master's Degree with scholarship must have the Bachelor's Degree with good grades. 3. Applicants under the age of 40 applying for the Doctoral Degree must have Master's Degree with excellent grades. B. Documents to be Submitted (two copies of each document) 1. Application Form for the Heilongjiang Provincial Government Scholarships 2. The notarized high school graduation certificate and academic record 3. Study or research plan in China written in Chinese or English 4. Recommendations of at least two professors or associate professors (This material is not required to apply for undergraduate study). 5. Original "Foreigner Physical Examination Record" 6. Passport copy C. The Content of Scholarship
Closing Date: 30 April
Funding: International office
Additional Information: www.china-admissions.com/chinese-scholarships/heilongjiang-government-scholarship-international-students/

For further information contact:

Room No. 209, the Admission Office of International Education College of Jiamusi University, No. 258 Xuefu Street, Jiamusi City, Heilongjiang Province, China.

Tel:	(86) 454 8603918
Fax:	(86) 454 8603918
Email:	jmsuadmission@163.com

John Carter Brown Library at Brown University

Box 1894, Brown University, Providence, RI 02912, United States of America.

Tel:	(1) 401 863 2725
Email:	JCBL_Information@Brown.edu
Website:	www.jcbl.org

The John Carter Brown Library, an independently funded and administered institution for advanced research in history and the humanities, is located on the campus of Brown University. The Library supports research focused on the colonial history of the Americas, including all aspects of the European, African, and Native American involvement.

Hodson Trust-John Carter Brown Library Fellowship

Purpose: The Hodson Trust - John Carter Brown Fellowship supports work by academics, independent scholars and writers working on significant projects relating to the literature, history, culture, or art of the Americas before 1830.
Type: Fellowship
Value: The stipend is US$5,000 per month for a total of US$20,000, plus housing and university privileges.
Length of Study: 4 months
Country of Study: Any country
Closing Date: 1 February
Additional Information: www.washcoll.edu/learn-by-doing/starr/Fellowships/hodson-brown-fellowship.php

JCB J. M. Stuart Brown Graduate Fellowship

Eligibility: The Stuart Fellow must have completed all preliminary exams and is expected to reside in Providence or nearby for the entire academic year in which the fellowship is

awarded. He or she is provided with work space in the Library. Time contributed to work on the Library project, which is a requirement of the fellowship, should average around one day/week.
Level of Study: Postgraduate
Type: Fellowship
Value: A stipend equivalent to the Graduate School stipend and up to US$1,000 in travel funds for supplementary dissertation research in other collections of primary materials.
Length of Study: 9 months
Frequency: Annual
Country of Study: Any country
Closing Date: 15 February
Additional Information: apply.interfolio.com/101571

Library Associates Fellowship

Purpose: The Hodson Trust - John Carter Brown Library Fellowship supports work by academics, independent scholars and writers working on significant projects relating to the literature, history, culture
Type: Fellowship
Value: The stipend is US$5,000 per month for a total of US$20,000
Length of Study: 2 Month
Frequency: Annual
Country of Study: Any country
Closing Date: 15 March
Additional Information: For more information on the fellowships and the sponsor institutions, please visit starrcenter.washcoll.edu and www.brown.edu/Facilities/John_Carter_Brown_Libraryjcblibrary.org/fellowships/apply

For further information contact:

Email:	jjohnson24@washcoll.edu OR applications_starrcenter@washcoll.edu

Norman Fiering Fund

Purpose: To support scholars in any area of research related to the Library's holdings
Eligibility: Open to scholars in any area of research related to the Library's holdings
Type: Funding support
Value: US$2,100 per month
Length of Study: 2–4 months
Country of Study: United States of America
Closing Date: 3 January
Additional Information: jcblibrary.org/fellowships/apply

For further information contact:

John Carter Brown Library, Box 1894, Providence, RI 02912, United States of America.

Email: JCBL_Fellowships@Brown.edu

Ruth and Lincoln Ekstrom Fellowship

Purpose: To sponsor historical research
Eligibility: Open to scholars engaged in predoctoral, post-doctoral or independent research. Graduate students must have passed their preliminary or general examinations at the time of application
Level of Study: Postdoctorate, Predoctorate, Research
Type: Fellowship
Value: US$2,100 per month
Length of Study: 2–4 months
Frequency: Annual
Country of Study: United States of America
Application Procedure: Applicants must complete an application form. Candidates should write to, or email the Director
Closing Date: 15 December
Funding: Private
No. of awards given last year: 1
Additional Information: jcblibrary.org/fellowships

John E Fogarty International Center (FIC) for Advanced Study in the Health Sciences

Building 31, 31 Center Drive, MSC 2220, Bethesda, MD 20892-2220, United States of America.

Tel: (1) 301 496 2075
Email: FICinfo@mail.nih.gov
Website: www.fic.nih.gov
Contact: Program Officer

The John E Fogarty International Center (FIC) for Advanced Study in the Health Sciences, a component of the National Institutes of Health (NIH), promotes international co-operation in the biomedical and behavioural sciences. This is accomplished primarily through long- and short-term fellowships, small grants and training grants. This compendium of international opportunities is prepared by the FIC with the hope that it will stimulate scientists to seek research enhancing experiences abroad.

Global Health Research Initiative Program for New Foreign Investigators (GRIP)

Purpose: To assist well-trained young investigators to contribute to health care advances in their home countries
Eligibility: Open to all well-trained young investigators. To verify eligibility, new foreign investigators should review the answers to Frequently Asked Questions. Please contact Dr Xingzhu Liu by email at xingzhu.liu@nih.gov with questions
Level of Study: Postgraduate
Type: Grant
Value: US$50,000 per year
Length of Study: 5 years
Frequency: Annual
Country of Study: Any country
Application Procedure: Application form on request
Funding: Foundation
Contributor: Fogarty International Center
Additional Information: Please see the website for further details www.fic.nih.gov/programs/Pages/new-foreign-investigators.aspxwww.fic.nih.gov/Programs/Info/Pages/grip-faqs.aspx

For further information contact:

Email: butrumb@mail.nih.gov

John E Fogarty Foreign Funded Fellowship Programs

Purpose: To allow United States scientists to conduct collaborative research abroad
Eligibility: Open to scientists who are United States citizens or permanent residents invited by foreign host scientists to participate in research projects of mutual interest
Level of Study: Postdoctorate
Type: Fellowship
Value: To cover the visiting scientist's individual expenses abroad
Length of Study: Usually up to 1 year, possible extension in some countries
Frequency: Annual
Country of Study: Other
Application Procedure: Applicants must complete an application form, available on request or downloadable from www.avh.de
Closing Date: 5 December
Additional Information: Because fellowships are intended to support an individual's expenses abroad, the foreign host is expected to have the resources to support the research project. Types of activities in which Fellows engage include collaboration in basic or clinical research and familiarisation with or

utilisation of special techniques and equipment not otherwise available to the applicant. The programmes do not provide support for activities which have as their principal purpose conducting brief observational visits, attending scientific meetings or formal training courses, or providing full-time clinical, technical or teaching services. Funding is provided by the Alexander von Humboldt Foundation (Germany), the Israeli Ministry of Health, the Japan Society for the Promotion of Science, the Japan Science and Technology Agency, the Swedish Medical Research Council, and the National Science Council of Taiwan. Candidates may apply to only one of these programmes during any given year www.fic.nih.gov/Programs/Info/Pages/grip-faqs.aspx

For further information contact:

Alexander von Humboldt Foundation, US Liaison Office, 1055 Thomas Jefferson Street NW, Suite 2030, Washington, DC 20007, United States of America.

Tel: (1) 202 296 2990
Fax: (1) 202 833 8514
Email: info@humboldtfoundation.org

John F. Kennedy Library Foundation

Columbia Point, Boston, MA 02125, United States of America.

Tel: (1) 866 514 1960
Email: Kennedy.library@nara.gov
Website: www.jfklibrary.org

The John F. Kennedy Library Foundation is a non-profit organization that provides financial support, staffing and creative resources for the John F. Kennedy Presidential Library and Museum whose purpose is to advance the study and understanding of President Kennedy's life and career, and the times in which he lived and to promote a greater appreciation of America's political and cultural heritage, the process of governing and the importance of public service.

Abba P. Schwartz Research Fellowship

Purpose: It is intended to support a scholar in the production of a substantial work in the areas of immigration, naturalization, or refugee policy, subjects of great personal and professional interest to Mr Schwartz

Eligibility: See award purpose
Level of Study: Postgraduate
Type: Fellowship
Value: A stipend of up to US$3,100
Frequency: Annual
Country of Study: United States of America
Application Procedure: Please submit the following documentation (1) an application form (pdf) accompanied by a brief proposal (three to four pages) in the form of a letter describing the planned research, its significance, the intended audience, and expected outcome; (2) two letters of recommendation from academic or other appropriate references; (3) a sample of your writing (approx. 10 pages); (4) a project budget; and (5) a CV
Closing Date: 30 September
Funding: Foundation
Contributor: John F. Kennedy Library Foundation
Additional Information: The estimated per diem cost of accommodations, meals, and incidentals for Boston is US$250 Please see the website for further details www.jfklibrary.org/archives/research-fellowships-grants/schwartz-fellowship

For further information contact:

Research Fellowship Coordinator, John F. Kennedy Presidential Library, Columbia Point, Boston, MA 02125, United States of America.

Email: Kennedy.Fellowships@nara.gov

Arthur M. Schlesinger, Jr. Fellowship

Purpose: To financially support scholars in the production of substantial work on the foreign policy of the Kennedy years
Eligibility: Open to citizens of the US only
Level of Study: Postgraduate
Type: Fellowships
Value: Up to US$5,000
Frequency: Annual
Country of Study: United States of America
Application Procedure: Applicants must submit application form, financial need analysis, essay, reference letters, and curriculum vitae. Applicants are strongly encouraged to contact the Kennedy Library for information about its collections and holdings before applying
Closing Date: 30 September
Funding: Foundation
Contributor: Schlesinger Fund
Additional Information: www.jfklibrary.org/archives/research-fellowships-grants/schlesinger-fellowship

For further information contact:

Research Fellowship Coordinator, John F. Kennedy Presidential Library, Columbia Point, Boston, MA 02125, United States of America.

Email: Kennedy.Fellowships@nara.gov

Marjorie Kovler Research Fellowship

Level of Study: Postgraduate
Type: Fellowship
Value: US$5,000
Frequency: Annual
Country of Study: United States of America
Application Procedure: www.jfklibrary.org/sites/default/files/2018-05/PDFResearchGrantApplicationForm.pdf
Closing Date: 30 September
Additional Information: www.jfklibrary.org/archives/research-fellowships-grants/kovler-fellowship

Theodore C. Sorensen Research Fellowship

Level of Study: Postgraduate
Type: Fellowship
Value: US$3,600
Frequency: Annual
Country of Study: United States of America
Application Procedure: www.jfklibrary.org/sites/default/files/2018-05/PDFResearchGrantApplicationForm.pdf
Closing Date: 30 September
Additional Information: www.jfklibrary.org/archives/research-fellowships-grants/sorensen-fellowship

John R. Mott Scholarship Foundation

John R. Mott Scholarship

Purpose: This award is for Italian students from the Calabria region attending college. Awards are given based on academic achievement and financial need
Eligibility: 1. Students native to the region of Calabria, Italy. 2. Students enrolled and who will be attending university or graduate school. 3. Students seeking an education leading to a degree or professional certification.
Level of Study: Graduate
Type: Scholarship
Value: US$10,000/year are awarded
Frequency: Annual

Country of Study: United States of America
Application Procedure: Applications are accepted between 9 February and 15 April. Applications will be available online from the John R. Mott Scholarship Foundation website. Applicants must complete the application online, and mail or fax the following materials to the foundation by the deadline official transcript from university or official completion certification and academic performance document from high school, and ISEE-U certification attesting to the tax liability of the family
Closing Date: 15 April
Funding: Foundation
Additional Information: mottscholarship.org/index.asp

For further information contact:

1860 19th St., N.W., Washington, DC 20009, United States of America.

Tel: (1) 202 483 2618
Email: scholarships@swe.org

Johns Hopkins University

615 N. Wolfe Street, Suite E1002, Baltimore, MD 21205, United States of America.

Tel: (1) 410 516 3400, 410 955 1680
Email: admiss@jhsph.edu
Website: webapps.jhu.edu/jhuniverse/information_about_hopkins/
Contact: Grants Co-ordinator

The vision of the Johns Hopkins Center for Alternatives to Animal Testing is to be a leading force in the development and use of reduction, refinement and replacement alternatives in research, testing and education to protect and enhance the health of the public.

Alan and Helene Goldberg In Vitro Toxicology Grants

Purpose: To be the leading force in the development and use of reduction, refinement, and replacement alternatives* in research, testing, and education to protect and enhance the health of the public.
Type: Grant
Value: US$40,000
Frequency: Annual

Country of Study: United States of America
Application Procedure: please use the Prepoposal Form: caat.jhsph.edu/programs/grants/proposalform.html
Closing Date: 15 April
Additional Information: caat.jhsph.edu/programs/grants/preproposal.html

Center for Alternatives to Animal Testing Grants Programme

Purpose: To promote and support research in the development of in vitro and other alternative techniques
Eligibility: No eligibility restrictions. Applicants' proposals must meet the goals of the CAAT Grants Program
Level of Study: Unrestricted
Value: For proposals relating to toxicology Up to US$25,000; proposals relating to developmental immunotoxicology Up to US$50,000
Length of Study: 1 year
Frequency: Annual
Country of Study: United States of America
Application Procedure: Applicants must complete a prepoposal. After review, selected applicants are invited to submit a full application
No. of awards offered: 30
Closing Date: 21 March
Funding: Private
No. of awards given last year: 12
No. of applicants last year: 30
Additional Information: Please see the website for further details caat.jhsph.edu/programs/grants/

For further information contact:

615 N Wolfe St W7032, Baltimore, MD 21205, United States of America.

Fax: (1) 410 614 2871
Email: caat@jhsph.edu

Greenwall Fellowship Program

Purpose: To provide an unparalleled opportunity for fellowship and faculty development training in bioethics and health policy
Eligibility: Open to applicants who have Doctoral degrees in medicine, nursing, philosophy, law, public health, biomedical sciences, social sciences or a related field
Level of Study: Postdoctorate
Type: Fellowship
Value: US$122,003

Length of Study: 2 years
Frequency: Annual
Study Establishment: Johns Hopkins University
Country of Study: United States of America
Application Procedure: Applicants must send a cover letter, a personal statement describing why they want to be a Greenwall Fellow, a copy of their curriculum vitae, 3 reference letters, official copies of undergraduate and graduate/professional school transcripts and copies of their written and/or published work
Closing Date: 1 December

For further information contact:

Email: fellows@ihsph.edu

Joint Institute for Laboratory Astrophysics (formerly Joint Institute for Laboratory Astrophysics)

440 B, University of Colorado, Boulder, CO 80309, United States of America.

Tel: (1) 303 492 7789
Email: jilavf@jila.colorado.edu
Website: www.colorado.edu
Contact: Programme Assistant

JILA's interests are at present research and applications in the fields of laser technology, optoelectronics, precision measurement, surface science and semiconductors, information and image processing, and materials and process science, as well as basic research in atomic, molecular and optical physics, precision measurement, gravitational physics, chemical physics, astrophysics and geophysical measurements. To provide an opportunity for persons actively contributing to these fields, JILA operates the Visiting Fellowship Programme as well as the Postdoctoral Research Associate Programme.

Joint Institute for Laboratory Astrophysics Postdoctoral Research Associateship and Visiting Fellowships

Purpose: To support additional training beyond the PhD and sabbatical research
Eligibility: There are no restrictions other than those that might be required by the grant that supports the research
Level of Study: Postdoctorate, Professional development
Type: Fellowship

Value: Varies

Length of Study: Visiting fellowships are for 4 to 12 months and Postdoctoral Research Associateships are for 1 year or more

Frequency: Annual

Country of Study: United States of America

Application Procedure: Applicants should download an application form, complete it, and send it (along with requested supporting materials) to the Visiting Scientists Program Assistant. All materials may be submitted via email to secretary via email

Closing Date: 1 November

Funding: Government

Contributor: Varies

Additional Information: Please see the website for further details jila.colorado.edu/students-postdocs/postdocs

For further information contact:

Visiting Scientists Program, 440 UCB, Boulder, CO 80309, United States of America.

Tel: (1) 303 492 5749
Email: secretary@jila.colorado.edu

Juvenile Diabetes Foundation International/The Diabetes Research Foundation

26 Broadway, 14th Floor, New York, NY 10004, United States of America.

Tel: (1) 1 800 533 CURE (2873)
Email: info@jdrf.org
Website: www.jdrf.org
Contact: Grant Administrator

JDRF remains dedicated to finding a cure for type 1 diabetes as our highest priority. In addition to focusing on specific research challenges and gaps that will lead to curing, better treating, and preventing type 1 diabetes. JDRF works to decrease barriers to commercial development of products for type 1 diabetes.

Advanced Postdoctoral Fellowships

Eligibility: MD, DMD, DVM, PhD, or equivalent. Must not be simultaneously serving an internship or residency.

Level of Study: Postdoctorate

Type: Fellowship

Value: US$95,000

Length of Study: 3 years

Frequency: Annual

Country of Study: United States of America

Closing Date: 31 January

Additional Information: grantcenter.jdrf.org/information-for-applicants/grant-mechanism-descriptions/advanced-post doctoral-fellowships/

Career Development Awards

Eligibility: MD, DMD, DVM, PhD, or equivalent and faculty position or equivalent

Level of Study: Postdoctorate

Type: Award

Value: US$150,000

Length of Study: 5 years

Frequency: Annual

Country of Study: United States of America

Closing Date: 30 April

Additional Information: grantcenter.jdrf.org/information-for-applicants/grant-mechanism-descriptions/career-develop ment-awards/

Conference Grants

Eligibility: Each criterion will be considered in the context of how it relates to JDRF research priorities: 1. How does the meeting/conference relate to JDRF goals? 2. What is the format and agenda? 3. What is the need for the meeting/conference? 4. What is the timeliness of the meeting/conference? 5. What are the qualifications of the organizers and proposed participants? 6. What is the past performance of the meeting/conference (when applicable)? 7. How appropriate is the meeting site? How appropriate is the budget?

Level of Study: Doctorate, Postdoctorate

Type: Grant

Value: Dollar amount awarded varies

Frequency: Annual

Country of Study: United States of America

Closing Date: 31 October

Additional Information: grantcenter.jdrf.org/information-for-applicants/grant-mechanism-descriptions/conference-grants/

For further information contact:

Email: mwhipple@jdrf.org

Early-Career Patient-Oriented Diabetes Research Awards

Eligibility: MD or MD-PhD, hold an appointment or joint appointment in a subspecialty of clinical medicine, and conduct human clinical research
Level of Study: Doctorate, Postdoctorate
Type: Award
Value: US$150,000
Length of Study: 5 years
Frequency: Annual
Country of Study: United States of America
Closing Date: 30 April
Additional Information: grantcenter.jdrf.org/information-for-applicants/grant-mechanism-descriptions/early-career-patient-oriented-diabetes-research-awards/

Industry Discovery & Development Partnerships

Eligibility: Biotechnology, pharmaceutical, device companies or other for-profit entities; PI should be a MD, DMD, DVM, PhD or equivalent, and hold a senior management position
Level of Study: Doctorate, Postdoctorate
Type: Grant
Value: As approved
Frequency: Annual
Country of Study: United States of America
Application Procedure: Applications may be submitted in response to periodic Requests for Applications (RFAs) or by invitation from JDRF on a rolling basis. All application materials must be submitted via JDRF's electronic portal, RMS360. All submissions are confidential.
Additional Information: grantcenter.jdrf.org/industry-discovery-development-partnerships/

For further information contact:

Email: olou@jdrf.org

Innovative Grants

Eligibility: MD, DMD, DVM, PhD or equivalent and faculty position or equivalent
Level of Study: Postgraduate
Type: Grant
Value: US$110,000 maximum/year for one year, including up to 10% for indirect costs.
Length of Study: 1 year
Frequency: Annual
Country of Study: Any country
Closing Date: 31 January

Additional Information: grantcenter.jdrf.org/information-for-applicants/grant-mechanism-descriptions/innovative-grants/

For further information contact:

Email: preawardsupport@jdrf.org

Postdoctoral Fellowships

Eligibility: MD, DMD, DVM, PhD, or equivalent. Must not be simultaneously serving an internship or residency
Level of Study: Doctorate, Postdoctorate
Type: Fellowship
Value: US$57,984 to US$69,060
Length of Study: 3 years
Frequency: Annual
Country of Study: United States of America
Closing Date: 31 January
Additional Information: grantcenter.jdrf.org/information-for-applicants/grant-mechanism-descriptions/postdoctoral-fellowships/

Strategic Research Agreement

Purpose: To support and fund research to find a cure for Type 1 diabetes
Eligibility: Required MD, DMD, DVM, PhD, or equivalent and faculty position or equivalent grantcenter.jdrf.org/information-for-applicants/grant-mechanism-descriptions/strategic-research-agreements/
Level of Study: Research
Type: Grant
Value: Varies
Length of Study: 3 years
Country of Study: United States of America
Closing Date: 1 February
Additional Information: Please check website for further details grantcenter.jdrf.org/information-for-applicants/grant-mechanism-descriptions/strategic-research-agreements/

For further information contact:

Email: support@smartsimple.com

Juvenile Diabetes Research Foundation - JDRF

Tel: (61) 2 9020 6100
Email: travelgrants@jdrf.org.au
Website: jdrf.org.au/

JDRF has transformed the understanding of Type 1 Diabetes (T1D). We have been part of every breakthrough in T1D care in the last 40 years. We drive innovation, demand action and stand with everyone facing life with T1D. We know research is the key to destroy T1D.

Career Support and Travel Grants

Eligibility: Applicants must be: 1. Undertaking research and/or working in an area relevant to T1D 2. Affiliated to an Australian University or Institution 3. Currently residing in Australia 4. Either presenting at a meeting/conference, visiting a lab or participating in a short training course 5. Attending between 30 April 2023 and 31 October 2023 6. Engaged with Australian Diabetes research for more than 12 months, however if this does not apply, contact Sonya Luu at travelgrants@jdrf.org.au to discuss.

Level of Study: Research

Type: Grant

Value: Up to AU$1,000 for virtual conferences and short training courses Up to AU$2,000 for domestic travel within Australia Up to AU$4,000 for international travel.

Frequency: Annual

Country of Study: Australia

Additional Information: jdrf.org.au/for-researchers/travel-grants/

For further information contact:

Email: travelgrants@jdrf.org.au

Conference Grants

Purpose: JDRF offers conference support grants to facilitate collaboration and information sharing within the local type 1 diabetes research community.

Eligibility: Meetings must be relevant to type 1 diabetes and demonstrate a focus on one or more of JDRF's therapeutic areas:1.Beta cell therapies 2. Immune therapies 3. Complications 4. Glucose control. In general, complimentary registration for a designated member of JDRF staff, or JDRF guests, is required for JDRF sponsorship of a meeting.

Level of Study: Research

Type: Grant

Value: Up to US$6,000

Frequency: Annual

Country of Study: United States of America

Application Procedure: jdrf.org.au/wp-content/uploads/2021/03/conference_application_form_2012_v3.docx

Additional Information: jdrf.org.au/for-researchers/conference-grants/

For further information contact:

Email: crn@jdrf.org.au

JDRF PhD Top-up Scholarships 2023

Purpose: The JDRF PhD Top-up scholarship is designed to support and encourage PhD students pursuing research in the field of type 1 diabetes in line with JDRF's mission - to treat, prevent and cure type 1 diabetes and its complications. The Top-Up will provide successful candidates with additional funding up to AU$6,000 per year, on top of their PhD Scholarship stipend, full-time or part-time, contingent on satisfactory progress.

Eligibility: The JDRF PhD Top-Up scholarship is available to domestic students in receipt of a Research Training Program Stipend (formerly Australian Postgraduate Award), NHMRC Postgraduate Award or University-funded scholarship. Students must be pursuing research relevant to JDRF's mission - to cure, treat and prevent type 1 diabetes and its complications. Applicants must be 1. Recipients of either a Research Training Program Stipend, NHMRC Postgraduate Award or a University-funded PhD scholarship 2. Not in receipt of any other PhD top-up funding 3. Pursuing research relevant to type 1 diabetes and its complications 4. Australian citizens or permanent residents currently residing in Australia

Level of Study: Postgraduate

Type: Scholarship

Value: The Top-Up will provide successful candidates with additional funding up to AU$6,000 per year, on top of their PhD Scholarship stipend, full-time or part-time, contingent on satisfactory progress.

Frequency: Annual

Country of Study: Australia

Application Procedure: The cut-off date for consideration of this scholarship is 500pm AEDT, 2nd May. Applications must be submitted on the following application form with headings in order 1. Details Summary - Please complete all fields within the application form. 2. Applicant Summary - Please complete all fields within the application form and adhere to the word limits of each question. 3. Letter confirming offer of a PhD Scholarship - Include a letter confirming your offer of a Research Training Program Stipend, NHMRC Postgraduate Award or a University-funded PhD scholarship. This should be pasted into the document. 4. Curriculum Vitae - 4 page limit. Please limit all information provided to that requested within the application form. 5. Academic transcript - Please provide a certified copy of your academic transcript. This should be pasted into the document. 6. NB Please note that acceptable persons who may certify a document are listed in Schedule 2 of the 'Statutory Declarations Regulations 2018' located here. 7. Certification of both the Applicant and their

Institution's Research Administration Office. 8. NB Electronic signatures are acceptable. Letters of Recommendation - In addition to the above, two letters of recommendation must be sent by referees before 500pm AEDT, 2nd May, directly to travelgrants@jdrf.org.au. Letters of recommendation should be e-mailed directly by the referee to maintain confidentiality. It is the applicant's responsibility to ensure that these letters are sent on time.

Closing Date: 2 May

Additional Information: jdrf.org.au/for-researchers/phd-top-ups/

Rebecca Davies Clinician Researcher Fellowship

Eligibility: 1. Hold a degree (see below) that allows them to undertake research into clinical or/and non-clinical areas. 1a. To have completed their MBBS or MD, or 1b. If an allied health care professional, have completed professional training and hold a Masters degree by research or have equivalent postgraduate research qualifications or experience. 2. Demonstrate strong commitment to research as per the following criteria: 2a. Be a clinician who has recently (5 years, relative to opportunity) completed a higher degree research (HDR; e.g., PhD) and intends to expand research commitments in the field of T1D; or, 2b. Be a clinician who has recently completed their professional training and intends to pursue a career in T1D research. It is expected that the Applicant will enrol in a PhD program prior to the completion of this Fellowship; or, Be a clinician currently enrolled in a PhD who intends to expand their research commitment outside of the work supported by their PhD. This Fellowship will not support research activity or salary/stipend for the PhD, however, additional research outside the scope of their PhD can be supported via this Fellowship. 3. Applicants must concurrently engage in research and clinical activity throughout the duration of this Fellowship. As such, Applicants must hold a clinical appointment and be actively engaged in patient care. 4. Applicants do not need to have held a formal research position, e.g., research assistant, research associate or post-doctoral. 5 This is a part-time research Fellowship designed to enable flexibility around the Fellow's clinical and research commitments. It is expected that the Fellow will dedicate between 0.2 and 0.4 FTE towards research supported by this Fellowship. An FTE lower than 0.2 will not be considered. 6. Applicants must be he named Principal Investigator. 7. Applicants must be supported by a nominated Mentor who is an established leader in a field of clinical research relevant to T1D. 8. Applications must be submitted by an Australian institution (e.g., an Australian university, college, hospital, laboratory, unit of state or local government, or an eligible Commonwealth government agency) affiliated with the Applicant or their Mentor. 9. The Institution submitting the application must provide a Research Office and a Finance Office contact. 10. Only one application may be submitted by an Applicant. 11 Although there are no citizenship requirements for this Fellowship, awardees must be eligible to work in Australia for the length of the proposed project. To assure continued excellence and diversity among applicants and awardees, JDRF encourages applications from individuals with disabilities, and members of minority groups underrepresented in the Australian T1D research landscape.

Level of Study: Research

Type: Fellowship

Value: Up to AU$150,000

Length of Study: 3 years

Frequency: Annual

Country of Study: Any country

Closing Date: 17 March

Additional Information: jdrf.org.au/for-researchers/rebecca-davies-clinician-researcher-fellowship/

For further information contact:

Email: dpawlak@jdrf.org.au

K

Karnatak University

Dr. B. H. Nagoor, Coordinator, Dr. D. C. Pavate Foundation, C/o Department of Economics, Karnatak University, Dharwad, Karnataka 580003, India.

Email: nagoor_bh@yahoo.co.in

Dr. D. C. Pavate Memorial Visiting Fellowship

Eligibility: To apply for the D. C. Pavate Memorial Visiting Fellowship, candidates must meet the following criteria 1. Be below the age of 40 years as on January 1 of the academic year. 2. Secured a PhD or a masters degree or equivalent with a minimum of first class. 3. For fellowships valid for Karnataka candidates A Karnataka candidate is any person who has studied at an educational institution in Karnataka or been employed in Karnataka for a minimum of 5 years continuously

Level of Study: Graduate

Type: Fellowship

Frequency: 3 times each year

Country of Study: Any country

Application Procedure: Application forms can be downloaded at www.kud.ac.in

Closing Date: 10 July

Funding: Private

Additional Information: www.indiaeducation.net/scholarships/dr-dc-pavate-memorial-fellowships.aspx

Keele University

Keele University, Keele, Staffordshire ST5 5BG, United Kingdom.

Tel: (44) 1782 734010
Email: admissions@keele.ac.uk
Website: www.keele.ac.uk

Keele University is committed to provide high quality teaching and research, with particular emphasis on multi-disciplinary and interdisciplinary studies, which are seen to be in the forefront of developments worldwide, promote networking, partnership and collaboration between disciplines and organisations at regional, national and international level, and develop the estate as a leading exemplar of a learning and working campus community of students, staff and business.

Keele MBA Programme

Length of Study: 1 year full-time and 2 years part-time
Application Procedure: Applicants must complete an application form

For further information contact:

Tel: (44) 1782 583425
Fax: (44) 1782 584272
Email: mna09@keele.ac.uk

Keio University

Garduate School of Business Administration, 2-1-1 Hiyoshi Honcho, Kohoku-ku, Yokohama 223-8523, Japan.

Tel: (81) 9 3962 4436
Contact: MBA Admissions Officer

Keio University is the first private university in Japan, founded in 1858 by Yukichi Fukuzawa, who is often called the intellectual father of modern Japan. Since then Keio University has developed a brilliant history of producing distinguished personalities in every field of society.

© Springer Nature Limited 2022
Palgrave Macmillan (ed.), *The Grants Register 2023*,
https://doi.org/10.1057/978-1-349-96053-8

Joint Japan World Bank Graduate Scholarship Program

Purpose: The Joint Japan/World Bank Graduate Scholarship Program (JJ/WBGSP) is open to women and men from developing countries with relevant professional experience and a history of supporting their countries' development efforts who are applying to a master degree program in a development-related topic

Eligibility: The applicant must meet the following eligibility criteria 1. Be a national of a World Bank member developing country (see above). 2. Not hold dual citizenship of a developed country. 3. Be in good health. 4. Hold a Bachelor (or equivalent) degree earned at least 3 years prior to the Application Deadline date. 5. Have 3 years or more of recent development-related experience after earning a Bachelor (or equivalent) degree. 6. Be employed in development-related work in a paid full- time position at the time of submitting the scholarship application. The only exception to this criterion is for developing country nationals from a country that will be on the updated list of Fragile and Conflict States provided to applicants in the Application Guidelines for each call for scholarships. 7. On or before the Scholarship Application Deadline date, be admitted unconditionally (except for funding) for the upcoming academic year to at least one of the JJ/WBGSP preferred university master's programs and located outside of the applicant's country of citizenship and country of residence listed at the time the call for scholarship applications open

Level of Study: Postgraduate

Type: Scholarship

Length of Study: 2 years

Frequency: Annual

Country of Study: Any country

Application Procedure: For scholarships to one of the preferred master's programs, you must first apply and be unconditionally accepted for admissions to one or more of the Preferred Program(s) to be considered for a JJ/WBGSP scholarship. The call for applications is open from 7 March to 11 April. For scholarships to one of the partner master's programs, you must apply for admission to one or more of the Partner Masters Degree Program(s). After reviewing submitted applications, each Partner Master Degree Program will identify a short list of eligible candidates who will then be invited by the JJ/WBGSP Secretariat to apply for a JJ/WBGSP scholarship

Closing Date: 28 February

Funding: Private

Additional Information: For further information, check the below website. www.ic.keio.ac.jp/en/study/jjwbgsp/index.html www.scholars4dev.com/2735/japan-world-bank-graduate-scholarships-for-development-related-studies/

For further information contact:

Email: ic-scholarship@adst.keio.ac.jp

Kennan Institute

Woodrow Wilson International Center for Scholars, One Woodrow Wilson Plaza, 1300 Pennsylvania Avenue North West, Washington, DC, 20004-3027, United States of America.

Tel: (1) 202 691 4100
Email: kennan@wilsoncenter.org
Website: www.wilsoncenter.org
Contact: Scholar Programs

The Kennan Institute for Advanced Russian Studies sponsors advanced research on the successor states to the USSR and encourages Eurasian studies with its public lecture and publication programmes, maintaining contact with scholars and research centres abroad. The Institute seeks to function as a forum where the scholarly community can interact with public policymakers.

James H. Billington Fellowship

Type: Fellowship

Value: monthly stipend of US$5,000

Country of Study: Any country

Application Procedure: To apply, please complete the attached application form according to the instructions and submit by email to kennan@wilsoncenter.org

Closing Date: 15 May

For further information contact:

Email: kennan@wilsoncenter.org

Title VIII-Supported Summer Research Grant

Purpose: To support United States citizens whose research in the social sciences or humanities focuses on the former Soviet Union, and who demonstrate a particular need to use the resources of the Washington, DC area

Eligibility: Open to academic participants with a doctoral degree or those who have nearly completed their dissertation. For non-academic participants, an equivalent level of professional development is required. Applicants must be United States citizens

Level of Study: Doctorate, Postdoctorate, Postgraduate, Predoctorate, Professional development, Research

Type: Scholarship
Value: US$7,000 for 2 months
Length of Study: Up to 62 days
Frequency: Dependent on funds available
Study Establishment: The Kennan Institute
Country of Study: United States of America
Application Procedure: Applicants must submit a concise description of their research project of 700–800 words, a curriculum vitae, a statement of preferred dates of residence in Washington, DC, and two letters of recommendation specifically in support of the research proposal. No application form required
No. of awards offered: 25
Closing Date: 31 January
Funding: Government
Additional Information: Please email kennan@wil soncenter.org or see our website with further details www. wilsoncenter.org/opportunity/kennan-institute-title-viii-supported-summer-research-scholarships

Kennedy Memorial Trust

3 Birdcage Walk, Westminster London SW1H 9JJ, United Kingdom.

Tel: (44) 20 7222 1151
Email: annie@kennedytrust.org.uk
Website: www.kennedytrust.org.uk
Contact: Ms Annie Thomas, Secretary

As part of the British national memorial to President Kennedy, the Kennedy Memorial Trust awards scholarships to British postgraduate students for study at Harvard University or the Massachusetts Institute of Technology. The awards are offered annually following a national competition and cover tuition costs and a stipend to meet living expenses.

Kennedy Scholarships

Subjects: Kennedy Scholarships are tenable across the range of graduate programs offered at both Harvard University and the Massachusetts Institute of Technology.
Purpose: Kennedy Scholarships are the UK's living memorial to President Kennedy. They are offered annually to enable British citizens who are graduates of UK universities to take graduate programs at Harvard University and the Massachusetts Institute of Technology.
Eligibility: Applicants must be British citizens who are, or will be, graduates of a UK university by the time of taking up the award. Applicants must have commenced their undergraduate studies no earlier than ten years prior to September 1st of year in which their intended postgraduate studies will begin.
Level of Study: Doctorate, Graduate, Postgraduate (MSc), Predoctorate, Professional development
Type: Scholarship
Value: Full tuition fees and health insurance plus a means-tested stipend for living expenses.
Length of Study: Typically one full academic year, starting in the Fall
Frequency: Annual
Study Establishment: Harvard University; Massachusetts Institute of Technology
Country of Study: United States of America
Application Procedure: Applications are made online and comprise a personal statement, an academic and professional history and the contact details for 2 referees who will be contacted automatically. See the website for full information.
No. of awards offered: 10
Closing Date: October
Funding: Private
Contributor: The Kennedy Memorial Trust is a British charity, dependent upon charitable donations
No. of awards given last year: 10
No. of applicants last year: 160
Additional Information: www.kennedytrust.org.uk/display. aspx?id=1848&pid=283

For further information contact:

Kennedy Memorial Trust, 3 Birdcage Walk, London SW1H 9JJ, United Kingdom.

Tel: (44) 207 2221151
Email: emily@kennedytrust.org.uk

Kidney Health Australia

Level 1, 25 North Terrace, GPO Box 9993, Adelaide, SA 5001, Australia.

Tel: (61) 8 8334 7555
Email: research@kidney.org.au
Website: www.kidney.org.au
Contact: Medical Director's Office

Founded in 1968, the Australian Kidney Foundation's mission is to be recognized as the leading non-profit national organization providing funding for, and taking the initiative in, the prevention of kidney and urinary tract diseases.

Australian Kidney Foundation Biomedical Scholarships

Purpose: To provide scholarships for individuals wishing to study full-time for the research degrees
Eligibility: Open to Australian applicants who are graduates, or proposing to graduate in the current academic year. Part-time students are not eligible
Level of Study: Doctorate, Postgraduate
Type: Scholarship
Value: AU$24,000 for science and AU$35,000 for medical
Length of Study: 2 or 3 years
Frequency: Annual
Country of Study: Any country
Closing Date: 31 August
Contributor: Kidney Health Australia

For further information contact:

Kidney Health Australia, GPO Box 9993, Adelaide, SA 5001, Australia.

Australian Kidney Foundation Medical Research Grants and Scholarships

Purpose: To support medical research
Eligibility: Open to Australian citizens who are graduates of Australian medical schools or overseas graduates who are eligible for Australian citizenship and for registration as medical practitioners in Australia
Level of Study: Doctorate, Postgraduate
Type: Scholarship
Value: Please contact the organization
Length of Study: Up to 3 years
Frequency: Annual
Study Establishment: Any approved medical centre, university or research institute
Country of Study: Australia
Application Procedure: See guidelines in website
Closing Date: 31 August
Additional Information: Please see the website for further details www.kidney.org.au/HealthProfessionals/MedicalRe searchFunding/tabid/633/Default.aspx

Investigator Driven Research Grants and Scholars

Purpose: To award investigators who have applied to the NHMRC for funding but have just missed the cut-off mark
Eligibility: Open to projects that are ranked as worthy of funding
Type: Scholarship
Frequency: Annual

Country of Study: Any country
Contributor: Kidney Health Australia

Kidney Research United Kingdom

Nene Hall, Lynch Wood Park, Cambridgeshire, Peterborough PE2 6FZ, United Kingdom.

Tel: (44) 300 303 1100
Email: grants@kidneyresearchuk.org
Website: www.kidneyresearchuk.org
Contact: Mrs Elaine Davies, Director of Research Operations

Kidney Research United Kingdom aims to advance and promote research into kidney and renal disease. These may include epidemiological, clinical or biological approaches to relevant problems. All research must be carried out in the United Kingdom.

Allied Health Professional Fellowship (clinical)

Purpose: To enable nurses and allied health professionals to undertake a renal research study and obtain a higher degree (Masters, DPhil or PhD)
Eligibility: Open to nurses and allied health professionals to undertake a renal research study with the object of obtaining a higher degree (Masters, DPhil or PhD). Work and employment must be in the United Kingdom
Level of Study: Doctorate, Postdoctorate, Postgraduate
Value: The salary will be based on the appropriate NHS or university scale, and an allowance for consumables and higher degree fees is included
Length of Study: 3 years at full time or 5 years at part time
Frequency: Annual
Country of Study: Any country
Application Procedure: Applicants must complete an online application
Closing Date: November

Kingdom of the Netherlands

Small Scale Support Program and Accountability Fund

Purpose: It support projects in countries with which the Netherlands does not have a development cooperation relationship, such as India

Eligibility: The Embassy receives a large number of project applications whereas the budget available is sufficient to support only a limited number of projects. Check the website link for further communication.

Level of Study: Graduate

Type: Funding support

Length of Study: 1–2 years

Frequency: Annual

Country of Study: Any country

Application Procedure: If your organization is working in India and provided that your project complies with the above mentioned criteria and is eligible to apply, please fill in the SSSP form. Organizations from Nepal and Bhutan, and projects in India with a focus on lobbying and advocacy have to use the Accountability form

Closing Date: 22 January

Funding: Private

Additional Information: www.netherlandsandyou.nl/your-country-and-the-netherlands/india/and-the-netherlands/small-scale-support-program

For further information contact:

Email: NDE-Projects@minbuza.nl

King's College London

Strand London WC2R 2LS, United Kingdom.

Bosco Tso & Emily Ng Scholarship

Purpose: The scholarship is intended to help support the winner with the cost of tuition fees and living expenses whilst studying

Eligibility: Eligible students must be 1. be undertaking the 1 year LLM Law programme at King's. 2. be able to demonstrate a need for financial assistance. 3. have provided a written personal statement. 4. be willing to provide an end of year report and a letter of thanks to the donor. There are few more conditions being implied for the scholarship. The award of a scholarship to an offer-holder will be conditional upon 1. the offer-holder accepting a place on the King's LLM programme and 2. the fulfilment by the offer-holder of all conditions, both academic and English Language, attached to his or her offer of a place at King's by 10 July

Level of Study: Graduate, Professional development

Type: Scholarship

Value: £22,500 (European Union/International) which intended towards tuition fees and others

Frequency: Annual

Country of Study: Any country

Application Procedure: Kindly access the application form with the below link. www.kcl.ac.uk/study/assets/pdf/fees-and-funding/postgraduate/bosco-tso-emily-ng-scholarship-2019.pdf

Closing Date: 3 July

Funding: Private

Additional Information: www.kcl.ac.uk/study/postgraduate/fees-and-funding/student-funding/postgraduate-taught-funding/2020-21/bosco-tso-emily-ng-scholarship2020

For further information contact:

King's College London, Strand, London WC2R 2LS, United Kingdom.

Email: funding@kcl.ac.uk

Claire Godfrey Postgraduate Fund

Purpose: The objective of the fund is to support postgraduate students at King's who are suffering unexpected, study-related, financial hardship

Eligibility: The fund is open to all home postgraduate students in financial hardship. All applicants will have to submit documentary evidence with their applications to verify their financial status

Level of Study: Postgraduate

Type: Funding support

Frequency: Annual

Country of Study: Any country

Application Procedure: To apply, you should download the form here. www.kcl.ac.uk/study/assets/pdf/fees-and-funding/postgraduate/claire-godfrey-postgraduate-fund.pdf

Closing Date: 30 April

Funding: Private

Additional Information: All applicants will be notified of the outcome of their application in May. The successful applicant will also receive payment at that time www.kcl.ac.uk/study/assets/pdf/fees-and-funding/postgraduate/claire-godfrey-postgraduate-fund.pdf

For further information contact:

King's College London, Strand, London WC2R 2LS, United Kingdom.

King's China Council Scholarships

Purpose: King's College London and the China Scholarship Council (CSC) hold an agreement to jointly fund PhD students to pursue research degrees at King's College London.

Type: Scholarship

Value: Up to £100,000

Closing Date: 5 January
Additional Information: www.kcl.ac.uk/study/doctoral-studies/funding

King's-HKU Joint PhD Scholarship

Purpose: King's College London ranked amongst some of the world's most prestigious universities. It is the research-intensive university with a global reputation for academic discovery and teaching. King's is in the top seven United Kingdom universities for research
Eligibility: 1. Be due to commence a full-time joint PhD programme run in collaboration between King's College London and the University of Hong Kong during the academic year. 2. Have applied to King's College London as the home institution. 3. Have submitted all the required application materials by the funding deadline
Level of Study: Postgraduate
Type: Scholarship
Value: £1,500
Length of Study: 4 year
Frequency: Annual
Country of Study: Any country
Closing Date: 31 May
Funding: International office
Additional Information: scholarship-positions.com/kings-hku-joint-phd-scholarship-for-international-students-in-the-uk/2019/03/11/

For further information contact:

Tel: (44) 20 7848 4568
Email: doctoralstudies@kcl.ac.uk

Norman Spink Scholarship

Purpose: The Norman Spink Scholarship Fund is a fund to help support all students who are able to demonstrate need of financial assistance, to undertake the one year LLM Law programme at King's specifically related to Tax Law
Eligibility: Eligible students must 1. be undertaking the 1 year LLM Law programme at King's. 2. be undertaking the LLM (Tax Law Pathway). 3. be able to demonstrate a need for financial assistance. 4. have provided a written personal statement. 5. be willing to provide an end of year report and a letter of thanks to the estate of the donor. 6. Applicants must have a confirmed place to study the one year LLM Law programme at King's in September. 7. be willing to provide an end of year report and a letter of thanks to the estate of the donor
Level of Study: Postgraduate
Type: Scholarship

Value: £10,000 will be awarded for European Union students
Frequency: Annual
Country of Study: Any country
Application Procedure: Provided your application form has been accurately completed and the appropriate documentary evidence supplied, you will be notified of the decision during June. 1. The award of a scholarship to an offer-holder will be conditional upon the offer-holder accepting a place on the King's LLM programme and. 2. the fulfilment by the offer-holder of all conditions, both academic and English Language, attached to his or her offer of a place at King's by 10 July
Closing Date: 3 July
Funding: Private
Additional Information: www.kcl.ac.uk/study/postgraduate/fees-and-funding/student-funding/postgraduate-taught-funding/2020-21/norman-spink-scholarship2020

For further information contact:

Tel: (44) 20 7848 4204
Email: funding@kcl.ac.uk

Santander Masters Scholarship

Purpose: King's will be offering one scholarship per Faculty to an eligible international student starting a postgraduate taught programme in September. Students may be undertaking study in any discipline
Eligibility: Eligible applicants must meet the following criteria 1. At the time of application, be a permanent resident of and ordinarily resident in one of the following Santander Network countries for at least 3 years prior to the start of the programme Belgium, Italy, France, Germany, Poland, Portugal, Spain and the United Kingdom. 2. Be undertaking a full-time postgraduate taught Masters degree programme, commencing September. 3. Hold a conditional or unconditional offer of a place on the relevant programme. 4. Have applied to King's no later than 31 March. 5. Fulfil the relevant academic and English Language proficiency requirements set by King's. 6. Complete and submit the necessary scholarship application form and supporting documentation by the stated deadline of 15 May
Level of Study: Postgraduate
Type: Scholarship
Value: £5,000
Length of Study: 1 year
Frequency: Annual
Country of Study: Any country
Application Procedure: In order to be considered for an award, candidates must 1. Submit a complete online admissions application (via apply.kcl.ac.uk/)

No. of awards offered: 4
Closing Date: 7 June
Funding: Private
Additional Information: www.kcl.ac.uk/study/postgradu ate/fees-and-funding/student-funding/postgraduate-taught-funding/2020-21/stem-education-teacher-scholarship-2020

For further information contact:

King's College London Strand, London WC2R 2LS, United Kingdom.

Tel: (44) 1334 46 2254
Email: funding@kcl.ac.uk

STEM Education Teacher Scholarship

Purpose: The STEM Education Teacher Scholarship is funded by Wipro Limited, a leading global information technology, consulting and business process services company
Eligibility: To be considered for a scholarship, on time of application, applicants MUST 1. Work in a state-funded school in United Kingdom (e.g. comprehensive, academy, free school). Including, primary, secondary and FE-levels. 2. Be a specialist teacher in Science, Mathematics, Computer Science or Geography. 3. Have completed, or is completing, their NQT year. 4. Have submitted an application for the MA in STEM Education
Level of Study: Professional development
Type: Scholarship
Value: 70% of the total fees
Frequency: Annual
Country of Study: Any country
Closing Date: 28 April
Funding: Private
Additional Information: www.kcl.ac.uk/study/postgradu ate/fees-and-funding/student-funding/postgraduate-taught-funding/2019-20/stem-education-teacher-scholarship2019

For further information contact:

King's College London, Strand, London WC2R 2LS, United Kingdom.

Kingston University

River House, 53–57 High Street, Kingston upon Thames, Surrey KT1 1LQ, United Kingdom.

Tel: (44) 20 8417 9000
Contact: Kingston University

The university's aim is to be internationally recognized for a creative approach to education that has practical outcomes which benefit people and communities.

Annual Fund Postgraduate Scholarships

Purpose: The aim is to encourage academic excellence and allow talented young graduates to continue to higher levels of learning and research, by offering a reduction in course fees for the most academically able applicants
Eligibility: Have already received an offer of a place to study at Kingston on an eligible course. Have first-class honours in a previous degree, or high 21 with additional evidence of academic excellence. Assessed as having Home/European Union fee status (not Overseas fee status). Students from outside the United Kingdom need to meet Kingston University's English language requirements – these depend on the course they are applying for
Level of Study: Postgraduate
Type: Scholarship
Value: £3,000 (full time courses) or £1,500 (part time courses).
Length of Study: Up to 2 years full time or 4 years part time
Frequency: Annual
Study Establishment: Kingston University
Country of Study: United Kingdom
Application Procedure: Completed application form 1. Academic letters of reference. 2. Copy of academic transcripts. 3. Copies of any certificates relevant to prizes or awards
No. of awards offered: 20
Closing Date: 17 July
Funding: Individuals
Contributor: Alumni of Kingston University
Additional Information: For more details, see the website: www.kingston.ac.uk/postgraduate/fees-and-funding/funding-your-course/scholarships/annual-fund-scholarship/

For further information contact:

Tel: (44) 20 8417 3299
Email: development@kingston.ac.uk

Klynveld Peat Marwick Goerdeler Foundation

3 Chestnut Ridge Road, Montvale, NJ 07645, United States of America.

Tel: (1) 201 307 7932
Email: acenglish@kpmg.com
Website: www.kpmgfoundation.org
Contact: Anita C. English, Scholarship Administrator

American Institute of Certified Public Accountants Fellowship for Minority Doctoral Students

Purpose: The AICPA Fellowship for Minority Doctoral Students ensures that CPAs of diverse backgrounds are visible in college and university classrooms. The program's goal is to increase the number of minority CPAs who serve as role models and mentors to young people in the academic environment and university classrooms

Eligibility: a) Applied to a PhD program and awaiting word on acceptance; b) been accepted into a PhD program; or c) already matriculated in a doctoral program and pursuing appropriate coursework; Earned a Master's Degree and/or completed at least 3 years of full-time experience in the accounting practice; 1. Minority student of Black or African American; Hispanic or Latino; or Native American ethnicity or Alaska Native; Native Hawaiian or Pacific Islander ethnicity. 2. Attend school on a full-time basis and plan to remain enrolled full-time until attaining PhD 3. Agree not to work full-time in a paid position or accept responsibility for teaching more than one course per semester as a teaching assistant, or dedicate more than one quarter of my time as a research assistant

Level of Study: Doctorate

Type: Scholarship

Value: US$12,000

Length of Study: Up to 5 years

Frequency: Annual

Study Establishment: A full-time AACSB-accredited university

Country of Study: United States of America

Application Procedure: Applicants must visit the website for further information and application forms

Closing Date: 30 May

Funding: Private

Additional Information: us.aicpa.org/career/diversityinitiatives/fmds

For further information contact:

Email: academics@aicpa.org

Korea Foundation

Fellowship Programme, 10th Floor, Diplomatic Center Building, 1376-1 Seocho-2-dong, Seocho-gu, Seoul, 137-863, Korea.

Tel: (82) 2 3463 5614
Email: fellow@kf.or.kr
Website: www.kf.or.kr
Contact: Ms Bo Myung KIM, Programme Officer

The Korea Foundation seeks to improve awareness and understanding of Korea worldwide as well as to foster co-operative relationships between Korea and foreign countries through a variety of exchange programmes.

Korea Foundation Fellowship for Field Research

Purpose: To promote Korean studies and support professional researchers in Korean studies by facilitating their research activities in Korea

Eligibility: Open to university professors and instructors, doctoral candidates, researchers and other professionals. Candidates must be proficient in Korean or English. In the case of Korean nationals, only those with foreign residency status and regular faculty positions at foreign universities are eligible to apply. Fellows in this programme must concentrate on their research and may not enrol in any language courses or other university courses during the fellowship period. Candidates who are receiving support from other organizations or programmes administered by the Korea Foundation are not eligible to receive this fellowship at the same time

Level of Study: Doctorate, Postdoctorate, Professional development, Research

Type: Fellowship

Value: Monthly stipend of KRW 2,000,000 to KRW 3,000,000

Length of Study: 1 month-12month

Frequency: Annual

Country of Study: Korea

Application Procedure: Applicants must complete an application form. Application forms are available from the Foundation and the website

No. of awards offered: 30

Closing Date: 31 July

Additional Information: en.kf.or.kr/?menuno=3795

For further information contact:

Email: hklee@kf.or.kr

Korea Foundation Fellowship for Korean Language Training

Purpose: To provide foreign scholars and graduate students who need systematic Korean language education with the opportunity to enrol in a Korean language programme at a language institute affiliated to a Korean university

Eligibility: Candidates must have a basic knowledge of, and an ability to communicate in, the Korean language. In the case of Korean nationals, only those with foreign residency status are eligible to apply. Candidates who are receiving support from other organizations or programmes administered by the

Korea Foundation are not eligible to receive this fellowship at the same time

Level of Study: Graduate, Postgraduate

Type: Fellowship

Value: (1) Living expenses (monthly basis), (2) Travel allowance KRW 300,000 (one-time benefit)

Length of Study: 6 months

Frequency: Annual

Study Establishment: A language institute affiliated to a Korean university

Country of Study: Korea

Application Procedure: Applicants must complete an application form are available from the Korean Foundation. Applicants must request an application form by supplying their curriculum vitae along with details of their including Korean language ability and previous study of Korean

No. of awards offered: 40

Closing Date: 31 May

Additional Information: en.kf.or.kr/?menuno=3792

For further information contact:

Email: koreanstudies@isop.ucla.edu

Korea Foundation Postdoctoral Fellowship

Purpose: To provide promising and highly qualified PhD recipients with the opportunity to conduct research at leading universities in the field of Korean studies so that they can further develop their scholarship as well as have their dissertations published as manuscripts

Eligibility: Open to non-Korean scholars who have received a PhD degree in a subject related to Korea within 5 years of their application, but do not currently hold a regular faculty position. Korean nationals with permanent resident status in foreign countries may apply. Candidates who are receiving support from other programmes administered by the Korea Foundation are not eligible to receive this fellowship at the same time

Level of Study: Doctorate, Postdoctorate

Type: Fellowship

Value: Stipend support for a 1-year period, of an amount to be determined based on the country, region and institution where the Fellow will conduct his or her research

Length of Study: 1 year

Frequency: Annual

Country of Study: Any country

Application Procedure: You will need to email a separate KI Korea Foundation application by the KI deadline, as well as, complete and submit the Korea Foundation application via the KF online portal by the Korea Foundation deadline. Be sure to verify and confirm the specific KF deadline by visiting the Korea Foundation website Complete application form must have the following details. For further information, check with the below link. www.kf.or.kr/

No. of awards offered: 10

Closing Date: 7 January

Additional Information: korea.fas.harvard.edu/korea-foundation-postdoctoral-fellowships-2

For further information contact:

Korea Institute, Harvard University, CGIS South Room S241, 1730 Cambridge Street, Cambridge MA 02138, United Kingdom.

Tel: (44) 617 496 2141

Email: cglover@fas.harvard.edu

Kosciuszko Foundation

The Kosciuszko Foundation, Inc., 15 East 65th Street, New York, NY 10065, United States of America.

Tel: (1) 212 734 2130

Email: addy@thekf.org

Website: www.thekf.org

The Kosciuszko Foundation, founded in 1925, is dedicated to promoting educational and cultural relations between the United States of America and Poland and increasing American awareness of Polish culture and history. In addition to its grants and scholarships, which total US$1,000,000 annually, the Foundation presents cultural programmes including lectures, concerts and exhibitions, promotes Polish culture in the United States of America and nurtures the spirit of multicultural co-operation.

Dr. Marie E. Zakrzewski Medical Scholarship

Purpose: The Dr. Marie E. Zakrzewski Medical Scholarship is awarded to a young woman of Polish ancestry for first, second, or third year of studies towards an M.D. degree at an accredited school of medicine in the United States.

Eligibility: citizens and legal permanent residents of the United States; must be of Polish descent; female resident of the state of Massachusetts; must be entering first, second or third year of studies towards an M.D. degree; GPA of 3.0 or higher is required; female candidates residing in New England will be considered if no eligible Massachusetts candidates apply.

Type: Scholarship
Value: US$3,500
Country of Study: Any country
No. of awards offered: 1
Closing Date: 31 January
Additional Information: www.thekf.org/kf/scholarships/tuition/mzms/

For further information contact:

Grants Department Kosciuszko Foundation, Inc. 15 East 65th Street New York, NY 10065, United States of America.

Email: tuitionscholarships@thekf.org

Jozef Tischner Fellowships

Purpose: To fund a Polish junior researcher in any academic discipline to work in Vienna on research projects of their choice related to one of the Institute for Human Sciences' (IWM) main research fields
Eligibility: Open to Polish citizens, permanent residents of Poland and Polish-American scholars with a recent PhD degree, not older than 35 years
Level of Study: Doctorate, Research
Type: Fellowship
Value: Fellowship and €8,000 stipend to cover accommodation, living expenses, travel, health insurance and incidentals during the stay
Length of Study: 6 months
Frequency: Annual
Study Establishment: The Institute for Human Sciences (IWM)
Country of Study: Austria
Application Procedure: Applicants must send the application by mail to address below
Closing Date: 1 December
Additional Information: www.iwm.at/fellowships/tischner/

For further information contact:

Fax: (43) 1 313 58 30
Email: fellowships@iwm.at

Polish National Alliance of Brooklyn, United States of America, Inc. Scholarship

Purpose: To fund qualified undergraduate students for full-time studies at accredited colleges and Universities in the United States
Eligibility: 1. Must be an undergraduate student 2. Must attend a university or a four-year college 3. Minimum 3.0

GPA 4. Citizenship requirements US 5. Must study full-time 6. Restricted to residents of New York 7. Must be affiliated with Polish National Alliance 8. Restricted by ethnic heritage Polish
Type: Scholarship
Value: US$2,000
Frequency: Annual
Study Establishment: At accredited colleges and universities in the United States
Country of Study: United States of America
Application Procedure: Submit application form, US$25 non-refundable application fee and supporting materials to the Kosciuszko foundation. E-mailed and faxed materials will not be considered
Closing Date: 12 March
No. of awards given last year: 1
Additional Information: www.petersons.com/scholarship/polish-national-alliance-of-brooklyn-usa-inc-scholarship-111_172414.aspx

For further information contact:

15 East 65th Street, New York, NY 10065, United States of America.

Email: Addy@thekf.org

Krist Law Firm, P.C

Email: scholarship@houstoninjurylawyer.com

The Krist Law Firm, P.C. National Scholarship

Purpose: Our Houston maritime lawyers are proud to announce that The Krist Law Firm, P.C. will be renewing our annual scholarship of US$10,000 to award an individual student the financial resources to accomplish their educational goals and prepare for future career aspirations!
Eligibility: 1. Be a United States citizen or permanent resident. 2. Be accepted to or currently enrolled in an accredited college, university, or graduate program within the United States. 3. Have a cumulative GPA of 3.0 or higher. 4. Demonstrate good character and high initiative
Level of Study: Graduate
Type: Scholarship
Value: US$10,000
Frequency: Annual
Country of Study: United States of America
Closing Date: 31 March
Funding: Foundation

Kungliga Tekniska högskolan Royal Institute of Technology

S-100 44 Stockholm, Sweden.

Tel: (46) 8 790 6000
Contact: KTH Royal Institute of Technology

KTH Royal Institute of Technology is a university in Stockholm, Sweden, specializing in engineering and technology, it ranks highest in northern mainland Europe in its academic fields.

Postdoctoral Scholarship in Solar Fuels at KTH

Purpose: A postdoctoral scholarship in Solar Fuels is available at the KTH Royal Institute of Technology
Eligibility: Students from Sweden can apply for this scholarship. If English is not your first language then you will need to show that your English language skills are at a high enough level to succeed in your studies
Type: Postdoctoral fellowship
Value: SEK 25,000 per month
Country of Study: Sweden
Application Procedure: Apply for this scholarship by e-mail
Closing Date: 26 February
Funding: Private
Additional Information: For more details please contact the website scholarship-positions.com/postdoctoral-scholarship-solar-fuels-kth-sweden/2018/02/19/

For further information contact:

Email: lichengs@kth.se

Kurt Weill Foundation for Music

7 East 20th Street, New York, NY 10003, United States of America.

Tel: (1) 212 505 5240
Email: kwfinfo@kwf.org

Website: www.kwf.org
Contact: Ms Elizabeth Blaufox, Assoc. Director of Programs

The Kurt Weill Foundation for Music is a non-profit, private foundation chartered to preserve and perpetuate the legacies of the composer Kurt Weill (1900–1950) and his wife, singer and actress Lotte Lenya (1898–1981). The Foundation awards grants and prizes, sponsors print and online publications, maintains the Weill-Lenya Research Center and administers Weill's copyrights.

Kurt Weill Prize

Purpose: To encourage distinguished scholarship in the disciplines of music, theater, dance, literary criticism and history addressing music theater since 1900 (including opera)
Eligibility: Open to nationals of any country
Level of Study: Unrestricted
Type: Prize
Value: US$5,000 to the author of the winning book entry; and a prize of US$2,000 to the author of the winning article entry.
Frequency: Every 2 years
Country of Study: Any country
Application Procedure: Applicants must submit five copies of their published work. Works must have been published within the 2 years preceding the award year. Please visit www.kwf.org
No. of awards offered: 2
Closing Date: 30 April
Funding: Private
Additional Information: www.kwf.org/pages/kurt-weill-prize.html

For further information contact:

Kurt Weill Foundation for Music, 7 East 20th Street, 3rd Floor, New York, NY 10003, United States of America.

Tel: (1) 212 505 5240 Ext. 204
Email: bsansone@kwf.org

K

L

La Trobe University

Research Services, Melbourne, VIC 3086, Australia.

Tel: (61) 1300 135 045
Email: rgs@latrobe.edu.au
Website: www.latrobe.edu.au/rgso

La Trobe is a university known for making a positive difference in the lives of our students, partners and communities.

Alumni Scholarship for the Master of Business Administration (MBA)

Purpose: Learn to lead business success in a connected world with support from La Trobe's Alumni Scholarship for the Master of Business Administration (MBA)
Eligibility: To be eligible to apply for this scholarship, applicants must: 1. be a domestic or international La Trobe (onshore or offshore) alumnus who has not completed or started an MBA with La Trobe 2. enrol and start your MBA before July 2023 3. not be a current MBA student
Level of Study: MBA
Type: Scholarship
Value: 25% fee reduction from the full-fee price of your course
Country of Study: Australia
Application Procedure: Domestic students: 1. Complete and submit your course application online. 2. We will assess your course application. If you have applied for an MBA and are eligible we will advise you in your offer letter if 3. you have been successful in being granted an Alumni Scholarship for the MBA. 4. If you wish to accept your Alumni Scholarship for the MBA you must accept the Terms and Conditions.; International students: 1. You must meet all conditions (if applicable) outlined in your course Letter of Offer. 2. Yo must accept your offer by paying the full acceptance deposit listed on your Letter of Offer and return your completed Offer Acceptance Form for International Students to La Trobe International, ensuring you also complete the Scholarship Details Section. 3. You must commence your course at La Trobe University by the date listed on your Letter of Offer to secure your scholarship, unless it is approved for you to defer your enrolment.
Funding: Government
Additional Information: Any questions? Contact us "www.latrobe.edu.au/study/contact" and we can help.

For further information contact:

Email: study@latrobe.edu.au

Destination Australia Scholarships - International Students

Purpose: The Destination Australia scheme seeks to attract and support international students looking to study in regional Australia. This scholarship offers students the opportunity to experience high-quality learning in regional Australia.
Eligibility: To be eligible to apply for this scholarship, applicants must: 1. Be an international student commencing their first year of study in an undergraduate or postgraduate coursework course in Semester 1 2023, Semester 1 2024, or Semester 1 2025. 2. Be studying full-time at one of La Trobe University's regional campuses. 3. Be residing in or intending to move to a regional area classified as RA2 to RA5, by the Australian Standard Geographical Classification Remoteness Area. (Check the 2016 box next the "ASGS Remoteness Areas").
Level of Study: Postgraduate, Undergraduate
Type: Scholarship
Value: AU$15000 per annum
Length of Study: Three years
Frequency: Annual

© Springer Nature Limited 2022
Palgrave Macmillan (ed.), *The Grants Register 2023*,
https://doi.org/10.1057/978-1-349-96053-8

Country of Study: Australia
Closing Date: 31 December
Funding: Government

For further information contact:

Email: LTIRecruitment@latrobe.edu.au

Early Bird Acceptance Grant - International Students

Purpose: International students applying for an undergraduate or postgraduate course to study at La Trobe University can be rewarded a one off grant for completing their admission process early
Eligibility: To be eligible to apply for this scholarship, applicants must 1. Be a citizen of a country other than Australia or New Zealand. 2. Be a new International student applying to study in any intake and 2023 3. Be a full fee-paying student (Non-sponsored). 4. Meet all the conditions outlined in the offer, accept the offer, and pay the required deposit mentioned on the offer, within a stated deadline. 5. Your course should be in the LTIS List of eligible courses.
Level of Study: Postgraduate
Value: 5% of the first-year tuition fees
Frequency: Annual
Country of Study: Any country
Closing Date: 31 December

For further information contact:

Email: LTIRecruitment@latrobe.edu.au

La Trobe – JSSAHER PhD Scholarship in Life Science and Public Health

Purpose: The aim of the project is to determine if the University and/or the Hospital have an effect on the microbial communities in the soils around them, including the amount and variation of multi-resistance organisms in the vicinity of the Hospital
Eligibility: Indian students are eligible to apply for this scholarship programme. Applicants need to fulfil the English language requirements at La Trobe University
Value: ₹25,000 per month in years 1 and 2, and ₹28,000 per month in year 3 and the first half of year 4 of candidature, to support your living costs Fee-relief scholarship (LTUFFRS) for up to four years (international candidates). There is the opportunity to travel to La Trobe University, Australia for up to six months during your candidature, including accessing a travel grant of up to AU$15,000 (pro rata for six months) (upon prior approval). Opportunities to work with outstanding researchers at La Trobe University and JSSAHER, and access to professional development programs through La Trobe's Research and Education Unit
Study Establishment: Scholarships are awarded in Life Science and Public Health. The focus of this research project is to analyze and monitor soil samples around JSSAHER and its JSS Hospital in Mysuru, India over the period of three years
Country of Study: Any country
Application Procedure: 1. Expression of Interest Send your CV, transcripts, certificates and relevant publications (if any) in a pdf file by email. You will be notified of the outcome of your expression of interest by email. 2. Interview If your expression of interest is successful, you will be invited to an interview with representatives of La Trobe on Skype and JSSAHER in person, separately. Interviews will take place at the JSSAHER campus in Mysuru, India. 3. Invitation to apply If you are shortlisted for the scholarship, you will be invited to formally apply for both the scholarship and for PhD candidature.
Closing Date: 31 March
Additional Information: For more details please visit the website scholarship-positions.com/la-trobe-jssaher-phd-scholarship-life-science-public-health-indian-students/2018/03/07/www.latrobe.edu.au/scholarships/la-trobe-jssaher-phd-scholarship-in-public-health

For further information contact:

Email: admissions@jssuni.edu.in

La Trobe Excellence Scholarships

Purpose: The scholarship offers a 50% reduction on annual tuition fees for international students, who will be studying undergraduate or postgraduate coursework programs for the entire duration of their course.
Eligibility: To be eligible to apply for this scholarship, applicants must: 1. The applicant must be a citizen and resident of India, Sri Lanka, Bangladesh, Nepal, Pakistan, Kenya, Mauritius and Vietnam. 2. La Trobe International Scholarship (LTIS) list of eligible courses. 3. Applicant must have an overall WAM achievement of 80% or above. 4. The applicant must commence their studies at any of the La Trobe University Victorian Campus in 2023. 5. The applicant must meet the University's English language requirements and all other conditions stated on the Offer Letter. 6. As a scholarship award recipient, the student should be willing to be an International student ambassador for La Trobe University during their studies.
Type: Scholarship
Value: 50% reduction in course fees
Frequency: Annual

Country of Study: Australia
Application Procedure: For application procedure, please visit www.latrobe.edu.au/contact
Closing Date: 14 August

For further information contact:

Email: LTISA@latrobe.edu.au; Vietnam@latrobe.edu.au

La Trobe Greater China Scholarship

Purpose: The La Trobe Greater China Scholarship is a scholarship available to cover tuition fees for high achieving International students accepted into our undergraduate and postgraduate programs.
Eligibility: To be eligible to apply for this scholarship, applicants must: 1. Be a citizen of China, Hong Kong, or Macau. 2. Be a new International student applying for 2023 or 2024 intakes. 3. Be a full fee-paying student (Non-sponsored). 4. Apply to a program in the LTIS List of eligible courses.
Level of Study: Postgraduate
Type: Scholarship
Value: Up to 30% reduction in course fees
Frequency: Annual
Country of Study: Any country
Application Procedure: Applicants will be automatically considered for the scholarship after submitting an application for an LTIS List of eligible course.
Closing Date: 31 December

For further information contact:

Email: LTIRecruitment@latrobe.edu.au

La Trobe International Scholarship

Purpose: La Trobe University values academic excellence. High achieving International students thinking about applying for an undergraduate or postgraduate course will be automatically be considered for this scholarship.
Eligibility: To be eligible to apply for this scholarship, applicants must 1. Be a citizen of a country other than Australia or New Zealand and be applying to start an undergraduate or postgraduate coursework program. 2. Be a new International students applying for 2023 or 2024 intakes. 3. Be a full-fee paying student (Non-sponsored). 4. Apply to a program in the LTIS List of eligible courses
Level of Study: Postgraduate
Type: Scholarship
Value: Up to 25% reduction in course fees
Country of Study: Any country

Application Procedure: Applicants will be automatically considered for the scholarship after submitting an application for an LTIS approved course. www.latrobe.edu.au/scholarships/other-scholarship-opportunities/courses-offering-international-scholarships.
Closing Date: 31 December

For further information contact:

Email: LTIRecruitment@latrobe.edu.au

La Trobe Jordan Scholarship

Purpose: The La Trobe Jordan Scholarship is a scholarship available to cover tuition fees for high achieving International students accepted into our undergraduate and postgraduate programs
Eligibility: To be eligible to apply for this scholarship, applicants must: 1. Be a citizen of Jordan. 2. Be a new International students applying for 2023 or 2024 intakes. 3. Be a full-fee paying student (Non-sponsored). 4. Apply to a program in the LTIS List of eligible courses.
Level of Study: Postgraduate
Type: Scholarship
Value: Up to 30% reduction in course fees
Country of Study: Any country
Application Procedure: Applicants will be automatically considered for the scholarship after submitting an application for an LTIS List of eligible course "www.latrobe.edu.au/scholarships/other-scholarship-opportunities/courses-offering-international-scholarships"
Closing Date: 31 December

For further information contact:

Email: LTIRecruitment@latrobe.edu.au

La Trobe Latin America Scholarship

Purpose: The La Trobe Latin America Scholarship is a scholarship available to cover tuition fees for high achieving International students accepted into our undergraduate and postgraduate programs
Eligibility: To be eligible to apply for this scholarship, applicants must: 1. Be a citizen of any country in Latin America. 2. Be a new International students applying for 2023 or 2024 intakes. 3. Be a full-fee paying student (Non-sponsored). 4. Apply to a program in the LTIS List of eligible courses.
Level of Study: Postgraduate
Type: Scholarship
Value: Up to 30% reduction in course fees
Country of Study: Any country

Application Procedure: Applicants will be automatically considered for the scholarship after submitting an application for a list of eligible course. www.latrobe.edu.au/scholarships/other-scholarship-opportunities/courses-offering-international-scholarships

Closing Date: 31 December

For further information contact:

Email: LTIRecruitment@latrobe.edu.au

La Trobe South Asia Scholarship

Purpose: The La Trobe South Asia Scholarship is a scholarship available to cover tuition fees for high achieving International students accepted into our undergraduate and postgraduate programs.

Eligibility: To be eligible to apply for this scholarship, applicants must: 1. Be a citizen of India, Sri Lanka, Nepal, Pakistan or Bangladesh. 2. Be a new International students applying for 2023 or 2024 intakes. 3. Be a full-fee paying student (Non-sponsored). 4. Apply to a program in the LTIS List of eligible courses.

Level of Study: Postgraduate

Type: Scholarship

Value: Up to 30% reduction in course fees

Country of Study: Any country

Application Procedure: Applicants will be automatically considered for the scholarship after submitting an application for an LTIS List of eligible course. www.latrobe.edu.au/scholarships/other-scholarship-opportunities/courses-offering-international-scholarships

Closing Date: 31 December

For further information contact:

Email: LTISA@latrobe.edu.au

La Trobe South East Asia Scholarship

Subjects: The La Trobe South East Asia Scholarship is a scholarship available to cover tuition fees for high achieving International students accepted into our undergraduate and postgraduate programs.

Eligibility: To be eligible to apply for this scholarship, applicants must: 1. Be a citizen of Cambodia, Indonesia, Malaysia, the Philippines or Vietnam 2. Be a new International students applying for 2023 or 2024 intakes. 3. Be a full-fee paying student (Non-sponsored). 4. Apply to a program in the LTIS List of eligible courses.

Level of Study: Postgraduate

Type: Scholarship

Value: Up to 30% reduction in course fees

Country of Study: Any country

Application Procedure: Applicants will be automatically considered for the scholarship after submitting an application for an LTIS List of eligible course. www.latrobe.edu.au/scholarships/other-scholarship-opportunities/courses-offering-international-scholarships

Closing Date: 31 December

For further information contact:

Email: LTIRecruitment@latrobe.edu.au

La Trobe Turkey Scholarship

Purpose: The La Trobe Turkey Scholarship is a scholarship available to cover tuition fees for high achieving International students accepted into our undergraduate and postgraduate programs.

Eligibility: To be eligible to apply for this scholarship, applicants must: 1. Be a citizen of Turkey. 2. Be a new International students applying for 2023 or 2024 intakes. 3. Be a full-fee paying student (Non-sponsored). 4. Apply to a program in the LTIS List of eligible courses.

Level of Study: Postgraduate

Type: Scholarship

Value: Up to 30% reduction in course fees

Country of Study: Any country

Application Procedure: Applicants will be automatically considered for the scholarship after submitting an application for an LTIS List of eligible course. www.latrobe.edu.au/scholarships/other-scholarship-opportunities/courses-offering-international-scholarships

Closing Date: 31 December

For further information contact:

Email: LTIRecruitment@latrobe.edu.au

La Trobe University Offshore Online Bursary

Purpose: La Trobe University is offering the OOB to students who have been disadvantaged by the Australian border closure. We understand that students commencing studies in their home countries are missing out on access to facilities and amenities which may impact their student experience. This is a top-up fee reduction of up to 35 per cent in recognition that students cannot experience the on-campus experience, services and facilities while they are offshore.

Eligibility: To be eligible, applicants must be: 1. a new, commencing or continuing international student studying offshore online due to border closures 2. a citizen or permanent resident of a country other than Australia or New Zealand 3. meet all the conditions in the offer letter for new students 4. self-funded or sponsored students 5. studying or intending to study a Bachelor's or Master's coursework program at La Trobe University and be adversely affected by the international (not interstate) border closures 6. studying online and must be offshore (outside Australia).

Level of Study: Postgraduate, Undergraduate

Type: Bursary

Value: Up to 35% reduction in subject tuition fees

Frequency: Annual

Country of Study: Australia

Application Procedure: New students will be automatically assessed for the bursary.

Closing Date: 31 March

Additional Information: For further inquiries: Current Students can contact Ask La Trobe latrobe-current.custhelp.com/app/ask

For further information contact:

Email: LTIRecruitment@latrobe.edu.au

La Trobe University OSHC Grant

Purpose: The La Trobe University OSHC grant is for prospective international students undertaking a postgraduate degree (2 years) at our Victorian campuses.

Eligibility: Be a new commencing international student applying to a postgraduate degree (2 years) at one of La Trobe's Victorian campuses commencing in Semester 2, Term 6, Summer 1 2023, or Semester 1 2024.

Level of Study: Postgraduate

Type: Grant

Value: AU$1400

Length of Study: 2 years

Frequency: Annual

Country of Study: Australia

Application Procedure: Complete the online application. The online application form will be distributed to students who have been made an offer

Closing Date: 31 March

For further information contact:

Email: LTIRecruitment@latrobe.edu.au

La Trobe – JSSAHER PhD Scholarship for Indian Students

Purpose: The aim of the project is to determine if the University and/or the Hospital have an effect on the microbial communities in the soils around them, including the amount and variation of multi-resistance organisms in the vicinity of the Hospital

Eligibility: 1. Indian students are eligible to apply for this scholarship programme. 2. Applicants should have a high level of achievement, including a first class honours degree or postgraduate degree or equivalent. 3. They will also need to fulfil the English language requirements at La Trobe University.

Value: ₹25,000 per month in years 1 and 2, and ₹28,000 per month in year 3 and the first half of year 4 of candidature, to support your living costs. There is the opportunity to travel to La Trobe University, Australia, for up to 6 months during your candidature, including accessing a travel grant of up to AU$15,000 (pro rata for six months) (upon prior approval)

Length of Study: 3.5 years

Country of Study: Any country

Application Procedure: For further details, please visit www.scholarshipsupdates.com/la-trobe-jssaher-phd-scholarship-for-indian-students-2018/

Closing Date: 15 March

For further information contact:

Jagadguru Sri Shivarathreeshwara University, JSS Medical Institutions Campus, Sri Shivarathreeshwara Nagara, Mysuru, Karnataka 570 015, India.

Tel: (91) 821 2548416/400
Fax: (91) 821 2548394
Email: admissions@jssuni.edu.in

Pathway to Victoria Scholarship

Purpose: Pathway to Victoria Scholarship Program has been made possible by funding from the Victorian Government through Study Melbourne.

Eligibility: Are you eligible to apply? 1. To be eligible to apply for this scholarship, applicants must: 2. be a new, international student commencing Trimester 3 2023 onwards. 3. be a citizen or permanent resident of a country other than Australia or New Zealand. 4. meet all entry requirements and accept the offer to study a pathway program at La Trobe College Australia. 5. receive a packaged Offer to commence an LTCA program in Trimester 3 2023 or any intake in 2024. 6. intend to study a La Trobe degree program in 2023 or 2024 (by 31 July 2024) immediately after completing their pathway program.

Level of Study: Postgraduate

Type: Scholarship

Value: AU$2500

Frequency: Annual

Country of Study: Australia
Application Procedure: New students will be automatically assessed when they apply to LTCA.
Closing Date: 3 October
Funding: Government

For further information contact:

Email: LTIRecruitment@latrobe.edu.au

Pathway to Victoria Scholarship

Subjects: Diploma, International Student
Purpose: Pathway to Victoria Scholarship Program has been made possible by funding from the Victorian Government through Study Melbourne.
Eligibility: To be eligible to apply for this scholarship, applicants must: 1. be a new, international student commencing Trimester 3 2023 onwards. 2. be a citizen or permanent resident of a country other than Australia or New Zealand. 3. meet all entry requirements and accept the offer to study a pathway program at La Trobe College Australia. 4. receive a packaged Offer to commence an LTCA program in Trimester 3 2023 or any intake in 2024. 5. intend to study a La Trobe degree program in 2023 or 2024 (by 31 July 2024) immediately after completing their pathway program.
Level of Study: Graduate
Type: Scholarship
Value: AU$2500
Frequency: Annual
Country of Study: Any country
Closing Date: 10 March

For further information contact:

Email: LTUGlobal@latrobe.edu.au

Regional Scholarship - International Students

Purpose: The Regional Scholarship is available to international students who are considering applying to study at one of our regional campus. This scholarship offers students the opportunity to experience high-quality learning in regional Australia.
Eligibility: To be eligible to apply for this scholarship, applicants must: 1. Be a citizen of a country other than Australia or New Zealand. 2. Be applying to an undergraduate or postgraduate coursework degree for any of the 2023 or 2024 intakes. 3. Be applying to any of the La Trobe University Regional Campus.
Level of Study: Postgraduate, Undergraduate
Type: Scholarship

Value: AU$5000
Frequency: Annual
Country of Study: Australia
Application Procedure: Applicants will be automatically considered for the scholarship after applying based on the eligibility of the course.
Closing Date: 31 December
Funding: Government

For further information contact:

Email: LTIRecruitment@latrobe.edu.au

Regional Victoria Experience Bursary

Purpose: The Regional Victoria Experience Bursary is a top-up bursary for high-achieving prospective international students who are willing to undertake an undergraduate or postgraduate coursework degree in one of our Regional Campuses.
Eligibility: Be a new commencing international student applying to study an undergraduate or postgraduate coursework program at one of La Trobe's regional campuses for 2023 or 2024 intakes. Limited bursaries are available.
Level of Study: Postgraduate, Undergraduate
Type: Scholarship
Value: AU$3000
Frequency: Annual
Country of Study: Australia
Closing Date: 31 December
Funding: Government

For further information contact:

Email: LTIRecruitment@latrobe.edu.au

Vice-Chancellor Excellence Scholarship - Vietnam

Purpose: La Trobe University values academic excellence. If you are a high-achieving international student and thinking about applying for a full-time undergraduate or postgraduate study, you can apply to receive a 100% scholarship for the duration of your studies at La Trobe.
Eligibility: To be eligible to apply for this scholarship, applicants must: 1. The applicant must be a citizen and resident of Vietnam 2. Be eligible for direct entry (no ELICOS or pathway) commencing an undergraduate or postgraduate coursework degree which is under the La Trobe International Scholarship List of eligible courses "www.latrobe.edu.au/scholarships/other-scholarship-opportunities/courses-offering-international-scholarships". 3. Be a full-fee paying student (Non-Sponsored) 4. The applicant must have an overall

WAM* (AQF Equivalent) of 80% or above. 5. The applicant must meet all the condition in the offer letter by the provided deadline.
Level of Study: Postgraduate, Undergraduate
Type: Scholarship
Value: 100% deduction on annual tuition fees
Frequency: Annual
Country of Study: Australia
Application Procedure: Applicants must submit a complete application for the course commencing in Semester 1 (March) or Semester 2 (July) intake of 2024 at La Trobe University. Applicants must also provide the following documents before the application closing date: 1. A detailed resume 2. A 4-5 minute video recording (in English) answering the below questions: a. Why should you be selected for this scholarship? b. Why have you chosen La Trobe University? c. What are your career goals? d. How would you like to make a difference to the world/community using this qualification? Applicants who have already applied for Semester 1 or Semester 2 of 2024 will be considered for the scholarship if they met the eligibility criteria. They must send their resume and video recording by the specified date.
Closing Date: 24 April

For further information contact:

Email: Vietnam@latrobe.edu.au

Vice-Chancellor Scholarship - India and Sri Lanka

Purpose: La Trobe University values academic excellence. If you are a high-achieving international student and thinking about applying for a full-time undergraduate or postgraduate study, you can apply to receive a 100% scholarship for the duration of your studies at La Trobe.
Eligibility: To be eligible to apply for this scholarship, applicants must: 1. The applicant must be a citizen and resident of India or Sri Lanka. 2. Be eligible for direct entry (no ELICOS or pathway) commencing an undergraduate or postgraduate coursework degree which is under the La Trobe International Scholarship (LTIS) list of eligible courses. 3. Be a full-fee paying student (Non-Sponsored) 4. The applicant must have an overall WAM* (AQF Equivalent) of 80% or above. 5. The applicant must meet all the conditions in the offer letter by the deadline provided.
Level of Study: Postgraduate, Undergraduate
Type: Scholarship
Value: 100% deduction on annual tuition fees
Frequency: Annual
Country of Study: Australia
Application Procedure: Applicants must submit a complete application for the course commencing in Semester 1 (March), Semester 2 (July) or Summer 1 (November) intake of 2024 at La Trobe University.; Applicants must also provide the following documents before the application closing date to apply for this scholarship. 1. A detailed resume 2. a 4-5 minute video recording answering the below questions a. Why should you be selected for this scholarship? b. Why have you chosen la Trobe University? c. What are your career goals? d. How would you like to make a difference to the world/community using this qualification?; Shortlisted candidates may be invited for an interview. Applicants who have already applied for Semester 1, Semester 2 or Summer 1 of 2024 will be considered for the scholarship if they met the eligibility criteria.
Closing Date: 22 August

For further information contact:

Email: LTISA@latrobe.edu.au

Lancaster University

Student Services, Lancaster University, Bailrigg, Lancaster LA1 4YW, United Kingdom.

Tel: (44) 1524 65201
Email: studentfunding@lancaster.ac.uk
Website: www.lancs.ac.uk/funding
Contact: Craig Lowe

Lancaster University is a campus university dedicated to excellence in teaching and research, offering a wide range of nationally and internationally recognized postgraduate courses. For updated information on all the University's funding opportunities, please see our website www.lancs.ac.uk/funding

Alumni Loyalty Scholarship

Type: Scholarship
Value: 20% fee reduction for 1st Class Hons degree holders 10% fee reduction for 2:1 Hons degree holders
Frequency: Annual
Country of Study: Any country

Alumni Postgraduate Scholarships

Eligibility: 1. Hold, or be expected to hold a Bachelor's degree (1 or 2.1), or Master's degree (merit or distinction)

from the University of Kent. 2. Hold an offer of a place for a full-time postgraduate research degree at University of Kent. 3. Demonstrate that they have made a contribution to the wider University community, for example, through Students' Union activities - societies, sports, volunteering - or acting as a student representative on University committees. 4. Have excellent written and oral communication skills and be able to Explain their research clearly and without jargon to non-experts, Convey their passion for their research to a wider audience, Convince the panel of their research's wider value, Your supporting statement should be no more than two A4 pages. Any statement exceeding this limit will not be accepted. Act as 'ambassadors' for both the University and their subjects. Be prepared to attend an interview in person at Canterbury on 5th May.

Level of Study: Postgraduate

Type: Studentship

Value: £1,000

Frequency: Annual

Application Procedure: In order to apply, you must complete an application form and submit your curriculum vitae and two references

Closing Date: 13 April

Contributor: Lancaster University Alumni

For further information contact:

Alumni & Development, Lancaster University, Bailrigg, Lancaster LA1 4YW, United Kingdom.

Tel: (44) 1524 592556

Email: s.nelhams@lancaster.ac.uk

Bowland College – Willcock Scholarships

Purpose: To provide financial assistance to undergraduate or postgraduate members of Bowland College who are in very good academic standing but who are facing long-term financial or other difficulties which are beyond their control and which jeopardise their continuing or commencing study at Lancaster University

Eligibility: All Bowland College students or alumni who would have difficulty achieving their full academic potential because of financial hardship may apply to the scholarship fund

Level of Study: Postgraduate

Type: Scholarship

Value: £2,500

Frequency: Annual

Application Procedure: Applications should be submitted to the Senior College Advisor

Closing Date: 27 April

For further information contact:

Bowland College Office Lancaster University, Bailrigg, Lancaster LA1 4YW, United Kingdom.

Tel: (44) 1524 594 506

Email: p.m.brown@lancaster.ac.uk

Cartmel College Postgraduate Studentship

Purpose: This is a scholarship for Cartmel College students and Alumni. The award is for postgraduate students who were Cartmel College students during their undergraduate degrees.

Level of Study: Masters Degree, Postgraduate, Research

Type: Studentship

Value: £1000 - two awards can be made each year.

Frequency: Annual

Country of Study: Any country

Application Procedure: A completed Cartmel College Postgraduate Studentship, academic reference and covering letter should be submitted to the Cartmel College Manager, A22 Cartmel College or emailed to cartmel@lancaster.ac.uk

Closing Date: 1 June

For further information contact:

Email: cartmel@lancaster.ac.uk

Cartmel College Scholarships

Purpose: Each year, Cartmel College offers a limited number of awards to its present or alumni members who are unable to obtain adequate grants from other bodies

Eligibility: All applications will be considered on their merit

Level of Study: Postgraduate

Type: Scholarship

Value: £500

Length of Study: Awards are tenable for 1 year

Frequency: Annual

Closing Date: 1 June

For further information contact:

Cartmel College Manager, A22 Cartmel College.

Email: cartmel@lancaster.ac.uk

County College Scholarships

Eligibility: Members of the County College who have completed a Lancaster degree and are proposing to commence postgraduate study at the university are eligible to apply to this scholarship fund. Selections are on the basis of academic merit and financial need

Level of Study: Postgraduate
Type: Scholarship
Value: £1,000
Length of Study: Awards are tenable for 1 year
Frequency: Annual
Country of Study: Any country
Closing Date: 1 June

County College Studentship

Subjects: All
Purpose: This is a studentship for County College students and alumni. The award for postgraduate students who were County College students during their undergraduate degrees.
Level of Study: Masters Degree, Postgraduate, Research
Type: Studentship
Value: £1,000
Frequency: Annual
Country of Study: United Kingdom
Application Procedure: The County College Studentship Application Form-Notes can be submitted from 1st April each year and must be returned to the Ali Moorhouse, County College, Lancaster University by the deadline of 1st June.
Closing Date: 1 June

Donald & Margot Watt Bursary Fund (FASS Only)

Subjects: Art, Design, English & Creative Writing, History, Philosophy, Religious Studies and Theatre Studies
Purpose: This fund is to be used to support undergraduate students who run into financial difficulty whilst at University
Eligibility: Students will be expected to complete feedback on how the award has assisted them so the information can be used to encourage other donors to support Lancaster students. This fund is for Undergraduate students studying one of the following seven disciplines Art, Design, English & Creative Writing, History, Philosophy, Religious Studies and Theatre Studies. (Those on joint degree schemes that include one of the specified subjects are also eligible)
Level of Study: Postgraduate
Type: Funding support
Value: Awards amounts of £500, £1,000, £1,500 or £2,000 depending on assessed financial need.
Frequency: Annual
Country of Study: Any country

Application Procedure: Please complete an Donald & Margo Watt Bursary Fund (FASS) application form and submit to The Base, University House. Application has to be processed in the physical format. Form detail is available on the official link. www.lancaster.ac.uk/student-based-services/money/funding/donald–margot-watt-bursary-fund-fass-only
Funding: Private

For further information contact:

Lancaster University, Bailrigg, Lancaster LA1 4YW, United Kingdom.

Tel: (44) 152 465 201
Email: studentfunding@lancaster.ac.uk

External Sources of Funding

Level of Study: Masters Degree, Postgraduate, Research, Undergraduate
Type: Funding support
Value: Variable according to source
Frequency: Annual
Country of Study: Any country

FfWG - Foundation Grants for Women Graduates

Purpose: FfWG offers Foundation Grants to help women graduates with their living expenses (not fees) while registered for study or research at an approved institution of higher education in Great Britain. The criteria are the proven needs of the applicant and their academic calibre.
Eligibility: Grants are offered to British and overseas students alike at postgraduate level. Any subject or field of study will be considered. There is no upper age limit. Evidence of ability to pay fees is required. Grant holders must submit a written report on their year's work within six weeks of the end of their academic year. The grants will be a contribution only towards the living expenses of one year's academic study or research.
Level of Study: Postgraduate, Research
Type: Scholarship
Value: The grants are not likely to exceed £4,000. All our grants are offered on a needs basis and therefore not all grants will be for £4,000
Length of Study: 1 year
Country of Study: Any country

For further information contact:

Email: jean.c@blueyonder.co.uk

FfWG - Foundation Grants for Women Graduates

Purpose: FfWG offers Foundation Grants to help women graduates with their living expenses (not fees) while registered for study or research at an approved institution of higher education in Great Britain
Level of Study: Masters Degree, Postgraduate, Research
Value: £4,000
Frequency: Annual
Country of Study: Any country

For further information contact:

Email: jean.c@blueyonder.co.uk

FfWG - Theodora Bosanquet Bursary for Women Graduates

Subjects: History and English Literature
Level of Study: Masters Degree, Postdoctorate, Research
Frequency: Annual
Country of Study: Any country
Closing Date: 31 October

For further information contact:

Mrs Jean F Collett Flatt, Grants Administrator.

Email: grants@ffwg.org.uk

Furness Studentship

Subjects: All
Purpose: Furness College offers annually a limited number of awards to present and former undergraduate members of the College who wish to commence postgraduate study at Lancaster University. The awards will take into consideration academic ability, financial hardship and an involvement in the College's Activities. Candidates may be required to attend an interview
Level of Study: Masters Degree, Postgraduate, Research
Type: Studentship
Value: £250
Country of Study: Any country
Application Procedure: A completed application form, academic reference and covering letter should be submitted to Jo Dickinson in the Furness College Office (A13, Furness College). Electronic copies can be sent to furnessoffice@lancaster.ac.uk
Closing Date: 28 May

For further information contact:

Email: furnessoffice@lancaster.ac.uk

Future Finance (Private Student Loans)

Subjects: All
Level of Study: Masters Degree, Postgraduate, Research, Undergraduate
Value: Loan entitlement will vary according to your circumstances
Country of Study: Any country

Geoffrey Leech Scholarships

Purpose: To mark the retirement of Professor Geoffrey Leech, the Department of Linguistics & English Language has established a scholarship fund in his honour
Eligibility: The Geoffrey Leech Scholarships are open to applicants who qualify to pay fees at the United Kingdom/European Union-fee rate. The scholarships will be awarded on a competitive basis; details of criteria applied may be found on the departmental website
Level of Study: Postgraduate
Type: Scholarship
Value: Covers the whole of the tuition fee at the appropriate rate
Frequency: Annual
Application Procedure: In order to be considered for these awards, applicants must write a formal request to be considered for the scholarship, in no more than 500 words to Postgraduate Secretary
No. of awards offered: 1
Closing Date: 28 February

For further information contact:

Email: postgraduatelinguistics@lancaster.ac.uk

Grizedale College Awards Fund

Purpose: Present and former undergraduate members of the college who wish to commence postgraduate study at Lancaster are eligible to apply for awards from this fund
Eligibility: The awards, in the form of grants, are made according to financial circumstances. The intended purpose of any grant awarded and any past or present contribution to college life are also taken into consideration
Level of Study: Postgraduate
Type: Award

Value: Up to £150 (depending on the number of applications received as there is a limit to the total funding available)
Frequency: Annual
Closing Date: 1 June

For further information contact:

Grizedale College, Lancaster University, Lancaster LA1 4YW, United Kingdom.

Tel: (44) 1524 592 190
Email: b.glass@lancaster.ac.uk

Heatherlea Bursary

Purpose: Heatherlea, one of Britain's leading wildlife-holiday operators, offers one annual bursary of £1,000 to a student applying for and studying on either the MSc in ecology and environment or the MSc in conservation science
Eligibility: The Environment Centre will consider suitable candidates automatically so students do not need to apply separately. This award is a bursary and will be awarded on the basis of the financial background/need of the applicant
Level of Study: Postgraduate
Type: Bursary
Value: £1,500
Frequency: Annual
Closing Date: 31 July

For further information contact:

Postgraduate Studies Office, Lancaster Environment Centre, Lancaster University, Library Avenue, Lancaster LA1 4YQ, United Kingdom.

Tel: (44) 1524 593 478
Email: pgadmissions@lancaster.ac.uk

Lancaster Enabling Access Fund

Subjects: All
Purpose: The Lancaster Enabling and Access Fund is offered to students who have incurred costs as a result of a disability or medical condition. The costs must be related to your studies and the fund cannot be used towards general living costs or personal care.
Level of Study: Masters Degree, Postgraduate, Undergraduate
Type: Funding support
Value: Between £50 and £500 per academic year.
Country of Study: Any country

Additional Information: www.lancaster.ac.uk/student-and-education-services/money/funding/lancaster-enabling-access-fund

For further information contact:

Email: disability@lancaster.ac.uk

Lancaster Opportunity and Access Fund (LOAF) (for UK, EU & International)

Subjects: All
Purpose: The Lancaster Opportunity and Access Fund is designed to help students who may require extra financial support. Any award from the fund is given as a grant and is non-repayable.
Level of Study: Masters Degree, Postgraduate, Research, Undergraduate
Type: Funding support
Value: Award amounts are limited for postgraduate students.
Frequency: Annual
Country of Study: Any country
Closing Date: 20 June

Lancaster University Peel Studentship Trust

Purpose: The awards are available for the support of students for first or higher degrees, in any subject. The period of the award is one academic year, although students can apply each year. The value of the award is determined by the Trustees in each case.
Eligibility: A pre-condition of application to the Peel Studentship Trust is that the applicant must be aged 21 or over on the first day of the first term for which they are seeking assistance. Both United Kingdom and non-United Kingdom students can apply for a grant. Applications are assessed on the basis of both academic merit and financial need
Level of Study: Postgraduate
Type: Studentship
Value: Up to £2,500 and paid in three termly instalments dependent on satisfactory academic progression.
Length of Study: 1 year
Frequency: Annual
Closing Date: 22 May
Contributor: The Peel Studentship Trust

Leverhulme Trade Charities Trust

Subjects: All
Eligibility: To be eligible to apply, you need to be: 1. a resident of the United Kingdom; 2. studying for a full-time

postgraduate degree at a recognised UK university; 3. the child, spouse, widow, widower or personally employed as a commercial traveller, pharmacist or grocer, and; 4. in 'financial need'.

Level of Study: Masters Degree, Postgraduate, Research, Undergraduate

Type: Award

Value: £5,000 a year

Frequency: Annual

Application Procedure: Apply online: www.leverhulme-trade.org.uk/

Closing Date: 15 October

Additional Information: www.lancaster.ac.uk/student-and-education-services/money/funding/leverhulme-trade-charities-trust

For further information contact:

Email: grants@leverhulme-trade.org.uk

Lone Parents Child Care Grant

Subjects: All

Eligibility: The grant is open to all lone parent students

Level of Study: Masters Degree, Postgraduate, Research, Undergraduate

Value: A maximum of £1,000 for any academic year

Frequency: Annual

Country of Study: Any country

Additional Information: You must be able to provide evidence of child care from a registered Childcare provider. Grants will be paid directly to the provider.

For further information contact:

Email: studentfunding@lancaster.ac.uk

Lonsdale College Travel Grant

Purpose: Lonsdale College offers Travel Awards to support undergraduate members of the College who propose to undertake an activity during the Summer vacation. Funds are awarded for voluntary activities which enhance or further your academic studies but which are not a compulsory part of your course. Please note that funds are not made available to final year students.

Eligibility: 1. These are cash grants available to assist Lonsdale students in travel projects where academic work would be advanced by such visits. 2. The visits must not be a compulsory part of the student's academic course. The grant will be considered a loan until a written report of

1,000 words has been completed and submitted to the college, no later than the fifth week of the following term

Level of Study: Postgraduate

Type: Travel grant

Value: Up to £250

Frequency: Annual

Country of Study: Any country

Application Procedure: Kindly contact Julie Shorrock for further information. For further information, refer the website link mentioned below. www.lancaster.ac.uk/student-based-services/money/funding/lonsdale-college-travel-grant

Funding: Private

For further information contact:

Julie Shorrock, Lonsdale College, Bailrigg, Lancaster LA1 4YN, United Kingdom.

Tel: (44) 1542 92296

PGR Hardship Fund (for UK, EU & International)

Subjects: All

Purpose: The University recognises there has been a significant impact from the Covid-19 pandemic on the PGR community. In particular, we are aware of a growing concern that there are increasing hardship issues for many PGR students, with their ability to earn from part-time employment both through the university and externally being constrained. In response to these concerns, the University has established a hardship fund to support PGR students who are in financial difficulty as a result of the pandemic.

Level of Study: Graduate

Type: Funding support

Frequency: Annual, if funds are available

Study Establishment: maximum of £4,000

Country of Study: Any country

Closing Date: 31 August

Postgraduate Access Awards (United Kingdom-Fee Only)

Purpose: Lancaster University is intending to offer up to six Postgraduate Access Awards from the Access to Learning Fund

Eligibility: Applicants should normally hold at least a 21 Honours degree

Level of Study: Postgraduate

Type: Award

Value: £500. These awards are intended to help towards living costs associated with undertaking full-time or part-

time postgraduate study (where part-time equals at least 50% of a full-time course). Awards are intended for students not otherwise in receipt of Government funding, but who are able to find finance for the remaining costs of their course
Frequency: Annual
Closing Date: July
Contributor: Access to learning fund

Robinson Scholarship

Purpose: As the scholarship will not cover all the costs of a course here at Lancaster, applicants should explain carefully their financial circumstances. This explanation should cover two aspects.
Level of Study: Masters Degree, Postgraduate, Research
Type: Scholarship
Value: £5,000
Frequency: Annual
Country of Study: Any country
Application Procedure: The successful candidate will be informed by 1st June, and will be required to pay a deposit of £1000 by 1st July.
Closing Date: 1 May

Sallie Mae Student Loans

Subjects: All
Level of Study: Masters Degree, Postgraduate, Research, Undergraduate
Type: Loan scholarship
Value: ariable depending on cost of attendance
Frequency: Annual
Country of Study: Any country
Additional Information: www.lancaster.ac.uk/student-and-education-services/money/funding/sallie-mae-student-loans

Social Work Bursary

Subjects: All
Purpose: The NHS Social Work Bursary is available for undergraduate and postgraduate study.
Eligibility: You must be studying, or intending to study, on a university based social work course approved by one of the following: 1. Social Work England (SWE) 2. the Scottish Social Services Council (SSSC) 3. Social Care Wales 4. the Northern Ireland Social Care Council (NISCC)
Level of Study: Masters Degree, Postgraduate, Research, Undergraduate
Length of Study: 1 year
Country of Study: Any country

Additional Information: www.lancaster.ac.uk/student-and-education-services/money/funding/social-work-bursary

For further information contact:

Email: nhsbsa.swb1@nhsbsa.nhs.uk

The Peel Trust Studentship

Purpose: The awards are available for the support of students for first or higher degrees, in any subject. The period of the award is one academic year, although students can apply each year. The value of the award is determined by the Trustees in each case.
Level of Study: Masters Degree, Postgraduate, Research, Undergraduate
Type: Scholarship
Value: Up to £2,500
Country of Study: Any country
Closing Date: 4 March
Additional Information: Please note that the selection process is made during the summer and successful applicants will be notified by August. www.latrobe.edu.au/scholarships/la-trobe-jssaher-phd-scholarship-in-public-health

For further information contact:

Email: studentfunding@lancaster.ac.uk

Le Cordon Bleu Australia

Days Road, Regency Park, SA 5010, Australia.

Tel: (61) 618 8346 3700/61 8 8348 3000
Email: australia@cordonbleu.edu
Website: www.lecordonbleu.com

Le Cordon Bleu, a global leader hospitality education, provides professional development for existing executives.

The Culinary Trust Scholarship

Purpose: Scholarships provides funds to qualified applicants for beginning, continuing, and specialty education courses at accredited culinary schools worldwide, as well as, independent study for research projects. Applicants must have at least, a minimum 3.0 GPA, must write an essay, submit two letters of recommendation

Eligibility: 1. Must be an undergraduate student, a graduate student or a postgraduate student. 2. Must attend a university, a four-year college, two-year college or a vocational-tech school. 3. Minimum 3.0 GPA. 4. Must be at least 18 years old. 4. Both full-time and part-time students. 5. Restricted to students studying Culinary Arts, Food Service/Hospitality, Food Science/Nutrition.

Level of Study: Postgraduate

Type: Partial scholarship

Value: AU$1,000, Low Amount Awarded; AU$5,000, High Amount Awarded; AU$90,000, Total Amount Awarded

Length of Study: 6 months

Frequency: Annual

Study Establishment: Le Cordon Bleu Australia, Adelaide

Country of Study: Australia

Application Procedure: Application form and full guidelines available from The Culinary Trust website

Closing Date: 1 March

Funding: Private

For further information contact:

PO Box 273, New York, NY 10013, United States of America.

Tel: (1) 888 345 4666
Fax: (1) 888 345 4666
Email: heather@theculinarytrust.org

Leeds International Pianoforte Competition

Leeds International Piano Competition, The University of Leeds, Leeds LS2 9JT, United Kingdom.

Tel: (44) 1132 446 586
Email: pianocompetition@leeds.ac.uk
Website: www.leedspiano.com

The Leeds International Pianoforte Competition is a member of the World Federation of International Music Competitions

Henry Rudolf Meisels Bursary Awards

Purpose: To award competitors accepted in the first stage of the competition

Eligibility: Open to candidates who are accepted to perform in the first stage of the competition

Level of Study: Professional development

Type: Scholarships and fellowships

Value: £100

Frequency: Every 3 years

Study Establishment: The University of Leeds

Country of Study: United Kingdom

Application Procedure: Entry by competitive audition. Application forms should be submitted by the closing date

No. of awards offered: 196

Closing Date: 1 February

Contributor: Henry Rudolf Meisels Bequest

No. of awards given last year: 71

No. of applicants last year: 196

Leiden University

Rapenburg 70, NL-2311 EZ Leiden, Netherlands.

Tel: (31) 71 527 27 27
Website: www.universiteitleiden.nl/

Leiden University was founded in 1575 and is one of Europe's leading international research universities. It has seven faculties in the arts, humanities and sciences, spread over locations in Leiden and The Hague. The University has over 6,700 staff members and 29,520 students. The motto of the University is 'Praesidium Libertatis' - Bastion of Freedom

CEU-Praesidium Libertatis Scholarship

Eligibility: 1. At the time of application you must be registered as a student at CEU. 2. You must obtain your degree from CEU in the academic year prior to the start of your master's programme at Leiden University.

Level of Study: Graduate, Masters Degree

Type: Scholarship

Length of Study: 1 year

Country of Study: Any country

Application Procedure: Complete all the following steps by 12 February at the latest 1. Submit an online application for admission to one of the eligible master's programmes in Leiden University's online application portal (uSis). 2. Pay Leiden University's €100 application fee. 3. Complete the scholarship application procedure at CEU. Note that your scholarship application will only be processed if you have submitted an application for admission to one of the eligible master's programmes in Leiden University's online application portal (uSis).

Closing Date: 11 February

For further information contact:

Tel: (36) 1 327 3000 ext. 2175
Email: TorokI@ceu.edu

Children's Rights Scholarship

Purpose: The Children's Rights Scholarship is intended for students who wish to follow the Master of Laws Advanced Studies programme in International Children's Rights and meet all criteria for admission

Eligibility: To be eligible for this scholarship you must 1. be a national of a country with medium (113-151) or low (152-189) ranking on the HDI Index (see www.hdr.undp.org/en/countries) 2. lack the financial means to follow the study programme without the assistance of a scholarship. 3. be highly motivated to follow the Master of Laws Advanced Studies programme in International Children's Rights.

Level of Study: Masters Degree
Type: Scholarship
Value: There are two scholarships available, each of €15 000. The scholarship takes the form of a contribution towards the tuition fee of €18,800
Length of Study: 1 year
Country of Study: Any country
Closing Date: 1 February

For further information contact:

Email: ICRscholarships@law.leidenuniv.nl

CSC-Leiden University Scholarship

Subjects: Archaeology, Humanities, Medicine/LUMC, Governance and Global Affairs, Law, Social and Behavioural Sciences, Science, Interfacultair Centrum voor Lerarenopleiding, Onderwijsontwikkeling en Nascholing (ICLON), African Studies Centre, International Institute for Asian Studies

Purpose: The China Scholarship Council (CSC) provides scholarships for outstanding Chinese master's students, recent graduates and young (academic) professionals who want to do a full-time PhD programme at Leiden University.

Eligibility: To be eligible for a CSC-Leiden University Scholarship, you must 1. be a citizen of the People's Republic of China at the time of application 2. be between 18 and 35 years old 3. hold a Master's degree or be in the process of obtaining a Master's degree 4. be (conditionally) admitted to the relevant graduate school at Leiden University 5. have a high level of English language proficiency 6. have a letter of acceptance for a PhD programme at Leiden University 7. satisfy the CSC selection criteria

Level of Study: Masters Degree
Type: Research scholarship
Value: 1. Full waiver of the application fee and bench fee for the PhD programme 2. Full waiver of the residence permit fee 3. Living allowance of €1,350 per month (including health insurance) 4. Return ticket from China to the Netherlands and vice versa 5. One-time contribution of €500 towards the costs of a health insurance 6. Supervision and personal research programme 7. 140 hours of academic training activities (training in the candidate's specialism, conference attendance etc.) 8. 140 hours of training activities focusing on transferable skills (such as academic integrity, giving presentations, academic English, time management, career orientation, entrepreneurship etc.) 9. Participation in at least 2 (inter) national conferences and/or seminars 10. Membership of faculty social clubs for PhD candidates 11. Printing costs of the dissertation

Length of Study: 48 months
Country of Study: Any country
Closing Date: 31 March

For further information contact:

Tel: (31) 71 527 7192
Email: scholarships@sea.leidenuniv.nl

Graça Machel scholarship

Purpose: The Graça Machel scholarship is intended for female South African students who wish to follow the Master of Laws Advanced Studies programme in International Children's Rights and meet all criteria for admission.

Eligibility: To be eligible for this scholarship you must 1. be a female national of South Africa. 2. lack the financial means to follow the study programme without the assistance of a scholarship. 3. be highly motivated to follow the Master of Laws Advanced Studies programme in International Children's Rights.

Level of Study: Masters Degree
Type: Scholarship
Value: There are two scholarships available, each of €30,000. The scholarship covers the tuition fee of €18,800 plus housing and living expenses
Length of Study: 1 year
Country of Study: Any country
Closing Date: 1 April

For further information contact:

Email: childrensrights@law.leidenuniv.nl

Kuiper-Overpelt Study Fund

Subjects: Law

Purpose: The Kuiper-Overpelt Study Fund is a scholarship programme for talented students from developing countries who wish to follow the Master of Laws Advanced Studies programme in International Children's Rights and meet all criteria for admission

Eligibility: To be eligible for this scholarship you must 1. be a national of a country with medium (113-151) or low (152-189) ranking on the HDI Index (see www.hdr.undp.org/en/countries). 2. lack the financial means to follow the study programme without the assistance of a scholarship. 3. be highly motivated to follow the Master of Laws Advanced Studies programme in International Children's Rights.

Level of Study: Masters Degree

Type: Scholarship

Value: The scholarships amount to €25,000, which covers the full tuition fee of €18,800 and part of the recipient's living costs

Length of Study: 1 year

Country of Study: Any country

Closing Date: 1 February

For further information contact:

Email: childrensrights@law.leidenuniv.nl

Leiden University Excellence Scholarships (LexS)

Subjects: Archaeology, Humanities, Medicine/LUMC, Governance and Global Affairs, Law, Social and Behavioural Sciences, Science, African Studies Centre, International Institute for Asian Studies

Purpose: The Leiden University Excellence Scholarship Programme (LExS) is open to outstanding Non-EU/EEA students enrolling in a full-time master's degree programme at Leiden University.

Eligibility: Students must have achieved excellent study results in their previous education, this being relevant to the Master's programme for which they are applying. As an indication, the student is amongst the top 10% of graduates in his/her previous study programme. Note proof of ranking is not required - this information is purely to indicate the level of competitiveness. Applicants must have a non EEA passport and may not be eligible for support under the Dutch system of study grants and loans (Studiefinanciering).

Level of Study: Masters Degree

Type: Scholarships

Value: The Leiden University Excellence Scholarship programme has 3 awards 1. €10,000 of the tuition fee 2. €15,000

of the tuition fee 3. Total tuition fee minus the statutory tuition fee

Country of Study: Netherlands

Application Procedure: You must first apply online for admissions to a Master's programme at Leiden University. In your application, you must indicate clearly that you would like to apply for the LExS scholarship and upload your letter of motivation for the LExS scholarship on the scholarship page. The deadline for programmes starting in September is 1 February (exception - LLM Advanced Studies programmes 1 March) while programmes starting in February has a deadline of 1 October. It is important to visit the official website (link found below) to access the online application form and for detailed information on how to apply for this scholarship

No. of awards offered: The number and type of award of the scholarship depends on the budget available for each Faculty department.

Closing Date: 1 February

For further information contact:

Email: scholarships@sea.leidenuniv.nl

Leiden University Fund - Lutfia Rabbani Scholarship Fund

Purpose: This fund is intended for students who have demonstrated exceptional academic excellence and a strong motivation to promote Euro-Arab dialogue.

Eligibility: The scholarship is intended for students who have been admitted to a one-year Master's programme at Leiden University and who are nationals of Algeria, Bahrain, Egypt, Iraq, Jordan, Kuwait, Lebanon, Libya, Morocco, Oman, Qatar, Saudi Arabia, Palestine, Syria, Tunisia, UAE, Yemen or Sudan.

Level of Study: Masters Degree

Type: Scholarship

Value: Up to €30,000 for one academic year (maximum), depending on tuition fees and budget.

Frequency: Annual

Country of Study: Any country

Closing Date: 31 March

For further information contact:

Lutfia Rabbani Foundation, P.O. Box 352, NL-2501 CJ The Hague, Netherlands.

Tel: (31) 70 365 88 41

Email: info@rabbanifoundation.org

Leiden University South Africa scholarship - University of Cape Town

Subjects: Archaeology, Humanities, Medicine/LUMC, Governance and Global Affairs, Law, Social and Behavioural Sciences, Science, Interfacultair Centrum voor Lerarenopleiding, Onderwijsontwikkeling en Nascholing (ICLON), African Studies Centre, International Institute for Asian Studies

Purpose: This Scholarship is intended for students of the University of Cape Town, South Africa, who would like to study at Leiden University for one or two semester as part of an exchange programme.

Eligibility: Applicants must: 1. be enrolled at the University of Cape Town. 2. be preselected for a scholarship by the University of Cape Town. 3. meet the standard admission requirements for exchange/study abroad students at Leiden University.

Level of Study: Masters Degree

Type: Scholarship

Value: Living allowance: €1,000 per month

Length of Study: 5 or 10 months

Frequency: Annual

Country of Study: South Africa

Application Procedure: 1. Submit your scholarship application to the University of Cape Town. Contact Ms Erin Pienaar for information on application procedures and deadlines. 2. Submit an online application for admission for an exchange/study abroad course at Leiden University

Closing Date: 15 October

Additional Information: www.universiteitleiden.nl/en/scholarships/sea/lu-southafrica-scholarship—university-of-cape-town

For further information contact:

Tel: (31) 71 527 7192
Email: scholarships@sea.leidenuniv.nl; erin.pienaar@uct.ac.za; exchange@sea.leidenuniv.nl

Leiden University South Africa scholarship - University of Pretoria

Subjects: Archaeology, Humanities, Medicine/LUMC, Governance and Global Affairs, Law, Social and Behavioural Sciences, Science, Interfacultair Centrum voor Lerarenopleiding, Onderwijsontwikkeling en Nascholing (ICLON), African Studies Centre, International Institute for Asian Studies

Purpose: This Scholarship is intended for students of the University of Pretoria, South Africa, who would like to study at Leiden University for one or two semester(s) as part of an exchange programme.

Eligibility: Applicants must: 1. be enrolled at the University of Pretoria. 2. be preselected for a scholarship by the University of Pretoria. 3. meet the standard admission requirements for exchange/study abroad students at Leiden University.

Level of Study: Masters Degree

Type: Scholarship

Value: Living allowance: €1,000 per month

Length of Study: Up to 10 months

Frequency: Annual

Country of Study: South Africa

Additional Information: www.universiteitleiden.nl/en/scholarships/sea/leiden-university-south-africa-scholarship—university-of-pretoria

For further information contact:

Tel: (31) 71 527 7192
Email: scholarships@sea.leidenuniv.nl; Mahlogonolo.Mphahlele@up.ac.za; exchange@sea.leidenuniv.nl

Leiden University South Africa scholarship - University of the Western Cape

Subjects: Archaeology, Humanities, Medicine/LUMC, Governance and Global Affairs, Law, Social and Behavioural Sciences, Science, Interfacultair Centrum voor Lerarenopleiding, Onderwijsontwikkeling en Nascholing (ICLON), African Studies Centre, International Institute for Asian Studies

Purpose: This Scholarship is intended for students of the University of Pretoria, South Africa, who would like to study at Leiden University for one or two semester(s) as part of an exchange programme.

Eligibility: Applicants must: 1. be enrolled at the University of Pretoria. 2. be preselected for a scholarship by the University of Pretoria. 3. meet the standard admission requirements for exchange/study abroad students at Leiden University.

Level of Study: Masters Degree

Type: Scholarship

Value: Living allowance: €1,000 per month

Length of Study: Up to 10 months

Frequency: Annual

Country of Study: South Africa

Application Procedure: 1. Submit your scholarship application to the University of Pretoria. Contact the International & Postgraduate Specialist Consultant: Europe Countries, Ms Mahlogonolo Mphahlele, for information on application procedures and deadlines. 2. Submit an online application for admission for an exchange/study abroad course at Leiden University.

Closing Date: 15 October

Additional Information: www.universiteitleiden.nl/en/schol arships/sea/leiden-university-southafrica-scholarship—unive rsity-of-the-western-cape

For further information contact:

Email: Mahlogonolo.Mphahlele@up.ac.za; exchange@sea.leidenuniv.nl

LUF International Study Fund (LISF)

Subjects: Archaeology, Humanities, Medicine/LUMC, Governance and Global Affairs, Law, Social and Behavioural Sciences, Science

Purpose: Leiden University students and recent graduates sometimes miss out on the regular exchange programmes, despite having an original plan for a project abroad. The LUF International Study Fund (LISF) can help them by securing funding for their project.

Level of Study: Masters Degree

Type: Scholarship

Value: Maximum of €1,500

Frequency: Annual

Country of Study: Any country

Additional Information: www.universiteitleiden.nl/en/schol arships/sea/luf-international-study-fund-lisf

For further information contact:

Leiden University Funds, Rapenburg 68, NL-2311 EZ Leiden, Netherlands.

Tel: (31) 71 513 0503

Email: lisf@luf.leidenuniv.nl

LUF-SVM Fund

Subjects: Archaeology, Humanities, Medicine/LUMC, Governance and Global Affairs, Law, Social and Behavioural Sciences, Science, Interfacultair Centrum voor Lerarenopleiding, Onderwijsontwikkeling en Nascholing (ICLON), African Studies Centre, International Institute for Asian Studies

Purpose: The Foundation for Packaging and the Environment (SVM) is offering eight scholarships, via the Leiden University Fund (LUF), for master students writing a thesis related to the theme of packaging and the environment

Eligibility: You must be registered as a master's student at Leiden University.

Level of Study: Masters Degree

Type: Research grant

Value: €4000 per awardee

Frequency: Annual

Country of Study: Any country

Application Procedure: Submit the following documents by email to cwb@luf.leidenuniv.nl, mentioning LUF-SVM Fund in the subject line: 1. A letter of motivation in which you explain why you believe your thesis proposal is worthy of a LUF/SVM fund scholarship. 2. Your thesis proposal related to the theme of packaging and the environment which includes: a. either an analytical of technical foundation; b. creative and innovative ideas; c. a description of the intended contribution of your master's thesis to the social discussion about packaging and environment. 3. A letter of recommendation written by your Leiden University thesis supervisor.

Additional Information: www.universiteitleiden.nl/en/schol arships/sea/luf-svm-fund

For further information contact:

Email: m.heijmen@luf.leidenuniv.nl

Mandela Scholarship Fund

Subjects: Archaeology, Humanities, Medicine/LUMC, Governance and Global Affairs, Law, Social and Behavioural Sciences, Science, Interfacultair Centrum voor Lerarenopleiding, Onderwijsontwikkeling en Nascholing (ICLON), African Studies Centre, International Institute for Asian Studies

Purpose: The Mandela Scholarship is intended for South African students, who want to study at Leiden University for one semester in order to extend their knowledge and contribute to the development of South Africa.

Eligibility: Applicants must be: 1. permanent residents of South Africa. 2. enrolled at a South African University. 3. motivated to upgrade or extend their knowledge in order to make a contribution towards the development of South Africa.

Level of Study: Masters Degree

Value: Living allowance: €1000 per month

Length of Study: maximum 5 months

Country of Study: South Africa

Application Procedure: 1. Submit an online application for admission for an exchange/study abroad course at Leiden University. 2. Once you have been admitted to an exchange/study abroad course, complete the Mandela scholarship application form. 3. Submit your completed scholarship application form as scanned email attachment to: scholarships@sea. leidenuniv.nl. Make sure to attach all required documents, namely: 1. Exchange/study abroad admission letter from Leiden University 2. Scholarship motivation letter 3. Recent transcript of records from your South African University

4. Up-to-date CV 5. Photocopy of your valid passport (s) 6. Two original letters of recommendation (one of which should be from an academic staff member) 7. Documentation showing the status of any other grants you have applied for 8. Proof of sufficient funds to support yourself in the Netherlands (the Mandela scholarship does not cover all expenses). This can take form of: a. a student grant letter showing the exact amount and duration of your grant, or b. a recent bank statement in your name, or c. a notary statement declaring that your parents have sufficient financial means to support you

Closing Date: 1 October

Additional Information: www.universiteitleiden.nl/en/schol arships/sea/mandela-scholarship-fund

For further information contact:

Email: scholarships@sea.leidenuniv.nl

Minerva Scholarship Fund

Subjects: Archaeology, Humanities, Medicine/LUMC, Governance and Global Affairs, Law, Social and Behavioural Sciences, Science, Interfacultair Centrum voor Lerarenopleiding, Onderwijsontwikkeling en Nascholing (ICLON)

Purpose: The Minerva Scholarship Fund Foundation (MSF) has provided Leiden University students of all disciplines with scholarships for study and research projects. The MSF also strives to support exceptional student projects overseas.

Eligibility: 1. You are registered as a Bachelor or Master student at Leiden University. 2. You do not need to be a member of L.S.V. Minerva. 3. The application pertains to an exceptional or prestigious study or research project in the Netherlands or abroad. 4. The project falls into one of the following categories: internship, study or research. PhD tracks and complete Master programmes are not eligible.

Level of Study: Masters Degree

Type: Scholarship

Value: €900 and €2000

Frequency: Annual

Country of Study: Any country

Application Procedure: 1. Download an application form from www.minervascholarshipfund.com. 2. Complete the form. 3. Check you have all the required documents. 4. Submit your complete application dossier to the address provided, before the deadline.

Closing Date: 15 December

Additional Information: www.universiteitleiden.nl/en/schol arships/sea/minerva-scholarship-fund

For further information contact:

Email: minervascholarshipfund@lsvminerva.nl;
assessorii@lsvminerva.nl

StuNed Scholarship

Purpose: The StuNed programme provides scholarships for Indonesian professionals and recent graduates wishing to follow a master's programme in the Netherlands, with the underlying objective of strengthening both human resources in Indonesia and Dutch-Indonesian relations.

Eligibility: 1. You must be unconditionally admitted to a 1- or 2-year master's programme at Leiden University. 2. You must be an Indonesian professional with at least two years of work experience OR a recent graduate with outstanding academic and non-academic achievements. 3. Your studies must have a clear relation to the StuNed underlying objectives of strengthening human resources in Indonesia and Dutch-Indonesian relations. 4. For further requirements visit the www.nesoindonesia.or.id/beasiswa/stuned

Level of Study: Masters Degree

Type: Scholarship

Country of Study: Any country

Closing Date: 8 March

For further information contact:

Email: stunedcontact@nesoindonesia.or.id

Trustee Funds (Curatorenfondsen)

Subjects: Archaeology, Humanities, Medicine/LUMC, Governance and Global Affairs, Law, Social and Behavioural Sciences, Science, Interfacultair Centrum voor Lerarenopleiding, Onderwijsontwikkeling en Nascholing (ICLON), African Studies Centre, International Institute for Asian Studies

Purpose: Trustee funds are intended to contribute towards the study costs of students who are going abroad for a study-related activity but are unable to fund the activity without additional financial support.

Eligibility: All students of Leiden University are eligible to submit a request.

Level of Study: Masters Degree

Type: Scholarship

Value: €700

Frequency: Annual

Country of Study: Any country

Application Procedure: Submit the following documents either by email (decanen@sea.leidenuniv.nl), in person at Plexus Student Centre 1. Letter of motivation 2. Budget 3. Curriculum vitae 4. Transcript of grades 5. Letter of recommendation 6. Statement from DUO (if applicable)

Additional Information: www.universiteitleiden.nl/en/schol arships/sea/trustee-funds-curatorenfondsen

For further information contact:

Email: decanen@sea.leidenuniv.nl

Leo Baeck Institute (LBI)

15 West 16th Street (Between 5th & 6th Avenues), New York, NY 10011, United States of America.

Tel: (1) 212 744 6400/212 294 8340
Email: lbaeck@lbi.cjh.org
Website: www.lbi.org
Contact: Secretary

The Leo Baeck Institute (LBI) is a research, study and lecture centre, a library and repository for archival and art materials. It is devoted to the preservation of original materials pertaining to the history and culture of German-speaking Jewry.

John A. S. Grenville PhD Studentship in Modern Jewish History and Culture

Purpose: The studentship is named after John A. S. Grenville (1928–2011), an eminent scholar of modern world history and German Jewish history
Eligibility: Check details on website
Level of Study: Doctorate
Type: Studentship
Value: The studentship amounts to £24,000 per year, from which tuition fees (Home/European Union students £3,996 full-time/£1,998 part-time and non-European Union/overseas students £12,600 full-time/£6,300 part-time) must be paid
Length of Study: 3 years
Frequency: Annual
Country of Study: United Kingdom
Application Procedure: Information on how to apply can be found at www.history.qmul.ac.uk/postgraduate/research-degrees/how-apply

For further information contact:

Email: d.wildmann@leobaeck.co.uk

Lepra Health in Action

28 Middleborough, Essex, Colchester CO1 1TG, United Kingdom.

Tel: (44) 1206 216 700
Email: lepra@lepra.org.uk

Website: www.lepra.org.uk
Contact: Programmes Department

LEPRA is a health development international organisation working to restore health, hope and dignity to people affected by leprosy and other diseases of poverty such as malaria, tuberculosis and HIV/AIDS, among others. LEPRA is currently working in India.

Medical Elective Funding and Annual Essay Competition

Purpose: To encourage United Kingdom-based medical students wishing to undertake a leprosy assignment overseas
Eligibility: Students in the United Kingdom of any nationality. LEPRA would also like to encourage medical students to apply for the annual essay competition
Level of Study: Graduate, Postgraduate
Type: Grant
Value: Dependent on funds available and up to United Kingdom £1,000 fund for essay competition
Length of Study: Up to 3 years
Study Establishment: As appropriate to the nature of the research or training
Country of Study: Any country
Application Procedure: Applicants must complete a research application pack, available on request. Applications must be submitted using the appropriate forms and should observe the time scales involved in the approval process
No. of awards offered: 5
Funding: Individuals
No. of awards given last year: 5
No. of applicants last year: 5

For further information contact:

Email: deeptyh@leprahealthinaction.org

LeTourneau University

2100 S. Mobberly Ave, Longview, TX 75602, United States of America.

Tel: (1) 903 233 3000
Email: admissions@james.letu.edu
Contact: MBA Admissions Officer

Dual Credit Scholarship

Purpose: The Dual Credit scholarship cannot be combined with or stacked onto any previously awarded merit based scholarships from LeTourneau

Eligibility: 1. Have passed a minimum of one LETU Dual Credit course before graduating high school. 2. Classes offered the summer directly preceding attendance to LETU cannot be used to qualify for this scholarship. 3. Minimum score of 20 on the ACT or 1030 on the SAT. 4. Minimum cumulative high school GPA of 2.5 (on an unweighted 4.0 scale). 5. Enroll full-time in the residential program at the Longview campus

Level of Study: Postgraduate

Type: Scholarship

Value: US$17,000 per year

Length of Study: Up to 4 years

Frequency: Annual

Country of Study: Any country

Application Procedure: Submit your online application for admission Send in your official high school transcript Send in your official test result (ACT or SAT) LETU ACT School Code 4120 LETU SAT School Code 6365 File your FAFSA to be considered for additional financial aid LETU FAFSA School Code 003584

Funding: Private

For further information contact:

Tel: (1) 903 233 4334

Email: SharleenHunt@letu.edu

Heritage Scholarship

Purpose: The Heritage Scholarship competition is designed to find students who will make an academic, spiritual, and personal impact on our campus from orientation through graduation and beyond. This "invitation only" event brings together the top students from all over the globe to LeTourneau University's Longview campus for a time of fun and competition

Eligibility: 1. The requirements to be invited to Heritage vary by the school at LeTourneau. 2. We are looking in the range of a 3.6+ GPA, and a score of 28+ composite on the ACT or 1260+ (critical reading plus math)

Level of Study: Postgraduate

Type: Scholarship

Value: US$100,000 over four years

Length of Study: Up to four years

Frequency: Annual

Country of Study: Any country

Application Procedure: With regard to the application procedure, kindly contact the director of admissions

Funding: Private

For further information contact:

Tel: (1) 509 865 8502

Email: financial_aid@heritage.edu

Leukaemia & Lymphoma Research

Leukaemia & Lymphoma Research, 39-40 Eagle Street, London WC1R 4TH, United Kingdom.

Tel: (44) 2075 042 200

Email: info@llresearch.org.uk

Website: www.llresearch.org.uk

Leukaemia research is devoted exclusively to leukaemia, Hodgkin's disease and other lymphomas, myeloma, myelodysplastic syndromes, aplastic anaemia and the myeloproliferative disorders. We are committed to finding causes, improving and developing new treatments and diagnostic methods as well as supplying free information booklets and answering written and telephone enquiries.

The Clinical Research Training Fellowship

Purpose: To train registrar grade clinicians in research and allow them to obtain a higher degree

Eligibility: Open to researchers of any nationality who work and reside in the United Kingdom

Level of Study: Research

Type: Fellowship

Value: £50,000–£100,000

Length of Study: 1–3 years

Study Establishment: Universities, medical schools, research institutes and teaching hospitals

Country of Study: United Kingdom

Application Procedure: Applicants must complete an application form

Closing Date: July

For further information contact:

Tel: (44) 20 7405 0101

Email: sdarling@lrf.org.uk

Leukaemia Foundation

P.O.BOX 1025, Lutwyche, QLD 4030, Australia.

Tel: (61) 3 9949 5831

Email: jridge@leukaemia.org.au

Website: www.leukaemia.org.au
Contact: Jacinta Ridge, Mission and Vision Project Officer

The Leukaemia Foundation is the peak body for blood cancers and is dedicated to the care and cure of patients and families living with leukaemia, lymphoma, myeloma and related blood disorders.

Leukaemia Foundation PhD Scholarships

Purpose: The Leukaemia Foundation is helping more medical and science graduates pursue a research career in blood cancer by combining resources and working in partnership with HSANZ to co-fund PhD scholarships.
Eligibility: Open to candidates who are citizens or permanent residents of Australia
Level of Study: Doctorate
Type: Scholarships
Value: AU$40,000
Length of Study: Three years
Frequency: Annual
Study Establishment: Research Institution in Australia
Country of Study: Australia
Application Procedure: Applicants can download the application forms from the website www.leukaemia.com/web/research/fellowships_phd.php
No. of awards offered: 22
Closing Date: 14 September
Funding: Foundation, Trusts
Contributor: Leukaemia Foundation
No. of awards given last year: 10
No. of applicants last year: 22
Additional Information: All queries should be directed to Dr Anna Williamson. Please see the website for further details www.leukaemia.com/web/research/researchgrants_applications.php
study-uk.britishcouncil.org/scholarships/chevening-scholarship

For further information contact:

Tel: (61) 1800 620 420
Email: awilliamson@leukaemia.org.au

Leukaemia Foundation Postdoctoral Fellowship

Purpose: To encourage and support young researchers and to foster cutting-edge research to improve the understanding of leukaemia and related malignancies and to benefit patients and families in the short-term or long-term

Eligibility: Open to candidates who have obtained a PhD no more than 3 years before the closing date for applications. Their PhD must be obtained by December of the year of application
Level of Study: Postdoctorate
Type: Fellowship
Value: AU$100,000 (75% salary plus 25% consumables) per year
Frequency: Annual
Country of Study: Australia
Application Procedure: Applicants can download the application form from the website
Closing Date: 27 July
Funding: Foundation
Contributor: Leukaemia Foundation
Additional Information: www.global-opportunities.net/scholarships-in-new-zealand/

For further information contact:

Advocacy and Patient Care, Leukaemia Foundation, National Research Program, PO Box 2126, Windsor, QLD 4030, Australia.

Email: awilliamson@leukaemia.org.au

Leukemia & Lymphoma Society

Career Development Program - Fellow

Subjects: Leukemia and Lymphoma
Purpose: The Leukemia & Lymphoma Society (LLS) offers career development awards to postdoctoral fellows and instructors, as well as early-career independent investigators, engaging in basic, clinical, or translational research to help understand and treat hematologic malignancies and relevant premalignant condicitons. Please verify in our Guidelines & Instructions which award is appropriate for your level of experience and apply to that category of the award.
Eligibility: You must be a promising investigator with less than 2.5 years of postdoctoral research training. This award encourages you to embark on an academic career involving basic or translational research in hematologic malignancies and/or relevant premalignant conditions under a research sponsor's direction. The proposal must be directly relevant to hematological malignancies and/or relevant pre-malignant conditions. In addition, your Sponsor(s) must be have the appropriate experience to mentor you as you engage in research of direct relevance to blood cancer.
Type: Fellowship
Value: US$60,000 per year
Length of Study: Three years

Frequency: Annual
Country of Study: Any country
Application Procedure: The CDP application will be completed in 3 phases Eligibility, Abstracts, and Full Application. See online for details
Closing Date: 1 May
Additional Information: www.lls.org/research/career-development-program

Career Development Program - Special Fellow

Subjects: Leukemia and Lymphoma
Purpose: The Leukemia & Lymphoma Society (LLS) offers career development awards to postdoctoral fellows and instructors, as well as early-career independent investigators, engaging in basic, clinical, or translational research to help understand and treat hematologic malignancies and relevant premalignant condicitons.
Eligibility: You must be a promising investigator with less than 2.5 years of postdoctoral research training. This award encourages you to embark on an academic career involving basic or translational research in hematologic malignancies and/or relevant premalignant conditions under a research sponsor's direction. The proposal must be directly relevant to hematological malignancies and/or relevant pre-malignant conditions. In addition, your Sponsor(s) must be have the appropriate experience to mentor you as you engage in research of direct relevance to blood cancer.
Type: Fellowship
Value: US$67,000 per year
Length of Study: Two or three years
Frequency: Annual
Country of Study: Any country
Application Procedure: The CDP application will be completed in 3 phases Eligibility, Abstracts, and Full Application. See online for details.
Closing Date: 1 May
Additional Information: www.lls.org/research/career-development-program

Leukemia Research Foundation (LRF)

Research Grants Administrator, Leukemia Research Foundation, 191 Waukegan Road, Suite 105, Northfield, IL 60091 1064, United States of America.

Tel: (1) 847 424 0600, 888 558 5385
Email: Linda@lrfmail.org
Website: www.allbloodcancers.org
Contact: Linda Kabot, Director of Programs

The Leukemia Research Foundation (LRF) was established in 1946. It aims to conquer leukemia, lymphoma and myelodysplastic syndromes by funding research into their causes and cures and to enrich the quality of life of those touched by these diseases.

Leukemia Research Foundation New Investigator Research Grant

Purpose: To enable an investigator to initiate and develop a project sufficiently to obtain continued funding from national agencies
Eligibility: Preference given to proposals that focus on leukemia, lymphoma and MDS. New Investigators are considered to be within seven years of their first independent position. Years as a resident physician, fellow physician, or post-doctoral fellow are considered to be training years. Questions regarding eligibility should be directed to our Research Grants Administrator. See the website for details regarding eligibility
Level of Study: Postgraduate
Type: Grant
Value: US$100,000
Length of Study: 1 year
Frequency: Annual
Country of Study: United States of America
Application Procedure: Applicants must submit application form, references, self-addressed stamped envelope and one paragraph abstract in lay terms
No. of awards offered: 73
Closing Date: 5 April
Funding: Private
Contributor: Leukaemia Research Foundation
No. of awards given last year: 10
No. of applicants last year: 73

For further information contact:

Leukemia Research Foundation, 820 Davis Street, Suite #420, IL 60201, United States of America.

Tel: (1) 847 424 0600
Fax: (1) 847 424 0606
Email: Info@LRFMail.org

Leverhulme Trust

Research Awards Advisory Committee, 1 Pemberton Row, London EC4A 3BG, United Kingdom.

Tel: (44) 2070 429 861
Email: agrundy@leverhulme.ac.uk

Website: www.leverhulme.ac.uk
Contact: Miss Anna Grundy, Grants Manger

The Trust, established by the Will of William Hesketh Lever, makes awards for the support of research and education. The Trust emphasizes individuals and encompasses all subject areas.

Early Career Fellowships

Purpose: The Fellowships are intended to assist those at a relatively early stage of their academic careers, and it is hoped that the appointment would lead to a more permanent position for the individual, either within the same or another institution
Eligibility: See website
Value: The Trust will contribute 100% of each Fellow's total salary costs up to a maximum of £50,000 in year one of the award. The Trust will then contribute 50% of the Fellow's total salary costs up to a maximum of £25,000 in years two and three, with the balance to be paid by the host institution. The Trust's maximum annual contribution will be pro-rated if the Fellowship is held on a part-time basis. Each Fellow may request up to £6,000 per annum in research expenses to further his or her research activities.
Country of Study: Any country
Closing Date: 24 February
Additional Information: www.leverhulme.ac.uk/early-career-fellowships

For further information contact:

Tel: (44) 20 7042 9863

Emeritus Fellowships

Purpose: The primary intention of the scheme is to support the facilitation, integration or completion of the applicant's own research output, rather than generally further support for his or her research group or research assistants.
Eligibility: See website
Level of Study: Research
Type: Fellowship
Value: The maximum value of a Fellowship is £24,000, to cover research expenses.
Length of Study: 3 and 24 months.
Frequency: Annual
Country of Study: Any country
Closing Date: May

Additional Information: www.leverhulme.ac.uk/emeritus-fellowships

For further information contact:

Anna Grundy.

Tel: (44) 20 7042 9861

International Fellowships

Eligibility: See website
Type: Fellowship
Value: The maximum value of a Fellowship is £50,000.
Length of Study: 3 and 24 months
Frequency: Annual
Country of Study: Any country
Additional Information: www.leverhulme.ac.uk/international_fellowships

For further information contact:

Bridget Kerr.

Tel: (44) 20 7042 9862

Leverhulme International Professorships

Purpose: The Trust has allocated at least £100 million over five years to fund these grants. Grants are for a period of five years.
Eligibility: Eligible institutions are universities in the UK. There are no restrictions on nationality of the professorial candidate but they must be working outside the UK at the time of application. Applications cannot be made retrospectively. Universities are expected to be actively engaged in the recruitment process at the time of the grant. Where an employment contract has already been signed, the candidate cannot be considered in this competition.
Type: Grant
Value: Up to £5 million for staff salaries and associated costs
Length of Study: 5 years
Frequency: Annual
Country of Study: Any country
Application Procedure: See website
Closing Date: 27 May
Additional Information: www.leverhulme.ac.uk/leverhulme-international-professorships

For further information contact:

Katharyn Lanaro.

Tel: (44) 20 7042 9878

Philip Leverhulme Prizes

Purpose: Philip Leverhulme Prizes have been offered since 2001 in commemoration of the contribution to the work of the Trust made by Philip Leverhulme, the Third Viscount Leverhulme and grandson of William Hesketh Lever, the founder of the Trust.

Eligibility: Nominees must hold either a permanent post or a long-term fellowship in a UK institution of higher education or research that would extend beyond the duration of the Philip Leverhulme Prize. Those otherwise without salary are not eligible to be nominated. Nominees should normally have been awarded their doctoral degree not more than ten years prior to the closing date for nominations. The award date is considered to be the date on which the degree was confirmed by the awarding institution. Prizes are awarded to individuals. The Trust Board will not consider making an award where two (or more) nominations are received for substantially the same body of work.

Level of Study: Masters Degree
Type: Prize
Value: Each prize is worth £100,000
Length of Study: 2 to 3 years
Frequency: Annual
Country of Study: Any country
Additional Information: www.leverhulme.ac.uk/philip-leverhulme-prizes

Research Fellowships

Purpose: Research Fellowships are open to experienced researchers, particularly those who are or have been prevented by routine duties from completing a programme of original research.

Eligibility: Applicants must: 1. hold a post in a UK institution of higher education, or in a museum, art gallery or comparable institution that will extend beyond the duration of the Fellowship 2. be experienced researchers, particularly those prevented by routine duties from undertaking or completing a research programme 3. be resident in the UK at the time of application 4. be a permanent member of the UK scholarly community and able to demonstrate an established track record in their chosen area of research

Level of Study: Masters Degree
Type: Fellowship
Value: The maximum value of a Fellowship is £60,000.
Length of Study: 3 and 24 months
Frequency: Annual
Country of Study: Any country
Closing Date: April
Additional Information: www.leverhulme.ac.uk/research-fellowships

For further information contact:

Anna Grundy.

Tel: (44) 20 7042 9861

Research Leadership Awards

Purpose: The aim is to support talented scholars who have successfully launched a university career but who need to build a research team of sufficient scale to tackle a distinctive research problem.

Eligibility: To be eligible to apply for the Research Leadership Awards scheme you must at the time of application: 1. Have had at least 2 years full-time or equivalent experience in a research and/or teaching post in a university after the date of your PhD award 2. Be at an early stage of your academic career such that the trajectory of your research contribution has not become firmly established 3. Have a contract with a university in the UK that extends beyond the end of the grant award (i.e. beyond 2027 for 4 year awards and 2028 for 5 year awards)

Level of Study: Masters Degree
Type: Award
Value: Up to £1 million
Length of Study: 4 to 5 years
Country of Study: Any country
Application Procedure: See website
Closing Date: 10 June
Additional Information: www.leverhulme.ac.uk/research-leadership-awards

For further information contact:

Tel: (44) 20 7042 9878
Email: grants@leverhulme.ac.uk

Research Project Grants

Purpose: For researchers based at universities, institutions of higher education or registered charities with university-equivalent research capacity, to undertake an innovative and original research project

Eligibility: See Website
Level of Study: Research
Type: Grant
Value: The maximum grant value is £500,000.
Length of Study: Up to five years
Frequency: Annual
Country of Study: Any country
Closing Date: 21 March

Additional Information: www.leverhulme.ac.uk/research-project-grants

For further information contact:

Tel: (44) 20 7042 9873

Study Abroad Studentship

Purpose: For students to study or undertake research at a centre of learning in any country except the UK or USA
Eligibility: Applicants must: 1. have been resident in the UK for at least three years at the time of application 2. hold an undergraduate degree (undergraduates are not eligible) 3. hold a degree from a UK institution (this may be either the undergraduate degree or a further degree held by the applicant). Those studying for a UK PhD who do not otherwise hold a degree from a UK institution may apply as long as they meet the other eligibility criteria 4. either be a student at the time of application or have been registered as a student within the last eight years 5. explain why their work requires residence overseas
Level of Study: Doctorate, Graduate, Postdoctorate, Postgraduate, Postgraduate (MSc), Predoctorate
Type: Studentship
Value: £21,000
Length of Study: 12–24 months
Frequency: Annual
Country of Study: Worldwide
Application Procedure: The 2023 round of awards will open in early September. Closing date in early January.
No. of awards offered: 25
Closing Date: May
Funding: Trusts
Contributor: The Leverhulme Trust
No. of awards given last year: 33
No. of applicants last year: 108

For further information contact:

Tel: (44) 2070429862

Visiting Professorships

Eligibility: Applications must be made by a member of academic staff, based in a UK university or other higher education institution, who will be responsible for coordinating the visit. The host academic's employing institution must also agree to administer the grant, if awarded, and to provide appropriate facilities for the Visiting Professor. Visitors who have previously held a Leverhulme Visiting Professorship can only apply if at least 7 years have elapsed since the last

one. The over-riding criteria for selection are: 1. the academic standing and achievements of the visitors in terms of their research and/or teaching 2. their potential for making a substantial contribution to skills in the host institution 3. the specific and systematic nature of the proposed programme while in the UK In special circumstances, the Trust Board is prepared to consider candidates who do not hold a university post. Collaborative research alone will not be a sufficient justification for a grant. The emphasis should be on the diffusion of skills and expertise. Priority will be given to new or recent collaborative ventures. Where a visit builds on an existing collaboration, the host should explain what the visit(s) will achieve over and above past outcomes. It is the intention that the visitor will provide a degree of expertise that is not otherwise available within the UK research base. Visiting Professors will be expected to offer a short course of "Leverhulme Lectures" to mark their residence in a UK institution. The Trust will not fund applications for research of which advocacy forms an explicit component. The Trust does not support research which is aimed principally at an immediate commercial application. The Trust will not fund applications in which the balance between assembling a data bank or database and the related subsequent research is heavily inclined to the former.
Level of Study: Masters Degree
Value: Minimum of £10,000 and a maximum of £150,000
Length of Study: 3 and 12 months
Frequency: Annual
Country of Study: Any country
Closing Date: 5 May
Additional Information: www.leverhulme.ac.uk/visiting-professorships

Library Company of Philadelphia

1314 Locust Street, Philadelphia, PA 19107, United States of America.

Tel: (1) 215 546 3181
Email: jgreen@librarycompany.org
Website: www.librarycompany.org
Contact: Fellowship Office

Founded in 1731, the Library Company of Philadelphia was the largest public library in America until the 1850s and contains printed materials on aspects of American culture and society in that period. It is a research library with a collection of 500,000 books, pamphlets, newspapers and periodicals, 75,000 prints, maps and photographs and 150,000 manuscripts.

Library Company of Philadelphia Dissertation Fellowships

Purpose: To promote scholarship by offering long-term dissertation fellowships
Eligibility: The fellowship Supports dissertation research in the collections of the Library Company and other Philadelphia repositones
Level of Study: Doctorate
Type: Fellowship
Value: US$25,000
Length of Study: 4–5 months
Frequency: As available
Country of Study: Any country
Application Procedure: Candidates are encouraged to enquire about the appropriateness of a proposed topic before applying. See website under fellowships
No. of awards offered: 45
Closing Date: 1 March
Funding: Private
No. of awards given last year: 6
No. of applicants last year: 45

For further information contact:

Email: fellowships@librarycompany.org

Library Company of Philadelphia Postdoctoral Research Fellowship

Purpose: To promote scholarship by offering long-term post-doctoral and advanced research fellowships
Eligibility: The fellowship supports both postdoctoral and advanced research in the collections of the Library Company and often Philadelphia repositories. Applicants must hold a doctoral degree
Level of Study: Postdoctorate, Research
Type: Fellowship
Value: US$40,000
Length of Study: 4.5 months (1 semester)
Frequency: Twice a year
Study Establishment: An independent research library
Country of Study: United States of America
Application Procedure: Candidates are encouraged to enquire about the appropriateness of a proposed topic before applying.
Closing Date: 1 November
Funding: Government, Private
Contributor: National Endowment for the Humanities; Andrew W Mellon Foundation

For further information contact:

Email: eguthrie@librarycompany.org

National Endowment for the Humanities Post-Doctoral Fellowships

Purpose: National Endowment for the Humanities Post-Doctoral Fellowships support research in residence at the Library Company on any subject relevant to its collections, which are capable of supporting research in a variety of fields and disciplines relating to the history of America and the Atlantic world form the 17th through the 19th centuries. NEH Fellowships are for individuals who have completed their formal professional training. Consequently, degree candidates and individuals seeking support for work in pursuit of a degree are not eligible to hold NEH-supported fellowships. Advanced degree candidates must have completed all requirements
Eligibility: NEH Fellowships are for individuals who have completed their formal professional training. Consequently, degree candidates and individuals seeking support for work in pursuit of a degree are not eligible to hold NEH-supported fellowships. Advanced degree candidates must have completed all requirements, except for the actual conferral of the degree, by the application deadline
Level of Study: Postdoctorate
Type: Fellowship
Value: The stipend is US$5,000 per month.
Length of Study: four to nine months
Frequency: Annual
Country of Study: Any country
Closing Date: 1 November

For further information contact:

Tel: (1) 215 546 3181
Email: jgreen@librarycompany.org

Program in Early American Economy and Society (PEAES) Post-Doctoral Fellowships

Purpose: The fellowships provide scholars the opportunity to investigate the history of commerce, finance, technology, manufacturing, agriculture, internal improvements, economic policy making and other topics.
Eligibility: Applicants may be citizens of any country, and they must hold a PhD.
Level of Study: Postdoctorate
Type: Fellowships
Value: The stipend is US$50,000 for the academic year or US$25,000 per semester
Country of Study: Any country
Closing Date: 1 September

Life Sciences Research Foundation (LSRF)

Life Sciences Research Foundation, PO Box 1482, Cockeysville, MD 21030-7482, United States of America.

Email: admin@lsrf.org
Website: www.lsrf.org

The Life Sciences Research Foundation (LSRF) solicits monies from industry, foundations and individuals to support postdoctoral fellowships in the life sciences. The LSRF recognizes that discoveries and the application of innovations in biology for the public's good will depend upon the training and support of the highest quality young scientists in the very best research environments. The LSRF awards fellowships across the spectrum of life sciences: biochemistry, cell, developmental, molecular, plant, structural, organismic population and evolutionary biology, endocrinology, immunology, microbiology, neurobiology, physiology and virology.

Life Sciences Research Foundation

Purpose: Three-year fellowships will be awarded on a competitive basis to graduates of medical and graduate schools in the biological sciences holding M.D., PhD, D.V.M. or D.D.S. degrees. Awards will be based solely on the quality of the individual applicant's previous accomplishments, and on the merit of the proposal for postdoctoral research. Persons doing a second postdoc are eligible only if they are transferring to a different supervisor's laboratory and embarking on a new project not connected to their previous research. All U.S. citizens are eligible to apply with no geographic restriction on the laboratory of their choice. Foreign applicants will be eligible for study in U.S. laboratories. LSRF fellows must carry out their research at nonprofit institutions. LSRF fellows may change projects, laboratories, and/or institutions during the fellowship as long as the eligibility rules listed here are not violated. A person holding a faculty appointment is not eligible to apply for an LSRF fellowship
Eligibility: Must be post-doctorals with less than five years from time of PhD awarded
Level of Study: Postdoctorate
Type: One fellowship
Value: US$58,000 stipend per year
Length of Study: 3 years
Frequency: Annual
Country of Study: Any country

Application Procedure: Application must be completed online
No. of awards offered: 800
Closing Date: 1 October
Funding: Foundation
No. of awards given last year: 27
No. of applicants last year: 800

Life Sciences Research Foundation Postdoctoral Fellowships

Purpose: Three-year fellowships will be awarded on a competitive basis to graduates of medical and graduate schools in the biological sciences holding M.D., PhD, D.V.M. or D.D.S. degrees. Awards will be based solely on the quality of the individual applicant's previous accomplishments, and on the merit of the proposal for postdoctoral research. Persons doing a second postdoc are eligible only if they are transferring to a different supervisor's laboratory and embarking on a new project not connected to their previous research. All U.S. citizens are eligible to apply with no geographic restriction on the laboratory of their choice. Foreign applicants will be eligible for study in U.S. laboratories. LSRF fellows must carry out their research at nonprofit institutions. LSRF fellows may change projects, laboratories, and/or institutions during the fellowship as long as the eligibility rules listed here are not violated. A person holding a faculty appointment is not eligible to apply for an LSRF fellowship.
Eligibility: Open to researchers of any nationality, who are graduates of medical or graduate schools in the biological sciences and who hold an MD or PhD degree. Awards will be based solely on the quality of the individual applicant's previous accomplishments and on the merit of the proposal for postdoctoral research
Level of Study: Postdoctorate
Type: Fellowship
Value: US$57,000 per year. The salary scale begins at US$43,000 for a first-year postdoctoral, US$45,000 for a second year, and US$47,000 thereafter. The fellow, not the advisor, will control expenditure of the remainder. It can be used for fringe benefits (up to US$2,000 per year), travel to the host institution, travel to visit the sponsor and to the LSRF annual meeting. However, its main purpose is to support the fellow
Length of Study: 3 years
Frequency: Annual
Study Establishment: Appropriate research institutions
Country of Study: Any country
Application Procedure: Electronic submission only. Please check website
No. of awards offered: 820

Closing Date: 1 January
Funding: Private
No. of awards given last year: 16
No. of applicants last year: 820
Additional Information: LSRF Fellows must carry out their research at non-profit institutions. The fellowship cannot be used to support research that has any patent commitment or other kind of agreement with a commercial profit-making company. Please see the website for further details www. lsrf.org/resources/resources-detail-view/LSRF-Awards-Postdoctoral-Fellowships

Linacre College

Linacre College, St. Cross Road, Oxford OX1 3JA, United Kingdom.

Tel:	(1) 1865 271650
Email:	accommodation@linacre.ox.ac.uk
Website:	www.linacre.ox.ac.uk

Brewer Street Scholarship

Subjects: Engineering
Purpose: The Brewer Street Scholarship was set up by former residents of Linacre accommodation in Brewer Street. Although the buildings are no longer in use by Linacre, this scholarship ensures that the Brewer Street name lives on in perpetuity. It is awarded on a competitive basis to an outstanding student who has gained a place at Oxford University.
Type: Scholarship
Value: £4,100
Length of Study: One year
Frequency: Annual
Country of Study: Any country
Application Procedure: Eligible students are automatically considered for this award.
No. of awards offered: 1

Carolyn and Franco Gianturco Scholarship in Music

Subjects: Musicology/Music
Purpose: Carolyn and Franco Gianturco Scholarship in Music is awarded to students reading or intending to read for a postgraduate degree in Musicology-related topics (not intended for performers or composers)
Type: Scholarship
Value: Full course fees and a stipend for living expenses

Length of Study: Period of fee liability
Frequency: Annual
Country of Study: Any country
Application Procedure: Eligible students are automatically considered for this award.
No. of awards offered: 1

Carolyn and Franco Gianturco Scholarship in Theoretical Chemistry

Purpose: The Department will select a scholarship holder from among all eligible students reading, or intending to read, for a Theoretical Chemistry degree (Theoretical and/or Computational Chemical Physics)
Level of Study: Masters Degree
Type: Scholarship
Value: £3,300
Length of Study: 3 years
Frequency: Annual
Country of Study: Any country
Application Procedure: Eligible candidates are automatically considered for this scholarship.
Closing Date: 2 March
Funding: Private

For further information contact:

St. Cross Road, Oxford OX1 3JA, United Kingdom.

Tel:	(44) 1865 271 650
Email:	support@linacre.ox.ac.uk

Clarendon Canadian National Scholarship

Subjects: Any
Purpose: This scholarship is open for students of Canadian nationality reading or intending to read for a postgraduate degree. The Canadian National Scholarship is generously funded by Canadian National, which operates Canada's largest railroad system.
Eligibility: The Scholar must have been admitted as a postgraduate student by a relevant Faculty of Oxford University, and must be, or become, a member of Linacre College.
Type: Scholarship
Value: £16,000.00
Length of Study: One year
Frequency: Annual
Country of Study: Canada
No. of awards offered: 1

Dapo Olagunju Scholarship

Subjects: MBA

Purpose: The scholarship has been funded by Mr Dapo Olagunju, who himself studied for an MBA when he was at Linacre, and is currently Managing Director for J P Morgan, West Africa. The scholarship is the sixth available for African students at Linacre, and is the first scholarship to be funded from Africa itself.

Eligibility: Open to candidates from Africa (with a preference for Nigeria) applying for the MBA. Eligible candidates who apply for a place on the MBA course will automatically be considered by the Saïd Business School Graduate Studies Board; no separate application is required. Any African country

Type: Scholarship

Value: £3,500

Length of Study: One year

Country of Study: Any country

Application Procedure: Eligible students are automatically considered for this award.

No. of awards offered: 1

Eldred Scholarship

Purpose: The Eldred Scholarship at Linacre College was established in 2012. It funds students from sub-Saharan Africa to study the MSc African Studies at Oxford

Eligibility: 1. You should be applying to start the MSc African Studies at Oxford and you must be ordinarily resident in sub-Saharan Africa. 2. You should be intending to return to your country of ordinary residence once your course is completed. Scholarships will be awarded on the basis of academic merit

Level of Study: Postgraduate (MSc)

Type: Scholarship

Value: £7,000. 100% of University and college fees, a grant for living costs and a return flight from your home country to United Kingdom

Frequency: Annual

Country of Study: Any country

Application Procedure: To apply this scholarship you don't need to provide a separated application for applying this scholarship. You are only required to apply the graduate study at the university

Funding: Private

For further information contact:

13 Bevington Rd, Oxford OX2 6LH, United Kingdom.

Email: african.studies@africa.ox.ac.uk

EPA Cephalosporin Scholarship

Subjects: Biological, medical & chemical sciences.

Purpose: The EPA Cephalosporin Scholarship is awarded in partnership with the Doctoral Training Centre and is tenable for one year

Level of Study: Doctorate

Type: Scholarship

Value: Full course fees and a stipend for living expenses

Length of Study: Period of fee liability

Frequency: Annual

Country of Study: Any country

Application Procedure: No separate application is required and eligible candidates are automatically considered for this scholarship.

No. of awards offered: 2

Norman & Ivy Lloyd Scholarship/Commonwealth Shared Scholarship

Subjects: Biodiversity, Conservation and Management; Environmental Change and Management; Water Science, Policy and Management

Purpose: The Norman and Ivy Lloyd Scholarship is jointly funded by Dr Keith Lloyd, in memory of his parents, and the Commonwealth Shared Scholarship scheme. It is available to support a student from any developing sub-Saharan African country wishing to study for one of the following MSc courses: Biodiversity, Conservation and Management; Water Science, Policy and Management; and Environmental Change and Management.

Level of Study: Masters Degree

Type: Scholarship

Value: Full course fees and a living expenses stipend

Length of Study: One year

Frequency: Annual

Country of Study: Any country

Application Procedure: Apply directly to Commonwealth Scholarship Commission (CSC) via website: cscuk.fcdo.gov.uk/scholarships/commonwealth-shared-scholarships-2022/

No. of awards offered: 1

Oxford Commonwealth Trapnell Scholarship

Subjects: Biodiversity, Conservation and Management; Environmental Change and Management; Water Science, Policy and Management

Purpose: The Trapnell Scholarship is a Commonwealth Shared Scholarship for a student from a developing African Commonwealth country to study an MSc on one of the following programmes: Biodiversity, Conservation and

Management; Water Science, Policy and Management; and Environmental Change and Management.

Level of Study: Masters Degree
Type: Scholarship
Value: Full course fees and a living expenses stipend
Length of Study: One year
Frequency: Annual
Country of Study: Any country
Application Procedure: Apply directly to Commonwealth Scholarship Commission (CSC) via website: cscuk.fcdo.gov.uk/scholarships/commonwealth-shared-scholarships-2022/
No. of awards offered: 1

School of Geography and the Environment Commonwealth Shared Scholarship

Subjects: Water Science, Policy & Management
Purpose: The scholarship is jointly funded by the School of Geography and the Environment(link is external) and the Commonwealth Shared Scholarship scheme.
Level of Study: Masters Degree
Type: Scholarship
Value: Full course fees and a living expenses stipend
Length of Study: One year
Frequency: Annual
Country of Study: Any country
Application Procedure: Apply directly to Commonwealth Scholarship Commission (CSC) via website: cscuk.fcdo.gov.uk/scholarships/commonwealth-shared-scholarships-2022/
No. of awards offered: 1

Showa Denko Environmental Scholarship

Subjects: Environmental Change and Management
Eligibility: Students who have applied for a place on the MSc in Environmental Change and Management are automatically considered for this scholarship. Preference will be given to a student from Sub-Saharan Africa or South America, but students with limited resources from other countries are not excluded.
Level of Study: Masters Degree
Type: Scholarship
Value: £9,500
Length of Study: One year
Frequency: Annual
Country of Study: United Kingdom
Application Procedure: Eligible students are automatically considered for this award
No. of awards offered: 1
Funding: Private

For further information contact:

Oxford University Centre for the Environment, Environmental Change Institute, South Parks Road, Oxford OX1 3QY, United Kingdom.

Lincoln Memorial University

School of Graduate Studies, Cumberland Gap Parkway, Harrogate, TN 37752, United States of America.

Tel: (1) 423 869 3611
Email: graduate@inetlmu.lmunet.edu
Contact: MBA Admissions Officer

Fulbright - Platinum Triangle Scholarship in Entrepreneurship

Purpose: The Fulbright Platinum Triangle Scholarship in Entrepreneurship is for a talented New Zealander in a knowledge economy-related fields to complete a Masters degree in the United States of America
Eligibility: New Zealand Citizen or Permanent Resident Students
Level of Study: Postgraduate
Type: Award
Length of Study: 4 year
Frequency: Varies
Application Procedure: Apply online www.fulbright.org.nz
Closing Date: 1 August
Funding: Foundation
Additional Information: For more information visit Fulbright: www.fulbright.org.nz/

For further information contact:

Email: info@fulbright.org.nz

Sasakawa Young Leaders Fellowship Fund Research Scholarship - Masters and PhD

Purpose: Applicants must be New Zealand Citizens of Permanent residents and be studying in the fields of Humanities or Social Sciences (or other areas provided the research has a Humanities/Social Science angle)
Eligibility: New Zealand Citizen or Permanent Resident Students
Level of Study: Postdoctorate
Type: Scholarship
Value: NZ$25,000

Frequency: Annual
Country of Study: New Zealand
Closing Date: 1 October
Funding: Foundation

For further information contact:

Email: info@lincoln.ac.nz

Zespri Innovation Scholarships

Purpose: The kiwifruit industry is New Zealand's largest horticultural exporter and Zespri is the leading global kiwifruit marketer. The Zespri Innovation Scholarships are offered to build awareness of the kiwifruit industry as an exciting career option, to encourage further research into kiwifruit and related fields and finally to encourage capability building
Eligibility: 1. New Zealand Citizen or Permanent Resident Students. 2. International Students
Level of Study: Postgraduate
Type: Scholarship
Value: Masters NZ$20,000pa (stipend) plus university fees PhD NZ$30,000pa (stipend) plus university fees
Length of Study: 1 year
Frequency: Annual
Country of Study: Any country
Application Procedure: Apply online www.zespri.com/Pages/InnovationScholarship.aspx
Closing Date: 31 July
Funding: Foundation

For further information contact:

Innovation Coordinator, 400 Maunganui Road, PO Box 4043, Mount Maunganui 3149, New Zealand.

Email: corporate.communications@zespri.com

Zonta International Canterbury Tertiary Education Scholarship

Purpose: To assist women in their completion of a tertiary course of study
Eligibility: New Zealand citizens who are living in Canterbury, or permanent residents
Level of Study: Graduate
Type: Grant
Value: NZ$3,000
Frequency: Annual
Country of Study: New Zealand
Application Procedure: Send the application to the address as mentioned in the address field

Closing Date: 10 March
Funding: Private

For further information contact:

Zonta International Canterbury Tertiary Education Scholarship, C/- Zonta Club of Christchurch South, PO Box 25196, Christchurch 8144, New Zealand.

Email: info@lincoln.ac.nz

Linnean Society of New South Wales

PO Box 137, Matraville, NSW 2036, Australia.

Tel: (61) 2 9662 6196
Email: linnsoc@acay.com.au
Website: www.acay.com.au/linnsoc
Contact: Grants Management Award

The Linnean Society of New South Wales is concerned with the publication of original scientific research papers and the encouragement of scientific research through grants and public lectures.

The Betty Mayne Scientific Research Fund for Earth Sciences

Purpose: The Linnean Society seeks donations from individuals, institutions or organisations sympathetic to the purposes for which the fund is currently being used. All such donations, which are tax-deductible, will be gratefully received by the Linnean Society of New South Wales and used to support original scientific research in Australasia. Give yourself a tax break and help a struggling research student, as most of the funds go to students
Eligibility: 1. Applications will be accepted from postgraduate students at recognised Australian Universities who are undertaking full-time or part-time higher degree studies with a geological emphasis. 2. Students enrolled in Honours degree courses at recognised Australian Universities, whether full- or part-time, may also be considered for an award. 3. Applications are also encouraged from amateur or professional geologists, whether in employment as such or not, who can demonstrate a level of achievement in original research in Earth Sciences, for example through a record of publications on the subject. 4. Projects proposed for support do not have to be restricted to Australian locations or specimens, but, given the Society's interests in the natural history of Australia, they

must demonstrate a strong Australian context 5. Money must be used for research purposes, which may include the purchase of equipment, laboratory, photographic or other consumables, and fieldwork or travel within Australasia

Level of Study: Graduate, Postgraduate
Type: Residency grant
Value: US$2,500
Closing Date: 1 March

For further information contact:

Email: secretary@linneansocietynsw.org.au

The Joyce W. Vickery Research Fund

Purpose: Grants from the Joyce W. Vickery Research Fund are intended to support worthy research in those fields of the Biological Sciences that fall within the range of interests of the Society, especially natural history research within Australia.
Level of Study: postgraduate and Honours degree
Value: Individual grants will not normally exceed US$2,500 for Members and US$1,500 for non-members
Frequency: Annual
Application Procedure: Applicants should email their signed applications
Closing Date: 1 March
Additional Information: linneansocietynsw.org.au/Vickery_Fund/Vickery_Fund.html

For further information contact:

Email: secretary@linneansocietynsw.org.au

Lock Heed Martin

Lockheed Martin Corporation Scholarship for Freshmen

Purpose: Lockheed Martin has launched a new scholarship program to provide opportunities to students who want to build their talents and change the world
Eligibility: 1. Applicants must not be receiving full funding for education (tuition, fees, and books or equivalent) from their school or another organization (e.g. members of the Armed Services attending United States military academies, students receiving full reimbursement from an employer). 2. Applicants must be enrolled in a program accredited by ABET. Accreditation information for specific programs is available online at main.abet.org/aps/Accreditedprogramsearch.aspx

Level of Study: Graduate
Type: Scholarship
Value: US$40,000 per student
Length of Study: 4 years
Frequency: Throughout the year
Country of Study: Any country
Application Procedure: This award is being provided by Society of Women Engineers (SWE). Applicants to the Lockheed Martin STEM Scholarship Program must meet the following eligibility requirements 1. United States Citizens. 2. Current high school seniors with a cumulative 3.5 or above GPA, or current college freshmen or sophomores with a cumulative 3.0 or above GPA. 3. Planning to enroll full-time at an accredited four-year college or university in the United States
No. of awards offered: 200
Closing Date: 1 April
Funding: Private
No. of applicants last year: 200

For further information contact:

130 East Randolph Street, Suite 3500, Chicago, IL 60601, United States of America.

London Goodenough Association of Canada

P.O. Box 5896, Toronto, ON M5W 1P3, Canada.

Email: admin@lgac.ca
Website: www.lgac.ca
Contact: Brian Cardie, Administrator

The London Goodenough Association of Canada (LGAC) is an association of Canadians who lived as graduate students at Goodebnough College in Mecklenburgh Square, London. The LGAC offers member events and provides a Scholarship Programme for Canadian graduate students studying in London and staying in London House or William Goodenough, the Goodenough College residence halls.

London Goodenough Association of Canada Scholarship Program

Purpose: To support Canadian nationals who wish to pursue their higher studies in London
Eligibility: Open to candidates who are full-time students enroled in an accredited graduate programme in London or undertaking theses research in London while enroled elsewhere

Level of Study: Postgraduate, Research
Type: Scholarships
Value: £6,000 each
Frequency: Annual
Study Establishment: The London Goodenough Association of Canada
Country of Study: United Kingdom
Application Procedure: Application form can be downloaded from the website. Candidates must also arrange to have all post-secondary institution transcripts and 3 letters of reference sent to the address below
Closing Date: 25 January
Funding: Foundation, Individuals
No. of applicants last year: 240
Additional Information: For further information contact Dr Kathleen McCrone at the above address. Please see the website for further details www.lgac.ca/scholarships

For further information contact:

The London Goodenough Association of Canada, Paul Zed, Chair, P.O. Box 5896, STN A, Toronto, ON M5W 1P3, Canada.

Email: admin@lgac.ca

London Mathematical Society

De Morgan House, 57-58 Russell Square, London WC1B 4HS, United Kingdom.

Tel: (44) 20 7637 3686
Email: lms@lms.ac.uk
Website: www.lms.ac.uk

The United Kingdom national learned society for the promotion and extension of mathematical knowledge, by means of publishing, grants, meetings and contribution to national debate on mathematics, research and education.

Cecil King Travel Scholarship

Purpose: To enable a young mathematician of outstanding promise to spend a period of 3 months undertaking study or research overseas
Eligibility: Nationals of the United Kingdom or Republic of Ireland, having recently completed a doctoral degree at a United Kingdom. university
Level of Study: Postdoctorate, Postgraduate

Type: Scholarship
Value: £6,000
Length of Study: 3 months
Frequency: Annual
Study Establishment: University or research institute
Country of Study: Any country
Application Procedure: Application forms are available on request from the society or can be downloaded from the website. Applications should be returned by post or email to Duncan Turton
Closing Date: 15 November
Funding: Trusts
Contributor: Cecil King Memorial Fund
No. of awards given last year: 2

For further information contact:

London Mathematical Society, De Morgan House, 57-58 Russell Square, Holborn, London WC1B 4HS, United Kingdom.

Email: Fellowships@lms.ac.uk

LMS Early Career Fellowships 2021-22 with support from the Heilbronn Institute for Mathematical Research (HIMR) and UKRI

Purpose: To support early career mathematicians in the transition between PhD and a postdoctoral position, the London Mathematical Society offers up to 8 Fellowships of between 3 and 6 months to mathematicians who have recently or will shortly receive their PhD.
Type: Scholarship
Country of Study: Any country
No. of awards offered: £1,300 per month plus a travel allowance
Closing Date: 14 January

For further information contact:

Email: fellowships@lms.ac.uk

London Metropolitan University

London Metropolitan University, 166-220 Holloway Road, London N7 8DB, United Kingdom.

Tel: (44) 20 7423 0000
Email: info@canoncollins.org.uk
Website: www.londonmet.ac.uk

London Metropolitan University is one of Britain's largest universities, which offers a wide variety of courses in a huge range of subject areas. The University aims to provide education and training that will help students to achieve their potential and London to succeed us a world city.

Canon Collins Trust Scholarships

Purpose: The key aim of the Scholarships Programme is to help build the human resources necessary for economic, social and cultural development in the southern African region and to develop an educated and skilled workforce that can benefit the wider community. Canon Collins Trust scholarship holders are thus expected to use the knowledge, training and skills acquired through their studies to contribute positively to the development of their home country

Eligibility: Open to nationals of South Africa, Namibia, Botswana, Swaziland, Lesotho, Zimbabwe, Zambia, Malawi, Angola and Mozambique who have been offered admission to the University

Level of Study: Postgraduate

Type: Scholarship

Value: Full-fee or half-fee waiver and support in the form of stipend, fares and books

Frequency: Annual

Study Establishment: London Metropolitan University

Country of Study: United Kingdom

Application Procedure: Application should be sent to the Canon Collins Trust and the Trust will forward it to the university. Please see the website to know how to apply. Applications that have been emailed or faxed or those that have been received after the deadline will not be considered

Closing Date: 3 March

Funding: Trusts

Contributor: Cannon Collins Educational Trust and Department of Applied Social Sciences

For further information contact:

22 The Ivories, 6 Northampton Street, London N1 2HY, United Kingdom.

Tel: (44) 20 7354 1462
Fax: (44) 20 7359 4875

International Students House/London Metropolitan Scholarship Scheme

Purpose: To support international students from selected countries with tuition fees and accommodation

Eligibility: Open to students from Afghanistan, Armenia, Bhutan, Cameroon, Cuba, East Timor, Gambia, Iran, Indonesia, Jordan, Kazakhstan, Lebanon, Namibia, Nepal, Sri Lanka, Tanzania, Tibet, Uganda, Uzbekistan, Vietnam, and Zimbabwe who have been offered admission to the University

Level of Study: MBA, Postgraduate

Type: Scholarship

Value: Free tuition and accommodation

Length of Study: 1–2 years

Study Establishment: London Metropolitan University

Country of Study: United Kingdom

Application Procedure: Please see the website www.londonmet.ac.uk/scholarships

Closing Date: 1 July

Funding: International office

Contributor: International Students House (ISH) and London Metropolitan University

No. of awards given last year: 1–5

For further information contact:

Scholarships International Office, London Metropolitan University, 166-220 Holloway Road, London N7 8DB, United Kingdom.

Email: international@londonmet.ac.uk

Savoy Educational Trust Scholarships

Purpose: To financially assist students wishing to pursue students in the field of Hospitality and Tourism

Eligibility: Open to applicants from any country in the world who have been offered admission to the University

Level of Study: Postgraduate

Type: Bursary

Value: Up to £9,000

Frequency: Annual

Study Establishment: London Metropolitan University

Country of Study: United Kingdom

Application Procedure: Please see the website www.londonmet.ac.uk/how

Closing Date: 31 October

Funding: Trusts

Contributor: Savoy Educational Trust

For further information contact:

Scholarship Department, c/o Student Recruitment Services, Room 210, London Metropolitan University, London N7 8DB, United Kingdom.

Email: epilepsy@savoy-foundation.ca

The Katrina Mihaere Scholarship

Purpose: To honour the memory of Katrina Mihaere, a former London Metropolitan Women's Tennis team member
Eligibility: Open to all women tennis players who have been offered admission to the University, with an excellent track record in women's sports
Level of Study: Postgraduate
Type: Scholarship
Value: Full tuition and accommodation
Frequency: Annual
Study Establishment: London Metropolitan University
Country of Study: United Kingdom
Application Procedure: Please see the website www. londonmet.ac.uk/how to apply. Applications that have been emailed or faxed or those that have been received after the deadline will not be considered
Closing Date: 31 October

For further information contact:

Email: i.jennings@londonmet.ac.uk

The ODASS Scheme

Purpose: To financially assist students of high academic merit from developing Commonwealth countries
Eligibility: Open to students from developing Commonwealth
Level of Study: Postgraduate
Type: Scholarship
Value: Full tuition fees and living allowance
Frequency: Annual
Study Establishment: London Metropolitan Society
Country of Study: United Kingdom
Application Procedure: See the website
Funding: Government
Contributor: British Government's Aid Programme

For further information contact:

22 College Street Suite 300, Toronto, ON M5G 1K2, Canada.

Email: info@acu.ac.uk

London School of Business & Finance

Buchanan House, 30 Holborn, London EC1N 2LX, United Kingdom.

Tel: (44) 20 3005 6336
Email: professionalenquiries@lsbf.org.uk
Website: www.lsbf.org.uk

Diversity Scholarship

Purpose: To ensure students originate from varied backgrounds creating an opportunity to form global corporate networks
Eligibility: Show a proven history of academic excellence. Meet the English requirements of the programme they are applying for. Provide proof of sufficient funds to pay the remaining course fees. Applicants must have already applied for a programme at LSBF. Applicants must be classified as an international student and not residing in the United Kingdom
Level of Study: Doctorate, MBA, Postgraduate
Type: Scholarship
Value: £1,000–8,000 (towards reducing tuition fees, not include a contribution to living costs, travel or other expenses)
Study Establishment: London School of Business & Finance
Country of Study: United Kingdom
Closing Date: 29 January
Additional Information: Size of awards vary according to each scholar's circumstances www.ish.org.uk/

For further information contact:

London School of Business and Finance, Postgraduate Admissions Office, 8/9 Holborn, London EC1N 2LL, United Kingdom.

Tel: (44) 14168002204
Fax: (44) 20 7823 2302

The Royal Bank of Scotland International Scholarship

Purpose: It aims at bridging international boundaries by providing Chinese business professionals with an opportunity to study a globally recognized degree in one of the world's financial centres
Eligibility: A national of the People's Republic of China, Hong Kong (SAR), Macau (SAR); a graduate with proven academic skills; committed to contribute to the socio-economic development of the People's Republic of China. Established in a career, with a track record of excellence and achievement, and the prospect of becoming a leader in his/her chosen field; have good English Language skills, as most United Kingdom Higher Education Institutions require a minimum IELTS of 6.5 for admission onto Postgraduate courses; have sufficient funds to meet your tuition fees and living expenses, after taking account of the possible award of the Bank of Scotland International Scholarship
Level of Study: Doctorate, MBA, Postgraduate
Type: Scholarship
Value: Cover tuition fees

Country of Study: United Kingdom
Application Procedure: Application form available at www. lsbf.org.uk
Closing Date: 28 August
Contributor: Bank of Scotland

For further information contact:

Email: info@lsbf.org.uk

London School of Economics and Political Science (LSE)

The London School of Economics and Political Science, Houghton Street, London WC2A 2AE, United Kingdom.

Tel: (44) 20 7405 7686
Email: c.s.lee2@lse.ac.uk
Website: www.lse.ac.uk

London School of Economics (LSE) was founded in 1895 by Beatrice and Sidney Webb. LSE has an outstanding reputation for academic excellence. LSE is a world class centre for its concentration of teaching and research across the full range of the social, political and economic sciences.

CR Parekh Fellowship

Purpose: To encourage research that is of social, economic, political and constitutional concern to India
Eligibility: Open to established Indian scholars who are below 40 years of age and hold a PhD or comparable qualifications and experience. The fellowship is not intended for students registered for a degree or diploma, nor is it intended for senior academics
Level of Study: Doctorate, Research
Type: Fellowship
Value: £1,500 per month
Length of Study: 3 months
Frequency: Annual
Country of Study: United Kingdom
Application Procedure: Applications should include a curriculum vitae and an outline of proposed research and the names and addresses of 2 referees who are familiar with their work, to be contacted by the chairman
Closing Date: 13 January
Additional Information: Applications will not be accepted via email or fax www.ish.org.uk/

For further information contact:

School of Economics & Political Science The Fellowships Selection Committee Asia Research Center, The Fellowships Selection Committee, Asia Research Center, London School of Economics & Political Science, Houghton Street, London WC2A 2AE, United Kingdom.

Email: arc@lse.ac.uk

Sir Ratan Tata Postdoctoral Fellowship

Purpose: To encourage research on contemporary social and economic concerns of South Asia
Eligibility: Applicants should be scholars in the social sciences with experience of research on South Asia. They should hold a PhD.
Level of Study: Research
Type: Fellowship
Value: £1,750
Length of Study: Up to 8 months
Frequency: Annual
Country of Study: United Kingdom
Application Procedure: Applications should include a curriculum vitae and an outline of proposed research and the names and addresses of 2 referees who are familiar with their work, to be contacted by the Chairman. Applications should be addressed to The Fellowships Selection Committee
Closing Date: 27 April
Additional Information: The fellowship is not intended for students registered for a degree or diploma, nor is it intended for senior academics. Applications will not be accepted via email or fax. Please see the website for further details www. ish.org.uk/

For further information contact:

The Fellowships Selection Committee, India Observatory, London School of Economics & Political Science, Houghton Street, London WC2A 2AE, United Kingdom.

Email: India.Observatory@lse.ac.uk

London School of Hygiene & Tropical Medicine - LSHTM

Tel: (44) 20 7636 8636
Website: www.lshtm.ac.uk/
Contact: Keppel Street, London, WC1E 7HT, United Kingdom.

Jeroen Ensink Memorial Fund Scholarship

Purpose: Jeroen Ensink was a Senior Lecturer in Public Health Engineering at the London School of Hygiene & Tropical Medicine (LSHTM) and a Programme Director for the MSc Public Health for Development between 2009 and 2015. Jeroen was passionately committed to a simple cause improving access to water and sanitation in countries where children continue to die needlessly due to the lack of these basic services. As a researcher and educator, his career crossed many continents, living and working in Asian and African countries, collaborating with numerous universities and international agencies. He was a natural educator and immensely popular with students in whom he invested much time and energy. He provided support and inspiration in equal measure and many of his students are now successful researchers and public health professionals in their own right. Following his death on 29 December 2015, LSHTM established a Memorial Fund in his name to support students from sub-Saharan Africa and South Asia who are committed to improving public health in low- or middle- income countries and wish to undertake the MSc Public Health for Development programme.

Eligibility: Applicants for the scholarship must 1. have been accepted onto the 2023–24 MSc Public Health for Development course; 2. have demonstrated a commitment to WASH (water, sanitation and hygiene); 3. be citizens of the ub-Saharan African or South Asian countries listed above; 4. have lived in one of the abovementioned developing countries and worked in activities related to public health for a minimum of 2 years; and 5. meet the LSHTM's minimum English language proficiency requirements.

Level of Study: Postgraduate

Value: A full scholarship covers full-time overseas tuition fees for 2023–24 (including the mandatory field trip fee); flights from the student's home country to the United Kingdom, and return on expiry of the scholarship (to be booked by the Scholarships team in Registry); and a tax free stipend (living allowance) of £17,175.00.

Country of Study: United Kingdom

Application Procedure: Applicants should follow both steps outlined below by the scholarship deadline. Step 1 Submit an application for study for the MSc Public Health for Development, via the LSHTM Admissions portal. Please ensure that all the necessary supporting documents have been uploaded to your study application before the Scholarship deadline. Applicants are encouraged to communicate with their referees as early as possible in the application process, notifying them of this deadline. It is the responsibility of the applicant to ensure that their references have been submitted by the scholarship closing date. Due to the introduction of a GBP 50.00 application fee at LSHTM, applicants are advised to apply early to allow time for this payment to be processed. Until the payment is processed applicants will be unable to submit an application for study. We would therefore recommend that applicants for this funding apply for their study/programme by 15 March in order to ensure that there are no processing delays which could impact on meeting the scholarship deadline. Please note that if you are applying for admission to LSHTM and are accepted, you will be asked to pay a deposit within 28 days. If you are applying for a scholarship at LSHTM, please email the Admissions team within this 28 day period, specifying the name of this scholarship and the expected decision date. This must be repeated for every scholarship for which you are applying. The admissions team will then apply an extension to the deposit deadline to match the decision deadline of the scholarship. Step 2 Submit a Scholarship Application, via the LSHTM's Online Scholarship Application portal, indicating that you are applying for the 2023–24 Jeroen Ensink Memorial Fund Scholarship. As part of this application you should upload a complete Curriculum Vitae (CV); and a statement of motivation of no more than 1,000 words. Your statement of motivation should address the following a brief biography of your life and career, clarifying your commitment to WASH; your reasons for choosing the MSc Public Health for Development; and your future plans and ambitions in the field of public health. Applicants must submit both CV and the statement of motivation with their scholarship application to be considered for this funding, even though they may have already submitted a statement with their application for admission. Applicants may choose to tailor this statement for the funding (and therefore submit something different to their standard MSc programme application statement). Applicants should be aware that their application for this scholarship award may be considered alongside the documents submitted for their application to the MSc Public Health for Development programme. Each applicant should submit only one Jeroen Ensink MSc Scholarship application. We would therefore encourage applicants to check carefully their online application and attachment before submission, as the first application submitted will be the one considered and there will be no opportunity to upload a statement of motivation or CV after submission. Applicants who have already submitted a completed 2023–24 London-based MSc Public Health for Development application for study and/or have been made an Offer of Admission for the 2023–24 London-based MSc Public Health for Development programme should apply for the scholarship by completing the scholarship application (Step 2 above) and submitting this by the scholarship deadline. Incomplete applications will not be considered for this funding. Incomplete applications include those with missing supplementary documentation at either/both Steps 1 and 2 above. By submitting an application for this funding applicants agree to its terms and conditions.

Closing Date: 30 March

London South Bank University

103 Borough Road, London SE1 0AA, United Kingdom.

Tel: (44) 20 7815 7815
Email: pgscholarships@lsbu.ac.uk
Website: www.lsbu.ac.uk

Vice-Chancellor's Scholarships

Purpose: This prestigious scholarship recognises applications from outstanding students who can demonstrate their skills and commitment to becoming future global leaders
Eligibility: 1. Be an international fee-paying undergraduate (including Level 0) or postgraduate taught degree offer holder, enrolling for the first time at Teesside University. 2. Submit an application for consideration.
Level of Study: Graduate, Postgraduate
Type: Scholarship
Value: £5,000
Frequency: Annual
Application Procedure: You will be invited to apply online via email after you firmly accept your unconditional or conditional offer to study at LSBU. We recommend you apply for your place at LSBU as soon as possible to ensure you have been made an offer by the scholarship deadline of July
Closing Date: 30 April
Funding: Individuals
Contributor: Donations from alumni and other supporters

Loren L Zachary Society for the Performing Arts

2250 Gloaming Way, Beverly Hills, CA 90210, United States of America.

Tel: (1) 310 276 2731
Email: info@zacharysociety.org
Website: www.zacharysociety.org
Contact: Mrs Nedra Zachary, President, Director of Competition

The Loren L Zachary Society for the Performing Arts was founded in 1972 by the late Dr Loren L Zachary, and Nedra Zachary. The purpose of the organization is to help further the careers of young opera singers by providing financial assistance and performance opportunities. The annual Loren L Zachary National Vocal Competition, now in its 46 year, has helped launch the International careers of many singers. For a complete list of winners and finalists visit the website.

Loren L Zachary National Vocal Competition for Young Opera Singers

Purpose: To assist in the development of the careers of young opera singers through competitive auditions with monetary awards
Eligibility: Competition is open to applicants ages 21–35. Singers must be prepared to pursue a professional operatic stage career, be present for all phases of the Competition, and reside in the United States or Canada
Level of Study: Professional development
Type: Competition
Value: The Top Award ranges from US$15,000 to US$18,000 and approximately US$50,000 will be distributed amongst the Finalists, each Finalist receiving a minimum of US$1,000 - US$2,000.
Frequency: Annual
Study Establishment: Must be thoroughly trained and be ready to pursue a professional operatic career
Country of Study: Any country
Application Procedure: Applicants must complete an application form accompanied by a proof of age and an application fee of US$50. For application forms and exact dates, singers should refer to www.zacharysociety.org or send a stamped, self-addressed envelope with letter
No. of awards offered: 300
Closing Date: 2 February
Funding: Individuals, Private, Trusts
No. of awards given last year: 10
No. of applicants last year: 300
Additional Information: All applicants are guaranteed an audition provided application is completed correctly with application fee. Applicants must be present at all phases of the auditions. Recordings are not acceptable. Preliminary and semifinal auditions take place in New York in February, and in Los Angeles in April.

For further information contact:

The Loren L. Zachary Society, 2250 Gloaming Way, Beverly Hills, CA 90210-1717, United States of America.

Tel: (1) 310 276 2731
Email: infoz@zacharysociety.org

Los Alamos National Laboratory (LANL)

PO Box 1663, MS P219, Los Alamos, NM 87545, United States of America.

Tel: (1) 505 667 4866
Email: bmontoya@lanl.gov
Website: www.lanl.gov

Los Alamos National Laboratory (LANL) is the largest institution in Northern New Mexico with more than 9,000 employees plus approximately 650 contractor personnel. From its origins as a secret Manhattan Project Laboratory, Los Alamos has attracted world-class scientists and applied their energy and creativity to solving the nation's most challenging problems.

Los Alamos Graduate Research Assistant Program

Purpose: To provide students with relevant research experience while they are pursuing a graduate degree
Eligibility: Applicant must be a graduate
Level of Study: Doctorate, Research
Type: Research
Value: US$33,300–44,600, including benefits, travel and moving expenses
Length of Study: Year or less
Frequency: Annual
Country of Study: Any country

For further information contact:

Email: errobinson@lanl.gov

Loughborough University

Leicestershire LE11 3TU, United Kingdom.

Tel: (44) 1509 222 222
Email: international-office@lboro.ac.uk
Website: www.lboro.ac.uk

With 3,000 staff and 12,000 students Loughbrough, with its impressive 410 acre campus, is one of the largest university's in the United Kingdom. Our mission is to increase knowledge through research, provide the highest quality of educational experience and the widest opportunities for students, advance industry and the profession, and benefit society.

Aziz Foundation Scholarships

Purpose: These scholarships aim to develop and empower graduates to bring positive change to British Muslim communites and beyond. They are designed to foster future leaders who aspire to make a positive contribution to society, raising aspirations and standards, and facilitating better representation of Muslim communities in civil society.
Eligibility: 1. have applied for a master's level programme (PGCE, PGDip and PGCert programmes are not considered) starting in the 2023/24 academic year. 2. dedicated to bettering Muslim communities and wider society. 3. experiencing financial barriers to pursing further study. 4. pursue a course that will benefit your career prospects and/or assist in the development of your current career geared towards community service. 5. willing to advocate on behalf of communities. 6. qualify for UK/EU tuition fee status.
Level of Study: Postgraduate
Type: Scholarship
Value: The Aziz Foundation is offering UK students 100% tuition fee scholarships for master's study at Loughborough University
Study Establishment: Loughborough University
Country of Study: United Kingdom
Closing Date: 1 June

For further information contact:

Email: scholarships@azizfoundation.org.uk

Daryl Jelinek Sporting Scholarship

Purpose: Daryl Jelinek studied at Loughborough University from 1980 to 1983, where he captained the rugby team as well as playing for England U23s. Daryl went on to play rugby for Blackheath, London Scottish, and the Anglo-Scots. When Daryl passed away in July 2018, the Daryl Jelinek Sporting Scholarship was established by Daryl's family and friends to create a legacy that will continue to help young people at Loughborough for many years to come.
Level of Study: Postgraduate
Type: Scholarship
Value: £2,000–£4,000
Frequency: Annual
Closing Date: 31 May

Dean's Award for Enterprise

Purpose: The award is highly competitive and will be given at the discretion of the Dean with the support of the Senior Leadership Team. Applicants must complete an application form outlining the business idea and are encouraged to include images and media content to support their application, such as a pitch slide deck or video

Eligibility: To be eligible to apply for the award, you must be an applicant to a Loughborough University London Postgraduate programme with a conditional/unconditional offer to study a full-time master's programme at Loughborough University London.

Level of Study: Masters Degree
Type: Award
Value: 90% off the full cost of tuition fees
Country of Study: Any country
Closing Date: 31 July

For further information contact:

Email: london@lboro.ac.uk

Design School Scholarships

Purpose: To assist students financially who want to study in the department
Eligibility: Outstanding academic achievement
Level of Study: Postgraduate
Type: Scholarship
Value: £500
Frequency: Annual
Study Establishment: Loughborough University
Country of Study: United Kingdom
Application Procedure: If full supporting documentation is supplied with your application to study in the department, you will be automatically considered for a scholarship. No separate scholarship application is required
Closing Date: 28 February

For further information contact:

Email: r.i.campbell@lboro.ac.uk

Development Trust Africa Scholarships

Purpose: The scholarships are funded through a combination of generous external funding and university funds. The University will award a limited number of scholarships and the standards required are very high
Eligibility: Applications will be initially shortlisted and the final decision on the awards will be made by a selection panel of senior staff at Loughborough. The selection panel will use the following eligibility criteria when assessing applications 1. currently domiciled (permanently living) in Africa 2. evidence of exceptional academic achievement (normally a first class honours degree) 3. commitment to return to your home

country on completion of postgraduate programme 4. evidence of the ability and commitment to make a significant contribution to your home country on your return 5. full understanding of the costs involved in coming to study and live in the UK 6. evidence of strong motivation and initiative to secure funds to cover the remainder of the costs involved.

Level of Study: Postgraduate
Type: Scholarship
Value: 100% of the course fees
Country of Study: Any country
Application Procedure: Apply here www.lboro.ac.uk/media/media/study/pg/2021/downloads/africa-scholarship-application-form-2021.docx
Closing Date: 30 April

For further information contact:

Email: International-office@lboro.ac.uk

Economic and Social Research Council Studentships

Purpose: To financially assist students to cover their living costs while undertaking a PhD.
Eligibility: Applicant must have been in full-time education in the United Kingdom throughout the 3 years preceding the start date of PhD course
Level of Study: Postgraduate
Type: Studentship
Value: The amount of funding is agreed each year by all the research councils and increase in line with inflation. Tuition fees are also paid
Length of Study: 1 year
Frequency: Annual
Study Establishment: Loughborough University
Country of Study: United Kingdom
Application Procedure: See website
Closing Date: 7 March
Funding: Government
Contributor: ESRC

For further information contact:

Email: l.e.child@lboro.ac.uk

Eli Lilly Scholarship

Purpose: To increase knowledge through research, provide the highest quality of educational experience and the widest opportunities for students, advance industry and the profession, and benefit society

Eligibility: Applicant must be a postgraduate in chemistry. See the website for details
Level of Study: Postgraduate
Type: Scholarships and fellowships
Value: £1,000
Length of Study: 1 year
Frequency: Annual
Study Establishment: Loughborough University
Country of Study: United Kingdom
Application Procedure: See website

For further information contact:

Tel: (44) 1509 263171
Email: l.e.child@lboro.ac.uk

Inspiring Success Scholarship

Purpose: The Inspiring Success Scholarship offers 100% off the full cost of tuition fees for selected unemployed and underemployed graduates, who obtained GCSE or A-level (or equivalent) qualifications from Hackney, Tower Hamlets, Newham or Waltham Forest.
Eligibility: All taught master's programmes
Level of Study: Masters Degree
Type: Scholarship
Value: 100% off the full cost of tuition fees
Country of Study: Any country
Closing Date: 31 July

For further information contact:

Email: london@lboro.ac.uk

Jean Scott Scholarships

Purpose: To support best qualified Loughborough University students
Eligibility: Open to the best qualified Loughborough University students entering MSc programmes in the Department of Economics
Level of Study: Postgraduate
Type: Scholarship
Value: A maximum of £5,000
Length of Study: 1 year
Frequency: Annual
Study Establishment: Loughborough University
Country of Study: United Kingdom
Application Procedure: See website

For further information contact:

Email: msc.economics@lboro.ac.uk

Loughborough Sports Scholarships

Purpose: To support elite athletes
Eligibility: Open to students who have excelled at least at junior international level (or equivalent) in their sport and have fulfilled the normal academic requirements for either undergraduate or postgraduate entry
Type: Scholarship
Value: Up to £5,000
Frequency: Annual
Study Establishment: Loughborough University
Country of Study: United Kingdom
Application Procedure: See website
Closing Date: 31 May

For further information contact:

Tel: (44) 1509 226108
Email: sports-scholars@lboro.ac.uk

Master of Business Administration Scholarships

Purpose: To support international Students who want to do MBA from University of Loughborough
Eligibility: Applicant may be a citizen of any country
Level of Study: MBA
Type: Scholarship
Value: Varies
Length of Study: Varies
Frequency: Annual
Study Establishment: Loughborough University
Country of Study: United Kingdom
Application Procedure: See website

For further information contact:

Email: exec.mba@lboro.ac.uk

Mathematical Sciences Scholarship

Level of Study: Postgraduate
Type: Scholarship
Value: 25% of the programme tuition fee which will be credited to the student's tuition fee account
Length of Study: 1–3 years
Frequency: Annual
Study Establishment: Loughborough University

Country of Study: United Kingdom
Application Procedure: See website

For further information contact:

Email: maths-admissions@lboro.ac.uk

School of Art and Design Scholarships

Level of Study: Postgraduate
Type: Scholarship
Value: £1,000 (tuition fee)
Length of Study: 1–3 years
Frequency: Annual
Study Establishment: Loughborough University
Country of Study: United Kingdom
Application Procedure: See website

For further information contact:

Email: R.Turner@lboro.ac.uk

School of Business and Economics Scholarships

Purpose: To assist financially the students who want to pursue a career in finance, international and marketing management
Eligibility: Applicants with a First Class Honours degree are eligible. A limited number of scholarships are available
Level of Study: Postgraduate
Type: Scholarship
Value: 50% of the tuition fee
Length of Study: 1 year
Frequency: Annual
Study Establishment: Loughborough University
Country of Study: United Kingdom
Application Procedure: See website

For further information contact:

Tel: (44) 1509 228278, 228844, 223291
Email: msc.management@lboro.ac.uk

Loughborough University Business School

Ashby Road, Leicestershire, Loughborough LE11 3TU, United Kingdom.

Tel: (44) 1509 223 398
Website: info.lut.ac.uk.departments/bs
Contact: Ms Gabriella Stenson, MBA Admissions Officer

Dean's Award for Enterprise Scholarship

Purpose: The award will be given at the discretion of the Dean, with the support of the Senior Leadership Team. Applicants are asked to produce a one-page submission of their business idea; though students are encouraged to include images and media content to support their application
Eligibility: To be eligible to apply for the award, you must be an applicant to a Loughborough University London Postgraduate programme with a conditional/unconditional offer to study a full-time master's programme at Loughborough University London.
Level of Study: Graduate
Type: Scholarship
Value: 90% tuition fee scholarship
Frequency: Annual
Country of Study: Any country
Closing Date: 31 July
Funding: Private

For further information contact:

Epinal Way, Leicestershire, Loughborough LE11 3TU, United Kingdom.

Tel: (44) 1509 222 222
Email: london@lboro.ac.uk

Loyola Marymount University

1 Loyola Marymount University Dr, Los Angeles, CA 90045, United States of America.

Tel: (1) 310 338 2700
Contact: Fellowships Office

Loyola Marymount University MBA Programme

Length of Study: 1–2 years
Application Procedure: Applicants must return a completed application form, two official undergraduate transcripts, a two page Statement of Intent, two letters of recommendation, test scores, and a fee of US$35

For further information contact:

Tel: (1) 310 338 2848
Fax: (1) 310 338 2899
Email: mbapc@imumail.lmu.edu

Ludwig-Maximilian University

Geschwister-Scholl-Platz 1, D-80539 Munich, Germany.

Tel: (49) 89 2180 0
Contact: Ludwig-Maximilians-Universität München

LMU is recognized as one of Europe's premier academic and research institutions. Since our founding in 1472, LMU has attracted inspired scholars and talented students from all over the world, keeping the University at the nexus of ideas that challenge and change our complex world.

Liaoning Medical University Postdoctoral Fellowship for International Students at MCMP

Purpose: The Munich Center for Mathematical Philosophy (MCMP) seeks applications for two 3-year postdoctoral fellowships. International students are eligible to apply for this fellowship
Eligibility: International students are eligible to apply for this fellowship. The official language at the MCMP is English and fluency in German is not mandatory
Type: Postdoctoral fellowship
Value: The fellowships are remunerated with 1. €853/month (paid out without deductions for tax and social security). The MCMP also provides funds to cover costs to attend some workshops and conferences
Study Establishment: LMU is especially interested in candidates with research interests in at least one of the following fields general philosophy of science, philosophy of physics, philosophy of the social sciences, philosophy of statistics, formal epistemology, formal philosophy of science, social epistemology, philosophy and psychology of reasoning and argumentation, agent-based modeling in philosophy, or decision theory
Country of Study: Any country
Application Procedure: Applications (including a cover letter that addresses, amongst others, one's academic background, research interests and the proposed starting date, a CV, a list of publications, a sample of written work of no more than 5,000 words, and a description of a planned research project of about 2,000 words) should be sent by email (in one PDF document) to office.hartmann-at-lrz.uni-muenchen.de. Hard copy applications are not accepted. Additionally, two confidential letters of reference addressing the applicant's qualifications for academic research should be sent to the same email address from the referees directly
Closing Date: 15 April

For further information contact:

Email: S.Hartmann@lmu.de

Lung Cancer Research Foundation

LCRF Research Grant on Disparities in Lung Cancer

Subjects: Lung cancer
Purpose: LCRF grant program provides funding for research into the prevention, diagnosis, treatment and cure of lung cancer.
Eligibility: Must be early- and mid-career investigators. icants from US-based and international institutions are eligible to apply and may hold any residency/citizenship status. Senior investigators with more than ten years experience since faculty appointment are generally not eligible for funding and are encouraged to mentor a junior team member through the application process. However, exceptions will be made for investigators with more than ten years experience in other disease areas or topics. Ineligible investigators with these or other special circumstances may request review by contacting the LCRF grants office (see Inquiries section below). For full details about eligibility, see website.
Type: Grant
Value: Maximum of US$150,000
Country of Study: United States of America
Closing Date: 7 May

For further information contact:

Email: grants@LCRF.org

Lupus Foundation of America

1300 Piccard Drive, Suite 200, Rockville, MD 20850, United States of America.

Tel: (1) 301 670 9292
Contact: Ms Arlise Davis, Executive Assistant

Gary S. Gilkeson Career Development Award

Purpose: To facilitate the professional development of rheumatology, nephrology, and dermatology fellows in the U.S. and Canada who are interested in lupus research.
Eligibility: U.S. citizen or legal resident of the U.S. or Canada
Value: Up to US$70,000 each

Length of Study: 2 years
Frequency: Annual
Country of Study: Any country
No. of awards offered: 4
Closing Date: 15 April
Additional Information: www.lupus.org/research/apply-for-funding

For further information contact:

Meghan Widmaier, Research and Grants Coordinator, Lupus Foundation of America, 2121 K Street, NW, Suite 200, Washington, DC 20037, United States of America.

Tel: (1) 202 349 1150
Email: widmaier@lupus.org

Gina M. Finzi Memorial Student Summer Fellowship Program

Purpose: To foster an interest among students in the areas of basic, clinical, translational, epidemiological, or behavioral research relevant to lupus.
Eligibility: 1. The project must be in one of the following areas focused on lupus research basic, clinical, translational, epidemiological, or behavioral research. 2. The applicant is responsible for identifying a supervising sponsor who is an established, tenure-track principal investigator who directs a laboratory dedicated at least in part to the investigation of lupus at an academic, medical, or research institution. 3. The institution where you re conducting your research must be in the U.S., Canada, or Mexico. 4. Undergraduates up to Medical Residents and/or PhDs' may apply. 5. Awards cannot be postponed for use in a later year or be carried out for two or more summers.
Level of Study: Research
Type: Fellowships
Value: US$4,000
Frequency: Annual
Country of Study: Any country
No. of awards offered: 6
Closing Date: 15 April

For further information contact:

Meghan Widmaier, Research and Grants Coordinator, Lupus Foundation of America, 2121 K Street, NW, Suite 200, Washington, DC 20037, United States of America.

Tel: (1) 202 349 1150
Email: widmaier@lupus.org

Lund University Global Scholarship

Purpose: The Lund University Global Scholarship programme seeks to recognise these students by awarding academic excellence grants. Scholarship recipients have a proven record of achieving consistently high grades in their previous studies and are assessed as being a good fit for our programmes
Eligibility: To be eligible to apply for a scholarship you must meet all of the following criteria 1. You must be a citizen of a country from outside the European Union/EEA (and Switzerland) and are required to pay a tuition fee. 2. You have made a complete application for Bachelor's or Master's level studies at Lund University in a regular application round for a minimum of one semester of study (30 ECTS). Note that priority is given to students who have ranked a programme at Lund University as the first choice in their application at universityadmissions.se
Level of Study: Graduate
Type: Scholarship
Value: US$35,000
Frequency: Dependent on funds available
Country of Study: Any country
Application Procedure: The selection process for scholarships is undertaken in parallel with the programme/course selection process. Priority will be given to students with high academic performance, who are assessed as a good fit for the programme, who demonstrate a strong commitment and desire to study at Lund University and have selected a programme/course at Lund University as their first choice/choices when applying at www.universityadmissions.se
Closing Date: 15 April
Funding: Private
Additional Information: Note that the opening date for this proposal is February www.lupus.org/research/apply-for-funding

For further information contact:

Meghan Widmaier, Research and Grants Coordinator, Lupus Foundation of America 2121 K, Street, NW, Suite 200, Washington, DC 20037, United States of America.

Email: Widmaier@lupus.org

Luton Business School University of Luton

MBA Programmes Putteridge Bury Hitchin Road, Luton, Bedfordshire LU2 8LE, United Kingdom.

Tel: (44) 1582 482555
Email: faculty-of-business@luton.ac.uk
Contact: MBA Admissions Officer

League of United Latin American Citizens National Educational Service Centers National Scholarship Fund

Purpose: Awards scholarships to Hispanic students who are enrolled or planning to enroll in accredited colleges or universities in the United States

Eligibility: Must be a full-time or part-time student. 1. Must be a Hispanic student. 2. Must be a United States citizen or permanent resident. 3. Must have a grade point average of 3.25 or higher. Must have applied to or be enrolled in a college, university, or graduate school, including two-year colleges or vocational schools that lead to an associate's degree

Level of Study: Graduate

Type: Funding support

Value: US$2,000

Frequency: Annual

Country of Study: Any country

Application Procedure: The applicants must send application and supporting materials to the LULAC council in his/her town. For a listing of participating councils, please visit www. lnesc.org/index.asp?Type=B_BASIC&SEC=A9E53 D4E-6 ADF-431B-A59A-E92DEDD44793

Closing Date: 31 March

Funding: Private

For further information contact:

2000 L St., N.W. Suite 610, Washington, DC 20036, United States of America.

Email: mbosques@lnesc.org

M

Maastricht University

Main administration building, Minderbroedersberg 4-6, NL-6211 LK Maastricht, The Netherlands.

Tel: (31) 43 388 2222
Website: www.maastrichtuniversity.nl/about-um
Contact: Maastricht University

Maastricht University (UM) is the most international university in the Netherlands and, with 20,000 students and 4,400 employees, is still growing. The university stands out for its innovative education model, international character and multidisciplinary approach to research and education.

Candriam Scholarship

Eligibility: 1. a full-time master's programme in Sustainability Science, Policy and society, or 2. a full-time master's programme in International Business- Sustainable Finance, or 3. a full-time master's programme in International Business – entrepreneurship & Business Development or 4. a full-time master's programme in Economics and Strategy in Emerging Markets at Maastricht University for the 2023–2024 academic year. You meet the specific admission requirements of the UM master programme to which you have applied. 1. You hold nationality in a country in the EU/EEA, Switzerland or Surinam; 2. You are a first generation student (we define first generation students as students from non-academic backgrounds. First generation students are the first in their families to follow higher education (university or university of applied sciences); their parents did not follow higher education).
Level of Study: Postgraduate
Type: Scholarship

Value: Tuition fee* €2,168 PA, Study materials €600 PA, Living expenses (per year)€11,400*p/m
Length of Study: 1 year
Frequency: Annual
Country of Study: Netherlands
Closing Date: 1 May
Additional Information: www.maastrichtuniversity.nl/support/your-studies-begin/coming-maastricht-university-abroad/scholarships/candriam-scholarship

For further information contact:

Email: master-sbe@maastrichtuniversity.nl

Fulbright / Maastricht University Award

Eligibility: Students of U.S. higher education institutions who wish to apply for a master's programme at UM. U.S. students currently residing in The Netherlands will not be considered for the Award, neither will U.S. students with both a U.S. and Dutch citizenship.
Level of Study: Postgraduate
Type: Scholarship
Value: €1,300 per nine months, €1,000 for international travel costs, Health benefits plan for illness and accidents, Travel cost
Length of Study: 1 year
Frequency: Annual
Country of Study: Netherlands
Closing Date: October
Additional Information: www.maastrichtuniversity.nl/support/your-studies-begin/coming-maastricht-university-abroad/scholarships/fulbright-maastricht#amount

For further information contact:

Email: scholarships@maastrichtuniversity.nl

© Springer Nature Limited 2022
Palgrave Macmillan (ed.), *The Grants Register 2023*,
https://doi.org/10.1057/978-1-349-96053-8

Maastricht University Holland Euregion Refugee Scholarship

Eligibility: 1. You hold nationality in a country outside the EU/EEA and are a refugee in Belgium or Germany 2. You can proof that you reside in the Euregion 3. You are willing to sign a consent form that you will not move to the Netherlands and agree to commute to Maastricht University 4. You have applied for admission to a full-time Master's programme at Maastricht University for the 2023–2024 academic year. Please note that the Master's programmes Medicine and Physician-Clinical Investigator are not eligible for the UM Holland Euregion Refugee Scholarship. 5. You meet the specific admission requirements of the UM Master's programme to which you have applied. 6. You have never participated in a degree-seeking higher education programme in the Netherlands.

Level of Study: Postgraduate
Type: Scholarship
Value: Tuition fees award €11.657*/€14.657*, Tuition fees student €2.143*, Pre-academic training-At cost.
Length of Study: 1 to 2 years
Frequency: Annual
Country of Study: Netherlands
No. of awards offered: 5
Additional Information: www.maastrichtuniversity.nl/sup port/your-studies-begin/coming-maastricht-university-abroad/ scholarships www.maastrichtuniversity.nl/support/your-studies-begin/coming-maastricht-university-abroad/scholar ships/maastricht-university-0#amount

For further information contact:

Email: scholarships@maastrichtuniversity.nl

Maastricht University Holland-High Potential scholarship

Eligibility: 1. You hold nationality in a country outside the EU/EEA, Switzerland or Surinam and meet the requirements for obtaining an entry visa and residence permit for the Netherlands. 2. You do not hold a double nationality from an EU/EEA country. 3. You have applied for admission to a full-time master programme at Maastricht University for the 2023/24 academic year. 4. You meet the specific admission requirements of the UM master programme to which you have applied. 5. You have never participated in a degree-seeking higher education programme in the Netherlands. Students who have completed exchange programmes in the Netherlands are welcome to apply. 6. You are not older than 35 years of age on 1 September 2023. 7. You have obtained excellent results during your prior education programmes, as demonstrated by your latest grade transcript or certified by academic excellence. If several applicants are equally quali-fied, UM will give preference to applicants whose academic transcript or certified letter of academic excellence demon-strate that they are among the top 5% of the 2023/24 scholar-ship programme applicants.

Level of Study: Postgraduate
Type: Scholarship
Value: €29,000
Frequency: Annual
Country of Study: Netherlands
No. of awards offered: 24
Closing Date: 1 February
Additional Information: www.maastrichtuniversity.nl/sup port/your-studies-begin/coming-maastricht-university-abroad/ scholarships/maastricht-university

For further information contact:

Email: hhp.scholarship@maastrichtuniversity.nl

Noord-Limburg Region Scholarship - FHML and SBE

Eligibility: The Noord-Limburg Region Scholarship will focus on the master's programme in Global Supply Chain Management and Change at the Maastricht University School of Business and Economics (SBE) and the two-year master's programme in Health Food Innovation Management of the Maastricht University Faculty of Health, Medicine and Life sciences (FHML). The Global Supply Chain Management and Change master is a one-year mas-ter's programme entirely taught in English at Maastricht University, Campus Venlo. Applicants must have been admitted to the Global Supply Chain Management and Change master programme starting in September 2023. The Health Food Innovation Management master is a -two-year master programme entirely taught in English at Maastricht University, Campus Venlo. Applicants must have been admitted to the two-year master's programme in Health Food Innovation Management starting in September 2023.

Level of Study: Postgraduate
Type: Scholarship
Value: Tuition fee refund*€2,168.00, Expenses/study mate-rials* €332.00.
Length of Study: 1 to 2 years
Frequency: Annual
Country of Study: Netherlands
Additional Information: www.maastrichtuniversity.nl/sup port/your-studies-begin/coming-maastricht-university-abroad/ scholarships/noord-limburg-region#amount

For further information contact:

Email: HFIM-admissions@maastrichtuniversity.nl

Orange Tulip Scholarship

Purpose: The Orange Tulip Scholarship (OTS) is intended for students from several Neso countries who want to study in the Netherlands. At Maastricht University the OTS grants are available for certain faculties combined win certain Neso countries.

Eligibility: All candidates must meet the following requirements: 1. You have the nationality of your Neso country and you live in this Neso country 2. You have a degree from a non-Dutch university 3. You have not previously studied or worked in the Netherlands 4. You have been admitted to a Master's programme at the corresponding Faculty for your Neso country.

Level of Study: MBA, Masters Degree, Postgraduate (MSc)

Type: Scholarship

Value: €13,800; €15,500 or €16,800 depending on the tuition of your study programme.

Length of Study: 1 to 2 years

Frequency: Annual

Country of Study: Netherlands

Application Procedure: Step 1: Register for one of the Master's programmes at the selected Faculty of Maastricht University for your Neso country. For further details on how to register for a Master's programme at UM, please see your prospective programme's webpage. Once you have submitted your application via Studielink, you will receive a student ID number for Maastricht University. Step 2: Apply for the OTS scholarship via the website of the Nuffic Neso office in your country. You can find the links to the right website if you click on your Neso country in the table above.

Closing Date: 1 April

Funding: Private

Additional Information: www.maastrichtuniversity.nl/support/your-studies-begin/coming-maastricht-university-abroad/scholarships/orange-tulip-scholarship#amount

For further information contact:

Bonnefantenstraat 2, NL-6211 KL Maastricht, Netherlands.

Email: scholarships@maastrichtuniversity.nl

UFL Jan de Limpens Scholarship

Eligibility: Eligible students have been admitted to the master's programme starting in September 2023. Candidates live and/or are born and raised in one of these selected villages: Amstenrade, Bingelrade, Brunssum, Doenrade, Jabeek, Merkelbeek, Oirsbeek, Schinveld and Sittard (places in Sittard before the municipal merger with Geleen).

Level of Study: Postgraduate

Type: Scholarship

Value: Tuition fee €2,186*, Expenses €332*.

Length of Study: 1 to 2 years

Frequency: Annual

Country of Study: Netherlands

Additional Information: www.maastrichtuniversity.nl/support/your-studies-begin/coming-maastricht-university-abroad/scholarships/ufl-jan-de-limpens

For further information contact:

Email: master-sbe@maastrichtuniversity.nl

UM Academic Achievement Scholarship

Eligibility: 1. You hold the nationality of a country outside the EU/EEA and Switzerland and meet the requirements for obtaining an entry visa and residence permit for the Netherlands. 2. You do not hold a double nationality from an EU/EEA country or Switzerland 3. You have completed or are in the process of completing your bachelor studies at UM with an average GPA of at least 8.5 4. You are not older than 35 years of age on 1 September 2023 5. You agree to become an UM ambassador during and after your studies, by committing to share your experiences during at least one (information) session for students and/or other stakeholders 6. You have have been (conditionally) admitted to one of the participating one-year master programmes at UM for the 2023–2024 academic year.

Level of Study: Postgraduate

Type: Scholarship

Value: The difference between the institutional and statutory tuition fee. Non-EU/EEA students who normally have to pay the institutional fee, now only need to pay the statutory tuition fee.

Length of Study: 1 year

Frequency: Annual

Country of Study: Netherlands

Closing Date: 1 February

Additional Information: www.maastrichtuniversity.nl/support/your-studies-begin/coming-maastricht-university-abroad/scholarships/um-academic-achievement#amount

For further information contact:

Email: scholarships@maastrichtuniversity.nl

M

UM Brightlands Talent Scholarship

Eligibility: 1. You hold the nationality of a country outside the EU/EEA and Switzerland and meet the requirements for obtaining an entry visa and residence permit for the Netherlands 2. You do not hold a double nationality from an EU/EEA country or Switzerland 3. You have never participated in a degree-seeking higher education programme in the Netherlands. Students who have completed exchange programmes in the Netherlands are welcome to apply 4. You are not older than 35 years of age on 1 September 2023 5. You agree to become an active Brightlands and UM ambassador during and after your studies, by committing to share your experiences during at least one (information) session for students and/or other stakeholders 6. You have have been (conditionally) admitted to the participating master's programmes at UM for the 2023–2024 academic year.
Level of Study: Postgraduate
Type: Scholarship
Value: Living expenses €11,400/€22,800, Health & liability insurance-At cost, Visa application costs €192* , Tuition fees-At cost.
Frequency: Annual
Country of Study: Netherlands
No. of awards offered: 4
Closing Date: 1 February
Additional Information: www.maastrichtuniversity.nl/support/your-studies-begin/coming-maastricht-university-abroad/scholarships/um-brightlands-talent

For further information contact:

Email: scholarships@maastrichtuniversity.nl

Macquarie University

Balaclava Road, North Ryde, NSW 2109, Australia.

Tel: (61) 2 9850 7111
Email: tgreen@ling.mq.edu.au
Website: www.mq.edu.au

Macquarie University began as a bold experiment in higher education. Built to break from traditions: to be distinctive, progressive, and to be transformational. Today our pioneering history continues to be a source of inspiration as we celebrate our place among the best and brightest minds. Our research is leading the way in ground-breaking discoveries. Our academics are at the forefront of innovation and, as accomplished researchers, we are embracing the opportunity to tackle the big issues of our time.

South Asia AU$10,000 Early Acceptance Scholarship

Eligibility: To be eligible for this scholarship, you must be a full-time international student studying a Bachelor or Master level degree on-campus (or online and/or offshore if impacted by COVID-19 border restrictions) and meet the following criteria: 1. Be a citizen of countries from South Asia. 2. Accept your Letter of Offer and pay the commencement fee by the Acceptance Deadline. 3. Adhere to the terms and conditions of this scholarship.
Level of Study: Postgraduate
Type: Scholarship
Value: AU$10,000 per year
Length of Study: Course duration
Frequency: Annual
Country of Study: Australia
Additional Information: mq.edu.au/study/admissions-and-entry/scholarships/international/south-asia-10-000-early-acceptance-scholarship

For further information contact:

Email: study@mq.edu.au

ASEAN AU$10,000 Early Acceptance Scholarship

Eligibility: To be eligible for this scholarship, you must be a full-time international student studying a Bachelor or Master level degree on-campus (or online and/or offshore if impacted by COVID-19 border restrictions) and meet the following criteria: Be a citizen of countries from the ASEAN region. Accept your Letter of Offer and pay the commencement fee by the Acceptance Deadline. Adhere to the terms and conditions of this scholarship.
Level of Study: Postgraduate
Type: Scholarship
Value: AU$10,000
Length of Study: 2 years
Frequency: Annual
Country of Study: Australia
Application Procedure: You have successfully lodged an application for the undergrad or postgrad degree you plan to study. You have met the eligibility criteria for the course you have applied for.
Additional Information: mq.edu.au/study/admissions-and-entry/scholarships/international/asean-10-000-early-acceptance-scholarship

For further information contact:

Email: study@mq.edu.au

Australian Eye and Ear Health Survey

Eligibility: 1. Completion of a Master of Research (MRes) with a grade of at least a Distinction level (75% or greater in second year; or 2. A Master of Philosophy; or 3. A two-year Masters degree with a major research component at Distinction level (75% or greater). Peer-reviewed research output may be taken into consideration for admission to the program. You must also demonstrate your suitability for entry to the program by: 1. Including a detailed research proposal. Providing evidence of the required level of English language proficiency.
Level of Study: Doctorate
Type: Scholarship
Value: AU$28,597 per annum
Length of Study: 3 years
Frequency: Annual
Country of Study: Australia
Closing Date: 28 February
Additional Information: www.mq.edu.au/research/phd-and-research-degrees/scholarships/scholarship-search/data/national-eye-and-hearing-health-survey

For further information contact:

Email: bamini.gopinath@mq.edu.au

Bangladesh Ministry of Public Affairs (MoPA)

Eligibility: To be eligible for this scholarship, you need to hold a full-offer letter for your undergraduate or postgraduate degree at Macquarie University in 2023 or 2024. You are also required to meet the following criteria: 1. Be a citizen of Bangladesh. 2. Secure admission for a program that is no longer than two sessions in duration (one year). 3. Adhere to the terms and conditions of the scholarship.
Level of Study: Postgraduate
Type: Scholarship
Value: 50% of total tuition fees
Length of Study: Course duration
Frequency: Annual
Country of Study: Australia
Additional Information: mq.edu.au/study/admissions-and-entry/scholarships/international/bangladesh-ministry-of-public-affairs-mopa

For further information contact:

Email: study@mq.edu.au

Beyond segments: towards a lexical model for tonal bilinguals

Eligibility: General requirements for the PhD posts: 1. MA/MSc degree in Psychology (Cognitive Science), Linguistics (esp. in Phonetics), Neuroscience, or other Science-related fields. 2. Strong experimental (e.g., programming) and data analysis skills. 3. Substantial experiences with Eye-trackers are desirable 4. Excellent communication skills in English. 5. Highly motivated, with the ability to conduct independent research.
Level of Study: Postgraduate
Type: Scholarship
Value: AU$28,854 per annum
Length of Study: 3 years
Frequency: Annual
Country of Study: Australia
Closing Date: 31 August
Additional Information: www.mq.edu.au/research/phd-and-research-degrees/scholarships/scholarship-search/data/Beyond-segments-towards-a-lexical-model-for-tonal-bilinguals

For further information contact:

Email: x.wang1@mq.edu.au

Centre for Lasers and Applications Scholarships

Purpose: To enable holders to pursue a research programme leading to the degree of MSc or PhD in experimental and theoretical laser studies.
Eligibility: Open to the Australian citizens, permanent residents, or citizens of overseas countries.
Level of Study: Postgraduate, Research
Type: Scholarship
Value: AU$19,231 (maximum per year). This award is to be used for living expenses.
Length of Study: 2 years (Masters) or 3 years (PhD)
Frequency: Annual
Study Establishment: Macquarie University
Country of Study: Australia
Application Procedure: Check website for further details.
Additional Information: Please see the website for details mailto: www.ru.nl/currentstudents/@1123620/orange-tulip-scholarship-india/

M

For further information contact:

Email: jpiper@ics.mq.edu.au

China Elite Scholarship

Eligibility: To be eligible for this scholarship, you must be a full-time international student studying a Bachelor or Master level degree on-campus (or online and/or offshore if impacted by COVID-19 border restrictions) and meet the following criteria: 1. Be a citizen of China. 2. Achieve a min 80 WAM for Postgrad or a min 95 ATAR (or equivalent) for Undergrad applications. 3. Adhere to the terms and conditions of the scholarship.
Level of Study: Postgraduate
Type: Scholarship
Value: AU$10,000
Frequency: Annual
Country of Study: Australia
Additional Information: mq.edu.au/study/admissions-and-entry/scholarships/international/china-elite-scholarship

For further information contact:

Email: study@mq.edu.au

China Key Partnership Cotutelle Stipend Scheme

Eligibility: The PhD scholarships are open to citizens of China who are studying at Macquarie University for 2 years during their Cotutelle PhD agreement.
Level of Study: Doctorate
Type: Scholarship
Value: a living allowance stipend of AU$28,597 p.a.
Length of Study: 2 years
Frequency: Annual
Country of Study: Australia
Closing Date: 31 December
Additional Information: www.mq.edu.au/research/phd-and-research-degrees/scholarships/scholarship-search/data/china-key-partnership-scholarship-kps

Co-designing culturally relevant end of life care in cancer

Level of Study: Doctorate
Type: Scholarship
Value: full-time stipend rate of AU$28,854 per annum
Length of Study: 3 years
Frequency: Annual

Country of Study: Australia
Closing Date: 28 February
Additional Information: www.mq.edu.au/research/phd-and-research-degrees/scholarships/scholarship-search/data/Co-designing-culturally-relevant-end-of-life-care-in-cancer

For further information contact:

Email: reema.harrison@mq.edu.au

COLFUTURO Scholarship

Eligibility: To be eligible for the scholarship, students must be a citizen of Colombia studying a postgraduate degree. Applicants also have to meet the following criteria: 1. Have a Macquarie University full offer as a full-fee paying international student. 2. Achieve a minimum WAM equivalent of 65 for Postgraduate applications. 3. Adhere to the terms and conditions of the scholarship.
Level of Study: Postgraduate
Type: Scholarship
Value: 50% of the tuition fees
Frequency: Annual
Country of Study: Australia
Additional Information: mq.edu.au/study/admissions-and-entry/scholarships/international/colfuturo-scholarship

For further information contact:

Email: study@mq.edu.au

Computational and methodological breakthroughs in high dimensional statistical modelling for complex data

Level of Study: Doctorate, Research
Type: Scholarship
Value: full-time stipend rate of AU$28,854 per annum.
Length of Study: 3 years
Frequency: Annual
Country of Study: Australia
Closing Date: 28 February
Additional Information: www.mq.edu.au/research/phd-and-research-degrees/scholarships/scholarship-search/data/20213605

For further information contact:

Email: samuel.muller@mq.edu.au

CONACYT Scholarship

Eligibility: To be eligible for the scholarship, students must be a citizen of Mexico studying a postgraduate degree. Applicants also have to meet the following criteria: 1. Have a Macquarie University full offer as a full-fee paying international student. 2. Achieve a minimum WAM equivalent of 65 for Postgraduate applications. 3. Adhere to the terms and conditions of the scholarship.
Level of Study: Postgraduate
Type: Scholarship
Value: 30% of total tuition fees
Frequency: Annual
Country of Study: Australia
Additional Information: mq.edu.au/study/admissions-and-entry/scholarships/international/conacyt-scholarship

For further information contact:

Email: study@mq.edu.au

Developing novel genetic disease models for dementia - Domestic

Eligibility: This scholarship is available to eligible candidates to undertake a MRes Year 2 + PhD Bundle program or direct entry 3-year PhD program. 1. You must be an Australian citizen or hold a permanent residency to be considered. 2. You must have completed an Honours in Biological/Medical Science (or equivalent). Excellent candidates may be considered for direct entry into the PhD program in accordance with HDR rules at Macquarie University.
Level of Study: Postdoctorate
Type: Scholarship
Value: Full-time stipend rate of A$28,854 per annum.
Length of Study: 4 years
Frequency: Annual
Country of Study: Australia
Closing Date: 30 June
Additional Information: www.mq.edu.au/research/phd-and-research-degrees/scholarships/scholarship-search/data/developing-novel-genetic-disease-models-for-dementia

For further information contact:

Email: Lars.ittner@mq.edu.au

Developing novel genetic disease models for dementia - International

Eligibility: This scholarship is available to eligible international candidates to undertake a MRes Year 2 + PhD Bundle program or direct entry 3-year PhD program. You must have completed an Honours in Biological/Medical Science (or equivalent). Excellent candidates may be considered for direct entry into the PhD program in accordance with HDR rules at Macquarie University
Level of Study: Predoctorate
Type: Scholarship
Value: full-time stipend rate of A$28,854 per annum
Length of Study: 4 years
Frequency: Annual
Country of Study: Australia
Closing Date: 30 June
Additional Information: www.mq.edu.au/research/phd-and-research-degrees/scholarships/scholarship-search/data/Developing-novel-genetic-disease-models-for-dementia-International

For further information contact:

Email: Lars.ittner@mq.edu.au

Doctor of Philosophy Scholarship-Artificial Intelligence in Medicine and Healthcare

Purpose: The aim of this research program is to investigate the future role of AI in healthcare and its social, ethical and technical implications.
Eligibility: Australian and international students can apply for these scholarships. If English is not your first language then you will need to show that your English language skills are at a high enough level to succeed in your studies.
Type: Scholarship
Value: The MQRTP full-time stipend rate is AU$27,082 per annum tax-exempt, for up to 3 years (indexed annually) The scholarship is comprised of a Tuition Fee Offset and a Living Allowance Stipend.
Frequency: Annual
Study Establishment: Scholarship is awarded to work on the project tiled, "Artificial Intelligence in Medicine and Healthcare"
Country of Study: Australia
Application Procedure: Applicants will need to complete an HDR Candidature and Scholarship Application Form and arrange for two academic referee reports to be submitted to the Higher Degree Research Office.
Closing Date: 31 July

For further information contact:

Email: annie.lau@mq.edu.au

Europe AU$10,000 Early Acceptance Scholarship

Eligibility: To be eligible for this scholarship, you must be a full-time international student studying a Bachelor or Master level degree on-campus (or online and/or offshore if impacted by COVID-19 border restrictions) and meet the following criteria: 1. Be a citizen of Russia, or one of the countries located in the European region. 2. Accept your Letter of Offer and pay the commencement fee by the Acceptance Deadline. 3. Adhere to the terms and conditions of this scholarship.
Level of Study: Postgraduate
Type: Scholarship
Value: AU$10,000
Length of Study: Course duration
Country of Study: Australia
Application Procedure: Applicants will be assessed automatically for this scholarship for admission to Macquarie University. Successful candidates will be made an offer as part of their Macquarie University offer. To be assessed for this scholarship, please ensure: 1. You have successfully lodged an application for the undergrad or postgrad degree you plan to study. 2. You have met the eligibility criteria for the course you have applied for.
Additional Information: mq.edu.au/study/admissions-and-entry/scholarships/international/europe-10-000-early-acceptance-scholarship

For further information contact:

Email: study@mq.edu.au

FIDERH Scholarship

Eligibility: To be eligible for the scholarship, students must be a citizen of Mexico studying a postgraduate degree. Applicants also have to meet the following criteria: 1. Have a Macquarie University full offer as a full-fee paying international student. 2. Achieve a minimum WAM equivalent of 65 for Postgraduate applications. 3. Adhere to the terms and conditions of the scholarship.
Level of Study: Postgraduate
Type: Scholarship
Value: 20% of total tuition fees
Frequency: Annual
Country of Study: Australia
Additional Information: mq.edu.au/study/admissions-and-entry/scholarships/international/fiderh-scholarship

For further information contact:

Email: study@mq.edu.au

FUNED Scholarship

Eligibility: To be eligible for the scholarship, students must be a citizen of Mexico studying a postgraduate degree. Applicants also have to meet the following criteria:1. Have a Macquarie University full offer as a full-fee paying international student. 2. Achieve a minimum WAM equivalent of 65 for Postgraduate applications. 3. Adhere to the terms and conditions of the scholarship.
Level of Study: Postgraduate
Type: Scholarship
Value: 25% of total tuition fees
Frequency: Annual
Country of Study: Australia
Additional Information: mq.edu.au/study/admissions-and-entry/scholarships/international/funed-scholarship

For further information contact:

Email: study@mq.edu.au

Global MBA Alumni Scholarship

Eligibility: To be eligible for this scholarship, you must be a full-time international student studying a Global MBA and meet the following criteria: 1. Be currently enrolled in the Global Master of Business Administration in 2023 or 2024. 2. Commence study in the session and year indicated in your scholarship letter of offer. 3. Adhere to the terms and conditions of the scholarship. Applicable course 1. Global Master of Business Administration
Level of Study: Postgraduate
Type: Scholarship
Value: 10% of total tuition fees
Length of Study: Course duration
Frequency: Annual
Country of Study: Australia
Additional Information: mq.edu.au/study/admissions-and-entry/scholarships/international/global-mba-alumni-scholarship

For further information contact:

Email: study@mq.edu.au

Indian Arts Partner Scholarship

Eligibility: To be eligible for this scholarship, you must be a full-time international student studying a Master level degree on-campus (or online and/or offshore if impacted by COVID-19 border restrictions) and meet the following criteria: 1. Be enrolled in an undergraduate program or be

a recent graduate from the aforementioned colleges. 2. You can't be a citizen of Australia or New Zealand, or hold permanent residency of Australia. 3. Achieve a minimum WAM equivalent of 65 for Postgraduate applications.
Level of Study: Postgraduate
Type: Scholarship
Value: 50% of the total tuition fee
Length of Study: Course duration
Frequency: Annual
Country of Study: Australia
Additional Information: mq.edu.au/study/admissions-and-entry/scholarships/international/indian-arts-partner-scholarship

For further information contact:

Email: study@mq.edu.au

Indigenous Macquarie University Research Excellence Scholarship

Level of Study: Doctorate
Type: Scholarship
Value: (MPhil) AU$38,854 per annum. plus an additional AU$10,000 pa as supplementary stipend. (PhD)AU$40,854 per annum. plus an additional AU$12,000 pa as supplementary stipend.
Frequency: Annual
Country of Study: Australia
Closing Date: 31 December
Additional Information: www.mq.edu.au/research/phd-and-research-degrees/scholarships/scholarship-search/data/annual-international-research-training-program-scholarship-irtp-and-international-macquarie-research-excellence-scholarship-program-imqres

For further information contact:

Email: tamika.worrell@mq.edu.au

Industrial Transformation Training Centre in Facilitated Advancement of Australia's Bioactive - Domestic

Eligibility: This scholarship is available to eligible candidates to undertake either a direct entry 3.5-year PhD program or a 4 year MRes+PhD programme.
Level of Study: Predoctorate
Type: Scholarship
Value: full-time stipend rate of AU$34,938 per annum
Length of Study: 3.5 to 4 years
Frequency: Annual
Country of Study: Australia

Closing Date: 1 March
Additional Information: www.mq.edu.au/research/phd-and-research-degrees/scholarships/scholarship-search/data/industrial-transformation-training-centre-in-facilitated-advancement-of-australias-bioactive

For further information contact:

Email: faab@mq.edu.au

Industrial Transformation Training Centre in Facilitated Advancement of Australia's Bioactive - International

Level of Study: Doctorate
Type: Scholarship
Value: full-time stipend rate of AU$34,938 per annum
Length of Study: 3.5 to 4 years
Frequency: Annual
Country of Study: Australia
Closing Date: 1 March
Additional Information: A tuition fee scholarship for exceptional international students may be provided by Macquarie University. www.mq.edu.au/research/phd-and-research-degrees/scholarships/scholarship-search/data/industrial-transformation-training-centre-in-facilitated-advancement-of-australias-bioactive-international

For further information contact:

Email: faab@mq.edu.au

International Road to Research Scholarship - Session 2 2023

Eligibility: Awards will only be available to applicants meeting the Eligibility and Selection Criteria who: 1. are onshore in Australia at the time of application. 2. intend to reside in Sydney, Australia during their candidature. 3. meet the English Language Requirement for MQ HDR Programs at the time of application. 4. are enrolling as full-time students. 5. meet the admission criteria for direct entry into MRes Year 2, for commencement in Session 2 2023 6. have a valid visa allowing you to commence your study in August 2023, at the time of application. Note that you will still be required to apply for a Student Visa prior to commencement, should your current visa not allow you to study in Australia until the end of the MRes program.
Level of Study: Postgraduate
Type: Scholarship
Value: AU$28,854 p.a. in 2023. Tuition-fee offset for 1 year maximum.

Length of Study: 1 year
Frequency: Annual
Country of Study: Australia
Application Procedure: To apply, please visit our How To Apply page: www.mq.edu.au/research/phd-and-research-degrees/how-to-apply
Closing Date: 1 May
Additional Information: www.mq.edu.au/research/phd-and-research-degrees/scholarships/scholarship-search/data/international-road-to-research-scholarship

Lab on bag: bioengineering a device for blood diagnostics

Eligibility: 1. Completion of a Master of Research (MRes) with a grade of at least a Distinction level (75% or greater in second year; or 2. A Master of Philosophy; or 3. A two-year Masters degree with a major research component at Distinction level (75% or greater). Peer-reviewed research output may be taken into consideration for admission to the program. You must also demonstrate your suitability for entry to the program by: 1. Including a detailed research proposal. 2. Providing evidence of the required level of English language proficiency.
Level of Study: Doctorate
Type: Scholarship
Value: AU$28,854 per annum
Length of Study: 3 years
Frequency: Annual
Country of Study: Australia
Closing Date: 31 March
Additional Information: www.mq.edu.au/research/phd-and-research-degrees/scholarships/scholarship-search/data/Lab-on-bag-bioengineering-a-device-for-blood-diagnostics

For further information contact:

Email: yuling.wang@mq.edu.au

Macquarie University AU$5,000 Regional Scholarship

Eligibility: To be eligible for this scholarship, you must be a full-time international student studying a Bachelor or Master level degree on-campus (or online and/or offshore if impacted by COVID-19 border restrictions) and meet the following criteria: Be a citizen of Mongolia, South Korea, Russia, Japan, Lebanon, or one of the countries located in either the ASEAN, South Asia, African, Latin American or European regions. Adhere to the terms and conditions of this scholarship.

Level of Study: Postgraduate
Type: Scholarship
Value: AU$5,000 per year
Length of Study: 2 years
Frequency: Annual
Country of Study: Australia
Additional Information: mq.edu.au/study/admissions-and-entry/scholarships/international/macquarie-university-5-000-regional-scholarship

For further information contact:

Email: study@mq.edu.au

Macquarie University Alumni Scholarship

Level of Study: Postgraduate
Type: Scholarship
Value: 10% of total tuition fees
Length of Study: Course duration
Frequency: Annual
Country of Study: Australia
Additional Information: mq.edu.au/study/admissions-and-entry/scholarships/international/macquarie-university-alumni-scholarship

For further information contact:

Email: study@mq.edu.au

Macquarie University Centre for the Health Economy (MUCHE) Industry Funded Higher Degree Research (HDR) scholarships

Eligibility: his scholarship is available to eligible candidates to undertake either the MRes Year 2 + PhD or direct entry PhD. To be eligible for a scholarship, applicants are expected to have a record of excellent academic performance and, preferably, additional relevant research experience and/or peer-reviewed research activity in line with the University's scholarship rating guidelines. Students must be willing and able to undertake research relevant to the Australian pharmaceutical sector and government. This is likely to be students with prior degrees related to health care fields, such as health economics, health policy, public health, epidemiology, health systems and informatics, and digital health. However, we encourage other students that have studied outside these fields to apply for the scholarship if they can demonstrate an innovative research idea that is relevant to the pharmaceutical sector and government. Students must have a high level of English language proficiency. To be considered for the bundled 2nd year

Master of Research plus PhD program, candidates must have a Masters degree (by coursework, inclusive of research methodology units) with a distinction average grade. To be considered for direct entry into the PhD program, candidates must have a Masters degree (by coursework) with distinction average results, and have: 1. completed Macquarie University Master of Research with at least 75 per cent in second year; or 2. completed a Master of Philosophy; or 3. completed a Masters (at least two years) from another institution with a major research component (a thesis component of approximately 50 per cent of the degree and 20,000 words) at distinction level. PhD candidates must also demonstrate their interest in health care related research, and their strong analytical and writing skills reflected in research output (i.e. peer reviewed publications). PhD candidates may be exempt from having to demonstrate a completed Master of Research, Master of Philosophy or Masters with a major research component, if they can demonstrate equivalence via their capacity to undertake independent research through publications in peer reviewed journals. Candidates may also be considered for both the Master of Research and a PhD (i.e., a four year scholarship bundle) if the prerequisites for direct entry into the PhD cannot be demonstrated, but prerequisites to the Master of Research can be demonstrated.

Type: Scholarship

Value: base stipend of AU$28,597 p.a. and a top-up stipend of AU$21,448 p.a, also a tuition-fee offset scholarship. AU$1,000 over the second year of the Master of Research and AU$10,000 over the course of the PhD for research related activities.

Length of Study: 3 to 4 years

Frequency: Annual

Country of Study: Australia

Application Procedure: Please note, at the start of your application you should select the scholarship type of "HDR Project/Supervisor Specific Scholarship". If you are an international candidate, please apply for scholarship reference 20201217. If you are a domestic candidate, please apply for scholarship reference 20201218. For information on how to apply, select the "How to Apply" button below: www.mq.edu.au/?a=519657

Closing Date: 31 December

Additional Information: www.mq.edu.au/research/phd-and-research-degrees/scholarships/scholarship-search/data/macquarie-university-centre-for-the-health-economy-muche-industry-funded-higher-degree-research-hdr-scholarships

For further information contact:

Email: martin.hoyle@mq.edu.au

Macquarie University Centre for the Health Economy (MUCHE) Industry Funded Higher Degree Research (HDR) scholarships-Domestic

Eligibility: his scholarship is available to eligible candidates to undertake either the MRes Year 2 + PhD or direct entry PhD. To be eligible for a scholarship, applicants are expected to have a record of excellent academic performance and, preferably, additional relevant research experience and/or peer-reviewed research activity in line with the University's scholarship rating guidelines. Students must be willing and able to undertake research relevant to the Australian pharmaceutical sector and government. This is likely to be students with prior degrees related to health care fields, such as health economics, health policy, public health, epidemiology, health systems and informatics, and digital health. However, we encourage other students that have studied outside these fields to apply for the scholarship if they can demonstrate an innovative research idea that is relevant to the pharmaceutical sector and government. Students must have a high level of English language proficiency. To be considered for the bundled 2nd year Master of Research plus PhD program, candidates must have a Masters degree (by coursework, inclusive of research methodology units) with a distinction average grade. To be considered for direct entry into the PhD program, candidates must have a Masters degree (by coursework) with distinction average results, and have: 1. completed Macquarie University Master of Research with at least 75 per cent in second year; or 2. completed a Master of Philosophy; or 3. completed a Masters (at least two years) from another institution with a major research component (a thesis component of approximately 50 per cent of the degree and 20,000 words) at distinction level. PhD candidates must also demonstrate their interest in health care related research, and their strong analytical and writing skills reflected in research output (i.e. peer reviewed publications). PhD candidates may be exempt from having to demonstrate a completed Master of Research, Master of Philosophy or Masters with a major research component, if they can demonstrate equivalence via their capacity to undertake independent research through publications in peer reviewed journals. Candidates may also be considered for both the Master of Research and a PhD (i.e., a four year scholarship bundle) if the prerequisites for direct entry into the PhD cannot be demonstrated, but prerequisites to the Master of Research can be demonstrated.

Level of Study: Research

Type: Scholarship

Value: a base stipend of AU$28,597 p.a. and a top-up stipend of AU$21,448 p.a, also a tuition-fee offset scholarship. AU$1,000 over the second year of the Master of Research and AU$10,000 over the course of the PhD for research.

Length of Study: 3 to 4 years

Frequency: Annual

Country of Study: Australia
Closing Date: 31 December

For further information contact:

Email: martin.hoyle@mq.edu.au

Macquarie University Higher Study Scholarship - Full time rate

Eligibility: In addition to academic excellence and financial hardship, consideration is given to factors including an Indigenous background, capacity to triumph over hardship, carer responsibilities, rural or remote background, non English-speaking background, long term disability or medical condition, or ongoing effects of trauma and abuse. | The successful applicant for this scholarship must be: 1. An Australian citizen or Permanent resident, or a New Zealand citizen 2. Studying or intending to study full-time or part time at the Honours or postgraduate coursework level in a Commonwealth Supported place or tuition fee place. (Note that students undertaking Graduate Certificate and Graduate Diploma study are not eligible for this scholarship.) 3. Able to demonstrate financial hardship; applicants need to be in receipt of Youth Allowance or any other means tested Commonwealth support payment. Applicable course 1. Postgraduate
Level of Study: Postgraduate
Value: AU$11,220
Length of Study: postgraduate course duration
Frequency: Annual
Country of Study: Australia
Additional Information: mq.edu.au/study/admissions-and-entry/scholarships/domestic/macquarie-university-higher-study-scholarship-full-time-rate

For further information contact:

Email: ask@mq.edu.au

Macquarie University Higher Study Scholarship - Part time rate

Eligibility: In addition to academic excellence and financial hardship, consideration is given to factors including an Indigenous background, capacity to triumph over hardship, carer responsibilities, rural or remote background, non English-speaking background, long term disability or medical condition, or ongoing effects of trauma and abuse. The successful applicant for this scholarship must be: 1. An Australian citizen or Permanent resident, or a New Zealand citizen

2. Studying or intending to study full-time or part time at the Honours or postgraduate coursework level in a Commonwealth Sup ported place or tuition fee place. (Note that students undertaking Graduate Certificate and Graduate Diploma study are not eligible for this scholarship.) 3. Able to demonstrate financial hardship; applicants need to be in receipt of Youth Allowance or any other means tested Commonwealth support payment. Applicable course 1. Postgraduate
Level of Study: Postgraduate
Type: Scholarship
Value: AU$5,610
Frequency: Annual
Country of Study: Australia
Additional Information: mq.edu.au/study/admissions-and-entry/scholarships/domestic/macquarie-university-higher-study-scholarship-part-time-rate

For further information contact:

Email: ask@mq.edu.au

Macquarie University PhD Scholarship in Knowledge Acquisition and Cognitive Modelling

Purpose: To enable students to undertake research in related fields.
Eligibility: Open to applicants who have completed, an Australian 4 year undergraduate degree with at least Second Class (Honours) division 1 in computing or a related field, or equivalent qualifications.
Level of Study: Postdoctorate, Postgraduate
Type: Scholarships
Value: AU$19,231 plus AU$5,000 top-up per year tax exempt.
Length of Study: 3 years
Frequency: Annual
Study Establishment: Macquarie University
Country of Study: Australia
Application Procedure: Applicants must download the form from the website.
Closing Date: 31 May
Additional Information: Additional Information can be obtained from the Higher Degree Research Unit by phoning (61) 2 9850 7277, by emailing or by downloading the form from the website mailto: pgschol@mq.edu.au

For further information contact:

Email: richards@mq.edu.au

Macquarie University Postgraduate Loyalty Scheme 10% sponsorship

Eligibility: An eligible student must: 1. Be attempting post-graduate study at Macquarie for the first time (either direct from their undergraduate degree or after taking a break) 2. be commencing their degree after 2022 3. be accepting a domestic fee-paying place, not a Commonwealth Supported Place 4. not be receiving any other Macquarie fee sponsorships 5. not be going into a Master of Chiropractic, Clinical Neuropsychology, Organisational Psychology, Clinical Psychology, Clinical Audiology, or Speech and Language Pathology; a Non Award course; a Higher Education Certificate course; or a Doctor of Medicine or Physiotherapy. Applicable course 1. Postgraduate
Level of Study: Postgraduate
Type: Scholarship
Value: 10% of course fee
Frequency: Annual
Country of Study: Australia
Additional Information: mq.edu.au/study/admissions-and-entry/scholarships/domestic/macquarie-university-postgraduate-loyalty-scheme-10-sponsorship

For further information contact:

Email: ask@mq.edu.au

Macquarie Vice-Chancellor's International Scholarships

Purpose: The Macquarie University Vice-Chancellor's International Scholarship is awarded to recognise academic excellence for international students. This highly competitive scholarship is based on academic merit and awarded to future students.
Eligibility: Applicants must 1. Be a citizen of a country other than Australia or New Zealand. 2. Meet the University's academic and English requirements for the course (must hold a full offer of admission by the application deadline). 3. Achieved a minimum GPA equivalent of 5.0 out of 7.0 for Postgraduate applications; or a minimum ATAR equivalent of 90 out of 100 for Undergraduate applications. 4. Applied for a program that is longer than one session in duration. 5. Commence study in session and year indicated in the scholarship offer letter, and commencement may not be deferred.
Level of Study: Postgraduate
Type: Scholarship
Value: AU$10,000
Length of Study: One-off
Frequency: Annual

Country of Study: Australia
Closing Date: 14 June
Funding: Private
Additional Information: mq.edu.au/study/admissions-and-entry/scholarships/international/vice-chancellor-s-international-scholarship

For further information contact:

Email: study@mq.edu.au

Mexican CONACYT-Macquarie University Postgraduate Research Scholarships

Purpose: Macquarie University has partnered with CONACYT (The National Council for Science and Technology of the United Mexican States) to promote the access of Mexican students to postgraduate studies at Macquarie University.
Eligibility: Scholarships are offered for up to 10 Mexican students accepted and enrolled in a research degree.
Level of Study: Doctorate
Type: Scholarship
Value: CONACYT – HDR tuition fees (70%), a living allowance/stipend, and annual support of overseas student health cover (OSHC). Macquarie University – HDR tuition fees (30%).
Length of Study: 2 to 3 years
Frequency: Annual
Country of Study: Australia
Closing Date: 31 December
Additional Information: www.mq.edu.au/research/phd-and-research-degrees/scholarships/scholarship-search/data/mexican-conacyt-macquarie-university-postgraduate

For further information contact:

Email: mcruzca@conacyt.mx

Mongolia AU$10,000 Early Acceptance Scholarship

Eligibility: To be eligible for this scholarship, you must be a full-time international student studying a Bachelor or Master level degree on-campus (or online and/or offshore if impacted by COVID-19 border restrictions) and meet the following criteria: 1. Be a citizen of Mongolia. 2. Accept your Letter of Offer and pay the commencement fee by the Acceptance Deadline. 3. Adhere to the terms and conditions of this scholarship.

M

Type: Scholarship
Frequency: Annual
Study Establishment: AU$10,000 per year
Country of Study: Australia
Additional Information: mq.edu.au/study/admissions-and-entry/scholarships/international/mongolia-10-000-early-acceptance-scholarship

For further information contact:

Email: study@mq.edu.au

Perovskite and quantum dot opto-electronic devices

Eligibility: The minimum requirement for admission to a PhD degree is: 1. Completion of a Master of Research (MRes) with a grade of at least a Distinction level (75% or greater in second year; or 2. A Master of Philosophy; or 3. A two-year Masters degree with a major research component at Distinction level (75% or greater). Peer-reviewed research output may be taken into consideration for admission to the program. You must also demonstrate your suitability for entry to the program by: 1. Including a detailed research proposal. 2. Providing evidence of the required level of English language proficiency. Entry to a PhD will also be assessed on availability of appropriate supervision and resources.
Level of Study: Doctorate
Type: Scholarship
Value: AU$28,854 per annum
Length of Study: 3 years
Frequency: Annual
Country of Study: Australia
No. of awards offered: 2
Closing Date: 31 May
Additional Information: www.mq.edu.au/research/phd-and-research-degrees/scholarships/scholarship-search/data/Perovskite-and-quantum-dot-opto-electronic-devices

For further information contact:

Email: shujuan.huang@mq.edu.au

Project Specific - Energy and Natural Resources Innovation and Technology Research Initiative (International)

Eligibility: The Master of Research equips students with intensive research preparation before beginning doctoral study. The minimum requirement for admission to an MRes degree is: 1. Bachelor or higher award from a recognised institution 2. MQ Graduates (from 2020 onwards): An overall WAM of 65+ and a WAM of 70+ at 300 level 3. All Other Applicants: Minimum overall GPA of 4.38 on a 7 point scale and GPA of 5.25 at 300 level 4. A research proposal (a short paragraph is sufficient). 5. A high level of English language proficiency.
Level of Study: Postgraduate
Type: Scholarship
Value: AU$28,597 per annum
Length of Study: 3 years
Frequency: Annual
Country of Study: Australia
Closing Date: 15 March
Additional Information: www.mq.edu.au/research/phd-and-research-degrees/scholarships/scholarship-search/data/project-specific-energy-and-natural-resources-innovation-and-technology-research-initiative-international

For further information contact:

Email: tina.solimanhunter@mq.edu.au

Project Specific Scholarship - Improving integrated pest management with genome editing

Eligibility: The Master of Research program equips students with intensive research preparation before beginning doctoral study. The minimum requirement for admission to an MRes degree is: 1. Bachelor or higher award from a recognised institution 2. MQ Graduates (from 2020 onwards): An overall WAM of 65+ and a WAM of 70+ at 300 level 3. All Other Applicants: Minimum overall GPA of 4.38 on a 7 point scale and GPA of 5.25 at 300 level 4. A research proposal (a short paragraph is sufficient). 5. A high level of English language proficiency.
Level of Study: Postgraduate
Type: Scholarship
Value: AU$28,854 per annum
Length of Study: 3 years
Frequency: Annual
Country of Study: Australia
Closing Date: 31 March
Additional Information: www.mq.edu.au/research/phd-and-research-degrees/scholarships/scholarship-search/data/Project-Specific-Scholarship-20203580

For further information contact:

Email: Maciej.maselko@mq.edu.au

Project Specific Scholarship - Investigating neuron-glia interactions in MND/ALS

Level of Study: Doctorate
Type: Scholarship
Value: full-time stipend rate of AU$28,854 per annum
Length of Study: 3 years
Frequency: Annual
Country of Study: Australia
Closing Date: 15 March
Additional Information: www.mq.edu.au/research/phd-and-research-degrees/scholarships/scholarship-search/data/project-specific-scholarship-investigating-neuron-glia-interactions-in-mndals

For further information contact:

Email: Marco.morsch@mq.edu.au

Raman LiDAR Spectroscopy Techniques for Remote Sensing of Subsurface Water Properties

Eligibility: The Scholarship will be awarded to a student who is an Australian Citizen. This scholarship is available to eligible candidates to undertake a direct entry 3-year PhD program.
Level of Study: Doctorate
Type: Scholarship
Value: stipend of AU$40,000 per annum with additional funding to support travel and project costs
Frequency: Annual
Country of Study: Australia
Closing Date: 15 March
Additional Information: www.mq.edu.au/research/phd-and-research-degrees/scholarships/scholarship-search/data/raman-lidar-spectroscopy-techniques-for-remote-sensing-of-subsurface-water-properties-from-numerical-modelling-to-the-field

For further information contact:

Email: Helen.pask@mq.edu.au

RuralKids GPS – delivering equitable care to children in rural NSW

Eligibility: The minimum requirement for admission to a PhD degree is: 1. Completion of a Master of Research (MRes) with a grade of at least a Distinction level (75% or greater in second year; or 2. A Master of Philosophy; or 3. A two-year Masters degree with a major research component at Distinction level (75% or greater). Peer-reviewed research output may be taken into consideration for admission to the program. You must also demonstrate your suitability for entry to the program by: 1. Including a detailed research proposal. 2. Providing evidence of the required level of English language proficiency.
Level of Study: Doctorate
Type: Scholarship
Value: AU$28,854 per annum
Frequency: Annual
Country of Study: Australia
Closing Date: 30 June
Additional Information: www.mq.edu.au/research/phd-and-research-degrees/scholarships/scholarship-search/data/AIHI-RuralKids-GPS

For further information contact:

Email: yvonne.zurynski@mq.edu.au

Saving Lives: Mapping the influence of Indigenous LGBTIQ+ creative artists - Domestic

Eligibility: This scholarship is available to eligible domestic candidates to undertake a 3-year Ph.D. program (FTE). Aboriginal and Torres Strait Islander candidates are eligible to receive an additional stipend of AU$12,000 per annum.
Level of Study: Doctorate
Type: Scholarship
Value: full-time stipend rate of AU$28,854 per annum. Aboriginal and Torres Strait Islander candidates are eligible to receive an additional stipend of AU$12,000 per annum.
Length of Study: 3 years
Frequency: Annual
Country of Study: Australia
Closing Date: 4 April
Additional Information: www.mq.edu.au/research/phd-and-research-degrees/scholarships/scholarship-search/data/saving-lives-mapping-the-influence-of-indigenous-lgbtiq-creative-artists-international2/saving-lives-mapping-the-influence-of-indigenous-lgbtiq-creative-artists-international

For further information contact:

Email: sandy.osullivan@mq.edu.au

Saving Lives: Mapping the influence of Indigenous LGBTIQ+ creative artists - International

Eligibility: This scholarship is available to eligible international candidates to undertake a 3-year Ph.D. program (FTE).

M

Level of Study: Doctorate
Type: Scholarship
Value: full-time stipend rate of AU$28,854 per annum
Length of Study: 3 year
Frequency: Annual
Country of Study: Australia
Closing Date: 4 April
Additional Information: www.mq.edu.au/research/phd-and-research-degrees/scholarships/scholarship-search/data/saving-lives-mapping-the-influence-of-indigenous-lgbtiq-creative-artists-international2

For further information contact:

Email: sandy.osullivan@mq.edu.au

SEP Scholarship

Eligibility: To be eligible for the scholarship, students must be a citizen of Mexico studying a postgraduate degree. Applicants also have to meet the following criteria: 1. Have a Macquarie University full offer as a full-fee paying international student. 2. Achieve a minimum WAM equivalent of 65 for Postgraduate applications. 3. Adhere to the terms and conditions of the scholarship.
Level of Study: Postgraduate
Type: Scholarship
Value: 50% of total tuition fees
Frequency: Annual
Country of Study: Australia
Additional Information: mq.edu.au/study/admissions-and-entry/scholarships/international/sep-scholarship

For further information contact:

Email: study@mq.edu.au

South Korea A$10,000 Early Acceptance Scholarship

Eligibility: To be eligible for this scholarship, you must be a full-time international student studying a Bachelor or Master level degree on-campus (or online and/or offshore if impacted by COVID-19 border restrictions) and meet the following criteria: 1. Be a citizen of South Korea. 2. Accept your Letter of Offer and pay the commencement fee by the Acceptance Deadline. 3. Adhere to the terms and conditions of this scholarship.
Level of Study: Postgraduate
Type: Scholarship
Value: AU$10,000 per year
Frequency: Annual

Country of Study: Australia
Additional Information: mq.edu.au/study/admissions-and-entry/scholarships/international/south-korea-10-000-early-acceptance-scholarship

For further information contact:

Email: study@mq.edu.au

Sponsored Student Grant

Eligibility: To be eligible for the scholarship, students must be in receipt of a fully funded external scholarship by Asian scholarship bodies. Applicants also have to meet the following criteria: 1. Have a Macquarie University full offer as a full-fee paying international student. 2. Adhere to the terms and conditions of the scholarship. 3. Achieve a min 65 WAM for Postgrad or a min 85 ATAR (or equivalent) for Undergrad applications.
Level of Study: Postgraduate
Type: Scholarship
Value: AU$5,000
Length of Study: One-off award
Frequency: Annual
Country of Study: Australia
Additional Information: mq.edu.au/study/admissions-and-entry/scholarships/international/sponsored-student-grant

For further information contact:

Email: study@mq.edu.au

Studying post-translational protein modifications in brain function and disease - Domestic

Eligibility: This scholarship is available to eligible candidates to undertake MRes Year2 +PhD Bundle program or a direct entry 3-year PhD program. 1. You must be an Australian citizen or hold a permanent residency to be considered. 2. You must have completed an Honours in Biological/Medical Science (or equivalent). Excellent candidates may be considered for direct entry into the PhD program in accordance with HDR rules at Macquarie University.
Level of Study: Doctorate, Predoctorate
Type: Scholarship
Value: full-time stipend rate of AU$28,854 per annum
Length of Study: 4 years
Frequency: Annual
Country of Study: Australia
Closing Date: 30 June
Additional Information: www.mq.edu.au/research/phd-and-research-degrees/scholarships/scholarship-search/data/

studying-post-translational-protein-modifications-in-brain-function-and-disease

For further information contact:

Email: Lars.ittner@mq.edu.au

Studying post-translational protein modifications in brain function and disease - International

Eligibility: You must have completed an Honours in Biological/Medical Science (or equivalent). Excellent candidates may be considered for direct entry into the PhD program in accordance with HDR rules at Macquarie University.
Level of Study: Postgraduate
Type: Scholarship
Value: full-time stipend rate of AU$28,854 per annum
Length of Study: 4 years
Frequency: Annual
Country of Study: Australia
Closing Date: 30 June
Additional Information: www.mq.edu.au/research/phd-and-research-degrees/scholarships/scholarship-search/data/Studying-post-translational-protein-modifications-in-brain-function-and-disease-International

For further information contact:

Email: Lars.ittner@mq.edu.au

Vice-Chancellors International Scholarship (VCIS) - Korea University

Eligibility: To be eligible for this scholarship, you must be a full-time international student studying a Master level degree on-campus (or online and/or offshore if impacted by COVID-19 border restrictions) and meet the following criteria: 1. Complete your Graduate Diploma at Korea University & hold a full-offer before application deadline. 2. Commence study in the session and year indicated in the scholarship letter of offer. 3. Adhere to the terms and conditions of the scholarship. Applicable course 1. Master of Translation and Interpreting Studies
Level of Study: Postgraduate
Type: Scholarship
Value: AU$7,500
Frequency: Annual
Country of Study: Australia
Additional Information: mq.edu.au/study/admissions-and-entry/scholarships/international/vice-chancellor-s-international-scholarship-vcis-korea-university

For further information contact:

Email: study@mq.edu.au

Vice-Chancellors International Scholarship (VCIS) - Pontificia Universidad Javeriana

Eligibility: To be eligible for this scholarship, you must be a full-time international student studying a Master level degree on-campus (or online and/or offshore if impacted by COVID-19 border restrictions) and meet the following criteria: 1. Achieve a minimum WAM equivalent of 65 for Postgraduate applications. 2. Commence study in the session and year indicated in your scholarship letter of offer. 3. Adhere to the terms and conditions of the scholarship.
Level of Study: Postgraduate
Type: Scholarship
Value: 15% of total tuition fees
Length of Study: Course duration
Frequency: Annual
Country of Study: Australia
Additional Information: mq.edu.au/study/admissions-and-entry/scholarships/international/vice-chancellor-s-international-scholarship-vcis-pontificia-universidad-javeriana

For further information contact:

Email: study@mq.edu.au

Walter Heywood Bryan Scholarship for International Students in Australia

Purpose: The aim of the WH Bryan Scholarship is to advance the understanding of Queensland Earth Sciences by addressing a globally significant problem leading to impactful outcomes, with the supported project to be led by an outstanding PhD candidate.
Eligibility: Australian and international students are eligible to apply. Students need to demonstrate that they have a good level of written and spoken English.
Type: Scholarship
Value: See the website.
Study Establishment: Scholarship is awarded in the field of Earth Sciences.
Country of Study: Australia
Application Procedure: The main written application is expected to be no more than 10 pages. Each application must be submitted from the host university.
Closing Date: 30 April
Additional Information: www.whbryanscholarship.org.au/

M

Magna Carta College

10, Innovation House, John Smith Dr, Oxford OX4 2JY,
United Kingdom.

Tel: (44) 1865 986787
Email: info@magnacartacollege.ac.uk
Website: www.magnacartacollege.ac.uk/about-us/
Contact: Innovation House

Magna Carta College is an independent business school, located
in Oxford, which has evolved from one founded 10 years ago by
senior Oxford academics. With its team of Oxbridge faculty and
experienced industry practitioners, Magna Carta College delivers
the highest quality business teaching, learning and insights, combining relevant, insightful, practical and theoretical experience
and research, to an international and richly diverse student body.

Global Ambassador Scholarship Programme (GASPR)

Purpose: GASPR is a global annual rolling scholarship programme and aims to give financial support for those who are
eager to improve their education.
Eligibility: Applicant should be 18+ years old and can be
citizen of any country in the world. Scholarships are only valid
during the June intake. The difference in tuition fee for the entire
programme must be paid in full before the commencement of
studies. Students must cover all other related costs on their own
(accommodation, meals, visa, medical insurance, etc.)
Type: Scholarship
Value: The scholarship provides discount on basic tuition fee.
Frequency: Annual
Country of Study: United Kingdom
Application Procedure: Applicants should send the application form along with the required documents to the email
address gaspr@magnacartacollege.org
Closing Date: 15 May
Additional Information: Successful scholarship candidates
will not be able to apply for further College awards and
payment plans: scholarships, discounts, installments, etc.,
www.magnacartacollege.org/programme/gaspr

Maine Restaurant Association

45 Melville St., Augusta, ME 04330, United States of
America.

Tel: (1) 207 623 2178
Website: www.mainerestaurant.com

Educational trade group of restaurants providing educational
and networking opportunities. Build relationships with key
people who manage and lead nonprofit organizations with
GuideStar Pro.

Russ Casey Scholarship

Purpose: This scholarship is available for Maine undergraduate
students who plan to pursue a career in culinary arts or hospitality. Culinary arts students will be given first consideration
Eligibility: 1. Must be a resident of Maine. 2. Must be a United
States citizen or permanent resident. 3. Must be a high school
senior or older to apply for this undergraduate award. 4. Must
be planning to pursue a culinary arts or hospitality-oriented
program. Culinary arts students will be given first consideration. 5. This award is for United States students
Level of Study: Graduate
Type: Scholarship
Value: US$1,000
Frequency: Annual
Country of Study: United States of America
Application Procedure: Applications are available on the
Maine Restaurant Association (MRA) website by searching
for "scholarship". In addition to a completed application, the
student must submit the following a high school transcript;
three letters of reference (two from teachers or counselors,
and one from a member of the Maine Restaurant Association); and a typed letter of not more than 300 words describing
his/her affiliation with the hospitality industry, why he/she is
applying for this scholarship, and his/her career goals. Applications and all supporting materials must be sent to the
address provided, and must be received by the deadline date
Closing Date: 28 April
Funding: Foundation

For further information contact:

45 Melville Street, Augusta, ME 04330, United States of
America.

Email: info@mainerestaurant.com

Managed Care Organization

8511 South Sam Houston Parkway East, Ste 200, Houston,
TX 77075, United States of America.

Tel: (1) 844 310 9791
Website: www.gallaghermalpractice.com/blog/

A managed care organization, by definition, is an organization that practices managed care principles. It is a health plan or health company which works to provide quality medical care at a cost-effective price. Healthcare organizations include providers such as hospitals, doctors and other medical professionals and facilities who work together on behalf of patients.

The James Madison Memorial Fellowship

Purpose: The James Madison Memorial Fellowship is a federal program that offers secondary level teachers (both pre-service and in-service) of history and government up to US$24,000 to complete a master's degree in history, political science, or related fields.

Eligibility: Fellowship applicants compete only against other applicants from the state of their legal residence. To be eligible to apply for a fellowship, you must: 1. Be a U.-S. citizen 2. Be a teacher, or plan to become a teacher, of American history, American government, or civics classes where you will teach topics on the Constitution at the secondary school level (grades 7–12). 3. Possess a bachelor's degree or plan to receive a bachelor's degree no later than August 31 of the year in which you are applying .

Level of Study: Graduate, Postgraduate

Type: Fellowship

Value: US$24,000

Frequency: Annual

Country of Study: United States of America

Application Procedure: 1. Applicants compete only against other applicants from the states of their legal residence. 2. Applicants are evaluated on their demonstrated commitment to a career teaching American history, American government, or civics classes where you will teach topics on the Constitution at the secondary school level; demonstrated intent to pursue and complete a program of graduate study that emphasizes the Constitution and offers instruction in that subject; demonstrated devotion to civic responsibility. 3. Demonstrated capacity for study and performance as classroom teachers, and their proposed courses of graduate study. 4. Applicants will be evaluated without regard to race, color, religion, sex, age, national origin, disability, political affiliation, marital status, sexual orientation or other non-merit factors.

No. of awards offered: 2

Closing Date: 1 March

Funding: Private

Additional Information: apply.scholarsapply.org/jamesmadison/

For further information contact:

1613 Duke Street, Alexandria, VA 22314, United States of America.

Email: Madison@scholarshipamerica.org

Manipal University in India

Tiger Circle Road, Madhav Nagar, Manipal, Karnataka 576104, India.

Email: mlsc@manipal.edu
Website: www.manipal.edu/sls-manipal/
Contact: Manipal University in India

Manipal Academy of Higher Education is synonymous with excellence in higher education. Over 28,000 students from 57 different nations live to learn and play in the sprawling University town, nestled on a plateau in Karnataka's Udupi district. It also has nearly 2,500 faculty and almost 10,000 other support and service staff, who cater to the various professional institutions in health sciences, engineering, management, communication and humanities which dot the Wi-Fi-enabled campus.

Doctor TMA Pai PhD Scholarships for International Students at Manipal University

Purpose: The Manipal Academy of Higher Education is currently accepting applications for Dr. TMA Pai PhD scholarship program. Indian and Foreign students are eligible to apply for this scholarship.

Eligibility: 1. Medicine & Dental MBBS / BDS / an undergraduate degree of atleast 5 year duration or MD / MS / MDS / PG Diploma from an institution recognized by MCI / DCI. 2. Pharmacy PharmD or PharmD Post Baccalaureate from an institution / university recognized by Pharmacy Council of India (PCI). 3. Others Master's Degree or equivalent from an institution / university recognized by UGC / respective regulatory body. 4. Candidates with Master's degrees or equivalent, from foreign universities will have to produce a certificate or recognition / equivalency by the Association of Indian Universities (AIU), as equivalent to the corresponding Indian degrees for the purpose of higher studies.

Level of Study: Doctorate, Postdoctorate

Type: Scholarship

Value: Rs. 30,000
Length of Study: 4 years
Frequency: Annual
Country of Study: India
Application Procedure: 1. Applicants with valid National Fellowships Candidates with UGC - CSIR - NET-JRF / ICMR - JRF / DBT - JRF / JEST / INSPIRE Fellowship or having qualified other UGC recognized National or State level eligibility test with a valid fellowship, at the time of admission are exempted from the All India PhD Manipal Entrance Test (MET). 2. Candidates interested in applying for the Dr. TMA Pai Scholarship MUST appear for the admission process through All India PhD Manipal Entrance Test (MET). 3. Candidates who work in research centres affiliated / collaborating with MAHE Manipal or work in funded projects within MAHE Manipal, are eligible to apply for Full-Time PhD program under this category.
No. of awards offered: 300
Closing Date: 31 December
Additional Information: As there are many areas of research and less number of scholarships, a few seats are available in the self - sponsored scheme (without scholarships). mahephd.azurewebsites.net/#no-back-button

For further information contact:

Email: cds.mahe@manipal.edu

March of Dimes

1550 Crystal Dr, Suite 1300, Arlington, VA 22202, United States of America.

Tel: (1) 888 663 4637
Email: researchgrantssupport@marchofdimes.com
Website: www.marchofdimes.com/professionals
Contact: March of Dimes National Office

March of Dimes leads the fight for the health of all mothers and babies. We believe that every baby deserves the best possible start. Unfortunately, not all babies get one. We are changing that. Now we're building on that legacy to level the playing field for all mothers and babies, no matter their age, socio-economic background or demographics. We support mothers throughout their pregnancy, even when everything doesn't go according to plan.

Basil O'Connor Starter Scholar Research Award

Purpose: This award is designed to support young scientists just embarking on their independent research careers and is limited, therefore, to those holding recent faculty appointments. The applicants' research interests should be consonant with those of the Foundation.
Eligibility: The Basil O'Connor Starter Scholar Research Award is intended to be an initial independent grant to young investigators. Eligibility is thus restricted. PhD applicants should be 4 to 8 years past their degree and must hold a full-time faculty position at their current institution. For MD or MD/PhD applicants, the same 4-8 year timeline applies, but begins upon completion of the last year of clinical training required for medical specialty board certification. Requests for exceptions (e.g. parental leave) should be directed to the Senior Vice President for Research & Global Programs.
Type: Award/Grant
Value: Up to US$150,000 including 10 percent indirect costs to sponsoring institutions
Length of Study: 2 years
Frequency: Annual
Country of Study: Any country
Application Procedure: Deans, Chairs of Departments, or Directors of Institutes/Centers should submit nominations for this award addressed to the Senior Vice President for Research and Global Programs.
Closing Date: 9 July
Additional Information: These grants do not cover the recipient's salary, but do provide salary support for technical help. Please email any enquiries regarding award www.researchfunding.duke.edu/basil-o%E2%80%99connor-starter-scholar-research-award

Marine Biological Association

The Laboratory, Citadel Hill, Plymouth, Devon PL1 2PB, United Kingdom.

Tel: (44) 1752 426493
Email: info@mba.ac.uk
Website: www.mba.ac.uk/
Contact: The Marine Biological Association

The Marine Biological Association (MBA) is one of the world's longest-running societies dedicated to promoting research into our oceans and the life they support. Since 1884 we have been providing a unified, clear, independent voice on behalf of the marine biological community and currently have a growing membership in over 40 countries.

MarTERA Call

Purpose: The overall goal of the MarTERA Cofund is to strengthen the European Research Area (ERA) in maritime and marine technologies and Blue Growth
Level of Study: Graduate
Type: Research grant
Frequency: Annual
Country of Study: Any country
Closing Date: 27 March
Funding: Private
Additional Information: www.martera.eu/joint-calls

For further information contact:

Email: f.aslan@fz-juelich.de

Peter Baker Fellowship

Purpose: The awards are intended for post-doctoral scientists interested in research in marine biology. Applications are particularly encouraged from those interested in physiological research. The Fellowship is provided by funds contributed by individuals and Scientific Societies from all over the world.
Level of Study: Doctorate, Postdoctorate, Research
Type: Fellowship
Value: Up to £3,000
Frequency: Annual
Country of Study: United Kingdom
Application Procedure: 1. Applications should be sent by e-mail to info@mba.ac.uk and one hard copy to the address shown below, to reach the MBA by 31st January in any one year. 2. A curriculum vitae, including a list of publications. 3. The names of two referees. 4. A detailed statement of the way in which the funds allocated for the Fellowship will be spent. Justifications for the number and timing of visits must also be given. 5. An undertaking from the candidate's employers that, if successful, the candidate will be given leave of absence to work at the Citadel Hill Laboratory. 6. A letter of support from the MBA Director confirming that the research can be accommodated at the MBA must accompany an application. In addition, collaboration with MBA scientists would be encouraged. 7. Usually one Fellowship will be awarded each year.
No. of awards offered: 1
Closing Date: 31 January
Funding: Individuals, Private, Trusts
Additional Information: On appointment the Fellow is expected to work at the Citadel Hill Laboratory, Plymouth, for a period of up to two months within a period of 2 years after appointment. On completion of the award the Fellow is required to submit a Final Report. www.mba.ac.uk/selfedit/peter-baker-fellowship-awards-grants

Marines' Memorial Association

609 Sutter Street, San Francisco, CA 94102, United States of America.

Tel: (1) 415 673 6672
Email: michaelallen@marineclub.com
Website: www.marineclub.com

The Marines' Memorial Association depends on donations to fulfill our mission to COMMEMORATE, EDUCATE and SERVE. The Foundation operates the Marines' Memorial Theatre and provides support to the Marines' Memorial Association.

The Marine Corps Scholarship

Purpose: To provide financial assistance to children of active and former members of the United States Marines Corps
Eligibility: Open to children of the MMA members scholastic aptitude, community involvement and civic spirit. Applicant must be Planning to attend an accredited undergraduate college or vocational/technical institution in the upcoming academic year. Applicant must have a maximum family adjusted gross income for the current tax year that does not exceed US$90,000. Non-taxable allowances are not included in determining adjusted gross income. Applicant must have A GPA of at least 2.0
Level of Study: Postgraduate
Type: Scholarship
Value: Varies
Length of Study: Renewable
Frequency: Annual
Country of Study: Any country
Application Procedure: See the website
Closing Date: 13 April
Funding: Foundation
Contributor: The Marine Corps Foundation
Additional Information: Please see the website for further details and if you have any questions, contact us by email or phone www.mcsf.org/

Marketing Science Institute (MSI)

1000 Massachusetts Avenue, Cambridge, Massachusetts 02138-5396, United States of America.

Tel: (1) 617 491 2060
Email: msi@msi.org
Website: www.msii.clients.bostonwebdevelopment.com/
               for-business/become-an-msi-member-company/

Founded in 1961, the Marketing Science Institute is a nonprofit, membership-based organization dedicated to bridging the gap between academic marketing theory and business practice. MSI is unique as the only research-based organization with an expansive network of practically-minded marketing academics from the best business schools all over the world.

Doctoral Dissertation Proposal Competition

Subjects: Marketing and Related Fields
Purpose: This competition recognizes marketing doctoral students who are working on research questions with important marketing, societal, and policy implications.
Eligibility: See website
Type: Research grant
Value: US$5,000
Frequency: Annual
Country of Study: Any country
No. of awards offered: Up to five
Closing Date: 31 July
No. of awards given last year: 2 winners
Additional Information: The competition is open to doctoral candidates in marketing and related fields (e.g., management, strategy, organizational behavior, consumer psychology, economics, etc.). The dissertation must be no more than fifty percent completed at the time of submission. Proposals will be judged on importance and potential contribution of the subject to business and academia; quality of conceptual development; feasibility and appropriateness of methodology; fit of research with MSI priorities; and creativity. Design aspects will play a particularly important role in the evaluation process. www.msi.org

Marshal Papworth

East of England Showground, Alwalton, Oundle Road, Peterborough, Cambridgeshire PE2 6XE, United Kingdom.

Tel: (44) 1733 363514
Email: slauridsen@eastofengland.org.uk.
Website: www.marshalpapworth.com

Our Fund takes its name from our late founder, Marshal Papworth, a well-respected Huntingdonshire farmer, who played a key role in the agricultural community, as well as being a proactive member of the East of England Agricultural Society. Born in 1939 to parents who farmed in Huntingdonshire Marshal began his farming career as a tenant farmer on Lord de Ramsey's 270 acre Townsend Farm in Upwood. An adventurous and visionary man, Marshal travelled extensively to Africa and Asia. It was during these trips that he saw the plight that communities in developing countries faced on a daily basis in sourcing food and safe water. Witnessing these difficulties, Marshal recognised the benefits that such communities could gain from being given the opportunity to embrace sustainable farming practices and learn valuable agricultural and horticultural skills. Marshal's untimely death in a flying accident was a huge loss to his family and friends, and to the communities in which he was involved. However, through his sincere generosity, his legacy has been able to live on by way of our Fund by providing scholarship opportunities for students in developing countries. Marshal's vision - helping students develop skills they can take back to their homelands and use for the benefit of their own communities - stands as true today as it did while he was alive, and through our work, continues to enrich the lives of people from developing countries around the world.

Marshal Papworth Scholarships in Agriculture for Developing Countries

Purpose: Marshal Papworth provides scholarships for students from developing countries for 1-year Masters degree programmes in agriculture or horticulture.
Eligibility: Applicants should be nationals of and resident in developing countries (countries with a GNI per capita below US$11500), and scholarship candidates who fully meet the criteria for the courses will be shortlisted for the scholarships against 3 main criteria academic excellence, professional experience (includes experience gained in a voluntary capacity) in community development and/or agricultural development, and the potential for contribution to development in their home country after completion of their degree programme. Applicants should be talented individuals who demonstrate that they have the potential, at the end of their Masters programme, to motivate people and communities in their home country towards positive change. Applicants must have a good command of the English Language.
Level of Study: Masters Degree
Type: Scholarships
Value: £19,000
Length of Study: 1 year
Frequency: Annual
Country of Study: United Kingdom

Application Procedure: Candidates for the Masters scholarships cannot apply directly to the Marshal Papworth Fund for the Masters programme. Rather, they have to apply directly to the participating universities. Once accepted into a course the university/college will select candidates they believe are eligible for a Marshal Papworth Scholarship and will forward the students application and CV onto the Marshal Papworth Fund directly for consideration. Applications for scholarships must be received from partnering universities/colleges no later than the end of the second week of April, or the last day before the Easter break, whichever is the former. To apply for the 10-week course at Harper Adams University starting in May, you must make an application through accredited organizations found at this link before their deadline. It is important to visit the official website (link found below) for detailed information on how to apply for this scholarship.

No. of awards offered: 15
Closing Date: April
Additional Information: www.marshalpapworth.com/our-scholarships/scholarship-details/

Marshall Aid Commemoration Commission

Woburn House, 20-24 Tavistock Square, London WC1H 9HF, United Kingdom.

Tel: (44) 20 7380 6704/3
Email: apps@marshallscholarship.org
Website: www.marshallscholarship.org

The Marshall Aid Commemoration Commission is responsible for the selection and placement of recipients of Marshall scholarships from the United States to the United Kingdom. The first awards were presented in 1954.

Marshall Scholarships

Purpose: To provide intellectually distinguished young Americans with the opportunity to study in the United Kingdom, and thus to understand and appreciate the British way of life.
Eligibility: Open to citizens of the United States of America who have graduated with a minimum grade point average of 3.7 or A from an accredited United States college not more than 2 years previously.
Type: Scholarship
Value: University fees, cost of living expenses, annual book grant, thesis grant, research and daily travel grants, fares to

and from the United States and, where applicable, a contribution towards the support of a dependent spouse.
Frequency: Annual
Country of Study: United Kingdom
Closing Date: October
No. of awards given last year: 37
No. of applicants last year: 900
Additional Information: Please see the website for further details www.marshallscholarship.org/apply

For further information contact:

11766 Wilshire Boulevard, Suite 1200, Los Angeles, CA 90025-6538, United States of America.

Tel: (1) 310 996 3028
Email: Atlanta@marshallscholarship.org

Marshall Sherfield Fellowships

Purpose: The aim of the Marshall Sherfield Fellowships is to introduce American scientists and engineers to the cutting edge of UK science and engineering.
Level of Study: post-doctoral
Type: Fellowship
Length of Study: 2 academic years
Frequency: Annual
Country of Study: United Kingdom
Closing Date: June
Additional Information: www.marshallscholarship.org/marshall-sherfield

For further information contact:

Woburn House, 20-24 Tavistock Square, London WC1H 9HF, United Kingdom.

Maryland Association of Certified Public Accountants

901 Dulaney Valley Road, Suite 800, Towson, MD 21204, United States of America.

Tel: (1) 800 782 2036
Email: team@macpa.org
Website: www.macpa.org/

MACPA has played a major role in shaping the CPA profession since its founding in 1901. Recognizing the importance of trustworthy financial information in a market-based economy, Maryland was the third state in the nation that created the professional designation of certified public accountant.

Maryland Association of Certified Public Accountants Scholarship

Purpose: United States students who are Maryland residents enrolled full time in a college or university in Maryland with a grade point average of 3.0 or higher committed to pursuing careers as CPAs are eligible for this award. Students must have completed 60 hours of college credit at the time of award, with six or more of those hours in accounting courses.

Eligibility: 1. Must attend a college or university in Maryland. 2. Must be a current college sophomore or older to apply for this undergraduate and graduate award. The applicant must have completed at least 60 total credit hours by the time of the award, of which at least six hours of credit are in accounting courses (including Accounting Principles I and II). 3. Must be a full-time student. 4. Must be a resident of Maryland. 5. Must be a United States citizen. 6. Must demonstrate commitment to pursuing a career as a certified public accountant. 7. Must have a grade point average of 3.0 or higher. 8. This award is for United States students.

Level of Study: Graduate

Type: Scholarship

Value: US$1,000

Frequency: Annual

Country of Study: United States of America

Application Procedure: Applications are available online from the Maryland Association of Certified Public Accountants (MACPA) website. In addition to the completed application, the applicant must submit the following a signed applicant's statement; a complete copy of the SAR (Student Aid Report) which is generated upon completion of the FAFSA (Free Application for Federal Student Aid); and an official, sealed transcript from the previous semester which shows cumulative grade point average, total credit hours completed and hours completed during the previous semester.

Closing Date: 15 April

Funding: Foundation

Additional Information: www.unigo.com/scholarships/all/macpa-scholarship/1627

For further information contact:

901 Dulaney Valley Road, Suite 800, Townson, MD 21204-2683, United States of America.

Tel: (1) 800 782 2036

Email: scholarships@swe.org

Massey University

Private Bag 11-222, Palmerston North 4442, New Zealand.

Tel: (64) 6 350 5701

Email: contact@massey.ac.nz

Website: www.massey.ac.nz/massey/

Massey University is a university based in Palmerston North, New Zealand, with significant campuses in Albany and Wellington. Massey University offers a range of undergraduate and postgraduate degrees, diplomas and certificates to students from around New Zealand.

Albert and Alexis Dennis Donation

Eligibility: You must: 1. be aged 65 years or older 2. be studying by distance

Level of Study: Postgraduate

Type: Scholarship

Value: NZ$1500

Length of Study: 1 year

Frequency: Annual

Country of Study: New Zealand

No. of awards offered: 1

Closing Date: 28 March

Additional Information: www.massey.ac.nz/massey/admission/scholarships-bursaries-awards/scholarship-bursary-award_home.cfm?id=CA9A5722-B70D-4235-8F2B-731AB01267D6

Alex C P Chu Trade for Training Scholarship

Eligibility: You must: 1. be studying a specific subject 2. be approved into an overseas internship or student exchange programme

Level of Study: Postgraduate

Type: Scholarship

Value: Varies

Length of Study: 1 year

Frequency: Annual

Country of Study: New Zealand

No. of awards offered: 1

Closing Date: 1 November

Additional Information: www.massey.ac.nz/massey/admission/scholarships-bursaries-awards/scholarship-bursary-award_home.cfm?id=F96F83FC-BC66-4432-9695-77319C155C98

Alex Lindsay awards

Eligibility: 1. You play an orchestral instrument 2. You are under 25 years of age on 30 September 2022 3. You are a New Zealand Citizen or a Permanent Resident
Level of Study: Postgraduate
Type: Scholarship
Value: NZ$10,000
Frequency: Annual
Country of Study: New Zealand
Closing Date: 31 July
Additional Information: www.nzso.co.nz/nzso-engage/learning/alex-lindsay-awards/

For further information contact:

Email: alex.lindsay.award@gmail.com

Alistair Betts Scholarship

Eligibility: Applicants must be studying postgraduate agribusiness at Massey University and undertaking research on a topic that affects New Zealand exports. Preference may be given to full time students, though self-funded part time students will also be considered
Level of Study: Postgraduate
Type: Scholarship
Value: NZ$5,000
Length of Study: 1 year
Frequency: Annual
Country of Study: New Zealand
No. of awards offered: 1
Closing Date: 10 March
Additional Information: www.massey.ac.nz/massey/admission/scholarships-bursaries-awards/scholarship-bursary-award_home.cfm?id=C8DAF00C-7C0B-4E7E-A6CB-9B2E1806A5D2

Allan Kay Undergraduate Memorial Scholarship

Purpose: The Allan Kay Undergraduate Memorial Scholarship helps students obtain a university education, especially those facing financial difficulties.
Eligibility: Applicants must: 1. be an enrolled Massey University student 2. be a New Zealand-born resident 3. be under 30 years old 4. be studying full-time.
Level of Study: Graduate
Type: Scholarship
Value: NZ$3,000
Length of Study: 1 year
Frequency: Annual

Country of Study: Any country
Application Procedure: The scholarship is awarded by the Trustees of the estate of Grace Edith Meliora Kay on the recommendation of the Applied Academic Programmes Scholarships Committee.
No. of awards offered: 6
Closing Date: 3 March
Funding: Private
Additional Information: www.massey.ac.nz/massey/admission/scholarships-bursaries-awards/other-scholarships/search-results/search-results_home.cfm?page=award_display&scholarship_id=166

For further information contact:

Massey University, Private Bag 11 222, Palmerston North 4442, New Zealand.

Email: K.Harrington@massey.ac.nz

Bailey Bequest Bursary

Eligibility: Applicants must be part-time or full-time students of Massey University who are enrolled internally or by distance for a postgraduate programme at any of the Massey University campuses.
Level of Study: Postgraduate
Type: Bursary
Value: NZ$3000
Frequency: Annual
Country of Study: New Zealand
Closing Date: 21 April
Additional Information: www.massey.ac.nz/massey/admission/scholarships-bursaries-awards/scholarship-bursary-award_home.cfm?id=763646FC-E2C5-4410-AF77-D8FB47175E1B

BayTrust Bruce Cronin Scholarship

Eligibility: Applicants must have links to the BayTrust geographical area. This area is shown on the BayTrust website www.baytrust.org.nz Applicants will be eligible if they were born in, or attended school in, or have whakapapa back to the area.
Level of Study: Postgraduate
Type: Scholarship
Value: NZ$5,000
Frequency: Annual
Country of Study: New Zealand
No. of awards offered: 2
Closing Date: 1 February

Additional Information: www.universitiesnz.ac.nz/scholar ships/baytrust-bruce-cronin-scholarship

Bell-Booth Dairy Research Scholarship

Eligibility: You must: 1. be an enrolled Massey University student 2. be studying dairy calf nutrition.
Level of Study: Postgraduate
Type: Scholarship
Value: NZ$3000
Frequency: Annual
Country of Study: New Zealand
No. of awards offered: 1
Closing Date: 10 March
Additional Information: www.massey.ac.nz/massey/admis sion/scholarships-bursaries-awards/scholarship-bursary-award_ home.cfm?id=E831747E-FCAF-4341-A988-45E7F20E13E6

Bing

Eligibility: Applicants will be: 1. New Zealand citizens or permanent residents. 2. undertaking full-time study at a NZ university. 3. in the thesis year of their Master's degree in the year of tenure.
Level of Study: Postgraduate
Type: Scholarship
Value: NZ$2,000
Frequency: Annual
Country of Study: New Zealand
Closing Date: 1 October
Additional Information: www.universitiesnz.ac.nz/scholar ships/bings-scholarship

Bowler Ravensdown Scholarship in Soil Science

Eligibility: You must: 1. be studying full time 2. be enrolled in a specific programme
Level of Study: Postgraduate
Type: Scholarship
Value: NZ$5,000
Length of Study: 1 year
Frequency: Annual
Country of Study: New Zealand
No. of awards offered: 1
Closing Date: 10 March
Additional Information: www.massey.ac.nz/massey/admis sion/scholarships-bursaries-awards/scholarship-bursary-award_ home.cfm?id=C96B37B1-DB3D-4406-A7D1-B83B477 06725

Bragato Research Fellowship

Eligibility: The Fellowship may be awarded to any student who has completed a Masters degree or Doctorate and who is involved in ongoing research. The applicant must be a New Zealand resident. The planned research must be at a university or other research institution in New Zealand or overseas, recognised for its research in subjects related to the wine industry. The research must be in a subject of benefit to the NZ industry.
Level of Study: Postgraduate
Type: Scholarship
Value: NZ$15,000
Frequency: Annual
Country of Study: New Zealand
Closing Date: 28 February
Additional Information: www.nzwine.com/en/events/ bragato-trust-scholarships/fellowship

Brian Aspin Memorial Scholarship

Eligibility: You must: 1. be a New Zealand citizen or permanent resident 2. be studying in specific subject areas
Level of Study: Postgraduate
Type: Scholarship
Value: NZ$5000
Frequency: Annual
Country of Study: New Zealand
No. of awards offered: 2
Closing Date: 9 March
Additional Information: www.massey.ac.nz/massey/admis sion/scholarships-bursaries-awards/scholarship-bursary-award_ home.cfm?id=7290A7C0-6F16-4D72-9A56-9D840C91E28C

C. Alma Baker Postgraduate Scholarship

Purpose: To encourage students enroling in Master or doctoral thesis programmes.
Eligibility: Open to candidates who are graduates and citizens of New Zealand. Awards are available for those intending to undertake postgraduate research either in New Zealand or overseas. Scholarships will be based on academic achievement.
Level of Study: Doctorate, Postgraduate
Type: Scholarship
Value: Maximum NZ$13,000 a year for a Master degree student and NZ$20,000 a year for a doctoral student.
Length of Study: 1 year for Master and up to 3 years for a Doctoral programme.
Frequency: Dependent on funds available
Country of Study: New Zealand

Application Procedure: Applicants must apply on the prescribed form to the Secretary, C. Alma Baker Trust. A certified copy of Academic Record, birth certificate, passport, or other proof of citizenship, and an outline of proposed research (not more than one page) must be enclosed with the application.

Closing Date: 1 February

Funding: Trusts

Additional Information: Do not send original documents as application and attachments will not be returned. Information provided will be used by the trust or its representatives only for awarding scholarships and may be subject to verification procedures as appropriate www.calmabakertrust.org/awards-grants-scholarships/postgraduate-scholarships

For further information contact:

C. Alma Baker Trust, C/o School of People, Environment & Planning Social Sciences Tower, Level 3, Massey University, Private Bag 11 222, Palmerston North 4442, New Zealand.

Email: calmabakertrust@drk.co.nz

C. Alma Baker Postgraduate Scholarship

Eligibility: Candidates must be New Zealand citizens, and graduates of a New Zealand university; awards are available for those intending to undertake postgraduate research either in New Zealand or overseas. At their discretion, the Trustees may make other educational awards from time to time.

Level of Study: Doctorate, Postgraduate

Type: Scholarship

Value: NZ$13,000 a year for a masterate student and NZ$20,000 a year for a doctoral student

Frequency: Annual

Country of Study: New Zealand

Closing Date: 1 February

Additional Information: www.calmabakertrust.org/awards-grants-scholarships/postgraduate-scholarships

For further information contact:

Email: calmabakertrust@drk.co.nz

Catherine Baxter Dairy Scholarship

Eligibility: You must: 1. be studying full-time 2. be an enrolled Massey University student 3. be studying in a specific subject area.

Level of Study: Postgraduate

Type: Scholarship

Value: NZ$5,000

Length of Study: 1 year

Frequency: Annual

Country of Study: New Zealand

No. of awards offered: 2

Closing Date: 10 March

Additional Information: www.massey.ac.nz/massey/admission/scholarships-bursaries-awards/scholarship-bursary-award_home.cfm?id=74571F98-BE48-4831-84FE-C051A632B87F

China Scholarship Council-Massey University PhD Scholars Programme

Level of Study: Postgraduate

Type: Scholarship

Value: Tuition fees and living allowance

Length of Study: 4 years

Frequency: Annual

Country of Study: New Zealand

Closing Date: 15 January

Additional Information: www.massey.ac.nz/massey/admission/scholarships-bursaries-awards/scholarship-bursary-award_home.cfm?id=A166B5BD-3364-4ADB-BA06-E0D7FF24FD0B

For further information contact:

Email: doctoral.applications@massey.ac.nz

Dilmah Tea International Study Award

Eligibility: You must: 1. be a new international student 2. be an employee or a family member of an employee of Dilmah Tea 3. meet the programme and admission entry requirements.

Level of Study: Postgraduate

Type: Scholarship

Value: NZ$2,500

Length of Study: 1 year

Frequency: Annual

Country of Study: New Zealand

No. of awards offered: 1

Closing Date: 1 May

Additional Information: www.massey.ac.nz/massey/admission/scholarships-bursaries-awards/scholarship-bursary-award_home.cfm?id=53881546-FCF0-46B8-8E0E-490EA36E61D5

Dreamfields Farm Agricultural Scholarship

Purpose: This scholarship was established in 2014, initially using money won by Bruce and Judy Woods from

Dreamfields Farm in Bay of Plenty for the Ballance Farm Environment Award. It is designed to encourage students from their local secondary schools to study agriculture at Massey University

Level of Study: Graduate
Type: Scholarship
Value: NZ$1,000
Length of Study: 1 year
Frequency: Varies
Country of Study: Any country
Application Procedure: Apply online
Closing Date: 3 March
Funding: Trusts
Additional Information: studyspy.ac.nz/scholarships/ 10171/dreamfields-farm-agricultural-scholarship

For further information contact:

Email: K.Harrington@massey.ac.nz

Energy Education Trust of New Zealand Masterate Scholarship

Eligibility: You must be: 1. a New Zealand citizen or permanent resident 2. enrolled full time 3. studying a master's with a minimum research component of 90 credits.
Level of Study: Postgraduate
Type: Scholarship
Value: NZ$8,000
Frequency: Annual
Country of Study: New Zealand
Closing Date: 31 March
Additional Information: www.massey.ac.nz/massey/admis sion/scholarships-bursaries-awards/scholarship-bursary-award_ home.cfm?id=ECCB5EBD-3581-47DF-BB4C-F10B7372CF10

For further information contact:

Email: scholarships@massey.ac.nz

FAR Postgraduate Scholarship

Eligibility: You must be: 1. enrolled full time 2. a New Zealand citizen or permanent resident 3. undertaking postgraduate research
Level of Study: Postgraduate
Type: Scholarship
Value: NZ$7,000
Frequency: Annual
Country of Study: New Zealand
No. of awards offered: 1
Closing Date: 15 March

Additional Information: www.massey.ac.nz/massey/admis sion/scholarships-bursaries-awards/scholarship-bursary-award_ home.cfm?id=7985EB49-7E04-4B32-9740-00675D5C3931

George Mason Sustainable Land Use Scholarship

Eligibility: You must: 1. be studying full-time 2. be studying in a specific subject area 3. be an enrolled Massey University student 4. be undertaking research relevant to land use in Taranaki.
Level of Study: Doctorate, Postgraduate
Type: Scholarship
Value: NZ$25,000
Frequency: Annual
Country of Study: New Zealand
Closing Date: 10 March
Additional Information: www.massey.ac.nz/massey/ admission/scholarships-bursaries-awards/scholarship-bursary-award_home.cfm?id=B8EECCF9-A40B-45A2-B1B4-E4900 1FB3DC4

Graduate Women Manawatu Postgraduate Scholarship

Eligibility: You must: 1. be female 2. be a New Zealand citizen or permanent resident 3. be willing to have your name and details published on the Graduate Women Manawatu Charitable Trust's website, should you be successful
Level of Study: Postgraduate
Type: Scholarship
Value: Up to US$25,000
Length of Study: 1 year
Frequency: Annual
Country of Study: New Zealand
No. of awards offered: 8 to 12
Closing Date: 31 March
Additional Information: www.massey.ac.nz/massey/admis sion/scholarships-bursaries-awards/scholarship-bursary-award_ home.cfm?id=4E12D7A7-49DE-44A7-AE81-D10EAE FA954B

Graduate Women North Shore Branch Scholarship

Eligibility: You must be: 1. a New Zealand citizen 2. female 3. enrolled internally at the Albany campus
Level of Study: Postgraduate
Type: Scholarship
Value: NZ$2,000 – NZ$10,000
Length of Study: 1 year

Frequency: Annual
Country of Study: New Zealand
No. of awards offered: 1
Closing Date: 31 March
Additional Information: www.massey.ac.nz/massey/admission/scholarships-bursaries-awards/scholarship-bursary-award_home.cfm?id=9D5C8342-0E73-4851-8188-F2B3F1CF8133

For further information contact:

Email: scholarship.applications@massey.ac.nz

Horizons Regional Council Sustainable Land Use Scholarships - Year 1 & Year 2 Students

Purpose: Horizons Regional Council provides the scholarships to encourage students who are interested in a career in an environmental field, to undertake study in soil science and farm management as part of their undergraduate degree. Applicants are expected to have a solid interest in environmental management, soil, and land use mapping. The scholarships are considered to be a good entry point for year three and postgraduate Horizons Regional Council Sustainable Land Use Advanced Scholarships
Level of Study: Graduate
Type: Scholarship
Value: NZ$5,000
Length of Study: 1 year
Frequency: Varies
Country of Study: Any country
Application Procedure: Apply online
No. of awards offered: 1
Closing Date: 13 April
Funding: Trusts
Additional Information: www.horizons.govt.nz/about-our-region-and-council/grants-and-sponsorship/sustainable-land-use-scholarships

For further information contact:

Private Bag 11025 Manawatu Mail Centre, Palmerston North 4442, New Zealand.

Tel: (64) 508 800 800
Email: help@horizons.govt.nz

Horticulture NZ Undergraduate Scholarships

Purpose: Horticulture New Zealand (HortNZ) and the Horticentre Trust has a number of scholarships available for undergraduate students studying towards a degree in areas of interest to the Horticulture Industry
Level of Study: Graduate
Type: Scholarship
Value: NZ$1,500. In addition, the top three applicants nationally will be awarded an added an additional NZ$3000 to support the individuals' studies.
Length of Study: 1 year
Frequency: Varies
Country of Study: Any country
Application Procedure: Apply online:forms.office.com/r/pE5RYTVvMi
Closing Date: 10 December
Funding: Trusts
Additional Information: www.hortnz.co.nz/our-work/people/horticulture-scholarships/

For further information contact:

Tel: (64) 494 9978
Email: schols@hortnz.co.nz

Hurley Fraser Postgraduate Scholarship

Purpose: To support postgraduate research in agriculture and horticulture.
Eligibility: Applicants must have enroled for a full-time postgraduate degree or a diploma in one of the Applied Sciences. The award is based on the candidate's academic attainment.
Level of Study: Graduate
Type: Scholarship
Value: Varies
Length of Study: 1 year
Study Establishment: Massey University
Country of Study: New Zealand
Application Procedure: Applicants must apply to the Scholarships Office, Graduate Research School on forms (ASSC.3) available from Massey Contact or can be downloaded from the website.
No. of awards offered: 1
Closing Date: 10 March
Contributor: John Alexander Hurley Scholarship and the Edith Fraser Agricultural and Horticultural Research Fund.
Additional Information: The award shall be paid in May. Applications will not be accepted more than 3 months in advance of the closing date www.studyspy.ac.nz/scholarships/10155/hurley-fraser-postgraduate-scholarship

For further information contact:

Tel: (64) 800 627 739
Email: Contact@massey.ac.nz

Leonard Condell Farming Postgraduate Scholarship

Purpose: Candidates must be New Zealand born graduates in science, agriculture or related disciplines (e.g. horticulture, veterinary science, food technology, biotechnology) and must enter fields of research for the benefit of some branch of agriculture in New Zealand.

Eligibility: There are two types of scholarships. (a) Postgraduate Scholarships Candidates must be New Zealand born graduates in science, agriculture or related disciplines (e.g. horticulture, veterinary science, food technology, biotechnology) and must enter fields of research for the benefit of some branch of agriculture in New Zealand. The emolument shall be up to NZ$3,000 per annum. (b) PhD Scholarships Candidates must be New Zealand born graduates in science, agriculture or related disciplines (e.g. horticulture, veterinary science, food technology, biotechnology) and must enter fields of research for the benefit of some branch of agriculture in New Zealand. The emolument shall be up to NZ$4,000 per annum.

Level of Study: Postgraduate
Type: Scholarship
Value: NZ$3,000
Length of Study: 1 year
Frequency: Annual
Country of Study: New Zealand
Application Procedure: All applications are acknowledged by email.
No. of awards offered: 1
Closing Date: 10 March
Funding: Individuals
Additional Information: Specific criteria is being added to the concern. Applications will NOT be accepted more than 3 months in advance of the closing date www.massey.ac.nz/massey/admission/scholarships-bursaries-awards/other-scholarships/search-results/search-results_home.cfm?page=award_display&scholarship_id=70

For further information contact:

Scholarships Office, (NSATS), Massey University, Private Bag 11-222, Palmerston North 4442, New Zealand.

Email: K.Harrington@massey.ac.nz

Massey University Doctoral Scholarship

Purpose: To fund research towards a PhD degree
Eligibility: You should: 1. be enrolled or be eligible to to enrol in doctoral study at Massey University 2. have a GPA of 7.0 or higher 3. be researching a topic of strategic value to the

University 4. agree to the conditions of the scholarship as outlined in the scholarship regulations.
Level of Study: Doctorate
Type: Scholarship
Value: NZ$75,000 plus fees
Length of Study: 3 years
Frequency: Annual
Study Establishment: Massey University
Country of Study: New Zealand
Application Procedure: www.massey.ac.nz/massey/fms/Research/Graduate%20Research%20School/Documents/Administration%20forms/Supervisor%20Support%20Template%20-%20Doctoral%20Scholarship.pdf?6F096322C6BB8E31DC225D51CFD062C4
Closing Date: 1 April
Additional Information: www.massey.ac.nz/massey/admission/scholarships-bursaries-awards/scholarship-bursary-award_home.cfm?id=83B45FEA-2E17-48C0-B717-CA5F15B27B6E

For further information contact:

Email: scholarships@massey.ac.nz

Sir Alan Stewart Postgraduate Scholarships

Purpose: To encourage new postgraduate enrolments from other tertiary institutions and to assist Massey students to progress from undergraduate to postgraduate study.
Eligibility: Applicant must be enroled or be intending to enrol full-time or part-time, in the year the award is to be made, in their initial year of a first postgraduate programme, undertaken either internally or extramurally and must be a New Zealand citizen or permanent resident who has completed an undergraduate degree at a New Zealand university.
Level of Study: Graduate
Type: Scholarship
Value: NZ$4,000 per year for full-time students and pro-rated for part-time students.
Length of Study: 1 year
Frequency: Annual
Study Establishment: Any Massey University campus
Country of Study: New Zealand
Application Procedure: Check website for further details.
No. of awards offered: 40
Closing Date: 1 December
Additional Information: Consideration will normally only be given to students with a B+ average or better. Full-time students may hold the scholarship only once. Part-time students may re-apply to the maximum of NZ$4,000 in a period of 4 years from first enrolment in the postgraduate programme. Applications will NOT be accepted more than

3 months in advance of the closing date www.scholarshipdb.
net/scholarships-in-New-Zealand/Sir-Alan-Stewart-Post
graduate-Scholarships-Massey-University=FABTZeXGB0
K9zyX_mH3hhA.html

Sir John Logan Campbell Agricultural Scholarship

Purpose: Sir John Logan Campbell was a successful Auckland businessman who lived from 1817 to 1912. He made many donations to the people of Auckland, including Cornwall Park. This scholarship has resulted from money gifted in 1925 from his endowment fund to help set up an agricultural teaching course in Palmerston North. It will be used to encourage 1st Year students from urban areas such as Auckland to begin a course in agriculture

Eligibility: The John Logan Campbell Agricultural Scholarship shall have a value determined each year from the interest earned on the capital and be open to 1st Year Massey University students who are enrolled full-time for the Bachelor of AgriCommerce degree, or the agriculture major within either the Bachelor of AgriScience degree or the Bachelor of Science degree

Level of Study: Graduate

Type: Scholarship

Value: Varies

Length of Study: 1 year

Frequency: Varies

Country of Study: Any country

Application Procedure: Apply online

No. of awards offered: 1

Closing Date: 3 March

Funding: Trusts

Additional Information: www.massey.ac.nz/massey/admission/scholarships-bursaries-awards/other-scholarships/search-results/search-results_home.cfm?page=award_display&scholarship_id=672

For further information contact:

Email: K.Harrington@massey.ac.nz

Sydney Campbell Undergraduate Scholarship

Purpose: The Sydney Campbell Scholarships are provided under the Will of the late Mr Sydney Campbell, Riverside Farm, Masterton, and are tenable at Massey University

Level of Study: Graduate

Type: Scholarship

Value: NZ$1,000

Length of Study: 1 year

Frequency: Varies

Country of Study: Any country

Application Procedure: Apply online

Closing Date: 3 March

Funding: Trusts

Additional Information: www.massey.ac.nz/massey/admission/scholarships-bursaries-awards/other-scholarships/search-results/search-results_home.cfm?page=award_display&scholarship_id=57

For further information contact:

Email: K.Harrington@massey.ac.nz

Turners and Growers Undergraduate Scholarships

Purpose: These scholarships are offered annually by T&G (formerly Turners and Growers) to assist students of high academic calibre to undertake a degree that will provide them with the education and training to support the sustainable development of the New Zealand horticultural industry

Level of Study: Graduate

Type: Scholarship

Value: NZ$3,000

Length of Study: 3 year

Frequency: Varies

Country of Study: Any country

Application Procedure: Apply online

No. of awards offered: 1

Closing Date: 3 March

Funding: Trusts

Additional Information: www.massey.ac.nz/massey/admission/scholarships-bursaries-awards/other-scholarships/search-results/search-results_home.cfm?page=award_display&scholarship_id=1207

For further information contact:

Email: K.Harrington@massey.ac.nz

Materials Research Society

9800 McKnight Road, Pittsburgh, PA 15237, United States of America.

Tel:	(1) 724 779 3003
Website:	www.mrs.org/
Contact:	Executive Director

The Materials Research Society is a growing, vibrant member-driven organization of over 11,200. It includes people from over 90 countries around the world–from the richest of nations to developing countries. Our members come from industry, academia and national labs, and their work touches on many fields, including chemistry, biology, physics and engineering. They have skills and expertise that range from technical and organizational, to advocacy and education.

The Material Handling Education Foundation

Purpose: The Material Handling Education Foundation, Inc.
Eligibility: For the academic term, the following students are eligible to apply 1. Students enrolled full time at a qualified four-year school in bachelors, masters or doctoral program that is on the target list of programs. Bachelors student must be classified as a junior or senior in the Fall term to be eligible. 2. Students from two-year, post-secondary schools (e.g., junior, community, or technical colleges) are eligible if the student has completed a minimum of two years of study and has been accepted as a transfer student to a target four-year baccalaureate program at a qualified school in the United States. 3. All applicants must be full-time students with a "B" grade point average in their major.
Level of Study: Graduate
Type: Scholarship
Frequency: Annual
Study Establishment: US$1,500 to US$6,000
Country of Study: United States of America
Application Procedure: The online application consists of three (3) letters of recommendation and all official transcripts must be received in the Foundation offices by 15 January. Official transcripts must be sent to the Foundation directly from the Registrar's office or equivalent office at the school.
Closing Date: 31 January
Funding: Private
Additional Information: www.mhi.org/mhefi/scholarship

For further information contact:

Tel: (1) 704 676 1190
Email: dvarner@mhi.org

Matsumae International Foundation (MIF)

4-14-46, Kamiogi, Suginami-ku, Tokyo 167-0043, Japan.

Tel: (81) 3 3301 7600
Email: contact@mif-japan.org
Website: www.mif-japan.org/fellowship/announcement/?hl=en

Dr. Shigeyoshi MATSUMAE who founded the Matsumae International Foundation. The Matsumae International Foundation aims to develop the future by contributing to the global friendship and goodwill through our enterprise which leaves peoples connecting Japan with the rest of the world. This is extremely important in the era of highly developed science and technologies, especially in these days of extremely tensed world affairs. Our activities are nothing fancy but we are happy to continue those activities based upon the enthusiasm from our supporters.

Matsumae International Foundation Research Fellowship Program

Purpose: Towards a greater understanding of Japan and a lasting world peace.
Eligibility: 1. Applicants must obtain an invitation (acceptance) letter from a host institution in Japan prior to application. 2. Applicants must hold Ph.D. (Doctoral degree). 3. Applicants must be at the age of 49 years old or younger at the time of application. 4. Applicants must have sufficient the English or Japanese languages ability. 5. Applicants should not have past or current experiences of staying in Japan (other than short-term stays such as for sightseeing or conferences) 6. Applicants must have an occupation in their home countries, return there upon completing their fellowship tenure, and should contribute to development of their own country.
Level of Study: Postdoctorate
Type: Fellowship
Value: JPY 220,000 per month
Length of Study: Between 3 months to 6 months
Frequency: Annual
Country of Study: Japan
Application Procedure: Applications are evaluated by the Screening Committee of MIF on the basis of academic value and the degree of perfection of the research projects.
No. of awards offered: 10
Closing Date: 20 June
Funding: Foundation
Additional Information: www.mif-japan.org/fellowship/announcement/?hl=en

For further information contact:

The Matsumae International Foundation, 4-14-46, Kamiogi, Suginami-ku, Tokyo 167-0043, Japan.

Tel: (81) 333 017 600
Email: application@mif-japan.org

Max Planck Institute

P.O Box 10 10 62, D-80084 Munich, Germany.

Tel:	(49) 89 2108 0
Email:	post@gv.mpg.de
Website:	www.mpg.de/en
Contact:	Max Planck Society

The Max Planck Society is a non-profit organization under private law in the form of a registered association. Its highest-ranking decision-making body is the Senate. Its members come from major sectors of academic and public life. Max Planck Society is mainly financed by public funds from the federal government. The federal and state governments jointly provide the subsidies for the budget of the Max Planck Society.

Criminology Scholarships for Foreign Researchers in Germany

Purpose: To pursue research programme.
Eligibility: Preference is given to those researchers whose work promotes and advances the goals of the research program and the research focuses of the Institute.
Level of Study: Doctorate, Postdoctorate, Research
Value: Doctoral scholarships €1,365 per month Post-doctoral scholarships €2,100 per month Research scholarships €2,300 per month.
Length of Study: 2 to 4 months
Country of Study: Germany
Closing Date: 31 May
Additional Information: www.scholarship-positions.com/criminology-scholarships-foreign-researchers-germany/2017/02/02/

Max Planck Institute for the History of Science Postdoctoral Fellowship in Germany

Purpose: The Max Planck Institute for the History of Science, Berlin is delighted to offer two postdoctoral fellows the opportunity to study in Germany starting on 1 September, for three years, with the employment contract.
Eligibility: Candidates of all nationalities are invited to apply; applications from women are especially welcome. The Max Planck Society is committed to promoting handicapped individuals and encourages them to apply. Candidates should hold a doctorate in the history of science or related field at the time the position begins (PhD awarded in 2016 or later).

Level of Study: Postdoctorate
Type: Fellowship
Value: Up to 1,365.00 EUR per month (Doctoral students) up to 2,500.00 EUR per month (Postdocs)
Frequency: Annual
Country of Study: Germany
Application Procedure: Your application should contain 1. Cover letter (indicating in which project you are interested). 2. Curriculum vitae including the list of publications. 3. Research prospectus (maximum 750 words). 4. Sample of writing. 5. Names and contact details of at least two referees.
Closing Date: 31 May
Funding: Private
Additional Information: csl.mpg.de/en/fellowships

For further information contact:

Max-Planck-Institut für Wissenschaftsgeschichte, Boltzmannstrasse 22, D-14195 Berlin, Germany.

Max Planck Institute for Dynamics and Self-Organization

Post office box 2853, D-37077 Göttingen, Germany.

Tel:	(49) 551 5176 0
Email:	info@ds.mpg.de
Website:	www.ds.mpg.de/en
Contact:	Max Planck Institute for Dynamics and Self-Organization

Max Planck Institute for Dynamics and Self-Organization is closely linked to the work of the famous physicist Ludwig Prandtl. Prandtl is regarded as the founder of fluid dynamics and especially made a name for himself with his boundary layer theory. However, now this field of research was put into the larger context of self-organized and nonlinear phenomena. This development led to the renaming of the institute on November 19th 2004. Since then the institute is called Max Planck Institute for Dynamics and Self-Organization.

Max Planck Institute-DS Gauss Postdoctoral Fellowships for International Students

Purpose: These prestigious positions are aimed at postdoctoral researchers who have shown exceptional promise in their doctoral or early postdoctoral work, which needs to be in a relevant field.

Eligibility: International students are eligible to apply for this fellowship. The candidate should hold a PhD/DPhil degree with a background in theoretical physics, applied mathematics, or related fields, have prior experience with non-equilibrium statistical physics of biological systems and soft matter, and be fluent in the English language.

Type: Postdoctoral fellowship

Value: The candidate should hold a PhD/DPhil degree with a background in theoretical physics, applied mathematics, or related fields, have prior experience with nonequilibrium statistical physics of biological systems and soft matter, and be fluent in the English language. The Gauss fellowship is limited to two years with the possibility of extension. Salary is in accordance with the German state public service salary scale (E13 TVöD-Bund) and the corresponding social benefits. The earliest starting date is 1 March

Study Establishment: The MPI-DS has recently appointed Oxford University theoretical physicist Prof. Ramin Golestanian as a new Director, and he is currently in the process of establishing the Department of Living Matter Physics. The new department will engage in a wide range of theoretical research aimed at a multi-scale understanding of the dynamics of living systems from a physical perspective

Country of Study: Germany

Application Procedure: Please apply online on our application portal. Applications in writing will not be sent back. Please send your CV, publication list, a statement of research interest and at least two letters of reference. Your statement of research interest should be commensurate with the position you are applying to. In addition to the description of your proposed research if relevant (depending on the position you are applying to), it should also briefly describe your past and current research interests and why you are interested in joining our department. The positions are open until they are filled. Once a position is filled, all applicants will be informed about the final decisions.

For further information contact:

Email: ramin.golestanian@ds.mpg.de

Max Planck Institute for European Legal History

Hansaallee 41, D-60323 Frankfurt, Germany.

Tel: (49) 69 789 78 0
Email: info@rg.mpg.de
Website: www.rg.mpg.de/en
Contact: Max Planck Institute for European Legal History

Max Planck Institute for European Legal History, The researchers of the Max Planck Institute for Legal History and Legal Theory located in Frankfurt am Main, engage in research on the history and theory of law. The scientific members of the Max Planck Society are the scientific members of the institutes, which usually consists of the directors, as well as the emeritus scientific members and external scientific members of the institutes.

Postdoctoral and Research Scholarships at MPIeR in Germany

Purpose: The Max Planck Institute for European Legal History (MPIeR) invites scholars from Germany and abroad to apply for Postdoctoral and Research Scholarships. The Institute will be awarding several scholarships for a research stay at the MPIeR.

Eligibility: 1. A university degree in law, humanities or social sciences that has been completed with above-average success is required. You have an excellent command of English, both spoken and written and are proficient in either French or German. Knowledge of African languages is not a requirement but will be considered as an asset. 2. Your curriculum vitae shows the potential to conduct research at an internationally high level. You work meticulously and are able to handle deadlines. You work independently and have a strong interest in interdisciplinary, archival and comparative work. You have the ability to play an active collaborative role in the research group.

Level of Study: Doctorate, Postdoctorate

Type: Scholarship

Value: Postdocs receive €2100.00 per month and research scholarship holders receive €2300.00 per month.

Frequency: Annual

Country of Study: Germany

Application Procedure: The application should be in English or German and should contain the following documents 1. Cover letter naming your research project and explaining to what extent your profile meets the selection criteria. 2. Names and addresses (by post and electronically) of three researchers who have agreed to issue you with a letter of reference. 3. Detailed CV containing a list of any publications you might have. 4. Copies of your school leaver's certificate and degree certificate. 5. Preliminary research project (up to five pages) fitting within one of the three themes. 6. Written sample of approx. 20 printed pages (e.g. master thesis sample, journal articles, book chapters, etc.).

Closing Date: 31 May

Additional Information: Please forward your application documents to your indicated reviewers. If you are shortlisted, we will request a review. If your application is convincing, we will invite you to a selection interview. www.scholarshipsads.com/postdoctoral-research-scholarships-mpier-germany-2019/

Max Planck Institute for Human Cognitive and Brain Sciences

Stephanstrasse 1A, D-04103 Leipzig, Germany.

Tel: (49) 341 9940 00
Email: info@cbs.mpg.de
Website: www.cbs.mpg.de/en
Contact: Max Planck Institute for Human Cognitive and Brain Sciences

The MPI for Human Cognitive and Brain Sciences provides an exciting framework for these topical and alluring theoretical domains, with the full gamut of cognitive and neuroscientific methodology available under one roof. Research at the Max Planck Institute for Human Cognitive and Brain Sciences revolves around human cognitive abilities and cerebral processes, with a focus on the neural basis of brain functions like language, emotions and human social behaviour, music and action.

Max Planck Institute-CBS Postdoctoral Position in Neuroscience of Pain Perception in Germany

Purpose: The aim of this research project is to understand how the multifaceted experience of pain is constructed from the interaction of external noxious input and internal expectations and predictions about pain.
Eligibility: International students are eligible to apply for the position. Applicants must have a PhD (or equivalent degree) in neuroscience, psychology, cognitive science or a related discipline (biology, physics, computer science, engineering, etc.)
Type: Postdoctoral fellowship
Value: Remuneration is based on the pay scale of the Max Planck Society. The Max Planck Society is committed to increasing the number of individuals with disabilities in its workforce and therefore encourages applications from such qualified individuals.
Study Establishment: Position is awarded to understand how the multifaceted experience of pain is constructed from the interaction of external noxious input and internal expectations and predictions about pain.
Country of Study: Germany
Application Procedure: To apply, please submit a cover letter stating personal qualifications, a curriculum vitae, contact information for two referees, a brief statement describing your research experience, your academic achievements and your motivation to apply for this position (1 page), and copies of up to three of your publications. Please submit your application via our online system.
Closing Date: 20 January
Additional Information: For more details please refer to the website www.scholarship-positions.com/mpi-cbs-postdoctoral-position-neuroscience-of-pain-perception-germany/2018/01/03/

For further information contact:

Email: eippert@cbs.mpg.de

Max Planck Research Group Neural Mechanisms of Human Communication

Max-Planck-Institut für Kognitions- und Neurowissenschaften, Stephanstrasse 1a, D-04103 Leipzig, Germany.

Tel: (49) 341 9940 2476
Email: kriegstein@cbs.mpg.de
Contact: Mrs Prof. Dr. Katharina von Kriegstein

The positions are funded by the ERC consolidator grant SENSOCOM. The aim of the SENSOCOM project is to investigate the role of auditory and visual subcortical sensory structures in analysing human communication signals and to specify how their dysfunction contributes to human communication disorders such as developmental dyslexia and autism spectrum disorders.

Doctor of Philosophy and Postdoctoral Positions - Investigating Sensory Aspects of Human Communication

Purpose: The aim of the SENSOCOM project is to investigate the role of auditory and visual subcortical sensory structures in analysing human communication signals and to specify how their dysfunction contributes to human communication disorders such as developmental dyslexia and autism spectrum disorders.
Eligibility: Applicants from Germany are eligible to apply.
Value: Not Known
Study Establishment: Positions are awarded in Investigating Sensory Aspects of Human Communication.
Country of Study: Germany

Application Procedure: To apply, please submit a CV, contact information of two references, a brief personal statement describing your qualifications and future research interests, copies of up to two of your publications. Please submit your application via our online system at www.tinyurl.com/yck4em3s

Additional Information: Please visit the website for more information, www.scholartechscience.com/2019/03/17/phd-and-postdoctoral-positions-investigating-sensory-aspects-of-human-communication-2018/

For further information contact:

Email: katharina.von_kriegstein@tu-dresden.de

Max Planck Society

P.O Box 10 10 62, D-80084 Munich, Germany.

Tel: (49) 89 2108 0
Email: post@gv.mpg.de
Website: www.mpg.de/en
Contact: Max Planck Society

The Max Planck Society is a British invention, proved to be a future-proof model, which was ultimately accepted by all of the Western Allies. The Max Planck Society was founded February 26, 1948 in Gottingen as successor organisation of the Kaiser Wilhelm Society.

Max-Planck-Society Research Scholarships

Purpose: To foster individual research projects, the Max Planck Society offers foreign researchers the possibility of obtaining a scholarship.

Type: Scholarship

Value: a Partial Funding €1365.00/month to €2,300/month depending upon the scholarship you earn

Country of Study: Any country

Application Procedure: For information concerning the application procedure, please email stipendien@mpicc.de

Closing Date: 15 August

Additional Information: Applications can be made either to the Department of Criminal Law (Prof. Dr. Dr. h.c. mult. Ulrich Sieber) or to the Department of Criminology (Prof. Dr. Dr. h.c. mult. Hans-Jörg Albrecht). Please clearly specify the chosen department in your application www.vergemagazine.com/program-search/funding/max-planck-institut-max-planck-society-research-scholarships.html

For further information contact:

Email: stipendien@mpicc.de

McGill University

845 Sherbrooke Street West, Montréal, QC H3A 0G4, Canada.

Tel: (1) 514 398 4066/4455
Email: graduate.admissions@mcgill.ca
Website: www.mcgill.ca

McGill University is Canada's best known university, renowned internationally for the highest standards in teaching and research and the outstanding record of achievement of professors and students. In fields like neurosciences, pain, cancer research and public policy to name but a few McGill is at the forefront of achievement nationally and internationally.

Boulton Fellowship

Purpose: To provide young scholars with an opportunity to pursue a major research project or to complete the research requirements for a higher degree.

Eligibility: Open to candidates who have completed the residency requirements for a doctoral degree in law.

Level of Study: Doctorate, Postdoctorate

Type: Fellowship

Value: C$50,000–55,000 per year

Length of Study: 1 year

Frequency: Annual

Study Establishment: McGill University

Country of Study: Canada

Application Procedure: Application details are listed on web page.

No. of awards offered: 20

Closing Date: 1 February

Funding: Trusts

No. of awards given last year: 1

No. of applicants last year: 20

Additional Information: www.scholarshipdesk.com/boulton-fellowship-programs-at-mcgill-university-in-canada/

For further information contact:

Faculty of Law Boulton Fund Administrators, McGill University, 3644 Peel Street, Montreal, QC H3A 1W9, Canada.

Email: staffappointments.law@mcgill.ca

Internal Studentships Past and Current Year

Purpose: Students who apply for a Faculty of Medicine Internal Studentship are automatically considered for every award for which they are eligible.

Eligibility: To be eligible for the studentship competition 1. Students must be registered full-time in a Faculty of Medicine graduate research training program. 2. At the time of application, student must be in MSc1 for Masters level students or between PhD1 and PhD4 for Doctoral level students. MSc 2 students must have already been accepted to fast-track.

Level of Study: Graduate

Type: Studentship

Value: Faculty of medicine will award an amount of C$10,000 for MSc students and C$12,000 for PhD students.

Frequency: Annual

Country of Study: Any country

Application Procedure: Listed amenities are required to process the internal studentship. 1. Studentship Application Form. 2. Publication List. 3. All graduate and undergraduate transcripts. 4. CGPA calculation. 5. Supervisor biosketch form. 6. 2 letters of support

Closing Date: August

Funding: Private

Additional Information: www.mcgill.ca/medhealthsci-gradstudies/funding-opportunities/graduate-students/internal-studentships

For further information contact:

McIntyre Medical Building, 3655 Promenade Sir William Osler, Montreal, QC H3G 1Y, Canada.

Email: submitgrad.med@mcgill.ca

McGill University PhD Studentships in Neurolinguistics

Purpose: To aid deserving students who wish to pursue a career in neuroscience.

Eligibility: Open to applicants who possess a First class (Honours) degree in linguistics, psychology, communication disorders or a related discipline, preferably with courses in psycho or neuro linguistics.

Level of Study: Postgraduate

Type: Studentship

Value: C$20,000 per year plus support for presenting work at research meetings.

Frequency: Annual

Study Establishment: McGill University

Country of Study: Canada

Application Procedure: Applicants must send their curriculum vitae and a detailed cover letter describing their research interests and academic goals.

Closing Date: 4 December

Additional Information: www.linguistlist.org/issues/17/17-2302.html

For further information contact:

McGill University, SCSD 1266, Avenue des Pins Ouest, Montreal, QC H3A 1A3, Canada.

Email: marc.pell@mcgill.ca

Media@McGill

Room 155, 853 Sherbrooke Street West, Montréal, QC H3A 0G5, Canada.

Tel: (1) 514 398 2850
Website: mediaatmcgill.ahcs@mcgill.ca
Contact: McCall McBain Arts Building

Media@McGill is a hub of interdisciplinary research, scholarship and public outreach on issues in media, technology and culture, located in the Department of Art History and Communication Studies at McGill University in Montreal, Canada.

Media@McGill Postdoctoral Fellowship

Purpose: Media@McGill's residential postdoctoral fellowships are awarded to scholars from the humanities and social sciences, working on any historical period

Eligibility: The Media@McGill Postdoctoral Fellowship is open to both national and international scholars who have completed their doctoral degree in a university other than McGill. Fluency in English is essential; working knowledge of French is an asset

Value: C$45,000 for 1 year

Study Establishment: Media@McGill

Country of Study: Canada

Closing Date: 3 February

Additional Information: scholarship-fellowship.com/mediamcgill-postdoctoral-fellowship/

For further information contact:

840 Dr Penfield, Room 231, Montreal, QC H3A 0G2, Canada.

Tel: (1) 514 398 1029

Medical Library Association (MLA)

65 East Wacker Place, Suite 1900, Chicago, IL 60601-7246, United States of America.

Tel:	(1) 312 419 9094
Email:	grants@mlahq.org
Website:	www.mlanet.org
Contact:	Maria Lopez, CAE, Executive Director

The Medical Library Association (MLA) is organized exclusively for scientific and educational purposes, and is dedicated to the support of health sciences research, education and patient care.

Eugene Garfield Research Fellowship

Purpose: To stimulate research into the history of information sciences to increase the underlying knowledge-base and enhance the current and future practice of the information professions, particularly health sciences librarianship and health informatics.

Eligibility: Health sciences librarians and information scientists, health professionals, researchers, educators, and administrators are eligible. Applicants must have a master's or doctor's degree or be enroled in a program leading to such a degree and demonstrate a commitment to the health sciences.

Type: Fellowship

Value: US$5,000

Length of Study: 1 year

Frequency: Annual

Country of Study: United States of America

Application Procedure: Applicants must submit a complete application, curriculum vitae, a detailed research proposal, and letter(s) of support from the applicant's home institution.

Closing Date: 1 December

Additional Information: www.mlanet.org/page/eugene-garfield-research-fellowship

MLA Doctoral Fellowship

Purpose: The MLA Doctoral Fellowship fosters and encourages superior students to conduct doctoral work in an area of health sciences librarianship or information sciences and to provide support to individuals who have been admitted to candidacy. The award supports research or travel applicable to the candidate's study within a twelve-month period. The award and may not be used for tuition.

Eligibility: 1. The applicant must be a member of MLA. 2. The applicant must be a graduate of an American Library Association-accredited school of library science or have equivalent graduate credentials in related information science disciplines (i.e., computer science, biomedical informatics). 3. The candidate must be a candidate in a doctoral program with an emphasis on biomedical and health-related information science. Preference will be given to applicants who have at least 75% of their course work completed and dissertation prospectus either approved or in the approval process. 4. The candidate must be a citizen of or have permanent residence status in the United States or Canada. 5. A past recipient of the MLA doctoral fellowship is ineligible.

Type: Fellowship

Value: US$2,000

Length of Study: 1 year

Country of Study: United States of America

Application Procedure: 1. The completed online application and all additional documentation must be received by December 1. 2. Two letters of reference are required. One reference must be from the applicant's advisor for the doctoral program in which he or she is enrolled, and the other must be from a person recognized for special competence or expertise in the proposal field. 3. The candidate is required to submit an informative summary and detailed budget for the doctoral project along with the application. 4. Once the doctoral fellowship is awarded, no changes may be made in budget or plans without prior approval from MLA. 5. The MLA doctoral fellowship will pay US$2,000 in one payment toward project expenses related travel expenses augmenting another larger, separately funded project relevant to health sciences librarianship and which is part of the requirements of a doctoral degree. 6. All publications and oral presentations by the grantee relevant to the project should acknowledge MLA support. 7. The period of disbursement will not exceed two years past the date of the MLA annual meeting at which the award is given. 8. Depending on the qualifications of the candidates, the jury may recommend that the fellowship not be awarded in a given year. 9. MLA will acknowledge applications upon receipt via email.

Closing Date: 1 December

Additional Information: www.mlanet.org/page/thomson-reuters/mla-doctoral-fellowship

Medical Research Council (MRC)

David Phillips Building, Polaris House, North Star Avenue, Swindon SN2 1FL, United Kingdom.

Tel:	(44) 20 7636 5422
Email:	joaune.mccallum@headoffice.mrc.ac.uk

Website: www.mrc.ac.uk
Contact: Medical Research Council

The Medical Research Council (MRC) offers support for talented individuals who want to pursue a career in the biomedical sciences, public health and health services research. It provides its support through a variety of personal award schemes that are aimed at each stage in a clinical or non-clinical research career.

Biomedical Catalyst: Developmental Pathway Funding Scheme (DPFS)

Purpose: To encourage clinicians to become involved in research and to promote research of relevance to the Royal College of Obstetricians and Gynaecologists.
Eligibility: Please note that there is no formal limit to the total amount that can be requested in a DPFS grant - all costs should be fully justified within a proposal and the Panel will assess value for money in the context of the proposed work.
Level of Study: Postgraduate, Research
Type: Fellowship
Value: £50,000–100,000 (estimated total funds is £80,000). Predoctoral level–the award provides a competitive personal salary, up to Specialist Registrar but not including NHS Consultant level, a Research Training Support Grant of up to £10,000 per year (items must be detailed and justified), and an annual travel allowance of £450. Postdoctoral level–the fellowship provides a competitive personal salary, up to Specialist Registrar but not including NHS consultant level, research expenses, and travel costs at an appropriate level for the research, under full economic costs (FEC). For full details of what funding includes at each level please see their website.
Length of Study: 1–3 years
Frequency: Annual
Study Establishment: A suitable university or similar institution.
Country of Study: United Kingdom
Application Procedure: Applicants must contact the Fellowships Section, Research Career Awards of the MRC for details.
No. of awards offered: 2
Closing Date: 24 November
Funding: Government
No. of applicants last year: 2
Additional Information: Please see the website for further details www.mrc.ukri.org/funding/browse/biomedical-catalyst-dpfs/biomedical-catalyst-developmental-pathway-funding-scheme-dpfs-submission-deadlines/

For further information contact:

Tel: (44) 20 7670 5485
Email: fellows@headoffice.mrc.ac.uk

Cell and oligonucleotide therapy fellowship with AstraZeneca

Eligibility: To be eligible for this award, you must: 1. have completed a PhD or equivalent higher research degree, or expect to have done so by the time you take up the award 2. have the support of an eligible research organisation where you will be based for the duration of the fellowship. There are no eligibility rules based on years of postdoctoral experience. However, you are not eligible to apply if: 1. you hold, or have held, an equivalent competitive fellowship that provides the opportunity to establish an independent research group 2. you have already established independent researcher status. 3. You must not have another UKRI fellowship application under consideration at the same time.
Level of Study: Doctorate
Type: Fellowship
Value: £500,000
Length of Study: 3 years
Country of Study: United Kingdom
Closing Date: 8 March
Additional Information: www.ukri.org/opportunity/cell-and-oligonucleotide-therapy-fellowship-with-astrazeneca/

For further information contact:

Email: fellows@mrc.ukri.org

Develop basic technologies in sensing and imaging

Eligibility: Institutions and researchers normally eligible for UKRI funding include: 1. higher education institutions 2. eligible independent research organisations (IROs) 3. public sector research establishments 4. UKRI funded labs and facilities.
Type: Grant
Value: £225,000
Length of Study: 18 months
Frequency: Annual
Country of Study: United Kingdom
Closing Date: 3 March
Additional Information: www.ukri.org/opportunity/develop-basic-technologies-in-sensing-and-imaging/

For further information contact:

Email: basictechnology@bbsrc.ukri.org

Develop new approaches to small molecule medicine

Eligibility: You must be a researcher working at one of these institutions: 1. UK higher education institution 2. UKRI unit or institute 3. eligible independent research organisation 4. eligible public sector research establishment.
Type: Grant
Value: £250,000
Country of Study: United Kingdom
Additional   Information: www.ukri.org/opportunity/develop-new-approaches-to-small-molecule-medicine/

For further information contact:

Email: highthroughputscreen@mrc.ukri.org

Environmental sustainability in life sciences and medical practice

Eligibility: You can apply if you meet at least one of the criteria below: 1. are employed at the submitting research organisation 2. hold a fixed-term contract that extends beyond the duration of the proposed project, and the host research organisation is prepared 3. to give you all the support normal for a permanent employee.
Level of Study: Postgraduate
Type: Grant
Value: £100,000
Length of Study: 1 year
Frequency: Annual
Country of Study: United Kingdom
Closing Date: 1 March
Additional   Information: www.ukri.org/opportunity/environmental-sustainability-in-life-sciences-and-medical-practice/

For further information contact:

Email: sustainableresearch@mrc.ukri.org

Experimental medicine

Eligibility: 1. higher education institutions 2. UKRI-approved independent research organisations or NHS bodies 3. government-funded organisations 4. MRC institutes

5. MRC units and partnership institutes (including overseas) 6. institutes and units funded by other research councils.
Level of Study: Research
Type: Grant
Value: 80% of your project's full economic cost.
Frequency: Annual
Country of Study: United Kingdom
Closing Date: 16 March
Additional   Information: www.ukri.org/opportunity/experimental-medicine/

For further information contact:

Email: experimental.medicine@mrc.ukri.org

International collaboration to address antimicrobial resistance

Eligibility: Standard UKRI eligibility and council full economic costings (fEC) rules apply. Please check the UK national annex in the opportunity documents for additional information. Applications must include a minimum of three eligible partners asking for funding from three different countries (at least two from EU member states or associated countries). Six project partners (including non-funded partners) maximum are permitted, rising to seven if partners from under represented countries (Lithuania, Poland or low- and middle-income countries) are included in the consortium.
Level of Study: Postgraduate
Type: Grant
Frequency: Annual
Country of Study: United Kingdom
Closing Date: 8 March
Additional   Information: www.ukri.org/opportunity/international-collaboration-to-address-antimicrobial-resistance/

For further information contact:

Email: amr@mrc.ukri.org

Medical Research Council Career Development Award

Eligibility: 1. have completed a PhD or equivalent 2. have the skills and experience that match those of the 'transition to independence' career stage in the MRC applicant skills and experience criteria, such as showing evidence of career progression and productivity across past appointments 3. have your own research plans which do not significantly overlap with those of their current group leaders or proposed sponsors 4. have the support of an eligible research organisation. There are no eligibility rules based on years of postdoctoral experience.

Level of Study: Doctorate, Postdoctorate
Type: Award
Value: We will fund your salary and project costs for up to five years. We will fund 80% of the full economic cost.
Length of Study: 5 years
Frequency: Annual
Country of Study: United Kingdom
Closing Date: 20 April
Funding: Private
Additional Information: www.ukri.org/opportunity/career-development-award/

For further information contact:

Email: fellows@mrc.ukri.org

Medical Research Council Clinical Research Training Fellowships

Eligibility: To be eligible you must: 1. be able to demonstrate ownership of your project and show ambition to follow a clinical academic career 2. be at an appropriate point in your clinical training to study for a PhD, with clear plans for completing your speciality training 3. request a minimum of 24 months funding full-time equivalent to complete your PhD 4. have the support of an eligible research organisation.

Level of Study: Doctorate, Postdoctorate, Research
Type: Fellowship
Value: We will fund your salary and project costs
Length of Study: 3 years
Frequency: Annual
Country of Study: United Kingdom
Closing Date: 6 April
Funding: Government
Additional Information: www.ukri.org/opportunity/clinical-research-training-fellowship/

For further information contact:

Email: fellows@mrc.ukri.org

Medical Research Council Clinician Scientist Fellowship

Purpose: To provide an opportunity for specialized or further research training leading to the submission of a PhD, DPhil, or MD.
Eligibility: To be eligible for the clinician scientist fellowship, you must: 1. have completed a PhD or equivalent 2. have the skills and experience that match those of the 'transition to

independence' career stage in the MRC applicant skil ls and experience criteria, such as showing evidence of career progression and productivity across past appointments 3. have your own research plans which do not significantly overlap with those of their current group leaders or proposed sponsors 4. have the support of an eligible research organisation. There are no eligibility rules based on years of postdoctoral experience.

Level of Study: Postdoctorate, Research
Type: Fellowship
Value: There's no limit on the amount of funding you can apply for. We will fund your salary and project costs for up to five years. We will fund 80% of the full economic cost.
Length of Study: Up to 5 years
Frequency: Annual
Study Establishment: A suitable university department or similar institution.
Country of Study: United Kingdom
Closing Date: 6 April
Funding: Government
Additional Information: www.ukri.org/opportunity/clinician-scientist-fellowship/

For further information contact:

Email: fellows@mrc.ukri.org

Medical Research Council Industrial CASE Studentships

Purpose: To provide an opportunity for outstanding clinical researchers who wish to consolidate their research skills and make the transition from postdoctoral research and training to becoming independent investigators
Eligibility: The scheme is open to hospital doctors, dentists, general practitioners, nurses, midwives and allied health professionals. All applicants must have obtained their PhD or MD in a basic science or clinical project, or expect to have received their doctorate by the time they intend to take up an award, and must not hold tenured positions
Level of Study: Postdoctorate, Research
Type: Fellowship
Value: £500,000
Length of Study: Up to 4 years
Frequency: Annual
Study Establishment: A suitable university department or similar institution
Country of Study: United Kingdom
Application Procedure: Applicants must submit a personal application. Forms and further details are available from the MRC
Closing Date: 30 September

M

Funding: Government
Additional Information: Please see the website for further details www.ukri.org/opportunity/science-and-technology-projects-industrial-case-studentship/

For further information contact:

Email: fellows@headoffice.mrc.ac.uk

Medical Research Council Senior Clinical Fellowship

Eligibility: You can apply if you are a registered healthcare professional. This includes, but is not limited to nurses, midwives, allied health, professionals, healthcare scientists, pharmacists, clinical psychologists, doctors, dentists, general practitioners.
Level of Study: Doctorate, Postdoctorate
Type: Fellowship
Value: There's no limit on the amount of funding you can apply for. We will fund project costs and 50% of your salary.
Length of Study: Up to 5 years
Frequency: Annual
Country of Study: United Kingdom
Application Procedure: You must apply using the Joint Electronic Submission (Je-S) system. We recommend you start your application early. You can save completed details in Je-S at any time and return to continue your application later. When applying select 'new document' then: 1. council: MRC 2. document type: fellowship proposal 3. scheme: fellowships, FEC 4. call: senior clinical fellowship (SCF) Apr 2022. You can find advice on completing your application in the Je-S handbook.
Closing Date: 6 April
Funding: Private
Additional Information: www.ukri.org/opportunity/senior-clinical-fellowship/

For further information contact:

Email: fellows@mrc.ukri.org.

Medical Research Council Senior Non-Clinical Fellowship

Purpose: Aim to develop outstanding medically and other clinically qualified professionals such that they become research leaders
Eligibility: 1. have completed a PhD or equivalent 2. have the skills and experience that match those of the 'transition to leadership' career stage in the MRC applicant skills and experience criteria, such as leading nationally competitive research and clear plans to develop into an internationally recognised leader in the field 3. be leading their own independent research group, as demonstrated by a strong track record of original and productive independent research and success in securing research funding 4. have the support of an eligible research organisation.
Level of Study: Postdoctorate, Research
Type: Fellowship
Value: There's no limit on the amount of funding you can apply for. We will fund project costs and 50% of your salary for up to five year
Length of Study: 5 years
Frequency: Annual
Country of Study: United Kingdom
Application Procedure: Applicants must submit a personal application. Forms and further details are available from the MRC
No. of awards offered: 8
Closing Date: 20 April
Funding: Government
Additional Information: www.ukri.org/opportunity/senior-non-clinical-fellowship/

For further information contact:

Email: fellows@mrc.ukri.org

Medical Research Council Special Training Fellowships in Health Services and Health of the Public Research

Purpose: To provide support for non-clinical scientists of exceptional ability to concentrate on a period of research
Eligibility: Open to nationals of any country. Applicants are expected to have proven themselves to be independent researchers, be well qualified for an academic research career and demonstrate the promise of becoming future research leaders. Applicants should normally hold a PhD or DPhil in a basic science project, have at least 6 years of relevant postdoctoral research experience and not hold a tenured position
Level of Study: Postdoctorate, Research
Type: Fellowship
Value: Competitive personal salary support is provided plus research support staff at the technical and postdoctoral level, research expenses, capital equipment and a travel allowance for attendance at scientific conferences
Length of Study: 7 years
Frequency: Annual
Study Establishment: A suitable university department or similar institution
Country of Study: United Kingdom

Application Procedure: Applicants must submit a personal application. Forms and further details are available from the MRC

Closing Date: 28 April

Funding: Government

No. of awards given last year: 3

No. of applicants last year: 24

Additional Information: Please see the website for further details mrc.ukri.org/skills-careers/fellowships/

For further information contact:

Email: fellows@headoffice.mrc.ac.uk

Medical Research Council/RCOG Clinical Research Training Fellowship

Purpose: To provide support for researchers wishing to gain further training in multidisciplinary research to address problems of direct relevance to the health services within the United Kingdom

Eligibility: You can apply if you're a registered healthcare professional. This includes, but is not limited to nurses, midwives, allied health, professionals, healthcare scientists, pharmacists, clinical psychologists, doctors, dentists, general practitioners, veterinarians. Types of applicants We welcome both predoctoral and postdoctoral applicants.

Level of Study: Postdoctorate, Predoctorate

Type: Fellowship

Value: We will fund your salary and project costs for three years.

Length of Study: 3 years

Frequency: Annual

Country of Study: United Kingdom

Application Procedure: Applicants must submit a personal application. Forms and further details are available from the MRC

Closing Date: 6 April

Funding: Government

Additional Information: www.ukri.org/opportunity/clinical-research-training-fellowship/

For further information contact:

Email: fellows@mrc.ukri.org

Partner with researchers in Switzerland

Eligibility: 1. is currently active at the time of the application deadline 2. has at least six months remaining from the start of the UK-Switzerland Partnering Award. 3. To apply for the languages theme, you must have held an eligible UKRI grant

within five years of the application deadline. The following applicants are eligible to apply: 1. principal or co-investigators on an active UKRI research grant 2. recipients of a research fellowship award from UKRI 3. principal or co-investigators on a UKRI funded institute research grant.

Value: £25,000

Length of Study: 1 year

Frequency: Annual

Country of Study: United Kingdom

Closing Date: 8 March

Additional Information: www.ukri.org/opportunity/partner-with-researchers-in-switzerland/

For further information contact:

Email: international@ukri.org

Reducing global health non-communicable disease risk for young people

Eligibility: You must: 1. be based at a UK research organisation eligible for UKRI funding 2. work in partnership with co-investigators based in low or middle income countries (LMICs) where the work will take place. Your research must: 1. take a life course approach 2. focus on people aged 10 to 24 in LMICs.

Type: Grant

Value: £5,000,000

Length of Study: 3 to 5 years

Country of Study: United Kingdom

Closing Date: 31 May

Additional Information: www.ukri.org/opportunity/reducing-global-health-non-communicable-disease-risk-for-young-people/

For further information contact:

Email: international@mrc.ukri.org

Medical Research Scotland

Princes Exchange, 1 Earl Grey Street, Edinburgh EH3 9EE, United Kingdom.

Tel:	(44) 131 659 8800
Email:	enquiries@medicalresearchscotland.org.uk
Website:	www.medicalresearchscotland.org.uk
Contact:	The Trust Administrator

Medical Research Scotland has launched a new digital learning series featuring inspiring young scientists encouraging S5 and S6 pupils to study STEM subjects. Each event will feature an inspiring young scientist at the cutting edge of their field as well as University lecturers and industry leaders from across medical research, science and technology. The young scientists featured are all studying at Scottish universities, thanks to funding from Medical Research Scotland.

Doctor of Philosophy Studentship

Purpose: To provide fully funded four year PhD Studentships, delivered collaboratively by a recognized Scottish University/Research Institution and a company working in medically-relevant research, which incorporate enhanced and tailored academic and commercial training and experience.

Eligibility: To be eligible, the Administering Institution must be a recognised Scottish University or Research Institution in which the student will be matriculated and which will award the PhD degree. There is no geographical requirement or restriction for the External Partner Organisation. There is no requirement or restriction on the subject or nature of the research, provided it addresses a question relevant to human health – the causation, prevention, diagnosis or treatment of illness or the development of medical or surgical appliances. At least three supervisors are required per PhD Studentship, including a Principal and a Second Supervisor from the Administering Institution and an External Partner Organisation Supervisor.

Level of Study: Postgraduate

Type: Studentship

Value: Up to £35,000 research expenses, £3,000 travel allowance

Length of Study: 4 years

Frequency: Annual

Study Establishment: Scottish Universities, Higher Education or research institutions recognized as such.

Country of Study: Scotland

Application Procedure: Applications must be submitted online, following the information available at www.medicalre searchscotland.org.uk/

No. of awards offered: 25

Contributor: Income from the original endowment fund, established when the charity came into being in 1953, invested and augmented by voluntary donations and bequests.

Additional Information: Applications must be submitted by a university and an appropriate company and not by prospective students medicalresearchscotland.org.uk/phd-studentships/

For further information contact:

Email: applications@medicalresearchscotland.org

Medical Research Scotland Sponsored Daphne Jackson Trust Fellowships

Purpose: To provide three year part time fellowships for those wishing to return to medical research at a Scottish University or Research Institution after a career break of three years or more. Fellowships are awarded in conjunction with the Daphne Jackson Trust.

Eligibility: To be eligible for consideration applicants must meet the following criteria: 1. have a good first degree in science, technology, engineering or mathematics (STEM) 2. have a PhD, or at least three years research experience (academic or industrial) prior to the career break (with evidence of scholarly outputs) 3. have had a career break of at least two years' duration taken for family, caring or health reasons 4. be resident in the UK with the right to remain in the UK indefinitely 5. have good command of English (spoken and written) 6. have good computer skills.

Level of Study: Postdoctorate, Professional development

Type: Fellowship

Value: £5,000 consumables per annum; and £1,500 extraordinary expenses

Length of Study: 3 years

Frequency: Annual

Country of Study: Scotland

Application Procedure: Applications must be submitted online, following the information available at www.medicalre searchscotland.org.uk/

Additional Information: www.medicalresearchscotland. org.uk/daphne-jackson-fellowships/

For further information contact:

The Daphne Jackson Trust, Department of Physics, University of Surrey, Guildford, Surrey GU2 7XH, United Kingdom.

Email: DJMFT@surrey.ac.uk

Meet The Composer, Inc.

90 John Street, Suite 312, New York, NY 10038, United States of America.

Tel: (1) 212 645 6949
Email: mtc@meetthecomposer.org
Website: www.newmusicusa.org

Meet The Composer's mission is to increase artistic and financial opportunities for American composers by fostering the creation, performance, dissemination and appreciation of their music.

Commissioning Music/United States of America

Purpose: To support the commissioning of new works
Eligibility: Open to citizens of the United States of America only. Organizations that have been producing or presenting for at least 3 years are eligible and may be dance, chorus, orchestra, opera, theatre and music-theatre companies, festivals, arts presenters, public radio and television stations, internet providers, soloists and small performing ensembles of all kinds, e.g. jazz, chamber, new music, etc
Level of Study: Professional development
Type: Grant
Value: Up to US$10,000–20,000
Frequency: Annual
Country of Study: United States of America
Application Procedure: Individuals cannot apply on their own. Host organizations must submit completed application forms and accompanying materials
No. of awards offered: 150-200
Closing Date: 19 March
Contributor: Offered in partnership with the National Endowment for the Arts
Additional Information: Please see the website for further details www.newmusicusa.org/grants/commissioning-music-usa/

For further information contact:

Tel: (1) 212 645 6040 ext 102
Email: swinship@newmusicusa.org

JP Morgan Chase Regrant Program for Small Ensembles

Purpose: To support small New York City-based ensembles and music organizations committed to performing the work of living composers and contemporary music
Eligibility: Open to organizations focused primarily or exclusively on new music and living composers, improvisers, sound artists or singer/songwriters
Level of Study: Professional development
Type: Grant
Value: US$1,000 to US$5,000
Frequency: Annual
Country of Study: United States of America
Application Procedure: Applicants must contact the organization
Funding: Commercial

Contributor: In partnership with JP Morgan Chase
Additional Information: jpmorganchaseco.gcs-web.com/static-files/3553e235-ead8-4320-bebe-8c4f5b5e7f65

For further information contact:

Email: east.giving@jpmchase.com

Melville Trust for Care and Cure of Cancer

Tods Murray LLP, Edinburgh Quay, 133 Fountain Bridge, Edinburgh EH8 9YL, United Kingdom.

Tel: (44) 131 650 1000
Email: melvilletrust@todsmurray.com
Contact: The Secretary

The trust supports work in the fields of research into care or cure of cancer. Whilst not taking a view on animal experimentation, the trust does not support research using animals for research.

Melville Trust for Care and Cure of Cancer Research Fellowships

Purpose: To fund innovative research work in the care or cure of cancer.
Eligibility: Applicants, who need not necessarily hold a medical qualification or have experience of research, should have formulated proposals for a research project which have been discussed with an established research worker in the field. The applicant should normally be under 30 years of age.
Level of Study: Research
Type: Fellowship
Value: £2,000
Length of Study: 1–3 year
Frequency: Annual
Study Establishment: One of the clinical or scientific departments in Lothian, Borders, Fife or Dundee.
Country of Study: Any country
Application Procedure: Applicants must complete an application form and then be interviewed.
No. of awards offered: 4
Closing Date: 28 February
Funding: Private
No. of awards given last year: 1
No. of applicants last year: 4

Additional Information: www.blogs.cs.st-andrews.ac.uk/
csblog/2019/07/03/the-melville-trust-for-the-care-and-cure-
of-cancer-phd-award/

For further information contact:

c/o Tods Murray LLP, Edinburgh Quay 133 Fountain Bridge,
Edinburgh EH3 9AG, United Kingdom.

Melville Trust for Care and Cure of Cancer Research Grants

Purpose: To fund innovative research work in cure or care of
cancer.
Eligibility: Applicants need not necessarily hold a medical
qualification or have experience of research. Research sup-
port by the Trust will be carried out in a clinical or
scientific department in Lothians, Borders, Fife or Dundee,
the head of which must signify his or her approval of the
application.
Level of Study: Research
Type: Grant
Value: Up to £25,000
Length of Study: 1–3 year
Frequency: Annual
Study Establishment: One of the clinical or scientific depart-
ments in Lothian, Borders, Fife or Dundee
Country of Study: Any country
Application Procedure: Applicants must complete an
application form.
No. of awards offered: 7
Closing Date: 28 February
Funding: Private
No. of awards given last year: 1
No. of applicants last year: 7
Additional Information: www.blogs.cs.st-andrews.ac.uk/
csblog/2019/07/03/the-melville-trust-for-the-care-and-cure-
of-cancer-phd-award/

Memorial Foundation for Jewish Culture

50 Broadway, 34th Floor, New York, NY 10004, United
States of America.

Tel: (1) 212 425 6606
Email: office@mfjc.org
Website: www.mfjc.org
Contact: Jeni S. Friedman, Executive Vice President

The Memorial Foundation for Jewish Culture is committed to
the creation, intensification, and dissemination of Jewish culture worldwide, the development of creative programs to
meet the emerging needs of Jewish communities globally,
and to serving as a central forum for identifying and
supporting innovative programs to insure the continuation
of creative Jewish life wherever Jewish communities exist.

Ephraim Urbach Post Doctoral Fellowship

Purpose: To assist recent recipients of the PhD in a field of
Jewish studies in publishing their first book, launching their
scholarly career, and/or furthering research in their area of
special interest.
Eligibility: Graduates of a PhD programme in a field of Jewish
studies who achieved superior grades, in graduate school, com-
pleted their dissertation with distinction, and who show prom-
ise of distinguished academic careers are eligible to apply.
Level of Study: Postgraduate
Type: Fellowship
Value: Up to US$10,000
Length of Study: 1 academic year
Frequency: Annual
Country of Study: Any country
Application Procedure: Applicants must be nominated by
the head of the department at which they completed their PhD
and must have received their PhD within 3 years of the date of
application. Applicants must write requesting an application.
Closing Date: 31 March
Additional Information: www.jewish-studies.org/member
ship2_en.ehtml

Memorial University of Newfoundland (MUN)

Memorial University of Newfoundland, St. John's, PO Box
4200, St Johns, NL A1C 5S7, Canada.

Tel: (1) 709 737 8000
Email: info@mun.ca
Website: www.mun.ca

Located in Canada's most easterly province, Newfoundland
and Labrador, Memorial University of Newfoundland offers
a diverse selection of Graduate programmes leading to
diplomas, Master's and Doctoral degrees in the arts, sciences,
professional and interdisciplinary areas of study. Their goal is
to promote excellence in all aspects of Graduate education in
order to assist students to fulfil their personal goals and to
prepare for a productive career.

School of Graduate Studies F. A. Aldrich Award

Purpose: To financially assist students with exceptional academic achievement to study further

Eligibility: Open to full-time Canadian students on the basis of exceptional academic achievement

Level of Study: Postdoctorate, Predoctorate

Type: Fellowship

Value: C$2,000

Frequency: Annual

Study Establishment: Memorial University of Newfoundland

Country of Study: Any country

Additional Information: Please see the website for details www.mun.ca/sgs/current/scholarships/internal_nominated. php#sgsaldrich www.med.mun.ca/getdoc/359e8c84-8b04-48de-a8c4-f180bb039c61/School-of-Graduate-Studies-FA-Aldrich-Fellowship.aspx

The Dr Ethel M. Janes Memorial Scholarship in Education

Purpose: To aid students who want to specialize in reading and language arts and to those who want to make a career in research and teaching in primary and elementary education.

Eligibility: Must be a full-time graduate student (not working more than 24 hours per week) in the area of Language and Literacy Studies for the Fall and Winter semesters.

Level of Study: Graduate

Type: Scholarship

Value: C$2,000

Frequency: Annual

Country of Study: Any country

Application Procedure: If you wish to be considered for this award please contact Darlene Flight (dflight@mun.ca).

Closing Date: 4 December

Additional Information: This scholarship will be awarded on the basis of academic standing in a first Memorial University of Newfoundland Education degree to a graduate student with a specialization in reading or language arts. In the event that in any given year no graduate student qualifies for the award, this scholarship will be awarded to an undergraduate student.

Training Graduate PhD Salary Award (TGP)

Purpose: Salary awards are offered to graduate students who are undertaking full-time research training in an area of clear relevance to arthritis and the Arthritis Society's new Strategic Plan 2020-2025 Accelerating Impact - Research Strategy which aims to identify research avenues that focus on areas of highest priority to patients and achieve the highest levels of scientific excellence and rigour. Applications must focus on innovative research efforts in the following priority areas.

Eligibility: 1. Be engaged in full-time training in research in a Canadian graduate school program leading to a PhD 2. Be within the first three years of a PhD training program at the time of the application deadline. 3. Be working on a research project with clear relevance relevance to the research priority areas in the Arthritis Society's 2020-25.

Level of Study: Postgraduate

Type: Award

Value: C$21,000

Country of Study: Canada

Application Procedure: All submissions will be screened for completeness and eligibility. Note that incomplete applications by the deadline will be deemed ineligible and withdrawn from the competition. It is the responsibility of the applicant to ensure that applications are complete at the time of submission.

Closing Date: 24 April

Additional Information: The intent is to augment the young investigators' training by providing a forum to share their research, gain knowledge on select topics such as consumer engagement in research, and provide networking and mentorship opportunities. www.scholarshipscanada.com/Scholarships/6862/Dr.-Ethel-M.-Janes-Memorial-Scholarship-in-Education-

Microsoft Research

One Microsoft Way, Redmond, WA 98052, United States of America.

Tel: (1) 800 642 7676
Email: latamint@microsoft.com
Website: www.research.microsoft.com

Microsoft Corporation became the first software company to create its own computer science research organization. It has developed into a unique entity among corporate research laboratories, balancing an open academic model with an effective process for transferring its research to product development teams.

Microsoft Fellowship

Purpose: To empower and encourage PhD students in the Asia-Pacific region to realize their potential in computer science-related research and to recognize and award outstanding PhD students.

Eligibility: Open to candidates who specialize in computer science, electronic engineering, information technology or applied mathematics and are in their first or second year of PhD programme and is enroled as a PhD student by the time of the nomination and has spent 6–18 months working towards a PhD.

Level of Study: Research

Type: Fellowships

Value: 100% of the tuition and fees, a stipend to cover living expenses while in school (US$28,000), travel allowance to attend professional conferences or seminars (US$4,000). See the website for details.

Length of Study: 2 years

Frequency: Annual

Country of Study: Any country

Application Procedure: Applicants must send the completed application form (downloaded from the website), 2 recommendation letters, curriculum vitae and a video or Power Point presentation with audio introduction (on compact disk), including statement of purpose, previous, on-going and future projects, research interests and accomplishments.

Closing Date: 9 October

Additional Information: www.microsoft.com/en-us/research/academic-program/phd-fellowship/#!asia-pacific For the next round of fellowships, check back the first week of May 2022.

For further information contact:

MS Fellow 2006 Committee Microsoft Research Asia 3F Beijing Sigma Center, No 49 Zhichun Road, Beijing, China.

Email: msfellow@microsoft.com

Microsoft Research European PhD Scholarship Programme

Purpose: To recognize and support exceptional students who show the potential to make an outstanding contribution to science.

Eligibility: Applicant must have been accepted by a university in Europe to start a PhD or will have completed no more than 1 year of their PhD by October.

Level of Study: Doctorate

Type: Scholarships

Value: €30,000 per year and a laptop with a range of software applications.

Length of Study: 3 years

Frequency: Annual

Country of Study: Any country

Closing Date: 31 March

Additional Information: All queries should be sent via email and please see the website for further details www.microsoft.com/en-us/research/academic-program/phd-scholarship-europe-middle-east-africa/ We will publish our next application dates in due course.

For further information contact:

Email: msrphd@microsoft.com

Middlesex University London

The Burroughs, Hendon, London NW4 4BT, United Kingdom.

Tel: (44) 20 8411 5000
Website: www.mdx.ac.uk

Established in 1878, Middlesex University is a public university that is associated with the Association of Commonwealth Universities, the European University Association, Coalition of Modern Universities, and Universities UK. Earlier, the university was known as the Middlesex Polytechnic University. It gained the status of a university in 1992.

International Merit Award

Purpose: Middlesex University is renowned for offering unrivalled support to international students and gives out scholarships and merit awards to international students totalling around £1,000,000 each year.

Eligibility: Open to any international postgraduate student in any subject.

Level of Study: Graduate, Postgraduate

Type: Award

Value: Up to £2,000

Frequency: Annual

Study Establishment: Middlesex University London

Country of Study: United Kingdom

Application Procedure: There is no separate application for this award; international students should apply for their chosen course through the normal application process. Awards will be given on a case-by-case basis which will be dependent on your course and application.

Contributor: Middlesex University London

Additional Information: Successful candidates will be notified at the point of offer for a programme of study and the award amount will be deducted from their tuition fees. NB:

Research students are not eligible for the International Merit Award www.studyabroad.shiksha.com/scholarships/international-merit-scholarship-master-of-engineering

For further information contact:

Tel: (61) 7 3138 8822
Email: sef.enquiry@qut.edu.au

Santander Formula Scholarship

Eligibility: Open to any undergraduate or postgraduate student from South America. Awarded to South American students demonstrating excellent academic potential. To be eligible students must Hold an offer of a place for a one-year postgraduate taught masters at the University of Glasgow, Be a national of Argentina, Belgium, Brazil, Chile, China, Colombia Germany, Ghana, Mexico, Poland, Peru, Portugal, Puerto, Rico, Russia, Singapore, South Korea, Spain, United Arab Emirates, United Kingdom, Uruguay, Venezuela United States of America.
Level of Study: Graduate, Postgraduate
Type: Scholarship
Value: £4,200 towards the students' fees
Study Establishment: Middlesex University London
Country of Study: United Kingdom
Application Procedure: Email the Americas and Caribbean regional office (info@mdxna.com)
Contributor: Middlesex University London
Additional Information: Please note that awards will be allocated based on application date so we encourage you to apply as soon as possible www.ufvinternational.com/en/santander-scholarships/formula-santander-international-scholarships/

For further information contact:

Email: support.team@postgraduatesearch.com

Santander Mobility Scholarship

Purpose: The Santander Universities Mobility Scholarship is available for students from Edinburgh Napier University participating in a single trimester or full year overseas exchange programme. Awards will be made to students who would ordinarily be unable to participate in their exchange without support from the scholarship.
Eligibility: Open to any undergraduate or postgraduate exchange student. Available for exchange students resident within the United Kingdom and countries listed in the Santander Universidades scheme*

Level of Study: Graduate, Postgraduate
Type: Scholarship
Value: £1,000 per month
Study Establishment: Middlesex University London
Country of Study: United Kingdom
No. of awards offered: 11
Contributor: Middlesex University London
Additional Information: *Countries involved in the Santander Universidades Scheme include; Argentina, Brazil, Belgium, Chile, China, Colombia, Germany, Ghana, Korea, Mexico, Poland, Portugal, Puerto Rico, Russia, Singapore, Spain, United States of America, United Kingdom, UAE, and Uruguay www.becas-santander.com/en/program/santander-universities-mobility-scholarship

For further information contact:

Dr Nosheen Rachel-Naseem, Student Exchange Manager, United Kingdom.

Tel: (44) 208 411 5962
Email: employability@mdx.ac.uk

Santander Work Based Learning Scholarship

Purpose: This award is available to Work Based Learning students who have demonstrated academic excellence. You must have applied, or be currently enrolled on an undergraduate or postgraduate/doctoral programme within the Institute for Work Based Learning
Eligibility: Open to any Work Based Learning student who has demonstrated academic excellence. You must have applied, or be currently enroled on an undergraduate or postgraduate/doctoral programme within the Institute for Work Based Learning
Level of Study: Doctorate, Graduate, Postgraduate
Type: Scholarship
Value: £750 to a maximum value of £1,500
Study Establishment: Middlesex University London
Country of Study: United Kingdom
Application Procedure: To apply, please fill in our Scholarship application form
Closing Date: 11 March
Contributor: Middlesex University London
Additional Information: www.plymouth.ac.uk/study/fees/scholarships-bursaries-and-funding/santander-scholarships

For further information contact:

Tel: (44) 208 411 5415
Email: scholarships@mdx.ac.uk

M

Significant Achievement in Sport

Purpose: This is for talented sports performers, who are keen to continue their sporting endeavours and compete for the University.
Eligibility: Any undergraduate or postgraduate student demonstrating a significant achievement in sport.
Level of Study: Postgraduate
Value: Ranging from £200 to £1,000
Country of Study: United Kingdom
Closing Date: 4 September
Additional Information: www.mdx.ac.uk/study-with-us/fees-and-funding/scholarships-and-bursaries

For further information contact:

Tel: (44) 208 411 5415
Email: scholarships@mdx.ac.uk

The Alumni Bursary

Eligibility: Available to United Kingdom/EU students who completed their first degree at Middlesex and have an offer for a further taught masters programme here. The bursary applies to self-financing students and students not eligible for funding from Student Finance United Kingdom. International (i.e. outside of the EU) alumni, not already receiving an International Merit Award or regional award, may be eligible to receive a 10% reduction in tuition fees when progressing to postgraduate study at Middlesex.
Level of Study: Graduate, Postgraduate
Type: Bursary
Value: Up to 20% of the tuition fee
Frequency: Dependent on funds available
Study Establishment: Middlesex University London
Country of Study: United Kingdom
Application Procedure: Find out more from your nearest regional office.
Contributor: Middlesex University London
Additional Information: Students already holding another Middlesex Scholarship (e.g. Academic Excellence Scholarship) are not entitled to the Alumni bursary www.london.ac.uk/applications/funding-your-study/alumni-bursary#terms-and-conditions-3425

For further information contact:

The Burroughs, London NW4 4BT, United Kingdom.

Tel: (44) 20 8411 6286
Email: scholarships@mdx.ac.uk

The David Caminer Postgraduate Scholarship in Business Computing

Eligibility: Open to any first year MSc student in the School of Science and Technology. The scholarships will be available to students who have demonstrated excellent academic potential. Applications are welcome from students who have fulfilled the admission criteria and been offered a place to study for a postgraduate degree based in the School of Science & Technology
Level of Study: Graduate, Postgraduate
Type: Scholarship
Value: £5,000
Frequency: Annual
Study Establishment: Middlesex University London
Country of Study: United Kingdom
Application Procedure: To apply, please fill in the Scholarship application form (www.mdx.hobsons.co.uk/emtinterestpage.aspx?ip=scholarship)
Closing Date: August
Contributor: Middlesex University London
Additional Information: A student will only be entitled to one award during his/her period of study with Middlesex University www.scholarship-positions.com/david-caminer-postgraduate-scholarship-in-business-computing-middlesex-university-uk-2014/2014/07/23/

For further information contact:

Email: studentship.research@mdx.ac.uk

Miles Morland Foundation

2nd Floor, Jubilee House, 2 Jubilee Place, London SW3 3TQ, United Kingdom.

Tel: (44) 2073491245
Email: mmf@milesmorlandfoundation.com
Website: www.milesmorlandfoundation.com

The MMF was set up by Miles Morland after a career investing in Africa through two companies he founded, Blakeney Management and DPI (Development Partners International). In the course of this career Miles has been surprised, entertained, impressed, and humbled by the energy, wit, entrepreneurialism and talent of the Africans he has got to know.

Miles Morland Foundation Writing Scholarship

Purpose: To help meet this need the MMF annually awards a small number of Morland Writing Scholarships, with the aim being to allow each Scholar the time to produce the first draft of a completed book. The Scholarships are open to anyone writing in the English language who was born in Africa, or both of whose parents were born in Africa

Eligibility: The Scholarships are open to anyone writing in the English language who was born in Africa, or both of whose parents were born in Africa. To qualify for the Scholarship a candidate must submit an excerpt from a piece of work of between 2,000 and 5,000 words, written in English that has been published and offered for sale,. This will be evaluated by a panel of readers and judges set up by the MMF. The work submitted will be judged purely on literary merit. It is not the purpose of the Scholarships to support academic or scientific research, or works of special interest such as religious or political writings. Submissions or proposals of this nature do not qualify.

Type: Scholarships

Value: £18,000, paid monthly

Length of Study: 12 Months

Frequency: Annual

Country of Study: United Kingdom

Closing Date: 18 September

Additional Information: www.milesmorlandfoundation.com/about-2/

For further information contact:

Email: scholarships@milesmorlandfoundation.com

Minerva Stiftung

Gesellschaft für die Forschung mbH, Hofgartenstrasse 8, D-80539 Munich, Germany.

Tel: (49) 89 2108 1420

Email: langegao@gv.mpg.de

Website: www.minerva.mpg.de

The Minerva Stiftung is the flagship of German-Israeli scientific cooperation. It is financed by the Federal Ministry of Education and Research, and works closely with leading universities and research facilities in Israel.

Minerva Fellowship

Eligibility: Applicants who are presently residing in Israel/Germany but are not nationals of either of the two countries must show a proven record of integration into the Israeli or German scientific community. An affiliation to a research institution in Israel or Germany is required together with a residency of 5 years or longer in either of the two countries. Conversely, if applicants are citizens of one country but have been living in the other for an extended period of time (more than 4 years) a scholarship in the second country cannot be granted since it would not truly support German-Israeli exchange.

Type: Fellowship

Value: Up to €800,00 (for spouses the limit is €300,00)

Length of Study: 6 months to 2 years

Country of Study: Germany

Closing Date: June

Additional Information: www.minerva.mpg.de/22157/application

For further information contact:

Email: minerva-team@gv.mpg.de

Minerva Short-Term Research Grants

Purpose: To fund scientific visits of Israeli scholars and scientists and to promote Israeli–German scientific co-operation.

Eligibility: Who can apply for the Minerva Short-Term Research Grant? 1. German or Israeli by citizens or 2. presently residing in Israel or Germany together with a proven affiliation to a research institution and a proven residency of 3 years or longer in either of the two countries; 3. student/member of a German university or research institution or 4. student/member of an Israeli university or public resp. governmental research institution; 5. under the age of 38 (parental leave will be taken into account); 6. not taking part in the Minerva Fellowship Programme; 7. not a Principal Investigator of a project within a BMBF-MOST Programme.

Level of Study: Research

Type: Grant

Value: Postdoc applicants €450,00

Length of Study: 1 to 8 weeks

Study Establishment: A German university or research institute.

Country of Study: Germany

Closing Date: 2 May

Additional Information: Flights are covered by a lump sum of up to €700.00 www.minerva.mpg.de/16320/application

For further information contact:

Minerva Foundation, Gesellschaft für die Forschung mbH, Hofgartenstraße 8, D-80539 München, Germany.

Tel: (49) 89 2108 1258

Fax: (49) 89 2108 1451

Email: michael.nagel@gv.mpg.de

Ministry of Education and Science Republic of Latvia (MESRL)

Valnuiela 2, LV-1050 Riga, Latvia.

Tel: (371) 722 6209
Email: info@izm.gov.lv
Website: www.izm.gov.lv

The ministry was established immediately after the proclamation of the Latvian state on 18 November 1918. Today the Ministry of Education and Science is the leading public administration institution in the Republic of Latvia in the field of education and science, as well as in the areas of sports, youth and state language policies.

Ministry of Education and Science of the Republic of Lithuania Scholarships for Studies and Research Work

Purpose: To encourage foreign students in studies and research work.
Eligibility: Open to candidates from Belarus, The Czech Republic, Flanders, Greece, Estonia, Italy, China, Lithuania, Mongolia, Poland, Spain and Hungary.
Level of Study: Research
Type: Scholarships
Value: Varies
Length of Study: 10 months
Frequency: Annual
Country of Study: Any country
Application Procedure: Applicants can download the application form from the website. The completed application form along with a curriculum vitae, letter of motivation, certified copies of education documents, letters of recommendation and photograph must be sent.
Closing Date: 15 May
Additional Information: www.topuniversities.com/student-info/scholarships/international-scholarships-students-developing-countries

For further information contact:

Tel: (371) 704 7876
Email: mara.katvare@izm.gov.lv

Ministry of Fisheries

Pastoral House, 25 The Terrace, PO Box 2526, Wellington 6140, New Zealand.

Tel: (64) 800 00 8333
Email: info@fish.govt.nz
Website: www.fish.govt.nz/en-nz/default.htm

Fisheries New Zealand works to ensure that fisheries resources are managed to provide the greatest overall benefit to New Zealanders. Our focus is the sustainability of New Zealand's wild fish stocks, aquaculture, and the wider aquatic environment, now and for future generations.

Ministry of Fisheries PG Scholarships in Quantitative Fisheries Science

Purpose: To allow graduate students to develop expertise in quantitative fisheries science and encourage postgraduate students to contribute to priority research areas identified by the New Zealand government.
Eligibility: Open to applicants with majors or minors in mathematics, statistics, biology, economics or computer science.
Level of Study: Postgraduate
Type: Scholarship
Value: NZ$30,000 per year for PhD and up to NZ$20,000 per year for Masters
Length of Study: 3 years (PhD) and up to 2 years (Masters)
Frequency: Annual
Country of Study: Any country
Application Procedure: Applicants should contact Rebecca Lawton for details.
Closing Date: 20 September
Contributor: In collaboration with NIWA
Additional Information: Research is most likely to be carried out a NIWA facility. Preference will be given to New Zealand citizens www.docplayer.net/161463027-Ministry-of-fisheries-niwa-postgraduate-scholarships-in-quantitative-fisheries-science.html

For further information contact:

Tel: (64) 4 819 4251
Email: rebecca.lawton@fish.govt.nz

Ministry of Foreign Affairs

Master Scholarships for International Students

Purpose: The aim of the Program is to foster cooperation among Italian Universities and Italian companies in order to promote their internationalization by sustaining higher education courses tailored to the needs of the labor market.

Eligibility: Candidates should submit an English language certificate as proof of their proficiency in English. Candidates should hold at least a B2 level certificate within the Common European Framework of Reference for Languages (CEFR). Proof of proficiency in Italian is not mandatory but will be taken into consideration in the selection process.

Value: Grantees will receive €888 monthly allowance every three months on their Italian bank account. The first instalment of the scholarship can only be received after the University enrollment according to the necessary administrative procedures. The last instalment of the scholarship can only be received after verification of conditions established under Article 6.2 of this Call. The scholarship only covers courses attended in Italy.

Study Establishment: Scholarships are awarded to study the subjects offered by the university

Country of Study: Italy

Application Procedure: Candidates must complete and submit the online application form.

Closing Date: 28 February

Additional Information: For more information please see the website www.scholarship-positions.com/master-scholarships-for-international-students-italy/2017/12/19

For further information contact:

Email: dgsp.iyt@esteri.it

Ministry of Foreign Affairs and International Cooperation

King Abdullah Bin Abdul Aziz Al Saud Street, Al Bateen - Abu Dhabi, United Arab Emirates.

Tel: (971) 80044444
Website: www.mofaic.gov.ae/en

The UAE Ministry of Foreign Affairs and International Cooperation (MoFAIC) provides document attestation services of all kinds. An attestation is a procedure that confirms the validity of a seal and signature on documents issued in UAE or abroad.

Ministry of Foreign Affairs and International Cooperation Scholarships for Foreign and Italian Students

Purpose: The Ministry of Foreign Affairs and International Cooperation (MAECI) offers grants in favor of foreign citizens in Italy and Italian citizens living abroad (IRE) in order to foster international cooperation in cultural, scientific and technological fields, to promote Italian language and culture and to support Italy's economic system in the world.

Eligibility: 1. Applicants who will meet the following requirements by the deadline of this call (October 2nd 2023, 2 p.m. C.E.T.) may apply for a grant. 2. According to the present call, only the candidates who have received a MAECI grant in the academic year 2022–2023 may apply, following the ordinary procedure, in order to continue or complete a multi-year study course. 3. Renewals are granted only to applicants who can prove to have given exams for a minimum of 15 credits (CFU) or, for Ph.D. students, presenting a letter from their tutor/supervisor stating the positive progress of their studies, in the previous academic year.

Level of Study: MBA, Masters Degree, Postgraduate (MSc)

Type: Scholarship

Value: €900 monthly allowance on a quarterly basis, which will be paid on their Italian bank account.

Length of Study: with in one year

Frequency: Annual

Country of Study: Italy

Application Procedure: Applicants must complete and submit the online application form available upon registration at the following link www.studyinitaly.esteri.it

Closing Date: 2 October

Additional Information: Applications will be evaluated by a Committee set up by the Italian Diplomatic Mission accredited in the applicant's country of origin. The relevant Diplomatic Mission will publish on its website the list of grantees. www.scholarship-positions.com/master-scholarships-for-international-students-italy/2017/12/19

Ministry of Foreign Affairs of the Republic of Indonesia

Directorate of Public Diplomacy, Tower Building, 12th Floor, Jl. Pejambon No. 6, Jakarta Pusat 10110, Indonesia.

Tel: (62) 21 344 15 08
Email: kontak-kami@kemlu.go.id
Website: www.kemlu.go.id

The first Cabinet of the Republic of Indonesia was formed after independence was proclaimed.

Indonesian Arts and Culture Scholarship

Purpose: The program serves to demonstrate Indonesia's commitment as an initiator of the establishment of South West Pacific Dialogue and as the originator member of

ASEAN in advancing the social culture cooperation in the region. The program also has an objective to encourage better understanding amongst participants from member countries.

Eligibility: 1. You should be single 2. Ages of 21 to 27 years old 3. Ensure you have at least a high school diploma 4. You should possess high interest and talent in the arts. 5. If you are an Arts students or have an academic history of Indonesian culture, you are also encouraged to apply; 6. Bearing in mind the intensity of the program, you are highly advised to ensure prime physical condition, particularly for female candidates so that you do not conceive prior to and during the program. 7. Endeavor to arrive in Indonesia a day before the Orientation Program; 8. Ensure you follow the whole program, including orientation program and Indonesian Channel; 9. Complete the application form (attached with the official link) and submit it with particulars as mentioned in the official link.

Level of Study: Postgraduate

Type: Scholarships and fellowships

Value: The scholarship will cover the following; Tuition fee (including extra-curricular activities); A round trip economy class ticket; Accommodation (board and lodging); Local transportation during the program; Health insurance (limited). All awardees are advised to have their own health insurance. Monthly allowance of Rp. 2,000,000.

Length of Study: 3 months

Frequency: Annual

Country of Study: Other

Country of Study: Indonesia

Application Procedure: 1. Candidates should be single, between the ages of 21 to 27 years-old with at least a high school diploma. 2. Candidates should possess high interest and talent in arts. Arts students or those with an academic history on Indonesian culture are encouraged to apply. 3. Bearing in mind the intensity of the program, candidates are highly advised to ensure prime physical mentally/psychologist conditions, particularly for female candidates to ensure that they do not conceive prior and during the program. 4. Participants must arrive in Indonesia a day before the Orientation Program. 5. Participants must follow the whole program, including orientation program and Indonesian Channel.

Closing Date: 14 February

Funding: Private

Additional Information: worldscholarshipforum.com/fully-funded-indonesian-arts-and-culture-scholarship/

For further information contact:

The Ministry of Foreign Affairs Directorate of Public Diplomacy Tower Building, 12th Floor, Jl. Taman Pejambon No. 6, Jakarta 10110, Indonesia.

Tel:	(62) 420 257 214 388
Email:	embassy@indonesia.cz

Minnesota Historical Society (MHS)

345 W. Kellogg Blvd., St. Paul, MN 55102, United States of America.

Tel:	(1) 651 259 3000
Email:	debbie.miller@mnhs.org
Website:	www.mnhs.org
Contact:	Ms Stacey Kennedy, Research Supervisor

The Minnesota Historical Society is a dynamic and widely recognized educational organization that is a trusted resource for history. It is highly valued for its historical resources, educational impact, service, advocacy and leadership. The vision of MNHS is to maximize the power of personal and community stories and shared history to enrich and transform lives.

Minnesota Historical Society Research Grant

Purpose: To support original research and interpretative writing by academics, independent Scholars and professional or non professional writers.

Eligibility: Open to applicants of any nationality with English reading and writing ability

Level of Study: Unrestricted

Type: Grant

Value: Varies. Up to US$1,500 for research that will result in an article, up to US$5,000 for research that will result in a book or up to US$1,000 for visiting Scholar grants.

Length of Study: Varies

Frequency: Twice a year

Country of Study: United States of America

Application Procedure: Applicants must complete an application form. Other documentation is also required. Guidelines and applications are available by writing to the given address, by sending an email or from the website

Closing Date: 10 April

Funding: Government

Contributor: The state of Minnesota

No. of awards given last year: 22

Additional Information: www.mnhs.org/preservation/legacy-grants

For further information contact:

Email:	grants@mnhs.org

Minnesota Ovarian Cancer Alliance (MOCA)

Minnesota Ovarian Cancer Alliance, 4604 Chicago Avenue, Minneapolis, MN 55407, United States of America.

Tel: (1) 612 822 0500
Email: info@mnovarian.org
Website: www.mnovarian.org/
Contact: Kathleen Gavin, Executive Director

Formed in 1999 by a group of ovarian cancer survivors, MOCA is a statewide non-profit that serves women and families from throughout the Upper Midwest.

National Early Detection of Ovarian Cancer Research Awards 2020

Purpose: The Minnesota Ovarian Cancer Alliance will award two grants to support research on early detection of ovarian cancer.
Eligibility: Research proposals may be for individual projects or part of a larger research project related to early detection of ovarian, primary peritoneal or fallopian tube cancer. Awards are available to researchers working anywhere in the U.S. Project funding is available for one year of activity.
Level of Study: Postgraduate
Type: Grant
Value: US$400,000
Frequency: Annual
Country of Study: United States of America
Application Procedure: Proposals must be paginated and include the following 1. Cover letter should include the grant title, the PI's name and direct contact information. 2. Abstract of proposed research, including rationale of the study (you do not need to include an explanation of why ovarian cancer is worthy of being studied or basic statistics on ovarian cancer as these are very familiar to all our reviewers), significance of research, explanation as to why this is innovative (if it is), aims, and a brief overview of research design and methods. 3. Summary of proposed research (one paragraph) which describes the proposed research in terms an educated layperson would understand and describes the significance of the research to the patient population. 4. Research proposal, not to exceed 6 pages. Additional supporting information may be provided in addendum form if deemed essential. Budget should include category of expense and include a rationale for each budget item. MOCA funds can be used for PI salary, conference travel and publication costs as deemed necessary by PI. Salary costs should be detailed. MOCA funds cannot be used for indirect costs. 5. Information about PI, including Biographical statement of personal career goals of PI (one page) 6. Contact information, including direct phone number and email address 7. Curriculum vitae (resume), including education, honors, professional experience, publications, grants Biographical sketch format is acceptable 8. Letter of recommendation from the relevant person overseeing the institution, department, or lab where the research will be conducted. 9. Project timeline detailing the expected chronological progress of research aims. 10. Review of similar studies, including similar studies underway or pending which might influence subject accrual or funding.
No. of awards offered: 4
Closing Date: 1 September
Additional Information: mnovarian.org/moca-research-awards-2020/

For further information contact:

Kathleen Gavin, Executive Director, Minnesota Ovarian Cancer Alliance, 4604 Chicago Avenue, Minneapolis, MN 55407, United States of America.

Email: kmicek@mnovarian.org

Missouri Department of Higher Education

301 W. High Street, P.O. Box 1469, Jefferson, MO 65101, United States of America.

Tel: (1) 573 751 2361
Email: info@dhewd.mo.gov
Website: dhewd.mo.gov/

The Missouri Department of Higher Education (MDHE) carries out the goals and administrative responsibilities for the state system of higher education. A board made up of citizens from each of the state's nine congressional districts-the Coordinating Board for Higher Education-oversees the Department of Higher Education.

Access Missouri Financial Assistance Program

Purpose: The Access Missouri Financial Assistance Program is a state program, administered through the Missouri Department of Higher Education, established to provide financial assistance to undergraduate student enrolled full-time at a participating Missouri school.

Eligibility: The EFC is calculated by the United States Department of Education using information provided on the FAFSA. Students should contact his/her school or the MDHE for additional details regarding his/her eligibility status.

Level of Study: Graduate

Type: Programme grant

Value: Award ranges U$1,300 and up to US$2,850 annually

Frequency: Annual

Country of Study: United States of America

Application Procedure: Submit your FAFSA each year by the deadlines in the Initial Students section under 'Am I Eligible'? The MDHE receives electronic FAFSA records for Missouri residents directly from the federal government. There is no state Access Missouri application to fill out.

Closing Date: 1 February

Funding: Private

Additional Information: dhewd.mo.gov/ppc/grants/accessmo.php#:~:text=Access%20Missouri%20is%20a%20need,Federal%20Student%20Aid%20(FAFSA).

For further information contact:

Missouri Department of Higher Education, 205 Jefferson Street, P.O. Box 1469, Jefferson City, MO 65102-1469, United States of America.

Tel: (1) 573 751 2361
Email: info@dhe.mo.gov

Missouri State University

College of Business, Glass Hall 223, 901 South National Avenue, Springfield, MO 65897, United States of America.

Tel: (1) 417 836 5000
Email: Info@MissouriState.edu
Website: www.mba.missouristate.edu
Contact: Dr Elizabeth Rozell, MBA Program Director

Missouri State University is a public university system with students who come from all over Missouri, the nation and the world. We are a close-knit community of passionate and steadfast learners committed to ethical leadership, cultural competence and community engagement. Those are the pillars of the university's unique public affairs mission, granted to us by the Missouri General Assembly.

The Robert W. and Charlotte Bitter Graduate Scholarship Endowment

Purpose: To assist a worthy graduate student in pursuing a master's of business administration or master's of accounting degree in College of Business.

Eligibility: Awarded annually to a student seeking an MBA or MACC, be enroled in 12 hours or enroled in 6 hours or more each semester if the student is a graduate assistant, have a combined formula score (200 grade point average plus Graduate Management Admission Test score) of 1,100 or higher and minimum 3.3 graduate grade point average, have completed a minimum of 24 hours or 15 hours, if the student is a graduate assistant, and have completed all prerequisite courses or be currently enroled in final prerequisite courses.

Level of Study: MBA

Type: Scholarship

Value: US$1,000

Length of Study: Varies

Frequency: Annual

Study Establishment: Missouri State University

Country of Study: United States of America

Application Procedure: Applicants must contact the organization for application details. Apply online (Check in November).

No. of awards offered: 121

Closing Date: 1 March

Funding: Foundation, Private

Contributor: The Robert W. and Charlotte Bitter Graduate Scholarship Endowment

No. of awards given last year: 1

No. of applicants last year: 121

Additional Information: Not renewable. Please contact the university for further information www.dhewd.mo.gov/ppc/grants/accessmo.php

For further information contact:

Email: ammsi@uonbi.ac.ke

Modern Language Association of America (MLA)

26 Broadway, 3rd Floor, New York, NY 10004-1789, United States of America.

Tel: (1) 646 576 5000
Website: www.mla.org
Contact: Annie Reiser

The Modern Language Association of America (MLA) is a non-profit membership organization that promotes the study and teaching of language and literature in English and foreign languages.

James Russell Lowell Prize

Purpose: The Committee on Honors and Awards of the Modern Language Association invites authors to compete for the fifty-fourth annual James Russell Lowell Prize, which will be awarded for a scholarly book published in 2022 by a current member of the association.

Eligibility: Books published in 2022; authors must be current members of the MLA.

Level of Study: Postdoctorate

Type: Prize

Value: Cash award and a certificate, will be presented to the winning author.

Frequency: Annual

Country of Study: United States of America

Application Procedure: Applicants must send six copies of the work. For detailed information about specific prizes, applicants should contact the MLA.

Closing Date: 1 March

Funding: Private

For further information contact:

Email: awards@mla.org

Katherine Singer Kovacs Prize

Purpose: The Committee on Honors and Awards of the Modern Language Association invites authors to compete for the thirty-first annual Katherine Singer Kovacs Prize for an outstanding book published in English or Spanish in the field of Latin American and Spanish literatures and cultures.

Eligibility: Open to books published the year preceding the year in which the prize is given. Competing books should be broadly interpretative works that enhance the understanding of the interrelations among literature, the arts and society. Authors need not be members of the MLA.

Level of Study: Postdoctorate

Type: Prize

Value: Cash award and a certificate, will be presented to the winning author.

Frequency: Annual

Country of Study: United States of America

Application Procedure: Applicants must send six copies of the work. For detailed information about specific prizes, applicants should contact the MLA.

Closing Date: 1 May

Funding: Private

Additional Information: The winning author will be contacted in September, and a public announcement will be made in early December. Because of the volume of submissions, we regret that we are unable to contact each entrant individually. www.dhewd.mo.gov/ppc/grants/accessmo.php

For further information contact:

Email: awards@mla.org

Modern Language Association Prize for a First Book

Purpose: To recognize an outstanding literary or linguistic study, or a critical biography

Eligibility: Open to books published in the year preceding the year in which the prize is given as the first book-length publication of a current MLA member

Level of Study: Postdoctorate

Type: Prize

Value: Cash award and certificate

Frequency: Annual

Country of Study: Any country

Application Procedure: Applicants must send six copies of the work. For detailed information about specific prizes, applicants should contact the MLA

Closing Date: 1 March

Funding: Private

Additional Information: www.mla.org/Resources/Career/MLA-Grants-and-Awards/Award-Submissions-and-Nominations/Competitions-for-MLA-Publication-Awards/Annual-Prizes-with-Competitions-in-2022/MLA-Prize-for-a-First-Book

For further information contact:

Email: awards@mla.org

Modern Language Association Prize for Independent Scholars

Purpose: To encourage the achievements and contributions of independent scholars

Eligibility: Open to books published in the year preceding the year in which the prize is given. At the time of publication of the book, the author must not be enroled in a programme leading to an academic degree or hold a tenured, tenure-accruing or tenure-track position in postsecondary education. Authors need not be members of the MLA

Level of Study: Postdoctorate

Type: Prize

Value: Cash award, certificate, and one-year membership in the association

Frequency: Annual

Country of Study: Any country

Application Procedure: Applicants must send six copies of the work. For detailed information about specific prizes, applicants should contact the MLA

Closing Date: 1 May

Funding: Private

Additional Information: www.mla.org/Resources/Career/MLA-Grants-and-Awards/Award-Submissions-and-Nominations/Competitions-for-MLA-Publication-Awards/Biennial-Prizes-with-Competitions-in-2022/MLA-Prize-for-Independent-Scholars

For further information contact:

Email: awards@mla.org

Monash Mount Eliza Business School

Kunyung Road, Mt Eliza, Melbourne, Victoria 3930, Australia.

Tel: (61) 3 9215 1100
Email: genmba@mteliza.edu.au
Website: www.monash.edu.au/intoff

Monash Business School is a global academy for leaders, innovators and change-makers. Monash Business School is a proud signatory to the Principles for Responsible Management Education. Monash Business School provides state-of-the-art research and teaching facilities, as well as a fully-catered function venue.

Monash Mt Eliza Business School Executive MBA Programme

Purpose: The Monash Global Executive MBA seeks to attract a cohort with gender, cultural, professional and sectoral diversity. A minimum of ten years' management experience is required. Applicants should be executives working in Australia, who can utilise program ideas in their roles and share their experiences in an executive-level peer-learning environment.

Eligibility: 1. An Australian bachelor's degree or an equivalent qualification 2. At least 10 years' management experience 3. Ability to contribute to executive-level learning.

Type: Programme

Country of Study: Any country

Application Procedure: Applicants must return a completed application form, a detailed curriculum vitae, full official academic transcripts, one passport photo, a reference from a sponsoring organisation, and an application fee of AU$495.

Additional Information: www.monash.edu/business/global-executive-mba/applications

For further information contact:

Email: cmccall@monashmteliza.edu.au

Monash University

Monash Graduate Education, Chancellery Building, 26, Sports Walk, Clayton, VIC 3800, Australia.

Tel: (61) 3 9905 3009
Email: mge.apply@monash.edu
Website: www.monash.edu/graduate-research

Monash University is one of Australia's largest universities, with 10 faculties covering every major area of intellectual activity, 6 campuses in Australia and an increasing global presence. Research at Monash covers the full spectrum from fundamental to applied research and ranges across the arts and humanities, social, natural, health and medical sciences and the technological sciences. The University is determined to preserve its strength in fundamental research, which underpins its successes in applied research, and to continue to make a distinguished contribution to intellectual and cultural life.

Alex Raydon Scholarship for Refugee or Migrant Students

Eligibility: 1. An Australian citizen 2. A New Zealand citizen 3. Australian permanent resident 4. Australian humanitarian visa holder.

Level of Study: Postgraduate

Type: Scholarship

Value: Up to AU$24,000

Frequency: Annual

Country of Study: Australia

No. of awards offered: 1
Closing Date: 4 March
Additional Information: www.monash.edu/study/fees-scholarships/scholarships/find-a-scholarship/alex-raydon-scholarship-refugee-migrant-students-5844A?international=true

Chin Communications Master of Interpreting and Translation Studies Scholarship

Eligibility: 1. An Australian citizen 2. A New Zealand citizen 3. Australian permanent resident 4. Australian humanitarian visa holder 5. An International student.
Level of Study: Postgraduate
Type: Scholarship
Value: AU$3250
Frequency: Annual
Country of Study: Australia
No. of awards offered: 2
Closing Date: 4 March
Additional Information: www.monash.edu/study/fees-scholarships/scholarships/find-a-scholarship/chin-communications-master-of-interpreting-scholarship-5778?international=true

Co-funded Monash Graduate Scholarship (CF-MGS)

Eligibility: Below is everything you need to know when applying for: 1. doctorates (PhD - including internal and external transfers); 2. research masters; 3. centrally managed scholarships; 4. Monash University Malaysia; 5. re-admission; 6. joint research awards; and 7. higher doctorates.
Level of Study: Doctorate
Type: Scholarship
Value: Up to AU$30,000
Frequency: Annual
Country of Study: Any country
No. of awards offered: Varies
Closing Date: 31 August
Additional Information: www.monash.edu/study/fees-scholarships/scholarships/find-a-scholarship/co-funded-monash-graduate-scholarship-cf-mgs?international=true

Colin and Eleanor Bourke Indigenous Postgraduate Scholarship

Eligibility: 1. An Australian citizen 2. Commencing or continuing student in a postgraduate (coursework) degree at a Monash campus in Australia. 3. To be eligible you must provide a Confirmation of Aboriginal and/or Torres Strait Islander Heritage certificate or a certified Statutory Declaration form to the William Cooper Institute. This can be emailed to wci-study@monash.edu. If you have any queries please contact the William Cooper Institute on 9902 4972.
Level of Study: Postgraduate
Type: Scholarship
Value: Up to AU$40,000
Frequency: Annual
Country of Study: Australia
No. of awards offered: 1
Closing Date: 4 March
Additional Information: www.monash.edu/study/fees-scholarships/scholarships/find-a-scholarship/colin-eleanor-bourke-indigenous-postgraduate-5725?international=true

Commonwealth Indigenous Support Scholarship

Eligibility: 1. Commencing or continuing student, enrolled in, or intending to enrol full-time in an undergraduate or postgraduate coursework degree at a Monash campus in Australia. 2. Have a low income 3. To be eligible you must provide a Confirmation of Aboriginal and/or Torres Strait Islander Heritage certificate or a certified Statutory Declaration form to the William Cooper Institute. This can be emailed to wci-study@monash.edu. If you have any queries please contact the William Cooper Institute on 9902 4972. 4. An Australian citizen.
Level of Study: Postgraduate
Type: Scholarship
Value: Up to AU$25,000
Frequency: Annual
Country of Study: Australia
Closing Date: 4 March
Additional Information: www.monash.edu/study/fees-scholarships/scholarships/find-a-scholarship/commonwealth-indigenous-support-scholarship-6096?international=true

Corrosion Research Postgraduate Scholarships

Eligibility: Open only to the citizens of Australia or New Zealand or permanent residents who have achieved Honours 2a in Materials Engineering/Science, Metallurgy, Physics, Chemistry, Chemical Engineering, or Mechanical Engineering or equivalent.
Level of Study: Postgraduate
Type: Scholarship
Value: AU$25,000 per year
Length of Study: 3 years
Frequency: Annual

Study Establishment: Monash University
Country of Study: Any country
Application Procedure: Applicants must apply directly to the scholarship provider. Check website for further details.
Contributor: ARC Discovery and Linkage grants in association with Victorian State Government ETIS Program.

For further information contact:

Department of Chemical Engineering, Monash University, Wellington Rd, Clayton, VIC 3800, Australia.

Tel: (61) 3 9905 3671
Email: raman.singh@eng.monash.edu.au

Doctor of Philosophy APA(I) Police-Mental Health Scholarship

Purpose: To investigate the police-mental health interface
Eligibility: Open only to the citizens of Australia or New Zealand or permanent residents who have achieved Honours 1 or equivalent, or Honours 2a or equivalent with an HI or H2A Honours Degree in a social sciences discipline.
Level of Study: Postgraduate, Research
Value: AU$25,118 per year
Length of Study: 3 years
Frequency: Dependent on funds available
Study Establishment: Monash University
Country of Study: Any country
Application Procedure: Applicants must apply directly to the scholarship provider.

For further information contact:

School of Psychology, Psychiatry, and Psychological Medicine, Australia.

Email: Kathy.Avent@med.monash.edu.au

Doctor of Philosophy Scholarship-Corrosion in Alumina Processing

Eligibility: Open only to the citizens of Australia or New Zealand or permanent residents who have achieved Honours 1 or equivalent, or Honours 2a or equivalent in chemical engineering/mechanical engineering/materials engineering/chemistry.
Level of Study: Postgraduate, Research
Type: Scholarship
Value: AU$25,118 per year
Length of Study: 3 years

Frequency: Annual
Study Establishment: Monash University
Country of Study: Any country
Application Procedure: Applicants must apply direct to faculty. Check website for further details.
Contributor: ARC

Dodson Indigenous Juris Doctor Scholarship

Eligibility: 1. you will need your Monash student ID, your applicant id and password, username and password check which supporting documentation you may need to provide 2. applications take 30 - 60 minutes to complete 3 . students employed full-time by Monash University, on a continuing basis or a fixed-term contract for 12 months or more, are 4. ineligible to apply for coursework scholarships and grants.
Level of Study: Doctorate
Type: Scholarship
Value: Up to AU$162,000
Frequency: Annual
Country of Study: Australia
Closing Date: 4 March
Additional Information: www.monash.edu/study/fees-scholarships/scholarships/find-a-scholarship/dodson-indigenous-juris-doctor-scholarship-5786Z?international=true

Engineering (Honours) Masters Accelerated Pathway

Eligibility: 1. an Australian citizen or a New Zealand citizen or holder of an Australian permanent resident visa or holder of a permanent humanitarian visa or an International student 2. an Australian Year 12 or IB school leaver 3. a commencing undergraduate student 4. enrolled or intending to enrol in (the Bachelor of Engineering and Master of Advanced Engineering or Master of Engineering pathway program) at a Monash campus in Australia.
Level of Study: Postgraduate
Type: Scholarship
Value: Up to AU$30,000.
Length of Study: 4 years
Frequency: Annual
Country of Study: Australia
No. of awards offered: 12
Closing Date: 4 March
Additional Information: www.monash.edu/engineering/future-students/undergraduate-study/engineering-honours-masters-accelerated-pathway

Faculty of Law Masters International Scholarship

Purpose: A scholarship which provides financial support to a commencing student within the Faculty of Law who will undertake a Masters degree.

Eligibility: You must be an International student. 1. Enrolling in an on-campus Masters degree offered in the Faculty of Law 2. Achieved in the top 5% of your previous studies or demonstrated outstanding achievement in a combination of your studies and your work based learning. 3. Applicants will be assessed on their entire academic record, with a distinction average (or equivalent) preferred.

Level of Study: MBA, Masters Degree, Postgraduate, Postgraduate (MSc)

Type: Scholarship

Value: AU$20,000 for one year only paid toward tuition fees.

Length of Study: 1 year

Frequency: Annual

Country of Study: Australia

Application Procedure: Every scholarship may have a different application process.

No. of awards offered: Varies

Closing Date: 13 June

No. of applicants last year: Varies

Additional Information: Award based on academic achievement. This scholarship cannot be deferred. www.monash.edu/study/fees-scholarships/scholarships/find-a-scholarship/faculty-of-law-masters-international-scholarship-6087Z#scholarship-details

Faculty of Law Masters International Scholarship

Purpose: A scholarship which provides financial support to a commencing student within the Faculty of Law who will undertake a Masters degree.

Eligibility: You must meet the following criteria: 1. Enrolling in an on-campus Masters degree offered in the Faculty of Law 2. Achieved in the top 5% of your previous studies or demonstrated outstanding achievement in a combination of your studies and your work based learning. 3. Applicants will be assessed on their entire academic record, with a distinction average (or equivalent) preferred.

Level of Study: Postgraduate

Type: Scholarship

Value: Up to AU$20,000

Frequency: Annual

Country of Study: Australia

Closing Date: 13 June

Additional Information: www.monash.edu/study/fees-scholarships/scholarships/find-a-scholarship/faculty-of-law-masters-international-scholarship-6087Z?international=true#scholarship-details

Information Technology Postgraduate Scholarship

Eligibility: 1. An Australian citizen. 2. A New Zealand citizen 3. Australian permanent resident 4. Australian humanitarian visa holder Additional requirements: 1. A full fee paying graduate (coursework) student in the Faculty of Information Technology at Clayton Campus, and 2. Minimum Weighted Average Mark (WAM) of 80 3. Continuing students must have completed a minimum of 18 but no more than 24 credit points of study (excluding advanced standing).

Level of Study: Postgraduate

Type: Scholarship

Value: Up to AU$24,000

Frequency: Annual

Country of Study: Australia

Closing Date: 4 March

Additional Information: www.monash.edu/study/fees-scholarships/scholarships/find-a-scholarship/information-technology-postgraduate-5750ZB?international=true

Master of Professional Engineering International Scholarship

Eligibility: Have an unconditional course offer, or a course offer conditional on meeting English requirements to enrol in the Master of Professional Engineering program at a Monash campus in Australia

Level of Study: Postgraduate

Type: Scholarship

Value: Up to AU$20,000

Length of Study: 2 years

Frequency: Annual

Country of Study: Australia

Application Procedure: 1. Scholarship cannot be deferred. 2. No application is required. All eligible students will be automatically assessed.

No. of awards offered: 10

Closing Date: 4 March

Additional Information: www.monash.edu/study/fees-scholarships/scholarships/find-a-scholarship/master-of-professional-engineering-international-scholarship-6136#scholarship-details

Maxwell King PhD Scholarship

Eligibility: 1. You must be one of the following: 2. An Australian citizen 3. A New Zealand citizen 4. Australian permanent resident 5. Australian humanitarian visa holder 6. An International student You must meet the following criteria:1. have submitted a scholarship application in the

M

current year; 2. be undertaking research in the study areas and faculties listed below; 3. meet Monash's competitive scholarship selection process requirements; and 4. meet Monash English language proficiency requirements.

Level of Study: Postgraduate
Type: Scholarship
Value: Up to AU$36,800
Frequency: Annual
Country of Study: Australia
Closing Date: 31 October
Additional Information: www.monash.edu/study/fees-scholarships/scholarships/find-a-scholarship/maxwell-king-phd-scholarship?international=true

For further information contact:

Email: mgro-apply@monash.edu

Santa Singh and Balwant Kaur Scholarship

Eligibility: 1. You must meet the following criteria: 2. An Indigenous Australian 3. Identify as female 3. A commencing or continuing undergraduate or postgraduate (coursework) student enrolled at a Monash campus in Australia. 4. Consideration will be given to students from one or more of Monash University's defined equity or personal disadvantage groups (for domestic students only) 5. from regional and remote areas of Australia 6. experiencing financial disadvantage 7. have a disability or long-term medical condition 8. experiencing difficult circumstances 9. A full time OR part time student
Level of Study: Postgraduate
Type: Scholarship
Value: AU$8000
Frequency: Annual
Country of Study: Australia
Closing Date: 4 March
Additional Information: www.monash.edu/study/fees-scholarships/scholarships/find-a-scholarship/santa-singh-and-balwant-kaur-scholarship-6156?international=true#scholarship-details

For further information contact:

Email: wci-study@monash.edu

Montessori St Nicholas Centre

4/4a Bloomsbury Square, London WC1A 2RP, United Kingdom.

Tel: (44) 20 7493 8300
Email: centre@montessori.org.uk
Website: www.montessori.org.uk

The Montessori St Nicholas Charity seeks to promote and provide exemplary Montessori education by means of training teachers, providing information, advice and support to schools, managing its own schools, and undertaking charitable projects to inform and sustain the Montessori community in the UK.

The Birts Scholarship

Purpose: To recognise and encourage research into Montessori teaching
Eligibility: United Kingdom Citizens holding a United Kingdom recognised degree
Level of Study: Graduate
Type: Scholarship
Value: £4–6,000
Length of Study: 2 years
Frequency: Annual
Country of Study: United Kingdom
Application Procedure: By application form from the charity and interview
No. of awards offered: 12
Closing Date: 1 July
Funding: Private
No. of awards given last year: 1
No. of applicants last year: 12

For further information contact:

Email: reception@montessori.org.uk

Morton Cure Paralysis Fund

5021 Vernon Avenue, Suite 145, Minneapolis, MN 55436, United States of America.

Tel: (1) 612 904 1420
Email: info@mcpf.org
Website: www.grantforward.com/sponsor/detail/morton-cure-paralysis-fund-1431

The Morton Cure Paralysis Fund has provided grants to fifty laboratories around the world. Here is the story of what those grants, your donations, have accomplished in one of those research centers. MCPF is compelled to find a cure for paralysis caused by spinal cord injury. We work to accelerate the pace of research through fundraising, and in turn award research grants to innovative scientists gathering proof of concept data. MCPF also provides emotional support and trustworthy research information to those affected by paralysis.

Morton Cure Paralysis Fund Research Grant

Subjects: Spinal cord injury and other disorders of the central nervous system

Purpose: The Morton Cure Paralysis Fund (MCPF) is committed to developing effective therapies (cures) for paralysis associated with spinal cord injury and other disorders of the central nervous system.

Type: Research grant

Value: Most research awards range from US$5,000 to US$75,000 and are based on one-year contracts

Length of Study: One or two years

Frequency: Annual

Country of Study: Any country

Application Procedure: Please provide the relevant information and send to info@mcpf.org

Closing Date: 31 October

Additional Information: A second year may be considered contingent upon the grantee submitting a six-month progress report, a 12-month progress report and a continuation application that is favorably reviewed by MCPF's Grant Committee. www.trdf.co.il/eng/kolkoreinfo.php?id=8352#:~:text=Developing%20effec tive%20therapies%20for%20paralysis,central%20nervous %20system%20(CNS).&text=*%20Evaluating%20new% 20therapies%20in%20clinical%20trial.

Motor Neurone Disease Association

6 Summerhouse Road, Moulton Park, Northampton NN3 6BJ, United Kingdom.

Tel: (44) 1604 250505
Email: enquiries@mndassociation.org
Website: www.mndassociation.org
Contact: Francis Crick House

Motor neurone disease (MND) describes a group of diseases that affect the nerves (motor neurones) in the brain and spinal cord that tell your muscles what to do. Select from the following for basic facts about the disease. MND is life-shortening and there is no cure. Although the disease will progress, symptoms can be managed to help achieve the best possible quality of life.

Motor Neurone Disease Association Non-Clinical Fellowship Awards

Purpose: Non-Clinical Research Fellowships provide the opportunity for post-doctoral scientists with relevant experience to apply for funding as principal investigator.

Eligibility: Fellowship awards may only be held at an institute in the UK and Ireland. At the time of application the prospective fellow may be based elsewhere 1. Junior Non-Clinical – applicants must have 2 – 6 years post-doctoral experience at the time of commencement of the award. 2. Exceptional final year PhD students may apply but should consult the Association prior to submitting a summary application. 3. Senior Non-Clinical – applicants must have 4 – 10 years post-doctoral experience at the time of commencement of the award.

Level of Study: Postdoctorate, Research

Type: Fellowship

Value: Grant of up to £270,000 (Junior Fellowship) or £440,000 (Senior Fellowship) for up to 4 years.

Length of Study: 4 years

Frequency: Annual

Country of Study: United Kingdom, Republic of Ireland

Application Procedure: 1. Applicants must submit a summary of their proposal, which is first checked for eligibility and considered by three members of the research advisory panel (RAP). 2. Full applications are invited thereafter and application forms are provided. 3. Full applications will be considered by a minimum of two independent external referees and then by the Biomedical Research Advisory Panel (BRAP).

No. of awards offered: Usually 2, tyically one senior and one junior

Closing Date: 30 April

Funding: Private, Trusts

Additional Information: We also have an established record of supporting studies in collaboration with other agencies, such as Marie Curie and NIHR to fund research into improved care for those living with MND. We will be keen to discuss opportunities for jointly funded initiatives. www. mndassociation.org/app/uploads/2019/02/Non-Clinical-Fellow ship-Guidelines-Summary-Application.pdf

Motor Neurone Disease Association PhD Studentship Award

Purpose: The essential purpose of the grant is to support the training of a graduate science student in order to achieve the qualification of PhD (or equivalent) in a subject of direct relevance to motor neurone disease. Such support will not normally exceed three years and applicants must be sure to submit proposals that are focused and compatible with a three year timescale.

Eligibility: 1. Studentship applications are invited from prospective supervisors, based in UK and Ireland laboratories. 2. Collaborative projects between departments are welcomed, provided the relative roles of the supervisors and departments are addressed. 3. Supervisors should recruit and nominate the student of their choice (subject to MND Association approval). 4. Students should hold, or expect to obtain, a first or upper second class honours degree.

Level of Study: Doctorate, Graduate, Postgraduate, Research
Type: Studentship
Value: Grant of up to £100,000 for up to 3 years.
Length of Study: 3 years
Frequency: Annual
Country of Study: United Kingdom, Republic of Ireland
Application Procedure: 1. Applicants must submit a summary of their proposal, which is first checked for eligibility and considered by three members of the research advisory panel (RAP). 2. Full applications are invited thereafter and application forms are provided. 3. Full applications are submitted to two or more independent referees and then to the RAP for consideration.
Closing Date: 30 April
Funding: Private, Trusts
Additional Information: Grantees of awards are mandated to make their peer reviewed papers directly arising from the grant available through open access. We also have a number of statements on research including research involving animals, stem cells, unproven treatments and our research knowledge strategy. www.postgraduatestudentships.co.uk/opportunity/motor-neurone-disease-association-phd-studentship/21962/

Motor Neurone Disease Association Research Project Grants

Purpose: We are committed to playing a key role in ending MND. Our biomedical research programme is delivering significant and measurable advances in understanding and treating the disease. We only fund research of the highest scientific excellence and greatest relevance to MND.

Eligibility: 1. Applicants can be based outside the UK and Ireland, provided the project is unique in concept or design (i.e. no similar research is being performed in the UK) and involves a significant aspect of collaboration with a UK institute.

Level of Study: Postdoctorate, Research
Type: Project grant
Value: Grant of up to £255,000 for up to 3 years.

Length of Study: 3 years
Frequency: Annual
Country of Study: United Kingdom
Application Procedure: Applicants must submit a summary of their proposal, which is first checked for eligibility and considered by three members of the research advisory panel (RAP). Full applications are invited thereafter and application forms are provided. Full applications are submitted to two or more independent referees and then to the RAP for consideration. Please see our research governance for information on our grant application processes. The summary application form for project grants will be available on our website from mid-September to be completed online.

No. of awards offered: Varies
Closing Date: 23 October
Funding: Private, Trusts
No. of applicants last year: Varies
Additional Information: Grantees of awards are mandated to make their peer reviewed papers directly arising from the grant available through open access. Research funded by the MND Association is guided by our terms and conditions. Applications for Healthcare Project Grants are also subject to external peer review and discussion by the Healthcare Research Advisory Panel (HRAP) and Board of Trustees. www.myresearchconnect.com/motor-neurone-disease-association-research-grants-open-for-application/

Mott MacDonald Charitable Trust

Administrativ Unit 10, "Skanderbeg" Street, Building no.6, Entrance no. 2, Apartment no. 11, Tirana, Albania.

Tel:	(355) 44 540 775
Email:	albania@mottmac.com
Website:	www.mottmac.com

The Mott MacDonald Group was formed in 1989 with the merger of two long-established and well-known international engineering consultancies – Mott, Hay & Anderson, renowned for its contribution to transportation engineering, and Sir M MacDonald & Partners, distinguished by a long tradition of water-related projects. Our long-term strategy to provide an all-inclusive engineering, management and development consultancy on a global scale features organic growth and planned acquisitions to increase our geographic spread, expand our range of services and introduce new expertise – all geared towards meeting the evolving needs of our customers around the world.

Mott MacDonald Charitable Trust Scholarships

Purpose: To enable a recipient to pursue studies and thus contribute to the advancement of engineering technology

Eligibility: Open to engineering students who wish to further their academic training at the postgraduate level. Students returning to academic training after a period of employment are preferred

Type: Scholarship

Value: Please consult the organization

Frequency: Annual

Study Establishment: Any university

Country of Study: United Kingdom

Application Procedure: Applicants must complete an application form, available on request from the main address

No. of awards offered: 129

Closing Date: 31 March

No. of awards given last year: 4

No. of applicants last year: 129

Additional Information: www.imperial.ac.uk/news/28194/mott-macdonald-charitable-trust-award-2008/

For further information contact:

Email: charitabletrust@mottmac.com

MQ Mental Health

Suite B, 6 Honduras Street, London EC1Y 0TH, United Kingdom.

Tel: (44) 300 030 8100
Email: info@mqfoundation.org
Website: www.mqmentalhealth.org/
Contact: MQ: Transforming Mental Health

MQ Trustees form the governing body of the charity and are accountable for management and trustworthiness of the charity as it performs its work for public benefit. Trustees serve a term of three years and the current MQ board is made up of experts in law, management, finance, fundraising and research. We champion and fund world-class research to transform the lives of everyone affected by a mental health condition. Between 2020 and 2025, we are honing our focus on the areas we believe are most vital and where we can have the greatest impact. After years of learning and listening, we believe this new five-year framework offers the opportunity for innovative and lasting change in the mental health landscape.

MQ Fellows Awards 2023

Purpose: The Fellows Award supports talented researchers with bold ideas from across the globe, who aspire to be the next generation leaders in mental health research, as they establish their independence. MQ seeks to fund a diverse research portfolio that reflects a bio-psycho-social approach to mental health. The MQ Fellows Awards are open to researchers anywhere in the world and from all disciplines related to mental health research. Research may involve theoretical, experimental, social sciences or medical humanities approaches. Projects should focus on genuine impact by charting, informing, developing and/or testing preventative or therapeutic interventions.

Eligibility: The MQ Fellows Award is designed to support early career researchers investigating questions that will ultimately improve the quality of life for people affected by mental illness. Applicants will have made an outstanding start to their research career as demonstrated by their research results and career track record to date. We are seeking applicants who are establishing their independence through their intellectual efforts and leadership. Researchers need to be fully committed to this path and at a career stage that demonstrates this commitment. Applicants will be able to demonstrate that they are either newly independent or will be independent by the time the awards are finalised in the summer of 2020. This award is not suitable for stand-alone 3-year post-doctoral research projects. Applicants must be early career researchers wishing to establish their independence with a PhD, DPhil, DClinPsy, MBBS, MD or equivalent have accumulated 3-7 years by January 2023 through whole-time-equivalent research experience, equivalent in nature to postdoctoral research be able to show that this award will help to establish your independence relative to your current position

Level of Study: postgraduate

Value: £225,000

Frequency: Annual

Country of Study: Any country

Application Procedure: Stage 1 Expression of Interest Applicants are required to complete and submit a Stage 1 Expression of Interest application form. This must be submitted through MQ's online application system by the deadline of Friday 3rd April at 1700 BST (GMT +1). The Stage 1 Expression of Interest is comprised of a short application, an abbreviated curriculum vitae form, and a statement of support and signature from the applicant's Head of Department (HoD). Please ensure that sufficient time is left to obtain HoD authorisation before the relevant deadline. Applications will be reviewed by the MQ Research Team and the MQ Fellows Award Panel. Applications that do not meet the submission criteria will not be processed further. Applicants will be informed of the results of Stage 1 review by the end of

M

May. Stage 2 Invited Proposal Shortlisted applicants will be invited to participate in Stage 2 of the process, by submitting a full application with a detailed scientific proposal including how PPI has been considered in the design of the project, along with a full budget. Applicants are asked to propose scientific mentor(s) for their project, who can be from any field, and whose research is pertinent to the proposed project. Deadline for invited proposals is Friday 3rd July at 1700 BST (GMT+1) Applications must have the support of your Head of Department and be approved by grants or finance officer before the deadline. Stage 2 Invited Proposals will be further reviewed, scored and ranked by the MQ Fellows Award Panel, external and lay reviewers. Those successful at this stage will be invited attend an interview. Stage 3 Invited Interview Finalists will be interviewed by the MQ Fellows Award Panel the week commencing 21st September, in London, UK. By submitting a Stage 2 Invited Proposal, applicants verify their ability to participate in the interview process, and be able to accept an offer of funding under the highlighted terms and conditions associated with the Award, should an offer be made. Final decisions for the 2023 MQ Fellows Awards will be made by the MQ Fellows Award Panel in October, on the basis of applicant's Stage 2 Invited Proposal, external review and performance at interview.

Closing Date: 3 April

Additional Information: www.mqmentalhealth.org/mq-announces-fellows-award-funding-call/#:~:text=Our%20Fellows%20Awards%20provide%20up,2020%20at%2017%3A00%20BST.

For further information contact:

Email: grants@mqmentalhealth.org

Multiple Sclerosis Society of Canada (MSSC)

250 Dundas Street West, Suite 500, Toronto, ON M5T 2Z5, Canada.

Tel: (1) 844 859 6789
Email: msnavigators@mssociety.ca
Website: www.mssociety.ca
Contact: MS Society of Canada

The MS Society provides services to people with multiple sclerosis and their families and funds research to find the cause and cure for this disease. We have a membership of over 7,000 and are the only national voluntary organization in Canada that supports both MS research and services. Since our founding in 1948, the core support of the MS Society has been from tens of thousands of dedicated individuals, companies and foundations in communities across Canada. The Society receives almost no funding from government.

Multiple Sclerosis Society of Canada Donald Paty Career Development Award

Purpose: To support the salary of an independent researcher whose research is relevant to MS.

Eligibility: This award is open to those that hold a doctoral degree (PhD, MD or equivalent) and who have recently completed their training in research and are in the early stages of independent research relevant to MS. Applicants must hold a Canadian university faculty appointment and either holds an operating grant from the MSSOC or another funding agency.

Level of Study: Postdoctorate

Value: The amount provided per year for the award is C$50,000

Length of Study: 3 years

Frequency: Annual

Study Establishment: A Canadian school of medicine/recognized institution

Country of Study: Canada

Application Procedure: All Applicants for regular research grants are required to use the website www.mscanadagrants.ca/ for the completion of their proposal. All components of the application must be submitted through the online system. No hard copies of any documentation will be accepted.

No. of awards offered: 5

Closing Date: 1 October

Funding: Private

No. of awards given last year: 1

No. of applicants last year: 5

Additional Information: www.vchri.ca/i/pdf/MS_Canada_FundingOpportunities_2013.pdf

For further information contact:

Email: msresearchgrants@mssociety.ca

Multiple Sclerosis Society of Canada Postdoctoral Fellowship Award

Purpose: To encourage research.

Eligibility: Open to qualified persons holding an MD or PhD degree and intending to pursue research work relevant to multiple sclerosis and allied diseases. The applicant must be associated to an appropriate authority in the field he or she wishes to study.

Level of Study: Postdoctorate

Type: Fellowship

Value: The amount provided per year for the award is C$39,000 for a PhD and C$48,500 for an MD.

Length of Study: 1 year, with the opportunity for 2 renewals at 1 year each.

Frequency: Annual

Study Establishment: A recognized institution which deals that problems relevant to multiple sclerosis

Country of Study: Other

Application Procedure: All Applicants for regular research grants are required to use the website www.mscanadagrants.ca/ for the completion of their proposal. All components of the application must be submitted through the online system. No hard copies of any documentation will be accepted.

No. of awards offered: 26

Closing Date: 1 October

Funding: Private

No. of awards given last year: 31

No. of applicants last year: 26

Additional Information: www.mssociety.ca/information-for-researchers/funding-opportunities/endms-research-and-training-network-awards-and-programs/endms-postdoctoral-fellowships

For further information contact:

Email: msresearchgrants@mssociety.ca

Murdoch University

90 South Street, Murdoch, Western Australia 6150, Australia.

Tel: (61) 8 9360 6000
Website: www.murdoch.edu.au/
Contact: Perth Campus

Murdoch University is a public research-intensive institution of higher education located in Perth. The institute is affiliated to Innovative Research Universities (IRU), Open Universities Australia (OUA) and Universities Australia (UA). With its main campus situated in Perth, it also operates satellite campuses in Dubai and Singapore. The university conducts teaching sessions in three separate campuses in Australia, i.e., the South Street Campus, Peel Campus and the Rockingham Campus. Located in a suburb, the South Street Campus forms the main campus of the university.

International Postgraduate Research Studentship (IPRS) at Murdoch University in Australia

Purpose: The purpose is to undertake the degree of Doctor of Philosophy (PhD) and Doctor of Education (EdD) at Murdoch

University in areas in which the University has specialized research strengths. Preference will be given to PhD candidates.

Eligibility: An applicant must provide evidence of having achieved Murdoch University English language proficiency requirements. These requirements are IELTS Academic 6.5 - no individual band less than 6.0 or TOEFL iBT 90 - no individual band less than 20. Exceptions are Nursing, Education and Pharmacy with an IELTS requirement of 7.0.

Level of Study: Doctorate

Type: Studentship

Value: The scholarships cover the research degree tuition fees and health insurance premiums.

Country of Study: Singapore

Application Procedure: Visit website www.our.murdoch.edu.au/Research-and-Innovation/Resources-for-students/Future-research-students/Admission-and-scholarships/International-student-scholarships/IPRS/

Closing Date: 30 September

Additional Information: Applicants who have had sustained contact with a potential academic research supervisor at Murdoch University prior to submission of their application will be considered favourably www.scholarship-positions.com/international-postgraduate-research-studentship-iprs-murdoch-university-australia/2017/01/28/

For further information contact:

Email: admin@scholarship-positions.com

International Welcome Scholarships (IWS)

Purpose: At Murdoch, we are proud of who we are and what we have to offer our students - a place where people from all over the world come together to make their mark, make a difference, overcome challenges and open their minds to new ways of thinking.

Eligibility: 1. You are an international, full fee-paying student. 2. You are starting studies at one of Murdoch's Western Australian campuses in 2022–2026 intakes. 3. You are starting studies in a Murdoch coursework degree (this is a bachelor, graduate certificate, graduate diploma or masters-by-coursework degree). 4. You are not receiving any other Murdoch scholarship. 5. You are not subject to any of these exclusions. 6. All bachelor degrees available to international students and delivered at one of Murdoch's Western Australian campus. 7. All graduate certificate, graduate diploma and masters by coursework degrees available to international students and delivered at one of Murdoch's Western Australian campus.

Level of Study: Postgraduate

Type: Scholarship

Value: AU$10,000.00

Length of Study: 4 years

Frequency: Annual

Country of Study: Australia

Application Procedure: 1. You do not need to apply for this scholarship as it is automatically awarded to students who meet all the eligibility criteria. 2. Application not required.

No. of awards offered: Multiple

Funding: Private

No. of applicants last year: Multiple

Additional Information: Each scholarship works as a partial fee-reduction; payments are deducted from each semester's tuition fee, for the duration of the scholarship. The amounts in these tables are maximum amounts, based on course duration. A student will only be eligible to receive instalments that match their course's duration. This may be less than the maximum. Further, a student who commences a course part-way through, due to advanced standing, will only be eligible to receive instalments corresponding with the remainder of the course. www.scholarship-positions.com/international-postgraduate-research-studentship-iprs-murdoch-university-australia/2017/01/28/

N

Nan Tien Institute

Nan Tien Institute - Wollongong Campus, 231 Nolan Street, Unanderra, NSW 2526, Australia.

Tel: (61) 1300 323 261
Email: info@nantien.edu.au
Website: www.nantien.edu.au

Nan Tien Institute (NTI) is a private, not for profit, government accredited higher education provider offering studies in the areas of Buddhist studies, health and wellbeing, within an environment that incorporates contemplative education. NTI offers postgraduate programs in Applied Buddhist Studies, Health and Social Wellbeing, Humanistic Buddhism, and Mental Health as well as customised Continuing Professional Development (CPD) programs and special interest subjects across the areas of meditation, mindfulness and health.

Hsing Yun Education Foundation (HYEF) Scholarship for Domestic Students

Purpose: To honour Venerable Master Hsing Yun, HYEF is offering this scholarship to assist high achieving domestic students to undertake the Graduate Certificate in Humanistic Buddhism course at Nan Tien Institute (NTI)
Eligibility: The applicant must have been admitted or been offered admission to the Graduate Certificate in Humanistic Buddhism at NTI. The applicant must be an Australian or New Zealand citizen, or a permanent resident of Australia.
Type: Scholarship
Value: Tuition fees, Vegetarian meals provided by Nan Tien Temple during the period of stay.
Frequency: Annual
Country of Study: Any country
No. of awards offered: 10
Closing Date: 15 April
Additional Information: www.nantien.edu.au/admissions/scholarships/

For further information contact:

Tel: (61) 2 4258 0700
Email: cholarships@nantien.edu.au

Hsing Yun Education Foundation (HYEF) Scholarship for International Students

Purpose: To honour Venerable Master Hsing Yun, HYEF is offering this scholarship to assist high achieving international students to undertake Applied Buddhist Studies and Humanistic Buddhism programs at Nan Tien Institute (NTI). We hope that people with similar visions can contribute to this great initiative.
Eligibility: 1. Master of Arts (Applied Buddhist Studies) 2. Graduate Diploma of Applied Buddhist Studies 3. Graduate Certificate in Applied Buddhist Studies 4. Graduate Certificate in Humanistic Buddhism
Type: Scholarship
Value: Tuition fees, accommodation, Vegetarian meals.
Country of Study: Any country
No. of awards offered: 10
Closing Date: 15 April
Additional Information: www.nantien.edu.au/admissions/scholarships/

For further information contact:

Tel: (61) 2 4258 0700
Email: scholarships@nantien.edu.au

Nan Tien Institute Postgraduate Scholarship

Eligibility: Open to Australian domestic students only.
Level of Study: Graduate, Postgraduate
Type: Scholarship
Value: AU$13,800.00 covers tuition costs only (not text books, learning materials or accommodation) plus research supervision.
Length of Study: Up to 3 years from commencement, unless otherwise agreed.
Frequency: Annual
Study Establishment: Nan Tien Institute
Country of Study: Australia
Application Procedure: Complete and submit the application form, along with your application for admission form by the closing date.
Closing Date: December
Contributor: Nan Tien Institute
Additional Information: Please check for more information at www.scholarshipdb.net/jobs-in-Australia/Nan-Tien-Institute-Postgraduate-Scholarship-Applied-Buddhist-Studies-Research-Pathway-Pgabssrp-Nan-Tien-Institute=Ox4iZhJ75RGUPAAlkGUTnw.html

For further information contact:

Tel: (61) 4258 0700

Nansen Fund

77 Saddlebrook Lane, Houston, TX 77024, United States of America.

Tel: (1) 713 686 3963
Contact: Fellowships Office

John Dana Archbold Fellowship

Purpose: To support educational exchange between the United States and Norway.
Eligibility: Eligibility is limited to those aged between 20 and 35, in good health, of good character, and citizens of the United States of America, who are not recent immigrants from Norway.
Level of Study: Postdoctorate, Postgraduate, Professional development
Type: Fellowship
Value: Grants vary, depending on costs and rates of exchange. The University of Oslo will charge no tuition and the Nansen Fund will pay up to US$10,000 for supplies, maintenance and travel. The maintenance stipend is sufficient to meet expenses in Norway for a single person. Air fare from the United States of America to Norway is covered
Length of Study: 1 year
Frequency: Every 2 years
Study Establishment: The University of Oslo
Country of Study: Norway
Application Procedure: Applicants must complete and submit an application form with references and transcripts.
Closing Date: 31 January
Additional Information: Every other year the Norway-America Association, the sister organisation of the Nansen Fund, offers fellowships for Norwegian citizens wishing to study at a university in the United States of America. For further information please contact The Norway-America Association. www.scholarshipdb.net/jobs-in-Australia/Nan-Tien-Institute-Postgraduate-Scholarship-Applied-Buddhist-Studies-Research-Pathway-Pgabssrp-Nan-Tien-Institute=Ox4iZhJ75RGUPAAlkGUTnw.html

For further information contact:

The Norway-American Association, Drammensveien 20c, N-0271 Oslo, Norway.

Tel: (47) 2 244 7716
Fax: (47) 2 244 7716
Email: cg.newyork@mfa.no

Nanyang Technological University (NTU)

50 Nanyang Avenue, 639798, Singapore.

Tel: (65) 67911744
Email: qsmanager@ntu.edu.sg
Website: www.ntu.edu.sg
Contact: Director

A research-intensive public university, Nanyang Technological University, Singapore (NTU Singapore) has 33,000 undergraduate and postgraduate students in the colleges of Engineering, Business, Science, and Humanities, Arts and Social Sciences, and its Graduate College. NTU's Lee Kong Chian School of Medicine was established jointly with Imperial College London.

Asia Journalism Fellowship

Eligibility: At least five years of professional journalism experience, not including student journalism, who are currently working as a journalist. Freelancers are eligible, if journalism is their main activity. Applicants should be residing in Asia and should be able to operate in English which is the working language of the programme. Journalists working in non-English media are welcomed, but they will have to show their proficiency in English through a telephone interview. Permission is required from their employers to be away for the full three months of the Fellowship

Type: Fellowship

Value: Stipend of Singaporean S$1,500 per month for the duration of the three month programme. Travel to and from Singapore will also be covered. There is no extra funding for spouses and children to visit. Free accommodation is provided in service apartments. Two or three Fellows share one apartment with kitchen to cook meals. Fellows will have access to the library, computer, internet and athletic facilities of the NTU campus. NTU will apply for Training Employment Passes for the Fellows to come to Singapore. Any visiting family members must handle their own entry permit applications

Country of Study: Singapore

Application Procedure: The mode of applying is electronically send to applications@ajf.sg

Closing Date: 25 October

Contributor: Temasek Foundation and Nanyang Technological University

Additional Information: The Fellowship brings around 15 journalists from across Asia to Singapore for three months www.ajf.sg/applying/

For further information contact:

Email: applications@ajf.sg

Asian Communication Resource Centre (ACRC) Fellowship Award

Purpose: To encourage in-depth research, promote cooperation and support scholars who wish to pursue research in communication, information and ICT-related disciplines in Asia

Eligibility: All applicants should possess or be working towards a postgraduate degree from a reputable academic institution and Applicants should be working on a research project in communication, media, information or related areas that would be able to exploit the materials in the ACRC

Level of Study: Postgraduate, Research

Type: Fellowships

Value: Up to US$1,500 (economy class return air ticket), on-campus accommodation will be provided and weekly allowance of US$210 will be provided

Length of Study: 1–3 months

Frequency: Annual

Application Procedure: Applicants can download the application form from the website and send in their completed application form along with a copy of their latest curriculum vitae

Closing Date: 1 October

Additional Information: www.liskw.wordpress.com/page/57/?arch__That

For further information contact:

Tel: (65) 6790 4577
Fax: (65) 6791 5214
Email: acrc_fellowship@ntu.edu.sg

Nanyang Technological University HASS International PhD Scholarship (HIPS) for Singaporean Students

Purpose: HIPS aims to encourage outstanding Singapore citizens and Singapore permanent residents to pursue an academic career in HASS by supporting their doctoral studies abroad.

Eligibility: Under HIPS, the successful candidates will be employed as University staff. They will be granted paid leave to pursue a sponsored PhD programme in an approved overseas university or in NTU with an extended period of research in an approved overseas partner university. Upon successful completion of the PhD programme, they will be appointed as tenure-track Assistant Professors of the University.

Type: Scholarship

Frequency: Annual

Application Procedure: Interested applicants should first get in touch with the relevant School and Division. Send all applications, through the respective Heads of Divisions/Groups and School Chairs, to Dean's Office (or to the Dean's office). Applicants who wish to submit their documents electronically should email their application form and complete dossier to Ms Chan Bee Kwang email BKCHAN@ntu.edu.sg

Closing Date: 31 December

Additional Information: All late and/or incomplete applications will not be considered. A check list is included in the application package www.cohass.ntu.edu.sg/Programmes/Pages/HIPS2020.aspx

For further information contact:

Email: wpseeto@ntu.edu.sg

Singapore Education – Sampoerna Foundation MBA in Singapore

Purpose: To help Indonesian citizens below 35 years pursue their MBA studies.

Eligibility: Applicant must be an Indonesian citizen under 35 years, hold a local Bachelor's degree from any discipline with a minimum GPA of 3.00 (on a 4.00 scale), have a minimum of 2 year full-time professional work experience after the completion of the undergraduate degree, currently not enrolled in graduate or post-graduate program, or obtained a Master's degree or equivalent; not be a graduate from overseas tertiary institutions, unless was on a full scholarship, not receive other equivalent award or scholarship offering similar or other benefits at the time of the award.

Level of Study: MBA

Type: Award

Value: US$70,000–150,000

Country of Study: Singapore

Closing Date: 1 February

Additional Information: www.postgraduatefunding.com/award-3961

Singapore International Graduate Award

Purpose: The Singapore International Graduate Award (SINGA) is a collaboration between the Agency for Science, Technology & Research (A*STAR), the Nanyang Technological University (NTU), the National University of Singapore (NUS) and the Singapore University of Technology and Design (SUTD).

Eligibility: Open for application to all international graduates with a passion for research and excellent academic results. Good skills in written and spoken English. Good reports from academic referees

Level of Study: Doctorate

Type: Award

Value: Tuition fees Monthly stipend of S$2,200 which will be increased to S$2,700 after the passing of the Qualifying Examination One-time airfare grant of up to S$1,500 One-time settling-in allowance of S$1,000

Length of Study: 4 years

Frequency: Annual

Country of Study: Singapore

Application Procedure: Online application form should be submitted. Go to Research Areas to browse the projects you are interested in. Valid Passport. A recent passport-sized

photo (in .jpeg or .png format). ALL transcripts need to be in English translation. Bachelor's and/or Master's academic transcripts. Bachelor's Degree certificate(s) / scroll(s) or a letter of certification from the university on your candidature if your degree certificate / scroll has not yet been conferred. 2 recommendation reports (to be completed and submitted online by the referees).

Closing Date: 1 June

Additional Information: 1. Please ensure that the information you provide during account registration in the application portal is accurate, as the information will be used for verification upon your first log-in. 2. Please do NOT mail any hard copy documents to the SINGA Office. 3. Please submit your applications as early as possible. This will provide ample time for your referees to submit their online recommendation reports before the application deadline, as only applications with 2 recommendation reports will be processed. 4. Please check and ensure that all data you have entered in the online application form is correct and accurate before you submit the application. Amendments to the application will NOT be possible after it is submitted. www.postgraduatefunding.com/award-3961

Spring Management Development Scholarship (MDS)

Purpose: To nurture the next generation of leaders for the trailblazing companies of tomorrow.

Eligibility: Those who are currently working in an SME or are interested to join one, are citizens or permanent residents of Singapore, have less than 5 years of working experience and successfully apply for one of the approved MBA programmes.

Level of Study: MBA

Type: Scholarship

Value: Full-time/Part-time MBA SPRING will provide grant value of up to 70 % of tuition fees, and other related expenses for full-time MBA scholars up to a maximum qualifying cost of S$52,000

Study Establishment: Nanyang Business School

Country of Study: Singapore

Application Procedure: Applicants will have to go through a joint selection process by SPRING and the participating SME, serve a 3 month internship in the SME prior to embarking on the approved MBA course (performance must be deemed satisfactory by the SME), and serve a bond of up to 2 years in the SME upon completion of studies. For more information on government assistance programmes, please contact the Enterprise One hotline at Tel (65) 6898 1800 or email enterpriseone@spring.gov.sg or visit their website at www.spring.gov.sg/mds

Funding: Private

Contributor: SPRING Singapore and small medium enterprises.

Additional Information: For more information on government assistance programmes, please contact the Enterprise One hotline at Tel: (65) 6898 1800 or email enterpriseone@spring.gov.sg or visit their website at www.spring.gov.sg/mds

For further information contact:

Tel: (65) 6898 1800
Email: enquiry@enterprisesg.gov.sg

The Lien Foundation Scholarship for Social Service Leaders

Purpose: To provide scholarships to support education and professional development.
Eligibility: The scholarship is open to candidates with academic excellence, notable performance record and the potential to take up leadership positions in voluntary welfare organizations.
Level of Study: Professional development
Type: Scholarship
Value: The award includes tuition fees, maintenance allowance (for full-time studies), book allowance and any other compulsory fees.
Country of Study: Any country
Application Procedure: For more information on the scholarship do visit the websites www.ncss.org.sg/lien
Closing Date: 22 June

For further information contact:

Email: Pamela_biswas@ncss.gov.sg

Narotam Sekhsaria Foundation

1st Floor, Nirmal Building, Nariman Point, Mumbai, Maharashtra 400021, India.

Tel: (91) 22 6132 6200
Email: pgscholarship@nsfoundation.co.in
Contact: Narotam Sekhsaria Foundation

Narotam Sekhsaria Foundation is a non-profit initiative created to support enterprising individuals and innovative organizations.

Narotam Sekhsaria Postgraduate Scholarship

Purpose: The aim of the scholarship is to help high achieving students to pursue postgraduate studies at prestigious Indian and international universities
Eligibility: 1. Applicant must be an Indian national, residing in India. 2. Applicant must be below 30 years of age as of January 31, 2023 3. Applicant must have graduated from an accredited Indian University. 4. Students in their final year of the degree course or those awaiting results are also eligible. 5. Students planning to pursue Postgraduate studies at top ranking institutions from Fall 2023 6. Students who have applied and are awaiting an acceptance from the university are also eligible to apply. 7. The award of scholarship is subject to securing admission.
Level of Study: Postgraduate
Type: Postgraduate scholarships
Value: The award of scholarship is subject to securing admission
Study Establishment: The scholarship is awarded in the fields offered by the university
Country of Study: India
Application Procedure: Applicants can apply through the registration process given below the link of scholarship page
Closing Date: 16 March
Additional Information: For more details please see the website pg.nsfoundation.co.in/
pg.nsfoundation.co.in/application-process/

For further information contact:

Tel: (91) 22 61326200
Email: pgscholarship@nsfoundation.co.in

National Academies

500 5th Street NW, Washington, DC 20001, United States of America.

Tel: (1) 202 334 2000
Email: infofell@nas.edu
Website: www.nationalacademies.org

The National Academies of Sciences, Engineering, and Medicine provide independent, objective advice to inform policy with evidence, spark progress and innovation, and confront challenging issues for the benefit of society.

Christine Mirzayan Science & Technology Policy Graduate Fellowship Program

Purpose: To engage students in science and technology policy

Eligibility: Graduate students and postdoctoral scholars and those who have completed graduate studies or postdoctoral research within the last 5 years are eligible to apply

Level of Study: Postgraduate

Type: Fellowship

Value: The stipend for a 10-week program is US$5,300

Length of Study: 12 weeks

Frequency: Annual

Country of Study: United States of America

Application Procedure: A completed application form must be submitted. Application forms are available on the website

Closing Date: 29 October

Additional Information: mirzayanfellow.nas.edu/

Jefferson Science Fellowship

Purpose: To offset the costs of temporary living quarters in the Washington, DC area

Eligibility: Applicants must be United States citizens and holding a tenured faculty position at a United States degree granting academic institution of higher learning. For terms and conditions as well as further details log on to the website.

Level of Study: Postgraduate

Value: The Jefferson Science Fellow will be paid a per diem of up to US$50,000 by the United States Department of State and US$10,000 will be made available to the Fellow for travel associated with their assignment(s).

Length of Study: 1 year

Frequency: Annual

Application Procedure: A complete nomination/application package consists of nomination/application form in PDF format and in word format; curriculum vitae (limit 10 pages); statements of qualifications (limit 2 pages each); and at least 3, and no more than 5, letters of recommendation from peers of the nominee/applicant.

Closing Date: October

Contributor: National Academies supported through a partnership between American philanthropic foundations, the United States STE academic community, professional scientific societies, and the United States Department of State.

Additional Information: Applicants should notify their institution while applying and encourage them to initiate a JSF/MOU as described on the website. Incomplete nomination/application packages, or those received after the deadline, will not be reviewed www.sites.nationalacademies.org/pga/jefferson/

For further information contact:

Tel: (1) 202 334 2643
Email: jsf@nas.edu

National Energy Technology Laboratory Methane Hydrates Fellowship Program (MHFP)

Purpose: The National Academies of Sciences, Engineering, and Medicine, in association with the U.S. Department of Energy's National Energy Technology Laboratory (NETL), administers a Research Fellowship Program designed to support the development of Methane Hydrate science and enable highly qualified graduate and postgraduate students to pursue advanced degrees and training in an area of increasing national interest.

Eligibility: M.S., Ph.D., and Postdoctoral applicants. Open to U.S. citizens only.

Level of Study: Doctorate, Postdoctorate, Postgraduate

Type: Fellowship

Value: Stipend Rates Master's Level (Fellow) begins at US$30,000 with a maximum 2-year tenure, PhD Level (Fellow) begins at US$35,000 with a maximum 3-year tenure and Postdoctoral Level (Research Associate) begins at US$60,000 with a maximum 2-year tenure, Travel Allowance of US$6,000.

Country of Study: United States of America

Application Procedure: The online application system will close on the deadline date at 500 PM Eastern Time. All application components, including letters of recommendation, must be submitted by this deadline. Access to the online application system will not be available to applicants and letter writers after this time.

Closing Date: 1 February

Additional Information: sites.nationalacademies.org/pga/rap/pga_050408

For further information contact:

Tel: (1) 304 285 4714
Email: richard.baker@netl.doe.gov

NRC Research Associate Programs (RAP)

Purpose: The National Academies of Sciences, Engineering, and Medicine administers competitive postdoctoral and senior research awards on behalf of U.S. federal research agencies and affiliated institutions with facilities at over 100 locations throughout the U.S. and abroad.

Eligibility: Awards are available for scientists and engineers at all stages of their career. Applicants should hold, or anticipate receiving, an earned doctorate in science or engineering.

Degrees from universities abroad should be equivalent in training and research experience to a degree from a U.S. institution. Many awards are open to foreign nationals as well as to U.S. citizens.

Level of Study: Postdoctorate, Research

Type: Award

Value: NRC Research Associates receive annual stipends ranging from US$45,000 to US$80,000 for recent doctoral recipients and are proportionally higher for Senior Associates.

Length of Study: More than 5 years

Frequency: Annual

Country of Study: Any country

Application Procedure: Apply online

Closing Date: 1 February

Funding: Government

Additional Information: sites.nationalacademies.org/PGA/RAP/index.htm

For further information contact:

The National Academies of Sciences, Engineering, and Medicine, 500 Fifth Street, NW, Washington, DC 20001, United States of America.

Tel: (1) 202 334 2000

NRC Research Associateship Programs (RAP)

Purpose: The NRC Research Associateship Programs (RAP) promote excellence in scientific and technological research conducted by the U.S. government through the administration of programs offering graduate, postdoctoral, and senior level research opportunities at sponsoring federal laboratories and affiliated institutions.

Eligibility: Awards are available for scientists and engineers at all stages of their career. Applicants should hold, or anticipate receiving, an earned doctorate in science or engineering. Degrees from universities abroad should be equivalent in training and research experience to a degree from a U.S. institution. Many awards are open to foreign nationals as well as to U.S. citizens.

Level of Study: Postdoctoral

Type: Award

Value: US$45,000 to US$80,000

Length of Study: 5 years

Frequency: Annual

Country of Study: United States of America

Application Procedure: An application is submitted through the NRC Research Associateship Programs online application system.

Closing Date: 1 February

Additional Information: sites.nationalacademies.org/PGA/RAP/index.htm

For further information contact:

NRC Research Associateship Programs, 500 Fifth Street, NW, Washington, DC 20001, United States of America.

Tel: (1) 202 334 2760
Email: rap@nas.edu

The Optical Society, Amplify Scholarship

Purpose: The Amplify Scholarship is awarded annually to 10 Black undergraduate or graduate level students. This grant is both merit and need-based. In addition to the funding, recipients gain access to our global network of mentors and the supporting companies.

Eligibility: Self-identify as Black Be currently enrolled as an undergraduate or graduate student at a university Undergraduates: have a major in physics, math or engineering and a demonstrated interest in optics and photonics. Graduates: have a major and/or concentration in optics or photonics demonstrated with your research and coursework. Demonstrate academic potential (GPA, publications, references, other awards/merits) Program requirements recognize and exclude career breaks from timelines (eg, eldercare; maternity or paternity leave)

Level of Study: Graduate

Type: Scholarship

Value: US$7,500 One-year Optica Student Membership Access to mentorship platform and connection with a mentor

Frequency: Annual

Country of Study: Any country

No. of awards offered: 10

Closing Date: 7 December

Contributor: 3DEO Gary Bjorklund Jason Eichenholz Fibertek Inc Optica Executive Team 2016-2020 Optica Ambassadors

Additional Information: www.optica.org/en-us/foundation/opportunities/scholarships/amplify_scholarship/

The Optical Society, Chang Pivoting Fellowship

Purpose: The Milton and Rosalind Chang Pivoting Fellowship provides unrestricted funding to talented, early-career optical scientists and engineers who believe their expertise can improve society outside of the lab. We encourage those with vision and exceptional talent to apply and pursue a newfound passion.

N

Eligibility: Be a current early career member who has received a terminal degree within the last five - seven years or will receive a terminal degree by the application deadline.
Type: Fellowship
Value: US$50,000
Length of Study: five - seven years
Frequency: Annual
Country of Study: Any country
Closing Date: 30 May
Additional Information: www.optica.org/en-us/foundation/opportunities/fellowships/milton_and_rosalind_chang_pivoting_fellowship/#SELECT

For further information contact:

Global Headquarters, 2010 Massachusetts Ave. NW, Washington, DC 20036, United States of America.

Tel: (1) 202 223 8130
Fax: (1) 202 223 1096
Email: info@optica.org

The Optical Society, Corning Women in Optical Communications Scholarship

Purpose: Celebrate excellence in women and their contributions to telecom and data center optics at OFC.
Eligibility: Be a current member Self Identify as a woman Be currently enrolled as a graduate student at a university Have a field of study/research focused on one of the following areas: optical components, devices and fiber, networks, applications and access or photonic systems and subsystems Demonstrate academic excellence (GPA, publications, references, other awards/merits) Program requirements recognize and exclude career breaks from career timelines (eg, eldercare; maternity or paternity leave)
Type: Scholarship
Value: US$3,000 scholarship, and up to US$2,000 toward travel expenses
Frequency: Annual
Country of Study: Any country
No. of awards offered: 3
Closing Date: 15 December
Contributor: Corning Incorporated.
Additional Information: www.optica.org/en-us/foundation/opportunities/scholarships/corning_women_in_optical_communications_scholarshi/

For further information contact:

Global Headquarters, 2010 Massachusetts Ave. NW, Washington, DC 20036, United States of America.

Tel: (1) 202 223 8130
Fax: (1) 202 223 1096
Email: info@optica.org

The Optical Society, Deutsch Fellowship

Purpose: This one-year multidisciplinary fellowship specifically fosters interactions between researchers from diverse fields of science and medicine and supports post-doctoral investigators pursuing training in either basic or clinical research. It is offered in partnership with the Massachusetts General Hospital (MGH) Wellman Center for Photomedicine
Eligibility: Select one or more positions available for the fellowship: 2023 Position Descriptions Hold a Ph.D., M.D. or M.D./Ph.D. degree Be at the postdoctoral training level at the time of the award and within 5 years of completion of your degree, excluding breaks in a career timeline (e.g., eldercare, maternity or paternity leave)
Level of Study: Postdoctorate
Value: One year fellowship
Length of Study: 5 Years
Country of Study: Any country
Application Procedure: Applications will be available at apply.optica.org
Closing Date: 15 June
Contributor: Massachusetts General Hospital (MGH) Wellman Center for Photomedicine
Additional Information: www.optica.org/en-us/foundation/opportunities/fellowships/thomas_f_deutsch_fellowship/

For further information contact:

Global Headquarters, 2010 Massachusetts Ave. NW, Washington, DC 20036, United States of America.

Tel: (1) 202 223 8130
Fax: (1) 202 223 1096
Email: info@optica.org

The Optical Society, Foundation Fellowships

Purpose: The Optical Society of America Foundation inspires future optics innovators, supports career development for optics students, recent graduates, and young professionals and recognizes distinguished achievement in the field through the presentation of awards and honors. OSAF Fellowships are intended to provide career enhancing experiences to recent PhDs through postdoctoral research at an OSAF sponsoring company.

Eligibility: Open to all nationalities; subject to visa requirements. Foreign nationals will be sponsored under a J-1 visa by the National Academy of Sciences.

Level of Study: Postgraduate

Type: Fellowship

Value: Stipend, health insurance allowance, relocation reimbursement, and funding for attendance and participation in OSA meetings and committees.

Length of Study: One year with the possibility of renewal for additional year(s) based on adequate research progress and availability of funds.

Additional Information: www.sites.nationalacademies.org/PGA/osaff/index.htm

For further information contact:

The Optical Society, Foundation Fellowships, 500 Fifth Street NW, Keck 516, Washington, DC 2000, United States of America.

Tel: (1) 202 334 3478

Email: OSAFFellowships@nas.edu

The Optical Society, Optica Women Scholars

Purpose: Empowering the next generation of women leaders in optics and photonics.

Eligibility: Self-identify as a woman. Be currently enrolled as an undergraduate or graduate student at a university. Undergraduates: have a major in optics, physics, math or engineering and a demonstrated interest in optics and photonics. Graduates: have a major and/or concentration in optics or photonics demonstrated with your research and coursework. Demonstrate academic potential (GPA, publications, references, other awards/merits). Program requirements recognize and exclude career breaks from timelines (eg, eldercare; maternity or paternity leave).

Level of Study: Graduate

Type: Scholarship

Value: US$10,000 One-year Optica Student Membership Access to mentorship platform and connection with a mentor

Frequency: Annual

Country of Study: Any country

No. of awards offered: 20

Closing Date: 15 March

Contributor: Marvell Semiconductors Inc Edmund Optics Joseph Goodman James Wyant

Additional Information: www.optica.org/en-us/foundation/opportunities/scholarships/optica_women_scholars/

National Aeronautics and Space Administration (NASA)

NASA Headquarters, Suite 5R30, Washington, DC 20546, United States of America.

Tel: (1) 202 358 0001

Email: hfinquiry@stsci.edu

Website: www.nasa.gov

Contact: Public Communications Office

The National Aeronautics and Space Administration is America's civil space program and the global leader in space exploration. The agency has a diverse workforce of just under 18,000 civil servants, and works with many more U.S. contractors, academia, and international and commercial partners to explore, discover, and expand knowledge for the benefit of humanity. With an annual budget of US$23.2 billion in Fiscal Year 2021, which is .5% of the overall U.S. federal budget, NASA supports more than 312,000 jobs across the United States, generating more than US$64.3 billion in total economic output (Fiscal Year 2019).

Hubble Fellowships for Postdoctoral Scientists

Purpose: The Hubble Fellowship Program provides an opportunity for highly qualified recent postdoctoral scientists to conduct independent research that is broadly related to the NASA Cosmic Origins scientific goals as addressed by any of the missions in that program the Hubble Space Telescope, Spitzer Space Telescope, Stratospheric Observatory for Infrared Astronomy (SOFIA), the Herschel Space Observatory, and the James Webb Space Telescope. The research will be carried out at United States Host Institutions chosen by each Fellow.

Eligibility: Applicants must have received a PhD or equivalent doctoral-level research degree in astronomy, physics, or a related discipline on or after 1 January (previous year). Graduate-student awardees who have not yet received their doctoral degree at the time of application must present evidence of having completed all requirements for the degree before commencing their Fellowships. Hubble Fellowships are open to citizens of the United States and to English-speaking citizens of other countries. Qualified applicants will receive consideration without regard to race, creed, color, age, gender, or national origin. Women and members of minority groups are strongly encouraged to apply. Incomplete applications and/or applications received after the deadline will not be considered.

Type: Fellowship

Value: An annual stipend of approx. US$67,000 plus benefits, and an additional allowance of US$16,000 per year for travel and other research costs. Funding will be provided initially for the first year of the Fellowship. Renewals for the second and third years will depend on annual performance reviews.

Length of Study: Up to 3 years

Frequency: Annual

Country of Study: United States of America

Closing Date: 4 November

Additional Information: The Hubble Fellowship Program is administered for NASA by the Space Telescope Science Institute (STScI), operated by the Association of Universities for Research in Astronomy, Inc., working in cooperation with astronomical institutions throughout the United States. Awards will be made to support each Hubble Fellow through a designated Host Institution www.stsci.edu/stsci-research/fellowships/nasa-hubble-fellowship-program

National Air and Space Museum (NASM), Smithsonian Institution

655 Jefferson Drive, SW, Washington, DC 20560, United States of America.

Tel: (1) 202 633 2214
Email: colette.williams@nasm.si.edu
Website: www.nasm.si.edu

The Smithsonian's National Air and Space Museum maintains the world's largest and most significant collection of aviation and space artifacts, encompassing all aspects of human flight, as well as related works of art and archival materials. It operates two landmark facilities that, together, welcome more than eight million visitors a year, making it the most visited museum in the country. It also is home to the Center for Earth and Planetary Studies.

A. Verville Fellowship

Subjects: History of aviation or space studies.

Purpose: The Verville Fellowship is a competitive nine- to twelve-month in-residence fellowship intended for the analysis of major trends, developments, and accomplishments in the history of aviation or space studies.

Eligibility: The A. Verville Fellowship is open to all interested candidates who can provide a critical analytical approach to major trends, developments, and accomplishments in some aspect of aviation and/or space history. Good writing skills are required. An advanced degree is not a requirement.

Level of Study: Research

Type: Fellowship

Value: An annual stipend of US$55,000

Length of Study: 12 months

Study Establishment: NASM

Country of Study: United States of America

Application Procedure: Before beginning your application, you must create an account. As you work on your application, you can save your progress and resume your application as needed. As part of the application, you will be required to include the following supplemental files 1. Three letters of reference. 2. A summary description, not longer than 250 words, of your proposed research. 3. A research proposal not more than 1,500 words. This statement should set forth your research plan, indicating the importance of the work both in relation to the larger discipline and to your own intellectual goals. The proposal must contain your evaluation of the contributions that Museum staff members are expected to make to your studies, and indicate what Museum collections, special facilities, and other resources are needed. In addition, the proposal must also provide justification for the research-related expenses included in the research budget. We encourage the inclusion of an annotated historiographical introduction to the subject field of your proposal. 4. An estimated schedule for each phase of the proposed research. 5. A curriculum vitae or resume, not longer than three pages, including pertinent publications, fellowships or accomplishments relevant to your proposal.

Closing Date: 1 December

Funding: Private

Additional   **Information**:   researchfunding.duke.edu/national-air-and-space-museum-verville-fellowship

For further information contact:

Office of Undergraduate Admissions, Box 90586, Durham, NC 27708, United States of America.

Tel: (1) 202 633 2648
Fax: (919) 668-1661
Email: NASM-Fellowships@si.edu

Charles A Lindbergh Chair in Aerospace History

Purpose: The Charles A. Lindbergh Chair in Aerospace History is a competitive 12-month fellowship open Oct 15, to senior scholars with distinguished records of publication who are at work on, or anticipate being at work on, books in aerospace history.

Level of Study: Research

Type: Fellowship
Value: US$100,000
Length of Study: 1 year
Frequency: Annual
Study Establishment: Smithsonian Institution
Country of Study: United States of America
Application Procedure: Before beginning your application, you must create an account. As you work on your application, you can save your progress and resume your application as needed. As part of the application, you will be required to include the following supplemental files 1. Three letters of reference. 2. A summary description, not longer than 250 words, of your proposed research. 3. A research proposal not more than 1,500 words. This statement should set forth your research plan, indicating the importance of the work both in relation to the larger discipline and to your own intellectual goals. The proposal must contain your evaluation of the contributions that Museum staff members are expected to make to your studies, and indicate what Museum collections, special facilities, and other resources are needed. In addition, the proposal must also provide justification for the research-related expenses included in the research budget. We encourage the inclusion of an annotated historiographical introduction to the subject field of your proposal. 4. An estimated schedule for each phase of the proposed research. 5. A curriculum vitae or resume, not longer than three pages, including pertinent publications, fellowships or accomplishments relevant to your proposal.
Closing Date: 1 November
Funding: Private
Contributor: Smithsonian restricted funds
Additional Information: www.airandspace.si.edu/support/get-involved/fellowships/charles-lindbergh-chair-aerospace-history

For further information contact:

Email: kinneyj@si.edu

Engen Conservation

Purpose: The Engen fellowship will introduce the candidate to conservation techniques for a wide range of composite objects, metals, organic materials, and painted surfaces. This fellowship is intended to contribute to the education of recent graduates by allowing them to delve into the complexities of working with modern composite materials, refine treatment process, learn management, and conduct a small-scale research project. The Fellow's independent research will be derived from our diverse collection materials. Fellows will be encouraged to publish or present their research at the end of their tenure. Access to other Smithsonian conservators, conservation scientists, and analytical capabilities at the Museum Conservation Institute (MCI) may also be available.
Eligibility: The ideal candidate will have a Master's degree in Objects Conservation from a recognized program and is able to multi-task, work collaboratively as well as conduct treatments and research independently. The candidate should have knowledge of ethical and professional principles and concepts related to the preservation of objects in a wide variety of media and knowledge of the theories, principles, techniques, practices, and methodologies used to examine, study, treat, and preserve historic objects. Applicants should have a proven record of research, writing ability, and proficiency in English language skills (written and spoken).
Level of Study: Research
Type: Fellowship
Value: US$5,000 research allowance and a US$43,000 stipend
Country of Study: United States of America
Application Procedure: Applications are submitted through the Smithsonian Online Academic Appointment System (SOLAA).
Closing Date: 15 February
Additional Information: We are excited about the opportunity to provide this fellowship experience and look forward to receiving your application. airandspace.si.edu/collections/conservation/fellowships

For further information contact:

Email: HorelickL@si.edu

Guggenheim Fellowship

Subjects: Space history
Purpose: The Guggenheim Fellowships are competitive three- to twelve-month in-residence fellowships for pre- or postdoctoral research in aviation and space history.
Eligibility: Applicants who have received a Ph.D. degree or equivalent within seven years of the beginning of the Fellowship period are eligible to apply for a Postdoctoral Guggenheim Fellowship. The limitation may be waived upon demonstration that a Fellowship appointment would further the applicant's research training. Recipients must have completed that degree at the time the Fellowship commences. Students who have completed preliminary course work and examinations and are engaged in dissertation research are eligible to apply for a Pre-doctoral Guggenheim Fellowship. All applicants must be able to speak and write fluently in English.
Level of Study: Research
Type: Fellowship

Value: An annual stipend of US$30,000 for predoctoral candidates and US$45,000 for postdoctoral candidates will be awarded, with limited additional funds for travel and miscellaneous

Study Establishment: NASM

Country of Study: United States of America

Application Procedure: Before beginning your application, you must create an account. As you work on your application, you can save your progress and resume your application as needed. As part of the application, you will be required to include the following supplemental files 1. Three letters of reference. 2. A summary description, not longer than 250 words, of your proposed research. 3. A research proposal not more than 1,500 words. This statement should set forth your research plan, indicating the importance of the work both in relation to the larger discipline and to your own intellectual goals. The proposal must contain your evaluation of the contributions that Museum staff members are expected to make to your studies, and indicate what Museum collections, special facilities, and other resources are needed. In addition, the proposal must also provide justification for the research-related expenses included in the research budget. We encourage the inclusion of an annotated historiographical introduction to the subject field of your proposal. 4. An estimated schedule for each phase of the proposed research. 5. A curriculum vitae or resume, not longer than three pages, including pertinent publications, fellowships or accomplishments relevant to your proposal.

Closing Date: 1 December

Additional Information: airandspace.si.edu/support/get-involved/fellowships/guggenheim

For further information contact:

Email: NASM-Fellowships@si.edu

National Air and Space Museum Aviation/Space Writers Award

Purpose: To support research on aerospace topics. The product created as a result of the grant must be in any form suitable for potential public dissemination in print, electronic, broadcast, or other visual medium, including, but not limited to, a book manuscript, video, film script, or monograph.

Type: Award

Value: US$5,000

Frequency: Annual

Application Procedure: 1. Maximum two-page, single-spaced proposal stating the subject of their research and their research goals 2. One- to two-page curriculum vitae 3. One-page detailed budget explaining how the grant will be spent.

Closing Date: March

Additional Information: www.airandspace.si.edu/support/get-involved/fellowships/aviation-space-writers-foundation-award

For further information contact:

National Air and Space Museum, Independence Ave at Sixth Street, SW, Rm 3313, MRC 312, P.O. Box 37012, Washington, DC 20013-7012, United States of America.

Email: NASM-Fellowships@si.edu

Postdoctoral Earth and Planetary Sciences Fellowship

Purpose: To support scientific research.

Level of Study: Postdoctorate

Type: Fellowship

Value: Stipend, compatible with National Research Council Awards.

Length of Study: 1 or more years

Frequency: Dependent on funds available

Study Establishment: NASM

Country of Study: United States of America

Application Procedure: Applicants must complete an application form.

Closing Date: 15 January

Funding: Private

Contributor: Smithsonian restricted funds

Additional Information: www.airandspace.si.edu/support/get-involved/fellowships/postdoctoral-earth-and-planetary-sciences

National Association for Core Curriculum, Inc.

1640 Franklin Avenue, Suite 104, Kent, OH 44240-4324, United States of America.

Tel: (1) 330 677 5008
Email: gvarsnacc@aol.com
Contact: Dr Gordon F Vars, Executive Secretary & Treasurer

The National Association for Core Curriculum, Inc. has promoted integrative person centred education at all levels since 1953.

Bossing-Edwards Research Scholarship Award

Purpose: To encourage research on core curriculum and other interdisciplinary or integrative approaches to education

Eligibility: Must be a postgraduate student: attend a university; by race for Black students; not be attending high school currently; study full-time; to students studying Nursing; be affiliated with National Black Nurses' Association

Level of Study: Doctorate, Postgraduate

Type: Scholarship

Value: US$2,500

Frequency: Dependent on funds available

Study Establishment: An appropriate institution

Country of Study: United States of America

Application Procedure: Applicants should write explaining intended research and how they meet the criteria of eligibility

No. of awards offered: 5

Closing Date: 1 May

No. of awards given last year: 1

No. of applicants last year: 5

Additional Information: www.petersons.com/scholarship/lynne-edwards-research-scholarship-111_228423.

For further information contact:

Email: canada@berkeley.edu

National Association for Gifed Children

1300 I Street, NW, Suite 400E, Washington, DC 20005, United States of America.

Tel: (1) 202 785 4268
Website: www.nagc.org/
Contact: National Association for Gifted Children

NAGC's mission is to support those who enhance the growth and development of gifted and talented children through education, advocacy, community building, and research. We aim to help parents and families, K-12 education professionals including support service personnel, and members of the research and higher education community who work to help gifted and talented children as they strive to achieve their personal best and contribute to their communities.

Davis Scholarship

Purpose: Lewis & Clark is pleased to announce its continuing commitment to the Davis United World College (UWC) Scholars program for the academic year

Level of Study: Postgraduate

Type: Scholarship

Value: US$20,000

Length of Study: 4 year

Frequency: Annual

Country of Study: Any country

Closing Date: 15 February

Funding: Foundation

Additional Information: www.lclark.edu/offices/international/financial_aid/davis_scholarship/

For further information contact:

Associate Dean of Students, Lewis & Clark College, 0615 SW Palatine Hill Road, Portland, OR 97219, United States of America.

Tel: (1) 503 768 7305
Fax: (1) 503 768 7301
Email: iso@lclark.edu

Distinguished Scholarship

Purpose: The National Association for Gifted Children (NAGC) annually presents the Distinguished Scholar Award to an individual who has made significant contributions to the field of knowledge regarding the education of gifted and talented individuals. This individual should have a continued record of distinguished scholarship and contributions to the field of gifted education for more than 10 years, and must show a record of ongoing scholarly productivity as recognized by experts in the field

Eligibility: 1. Evidence of research in the field of gifted and talented. 2. Evidence that the contributions reflect a continuous and noted record of involvement in the field of gifted and talented education. 3. Evidence of recognition by peers of the importance of the above-mentioned contributions

Level of Study: Postgraduate

Type: Scholarship

Value: US$30,000

Length of Study: 4 year

Frequency: Annual

Country of Study: Any country

Closing Date: 1 February

Funding: Foundation

Additional Information: www.nagc.org/about/awards-recognition/distinguished-scholar-award

Goodrich Scholarship Program

Purpose: Goodrich students establish a dynamic presence on campus. They come hungry, ready to learn and eager to join the UNO community. Many recipients are the first in their families to attend college. They come from underrepresented populations and have earned an opportunity to continue their education.
Type: Scholarship
Value: Financial aid in the form of tuition and general fees.
Frequency: Annual
Country of Study: United States of America
Application Procedure: The Goodrich scholarship is both merit-and-need-based. Merit and financial aid are evaluated based on a composite of selection criteria, including 1. Application data 2. Financial analysis 3. Academic record 4. In-person interview 5. English Placement and Proficiency Exam (EPPE) 6. Personal life-experience essay 7. References
Closing Date: 1 March

For further information contact:

UNO Campus, 6001 Dodge Street, CPACS 123, Omaha Nebraska, NE 68182, United States of America.

Tel: (1) 402 554 2274
Email: unogoodrich@unomaha.edu

Javits-Frasier Scholars Program

Subjects: Teachers, school counselors, or school psychologists.
Purpose: The Javits-Frasier Teacher Scholars program is a unique professional development opportunity for teachers, school counselors/psychologists, and others who work in Title I schools and are passionate about helping all gifted children.
Eligibility: 1. Teachers, school counselors, or school psychologists should apply. Educators from culturally and ethnically diverse backgrounds are especially encouraged to apply. 2. Applicant must work in a Title I School. 3. Applicant has not previously attended an NAGC Convention. 4. Applicant must be new (1-2 years of experience) to teaching and/or new to gifted/talented education.
Type: Scholarship
Frequency: Annual
Country of Study: United States of America
Application Procedure: 1. Personal Contact & School Information (school demographic information will be available in the school report card or through your state's department of education). 2. Personal Statement (no more than two [2] single-spaced pages). 3. Professional Resume 4. One (1) Administrative Recommendation (Have your administrator recommender go to www.nagc.org/javits-frasier-scholar-

recommendation. 5. One (1) Recommendation form from another source (Have the recommender go to www.nagc.org/javits-frasier-scholar-recommendation
Closing Date: 14 May

National Association of Teachers of Singing (NATS)

9957 Moorings Drive, Suite 401, Jacksonville, FL 32257, United States of America.

Tel: (1) 904 992 9101
Email: info@nats.org
Website: www.nats.org

The National Association of Teachers of Singing (NATS) is now the largest association of teachers of singing in the world. NATS offers a variety of lifelong learning experiences to its members, such as workshops, intern programmes, master classes, and conferences, all beginning at the chapter level and progressing to national events.

Emerging Leaders Awards

Purpose: Designed to recognize and support NATS teachers with no more than 10 years of teaching experience, this grant will help selected recipients attend sessions, network with colleagues, and enjoy all the benefits available at the NATS Conference.
Eligibility: Applicants must be FULL members in good standing, with no more than 10 years of full-time teaching, or the part-time equivalent. Applicants should be active in NATS Chapter and Regional activities. Prior participants in the NATS Intern Program and winners of the YOUNG LEADERS AWARD will not be eligible to apply.
Type: Award
Value: Up to US$750
Country of Study: Any country
Closing Date: 21 January
Additional Information: www.nats.org/emerging-leaders-awards.html

For further information contact:

National Association of Teachers of Singing, 9957 Moorings Drive, Suite 401, Jacksonville, FL 32257, United States of America.

Tel: (1) 904 992 9101
Fax: (1) 904 262 2587

Joan Frey Boytim Awards for Independent Teachers

Purpose: In summer 2015, the NATS Foundation announced a new opportunity for independent teachers.

Eligibility: The applicant must be a NATS member in good standing at the time of application and time of conference; The applicant must never have attended a NATS National Conference previously; Applicant must teach at least 5 private students per week; Applicant must not work for a college or university as a voice instructor;

Type: Award

Value: US$1,000

Country of Study: Any country

No. of awards offered: 14

Closing Date: 1 February

Additional Information: www.nats.org/independent-teacher-fellowship.html

For further information contact:

National Association of Teachers of Singing, 9957 Moorings Drive, Suite 401 Jacksonville, FL 32257, United States of America.

Tel: (1) 904 992 9101
Fax: (1) 904 262 2587

National Association of Teachers of Singing Art Song Competition Award

Purpose: To stimulate the creation of quality vocal literature through the cooperation of singer and composer.

Eligibility: 1. A song cycle, group of songs, or extended song approximately 20' in length-13' to 25' acceptable. (Genres other than the classical "art song" are discouraged.) 2. For single voice and single instrument (neither synthesized) Solo instruments, other than piano, may be used as the collaborative/accompanying instrument with the voice. The genre and style remains that of the art song. Compositions must be scored for voice and ONE accompanying instrument, i.e., voice & piano, voice & flute, voice & violin, etc. ("Compositions may not be scored for three or more instruments, i.e. voice, piano, & violin; voice, guitar, & flute; etc.") 3. To a text written in English, for which the composer has secured copyright clearance-only text setting permission necessary. (If the poem is not in the public domain, the composer must be able to show proof that the proper rights from the appropriate person in control of the copyright-either the poet, the poet's estate or the publisher-have been secured.) 4. Composed within the past two years.

Type: Cash prize

Value: 1st place - US$2,000 plus the composer's expenses (US$500 airfare reimbursement plus hotel) and for 2nd place - US$1,000.

Country of Study: United States of America

Application Procedure: All applications for the Art Song Composition Award are submitted electronically via www.NATS.org.

Closing Date: 1 December

For further information contact:

Email: cmikkels@valdosta.edu

NATS Artist Awards

Purpose: The NATS Artist Awards (NATSAA) competition is designed to assist singers prepared to launch a professional career and, to that end, substantial monetary and performance prizes are offered.

Eligibility: 1. Applicant must be at least 21 but not more than 35 years of age on the deadline entry date September 13, 2023. 2. The applicant's most recent teacher must be a full or associate member of NATS (in good standing) with whom the applicant must have studied continuously for at least one academic year. 3. The applicant must be a full or associate member of NATS in good standing for at least one year prior to September 13, 2023.

Type: Award

Value: A total of over US$50,000 in cash and other prizes is awarded!

Frequency: Annual

Country of Study: United States of America

Application Procedure: All applications must be submitted electronically.

No. of awards offered: 6

Closing Date: 13 September

No. of applicants last year: 6

Van L. Lawrence Fellowship

Purpose: The Van L. Lawrence Fellowship was created to honor Van L. Lawrence, M.D. for his outstanding contribution to voice, and particularly to recognize the importance of the interdisciplinary education he fostered among laryngologists and singing teachers

Eligibility: Candidates for the Van L. Lawrence Fellowship must be members of National Association of Teachers of Singing and actively engaged in teaching. The Fellowship will be awarded to candidates who have demonstrated excellence in their professions as singing teachers, and who have shown interest in, and knowledge of, voice science.

Type: Fellowship
Value: US$2,000
Country of Study: Any country
Closing Date: 15 November
Additional Information: www.nats.org/van-lawrence-fellowship.html

For further information contact:

National Association of Teachers of Singing, 9957 Moorings Drive, Suite 401, Jacksonville, FL 32257, United States of America.

Tel: (1) 904 992 9101
Fax: (1) 904 262 2587

National Breast Cancer Foundation (NBCF)

GPO Box 4126, Sydney, NSW 2001, Australia.

Tel: (61) 1300 737 086
Email: info@nbcf.org.au
Website: www.nbcf.org.au
Contact: National Breast Cancer Foundation

The National Breast Cancer Foundation (NBCF) is Australia's leading national body funding game-changing breast cancer research with money raised entirely by the Australian public. Since NBCF's inception in 1994, the five-year survival rates for breast cancer has increased from 76% to 91%. It's proof our strategy is working. Identifying new and effective models of funding and ensuring that we don't stand alone but work collaboratively and creatively to achieve our mission of Zero Deaths by breast cancer by 2030.

National Breast Cancer Foundation Doctoral Scholarship

Purpose: To provide outstanding graduates with a strong interest in breast cancer research with an opportunity to pursue full-time PhD studies at an Australian University
Eligibility: Open to applicants who are permanent residents of Australia
Level of Study: Doctorate, Postgraduate, Research
Type: Scholarship
Value: Scholars will receive a stipend of approx. AU$33,240
Length of Study: 3 years
Frequency: Annual

Country of Study: Australia
Application Procedure: The applications are judged under peer review by experts in the field for their scientific merit and contribution to either new knowledge or building on existing knowledge of breast cancer
No. of awards offered: 15
Funding: Foundation
Contributor: Australian community and corporate funding
No. of awards given last year: 4
No. of applicants last year: 15

For further information contact:

Email: lhan.gannon@nbcf.org.au

Novel Concept Awards

Purpose: To provide investigators with the opportunity to pursue serendipitous observations and explore new, innovative, and untested ideas
Eligibility: Open to applicants undertaking research in the entire continuum of breast cancer research. Residing in Australia throughout the funding period. Must meet all eligibility criteria outlined in guidelines and application form. Please check at www.nbcf.org.au
Level of Study: Unrestricted
Type: Research grant
Value: Maximum value of AU$100,000 per grant per year
Length of Study: 1–2 years
Country of Study: Australia
Application Procedure: Please contact the Research Administrator or check the website for further details
No. of awards offered: 35
Closing Date: 20 June
Funding: Foundation, Trusts
Contributor: NBCF, Australian Community and Corporate
No. of awards given last year: 12
No. of applicants last year: 35
Additional Information: Each year NBCF board will decide when to call for application and closing dates in late February www.unomaha.edu/womens-club/scholarships.php

Pilot Study Grants

Purpose: To financially assist investigators to obtain preliminary data regarding methodology, effect sizes and possible findings relating to new research ideas relevant to breast cancer
Eligibility: Applicants must be Australian citizens, or be graduates from overseas with permanent Australian resident

status, must reside in Australia throughout the funding period and not under bond to any foreign government
Level of Study: Research, Unrestricted
Type: Grant
Value: A maximum of AU$100,000 for up to 2 years
Length of Study: Up to 2 years
Frequency: Every 2 years
Country of Study: Australia
Application Procedure: Check website for further details
No. of awards offered: 76
Closing Date: 10 May
Funding: Foundation
Contributor: Australian Community and Corporate
No. of awards given last year: 3
No. of applicants last year: 76
Additional Information: NBCF Board will decide whether to offer this grant scheme again when they meet annual in late February researchfunding.duke.edu/pilot-study-grants

National Bureau of Asian Research (NBR)

1414 NE 42nd Street, Suite 300, Seattle, WA 98105, United States of America.

Tel: (1) 206 632 7370
Email: nbr@nbr.org
Website: www.nbr.org
Contact: George F Russell

NBR is an independent research institution based in Seattle and Washington, D.C. We bring world-class scholarship to bear on the evolving strategic environment in Asia through original, policy-relevant research, and we invest in our future by training the next generation of Asia specialists.

The Next Generation: Leadership in Asian Affairs Fellowship

Purpose: The Next Generation Leadership in Asian Affairs Fellowship (Next Generation) is a post-master's degree one-year program that is cultivating a new generation of Asian affairs specialists committed to and capable of bridging the gap between the best scholarly research and the pressing needs of U.S. foreign policy toward a rapidly changing Asia.
Eligibility: Eligible applicants must be U.S. citizens or permanent residents.
Level of Study: Research
Type: Fellowships

Value: Each fellow will receive a US$32,500 fellowship award (with benefits), as well as a reimbursement for some relocation expenses.
Length of Study: 1 year
Frequency: Annual
Country of Study: United States of America
Closing Date: 15 January
Funding: Corporation, Foundation, Government
Additional Information: www.honorsociety.org/scholarships/next-generation-leadership-asian-affairs-fellowship

For further information contact:

Tel: (1) 866 313 6311
Email: nextgen@nbr.org

National Cattleman Foundation

9110 E Nichols Ave Ste 300, Centennial, CO 80112, United States of America.

Tel: (1) 303 850 3457
Email: ncf@beef.org
Website: www.nationalcattlemensfoundation.org/
Contact: General Foundation Information & Scholarships

The American Cattlemen's Foundation was first organized in 1972 with the stated purpose of providing "Charitable, scientific and educational activities to benefit the cattle industry." The foundation was later renamed the National Cattlemn's Foundation (NCF).

Continuing Medical Education Beef Industry Scholarship

Subjects: Beef industry, which may include education, communications, production, and research.
Purpose: The CME Beef Industry Scholarships are awarded to students pursuing careers in the beef industry, which may include education, communications, production, and research. The purpose of this program is to identify and encourage talented and thoughtful students who will emerge as industry leaders.
Eligibility: 1. Be a graduating high school senior or full-time undergraduate student who will be enrolled in a two- or four-year institution for the 2023–2024 school year. 2. Have demonstrated a commitment to a career in the beef industry through classes, internships or life experiences. 3. Include a Letter of Intent-write a one-page letter expressing/indicating

your future career goals related to the beef industry. 4. Write an original essay-750 words or less describing an issue confronting the beef industry and offering a solution(s). 5. Provide two Letters of Recommendation-two letters of reference from current or former instructors or industry professionals. 6. Previous scholarship winners are eligible to apply.

Level of Study: Graduate
Type: Scholarship
Value: US$1,500
Length of Study: 2–4 years
Frequency: Annual
Country of Study: United States of America
Closing Date: 13 November
Funding: Foundation, Private
Additional Information: www.nationalcattlemens foundation.org/scholarships/cme-beef-industry-scholarship

For further information contact:

9110 East Nichols Ave., Suite #300, Centennial, CO 80112, United States of America.

National Education Association (NEA) Foundation

1201 16th Street, North West, Washington, DC 20036, United States of America.

Tel: (1) 202 822 7840
Email: NEAFoundation@nea.org
Website: www.neafoundation.org

The NEA Foundation offers programs and grants that support public school educators' efforts to close the achievement gaps, increase student achievement, salute excellence in education and provide professional development.

Envision Equity Grants

Purpose: Envision Equity Grants enable educators to test creative new ideas and innovations, demonstrating exemplary teaching and learning
Type: Grant
Value: US$1,500 and US$5,000
Length of Study: 12 Months
Country of Study: Any country
Closing Date: 1 February

Additional Information: www.neafoundation.org/for-educators/envision-equity-grants/

For further information contact:

1201 16th Street, NW Washington, DC 20036, United States of America.

Tel: (1) 202 822 7840
Fax: (1) 202 822 7779

Learning & Leadership Grants

Purpose: Educators frequently need outside resources to engage in meaningful professional development due to limited district funding. Through our Learning & Leadership grants, we support the professional development of NEA members by providing grants
Eligibility: Applicants must be teachers, education support professionals, or specialized instructional support personnel and must be current NEA members. Current NEA Foundation grantees are ineligible for this funding opportunity. A successful proposal will also make an individual ineligible for other NEA Foundation funding opportunities, until the grant is successfully completed and closed out.
Type: Grant
Value: US$1,500 and US$5,000
Length of Study: 12 Months
Country of Study: Any country
Closing Date: 1 February
Additional Information: www.neafoundation.org/for-educators/learning-and-leadership-grants/

For further information contact:

1201 16th Street, NW Washington, DC 20036, United States of America.

Tel: (1) 202 822 7840
Fax: (1) 202 822 7779

Student Achievement Grants

Purpose: The NEA Foundation believes public education should stimulate students' curiosity and excitement about learning and help them become successful 21st-century global citizens.
Eligibility: Applicants must be teachers, education support professionals, or specialized instructional support personnel and must be current NEA members.
Type: Grant
Value: US$1,500 and US$5,000

Length of Study: 12 months
Frequency: Annual
Country of Study: United States of America
Closing Date: 1 February
Additional Information: www.neafoundation.org/for-educators/student-success-grants/

National Endowment for the Humanities (NEH)

400 7th Street, SW, Washington, DC 20506, United States of America.

Tel:	(1) 202 606 8400
Email:	questions@neh.gov
Website:	www.neh.gov

The National Endowment for the Humanities (NEH) is an independent federal agency created in 1965. It is one of the largest funders of humanities programs in the United States. NEH grants typically go to cultural institutions, such as museums, archives, libraries, colleges, universities, public television, and radio stations, and to individual scholars.

Awards for Faculty at Historically Black Colleges and Universities

Subjects: Archaeological Report; Article; Basic research leading to improvement of existing course; Basic research related to goals and interests of the institution or community; Book; Digital Material and Publication; Edition; Other Scholarly Resource; Translation
Purpose: The NEH Awards for Faculty program seeks to strengthen the humanities at Historically Black Colleges and Universities (HBCUs) by encouraging and expanding humanities research opportunities for individual faculty and staff members. Awards support individuals pursuing scholarly research that is of value to humanities scholars, students, and/or general audiences.
Eligibility: humanities research in primary and secondary materials leading to the development of books, monographs, peer-reviewed articles, e-books, digital materials, translations with annotations or a critical apparatus, critical editions, or other scholarly resources humanities research related to institutional or community goals or interests, such as projects that draw on institutional or community archival collections, or the development of materials in support of culture or language preservation and revitalization humanities research leading to the improvement of an existing undergraduate course,

including the development of humanities resources (for example, oral histories, identification of previously unavailable primary sources, historical or literary collections)
Type: Award
Value: US$5,000 per month
Length of Study: Two to twelve months
Country of Study: Any country
Closing Date: 13 April
Additional Information: www.neh.gov/grants/research/awards-faculty-historically-black-colleges-and-universities

For further information contact:

400 7th Street, SW Washington, DC 20506, United States of America.

Tel:	(1) 202 606 8200
Email:	FacultyAwards@neh.gov

Awards for Faculty at Tribal Colleges and Universities

Subjects: Archaeological Report; Article; Basic research leading to improvement of existing course; Basic research related to goals and interests of the institution or community; Book; Digital Material and Publication; Edition; Other Scholarly Resource; Translation
Purpose: The Awards for Faculty program seeks to strengthen the humanities at Tribal Colleges and Universities by encouraging and expanding humanities research opportunities for individual faculty and staff members.
Eligibility: earch related to tribal or institutional priorities, goals or interests, such as projects that draw on cultural or institutional archival collections the development of materials in support of sustaining, preserving and revitalizing culture or language research leading to the improvement of an existing undergraduate or graduate course travel to and research in archival or cultural collections with significant holdings in the researcher's area of expertise or in an area of tribal or institutional priority or interest
Type: Award
Value: US$5,000 per month
Length of Study: Two to twelve months
Country of Study: Any country
Closing Date: 13 April
Additional Information: www.neh.gov/grants/research/awards-faculty-tribal-colleges-and-universities

For further information contact:

400 7th Street, SW Washington, DC 20506, United States of America.

N

Tel: (1) 202 606 8200
Email: FacultyAwards@neh.gov

Fellowships for Advanced Social Science Research on Japan

Purpose: The Fellowships for Advanced Social Science Research on Japan program is a joint activity of the Japan-United States Friendship Commission (JUSFC) and the National Endowment for the Humanities (NEH). The goals of the program are to promote Japan studies in the United States, to encourage U.S.-Japanese scholarly exchange, and to support the next generation of Japan scholars in the United States.
Type: Fellowship
Value: US$60,000 (US$5,000 per month)
Length of Study: Six to twelve months
Country of Study: Any country
Closing Date: 27 April
Additional Information: www.neh.gov/grants/research/fellowships-advanced-social-science-research-japan

For further information contact:

400 7th Street, SW Washington, DC 20506, United States of America.

Tel: (1) 202 606 8200
Email: fellowships@neh.gov

Fellowships Open Book Program

Subjects: Digital Material and Publication
Purpose: The Fellowships Open Book Program is a limited competition designed to make outstanding humanities books available to a wide audience. By taking advantage of low-cost e-book technology, the program will allow teachers, students, scholars, and the public to read humanities books that can be downloaded or redistributed for no charge.
Eligibility: Organizations
Type: Fellowship
Value: US$5,500
Length of Study: Up to 18 months
Country of Study: Any country
Closing Date: 15 March
Additional Information: www.neh.gov/grants/odh/FOBP

For further information contact:

Email: odh@neh.gov

National Endowment for the Humanities Fellowships

Purpose: NEH Fellowships are competitive awards granted to individual scholars pursuing projects that embody exceptional research, rigorous analysis, and clear writing. Applications must clearly articulate a projects value to humanities scholars, general audiences, or both.
Eligibility: The Fellowships program accepts applications from individuals who meet the following requirements. 1. Citizenship 2. Currently enrolled students.
Level of Study: Postdoctorate
Type: Fellowship
Value: US$60,000 (US$5,000 per month)
Length of Study: Six to twelve months
Frequency: Annual
Country of Study: United States of America
Application Procedure: Applicants are required to apply online through www.Grants.gov Workspace.
Closing Date: 14 April
Funding: Government

For further information contact:

Tel: (1) 202 606 8200
Email: fellowships@neh.gov

NEH-Mellon Fellowships for Digital Publication

Purpose: Through NEH-Mellon Fellowships for Digital Publication, the National Endowment for the Humanities and The Andrew W. Mellon Foundation jointly support individual scholars pursuing interpretive research projects that require digital expression and digital publication.
Type: Fellowship
Value: US$5,000 per month
Length of Study: Six to twelve months
Country of Study: Any country
Closing Date: 20 April
Additional Information: www.neh.gov/grants/research/neh-mellon-fellowships-digital-publication

For further information contact:

400 7th Street, SW Washington, DC 20506, United States of America.

Tel: (1) 202 606 8200
Email: fellowships@neh.gov

Scholarly Editions and Scholarly Translations

Purpose: The Scholarly Editions and Scholarly Translations program provides grants to organizations to support collaborative teams who are editing, annotating, and translating foundational humanities texts that are vital to learning and research but are currently inaccessible or are available only in inadequate editions or translations.
Eligibility: Projects must be undertaken by at least two scholars working collaboratively. While international collaboration is permitted, projects must maintain an equitable balance between scholars at U.S. institutions and scholars at non-U.S. institutions.
Type: Scholarship
Value: US$300,000; up to US$450,000
Length of Study: One to three years
Country of Study: Any country
Closing Date: 24 December
Additional Information: www.neh.gov/grants/research/scholarly-editions-and-translations-grants

For further information contact:

Tel: (1) 202 606 8200
Email: editions@neh.gov

National Foundation for Infectious Diseases (NFID)

7201 Wisconsin Avenue, Suite 750, Bethesda, MD 20814, United States of America.

Tel: (1) 301 656 0003
Email: info@nfid.org
Website: www.nfid.org

The National Foundation for Infectious Diseases (NFID) is a non-profit, non-governmental organization whose mission is public and professional education and promotion of research on the causes, treatment and prevention of infectious diseases.

National Foundation for Infectious Diseases Postdoctoral Fellowship in Nosocomial Infection Research and Training

Purpose: To encourage a qualified physician researcher to become a specialist and investigator in the field of nosocomial infections

Eligibility: Open to citizens of the United States
Level of Study: Postgraduate
Type: Fellowship
Value: US$40,000
Frequency: Annual
Country of Study: United States of America
Application Procedure: Applicants must submit their application form and curriculum vitae
Closing Date: 6 January
Additional Information: Contact Grants Manager. Priority will be given to Fellows in or entering into infectious diseases training www.neh.gov/grants/research/fellowships

For further information contact:

Email: nfid@aol.com

National Health and Medical Research Council (NHMRC)

NHMRC, GPO Box 1421, Canberra, ACT 2601, Australia.

Tel: (61) 2 6217 9000
Email: grantnet.help@nhmrc.gov.au
Website: www.nhmrc.gov.au
Contact: Executive Director

At NHMRC we are excited by the huge potential benefits of the research we fund and by the opportunities we have to ensure Australians have access to evidence-based, authoritative health advice.

National Health and Medical Research Council Equipment Grants

Purpose: To provide funding support for the purchase of items of equipment required for biomedical research.
Eligibility: Open to individuals, groups or institutions which are normally eligible for NHMRC support. Grants will be made on the basis of scientific merit, taking into consideration factors including whether the applicants hold NHMRC grants, the institutional ranking of the application, and institutional or regional availability of major equipment.
Level of Study: Unrestricted
Type: Grant
Value: AU$10,000 to cover the cost of equipment in excess.
Frequency: Annual
Country of Study: Australia

Application Procedure: Applicants must complete an application form
Funding: Government

For further information contact:

MDP 33, Project Grants Office, GPO Box 9848, Canberra, ACT 2601, Australia.

Tel: (61) 2 6289 8278
Fax: (61) 2 6289 8617
Email: jean.sewell@hhlgcs.ausgovhhcs.telememo.au

National Health and Medical Research Council Public Health Travelling Fellowships

Purpose: To enable Fellows to make postgraduate study tours abroad or within Australia, which relate to their work and speciality and which will be of benefit to public health in Australia.
Eligibility: Open to all personnel working in the field of public health, who are suitably qualified at a level appropriate for fulfilment of the objectives of the study and for implementation of its benefits. The applicant may be employed in government or industry, or may be self-employed. Preference will be given to those applicants who would not normally, in the course of their employment, have the opportunity, as part of their normal duties, for overseas travel and experience.
Level of Study: Unrestricted
Type: Other
Value: Not exceeding AU$19,700 plus an agreed annual allowance to cover cost increases.
Length of Study: 2–12 months
Frequency: Annual
Country of Study: Any country
Application Procedure: Please write for details
No. of awards offered: 18
Closing Date: 31 July
Funding: Government
No. of awards given last year: 8
No. of applicants last year: 18
Additional Information: Preference will be given to public health practitioners www.neh.gov/grants/research/fellowships

For further information contact:

Secretariat & Training Awards, GPO Box 9848, Canberra, ACT 2601, Australia.

Tel: (61) 2 6289 7945
Fax: (61) 2 6289 6957
Email: trevorlord@hhlgcs.ausgovhhcs.telememo.au

National Health and Medical Research Council Research Project Grants

Purpose: To provide support for work on problems which are likely to be capable of solution in a reasonably short period of time
Eligibility: Open to Australian researchers only
Level of Study: Unrestricted
Type: Grant
Value: To cover salary, equipment, maintenance and other specific expenses
Frequency: Annual
Country of Study: Australia
Application Procedure: Applicants must complete an application form
No. of awards offered: 1299
Closing Date: 6 March
Funding: Government
No. of awards given last year: 406
No. of applicants last year: 1299

For further information contact:

Project Grants Office, GPO Box 9848, Canberra, ACT 2601, Australia.

Tel: (61) 2 6289 6974
Fax: (61) 2 6289 8617
Email: elizabeth.hoole@hhlgcs.ausgovhhcs.telememo.au

R Douglas Wright Awards

Purpose: To provide outstanding researchers at an early stage in their career with an opportunity for independent research together with improved security
Eligibility: Open to applicants who have completed postdoctoral research training or have equivalent experience, and are seeking to establish themselves in a career in medical research in Australia
Level of Study: Postdoctorate, Professional development
Type: Award
Value: Salary in the range of Senior Research Officer Level 1 to Senior Research Officer Level 4, with annual increments, plus an allowance of AU$10,000 per year
Length of Study: 4 years
Frequency: Annual
Study Establishment: Australian research institutions
Country of Study: Australia
Application Procedure: Applicants must complete an application form, available from Ms H Murray
No. of awards offered: 43
Closing Date: 30 April

Funding: Government
No. of awards given last year: 6
No. of applicants last year: 43
Additional Information: staff.unimelb.edu.au/mdhs/research-development/research-collaboration-and-funding/faculty-trust-fellowships/r-douglas-wright-research-fellowship

For further information contact:

Fellowships Unit - Mail Drop Point, 33GPO Box 9848, Canberra, ACT 2601, Australia.

Tel: (61) 2 6289 5034
Fax: (61) 2 6289 1329
Email: helen.murray@hhlgcs.ausgovhhcs.telememo.au

Targeted Call for Research into Healthy Ageing of Aboriginal and Torres Strait Islander Peoples

Purpose: The aim of implementing this call is to provide funding for rigorous, culturally-informed research into improving the health and experiences of ageing in older Aboriginal and Torres Strait Islander peoples. Quality evidence generated from research will allow for better planning, funding and implementation of policies and services to achieve and support healthy ageing for Aboriginal and Torres Strait Islander peoples
Eligibility: Applications for NHMRC funding are subject to the general eligibility requirements set out in the NHMRC Funding Rules. Additional eligibility requirements are in scheme-specific funding rules. Institutions must be an NHMRC approved Administering Institution to be eligible to receive and administer NHMRC funding - refer to the NHMRC website for a list of approved Administering Institutions
Level of Study: Graduate
Type: Grant
Value: Total value available is AU$5,000,000
Frequency: Annual
Country of Study: Any country
Application Procedure: Official website to apply electronically for the grant application is www.nhmrc.gov.au/grants-funding-administering-grants
Closing Date: 15 August
Funding: Private
Additional Information: Applications must be submitted electronically using NHMRC's online Research Grants Management System (RGMS). Official link for the following grant is www.nhmrc.gov.au/grants-funding-administering-grants

www.nhmrc.gov.au/funding/find-funding/targeted-call-research-healthy-ageing-aboriginal-and-torres-strait-islander-peoples

For further information contact:

Email: help@nhmrc.gov.au

National Heart, Lung, and Blood Institute

Building 31, 31 Center Drive, Bethesda, MD 20892, United States of America.

Tel: (1) 877 645 2448
Website: www.nhlbi.nih.gov/

The NHLBI's Strategic Vision rests on four mission-driven goals that will benefit from sustained Institute focus. Eight objectives organize the 132 Research Priorities. The goals are Understand Human Biology, Reduce Human Disease, Develop Workforce and Resources and Advance Translational Research.

Immersive Training in the Glycosciences - Fellowship

Subjects: Glycosciences
Purpose: The ultimate goal of the program is to transform the study of glycoscience from a specialized domain into mainstream biology. This fellowship is expected to provide scholars with an unparalleled opportunity to participate in cross-disciplinary research, obtain advanced knowledge, skills, and professional exposure within the glycosciences, as well as to develop a research portfolio from which to launch independent careers.
Eligibility: Scholars must be citizens or non-citizen nationals of the United States or have been lawfully admitted for permanent residence at the time of appointment. At the time of appointment scholars should hold an M.D. and/or PhD degree.
Type: Fellowship
Value: Salary support of up to US$100,000 per year (inclusive of benefits), research supplies, and travel. Rigorous training in the Glycosciences (didactic and technical) will be provided.
Length of Study: 9 Months
Study Establishment: John Hopkins University
Country of Study: United States of America
Closing Date: 15 June

Additional   Information: glycocareers.cclinic.jhu.edu/styled/index.html

For further information contact:

Email: GlycoED@jhmi.edu

National Institute for Health and Care Excellence (NICE)

2nd Floor, 2 Redman Place, London E20 1JQ, United Kingdom.

Tel: (44) 300 323 0140
Email: nice@nice.org.uk
Website: www.nice.org.uk
Contact: National Institute for Health and Care Excellence

We provide national guidance and advice to improve health and social care. The history, structure and key responsibilities of NICE. Contains governance information, up-to-date policies, procedures and publications. Our guidance, advice, quality standards and information services for health, public health and social care. Contains resources to help maximise use of evidence and guidance.

National Institute for Health and Care Excellence Scholarships

Purpose: NICE Scholarships are one-year opportunities for qualified health and social care professionals to find out about the inner workings of NICE and undertake a supported improvement project, related to NICE guidance, within their local organization
Eligibility: NICE Scholarships are typically awarded to specialist registrars, senior nurses, pharmacists and allied health professionals, service improvement leads, public health and social care specialists and health service managers. In addition to their project-based activities, NICE Scholars are expected to act as local ambassadors for clinical and public health and social care excellence; promote the principles and the recommendations of NICE guidance-through teaching activities, for example
Type: Scholarship
Value: NICE Scholars are supported in their project via a series of workshops, access to a very experienced senior mentor and contact with the expert teams at NICE. NICE

Scholars are not paid. NICE will, however, meet all reasonable expenses (e.g. travel, accommodation) incurred in the course of carrying out Scholarship activities
Length of Study: 1 year
Frequency: Annual
Country of Study: United Kingdom
Application Procedure: The mode of applying is by post
Closing Date: 1 November
Additional Information: Scholars are expected to devote approximately 7.5 hours per week to their Scholarship project. For detailed information, visit www.nice.org.uk/getinvolved/nice_fellows_and_scholars/scholars/NICEScholarships.jsp
scientistsolutions.com/forum/jobs-clinicaldiagnostic/national-institute-health-and-care-excellence-scholarships

---

National Institute of General Medical Sciences (NIGMS)

45 Center Drive, MSC 6200, Bethesda, MD 20892-6200, United States of America.

Tel: (1) 301 496 7301
Email: info@nigms.nih.gov
Website: www.nigms.nih.gov
Contact: Ms Jilliene Drayton, Information Development Specialist

The National Institute of General Medical Sciences (NIGMS) supports basic research that increases our understanding of biological processes and lays the foundation for advances in disease diagnosis, treatment, and prevention. NIGMS-funded scientists investigate how living systems work at a range of levels from molecules and cells to tissues and organs, in research organisms, humans, and populations.

High-End Instrumentation (HEI) Grant Program

Purpose: The High-End Instrumentation (HEI) Grant Program encourages applications from groups of NIH-supported investigators to purchase or upgrade a single item of high-end, specialized, commercially available instruments or integrated systems.
Eligibility: Higher Education Institutions Public/State Controlled Institutions of Higher Education Private Institutions of Higher Education The following types of Higher Education Institutions are always encouraged to apply for NIH support as Public or Private Institutions of Higher Education:

Hispanic-serving Institutions Historically Black Colleges and Universities (HBCUs) Tribally Controlled Colleges and Universities (TCCUs) Alaska Native and Native Hawaiian Serving Institutions Asian American Native American Pacific Islander Serving Institutions (AANAPISIs) Nonprofits Other Than Institutions of Higher Education Nonprofits with 501(c)(3) IRS Status (Other than Institutions of Higher Education) Nonprofits without 501(c)(3) IRS Status (Other than Institutions of Higher Education)

Type: Grant

Value: The minimum award is US$600,001. the maximum award is US$2,000,000.

Frequency: Annual

Country of Study: Any country

Closing Date: 1 June

Additional Information: grants.nih.gov/grants/guide/pa-files/PAR-22-079.html

For further information contact:

Karen Brummett Office of Research Infrastructure Programs (ORIP)

Tel: (1) 301 945 7573
Email: GrantsInfo@nih.gov

National Institute of General Medical Sciences Research Project Grants (R01)

Purpose: To support a discrete project related to the investigator's area of interest and competence.

Eligibility: Research project grants may be awarded to nonprofit organizations and institutions; governments and their agencies; occasionally, though rarely, to individuals who have access to adequate facilities and resources for conducting the research; and to profit-making organizations. Foreign institutions and international organizations are also eligible to apply for these grants.

Level of Study: Postgraduate

Type: Grant

Value: These grants may provide funds for reasonable costs of the research activity, as well as for salaries, equipment, supplies, travel and other related expenses.

Frequency: Annual

Country of Study: United States of America

Application Procedure: Applicants must contact the Office of Extramural Outreach for details.

Closing Date: 5 February

Funding: Government

Additional Information: grants.nih.gov/grants/funding/r01.htm

For further information contact:

Office of Extramural Outreach, NIH 6701 Rockledge Drive Msc 7760, Bethesda, MD 20892-7760, United States of America.

Tel: (1) 301 435 0714
Email: grantsinfo@nih.gov

National Road Safety Authority Individual Postdoctoral Fellowships (F32)

Purpose: NIGMS welcomes NRSA applications from eligible individuals who seek postdoctoral biomedical research training in areas related to the scientific programmes of the Institute

Eligibility: Open to applicants who have received the doctoral degree (domestic or foreign) by the beginning date of the proposed award

Level of Study: Postdoctorate

Type: Award

Value: NIGMS provides an annual stipend to postdoctoral fellows, and an institutional allowance to cover training-related expenses. The stipend, tuition/fees and institutional allowance are detailed at

Length of Study: Up to 3 years

Frequency: Annual

Study Establishment: The institutional setting may be domestic or foreign, public or private

Country of Study: Any country

Application Procedure: Applicants must write to the main address for details or telephone Dr Michael Sesma, at (1) 301 594 2772. Further details are also available from the website www.nigms.nih.gov

Closing Date: 8 April

Funding: Government

Additional Information: www.nigms.nih.gov/training/indivpostdoc/Pages/PostdocFellowshipDescription.aspx

National Institutes of Health

9000 Rockville Pike, Bethesda, MA 20892, United States of America.

Tel: (1) 301 496 4000
Website: www.nih.gov
Contact: Dr Belinda Seto, Acting Deputy Director for Extramural Research

The National Institutes of Health (NIH), a part of the U.S. Department of Health and Human Services, is the nation's medical research agency - making important discoveries that improve health and save lives. Life expectancy in the United States has jumped from 47 years in 1900 to 78 years as reported in 2009, and disability in people over age 65 has dropped dramatically in the past 3 decades. In recent years, nationwide rates of new diagnoses and deaths from all cancers combined have fallen significantly.

Hitchings-Elion Postdoctoral Fellowships for United States Scientist

Purpose: The purpose of these fellowships is to promote scientific collaboration between British and American scientists for the conduct of biomedical and behavioral research. The Hitchings-Elion Fellowships will support two years of collaborative research by a U.S. scientist at a sponsor's laboratory in the United Kingdom and a third year at a sponsor's laboratory in the United States.

Eligibility: The applicant must be a United States citizen or permanent United States resident, hold a doctorate level degree in one of the medical or veterinary clinical, behavioral, or biomedical sciences, and be within ten years of the last doctoral degree.

Level of Study: Research

Type: Fellowship

Value: stipend allowance 13,661 pounds, maximum of 20,868 pounds, US$7,500 per annum for research expenses

Frequency: Annual

Country of Study: United States of America

Application Procedure: The administration of the program will be integrated into the administration of other Fogarty International Center fellowship activities and the application receipt processes of the Division of Research Grants, NIH. The initial review of applications will be conducted by a special FIC study section. Application kits and information may be obtained from the Fogarty International Center at the address listed below. In addition to biographical data, references, and letters of invitation from the United Kingdom and U.S. sponsors, a description of the proposed activities in the United Kingdom and the U.S. and the benefit expected of the experiences will be required. While it is the applicant's responsibility to arrange for his or her research program with the United Kingdom and U.S. sponsors, it may be done directly or through correspondence by a senior U.S. scientist. In the United Kingdom, host institutions may include universities or government laboratories.

Closing Date: 10 May

Funding: Private

Additional Information: www.grants.nih.gov/grants/guide/pa-files/PA-92-030.html

For further information contact:

Chief, International Research and Awards Branch Fogarty International Center, Building 31, Room B2C21, Bethesda, MD 20892, United States of America.

Tel: (1) 301 496 1653

Ruth L. Kirschstein National Research Service Award (NRSA) Individual Postdoctoral Fellowship

Subjects: 1. Engineering and Physical Sciences 2. Environmental & Life Sciences 3. Medical 4. Medical - Basic Science 5. Medical - Clinical Science 6. Medical - Translational 7. Social Sciences

Purpose: The purpose of the Ruth L. Kirschstein National Research Service Award (NRSA) Individual Postdoctoral Fellowship (Parent F32) is to support research training of highly promising postdoctoral candidates who have the potential to become productive, independent investigators in scientific health-related research fields relevant to the missions of the participating NIH Institutes and Centers. Applications are expected to incorporate exceptional mentorship.

Level of Study: Postdoctoral

Type: Fellowships

Value: Stipend, allowance & tuition

Frequency: Annual

Country of Study: Any country

Closing Date: 8 January

Additional Information: www.grants.nih.gov/grants/guide/pa-files/PA-19-188.html

National Library of Medicine (NLM)

8600 Rockville Pike, Bethesda, MD 20894, United States of America.

Tel: (1) 301 594 5983
Email: NLMCommunications@nih.gov
Website: www.nlm.nih.gov
Contact: Mr Dwight Mawrery, Grants Management Officer

The National Library of Medicine (NLM), on the campus of the National Institutes of Health in Bethesda, Maryland, has been a center of information innovation since its founding in 1836. The world's largest biomedical library, NLM maintains and makes available a vast print collection and produces electronic information resources on a wide range of topics that are searched billions of times each year by millions of people around the globe. It also supports and conducts research, development, and training in biomedical informatics and health information technology. In addition, the Library coordinates a 6,500-member Network of the National Library of Medicine that promotes and provides access to health information in communities across the United States.

National Library of Medicine Fellowship in Applied Informatics

Purpose: The National Library of Medicine (NLM) wishes to increase the national pool of health professionals capable of managing the knowledge and techniques of medical informatics in health science organizations. Medical informatics provides the theoretical and scientific basis for the application of computer and automated information systems to biomedicine.

Eligibility: Open to individuals with a BA, BSc, MA, MSc or PhD in a field related to health, who are United States nationals or permanent residents of the United States of America.

Level of Study: Doctorate, Graduate, Postdoctorate, Postgraduate

Type: Fellowship

Value: Up to US$58,000 per year, based on the salary or remuneration the individual would have been paid from their home institution.

Length of Study: Varies

Frequency: Annual

Study Establishment: Universities, colleges, hospitals, laboratories, units of State and certain agencies of the Federal Government in the United States.

Country of Study: United States of America

Application Procedure: Applications must be submitted by an organisation on behalf of the individual seeking the grant, on the standard grant application form PHS 416-1 (rev 8/95)

Closing Date: 10 May

Additional Information: The NLM encourages potential applicants to clarify any issues or questions. For enquiries regarding programmatic issues, please contact Mr Peter Clepper, Program Officer. For enquiries regarding Division of Nursing programmatic issues, please contact the Division of Nursing. For enquiries regarding fiscal matters, please contact Ms Shelley Carow, Grants Management Officer. www.grants.nih.gov/grants/guide/pa-files/PA-92-090.html

For further information contact:

Division of Nursing, Parklawn Building, Room 9-36, 5600 Fishes Lane, Rockville, MD 20852, United States of America.

Tel: (1) 301 443 5786
Fax: (1) 301 443 8586

National Library of Medicine Investigator Initiated Project Grant

Purpose: To support individual investigators and their colleagues to pursue a discreet, circumscribed line of investigation to its logical conclusion.

Type: Project grant

Length of Study: Up to 3 years

Frequency: 3 times each year

Study Establishment: United States universities or research institutions.

Country of Study: United States of America

Application Procedure: Applications must be submitted on the PHS form 398 (ref 5/95).

Closing Date: 15 February

Additional Information: www.grants.nih.gov/grants/guide/pa-files/PA-96-001.html

For further information contact:

Division of Extramural Programmes, National Library of Medicine, Rockledge One Building, 6705 Rockledge Drive Suite 301, Bethesda, MD 20817, United States of America.

Tel: (1) 301 594 4882
Fax: (1) 301 402 2952
Email: bean@nlm.nih.gov

National Library of Medicine Postdoctoral Informatics Research Fellowships

Purpose: To promote researchers interested in informatics research training wishing to identify their own mentor and host institution.

Eligibility: Open to applicants who have a PhD relevant to biomedicine or computer science or an equivalent degree from an accredited domestic or foreign institution.

Level of Study: Postdoctorate

Type: Fellowship

Value: Based on established NIH schedules.

Frequency: Annual

Study Establishment: United States universities or research institutions.

Country of Study: United States of America

Application Procedure: Applicants must contact the organisation.

Additional Information: For a complete list of NLM factsheets, please contact Factsheets, Office of Public

Information. www.grants.nih.gov/grants/guide/pa-files/PA-96-001.html

For further information contact:

Factsheets Office of Public Information National Library of Medicine, 8600 Rockville Pike, Bethesda, MD 20894, United States of America.

Fax: (1) 301 496 4450
Email: publicinfo@nlm.nih.gov

National Library of Medicine Publication Grant Program

Purpose: To provide assistance for the preparation of book length manuscripts and, in some cases, the publication of important scientific information needed by United States health professionals.
Eligibility: Open to public or private, non-profit institutions and individuals, who are involved in research.
Type: Project grant
Value: US$35,000 direct costs per year over a period of three years maximum.
Length of Study: 1–3 years
Frequency: 3 times each year
Country of Study: United States of America
Application Procedure: Applications must be submitted on the PHS FORM 398 (Rev 5/95) grant application kit.
Closing Date: 1 October
Additional Information: Potential applicants are strongly encouraged to discuss projects early with the Program staff, who will discuss programme status and experience with them, provide additional information in response to specific application plans and review draft proposals for completeness if desired. For a complete list of NLM Factsheets, please contact Factsheets, Office of Public Information. www.grants.nih.gov/grants/guide/pa-files/PA-96-001.html

For further information contact:

Fax: (1) 301 402 2952
Email: sparks@nlm.nih.gov

NLM Research Grants in Biomedical Informatics and Data Science

Purpose: The National Library of Medicine (NLM) supports innovative research and development in biomedical informatics and data science. The scope of NLM's interest in these research domains is broad, with emphasis on new methods and approaches to foster data driven discovery in the biomedical and clinical health sciences as well as domain-independent, reusable approaches to discovery, curation, analysis, organization and management of health-related digital objects. Biomedical informatics and data science draw upon many fields, including mathematics, statistics, information science, computer science and engineering, and social/behavioral sciences
Eligibility: Higher Education Institutions Public/State Controlled Institutions of Higher Education Private Institutions of Higher Education State Governments County Governments City or Township Governments Special District Governments Indian/Native American Tribal Governments (Federally Recognized) Indian/Native American Tribal Governments (Other than Federally Recognized) Eligible Agencies of the Federal Government U.S. Territory or Possession
Type: Grant
Value: US$250,000
Frequency: Annual
Country of Study: Any country
Closing Date: 5 February
Additional Information: www.nlm.nih.gov/ep/GrantResearch.html

National Multiple Sclerosis Society (MS)

National MS Society, P.O. Box 4527, New York, NY 10163, United States of America.

Tel: (1) 310 479 4456
Website: www.nationalmssociety.org/

The National Multiple Sclerosis Society (NMSS) is a non-profit organization based in New York City with chapters located throughout the United States. The organization funds research, advocates for social and political change, provides education, and sponsors services that help people with multiple sclerosis and their families.

Biostatistics/Informatics Junior Faculty Award

Purpose: As part of our commitment to building a workforce of research leaders to drive pathways to MS cures, the National MS Society established a junior faculty award in biostatistics/ informatics/computational biology, with funding from the Marilyn Hilton MS Research Fund.

Eligibility: Eligible candidates hold a doctoral degree (Ph.D. or equivalent) in biostatistics, data science, or informatics, and are within five years of completion of their terminal degree. They must have been offered or hold an academic appointment at the assistant professor (or equivalent) level at the initiation of the award.

Type: Award

Value: Up to US$20,000

Frequency: Annual

Country of Study: Any country

Closing Date: 18 August

Additional Information: www.nationalmssociety.org/For-Professionals/Researchers/Society-Funding/Training-Grants-and-Fellowships/Biostatistics-Informatics-Junior-Faculty-Award

Career Transition Fellowships

Purpose: The Society's Career Transition Fellowship addresses this need by fostering the development and productivity of young scientists who have potential to make significant contributions to MS research and help ensure the future and stability of MS research. The Career Transition Fellowship targets current postdoctoral trainees who demonstrate both commitment and exceptional potential to conduct MS-related research.

Eligibility: Applicants must hold a doctoral degree (M.D., PhD or equivalent) and must be in a research-oriented postdoctoral training program. Individuals with less than two or more than five years of postdoctoral research experience at the time of application are ineligible for this award.

Type: Fellowships

Value: US$550,000

Length of Study: 5 years

Frequency: Annual

Country of Study: Any country

Application Procedure: The application process for this award involves two levels of review, preliminary and full applications. To submit a proposal for research support, investigators must first register with our Apply Online site (www.nmss.fluxx.io) and complete a pre-application. Staff will review the pre-applications and selected applicants will be invited to submit a full proposal.

Closing Date: 18 August

Additional Information: www.nationalmssociety.org/For-Professionals/Researchers/Society-Funding/Training-Grants-and-Fellowships/Career-Transition-Fellowships

For further information contact:

Email: Douglas.Landsman@nmss.org

MS Clinical Mentorship for Medical Students

Purpose: to raise awareness of the challenges experienced by people with MS to generate interest in a career in MS care

Eligibility: he student must make their own living arrangements. They must also have their own daily transportation and the ability to travel to the assigned mentorship sites. The mentorship is open to all graduate students attending school who are U.S. citizens or candidates lawfully admitted to the U.S. for permanent residence.

Type: Studentship

Value: US$2,500

Country of Study: Any country

Closing Date: 1 March

Additional Information: www.nationalmssociety.org/For-Professionals/Researchers/Society-Funding/Training-Grants-and-Fellowships/MS-Clinical-Mentorship-for-Students

For further information contact:

Tel: (1) 800 344 4867

National Research Council (NRC)

500 Fifth Street NW, Washington, DC 20001, United States of America.

Tel: (1) 202 334 2644

The National Research Council was organized by the National Academy of Sciences in 1916 to associate the broad community of science and technology with the Academy's purposes of further knowledge and advising the federal government. The Council has become the principal operating agency of both the National Academy of Sciences and the National Academy of Engineering in providing services to the government, the public, and the scientific and engineering communities.

Christine Mirzayan Science & Technology Policy Graduate Fellowship Program

Subjects: Social/behavioral sciences, health and medicine, physical or biological sciences, engineering, law/business/public administration, or relevant interdisciplinary fields.

Purpose: The fellowship program, which operates under the auspices of the Policy and Global Affairs Division, a program unit within the Academies, is designed to engage early career professionals in the analytical processes that inform U.S. science and technology policy. Fellows obtain the essential skills and knowledge needed to work in science policy at the federal, state, or local levels.

Eligibility: Graduate and professional school students and those who have completed graduate studies within the last five years may apply. Areas of study may include social/behavioral sciences, health and medicine, physical or biological sciences, engineering, law/business/public administration, or relevant interdisciplinary fields.

Type: Fellowship

Value: A stipend is provided to offset expenses during the fellowship period.

Length of Study: 12 weeks

Country of Study: Any country

Application Procedure: 1. Apply using the register/login buttons at the top right of this page under "How to Apply". If you are a first time visitor, click the 'register' button. If you have applied in the past or already started your application, click Log In. 2. Review your eligibility. This is an early career fellowship program. Graduate and professional school students and those who have completed graduate studies (degree awarded) within the last five years may apply. Areas of study may include social/behavioral sciences, health and medicine, physical or biological sciences, engineering, law/business/public administration, or relevant interdisciplinary fields. 3. Review Prospective Units and select up to 7 that interest you. 4. Review all sections of the application prior to submission. 5. Notify Referees. TWO references are required. These must be relevant to your academic, professional, volunteer, or other related experience. Towards the beginning of the application form, you will be asked to provide an email address for each referee. Complete this section right away to ensure that your referees have adequate time to submit their reference before the application deadline. Mailed reference letters will NOT be accepted. 6. In order to submit your application successfully, you must upload ALL required materials, ensure that your recommendation letters are attached, and hit the SUBMIT button by the deadline.

Additional Information: www.mirzayanfellow.nas.edu/

For further information contact:

500 5th Street, NW, Keck 574, Washington, DC 20001, United States of America.

Tel:	(1) 202 334 2455
Email:	policyfellows@nas.edu

National Research Foundation (NRF)

PO Box 2600, Pretoria 0001, South Africa.

Tel:	(27) 12 481 4209
Email:	haveline@nrf.ac.za
Website:	www.nrf.ac.za
Contact:	Ms HA Michau, Manager, Student Support

The NRF is an independent statutory body established through the National Research Foundation Act (Act No 23 of 1998), following a system-wide review conducted for the Department of Arts, Culture, Science and Technology (DACST). The new entity incorporated the functions of the research funding agencies that were previously servicing various sections of the research community, namely the former Centre for Science Development (CSD) of the Human Sciences Research Council (HSRC) and the former Foundation for Research Development (FRD) that included several National Research Facilities.

Innovation Masters and Doctoral Scholarships

Eligibility: Scholarships are open to South African citizens, South African permanent residents as well as a limited percentage of non-South African citizens registered at a South African public university.

Level of Study: Postgraduate

Type: Scholarship

Value: Masters scholarships worth R80,000 per annum and doctoral scholarships worth R110,000 per annum.

Country of Study: South Africa

Application Procedure: Please check website for more details.

Closing Date: 7 August

Contributor: Funded by Department of Science and Technology (DST) and managed by the National Research Foundation (NRF).

For further information contact:

Email:	futurestudents@bournemouth.ac.uk

National Research Foundation Fellowships for Postdoctoral Research

Purpose: To foster postdoctoral research in the natural and applied sciences, engineering, social sciences and the humanities.

Eligibility: Open to any nationals who have received their PhD within the last 5 years.
Level of Study: Postdoctorate
Type: Fellowship
Value: Up to R60,000 plus a contribution of R10,000 towards the running cost of the project.
Length of Study: Up to 2 years
Frequency: Twice a year
Study Establishment: Any university, technikon or research institute for full-time research
Country of Study: South Africa
Application Procedure: Applicants must complete and submit an application form, full academic record and the names of referees. Forms are available from the bursary offices of universities and technikons or can be downloaded from the website.
No. of awards offered: 150
Closing Date: 31 July
Funding: Government
No. of awards given last year: 50
No. of applicants last year: 150

For further information contact:

Email: fellowships@twas.org

National Research Foundation Free-standing Masters and Doctoral Scholarships

Eligibility: Scholarships are open to South African citizens, South African permanent residents as well as a limited percentage of non-South African citizens registered at a South African public university. All applicants for full-time Masters or Doctoral studies in South Africa must be registered or intending to register at a South African public university. Applicants that already hold a degree at the level for which they are applying for funding are not eligible.
Level of Study: Doctorate
Type: Scholarship
Value: Masters scholarships worth R50,000 per year and doctoral scholarships worth R70,000 per year.
Frequency: Annual
Country of Study: South Africa
Application Procedure: Applications must be submitted through an online application process to the NRF.
Closing Date: 7 August
Funding: International office

For further information contact:

Email: CGSMSFSS-SEEMSBESC@cihr-irsc.gc.ca

National Research Foundation Targeted Research Awards Competitive Industry Programme

Purpose: To support research in priority areas where expertise is lacking.
Eligibility: Open to South African citizens only, who qualify for postgraduate support. Postdoctoral support is available for any nationality.
Level of Study: Doctorate, Postdoctorate, Postgraduate
Type: Research grant
Value: From a total of approximately R20 million per year.
Frequency: Annual
Study Establishment: Any tertiary educational institution in South Africa.
Country of Study: Other
Application Procedure: Applicants must complete an electronic application form. For further information please contact Ms Jill Sawers.
No. of awards offered: 200
Closing Date: 31 July
Funding: Government
No. of awards given last year: 181
No. of applicants last year: 200
Additional Information: Joint ventures and collaboration with industry are strongly encouraged. www.mirzayanfellow.nas.edu/

For further information contact:

Tel: (27) 12 481 4104
Email: jill@frd.ac.za

National Research Foundation Visiting Fellowships

Purpose: To strengthen areas of expertise needed in South Africa.
Eligibility: Open to senior scientists of any nationality
Level of Study: Postdoctorate
Type: Fellowship
Value: To cover air fares and accommodation.
Length of Study: Up to 3 months
Frequency: Annual, if funds are available
Study Establishment: Any South African university, technikon, museum or scientific society.
Country of Study: South Africa
Application Procedure: Applications should be submitted by a South African counterpart attached to a South African university, technikon, museum or scientific society.

For further information contact:

Meiring Naude Rd, Gauteng, Pretoria 0184, South Africa.

Tel: (27) 12 481 4122
Email: ferdi@frd.ac.za

Vrije University Amsterdam-NRF Desmond Tutu Doctoral Scholarships

Eligibility: Be in possession of a research Master's degree, or be in the process of completing requirements for such a degree. Should be South African citizens or permanent residents.
Level of Study: Postgraduate
Type: Scholarship
Value: R240,000
Length of Study: The VUA-NRF Desmond Tutu Training Programme provides funding for up to four (4) years of study, depending on satisfactory progress each year.
Country of Study: South Africa
Application Procedure: Check website for more details.
Closing Date: 17 July
Contributor: Vrije Universiteit Amsterdam (VUA)

For further information contact:

Email: danielle.nel@nrf.ac.za

National Science Foundation (NSF)

2415 Eisenhower Avenue, Alexandria, VA 22314, United States of America.

Tel: (1) 703 292 5111
Email: info@nsf.gov
Website: www.nsf.gov
Contact: Division Director

The National Science Foundation (NSF) is an independent federal agency created by Congress in 1950 to promote the progress of science; to advance the national health, prosperity, and welfare; to secure the national defense. NSF is vital because we support basic research and people to create knowledge that transforms the future.

Cultural Anthropology Program Senior Research Awards

Purpose: The primary objective of the Cultural Anthropology Program is to support fundamental, systematic anthropological research and training to increase understanding of the causes, consequences, and complexities of human social and cultural variability.
Eligibility: The categories of proposers eligible to submit proposals to the National Science Foundation are identified in the NSF Proposal & Award Policies & Procedures Guide.
Level of Study: Graduate
Type: Award
Value: US$4,000,000
Frequency: Annual
Country of Study: Any country
No. of awards offered: 30–40
Closing Date: 15 August
Funding: Foundation
Additional Information: The Cultural Anthropology Program cannot support research that takes as its primary objective improved clinical practice, applied policy, or other immediate application www.nsf.gov/funding/pgm_summ.jsp?pims_id=505513

For further information contact:

Tel: (1) 703 292 7783
Email: jmantz@nsf.gov

Directorate for Education and Human Resources Core Research

Purpose: The ECR program places emphasis on the rigorous development of theory and accumulation of knowledge to inform efforts to address challenges in STEM interest, learning, and participation, for all groups and all ages in formal and informal settings. This emphasis includes research on advancing evaluative methodologies to support research efforts funded through ECR
Level of Study: Graduate
Type: Research
Value: Level I proposals may request up to US$500,000; Level II proposals may request up to US$1,500,000; Level III proposals may request up to US$2,500,000
Frequency: Annual
Country of Study: Any country
No. of awards offered: 40 Estimated number of awards description- approximately 15 awards at level I; 12 awards at level II; 5 awards at level III, and 9 other awards.
Closing Date: 6 October
Funding: Foundation
Additional Information: 1. Level 1 and Level 2 proposals have a maximum grant duration of three years. 2. Level 3 proposals have a maximum grant duration of five years. ECR Proposals may fall within three levels of funding. Level 1 Proposals: have a maximum award size of US$5,00,000.

Synthesis proposals may only be budgeted at Level 1 or 2. Level 2 Proposals: have a maximum award size of US$1,500,000. Synthesis proposals may only be budgeted at Level 1 or 2. Level 3 Proposals: have a maximum award size of US$2,500,000 www.nsf.gov/funding/pgm_summ.jsp?pims_id=504924

For further information contact:

Email: ECR@nsf.gov

Enabling Discovery through GEnomic Tools (EDGE)

Purpose: Enabling Discovery through GEnomics (EDGE) program, the National Science Foundation (NSF) and the National Institutes for Health (NIH) support research to advance understanding of comparative and functional genomics. The EDGE program supports the development of innovative tools, technologies, resources, and infrastructure that advance biological research focused on the identification of the causal mechanisms connecting genes and phenotypes. The EDGE program also supports functional genomic research that addresses the mechanistic basis of complex traits in diverse organisms within the context (environmental, developmental, social, and/or genomic) in which they function.

Eligibility: The categories of proposers eligible to submit proposals to the National Science Foundation are identified in the NSF Proposal & Award Policies & Procedures Guide (PAPPG), Chapter I.E.

Level of Study: Graduate

Type: Award

Value: US$10,000,000

Frequency: Annual

Country of Study: Any country

Application Procedure: Step 1 Download a Grant Application Package and Application Instructions link and enter the funding opportunity number, (the program solicitation number without the NSF prefix) and press the Download Package button.

No. of awards offered: 10 to 15

Closing Date: 17 February

Funding: Private

Additional Information: www.nsf.gov/pubs/2021/nsf21546/nsf21546.htm

For further information contact:

2415, Eisenhower Avenue, Alexandria, VA 22314, United States of America.

Tel: (1) 301 312 3276
Email: jennifer.troyer@nih.gov

Faculty Early Career Development Program (CAREER)

Purpose: The Faculty Early Career Development (CAREER) Program is a Foundation-wide activity that offers the National Science Foundation's most prestigious awards in support of early-career faculty who have the potential to serve as academic role models in research and education and to lead advances in the mission of their department or organization. Activities pursued by early-career faculty should build a firm foundation for a lifetime of leadership in integrating education and research. NSF encourages submission of CAREER proposals from early-career faculty at all CAREER-eligible organizations and especially encourages women, members of underrepresented minority groups, and persons with disabilities to apply.

Level of Study: Foundation programme

Type: Award

Value: subject to availability of funds.

Frequency: Annual

Country of Study: Any country

No. of awards offered: 500

Closing Date: 25 July

Funding: Foundation

Additional Information: www.nsf.gov/funding/pgm_summ.jsp?pims_id=503214

For further information contact:

Tel: (1) 703 292 5111
Email: nsf-ccc@nsf.gov

Macrosystems Biology and NEON-Enabled Science (MSB-NES)

Purpose: The Macrosystems Biology and NEON-Enabled Science (MSB-NES) Research on Biological Systems at Regional to Continental Scales program will support quantitative, interdisciplinary, systems-oriented research on biosphere processes and their complex interactions with climate, land use, and changes in species distribution at regional to continental scales as well as training activities to broaden participation of researchers in Macrosystems Biology and NEON-Enabled Science.

Type: Award

Value: US$300,000

Length of Study: (MRA)-5 years; (MSA)-3 years

Frequency: Annual

Country of Study: Any country

No. of awards offered: 15–25

Closing Date: 14 November

Additional Information: www.nsf.gov/funding/pgm_summ.jsp?pims_id=503425

For further information contact:

Tel: (1) 703 292 7186
Email: mkane@nsf.gov

National Science Foundation Research Traineeship (NRT) Program

Purpose: The NSF Research Traineeship (NRT) program seeks proposals that explore ways for graduate students in research-based master's and doctoral degree programs to develop the skills, knowledge, and competencies needed to pursue a range of STEM careers. The program is dedicated to effective training of STEM graduate students in high priority interdisciplinary or convergent research areas, through a comprehensive traineeship model that is innovative, evidence-based, and aligned with changing workforce and research needs.
Level of Study: Doctorate, Masters Degree
Type: Grant
Value: 14–16 awards US$3,000,000 4–6 awards US$2,000,000
Length of Study: 5 years
Frequency: Annual
Country of Study: Any country
No. of awards offered: 18 to 20
Closing Date: 6 September
Funding: Foundation
Additional Information: www.nsf.gov/funding/pgm_summ.jsp?pims_id=505015

For further information contact:

Tel: (1) 703 292 8072
Email: ddenecke@nsf.gov

Robert Noyce Teacher Scholarship Program

Purpose: The National Science Foundation Robert Noyce Teacher Scholarship Program seeks to encourage talented science, technology, engineering, and mathematics (STEM) majors and professionals to become K-12 mathematics and science (including engineering and computer science) teachers. The program invites creative and innovative proposals that address the critical need for recruiting and preparing highly effective elementary and secondary science and mathematics teachers in high-need local educational agencies.

Level of Study: Graduate
Type: Scholarship
Value: Up to US$3,000,000
Length of Study: 6 years
Frequency: Annual
Study Establishment: This program provides educational opportunities for Undergraduate Students, Graduate Students, K-12 Educators.
Country of Study: Any country
No. of awards offered: 55 to 70
Closing Date: 30 August
Funding: Private
Additional Information: www.nsf.gov/funding/pgm_summ.jsp?pims_id=5733

For further information contact:

Tel: (1) 703 292 4657
Email: srichard@nsf.gov

Scalable Parallelism in the Extreme (SPX)

Purpose: The Scalable Parallelism in the Extreme (SPX) program aims to support research addressing the challenges of increasing performance in this modern era of parallel computing. This will require a collaborative effort among researchers in multiple areas, from services and applications down to micro-architecture.
Eligibility: Proposals may only be submitted by the following 1. Institutions of Higher Education (IHEs) - Two- and four-year IHEs (including community colleges) accredited in, and having a campus located in the United States, acting on behalf of their faculty members. 2. Non-profit, non-academic organizations Independent museums, observatories, research labs, professional societies and similar organizations in the United States associated with educational or research activities.
Level of Study: Graduate
Type: Grants, work-study (not just grants)
Frequency: Annual
Country of Study: Any country
Closing Date: 17 January
Funding: Private
Additional Information: www.nsf.gov/funding/pgm_summ.jsp?pims_id=505348&org=NSF

For further information contact:

Tel: (1) 703 292 7885
Email: abanerje@nsf.gov

National Sea Grant College

1315 East-West Highway, Silver Spring, MD 20910, United States of America.

Tel:　　(1) 301 734 1066
Email:　sgfellow@ucsd.edu
Website:　www.seagrant.noaa.gov
Contact:　Jim Eckman, Director

The National Sea Grant College program was established by the U.S. Congress in 1966 and works to create and maintain a healthy coastal environment and economy. The Sea Grant network consists of a federal/university partnership between the National Oceanic and Atmospheric Administration (NOAA) and 34 university-based programs in every coastal and Great Lakes state, Puerto Rico, and Guam. The network draws on the expertise of more than 3,000 scientists, engineers, public outreach experts, educators and students to help citizens better understand, conserve and utilize America's coastal resources.

Sea Grant/NOAA Fisheries Graduate Fellowship

Purpose: To encourage qualified applicants to pursue careers in either population and ecosystem dynamics and stock assessment or in marine resource economics. To increase available expertise related to these fields. To foster closer relationships between academic scientists and NOAA Fisheries. To provide real-world experience to graduate students and accelerate their career development.
Eligibility: The NMFS-Sea Grant Fellowships are available to U.S. citizens who are graduate students enrolled in Ph.D. degree programs in academic institutions in the United States and its territories. Only U.S. citizens are eligible to apply.
Level of Study: Postdoctorate
Type: Fellowship
Value: Up to US$54,166
Length of Study: 3 years
Frequency: Annual
Country of Study: United States of America
Application Procedure: Applicants are strongly encouraged to reach out to the Sea Grant program in their state/territory at least one month prior to the state application deadline to receive application support and provide notification of intent to apply.
No. of awards offered: stipend, tuition, fees, equipment, supplies, and travel necessary
Closing Date: 27 January

Funding: Government
Additional Information: www.seagrant.noaa.gov/NMFS-SG-Fellowship

For further information contact:

Tel:　　(1) 240 507 3712
Email:　OAR.SG.Fellows@noaa.gov

National Sun Yat-Sen University (NSYSU)

70 Lien-hai Road, Kaohsiung 804, Taiwan.

Tel:　　(886) 7 525 2633
Website:　www.oia.nsysu.edu.tw

National Sun Yat-sen University (NSYSU) is one of the few universities in the world to feature its very own on-campus beach. Built in the coastal city of Kaohsiung which boasts almost year-round sunshine, the campus is bordered to the east by the slopes of the beautifully-named Longevity mountain and to the west by the sandy beach, clear blue water and coral reefs of Sizi Bay and beyond that the Strait of Taiwan.

National Sun Yat-sen University International Fellowship

Purpose: To pursue academic excellence combining theory and practice.
Eligibility: Open to candidates who are pursuing their Master's or Doctoral degrees.
Level of Study: Doctorate, Postgraduate
Type: Fellowships
Value: Varies
Length of Study: 2–3 months
Frequency: Annual
Country of Study: Any country
Application Procedure: Applications along with a curriculum vitae, research proposal, name of the corresponding member in the Kuroshio Research Group and 2 letters of recommendation must be mailed.
Additional Information: "Recommendation to Kuroshio Application" must appear as the subject line. www.seagrant.noaa.gov/NMFS-SG-Fellowship

For further information contact:

Email:　keryea@mail.nsysu.edu.tw

N

National Tax Association

1100 Vermont Avenue, NW, Suite 650, Washington, DC 20005, United States of America.

Tel: (1) 202 737 3325
Email: nta@ntanet.org
Website: ntanet.org/

The National Tax Association serves as the leading association of scholars and professionals dedicated to advancing the theory and practice of public finance, including public taxing, spending and borrowing. The National Tax Association is a nonpartisan, nonpolitical educational association. As a 501(c)(3) organization, the NTA does not promote any particular tax program or policy. The enormous public benefit that can come from sound tax policy and wise administration of public finances is a prime reason for the work of NTA.

Tax Institute of America Doctoral Dissertations in Government and Taxation

Subjects: Finance
Purpose: To award original, innovative, clear and analytical dissertations written by scholars and practitioners of government finance.
Eligibility: The award will be granted to exceptional dissertations written by scholars and practitioners of government finance.
Type: Award
Value: The winning entry will receive US$2,000 and the opportunity to publish a paper based on the dissertation in the National Tax Journal. There will also be two honorable mentions of US$1,000 each for outstanding entries.
Country of Study: Any country
Closing Date: 30 June
Additional Information: ntanet.org/awards/phd-dissertation-award/

National Tour Association

101 Prosperous Place, Suite 190, Lexington, KY 40509, United States of America.

Tel: (1) 859 264 6540
Website: ntaonline.com/

NTA is the leading business association for companies and organizations that serve customers traveling to, from and within North America. Our 700 buyer members are tour operators and travel planners who package travel product domestically and around the world. Our seller members - 500 destinations and 1,100 tour suppliers - represent product in all 50 U.S. states, each Canadian province and more than 40 other countries.

National Tour Association (NTA) Luray Caverns Graduate Research Scholarship

Purpose: To aid graduate students who are conducting tourism-related research.
Eligibility: 1. Applicants can be permanent residents of any country but must be enrolled at an accredited U.S. or Canadian four-year postsecondary institution. 2. They must be entering or returning graduate students who are conducting research that focuses on tourism. They must have a proven commitment to the tourism industry, and must have a GPA of 3.0 or higher on a four-point scale. Selection is based on the strength of the research project.
Level of Study: Graduate
Type: Scholarship
Value: US$3,000
Frequency: Annual
Country of Study: Any country
Application Procedure: Applications are available online. An application form, proof of residency, a personal essay, a resume, a research proposal, an official transcript and one letter of recommendation are required.
No. of awards offered: 1
Closing Date: 3 April
Funding: Private
Additional Information: www.chegg.com/scholarships/national-tour-associationluray-caverns-graduate-research-scholarship-2345

National Union of Teachers (NUT)

Hamilton House, Mabledon Place, London WC1H 9BD, United Kingdom.

Tel: (44) 20 7388 6191
Email: enquiries@neu.org.uk
Website: www.teachers.org.uk
Contact: Ms Angela Bush

First established at King's College London and once the largest teachers' union in the UK, the NUT merged with the ATL (Association of Teachers and Lecturers) in September 2017 to form the National Education Union.

National Union of Teachers Page Scholarship

Purpose: To promote the exchange of educational ideas between Britain and America.

Eligibility: Open to teaching members of the NUT aged 25–60 years, although 25–55 is preferred.

Level of Study: Graduate

Type: Scholarship

Value: Each up to £1,700 pro rata daily rate with complete hospitality in the United States of America provided by the English- Speaking Union of the United States of America.

Length of Study: 2 weeks. The scholarship must be taken during the American academic year, which is September–May.

Frequency: Annual

Country of Study: United States of America

Application Procedure: Applicants must complete an application form. An outline and synopsis of the project must accompany the form along with a curriculum vitae and scholastic and personal testimonials.

No. of awards offered: 100

Funding: Private

No. of awards given last year: 2

No. of applicants last year: 100

Additional Information: It is a discontinued award type. The scholarship is limited to the individual teacher and neither the spouse nor partner can be included in the travel, accommodation or study arrangements. Recipients are required to report on their visit to teacher groups and educational meetings in the United States and on their return home. www. chegg.com/scholarships/national-tour-associationluray-cav erns-graduate-research-scholarship-2345

For further information contact:

Tel: (44) 1 812 277 9670
Fax: (44) 20 7388 6191

National University of Ireland Galway

Postgraduate Admission Office, University Road, Galway, H91 TK33, Ireland.

Tel: (353) 91 524 411
Email: info@it.nuigalway.ie

Website: www.nuigalway.ie
Contact: Mairead Faherty

NUI Galway has grown massively in size and reputation over the past 175 years, with a student population today of over 18,000. According to QS World University Rankings, we are ranked 259 in the world and have been increasing our global reach and reputation over the past decade.

Charles Parsons Energy Research Award

Purpose: To focus on investigation and optimization of electron transfer reactions in biological fuel cells that can generate energy from diverse substrates. To focus the research on applications of pure- and mixed-culture microbial fuel cells, and biocatalytic enzyme-based fuel cells.

Eligibility: Open to engineering graduates.

Level of Study: Doctorate

Type: Research award

Value: Salary scale €55,000–80,486 per year for researchers, stipend of €18,000 per year plus tuition fees for PhD studentship and undergraduate engineering students €1,500 per month.

Application Procedure: Applicants should include a curriculum vitae and the names of two academic referees.

Closing Date: October

Additional Information: The research will involve liaison with international collaborators, bench research and reporting. To this end, good inter-personal, written communication and networking skills are advantageous. www.chegg. com/scholarships/national-tour-associationluray-caverns-graduate-research-scholarship-2345

For further information contact:

Email: donal.leech@nuigalway.ie

Hardiman PhD Scholarships

Purpose: The Scholarships offer opportunities for suitably qualified individuals to pursue a Structured PhD focused on the five key areas of research in which the University offers leading expertise; Engaging with our partners locally, nationally and worldwide, we invite ambition in research that underpins the following areas 1. Enhancing policy and society 2. Enriching creativity and culture 3. Improving health and wellbeing 4. Realising potential through data and enabling technologies 5. Sustaining our planet and people.

N

Eligibility: 1. Successful applicants will be expected to have a first or upper second class honours primary degree or equivalent. 2. Applications will not be accepted from persons currently registered as PhD students. 3. English Language Requirements - please go to this webpage www.nuigalway. ie/international-students/entry-requirements/
Level of Study: Postgraduate
Type: Scholarship
Value: stipend of €18,500
Length of Study: 4 years
Country of Study: Any country
Application Procedure: Applicants must read the Applicant's Guide prior to completing the application form.
Closing Date: 11 February
Additional Information: www.nuigalway.ie/hardiman-scholarships/

For further information contact:

Email: hrscholar@nuigalway.ie

PhD Student Scholarship in Atmospheric Science

Purpose: To study the effect of ambient relative humidity on aerosol radiative parameters aerosol light scattering coefficient and aerosol absorption coefficient
Eligibility: Open to candidates who have obtained a good Honours Degree (grade 2.1 at least) in physics or in a cognate subject.
Level of Study: Doctorate
Type: Scholarship
Value: Stipend and tuition fees
Length of Study: 3 years
Country of Study: Ireland
Application Procedure: Applicants must submit a covering letter, curriculum vitae and the names of at least two referees.

For further information contact:

Tel: (353) 91 492 704
Fax: (353) 91 495 515
Email: gerard.jennings@nuigalway.ie

Student Research Scholarship in Occupational Hygiene

Purpose: To enhance GSK's exposure assessment strategy, to look at current occupational hygiene data collected from across all GSK sites and to apply Bayesian statistics to optimize the exposure assessment strategy.

Eligibility: Open to candidates who have obtained an Honours Degree (2.1 minimum) in a science or engineering discipline. Ideally, the candidate should have a sound understanding of mathematics/statistics, combined with an understanding of exposure assessment.
Level of Study: Postgraduate
Type: Scholarship
Value: Monthly stipend
Country of Study: Ireland
Application Procedure: Applicants must submit a covering letter, a curriculum vitae and the names of at least two referees.
Closing Date: 31 August
Contributor: GlaxoSmithKline (GSK)

For further information contact:

Department of Experimental Physics, National University of Ireland, University Road, Galway, H91 TK33, Ireland.

Email: marie.coggins@nuigalway.ie

Taught Postgraduate Scholarships

Purpose: NUI Galway has established a Postgraduate Scholarship Scheme to support and facilitate students wishing to register for a Fulltime Taught Postgraduate Masters programme in the academic.
Eligibility: In order to be eligible for the award of a scholarship, students must 1. Have submitted a valid online scholarship application form by the deadline; 2. Be registered in Year 1 of a Fulltime Taught Masters programme for the academic year subsequent to the scholarship application (repeat students are not eligible to apply); 3. Have attained a first class honours (or equivalent) in a Level 8 primary degree.
Level of Study: Postgraduate
Type: Scholarship
Value: €1,500 per student
Country of Study: Any country
Application Procedure: Applications must be made using the online application form.
Closing Date: 16 August
Additional Information: The Admissions Office will review applications and will verify submitted documentary evidence provided, during the summer months. Once the applicant is notified of her/his eligibility, they will then be required to complete the registration requirements of the University by the due date. www.nuigalway.ie/media/registry/admissions/files/Scholarship_criteria.pdf

National University of Ireland, Maynooth

Co. Kildare, Maynooth, W23 X021, Ireland.

Tel:	(353) 1 708 3868
Email:	international.office@mu.ie
Website:	www.maynoothuniversity.ie/

The Maynooth University International Office supports over 1000 students of different nationalities and cultures, and facilitates the applications of international undergraduate and postgraduate students from outside of the European Union to study at the University. In addition the Office coordinates and provides support to approximately 600 visiting students from North America and the European Union each year, while also encouraging all current Maynooth students to incorporate a period of study or work placement abroad into their degree.

John and Pat Hume Doctoral Scholarships

Purpose: John & Pat Hume doctoral awards will be offered to successful doctoral applicants with demonstrated excellence in academic course work and research. Consideration will be given to the relevance of the proposed doctoral research to departmental and university research priorities. Applicants will also be expected to have some prior non-academic engagement such as volunteering, outreach activities or similar, in line with the university's strategic plan.

Eligibility: The minimum standards for eligibility for MU John & Pat Hume doctoral awards of any type are 1. All applicants must have a first class or upper second-class honours bachelor's degree, or the equivalent, in the discipline of the department of application, or in a cognate discipline approved by the proposed supervisor. 2. If undergraduate examination results are not known at the time of application, Maynooth University may make a provisional offer of a scholarship on condition that the scholar's bachelor's (equivalent) degree result is a first class or upper second-class honours. 3. If a scholar does not have a first class or upper second-class honours bachelor's degree (or equivalent), they must possess a master's degree in the discipline of the department of application or cognate discipline as approved by proposed supervisor. 4. Applicants of any nationality are eligible to apply.

Level of Study: Doctorate

Type: Scholarship

Value: The maximum duration of €20,500 and €10,000 scholarships is four years.

Length of Study: 4 years

Country of Study: Any country

Application Procedure: Completed and signed applications should be submitted via the online application system.

Closing Date: 12 April

Additional Information: www.maynoothuniversity.ie/graduate-studies/john-pat-hume-doctoral-awards

For further information contact:

John Hume Building, 3rd Floor, Maynooth University, Co. Kildare, Ireland.

Email:	humephdscholarship@mu.ie

John and Pat Hume Research Scholarships

Purpose: To build on excellence in areas across the arts, humanities, social sciences, sciences and engineering.

Eligibility: Applicants must have a First or Upper Second-Class Honours Primary Degree (or equivalent) from Ireland, the European Union or from any overseas university and intend to pursue a PhD degree at the University. Those who have commenced a research degree at NUI Maynooth prior to application will not be eligible.

Level of Study: Postgraduate, Research

Type: Scholarship

Value: €5,000 per year plus payment of fees at European Union level. In some cases an additional fund of €3,000 is also provided to the student researcher for activities undertaken in support of the Department including tutorials and laboratory demonstration.

Length of Study: Up to 4 years

Frequency: Annual

Study Establishment: NUI Maynooth

Country of Study: Ireland

Application Procedure: Applicants must first make contact with a NUI Maynooth department or centre to discuss their suitability for a PhD programme. A list of departmental contacts is available on the website. Application for the scholarship can then be filed.

Closing Date: May

No. of awards given last year: 30

Additional Information: Supplement the scholarship with an additional €3,000 for tutorial or demonstrating duties www.maynoothuniversity.ie/study-maynooth/postgraduate-studies/fees-funding-scholarships/john-and-pat-hume-doctoral-awards.

For further information contact:

Tel:	(353) 1 708 6018
Fax:	(353) 1 708 3359
Email:	pgdean@nuim.ie

Maynooth University Teaching Studentships

Purpose: Funded student teaching assistant opportunities are offered across a range of disciplines at Maynooth University. Successful applicants will commence PhD Doctoral studies at Maynooth University in the Autumn semester and will have 5 years to complete their PhD.
Level of Study: Postdoctorate
Type: Scholarship
Value: 1. Full annual tuition fees support (approximately €6,200 per annum); 2. A fixed stipend of €9,007 per annum.
Length of Study: 5 years
Country of Study: Ireland
Additional Information: In addition to their PhD research, the recipient of the Teaching Studentship will support the teaching and assessment duties of their Department up to a maximum of 455 hours per annum. www.maynoothu niversity.ie/study-maynooth/postgraduate-studies/fees-funding-scholarships/maynooth-university-teaching-studentship#main-content

Taught Master's Scholarships

Eligibility: 1. 60 Taught Master's scholarships of €2000 each will be awarded to student across all disciplines in recognition of academic excellence. 2. All applicants must have achieved a minimum 2.1 honours undergraduate degree. 3. Open to both EU and Non-EU applicants. 4. Graduates or current students of PhD or Master's programmes are not eligible to apply. Prospective students interested in research programmes should apply instead for the Maynooth University John and Pat Hume Doctoral Research Awards.
Level of Study: Postgraduate
Type: Scholarship
Value: €2000
Country of Study: Ireland
Application Procedure: Terms and Conditions and application details will be available soon.
Closing Date: 30 June
No. of applicants last year: 60
Additional Information: www.maynoothuniversity.ie/study-maynooth/postgraduate-studies/fees-funding-scholar ships/taught-masters-scholarships

For further information contact:

Email: tmscholarships@mu.ie

National University of Singapore (NUS)

21 Lower Kent Ridge Road, 119077, Singapore.

Tel: (65) 6516 6666
Email: research@nus.edu.sg
Website: www.nus.edu.sg

The National University of Singapore aspires to be a vital community of academics, researchers, staff, students and alumni working together in a spirit of innovation and enterprise for a better world. Our singular focus on talent will be the cornerstone of a truly great university that is dedicated to quality education, influential research and visionary enterprise, in service of country and society.

Asian Development Bank-Japan Scholarship Program

Purpose: To find further study in public policy implementation
Eligibility: Open to residents of Asian Development Bank member countries currently enroled at NUS. Upon completion of their study programmes, scholars are expected to contribute to the economic and social development of their home countries. Check website for further details
Level of Study: Postgraduate
Type: Scholarship
Value: S$250 per semester (one-time book allowance), tuition, health insurance, examination and other approved fees. Cost of travel from home country to Singapore on award of the scholarship and from Singapore to home country on graduation
Length of Study: 2 years for Master in public policy
Frequency: Annual
Study Establishment: Lee Kuan Yew School of Public Policy, National University of Singapore
Country of Study: Singapore
Application Procedure: Application form with 3 photographs attached, certificate of citizenship (or a copy of your valid passport), research and/or work experience, two confidential letters of recommendation
No. of awards offered: 350
Closing Date: 12 July
Funding: Government
Contributor: Government
No. of awards given last year: 3
No. of applicants last year: 350
Additional Information: www.ait.ac.th/admissions/scholar ships/asian-development-bank-japan-scholarship-program/

Law/Faculty Graduate Scholarship (FGS)

Purpose: To reward an outstanding student of the faculty of Law

Eligibility: Outstanding applicants of any nationality (including Singapore citizens and permanent residents) may be awarded the FGS to pursue the LLM coursework degrees LLM, LLM (Asian Legal Studies), LLM (Corporate & Financial Services Law), LLM (Intellectual Property & Technology Law), LLM (International & Comparative Law), LLM (Maritime Law)

Level of Study: Postgraduate

Type: Scholarship

Value: The scholarship will cover tuition fees

Frequency: Annual

Study Establishment: National University of Singapore

Country of Study: Singapore

Lee Kuan Yew School of Public Policy Graduate Scholarships (LKYSPPS)

Purpose: To find further study in public policy and administration implementation

Eligibility: Open to all nationalities (except Singapore)

Level of Study: Postgraduate

Type: Scholarship

Value: A monthly stipend, a one-time book allowance, a one-time settling-in allowance, shared housing, tuition, health insurance, examination and other approved fees, cost of travel from home country to Singapore on award of the scholarship and from Singapore to home country on graduation

Length of Study: 1 year (for public administration) and 2 years (for public policy)

Frequency: Annual

Study Establishment: Lee Kuan Yew School of Public Policy, National University of Singapore

Country of Study: Singapore

Application Procedure: Apply online

Funding: Government

Contributor: Government

For further information contact:

Email: LKYSPPmpp@nus.edu.sg

Master of Business Administration Programme

Application Procedure: Applicants must complete an application form supplying US$15 fee.

Closing Date: 1 April

For further information contact:

Graduate School of Business, MBA Programme, FBA2, Level 5, Room 6, 17 Law Link, 117592, Singapore.

Tel: (65) 6874 6149
Fax: (65) 6778 2681
Email: fbagrad@nus.edu.sg

National University of Singapore Design Technology Institute Scholarship

Eligibility: Open to all nationalities with good Bachelor's degree with Honours in Engineering or Science.

Level of Study: Postgraduate

Type: Scholarship

Value: A monthly stipend S$1,500 with a possible monthly top-up of S$500 and all approved NUS fees.

Length of Study: 2 years

Frequency: Annual

Study Establishment: National University of Singapore

Country of Study: Singapore

Closing Date: November

Additional Information: DTI Scholars who are international students will be required to serve a 2 years bond in Singapore upon graduation. www.ait.ac.th/admissions/scholarships/asian-development-bank-japan-scholarship-program/

For further information contact:

Tel: (65) 6874 1227
Fax: (65) 6873 2175
Email: dtibox@nus.edu.sg

Singapore-MIT Alliance Graduate Fellowship

Purpose: The SMA Graduate Fellowship is established by the Singapore Ministry of Education in January 2009 to attract the best and most talented PhD students from Singapore, the region and beyond, and educate them to be future leaders in the areas of science and technology. The selection of candidates will take place twice a year, in time for the start of the semesters in August and January

Eligibility: The Scholarships are open to students of all nationalities who gain admission to any PhD programme at the University whose research interest fits within one or more of the projects currently being carried out in one of the SMART Interdisciplinary Research Groups (IRGs)

Level of Study: Graduate, Postgraduate

Type: Fellowship

Value: A monthly stipend of Singaporean S$3,200; Tuition fees at NUS; and Scholarship allowance of up to S$12,000 to help cover the expenses associated with a 6-month research residency at MIT

Length of Study: The award is tenable for 1 year in the first instance; but subject to the scholar's satisfactory progress, it may be renewed each semester. The maximum period of award is 4 years

Frequency: Annual

Study Establishment: National University of Singapore and Nanyang Technological University

Country of Study: Singapore

Application Procedure: Applicants must apply separately to both MIT and NUS/NTU for the dual degrees and only to NUS or NTU for direct PhD degree; applicants must also apply directly to SMA for an SMA Graduate Fellowship

No. of awards offered: 120

Closing Date: March

Funding: Government

Contributor: A*Star, Economic and Development Board (EDB), Ministry of Education (MOE), National University of Singapore (NUS) and Nanyang Technological University (NTU)

No. of applicants last year: 120

Additional Information: smart.mit.edu/fellowships/for-graduates-smart-graduates

For further information contact:

Tel: (65) 6516 4787
Fax: (65) 6775 2920
Email: smart@nus.edu.sg

Natural Environment Research Council (NERC)

Polaris House, North Star Avenue, Swindon SN2 1EU, United Kingdom.

Tel: (44) 1793 411500
Website: www.nerc.ac.uk/funding
Contact: Studentships & Training Awards Group (STAG)

NERC - the Natural Environment Research Council - is the driving force of investment in environmental science in the UK. NERC advances the frontier of environmental science by commissioning new research, infrastructure and training that delivers valuable scientific breakthroughs. We do this because understanding our changing planet is vital for our wellbeing and economic prosperity.

Natural Environment Research Council Independent Research Fellowships (IRF)

Purpose: To develop scientific leadership among the most promising early-career environmental scientists, by giving all Fellows 5 year's support, which will allow them sufficient time to develop their research programmes, and to establish international recognition

Eligibility: Open to any nationality, and may be held in any area of the NERC remit, but the fellowship must be based at an eligible United Kingdom Research Organization. Applicants may not have a permanent academic position in a university or equivalent organization. Applicants must expect to submit their PhD thesis before the fellowship interview would take place (April following the closing date) and, if successful, would not be able to take up the fellowship until the intent to award the PhD has been confirmed by the awarding university. Applicants may have up to a maximum of 8 years of full-time postdoctoral research experience between the PhD certificate date and the closing date of the fellowship competition to which they are applying. The eight year window is based on full-time working. Where applicants have worked part-time or had research career breaks, the eight year window would be extended accordingly

Level of Study: Research

Type: Fellowship

Value: Includes 80% of the full economic cost (FEC) of the proposal. NERC will provide funding for the fellow

Length of Study: 5 years

Frequency: Annual

Study Establishment: Universities and other approved research institutes

Country of Study: United Kingdom

Application Procedure: Please refer to the Research Grants and Fellowships Handbook at www.nerc.ac.uk/funding/available/fellowships/apply/

Closing Date: December

Funding: Government

No. of awards given last year: 14

Additional Information: microsites.ncl.ac.uk/nubsstaffblog/2019/06/25/nerc-independent-research-fellowships/

For further information contact:

Email: Fellowships@nerc.ac.uk

Natural Environment Research Council Research Grants

Purpose: To support a specific investigation in which the applicant will be engaged personally, to enter promising new or modified fields of research, or to take advantage of developments in apparatus offering improved techniques in promising lines of research already established

Eligibility: Open to research workers ordinarily resident in the United Kingdom who are also members of the academic staff of universities, colleges and similar institutions within the United Kingdom recognised by the NERC. Research assistants and technicians are not eligible to apply. Holders of Research Council Fellowships at an Institute of Higher Education are eligible to apply for research grants

Level of Study: Postdoctorate, Professional development

Type: Grant

Value: The Standard Research Grant offers amounts over £30,000, for periods not usually in excess of three years. The Small Research Grant offers a more rapid response for applications costing £2,000-30,000. Applications for less than £2,000 will not be accepted. The new investigator scheme offers up to the £50,000

Frequency: Throughout the year

Study Establishment: Any approved Institute of Higher Education in the United Kingdom

Country of Study: United Kingdom

Application Procedure: Applicants must complete an application form, available on request. Application forms and further information can be found on the NERC website

Closing Date: 1 October

Funding: Government

No. of awards given last year: 307

For further information contact:

Email: researchcareers@nerc.ac.uk

Natural Hazards Center-University of Colorado

482 UCB, Boulder, CO 80309-0482, United States of America.

Tel: (1) 303 492 6818
Email: hazctr@colorado.edu
Website: www.colorado.edu/hazards

The mission of the Natural Hazards Center at the University of Colorado at Boulder is to advance and communicate knowledge on hazards mitigation and disaster preparedness, response and recovery. Using an all hazards and interdisciplinary framework, the Center fosters information- sharing and integration of activities among researchers, practitioners and policy makers from around the world, supports and conducts research and provides educational opportunities for the next generation of hazards scholars and professionals.

Annual Hazards and Disasters Student Paper Competition

Purpose: The Natural Hazards Center created the Annual Hazards and Disasters Student Paper Competition for undergraduate and graduate students in 2004 as a way to recognize and promote the next generation of hazards and disaster researchers.

Eligibility: Author(s) must be enrolled as an undergraduate or graduate student for at least one term in the 2022–23 academic year. Papers must be authored by one or more students and cannot be co-authored by faculty or colleagues who are not students. Papers cannot be under consideration or accepted for publication at the time of submission. Papers presented or submitted for presentation at professional meetings are allowable. Papers must be edited, double-spaced (including references), and less than 25 pages, including notes, references, and tables. Single-spaced papers or papers over 25 pages will be disqualified. Papers must include a brief abstract that provides an overview of the paper. Submissions should be submitted in a Word document format using 12-point Arial font. Winning submissions will be edited for Natural Hazards Center style and length before publication

Type: Competition

Value: winner each will receive US$100

Frequency: Annual

Country of Study: Any country

Closing Date: 15 May

Additional Information: hazards.colorado.edu/awards/paper-competition

For further information contact:

Natural Hazards Center, 483 UCB, Boulder, CO 80309-0483, United States of America.

Tel: (1) 303 735 5844
Email: hazctr@colorado.edu

Dissertation Fellowship in Hazards, Risks, and Disaster

Purpose: To provide financial support for research that is crucial to advancing the knowledge in the hazards field, as well as ensure that the next generation of interdisciplinary

N

hazards professional has a source of financial and academic support to foster sound development

Eligibility: Open to candidates who already have a dissertation at an institution in the United States. Non-United States citizens may apply as long as the Doctorate degree will be granted by a United States institution

Level of Study: Postgraduate

Type: Fellowships

Value: US$10,000

Frequency: Annual

Country of Study: United States of America

Application Procedure: The applicant must submit a curriculum vitae along with a dissertation summary

Closing Date: September

Additional Information: freestudiesabroad.blogspot.com/2006/06/dissertation-fellowship-in-hazards.html

For further information contact:

Email: periship@riskinstitute.org

Natural Sciences and Engineering Research Council of Canada (NSERC)

Ontario Regional Office, 350 Albert Street, 16th floor, Ottawa, ON K1A 1H5, Canada.

Tel: (1) 877 767 1767
Email: nserc-ontario@nserc-crsng.gc.ca
Website: www.nserc.ca
Contact: Corporate Account Executive

The Natural Sciences and Engineering Research Council of Canada funds visionaries, explorers and innovators who are searching for the scientific and technical breakthroughs that will benefit our country. We are Canada's largest supporter of discovery and innovation. We work with universities, colleges, businesses and not-for-profits to remove barriers, develop opportunities and attract new expertise to make Canada's research community thrive. We give Canadian scientists and engineers the means to go further because we believe in research without borders and beyond frontiers.

Canada Graduate Scholarships – Michael Smith Foreign Study Supplements Program

Purpose: The Canada Graduate Scholarships - Michael Smith Foreign Study Supplements (CGS-MSFSS) support high-calibre Canadian graduate students in building global linkages and international networks through the pursuit of exceptional research experiences at research institutions abroad. By accessing international scientific research and training, CGS-MSFSS recipients will contribute to strengthening the potential for collaboration between Canadian and foreign institutions.

Eligibility: 1. Have accepted or currently hold one of the following CGS a. Joseph-Armand Bombardier (SSHRC). b. Alexander Graham Bell (NSERC). c. Frederick Banting and Charles Best (CIHR). d. Vanier (if eligible). 2. Undertake your proposed trip abroad no earlier than the competition deadline date; 3. Not hold, or have held, any other CGS-MSFSS during the course of your graduate studies.

Level of Study: Postgraduate

Type: Award

Value: Up to C$6,000 for a period of research study abroad

Frequency: Annual

Country of Study: Canada

Application Procedure: You will be required to provide the following information 1. The name and contact information of your CGS or Vanier CGS research supervisor and of the proposed host supervisor. 2. The name and location of the proposed host institution. 3. A maximum two-page description of your intended research activities during your research study period abroad (including objectives, methodology, timelines and expected outcomes) and how they relate to your main graduate research topic, and a description of the potential benefits you will derive from the host institution in relation to your current research objectives. 4. A budget that provides estimates for costs of travel, living and other expenses during your research study period abroad. 5. A letter from your CGS or Vanier CGS research supervisor detailing their support for your research study period abroad and confirming that your proposed research aligns with the research from your CGS award (maximum one page). 6. A letter from your host supervisor detailing their support for your research study period abroad and the resources they have available-financial (if any), supervision time, equipment, library access, etc.-to support your planned research activities (maximum one page)

No. of awards offered: A total of 250 awards, in which 45 for CIHR, 80 for NSERC and 125 for SSHRC.

Closing Date: 10 October

Additional Information: www.nserc-crsng.gc.ca/Students-Etudiants/PG-CS/CGSForeignStudy-BESCEtudeEtranger_eng.asp#applicationinstructions

For further information contact:

Email: schol@nserc-crsng.gc.ca

Canada Graduate Scholarships-Master's (CGS M) Program

Purpose: The objective of the Canada Graduate Scholarships – Master's (CGS M) program is to help develop research skills and assist in the training of highly qualified personnel by supporting students who demonstrate a high standard of achievement in undergraduate and early graduate studies.

Eligibility: 1. Open to be a Canadian citizen or a permanent resident of Canada, as of the application deadline date. 2. Be enrolled in, have applied for or will apply for full-time admission to an eligible graduate program at the master's or doctoral level at a Canadian institution with a CGS M allocation. 3. Respect the internal deadline to apply for admission for your intended program of study contact the faculty of graduate studies (or its equivalent) at the selected Canadian institution(s) for more detailed information. 4. Not have previously held a CGS M. 5. Have achieved a first-class average**, as determined by the host institution, in each of the last two completed years of study (full-time equivalent) 6. Submit a maximum of one scholarship application per academic year to either CIHR, NSERC or SSHRC

Level of Study: Postgraduate
Type: Scholarship
Value: C$17,500
Length of Study: 1 year
Frequency: Annual
Country of Study: Canada
Application Procedure: To apply to the CGS M program, applicants must complete and submit an application to up to three institutions using the research portal. Applicants should consult the Canada Graduate Scholarships - Master's program Instructions for completing an application.
No. of awards offered: 3,000
Closing Date: 1 December
Funding: Government
Contributor: CIHR, NSERC and SSHRC
Additional Information: www.nserc-crsng.gc.ca/Students-Etudiants/PG-CS/CGSM-BESCM_eng.asp

For further information contact:

Email: schol@nserc-crsng.gc.ca

Canada Postgraduate Scholarships (PGS)

Eligibility: Open to a Canadian citizen or a permanent citizen of Canada, with a university degree in science or engineering, intending to pursue year full-time graduate study and research at the Master's or Doctorate level in one of the areas supported by NSERC with a first-class average in each of the last two completed years of study.
Level of Study: Postgraduate

Type: Fellowship
Value: C$17,300 (Masters) per year for 1 year and C$21,000 (Doctoral) per year for a period of 2–3 years.
Length of Study: 1 year
Frequency: Annual
Country of Study: Canada
Application Procedure: Check website for further details
Closing Date: 15 October
Contributor: Natural Sciences and Engineering Research Council of Canada (NSERC)

For further information contact:

Scholarships and Fellowships Division National Sciences and Engineering Research Council of Canada, 350 Albert Street (for courier mailings, add 10th Floor), Ottawa, ON K1A 1H5, Canada.

Fax: (1) 613 996 2589
Email: schol@nserc.ca

Defence Research and Development Canada Postgraduate Scholarship Supplements

Purpose: To encourage and support graduates to carry out research of interest to DRDC; to increase contact between DRDC researchers and those at Canadian universities; and to foster graduate training potential candidates for possible employment at DRDC.
Eligibility: Open to candidates possessing a CGS, PGS or IPS award.
Level of Study: Postgraduate
Type: Scholarship
Value: C$5,000 per year
Length of Study: 2 years
Frequency: Annual
Country of Study: Canada
Application Procedure: Applicants must submit a copy Notification of Award document from NSERC, a copy of successful scholarship application (Form 200), and a statement of interest in R&D for defence/national security. Check website for further details.
Closing Date: 1 June
Contributor: Defence Research and Development Canada.

For further information contact:

DRDC Postgraduate Scholarship Supplements Program, Department of National Defence, 305 Rideau Street, Ottawa, ON K1N 5Y6, Canada.

Tel: (1) 613 992 0563
Fax: (1) 613 996 7063
Email: hr-rh@drdc-rddc.gc.ca

Japan Society for the Promotion of Science Postdoctoral Fellowships

Purpose: The Japan Society for the Promotion of Science (JSPS) has established the JSPS Postdoctoral Fellowships for Foreign Researchers. A limited number of promising early career researchers are given the opportunity, through this fellowship, to conduct research in Japanese universities and in designated research institutions and laboratories. NSERC is responsible for recommending Canadian nominees for JSPS Postdoctoral Fellowships.

Eligibility: be a Canadian citizen or a permanent resident of Canada not have Japanese nationality or be a permanent resident of Japan hold or expect to hold a doctorate degree in one of the fields of research that NSERC supports prior to the proposed start date of the postdoctoral fellowship not hold, or have held, any other JSPS Postdoctoral fellowship

Type: Fellowship

Value: Airfare, Maintenance Allowance ¥362,000 per month, A settling-in allowance of ¥200,000, Overseas travel insurance, etc.

Frequency: Annual

Country of Study: Any country

Closing Date: 1 February

Additional Information: www.nserc-crsng.gc.ca/Students-Etudiants/PD-NP/JSPS-SJPS_eng.asp#value

NSERC Indigenous Student Ambassadors

Purpose: The NSERC Indigenous Student Ambassadors (NISA) grant aims to engage Indigenous students and fellows in promoting interest and participation in the natural sciences and engineering (NSE) by visiting Indigenous communities and schools in Canada and sharing their research and education experiences or participating in science promotion events and activities.

Eligibility: 1. Open to a Canadian citizen or permanent resident of Canada. 2. An Indigenous person. 3. Registered full time in a degree program in the NSE at an eligible institution or be employed at an eligible institution as a postdoctoral fellow in the NSE at the time your application is submitted.

Level of Study: Postgraduate

Type: Award

Value: Up to C$5,000

Country of Study: Canada

Application Procedure: Applications must be submitted electronically using NSERC's ICSP Secure Submission Site. The application must be submitted in Portable Document Format (PDF) as a single document.

Funding: Government

Additional Information: If your activity is planned for March or April, please submit your application earlier than two months in advance due to a potential delay of your payment as a result of NSERC's fiscal year-end processes. www.nserc-crsng.gc.ca/students-etudiants/pg-cs/index_eng.asp

For further information contact:

Email: ambassadors@nserc-crsng.gc.ca

NSERC Postgraduate Scholarships-Doctoral program

Purpose: The NSERC Postgraduate Scholarships - Doctoral (PGS D) program provides financial support to high-calibre scholars who are engaged in an eligible doctoral program (see Eligibility criteria for students and fellows) in the natural sciences or engineering. This support allows these scholars to fully concentrate on their studies and seek out the best research mentors in their chosen fields.

Eligibility: 1. Be a Canadian citizen or a permanent resident of Canada, as of the application deadline date. 2. Have completed no more than 24 months of full-time study in their doctoral program by December 31 of the calendar year of application if previously enrolled in a master's program. 3. Have completed no more than 36 months of full-time study in their doctoral program by December 31 of the calendar year of application if enrolled in a joint program; for example, MD/PhD, MA/PhD. 4. Have completed no more than 36 months of full-time study in their doctoral program by December 31 of the calendar year of application if enrolled directly from a bachelor's to a PhD program (with no time spent in a master's program).

Level of Study: Postgraduate

Type: Scholarship

Value: C$21,000 per year

Length of Study: 3 years

Country of Study: Canada

Application Procedure: Refer to the CGS D program description for information on applying to the PGS D program www.nserc-crsng.gc.ca/Students-Etudiants/PG-CS/CGSD-BESCD_eng.asp

Closing Date: 17 October

Additional Information: www.nserc-crsng.gc.ca/Students-Etudiants/PG-CS/BellandPostgrad-BelletSuperieures_eng.asp

Netherlands Organization for Scientific Research (NWO)

Lann van Nieuw Oost Indie 300, PO Box 93138, NL-2509 The Hague AC, Netherlands.

Tel:	(31) 70 344 0640
Email:	nwo@nwo.nl
Website:	www.nwo.nl
Contact:	F.A.O. Grants Department

The Dutch Research Council (NWO) is one of the most important science funding bodies in the Netherlands and realises quality and innovation in science. Each year, NWO invests almost 1 billion euros in curiosity-driven research, research related to societal challenges and research infrastructure. The Dutch Research Council advances world-class scientific research. NWO facilitates excellent, curiosity-driven disciplinary, interdisciplinary and multidisciplinary research.

Rubicon Programme

Purpose: Rubicon aims to encourage talented researchers who recently received their PhD to spend some time at top research institutes outside the Netherlands to further their scientific career. Rubicon bridges the phase between obtaining a PhD and being eligible for funding from the Talent Scheme.
Eligibility: Postgraduates who are currently engaged in doctoral research or who have been awarded a doctorate in the twelve months. Women especially are urged to apply.
Level of Study: Postdoctorate
Type: Award
Value: €2,278,333 a year
Length of Study: Up to 2 years
No. of awards offered: Varies
Closing Date: 30 November
Additional Information: www.nwo.nl/en/calls/rubicon-2021-1

For further information contact:

Tel: (31) 70 3440989

WOTRO DC Fellowships

Purpose: To support high-quality PhD and postdoctorate research projects.

Eligibility: Open to project researchers with the appropriate degrees.
Level of Study: Doctorate
Type: Fellowship
Value: A contribution to personal living costs and research costs
Length of Study: 4 years for PhD research and 2 years for postdoctorate research
Frequency: Annual
Application Procedure: Applications must be formally submitted by a senior researcher employed at a Dutch research institution, together with a senior researcher from the home country as a co-applicant and as part of the supervising them.
Contributor: WOTRO

For further information contact:

Tel:	(31) 70 344 0945
Email:	dijk@nwo.nl

Neurosurgery Research & Education Foundation (NREF)

5550 Meadowbrook Industrial Ct., Rolling Meadows, IL 60008, United States of America.

Email:	info@nref.org
Website:	www.nref.org/

Cerebrovascular Traveling Fellowship

Purpose: The objective of the grant is to fund travel of mid-career (see eligibility below) fellowship-trained cerebrovascular/endovascular specialist (applicant/fellow) to another institution (host) for five (5) days.
Eligibility: Applicant/Fellow: Fellowship-trained cerebrovascular/endovascular specialist, board certified in his/her specialty and holds a CAST certificate in neuroendovascular surgery or is able to demonstrate significant open cerebrovascular experience and practice, who has practiced independently for at least five (5) years and is a dues-paying member in good standing of the AANS/CNS Joint Cerebrovascular Section or the Society of NeuroInterventional Surgery (SNIS). Host: Any practice that demonstrates significant volumes and outcomes in the area that the applicant is seeking experience. The presence of a CAST-approved fellowship training program may be used as an indicator of such practice focus but may not be sufficient. The selection committee will

reserve the right to make a final decision regarding the eligibility of a specific applicant or host.

Type: Fellowship
Value: stipend of US$5,000, travel and lodging expenses up to US$2,500, award of US$1,000.
Length of Study: 5 Days
Frequency: Annual
Country of Study: Any country
Closing Date: 1 December
Additional Information: www.nref.org/-/media/Files/ NREF/CV_Traveling_Fellowship-Application_Instructions_ and_FAQs.ashx

For further information contact:

Lauren Coleman NREF Development Coordinator.

Tel: (1) 847 378 0535
Email: lcoleman@nref.org

CV Section/CNS Foundation Young Investigator Research Grant

Purpose: The objective of the grant is to provide sustained research startup funding for early-stage academic neurosurgeon-scientists in the field of cerebrovascular disease.
Eligibility: Board-eligible cerebrovascular and/or endovascular fellowship-trained neurosurgeon, in the first three (3) years of full-time faculty position at the start of the funding period. Applicant must be an active member in good standing of the AANS/CNS Cerebrovascular Section ("CV Section"). Fellows may apply in the final year of fellowship, as long as a faculty position is confirmed prior to the start of the funding period. Faculty position must be at a teaching institution in North America.
Type: Grant
Value: US$50,000 per year for three (3) years; total US$150,000 of direct costs.
Length of Study: Three years
Country of Study: Any country
Closing Date: 31 March
Additional Information: www.nref.org/-/media/Files/ NREF/2022_CV_Section_Research_Grant-Application_ Instructions_and_FAQs.ashx

For further information contact:

Tel: (1) 847 378 0500
Email: info@nref.org

Directed Residency Scholarships

Purpose: The objective of the scholarship grant is to fund clinical scholarships in a subspecialty of neurosurgery
Eligibility: Neurosurgical residents in ACGME-accredited neurosurgery residency training programs interested in expanded subspecialty exposure with a rotation away from their home program prior to their Chief Resident year. Rotation must be spent in a neurosurgery residency program with Accreditation Council for Graduate Medical Education (ACGME) certification or the international equivalent. The applicant institution must provide proof of qualification as a non-profit, charitable entity (IRS determination letter).
Type: Scholarship
Value: US$30,000
Length of Study: Three (3) months to one (1) year
Country of Study: Any country
Closing Date: 1 December
Additional Information: www.nref.org/-/media/files/nref/ NREFDirectedResidencyScholarshipApplicationInstructions andFAQs82721

For further information contact:

Lauren Coleman Kathryn A. Dattomo, MNA, CAE, CFRE NREF Development Coordinator.

Tel: (1) 847 378 0535
Email: kam@nref.org

NREF Clinical Fellowship Grant

Purpose: The objective of the fellowship grant is to fund post-residency clinical fellowships in the specialty of neurosurgery. Any academic institution or group practice with an established neurosurgery residency program in North America that qualifies as a non-profit, charitable entity may apply. A for-profit entity is not eligible unless affiliated with a non-profit entity. The NREF strongly encourages institutions to be accredited by CAST, but exceptions may be considered by the selection committee.
Eligibility: Applicants must be neurosurgeons, no more than two years from having completed their neurosurgical residency training, and/or clinical fellowship, who are full-time faculty in North American teaching institutions.
Level of Study: Postdoctorate
Type: Award
Value: Up to US$75,000
Length of Study: 1 year

Frequency: Annual

Country of Study: Any country

Application Procedure: Complete an application for each subspecialty for which funding is requested. However, based on an evaluation of proposals from recent awardees, here are factors to consider when applying 1. Is the training environment supportive? Does the institution offer strong mentorship? 2. Does the institution have Accreditation Council for Graduate Medical Education (ACGME) certification for neurosurgery residency program or the Canadian equivalent? 3. Has the institution applied for CAST accreditation, but not yet received CAST accreditation? Have they submitted a copy of the CAST accreditation request with the application? The NREF strongly encourages institutions to be accredited by CAST, but exceptions may be considered by the selection committee. 3. NOTE Including these elements should not be interpreted as a guarantee of an award.

Closing Date: 1 December

Funding: Private

Contributor: Corporations and membership

Additional Information: www.nref.org/-/media/Files/NREF/2022-23_CFG_Application_Instructions-FAQs.ashx

For further information contact:

5550 Meadowbrook Industrial Ct., Rolling Meadows, IL 60008, United States of America.

Tel: (1) 847 378 0535
Email: lcoleman@nref.org

NREF Research Fellowship Grant

Purpose: Open to residents only, the NREF Research Fellowship Grant provides funding for neurosurgeons preparing for academic careers as clinician investigators. Applicants must be physicians who are currently accepted into an approved residency training program in neurological surgery within North America. One hundred percent of the resident's research effort during the funding period of this grant should be devoted to the project.

Eligibility: Applicants must be neurosurgeons, no more than two years from having completed their neurosurgical residency training, and/or clinical fellowship, who are full-time faculty in North American teaching institutions.

Level of Study: Postdoctorate

Type: Award

Value: Up to US$50,000

Length of Study: 1 year

Frequency: Annual

Country of Study: Any country

Application Procedure: Complete an application for each category for which funding is requested. The format of the application is flexible. However, based on an evaluation of proposals from recent awardees, here are factors to consider when applying 1. Does the research have potential for extramural funding? Is there strong preliminary data? 2. Does the project represent a new direction from existing research efforts? Is the study innovative? 3. What is the societal impact and potential applications of the research? Would a positive outcome contribute to the field? 4. Are the goals, objective and anticipated results clearly defined, logical and well-described in the proposal? Is the scope of the project realistic for timeframe? 5. Is the research environment supportive? Does the institution offer strong mentorship? 6. NOTE Including these elements should not be interpreted as a guarantee of an award.

Closing Date: 1 November

Funding: Private

Contributor: Corporations and membership

Additional Information: www.nref.org/research/medical-student-fellowships

For further information contact:

5550 Meadowbrook Industrial Ct., Rolling Meadows, IL 60008, United States of America.

Tel: (1) 847 378 0535
Email: lcoleman@nref.org

NREF Young Clinician Investigator Award

Purpose: The NREF Young Clinician Investigator Award supports junior faculty pursuing careers as clinical investigators. Applicants must be neurosurgeons, no more than two years from completing neurosurgical residency training or clinical fellowship, who are full-time faculty in North American teaching institutions. Fifty percent of the young clinician investigator's efforts during the funding period of this grant should be devoted to research, but exceptions can be considered.

Eligibility: Applicants must be neurosurgeons, no more than two years from having completed their neurosurgical residency training, and/or clinical fellowship, who are full-time faculty in North American teaching institutions.

Level of Study: Postdoctorate

Type: Award

Value: Up to US$50,000
Length of Study: 1 year
Frequency: Annual
Country of Study: Any country
Application Procedure: Complete an application for each category for which funding is requested. The format of the application is flexible. However, based on an evaluation of proposals from recent awardees, here are factors to consider when applying 1. Does the research have potential for extramural funding? Is there strong preliminary data? 2. Does the project represent a new direction from existing research efforts? Is the study innovative? 3. What is the societal impact and potential applications of the research? Would a positive outcome contribute to the field? 4. Are the goals, objective and anticipated results clearly defined, logical and well-described in the proposal? Is the scope of the project realistic for timeframe? 5. Is the research environment supportive? Does the institution offer strong mentorship? 6. NOTE Including these elements should not be interpreted as a guarantee of an award.
Closing Date: 1 November
Funding: Private
Contributor: Corporations and membership
Additional Information: www.nref.org/-/media/Files/NREF/2022-23_RG-YCI_Application_Instructions-FAQs.ashx

For further information contact:

5550 Meadowbrook Industrial Ct., Rolling Meadows, IL 60008, United States of America.

Tel: (1) 847 378 0535
Email: lcoleman@nref.org

The William P. Van Wagenen Fellowship

Purpose: The William P. Van Wagenen Fellowship was established by the estate of Dr. Van Wagenen, one of the founders and the first President of the Harvey Cushing Society, now the AANS.
Eligibility: Application should be submitted with letters of reference, including one from the applicant's Program Director. A letter from the proposed sponsor and documentation of intent to pursue an academic career, while not required, will strengthen the application.
Type: Fellowship
Value: Up to US$120,000 stipend, travel and living allowance of US$6,000, US$15,000 of research support, US$5,000 for medical insurance.
Frequency: Annual
Country of Study: Any country

Closing Date: 1 October
Additional Information: www.aans.org/en/Trainees/Grants-and-Fellowships/Van-Wagenen-Fellowship

New England Culinary Institute (NECI)

Admissions Office, 56 College Street, Montpelier, VT 05602, United States of America.

Tel: (1) 877 223 324
Website: www.neci.edu

New England Culinary Institute (NECI) opened in 1980, the school offered an experience that was different from any other culinary school. NECI is small and intimate by design. NECI is student centered and students participate in shared governance. A NECI education propels you out into the real world, building your professional network and finding your place in the fascinating food and beverage industry. A NECI education opens a world of possibilities!

Cabot Scholarships

Purpose: To encourage and support students who are committed to furthering their education and enhancing their careers in the restaurant and food service industry
Eligibility: Open to candidates who are current resident of Vermont, New York, Maine, New Hampshire, Connecticut, Rhode Island or Massachusetts
Level of Study: Professional development
Type: Scholarship
Value: US$100,000
Length of Study: 1 year
Frequency: Annual
Study Establishment: New England Culinary Institute
Country of Study: United States of America
Application Procedure: Applicant must submit a complete application form to New England Culinary Institute
Closing Date: 18 January
Additional Information: www.cabotschools.org/news/10159/cabot+scholarship+foundation+application++deadline+20212022

For further information contact:

Tel: (1) 501 843 3562
Email: lindac@neci.edu

New South Wales Architects Registration Board

NSW Architects Registration Board, Level 2, 156 Gloucester Street, Sydney, NSW 2000, Australia.

Tel: (61) 2 9241 4033
Email: mail@architects.nsw.gov.au
Website: www.architects.nsw.gov.au
Contact: Ms Mae Cruz, Deputy Registrar

The NSW Architects Registration Board (ARB) administers the Architects Act - the legislation regulating architects in NSW. When the Act was introduced in to NSW parliament, the aim was a community actively discussing architecture that is contributing to its wellbeing, a community that is serviced by architects who have a robust professional framework and a flexible system of professional discipline.

Byera Hadley Travelling Scholarships

Purpose: The purpose of the Byera Hadley Travelling Scholarships (BHTS) is to provide financial support for the promotion and encouragement of students and/or graduates in architecture to undertake a course of study, research, or other activity approved by the Board.
Eligibility: Applicants for the Scholarship must be a student or a graduate of an accredited architecture program offered by a NSW university.
Level of Study: Masters Degree, Research
Type: Scholarship
Value: US$30,000
Frequency: Annual
Country of Study: Any country
Closing Date: 31 August
Additional Information: www.architects.nsw.gov.au/download/Byera%20Hadley%20Application%20Form.pdf?v=20210521

For further information contact:

Tel: (61) 2 9241 4033
Email: mail@architects.nsw.gov.au

Client Service Excellence Award

Purpose: To encourage excellence in the professional services offered by architects

Eligibility: Open to all architects registered in New South Wales (NSW) who have completed projects in the last 2 years in NSW not exceeding AU$4 million
Level of Study: Unrestricted
Type: Award
Value: AU$5,000
Frequency: Annual
Country of Study: Any country
Application Procedure: For further information about the Client Service Excellence Award contact the Registrar of the NSW Architects Registration Board on (61) 2 9241 4033. Check website for further details
Closing Date: 28 September
Contributor: Victorian Architects Registration Board
Additional Information: Architect, architect corporations, and firms should have two nominations from clients www.nserc-crsng.gc.ca/Students-Etudiants/PG-CS/BellandPostgrad-BelletSuperieures_eng.asp

For further information contact:

Email: awards@rcsa.com.au

New South Wales Ministry of the Arts

Level 9 St James Centre, 111 Elizabeth Street, PO Box A226, Sydney, NSW 1235, Australia.

Tel: (61) 1800 358 594, (61) 2 8218 2222
Email: mail@arts.nsw.gov.au
Website: www.arts.nsw.gov.au

New South Wales Ministry of the Arts works closely with the State's 8 major cultural institutions, providing policy advice to Government on their operations.

Western Sydney Artists Fellowship

Purpose: To encourage artists and students in the field of creative arts
Eligibility: Open to applicants who are residents of Western Sydney or whose practice is located primarily in Western Sydney
Level of Study: Postgraduate
Type: Fellowship
Value: AU$5,000–25,000
Length of Study: 1 year
Frequency: Annual

Study Establishment: New South Wales, Sydney Western Suburbs
Country of Study: Australia
Closing Date: September

For further information contact:

Email: mail@create.nsw.gov.au

New York Foundation for the Arts (NYFA)

20 Jay Street, Suite 740, Brooklyn, NY 11201, United States of America.

Tel: (1) 212 366 6900
Website: www.nyfa.org

New York Foundation for the Arts (NYFA) is a 501(c)(3) service organization that provides artists, emerging arts organizations, arts administrators, and students with critical support, professional development tools, and resources for defining and achieving career success.

"Made in NY" Women's Film, TV and Theatre Fund

Purpose: "Made in NY" Women's Film, TV and Theatre Fund provides grants to encourage and support the creation of film, television, digital, and live theatre content that reflects the voices and perspectives of all who identify as women
Eligibility: In addition to being made by, for, or about all who identify as women, projects are eligible if they feature a strong female perspective; and/or include a female director; and/or include a meaningful female producer credit; and/or include a meaningful female writing credit; and/or include a female protagonist(s). Projects must also meet the "Made in NY" criteria as described in the program guideline.
Level of Study: Unrestricted
Type: A variable number of grants
Value: US$20,000–US$50,000
Frequency: Annual
Country of Study: Any country
Application Procedure: All applications must be submitted online at apply.nyfa.org/submit. Applications open in the summer, and close in the fall

No. of awards offered: 568
Closing Date: October
Funding: Government
Contributor: The City of New York Mayor's Office of Media and Entertainment (MOME)
No. of awards given last year: 60
No. of applicants last year: 568

Canadian Women Artists' Award

Purpose: The Canadian Women Artists' Award is open to emerging or early career artists in New York State. The C$5,000 award is designed to provide financial support to an emerging or early career artist working in any discipline, and can be used in any manner the recipient deems necessary to further their artistic goals.
Eligibility: The Canadian Women Artist's Award is open to women artists who meet the following requirements Must be a Canadian citizen, and able to provide proof of citizenship with legal documentation upon receipt of the award; Must be between the ages of 21 and 35 before the application deadline; Must be a current resident of New York, New Jersey, or Connecticut; Must apply in only one of the eligible discipline categories; Must be the originators of the work, i.e. choreographers or playwrights; not awarded to interpretative artists such as dancers or actors; Must not be a previous recipient of the Canadian Women Artist's Award; Must not be a NYFA employee, member of the NYFA Board of Trustees or Artists' Advisory Committee, and/or an immediate family member of any of the previous.
Level of Study: Unrestricted
Type: Award
Value: C$5,000
Frequency: Annual
Country of Study: Any country
Application Procedure: All applicants must apply online at www.apply.nyfa.org/submit. The application cycle runs through the Spring, opening in March and closing in May.
No. of awards offered: 82
Closing Date: May
Funding: Foundation, Private
Contributor: The Canadian Women's Club (CWC) of New York
No. of awards given last year: 1
No. of applicants last year: 82
Additional Information: www.nyfa.org/awards-grants/canadian-women-artists-award/

New York State Council on the Arts/New York Foundation for the Arts Artist Fellowship

Purpose: This grant is awarded in fifteen different disciplines over a three-year period (five categories a year) and the application is free to complete. The NYSCA/NYFA Artist Fellowship is not a project grant, but is intended to fund an artist's vision or voice, at all levels of their artistic development.

Eligibility: 1. 25 years or older 2. Current residents of New York State and/or one of the Indian Nations located in New York State 3. Must have maintained New York State residency, and/or residency in one of the Indian Nations located therein, for at least the last two consecutive years 4. Cannot be enrolled in a degree-seeking program of any kind 5. Are the originators of the work, i.e. choreographers or playwrights, not interpretive artists such as dancers or actors 6. Did not receive a NYSCA/NYFA Artist Fellowship in any discipline in the past five consecutive years 7. Cannot submit any work samples that have been previously awarded a NYSCA/NYFA Artist Fellowship 8. While collaborating artists are eligible to apply, the total number of collaborators cannot exceed three 9. Are not a current NYFA employee or have been in the last 12 months, a member of the NYFA Board of Trustees or Artists' Advisory Committee, immediate family member of any of the aforementioned, or an immediate family member of a 2023–2024 panelist 10. Artists that have been awarded five NYSCA/NYFA Artist Fellowships receive Emeritus status and are no longer eligible for the award.

Type: Fellowship

Value: US$7,000

Length of Study: Unrestricted

Frequency: Annual

Country of Study: Any country

Application Procedure: NYFA only accepts applications online via www.apply.nyfa.org/submit

Additional Information: www.nyfa.org/awards-grants/artist-fellowships/

For further information contact:

New York Foundation for the Arts, 20 Jay Street, Suite 740, Brooklyn, NY 11201, United States of America.

Rauschenberg Emergency Grants

Purpose: New York Foundation for the Arts (NYFA) is proud to partner with the Robert Rauschenberg Foundation to administer a new emergency grant program called Rauschenberg Emergency Grants. This marks the first phase of a program that will be in the tradition of Change, Inc., a non-profit foundation established in 1970 by Robert Rauschenberg to assist professional artists of all disciplines in need of emergency medical aid.

Eligibility: Open to visual and media artists and choreographers. If you aren't sure if your artistic discipline fits within these guidelines, please contact emergencyfunds@nyfa.org. 1. Open to artists who are U.S. citizens or permanent residents in the United States, District of Columbia, or U.S. Territories. 2. Applicants must demonstrate current and ongoing activity in artistic discipline/s. 3. Applicants cannot be enrolled in any degree-seeking program.

Type: Grant

Value: US$5,000 ($100,000)

Frequency: Annual

Country of Study: Any country

No. of awards offered: 20

Closing Date: 31 July

Additional Information: www.nyfa.org/awards-grants/rauschenberg-dancer-emergency-grants/

For further information contact:

New York Foundation for the Arts, 20 Jay Street, Suite 740, Brooklyn, NY 11201, United States of America.

Email: emergencyfunds@nyfa.org

Recharge Foundation Fellowship for New Surrealist Art

Purpose: The New York Foundation for the Arts (NYFA) created the Recharge Foundation Fellowship for New Surrealist Art, a US$5,000 award for painters living in the United States and U.S. Territories who are working in the New Surrealist style. The award program is administered by NYFA with funding provided by the Gu Family of the Recharge Foundation.

Type: Award

Value: US$5,000

Frequency: Annual

Application Procedure: The JGS Fellowship for Photography is open to New York State photography artists, living and working anywhere in the following regions of New York State Western New York, Finger Lakes, Southern Tier, Central New York, North Country, Mohawk Valley, Capital District, Hudson Valley, and Long Island. 1. Applicants must work in photography. 2. Applicants can work in traditional and experimental photography or any form in which photography or photographic techniques are pivotal, if not exclusive.

3. Applicants must be a current full-time resident of New York State and have lived full-time in one of the regions listed above for a minimum of 12 months at the time applications close. 4. Applicant must be at least 25 years of age at the time the application closes. 5. Students in bachelor's or master's degree programs of any kind are not eligible to apply. 6. All past recipients of any NYFA grant or Fellowship are eligible to apply. 7. NYFA employees, members of the NYFA Board of Trustees or Artists' Advisory Committee, and/or an immediate family member of any of the above cannot apply.

Closing Date: 15 May

Additional Information: www.nyfa.org/Content/Show/The-Recharge-Foundation-Fellowship-for-New-Surrealist-Art

New York University

27 West Fourth Street, New York, NY 10003, United States of America.

Tel: (1) 212 998 4550
Website: www.nyu.edu/

NYU has been an innovator in higher education, reaching out to an emerging middle class, embracing an urban identity and professional focus, and promoting a global vision that informs its 19 schools and colleges. Today, that trailblazing spirit makes NYU one of the most prominent and respected research universities in the world, featuring top-ranked academic programs and accepting fewer than one-in-five undergraduates.

Provost's Postdoctoral Fellowship Program

Purpose: New York University's Provost's Postdoctoral Fellowship Program was created to attract and support a wide range of brilliant young scholars and educators from diverse backgrounds whose research experience, life experience, and employment background can significantly contribute to academic excellence. The program provides fellows with faculty mentoring, professional development, and academic networking opportunities. The ultimate goal of the program is for participants to join the ranks of faculty at competitive institutions.

Eligibility: 1. Successfully complete their two-year fellowship assignment at NYU 2. Dedicate their scholarship towards producing high quality research 3. Regularly meet and collaborate with their mentors 4. Actively participate in professional advancement events.

Level of Study: Postgraduate

Type: Fellowship

Value: US$62,000 nine-month salary, research allowance ($2,000), one-time relocation fees (up to US$3,000)

Frequency: Annual

Country of Study: Any country

Closing Date: 22 November

Funding: Private

Additional Information: www.nyu.edu/faculty/faculty-diversity-and-inclusion/mentoring-and-professional-development/provosts-postdoctoral-fellowship-program/about.html

For further information contact:

383 Lafayette Street, New York, NY 10003, United States of America.

Email: admissions.ops@nyu.edu

University Distinguished Teaching Awards

Purpose: Established in 1987, the Distinguished Teaching Award (DTA) highlights New York University's commitment to teaching excellence and is given annually to selected outstanding members of the faculty. Recipients are presented with a research stipend.

Eligibility: Only full-time faculty members with at least ten years of service at NYU. Please note that while current adjuncts are not eligible for consideration, current full-time faculty may count past adjunct service towards the ten-year eligibility requirement. Past winners of the award may not be renominated. Please review the list of previous winners before nominating. Faculty members must hold one of the following job titles: Professor, Associate Professor, Assistant Professor Clinical Professor, Clinical Associate Professor, Clinical Assistant Professor Research Professor, Research Associate Professor, Research Assistant Professor Industry Assistant Professor, Industry Associate Professor, Industry Full Professor, Lecturer and Senior Lecturer Master Teacher, Teacher Arts Professor, Arts Associate Professor, Arts Assistant Professor

Type: Award

Value: Recipients are presented with a research stipend.

Frequency: Annual

Country of Study: Any country

Closing Date: 16 February

Additional Information: docs.google.com/document/d/1ZhfsctdkTnFmr9GLKUP9kp1vSlBWNXlJl_KSmGfMfx8/edit#

For further information contact:

Email: facultyadvance@nyu.edu.

New York University Academic and Science

Tel: (1) 212 998 6880
Email: cas.alumni@nyu.edu

NYU has been an innovator in higher education, reaching out to an emerging middle class, embracing an urban identity and professional focus, and promoting a global vision that informs its 19 schools and colleges. The core of New York University is the academic enterprise. The best students and faculty are drawn to the University by the allure of being part of a compelling intellectual and creative enterprise - a community of scholars characterized by collaboration, innovation, and incandescent teaching.

Rangel Graduate Fellowship Program

Subjects: Foreign Service
Purpose: The Rangel Graduate Fellowship is a program that aims to attract and prepare outstanding young people for careers in the Foreign Service of the U.S. Department of State in which they can help formulate, represent and implement U.S. foreign policy.
Eligibility: 1. Applicants must be seeking admission to enter graduate school in the fall for a two-year program at a United States university in an area of relevance to the Foreign Service. They can be in their senior year of their undergraduate studies, graduating by June, or they can be college graduates. 2. Applicants must have a cumulative grade point average of 3.2 or higher on a 4.0 scale at the time of application. 3. Applicants must be United States citizen.
Level of Study: Masters Degree
Type: Fellowship
Value: Up to US$42,000 annually for a two year period for tuition, room, board, books and mandatory fees.
Frequency: Annual
Country of Study: United States of America
Application Procedure: Applicants apply to two-year graduate programs at U.S. universities simultaneously with their application to the Rangel Program.
No. of awards offered: 45
Closing Date: 14 October
Funding: Private
Additional Information: www.rangelprogram.org/graduate-fellowship-program/

For further information contact:

2218 6th Street NW, Washington, DC 20059, United States of America.

Tel: (1) 202 806 4367
Email: rangelprogram@howard.edu

New Zealand Aid Programme

195 Lambton Quay, Private Bag 18 901, Wellington 6160, New Zealand.

Tel: (64) 4 439 8000
Contact: Ministry of Foreign Affairs and Trade

The purpose of New Zealand's aid is to develop shared prosperity and stability in the Pacific and beyond, drawing on the best of New Zealand's knowledge and skills. We support sustainable development in developing countries to reduce poverty and contribute to a more secure, equitable and prosperous world.

New Zealand Pacific Scholarships

Purpose: A particular focus of NZPS is to increase the number of young pacific people studying in New Zealand and to build a new generation of Pacific leadership with strong links to New Zealand
Type: Scholarship
Country of Study: Any country
Application Procedure: For application procedure, please refer website www.mfat.govt.nz/en/aid-and-development/scholarships/how-to-apply/
Closing Date: 28 March
Additional Information: scholarship-positions.com/new-zealand-pacific-scholarships-for-pacific-countries/2011/06/11/

For further information contact:

Email: studentinfo@auckland.ac.nz

Newberry Library

60 West Walton Street, Chicago, IL 60610-3380, United States of America.

Tel: (1) 312 943 9090
Email: research@newberry.org
Website: www.newberry.org
Contact: Research and Education

The Newberry Library supports and inspires research, teaching, and learning in the humanities. The Newberry collection some 1.6 million books, 600,000 maps, and 5 million manuscript pages is a portal to more than six centuries of human history, from the Middle Ages to the present. We connect researchers and visitors with our collection in the Newberry's reading rooms, exhibition galleries, program spaces, classrooms, and online digital resources.

Associated Colleges of the Midwest/the Great Lakes Colleges Association Faculty Fellowships

Purpose: This fellowship supports faculty from the colleges of the Associated Colleges of the Midwest and the Great Lakes Colleges Association, Inc.

Eligibility: Applicants can come from any of the colleges in ACM or GLCA, from any discipline.

Type: Fellowship

Value: Fellows teach a small group of select undergraduate students in an advanced research seminar.

Application Procedure: Potential applicants should contact Joan Gillespie at the ACM.

Closing Date: 15 March

Additional Information: For more information, visit the Associated Colleges of the Midwest's call for proposals at www.acm.edu/programs/14/newberry/index.html

For further information contact:

535 West William, Suite 301, Ann Arbor, Michigan 48103, United States of America.

Tel: (1) 734 661 2350

Long-Term Fellowships

Purpose: Long-Term Fellowships are intended to support individual scholarly research and promote serious intellectual exchange through active participation in the Newberry's scholarly activities, including Fellows' Seminars and Weekly Colloquium.

Eligibility: Long-Term Fellowships are open only to post-doctoral scholars who have been awarded the PhD degree or other equivalent terminal degree by the Newberry's application deadline. United States citizens are eligible for all Newberry Fellowships. Permanent United States residents who have had at least three years of continuous residence in the U.S. are eligible for all fellowships. Recent United States residents who have had less than three years of continuous residence in the U.S. are eligible for all fellowships except the National Endowment for the Humanities (NEH) Fellowships. Citizens of foreign nations are eligible for all fellowships except the National Endowment for the Humanities (NEH) Fellowships. Only applicants of North

American Indian heritage are eligible for the Susan Kelly Power and Helen Hornbeck Tanner and Frances C. Allen Fellowships.

Level of Study: Postgraduate

Type: Fellowships

Value: US$5,000 per month

Length of Study: 4 to 9 months

Frequency: Annual

Study Establishment: The Newberry Library

Country of Study: United States of America

Application Procedure: For more information on eligibility, guidelines, and the application process, please visit www.newberry.org/how-apply. Fellowship applicants are required to submit the following material 1. A project abstract of no more than 300 words (approximately 2000 characters) that communicates the significance of the project to the Newberry's review panel, which consists of humanities scholars with wide areas of expertise. 2. A project description of no more than 1500 words. 3. A current Curriculum Vitae (CV) of no more than 5 pages. 4. Letter(s) of recommendation.

Closing Date: 1 November

Funding: Private

Additional Information: www.newberry.org/long-term-fellowships

Rudolph Ganz Fellowship

Purpose: The Rudolph Ganz Fellowship is a new opportunity at the Newberry Library. The fellowship is intended to support research using the Rudolph Ganz Papers and other late nineteenth- and early twentieth-century materials related to Chicago music in that period. The Rudolph Ganz Papers include the musical compositions of this world-renowned concert pianist, composer, conductor, and educator, as well as articles, speeches, lectures and essays by him, and two recordings. Also in the collection is correspondence to and from prominent musical figures, family correspondence, clippings, photographs, programs, and some artifacts.

Eligibility: Applicants must demonstrate a specific need for the Newberry's collection. For additional information about eligibility requirements and application guidelines, please check the website www.newberry.org/fellowships

Type: Scholarship

Value: Short-Term Fellowships are generally awarded for one continuous month in residence at the Newberry, with stipends of US$2,500 per month

Country of Study: United States of America

Closing Date: 15 December

Additional Information: www.networks.h-net.org/node/73374/announcements/85457/rudolph-ganz-fellowship

Weiss/Brown Publication Subvention Award

Subjects: Music, theater, cultural studies, or French or Italian literature.

Purpose: The purpose of this award is to enable the publication of works of the highest quality either by making it possible to publish a work in a particularly appropriate way (with special typography plates, or appendices, for example) that would otherwise be prohibitively expensive; or by significantly reducing the cover price, allowing the publication to reach a wider audience.

Eligibility: 1. United States citizens are eligible for all Newberry Fellowships. 2. Permanent United States residents who have had at least three years of continuous residence in the U.S. are eligible for all fellowships. 3. Recent United States residents who have had less than three years of continuous residence in the U.S. are eligible for all fellowships except the National Endowment for the Humanities (NEH) Fellowships. 4. Citizens of foreign nations are eligible for all fellowships except the National Endowment for the Humanities (NEH) Fellowships. 5. Only applicants of North American Indian heritage are eligible for the Susan Kelly Power and Helen Hornbeck Tanner and Frances C. Allen Fellowships.

Type: Award

Value: Up to US$8,000

Frequency: Annual

Country of Study: United States of America

Application Procedure: For more information, please see www.newberry.org/how-apply. Fellowship applicants are required to submit the following material 1. A project abstract of no more than 300 words (approximately 2000 characters) that communicates the significance of the project to the Newberry's review panel, which consists of humanities scholars with wide areas of expertise. 2. A project description of no more than 1500 words. 3. A current Curriculum Vitae (CV) of no more than 5 pages. 4. Letter(s) of recommendation.

Closing Date: 15 February

Additional Information: www.newberry.org/publication-subvention

Newcastle University

Manager, Student Financial Support, Newcastle University, King's Gate, Newcastle upon Tyne NE1 7RU, United Kingdom.

Tel: (44) 191 208 6000
Website: www.ncl.ac.uk/
Contact: Mrs Rencesova Irena, Student Financial Support Officer

Newcastle University experts are protecting cultural property and preserving unique archives around the world We are a world-leading university, advancing knowledge, providing creative solutions, and addressing global problems.

Advancing Women in Leadership Scholarship (MBA)

Purpose: The scholarship will support innovative business women who aspire to higher levels of influence and professional development.

Eligibility: 1. Applicant must hold a conditional or unconditional offer of admission to the Full-time MBA programme of 2023 entry. 2. Applicant must have substantive managerial experience (normally 6 years or more, minimum 3 years). 3. Applicant must Hold the equivalent of 60% in honours degree, or Demonstrate relevant work experience above the minimum plus significant career progression may also be considered. 4. Applicants must perform well at interview. 5. Applicant must hold English language qualification of IELTS 6.5 or its equivalent with no subskill below 6.0.

Level of Study: MBA

Type: Scholarship

Value: A full fee award of £22,800, payable towards the cost of tuition fees.

Frequency: Annual

Study Establishment: Newcastle University Business School

Country of Study: Any country

Application Procedure: Applications and essays will be reviewed by a panel of judges. Candidates need to complete the online application form. www.forms.ncl.ac.uk/view.php?id=2981403

Closing Date: 5 April

Funding: Private

Contributor: Newcastle University Business School

Additional Information: www.scholarshubafrica.com/34923/advancing-women-leadership-scholarship-mba-newcastle-university-uk/

For further information contact:

Tel: (44) 191 208 1589
Email: mba@ncl.ac.uk

British Marshall Scholarships

Purpose: The British Marshall Scholarships will finance two years of postgraduate and occasionally, undergraduate study in the UK. The scholarships cover fares to and from the United States, university tuition fees, cost of living expenses, book, thesis, research and daily travel allowances, and where applicable, a contribution towards the support of a dependent spouse.

Eligibility: You may be eligible to apply for one of 40 competitive awards if you meet the following criteria 1. You are a United States citizen (at the time you take up your Scholarship). 2. Hold a first degree from an accredited four-year college or university in the United States with a minimum GPA of 3.7. 3. Aged under 26.

Level of Study: Postgraduate

Type: Scholarship

Value: Varies

Length of Study: Two years duration.

Frequency: Annual

Country of Study: United Kingdom

Application Procedure: For further information about the scholarship and details on eligibility and applications, contact the Marshall Aid Commemoration Commission.

No. of awards offered: 40

Funding: Private

Contributor: The Marshall Aid Commemoration Commission.

Additional Information: www.ncl.ac.uk/postgraduate/funding/sources/internationalnoneustudents/bmarshall.html

For further information contact:

Woburn House 20-24 Tavistock Square, London WC1H 9HF, United Kingdom.

Email: apps@marshallscholarship.org

European Excellence Scholarship (MBA)

Purpose: Our MBA provides an inclusive, diverse and collaborative learning community that educates and develops our students to be creative, innovative, enterprising and global in their outlook.

Eligibility: To be eligible for this full-fee scholarship you must meet the following criteria 1. Completed the scholarship application form including submitting an essay of no more than 1,500 words in response to the question listed. Submissions need to be in English. 2. Hold a conditional or unconditional offer of admission to the Full-time MBA programme entry. 3. Have substantive managerial experience (minimum 3 years prior to starting the MBA) preferably hold the equivalent of a United Kingdom 21 honours degree (however, applicants who do not meet this requirement but can demonstrate relevant work experience above the minimum plus significant career progression may also be considered). 4. Perform well at interview across all competency areas. 5. Hold an English language

qualification of IELTS 6.5 or its equivalent with no subskill below 6.0 (if your first language is not English). 6. Be assessed as an European Union student for fee paying purposes.

Level of Study: Postgraduate

Type: Scholarship

Frequency: Annual

Country of Study: Any country

Application Procedure: Applications and essays will be reviewed by a panel of judges. Candidates need to complete the online application form.

Closing Date: 5 April

Funding: Private

Additional Information: www.ncl.ac.uk/business-school/courses/scholarships/mba/

For further information contact:

Tel: (44) 191 208 1589
Email: mba@ncl.ac.uk

Humanities and Social Sciences Postgraduate Scholarships

Purpose: The Faculty of Humanities and Social Sciences at Newcastle University is pleased to offer Humanities and Social Sciences Postgraduate scholarships to assist non-UK European Union nationals to study a postgraduate Master's degree.

Eligibility: To be considered for awards applicants must 1. Hold the equivalent of a first class UK honours degree. 2. Have an offer for an eligible, full time, taught postgraduate degree programme within the Faculty of Humanities and Social Sciences. Applicants applying to Newcastle University Business School are not eligible for these awards. 3. Must be non UK European Union nationals and must be classed as EU for fee paying purposes. 4. Eligible candidates will be assessed as part of their academic application.

Level of Study: Postgraduate

Type: Scholarship

Value: £2,000 tuition fee awards.

Frequency: Annual

Country of Study: United Kingdom

Application Procedure: Eligible candidates will automatically be considered for a Humanities and Social Sciences Postgraduate Scholarship as part of their academic course application.

Closing Date: September

Funding: Private

Additional Information: www.ncl.ac.uk//postgraduate/funding/sources/ukeustudents/hsspgs20.html

Indonesia Endowment Fund for Education (LPDP)

Purpose: The Indonesia Endowment Fund (LPDP) provides funding for high achieving Indonesian students undertaking Master's or PhD study. It forms part of the Indonesian government's aim to nurture young talented individuals, enabling them to become future leaders

Eligibility: For detailed information about the eligiblity, check the website

Level of Study: Postgraduate

Type: Funding support

Value: The scholarship covers tuition fees and living expenses

Frequency: Annual

Study Establishment: Ministry of Finance and Minister of Research, Technology and Higher Education

Country of Study: Any country

Application Procedure: For detailed information grants, check the following link, www.lpdp.kemenkeu.go.id

Closing Date: October

Funding: Private

Contributor: Lembaga Pengelolaan Dana Pendidikan (LPDP)

Additional Information: www.ncl.ac.uk/postgraduate/funding/sources/internationalnoneustudents/lpdp19.html

For further information contact:

Email: cso.lpdp@kemenkeu.go.id

International Family Discounts (IFD)

Purpose: We offer discounts to encourage relatives of our current international students, and past international graduates, to pursue their studies at Newcastle University.

Eligibility: 1. This discount is only available to students studying at the Newcastle city campus. 2. The University offers partial discounts to close relatives (husband, wife, brother, sister, mother, father, son or daughter) of students and graduates, who have been assessed as International for fees purposes, and who wish to pursue their studies at Newcastle University in currently studying here. 3. Students may only apply for a discount if they are registered as a student at the University or after they have been offered a place to study on their chosen degree programme, and have been assessed as International for fees purposes.

Level of Study: Postgraduate

Type: Award

Value: 10% of the tuition fee per year.

Length of Study: Duration of the degree programme.

Frequency: Annual

Country of Study: Any country

Application Procedure: Please complete the online International Family Discount application form in accordance with the IFD regulations.

Funding: Private

Additional Information: www.ncl.ac.uk/postgraduate/funding/sources/internationalnoneustudents/ifd.html

For further information contact:

Newcastle upon Tyne NE1 7RU, United Kingdom.

Tel: (44) 191 208 5537
Email: scholarship.applications@ncl.ac.uk

Master of Arts (Taught Masters) Scholarships in the School of Modern Languages

Purpose: The School of Modern Languages is offering competitive scholarships to outstanding applicants for the following programmes MA programmes in Translating and Interpreting (Chinese) MA in Professional Translating for European Languages (French, German, Italian, Spanish) MA Film Theory and Practice.

Eligibility: Home, European Union and International Students are eligible to apply.

Level of Study: Postgraduate

Type: Scholarship

Value: £5,000

Frequency: Annual

Country of Study: Any country

Application Procedure: In order to apply for the scholarship, check the website. www.ncl.ac.uk/sml/study/funding/#currentopportunities

Closing Date: 7 June

Funding: Private

Contributor: SML Postgraduate Officer

For further information contact:

Tel: (44) 191 208 5867
Email: modlang.pgadmin@ncl.ac.uk

Master of Arts in Art Museum and Gallery Studies Scholarship

Purpose: The Art Museum and Gallery Studies MA provides students with the opportunity to develop skills as a curator or gallery educator in the fields of both historical and contemporary art.

Eligibility: The studentships are open to United Kingdom, European Union and international applicants who hold, or expect to achieve a minimum of a 2.1 Honours degree

N

(or international equivalent) in fine art or an art related subject. We welcome applications from all sections of the community regardless of race, ethnicity, gender or sexuality, and wish to encourage applications from traditionally underrepresented groups in United Kingdom higher education. International students If your first language is not English you must also meet our English language requirements.

Level of Study: Professional development
Type: Scholarship
Value: £3,000
Frequency: Annual
Country of Study: Any country
Application Procedure: You must apply through the University's online postgraduate application system. To do this please 'Create a new account'. All relevant fields should be completed, but fields marked with a red asterisk must be completed. The following information will help us to process your application. You will need to 1. Insert the programme code 4138F in the programme of study section. 2. Select 'Art Museum and Gallery Studies (full time)' as the programme of study. 3. Insert the studentship code SAC025 in the studentship/partnership reference field. 4. Attach a personal statement of no more than 500 words outlining. i. Your preparedness to undertake the Art Museum and Gallery Studies MA. ii. Your aspirations for a career in the art museum and gallery sector.
Closing Date: 30 April
Funding: Private
Additional Information: www.ncl.ac.uk/postgraduate/courses/degrees/art-museum-gallery-studies-ma-pgdip/#profile

For further information contact:

Email: gerard.corsane@ncl.ac.uk

Master of Business Administration Business Excellence Scholarships

Purpose: The main aim of this programme is to provide financial help and support candidates in achieving their career goals by providing awards of £8,000, payable towards the cost of tuition fees. So, all the interested candidates can apply for the programme.
Eligibility: 1. Eligible Countries Applications are accepted from around the world. 2. Eligible Course or Subjects MBA degree programme in Business Excellence at the Newcastle University. 3. Must hold a conditional or unconditional offer of admission to the MBA programme. 4. Must have substantive managerial experience (normally four years or more, minimum of three years). 5. Must preferably hold the

equivalent of a UK 21 honours degree. 6. Must have to perform well at interview across all competency areas.
Level of Study: MBA
Type: Scholarship
Value: £8,000
Frequency: Annual
Study Establishment: Newcastle University Business School
Country of Study: Any country
Application Procedure: To be considered for the programme applicants must have to take admission at the university. After that No other application required. All candidates will be assessed at the time of interview for this Scholarship. Applicants must submit the following documents previous year degree, a CV, Certificates to confirm your degree or highest qualification - if your degree is complete, a copy of passport, and a personal statement. Interested students must be met out of the university admission requirement page. University's programs are in the English Language; if the student hasn't met the English Level requirements, he/she will be required to take the English Proficiency Exam.
No. of awards offered: Various
Funding: Private
Additional Information: www.scholarship-positions.com/mba-business-excellence-scholarships-at-newcastle-university-in-the-uk/2020/11/18/

For further information contact:

Northways Parade, 28 College Cres, London NW3 5DN, United Kingdom.

Tel: (44) 756 390 4978
Email: mba@ncl.ac.uk

Newcastle University - English Language Excellence Scholarships (Business School Masters)

Purpose: Newcastle University Business School offers a number of partial scholarship awards to outstanding and high-quality Masters students each year to assist them to study for a Masters degree.
Eligibility: You will be considered for an English Language Excellence Scholarship if you hold an unconditional offer for one of the following Masters courses 1. Arts, Business and Creativity MA. 2. Innovation, Creativity and Entrepreneurship MSc. 3. Global Human Resource Management MSc. 4. International Economics and Finance MSc. 5. Banking and Finance MSc. 6. Finance MSc. 7. Quantitative Finance and Risk Management MSc. 8. International Business Management MSc. 9. International Marketing

MSc. 10. Operations, Logistics and Supply Chain Management MSc. 11. Accounting, Finance and Strategic Investment MSc. 12. International Financial Analysis MSc. 13. E-Business MSc. 14. E-Business (Information Systems) MSc. 15. E-Business (E-Marketing) MSc.

Level of Study: Postgraduate

Type: Scholarship

Value: Partial awards of £5,000 towards the cost of tuition fees.

Frequency: Annual

Country of Study: Any country

Application Procedure: Regulations and application details are available on the below link, www.ncl.ac.uk/media/wwwnclacuk/postgraduate/funding/files/English%20Language%20Excellence%20Scholarships%20Regulations%202019%20Entry.pdf

Funding: Private

For further information contact:

Tel: (44) 191 208 1503
Email: nubs@ncl.ac.uk

Newcastle University - United States of America Athlete Scholarship

Purpose: Newcastle University offers partial scholarship awards to encourage USA and Canadian athletes to undertake Master's level study. Awards have a value of £4000–£8000 payable to the student's tuition fee account (40% or 20% fee reduction) and include a comprehensive support package including Free gym membership, Unlimited strength and conditioning support, Professional coaching, Physiotherapy and sports massage, Lifestyle support and mentoring.

Eligibility: Applicants should ideally have NCAA D1- D3 playing experience in one of the following sports Basketball, Lacrosse, Volleyball, Tennis, Golf, Women's Soccer, Waterpolo. They must also be 1. Registered at Newcastle University for the academic year. 2. Registered for one of the following eligible Master's courses MA; MBA; MClinRes; MEd; MMedEd; LLM; LLM (by research); MLitt; MMus; MPH; MRes; MSc. 3. Defined as international for fee purposes. 4. Resident in the USA or Canada. 5. Registered to study at Newcastle University city centre campus. 6. Students new to the University and not those transferring or repeating courses.

Level of Study: Graduate

Type: Scholarship

Value: 40% or 20% fee reduction. £4,000 - £8,000 payable towards the first year of tuition fees and a comprehensive support package on eligible Master's courses.

Length of Study: September for one year of study.

Frequency: Annual

Country of Study: Any country

Application Procedure: Complete the application form using the following www.ncl.ac.uk/sport/performance/scholarships/application/

No. of awards offered: 20 at 40% 10 at 20%

Closing Date: 31 July

Funding: Private

Contributor: Newcastle University

For further information contact:

Tel: (44) 191 208 5230
Email: performance.sport@ncl.ac.uk

Newcastle University - Vice-Chancellor's Excellence Scholarships - Postgraduate

Purpose: Newcastle University is pleased to offer 39 Vice-Chancellor's Excellence Scholarships (VCES) for outstanding international applicants who apply to commence full-time Master's studies. There are 37 50% tuition fee scholarships and 2 100% tuition fee scholarships.

Eligibility: To be considered for the 50% scholarships applicants must 1. Be a national of one of the following countries Algeria, Argentina, Brazil, Canada, Chile, China, Colombia, Ecuador, Egypt, India, Indonesia, Jordan, Lebanon, Malaysia, Mexico, Morocco, Peru, Thailand, Turkey, United States of America, Venezuela. 2. Be assessed as international for fee purposes. 3. Hold an offer for an eligible Master's degree programme at the University's Newcastle city centre campus for the academic year. 4. Already have or expect to receive the equivalent of an upper second class United Kingdom honours degree or above.

Level of Study: Postgraduate

Type: Scholarship

Value: 50% and 100% of tuition fees

Length of Study: September for the full duration of the degree programme.

Frequency: Annual

Study Establishment: Newcastle University

Country of Study: Any country

Application Procedure: Online application form is available on the below web link path. www.app.geckoform.com/public/#/modern/FOEU01c3uP6v8lEi

No. of awards offered: 39

Closing Date: 27 May

Funding: Private

Contributor: Newcastle University

Additional Information: www.ncl.ac.uk/postgraduate/funding/sources/internationalnoneustudents/vces21.html

For further information contact:

Tel: (44) 191 208 5537/8107
Email: scholarship.applications@ncl.ac.uk

Newcastle University International Postgraduate Scholarship (NUIPS)

Purpose: To provide a partial scholarship for international students.
Eligibility: Candidates for scholarships must already have been offered a place to study at Newcastle University. See webpages www.ncl.ac.uk/postgraduate/funding/search/list/nuips
Level of Study: Postgraduate
Type: Partial scholarship
Value: £2,000 per year
Length of Study: 1st year of study only
Frequency: Annual
Study Establishment: Newcastle University
Country of Study: United Kingdom
Application Procedure: All eligible applicants who are offered a place to study at Newcastle University are invited to apply for one of these scholarships. Applicants must check the website for details or contact the Student Financial Support Team.
No. of awards offered: 800
Closing Date: 27 May
Contributor: Newcastle University
No. of awards given last year: 100
No. of applicants last year: 800
Additional Information: www.scholarshipsads.com/newcastle-university-international-postgraduate-scholarship-nuips-uk/

For further information contact:

Email: international-scholarships@ncl.ac.uk

Newcastle University Overseas Research Scholarship (NUORS)

Purpose: Newcastle University is committed to offering support to the very best international students hoping to pursue a programme of research. We are pleased to offer a small number of University funded NUORS awards for outstanding international students who apply to commence PhD studies in any subject.
Eligibility: You could be eligible to apply for a NUORS award if 1. You have been offered a place on a PhD research programme. 2. You have been assessed as international/overseas for fees purposes, and are wholly or partially self-

financing. 3. Applicants must already have been offered a place on a PhD research programme before applying.
Level of Study: Postgraduate
Type: Scholarship
Value: This award covers the difference between home and overseas fee rates (value to be determined).
Length of Study: The award is valid for the normal duration of the PhD (not longer than 3 years).
Frequency: Annual
Country of Study: Any country
Application Procedure: You must have already applied for and been offered a place to study at Newcastle University before you apply for a NUORS award. Please complete the online NUORS application form and in accordance with the NUORS regulations. You will also be required to provide details of an academic referee; the University will then contact your referee directly.
No. of awards offered: 18
Closing Date: 23 April
Funding: Private
Contributor: Newcastle University
Additional Information: www.ncl.ac.uk/postgraduate/funding/sources/internationalnoneustudents/nuors21.html

For further information contact:

Newcastle upon Tyne NE1 7RU, United Kingdom.

Tel: (44) 191 208 5537/8107
Email: scholarship.applications@ncl.ac.uk

Newcastle University Scholarship – Thailand - GREAT

Purpose: This year, in partnership with the British Council and the GREAT Britain Campaign, Newcastle University is offering scholarships to students in Thailand applying for postgraduate taught courses listed below. This scholarship scheme is part of the "GREAT Scholarships - East Asia" campaign, which has been launched by the British Council together with 28 United Kingdom universities to support more students in East Asia to get access to the excellent United Kingdom higher education opportunities
Eligibility: To be considered for awards applicants must 1. Must be passport holders of Thailand. 2. Be assessed as international for fee purposes. 3. Hold an offer for an eligible Master's degree programme listed below. 4. MSc Sustainable Chemical Engineering. 5. MSc REFLEX (Renewable Energy Flexible Training Programme).
Level of Study: Postgraduate
Type: Scholarship

Value: Full tuition fees
Frequency: Annual
Study Establishment: Newcastle University
Country of Study: Any country
Application Procedure: Applications must be submitted using the application form. Other applications will not be accepted. Application link is available below www.app. geckoform.com/public/#/modern/FOEU01c3zJ6qAVgh
Closing Date: 30 April
Funding: Private
Contributor: British Council and Newcastle University
Additional Information: www.app.geckoform.com/public/ #/modern/FOEU01c3zJ6qAVgh, www.wemakescholars. com/scholarship/newcastle-university-great-scholarships-thailand

For further information contact:

Email: scholarship.applications@newcastle.ac.uk

Newcastle Vice-Chancellor's Global Scholarships - Postgraduate

Purpose: Newcastle University is pleased to offer 5 Vice-Chancellor's Global Scholarships (VCGS) for outstanding international applicants who apply to commence full-time Master's studies.
Eligibility: To be considered for the Vice-Chancellor's Global Scholarships applicants must 1. Be assessed as international for fee purposes. 2. Hold an offer for an eligible Master's degree programme at the University's Newcastle city centre campus for the academic year. 3. Already have or expect to receive the equivalent of an upper second class United Kingdom honours degree or above.
Level of Study: Postgraduate
Type: Scholarship
Value: £4,000
Length of Study: September for the full duration of degree programme.
Frequency: Annual
Country of Study: Any country
Application Procedure: Applications must be submitted using the online application form. Other applications will not be accepted.
No. of awards offered: 5
Closing Date: 29 April
Funding: Private
Contributor: Newcastle University

For further information contact:

Tel: (44) 191 208 5537/8107
Email: scholarship.applications@ncl.ac.uk

Postgraduate Master's Loan Scheme (Students from United Kingdom and non-United Kingdom European Union Countries)

Purpose: The Loan is non means-tested and is considered as a contribution towards your tuition fees and living expenses. It is available to students under the age of 60. If you already have a Master's level qualification (including an integrated Master's), an equivalent qualification or a higher level qualification, you will not be eligible to receive the Master's Student Loan. This applies even if your previous qualification was entirely self-funded and/or achieved outside the UK. If you already have a lower postgraduate qualification, such as a Postgraduate Diploma or Postgraduate Certificate, you will be eligible to receive the loan if you choose to undertake a standalone Master's course.
Eligibility: 1. Taught and research Master's courses in all disciplines (online and campus-based) will normally be eligible, e.g. MA, MSc, MRes, MEd, MBA, LLM, MLitt, MFA. 2. You can receive a loan for an MPhil. However, this programme must lead to a standalone. Master's degree and not be part of a longer PhD programme. 3. You will not be entitled to receive the Postgraduate Loan if you are eligible to receive healthcare funding from any of the following organisations. i. National Health Service (NHS). ii. Department of Health (DOH). iii. Student Awards Agency Scotland (SAAS). 4. Doctoral degrees (eg PhD, EngD, Integrated PhDs), PG Certificates, PG Diplomas, PGCE's and Master's courses that are currently funded by the undergraduate support system, eg Master of Architecture (MArch), will not be eligible for the Loan. 5. You will not be eligible for the Postgraduate Loan if you are studying towards top-up credits to a gain a Master's qualification after studying a PG Certificate or PG Diploma
Level of Study: Postgraduate
Type: Award
Value: £11,570
Frequency: Annual
Country of Study: Any country
Application Procedure: The application cycle is still open. The quickest way to apply is online. www.gov.uk/masters-loan/apply
Closing Date: June
Funding: Private
Additional Information: www.ncl.ac.uk/postgraduate/ funding/sources/ukeustudents/mastersloan.html

For further information contact:

Email: ltds@ncl.ac.uk

N

Postgraduate Masters Scholarships in the School of Geography, Politics and Sociology

Purpose: The scholarships are open to United Kingdom, European Union and international applicants who Hold an offer of admission on one of the eligible programmes Hold, or expect to achieve, at least a 2.1 honours degree (or international equivalent), in a related discipline

Eligibility: The scholarships are open to United Kingdom, European Union and international applicants who 1. Hold an offer of admission on one of the eligible programmes. 2. Hold, or expect to achieve, at least a 2.1 honours degree (or international equivalent), in a related discipline

Level of Study: Postgraduate

Type: Scholarship

Value: £7,410

Frequency: Annual

Country of Study: Any country

Closing Date: 7 June

Funding: Private

Additional Information: www.ncl.ac.uk/gps/about/funding/schoolfunding/#phdscholarships

For further information contact:

Email: gps.pgr@ncl.ac.uk

Postgraduate Opportunity Scholarships

Purpose: The scholarships are available as part of Newcastle University's Postgraduate Support Scheme for Master's students. They have been designed to enable students from under-represented groups to progress to higher level study

Eligibility: Postgraduate Opportunity Scholarships are available only to students applying to Newcastle University who meet the following criteria have been offered a place to study full time for one year or a maximum of two years part time on one of the University's eligible taught or research Master's courses commencing in September. are United Kingdom students progressing from undergraduate courses for which they were charged the higher tuition fee applying and falling into the following categories 1. A student living in United Kingdom when they entered undergraduate study at any United Kingdom institution. 2. A student living in Scotland when they entered undergraduate study at any English, Northern Irish or Welsh institution. 3. A student living in Northern Ireland when they entered undergraduate study at any English, Scottish or Welsh institution.

Level of Study: Postgraduate

Type: Scholarship

Frequency: Annual

Country of Study: Any country

Application Procedure: To apply for the Postgraduate Opportunity Scholarship, please complete the online application form. Check the following link. www.app.geckoform.com/public/#/modern/FOEU01c3RUfcdPr6%20

Closing Date: 28 June

Funding: Private

Additional Information: In order to be considered for a Postgraduate Opportunity Scholarship, you must have already applied to the University for an eligible taught or research Master's course and received an offer of a place by this date www.ncl.ac.uk/postgraduate/funding/sources/ukeustudents/pos20.html

For further information contact:

Email: uk.postgraduate-scholarships@ncl.ac.uk

Regional Impact Scholarship (MBA)

Purpose: To support aspiring and established leaders from the region to continue their professional development. The Regional Impact Scholarship is aimed at MBA candidates who can demonstrate their potential to the economy and society of the North East of United Kingdom

Eligibility: To be eligible for this full-fee scholarship you must meet the following criteria 1. Completed the scholarship application form including submitting an essay of no more than 1,500 words in response to the question listed. Submissions need to be in English. 2. Hold a conditional or unconditional offer of admission to the Full-time MBA programme of current year entry. 3. Have substantive managerial experience (minimum 3 years prior to starting the MBA). 4. Preferably hold the equivalent of a United Kingdom 21 honours degree (however, applicants who do not meet this requirement but can demonstrate relevant work experience above the minimum plus significant career progression may also be considered). 5. Perform well at interview across all competency areas hold an English language qualification of IELTS 6.5 or its equivalent with no subskill below 6.0 (if your first language is not English).

Level of Study: Postgraduate

Type: Scholarship

Value: A full fee award of £22,800, payable towards the cost of tuition fees

Frequency: Annual

Country of Study: United Kingdom

Application Procedure: Applications and essays will be reviewed by a panel of judges. Candidates need to complete the online application form. www.forms.ncl.ac.uk/view.php?id=2981068

Closing Date: 5 April

Funding: Private

Additional Information: www.ncl.ac.uk/business-school/courses/scholarships/mba/

For further information contact:

Tel: (44) 191 208 1589
Email: mba@ncl.ac.uk

Newcastle University in the United Kingdom

Newcastle upon Tyne, Tyne and Wear NE1 7RU, United Kingdom.

Tel: (44) 191 208 6000
Website: www.ncl.ac.uk/
Contact: Newcastle University

Newcastle University experts are protecting cultural property and preserving unique archives around the world

13 PhD International Studentships at Northumbria University in UK

Purpose: This is a 3.5 years funded studentship available to Home/EU/ Worldwide students who will commence the PhD study at the university in the UK.
Eligibility: Eligible Countries: Applications are accepted from around the world. Acceptable Course or Subjects: PhD degree will be awarded in any subject offered by the university Admissible Criteria: To be eligible, the applicants must meet all the following criteria: You must have or expect to gain a First Class or high 2:1 Honours degree or international equivalent in a relevant subject or subject relevant to the proposed PhD project. Enthusiasm for research, the ability to think and work independently, excellent analytical skills, and strong verbal and written communication skills are also essential requirements.
Level of Study: Postdoctorate
Type: Studentship
Value: Full tuition fees, living allowance of £15,609.
Length of Study: 3.5 Years
Frequency: Annual
Country of Study: Any country
No. of awards offered: 13
Closing Date: 24 January
Additional Information: scholarship-positions.com/13-phd-international-studentships-at-northumbria-university-in-uk/2022/01/19/

For further information contact:

Northways Parade, 28 College Cres, London NW3 5DN, United Kingdom.

Tel: (44) 756 390 4978
Email: help@scholarship-positions.com

40 Fully-Funded Postgraduate Scholarships at Newcastle University in the United Kingdom

Purpose: Students need a good level of English language to study at Newcastle University. English will be the main language you use socially and for study. If English is not their first language they will need to provide a recognised English language test or qualification
Eligibility: Citizens of China, United States of America, Canada, India, Indonesia, Malaysia, Thailand, Singapore, Jordan, Lebanon, Egypt, Turkey, Algeria, Morocco, India, Nigeria, Ghana, Kenya and Uganda are eligible to apply
Type: Postgraduate scholarships
Value: 50% or 100% of tuition fees
Study Establishment: Scholarships are awarded to study the subjects offered by the university
Country of Study: United Kingdom
Application Procedure: International preparation courses and graduate diplomas have a different application method. Students apply online through partner INTO. Applications must be submitted using the online application form
Closing Date: 29 June
Additional Information: For more details please browse the website scholarship-positions.com/fully-funded-postgraduate-scholarships-newcastle-university-uk/2017/11/14/

For further information contact:

Email: scholarship.applications@ncl.ac.uk

International PhD Fellowships in Environmental Chemistry, Denmark

Subjects: PhD degree study in the Department of Plant and Environmental Sciences
Purpose: The University of Copenhagen has collaborated with the Department of Ecoscience at Aarhus University to offer the International PhD fellowships in Environmental Chemistry.
Eligibility: Professional qualifications relevant to the PhD project: Relevant publications; Relevant work experience; Other relevant professional activities; The curious mindset with a strong interest in biogeochemistry as the basis for

developing solutions for sustainable and climate-smart land use; Good language skills

Level of Study: Postdoctorate
Type: Fellowship
Country of Study: Any country
Closing Date: 30 January
Contributor: Department of Ecoscience at Aarhus University
Additional Information: scholarship-positions.com/international-phd-fellowships-in-environmental-chemistry-denmark/2022/01/27/

For further information contact:

Newcastle upon Tyne NE1 7RU, United Kingdom.

Tel: (44) 191 208 6000
Email: scholarship.applications@ncl.ac.uk

International PhD Student Positions in Mathematics, Sweden

Purpose: Awards are another resource to help students afford the degree. To cover educational expenses, the University of Gothenburg is offering International PhD Student Positions in Mathematics.
Eligibility: Eligible Countries: All countries candidates can join this program. Acceptable Course or Subjects: The PhD scholarship will be awarded in Mathematics Admissible Criteria: The eligibility for academic positions is given in the Swedish Higher Education Ordinance. To qualify for the position, you must have obtained a master's degree or a 4-year bachelor's degree, or expect to complete that degree by the time the employment starts.
Level of Study: Postdoctorate
Type: Studentship
Value: Salary
Length of Study: 4 Years
Frequency: Annual
Country of Study: Any country
No. of awards offered: 3
Closing Date: 25 January
Additional Information: scholarship-positions.com/international-phd-student-positions-in-mathematics-sweden/2022/01/21/

For further information contact:

Newcastle upon Tyne NE1 7RU, United Kingdom.

Tel: (44) 191 208 6000
Email: scholarship.applications@ncl.ac.uk

PhD (via MPhil) International Studentships in Cyber Security in UK

Subjects: School of Psychology and Computer Science
Purpose: The University of Central Lancashire is offering financial support to high-potential students through its PhD (via MPhil) Studentships in Cyber Security in the UK.
Eligibility: Eligible Countries: All nationalities Acceptable Course or Subjects: PhD degree in Towards Securing Connected and Autonomous Vehicles (CAV) infrastructure to mitigate Virtual Vehicle Hijacking Admissible Criteria: To be eligible, the applicants must meet all the given criteria: Applicants must have to enroll in the PhD degree programme
Level of Study: Postdoctorate
Type: Studentship
Value: £15,609 per year
Country of Study: Any country
Closing Date: 23 February
Additional Information: scholarship-positions.com/phd-via-mphil-international-studentships-in-cyber-security-in-uk/2022/01/25/

For further information contact:

Newcastle upon Tyne NE1 7RU, United Kingdom.

Tel: (44) 191 208 6000
Email: scholarship.applications@ncl.ac.uk

PhD Excellence Scholarships for International Students at Walailak University, Thailand

Purpose: Walailak University is pleased to announce the PhD Excellence Scholarships to help foreign students conduct studies in order to develop new knowledge in Thailand.
Eligibility: Eligible Countries: Foreign and home country national students are eligible to apply. Eligible Course or Subjects: International PhD programmes offered at Walailak are eligible to be applied for. Eligibility Criteria: To be eligible, the applicants must meet all the following/given criteria: The applicants must have at least 2 research articles written by scholarship recipients MUST be published or have been formally accepted for publication in peer-review academic journals indexed in the Scopus database ranked in the 1stquartile (Q1) or 2nd quartile (Q2).
Level of Study: Postdoctorate
Type: Scholarship
Value: Tuition fee
Frequency: Annual
Country of Study: Any country

Additional Information: scholarship-positions.com/phd-excellence-scholarships-for-international-students-at-walailak-university-thailand/2022/01/19/

For further information contact:

Northways Parade, 28 College Cres, London NW3 5DN, United Kingdom.

Tel: (44) 756 390 4978
Email: help@scholarship-positions.com

PhD International Scholarships in Quantitative Genetics of Senescence in Seychelles Warblers, Netherlands

Purpose: The University of Groningen is looking for a student who wishes to design their PhD research project researching the Genomics of Senescence. It has established the PhD Scholarships in Quantitative Genetics of Senescence in Seychelles Warblers in the Netherlands
Eligibility: Eligible Countries: Home country national and international students can both apply. Eligible Course or Subjects: PhD degree studies in Quantitative genetics of senescence in Seychelles warblers at Groningen can be undertaken. Eligibility Criteria: To be eligible, the applicants must meet all the following/given criteria: The applicants must have experience extracting and analyzing data from databases (e.g., Access) or large datasets (training provided).
Level of Study: Postdoctorate
Type: Scholarship
Value: € 2,249
Length of Study: 4 Years
Frequency: Annual
Country of Study: Any country
Closing Date: 30 January
Contributor: University of Groningen
Additional Information: scholarship-positions.com/phd-international-scholarships-in-quantitative-genetics-of-senescence-in-seychelles-warblers-netherlands/2022/01/24/

For further information contact:

Newcastle upon Tyne NE1 7RU, United Kingdom.

Tel: (44) 191 208 6000
Email: scholarship.applications@ncl.ac.uk

PhD International Studentships in Control of Mitosis in Calcium in Mammalian Cells, UK

Purpose: This funding scheme aims to cover the costs of studying for a PhD degree in the Biological and Medical Sciences at the Faculty of Health and Life Sciences at the University of Liverpool.
Eligibility: Eligible Countries: All students from all countries can apply. Eligible Course or Subjects: PhD study programmes in Biological and Medical Sciences at the University of Liverpool. Eligibility Criteria: To be eligible, the applicants must meet all the following/given criteria: The applicants must be self-funded students.
Level of Study: Postdoctorate
Type: Studentship
Value: £24,250 and £4,500
Frequency: Annual
Country of Study: Any country
Closing Date: 3 May
Additional Information: scholarship-positions.com/phd-international-studentships-in-control-of-mitosis-in-calcium-in-mammalian-cells-uk/2022/01/21/

For further information contact:

Newcastle upon Tyne NE1 7RU, United Kingdom.

Tel: (44) 191 208 60008
Email: scholarship.applications@ncl.ac.uk

PhD International Studentships in Physical Layer Algorithm Design in 6G Non-Terrestrial Communications, UK

Purpose: The role will include both theoretical and applied research in the well-equipped 6GIC/ICS at the University of Surrey. Future wireless communication networks are expected to provide a much more satisfying service to people by building uninterrupted and ubiquitous connectivity to everyone, everything, and everywhere with ultra-high data rate, extremely high reliability, and low latency.
Eligibility: Eligible Countries: All nationalities. Eligible Course or Subjects: PhD degree in Physical layer algorithm design in 6G non-terrestrial communications Eligibility Criteria: To be eligible, the applicants must meet all the following/given criteria: The applicants must be the UK or international students holding a relevant master's degree qualification.
Level of Study: Postdoctorate
Type: Studentship
Value: Tuition fee
Frequency: Annual

Country of Study: Any country
Closing Date: 27 January
Contributor: University of Surrey.
Additional Information: scholarship-positions.com/phd-international-studentships-in-physical-layer-algorithm-design-in-6g-non-terrestrial-communications-uk/2022/01/27/

For further information contact:

Newcastle upon Tyne NE1 7RU, United Kingdom.

Tel: (44) 191 208 6000
Email: scholarship.applications@ncl.ac.uk

PhD Studentship in Liquid Metal Catalysts for Green Fuels, Australia

Purpose: This studentship is open to all applicants that wish to work on a project that will investigate novel catalytic systems with applications in CO2 reduction
Eligibility: Eligible Countries: Australian national and other international students can apply. Eligible Course or Subjects: PhD study in Liquid Metal Catalysts for Green Fuels and Co2 Mitigation at RMIT is eligible to apply for. Eligibility Criteria: To be eligible, the applicants must meet all the following/given criteria: The applicants must meet the university's research degree requirements.
Level of Study: Masters Degree
Type: Studentship
Value: US$31,000 per annum
Length of Study: 3 Years
Frequency: Annual
Country of Study: Any country
No. of awards offered: 1
Additional Information: scholarship-positions.com/phd-studentship-in-liquid-metal-catalysts-for-green-fuels-australia/2022/01/20/

For further information contact:

Northways Parade, 28 College Cres, London NW3 5DN, United Kingdom.

Tel: (44) 756 390 4978
Email: help@scholarship-positions.com

Sam and Nina Narodowski PhD International Scholarships in Australia

Purpose: Aiming to support new commencing PhD candidates financially throughout their PhD study, RMIT University has decided to award deserving students the Sam and Nina Narodowski PhD Scholarships in Australia
Eligibility: Eligible Countries: Domestic and International students are both eligible to apply. Eligible Course or Subjects: PhD study programme in Food Production and Agribusiness, Sustainability and Environment or Clothing Textiles and Health Disability and Aged Care, Urban Transport and Social Planning or Migration and Settlement Services at RMIT can be applied for. Eligibility Criteria: To be eligible, the applicants must meet all the following/given criteria: The applicants must meet the eligibility criteria for admission into the PhD program.
Level of Study: Postdoctorate
Type: Scholarship
Value: US$33,000 per annum
Frequency: Annual
Country of Study: Any country
No. of awards offered: 2
Closing Date: 1 March
Additional Information: scholarship-positions.com/sam-and-nina-narodowski-phd-international-scholarships-in-australia/2022/01/24/

For further information contact:

Newcastle upon Tyne NE1 7RU, United Kingdom.

Tel: (44) 191 208 6000
Email: scholarship.applications@ncl.ac.uk

School of Social Sciences and Humanities International PhD Studentships in UK

Purpose: Applications are welcomed from high calibre students wishing to apply for the International PhD Studentships based in the School of Social Sciences and Humanities at Loughborough University.
Eligibility: Eligible Countries: Applications are accepted from around the world. Eligible Course or Subjects: PhD degree programme in creative arts by the university. Eligibility Criteria: To be eligible, the applicants must have first-class honours, upper second-class honours, and lower second-class honours
Level of Study: Postdoctorate
Type: Studentship
Value: £15609 per annum
Frequency: Annual
Country of Study: Any country
Closing Date: 13 March
Contributor: Loughborough University

Additional Information: scholarship-positions.com/school-of-social-sciences-and-humanities-international-phd-student ships-in-uk/2022/01/22/

For further information contact:

Newcastle upon Tyne NE1 7RU, United Kingdom.

Tel: (44) 191 208 6000
Email: scholarship.applications@ncl.ac.uk

Test Scholarships for International Students at Free University of Berlin, Germany

Purpose: International students alone can make applications for this scholarship scheme. PhD degree programme applicants are eligible.
Eligibility: Eligible Countries: All international students are eligible to apply. Eligible Course or Subjects: Students can undertake PhD degree study programmes at FU Berlin. Eligibility Criteria: To be eligible, the applicants must meet all the following/given criteria: The applicants must submit a project report to the Center for International Cooperation within six weeks of project completion.
Level of Study: Postdoctorate
Type: Scholarship
Value: EURO 1,300
Length of Study: 3 Months
Frequency: Annual
Country of Study: Any country
Closing Date: 1 April
Additional Information: scholarship-positions.com/test-scholarships-for-international-students-at-free-university-of-berlin-germany/2022/01/21/

For further information contact:

Newcastle upon Tyne NE1 7RU, United Kingdom.

Tel: (44) 191 208 6000
Email: scholarship.applications@ncl.ac.uk

University of Copenhagen International PhD Fellowships in Food Biotechnology, Denmark

Subjects: Department of Food Science
Purpose: The PhD position aims to explore the potential to release and extract seed storage proteins in a mild, controlled, and sustainable way by using enzymatic methods inspired by the pea plant's mechanism to mobilize the storage proteins during germination.

Eligibility: Eligible Countries: All nationalities Acceptable Course or Subjects: PhD program in Microbial Interactions Admissible Criteria: To be eligible for the regular PhD programme, you must have completed a degree programme, equivalent to a Danish master's degree (180 ECTS/3 FTE BSc + 120 ECTS/2 FTE MSc) related to the subject area of the project, e.g. biochemistry, molecular biology, biotechnology or bioengineering.
Level of Study: Postdoctorate
Type: Fellowship
Value: DKK 27,871.40 per month
Country of Study: Any country
Closing Date: 27 January
Additional Information: scholarship-positions.com/university-of-copenhagen-international-phd-fellowships-in-food-biotechnology-denmark/2022/01/25/

For further information contact:

Newcastle upon Tyne NE1 7RU, United Kingdom.

Tel: (44) 191 208 6000
Email: scholarship.applications@ncl.ac.uk

University of Newcastle International PhD Scholarships in Geomicrobial Biosensors, Australia

Purpose: The educational programme is available for highly motivated domestic and international students to apply for this PhD degree programme.
Eligibility: An applicant for admission to candidature for a Doctoral Degree (Research) shall: Have satisfied all of the requirements for admission to the degree of Bachelor with Honours Class 1 or Honours Class II, Division 1 or any other degree approved for this purpose by the Assistant Dean (Research Training); or Have satisfied all of the requirements for admission to the degree of Bachelor in the University or any other degree approved for this purpose by the Assistant Dean (Research Training), and have achieved by subsequent work and study a standard recognized by the Assistant Dean (Research Training) as equivalent to at least Honours Class II, Division 1; or In exceptional cases, submit evidence of possessing such other academic or professional qualifications and experience as may be approved by the Assistant Dean (Research Training) on the recommendation of the relevant School; or In the disciplines of education, medical physics, nursing, social work, social sciences and surgery have completed a minimum standard of professional experience as required by the Assistant Dean (Research Training) on the recommendation of the School;

An Australian honours degree with Class 1 or Class 2 division
Type: Scholarship
Value: US$28,092
Frequency: Annual
Country of Study: Any country
Closing Date: 28 February
Additional Information: scholarship-positions.com/university-of-newcastle-international-phd-scholarships-in-geomicrobial-biosensors-australia/2022/01/20/

For further information contact:

Newcastle upon Tyne NE1 7RU, United Kingdom.

Tel: (44) 191 208 6000
Email: scholarship.applications@ncl.ac.uk

Newcomen Society of the United States

211 Welsh Pool Road, Suite 240, Exton, PA 19341, United States of America.

Tel: (1) 610 363 6600
Email: mstoner@newcomen.org
Website: www.newcomen.org
Contact: Ms Marcy J. Stoner, Executive Assistant

The Newcomen Society of the United States is a non-profit business educational foundation that studies and supports outstanding achievement in American business.

Harvard/Newcomen Postdoctoral Award

Purpose: To improve the scholar's professional acquaintance with business and economic history, to increase his or her skills as they relate to this field, and to enable him or her to engage in research that will benefit from the resources of the Harvard Business School and the Boston scholarly community.
Eligibility: Open to Scholars who have received a PhD in history, economics or a related discipline within the past 10 years, and who would not otherwise be able to attend Harvard Business School.
Level of Study: Postdoctorate
Type: Award

Value: US$46,000
Length of Study: 1 year
Frequency: Annual
Study Establishment: Harvard Business School in Cambridge, Massachusetts.
Country of Study: United States of America
Application Procedure: Applicants must contact Harvard University for further details.
Closing Date: 15 March

For further information contact:

Graduate School of Business Administration, Straus Professor of Business History Harvard University, Soldiers Field Road, Boston, MA 02163, United States of America.

Tel: (1) 617 495 6354
Email: tmccraw@hbs.edu

RMIT- CSIRO PhD International Scholarship in Mineral Resources and Environmental Science, Australia

Purpose: RMIT University is looking for excellent, highly motivated early-career researchers that are keen on studying in Australia to apply for the CSIRO PhD International Scholarship in Mineral Resources and Environmental Science
Eligibility: Eligible Countries: Australian or international students are eligible. Acceptable Course or Subjects: PhD degree in Chemical and Rheological Assessment of Rejuvenated Asphalt Material. Admissible Criteria: To be eligible, the candidates must meet all the following criteria: Applicants with an honours degree or graduates with a research master in experimental and analytical work with a civil engineering or chemical engineering background are invited to apply. Previous experience in the rheology and chemistry of bituminous products is highly regarded.
Level of Study: Postdoctorate
Type: Scholarship
Value: US$31,260 per annum
Length of Study: 3 years
Frequency: Annual
Country of Study: Any country
No. of awards offered: 1
Additional Information: scholarship-positions.com/rmit-csiro-phd-international-scholarship-in-mineral-resources-and-environmental-science-australia/2022/01/21/

For further information contact:

Northways Parade, 28 College Cres, London NW3 5DN, United Kingdom.

Tel: (44) 756 390 4978

North Atlantic Treaty Organization (NATO)

Public Diplomacy Division, Office Nb 106, Boulevard Leopold III, B-1110 Brussels, Belgium.

Tel: (32) 2 811 4000
Website: www.nato.int
Contact: Academic Affairs Officer

NATO's purpose is to guarantee the freedom and security of its members through political and military means. NATO promotes democratic values and enables members to consult and cooperate on defence and security-related issues to solve problems, build trust and, in the long run, prevent conflict.

Manfred Wörner Fellowship

Purpose: To honour the memory of the late Secretary General by focusing attention on his leadership in the transformation of the alliance, including efforts at extending NATO's relations with CEE countries and promoting the principles and image of the Transatlantic partnership.
Eligibility: Open to applicants who are citizens of the EAPC countries with proven experience to carry out an important scholarly endeavour within the time limit of the Fellowship.
Level of Study: Professional development
Type: Fellowship
Value: €5,000 (including all travel costs)
Frequency: Annual
Country of Study: Any country
Application Procedure: Application forms can be downloaded from the NATO website.
Closing Date: 25 January
Funding: Government
Additional Information: GMF invites all interested parties to apply. New awards will be made after March 1.

For further information contact:

Fax: (32) 2 707 5457
Email: leadershipprograms@gmfus.org

North Central College

Graduate Programs MBA Program, 30 North Brainard Street, Naperville, IL 60540, United States of America.

Tel: (1) 630 637 5100
Email: grad@noctrl.edu
Website: www.noctrl.edu
Contact: MBA Admissions Officer

Since 1861, North Central has been a place where new ideas lead to unlimited possibilities. We're an independent college dedicated to the power of the liberal arts and sciences to transform students into leaders both in their careers and communities. Our nearly 3,000 students study across more than 65 undergraduate and graduate programs, with their education made richer by supportive faculty and staff, world-class facilities and countless opportunities to learn beyond the classroom.

North Central Association for Counselor Education and Supervision Research Grant Awards

Purpose: The call for proposals is to fund studies that increase understanding of the counselor education profession (including research, teaching, supervision, leadership and advocacy). Research grant awards will be presented at the business meeting at the NCACES.
Eligibility: Proposed topic is within the scope of this Research Award program. Need for the proposed topic is clearly outlined through review of the research. Objectives are clear and attainable in the proposed study. Methodology proposed is appropriate for the research questions. Outcomes are consistent with objectives and method. Research proposed adheres to ACA/ACES ethical standards for research with human subjects.
Level of Study: Graduate
Type: Study grant
Value: US$1,000
Frequency: Annual
Country of Study: Any country
Application Procedure: The competition is open to both professional and student members of NCACES. The primary investigator must be an ACES/NCACES member at the time the application is submitted. Individuals may submit (or be part of a submission team) for only one proposal. www.ncaces.org/awards/general/gsubmit

N

No. of awards offered: 3
Closing Date: 29 June
Funding: Private

North Dallas Bank & Trust Company

P.O. Box 801826, Dallas, TX 75380-1826, United States of America.

Tel: (1) 972 716 7100
Email: customer.service@ndbt.com
Website: www.ndbt.com/

North Dallas Bank & Trust aims to provide banking for smarter choices in business and life. This means engaging with our customers and communities through personalized and excellent service, returning a fair and reasonable profit to our shareholders, acting at all times with dignity, honor and respect and providing an environment in which each of our employees can excel in the spirit of mutual respect, accountability, creativity and teamwork.

James W. Tyra Memorial Scholarship

Purpose: High school seniors who have a grade point avearage of 3.0 or higher and are in the top 25 percent of their graduating class are eligible for this award. Students must be attending high schools located inside the North Dallas Bank & Trust Company service area and have a annual family income no higher than US$58,720.
Level of Study: Graduate
Type: Scholarship
Value: US$4,000
Frequency: Annual
Country of Study: United States of America
Application Procedure: Application requirements for the James W. Tyra Memorial Scholarship are Application form. Official Transcript. Recommendation letters (2). Personal statement.
No. of awards offered: 2
Closing Date: 1 April
Funding: Private
Additional Information: Applicants must demonstrate financial need. Selection will be judged by an internal North Dallas Bank committee, representing a cross-section of the bank's communities. The decision of the committee will be final. The bank will notify all recipients. Family members and employees of North Dallas Bank and its affiliates are not

eligible. www.gmfus.org/transatlantic-leadership-initiatives/manfred-w%C3%B6rner-seminar

North West Cancer Research Fund

200 London Road, Liverpool L3 9TA, United Kingdom.

Tel: (44) 151 709 2919
Email: info@nwcr.org
Website: www.nwcr.org/
Contact: Mr A W Renison, General Secretary

As the only independent charity dedicated to tackling cancer across the North West and North Wales, our goal is simple: to put our region's cancer needs first.

North West Cancer Research Fund Research Project Grants

Purpose: To support fundamental research into the cause of cancers and the mechanisms by which cancers arise and exert their effects.
Eligibility: Open to candidates undertaking cancer research studies at one of the universities named below in the Northwest. Grants are only available for travel costs associated with currently funded 3-year cancer research projects. No grants are awarded for buildings or for the development of drugs.
Level of Study: Research
Type: Project
Value: Approx. £35,000 per year
Length of Study: Usually 3 years
Frequency: Dependent on funds available
Study Establishment: The University of Liverpool, Lancaster University and the University of Wales, Bangor
Country of Study: Any country
Application Procedure: The NWCRF Scientific Committee meets twice a year. All applications are subject to peer review.
No. of awards offered: 50
Closing Date: 1 October
Funding: Individuals, Private
Contributor: Voluntary donations
No. of awards given last year: 10
No. of applicants last year: 50

For further information contact:

NWCRF Scientific Committee, Department of Medicine, Duncan Building, Daulby Street, Liverpool L7 8XW, United Kingdom.

Email: ricketts@liverpool.ac.uk

NWCR & Tenovus PhD Studentship Award

Purpose: We invite applications from principal investigators, with a track record of successful PhD supervision, to submit proposals for this jointly funded research award. NWCR and Tenovus Cancer Care (Tenovus) seek to fund a health services PhD research award which will aim to impact cancer policy or practice through the targeted area of psycho-social oncology.
Level of Study: Research
Value: Maximum funding budget of up to £75,000
Length of Study: 3 years
Closing Date: 22 June
Funding: Individuals, Private

Northeast Florida Phi Beta Kappa Alumni Association

1606 New Hampshire Ave NW, Washington, DC 20009, United States.

Northeast Florida Phi Beta Kappa Alumni Association Scholarship

Purpose: The Fall Program provides a social and intellectual opportunity for members and their guests.
Eligibility: Winners will be honored at the association's Spring Banquet. For further details, see the website.
Level of Study: Postgraduate
Type: Scholarship and Research award
Value: US$2,000
Frequency: Annual
Country of Study: Any country
Application Procedure: Application information is available online at the Phi Beta Kappa Alumni Association of Northeast Florida website.
Closing Date: 1 March
Funding: Private
Additional Information: www.unigo.com/scholarships/merit-based/merit-scholarships/northeast-florida-phi-beta-kappa-alumni-association-scholarship

For further information contact:

1606 New Hampshire Ave NW, Washington, DC 20009, United States of America.

Tel: (1) 2022653808
Email: mroberts@unf.edu

Northeastern University

Graduate School of Business Administration, 350 Dodge Hall, 360 Huntington Ave, Boston, MA 02115, United States of America.

Tel: (1) 617 373 2000
Email: gsba@neu.edu
Contact: MBA Admissions Officer

Located in Boston and founded in 1898, Northeastern is a private, nonprofit university that offers degree programs at the undergraduate and graduate levels. Home to more than 35 specialized research and education centers, we are a leader in worldwide experiential learning, urban engagement and interdisciplinary research that responds to global and societal needs.

Expanding Capacity in Quantum Information Science and Engineering (ExpandQISE)

Purpose: The NSF Expanding Capacity in Quantum Information Science and Engineering (ExpandQISE) program aims to increase research capacity and broaden participation in Quantum Information Science and Engineering (QISE) and related disciplines through the creation of a diversified investment portfolio in research and education that will lead to scientific and engineering breakthroughs, while securing a talent pipeline in a field where workforce needs of industry, government and academia continue to outgrow the available talent.
Type: Award
Value: Track1-$800,000; Track 2-$5,000,000.
Length of Study: 3-5 years
Country of Study: Any country
No. of awards offered: 50 to 62
Closing Date: 6 May
Additional Information: beta.nsf.gov/funding/opportunities/expanding-capacity-quantum-information-science-and-engineering-expandqise

For further information contact:

360 Huntington Ave, Boston, MA 02115, United States of America.

Tel: (1) 617 373 2000
Email: beta-nsf-feedback@nsf.gov

National Robotics Initiative 2.0: Ubiquitous Collaborative Robots (NRI-2.0)

Purpose: The goal of the National Robotics Initiative (NRI) is to support fundamental research that will accelerate the development and use of robots in the United States that work beside or cooperatively with people

Eligibility: 1. An investigator may participate as PI, co-PI, or Senior Personnel in no more than two proposals submitted in response to this solicitation each year. 2. In the event that an individual exceeds this limit, proposals received within the limit will be accepted based on earliest date and time of proposal submission (i.e., the first two proposals received will be accepted and the remainder will be returned without review). No exceptions will be made. 3. The above limit applies only to proposals to the NRI-2.0 solicitation, not to the totality of proposals submitted to NSF

Level of Study: Graduate

Type: Grant

Value: US$250,000 to US$1,500,000

Length of Study: 4 Years

Frequency: Annual

Country of Study: Any country

No. of awards offered: 15–30

Closing Date: 22 February

Funding: Private

Additional Information: www.nsf.gov/funding/pgm_summ.jsp?pims_id=503641

For further information contact:

360 Huntington Ave, Boston, MA 02115, United States of America.

Tel: (1) 617 373 2000
Email: beta-nsf-feedback@nsf.gov

Northumbria University

Newcastle City Campus, Sutherland Building, Newcastle upon Tyne NE1 8ST, United Kingdom.

Tel: (44) 191 232 6002
Website: www.northumbria.ac.uk/

Northumbria is a research-rich, business-focused, professional university with a global reputation for academic excellence. It is based in the heart of Newcastle upon Tyne, which is regularly voted the best place in the UK for students

Dean's Award Scholarship

Purpose: Scholarships are available for pursuing full-time or part-time LPC or LLM LPC programme

Eligibility: For eligibility details, please visit website

Value: £1,000 with 90% off tuition fees

Country of Study: Any country

Application Procedure: Applications must be must be sent via email

Closing Date: 31 July

Contributor: Northumbria University

Additional Information: For more details, please visit website www.northumbria.ac.uk/study-at-northumbria/fees-funding/pg-fees-funding/2018-deans-award-lpc/ www.northumbria.ac.uk/study-at-northumbria/fees-funding/pg-fees-funding/2018-deans-award-bptc/

For further information contact:

Email: gradadms@mtu.edu

Norway – the Official Site in the United States

2720 34th Street NW, Washington, DC 20008, United States of America.

Tel: (1) 202 333 6000
Email: cg.newyork@mfa.no
Website: www.norway.org
Contact: Grants and Scholarships Department

Al Fog Bergljot Kolflats Stipendfond

Purpose: To provide a stipend for those who want to take a trip to the United States to get practical experience within their fields of interest.

Eligibility: Open to Norwegian citizens only, especially for a Norwegian engineer or architect. The applicant must have worked for at least 3 years after graduation, and he/she must present a detailed plan for the trip when they apply. Also, a budget for the trip must be included as well as references.

Level of Study: Postgraduate

Value: Up to 40,000 NOK.

Length of Study: 3 years

Country of Study: Any country

Closing Date: 1 April

Additional Information: noram.no/noram_stipend/andre-stipend/

For further information contact:

The Norway–America Association, Rådhusgaten 23B, N-0158 Oslo, Norway.

Tel: (47) 233 571 60
Fax: (47) 233 571 75
Email: info@noram.no

American-Scandinavian Foundation Scholarships (ASF)

Purpose: To encourage Scandinavians to undertake advanced study and research programmes in the United States
Eligibility: Applicants must be citizens of Denmark, Finland, Iceland, Norway or Sweden and have completed their undergraduate degree. They should be fluent in English. Citizens of Finland, Iceland and Norway must apply through the sister-societies in their home country
Level of Study: Postgraduate
Type: Fellowship
Value: The American-Scandinavian Foundation (ASF) offers over US$500,000
Length of Study: 1 year
Frequency: Annual
Country of Study: United States of America
Application Procedure: Applicants must complete an application on ASF application forms. More information available on our website - www.amscan.org/fellowships-and-grants/fellowships-and-grants-for-advanced-study-or-research-in-the-usa/
Funding: Foundation
Additional Information: www.amscan.org/fellowships-and-grants/fellowshipsgrants-to-study-in-scandinavia/

For further information contact:

58 Park Ave, New York, NY 10016, United States of America.

Tel: (1) 212 879 9779
Fax: (1) 212 249 3444
Email: grants@amscan.org

John Dana Archbold Fellowship Program

Purpose: To support educational exchange between the United States of America and Norway.
Eligibility: Open to citizens of the United States of America citizens aged 20–35, in good health and of good character. Qualified applicants must show evidence of a high level of competence in their chosen field, indicate a seriousness of

purpose, and have a record of social adaptability. There is ordinarily no language requirement.
Level of Study: Postgraduate, Professional development, Research
Type: Fellowship
Value: US$23,000
Length of Study: 1 year
Frequency: Annual
Study Establishment: University of Oslo International Summer School
Country of Study: United States of America
Application Procedure: Applicants must write to the Nansen Fund, Inc. for an application form
Closing Date: 1 November
Funding: Private
Additional Information: The University of Oslo International Summer School offers orientation and Norwegian languages courses 6 weeks before the start of the regular academic year. For Americans, tuition is paid. Attendance is required. Americans visit Norway in even-numbered years and Norwegians visit the United States of America in odd-numbered years. For further information please contact the Nansen Fund, Inc. www.amscan.org/fellowships-and-grants/fellowshipsgrants-to-study-in-scandinavia/

For further information contact:

Rådhusgata 23B, N-0158 Oslo, Norway.

Tel: (47) 23 35 71 60

Memorial Fund of 8 May

Purpose: To promote cultural exchange between foreign countries and Norwegian residential experiential colleges by providing scholarships for residence, and to help prepare young people for everyday life in the community.
Eligibility: Open to candidates aged 18–22 years who do not have a permanent residence in Norway, and do not hold a Norwegian passport. Candidates must be planning to return to their home country after a year in Norway. Candidates must be aware of the kind of education the Memorial Fund bursaries cover, that being a year in a Norwegian residential colleges, not admission to education on a higher level, such as a university, or specialized training.
Type: Scholarship
Value: The scholarship will cover board and lodging. In addition it is possible to apply for extra funds. Applicants from some countries may apply for required books and excursions arranged by the school. Also, extra support may be provided for short study trips and short courses before or after the school year. A fixed amount towards spending

money may also be given. Normally the students must pay their own travelling expenses. The colleges do not charge tuition fees.

Length of Study: 1 year

Frequency: Annual

Study Establishment: Norwegian residential experiential colleges.

Country of Study: Norway

Application Procedure: Applicants must request more information and application forms from the Memorial Fund of 8 May or to the nearest Norwegian Embassy. Applicants who require a scholarship to attend a Norwegian college should not apply to a them directly. In this case, the Board will place successful applicants at a college school based on their hobbies and interest. Residence permits must be applied for by each individual student when a scholarship has been granted.

No. of awards offered: 700

Closing Date: 1 November

No. of awards given last year: 25

No. of applicants last year: 700

Additional Information: A residential experiential college is a 1-year independent residential school, primarily for young adults, offering many non-traditional subjects of study. Each college has its own profile, but as a group, the Norwegian colleges teach classes covering almost all areas, including history, arts, crafts, music, sports, philosophy, theatre, photography etc. www.grad.uchicago.edu/fellowship/john-dana-archbold-fellowship-in-norway/

For further information contact:

IKF, Grensen 9a, N-0159 Oslo, Norway.

Email: ikf@ikf.no

Norwegian Emigration Fund

Purpose: To support for advanced or specialized study in Norway

Eligibility: Open to citizens and residents of the United States of America. The fund may also give grants to institutions in the United States of America whose activities are primarily centred on the subjects mentioned

Level of Study: Doctorate, Graduate, Professional development

Type: Grant

Value: NOK 5,000–20,000

Frequency: Annual

Country of Study: Norway

Application Procedure: Applicants must complete an application form and return it clearly marked Emigration Fund to Nordmanns-Forbundet. Applications as well as enclosures will not be returned

Closing Date: 1 February

Funding: Government

For further information contact:

Email: norseman@online.no

Norwegian Marshall Fund

Purpose: To provide financial support for Americans to come to Norway to conduct postgraduate study or research in areas of mutual importance to Norway and the United States of America, thereby increasing knowledge, understanding and strengthening the ties of friendship between the two countries.

Eligibility: Open to citizens of the United States of America, who have arranged with a Norwegian sponsor or research institution to pursue a research project or programme in Norway. Under special circumstances, the awards can be extended to Norwegians for study or research in the United States of America.

Level of Study: Postgraduate

Type: Award

Value: US$1,500–4,500 or NOK10,000–30,000

Length of Study: Varies

Frequency: Annual

Country of Study: Norway

Application Procedure: Applicants must contact the Norway-America Association to receive an application. Application forms must be typewritten either in English or Norwegian and submitted in duplicate, including all supplementary materials. Each application must also be accompanied by a letter of support from the project sponsor or affiliated research institution in Norway. There is an application fee of Norwegian Krone 350.

No. of awards offered: 5–15

Closing Date: 15 March

Funding: Private

Additional Information: www.postgraduatefunding.com/award-2647

For further information contact:

Rådhusgata 23B, N-0158 Oslo, Norway.

Tel: (47) 23 35 71 60

Norwegian Thanksgiving Fund Scholarship

Purpose: To provide eligible students to pursue their studies.

Eligibility: The applicant must be a US citizen doing graduate level work in Norway. The student must be working on social medicine, Norwegian culture, fisheries, geology, glaciology or astronomy at a Norwegian university.

Level of Study: Graduate

Type: Scholarship

Value: US$3,000

Frequency: Annual

Country of Study: Any country

Application Procedure: Candidates must contact the American Scandinavian Foundation.

No. of awards offered: 1

Closing Date: 15 March

Contributor: Former Norwegian students and friends

SCHOLARSHIPS FOR AMERICANS TO STUDY IN NORWAY

Purpose: The purpose of the scholarships is to provide financial support for Americans to study in Norway. By supporting post-graduate study or research in areas of mutual importance to Norway and the United States, we hope to bring the two countries closer.

Eligibility: The applicant must be American citizen, planning to study/currently studying in Norway.

Type: Scholarship

Value: NOK 10 000– 40 000.

Frequency: Annual

Country of Study: Any country

No. of awards offered: 10

Closing Date: 1 April

Additional Information: noram.no/en/scholarship-americans/

For further information contact:

The Norway-America Association Rådhusgaten 23 B, N-0158 Oslo, Norway.

Tel: (47) 23 35 71 60

Email: info@noram.no

The Norway-America Association Awards

Purpose: Norwegians who wish to study in the United States on the graduate level.

Eligibility: Open to Norwegian who wish to study in the United States on the graduate level, must have completed their Bachelor's Degree before applying for these scholarships. The applicants must also be members of the Norway-America Association, and the membership fee is NOK 200 per year.

Level of Study: Graduate, Research

Type: Award

Value: US$2,000–US$20,000

Frequency: Annual

Country of Study: United States of America

Application Procedure: Check website for further details

Closing Date: 22 September

The Norway-America Association Graduate & Research Stipend

Purpose: To give the student substantial financial support for 1 year of studies in the United States.

Eligibility: Open to Norwegians and members of the Norway-America Association, and he/she must pay NOK 250 in administrative fees and are currently living in Norway, and intend to return to Norway after their graduation.

Level of Study: Graduate, Research

Type: Award

Value: US$2,000–US$25,000

Country of Study: Norway

Application Procedure: Check website for further details.

Closing Date: 22 September

The Professional Development Award

Purpose: To help established professionals with a higher education who want to study within their own field of interest.

Eligibility: Open to Norwegian professionals who worked for at least 3 years after finishing his or her education as well as planning on doing special research or further study in their fields.

Level of Study: Postgraduate

Type: Award

Value: US$250 and maximum of US$1,000

Frequency: Annual

Country of Study: Any country

Application Procedure: Check website for further details.

No. of awards offered: 2

Additional Information: Candidates must be invited to apply for this award. There is also an administrative fee of NOK 250, which must be deposited in bank account with number 7878.05.23025. Please contact the American-Scandinavian Foundation or the Norway-America Association directly in order to find the appropriate scholarship. www.grad.uchicago.edu/fellowship/john-dana-archbold-fellowship-in-norway/

The Torskeklubben Stipend

Purpose: To promote Norwegian-American relations through helping Norwegians come to the United States to study.
Eligibility: Open to Norwegians and must already be accepted at the Graduate School at the University of Minnesota before applying for the award.
Level of Study: Graduate
Type: Award
Value: US$15,000
Frequency: Annual
Country of Study: Norway
Application Procedure: Application forms are available upon request from the Norway-America Association and the Graduate School at the University of Minnesota or it can be downloaded from the website.
Closing Date: 1 March
Funding: Private

For further information contact:

2720 34th Street NW, Washington, DC 20008, United States of America.

Tel: (1) 202 333 6000

Novo Nordisk A/S

Novo Alle 1, DK-2880 Bagsvaerd, Denmark.

Tel: (45) 44 44 88 88
Website: www.novonordisk.com
Contact: Director

Novo Nordisk A/S develops, produces, and markets pharmaceutical products. The Company focuses on diabetes care and offers insulin delivery systems and other diabetes products. Novo Nordisk also works in areas such as haemostatis management, growth disorders, and hormone replacement therapy. The Company offers educational and training materials. Novo Nordisk markets worldwide.

National Fellowship and Scholarship for Higher Education of ST Students

Purpose: National Fellowship and Scholarship for Higher Education of ST Students is offered by Ministry of Tribal Affairs. This is a central sector scheme for the ST students who are selected for pursuing MPhil and PhD. The application form is available online and students can apply via the link given on this page. The scholarship has emerged as two different schemes i.e. Rajiv Gandhi National Fellowship for ST students and top class education for ST students. The fellowship covers under Rajiv Gandhi National Fellowship programme and scholarship is covered by top-class education.
Eligibility: 1. Candidates must belong to ST category. 2. Candidates should get registered for the full-time Mphil and PhD course. 3. Scholarship, the students must have taken admission in their notified institution. 4. Family income should not exceed more than 6 Lac P/A.
Level of Study: Postdoctorate
Type: Scholarship
Value: Tuition Fees, Books & Stationery-Rs.3000/-; Living expenses-2200/- per month; Computer & Accessories-Rs.45000/
Frequency: Annual
Country of Study: Any country
No. of awards offered: 1000
Closing Date: 15 December
Funding: Foundation
Additional Information: www.vikaspedia.in/education/policies-and-schemes/scholarships/p-g-and-above-scholarships/national-fellowship-and-scholarship-for-higher-education-of-st-students

For further information contact:

Novo Alle 1, 2880 Bagsværd, Denmark.

Tel: (45) 44 44 88 88
Email: info@vidhyaa.in

Novo Nordisk Foundation

Tuborg Havnevej 19, DK-2900 Hellerup, Denmark.

Tel: (45) 3527 6600
Email: info@novonordiskfonden.dk
Contact: Kirsten Klüver, Grant Administrator

The Novo Nordisk Foundation dates back to 1922, when Nobel laureate August Krogh returned home from the United States and Canada with permission to produce insulin in the Nordic countries. This marked the beginning of the development of world-class diabetes medicine and a subsequent Danish business and export venture. It also led to the establishment of several foundations that, many years later, merged into today's Novo Nordisk Foundation.

Postdoc Fellowship for Research Abroad - Bioscience and Basic Biomedicine

Purpose: The Novo Nordisk Foundation invites young, ambitious researchers in Denmark to apply for a post-doctoral fellowship to conduct research outside of Denmark, with the purpose of obtaining knowledge, training and research experience in an international research environment. Associating the fellow to a Danish research institution throughout the fellowship, and thereby facilitating the return to, and integration in, the Danish academic research environment.

Eligibility: The applicant will carry out research at least 3 years abroad, followed by up to 1 year in Denmark. Has obtained a PhD degree within 5 years of the fellowship start date. Can apply as a PhD-student if the supervisor signs a declaration stating that the applicant is expected to graduate before the start date of the fellowship. Can apply if he/she has already started a postdoctoral stay abroad. However, the time spent as postdoc abroad must not exceed 1 year at the time of application. Has established contact with the laboratory abroad and has support from the principle investigator/lab head at the foreign research institution. Has considerable prior association to the Danish education or research community.

Level of Study: Postdoctorate

Type: Fellowship

Value: The Novo Nordisk Foundation awards DKK 1 million per year, that is, for a total of up to DKK 4 million/fellowship.

Length of Study: 4 years

Frequency: Annual

Country of Study: Denmark

Application Procedure: The applicant has to submit application via the foundation's application system (the green 'Apply' button at the top of the screen) from the indicated 'Application opens' date.

No. of awards offered: 3

Closing Date: 11 January

Contributor: Novo Nordisk Foundation

No. of applicants last year: 3

Additional Information: For more information refer: www.novonordiskfonden.dk/sites/default/files/information_and_guidelines_for_applicants_postdoc_fellowship_for_researc.pdf
www.novonordiskfonden.dk/en/grants/postdoc-fellowship-for-research-abroad-bioscience-and-basic-biomedicine/

For further information contact:

Tuborg Havnevej 19, 2900 Hellerup, Denmark.

Tel: (45) 35 27 66 00

Nuffic

Kortenaerkade 11, 2518 AX Den Haag, PO Box 29777, NL-2502 LT The Hague, Netherlands.

Tel: (31) 70 4260 260
Email: nuffic@nuffic.nl
Website: www.nuffic.net

We are Nuffic, the Dutch organization for internationalization in education. From primary and secondary education to MBO, higher education and research, and adult education.

Netherlands Organization for International Cooperation in Higher Education-Natural Family Planning Fellowships for PhD Studies

Purpose: To allow candidates to pursue a PhD at one of 18 Dutch universities and institutes for international education.

Eligibility: Candidate must be a national of one of 61 developing countries and have been admitted to a Dutch institution as a PhD fellow. Priority will be given to female candidates and candidates from sub-Saharan Africa.

Level of Study: Doctorate

Type: Fellowship

Value: €595–1190

Length of Study: 4 years

Frequency: Annual

Country of Study: Any country

Application Procedure: After being accepted for admission to a Dutch institution, the candidate may submit a request for a PhD fellowship. Applicant must present a completed NFP PhD study application form to the Netherlands embassy or consulate in his/her own country. The application must be accompanied by the necessary documentation and by a research proposal that is supported by the supervisor(s). Form can be downloaded from website.

No. of awards offered: Varies

Closing Date: 1 February

No. of applicants last year: Varies

Additional Information: www.european-funding-guide.eu/other-financial-assistance/14452-nfp-fellowships-phd-studies

N

Office of International Affairs at Ohio State University (OIA)

140 Enarson Classroom Building, 2009 Millikin Rd, Columbus, OH 43210, United States of America.

Tel:	(1) 614 292 6101
Email:	bock.126@osu.edu
Website:	oia.osu.edu/
Contact:	Jennifer Bock, Student Immigration Coordinator

The Office of International Affairs provides leadership and international expertise to ensure a coordinated and dynamic strategy for university-wide global engagement. To further Ohio State's international goals and to advance the university's reputation world-wide, the Office of International Affairs facilitates international experiences for students and faculty, supports academic programs and research, coordinates international partnerships, administers grants and scholarships for global engagement and contributes to enriching the Ohio State experience for the university's international student and scholar population. The Office of International Affairs falls under the umbrella of the Office of Academic Affairs, which has responsibility for the administration and coordination of all academic areas of the university.

Everett And Florence Drumright Scholarship

Purpose: The awarding of scholarships is based on a combination of academic merit and financial need. Students in all fields are eligible
Eligibility: Check the official website.
Level of Study: Graduate
Type: Scholarship
Value: US$1,000
Frequency: Annual

Country of Study: Any country
Funding: Private

For further information contact:

509 University Hall (M/C 590), 601 South Morgan Street, Chicago, IL 60607-7128, United States of America.

Tel:	(1) 312 996 5455
Email:	oia@uic.edu

Office of Research & Graduate Education Pfizer Inc

A-300 HSC, Box 35640, Washington, D.C. 20001–20098, United States of America.

Tel:	(1) 800 201 1214
Contact:	Dr Albert Berger

Pfizer's Medical and Academic Partnerships provide support for researchers in a range of medical disciplines.

Pfizer Scholar

Purpose: To support research bridging the basic science of epidemiology with clinical medicine
Eligibility: Applicants must have completed their clinical training and demonstrate the motivation and ability to conduct original research
Level of Study: Postgraduate
Type: Grant
Value: US$65,000 per year
Length of Study: 3 years
Frequency: Annual

© Springer Nature Limited 2022
Palgrave Macmillan (ed.), *The Grants Register 2023*,
https://doi.org/10.1057/978-1-349-96053-8

Study Establishment: A United States medical school
Country of Study: United States of America
Application Procedure: Online via the website
Closing Date: 9 January
Funding: Commercial
No. of awards given last year: 2
Additional Information: Grantees must plan to conduct their research at a United States academic institution with an experienced mentor www.collegescholarships.org/scholarships/companies/pfizer.htm

For further information contact:

Email: mzebrowski@metrohealth.org

Pfizer Scholars Grants in Pain Medicine

Purpose: To support physician scientists who wish to pursue basic biomedical research in an academic setting
Level of Study: Postgraduate
Type: Scholarship
Value: US$65,000 per year
Length of Study: 2 years
Frequency: Annual
Study Establishment: United States academic medical institution
Country of Study: United States of America
Application Procedure: Online via the website
Closing Date: 9 January
Funding: Commercial
Additional Information: Applicants will be selected for the quality of their research proposals, mentioning program and potential for advancing pain medicine www.collegescholarships.org/scholarships/companies/pfizer.htm

For further information contact:

Email: mzebrowski@metrohealth.org

Ohio Arts Council

Rhodes State Office Tower, 30 E. Broad Street, 33rd Floor, Columbus, OH 43215-3414, United States of America.

Tel: (1) 614 466 2613
Email: communications@oac.ohio.gov
Website: oac.ohio.gov/

The Ohio Arts Council is a state agency that funds and supports quality arts experiences to strengthen Ohio communities culturally, educationally and economically. It was created in 1965 to foster and encourage the development of the arts and assist the preservation of Ohio's cultural heritage.

Ohio Arts Council Individual Excellence Awards

Purpose: The Individual Excellence Awards program recognizes outstanding accomplishments by artists in a variety of disciplines. Individual artists will be supported through programs that recognize excellence, preserve cultural traditions, and offer developmental support.
Eligibility: Creative artists who are residents of Ohio may apply to this program. Applicants must have lived in Ohio for one year prior to the deadline, and must remain in the state throughout the grant period. Applicants must be at least eighteen years of age.
Level of Study: Postgraduate
Type: Award/Grant
Value: US$4,000
Frequency: Annual
Country of Study: United States of America
Application Procedure: Individual Excellence Awards program applications must be submitted via the ARTIE system (ohioartscouncil.smartsimple.com/s_Login.jsp) refer to ARTIE Individual Artist Grant Applications oac.ohio.gov/Portals/0/grants/Guidelines/Guidelines_ARTIE_Inds.pdf) for a description of the process.
Closing Date: 1 September
Funding: Government
Additional Information: NOTE: Up to two artists who worked together to create a body of work, and who plan to continue working together, may apply collaboratively, with each artist retaining creative ownership of the completed artwork. If awarded an Individual Excellence Award, the collaborative applicants split the award equally. Collaborative artists must each submit an application with the same narrative on each application, and each must submit the same required support materials. For more details please refer oac.ohio.gov/grants#4436-individual-artists, oac.ohio.gov/Portals/0/grants/Guidelines/Individual_Excellence.pdf

For further information contact:

30 E. Broad Street, 33rd Floor, Columbus, OH 43215-3414, United States of America.

Tel: (1) 614 728 4421
Email: katie.davis@oac.ohio.gov

Omohundro Institute of Early American History and Culture

Omohundro Institute, P.O. Box 8781, Williamsburg, VA 23187-8781, United States of America.

Tel: (1) 757 221 1114
Email: OIdirector@wm.edu; oieahc@wm.edu
Website: oieahc.wm.edu/
Contact: Karin Wulf, Executive Director

The Omohundro Institute of Early American History and Culture supports scholars and scholarship focused on the expansive field of early American history. The OI is an independent research organization sponsored by William and Mary. Our scope encompasses the history and cultures of North America from circa 1450 to 1820 and includes related developments in Africa, the British Isles, the Caribbean, Europe, and Latin America.

Omohundro Institute-NEH Postdoctoral Fellowship

Purpose: The Omohundro Institute of Early American History & Culture (OI) is pleased to announce an expanded residential postdoctoral fellowship program in any area of early American studies and funded by a grant from the National Endowment of the Humanities' Fellowship Programs at Independent Research Institutions (FPIRI) program
Eligibility: Applicants must have met all requirements for the doctorate, including a successful defense, by the application deadline. Foreign nationals must have been in continuous residence in the United States for the three years immediately preceding the date of application for the fellowship in order to be eligible for NEH funding.
Level of Study: Postdoctorate
Type: Fellowship
Value: US$5,000 per month
Length of Study: 1 Year
Frequency: Annual
Study Establishment: Omohundro Institute
Country of Study: United States of America
Application Procedure: You will need the following documents in PDF format in order to complete your application 1. Curriculum Vitae. 2. Abstract (a one-paragraph summary of your project). 3. Statement of proposed work (4 to 7 pages). 4. Manuscript (up to 100 pages). 5. Three references. You will need to provide contact information for the three scholars who have agreed to serve as references for you. All letters of recommendation should be addressed to Chair, OI-NEH

Postdoctoral Fellowship Committee and sent by email to oieahc@wm.edu. Apply online oieahc.wm.edu/postdoctoral-fellowship-application/
No. of awards offered: 2
Closing Date: 1 November
Funding: Foundation
Contributor: Omohundro Institute and National Endowment of the Humanities
Additional Information: Please note that all recipients of Omohundro Institute fellowships are expected to provide an ORCID identifier. For more information: oieahc.wm.edu/fellowships/neh/

For further information contact:

P.O. Box 8781, Williamsburg, VA 23187-8781, United States of America.

Email: oieahc@wm.edu

Oncology Nursing Society Foundation (ONS)

125 Enterprise Drive, Pittsburgh, PA 15275-1214, United States of America.

Tel: (1) 866 257 4667
Email: info@onfgivesback.org
Website: www.onsfoundation.org/
Contact: Director of Research

The mission of the Oncology Nursing Foundation is to support cancer nursing excellence. The Oncology Nursing Foundation is a national public, non-profit, tax-exempt, charitable organization headquartered in Pittsburgh, PA and dedicated to oncology nurses from around the world. This funding has translated to career development awards, academic scholarships, research grants, a myriad of specialized educational initiatives, as well as nurse wellness support.

Doctoral Scholarships

Purpose: To provide scholarships to registered nurses who are interested in and committed to oncology nursing to continue their education by pursuing a research doctoral degree (PhD or DNSc) or clinical doctoral degree (DNP).
Eligibility: 1. The candidate must be currently enrolled in (or applying to) a Ph.D. or DNP nursing degree program for the 2023–2024 academic year (starting fall 2023.). 2. The

candidate must have a current license to practice as a registered nurse and must have a commitment to oncology nursing. 3. The candidate must provide a letter of reference from the current work supervisor or academic advisor on organizational letterhead, signed by the individual providing recommendation. The letter must address the applicant's ability to perform doctoral-level work.

Level of Study: Doctorate
Type: Scholarship
Value: US$5,000 and US$7,500
Frequency: Dependent on funds available
Country of Study: Any country
Application Procedure: Two professional letters of support are required. One of these letters must address the applicant's ability to perform doctoral level work. Apply Online. Required: Submit US$5 application fee (www.ons.org/store/oncology-nursing-foundation-academic-scholarship-application-fee) payable to Oncology Nursing Foundation through ONS. www.onsfoundation.org/funding-for-nurses/education/doctoral-scholarships
Closing Date: 30 January

For further information contact:

Tel: (1) 866 257 4667
Email: info@onfgivesback.org

Master's Scholarships

Purpose: To provide scholarships to registered nurses who are interested in and committed to oncology nursing to continue their education by pursuing a master's degree in nursing.
Eligibility: 1. The candidate must be enrolled in (or applying to) a master's degree program at an accredited institution in the 2023–2024 academic year (starting fall 2023) and in good academic standing 2. The candidate must be a registered nurse. 3. The candidate must have a commitment to oncology nursing 4. The candidate must provide a letter of reference.
Level of Study: Masters Degree
Type: Scholarship
Value: US$5,000 each
Frequency: Dependent on funds available
Country of Study: Any country
Application Procedure: Required: Submit a US$5 application fee made payable to Oncology Nursing Foundation through ONS. www.ons.org/store/oncology-nursing-foundation-academic-scholarship-application-fee?pk_vid=df08 5644dbc1665116430923107b580c
Closing Date: 30 January
No. of awards given last year: 39

For further information contact:

Tel: (1) 866 257 4667
Email: info@onfgivesback.org

Oncology Doctoral Scholarships

Purpose: To provide scholarships to registered nurses who are interested in and committed to oncology nursing to continue their education by pursuing a research doctoral degree (PhD or DNSc) or clinical doctoral degree (DNP).
Eligibility: 1. The candidate must be currently enrolled in (or applying to) a PhD, DNSc or DNP nursing degree program for the 2023–2024 academic year (starting fall 2023). 2. The candidate must have a current license to practice as a registered nurse and must have an interest in and commitment to oncology nursing.
Level of Study: Graduate
Type: Scholarship
Value: US$5,000 and US$7,500
Frequency: Annual
Country of Study: Any country
Application Procedure: 1. Two professional letters of support are required. One of these letters must address the applicant's ability to perform doctoral level work. 2. At the end of each year of scholarship participation, the nurse shall submit a summary describing the education activities in which he/she participated. Apply Online. Required: Submit US$5 application fee (www.ons.org/store/oncology-nursing-foundation-academic-scholarship-application-fee) payable to Oncology Nursing Foundation through ONS. www.onsfoundation.org/funding-for-nurses/education/doctoral-scholarships
Closing Date: 31 January
Funding: Foundation, Private
Additional Information: NOTE: An individual cannot receive this award more than one time. www.onsfoundation.org/funding-for-nurses/education/doctoral-scholarships

For further information contact:

Email: info@onfgivesback.org

Oncology Nursing Society Breast Cancer Research Grant

Purpose: To increase breast cancer awareness in communities by supporting nurse-directed and community-focused educational programs.
Eligibility: 1. Program must be an ONS Chapter activity and focus on community education. 2. Grant is not intended to support work-based community education programs. Program cannot limit attendance to an institution, hospital, or

hospital network, or nurse work setting. 3. Individual programs and/or Chapters can only receive one grant.

Level of Study: Research

Type: Grant

Value: Up to US$1,000

Frequency: Annual

Country of Study: United States of America

Application Procedure: Apply Online First-time users must create an account using the link below. Returning users may access the application directly. 1. Register by creating a username and password on the Closerware Grantmaker site. 2. Access the online application. www.closerware.com/intake/bo/grant/ApplicationEdit.do?ownerKey=onsf&intakeFormId=36&opportunityId=8295

Funding: Foundation

Contributor: ONS Foundation

Additional Information: Open applications accepted but must be received by the Oncology Nursing Foundation no later than two weeks prior to the program start date. Applications will remain open until funds are expended. For more details please refer: www.onfgivesback.org/funding-nurses/chapter-funding/breast-cancer-community-education-grants-ons-chapters

For further information contact:

125 Enterprise Drive, Pittsburgh, PA 15275, United States of America.

Email: info@onfgivesback.org

Oncology Nursing Society Foundation Research Grant Awards

Purpose: To support oncology nursing research addressing cancer health disparities, including in the topic areas of breast, colorectal, lung or prostate cancer. To support oncology nursing research in symptom science addressing the adverse effects of immunotherapy and emerging therapies used in the treatment of cancer patients. Symptom science in immunotherapy and emerging therapies has been identified as one of the top cancer nursing research priorities in need of new knowledge.

Eligibility: The principal investigator must be a registered nurse actively involved in some aspect of cancer patient care, education or research and be PhD or DNSc prepared that has received and completed at least one research study of at least US$50,000 as PI.

Level of Study: Postgraduate

Type: Grant

Value: Grant up to US$100,000 will be awarded with funding period of up to two years for Addressing Cancer Health Disparities Through Evidence-Based Cancer Nursing Research. Grant up to US$150,000 will be awarded with funding period of up to two years for Addressing the Adverse Effects of Immunotherapy and Emerging Therapies on Cancer Patients

Frequency: Annual

Country of Study: United States of America

Application Procedure: Apply online www.onsfoundation.org/funding-for-nurses/research/research-grant

Closing Date: 17 May

Funding: Foundation

Additional Information: For more information, contact the ONS Foundation Research Department www.onsfoundation.org/funding-for-nurses/research/research-grant

For further information contact:

Email: info@onfgivesback.org

Oncology Research Grant

Purpose: To support rigorous scientific oncology nursing research. Research projects may include investigator-initiated research, pilot or feasibility studies, supplements to current funded projects, or developing a new aspect of a program of research. Funding preference is given to projects that involve nurses in the design and conduct of the research activity and that promote theoretically based oncology practice.

Eligibility: The principal investigator (individual primarily responsible for implementing the proposal and reporting to Oncology Nursing Foundation) must be a registered nurse actively involved in some aspect of cancer patient care, education, or research and be PhD or DNSc prepared (only one PI can appear on the grant).

Level of Study: Graduate

Type: Research grant

Value: US$50,000 over 2 years. At least one member of the research team must have received and completed research study funding of at least US$100,000 as PI

Frequency: Annual

Country of Study: Any country

Application Procedure: Apply online www.onsfoundation.org/funding-for-nurses/research/research-grant

Closing Date: 15 April

Funding: Private

For further information contact:

Tel: (1) 866 257 4667

Email: info@onfgivesback.org

Sandy Purl Mentorship Scholarship

Purpose: To support an additional ONS Chapter member to attend the ONS Chapter Leadership Workshop.

Eligibility: 1. Must be a current ONS Chapter Board or committee member supported by a Chapter Leader Sponsor. (A Chapter Leader Sponsor is a current Chapter Board member who has agreed that the applicant has the approval of the Chapter to attend). 2. Chapter Leaders Sponsors may support more than one individual, however the grant is restricted to support only one individual. 3. Applicants must share their goal for attending the Chapter Leadership Workshop and how they plan to use the information they gained by attending. Applicants must identify the other Chapter member who is attending the Chapter Leadership Workshop

Level of Study: Graduate

Type: Scholarship

Value: Up to US$1,000

Frequency: Annual

Country of Study: Any country

Application Procedure: Apply online www.onfgivesback. org/apply-now. Kindly view the following link for further details www.onfgivesback.org/funding-nurses/chapter-funding/ sandy-purl-mentorship-scholarship

Closing Date: 15 May

Funding: Private

Additional Information: Note: An individual cannot receive this award more than one time. www.onfgivesback.org/ funding-nurses/chapter-funding/sandy-purl-mentorship-scholarship

For further information contact:

Email: info@onfgivesback.org

Ontario Council on Graduate Studies (OCGS)

Council of Ontario Universities, 180 Dundas St West, Suite 1800, Toronto, ON M5G 1Z8, Canada.

Tel: (1) 416 979 2165 ext 218
Email: ktodic@cou.ca
Website: cou.ca/members-groups/affiliates/ocav/ocgs/
Contact: Katarina Todic, Senior Policy Analyst, Policy and Sector Collaboration

The Ontario Council on Graduate Studies (OCGS) is an affiliate of the Council of Ontario Universities (COU). The Ontario Council on Graduate Studies seeks to highlight the importance of graduate education in Ontario, develop and implement best practices in the delivery of graduate education, and advocate for continuing improvement in graduate programs.

Women's Health

Purpose: The community of women's health scholars fostered by this Awards program will excel, according to internationally accepted standards of scientific excellence, in the creation of new knowledge about women's health and its translation into improved health for women, more effective health services and products for women, and a strengthened heath care system.

Eligibility: 1. To be eligible for an Ontario Women's Health Scholars award, an applicant must be a Canadian citizen or a permanent resident of Canada at the time of the application deadline. 2. To be eligible for a master's award, an applicant must be registered as a full-time student in a master's program at an Ontario university at the beginning of the award period (i.e., fall 2023), and must remain registered as a full-time student throughout the term of the award; a master's student remains eligible until the end of the sixth term of full-time study. 3. To be eligible for a doctoral award, an applicant must be registered as a full-time student in a doctoral program at an Ontario university at the beginning of the award period and must remain registered as a full-time student throughout the term of the award; a doctoral student remains eligible until the end of the 15th term of full-time study. 4. To be eligible for a postdoctoral award, an applicant must be engaged in full-time research at an Ontario university at the time of taking up the award, and must have completed all requirements for the doctoral degree by May 31, 2023 and normally no earlier than January 31, 2020). In cases where an applicant completed all requirements for the doctoral degree before this date, an explanation of extenuating circumstances (e.g., childrearing responsibilities) must accompany the application.

Level of Study: Doctorate, Masters Degree, Postdoctorate

Type: Award

Value: 1. Master's Awards - C$25,000 plus C$1,000 research allowance. 2. Doctoral Awards - C$35,000 plus C$2,000 research allowance. 3. Postdoctoral Awards - C$50,000 plus C$5,000 research allowance.

Frequency: Annual

Country of Study: Canada

Application Procedure: Application forms are available at cou.ca/resources/awards/, or from the offices of the Deans of Graduate Studies in Ontario universities. A complete application requires 1. an application form completed by the applicant; 2. the applicant's curriculum vitae, which should include information regarding the eligibility criteria; 3. a statement of no more than 1,000 words describing the research to be undertaken during the period of graduate or postdoctoral study and any progress already made in this research, and a non-technical summary of no more than 500 words, both written by the applicant (one additional page is allowed for diagrams, bibliography, etc.). For more details please refer https://cou.ca/wp-content/uploads/2021/09/OWHS-Awards-Announcement-2022-23-English.pdf

No. of awards offered: 8

Closing Date: 29 January

Funding: Government

Contributor: Ontario Ministry of Health and Long-Term Care

No. of awards given last year: 9

Additional Information: Please see the website for further details cou.ca/resources/awards/

For further information contact:

Tel: (1) 416 979 2165 ext 235

Email: SeniorDirectorQA@cou.ca

Ontario Federation of Anglers & Hunters (OFAH)

4601 Guthrie Drive, PO Box 2800, Peterborough, ON K9J 8L5, Canada.

Tel: (1) 705 748 6324

Email: ofah@ofah.org

Website: www.ofah.org/

The Ontario Federation of Anglers & Hunters (OFAH), Canada's largest nonprofit, charitable fish and wildlife conservation organization. The Ontario Federation of Anglers and Hunters (OFAH) will strive to ensure the protection of our hunting and fishing heritage and the enhancement of hunting and fishing opportunities; encourage safe and responsible participation; and champion the conservation of Ontario's fish and wildlife resources, which so enrich our lives.

OFAH/Fleming College Fish & Wildlife Scholarship

Eligibility: The OFAH/Fleming College Fish & Wildlife Scholarship is open to Fleming College students who: 1. are in their final year of the Fish and Wildlife Program (Technician or Technology Graduate); 2. are continuing further studies in a related University Degree or College Diploma program (e.g. third-year Fish and Wildlife

3. Technology, or Ontario College Graduates Certificates – Aquaculture, and Conservation and Environmental Law Enforcement Programs, etc.); and 4. have a minimum GPA of 3.0

Type: Scholarship

Value: Value of US$2,000

Country of Study: Any country

Application Procedure: Send all supporting documents and your application to: Dean/Campus Principal Office School of Environmental & Natural Resource Sciences, Frost Campus Fleming College SENRS_deansoffice@flemingcollege.ca; Reference: OFAH/Fleming College Fish & Wildlife Scholarship

Closing Date: 18 February

For further information contact:

Chris Robinson, Program Manager, Ontario Federation Anglers and Hunter.

Tel: (1) 705 748 6324 Ext 240

Email: SENRS_deansoffice@flemingcollege.ca; chris_robinson@ofah.org

Oil Natural Air Forced/OFAF Zone 6 Wildlife Research Grant

Purpose: To financially support students who wish to pursue their research work in wildlife research

Level of Study: Research

Type: Fellowship

Value: C$2,000

Frequency: Annual

Country of Study: Canada

Application Procedure: 1. Applicants must submit a complete application form, research proposal consisting of abstract, introduction, methods, results anticipated, literature cited and budget, a curriculum vitae, transcripts. 2. Should submit letter from supervising professor supporting the intended research projects

Ontario Federation of Anglers & Hunters/Oakville and District Rod & Gun Club Conservation Research Grant

Purpose: The OFAH is committed to supporting students and their research, which provides the science needed to inform and support sound fish and wildlife conservation management in Ontario. Preference will be given to projects utilizing the funds for equipment and field support.

Eligibility: Any graduate or post-graduate university student currently researching a fish and wildlife topic, and whose findings would benefit Ontario's fish and/or wildlife management.

Level of Study: Research

Type: Research grant

Value: C$4,000

Frequency: Annual

Country of Study: Canada

Application Procedure: Apply online www.ofah.org/pro grams/ofah-student-research-grants/

Closing Date: 12 February

Additional Information: For more details: www.ofah.org/programs/ofah-student-research-grants/

For further information contact:

Ontario Federation of Anglers & Hunters, PO Box 2800 / 4601 Guthrie Dr, Peterborough, ON K9J 8L5, Canada.

Tel: (1) 705 748 6324

Ontario Ministry of Education and Training

Ministry of Education, 315 Front Street, 14th Floor, Toronto, Ontario M7A 0B8, Canada.

Tel: (1) 416 325 2929
Email: Ingrid.E.Anderson@ontario.ca
Website: www.ontario.ca/page/education-and-training
Contact: Ingrid Anderson, Communications Branch

Ontario Ministry of Education and Training works to make Ontario's publicly funded education and child care systems the world's best, where all children and students have the opportunity to achieve success.

Ontario Ministry of Education and Training Graduate Scholarship Programme

Purpose: OGS is a merit-based scholarship. Students in graduate studies at the master's and doctoral levels can apply for a merit-based scholarship through the Ontario Graduate Scholarship (OGS) Program. Awards are available to graduate students for all disciplines of academic study at participating schools in Ontario.

Eligibility: 1. You'll be in graduate studies in the master's or doctoral level. 2. You'll be enrolled in a full-time program for 2 or more terms (21 to 52 weeks in total) for the academic year you're submitting your application. 3. You'll be attending one of the participating Ontario school in following link osap.gov.on.ca/OSAPPortal/en/A-ZListofAid/PRDR019245.html

Level of Study: Doctorate, Masters Degree

Type: Scholarship

Value: C$10,000 for 2 consecutive study terms and C$15,000 for 3 consecutive study terms. OGS award is issued for 1. a minimum of 1 academic year (2 or 3 consecutive academic terms). 2. a maximum of 2 years (up to 6 consecutive academic terms). OGS awards maximums for Master's students 2 academic years, for Doctoral students 4 academic years and for Lifetime limit (all students) 6 academic years

Frequency: Annual

Study Establishment: A university in Ontario

Country of Study: Canada

Application Procedure: Use your school's OGS application. If you're applying to more than one graduate program at different schools, submit an OGS application for each school. Contact the Graduate Studies Office at the school you're planning to attend for details on their application process. Please refer osap.gov.on.ca/OSAPPortal/en/A-ZListofAid/PRDR019245.html

Funding: Government

Contributor: The Ministry of Training, Colleges and Universities

Additional Information: Each award is jointly funded by the Province of Ontario (two thirds) and the school offering the award (one third). For more information please refer osap.gov.on.ca/OSAPPortal/en/A-ZListofAid/PRDR019245.html

Ontario Student Assistance Program (OSAP)

Student Financial Assistance Branch, Ministry of Colleges and Universities, PO Box 4500, 189 Red River Road, 4th Floor, Thunder Bay, ON P7B 6G9, Canada.

Tel: (1) 807 343 7260
Email: webmaster.tcu@ontario.ca
Website: www.ontario.ca/page/osap-ontario-student-assistance-program

Minister of Education and the Minister of Training, Colleges and Universities are responsible for the administration of laws relating to education and skills training in Ontario.

Ontario Graduate Scholarship Program

Purpose: Students in graduate studies at the master's and doctoral levels can apply for a merit-based scholarship through the Ontario Graduate Scholarship (OGS) Program. Each award is jointly funded by the Province of Ontario (two thirds) and the school offering the award (one third).

Eligibility: Candidates must be citizens or permanent residents of Canada. To be considered, you must also meet the following criteria 1. You'll be in graduate studies in the master's or doctoral level. 2. You'll be enrolled in a full-time program for 2 or more terms (21 to 52 weeks in total) for the academic year you're submitting your application. 3. You'll be attending one of the participating Ontario school in website

Level of Study: Doctorate, Masters Degree, Postgraduate

Type: Scholarships

Value: C$10,000 for 2 consecutive study terms and C$15,000 for 3 consecutive study terms. Each OGS award is issued for 1. a minimum of 1 academic year (2 or 3 consecutive academic terms). 2. a maximum of 2 years (up to 6 consecutive academic terms).

Length of Study: Master's students: 2 academic years; Doctoral students: 4 academic years; Lifetime limit (all students): 6 academic years

Frequency: Annual

Country of Study: Canada

Application Procedure: Use your school's OGS application. They are normally available in October. If you're applying to more than one graduate program at different schools, submit an OGS application for each school. Contact the Graduate Studies Office (cou.ca/resources/graduate-studies/) at the school you're planning to attend for details on their application process

Funding: Government, Private

Additional Information: For more details: osap.gov.on.ca/OSAPPortal/en/A-ZListofAid/PRDR020870.html

Open Society Foundation - Sofia

56 Solunska Str., BG-1000 Sofia, Bulgaria.

Tel:	(359) 2 930 6619
Email:	info@osi.bg
Website:	osis.bg/?page_id=849&lang=en
Contact:	Ms Iliana Bobova, Education Consultant

Open Society Institute – Sofia is a non-governmental organization, acting for the public benefit, defending the values of the open society in Bulgaria and supporting the integration of the country to the European Union. The Institute is founded in 1990, thanks to a donation of Mr. George Soros. To promote, develop and support the values, dispositions and practices of the open society in Bulgaria.

Open Society Institute's Global Supplementary Grant Program (Grant SGP)

Purpose: To enable qualified students to pursue doctoral studies in the humanities and social sciences

Eligibility: Open to candidates from selected countries from Eastern and Central Europe and the former Soviet Union. Bulgarian nationals under the age of 40 who have been accepted into a full-time doctoral programme at an accredited university in Western Europe, Asia, Australia or North America and have already been awarded partial or full tuition, room and board stipends or other types of financial aid are also eligible

Level of Study: Doctorate

Type: Grant

Value: 50% of tuition and fees or living expenses or additional expenses

Length of Study: Up to 1 year of study with the option to apply for a second year

Frequency: Annual

Study Establishment: Accredited universities

Country of Study: Other

Application Procedure: Applicants must complete an application form and provide the required supporting documents

Closing Date: 1 April

Funding: Private

Contributor: The Open Society Institute in New York

No. of awards given last year: 22

Additional Information: Programme availability and format are reviewed on an annual basis. Changes may occur from year to year. For the most up to date information please contact the Open Society Institute in New York www.european-funding-guide.eu/scholarship/12229-open-society-foundations%C2%A0-%E2%80%93-global-supplementary-grant-program

For further information contact:

Open Society Institute, Network Scholarship Programs, 400 West 59th Street, New York, NY 10019, United States of America.

Tel:	(1) 212 548 0175
Fax:	(1) 212 548 4652
Email:	vjohnson@sorosny.org

Oxford Colleges Hospitality Scheme for East European Scholars

Purpose: To enable overseas scholars to work in Oxford or Cambridge libraries or to consult Oxbridge specialists in their subjects

Eligibility: Open to Scholars from Eastern and Central Europe, who have a good knowledge of English and who are in the process of completing work for an advanced degree, or who are working on a book, or a new course of lectures

Level of Study: Professional development

Type: Scholarship

Value: Full scholarship

Length of Study: 1–3 months

Frequency: Annual

Study Establishment: The University of Oxford and the University of Cambridge

Country of Study: United Kingdom

Application Procedure: Applicants must submit a completed application form, a curriculum vitae, a list of publications and two recommendation letters

No. of awards offered: 45

Closing Date: November

Funding: Government, Private

Contributor: FCO, OSI-Budapest, University of Oxford

No. of awards given last year: 7

No. of applicants last year: 45

Additional Information: Programme availability and format are reviewed on an annual basis. Changes may occur from year to year. For the most up to date information, please contact the Open Society Institute in Budapest www.eac.md/scholarships/soros/oxford_hospitality/index.html

For further information contact:

Open Society Institute, Network Scholarship Programmes, Nador Utca 11, H-1051 Budapest, Hungary.

Email: mariefergusonsmith@hotmail.com

Soros Equality Fellowship

Purpose: Open Society-U.S.'s Soros Equality Fellowship seeks to support emerging midcareer professionals whom we believe will become long-term innovative leaders impacting racial justice.

Eligibility: Applicants must be able to devote at least 35 hours per week to the project if awarded a Fellowship; and the project must be the applicant's only full-time work during the course of the Fellowship.

Type: Fellowship

Value: US$130,000 stipend

Length of Study: 18 months

Country of Study: Any country

Application Procedure: See: www.opensocietyfoundations.org/uploads/423f3678-1988-4ed7-8e19-702da82e2ee9/2022-soros-equality-fellowship-guidelines-20211129.pdf

Closing Date: 14 February

Funding: Individuals

For further information contact:

Email: equality.fellowships@opensocietyfoundations.org

Soros Justice Fellowships

Purpose: Open Society-U.S.'s Soros Justice Fellowships fund outstanding individuals to undertake projects that advance reform, spur debate, and catalyze change on a range of issues facing the U.S. criminal justice system.

Eligibility: All projects must, at a minimum, relate to one or more of the following U.S. criminal justice reform goals: reducing the number of people who are incarcerated or under correctional control, challenging extreme punishment, and promoting fairness and accountability in our systems of justice. Please carefully review the complete guidelines for more details on the specific requirements for each category of fellowships.

Type: Fellowship

Frequency: Annual

Country of Study: United States of America

Application Procedure: Applications must be submitted online via the application

Closing Date: 8 February

Funding: Individuals

For further information contact:

Email: sorosjusticefellowships@opensocietyfoundations.org

Organization for Autism Research (OAR)

2111 Wilson Boulevard, Suite 401, Arlington, VA 22201, United States of America.

Tel: (1) 866 366 9710

Email: info@researchautism.org

Website: researchautism.org/

Contact: 2111 Wilson Boulevard, Suite 401 Arlington, VA 22201

Organization for Autism Research, better known as OAR. OAR was founded in December 2001 by seven individuals whose lives and families had been directly impacted by autism. The studies we fund and the information resources we provide have meaning in the day-to-day lives of persons with autism and their families. Rather than fund research relative to cause and cure, we funds pilot studies on topics of more every day relevance such as education, parent and teacher training, communication, self-care, social skills, employment, behavior and adult and community issues. In pursuing its efforts to change lives, our ultimate focus is quality of life.

Applied Research Competition

Purpose: Since 2002, the Organization for Autism Research has proudly contributed more than US$4.2 million in research grants. OAR is currently accepting proposals for its Applied Research Competition. Our Scientific Council, augmented by highly qualified professionals from the autism community, select and fund the most promising research proposals through three rounds of review pre-proposals, full proposals, and final selection.

Eligibility: International researchers are eligible to apply. At least one member of the research team must hold a Ph.D., M.D., or equivalent degree and maintain a faculty position or equivalent at a college, university, medical school, or other research facility.

Level of Study: Doctorate, Postgraduate

Type: Grant

Value: Grant awards for US$40,000 each

Length of Study: 1-2 year

Frequency: Annual

Country of Study: United States of America

Application Procedure: OAR's Scientific Council and adjunct review panel will evaluate the proposals OAR receives for scientific and technical merit. Applicants must visit the website researchautism.org/research-grants/apply-for-a-grant/applied-research/. Apply online researchautism.smapply.io/prog/applied_research_competition/

No. of awards offered: 8

Closing Date: 3 December

Additional Information: In June, OAR will invite selected applicants to submit full proposals, complete the final review in November, and announce grant recipients in December. For more details: researchautism.org/research-grants/apply-for-a-grant/applied-research/

For further information contact:

Tel:		(1) 703 243 9762

Email:	research@researchautism.org

Organization of American Historians (OAH)

Data Protection Officer, Organization of American Historians, 112 North Bryan Avenue, Bloomington, Indiana 47408-4141, United States of America.

Tel:		(1) 812 855 7311

Email:	oah@oah.org

Website:	www.oah.org/

Founded in 1907, the Organization of American Historians (OAH) is the largest professional society dedicated to the teaching and study of American history. The mission of the organization is to promote excellence in the scholarship, teaching, and presentation of American history, and to encourage wide discussion of historical questions and the equitable treatment of all practitioners of history.

ALA Library History Round Table Davis Article Award

Subjects: The round table is particularly interested in articles that place the subject within its broader historical, social, cultural, and political context and make interdisciplinary connections with print culture and information studies.

Purpose: The Library History Round Table (LHRT) of the American Library Association (ALA) invites submissions for the Donald G. Davis Article Award. The Davis Award is given every even-numbered year to the best article written in English in the field of United States and Canadian library history.

Type: Award

Frequency: Annual

Country of Study: Any country

No. of awards offered: 1

Closing Date: 16 February

For further information contact:

Email:	julie8park@gmail.com

Avery O. Craven Award

Purpose: Since 1985, the Avery O. Craven Award has been presented annually by the OAH for the most original book on the coming of the Civil War, the Civil War years, or the Era of

Reconstruction, with the exception of works of purely military history.

Eligibility: Each entry must be published during the period mentioned in the website.

Type: Award

Frequency: Annual

Country of Study: Any country

Application Procedure: One copy of each entry, clearly labeled must be mailed directly to the committee members listed below. Each committee member must receive all submissions. Applicants must visit the website www.oah.org/awards/book-awards/civil-war-and-reconstruction-award/

Closing Date: 1 October

No. of awards given last year: 1

Additional Information: For more information www.oah.org/awards/book-awards/avery-o-craven-award/. www.oah.org/awards/book-awards/civil-war-and-reconstruction-award/

For further information contact:

Diane Miller Sommerville, Committee Chair, 18 East Country Gate Place, Vestal, NY 13850, United States of America.

China Residency Program

Purpose: Thanks to a generous grant from the Ford Foundation, the Organization of American Historians and the American History Research Association of China (AHRAC) are pleased to announce the third year of the teaching seminars in the People's Republic of China

Eligibility: The OAH International Committee seeks applications from OAH members with strong records of research and teaching excellence who are interested in leading an advanced seminar in the People's Republic of China, focused on one of the following three topics: constitutional history, cultural/gender history or history of the American West

Level of Study: Research

Type: Residency

Length of Study: 3 week-long intensive seminars

Frequency: Annual

Country of Study: United States of America

Application Procedure: The application consists of a short (3–5 pages) curriculum vitae, the name and contact information of 3 references who can speak to the applicant's teaching and scholarship, and an outline of the proposed intensive week-long seminar. Applications should be submitted electronically, in Microsoft Word format, to prizes@oah.org. Please indicate, China Residency Program in the subject line. If you do not receive an email confirmation that your application has been received within 3 days, please contact the OAH Committee Coordinator at khamm@oah.org

Additional Information: www.oah.org/programs/residencies/china/

Civil War and Reconstruction Book Award

Purpose: The Civil War and Reconstruction Book Award is given annually by the Organization of American Historians to the author of the most original book on the coming of the Civil War, the Civil War years, or the Era of Reconstruction.

Level of Study: Graduate

Type: Award

Value: US$500

Frequency: Annual

Country of Study: Any country

Application Procedure: One copy of each entry, clearly labeled "2024 Civil War and Reconstruction Book Award Entry," must be mailed directly to the committee members listed below. Each committee member must receive all submissions postmarked by October 1, 2023.

No. of awards offered: 1

Closing Date: 1 October

No. of awards given last year: 1

No. of applicants last year: 42

Darlene Clark Hine Award

Purpose: The Darlene Clark Hine Award is given annually by the Organization of American Historians to the author of the best book in African American women's and gender history.

Level of Study: Postgraduate

Type: Award

Value: US$2,000

Frequency: Annual

Country of Study: Any country

No. of awards offered: 1

Closing Date: 1 October

Funding: Private

No. of awards given last year: 1

No. of applicants last year: 20

Additional Information: www.oah.org/awards/book-awards/darlene-clark-hine-award/

David Montgomery Award

Purpose: The David Montgomery Award is given annually by the OAH with co-sponsorship by the Labor and Working-Class History Association (LAWCHA) for the best book on a topic in American labor and working-class history.

Eligibility: Eligible works shall be written in English and deal with United States history in significant ways but may include comparative or transnational studies that fall within these guidelines.

Type: Award

Value: US$500

Frequency: Annual

Country of Study: Any country

Application Procedure: One copy of each entry, clearly labeled "David Montgomery Award Entry," must be mailed directly to the committee members listed website. Please refer www.oah.org/awards/book-awards/david-montgomery-award/

No. of awards offered: 1

Closing Date: 1 October

No. of awards given last year: 1

No. of applicants last year: 35

Additional Information: www.oah.org/book-awards/david-montgomery-award/

For further information contact:

David Roediger, Committee Chair, 1501 Rhode Island, Lawrence, KS 66044, United States of America.

David Thelen Award

Purpose: The David Thelen Award honors the best article on American history written in a language other than English.

Eligibility: Articles published between January 1, and December 31, as well as previously unpublished articles, are eligible for consideration. Submissions should be carefully argued and well written. They should offer an original perspective on colonial American and/or U.S. history. Manuscripts should be framed for and addressed to readers outside the U.S. and written in a language other than English.

Type: Award

Value: US$500

Frequency: Every 2 years

Country of Study: Any country

Application Procedure: Technical requirements and submission process 1. Length: Equivalent to approximately 5,000–15,000 words when translated into English. 2. Languages: Other than English. 3. Submissions must include a brief abstract (written in English) explaining how the manuscript meets the criteria stated above. Submissions must be clearly labeled "2024 David Thelen Award Entry." An electronic version of the manuscript must be sent to e-mail address. One hard copy must be mailed to the address. The application should also include the following information: 1. Author's name. 2. Mailing address. 3. Institutional affiliation. 4. E-mail address. 5. Language of submitted article.

Closing Date: 1 May

No. of awards given last year: 1

No. of applicants last year: 6

Additional Information: Please check at www.oah.org/awards/article-essay-awards/david-thelen-award/

For further information contact:

Benjamin H. Irvin, Chair, 2022 David Thelen Award Committee, Executive Editor, Journal of American History, 1215 East Atwater Avenue, Bloomington, IN 47401, United States of America.

Email: jahms@oah.org

Ellis W. Hawley Prize

Purpose: The Ellis W. Hawley Prize is given annually by the Organization of American Historians to the author of the best book-length historical study of the political economy, politics, or institutions of the United States, in its domestic or international affairs, from the Civil War to the present. The prize honors Ellis W. Hawley, Emeritus Professor of History, University of Iowa, an outstanding historian of these subjects.

Eligibility: Eligible works shall include book-length historical studies, written in English and published during a given calendar year

Type: Prize

Value: US$500

Frequency: Annual

Country of Study: Any country

Application Procedure: One copy of each entry, clearly labeled "2024 Ellis W. Hawley Prize Entry," must be mailed directly to the committee members listed below. Each committee member must receive all submissions postmarked by October 1, 2023.

No. of awards offered: 1

Closing Date: 1 October

Contributor: OAH

No. of awards given last year: 1

No. of applicants last year: 78

Additional Information: For more details please check at www.oah.org/awards/book-awards/ellis-w-hawley-prize/

For further information contact:

Email: eyellin@richmond.edu

Erik Barnouw Award

Purpose: Awards are given annually by the Organization of American Historians in recognition of outstanding programming on television, or in documentary film, concerned with

American history, the study of American history, and/or the promotion of American history.

Eligibility: Only films and video programs released January 1 through December 31 are eligible for entry.

Type: Award

Value: US$500

Frequency: Annual

Country of Study: Any country

Application Procedure: Applicants should visit the website for complete application requirements. One copy of each entry, clearly labeled must be sent directly to the committee members listed in website. Each committee member must receive all submissions. www.oah.org/awards/uncategorized-awards/erik-barnouw-award/

No. of awards offered: 2

Closing Date: 7 January

No. of awards given last year: 1

No. of applicants last year: 42

Additional Information: Please check at www.oah.org/awards/uncategorized-awards/erik-barnouw-award/

For further information contact:

Daniel Blake Smith (Committee Chair), DBS Films, 5234 Nottingham Avenue, Saint Louis MO 63109-2963, United States of America.

Email:　dblakesmitty13@gmail.com; Eduardo.Pagan@asu.edu

Frederick Jackson Turner Award

Purpose: The Frederick Jackson Turner Award is given annually by the Organization of American Historians to the author of a first scholarly book dealing with some aspect of American history.

Eligibility: The rules and terms of the competition are as follows 1. Eligible books must be published during the calendar year preceding that in which the award is given; 2. The author may not have previously published a book-length work of history; 3. Submissions will be made by publishers, who may submit such books as they deem eligible; 4. Co-authored works are eligible, as long as neither author has previously published a book of history; 5. Authors who have previously co-authored a book of history are not eligible.

Type: Award

Value: US$1,000

Frequency: Annual

Country of Study: Any country

Application Procedure: One copy of each entry, clearly labeled "2024 Frederick Jackson Turner Award Entry" must be mailed directly to the committee members listed below and

must include a complete list of the author's publications OR a statement from the publisher verifying this is the author's first book. No submission will be considered without this proof of eligibility. Each committee member must receive all submissions postmarked by October 1, 2023.

No. of awards offered: 1

Closing Date: 1 October

No. of awards given last year: 1

No. of applicants last year: 81

Germany Residency Program

Purpose: Thanks to a generous grant from the Fritz Thyssen Foundation, the OAH International Committee is pleased to announce the continuation of the Residency Program in American History–Germany (Germany Residency Program) at the University of Tübingen

Eligibility: The committee seeks applications from OAH members who are established scholars affiliated with an American or Canadian University interested in leading an advanced undergraduate/graduate student seminar in Tübingen. The seminar will cover a topic of U.S. History or the History of Transatlantic Relations of an applicant's design. All fields and methodologies are welcome. The language of instruction is English.

Type: Residency

Value: The Residency Program will provide round-trip air-fare, housing for thirty days, a modest honorarium (around US$1,000), support by a graduate assistant, and office space.

Length of Study: 4 to 5 Weeks

Frequency: Annual

Country of Study: Any country

Application Procedure: The application process for the Germany residency program requires a short CV and an outline of the planned seminar. The application materials must be sent electronically (PDF) to germanyresidency@oah.org. Please indicate "Germany Residency Program" in the subject line.

Closing Date: 1 October

Contributor: OAH

No. of awards given last year: 1

Additional Information: For more details, please visit: www.oah.org/awards/residencies/germany/

For further information contact:

Email:　georg.schild@uni-tuebingen.de

Huggins-Quarles Award

Purpose: For graduate students of color to assist them with expenses related to travel to research collections for the completion of the PhD dissertation. These awards were established to promote greater diversity in the historical profession.

Eligibility: 1. Applicant must be advanced ABD. 2. Applicant must be ALANA (African American, Latino/a, Asian American, Native American) scholar. 3. Applicant's dissertation must focus on U.S. history.

Level of Study: Doctorate

Type: Award

Value: US$1,500 for one award/US$750 each for two awards

Frequency: Annual

Country of Study: Any country

Application Procedure: To apply, the student should submit the following items in one PDF document and in the following order: 1. cover letter, which should also indicate the candidate's progress on the dissertation, including ABD status. 2. CV. 3. abstract: a five-page dissertation proposal (double spaced), which should include a definition of the project, an explanation of the project's significance and contribution to the field, and a description of the most important primary sources. 4. a one-page itemized budget explaining travel and research plans. Each application must include a letter from the dissertation adviser attesting to the student's status and the ways in which the Huggins-Quarles Award will facilitate the completion of the dissertation project. Advisers should e-mail their letters separately to the committee chair. Please refer www.oah.org/awards/dissertation-awards/huggins-quarles-award/

No. of awards offered: 2

Closing Date: 1 January

No. of awards given last year: 1

No. of applicants last year: 7

Additional Information: Please check at www.oah.org/awards/dissertation-awards/huggins-quarles-award/

For further information contact:

Email: francoise_hamlin@brown.edu

James A. Rawley Prize

Purpose: The James A. Rawley Prize is given annually by the Organization of American Historians to the author of the best book dealing with the history of race relations in the United States. The prize is given in memory of Professor James A. Rawley, Carl Adolph Happold Professor of History Emeritus at the University of Nebraska, Lincoln.

Eligibility: Each entry must be published during the period.

Type: Prize

Value: US$1,000

Frequency: Annual

Country of Study: Any country

Application Procedure: One copy of each entry, clearly labeled "2024 James A. Rawley Prize Entry," must be mailed directly to the committee members listed below. Each committee member must receive all submissions postmarked by October 1, 2023.

No. of awards offered: 1

Closing Date: 1 October

Contributor: OAH

No. of awards given last year: 1

No. of applicants last year: 80

Additional Information: Please check at www.oah.org/awards/book-awards/organization-of-american-historians-oah-james-a-rawley-prize/

For further information contact:

Deborah Cohen, Committtee Chair, 3943 Fairview Avenue, St. Louis, MO 63116, United States of America.

Japanese Residencies for United States of America Historians

Purpose: The purpose of this program is to facilitate scholarly dialogue and contribute to the expansion of scholarly networks among students and professors of American history in both countries.

Eligibility: Applicants must be members of the OAH, have a PhD, and be scholars of American history. Applicants from previous competitions are welcome to apply again.

Type: Residency

Value: Round-trip airfare to Japan, housing, and modest daily expenses are covered by the award (note if the host university is unable to provide housing, award recipients are expected to use the daily stipend to pay hotel expenses)

Length of Study: 2 weeks

Frequency: Annual

Country of Study: Japan

Application Procedure: Please send all materials (in one PDF labeled with your name) and indicate "Japan Residencies Program-[UNIVERSITY NAME]" in the subject line. If you would like to apply for both residencies, please send a separate application for each. 1. A two-page curriculum vitae emphasizing teaching experience and publications. 2. The institution for which you would like to be considered. 3. A personal statement, no longer than two pages, describing your interest in this program and the issues that your own scholarship and teaching have addressed. Please devote one or two paragraphs to why you understand this residency to be central to your development as a scholar in the world community. You may include comments on any previous collaboration or work with non-U.S. academics or students. If you wish, you may comment on your particular interest in Japan.

O

4. A letter of recommendation, to be solicited by the applicant and sent directly by the recommender to OAH (japanresidency@oah.org), which should also address the applicant's teaching skill. The subject line of the e-mail should say "Recommendation for [NAME OF APPLICANT].".

No. of awards offered: 2

Additional Information: For more detials, please visit: www.oah.org/awards/residencies/japan/

For further information contact:

Email: japanresidency@oah.org

John D'Emilio LGBTQ History Dissertation Award

Purpose: The John D'Emilio LGBTQ History Dissertation Award is given annually by the Organization of American Historians to the best PhD dissertation in U.S. LGBTQ history. The award is named for John D'Emilio, pioneer in LGBTQ history.

Type: Award

Value: US$500

Length of Study: 1 Year

Frequency: Annual

Country of Study: Any country

Application Procedure: Please send an electronic attachment (PDF) of your complete dissertation, abstract, and table of contents in one e-mail to all three committee members listed below. The subject line should be 2024 John D'Emilio LGBTQ History Dissertation Award.

No. of awards offered: 1

Closing Date: 1 October

No. of awards given last year: 1

No. of applicants last year: 9

John Higham Research Fellowship

Purpose: This fellowship is open to all graduate students writing doctoral dissertations for a PhD in American history. Applicants pursuing research in those fields most congenial to the research and writing interests of John Higham will receive special consideration

Level of Study: Graduate

Type: Fellowship

Value: US$3,000

Frequency: Annual

Country of Study: Any country

Application Procedure: Applications should include the following components 1. Project proposal of no more than 1,000 words describing the applicant's research project and detailing how the funds will be used. 2. An updated curriculum vitae with a list of the names and addresses of references. 3. Two signed letters of recommendation on official letterhead submitted independently by referees. Letters in the form of a signed PDF should be e-mailed to the chair of the John Higham Research Fellowship Committee at the address listed below. We ask that recommenders use the subject line "Recommendation for [APPLICANT'S NAME].". Complete all application components (including project proposal, names and addresses of recommenders, and curriculum vitae), in a recent version of Microsoft Word or PDF (preferable), and e-mail the entire electronic file to the chair of the John Higham Research Fellowship Committee at the address listed in website. For more details please refer www.oah.org/awards/uncategorized-awards/john-higham-fellowship/

No. of awards offered: 2

Closing Date: 1 November

Funding: Private

No. of awards given last year: 2

No. of applicants last year: 25

Additional Information: Applicants pursuing research in those fields most congenial to the research and writing interests of John Higham will receive special consideration. These topics include U.S. social and intellectual history broadly considered, with preference given to research projects on American immigration and ethnic history as well as American historiography, and the cultural history of the nineteenth-century U.S. www.oah.org/awards/uncategorized-awards/john-higham-fellowship/

For further information contact:

Patrick Chung, University of Maryland, College Park, MD 20742, United States of America.; Julian Lim, Arizona State University, Phoenix, AZ 85004, United States of America.

Tel: (1) 812 855 7311
Email: pchung10@umd.edu

Lawrence W. Levine Award

Purpose: The Lawrence W. Levine Award is given annually by the Organization of American Historians to the author of the best book in American cultural history.

Type: Award

Frequency: Annual

Country of Study: Any country

Application Procedure: One copy of each entry, clearly labeled "2024 Lawrence W. Levine Award Entry," must be mailed directly to the committee members listed in website. Applicants should contact by e-mail for mailing address. Please refer www.oah.org/awards/book-awards/lawrence-w-levine-award/.

Closing Date: 1 October
Additional Information: Please check at www.oah.org/awards/book-awards/lawrence-w-levine-award/

For further information contact:

112 N. Bryan Avenue, Bloomington, IN 47408-4141, United States of America.

Email: kah@umich.edu

Lerner-Scott Prize

Purpose: The Lerner-Scott Prize is given annually by the Organization of American Historians for the best doctoral dissertation in U.S. women's history.
Eligibility: All
Level of Study: Postdoctorate
Type: Award
Value: US$1,000
Frequency: Annual
Country of Study: Any country
Application Procedure: Please send an electronic attachment (PDF) of your complete dissertation (including abstract and table of contents) to the committee listed below by midnight (PST) on October 1, 2021 with "2024 OAH Lerner-Scott Prize Entry" in the subject line.
No. of awards offered: 1
Closing Date: 1 October
No. of awards given last year: 1
No. of applicants last year: 12

Liberty Legacy Foundation Award

Purpose: Inspired by OAH President Darlene Clark Hine's call in her 2002 OAH presidential address for more research on the origins of the civil rights movement in the period before 1954, the Liberty Legacy Foundation Award is given annually by the Organization of American Historians to the author of the best book by a historian on the civil rights struggle from the beginnings of the nation to the present.
Type: Award
Value: US$2,000
Frequency: Annual
Country of Study: Any country
Application Procedure: One copy of each entry, clearly labeled "2024 Liberty Legacy Foundation Award Entry", must be mailed directly to the committee members listed below. Each committee member must receive all submissions postmarked by October 1, 2023.

No. of awards offered: 1
Closing Date: 1 October
Contributor: OAH
No. of awards given last year: 1
No. of applicants last year: 41

Louis Pelzer Memorial Award

Purpose: The Louis Pelzer Memorial Award Committee of the Organization of American Historians invites candidates for graduate degrees to submit essays for the Louis Pelzer Memorial Award competition. Essays may deal with any period or topic in the history of the United States.
Level of Study: Graduate
Type: Award
Value: US$500
Frequency: Annual
Country of Study: Any country
Application Procedure: Essays, including footnotes, should not exceed 10,000 words. An abstract and the electronic version of the essay should be sent to jahms@oah.org with "2024 Louis Pelzer Memorial Award Entry" noted in the subject line, and one hard copy should be submitted to the address below. Because manuscripts are judged anonymously, the author's name and graduate program should appear only on a separate cover page.
No. of awards offered: 1
Closing Date: 1 November
No. of awards given last year: 1
No. of applicants last year: 21

For further information contact:

Benjamin H. Irvin, Executive Editor, OAH/Editor, Journal of American History, Journal of American History, 1215 East Atwater Avenue, Bloomington, IN 47401, United States of America.

Email: jahms@oah.org

Mary Nickliss Prize in United States Women's and/or Gender History

Purpose: The Mary Nickliss Prize is given for "the most original" book in United States Women's and/or Gender History (including North America and the Caribbean prior to 1776). The best book recognizes the ideas and originality of the significant historical scholarship being done by historians of United States Women's and/or Gender History and makes a significant contribution to the understanding of United States Women's and/or Gender History

Eligibility: Each entry must be published during the calendar year preceding that in which the award is given.

Type: Award

Value: US$1,000

Frequency: Annual

Country of Study: Any country

Application Procedure: One copy of each entry, clearly labeled "Mary Nickliss Prize Entry" must be mailed directly to the committee members listed in website. Each committee member must receive all submissions postmarked by 1 October. If a book carries a copyright date that is different from the publication date, but the actual publication date falls during the correct timeframe making it eligible, please include a letter of explanation from the publisher with each copy of the book sent to the committee members. Applicants should contact by e-mail for mailing address

No. of awards offered: 1

Closing Date: 1 October

No. of awards given last year: 2

No. of applicants last year: 48

Additional Information: www.oah.org/awards/book-awards/mary-nickliss-prize/

For further information contact:

112 N. Bryan Avenue, Bloomington, IN 47408-4141, United States of America.

Email: mchavezgarcia@history.ucsb.edu

Merle Curti Award in American Intellectual History

Purpose: To recognise books in the fields of american social, intellectual, and/or cultural history

Type: Award

Value: US$500

Frequency: Annual

Country of Study: Any country

Application Procedure: Applicants must send a copy of each entry to the committee members. Publishers are urged to enter one or more books in the competition. For further application details, candidates should visit the website

No. of awards offered: 73

Closing Date: 1 October

Contributor: OAH

No. of awards given last year: 1

Additional Information: www.oah.org/awards/book-awards/merle-curti-award-intellectual-history/

Merle Curti Intellectual History Award

Purpose: For the best book in American intellectual history.

Type: Award

Value: US$500

Frequency: Annual

Country of Study: Any country

Application Procedure: One copy of each entry, clearly labeled "2024 Merle Curti Intellectual History Award Entry," must be mailed directly to the committee members listed below. Each committee member must receive all submissions postmarked by October 1, 2023.

No. of awards offered: 1

Closing Date: 1 October

Contributor: OAH

No. of awards given last year: 1

No. of applicants last year: 45

Additional Information: Please check at www.oah.org/awards/book-awards/merle-curti-award-social-history/

Merle Curti Social History Award

Purpose: One award is given annually to the author of the best book in American social history. Merle Curti was president of the OAH 1951-1952.

Level of Study: Graduate

Type: Award

Value: US$500

Frequency: Annual

Country of Study: Any country

Application Procedure: 1. One copy of each entry, clearly labeled "Merle Curti Social History Award Entry," must be mailed directly to the committee members listed below. Each committee member must receive all submissions postmarked by 1 October. 2. Bound page proofs may be used for books to be published after 1 October and before 1 January. If a bound page proof is submitted, a bound copy of the book must be received by each committee member postmarked no later than 7 January. (Please see "Submission Policy") 3. If a book carries a copyright date that is different from the publication date, but the actual publication date falls during the correct timeframe making it eligible, please include a letter of explanation from the publisher with each copy of the book sent to the committee members.

No. of awards offered: 1

Closing Date: 1 October

Funding: Private

No. of awards given last year: 1

No. of applicants last year: 81

Additional Information: The final decision will be made by the Merle Curti Social History Award Committee by February. The winner will be provided with details regarding the OAH Annual Meeting and awards presentation. www.oah.org/awards/book-awards/merle-curti-award-social-history/

Presidents' Travel Fund

Purpose: The fund provides travel stipends to five graduate students and recent PhDs in history (no more than four years from date of degree) whose papers or panels/sessions have been accepted by the OAH Program Committee for inclusion on the annual meeting program

Eligibility: PhDs in history (no more than four years from date of degree) whose papers or panels/sessions have been accepted by the OAH Program Committee for inclusion on the annual meeting program. For more details, check the website.

Level of Study: Doctorate

Type: Travel grant

Value: The fund provides travel stipends of up to US$750

Frequency: Annual

Country of Study: Any country

Application Procedure: Please e-mail your paper title or panel title, with an abstract and a CV (indicating your anticipated year of completion of the PhD or the year your PhD was granted), and a paragraph describing why it is important for you to attend the meeting (besides presenting your paper if you are doing so) as a PDF to the OAH Presidents' Travel Fund for Emerging Historians Committee . For further information, check the websitre

No. of awards offered: 5

Closing Date: 1 December

Additional Information: For more information: www.oah.org/awards/travel-grants/presidents-travel-fund/

For further information contact:

Email: presidentstravelfund@oah.org

Ray Allen Billington Prize

Purpose: The Ray Allen Billington Prize is awarded biennially by the Organization of American Historians to the author of the best book on the history of native and/or settler peoples in frontier, border, and borderland zones of intercultural contact in any century to the present and to include works that address the legacies of those zones.

Eligibility: Author of the best book on the history of native and/or settler peoples in frontier, border, and borderland zones of intercultural contact in any century to the present and to include works that address the legacies of those zones.

Type: Award

Value: US$1,000

Frequency: Every 2 years

Country of Study: Any country

Application Procedure: Applicants must visit the website www.oah.org/awards/book-awards/ray-allen-billington-prize/

No. of awards offered: 1

Closing Date: 3 October

Contributor: OAH

No. of awards given last year: 1

No. of applicants last year: 62

Additional Information: Please check at www.oah.org/awards/book-awards/ray-allen-billington-prize/

For further information contact:

Andrés Reséndez (Committee Chair), University of California, Davis, Department of History, One Shields Avenue, Davis CA 95616-5270, United States of America.

Email: adubcovs@ucr.edu

Richard W. Leopold Prize

Purpose: The Richard W. Leopold Prize is given biennially by the Organization of American Historians to the author or editor of the best book on foreign policy, military affairs, historical activities of the federal government, documentary histories, or biography written by a U.S. government historian or federal contract historian.

Eligibility: U.S Government or Federal Contract Historians (current or former)

Type: Prize

Value: US$1,500

Frequency: Every 2 years (even-numbered years)

Country of Study: Any country

Application Procedure: Verification of current or past employment with the U.S. government (in the form of a letter or e-mail sent to the publisher from the office that employs or has employed the author) must be included with each entry for the Leopold Prize. One copy of each entry, clearly labeled "2024 Richard W. Leopold Prize Entry," must be mailed directly to the committee members listed. Applicants should contact by e-mail for mailing address. Applicants must visit the website www.oah.org/awards/book-awards/richard-w-leopold-prize/

Closing Date: 1 October

Funding: Government

No. of awards given last year: 1

No. of applicants last year: 7

Additional Information: Please check at www.oah.org/awards/book-awards/richard-w-leopold-prize/

For further information contact:

Rebecca Tinio McKenna, Department of History, University of Notre Dame, 434 Decio Hall, Notre Dame, IN 46556, United States of America.

Email: mbradley@uchicago.edu

Society of American Archivists' Mosaic Scholarship Opportunity

Purpose: The Mosaic Scholarship was established to provide financial and mentoring support to minority students pursuing graduate education in archival science, to encourage students to pursue careers in archives, and to promote the diversification of the American archival profession.

Eligibility: 1. The applicant must be a citizen or permanent resident of the United States or Canada. 2. The applicant must be of American Indian/Alaska Native, Asian, Black/African American, Hispanic/Latino, Middle Eastern/North African, or Native Hawaiian/Other Pacific Islander descent. 3. The applicant must be currently enrolled in a graduate program or a multi-course program in archival administration, or have applied to such a program for the next academic year. (The graduate program must offer at least three courses in archival science or be listed in the current SAA Directory of Archival Education (www2.archivists.org/dae). If the program is not listed in the SAA Directory of Archival Education, the applicant must provide proof of the three-course standard by submitting copies of course descriptions from the institution's current course catalog.) 4. The applicant shall have completed no more than half of the credit requirements toward her/his graduate degree at the time of the award (i.e., June 1). 5. The applicant must be enrolled in a graduate program and begin school no later than September 1 or the fall semester/quarter immediately following the award. Otherwise the award will be rescinded. 6. Applicants may have full-time or part-time status.

Type: Scholarship
Value: US$5,000 each
Length of Study: one-year
Frequency: Annual
Country of Study: Any country
Application Procedure: Apply online:app.smarterselect.com/program/apply/45830?apply=true
No. of awards offered: 2

Tachau Teacher of the Year Award

Purpose: The Mary K. Bonsteel Tachau Teacher of the Year Award is given annually by the Organization of American Historians in recognition of the contributions made by precollegiate teachers to improve history education within the field of American history

Eligibility: Precollegiate teachers engaged at least half time in U.S. history teaching, whether in history or social studies, are eligible. Successful candidates shall demonstrate exceptional ability in one or more of the following kinds of activities 1. Initiating or participating in projects which involve students in historical research, writing, or other means of representing their knowledge of history. 2. Initiating or participating in school, district, regional, state, or national projects which enhance the professional development of history teachers. 3. Initiating or participating in projects to build bridges between precollegiate and collegiate history or social studies teachers. 4. Working with museums, historical preservation societies, or other public history associations to enhance the place of public history in precollegiate schools. 5. Developing innovative history curricula which foster a spirit of inquiry and emphasize critical skills. 6. Publishing or otherwise publicly presenting scholarship that advances history education or historical knowledge.

Type: Award
Value: US$500
Frequency: Annual
Country of Study: Any country
Application Procedure: Applicants must visit the website www.oah.org/awards/uncategorized-awards/tachau-teacher-of-the-year-award/. Please fill out the nomination form here. www.oah.org/awards/uncategorized-awards/tachau-teacher-of-the-year-award/submission-form/
Closing Date: 1 November
No. of awards given last year: 1
No. of applicants last year: 9
Additional Information: Please check at www.oah.org/awards/uncategorized-awards/tachau-teacher-of-the-year-award/

The Japan Residencies Program

Purpose: The purpose of this program is to facilitate scholarly dialogue and contribute to the expansion of scholarly networks among students and professors of American history in both countries.

Eligibility: Applicants must be members of the OAH, have a PhD, and be scholars of American history. Applicants from previous competitions are welcome to apply again.

Type: Residency
Value: Round-trip airfare to Japan, housing (if the host university cannot offer housing, applicants are expected to pay hotel expenses from the daily stipend) and modest daily expenses
Length of Study: 2 weeks

Frequency: Annual
Country of Study: Any country
Application Procedure: Please send all materials (in one PDF labeled with your name) and indicate "2024 Japan Residencies Program-[UNIVERSITY NAME]" in the subject line. If you would like to apply for both residencies, please send a separate application for each. 1. A two-page curriculum vitae emphasizing teaching experience and publications. 2. The institution for which you would like to be considered. 3. A personal statement, no longer than two pages, describing your interest in this program and the issues that your own scholarship and teaching have addressed. Please devote one or two paragraphs to why you understand this residency to be central to your development as a scholar in the world community. You may include comments on any previous collaboration or work with non-U.S. academics or students. If you wish, you may comment on your particular interest in Japan. 4. A letter of recommendation, to be solicited by the applicant and sent directly by the recommender to OAH (japanresidency@oah.org), which should also address the applicant's teaching skill. The subject line of the e-mail should say "Recommendation for [NAME OF APPLICANT].".
No. of awards offered: 2
Additional Information: For more detials, please visit: www.oah.org/awards/residencies/japan/

For further information contact:

Email: japanresidency@oah.org

Willi Paul Adams Award

Purpose: The Willi Paul Adams Award is given biennially by the Organization of American Historians to the author of the best book on American history published in a language other than English.
Eligibility: Please write a one- to two-page essay (in English, along with the title in English) explaining why the book is a significant and original contribution to our understanding of American history, and include a summary of the book's main argument.
Type: Award
Value: US$1,250
Frequency: Every 2 years
Country of Study: Any country
Application Procedure: Please write a one- to two-page essay (in English, along with the title in English) explaining why the book is a significant and original contribution to our understanding of American history, and include a summary of the book's main argument. The application should also include the following information 1. Name. 2. Mailing address. 3. Institutional affiliation. 4. Fax number. 5. E-mail address. 6. Language of submitted book. 7. Table of contents in English. Copies of the book and essay will be reviewed by contributing editors of the Journal of American History who are proficient in the language of the submission as well as by referees (proficient in the language of the submitted book) who are experts on its subject matter. Three copies of the essay and book, clearly labeled "2024 OAH Willi Paul Adams Award Entry," must be mailed to the address
No. of awards offered: 1
Closing Date: 2 May
Contributor: OAH
No. of awards given last year: 1
No. of applicants last year: 4
Additional Information: Please check at www.oah.org/awards/book-awards/willi-paul-adams-award/

For further information contact:

Willi Paul Adams Award Committee, c/o Organization of American Historians, 112 North Bryan Avenue, Bloomington IN 47408-4141, United States of America.

Email: khamm@oah.org

Organization of American States (OAS)

17th Street and Constitution Ave., NW, Washington, D.C. 20006-4499, United States of America.

Tel: (1) 202 370 5000
Email: Scholarships@oas.org
Website: www.oas.org/en/

The Organization of American States is the world's oldest regional organization came into being in 1948 with the signing in Bogotá, Colombia, of the Charter of the OAS, which entered into force in December 1951. The Organization uses a four-pronged approach to effectively implement its essential purposes, based on its main pillars: democracy, human rights, security, and development.

Stanton-Horton Award for Excellence in National Park Service History

Purpose: The award recognizes excellence in National Park Service historical efforts that make the NPS a leader in promoting public understanding of and engagement with American history. Please share with us exemplary projects that encourage civic dialogue in all areas of public history

Level of Study: Graduate
Type: Award
Frequency: Annual
Country of Study: Any country
Application Procedure: For further details on the application process, kindly check with the website.
Closing Date: 15 December
Funding: Private

For further information contact:

Email: david_osborne@partner.nps.gov; april_
             antonellis@nps.gov; hagertyed357@gmail.com

Oriel College

Oriel College, Oriel Square, Oxford OX1 4EW, United Kingdom.

Tel: (44) 1865 276555
Email: lodge@oriel.ox.ac.uk
Website: www.oriel.ox.ac.uk/

Oriel College is the fifth oldest of the University of Oxford's constituent colleges, founded in 1326. Situated in the heart of Oxford. The College prides itself on being a welcoming academic community, home to world-class teaching, learning and research.

David N. Lyon Scholarship in Politics – The Politics of Sex and Gender Equality in Diverse Societies

Purpose: This scholarship will support one student to undertake research at Oriel into the politics of sex and gender equality in diverse societies in the field of Politics, broadly construed. These questions reward investigation from a number of different approaches: historical and contemporary, theoretical and empirical.
Level of Study: Postgraduate
Value: £8,500 per year
Country of Study: Any country
Closing Date: 31 December
Funding: Private

For further information contact:

Joseph Cole, Academic Registrar, Oriel College, Oxford OX1 4EW, United Kingdom.

Email: teresa.bejan@oriel.ox.ac.uk

Oriel College: Oriel Graduate Scholarships

Purpose: Postgraduate students are an integral part of the Oriel community, and the College seeks to provide financial support and teaching opportunities to help students achieve their goals. To support postgraduate student focused on artificial intelligence research as part of a DPhil course in either Engineering Science or Computer Science.
Eligibility: Open to current graduate students at Oriel College
Level of Study: Postgraduate
Type: Scholarship
Value: Award of £5,000 for up to three years
Frequency: Annual
Country of Study: Any country
Application Procedure: Applicants should make a direct DPhil application to the Department of Engineering Science or Department of Computer Science, following the University's admissions procedures and course deadlines. Applicants should list Oriel College as their first-choice college and note the Oriel Graduate Scholarship in Artificial Intelligence on their application form. Please note that all applications should go through the University of Oxford online application system and applications should not be made to Oriel College directly.
Funding: Private
Additional Information: www.oriel.ox.ac.uk/about-college/news-events/news/open-applications-oriel-graduate-scholarship-artificial-intelligence

For further information contact:

Tel: (44) 1865 276555
Email: info@yaldahakimfoundation.org; lodge@oriel.ox.ac.uk

Orthopaedic Research and Education Foundation (OREF)

9400 W. Higgins Road, Suite 215, Rosemont, IL 60018-4975, United States of America.

Tel: (1) 847 698 9980
Email: communications@oref.org
Website: www.oref.org/

The Orthopaedic Research and Education Foundation (OREF) is a charitable organization committed to improving lives by supporting excellence in orthopaedic research. OREF is dedicated to being the leader in supporting research that improves function, eliminates pain and restores mobility, and is the premier orthopaedic organization funding research across all specialties. As the leading grant making resource for new investigators, OREF provides important financial support that helps them build a strong foundation for their research careers.

Grants Programs

Subjects: Orthopaedic research
Purpose: Orthopaedic Research and Education Foundation offers both Investigator-Initiated and Research Specific Grants. Read each program for details.
Eligibility: OREF invites applications for funding for qualified, clinically relevant orthopaedic research projects. Please visit website.
Type: Grant
Value: 1. US$300,000 over 2 years for OREF Total Joint Replacement Research Grant in Memory of Jorge O. Galante, MD. 2. US$50,000 for OREF New Investigator Grant. 3. US$50,000 for OREF Multimodal Musculoskeletal Perioperative Pain Management Grant. 4. US$20,000 for Friedenberg Mentored Clinician Scientist Grant. 5. US$100,000 over 2 years for OREF and The Aircast Foundation Orthopaedic Research Grant. 6. US$300,000 over 3 years for OREF Career Development Grant. 7. US$5,000 for Resident Research Project Grant Round 2.
Frequency: Annual
Country of Study: Any country
Application Procedure: Please visit www.oref.org/grants-and-awards/grant-programs
Closing Date: 11 May
Additional Information: Grant programs for funding will be offered in two cycles with RFAs going live in November or May. There are research-specific grants as well as investigator-initiated grants. See website for details. www.oref.org/grants-and-awards/grant-programs

For further information contact:

Tel: (1) 847 430 5109
Email: grants@oref.org

OREF Mentored Clinician-Scientist Grant

Subjects: Orthopaedic research
Purpose: The objective of this grant is to promote the development of new clinician-scientists who have demonstrated success as both a clinician and a researcher. This will allow the investigators to spend dedicated time in research for a period of up to five years to develop a long and productive career in academic surgery.

Eligibility: 1. Orthopaedic surgeons licensed to practice and working at an institution in the United States. 2. Applicants who have demonstrated success in research by receiving extramural research funding under one or more K08 or K23 awards from the National Institutes of Health or an equivalent funding source. 3. Recipients with multiyear NIHK08 or K23 awards may reapply to continue support
Level of Study: Junior Faculty
Type: Grant
Value: US$20,000, subject to annual review and available funds.
Length of Study: 5 Years
Frequency: Annual
Country of Study: Any country
Application Procedure: To Access the Request for Application, you will need a proposalCENTRAL account. If you don't already have one, go to proposalCENTRAL by clicking the button below, then click the "Create an Account" link. See website.
Closing Date: 11 May
Additional Information: www.oref.org/grants-and-awards/grant-programs/general-grants/friedenberg-mentored-clinician-scientist-grant

For further information contact:

Email: grants@oref.org

Otaru University of Commerce

Business Administration, 3-5-21,Midori, Otaru-shi, Hokkaido 047-8501, Japan.

Website: english.otaru-uc.ac.jp/
Contact: MBA Admissions Officer

Otaru University of Commerce is located in a historical city which was once a commercial center in the pioneering era of Hokkaido and one of the main ports in Japan. The university was established in this city to support the development of international trade. It has kept its fame during its history of ninety years because of its academic achievement, and distinguished graduates.

Bamforth Postgraduate Scholarship

Purpose: Doctoral scholarships are awarded by the University Council, on the recommendation of the Senate, to candidates proceeding to a course of supervised doctoral study at this University. These scholarships are normally available only to students seeking to obtain their first doctoral qualification. Candidates may be awarded one University of Otago doctoral scholarship only

Eligibility: In the case of an applicant for a doctoral scholarship who has completed a Master's degree by papers and thesis (at least 0.75 EFTS), the grades of all relevant advanced level papers counting towards the award of the degree and the thesis will be taken into account. An explanation of the time taken for completion of the thesis may be requested and considered by the Scholarships and Prizes Committee if the thesis has taken more than 2 EFTS (2 fulltime years) to complete

Level of Study: Postgraduate

Type: Scholarship

Value: NZ$28,600 stipend per annum

Length of Study: 3 year

Frequency: Annual

Country of Study: New Zealand

Funding: Foundation

For further information contact:

Email: scholarships@otago.ac.nz

Ovarian Cancer Research Fund

14 Pennsylvania Plaza, Suite 2110, New York, NY 10122, United States of America.

Tel: (1) 212 268 1002
Email: info@ocrahope.org
Website: ocrahope.org/

Ovarian Cancer Research Alliance (OCRA) is the leading organization in the world fighting ovarian cancer from all fronts, including in the lab and on Capitol Hill, while supporting women and their families. OCRA's ongoing investment in the most promising scientific research is funding discoveries, creating new treatments, and hastening desperately needed breakthroughs.

Ann and Sol Schreiber Mentored Investigator Award

Subjects: Ovarian cancer research

Purpose: The Ann and Sol Schreiber Mentored Investigator Award provides funding for trainees (post-doctoral fellows or clinical fellows) who are working under the supervision of a mentor who is a recognized leader in the field of ovarian cancer research.

Eligibility: Applicants must have an MD or a PhD degree.

Level of Study: Doctorate, Postdoctorate

Type: Award

Value: The award provides a total of US$75,000 to be used over one or two years

Length of Study: One or two years

Country of Study: Any country

Application Procedure: Requests for Proposals (RFPs) are issued every spring. We use a two step application and peer review process. Letters of Intent (LOIs) are due in May and undergo a rigorous peer review by our Scientific Advisory Committee. After LOI review, a subset of those applicants are invited to submit full applications. Full applications are due in July. Final grant notifications are made in October. RFPs are available for future grant cycles, please send an email to grants@ocrahope.org.

Closing Date: May

No. of awards given last year: 10

Additional Information: ocrahope.org/grant/ann-schreiber-mentored-award/

For further information contact:

Email: grants@ocrahope.org

Oxford Brookes University, School of Business

Headington Campus, Oxford OX3 0BP, United Kingdom.

Tel: (44) 1865 485858
Email: business@brookes.ac.uk
Website: www.brookes.ac.uk/business/

Oxford Brookes Business School is a place of inspiration and transformation. Our students embark on a supported journey of learning and self-development to become highly effective practitioners and responsible leaders operating in global markets.

Oxford Brookes University MBA Programme

Purpose: These scholarships aim to support those who are based in lower-income countries, to provide enhanced opportunities and to celebrate the truly global reach of our MBA programme.

Eligibility: They are offered to all students who live and work in specific countries based on the UN Development Index. Please visit website

Type: Scholarship

Value: £2,000

Country of Study: Any country

Application Procedure: Please apply using our application form. www.brookes.ac.uk/courses/postgraduate/oxford-brookes-mba

Additional Information: These scholarships do not apply to ACCA members, who already receive a substantial discount on the Oxford Brookes Global MBA fees. www.brookes.ac.uk/courses/postgraduate/oxford-brookes-mba

For further information contact:

Tel: (44) 1865 48 58 00

Email: mbaoxford@brookes.ac.uk

P

Paloma O Shea Santander International Piano Competition

C / Luis Martinez 21, E-39005 Santander, Spain.

Tel:	(34) 942 31 14 51
Email:	concurso@albeniz.com
Website:	www.santanderpianocompetition.com
Contact:	Foundation Albeniz

Non-profit institution founded in 1987. It directs and governs the set of programs sponsored by the Albeniz Foundation in Cantabria. Organization 19th International Piano Competition of Santander.

Gold, Silver and Bronze Medals

Subjects: Musical instrument (piano)
Purpose: To give support to young pianists of Exceptional talents.
Eligibility: Competition is open to all pianists born on 1st January, 1994 and after
Level of Study: Unrestricted
Type: Prize
Value: Cash prizes totalling more than €90,000
Frequency: Annual
Study Establishment: ANY
Country of Study: Any country
Application Procedure: Online application for the 2023 competition www.santanderpianocompetition.com available from June
No. of awards offered: 7
Closing Date: November
Funding: Commercial, Foundation, Government, Private
No. of applicants last year: 241

Additional Information: Cash prizes totalling more than €90,000; concerts in Spain and abroad; CD recording; online promotion campaign www.brookes.ac.uk/courses/postgradu ate/oxford-brookes-mba/

For further information contact:

Calle Luis Martínez, 21, Santander, E-39005 Cantabria, Spain.

Paralyzed Veterans of America (PVA)

801 Eighteenth Street NW, Washington, DC, 20006-3517, United States of America.

Tel:	(1) 800 424 8200
Email:	info@pva.org
Website:	www.pva.org
Contact:	Paralyzed Veterans of America

PVA was originally founded by a band of service members who came home from World War II with spinal cord injuries. They returned to a grateful nation, but also to a world with few solutions to the major challenges they faced. Paralyzed Veterans of America, a congressionally chartered veterans service organization founded in 1946, has developed a unique expertise on a wide variety of issues involving the special needs of our members - veterans of the armed forces who have experienced spinal cord injury or dysfunction.

Paralyzed Veterans of America Fellowships in Spinal Cord Injury Research

Purpose: The Research Foundation is focused on funding projects grounded in basic laboratory science and the education of scientists working on breakthroughs directed toward a cure for paralysis, secondary health effects and technologies associated with spinal cord injury or disease (SCI/D).

Eligibility: 1. Eligible grantee institutions must be located in the United States or Canada. 2. However, investigators and fellows are not required to be U.S. or Canadian citizens. 3. All grant applicants must have a professional degree Ph.D. or M.D. preferred. 4. Senior fellows are encouraged to apply as principal investigators. 5. Post-doctoral scientists are eligible to apply for fellowship support within four years of receiving a Ph.D. or completing M.D. residency. 6. Graduate students can participate in Foundation-related research and be paid from a Foundation award. 7. However, graduate students cannot apply for a Foundation grant as a fellow or as a principal investigator.

Level of Study: Postdoctorate, Postgraduate, Research
Type: Fellowship
Value: US$746,293
Length of Study: Two-year period
Frequency: Annual
Country of Study: United States of America
No. of awards offered: 5
Closing Date: 1 July
Funding: Foundation
No. of applicants last year: 83
Additional Information: The grants for FY2023 are funded in three categories: basic science, clinical applications, and design and development. www.brookes.ac.uk/courses/post graduate/oxford-brookes-mba/

For further information contact:

Tel: (1) 202 416 7611
Email: LindsayP@pva.org

Research Grants & Fellowships

Eligibility: Eligible grantee institutions must be located in the United States or Canada. However, investigators and fellows are not required to be U.S. or Canadian citizens. All grant applicants must have a professional degree: Ph.D. or M.D. preferred. Senior fellows are encouraged to apply as principal investigators. Post-doctoral scientists are eligible to apply for fellowship support within four years of receiving a Ph.D. or completing M.D. residency. Graduate students can participate in Foundation-related research and be paid from a Foundation award. However, graduate students cannot apply for a Foundation grant as a fellow or as a principal investigator.

Level of Study: Postgraduate
Type: Fellowship or Grant

Value: US$796,402
Country of Study: Any country
Application Procedure: Lindsay Perlman, Associate Director, Research and Education
Closing Date: 1 January

For further information contact:

Tel: (1) 202 416 7611
Email: LindsayP@pva.org

Parapsychology Foundation, Inc.

PO Box 1562, New York, NY 10021, United States of America.

Tel: (1) 212 628 1550
Email: office@parapsychology.org
Website: www.parapsychology.org
Contact: Parapsychology Foundation

The Parapsychology Foundation is a not-for-profit foundation which provides a worldwide forum supporting the scientific investigation of psychic phenomena. The Foundation gives grants, publishes pamphlets, monographs, conference proceedings and the International Journal of Parapsychology, hosts the Perspectives Lecture Series, conducts the Outreach Program, maintains the Eileen J. Garrett Library with its collection of more than 12,000 volumes and 100 periodicals on parapsychology and related topics, and is proud of its quality paperback imprint, Helix Press.

Eileen J Garrett Scholarship

Purpose: To assist students attending an accredited college or university in pursuing the academic study of the science of parapsychology
Eligibility: 1. Must be an undergraduate student, a graduate student or a postgraduate student. 2. Must attend a university, a four-year college or two-year college. 3. Citizenship requirements US. 4. Must not be attending high school currently. 5. Must study full-time. 6. Restricted to students studying Social Sciences.
Level of Study: Unrestricted
Type: Scholarship
Value: US$3,000
Length of Study: 1 year
Frequency: Annual
Study Establishment: An accredited college or university

Country of Study: Any country

Application Procedure: Applicants must submit samples of writings on the subject with an application form from the Foundation. Letters of reference are required from three individuals, familiar with the applicant's work and/or studies in parapsychology

Closing Date: 15 July

Additional Information: www.petersons.com/scholarship/eileen-j-garrett-scholarship-for-parapsychological-research-111_150558.aspx

For further information contact:

PO Box 1562, New York, NY 10021-0043, United States of America.

Tel: (1) 212 628 1550
Fax: (1) 212 628 1559

Paris School of International Affairs (PSIA)

28 Rue des Saints-Peres, F-75007 Paris, France.

Website: www.sciencespo.fr/psia/

At Sciences Po's Paris School of International Affairs (PSIA), our goal is to train and shape global actors to understand and respond to the complexities of our world. Attracting the best and brightest students worldwide, PSIA has a population of 1500 students representing over 110 countries. With 70% of courses taught in English, students may take a full course of study in English.

Kuwait Program at Sciences Po Excellence Scholarship for Arab Students and Kuwait Nationals

Purpose: The Kuwait Excellence Scholarship program supports outstanding students coming from the Arab world and Kuwait to pursue Master's level graduate studies at Sciences Po. Multiple scholarships will be awarded to the best candidates on a competitive basis.

Eligibility: 1. Nationals from Arab countries, Kuwaiti National including the Gulf Region, may apply. 2. Applicants must: a. be first-time degree-seeking students in France. b. submit a full application to Sciences Po for the 2023/2024 intake (including all supporting documents and references) via the Sciences Po Admissions Portal. c. apply to any of the 7 graduate schools of Sciences Po, in any of the two-year Master programs. 3. Students applying to a dual degree program are not eligible. Students applying to a one-year Master program are not eligible.

Level of Study: MBA, Masters Degree, Postgraduate, Postgraduate (MSc)

Type: Scholarship

Value: For Arab students: Each recipient is awarded up to 20,000 Euros for two years of study. For Kuwait Nationals: 25,000 Euros for the two years of study.

Length of Study: 2 years

Frequency: Annual

Country of Study: United States of America

Application Procedure: 1. To apply, please send the following materials by email to program.kuwait@sciencespo.fr with "Kuwait Excellence Scholarship Application 2023/2024" in the subject line: CV in English, cover letter in English of 1000 words addressed to the members of the joint selection committee (this letter must be different from your letter of motivation to Sciences Po, describing your motivations for applying to the Kuwait Excellence Scholarship). copy of passport.

No. of awards offered: Multiple

Closing Date: 14 February

No. of applicants last year: Multiple

For further information contact:

27, rue Saint Guillaume, F-75337 Paris Cedex 07, France.

Tel: (33) 1 45 49 50 50
Email: program.kuwait@sciencespo.fr

Parkinson's United Kingdom

215 Vauxhall Bridge Road, London SW1V 1EJ, United Kingdom.

Tel: (44) 20 7931 8080
Email: hello@parkinsons.org.uk
Website: www.parkinsons.org.uk

We have come a long way since 1969, when Mali Jenkins founded the Parkinson's Disease Society - now Parkinson's UK. Together we will find a cure, and improve life for everybody affected by Parkinson's. Our core values show the way we all work together to bring forward the day when no one fears Parkinson's.

Clinician Scientist Fellowship

Purpose: To support MDs and other health professionals studying for a PhD.
Level of Study: Doctorate
Type: Fellowship
Value: Up to £250,000
Length of Study: 3 years
Frequency: Annual
Country of Study: United Kingdom
Application Procedure: Please see website
Additional Information: mrc.ukri.org/skills-careers/fellowships/clinical-fellowships/clinician-scientist-fellowship-csf/

For further information contact:

Email: cindy@cmscfoundation.org

Parkinson's UK drug accelerator grant

Purpose: These awards will help pioneer and accelerate novel drug development for the treatment of Parkinson's, providing researchers the opportunity to plug essential gaps in existing datasets to get their projects/compounds ready to enter full scale drug discovery with an industry partner or the Parkinson's Virtual Biotech. We are looking for projects that will have a clear focus on translational drug development to make a difference to those affected by Parkinson's.
Eligibility: 1. Grants are tenable only at a UK university, NHS Trust or small start-up biotech companies. 2. Principal applicants should hold employment contracts that extend beyond the period of the grant. 3. Co-applicants and collaborators may be based at institutions outside the UK or biotech companies.
Value: There is no minimum value and the maximum award amount is £50,000
Length of Study: Maximum of 12 months
Country of Study: Any country
Application Procedure: Apply online
Closing Date: 24 March

For further information contact:

Email: researchapplications@parkinsons.org.uk

Parkinson's UK non-drug approaches grant

Eligibility: 1. Grants are tenable only at a UK university, NHS Trust, statutory social care organisation or other research institution. 2. Principal applicants should hold employment contracts that extend beyond the period of the grant. 3. Co-applicants and collaborators may be based at institutions outside the UK or biotech companies.
Value: There is no minimum value and the maximum award amount is £200,000.
Length of Study: Maximum of 2 years.
Country of Study: Any country
No. of awards offered: 2
Closing Date: 14 September
No. of awards given last year: 8
No. of applicants last year: 19

For further information contact:

Email: researchapplications@parkinsons.org.uk

Parkinson's UK project grant

Purpose: Our project grants tackle major Parkinson's research challenges with groundbreaking studies that get right to the heart of complex problems.
Eligibility: 1. Grants are tenable only at a UK university, NHS Trust, statutory social care organisation or other UK research institution. 2. Principal applicants should hold employment contracts that extend beyond the period of the grant. 3. Co-applicants and collaborators may be based at institutions outside the UK or at pharmaceutical or biotech companies.
Level of Study: Research
Type: Grant
Value: Up to £400,000
Length of Study: Maximum of 3 years
Country of Study: Any country
No. of awards offered: 4
Closing Date: 2 February
No. of awards given last year: 19
No. of applicants last year: 30

Paul & Daisy Soros Fellowships for New Americans

11 West 42nd Street, 3rd floor, New York, NY 10036, United States of America.

Tel: (1) 212 405 8234
Email: pdsoros_fellows@sorosny.org
Website: www.pdsoros.org

In its near 20 year history, The Paul & Daisy Soros Fellowships for New Americans has built a community of

655 immigrants and children of immigrants. The Fellowship has supported New Americans with heritage in 89 countries. India, China, and Mexico are the most well represented.

The Paul & Daisy Soros Fellowship for New Americans

Purpose: To provide opportunities for continuing generations of able and accomplished New Americans to achieve leadership in their chosen fields
Eligibility: Open to New Americans resident aliens (Green Card Holders) naturalized United States citizens and/or children of 2 naturalized parents
Level of Study: Postdoctorate
Type: Fellowship
Value: US$25,000 up to US$20,000 in tuition support for each year
Length of Study: 2 years
Study Establishment: Any accredited graduate University in the United States
Country of Study: United States of America
Application Procedure: Apply online
No. of awards offered: 77
Closing Date: 12 November
Funding: Private
Contributor: Paul and Daisy Soros
No. of awards given last year: 30
No. of applicants last year: 77
Additional Information: https://www.pdsoros.org/apply

For further information contact:

Email: pdsoros@pdsoros.org

Paul Lowin Prizes

Perpetual Trustees Australia Limited, 39 Hunter Street, Sydney, NSW 2000, Australia.

Email: lowinprizes@perpetual.com.au
Website: www.paullowin.perpetual.com.au

The Paul Lowin Prizes are administered by the Perpetual Trustees Australia Limited, which is a public trustee company operating in all mainland states of Australia. Income generated from investment of this capital is distributed annually to charitable organisations to fulfil the intent of the trusts under management.

Paul Lowin Prizes - Song Cycle Prize

Purpose: To recognise original composition. For the purposes of the competition, a song cycle is music suitable for chamber performance
Eligibility: The composer must be at least 18 years of age and an Australian citizen or a resident of Australia for not less than three years prior to the closing date
Level of Study: Unrestricted
Type: Prize
Value: AU$15,000
Frequency: Every 2 years
Country of Study: Any country
Application Procedure: Applicants must refer to the website for details
No. of awards offered: 10
Closing Date: 30 June
Funding: Private
No. of awards given last year: 1
No. of applicants last year: 10
Additional Information: Works should use no more than one-eight independent vocal lines, which may be accompanied by up to 10 instrumental players. The text of the work may have a unifying theme, and the composer and the author of the text may or may not be different people, but the author of the text is not eligible for the prize. The work may be no less than 15 minutes and no more than 60 in duration taitmemorialtrust.org/tag/paul-lowin-song-cycle-prize/

For further information contact:

Australian Music Centre, Level 4, The Arts Exchange, 18 Hickson Road, Dawes Point, NSW 2000, Australia.

Email: info@australianmusiccentre.com.au

Peninsula School of Medicine and Dentistry

Plymouth Science Park, Research Way, Plymouth PL6 8BT, United Kingdom.

Email: info@psmd.ac.uk
Website: www.pcmd.ac.uk

Peninsula College of Medicine and Dentistry (PCMD) is a Medical and Dental school in England, run in partnership with the University of Exeter, the University of Plymouth and the NHS in Devon and Cornwall.

Peninsula College of Medicine and Dentistry PhD Studentships

Purpose: To attract PhD candidates of outstanding ability to join their exciting and rapidly expanding programme of internationally rated research
Eligibility: Open to the suitably qualified graduates
Level of Study: Doctorate
Type: Studentship
Value: £13,290 (Research Council Rate)
Frequency: Dependent on funds available
Study Establishment: Peninsula College of Medicine & Dentistry
Country of Study: United Kingdom
Application Procedure: Check website for the details
Closing Date: 8 November
Contributor: Various sources
Additional Information: scholarship-positions.com/studentship-peninsula-college-of-medicine-dentistry/2007/10/31/

Penn State, College of Communications

201 Carnegie Building, State College, PA 16803, United States of America.

Tel: (1) 814 863 1484
Website: www.bellisario.psu.edu/

The Donald P. Bellisario College of Communications at Penn State provides the opportunities and resources of a large university with the personalized feel and support of a small school. As one of the largest accredited programs of its kind in the nation, students can find a place where they can fit and succeed.

Call for Proposals: Narratives in Public Communications

Purpose: Donald P. Bellisario College of Communications at Penn State has announced its annual Page/Johnson Legacy Scholar Grant competition for the study of integrity in public communication. This year, the Center is issuing three research calls 1. Proposals for research projects on Corporate Social Advocacy. 2. Proposals for research projects on Ethics of Care. 3. Proposals for curriculum development on Activism.

Eligibility: This call therefore seeks grant proposals that will examine the uses and implications of stories and storytelling in public communications.
Level of Study: Graduate
Type: Grant
Value: US$2,000
Frequency: Annual
Country of Study: United States of America
Application Procedure: Check the application procedure at the link below. The proposal requires the below information to process further 1. Narrative (up to 5 pages). 2. Abstract (1 page). 3. Coversheet (1 page). 4. Budget (1 page). 5. Curriculum Vitae or Professional Resume. bellisario.psu.edu/page-center/grants/legacy-scholar-grants/guidelines-for-grant-applications.
No. of awards offered: 3
Closing Date: 15 January
Funding: Private
Additional Information: Other ideas for topics related to activism and public relations will also be accepted. Modules that center the voices and experiences of marginalized publics are especially encouraged.

Perkins School of Theology

Southern Methodist University, PO Box 750133, Dallas, TX 75275-0133, United States of America.

Tel: (1) 214 768 8436
Email: theology@smu.edu
Website: www.smu.edu/perkins

Perkins School of Theology is one of the 13 seminaries of The United Methodist Church and one of only five university-related United Methodist theological schools, located in the heart of Dallas, Texas, with an extension program in Houston/Galveston. The primary mission of Perkins School of Theology, as a community devoted to theological study and teaching in the service of the church of Jesus Christ, is to prepare women and men for faithful leadership in Christian ministry.

Diaconia Graduate Fellowships

Purpose: This fellowship was established to support deacons in full or provisional membership and diaconal ministers planning to teach or serve as an administrator in a school of theology, college, or university or in another institution or agency of the church. Applicants must be graduate students at an accredited academic institution. Demonstration of academic ability and financial need is a must.

Eligibility: 1. Applicant must be a full-time doctoral student in an accredited academic institution and have been accepted for work in a doctoral program (preferably Ph.D.) prior to the year for which the award is granted in an institution. 2. Applicant must be a full-time doctoral student in an accredited academic institution. 3. Applicant must be an ACTIVE, full member of The United Methodist Church for at least ONE year. Membership is determined by the date the applicant was confirmed and took membership vows with a United Methodist church.

Level of Study: Doctorate, Graduate
Type: Fellowships
Value: US$1,000 - US$10,000
Frequency: Annual
Country of Study: United States of America
Application Procedure: 1. Award selection is based on intellectual competence, academic achievements, promise of usefulness, personal qualities, and clarity of spiritual purpose and commitment. 2. A completed online application.
No. of awards offered: 1
Closing Date: March

For further information contact:

Tel: (1) 615 340 7344
Email: umscholar@gbhem.org

Petro Jacyk Central & East European Resource Centre (PJRC)

130 St George St, Room 3008 (3rd floor), Toronto, Ontario M5S 1A5, Canada.

Tel: (1) 416 978 0588
Email: jacyk.centre@utoronto.ca
Website: pjrc.library.utoronto.ca/content/

Petro Jacyk's contributions to the University of Toronto Library include funding the microfilming of the Peter Jacyk Collection of Ukrainian Serials in 1983, establishing an endowment to support annual subscriptions to Ukrainian periodicals in 1994, and support for the creation of the Petro Jacyk Central and East European Resource Centre in 1995.

Petro Jacyk Program

Purpose: The objective of the Post-Doctoral Fellowship is to support annually one of the most promising junior scholars studying contemporary Ukraine and thereby to advance academic understanding of Ukrainian politics, culture, and society
Eligibility: The Petro Jacyk Post-Doctoral Fellowship is available to junior scholars in the social sciences and humanities with a research and teaching focus on contemporary Ukraine. The fellowship is open to recently awarded PhDs (persons holding doctorates for no more than three years at the time of application)
Level of Study: Postdoctorate
Type: Fellowship
Value: C$40,000, which includes payment for teaching a semester-long course, and separately an allowance of up to C$2,500 for research and travel expenses
Length of Study: 1 year
Study Establishment: University of Toronto
Country of Study: Canada
Application Procedure: Please send applications by email to the Foundation at pjef@bellnet.ca and the Petro Jacyk Program for the Study of Ukraine at the University of Toronto at jacyk.program@utoronto.ca simultaneously
Closing Date: 1 February
Contributor: Petro Jacyk Education Foundation
Additional Information: For more information on the post-doctoral fellowship, please visit our website. www.science-community.org/en/node/161353

Pfizer

235 East 42nd Street, New York, NY 10017, United States of America.

Tel: (1) 212 733 2323
Email: MAPinfo@clinicalconnexion.com
Website: www.pfizermap.com

Pfizer supports the global healthcare community's independent initiatives to improve patient outcomes in areas of unmet medical need that are aligned with Pfizer's medical and/or scientific strategies.

Acromegaly/Growth Hormone Excess Research

Purpose: Pfizer Global Medical Grants (GMG) supports the global healthcare community's independent initiatives (e.g., research, quality improvement or education) to improve patient outcomes in areas of unmet medical need that are aligned with Pfizer's medical and/or scientific strategies. Pfizer's GMG competitive grant program involves a publicly posted Request for Proposal (RFP) that provides detail regarding a specific area of interest, sets timelines for review and approval, and uses an external review panel (ERP) to make final grant decisions. Organizations are invited to submit an application addressing the specific gaps in research, practice or care as outlined in the specific RFP. For all Investigator Sponsored Research (ISRs) and general research grants, the grant requester (and ultimately the grantee) is responsible for the design, implementation, sponsorship, and conduct of the independent initiative supported by the grant, including compliance with any regulatory requirements. Pfizer must not be involved in any aspect of study protocol or project development, nor the conduct or monitoring of the research program.

Eligibility: The institution and principal investigator (PI) must be based in one of the eligible countries noted above. 1. Only organizations are eligible to receive grants, not individuals or medical practice groups. 2. The applicant (PI) must have a medical or postdoctoral degree (MD, PhD, or equivalent), an advanced nursing degree (BSN with a MS/PhD), or a degree in Pharmacy, Physiotherapy, or Social Work. 3. Applicant must be affiliated with a host institution 4. Both early career and experienced investigators are encouraged to apply and consideration will be given to all proposals meeting the selection criteria

Level of Study: Postgraduate

Type: Grant

Value: Individual projects requesting up to US$100,000 will be considered. Pfizer anticipates awarding up to 1 grant 1. The amount of the grant Pfizer will be prepared to fund for any project will depend upon the external review panel's evaluation of the proposal and costs involved, and will be stated clearly in the approval notification

Frequency: Annual

Country of Study: United States of America

Application Procedure: 1. Please go to www.cybergrants. com/pfizer/Research and sign in. First-time users should click "Create your password". Requirements for submission 2. Select the following Competitive Grant Program Name RD LAcromegaly/Growth Hormone Excess Research US 3. Complete all required sections of the online application. See Appendix A for additional details 4. If you encounter any technical difficulties with the website, please click the "Technical Questions" link at the bottom of the page

No. of awards offered: 1

Closing Date: 28 May

Additional Information: www.pfizer.com/purpose/ independent-grants/competitive-grants

For further information contact:

Email: amanda.j.stein@pfizer.com

Breast Cancer Competitive Research Grant Program

Purpose: Pfizer Global Medical Grants (GMG) supports the global healthcare community's independent initiatives (e.g., research, quality improvement or education) to improve patient outcomes in areas of unmet medical need that are aligned with Pfizer's medical and/or scientific strategies. Pfizer's GMG competitive grant program involves a publicly posted Request for Proposal (RFP) that provides detail regarding a specific area of interest, sets timelines for review and approval, and uses an external review panel (ERP) to make final grant decisions. Organizations are invited to submit an application addressing the specific gaps in research, practice or care as outlined in the specific RFP. For all Investigator Sponsored Research (ISRs), general research and medical education grants, the grant requester (and ultimately the grantee) is responsible for the design, implementation, sponsorship, and conduct of the independent initiative supported by the grant, including compliance with any regulatory requirements. Pfizer must not be involved in any aspect of study protocol or project development, nor the conduct or monitoring of the project.

Eligibility: The principal investigator (PI) and institution must be based in one of the eligible regions noted above. 1. The applicant (PI) must have a medical or postdoctoral degree (MD, PhD, or equivalent). 2. Applicant must be affiliated with a host institution. 3. Both early career and experienced investigators are encouraged to apply and consideration will be given to all proposals meeting the selection criteria. 4. If the project involves multiple departments within an institution and/or between different institutions/ organizations/associations, all institutions must have a relevant role and the requesting organization must have a key role in the project.

Level of Study: Postgraduate

Type: Grant

Value: A total of US$3 million is allocated to this grants program. 1. Applications will be reviewed by an independent review panel. Up to 15 projects will be selected for funding. 2. The amount of the grant Pfizer will be prepared to fund for any project will depend upon the external review panel's evaluation of the proposal and costs involved, and will be stated clearly in the approval notification.

Frequency: Annual

Country of Study: United States of America

Application Procedure: Please go to www.cybergrants.com/ pfizer/Research and sign in. Firsttime users should click "REGISTER NOW". Requirements for submission 1. Select the following Competitive Grant Program Name Breast Cancer Competitive Research for AfME, Asia, LatAm 2. Complete all required sections of the online application. See Appendix A for additional details. All applications must be in English. 3. If you encounter any technical difficulties with the website, please click the "Technical Questions" link at the bottom of the page

Closing Date: 7 April

Additional Information: www.pfizer.com/purpose/ independent-grants/competitive-grants

For further information contact:

Email: Jessica.Romano@pfizer.com

Growth Hormone Research

Purpose: Pfizer Global Medical Grants (GMG) supports the global healthcare community's independent initiatives (e.g., research, quality improvement or education) to improve patient outcomes in areas of unmet medical need that are aligned with Pfizer's medical and/or scientific strategies. Pfizer's GMG competitive grant program involves a publicly posted Request for Proposal (RFP) that provides detail regarding a specific area of interest, sets timelines for review and approval, and uses an external review panel (ERP) to make final grant decisions. Organizations are invited to submit an application addressing the specific gaps in research, practice or care as outlined in the specific RFP. For all Investigator Sponsored Research (ISRs) and general research grants, the grant requester (and ultimately the grantee) is responsible for the design, implementation, sponsorship, and conduct of the independent initiative supported by the grant, including compliance with any regulatory requirements. Pfizer must not be involved in any aspect of study protocol or project development, nor the conduct or monitoring of the research program.

Eligibility: The institution and principal investigator (PI) must be based in one of the eligible countries noted above. 1. Only organizations are eligible to receive grants, not individuals or medical practice groups. 2. The applicant (PI) must have a medical or postdoctoral degree (MD, PhD, or equivalent), an advanced nursing degree (BSN with a MS/PhD), or a degree in Pharmacy, Physiotherapy, or Social Work. 3. Applicant must be affiliated with a host institution 4. Both early career and experienced investigators are encouraged to apply and consideration will be given to all proposals meeting the selection criteria

Level of Study: Postgraduate

Type: Grant

Value: Individual projects requesting up to US$100,000 will be considered. Pfizer anticipates awarding up to one grant. The amount of the grant Pfizer will be prepared to fund for any project will depend upon the external review panel's evaluation of the proposal and costs involved, and will be stated clearly in the approval notification

Frequency: Annual

Country of Study: United States of America

Application Procedure: Please go to www.cybergrants.com/ pfizer/Research and sign in. First-time users should click "Create your password". Requirements for submission 1. Select the following Competitive Grant Program Name RD LPediatric Growth Hormone Deficiency Research US 2. Complete all required sections of the online application. See Appendix A for additional details 3. If you encounter any technical difficulties with the website, please click the "Technical Questions" link at the bottom of the page

No. of awards offered: 1

Closing Date: 28 May

Additional Information: www.pfizer.com/purpose/ independent-grants/competitive-grants

For further information contact:

Email: amanda.j.stein@pfizer.com

Global Hemophilia ASPIRE

Purpose: Projects that will be considered for Pfizer support will focus on the following areas in Gene Therapy for Hemophilia A or B Basic Science of Gene Therapy for Hemophilia; Basic Science of TFPI & Anti-TFPI Monoclonal Antibodies; ross talk among regulators (e.g., Protein S being a co-factor for both Protein C and TFPI); AND Patients with MILD Hemophilia A or B.

Eligibility: The applicant (PI) must have a medical or postdoctoral degree (MD, PhD, or equivalent), an advanced nursing degree (BSN with a MS/PhD), or a degree in Pharmacy, Physiotherapy, or Social Work.

Level of Study: Masters Degree, Postdoctorate, Postgraduate, Postgraduate (MSc)

Type: Grant

Value: US$90,000

Length of Study: 1 to 2 year

Frequency: Annual

Country of Study: Any country

Closing Date: 1 March

Additional Information: cdn.pfizer.com/pfizercom/2021-11/2022-RD-G_GlobalHemophiliaASPIRE.pdf?i9KTO8LQ kwd0.6WPjji0GapVHAvXbc9h

For further information contact:

Email: amanda.j.stein@pfizer.com

Pfizer Scholar

Purpose: To support cancer development in epidemiology
Eligibility: Open to individuals who are pursuing research in epidemiology relevant to human health
Level of Study: Postgraduate
Type: Grant
Value: US$130,000
Length of Study: 2 years
Frequency: Annual
Country of Study: Any country
Application Procedure: A completed application form must be submitted
Closing Date: 6 January
Funding: Commercial
Additional Information: www.collegescholarships.org/scholarships/companies/pfizer.htm

For further information contact:

Email: mzebrowski@metrohealth.org

Pfizer Scholars Grants in Clinical Epidemiology

Purpose: To support the career development of junior faculty
Eligibility: Citizens or permanent residents of the United States of America who have a doctoral degree, relevant research experience and postdoctoral clinical training appropriate for the proposed research are encouraged to apply. The applicant should hold a junior faculty position (with 2 years of appointment as an instructor, an assistant professor or an equivalent junior faculty rank) at an accredited academic medical institution
Level of Study: Professional development
Type: Grant
Value: US$195,000
Length of Study: 3 years
Frequency: Annual
Country of Study: United States of America
Application Procedure: Applicants must visit the website for full details on the application process
Closing Date: 5 January
Funding: Corporation
Contributor: Pfizer Inc

For further information contact:

Email: mzebrowski@metrohealth.org

Pfizer Scholars Grants in Clinical Psychiatry

Purpose: To support the development of junior faculty
Eligibility: Citizens or permanent residents of the United States of America who are junior faculty with a doctoral degree (with 2 years of appointment as an instructor, an assistant professor or an equivalent junior faculty rank) at an accredited academic medical institution are encouraged to apply
Level of Study: Professional development
Type: Grant
Value: US$130,000
Length of Study: 2 years
Frequency: Annual
Country of Study: United States of America
Application Procedure: Applicants must visit the website for full details
Closing Date: 5 January
Funding: Corporation
Contributor: Pfizer Inc

For further information contact:

Email: mzebrowski@metrohealth.org

Pfizer Scholars Grants in Clinical Rheumatology

Purpose: To support the career development of junior faculty
Eligibility: Citizens or permanent residents of the United States of America who have a doctoral degree, relevant research experience and postdoctoral clinical training appropriate for the proposed research are encouraged to apply. The applicant should hold a junior faculty position (with 2 years of appointment as an instructor, an assistant professor or an equivalent junior faculty rank) at an accredited academic medical institution
Level of Study: Professional development
Type: Grant
Value: Up to US$130,000
Length of Study: 2 years
Frequency: Annual
Country of Study: United States of America
Application Procedure: Applicants must visit the website for details on the application process
Closing Date: 24 February
Funding: Corporation
Contributor: Pfizer Inc
Additional Information: researchfunding.duke.edu/2020-rheumatology-fellowship-competitive-grant-program

For further information contact:

Email: Amanda.solis@pfizer.com

Pfizer Scholars Grants in Pain Medicine

Purpose: To support the career development of junior faculty
Eligibility: Citizens or permanent residents of the United States of America who have a doctoral degree, relevant research experience are encouraged to apply. The applicant should hold a junior faculty position (with 2 years of appointment as an instructor, an assistant professor or an equivalent junior faculty rank) at an accredited academic medical institution
Level of Study: Professional development
Type: Grant
Value: US$130,000
Length of Study: 2 years
Frequency: Annual
Country of Study: United States of America
Application Procedure: Applicants must visit the website for details on the application process
Closing Date: 5 January
Funding: Corporation
Contributor: Pfizer Inc

For further information contact:

Email: mzebrowski@metrohealth.org

Pfizer Visiting Professorships Program

Purpose: To create opportunities for selected institutions to invite a distinguished expert for three days of teaching
Eligibility: Open to accredited medical schools and/or affiliated teaching hospitals
Level of Study: Postgraduate
Type: Grant
Value: US$7,500 each
Frequency: Annual
Country of Study: Any country
Application Procedure: Applications available online
Closing Date: 12 February
Additional Information: researchfunding.duke.edu/pfizer-visiting-professorship-program

For further information contact:

Email: mzebrowski@metrohealth.org

Transthyretin Amyloidosis (ATTR) Competitive Grant Program/ ASPIRE

Subjects: Transthyretin Amyloidosis (ATTR) including cardiomyopathy, peripheral neuropathy, and mixed phenotypes

Purpose: The intent of this Request for Proposal (RFP) is to improve the care of patients with ATTR by improving our understanding of disease epidemiology, pathophysiology, early diagnosis, prognosis, and emerging treatment paradigms.
Eligibility: Only organizations are eligible to receive grants, not individuals or medical practice groups. The principal investigator (PI) and institution must be based in one of the eligible countries noted above. The applicant (PI) must have a medical or postdoctoral degree (MD, PhD, or equivalent), an advanced nursing degree (BSN with a MS/PhD), or a degree in Pharmacy, Physiotherapy, or Social Work. Applicant must be affiliated with a host institution. Both early career and experienced investigators are encouraged to apply and consideration will be given to all proposals meeting the selection criteria
Type: Grant
Value: Up to US$75,000
Country of Study: United States of America
Application Procedure: Go to www.cybergrants.com/pfizer/ Research and sign in. First-time users should click "REGISTER NOW"
No. of awards offered: Up to four
Closing Date: 17 May

Phi Beta Kappa Society

1606 New Hampshire Avenue, NW, Washington, DC 20009, United States of America.

Tel: (1) 202 265 3808
Email: info@pbk.org
Website: www.pbk.org

Since 1776, Phi Beta Kappa has championed education in the arts and sciences, fostered freedom of thought, and recognized academic excellence. Phi Beta Kappa grew along with American higher education into an organization grounded in liberal arts and sciences learning and freedom of inquiry.

The Mary Isabel Sibley Fellowship

Purpose: This fellowship was designed to reward women pursuing graduate work in one of two fields of study, French or Greek, with the experience of researching and living abroad.
Eligibility: The fellowship is intended, according to the donor's wishes, for women in the early stages of their research careers who 1. Demonstrate ability to carry on original

research. 2. Hold a doctorate/have fulfilled all requirements for doctorate except the dissertation (ABD). 3. Plan to devote full-time work to research during the fellowship year. Under appropriate circumstances, if approved by Phi Beta Kappa, candidates may hold other positions concurrently with the Sibley Fellowship.

Level of Study: Research

Type: Fellowship

Value: US$20,000

Length of Study: 1 year, non-renewable

Frequency: Annual

Country of Study: Any country

Application Procedure: Applications must include 1. A work proposal. 2. Transcripts from all institutions (Transcripts do not need to come directly from the institution). 3. Three letters of recommendation should be uploaded directly by each recommender at this link.

Closing Date: 1 January

Funding: Private

Additional Information: The stipend is typically paid in two installments, the first on July 1 of the award year, and the second on January 1 of the following year. researchfunding. duke.edu/pfizer-visiting-professorship-program

For further information contact:

Email: hkelly@pbk.org

PhRMA Foundation

950 F Street, N.W. Suite 300, Washington, DC 20004, United States of America.

Tel: (1) 202 572 7756
Email: foundation@phrma.org.
Website: www.phrmafoundation.org/
Contact: PhRMA Foundation

The PhRMA Foundation works to improve public health by proactively investing in innovative research, education and value-driven health care. Supporting and encouraging young scientists to pursue novel projects to advance innovative and transformative research efforts. Using data, sound methodologies and advanced technology to inform decisions.

Patient-Centered Outcomes Challenge Award

Subjects: Health economics, outcomes research, clinical sciences, health care evaluation, public health

Purpose: The PhRMA Foundation is committed to driving real change in health care delivery and recognizes the benefit of shared knowledge.

Level of Study: Postdoctorate, Postgraduate (MSc)

Type: Award

Value: The winner will receive US$50,000; The runner up will receive US$25,000; Third place will receive US$5,000

Frequency: Annual

Country of Study: Any country

Closing Date: 1 March

Postdoctoral Fellowship in Health Outcomes Research

Purpose: To seek further development and refine their research skills through formal postdoctoral training. These fellowships are designed for individuals engaged in a multidisciplinary research training program that will create or extend their credentials.

Eligibility: 1. Applicants (U.S. and non-U.S. citizens) attending schools of medicine, pharmacy, public health, nursing, and dentistry are eligible for this award. 2. Applicants (U.S. and non-U.S. citizens) must have a firm commitment from a sponsor (a.k.a. mentor) at an accredited U.S. university. 3. Applicants must hold a PhD, PharmD, or MD degree. 4. If you do not hold one at the time of application submission, please state in your extended letter when you expect to receive it, as it must be received before funding could begin. 5. Applicants are encouraged to apply at the earliest point possible in their postdoctoral research. 6. Applicants requesting funds to continue an existing postdoctoral program for a third to fifth year will not be considered, nor will preference be given to those applying for funds to support postdoctoral work in the laboratory where their graduate work was performed. 7. Applicants must write and submit a research plan and provide the mentor's research record, as well as a description of how the mentoring experience will enhance their career development in Health Outcomes Research.

Level of Study: Doctorate, Masters Degree, Postdoctorate, Postgraduate (MSc)

Type: Fellowship

Value: US$60,000 per year

Length of Study: two-year

Frequency: Annual

Country of Study: United States of America

Application Procedure: We look forward to receiving your application. Items needed 1. General Registration Information 2. Applicant Biosketch (should be NIH or NSF format) 3. Extended Letter 4. Project/Research Title 5. Project/Research Abstract 6. Project/Research Description 7. Transcripts

Closing Date: 10 February

Additional Information: The application portal will permit you to review your application and the status of your letters of support before your final submission. Be sure to check it frequently and do not wait until the last minute. The application portal will not permit the application to be submitted until the letters of support have been uploaded. researchfunding. duke.edu/pfizer-visiting-professorship-program

Postdoctoral Fellowship in Translational Medicine

Purpose: This award supports individuals engaged in multidisciplinary/collaborative research training programs that will extend their credentials in Translational Medicine. To support research that can readily translate into positively impacting patients and physicians.

Eligibility: 1. Applicants (U.S. and non-U.S. citizens) must have a firm commitment from a sponsor (a.k.a. mentor) at an accredited U.S. university or research institution. 2. Applicants must hold a PhD, DSc, DEng, or MD degree, and seek to further develop and refine their skills and understanding of Translational Medicine through postdoctoral training. If you do not hold one at the time of application submission, please state in your extended letter when you expect to receive it, as it must be received before funding could begin. 3. Applicants are encouraged to apply at the earliest point possible in their postdoctoral research. 4. Applicants must write and submit a research plan and provide the mentor's research record, as well as a description of how the mentoring experience will enhance the applicant's career development in Translational Medicine. 5. A key component of Translational Medicine involves collaborative programs that span non-clinical and clinical domains, potentially involving multiple laboratories, advisers, and institutions.

Level of Study: Doctorate, Masters Degree, Postdoctorate

Type: Fellowship

Value: US$60,000

Length of Study: Two years

Frequency: Annual

Country of Study: United States of America

Application Procedure: Items needed 1. General Registration Information 2. Applicant Biosketch (should be NIH or NSF format) 3. Extended Letter 4. Project/Research Title 5. Project/Research Abstract 6. Research Plan

Closing Date: 10 February

Additional Information: An individual may not simultaneously hold or interrupt any other fellowship providing stipend support while the PhRMA Foundation fellowship is active. PhRMA Foundation funds may not be used for indirect costs to the university. researchfunding.duke.edu/pfizer-visiting-professorship-program

Pierre Elliott Trudeau Foundation

600 - 1980 Sherbrooke Street West, Montreal, Quebec H3H 1E8, Canada.

Tel: (1) 514 938 0001
Email: competition@trudeaufoundation.ca
Website: www.trudeaufoundation.ca/

The Pierre Elliott Trudeau Foundation is an independent and non-partisan charity established in 2001 as a living memorial to the former prime minister. The Pierre Elliott Trudeau Foundation represents much more than a Scholarship. We are a gateway for bold, cutting-edge doctoral researchers to become Engaged Leaders who have meaningful impact in their communities and institutions.

Pierre Elliott Trudeau Foundation Doctoral Scholarships

Purpose: This three-year leadership program is designed to train engaged leaders, equipping outstanding doctoral candidates with the skills to translate their ideas into action, for the betterment of their communities, Canada, and the world. Up to 16 doctoral Scholars are selected each year and receive generous funding for their studies in addition to leadership training in the context of Brave Spaces.

Eligibility: 1. You must be already accepted into or in year one, two, or three of a full-time doctoral program in the humanities or social sciences. 2. Your doctoral work must relate to at least one of the Foundation's Four Themes Human Rights and Dignity, Responsible Citizenship, Canada and the World, People and their Natural Environment. 3. Be a Canadian citizen studying at a Canadian or foreign institution, or a non-Canadian (permanent resident or foreign national) enrolled in a doctoral program at a Canadian institution.

Level of Study: Doctorate, Postdoctorate

Type: Scholarship

Value: Up to C$40,000 per year

Length of Study: 3 years

Frequency: Annual

Country of Study: Canada

Application Procedure: In order to complete your application, you will need to provide 1. Demographic information on yourself The Foundation gathers demographic information for statistical purposes, in order to fulfill its commitment to diversity and inclusion. This information will only be used by the Pierre Elliott Trudeau Foundation. 2. Essay Questions Provide answers (200 to 400 words) to four essay questions.

3. Doctoral Projects and Themes Provide information on your doctoral project, with answers ranging from 200 to 400 words in length. 4. Upload Transcripts Upload transcripts for all your post-secondary education, except information related to CEGEP in Quebec, should you have attended CEGEP in Quebec.

No. of awards offered: three years

Closing Date: 5 January

Additional Information: The Foundation reviews all applications and shortlisted candidates are invited to group interviews. Finalists proceed to interviews with the Application and Nomination Review Committee, who ultimately recommend their choices to the Board of Directors for final approval. researchfunding.duke.edu/pfizer-visiting-professorship-program

Pine Tree State 4-H Foundation

York Complex #1, Orono, ME 04469, United States of America.

Tel: (1) 207 581 3739
Email: angela.martin@maine.edu
Website: extension.umaine.edu/4hfoundation/

Since 1961 the Maine 4-H Foundation has played an active role in supporting the University of Maine Cooperative Extension 4-H program. With your help it will continue to do so for many years into the future.

Azure Dillon 4-H Memorial Scholarship

Purpose: The purpose of scholarship is for the graduating high school seniors and for the female members.

Eligibility: 1. This scholarship is available for female 4-H members in Maine who are active in 4-H activities. 2. Students must be graduating high school seniors or have previously graduated from high school but delayed going to college for no more than one year.

Level of Study: Graduate

Type: Scholarship

Value: US$1,000

Frequency: Annual

Country of Study: United States of America

Application Procedure: Application requirements for the Azure Dillon 4-H Memorial Scholarship are 1. Recommendation letter 2. Application form 3. Official Transcript 4. Story 5. Resume

No. of awards offered: 1

Closing Date: 1 March

Funding: Private

Additional Information: Scholarships are awarded based on a combination of demonstrated academic and 4-H excellence. Recipients will be requested to attend the foundation's annual meeting to receive their scholarship in person. researchfunding.duke.edu/pfizer-visiting-professorship-program

Plymouth University

Drake Circus, Plymouth, Devon PL4 8AA, United Kingdom.

Tel: (44) 1752 600 600
Email: india@plymouth.ac.uk
Website: www.plymouth.ac.uk

The University of Plymouth is a public university that was established in 1862 as a polytechnic institute. The institute gained the status of a university in 1992 and is also the first contemporary university to start a private medical and dental school. It is affiliated to ACU, EUA, CHUC, and Universities UK. The university has academic collaborations with several renowned institutes including GSM London, Highlands College, Weymouth College, Strode College, City of Bristol College, and Exeter College.

International Postgraduate Gaza Scholarships

Purpose: These scholarships will be awarded on a competitive basis to prospective masters students.

Eligibility: To be considered for the scholarship you must 1. be a citizen of Gaza. 2. be self-funding and classified as overseas for tuition fee purposes. 3. hold a conditional or unconditional offer from the University of Sheffield before the specified deadline to study a full-time postgraduate taught Master's course starting in September 2023.

Level of Study: Postgraduate, Postgraduate (MSc)

Type: Scholarship

Value: Each scholarship will be for a fee discount of £5,000 on a masters programme at Plymouth University.

Frequency: Annual

Country of Study: United Kingdom

Application Procedure: Please send completed application form as an attachment to internationalscholarships@plymouth.ac.uk along with a copy of your offer letter; a copy of final transcript/marks sheet from undergraduate degree (if final transcript is not available at the time of application please send the most recent

or provisional results); a reference letter, from a suitable source, supporting this scholarship application (please do not supply the same reference as that submitted with the postgraduate application). www.plymouth.ac.uk/uploads/production/document/path/5/5758/GazaScholarship2016.docx
Closing Date: 31 May

For further information contact:

Tel: (44) 114 222 1319
Email: financialhelp@sheffield.ac.uk

International Student Merit Scholarship

Purpose: This scholarship is available to international students who have met the conditions of their University of Plymouth offer of study for the following programmes MSc Advanced Psychology, MSc/PgDip Psychology.
Eligibility: Applicants must have received a conditional offer of a place for a postgraduate taught programme commencing in September and be holding the equivalent of a United Kingdom university 1 class Bachelors degree in a relevant subject.
Level of Study: Masters Degree, Postgraduate, Postgraduate (MSc)
Type: Scholarship
Value: £2,500
Frequency: Annual
Country of Study: United Kingdom
Application Procedure: Applicants can apply via email. For detailed information, please visit website.
Closing Date: 31 May
Additional Information: Please check at website www.sheffield.ac.uk/international/fees-and-funding/scholarships/undergraduate/international-undergraduate-merit-scholarship

For further information contact:

The University of Sheffield, Western Bank, Sheffield S10 2TN, United Kingdom.

Tel: (44) 114 222 2000

International Student PGT Scholarship

Purpose: Scholarships are available for international students who wish to study postgraduate taught degree courses.
Eligibility: 1. Applicants should hold a conditional offer of a place on a postgraduate taught degree programme at Plymouth University. 2. The University will automatically consider applicants with relevant Bachelor degree grades as stipulated in the list. Please note this eligibility criteria list is not exhaustive and graduates from all non-EU countries will be considered for these scholarships. 3. The Bachelor's degree must be the equivalent of a United Kingdom Honours degree, as specified by United Kingdom NARIC.
Level of Study: Postgraduate, Postgraduate (MSc)
Type: Scholarship
Value: £1,500
Frequency: Annual
Country of Study: United Kingdom
Application Procedure: If the student has applied for a postgraduate taught degree programme, they will automatically be considered for this scholarship if their final transcript or marks sheet was submitted with their application.
Closing Date: 31 May
Additional Information: studyabroad.shiksha.com/scholarships/school-of-management-pgt-scholarship-ma-international-development-management

For further information contact:

Tel: (44) 1274 236637
Email: scholarships@bradford.ac.uk

Poets Essayists Novelists American Center

588 Broadway, Suite 303, New York, NY 10012, United States of America.

Tel: (1) 212 334 1660
Email: pen@pen.org
Website: www.pen.org

PEN America stands at the intersection of literature and human rights to protect free expression in the United States and worldwide. We champion the freedom to write, recognizing the power of the word to transform the world. Our mission is to unite writers and their allies to celebrate creative expression and defend the liberties that make it possible.

The PEN Translation Fund Grants

Purpose: Its purpose is to promote the publication and reception of translated international literature in English.
Eligibility: 1. The PEN/Heim Translation Fund provides grants to support the translation of book-length works of fiction, creative nonfiction, poetry, or drama that have not previously appeared in English in print or have appeared only in an outdated or otherwise flawed translation. 2. Works should be translations-in-progress, as the grant

aims to provide support for completion. 3. There are no restrictions on the nationality or citizenship of the translator, but the works must be translated into English. 4. The Fund seeks to encourage translators to undertake projects they might not otherwise have had the means to attempt. 5. Works with multiple translators, literary criticism, and scholarly or technical texts do not qualify. 6. Translators who have previously been awarded grants by the Fund are ineligible to reapply for three years after the year in which they receive a grant. 7. Please note that projects that have been previously submitted and have not received a grant are unlikely to be reconsidered in a subsequent year.

Level of Study: Unrestricted

Type: Grant

Value: US$2,000-US$4,000 to nearly 200 translations from over 35 languages.

Frequency: Annual

Country of Study: Any country

Application Procedure: The application will require the following materials. Please use a standard 12pt font with 1 inch margins 1. A 1-2 page, single-spaced statement outlining the work and describing its importance. 2. A biography and bibliography of the author, including information on translations of his or her work into other languages. 3. A CV of the translator, no longer than 3 pages. 4. If the book is not in the public domain and the project is not yet under contract, please include a photocopy of the copyright notice on the original (the copyright notice is a line including the character, a date, and the name of the copyright holder, which appears as part of the front matter in every book), and a letter from the copyright holder stating that English-language rights to the book are available. A letter or copy of an email from the copyright holder is sufficient. 5. If the translation is currently under contract with a publisher, please submit a copy of the contract. 6. An 8-10 page, single-spaced sample of the translation. For prose, this should be within the range of 3,000-5,000 words. For poetry, please include 1-2 poems per page, within the 8-10 page range. 7. The same passage in the original language (and, if the work has been previously translated, the same passage in the earlier version).

Closing Date: 1 June

Additional Information: Translation Fund received a large number of applications from a wide array of languages of origin, genres, and time periods. From this vast field of applicants, the Fund Advisory Board has selected 11 projects, spanning 10 different languages, including Russian, Italian, Korean, French, Portuguese, Galician, Vietnamese, Hindi, and Spanish. PEN America has awarded grants to nearly 200 winning projects to date. studyabroad.shiksha.com/schol arships/school-of-management-pgt-scholarship-ma-international-development-management

For further information contact:

Email: awards@pen.org.

Polycystic Kidney Disease Foundation

1001 E 101st Terrace Suite 220, Kansas City, MO 64131, United States of America.

Tel:	(1) 816 931 2600
Email:	pkdcure@pkdcure.org
Website:	www.pkdcure.org
Contact:	PKD Foundation

We are the only organization in the U.S. solely dedicated to finding treatments and a cure for polycystic kidney disease (PKD). We fund research, education, advocacy, support, and awareness on a national and local level. We fund basic and clinical research, nephrology fellowships, and scientific meetings. We fund research, advocate for patients, and build a community for all impacted by PKD.

Polycystic Kidney Disease Foundation Grant-In-Aid

Purpose: The principal goal of our research grant program is the development of clinical interventions for the treatment of PKD. This program funds basic laboratory research aimed at increasing understanding of the genetic and pathological processes involved in PKD as well as research with an obvious or direct potential to accelerate the development of potential therapies.

Eligibility: 1. Applicants must have an M.D., Ph.D. or equivalent degree and hold a faculty appointment at the institution where the research will be conducted at the time of award. 2. Applicants need not be United States citizens. 3. No fellowships will be awarded under this RFA, although salary support for personnel working on the project may be requested. 4. Applicants may only submit one grant proposal per funding cycle.

Level of Study: Doctorate, Masters Degree, Postdoctorate

Type: Research grant

Value: Award amounts will equal US$80,000 direct costs per year for two years, for a total grant award of US$160,000 (or US$240,000 for a three-year Young Investigator Award).

Length of Study: 2 or 3 years

Frequency: Annual

Country of Study: Any country

Application Procedure: 1. Applicants will be asked to submit a project proposal, letters of support, and budget details through the Proposal Central platform. 2. If the application is a resubmission, a response to reviewers will be requested. 3. If eligible, applicants may also submit justification to be considered for the Young Investigator Award.

Closing Date: 19 January

Funding: Foundation, Individuals, Private

Additional Information: Applicants are restricted to one application resubmission and will be asked to provide a one-page response to reviewer comments. Thereafter, the application must be submitted as a new application. Grantees must submit an annual Progress Report to be submitted along with a Financial Report. studyabroad.shiksha.com/scholar ships/school-of-management-pgt-scholarship-ma-international-development-management

Population Council

One Dag Hammarskjold Plaza, New York, NY 10017, United States of America.

Tel: (1) 877 339 0500
Email: pubinfo@popcouncil.org
Website: www.popcouncil.org

The Population Council conducts research to address critical health and development issues. Our work allows couples to plan their families and chart their futures. We conduct research and programs in more than 50 countries. Our New York headquarters supports a global network of offices in Africa, Asia, Latin America, and the Middle East.

Health and Population Innovation Fellowship Program

Purpose: To support mid-career individuals who have innovative ideas and the capacity to help shape public debate in the field of population, rights and reproductive health

Level of Study: Postdoctorate, Professional development

Type: Fellowship

Length of Study: 1 year

Frequency: Annual

Study Establishment: The Population Council, New Delhi

Country of Study: India

Application Procedure: Request application form

Closing Date: 15 September

Funding: Foundation

Contributor: John D. and Catherine T. MacArthur Foundation

No. of awards given last year: 12

Additional Information: nursing.duke.edu/centers-institutes/center-nursing-research/postdoctoral-fellowship-health-innovation

For further information contact:

Zone 5A, Ground Floor India Habitat Centre, Lodi Road, New Delhi, Delhi 110003, India.

Tel: (91) 11 2464 2901
Fax: (91) 11 2464 2903
Email: fellowships@pcindia.org

Transmission of Immunodeficiency Viruses: Postdoctoral Research Position

Additional Information: www.niaid.nih.gov/about/postdoctoral-research-training

For further information contact:

Center for Biomedical Research Population Council, 1230 York Avenue, New York, NY 10065, United States of America.

Tel: (1) 212 327 7794
Fax: (1) 212 327 7764
Email: mpope@popcouncil.org

Prehistoric Society

Institute of Archaeology, University College London, 31-34 Gordon Square, London WC1H 0PY, United Kingdom.

Email: prehistoric@ucl.ac.uk
Website: www.prehistoricsociety.org

The Prehistoric Society's interests are world-wide and extend from the earliest human origins to the emergence of written records. Founded in 1935, we currently have around 1500 members in over 40 countries. The Society is registered in England and Wales as a company limited by guarantee and is a registered charity.

P

Collections Study Award

Eligibility: The award will be available to partnerships between a museum and a named early-stage researcher (post-graduate, post-doctorate or equivalent experience) and both parties will be eligible for a contribution to the costs incurred. Third-party ('external') costs will also be eligible where essential to the successful outcome of the project. Applications may be submitted by the named researcher or by the museum. The named researcher is required to be a member of the Prehistoric Society.

Level of Study: Postdoctorate, Postgraduate
Type: Award
Value: Up to £3000
Frequency: Annual
Country of Study: Any country
Closing Date: 31 January
Funding: Private

For further information contact:

Email: admin@prehistoricsociety.org

Prehistoric Society Conference Fund

Purpose: It's aim is to further the development of prehistory as an international discipline. To offer funding to those who might not otherwise be able to travel to an international conference.
Eligibility: There are no eligibility restrictions.
Level of Study: Unrestricted
Type: Scholarship
Value: £200–300
Frequency: Annual
Country of Study: Any country
Application Procedure: Applications from both members and non-members will be considered. Applications may also be made by conference organisers, on behalf of attending scholars. Please check website for application www.prehistoricsociety.org/grants/conference_fund/
Closing Date: 31 January
Funding: Private
Additional Information: www.prehistoricsociety.org/grants/conference_fund/

For further information contact:

Administrative Assistant, Prehistoric Society, Institute of Archaeology, 31-34 Gordon Square, London WC1H 0PY, United Kingdom.

Email: admin@prehistoricsociety.org

Research Fund

Purpose: The Research Grant aims to offer small "pump-primer" grants to projects in their early stages. A further aim is to give preference to projects showing innovation in the field of prehistory research and to those scholars in the earliest stages of their research careers.
Eligibility: The Research Fund is open only to members of the Prehistoric Society. The Prehistoric Society cannot accept applications for salaries or student funding. Post-excavation work relating to excavations not originally sponsored by the Society will only be considered in situations of exceptional research potential that exceed reasonable, initial planning expectations. Where applications are being made to help fund an excavation, the Society will only consider funding the project to assessment stage. The society may, however, consider an application to fund post-excavation work in the following year.
Level of Study: Unrestricted
Type: Award
Value: £100-£1,500 per award
Frequency: Annual
Country of Study: Any country
Application Procedure: Applications will only be considered from members of the society.
Closing Date: 31 January
Funding: Private
Additional Information: www.prehistoricsociety.org/grants/research_fund/

For further information contact:

Administrative Assistant, Prehistoric Society, Institute of Archaeology, 31-34 Gordon Square, London WC1H 0PY, United Kingdom.

Email: admin@prehistoricsociety.org

The John and Bryony Coles Bursary (Student Travel Award)

Purpose: The purpose of the bursary is to permit the recipients to travel abroad (i.e. outside their countries of residence and registered study) to gain a better understanding of prehistoric archaeology, through the active study of archaeology, whether by taking part in excavations, surveys or other fieldwork, by working in museums, or by travelling to visit sites.
Eligibility: Applicants must be registered students of archaeology (either part or full time) in the later stages of undergraduate study or in the early years of postgraduate study, or other equivalent status, without restriction on age. All applicants must provide proof of their student status (i.e. a letter from their institution). Student cards will not be accepted.
Level of Study: Unrestricted

Type: Award
Value: £200 and £300 each are usually given each year.
Frequency: Annual
Country of Study: Any country
Application Procedure: Applications will only be considered from members of the society.
Closing Date: 31 January
Funding: Private
Additional Information: www.prehistoricsociety.org/grants/the_john_and_bryony_coles_bursary_student_travel_award/

For further information contact:

Administrative Assistant, Prehistoric Society, Institute of Archaeology, 31-34 Gordon Square, London WC1H 0PY, United Kingdom.

Email: admin@prehistoricsociety.org

President's Commission on White House Fellowships

1600 Pennsylvania Ave NW, Washington, DC 20500, United States of America.

Tel: (1) 202 395 4522
Email: comments@whitehouse.gov
Website: www.whitehouse.gov/fellows
Contact: The White House

The White House is where the President and First Family of the United States live and work - but it's also the People's House, where we hope all Americans feel a sense of inclusion and belonging. Thousands of people work in the West Wing, the East Wing, the Cabinet, and the Executive Office of the President.

White House Fellowships

Purpose: The purpose of the White House Fellows program is to provide gifted and highly motivated emerging leaders with some first-hand experience in the process of governing the Nation and a sense of personal involvement in the leadership of society.
Eligibility: 1. Applicants must be U.S. citizens. 2. Employees of the Federal government are not eligible unless they are career military personnel. 3. Applicants must have completed their undergraduate education by the time they begin the application process. 4. There are no formal age restrictions. However, the Fellowship program was created to give selected Americans the experience of government service early in their careers.
Level of Study: Postgraduate
Type: Fellowships
Length of Study: 1 year
Frequency: Annual
Country of Study: United States of America
Application Procedure: 1. If you have additional questions about the program, please contact our program office at whitehousefellows@who.eop.gov. 2. If you encounter technical difficulties with your application, please contact WHFApplication@opm.gov.
Closing Date: 6 January
Funding: Government
Additional Information: At least one recommendation should be from an individual that can speak to your professional competence and accomplishments in your field. At least one recommendation should come from someone with knowledge of your community and civic activities. In addition, one recommendation should be from your current supervisor, if applicable. A recommendation from a prior supervisor is acceptable, but a current supervisor is preferred.

For further information contact:

Email: whitehousefellows@who.eop.gov

Prime Minister's Research Fellowship

Hauz Khas, New Delhi, 110 016, India.

Email: pmrfsupport@iitd.ac.in
Website: dec2020.pmrf.in/

Prime Minister's Research Fellowship scheme aims to attract the talent pool of the country to doctoral programmes of Indian Institute of Science (IISc), Indian Institutes of Science Education & Research (IISERs), Indian Institutes of Technology (IITs), National Institute of Technology (NITs) and Central Universities for carrying out research in cutting edge science and technology domains, with focus on national priorities.

Prime Minister's Research Fellowship Scheme

Purpose: The aim of this fellowship is to promote technical research studies and attract meritorious students to pursue doctoral programmes at leading institutions in India. Selected students will get admission in Ph.D. programmes at IISc/IISERs/IITs and Central Universities.

Eligibility: To be eligible, an applicant must 1. Apply for a PhD programme at one of the PMRF granting institutes either through direct entry channel or lateral entry channel. For Direct Entry Channel the following criteria 1. Have completed or been pursuing the final year of 4- (or 5) year undergraduate or 5-year integrated M.Tech or 5-year integrated M.Sc. or 2-year M. Sc. or 5-year undergraduate-postgraduate dual degree programs in Science and Technology streams from IISc/IITs/NITs/IISERs/IIEST and centrally funded universities with a CGPA/CPI of at least 8.0 (on a 10 point scale). 2. Have completed or been pursuing the final year of 4- (or 5) year undergraduate or 5-year integrated M.Tech or 5-year integrated M.Sc. or 2-year M.Sc. or 5-year undergraduate-postgraduate dual degree programs in Science and Technology streams from any other (not covered in the first point) Institute/University recognized in India with a CGPA/CPI of at least 8.0 (on a 10-point scale). 3. Have qualified GATE and be pursuing or have completed M.Tech./MS by Research at one of PMRF granting institutions having a minimum CGPA or CPI of 8.0 (on a 10-point scale) at the end of the first semester with a minimum of four courses. For Lateral Entry Channel the following criteria are 1. Be pursuing PhD in one of the PMRF granting institutions and have completed at most 12 months in the PhD programme (if they have joined the programme with a Master's degree), OR have completed at most 24 months in the PhD programme (if they have joined the programme with a Bachelor's degree). 2. Have completed at least four courses in the PhD programme, each of which should be a full-semester course. 3. Have obtained an aggregate CGPA of 8.5 (out of 10) or higher.

Level of Study: MBA, Masters Degree, Postgraduate, Postgraduate (MSc), Undergraduate

Type: Fellowship

Value: Up to ₹80,000

Frequency: Annual

Country of Study: India

Application Procedure: 1. Click the 'Apply Online' button below. 2. Then click the 'Apply Now' button. 3. Register on the site, if not registered. 4. Log in to begin the application process. 5. Fill the required details in the online application form. 6. Upload the necessary documents as part of the application process. 7. Click on the 'Submit' button to complete the application process.

Closing Date: December

Funding: Government

Additional Information: Screening of scholarship applications based on academic records (merit) and financial need.

Candidates may also have to give a telephonic interviews for further shortlisting. At certain stage, a candidate may also need to give a face to face interview. (only if required) www.prehistoricsociety.org/grants/the_john_and_bryony_coles_bursary_student_travel_award/

Prince Charles Hospital Foundation's

GPO Box 3175, Brisbane, QLD 4001, Australia.

Tel: (61) 1800 501 269
Email: info@thecommongood.org.au
Website: www.thecommongood.org.au

The Common Good is all of us working together to give precious time to researchers, so they can give more time to us and those we love to live happier, healthier, longer lives.

Prince Charles Hospital Foundation's PhD Scholarship

Purpose: The aim of the scholarship is to support educational academic research and high-quality research training at TPCH or in the significant partnership with TPCH and its associated community programs. The scholarship provides the applicant with a living stipend to undertake research at or in significant association with, The Prince Charles Hospital

Eligibility: Applicants from Australia are eligible to apply for the scholarship. Applicants must be enrolled, or soon to be enrolled, full-time in a PhD program at an Australian University

Type: Scholarship

Value: The scholarship will be valued at AU$27,082 per annum. The scholarship provides the applicant with a living stipend to undertake research at or insignificant association with, The Prince Charles Hospital

Country of Study: Australia

Application Procedure: See the website

Closing Date: 23 January

For further information contact:

Email: Stephanie.Yerkovich@tpchfoundation.org.au

Q

Qalaa Holdings Scholarship Foundation (QHSF)

Qalaa Holdings Scholarship Foundation, P.O Box: 29, Cairo EG-11516, Egypt.

Tel: (20) 2 2794 5553
Email: info@qalaascholarships.org
Website: qalaascholarships.org/

The Qalaa Holdings Scholarship Foundation was created in 2007, out of a strong will to contribute to national development through creating high caliber professionals to help enhance Egypt's growth in all sectors. The Foundation is funded by an endowment from Qalaa Holdings to grant academic scholarships for talented and promising young Egyptian men and women to pursue master degrees abroad in all fields of study.

Citadel Capital Scholarship

Purpose: The Citadel Capital Scholarship Foundation was created in 2007, out of a strong will to contribute to national development through creating high caliber professionals to help enhance Egypt's growth in all sectors
Eligibility: Students from Egypt can apply for this Citadel Capital Scholarship
Level of Study: Postgraduate
Type: Scholarship
Value: US$50,000
Frequency: Annual
Country of Study: Egypt
Application Procedure: Application form is only accepted by postal mail or through the FedEx account.
Closing Date: 15 April

For further information contact:

Qalaa Holdings Scholarship Foundation, P.O Box: 29, Cairo EG-11516, Egypt.

Email: info@citadelscholarships.org

Queen Elisabeth International Music Competition of Belgium

20 rue aux Laines, B-1000 Brussels, Belgium.

Tel: (32) 2 213 4050
Email: info@queenelisabethcompetition.be
Website: queenelisabethcompetition.be/
Contact: Secretariat

One of the most demanding and also one of the most widely publicised international competitions, the Queen Elisabeth Competition, ever since its creation in 1937, has established itself as a springboard for young violinists, pianists, singers, and cellists on the threshold of an international career. The Competition aims, above all, to serve as an intermediary between those young virtuosos and the world's great musical venues.

Queen Elisabeth International Music Competition of Belgium

Purpose: To provide career support for young pianists, singers, violinists and cellists
Eligibility: Open to musicians of any nationality who are at least 17 years of age and not older than 30 years for violin,

© Springer Nature Limited 2022
Palgrave Macmillan (ed.), *The Grants Register 2023*,
https://doi.org/10.1057/978-1-349-96053-8

piano, singing and cellists. The competition is made up of a first round, a semi-final and a final round
Level of Study: Unrestricted
Type: Competition
Value: Prizes, awards and certificates along with cash prizes will be awarded
Frequency: Annual
Country of Study: Any country
Application Procedure: Applicants must obtain an application form from the Secretariat of the Competition or via the website
No. of awards offered: Unrestricted
Closing Date: November
Funding: Private
No. of applicants last year: Unrestricted
Additional Information: queenelisabethcompetition.be/en/competitions/cello-2022/

Queen Margaret University

Queen Margaret University Drive, Musselburgh, Edinburgh EH21 6UU, United Kingdom.

Tel: (44) 131 474 0000
Email: rilo@qmu.ac.uk
Website: www.qmuc.ac.uk
Contact: Professor Anthony Cohen, Principal

We aim to shape a better world through education, research and innovation. In doing so, we enable individuals and communities to flourish. Our person-centred approach to learning makes us stand out from other universities, along with our focus on making society better. Our academic offering also distinguishes us. We dedicate ourselves to subjects where we can offer a distinctive offering - in healthcare; social sciences; creative arts; business, management and enterprise; and primary and secondary teaching.

Students Awards Agency for Scotland Postgraduate Students' Allowances Scheme (PSAS)

Purpose: Under the scheme, students may receive support for certain full-time vocational courses, mostly at diploma level.
Eligibility: To be eligible for postgraduate support students must meet the residence and previous study conditions; and take an eligible course.

Level of Study: Postgraduate
Type: Award
Value: £10,000
Frequency: Annual
Study Establishment: Queen Margaret University College
Country of Study: United Kingdom
No. of awards offered: 7
Closing Date: 8 April
Contributor: Students Awards Agency for Scotland (SAAS)
Additional Information: www.postgraduatestudentships.co.uk/opportunity/postgraduate-student-allowance-scheme/22237

Queen Mary, University of London

Admissions and Research Student Office, Mile End Road, London E1 4NS, United Kingdom.

Tel: (44) 20 7882 5555
Email: admissions@qmul.ac.uk
Website: www.qmul.ac.uk

Queen Mary has a long, proud and distinctive history built on four historic institutions stretching back to 1785 and beyond. Our founding institutions are: St Bartholomew's Hospital Medical College, London Hospital Medical College, Westfield College and Queen Mary College.

ANID (Becas Chile)

Subjects: PhD or Masters study in any subject
Purpose: Queen Mary has an agreement with ANID Becas Chile (formerly known as CONICYT), which allows us to offer funding for postgraduate students (Master's and PhDs). This co-funded scholarship is available across all of our full-time Masters and PhD programmes.
Level of Study: Masters Degree, Postdoctorate
Type: Award
Value: Tuition fee, stipend and airfare.
Frequency: Annual
Country of Study: Other
Country of Study: Chile
No. of awards offered: Variable

For further information contact:

Email: f.mckay@qmul.ac.uk

ANII Becas

Purpose: ANII and Queen Mary have formally partnered to fund Uruguayan Master's and Doctoral students to study at Queen Mary.
Level of Study: Masters Degree, Postdoctorate
Type: Scholarships
Value: US$20,000 per year
Frequency: Annual
Country of Study: United Kingdom
Application Procedure: Applicants should first apply to Queen Mary for admission and then to ANII for the scholarship.
No. of awards offered: Up to 5
Closing Date: 16 March
Additional Information: www.qmul.ac.uk/scholarships/items/anii-becas.html

For further information contact:

Queen Mary University of London, Mile End Road, London E1 4NS, United Kingdom.

Email: scholarships@qmul.ac.uk

Associate Alumni Bursary

Subjects: All Taught Masters courses in Humanities and Social Sciences
Purpose: Queen Mary offers students who have studied as an Associate Student a bursary of 20% reduction on tuition fees when returning for a postgraduate taught programme from September 2023. This award is automatically awarded and students are not required to submit a formal application.
Eligibility: 1. Must have studied on an Associate Student Programme in the last three academic years - the scheme is currently open to students who have studied with us between September 2014 - present. 2. The scholarship is available for students applying for programmes running until September 2023. 3. Must have successfully completed their semester or year abroad at Queen Mary. 4. Must enrol on a postgraduate taught programme in the Faculty of Humanities and Social Sciences.
Level of Study: Postgraduate
Type: Award
Value: 20% tuition fee discount
Frequency: Annual
Country of Study: Any country
Application Procedure: Students should submit an application for their programme of study using the following application link www.qmul.ac.uk/postgraduate/taught/applyfortaughtprogrammes/ and inform us via email following submitting the application to scholarships@qmul.ac.uk
No. of awards offered: Unlimited
Additional Information: www.qmul.ac.uk/scholarships/items/associate-alumni-bursary.html

For further information contact:

Queen Mary University of London, Mile End Road, London E1 4NS, United Kingdom.

Email: scholarships@qmul.ac.uk

B.A. Krukoff Fellowship in Systematics

Subjects: MSc Plant and Fungal Taxonomy, Diversity and Conservation
Purpose: The bursary is provided by the Bentham-Moxon Trust B.A. Krukoff Fund to support a student wishing to focus their MSc research project on Tropical African botany. The bursary itself will be administered by RBG Kew.
Eligibility: Applicants must: 1. Have received an offer of a place on the Kew/QMUL Plant and Fungal Taxonomy Diversity and Conservation MSc programme for the 2023–24 academic year. Applicants who have received a conditional offer are also eligible to apply but, if awarded the bursary, they must fulfil all conditions of the offer no later than 31 August 2023. 2. Demonstrate their experience in Tropical African botany*. 3. Demonstrate how they will continue to work and have an impact in Tropical African Botany* after they complete the course. *Note - In this context, we consider tropical Africa to comprise those countries that are members of the African Union, as per the following list of qualifying countries. The bursary recipient must: 1. Be eligible to study in the UK. All applicants are advised to check the UK visa requirements and application processes as early as possible, to ensure that they fulfil any requirements before the start of the course in September 2023. 2. Not be in receipt of any other bursaries or grants for completion of an MSc in the 2023–24 academic year.
Type: Fellowship
Value: Full tuition fees, and up to £21,000 maintenance and travel costs
Country of Study: Any country
No. of awards offered: 1
Closing Date: 31 March

For further information contact:

Email: kewmsc@kew.org

BASF (Ludwigshafen/Germany)

Purpose: BASF (Ludwigshafen/Germany) are offering three fee waivers
Level of Study: Masters Degree
Type: Scholarships
Value: £9,950 each
Frequency: Annual
Country of Study: United Kingdom
No. of awards offered: 2
Closing Date: 1 May
Additional Information: For further information about the programme, and to apply, please visit: www.qmul.ac.uk/postgraduate/taught/coursefinder/courses/121436.html www.qmul.ac.uk/scholarships/items/basf-ludwigshafengermany-.html

For further information contact:

Queen Mary University of London, Mile End Road, London E1 4NS, United Kingdom.

Tel: (44) 20 7882 5555
Email: r.goerner@qmul.ac.uk

Blockchain in Business and Society Scholarships

Subjects: MSc Blockchain in Business and Society Scholarships
Eligibility: 1. You must have achieved, or be on track to achieve, a UK 2:1 degree (Upper Second) or an overseas equivalent degree. Information on the comparability of international qualifications can be found on the Entry Requirements section under the listings for each programme in the course finder. Please note this information is only intended as a guide and the final decision on equivalency of overseas qualifications will be made by the School of Business and Management. 2. This scheme is available only to students who apply for and enrol on an MSc Blockchain in Business and Society taught in the School of Business and Management in the 2023/24 academic year. 3. Preference will be given to those students studying for their first postgraduate degree. 4. Your fee status must have been confirmed as 'Overseas' by Queen Mary and must remain 'Overseas' throughout the programme. This award is not available to applicants assessed as 'Home' for fee status purposes, regardless of domicile. 5. You must be enrolled on a full time programme. 6. You must not be in receipt of any other University scholarship or full-fee scholarship from any other source. 7. If you are awarded the scholarship it will be deducted directly from tuition fees payable to the University. You must be able to finance the remainder of your tuition fees and living expenses. 8. Successful applicants must accept the scholarship and pay a tuition fee deposit of £2,000 by the dates stipulated in the scholarship offer email. Failure to do so could lead to the withdrawal of the award. 9. The scholarship will be confirmed when you are placed at Queen Mary (your admissions status is 'unconditional firm' (UF)). 10. The scholarship is awarded by Queen Mary in line with the eligibility criteria and application requirements published above. We reserve the right to withdraw the scholarship if your fee status changes to Home or if you otherwise become ineligible for the award.
Level of Study: Masters Degree
Type: Scholarship
Value: £15,000
Frequency: Annual
Country of Study: Any country
No. of awards offered: 2
Additional Information: Eligible students will contacted by Queen Mary after receiving an offer and invited to apply for a scholarship. We will consider applicants that have achieved a UK 2:1 degree (Upper Second) (or equivalent), and those who are on course to achieve a 2:1.

Business and Management Postgraduate Scholarships

Subjects: MSc and MA programmes in the School of Business and Management
Purpose: Business and Management Postgraduate Scholarships are £3000 awards for outstanding students enrolling on a full time Master's programme in the School of Business and Management in September.
Eligibility: Eligible students will be contacted by Queen Mary after receiving an offer and invited to apply for a scholarship. We will consider applicants that have achieved a UK first class honours degree (or equivalent), and those who are on course to achieve a First. Applicants must be domiciled in one of the eligible countries.
Level of Study: Masters Degree
Type: Scholarships
Value: £5000
Frequency: Annual
Country of Study: United Kingdom
Application Procedure: There is no separate application for this scholarship. We will consider all applicants that have achieved a UK first class honours degree (or equivalent), and those who are on course to achieve a First. Applicants must be domiciled in one of the eligible countries.
No. of awards offered: 12
Additional Information: www.qmul.ac.uk/scholarships/items/business-and-management-postgraduate-scholarships.html

For further information contact:

Queen Mary University of London, Mile End Road, London E1 4NS, United Kingdom.

Email: Scholarships@qmul.ac.uk

Business and Management Postgraduate Scholarships

Subjects: MSc and MA programmes in the School of Business and Management (see below for full list)
Purpose: Business and Management Postgraduate Scholarships
Level of Study: Masters Degree, Postgraduate
Type: Scholarship
Value: £5000
Frequency: Annual
Country of Study: Any country
No. of awards offered: 12

Children of Alumni Award

Subjects: The Children of Alumni Loyalty Award is those enrolling on a full Bachelors, Master's or Doctoral degree programme
Purpose: The Children of Alumni Loyalty Award gives £1000 of year-1 overseas fees for children of international alumni.
Eligibility: To be eligible you must: 1. be enrolling on a full Bachelors, Master's or Doctoral degree 2. be the child of a Queen Mary alumnus 3. be paying at least £1000 of your fees (i.e. not full sponsored) 4. be an overseas fee payer (i.e. not paying the cheaper "Home Fee" rate)
Level of Study: Masters Degree, Postgraduate, Undergraduate
Type: Award
Value: £1000 one-off fee discount
Country of Study: Any country
No. of awards offered: Unlimited

China Scholarship Council Scholarships

Subjects: All PhDs in the Faculties of Science and Engineering and Humanities and Social Sciences
Purpose: Queen Mary will provide scholarships to cover all tuition fees, whilst the CSC will provide living expenses and one return flight ticket to successful applicants. This scholarship is available to both new and continuing (current 1st year) students.

Level of Study: Postdoctorate
Type: Scholarship
Value: Full tuition fee waiver and living stipend (£1350/month)
Length of Study: 4 years
Frequency: Annual
Country of Study: Any country
No. of awards offered: 60
Closing Date: 30 January

For further information contact:

Email: international-partnerships@qmul.ac.uk

Colfuturo Scholarships

Subjects: Any Masters course and any PhD programme except those in Medicine and Dentistry
Purpose: COLFUTURO is a Colombian non-profit foundation that was established in 1991 with the support of the National Government and some of the most important companies of the private sector in the country at that time. Its main objective is to provide financial support and increase the possibilities of Colombian citizens to access high-quality postgraduate study programs abroad.
Eligibility: See website: www.colfuturo.org
Type: Award
Value: Up to US$50,000
Length of Study: 2 years
Country of Study: Colombia
No. of awards offered: 3 PhD awards and an unlimited number of Master's awards.
Closing Date: 28 February

For further information contact:

Email: scholarships@qmul.ac.uk

DeepMind Scholarship

Subjects: MSc in Artificial Intelligence (FT) MSc in Computer Science (FT) MSc in Machine Learning for Visual Data Analytics (FT) MSc Computer Games (FT)
Purpose: The DeepMind Scholarship at Queen Mary University of London is a programme to support and encourage underrepresented groups to pursue postgraduate education in the field of Artificial Intelligence, Machine Learning and Computer Science. The scholarships are for female and/or black students as these students are currently underrepresented in these areas of study.
Eligibility: To be eligible to apply for a DeepMind Scholarship you must: 1. Be a UK or International student.

2. Identify as female or have one of the following categories of ethnicity: Black African; Black Caribbean; Black Other; Mixed – White and Black Caribbean; Mixed – White and Black African; or Other mixed background (to include Black African, Black Caribbean or Black Other). 3. Have a confirmed offer to study on one of the following programmes in September 2023: MSc in Artificial Intelligence (Full Time), MSc Computer Science (Full Time), MSc Computer Games (Full Time), and MSc in Machine Learning for Visual Data Analytics (Full Time) at Queen Mary University of London.

Level of Study: Masters Degree

Type: Scholarship

Value: Each DeepMind Scholarship will cover the cost of tuition fees, £11,850 (International fees - £27,250), a living allowance of £15,480, an annual £2,000 travel scholarship and a one-off equipment grant of £1,500.

Frequency: Annual

Country of Study: Any country

Application Procedure: 1. First, please check your eligibility to apply. The panel will not consider any applications that do not meet eligibility criteria, and awards may be withdrawn if applicants are later found not to have met eligibility criteria or to have provided false information. 2. Please download, complete and submit the application form to ioc@qmul.ac.uk. Download the DeepMind Scholarship Application Form 2023 [www.qmul.ac.uk/media/eecs/ioc/scholarship-application-forms/2022_AF_The-DeepMind-Scholarship-in-the-School-of-Electronic-Engineering-and-Computer-Science-2022.docx] here. 3. To complete your application, you will need to provide: A copy of your offer letter to study on one of the following programmes at Queen Mary: MSc in Artificial Intelligence (Full Time), MSc Computer Science (FT), MSc Computer Games, or MSc in Machine Learning for Visual Data Analytics (FT) programme. A completed application form, including a short statement of no more than 500 words detailing why you should be considered for the award and what motivated your interest in this area of study at Queen Mary University of London.

No. of awards offered: 4

Closing Date: 13 July

For further information contact:

Email: ioc@qmul.ac.uk

Dhaka PhD Scholarships

Subjects: Any PhD in the Faculty of Science and Engineering

Purpose: This award covers full tuition fees and if the scholar is a current Faculty member at University of Dhaka they will receive their basic salary to cover living expenses. Any

shortfall between the salary and living expenses set by UKVI will need to be covered by the student.

Level of Study: Masters Degree, Postdoctorate

Type: Scholarship

Value: Full tuition fees and partial living stipend.

Frequency: Annual

Country of Study: Any country

No. of awards offered: 3

Closing Date: 31 January

Herchel Smith Scholarship in Intellectual Property

Purpose: The award will cover all tuition fees whether at the Home/EU rate or the overseas rate. It is therefore open to both UK and non-EU applicants.

Eligibility: New PhD students undertaking full-time research in the area of Intellectual Property (IP) can apply for a Herchel Smith Scholarship to start in the academic year. Open to both United Kingdom and non-European Union applicants

Level of Study: Postdoctorate

Type: Scholarship

Value: £17,000

Length of Study: 3 years

Frequency: Annual

Country of Study: United Kingdom

Application Procedure: Submit online application.

Closing Date: 2 June

Additional Information: www.scholarshiproar.com/intellectual-property-phd/

For further information contact:

Email: g.skehan@qmul.ac.uk

Historic Royal Palaces Heritage Scholarships

Purpose: Historic Royal Palaces (HRP) wishes to make careers in the heritage sector more accessible to people from UK-resident Black, Asian, and Minority Ethnic (BAME) communities to help ensure everyone feels the palaces are for them and make them accessible and relevant for all.

Eligibility: The scholarships will cover your part-time course fees

Level of Study: Masters Degree, Postgraduate

Type: Scholarships

Value: Part-time course fees and a living allowance of £12,273 per annum

Frequency: Annual

Country of Study: United Kingdom

No. of awards offered: 2

Closing Date: 3 July

Additional Information: www.qmul.ac.uk/scholarships/items/historic-royal-palaces-heritage-scholarships.html

For further information contact:

Queen Mary University of London, Mile End Road, London E1 4NS, United Kingdom.

Email: john.davis@hrp.org.uk

Marshall Scholarships

Purpose: The QMUL Marshall Scholarship offers support for candidates wishing to pursue up to two years of postgraduate study, on any Masters or PhD programme across the University. A third year of funding may be available for students engaged in doctoral degrees.
Eligibility: The award is open to US citizens
Level of Study: Masters Degree, Postgraduate
Type: Scholarships
Value: Full tuition and living costs.
Frequency: Annual
Country of Study: United Kingdom
Application Procedure: Applications are made online directly to the www.marshallscholarship.org/applications/apply
No. of awards offered: Up to 2 each year
Closing Date: September
Additional Information: www.qmul.ac.uk/scholarships/items/marshall-scholarships.html

For further information contact:

Queen Mary University of London, Mile End Road, London E1 4NS, United Kingdom.

Tel: (1) 202 538 3885
Email: americas@qmul.ac.uk

Snowdon Masters Scholarship

Purpose: The Snowdon Masters Scholarship has been designed to identify and accelerate talented disabled students through higher education, creating the influencers of the future.
Eligibility: 1. Exceptional leaders, with the ability to create change within and beyond their academic field 2. Individuals that have shown excellence within their chosen subjects 3. Those that have demonstrated leadership potential with a proven drive for success 4. Ability to create change and drive disability issues 5. Proven achievements in academia, employment or voluntary activities.

Level of Study: Masters Degree
Type: Scholarships
Value: Up to £30,000
Length of Study: 1 year
Frequency: Annual
Country of Study: Any country
Application Procedure: Apply online
Closing Date: 1 April
Contributor: Snowdon Trust
Additional Information: www.qmul.ac.uk/scholarships/items/snowdon-masters-scholarship.html

For further information contact:

Queen Mary University of London, Mile End Road, London E1 4NS, United Kingdom.

Queen's Nursing Institute

3 Albemarle Way, London EC1V 4RQ, United Kingdom.

Tel: (44) 20 7549 1400
Email: rosemary.cook@qni.org.uk
Website: www.qni.org.uk

The Queen's Nursing Institute is a registered charity dedicated to improving the nursing care of people in the home and community. We promote excellent nursing care for everyone, where and when they need it, provided by nurses and their teams with specific skills and knowledge. Through our national network of Queen's Nurses, who are committed to the highest standards of care.

Queen's Nursing Institute Fund for Innovation and Leadership

Purpose: Implementation of good practice, or a project or an idea, within the community
Level of Study: Graduate, Postgraduate
Type: A variable number of grants
Value: Up to £5,000
Length of Study: 1 year
Frequency: Annual
Country of Study: United Kingdom
Closing Date: 17 October
No. of awards given last year: 12
Additional Information: This content is password protected. To view it please enter your password. www.qni.

org.uk/explore-qni/nurse-led-projects/fund-for-innovation-ld-leaders-2/

Queen's University of Belfast

University Road, Belfast Northern Ireland BT7 1NN, United Kingdom.

Tel: (44) 28 9024 5133
Email: pg.office@qub.ac.uk
Website: www.qub.ac.uk/

The Queen's University of Belfast has provided a stimulating environment for postgraduate students since the 1850s. It has a reputation as a centre of academic excellence, embracing the most effective technologies and techniques of the 21 century. Queen's has 14 subjects in the top 200 in the world. Queen's currently has over 2,600 international students from 85 different countries and we're ranked 22nd in the world for international outlook.

International Office Postgraduate Scholarship

Purpose: This award is exclusively for new International students beginning their first year of full-time postgraduate taught study at Queen's University Belfast in the academic year who meet the conditions of their academic offer.
Eligibility: If you are holding an offer for an eligible programme and meet the criteria as set out in these terms & conditions, you will automatically be awarded an International Office Postgraduate Taught Scholarship upon enrolment.
Level of Study: Postgraduate
Type: Award
Value: Year one award of £2,000 (fee rate 1) or £3,000 (fee rate 2)
Length of Study: 1 year
Frequency: Annual
Country of Study: United Kingdom
Application Procedure: No application necessary.
Funding: International office
Additional Information: www.qub.ac.uk/International/International-students/International-scholarships/taught-masters-scholarships/

For further information contact:

Email: internationalscholarships@qub.ac.uk

International PhD Awards

Subjects: Arts, Humanities and Social Sciences
Purpose: To support more International and EU students the Faculty of Arts, Humanities and Social Sciences (AHSS) is offering 2 PhD scholarships for September entry.
Eligibility: To qualify for an international/EU scholarship, students must be in receipt of an offer to study for a PhD degree at Queen's University Belfast within the Faculty of Arts, Humanities and Social Sciences and meet the eligibility criteria below 1. Students must not be in receipt of funding from any other organisation. 2. Students must be in a position to commence their studies in September. 3. Students must be classified as international fee paying students paying the international tuition fee rate OR be classified as EU fee paying students paying the EU tuition fee rate in order to be considered for these awards. 4. Students must hold an offer of a place on a full-time programme at the Queen's University Belfast campus, starting in the academic year 2023–2024 and meet any academic and language conditions attached to their offer as stated in their offer letter.
Level of Study: Postgraduate
Type: Award
Length of Study: 3 years
Frequency: Annual
Country of Study: Any country
Application Procedure: Please complete an application for admission to PhD study via the Direct Application Portal.
No. of awards offered: 2
Closing Date: 22 January
Additional Information: uwaterloo.ca/graduate-studies-postdoctoral-affairs/awards/international-doctoral-student-award-idsa

For further information contact:

Email: G.ODonnell@qub.ac.uk

Kyle Scholarship

Purpose: This postgraduate scholarship has been established by Terence Kyle, former chief executive of Linklaters. Terence Kyle was educated at Christ's College, Cambridge University, graduating with an MA in Classics and Law in 1969. Prior to attending university, Terence went to school in Belfast and is a keen supporter of Queen's University Belfast in its efforts to provide increased opportunity for postgraduate study.
Eligibility: To be eligible for the scholarship an applicant must 1. Be classified in residency terms for fees at UK or

EU status only; 2. Have received an offer of study for the postgraduate LLM International Business Law programme in the School of Law.

Level of Study: Postgraduate

Type: Scholarship

Value: £5,000

Frequency: Annual

Country of Study: United Kingdom

Application Procedure: Applicants for the Kyle Scholarship should also submit a written statement outlining, in not more than 750 words: 1. Why they want to undertake the LLM International Business Law at Queen's; 2. What they hope to achieve through this opportunity and the impact they think this will have on their career and/or future ambitions. This statement should be submitted to law.office@qub.ac.uk by the stipulated deadline.

No. of awards offered: 1

Closing Date: 9 July

Additional Information: www.qub.ac.uk/Study/funding-scholarships/ahss/SchoolofLaw/TheKyleScholarship.html

For further information contact:

4501 W. 38th Street, Indianapolis IN 46254, United Kingdom.

Email: law.office@qub.ac.uk

Leverhulme (LINCS) PhD Scholarship

Purpose: To support pioneering research at the interface between the social sciences and electronic engineering and computer science

Eligibility: 1. Applicants must hold a minimum 2 Class Upper Degree (21) or equivalent qualification in a relevant Technology, Social Science or Humanities Based subject. 2. Applicants must be a United Kingdom or European Union citizen. 3. Applications from non-United Kingdom or non-European Union citizens may be accepted on an exceptional basis but additional funding to cover International student fees is not available and must be secured by the applicant prior to starting. 4. Applicants must be proficient in both writing and speaking in English

Type: Scholarship

Value: Full tuition fees at standard United Kingdom rates (currently £4,195 per annum) for 3 years; a maintenance award at the Research Councils United Kingdom national rate. £1,000 per annum research training and expenses to fund the costs of study abroad, conference attendance and fieldwork

Frequency: Annual

Country of Study: United Kingdom

Closing Date: 15 January

Additional Information: worldscholarshipforum.com/fully-funded-leverhulme-scholarship-queens-university-belfast-uk-20182019/

Mary McNeill Scholarship in Irish Studies

Purpose: Two scholarships to the value of £3,000 each are available for well–qualified students enrolling in the one-year MA in Irish Studies at the Queen's University of Belfast in September. This scholarship is open only to residents of the USA or Canada, enrolling as overseas students on this MA course, and will take the form of a fee bursary covering part of their student fees.

Eligibility: Open to well-qualified United States of America or Canadian students enrolled in the MA (Irish Studies) programme

Level of Study: Postgraduate

Type: Scholarship

Value: £5000

Frequency: Annual

Study Establishment: Queen's University of Belfast

Country of Study: United Kingdom

Application Procedure: Applications will be judged by a panel chaired by the Director of Irish Studies on the basis of academic merit and reasons for taking the course. Download an Application Form McNeill Bursary Form

No. of awards offered: 2

Closing Date: 22 April

Additional Information: www.qub.ac.uk/schools/IrishStudiesGateway/Study/MAIrishStudies/FeesFundingAccommodation/

PhD Studentships in Astrophysics Research Centre

Subjects: Astrophysics

Purpose: These scholarships are available for students wishing to undertake a PhD in the Astrophysics Research Centre

Level of Study: Postgraduate

Type: Scholarship

Value: fully funded PhD studentships

Length of Study: 3 years

Frequency: Annual

Country of Study: United Kingdom

Application Procedure: Applications for post-graduate studies must be made via the QUB portal

Closing Date: 26 January

Contributor: Queen's University Belfast

For further information contact:

Email: e.demooij@qub.ac.uk

Queen's Loyalty Scholarship

Purpose: The Queen's Loyalty Scholarship is a 20% reduction on first year gross tuition fees available exclusively to students who have been assessed as paying International tuition fee rates and are Queen's University Belfast alumni or Exchange, Study Abroad or International Summer School students progressing to a full duration postgraduate programme at the Queen's University Belfast campus in the academic year.

Eligibility: 1. Students must hold an offer of a place on a full-time and complete duration programme at the Queen's University Belfast campus, starting in the academic year and prior to commencement of study have met any academic and language conditions attached to their offer as stated in their offer letter. 2. Students must register on their degree programme by the start date outlined in their offer.

Level of Study: Postgraduate

Type: Scholarship

Value: 20% tuition fee reduction on year 1

Frequency: Annual

Country of Study: United Kingdom

Application Procedure: Students must complete an application form via the Queen's University Belfast website to verify their previous programme of study.

Closing Date: 31 October

Additional   Information: www.qub.ac.uk/International/International-students/International-scholarships/postgraduate-research-scholarships/queens-loyalty-scholarship/

For further information contact:

Queen's University Belfast 2020, University Road, Belfast BT7 1NN, Northern Ireland, United Kingdom.

Email: internationalscholarships@qub.ac.uk

Vice-Chancellor's International Attainment Scholarship

Purpose: Four scholarships offering a 50% reduction on full international tuition fee rates available to exceptionally talented international students starting full-time undergraduate studies in the academic year.

Eligibility: Students must hold an offer for a place on a full-time eligible undergraduate programme starting in the academic year 2021/22 at the Queen's University Belfast campus which has been confirmed as their FIRM choice by their UCAS deadline, and prior to commencement of study have met any academic and language conditions attached to their offer as stated in their offer letter.

Level of Study: Undergraduate

Type: Scholarship

Value: 50% reduction on full tuition fees paid for all years of a programme, up to a maximum of four years (including advanced entry into Year 2 or Year 3)

Length of Study: 4 years

Frequency: Annual

Country of Study: United Kingdom

Application Procedure: Applicants must complete the online application form and submit a video as detailed on the application form within the deadline. response.questback.com/isa/qbv.dll/bylink?p=NbqJlAKfOA7uB8uLPyAWIBPaJT9X8Rt2ZU6dCPk3ktx2A6BtrtoMyVhwNC2W6u3zrTUU5-dZvI2RDT4JZsIEqQ2

No. of awards offered: 4

Closing Date: 8 June

Additional   Information: www.qub.ac.uk/International/International-students/International-scholarships/undergraduate-scholarships/vice-chancellors-international-attainment-scholarship/

For further information contact:

Queen's University Belfast 2020, University Road, Belfast BT7 1NN, Northern Ireland, United Kingdom.

Email: internationalscholarships@qub.ac.uk

Queensland University of Technology (QUT)

Research Students Centre, GPO Box 2434, Brisbane, QLD 4001, Australia.

Tel: (61) 3138 2000
Email: askqut@qut.edu.au
Website: www.qut.edu.au/

Queensland University of Technology (QUT) is a major Australian university with a truly global outlook. Home to nearly 50,000 students, we're providing real-world infrastructure, learning and teaching, and graduate skills to the next generation of change-makers.

Australian Postgraduate Award Industry Scholarships within Integrative Biology

Eligibility: Open to citizens of Australia or permanent residents having Honours 1 Degree or equivalent
Level of Study: Postgraduate
Type: Scholarship
Value: AU$25,627
Length of Study: 3 years
Frequency: Annual
Application Procedure: Check website for further details
Closing Date: 2 March
Additional Information: https://www.postgraduatefunding.com/award-4239

For further information contact:

School of Integrative Biology, 286 Morrill Hall, MC-120 University of IL 505 S. Goodwin Ave., Urbana, IL 61801, United States of America.

Email: susanne.schmidt@uq.edu.au

Australian Research Council Australian Postgraduate Award Industry – Alternative Engine Technologies

Purpose: The multidisciplinary nature of the project will provide the student with a significant intellectual challenge, to assimilate the required background research and to integrate this knowledge to achieve the aims of the current project
Eligibility: Open to citizens of Australia or New Zealand or permanent residents who have achieved Honours 1 or equivalent, or Honours 2a or equivalent
Level of Study: Postdoctorate, Postgraduate
Type: Scholarship
Value: AU$26,140 per year
Length of Study: 3 years
Frequency: Annual
Country of Study: Australia
Application Procedure: Check website for further details
Closing Date: 28 September
Additional Information: Please check website for more details scholarship-positions.com/australian-postgraduate-award-industry-apai-phd-scholarship/2009/03/31/

For further information contact:

Tel: (61) 7 3138 5174
Email: rong.situ@qut.edu.au

Institute of Health and Biomedical Innovation Awards

Purpose: To support living expenses
Eligibility: Open for citizens of Australia or permanent residents who have achieved Honours 1 or equivalent, or Honours 2a or equivalent
Level of Study: Doctorate, Postgraduate
Type: Award
Value: AU$36,140
Length of Study: 2 years (Masters) or 3 years (PhD)
Frequency: Annual
Country of Study: Australia
Application Procedure: Check website for further details
Closing Date: 12 October

For further information contact:

Tel: (61) 7 3138 6056
Fax: (61) 7 3138 6039
Email: s.winn@qut.edu.au

International Postgraduate Research Scholarship at Queensland University of Technology

Purpose: We are building research excellence by supporting students of exceptional research potential with QUTPRAs. The number of QUTPRAs offered varies from year to year.
Eligibility: Applicant must apply for and be accepted into a PhD or professional doctorate.
Level of Study: Postgraduate
Type: Postgraduate scholarships
Value: AU$28,597
Frequency: Annual
Country of Study: Australia
No. of awards offered: Varies
Additional Information: www.qut.edu.au/study/fees-and-scholarships/scholarships/qut-postgraduate-research-award-qutpra-international

Q

R

Radboud University Nijmegen

Houtlaan 4, NL-6525 XZ Nijmegen, The Netherlands.

Tel: (31) 24 361 61 61
Email: info@communicatie.ru.nl
Website: www.ru.nl/english/

Radboud University Nijmegen was established on 17 October 1923 under the name Catholic University Nijmegen. With their own university, Dutch Catholics sought to promote the emancipation of Roman Catholics in the Netherlands, who at that time were strongly underrepresented in public administration, the legal profession, medicine and other sectors. The Radboud Foundation was the body behind this initiative. Today, Radboud University continues its commitment to the emancipation of certain groups. For example, the University has an above average percentage of female professors, compared to other Dutch universities. And of all the general universities, it has the highest relative number of students for whom neither parent had a university education (source: WO-instroommonitor, 1999-2000 t/m 2014-2015).

Radboud Scholarship Programme

Purpose: The Radboud Scholarship Programme is a very selective scholarship programme. It offers talented, highly motivated, non-EEA students with outstanding study results the opportunity to be awarded a scholarship for a complete English-taught Radboud University Master's degree programme.
Eligibility: You can apply for a Radboud Scholarship if you 1. Hold a non-EU/EEA passport. 2. Are not eligible for the lower EEA tuition fee for other reasons. 3. Have (will obtain) a Bachelor's degree achieved outside the Netherlands, have no degrees achieved in the Netherlands and did not receive any previous education in the Netherlands (exchange programmes excluded, provided that they are part of the bachelor degree achieved outside the Netherlands). 4. Meet the English language proficiency requirement for the Master's programme of your choice. 5. Have been fully admitted to the English-taught Master's degree programme starting 1 September as stated in the formal letter of admission. 6. Are able to comply with the conditions for obtaining a visa for the Netherlands. 7. Are enrolled at Radboud University as a full-time student for the academic year and Master's degree programme for which the scholarship will be awarded.
Level of Study: Masters Degree
Type: Scholarship
Value: The Scholarship will reduce your tuition fee to €2,209
Frequency: Annual
Country of Study: Any country
Application Procedure: You can apply by indicating during your application for admission (www.ru.nl/english/education/masters-programmes/application-procedure-master-pre-master/) for a Master's programme in the OSIRIS Application system that you wish to apply for a Radboud Scholarship. You will then be requested to upload three additional documents two reference letters and a curriculum vitae. For more details please visit website.
No. of awards offered: 37
Closing Date: 28 February
Funding: Private
Additional Information: For more information: www.ru.nl/english/education/masters-programmes/international-masters-students/financial-matters/scholarships-grants/read_more/rsprogramme/

For further information contact:

Houtlaan 4, NL-6525 XZ Nijmegen, Netherlands.

Tel: (31) 24 361 60 55
Email: scholarships@ru.nl; internationaloffice@io.ru.nl

Radboud Scholarship Programme for International Students

Purpose: The Radboud Scholarship Programme is a very selective scholarship programme. It offers talented, highly motivated, non-EEA students with outstanding study results the opportunity to be awarded a scholarship for a complete English-taught Radboud University Master's degree programme.

Eligibility: You are eligible to apply for a Radboud Scholarship if you 1. Hold a non-EU/EEA passport. 2. Are not eligible for the lower EEA tuition fee for other reasons. 3. Have (will obtain) a Bachelor's degree achieved outside the Netherlands, have no degrees achieved in the Netherlands and did not receive any previous education in the Netherlands (exchange programmes excluded, provided that they are part of the bachelor degree achieved outside the Netherlands). 4. Meet the English language proficiency requirement for the Master's programme of your choice. 5. Have been fully admitted to the English-taught Master's degree programme starting 1 September as stated in the formal letter of admission. 6. Are able to comply with the conditions for obtaining a visa for the Netherlands. 7. Are enrolled at Radboud University as a full-time student for the academic year and Master's degree programme for which the scholarship will be awarded.

Level of Study: Masters Degree

Type: Scholarships

Value: A partial scholarship will reduce your tuition fee to €2,209.

Frequency: Annual

Country of Study: Netherlands

Application Procedure: You can apply by indicating during your application for admission for a Master's programme in the OSIRIS Application system that you wish to apply for a Radboud Scholarship. You will then be requested to upload three additional documents two reference letters and a curriculum vitae. For details please vist website.

No. of awards offered: 37

Closing Date: 28 February

Additional Information: www.ru.nl/english/education/masters-programmes/financial-matters/scholarships-grants/read_more/rsprogramme/. www.scholars4dev.com/6127/radboud-university-scholarships-for-international-students/

For further information contact:

Houtlaan 4, NL-6525 XZ Nijmegen, Netherlands.

Tel: (31) 24 361 6161
Email: scholarships@ru.nl

Radboud Scholarships Programme for Masters Students

Purpose: The Radboud Scholarship Programme is a very selective scholarship programme. It offers talented, highly motivated, non-EEA students with outstanding study results the opportunity to be awarded a scholarship for a complete English-taught Radboud University Master's degree programme.

Eligibility: You are eligible to apply for a Radboud Scholarship if you 1. Hold a non-EU/EEA passport. 2. Are not eligible for the lower EEA tuition fee for other reasons. 3. Have (will obtain) a Bachelor's degree achieved outside the Netherlands, have no degrees achieved in the Netherlands and did not receive any previous education in the Netherlands (exchange programmes excluded, provided that they are part of the bachelor degree achieved outside the Netherlands). 4. Meet the English language proficiency requirement for the Master's programme of your choice. 5. Have been fully admitted to the English-taught Master's degree programme starting 1 September as stated in the formal letter of admission. 6. Are able to comply with the conditions for obtaining a visa for the Netherlands. 7. Are enrolled at Radboud University as a full-time student for the academic year and Master's degree programme for which the scholarship will be awarded.

Level of Study: Masters Degree

Type: Scholarship

Value: A partial scholarship will reduce your tuition fee to €2,209

Frequency: Annual

Country of Study: The Netherlands

Application Procedure: You can apply by indicating during your application for admission for a Master's programme in the OSIRIS Application system that you wish to apply for a Radboud Scholarship. You will then be requested to upload three additional documents two reference letters and a curriculum vitae. For details please vist website.

No. of awards offered: 37

Closing Date: 28 February

Additional Information: For more information about the scholarship programme, you may contact the International Office via scholarships@ru.nl. www.ru.nl/english/education/masters-programmes/international-masters-students/financial-matters/scholarships-grants/read_more/rsprogramme/

For further information contact:

Houtlaan 4, NL-6525 XZ Nijmegen, Netherlands.

Tel: (31) 24 361 6161
Email: scholarships@ru.nl

Radcliffe Institute for Advanced Study

10 Garden Street, Fay House, Suite 330, Cambridge, MA 02138, United States of America.

Tel:	(1) 617 496 3078
Email:	info@radcliffe.harvard.edu; jane_huber@radcliffe.harvard.edu
Website:	www.radcliffe.harvard.edu/
Contact:	Jane F. Huber, Director of Communications

The Radcliffe Institute for Advanced Study at Harvard University, known as Harvard Radcliffe Institute, is one of the world's leading centers for interdisciplinary exploration. Harvard Radcliffe Institute is an interdisciplinary community of students, scholars, researchers, practitioners, artists, and others committed to pursuing curiosity-driven research, expanding human understanding, and grappling with questions that demand insight from across disciplines.

Radcliffe Institute Fellowship

Purpose: The Fellowship Program annually selects and supports artists, scholars, and practitioners who bring both a record of achievement and exceptional promise to the Institute.

Eligibility: Applicants may apply as individuals or in a group of two to three people working on the same project. For eligibility guidelines, please refer website www.radcliffe.harvard.edu/radcliffe-fellowship

Level of Study: Doctorate

Type: Fellowship

Value: 1. A stipend with the possibility of an additional US$750 for travel related to conferences and job interviews. (The stipend for last year was US$32,000). 2. Tuition and health fees. 3. Private work space at the Radcliffe Institute's Byerly Hall.

Frequency: Annual

Country of Study: United States of America

Application Procedure: A complete application with all necessary documents must be uploaded to CARAT. Applicants for Radcliffe Institute Dissertation Completion Fellowships must include a brief statement describing how an affiliation with the Radcliffe Institute Fellowship Program would benefit them; a two-page resume; a dissertation abstract and a table of contents; two letters of recommendation, one of which must be written by the dissertation advisor; and two faculty evaluation forms. Apply via CARAT www.pin1.harvard.edu/cas/login?service=https%3A%2F%2Fcarat.fas.harvard.edu%2Flogin%2Fcas.

No. of awards offered: 50

Closing Date: 12 February

Additional Information: www.radcliffe.harvard.edu/radcliffe-fellowship

For further information contact:

Radcliffe Institute Fellowship Program, 8 Garden Street, Byerly Hall, Cambridge, MA 02138, United States of America.

Tel:	(1) 617 495 8212 or (1) 617 495 8213
Email:	fellowships@radcliffe.harvard.edu; claudia_rizzini@radcliffe.harvard.edu

Radiological Society of North America, Inc. (RSNA)

820 Jorie Blvd., Suite 200, Oak Brook, IL 60523-2251, United States of America.

Tel:	(1) 630 571 2670
Email:	customerservice@rsna.org
Website:	www.rsna.org/
Contact:	Mr Scott Walter, Assistant Director, Grant Administration

The Radiological Society of North America (RSNA) is a non-profit organization with over 52,000 members from 153 countries around the world. We provide high-quality educational resources, including continuing education credits toward physicians' certification maintenance, host the world's largest radiology conference and publish five top peer-reviewed journals. Our Research and Education Foundation, which has funded US$66 million in grants since its inception, our solutions to support standards development or educational outreach to low-resource nations.

Medical Student Research Grant

Subjects: Projects may include any of the following 1. Hypothesis-driven basic science. 2. Clinical investigation. 3. Drug, device or therapy development. 4. Comparative effectiveness. 5. Evidence-based radiology. 6. Ethics and professionalism. 7. Quality improvement. 8. Clinical practice efficiency. 9. Imaging informatics

Purpose: This R&E Foundation grant gives medical students the opportunity to gain research experience in medical imaging while they're still in school. Recipients will define objectives, develop research skills and test hypotheses, all before even choosing a residency program. Ultimately, this experience gives students a chance to consider academic radiology as a future career option.

Eligibility: Any area of research in the radiologic sciences is eligible for funding. 1. You must be an RSNA member to apply for the Medical Student Research Grant. If you're a non dues-paying member, your scientific advisor or your co-investigator must be a dues-paying member. 2. You must be a full-time medical student at an accredited North American medical school. 3. You must commit to work full-time for at least 10 weeks on your research project. 4. Your research project must take place in a department of radiology, radiation oncology or nuclear medicine in a North American medical institution, but this doesn't have to be the same institution where you're enrolled as a student. 5. You cannot have been a principal investigator on a grant or contract totaling more than US$60,000 in a single year. This includes single and combined grants and contracts from government, private and commercial sources. 6. You and your principal investigators cannot be employed by any for-profit, commercial company in the radiologic sciences. 7. You cannot submit more than one grant application to the RSNA R&E Foundation a year, and cannot have a concurrent RSNA grant. 8. Funding from other grant sources must be approved by foundation staff if it wasn't described in the original research plan.

Level of Study: Research

Type: Research grant

Value: Grant recipients receive US$3,000, which is matched by the sponsoring department, equaling US$6,000 total. It is to be used as a stipend for the medical student

Frequency: Annual

Country of Study: Any country

Application Procedure: For more detailed information, including application instructions, please review the policies and procedures (PDF) for this grant www.rsna.org/-/media/ Files/RSNA/Research/Funding-opportunities/Research-grants/ Medical-student-research-grant/RMS-Policies-Procedures. ashx?la=en&hash=6C20E6B88B64C5C37A08819E944 375D34F317DF8. To apply for this grant, please log in and use our online grant application system.

No. of awards offered: 10

Closing Date: 3 February

Funding: Private

Additional Information: For more information: www.rsna. org/research/funding-opportunities/research-grants/medical-student-research-grant

For further information contact:

820 Jorie Blvd # 200, Oak Brook, IL 60523, United States of America.

Tel: (1) 630 571 7816
Email: grants@rsna.org

Radiological Society of North America Education Seed Grant

Purpose: To provide funding opportunities for individuals with an active interest in radiologic education

Eligibility: Applicants must hold a faculty position in a department of radiology, radiation oncology, or nuclear medicine within a North American, educational institution and must have completed advanced training and be certified by the American Board of Radiology (or equivalent), or on track for certification. Applicants must not have received grant/contract amounts totaling US$50,000 or more in a single calendar year as principal investigator

Level of Study: Research

Type: Grant

Value: Up to US$40,000 to support the preliminary or pilot phase of education projects, not to supplement major funding already secured. No salary support for the principal investigator will be provided

Frequency: Annual

Country of Study: Any country

Application Procedure: Application can be submitted online

Closing Date: 10 January

Funding: Foundation

For further information contact:

Email: rmurray@rsna.org

Radiological Society of North America Institutional Clinical Fellowship in Cardiovascular Imaging

Purpose: To provide opportunities for radiologists early in their careers to gain experience and expertise in cardiovascular imaging

Eligibility: Open to citizens or permanent residents of a North American country who have completed their residency training in the radiological sciences. Fellows must also hold an MD or the equivalent as recognized by the American Medical Association and must be ACGME-certified in radiology or be eligible to sit for such certification

Type: Fellowship

Value: US$50,000 per year paid to a department. The Foundation does not pay overhead or indirect costs

Length of Study: 3 years

Frequency: Annual

Country of Study: Any country

Application Procedure: Applications must be submitted by a department in preparation for the recruitment of a Fellow into an existing cardiovascular imaging training programme. Application forms are available from the website

Closing Date: 1 June

For further information contact:

Department of Radiology Northwestern University Feinberg School of Medicine, Cardiovascular Imaging Fellowship Program, 676 N. Saint Clair St., Suite 800, Chicago, IL 60611, United States of America.

Email: bcartalino@rsna.org

Radiological Society of North America Medical Student Grant Program

Purpose: This R&E Foundation grant gives medical students the opportunity to gain research experience in medical imaging while they're still in school. Recipients will define objectives, develop research skills and test hypotheses, all before even choosing a residency program. Ultimately, this experience gives students a chance to consider academic radiology as a future career option.

Eligibility: You must be an RSNA member to apply for the Medical Student Research Grant. If you're a non dues-paying member, your scientific advisor or your co-investigator must be a dues-paying member. You must also meet the following criteria 1. You must be a full-time medical student at an accredited North American medical school. 2. You must commit to work full-time for at least 10 weeks on your research project. 3. Your research project must take place in a department of radiology, radiation oncology or nuclear medicine in a North American medical institution, but this doesn't have to be the same institution where you're enrolled as a student. 4. You cannot have been a principal investigator on a grant or contract totaling more than US$60,000 in a single year. This includes single and combined grants and contracts from government, private and commercial sources. 5. You and your principal investigators cannot be employed by any for-profit, commercial company in the radiologic sciences. 6. You cannot submit more than one grant application to the RSNA R&E Foundation a year, and cannot have a concurrent RSNA grant. 7. Funding from other grant sources must be approved by foundation staff if it wasn't described in the original research plan. For UIM applicants please refer website.

Level of Study: Research

Type: Grant

Value: Grant recipients receive US$3,000, which is matched by the sponsoring department, equaling US$6,000 total as stipend for the medical student.

Length of Study: 1 year

Frequency: Annual

Country of Study: Any country

Application Procedure: To apply for this grant, please log in and use our online grant application system. For more detailed information, including application instructions, please review the policies and procedures (PDF) for this grant. www.rsna.org/-/media/Files/RSNA/Research/Funding-opportunities/Research-grants/Medical-student-research-grant/RMS-Policies-Procedures.ashx?la=en&hash=6C20E6B88B64C5C37A08819E944375D34F317DF8

No. of awards offered: 10

Closing Date: 3 February

Funding: Foundation

Additional Information: www.rsna.org/research/funding-opportunities/research-grants/medical-student-research-grant

For further information contact:

820 Jorie Blvd # 200, Oak Brook, IL 60523, United States of America.

Tel: (1) 630 571 7816
Email: grants@rsna.org

Radiological Society of North America Research Resident Program

Purpose: To provide opportunities for individuals to gain further insight into scientific investigation, and to develop competence in research and educational techniques and methods

Eligibility: Open to citizens or permanent residents of a North American country. Applicants should be in residency training so that the award can occur during any year after the 1st year of training and should have an academic degree acceptable for a radiology residency

Level of Study: Postgraduate

Type: Grant

Value: US$30,000 designed to replace a portion of the resident

Length of Study: 1 year, non-renewable

Frequency: Annual

Country of Study: Any country

Application Procedure: Applicants must complete an application form, available from the website

Closing Date: 1 April

Additional Information: www.rsna.org/research/research-awards/roentgen-resident-fellow-research-award#:~:

text=Eligibility,with%20an%20ACGME%2Dapproved%20program.&text=Nominations%20are%20limited%20to%20one,nuclear%20medicine%20program%20per%20year.

For further information contact:

820 Jorie Blvd., Suite 200, Oak Brook, IL 60523-2251, United States of America.

Tel: (1) 6305712670
Email: REfoundation@rsna.org

Radiological Society of North America Research Resident/Fellow Program

Purpose: To provide young investigators an opportunity to gain further insight into scientific investigation and to gain competence in research techniques and methods in anticipation of establishing a career in academic radiologic science.
Eligibility: Any resident or fellow may apply for this grant, as long as you are an RSNA member. If you're a non dues-paying member, your scientific advisor or your co-investigator must be a dues-paying member. You must also meet the criteria listed in website www.rsna.org/research/funding-opportunities/research-grants/resident-fellow-research-grant
Level of Study: Research
Type: Fellowship
Value: Resident grant recipients receive US$30,000 for a one year project, and fellow grant recipients receive US$50,000 for a one year project
Length of Study: 1 year
Frequency: Annual
Country of Study: Any country
Application Procedure: To apply for this grant, please log in and use our online grant application system. Please refer website.
Closing Date: 15 January
Funding: Foundation
Additional Information: For more detailed information, including application instructions, please review the policies and procedures (PDF) for this grant. www.rsna.org/research/funding-opportunities/research-grants/resident-fellow-research-grant

For further information contact:

Keshia Osley, Assistant Director, Grant Administration Radiological Society of North America, United States of America.

Tel: (1) 630 571 7816
Email: grants@rsna.org

Radiological Society of North America Research Scholar Grant Program

Purpose: This R&E Foundation grant supports junior faculty members who have completed resident and fellowship programs, but haven't been recognized as independent investigators
Eligibility: As a junior radiology faculty member, you may apply for the Research Scholar Grant, as long as you are an RSNA member and meet the following criteria 1. You must hold a full-time faculty position in a department of radiology, radiation oncology or nuclear medicine within a North American educational institution. 2. You must have been hired within the last 5 years with an academic rank of instructor, assistant professor or an equivalent title. 3. You must have completed advanced training and be certified by either the American Board of Radiology (ABR), The Royal College of Physicians and Surgeons of Canada or are on track for certification. 4. You cannot have been a principal investigator on a grant or contract totaling more than US$60,000 in a single year. This includes single and combined grants and contracts from government, private and commercial sources. 5. You and your principal investigators cannot be employed by any for-profit, commercial company in the radiologic sciences. 6. You cannot submit more than one grant application to the RSNA R&E Foundation a year and cannot have a concurrent RSNA grant. 7. Funding from other grant sources must be approved by Foundation staff if it wasn't described in the original research plan. 8. You cannot have previously accepted any of the following grants ARRS Scholar Award, AUR GE-Radiology Research Academic Fellowship (GERRAF), RSNA Research Scholar Grant.
Level of Study: Doctorate, Postdoctorate
Type: Research grant
Value: Grant recipients receive US$75,000 a year for two years to be used as salary support. An additional US$1,000 will be paid to the institution each year to help cover costs associated with the Scholar Advisor Program.
Length of Study: 2 years
Frequency: Annual
Country of Study: Any country
Application Procedure: To apply for this grant, please log in and use our online grant application system. For more detailed information, including application instructions, please review the policies and procedures (PDF) for this grant. www.rsna.org/-/media/Files/RSNA/Research/Funding-opportunities/Research-grants/Research-scholar-grant/RSCH-Policies-Procedures.ashx?la=en&hash=EBC6B6F14D35771AC5ACF26CC402672E0E215E0B
Closing Date: 15 January
Funding: Private
Additional Information: www.rsna.org/research/funding-opportunities/research-grants/research-scholar-grant

For further information contact:

Keshia Osley, Assistant Director, Grant Administration Radiological Society of North America, 820 Jorie Boulevard, Oak Brook, IL 60523, United States of America.

Email: grants@rsna.org

Research Scholar Grant

Purpose: This R&E Foundation grant supports junior faculty members who have completed resident and fellowship programs, but haven't been recognized as independent investigators.

Eligibility: Any junior radiology faculty member may apply for the Research Scholar Grant, as long as you are an RSNA member and meet the following criteria 1. You must hold a full-time faculty position in a department of radiology, radiation oncology or nuclear medicine within a North American educational institution. 2. You must have been hired within the last 5 years with an academic rank of instructor, assistant professor or an equivalent title. 3. You must have completed advanced training and be certified by either the American Board of Radiology (ABR), The Royal College of Physicians and Surgeons of Canada or are on track for certification. 4. You cannot have been a principal investigator on a grant or contract totaling more than US$60,000 in a single year. This includes single and combined grants and contracts from government, private and commercial sources. 5. You and your principal investigators cannot be employed by any for-profit, commercial company in the radiologic sciences. 6. You cannot submit more than one grant application to the RSNA R&E Foundation a year and cannot have a concurrent RSNA grant. 7. Funding from other grant sources must be approved by Foundation staff if it wasn't described in the original research plan. 8. You cannot have previously accepted any of the following grants ARRS Scholar Award, AUR GE-Radiology Research Academic Fellowship (GERRAF), RSNA Research Scholar Grant.

Level of Study: Research

Type: Research grant

Value: Grant recipients receive US$75,000 a year for two years to be used as salary support. An additional US$1,000 will be paid to the institution each year to help cover costs associated with the Scholar Advisor Program.

Length of Study: 2 Year

Frequency: Annual

Country of Study: Any country

Application Procedure: To apply for this grant, please log in and use our online grant application system. For more detailed information, including application instructions, please review the policies and procedures (PDF) for this grant. www.rsna. org/-/media/Files/RSNA/Research/Funding-opportunities/ Research-grants/Research-scholar-grant/RSCH-Policies-Procedures.ashx?la=en&hash=EBC6B6F14D35771AC5 ACF26CC402672E0E215E0B

Closing Date: 15 January

Funding: Private

Additional Information: www.rsna.org/research/funding-opportunities/research-grants/research-scholar-grant

For further information contact:

Keshia Osley, Assistant Director, Grant Administration Radiological Society of North America, United States of America.

Tel: (1) 630 571 7816
Email: grants@rsna.org

Research Seed Grant

Purpose: This R&E Foundation Research Seed Grant gives investigators around the world the chance to define objectives and test hypotheses in preparation for larger grant applications at corporations, foundations and government agencies.

Eligibility: Any investigator from anywhere in the world with an academic appointment may apply for this grant, as long as you are an RSNA member. If you're a non dues-paying member, your scientific advisor or your co-investigator must be a dues-paying member. You must also meet the following criteria For all applicants; 1. You must hold a full-time faculty position in a radiology, radiation oncology or nuclear medicine department at an educational institution. 2. If you aren't currently a full-time faculty member, but will be by the time funding starts, a letter from the department chair must be included in your application. 3. You cannot have been a principal investigator on a grant or contract totaling more than US$60,000 in a single year. This includes single and combined grants and contracts from government, private and commercial sources. 4. You and your principal investigators cannot be employed by any for-profit, commercial company in the radiologic sciences. 5. You cannot submit more than one grant application to the RSNA R&E Foundation a year and cannot have a concurrent RSNA grant. 6. Funding from other grant sources must be approved by foundation staff if it wasn't described in the original research plan. For North American applicants; You must have completed advanced training and be certified by the American Board of Radiology (ABR) or The Royal College of Physicians and Surgeons of Canada or are on track for certification. For international applicants; You must have completed advanced training and be certified by the radiology board in your country.

Level of Study: Research

Type: Research grant
Value: Up to US$40,000
Length of Study: 1 year
Frequency: Annual
Country of Study: Any country
Application Procedure: To apply for this grant, please log in and use our online grant application system. For more detailed information, including application instructions, please review the policies and procedures (PDF) for this grant. www.rsna. org/-/media/Files/RSNA/Research/Funding-opportunities/ Research-grants/Research-seed-grant/RSD-Policies-Procedures. ashx?la=en&hash=D3C54D1B3927EAFB319EE2B897A132 6E33044C9D
Closing Date: 15 January
Funding: Private
Additional Information: www.rsna.org/research/funding-opportunities/research-grants/research-seed-grant

For further information contact:

Keshia Osley, Assistant Director, Grant Administration Radiological Society of North America, United States of America.

Tel: (1) 630 571 7816
Email: grants@rsna.org

Ragdale

1260 North Green Bay Road, Lake Forest, IL 60045, United States of America.

Tel: (1) 847 234 1063
Email: info@ragdale.org
Website: www.ragdale.org/

Ragdale is a nonprofit artists' community located on the former country estate of architect Howard Van Doren Shaw. Our residents represent a cross-section of ages, cultures, experience, and mediums for a diverse and vibrant community.

Sybil Shearer Fellowship: Dancemakers

Purpose: This fellowship opportunity to dancemakers will support an individual choreographer and/or dance artist by offering residency at Ragdale along with a cash stipend, the creation of a brief video documentary/interview, and the presentation of a public program. The residency may be awarded to a collaborative duo if they share a live/work studio. Open to emerging and established practitioners. This fellowship is made possible by the Morrison-Shearer Foundation.

Eligibility: Ragdale encourages applications from artists representing the widest possible range of perspectives and demographics, and to that end, emerging as well as established artists are invited to apply. While there are no publication, exhibition or performance requirements for application, applicants should be working at the professional level in their fields. Ragdale encourages artists of all backgrounds to apply.
Type: Fellowship
Value: 18-day or 25-day residency at Ragdale along with a cash stipend of US$500
Length of Study: 18-day or 25-day
Frequency: Annual
Country of Study: Any country
Application Procedure: All applicants submit electronic materials through the Submittable application portal. Please note the following requirements to complete your application 1. A completed online application form. 2. Two current letters of reference OR surveys completed by people who know you personally and can address your professional capacity and suitability for a residency in a working community with other artists. Reference letters and survey responses are confidential and are submitted electronically through Submittable when you submit your application. Letters of reference/ Reference Surveys are due 1159 PM CST June 1. A 10-15 minute survey option has been added to residency applications. Instructions for completing the survey or letter of recommendation will be automatically sent to your references when you submit your application. 3. A one-page artist's statement and work plan explaining your work and what you plan to do while in residence. 4. A one-page CV or resume that summarizes your professional background. 5. Work samples that show previous work from the past 2-3 years. All media is acceptable. Most electronic file types and sizes are accepted. 6. Some fellowships require an eligibility statement of 500 words or less. Please refer www.ragdale.org/residencies
Closing Date: 15 May
Funding: Private
Additional Information: www.ragdale.org/fellowships

For further information contact:

Email: info@ragdale.org

Rebecca Skelton Fund

Dance Department Administrator, University of Chichester, Bishop Otter Campus, College Lane, Chichester, Sussex PO19 6PE, United Kingdom.

Tel: (44) 1243 812137
Email: rebeccaskeltonfund@chi.ac.uk

Website: www.rebeccaskeltonfund.org
Contact: The Rebecca Skelton Fund Administrator

The fund provides financial assistance towards the cost of postgraduate dance study in experiential/creative work to include dance improvization and those training methods such as Skinner Releasing Technique, Alignment Therapy, Feldenkrais Technique, Alexander Technique and other body-mind practices that focus on an inner awareness and use the proprioceptive communication system or an inner sensory mode.

The Rebecca Skelton Scholarship

Purpose: To assist students to pursue a course of specific or advanced performance studies or an appropriate dance research and performance
Eligibility: Open to anyone pursuing dance studies at postgraduate level
Level of Study: Doctorate, Postdoctorate, Postgraduate, Professional development, Research
Type: Scholarships and fellowships
Value: UK £500
Frequency: Annual
Country of Study: United Kingdom
Application Procedure: Application form on request
No. of awards offered: 1-4
Closing Date: 12 January
Funding: Foundation
Contributor: The Rebecca Skelton Fund
No. of awards given last year: 5
No. of applicants last year: 9

For further information contact:

Email: artsresearch@chi.ac.uk

Regent's Park College

Pusey Street, Oxford OX1 2LB, United Kingdom.

Tel: (44) 1865 288120
Email: enquiries@regents.ox.ac.uk
Website: www.rpc.ox.ac.uk/

Regent's Park College is a small, dynamic community at the heart of the City and University of Oxford, specialising in the Arts and Humanities. The College offers places in a range of Arts and Humanities disciplines, with an outstanding record in Theology, Philosophy, History and English, as well as preparing men and women for ordained ministry in the Baptist Union of Great Britain. Everyone admitted to read for a degree is matriculated into the University and has full access to its rich resources. The College also has award-winning tutors, who are teaching members of multiple faculties and departments, encouraging students to aim high and providing excellent academic support.

Greyfriars Postgraduate Scholarship

Purpose: Regent's Park College is offering a postgraduate scholarship worth up to £2000 for a UK student who is currently engaged in, or has been accepted for, masters-level studies in a humanities subject at the University of Oxford.
Eligibility: The holder of the scholarship is required to be, or to become, a member of Regent's Park College, Oxford.
Level of Study: Masters Degree
Type: Scholarship
Value: Up to £2000
Country of Study: Any country
Closing Date: 6 May
Additional Information: www.rpc.ox.ac.uk/study-here/postgraduate-study/scholarships/

For further information contact:

Pusey St, Oxford OX1 2LB, United Kingdom.

Tel: (44) 1865 288120
Email: academic.administrator@regents.ox.ac.uk

Regent's Park College: Aziz Foundation Scholarship

Purpose: In association with Regent's Park College, the Aziz Foundation is offering a scholarship for a student who is undertaking, or has been accepted for, a Master's degree in the humanities, arts or social sciences at the University of Oxford.
Eligibility: The holder of the scholarship is required to be, or to become, a member of Regent's Park College, Oxford. In addition to the academic requirements of the University, applicants should 1. Be active within a Muslim community and their wider community, and demonstrate a desire to develop intellectual skills within a multi-faith and secular environment; 2. Be able to demonstrate long-term commitment to community/societal development and working for good relations through effecting public policy; and 3. Be

eligible for Home fee status at the University. For more details visit website.

Level of Study: Masters Degree
Type: Scholarship
Value: Up to £25,000
Length of Study: 2 Year
Frequency: Annual
Country of Study: Any country
Application Procedure: 1. Covering letter, explaining which course the candidate is intending to apply for and, if relevant, its focus/specialism; 2. Current CV (up to 2 pages), detailing qualifications and work history; 3. Statement (up to 1000 words), explaining how the candidate meets the criteria, particularly with regard to community engagement and involvement, and how they hope to use this scholarship for their future work; 4. Copy of the candidate's University application (it is possible to download this once completed). Send application materials to Jennifer Taylor, Academic Administrator by email.
No. of awards offered: 1
Closing Date: 31 March
Funding: Private
Additional Information: www.rpc.ox.ac.uk/study-here/postgraduate-study/scholarships/

For further information contact:

Regent's Park College, Pusey Street, Oxford, OX1 2LB, United Kingdom.

Tel: (44) 1865 288120
Email: academic.administrator@regents.ox.ac.uk

The Pamela Sue Anderson Studentship for the Encouragement of the Place of Women in Philosophy

Purpose: Regent's Park College is offering a postgraduate studentship who is currently engaged in or has been accepted for post graduate study in the University of Oxford
Eligibility: The holder of the scholarship is required to be, or to become, a member of Regent's Park College, Oxford.
Level of Study: Postgraduate
Type: Studentship
Value: Up to £4,000
Frequency: Annual
Study Establishment: University of Oxford
Country of Study: Any country
Application Procedure: 1. Covering letter, explaining how the candidate's proposed research relates to the vision of the studentship; 2. Current CV, including the names and contact details of two referees; 3. Research proposal; 4. Writing

sample of no more than 5,000 words. Send application materials to Jennifer Taylor, Academic Administrator by email.
No. of awards offered: 1
Closing Date: 29 April
Funding: Private
Additional Information: www.rpc.ox.ac.uk/study-here/postgraduate-study/scholarships/

For further information contact:

Pusey Street, Oxford, OX1 2LB, United Kingdom.

Tel: (44) 1865 288120
Email: academic.administrator@regents.ox.ac.uk

The Tim Collins Scholarship for the Study of Love in Religion

Purpose: The Project for the Study of Love in Religion is offering a scholarship worth £5,000 per annum for a student at Oxford who is writing, or intending to write a thesis that relates in some way to the place or meaning of love in religion.
Eligibility: DPhil in Theology (Full-time or Part-time); Philosophy; Oriental Studies; Anthropology; Archaeology; Archaeology (Part-time) (Continuing Education); Archaeological Science; Ancient History (Full-time or Part-time); Classical Languages and Literature (Full-time or Part-time); General Linguistics and Comparative Philology; Classical Archaeology; International Development; Education (Full-time or Part-time); English (all subjects); English Local History (Part-time); Geography and the Environment; Fine Art (Full-time or Part-time); Continuing Education (Part-time); History of Art (Full-time or Part-time); History (History of Science and Medicine and Economic and Social History); History (HSM and ESH) (Part-time); History (Full-time and part-time); Literature and Arts; Law; Socio-Legal Studies; Music (Part-time); Politics; Medieval and Modern Languages (Full-time and Part-time); Sustainable Urban Development; Social Policy; Social Intervention; Sociology; Economics; International Relations.
Level of Study: Research
Type: Scholarship
Value: £5,000 per annum
Frequency: Annual
Country of Study: Any country
Closing Date: 30 June
Additional Information: www.rpc.ox.ac.uk/study-here/postgraduate-study/scholarships/

For further information contact:

Pusey St, Oxford OX1 2LB, United Kingdom.

Tel: (44) 1865 288120
Email: academic.administrator@regents.ox.ac.uk

Regent's University London

Inner Circle, Regent's Park, London NW1 4NS, United Kingdom.

Tel: (44) 20 7487 7700
Email: enquiries@regents.ac.uk
Website: www.regents.ac.uk/
Contact: Regent's University London

Regent's University London is a private non-profit university located in London, United Kingdom. Regent's University is only the second institution in the United Kingdom to be granted the status of a private university.

Greyfriars Postgraduate Scholarship

Purpose: In recognition of the historic commitment of the Greyfriars and of Regent's Park College to philanthropy and the inclusion of those whose life chances have been limited through no fault of their own, preference will be given to applicants whose financial needs are greatest and may otherwise prohibit their studies. The intention is that the Scholarship be applied to student fees.
Level of Study: Postgraduate
Type: Scholarship
Value: Up to £2,000
Frequency: Annual
Country of Study: Any country
Application Procedure: 1. Covering letter, including an explanation of any special circumstances in relation to financial need that may otherwise prohibit or make it difficult to undertake postgraduate studies at Oxford University. Also state any other postgraduate grants or scholarships applied for and awarded; 2. Current CV, including the names and contact details of two referees; 3. Research proposal
Closing Date: 6 May
Funding: Private
Additional Information: www.rpc.ox.ac.uk/study-here/postgraduate-study/scholarships/

For further information contact:

Inner Cir, London NW1 4NS, United Kingdom.

Tel: (44) 20 7487 7700
Email: academic.administrator@regents.ox.ac.uk

Robert McKee International Screenwriting Scholarships

Level of Study: Graduate
Type: Scholarship
Value: £7,000
Country of Study: Any country
Closing Date: 30 June
Additional Information: www.regents.ac.uk/study/scholarships-funding-and-bursaries/robert-mckee#overview

For further information contact:

Email: contact@mckeestory.com

The Dean of Humanities, Arts & Social Sciences Excellence Scholarship

Purpose: The Dean of the Faculty of Humanities, Arts & Social Sciences has established three scholarships that celebrate the University's independent, cosmopolitan and enterprising spirit
Level of Study: Graduate
Type: Scholarship and award
Value: The Scholarship award will cover a quarter of the tuition fees for the selected course
Frequency: Annual
Country of Study: Any country
Application Procedure: Applications must be emailed to scholarships@regents.ac.uk
No. of awards offered: 3
Closing Date: 31 May
Funding: Private
Additional Information: For any queries, please contact: Regent's University London, Tel: (44) 20 7487 7505, Email: enquiries@regents.ac.uk www.regents.ac.uk/study/scholarships-funding-and-bursaries/the-dean-of-humanities-arts-social-sciences-excellence-scholarship

For further information contact:

Email: scholarships@regents.ac.uk

Regional Institute for Population Studies

University of Ghana, PO Box 96, Legon, Accra, Ghana.

Tel: (233) 302 906800
Email: rips@ug.edu.gh
Website: www.rips-ug.edu.gh/
Contact: Director

R

The Regional Institute for Population Studies (RIPS) was established in 1972 jointly by the United Nations in partnership with the Government of Ghana, and is located at the University of Ghana. Since its establishment, the Institute has served as a regional centre for teaching and research training at the post-graduate level of population scientists in English-speaking countries in Africa. The Institute enjoyed enormous funding from the United Nations Population Fund (UNFPA), was the leading demographic research and teaching centre has trained more than 600 population scientists since its inception in 1972. RIPS is committed to training and development of the intellect, independence and character of the most competitive graduate students and faculty from across the continent and the globe and playing a leading role in research in population health by ardently pursuing excellence in education.

Respective Government Fellowships

Purpose: To enable fellows to obtain advanced training through study or research leading to a Master of Arts, Master of Philosophy or PhD degree

Eligibility: Open to English speaking Sub-Saharan Africans, nominated by their governments, who are capable of pursuing a course of study or research using English as a medium of expression. Candidates should have a good first degree in population studies for the Master of Arts degree course or the Master of Population Studies degree, a Master of Arts in population studies or its equivalent for the Master of Philosophy degree, a Master of Philosophy in population studies or its equivalent for a PhD course

Level of Study: Doctorate, Postgraduate

Type: Fellowship

Value: Approx. US$13,840 per year including stipend, fees, costs for books, minor equipment and production of dissertations and theses

Length of Study: At least 1 year for Master of Arts, at least 18 months for MPhil and 36 months for PhD

Frequency: Annual

Study Establishment: Regional Institute for Population Studies at the University of Ghana

Country of Study: Ghana

Application Procedure: United Nations Fellows must complete an application form, available at any United Nations Development Programme Office in the capital city of each English speaking Sub Saharan African country, through which all applications should be routed. Applications must be filled out in triplicate and submitted together with the relevant admission requirement through the government ministry responsible for recruiting candidates for the Institute. Non United Nation Fellows should send an application letter

directly to the Director of the Institute. All seven students were sponsored through country programme budgets of governments of three of the member states of the Institute

No. of awards offered: 22

Closing Date: 30 June

Funding: Government

No. of awards given last year: 13

No. of applicants last year: 22

Additional Information: 20 of last year's candidates were sponsored directly by the Institute and 10 through country programme budgets of governments of four of the member states of the Institute www.regents.ac.uk/study/scholarships-funding-and-bursaries/the-dean-of-humanities-arts-social-sciences-excellence-scholarship

For further information contact:

Tel:	(233) 21 773 8906
Fax:	(233) 21 772 829
Email:	fo.gha@undp.org

Religious Scholarships

513 Central Avenue, Suite 300, Highland Park, IL 60035, United States of America.

Website: www.scholarships.com/financial-aid/college-scholarships/scholarships-by-type/religious-scholarships/

Religious scholarships reward students who are actively involved with faith-related activities, pursuing religious-affiliated careers or ministry work, or even those who simply belong to the church. If you are active in your church community or strong in your religious faith, there are religious scholarships for you. Providing scholarship opportunities and financial aid are ideal ways for churches and religious organizations to show their commitment to helping its members go to college. Religious organizations sponsor a variety of national, regional, and local scholarships.

American Atheists Chinn Scholarships

Purpose: American Atheists celebrates activism by awarding scholarships to students who engage in atheist activism in their communities and schools. American Atheists is proud to award Chinn Scholarships for LGBTQ Atheist Activism that recognize atheist activism in the area of LGBTQ equality

Eligibility: 1. You do not have to be a U.S. citizen to be awarded a scholarship, but you do have to attend a U.S.-based institution. 2. Scholarships are open to current college or vocational students and to high school students entering college in the upcoming year. 3. Full-time graduate and law school students are also eligible. 4. Applicants for all awards must be atheists and must have a cumulative GPA of 2.5 or higher in academic subjects. 5. Applicants of all races, ethnicities, genders, and sexual orientations are encouraged to apply.
Level of Study: Graduate
Type: Scholarship
Value: US$1,000
Length of Study: 1 year
Frequency: Annual
Country of Study: Any country
Application Procedure: Apply online. For more information or to apply, please visit the scholarship provider's website. www.atheists.org/activism/scholarships/
No. of awards offered: 8
Closing Date: 15 April
Funding: Foundation
Contributor: American Atheists
Additional Information: www.scholarships.com/financial-aid/college-scholarships/scholarship-directory/religion/atheist/american-atheists-scholarships

For further information contact:

P.O. Box 158, Cranford, NJ 07016, United States of America.

Tel: (1) 908 276 7300
Email: scholarships@atheists.org

American Atheists O'Hair Award

Purpose: American Atheists celebrates activism by awarding scholarships to students who engage in atheist activism in their communities and schools. American Atheists awards O'Hair Scholarships to atheist students in the United States.
Eligibility: 1. You do not have to be a U.S. citizen to be awarded a scholarship, but you do have to attend a U.S.-based institution. 2. Scholarships are open to current college or vocational students and to high school students entering college in the upcoming year. 3. Full-time graduate and law school students are also eligible. 4. Applicants for all awards must be atheists and must have a cumulative GPA of 2.5 or higher in academic subjects. 5. Applicants of all races, ethnicities, genders, and sexual orientations are encouraged to apply.
Level of Study: Graduate

Type: Award
Value: US$1,000
Length of Study: 1 year
Frequency: Annual
Country of Study: New Zealand
Application Procedure: Apply online. For more information or to apply, please visit the scholarship provider's website. www.atheists.org/activism/scholarships/
No. of awards offered: 8
Closing Date: 15 April
Funding: Foundation
Contributor: American Atheists
Additional Information: www.scholarships.com/financial-aid/college-scholarships/scholarship-directory/religion/atheist/american-atheists-scholarships

For further information contact:

Scholarship Committee, P.O. Box 158, Cranford, NJ 07016, United States of America.

Tel: (1) 908 276 7300
Email: scholarships@atheists.org

Anna Schiller Scholarship

Purpose: Anna Schiller Memorial Scholarship provides educational resources to a graduating Rockford Christian High School senior to further their education. Rockford Christian High School graduating senior who demonstrates a strong commitment to improving the quality of life for people in their school, community and/or world at large through their community service and demonstrates the same strong love for others that Anna exemplified through her life
Eligibility: Applicants must 1. Be a graduating senior from Rockford Christian High School; 2. Demonstrate a strong commitment to improving the quality of life of others; 3. Demonstrate the same joyful spirit, kind and compassionate love for others that Anna exemplified through her life; and 4. Have a minimum GPA of 2.0/4.0.
Level of Study: Graduate
Type: Scholarship
Frequency: Annual
Country of Study: United States of America
Application Procedure: Apply online. For more information or to apply, please visit the scholarship provider's website. www.cfnil.org/scholarships/anna-schiller-scholarship
Closing Date: 1 February
Funding: Foundation
Additional Information: www.scholarships.com/financial-aid/college-scholarships/scholarship-directory/religion/christian/anna-schiller-scholarship

For further information contact:

Scholarship Committee, 946 N. Second Street, Rockford, IL 61107, United States of America.

Tel: (1) 779 210 8209
Email: cstahly@cfnil.org

Associated Women for Pepperdine (AWP) Scholarship

Purpose: The Associated Women for Pepperdine (AWP) was established in 1958 and is the largest, most active women's group supporting colleges and universities in Southern California. For over 50 years members have been primary contributors to scholarships for Christian students and have forged a strong link between the University and the Churches of Christ across the country
Eligibility: Applicants must meet the following criteria 1. Be a current, active member of a Church of Christ congregation. 2. Submit the general Pepperdine admission application by the January 5 deadline. 3. Submit the Free Application for Federal Student Aid (FAFSA) (studentaid.gov/h/apply-for-aid/fafsa) by February 15. 4. Submit an additional recommendation from a Church of Christ leader (minister, youth minister, elder, or deacon) by February 15.
Type: Scholarship
Value: US$5,000
Frequency: Annual
Country of Study: United States of America
Application Procedure: Apply online
Closing Date: 15 February
Funding: Foundation
Contributor: The Associated Women for Pepperdine (AWP)
Additional Information: www.seaver.pepperdine.edu/admission/financial-aid/undergraduate/assistance/awp-scholarship-exception.htm www.scholarships.com/financial-aid/college-scholarships/scholarships-by-type/federal-scholarships/associated-women-for-pepperdine-awp-scholarship/

For further information contact:

Scholarship Committee, 24255 Pacific Coast Hwy, Malibu, CA 90263, United States of America.

Tel: (1) 310 506 4000

Republic of South Africa

Tel: (27) 12 312 5372
Email: internationalscholarships@dhet.gov.za
Website: www.internationalscholarships.dhet.gov.za/

There are a number of scholarship opportunities currently available for South African students to undertake studies, research and exchanges in other countries. The Department of Higher Education and Training (DHET) coordinates several such scholarships, while others are managed by other international, national and provincial departments or government agencies. Scholarships are for South African citizens and require a commitment to return to South African upon completion of studies.

Azerbaijan: Azerbaijan Diplomatic Academy University Scholarship

Purpose: The Government of the Republic of Azerbaijan and ADA University are offering scholarships to foreign students. The ADA University is committed to grooming world class leaders
Eligibility: Be South African citizens in good health, with a strong academic record. 1. Meet the entry criteria for their selected programme at the ADA University. 2. Meet the minimum academic requirement for entry into a similar programme at a South African university. 3. Applicants must be proficient in English
Level of Study: Postgraduate
Type: Scholarship
Value: Offers tuition fees, travel expenses, medical benefits and monthly stipend
Frequency: Annual
Country of Study: Any country
Application Procedure: Information on the application process is available on the website. www.ada.edu.az/en-us/pages/admission_fellowships.aspx
Closing Date: 1 July
Funding: Private
Additional Information: www.dhet.gov.za/international Scholarships/AZERBAIJAN2.html

For further information contact:

Email: admissions@ada.edu.az

Research Corporation for Science Advancement

4703 East Camp Lowell Drive, Suite 201, Tucson, AZ 85712, United States of America.

Tel: (1) 520 571 1111
Email: awards@rescorp.org
Website: rescorp.org/
Contact: Editor, Science Advancement Programme

Research Corporation for Science Advancement (RCSA) is a foundation providing catalytic funding for innovative scientific research and the development of academic scientists since 1912. RCSA is a private foundation that aids basic research in the physical sciences (astronomy, chemistry, physics, and related fields) at colleges and universities through its Cottrell Scholar and Scialog programs. It supports research independently proposed by faculty members and convenes conferences. RCSA is a strong supporter of improvements in science education.

Research Corporation (United States of America) Research Innovation Awards

Purpose: To assist innovative research programmes for faculty of PhD granting departments
Eligibility: Open to faculty members whose first tenure track position began in either the preceding or the current calendar year are eligible to apply
Level of Study: Doctorate
Type: Research grant
Value: US$35,000 for equipment and supplies, graduate stipends and some other expenses. The award does not cover overheads
Frequency: Annual
Study Establishment: Research universities with PhD granting departments of physics, chemistry and astronomy
Country of Study: United States of America or Canada
Application Procedure: Applicants must complete an application form. Guidelines and an application request forms are available from the website
No. of awards offered: 200
Closing Date: 1 May
Funding: Private
Contributor: Foundation endowment
No. of awards given last year: 45
No. of applicants last year: 200

For further information contact:

Email: awards@ria.ie

Research Council of Norway

Drammensveien 288, N-0283 Oslo, Norway.

Tel: (47) 22 03 70 00
Email: post@forskningsradet.no
Website: www.forskningsradet.no/en/

The Research Council works to promote research and innovation of high quality and relevance and to generate knowledge in priority areas to enable Norway to deal with key challenges to society and the business sector.

Collaborative Project in Global Health

Subjects: Global development and international relations
Purpose: The purpose of this call for proposals is to support research on health improvements for disadvantaged populations in low- and lower-middle income countries (LLMICs). The research must be relevant to Sustainable Development Goal 3 'Good health for all' and its targets. Projects where it is expedient and beneficial to establish collaboration outside academia should apply under this call.
Eligibility: The call is open to approved Norwegian research organisations in effective collaboration with relevant actors from public sector bodies, non-governmental organisations and/or other private organisations.
Value: NOK 48,000,000
Length of Study: 32-72 months
Country of Study: Any country
No. of awards offered: 5
Closing Date: 9 February
Additional Information: www.forskningsradet.no/en/call-for-proposals/2022/collaborative-project-global-health/

For further information contact:

Drammensveien 288, N-0283 Oslo, Norway.

Tel: (47) 22 03 70 00

Collaborative Project relating to Antimicrobial Resistance from a One Health Perspective

Subjects: Cross-cutting topics
Purpose: The purpose of this call is to generate new knowledge about measures that can help us to understand, handle and prevent the development of antimicrobial resistance (AMR) from a One Health perspective, both nationally and internationally. The call is open to approved Norwegian research organisations in collaboration with non-research organisations from Norway and/or developing countries (LLMIC countries), India and China.
Eligibility: The call is open to approved Norwegian research organisations in effective collaboration with relevant actors from public sector entities, non-governmental organisations, the business sector and/or other private organisations.
Value: NOK 60,000,000
Length of Study: 24-48 months
Country of Study: Any country
No. of awards offered: 5

R

Closing Date: 9 February

Additional Information: www.forskningsradet.no/en/call-for-proposals/2022/collaborative-project-antimicrobial-resistance/

For further information contact:

Drammensveien 288, N-0283 Oslo, Norway.

Tel: (47) 22 03 70 00

Collaborative Project to Meet Societal and Industry-related Challenges

Subjects: Cross-cutting topics, Democracy, Administration and renewal, Energy, Transport and low emissions, Oceans, Health, Land-based food, The environment and bioresources, Enabling technologies, Petroleum, Education and competence, Welfare, Culture and society

Purpose: The purpose of this call is to develop new knowledge and generate research competence needed by society or the business sector to address important societal challenges. The projects are to encourage and support collaboration between research organisations and stakeholders from outside the research sector that represent societal and/or industry-related needs for knowledge and research competence.

Eligibility: The call is open to approved Norwegian research organisations in effective cooperation with relevant actors from public sector entities, non-governmental organisations, the business sector and/or other private organisations.

Value: NOK 1,028,000,000

Length of Study: 24-48 months

Frequency: Annual

Country of Study: Any country

No. of awards offered: 5

Closing Date: 9 February

Additional Information: www.forskningsradet.no/en/call-for-proposals/2022/collaborative-project-industry/

For further information contact:

Drammensveien 288, N-0283 Oslo, Norway.

Tel: (47) 22 03 70 00

Knowledge-building Project for Industry

Subjects: Energy, transport and low emissions; Petroleum

Purpose: The purpose of this call is to develop new knowledge and generate competence in the research organisations needed by society or the business sector to address important societal challenges. The projects are to encourage and support

collaboration between research organisations and stakeholders from outside the research sector that represent societal and/or industry-related needs for knowledge and research competence.

Eligibility: The call is open to approved Norwegian research organisations in effective cooperation with relevant actors from public sector entities, non-governmental organisations, the business sector and/or other private organisations.

Value: NOK 305,000,000

Length of Study: 24-60 months

Country of Study: Any country

No. of awards offered: 5

Closing Date: 9 February

Additional Information: www.forskningsradet.no/en/call-for-proposals/2022/knowledge-building-project-industry/

For further information contact:

Drammensveien 288, N-0283 Oslo, Norway.

Tel: (47) 22 03 70 00

Research Council of Norway Senior Scientist Visiting Fellowship

Purpose: To enable Norwegian research institutions to receive foreign scientists to participate in research groups, discuss research arrangements and give lectures within their special fields

Eligibility: Open to well established and internationally recognised scientists who are at a professional or equivalent level

Level of Study: Professional development

Type: Fellowship

Value: NOK 25,000 per month for the first two months, NOK 10,000 for each succeeding month. Travelling expenses may also be defrayed

Length of Study: 1–12 months

Frequency: Annual

Study Establishment: A Norwegian research institution

Country of Study: Norway

Application Procedure: Applications must be filed by Norwegian institutions, so individual scientists should contact the Norwegian research institution or university department of their choice

Funding: Government

Additional Information: The Research Council of Norway also administers the following: Research Programmes of the European Union (EU), Bilateral Scholarship Agreements, and the Nordic Scheme for the Baltic Countries and North West Russia   www.dhet.gov.za/internationalScholarships/AZER BAIJAN2.html

For further information contact:

Email: post@forskningsradet.no

Researcher Project for Scientific Renewal

Subjects: Ground-breaking research, Cross-cutting topics, Global development and international relations, Oceans, Health, Climate and polar research, Petroleum, Sámi society and culture, Education and competence, Welfare, culture and society

Purpose: Funding is intended to support scientific renewal and development in research that can help to advance the international research front. This call is therefore targeted towards researchers who have demonstrated the ability to conduct research of high scientific quality. Grant proposals will be accepted for projects within all disciplines and research areas.

Eligibility: Only approved Norwegian research organizations may apply

Type: Research grant

Value: NOK 1 467 000 000

Length of Study: 36-72 months

Country of Study: Any country

Closing Date: 2 February

Additional Information: www.forskningsradet.no/en/call-for-proposals/2022/researcher-project-scientific-renewal/

For further information contact:

Drammensveien 288, N-0283 Oslo, Norway.

Tel: (47) 22 03 70 00

Researcher Project for Young Talents

Subjects: Ground-breaking research, Oceans, Climate and polar research

Purpose: Funding is intended to give talented young researchers, under the age of 40 in all disciplines and thematic areas, the opportunity to pursue their ideas and lead a research project. This call is targeted towards researchers in the early stages of their careers, 2–7 years after defence of an approved doctorate, who have demonstrated the potential to conduct research of high scientific quality.

Eligibility: Only approved Norwegian research organizations may apply

Level of Study: Research

Type: Grant

Value: NOK 3,06,000,000

Length of Study: 36-48 months

Country of Study: Any country

Closing Date: 2 February

Additional Information: www.forskningsradet.no/en/call-for-proposals/2022/researcher-project-young-talents/

For further information contact:

Drammensveien 288, N-0283 Oslo, Norway.

Tel: (47) 22 03 70 00

Three-year Researcher Project with International Mobility

Purpose: Funding is intended to increase international mobility and promote career development among researchers at an early stage in their careers, as well as to facilitate knowledge transfer to research groups in Norway. The call is targeted towards researchers at the post-doctoral level who are to spend two years at a research organisation abroad and the third year at a research organisation in Norway. Grant proposals will be accepted for projects within all disciplines and research areas.

Eligibility: Only approved Norwegian research organizations may apply

Level of Study: Research

Type: Research grant

Value: NOK 40,000,000

Length of Study: 36-36 months

Frequency: Annual

Country of Study: Any country

Closing Date: 2 February

Additional Information: www.forskningsradet.no/en/call-for-proposals/2022/researcher-project-international-mobility/

For further information contact:

Drammensveien 288, N-0283 Oslo, Norway.

Tel: (47) 22 03 70 00

Reserve Bank of New Zealand

2 The Terrace, PO Box 2498, Wellington 6140, New Zealand.

Tel: (64) 4 472 2029
Email: rbnz-info@rbnz.govt.nz
Website: www.rbnz.govt.nz/

The Reserve Bank of New Zealand is New Zealand's central bank. They promote a sound and dynamic monetary and financial system. They work towards our vision by operating monetary policy to achieve and maintain price stability, assisting the functioning of a sound and efficient financial system, meeting the currency needs of the public, overseeing and operating effective payments systems and providing effective support services to the Bank.

Māori and Pacific Islands Scholarship

Purpose: Enabling and supporting diversity in our talent, pipeline is important to the Bank. One of the ways we do this is by offering Maori and Pacific Island scholarships, to those studying towards the afore mentioned qualifications.
Eligibility: The scholarships are available each year to students majoring in Economics, Finance, Mathematics, Law and Accounting studies, who attained at least a B+ grade point average and who intend to continue studying to Honours or Master's level. Please note that students who are entering their first year of university are not eligible. We're looking for future leaders who're interested in becoming well-rounded central bankers and who demonstrate our values of integrity, innovation and inclusion. A key focus for us is attracting diversity of thought and experience, to enable our vision of 'Great Team, Best Central Bank'
Type: Scholarship
Value: US$3,000 for each of the first year and second years of study and US$5,000 in the final year of study.
Frequency: Annual
Country of Study: Any country
Closing Date: 13 February
Additional Information: www.rbnz.govt.nz/grads/scholarships#maori-pacific-scholarship

For further information contact:

2 The Terrace, Wellington Central, Wellington 6140, New Zealand.

Tel: (64) 4 472 2029

Reserve Bank of New Zealand Scholarships

Purpose: The RBNZ scholarships is open to all students.
Eligibility: The scholarships are available each year to students majoring in Economics, Finance, Mathematics, Law and Accounting studies, who attained at least a B+ grade point average and who intend to continue studying to Honours or Master's level.
Type: Scholarship
Value: US$3,000 for each of the first year and second years of study and US$5,000 in the final year of study
Country of Study: Any country
Closing Date: 13 February

Additional Information: www.rbnz.govt.nz/grads/scholarships#maori-pacific-scholarship

For further information contact:

2 The Terrace, Wellington Central, Wellington 6140, New Zealand.

Tel: (64) 4 472 2029
Email: recruitment@rbnz.govt.nz

Reserve Bank of New Zealand Scholarships for International Students

Purpose: The Reserve Bank of New Zealand offers scholarships for students studying at a New Zealand University. The scholarships are available each year to students majoring in Economics, Finance, Mathematics, Law and Accounting studies, who intend to continue studying to Honours or Master's level.
Eligibility: 1.To be eligible, applicants must be studying full-time at a New Zealand University and are a NZ Citizen or have NZ Permanent Residency status. 2. The RBNZ scholarships is open to all students. 3. The scholarships are available each year to students majoring in Economics, Finance, Mathematics, Law and Accounting studies, who attained at least a B+ grade point average and who intend to continue studying to Honours or Master's level.
Type: Scholarship
Value: The scholarship is valued at NZ$3,000 for each of the first year and second years of study and NZ$5,000 in the final year of study. These funds will be paid fortnightly during the academic year.
Frequency: Annual
Country of Study: New Zealand
Application Procedure: Please complete our online application. As part of this, you will need to provide the following information: 1. Your CV. 2. A copy of your official academic transcript. 3. A recent essay or assessment (to demonstrate your written work) you have submitted as part of your degree. 4. Details of 2 - 3 referees who are able to give verbal references.
Closing Date: 13 February
Contributor: Any New Zealand University
Additional Information: Please note that students who are entering their first year of university are not eligible. www.rbnz.govt.nz/grads/scholarships#rbnz-scholarship

For further information contact:

2 The Terrace, Wellington Central, Wellington 6140, New Zealand.

Tel: (64) 4 472 2029
Email: working@rbnz.govt.nz

The Roger Perry Memorial Scholarship

Purpose: The Roger Perry Memorial scholarship is for those students entering their final year of study and working towards Honours or Masters. This scholarship has been established as an enduring recognition of the immense contribution Roger made to the Reserve Bank.
Eligibility: The scholarships are available each year to students majoring in Economics, Finance, Mathematics, Law and Accounting studies, who attained at least a B+ grade point average and who intend to continue studying to Honours or Master's level.
Type: Scholarship
Value: US$10,000
Country of Study: Any country
Closing Date: 13 February
Additional Information: www.rbnz.govt.nz/grads/scholarships#maori-pacific-scholarship

For further information contact:

2 The Terrace, Wellington Central, Wellington 6140, New Zealand.

Tel: (64) 4 472 2029
Email: recruitment@rbnz.govt.nz

Women in Central Banking Scholarship

Purpose: This scholarship is aimed at increasing opportunities for women in central banking and forms part of our wider commitment to diversity and inclusion.
Eligibility: The scholarships are available each year to students majoring in Economics, Finance, Mathematics, Law and Accounting studies, who attained at least a B+ grade point average and who intend to continue studying to Honours or Master's level.
Type: Scholarship
Value: US$3,000 for each of the first year and second years of study and US$5,000 in the final year of study
Frequency: Annual
Country of Study: Any country
Closing Date: 13 February
Additional Information: www.rbnz.govt.nz/grads/scholarships#maori-pacific-scholarship

For further information contact:

2 The Terrace, Wellington Central, Wellington 6140, New Zealand.

Tel: (64) 4 472 2029
Email: recruitment@rbnz.govt.nz

Resuscitation Council (United Kingdom)

5th Floor, Tavistock House North, Tavistock Square, London WC1H 9HR, United Kingdom.

Tel: (44) 20 7388 4678
Website: www.resus.org.uk/
Contact: Dr Sara Harris, Assistant Director

Resuscitation Council UK is the national expert in resuscitation. Formed in 1983, Resuscitation Council UK is committed to ensuring that survival rates for in and out of hospital cardiac arrest improve. We're doing this by driving CPR education, and encouraging everyone, from healthcare workers to the general public, to learn life-saving resuscitation skills.

Resuscitation Council (United Kingdom) Research & Development Grant

Purpose: The purpose of this grant funding is to support high-quality medical education research and/or clinical research involving people (patients, staff, relatives), and the generation of new knowledge in resuscitation science and education. The purpose is also to support future resuscitation specialists developing their interest and expertise through high quality research.
Eligibility: 1. Applications must be methodologically robust. Advice on research design may be available from the regional NIHR Research Design Services. 2. RCUK does not fund animal research or purely basic science research. 3. Project proposers and project leads must be based in the UK. 4. Applications where the applicant is registered for a higher degree (e.g. MSc by Research, MPhil, PhD will be considered if associated with high quality research. 5. Applicants should have a credible track record of conducting such research projects or have appropriate supervision. 6. The lead investigator must hold a tenured position within an official health or social care setting, NHS setting or UK university organisation. 7. The research project should normally be completed within 1-3 years.
Level of Study: Doctorate, Masters Degree, Postgraduate, Research

Type: Grant
Value: £20,000
Frequency: Annual
Country of Study: United Kingdom
Application Procedure: Applications should be submitted by a department or institution for a defined project to be undertaken by a specified individual. The researcher must be working within an official health or social care setting, NHS setting or UK university organisation within the UK and hold qualifications appropriate to their grade. Such individuals will usually be doctors, nurses, resuscitation officers or other professions allied to medicine. If the application is submitted by the supervisor of the research project the CV and reference will be required in respect of the appointed individual. Applications must be submitted using the RCUK Research and Development Grant applications online system.
Closing Date: 6 January
Additional Information: For more details www.resus.org. uk/about-us/resuscitation-research

For further information contact:

Email: research@resus.org.uk

Rheumatology Research Foundation

2200 Lake Boulevard NE, Atlanta, GA 30319, United States of America.

Tel: (1) 404 365 1373
Email: foundation@rheumatology.org
Website: www.rheumresearch.org/
Contact: Sarah Barksdale, Senior Specialist, Awards and Grants

The Rheumatology Research Foundation is the largest private funding source for rheumatology research & training in the U.S. The mission of the Rheumatology Research Foundation is to advance research and training to improve the health of patients living with rheumatic disease. We award grants to scientists conducting innovative research that will lead to a future with more options for patients with rheumatic disease to live longer, healthier lives.

American College of Rheumatology REF Rheumatology Scientist Development Award

Purpose: To encourage qualified physicians without significant prior research experience to embark on careers in biomedical and/or clinical research in arthritis and rheumatic diseases

Eligibility: Candidates must be an ACR or ARHP member, have a doctoral level degree, must be clinician scientists
Level of Study: Doctorate, Postdoctorate, Professional development, Research
Type: Award
Value: US$50,000 for first year, US$75,000 for second year and US$100,000 for third year
Length of Study: 3 years
Frequency: Annual
Country of Study: United States of America
Application Procedure: Application forms are available on the website
No. of awards offered: 12
Closing Date: 1 June
Funding: Foundation
Contributor: Centocor Inc
Additional Information: For any questions regarding eligibility, contact the REF www.rheumresearch.org/career-development-research-awards

For further information contact:

Email: Foundation@rheumatology.org

American College of Rheumatology/REF Arthritis Investigator Award

Purpose: To provide support to physicians and scientists in research fields related to arthritis for the period between the completion of postdoctoral fellowship training and establishment as an independent investigators
Level of Study: Research
Type: Award
Value: US$75,000 for the first 2 years and US$90,000 per year after renewal
Length of Study: 2–4 years
Frequency: Annual
Country of Study: United States of America
Application Procedure: Application forms are available on the website
Closing Date: 1 September
Funding: Foundation
Contributor: The Arthritis Foundation

For further information contact:

Email: acrnominations@rheumatology.org

Amgen Fellowship Training Award

Purpose: The purpose of this award is to help ensure an adequate supply of (a) rheumatology providers meeting the needs of children and adults with rheumatic diseases in all areas of the country and (b) rheumatology educators and investigators to train future clinicians and advance research in rheumatic and musculoskeletal diseases. The Amgen Fellowship Training Award may be used to support the salary of any fellow in an ACGME-accredited rheumatology fellowship training program.

Eligibility: Applicant (Program Director) must be an ACR or ARP member at the time of submission and for the duration of the award. 1. Only Program Directors at ACGME-accredited institutionsin good standing may apply. 2. The rheumatology fellowship training Program Director at the institution will be responsible for the overall direction, management and administration of the program. 3. By submitting an application, the Program Director and sponsoring institution agree funds will be used ONLY for salary support of one fellow in their first or second year (or third year fellow in pediatric rheumatology). 4. Multiple applications from a single institution will not be permitted unless they are for separate training programs (e.g., adult and pediatric rheumatology). 5. Programs may not apply for the Amgen Fellowship Training Award and Fellowship Training Award- Workforce Expansion within the same application cycle. 6. Current recipients of the Fellowship Training Award for Workforce Expansion are not eligible to apply for this award. 7. Supported fellows do not need to be U.S. citizens or non-citizen nationals. If you have questions about your eligibility, please inquire by email.

Type: Award

Value: US$50,000

Length of Study: 1 year

Frequency: Annual

Country of Study: United States of America

Application Procedure: All applications must be submitted online by 5 PM ET on the deadline day through ProposalCentral at proposalcentral.com/. Before starting the online application, you will be required to create a Professional Profile in ProposalCentral, if you have not already. To do so, visit this link (proposalcentral.com/register.asp) to begin creating your account. Please refer website.

Closing Date: 2 May

Contributor: Amgen, Inc

Additional Information: www.rheumresearch.org/education-and-training-awards

Career Development Bridge Funding Award: K Bridge

Purpose: The purpose of this award is to provide bridge funding for promising investigators as they are revising outstanding individual career development award applications (i.e., applications for NIH K series awards or VA CDA-2 awards or any equivalent career development awards). Through this bridge funding award, the Foundation will support young faculty members so that they have the highest likelihood of achieving success in obtaining longerterm career development awards.

Eligibility: 1. All applicants must meet citizenship/permanent resident status and other eligibility requirements as outlined in the Awards and Grants policies. 2. Applicants must be ACR or ARP members with an MD, DO, PhD or equivalent doctoral level degree from an accredited institution. 3. The Foundation does not currently support non-MD/DO scientists working on basic science research. 4. Bridge funds are not intended to bridge the period between review and funding. 5. Previous recipients of this award are not eligible to apply. 6. In addition to an excellent application, applicantsmust be capable of becoming independent researchers with a clear and firm institutional commitment to their career development, including a faculty position and other supporting resources.

Level of Study: Professional development

Type: Award

Value: Up to US$75,000

Length of Study: 1 year

Frequency: Annual

Country of Study: United States of America

Application Procedure: All applications must be submitted by 5 PM ET on the deadline day through ProposalCentral proposalcentral.com/. Before starting the online application, you will be required to create a Professional Profile in ProposalCentral, if you have not already. To do so, visit this link to begin creating your account. proposalcentral.com/register.asp. Please refer website.

Closing Date: 1 June

Funding: Foundation

Additional Information: For more details: www.rheumresearch.org/career-development-research-awards. www.rheumresearch.org/file/FY22_Career-Development-Bridge-Funding-Award_K-Bridge_3.3.2021.pdf

Career Development Bridge Funding Award: K Supplement

Purpose: The NIH K Series and VA CDA awards provide limited resources to cover research costs, such as essential laboratory supplies or supportstaff (e.g. salary support for research technician, database assistant or statistician), which are crucial to the successful transition of junior investigators to independent investigators. This award is designed to address the needs of these investigators and serve as a supplement to the NIH individual K series, VA CDA, or equivalent 4- or 5-year award mechanism.

Eligibility: 1. All applicants must meet citizenship/permanent resident status and other eligibility requirements as outlined in the Awards and Grants policies. 2. Applicants must be ACR or ARPmembers with an MD, DO, PhD or equivalent doctoral level degree from an accredited institution. ACR members must meet the following criteria: a. Applicant must be an

NIH K08, K23, K25, VA CD, or equivalent 4- or 5-year award recipient. The applicant must be in years 2, 3 or 4 of their award at the time of application. b. Have earned a DO, MD, MD/PhD, or DO/PhD degree or be currently enrolled in an ACGME accredited clinical training program. c. MDs and DOs who are not licensed to perform clinical care may not apply. ARP members must meet the following criteria: a. Applicant must be an NIH K01, K08, K23, K25, VA CD, or equivalent 4- or 5-year award recipient. The applicant must be in years 2, 3 or 4 of their award at the time of application. b. Have earned a PhD, DSc, or equivalent doctoral degree. 3. The Foundation does not currently support non- MD/DO scientists working on basic science research. 4. In addition to an excellent application, applicants must be capable of becoming independent researchers with a clear and firm institutional commitment to their career development, including a faculty position and other supporting resources.

Level of Study: Doctorate, Professional development, Research

Type: Award

Value: US$100,000 (up to US$50,000 per year for 2 years)

Length of Study: 2 years

Frequency: Annual

Country of Study: United States of America

Application Procedure: All applications must be submitted by 5 PM ET on the deadline day through ProposalCentral. proposalcentral.com/. Please visit website.

Closing Date: 2 August

Funding: Foundation

Additional Information: For more details: www. rheumresearch.org/career-development-research-awards. www. rheumresearch.org/file/FY22_Career-Development-Bridge-Funding-Award_K-Supplement_2.16.21.pdf

For further information contact:

Email: Foundation@rheumatology.org

Career Development Bridge Funding Award: R Bridge

Purpose: The purpose of this award is to provide funding to NIH R01, VA Research Career Scientist (RCS) or Merit Award applicants whose application received a priority score but was not funded, and who are at risk of running out of research support.

Eligibility: 1. All applicants must meet citizenship/permanent resident status and other eligibility requirements as outlined in the Awards and Grants policies. 2. Applicants must be ACR or ARP members with an MD, DO, PhD or equivalent doctoral level degree from an accredited institution. ACR members must meet the following criteria: a. Applicants must have

less than one year (or a lapse) remaining on one of the following awards NIH K08, K23, K25, K99/R00, VA CDA, institutional K, or Rheumatology Research Foundation Investigator Award. b. Have earned a DO, MD, MD/PhD, or DO/PhD degree and have completed a Rheumatology fellowship. c. MDs and Dos who are not licensed to perform clinical care in the U.S. may not apply. ARP members must meet the following criteria: a. Applicants must have less than one year (or a lapse) remaining on one of the following awards NIH K01, K08, K23, K25, K99/R00, VA CDA, institutional K, or Rheumatology Research Foundation Investigator Award. b. Have earned a PhD, DSc, or equivalent degree. 3. The Foundation does not currently support non- MD/DO scientists working on basic science research. 4. Previous recipients of an NIH R01 or VA RCS/ORD are not eligible to apply. 5. Applicants must have received a priority score, summary statement, and funding decision on their NIH R01 or VA RCS/ORD award. Applicants whose career development applications were triaged, and therefore, not discussed during peer review, are not eligible. Bridge funds are not intended to bridge the period between review and funding. 6. Applications from individuals from groups underrepresented (diversity. nih.gov/about-us/population-underrepresented) in medicine are particularly encouraged. 7. Previous recipients of this award are not eligible to apply. 8. In addition to an excellent application, applicants must be capable of becoming independent, researchers with a clear and firm institutional commitment to their continued career development, including a faculty position and other supporting resources.

Level of Study: Doctorate, Masters Degree, Postdoctorate

Type: Award

Value: US$200,000 (Up to US$100,000 per year for 2 years)

Length of Study: 2 years

Frequency: Annual

Country of Study: United States of America

Application Procedure: All applications must be submitted by 5 PM ET on the deadline day through ProposalCentral. proposalcentral.com/. Please visit website.

Closing Date: 1 June

Additional Information: For more information: www. rheumresearch.org/career-development-research-awards. www. rheumresearch.org/file/FY22_Career-Development-Bridge-Funding-Award_R-Bridge_3.3.2021.pdf

Career Development in Geriatric Medicine Award

Purpose: To support career development for junior faculty in the early stages of their research career

Eligibility: To be eligible for the award, the candidate must be a member of the ACR; have completed a rheumatology fellowship leading to certification by the ABIM and be within the first 3 years of his/her faculty appointment; and possess a faculty appointment at the time of the award. Award applicant must be a citizen or non-citizen national of the United States of America, or be in lawful possessions of a permanent resident card. Individuals on temporary (J1, H1) or student visas are not eligible

Level of Study: Doctorate, Professional development, Research

Type: Research award

Value: US$75,000 per year plus US$3,000 in travel grants

Length of Study: 2 years

Frequency: Annual

Country of Study: United States of America

Application Procedure: Application forms are available on website www.rheumatology.org/foundation/index.asp

No. of awards offered: 1

Closing Date: 1 December

Funding: Foundation

Contributor: Association of Subspecialty Professors

No. of awards given last year: 1

No. of applicants last year: 1

Additional Information: www.rheumresearch.org/career-development-research-awards

For further information contact:

Email: ysong@hrsa.gov

Clinician Scholar Educator Award

Purpose: The purpose of the Clinician Scholar Educator (CSE) Award is to enhance education in musculoskeletal diseases for future doctors and rheumatology health professionals. Recipients of the award have demonstrated that they want to develop a career in education and are devoted to providing effective and efficient training. Recipients of the CSE Award devote themselves to developing products and processes using new technologies and methods to better train future rheumatologists.

Eligibility: 1. Applicant must meet citizenship and other eligibility requirements as outlined in the Awards and Grants policies. 2. Must propose educational projects related to rheumatic disease. 3. Applicant must be affiliated with an accredited graduate or medical school. 4. Applicant must be able to devote at least 25 percent full-time effort (including this project and other educational endeavors) to educational and scholarly activity for the duration of the award. Note this time is independent of any program administrative time for teaching faculty, Assistant Program Directors or Program Directors. 5. Applicant must be an ACR or ARP member at the time of submission and for the duration of the award. For ACR members must meet the following criteria 1. Have

earned a DO, MD, or MD/PhD degree and completed a Rheumatology fellowship by the time of award start, 2. Have experience in the education or training of medical students, and/or residents and fellows, 3. Be licensed to perform clinical care, 4. Have experience seeing patients AND currently see patients; For ARP members must meet the following criteria 1. Have earned an advanced degree (Masters or above), 2. Have experience in the education or training of health professionals, 3. Have experience seeing patients AND currently see patients.

Type: Award

Value: Up to US$60,000 per year for 3 years (US$50,000 per year for salary and up to US$10,000 supplemental funding)

Length of Study: 3 years

Frequency: Annual

Country of Study: United States of America

Application Procedure: All applications must be submitted online by 5 PM ET on the deadline day through ProposalCentral at proposalcentral.com/. If you have any questions about your eligibility or submitting your application, please contact Award & Grants staff. Before starting the online application, you will be required to create a Professional Profile in ProposalCentral. Please refer website www.rheumresearch.org/education-and-training-awards

Closing Date: 2 May

Additional Information: www.rheumresearch.org/education-and-training-awards

Fellowship Training Award

Purpose: The purpose of this workforce expansion award is to help ensure an adequate supply of rheumatology providers meeting the needs of children and adults with rheumatic diseases in all areas of the country, particularly those currently underserved.

Eligibility: 1. The Fellowship Training Award for Workforce Expansion may be used to support the salary of any fellow in an ACGME-accredited rheumatology fellowship training program meeting any of the criteria below a. Program has been unable to fill all of its ACGME-approved slots due to funding constraints, b. An existing program that is creating a new slot, c. A new ACGME-accredited program (prepared to participate in the NRMP match for the first year of funding). 2. Applicant (Program Director) must be an ACR or ARP member at the time of submission and for the duration of the award. 3. Only Program Directors at ACGME-accredited institutions in good standing may apply. 4. The rheumatology fellowship training Program Director at the institution will be responsible for the overall direction, management and administration of the program. 5. By submitting an application, the Program Director and sponsoring institution agree funds will be used ONLY for salary support of one fellow in their first or second year (or third year fellow in pediatric rheumatology). 6. Multiple applications from a single institution will not be permitted unless they are for separate training programs (e.g. adult and pediatric rheumatology). 7. Programs may not apply for the Amgen Fellowship Training Award and Fellowship Training Award for Workforce Expansion within the same application cycle. Preference will be given to programs not supported by fellowship training awards granted by other organizations. 8. If there is no fellow available to appoint to this award between July 1 and June 30, recipient may request a one-year deferral. 9. Supported fellows do not need to be U.S. citizens or non-citizen nationals.

Type: Award

Value: US$100,000 for adult programs; US$150,000 for pediatric programs

Length of Study: 2 Years or 3 Years

Frequency: Annual

Country of Study: United States of America

Application Procedure: All applications must be submitted online by 5 PM ET on the deadline day through ProposalCentral at proposalcentral.com/. Please refer www. rheumresearch.org/file/FY23-Fellowship-Training-Award-for-Workforce-Expansion_2.16.21.pdf

Closing Date: 3 May

Additional Information: For more information www. rheumresearch.org/education-and-training-awards, www. rheumresearch.org/file/FY23-Fellowship-Training-Award-for-Workforce-Expansion_2.16.21.pdf

For further information contact:

Email: foundation@rheumatology.org

Health Professional Online Education Grant

Purpose: The purpose of this award is to increase the knowledge and skills of non-physician rheumatology health professionals to meet the needs of a growing rheumatology patient population by reimbursing the cost of registration for the Advanced Rheumatology Courses or the Fundamentals of Rheumatology Courses.

Eligibility: 1. Applicants must meet citizenship and other eligibility requirements as outlined in the Awards and Grants Policies. 2. Applicants must be ARP members at the time of submission and for the duration of the award. 3. Nurse practitioners, physician assistants, nurses, pharmacists, physical therapists, occupational therapists, social workers, psychologists, practice management staff, other licensed non-physician health professionals with an interest in rheumatology.

Type: Grant

Value: Up to US$1,776 for the Advanced Rheumatology Courses or up to US$750 Fundamentals of Rheumatology Courses.

Frequency: Annual

Country of Study: United States of America

Application Procedure: All applications must be submitted by 5 PM ET on the deadline day through ProposalCentral at proposalcentral.com/. Please refer www.rheumresearch.org/file/HPOEG-21.pdf

Closing Date: 1 May

Additional Information: For more information www. rheumresearch.org/file/awards/2019/FY20-HPOEG-RFA_ FINAL.pdf

Innovative Research Award

Purpose: Supporting innovative research ideas is essential to better understanding rheumatic diseases, their cause, and the best way to treat them. The Innovative Research Award provides independent academic investigators with the funding they need to pursue ideas that could lead to important breakthroughs in discovering new treatments and, one day, a cure. This award provides essential support for innovative studies focused on generating new insights into the cause, progression, treatment, and outcomes of rheumatic and musculoskeletal diseases.

Eligibility: To be eligible for this award, the applicant must: 1. Be a member of the ACR or ARP at the time of submission and for the duration of the award, 2. Hold a doctoral-level degree (MD, PhD, DO, MBBS or equivalent), 3. Have a faculty appointment (instructor, assistant professor, etc.) at an academic center or research institution at the time of application and for the duration of the award, 4. Must exhibit evidence of research independence, scientific productivity and career accomplishments, 5. Be able to devote a minimum of 20% full-time professional research effort to the project (see details in Award Eligibility and Guidelines in website), 6. Meet citizenship and other eligibility requirements as outlined in the Awards and Grants policies.

Level of Study: Doctorate, Postdoctorate, Professional development

Type: Award

Value: Up to US$400,000 for two years (maximum US$200,000 per year)

Length of Study: 2 years

Frequency: Annual

Country of Study: United States of America

Application Procedure: All applications must be submitted by 5 PM ET on the deadline day through ProposalCentral at www.proposalcentral.com/ Please refer website. www. rheumresearch.org/innovative-research-award

Closing Date: December

Funding: Foundation
Additional Information: www.rheumresearch.org/ innovative-research-award

Innovative Research Award for Community Practitioners

Purpose: Through our innovative research program, the Foundation is committed to funding research ideas that are essential to improve understanding of rheumatic diseases, including their causes and optimal treatments. The Innovative Research Award for Community Practitioners will enable research that has the potential to improve treatment of rheumatic diseases, patient outcomes, and/or quality of care. This award is targeted to community practitioners who, in addition to being engaged in patient care, conduct or are interested in conducting research.
Eligibility: To be eligible for this award, the applicant must 1. Be a member of the ACR or ARP at the time of submission and for the duration of the award; 2. Hold a doctoral-level degree (MD, DO, PhD, DNP, PsyD, EdD); 3. Have a current license to practice medicine or other interprofessional specialty and be in good medical standing; 4. Be employed in a community practice setting including a. Solo practice. b. Single specialty group practice. c. Multi-specialty group practice. d. Hospital system-based practice. 5. Have the ability to manage a grant award administratively and fiscally, 6. Demonstrate certification of training in human subjects research and the ability to obtain human subjects research approval and oversight for the proposed research for the duration of the award; 8. Meet citizenship and other eligibility requirements as outlined in the Awards and Grants policies.
Level of Study: Doctorate, Postdoctorate, Professional development, Research
Type: Award
Value: US$50,000 to US$200,000 per year, for up to two years
Length of Study: 2 years
Frequency: Annual
Country of Study: United States of America
Application Procedure: All applications must be submitted by 5 PM ET on the deadline day through ProposalCentral at www.proposalcentral.com/ Please refer website www. rheumresearch.org/innovative-research-award
Closing Date: 1 June
Funding: Foundation
Additional Information: For more information: www. rheumresearch.org/document.doc?id=491

For further information contact:

Award and Grants staff, United States of America.

Email: Foundation@rheumatology.org

Lawren H. Daltroy Health Professional Preceptorship

Purpose: The Lawren H. Daltroy Preceptorship in Health Communication was established with the aim of improving patient-clinician interactions and communications. Dr. Daltroy was an internationally recognized authority on health education and enhancing communication between physicians and patients. He performed groundbreaking studies on patient selfmedication in hospitals, spousal support for cardiac patients and worksite health education. This award provides resources to support the training, career development, and/or enhancement of research skills of researchers and clinicians.
Eligibility: 1. Preceptee must meet citizenship and other eligibility requirements as outlined in the Awards and Grants policies. 2. Preceptor must be an ACR or ARP member. 3. This mentored award is intended for trainees and junior researchers or health professionals with no current or prior R01 or R01-equivalent funding. Both ACR and ARP members are eligible to apply.
Level of Study: Professional development, Research
Type: Award
Value: Up to US$15,000 for one year
Length of Study: 1 year
Frequency: Annual
Country of Study: United States of America
Application Procedure: All applications must be submitted by 5 PM ET on the deadline day through Proposal Central at www.proposalcentral.com/. Please refer www. rheumresearch.org/file/FY22-Lawren-H.-Daltroy-Health-Professional-Preceptorship.pdf.
Closing Date: 3 May
Funding: Corporation
Contributor: Funding for this award is made possible through an endowment established by Rheuminations, Inc.
Additional Information: Please check website www. rheumresearch.org/preceptorships#LHDP

For further information contact:

Email: Foundation@rheumatology.org

Medical and Graduate Student Preceptonship

Purpose: The purpose of the preceptorship program is to introduce medical and graduate students to rheumatology-related health care by supporting a 4-Week or 8-Week, full-time clinical or research experience in the broad area of rheumatic disease.
Eligibility: 1. Preceptor must be an ACR or ARP member at the time of submission and for the duration of the award

(students are not required to be members). 2. A preceptor may be eligible to receive the award multiple times; however, they must work with a different student each time. 3. Students enrolled in LCME or AOA COCA accredited medical schools, undergraduate students who have been accepted into medical school, students enrolled in an accredited graduate school, or undergraduate students who have been accepted into graduate school, are eligible to apply. 4. Students may apply during any year of their medical or graduate studies and must have identified a preceptor by the time of the application. 5. Individuals who are personally related to the proposed student are not eligible to serve as the student's preceptor.

Level of Study: Research

Type: Award

Value: US$4,000 for an at least 8-week research or clinical preceptorship to be completed within 12 months of award start date or US$2,000 for an atleast 4-week clinical preceptorship to be completed within 12 months of award start date.

Length of Study: 4-Week or 8-Week

Frequency: Annual

Country of Study: United States of America

Application Procedure: Applicants have the option to select Clinical or Research when applying. All applications must be submitted by 5 PM ET on the deadline day through ProposalCentral at www.proposalcentral.com/. For details please refer www.rheumresearch.org/file/FY22-Medical–Graduate-Student-Preceptorship.pdf

No. of awards offered: 3

Closing Date: 1 May

Funding: Private

Contributor: Marc R. Chevrier, MD, PhD, FACR, Lupus Research Memorial Fund

Additional Information: www.rheumresearch.org/file/FY21-Medical–Graduate-Student-Preceptorship_FINAL.pdf

Mentored Nurse Practitioner/Physician Assistant Award for Workforce Expansion

Purpose: The purpose of the Mentored Nurse Practitioner/ Physician Assistant (NP/PA) Award for Workforce Expansion is to increase the supply of rheumatology healthcare providers to better meet the needs of people with rheumatic diseases across the United States, particularly in geographically underserved areas. This award provides resources and the framework of knowledge, skills, and attitudes needed by NP/PAs, new to rheumatology, to facilitate their integration into a rheumatology practice under the supervision of a rheumatologist.

Eligibility: 1. Eligible applicant ("Mentor") must be a board-certified rheumatologist employed in clinical rheumatology practice. The NP or PA does not have to be identified at the time of application but must be identified at the time of award contract. Eligible NP/PA must be new to the field of rheumatology (employed in a rheumatology practice setting for fewer than 18 months). 2. Mentor must meet citizenship and other eligibility requirements as outlined in the Awards and Grants policies. 3. Mentor must be an ACR member at the time of submission and for the duration of the award. 4. Mentor is eligible to receive the award multiple times; however, the mentor must work with a new NP or PA each time. The mentor may have only one active NP/PA award at a time. 5. NP or PA must be a graduate from a program accredited by either the Commission on Collegiate Nursing Education (CCNE) or the Accreditation Review Commission on Education for the Physician Assistant. 6. NP or PA must have current state licensure. 7. NP or PA must have national Board certification by one or more of the following a. American Nurses Credentialing Center b. American Academy of Nurse Practitioners c. Pediatric Nursing Certification Board d. National Certification Corporation e. National Commission on Certification of Physician Assistants 8. NP or PA must be a member of the Association for Rheumatology Professionals for the duration of the award.

Type: Award

Value: US$25,000

Length of Study: 1 year

Frequency: Annual

Country of Study: United States of America

Application Procedure: All applications must be submitted online. For more details visit www.rheumresearch.org/file/awards/04-education-and-training/FY22-Mentored-Nurse-Practitioner-Physician-Assistant-Award-for-Workforce-Expansion_FINAL.pdf

Closing Date: 1 March

Contributor: Rheumatology Research Foundation

Additional Information: For more information: www.rheumresearch.org/education-and-training-awards

Paula de Merieux Fellowship Training Award

Purpose: Paula de Merieux grant is awarded to support a trainee who belongs to an underrepresented minority within rheumatology, or is a woman. For the purposes of this program, "underrepresented minority within rheumatology" shall mean Black, Hispanic, or Native American.

Eligibility: 1. To qualify, the trainee must be a member of an underrepresented minority within rheumatology, or a woman. 2. Applicant (Program Director) must be an ACR or ARP member at the time of submission and for the duration of the award. 3. Only Program Directors at ACGME-accredited institutionsin good standing may apply. 4. The rheumatology fellowship training Program Director at the institution will be responsible for the overall direction, management and administration of the program. 5. By submitting an application, the Program Director and sponsoring institution agree funds will be used ONLY for salary support of one fellow in their first orsecond year (or third year fellow in pediatric rheumatology). 6. Multiple applicationsfrom a single institution will not be permitted unless they are for separate training programs (e.g., adult and pediatric rheumatology). 7. Programs may not apply for the Amgen Fellowship Training Award and Fellowship Training Award- Workforce Expansion within the same application cycle. 8. Current recipients of the Fellowship Training Award for Workforce Expansion are not eligible to apply for this award. 9. Supported fellows do not need to be U.S. citizens or non-citizen nationals.

Type: Award
Value: US$50,000
Length of Study: 1 year
Frequency: Annual
Country of Study: United States of America
Application Procedure: All applications must be submitted online by 5 PM ET on the deadline day through ProposalCentral at www.proposalcentral.com/. Please refer www.rheumresearch.org/file/FY23_Fellowship-Training-Award-PDM_2.16.21.pdf
No. of awards offered: 1
Closing Date: 3 May
Funding: Private
Contributor: Paula de Merieux estate
Additional Information: For more details: www.rheumresearch.org/file/FY23_Fellowship-Training-Award-PDM_2.16.21.pdf

For further information contact:

Email: foundation@rheumatology.org

Rheumatology Future Physician Scientist Award

Purpose: The purpose of this pre-doctoral scholar award is to enhance the research training of promising students who are enrolled in a combined MD/PhD or DO/PhD dual-doctoral degree training program and who intend careers as physician-scientists. This grant mechanism aims to support the nation's top emerging physician scientists and promote their interest in investigative careers in rheumatology. This award will support dissertation research projects in scientific health-related fields relevant to the mission of the Rheumatology Research Foundation. The research training experience is expected to tangibly enhance the individuals' potential to develop into a productive, independent physician-scientist in the field of rheumatology.
Eligibility: The Foundation encourages applications from students early in the research training phase of their dual degree training so that they can substantively benefit from

the mentored research training opportunities. 1. Applicant must meet citizenship and other eligibility requirements as outlined in the Awards and Grants policies. 2. The applicant must have a baccalaureate degree, show evidence of high academic performance in the sciences, and commitment to a career as an independent physician-scientist. Applicants should demonstrate a strong interest in pursuing a career in rheumatology research. 3. This program is specifically designed to support combined, dual-degree training leading to award of both a health professional doctoral degree (MD, DO) that would make the awardee eligible for future training as a rheumatologist; and a research doctoral degree (PhD) from an accredited program. Thus, the applicant must be enrolled in an MD/PhD or DO/PhD program. The entirety of the award period must be devoted to full-time graduate research training leading to the doctoral research degree. This award will not support full-time clinical training during the years of the MD/PhD or DO/PhD program. Program-required preceptorships during graduate training are allowed. 4. To encourage timely completion of dual degree training, this award is generally not intended to support students after year 5 of their training program. Ideally, support will be for 2 years during years 3-6 of the dual degree program (after the initial 2 years of classwork but prior to the clinical rotations/ medical training). 5. The applicant must have identified a dissertation research project and a primary mentor. The primary mentor must be a faculty member actively engaged in basic, translational, clinical or health services research with a strong record of peer-reviewed research relevant to rheumatology. 6. The primary mentor must be a member of the American College of Rheumatology (ACR) at the time of the application and for the duration of the award.

Level of Study: Doctorate, Postgraduate, Professional development, Research
Type: Award
Value: Up to US$30,000 per year in direct costs (maximum US$60,000 over 2 years)
Length of Study: 2 years
Frequency: Annual
Country of Study: United States of America
Application Procedure: All applications must be submitted by 5 PM ET on the deadline day through ProposalCentral at www.proposalcentral.com/. Please refer www.rheumresearch.org/file/FY23-Rheumatology-Future-Physician-Scientist-Award.pdf
Closing Date: 1 December
Additional Information: For more details: www.rheumresearch.org/file/FY23-Rheumatology-Future-Physician-Scientist-Award.pdf

For further information contact:

Email: foundation@rheumatology.org

R

Scientist Development Award

Purpose: This award is designed for individuals in the early stages of their career (typically Fellows) or those without significant prior research experience who plan to embark on careers in rheumatic diseases. The purpose of this award is to provide support for a structured research training program for rheumatologists or health professionals in the field of rheumatology.

Eligibility: 1. Applicant must meet citizenship and other eligibility requirements as outlined in the Awards and Grants policies. 2. Applicant must be an ACR or ARP member at the time of submission and for the duration of the award. For ACR members must meet the following criteria: a. Have earned a DO, MD, or degree and by the start of the award term have completed at least one year of training in an ACGME accredited rheumatology training program. b. Individuals more than 4 years from the beginning of fellowship (or 5 years for pediatric rheumatologists) at the time of award start date may not apply. c. MDs and DOs who are not licensed to perform clinical care may not apply. For ARP members must meet the following criteria a. Have earned a PhD, DSc, or equivalent doctoral degree. b. Must be within 3 years of terminal degree at the time of award start date. 3. The Foundation does NOT currently support non-MD/DO scientists working on basic science projects. 4. Applicant must be affiliated with an accredited graduate or medical school. 5. Applicant must be able to commit a minimum of 75 percent full-time professional effort to research, academic career development, and other research related activities. Candidates may not spend more than 25 percent in clinical and/or teaching activities. It is expected that about 50 percent full-time professional effort will be spent on the Foundation funded project. 6. Receive acceptance by a mentor who will oversee the training and research experience. 7. Former or current recipients of research grants (at the K level or higher, including institutional K) and past awardees of this or equivalent Foundation grants are NOT eligible to apply. 8. Applicants may not apply for the Investigator Award in the same funding cycle. 9. Individuals may not apply for more than one Scientist Development Award per funding cycle. 10. Investigators interested in using data from the ACR's RISE registry as part of their proposed research project need to get their data use request approved before applying for funding. Please visit RISE for Research (www.rheumatology.org/I-Am-A/Rheumatologist/RISE-Registry/RISE-for-Research) for more information on RISE data. RISE data requests should be submitted at least 2 months prior to the Foundation's application deadline.

Level of Study: Professional development
Type: Award
Value: Up to US$125,000 for the first 2 years (up to US$50,000 for year 1 and up to US$75,000 for year 2), competitive renewal for year 3 up to US$100,000.

Length of Study: 3 Years
Frequency: Annual
Country of Study: United States of America
Application Procedure: All applications must be submitted by 5 PM ET on the deadline day through ProposalCentral at www.proposalcentral.com/. Please refer www.rheumresearch.org/file/FY23-Scientist-Development-Award_2.16.21.pdf
Closing Date: 1 June
Funding: Foundation
Contributor: Rheumatology Research Foundation
Additional Information: For more information: www.rheumresearch.org/career-development-research-awards. www.rheumresearch.org/file/FY23-Scientist-Development-Award_2.16.21.pdf

For further information contact:

Email: foundation@rheumatology.org

Rhode Island Foundation

One Union Station, Providence, RI 02903, United States of America.

Tel: (1) 401 274 4564
Email: info@rifoundation.org
Website: rifoundation.org/

The Foundation was organized at the Rhode Island Hospital Trust Co. in June 1916 by a small group of prominent Rhode Islanders. For more than 100 years, the Rhode Island Foundation has been dedicated to improving the lives of Rhode Islanders. We partner with generous individuals, families, organizations, and corporations that share our commitment to the state, as well as with non-profit organizations that provide the "boots-on-the-ground" services that make Rhode Island a better place to live, work, and play.

AAA Northeast Scholarship

Purpose: The scholarship program provides financial assistance to children and legal dependents of current employees of AAA Northeast who have been employed full-time for at least one year at the time of application (initial or renewal).

Eligibility: Are the child and legal dependent of a current AAA Northeast employee who has been employed full-time for at least one year at the time of application. Are a high school senior or first, second, or third-year student at an accredited post-secondary institution enrolling full-time in an associate or bachelor's degree program. If a high-school senior, you must enroll in and attend such institution in the first academic term following graduation from high school. Demonstrate academic achievement as evidenced by a GPA of at least 2.5 on a 4.0 scale (or its equivalent). Demonstrate unmet financial need. Demonstrate good character and potential as evidenced by the application responses and a required essay of up to 300 words.

Type: Scholarship
Value: US$2,500
Frequency: Annual
Country of Study: Any country
No. of awards offered: 12
Closing Date: 15 April
Additional Information: rifoundation.org/grants-scholar ships/browse-scholarships/aaa-northeast-scholarship

For further information contact:

1 Union Station, Providence, RI 02903, United States of America.

Tel: (1) 401 274 4564

Carter Roger Williams Scholarship

Purpose: This annual scholarship program is intended to inspire students and their parents to think big about what's possible for their future. Students who appreciate and embody Roger Williams's values and legacy are encouraged to apply.
Eligibility: Currently reside in Rhode Island; Be current seniors at any high school (public, independent, or private) in Rhode Island; and Have been accepted by an accredited post-secondary institution (by the date of the award).
Type: Scholarship
Value: US$20,000
Frequency: Annual
Country of Study: Any country
Closing Date: 28 February
Additional Information: rifoundation.org/grants-scholar ships/browse-scholarships/carterscholarship

For further information contact:

1 Union Station, Providence, RI 02903, United States of America.

Tel: (1) 401 274 4564

Cataract Fire Company #2 Scholarship

Purpose: This scholarship is open to residents of Warwick, Rhode Island, who are entering their first year of a two-year, four-year, or vocational/technical postsecondary institution.
Eligibility: 1. Must be a High school seniors. 2. Must be a Warwick, Rhode Island residents. 3. Academic excellence not necessary, preference given to students not in the top 10% of their graduating class. 4. Students must demonstrate financial need.
Level of Study: Graduate
Type: Scholarship
Value: US$1,500 - US$2,000; non-renewable
Frequency: Annual
Country of Study: United States of America
Application Procedure: Applications must be submitted through Rhode Island Foundation Online Application System.
Closing Date: 11 April
Funding: Foundation
Additional Information: rifoundation.org/grants-scholarships/browse-scholarships#cataract-fire-company-2-scholarship

For further information contact:

1 Union Station, Providence, RI 02903, United States of America.

Tel: (1) 401 427 4028
Email: kriley@rifoundation.org

Major Jeremiah P. Murphy Scholarship

Purpose: This scholarship is open to children of active, retired, or deceased Providence (RI) police officers who are or will be attending postsecondary institutions offering two-year associate's or four-year college degree
Eligibility: 1. Children of active, retired, or deceased Providence police officers. 2. Attending post-secondary institutions offering two-year associate or four-year college degree.
Type: Scholarship
Value: US$1,000 - US$2,500; renewable
Frequency: Annual
Country of Study: United States of America
Application Procedure: Applications must be submitted through Rhode Island Foundation Online Application System.
Closing Date: 4 April
Additional Information: www.rifoundation.org/grants-scholarships/browse-scholarships?l=54&s=1&q=Jeremiah+

For further information contact:

1 Union Station, Providence, RI 02903, United States of America.

Tel: (1) 401 427 4028
Email: kriley@rifoundation.org

Michael P. Metcalf Memorial Fund and Christine T. Grinavic Adventurer

Purpose: These funds provide grants to college students to subsidize experiences intended to broaden their perspective and enhance personal growth.
Eligibility: Applications will be accepted from college freshmen, sophomores, juniors, and seniors who are legal residents of Rhode Island.
Type: Scholarship
Value: US$2,000 to US$5,000
Country of Study: Any country
Closing Date: 22 February
Additional Information: rifoundation.org/grants-scholarships/browse-scholarships/metcalf-memorial-fund-and-grinavic-adventurers-fund

For further information contact:

1 Union Station, Providence, RI 02903, United States of America.

Tel: (1) 401 274 4564

Nursing Scholarships

Purpose: The Foundation awards scholarships from five nursing funds each year. One application may be used to apply for all five programs, as long as an applicant qualifies for at least one of the programs described below.
Eligibility: To be eligible you must be either a Rhode Island resident or attending a nursing program in Rhode Island.
Type: Scholarship
Value: US$500 to US$5000
Country of Study: Any country
Closing Date: 18 April
Additional Information: rifoundation.org/grants-scholarships/browse-scholarships/nursing-scholarships

For further information contact:

1 Union Station, Providence, RI 02903, United States of America.

Tel: (1) 401 274 4564

Rhodes College

2000 North Parkway, Memphis, TN 38112, United States of America.

Tel: (1) 901 843 3000
Email: adminfo@rhodes.edu
Website: www.rhodes.edu/

Rhodes College was founded in 1848 in Clarksville, Tennessee. Rhodes College aspires to graduate students with a life-long passion for learning, a compassion for others, and the ability to translate academic study and personal concern into effective leadership and action in their communities and the world.

Emerson National Hunger Fellows Program

Purpose: The Emerson Hunger Fellow Program is a social justice program that trains, inspires, and sustains leaders.
Eligibility: US citizen or permanent resident; BA or equivalent by beginning of grant period, language proficiency
Type: Scholarship
Value: US$16,000 annual living allowance; Health insurance; Travel expenses; Housing during field placement; US$3,500 end of service award; US$4,000 housing subsidy in DC; Relocation subsidies.
Frequency: Annual
Country of Study: Any country
Closing Date: 14 January
Additional Information: www.rhodes.edu/academics/postgraduate-scholarships/scholarship-opportunities#Carnegie

For further information contact:

Rhodes College, 2000 North Parkway, Memphis, TN 38112, United States of America.

Tel: (1) 800 844 5969

Lilly Fellows Program in the Humanities and the Arts

Subjects: Eligible disciplines are: art; art history; creative writing; history; interdisciplinary studies; languages and literature; music; music history; philosophy; religion; rhetoric; theater history; theater arts, and theology.

Purpose: Nominees must have earned or be in the process of earning a baccalaureate degree from a LFP network institution.
Eligibility: Eligibility is open to seniors graduating during the current academic year, or to anyone having received a baccalaureate from a network institution within the last five years. Nominees must be U.S. Citizens
Type: Fellowship
Value: US$3,000 stipend
Length of Study: 5 Years
Frequency: Annual
Country of Study: Any country
Closing Date: 6 October
Additional Information: www.rhodes.edu/academics/postgraduate-scholarships/scholarship-opportunities#Fulbright

For further information contact:

Rhodes College, 2000 North Parkway, Memphis, TN 38112, United States of America.

Tel: (1) 800 844 5969

Watson Fellowship

Purpose: To offer college graduates a year of independent study and travel outside the United States
Eligibility: Candidates must be a graduating senior.
Type: Fellowship
Value: US$36,000
Length of Study: 1 year
Frequency: Annual
Country of Study: Any country
Application Procedure: 1. Ensure eligibility. 2. Meet with your campus advisor. 3. Complete the application including a. Your Personal Statement - What has convinced you to apply for the Watson? What do you hope to benefit from the year? b. Your Project Proposal - Your project must sustain your interest amidst the highs and lows of a year in unfamiliar places. What is your plan for the 12-month period? What opportunities and challenges are unique to your project? 4. 2 Recommendations. 5. Transcript. 6. Complete the campus selection process.
Closing Date: 4 October
Contributor: Thomas J. Watson Foundation
Additional Information: www.rhodes.edu/academics/experiential-and-applied-learning/postgraduate-scholarships/internal-and-national-deadlines

For further information contact:

2000 North Pkwy, Memphis, TN 38112, United States of America.

Tel: (1) 901 843 3249
Email: saxer@rhodes.edu

Rhodes Trust

Rhodes House, South Parks Road, Oxford OX1 3RG, United Kingdom.

Tel: (44) 1865 270901
Email: admin@rhodeshouse.ox.ac.uk
Website: www.rhodeshouse.ox.ac.uk/
Contact: Porters' Lodge

The Rhodes Trust, based at the University of Oxford, brings together and develops exceptional people from all over the world, and in all fields of study, who are impatient with the way things are and have the courage to act. The Rhodes Trust is an educational charity which supports exceptional students from around the world to study at the University of Oxford.

Rhodes Scholarship

Purpose: Rhodes Scholarships are the oldest and perhaps most prestigious international scholarship programme in the world, enabling outstanding young people from around the world to undertake full-time postgraduate study at the University of Oxford.
Eligibility: The broad eligibility criteria of the Rhodes Scholarship; definitive eligibility criteria are listed in the relevant Information for Candidates document for your country/region. www.rhodeshouse.ox.ac.uk/scholarships/application-overview/#number-1.
Level of Study: Postgraduate
Type: Scholarship
Length of Study: 2 year
Frequency: Annual
Country of Study: United Kingdom
Application Procedure: Apply online. Please visit website www.rhodeshouse.ox.ac.uk/scholarships/application-overview/.
No. of awards offered: 100
Funding: Trusts
Additional Information: For more information: www.rhodeshouse.ox.ac.uk/scholarships/the-rhodes-scholarship/

For further information contact:

Email: scholarship.queries@rhodeshouse.ox.ac.uk

Rhodes University

PO Box 94, Makhanda, Eastern Cape 6140, South Africa.

Tel:	(27) 46 603 8111
Email:	communications@ru.ac.za
Website:	www.ru.ac.za/
Contact:	John Gillam, Manager

Founded in 1904, the University has a well-established reputation for academic excellence. With just over 8200 students, Rhodes is a small University, which enjoys the distinction of having among the best undergraduate pass and graduation rates in South Africa, outstanding postgraduate success rates, and the best research output per academic staff member.

Andrew W. Mellon Foundation Masters & Doctoral Scholarships

Purpose: The focus of Dr Thando Njovane's project is History, Memory and Trauma in African Fiction. Working within this interdisciplinary lense, the project investigates how works of fiction may help us theorise trauma, history and memory from an African perspective. This may include comparative studies with other postcolonial, post-conflict and/or African-American fictions in which questions of race and/or embodiment feature prominently.
Eligibility: Preference will be given to designated groups. Honours degree in English literature/Literary Studies for MA applicants, and MA in English literature/Literary Studies for PhD applicants (candidates must have studied or show a keen interest in African literature or comparative postcolonial literature). Candidates may select to work on either the short story, novels or poetry.
Level of Study: Masters Degree, Postdoctorate
Type: Scholarship
Value: MA scholarship (two years): R105,000 per annum PhD scholarship (three years): R135,000 per annum
Country of Study: Any country
Closing Date: 5 November
Contributor: Dr Thando Njovane, Department of Literary Studies in English, Rhodes University, Makhanda
Additional Information: www.ru.ac.za/researchgateway/postgraduates/funding/internal/

For further information contact:

PO Box 94 Makhanda (Grahamstown) 6140 Eastern Cape, South Africa.

Tel: (27) 46 603 8111

Global Partnership Network Masters Scholarships

Subjects: The politics of NGO work; Post-development thinking and Africa; and/or Alternative knowledge production about Africa.
Purpose: The Global Partnership Network (GPN) funds research on development cooperation, the global economy, and knowledge production.
Eligibility: In line with the GPN scholarship requirements, preference will be given to candidates from countries in the Global South (including but not limited to South Africa)
Type: Scholarship
Value: R100 000.00 per annum
Length of Study: Two years
Frequency: Annual
Country of Study: Any country
Closing Date: 30 September
Additional Information: www.ru.ac.za/researchgateway/postgraduates/funding/internal/

For further information contact:

Drosty Rd, Grahamstown, Makhanda, 6139, South Africa.

Tel:	(27) 46 603 8111
Email:	s.matthews@ru.ac.za or pgfunding@ru.ac.za

GUS LIPSCHITZ BURSARY

Purpose: This Bursary was established in 2021 by the family of the late Gustav Lipschitz. He was a graduate of Rhodes University (BCom 1941 (majoring in Accounting an Economics) and MCom Economics 1946). He had a strong belief in education and this bursary is established in his memory.
Eligibility: Acceptance for postgraduate course (full-time in attendance) in Economics at Rhodes University, proven financial need and academic merit.
Type: Bursary
Value: R130,000
Length of Study: Maximum of two years.
Frequency: Annual
Country of Study: Any country
Closing Date: 30 September
Additional Information: www.ru.ac.za/researchgateway/postgraduates/funding/internal/

For further information contact:

PO Box 94 Makhanda (Grahamstown) 6140 Eastern Cape, South Africa.

Tel: (27) 46 603 8111

Guy Butler Research Award

Subjects: English Language, English Literature, English-in-Education, South African English Drama, South African Journalism in English, Cultural studies focusing on English-related topics in Southern Africa and research in the area of English bilingualism, as an additional language.

Purpose: Rhodes University invites all students with a strong academic record (grades 70% and above) who intend pursuing full-time Postgraduate studies in 2023, to apply for the Guy Butler Research Award.

Eligibility: Applicants must pursue research in one of the following fields: English Language, English Literature, English-in-Education, South African English Drama, South African Journalism in English, Cultural studies focusing on English-related topics in Southern Africa and research in the area of English bilingualism, as an additional language. Period: Initially for one year, but renewable depending on satisfactory progress for a further year at Masters level and two years at Doctoral level. Tenable: Full-time attendance and registration at Rhodes University (Departments of English, English Languages and Linguistics and ISEA).

Level of Study: Doctorate, Masters Degree, Postgraduate
Type: Award
Value: Honours - R80,000; Masters - R90,000; Doctoral - R100,000
Frequency: Annual
Country of Study: Any country
Closing Date: 11 October
Additional Information: www.ru.ac.za/researchgateway/postgraduates/funding/internal/

For further information contact:

Drosty Rd, Grahamstown, Makhanda, 6139, South Africa.

Tel: (27) 46 603 8111
Email: pgfunding@ru.ac.za

Hobart Houghton Research Fellowship

Purpose: The Fellowship is intended to promote work relevant to the economic problems of the Eastern Cape, and which could contribute to the development of the region. Funding for the establishment of the Fellowship has been provided by Hobart Houghton's former students and associates and by the Liberty Life Educational Foundation.

Eligibility: Prospective Fellows should have had research experience, and hold at least a Masters degree in Economics or Agricultural Economics. They should have a sound knowledge of economic analysis and be capable of independent, innovative work. Candidates may either be established scholars (possibly on sabbatical leave) or young, promising economists.

Level of Study: Research
Type: Fellowship
Value: A typical package includes return airfare to Grahamstown, accommodation in university visitor's flats, plus a monthly cost of living stipend, all determined by the availability of funds and the background and status of the fellow. Limited funds will be available for travel and other research expenses
Length of Study: 6-8 weeks
Frequency: Annual
Study Establishment: Rhodes University, Grahamstown
Country of Study: South Africa
Application Procedure: The Hobart Houghton Fellowship Application Form should include a full statement of research interest.
Closing Date: 30 September
Funding: Foundation, Private
Contributor: Hobart Houghton's former students and associates and by the Liberty Life Educational Foundation
Additional Information: www.ru.ac.za/economics/hobarthoughtonresearchfellowship/

For further information contact:

Email: h.nel@ru.ac.za

Makabongwe Ndzwayiba Bursary

Purpose: This Bursary was established in 2012 by the Vice-Chancellor in memory of the late Makabongwe Ndzwayiba who passed away after a long and courageous battle against cancer. He spent three very successful years in Winchester House, Allan Webb Hall at Rhodes University. An outstanding student, a sub-warden and Community Engagement representative, Makabongwe was an inspiration to all who came to know him.

Eligibility: Acceptance for Honours in Economics, proven financial need, demonstrable hardships overcome and leadership in assisting in the "upliftment" of local communities.
Type: Bursary
Value: R37,000 per annum.
Frequency: Annual
Country of Study: Any country
Closing Date: 22 October
Additional Information: www.ru.ac.za/researchgateway/postgraduates/funding/internal/

For further information contact:

Drosty Rd, Grahamstown, Makhanda, 6139, South Africa.

R

Tel: (27) 46 603 8111
Email: pgfunding@ru.ac.za

Nicholas Iain Paumgarten Scholarship for Postgraduate Studies in Accounting

Purpose: This scholarship for Postgraduate studies in Accounting has been established through the generous support from the family of the late Nicholas Iain Paumgarten. His special interests were music, fishing, nature, spending time with family and friends.
Eligibility: South African citizenship, Full-time (in attendance) Honours, HDAC or Masters in Accounting Academic merit In addition, the Committee will consider the applicant's active participation in sporting, cultural and altruistic activities during their undergrad while still managing to maintain an academic record that makes them eligible for Honours/HDAC or Masters. Academic CV Certified copies of academic transcripts Motivation/Essay not exceeding 300 words explaining why you have chosen your field of study & what you propose to do in South Africa once qualified.
Level of Study: Postgraduate
Type: Scholarship
Value: R50 000-00
Length of Study: ONE year
Country of Study: Any country
Closing Date: 15 October
Additional Information: www.ru.ac.za/research/postgraduates/funding

For further information contact:

Drosty Rd, Grahamstown, Makhanda, 6139, South Africa.

Tel: (27) 46 603 8111
Email: pgfunding@ru.ac.za

Rhodes University African Studies Centre (RASC)

Subjects: All research projects must align to at least one of the following themes: (1) Moralities; (2) Knowledge; (3) Arts and Aesthetics; (4) Mobilities; (5) Affiliations; and (6) Learning.
Purpose: We are pleased to announce the launch of the RHODES UNIVERSITY AFRICAN STUDIES CENTRE (RASC) DOCTORAL SCHOLARSHIPS IN AFRICAN STUDIES.
Level of Study: Doctorate
Type: Scholarship

Value: R120,000
Study Establishment: African Studies
Country of Study: Any country
Closing Date: 19 November
Additional Information: For additional information about the Rhodes University African Studies Centre, visit our website: www.ru.ac.za/africanstudiescentre/

For further information contact:

Drosty Rd, Grahamstown, Makhanda, 6139, South Africa.

Tel: (27) 46 603 8111

Ruth First Scholarship

Purpose: The Ruth First Scholarship is intended to support candidates whose research is in the spirit of the life and work of Ruth First, whose research poses difficult social questions, and who are interested in linking knowledge and politics and scholarship and action.
Eligibility: All Doctoral and Masters candidates accepted at Rhodes University in the focus areas of this scholarship will be eligible to apply. South African and Mozambican black and women candidates will be particularly encouraged to apply.
Level of Study: Doctorate, Masters Degree
Type: Scholarship
Value: R120,000 per annum for PhD or R100,000 per annum for Masters.
Frequency: Annual
Study Establishment: Rhodes University, Grahamsdown
Country of Study: South Africa
Application Procedure: Ruth First Scholarship Application Process downloadable from www.ru.ac.za/researchgateway/postgraduates/funding/internal/. Submit a SINGLE PDF document clearly marked as your "surname_RFirst_Schol.pdf" no later than the closing date to pgfunding@ru.ac.za
Closing Date: 4 March
Funding: Private
Contributor: Donor and Investments
No. of awards given last year: 1
No. of applicants last year: 126
Additional Information: www.ru.ac.za/researchgateway/postgraduates/funding/internal/

For further information contact:

Jaine Roberts, South Africa.

Tel: (27) 46 603 8755
Email: j.roberts@ru.ac.za; pgfunding@ru.ac.za

Robert Wood Johnson Foundation

50 College Road East, Princeton, NJ 08540-6614, United States of America.

Tel: (1) 609 627 6000
Website: www.rwjf.org/

The Robert Wood Johnson Foundation (RWJF) is working alongside others to build a national Culture of Health. Our goal is to help raise the health of everyone in the United States to the level that a great nation deserves, by placing well-being at the center of every aspect of life. Since 1972, RWJF supported research and programs targeting some of America's most pressing health issues—from substance abuse to improving access to quality health care.

Clinical Scholars

Purpose: Clinical Scholars is a three-year, team-based program for a wide variety of health professionals in community, clinical, or academic settings. By the end of the program, fellows will have gained the skills they need to appraise, synthesize, use the best evidence to guide practice and inform policy in addressing complex health problems in their teams, organizations, and community

Eligibility: Clinical Scholars is a team-based program for a wide variety of health professionals in community, clinical, or academic settings (e.g., audiologists, clinical counselors, dentists, dieticians, nurses, nurse practitioners, nutritionists, occupational therapists, pharmacists, physical therapists, physicians, physician assistants, psychologists, social workers, speech therapists, veterinarians). The team must be sponsored by an applicant organization that will manage the award.

Level of Study: Masters Degree
Type: Scholarships
Value: Grant funds based on team size (from up to US$315,000 for a three-person to US$525,000 for a five-person team)
Length of Study: 3 Year
Country of Study: United States of America
Application Procedure: Application procedure furnised @ www.rwjf.org/en/library/funding-opportunities/2020/clinical-scholars.html
No. of awards offered: 35
Closing Date: 11 March
Additional Information: www.rwjf.org/en/library/funding-opportunities/2020/clinical-scholars.html

For further information contact:

Melissa Green, MPH, deputy director for Recruitment and Communications, United States of America.

Tel: (1) 919 843 3304
Email: clinical.scholars@unc.edu

Harold Amos Medical Faculty Development Program

Purpose: The Harold Amos Medical Faculty Development Program (AMFDP) offers four-year postdoctoral research awards to physicians, dentists, and nurses from historically marginalized backgrounds. Scholars should be committed to working toward eliminating health disparities by achieving senior rank in academic medicine, dentistry, or nursing.
Eligibility: Applicants must be physicians, dentists, or nurses who 1. are from historically marginalized backgrounds; 2. are U.S. citizens, permanent residents at the time of application, or individuals granted Deferred Action for Childhood Arrivals (DACA) status by the U.S. Citizenship and Immigration Services at the time of application (changes in federal policy or law may necessitate that we consider adjustments in eligibility and grant terms); 3. are completing or have completed their formal clinical training (we will give preference to those who have recently completed their formal clinical training or–in the case of nurses–their research doctorate); 4. are not related by blood or marriage to any Officer or Trustee of the Robert Wood Johnson Foundation, or a descendant of its founder, Robert Wood Johnson. 5. Federal, state, tribal, and local government employees who are not considered government officials under Section 4946 of the Internal Revenue Code are eligible to apply. 6. Physicians must be Board-eligible to apply for this program. A dental applicant must be a general dentist with a master's or a doctoral degree or have completed advanced dental education. Nurse applicants must be registered nurses with a research doctorate in nursing or a related discipline completed by the application deadline. 7. Detailed research plans and budgets for selected finalists must be submitted by the university, school of medicine, dentistry, nursing, or research institution with which the prospective scholar will be affiliated during the term of the fellowship. 8. The university, school, or research institution must meet the following criteria a. Be either a public entity or nonprofit organization that is tax-exempt under Section 501(c)(3) of the Internal Revenue Code and is not a private foundation or nonfunctionally integrated Type III supporting organization; b. Be based in the United States or its territories.
Level of Study: Doctorate, Postdoctorate
Type: Scholarships

R

Value: RWJF will fund up to 10 four-year awards of up to US$420,000 each. Scholars will receive an annual stipend of up to US$75,000 each, complemented by a US$30,000 annual grant to support research activities.

Length of Study: 4 Year

Country of Study: United States of America

Application Procedure: Apply online.

No. of awards offered: 10

Closing Date: 17 March

No. of awards given last year: 88

Additional Information: https://www.rwjf.org/en/library/funding-opportunities/2022/harold-amos-medical-faculty-development-program.html

For further information contact:

Harold Amos Medical Faculty Development Program, 340 W. 10th St., Suite FS5110, Indianapolis, IN 46202, United States of America.

Tel: (1) 317 278 0500

Email: amfdp@indiana.edu

Health Policy Research Scholars

Purpose: Health Policy Research Scholars (HPRS) is a four-year national leadership development program for full-time doctoral students from nonclinical, academic disciplines-who want to improve health, well-being, and equity; challenge long-standing, entrenched systems; exhibit new ways of working; and collaborate across disciplines and sectors.

Level of Study: Doctorate

Type: Scholarships

Value: Stipend of US$30,000 each per year paid to their home institutions, for up to four years or until they complete their doctoral program (whichever is sooner). Scholars will also be eligible for competitive dissertation grants of up to US$10,000 each, as well as competitive conference and research dissemination grants, awarded by the national program center directly to the scholars. Administrative fee Home institutions may include an administrative fee of US$1,000 per year, US$4,000 in total to the grant amount to cover the administrative costs of managing the award.

Country of Study: United States of America

Application Procedure: Apply online

No. of awards offered: 40

Closing Date: 17 March

Additional Information: www.rwjf.org/en/library/funding-opportunities/2021/health-policy-research-scholars.html

For further information contact:

Johns Hopkins Bloomberg School of Public Health, United States of America.

Tel: (1) 410 502 5530

Email: hprs@jhu.edu

Interdisciplinary Research Leaders

Purpose: Interdisciplinary Research Leaders (IRL) is a three-year national leadership development program that aims to foster and support new interdisciplinary, action-oriented research collaborations. Achieving health equity–especially for communities of color, those in low socioeconomic positions, and Native populations–is a core value of the program. The aim for the 2023 IRL program is to generate high-quality, community-engaged research useful for dismantling structural racism and improving health and health equity.

Eligibility: 1. Be at least 21 years old as of September 1. 2. Be a U.S. citizen, permanent resident, or individual granted Deferred Action for Childhood Arrivals (DACA) status by the U.S. Citizenship and Immigration Services at the time of application. As federal policy or laws change, we may need to consider adjustments in eligibility and grant terms.

Type: Fellowship

Value: 1. Stipend US$25,000 per fellow for each year of the three-year program, US$75,000 in total. An optional administrative fee of US$1,000 per year, US$3,000 in total, to cover the sponsoring organization's administrative costs of managing the grant will be available. 2. Research project grant US$125,000 for the specific research project that each team will carry out. 3. Travel expenses for all required program meetings and trainings will be paid directly by the national leadership program center or RWJF.

Length of Study: 3 Year

Country of Study: Any country

Application Procedure: For the cohort, we will select up to 15 teams of three midcareer individuals each (two researchers and a community partner) from diverse disciplinary backgrounds or scientific perspectives. Apply online.

No. of awards offered: 45

Closing Date: 5 May

Additional Information: The following individuals are not eligible to apply or be part of an Interdisciplinary Research Leaders team: 1. Federal, state, tribal and local government employees who are considered government officials under Section 4946 of the Internal Revenue Code. 2. Individual candidates who are related by blood or marriage to any Officer or Trustee of the Robert Wood Johnson Foundation, or be a descendant of its founder, Robert Wood Johnson. 3. Individuals who are receiving support from other research fellowships/traineeships; this includes NIH K award. For more details: www.rwjf.org/en/library/funding-opportunities/2021/interdisciplinary-research-leaders.html

For further information contact:

IRL National Program Center, United States of America.

Tel: (1) 844 210 9072
Email: researchleaders@umn.edu

Roberta Sykes Indigenous Education Foundation

100 Botany Road, Alexandria, NSW 2015, Australia.

Tel: (61) 2 9310 8402
Email: scholarships@aurorafoundation.com.au
Website: www.robertasykesfoundation.com/
Contact: The Roberta Sykes Indigenous Education Foundation

The Roberta Sykes Indigenous Education Foundation partners with the Aurora Education Foundation to support Aboriginal and Torres Strait Islander students to undertake postgraduate study abroad. This support falls under two broad categories: Scholarships to study full time postgraduate programs at recognised overseas universities and Bursaries to study Short Executive Programs at leading overseas academic institutions.

Roberta Sykes Bursary

Purpose: The Roberta Sykes Indigenous Education Foundation provides partial funding for Indigenous Australians to undertake short, executive education courses at leading overseas academic institutions.

Eligibility: Applicants must 1. Be of Aboriginal or Torres Strait Islander descent, identify as Aboriginal and/or Torres Strait Islander and be accepted as such by the community in which they live or have lived. 2. Provide confirmation of Aboriginal or Torres Strait Islander descent through a signed statement (including common seal) from the Aboriginal or Torres Strait Islander Heritage Association, Aboriginal or Torres Strait Islander Corporation or Land Council of your ancestors. If applicable, candidates are encouraged to provide a written statement from the Aboriginal or Torres Strait Islander Heritage Association, Aboriginal or Torres Strait Islander Corporation or Land Council of the community in

which they live or have lived and/or are connected to. 3. Be accepted into an executive program at a recognised overseas academic institution. 4. Be able to demonstrate that their studies will be of benefit to their community upon their return to Australia.

Type: Bursary
Value: The value of the Bursary is up to AU$20,000
Country of Study: Australia
Application Procedure: To apply you will need to submit 1. A completed application form. Please contact scholarships@aurorafoundation.com.au for an application form. 2. A personal statement outlining mentioned in website. 3. Your curriculum vitae. 4. Academic transcript/s if you completed your studies in the last 6 years. 5. Three written references, which highlight your capabilities, your past contribution to the Indigenous community, and the perceived future benefit of doing your chosen course. These should be a. One academic/professional; b. One from an Elder in your community, (which should highlight your connection to the community); c. One personal. 6. A written statement confirming Aboriginal or Torres Strait Islander heritage. In addition, applicants are required to provide a signed statement in writing from the Aboriginal Heritage Association, Aboriginal Corporation or Land Council of the community in which they live or have lived, also confirming the above. 7. A passport sized photo. 8. A financial budget. Please check your application thoroughly as any errors may delay the process. You can send your application to the Scholarships Team at Aurora.
Closing Date: 8 November
Additional Information: www.robertasykesfoundation.com/roberta-sykes-bursary.html

For further information contact:

International Scholarships Coordinator, Aurora Education Foundation, Australia.

Email: scholarships@aurorafoundation.com.au

Roberta Sykes Scholarship

Purpose: The Roberta Sykes Scholarship provides partial funding to Aboriginal and/or Torres Strait Islander postgraduate students who wish to undertake studies at recognised overseas universities.

Eligibility: Applicants must 1. Usually have an undergraduate degree with a strong academic record. 2. Be accepted into a postgraduate coursework or research degree at a recognised overseas university. 3. Be of Aboriginal and/or Torres Strait Islander descent, identify as Aboriginal and/or Torres Strait Islander and be accepted as such by the community in which they live or have lived. 4. Be able to demonstrate that

R

alongside a Roberta Sykes Scholarship, they will have sufficient funds to support themselves during the course of their postgraduate degree (such as through another scholarship, private sponsorship or personal funds). 5. Be able to demonstrate that their studies will be of benefit to their community upon their return to Australia. 6. Applications for part-time study will be considered in special circumstances.

Type: Scholarship

Value: The value of the Scholarship is up to AU$30,000 per year

Country of Study: Australia

Application Procedure: Applicants need to apply directly to the overseas academic institution first, and then to the Trust for a Scholarship. To apply, you will need to submit 1. A completed application form downloadable from website. 2. A personal statement outlining a. Why you want to do the course. b. How you identify with the Aboriginal and/or Torres Strait Islander community in which you live or have lived and past contributions you have made within the community. c. Ways in which undertaking your chosen course will benefit the Aboriginal and/or Torres Strait Islander community, and future contributions you plan to make to the Aboriginal and/or Torres Strait Islander community (and wider community) following completion of the course. 3. Your curriculum vitae. 4. Academic transcript(s). 5. Four written references, which highlight you capabilities, your past contribution to the Indigenous community, and the perceived future benefit of doing your chosen course. These should be a. Two academic; b. One from and Elder in your community (which should highlight your connection to the community); c. One personal. 6. Confirmation of Aboriginal or Torres Strait Islander descent through a signed statement (including common seal) from and Aboriginal or Torres Strait Islander Heritage Association, Aboriginal or Torres Strait Islander Corporation or Land Council .

Closing Date: 8 November

Additional Information: www.robertasykesfoundation.com/roberta-sykes-scholarship.html

For further information contact:

Email: scholarships@aurorafoundation.com.au

The Annual Aurora Indigenous Scholars International Study Tour

Purpose: The Study Tour takes place from around mid-October to the end of November each year, taking Aboriginal and/or Torres Strait Islander university students and graduates to visit leading universities in the US and the UK. The Study Tour not only offers invaluable opportunities for students to gain insight into the realities of undertaking postgraduate study at these leading institutions but also provides the opportunity to travel with a group of like-minded students. The Study Tour involves meetings with key academics and administrators at each university, as well as current students in the areas of the participants' interest.

Eligibility: Applicants must 1. Identify as Aboriginal and/or Torres Strait Islander; 2. Have graduated from your first degree, or have completed at least two years of your undergraduate degree; 3. Have a distinction average or an Honours degree; 4. Have a strong interest in postgraduate study overseas; 5. Be willing to act as an ambassador of the program while overseas and on your return to Australia, committing to 5 Outreach events with school and university students.

Level of Study: Postgraduate

Type: Scholarship

Value: Costs associated with travel, accommodation and meals are covered

Frequency: Annual

Country of Study: Australia

Application Procedure: You can apply for this scholarship internally through this Portal and need to attach the following documents to your application 1. Personal Statement/Cover letter, explaining your background, career aspirations and reasons for wanting to go on the Study Tour. 2. A Curriculum Vitae. 3. An official Academic Transcript of all university results (including mid-year results, if available). 4. Confirmation of Aboriginal and/or Torres Strait Islander descent through a signed statement (including common seal) from a Aboriginal or Torres Strait Islander Heritage Association, Aboriginal or Torres Strait Islander Corporation or Land Council. 5. A high-resolution headshot. 6. Copy of your passport bio-data page. You will need to arrange for three written references (two of which should be academic references) to be forwarded by your referees directly to scholarships@aurorafoundation.com.au. For more information please refer to the reference criteria document (attached as a pdf on downloads section).

Closing Date: May

Additional Information: For further information on the Study Tour, please visit the Aurora Education Foundation website www.robertasykesfoundation.com/aurora-indigenous-scholars-international-study-tour.html

For further information contact:

Aurora Scholarships Team, Australia.

Email: scholarships@aurorafoundation.com.au

The Roberta Sykes Harvard Club Scholarship

Purpose: The purpose of the award is to promote fellowship amongst alumni and to assist Australians wishing to study at Harvard.

Eligibility: For eligibility details, please visit www.robertasy kesfoundation.com/roberta-sykes-scholarships.html. Usually have an undergraduate degree with a strong academic record; Be accepted into a postgraduate coursework or research degree at a recognised overseas university; Be of Aboriginal and/or Torres Strait Islander descent, identify as Aboriginal and/or Torres Strait Islander and be accepted as such by the community in which they live or have lived; Be able to demonstrate that alongside a Roberta Sykes Scholarship, they will have sufficient funds to support themselves during the course of their postgraduate degree (such as through another scholarship, private sponsorship or personal funds); Be able to demonstrate that their studies will be of benefit to their community upon their return to Australia

Type: Scholarship

Value: The Scholarship is valued at approximately AU$14,000 and includes 1. All tuition fees for one of two Harvard Graduate School of Education programs - either 'Improving Schools The Art of Leadership' or 'Leadership An Evolving Vision' 2. Travel insurance; 3. Economy return airfares ex-your nearest capital city; and 4. Accommodation for the duration of the course.

Country of Study: Australia

Application Procedure: Apply online.

Contributor: Roberta Sykes Harvard Club

Additional Information: For further details www.robertasy kesfoundation.com/harvard-club-roberta-sykes-scholarship. html

For further information contact:

Scholarships Manager, Aurora Education Foundation, Australia.

Tel: (61) 2 9310 8403
Email: scholarships@aurorafoundation.com.au

Rotterdam School of Management Erasmus University

Burgemeester Oudlaan 50, Rotterdam, NL-3062 PA, The Netherlands.

Tel: (31) 10 408 2222
Email: info@rsm.nl
Website: www.rsm.nl/
Contact: Denise Chasney van Dijk, Financial Aid Manager

Rotterdam School of Management, Erasmus University (RSM) has firmly established its reputation over almost 50 years as one of Europe's most international and innovative business schools. RSM's primary focus is on developing business leaders with international careers who can become a force for positive change by carrying their innovative mindset into a sustainable future. Our first-class portfolio of bachelor, master, MBA, PhD and executive programmes encourage people to become critical, creative, caring and collaborative thinkers and doers.

Rotterdam School of Management Master of Business Administration Asia & Australia Regional Scholarship

Purpose: To assist candidates from the Asia & Australasia Region in financing their MBA study in the Netherlands

Eligibility: The scholarship is open to high potential candidates who are a citizen or hold permanent residence status in one of the following listed countries Australia, Bangladesh, Bhutan, Brunei, Burma, Cambodia, China, Fiji, Hong Kong, India, Indonesia, Japan, Kiribati, Laos, Macau, Malaysia, Micronesia, Mongolia, Nepal, New Zealand, Palau, Papua New Guinea, Philippines, Samoa, Singapore, Solomon Islands, Sri Lanka, Thailand, Timor-Leste, Tonga, Tuvalu, Vietnam, Yemen

Level of Study: MBA

Type: Scholarship

Value: 20% tuition fee waiver

Length of Study: 12 months

Frequency: Annual

Study Establishment: Erasmus University

Country of Study: Netherlands

Application Procedure: Complete application form to be considered

No. of awards offered: 36

Closing Date: 30 September

Funding: Private

Contributor: RSM Erasmus University

No. of awards given last year: 1

No. of applicants last year: 36

Additional Information: Eligible to nationals of Asia and Australasia www.robertasykesfoundation.com/harvard-club-roberta-sykes-scholarship.html

Rotterdam School of Management, Erasmus Graduate School of Business

Burgemeester Oudlaan 50, Rotterdam, NL-3062 PA, The Netherlands.

Tel: (31) 10 408 2222
Email: info@rsm.nl
Website: www.rsm.nl/

R

Rotterdam School of Management, Erasmus University (RSM) has firmly established its reputation over almost 50 years as one of Europe's most international and innovative business schools. RSM's primary focus is on developing business leaders with international careers who can become a force for positive change by carrying their innovative mindset into a sustainable future. Our first-class portfolio of bachelor, master, MBA, PhD and executive programmes encourage people to become critical, creative, caring and collaborative thinkers and doers.

Erasmus Trustfonds Scholarship

Purpose: The Erasmus Trustfonds was founded to support research and education projects, organised by the Erasmus University Rotterdam (EUR). The scholarship is aimed at excellent EU/EEA master's students. One Erasmus Trustfonds Scholarship has been allotted for RSM.

Eligibility: Your nationality is EEA. You are a prospective student, starting your studies in the academic year 2023/2024; You are applying for a full-time master's programme at RSM; You meet the specific requirements of the programme you are applying for; You do not already have a degree from an educational institution in the Netherlands (excluding exchange programmes in the Netherlands).

Type: Scholarship

Value: € 15,000

Length of Study: 12 months

Country of Study: Any country

Closing Date: 1 March

Additional Information: www.rsm.nl/master/msc-programmes/scholarships/scholarships/?tx_rsmfinancialaid%5Bidentifier%5D=614&cHash=2dcbcdb4ed6ab17200e76f0f57825f4e

For further information contact:

Burgemeester Oudlaan 50, NL-3062 PA Rotterdam, Netherlands.

Tel: (31) 10 408 2222

Holland Government Scholarship/Upcoming Year for School of Management

Purpose: The Erasmus University Holland Scholarship is financed by the Dutch Ministry of Education, Culture and Science as well as Rotterdam School of Management, Erasmus University. This scholarship is meant for international students from outside the European Economic Area (EEA) who want to do their master's at RSM.

Eligibility: To be eligible, fulfill the following 1. Your nationality is non-EEA; 2. You are a prospective student, starting your studies in the current academic year; 3. You are applying for a full-time master's programme at RSM; 4. You meet the specific requirements of the programme you are applying for; 5. You do not have a degree from an educational institution in the Netherlands (excluding exchange programmes in the Netherlands).

Level of Study: Masters Degree

Type: Scholarship

Value: €10,000

Length of Study: 12 months

Frequency: Annual

Country of Study: Any country

Application Procedure: First step is to register for the Master programme in Studielink. Once you have registered yourself, you will receive a link to our Online Application Form (OLAF). Required documents 1. A scholarship application letter in OLAF of maximum 1 A4 size page, including the following information a. an explanation why you would need a scholarship, comprising a description of your current financial situation; b. an explanation why you would deserve a scholarship, comprising a description of academic excellence and if applicable other merits. 2. A budget plan using this template www.rsm.nl/fileadmin/Images_NEW/Master/Admissions/Budget_Plan_RSM_MSc.pdf. 3. If applicable certified copies of other scholarships granted. Please note that we can only take a scholarship application into consideration if it is complete and meets all of the requirements. This includes a GMAT score, English language test results, a scholarship application letter and a budget plan.

Closing Date: 1 February

Funding: Government, Private

Contributor: The Dutch Ministry of Education, Culture and Science

Additional Information: The scholarship amount will be paid in 10 installments after you have paid the full tuition fee amount. www.rsm.nl/master/msc-programmes/scholarships/scholarships/?tx_rsmfinancialaid%5Bidentifier%5D=607&cHash=4f21fd9a7db8ae5e813341cceef75da9

For further information contact:

Burgemeester Oudlaan 50, NL-3062 PA Rotterdam, Netherlands.

Tel: (31) 10 408 2222
Email: scholarships@rsm.nl

Royal Academy of Engineering

Prince Philip House, 3 Carlton House Terrace, London SW1Y 5DG, United Kingdom.

Tel: (44) 20 7766 0600
Email: research@raeng.org.uk
Website: www.raeng.org.uk/
Contact: Dr Mark Bambury, Scheme Manager

The Royal Academy of Engineering is a charity that harnesses the power of engineering to build a sustainable society and an inclusive economy that works for everyone. In collaboration with our Fellows and partners, we're growing talent and developing skills for the future, driving innovation and building global partnerships, and influencing policy and engaging the public.

ExxonMobil Excellence in Teaching Awards

Purpose: To encourage able young engineering and Earth science lecturers to remain in the education sector in their early years
Eligibility: Open to well-qualified graduates, preferably with industrial experience and full-time lecturing posts at Institutes of Higher Education in the United Kingdom. Applicants should have been in their current posts for at least 1 year. The post must include the teaching of chemical, petroleum or mechanical engineering to undergraduates through courses that are accredited for registration with professional bodies for qualifications such as chartered engineer. For applicants whose career path has been graduation at the age of 22 years, followed by academic or industrial posts, the age limit is generally 32 years (at the closing date). Older candidates who have taken time out, e.g. for industrial experience, parenthood or voluntary service, will also be considered. Applicants should preferably be chartered engineers, or of equivalent professional status, or should be making progress towards this qualification
Level of Study: Postdoctorate
Type: Fellowship
Value: A range of benefits in addition to the £10,000 prize
Length of Study: 12 months
Frequency: Annual
Study Establishment: The applicant's current university in the United Kingdom
Country of Study: United Kingdom

Application Procedure: Applicants must complete an application form
Closing Date: 31 October
Funding: Commercial
Contributor: Exxon Mobile
Additional Information: A brochure is available on request. Enquiries about Exxon mobile university contacts should be sent via email and please see the website for further details

For further information contact:

Email: bowbricki@raeng.co.uk

Royal Academy Engineering Professional Development

Purpose: To ensure that the stills and knowledge of employees reflect the very latest in technological advances
Eligibility: Open to United Kingdom citizens with a degree or HND/HNC in engineering or a closely allied subject. OND/ONC or City and Guilds Full Technological Certificate or NVQ level III qualifications are acceptable provided the individual has substantial industrial experience
Level of Study: Professional development
Type: Grant
Value: £10,000 and £5,000 and prospective applicants should indicate for which level of award they are applying
Length of Study: 1 year
Frequency: Annual
Country of Study: United Kingdom
Application Procedure: For further information please contact the scheme manager lan Bowbrick at the Academy
Closing Date: 24 October

For further information contact:

Email: lan.bowbrick@raeng.org.uk

Royal Academy Sir Angus Paton Bursary

Purpose: To study water and environmental management
Eligibility: The bursary supports a suitably qualified engineer study a full-time Masters' degree course specifically related to water resources engineering or some other environmental technology
Level of Study: Postgraduate
Type: Bursary
Value: £8,000
Length of Study: 1 year

Frequency: Annual
Country of Study: United Kingdom
Application Procedure: For further information please contact the scheme manager Ian Bowbrick at the Academy
Funding: Private
Contributor: Sir Angus Paton
Additional Information: www.raeng.org.uk/publications/other/panasonic-trust-fellowships-guidance-notes

For further information contact:

Email: ian.bowbrick@raeng.org.uk

Royal Academy Sir Henry Royce Bursary

Eligibility: Open to qualified engineers enrolled on part-time modular Master's courses
Level of Study: Postgraduate
Type: Bursary
Value: £1,000
Length of Study: 1 year
Frequency: Annual
Country of Study: United Kingdom
Application Procedure: For further information please contact the scheme manager Ian Bowbrick at the Academy
Funding: Foundation
Contributor: Sir Henry Royce Memorial Foundation
Additional Information: Each awardee will receive a commemorative certificate and, on successful completion of their studies and award of the degree, a medal from the Sir Henry Royce Memorial Foundation www.raeng.org.uk/publications/other/issue-10

For further information contact:

Email: ian.bowbrick@raeng.org.uk

Sainsbury Management Fellowships

Purpose: The Sainsbury Management Fellowship scheme, funded by the Gatsby Charitable Foundation, enables engineers of high career potential to undertake full time MBA courses at major international business schools. The overall objective of the scheme is to improve the economic performance of UK engineering, manufacturing and construction businesses by providing a resource of highly-motivated engineers who have complemented their technical qualifications and skills with a first-class business education in an international environment.
Eligibility: 1. Applicants must have a confirmed place on a full-time MBA programme at one of the 14 eligible business schools 2. You may apply before a place is confirmed but will

not be invited to interview until a Business school place is confirmed 3. Applicants must have a first degree in an engineering, allied technology or science discipline, preferably a first or upper second class 4. Applicants must demonstrate a strong commitment to both UK engineering/business/industry and their respective engineering communities 5. Applicants must be a UK / EU / EEA citizen, normally domiciled in the United Kingdom 6. Applicants do not need to have Chartered Engineer status (or equivalent), however this qualification or progress towards it will be viewed favourably 7. Applicants would usually have 4-10 years professional experience post-degree
Level of Study: Postgraduate
Type: Fellowships
Value: £50,000 to cover tuition fee.
Frequency: Annual
Country of Study: United Kingdom
Application Procedure: Applying for a Sainsbury Management Fellowship, please contact Veronica Frincu
Closing Date: 4 April
Funding: Foundation
Contributor: Gatsby Charitable Foundation
Additional Information: For more details: www.raeng.org.uk/grants-prizes/grants/schemes-for-students/sainsbury-management-fellowship

For further information contact:

3 Carlton House Terrace, St. James's, London SW1Y 5DG, United Kingdom.

Tel: (44) 20 7766 0625
Email: veronica.frincu@raeng.org.uk

Royal Agricultural University

Royal Agricultural University, Gloucestershire, Cirencester GL7 6JS, United Kingdom.

Tel: (44) 1285 652531
Email: international@rau.ac.uk
Website: www.rau.ac.uk/

The Royal Agricultural University has always been at the forefront of agricultural education since 1845. Today, the RAU has more than 1,100 students studying agriculture, business, environment, equine science, farm management, food, real estate and rural land management. The University, which is based in Cirencester, Gloucestershire, prides itself on its links with industry and all courses are designed to meet the demands of the employment market for land-based expertise, both in the UK and worldwide.

Africa Land and Food Masters Fellowship

Eligibility: Fellowships are open to Africans from Sub-Saharan Africa who have experience in agriculture, agri-business, food or natural resource management; an interest in land reform; and a desire to make a strategic and sustainable contribution to Africa's development
Level of Study: Postgraduate
Type: Fellowship
Value: Since the Fellowship was launched in 2005, over £1,800,000 has been generously provided by the private sector, foundations and charities in support of the programme
Country of Study: United Kingdom
Application Procedure: Nationals from sub-Saharan Africa are invited to apply for a Fellowship
Closing Date: 31 October
Funding: International office

Royal College of Midwives

10-18 Union Street, London SE1 1SZ, United Kingdom.

Tel: (44) 207 3123 535
Email: info@rcm.org.uk
Website: www.rcm.org.uk/

The RCM was established in 1881 as the Matron's Aid or Trained Midwives Registration Society, but has existed under its present name since 1947. A charity for maintaining and improving standards of professional midwifery. The Trust conducts and commissions research, publishes information, provides education and training and organises conferences, campaigns and other events.

Royal College of Midwives Annual Midwifery Awards

Purpose: To recognize and celebrate innovation in midwifery practice, education and research
Eligibility: Applicants may be individuals or small groups but should meet the criteria of 1 of the 10 categories. Check the website for complete details
Level of Study: Postgraduate, Professional development, Research
Type: Award

Value: Varies (up to £20,000 in total)
Frequency: Annual
Application Procedure: Applicants must apply in writing or email to the address given below. The application must be accompanied by a 500-word description of the project. Short-listed candidates will be asked to attend an interview
No. of awards offered: 82
Closing Date: 1 November
Funding: Commercial
Contributor: Several
No. of awards given last year: 12 awards in 12 categories plus a midwife award
No. of applicants last year: 82

For further information contact:

Gothic House, 3 The Green, Richmond, Surrey TW9 1PL, United Kingdom.

Email: mail@chamberdunn.co.uk

Ruth Davies Research Bursary

Purpose: To promote and develop midwifery research and practice
Eligibility: Open to practicing midwives who are RCM members, who have basic knowledge, skills and understanding of the research process, have access to research support in their trust or Institutes of Higher Education and who have been in practice for 2 years or more
Level of Study: Doctorate, Graduate, Postdoctorate, Postgraduate, Predoctorate, Professional development, Research
Type: Bursary
Value: £5,000 per bursary
Length of Study: 1 year
Frequency: Annual
Country of Study: United Kingdom
Application Procedure: Applicants must submit a succinct curriculum vitae covering the previous 5 years, a research proposal of no more than 2,500 words and letters of support from both employers and academics who are familiar with the applicant's work
No. of awards offered: 4 shortlisted
Closing Date: 30 July
Funding: Commercial
Contributor: Bounty
No. of awards given last year: 3
No. of applicants last year: 4 shortlisted
Additional Information: www.pdfslide.net/documents/ruth-davies-bursary-2010.html,   www.rcm.org.uk/news-views/rcm-opinion/a-new-pathway-to-parenthood/

R

For further information contact:

Tel: (44) 20 7312 3463
Email: marlyn.gennace@rcm.org.uk

Royal College of Nursing Foundation

20 Cavendish Square, London W1G 0RN, United Kingdom.

Tel: (44) 20 7647 3645
Email: rcnfoundation@rcn.org.uk
Website: rcnfoundation.rcn.org.uk/
Contact: Ms Grants Officer Awards Officer

In 2010, the Royal College of Nursing (RCN) set up an independent charity – the RCN Foundation. The RCN Foundation is here to support every member of the nursing team as they care for patients and improve the UK's health and wellbeing.

Education Grants

Subjects: Nursing
Purpose: We offer two types of education grants professional development grants and student grants
Eligibility: Open to nurses, midwives and HCAs in United Kingdom
Level of Study: Doctorate, Postgraduate
Type: Award
Value: Up to £1,600 for professional development grants, £2,500 for student grants
Length of Study: Unrestricted
Frequency: Twice a year
Study Establishment: Unrestricted
Country of Study: United Kingdom
Application Procedure: Online rcnfoundation.rcn.org.uk/apply-for-funding/educational-grants
No. of awards offered: Up to 100
Closing Date: October
Funding: Private
No. of awards given last year: 69
No. of applicants last year: 771
Additional Information: rcnfoundation.rcn.org.uk/apply-for-funding/educational-grants

For further information contact:

Email: grants@rcnfoundation.org.uk

Mary Seacole Leadership and Development Awards

Purpose: To provide funding for a project, or other educational/development activity that benefits the health needs of people from black and minority ethnic communities
Eligibility: Open to nurses, midwives and health visitors in United Kingdom
Level of Study: Doctorate, Graduate, Postdoctorate, Postgraduate, Predoctorate, Professional development, Research
Type: Award
Value: Up to £12,500 for Mary Seacole Leadership Award and up to £6,250 for Mary Seacole Development Award
Length of Study: Unrestricted
Frequency: Annual
Study Establishment: Unrestricted
Country of Study: United Kingdom
Application Procedure: Applicants must send a stamped addressed envelope to the Royal College of Nursing (RCN) to obtain details and an application form
No. of awards offered: 16
Closing Date: 23 March
Funding: Government
Contributor: Department of Health
No. of awards given last year: 6
No. of applicants last year: 16
Additional Information: www.rcn.org.uk/professional-development/scholarships-and-bursaries/mary-seacole-awards

For further information contact:

Email: governance.support@rcn.org.uk

Royal College of Obstetricians and Gynaecologists (RCOG)

10-18 Union Street, London SE1 1SZ, United Kingdom.

Tel: (44) 20 7772 6200
Email: info@rcog.org.uk
Website: www.rcog.org.uk/

The Royal College of Obstetricians and Gynaecologists (RCOG) founded in 1929, works to improve health care for women everywhere, by setting standards for clinical practice, providing doctors with training and lifelong learning, and advocating for women's health care worldwide.

American Gyneocological Club/Gynaecological Visiting Society Fellowship

Purpose: Through generous funding from the American Gynaecological club and the Gynaecological Visiting Society of Great Britain, the RCOG can offer to an individual to visit and gain knowledge from a specific centre offering new techniques of clinical management within O&G.

Eligibility: This award is open to Trainees in the UK and Republic of Ireland and their equivalents in the US in alternating years. For the current year, the award is only open to applicants from the UK and Republic of Ireland. The award may only be used for the purpose outlined in your original application. Travel must take place within 12 months of the award being made.

Type: Fellowship
Value: Up to £1,200
Frequency: Annual
Country of Study: Any country
Application Procedure: Please complete the online application via Oxford Abstracts app.oxfordabstracts.com/login?redirect=/stages/2098/submitter. This application is hosted by Oxford Abstracts platform. Please register for an account using your email address. For further guidance on how to submit your application, please see Oxford Abstracts' guidance on making a submission oxfordabstracts.freshdesk.com/support/solutions/articles/8000072762-making-a-submission.
Closing Date: 30 April
Additional Information: www.rcog.org.uk/en/careers-training/awards-grants-prizes/american-gynecological-clubgynaecological-visiting-society-fellowship/

For further information contact:

Email: awards@rcog.org.uk

Annual Academic Award

Purpose: The award recognises distinguished service to academic obstetrics and gynaecology.
Eligibility: 1. Outstanding contribution to the academic aspects of our speciality (scientific discovery, pre-clinical and clinical research, academic education and training). 2. UK RCOG Fellows or Members, RCOG Fellows ad eundem or others of equivalent academic distinction (professorial level), at the discretion of the Academic Board. 3. Award exclusions Current members of the Academic Board. 4. Nominators to be UK Fellows. 5. Nominees can self-nominate with the support of 2 UK Fellows.
Type: Award

Frequency: Annual
Country of Study: Any country
Application Procedure: Please complete the nomination form word document downloadable from website. www.rcog.org.uk/en/careers-training/awards-grants-prizes/annual-academic-award/. Please ensure that the nominee is aware of this nomination. Please email the nomination form, written statement and abbreviated CV to awards@rcog.org.uk
Closing Date: 30 April
Additional Information: For more information: www.rcog.org.uk/en/careers-training/awards-grants-prizes/annual-academic-award/

For further information contact:

Email: academic@rcog.org.uk

Bernhard Baron Travelling Fellowship

Purpose: The Bernhard Baron Charitable Trust has generously endowed to the RCOG two travel scholarships in obstetrics and gynaecology for Fellows and Members of the College worth up to £6000 each
Eligibility: 1. Travel must take place within 12 months of the award being made. 2. The award may only be used for the purpose outlined in your original application. 3. A detailed report (maximum 1,000 words), including pictures if necessary, must be submitted to the RCOG Awards Administrator within eight weeks after the elective
Level of Study: Postdoctorate
Type: Fellowships
Value: Up to £6,000
Length of Study: 1 year
Frequency: Annual
Country of Study: Any country
Closing Date: 31 May
Funding: Foundation

For further information contact:

27 Sussex Place Regent's Park, London NW1 4RG, United Kingdom.

Fax: (44) 20 7723 0575
Email: awards@rcog.org.uk

Bruggeman Postgraduate Scholarship in Classics

Purpose: Doctoral scholarships are awarded by the University Council, on the recommendation of the Senate, to candidates proceeding to a course of supervised doctoral study at this University. These scholarships are normally available only to students seeking to obtain their first doctoral qualification

Level of Study: Postgraduate

Type: Scholarship

Value: NZ$25,000

Frequency: Annual

Country of Study: New Zealand

Funding: Foundation

For further information contact:

Email: scholarships@otago.ac.nz

Calcutta Eden Hospital Annual Prize

Purpose: The Calcutta (Kolkata) Eden Hospital is notable because it is where the highly reputed Professor Green Armytage spent his professional career for 25 years. During his tenure, he designed 'uterine haemostatic forceps' which are still widely used around the world in caesarean sections. The Kolkata Eden Hospital, a major maternity and gynaecological hospital and part of the Kolkata Medical College Hospital was the medical school of Mr Prabhat Chattopadhyay FRCOG. His generosity has enabled the RCOG to offer an annual prize to final year medical students or junior doctors (FY1) in the UK and Republic of Ireland.

Eligibility: This prize is open to final year medical students or FY1 junior doctors in the UK and Republic of Ireland. The prize is awarded for the best submission of an article that outlines your insight into any aspect of obstetrics and gynaecology undertaken during your training.

Type: Prize

Value: £350 of Book tokens

Frequency: Annual

Country of Study: Any country

Application Procedure: Please complete the online application via Oxford Abstracts app.oxfordabstracts.com/login?redirect=/stages/2100/submitter. This application is hosted by Oxford Abstracts platform. Please register for an account using your email address. For further guidance on how to submit your application, please see Oxford Abstracts' guidance on making a submission oxfordabstracts.freshdesk.com/support/solutions/articles/8000072762-making-a-submission.

Closing Date: 30 April

Additional Information: For more information: www.rcog.org.uk/en/careers-training/awards-grants-prizes/kolkata-eden-hospital/

For further information contact:

Email: awards@rcog.org.uk

Eden Travelling Fellowship in Obstetrics and Gynaecology

Purpose: The RCOG through the generous endowment of the late Dr Thomas Watts is able to offer a travel fellowship. The winner can use the funds to visit another O&G department or a related discipline to gain additional O&G knowledge and experience.

Eligibility: This Fellowship is open to medical graduates (who graduated within the last 2 years) who are currently undertaking a research project. This award may only be used for the purposes outlined in your original application.

Type: Travelling fellowship

Value: Up to £5,000

Frequency: Annual

Country of Study: Any country

Application Procedure: Please complete the online application via Oxford Abstracts app.oxfordabstracts.com/login?redirect=/stages/2102/submitter. This application is hosted by Oxford Abstracts platform. Please register for an account using your email address. For further guidance on how to submit your application, please see Oxford Abstracts' guidance on making a submission oxfordabstracts.freshdesk.com/support/solutions/articles/8000072762-making-a-submission.

Closing Date: 30 April

Additional Information: For more details: www.rcog.org.uk/en/careers-training/awards-grants-prizes/eden-travelling-fellowship-in-obstetrics-and-gynaecology/

For further information contact:

Email: awards@rcog.org.uk

Edgar Gentilli Prize

Purpose: Through the kind and generous bequest of the late Mr and Mrs Gilbert Edgar, the RCOG is delighted to offer this award to the candidate who submits the best piece of original work on the cause, nature, recognition and treatment of any form of cancer of the female genital tract.

Eligibility: 1. The Edgar Gentilli Prize is open to both members and non-members of the RCOG. 2. Applicants should submit results of their research by way of an original manuscript, adequately referenced and written in a format comparable to that used for submission to a learned journal, or by means of a reprint of the published article.

Type: Prize

Value: First prize £750 and Second prize £250

Frequency: Annual

Country of Study: Any country

Application Procedure: Please complete the online application via Oxford Abstracts app.oxfordabstracts.com/login? redirect=/stages/2102/submitter. This application is hosted by Oxford Abstracts platform. Please register for an account using your email address. For further guidance on how to submit your application, please see Oxford Abstracts' guidance on making a submission oxfordabstracts.freshdesk.com/ support/solutions/articles/8000072762-making-a-submission. Applicants must submit a maximum of 2,000 words, with a maximum of 10 references. Applications that are over the word limit will be marked down.

No. of awards offered: 2

Closing Date: 30 April

Additional Information: For more details: www.rcog.org. uk/en/careers-training/awards-grants-prizes/edgar-gentilli-prize/

For further information contact:

Email: awards@rcog.org.uk

Elizabeth Garrett Anderson Hospital Charity Travelling Fellowship in Memory of Anne Boutwood

Purpose: Through the generosity of the EGA Hospital Charity, we award a prize of £5,000 to one United Kingdom trainee in the field of obstetrics and gynaecology in memory of Miss Anne Boutwood FRCOG

Eligibility: 1. Travel must take place within 12 months of the award being made. 2. The award may only be used for the purpose outlined in your original application. 3. A detailed report (maximum 1,000 words), including pictures if necessary, must be submitted to the RCOG Awards Administrator within eight weeks after the elective

Level of Study: Postgraduate

Type: Fellowship

Value: £5,000

Frequency: Annual

Country of Study: Any country

Closing Date: 31 May

Funding: Foundation

For further information contact:

Email: awards@rcog.org.uk

Endometriosis Millenium Fund

Purpose: The RCOG is proud to support the Organising Committee of the World Congress of Endometriosis who, through a generous donation, have established the Endometriosis Millennium Fund. Available to RCOG Members and Trainees working in the UK and Republic of Ireland, the RCOG is able to offer in order to stimulate and encourage research (clinical or laboratory based) in the field of endometriosis.

Eligibility: The Fund is available to RCOG members and trainees working in the British Isles. Applications are invited for the following 1. To provide monies to fund a pilot project, clinical or laboratory based in the field of endometriosis, or to provide monies to fund an extension of an existing project researching endometriosis, or 2. To provide a contribution towards a travelling fellowship to attend a recognised training centre, preferably overseas, to obtain surgical training in the management of cases of endometriosis, beyond the skills expected of core training. 3. If the application is for travel funding, travel must take place within 12 months of the award being made. 4. The award may only be used for the purpose outlines in your original application. 5. Clinicians are encouraged, with the use of the funds to acquire extra clinical skills in order to more efficiently manage patients with the disease.

Level of Study: Postgraduate

Type: Funding support

Value: Up to £5,000

Frequency: Annual

Country of Study: Any country

Application Procedure: Please complete the online application via Oxford Abstracts app.oxfordabstracts.com/login? redirect=/stages/2102/submitter. This application is hosted by Oxford Abstracts platform. Please register for an account using your email address. For further guidance on how to submit your application, please see Oxford Abstracts' guidance on making a submission oxfordabstracts.freshdesk.com/ support/solutions/articles/8000072762-making-a-submission.

Closing Date: 30 April

Additional   Information: www.rcog.org.uk/en/careers-training/awards-grants-prizes/endometriosis-millennium-fund/

For further information contact:

Email: awards@rcog.org.uk

Ethicon Foundation Fund Travelling Fellowship

Purpose: The objective of the Ethicon Foundation Fund Travelling Fellowship, established through the generosity of Ethicon Limited, is to promote international goodwill in medicine and surgery by means of grants to assist the overseas travel of surgeons

Eligibility: 1. Applicants must be MRCS(Glasg) or FRCS (Glasg) and in a higher training post in the United Kingdom, or equivalent elsewhere in the world. 2. The proposed work experience, research or other study should be of clear benefit to the individual's training and to the NHS- or equivalent- on

R

return. 3. Periods abroad should generally be between 1-12 months. 4. Awards will not be given for the sole purpose of attending meetings, or conferences to present papers or for undertaking a series of brief visits to multiple centres

Level of Study: Postgraduate

Type: Travel grant

Value: Up to £900

Frequency: Annual

Country of Study: Any country

Application Procedure: Download and complete the application form and return the completed form to the address given. Make sure to include in your application Your CV A signed letter of support from your current supervisor A signed letter from the centre you will be visiting confirming that you are welcome

No. of awards offered: 10

Closing Date: 30 April

No. of awards given last year: 6

No. of applicants last year: 10

Additional Information: Travel must take place within 6 months of the award being made. www.rcpsg.ac.uk/awards-and-scholarships/ethicon-foundation-fund-travelling-fellowship

For further information contact:

Royal College of Physicians and Surgeons of Glasgow, 232 - 242 St Vincent Street, Glasgow G2 5RJ, United Kingdom.

Tel: (44) 141 221 6072
Fax: (44) 141 221 1804
Email: scholarships@rcpsg.ac.uk

Ethicon Student Elective Award

Purpose: The RCOG, with the kind and generous support of Ethicon, is pleased to offer funding towards approved student medical electives in obstetrics and gynaecology taking place between autumn current and upcoming year.

Eligibility: This award is open to students wishing to pursue a career in obstetrics and gynaecology. Applicants undertaking/planning to undertake their elective in a subject associated with this specialty in a low-resource country are particularly encouraged to apply. The successful applicants will have submitted a well-planned and well-presented application demonstrating clear objectives and detailed information about the project they wish to undertake. 1. The award may only be used for the purpose outlined in your original application. 2. Travel must take place within 12 months of the award being granted. 3. Retrospective applications will not be accepted.

Type: Award

Value: Up to £500

Frequency: Annual

Country of Study: Any country

Application Procedure: Please complete the online application via Oxford Abstracts app.oxfordabstracts.com/login? redirect=/stages/2098/submitter. This application is hosted by Oxford Abstracts platform. Please register for an account using your email address. For further guidance on how to submit your application, please see Oxford Abstracts' guidance on making a submission oxfordabstracts.freshdesk.com/support/solutions/articles/8000072762-making-a-submission

Closing Date: 30 April

Funding: Private

Additional Information: www.rcog.org.uk/en/careers-training/awards-grants-prizes/ethicon-student-elective-award/

For further information contact:

Email: awards@rcog.org.uk

Florence and William Blair Bell Research Fellowship

Purpose: The funding has been donated in order to stimulate and encourage research (clinical or laboratory based) in the field of O&G. Clinicians are encouraged, with the use of funds, to acquire extra clinical or research skills to improve patient management or develop their postdoctoral research.

Eligibility: The research fellowship will be awarded to a Member or Trainee on the RCOG Trainees' Register pre-CCT in obstetrics and gynaecology within a year of MD or PhD award at the time of application. 1. If the application is for travel funding, travel must take place within 12 months of the award being made. 2. The award may only be used for the purpose outlined in your original application. 3. A detailed report (maximum 1,000 words), including pictures if appropriate, must be submitted to the RCOG Awards at the end of the grant period. 4. An undertaking must be given that the source of the grant will be acknowledged in any related publications

Level of Study: Doctorate, Postdoctorate, Postgraduate

Type: Fellowship

Value: Up to £5,000

Frequency: Annual

Country of Study: Any country

Application Procedure: Please complete the online application via Oxford Abstracts app.oxfordabstracts.com/login? redirect=/stages/2102/submitter. This application is hosted by Oxford Abstracts platform. Please register for an account using your email address. For further guidance on how to submit your application, please see Oxford Abstracts' guidance on making a submission oxfordabstracts.freshdesk.com/support/solutions/articles/8000072762-making-a-submission.

No. of awards offered: 1
Closing Date: 30 April
Additional Information: www.rcog.org.uk/en/careers-training/awards-grants-prizes/florence-and-william-blair-bell-research-fellowship/

For further information contact:

Email: awards@rcog.org.uk

Green-Armytage and Spackman Travelling Scholarship

Purpose: Through the generosity of the late Mr V B Green-Armytage and of the late Colonel W C Spackman, Council is able to award a biennial travelling scholarship up to £4,000 to a Fellow or Member of the College
Eligibility: Applicants should have shown a special interest in some particular aspect of obstetrical or gynaecological practice. The donors' wishes are that the awards should be used for the purpose of visiting centres where similar work is being carried out. Your application will be judged on the following criteria 1. Presentation well planned and presented. 2. Relevance of project to career development in O&G. 3. Level of involvement. 4. References. 5. Value to the NHS/local community. 6. Value to personal development
Level of Study: Postgraduate
Type: Scholarship
Value: £4,000
Frequency: Annual
Country of Study: Any country
Application Procedure: Applicants must include information on qualifications, areas of interest and/or publications in a specified area, centres to be visited with confirmation from the head of that centre, estimated costs and the names of two referees
Closing Date: 24 May
Funding: Private
Additional Information: www.register-of-charities. charitycommission.gov.uk/charity-search/-/charity-details/7842/linked-charity-overview

Herbert Erik Reiss Memorial Case History Prize

Purpose: The Herbert Erik Reiss is comprised of prizes which are available for FY1 and FY2 doctor or specialist training Years 1 and 2 in the UK and the republic of Ireland.
Eligibility: Open to FY1 and FY2 doctors or Specialist Training Years 1 and 2 in the UK and the Republic of Ireland. The prizes are awarded to candidates who submit the most outstanding presentation of clinical case, including critical assessment and literature research on a topic in obstetrics and gynaecology.
Type: Prize
Value: First prize £400 and Second prize £200
Frequency: Annual
Country of Study: Any country
Application Procedure: Please complete the online application via Oxford Abstracts app.oxfordabstracts.com/login?redirect=/stages/2100/submitter. This application is hosted by Oxford Abstracts platform. Please register for an account using your email address. For further guidance on how to submit your application, please see Oxford Abstracts' guidance on making a submission oxfordabstracts.freshdesk.com/support/solutions/articles/8000072762-making-a-submission
No. of awards offered: 2
Closing Date: 30 April
Additional Information: For more details: www.rcog.org.uk/en/careers-training/awards-grants-prizes/herbert-erik-reiss-memorial-case-history-prize/

For further information contact:

Email: awards@rcog.org.uk

John Lawson Prize

Purpose: The prize will be awarded through the kind generosity of the late Mr John Lawson FRCOG, for the best article on obstetric and/or gynaecological work carried out in Africa between the tropics of Capricorn and Cancer.
Eligibility: This award is open to Members and non-members of the RCOG. The record of work can be submitted by way of an original manuscript, adequately referenced and written in a format comparable to that used for submission to a learned journal, or by means of a reprint of the published article.
Type: Prize
Value: £150
Frequency: Annual
Country of Study: Any country
Application Procedure: Please complete the online application via Oxford Abstracts app.oxfordabstracts.com/login?redirect=/stages/2102/submitter. This application is hosted by Oxford Abstracts platform. Please register for an account using your email address. For further guidance on how to submit your application, please see Oxford Abstracts' guidance on making a submission oxfordabstracts.freshdesk.com/support/solutions/articles/8000072762-making-a-submission. A maximum of 2,000 words with a maximum of 10 references should be submitted. Applications that are over the word limit will be marked down.
Closing Date: 30 April

R

Additional Information: www.rcog.org.uk/en/careers-training/awards-grants-prizes/john-lawson-prize/

For further information contact:

Email: awards@rcog.org.uk

Malcolm Black Travel Fellowship

Purpose: The purpose of the fellowship is to enable a College Member of up to 5 years' standing or a Fellow at the time of application, to travel either to the British Isles or from the British Isles abroad, for a period of time to attend postgraduate training courses or to visit centres of research or of particular expertise within the specialty of obstetrics and gynaecology.
Eligibility: This Fellowship is open to college Members and Fellows
Level of Study: Postgraduate
Type: Fellowship
Value: This biennial travel fellowship awards up to £1,000 to RCOG Members and Fellows
Length of Study: 12 months
Frequency: Annual

Overseas Fund

Purpose: The purpose of this fund is to make grants available to International Fellows and Members of the College working in obstetrics and gynaecology overseas who wish to travel to the UK for further training.
Eligibility: The award may only be used for the purpose outlined in the original application. Travel must take place within 12 months of the award being made.
Type: Travel grant
Value: Up to £2,500 of grants towards travel, accommodation and subsistence
Frequency: Annual
Country of Study: Any country
Application Procedure: Please complete the online application via Oxford Abstracts app.oxfordabstracts.com/login? redirect=/stages/2102/submitter. This application is hosted by Oxford Abstracts platform. Please register for an account using your email address. For further guidance on how to submit your application, please see Oxford Abstracts' guidance on making a submission oxfordabstracts.freshdesk.com/ support/solutions/articles/8000072762-making-a-submission.
Closing Date: 30 April
Additional Information: www.rcog.org.uk/en/careers-training/awards-grants-prizes/overseas-fund/

Peter Huntingford Memorial Prize

Purpose: The British Pregnancy Advisory Service (BPAS) has generously endowed the Peter Huntingford Memorial Prize to mark the late Professor Peter Huntingford's contribution to O&G.
Eligibility: This award is for FY1 or FY2 doctors across the UK and Republic of Ireland. The prize will be awarded to the best presentations of either 1. A case history focused on women with complications of pregnancy and giving birth. 2. A clinical audit of report of a research project with any aspect of sexual health and fertility control in which they have been directly involved.
Type: Prize
Value: First prize £150 and Second prize £75
Frequency: Annual
Country of Study: Any country
Application Procedure: Please complete the online application via Oxford Abstracts app.oxfordabstracts.com/login? redirect=/stages/2100/submitter. This application is hosted by Oxford Abstracts platform. Please register for an account using your email address. For further guidance on how to submit your application, please see Oxford Abstracts' guidance on making a submission oxfordabstracts.freshdesk.com/ support/solutions/articles/8000072762-making-a-submission
No. of awards offered: 2
Closing Date: 30 April
Contributor: British Pregnancy Advisory Service (BPAS)
Additional Information: For more information: www.rcog. org.uk/en/careers-training/awards-grants-prizes/peter-huntingford-memorial-prize/

For further information contact:

Email: awards@rcog.org.uk

Professor Geoffrey Chamberlain Award

Purpose: This award was established in memory of Professor Geoffrey Chamberlain who was a President of the College, Editor-in-Chief of BJOG and Head of the O&G Department at St George's Hospital London. The award consists of two separate awards.
Eligibility: 1. The first award is open to Trainees in the sub-continent Nepal, Bhutan, Pakistan, India, Bangladesh or Sri Lanka. (Not open for current year.). 2. The second award is open to all Trainees worldwide. The essay for the second award should be no more than 800 words and must be adequately referenced and written in a format comparable to that used for submission to a learned journal. Applications that are over the word limit will be marked down.
Type: Award

Value: First award £1,000 will be awarded every 3 years, Second award £150 will be awarded an annual basis

Frequency: Annual

Country of Study: Any country

Application Procedure: Please complete the online application via Oxford Abstracts app.oxfordabstracts.com/login? redirect=/stages/2102/submitter. This application is hosted by Oxford Abstracts platform. Please register for an account using your email address. For further guidance on how to submit your application, please see Oxford Abstracts' guidance on making a submission oxfordabstracts.freshdesk.com/support/solutions/articles/8000072762-making-a-submission.

Closing Date: 30 April

Additional Information: For more details: www.rcog.uk/en/careers-training/awards-grants-prizes/professor-geoffrey-chamberlain-award/

For further information contact:

Email: awards@rcog.org.uk

Royal College of Obstetricians and Gynaecologists Edgar Research Fellowship

Purpose: To encourage research, especially into chorion carcinoma or other forms of malignant disease

Eligibility: Open to candidates of high academic standing either in obstetrics and gynaecology, or related fields

Level of Study: Postgraduate

Type: Fellowship

Value: Up to a maximum of £35,000

Length of Study: Initially for 1 year's research but a further year's funding may be offered

Frequency: Annual

Country of Study: Any country

Application Procedure: Please contact the Research Administrator at the WellBeing address

Closing Date: December

Additional Information: In making the award the Council of the College will bear in mind the original intention of the fellowship, which was to encourage research into chorion carcinoma or other forms of malignant disease. Where applications of equal merit are received, priority will be given to the project most closely related to this condition. Fellows are required to submit a report on the work carried out as soon as the tenure of the fellowship is completed. www.rcog.org.uk/en/careers-training/academic-og/research-funding-opportunities/mrcrcog-clinical-research-training-fellowship/

For further information contact:

WellBeing 27 Sussex Place Regent's Park, London NW1 4SP, United Kingdom.

Tel: (44) 20 7772 6338

Fax: (44) 20 7724 7725

Email: mary.stanton@wellbeing.org.uk

Royal College of Obstetricians and Gynaecologists Research Training Fellowships

Purpose: To further the training of a young medical graduate in research techniques and methodology in a subject in a subject of direct or indirect relevance to obstetrics and gynaecology

Eligibility: Candidates will have had their basic training in obstetrics and gynaecology, preferably having passed their MRCOG. Candidates will be expected to enrol for a higher degree

Type: Fellowship

Value: Up to a maximum of three years salary

Length of Study: Up to 3 years

Frequency: Annual

Application Procedure: Enquiries about this award should be directed to The Research Administrator, WellBeing

Closing Date: October

Additional Information: www.rcog.org.uk/en/careers-training/academic-og/research-funding-opportunities/mrcrcog-clinical-research-training-fellowship/

For further information contact:

WellBeing 27 Sussex Place Regent's Park, London NW1 4SP, United Kingdom.

Tel: (44) 20 7772 6338

Fax: (44) 20 7724 7725

Email: mary.stanton@wellbeing.org.uk

Royal College of Obstetricians and Gynaecologists WellBeing Grants

Purpose: To fund research into all aspects of Obstetrics and Gynaecology with emphasis on increasing safety of childbirth for mother and baby and prevention of handicap

Eligibility: Open to specialists in any obstetrics and gynaecology inter-related field

Level of Study: Professional development, Research

Type: Grant

Value: Maximum of £80,000 over three years, with not more than £45,000 in the first year

Frequency: Annual

Application Procedure: Applicants must write for details

Funding: Private

Additional Information: www.rcog.org.uk/en/careers-training/academic-og/research-funding-opportunities/

For further information contact:

WellBeing 27 Sussex Place Regent's Park, London NW1 4SP, United Kingdom.

Tel: (44) 20 7772 6338
Fax: (44) 20 7724 7725
Email: mary.stanton@wellbeing.org.uk

Sims Black Travelling Proffesorship

Purpose: The purpose of the Sims Black Travelling Professorship is to Contribute to postgraduate education by presenting lectures, participating in seminars, group discussions and clinical demonstrations (if appropriate)
Eligibility: Check for the eligibility through the below link.
Level of Study: Postgraduate
Type: Professorship
Frequency: Annual
Closing Date: 31 January
Funding: Private

For further information contact:

10-18 Union Street, London, SE1 1SZ, United Kingdom.

Tel: (44) 20 7772 6200
Fax: (44) 20 7723 0575
Email: awards@rcog.org.uk

Target Ovarian Cancer Essay Prize

Purpose: The Target Ovarian Cancer essay prize is supported by The Royal College of Obstetricians and Gynaecologists. The prize is open to all undergraduate medical students across the United Kingdom. Its aim is to encourage students to read more widely on ovarian cancer, to think about some of the current issues and learn about recent research.
Eligibility: Open to all undergraduate medical students studying at a UK medical school. Applicants must submit an essay of up to 2,000 words including a maximum of three figures and/or tables (a 10 per cent margin either side will be applied). Applicants should include no more than ten references. Submit an essay that addresses one of the following: 1. Abdominal symptoms presenting in primary care: when to consider ovarian cancer in the differential diagnosis and how to avoid common misdiagnosis? 2. Describe the value of CA125 as a diagnostic tool for ovarian cancer and how NICE guidelines for primary care could be revised to reflect latest findings.

3. How can health care services be best organised to support the early diagnosis of ovarian cancer?
Level of Study: Undergraduate
Type: Prize
Value: First prize £750, Second prize £500 and Third prize £250
Frequency: Annual
Country of Study: Any country
Application Procedure: Please complete the online application via Oxford Abstracts app.oxfordabstracts.com/stages/2103/submitter. This application is hosted by Oxford Abstracts platform. Please register for an account using your email address. For further guidance on how to submit your application, please see Oxford Abstracts' guidance on making a submission oxfordabstracts.freshdesk.com/support/solutions/articles/8000072762-making-a-submission.
No. of awards offered: 3
Closing Date: 26 June
Contributor: Annette Mills Charitable Trust
Additional Information: For more information: www.rcog.org.uk/en/careers-training/awards-grants-prizes/target-ovarian-cancer-essay-prize/

For further information contact:

Email: essay@targetovariancancer.org.uk

Tim Chard Chase History Prize

Purpose: The Tim Chard Case History Prize has been generously endowed by the Bart's and The London school of Medicine to further the contribution of the late professor Tim Chard in obstetrics and gynaecology. To award students showing the greatest understanding of a clinical problem in obstetrics and gynaecology.
Eligibility: The prize is open to all medical students from the UK and the Republic of Ireland. 1. The successful applicants will show the greatest understanding of a clinical problem in O&G by submitting a case history with an intelligent discussion. 2. The successful applicants are invited to present their submission in a short lecture or a poster presentation at an RCOG event.
Type: Prize
Value: First prize £500, Second prize £250 and Third prize £150
Frequency: Annual
Country of Study: Any country
Application Procedure: Please complete the online application via Oxford Abstracts app.oxfordabstracts.com/login?redirect=/stages/2100/submitter. This application is hosted by Oxford Abstracts platform. Please register for an account using your email address. For further guidance on how to

submit your application, please see Oxford Abstracts' guidance on making a submission oxfordabstracts.freshdesk.com/support/solutions/articles/8000072762-making-a-submission

No. of awards offered: 3
Closing Date: 30 April
Funding: Private
Contributor: Bart's and The London school of Medicine
Additional Information: For more information: www.rcog.org.uk/en/careers-training/awards-grants-prizes/tim-chard-case-history-prize/

For further information contact:

Royal College of Obstetricians and Gynaecologists, United Kingdom.

William Blair Bell Memorial Lecture

Purpose: William Blair Bell, the first president of the RCOG, called for the award of an annual lectureship in a gynaecological or obstetric subject to a developing clinician scientist. The purpose of the lectureship is to allow a clinician or scientist who is at any stage of their career between award of an MD /PhD and the completion of their second year as a Senior Lecturer or its equivalent (e.g. Clinician Scientist), at the time of application, to give a lecture describing research in any area pertaining to Women's Health at the RCOG Annual Academic Meeting.
Eligibility: 1. Clinician or scientist between the award of their MD/PhD thesis and completion of their second year as a Senior Lecturer or its equivalent. 2. Proposed lecture describes their personal research in any area pertaining to Women's Health. 3. Applicants must declare that the lecture is entirely their own work and whether they have applied for other prizes for the same work.
Level of Study: Doctorate, Postgraduate
Type: Lectureship/Prize
Value: The winner of the lecture will be awarded a free place at the RCOG's Annual Academic Meeting and will have the opportunity to present a lecture.
Frequency: Annual
Country of Study: Any country
Application Procedure: Please complete the online application via Oxford Abstracts app.oxfordabstracts.com/login?redirect=/stages/2102/submitter. This application is hosted by Oxford Abstracts platform. Please register for an account using your email address. For further guidance on how to submit your application, please see Oxford Abstracts' guidance on making a submission oxfordabstracts.freshdesk.com/support/solutions/articles/8000072762-making-a-submission.
Closing Date: 30 April

Funding: Foundation
Additional Information: www.rcog.org.uk/en/careers-training/awards-grants-prizes/william-blair-bell-memorial-lecture/

For further information contact:

Email: awards@rcog.org.uk

Women's Visiting Gynaecological Club Prize

Purpose: Through the generosity of the Women's Visiting Gynaecological Club, the RCOG is able to offer prize to a medical student in the UK or Republic of Ireland towards an overseas elective in obstetrics and gynaecology.
Eligibility: This prize is awarded to a medical student who presents an application that best articulates the rationale and objectives for wanting to complete an overseas elective. The award may only be used for the purposes outlines in the original application. Travel must take place within 12 months of the award being made.
Type: Prize
Value: £500
Frequency: Annual
Country of Study: Any country
Application Procedure: Please complete the online application via Oxford Abstracts. app.oxfordabstracts.com/login?redirect=/stages/2098/submitter. This application is hosted by Oxford Abstracts platform. Please register for an account using your email address. For further guidance on how to submit your application, please see Oxford Abstracts' guidance on making a submission oxfordabstracts.freshdesk.com/support/solutions/articles/8000072762-making-a-submission
No. of awards offered: 1
Closing Date: 30 April
Additional Information: For more information www.rcog.org.uk/en/careers-training/awards-grants-prizes/womens-visiting-gynaecological-club-prize/

For further information contact:

Email: awards@rcog.org.uk

Royal College of Ophthalmologists

18 Stephenson Way, Euston, London NW1 2HD, United Kingdom.

Tel: (44) 20 3770 5327
Email: communications@rcophth.ac.uk; liz.price@rcophth.ac.uk

R

Website: www.rcophth.ac.uk/
Contact: Vanda Fadda, Deputy Head of Education and
                Training

The College was originally formed from the Ophthalmological Society of the United Kingdom and the Faculty of Ophthalmologists. The Royal Charter creating the College of Ophthalmologists was granted on the 14 April 1988 and the Royal Licence was granted five years later. The Royal College of Ophthalmologists believes that everyone should have access to high quality eye care. The College acts as the voice of the profession, set the curriculum and examinations for trainee ophthalmologists, provide training in eye surgery, maintain standards in the practice of ophthalmology, and promote research and advance science in the specialty. Ophthalmologists are at the forefront of eye health services because of their extensive training and experience.

Bayer Educational Grant Awards

Purpose: Supporting ophthalmologists to present work at educational meetings in the United Kingdom and overseas
Eligibility: Application from any grade of ophthalmologist working in the United Kingdom. Members and fellows of the Royal College of Ophthalmologists
Level of Study: Postgraduate
Type: Travel award
Value: Varies
Country of Study: United Kingdom
No. of awards offered: 37
Closing Date: 28 February
Funding: Commercial
Contributor: Bayer HealthCare, Bayer plc
No. of awards given last year: 11
No. of applicants last year: 37
Additional Information: www.fund.bayer.us/grant/2016/7/1/education

For further information contact:

Email: helen.sonderegger@rcophth.ac.uk

Essay Prize for Foundation Doctors

Purpose: Entries are now invited to the Essay Prize for Foundation Doctors on the essay "Discuss the impact of multi professional working on eye care"
Eligibility: 1. The competition is open to all those currently in a United Kingdom Foundation Programme. (F1, F2) at the time of submission, as well as those who have completed the United Kingdom Foundation Programme but have not yet achieved an OST1 post. 2. Entries are invited on the essay "Discuss the impact of multi professional working on eye care"
Level of Study: Postgraduate
Type: Grant
Frequency: Annual
Country of Study: Any country
Application Procedure: Essays of up to 1,500 words should be submitted to education@rcophth.ac.uk
Closing Date: 7 October
Funding: Private
Additional Information: www.rcophth.ac.uk/wp-content/uploads/2019/02/Essay-prize-for-foundation-doctors-2019-1.pdf,   www.rcophth.ac.uk/professional-resources/awards-and-prizes/

For further information contact:

18 Stephenson Way, Kings Cross, London NW1 2HD, United Kingdom.

Email: education@rcophth.ac.uk

Keeler Scholarship

Purpose: To enable the scholar to study, research or acquire special skills, knowledge or experience at a suitable location in the United Kingdom or elsewhere for a minimum period of 6 months
Eligibility: Applicants must be Fellows, Members or Affiliates of the Royal College of Ophthalmologists, those Fellows, Members and Affiliates being in good standing. Potential applicants who have received substantial (usually meaning amounts greater than the value of the scholarship) funding for their project are not eligible for the Keeler Scholarship. The trustees will give special consideration to candidates intending to make a career in ophthalmology in the United Kingdom. Applicants may apply retrospectively but should not be more than 3 months into the fellowship for which they are applying for support by 10 February (application closing date)
Level of Study: Postgraduate
Type: Scholarship
Value: Up to £30,000
Length of Study: 2 years
Frequency: Annual
Country of Study: Any country
Application Procedure: 5 copies each of the application form duly completed and the candidate's curriculum vitae should be submitted
Closing Date: 10 February

Funding: Private
Contributor: Keeler Ltd
Additional Information: Funds will be paid to the Scholar two months before the start date of the project or fellowship. www.eyedocs.co.uk/ophthalmology-clinical-awards/1078-keeler-scholarship, www.rcophth.ac.uk/professional-resources/awards-and-prizes/

For further information contact:

The Royal College of Ophthalmologists Education and Training Department – Awards and Prizes, 18 Stephenson Way, Kings Cross, London NW1 2HD, United Kingdom.

Nettleship Medal

Eligibility: The applicant should be British, a member of The Royal College of Ophthalmologists, and the work must be undertaken under the auspices of a British institution.
Type: Monetary award and medal
Value: £500.00
Country of Study: Any country
Closing Date: 7 January
Additional Information: www.rcophth.ac.uk/news-views/2022-nettleship-medal/

For further information contact:

18 Stephenson Way, London NW1 2HD, United Kingdom.

Email: laurelle.bygraves@rcophth.ac.uk.

Patrick Trevor-Roper Undergraduate Award

Purpose: Applications are invited for the Patrick Trevor-Roper Award, which is open to all undergraduate medical students from the United Kingdom and Ireland who have an interest in the specialty. The money may be used to fund electives in Ophthalmology, and may be spent on traveling or subsistence
Eligibility: Medical Undergraduates
Level of Study: Postgraduate
Type: Award
Value: £550
Frequency: Annual
Country of Study: Any country
Application Procedure: Please post 4 hard copies of your application form and CV to The Royal College of Ophthalmologists, Education and Training Department – Awards and Prizes, 18 Stephenson Way, NW1 2HD, London, United Kingdom
Closing Date: 31 May

Funding: Private
Additional Information: www.eyedocs.co.uk/undergraduate-ophthalmology-awards/1076-patrick-trevor-roper-award, www.rcophth.ac.uk/professional-resources/awards-and-prizes/

For further information contact:

The Royal College of Ophthalmologists, Education and Training Department – Awards and Prizes, 18 Stephenson Way, Kings Cross, London NW1 2HD, United Kingdom.

Email: education@rcophth.ac.uk

The Ulverscroft David Owen Award

Purpose: The Ulverscroft Foundation gives financial help to Universities that research the causes of eye diseases; funds eye clinics, hospitals, schools, libraries and other organisations which help visually impaired people.
Eligibility: The first author and senior author should apply together. Either the first or lead author must be an ophthalmologist. At least one of the authors must be a member of the RCOphth. The applicants should be based and have undertaken the research reported at a British institution. The paper must have been published in a peer reviewed scientific journal after 1 January 2020.
Type: Award
Value: £500
Country of Study: Any country
Closing Date: 7 January
Additional Information: www.rcophth.ac.uk/news-views/ulverscroft-david-owen-award-2022/

For further information contact:

18 Stephenson Way, London NW1 2HD, United Kingdom.

Email: aurelle.bygraves@rcophth.ac.uk.

Royal College of Ophthalmologists-Bayer Research

18 Stephenson Way, London NW1 2HD, United Kingdom.

Tel: (44) 20 3770 5341
Email: gareth.brennan@rcophth.ac.uk
Website: www.rcophth.ac.uk/
Contact: Gareth Brennan, Education and Training Administrator

The Royal College of Ophthalmologists believes that everyone should have access to high quality eye care. We champion excellence in the practice of ophthalmology through standards in training, education and assessment of ophthalmologists; supporting the promotion of research and innovation throughout the ophthalmic community.

Royal College of Ophthalmologists-Bayer Research Award

Purpose: The Royal College of Ophthalmologists and Bayer have come together in a partnership to launch a grant to promote research in ophthalmology
Eligibility: Any Ophthalmic Specialist Trainee, Member or Fellow of The RCOphth with an interest in research
Level of Study: Postgraduate
Type: Award
Value: £8,000
Frequency: Annual
Country of Study: Any country
Closing Date: 30 March
Funding: Foundation

For further information contact:

Email: education@rcophth.ac.uk

Royal College of Organists (RCO)

PO Box 7328, New Milton, Hampshire BH25 9DU, United Kingdom.

Tel: (44) 20 3865 6998
Email: admin@rco.org.uk
Website: www.rco.org.uk/

The College was established in 1864, the result of an idea by Richard Limpus, organist of St Michael's, Cornhill in the City of London. The Royal College of Organists has supported and represented organists and choral directors for more than 150 years. With members in nearly 40 countries around the world, we work together to promote the best in organ playing and choral directing, to encourage anyone who is interested to learn more about this fascinating and versatile musical instrument, and to explore its history and repertoire.

Royal College of Organists Scholarships and Awards

Purpose: To assist organists with professional playing
Eligibility: Open to members of the College. Only in exceptional circumstances will awards be made to non members. Membership is open to all upon payment of an annual subscription
Level of Study: Unrestricted
Type: Grant
Length of Study: 2 year, renewable
Frequency: Annual
Study Establishment: Varies
Country of Study: Any country
Application Procedure: Applicants must write for an application form
Closing Date: 17 February
Funding: Private
Contributor: College trusts
Additional Information: www.rca.ac.uk/studying-at-the-rca/fees-funding/financial-help-/preentry-scholarships-and-awards/

For further information contact:

Tel: (44) 207 590 4108
Email: scholarships@rca.ac.uk

Royal College of Organists Various Open Award Bequests

Purpose: To assist students who are training to become organists and/or choral directors.
Eligibility: Students in serious organ study, and in particular study devoted to the attainment of the College's diplomas
Type: Award
Value: Various; each award usually between £100 and £400
Frequency: Annual
Country of Study: Any country
Application Procedure: Applications for an RCO award should be made through this form RCO Awards & Bursaries Application Form downloadable from website. This application form should be accompanied by a letter of recommendation from your current organ teacher or suitable person. Please print and complete this Bursary Application form either post to Andrew McCrea or send by e-mail as a scanned file to andrew.mccrea@rco.org.uk.

Closing Date: 1 February

Additional Information: Open Awards Group A: 1. Mrs Alice Bonwick Bequest; 2. Miss Agnes Ethel Freeth Bequest; 3. Mrs Nellie Parnaby Bequest; 4. Noel Bonavia-Hunt Bequest. For more information www.rco.org.uk/education_scholarships.php#awards

For further information contact:

Andrew McCrea, Director of Academic Development, Royal College of Organists, RCO Bookings and Accounts, PO Box 7328, New Milton BH25 9DU, United Kingdom.

Email: andrew.mccrea@rco.org.uk

Royal College of Organists Various Open Awards

Purpose: These awards, each of which is available to more than one applicant, will normally be made to full-time music students (i.e. students pursuing to some extent organ and/or choral directing studies) at postgraduate level. They may also be used towards the cost of additional courses or lessons for which the holder receives little or no other funding, and may be used in this country or abroad.

Eligibility: Full-time music students (i.e. students pursuing to some extent organ and/or choral directing studies) at postgraduate level.

Level of Study: Postgraduate

Type: Award

Value: Various; each award from at least £400

Country of Study: Any country

Application Procedure: Applications for an RCO award should be made through this form RCO Awards & Bursaries Application Form downloadable from website. This application form should be accompanied by a letter of recommendation from your current organ teacher or suitable person. Please print and complete this Bursary Application form, either post or send by e-mail as a scanned file to Andrew McCrea.

Closing Date: 1 February

Additional Information: Open Awards Group B: 1. Lady Aline Cholmondeley Award. 2. Barbara Maude Osborne Award. 3. Samuel Paterson Baird Award. www.rco.org.uk/education_scholarships.php

For further information contact:

Andrew McCrea, Director of Academic Development, Royal College of Organists, RCO Bookings and Accounts, PO Box 7328, New Milton BH25 9DU, United Kingdom.

Email: andrew.mccrea@rco.org.uk

The Harry Moreton Memorial Scholarship

Purpose: The Scholarship grants towards graduate and post-graduate studies in the UK or abroad and also for grants towards local courses of organ lessons with teachers approved by the College.

Eligibility: Tenable only by students whose home is in either Devon or Cornwall.

Level of Study: Graduate, Postgraduate

Type: Scholarship

Value: At least £800 per annum

Country of Study: Any country

Application Procedure: Applications for an RCO award should be made through this form RCO Awards & Bursaries Application Form downloadable from website. This application form should be accompanied by a letter of recommendation from your current organ teacher or suitable person. Please print and complete this Bursary Application form, either post or send by e-mail as a scanned file to Andrew McCrea.

Closing Date: 1 May

Additional Information: www.rco.org.uk/education_scholarships.php

For further information contact:

Andrew McCrea, Director of Academic Development, Royal College of Organists, RCO Bookings and Accounts, PO Box 7328, New Milton BH25 9DU, United Kingdom.

Email: andrew.mccrea@rco.org.uk

The Leonard Freestone Scholarship

Purpose: This scholarship is available to a student pursuing postgraduate (taught or research based) course related to organ playing and/or choral direction.

Level of Study: Postgraduate

Type: Scholarship

Value: £4,750 per annum

Length of Study: 3 Years

Frequency: Annual

Country of Study: United Kingdom

Application Procedure: Applications for an RCO award should be made through this form RCO Awards & Bursaries Application Form downloadable from website. This application form should be accompanied by a letter of recommendation from your current organ teacher or suitable person. Please print and complete this Bursary Application form, either post or send by e-mail as a scanned file to Andrew McCrea.

Closing Date: 1 May

Additional Information: www.rco.org.uk/education_schol arships.php

For further information contact:

Andrew McCrea, Director of Academic Development, Royal College of Organists, RCO Bookings and Accounts, PO Box 7328, New Milton BH25 9DU, United Kingdom.

Email: andrew.mccrea@rco.org.uk

The Peter Wiles Scholarship

Purpose: This scholarship is available annually to a student in higher education pursuing postgraduate course related to organ playing and/or choral direction, or pursuing vocational training as an organist and/or choral director.
Level of Study: Postgraduate
Type: Scholarship
Value: £1,500 per annum
Frequency: Annual
Country of Study: United Kingdom
Application Procedure: Applications for an RCO award should be made through this form RCO Awards & Bursaries Application Form downloadable from website. This application form should be accompanied by a letter of recommendation from your current organ teacher or suitable person. Please print and complete this Bursary Application form, either post or send by e-mail as a scanned file to Andrew McCrea.
Closing Date: 1 May
Additional Information: www.rco.org.uk/education_schol arships.php

For further information contact:

Andrew McCrea, Director of Academic Development, Royal College of Organists, RCO Bookings and Accounts, PO Box 7328, New Milton BH25 9DU, United Kingdom.

Email: andrew.mccrea@rco.org.uk

Royal College of Physicians and Surgeons of Canada (RCPSC)

Office of Fellowship Affairs, 774 Echo Drive, Ottawa, ON K1S 5N8, Canada.

Tel: (1) 613 730 8177
Email: feedback@royalcollege.ca
Website: www.royalcollege.ca/
Contact: Dr James Hickey, FRCPC, Director

In June 1929, a special act of Parliament established the Royal College of Physicians and Surgeons of Canada to oversee postgraduate medical education. We serve patients, diverse populations and our Fellows by setting the standards in specialty medical education and lifelong learning, and by advancing professional practice and health care. The Royal College sets the highest standards for specialty medical education in Canada. The Royal College distributes more than C$1 million a year in awards, grants, fellowships and visiting professorship programs. Funds are provided by member donations, through a portion of membership dues, through the Royal College's Education Fund and from private endowments.

Canadian Research Awards for Specialty Residents (Medicine, Surgery)

Purpose: We serve patients, diverse populations and our Fellows by setting the standards in specialty medical education and lifelong learning, and by advancing professional practice and health care.
Additional Information: www.vascular.org/career-tools-training/awards-and-scholarships/resident-research-award

For further information contact:

774 Echo Drive, Ottawa, ON K1S 0R4, Canada.

Fax: (1) 613 730 8830
Email: llocas@rcpsc.edu

Duncan Graham Award for Outstanding Contribution to Medical Education

Purpose: One of the notable and outstanding awards that The Royal College of Physicians and Surgeons of Canada may bestow upon an individual is the Duncan Graham Award in Medical Education.
Eligibility: The Award is conferred upon any individual, whether physician or not, in recognition of outstanding contribution to medical education.
Type: Award
Value: US$1,000
Country of Study: Any country
Closing Date: 30 September
Additional Information: www.royalcollege.ca/rcsite/awards-grants/awards/duncan-graham-award-lifelong-contribution-medical-education-e

For further information contact:

Email: awards@royalcollege.ca

International Medical Educator of the Year Award

Purpose: This award is given annually to an international medical educator who has demonstrated a commitment to enhancing residency education as evidenced by innovation and impact beyond their program.

Eligibility: A nominee must be a current medical educator of a postgraduate program residing outside of Canada.

Type: Award

Country of Study: Any country

Closing Date: 8 April

Additional Information: www.royalcollege.ca/rcsite/awards-grants/awards/international-medical-educator-year-award-e

For further information contact:

Tel: (1) 613 730 8177

Email: icreawards@royalcollege.ca

International Resident Leadership Award

Purpose: This award is given to an international resident who has demonstrated leadership in specialty education and encourages the development of future leaders in medicine. Up to two awards will be presented annually. Award winners receive a plaque recognizing their contribution as well as travel and registration to the International Conference on Residency Education.

Eligibility: The resident must be enrolled in a postgraduate medical or surgical training program outside of Canada

Type: Award

Country of Study: Any country

Closing Date: 8 April

Additional Information: www.royalcollege.ca/rcsite/awards-grants/awards/international-resident-leadership-award-e

For further information contact:

Tel: (1) 613 730 8177

Email: icreawards@royalcollege.ca

James H. Graham Award of Merit

Purpose: This honorary award of merit was named for Dr. James H. Graham, secretary-general of the Royal College from 1953 to 1979. In 1987, the Council of The Royal College of Physicians and Surgeons of Canada recommended that an award of merit be given to a person whose outstanding career achievements reflect the aims and objectives of the Royal College.

Eligibility: This person need not be a physician. Self-applications are ineligible. The recipient's career achievements must be outstanding, enduring, and must be reflective of the Royal College strategic priorities. Potential candidates, who need not be physicians, could be long-serving contributors in a wide variety of areas

Type: Award

Value: The recipient will be presented with an engraved memento at Royal College event.

Country of Study: Any country

Closing Date: 30 September

Additional Information: www.royalcollege.ca/rcsite/awards-grants/awards/james-h-graham-award-merit-commitment-royal-college-e

For further information contact:

Email: awards@royalcollege.ca

Kristin Sivertz Resident Leadership Award

Purpose: This award is given to a resident who has demonstrated leadership in Canadian specialty education and encourages the development of future leaders in medicine. Up to two awards will be presented annually. Award winners will receive a plaque recognizing their contribution as well as complimentary travel and registration to the International Conference on Residency Education.

Eligibility: The resident must be enrolled in a Royal College-accredited residency program.

Type: Award

Country of Study: Any country

Closing Date: 8 April

Additional Information: www.royalcollege.ca/rcsite/awards-grants/awards/kristin-sivertz-resident-leadership-award-e

For further information contact:

Tel: (1) 613 730 8177

Email: icreawards@royalcollege.ca

Program Administrator Award for Excellence

Purpose: This award is given to a residency Program Administrator who has demonstrated a commitment to excellence in supporting all aspects of residency education, and works with all aspects of the program and with peers to exemplify the professional role of the Program Administrator and may be evidenced by innovation and/or improved or newly implemented processes within their program(s).

Eligibility: 1. Nominee must be a current postgraduate residency Program 2. Administrator Current members of the Royal College Program 3. Administrator Conference Steering Committee are not eligible 4. Self-nominations are not accepted 5. Individuals may be re-nominated in subsequent years; however, previous winners of the award will not be eligible to win again.

Type: Award

Country of Study: Any country

Closing Date: 8 April

Additional Information: www.royalcollege.ca/rcsite/awards-grants/awards/program-administrator-award-for-excellence-e

For further information contact:

Tel: (1) 613 730 8177

Email: paconference@royalcollege.ca

Royal College AMS Donald Richards Wilson Award for CanMEDS Integration

Purpose: The Royal College of Physicians and Surgeons of Canada, in collaboration with Associated Medical Services, Inc. has established an award to honour and acknowledge the contribution of Dr. Donald R. Wilson (President, RCPSC, 1988-1990) to medical education.

Eligibility: Any medical educator (not necessarily a Fellow) or an identified leader of a team, program, or department who has demonstrated excellence in integrating the CanMEDS roles into a Royal College or other health related training programs. Nominations should be accompanied by a statement describing: the relevant educational program; how the particular innovations have been implemented; the impact of the innovations for integrating CanMEDS roles into the program. A curriculum vitae along with two letters of support are required: one from the Dean of Medicine, or the Dean responsible for postgraduate education; and a second from an individual acquainted with the particulars of the innovation leading to the program changes. Self-applications are ineligible.

Type: Award

Value: US$2,000

Country of Study: Any country

Closing Date: 30 September

Additional Information: www.royalcollege.ca/rcsite/awards-grants/awards/royal-college-associated-medical-services-donald-r-wilson-award-e

For further information contact:

Email: awards@royalcollege.ca

Royal College Award for Early-Career Leadership

Purpose: The Award for Early-Career Leadership honours new Royal College Fellows (with 7 or fewer years of post-training full-time practice) who have shown outstanding leadership, initiative, service and/or innovation in areas aligned with one of three key areas of the Royal College mandate: Medical Education and/or Continuing Professional Development (CPD);Health Policy / Health Systems Professional Practice / Patient Care

Eligibility: The nominee must currently be a Fellow of the Royal College, and has been so for at least one year; Has been in full-time practice (clinical or academic) for not more than seven years post-training (not including any leaves of absence such as maternity leave); Self-applications are ineligible; Unsuccessful nominees may be re-submitted, however recipients are not eligible for future nomination.

Type: Award

Value: US$1,000.

Country of Study: Any country

Closing Date: 30 September

Additional Information: www.royalcollege.ca/rcsite/awards-grants/awards/early-career-leadership-in-medical-education-e

For further information contact:

Email: awards@royalcollege.ca

Royal College Dr. Thomas Dignan Indigenous Health Award

Purpose: The Royal College Dr. Thomas Dignan Indigenous Health Award was founded in 2014 in honour of the late Thomas Dignan, CM, OOnt, MD, co-chair of the Indigenous Health Committee of the Royal College.

Eligibility: The award may be bestowed upon physicians, residents or medical students who self-identify as Indigenous, Aboriginal, First Nations, Inuit or Métis and are Canadian residents (International applicants are not eligible). The award may be bestowed upon Elders and Knowledge Keepers who self-identify as Indigenous, Aboriginal, First Nations, Inuit or Métis and are Canadian residents (International applicants are not eligible). Nominators will be asked to describe the nominee's exceptional contribution, as well as to provide a curriculum vitae for the nominee and at least two letters of support. It is strongly preferred but not essential that at least one of the letters be from a Fellow of the Royal College. Self-applications are ineligible.

Type: Award

Value: US$1,000, Travel and related expenses

Country of Study: Any country

Closing Date: 30 September
Additional Information: www.royalcollege.ca/rcsite/awards-grants/awards/royal-college-dr-thomas-dignan-indigenous-health-award-e

For further information contact:

Email: awards@royalcollege.ca

Royal College of Surgeons

35-43 Lincoln's Inn Fields, London WC2A 3PE, United Kingdom.

Tel: (44) 20 7405 3474
Email: reception@rcseng.ac.uk
Website: www.rcseng.ac.uk/

The Royal College of Surgeons of England is a professional membership organisation and registered charity, which exists to advance patient care. We support over 25,000 members in the UK and internationally by improving their skills and knowledge, facilitating research and developing policy and guidance. The College was set up by Royal Charter in 1800 and has a unique heritage and collections, including the Hunterian Museum, surgeons' library and Wellcome Museum of Anatomy and Pathology. The RCS relies heavily on charitable support to fund surgical research, training and conserving our heritage collections. Legacies and support from grant-giving trusts, companies and individuals play a crucial role in maintaining and improving surgical care for patients.

Ethicon Travel Award

Purpose: Ethicon Foundation Fund travel awards for overseas visits are awarded to fellows and members of the College who are in good standing
Eligibility: Applicants must demonstrate that the period overseas relates directly to their home country's surgical training scheme's objectives and/or an opportunity to obtain relevant surgical experience that is not normally available in their home country. They must have obtained prior approval for the visit from the appropriate training authority in the country of application where appropriate. UK trainees must produce confirmation/evidence of prospective approval from the GMC if the post is to count towards the award of a Certificate of Completion of Training (CCT).
Type: Award

Value: The awards are for travel costs only, economy class travel, up to a value of £1,000
Length of Study: 3-12 Months
Frequency: Annual
Country of Study: United Kingdom
Application Procedure: Please email the following documents to Linda at lslater@rcseng.ac.uk. 1. Completed application form (download from website). 2. A letter of support from the head of department, or consultant, under whom the applicant is currently working. 3. A letter of support from another, independent referee. 4. Confirmation from the Institute you are visiting.
Closing Date: 17 March
Contributor: Ethicon Foundation Fund
Additional Information: As a condition of the award, successful applicants are required to submit a report of their visit within two months of return. Applicants who do not submit a report may have the award withdrawn. For more information www.rcseng.ac.uk/standards-and-research/research/fellowships-awards-grants/awards-and-grants/travel-awards/ethicon-grants/

For further information contact:

38-43 Lincoln's Inn Fields, London WC2A 3PE, United Kingdom.

Tel: (44) 20 7405 3474
Email: lslater@rcseng.ac.uk

Royal College of Surgeons of United Kingdom

35-43 Lincoln's Inn Fields, London WC2A 3PE, United Kingdom.

Tel: (44) 20 7405 3474
Email: reception@rcseng.ac.uk
Website: www.rcseng.ac.uk
Contact: Miss Bumbi Singh, Research Department

The Royal College of Surgeons of England is a professional membership organisation and registered charity, which exists to advance patient care. The College was set up by Royal Charter in 1800 and has a unique heritage and collections, including the Hunterian Museum, surgeons' library and Wellcome Museum of Anatomy and Pathology. We support over 25,000 members in the UK and internationally by improving their skills and knowledge, facilitating research and developing policy and guidance.

Ethicon Foundation Fund

Purpose: Ethicon Foundation Fund travel awards for overseas visits are awarded to fellows and members of the College who are in good standing.

Eligibility: Applicants must demonstrate that the period overseas relates directly to their home country's surgical training scheme's objectives and/or an opportunity to obtain relevant surgical experience that is not normally available in their home country. They must have obtained prior approval for the visit from the appropriate training authority in the country of application where appropriate. UK trainees must produce confirmation/evidence of prospective approval from the GMC if the post is to count towards the award of a Certificate of Completion of Training (CCT).

Type: Travel grant

Value: The awards are for travel costs only, economy class travel, up to a value of £1,000.

Frequency: Annual

Country of Study: Any country

Application Procedure: Please email the following documents to Linda at lslater@rcseng.ac.uk 1. Completed application form (download from website). 2. A letter of support from the head of department, or consultant, under whom the applicant is currently working. 3. A letter of support from another, independent referee. 4. Confirmation from the Institute you are visiting.

Closing Date: 17 March

Additional Information: As a condition of the award, successful applicants are required to submit a report of their visit within two months of return. Applicants who do not submit a report may have the award withdrawn. For more information www.rcseng.ac.uk/standards-and-research/research/fellowships-awards-grants/awards-and-grants/travel-awards/ethicon-grants/

For further information contact:

38-43 Lincoln's Inn Fields, London WC2A 3PE, United Kingdom.

Tel: (44) 20 7405 3474
Email: lslater@rcseng.ac.uk

Royal Geographical Society (with the Institute of British Geographers)

1 Kensington Gore, London SW7 2AR, United Kingdom.

Tel: (44) 20 7591 3000
Email: enquiries@rgs.org

Website: www.rgs.org/
Contact: Juliette Scull, Grants Officer

The Royal Geographical Society (with the Institute of British Geographers) is the UK's learned society and professional body for geography. We advance geography and support geographers in the UK and across the world. As a charity, learned society and professional body, we reach millions of people each year through our work in advancing geography and supporting geographers. With over two million items, our Collections provide an unparalleled resource tracing 500 years of geographical discovery and research. Equality, diversity and inclusion are core values for the Society and for the practice, study and teaching of geography.

30th International Geographical Congress Award

Purpose: To assist with the cost of attending a conference organised by a geographical scientific Union or Association formally affiliated with the International Science Council (ISC)

Eligibility: Applicants must be UK/EU nationals. Applicants are early career researchers (post PhD) currently affiliated with a UK Higher Education Institution. Preference will be given to applicants within 6 years of completion of a PhD, presenting papers and seeking to cover travel expenses, although help with conference fees, accommodation, and maintenance costs will also be considered. Applicants must demonstrate the geographical nature of both the conference and the work they will present.

Level of Study: Research

Type: Award

Value: Up to £750

Frequency: Annual

Country of Study: Any country

Application Procedure: All prospective grant applicants should read our Advice and Resources pages, which include more information about the grants programme, its conditions, and what is expected if your application is successful. Please download application form from website and send your completed application form by email.

No. of awards offered: 5

Closing Date: 31 October

Additional Information: Priority will be given for conferences outside Europe and North America. Attendance at AAG, CAG or the RGS-IBG Annual Conference is not eligible for support from this award. For more details www.rgs.org/in-the-field/in-the-field-grants/research-grants/thirtieth-international-geographical-congress/

For further information contact:

Grants Officer, Royal Geographical Society (with IBG), United Kingdom.

Tel: (44) 20 7591 3073
Email: grants@rgs.org

Environment and Sustainability Research Grants

Purpose: To support researchers investigating some of the bigger issues in environmental sustainability.

Eligibility: Applicants may be researches of any nationality but must be affiliated with a UK Higher Education Institution. Individuals or groups may apply.

Type: Grant
Value: £15,000
Frequency: Annual
Country of Study: Any country
Application Procedure: All prospective grant applicants are encouraged to read our Advice and Resources pages from website, which include more information. Please download application from website and send your application by email to grants@rgs.org
No. of awards offered: 3
Closing Date: 22 February
Contributor: Deutsche Post-Stiftung and SUN Institute Environment and Sustainability
No. of awards given last year: 4
Additional Information: For more information www.rgs.org/in-the-field/in-the-field-grants/research-grants/environment-and-sustainability-research-grants/

For further information contact:

Grants Officer, United Kingdom.

Tel: (44) 207 591 3073
Email: grants@rgs.org

Geographical Club Award

Purpose: The Geographical Club Award is given through the RGS-IBG Postgraduate Research Awards scheme to support PhD students undertaking geographical fieldwork or other forms of data collection in the UK or overseas.

Eligibility: Applicants must be registered at a UK Higher Education Institution. Preference is given to students who do not receive full funding from a research council, university or comparable levels of support from other sources for fieldwork and data collection.

Level of Study: Doctorate, Postgraduate

Type: Award
Value: £1,000
Frequency: Annual
Country of Study: Any country
Application Procedure: All prospective grant applicants are encouraged to read our Advice and Resources pages, which include more information about the grants programme, its conditions, how to apply for a grant. Please download application form from website and send your completed application by email to grants@rgs.org
No. of awards offered: 2
Closing Date: 23 November
No. of awards given last year: 2
Additional Information: www.rgs.org/in-the-field/in-the-field-grants/students/phd/geographical-club-award-(1)/

For further information contact:

Grants Officer, United Kingdom.

Tel: (44) 207 591 3073
Email: grants@rgs.org

Innovative Geography Teaching Grants

Purpose: The aim is to serve both geography pupils and the wider teaching community through the creation of teaching materials. The materials produced will be published on the Society's website.

Eligibility: Two supporting statements are required. One referee statement must be signed by the Head of Department, Head Teacher or Employer of the lead applicant.

Type: Grant
Value: £1,000
Country of Study: Any country
No. of awards offered: 2
Closing Date: 15 February
Additional Information: www.rgs.org/in-the-field/in-the-field-grants/teacher-grants/innovative-teaching-geography-grants/

For further information contact:

1 Kensington Gore, South Kensington, London SW7 2AR, United Kingdom.

Tel: (44) 20 7591 3000
Email: grants@rgs.org.

Ray Y. Gildea Jr Award

Purpose: The Ray Y Gildea Jr Award supports innovation in teaching and learning in higher and secondary education.

Eligibility: Applicants must be UK or USA nationals and must be currently employed in the higher education (college) sector and/or secondary school level, either in the UK or the USA, actively teaching students.

Type: Grant

Value: Up to £1,000

Frequency: Annual

Country of Study: Any country

Application Procedure: All prospective grant applicants are encouraged to read our Advice and Resources pages from website, which include more information about the grants programme, its conditions, how to apply for a grant. Please download application form from website and send your completed application by email to grants@rgs.org

Closing Date: 30 November

Additional Information: For more information www.rgs.org/in-the-field/in-the-field-grants/teacher-grants/ray-y-gildea-jr-award/

For further information contact:

Grants Officer, United Kingdom.

Tel: (44) 207 591 3073
Email: grants@rgs.org

Walters Kundert Fellowship

Purpose: The Walters Kundert Fellowship offers awards to support field research in physical geography within Arctic and/or high mountain environments, with preference for field studies that advance the understanding of environmental change past or present.

Eligibility: Applications are open to post-PhD researchers affiliated with a UK university or research institute, or Fellows and members of the Society who are employed outside the UK.

Level of Study: Postdoctorate, Research

Type: Grant

Value: £10,000

Frequency: Annual

Country of Study: Any country

Application Procedure: All prospective grant applicants are encouraged to read our Advice and Resources pages from website, which include more information about the grants programme, its conditions, how to apply for a grant. Please download application from website and send your completed application by email to grants@rgs.org

No. of awards offered: 1

Closing Date: 23 November

No. of awards given last year: 1

Additional Information: For more information www.rgs.org/in-the-field/in-the-field-grants/research-grants/kundert-fellowship/

For further information contact:

Grants Officer, United Kingdom.

Email: grants@rgs.org

Royal Holloway, University of London

Egham Hill, Egham, Surrey TW20 0EX, United Kingdom.

Tel: (44) 1784 434 455
Email: international@royalholloway.ac.uk
Website: www.royalholloway.ac.uk/
Contact: Ms Claire Collingwood, Schools & International Liaison Officer

Royal Holloway is formed from two colleges, Bedford College in London and Royal Holloway College was founded by two social pioneers, Elizabeth Jesser Reid and Thomas Holloway. In 1900, the colleges became part of the University of London and in 1985 they merged to form what is now known as Royal Holloway. As one of the UK's leading research-intensive universities, we are home to some of the world's foremost authorities in the sciences, arts, business, economics and law. As teachers and researchers they change lives, expand minds and help current and future leaders understand power and responsibility.

American Foundation of RHBNC International Excellence Scholarship

Purpose: This scholarship is available to students from the United States with outstanding academic ability studying any taught Masters course.

Eligibility: Applicant must be a US citizen applying for a full-time taught Masters course with a current grade average in the range of a First Class full-time Honours degree, or equivalent (PDF link available in website). You must provide a supporting statement of no longer than 400 words, which should include 1. academic achievements you are particularly proud of and why these really matter to you; 2. why you have chosen to do the degree you have applied for; 3. what your future aspirations are and how the scholarship will help you to achieve your future goals. As well as your statement, you will need to upload your most recent grades transcript from your undergraduate degree.

Level of Study: Masters Degree
Type: Scholarships
Value: £3,000
Frequency: Annual
Country of Study: United Kingdom
Application Procedure: Apply via our online system Royal Holloway Direct (admissions.royalholloway.ac.uk/#/login), where you will be able to complete your statement and upload any required documents including your grades transcript.
Closing Date: 11 July
Additional Information: For further details www.royalholloway.ac.uk/studying-here/fees-and-funding/postgraduate/scholarships/american-foundation-of-rhbnc-international-excellence-scholarship/

For further information contact:

Egham Hill, Egham TW20 0EX, United Kingdom.

Tel: (44) 1784 414944
Email: study@royalholloway.ac.uk

Bedford Society Scholarship

Purpose: The scholarships are awarded to new full-time or part-time students with Home or International fee status who are studying for a taught Masters degree within one of the academic departments listed. The scholarships are funded by the alumni and friends of Bedford College, one of the founding colleges of Royal Holloway and Bedford New College. Formed in 2013, the Bedford Society aims to ensure the spirit of Bedford College lives on by providing new scholars with access to financial support and opportunities for networking.
Eligibility: You must have achieved, or be on target to achieve, a First Class Honours degree or equivalent (PDF link available in website). You must have a conditional or unconditional offer to study a Masters course within 1. Department of Classics. 2. Department of English. 3. Department of History. 4. Department of Languages, Literatures and Cultures. 5. Department of Economics. 6. Department of Law and Criminology. 7. Department of Politics, International Relations and Philosophy. 8. Department of Social Work. 9. Department of Biological Sciences. 10. Department of Earth Sciences. 11. Department of Geography. 12. Department of Psychology.
Level of Study: Masters Degree
Type: Scholarships
Value: Scholarships are offered as a tuition fee reduction of £8,100.

Country of Study: United Kingdom
Application Procedure: You must apply via our online system Royal Holloway Direct admissions.royalholloway.ac.uk/#/login, where you will be able to complete your statement and upload any required documents including your grades transcript. You must provide a supporting statement of no more than 400 words, which should include 1. Academic achievements you are particularly proud of and why these really matter to you. 2. Why you have chosen to do the degree you have applied for. 3. What your future aspirations are and how the scholarship will help you to achieve your future goals. 4. It should also demonstrate an enthusiastic and authentic spirit of enquiry and indicate clearly how this scholarship would help you share and advance knowledge of future generations. As well as your statement, you will need to upload your most recent grades transcript from your undergraduate degree.
No. of awards offered: 3
Closing Date: 11 July
Funding: Private
Contributor: Bedford College
Additional Information: For more information vist www.royalholloway.ac.uk/studying-here/fees-and-funding/postgraduate/scholarships/bedford-society-scholarships/

For further information contact:

Egham Hill, Egham TW20 0EX, United Kingdom.

Tel: (44) 1784 414944
Email: study@royalholloway.ac.uk

Brian Harris Scholarship

Purpose: The scholarship was established by entrepreneur Brian Harris to provide an opportunity for a student from a low-income background to study a Masters degree in History.
Eligibility: 1. You must be a full or part-time student from the UK applying for one of the following Masters degrees a. MA History. b. MA Public History. 2. To be eligible for the scholarship your focus of study, including the MA dissertation, must be on British and/or European History. 3. You are expected to have achieved, or be on target to achieve, at least a 2 1 degree or equivalent, with preference given to those with, or expected to achieve, a First Class Honours Degree. 4. You must be able to demonstrate financial need. 5. You must also hold a conditional or unconditional offer to study at Royal Holloway.
Level of Study: Postgraduate
Type: Scholarship
Value: £10,000

Frequency: Annual

Country of Study: United Kingdom

Application Procedure: You will need to apply using our online system Royal Holloway Direct admissions. royalholloway.ac.uk/#/login. You must provide a supporting statement of up to 1,000 words which should include 1. How and why you feel you qualify for the scholarship. 2. What you want to achieve by completing a Masters in History. 3. Details of your career plans and how your degree will help you fulfil your goals. 4. Details of what you think you gained from your undergraduate degree. 5. Details of your educational background prior to your undergraduate degree. 6. Details of both your academic and personal background, including financial need. 7. Evidence of resilience e.g. an example of a difficult period in your life, how you overcame it and what you learnt from your experience. 8. How you will give back to the university community. You must also provide 1. Evidence of the financial support you received at undergraduate level and the basis on which this was received and why. The sources this could be from are Student Finance England, Student Awards Agency Scotland, Student Finance Wales, Student Finance Northern Ireland, or a university-funded bursary (where this has been awarded on the basis of financial need). 2. Evidence of having achieved or expected to achieve a 21 or First Class undergraduate degree or equivalent. 3. An up-to-date CV. 4. You must provide two written academic references (up to 200 words each). These must be from academics who have previously supported, taught or worked with you. Please ask your reference to email their statement to RHPS@rhul.ac.uk directly. 5. The piece of work from your undergraduate degree that you are most proud of.

No. of awards offered: 2

Closing Date: 30 April

Additional Information: For more information www. royalholloway.ac.uk/studying-here/fees-and-funding/post graduate/scholarships/brian-harris-scholarship/

For further information contact:

Egham Hill, Egham TW20 0EX, United Kingdom.

Tel: (44) 1784 434455
Email: study@rhul.ac.uk

RHBNC Trust Scholarship

Purpose: These scholarships provide a tuition fee reduction and are for new full-time or part-time taught Masters students with Home or International status, studying for a postgraduate degree within one of the academic departments listed.

Eligibility: You must have achieved, or be expected to achieve, a First Class Honours degree or equivalent. This scholarship is open to Home and International fee paying students with a conditional or unconditional offer to study a course within 1. School of Business and Management. 2. Department of Drama, Theatre and Dance. 3. Department of Media Arts. 4. Department of Music. 5. Department of Computer Science. 6. Department of Electronic Engineering. 7. Department of Information Security. 8. Department of Mathematics. 9. Department of Physics. Only students applying to study for their first Masters degree will be considered for this scholarship.

Level of Study: Masters Degree, Postgraduate

Type: Scholarships

Value: Tuition fee reduction of £7,000

Frequency: Annual

Country of Study: United Kingdom

Application Procedure: You must apply via our online system Royal Holloway Direct admissions.royalholloway. ac.uk/#/login, where you will be able to complete your statement and upload any required documents including your grades transcript. You must provide a supporting statement of no more than 400 words, which should include 1. Academic achievements you are particularly proud of and why these really matter to you. 2. Why you have chosen to do the degree you have applied for. 3. What your future aspirations are and how the scholarship will help you to achieve your future goals. As well as your statement, you will need to upload your most recent grades transcript from your undergraduate degree.

Closing Date: 11 July

Additional Information: For more information www. royalholloway.ac.uk/studying-here/fees-and-funding/post graduate/scholarships/rhbnc-trust-scholarship/

For further information contact:

Egham Hill, Egham TW20 0EX, United Kingdom.

Tel: (44) 1784 434455
Email: study@royalholloway.ac.uk

Royal Holloway, University of London MBA Programme

Application Procedure: Applicants must complete an application form

Closing Date: 30 June

Additional Information: studyabroad.shiksha.com/uk/uni versities/royal-holloway-university-of-london/mba-inter national-management

For further information contact:

School of Management Royal Holloway University of London, Egham TW20 0EX, United Kingdom.

Tel: (44) 1784 443 780
Fax: (44) 1784 439 854
Email: school-management@rhul.ac.uk

Royal Horticultural Society (RHS)

80 Vincent Square, London SW1P 2PE, United Kingdom.

Tel: (44) 20 3176 5800
Email: customercare@rhs.org.uk
Website: www.rhs.org.uk/
Contact: Secretary of RHS Bursaries Committee

The Royal Horticultural Society is the world's leading gardening charity. We aim to enrich everyone's life through plants, and make the UK a greener and more beautiful place - we are committed to inspiring everyone to grow. As a charity, we want to inspire a passion for gardening and growing plants, promote the value of gardens, demonstrate how gardening is good for us and explain the vital role that plants play.

Blaxall Valentine Bursary Fund

Purpose: To help finance horticultural study tours and projects that will provide real benefits to horticulture.
Eligibility: Open to applicants worldwide, but preference is given to UK citizens. Financial sponsorship will be available to both professional and amateur horticulturists and consideration for an award is not restricted to RHS members. Proposals may be made by individuals or group of individuals.
Level of Study: Unrestricted
Type: Bursary
Value: Funds are limited. High-cost projects are expected to receive supplementary finance from other sources, including personal contributions
Frequency: Annual
Country of Study: Any country
Application Procedure: Applicants must complete an application form downloaded from the RHS website www.rhs.org.uk/bursaries.
Closing Date: 30 September
Funding: Private
Additional Information: Please contact at for applying and deadline. mailto: bursaries@rhs.org.uk

Royal Horticultural Society Financial Awards

Purpose: To help finance horticulture-related projects and to further the interests of horticultural education along with horticultural work experience
Eligibility: Submissions are welcomed from applicants worldwide, but preference is given to United Kingdom and Commonwealth citizens. Applicants should preferably be within the age bracket of 20 and 35 years and satisfy the Society that their health enables them to undertake the project proposed. Financial sponsorship will be available to both professional and amateur horticulturists, and consideration for an award is not restricted to RHS members. Proposals may be made by individuals or groups
Level of Study: Unrestricted
Type: Bursary
Value: Funds are limited. High-cost projects are expected to receive supplementary finance from other sources, including personal contributions
Frequency: Annual
Country of Study: Any country
Application Procedure: Applicants must complete an application form, available on request. Candidates may be called for interview
Closing Date: 30 September
Funding: Private
No. of awards given last year: 6
Additional Information: Recipients must submit a brief factual report within 3 months of completion, along with an outline of achievements or difficulties, including any unusual problems, e.g. medical or political, and an account of expenses mailto: bursaries@rhs.org.uk

Royal Horticulture Society Bursary Scheme

Purpose: To broaden skills, increase knowledge and enhance career opportunities related to Horticulture
Eligibility: United Kingdom citizens may apply for projects worldwide. Others may only apply for projects based in the United Kingdom
Level of Study: Unrestricted
Type: Bursary
Value: Funds are limited. High-cost projects are expected to receive supplementary finance from other sources
Frequency: Annual
Country of Study: United Kingdom
Application Procedure: Applicants must complete an application form downloadable from the RHS website www.rhs.org.uk/bursarie
Closing Date: 15 December
Funding: Private
Additional Information: www.rhs.org.uk/education-learning/bursaries-grants

R

For further information contact:

RHS Garden, Wisley, Woking, Surrey GU23 6QB, United Kingdom.

Email: bursanes@rhs.org.uk

Royal Institution of Chartered Surveyors Education Trust

Royal Institution of Chartered Surveyors, RICS, Parliament Square, London SW1P 3AD, United Kingdom.

Tel: (44) 24 7686 8555
Email: contactrics@rics.org
Website: www.rics-educationtrust.org

The Royal Institution of Chartered Surveyors (RICS) is the professional institution for the surveying profession.

Royal Institution of Chartered Surveyors Education Trust Award

Eligibility: Open to chartered surveyors and others carrying out research studies in relevant subjects
Level of Study: Unrestricted
Type: Research grant
Value: Up to £7,500
Country of Study: Any country
Application Procedure: Applicants must complete an application form, available to download online at www.rics-educationtrust.org
No. of awards offered: 40
Closing Date: 6 March
Funding: Commercial
Contributor: RICS
No. of awards given last year: 20
No. of applicants last year: 40
Additional Information: www.rics.org/en-in/news-insight/research/research-trust/

Royal Irish Academy

19 Dawson Street, Dublin 2, D02 HH58, Ireland.

Tel: (353) 1 609 0600
Email: info@ria.ie

Website: www.ria.ie/
Contact: Ms Laura Mahoney, Assistant Executive Secretary

The Royal Irish Academy is Ireland's leading body of experts in the sciences and humanities. We identify and recognise Ireland's world class researchers. It was founded in 1785, with the Earl of Charlemont as first president. Its royal charter, granted the following year, declared its aims to be the promotion and investigation of the sciences, polite literature, and antiquities, as well as the encouragement of discussion and debate between scholars of diverse backgrounds and interests. We support scholarship and promote awareness of how science and the humanities enrich our lives and benefit society. The Academy is run by a Council of its members. Membership is by election and considered the highest academic honour in Ireland.

R.J. Hunter Research Bursary Scheme

Purpose: The R.J. Hunter Grants Scheme was established in 2014 using funding generously made available by his daughter, Ms Laura Hunter Houghton, through the Community Foundation for Northern Ireland.
Type: Bursary
Value: Maximum of €2,500
Country of Study: Any country
Closing Date: 2 February
Additional Information: www.ria.ie/grants-and-awards/rj-hunter-research-bursary-scheme

For further information contact:

Email: grants@ria.ie

Royal Irish Academy Senior Visiting Fellowships

Purpose: To enable a new scientific research technique or development to be introduced into the Republic of Ireland
Eligibility: Open to senior researchers from member countries of the Organisation for Economic Co-operation and Development (OECD) only
Level of Study: Postdoctorate, Professional development
Type: Fellowship
Value: Varies
Frequency: Annual
Country of Study: Other
Application Procedure: Applicants must complete an application form
Closing Date: 15 October

Funding: Government

No. of awards given last year: 10

Additional Information: Senior Visiting Fellowships are made on behalf of the Irish government www.rics.org/en-in/news-insight/research/research-trust/

For further information contact:

Email: grants@ria.ie

Royal Literary Fund RLF

3 Johnson's Court, off Fleet Street, London EC4A 3EA, United Kingdom.

Tel: (44) 20 7353 7150
Email: rlitfund@btconnect.com
Website: www.rlf.org.uk/
Contact: Steve Cook, Fellowship Officer

The Royal Literary Fund is a British charity that has been supporting authors since 1790. The Royal Literary Fund is a benevolent fund for professional published authors; it is funded exclusively by bequests and donations from writers and others who wish to help writers. We provide grants and pensions to writers in financial difficulty: novelists, poets, playwrights, screenwriters and translators. As writers struggle in the current situation, we are here to help. We also run education programmes where writers deploy their talents for the wider benefit. Our Fellowship scheme funds writers to work one-to-one with university students. We also provide writing development workshops to schools and our community projects nurture resilience, engagement and empowerment.

Royal Literary Fund Grant

Purpose: To support prolific writers suffering financial hardship

Eligibility: You are eligible to apply for financial assistance if you have published several works.

Type: Grant

Value: £15,000

Length of Study: 36 weeks

Frequency: Annual

Country of Study: United Kingdom

Application Procedure: The application form requests details of income and expenditure and applicants are requested to send copies of published work with the completed form. For application form please contact Eileen Gunn and provide a list of your publications including names of publishers, dates, and whether sole author.

Closing Date: 8 April

Additional Information: www.rlf.org.uk/helping-writers/fellowships/

For further information contact:

The Royal Literary Fund, 3 Johnson's Court, London EC4A 3EA, United Kingdom.

Tel: (44) 20 7353 7159

Royal Melbourne Institute of Technology University

Info Corner - Office for Prospective Students, GPO Box 2476, Melbourne, VIC 3001, Australia.

Tel: (61) 3 9925 2000
Email: study@rmit.edu.au
Website: www.rmit.edu.au/

RMIT was established in 1887 as the Working Men's College with the aim of bringing education to the working people of Melbourne. RMIT University has excellent opportunities for talented employees across academic, professional, teaching and research areas. RMIT is a world leader in Art and Design; Architecture; Education; Engineering; Development; Computer Science and Information Systems; Business and Management; and Communication and Media Studies.

Aboriginal Social and Emotional Wellbeing Scholarship

Purpose: For Aboriginal and/or Torres Strait Islander students working, or intending to work in the social and emotional well-being workforce, enrolled in related programs; worth up to US$135,000 for tuition fees, SSAF and financial support.

Eligibility: Identify as Aboriginal and/or Torres Strait Islander have applied for admission or be continuing study in one of the following programs at RMIT with enrolments in semester 1, 2023: 1. Bachelor of Applied Science (Psychology) 2. Bachelor of Social Science (Psychology) 3. Bachelor of Applied Science (Psychology) (Honours) 4. Bachelor of Social Work (Honours) 5. Bachelor of Youth Work and Youth Studies 6. Graduate Certificate in

Domestic and Family Violence 7. Online Graduate Diploma in Psychology 8. Graduate Diploma in Mental Health Nursing 9. Master of Mental Health Nursing 10. Master of Clinical Psychology 11. Master of Social Work 12. be an Australian citizen or permanent resident13. be currently employed by an ACCO or a mainstream health organisation in a Victorian Aboriginal SEWB (social and emotional well-being) team or role OR 14. if not currently employed, intend to work in a Victorian Aboriginal SEWB team or role in the future.

Type: Scholarship

Value: US$10,000 per annum, US$5,000 per annum

Length of Study: eight years

Country of Study: Any country

Closing Date: 30 January

Additional Information: www.rmit.edu.au/students/careers-opportunities/scholarships/coursework/sewb

For further information contact:

Tel: (61) 3 9925 2811

Email: scholarships@rmit.edu.au

Arcadia Landscape Architecture Scholarship in Landscape Architecture Design

Purpose: For Aboriginal and/or Torres Strait Islander student commencing a Bachelor of Landscape Architecture Design. If you are an Australian Aboriginal and/or Torres Strait Islander student commencing a Bachelor of Landscape Architecture Design, this scholarship could provide assistance for three years.

Eligibility: 1. Be an Aboriginal and/or Torres Strait Islander student 2. Be an Australian citizen 3. Be commencing full-time study in semester 1, 2023 in your first year of the Bachelor of Landscape Architecture Design (BP256) at RMIT University.

Type: Scholarship

Value: The scholarship provides US$5,000 per year

Length of Study: 3 Years

Frequency: Annual

Country of Study: Any country

Closing Date: 14 January

Additional Information: www.rmit.edu.au/students/careers-opportunities/scholarships/coursework/arcadia

For further information contact:

124 La Trobe St, Melbourne, VIC 3000, Australia.

Tel: (61) 3 9925 2000

Email: scholarships@rmit.edu.au

Interior Design-Masters of Arts by Research

Purpose: To offer a space within which candidates develop and contribute to the knowledge and possibilities of interior design

Eligibility: Open to the candidates of any country who have a First Degree of RMIT with at least a credit average in the final undergraduate year or a deemed equivalent by RMIT to a First Degree of RMIT with at least a credit average in the final undergraduate year or evidence of experience

Level of Study: Postgraduate

Length of Study: 2 years full-time (Masters) and 4 years part-time (PhD)

Application Procedure: Check website for further details

Closing Date: 31 October

Funding: Government

Contributor: Commonwealth Government

Additional Information: Please check the website for more details www.rlf.org.uk/

For further information contact:

Tel: (61) 3 9925 2819

Email: suzie.attiwill@rmit.edu.au

Royal Melbourne Institute of Technology PhD Scholarship in the School of Electrical and Computer Engineering

Eligibility: To be eligible for this scholarship, you must be enroled in a higher degree by research (HDR) at the RMIT School of Electrical and Computer Engineering; be a top ranking student using the RMIT University Scholarships Ranking Model; awarded an APA or RMIT PhD Scholarship and/or an RTS place; be aligned to one of the school's areas of strategic focus; not previously have held any Electrical and Computer Engineering (ECE) scholarship over the past 3 years (or more); demonstrate excellent academic results and research capability

Type: Scholarship

Value: AU$12,000

Frequency: Annual

Country of Study: Australia

Application Procedure: International applicants are expected to apply for the RMIT International PhD Scholarship. If successful, the school may supplement the scholarship stipend

Additional Information: Preference will be given to PhD students but high ranking Masters by Research students may also be eligible for the top-up scholarship www.rmit.edu.au/study-with-us/levels-of-study/research-programs/phd/phd-electrical–electronic-engineering-dr220

For further information contact:

Tel: (61) 3 9925 3174
Email: elecengresearch@rmit.edu.au

Royal Over-Seas League ARTS

Over-Seas House, Park Place, St James's Street, London SW1A 1LR, United Kingdom.

Tel: (44) 20 7408 0214
Email: roslarts@rosl.org.uk
Website: www.rosl.org.uk/rosl-arts
Contact: Mandy Murphy, Administrative Assistant

The Royal Over-Seas League is dedicated to championing international friendship and understanding throughout the Commonwealth and beyond. A not-for-profit private members' club, we've been bringing like-minded people together since our launch in 1910. ROSL is a self-funded organisation which operates under a Royal Charter. ROSL ARTS A cultural organisation providing performance opportunities, and support for young musicians and artists throughout the commonwealth. ROSL's renowned ARTS programme has worked for nearly 70 years to support the careers of emerging talent in the fields of music, visual arts and literature, and the programme continues to grow. We run competitions, scholarships, residencies and concerts and events at our headquarters in London and around the world.

Royal Over-Seas League Annual Music Competition

Purpose: To support and promote young Commonwealth musicians
Eligibility: The age limit for all competitors is 30 years. The solo awards are open to UK and Commonwealth citizens, and at least one member of an ensemble must also be a UK or Commonwealth citizen.
Level of Study: Professional development
Type: Competition
Value: The competition offers more than £75,000 in awards with a £15,000 first prize for solo performers and chamber ensemble awards of £10,000. The winners of the Wind and Brass, Singers, Strings, and Keyboard solo sections and the collaborative piano prize receive £5,000 each.
Frequency: Annual
Country of Study: Any country

Application Procedure: Applicants must see the website www.rosl.org.uk/amc/for-applicants
Closing Date: 6 January
Funding: Commercial, Individuals, Private, Trusts
No. of awards given last year: 19
No. of applicants last year: 500
Additional Information: www.rosl.org.uk/amc/for-applicants

For further information contact:

Royal Over-Seas League St James's St, Over-Seas House, Park Pl, London SW1A 1LR, United Kingdom.

Email: head-conmus@uwa.edu.au

Royal Over-Seas League Travel Scholarship

Purpose: To support and promote young United Kingdom and Commonwealth artists
Eligibility: Open to citizens of Commonwealth, including the United Kingdom, and former Commonwealth countries, who are up to 35 years of age, on year of application
Level of Study: Graduate, Postgraduate, Professional development, Unrestricted
Value: £3,000
Frequency: Annual
Country of Study: United Kingdom or Commonwealth
Application Procedure: Applicants must see the website www.roslarts.co.uk
No. of awards offered: 450
Closing Date: 31 March
Funding: Commercial, Private, Trusts
No. of awards given last year: 5
No. of applicants last year: 450
Additional Information: Each artist may be represented by one recent work only, any medium. Works must not exceed 152 cm in their largest dimension, inclusive of frame www.student.uwa.edu.au/faculties/able/music-students/prizes/royal-over-seas-league-travel-scholarship

For further information contact:

Email: Membership@rosl.org.uk

Royal Scottish Academy (RSA)

The Mound, Edinburgh EH2 2EL, United Kingdom.

Tel: (44) 131 624 6110
Email: info@royalscottishacademy.org

Website: www.royalscottishacademy.org/
Contact: Secretary

The Royal Scottish Academy (RSA) was founded in 1826 by a group of eleven eminent artists. The RSA runs a year-round programme of exhibitions, artist opportunities and related educational talks and events which support artists at all stages of their careers. Over the last decade, every aspect of the RSA has been interrogated to ensure that the Academy remains relevant to the needs of today's artists and architects. Importantly, the Academy continues to evolve, electing new Members, exhibiting new work, developing its collections and supporting and promoting excellence in contemporary Scottish art and architecture.

The Barns-Graham Travel Award

Subjects: Painting, sculpture or printmaking
Purpose: The RSA Barns-Graham Travel Award provides a travel and research opportunity for graduating and postgraduate students.
Eligibility: 1. Entrants must be painters, printmakers or sculptors. 2. Entrants must either be graduating in current year or currently studying at postgraduate level at one of the following art schools in Scotland Aberdeen, Dundee, Edinburgh, Glasgow, and UHI.
Level of Study: Postgraduate
Type: Travel award
Value: £2,000
Frequency: Annual
Country of Study: Scotland
Application Procedure: Apply online. royalscottishacademy.submittable.com/submit. A collaborative application must only include one CV and be in keeping with the exact same guidelines and limits as a single artist application.
No. of awards offered: 1
Closing Date: 3 April
Funding: Trusts
Contributor: Barns-Graham Charitable Trust
No. of awards given last year: 1
Additional Information: Please see the website for further details www.royalscottishacademy.org/artist/rsa-barns-graham-travel-award/

For further information contact:

The Mound, Edinburgh EH2 2EL, United Kingdom.

Tel: (44) 131 624 6110
Email: opportunities@royalscottishacademy.org

The Royal Scottish Academy John Kinross Scholarships to Florence

Purpose: The RSA John Kinross Scholarships are for final year and postgraduate artists and architects to spend a period of 6 to 12 weeks in Florence to research and develop their practice.
Eligibility: 1. Visual Art Applications are invited from students in their Honours or post-graduate years of study at one of the following art schools in Scotland (Aberdeen, Dundee, Edinburgh, Glasgow, and UHI). 2. Architecture Applicants must be RIBA Part 2 students in their final year, or currently attending a Masters programme, at one of the six Scottish Schools of Architecture. Group work is not admissible.
Level of Study: Masters Degree, Postgraduate
Type: Scholarship
Value: £3000 (Ten artists receive an initial payment of £2,800 for travel, accommodation and subsistence, with the remaining £200 awarded on the satisfactory completion of the scholarship.)
Length of Study: 6 to 12 weeks
Frequency: Annual
Country of Study: Scotland
Application Procedure: Apply online: royalscottishacademy.submittable.com/submit
No. of awards offered: 10
Closing Date: 3 April
No. of awards given last year: 10
Additional Information: For more details www.royalscottishacademy.org/artist/the-rsa-john-kinross-scholarships/

For further information contact:

The Mound, Edinburgh EH2 2EL, United Kingdom.

Tel: (44) 131 624 6110
Email: opportunities@royalscottishacademy.org

The Royal Scottish Academy William Littlejohn Award for Excellence and Innovation in Water-Based Media

Purpose: To provide young professional artists who are Scottish or have studied in Scotland, with a period for personal development and the exploration of new directions
Eligibility: Entrants must be working in water-based media (any pigment mixed with water), entrants must be born or have been resident in Scotland for at least 3 years, in the case of students applying, entrants must either be graduating in current year or studying at postgraduate level at one of the following art schools in Scotland (Aberdeen, Dundee, Edinburgh, Glasgow, and Moray)

Level of Study: Postgraduate
Type: Residency
Value: £2,000
Frequency: Annual
Study Establishment: Hospitalfield House, Arbroath
Country of Study: Scotland
Application Procedure: Applicants must contact the RSA
Closing Date: 12 June
Funding: Private
Contributor: The Bequest Fund administered by the RSA
Additional Information: www.royalscottishacademy.org/artist/the-william-littlejohn-award/

For further information contact:

Email: opportunities@royalscottishacademy.org

THE RSA DAVID MICHIE TRAVEL AWARD

Purpose: The RSA David Michie Travel Award (£2,500) provides a travel and research opportunity for graduating and postgraduate drawing and painting students
Eligibility: Entrants must be graduating artists and post graduates whose area of practice is drawing and/or painting. Entrants must either be graduating in 2023 or currently studying at postgraduate level at one of the following art schools in Scotland: Aberdeen, Dundee, Edinburgh, Glasgow, and UHI.
Type: Award
Value: £2,500
Country of Study: Any country
Closing Date: 3 April
Contributor: Michie Family and administered by the Royal Scottish Academy
Additional Information: https://www.royalscottishacademy.org/opportunities/rsa-david-michie-award/

For further information contact:

The Mound, Edinburgh EH2 2EL, United Kingdom.

Tel: (44) 131 624 6110
Email: opportunities@royalscottishacademy.org

Royal Society

6-9 Carlton House Terrace, London SW1Y 5AG, United Kingdom.

Tel: (44) 207 451 2500
Email: webmanager@royalsociety.org

Website: royalsociety.org/
Contact: Charles Fleming Publishing Award

The Royal Society is a Fellowship of many of the world's most eminent scientists and is the oldest scientific academy in continuous existence. The Society's fundamental purpose, reflected in its founding Charters of the 1660s, is to recognise, promote, and support excellence in science and to encourage the development and use of science for the benefit of humanity. The Society has played a part in some of the most fundamental, significant, and life-changing discoveries in scientific history and Royal Society scientists continue to make outstanding contributions to science in many research areas.

Charles Fleming Publishing Award

Purpose: To support the preparation of scientific books and relevant publications.
Eligibility: The fund will give preference to those who do not normally have access to funds through their place of employment for assisting with the writing and publication of their research or a review of a particular area of scientific endeavour.
Level of Study: Post graduate
Type: Award
Value: Up to NZ$8,000
Frequency: Annual
Country of Study: New Zealand
Application Procedure: A Charles Fleming Publishing Fund Application form (downloaded from website) must be completed. Applicants should: 1. Describe the project for which the funding is being applied, and explain how funding will assist in meeting its objectives (1000 words maximum). Please include start and estimated end dates for the project. 2. Include a budget with details of other funding received or applied for. 3. Include a brief Curriculum Vitae (1 page) plus a list of any refereed publications for the previous 5 years. 4. Include contact details. Please email the application to awards@royalsociety.org.nz.
No. of awards offered: 1
Closing Date: 31 March
No. of awards given last year: 2
Additional Information: www.royalsociety.org.nz/what-we-do/funds-and-opportunities/charles-fleming-fund/charles-fleming-publishing-award/#:~:text=Annual%20award%20worth%20up%20to,of%20the%20Academy%20Executive%20Committee.

R

For further information contact:

11 Turnbull St Thorndon, Wellington, 6011 Aotearoa, New Zealand.

Email: awards@royalsociety.org.nz

Charles Fleming Senior Scientist Award

Purpose: To support the research of a senior scientist at a university, Crown Research Institute, polytechnic or other research organisation in New Zealand, and that of their research group.

Eligibility: The fund will give preference to requests for research expenses over and above those that a university or Crown Research Institute in New Zealand would normally be expected to cover. Examples include expenses to 1. Cover a visit to an institution in New Zealand or overseas; 2. Expenses related to specialist assays or methodologies; 3. Research assistance to carry out a specific task; or 4. Expenses relating to a visit to the research group of a visitor.

Level of Study: Post Doctoral

Type: Grant

Value: Up to NZ$10,000

Frequency: Annual

Country of Study: New Zealand

Application Procedure: A Senior Scientist Application Form (downloaded from website) must be completed. Applicants should provide the following information 1. Project description (suitable for a non-specialist scientist; one page maximum); 2. Method, resources, collaboration (one page maximum, excluding references); 3. Expected outcomes from this project (This section should NOT be used to discuss scientific outcomes which should be covered in the previous two sections; one page maximum.); 4. Researcher experience; 5. Curriculum Vitae (one page maximum for each named research person); 6. Budget details and justification; 7. Approvals. Please email the application.

No. of awards offered: 1

Closing Date: 31 March

No. of awards given last year: 1

Additional Information: www.royalsociety.org.nz/what-we-do/funds-and-opportunities/charles-fleming-fund/charles-fleming-senior-scientist-award/

For further information contact:

11 Turnbull St Thorndon, Wellington, 6011 Aotearoa, New Zealand.

Email: awards@royalsociety.org.nz

Global Challenges Research Fund Challenge-led Grants (GCRF)

Purpose: The scheme provided funding to support research consortia involving groups in the UK and developing countries to address global challenges.

Eligibility: 1. Your proposed research must address two or more GCRF thematic areas. The proposal must ultimately benefit the economic development and welfare of developing countries (i.e. be compliant with the ODA guidelines). 2. Your proposal must fall within the remit of the United Kingdom academies and must be interdisciplinary. The consortia must consist of one United Kingdom research group and two research groups from developing countries

Level of Study: Graduate

Type: Grant

Country of Study: Any country

Application Procedure: Application should be submitted through the Royal Society's grants and awards management system (Flexi-Grant®). The weblink is www.grants.royalsociety.org/

Closing Date: 11 September

Funding: Private

Additional Information: royalsociety.org/grants-schemes-awards/grants/challenge-led-grants/

For further information contact:

Email: ChallengeGrants@royalsociety.org

Hutton Fund

Subjects: Zoology, Botany, Geology

Purpose: To encourage research in New Zealand zoology, botany and geology.

Eligibility: Please note that funding is not available for fees, thesis production or conference attendance.

Type: Grant

Value: NZ$1,000

Frequency: Annual

Country of Study: New Zealand

Closing Date: 31 March

Additional Information: www.royalsociety.org.nz/what-we-do/funds-and-opportunities/hutton-fund/

For further information contact:

Email: awards@royalsociety.org.nz

Olga Kennard Research Fellowship Scheme

Purpose: The Royal Society Olga Kennard Research Fellowship is a privately funded award through the University

Research Fellowship for early career researchers working in the field of crystallography. This award is supported by a donation in the name of Professor Olga Kennard OBE FRS by the Cambridge Crystallographic Data Centre.

Eligibility: Applicants must be citizens of the EU, Norway, Israel or Switzerland. There are no UK residency requirements for this appointment. Applicants must have at least three years' postdoctoral experience and should be at least 26 years but should not have passed their 40th birthday on 1 October in the year of application

Level of Study: Postdoctorate

Type: Fellowship

Value: Salary with London allowance where appropriate, together with annual research expenses, travel expenses and a contribution to baggage costs for overseas applicants

Length of Study: 5 years

Study Establishment: Appropriate university departments

Country of Study: United Kingdom

Application Procedure: Applications can only be submitted online on the Royal Society's E-gap system. For further information on this scheme or the E-gap process, submit an enquiry to ukgrants@royalsoc.ac.uk

No. of awards offered: 1

Additional Information: Further information is available on the website www.vrijmetselaarsgilde.eu/Maconnieke%20Encyclopedie/RMAP~1/TRS/fell_okr.htm, www.royalsociety.org/people/olga-kennard-11735/, www.royalsociety.org/grants-schemes-awards/grants/university-research/jon-agirre/

For further information contact:

Tel: (44) 207 451 2547
Email: ukresearch.appointments@royalsoc.ac.uk

Raewyn Good Study Award for Māori and Pasifika Social Science Research

Subjects: Social Science

Purpose: For Māori and Pasifika postgraduate student undertaking a Master's which involves social sciences research.

Eligibility: Māori and Pasifika postgraduate students at any New Zealand university/wānanga

Level of Study: Postgraduate

Type: Grant

Value: NZ$6,000

Length of Study: 1 year

Frequency: Annual

Country of Study: New Zealand

No. of awards offered: 1

Closing Date: 31 August

Funding: Foundation

Additional Information: www.royalsociety.org.nz/what-we-do/funds-and-opportunities/raewyn-good-study-award/

For further information contact:

Email: awards@royalsociety.org.nz

RHT Bates Postgraduate Scholarship

Subjects: Physical Sciences and Engineering

Purpose: For a PhD in the Physical Sciences and Engineering in a New Zealand university.

Eligibility: Applicants must have physical sciences or engineering as a significant part of their undergraduate degree. For the purposes of this scholarship, physical sciences shall be deemed to mean physics, chemistry and mathematical and information sciences. At the time of application students must be engaged in postgraduate studies (honours, masters or doctorate). Students in their final year of undergraduate study are ineligible to apply.

Level of Study: Postgraduate

Type: Grant

Value: NZ$6,000

Frequency: Annual

Country of Study: New Zealand

No. of awards offered: 1

Closing Date: 31 August

Additional Information: www.royalsociety.org.nz/what-we-do/funds-and-opportunities/r-h-t-bates-postgraduate-scholarship/

For further information contact:

Email: awards@royalsociety.org.nz

Royal Society South East Asia Rainforest Research Project - Travel Grants

Eligibility: Open to scientists and nationals of European Union countries and South East Asia countries who are PhD or MSc students

Level of Study: Postgraduate

Type: Travel grant

Value: Economy air fare plus two weeks subsistence for European scientists travelling to South East Asia or three months subsistence for South East Asian scientists travelling to Europe

Length of Study: Varies

Country of Study: Other

Application Procedure: Applicants must apply for information, available on request from Programme Research Coordinator, Dr Stephen Sutton email sutton@hh.edi.co.uk

Additional Information: Further information available on request www.royalsociety.org.nz/what-we-do/funds-and-opportunities/raewyn-good-study-award/

For further information contact:

Department of Zoology, University of Cambridge, Downing Street, Cambridge CB2 3EJ, United Kingdom.

Fax: (44) 8 988 4046
Email: ajdavis@pc.jaring.my

Sir Henry Dale Fellowships

Purpose: This scheme is for outstanding post-doctoral scientists wishing to build their own UK-based, independent research career addressing an important biomedical question. It supports research ranging from molecules and the cells vital to life, to the spread of diseases and vectors of disease around the world, to public health research.
Eligibility: You can apply for a Small Grant if you're a humanities or social science researcher with a compelling research vision and you want to do one or more of the following 1. Build your professional network. 2. Develop a new research agenda. 3. Increase the impact of your work
Level of Study: Postdoctorate, Research
Type: Research grant
Value: The scheme covers 1. A basic salary for the Fellow, as determined by the host organisation. 2. Wellcome Trust fellowship supplement of £7,500 per annum for your personal support. 3. Research expenses, normally including research post (postdoctoral research assistant or technician)
Length of Study: 5 Years
Frequency: Every 5 years
Country of Study: Any country
Application Procedure: Applications should be submitted through the Wellcome Trust Grant Tracker (WTGT) wtgrants. wellcome.org/Login.aspx?ReturnUrl=%2f
Closing Date: 21 March
Additional Information: This scheme is not open to individuals who wish to combine research with a continuing clinical career in medicine, psychology, dentistry or veterinary practice. For more information royalsociety.org/grants-schemes-awards/grants/henry-dale/

For further information contact:

Tel: (44) 207 451 2500
Email: grants@royalsociety.org

Skinner Fund

Subjects: History, art, culture, physical and social anthropology of the Māori and other Polynesian people
Purpose: To encourage research in the study of the history, art, culture, physical and social anthropology of the Māori and other Polynesian people

Eligibility: The results of research aided by grants from the fund, shall, where possible, be published in New Zealand, with due acknowledgement of the source of financial assistance, and one copy of any report stemming from such research shall be sent to the Society.
Type: Grant
Value: NZ$1,000
Frequency: Annual
Country of Study: New Zealand
Closing Date: 31 March
Additional Information: www.royalsociety.org.nz/what-we-do/funds-and-opportunities/skinner-fund/

For further information contact:

Email: awards@royalsociety.org.nz

The Sir Hugh Kawharu Masters Scholarship for Innovation in Science

Subjects: Sciences
Purpose: Supporting and encouraging masters level study by Māori in the sciences
Eligibility: To be eligible applicants must be enrolled full-time in a one or two year masters degree in a science discipline; and be persons of Māori descent able to explain their tribal connections.
Level of Study: Masters
Type: Scholarship
Value: NZ$10,000
Length of Study: 1-2 Years
Frequency: Annual
Country of Study: New Zealand
No. of awards offered: 1
Funding: Foundation
Contributor: Sir Hugh Kawharu Foundation
Additional Information: www.royalsociety.org.nz/what-we-do/funds-and-opportunities/the-sir-hugh-kawharu-masters-scholarship-for-innovation-in-science/

For further information contact:

Email: awards@royalsociety.org.nz

Royal Society of Chemistry

Thomas Graham House (290), Science Park, Milton Road, Cambridge CB4 0WF, United Kingdom.

Tel: (44) 1223 420066
Website: www.rsc.org/

Our origins can be traced through the history of our predecessor societies: the Chemical Society, the Society for Analytical Chemistry, the Royal Institute of Chemistry and the Faraday Society. These four bodies merged in 1980 to form The Royal Society of Chemistry, which was granted a new Royal Charter in 1980. The Royal Society of Chemistry's purpose is to advance excellence in the chemical sciences – to improve the lives of people around the world now and in the future. As a not-for-profit organisation, we invest our surplus income to achieve our charitable objectives in support of the chemical science community and advancing excellence in the chemical sciences.

Royal Society of Chemistry Journals Grants for International Authors

Purpose: To allow international authors to visit other countries in order to collaborate in research, exchange research ideas and results, and to give or receive special expertise and training
Eligibility: Open to anyone with a recent publication in any of the Society's journals. Those from the United Kingdom or Republic of Ireland are excluded
Level of Study: Professional development
Type: Grant
Value: Up to £2,500 cover travel and subsistence (but not research related costs) and are available
Length of Study: Normally 1–3 months
Country of Study: Any country
Application Procedure: Candidates must apply for application forms, together with full details, from the International Affairs Officer
No. of awards offered: 107
Closing Date: 1 October
No. of awards given last year: 83
No. of applicants last year: 107
Additional Information: Please see the website for further details pubs.rsc.org/en/content/articlehtml/2003/dt/b211852c

Royal Society of Edinburgh

22-26 George Street, Edinburgh EH2 2PQ, United Kingdom.

Tel: (44) 131 240 5000
Email: scarcassonne@therse.org.uk
Website: www.rse.org.uk/
Contact: Sasha Carcassonne, Research Awards Officer

The RSE is an educational charity, registered in Scotland, operating on a wholly independent and non-party-political basis and providing public benefit throughout Scotland. The RSE was created in 1783 by Royal Charter for "the advancement of learning and useful knowledge" and since then have drawn upon the considerable strengths and varied expertise of our Fellows, of which there are currently around 1600, who are based in Scotland, the rest of the UK and beyond.

Royal Society of Edinburgh Personal Research Fellowships

Purpose: To provide outstanding researchers, who have the potential to become leaders in their chosen field, with the opportunity to build an independent research career
Eligibility: Open to persons of all nationalities who have 2 to 6 years postdoctoral experience. They must also show that they have the capacity for innovative research and the potential to become leaders in their field
Level of Study: Doctorate
Value: Salary up to £55k plus research costs of £10k per year
Length of Study: 3-12 months
Frequency: Annual
Study Establishment: Any Higher Education Institution in Scotland
Country of Study: Scotland
Application Procedure: Applicants must complete an application form, available on the RSE website. Applicants should negotiate directly with their host institution
No. of awards offered: 53
Closing Date: 24 March
Contributor: Scottish Government, BP and Caledonian Research Fund
No. of awards given last year: 3
No. of applicants last year: 53
Additional Information: Please note: this scheme is no longer running. www.rse.org.uk/awards/rse-personal-research-fellowships/

For further information contact:

22-26 George Street, Edinburgh EH2 2PQ, United Kingdom.

Email: schooloffice-ls@dundee.ac.uk

RSE FULBRIGHT SCHOLAR AWARD

Purpose: We are delighted to accept applications for the 2022/2023 round of the RSE Fulbright Scholar Award, in partnership with the US-UK Fulbright Commission.
Eligibility: You are a resident in the UK and have a clear and continuing connection with Scotland and that you hold a PhD (or equivalent professional training or experience) in a relevant area before departure to the US.
Type: Award

Value: US$5,000 per month
Length of Study: Maximum 3 months
Country of Study: Any country
Closing Date: 8 November
Additional Information: rse.org.uk/funding-collaboration/award/fulbright-rse-scholar-award/

For further information contact:

Tel: (44) 131 240 5000
Email: fulbrightprogrammes@fulbright.org.uk.

RSE Research Network Grants

Purpose: RSE Research Network Grants are designed to create and/or to consolidate collaborative partnerships over a two-year period.
Eligibility: The awards are open to applications from Principal Investigators from all academic disciplines and all career stages who are eligible as one of the following: a full or part-time academic in any academic discipline and are tenured and/or salaried staff of a Higher Education Institution (HEI), Research Institute (RI) or Cultural Institution (CI) in Scotland. Applicants must be on open-ended, continuing, or fixed-term contracts which extend three months beyond the end date of the envisaged grant period. The RSE grant cannot be used to extend an applicant's contract. a retired academic in any academic field who retains demonstrable links with a Scottish HEI, RI or CI with a demonstrable commitment to teaching and research within that institution. a full or part-time practitioner or research-active member of staff in any academic field employed by a Scottish Cultural Institution with a demonstrable commitment to teaching and research within that institution. Applicants on short or fixed-term contracts should ensure their contracts extend for at least three months after the end of the proposed project. Early career researchers on staged contracts to permanent lectureship positions are eligible but must be in contract for the duration of the award. Joint applications are accepted for the RSE Research Network Grants where there is evidence of the partners having worked together successfully previously to bring together complementary skills and expertise. Collaborations may be between Scottish or overseas HEIs and/or practitioners, policy makers, Research Institutions and Cultural Institutions provided that: the lead applicant is based in Scotland; the key principles of the awards scheme are recognised; and the application is interdisciplinary. A new application will not be considered when a report on a previous RSE grant is overdue.
Type: Grant
Value: £20,000
Length of Study: 24 months
Country of Study: Any country

Closing Date: 24 March
Additional Information: rse.org.uk/funding-collaboration/award/rse-research-network-grants/

For further information contact:

Email: Awards@theRSE.org.uk

RSE Research Workshop Grants

Purpose: RSE Research Workshop Grants are designed to encourage collaborative investigation into a research proposition at an early stage of development.
Eligibility: The awards are open to applications from Principal Investigators from all academic disciplines and all career stages who are eligible as one of the following: a full or part-time academic in any academic discipline and are tenured and/or salaried staff of a Higher Education Institution (HEI), Research Institute (RI) or Cultural Institution (CI) in Scotland. Applicants must be on open-ended, continuing, or fixed-term contracts which extend three months beyond the end date of the envisaged grant period. The RSE grant cannot be used to extend an applicant's contract. a retired academic in any academic field who retains demonstrable links with a Scottish HEI, RI or CI with a demonstrable commitment to teaching and research within that institution. a full or part-time practitioner or research-active member of staff in any academic field employed by a Scottish Cultural Institution with a demonstrable commitment to teaching and research within that institution. Applicants on short or fixed-term contracts should ensure their contracts extend for at least three months after the end of the proposed project. Early career researchers on staged contracts to permanent lectureship positions are eligible but must be in contract for the duration of the award. Joint applications are accepted for the RSE Research Workshop Grants where there is evidence of the partners having worked together successfully previously to bring together complementary skills and expertise. Collaborations may be between Scottish or overseas HEIs and/or practitioners, policy makers, Research Institutions and Cultural Institutions provided that: the lead applicant is based in Scotland; the key principles of the awards scheme are recognised; and the application is interdisciplinary. A new application will not be considered when a report on a previous RSE grant is overdue.
Type: Grant
Value: £10,000
Length of Study: 12 months
Country of Study: Any country
Closing Date: 24 March
Additional Information: rse.org.uk/funding-collaboration/award/rse-research-workshop-grants/

For further information contact:

Email:　Awards@theRSE.org.uk

RSE Small Research Grants

Purpose: RSE Small Research Grants are designed to support personally conducted high-quality research. The awards are available to cover eligible costs arising from a defined research project.

Eligibility: The awards are open to applications from Principal Investigators from all academic disciplines and all career stages who are eligible as one of the following: a full or part-time academic in any academic discipline and are tenured and/or salaried staff of a Higher Education Institution (HEI), Research Institute (RI) or Cultural Institution (CI) in Scotland. Applicants must be on open-ended, continuing, or fixed-term contracts which extend three months beyond the end date of the envisaged grant period. The RSE grant cannot be used to extend an applicant's contract. a retired academic in any academic field who retains demonstrable links with a Scottish HEI, RI or CI with a demonstrable commitment to teaching and research within that institution. a full or part-time practitioner or research-active member of staff in any academic field employed by a Scottish Cultural Institution with a demonstrable commitment to teaching and research within that institution. Applicants on short or fixed-term contracts should ensure their contracts extend for at least three months after the end of the proposed project. Early career researchers on staged contracts to permanent lectureship positions are eligible but must be in contract for the duration of the award. Collaborations may be between Scottish or overseas HEIs and/or practitioners, policymakers, Research Institutions and Cultural Institutions provided that: the lead applicant is based in Scotland; the key principles of the awards scheme are recognised; and the application is interdisciplinary. A new application will not be considered when a report on a previous RSE grant is overdue.

Type: Grant

Value: £500-£5,000

Length of Study: 12 months

Country of Study: Any country

Closing Date: 24 March

Additional Information: rse.org.uk/funding-collaboration/award/rse-small-grants/

For further information contact:

Tel:　(44) 131 240 5000

Email:　Awards@theRSE.org.uk

Royal Society of Medicine (RSM)

1 Wimpole Street, London W1G 0AE, United Kingdom.

Tel:　　(44) 20 7290 2900
Email:　info@rsm.ac.uk
Website:　www.rsm.ac.uk/
Contact:　Awards Manager, Alademic Department

The Royal Society of Medicine is a leading provider of high-quality continuing postgraduate education and learning to the medical profession. Its mission is to advance health, through education and innovation. Independent and apolitical, the RSM also aims to actively encourage and support those who are entering medicine and healthcare.

Adrian Tanner Prize

Purpose: To encourage surgical trainees to submit the best clinical case reports

Eligibility: Open to all surgical trainees.

Type: Prize

Value: £250

Frequency: Annual

Study Establishment: Royal Society of Medicine–Surgery section

Country of Study: United Kingdom

Application Procedure: Apply online www.rsm.ac.uk/prizes-and-awards/prizes-for-trainees/. Clinical case reports should be submitted for this prize focusing upon the multidisciplinary nature of the care of a surgical patient. The report should be no longer than 500 words and have a maximum of 5 references. Abstracts previously presented at another meeting should be declared.

Closing Date: 1 June

Additional Information: www.rsm.ac.uk/prizes-and-awards/prizes-for-trainees/

Alan Emery Prize

Purpose: To reward the best published research article in Medical Genetics in the past 2 years

Eligibility: Open to candidates in an accredited training or research post in the United Kingdom

Type: Prize

Value: £500 or £300 or 1 year membership of Royal Society of Medicine

Frequency: Annual

Application Procedure: Candidates must submit full copy of the article, curriculum vitae or covering letter explaining the significance of the publication
No. of awards offered: 7
Closing Date: 5 March
No. of awards given last year: 1
No. of applicants last year: 7

For further information contact:

Email: genetics@rsm.ac.uk

BMDST-RSM Student Elective Awards

Purpose: Medical and dental students of UK and other EU medical and dental schools intending to go on an elective including a research element in the next academic year
Eligibility: Medical and dental students of UK and other EU medical and dental schools intending to go on an elective including a research element in the next academic year
Type: Award
Value: Successful applicants will receive funding
Country of Study: Any country
Closing Date: 31 July
Additional Information: www.rsm.ac.uk/prizes-and-awards/prizes-for-students/

For further information contact:

1 Wimpole St, London W1G 0AE, United Kingdom.

Tel: (44) 20 7290 2900

Cardiology Section Presidents Prize

Purpose: The President's prize will be given for original research from specialist registrars in cardiology.
Eligibility: Open to Cardiology trainees who have received all or part of their training at recognised centres in the UK are eligible.
Level of Study: Research
Type: Prize
Value: 1st prize Medal and £1,000 and 2nd prize £500
Frequency: Annual
Country of Study: United Kingdom
Application Procedure: Please submit an abstract of no more than 200 words, based on a subject which represents original work. Apply online www.shocklogic.com/scripts/jmevent/Abstract.asp?Client_Id=%27RSM%27&Project_Id=%2706CDP234%27&System_Id=1
Closing Date: 9 April

Additional   Information: www.rsm.ac.uk/prizes-and-awards/prizes-for-trainees/

Catastrophes & Conflict Forum Medical Student Essay Prize

Eligibility: Open to candidates who are enroled full-time at a United Kingdom medical school
Level of Study: Postgraduate
Type: Prize
Value: £250 plus encouragement and advice on submitting the essay for publication in the JRSM
Frequency: Annual
Study Establishment: Royal Society of Medicine
Country of Study: United Kingdom
Application Procedure: Candidates should submit an essay no longer than 1,500 words, emailed in Word format
No. of awards offered: 9
Closing Date: 1 March
No. of awards given last year: 2
No. of applicants last year: 9

For further information contact:

Email: catastrophes@rsm.ac.uk

Clinical Forensic and Legal Medicine Section Poster Competition

Purpose: Postgraduate students who have been working for qualifications in forensic and legal medicine or medical law to present a case or a poster in clinical studies
Eligibility: Open to anyone who is undertaking or has completed a post graduate qualification in a clinical forensic or legal field related to forensic medicine.
Level of Study: Postgraduate
Type: Prize
Value: £250
Frequency: Annual
Country of Study: United Kingdom
Application Procedure: Apply online www.shocklogic.com/scripts/jmevent/Abstract.asp?Client_Id=%27RSM%27&Project_Id=%2706CLP387%27&System_Id=1
Closing Date: 7 September
Additional Information: Students studying other specialities may submit their work to be considered for presentation purposes but are NOT eligible for the prize. All presenters will receive a certificate after the event. www.rsm.ac.uk/prizes-and-awards/prizes-for-trainees/

Clinical Forensics and Legal Medicine: postgraduate poster prize

Eligibility: Postgraduate students who have been working for qualifications in forensic and legal medicine or medical law.
Type: Prize
Value: £250
Country of Study: Any country
Closing Date: 7 September
Additional Information: www.rsm.ac.uk/prizes-and-awards/prizes-for-students/

For further information contact:

1 Wimpole St, London W1G 0AE, United Kingdom.

Tel: (44) 20 7290 2900

Clinical Immunology & Allergy President's Prize

Purpose: To support training grade doctors, young scientists and medical students with an immunological or allergy component of their clinical research.
Eligibility: Open to training grade doctors and young scientists (not above Specialist Registrar, Grade B Clinical Scientist or equivalent grade) with an immunological or allergy component of their clinical research
Level of Study: Research
Type: Prize
Value: £300 (First prize); two prizes of £100 (Second prize)
Frequency: Annual
Country of Study: United Kingdom
Application Procedure: Check website for further details
No. of awards offered: 3
Closing Date: 19 January
No. of awards given last year: 3
Additional Information: www.rsm.ac.uk/prizes-and-awards/prizes-for-trainees/

Clinical Neurosciences Gordon Holmes Prize

Purpose: To award a research prize in clinical neurosciences
Eligibility: Trainees in neurosciences, including neurology, neurosurgery, neurophysiology, neuropathology or neuroradiology
Type: Prize
Value: £300
Frequency: Every 2 years
Country of Study: Any country
Application Procedure: Please check the website www.rsm.ac.uk/prizes-awards/trainees.aspx

Closing Date: 7 March
Additional Information: www.rsm.ac.uk/prizes-and-awards/prizes-for-trainees/

For further information contact:

Email: cns@rsm.ac.uk

Clinical Neurosciences President's Prize

Purpose: To encourage clinical neurosciences case presentation
Eligibility: Open to Trainees in all areas of clinical neurosciences, including neurology, neurosurgery, neurophysiology, neuropsychiatry, neuropathology or neuroradiology.
Type: Prize
Value: 1. Official President's prize Best oral presentation of case report(s) £300. 2. Live popular vote prize Certificate
Frequency: Every 2 years
Country of Study: United Kingdom
Application Procedure: The Clinical Neurosciences Section would like to welcome summary abstracts of up to 250 words of a clinical paper on an unusual case report or a short case series which should not be derived from a supervised research project. Please ensure your abstract is anonymous - i.e. your name and the name of the institution are not mentioned or included in the text.
Closing Date: 25 January
Additional Information: Please note: An individual can submit more than one case report but no more than one abstract will be eligible - abstract receiving the highest mark will be selected. www.rsm.ac.uk/prizes-and-awards/prizes-for-trainees/

Coloproctology John of Arderne Medal

Purpose: To award the presenter of the best paper presented at the short papers meeting of the section of coloproctology.
Eligibility: Open to all coloproctology and surgery trainees and medical students.
Type: Award
Value: The John of Arderne medal and a travelling fellowship
Frequency: Annual
Study Establishment: Varies
Country of Study: Any country
Application Procedure: Apply online. Abstracts should state briefly and clearly the purpose, methods, results and conclusions of the work and must not exceed 200 words.
Closing Date: 18 November
Additional Information: www.rsm.ac.uk/prizes-and-awards/prizes-for-trainees/

Critical Care Medicine Section: Audit and Quality Improvement Project Prize

Eligibility: All UK & Eire junior doctors in Intensive Care Medicine
Type: Prize
Value: annual subscription to CRIT-IQ (an excellent resource for the FFICM) and 1 year free RSM membership.
Country of Study: Any country
No. of awards offered: 3
Closing Date: 20 January
Additional Information: www.rsm.ac.uk/prizes-and-awards/prizes-for-trainees/

For further information contact:

1 Wimpole St, London W1G 0AE, United Kingdom.

Tel: (44) 20 7290 2900

Dermatology Clinicopathological Meetings

Eligibility: Open to all dermatology trainees.
Type: Prize
Value: First prize £50 and RSM certificate
Frequency: Annual
Country of Study: United Kingdom
No. of awards given last year: 1
Additional Information: For more details, please refer the website: www.rsm.ac.uk/prizes-and-awards/prizes-for-trainees/

Dermatology Section: Trainee Research Prize

Eligibility: All dermatology trainees in the United Kingdom and Ireland. Newly qualified consultants whose research was completed as a trainee in the year before the submission date.
Type: Prize
Value: First prize: £250
Country of Study: Any country
Closing Date: 10 March
Additional Information: www.rsm.ac.uk/prizes-and-awards/prizes-for-trainees/

For further information contact:

1 Wimpole St, London W1G 0AE, United Kingdom.

Tel: (44) 20 7290 2900

Dermatology Section: Hugh Wallace Essay Prize

Eligibility: Dermatology registrars.
Type: Prize
Value: First prize: £250
Country of Study: Any country
Closing Date: 10 March
Additional Information: www.rsm.ac.uk/prizes-and-awards/prizes-for-trainees/

For further information contact:

1 Wimpole St, London W1G 0AE, United Kingdom.

Tel: (44) 20 7290 2900

Ellison-Cliffe Travelling Fellowship

Purpose: The award is intended to cover expenses for travel abroad, to one or two centres, for a period of not less than six months, in pursuit of further study, research or clinical training relevant to the applicant's current interests.
Eligibility: Fellows of the Royal Society of Medicine who are of specialist registrar or lecturer grade or equivalent, or who are consultants within three years of their first consultant appointment.
Type: Prize
Value: First prize: £15,000
Country of Study: Any country
Closing Date: 4 October
Additional Information: www.rsm.ac.uk/prizes-and-awards/travel-grants-and-bursaries/

For further information contact:

1 Wimpole St, London W1G 0AE, United Kingdom.

Tel: (44) 20 7290 2900

Emergency Medicine section: Innovation in ED education for students

Subjects: Students, nurses and doctors all grades working in Emergency Departments
Purpose: The aim of this prize is to recognise and promote educational initiatives in Emergency Departments.
Eligibility: The top 3 entrants will be invited to deliver a presentation on their initiative at a designated Emergency Medicine Section meeting at the Royal Society of Medicine.
Type: Prize
Value: £100
Country of Study: Any country

No. of awards offered: 3
Closing Date: 3 April
Additional Information: www.rsm.ac.uk/prizes-and-awards/
travel-grants-and-bursaries/

Emergency Medicine section: Innovation in ED education for trainers

Purpose: The aim of this prize is to recognise and promote educational initiatives in Emergency Departments.
Eligibility: Students, nurses and doctors all grades working in Emergency Departments
Type: Prize
Value: £100
Country of Study: Any country
No. of awards offered: 3
Closing Date: 3 April
Additional Information: www.rsm.ac.uk/prizes-and-awards/
prizes-for-trainees/

For further information contact:

1 Wimpole St, London W1G 0AE, United Kingdom.

Tel: (44) 20 7290 2900

Emergency Medicine section: Innovation in ED education Prize

Purpose: The aim of this prize is to recognize and promote educational initiatives in Emergency Departments.
Eligibility: Students, nurses and doctors all grades working in Emergency Departments
Type: Prize
Value: £100 will be awarded
Country of Study: Any country
No. of awards offered: 3
Closing Date: 3 April
Additional Information: www.rsm.ac.uk/prizes-and-awards/
prizes-for-students/

For further information contact:

1 Wimpole St, London W1G 0AE, United Kingdom.

Tel: (44) 20 7290 2900

Emergency Medicine Section: Students' Prize for students

Purpose: This prize is to contribute towards the cost of an elective abroad, with the intention of gaining experience in the practice of emergency medicine.

Eligibility: Medical students
Type: Prize
Value: £1 x £250 and one year
Country of Study: Any country
Closing Date: 3 April
Additional Information: www.rsm.ac.uk/prizes-and-awards/
prizes-for-students/

For further information contact:

1 Wimpole St, London W1G 0AE, United Kingdom.

Tel: (44) 20 7290 2900

Emergency Medicine Section: Students' Prize for trainers

Purpose: This prize is to contribute towards the cost of an elective abroad, with the intention of gaining experience in the practice of emergency medicine.
Eligibility: Medical students
Type: Prize
Value: £1 x £250 and one year
Country of Study: Any country
Closing Date: 3 April
Additional Information: www.rsm.ac.uk/prizes-and-awards/
prizes-for-trainees/

For further information contact:

1 Wimpole St, London W1G 0AE, United Kingdom.

Tel: (44) 20 7290 2900

Epidemiology & Public Health Young Epidemiologists Prize

Purpose: To reward outstanding papers in epidemiology and public health section
Eligibility: Open to any medical and non-medical epidemiologist or public health practitioner under the age of 40 years.
Type: Award
Value: First prize £250
Frequency: Annual
Country of Study: United Kingdom
Application Procedure: Download the application form from website. Submit a 1,000-word paper addressing a public health issue which relates to a project conducted. Your paper should include an introduction, methodology used and results, discussion headings and a conclusion.
Additional Information: www.rsm.ac.uk/prizes-and-awards/prizes-for-trainees/

Gastroenterology & Hepatology Section: Gut Club Prize

Eligibility: Medical students and pre-registrar junior doctors
Type: Prize
Value: 1st prize - £100 and 50% discount on RSM membership for 1 year; Other: Runners-up will receive 50% discount on RSM membership for 1 year
Country of Study: Any country
Closing Date: 10 February
Additional Information: www.rsm.ac.uk/prizes-and-awards/prizes-for-students/

For further information contact:

1 Wimpole St, London W1G 0AE, United Kingdom.

Tel: (44) 20 7290 2900

General Practice with Primary Healthcare John Fry Prize

Purpose: To award best examples of practice-based research involving members of the primary health and social community, demonstrating and promoting effective team work
Eligibility: Open to GP registrars, postgraduate students based in primary care, medical students and other undergraduates from professional groups involved in primary care and patients with experiences from primary care.
Type: Prize
Value: £300
Frequency: Annual
Country of Study: United Kingdom
Application Procedure: Title of the essay: When Dr John Fry started his pioneering research he was a single handed GP. Today general practice is delivered by the primary care team comprising a broad group of healthcare professionals. Giving referenced examples, show how this has influenced current research in primary care. The essay submission should be between 2500-3000 words and well referenced. Apply online https://www5.shocklogic.com/scripts/jmevent/Abstract.asp?Client_Id=%27RSM%27&Project_Id=%2706GPQ231%27&System_Id=1
Closing Date: 1 July
Additional Information: www.rsm.ac.uk/prizes-and-awards/prizes-for-students/

For further information contact:

RSM, 1 Wimpole Street, Marylebone, London W1G 0AE, United Kingdom.

Geriatrics & Gerontology Section: Clinical audit and governance prize

Eligibility: The prize is open to all trainees involved in the field of geriatrics and care of older people - including trainee nurses, allied health professionals and social workers.
Type: Prize
Value: First prize - for best oral presentation: £100 and certification recognition and a 1-year membership to the British Geriatrics Society; First prize - for best poster presentation: £50 and certification recognition and a 1-year membership to the British Geriatrics Society.
Country of Study: Any country
Closing Date: 14 February
Additional Information: www.rsm.ac.uk/prizes-and-awards/prizes-for-trainees/

For further information contact:

1 Wimpole St, London W1G 0AE, United Kingdom.

Tel: (44) 20 7290 2900

Geriatrics & Gerontology Section: President's Essay Prize for students

Eligibility: Students or postgraduates of 5 years standing from disciplines involved in the care of older people
Type: Prize
Value: One year
Country of Study: Any country
Closing Date: 30 April
Additional Information: www.rsm.ac.uk/prizes-and-awards/prizes-for-students/

For further information contact:

1 Wimpole St, London W1G 0AE, United Kingdom.

Tel: (44) 20 7290 2900

Geriatrics & Gerontology Section: President's Essay Prize for trainers

Eligibility: Students or postgraduates of 5 years standing from disciplines involved in the care of older people
Type: Prize
Value: One year
Country of Study: Any country
Closing Date: 30 April
Additional Information: www.rsm.ac.uk/prizes-and-awards/prizes-for-trainees/

For further information contact:

1 Wimpole St, London W1G 0AE, United Kingdom.

Tel: (44) 20 7290 2900

Geriatrics & Gerontology Section: Trainees' prize, clinical presentations

Eligibility: Trainees in elderly medicine and old age psychiatry
Type: Prize
Value: First prize - for best oral presentation: £100; First prize - for best poster presentation: £50
Country of Study: Any country
Closing Date: 13 October
Additional Information: www.rsm.ac.uk/prizes-and-awards/prizes-for-students/

For further information contact:

1 Wimpole St, London W1G 0AE, United Kingdom.

Tel: (44) 20 7290 2900

Geriatrics & Gerontology Section: Trainees' prize, clinical presentations for trainers

Eligibility: Trainees in elderly medicine and old age psychiatry
Type: Prize
Value: First prize - for best oral presentation: £100 ; First prize - for best poster presentation: £50
Country of Study: Any country
Closing Date: 13 October
Additional Information: www.rsm.ac.uk/prizes-and-awards/prizes-for-trainees/

For further information contact:

1 Wimpole St, London W1G 0AE, United Kingdom.

Tel: (44) 20 7290 2900

History of Medicine Society: Norah Schuster Essay Prize

Purpose: This prize will be awarded for the best essay or essays submitted on any subject related to the history of medicine, including medical science.

Eligibility: Pre-clinical, clinical medical and dental students. Please note that you must be a medical student to be eligible to submit for this prize.
Type: Prize
Value: £100 Amazon voucher and a year's membership of the RSM
Country of Study: Any country
Closing Date: 17 January
Additional Information: www.rsm.ac.uk/prizes-and-awards/prizes-for-students/

For further information contact:

1 Wimpole St, London W1G 0AE, United Kingdom.

Tel: (44) 20 7290 2900

Laryngology & Rhinology Section: Short Paper and Poster Prize

Eligibility: All trainees and consultants within 2 years of appointment in the UK and Ireland.
Type: Prize
Value: 1st: £250 and a year's free RSM membership 2nd: £100 and a year's free RSM membership 3rd: £50 and a year's free RSM membership
Country of Study: Any country
Closing Date: 25 March
Additional Information: www.rsm.ac.uk/prizes-and-awards/prizes-for-trainees/

For further information contact:

1 Wimpole St, London W1G 0AE, United Kingdom.

Tel: (44) 20 7290 2900

Laryngology & Rhinology Section: Rhinology Essay Prize

Purpose: This prize is to be awarded for an original essay on 'The nasal septum should never be touched before the age of sixteen. Discuss.'
Eligibility: All trainees and consultants within 1-2 years of appointment in the UK or Republic of Eire
Type: Prize
Value: £1,000
Country of Study: Any country
Closing Date: 25 March
Additional Information: www.rsm.ac.uk/prizes-and-awards/prizes-for-trainees/

Laryngology & Rhinology Travel and Equipment Grants

Purpose: To assist with the cost of travel to overseas centres

Eligibility: Open to trainee RSM members with an interest in laryngology and rhinology who live–more than 50 miles from the RSM.

Level of Study: Postdoctorate

Type: Travel grant

Value: A grant of up to £100 towards attending a Laryngology and Rhinology meeting at the RSM

Frequency: Annual

Country of Study: United Kingdom

Application Procedure: Applicants should submit a letter of no more than two A4 pages in length detailing their expenses and which Laryngology & Rhinology meeting they would like to attend and why. Email your application letter to laryngology@rsm.ac.uk

Additional Information: Applications will be accepted up to two weeks before each meeting. www.rsm.ac.uk/prizes-and-awards/travel-grants-and-bursaries/

Maternity & the Newborn Forum: Basil Lee Bursary for Innovation in Communication

Purpose: This bursary is to honour Basil Lee a GP who was a founding member of the Forum and an innovator in maternity care.

Eligibility: Students, trainees and other professionals who specialise in maternity and/or surrounding disciplines who are registered in the UK. Please note those who work for commercial operations will not be eligible for the bursary. This bursary is to enable the successful applicant to develop their new media skills which relate to the subject of maternity care or care of the newborn.

Type: Bursary

Value: £500 and a year's free RSM membership for students

Country of Study: Any country

Closing Date: 28 March

Additional Information: www.rsm.ac.uk/prizes-and-awards/travel-grants-and-bursaries/

Maternity & the Newborn Forum: Wendy Savage Bursary

Purpose: This bursary is to honour Wendy Savage, a long-standing member of the Forum and an innovator in maternity care.

Eligibility: Students, trainees and other professionals who specialise in maternity and/ or surrounding disciplines who are registered in the UK. Please note those who work for commercial operations will not be eligible for the bursary. The bursary is to enable the successful applicant to attend a conference to present a paper based on their research in the field of maternity care or care of the newborn.

Value: One prize of £750 to cover overseas travel or £500 to cover travel within the UK and a year's free RSM membership for students

Country of Study: Any country

Closing Date: 4 February

Additional Information: www.rsm.ac.uk/prizes-and-awards/travel-grants-and-bursaries/

Military Medicine Colt Foundation Research Prize

Purpose: To recognize the best abstract by a serving military medical officer

Eligibility: Open to medical officers in any training grade in general practice, occupational medicine, public health or hospital-based specialties.

Level of Study: Postgraduate

Type: Prize

Value: First prize £200 and Second prize Five £100 prizes

Frequency: Annual

Study Establishment: Royal Society of Medicine

Country of Study: United Kingdom

Application Procedure: Candidates should email the abstracts.

No. of awards offered: 6

Closing Date: 6 November

Funding: Foundation

Contributor: Colt Foundation

Additional Information: www.rsm.ac.uk/prizes-and-awards/prizes-for-trainees/

For further information contact:

Email: united.services@rsm.ac.uk

Nephrology Section Rosemarie Baillod Clinical Award

Purpose: To support trainees and research fellows in the area of clinical research, case series or individual case history in nephrology.
Eligibility: Open to any trainees or fellows training in nephrology and wider specialties.
Level of Study: Research
Type: Research award
Value: £200
Frequency: Annual
Country of Study: United Kingdom
Application Procedure: Trainees and research fellows are invited to submit clinical abstracts in the area of clinical research, case series or individual case histories. Clinical cases or pedigrees should demonstrate novel clinical findings, illustrate classic conditions in new or unusual ways, and illuminate or expand knowledge concerning physiology, cell biology, genetics, radiology, or molecular mechanisms. Abstracts should be no more than 300 words. Submissions will be shortlisted for oral presentation at a Section meeting. The prize will be awarded to the best 15 minute presentation.
Additional Information: www.rsm.ac.uk/prizes-and-awards/prizes-for-trainees/

Obstetrics & Gynaecology Section: Dame Josephine Barnes Award

Eligibility: All medical students
Type: Prize
Value: £100
Country of Study: Any country
Closing Date: 21 January
Additional Information: www.rsm.ac.uk/prizes-and-awards/prizes-for-students/

For further information contact:

1 Wimpole St, London W1G 0AE, United Kingdom.

Tel: (44) 20 7290 2900

Obstetrics & Gynaecology Section: Herbert Reiss Trainees' Prize

Eligibility: SpRs in obstetrics and gynaecology
Type: Prize

Value: Oral first prize: £150 Oral second prize: £100 Poster first prize: £100 Poster second prize: £75
Country of Study: Any country
Closing Date: 14 January
Additional Information: www.rsm.ac.uk/prizes-and-awards/prizes-for-trainees/

For further information contact:

1 Wimpole St, London W1G 0AE, United Kingdom.

Tel: (44) 20 7290 2900

Occupational Medicine Section Malcolm Harrington Prize

Purpose: To award the work that is most likely to advance the study of occupational medicine in its broadest sense
Eligibility: Open to occupational physician in training or within an year of achieving specialist accreditation
Type: Prize
Value: £250
Frequency: Annual
Application Procedure: Candidates should submit an abstract of their own work (no longer than 200 words)
No. of awards offered: 9
Closing Date: 9 March
Funding: Private
Contributor: Professor Harrington
No. of awards given last year: 1
No. of applicants last year: 9

For further information contact:

Email: occupational@rsm.ac.uk

Oncology Section Sylvia Lawler Prize

Purpose: To encourage scientists and clinicians in training to present the best scientific paper and best clinical paper on oncology
Eligibility: Open to all clinicians in training
Type: Prize
Value: £250 to oral presenters
Frequency: Annual
Country of Study: United Kingdom
Application Procedure: Abstracts of no more than 200 words are invited from clinicians in training, themed on a clinical research project. Apply online www.rsm.ac.uk/prizes-and-awards/prizes-for-trainees/.
No. of awards offered: 6
Closing Date: 25 April

Additional Information: The top 6 abstracts (3x clinical, 3x scientific) will be selected for oral presentations; a panel of judges will determine the best oral presentation and 1 applicant will be awarded the Sylvia Lawler Prize for the best scientific paper and 1 applicant will be awarded the Sylvia Lawler Prize for the best clinical paper. www.rsm.ac.uk/prizes-and-awards/prizes-for-trainees/

Ophthalmology Section Travelling Fellowships

Purpose: To enable British ophthalmologists to travel abroad with the intention of furthering the study or advancement of ophthalmology, or to enable foreign ophthalmologists to visit the United Kingdom for the same purpose
Eligibility: Open to British based ophthalmologists travelling abroad and foreign ophthalmologists travelling to the UK.
Level of Study: Professional development
Type: Travelling fellowship
Value: Up to the value of £1,000 towards travelling abroad to further the study or advancement of ophthalmology.
Frequency: Every 2 years
Country of Study: Any country
Application Procedure: Submit a CV and an application letter detailing the intended purpose of travelling abroad, along with a budget outline of your travelling costs and any supporting statements and letters. Apply online www.shocklogic.com/scripts/jmevent/Abstract.asp?Client_Id=%27RSM%27&Project_Id=%2706OPP25A%27&System_Id=1
Closing Date: 1 May
Additional Information: Travelling Fellows may be required by the Ophthalmology Section Council to lecture at an Ophthalmology meeting on their experiences during the period of the award. www.rsm.ac.uk/prizes-and-awards/travel-grants-and-bursaries/

Oral & Maxillofacial Surgery Section: Short Paper Prize

Eligibility: All trainees in relevant specialties - to be eligible for the prize the candidate must be registered with the General Medical Council and/or the General Dental Council in the United Kingdom or be studying medicine or dentistry at a United Kingdom university. The candidate need not be a member of the Royal Society of Medicine. Candidates must register for and attend the meeting if short-listed.
Type: Prize
Value: £100
Country of Study: Any country
Closing Date: 11 September
Additional Information: www.rsm.ac.uk/prizes-and-awards/prizes-for-trainees/

For further information contact:

1 Wimpole St, London W1G 0AE, United Kingdom.

Tel: (44) 20 7290 2900

Oral & Maxillofacial Surgery Section: UMAX Poster Prize for students

Eligibility: All trainees without dual qualification including students as well as singly-qualified and second degree medical and dental students
Type: Prize
Value: 1 year
Country of Study: Any country
Closing Date: 26 February
Additional Information: www.rsm.ac.uk/prizes-and-awards/prizes-for-students/

For further information contact:

1 Wimpole St, London W1G 0AE, United Kingdom.

Tel: (44) 20 7290 2900

Oral & Maxillofacial Surgery Section: UMAX Poster Prize for trainers

Eligibility: All trainees without dual qualification including undergraduate students as well as singly-qualified and second degree medical and dental students
Type: Prize
Value: 1 year's RSM membership
Country of Study: Any country
Closing Date: 26 February
Additional Information: www.rsm.ac.uk/prizes-and-awards/prizes-for-trainees/

For further information contact:

1 Wimpole St, London W1G 0AE, United Kingdom.

Tel: (44) 20 7290 2900

Orthopaedics Section FOSC (Future Orthopaedic Surgeons Conference) prize for research for students

Eligibility: 1. Medical Students 2. Foundation 1 and 2 doctors 3. Core surgical trainees
Type: Prize

Value: £100 cash prize for 1st place + and a 1-year subscription to the RSM £50 for the Runner up and a 1-year subscription to the RSM, which will be awarded at the FOSC
Country of Study: Any country
Closing Date: 28 January
Additional Information: www.rsm.ac.uk/prizes-and-awards/prizes-for-students/

For further information contact:

1 Wimpole St, London W1G 0AE, United Kingdom.

Tel: (44) 20 7290 2900

Orthopaedics Section FOSC (Future Orthopaedic Surgeons Conference) prize for research for trainers

Eligibility: 1. Medical Students 2. Foundation 1 and 2 doctors 3. Core surgical trainees
Type: Prize
Value: £100 cash prize for 1st place + and a 1-year subscription to the RSM £50 for the Runner up and a 1-year subscription to the RSM, which will be awarded at the FOSC
Country of Study: Any country
Closing Date: 28 January
Additional Information: www.rsm.ac.uk/prizes-and-awards/prizes-for-trainees/

For further information contact:

1 Wimpole St, London W1G 0AE, United Kingdom.

Tel: (44) 20 7290 2900

Orthopaedics Section President's Prize Papers

Purpose: To encourage research in the area of Orthopaedics
Eligibility: Open to medical students and trainees.
Type: Prize
Value: First prize £600, Second prize £400 and Third prize £200
Frequency: Annual
Study Establishment: Royal Society of Medicine
Country of Study: United Kingdom
Application Procedure: Submit a 300-word abstract describing original (not previously published) work exploring clinical case studies and case reports. Apply online
No. of awards offered: 3
Closing Date: 20 October
Additional Information: www.rsm.ac.uk/prizes-and-awards/prizes-for-trainees/

Orthopaedics Section: President's Prize

Eligibility: Students and trainees
Type: Prize
Value: First prize: £600 Second prize: £400 Third prize: £200
Country of Study: Any country
Closing Date: 14 January
Additional Information: www.rsm.ac.uk/prizes-and-awards/prizes-for-trainees/

For further information contact:

1 Wimpole St, London W1G 0AE, United Kingdom.

Tel: (44) 20 7290 2900

Otology Section Norman Gamble Grant

Purpose: This prize is awarded to the best original work in otology in the preceding four years, as evidenced by published papers.
Eligibility: Open to British citizens, both lay and medics.
Level of Study: Unrestricted
Type: Prize grant
Value: £100
Frequency: Annual
Country of Study: United Kingdom
Application Procedure: Submissions should include copies of these papers, along with a supporting letter from a proposer or a cover letter from the researcher themselves. Apply online
Closing Date: 1 May
Additional Information: www.rsm.ac.uk/prizes-and-awards/prizes-for-trainees/

Otology Section: Matthew Yung Short Paper and Poster Prize

Eligibility: All trainees and consultants within 2 years of appointment
Type: Prize
Value: 1st place: £1,000 to be used in support of travel to centres of otology overseas 2nd place: CWJ Short Fellowship to the International Otology Course at the Causse clinic in Beziers, France sponsored by the TWJ Foundation Poster prize: ENT book to be confirmed
Country of Study: Any country
Closing Date: 21 January
Additional Information: www.rsm.ac.uk/prizes-and-awards/prizes-for-trainees/

For further information contact:

1 Wimpole St, London W1G 0AE, United Kingdom.

Tel: (44) 20 7290 2900

Otology Section: Training Scholarships

Eligibility: RSM Trainee Members interested in Otology
Type: Prize
Value: Up to £1,000
Country of Study: Any country
Closing Date: 26 January
Additional Information: www.rsm.ac.uk/prizes-and-awards/prizes-for-trainees/

For further information contact:

1 Wimpole St, London W1G 0AE, United Kingdom.

Tel: (44) 20 7290 2900

Paediatrics & Child Health Section Trainees Tim David Prize

Purpose: To encourage research in the area of Paediatrics and Child Health
Eligibility: Open to medical trainees.
Level of Study: Research
Type: Prize
Value: First prize: £250 and a year's free RSM membership Second prize: £200 Third prize: £150
Frequency: Annual
Country of Study: United Kingdom
Application Procedure: Submit a 750-word case report on a general paediatric case. A maximum of four general paediatric case reports will be shortlisted to presented at a Paediatrics & Child Health meeting. Apply online
Closing Date: 14 December
Additional Information: www.rsm.ac.uk/prizes-and-awards/prizes-for-trainees/

Paediatrics & Child Health Section: President's Prize for students

Eligibility: Students and paediatrics trainees.
Type: Prize
Value: First prize: £250 Second prize: £150 The two runner ups will receive a £20 Amazon voucher
Country of Study: Any country
Closing Date: 18 January

Additional Information: www.rsm.ac.uk/prizes-and-awards/prizes-for-students/

For further information contact:

1 Wimpole St, London W1G 0AE, United Kingdom.

Tel: (44) 20 7290 2900

Paediatrics & Child Health Section: President's Prize for trainers

Eligibility: Students and paediatrics trainees.
Type: Prize
Value: First prize: £250 Second prize: £150 The two runner ups will receive a £20 Amazon voucher
Country of Study: Any country
Closing Date: 18 January
Additional Information: www.rsm.ac.uk/prizes-and-awards/prizes-for-trainees/

For further information contact:

1 Wimpole St, London W1G 0AE, United Kingdom.

Tel: (44) 20 7290 2900

Paediatrics & Child Health Section: Sam Tucker Fellowship

Eligibility: Individuals for whom less than ten years have elapsed since they obtained their primary medical qualification
Type: Prize
Value: £250 and membership of the RSM as a trainee
Length of Study: Six years
Country of Study: Any country
Closing Date: 3 April
Additional Information: www.rsm.ac.uk/prizes-and-awards/prizes-for-trainees/

Pain Medicine Section: Andrew Lawson Prize

Eligibility: All medical students and trainees in pain medicine up to APT level, submissions from trainees of other specialities will also be accepted.
Type: Prize
Value: First prize: £200 and one year free RSM membership and free attendance to the meeting Second prize: £100 Third prize: £50
Country of Study: Any country

Closing Date: 16 November
Additional Information: www.rsm.ac.uk/prizes-and-awards/prizes-for-students/

For further information contact:

1 Wimpole St, London W1G 0AE, United Kingdom.

Tel: (44) 20 7290 2900

Pain Medicine Section: Andrew Lawson Prize for trainers

Eligibility: All medical students and trainees in pain medicine up to APT level, submissions from trainees of other specialities will also be accepted.
Type: Prize
Value: First prize: £200 and one year free RSM membership and free attendance to the meeting Second prize: £100 Third prize: £50
Country of Study: Any country
Closing Date: 16 November
Additional Information: www.rsm.ac.uk/prizes-and-awards/prizes-for-trainees/

For further information contact:

1 Wimpole St, London W1G 0AE, United Kingdom.

Tel: (44) 20 7290 2900

Palliative Care Section MSc/MA Research Prize

Purpose: To support healthcare students and healthcare professionals with master's level research projects, quality improvement or audit in the field of palliative medicine.
Eligibility: Open to Healthcare students and healthcare professionals with master's level research projects, quality improvement or audit in the field of palliative medicine
Level of Study: Masters Degree
Type: Prize
Value: 1st prize - £250 plus a year's free membership, 2nd prize - £100, 3rd prize - £50 and Poster prize - £50
Frequency: Annual
Application Procedure: Submissions of abstracts for poster and/or oral presentations to showcase current research in palliative care from master's research or quality improvement/audit projects (no more than 300 words). Apply online.
No. of awards offered: 4
Closing Date: 15 October
Additional Information: www.rsm.ac.uk/prizes-and-awards/prizes-for-students/

Patient Safety Section: Student and Trainees' Prize

Eligibility: All students and trainees.
Type: Prize
Value: Oral presentation: A year's free RSM membership Poster presentation: £50
Country of Study: Any country
Closing Date: 22 November
Additional Information: www.rsm.ac.uk/prizes-and-awards/prizes-for-trainees/

For further information contact:

1 Wimpole St, London W1G 0AE, United Kingdom.

Tel: (44) 20 7290 2900

Psychiatry Section Mental Health Foundation Research Prize

Purpose: This prize is to be awarded for the most outstanding published paper reporting original research work by the principal author in the last year.
Eligibility: Open to Juniors (excluding consultants or senior academic staff)
Type: Prize
Value: £750 and £100
Frequency: Annual
Country of Study: United Kingdom
Application Procedure: Entries should consist of a covering letter explaining, the significance of the publication and attachments of 1. The published article or the article and a letter of acceptance from the publisher. 2. A short CV of the applicant. Apply online.
Closing Date: 4 March
Additional Information: www.rsm.ac.uk/prizes-and-awards/prizes-for-trainees/

Radiology Section: Finzi Prize

Eligibility: All SpRs radiologists and radiotherapists training in the UK and Northern Ireland with a limit of one paper from each hospital
Type: Prize
Value: First prize: £500
Country of Study: Any country
Closing Date: 7 February
Additional Information: www.rsm.ac.uk/prizes-and-awards/prizes-for-trainees/

R

For further information contact:

1 Wimpole St, London W1G 0AE, United Kingdom.

Tel: (44) 20 7290 2900

Radiology: BSHNI eposter presentations

Eligibility: All delegates (the presenting author should register for the meeting)
Type: Prize
Value: First prize £150 (for each category) Second prize £75 (for each category)
Country of Study: Any country
Closing Date: 5 May
Additional Information: www.rsm.ac.uk/prizes-and-awards/prizes-for-trainees/

For further information contact:

1 Wimpole St, London W1G 0AE, United Kingdom.

Tel: (44) 20 7290 2900

Respiratory Medicine Section: Foundation Year and Internal Medicine Trainee Award

Eligibility: Junior doctors currently in foundation training or SHO level (IMT trainees, JCF, trust-grade SHO)
Type: Prize
Value: £100 and one free admission to an RSM Respiratory Section event
Country of Study: Any country
Closing Date: 1 December
Additional Information: www.rsm.ac.uk/prizes-and-awards/prizes-for-trainees/

For further information contact:

1 Wimpole St, London W1G 0AE, United Kingdom.

Tel: (44) 20 7290 2900

Respiratory Medicine Section: Respiratory Specialist Registrar Award

Eligibility: ST3 and above who have received all or part of their training in the UK. Registrars from any speciality may apply.
Type: Prize
Value: £100 and one free admission to an RSM Respiratory Section event

Country of Study: Any country
Closing Date: 1 December
Additional Information: www.rsm.ac.uk/prizes-and-awards/prizes-for-trainees/

For further information contact:

1 Wimpole St, London W1G 0AE, United Kingdom.

Tel: (44) 20 7290 2900

Respiratory Medicine Section: Student Award

Eligibility: All current UK medical students and FY1 doctors who completed the research whilst at medical school.
Type: Prize
Value: £100 and one year's free RSM membership
Country of Study: Any country
Closing Date: 1 December
Additional Information: www.rsm.ac.uk/prizes-and-awards/prizes-for-students/

For further information contact:

1 Wimpole St, London W1G 0AE, United Kingdom.

Tel: (44) 20 7290 2900

Rheumatology & Rehabilitation Section: Barbara Ansell Prize

Eligibility: Specialist registrars and research fellows in all specialities
Type: Prize
Value: First prize: £200; Second prize: £100; Third prize: £50
Country of Study: Any country
Closing Date: 9 May
Additional Information: www.rsm.ac.uk/prizes-and-awards/prizes-for-trainees/

For further information contact:

1 Wimpole St, London W1G 0AE, United Kingdom.

Tel: (44) 20 7290 2900

Rheumatology & Rehabilitation Section: Eric Bywaters Prize

Eligibility: Specialist registrars, research fellows, scientists and allied health professionals in all specialities

Type: Prize
Value: First prize: £200 Second prize: £100 Third prize: £50
Country of Study: Any country
Closing Date: 9 May
Additional Information: www.rsm.ac.uk/prizes-and-awards/prizes-for-trainees/

For further information contact:

1 Wimpole St, London W1G 0AE, United Kingdom.

Tel: (44) 20 7290 2900

Sexuality & Sexual Health Section: Medical Student Essay Prize

Eligibility: Medical students, all medical specialities, all training levels and allied health professionals.
Type: Prize
Value: First prize: £250 and a year
Country of Study: Any country
Closing Date: 16 February
Additional Information: www.rsm.ac.uk/prizes-and-awards/prizes-for-students/

For further information contact:

1 Wimpole St, London W1G 0AE, United Kingdom.

Tel: (44) 20 7290 2900
Email: sexmed@rsm.ac.uk.

Sexuality & Sexual Health Section: Trainee Essay Prize

Eligibility: Medical students, all medical specialities, all training levels and allied health professionals.
Type: Prize
Value: First prize: £250 and a year's free RSM membership Second prize: A year's free RSM membership
Country of Study: Any country
Closing Date: 16 February
Additional Information: www.rsm.ac.uk/prizes-and-awards/prizes-for-trainees/

For further information contact:

1 Wimpole St, London W1G 0AE, United Kingdom.

Tel: (44) 20 7290 2900

Sleep Medicine Section: Student Essay Prize

Type: Prize
Value: First prize: £300; Second prize: £200 Third prize: £100
Country of Study: Any country
Application Procedure: Pre-clinical, clinical medical and dental students
Closing Date: 7 December
Additional Information: www.rsm.ac.uk/prizes-and-awards/prizes-for-students/

For further information contact:

1 Wimpole St, London W1G 0AE, United Kingdom.

Tel: (44) 20 7290 2900

Surgery Section Norman Tanner Prize and Glaxo Travelling Fellowship

Purpose: To encourage clinical registrars submit the best clinical paper
Eligibility: Open to all surgical trainees.
Type: Prize
Value: £250 and the Norman Tanner Medal
Frequency: Annual
Country of Study: United Kingdom
Application Procedure: Candidates must submit clinically oriented papers detailing original clinical research, multi-disciplinary care and audit leading to improved patients' care. Submissions should be no longer than 500 words +/- 10%. Apply online.
Closing Date: 1 November
Additional Information: www.rsm.ac.uk/prizes-and-awards/prizes-for-trainees/

Trainees' Committee John Glyn Trainees' Prize

Purpose: The John Glyn trainees audit prize is awarded for an audit project undertaken during training.
Eligibility: Open to trainees working in any hospital or primary care specialty.
Type: Prize
Value: Oral presentation: 1st - £250, 2nd - £100 Poster presentation: 1st - £100, 2nd - £50
Frequency: Annual
Country of Study: Any country
Application Procedure: Submit a 200-word abstract describing an audit project that was undertaken during your training.

The abstract should include the objective, methods used and results, discussion topics and conclusion. Applicants must be the primary authors of the original project. Apply online www.shocklogic.com/scripts/jmevent/Abstract.asp?Client_Id=%27RSM%27&Project_Id=%2706TRN224%27&System_Id=1

Closing Date: 30 June

Additional Information: www.rsm.ac.uk/prizes-and-awards/prizes-for-trainees/

Urology Professor Geoffrey D Chisholm CBE Communication Prize

Purpose: To reward the best abstract at the Short Papers Prize Meeting

Eligibility: Open to urological trainees.

Type: Prize

Value: First prize: £2000 towards the urology overseas scientific winter meeting in 2022 Second prize: £750 towards the urology overseas scientific winter meeting in 2022 or Campbell's Urology Third prize: £500 towards the urology overseas scientific winter meeting in 2022 or Smith's Urology

Frequency: Annual

Country of Study: Any country

Application Procedure: Please send a brief abstract of no more than 200 words summarising your planned presentation. Apply online.

Closing Date: 24 Maech

Additional Information: www.rsm.ac.uk/sections/urology-section/, www.rsm.ac.uk/prizes-and-awards/prizes-for-trainees/

Urology Section Professor John Blandy Essay Prize for Medical Students

Purpose: To enable the holder to enhance his or her knowledge and experience by visiting an overseas unit

Eligibility: Medical students

Type: Fellowship

Value: A bursary of £1,000 and an RSM award certificate

Frequency: Annual

Closing Date: 8 March

Additional Information: Candidates must be available on the May 16th for presentation of their short paper to be eligible for this prize www.baus.org.uk/professionals/sections/essay_competition.aspx

For further information contact:

Email: urology@rsm.ac.uk

Urology Section Winter Short Papers Prize (Clinical Uro-Radiological Meeting)

Purpose: To reward the best clinicopathological short paper

Eligibility: Open to UK-based Urology Specialty or urologically inspired core surgical trainees.

Type: Prize

Value: 1. First prize £2,000 towards attending the Urology Section overseas winter meeting. 2. Second prize Campbell's Urology and RSM certificate. 3. Third prize Smith's Urology and RSM certificate.

Frequency: Annual

Country of Study: United Kingdom

Application Procedure: Submit a 250-word abstract on a topic such as latest academic or clinical research topics, interesting case collections in the context of diagnosis and management or audit projects and their application to urological practice. Apply online.

Closing Date: 18 September

Additional Information: Submissions must not have been presented previously at any national or international meeting. www.rsm.ac.uk/sections/urology-section/,   www.rsm.ac.uk/prizes-and-awards/prizes-for-trainees/

Urology Section: Malcolm Coptcoat spring short papers prize

Purpose: The Malcolm Coptcoat Prize was established in the early 2000s to celebrate the enormous contribution of Malcolm Coptcoat to British Urology during his relatively short professional career. He was a great innovator and a pioneer of laparoscopic urology in the UK.

Eligibility: Urological trainees

Type: Prize

Value: First prize: Up to £2,000; Second prize: £750; Third prize: £500

Country of Study: Any country

Closing Date: 15 February

Additional   Information: www.rsm.ac.uk/prizes-and-awards/prizes-for-trainees/

For further information contact:

1 Wimpole St, London W1G 0AE, United Kingdom.

Tel: (44) 20 7290 2900

Urology Section: Secretary's Prize

Eligibility: All pre-SpRs training grades

Type: Prize
Value: First prize: £200 plus an RSM certificate
Country of Study: Any country
Closing Date: 24 March
Additional Information: www.rsm.ac.uk/prizes-and-awards/prizes-for-trainees/

For further information contact:

1 Wimpole St, London W1G 0AE, United Kingdom.

Tel: (44) 20 7290 2900

Urology: A career in urology – poster prize

Eligibility: Medical students and doctors not yet in core or specialist training
Type: Prize
Value: 12-month free print and online subscription to the Journal of Clinical Urology and certificate
Country of Study: Any country
Closing Date: 15 February
Additional Information: www.rsm.ac.uk/prizes-and-awards/prizes-for-trainees/

For further information contact:

1 Wimpole St, London W1G 0AE, United Kingdom.

Tel: (44) 20 7290 2900

Venous Forum Spring Meeting Prizes

Purpose: To recognize the best original paper in the field of venous disease
Eligibility: Open to medical students and trainees.
Type: Prize
Value: First prize £250, Second prize £200, Third prize £150 and Poster prize £200
Frequency: Annual
Country of Study: United Kingdom
Application Procedure: Submit a 250-word abstract on a topic relating to the Venous Forum annual meeting. The abstract should be structured to include aims, methods, results and conclusions. Apply online.
No. of awards offered: 4
Closing Date: 1 March
Additional Information: www.rsm.ac.uk/sections/venous-forum/, www.rsm.ac.uk/prizes-and-awards/prizes-for-trainees/

Royal Town Planning Institute (RTPI)

41 Botolph Lane, London EC3R 8DL, United Kingdom.

Tel: (44) 370 774 9494
Email: contact@rtpi.org.uk
Website: www.rtpi.org.uk/

The Royal Town Planning Institute (RTPI) was founded in 1914 and is a registered charity, leading membership organisation and a Chartered Institute responsible for maintaining professional standards and accrediting world class planning courses nationally and internationally.

George Pepler International Award

Purpose: The George Pepler International Award is a bursary granted biennially to a person in their first ten years of post-qualification experience wishing to undertake a short period of study (3-4 weeks) on a particular aspect of spatial planning. The study consists of live blog posts, images and video during the visit and a written report at completion.
Eligibility: Open to those that are wishing to travel to either the UK or anywhere in the world that supports their study.
Level of Study: Professional development, Research
Type: Bursary
Value: Up to £1,500
Length of Study: 3-4 weeks
Frequency: Every 2 years
Country of Study: Any country
Application Procedure: Applicants must submit a statement showing the nature of the study visit proposed, together with an itinerary. Application forms are available on request from the RTPI
Closing Date: 31 March
Funding: Private
Contributor: Trust fund
No. of awards given last year: 1
No. of applicants last year: 20
Additional Information: At the conclusion of the visit the recipient must submit a report. Please see the website for further details www.rtpi.org.uk/events-training-and-awards/awards/george-pepler-award/

For further information contact:

Email: marketing@rtpi.org.uk

Rural Health Information Hub

School of Medicine and Health Sciences, Suite E231, 1301 N. Columbia Road, Stop 9037, Grand Forks, ND 58202-9037, United States of America.

Tel:	(1) 800 270 1898
Email:	info@ruralhealthinfo.org
Website:	www.ruralhealthinfo.org/

The Rural Health Information Hub, formerly the Rural Assistance Center, is funded by the Federal Office of Rural Health Policy to be a national clearinghouse on rural health issues. We are committed to supporting healthcare and population health in rural communities.

National Board for Certified Counselors Minority Fellowship Program for Mental Health Counselors

Purpose: The NBCC Foundation provides fellowships for master's and doctoral degree-level counseling students from minority backgrounds. The purpose of the program is to ensure that the behavioral health needs of all Americans are met, regardless of language or culture, thereby reducing health disparities and improving overall community health and well-being. For the purpose of this program, minorities include racial, ethnic, cultural, religious, gender, sexual orientation, rural, and military groups.

Eligibility: Eligible applicants are U.S. citizens or permanent residents that are currently enrolled and in good standing in an accredited graduate level counseling program. Other specific eligibility and service requirements are listed in the application instructions for master's level fellowships and doctoral level fellowships. Please check the website link for further details

Level of Study: Doctorate, Masters Degree

Type: Fellowship

Value: For master's degree-level students US$10,000, plus travel expenses to participate in other program-related training. For doctoral degree-level students US$20,000, plus travel expenses to participate in other program-related training.

Frequency: Annual

Country of Study: Any country

Application Procedure: Links to application instructions are available on the program website www.nbccf.org/programs/scholarships. Choose either master's level fellowships or doctoral level fellowships. A link to the online application portal is available at the bottom of each page.

No. of awards offered: 50

Closing Date: 15 December

Funding: Foundation

Contributor: National Board for Certified Counselors (NBCC) Foundation

Additional Information: www.ruralhealthinfo.org/funding/4510. www.nbccf.org/Assets/Scholarships/MFP_MHC_Masters_Fellowship_Eligibility_2020-2021.pdf www.nbccf.org/Assets/Scholarships/MFP_MHC_Doctoral_Fellowship_Eligibility_2020-2021.pdf

For further information contact:

NBCCF, 3 Terrace Way, Greensboro, NC 27403, United States of America.

Tel:	(1) 336 232 0376
Email:	foundation@nbcc.org

Rural Maternity Care Research

Suite 530-1501 West Broadway, Vancouver, BC V6J 4Z6, Canada.

Tel:	(1) 604 742 1796
Email:	leslie@ruralmatresearch.net
Website:	www.ruralmatresearch.net

Rural Maternity Care Research is a team of academic and community based researchers interested in rural maternity care. They believe their diversity of expertise, backgrounds and interests enhance their ability to comprehensively investigate the complexity of challenges and opportunities for rural maternity care in British Columbia.

Rural Maternity Care Doctoral Student Fellowship

Purpose: To enable a motivated Doctoral student researcher to join the interdisciplinary team investigating rural maternity care in British Columbia

Eligibility: Open to citizens or permanent residents of Canada who are registered in a Doctoral programme in Canada

Level of Study: Doctorate

Type: Fellowship

Value: Up to C$45,000 (benefits included)

Length of Study: 18 months

Frequency: Annual

Country of Study: Canada

Application Procedure: Applicants must include the following documents in the application cover letter, transcripts, curriculum vitae, contact information of 3 research referees and sample of the candidates writing preferably from an article published in a referred journal

Closing Date: 1 October

Additional Information: The fellow will be provided with office space in Vancouver, as well as access to and use of internet, printers and telephone and fax lines. Candidates from all academic disciplines are invited to apply. Candidates who may be completing coursework for their PhD programme, will be expected to contribute sufficient time to the RM-NET to develop a research focus area www.multicare.org/rural-fellowship/

For further information contact:

Email: clin2@cw.bc.ca

Ryerson University

350 Victoria Street, Toronto, ON M5B 2K3, Canada.

Tel: (1) 416 979 5000
Website: www.ryerson.ca/

Ryerson University is currently recognized as a leading institution for research and innovation, being ranked the top institution for undergraduate research in Canada. At Ryerson University we're dedicated to creating a culture of action. We believe that education and experience go hand-in-hand. What our students learn in the classroom is enhanced by real-world knowledge through internships and co-ops, or amplified through zone learning, specialized minors and graduate programs.

Autism Scholars Award

Purpose: With the support of the Ministry of Training, Colleges and Universities, a scholar awards program in autism has been established to ensure that Ontario attracts and retains pre-eminent scholars. The community of autism scholars fostered by this awards program will excel, according to internationally accepted standards of scientific excellence, in the creation of new knowledge concerning child autism, and its translation into improved health for children, more effective services and products for children with autism, and increase the province's capacity in diagnosis and assessment of autism and a strengthened treatment system.

Eligibility: 1. An applicant must be a. A Canadian citizen or a permanent resident of Canada at the time of the application

deadline. b. Registered as a full-time student in a master's or doctoral program at an Ontario university at the beginning of the award period, and remain registered as a full-time student throughout the term of the award. 2. A master's student remains eligible until the end of the sixth term of full-time study. 3. A doctoral student remains eligible until the end of the 15th term of full-time study. 4. During the year an Autism Scholars Award is held, the recipient is precluded from holding any other award that offers financial support of more than C$20,000 for that same year (subject to the university's own policies).

Level of Study: Doctorate, Masters Degree
Type: Award
Value: Master's awards - C$18,000, Doctoral awards - C$20,000
Frequency: Annual
Country of Study: Any country
Application Procedure: Each applicant must submit an electronic copy of the following documents in a single PDF package by December 1st to Natasha Mills. 1. The completed application form. 2. A curriculum vitae (including information concerning eligibility criteria). 3. A statement of research to be undertaken during the period of graduate study (maximum 1,000 words). There must also be an additional non-technical summary (maximum 500 words). These statements must be written by the candidate.
Closing Date: 1 December
Funding: International office
Additional Information: For further information visit www.ryerson.ca/graduate/future-students/financing-your-studies/scholarships-awards/autism-scholars-award/

For further information contact:

Natasha Mills, Canada.

Email: natasha.mills@ryerson.ca

C. Ravi Ravindran Outstanding Doctoral Thesis Award

Purpose: The C. Ravi Ravindran Outstanding Doctoral Thesis Award was established in 2008 (the 60th year of the creation of Ryerson as an educational institution) by his family in recognition of his long and distinguished industrial and academic career. This Award recognizes the excellence of the winning doctoral dissertation from the points of originality, contribution to better understanding of the theory, philosophy, science, practice or their interrelationship, application of theory and impact on society, industry or some aspect of national value.

Eligibility: 1. Registration as a graduate studies student in a program of study leading to a PhD 2. One student may be nominated by a program director from each PhD program. 3. A nominated student must have applied to graduate at the upcoming fall graduation convocation ceremonies or have already graduated at the spring graduation convocation ceremonies.

Level of Study: Doctorate

Type: Award

Value: C$2,500

Frequency: Annual

Application Procedure: Please email your nomination to Natasha Mills.

No. of awards offered: 1

Closing Date: 1 September

Funding: Foundation

Additional Information: For more information: www. ryerson.ca/graduate/future-students/financing-your-studies/ scholarships-awards/ravindran-outstanding-doctoral-thesis/

For further information contact:

Natasha Mills, Canada.

Email: natasha.mills@ryerson.ca

Canada's Distinguished Dissertation Awards

Purpose: The CAGS/ProQuest Distinguished Dissertation Awards recognize Canadian doctoral dissertations that make unusually significant and original contributions to their academic field. They were established in 1994 and are presented annually

Eligibility: Eligible Dissertations include 1. A dissertation in any discipline in engineering, medical sciences, and natural sciences completed and accepted by the Graduate School between 1 January and 31 December. 2. A dissertation in any discipline in the fine arts, humanities, and social sciences completed and accepted by the Graduate School between 1 January and 31 December.

Level of Study: Graduate

Type: Award

Value: C$1,500 prize, a Citation Certificate, and travel expenses of up to C$1,500 to attend the CAGS Annual Conference

Frequency: Annual

Country of Study: Any country

Application Procedure: Complete nomination packages must be received by YSGS as a single PDF document from the nominating program, 1. A letter from the student's supervisor or program director describing the reasons for the nomination, and why the dissertation constitutes a significant

piece of original work. 2. A copy of the external examiner's pre-defence report. The examiner's report must be dated and signed or otherwise authenticated by the Dean of Graduate Studies. 3. An abstract of the dissertation, not exceeding 350 words, written by the candidate in non-technical language. 4. An up-to-date c.v. of the nominee. Please submit required documents to Natasha Mills.

Closing Date: 30 April

Funding: International office

Additional Information: For further details: www.ryerson. ca/graduate/future-students/financing-your-studies/scholar ships-awards/distinguished-dissertation-awards/

For further information contact:

Natasha Mills, Canada.

Email: info@cags.ca; natasha.mills@ryerson.ca

Doctoral Completion Award

Purpose: Funding amount is determined on a year-to-year basis and is a one-time-only award

Eligibility: 1. Satisfactory progress reports. 2. Comprehensive examination process. 3. Dissertation research proposal. 4. Those students who have a very high probability (ie. 90%) to complete in their 4th year

Level of Study: Graduate

Type: Award

Value: Up to US$10,000

Frequency: Annual

Country of Study: Any country

Closing Date: 19 November

Funding: International office

Additional Information: www.sgs.utoronto.ca/awards/ doctoral-completion-award-dca/

Edward S. Rogers Sr. Graduate Student Fellowships

Purpose: The Edward S. Rogers Sr. Graduate School Fellowship, first awarded in 2001, was established by Ted and Loretta Rogers to honour the contributions of Edward S. Rogers Sr. to the Canadian communications industry. The fellowships are available annually to recognize the accomplishments of master's and doctoral level students in the Communication and Culture program who have demonstrated outstanding academic accomplishments in the communications field.

Eligibility: All Canadian PhD students in the Communication & Culture program.

Level of Study: Graduate
Type: Fellowship
Value: US$20,000
Frequency: Annual
Country of Study: Any country
Additional Information: www.ryerson.ca/graduate/future-students/financing-your-studies/scholarships-awards/rogers-graduate-student-fellowships/

For further information contact:

Email: grdadmit@ryerson.ca

Fulbright Canada Scholarship

Purpose: The mandate of Fulbright Canada is to enhance mutual understanding between the people of Canada and the United States of America by providing support to outstanding graduate students, faculty, professionals, and independent researchers. These individuals conduct research, lecture, or enroll in formal academic programs in the other country. In doing so, Fulbright Canada aims to grow intellectual capacity, increase productivity, and assist in the shaping of future leaders in both countries.
Eligibility: 1. Be a Canadian citizen (Permanent residence is not sufficient). 2. Hold a Bachelor's degree prior to the proposed start date of the grant. 3. Be proficient in English. 4. Be in compliance with all J. William Fulbright Foreign Scholarship Board (FFSB) guidelines. 5. Be in compliance with all governmental regulations regarding visas, immigration, travel and residence.
Level of Study: Graduate
Type: Scholarship
Value: US$15,000
Frequency: Annual
Country of Study: Any country
Application Procedure: Applicants interested in applying for a Traditional Fulbright Student award are asked to complete an online application through the Embark system www.fulbright.ca/programs/canadian-students/traditional-awards/how-to-apply-traditional-fulbright-student-awards.html
Closing Date: 15 November
Funding: International office
Additional Information: www.ryerson.ca/graduate/future-students/financing-your-studies/scholarships-awards/fulbright-canada-scholarship/

Governor General Gold Medal

Purpose: The Governor General Gold Medal (GGGM), Ryerson University's most prestigious academic award, is awarded annually to the graduate student who achieves the highest academic standing in a graduate degree program
Eligibility: All master's and doctoral program students, who are in their first Master's or Doctoral program respectively, are eligible for this award. The student must have completed his/her program within the normal time frame (as deemed by the Yeates School of Graduate Studies)
Level of Study: Graduate
Type: Award
Value: No nominal value
Frequency: Annual
Country of Study: Any country
Application Procedure: Candidates must be nominated by their program. Please direct inquiries to Natasha Mills
Closing Date: 3 September
Funding: International office
Additional Information: www.ryerson.ca/graduate/future-students/financing-your-studies/scholarships-awards/governor-general-gold-medal/

For further information contact:

Natasha Mills, Canada.

Email: natasha.mills@ryerson.ca

Graduate Student Stipend

Purpose: A graduate student stipend provides financial support to a graduate student while completing their graduate studies. Normally the stipend is paid from the research funding of a faculty supervisor. Stipends are not payment for employment
Level of Study: Graduate
Type: Stipendiary
Value: Dollar amounts vary by program and/or discipline
Frequency: Annual
Country of Study: Any country
Funding: International office
Additional Information: www.ryerson.ca/graduate/future-students/financing-your-studies/scholarships-awards/graduate-stipend/

For further information contact:

Email: grdadmit@ryerson.ca

John Charles Polanyi Prizes

Purpose: In honour of the achievement of John Charles Polanyi, recipient of the 1986 Nobel Prize in Chemistry, the Government of the Province of Ontario has established a fund to provide annually up to five (5) prizes to outstanding

R

researchers in the early stages of their careers who are continuing to postdoctoral studies or have recently started a faculty appointment at an Ontario university. The John Charles Polanyi Prizes are available in the areas broadly defined as Physics, Chemistry, Physiology or Medicine, Literature and Economic Science

Eligibility: An applicant must 1. Be normally resident in Ontario; 2. Have received their doctoral degree from any recognized university in the world on or after September 1, 2017, or, if the doctoral degree has not yet been awarded, be confident that they will have completed all degree requirements by May 31, current year (an applicant who was on parental leave between the time of completion of the doctorate and the time of application may have their period of eligibility extended by six months); 3. Either be planning to continue to post-doctoral studies, or hold a faculty appointment, in a recognized publicly assisted university in Ontario.

Level of Study: Postdoctorate

Type: Grant

Value: Prizes have a value of US$20,000 each.

Frequency: Annual

Country of Study: Any country

Application Procedure: All applicants must submit an electronic copy of the following documents in a single PDF package by December 1st to Natasha Mills. 1. The completed application form. 2. Curriculum vitae, including information concerning the application. Updates to curriculum vitae will not be accepted after submission. 3. A brief summary of the doctoral thesis (1 page, to be written by the applicant). 4. A statement of research (or writing) to be undertaken during the period of the award (maximum of 2 pages, plus an additional 1 page for diagrams, bibliography, etc., to be prepared by the applicant). 5. A non-technical summary (maximum 500 words, to be written by the applicant). 6. Confidential letters from four assessors. These should focus on an evaluation of the applicant's research (or writing) to date, and the research (or writing) being undertaken. The applicant must ask for the appraisals to be transmitted electronically directly to the Dean of Graduate Studies. Two of the assessors must not have been associated with the candidate as either a supervisor, or a member of the applicant's supervisory committee, or a co-author and should preferably be from another university.

No. of awards offered: 5

Closing Date: 1 December

Funding: Government

Contributor: The Government of the Province of Ontario

Additional Information: www.ryerson.ca/graduate/future-students/financing-your-studies/scholarships-awards/john-charles-polanyi-prizes/

For further information contact:

Email: natasha.mills@ryerson.ca

Sandbox Student Grant Program

Purpose: The DMZ Sandbox Student Grant Program (also known as the "Grant Program") will financially support and provide eligible Ryerson led startups with the crucial grant funding and mentorship they need

Eligibility: The Sandbox Student Grant Program is open to Ryerson students registered in a; full-time academic program or a recent graduates (up to eight months after date of; graduation) from a full-time academic program who meet the following eligibility. requirements

Level of Study: Postgraduate

Type: Grant

Value: Up to US$15,000

Frequency: Annual

Country of Study: Any country

Closing Date: 17 February

Funding: International office

Additional Information: www.ryerson.ca/news-events/events/2019/03/sandbox-student-grant-pitch-competition/, startupheretoronto.com/partners/ryerson-university/sandbox-student-grant-program/

For further information contact:

Email: sandbox@ryerson.ca

Senior Women Academic Administrators of Canada Awards

Purpose: The Senior Women Academic Administrators of Canada (SWAAC), organization was founded in 1987 to provide a forum and a collective voice for women in senior administrative ranks in Canadian universities, colleges and technical institutes. The primary purpose of SWAAC is the promotion of female leadership in Canadian universities, colleges and technical institutes.

Eligibility: Women registered in master's or PhD programs at any Member Institution of Universities Canada within a designated region are eligible to be nominated. 1. Outstanding academic performance. 2. Evidence of leadership, including but not limited to such things as a. Executive positions in student organizations; b. Participation on committees (student committees and university committees); c. Organization of special events, conferences, etc.; d. Involvement in advocacy groups; e. Involvement in volunteer organizations, within the campus setting and/or in the general community.

Level of Study: Doctorate, Graduate, Masters Degree

Type: Award

Value: US$3,000

Frequency: Annual

Application Procedure: Applicants must provide the following 1. Biographical data - includes information about former and current studies, areas of interest, research, publications, other awards, interests outside the university, and community or volunteer work. It's usually in a narrative form, about 1-2 pages in length, and is an opportunity for the nominee to tell the adjudication committee some things about herself, and to explain at greater length her background/interests/passions/ambitions/volunteer work. 2. Curriculum vitae. 3. All post-secondary transcripts. 4. Three letters of reference.

No. of awards offered: 4

Closing Date: 3 December

Funding: Foundation

Contributor: The Senior Women Academic Administrators of Canada (SWAAC)

Additional Information: www.ryerson.ca/graduate/future-students/financing-your-studies/scholarships-awards/swaac-awards/

For further information contact:

Email: natasha.mills@ryerson.ca

Social Sciences and Humanities Research Council Impact Awards

Purpose: SSHRC Impact Awards are designed to build on and sustain Canada's research-based knowledge culture in all research areas of the social sciences and humanities. The awards recognize outstanding researchers and celebrate their research achievements, research training, knowledge mobilization, and outreach activities funded partially or entirely by SSHRC.

Eligibility: A nominee must 1. Be a citizen or permanent resident of Canada at the time of nomination; 2. Be an active social sciences and humanities researcher or student; 3. Hold or have held SSHRC funding pertinent to the award category; 4. Be in good standing with SSHRC; 5. Be affiliated with an eligible institution; and 6. If the recipient of an award, maintain affiliation with an eligible institution for the duration of the award. Nominees 1. Cannot nominate themselves; 2. Can be nominated in two sequential years for the same award, following which two years must pass before they can next be nominated in the same category; 3. Can be nominated in only one category in any year; and 4. Can be nominated in a subsequent year for a different SSHRC Impact Award. To be eligible to hold an award, winning institutions must provide SSHRC with a promotion strategy (two pages maximum) outlining a proposed approach for promoting and celebrating the impact and outcomes of the award winners' and project's achievements.

Type: Award

Value: C$50,000 or C$100,000

Frequency: Annual

Country of Study: Any country

Application Procedure: Every nomination package must include all of the components listed below 1. Institutional nomination letter and rationale (three pages maximum). 2. Information supporting the nomination. 3. SSHRC CVs and consent forms. 4. Letters of support, two pages maximum each, from three referees. Please visit website for more information.

Contributor: Social Sciences and Humanities Research Council

Additional Information: www.ryerson.ca/graduate/future-students/financing-your-studies/scholarships-awards/sshrc-impact-awards/

For further information contact:

Social Sciences and Humanities Research Council, 350 Albert Street, P.O. Box 1610, Ottawa, ON K1P 6G4, Canada.

Tel: (1) 613 943 7777

Email: impactawards-priximpacts@sshrc-crsh.gc.ca

The Dennis Mock Graduate Scholarship

Purpose: The Dennis Mock Graduate Scholarship is available annually to recognize the accomplishments of a first-year Master's student. This award was established in the name of Dennis Mock to honour his commitment to higher education, to recognize his leadership and dedication demonstrated during his 28 years at Ryerson, and to acknowledge his role in developing graduate studies at the university, as vice-president, academic. The funds have been provided by the Peter Bronfman Scholarship Program and the Ontario Student Opportunities Trust Fund.

Eligibility: Students must meet the following criteria 1. Completion of an undergraduate degree program at Ryerson; 2. Full-time enrollment in the first year of a master's program at Ryerson, with a course load of at least two graded, one-term courses in the fall term; 3. First time enrollment in a graduate program; 4. Canadian Citizen or Permanent Resident; 5. Must meet the Ontario Residency Requirement (see application form for details) and Demonstrated financial need.

Level of Study: Graduate

Type: Scholarship

Value: C$5,000

Frequency: Annual

Country of Study: Any country

Application Procedure: Download and complete the application PDF file Dennis Mock Graduate Scholarship Application from website. Please email applications to g2guerci@ryerson.ca. The following must be included along with your application form 1. Graduate student budget form. 2. A grade report; RAMSS web version will suffice. 3. A progress report for fall 2022, signed by your Supervisor. Some programs/streams do not utilize progress reports. Please provide a note from your Program Director (www.ryerson.ca/graduate/contact/#tab-1466025665344-program-contacts) indicating this. 4. Please contact your Program Administrator (www.ryerson.ca/graduate/contact/#tab-1466025665344-program-contacts) if you require assistance regarding your grade report and progress report.

Closing Date: 15 March

Funding: Private, Trusts

Contributor: Peter Bronfman Scholarship Program and the Ontario Student Opportunities Trust Fund

Additional Information: NOTE: Incomplete applications will not be considered. Paper applications will NOT be accepted. www.ryerson.ca/graduate/future-students/financing-your-studies/scholarships-awards/dennis-mock-graduate-scholarship/

For further information contact:

Email: g2guerci@ryerson.ca

The Dennis Mock Student Leadership Award

Purpose: The Dennis Mock Student Leadership Awards recognize graduating students who have made outstanding voluntary extracurricular contributions to their school or academic program department, their faculty, or to Ryerson University as a whole. The awards acknowledge and encourage student participation in university affairs.

Eligibility: 1. Students who graduated in Fall or will be graduating in Spring. 2. In a full-time or part-time Ryerson degree program. 3. Clear academic standing at the time of nomination. 4. Leadership on committees, or influence on student or university affairs. 5. Improvement in the quality of life of students. 6. Encouragement of fellow students to become involved in extracurricular activities; although external involvement is encouraged, activities should be focused on the Ryerson campus or community. 7. Contribution to the sense of community at Ryerson.

Level of Study: Graduate

Type: Award

Frequency: Annual

Country of Study: Any country

Application Procedure: 1. Program/Faculty-level one recipient per program is recommended Faculty/staff do not need to submit formal nomination applications to our office - names of meritorious graduands is sufficient. 2. University-wide nominations will be accepted via the google formDennis

Mock Student Leadership Awards - University-wide Application Form downloadable from website. Submit program/faculty recipients to YSGS.

Closing Date: 19 March

Additional Information: www.ryerson.ca/graduate/future-students/financing-your-studies/scholarships-awards/dennis-mock-student-leadership-award/

For further information contact:

Yeates School of Graduate Studies, 1 Dundas St. West (11th floor), Toronto, ON M5B 2K3, Canada.

Tel: (1) 416 979 5365
Email: awards@ryerson.ca

The Geoffrey F. Bruce Fellowship in Canadian Freshwater Policy

Purpose: Geoffrey F. Bruce was a distinguished Canadian, dedicated public servant and diplomat who devoted his career to advancing multilateral cooperation in pursuit of environmental protection and sustainable development practices. Geoffrey was passionate about the stewardship of Canadian water resources. The Geoffrey F. Bruce Fellowship is designed to generate research recommendations that shape public policy related to freshwater resources in Canada. Research projects should be rooted in the social sciences and contribute to interdisciplinary analysis and discussion of freshwater governance and policy in Canada.

Eligibility: 1. Projects must align with the spirit of the fellowship and relevant research areas. 2. Students at Ryerson University. 3. Graduate students involved in collaborative research co-supervised by Ryerson faculty.

Level of Study: Graduate

Type: Fellowship

Value: C$25,000

Length of Study: 2 year

Frequency: Annual

Country of Study: Any country

Application Procedure: Interested applicants should submit an application package by September 30 including 1. Resume 2. Transcripts; 3. Statement of interest; 4. Two (2) letters of reference. All application documents can be submitted to Dr. Carolyn Johns.

No. of awards offered: 2

Closing Date: 30 September

Additional Information: For more information www.ryerson.ca/graduate/future-students/financing-your-studies/scholarships-awards/geoffrey-bruce-fellowship/

For further information contact:

Dr. Carolyn Johns, Chair, Geoffrey F. Bruce Fellowship, Selection Committee, Ryerson University, 350 Victoria Street, Toronto, ON M5B 2K3, Canada.

Email: cjohns@ryerson.ca

The Hydro One Aboriginal Award for Graduate Studies in Public Policy and Administration

Purpose: The Hydro One Aboriginal Award for Graduate Studies in Public Policy and Administration provides financial assistance and recognizes the academic achievement of an Aboriginal student entering the Master of Arts in Public Policy and Administration program at Ryerson University.

Eligibility: To be eligible for this award, students must be of Aboriginal descent. In keeping with the admission requirements of the Master of Arts in Public Policy and Administration program and the requirements of the Ontario Trust for Student Support initiative (OTSS), the applicant must also have 1. A four year degree with a least a B+ average in the last two years of study; 2. Demonstrated competence in the English Language; 3. Canadian citizenship or be a protected person; 4. Ontario residency (in accordance with OTSS requirements); and 5. Demonstrated financial need as determined by Ryerson University.

Level of Study: Graduate

Type: Award

Value: Up to US$10,000

Frequency: Annual

Country of Study: Any country

Application Procedure: Applicants will need to supply A one-page cover letter describing why they are an ideal candidate. The letter should address the applicant's reasons for pursuing graduate studies in this program, research interests which the applicant may wish to pursue, how the applicant's previous studies and experience have prepared him/her for the MA program, and the applicant's career objectives and how this program relates to them. 2. Three Letters of support from both academic and community-based references. A student may substitute one letter from an employer for one of the academic references. A letter of recommendation from an Aboriginal community or organization supporting the applicant's future contributions may enhance the award application. 3. Resume. 4. OTSS budget form.

No. of awards offered: 2

Funding: Private, Trusts

Contributor: Hydro One Networks Inc. and the Ontario Trust for Student Support (OTSS)

Additional Information: Applicants may be self-nominated, nominated by their peers or nominated by faculty or staff from the Department of Politics and Public Administration. Contact the program for deadline. The Committee will prepare a ranked list of qualified award recipients and will make the final selection of the recipient based on the weighted criteria. If, in the opinion of the selection committee, no applicants meet the outlined criteria, the award shall not be given to any applicant that year. www.ryerson.ca/graduate/future-students/financing-your-studies/scholarships-awards/hydro-one-aboriginal-award/

For further information contact:

Tuna Baskoy, PhD, Department Chair, Ryerson University, Department of Politics & Public Administration, 350 Victoria Street JOR-700, Toronto, ON M5B 2K3, Canada.

Tel: (1) 416 979 5000 Ext 552702
Email: tbaskoy@ryerson.ca

The Pierre Elliott Trudeau Foundation Scholarship

Purpose: The award supports interdisciplinary research and original fieldwork by providing a substantial yearly allowance for research and travel, enabling the Scholars to gain first-hand contact with the diverse communities that can enrich their studies. Moreover, each Scholar is paired with a distinguished Trudeau Mentor selected by the Foundation among the most eminent Canadian practitioners in all sectors of public life. The Scholarship also offers the opportunity to interact with an exceptional community of leaders and committed individuals in every field of the social sciences and humanities, to participate in events organized by the Foundation and to hold their own workshops, through available financial support.

Eligibility: 1. Be a Canadian citizen or landed immigrant applying to a doctoral program in the social sciences and humanities or registered full-time in the first or second year of such a program at a Canadian university. OR; 2. Be a Canadian citizen applying to a doctoral program in the social sciences and humanities or registered full-time in the first or second year of such a program at a foreign university. OR; 3. Be a foreign national [with a preference for candidates from the developing world] applying to a doctoral program in the social sciences and humanities or registered full-time in the first or second year of such a program at a Canadian university. 4. Present a research project linked to one of the Foundation's four themes (Human rights and dignity; Responsible citizenship; Canada in the world; People and their natural environment). 5. Be nominated by a university.

Level of Study: Graduate

Type: Scholarship

R

Value: Annual value up to US$60,000 (including an annual travel allowance of US$20,000) per Scholar for a maximum of three years
Length of Study: 3 year
Frequency: Annual
Country of Study: Any country
Application Procedure: Interested students must complete and submit their electronic application package through the Trudeau Foundation website online application system by the internal deadline stated above. Create an account and follow instructions fdnpetf.smartsimple.ca/s_Login.jsp.
Closing Date: 5 January
Funding: International office
Additional Information: Ryerson can offer editorial support if applications are submitted to natasha.mills@ryerson.ca for review by December 14. www.ryerson.ca/graduate/future-students/financing-your-studies/scholarships-awards/trudeau-foundation/

For further information contact:

Natasha Mills, Coordinator, Graduate Scholarships and Awards, Yeates School of Graduate Studies, Ryerson University, 1 Dundas St. West (11th floor), Toronto, ON M5B 2K3, Canada.

Tel: (1) 416 979 5000 ext. 3648
Email: natasha.mills@ryerson.ca

The W. L. Mackenzie King Scholarships

Purpose: The Mackenzie King Scholarships were established as an independent trust under the will of the late Rt. Hon. William Mackenzie King (1874-1950). Two classes of Mackenzie King Scholarship are available to graduates of Canadian universities the Open Scholarship and the Travelling Scholarship. Both are to support graduate study.
Eligibility: 1. The Mackenzie King Open Scholarship is open to graduates of any Canadian university who engage in (commence or continue) graduate study (master's or doctoral) in any field, in Canada or elsewhere. 2. The Mackenzie King Travelling Scholarship is open to graduates of any Canadian university who engage in (commence or continue) postgraduate study (master's or doctoral) in the United States or the United Kingdom, of international relations or industrial relations (including the international or industrial relations aspects of law, history, politics and economics).
Level of Study: Doctorate, Masters Degree
Type: Scholarship
Value: 1. The Mackenzie King Open Scholarship - US$8,500 (value subject to change). 2. The Mackenzie King Travelling Scholarship - US$10,500 (value subject to change).
Frequency: Annual
Country of Study: Any country
Application Procedure: 1. The completed and signed application form (including attached sheets A and B as described on that form). 2. Three letters of reference from persons who have an intimate knowledge of your record and ability and are able to give a critical evaluation of your plans for graduate study. Note At least two of these testimonials must be from persons under whom you have taken your major work at university, or from senior colleagues with whom you have been associated in academic teaching or research. 3. Information for Referees Reference letters must be signed, dated, on letterhead and sent directly by the referee(s) to Natasha Mills - natasha.mills@ryerson.ca in a PDF format. 4. Certified copies or official transcripts of marks and other academic records from each university you have attended. If a transcript is not available, you may substitute a certified statement by the Registrar or the Faculty concerned. Each applicant must submit an electronic copy of their application (completed application form and certified or official transcripts) in a single PDF package by February 1 to Natasha Mills
No. of awards offered: 5
Closing Date: 1 February
Additional Information: Note: This is the internal YSGS Ryerson deadline for all candidates to submit their application packages. www.ryerson.ca/graduate/future-students/financing-your-studies/scholarships-awards/mackenzie-king/

For further information contact:

Email: natasha.mills@ryerson.ca

S

Sacramento State

6000 J Street, Sacramento, CA 95819, United States of America.

Tel:	(1) 916 278 6011
Email:	infodesk@csus.edu
Website:	www.csus.edu
Contact:	Timothy Hodson, Executive Director

Center for California Studies, CSU-Sacramento, California Legislature (CSUS) was founded in 1984. It is located on the capital campus of the California State University. Center for California Studies is a public service, educational support and applied research institute of CSUS. It is dedicated to promoting a better understanding of California's government, politics, people, cultures and history.

California Senate Fellows

Purpose: The California Senate Fellows program was established in 1973 to provide participants with insight into the legislative process. The fellowship program's primary goals include exposing people with diverse life experiences and backgrounds to the legislative process and providing research and other professional staff assistance to the Senate.
Eligibility: Anyone who will be at least 20 years of age and a graduate of a four-year college or university is eligible to apply. There is no preferred major. Individuals with advanced degrees and those in mid-career are encouraged to apply. Although no previous political or legislative experience is necessary, applicants should have a strong interest in public policy and politics. A five-week orientation provides background on state government, the legislative process, and major policy issues.
Level of Study: Professional development

Type: Fellowships
Value: Fellows receive a monthly stipend of US$2964 plus full health, vision and dental benefits.
Length of Study: 11 months
Frequency: Annual
Country of Study: United States of America
Application Procedure: Applicants can download the application form from the website
No. of awards offered: 18
Closing Date: 7 February
Funding: Government
Additional Information: sfela.senate.ca.gov/home

For further information contact:

Email: Jamie.Taylor@sen.ca.gov

Jesse M. Unruh Assembly Fellowship Program

Purpose: The Assembly Fellowship seeks highly motivated individuals who are passionate about the state of California, public policy and politics. Fellowship alumni have gone on to positions of leadership in both the public and private sectors, including federal, state, and local elected office. The program successfully provides fellows with the professional development, support and mentorship needed to continue legislative work post-fellowship while also developing transferrable skills that can be applied to other career or academic pursuits.
Eligibility: 1. Be at least 20 years of age by September 1st of the fellowship year. 2. Have a bachelor's degree by September 1st of the fellowship year and either a cumulative undergraduate GPA of 2.5 or higher or a GPA of 2.5 or higher in the last 60 (semester) or 90 (quarter) units. 3. Demonstrated interest in state government and public policy. 4. Be authorized to work in the United States for the duration of the fellowship program.
Type: Fellowship

© Springer Nature Limited 2022
Palgrave Macmillan (ed.), *The Grants Register 2023*,
https://doi.org/10.1057/978-1-349-96053-8

Value: Monthly stipend of US$2,964 and health, dental and vision benefits
Length of Study: 11 months
Frequency: Annual
Study Establishment: Center for California Studies
Country of Study: United States of America
Application Procedure: Applicants must submit the following by the February deadline 1. Completed online application at www.csus.edu/calst/assembly. 2. College transcript(s). 3. Personal statement and policy statement. 4. Three current, original letters of recommendation.
Closing Date: February
Additional Information: www.assembly.ca.gov/fellowship

For further information contact:

Email: Pam.Chueh@asm.ca.gov

Saint Louis University

1 N. Grand Blvd., St Louis, MO 63103, United States of America.

Tel: (1) 314 977 2500
Email: admission@slu.edu
Website: www.slu.edu/
Contact: MBA Admissions Officer

Saint Louis University is one of the nation's oldest and most prestigious Catholic universities. SLU, which also has a campus in Madrid, Spain, is recognized for world-class academics, life-changing research, compassionate health care, and a strong commitment to faith and service.

Saint Louis University International MBA Programme

Length of Study: More than 2 years
Country of Study: Any country
Application Procedure: Applicants must return a completed application, with personal essays, a non-refundable US$55 application fee, two letters of recommendation, official transcripts from all previously attended colleges and universities, Graduate Management Admission Test score, and a curriculum vitae. Overseas students must also provide evidence of financial support and a TOEFL score
Closing Date: 15 April

For further information contact:

Institute of International Business, International Option MBA.

Tel: (1) 314 977 3630
Fax: (1) 314 977 7188
Email: biib@slu.edu

Samuel H. Kress Foundation

174 East 80th Street, New York, NY 10075, United States of America.

Tel: (1) 212 861 4993
Email: info@kressfoundation.org
Website: www.kressfoundation.org/
Contact: Wyman Meers, Program Administrator

The Samuel H. Kress Foundation devotes its resources to advancing the study, conservation, and enjoyment of the vast heritage of European art, architecture, and archaeology from antiquity to the early 19th century. Our mission at the Samuel H. Kress Foundation (est. 1929) is to sustain and carry out the original vision of our founder, Samuel H. Kress (1863-1955).

Kress Conservation Fellowships

Purpose: The purpose of the Kress Conservation Fellowship program is to provide a wide range of post-graduate fellowship opportunities that will help develop the skills of emerging conservators.
Eligibility: Applications must be made by the museum or conservation facility at which the fellowship will be based. Prior to beginning the fellowship, fellows should have completed a masters-level degree in conservation. The fellowship candidate may be identified in advance of application by the host institution or recruited subsequently.
Level of Study: Postgraduate
Type: Fellowship
Value: US$37,000
Length of Study: 9 to 12 months
Frequency: Annual
Country of Study: United States of America
Application Procedure: The Kress Conservation Fellowships are administered by the Foundation for Advancement in Conservation (FAIC). Please visit the FAIC website

for detailed application instructions. For answers to additional questions, you may also wish to review the Fellowship FAQs.

No. of awards offered: 6
Closing Date: 22 January
Funding: Foundation
Contributor: Foundation for Advancement in Conservation (FAIC)
Additional Information: www.kressfoundation.org/Programs/Fellowships/Conservation-Fellowships

For further information contact:

The Foundation of the American Institute for Conservation of Historic and Artistic Works, United States of America.

History of Art Institutional Fellowships

Subjects: History
Purpose: The Kress History of Art Institutional Fellowships are intended to provide promising emerging art historians with the opportunity to experience just this kind of immersion.
Eligibility: Restricted to pre-doctoral candidates in the history of art and related disciplines (such as archaeology, architecture, or classics). Nominees must be U.S. citizens or individuals matriculated at an American university. Dissertation research must focus on European art from antiquity to the early 19th century and applicants must be ABD by the time their fellowship begins. Candidates must be nominated by their academic department.
Level of Study: Postdoctorate
Type: Fellowship
Value: US$30,000
Length of Study: 2 year
Frequency: Annual
Country of Study: United States of America
Application Procedure: Individuals must apply for a Kress Institutional Fellowship using the Foundation's online grantmaking portal.
No. of awards offered: 6
Closing Date: 30 November
Funding: Foundation
Additional Information: www.kressfoundation.org/Programs/Fellowships/History-of-Art-Institutional-Fellowships

For further information contact:

174 East 80th Street, New York, NY 10075, United States of America.

Interpretive Fellowships at Art Museums

Subjects: Mentored professional development opportunity within American art museums
Purpose: The purpose of the Kress Interpretive Fellowships at Art Museums program is to provide a new kind of mentored professional development opportunity within American art museums.
Eligibility: Application must be made by the art museum proposing to host a Kress Interpretive Fellow. These Interpretive Fellowships are intended as an opportunity for individuals who have completed a degree (B.A., M.A., or Ph.D.) in art history, art education, studio art or museum studies and who are pursuing or contemplating graduate study or professional placement in these or related fields. The appropriate level of educational achievement will be determined by the host museum and be dependent upon the needs of the proposed fellowship project. The Fellowship candidate may be identified in advance of application by the host institution or recruited subsequently.
Type: Fellowship
Value: US$30,000
Length of Study: 9-12 month
Frequency: Annual
Country of Study: United States of America
Application Procedure: Applicants who do not already have access to the grantmaking portal must register for access at kressfoundation.fluxx.io.
Closing Date: 1 April
Additional Information: www.kressfoundation.org/Programs/Fellowships/Interpretive-Fellowships-at-Art-Museums

San Antonio Nathan Shock Center

15355 Lambda Drive San, Antonio, TX 78245, United States of America.

Tel: (1) 210 562 6140
Website: nathanshock.barshop.uthscsa.edu/

The San Antonio Nathan Shock Center has, for nearly 25 years, provided critical support to investigators locally, nationally and abroad. With its existing and growing intellectual capital, the San Antonio Nathan Shock Center is poised to provide (1) an enhanced platform to conduct horizontally-integrated (lifespan, healthspan, pathology) transformative research in the biology of aging, and (2) a springboard for advanced educational and training activities.

Awards Supported by the San Antonio Nathan Shock Center

Subjects: Biomedical and Clinical; physiology; pharmacology; pathology

Purpose: To support the research of any investigator who is developing a new project in the basic biology of aging.

Eligibility: Any investigator who is eligible to receive NIH grants according to the rules of their home institution.

Type: Research grant

Value: Contingent on the availability of funds

Frequency: Annual, if funds are available

Study Establishment: Any US Academic Institution

Country of Study: United States of America

Application Procedure: The projects should utilize one or more Cores of the Center. Projects that propose creative uses of more than one Core are encouraged. Center Cores and their capabilities are listed at nathanshock.barshop.uthscsa.edu Applications must include a one-page hypothesis and specific aims of your project. Include a title for your project. This can be very brief, sufficient for the reader to understand the importance of what is being proposed. Specifics such as numbers of animals, etc., are not initially needed because this will be determined in conjunction with the Core Leaders if the proposal is selected for further consideration. Please indicate which Cores of the Center will be needed for your studies. It is strongly suggested that you contact the Core Leaders (see above) in advance of submitting your proposal. If you have consulted with one or more Core Leaders during the development of your proposal, please state it in your application. Please include your NIH biosketch and the biosketches of any proposed collaborators. A budget is not initially required. If your proposal is selected for further consideration, a budget will be developed based on a power analysis of the number of samples, animals, etc., that will be needed for the successful development of your project. The budget will be used for internal planning purposes only. Costs of the entire project, including purchase of animals and their housing, will be borne by the San Antonio Shock Center. Some parts of the project may be more appropriately performed in the applicant's lab, in which case it will be expected that the PI will bear the cost of those studies.

Closing Date: 15 April

San Francisco Foundation (SFF)

One Embarcadero Center, Suite 1400, San Francisco, CA 94111, United States of America.

Tel: (1) 415 733 8500
Email: info@sff.org
Website: www.sff.org

The San Francisco Foundation is one of the nation's largest community foundations - a grantmaking public charity dedicated to improving life within a specific local region. Our mission is to mobilize resources and act as a catalyst for change to build strong communities, foster civic leadership, and promote philanthropy in the San Francisco Bay Area.

Koshland Young Leader Awards

Purpose: It recognizes young leaders who balance extraordinary challenges, including family separation and homelessness, yet continue to show academic promise and community leadership.

Eligibility: Candidates must be a junior with San Francisco Unified School District (SFUSD). Competitive candidates have demonstrated academic excellence (at least a 3.0 cumulative GPA), are college bound, and embrace a commitment to strengthening their families and communities despite facing formidable life challenges, such as economic and family responsibilities.

Level of Study: Postgraduate

Type: Award

Value: US$10,000

Frequency: Annual

Country of Study: United States of America

Application Procedure: Applicants must submit the online application form (forms.office.com/Pages/ResponsePage. aspx?id=0zmWfMTB0U2Rg_UGH1hstGGfr7fLkqVKkQzxw 1uPOy1UQU8yVzdVU1dFRzdaSEJNU1I2WEgzVjU1Ty4u)

No. of awards offered: 11

Closing Date: 19 April

Funding: Foundation

Contributor: San Francisco Foundation

No. of awards given last year: 11

Additional Information: sff.org/what-we-do/leadership-programs-awards/kyla/

San Francisco State University (SFSU)

1600 Holloway Avenue, San Francisco, CA 94132, United States of America.

Tel: (1) 415 338 1111
Email: outreach@sfsu.edu
Website: sfsu.edu/

SF State is a major public urban university, situated in one of the world's great cities. Building on a century-long history of commitment to quality teaching and broad access to under-graduate and graduate education, the University offers comprehensive, rigorous, and integrated academic programs that require students to engage in open-minded inquiry and reflection. SF State encourages its students, faculty, and staff to engage fully with the community and develop and share knowledge.

Robert Westwood Scholarship

Purpose: To assist SFSU students who are living with HIV and plan to make a contribution in any field to communities affected by HIV

Level of Study: Postgraduate

Type: Scholarship

Value: US$1,000

Frequency: Annual

Study Establishment: San Francisco State University

Country of Study: United States of America

Application Procedure: Applicants must submit a copy of the most recent SFSU academic transcript, along with a brief, typed essay discussing plans to incorporate academic work and degree at SFSU with service in the HIV community or in the area of HIV prevention

Closing Date: 7 May

Additional Information: Applicants must submit a verification from the physician sfsu.academicworks.com/opportunities/2089

For further information contact:

Tel: (1) 415 338 7339

Email: mritter@sfsu.edu

Sanskriti Pratishthan

Head Office C-11 Qutab Institutional Area, New Delhi, 110016, India.

Tel: (91) 8130968700

Email: kendra@sanskritifoundation.org

Website: www.sanskritifoundation.org

Sanskriti Pratishthan is a non-profit organization that was established in 1978. Sanskriti Pratishthan perceives its role as that of a catalyst, in revitalizing cultural sensitivity in contemporary times.

Geddes Scholarship

Purpose: The objective of the scholarship is to promote and advance interest in and understanding of Patrick Geddes' principles of town planning. This scholarship will provide an opportunity to create awareness among young planners and architects of Geddes' principle of 'place, work, and folk'.

Eligibility: The scholarship is only open to Indian Nationals in the age group of 20 to 30. The applicant must be a student of planning and architecture at a graduate/postgraduate/research level from a recognized university or institution and/or young practicing professionals. The applicants can be an individual or can be a collaborative work of a group of individuals.

Level of Study: Professional development

Type: Scholarships

Value: ₹45,000 will be given in two phases

Length of Study: 6 months

Frequency: Annual

Country of Study: India

Application Procedure: Applications are accepted round the year for the next year's fellowship.

Funding: Foundation

Additional Information: www.sanskritifoundation.org/Geddes-Fellowship.htm

For further information contact:

Sanskriti Kendra / Sanskriti Museums, Anandagram, Mehrauli Gurgaon Road, Opposite Metro Pillar No. 165, Nearest Metro Station Arjangarh, New Delhi, 110047, India.

Tel: (91) 11 2696 3226, 2652 7077 / 8130968700

Email: info@sanskritifoundation.org

Kalakriti Fellowship in Indian Classical Dance

Purpose: The purpose of the Fellowship is to encourage young artists to develop their potential and enhance their skills through intensive practice and or incorporating different facets of their art.

Eligibility: The fellowship is only open to Indian Nationals in the age group of 25 to 40. While this fellowship specially encourages women applicants, all proposals that further the objectives of the program are welcome. The candidate should have at least ten years of initial training in Indian classical dance. The fellow would be required to have given at least 2-3 solo performances to his/her credit in recognized forums. The candidate will be required to take guidance from another senior guru and enhance the existing style. It would be a residency programme for a period of three months, which can be spread over the period of ten months. This will require the candidate to take consent from her current guru and the guru he/she would want to go to.

Level of Study: Professional development

Type: Fellowships

Value: ₹50,000 in two instalments

Length of Study: 10 months

Frequency: Annual

Country of Study: India

Application Procedure: Candidates should send their two page CV and a write up of approximately 500 words explaining their project. Full postal and telephonic contact details together with any e-mail address should be submitted to facilitate contact. Few samples of previous work, project or performances should be submitted. The names and contact addresses/telephones of two referees should also be sent. The application should bear the title 'Sanskriti - Kalakriti Fellowship' on the envelope when sent by post and in subject line if sent through email on fellowships@sanskritifoundation.org

Funding: Foundation

Additional Information: www.sanskritifoundation.org/Kalakriti-Fellowship.htm

For further information contact:

Mehrauli Gurgaon Road, Opposite Metro Pillar No. 165, Nearest Metro Station Arjangarh, New Delhi, 110047, India.

Email: fellowships@sanskritifoundation.org

Madhobi Chatterji Memorial Fellowship

Purpose: The objective of the Fellowship is to encourage promising young artists to develop their potential and perfect their skills by providing them the resources and time to dedicate to the art.

Eligibility: The Fellowship is open to Indian Nationals from any genre of Indian classical music (vocal or instrumental) or dance (any form or choreography). Proposals that further the objectives of the program are welcome. The candidate should have at least some years of formal training in Indian classical music or dance. The fellow would be required to have given at least 2-3 solo performances to his/her credit.

Level of Study: Professional development

Type: Fellowships

Value: The grant of ₹100,000 will be given in two instalments

Length of Study: 10 Months

Frequency: Annual

Country of Study: India

Application Procedure: The application should bear the title 'Sanskriti - Kalakriti Fellowship' on the envelope when sent

by post and in the subject line if sent through email on fellowships@sanskritifoundation.org. Applications are accepted round the year for the next year's fellowship.

Funding: Foundation

Additional Information: www.sanskritifoundation.org/Madhobi-Chatterji-Memorial.htm

For further information contact:

Sanskriti Kendra / Sanskriti Museums, Anandagram, Mehrauli Gurgaon Road, Opposite Metro Pillar No. 165, Nearest Metro Station Arjangarh, New Delhi, 110047, India.

Email: fellowships@sanskritifoundation.org

Mani Mann Fellowship

Purpose: This Fellowship has been instituted to encourage promising young artists to advance in their field. This fellowship will enable the recipient to have the resources and time to dedicate to the art.

Eligibility: The fellowship is only open to Indian Nationals in the age group of 25 to 40. While this fellowship specially encourages women applicants, all proposals that further the objectives of the program are welcome. The applicant must hold a degree/diploma from a recognized university or institution in the field and/or the candidate should have at least ten years of initial training in Indian classical music. The fellow would be required to have given at least 2-3 solo performances to his/her credit in recognized forums. The candidate will be required to take guidance from another senior guru and enhance the existing style. It would be a residency programme for a period of three months, which can be spread over the period of one year.

Level of Study: Professional development

Type: Fellowships

Value: ₹100,000 will be given in two phases

Length of Study: 1 year

Frequency: Annual

Country of Study: India

Application Procedure: The application should bear the title 'Mani Mann Fellowship' on the envelope when sent by post and in subject line if sent through email on fellowships@sanskritifoundation.org. Applications are accepted round the year for the next year's fellowship.

Funding: Foundation

Additional Information: www.sanskritifoundation.org/Mani-Mann-Fellowship.htm

For further information contact:

Sanskriti Kendra / Sanskriti Museums, Anandagram, Mehrauli Gurgaon Road, Opposite Metro Pillar No. 165, Nearest Metro Station Arjangarh, New Delhi, 110047, India.

Email: fellowships@sanskritifoundation.org

Prabha Dutt Fellowship

Purpose: The purpose of the fellowship is to encourage young mid career women journalists to develop their potential by pursuing meaningful projects without having to work under the pressures of short deadlines.

Eligibility: The fellowship is only open to women who are Indian Nationals in the age group of 25 to 40 years. It is exclusively for print journalists. The fellows will be required to publish a stipulated number of articles in established publications. The fellow may work on a book or monograph for subsequent publication within the given time frame.

Level of Study: Professional development

Type: Fellowships

Value: ₹1,00,000 including travel expenses

Length of Study: 10 months

Frequency: Annual

Country of Study: India

Application Procedure: Candidates should send a two page CV and a write up of about 250 - 300 words explaining their project. Full postal and telephonic contact details together with any e-mail id should be submitted to facilitate contact. Five published work samples should be submitted. The names and contact addresses/telephones of two referees should also be sent. The application should bear the title 'Sanskriti - Prabha Dutt Fellowship' on the envelope when sent by post or can be emailed on fellowships@sanskritifoundation.org with 'Sanskriti - Prabha Dutt Fellowship' in the subject line. Applications are accepted through the year for the next year's fellowship.

Funding: Foundation

Additional Information: www.sanskritifoundation.org/prabha-dutt-fellowship.htm

For further information contact:

Sanskriti Kendra / Sanskriti Museums, Anandagram, Mehrauli Gurgaon Road, Opposite Metro Pillar No. 165, Nearest Metro Station Arjangarh, New Delhi, 110047, India.

Email: fellowships@sanskritifoundation.org

Pt. Vasant Thakar Memorial Fellowship

Purpose: The objective of the Fellowship is to recognize and provide a platform to excellent but lesser known artists and to bring them to larger audiences.

Eligibility: The fellowship is open to Indian nationals from any genre of Indian classical music (vocal or instrumental). Proposals that further the objectives of the program are welcome. The duration of the fellowship will be 10 months followed by a performance in Delhi.

Level of Study: Professional development

Type: Fellowships

Value: ₹1,00,000 will be given in two instalments

Length of Study: 10 months

Frequency: Annual

Country of Study: India

Application Procedure: All candidates should mail their CV and a short synopsis of their project proposal to Sanskriti Head Office. The application should bear the title 'Sanskriti-Pt Vasant Thakar Memorial Fellowship' on the envelope when sent by post or can be emailed at fellowships@sanskritifoundation.org with the subject line 'Sanskriti- Pt Vasant Thakar Memorial Fellowship' Applications are accepted through the year for the next year's fellowship.

Funding: Foundation

Additional Information: www.sanskritifoundation.org/Pt-Vasant-Thakar-Memorial-Fellowship.htm

For further information contact:

Sanskriti Kendra / Sanskriti Museums, Anandagram, Mehrauli Gurgaon Road, Opposite Metro Pillar No. 165, Nearest Metro Station Arjangarh, New Delhi, 110047, India.

Email: fellowships@sanskritifoundation.org

Sasakawa Fund

School of Economics, University of São Paulo 908, FEA 1, room D105, São Paulo, Buntantã, SP 055 (080) 10, Brazil.

Tel: (55) 11 3091 6075
Email: sylff@usp.br

Generally known as SYLFF, The Ryoichi Sasakawa Young Leaders Fellowship Fund, established in 1987, aims to nurture future leaders who will transcend the geopolitical, religious, ethnic, and cultural boundaries and actively participate in the world community for peace and the well-being of humankind.

Sasakawa Young Leader Fellowship (SYLFF) Program

Subjects: Humanities and Social Sciences
Purpose: The Ryoichi Sasakawa Young Leaders Fellowship Fund, or SYLFF, is a fellowship program initiated in 1987 to support students pursuing graduate studies in the humanities and social sciences.
Eligibility: Open to postgraduate students from the university of Sao Paulo with research projects proposals that relate to approved subject areas and aim to assist Brazil in its global insertion
Level of Study: Postgraduate
Type: Fellowship
Length of Study: 2 years
Frequency: Annual
Study Establishment: São Paulo University
Country of Study: Japan
Funding: Foundation
Contributor: The Tokyo Foundation
No. of awards given last year: 9
Additional Information: www.sylff.org/about/

For further information contact:

Email:　sylff@tkfd.or.jp

Savoy Foundation

230 Foch Street, Saint-Jean-sur-Richelieu, QC J3B 2B2, Canada.

Tel:　　　(1) 450 358 9779
Email:　　epilepsy@savoy-foundation.ca
Website:　savoy-foundation.ca/
Contact:　Vivian Downing, Assistant to Vice President/ Secretary

The Savoy Foundation is a non-profit organization established by the Savoy family with the stated mission to raise funds to be used for the sole purpose of financing research into epilepsy. The Foundation works principally with Canadian researchers or with foreign nationals who conduct projects in Canada.

Savoy Foundation International Grant

Purpose: To improve the situation of people with epilepsy where medical care is not readily available.

Eligibility: Only available to clinicians and established scientists
Level of Study: Postdoctorate, Postgraduate, Research
Type: Research grant
Value: Up to C$30,000
Length of Study: 1 year
Frequency: Annual
Study Establishment: An affiliated University
Country of Study: Any country
Application Procedure: Applicants must contact the Foundation or visit the website for application forms and further information
No. of awards offered: 1
Closing Date: 15 January
Funding: Private
Contributor: The Savoy Foundation endowments
No. of awards given last year: 1
No. of applicants last year: 1
Additional Information: One grant is available per year. All applications are evaluated by the medical board of the Savoy Foundation for epilepsy www.savoy-foundation.ca/

Savoy Foundation Postdoctoral and Clinical Research Fellowships

Purpose: Awarded to scientists or medical specialists (Ph.D. or M.D.) wishing to carry out a full-time research project, which must be focused on epilepsy.
Eligibility: Candidates must be scientists or medical specialists with a PhD or MD
Level of Study: Postgraduate, Research
Type: Fellowship
Value: The fellow with the highest marks will be awarded C$1,500.
Length of Study: 1 year (non-renewable)
Frequency: Annual
Country of Study: Canada
Application Procedure: Applicants must contact the Foundation or visit the website for application forms and further information
No. of awards offered: 2-3
Closing Date: 31 January
Funding: Foundation
Contributor: The Savoy Foundation endowments
Additional Information: www.savoy-foundation.ca/doc toral.html

Savoy Foundation Research Grants

Purpose: These grants will be awarded for the following purposes 1. Launching of a project operating costs in the expectation of funds already requested from government agencies. In this category, the description of the project should bear mainly on the initial stages (and/or reorientation) rather than the whole research program. 2. Pre-research. 3. Pursuit or completion of a project. 4. Contribution to the funding of a research project of particular interest in the field of epilepsy. 5. Contribution to the funding of a scientific activity (e.g. workshop, symposium) related to the field of epilepsy.

Level of Study: Research
Type: Research grant
Value: Up to C$5,000
Frequency: Annual
Country of Study: Canada
Application Procedure: Applicants must contact the Foundation or visit the website for application forms and further information
No. of awards offered: 2-3
Closing Date: 31 January
Funding: Foundation, Private
Contributor: The Savoy Foundation endowments
Additional Information: savoy-foundation.ca/en/research Programs

Savoy Foundation Studentships

Purpose: To meritorious applicants wishing to acquire training and pursue research in a biomedical discipline, the health sciences or social sciences related to epilepsy in an MSc or PhD program.
Eligibility: Candidates must have a good university record, e.g. a BSc, MD or equivalent diploma and have ensured that a qualified researcher affiliated to a university or hospital will supervise his or her work. Concomitant registration in a graduate programme is encouraged. The awards are available to Canadian citizens or for projects conducted in Canada
Level of Study: Doctorate, Postgraduate, Predoctorate
Type: Studentship
Value: The stipend will be C$15,000 per year for masters studies and C$17,000 for PhD studies. The student with the highest mark will receive in addition the prestigious Van Gelder-Savoy award worth C$1,500.
Length of Study: 1
Frequency: Annual
Country of Study: Canada
Application Procedure: Applicants must contact the Foundation or visit the website for application forms and further information
No. of awards offered: 2-3
Closing Date: 31 January
Funding: Foundation

Contributor: The Savoy Foundation endowments
Additional Information: www.savoy-foundation.ca/student ship.html

---

Scholarship Foundation of the League of Finnish-American Societies

Mechelininkatu 10, Helsinki, FI-00100 Helsinki, Finland.

Tel: (358) 9 4133 3700
Email: sayl@sayl.fi
Website: www.sayl.fi
Contact: Ms Tuula Nuckols, Project Manager

American Society of Naval Engineers (ASNE) Scholarship

Purpose: The American Society of Naval Engineers began its scholarship program in 1979 in order to promote the profession of naval engineering and to encourage college students to enter the field. Since the inception of the Scholarship Program, ASNE has since awarded more than 500 scholarships to undergraduate and graduate students interested in pursuing an education and career in naval engineering.
Eligibility: You must be a United States citizen to be eligible for an ASNE Scholarship. Graduate candidates must be a member of ASNE to apply for a scholarship. Student membership applications can be submitted with the scholarship application. Undergraduate candidates do not have to be a member of ASNE to apply.
Level of Study: Professional development
Type: Scholarship
Value: US$4,000
Frequency: Annual
Country of Study: United States of America
Application Procedure: www.navalengineers.org/Portals/ 16/Students/Scholarship/ASNE_Scholarship_Application_ 2022-2023.pdf
Closing Date: 7 February
Funding: Private
Additional Information: www.navalengineers.org/Educa tion/Scholarships

For further information contact:

1452 Duke Street, Alexandria, VA 22314, United States of America.

Email: scholarships@navalengineers.org

School of American Research

PO Box 2188, Santa Fe, NM 87504-2188, United States of America.

Tel: (1) 505 954 7200
Website: sarweb.org/
Contact: Grants Management Officer

Founded in 1907, SAR is a residential center focused on the cultivation of innovative research in anthropology, broadly defined, as well as the work of Native American artists and writers. To become the preeminent institution that fosters understanding of humankind through scholarly and artistic creativity.

School of Oriental and African Studies (SOAS)

University of London, 10 Thornhaugh Street, Russell Square, London WC1H 0XG, United Kingdom.

Tel: (44) 20 7637 2388
Website: www.soas.ac.uk/
Contact: Miss Alicia Sales, Scholarships Officer, Registry

SOAS University of London is the leading higher education institution in Europe specialising in the study of Asia, Africa and the Near and Middle East. SOAS is a remarkable institution. With our vast repository of knowledge and expertise on our specialist regions, we are uniquely placed to inform and shape current thinking about the economic, political, cultural, security and religious challenges of our world. Our programmes are taught by respected academics engaged in fieldwork and research which influences government policy and the lives of individuals across the globe. SOAS scholars grapple with the pressing issues confronting two-thirds of humankind today: democracy, development, economy, finance, public and corporate policy, human rights, migration, identity, legal systems, poverty, religion, and social change.

Academy of Korean Studies Postgraduate Bursaries

Eligibility: Open to United Kingdom/European Union and overseas applicants. See the website for details
Level of Study: Postgraduate

Type: Bursary
Value: Up to £6,000 towards tuition fees
Length of Study: 1 year
Frequency: Annual
Study Establishment: SOAS
Country of Study: United Kingdom
Application Procedure: See website www.soas.ac.uk/scholarships
Closing Date: 24 May
Funding: Private
Contributor: Academy of Korean Studies
No. of awards given last year: 1
Additional Information: If you have any questions about the bursary application, please contact the Scholarships Officer www.petersons.com/scholarship/babe-ruth-scholarship-program-111_179153.aspx

For further information contact:

Email: ak49@soas.ac.uk

Allan and Nesta Ferguson Scholarships

Eligibility: 1. Be nationals of and resident in an African country, 2. Hold an undergraduate degree at the first class level, 3. New scholarship applicants must have applied to SOAS but are not required to have received an offer of admissions by the scholarship deadline. An offer will need to have been received by the time the relevant panel meets to discuss scholarship applications, 4. Applicants must meet the English language condition of their offer of admission to study at SOAS as soon as possible but no later than 1 June 2023. If your offer is conditional on English, please arrange your English test and ensure you meet the English requirement as soon as possible. 5. Please note that most scholarships do not cover funding or even allow for Pre-sessionals. Please check the wording of your scholarship offer carefully to see if you are eligible for a Pre-sessional course or whether you need to achieve SOAS direct entry scores by the deadline specified in your scholarship terms and conditions.
Level of Study: Postgraduate
Type: Scholarship
Value: £30,555
Frequency: Annual
Country of Study: United Kingdom
Closing Date: 1 May
Additional Information: www.soas.ac.uk/registry/scholarships/allan-and-nesta-ferguson-scholarships.html

For further information contact:

Email: scholarships@soas.ac.uk

Alphawood Scholarships at SOAS 2023/24

Eligibility: To be considered for an Alphawood Scholarship, you must have received an offer for your programme of study from the SOAS Department of Art and Archaeology by the time that the Scholarships are awarded in March 2023.
Level of Study: Postgraduate
Type: Scholarship
Value: Tuition fees will be paid in full for the MA. an allowance of £16,539 per year
Frequency: Annual
Country of Study: United Kingdom
Closing Date: 14 January
Additional Information: www.soas.ac.uk/saaap/alphawood-scholarships/

For further information contact:

Email: alphawoodscholarships@soas.ac.uk

Arts and Humanities Research Council Studentships

Purpose: Up to 56 Arts and Humanities studentships available from CHASE Doctoral Training Partnership. CHASE Studentships are for PhD-level study only and successful applicants will have their fees paid, as well as receiving a stipend to cover living expenses (where eligible, see below) and access to further funds for skills training and research.
Eligibility: CHASE AHRC funding is only available to Home or EU students. Both Home and EU students must satisfy the standard research council eligibility criteria. Please see page 12 of the Research Councils Terms and Conditions for Training Grants to check eligibility.
Level of Study: Postgraduate
Type: Studentship
Value: Maintenance plus approved tuition fees
Frequency: Annual
Study Establishment: SOAS
Country of Study: United Kingdom
Application Procedure: You must apply for the CHASE studentships via the studentship application. (www.chase.ac.uk/apply)
No. of awards offered: 56
Closing Date: 28 January
Funding: Government
Additional Information: www.soas.ac.uk/registry/scholarships/ahrc-chase.html

For further information contact:

Tel: (44) 20 7074 5083
Email: scholarships@soas.ac.uk

Bernard Buckman Scholarship

Purpose: The Bernard Buckman Scholarship was established in 1992 with generous support by Mrs Buckman in memory of her late husband who was a Governor of the School. There is one Bernard Buckman Scholarship available.
Eligibility: 1. Open to applicants paying fees at the UK/EU rate only. 2. Applicants must possess a good honours degree from a UK university or an equivalent institution recognised by SOAS. 3. Applicants must have an offer of admission to pursue the full-time MA Chinese Studies or MA Advanced Chinese Studies programme at SOAS by the scholarship application deadline. 4. Applicants must meet the English language condition of their offer of admission to study at SOAS. If your offer is conditional on English, please arrange your English test and ensure you meet the English requirements as soon as possible.
Level of Study: Postgraduate
Type: Scholarship
Value: £6,000
Frequency: Annual
Study Establishment: SOAS
Country of Study: United Kingdom
Application Procedure: Candidates can apply for this scholarship via the online scholarship application form.
No. of awards offered: 2
Closing Date: 30 April
Funding: Private
Additional Information: www.soas.ac.uk/registry/scholarships/bernard-buckman-scholarship.html

For further information contact:

Thornhaugh Street, Russell Square, London WC1H 0XG, United Kingdom.

Tel: (44) 20 7074 5094/5091
Email: scholarships@soas.ac.uk

Brough Sanskrit Awards

Purpose: There are 3 awards of up to £1,200 for SOAS postgraduate research and master's students who use Sanskrit in their work and will use the funds for research activity such as fieldwork trips.
Eligibility: 1. The funding is for students who use Sanskrit in their work. Evidence of this should be provided in your application. 2. We cannot normally hold an award over into the next academic year if a candidate does not make the trip or attend the conference or workshop when intended a re-application has to be made. 3. For research degree applicants only 4. Any student accepting a Brough Sanskrit award

for fieldwork, workshops and conference must be enrolled 5. The student must submit a brief report, signed by the supervisor, to the Scholarships Officer within one month of the end of the fieldwork visit, conference or workshop. 6. Retrospective applications for a Brough Sanskrit Award will be considered but will not be given priority. 7. If you have already had a Brough Sanskrit Award, you can be considered for another award in a different academic year. 8. For conference funding, priority may be given to students who have been invited to present a paper at the conference

Level of Study: Postgraduate

Type: Award

Value: £1,200

Length of Study: 1 year

Frequency: Annual

Study Establishment: SOAS

Country of Study: United Kingdom

Application Procedure: Please apply online via the on-line application form. (docs.google.com/forms/d/e/1FAIpQLSciNs4iyr1IJ293OUamoABPLWifocGTDFPpANCHyvgCIxVgVw/viewform)

No. of awards offered: 3

Closing Date: 9 April

Additional Information: www.soas.ac.uk/registry/scholarships/brough-sanskrit-awards.html

For further information contact:

SOAS University of London, 10 Thornhaugh Street, Russell Square, London WC1H 0XG, United Kingdom.

Email: scholarships@soas.ac.uk

CSJR Postgraduate Student Bursary

Purpose: The Centre for the Study of Japanese Religions offers a CSJR Postgraduate Student Bursary in Japanese Religions to be held at SOAS, University of London.

Eligibility: 1. Applicants must possess an outstanding academic record. 2. Taught Masters (MA) applicants must focus on Japanese Religions / Japanese Buddhism. Evidence of this should be included in the statement of their application and reflected in their choice of modules. 3. Taught Masters (MA) and Research Degree (MPhil/PhD) applicants should give evidence in the statement of their application of their ability to use sources in Japanese. 4. Open to UK/EU and Overseas candidates. 5. Applicants must have an offer of admission for one of the eligible programmes at SOAS by the scholarship application deadline. 6. Applicants must meet the English language condition of their offer of admission to study at SOAS as soon as possible but no later than 1 June

Level of Study: Postgraduate

Type: Bursary

Value: £5,000 for one year

Length of Study: 1 year

Frequency: Annual

Study Establishment: SOAS

Country of Study: United Kingdom

Application Procedure: You must apply for this scholarship via the on-line application form. (docs.google.com/forms/d/e/1FAIpQLSfJoH5lA2_Opi7_nMY-f_58-PBXlxnZfM7peotowp9q0kLoZg/viewform).

Closing Date: 28 May

Funding: Foundation

Additional Information: www.soas.ac.uk/registry/scholarships/csjr-postgraduate-student-bursary.html

For further information contact:

SOAS University of London, 10 Thornhaugh Street, Russell Square, London WC1H 0XG, United Kingdom.

Tel: (44) 20 7074 5094/ 5091

Email: scholarships@soas.ac.uk

Felix Scholarship

Subjects: Any full time PhD programme or Taught Masters programmes

Purpose: A number of Felix Scholarships will be available to Indian nationals with first class degrees to pursue graduate studies at SOAS, University of London.

Eligibility: 1. Must be Indian nationals and not currently be living or studying outside of India. 2. Must not have previously studied for one year or more outside India. 3. Felix Master's Alumni who have obtained a distinction at Masters may apply for a PhD Felix scholarship. 4. Candidates must have at least a first class Bachelor's degree from an Indian University or comparable institution. We may give priority applicants with a higher first class Bachelor's degree. 5. Exceptionally those with an upper second-class degree at the Bachelor's level may be considered for PhD if they hold a first class degree at the Master's level.

Level of Study: Doctorate, Postgraduate

Type: Scholarship

Value: Covers the full cost of tuition fees; living costs and a return air fare

Frequency: Annual

Study Establishment: SOAS

Country of Study: United Kingdom

Closing Date: 28 January

Funding: Private

Contributor: Felix Scholarship Trust

Additional Information: www.soas.ac.uk/registry/scholar ships/felix-scholarships.html

For further information contact:

Tel: (44) 20 7074 5094/5091
Email: scholarships@soas.ac.uk

Hong Kong and Shanghai Banking Corporation School of Oriental and African Studies Scholarships

Purpose: To support United Kingdom or European Union fee payers commencing a full-time master's course in Sinology or Chinese literature.
Eligibility: Applicants must possess or be about to complete a good honours degree, preferably first class, from a United Kingdom institution or overseas equivalent
Level of Study: Postgraduate
Type: Scholarship
Value: £16,650 plus tuition fees at the home European Union rate
Length of Study: 1 year
Frequency: Annual
Study Establishment: SOAS
Country of Study: United Kingdom
Application Procedure: Candidates can apply for this scholarship via the online scholarship application form. For enquiries, please contact Scholarships Officer
Closing Date: 22 March
Funding: Trusts
Contributor: HSBC educational trust
No. of awards given last year: 2
Additional Information: www.soas.ac.uk/registry/scholar ships/hsbc-soas-scholarships.html

For further information contact:

Tel: (44) 20 7074 5094/5091

International Postgraduate Scholarships

Purpose: The International Postgraduate Scholarship is designed to award new entry Postgraduate students with outstanding academic performance.
Eligibility: 1. Accepted an offer to study a Postgraduate taught (on-campus) degree. 2. Overseas fee-paying student who is a national of China, Hong Kong, or Taiwan. 3. Minimum UK upper second-class (21) or international equivalent.
Level of Study: Postgraduate
Type: Scholarship
Value: £3,000

Frequency: Annual
Study Establishment: SOAS
Country of Study: United Kingdom
Application Procedure: Apply for the International Scholarship via the online form. (docs.google.com/forms/d/e/ 1FAIpQLSd3dRxz_SdPARVCzG8AeNOBPXelEw2ItS2ho dRD1qO7wBL3kQ/viewform)
No. of awards offered: 15
Closing Date: 31 May
Funding: Foundation
Additional Information: www.soas.ac.uk/registry/scholar ships/international-postgraduate-scholarship-east-asia.html

For further information contact:

SOAS University of London, 10 Thornhaugh Street, Russell Square, London WC1H 0XG, United Kingdom.

Tel: (44) 20 7074 4700
Email: study@soas.ac.uk

Shapoorji Pallonji Scholarships

Purpose: The Shapoorji Pallonji Scholarships will provide a contribution to fees and living costs calibrated according to merit and availability of funds.
Eligibility: 1. Applicants for the MA Scholarships must possess or expect to be awarded a First Class Honours Degree or equivalent. Applicants with a non UK masters degree must be in the top rank as evidenced by references and transcripts. Applicants with a 2.1 may also apply but will not be given preference. 2. Applicants for the MPhil/ PhD scholarships must possess or expect to be awarded a Masters degree with a mark of Distinction from a UK university. Applicants with a non UK masters degree must be in the top rank as evidenced by references and transcripts. Applicants with a mark of merit may also apply but will not be given preference. 3. Applicants for the MPhil/PhD scholarships must have demonstrated in the research proposal of their application for admission that their research is in one of the following subject areas i) Zoroastrianism, both ancient and modern ii) Zoroastrianism with Avestan, Pahlavi, Persian or Gujarati languages. 4. Applicants for the MA scholarship must complete the compulsory 60 credit dissertation in Zoroastrianism and the 30-credit module Zoroastrianism, Historical and Contemporary Perspectives. In addition to this, applicants may wish to take one further 30-credit language module (e.g. Avestan language module). 5. The scholarship is open to UK/EU and overseas fee-paying full time students.
Level of Study: Postgraduate
Type: Scholarship

S

Value: contribution to fees and living costs calibrated according to merit and availability of funds.

Length of Study: The MPhil/PhD scholarship is paid for 3 years. The MA is paid for one year (or over two years if part-time).

Frequency: Annual

Study Establishment: SOAS

Country of Study: United Kingdom

Application Procedure: Applicants must submit a complete on-line application for admission and as soon as possible and no later than the studentship deadline.

Closing Date: 1 May

Funding: Foundation

Additional Information: www.soas.ac.uk/registry/scholar ships/shapoorji-pallonji-scholarships-.html

For further information contact:

SOAS University of London, 10 Thornhaugh Street, Russell Square, London WC1H 0XG, United Kingdom.

Tel:	(44) 20 7074 5094/ 5091
Email:	scholarships@soas.ac.uk

SOAS Master's Scholarship

Purpose: The SOAS Masters Scholarships are designed to recognise applicants with outstanding academic achievements.

Eligibility: 1. UK 'Home fees' applicants only. 2. Holding offer (conditional or unconditional) for full-time Postgraduate Taught (on campus) programmes. Part-time programmes are not eligible. 3. Assessed on academic merit and work experience.

Level of Study: Postgraduate

Type: Scholarship

Value: £4,000

Length of Study: 1 year, non-renewable

Frequency: Annual

Study Establishment: SOAS

Country of Study: United Kingdom

Application Procedure: Applicants must submit a complete online application for admission. (www.soas.ac.uk/admis sions/pg/howtoapply/)

No. of awards offered: 44

Closing Date: 30 April

Funding: Government

Additional Information: www.soas.ac.uk/registry/scholar ships/soas-alumni-scholarship.html

For further information contact:

Tel:	(44) 20 7074 5094/5091
Email:	scholarships@soas.ac.uk

SOAS Research Scholarship

Purpose: To support full-time research study at SOAS

Eligibility: 1. Any full-time MPhil/PhD programme (new admissions only). 2. Be UK-permanent residents (UK fee-paying students) from the following ethnic group: 3. Black (Black or Black British African, Black or Black British Caribbean, Black or Black British other or Mixed Black or Black British).

Level of Study: Doctorate

Type: Scholarship

Value: £17,285

Length of Study: 3 years

Frequency: Annual

Study Establishment: SOAS

Country of Study: United Kingdom

Application Procedure: Applicants must complete and submit an application form that can be downloaded from the website

Closing Date: 30 April

Funding: Government

No. of awards given last year: 4

Additional Information: For enquiries, please contact Scholarships Officer www.afterschoolafrica.com/35577/ soas-research-studentships/

For further information contact:

Email:	scholarships@soas.ac.uk

SOAS Sanctuary Scholarship

Purpose: The SOAS Sanctuary scheme to support displaced people

Eligibility: 1. Any full-time undergraduate degree of 3 years duration 2. Any full-time one year or part-time two year postgraduate taught Master's degree on campus (not distance learning) 3. In addition, a package of support will be provided to contribute towards the living costs (which includes accommodation, travel and study materials) for the student to take up their place.

Level of Study: Postgraduate

Type: Scholarship

Value: Full tuition fee waiver

Frequency: Annual

Study Establishment: SOAS

Country of Study: United Kingdom

Closing Date: 30 June

Funding: Foundation

Additional Information: www.soas.ac.uk/registry/scholar ships/soas-sanctuary-scholarships-202021.html

For further information contact:

SOAS University of London, 10 Thornhaugh Street, Russell Square, London WC1H 0XG, United Kingdom.

Tel: (44) 20 7074 5094
Email: scholarships@soas.ac.uk

Sochon Foundation Scholarship

Purpose: The Sochon Foundation has generously provided SOAS with scholarships for students undertaking a full-time post-graduate programmes in Korean Studies.
Eligibility: 1. Open to UK/EU and overseas applicants. Priority will be given to Overseas applicants. 2. Applicants must have an offer of admission to the degree programme by the scholarship application deadline. 3. Applicants must meet the English language condition of their offer of admission to study at SOAS as soon as possible. If your offer is conditional on English, please arrange your English test and ensure you meet the English requirements as soon as possible.
Level of Study: Postgraduate
Type: Scholarship
Value: £9,000
Length of Study: 1 year
Frequency: Annual
Study Establishment: SOAS
Country of Study: United Kingdom
Application Procedure: Applicants must apply for this scholarship via the online scholarship application.
Closing Date: 1 May
Funding: Foundation
Additional Information: www.soas.ac.uk/registry/scholar ships/sochon-foundation-scholarship.html

For further information contact:

Tel: (44) 20 7074 5091/5094
Email: scholarships@soas.ac.uk

Tibawi Trust Awards

Purpose: Dr Abdul-Latif Tibawi left a gift in his will to establish a Trust for a postgraduate award. The award is to assist Palestinians undertaking a postgraduate course at SOAS and may be used towards conference visits or fieldwork in the UK or Overseas.
Eligibility: 1. Any postgraduate degree programme at SOAS. 2. Candidates must be of Palestinian origin. 3. Candidates must be enrolled in a programme at SOAS.
Level of Study: Postgraduate
Type: Award

Value: Up to £1,300 each
Frequency: Annual
Study Establishment: SOAS
Country of Study: United Kingdom
Application Procedure: 1. Applications must be received no later than 1500 (UK time) on 5 June. 2. Late applications will not be considered.
No. of awards offered: 2
Closing Date: 4 June
Funding: Foundation
Additional Information: www.soas.ac.uk/registry/scholar ships/tibawi-trust-award.html

For further information contact:

SOAS University of London, 10 Thornhaugh Street, Russell Square, London WC1H 0XG, United Kingdom.

Tel: (44) 20 7074 5094/ 5091
Email: scholarships@soas.ac.uk

VP Kanitkar Memorial Scholarship

Purpose: The V P Kanitkar Memorial Scholarships are available for postgraduates to support a taught masters in Religious Studies with reference to Hinduism and a taught masters in Anthropology with reference to Hindu culture in South Asia. Each scholarship covers the cost of tuition fees and provides a maintenance.
Eligibility: 1. The scholarship is open to UK/EU and overseas applicants. 2. Applicants must possess or expect to be awarded a First Class Honours Degree or equivalent. Students with a non-UK degree to be adjudged in the top rank by their referees and transcript. 3. Applicants must have an offer of admission to pursue one of the full-time eligible taught masters programmes by the scholarship application deadline, that is, by 16 April.
Level of Study: Postgraduate
Type: Scholarship
Value: Each scholarship covers the cost of tuition fees and provides a maintenance
Frequency: Annual
Study Establishment: SOAS
Country of Study: United Kingdom
Application Procedure: Applicants must submit a complete on-line application for admission. (www.soas.ac.uk/admis sions/pg/howtoapply/)
Closing Date: 1 May
Funding: Foundation
Additional Information: www.soas.ac.uk/registry/scholar ships/soas-open-scholarship.html

SOAS University of London, 10 Thornhaugh Street, Russell Square, London WC1H 0XG, United Kingdom.

Tel: (44) 20 7074 5094/5091
Email: scholarships@soas.ac.uk

William Ross Murray Scholarship

Purpose: To support a student of high academic achievement from a developing country unable to pay overseas tuition fees and attend the full-time LLM degree at SOAS
Eligibility: 1. Must be domiciled in a developing country. 2. Possess a good honours degree, preferably first class, from a UK institution or overseas equivalent. 3. Have an unconditional offer of admission to pursue the full-time LLM at SOAS by the scholarship application deadline. If your offer is conditional, please ensure you meet the conditions and receive an unconditional offer by the deadline.
Level of Study: Postgraduate
Type: Scholarship
Value: Overseas tuition fees. Free accommodation at International Student House and food vouchers
Length of Study: 1 year
Frequency: Annual
Study Establishment: SOAS
Country of Study: United Kingdom
No. of awards offered: 1
Closing Date: 20 February
Funding: Foundation
No. of awards given last year: 1
Additional Information: www.afterschoolafrica.com/159/william-ross-murray-scholarship/

Science and Engineering Research Board

5 & 5A, Lower Ground Floor, Vasant Square Mall, Sector-B, Pocket-5, Vasant Kunj, New Delhi, 110070, India.

Tel: (91) 11 40000398
Website: serb.gov.in/
Contact: Science and Engineering Research Board

One of the most notable developments in the S&T sector in the XI Plan has been the setting up of the Science and Engineering Research Board (SERB) through an Act of Parliament, viz. the Science and Engineering Research Board Act, 2008. Promoting basic research in Science and Engineering and to provide financial assistance to persons engaged in such research, academic institutions, research and development laboratories, industrial concerns and other agencies for such research and for matters connected therewith or incidental thereto are the primary and distinctive mandate of the Board. SERB aims to build up best management systems which would match the best global practices in the area of promotion and funding of basic research.

J C Bose National Fellowship

Subjects: All areas of Science
Purpose: The JC Bose fellowship is awarded to active scientists in recognition for their outstanding performance. The fellowship is scientist-specific and very selective.
Eligibility: 1. Should be an active scientist with a record of outstanding performance apparent from the award of SS Bhatnagar prize and or fellowship of science academies (including engineering, agriculture and medicine). 2. The scientist should be in service at the time of nomination to this fellowship. 3. The nominee should be an Indian national working in institutions in India. 4. The nominee should not be receiving any other fellowship from any other Government sources.
Level of Study: Postgraduate
Type: Fellowship
Value: The fellowship amount is ₹25,000 per month in addition to regular income. Research grant of ₹15.00 lakh per annum. Overhead of ₹1.00 lakh per annum to the host institute.
Length of Study: 5 years
Frequency: Twice a year
Country of Study: India
Application Procedure: Nominator should first register into the online website. www.serbonline.in/SERB/Registration
Funding: Government
Additional Information: serb.gov.in/jcbn.php

For further information contact:

Science and Engineering Research Board, 5 & 5A, Lower Ground Floor, Vasant Square Mall, Plot No. A, Community Centre, Sector-5, Pocket-5, Vasant Kunj, New Delhi, 110070, India.

National Post Doctoral Fellowship (N-PDF)

Purpose: The SERB-National Post Doctoral Fellowship (N-PDF) is aimed to identify motivated young researchers and provide them support for doing research in frontier areas of science and engineering. The fellows will work under a mentor, and it is hoped that this training will provide them a platform to develop as an independent researcher

Eligibility: 1. The applicant should be an Indian citizen. 2. The applicant must have obtained Ph.D./M.D./M.-S. degree from a recognized University. Those who have submitted their PhD/M.D/M.S thesis and are awaiting award of the degree are also eligible to apply. However, such candidates, if selected, will be offered lower fellowship amount till they qualify the eligible degree. 3. The upper age limit for the fellowship is 35 years at the time of the submission of application, age will be calculated by taking the date of closure of the respective call. Age relaxation of 5 (five) years will be given to candidates belonging to SC/ST/OBC/Physically Challenged & Women candidates. 4. NPDF can be availed only once by a candidate in his/her career. 5. Mentor must hold a regular academic / research position in a recognized institution in India. Should hold Ph.D. degree in Science or Engineering. 6. A mentor shall not have more than two SERB NPDF fellows at any given time.

Level of Study: Postdoctorate

Type: Fellowship

Value: Fellowship ₹55,000 per month + HRA. Research Grant ₹200,000 per annum. Overheads ₹100,000 per annum

Length of Study: 2 years

Frequency: Annual

Country of Study: India

Application Procedure: Applicants should first register into the online website www.serbonline.in. For details one may visit serbonline.in/SERB/npdf?HomePage=New.

Funding: Government

Additional Information: serb.gov.in/npdf.php

Prime Minister's Fellowship Scheme for Doctoral Research

Purpose: This scheme is aimed at encouraging young, talented, enthusiastic and result-oriented scholars to take up industry-relevant research. Under this scheme, full-time PhD scholars get double the money that they would otherwise get for doing research.

Level of Study: Research

Type: Fellowship

Value: ₹36,400 per month

Length of Study: 4 years

Frequency: Annual

Country of Study: India

No. of awards offered: 100

Funding: Government

Contributor: Department of Science & Technology (DST) and Science & Engineering Research Board (SERB) with The Confederation of Indian Industry (CII)

Additional Information: www.primeministerfellow shipscheme.in/about-the-scheme

For further information contact:

Email: shalini.sharma@cii.in

Ramanujan Fellowship

Subjects: Researchers scientists/engineers

Purpose: The scheme provides support to active researchers/ scientists/engineers who want to return to India from abroad and contribute their work for the country.

Eligibility: 1. The Fellowship is open to brilliant Indian scientists and engineers working abroad and are below the age of 40 years. 2. The nominee should possess a higher degree or equivalent, such as Ph.D. in Science/ Engineering, Masters in Engineering or Technology/ MD in Medicine, etc. and have adequate professional experience. 3. These Fellowships are very selective and only those who have a proven/ outstanding track-record as evident from their research publications and recognition's would be eligible. 4. In case of selection of the candidate for regular position in the University/ Institute, the candidate will not be eligible for receiving grant under the Ramanujan Fellowship. 5. The Fellowship is only for those scientists who are not holding any permanent/ tenuretrack/ contractual position in any Indian Institute/ University. 6. The nominee should be working abroad at the time of nomination.

Level of Study: Postgraduate

Type: Fellowship

Value: Fellowship will be ₹1,35,000 per month. Research grant of ₹7,00,000 per annum and ₹60,000 per annum as overhead charges

Length of Study: 5 years

Frequency: Annual

Country of Study: India

Application Procedure: Nominee need to register in SERB online portal, www.serbonline.in

Funding: Government

Additional Information: serb.gov.in/rnf.php

For further information contact:

Science and Engineering Research Board, 5 & 5A, Lower Ground Floor, Vasant Square Mall, Plot No. A, Community Centre, Sector-5, Pocket-5, Vasant Kunj, New Delhi, 110070, India.

S.N Bose Scholar Program

Purpose: S.N Bose Scholar Program is organized by the Science and Engineering Board (SERB), Department of science and technology (DST), Govt. of India, Indo–US Technology Forum and Win Step Forward. The scholarship envisages providing a world-class research platform in top US universities. It also aims at making Indo-US long-term collaboration in the field of research

Eligibility: 1. Students pursuing a Bachelor's or Master's degree program from a recognized institution of India can apply for this scheme. 2. The disciplines of pursuing UG and PG degree are Atmospheric and Earth Sciences, Chemical Sciences, Engineering Sciences, Mathematical and Computational Sciences, and Physical Sciences. 3. Candidates who are studying PhD cannot apply

Level of Study: Postdoctorate

Type: Scholarship

Length of Study: 1 year

Frequency: Annual

Closing Date: May

Funding: Foundation

Additional Information: The program will not be accepting applications for this year. www.iusstf.org/program/for-indian-students

For further information contact:

Indo-US Science and Technology Forum, Fulbright House, 12, Hailey Road, New Delhi, 110001, India.

Tel:	(91) 11 42691712
Email:	bose@indousstf.org

Science and Engineering Research Board Distinguished Fellowship

Purpose: This fellowship is especially to encourage and provide financial support to those senior scientists who find it difficult to continue their research because of financial limitations, and those who are forced to stop their research against their will.

Eligibility: Superannuated scientist who is active in research. Must have received recognition for his/her work from National and/or International scientific bodies

Level of Study: Research

Type: Fellowship

Value: A research grant of ₹5,00,000 per annum and a fellowship amount of ₹60,000 per month will be given to each fellow

Length of Study: 3 years

Country of Study: India

Application Procedure: Call for nomination is made from time to time. Nominations are accepted only when the call is made

No. of awards offered: 20

Closing Date: 30 November

Funding: Government

Additional Information: www.scholarshipsinindia.com/fellowship/serb-distinguished-fellowship.html

For further information contact:

Email: keerti.serb@gmail.com

Science and Engineering Research Board Overseas Postdoctoral Fellowship (OPDF)

Purpose: SERB Overseas Postdoctoral fellowship (SERB-OPDF) aims to build national capacity in frontier areas of Science and Engineering, which are of interest to India by providing postdoctoral fellowship

Eligibility: The applicant should have completed PhD in science and engineering not earlier than the preceding 2 years from recognized institutions in India. For researchers who are in regular employment, the 2 years period may be relaxed

Level of Study: Postdoctorate

Type: Fellowship

Length of Study: 1 year, extendable to 1 more year subject to good performance

Application Procedure: The format, guidelines and other details of the SERB-OPDF Program details are also available at www.dst.gov.in

Additional Information: The programme admits candidates in identified areas and sends them to top institutions around the globe, other than United States of America and also to institutions where internationally acclaimed scientists are working www.serb.gov.in/opf.php

Science and Engineering Research Board Women Excellence Award

Purpose: SERB Women Excellence Award is a one-time award given to women scientists below 40 years of age and who have received recognition from any one or more of the following national academies such as Young Scientist Medal, Young Associate etc.

Level of Study: Research

Type: Award

Value: ₹5,00,000 per annum

Length of Study: 3 years

Frequency: Annual

Country of Study: India

Application Procedure: A copy of the proposal (in one file in PDF) may also be sent by email to shilpipaul@serb.gov.in

Funding: Government

Additional Information: The call for proposals will be notified through the website annually. Women Scientists who have received the award earlier are not eligible to apply again serb.gov.in/wea.php

For further information contact:

Email: shilpipaul@serb.gov.in

Science and Technology Facilities Council (STFC)

Polaris House, North Star Avenue, Swindon SN2 1SZ, United Kingdom.

Tel: (44) 1793 442 000
Email: enquiries@stfc.ac.uk
Website: stfc.ukri.org/

STFC's Strategic Context and Future Opportunities takes into account the Government's renewed focus on the importance of UK Industrial Strategy and the impact of the UK's decision to leave the European Union. We have also taken the opportunity to consider STFC's contribution to UK Research and Innovation's (UKRI's) ambitions. This replaces our existing Corporate Strategy but provides a current document on which to base our engagement with stakeholders.

Daphne Jackson Fellowships

Purpose: Daphne Jackson fellowships are retraining fellowships open to all researchers across science, technology, engineering, mathematics, social sciences, arts and humanities, and other related disciplines. Daphne Jackson Fellowships are retraining fellowships for anyone who has taken a break of two years or more from research for family, caring or health reasons.

Eligibility: 1. A career break of at least two years' duration, taken for family, health or caring reasons. 2. A good first degree in a research subject. 3. A PhD, or at least three years research experience (academic or industrial) prior to the career break (with evidence of research impacts and outcomes). 4. UK residency status / right to remain in the UK indefinitely and based in the UK on application. 5. Good command of English (spoken and written). 6. Good computer skills. 7. Your application will be stronger if you also have post-doctoral experience and research impacts and outcomes.

Level of Study: Research

Type: Fellowship

Frequency: Annual

Country of Study: United Kingdom

Application Procedure: There are two main application routes for Daphne Jackson Fellowships. Whichever route you choose, please read 'Are you eligible to apply for a Fellowship' and 'Application process' before submitting your application. (daphnejackson.org/about-fellowships/apply-here/)

Funding: Government

Contributor: Daphne Jackson Trust

Additional Information: Please refer to the website for more details: www.daphnejackson.org/fellowships/applicationprocess/
daphnejackson.org/about-fellowships/application-process/

For further information contact:

Department of Physics, The Daphne Jackson Trust, University of Surrey, Guildford GU2 7XH, United Kingdom.

Tel: (44) 1483 689166
Email: djmft@surrey.ac.uk

Develop early-stage research outputs for commercial application: STFC follow-on fund Feb 2023

Eligibility: You must: 1. be employed at an eligible research organisation 2. have held, or hold, STFC funding from our core science programme. The STFC core science programme consists of: 1. nuclear physics 2. particle physics and particle astrophysics 3. astronomy and space science 4. accelerators 5. computing in support of these. If you have received funding from the STFC core science programme but not as a principal investigator or a co-investigator, you are still eligible for this scheme. This could, for example, include postdoctoral research assistants and PhD students.

Level of Study: Postgraduate

Type: Grant

Value: Up to £200,000. STFC will fund 80% of the full economic cost.

Length of Study: 18 months.

Frequency: Annual

Country of Study: United Kingdom

Closing Date: 2 February

Additional Information: www.ukri.org/opportunity/develop-early-stage-research-outputs-for-commercial-application-stfc-follow-on-fund-feb-2022/

For further information contact:

Email: wendy.carr@stfc.ac.uk

Ernest Rutherford Fellowship

Purpose: The Ernest Rutherford Fellowships will enable early career researchers with clear leadership potential to establish a strong, independent research programme
Eligibility: Ernest Rutherford Fellowships are intended for early career researchers who do not have a permanent academic position. You are not eligible if you currently hold a permanent academic position or the equivalent in institutions other than universities. Fellowships are open to applicants of any nationality
Level of Study: Research
Type: A variable number of fellowships
Value: Fund the proposal at 80% of the full economic cost
Length of Study: 5 years
Frequency: Annual
Country of Study: United Kingdom
Application Procedure: Please refer to the application details on the STFC website stfc.ukri.org/funding/fellowships/ernest-rutherford-fellowship/
No. of awards offered: 160
Closing Date: 16 September
Funding: Government
No. of awards given last year: 11
No. of applicants last year: 160
Additional Information: stfc.ukri.org/funding/fellowships/ernest-rutherford-fellowship/

For further information contact:

Email: fellowships@stfc.ukri.org

Industrial CASE Studentships

Purpose: Provides support for PhD students to work in collaboration with a non-academic partner on projects that aim to apply technologies or techniques developed within the programme into other areas
Eligibility: Organisations eligible to receive STFC grant funding
Level of Study: Postgraduate
Type: Studentship
Value: Stipend, fees, research training and fieldwork travel
Length of Study: 3.5 years
Frequency: Annual
Country of Study: United Kingdom
Application Procedure: Call opens in August. Applications must be submitted by the academic partner through the Je-S

system. Proposals may be led by either the academic supervisor at an eligible United Kingdom University or research institute or supervisor/supervisors at the non-academic partner organisation, but the application process must be completed by the academic partner, who will then be the recipient of the award
Closing Date: October
Funding: Commercial
Additional Information: stfc.ukri.org/funding/studentships/industrial-case-studentships/

For further information contact:

Email: studentships@stfc.ukri.org

Industrial CASE-Plus Studentship

Purpose: Industrial CASE-Plus extends the Industrial CASE competition to help students become more effective in promoting technology transfer, should their chosen career path take them into either academic research or industry.
Eligibility: Proposals should be submitted by a supervisor from a research organisation eligible to be the academic partner through Je-S. Proposals may be led by either the academic supervisor at an eligible UK university or research institute or supervisor/supervisors at the non-academic partner organisation. The application process must be completed by the academic partner, who will then be the recipient of the award. Before preparing and submitting a proposal it is essential you ensure the non-academic partner and academic institution are both eligible.
Level of Study: Postgraduate
Type: Grant
Value: £500,000
Length of Study: 3.5 years
Frequency: Annual
Study Establishment: Science and Technology Facilities Council
Country of Study: United Kingdom
Closing Date: 30 September
Funding: Government
Additional Information: stfc.ukri.org/funding/studentships/types-of-postgraduate-studentship/

For further information contact:

Email: studentships@stfc.ukri.org.

PPARC Communications/Media Programme

Purpose: To support students undertake communications training

Eligibility: Either (a) Upper second class honours (2:1) degree or equivalent in social science, or (b) Upper second class (2:1) degree or equivalent in another field with professional experience in the media and communications field
Level of Study: Postgraduate
Type: Bursary
Value: £24,456
Length of Study: 12 months full-time, 24 months part-time
Frequency: Annual
Study Establishment: Any approved university
Country of Study: United Kingdom
Application Procedure: Contact the PPARC Science and Society team
Additional Information: www.lse.ac.uk/study-at-lse/Graduate/Degree-programmes-2020/MSc-Media-and-Communications

For further information contact:

Tel:　　(44) 1793 442030
Email:　pr.pus@pparc.ac.uk

PPARC Royal Society Industry Fellowships

Purpose: To enhance interaction between those in industry and the research base, to the benefit of United Kingdom industry
Eligibility: Open to senior academic scientists and industrial employees with a project proposal central to their own research programme for which a collaborative effort would bring benefits
Level of Study: Postdoctorate
Type: Fellowship
Value: Varies
Length of Study: 6 months–2 years full-time, or part-time over a period of up to 4 years
Frequency: Annual
Study Establishment: An appropriate academic institution or position in the industry
Country of Study: United Kingdom
Application Procedure: Applicants must find a suitable industrial or academic partner to host their project before submitting an application. Applications and further information are available from the Research Appointments Department of The Royal Society
Closing Date: December
Funding: Commercial, Private
Contributor: The Royal Society, EPSRC, BBSRC, Rolls-Royce and PPARC
Additional Information: Apart from the Royal Society Fellowships Programme the following fellowship programmes are administered by the PPARC in collaboration with other

partners: The European Organisation for Nuclear Research (CERN) Fellowships, The European Space Agency (ESA) Fellowships, The Anglo-Australian Postdoctoral Research Fellowships, and the Daphne Jackson Fellowships. Further information on these programmes is available on the PPARC website royalsociety.org/grants-schemes-awards/grants/industry-fellowship/

For further information contact:

Research Appointments Department The Royal Society, 6 Carlton House Terrace, St. James's, London SW1Y 5AR, United Kingdom.

Tel:　　(44) 20 7451 2542
Email:　ukresearch.appointments@royalsoc.ac.uk

PPARC Standard Research Studentship

Purpose: To enable promising scientists and engineers to continue training
Eligibility: Advice on eligibility should be sought from the Registrar's Office
Level of Study: Postgraduate
Type: Studentship
Value: Tuition fees only
Length of Study: 3 years
Frequency: Annual
Country of Study: United Kingdom
Application Procedure: Contact the PPARC
Closing Date: 31 March

For further information contact:

Tel:　　(44) 1793 442026
Email:　steve.cann@pparc.ac.uk

Science and Technology Facilities Council Postgraduate Studentships

Subjects: Particle physics, accelerator science, nuclear physics, particle astrophysics, solar system science and astronomy.
Purpose: STFC postgraduate studentships are awarded to enable promising scientists and engineers to continue training beyond a first degree.
Eligibility: Open to postgraduates from the UK and EU countries. All studentship projects supported through STFC funding must fall within STFC remit.
Level of Study: Postgraduate
Type: Studentship
Value: Stipend (excluding fees only students), approved fees, research training support grant, conference and

U.K. fieldwork element, fieldwork expenses, long term attachments, other allowances (where applicable).
Length of Study: 3.5 years
Frequency: Annual
Country of Study: United Kingdom
Application Procedure: If you are interested in applying for an STFC-funded PhD, please contact the institution at which you wish to undertake a research degree directly.
No. of awards offered: Approx. 220
Closing Date: 31 March
Funding: Government
Additional Information: Please check at www.stfc.ac.uk/funding/studentships/types-of-postgraduate-studentship/.

For further information contact:

Email: studentships@stfc.ukri.org

University of Canterbury Pasifika Doctoral Scholarship

Purpose: This scholarship supports Pasifika students for study towards a research doctoral degree at the University of Canterbury
Eligibility: 1. Candidates must be Pasifika. 2. Intending students who already hold a research doctoral degree are not eligible for the scholarship. 3. Students may not take up the scholarship until any non-academic requirements for the qualifying degree have been completed and credited. Offers of scholarships to candidates whose qualifying degree is the BE (Hons) are conditional on the completion and crediting of ENGR 200 no later than 12 months after the formal offer of a place in a doctoral programme has been accepted.
Level of Study: Doctorate
Type: Scholarship
Value: Up to US$21,000 per annum plus tuition fees at domestic rate
Length of Study: Up to 3 years
Frequency: Annual
Country of Study: New Zealand
Application Procedure: You may apply through this webpage approximately 8 weeks before applications close. If it's possible to apply on-line for this scholarship there will be a link above to the on-line system. If the link is not provided, please download and complete the application form located below. However, if the scholarship is managed by Universities NZ or another department of the University an External Website link will appear below and application instructions will be available through that link. Apply through online link. www.canterbury.ac.nz/scholarshipsearch/ScholarshipDetails.aspx
No. of awards offered: 2

Closing Date: 15 May
Funding: Private
Additional Information: www.canterbury.ac.nz/scholarship search/ScholarshipDetails.aspx?ScholarshipID=6935.1640

For further information contact:

Email: scholarships@canterbury.ac.nz

Science Foundation Ireland

Three Park Place, Hatch Street Upper, Dublin 2 D02 FX65, Ireland.

Tel: (353) 1 607 3200
Email: info@sfi.ie
Website: www.sfi.ie/
Contact: Professor Mark W. J. Ferguson, Director

SFI funds oriented basic and applied research in the areas of science, technology, engineering and mathematics. SFI began with an intensive study commissioned by the Irish Government in 1998. Dozens of leaders in Government, academia, and industry assessed the Irish economy, from pharmaceuticals to life science, from transportation to manufacturing. SFI provides awards to support scientists and engineers working in the fields of science and engineering that underpin biotechnology, information and communications technology and sustainable energy and energy-efficient technologies.

President of Ireland Young Research Award (PIYRA)

Purpose: The purpose of the PIYRA programme is to recruit and retain outstanding early career investigators with leadership potential. Its aim is to enable those at an earlier career stage who already hold permanent academic positions to advance their careers and build up their research teams and activities; to allow researchers in temporary positions to advance their careers and provide them with enhanced opportunities to move into a permanent academic position; to enable the award holder, together with his/her team, to carry out their work in Ireland's public research bodies; to offer funding opportunities that help third-level institutions attract and develop researchers and their careers; to allow earlier-career investigators of all nationalities to enhance their experience in Irish HEIs and to allow those employed outside of Ireland to return to work in an Irish HEI

Eligibility: The lead applicant must have completed a minimum of 36 months of active postdoctoral research. The lead applicant must have been awarded a PhD or MD within the last 8 years, in the normal case, or up to a maximum of 12 and a half years for applicants who have taken documented eligible leave, as described below. The lead applicant has an exceptional record of internationally recognized independent research accomplishments for their career stage. The lead applicant must be an individual who will be recognized by the research body upon receipt of the SFI grant as an independent investigator who will have an independent office and research space at the host research body for which he/she will be fully responsible for at least the duration of the SFI grant

Level of Study: Postdoctorate, Research

Type: Grant

Value: Up to €1,000,000 of total value (inclusive of the host institution contribution) in direct costs

Length of Study: 5 years

Frequency: Annual

Study Establishment: Host Research Bodies must be situated in the Republic of Ireland. Research Bodies will include Universities, Institutes of Technology and independent not-for-profit public research organizations that receive a significant share of their total funding from public sources

Country of Study: Ireland

Application Procedure: Applicants are invited to submit the following documentation expression of Interest and if invited to do so after the Expression of Interest evaluation stage; full proposal. Application must be submitted via an eligible research body. Application must be submitted online via SESAME

Closing Date: December

Funding: Government

Contributor: Science Foundation Ireland

Additional Information: www.sfi.ie/funding/funding-calls/sfi-president-of-ireland/

Science Foundation Ireland Career Development Award (CDA)

Purpose: The SFI Career Development Award (CDA) aims to support early- and mid-career researchers who already hold a salaried, independent research post and who are looking to expand their research activities. Its aims is to support excellent scientific research that has potential economic and societal impact; to enable those at an earlier career stage who already hold permanent academic positions to advance their careers and build up their research teams and activities; to allow researchers in temporary positions to advance their careers and provide them with enhanced opportunities to move into a permanent academic position; to provide the

support and infrastructure to carry out novel research in areas that underpin SFI's legal remit; to enable the award holder, together with his/her team, to carry out their work in Ireland's public research bodies, including Universities and Institutes of Technology; to offer funding opportunities that help third-level institutions attract and develop researchers and their careers; to allow earlier-career investigators of all nationalities to enhance their experience in Irish HEIs

Eligibility: The applicant will be a researcher with 3–15 years of relevant experience beyond the award of their doctoral degree, who at the time of application will be either in a permanent, full-time academic position (either within the institution at which they wish to base their CDA-funded research or another elsewhere in Ireland or overseas), or employed on a temporary (fixed-term) contract where it is evident that the role being carried out is an independent research position (i.e., Postdoctoral Research Associates (or equivalent) or Research Fellows working under the guidance of a supervisor and who have never held an independent position are not eligible to apply to the CDA Programme)

Level of Study: Research

Type: Award

Value: Between €300,000 and €500,000 direct costs

Length of Study: 4 years

Frequency: Every 2 years

Study Establishment: Host Research Bodies must be situated in the Republic of Ireland. Research Bodies will include Universities, Institutes of Technology and independent not-for-profit public research organizations that receive a significant share of their total funding from public sources

Country of Study: Ireland

Application Procedure: Application must be submitted via an eligible research body. Application must be submitted online via SESAME (www.sfi.ie/funding/award-management-system)

Closing Date: 10 December

Funding: Government

Contributor: Science Foundation Ireland

No. of awards given last year: 20

Additional Information: Please write to cda@sfi.ie www.sfi.ie/funding/funding-calls/sfi-career-development-award/

For further information contact:

Email: cda@sfi.ie

Science Foundation Ireland Investigator Programme

Purpose: To fund scientific research projects of excellence in focused areas. To build capacity, expertise and relationships so as to enable researchers to compete in future SFI Research Centre Programmes or in other funding programmes such as ERC and Horizon 2020. To encourage researchers to build capacity, expertise, collaborations and relationships in areas of strategic economic importance through themed calls. To facilitate partnerships with other agencies. To support collaborations and partnerships between academia and industry

Eligibility: The lead applicant and any co-applicant(s) must hold a PhD/MD or equivalent for at least 5 years by the proposal deadline. The lead applicant and any co-applicant(s) are required to have demonstrated that they are each senior author on at least 10 international peer reviewed articles. The lead applicant and any co-applicant(s) are required to have demonstrated research independence through securing at least one independent research grant as a lead investigator or as co-investigator

Level of Study: Research

Type: Grant

Value: €400,000–2,500,000 per year

Length of Study: 3–5 years

Frequency: Annual

Study Establishment: Host Research Bodies must be situated in the Republic of Ireland. Research Bodies will include Universities, Institutes of Technology and independent not-for-profit public research organizations that receive a significant share of their total funding from public sources

Country of Study: Ireland

Application Procedure: Application must be submitted via an eligible research body. Application must be submitted online via SESAME (www.sfi.ie/funding/award-management-system)

Closing Date: 26 June

Funding: Government

Contributor: Science Foundation Ireland

No. of awards given last year: 40

Additional Information: www.sfi.ie/funding/funding-calls/sfi-investigators-programme/

For further information contact:

Email: investigators@sfi.ie

Starting Investigator Research Grant (SIRG)

Purpose: The SIRG programme supports excellent postdoctoral researchers who wish to take steps towards a fully independent research career. Aims to support excellent scientific research that has potential economic and societal impact. To enable those at an early career stage to establish themselves as independent researchers; to provide the support and infrastructure to carry out novel research in areas that underpin SFI's legal remit; to gain important experience towards a full-time academic position, including the supervision of the postgraduate student supported by the award; to enable the award holder, together with his/her postgraduate student, to carry out their work in Ireland's public research bodies, including Universities and Institutes of technology; to offer funding opportunities that help third-level institutions attract and develop researchers and their careers; to allow early-career investigators of all nationalities to enhance their experience in Irish HEIs; to allow early-career investigators who have been employed outside of Ireland to return to work in an Irish HEI

Eligibility: The applicant will be a researcher with 3 to 8 years of relevant experience beyond the award of their doctoral, who is currently employed as a Postdoctoral Research Associate (or equivalent) or a Research Fellow under the guidance of a named supervisor, and who has never previously held an independent research position of any kind where they were primarily responsible for a research team and its financial support. Allowances will be made for documented leave, including maternity leave, paternity leave, parental leave, military service, sick/disability leave and carer's leave

Level of Study: Research

Type: Grant

Value: €425,000 direct costs over a period of four years

Length of Study: 4 years

Study Establishment: Host Research Bodies must be situated in the Republic of Ireland. Research Bodies will include Universities, Institutes of Technology and independent not-for-profit public research organizations that receive a significant share of their total funding from public sources

Country of Study: Ireland

Application Procedure: Application must be submitted via an eligible research body. Application must be submitted online via SESAME

Closing Date: 26 November

Funding: Government

Contributor: Science Foundation Ireland

No. of awards given last year: 20

Additional Information: www.sfi.ie/funding/funding-calls/sirg/

For further information contact:

Email: sirg@sfi.ie

Sciences Po

27, rue Saint Guillaume, Cedex 07, F-75337 Paris, France.

Tel: (33) 1 45 49 50 50
Website: www.sciencespo.fr/en/
Contact: Sciences Po

Sciences Po's international dimension was established in its founding documents. Driven forward by this vocation for more than 150 years, today Sciences Po stands out as a world-class university. Sciences Po has within its network over 478 partner universities.

David Gritz Scholarship

Purpose: the David Gritz Scholarship is meant to attract undergraduate and graduate Israeli citizens who wish to study at Sciences Po

Eligibility: The scholarship is awarded every year to 1 Israeli citizen. The candidates must be admitted to an undergraduate or a masters programme or have submitted an application for admission to Sciences Po

Level of Study: Postgraduate

Type: Scholarship

Value: €15,000 per year

Length of Study: 1 year

Country of Study: France

Application Procedure: Applicants must send the forms to caterina.sabbatini@sciencespo.fr

Closing Date: 1 June

Contributor: Sciences Po Foundation

Additional Information: For more details contact Caterina Sabbatini-Clec'h, caterina.sabbatini@sciencespo.fr www.sciencespo.fr/students/en/finance/financial-aid/bourse-david-gritz.html

For further information contact:

Tel: (33) 1 45 49 55 46
Email: lea.albrieux@sciencespo.fr

Emile Boutmy Scholarships

Purpose: Sciences Po created the Emile Boutmy Scholarships after the founder of Sciences Po in order to attract the very best international students from outside of the European Union who are first time applicants and who have been admitted to an undergraduate or master's programme offered at the University

Eligibility: To be eligible for the scholarship, students must be first time applicants from a non-European Union state, whose household does not file taxes within the European Union, and who have been admitted to the Undergraduate or Master's programme.

Level of Study: Postgraduate

Type: Scholarship

Value: €12,200 per year

Length of Study: 2 years

Frequency: Annual

Country of Study: France

Application Procedure: It is important to visit the official website to access the application form and for detailed information on how to apply for this scholarship. Students must indicate that they are applying for the Emile Boutmy scholarship in their Sciences Po application

Closing Date: 30 November

Contributor: Science Po Foundation

Additional Information: www.sciencespo.fr/students/en/fees-funding/financial-aid/emile-boutmy-scholarship.html

KSP Fund for Innovative Projects

Purpose: The KSP Fund for Innovative Projects supports extra-curricular student-led initiatives taking place in countries of the Arab World and the Gulf Region. It is aimed at fostering innovation and providing funding for the realization of creative ideas benefiting the region in all sectors

Level of Study: Postgraduate

Value: €5,000–€10,000

Application Procedure: To apply, please send the following materials with 'KSP Fund for Innovative Projects' in the subject line, by email to the Kuwait Program Assistant fatima.iddahamou@sciencespo.fr

Closing Date: 28 February

Additional Information: Proposed projects must take place in a country of the Arab World or the Gulf Region. For further details, please contact Kuwait Program Assistant, Fatima Iddahamou: mailto: fatima.iddahamou@sciencespo.fr

For further information contact:

Email: kancelaria@ksplegal.pl

KSP Joint Research Projects

Purpose: KSP Joint Research Projects are funded by the Kuwait Program at Sciences Po to foster research links between faculty members at Sciences Po and in Kuwait, in the interest of building a unique scholarly network

Level of Study: Research

Value: Up to €50,000

Length of Study: 1 year

Application Procedure: Application files should be sent to the Kuwait Program Manager at mariezenaide.jolys@sciencespo.fr

Closing Date: 31 October

Funding: Foundation

Contributor: Sciences Po and the Kuwait Foundation for the Advancement of Sciences (KFAS)

S

Additional Information: For details, please check the website: www.sciencespo.fr/psia/kuwait-program www.cnr.it/en/joint-research-projects

For further information contact:

Email: info@itsr.ir

Kuwait Excellence Scholarship for Arab students and Kuwait Nationals

Purpose: The Kuwait Excellence Scholarship program supports outstanding students coming from the Arab world and Kuwait to pursue Master's level graduate studies at Sciences Po. Multiple scholarships will be awarded to the best candidates on a competitive basis.
Eligibility: 1. Applicants must be first-time degree-seeking students in France. 2. Nationals from Arab countries, including the Gulf Region, may apply. 3. Kuwaiti National
Level of Study: Masters Degree
Type: Scholarship
Value: Arab students £10 000 per year (ie. £20 000 for two years of study). and for Kuwait students £12,500 per year (i.e. £25,000 for the two years of study).
Country of Study: France
Application Procedure: To apply, please send the following materials by email to program.kuwait@sciencespo.fr with Kuwait Excellence Scholarship Application for Kuwaiti Nationals in the subject line.
Closing Date: 14 February
Additional Information: www.sciencespo.fr/kuwait-program/student-activities/scholarship/

For further information contact:

Email: program.kuwait@sciencespo.fr

Scope

East Press Centre, 14 East Bay Lane, London E15 2GW, United Kingdom.

Tel: (44) 808 800 3333
Email: helpline@scope.org.uk
Website: www.scope.org.uk/
Contact: Mr Richard Parnell, Research & Public Policy Manager

We provide practical information and emotional support when it's most needed. Campaign relentlessly to create a fairer society. We won't stop until we achieve a society where all disabled people enjoy equality and fairness. We're a strong community of disabled and non-disabled people with a shared vision of equality.

Seoul National University

1 Gwanak-ro, Gwanak-gu, Seoul 08826, Korea.

Tel: (82) 822 880 6971, 6977
Email: snuadmit@snu.ac.kr
Website: en.snu.ac.kr/
Contact: MBA Admissions Officer

Seoul National University becomes the first comprehensive university of independent Korea, founded with the primary aim of producing intellectual elites who would lead the newly liberated country. Aided by countries all over the world, the University makes a rapid recovery, propelled by the Korean people's collective desires for a strong education for the young generation.

Korea Foundation Fellowship

Eligibility: Preference is given to Korean nationals residing abroad
Level of Study: Postdoctorate, Postgraduate, Research
Type: Fellowship
Value: To be determined by the review committee
Length of Study: 1 academic year
Frequency: Annual
Study Establishment: Seoul National University
Country of Study: Korea
Application Procedure: Contact the Office of international Affairs
Closing Date: January
Funding: Foundation
Contributor: The Korean Foundation
Additional Information: en.snu.ac.kr/admission/undergraduate/scholarships/before_admission

For further information contact:

Tel: (82) 2 880 8635
Fax: (82) 2 880 8632
Email: yss@snu.ac.kr

Korea-Japan Cultural Association Scholarship

Eligibility: Japanese students enroled in undergraduate programs who are not in 1st-year
Level of Study: Postdoctorate, Postgraduate, Research
Type: Scholarship
Value: KRW 3,500,000
Length of Study: 1 academic year
Frequency: Annual
Study Establishment: Seoul National University
Country of Study: Korea
Application Procedure: Contact the Office of International Affairs
Closing Date: March
Funding: Foundation
Contributor: Korea-Japan Cultural Association
Additional Information: en.snu.ac.kr/about/overview/vision

For further information contact:

The Office of International Affairs, Korea.

Tel: (82) 2 880 8638
Fax: (82) 2 880 8632
Email: sjlim@snu.ac.kr

Overseas Koreans Scholarship

Purpose: To support students with an outstanding academic record
Eligibility: Preference is given to Korean students with majors related to Korean studies, in particular language, literature, medicine, education or IT, which are beneficial to the development of Korea. Overseas Korean students who wish to take graduate degrees at SNU.
Level of Study: Postdoctorate, Postgraduate, Research
Type: Scholarship
Value: KRW 900,000, full tuition exemption for 8 months, airfare for one economic round trip, medical insurance, Korean language training
Length of Study: 1 year
Frequency: Annual
Country of Study: Any country
Application Procedure: Contact the Overseas Korean Foundation
Closing Date: March
Additional Information: en.snu.ac.kr/about/overview/vision

For further information contact:

Education Department Overseas Korean Foundation, Seocho 2-dong, Seocho-gu, South Korea.

Tel: (82) 64 786 0274
Fax: (82) 2 3415 0118
Email: scholarship@okf.or.kr

Shastri Indo-Canadian Institute

1418 Education Tower, 2500 University Drive, N.W., Calgary, AL T2N-1N4, Canada.

Tel: (1) 403 220 7467
Email: sici@ucalgary.ca
Website: shastriinstitute.org/
Contact: Programme Officer India Studies

The Shastri Indo-Canadian Institute is a binational organization that promotes understanding between India and Canada through academic activities and exchanges. The Shastri Institute is funded by and partners closely with government bodies in both India and Canada. The Institute aims to achieve gender equality and reduce poverty by focusing programming on sustainable development and other United Nations Millennium Development Goals.

Sher-Gil-Sundaram Arts Foundation

3/9, Sector 3, Shanti Niketan, New Delhi, 110021, India.

Tel: (91) 11 46170894
Email: contact@ssaf.in
Website: ssaf.in/

The Sher-Gil Sundaram Arts Foundation (SSAF) seeks to enable conjunctions of artistic and cultural practice that deal with historical memory, and to build expectations for the future. It commits itself to advancing creative independence for art that is founded on freedom of expression, and which is secular. It will work in solidarity with initiatives addressing concerns of the marginalized; it will support alternative and heterodox practices.

Sher-Gil Sundaram Arts Foundation: Installation Art Grant

Purpose: The SSAF Installation Art Grant is premised on the fact that Indian art has been energized since the 1990s by what is broadly termed installation art, but that there is, till today, limited infrastructural and institutional support for such projects

Eligibility: 1. Individuals of Indian origin residing in India, or collectives whose members are Indian nationals residing in India. Preference will be given to applicants who lack access to networks of national and international sponsorships. 2. Artists who currently do not hold a grant or a residency where the proposed project has been developed.

Level of Study: Postgraduate

Type: Grant

Value: ₹8 lakhs

Length of Study: 18 months

Frequency: Annual

Country of Study: India

Application Procedure: The SSAF Installation Art Grant invites applications from artists or artists' collectives of Indian origin residing in India. Preference will be given to applicants who lack access to networks of national and international sponsorships. The SSAF Installation Art Grant will support an individual artist or an artists' collective to conceptualize and produce a new work within the parameters of installation art.

Closing Date: 20 February

Funding: Foundation

Additional Information: ssaf.in/grant-details-ssaf-open-call/

For further information contact:

Email: ssaf.installationart@gmail.com

Shorenstein Asia-Pacific Research Center (APARC)

616 Jane Stanford Way, Stanford, CA 94305-6055, United States of America.

Tel: (1) 650 723 9741
Website: aparc.fsi.stanford.edu/

The Walter H. Shorenstein Asia-Pacific Research Center is Stanford University's hub for contemporary Asia studies. The Walter H. Shorenstein Asia-Pacific Research Center (Shorenstein APARC) addresses critical issues affecting the countries of Asia, their regional and global affairs, and U.S.-Asia relations. As Stanford University's hub for the interdisciplinary study of contemporary Asia, we produce policy-relevant research, provide education and training to students, scholars, and practitioners, and strengthen dialogue and cooperation between counterparts in the Asia-Pacific and the United States.

Shorenstein Fellowships in Contemporary Asia

Purpose: Each year the Walter H. Shorenstein Asia-Pacific Research Center (Shorenstein APARC) offers two postdoctoral fellowship positions to junior scholars for research and writing on contemporary Asia. The primary research areas focus on political, economic, or social change in the Asia-Pacific region (including Northeast, Southeast, and South Asia), or on international relations and international political economy in the region. The fellowships are made possible through the generosity of APARC's benefactor, Walter H. Shorenstein.

Eligibility: 1. Applicants must be recent Ph.D.s and cannot be more than 3 years past the awarding of their doctoral degree when the fellowship begins. 2. Must have dissertation submission and approval for conferral by June 30. 3. Certification of degree completion and conferral must be submitted no later than August 31.

Level of Study: Doctorate, Postdoctorate

Type: Fellowships

Value: Approximately US$60,000 (annual rate of US$72,000) + US$2,000 for research expenses.

Length of Study: 10 months

Frequency: Annual

Country of Study: Asia

Application Procedure: Apply through Online.

No. of awards offered: 2

Closing Date: 3 January

Funding: Private

Additional Information: aparc.fsi.stanford.edu/education/fellowship-and-training-opportunities/shorenstein-postdoctoral-fellowship

For further information contact:

Email: shorensteinfellowships@stanford.edu

Shuttleworth Foundation Trust

PO Box 4615, Durbanville, 7551, South Africa.

Website: shuttleworthfoundation.org/

The Shuttleworth Foundation is a small social investor that provides funding to dynamic leaders who are at the forefront of social change. We look for social innovators who are helping to change the world for the better and could benefit from a social investment model with a difference. We identify amazing people, give them a fellowship grant, and multiply the money they put into their own projects by a factor of ten or more.

Sickle Cell Disease Foundation of California

3602 Inland Empire Blvd, Suite B140, Ontario, CA 91764, United States of America.

Tel: (1) 909 743 5226
Email: info@scdfc.org
Website: www.scdfc.org/

The Sickle Cell Disease Foundation provides life-enhancing education, services and programs for individuals living with sickle cell disease. Our mission is "to improve the whole lives of those living with sickle cell disease across the nation by destroying barriers, cultivating unprecedented partnerships & employing innovative strategies to deliver impactful advocacy initiatives & life-enhancing programs, while fostering new research & therapies to eradicate sickle cell disease."

Sidney Sussex College

Cambridge University, Sidney Street, Cambridge CB2 3HU, United Kingdom.

Tel: (44) 1223 338800
Email: gradtutor@sid.cam.ac.uk
Website: www.sid.cam.ac.uk
Contact: Sidney Sussex College Tutor for Graduate Students

Sidney Fellows and students from 1596 have made a huge impact on all aspects of the nation's culture, religion, politics, business, legal and scientific achievements. It has also found time to produce soldiers, political cartoonists, alchemists, spies, murderers, ghosts and arsonists as well as media personalities, film and opera directors, a Premiership football club chairman, best-selling authors, the man who introduced soccer to Hungary, the 1928 Grand National winner and, so they say, Sherlock Holmes.

Evan Lewis-Thomas Law Studentships

Purpose: Evan Lewis-Thomas Law Studentship (for research or advanced courses in Law or cognate subjects) There are three current award-holders (PhD, Law).
Eligibility: There are no eligibility restrictions. Candidates must have shown proficiency in Law and Jurisprudence, normally by obtaining a university degree in Law by August, and they must be or become candidates for the PhD Degree, the Diploma in Legal Studies, the Diploma in International Law, the MPhil Degree (1 year course) in Criminology, or the LLM Degree. Students from other Cambridge Colleges may apply, but if successful they would be expected to transfer their membership to Sidney Sussex College. In the competition for the studentship, no preference will be given to candidates who nominate Sidney Sussex College as their college of first or second choice on their application form
Level of Study: Postgraduate
Type: Studentship
Value: The value depends on the candidate's needs in the light of support from other sources and on the availability of income from the Evan Lewis Thomas Fund.
Length of Study: 1–3 years
Frequency: Annual
Study Establishment: The University of Cambridge
Country of Study: United Kingdom
Application Procedure: Further details of these competitions, including deadlines, can be found at www.admin.cam.ac.uk/students/studentregistry/fees/funding/index.htm
Funding: Private
Contributor: Sidney Sussex College
Additional Information: www.sid.cam.ac.uk/apply/postgraduate-study/studentships-and-funding

For further information contact:

Sidney Street, Cambridge CB2 3HU, United Kingdom.

Email: graduate.funding@admin.cam.ac.uk

Sievert Larsson Foundation

Box 23415, CY-1683 Nicosia, Cyprus.

Email: info@sievertlarssonscholarships.org
Website: www.sievertlarssonscholarships.org/
Contact: The Sievert Larsson Scholarship Foundation

The Sievert Larsson Scholarship Foundation's primary purpose is to facilitate the education of promising students from disadvantaged backgrounds. The Foundation will also facilitate the education of a few high calibre students that have exhibited excellence through their academic achievements.

The Sievert Larsson Scholarship

Purpose: To support students who come from financially vulnerable homes and who would not otherwise have the opportunity to study in Sweden

Eligibility: 1. Citizens of Thailand. 2. Students with a completed or soon to be completed Bachelor's Degree (equivalent to a Swedish Kandidatexamen) with a minimum grade of 3.0 (CGPA) from a prestigious Thai University*

Level of Study: Postgraduate

Type: Scholarship

Value: Version 1: Full tuition fee waiver (covers 100% of the tuition fees) during the 2-year programme (4 semesters). Version 2: Full tuition fee waiver (covers 100% of the tuition fees) and SEK 230,000 for costs of living during the 2-year programme (4 semesters)

Length of Study: 2 years

Frequency: Annual

Study Establishment: Chalmers University of Technology

Country of Study: Thailand

Application Procedure: Applications for the Sievert Larsson Scholarship are made online via the Chalmers scholarship application form

Closing Date: 17 January

Contributor: The Sievert Larsson Foundation

Additional Information: www.chalmers.se/en/education/fees-finance/Pages/The-Sievert-Larsson-Scholarship.aspx

For further information contact:

Email: charlotte.salmenius@chalmers.se

Sigma Theta Tau International

550 W. North Street,, Indianapolis, IN 46202, United States of America.

Tel: (1) 888 634 7575
Email: memserv@sigmanursing.org
Website: www.sigmanursing.org/
Contact: Tonna M.Thomas, Grants Coordinator

Sigma Theta Tau International exists to promote the development, dissemination and utilization of nursing knowledge. It is committed to improving the health of people worldwide through increasing the scientific base of nursing practice. In support of this mission, the society advances nursing leadership and scholarship, and furthers the utilization of nursing research in healthcare delivery as well as in public policy.

Sigma Theta Tau International/Association of Operating Room Nurses Foundation Grant

Purpose: The AORN Foundation awards scholarships to students who are pursuing a career in perioperative nursing, and to registered nurses who are continuing their education in perioperative nursing by pursuing a bachelor's, master's or doctoral degree.

Level of Study: Doctorate

Type: Grant

Frequency: Annual

Country of Study: United States of America

Application Procedure: Applicants should submit a completed application package for the relevant institution for that year

Closing Date: 15 June

Funding: Private

Additional Information: www.aorn.org/aorn-foundation/foundation-scholarships

For further information contact:

Association of Operating Room Nurses, 2170 South Parker Road, Suite 300, CO 80231, United States of America.

Tel: (1) 800 755 2676
Email: foundation@aorn.org

Sigma Theta Tau International/Association of Perioperative Registered Nurses Foundation Grant

Purpose: To encourage qualified nurses to conduct research related to perioperative nursing practice and contribute to the development of perioperative nursing science.

Eligibility: 1. Principal investigator is required to be a registered nurse (with a current license) in the perioperative setting or a registered nurse who demonstrates interest in or significant contributions to perioperative nursing practice. 2. Principal investigator must have, at a minimum, a master's degree in nursing. 3. Membership in either organization is acceptable but not required.

Type: Grant
Value: US$5,000 (max)
Frequency: Annual
Country of Study: United States of America
Application Procedure: All applications are accepted by AORN. View additional details. (www.aorn.org/guidelines/clinical-resources/nursing-research)
No. of awards offered: 1
Closing Date: 31 August
Contributor: The Association of Perioperative Registered Nurses and Sigma Theta Tau International
Additional Information: www.sigmanursing.org/advance-elevate/research/research-grants/association-of-perioperative-registered-nurses-(aorn)-grant

For further information contact:

2170 S. Parker Road, Suite 400, Denver, CO 80231-571, United States of America.

Tel: (1) 303 755 6304 ext. 207
Fax: (1) 800 755 2676 ext. 207
Email: lspruce@aorn.org

Sigma Theta Tau International/Rehabilitation Nursing Foundation Grant

Purpose: The Sigma Theta Tau International/Rehabilitation Nursing Foundation (RNF) Grant encourages research related to rehabilitation nursing.
Eligibility: The applicant must be a registered nurse in rehabilitation or a registered nurse who demonstrates interest in and significantly contributes to rehabilitation nursing. Proposals that address the clinical practice, educational or administrative dimensions of rehabilitation nursing are requested. Quantitative and qualitative research projects will be accepted for review. The principal investigator must have a Master's degree in nursing and an ability to complete the project within 2 years of initial funding
Level of Study: Doctorate, Postdoctorate, Postgraduate, Predoctorate
Type: Research grant
Value: Up to US$4,500
Length of Study: 1 year
Frequency: Annual
Application Procedure: Applicants must write to the Rehabilitation Nursing Foundation for details
Closing Date: 1 March
Funding: Foundation, Private
Contributor: The Rehabilitation Nursing Foundation and Sigma Theta Tau International

Additional Information: The funding month is the following January www.sigmanursing.org/advance-elevate/research/research-grants/rehabilitation-nursing-foundation-grant-(rna)

For further information contact:

Rehabilitation Nursing Foundation, 4700 West Lake Avenue, Glenview, IL 60025, United States of America.

Tel: (1) 800 229 7530
Fax: (1) 847 375 4710
Email: info@rehabnurse.org

Silicon Valley Community Foundation

2440 West El Camino Real, Suite 300, Mountain View, CA 94040-1498, United States of America.

Tel: (1) 650 450 5400
Email: donate@siliconvalleycf.org
Website: www.siliconvalleycf.org/

Silicon Valley Community Foundation is a regional catalyst, connector and collaborator. We bring the resources and skills of donors, business, government and community to solve some of our region's toughest challenges. We promote philanthropy in our region and support philanthropists to invest with impact. Through advocacy, research, policy and grantmaking, we seek systemic solutions to drive enduring community change.

Western Digital Scholarship Program

Subjects: Science
Purpose: For students pursuing a Bachelor of Science degree in a STEM major, particularly those from underrepresented populations and/or those demonstrating financial need or hardship. A portion of the scholarships awarded through this fund are reserved for the dependents of Western Digital employees.
Eligibility: 1. Legal dependent of a Western Digital Employee with an Employee Level of 109 or below. 2. Undergraduate student enrolled on a full-time basis at an accredited four year college / university. 3. Minimum grade point average of 3.0 on a 4.0 scale or equivalent. 4. Financial need or hardship.
Level of Study: Graduate
Type: Scholarship
Value: US$5,000

Frequency: Annual
Country of Study: United States of America
No. of awards offered: Up to 500 one-time scholarships
Closing Date: 24 March
Funding: Foundation
Additional Information: www.siliconvalleycf.org/scholar ships/westerndigital

Simon Fraser University

8888 University Drive, Burnaby, BC V5A 1S6, Canada.

Tel:	(1) 778 782 8019
Email:	sfubeedie_undergrad@sfu.ca
Website:	beedie.sfu.ca/
Contact:	Ms Preet Virk, Manager, Donor Relations

Since the creation of Canada's first Executive MBA in 1968, Simon Fraser University's Beedie School of Business has emerged as a dynamic teaching and learning setting with a reputation for producing global-class research for the knowledge economy. Our undergraduate, graduate and PhD programs demonstrate a spirit of innovation, flexibility and relevance. Supported by extensive partnerships with public, private and not-for-profit organizations, our goal is to produce broadly educated, enterprising and socially responsible managers capable of making lasting contributions to their communities.

Natural Sciences and Engineering Research Council of Canada - Postdoctoral Fellowship Program

Purpose: The Postdoctoral Fellowships (PDF) program provides support to a core of the most promising researchers at a pivotal time in their careers. The fellowships are also intended to secure a supply of highly qualified Canadians with leading-edge scientific and research skills for Canadian industry, government and academic institutions.
Eligibility: 1. Be a Canadian citizen or a permanent resident of Canada. 2. Hold or expect to hold a doctorate in one of the fields of research that NSERC supports.
Level of Study: Postdoctorate
Type: Fellowship
Value: C$45,000 per year
Length of Study: 2 years
Frequency: Annual
Study Establishment: Simon Fraser University (SFU)
Country of Study: Canada

Application Procedure: You can apply for a PDF by completing and submitting form 201, and attaching supporting documents if necessary. For further information, check with the below link., www.nserc-crsng.gc.ca/OnlineServices-ServicesEnLigne/Index_eng.asp
Closing Date: 17 October
Additional Information: www.nserc-crsng.gc.ca/Students-Etudiants/PD-NP/PDF-BP_eng.asp

For further information contact:

350 Albert Street, 16th Floor, Ottawa, ON K1A 1H5, Canada.

Email: schol@nserc-crsng.gc.ca

Natural Sciences and Engineering Research Council of Canada Industrial Post-Graduate Scholarships (IPS)

Purpose: The NSERC Postgraduate Scholarships – Doctoral (PGS D) program provides financial support to high-calibre scholars who are engaged in an eligible doctoral program in the natural sciences or engineering. This support allows these scholars to fully concentrate on their studies and seek out the best research mentors in their chosen fields.
Eligibility: Open to highly qualified science and engineering graduates
Level of Study: Postgraduate
Type: Scholarship
Value: C$21,000 per year for three years
Length of Study: 3 years
Frequency: Annual
Country of Study: Canada
Application Procedure: Form 201 - Application for a Postgraduate Scholarship or Postdoctoral Fellowship. To create or access an application, select online system login. (www.nserc-crsng.gc.ca/OnlineServices-ServicesEnLigne/Index_eng.asp)
Closing Date: 17 October
Additional Information: www.nserc-crsng.gc.ca/Students-Etudiants/PG-CS/BellandPostgrad-BelletSuperieures_eng.asp

For further information contact:

Office of the Dean of Graduate Studies, Canada.

Winter Pilot Award

Purpose: The goal of the Pilot Award is to provide early support for exploratory ideas, particularly those with novel hypotheses.

Eligibility: All applicants and key collaborators must hold a Ph.D., M.D. or equivalent degree and have a faculty position or the equivalent at a college, university, medical school or other research facility. Applications may be submitted by domestic and foreign nonprofit organizations; public and private institutions, such as colleges, universities, hospitals, laboratories, and units of state and local government; and eligible agencies of the federal government. There are no citizenship or country requirements.

Level of Study: Postgraduate

Type: Award

Value: The total budget of a Pilot Award is US$300,000 or less

Length of Study: 2 years

Frequency: Annual

Country of Study: United States of America

Application Procedure: Applications must be completed electronically and submitted using forms provided at proposalCENTRAL. Please log in as an applicant, go to the "Grant Opportunities" tab, scroll to Simons Foundation and click "Apply Now" for the Simons Foundation Autism Research Initiative – Pilot Award program.

Closing Date: 17 March

Additional Information: www.sfari.org/grant/pilot-awards-request-for-applications/

For further information contact:

Email: sfarigrants@simonsfoundation.org

Simons Foundation

160 Fifth Avenue, 7th Floor, New York, 10010, United States of America.

Tel: (1) 646 654 0066
Website: www.simonsfoundation.org/

The Simons Foundation's mission is to advance the frontiers of research in mathematics and the basic sciences. The Simons Foundation's support of science takes two forms: We support research by making grants to individual investigators and their projects through academic institutions, and, with the launch of the Flatiron Institute in 2016, we now conduct scientific research in-house, supporting teams of top computational scientists.

Bridge to Independence Award Program

Purpose: SCGB's Bridge to Independence (BTI) Award aims to facilitate the transition of the next generation of systems and computational neuroscientists to research independence.

Eligibility: 1. Applicants must hold a Ph.D., M.D., or equivalent degree. 2. Applicants must be currently in non-independent, mentored training positions, as recognized by their institution. 3. Applicants must be actively seeking a tenure-track position at an institution of higher education during the next job cycle. 4. Applicants are not eligible if they are recipients of other career development awards with similar budgetary scopes as the SCGB BTI Award. 5. Applicants must not have accepted a formal offer for a tenure-track faculty position. 6. There are no citizenship requirements.

Level of Study: Postdoctorate

Type: Award

Value: US$495,000 over three years, as well as a designated US$10,000 gift

Length of Study: 3 years

Frequency: Annual

Country of Study: United States of America or Canada

Application Procedure: The Simons Foundation uses an electronic grants submission process. All interested grant applicants must submit their applications online through proposalCENTRAL. (proposalcentral.com/)

Closing Date: 28 February

Additional Information: www.simonsfoundation.org/grant/bridge-to-independence-award/?tab=rfa

For further information contact:

Tel: (1) 800 875 2562
Email: pcsupport@altum.com

Singapore-MIT Alliance for Research and Technology

1 CREATE Way, #10-01 & #09-03, CREATE Tower, 138602, Singapore.

Tel: (65) 6516 8603
Website: smart.mit.edu/

The Singapore-MIT Alliance for Research and Technology (SMART) is a major research enterprise established by the Massachusetts Institute of Technology (MIT) in partnership with the National Research Foundation of Singapore (NRF) in 2007. SMART is the first entity in the Campus for Research

Excellence and Technological Enterprise (CREATE) developed by NRF.

Sir Richard Stapley Educational Trust

The Sir Richard Stapley Educational Trust, Clerk SRSET, PO Box 76132, London E8 9HE, United Kingdom.

Email: admin@stapleytrust.org
Website: www.stapleytrust.org/
Contact: The Administrator

Founded in 1919 by the businessman and philanthropist Sir Richard Stapley (1843-1920), the Sir Richard Stapley Educational Trust supports the work of students of proven academic merit, and in financial need, who are pursuing further degrees or certain postgraduate qualifications at an institution in the UK. Open to students from all countries, applicants must be living in the UK at the time of applying, as well as during their course of study. The Trust supports courses in medicine, dentistry or veterinary studies taken as a second degree, as well as certain postgraduate courses in any subject.

Sir Richard Stapley Educational Trust Grants

Purpose: To support postgraduate study
Eligibility: Open to graduates holding a First Class (Honours) degree or a good Second Class (Honours) degree (65% or above, or its overseas equivalent, or a Masters or PhD) and who are more than 24 years of age on October 1st of the proposed academic year. Students in receipt of a substantial award from local authorities, the NHS Executive, Industry, Research Councils, the British Academy or other similar public bodies will not normally receive a grant from the Trust. Courses not eligible include electives, diplomas, placements, professional training and intercalated degrees. The Trust does not support students for full-time PhD studies beyond year 3, or part-time PhD studies beyond year 6. Applicants must already be resident in the United Kingdom at the time of application
Level of Study: Postgraduate
Type: Grant
Value: £500 and £1,300
Length of Study: Grants are awarded for 1 full academic year in the first instance
Frequency: Annual
Study Establishment: Any appropriate University
Country of Study: United Kingdom

Application Procedure: Electronic applications are available in early January. The trust will consider either the first 300 complete applications or all applications received on or before deadline
No. of awards offered: 300
Closing Date: March
Funding: Trusts
No. of awards given last year: 133
No. of applicants last year: 300
Additional Information: www.stapleytrust.org/applications

Sir William Lister/Dorey Bequest

18 Stephenson Way, London NW1 2HD, United Kingdom. The award is for ophthalmologists in training who are citizens of the United Kingdom as well as Members and Fellows of the Royal College of Ophthalmologists, in good standing.

Sir William Lister/Dorey Bequest

Purpose: The award is for ophthalmologists in training who are citizens of the United Kingdom as well as Members and Fellows of the Royal College of Ophthalmologists, in good standing. The number and value of the awards will be determined by the state of the funds and the candidate's requirements;
Eligibility: 1. UK citizen 2. Members/Fellows of RCO in good standing
Level of Study: Postgraduate
Type: Grant
Value: £300 to £600
Frequency: Annual
Country of Study: United Kingdom
Application Procedure: Retrospective applications will not be considered. All award recipients are required to submit a written report within three months of the completion of their Fellowship/research, to be circulated to the RCOphth Education Committee and the awarding body.
No. of awards offered: Varies
Closing Date: September
Funding: Private
Additional   Information: www.eyedocs.co.uk/ophthalmology-travel-awards/1110-dorey-bequest-and-sir-william-lister-travel-awards

For further information contact:

Email: training@rcophth.ac.uk

Smeal College of Business

351 Business Building, University Park, Pennsylvania 16802, United States of America.

Tel: (1) 814 865 7669
Website: www.smeal.psu.edu/

The Penn State Smeal College of Business is a vibrant intellectual community offering highly ranked undergraduate, graduate, doctoral, and executive education opportunities to more than 6,000 students from across the country and around the world. Since our introduction in 1953, we have prepared 95,000 students for professional success, annually adding to Penn State's vast alumni network. We are a destination of choice for top global organizations seeking talent that will make a positive difference.

Edward & Susan Wilson Graduate Scholarship in Business

Subjects: Business
Purpose: The purpose of this program is to identify and honor full-time graduate students enrolled or planning to enroll in Smeal College of Business.
Eligibility: Consideration for this scholarship shall be given to all full-time graduate students who are currently enrolled or are planning to enroll in Smeal College of Business and have achieved superior academic standing.
Type: Scholarship
Value: The amount of the awards will depend on the performance of the endowment.
Study Establishment: Smeal College of Business, The Pennsylvania State University
Country of Study: United States of America
Application Procedure: Nominations should be made by the Department Chair (attach copy of transcript and resume) and send to Hans Baumgartner, 483-A Business Building.
Closing Date: 1 May
Additional Information: phdstudents.smeal.psu.edu/scholarship-fellowship-opportunities/internal-awards/wilson.html

For further information contact:

The Pennsylvania State University, 483-A Business Building, University Park, PA 16802, United States of America.

Jeanne and Charles Rider Graduate Fellowship

Subjects: Business
Purpose: The purpose of this fellowship shall be to recognize and support outstanding graduate students enrolled or planning to enroll in The Smeal College of Business Administration.
Eligibility: Selection is based on academic merit.
Type: Fellowship
Value: To be determined
Length of Study: One academic year and may be renewed for subsequent years providing the recipient continues to meet the conditions of eligibility and funds are available.
Study Establishment: Smeal College of Business, The Pennsylvania State University
Country of Study: United States of America
Application Procedure: Nominations should be made by Department Chair to Hans Baumgartner, PhD Director. Recipient shall be selected by the Graduate Fellowship Committee.
No. of awards offered: To be determined
Closing Date: 1 May
Additional Information: phdstudents.smeal.psu.edu/scholarship-fellowship-opportunities/internal-awards/rider.html

For further information contact:

483-A Business Building, University Park, PA 16802, United States of America.

Ossian R. MacKenzie Teaching Award

Subjects: Business Administration
Purpose: The purpose of this program is to identify and honor an exceptional doctoral candidate who demonstrates a high degree of promise toward making significant teaching contributions in business administration.
Eligibility: Be an exceptional doctoral candidate with demonstrable experience working towards a career teaching business administration.
Level of Study: Doctorate
Type: Award
Value: The amount of each award shall be determined by a selection committee and shall depend upon the amount of income earned by the Ossian R. MacKenzie Doctoral Award Fund.
Length of Study: One academic year
Frequency: Annual
Study Establishment: Smeal College of Business, The Pennsylvania State University
Country of Study: United States of America

S

Application Procedure: To nominate a graduate student, faculty are encouraged to send their letters of recommendation to 351 Business Building.

Closing Date: 1 May

Peter E. Liberti and Judy D. Olian Scholarship

Subjects: Business

Purpose: The purpose of this scholarship shall be to provide recognition and financial assistance to outstanding PhD students enrolled or planning to enroll in The Smeal College of Business.

Eligibility: Selection is based on superior academic records or who manifest promise of outstanding academic success.

Level of Study: Postdoctorate

Type: Scholarship

Value: To be determined.

Length of Study: One academic year and may be renewed for subsequent years providing the recipient continues to meet the conditions of eligibility and funds are available.

Frequency: Annual

Study Establishment: Smeal College of Business, The Pennsylvania State University

Country of Study: United States of America

Application Procedure: Nominations should be made by Department Chair to Hans Baumgartner, PhD Director. Recipient shall be selected by the Graduate Fellowship Committee.

No. of awards offered: 2

Closing Date: 1 May

Additional Information: phdstudents.smeal.psu.edu/scholarship-fellowship-opportunities/internal-awards/liberti.html

For further information contact:

483-A Business Building, University Park, PA 16802, United States of America.

Smithsonian Environmental Research Center (SERC)

Smithsonian Institution, PO Box 28, 647 Contees Wharf Road, Edgewater, MD 21037-0028, United States of America.

Tel: (1) 443 482 2217
Email: gustafsond@si.edu
Website: serc.si.edu/
Contact: Daniel E Gustafson, Jr, Professional Training & Volunteer Coordinator

The Smithsonian Environmental Research Center (SERC) provides science-based knowledge to meet critical environmental challenges. SERC leads objective research on coastal ecosystems where land meets the sea to inform real-world decisions for wise policies, best business practices, and a sustainable planet.

Postdoctoral Fellowships

Purpose: The Smithsonian Institution offers several Postdoctoral Fellowships annually to outstanding early career scientists.

Eligibility: Applicants currently working at SERC should dedicate one page of the proposal to describing their research progress. This progress report should include publications and presentations at conferences and meetings.

Level of Study: Postdoctorate

Type: Fellowship

Value: US$55,000 plus health, relocation and research expenses

Length of Study: 1 year

Frequency: Annual

Country of Study: United States of America

Closing Date: 1 November

Additional Information: serc.si.edu/fellowships

Predoctoral Fellowships

Purpose: Predoctoral fellowships are offered for students enrolled in a university as candidates for a Ph.D. or equivalent doctoral candidates who have completed preliminary course work and examinations.

Eligibility: Applicants currently working at SERC should dedicate one page of the proposal to describing their research progress. This progress report should include publications and presentations at conferences and meetings.

Level of Study: Predoctorate

Type: Fellowship

Value: US$40,000 plus allowances

Length of Study: 1 year

Frequency: Annual

Country of Study: United States of America

Closing Date: 1 November

Additional Information: serc.si.edu/fellowships

Smithsonian Environmental Research Center Graduate Student Fellowship

Subjects: Research Topics Include Biodiversity & Conservation, Biological Invasions, Ecosystems Ecology,

Environmental Pollution, Food Webs, Global Change, Parasite & Disease Ecology and Watersheds & Land Use

Purpose: Graduate student fellowships are offered for students formally enrolled in a graduate program who have completed at least one semester and not yet been advanced to candidacy if in a Ph.D. program.

Eligibility: Students must be formally enroled in a graduate program of study at a degree granting institution must have completed at least one full-time semester. Intended for students who have not yet been advanced to candidacy if in a doctoral program.

Level of Study: Graduate

Type: Fellowship

Value: US$8,000

Length of Study: 10 weeks

Frequency: Annual

Country of Study: United States of America

Application Procedure: Complete online fellowship application form with the Smithsonian Office of Fellowships and Internships (click "Smithsonian Institution Fellowship Program" for application instructions)

Closing Date: 1 November

Additional Information: serc.si.edu/fellowships

Smithsonian Institution-National Air and Space Museum

655 Jefferson Drive, SW, Washington, DC 20560, United States of America.

Tel: (1) 202 633 2214
Email: NASM-Fellowships@si.edu
Website: airandspace.si.edu/
Contact: Ms Collette Williams, Fellowships Programme Coordinator

The Smithsonian's National Air and Space Museum maintains the world's largest and most significant collection of aviation and space artifacts, encompassing all aspects of human flight, as well as related works of art and archival materials. It operates two landmark facilities that, together, welcome more than eight million visitors a year, making it the most visited museum in the country. It also is home to the Center for Earth and Planetary Studies.

Charles A Lindbergh Chair in Aerospace History

Subjects: Aerospace History

Purpose: The Charles A. Lindbergh Chair in Aerospace History is a competitive 12-month fellowship open Oct

15, to senior scholars with distinguished records of publication who are at work on, or anticipate being at work on, books in aerospace history.

Eligibility: Open to senior scholars with distinguished records of publication who are at work on, or anticipate being at work on, books in aerospace history

Type: Fellowship

Value: US$100,000

Length of Study: 12 months

Country of Study: United States of America

Closing Date: 1 December

Additional Information: airandspace.si.edu/support/get-involved/fellowships/charles-lindbergh-chair-aerospace-history

For further information contact:

Email: kinneyj@si.edu

The Aviation Space Writers Foundation Award

Purpose: The product created as a result of the grant must be in any form suitable for potential public dissemination in print, electronic, broadcast, or other visual medium, including, but not limited to, a book manuscript, video, film script, or monograph. Potential topics might be contemporary aviation or space events that are of interest to the general public; significant persons, historical events, or trends that illuminate the history of human flight in air and space; records; or compendia of aerospace source material.

Type: Grant

Value: US$5,000

Frequency: Every 2 years

Country of Study: United States of America

Application Procedure: Candidates should submit the online Aviation Space Writers Foundation Award Application form, including 1. a maximum two-page, single-spaced proposal stating the subject of their research and their research goals; 2. a one to two-page curriculum vitae; and 3. a one-page detailed budget explaining how the grant will be spent

Closing Date: 15 January

Additional Information: Award winners are required to provide a summary report in the form of a memorandum to Ms Collette Williams that outlines how the grant was used to accomplish the goals of the project airandspace.si.edu/support/get-involved/fellowships/aviation-space-writers-foundation-award

For further information contact:

Independence Ave at Sixth Street, SW, Rm 3313, MRC 312, P.O. Box 37012, Washington, DC 20013-7012, United States of America.

Smithsonian National Air and Space Museum

655 Jefferson Drive, SW, Washington, DC 20560, United States of America.

Tel: (1) 202 633 2214
Website: airandspace.si.edu/
Contact: Miss Collette Williams

The Smithsonian's National Air and Space Museum maintains the world's largest and most significant collection of aviation and space artifacts, encompassing all aspects of human flight, as well as related works of art and archival materials. It operates two landmark facilities that, together, welcome more than eight million visitors a year, making it the most visited museum in the country. It also is home to the Center for Earth and Planetary Studies.

A. Verville Fellowship

Purpose: To pursue programs of research and writing professional in tone and substance, but addressed to an audience with broad interests
Eligibility: The A. Verville Fellowship is open to all interested candidates who can provide a critical analytical approach to major trends, developments, and accomplishments in some aspect of aviation and/or space history. Good writing skills are required. An advanced degree is not a requirement.
Type: Fellowship
Value: US$55,000 per year
Length of Study: 9 months to 1 year
Country of Study: United States of America
Application Procedure: All applications for the Verville Fellowships must be submitted electronically through the Smithsonian Online Academic Appointment System (SOLAA) (solaa.si.edu/solaa/#/public)
Closing Date: 1 December
Additional Information: airandspace.si.edu/support/get-involved/fellowships/verville

For further information contact:

Email: NASM-Fellowships@si.edu

Charles A. Lindbergh Chair in Aerospace History

Purpose: The Charles A. Lindbergh Chair in Aerospace History is a competitive 12-month fellowship open 15 October, to senior scholars with distinguished records of publication who are at work on, or anticipate being at work on, books in aerospace history
Eligibility: The Lindbergh Chair is open to established and recognized senior scholars with distinguished records of publication who are at work on, or anticipate being at work on, books in aerospace history
Type: Award
Value: US$100,000 per year
Length of Study: 1 year
Frequency: Annual
Country of Study: United States of America
Application Procedure: All applications for the Lindbergh Fellowships must be submitted electronically through the Smithsonian Online Academic Appointment System (SOLAA)
Closing Date: 1 December
Additional Information: airandspace.si.edu/support/get-involved/fellowships/charles-lindbergh-chair-aerospace-history

For further information contact:

Email: kinneyj@si.edu; neufeldm@si.edu

Engen Conservation

Purpose: The Engen fellowship will introduce the candidate to conservation techniques for a wide range of composite objects, metals, organic materials, and painted surfaces. This fellowship is intended to contribute to the education of recent graduates by allowing them to delve into the complexities of working with modern composite materials, refine treatment process, learn management, and conduct a small-scale research project. The Fellow's independent research will be derived from our diverse collection materials. Fellows will be encouraged to publish or present their research at the end of their tenure. Access to other Smithsonian conservators, conservation scientists, and analytical capabilities at the Museum Conservation Institute (MCI) may also be available.
Eligibility: The ideal candidate will have a Master's degree in Objects Conservation from a recognized program and is able to multi-task, work collaboratively as well as conduct treatments and research independently. The candidate should have knowledge of ethical and professional principles and concepts related to the preservation of objects in a wide variety of media and knowledge of the theories, principles,

techniques, practices, and methodologies used to examine, study, treat, and preserve historic objects.

Type: Award

Value: US$43,000 per year in addition to US$5,000 for Research allowance

Length of Study: 1 year

Frequency: Annual

Country of Study: United States of America

Application Procedure: Applications are submitted through the Smithsonian Online Academic Appointment System (SOLAA)

Closing Date: 15 February

Additional Information: For further queries, please contact CollumM@si.edu
airandspace.si.edu/collections/conservation/fellowships

For further information contact:

Email: HorelickL@si.edu

Guggenheim Fellowships

Purpose: To pursue programs of research and writing that support publication of works that are scholarly in tone and substance and intended for publication as articles in peer-reviewed journals or in book form from a reputable publisher (in the case of post postdoctoral applicants) or in a doctoral dissertation (in the case of pre-docs)

Eligibility: Predoctoral applicants should have completed preliminary course work and examinations and be engaged in dissertation research. Postdoctoral applicants should have received their PhD within the past seven years.

Level of Study: Postdoctorate, Predoctorate

Type: Fellowship

Value: US$30,000 for predoctoral candidates and US$45,000 for postdoctoral candidates

Length of Study: 1 year

Frequency: Annual

Country of Study: United States of America

Application Procedure: All applications for the Guggenheim, Verville and Lindbergh Fellowships must be submitted electronically through the Smithsonian Online Academic Appointment System (SOLAA)

Closing Date: 1 December

Additional Information: airandspace.si.edu/support/get-involved/fellowships/guggenheim

For further information contact:

John Simon Guggenheim Memorial Foundation, 90 Park Avenue, New York, NY 10016, United States of America.

Email: NASM-Fellowships@si.edu

National Air and Space Museum

Purpose: To support research on aerospace topics

Value: US$5,000

Frequency: Every 2 years

Country of Study: United States of America

Closing Date: 15 January

Additional Information: airandspace.si.edu/visit

For further information contact:

MRC 312, National Air and Space Museum, Smithsonian Institution, Washington, DC 20013-7012, United States of America.

Email: karafantisl@si.edu

Smithsonian Tropical Research Institution (STRI)

Roosvelt Avenue, Tupper Building 401, Balboa, Ancón, Panamá, República de Panamá, Washington, DC 20521-9100, United States of America.

Tel: (1) 507 212 8000

Email: fellows@si.edu

Website: www.stri.org

The Smithsonian Tropical Research Institute was founded with the purpose of increasing and sharing knowledge about the past, present and future of tropical ecosystems and their relevance to human welfare. This work began in Panama in 1910, when the Smithsonian led one of the world's first major environmental impact studies, which surveyed and catalogued the flora and fauna of the lowland tropical forests that would be flooded with the creation of the Panama Canal. A century later, the Smithsonian in Panama is a standard-setting global platform for groundbreaking research on tropical forests and marine ecosystems and their astounding biodiversity.

STRI Postdoctoral Research in Hydrology

Eligibility: Open to applicants with a PhD in spatial analysis applied to soils or hydrology, hands-on programming skills, fluency in English and Spanish

Level of Study: Postdoctorate

Type: Research grant

Value: Minimum salary of US$40,000
Length of Study: 2 years
Frequency: Annual
Country of Study: United States of America
Application Procedure: Applicants should send an electronic copy of the current curriculum vitae, statement of research accomplishments and goals, names and contact information of three references, and reprints to Helmut Elsenbeer. Review of applications begins by July 15th
Additional Information: stri.si.edu/academic-programs/fellowships

For further information contact:

Email: ElsenbeerH@si.edu

STRI Tropical Forest/Restoration Ecologist

Purpose: To support a long-term study to understand the ecosystem services provided by forests within the Panama Canal Watershed
Eligibility: Open to applicants with a PhD in forestry, forest ecology, restoration ecology, or a closely related field, a proven ability to develop research programs and publish in scientific journals, ability to work well in teams, and preferred with Spanish language skills
Level of Study: Doctorate
Value: US$40,000 per year
Frequency: Annual
Application Procedure: Applicants should send a letter detailing qualifications and interest in the position, curriculum vitae, and contact information for three references to Adriana Sautu. For questions related to the position, please contact Jefferson Hall (hallje@si.edu)
Closing Date: 1 August
Additional Information: The successful candidate will work in a multidisciplinary team to design landscape treatments and the vegetation monitoring program for focal research catchments. She will synthesize data from the Native Species Reforestation Project (PRORENA) growth trials to inform species selection for native species reforestation treatments and for publication. The Research Fellow will be expected to develop his/her own research program in association with this project stri.si.edu/academic-programs/fellowships

For further information contact:

Email: sautua@si.edu

Social Science Research Council (SSRC)

One Pierrepont Plaza, 15th Floor, 300 Cadman Plaza West, Brooklyn, NY 11201, United States of America.

Tel: (1) 212 377 2700
Email: info@ssrc.org
Website: www.ssrc.org/
Contact: Director

The Social Science Research Council (SSRC) is an independent, international, nonprofit organization founded in 1923. It fosters innovative research, nurtures new generations of social scientists, deepens how inquiry is practiced within and across disciplines, and mobilizes necessary knowledge on important public issues.

African Peacebuilding Network (APN) Residential Postdoctoral Fellowship Program

Purpose: To support independent African research and its integration into regional and global policy communities
Eligibility: Applicants must be African citizens currently residing in an African country. Researchers based in conflict-affected African countries or those recently emerging from conflict are especially encouraged to apply. Applicants must hold a faculty or research position at an African university and have completed their PhD within 7 years of the application deadline
Level of Study: Research
Type: Fellowships
Value: A maximum of US$20,000
Frequency: Annual
Application Procedure: All applications must be uploaded through our online portal. For enquiries or technical questions pertaining to the portal, please contact APN staff (apn@ssrc.org)
Closing Date: December
Additional Information: If you have questions, please contact APN program staff by telephone at (1) 212 377 2700 or by email at apn@ssrc.org
www.ssrc.org/programs/component/apn/residential-postdoctoral-fellowships/

For further information contact:

Email: apn@ssrc.org

African Peacebuilding Network Fellowships

Eligibility: All applicants must be African citizens currently residing in an African country. This competition is open to African academics, as well as policy analysts and practitioners. Applicants who are academics must hold a faculty or research position at an African university or research organization, and have a PhD obtained no earlier than January 2012.
Level of Study: Postdoctorate
Type: Fellowship
Value: US$15,000 each
Frequency: Annual
Country of Study: United States of America
Application Procedure: All applications must be uploaded through our Online Open Water portal ssrc.secure-platform. com/.
No. of awards offered: 18
Closing Date: 1 February
Additional Information: www.ssrc.org/programs/african-peacebuilding-network/apn-individual-research-fellowships/

For further information contact:

Email: apn@ssrc.org

Berlin Program Fellowship

Purpose: To support doctoral dissertation research as well as postdoctoral research leading to the completion of a monograph
Eligibility: Applicants for a dissertation fellowship must be full-time graduate students who have completed all coursework required for the PhD and must have achieved ABD status by the time the proposed research stay in Berlin begins. Also eligible are United States of America and Canadian PhD's who have received their doctorates within the past two calendar years
Level of Study: Postdoctorate
Type: Fellowship
Value: €1,100 per month for dissertation fellows, €1,400 per month for postdoctoral fellows
Length of Study: 10 months–1 year
Frequency: Annual
Study Establishment: Freie Universität Berlin
Country of Study: Germany
Closing Date: 25 March
Additional Information: grad.uchicago.edu/fellowship/berlin-program-for-advanced-german-and-european-studies-fellowship/

For further information contact:

Berlin Program for Advanced German and European Studies, Freie Universität Berlin, Kaiserswerther Str. 16-18, D-14195 Berlin, Germany.

Tel: (49) 30 838 56671
Fax: (49) 30 838 56672
Email: bprogram@zedat.fu-berlin.de

ESRC/SSRC Collaborative Visiting Fellowships

Purpose: To encourage communication and cooperation between social scientists in Great Britain and the Americas
Eligibility: Open to PhD scholars in the Americas, ESRC-supported centres, and holders of large grants awards or professorial fellowships in Britain
Level of Study: Doctorate, Research
Type: Fellowship
Value: Up to US$9,500
Length of Study: 1–3 months
Frequency: Annual
Application Procedure: Check website for further details
Closing Date: 16 April
Additional Information: www.scholarshipsinindia.com/esrc-ssrc.html

For further information contact:

Email: international@esrc.ac.uk

Japan Society for the Promotion of Science (JSPS) Fellowship

Purpose: To provide qualified researchers with the opportunity to conduct research at leading universities and other research institutions in Japan
Eligibility: 1. Scholars who have previously been awarded a fellowship under the JSPS Postdoctoral Fellowship Program for Foreign Researchers are not eligible. However, previous short-term fellowship recipients may apply for the long-term fellowship. 2. JSPS does not extend fellowships to scholars employed in institutions under the jurisdiction of the U.S. Department of Defense. 3. Japanese nationals are not eligible. 4. Japanese permanent residents are not eligible. 5. Those who have resident cards with mailing addresses in Japan at the application deadline are not eligible for the short-term fellowship.
Level of Study: Doctorate, Postdoctorate, Research
Type: Fellowship

S

Value: Round-trip international airfare for fellows originating in the U.S.; Insurance coverage for accidents and illness; A monthly stipend of ¥362,000 for fellows with a PhD at the start of their tenure and ¥200,000 for fellows without it. A settling-in allowance of ¥200,000 for fellowships over three months in duration; Additional research expenses may be made available for long-term fellows only.
Length of Study: 1 month to 2 years
Frequency: Annual
Study Establishment: An approved institution
Country of Study: Japan
Application Procedure: Applicants must submit the application, including all supporting documents, through the portal (www.ssrc.org/fellowships/jsps-fellowships)
No. of awards offered: 11
Closing Date: 5 January
Funding: Government
Contributor: The Japan Society for the Promotion of Science
Additional Information: www.ssrc.org/fellowships/view/jsps-fellowship/

Mellon Mays Predoctoral Research Grants

Purpose: The Graduate Initiatives Program offers three predoctoral grant opportunities the Graduate Studies Enhancement Grant (GSE), the Predoctoral Research Development Grant (PRD), and the Dissertation Completion Grant (DCG). These grants are only open to Ph.-D. students who were selected as Mellon Mays Undergraduate Fellows.
Eligibility: Applicants must be a Mellon fellow enroled in a doctoral program. Applicants must have been selected as Mellon Mays Fellows as undergraduates. Fellows may apply for one grant per year and must be enroled in a doctoral program in one of the fields listed in the website or have filed a petition for inclusion of another field
Level of Study: Predoctorate
Type: Grant
Value: Maximum of US$6,500 and in GSE up to US$2,000; PRD up to US$3,000; DCG up to US$2,500.
Country of Study: United States of America
Application Procedure: Applicants should use the online application portal to apply. For detailed information, please visit www.ssrc.org/fellowships/mellon-mays-predoctoral-research-grants/
Closing Date: 1 November
Additional Information: www.ssrc.org/fellowships/view/mellon-mays-predoctoral-research-grants/

Religion, Spirituality, and Democratic Renewal Fellowship

Purpose: The Religion, Spirituality, and Democratic Renewal (RSDR) Fellowship of the Social Science Research Council (SSRC) aims to bring knowledge of the place of religion and spirituality into scholarly and public conversations about renewing democracy in the United States. These fellowships are offered by the SSRC Program on Religion and the Public Sphere with the support and partnership of the Fetzer Institute.
Eligibility: The RSDR fellowship program invites proposals for research at the intersection of religion, spirituality, and democracy in the United States. The fellowships offer research support over a period of up to 12 months to doctoral students who have advanced to candidacy and to postdoctoral researchers within five years of their PhD.
Type: Fellowship
Length of Study: 12 Months
Study Establishment: Doctoral candidates will receive up to US$15,000 and postdoctoral researchers up to US$18,000
Country of Study: United States of America
Closing Date: 14 April
Additional Information: www.ssrc.org/programs/religion-and-the-public-sphere/religion-spirituality-and-democratic-renewal-fellowship/

For further information contact:

Email: religion@ssrc.org

Social Science Research Council Abe Fellowship Program

Purpose: To encourage international multidisciplinary research on topics of pressing global concern and to foster the development of a new generation of researchers who are interested in policy-relevant topics of long-range importance and who are willing to become key members of a bilateral and global research network built around such topics
Eligibility: Open to citizens of Japan and the United States of and to other nationals who can demonstrate serious and long-term affiliations with research communities in Japan or the United States. Applicants must hold a PhD or have attained an equivalent level of professional experience. Applications from researchers in non-academic professions are welcome
Level of Study: Postdoctorate
Type: Fellowship
Value: Research and travel expenses as necessary for the completion of the research project in addition to limited salary replacement

Length of Study: Up to 1 year
Frequency: Annual
Study Establishment: An appropriate institution
Country of Study: United States of America
Application Procedure: Applicants must submit an online application along with a writing sample, letter of reference and an optional language evaluation form
No. of awards offered: 60–100
Closing Date: 1 September
Funding: Foundation
Contributor: The Japan Foundation Center for Global Partnership
No. of awards given last year: 14
No. of applicants last year: 60 to 100
Additional Information: In addition to working on their research projects, Fellows will attend annual conferences and other events sponsored by the program, which will promote the development of an international network of scholars concerned with research on contemporary policy issues. Funds are provided by the Japan Foundation Center for Global Partnership www.jpf.go.jp/cgp/e/fellow/abe/index. html

For further information contact:

Japan Foundation Center for Global Partnership, 4-16-3 Yotsuya, Shinjuku-ku, Tokyo 160-0004, Japan.

Tel: (81) 3 5369 6085
Fax: (81) 3 5369 6142
Email: abe@ssrc.org

Social Science Research Council Eurasia Program Postdoctoral Fellowships

Purpose: To support research and/or publication records and to further the recipients academic career
Eligibility: Applicants for Postdoctoral Fellowships must have the PhD in hand at the time of application (ABDs will not be considered), and must have received the degree no more than 5 years prior to the application deadline. They must be citizens or permanent residents of the United States of America. Detailed information on eligibility criteria and conditions of awards will be in the application materials
Level of Study: Doctorate
Type: Fellowship
Value: Up to US$20,000
Length of Study: 18–24 months
Frequency: Annual
Application Procedure: Awards are made on the basis of evaluations and recommendations by the Title III Program

Committee, an interdisciplinary committee and composed of scholars of the region. The committee rewards proposals with clarity of argument, purpose, theory, and method, written in a style accessible to readers outside the applicant's discipline. Applicants must submit a completed application, a narrative statement, a curriculum vitae and references. Full information is available online
No. of awards offered: Approx. 30
Closing Date: 13 November
Funding: Government
Contributor: United States Department of State under the Program for Research and Training on Eastern Europe and the Independent States of the Former Soviet Union (Title VIII)
No. of awards given last year: Approx. 3
No. of applicants last year: Approx. 30
Additional Information: No funding is available for research on the Baltic States www.ssrc.org/programs/view/ eurasia-program/

For further information contact:

Email: eurasia@ssrc.org

Social Science Research Council Eurasia Program Predissertation Training Fellowships

Purpose: To provide graduate students with the opportunity to enhance their research skills in the field of Eurasian Studies
Eligibility: Applicants for Predissertation Training Fellowships must be enrolled in a doctoral programme in the social sciences or humanities or equivalent degree, but not yet advanced to the PhD candidacy. ABD's are not eligible for these fellowships. They must be citizens or permanent residents of the United States of America. Detailed information on eligibility criteria and conditions of awards will be available in the application materials
Level of Study: Doctorate, Graduate
Type: Fellowship
Value: Up to US$7,000
Length of Study: Up to 9 months
Frequency: Annual
Country of Study: United States of America
Application Procedure: Awards are made on the basis of evaluations and recommendations by the Title VIII Program Committee, an interdisciplinary committee composed of scholars of the region. The committee rewards proposals with clarity of argument, purpose, theory, and method, written a style accessible to readers outside the applicant's discipline. Applicants must submit a completed application, a narrative statement, transcripts, a course list and language evaluation form and references. Full information is available online

No. of awards offered: Approx. 20
Closing Date: 13 November
Funding: Government
Contributor: United States Department of State under the Program for Research and Training on Eastern Europe and the Independent States of the Former Soviet Union (Title VIII)
No. of awards given last year: 2
No. of applicants last year: Approx. 20
Additional Information: No funding is available for research on the Baltic States www.ssrc.org/programs/view/eurasia-program/

For further information contact:

Email: eurasia@ssrc.org

Social Science Research Council Eurasia Program Teaching Fellowships

Purpose: To encourage and support faculty members at all career levels in their efforts to impart their own knowledge and expertise to their students
Eligibility: Applicants for the Teaching Fellowships must have the PhD in hand and currently be teaching full-time in an accredited United States of America university, and the must be citizens or permanent residents of the United States of America. The home institution of the teaching fellowship recipient is expected to provide a letter of intent stating that the institution or relevant department intends to support the implementation of the Fellow's new course into the offered curriculum at least once within a period of no more than 2 years. Detailed information on eligibility criteria and conditions of awards will be available in the application materials
Level of Study: Postdoctorate
Type: Fellowship
Value: US$10,000
Length of Study: Maximum 2 years
Frequency: Annual
Country of Study: United States of America
Application Procedure: Awards are made on the basis of evaluations and recommendations by the Title III Programme Committee, an interdisciplinary committee and composed of scholars of the region. The committee rewards proposals with clarity of argument, purpose, theory, and method, written in a style accessible to readers outside the applicant's discipline. Applicants must submit a completed application, a narrative statement, a curriculum vitae and references. Full information is available online
No. of awards offered: 15
Closing Date: 1 November
Funding: Government
Contributor: United States Department of State (Title VIII)

No. of awards given last year: 3
No. of applicants last year: 15
Additional Information: www.ssrc.org/programs/view/eurasia-program/

For further information contact:

Email: eurasia@ssrc.org

Social Science Research Council International Dissertation Research Fellowship

Purpose: To support distinguished graduate students in the humanities and social sciences conducting dissertation research outside the United States
Eligibility: The program is open to graduate students in the humanities and humanistic social sciences regardless of citizenship enrolled in PhD programs in the United States. Applicants to the 2023 IDRF competition must complete all PhD requirements except on-site research by the time the fellowship begins or by December 2023, whichever comes first.
Level of Study: Doctorate
Type: Fellowship
Value: US$23,000
Length of Study: 6 to 12 months
Frequency: Annual
Country of Study: United States of America
No. of awards offered: 60
Closing Date: December
Funding: Private
Additional Information: https://www.ssrc.org/programs/idrf/international-dissertation-research-fellowship/

For further information contact:

Email: idrf@ssrc.org

Social Science Research Council Summer Institute on International Migration

Purpose: To enable attendance at a workshop/conference training young scholars in the field of migration studies
Eligibility: Open to advanced doctoral candidates currently involved in research or writing for their dissertations and recent PhDs revising their dissertations for publication or initiating new research
Level of Study: Postdoctorate, Postgraduate, Predoctorate
Type: Award
Value: Flights, meals and lodging necessary for participation in the institute are fully subsidized

Length of Study: 1 Week
Frequency: Dependent on funds available
Study Establishment: The University of California at Irvine
Country of Study: United States of America
Application Procedure: Applicants must download the application form from the website www.cri.uci.edu
No. of awards offered: 250
Closing Date: 18 February
Funding: Private
Contributor: UCT and SSRC
No. of awards given last year: 20
No. of applicants last year: 250
Additional Information: The Institute is a collaboration between the SSRC and the Center for Research on Immigration, Population and Public Policy (CRI) at the University of California, Irvine www.ssrc.org/programs/view/migration-program/

For further information contact:

Center for Research on International Migration, United States of America.

Tel: (1) 949 824 1361
Email: cbramle@uci.edu

SSRC/ACLS Eastern European Program Dissertation Fellowships

Purpose: To fund dissertation research
Eligibility: Open to United States citizens or permanent legal residents
Level of Study: Postgraduate
Type: Varies
Value: Up to US$15,000 plus expenses
Length of Study: 1 academic year
Frequency: Annual, if funds are available
Study Establishment: Any university or institution
Country of Study: Other
Application Procedure: Applicants must contact the American Council of Learned Societies (ACLS) for further information
Closing Date: November
Additional Information: The product of the proposed work must be disseminated in English www.ssrc.org/programs/view/eurasia-program/

For further information contact:

228 East 45th Street, New York, NY 10017, United States of America.

Email: grants@acls.org

Social Sciences and Humanities Research Council of Canada (SSHRC)

350 Albert Street, PO Box 1610, Ottawa, ON K1P 6G4, Canada.

Tel: (1) 613 992 0691
Email: award@sshrc-crsh.gc.ca
Website: www.sshrc-crsh.gc.ca/

The Social Sciences and Humanities Research Council (SSHRC) is the federal research funding agency that promotes and supports postsecondary-based research and research training in the humanities and social sciences. Through its Talent, Insight and Connection programs, and through partnerships and collaborations, SSHRC strategically supports world-leading initiatives that reflect a commitment to ensuring a better future for Canada and the world. SSHRC also oversees the delivery of a number of tri-agency programs, including the Canada Research Chairs and other research chairs programs, and the New Frontiers in Research Fund, which supports international, interdisciplinary, fast-breaking and high-risk research

Aid to Scholarly Journals

Purpose: To promote the sharing of research results by assisting the publication of individual works that make an important contribution to the advancement of knowledge
Eligibility: Applicants must consult the Canadian Federation for the Humanities and Social Sciences website for eligibility requirements
Level of Study: Postdoctorate, Research
Type: Grant
Value: Up to US$30,000 per year
Length of Study: 3 years
Frequency: Annual
Country of Study: Canada
Application Procedure: Applicants must refer to the website or email the Humanities and Social Sciences Federation of Canada
Closing Date: 2 June
Funding: Government
Additional Information: The program is administered on behalf of SSHRC by the Humanities and Social Sciences Federation of Canada www.sshrc-crsh.gc.ca/news_room-salle_de_presse/latest_news-nouvelles_recentes/2018/aid_to_scholarly_journals-aide_aux_revues_savantes-eng.aspx

S

For further information contact:

The Humanities and Social Sciences Federation of Canada, 151 Slater Street, Ottawa, ON K1P 5H2, Canada.

Tel: (1) 613 238 6112 ext 350
Email: scholarlyjournals@sshrc-crsh.gc.ca

Canada Graduate Scholarships – Doctoral program

Eligibility: To be eligible to apply, you must: 1. be a Canadian citizen, a permanent resident of Canada or a Protected Person under subsection 95(2) of the Immigration and Refugee Protection Act (Canada), as of the application deadline 2. have completed no more than 24 months of full-time study in your doctoral program by December 31 of the calendar year of application if previously enrolled in a graduate program 3. have completed no more than 36 months of full-time study in your doctoral program by December 31 of the calendar year of application if enrolled in a joint program; for example, MD/PhD, MA/PhD. 3a. if you fall into this category, you have access to the 36-month window whether or not you were previously enrolled in a Master's program 4. have completed no more than 36 months of full-time study in your doctoral program by December 31 of the calendar year of application if enrolled directly from a bachelor's to a PhD program (not previously enrolled in a graduate program) 4a. direct-entry applicants must be enrolled in their doctoral program at the time of application.
Level of Study: Doctorate
Type: Scholarship
Value: C$35,000
Length of Study: 3 years
Frequency: Annual
Country of Study: Canada
Closing Date: 17 October
Additional Information: www.nserc-crsng.gc.ca/Students-Etudiants/PG-CS/CGSD-BESCD_eng.asp

For further information contact:

Email: fellowships@sshrc-crsh.gc.ca

Canada Graduate Scholarships – Master's program

Purpose: The objective of the Canada Graduate Scholarships – Master's (CGS M) program is to help develop research skills and assist in the training of highly qualified personnel by supporting students who demonstrate a high standard of achievement in undergraduate and early graduate studies.

Eligibility: To be eligible to apply, you must: 1. be a Canadian citizen, a permanent resident of Canada or a Protected Person under subsection 95(2) of the Immigration and Refugee Protection Act (Canada) as of the application deadline date 2. be enrolled in, have applied for or will apply for full-time admission to an eligible graduate program at the Master's or Doctoral level at a Canadian institution with a CGS M allocation. 3. respect the internal deadline to apply for admission for your intended program of study—contact the faculty of graduate studies (or its equivalent) at the selected Canadian institution(s) for more detailed information 4. have completed the following:, as of December 31 of the year of application: 4a. either between 0 and 12 months of full-time studies (or full-time equivalent) in the program for which you are requesting funding or 4b. between 4 and 12 months of full-time study (or full-time equivalent) in an eligible master's program for which the degree requirements will be completed before activation of the award, allowing it to be activated during the first 12 months of the subsequent doctoral program for which you are requesting funding.
Level of Study: Postgraduate
Type: Scholarship
Value: C$17,500
Length of Study: 1 year
Frequency: Annual
Country of Study: Canada
Closing Date: 1 December
Additional Information: www.nserc-crsng.gc.ca/Students-Etudiants/PG-CS/CGSM-BESCM_eng.asp

For further information contact:

Email: fellowships@sshrc-crsh.gc.ca

Canadian Forest Service Graduate Supplements

Purpose: To promote Canadian doctoral research into forestry, to encourage the use of Canadian Forest Service (CFS) centres and to increase contacts between CFS researchers and Canadian universities
Eligibility: Open to SSHRC Doctoral Fellows who are conducting research in an area related to forestry in Canada and who are in the 3rd or 4th year of their programme. Candidates must have at least one CFS scientist on their supervisory committee and must carry out all or part of their research at a CFS forestry centre
Level of Study: Doctorate, Predoctorate, Research
Type: Supplement or Fellowship
Value: C$5,000 supplement to the C$20,000 doctoral fellowship
Length of Study: Up to 2 years
Frequency: Annual
Country of Study: Canada

Application Procedure: Applicants must visit the website
Funding: Foundation, Government
Contributor: The Canadian Forest Service

For further information contact:

Canadian Forest Service Graduate Supplements Science Branch, Natural Resources Canada, 580 Booth Street, Ottawa, ON K1A 0E4, Canada.

Tel: (1) 613 947 8992
Fax: (1) 613 947 9090
Email: mlamarch@nrcan.gc.ca

Canadian Tobacco Control Research Initiative Planning Grants

Purpose: To support investigators in developing strong proposals for grants in tobacco control research
Eligibility: Open to experts in programme and policy development as well as researchers
Level of Study: Research
Type: Grant
Value: Up to C$30,000
Length of Study: Up to 1 year
Frequency: Dependent on funds available
Country of Study: Canada
Application Procedure: Applicants must complete an application form available with instructions on the National Cancer Institute of Canada website www.ncic.cancer.ca
Closing Date: 1 March
Funding: Government, Private
No. of awards given last year: 6
Additional Information: www.idrc.ca/en/funding

For further information contact:

Research Programs Department National Cancer Institute of Canada (NCIC), 10 Alcorn Avenue Suite 200, Toronto, ON M5V 1L9, Canada.

Tel: (1) 416 961 7223
Email: mwosnick@cancer.ca

SSHRC Doctoral Fellowships

Purpose: This support allows scholars to fully focus on their doctoral studies, to seek out the best research mentors in their chosen fields, and to contribute to the Canadian research ecosystem during and beyond the tenure of their awards.
Eligibility: To be eligible to apply, an applicant must: 1. be a Canadian citizen or a permanent resident of Canada or a "protected person" under subsection 95(2) of Canada's

Immigration and Refugee Protection Act by the application deadline ; 2. not have already received a doctoral-level scholarship or fellowship from the Canadian Institutes of Health Research (CIHR), the Natural Sciences and Engineering Research Council (NSERC) or SSHRC; 3. not have submitted more than one scholarship or fellowship (Masters or Doctoral) application per academic year to either CIHR , NSERC or SSHRC—nominations to the Vanier CGS program do not count toward this limit (see SSHRC's regulations on multiple applications and on holding multiple awards for more information); and 4. have completed no more than 48 months of full-time study in their doctoral program by December 31 of the calendar year of application.
Level of Study: Doctorate
Type: Fellowship
Value: C$20,000 per year up to a total of C$80,000
Length of Study: 1 to 4 years
Frequency: Annual
Country of Study: Canada
Closing Date: 17 October
Additional Information: Both the SSHRC Doctoral Fellowships and the Canada Graduate Scholarships—Doctoral Program (CGS D) are offered through one annual national competition. Applicants need to submit only one application to be considered for one or both awards. As each award has notable differences, applicants must read the descriptions for each award carefully to determine if they are eligible to apply and hold each award. Applicants eligible for both the SSHRC Doctoral Fellowships and CGS D Scholarships will automatically be considered for both awards. www.sshrc-crsh.gc.ca/funding-financement/programs-programmes/fellowships/doctoral-doctorat-eng.aspx

For further information contact:

Email: fellowships@sshrc-crsh.gc.ca

SSHRC Impact Awards

Purpose: SSHRC Impact Awards are designed to build on and sustain Canada's research-based knowledge culture in all research areas of the social sciences and humanities.
Eligibility: A nominee must: 1 . be a citizen or permanent resident of Canada, or a "protected person" under subsection 95(2) of Canada's 2. Immigration and Refugee Protection Act, by the nomination deadline; 3. be an active social sciences and humanities researcher or student; 4 . hold or have held SSHRC funding relevant to the award category; 5. be in good standing with SSHRC; be affiliated with an eligible institution; and 6 . maintain affiliation with an eligible institution for the duration of the Impact Award.
Type: Award
Value: C$50,000 or C$100,000

Frequency: Annual
Country of Study: Canada
Closing Date: 1 April
Additional Information: www.sshrc-crsh.gc.ca/funding-financement/programs-programmes/impact_awards-prix_impacts-eng.aspx

For further information contact:

Email: impactawards-priximpacts@sshrc-crsh.gc.ca

SSHRC Postdoctoral Fellowships

Purpose: These fellowships support the most promising Canadian new scholars in the social sciences and humanities, and assist them in establishing a research base at an important time in their research careers.
Eligibility: To apply to this funding opportunity, applicants must: 1. be a citizen or permanent resident of Canada or a "protected person" under subsection 95(2) of Canada's Immigration and Refugee Protection Act by the application deadline; 2. not hold a permanent faculty position or a faculty position leading to permanency; 3. have finalized arrangements for affiliation with a recognized university or research institution; 4. not have applied more than twice before to the SSHRC Postdoctoral Fellowships funding opportunity;
Level of Study: Postdoctorate
Type: Fellowship
Value: C$45,000 per year
Length of Study: 1 to 2 years
Frequency: Annual
Country of Study: Canada
Closing Date: 15 September
Additional Information: www.sshrc-crsh.gc.ca/funding-financement/programs-programmes/fellowships/postdoctoral-postdoctorale-eng.aspx

For further information contact:

Email: fellowships@sshrc-crsh.gc.ca

Society for Academic Emergency Medicine Foundation

1111 East Touhy Ave, Suite 540, Des Plaines, IL 60018, United States of America.

Tel: (1) 847 813 9823
Website: www.saem.org/saem-foundation/
        lowerfootermenu/

The Society for Academic Emergency Medicine (SAEM) is the founding member and parent organization of the SAEM Foundation. SAEM serves over 6,500 members and has a mission to create and promote scientific discovery, advancement of education, and the highest professional and ethical standards for clinicians, educators, and researchers.

Education Research Grant

Subjects: Emergency medicine
Purpose: The SAEMF Education Research Grant strives to foster innovation in teaching, education, and educational research in emergency medicine for faculty-, fellow-, resident- and medical student-level learners. The mission of the grant is to develop the academic potential of the selected fellow by providing support for a dedicated two-year training period, including pursuit and preferably completion of an advanced degree in education.
Eligibility: An applicant for the Education Research Grant must Be a member of SAEM in good standing at application deadline and during the entire award period. Be board eligible or certified by the American Board of Emergency Medicine or American Board of Osteopathic Emergency Medicine and practicing in an emergency care setting. Senior/final year residents (3rd or 4th year, as applicable to the applicant's residency program) in good standing to graduate from an ACGME accredited emergency medicine residency program may also apply but must complete their residency program before the start of the award period. Not have completed more than one year of an education fellowship at the start of the award period. Not have received an Education Research Grant (formerly Education Fellowship grant) previously. Express and, if possible, provide evidence of a commitment to leadership in emergency medicine education in his/her current or prior work, or show potential for serving as a future leader in emergency medicine education. Demonstrate a sustained interest in and commitment to emergency medicine education and an education career. This demonstrated commitment may include previous participation in educational activities related to emergency medicine or another field, peer-reviewed publications, current or previous educational research, presentations of educational scholarly activity at scientific meetings, and engagement in local, regional, national and international activities focused on research and emergency medicine-focused education. Applicants will be judged and scored according to their expressed and demonstrated commitment to these areas. Greater consideration and potentially higher scores will be given to applicants who can demonstrate this commitment. Demonstrate evidence of involvement in

SAEM activities and functions. Demonstrated involvement includes number of years as a member of SAEM and participation in SAEM activities and functions (e.g., SAEM presentations and committee membership). Applicants will be judged and scored according to their expressed and demonstrated commitment to SAEM. Greater consideration and potentially higher scores will be given to applicants who can demonstrate this commitment.

Type: Grant

Value: Up to US$50,000 per year for two years

Length of Study: 2 years

Frequency: Annual

Country of Study: United States of America

Closing Date: 1 August

Additional Information: www.saem.org/saem-foundation/grants/funding-opportunities/what-we-fund/education-fellowship-grant

For further information contact:

Email: grants@saem.org

Research Training Grant

Subjects: Emergency medicine

Purpose: The SAEMF Research Training Grant is intended to provide funding to support the development of a scientist in emergency medicine.

Eligibility: Applicants should be a member of SAEM in good standing at application deadline and during the entire award period. Have an advanced/doctoral or terminal educational degree (e.g., MD, DO, PhD, PharmD, DSc or equivalent). Hold a university appointment (e.g., faculty, fellow, or similar) in or be actively involved (e.g., have an adjunct appointment) with a department or division of emergency medicine or pediatric emergency medicine at the start of the Research Training Grant award period. Emergency medicine residents in their final year of residency may apply for the Research Training Grant, subject to the same stipulation of holding a university appointment at the start of the Research Training Grant award period. The applicant may work as a clinician at an institution other than the host institution or the institution at which the project will be conducted. Not have previously received a SAEMF Research Training Grant, an Emergency Medicine Foundation (EMF) Research Fellowship grant or other EMF grant with similar purpose as the SAEMF Research Training Grant, a federally funded individual career development award (K-series or VA CDA), or a similar research training grant from another entity, prior to the start of the Research Training Grant period. If an applicant has received funding

for an institutional training grant (K12, KL2 or similar), he/she should provide a detailed description of the currently funded project and any similarities or overlap with the SAEMF application.

Level of Study: Research

Type: Grant

Value: The Research Training Grant will provide a total of up to US$150,000 per year for two years, contingent on the availability of funds from the SAEMF. The SAEMF Research Training Grant funds only may be used for the applicant's salary. Fringe benefits are permissible in addition to salary, but the total of salary and fringe benefits may not exceed US$150,000 per year for two years. No additional costs, such as project costs, tuition, travel, and indirect costs, are supported by SAEMF; any other costs are the responsibility of the fellow's host institution or another group specified in the application.

Length of Study: 2 years

Frequency: Annual

Application Procedure: All application components, including letters of support, must be submitted through the SAEM Foundation Grant Portal. (auth.saem.org/openid/authenticate?state=7e5c1964-30bd-11ea-bf93-002590ebe516&redirect_uri=https%3A%2F%2Fsaem.smapply.io%2Fsso%2Foauth%2F&response_type=code&client_id=39b29911-9e25-4416-b0cb-bd33a0d2dd45)

Closing Date: 1 August

Additional Information: www.saem.org/saem-foundation/grants/funding-opportunities/what-we-fund/research-training-grant

Society for Promotion of Roman Studies

Room 252, South Block, Senate House, Malet Street, London WC1E 7HU, United Kingdom.

Tel: (44) 20 7862 8727

Email: office@romansociety.org

Website: www.romansociety.org/

Contact: Dr Fiona Haarer, Secretary of Society

The Society for the Promotion of Roman Studies - The Roman Society - was founded in 1910 as the sister society to the Society for the Promotion of Hellenic Studies. The Roman Society is the leading organisation in the United Kingdom for those interested in the study of Rome and the Roman Empire. Its scope is wide, covering Roman history, archaeology, literature and art down to about A.D. 700. It has a broadly based membership, drawn from over forty countries and from all ages and walks of life.

Hugh Last Fund and General Fund

Purpose: To assist in the undertaking, completion, or publication of works relating to the general scholarly purposes of the Roman Society, excluding expenses in connection with archaeological projects. The Hugh Last Fund also excludes travelling, hotel, conference, or other living expenses of scholars

Level of Study: Postdoctorate

Type: Funding support

Value: Varies £500 or £1,000

Frequency: Annual

Country of Study: United Kingdom

Application Procedure: Applications should be made using the application form – the completed application should not exceed two sides of A4. Applicants should give a concise and clear outline of the project, including publication plans if relevant, and itemise the costs requested. They must declare any other applications being made for the same project. Completed applications should be sent to the Secretary by email office@romansociety.org

Closing Date: 31 January

Additional Information: Individuals may not make more than one application in any year www.romansociety.org/Grants-Prizes/Hugh-Last-Fund-General-Fund

Society for the Arts in Religious and Theological Studies (SARTS)

United Theological Seminary of the Twin Cities, 3000 5th Street NW, New Brighton, MN 55112, United States of America.

Tel: (1) 651 255 6117, 651 255 6190
Email: wyates@unitedseminary-mn.org
Website: www.societyarts.org/
Contact: Wilson Yates

The Society for the Arts in Religious and Theological Studies had its charter meeting at the 2002 AAR/SBL (American Academy of Religion/Society of Biblical Literature) conference. The Society was organized to provide a forum for scholars and artists interested in the intersections among theology, religion, spirituality, and the arts, to share thoughts,

challenge ideas, strategize approaches in the classroom, and to advance the discipline in theological and religious studies curricula.

Luce Fellowships

Purpose: To enhance and expand the conversation on theology and art

Eligibility: Open to candidates teaching theology as a faculty member at an accredited postsecondary educational institution or graduate students

Level of Study: Graduate, Research

Type: Fellowships

Value: Awards are up to US$3,000 each

Length of Study: 1 year

Frequency: Annual

Country of Study: United States of America

Application Procedure: Applicants must submit an information sheet, curriculum vitae, a project abstract, a formal proposal, a budget and 2 letters of recommendation

Closing Date: 20 February

Additional Information: www.societyarts.org/fellowships.html

For further information contact:

University of St Thomas, Mail JRC 153 2115 Summit Avenue, MN 55105, United States of America.

Email: office@societyarts.org

Society for the Psychological Study of Social Issues (SPSSI)

700 7th St SE,, Washington, DC 20002, United States of America.

Tel: (1) 877 310 7778
Email: spssi@spssi.org
Website: www.spssi.org/
Contact: Anila Balkissoon, Executive Director

The Society for the Psychological Study of Social Issues is an organization of social scientists that has historically brought research to bear on a wide array of societal problems. SPSSI was organized during the Depression of the 1930s, in an attempt to bring together a "national group of socially minded psychologists" to address social and economic issues (Finison, 1979). While maintaining its status as an independently incorporated society, SPSSI also became an affiliated organization of the American Psychological Association from 1937 to 1945, and Division 9 of the APA from 1945 to the present (Kimmel, 1997).

Society for the Psychological Study of Social Issues Grants-in-Aid Program

Purpose: To support scientific research in social problem areas related to the basic interests and goals of SPSSI

Eligibility: Applicant must be a member of SPSS-I. Applicants may submit only one application per deadline. If applied to the Clara Mayo Grant in the same award year he/she is not eligible for GIA. Individuals may submit a joint application

Level of Study: Doctorate, Graduate, Postdoctorate, Postgraduate

Type: Grant

Value: The usual grant from SPSSI is for up to US$2,000 for post-doctoral work and up to US$1,000 for pre-doctoral work.

Frequency: Twice a year

Country of Study: Any country

Application Procedure: The application should include 1. A cover sheet with the applicant's name, address, phone number, email address and title of the proposal. 2. An abstract of 100 words or less summarizing the proposed research. 3. Project purposes, theoretical rationale, and research methodology and analytical procedures to be employed. 4. Relevance of research to SPSSI goals and Grants-in-Aid criteria. 5. Status of human subjects review process (which must be satisfactorily completed before grant funds can be forwarded). 6. Curriculum vitae of investigator (a faculty sponsor's recommendation must be provided if the investigator is a graduate student; support is seldom awarded to students who have not yet reached the dissertation stage). 7. Specific amount requested, including a budget. For co-authored submissions, please indicate only one name and institution to which a check should be jointly issued if selected for funding

Closing Date: 15 October

Funding: Private

Additional Information: www.spssi.org/index.cfm?fuseaction=page.viewpage&pageid=730

For further information contact:

Email: awards@spssi.org

The Clara Mayo Grants

Purpose: The Clara Mayo Grant program was set up to support Masters' theses or pre-dissertation research on aspects of sexism, racism, or prejudice, with preference given to students enrolled in a terminal Master's program.

Eligibility: Individuals who are SPSSI members and who have matriculated in graduate programs in psychology, applied social science, and related disciplines. A student who is applying for a Grants-In-Aids may not apply for the Clara Mayo award in the same award year. Applicants may submit only one Clara Mayo grant application per calendar year.

Level of Study: Research

Type: Grant

Value: US$1,000

Frequency: Twice a year

Country of Study: United States of America

Application Procedure: Apply online. Online submissions are the preferred method. Please limit the number and size of files uploaded when applying online.

No. of awards offered: 6

Closing Date: 15 October

Additional Information: www.spssi.org/index.cfm?fuseaction=page.viewpage&pageid=727

For further information contact:

Email: awards@spssi.org

Society for the Scientific Study of Sexuality (SSSS)

1874 Catasauqua Road, #208, Allentown, PA 18109, United States of America.

Tel: (1) 610 443 3100
Email: Thesociety@SexScience.org
Website: www.sexscience.org/
Contact: Dawn Laubach, Director of Operations

The Society for the Scientific Study of Sexuality is dedicated to advancing knowledge of sexuality and communicating scientifically based sexuality research and scholarship to professionals, policy makers, and the general public. SSSS fosters a worldwide community of diverse professionals committed to a scholarly and scientific approach to acquiring and disseminating accurate knowledge of sexuality.

Society for the Scientific Study of Sexuality Student Research Grants

Purpose: The Society for the Scientific Study of Sexuality (SSSS) has a strong commitment to "the next generation" through the support of a vigorous student membership program, and as a member benefit to its students, SSSS offers two grants to be awarded each year - one to a graduate student and one to an undergraduate student.
Eligibility: Applicants must be a member of the SSSS
Level of Study: Graduate, Undergraduate
Type: Grant
Value: Graduate Student Research Grant up to US$1,500 and for Undergraduate Student Research Grant up to US$1,000. Both US$500 for travel
Length of Study: 1 year
Frequency: Annual
Country of Study: Any country
Application Procedure: Contact the society or check website for details
Contributor: The Foundation for the Scientific study of sexuality
Additional Information: www.sexscience.org/content.aspx?page_id=22&club_id=173936&module_id=455311

For further information contact:

Email: TheSociety@SexScience.org

Society of Apothecaries of London

Apothecaries Hall, Black Friars Lane, London EC4V 6EJ, United Kingdom.

Tel: (44) 20 7236 1189
Email: clerksec@apothecaries.org
Website: www.apothecaries.org/
Contact: Wallington Smith, Clerk

The Worshipful Society of Apothecaries lies at the heart of the early foundations of modern-day medicine and remains an important, active and innovative medical institution today. The Society plays a key role in the advancement of specialist areas of medicine, and in the ongoing post-graduate education and qualification of practitioners. Steeped in history and tradition, the Society was founded by Royal Charter in 1617 and is one of the few livery companies in the City of London to remain professionally based with over 85 per cent of its membership belonging to professions allied to medicine.

Gillson Scholarship in Pathology

Purpose: To encourage original research in any branch of pathology
Eligibility: Open to candidates under 35 years of age who are either licenciates or freemen of the Society, or who will obtain the licence or the freedom within 6 months of election to the scholarship
Level of Study: Postgraduate
Type: Scholarship
Value: £1,800 in total. Payments are made twice annually for the duration of the scholarship
Length of Study: 3 years, renewable for a second term of 3 years
Frequency: Every 3 years
Country of Study: Any country
Application Procedure: Applicants must submit two testimonials and present evidence of their attainments and capabilities as shown by any papers already published, and a detailed record of any pathological work already done. Candidates should also state where the research will be undertaken
Closing Date: 1 December
Funding: Private
Additional Information: Preference is given to the candidate who is engaged in the teaching of medical science or in its research. Scholars are required to submit an interim report at the end of the first 6 months of tenure, and a complete report 1 month prior to the end of the 3rd year. Any published results should also be submitted to the Society phd.northeastern.edu/opportunity/society-for-the-scientific-study-of-sexuality-ssss-graduate-research-grant/

For further information contact:

Email: admin@scholarship-positions.com

Society of Architectural Historians (SAH)

1365 North Astor Street, Chicago, IL 60610, United States of America.

Tel: (1) 312 573 1365
Email: info@sah.org
Website: www.sah.org/

SAH is an international not-for-profit membership organization that promotes the study and preservation of the built environment worldwide. The society serves scholars, professionals in allied fields and the interested general public.

American Council of Learned Societies Digital Extension Grants

Purpose: ACLS invites applications for ACLS Digital Extension Grants, made possible by the generous assistance of The Andrew W. Mellon Foundation. This program supports digitally based research projects in all disciplines of the humanities and related social sciences. It is hoped that these grants will advance humanistic scholarship by enhancing established digital projects and extending their reach to new communities of users

Eligibility: The project must be hosted by an institution of higher education in the United States. The project's principal investigator must be a scholar in a field of the humanities and the; humanistic social sciences. The principal investigator must have a PhD degree conferred prior to the application; deadline. (An established scholar who can demonstrate the equivalent of the PhD in publications and professional experience may also qualify.)

Level of Study: Graduate

Type: Grant

Length of Study: 12 to 18 months

Frequency: Annual

Country of Study: Any country

Application Procedure: 1. Applicants must list current and past funding sources for their projects; in the case of joint funding sources for the project. 2. Applicants should indicate clearly in their budget plans how each source of project funding will be used during the ACLS grant period. 3. Awards provide funding of up to US$150,000 for project costs. A portion of grant funds must go towards collaborations with new project partners who could benefit from access to the infrastructure at the project's host site or from substantive participation in the development of the project. 4. Grants may be used to cover salary replacement, staffing, equipment, and other costs. 5. Tenure 12–18 months, to be initiated between 1 July and 31 December

Closing Date: 31 December

Funding: Private

Additional Information: www.acls.org/programs/digitalextension/

For further information contact:

Email: fellowships@acls.org

Edilia and François-Auguste de Montequin Fellowship in Iberian and Latin American Architecture

Purpose: To fund travel for research into Spanish, Portuguese and Ibero American architecture

Eligibility: Open to SAH members who are junior scholars, including graduate students

Level of Study: Doctorate, Postdoctorate, Postgraduate

Type: Fellowship

Value: US$2,000 for junior scholars awarded each year and US$6,000 for senior scholars offered every 2 years

Application Procedure: Applicants must complete an application form, available on request by writing to SAH for guidelines or visiting the SAH website

No. of awards offered: 5

Closing Date: 16 October

Funding: Private

No. of awards given last year: 1

No. of applicants last year: 5

Additional Information: eahn.org/2017/08/fellowship-edilia-and-francois-auguste-de-montequin-fellowship/

For further information contact:

Email: vnelson@unm.edu

Sally Kress Tompkins Fellowship

Purpose: To enable an architectural history student to work as an intern on an Historic American Buildings Survey project, during the summer

Eligibility: Open to architectural history and historic preservation students

Level of Study: Doctorate, Postdoctorate, Postgraduate

Type: Fellowship

Value: US$10,000

Length of Study: 12 weeks

Frequency: Annual

Country of Study: United States of America

Application Procedure: Applicants must submit an application including a sample of work, a letter of recommendation from a faculty member, and a United States Government Standard Form 171, available from HABS or most United States government personnel offices. Applications should be sent to the Sally Kress Tompkins Fellowship. Applicants not selected for the Tomkins Fellowship will be considered for other HABS Summer employment opportunities. For more information, please contact Lisa P. Davidson, HABS/HAER Co-ordinator

Closing Date: 31 December

Funding: Government

No. of awards given last year: 1

Additional Information: researchfunding.duke.edu/sally-kress-tompkins-fellowship

For further information contact:

National Park Service The Sally Kress Tompkins Fellowship c/o HABS/HAER, 1201 Eye Street, 7th floor NW, Washington, DC 20005, United States of America.

Tel: (1) 202 354 2179
Fax: (1) 202 371 6473
Email: lisa.davidson@nps.gov

Society of Naval Architects and Marine Engineers

99 Canal Center Plaza, Suite 310, Alexandria, VA 22314, United States of America.

Tel: (1) 703 997 6701
Email: sname@sname.org
Website: www.sname.org/

SNAME is an internationally recognized non-profit, professional society of individual members serving the maritime and offshore industries and their suppliers. For many, SNAME has been absolutely essential to career development and success in the industry.

John W. Davies Scholarship

Subjects: Marine transportation, development of offshore resources, eco-systems interaction with development of Arctic/cold ocean resources, climate change impact in marine cold regions, or special areas of research for Arctic/cold ocean environments.

Purpose: The competition is open to any full time graduate student at a recognized University in Canada or the US State of Alaska whose research will assist in providing solutions to problems encountered in the Arctic or in cold ocean environments.

Eligibility: The competition is open to any full time graduate student at a recognized University in Canada or the US State of Alaska

Type: Scholarship

Value: C$3,000

Study Establishment: Any recognized University in Canada or the US State of Alaska

Country of Study: United States of America or Canada

Application Procedure: An abstract of approximately 500 words is to be submitted explaining the objectives of the research being undertaken, progress to date, and how this research is to be applied in the Arctic or to cold ocean environments. Applicants are also encouraged to describe how their research is placed within the context of broader Arctic issues. In addition, the selection panel will require a resume, a transcript of marks, sent by the university directly to the Awards Committee (for the most recent degree completed and degree in progress), and three letters of reference, two of which being former or current professors, to be sent by the referees directly to the Awards Committee.

Closing Date: 26 June

Additional Information: www.sname.org/arcticsection/home

Society of Women Engineers (SWE)

130 East Randolph Street, Suite 3500, Chicago, IL 60601, United States of America.

Tel: (1) 312 596 5223
Email: hq@swe.org
Website: swe.org/
Contact: Ms Karen Horting, Executive Director

The Society of Women Engineers (SWE) was founded in 1950, and is a non-profit educational service organization. SWE is the driving force that establishes engineering as a highly desirable career aspiration for women. SWE empowers women to succeed and advance in those aspirations and be recognized for their life-changing contributions and achievements as engineers and leaders.

Society of Women Engineers Past Presidents Scholarships

Purpose: Past Presidents Scholarship is open to sophomore, junior, senior undergraduate and graduate students taking up engineering or engineering technology related majors. Two scholarships worth US$2000 will be given to the chosen recipients

Eligibility: United States of America citizenship is required

Level of Study: Doctorate, Graduate, Postgraduate

Type: Scholarship
Value: US$2,000
Frequency: Annual
Country of Study: United States of America
Application Procedure: Application forms are available from the website
Closing Date: February
Funding: Private
No. of awards given last year: 2
Additional Information: www.smartscholar.com/scholar ship/past-presidents-scholarship-swe/

For further information contact:

Email: scholarships@swe.org

Södertörn University

SE-141 89 Huddinge, Sweden.

Contact: Södertörn University Registrar

Sodertorn University is a public university located in Flemingsberg, which is located in Huddinge Municipality, and the larger area called Södertörn, in Stockholm County, Sweden. In 2013, it had about 13,000 full-time students.

Södertörn University Tuition Fee Waive

Purpose: Södertörn University is offering tuition fee waiver for pursuing master's programme studies
Eligibility: Students who have applied for a one or two-year Master's programme at Södertörn University may submit an application for a tuition fee waiver
Level of Study: Postgraduate
Length of Study: 1 to 2 years
Country of Study: Sweden
Application Procedure: Send the application form along with necessary supporting documents to the following email address registrator@sh.se
Closing Date: 10 March
Additional Information: scholarship-fellowship.com/ sodertorn-university-tuition-fee-waiver/

For further information contact:

Email: studentservice@sh.se

Soil and Water Conservation Society (SWCS)

945 SW Ankeny Road, Ankeny, IA 50023, United States of America.

Tel: (1) 515 289 2331
Email: swcs@swcs.org
Website: www.swcs.org/

The Soil and Water Conservation Society (SWCS) fosters the science and the art of soil, water and related natural resource management to achieve sustainability. The SWCS promotes and practices an ethic recognizing the interdependence of people and the environment.

The Kenneth E. Grant Scholarship

Purpose: The Kenneth E. Grant Research Scholarship provides financial aid to members of SWCS for interdisciplinary graduate-level research on a conservation topic that will extend the SWCS mission of fostering the science and the art of soil, water, and related natural resource management research.
Eligibility: 1. Applicants must be a member of SWCS for at least one year prior to the application deadline. 2. Have demonstrated integrity, ability, and competence to complete the specified study topic.
Level of Study: Postgraduate
Type: Grant
Value: US$500
Frequency: Annual
Country of Study: United States of America
Application Procedure: 1. Provide responses to the questions within this application. 2. Provide a research project proposal (three pages maximum) that supports completing a specified research project related to this year's research topic (see above). Included in the proposal should be material supporting your ability to meet the eligibility requirements outlined above. 3. Provide a proposed research project budget. 4. Upload the project proposal and project budget in this application. (swcs. formstack.com/forms/2021_grant_scholarship)
No. of awards offered: 1
Closing Date: 23 April
Additional Information: https://seas.umich.edu/student-ser vices/financial-aid/funding/kenneth-e-grant-research-scholarship

For further information contact:

Email: awards@swcs.org

S

South African Association of Women Graduates (SAAWG)

SAAWG NATIONAL OFFICE, Suite 329, Rondebosch, 7701, South Africa.

Tel: (27) 11 883 4847
Email: medwards@netactive.co.za
Website: www.ifuw.org/southafrica
Contact: Miss Margaret Edwards, National President

The South African Association of Women Graduates (SAAWG) promotes the tertiary education of women and their self-development over their life span. It seeks and facilitates equity for women graduates, cross-cultural insights and co-operation and societal advancement. Its great underlying purpose is world peace, brought about through education and international friendship. SAAWG is affiliated to the International Federation of University Women (IFUW) and is a member of the Federation of University Women of Africa (FUWA).

Hansi Pollak Scholarship

Purpose: To assist postgraduate study or research devoted to the practical purpose of ameliorating social conditions in South Africa
Eligibility: Open to South African women graduates of all races who are, or have become, members of the Association
Level of Study: Doctorate, Postgraduate
Type: Scholarship
Value: R6,000 paid in 6-month installments
Length of Study: 2 years, non-renewable
Frequency: Every 2 years
Study Establishment: Any recognized university
Country of Study: Any country
Application Procedure: Applicants must write for application forms
No. of awards offered: 50
Closing Date: 25 March
Funding: Private
No. of awards given last year: 1
No. of applicants last year: 50
Additional Information: Fellows must spend at least 2 years in South Africa after completing a Master's or doctoral degree, in order to put into practice the results of the research www.instrumentl.com/grants/south-african-association-of-women-graduates-hansi-pollak-fellowship

For further information contact:

Post Suite 329, Private Bax X18, South Africa.

Email: hbowen@telkomsa.net

Isie Smuts Research Award

Purpose: To assist postgraduate women in research
Eligibility: 1. For a female applicant undertaking postgraduate studies/research in any field. 2. Applicants must be studying in South African Universities or Universities of Technology. 3. There is option for renewal of scholarship.
Level of Study: Postgraduate
Type: Award
Value: R1,300
Frequency: Annual
Study Establishment: Any university
Country of Study: South Africa
Application Procedure: Applicants must write to Miss V Henley
Closing Date: 25 March
Funding: Private
No. of awards given last year: 1
Additional Information: www.instrumentl.com/grants/south-african-association-of-women-graduates-isie-smuts-award

For further information contact:

Email: fellowships@saawg.org

South African Association of Women Graduates International Fellowship

Purpose: To assist women, who wish to study in South Africa
Eligibility: Open to members of the International Federation of University Women, foreign students enrolled at a South African university for at least one year for postgraduate research
Level of Study: Postgraduate
Type: Fellowship
Value: At least R1,000
Length of Study: Not less than 6 months
Frequency: Every 3 years
Study Establishment: A university
Country of Study: South Africa
Application Procedure: Applicants must write for application forms
Closing Date: 25 March

Funding: Private

Additional Information: The award is made when a suitable applicant applies www.saawg.org/Bursaries.html

For further information contact:

Email: fellowships@saawg.org

South African Council for English Education (SACEE)

1261 Storey Street, Queenswood, 0186, South Africa.

Tel: (27) 82 4488 372
Email: sacee.national@gmail.com
Website: sacee.org.za/
Contact: Treasurer/Secretary

The South African Council for English Education is a registered non-profit association mainly consisting of voluntary members. SACEE was established in 1955 by a small group of people who were dedicated to the protection of English usage. Our mission statement - to support the teaching, learning and appreciation of English. Today, through a network of branches and membership, the Council succeeds in initiating and sustaining a wide variety of worthwhile activities and projects, undertaken voluntarily by members and aimed at benefiting teachers, learners and college and university students. SACEE provides a practical means for individuals and organisations to participate in the development of skills and in the enjoyment of the English language. SACEE draws together people with an appreciation of the richness of the language, a concern for clarity of thought and a respect for the multilingual diversity of South Africa.

South African Council for English Education's EX-PCE Bursary

Purpose: The bursary is available for course fees, the purchase of books, printing costs and, at the Bursary Committee's discretion, any other incidental expenses which may be incurred. The applicant will need to show that he/she is a 'deserving' case.
Eligibility: Applicants must be South African citizens or residents. The applicant's normal place of residence must be in the PRETORIA area.

Level of Study: Postgraduate
Type: Bursary
Value: Course fees, the purchase of books, printing costs
Frequency: Annual
Study Establishment: Any academic institution
Country of Study: South Africa
Application Procedure: All completed application forms, together with required documentation must be e-mailed back to SACEE National Office (sacee.national@gmail.com) within the stated time limits
Closing Date: 31 July
Funding: Private
Additional Information: sacee.org.za/bursary-news/

For further information contact:

Email: sacee@iburst.co.za

South African Institute of International Affairs (SAIIA)

Jan Smuts House, PO Box 31596, Johannesburg, Braamfontein, 2017, South Africa.

Tel: (27) 11 339 2021
Email: info@saiia.org.za
Website: saiia.org.za/
Contact: Mr Jonathan Stead, Director of Operations

The South African Institute of International Affairs (SAIIA) is an independent public policy think tank advancing a well governed, peaceful, economically sustainable and globally engaged Africa.

Southern African-Nordic Center (SANORD)

SANORD Central Office, University of the Western Cape, Private Bag x17, Bellville, ZA 7535, South Africa.

Website: sanord.uwc.ac.za/

The Southern African-Nordic Centre is a non-profit membership organization of institutions of higher education and research for all Nordic countries and southern Africa.

Southern Cross University

Graduate Research College, PO Box 157, Lismore, NSW 2480, Australia.

Tel: (61) 2 6620 3876
Email: jrussell@scu.edu.au
Website: www.scu.edu.au
Contact: Mr John Russell, Administrative Officer

Southern Cross University is one of Australia's most modern, creative and innovative universities founded on traditions of academic excellence, with national and international industry links. The University's courses emphasize real-world skills and vocational training, and are designed to give graduates a competitive edge in today's demanding employment market.

Master of Business Administration Programme

Length of Study: Please contact the Organisation
Application Procedure: Applicants must complete the application form, supply evidence of any previous academic qualifications, as well as a curriculum vitae and a letter of support from your employer
Closing Date: 30 November

For further information contact:

Fax: (61) 2 6620 3227
Email: intoff@scu.edu.au

Space Environment Research Centre (SERC)

AITC2 Mount Stromlo Observatory, Cotter Road, Weston Creek, ACT 2611, Australia.

Tel: (61) 7 3365 1111
Website: www.serc.org.au/

SERC brings together expertise and resources from leading universities, international space agencies and commercial research providers to mitigate and ultimately remove the risk of space debris collisions.

Space Environment Research Centre Scholarships

Purpose: The CRC for Space Environment Management (SEMCRC), managed by the Space Environment Research Centre (SERC) has been established to build on Australian and international expertise. Students can receive additional support and opportunities provided by the Space Environment Research Centre. Successful scholarship candidates will also have the opportunity to apply for exciting short-term placements in space research centres internationally and within Australia
Eligibility: Consideration of all candidates will be given based on academic merit, relevance of studies to SERC objectives and potential for long-term contribution to research outcomes. Priority is given to students with first class honours (or equivalent) from participating countries, currently Australia, Japan and the United States of America
Level of Study: Graduate, Postgraduate
Type: Scholarship
Value: Will cover an additional support and opportunities provided by the Space Environment Research Centre and an opportunity to apply for exciting short-term placements in space research centres internationally and within Australia.
Country of Study: Australia
Application Procedure: Applicants can apply through online system at the link scholarships.uq.edu.au/scholarship/space-environment-research-centre-scholarships
Closing Date: 31 December
Additional Information: The applicant is or will be enrolled in academic studies at a reputable Australian University. In the case of an international applicant, the applicant is required to have a valid passport, appropriate visa and may not be from a country subject to Trade Controls www.scholarshipsads.com/space-environment-research-centre-scholarships-international-students-australia-2017/

For further information contact:

Email: admissions@gradschool.uq.edu.au

Spencer Foundation

The Spencer Foundation, 625 N Michigan Ave, Suite 1600, Chicago, IL 60611, United States of America.

Tel: (1) 312 337 7000
Website: www.spencer.org/
Contact: Fellowships Office

The Spencer Foundation has been a leading funder of education research since 1971 and is the only national foundation focused exclusively on supporting education research.

Research Grants on Education: Small

Purpose: The Small Research Grants Program supports education research projects that will contribute to the improvement of education, broadly conceived, with budgets up to US$50,000 for projects ranging from one to five years

Eligibility: Proposals to the Research Grants on Education program must be for academic research projects that aim to study education. Proposals for activities other than research are not eligible (e.g., program evaluations, professional development, curriculum development, scholarships, capital projects). Additionally, proposals for research studies focused on areas other than education, are not eligible

Level of Study: Postgraduate

Type: Grant

Value: US$50,000

Frequency: Annual

Country of Study: United States of America

Application Procedure: The application process begins with a full proposal; there is no requirement to submit a letter of intent or intent to apply form. Full Proposal Guidelines Small Grant proposals must be submitted through an online application form following the guidelines below. Step 1 - Registration. Step 2 - My Profile. Step 3 - Start a Proposal. Step 4 - Small Grant Proposal Elements. Step 5 - Proposal Summary. Application could be processed as follows.

Closing Date: 12 April

Funding: Private

Additional Information: www.spencer.org/grant_types/small-research-grant

For further information contact:

625 N Michigan Ave, Suite 1600, Chicago, IL 60611, United States of America.

Email: smallgrants@spencer.org

Spencer Foundation Dissertation Fellowship Program

Purpose: The fellowship is designed to provide fellows with support for the writing phase of the dissertation and to alleviate the need for significant other employment.

Type: Fellowship

Value: US$27,500

Frequency: Annual

Country of Study: United States of America

No. of awards offered: 35

Closing Date: 7 October

Additional Information: www.spencer.org/grant_types/dissertation-fellowship

For further information contact:

Email: fellows@spencer.org

Spinal Research

80 Coleman Street, London EC2R 5BJ, United Kingdom.

Tel: (44) 20 7653 8935
Email: info@spinal-research.org
Website: spinal-research.org/

Spinal Research is the UK's leading charity funding medical research around the world to develop effective treatments for paralysis caused by spinal cord injury. Spinal Research raises money to fund research into clinical treatments including vital scientific research such as clinical tools to better understand the injury caused, and for the devastating effects on daily living such as breathing, hand movement, and bladder and bowel control.

International Spinal Research Trust

Purpose: Healthcare Innovations that could have a significant impact on bladder, bowel and sexual function. The aim of the call is to support high-quality clinical research that develops and tests innovative ways to recover bladder, bowel or sexual function after spinal cord injury.

Eligibility: Any application is expected to have direct relevance to the fields of research discussed in the following published articles on the ISRT Research Strategy, copies are available Adams et al. International Spinal Research Trust Research Strategy a discussion document. Spinal Cord (2007) 45 2-14.

Level of Study: Graduate

Type: Grant

Value: Up to £250,000

Length of Study: 3 years

Frequency: Annual
Closing Date: 8 May
Funding: Private

For further information contact:

International Spinal Research Trust, 80 Coleman Street, London EC2R 5BJ, United Kingdom.

Email: research@spinal-research.org

Solomon Awards

Purpose: The Solomons' award is to help endorse quality experimental medicine, translational and reverse translational research in the UK within the field of spinal cord injury. The purpose of the award is to support the development of an early career clinical researcher with either a science or medical training background.
Eligibility: The call is initially open to applicants from clinical units and allied research institutions that have an evident traumatic spinal cord injury case mix or demonstrable interest in SCI clinical research.
Level of Study: Research
Type: Award
Value: £10,000
Frequency: Annual
Country of Study: United Kingdom
Application Procedure: Our Solomons' awards are ongoing and open for applications. You can apply by completing our online application.
Additional Information: spinal-research.org/type-grant

St Cross College

61 St. Giles', Oxford OX1 3LZ, United Kingdom.

Tel: (44) 1865 278490
Email: master@stx.ox.ac.uk
Website: www.stx.ox.ac.uk/

St Cross College is a graduate college of the University of Oxford. It offers an outstanding academic environment dedicated to the pursuit of excellence within the Collegiate University. The St Cross College community is diverse with over 60% of students hailing from overseas; the common room is a wonderful mixture of language and cultures.

Clarendon Scholarship

Level of Study: Postgraduate
Type: Scholarship
Value: course fees in full-
Frequency: Annual
Country of Study: United Kingdom
Closing Date: January
Additional Information: www.ox.ac.uk/clarendon

Godfrey Tyler Scholarship in Economics

Eligibility: No separate application is required and all eligible offer-holders will be considered for this award.
Level of Study: Doctorate, Research
Type: Scholarship
Value: covers the full cost of the course fee for both Home/ROI and overseas students for three years, together with an annual stipend for living costs.
Length of Study: 3 years
Frequency: Annual
Country of Study: United Kingdom
Closing Date: January
Additional Information: www.stx.ox.ac.uk/godfrey-tyler-scholarship-in-economics

HAPP MSc Scholarship in the History of Science

Subjects: History of Science, Medicine and Technology
Purpose: The successful scholar and will be expected to engage with the termly activities of the St Cross Centre for the History and Philosophy of Physics (HAPP).
Eligibility: Applicants must have applied to study for an MSc in History of Science, Medicine and Technology
Level of Study: Masters Degree
Type: Scholarship
Value: £10,000 per annum.
Length of Study: 1 year
Frequency: Annual
Country of Study: Any country
Application Procedure: No separate application is required and all eligible offer-holders will be considered for these awards.
Closing Date: October
Funding: Private
Additional Information: www.stx.ox.ac.uk/happ-msc-scholarship-in-the-history-of-science

For further information contact:

Email: joanna.ashbourn@stx.ox.ac.uk

HAPP Scholarship in the History & Philosophy of Physics

Eligibility: To be considered for this Scholarship, applicants must have applied to study for a DPhil in the History of Physics in the Faculty of History or a DPhil in the Philosophy of Physics in the Faculty of Philosophy by the relevant 2024 admissions deadline.
Level of Study: Postgraduate
Type: Scholarship
Value: full fee liability and has a value of £10,000 per annum
Length of Study: 3 year
Frequency: Annual
Country of Study: United Kingdom
Application Procedure: No separate application is required and all eligible offer-holders will be considered automatically.
Additional Information: www.stx.ox.ac.uk/happ-scholarship-physics

Humanities St Cross College UK BAME PGT Studentship

Eligibility: Applicants must apply to the University of Oxford for admission to a Master's degree in the Humanities by the January 2023 application deadline.
Level of Study: Postgraduate
Type: Studentship
Value: All tuition fees and provide a grant for living expenses at UK Research Council rates
Frequency: Annual
Country of Study: United Kingdom
Application Procedure: No separate application is required to be considered for this award. All eligible applicants will be considered automatically.
Closing Date: January
Additional Information: www.stx.ox.ac.uk/humanities-st-cross-college-uk-bame-pgt-studentship

Hélène La Rue Scholarship in Music

Eligibility: All applicants who have submitted their DPhil course application by the relevant 2023 admissions deadline and who subsequently hold a College place offer from St Cross College will be considered automatically.
Level of Study: Doctorate, Research
Type: Scholarship
Value: a value of £6,000, which includes a grant of up to £500 per annum for travel and research expenses
Frequency: Annual
Country of Study: United Kingdom

Additional Information: www.stx.ox.ac.uk/helene-la-rue-scholarship-in-music

Jan-Georg Deutsch Scholarship in African Studies

Eligibility: No separate application is required and all eligible offer-holders will be considered for this award.
Level of Study: Postgraduate
Type: Scholarship
Value: value of £10,000
Frequency: Annual
Country of Study: United Kingdom
Additional Information: www.stx.ox.ac.uk/jan-georg-deutsch-scholarship-in-african-studies

Law Faculty Scholarships

Eligibility: To be considered for these scholarships, applicants must have applied to study for a Master's-level course by the January 2023 deadline.
Level of Study: Postgraduate
Value: £10,000
Length of Study: 1 year
Frequency: Annual
Country of Study: United Kingdom
Application Procedure: No separate application is required and all eligible offer-holders will be considered for these awards.
Closing Date: January
Additional Information: www.stx.ox.ac.uk/law-faculty-scholarships

Lorna Casselton Memorial Scholarships in Plant Sciences

Eligibility: The Scholarships are awarded purely on the basis of academic merit. To be considered for these Scholarships, applicants must have applied for a DPhil in Interdisciplinary Bioscience by the January application deadline. No separate application is required and all eligible offer-holders will be considered for these awards.
Level of Study: Doctorate, Research
Type: Scholarship
Value: cover the annual cost of the course fee and the standard UKRI stipend for annual living costs
Frequency: Annual
Country of Study: United Kingdom
Additional Information: www.stx.ox.ac.uk/lorna-casselton-memorial-scholarships-in-plant-sciences

S

MPhil Scholarships in the Humanities and Social Sciences

Purpose: St Cross College offers two MPhil Scholarships for students studying at the University of Oxford for an MPhil degree in any of the humanities and social science disciplines or for the BPhil degree in Philosophy

Eligibility: To be considered for these scholarships, applicants must have applied to study for a Master's-level course

Level of Study: Postgraduate

Type: Scholarship

Value: £5,000 per annum

Length of Study: 2 years

Frequency: Annual

Country of Study: United Kingdom

Application Procedure: No separate application is required and all eligible offer-holders will be considered for these awards.

Closing Date: January

Funding: Private

Additional Information: www.stx.ox.ac.uk/mphil-scholarships-in-the-humanities-and-social-sciences

For further information contact:

Email: joanna.ashbourn@stx.ox.ac.uk

MSc Scholarships in Sustainability, Enterprise and the Environment

Eligibility: To be considered for these scholarships, applicants must have applied to study for the MSc in Sustainability, Enterprise and the Environment at the University of Oxford by the January 2023 deadline.

Level of Study: Postgraduate

Type: Scholarship

Value: £10,000

Frequency: Annual

Country of Study: United Kingdom

Application Procedure: No separate application is required and all eligible offer-holders will be considered for this award.

Closing Date: January

Additional Information: www.stx.ox.ac.uk/msc-in-sustainability-enterprise-and-the-environment

St Cross MSc Scholarship in Biodiversity, Conservation and Management

Eligibility: To be considered for this Scholarship, applicants must have applied to study for the MSc in Biodiversity, Conservation and Management by the January 2023 application deadline.

Level of Study: Postgraduate

Type: Scholarship

Value: £20,000

Frequency: Annual

Country of Study: United Kingdom

Closing Date: January

Additional Information: www.stx.ox.ac.uk/st-cross-msc-scholarship-in-biodiversity-conservation-and-management

St Cross MSc Scholarship in Global Health Science and Epidemiology

Eligibility: To be considered for this Scholarship, applicants must have applied to study for the MSc in Global Health Science and Epidemiology by the December 2023 application deadline.

Level of Study: Postgraduate

Type: Scholarship

Value: the MSc course fee as well as providing a one-year maintenance grant to the value of the annual UKRI living allowance.

Frequency: Annual

Country of Study: United Kingdom

Closing Date: December

Additional Information: www.stx.ox.ac.uk/st-cross-msc-scholarship-in-global-health-science-and-epidemiology

The Robin & Nadine Wells Scholarship

Type: Scholarship

Value: £7,500

Length of Study: 1 year

Frequency: Annual

Country of Study: United Kingdom

Closing Date: March

Additional Information: www.stx.ox.ac.uk/the-robin

St John's College

St Johns Street, Cambridge CB2 1TP, United Kingdom.

Tel: (44) 1223 338600
Email: graduate-office@joh.cam.ac.uk
Website: www.joh.cam.ac.uk/

St John's is one of 31 Colleges at the University of Cambridge. Colleges are self-governing; while they are part of the

University (subject to University regulations) they select their own students and have their own internal procedures. Although students receive the same outstanding education whichever College they attend, each has its own unique history, environment and identity.

The Louis Cha Scholarship

Subjects: Literature and History

Purpose: Louis Cha Scholarship enables a student to undertake research in the University of Cambridge in literature, history, and culture of early and dynastic China (pre-1912).

Eligibility: 1. St John's College proposes to award a Louis Cha Scholarship commencing in October. 2. The successful applicant will be selected from those who have obtained a place at St John's College Cambridge to read for the MPhil or PhD degree in a relevant subject

Level of Study: Masters Degree, Postgraduate

Type: Scholarship

Value: A maintenance grant of £15,200 per annum and the approved University Composition fee

Length of Study: 3 years

Frequency: Annual

Country of Study: United Kingdom

Application Procedure: 1. Candidates should apply to the University of Cambridge through the University's Graduate Admissions Office at the Board of Graduate Studies for admission as a graduate student, specifying St John's as their first choice of College For further information

Closing Date: 30 November

Funding: Private

Additional Information: www.joh.cam.ac.uk/louis-cha-scholarship

For further information contact:

The Graduate Office St John's College, Cambridge CB2 1TP, United Kingdom.

St. Baldricks Foundations

1333 South Mayflower Avenue, Suite 400, Monrovia, CA 91016, United States of America.

Tel: (1) 888 899 2253
Email: sbinfo@stbaldricks.org
Website: www.stbaldricks.org/

The St. Baldrick's Foundation is a volunteer and donor powered charity committed to supporting the most promising research to find cures for childhood cancers and give survivors long and healthy lives.

Research Grants

Purpose: The St. Baldrick's Foundation is a volunteer and donor powered charity committed to supporting the most promising research to find cures for childhood cancers and give survivors long and healthy lives. Since the Foundation's first grants as an independent charity in 2005, St. Baldrick's has invested more than US$300 million in childhood cancer research grants worldwide.

Eligibility: Applicants need not be American citizens; however, they must work at an academic, medical, or research institution within the United States. 1. Institutions that are actively involved in (sponsor, promote, or participate in) non-St. Baldrick's head-shaving fundraising events are not eligible to apply for St. Baldrick's funding. 2. St. Baldrick's funds may not be used for human embryonic stem cell research. 3. All awards will be payable to the Scholar's academic institution, non-profit research institution, or laboratory. 4. Applicants should hold a PhD, M.D., or D.O. degree in a field of research specialty by the date the award becomes effective. 5. Applicants must currently hold (for no longer than 7 years at the time the award begins), or will hold by start of the award, a title that is considered by the institution to be a fulltime, faculty position. Situations may occur where the institutions definition of "faculty" may differ from the Foundation's definition, this should be fully explained in the Scholar Applicant Checklist (required at LOI stage). 6. This is an early-career award. The Scholar award is intended to develop the independent pediatric cancer research careers of highly qualified investigators, not to support well established or senior investigators. 7. Scholars may receive funding from other sources to support their research. However, no other comparable or higher (monetary value) career development award may be held prior to or at the time the award begins. Scientific or budgetary overlap with other funded projects is not allowed. In the event of comparable or higher (monetary value) career development funding after the LOI has been approved, the Scholar must give up the remainder of their St. Baldrick's award, unless otherwise approved by the St. Baldrick's Foundation. 8. Applicants holding or awarded R01s at the time of the LOI are not eligible to apply. Applicants cannot hold a NIH K-award at the time that they apply (institutional K12 funding is allowable). 9. Applicants must have an appropriate sponsor who provides supervision, facilities, and research support. If appropriate for the project, applicants may have more than one (1) sponsor. 10. Research projects must have direct applicability and relevance to pediatric cancer. They may be in any discipline of basic, clinical, translational, or epidemiological research.

Level of Study: Postgraduate

Type: Grant

Value: This award is granted for three years with an opportunity to apply for an additional two years of funding based upon the demonstration of significant accomplishment. (Years 3-5, if funded, will be up to US$115,000/year).

Frequency: Annual

Country of Study: United States of America

Application Procedure: Category/Cycle specific LOI Instructions/Requirements are available in ProposalCENTRAL upon starting the LOI and on the St. Baldrick's website (stbaldricks.org/for-researchers). 1. LOI, application, and required documents must be submitted by the Principal Investigator, in English, online through ProposalCENTRAL (proposalcentral.altum.com) before 5 p.m. EST on the deadline. 2. All application instructions and templates/requirements will be available in ProposalCENTRAL upon approval of an LOI. 3. Applicants can enable other users to access their proposal (e.g., department or grants administrators) in the full proposal section of ProposalCENTRAL. 4. It is the responsibility of the applicant to ensure and to verify that the application is received by the deadline date and that the application is complete and correct prior to submission. 5. Eligible current St. Baldrick's Scholars applying for extended funding will be contacted by the St. Baldrick's Foundation Grants Administration staff with instructions for applying. Applications will be submitted via ProposalCENTRAL and reviewed for progress. Grantees can email Grants@StBaldricks.org with further questions about the optional funding. 6. St. Baldrick's Foundation funds biomedical research to better understand the causes of pediatric cancers and to advance its prevention, treatment, and cure. The main output of this research is new knowledge. To ensure this knowledge can be accessed, read, applied, and built upon in fulfillment of our goals, St. Baldrick's Foundation encourages researchers to share data with the research community in accordance with the NIH policy on data sharing and expects its grantees to publish their findings, including but not limited to publication in peer reviewed journals. Applicants will be asked about data sharing plans as part of the application. 7. All application evaluations are considered confidential and are available to scientific reviewers, the Foundation's Board of Directors, and the administrative personnel of the St. Baldrick's Foundation only. 8. Resubmissions Applicants with resubmissions have the option to check a box in ProposalCENTRAL on the title page of the application stating that it is a resubmission. Resbumissions are not marked in the Letter of Intent stage. You may mention it is a resubmission in your LOI. Applicants with a resubmission are asked to address the reviewer comments in the appendix. Be sure that the document addressing previous reviewer comments is listed in the table of contents for your appendix. Resubmission applicants will not have all three of the same

reviewers. St. Baldrick's does ask at least one of the previous reviewers to re-review the resubmission. Once marked as a resubmission in ProposalCENTRAL, new reviewers will have access to the past reviewer comments. Resubmissions are still required to go through limited submission decisions per the institution.

Closing Date: 27 March

Additional Information: www.stbaldricks.org/for-researchers

For further information contact:

Email: Laura@StBaldricks.org

St. Baldrick's International Scholars

Purpose: This three (3) year award, with an option for two (2) additional years based on progress, is to train researchers from low- and middle- income countries (as classified by the World Bank) to prepare them to fill specific stated needs in an area of childhood cancer research upon returning to their country of origin. Recipients are called St. Baldrick's International Scholars.

Eligibility: Applicants need not be American citizens; however, they must work at an academic, medical, or research institution within the United States. 1. A program/institution is defined as an entity essentially operating under one management. o Any questions or questionable situations will be reviewed by a subset of the Scientific Advisory Board of St. Baldrick's. Questions can be emailed to Grants@Stbaldricks.org, please include a copy of the potential Scholar's biosketch. 2. Institutions that are actively involved in (sponsor, promote, or participate in) non-St. Baldrick's head-shaving fundraising events are not eligible to apply for St. Baldrick's funding. 3. St. Baldrick's funds may not be used for human embryonic stem cell research. 4. All awards will be payable to the Scholar's academic institution, non-profit research institution, or laboratory. 5. Applicants should hold a PhD, M.D., or D.O. degree in a field of research specialty by the date the award becomes effective. 6. Applicants must currently hold (for no longer than 7 years at the time the award begins), or will hold by start of the award, a title that is considered by the institution to be a fulltime, faculty position. o Situations may occur where the institutions definition of "faculty" may differ from the Foundation's definition, this should be fully explained in the Scholar Applicant Checklist (required at LOI stage). 7. This is an early-career award. The Scholar award is intended to develop the independent pediatric cancer research careers of highly qualified investigators, not to support well established or senior investigators. 8. Scholars may receive funding from other sources to support their research. However, no other comparable or higher (monetary value) career development award may be held prior to or at the time the award begins. Scientific or budgetary overlap with other funded projects is not allowed. o In the event of comparable or higher (monetary value) career development funding after the LOI has been approved, the Scholar must give up the remainder of their St. Baldrick's award, unless otherwise approved by the St. Baldrick's Foundation. 10. Applicants holding or awarded R01s at the time of the LOI are not eligible to apply. Applicants cannot hold a NIH K-award at the time that they apply (institutional K12 funding is allowable). See "Conditions of Award" below regarding other awards received after the LOI is approved. 11. Applicants must have an appropriate Sponsor who provides supervision, facilities, and research support. If appropriate for the project, applicants may have more than one (1) Sponsor. 12. Research projects must have direct applicability and relevance to pediatric cancer. They may be in any discipline of basic, clinical, translational, or epidemiological research.

Level of Study: Postgraduate

Type: Grant

Value: This award is granted for three years with an opportunity to apply for an additional two years of funding based upon the demonstration of significant accomplishment. (Years 3-5, if funded, will be up to US$115,000/year).

Length of Study: 3 year

Frequency: Annual

Country of Study: United States of America

Application Procedure: Category/Cycle specific LOI Instructions/Requirements are available in ProposalCENTRAL upon starting the LOI and on the St. Baldrick's website (stbaldricks.org/for-researchers). 1. LOI, application, and required documents must be submitted by the Principal Investigator, in English, online through ProposalCENTRAL (proposalcentral.altum.com) before 5 p.m. EST on the deadline. 2. All application instructions and templates/requirements will be available in ProposalCENTRAL upon approval of an LOI. 3. Applicants can enable other users to access their proposal (e.g., department or grants administrators) in the full proposal section of ProposalCENTRAL. 4. It is the responsibility of the applicant to ensure and to verify that the application is received by the deadline date and that the application is complete and correct prior to submission. 5. Eligible current St. Baldrick's Scholars applying for extended funding will be contacted by the St. Baldrick's Foundation Grants Administration staff with instructions for applying. Applications will be submitted via ProposalCENTRAL and reviewed for progress. Grantees can email Grants@StBaldricks.org with further questions about the optional funding. 1. St. Baldrick's Foundation funds biomedical research to better understand the causes of pediatric cancers and to advance its prevention, treatment, and cure. The main output of this research is new knowledge. To ensure this knowledge can be accessed, read, applied, and built upon in fulfillment of our goals, St. Baldrick's Foundation encourages researchers to share data with the research community in accordance with the NIH policy on data sharing and expects its grantees to publish their findings, including but not limited to publication in peer reviewed journals. Applicants will be asked about data sharing plans as part of the application. 2. All application evaluations are considered confidential and are available to scientific reviewers, the Foundation's Board of Directors, and the administrative personnel of the St. Baldrick's Foundation only. 3. Resubmissions Applicants with resubmissions have the option to check a box in ProposalCENTRAL on the title page of the application stating that it is a resubmission. Resbumissions are not marked in the Letter of Intent stage. You may mention it is a resubmission in your LOI. Applicants with a resubmission are asked to address the reviewer comments in the appendix. Be sure that the document addressing previous reviewer comments is listed in the table of contents for your appendix. Resubmission applicants will not have all three of the same reviewers. St. Baldrick's does ask at least one of the previous reviewers to re-review the resubmission. Once marked as a resubmission in ProposalCENTRAL, new reviewers will have access to the past reviewer comments. Resubmissions are still required to go through limited submission decisions per the institution.

Closing Date: 18 February

Additional Information: www.stbaldricks.org/file/Research/2022-SBF-International-Scholar-Guidelines.pdf

For further information contact:

Tel: (1) 626 792 8247 (ext. 236)
Email: Laura@StBaldricks.org

St. Baldrick's Scholars

Purpose: The Scholar (Career Development) Award is meant to help develop the independent research of highly qualified individuals still early in their careers. Recipients are called St. Baldrick's Scholars.

Eligibility: Applicants need not be American citizens; however, they must work at an academic, medical, or research institution within the United States. 1. A program/institution is defined as an entity essentially operating under one management. o Any questions or questionable situations will be reviewed by a subset of the Scientific Advisory Board of St. Baldrick's. Questions can be emailed to Grants@Stbaldricks.org, please include a copy of the potential Scholar's biosketch. 2. Institutions that are actively involved in (sponsor, promote, or participate in) non-St. Baldrick's head-shaving fundraising events are not eligible to apply for St. Baldrick's funding. 3. St. Baldrick's funds may not be used for human embryonic stem cell research. 4. All awards will be payable to the Scholar's academic institution, non-profit research institution, or laboratory. 5. Applicants should hold a PhD, M.D., or D.O. degree in a field of research specialty by the date the award becomes effective. 6. Applicants must currently hold (for no longer than 7 years at the time the award begins), or will hold by start of the award, a title that is considered by the institution to be a fulltime, faculty position. o Situations may occur where the institutions definition of "faculty" may differ from the Foundation's definition, this should be fully explained in the Scholar Applicant Checklist (required at LOI stage). 7. This is an early-career award. The Scholar award is intended to develop the independent pediatric cancer research careers of highly qualified investigators, not to support well established or senior investigators. 8. Scholars may receive funding from other sources to support their research. However, no other comparable or higher (monetary value) career development award may be held prior to or at the time the award begins. Scientific or budgetary overlap with other funded projects is not allowed. o In the event of comparable or higher (monetary value) career development funding after the LOI has been approved, the Scholar must give up the remainder of their St. Baldrick's award, unless otherwise approved by the St. Baldrick's Foundation. 9. Applicants holding or awarded R01s at the time of the LOI are not eligible to apply. Applicants cannot hold a NIH K-award at the time that they apply (institutional K12 funding is allowable). See "Conditions of Award" below regarding other awards received after the LOI is approved. 10. Applicants must have an appropriate Sponsor who provides supervision, facilities, and research support. If appropriate for the project, applicants may have more than one (1) Sponsor. 11. Research projects must have direct applicability and relevance to pediatric cancer. They may be in any discipline of basic, clinical, translational, or epidemiological research.

Level of Study: Postgraduate

Type: Fellowship

Value: This award is granted for three years with an opportunity to apply for an additional two years of funding based upon the demonstration of significant accomplishment. (Years 3-5, if funded, will be up to US$115,000/year).

Frequency: Annual

Country of Study: United Kingdom

Application Procedure: Category/Cycle specific LOI Instructions/Requirements are available in ProposalCENTRAL upon starting the LOI and on the St. Baldrick's website (stbaldricks.org/for-researchers). 1. LOI, application, and required documents must be submitted by the Principal Investigator, in English, online through ProposalCENTRAL (proposalcentral.altum.com) before 5 p.m. EST on the deadline. 2. All application instructions and templates/requirements will be available in ProposalCENTRAL upon approval of an LOI. 3. Applicants can enable other users to access their proposal (e.g., department or grants administrators) in the full proposal section of ProposalCENTRAL. 4. It is the responsibility of the applicant to ensure and to verify that the application is received by the deadline date and that the application is complete and correct prior to submission. 5. Eligible current St. Baldrick's Scholars applying for extended funding will be contacted by the St. Baldrick's Foundation Grants Administration staff with instructions for applying. Applications will be submitted via ProposalCENTRAL and reviewed for progress. Grantees can email Grants@StBaldricks.org with further questions about the optional funding. 1. St. Baldrick's Foundation funds biomedical research to better understand the causes of pediatric cancers and to advance its prevention, treatment, and cure. The main output of this research is new knowledge. To ensure this knowledge can be accessed, read, applied, and built upon in fulfillment of our goals, St. Baldrick's Foundation encourages researchers to share data with the research community in accordance with the NIH policy on data sharing and expects its grantees to publish their findings, including but not limited to publication in peer reviewed journals. Applicants will be asked about data sharing plans as part of the application. 2. All application evaluations are considered confidential and are available to scientific reviewers, the Foundation's Board of Directors, and the administrative personnel of the St. Baldrick's Foundation only. 3. Resubmissions Applicants with resubmissions have the option to check a box in ProposalCENTRAL on the title page of the application stating that it is a resubmission. Resbumissions are not marked in the Letter of Intent stage. You may mention it is a resubmission in your LOI. Applicants with a resubmission are asked to address the reviewer comments in the appendix. Be sure that the document addressing previous reviewer comments is listed in the table of contents for your appendix. Resubmission applicants will not have all three of the same reviewers. St. Baldrick's does ask at least one of the previous reviewers to re-review the resubmission. Once marked as a resubmission in ProposalCENTRAL, new reviewers will have access to the past reviewer comments. Resubmissions are still required to go through limited submission decisions per the institution.

Closing Date: 19 February

Additional Information: www.stbaldricks.org/file/Research/2021-SBF-Scholar-Guidelines.pdf

For further information contact:

Email: Laura@StBaldricks.org

St. Catherine's College - University of Oxford

Manor Road, Oxford OX1 3UJ, United Kingdom.

Tel: (44) 1865 271 700
Email: admissions@stcatz.ox.ac.uk
Website: www.stcatz.ox.ac.uk/
Contact: Mrs Ben Nicholas, Graduate Funding Administrator

St Catherine's College is the largest college within Oxford University and teaches both undergraduate and graduate students. Although one of the youngest Oxford colleges, we can trace our roots back to 1868, when a 'Delegacy for Non-Collegiate Students' was formed. This Delegacy enabled students to gain an Oxford education without the prohibitive costs of college membership. This founding ethos of inclusion is still evident today, and the College has an open, friendly and diverse community amongst its Students, Fellows and Alumni.

Alan Tayler Scholarship (Mathematics)

Eligibility: For Overseas and EU fee status students who in October 2023 will be reading for an Oxford University DPhil degree in the Mathematical Institute.
Level of Study: Postgraduate
Type: Scholarship
Value: £5,000 per annum
Length of Study: 3 years
Frequency: Annual
Country of Study: United Kingdom
No. of awards offered: 1
Closing Date: 11 March
Additional Information: www.stcatz.ox.ac.uk/prospective-students/postgraduate-admissions/student-finance-and-scholarships/

Allen Senior Scholarship (Music)

Eligibility: For students who in October 2023 will be reading for an Oxford University graduate degree (MSt, MPhil or DPhil) in Music.
Type: Scholarship
Value: £3,300 per annum

Length of Study: 1 year
Frequency: Annual
Country of Study: United Kingdom
No. of awards offered: 1
Closing Date: 11 March
Additional Information: www.stcatz.ox.ac.uk/prospective-students/postgraduate-admissions/student-finance-and-scholarships/

Berlinski-Jacobson Graduate Scholarship (Humanities & Social Sciences)

Eligibility: For students who in October will be reading for any Oxford University graduate degree in the Arts (Humanities Division and Social Science Division) for which St Catherine's admits graduate students
Level of Study: Graduate
Type: Scholarship
Value: £4,000 per annum
Length of Study: 3 years
Frequency: Every 3 years
Country of Study: United Kingdom
Closing Date: 11 March
Funding: Private
Additional Information: studyqa.com/scholarships/view/257

For further information contact:

Email: development.office@stcatz.ox.ac.uk

Overseas Scholarship

Eligibility: For Overseas fee status students who in October 2023 will be reading for any Oxford University research degree (DPhil, MLitt, or MSc by Research) for which St Catherine's admits graduate students.
Level of Study: Postgraduate
Type: Scholarship
Value: £3,300 per annum
Length of Study: 3 years
Frequency: Annual
Country of Study: United Kingdom
No. of awards offered: 2
Closing Date: 11 March
Additional Information: www.stcatz.ox.ac.uk/prospective-students/postgraduate-admissions/student-finance-and-scholarships/

St. Mary's University

Waldegrave Rd, Strawberry Hill, Twickenham TW1 4SX, United Kingdom.

Tel: (44) 20 8240 4000
Email: scholarships@stmarys.ac.uk
Website: www.stmarys.ac.uk/

St Mary's has a long and distinguished history and a very modern outlook. With an original intake of just six students, St Mary's has now grown to around 6,000 undergraduate and postgraduate students across the four academic Schools.

Centre for Bioethics and Emerging Technologies PhD Funding

Purpose: The Centre for Bioethics and Emerging Technologies (CBET) at St Mary's University, Twickenham, offers a fully funded, full-time three year PhD programme commencing in October to support the successful applicant's research in bioethics
Eligibility: 1. The successful applicant would also expected to be involved with CBET activities, including conference organization and undergraduate teaching after a mandatory induction course. 2. The successful candidate may if they wish, carry out work with the Catholic Bishops' Conference of England and Wales. 3. It is also highly desirable that the successful applicant be located within the Greater London area during their studies
Level of Study: Graduate
Type: Funding support
Value: Provide full-time PhD fees at the current home/European Union rate of £4,375 p.a. and a bursary of £13,000 p.a
Length of Study: Up to 3 years
Frequency: Annual
Country of Study: United Kingdom
Application Procedure: To apply, download and complete a full registration PhD application and send it together with your 3,000-4,000 word research proposal, two academic references from your chosen referees, copies of your Master's qualification(s), a current CV and a covering letter stating the reasons you wish to be considered for the bursary to the physical address mentioned below
Closing Date: 26 April
Funding: Private

For further information contact:

Email: maggie.mayer@stmarys.ac.uk

Stanford University

450 Serra Mall, Stanford, CA 94305, United States of America.

Tel: (1) 650 723 2300
Website: www.stanford.edu

Stanford University, located between San Francisco and San Jose in the heart of California's Silicon Valley, is one of the world's leading teaching and research universities. Since its opening in 1891, Stanford has been dedicated to finding solutions to big challenges and to preparing students for leadership in a complex world.

School of Medicine Dean's Postdoctoral Fellowship

Purpose: The School of Medicine Dean's Postdoctoral Fellowships encourage and support young investigators in the first two years of their postdoctoral research training at the School of Medicine and who are under the mentorship of faculty in the School of Medicine. With the goal to support current postdocs and to facilitate the recruitment of new scholars, the Dean's Fellowship is often used as seed money while outside funds are sought.
Eligibility: 1. Applicants must be postdoctoral scholars at the School of Medicine at the time the award begins. If applicant is not a postdoc at the application deadline, additional documents must be submitted with application. 2. Faculty sponsors must be appointed in the School of Medicine. Acting, consulting, and courtesy appointees are ineligible. 3. Awardees cannot be enrolled in a degree-granting program while funded. 4. Applicants in the first one or two years of postdoctoral research training are preferred. 5. Foreign fellows must have visas that allow stipend support (typically a J-1 & F-1 OPT). H1-B and TN visa holders are ineligible. Citizenship is not a selection factor. 6. This is a one-year fellowship and applications for a second year of funding will not be reviewed.
Level of Study: Postdoctorate
Type: Fellowship
Value: Stipend is US$$32,784 for the entire award period.
Length of Study: 2 years
Frequency: Annual

Country of Study: Any country

Application Procedure: Complete applications must be submitted online by the deadline. Start applications early to allow enough time for the system to solicit the required form from your faculty mentor which is due at the same time as your application. Applications due by 1159 PM PST on deadline date. A complete application consists of 1. Complete online application form. 2. NIH Biosketch. 3. Research proposal Two page limit, including graphics/tables. Proposals are written by the fellow and reviewed by the faculty sponsor. Proposals must include a brief statement of proposed investigation including background, goals, hypothesis, and experimental methods. Use 1-inch margins and 12-point font. Include title of project on both numbered pages. Include references only if they are part of your two-page proposal. 4. Faculty Sponsor's Recommendation Form & Agreement. 5. Offer Letter only if not currently appointed as a postdoctoral scholar in the School of Medicine. This application does not go through RMG or OSR at Stanford.

Closing Date: 11 October

Additional Information: postdocs.stanford.edu/current/fellowship/deans

For further information contact:

1265 Welch Rd., Suite 100, Stanford, CA 94305-5402, United States of America.

Email: kwheller@stanford.edu

Stanford Postdoctoral Recruitment Initiative in Sciences and Medicine (PRISM)

Purpose: PRISM invites students to explore our training environment and to consider whether advanced training at Stanford would support their career goals. Postdoctoral training is a critical period for establishing research independence. At Stanford, postdocs work alongside top scientists and at the same time develop their professional skills, explore career options, and prepare for independent careers. Stanford has one of the largest postdoc populations in the country and a strong commitment to making the postdoc experience the best it can possibly be.

Eligibility: 1. Eligible for NIH T-32 training grants, which are limited to US Citizens or Permanent Residents, by the time they will begin their postdoctoral appointment. 2. Currently at any institution in the US. Applications from students in Canada, Mexico, Puerto Rico, etc., may also be considered, pending funding availability. Travel funds are not available for those currently located overseas. 3. Intend to complete their PhD within 15 months of PRISM, though later

graduation dates may be considered, at the discretion of the faculty or program.

Level of Study: Postgraduate

Type: Grant

Value: Travel funding through PRISM varies by School

Frequency: Annual

Country of Study: United States of America

Application Procedure: The PRISM Application consists of 2 parts, the Stanford Postdoc Diversity Common Application and the PRISM Application. (postdocs.stanford.edu/prism-application-guide)

Closing Date: 7 February

Additional Information: postdocs.stanford.edu/PRISM

For further information contact:

1265 Welch Rd., Suite 100, Stanford, CA 94305-5402, United States of America.

Email: stanfordprism@stanford.edu

The Helena Anna Henzl-Gabor Young Women in Science Fund for Postdoctoral Scholars Travel Grant

Purpose: The Helena Anna Henzl-Gabor Young Women in Science Fund for Postdoctoral Scholars Travel Grant is open to currently appointed Stanford postdoctoral scholars in the School of Medicine and School of Humanities & Sciences who have demonstrated a positive attitude through professional teamwork and collaborations of men and women. The Henzl-Gabor Travel Grant supports travel (airline tickets, accommodations, and registration expenses) for participation at scientific conferences. These travel grants are meant to help defray the costs of attending a national or international meeting for travel taking place during the period of December 1 - November 30

Eligibility: Applicants must have completed an MD or PhD degree within the past six years of fund application submission. Awards may be given in amounts up to US$2,000 based on the detailed expenses submitted. Total awards given and funding levels may vary depending on the size and strength of the applicant pool

Level of Study: Postgraduate

Type: Grant

Frequency: Annual

Closing Date: 22 October

Funding: Foundation

Additional Information: ***COVID19 UPDATE: As the award is a travel award, it is being put on hold until the pandemic is resolved. Please check back from time to time for updates.*** postdocs.stanford.edu/PRISM

S

For further information contact:

1265 Welch Rd., Suite 100, Stanford, CA 94305-5402, United States of America.

The Katharine McCormick Advanced Postdoctoral Scholar Fellowship to Support Women in Academic Medicine

Purpose: The Katharine McCormick Advanced Postdoctoral Fellowships are for advanced postdoctoral scholars who are pursuing faculty careers in academic medicine. The program aims to provide a bridge of the gap of support for advanced postdoctoral trainees who are competitive, yet have not yet been selected, for faculty positions

Eligibility: Eligibility requirements; Only individuals who are currently appointed as Postdoctoral Scholars at Stanford University are eligible to apply. Instructors and Research Associates may not apply. The applicant may be a United States citizen, permanent resident, or foreign national. Foreign scholar applicants must be a holder of a J1 visa or an F1 visa in OPT status. Applicants who hold H1B, TN, J2, O-1 or other visas are ineligible. The scholar's faculty mentor must have a primary appointment in the School of Medicine. Acting, consulting and courtesy faculty are not eligible. Commitment on the part of the applicant and his/her faculty mentor to hold monthly mentorship meetings with a focus on topics related to the job search process and starting out as an assistant professor. Candidate's willingness to make a presentation of their work to a large scientific audience. A progress report is required at the end of the fellowship

Level of Study: Graduate

Type: Fellowship

Value: US$65,000

Frequency: Annual

Country of Study: United Kingdom

Application Procedure: Application Process Complete online application Applicant's NIH Biosketch (uploaded by applicant online) Applicant's complete curriculum vitae (uploaded by applicant online) Research proposal (uploaded by applicant online) Two page limit, including any graphics or charts. The research proposal must be written by the fellow and reviewed by the faculty sponsor. These two pages should include a brief statement of proposed investigation in the following sections Background, Goals, Hypothesis, and Experimental methods. If the applicant chooses to include references in the two pages, the reference should include enough information to allow the reviewer to look up the paper. Three letters of reference. One letter is required from the faculty sponsor (mentor) at Stanford. Two letters are required from other faculty, at Stanford or elsewhere, who are familiar with the candidate's work and will likely serve as

references for the candidate's anticipated job search. Letters will be submitted online by the reference writer directly to the application. Letters are due the s

Closing Date: 16 January

Funding: Private

Additional Information: postdocs.stanford.edu/current/fellowship/katharine-mccormick-advanced-postdoctoral-scholar-fellowship-support-women#:~:text=Fellowships%20are%20awarded%20to%20women,are%20appointed%20in%20the%20SoM.

For further information contact:

1265 Welch Rd., Suite 100, Stanford, CA 94305-5402, United States of America.

Email: kwheller@stanford.edu

The Walter V. and Idun Berry Postdoctoral Fellowship Program

Purpose: The fellowships aims to enhance research which utilizes the most advanced technologies and methodologies available to improve the health and wellness of children, including the latest opportunities in molecular and genetic medicine

Eligibility: 1. The applicant must be appointed as a postdoctoral scholar at the Stanford University School of Medicine at the time the award begins. If the applicant is not an appointed postdoctoral scholar at the time of the application deadline, additional documents must be submitted with the application (see application checklist below). Instructors and Research Associates may not apply. 2. Applicants must also hold an MD, PhD and/or a DVM/VMD degree(s); selection preference will be given to physician scientists. 3. The faculty mentor/sponsor must be appointed in the School of Medicine. Acting, consulting and courtesy appointees are not eligible. 4. Foreign scholars may have J-1 or F-1 OPT (receiving stipends), or H1B visas (receiving the award as salary). Citizenship is not a selection factor. 5. Applicants must be available for an interview on the interview date listed on this website

Level of Study: Postgraduate

Type: Fellowship

Value: US$76,000/year

Frequency: Annual

Country of Study: United States of America

Application Procedure: 1. Complete online application form (application visible only when application period is open). 2. Applicant's NIH Biosketch (uploaded by applicant online). 3. Research Proposal (two page limit, including any graphics, charts or references). The research proposal must be written by the postdoc and reviewed by the faculty sponsor. These two pages should include a brief statement of proposed investigation in the following sections Background, Goals, Hypothesis, and Experimental methods. Formatting guidelines require at least 1-inch margins at the top, bottom, left and right; and 12 point or larger font Times New Roman, Times Roman, Arial, Helvetica, or Verdana. Include title of project and your name on both pages and number pages. If the applicant choses to include references, the reference should include enough information to allow the reviewer to look up the paper. 4. Three letters of recommendation one from the sponsoring Faculty Mentor at Stanford, and two additional letters from other recommenders. Letters are due the same day as the application, so please request these letters at the beginning of the application process via the online application

Closing Date: 6 June

Funding: Private

Additional Information: postdocs.stanford.edu/current/fellowship/walter-v-and-idun-berry-postdoctoral-fellowship-program

For further information contact:

Email: postdocaffairs@stanford.edu

Stanley Smith (United Kingdom) Horticultural Trust

770 Tamalpais Drive, Suite 309, Corte Madera, CA 94925, United States of America.

Tel: (1) 415 332 0166
Website: smithht.org/
Contact: Dr James Cullen, Director

The Stanley Smith Horticultural Trust was created in 1970 by May Smith, in honor of her late husband and in fulfillment of his vision. The Trust stewards Stanley Smith's philanthropic legacy, and seeks to nurture in others his enthusiasm for ornamental horticulture.

Stanley Smith (UK) Horticultural Trust Awards

Eligibility: Offered to charities, community and voluntary organisations and institutions for projects that meet the objectives of the Trust:: 1. to promote horticulture; 2. to promote the conservation of the physical and natural environment by promoting biological diversity 3. to promote the creation, development, preservation and maintenance of gardens (preference will normally, but not exclusively, be given 4. to gardens accessible to the public); and 5. the advancement of horticultural education.

Level of Study: Unrestricted
Type: Grant
Value: £3,000 to £4,000
Length of Study: Dependent on the nature of the project
Frequency: Annual
Country of Study: United Kingdom
Application Procedure: Applicants must apply to the Trust. Trustees allocate awards in Spring and Autumn
No. of awards offered: 200
Closing Date: 15 August
Funding: Private
Contributor: Donations
No. of awards given last year: 30
No. of applicants last year: 200
Additional Information: www.fundingforall.org.uk/funds/stanley-smith-uk-horticultural-trust/

For further information contact:

Email: tdaniel@calacademy.org

State Secretariat for Education, Research and Innovation SERI

Einsteinstrasse 2, CH-3005 Bern, Switzerland.

Email: sgs@sbfi.admin.ch
Website: www.sbfi.admin.ch

SERI is the national contact point for the recognition of professional qualifications in Switzerland.

Swiss Government Excellence Scholarships for Foreign Scholars and Artists

Purpose: The Swiss government, through the Federal Commission for Scholarships for Foreign Students (FCS), awards various postgraduate scholarships to foreign scholars and researchers
Eligibility: These scholarships provide graduates from all fields with the opportunity to pursue doctoral or postdoctoral research in Switzerland at one of the public funded universities or recognised institutions
Level of Study: Doctorate, Postdoctorate
Type: Scholarship
Frequency: Annual

Country of Study: Any country

Additional Information: Please check www.sbfi.admin.ch/scholarships_eng
www.sbfi.admin.ch/sbfi/en/home/education/scholarships-and-grants/swiss-government-excellence-scholarships.html

For further information contact:

Tel: (41) 446326161
Email: exchange@ethz.ch

Statistical Society of Canada

219 - 1725 St. Laurent Blvd., Ottawa, ON K1G 3V4, Canada.

Tel: (1) 613 627 3530
Email: info@ssc.ca
Website: ssc.ca/
Contact: Sudhir Paul, Chair, Pierre Robillard Award

The Statistical Society of Canada provides a forum for discussion and interaction among individuals involved in all aspects of the statistical sciences. It publishes a newsletter, Liaison as well as a scientific journal, The Canadian Journal of Statistics. The Society also organizes annual scientific meetings and short courses on professional development.

Pierre Robillard Award

Purpose: The aim of the Pierre Robillard Award is to recognize the best PhD thesis defended at a Canadian university in a given year and written in the fields covered by The Canadian Journal of Statistics.
Eligibility: Open to all postgraduates who have made a potential impact on the statistical sciences
Level of Study: Doctorate, Postgraduate
Type: Award
Value: The award consists of a certificate, a monetary prize, and a one-year membership in the SSC.
Frequency: Annual
Country of Study: Canada
Application Procedure: Applicants must submit four copies of the thesis together with a covering letter from the thesis supervisor
Closing Date: 31 January

Additional Information: ssc.ca/en/award/pierre-robillard-award

For further information contact:

Department of Mathematical and Statistical Sciences University of Alberta, 632 Cab, AB T6G 2G1, Canada.

Tel: (1) 780 492 4230
Fax: (1) 780 492 6826
Email: kc.carriere@ualberta.ca

Stellenbosch University

Private Bay XI, Matieland, 7602, South Africa.

Tel: (27) 21 808 9111
Email: info@sun.ac.za
Website: www.sun.ac.za

Stellenbosch University (SU) is home to an academic community of 29 000 students (including 4 000 foreign students from 100 countries) as well as 3 000 permanent staff members (including 1 000 academics) on five campuses. The historical oak-lined university town amongst the Boland Mountains in the winelands of the Western Cape creates a unique campus atmosphere, which attracts local and foreign students alike. On the main campus, paved walkways wind between campus buildings – some dating from previous centuries; others just a few years old. Architecture from various eras attests to the sound academic foundation and establishment of an institution of excellence. This, together with the scenic beauty of the area; state-of-the-art, environmentally friendly facilities and technology, as well as visionary thinking about the creation of a sustainable 21st-century institution, makes for the unique character of Stellenbosch University..

Harry Crossley Doctoral Fellowship

Purpose: To reward academically above-average students
Eligibility: Individuals are not eligible who will be employed for more than 20 hours per week; who will register for part-time courses, the 4th year of an undergraduate degree, the LLB, postgraduate certificates and postgraduate diplomas and who will register for degrees in disciplines in Religious Studies and Political Studies
Level of Study: Doctorate
Type: Fellowship

Value: R80,000
Length of Study: 2 years
Frequency: Annual
Study Establishment: Stellenbosch University
Country of Study: South Africa
Application Procedure: Request application
No. of awards offered: 350
Closing Date: 29 September
Funding: Foundation
Contributor: Harry Crossley Foundation
No. of awards given last year: 50
No. of applicants last year: 350
Additional Information: www.validate-network.org/event/the-harry-crossley-foundation-research-fellowships-2020

For further information contact:

Level 3, Otto Beit Building, Upper Campus Rondebosch, 7700, South Africa.

Tel:	(27) 21 650 3622
Fax:	(27) 21 808 2739
Email:	pgfunding@uct.ac.za

Harry Crossley Master

Purpose: To reward academically above-average students
Eligibility: To full-time students registered at Stellenbosch University in any postgraduate degree programme except theology and political science
Level of Study: Doctorate, Postgraduate
Type: Bursary
Value: R 75,000 (Honours), R 80,000 (Master)
Length of Study: 1 year
Frequency: Annual
Study Establishment: Stellenbosch University
Country of Study: South Africa
No. of awards offered: 500
Closing Date: 15 October
Funding: Foundation
Contributor: Harry Crossley Foundation
No. of awards given last year: 30
No. of applicants last year: 500
Additional Information: Please see the website further details www.scholarshubafrica.com/41257/harry-crossley-foundation-research-fellowship-uct-south-africa/

For further information contact:

Tel:	(27) 21 808 4208
Fax:	(27) 21 808 3799
Email:	usbritz@sun.ac.za

Stellenbosch Fellowship in Polymer Science

Purpose: To fund further study in Polymer Science and synthetic Polymer chemistry
Eligibility: Open to students with a PhD in Polymer Science or Environmental Engineering and experience in membranes, membrane operations, polymer brushes, grafts and other nano particles
Level of Study: Postdoctorate
Type: Fellowship
Length of Study: 1 year
Frequency: Annual
Study Establishment: University of Stellenbosch
Country of Study: South Africa
Application Procedure: Request application.

For further information contact:

Department of Chemistry Division of Polymer Science University of Stellenbosch, Private Bag X1, Matieland, 7602, South Africa.

Email:	rds@sun.ac.za

Stellenbosch Merit Bursary Award

Purpose: To reward academically above-average students
Eligibility: Available to full-time students registered at Stellenbosch University in any postgraduate degree programme
Level of Study: Postgraduate
Type: Bursary
Value: R 4,100 to 34,700
Length of Study: Up to 2 years
Frequency: Annual
Study Establishment: Stellenbosch University
Country of Study: South Africa
Application Procedure: Students must submit an application and a certified copy of a complete, official academic record
No. of awards offered: Approx. 700
Closing Date: 6 December
Contributor: Stellenbosch University
No. of awards given last year: 340
No. of applicants last year: Approx. 700
Additional Information: www.sun.ac.za/english/learning-teaching/undergraduate-bursaries-loans/su-funding/merit-bursaries

For further information contact:

Office for postgraduate student funding, Postgraduate and International Office Stellenbosch Central, Wilcocks Building, Room 3015, Stellenbosch, 7600, South Africa.

Tel:　　　(27) 21 808 4208
Fax:　　　(27) 21 808 3799
Email:　　postgradfunding@sun.ac.za

Stellenbosch Postdoctoral Research Fellowship in Geology

Purpose: To finance a student interested in Archaen tectonics and applied structural geology of high-grade metamorphic granite-gneiss terrains
Eligibility: Open to students with a PhD in geology obtained within the past 5 years, with a background in regional mapping and structural geology
Level of Study: Postdoctorate
Type: Fellowship
Value: R60,000 per annum
Length of Study: 2 years
Frequency: Annual
Study Establishment: University of Stellenbosch
Country of Study: South Africa
Application Procedure: Submit a covering letter, curriculum vitae and all research outputs
Closing Date: 21 March
Additional Information: www.researchersjob.com/research-fellowship/

For further information contact:

Fax:　　　(27) 21 808 3129
Email:　　akister@sun.ac.za

Stellenbosch Rector's Grants for Successing Against the Odds

Purpose: To award students who have achieved exceptional success despite difficult circumstances
Eligibility: Open to candidates who satisfy the admission requirements of the University and who can provide proof of exceptional achievement despite handicaps and/or specific physical, educational or social challenges
Level of Study: Postgraduate
Type: Grant
Value: R70, 000 per year
Length of Study: 1 to 3 years
Frequency: Annual
Study Establishment: Stellenbosch University

Country of Study: South Africa
Application Procedure: Students must submit a complete application form accompanied by a curriculum vitae and 2 references
No. of awards offered: 3
Closing Date: 10 September
Funding: Foundation
Contributor: Andrew Mellon Foundation
No. of awards given last year: 3
No. of applicants last year: 100

For further information contact:

Tel:　　　(27) 21 8084208
Fax:　　　(27) 21 808 2739
Email:　　beursnavrae_nagraads@sun.ac.za

Stockholm School of Economics

PO Box 6501, SE-11383 Stockholm, Sweden.

Tel:　　　(46) 8 736 9000
Email:　　info@hhs.se
Website:　www.hhs.se/

The Stockholm School of Economics is an academic hub for ambitious students and researchers from all over the world. By working closely with corporate partners and society at large, SSE has been creating opportunities for its graduates for over 100 years.

Consejo Nacional de Ciencia y Tecnologia (CONACYT) Scholarships

Eligibility: Open to Mexican students only
Level of Study: MBA
Type: Scholarship
Value: All agreed fees
Length of Study: 1 year
Frequency: Annual
Country of Study: Sweden
Application Procedure: Contact the Foundation
Funding: Foundation
Contributor: CONACYT
Additional Information: www.sussex.ac.uk/study/phd/doctoral/funding-support-international/conacyt

For further information contact:

Email:　　ochoa@buzon.main.conacyt.mx

Petra Och Kail Erik Hedborgs Stiftelse Scholarship

Level of Study: MBA
Type: Scholarship
Value: All tuition fees and travel costs
Length of Study: 1 year
Frequency: Annual
Country of Study: Sweden
Application Procedure: Contact the institute
Funding: Private
Additional Information: www.pkhedborg.com/english.html

For further information contact:

Tel: (46) 8 765 6327
Email: info@pkhedborg.com

The Swedish Foundation for International Cooperation in Research and Higher Education (STINT) Scholarship

Eligibility: Open to Brazilian nationals only
Level of Study: MBA
Type: Scholarship
Length of Study: 1 year
Frequency: Dependent on funds available
Country of Study: Sweden
Application Procedure: Contact the institute
Closing Date: 31 May
Funding: Government
Contributor: STINT
Additional Information: www.european-funding-guide.eu/scholarship/5175-initiation

For further information contact:

STINT, Wallingatan 2, Stockholm, SE-111 60, Sweden.

Tel: (46) 46 8662 7690
Fax: (46) 46 8661 9210
Email: info@stint.se

Strathclyde University

16 Richmond Street, Glasgow G1 1XQ, United Kingdom.

Tel: (44) 141 552 4400
Website: www.strath.ac.uk/

Based in the heart of the City of Glasgow, Strathclyde University is a leading technological university with around 23,000 students from more than 100 nations. With an international reputation for teaching excellence, the university has a five-star Overall Rating in the QS Stars University Ratings, and seven Times Higher Education awards in as many years.

Carnegie Trust: St Andrew's Society Scholarships

Eligibility: Candidates must be Scottish by birth or descent, and will be expected to have current knowledge of Scotland and Scottish current affairs, and of the Scottish tradition generally. The Society expects its scholars to be good ambassadors for Scotland. Candidates must also be: 1. either graduates of a Scottish university, Glasgow School of Art, Royal Conservatoire of Scotland, or of Oxford or 2. Cambridge, who have completed their first degree course (so as to be qualified to graduate) not earlier than 2021; or students of a Scottish university, Glasgow School of Art, Royal Conservatoire of Scotland, or of Oxford or Cambridge, who expect to complete their first degree course (so as to be qualified to graduate) in 2022. Preference will be given to candidates who have no previous experience of the United States and for whom a period of study there can be expected to be a life-changing experience. Selection will be on the basis of an all-round assessment, including character, experience and academic achievement.
Level of Study: Postgraduate
Type: Scholarship
Value: US$35,000 each
Frequency: Annual
Country of Study: United States of America
No. of awards offered: 2
Closing Date: 28 February
Additional Information: www.strath.ac.uk/studywithus/scholarships/carnegietrust-standrewssocietyscholarships/

For further information contact:

Email: shona.cameron@strath.ac.uk

Faculty of Science Masters Scholarship for International Students

Eligibility: In order to be considered for a Faculty of Science International Masters Scholarship, candidates must: 1. Be a new, international fee-paying student holding an offer of admission for a full-time, taught masters degree in the Faculty of Science for the 2023/2024 academic year. 2. Be self-funded. Students who receive full scholarships, for example from a government office or embassy, will not be eligible.
Level of Study: Postgraduate
Type: Scholarship
Value: £4,000 to £5,000

Frequency: Annual
Country of Study: United Kingdom
Closing Date: 31 July
Additional Information: www.strath.ac.uk/studywithus/scholarships/sciencescholarships/facultyofsciencemastersscholarshipsforinternationalstudents202223/

For further information contact:

Email: science-scholarships@strath.ac.uk

Mature Students Hardship Fund

Eligibility: Applicants: 1. Are aged 21 or over at the start of their current course of study. 2. Started their course with an appropriate funding arrangement in place but have fallen into hardship 3. If eligible, have applied to the Discretionary Fund for support 4. If eligible, have applied for all statutory funding (student loan, bursary, cost of living grant) 5. Or they have been recommended for support from the Fund by the Student Support Team on the basis of urgent or exceptional circumstances 6. A payment from the fund will make a significant contribution to the student's ability to continue their studies successfully.
Level of Study: Postgraduate
Type: Award
Value: £500 to £1000
Frequency: Annual
Country of Study: Scotland
Closing Date: 1 January
Additional Information: www.strath.ac.uk/studywithus/scholarships/maturestudentshardshipfund/

For further information contact:

Email: financial-support@strath.ac.uk

MSc Psychology with a specialisation in Business Scholarship

Eligibility: To be eligible for this award applicants must: 1. Be available to commence their academic studies by the start of the academic year in September 2023. 2. Hold an unconditional academic offer to the MSc Psychology with a specialisation in Business at the University of Strathclyde (full-time, part-time and flexible route included).
Level of Study: Postgraduate
Type: Scholarship
Value: £6,700
Frequency: Annual
Country of Study: United Kingdom

Closing Date: 31 August
Additional Information: www.strath.ac.uk/studywithus/scholarships/humanitiessocialsciences/psychologicalscienceshealth/mscpsychologywithaspecialisationinbusinessscholarship/

For further information contact:

Email: hass-pg-enquiries@strath.ac.uk

Strathclyde Research Studentship Scheme (SRSS)

Eligibility: Funding is provided for students with a good honours degree at a first- or upper second-class level, awarded within a relevant cognate discipline. Faculties may stipulate a first class honours degree
Level of Study: Postgraduate
Type: Scholarship
Value: Home fees and stipend at UKRI rate
Length of Study: 3 to 3.5 years
Frequency: Annual
Country of Study: United Kingdom
No. of awards offered: 150
Additional Information: www.strath.ac.uk/studywithus/scholarships/

University of Strathclyde Performance Sport Scholarship

Eligibility: All applicants must be competing in a Sport Scotland-recognised sport, and priority will be given to students competing in a BUCS-sport who can demonstrate the potential to contribute toward the University's objective of being ranked in the top 20 in the UK. In addition, all applicants should be competing at least at junior, if not senior, International level.
Level of Study: Postgraduate
Type: Bursary
Value: Up to £1,000 (+ up to £3,750* in-kind support)
Length of Study: 1 year
Frequency: Annual
Country of Study: Scotland
Closing Date: 25 April
Additional Information: www.strath.ac.uk/studywithus/scholarships/performancesportscholarship/

For further information contact:

Email: dave.sykes@strath.ac.uk

Stroke Association

Stroke House, 240 City Road, London EC1V 2PR, United Kingdom.

Tel: (44) 20 7566 1543
Email: research@stroke.org.uk
Website: www.stroke.org.uk
Contact: Rachael Sherrington, Research Awards Officer

The Stroke Association funds research into stroke prevention, treatment, rehabilitation, and long term care. It also helps stroke patients and their families directly through community services. It campaigns, educates and informs to increase knowledge of stroke at all levels of society and it acts as a voice for everyone affected by stroke.

Priority Programme Awards

Purpose: This new funding stream is aimed at addressing the gaps in research in the following areas
Type: Award
Value: Up to the amount of £450,000
Length of Study: 3 to 5 years
Frequency: Annual
Country of Study: Any country
Closing Date: January
Additional Information: These awards will be made in July. Please contact research@stroke.org.uk
www.stroke.org.uk/research/our-funding-schemes/priority-programme-awards

The Stroke Association Research Project Grants

Purpose: To advance research into stroke
Eligibility: 1. Stroke Association Awards must be carried out at Universities, NHS Trusts, Statutory Social Care Organisations or other Research Institutions within Great Britain and Northern Ireland. 2. The lead applicant must be a senior researcher holding a PhD (or equivalent) with a track record of managing grants, delivering research studies and a strong publication record. 3. The salary of the lead applicant has to be guaranteed for the duration of the proposed programme; the Lead applicant's salary cannot be requested in the budget. 4. For this funding call Masters, PhD studentships, and clinical fellowships are not eligible to be included in the budget.
Level of Study: Research
Type: Project grant
Value: Up to £250,000

Length of Study: 3 to 5 years
Frequency: Annual
Study Establishment: A suitable university or hospital in the United Kingdom
Country of Study: United Kingdom
Application Procedure: Application forms are available from the website
No. of awards offered: 20
Closing Date: 4 February
Funding: Private, Trusts
Contributor: Donations
No. of awards given last year: 3
No. of applicants last year: 20
Additional Information: Please visit www.stroke.org.uk/research/looking-funding/project-grants
www.stroke.org.uk/research/our-funding-schemes/project-grants

Sugar Research Australia - SRA

50 Meiers Road, Indooroopilly QLD 4068 PO Box 86, Indooroopilly, QLD 4068, Australia.

Tel: (61) 7 3331 3333
Website: sugarresearch.com.au/

Sugar Research Australia invests in and manages a portfolio of research, development and adoption projects that drive productivity, profitability and sustainability for the Australian sugarcane industry.

Sugar Industry Postgraduate Research Scholarships (SPRS)

Purpose: Sugar Research Australia (SRA) invests in and manages a portfolio of research, development and adoption (RD&A) projects that drive productivity, profitability and sustainability for the Australian sugarcane industry. SRA also invests significantly in industry capability with the ongoing future success of the sugar industry dependent upon improving the capability of existing industry employees. With respect to research funding and encouraging young scientists into our industry, SRA makes available a number of SPRS awards every year, tenable at Australian universities and institutions, for postgraduate research study. The purpose of these awards is to enable qualified graduates to undertake Research Doctorate or Research Masters study and to facilitate research and training in areas of value to the Australian sugarcane industry.

S

Eligibility: The purpose of the SPRS is to enable high calibre students to undertake a Masters or PhD research degree in disciplines relevant to the future of the Australian sugar industry. Scholarships are available for three years for PhD studies and two years for Research Masters studies and are awarded on the basis of academic excellence. Applicants should consult the SRA Strategic Plan document available on the SRA website and focus on inventive projects that address at least one of the following eight key focus areas of investment 1. Optimally-adapted varieties, plant breeding and release 2. Soil health, nutrient management and environmental sustainability 3. Pest, disease and weed management 4. Farming systems and harvesting 5. Milling efficiency and technology 6. Product diversification and value addition 7. Knowledge and technology transfer and adoption 8. Collaboration and capability development To be eligible for a full SPRS or a top-up scholarship, the candidate must be a citizen or permanent resident of Australia and must have acceptance at a recognised research institution. The principal supervisor for the postgraduate study program must provide evidence that the host organisation supports the project and the applicant's candidature for the relevant study program. Awards are tenable at Australian universities/institutions; however for applicants of proven ability who are undertaking a PhD, training at overseas institutions may be approved where benefits will return to the Australian sugar industry and where overseas supervision will confer additional benefit. Awards are conferred on the student based on merit, with the evaluation criteria set out within this document. Generic applications from prospective supervisors requesting support for postgraduate research projects without identifying a specific candidate will not be considered. The SPRS award offers supplementary or full scholarships, the number and value of which are at the discretion of SRA. For a higher probability of success, the applicant is encouraged to also apply for a Research Training Program (RTP) scholarship or equivalent through their host university. Preference will be given to applicants who receive an RTP or equivalent scholarship. Successful applicants not holding an RTP scholarship or any other base scholarship will be provided a tax-free stipend of AU$32,000 per annum (exclusive of GST). Successful applicants with an RTP scholarship will be provided a tax free top-up set at a maximum of 75% of the RTP stipend rate which is determined by the Australian Government Department of Education and Training each year. All successful applicants will also be provided with an additional budget of AU$10,000 (excluding GST) per year to support research project operating expenses.

Level of Study: Postgraduate
Type: Scholarship
Value: AU$32,000
Length of Study: 2 to 3 years
Frequency: Annual
Country of Study: Australia

Application Procedure: The SRA SugarNet online submission system must be used for all SPRS applications. This can be accessed at sugarnet.sugarresearch.com.au. Applications will not be considered to be complete until the curriculum vitae (CV), certified copies of the academic record and academic transcript, letters of reference from at least two referees and proof of nationality or permanent residence visa are uploaded through SugarNet to accompany the application. The project title needs to be a concise statement of the aim of the proposed research project. The title, objectives and outcomes expected from the project may be published in the SRA Annual Report. Candidates are encouraged to consult their Principal Supervisor when completing this section of the online submission form. No additional information or attachments (such as images, diagrams, flow-charts, tables etc.) should be included unless a prior arrangement has been made with SRA

Closing Date: 31 October
Additional Information: www.worldwidecancerresearch.org/for-researchers/our-funding-criteria/

For further information contact:

Email: fundingunit@sugarresearch.com.au.

Swansea University

Singleton Park, Swansea Wales SA2 8PP, United Kingdom.

Tel:	(44) 1792 205 678
Email:	sro@swansea.ac.uk
Website:	www.swan.ac.uk
Contact:	Dr Mark Skippen, Senior Postgraduate Recruitment Officer

Swansea University is a United Kingdom top 30 institution for research excellence (REF2014) that has been providing the highest quality postgraduate teaching since 1920. Our campuses are situated on the sandy beach of Swansea Bay. We have taught and research postgraduate funding for United Kingdom, European Union and international students: www.swansea.ac.uk/postgraduate/scholarships

International Excellence Scholarships

Eligibility: 1. Applicants must be non UK nationals and classed as overseas fee payers. If the fee status of the applicant changes after the scholarship application is made, then the University will need to remove the scholarship. 2. Applicants must have applied for and received an offer to study at Swansea University at Undergraduate or Master's level. 3. Students studying for a PhD, MPhil, Masters by Research, Graduate Diploma in Law, Postgraduate Diploma, Postgraduate Certificate or Erasmus Mundus programme are not eligible to apply for this scholarship. 4. Students on BSc, BA, BEng, LLB, MEng, MSci, MSc, MPharm, MBBCh, MA, LLM, MRes (not the same as Masters by Research) are eligible. 5. Students progressing from 'The College Swansea University' and students currently studying at the University are not eligible to apply for this scholarship. 6. Alumni are eligible to apply.

Level of Study: Postgraduate
Type: Scholarship
Value: Approx. £4,000
Length of Study: 1 year (Masters)
Frequency: Annual
Study Establishment: Swansea University
Country of Study: United Kingdom
Application Procedure: Complete application form, available online at website
Closing Date: 20 August
Additional Information: Please contact at international@swansea.ac.uk studyabroad.shiksha.com/scholarships/international-excellence-scholarship-masters

For further information contact:

Tel: (44) 1245 493131
Email: scholarships@brunel.ac.uk

MRes Scholarships

Purpose: An MRes Scholarship includes a fee waiver for one year. Associated costs – such as fieldwork and conference attendance – may also be awarded if approved by the faculty during your research.
Eligibility: Candidates must demonstrate outstanding academic potential with preferably a 1st class honours degree and/or a Master's degree with distinction or equivalent Grade Point Average. An IELTS (Academic) score of 6.5 minimum (with a minimum 6.0 in each component) is essential for candidates for whom English is not their first language.
Type: Scholarship
Value: Each scholarship is worth £2,500, to be used towards the cost of tuition fees
Length of Study: 1 year
Country of Study: United Kingdom
Application Procedure: To apply, click the green Apply Now button on the Scholarship page and complete our online application form. science-scholarships@swansea.ac.uk

Additional Information: www.bournemouth.ac.uk/study/postgraduate-research/fees-funding/studentships-scholarships/mres-scholarships

For further information contact:

Macquarie University, NSW 2109, Australia.

Email: science-scholarships@swansea.ac.uk

PhD Fees-only Bursaries

Eligibility: Open to good Master's graduates from the United Kingdom/European Union who will be commencing PhD studies at Swansea University
Level of Study: Doctorate
Type: Scholarship
Value: Covers United Kingdom/European Union tuition fees
Length of Study: 3 years
Frequency: Annual
Study Establishment: Swansea University
Country of Study: United Kingdom
Application Procedure: Please contact us for an application form
No. of awards given last year: 10

For further information contact:

Email: admissions-enquiries@swansea.ac.uk

Swansea University Masters Scholarships

Eligibility: Open to students from the United Kingdom/European Union who will be starting an eligible master's course at Swansea University for the first time in September
Level of Study: Postgraduate
Type: Scholarship
Value: £2,900 towards tuition fees
Length of Study: 1 year full time or 2 to 3 years part-time
Frequency: Annual
Study Establishment: Swansea University
Country of Study: United Kingdom
Application Procedure: Eligible students are sent an application form when offered a place on a course
Closing Date: 17 July
No. of awards given last year: 100
Additional Information: www.swansea.ac.uk/science/postgraduatescholarships/swansea-science-masters-scholarships/

S

For further information contact:

Postgraduate Admissions Office Swansea University, Singleton Park, Sketty, Swansea SA2 8PP, United Kingdom.

Email: science-scholarships@swansea.ac.uk

Swansea University PhD Scholarships

Eligibility: Open to good Master's graduates from the United Kingdom/European Union who will be commencing PhD studies at Swansea University
Level of Study: Doctorate, Postgraduate
Type: Scholarship
Value: Annual stipend at Rcuk level (approx.£14,000)
Length of Study: 3 years
Frequency: Annual
Study Establishment: Swansea University
Country of Study: United Kingdom
Application Procedure: Please see individual scholarship listings on our website www.swansea.ac.uk/postgraduate/scholarships/research
No. of awards given last year: 15

For further information contact:

Postgraduate Admissions Office Swansea University, Singleton Park, Sketty, Swansea SA2 8PP, United Kingdom.

Email: postgraduate.admissions@swansea.ac.uk

Swansea University Research Excellence Scholarship

Purpose: The project aims to create novel approaches to contemporary challenges in theoretical and applied ecological and evolutionary biosciences
Level of Study: Doctorate
Type: Scholarship
Value: The scholarship covers the full cost of United Kingdom/European Union tuition fees, plus an annual stipend of £14,553 (in line with the RCUK stipend amount) for 3 years. There will also be £1,000 per annum available for research expenses such as travel, accommodation, field trips and conference attendance
Frequency: Annual
Country of Study: United Kingdom
No. of awards offered: 14
Closing Date: 8 January
Contributor: Swansea University
Additional Information: To apply please complete and return the following documents to Dr Vivienne Jenkins

(pgrsures-at-swansea.ac.uk) using the quote reference COS2 www.postgrad.com/news/Applications-open-for-Swansea-University-Research-Excellence-Scholarships-SURES/2563/

For further information contact:

Email: pgrsures@swansea.ac.uk

The James Callaghan Scholarships

Eligibility: Research students from Commonwealth member countries are eligible to apply. Awards are available for full-time or part-time MPhil or PhD studies
Level of Study: Doctorate, Predoctorate
Type: Scholarship
Value: £1,700 (full-time) and £850 (half-time)
Length of Study: 1 year (MPhil) and 3 years (PhD)
Frequency: Annual
Study Establishment: Swansea University
Country of Study: United Kingdom
Application Procedure: Please contact us for an application form
Closing Date: 1 June
Additional Information: www.advance-africa.com/The-James-Callaghan-Scholarships.html

For further information contact:

Postgraduates Admissions Office Swansea University, Singleton Park, Sketty, Swansea SA2 8PP, United Kingdom.

Email: postgraduate.admissions@swansea.ac.uk

Swedish Institute

Swedish Institute, Virkesvägen 2, SE-120 30 Stockholm, Sweden.

Tel: (46) 8 453 7800
Email: si@si.se
Website: si.se/en/
Contact: The Swedish Institute

SISS is the Swedish government's international awards scheme aimed at developing global leaders. It is funded by the Ministry for Foreign Affairs of Sweden and administered by the Swedish Institute (SI). The programme offers a unique opportunity for future leaders to develop professionally and academically, to experience Swedish society and culture, and to build a long-lasting relationship with Sweden and with each other.

Swedish Institute Scholarships for Global Professionals (SISGP)

Purpose: The Swedish Institute (SI) Scholarships for Global Professionals aims to develop future global leaders that will contribute to the United Nations 2030 Agenda for Sustainable Development and contribute to a positive and sustainable development in their home countries and regions.

Eligibility: You must be a citizen of a country that is eligible for SI scholarships. However, you do not need to reside in the country at the time of the application. You must be liable to pay tuition fees to Swedish universities, have followed the steps of University Admissions and be admitted to one of the eligible Master's programmes by the 7 April. Please note that the Master's programmes you apply for must be eligible for SI scholarships. We give priority to programmes within certain subject areas, depending on your country of citizenship. Work experience: You must have minimum of 3,000 hours of demonstrated employment. - Leadership experience: You must have demonstrated leadership experience from your current or previous employment, or from civil society engagement.

Level of Study: Masters

Type: Scholarship

Value: Living expense of SEK 10,000 and travel allowance of SEK 15,000

Length of Study: One academic year (2 sememsters)

Frequency: Varies

Country of Study: Any country

Application Procedure: A complete application must consist of 1. A completed motivation letter. 2. A CV. 3. Two valid and completed letters of reference. 4. Valid and completed proof of work and leadership experience. 5. A copy of your valid passport

Closing Date: 28 February

Funding: Private

Additional Information: For further information, visit the website. si.se/en/apply/scholarships/swedish-institute-scholarships-for-global-professionals/ www.opportunitiesforafricans.com/swedish-institute-scholarships-for-global-professionals-sisgp-2020-2021/

For further information contact:

Slottsbacken 10, SE-111 30 Stockholm, Sweden.

Swedish Institute Scholarships for the Western Balkans Programme

Purpose: The SI Scholarships for the Western Balkans Programme aims at supporting advanced level studies and research within the field of social sciences in order to forge closer links between the Western Balkans and the European Union, and to contribute to strengthened democracy in the region

Eligibility: The scholarships are intended for PhD students and postdoctoral researchers from Albania, Bosnia-Herzegovina, Kosovo, Macedonia (FYROM), Montenegro and Serbia conducting part of their studies/research in Sweden within the field of social sciences with a special focus on any of the following thematic areas: 1 . Democratic accountability;2. Gender equality, anti-discrimination; 3. Human rights, tolerance, minority groups; 4 Independent media; 5. Pluralistic civil society; 6 .Rule of law; 7. Transparency, anti-corruption.

Level of Study: Doctorate, Postdoctorate

Type: Scholarship

Value: SEK 15,000 per month for PhD students, and SEK 18,000 per month for postdoctoral researchers and senior scientists

Length of Study: 1 year

Frequency: Annual

Country of Study: Sweden

Application Procedure: Online application portal

Closing Date: 10 January

Contributor: Ministry for Foreign Affairs of Sweden and administered by the Swedish Institute (SI)

Additional Information: Please contact mailto: sischolarships@si.se

For further information contact:

Email: sischolarships@si.se

Swedish-Turkish Scholarship Programme for PhD Studies and Postdoctoral Research

Purpose: The Swedish-Turkish Scholarship Programme aims at supporting advanced level studies and research in order to forge closer links between Turkey and the European Union, and to contribute to strengthened democracy and a greater respect for human rights

Eligibility: The scholarships are intended for PhD students and postdoctoral researchers from Turkey conducting part of their studies/research in Sweden within the field of social sciences. You should not be a resident for more than 2 year in Sweden

Level of Study: Doctorate, Postdoctorate

Type: Scholarship

Value: SEK 15,000 per month for PhD students, and SEK 18,000 per month for postdoctoral researchers and senior scientists

Length of Study: 1 year

Frequency: Annual
Country of Study: Sweden
Closing Date: 1 November
Contributor: Ministry for Foreign Affairs of Sweden and administered by the Swedish Institute (SI)
Additional Information: Please contact scholarization. blogspot.com/2010/07/swedish-turkish-scholarship-program. html

For further information contact:

Email: sischolarships@si.se

The Swedish Institute Study Scholarships (SISS)

Purpose: SISS is the Swedish government's international awards scheme aimed at developing global leaders
Eligibility: Applicants must be from an eligible country and have at least 3,000 hours of experience from full-time/part-time employment, voluntary work, paid/unpaid internship, and/or position of trust. Applicants must display academic qualifications and leadership experience. In addition, applicants should show an ambition to make a difference by working with issues which contribute to a just and sustainable development in their country, in a long term perspective. The travel grant is a one-time payment of SEK 15,000
Level of Study: Foundation programme
Type: Scholarship
Value: The scholarship covers both tuition fees (paid directly to the Swedish university/university college by the Swedish Institute) and living expenses to the amount of SEK 10,000 per month. There are no additional grants for family members
Length of Study: The scholarship is intended for full-time master's level studies of one or two years, and is only awarded for programmes starting in the autumn semester. The scholarship covers the whole duration of the master's programme
Country of Study: Any country
Closing Date: 19 February
Funding: Government
Contributor: Ministry for Foreign Affairs of Sweden
Additional Information: si.se/en/apply/scholarships/ swedish-institute-scholarships-for-global-professionals/

The Swedish Institute Study Scholarships for South Africa

Purpose: The programme offers a unique opportunity for future leaders to develop professionally and academically, to experience Swedish society and culture, and to build a long-lasting relationship with Sweden and with each other

Eligibility: Only citizens of South Africa are eligible for SISSA.
Level of Study: Masters Degree
Type: Scholarship
Value: The scholarship covers both tuition fees, Living expenses of SEK 10,000/month and Travel grant of SEK 15,000
Length of Study: Whole duration of the master's programme
Country of Study: Sweden
Application Procedure: Online application
No. of awards offered: 10
Closing Date: 19 February
Contributor: Ministry for Foreign Affairs of Sweden and administered by the Swedish Institute (SI)
Additional Information: si.se/en/apply/scholarships/ swedish-institute-scholarships-for-south-africa/

For further information contact:

Email: sischolarships@si.se

Visby Programme Scholarships

Purpose: The aim of the Visby Programme is to support individual mobility, thereby contributing to increased contacts and collaborations between actors in Sweden and countries in the EU Eastern Partnership and Russia. The goal is to build an integrated, knowledge-based and research-intense region, centred on the Baltic Sea while also including EU Eastern Partnership countries and Russia
Eligibility: The candidates who are interested in applying for Masters degree program at university must possess a full time bachelor's degree from an accredited university in their nation with good academic score as the allotment of scholarships are completely merit based and the candidate should demonstrate good leadership skills and good oral and written skills in the languages that are mentioned compulsory to obtain education from Sweden.
Level of Study: Doctorate, Postdoctorate
Type: Scholarship
Value: monthly grant of SEK 9,000 covers tuition fees, insurance, travel expenses of SEK 5,000
Country of Study: Any country
No. of awards offered: 50
Closing Date: 9 February
Additional Information: Please contact scholarship-fellowship.com/visby-programme-scholarships-for-masters-level-studies/

For further information contact:

Email: markus.boman@si.se

Swedish Natural Science Research Council (NFR)

Box 7142, SE-10387 Stockholm, Sweden.

Tel: (46) 85 464 400
Email: gfar-secretariat@fao.org
Website: www.gfar.net/
Contact: Grants Management Officer

GFAR makes agri-food research and innovation systems more effective, responsive and equitable, towards achieving Sustainable Development Goals. Partners in GFAR, at national, regional and international levels, advocate for, and catalyse Collective Actions that strengthen and transform agri-food research and innovation systems

NFR FRN Grants for Scientific Equipment

Purpose: To assist researchers
Eligibility: Open to individuals holding a research grant from any Swedish research council
Level of Study: Research
Type: A variable number of grants
Value: Up to SEK 10,000,000
Length of Study: Dependent on the requirements of the projects
Frequency: Annual
Study Establishment: Universities
Country of Study: Sweden
Application Procedure: Applicants must contact the organisation for details
Funding: Government

For further information contact:

Tel: (46) 84 544 254
Email: lars@nfr.se

NFR Travel Grants

Purpose: To give financial support to researchers attending conferences or wishing to undertake short-term research abroad
Eligibility: Open to Swedish researchers and foreign national researchers who have completed their PhD at a Swedish university and have embarked on postdoctoral studies
Level of Study: Postdoctorate, Research
Type: Travel grant
Value: Travelling expenses and subsistence

Length of Study: Up to 2 months
Frequency: Throughout the year
Study Establishment: Universities or academic institutions abroad
Country of Study: Sweden
Application Procedure: Applicants must complete an application form
Closing Date: 15 August
Funding: Government

For further information contact:

Tel: (46) 84 544 229
Email: elisa@nfr.se

Swinburne University of Technology

PO Box 218, Hawthorn, VIC 3122, Australia.

Tel: (61) 3 9214 8000
Email: webmaster@swin.edu.au
Website: www.swinburne.edu
Contact: MBA Admissions Officer

It provides career-orientated education and as a university with a commitment to research. The University maintains a strong technology base and important links with industry, complemented by a number of innovative specialist research centres which attract a great deal of international interest. A feature of many Swinburne undergraduate courses is the applied vocational emphasis and direct industry application through Industry Based Learning (IBL) programs. Swinburne was a pioneer of IBL program which places students directly in industry for vocational employment as an integral part of the course structure. Swinburne is committed to the transfer of lifelong learning skills. It is heavily involved in international initiatives and plays a significant part in the internationalization of Australia's tertiary education system.

Chancellor's Research Scholarship

Purpose: To award students of exceptional research potential to undertake a higher degree by research (HDR)
Eligibility: Open to a local or an international student undertaking a higher degree by research (HDR) with Bachelor Degree with First Class Honours. For further details, please check the website
Level of Study: Doctorate, Postgraduate
Type: Research scholarship

Value: An annual stipend of US$30,000, an Establishment Grant of up to US$3,000, up to US$5,000 for a 6-month overseas placement, up to US$840 thesis allowance, Tuition fees and Relocation allowance
Length of Study: 3 years
Frequency: Annual
Application Procedure: Check website for further details
Additional Information: Please refer website for details: www.swinburne.edu.au/study/options/scholarships/215/chancellors-research-scholarship-/

For further information contact:

Building 60Wm, Level 7, 60 William Street, Hawthorn Campus, VIC 3122, Australia.

Tel: (61) 9214 5547 or 9214 8744
Email: HDRscholarships@swin.edu.au

PhD in Mechatronics

Purpose: To provide full time scholarships to undertake the degree of Doctor of Philosophy (PhD) at the Faculty of Engineering and Industrial Sciences of Swinburne University of Technology
Eligibility: Applicants should have completed an undergraduate course in engineering preferably in mechatronics or electrical engineering. Candidates with a Masters Degree in a related area or with previous research experience will be given priority
Level of Study: Doctorate
Type: Scholarship
Value: AU$19,616 per year
Length of Study: 3 years
Country of Study: Australia
Application Procedure: Check website for further details
Closing Date: 20 July

For further information contact:

Swinburne University of Technology, PO Box 218, VIC 3122, Australia.

Tel: (61) 61 3 9214 5659
Email: arad@swin.edu.au

Swinburne University Postgraduate Research Award (SUPRA)

Purpose: To assist with general living costs

Eligibility: Applicants must hold a bachelor's degree with first-class honours or equivalent.
Level of Study: Doctorate, Research
Type: Research award
Value: A$27,082 Annual stipend A$27,082 (indexed) (2018 rate) for three years (with possible 6 month extension). Tuition fees for up to four years. Thesis allowance
Length of Study: 3 years (Research Doctorate)
Country of Study: Australia
Application Procedure: Complete an application for admission to research higher degree candidature and scholarship and mail/courier or you can scan your application forms in and email them
Closing Date: October
Additional Information: www.swinburne.edu.au/study/options/scholarships/221/swinburne-university-postgraduate-research-award/

For further information contact:

Tel: (61) 9214 5547 or 9214 8744
Email: ehill@swin.edu.au

Vice Chancellor's Centenary Research Scholarship (VCRS)

Purpose: To assist with general living costs
Eligibility: Open to domestic or an international student who have completed a Bachelor degree with First Class Honours and are of exceptional research potential undertaking a higher degree by research (HDR). For further details, please check the website
Level of Study: Research
Type: Research scholarship
Value: The value of the VCRS will be up to US$35,000 (tax-exempt) over a maximum period of up to 3.5 full-time years, payable at the rate of US$5,000 per year for the 1st year and US$12,000 per year for the remaining 2.5 years
Length of Study: 3 years
Country of Study: Australia
Application Procedure: Check website for further details

For further information contact:

Building 60Wm, Level 7, 60 William Street, Hawthorn Campus, VIC 3122, Australia.

Tel: (61) 9214 5547 or 9214 8744
Email: ehill@swin.edu.au

Swiss National Science Foundation (SNSF)

Wildhainweg 20, PO Box CH-3001 Berne, Switzerland.

Tel: (41) 31 308 2222
Email: com@snf.ch
Website: www.snf.ch/
Contact: Dr Benno G Frey, Office for Fellowship
               Programmes

The Swiss National Science Foundation (SNSF) supports scientific research at Swiss universities and other scientific institutions and awards fellowships to Swiss scientists or scientists living in Switzerland. The SNSF was established in 1952 as a private foundation entrusted with the promotion of basic non commercial research. While the SNSF supports research through grants given to established or promising researchers, it does not maintain its own research institutions. The main objectives of the SNSF are to support basic research in all areas of academic research and to support young scientists and researchers, with the intent of ensuring the continuing high quality of teaching and research in Swiss higher education. In addition to the general research funding, the SNSF is responsible for the National Research Programmes (NRP).

Swiss National Science Foundation Fellowships for Prospective Researchers

Purpose: To promote holders of MA or PhD degrees, who have had at least one year's experience in active research after the completion of their degree
Eligibility: Open to promising young scholars under the age of 33 who are Swiss nationals or permanent residents of Switzerland, hold an MA or PhD and can demonstrate at least one year's experience in active research. An exception to the age restriction (to a maximum of two years) can be made for candidates from clinical disciplines, or candidates who have interrupted their scientific careers due to family obligations. The main condition for such an exception is that the candidate has reached a high scientific level and will in the future pursue an active career in science and research. A high priority will be given to candidates who plan to return to Switzerland
Level of Study: Postdoctorate, Predoctorate
Type: A variable number of fellowships
Value: US$35,000 (tax-exempt)
Length of Study: 3.5 years

Frequency: Annual
Study Establishment: Universities worldwide
Country of Study: Australia
Application Procedure: Applicants must complete an application form, available from the Local Research Commission. Candidates with a degree from a Swiss university should contact the Research Commission of their institution. Candidates with Italian as their native language, who have completed their studies in a foreign country should contact the Research Commission for the Italian speaking part of Switzerland. Swiss candidates who are residents of foreign countries, hold a degree from a foreign university, but who intend to return to Switzerland should contact the Swiss scientific academy responsible for their area of research
Additional Information: For further information please contact Benno Frey or Laurence at the Office for Fellowship Programmes, or refer to the website www.snf.ch/SiteCollectionDocuments/stip_ang_weisungen_mySNF_e.pdf

For further information contact:

Email: ehill@swin.edu.au

Syracuse University

900 South Crouse Ave, Syracuse, NY 13244, United States of America.

Tel: (1) 315 443 1870
Website: www.syracuse.edu/

New information and technology. New worldviews and attitudes. New breakthroughs and challenges. It's all happening right now. And Syracuse University is in the middle of it all. In a world undergoing extraordinary transformation, leadership and innovation are more critical than ever. Our students work alongside leading scholars and have access to hands-on research and learning opportunities-all of which prepare them to shape their communities and become the change-makers of tomorrow.

Syracuse University Executive MBA Programme

Length of Study: 2 years
Application Procedure: Applicants must return a completed 'Independent Study MBA' application form
Closing Date: 7 May
Additional Information: onlinebusiness.syr.edu/mba/

For further information contact:

School of Management, Suite 100, Crouse-Hinds School of Management, Syracuse, NY 13244, United States of America.

Tel: (1) 315 443 3006
Fax: (1) 315 443 5389
Email: grad@gwmail.syr.edu

Syracuse University MBA

Purpose: All Syracuse MBA scholarships are awarded based on merit and the qualifications shown on a student's admission application. Applicants are not required to apply separately for merit-based scholarships
Eligibility: To be eligible for the MBA admission, listed below are the requirements. 1. A United States bachelor's degree or its equivalent from an accredited college or university Completed application. 2. Recommended minimum GPA is 3.0 on a 4.0 scale. 4. GMAT or GRE exam. 5. Recommended minimum GMAT score is 600. The 2016 entering class average was 623. 6. For those with GRE scores you can convert them to GMAT through the website www.ets.org/gre/institutions/about/mba/comparison_tool. 7. Program code for GMAT is NG0-SB-40. 8. Institution code for GRE is 2823. 9. English exam (for international students). 10. Minimum total score for TOEFL is 100, IELTS 7.0, PTE 68. 11. Preferred speaking score for TOEFL is 24, IELTS 7.5, PTE 65. 12. Institution code for TOEFL is 2823, department code is 02 if required. 13. PTE Academic program code is 5LD-BQ-15. 14. IELTS Whitman downloads IELTS scores that have been transmitted to our e-download account
Length of Study: 1 to 2 years
Country of Study: Any country
Application Procedure: Applicants must complete the application form (including the specified number of photocopies) with official academic transcripts, two letters of recommendation, personal essays, requested financial documents, Graduate Management Admission Test and TOEFL (if applicable)

scores, and a fee of US$50. Applications may be fully completed online
Additional Information: whitman.syr.edu/programs-and-academics/programs/whitman-mba-experience/fulltime-mba-experience/index.aspx

For further information contact:

School of Management Syracuse University, Suite 100, Crouse-Hinds School of Management, Syracuse, NY 13244, United States of America.

Tel: (1) 315 443 4492
Fax: (1) 315 443 3423
Email: lescis@syr.edu

System for Analysis Research and Training (START)

International START Secretariat, 2000 Florida Avenue NW Suite 200, Washington, DC 20009, United States of America.

Tel: (1) 202 462 2213
Email: START@agu.org
Website: www.start.org
Contact: Professor Roland Fuchs, Director

START was founded in 1992 to strengthen capacities for global environmental change science in Africa and Asia that addresses critical sustainability challenges. Our programs and partnerships provide opportunities for training, research, education and networking that strengthen scientific skills and inspire leadership. A world in which developing countries strengthen their capacities to use science to advance sustainability. To increase opportunities for research, education and training that strengthen scientific capacities in developing countries to understand, communicate and motivate action on critical global environmental change challenges.

T

Tante Marie's Cooking School

271 Francisco Street, San Francisco, CA 94133, United States of America.

Tel: (1) 415 788 6699
Email: peggy@tantemarie.com
Website: www.tantemarie.com

Mary Risley started Tante Marie's Cooking School as a full-time School over 30 years ago. In 1997, she was honored as the Cooking Teacher of the Year by BON APPETIT magazine. Mary Risley's career has spanned over 40 years of teaching people to cook. Tante Marie's Kitchen focusses on her passion of keeping the fun in cooking.

Tanzania Communications Regulatory Authority (TCRA)

20 Sam Nujoma Road, P.O Box 474, Dar es Salaam, 14414, Tanzania.

Tel: (255) 22 219 9760 8
Email: dg@tcra.go.tz
Website: www.tcra.go.tz

The Tanzania Communications Regulatory Authority (TCRA) is a quasi-independent Government body responsible for regulating the communications and broadcasting sectors in Tanzania. It was established under the TCRA Act no. 12 of 2003 to regulate the electronic communications, and postal services, and management of the national frequency spectrum in the United Republic of Tanzania.

Tanzania Communications Regulatory Authority ICT Scholarship

Purpose: The scholarship offers Tanzania students the opportunity to obtain degrees in the Information and Communication Technologies (ICT) and related areas
Eligibility: The scholarship will be awarded on the basis of academic merit and an interview to be conducted by the Scholarship Panel
Level of Study: Postgraduate
Type: Scholarship
Length of Study: All scholarships are provided for the specified duration of a particular degree course
Country of Study: Tanzania
Closing Date: 20 July
Funding: International office
Additional Information: Tanzanian students can apply for these ICT scholarships www.tcra.go.tz/images/headlines/ScholarshipAdvertReadvertisement2015-16.pdf

Tata Trusts

Bombay House, 24, Homi Mody Street, Mumbai 400 001, India.

Tel: (91) 22 6665 8282
Email: talktous@tatatrusts.org
Website: www.tatatrusts.org/

The Tata Trusts symbolise humanitarianism and personify the prodigious force that advances new frontiers of social and economic development. Tata Trusts have constantly endeavoured to achieve societal and economic development for attaining self-sustained growth relevant to the nation. They support an assortment of causes such

© Springer Nature Limited 2022
Palgrave Macmillan (ed.), *The Grants Register 2023*,
https://doi.org/10.1057/978-1-349-96053-8

as health, nutrition, education, water and sanitation, livelihoods, social justice and inclusion, skilling, migration and urbanisation, environment, digital literacy, sports, arts, craft and culture, and disaster management to name a few.

Lady Meherbai D. TATA Education Trust

Purpose: The Lady Meherbai D Tata Education Trust awards scholarships to Indian women graduates of recognised universities to pursue higher education abroad, towards the tuition fee.

Eligibility: Indian women graduates from a recognised university. 1. Should have a consistently remarkable academic record. 2. Must have applied for admission / secured admission to reputed accredited universities or institutions in the United States, United Kingdom or Europe for the current academic year. 3. Preference will be given to candidates with a minimum of 2 years of work experience in the requisite fields of study.

Level of Study: Graduate

Type: Grant

Value: Scholarship amount of ₹600,000 per student is awarded, depending on the performance of candidate.

Frequency: Annual

Country of Study: Any country

Application Procedure: Applications have to be processed through mailing process. Application forms will be emailed to the students on request from 11 March to 19 April. Application forms will be emailed to the applicants upon submission of a neatly typed letter / email giving details of 1. The course they wish to pursue. 2. The university they will be attending. 3. The course fee required. 4. Sources of funding. 5. Their current profile along with documents for the same.

Closing Date: 10 May

Funding: Private

Additional Information: Students shortlisted for the interviews and scholarships awarded would be solely at the discretion of the Trustees of the Lady Meherbai D Tata Education Trust www.tatatrusts.org/upload/scholarship-announcement-2019-2020.pdf

For further information contact:

Bombay House, 24, Homi Mody Street, Mumbai, Maharashtra 400 001, India.

Email: igpedulmdtet@tatatrusts.org

Te Pôkai Tara Universities New Zealand

PO Box 11915, Manners Street, Wellington 6142, New Zealand.

Tel: (64) 404 381 8500
Email: kiri@nzvcc.ac.nz
Website: www.nzvcc.ac.nz
Contact: Kiri Manuera, Scholarships Manager

The New Zealand Vice Chancellors Committee (NZVCC) was established by the Universities Act 1961, which replaced the Federal University of New Zealand with separate institutions. Today the Committee represents the interests of New Zealand's 8 universities. The NZVCC represents the interests of the New Zealand university system to government, its agencies and the public through a range of forums and communications from joint consultative groups to electronic and print publications.

William Georgetti Scholarships

Purpose: To encourage postgraduate study and research in a field that is important to the social, cultural or economic development of New Zealand.

Eligibility: Applicants must: 1. Have resided in New Zealand for a period of at least five years immediately preceding the year of selection (refer to the Regulations for further information). 2. Be of good moral character and repute. 3. Be of good health. 4. Hold a degree from a university in New Zealand or elsewhere or any other academic qualification of a university or other institution of learning (in New Zealand or elsewhere) reasonably equivalent in the opinion of the Scholarship Board to a degree of a university in New Zealand.

Level of Study: Postgraduate

Type: Scholarship

Value: NZ$45,000 per year

Frequency: Annual

Study Establishment: Suitable universities

Country of Study: Any country

Application Procedure: Apply online: universitiesnz.communityforce.com/

Closing Date: 1 February

Funding: Private

Contributor: The Georgetti Trust

Additional Information: Further information is available on request. www.universitiesnz.communityforce.com/www.universitiesnz.ac.nz/scholarships/william-georgetti-scholarship

For further information contact:

Email: scholarshipscf@universitiesnz.ac.nz

Technical University of Denmark (DTU)

Anker Engelunds Vej 1 Bygning 101A, DK-2800 Lyngby, Denmark.

Tel: (45) 45 25 11 56
Email: oerstedpostdoc@adm.dtu.dk
Website: www.dtu.dk/

DTU is recognized internationally as a leading university in the areas of the technical and the natural sciences, renowned for our business-oriented approach, our focus on sustainability, and our amazing study environment. DTU has a vision for a better world, and we invite the world to join us in realizing that vision.

Technische Universiteit Delft (TUD)

Post bus 5, NL-2600 AA Delft, Netherlands.

Tel: (31) 15 278 9111
Email: info@tudelft.nl
Website: www.tudelft.nl/msc

Founded in 1842, the Delft University of Technology is the oldest, largest, and most comprehensive technical university in the Netherlands. It is an establishment of both national importance and significant international standing. Renowned for its high standard of education and research, TU Delft collaborates with other educational establishments and research institutes, both within and outside of the Netherlands. TU Delft aims at being an, interactive partner to social issues, committed to answering its multifaceted demands and initiating changes to benefit people in the future.

The Shell Centenary Scholarship Fund, Netherlands

Purpose: To give students the opportunity to study at the TUD and gain skills that will make a long-term contribution to the further development of their countries

Eligibility: Open to candidates who are nationals of and resident in any country other than the ones listed in the official website and aged 35 years or under, intending to study a subject that will be of significant value in aiding the sustainable development of their home country, fluent in spoken and written English, and neither a current nor former employee of the Royal Dutch/Shell Group of companies
Level of Study: Postgraduate
Type: Scholarship
Value: Full-cost scholarship including tuition fees, international travel, living allowances and health insurance
Length of Study: 2 years
Frequency: Annual
Country of Study: Netherlands
Application Procedure: Applicants must have been admitted to a MSc programme of TU Delft, the International Office will subsequently send you the application form by email, the International Office will check your application on the basis of the Royal Dutch/Shell criteria
Closing Date: 15 December
Contributor: TUD with support from The Shell Centenary Scholarship Fund (TSCSF)

For further information contact:

Tel: (31) 15 278 5690
Email: msc2@tudelft.nl

Tel Aviv University (TAU)

PO Box 39040, Tel Aviv 6997801, Israel.

Tel: (972) 3 640 8111
Email: tauinfo@post.tau.ac.il
Website: www.tau.ac.il

Tel Aviv University (TAU) was founded in 1956 and is located in Israel's cultural, financial and industrial heartland, TAU is the largest university in Israel and the biggest Jewish university in the world. TAU offers an extensive range of programmes in the arts and sciences.

Tel Aviv University Scholarships

Purpose: To encourage innovative and interdisciplinary research that cuts across traditional boundaries and paradigms.

Eligibility: Open to candidates who have registered for their Doctoral or Postdoctoral degree.
Level of Study: Doctorate, Postdoctorate
Type: Scholarships
Value: Minimum award amount is US$500
Frequency: Annual
Application Procedure: Applicants can download the application form from the website. The completed application form along with a curriculum vitae and a description of research project with a list of publications is to be sent.
Closing Date: 30 April
Additional Information: Applications if sent by email, must be directed to ddprize@post.tau.ac. il www.international.tau. ac.il/scholarship_programs

For further information contact:

The Lowy School for Overseas Students, Tel-Aviv University, Center Building, Israel.

Email: scholarship@tauex.tau.ac.il

Texas LBJ School

2300 Red River St., Stop E2700, Sid Richardson Hall, Unit 3, Austin, TX 78712-1536, United States of America.

Tel: (1) 512 471 3200
Email: lbjdeansoffice@austin.utexas.edu
Website: www.lbj.utexas.edu/

The LBJ School boasts of a dynamic community of students, faculty and staff all working toward the same goal of making an impact on the world. Sitting in on an actual LBJ class can be a great way to get a feel for the community and the program. Use the course schedule to find a course that interests you, and email the concerned professor directly for more details.

Barbara Jordan Baines Report Fellowship Fund

Purpose: The Barbara Jordan Baines Report Fellowship Fund is available to students interested in gaining skills in policy writing and storytelling, as well as exercising leadership through managing the student-run publication.
Eligibility: The Baines Report Fellowship supports a master's student pursuing skills in writing about public policy and experience in news media and content creation. Preference will be given to applicants with prior writing or

journalism experience. All currently enrolled full-time LBJ School Master's students who are in good academic standing are eligible to apply.
Level of Study: Graduate
Type: Funding support
Value: Students are eligible up to US$750 fund and US$500 toward travel funds.
Frequency: Annual
Country of Study: Any country
Application Procedure: Apply using the common Current Student Endowed Fellowship Application form, located on the right side of this page. Students must also submit a current resume, a letter of interest, two writing samples and one well-planned story idea. Final candidates may be interviewed. For further details, check the following link www.lbj.utexas.edu/sites/default/files/BJBREligCriteria.pdf
Funding: Private
Additional Information: In addition, both the fall and spring fellowship awards provide US$500 towards travel to attend the Journal of Public and International Affairs (JPIA) reading weekend in February, contingent on JPIA's invitation. JPIA provides main meals and lodging www.lbj.utexas.edu/lbj-school-fellowships#Baines%20Report

For further information contact:

Lyndon B. Johnson School of Public Affairs, The University of Texas at Austin, P.O. Box Y, Austin, TX 78713-8925, United States of America.

Email: lbjdeansoffice@austin.utexas.edu

Elspeth D. Rostow Memorial Graduate Fellowship

Purpose: The LBJ Foundation is supporting the LBJ School of Public Affairs through the Elspeth Rostow Memorial Fellowship Fund.
Eligibility: To be considered for this fellowship, applicants must be degree-seeking master's students who have completed one year of full-time study at the LBJ School with a cumulative GPA of 3.0 or above. There are no exceptions to these requirements.
Level of Study: Graduate
Type: Fellowship
Value: US$3,000.
Frequency: Annual
Country of Study: Any country
Application Procedure: 1. Complete the Elspeth D. Rostow Memorial Graduate Fellowship application. 2. Submit a one-page statement describing your public service related commitments since enrolling in the LBJ School. Your statement should describe the needs of the community served, how the

project pursued addressed those needs, the role you personally played in the public service activities, and the time commitment of the activity. 3. A current resume.

Closing Date: November
Funding: Private
Additional Information: www.lbj.utexas.edu/sites/default/files/RostowCriteria.pdf

For further information contact:

Email: lbjdeansoffice@austin.utexas.edu

Michael and Alice Kuhn Summer Fellowships

Purpose: The Kuhn Fellowship grant, made possible by the Michael and Alice Kuhn Foundation, awards each grantee US$6,000 to cover living expenses during their summer internship.

Eligibility: 1. A selection committee will review applications on a rolling basis and recommend applicants with demonstrated commitment to the goals of the Kuhn Summer Fellowship Program to promote social justice and fight poverty. 2. Students with diverse backgrounds receive priority consideration. 3. The selection committee may make requests in addition to the online application, such as official UT transcripts and/or interviews. 4. The selection committee will make its recommendations to the LBJ School leadership. Final selection is at the discretion of school leadership.

Level of Study: Graduate
Type: Fellowship
Frequency: Annual
Country of Study: Any country
Application Procedure: The student's summer work must be done for a nonprofit organization in Central Texas or the United States whose mission is related to social justice and alleviating poverty. There is an interest in supporting students whose placements involve leadership opportunities in the areas of public and legislative advocacy, program-related management, as well as opportunities to work with executive team members on strategic priorities and projects. Students will be asked to link to a Google Drive PDF copy of their 1. Resume. 2. Relevant three- to five-page writing sample from school or professional setting. 3. Offer letter from the nonprofit confirming the internship and description of work.

Closing Date: 30 April
Funding: Commercial, Private
Additional Information: www.lbj.utexas.edu/michael-and-alice-kuhn-summer-fellowships

For further information contact:

Email: LBJFellowships@austin.utexas.edu

Terrell Blodgett Fellowship for Government Services in Urban Management and Finance

Purpose: The Blodgett Fellowship is awarded annually on a competitive basis as part of the internship fellowship process.

Eligibility: The Blodgett Fellowship is awarded annually on a competitive basis as part of the internship fellowship process. First-year master's students pursuing an internship in local government and/or city management are eligible to apply. To be considered for this fellowship, applicants must be degree-seeking master's stundents.

Level of Study: Graduate
Type: Fellowship
Frequency: Annual
Country of Study: Any country
Application Procedure: To apply, students must complete the LBJ internship fellowship application and submit it along with their approved internship request form, a letter from the agency supervising the internship, a one-page essay on career goals, and a current resume. Using the following link for further information. www.blodgettfellows.org/

Closing Date: April
Funding: Private
Additional Information: www.lbj.utexas.edu/sites/default/files/Blodgett%20Criteria%20PDF.pdf

For further information contact:

Email: lbjwriting@austin.utexas.edu

The Churchill Fellowship

Website: www.churchillfellowship.org
Contact: Communications Director

Churchill Fellowship

Subjects: Churchill Fellowships explore the whole spectrum of challenges facing the UK. They are focussed around eight universal themes in society: Arts and culture, Community and citizenship, Economy and enterprise, Education and skills, Environment and resources, Health and wellbeing, Governance and public provision, and Science and technology. There is also an Open category for anything else.

Purpose: Churchill Fellowships fund UK citizens from all areas of society to travel overseas for 4-8 weeks in search of practical solutions for today's most pressing problems. On their return, Fellows are helped to make change happen in their community or sector in the UK.

Eligibility: Open to all UK citizens resident in the UK aged 18 years and above, regardless of their qualifications or background. We do not fund gap year activities, courses, volunteering, academic studies, degree placements, internships, medical electives or post-graduate studies.
Level of Study: Unrestricted
Type: Fellowship
Value: Average award is £7,000
Length of Study: 4 - 8 weeks
Frequency: Annual
Country of Study: Any country
Application Procedure: Applications must be made using the online form: churchilltrust.force.com/app/s/
No. of awards offered: Up to 150 each year
Funding: Private, Trusts
No. of awards given last year: 141
No. of applicants last year: 1405
Additional Information: To hear when applications open, you can sign up for application alerts on our website at www.churchillfellowship.org

For further information contact:

The Winston Churchill Memorial Trust, GPO Box 1536, Canberra ACT 2601, Australia.

Email: office@churchillfellowship.org

The Community Foundation of South Alabama

P.O. Box 990, Alabama 36601-0990, United States of America.

Tel: (1) 251 438 5591
Email: lbolton@communityfoundationsa.org
Website: www.communityfoundationsa.org/

The Community Foundation of South Alabama is an Alabama not-for-profit corporation approved by the Internal Revenue Service as a publicly supported organization. We recognize the stewardship of the assets entrusted to us as one of our most important responsibilities.

Harry & Lula McCarn Nurses Scholarship

Subjects: Nursing Administration or other field of nursing
Purpose: To offer financial assistance to a student pursuing a Master's degree in Nursing Administration or a related field.

Eligibility: For a student living in Mobile or Baldwin Counties and pursuing a Master's degree in Nursing Administration or other field of nursing in the USA. Applicants must have a minimum 3.0 GPA.
Type: Scholarship
Study Establishment: University of South Alabama
Country of Study: United States of America
Additional Information: www.communityfoundationsa.org/apply-for-a-scholarship

The Foundation for Advancement of Diversity in IP Law

1400 Crystal Drive, Suite 600, Arlington, VA 22202, United States of America.

Tel: (1) 703 412 1313
Email: admin@diversityinIPlaw.org
Website: www.diversityiniplaw.org/

For nearly two decades the Foundation, formerly the American Intellectual Property Law Education Foundation, has worked for the advancement of diversity in the IP profession. In addition to the program's historic focus on underrepresented racial and ethnic group members already in law school, the Foundation's Scholar Program is now tailored to support underrepresented individuals who are seeking law school admission in order to explore a career in patent law.

AIPLEF Sidney B. Williams Scholarship

Subjects: Law
Purpose: The Foundation for Advancement of Diversity in IP Law is a charitable organization whose mission is to increase the diversity of the IP bar by providing scholarships and mentoring to underrepresented minority law school students pursuing careers in IP law.
Eligibility: Be enrolled as an entering law school (1L) student. Have proven academic performance at the undergraduate, graduate, and law school levels (if applicable). Have a financial need. Have record of leadership, community activities, and/or special accomplishments. Demonstrate intent to engage in the full-time practice of patent law. Are currently enrolled in or have been accepted to an ABA-accredited law school.
Type: Scholarship
Value: Students will be selected to receive a three-year scholarship of up to US$30,000 (US$10,000 per academic year,

US$5,000 per semester, which can only be applied to verifiable costs associated with average tuition and usual fees).

Length of Study: Three years

Country of Study: United States of America

Additional Information: The curriculum of law school, as it relates to intellectual property law, is not considered in awarding scholarships. Applicants related to a trustee of AIPLEF, a council member of the ABA-IPL Section, Officer or member of the Board of Directors of the AIPLA, or a member of the AIPLEF Scholarship Committee are ineligible to apply. Scholarship recipients are required to attend law school, day or evening, on either a full-time or part-time enrollment basis, and to maintain a grade point average of "B" (3.0) or better. Scholarship recipients are required to join and maintain membership in AIPLA. www.communityfoundationsa.org/apply-for-a-scholarship

The Gerda Henkel Foundation

Malkastenstrasse 15, D-40211 Dusseldorf, Germany.

Tel:	(49) 211 93 65 24 0
Email:	info@gerda-henkel-stiftung.de
Website:	www.gerda-henkel-stiftung.de/en/

The Gerda Henkel Foundation was established in June 1976 by Lisa Maskell in memory of her mother Gerda Henkel as an incorporated foundation under civil law, headquartered in Düsseldorf. The Gerda Henkel Foundation concentrates its support on the historical humanities. In connection with funded projects, the Foundation also provides assistance for social support measures as part of complementary projects.

Lost Cities Funding Programme

Subjects: Abandoned cities

Purpose: The aim of the program is to describe the tangible cultures of interpretation, knowledge and perception within these different contexts. Lost Cities are part of a distinct culture of memory, for example, which serves for the negotiation of identities, the preservation of knowledge cultures, the formulation of criticism of progress, or the construction of mythical or sacral topographies as part of a veritable "ruin cult". On this basis, the focus here should not be on the question of which factors led to the city's abandonment. Rather, it is the abandoned cities themselves that are of particular interest, as well as the different forms of their interpretation, instrumentalization and coding in various cultures and time frames.

Eligibility: Eligible to apply are post-doctoral researchers based in a university and working in the area of the humanities and the social sciences. Funding can be provided for projects with a thematic focus being addressed by a group of researchers. The Foundation uses the term "group of researchers" to mean associations of at least two researchers actively involved in the project work which is to be funded by means of scholarships from the Foundation and who are carrying out research into the same issues. Applications can only be made for PhD or research scholarships. Applications for a research scholarship by the applicant (project leader) are also possible. A maximum total of three scholarships per group of researchers can be applied for, as well as funds for travel and materials. A fundamental prerequisite for a grant is that project staff conduct their own research, which is published under their name. Other contributors who are not financed by scholarships can also be involved in the project. Scholarship applications made by individual researchers outside of the group are not accepted. The funding programme also provides for the project partners to participate in a public "workshop discussion on Lost Cities" organised by the Foundation.

Type: Grant

Value: €2,300 monthly scholarship, plus a bonus €400 grant for one child and €100 for each further child

Length of Study: 36 months

Country of Study: Any country

Closing Date: 2 June

Additional Information: The Foundation generally accepts applications for research projects made by universities, other research institutes or comparable institutions as well as by one or several Postdocs or scholars with Post Doctoral Lecture Qualification. www.gerda-henkel-stiftung.de/en/lost_cities

The Lynde and Harry Bradley Foundation

1400 N. Water Street, Suite 300, Milwaukee, WI 53202, United States of America.

Tel:	(1) 414 291 9915
Website:	www.bradleyfdn.org/

The Bradley Foundation envisions a nation invigorated by the principles and institutions that uphold our unalienable rights to life, liberty, and the pursuit of happiness. The Bradley Foundation seeks to further those beliefs by supporting the study, defense, and practice of the individual initiative and ordered liberty that lead to prosperity, strong families, and vibrant communities.

Grants

Subjects: Projects may address any arena of public life economics, politics, culture or civil society. As such, support is provided to schools of business, economics, public policy and more for activities including research, general operating expenses, graduate and post-graduate fellowships, seminars and speakers programs.

Purpose: Supports projects that "nurture a solid foundation of competent, self-governing citizens, who are capable of and responsible for making the major political, economic and moral decisions that shape their lives."

Eligibility: See website.

Type: Grant

Value: Varies

Country of Study: Any country

Application Procedure: The application process proceeds in two stages. First, brief letters of inquiry are required. If the foundation determines the project to be within its policy guidelines, the applicant will receive a brochure with further application instructions.

Closing Date: 1 December

Additional Information: www.bradleyfdn.org

The Marfan Foundation

22 Manhasset Avenue, Port Washington, NY 11050, United States of America.

Tel: (1) 516 883 8712
Email: research@marfan.org
Website: www.marfan.org/
Contact: Josephine Grima, PhD Chief Science Officer The Marfan Foundation

The Marfan Foundation's mission is to save lives and improve the quality of life of individuals with Marfan syndrome and other genetic aortic conditions. Our values in our mission to save and improve lives, we hold a number of core beliefs and values that drive everything we do: We put families at the heart of what we do. Marfan syndrome and related conditions affect not only individuals but also the people who love them. We stand with and for the whole community.

Faculty Grant Program

Purpose: We provide financial support for investigators studying any or all disciplines involving Marfan syndrome and related conditions.

Eligibility: The principal investigator must hold an MD, DO, PhD, ScD, DDS, DVM or equivalent degree. The investigator must have proven ability to pursue independent research as evidenced by original research publications in peer-reviewed journals and should hold a position of Associate Professor or above. Faculty members with less experience who have obtained an NIH R-01 grant are also eligible for the faculty grant award. Work can be performed in the U.S. or internationally and non U.S. appointments are acceptable.

Level of Study: Postgraduate

Type: Grant

Value: The Marfan Foundation will award up to three 2-year US$100,000 grant.

Frequency: Annual

Country of Study: Any country

Application Procedure: The application must be submitted electronically, including the application forms, additional pages, and appendices, as a single PDF file, via The Marfan Foundation website, www.marfan.org. Please name your application using the following format FacultyGrant_Lastname_FirstName.pdf Example FacultyGrant_Smith_Jane.pdf The application forms may be completed by using the free Adobe Reader program. If you do not already have it, you can download it at www.adobe.com/products/reader. html. The Title Page form requires dated signatures; you may either insert a digital signature and date or print the form and then scan it to include in your application PDF. Additional pages should be typed single-spaced using a font size of at least a 10 points and with one inch margins. Pages should be numbered at the bottom. Appendices should not be used to subvert the page limitation on the grant, however, figures, tables, diagrams and photographs can be placed in the appendices. Please present the proposal in the order that follows THE MARFAN FOUNDATION FACULTY GRANT GUIDELINES 5 1. Title Page 1 page Application form provided 2. Table of Contents 1 page Application form provided 3. Project Abstract and Lay Person Summary 1 page each On a single page, describe precisely and clearly the nature, objective, methods of procedure and significance of the proposed research project, and how it relates to the goal of providing a better understanding of Marfan syndrome, EDS, LDS, and other related disorders and/or improving the treatment or diagnosis of Marfan syndrome, EDS, LDS, and other related disorders (limit 300 words). Rewrite the abstract in abbreviated form in terms suitable for presentation to lay persons (limit 500 words). 4. Research Plan 3 pages a. Include Goals and Objectives; Rationale; Methodology; Evaluation. (Figures may be placed in appendix if needed). b. Please comment upon the importance of funding i. Will this funding allow you to pursue studies that would otherwise not be performed? Is funding meant to supplement other sources of support? ii. Do you anticipate that this funding will increase your competitiveness for other funding sources? c. Please comment upon the significance of the work that you propose i. Is it similar to or a direct extension of work that has been or is being performed elsewhere? ii. Does the work complement or extend other studies that are being performed at your institution? iii. How novel are the studies that you describe? iv. Would such a proposal be competitive for NIH funding in its current form, or would you require additional preliminary data? v. Do you anticipate that the support would lead to the generation of physical resources that might be useful to other investigators in the field? vi. If so, would you be willing to make them widely available? 5. Budget and Justification List full budget with amount requested. Include a. Names, titles, time/percentage effort of all participants, requested salaries and fringe benefits and total amount required. b. Statement that the institution or other funding sources will absorb indirect costs. c. A written budget justification. 6 The budget justification should be suited to the proposal. It is important that the investigators match the dollar award with the actual project. If funding from other sources is being used to cover certain parts of the study, please elaborate on what parts of the budget will not be completed with Foundation funding and what the approximate costs of the full project would be. No overhead or indirect costs will be considered. List the additional sources of funding if budget exceeds proposal amount. 6. Other Support 2 pages List other support received by principal and co-investigators for any projects (include yearly and total budget and duration of any grants) a. Current b. Pending c. Description (in a paragraph, describe each current or pending grant and whether it has scientific or budgetary overlap with the present proposal). 7. Biographical Sketches 5 pages each. Using the supplied form, please provide biographical sketches for key personnel. Indicate the total number of publications in each of the (2) categories referenced articles and invited works. If you prefer, you may use the NIH biosketch form instead. 8. Facilities Description 1 page Describe the research facilities (laboratory space, clinical population, etc) available for the project. 9. Appendix a. Figures, tables etc. b. Literature cited c. Human subjects experimental approval d. Vertebrate animal experimental approval Letters of support.

Closing Date: January

For further information contact:

Email: jgrima@marfan.org

The National Academies of Sciences, Engineering and Medicine

500 Fifth St., N.W., Washington, DC 20001, United States of America.

Tel: (1) 202 334 2000
Email: worldwidewebfeedback@nas.edu
Website: www.nationalacademies.org/

The National Academies of Sciences, Engineering, and Medicine provide independent, objective advice to inform policy with evidence, spark progress and innovation, and confront challenging issues for the benefit of society.

Gulf Research Program Science Policy Fellowships

Subjects: Science policy
Purpose: The Gulf Research Program's Science Policy Fellowship program helps scientists hone their skills by putting them to practice for the benefit of Gulf Coast communities and ecosystems. Fellows gain first-hand experience as they spend one year on the staff of federal, state, local, or non-governmental environmental, natural resource, oil and gas, and public health agencies in the Gulf of Mexico region.
Eligibility: Applicants must: 1. Be currently enrolled in a doctoral program or hold an eligible degree, including MA/MS, MPH/MSPH, PhD, ScD, EngD, MD, DrPH, and DVM. For applicants not currently enrolled in a doctoral program, eligible degrees must be completed by August 15, 2023, and conferred by December 31, 2023. Applicants currently enrolled in a doctoral program must take a leave of absence for the duration of the fellowship. 2. Come from an area of research – including social and behavioral sciences, health sciences and medicine, engineering and physical sciences, earth and life sciences, and interdisciplinary scientific fields – relevant to the charge of the Gulf Research Program to focus on "human health and environmental protection including issues relating to offshore oil drilling and hydrocarbon production and transportation in the Gulf of Mexico and on the United States' outer continental shelf." 3. Be a U.S. citizen, U.S. national, or lawful permanent resident. 4. Not be currently employed by the U.S. federal government. Full-time, paid, permanent federal employees are not eligible for the fellowship.
Type: Fellowship
Value: Fellows who have completed an MA, MS, or MPH degree or who are currently enrolled in a doctoral program will receive an annual stipend of US$45,000. Fellows who have completed a PhD, ScD, MD, or DVM will receive an annual stipend of US$55,000. Stipends will be paid directly to the fellow in monthly disbursements.
Frequency: Annual
Country of Study: Any country
Application Procedure: Applications submitted through the online application system.
Closing Date: 2 March

For further information contact:

Email: GulfFellowships@nas.edu

The Gulf Research Program's Early-Career Research Fellowship

Purpose: The Gulf Research Program's Early-Career Research Fellowship supports emerging scientific leaders as they take risks on research ideas not yet tested, pursue unique collaborations, and build a network of colleagues who share their interest in improving offshore energy system safety and the well-being of coastal communities and ecosystems.

Eligibility: The Human Health and Community Resilience track goal focuses on contributing to the advancement of health equity in the Gulf of Mexico region or Alaska by considering the social determinants of health. Applicants must, at the time of application: 1. Hold a permanent, fully independent position as an investigator, faculty member, clinician scientist, or scientific team lead in industry, academia, or a research organization. A postdoc is not considered a fully independent position. 2. Be an early-career scientist who has received their eligible degree within the past 10 years (on or after September 1, 2012). 3. Hold a doctoral degree (e.g., PhD, ScD, EngD, MD, DrPH) in the social and behavioral sciences, health sciences and medicine, engineering and physical sciences, earth and life sciences, or interdisciplinary scientific fields relevant to the charge of the Gulf Research Program. 4. Be affiliated with a non-federal U.S. institution that has a valid tax ID number. 5. Not be currently employed by the U.S. federal government.

Value: US $76,000

Country of Study: Any country

Application Procedure: See website: www.nationala cademies.org/our-work/early-career-research-fellowship/for-applicants

Closing Date: 12 January

For further information contact:

Email: GulfFellowships@nas.edu

The National GEM Consortium

1430 Duke Street, Alexandria, VA 22314, United States of America.

Tel: (1) 703 562 3646
Email: info@gemfellowship.org
Website: www.gemfellowship.org/

The mission of The National GEM Consortium is to enhance the value of the nation's human capital by increasing the participation of underrepresented groups at the master's and doctoral levels in engineering and science.

MS Engineering and Science Fellowship Program

Subjects: Engineering

Purpose: The objective of this program is to promote the benefits of a Masters degree within industry.

Type: Fellowship

Value: 1. US$4,000 living stipend per full-time semester up to 4 semesters (US$8K per academic year – 3 quarters) 2. Minimum US$16,000 total stipend over the entire Master's program 3. Up to two paid summer internships with a GEM Employer Member 4. Full tuition and fees provided by a GEM University Member

Country of Study: United States of America

Application Procedure: See website.

Additional Information: www.gemfellowship.org/students/gem-fellowship-program/

PhD Engineering and Science Fellowship

Subjects: Engineering

Purpose: The objective of this program is to offer doctoral fellowships to underrepresented minority students who have either completed, are currently enrolled in a Master's in an Engineering program, or received admittance into a PhD program directly from a Bachelor's degree program.

Type: Fellowship

Value: During the first academic year of being awarded the GEM Fellowship, the GEM Consortium remits a stipend and a cost of instruction grant to the institution where the fellow is enrolled. Thereafter, up to the fifth year of the doctoral program, continued financial support of the GEM Fellow is borne by the GEM University through alternative sources of funding such as institutional awards, assistantships or other external fellowships. Fellows recieve US$16,000 stipend in the first academic year of the GEM Fellowship; GEM Member University provides a living stipend up to the 5th year of the PhD program, equivalent to other funded doctorate students in the department; a minimum of one paid summer internship with a GEM Employer Member; full tuition and fees at a GEM University Member

Country of Study: Any country

Application Procedure: See website.

PhD Science Fellowship

Subjects: Chemistry, physics, earth sciences, mathematics, biological sciences, and computer science.

Purpose: The goal of this program is to increase the number of minority students who pursue doctoral degrees in the natural science disciplines

Eligibility: Applicants to this program are accepted as early as their senior undergraduate year, as well as candidates currently enrolled in a Master's of Engineering program and working professionals.

Type: Fellowship

Value: During the first academic year of being awarded the GEM Fellowship, the GEM Consortium remits a stipend and a cost of instruction grant to the institution where the fellow is enrolled. Thereafter, up to the fifth year of the doctoral program, continued financial support of the GEM Fellow is borne by the GEM University through alternative sources of funding such as institutional awards, assistantships or other external fellowships. Fellows recieve US$16,000 stipend in the first academic year of the GEM Fellowship; GEM Member University provides a living stipend up to the 5th year of PhD program, equivalent to other funded doctorate students in the department; a minimum of one paid summer internship with a GEM Employer Member; full tuition and fees at a GEM University Member

Country of Study: Any country

Application Procedure: See website.

Closing Date: 15 November

Additional Information: Fellowships offered through this program are portable and may be used at any participating GEM Member University where the GEM Fellow is admitted. www.gemfellowship.org/students/gem-fellowship-program/

The National Hispanic Scholarship Fund

P.O. Box 160113, Orlando, FL 32816-0113, United States of America.

Tel: (1) 407 823 2827
Website: www.hsf.net/

Founded in 1975, the Hispanic Scholarship Fund empowers students and parents with the knowledge and resources to successfully complete a higher education, while providing support services and scholarships. HSF empowers students and parents with the knowledge and resources to successfully complete a higher education, while providing support services and scholarships to as many exceptional students, HSF Scholars, and Alumni as possible. Hispanics are a highly educated and influential community of courageous leaders, thriving and positively shaping all areas of a strong American society, from science and technology to entertainment, from finance to government.

HSF Scholarship

Subjects: All

Purpose: The HSF Scholarship is designed to assist students of Hispanic heritage obtain a university degree.

Eligibility: 1. Must be of Hispanic heritage 2. U.S. citizen, permanent legal resident, or DACA 3. Minimum of 3.0 GPA on a 4.0 scale (or equivalent) for high school students; minimum of 2.5 GPA on a 4.0 scale (or equivalent) for college and graduate students 4. Plan to enroll full-time in an accredited, public or not-for-profit, four-year university, or graduate school, in the US, for the 2023–2024 academic year 5. Submit the FAFSA or state-based financial aid forms (if applicable)

Type: Scholarship

Value: Award amounts range from US$500 - US$5,000, based on relative need.

Country of Study: United States of America

No. of awards offered: 10,000

Additional Information: www.hsf.net

The Thomas R. Pickering Foreign Affairs Fellowship Program

2216 6th Street NW, Washington, DC 20059, United States of America.

Tel: (1) 202 806 6495
Email: pickeringfellowship@howard.edu
Website: pickeringfellowship.org/

The Thomas R. Pickering Foreign Affairs Fellowship Program is a program funded by the U.S. Department of State, administered by Howard University, that attracts and prepares outstanding young people for Foreign Service careers in the U.S. Department of State. It welcomes the application of members of minority groups historically underrepresented in the State Department, women, and those with financial need. Based on the fundamental principle that diversity is a strength in our diplomatic efforts, the program values varied backgrounds, including ethnic, racial, social, and geographic diversity.

The Thomas R. Pickering Foreign Affairs Fellowship

Subjects: Public policy, international affairs, public administration, business, economics, political science, sociology, or foreign languages.

Purpose: Prepares outstanding young people for Foreign Service careers in the U.S. Department of State. It welcomes the application of members of minority groups historically underrepresented in the State Department, women, and those with financial need.

Eligibility: Must be seeking admission to a two-year, full-time, on-campus, Master's degree program at a U.S.-based graduate institution in an academic field relevant to the work of the Foreign Service. Must have a cumulative grade point average of 3.2 or higher on a 4.0 scale.

Type: Fellowship

Value: US$37,500 annually for a two-year period for tuition, room, board, books, and mandatory fees for completion of two-year Master's degrees. This includes up to US$21,500 per year for tuition and mandatory fees and an academic year stipend of US$16,000.

Length of Study: Two years

Frequency: Annual

Study Establishment: Howard University

Country of Study: United States of America

No. of awards offered: 30

Closing Date: September

Additional Information: Law degrees do not satisfy this requirement. Fellows are expected to maintain a cumulative GPA of 3.2 throughout their period of study. Applicants apply to two-year graduate programs at U.S.-based universities simultaneously with their application to the Pickering Program. www.pickeringfellowship.org/

The White House

1600 Pennsylvania Ave NW, Washington, DC 20500, United States of America.

Website: www.whitehouse.gov/

The White House is where the President and First Family of the United States live and work, but it's also the People's House, where we hope all Americans feel a sense of inclusion and belonging.

The White House Fellowship

Subjects: All

Purpose: The White House Fellowship is a highly competitive opportunity to participate in and learn about the Federal Government from a unique perspective.

Eligibility: See website.

Type: Fellowship

Value: The work assignment provides the Fellow the opportunity to observe closely the process of public policy development and to come away with a sense of having participated in the governmental process as well as having made an actual contribution to the business of government.

Country of Study: Any country

Closing Date: 1 February

Additional Information: Fellows typically spend a year working as full-time, paid special assistants to senior White House Staff, the Vice President, Cabinet Secretaries and other top-ranking government officials. Fellows also participate in an education program consisting of roundtable discussions with renowned leaders from the private and public sectors, and trips to study U.S. policy in action both domestically and internationally. pickeringfellowship.org/

Third World Academy of Sciences (TWAS)

TWAS Executive Director ICTP Enrico Fermi Building, Room 108, Via Beirut 6, I-34151 Trieste, Italy.

Tel: (39) 40 2240 327
Email: edoffice@twas.org
Website: www.twas.org

The Third Word Academy of Sciences (TWAS) is an autonomous international organization that promotes and supports excellence in scientific research and helps build research capacity in the South.

Council of Scientific and Industrial Research/ TWAS Fellowship for Postgraduate Research

Purpose: To enable scholars from developing countries (other than India) who wish to pursue postgraduate research to undertake research in laboratories or institutes of the CSIR

Eligibility: Candidates must have a Master's or equivalent degree in science or engineering and should be a regular employee in a developing country (other than India) and be holding a research assignment.

Level of Study: Postgraduate

Type: Fellowship

Value: Monthly stipend to cover for living costs, food and health insurance.

Length of Study: Up to 4 years

Frequency: Annual

Study Establishment: CSIR research laboratories or institutes.
Country of Study: India
Application Procedure: One copy of the application should be sent to TWAS and three copies to CSIR. Application forms are available on request or from the website.
Closing Date: 31 July
Funding: Government
Contributor: CSIR (India), the Italian Ministry of Foreign Affairs and the Directorate General for Development Co-operation
No. of awards given last year: 8

For further information contact:

International S&T Affairs Directorate, Council for Scientific and Industrial Research (CSIR), Anusandhan Bhavan, 2 Rafi Marg, New Delhi, Delhi 110001, India.

Tel: (39) 040 2240 314, (91) 11 2331 6751
Fax: (91) 11 2371 0618, (39) 040 2240 689
Email: fellowships@twas.org; anuradha@csir.res.in

OWSD PhD Fellowships for Women Scientists

Purpose: The PhD fellowship for women scientists from Science and Technology Lagging Countries (STLCs) supports them to undertake PhD research in the Natural, Engineering and Information Technology sciences at a host institute in the South.
Eligibility: For details, please go to the relevant OWSD website: owsd.net/career-development/phd-fellowship
Level of Study: Postgraduate
Type: Fellowship
Length of Study: Up to 4 years
Frequency: Annual
Country of Study: Any country
Closing Date: 15 April

Seed Grant for New African Principal Investigators (SG-NAPI)

Subjects: Agriculture, Biology, Chemistry, Earth Sciences, Engineering, Information Computer Technology, Mathematics, Medical Sciences and Physics
Purpose: With the support of the German Federal Ministry of Education and Research (BMBF), TWAS launches a new programme to strengthen the capacity of African countries lagging in science and technology. The new programme is aimed at young scientists who are getting established in their country or about to return home to an academic position.

Under this scheme, grants are awarded to promising high-level research projects in Agriculture, Biology, Chemistry, Earth Sciences, Engineering, Information Computer Technology, Mathematics, Medical Sciences and Physics carried out in African countries lagging in science and technology identified by TWAS.
Eligibility: 1. Applying Principal Investigator must be a national of an eligible country, who holds a PhD and has good research experience. The grant should operate within a university or a research institution in one of the African countries lagging in science and technology. The PI must be 40 years or under. Any applicant turning 41 years in the year of application is not eligible. 2. The PI must have obtained their Ph.D. within the last 5 years in a country other than their home country. 3. The PI must have returned to their home country (refer to list in the guidelines) within the last 36 months or before the end of 2022. 4. The PI must hold, be offered or be in the process of accepting a position at an academic and/or research institution (including international research centers) in their home country. 5. The PI must be national of an eligible African country that is lagging in science and technology (refer to list in the giudelines). 6. Applicant must at the time of application NOT have an active research grant with TWAS or OWSD Early Career Women Scientists (ECWS) Fellowship. 7. Applications from women scientists and those working in Least Developed Countries are especially encouraged. 8. The applicant must submit a strong Research Proposal (you may find further information on how to write a strong proposal by visiting AuthorAID). Please be advised that applicants may apply for only one programme per calendar year in the TWAS and OWSD portfolio. Applicants will not be eligible to visit another institution in that year under the TWAS Visiting Scientists or the Visiting Professor programmes. One exception: The head of an institution who invites an external scholar to share his/her expertise under the TWAS Visiting Professor programme or the TWAS Visiting Expert programme may still apply for another programme.
Level of Study: Postdoctorate
Type: Grant
Value: Maximum of US$67,700
Frequency: Annual
Country of Study: Any country
Application Procedure: SG-NAPI grant applications, once the call opens, will need to be submitted online by clicking on the "Apply Now" link at the bottom of this page. Please note the link will only be active once the call opens and not before (or after it is closed).

For further information contact:

Email: sgnapi@twas.org

The Council of Scientific and Industrial Research/ TWAS Fellowship for Postdoctoral Research

Subjects: 01-Agricultural Sciences, 02-Structural, Cell and Molecular Biology, 03-Biological Systems and Organisms, 04-Medical and Health Sciences incl. Neurosciences, 05-Chemical Sciences, 06-Engineering Sciences incl. Computing and IT, 07-Astronomy, Space and Earth Sciences, 08-Mathematical Sciences, 09-Physics

Purpose: To enable scholars from developing countries (other than India) who wish to pursue postdoctoral research to undertake research in laboratories or institutes of the CSIR.

Eligibility: The minimum qualification requirement is a PhD degree in science or technology. Applicants must be regular employees in a developing country (but not India) and should hold a research assignment. Be a maximum age of 45 years on December 31st of the application year.

Level of Study: Postdoctorate

Type: Fellowship

Value: Monthly stipend to cover for living costs, food and health insurance.

Length of Study: Up to 12 months

Frequency: Annual

Study Establishment: CSIR research laboratories or institutes

Country of Study: India

Application Procedure: Applicants must complete an application form, available on request or from the website.

Closing Date: 31 July

Funding: Government

Contributor: CSIR (India), the Italian Ministry of Foreign Affairs and the Directorate General for Development Co-operation.

No. of awards given last year: 4

Additional Information: CSIR is the premier civil scientific organization of India, which has a network of research laboratories covering wide areas of industrial research www.twas. org/opportunity/twas-csir-postdoctoral-fellowship-programme

For further information contact:

Tel: (39) 040 2240 314, (91) 11 2331 6751
Fax: (91) 11 2371 0618, (39) 040 2240 689
Email: fellowships@twas.org, anuradha@csir.res.in

TWAS-COMSTECH Science in Exile PhD fellowship programme for displaced and refugee scientists

Subjects: 01-Agricultural Sciences 02-Structural, Cell and Molecular Biology 03-Biological Systems and Organisms 04-Medical and Health Sciences incl. Neurosciences 05-Chemical Sciences 06-Engineering Sciences incl.

Computing and IT 07-Astronomy, Space and Earth Sciences 08-Mathematical Sciences 09-Physics

Purpose: UNESCO-TWAS has partnered with the Ministerial Standing Committee on Scientific and Technological Cooperation of the Organization of Islamic Cooperation (COMSTECH) for the UNESCO-TWAS-COMSTECH Science in Exile Fellowship Programme for displaced and refugee scholars and scientists. The PhD Fellowship Programme aims to provide displaced and refugee scholars and scientists who have not yet found a safe and long-term host country to pursue doctoral studies in Pakistan, at institutions members of the COMSTECH Consortium of Excellence (CCoE).

Eligibility: Applicants for these fellowships must meet the following criteria: 1. They must be displaced or refugee scholars and scientists. 2. They must be currently living in Pakistan and holding the right to live and study in the country, OR able to travel to Pakistan. 3. Please note that the Programme is not suitable for scholars at risk who need specific assistance to leave their home country. Awardees are responsible for arranging the logistics and safety of their own relocation. Please note there is only a very small number of competitive travel bursaries available. 3. They must hold a Master's Degree as well as a Bachelors in the field of natural sciences, applied sciences, engineering and technology, health sciences, software engineering and computer.

Level of Study: Postdoctorate, Postgraduate (MSc)

Type: Fellowship

Length of Study: Up to 12 months

Frequency: Annual

Country of Study: Any country

Application Procedure: Applicants may apply for only one of the two types of the UNESCO-TWAS – COMSTECH Science in Exile Fellowships Programme. To learn about the Postdoctoral fellowships, please visit: twas.org/opportunity/twas-comstech-postdoctoral-fellowship-programme-displaced-and-refugee-scientists

Closing Date: 4 February

For further information contact:

Email: displacedscientists@twas.org, events@comstech.org

TWAS-SN Bose Postgraduate Fellowship Programme

Subjects: Chemical Sciences, Mathematical Sciences, Physics

Purpose: TWAS-SN Bose Postgraduate Fellowships are tenable at the S.N. Bose National Centre for Basic Sciences in Kolkata, India for studies leading towards a PhD degree in the physical sciences for four years with the possibility of a one-year extension.

Eligibility: 1. Be a maximum age of 35 years on 31 December of the application year; 2. Be nationals of a developing country (other than India); 3. Must not hold any visa for temporary or permanent residency in India or any developed country; 4. Hold a Masters Degree in physics, mathematics or physical chemistry. S/He must have completed at least a total 5 years of undergraduate and postgraduate studies in a recognized university or institute. 5. Provide evidence of proficiency in English, if medium of education was not English; 6. Provide evidence that s/he will return to her/his home country on completion of the fellowship; 7. Not take up other assignments during the period of her/his fellowship; 8. Be financially responsible for any accompanying family members.

Level of Study: Postgraduate

Type: Fellowship

Length of Study: 5 years

Frequency: Annual

Study Establishment: S.N. Bose National Centre for Basic Sciences

Country of Study: Any country

Closing Date: 31 July

For further information contact:

Tel: (91) 33 2335 5706

Fax: (91) 33 2335 3477

Email: deanap@bose.res.in, studentsprogramme@boson. bose.res.in, fellowships@twas.org

Thomson Foundation

Thomson Foundation, 46 Chancery Lane, London WC2A 1JE, United Kingdom.

Tel: (44) 29 2035 3060

Email: enquiries@thomfound.co.uk

Website: www.thomsonfoundation.co.uk

The Thomson Foundation provides practical, intensive training both in the United Kingdom and abroad, along with a wide range of consultancies to journalists, managers, technicians and production staff in television, radio and the press.

Thomson Foundation Scholarship

Purpose: To enable recipients to attend Thomson Foundation training courses in Britain.

Eligibility: Open to professional journalists and broadcasters with at least 3 years of full-time experience.

Level of Study: Professional development

Type: Scholarship

Value: Varies

Length of Study: Varies, usually a 12-week Summer course or a shorter 4-week course.

Study Establishment: The Thomson Foundation

Country of Study: United Kingdom

Application Procedure: Applicants must complete an application form, available from the Foundation, for the courses they wish to apply for

No. of awards offered: 20

Closing Date: 15 April

Funding: Government, Private

Contributor: The British Foreign Office Chevening Scholarship Scheme.

No. of awards given last year: 6

No. of applicants last year: 20

Additional Information: Annual 3-month courses in television, radio and press journalism run from June to September Webpage not open www.twas.org/opportunity/twas-csir-postdoctoral-fellowship-programme

For further information contact:

Email: enquiries@thomsonfoundation.org

Thurgood Marshall College Fund (TMCF)

901 F Street NW, Suite 300, Washington, DC 20004, United States of America.

Tel: (1) 202 507 4851

Email: info@tmcfund.org

Website: www.thurgoodmarshallfund.org

The Thurgood Marshall College Fund (TMCF) was established in 1987 to carry on Justice Marshall's legacy of equal access to higher education by supporting exceptional merit scholars attending America's public historically Black colleges and universities. More than 5,000 Thurgood Marshall Scholars have graduated and are making valuable contributions to science, technology, government, human service, business, education and various communities

Center for Advancing Opportunity Doctorial Fellowship

Subjects: Education, criminal justice, and entrepreneurship

Purpose: CAO supports faculty and students at Historically Black Colleges and Universities (HBCUs) and other post-secondary institutions to develop research-based solutions to the most challenging issues. Our constituency is people living in fragile communities and they are members of all races, ethnicities, and religions.

Eligibility: Must be a current doctoral student at an accredited college or university. Must have received a four-year undergraduate degree from an HBCU, have a current cumulative grade point average of 3.0 or higher, be able to demonstrate leadership abilities and be able to demonstrate a financial need.

Type: Fellowship

Value: Scholars will be selected to receive a scholarship up to US$15,000 for the academic school year (US$7,500 per semester which can only be applied to verifiable costs associated with average tuition and usual fees).

Study Establishment: A Historically Black College and University (HBCU).

Country of Study: United States of America

No. of awards offered: Up to five

CVS Health Pharmacy Scholarship

Purpose: To offer financial assistance to outstanding students attending one of the three pre-selected publicly-supported Historically Black College and University (HBCU) and Predominantly Black Institution (PBI) Pharmacy Schools within the TMCF 47 member-school network.

Eligibility: Must be enrolled as a full-time graduate or doctoral student. Must have a current grade point average of 3.0 or higher. Must demonstrate outstanding financial need and must demonstrate leadership ability through a variety of measures.

Type: Scholarship

Value: One-year scholarship up to US$5,000 which will be used to cover the costs of tuition and fees, on-campus room and board, and required textbooks purchased from member schools.

Study Establishment: Florida A & M University, Pharmacy School; University of Maryland Eastern Shore, Pharmacy School; and Texas Southern University, Pharmacy School.

Country of Study: United States of America

Additional Information: The recipient must be willing to apply for a CVS Health Summer internship. www.twas.org/opportunity/twas-csir-postdoctoral-fellowship-programme

Thurgood Marshall College Fund Scholarships

Purpose: The Thurgood Marshall College Fund (TMCF) is proud to offer financial assistance to outstanding students attending one of the publicly-supported Historically Black

Colleges and Universities (HBCUs) and Predominantly Black Institutions (PBIs) within the TMCF 47 member-school network.

Eligibility: See website: www.tmcf.org/students-alumni/scholarship/2021-2022-tmcf-all-around-access-scholarship/

Type: Scholarship

Value: Varies

Frequency: Annual

Country of Study: Any country

Application Procedure: All Applicants Must: Answer the following statement. (Video Question): How will your education benefit you, your family, and the community?

Closing Date: 28 February

Additional Information: Refer to the website for details: www.tmcf.org/students-alumni/scholarship/2021-2022-tmcf-all-around-access-scholarship/

For further information contact:

AIPLEF Scholarship, 80 Maiden Lane, Suite 2204, New York, NY 1138, United States of America.

Email: jessica.barnes@tmcfund.org

WGRG Foundation Terri Grier Memorial Scholarship

Subjects: Public policy, public administration, political science, community engagement or other advocacy disciplines.

Purpose: To offer financial aid towards books, tuition and/or other college expenses.

Eligibility: Must be a member of an ethnic minority group African-American (Black), Asian and Pacific Islanders, Hispanic/Latin (Black, White or Asian), Indians (Western and Eastern). Must be a high school senior and/or enrolled in an accredited college or university in the year of the award; demonstrate a 3.0 or higher GPA; demonstrate leadership skills through participation in community/public service, issue advocacy, research, extracurricular, and/or other activities; demonstrate the courage of conviction, persistence, and determination in the pursuit of his or her goals; and demonstrate a commitment to a career in government or the non-profit and advocacy sectors.

Type: Scholarship

Value: At least US$5,000.00 towards your books, tuition and/or other college expenses.

Country of Study: United States of America

Application Procedure: Must complete the online application form; select one individual to complete a reference survey to be submitted by either an educator/college professor, administrator, counselor, employer, or individual with significant knowledge of the applicant's experience and public service engagement; provide an official and recent academic transcript with cumulative grade point average and a class standing/rank; submit a personal essay - in your essay, please answer the question directly in the application.

Toxicology Education Foundation (TEF)

626 Admiral Drive, Ste. C, PMB 221, Annapolis, MD 21401, United States of America.

Tel: (1) 443 321 4654
Email: tefhq@toxedfoundation.org
Website: www.toxedfoundation.org

The mission of TFE is to encourage, support and promote charitable and educational activities that increase the public understanding of toxicology.

Alleghery-ENCRC Student Research Award

Purpose: To support a student's thesis, dissertation and summer research project in toxicology and to encourage them to formulate and conduct meaningful research
Eligibility: Open to students who are members in good standing of AE-SOT. The student's advisor must also be a member in good standing and submit a letter concerning availability
Level of Study: Graduate
Type: Award
Value: Up to US$1,000
Frequency: Annual
Country of Study: United States of America
Application Procedure: Applicants must send four copies of completed application form along with a project description and budget
Closing Date: 30 May

For further information contact:

CDC/NIOSH MS 2015, 1095 Willowdale Road, Morgantown, WV 26505, United States of America.

Email: LBattelli@cdc.gov

Colgate-Palmolive Grants for Alternative Research

Purpose: To identify and support efforts that promote, develop, refine or validate scientifically acceptable animal alternative methods to facilitate the safety assessment of new chemicals and formulations

Level of Study: Research
Type: Research grant
Value: Plaque and maximum award of US$40,000
Frequency: Annual
Country of Study: United States of America
Application Procedure: Application is available online. A research plan, budget, curriculum vitae and a letter from the institution must be sent
Closing Date: 9 October
Funding: Private
Contributor: Colgate-Palmolive
No. of awards given last year: 5
Additional Information: www.toxicology.org/awards/sot/awards.aspx?AwardID=79

For further information contact:

Colgate-Palmolive Grants for Alternative Research, Society of Toxicology, 11190 Sunrise Valley Dr, Suite 300, Reston, VA 20191, United States of America.

Food Safety SS Burdock Group Travel Award

Purpose: To cover travel expenses for a student to attend the Annual Meeting
Eligibility: Open to full-time graduate students with research interests in toxicology. Students in their early graduate training, who have not attended any SOT Annual Meeting are encouraged to apply
Level of Study: Graduate
Value: Up to US$1000 per student
Frequency: Annual
Country of Study: United States of America
Application Procedure: Applicants must send a letter of request indicating that he/she is enroled in good standing in a doctoral training programme. The applicant must also state how the research and training relate to food safety
Closing Date: 15 January

For further information contact:

Email: tberdum@burdockgroup.com

Regulation and Safety SS Travel Award

Purpose: To help defray the costs of travel to the SOT meeting
Eligibility: Open to students submitting a poster or making a presentation at the SOT meeting
Type: Travel award
Value: US$1,500 each
Frequency: Annual

Country of Study: United States of America
Application Procedure: Applicants must fill an application form and an abstract of work preserved
Closing Date: 15 December

For further information contact:

Email: jtmacgror@earthlink.net

Robert L. Dixon International Travel Award

Purpose: To financially assist students studying in the area of reproductive toxicology.
Eligibility: Open to applicants enroled full-time in a PhD programme studying reproductive toxicology and are student members of SOT.
Level of Study: Doctorate, Graduate
Type: Award
Value: Includes a stipend of US$2,000 for travel costs to enable students to attend the International Congress of Toxicology meeting.
Frequency: Every 3 years
Country of Study: United States of America and abroad
Application Procedure: Applicants must submit a completed application form, reference letter, graduate transcripts and lists of complete citations of the original work.
Closing Date: 9 October
Contributor: Toxicology Education Foundation
Additional Information: www.toxedfoundation.org/travel-awards/

For further information contact:

Email: crzymama17@gmail.com

Transport Research Laboratory

Crowthorne House, Nine Mile Ride, Wokingham, Berkshire RG40 3GA, United Kingdom.

Website: trl.co.uk/

Transport Research Laboratory, provides impartial world-class research, consultancy, testing and certification for all aspects of transport. Commercially independent, we work with public and private sector organisations to help understand, shape and inform transport decisions. With over 80 years of experience and knowledge embedded within its history and a number of world-renowned experts under our roof, it has positioned itself at the forefront of the future of transport.

A Master of Science Degree Scholarship

Purpose: To financially support postgraduate study
Eligibility: Open to part-time self-financing students only. Applicants must have applied for a place for graduate study at UCL
Level of Study: Postgraduate
Type: Scholarship
Value: United Kingdom/European Union tuition fees
Length of Study: Full time 1 year, Part time 2-3 years
Frequency: Annual
Study Establishment: University College London
Country of Study: United Kingdom
Application Procedure: Applicants should contact the department. If the applicants have not applied to UCL they complete a graduate application form and enclose it with the scholarship application

For further information contact:

Tel: (44) 20 7288 3548
Fax: (44) 20 7288 3322
Email: p.taylor@chime.ucl.ac.uk

Tropical Agricultural Research and Higher Education Center (CATIE)

Cartago, Turrialba 30501, Costa Rica.

Tel: (506) 2558 2106
Email: posgrado@catie.ac.cr
Website: www.catie.ac.cr
Contact: Dean of the Graduate School

The Tropical Agricultural Research and Higher Education Center (CATIE) is an international, non-profit, regional, scientific and educational institution. Its main purpose is research and education in agricultural sciences, natural resources and related subjects in the American tropics, with emphasis on Central America and the Caribbean.

Scholarship Opportunities Linked to CATIE

Purpose: To develop specialized intellectual capital in clean technology, tropical agriculture, natural resources management and human resources in the American tropics
Eligibility: Priority is given to citizens of Belize, Guatemala, El Salvador, Honduras, Nicaragua, Panama, Costa Rica,

Mexico, Venezuela, Colombia, the Dominican Republic, Bolivia and Paraguay

Level of Study: Doctorate, Postgraduate

Type: Scholarship

Value: Tuition and fees

Length of Study: 2 years for a Master

Frequency: Annual

Country of Study: Costa Rica

Application Procedure: Applicants must undertake an admission process that constitutes 75% for curricular evaluation and 25% for a domiciliary examination. Please refer to the CATIE website for full instructions

No. of awards offered: 350

Funding: Foundation, Government, International office, Private

Contributor: ASDI, OAS, CATIE, DAAD, CONACYT (Mexico), Ford Foundation, Kellogg Foundation, Joint/Japan World Bank. USAID provided the original donation for the endowment financing the Scholarship-Loan Program, SENACYT and Belgium Cooperation

No. of awards given last year: 32 in the Scholarship-Loan Program. Over 25 students received funding from alternative sources

No. of applicants last year: 350

Trust Company

Level 15, 20 Bond Street, GPO Box 4270, New South Wales, Sydney, NSW 2001, Australia.

A trust company is a legal entity that acts as a fiduciary, agent, or trustee on behalf of a person or business for a trust. A trust company is typically tasked with the administration, management, and the eventual transfer of assets to beneficiaries.

Miles Franklin Literary Award

Purpose: To reward the novel of the year that is of the highest literary merit and presents Australian life in any of its phases

Eligibility: Refer to the application form. The novel must have been first published in any country in the year preceding the award. Biographies, collections of short stories, children's books and poetry are not eligible. All works must be in English

Level of Study: Unrestricted

Type: Award

Value: AU$60,000

Frequency: Annual

Country of Study: Any country

Application Procedure: Applicants must complete an application form and send six copies of their novel

Funding: Trusts

Contributor: The estate of the late Miss SMS Miles Franklin

No. of awards given last year: 1

Additional Information: If there is no novel worthy of the prize, the award may be given to the author of a play. Please refer to the website for further details: www.milesfranklin.com.au/

For further information contact:

Email:　trustawards@thetrustcompany.com.au

TU Delft

Postbus 5, NL-2600 AA Delft, Netherlands.

Tel:　　　(31) 15 27 89111

Email:　　info@tudelft.nl

Website:　www.tudelft.nl/en/

Delft University of Technology is a public legal entity in accordance with the Higher Education and Research Act. The main tasks include providing scientific education, conducting scientific research, transferring knowledge to society and promoting social responsibility.

Justus & Louise van Effen Excellence Scholarships

Purpose: The Foundation Justus & Louise van Effen was established with the aim of stimulating excellent international MSc students and financially supporting them in their wish to study at TU Delft

Eligibility: Excellent international applicants (conditionally) admitted to one of the 2-year Regular TU Delft's MSc programmes. With a cumulative grade point average (GPA) of 80% or higher of the scale maximum in the bachelor's degree from an internationally renowned university outside The Netherlands

Level of Study: Graduate

Type: Scholarship

Value: €30.000 per year for Non-EU students and €11.500 per year for EU/EFTA students

Frequency: Annual

Country of Study: Any country

Application Procedure: Apply it online. Check with the below link for further information. www.tudelft.nl/en/education/admission-and-application/msc-international-diploma/1-admission-requirements/

No. of awards offered: 2

Closing Date: 1 December

Funding: Private

Additional Information: Membership to the Scholarship club giving access to personal development, workshops, seminars, etc www.tudelft.nl/en/education/practical-matters/scholarships/justus-louise-van-effen-excellence-scholarships/

For further information contact:

NL-2600 AA Delft, Netherlands.

Email: info@tudelft.nl

Turkiye Scholarships Burslari

Oguzlar Mah. Mevlana Boulevard No: 145, Balgat, TR-06520 ANKARA, Turkey.

Tel: (90) 850 455 0 982

Email: info@turkiyeburslari.gov.tr

Website: www.turkiyeburslari.gov.tr/

Through international students studying in Turkey, Turkey's aim is to raise generations that will produce solutions to problems of their countries as well as our world, have equality of opportunity and a supra-national perspective. Turkiye Scholarships is a scholarship program which not only provides financial support but also ensures university placement for students in their intended program of application. With this feature, it differs from other scholarship programs in the world. Apart from university education, it is aimed to provide students with the benefits of social, cultural and academic extra- curricular programs and activities while they are in Turkey.

Turkey Government Scholarships

Purpose: Winning this Turkish scholarship gives the chance to experience a 4-year undergraduate, master or doctoral program at the partner Turkish Universities and that too in English

Eligibility: 1. There is also a strict criterion when it comes to the age of the applicant. 2. For the undergraduate degree, the candidates should not be born earlier than January 1997. 3. While for Master's degree the candidates must not be born before January 1988. For PhDs the date is January 1983 and for Research program the applicants should be born before January 1973. 4. 70% marks required for the application of an undergraduate program. 5. 75% marks required for the application of PhD and Masters. 6. 90% marks required for the application of Medical School programs. 7. Anyone holding Turkish citizenship or having previously held Turkish citizenship cannot apply for the program. 8. Students who are already studying in Turkey are not able to apply for the Scholarship. 9. Students who are selected must present their documents if they are asked otherwise they will not be entertained

Level of Study: Postgraduate, Undergraduate

Type: Scholarship

Value: Free Accomodation, No tuition fees, Health expense, Travel Expenses, Language Course Requirement.

Frequency: Annual

Country of Study: Any country

Application Procedure: Turkey scholarship will be applied with the following terms. 1. University Entrance Exam Grade. 2. Diploma Grade. 3. Average Grades. 4. High School Graduation. 5. International Test Score. 6. CGPA

Closing Date: 20 February

Funding: Private

For further information contact:

Email: intoffice@agu.edu.tr

U

UHasselt University

Hasselt University, Martelarenlaan 42, B-3500 Hasselt, Belgium.

Tel: (32) 11 268 111
Website: www.uhasselt.be/

Civic university, UHasselt, is more than its seven faculties, four research institutes, three research centres, 6,500 students and 1,400 researchers and staff. As civic university, we are strongly committed to the Region and the world. Better through education, research and technology transfer.

Master Mind Scholarships

Purpose: The Flemish Ministry of Education awards scholarships to outstanding students for Master programmes in Flanders and Brussels. The programme aims to promote Flanders and Brussels as a top study destination

Eligibility: 1. Only students who are currently not enrolled at a Flemish higher education institution are eligible. The only exception is made for international students who are enrolled in a preparatory programme only in order to start a master's programme in September. 2. Students who enrol for only a preparatory programme, a bridging programme or a distance learning programme are not eligible. 3. All nationalities can apply, but the previous degree obtained should be from a higher education institution located outside Flanders. 4. Students can not combine this scholarship with another scholarship from the Flemish government or an Erasmus Mundus scholarship.

Level of Study: Masters Degree

Type: Scholarships

Value: The Flemish Ministry of Education awards scholarships of €8.000 per academic year to outstanding students for master programmes in Flanders. A number of scholarships are reserved for students from certain countries: Japan (3), Mexico (3), Palestine (2) and USA (5). More information about the study programmes offered by Hasselt University can be found on our website (UHasselt - Study Programmes).

Frequency: Annual

Country of Study: Belgium

Application Procedure: 1. 2 recommendation letters from professors of your (previous) Home university, University or recent employer written in English. Please merge the 2 letters in 1 PDF document and upload the document here. 2. Students applying for Master of Management or Master of Transportation Sciences also have to upload their admission letter from Hasselt University.

No. of awards offered: 13

Closing Date: 15 March

Funding: Government

Additional Information: docs.google.com/forms/d/e/1FAIpQLSeJS9EqhiB40XPetlXwav-UXP7HjSNbLMeZZeHxV4LpLYLSyg/viewform?usp=sf_link

Union College

Union College Board of Trustees Scholarship

Purpose: This scholarship is worth full tuition

Eligibility: 1. Must attend a college or university in the state of Nebraska. 2. Must be an incoming freshman. 3. Must enroll full-time. 4. Must have a grade point average of 3.9 or higher (or a GED score of 750 or higher). 5. Must have an ACT score of 32 or higher OR an SAT score of 1,500 or higher

Level of Study: Graduate

Type: Scholarship

Value: US$21,250

Length of Study: Varies. Addition of years is possible

Frequency: Annual

© Springer Nature Limited 2022
Palgrave Macmillan (ed.), *The Grants Register 2023*,
https://doi.org/10.1057/978-1-349-96053-8

Country of Study: Any country

Application Procedure: 1. Admissions information is available on the Union College website by clicking on the 'Admissions Policy' link. Admissions applications are available in online and PDF formats. 2. In addition to a completed application, each student must submit an official high school transcript and ACT/SAT scores. 3. Students whose first language is not English must also submit TOEFL (Test of English as a Foreign Language) scores. 4. Admissions applications are available in online and PDF formats. In addition to a completed application, each student must submit an official high school transcript and ACT/SAT scores

Closing Date: 1 April

Funding: Private

Additional Information: www.unigo.com/scholarships/all/union-college-board-of-trustees-scholarship/1005990

For further information contact:

3800 S. 48th St., Lincoln, NE 68506-4386, United States of America.

Tel: (1) 402 486 2600
Email: enroll@ucollege.edu

United Nations Educational, Scientific and Cultural Organization (UNESCO)

7 place de Fontenoy, F-75352 Paris, France.

Tel: (33) 1 45 68 10 00 ext. 81507
Contact: Ms F Abu-Shady, Director, Equipment & Fellowships Division

As early as 1951, a programme to promote and develop youth exchange for educational purposes has existed in UNESCO. The Organization continued its action under the Fellowships Programme to respond to the needs of Member States in the field of human resources development and capacity building. This programme has up to date enabled more than 52,000 fellows from around the world to study in different countries contributing to intellectual solidarity, international cooperation and mutual understanding.

United Nationals Educational Scientific Cultural Organization Individual Fellowships

Purpose: To provide opportunities to further primarily higher education or research generally abroad, and to acquire international experience in fields of study for which appropriate facilities are not available in the country of origin

Eligibility: Open to nationals of UNESCO member states and associate members

Level of Study: Doctorate, Postdoctorate, Postgraduate, Professional development

Type: Fellowship

Value: Monthly allowance usually based on UN stipend scale, plus travel, tuition, books and small equipment costs

Length of Study: No more than 9 months

Frequency: Dependent on funds available

Country of Study: Other

Application Procedure: Application through national authorities specially designated by UNESCO member states (usually National Commission for UNESCO or appropriate Ministry). Direct applications will not be considered.

United Nations Educational, Scientific and Cultural Organization(UNESCO)/International Sustainable Energy DeISEDC Co-Sponsored Fellowships Programme

Purpose: To enhance the capacity-building and human resources development in the area of sustainable and renewable energy sources in developing countries and countries in transition

Eligibility: Holder of at least a BSc degree or BA in Economics; proficient in English language; not more than 35 years of age

Level of Study: Postgraduate

Value: Exempt of paying tuition fees for the entire duration, US$450 is intended to cover living expenses, one-time travel allowance amounting to US$100, cover the cost of the round-trip international travel

Length of Study: This is a four weeks fellowship programme

Country of Study: Any country

Application Procedure: All applications should be endorsed by the National Commission for UNESCO and must be duly completed in English or French

No. of awards offered: 20

Closing Date: 3 April

Contributor: UNESCO/ISEDC

Additional Information: www.scholars4dev.com/24922/unesco-isedc-co-sponsored-fellowships-programme/

For further information contact:

Email: info@oppurtunitydesk.org

United Nations International School of Hanoi

G9 Ciputra Lac Long Quan Road, Tay Ho District, Vietnam.

Tel: (84) 4 3758 1551
Email: info@unishanoi.org
Website: www.unishanoi.org

United Nations International School of Hanoi's mission is to encourage students to be independent, lifelong learners who strive for excellence and become responsible stewards of our global society and natural environment, achieved within a supportive community that values diversity and through a programme reflecting the ideals and principles of the United Nations.

United Nations University - Institute for the Advanced Study of Sustainability (UNU - IAS)

5-53-70 Jingumae, Shibuya-ku, Tokyo 150-8925, Japan.

Tel: (81) 3 5467 1212
Website: ias.unu.edu/

PhD in Sustainability Science

Purpose: The Japan Foundation for UNU (JFUNU) Scholarship is available for outstanding applicants from developing countries who can demonstrate a need for financial assistance and who are granted admissions to the PhD Programme in Sustainability Science at United Nations University Institute for the Advanced Study of Sustainability (UNU-IAS).
Eligibility: Applicants for the PhD in Sustainability Science are required to have met ALL of the following requirements by the application deadline in order to be considered 1. Strong interest in sustainability studies; 2. Demonstrated commitment to study and understand global issues; 3. A completed Master's degree in disciplines related to sustainability studies and a minimum of 2 years of practical field experience related to UNU-IAS research themes OR Two completed Master's degrees, at least one of which must be in disciplines related to sustainability studies; 4. A GPA of 3.5 or above on a 4.0 scale on at least one of the Master's degrees earned; and 5. English language proficiency; 6. Applicants must be from developing countries who can demonstrate a need for financial assistance; 7. Applicants who are currently living in Japan under a working visa are NOT eligible for the scholarship;

8. Applicants who want to pursue a second PhD degree at UNU-IAS are not eligible for the scholarship.
Level of Study: Postgraduate
Value: The scholarship provides a monthly allowance of ¥120,000 for living expenses for a maximum of 36 months. Travel costs to and from Japan, visa handling fees, and health/accident insurance costs must be covered by the student. The tuition fees are fully waived for the scholarship recipients
Country of Study: Japan
Application Procedure: It is important to visit the official website (link found below) to access the application form and for detailed information on how to apply for this scholarship. ias.unu.edu/en/admissions/degrees/phd-in-sustainability-science-2020.html#overview
Closing Date: 9 April
Additional Information: ias.unu.edu/en/admissions/degrees/phd-in-sustainability-science-2022.html#requirements

United States Center for Advanced Holocaust Studies

United States Holocaust Memorial Museum, 100 Raoul Wallenberg Place South West, Washington, DC 20024-2126, United States of America.

Tel: (1) 202 488 0400 / 202 314 7802
Email: vscholars@ushmm.org
Website: www.ushmm.org
Contact: Ms Jo-Ellyn Decker, Program Coordinator

The United States Holocaust Memorial Museum is the United State's national institution for the documentation, study and interpretation of Holocaust history, and serves as the country's memorial to the millions of people murdered during the Holocaust. The Center for Advanced Holocaust Studies fosters research in Holocaust and genocide studies.

United States Commission on International Religious Freedom (USCIRF)

732 N. Capitol Street, N.W., Suite A714, Washington, DC 20401, United States of America.

Tel: (1) 202 523 3240
Email: communications@uscirf.gov
Website: www.uscirf.gov

United States Commission on International Religious Freedom is an independent, bipartisan United States of America federal government commission, the first of its kind in the world, that monitors the universal right to freedom of religion or belief abroad. USCIRF reviews the facts and circumstances of religious freedom violations and makes policy recommendations to the President, the Secretary of State, and Congress. USCIRF Commissioners are appointed by the President and the Congressional leadership of both political parties.

United States Institute of Peace (USIP)

2301 Constitution Avenue, NW, Washington, DC 20037, United States of America.

Tel: (1) 202 457 1700
Email: grant_program@usip.org
Website: www.usip.org
Contact: Ms Cornelia Hoggart, Senior Programme
                    Assistant

The United States Institute of Peace (USIP) is mandated by the Congress to promote education and training, research and public information programmes on means to promote international peace and resolve international conflicts without violence. The Institute meets this mandate through an array of programmes, including grants, fellowships, conferences and workshops, library services, publications and other educational activities.

Jennings Randolph Program for International Peace Dissertation Fellowship

Purpose: To support dissertations that explore the sources and nature of international conflict, and strategies to prevent or end conflict and to sustain peace
Eligibility: Open to applicants of all nationalities who are enroled in an accredited college or university in the United States of America. Applicants must have completed all requirements for the degree except the dissertation by the commencement of the award
Level of Study: Doctorate
Type: Fellowships
Value: Stipends of up to US$20,000 per academic year
Length of Study: 1 year
Frequency: Annual
Study Establishment: The student's home university or site of fieldwork
Country of Study: United States of America

Application Procedure: Application Applications must be submitted through the FLUXX online application system. On the application form, please indicate the scholarship for which you would like to be considered the USIP Peace Scholar fellowship only; Minerva Research Initiative Peace and Security Fellowship only; or no preference. 1. Both fellowships have the same application form, deadline, award amount, and selection process; the only difference between the USIP and Minerva Fellowships is the source of funding. 2. Three letters of recommendation must be attached to your application in the FLUXX system. One letter must be from your dissertation advisor and two from current professors.
Closing Date: 15 October
Funding: Government
No. of awards given last year: 10
Additional Information: The programme does not support work involving partisan political and policy advocacy or policy making for any government or private organization www.usip.org/grants-fellowships/fellowships/jennings-rando lph-peace-scholar-dissertation-fellowship-program

For further information contact:

Tel: (1) 202 429 3853
Email: jrprogram@usip.org

Jennings Randolph Program for International Peace Senior Fellowships

Purpose: To use the recipient's existing knowledge and skills towards a fruitful endeavour in the international peace and conflict management field, and to help bring the perspectives of this field into the Fellow's own career
Eligibility: Open to outstanding practitioners and scholars from a broad range of backgrounds. The competition is open to citizens of any country who have specific interest and experience in international peace and conflict management. Candidates would typically be senior academics, but applicants who hold at least a Bachelor's degree from a recognized university will also be considered
Type: Fellowship
Value: A stipend, an office with computer and voicemail and a part-time research assistant
Length of Study: Up to 10 months
Frequency: Annual
Study Establishment: USIP
Country of Study: United States of America
Application Procedure: Applicants must complete a web-based application form, available on request from the Institute or from the website
No. of awards offered: 136
Closing Date: January

No. of awards given last year: 10
No. of applicants last year: 136

For further information contact:

Tel: (1) 202 429 3886
Email: jrprogram@usip.org

United States-India Educational Foundation (USIEF)

Fulbright House, 12 Hailey Road, New Delhi, Delhi 110001, India.

Tel: (91) 11 2332 8944/48
Email: info@fulbright-india.org
Website: www.fulbright-india.org
Contact: Programme Officer

The activities of the United States Educational Foundation in India (USEFI) may be broadly categorized as the administration of the Fulbright Exchange Fellowships for Indian and United States of America scholars and professionals, and the provision of educational advising services to help Indian students wishing to pursue higher education in the United States. USEFI also works for the promotion of dialogue among fulbrighters and their communities as an outgrowth of educational exchange.

Fulbright Distinguished Awards in Teaching Program for International Teachers

Purpose: It is part of the overall Fulbright Program, named in honor of Senator J. William Fulbright, which promotes mutual understanding among people of the United States and other countries
Eligibility: 1. Be a citizen of India and reside in India at the time of application. 2. Live and teach in the states of Arunachal Pradesh, Assam, Bihar, Jharkhand, Manipur, Meghalaya, Mizoram, Nagaland, Sikkim, Tripura, West Bengal, Chandigarh, Delhi, Haryana, Himachal Pradesh, Jammu and Kashmir, Ladakh, Punjab, Rajasthan, Uttarakhand and Uttar Pradesh; 3. Hold at least a bachelor's degree. A teacher training degree is preferred. 4. Be a full-time teacher teaching any subject at any level (primary, middle, secondary or senior secondary). 5. Have completed at least five years of full-time teaching experience at the program start. 6. Primary and secondary level library media specialists, guidance counselors, curriculum specialists, special education coordinators,

and administrators who spend at least fifty percent of their time teaching or working directly with students may also apply to the program. 7. Teacher trainers are eligible to apply. 8. Demonstrate good English language competence. 9. Demonstrate a commitment to continue teaching or working in their field after completion of the program. Candidates should be planning to continue working in elementary or secondary education for at least five years after the conclusion of the program.
Type: Award
Frequency: Annual
Country of Study: Any country
Application Procedure: You must submit an application online. Click fulbright.irex.org/ to access the online application
Closing Date: 10 March
Additional Information: www.usief.org.in/Distinguished-Fulbright-Awards-Teaching-Program.aspx

For further information contact:

Tel: (91) 8754486955
Email: usiefchennai@usief.org.in

Fulbright Indo-American Environmental Leadership Program

Purpose: To provide funding for Indian environment professionals to explore future links between American and Indian organisations with common agendas
Eligibility: Open to all Indian mid-level environment professionals with at least five years of professional experience in the respective field and a Master's or professional degree of at least four years duration. Applicants will preferably be under 50 years of age. Special attention will be given to applicants who can demonstrate involvement in co-operative efforts between academia, research institutions, government, industry and non governmental organisations to make practical contributions to environmental policies and programmes
Level of Study: Postdoctorate, Professional development
Type: Internship
Value: Round-trip travel from India to the United States of America, a monthly stipend, professional allowance, settling-in allowance plus health insurance. No allowance or travel is provided for dependants
Length of Study: 4 and 8 weeks
Frequency: Annual
Study Establishment: Selected Fellows will be placed at environmental public, private, non governmental organisations, academic institutions, research centres or environment related government agencies
Country of Study: United States of America

Application Procedure: Applicants must obtain an application form either in person from USEFI offices or by sending a stamped addressed envelope to the nearest local USEFI office. The envelope should be superscribed USEFI-IAELP. Application forms can also be downloaded from the website or requested via email specifying the relevant fellowship category. Although USEFI does not require applicants to have a letter of affiliation from a United States institution at the time of applying, it encourages all applicants to correspond, in advance, with potential host institutions

Closing Date: 15 July

Additional Information: If the applicant is successful but unable to arrange an affiliation or name an institution in the United States of America with which to be affiliated, USEFI will help secure placement. The programme will combine short-term practical training/internship with opportunities for networking with American counterpart organisations www.usief.org.in/Distinguished-Fulbright-Awards-Teaching-Program.aspx

For further information contact:

Email: lakshmi@fulbright-india.org

Fulbright-Nehru Doctoral Research Fellowships

Purpose: The Fulbright-Nehru Academic and Professional Excellence Fellowships aim to provide Indian faculty, researchers, and professionals the opportunity to teach, conduct research, or carry out a combination of teaching and research at a U.S. institution

Eligibility: 1. Faculty/researchers must have a PhD degree or equivalent published work with at least five years of relevant teaching/research experience; 2. Professionals outside academe must have a master's degree or equivalent published work with recognized professional standing and at least five years relevant experience; 3. The applicant should upload a recent significant publication (copy of paper/article) in the online application; and 4. If the applicant is employed, s/he must follow the instructions carefully regarding Letter of Support from Home Institution. The employer must indicate that leave will be granted for the fellowship period. The applicant must obtain the endorsement from the appropriate administrative authority on the Letter of Support from Home Institution. The applicant can download the Letter of Support from Home Institution from the USIEF website.

Level of Study: Doctorate

Type: Fellowship

Value: The fellowships provide J-1 visa support, a monthly stipend, Accident and Sickness Program for Exchanges per U.S. Government guidelines, round-trip economy class air travel, applicable allowances and modest affiliation fees

Length of Study: 6 to 9 months

Frequency: Annual

Country of Study: United States of America

Application Procedure: Applications must be submitted online at https://apply.iie.org/ffsp2023

Closing Date: 15 July

Additional Information: www.usief.org.in/Fulbright-Nehru-Doctoral-Research-Fellowships.aspx

For further information contact:

Email: dr@usief.org.in

Fulbright-Nehru Master's Fellowships

Purpose: The Fulbright-Nehru Master's Fellowships are designed for outstanding Indians to pursue a master's degree program at select United States of America colleges and universities in the areas of Arts and Culture Management including Heritage Conservation and Museum Studies; Environmental Science/Studies; Higher Education Administration; International Legal Studies;

Eligibility: In addition to the General Prerequisites, the applicants: 1. must have completed an equivalent of a U.S. bachelor's degree from a recognized Indian university with at least 55% marks. Applicants must either possess a four-year bachelor's degree; or a completed master's degree, or a full-time postgraduate diploma from a recognized Indian institution, if the bachelor's degree is of less than four years' duration; 2. must have at least three years' full-time (paid) professional work experience relevant to the proposed field of study by the application deadline; 3. should demonstrate experience in leadership and community service; 4. must not have another degree from a U.S. university or be enrolled in a U.S. degree program; and 5. if employed, should follow the instructions carefully regarding employer's endorsement. If applicable, obtain the endorsement from the appropriate administrative authority on the FNMasters Employer's Endorsement Form. The employer must indicate that leave will be granted for the fellowship period.

Level of Study: Postgraduate

Type: Fellowship

Value: The fellowship will provide the following benefits 1. J-1 visa support; 2. Round-trip economy class air travel from fellow's home city to the host institution in the U.S.; 3. Funding for tuition and fees, living and related costs; 4. and Accident and sickness coverage per U.S. Government guidelines.

Length of Study: 1 to 2 years

Frequency: Annual

Country of Study: Any country

Application Procedure: Applications must be submitted online at https://apply.iie.org/ffsp2023/

Closing Date: 16 May

Additional Information: IMPORTANT: 1. You can apply for only ONE Fulbright-Nehru fellowship category during a competition cycle. 2. Plagiarism in the application will lead to disqualification. 3. Unless otherwise specified, Fulbright-Nehru applications are to be submitted online. 4. Applications received after the deadline will NOT be considered. 5. Extensions and Transfer of visa sponsorship will not be permitted. www.usief.org.in/Fulbright-Nehru-Fellowships.aspx

For further information contact:

Email: masters@usief.org.in

Fulbright-Nehru Postdoctoral Research Fellowships

Purpose: These fellowships are designed for Indian faculty and researchers who are in the early stages of their research careers in India

Eligibility: In addition to the General Prerequisites, the applicant: 1. must have a PhD or a DM degree within the past four years. The applicant is required to upload his/her PhD or DM degree/provisional certificate on the online application; 2. must be published in reputed journals and demonstrate evidence of superior academic and professional achievement. S/he must upload a recent significant publication (copy of paper/article) on the online application; and 3. if applicant is employed, please follow the instructions carefully regarding Letter of Support from Home Institution. If applicable, please obtain the endorsement from the appropriate administrative authority on the FNPostdoc Letter of Support from Home Institution. The employer must indicate that leave will be granted for the fellowship period. The applicant can download the FNPostdoc Letter of Support from Home Institution from the USIEF website. Candidates working under government-funded projects are also required to get endorsement from their affiliating institutions in India.

Level of Study: Doctorate, Postdoctorate, Postgraduate

Type: Fellowship

Value: These fellowships provide J-1 visa support, a monthly stipend, Accident and Sickness Program for Exchanges per U.S. Government guidelines, round-trip economy class air travel, a modest settling-in allowance, and a professional allowance

Length of Study: 8 to 24 months

Frequency: Annual

Country of Study: Any country

Application Procedure: Applications must be submitted online at https://apply.iie.org/fvsp2023

Closing Date: 17 August

Funding: Private

Additional Information: www.usief.org.in/Fulbright-Nehru-Postdoctoral-Research-Fellowship.aspx

For further information contact:

Email: postdoc@usief.org.in

United States-United Kingdom Fulbright Commission

188 Kirtling Street, London SW8 5BN, United Kingdom.

Tel:	(44) 2074 046 880
Email:	programmes@fulbright.co.uk
Website:	www.fulbright.co.uk
Contact:	Mr Michael Scott-Kline, Director

The United States-United Kingdom Fulbright Commission has a programme of awards offered annually to citizens of the United Kingdom and United States of America.

The Fulbright-Edinburgh University Award

Purpose: To enable a United States citizen to pursue postgraduate study in the United Kingdom at the University of Bristol

Eligibility: Applicant must be a United States citizen (resident anywhere but the United Kingdom), and a graduating senior, holding a BS/BA degree, master's or doctoral degree candidate, young professional or artist

Level of Study: Doctorate, Graduate, Postgraduate

Type: Award/Grant

Value: £2,625 per month

Frequency: Annual

Country of Study: United Kingdom

Application Procedure: Please visit the website us.fulbrightonline.org/applynow.html

Closing Date: 18 October

For further information contact:

Tel:	(44) 131 651 4221
Email:	Robert.Lawrie@ed.ac.uk

U

Universities Canada

Tel: (1) 613 563 3961 ext. 259
Email: tanaka@univcan.ca
Contact: Gabrielle Leblanc, Program Officer

Universities Canada manages government-funded international partnership programs and more than 130 scholarship programs on behalf of private sector companies.

ConocoPhillips Canada Centennial Scholarship Program

Purpose: To support young Canadian visionaries who have a drive to make a difference in the future. The scholarship programme encourages individuals with academic excellence and demonstrated leadership
Eligibility: Canadian citizens or permanent residents of Canada
Level of Study: Postgraduate
Type: Scholarship
Value: C$2,500 to C$10,000
Length of Study: 2 years
Frequency: Annual
Country of Study: Canada
Closing Date: 31 May
Additional Information: For more information, please contact   awards@univcan.cawww.scholarshipdesk.com/conocophillips-canada-centennial-scholarship/

For further information contact:

Email: ucawards@ucalgary.ca

Fessenden-Trott Scholarship

Eligibility: 1. Be entering the second year of their first bachelor degree on a full-time basis in September. 2. Have Canadian citizenship or permanent residency by June 14th in the year of application. 3. Have completed the first year of their first bachelor degree program in a Canadian educational institution. 4. Have attained a high academic standing as defined by the nominating institution. 5. Be nominated by a Canadian educational institution where the first year of the first bachelor degree studies has been completed.
Type: Scholarship
Value: C$9,000
Length of Study: 3 years
Country of Study: Canada

Closing Date: 1 April
Additional Information: For more information, please contact awards@univcan.cascholartree.ca/scholarship/fessenden-trott-scholarship-program/0WPlIx3yy

For further information contact:

Tel: (1) 613 563 1236
Email: awards@aucc.ca

Multiple Sclerosis Society of Canada Scholarship Programs: John Helou Scholarship

Purpose: To encourage academic excellence and the pursuit of higher education among students who are directly affected by multiple sclerosis
Eligibility: Candidates must be female Canadian citizens or permanent residents
Level of Study: Postgraduate
Type: Fellowship
Value: C$25,000 over four years
Length of Study: 4 years
Frequency: Annual
Country of Study: Canada
Application Procedure: Applicants must submit their own application electronically through the online platform www.fwis.fr
Closing Date: 31 March
Additional Information: www.wrdsb.ca/learning/programs/secondary-school-information/scholarships/national-scholarships/john-helou-scholarship-ms-society/

For further information contact:

Email: lindsay.gulin@mssociety.ca

Tanaka Fund Program

Purpose: The Tanaka Fund Program provides institutional support for the enhancement of Japanese language study opportunities at Canadian universities. It aspires to promote and help improve Japanese language education, and to support institutional program development
Type: Grant
Value: US$50,000 is available for this year's awards and Grants up to a maximum of US$10,000 are available
Length of Study: 3 Months
Country of Study: Canada
Closing Date: 7 January
Additional Information: For further details, please contact tanaka@univcan.cawww.univcan.ca/programs-and-scholarships/tanaka-fund-program/

Universities Federation for Animal Welfare (UFAW)

The Old School, Brewhouse Hill, St Albans AL4 8AN, United Kingdom.

Tel: (44) 15 8283 1818
Email: ufaw@ufaw.org.uk
Website: www.ufaw.org.uk

The Universities Federation for Animal Welfare (UFAW), the international animal welfare science society, is a United Kingdom registered scientific and educational charity that brings together the animal welfare science community, educators, veterinarians and all concerned about animal welfare worldwide in order to achieve advances in the well-being of farm, companion, laboratory and captive wild animals, and for those animals with which we interact in the wild.

Universities Federation for Animal Welfare Student Scholarships

Purpose: To encourage students to develop their interests in animal welfare and their abilities for animal welfare research
Eligibility: Applications are welcome from individuals studying at universities or colleges in the United Kingdom or an overseas institution at which there is a UFAW University Links representative. Students will usually be undertaking courses in the agricultural, biological, medical, psychological, veterinary or zoological sciences. Any student in the UK or overseas where we have a UFAW University Link
Level of Study: Postgraduate
Type: Scholarship
Value: £200 per week for student and £200 plus £800 maximum project costs to the department.
Length of Study: Funding provided for a maximum of 8 weeks (although project duration may be longer)
Frequency: Annual
Country of Study: United Kingdom
Country of Study: Any student in the UK or overseas where we have a UFAW University Link
Application Procedure: Applicants must complete a UFAW Animal Welfare Student Scholarship application form available for download from the UFAW website www.ufaw.org.uk
Closing Date: 28 February
Funding: Private
Additional Information: www.ufaw.org.uk/animal-welfare-student-scholarships/animal-welfare-student-scholarships

For further information contact:

Wendy Goodwin, UFAW, The Old School, Brewhouse Hill,, Wheathampstead, Hertfordshire AL4 8AN, United Kingdom.

Tel: (44) 1582 831818
Email: grants@ufaw.org.uk

Universities New Zealand

Universities NZ – Te Pokai Tara, Level 9, 142 Lambton Quay, Wellington, PO Box 11915, Wellington 6142, New Zealand.

Tel: (64) 4 381 8500

Universities New Zealand was established under the Education Act 1961 as the New Zealand Vice-Chancellors' Committee. Since 2010 we have operated as Universities New Zealand.

Auckland Council Research Scholarship in Urban Economics

Purpose: The purpose of this scholarship is to encourage and support postgraduate research into urban economics that has particular relevance to local government in New Zealand
Eligibility: 1. At the time of application, candidates must be enrolled or planning to enrol in a postgraduate programme at a New Zealand university (applicants may be enrolled as full-time students). 2. The postgraduate programme must be in the area of urban economics. Universities NZ and Auckland Council reserve the right to determine the eligibility of a particular area of study. 3. A thesis, dissertation, or research report must be a requirement of the postgraduate programme
Level of Study: Postgraduate
Type: Scholarship
Value: NZ$3,000
Length of Study: 1 year
Frequency: Annual
Country of Study: Any country
Application Procedure: Candidates must complete an application using the Universities NZ scholarships application website universitiesnz.communityforce.com/ Each year Auckland Council may grant one scholarship with an award of NZ$3,000. For candidates who are enrolled on a part-time basis, the value of the award will be NZ$1,500
No. of awards offered: 1
Closing Date: 1 February
Funding: Private

U

Additional Information: Application link to fill the basic information is universitiesnz.communityforce.com/Login.aspx www.universitiesnz.ac.nz/scholarships/auckland-council-research-scholarship-urban-economics

For further information contact:

Email: scholarships-cf@universitiesnz.ac.nz

BayTrust Bruce Cronin Scholarship

Purpose: The scholarship is to support postgraduate study at masters or doctoral level at a New Zealand university.
Eligibility: Applicants must have links to the BayTrust geographical area. This area is shown on the BayTrust website www.baytrust.org.nz Applicants will be eligible if they were born in, or attended school in, or have whakapapa back to the area.
Level of Study: Postgraduate
Type: Scholarship
Value: NZ$5,000. each
Length of Study: 1 year
Frequency: Annual
Country of Study: New Zealand
No. of awards offered: 2
Closing Date: 1 February
Additional Information: www.universitiesnz.ac.nz/scholarships/baytrust-bruce-cronin-scholarship

Freyberg Scholarship

Purpose: Freyberg Scholarships are awarded to encourage graduate study into areas relevant to national security. Study should be undertaken at a recognised institution in New Zealand or an Asia-Pacific country, including Canada and the United States
Eligibility: Applicants must be New Zealand citizens or permanent residents who meet the following academic requirements they should normally have obtained at least second class honours, division A, or equivalent in their qualifying degree and have completed academic studies in political science, history, economics or some other discipline that may be considered an appropriate foundation for such study
Level of Study: Postgraduate
Type: Scholarship
Value: NZ$70,000 will be made annually for the award of one or more scholarship
Frequency: Annual
Country of Study: New Zealand
Country of Study: Any approved course

Application Procedure: Apply online. Check the below link for further information. www.universitiesnz.ac.nz/scholarships/freyberg-scholarship
No. of awards offered: Up to 3
Closing Date: 1 October
Additional Information: www.universitiesnz.ac.nz/scholarships/freyberg-scholarship

For further information contact:

Email: scholarships-cf@universitiesnz.ac.nz

Gordon Watson Scholarship

Purpose: This scholarship is to enable New Zealanders to study international relationships or social and economic conditions at a university overseas. Candidates will be planning to study at Masters or PhD level.
Eligibility: Applicants must have graduated or be graduating with an Honours or Masters degree in arts, science, commerce, law or divinity from a New Zealand university, and be New Zealand citizens or permanent residents.
Level of Study: Postgraduate
Type: Scholarship
Value: NZ$12,000 per year
Length of Study: 3 years
Frequency: Annual
Country of Study: New Zealand
Application Procedure: Apply online www.universitiesnz.ac.nz/scholarships/gordonwatson
Closing Date: 1 April
Funding: Private
Additional Information: Please note that to be eligible a planned Masters degree must have a substantial research component, i.e. at least half www.universitiesnz.ac.nz/scholarships/gordon-watson-scholarship

For further information contact:

Tel: (64) 3 369 3999
Email: scholarships-cf@universitiesnz.ac.nz

Henry Kelsey Scholarship

Eligibility: Applicants will: 1. be New Zealand citizens or permanent residents and 2. have a Bachelor degree or equivalent, with honours where they are awarded, in a field appropriate to their intended doctoral study.
Level of Study: Doctorate
Type: Scholarship
Value: NZ$10,000 per annum
Length of Study: 3 years

Frequency: Annual
Country of Study: New Zealand
Application Procedure: Apply online here.: universitiesnz. communityforce.com/Login.aspx
No. of awards offered: 1
Closing Date: 1 October
Additional Information: www.universitiesnz.ac.nz/scholar ships/henry-kelsey-scholarship

Kia Ora Foundation Patricia Pratt Scholarship

Purpose: The purpose of the Kia Ora Foundation Patricia Pratt Scholarship is to assist outstanding New Zealand musical performers who have completed the equivalent of an honours degree in any field of musical performance in New Zealand to continue their musical development at a renowned international music school or conservatorium. The scholarship will be awarded for classical music performance including vocal or instrumental performance or conducting.
Eligibility: Applicants will be New Zealand citizens. Applicants may apply from outside New Zealand but must have resided in New Zealand for at least three of the last five years immediately preceding the year of selection. Applicants will have recently completed the requirements for an honours degree in musical performance at a New Zealand university (or an equivalent musical qualification).
Type: Scholarship
Value: NZ$70,000 per annum
Length of Study: 2 years
Country of Study: New Zealand
Closing Date: 1 March
Additional Information: www.universitiesnz.ac.nz/scholar ships/kia-ora-foundation-patricia-pratt-scholarship

Kiwi Music Scholarship

Purpose: This scholarship is to assist outstanding New Zealand musical performers or conductors to continue their musical development either in New Zealand or overseas.
Eligibility: Applicants will be New Zealand citizens who are normally resident in New Zealand. Applicants will have completed or are completing an honours or masters degree in musical performance (including vocal performance) or conducting at a New Zealand university, or an equivalent musical qualification.
Level of Study: Postgraduate
Type: Scholarship
Value: NZ$50,000 to NZ$60,000.
Frequency: Annual
Country of Study: New Zealand

Closing Date: 1 March
Additional Information: www.universitiesnz.ac.nz/scholar ships/kiwi-music-scholarship

New Zealand Law Foundation Ethel Benjamin Scholarship (For Women)

Purpose: To support postgraduate research in law that will protect and promote the interests of the public in relation to legal matters in New Zealand.
Eligibility: A scholarship may be awarded to any woman scholar who is: 1. a New Zealand citizen or permanent resident 2. the holder of a New Zealand university law degree (unless there are exceptional circumstances the award would normally be made to candidates who have gained the qualifying degree within the past five years) 3. accepted into a postgraduate course in law at either a New Zealand or an overseas university acceptable to the Selection Committee.
Level of Study: Postgraduate
Type: Scholarship
Value: Up to NZ$20,000 for study in New Zealand and up to NZ$30,000 for study overseas
Frequency: Annual
Country of Study: New Zealand
Application Procedure: Applications for the scholarship is an online application process.universitiesnz.communityforce. com/Login.aspx
No. of awards offered: 3
Closing Date: 1 March
Additional Information: www.universitiesnz.ac.nz/scholar ships/new-zealand-law-foundation-ethel-benjamin-scholarship-women

Shirtcliffe Fellowship

Eligibility: Applicants must be: 1. New Zealand citizens 2. ordinarily resident in New Zealand 3. New Zealand university graduates 4. planning to register or be currently registered as a doctoral candidate at a university in New Zealand or other Commonwealth country.
Level of Study: Predoctorate
Type: Scholarship
Value: NZ$5,000 per year
Length of Study: 3 years
Frequency: Annual
Country of Study: New Zealand
No. of awards offered: 1
Closing Date: 1 April
Additional Information: www.universitiesnz.ac.nz/scholar ships/shirtcliffe-fellowship

U

William Georgetti Scholarship

Eligibility: Applicants must: 1. Have resided in New Zealand for a period of at least five years immediately preceding the year of selection (refer to the Regulations for further information). 2. Be of good moral character and repute. 3. Be of good health. 4. Hold a degree from a university in New Zealand or elsewhere or any other academic qualification of a university or other institution of learning (in New Zealand or elsewhere) reasonably equivalent in the opinion of the Scholarship Board to a degree of a university in New Zealand.
Level of Study: Doctorate, Postdoctorate
Type: Scholarship
Value: Up to NZ$20,000 per year for Masters study and NZ$30,000 per year for doctoral study. NZ$45,000 per year for those students studying overseas.
Length of Study: 3 years
Frequency: Annual
Country of Study: New Zealand
Closing Date: 1 February
Additional Information: www.universitiesnz.ac.nz/scholarships/william-georgetti-scholarship

For further information contact:

Email: scholarshipscf@universitiesnz.ac.nz

University College Birmingham

Summer Row, Birmingham B3 1JB, United Kingdom.

Tel: (44) 12 1604 1000
Email: Registry@bcftcs.ac.uk
Website: www.ucb.ac.uk
Contact: Student Scholarships

Target Recruitment Partial Fee Waiver

Purpose: To reduce tuition fee for new international students
Eligibility: Applicants must refer to the website for details
Level of Study: Postgraduate
Type: Scholarships
Value: Up to £1,000
Length of Study: 1 year
Frequency: Annual
Study Establishment: University College Birmingham
Country of Study: United Kingdom
Additional Information: Applications can be considered for entry in Semester 1 (Late September/Early October) or Semester 2 (Late January/Early February). Applications should be made at least 2 months prior to the entry date. No applications are necessary. Partial Fee Waivers will be noted in all offer letters sent to applicants from relevant countries. For more information contact the International Student Office - https://www.ucb.ac.uk/student-support/financial-support/scholarships-and-waivers/#scholarships

For further information contact:

Email: international@ucb.ac.uk

University College London

Gower Street, London WC1E 6BT, United Kingdom.

Tel: (44) 20 7679 2000
Website: www.ucl.ac.uk

Just 175 years ago, the benefits of a university education in United Kingdom were restricted to men who were members of the Church of United Kingdom; University College London (UCL) was founded to challenge that discrimination. UCL was the first university to be established in United Kingdom after Oxford and Cambridge, providing a progressive alternative to those institutions social exclusivity, religious restrictions and academic constraints. UCL is the largest of over 50 colleges and institutes that make up the federal University of London.

The Bartlett Promise PhD Scholarship

Eligibility: Candidates must: 1. be UK domiciled with home fee status or a forced migrant (as defined by UCL). 2. have an offer of admission to a Bartlett PhD programme for study in 2023/24 and 3. must not have completed a PhD at UCL or anywhere else previously.
Level of Study: Doctorate
Type: Scholarship
Value: Full fees, plus £17,631 maintenance
Frequency: Annual
Country of Study: United Kingdom
No. of awards offered: 4
Closing Date: 29 April
Additional Information: www.ucl.ac.uk/bartlett/study/funding-and-scholarships/bartlett-promise-scholarship/bartlett-promise-phd-scholarship

For further information contact:

Email: bartlett.promise@ucl.ac.uk

A C Gimson Scholarships in Phonetics and Linguistics

Purpose: To financially support MPhil/PhD research
Eligibility: United Kingdom, European Union and overseas students are eligible to apply
Level of Study: Doctorate, Postgraduate, Research
Type: Scholarship
Value: £1,000
Frequency: Annual
Study Establishment: University College London
Country of Study: United Kingdom
Application Procedure: Applicants should write indicating their intention to compete for the bursaries to the department
Closing Date: 1 June

For further information contact:

Tel: (44) 20 7679 4245
Email: n.wilkins@ucl.ac.uk

Alfred Bader Prize in Organic Chemistry

Purpose: To financially support MPhil/PhD research
Eligibility: Applicants must contact the department
Level of Study: Doctorate, Postgraduate, Research
Type: Scholarship
Value: £1,000
Frequency: Annual
Study Establishment: University College London
Country of Study: United Kingdom
Application Procedure: Applicants must contact the department
Closing Date: 1 May

For further information contact:

Tel: (44) 20 7679 4650
Fax: (44) 20 7679 7463
Email: m.l.jabore@ucl.ac.uk

Archibald Richardson Scholarship for Mathematics

Purpose: To financially support students to pursue MPhil/PhD research
Eligibility: United Kingdom, European Union and overseas applicants are eligible to apply. All applicants who firmly accept a place for MPhil/PhD research in pure Mathematics department will be considered
Level of Study: Doctorate, Postgraduate, Research

Type: Scholarship
Value: £3,000
Frequency: Annual
Study Establishment: University College London
Country of Study: United Kingdom
Application Procedure: All applicants who firmly accept a place for MPhil/PhD research in pure mathematics will be considered automatically
Closing Date: 15 May
Additional Information: www.european-funding-guide.eu/other-financial-assistance/14077-archibald-richardson-scholarship-mathematics%C2%A0

For further information contact:

Tel: (44) 20 7679 2839
Fax: (44) 20 7383 5519
Email: h.higgins@ucl.ac.uk

Arnold Hugh William Beck Memorial Scholarship

Purpose: To financially support research Master's and MPhil/PhD students
Eligibility: Applicants should have applied for a place for graduate study at University College London. A past or current holder of the scholarship may apply again for the scholarship but such applications will be considered in open competition with other applicants. No individual may hold the scholarship for more than three years in total
Level of Study: Doctorate, Postgraduate, Research
Type: Scholarship
Value: £6,500
Frequency: Annual
Study Establishment: University College London
Country of Study: United Kingdom
Application Procedure: Applicants should send an academic curriculum vitae and a letter of more than 500 words describing their areas of interest in the discipline to the address given below. If the applicant has not applied to UCL, they must complete a graduate application form and enclose it with the scholarship application
Closing Date: 15 August
Additional Information: www.european-funding-guide.eu/other-financial-assistance/14156-ahw-beck-memorial-scholarship

For further information contact:

Tel: (44) 20 7679 7306
Email: p.johnson@ee.ucl.ac.uk

U

Bartlett School of Planning Centenary Scholarship

Eligibility: Students who have applied to study one of the eight eligible degree programmes concerned (MSc Housing and City Planning; MSc Infrastructure Planning, Appraisal and Delivery; MSc International Planning; MSc Spatial Planning; MSc Sustainable Urbanism; MSc Transport and City Planning; MSc Urban Regeneration; MRes Inter-disciplinary Urban Design; MPlan City Planning, i.e. all Masters programmes except International Real Estate and Planning or Urban Design and City Planning).
Level of Study: Postgraduate
Type: Scholarship
Value: £9,200
Length of Study: 1 year
Frequency: Annual
Study Establishment: University College London
Country of Study: United Kingdom
Application Procedure: Application form: www.ucl.ac.uk/bartlett/planning/sites/bartlett_planning/files/scholarshipapplicationform2022_1.doc
No. of awards offered: 6
Closing Date: 30 June
Funding: Individuals
No. of awards given last year: 6
Additional Information: www.ucl.ac.uk/bartlett/planning/funding-and-scholarships

For further information contact:

Tel: (44) 20 3108 6682
Email: a.n.patel@ucl.ac.uk

Bentham Scholarships

Purpose: To financially support prospective LLM students
Eligibility: Applicants must be overseas students from outside the European Union. An applicant must have accepted an offer (either conditional or unconditional) to read for the LLM at UCL to be eligible
Level of Study: Postgraduate
Type: Scholarship
Value: £16,000
Length of Study: 4 years
Frequency: Annual
Study Establishment: University College London
Country of Study: United Kingdom
Application Procedure: There is no application procedure. All eligible students will automatically be considered if they have firmly accepted their offer of admission by May 31st
Closing Date: 30 April

Additional Information: www.ucl.ac.uk/political-science/study/post-graduate-research/funding-opportunities/departmental-scholarships

For further information contact:

Tel: (44) 20 7679 1441
Fax: (44) 20 7209 3470
Email: polsci.admissions@ucl.ac.uk

Bioprocessing Graduate Scholarship

Purpose: To financially support study leading to an MPhil/PhD.
Eligibility: Open to students resident outside the United Kingdom and pursuing the MSc or MPhil or PhD research in the department of biomedical engineering
Level of Study: Doctorate, Postgraduate
Type: Scholarship
Value: Up to a maximum of £11,000 per year. This sum can be set against tuition fees and/or be received as maintenance allowance payable in quarterly installments
Length of Study: Maximum of 4 calendar years
Frequency: Annual
Study Establishment: University College London
Country of Study: United Kingdom
Application Procedure: Applicants must contact the department at the address given below
No. of awards offered: 8
Closing Date: 15 February
Funding: Trusts
No. of applicants last year: 8
Additional Information: www.scholarshipsads.com/category/subject/bioprocessing/

For further information contact:

Tel: (44) 20 7679 3796
Email: nigelth@ucl.ac.uk

Brain Research Trust Prize

Purpose: To financially support MPhil/PhD research students
Eligibility: Open to United Kingdom, European Union and overseas students. Overseas fee-paying students should be aware that only home tuition fee (European Union rates) is included in the award
Level of Study: Doctorate, Postgraduate, Research
Type: Studentship
Value: Stipend, tuition fees at United Kingdom/European Union rate and travel budget
Length of Study: Up to 3 years

Frequency: Annual
Study Establishment: University College London Institute of Neurology
Country of Study: United Kingdom
Application Procedure: Applicants should contact the UCL Institute of Neurology. Please submit full curriculum vitae, references and statement of research interests indicating how these would complement projects on offer
Funding: Government, Trusts
Contributor: The Brian Research Trust

For further information contact:

Cell Signalling Laboratory, Institute of Neurology, UCL, 1 Wakefield Street, London WC1N 1PJ, United Kingdom.

Tel: (44) 20 7679 4031
Email: phdstudentship@ion.cl.ac.uk

Brown Family Bursary

Eligibility: Candidates must fulfil all of the following criteria: 1. be ordinarily resident in the UK; 2. be in financial need (as determined by the UCL Student Funding Office); 3. hold an offer to study a full-time Master's degree at UCL in 2023/24 for one of the following programmes: MSc Environment and Sustainable Development MSc Sustainable Resources: Economics, Policy and Transitions MSc Climate Change MPA Sustainable Infrastructures and Public Policy MPA Energy, Technology and Public Policy MSc Environmental Systems Engineering MSc Global Management of Natural Resources MSc Materials for Energy and Environment MSc Biodiversity and Global Change MSc Ecology and Data Science.
Level of Study: Postgraduate
Type: Bursary
Value: £15,000 (for one year)
Length of Study: 1 year
Frequency: Annual
Country of Study: United Kingdom
No. of awards offered: 1
Closing Date: 9 June
Additional Information: www.ucl.ac.uk/scholarships/brown-family-bursary

Child Health Research Appeal Trust Studentship

Purpose: To fund graduate students for MPhil/PhD research
Eligibility: Open to committed individuals wishing to do research in a clinical context, who expect to graduate with a United Kingdom first class or upper second class honours degree or equivalent from abroad

Level of Study: Doctorate, Postgraduate
Type: Studentship
Value: Tuition fees at the United Kingdom/European Union student rate, a stipend equivalent to MRC levels and £3,000 towards research costs
Length of Study: 3 years
Frequency: Annual
Study Establishment: UCL Institute of Child Health
Country of Study: United Kingdom
Application Procedure: Studentships are advertised on the department's vacancy website between November–January each year. Applicants should refer to www.ich.ucl.ac.uk/ich/humanresources/
Closing Date: January
Funding: Trusts
No. of awards given last year: Up to 4

For further information contact:

Email: chratapps@ich.ucl.ac.uk

Common Wealth Shared Scholarship Scheme (CSSS)

Purpose: The aim of the Commonwealth Shared Scholarship Scheme (CSSS) is to assist students from developing Commonwealth countries who are of excellent academic calibre but for financial reasons would not otherwise be able to afford to study in the United Kingdom.
Eligibility: 1. Be a Commonwealth citizen, refugee, or British Protected Person; 2. Be permanently resident in an eligible Commonwealth country; 3. Be available to start your academic studies in the UK by the start of the UK academic year in September/October 2021; 4. By September 2021, hold a first degree of either first or upper second class (21) classification, or lower second class (22) classification plus a relevant postgraduate qualification (usually a Master's degree). If you are applying for a second UK Master's degree, you will need to provide justification as to why you wish to undertake this study; 5. Not have studied or worked for one (academic) year or more in a high-income country; 6. Be unable to afford to study in the UK without this scholarship;
Level of Study: Postgraduate
Type: Scholarship
Value: Tuition fees, living costs, flights to UK
Length of Study: 1 year
Frequency: Annual
Study Establishment: University College London
Country of Study: United Kingdom
Application Procedure: 1. You must separately apply for admission to UCL for one of the eligible programmes through the standard admissions procedure. 2. You must apply for the

scholarship on the Commonwealth Scholarship Commission Electronic Application System (EAS) online following the procedures described on their website.

Closing Date: 9 April

Contributor: Department for International Development (DFID) and UCL

No. of awards given last year: 3

Additional Information: Preference is given to candidates unable to afford the cost of studying abroad by themselves. Candidates are expected to return to their home countries to work or study as soon as the award ends www.ucl.ac.uk/scholarships/commonwealth-shared-scholarship-scheme

For further information contact:

Tel: (44) 20 7679 1111
Fax: (44) 20 7679 1112
Email: dpu@ucl.ac.uk

Dawes Hicks Postgraduate Scholarships in Philosophy

Purpose: To financially support postgraduate research

Eligibility: United Kingdom, European Union and overseas students are eligible to apply

Level of Study: Postgraduate, Research

Type: Scholarship

Value: Up to £5,000

Frequency: Annual

Study Establishment: University College London

Country of Study: United Kingdom

Application Procedure: No separate application is required. All who are admitted to research programmes in philosophy will automatically be considered for the scholarship. Any queries should be directed to the department

Additional Information: Decisions regarding this award will be made in September www.european-funding-guide.eu/other-financial-assistance/14159-dawes-hicks-postgraduate-scholarships-philosophy

For further information contact:

Tel: (44) 20 7679 4451
Email: r.madden@ucl.ac.uk

Department of Communities and Local Government (formally Office of the Deputy Prime Minister)

Purpose: To financially support full-time study

Eligibility: Open to candidates who take up full time study only with residence restrictions, already holding or offer for

the MSC spatial planning or MSC international planning, 21 or equivalent (except in exceptional circumstances)

Level of Study: Postgraduate

Type: Bursary

Value: Tuition fees at United Kingdom/European Union rate plus (For United Kingdom/European Union nationals only) along with a monthly stipend of £500

Length of Study: 1 year

Frequency: Annual

Study Establishment: University College London

Country of Study: United Kingdom

Application Procedure: Applications are available from www.esrc.ac.uk (ESRC) and should be sent to the department. Potentially eligible candidates will be contacted by the department

No. of awards offered: 16

Funding: Government

Contributor: Department of Communities and Local Government

No. of awards given last year: 7

No. of applicants last year: 16

For further information contact:

Tel: (44) 20 7679 7501
Email: j.hillmore@ucl.ac.uk

Digital Media Programme Bursary

Eligibility: Candidates must fulfil all of the following criteria: 1. Be ordinarily resident in the UK and eligible to pay Home fee rate; 2. Hold an offer to study an MA Digital Media: Critical Studies, MA Digital Media: Education, or MA Digital Media: Production in at UCL in 2022/23.

Level of Study: Postgraduate

Type: Bursary

Value: £5,000 (for one year)

Length of Study: 1 year

Frequency: Annual

Country of Study: United Kingdom

Closing Date: 9 June

Additional Information: www.ucl.ac.uk/scholarships/digital-media-programme-bursary

Follett Scholarship

Purpose: To financially support MPhil/PhD research

Eligibility: United Kingdom, European Union and overseas students are eligible to apply

Level of Study: Doctorate, Postgraduate, Research

Type: Scholarship

Value: Up to £13,000 towards fees and/or maintenance
Frequency: Annual
Study Establishment: University College London
Country of Study: United Kingdom
Application Procedure: No separate application is required. Applicants who are admitted to research programmes in philosophy will automatically be considered for the scholarship. Any queries should be directed to the department
Closing Date: July
Additional Information: www.european-funding-guide.eu/other-financial-assistance/14161-follett-scholarship

For further information contact:

Tel: (44) 20 7679 4451
Fax: (44) 20 7679 3336
Email: r.madden@ucl.ac.uk

Gaitskell MSc Scholarship

Purpose: To financially support full-time Master's study in the Department of Economics
Eligibility: Open to candidates who have applied for a place for graduate study at UCL and are not already receiving full financial support from other sources for fees and living costs
Level of Study: Postgraduate
Type: Scholarship
Value: £5,000
Frequency: Annual
Study Establishment: University College London (UCL)
Country of Study: United Kingdom
Application Procedure: Applications not needed. All applicants to the department are automatically considered
Additional Information: www.european-funding-guide.eu/other-financial-assistance/14086-gaitskell-msc-scholarships

For further information contact:

Tel: (44) 20 7679 5861
Fax: (44) 20 7616 2775
Email: d.fauvrelle@ucl.ac.uk

Gay Clifford Fees Award for Outstanding Women Students

Purpose: The Gay Clifford Awards for Outstanding Women Students aims to enable female students to pursue full-time Master's degree studies in the departments of Economics or Philosophy.
Eligibility: Candidates can be from any country, but must fulfil the following criteria: 1. identify as female; AND 2. hold an offer to study a full-time Master's degree at UCL in 2023/24 in the departments of Economics, or Philosophy.
Level of Study: Postgraduate
Type: Scholarship
Value: £10,000 (for one year)
Length of Study: 1 year
Frequency: Annual
Study Establishment: University College London
Country of Study: United Kingdom
Application Procedure: Applicants should refer to the website for further information about the application procedures and deadlines
No. of awards offered: 2
Additional Information: www.ucl.ac.uk/scholarships/gay-clifford-awards-outstanding-women-students

For further information contact:

Tel: (44) 20 7679 2005/4167
Email: studentfunding@ucl.ac.uk

Graduate Research Scholarships

Eligibility: In order to APPLY, you must: 1. have submitted an application to, or currently be registered on, a full- or part-time research degree programme at UCL by the scholarship deadline; 2. holding or expected to achieve at least an upper second-class Honours UK undergraduate degree or equivalent qualification.
Level of Study: Postgraduate
Type: Scholarship
Value: UK rate fees and maintenance stipend
Frequency: Annual
Country of Study: Any country
No. of awards offered: 1 year
Closing Date: 14 January
Additional Information: www.ucl.ac.uk/scholarships/graduate-research-scholarships

Graduate Research Scholarships for Cross-disciplinary Training (One-Year)

Eligibility: Eligible candidates must: 1. be in receipt of an offer of admission to or currently registered at UCL on a full-time MPhil/PhD or EngD research programme*, and; 2. provide proof of three years of guaranteed funding for their normal MPhil/PhD or EngD programme. *Please note, students must be in the research phase of their degree and still paying fees. Students who have entered CRS are not eligible to apply.
Value: Full fees and maintenance stipend

Country of Study: United Kingdom
Closing Date: 28 January
Additional Information: www.ucl.ac.uk/scholarships/graduate-research-scholarships-cross-disciplinary-training-one-year

For further information contact:

Email: studentfundingadvice@ucl.ac.uk

GREAT Scholarship

Eligibility: Candidates must be citizens of China, Singapore and Vietnam. Hold an offer to study a full-time Master's degree at UCL in 2023/24
Level of Study: Postgraduate
Type: Scholarship
Value: £10,000 (one year only)
Length of Study: 1 year
Frequency: Annual
Country of Study: United Kingdom
Closing Date: 31 May
Additional Information: www.ucl.ac.uk/scholarships/great-scholarship

For further information contact:

Email: studentfunding@ucl.ac.uk

GREAT Scholarship for Justice and Law

Eligibility: Candidates must be citizens of Pakistan. Hold an offer to study a full-time Master's degree at UCL in 2023/24
Type: Scholarship
Value: £10,000 (one year only)
Length of Study: 1 year
Country of Study: United Kingdom
Closing Date: 31 May
Additional Information: www.ucl.ac.uk/scholarships/great-scholarship-justice-and-law

For further information contact:

Email: studentfunding@ucl.ac.uk

Ian Karten Charitable Trust Scholarship (Hebrew and Jewish Studies)

Purpose: To financially support postgraduate study

Eligibility: Applicants must have applied for a place for graduate study at UCL in the Department of Hebrew and Jewish Studies
Level of Study: Graduate, Postgraduate
Type: Scholarship
Value: £1,000 each
Frequency: Annual
Study Establishment: University College London
Country of Study: United Kingdom
Application Procedure: Applicants should contact the department. If the applicants have not applied to UCL they must complete a graduate application form and enclose it with the scholarship application
Closing Date: 1 June
Funding: Trusts

For further information contact:

Tel: (44) 20 7679 3028
Fax: (44) 20 7209 1026
Email: n.f.lochery@ucl.ac.uk

Ian Karten Charitable Trust Scholarship (Microbiology)

Purpose: To financially support postgraduate study
Eligibility: Applicants must be United Kingdom nationals aged 30 years or under at the start of their intended academic year of study
Level of Study: Postgraduate
Type: Scholarship
Value: £2,500
Frequency: Annual
Study Establishment: University College London
Country of Study: United Kingdom
Application Procedure: Applicants should contact the department

For further information contact:

Email: t.mchugh@rfc.ucl.ac.uk

Ian Karten Charitable Trust Scholarship (Neuroscience)

Purpose: To financially support postgraduate study in neuroscience
Eligibility: Applicants must be United Kingdom nationals aged 30 years or under on October 10th in the intended year of entry
Level of Study: Postgraduate

Type: Scholarship
Value: £2,750
Frequency: Annual
Study Establishment: University College London
Country of Study: United Kingdom
Application Procedure: Applicants must contact the department

For further information contact:

Department of Anatomy and Developmental Biology, Gower St, London WC1E 6BT, United Kingdom.

Tel: (44) 20 7679 7740
Fax: (44) 20 7679 7349
Email: anatpgenquires@anatomy.ucl.ac.uk

Institute of Education, University of London Centenary Masters Scholarships

Purpose: IOE is offering Centenary Masters Scholarships for students who plan to work either in their home country, or another, to improve the circumstances of disadvantaged, excluded or underachieving citizens.
Eligibility: 1. Be citizens and residents of a low or middle income country with a GNI not higher than US$8000 per capita (as per the World Bank GNI per capita classification tables) 2. Have an offer to study a full time masters degree in London at the UCL Institute of Education (September/October start). 3. Not have studied or lived in the UK before.
Level of Study: Postdoctorate
Type: Scholarship
Value: US$8,000
Length of Study: 1 year
Frequency: Annual
Country of Study: Any country
Application Procedure: To be eligible for the scholarship, you must have an offer to study a full time masters degree in London at the UCL Institute of Education. If you fulfill all the criteria, please email IOEinternational[at] ucl.ac.uk to request a scholarship application form. Please include in your email your student ID number. The deadline to apply for these scholarships is 4 May (5pm London time).
Closing Date: 3 May
Funding: Foundation
Additional Information: www.ucl.ac.uk/ioe/about-ioe/global-reach/scholarships-and-funding

For further information contact:

Email: IOEinternational@ucl.ac.uk

Jackson Widening Participation Scholarship

Eligibility: Candidates must fulfil all of the following criteria:1. be ordinarily resident in the UK and eligible to pay Home fee rate; 2. hold an offer to study an MSc Social Epidemiology in 2022/23.
Level of Study: Postgraduate
Type: Scholarship
Value: £6,000 (for one year)
Length of Study: 1 year
Frequency: Annual
Country of Study: United Kingdom
No. of awards offered: 1
Closing Date: 9 June
Additional Information: www.ucl.ac.uk/scholarships/jackson-widening-participation-scholarship

For further information contact:

Email: rebecca.lacey@ucl.ac.uk

Jacobsen Scholarship in Philosophy

Purpose: To financially support MPhil/PhD research
Eligibility: Open to United Kingdom, European Union and overseas students
Level of Study: Doctorate, Postgraduate, Research
Type: Scholarship
Value: Up to £9,500
Frequency: Annual
Study Establishment: University College London
Country of Study: United Kingdom
Application Procedure: No separate application is required. Applicants who are admitted to research programmes in philosophy will automatically be considered for the scholarship. Any queries should be directed to the department
Additional Information: Decisions regarding this award will be made in September www.european-funding-guide.eu/other-financial-assistance/14162-jacobsen-scholarship-philosophy

For further information contact:

Tel: (44) 20 7679 7115
Email: r.madden@ucl.ac.uk

James Joseph Sylvester Scholarship

Purpose: To financially support MPhil/PhD research
Eligibility: United Kingdom, European Union and overseas students are eligible to apply
Level of Study: Doctorate, Postgraduate, Research
Type: Scholarship

U

Value: Up to £3,000
Frequency: Annual
Study Establishment: University College London
Country of Study: United Kingdom
Application Procedure: Applicants must contact the department
Closing Date: 15 May

For further information contact:

Department of Mathematics, University College London, Gower Street, London WC1E 6BT, United Kingdom.

Tel: (44) 20 7679 2839
Fax: (44) 20 7383 5519
Email: h.higgins@ucl.ac.uk

Jevons Memorial Scholarship in Economic Science

Purpose: To financially support MPhil/PhD study
Eligibility: Candidates must have graduated or be a candidate for graduation in the term in which the award is made. Previous tenure of the scholarship does not debar candidate from competing on a second occasion. Normally the scholar elected must pursue a course of study and research for a higher degree at UCL
Level of Study: Doctorate, Postgraduate
Type: Scholarship
Value: £55
Frequency: Annual
Study Establishment: University College London
Country of Study: United Kingdom
Application Procedure: Applicants should send particulars of the research work they intend to pursue plus an academic curriculum vitae to the department. If the applicant has not applied to UCL, they must complete a graduate application form and enclose it with the scholarship application
Closing Date: 15 May

For further information contact:

Tel: (44) 20 7679 5861
Fax: (44) 20 7916 2775
Email: d.fauvrelle@ucl.ac.uk

John Carr Scholarship for Students from Africa and the Caribbean

Purpose: To financially support prospective LLM students
Eligibility: Applicants must be overseas students from Africa and the Caribbean. An applicant must have accepted an offer

(either conditional or unconditional) to read for the LLM at UCL to be eligible
Level of Study: Postgraduate
Type: Scholarship
Value: £2,000
Frequency: Annual
Study Establishment: University College London
Country of Study: United Kingdom
Application Procedure: There is no application procedure. All eligible students who have accepted the offer of admission by March 31st will automatically be considered
Closing Date: 2 March
Additional Information: The scholarships will be based on academic merit. The faculty will only consider those applicants who have firmly accepted their offer of admission to the LLM by May 31st www.european-funding-guide.eu/other-financial-assistance/14064-john-carr-scholarship-students-africa-and-caribbean

For further information contact:

Tel: (44) 20 7679 1441
Fax: (44) 20 7209 3470
Email: graduatelaw@ucl.ac.uk

John Hawkes Scholarship

Purpose: The primary purpose is to support third year study in pure mathematics but a secondary purpose when there is no suitable candidate or candidates for the whole sum available, is to support a graduate research student
Eligibility: All students registered or accepted for MPhil/PhD research in pure mathematics will be considered for the scholarship.
Level of Study: Doctorate, Postgraduate, Research
Type: Scholarship
Value: Up to £12,000 per annum
Length of Study: 3 years
Frequency: Annual
Study Establishment: University College London
Country of Study: United Kingdom
Application Procedure: Please see the detail instruction at the link www.ucl.ac.uk/prospective-students/scholarships/graduate/deptscholarships/mathematics
Closing Date: 1 May
Additional Information: www.ucl.ac.uk/prospective-students/scholarships/graduate/deptscholarships/mathematics

For further information contact:

Tel: (44) 20 7679 2839
Fax: (44) 20 7383 5519
Email: h.higgins@ucl.ac.uk

Joseph Hume Scholarship

Purpose: To financially support LLM students or MPhil/PhD research
Eligibility: For all LLM or MPhil/PhD research students in the Department of Laws
Level of Study: Doctorate, Postgraduate, Research
Type: Scholarship
Value: £1,600
Frequency: Annual
Study Establishment: University College London
Country of Study: United Kingdom
Application Procedure: There is no application procedure. All eligible students will automatically be considered
Closing Date: 23 March
Additional Information: Please check the website for further details www.laws.ucl.ac.uk/study/graduate/applying/funding-scholarships/ www.european-funding-guide.eu/other-financial-assistance/14068-joseph-hume-scholarship

For further information contact:

Tel: (44) 20 7679 1441
Fax: (44) 20 7209 3470
Email: graduatelaw@ucl.ac.uk

Keeling Scholarship

Purpose: To financially support MPhil/PhD research
Eligibility: United Kingdom, European Union and overseas students are eligible to apply
Level of Study: Doctorate, Postgraduate, Research
Type: Scholarship
Value: Up to £1,000
Length of Study: 3 years
Frequency: Annual
Study Establishment: University College London
Country of Study: United Kingdom
Application Procedure: No separate application is required. Applicants who are admitted to research programmes in philosophy will automatically be considered for the scholarship. Any queries should be directed to the department
Closing Date: 31 January
Additional Information: www.ucl.ac.uk/philosophy/keeling/scholarship

For further information contact:

Tel: (44) 20 7679 7115
Email: r.madden@ucl.ac.uk

Liver Group PhD Studentship

Purpose: To financially support students to pursue MPhil/PhD research
Eligibility: Open to United Kingdom and European Union applicants holding a relevant First or Upper Second Class
Level of Study: Doctorate, Postgraduate, Research
Type: Scholarship
Value: Home student fees plus a maintenance allowance (1st year approx. £14,500)
Length of Study: 3 years
Frequency: Dependent on funds available
Study Establishment: Royal Free and University College Medical School, UCL-Hampstead campus
Country of Study: United Kingdom
Application Procedure: Applicants should contact the department
Funding: Foundation
Contributor: The Liver Group Charity
No. of awards given last year: 1

For further information contact:

Centre for Hepatology, Department of Medicine (Royal Free Campus), Royal Free and University College Medicine School, Rowland Hill Street, London NW3 2PF, United Kingdom.

Tel: (44) 20 7433 2854
Fax: (44) 20 7433 2852
Email: c.selden@rfc.ucl.ac.uk

Master of the Rolls Scholarship For Commonwealth Students

Purpose: To financially support prospective LLM students
Eligibility: Applicants must be overseas students from the Commonwealth countries. An applicant must have accepted an offer (either conditional or unconditional) to read for the LLM at UCL
Level of Study: Postgraduate
Type: Scholarship
Value: £2,000
Frequency: Annual
Study Establishment: University College London
Country of Study: United Kingdom
Application Procedure: There is no application procedure. All eligible students who firmly accept the offer of admission by May 31st will be automatically considered
No. of awards given last year: 1
Additional Information: The scholarships will be based on academic merit. The faculty will only consider those

applicants who have firmly accepted their offer of admission to the LLM by May 31st www.european-funding-guide. eu/other-financial-assistance/14063-master-rolls-scholarship-commonwealth-students

For further information contact:

Tel: (44) 20 7679 1441
Fax: (44) 20 7209 3470
Email: graduatelaw@ucl.ac.uk

Master's Degree Awards in Archaeology

Subjects: Archaeology.
Purpose: To financially support MA and MSc programmes in the Institute of Archaeology.
Eligibility: Open to students on MA and MSc programmes in UCL's institute of archaeology.
Level of Study: Postgraduate
Type: Scholarship
Value: Approx. £1,000
Length of Study: 1 year full-time, 2 years part-time
Frequency: Annual
Study Establishment: University College London
Country of Study: United Kingdom
Application Procedure: Applicants must contact the department.
No. of awards offered: 10
Closing Date: March
No. of applicants last year: 46
Additional Information: www.ucl.ac.uk/archaeology/study/ graduate-taught-programmes

For further information contact:

Tel: (44) 20 7679 7499
Email: l.daniel@ucl.ac.uk

Master's Degree Awards in Biochemical Engineering

Purpose: To financially support postgraduate study
Eligibility: Open to United Kingdom/European Union resident applicants only
Level of Study: Postgraduate
Type: Scholarship
Value: A full award amounts to £9,000 plus tuition fees
Frequency: Annual
Study Establishment: University College London
Country of Study: United Kingdom
Application Procedure: Applicants must contact the department at the address given below or the British Council Office in Colombo

Closing Date: 1 July
Additional Information: The scholarships may be partly or fully funded https://www.ucl.ac.uk/prospective-students/grad uate/taught-degrees/biochemical-engineering-msc

For further information contact:

Tel: (44) 20 7679 3796
Email: nigelth@ucl.ac.uk

Member Scholarship in Statistics

Purpose: To financially support full-time graduate study and research
Eligibility: Applicants should have graduated from UCL or be a candidate for graduation in the term in which the award is made. United Kingdom, European Union and overseas students are eligible to apply
Level of Study: Postgraduate, Research
Type: Scholarship
Value: £55
Frequency: Annual
Study Establishment: University College London
Country of Study: United Kingdom
Application Procedure: Applicants should write to the department indicating their intention to compete for the scholarship

For further information contact:

Tel: (44) 20 7679 1872
Fax: (44) 20 7383 4703
Email: marion@stats.ucl.ac.uk

Monica Hulse Scholarship

Purpose: This Scholarship, founded in 2004, is funded from a regular lifetime gift from Dr Paul Hulse, alumnus of UCL, in memory of his mother, Monica Hulse (1934-1999). One scholarship is awarded annually to a prospective graduate student from any country admitted to the Department of Mathematics for full-time Master's study or MPhil/PhD research
Eligibility: 1. University College London - Monica Hulse Scholarships in UK, is available to candidates from all nationalities. 2. Candidates intending to pursue their masters or PhD studies can apply. 3. The applicants of University College London - Monica Hulse Scholarships in UK, must be enrolled in a full-time program in the Department of Mathematics at UCL. 4. Candidates are not permitted to receive any other special funding
Level of Study: Doctorate, Masters Degree, Postgraduate, Research
Type: Scholarship

Value: £1,000
Length of Study: 1 year
Frequency: Annual
Country of Study: United Kingdom
Application Procedure: Candidates wishing to apply for the Scholarship must send written notice of their intention to apply for the Scholarship, along with an academic CV, to the Graduate Tutor in the Department of Mathematics. Applicants should not normally be in receipt of any other special funding (other than in exceptional circumstances).
Closing Date: 31 May
Funding: Private
No. of awards given last year: 1

For further information contact:

Email: h.higgins@ucl.ac.uk

National Health Service Bursaries

Purpose: To financially support postgraduate study
Eligibility: Open to United Kingdom and European Union applicants only who have applied for a place for graduate study at UCL
Level of Study: Postgraduate
Type: Bursary
Value: United Kingdom/European Union tuition fees. United Kingdom residents will also normally be eligible for a means tested bursary
Frequency: Annual
Study Establishment: University College London
Country of Study: United Kingdom
Application Procedure: There is no separate bursary application form. Application procedure is an automatic process once an offer of a place has been made
Additional Information: When an offer of a place has been made, the NHS Student Grants unit will contact the applicant directly www.scholarshipdesk.com/monica-hulse-scholarship/

For further information contact:

Tel: (44) 20 7679 4202
Email: n.wilkins@ucl.ac.uk

Nederlandse Taalunie Scholarship

Purpose: To financially support postgraduate study
Eligibility: Applicants must have applied for a place for graduate study at UCL
Level of Study: Postgraduate
Type: Scholarship
Value: £2,500
Frequency: Annual

Study Establishment: University College London
Country of Study: United Kingdom
Application Procedure: Applicants should contact the department. If the applicant has not applied to UCL, they must complete a graduate application form and enclose it with the scholarship application
Closing Date: 15 July

For further information contact:

Tel: (44) 20 7679 3117
Fax: (44) 20 7616 6985
Email: t.hermans@ucl.ac.uk

Perren Studentship

Purpose: To financially support graduate study and research
Eligibility: Open to U.K. and EU applicants only who have applied for a place for graduate study at UCL.
Level of Study: Postgraduate, Research
Type: Studentship
Value: United Kingdom/European Union tuition fees. United Kingdom residents will also normally be eligible for a means tested bursary.
Frequency: Annual
Study Establishment: University College London
Country of Study: United Kingdom
Application Procedure: Applicants should provide particulars of their academic record and of the work that they intend to pursue to the department
Closing Date: 15 May
Funding: Trusts
Contributor: Perren Fund

For further information contact:

Tel: (44) 20 7679 473
Email: lahauestar@ucl.ac.uk

Professor Sir Malcolm Grant Postgraduate Scholarship

Eligibility: Candidates must fulfil all of the following criteria: 1. be ordinarily resident in the UK and eligible to pay Home fee rate; 2. have successfully completed or be currently completing undergraduate studies at UCL; 3. hold an offer to study a full-time Master's degree at UCL in 2023/24.
Level of Study: Postgraduate
Type: Scholarship
Value: £25,000 (for one year)
Length of Study: 1 year
Frequency: Annual
Country of Study: United Kingdom

U

Closing Date: 9 June
Additional Information: www.ucl.ac.uk/scholarships/
professor-sir-malcolm-grant-postgraduate-scholarship

R B Hounsfield Scholarship in Traffic Engineering

Purpose: To financially support MPhil/PhD research in Traffic Engineering in the Department of Civil and Environmental Engineering
Eligibility: Candidates should hold or expect to obtain a First Class (Honours) Degree or equivalent and should have been offered a place at UCL and have firmly accepted that offer or be intending to do so
Level of Study: Doctorate, Postgraduate, Research
Type: Scholarship
Value: Not less than £120
Frequency: Dependent on funds available
Study Establishment: University College London
Country of Study: United Kingdom
Application Procedure: Enquiries should be directed to the department
Closing Date: 15 May
Additional Information: If the applicant has not already applied to UCL, please complete a graduate application form and enclose it with the scholarship application www. scholarshipdesk.com/monica-hulse-scholarship/

For further information contact:

Tel: (44) 20 7679 2710
Fax: (44) 20 7380 0986
Email: civeng.admissions@ucl.ac.uk

Research Degree Scholarship in Chemical Engineering

Purpose: To financially support MPhil/PhD research
Level of Study: Doctorate, Postgraduate, Research
Type: Scholarship
Value: £2,000
Frequency: Annual
Study Establishment: University College London
Country of Study: United Kingdom
Application Procedure: Applicants must contact the department

For further information contact:

Tel: (44) 20 7679 3835
Fax: (44) 20 7383 2348
Email: h.mahgerefteh@ucl.ac.uk

Research Degree Scholarships in Anthropology

Purpose: To financially support research in the field of anthropology
Eligibility: Please contact the Department of Anthropology for details
Level of Study: Doctorate, Postgraduate, Research
Type: Scholarship
Value: United Kingdom/European Union tuition fees
Frequency: Annual
Study Establishment: University College London
Country of Study: United Kingdom
Application Procedure: Applicants must contact the department
No. of awards offered: 12
Closing Date: 30 April
No. of awards given last year: 4
No. of applicants last year: 12

For further information contact:

Tel: (44) 20 7679 8622
Fax: (44) 20 7679 8632
Email: ucsapga@ucl.ac.uk

Richard Chattaway Scholarship

Purpose: To financially support MPhil/PhD study
Eligibility: This scholarship is open to candidates from any country however candidates need to apply to a graduate programme in History by the relevant deadline to be eligible
Level of Study: Doctorate, Postgraduate
Type: Scholarship
Value: £2,000
Length of Study: 1 year
Frequency: Annual
Study Establishment: University College London
Country of Study: United Kingdom
Application Procedure: Applicants must contact the department. If the applicants have not already applied to UCL they must complete a graduate application form and enclose it with the scholarship application. Applicants must include particulars of the research work they intend to pursue in the event of the scholarship being awarded to them
Closing Date: 15 May
Funding: Individuals
Contributor: Private donation in honour of Richard Chattaway
No. of awards given last year: 1
Additional Information: https://www.ucl.ac.uk/history/prospective-students/graduate-research/history-mphilphd-funding

For further information contact:

Email: n.miller@ucl.ac.uk

Royal National Orthopaedic Hospital Special Trustees Research Training Scholarship

Purpose: To give orthopaedic specialists of the future an early exposure to the first-class research culture at Stanmore

Eligibility: Open to students enrolled in the MSc in Surgical Sciences programme undertaking a research project at the Royal National Orthopaedic Hospital/Institute of Orthopaedic and Musculoskeletal Science.

Level of Study: Postgraduate

Type: Scholarship

Value: A stipend, tuition and bench fees

Frequency: Annual

Study Establishment: Royal National Orthopaedic Hospital, Stanmore

Country of Study: United Kingdom

Application Procedure: Once students have been accepted by a supervisor, they should contact the R&D office, Royal National Orthopaedic Hospital. Applicants will be asked to send an outline of the research project and their curriculum vitae. Applicant should contact the department at the address given below

Funding: Private

Contributor: The RNOH Special Trustees and the R&D Subcommittee

Additional Information: Recipients of the scholarships must present their research findings at a symposium to be held at the RNOH. The R&D Director and the Non-Executive Director for research will review applications www.european-funding-guide.eu/other-financial-assistance/14163-keeling-scholarship

For further information contact:

Royal National Orthopaedic Hospital, Brockley Hill, Stanmore, Middlesex HA7 4LP, United Kingdom.

Tel: (44) 20 8909 5752
Email: lphilpots@rnoh.nhs.uk

Score Africa/Allan & Nesta Ferguson Charitable Trust Scholarship

Purpose: To financially assist African nationals to undertake MSc/PhD studies at the Centre for International Health and Development (CIHD) at UCL

Eligibility: Applicants should refer to the website for full details on eligibility

Level of Study: Postgraduate

Type: Scholarship

Value: £30,555

Frequency: Annual

Country of Study: Any country

Application Procedure: Applicants should refer to the website for further information on application procedures, forms and deadlines

No. of awards offered: 10

Closing Date: 30 April

For further information contact:

Tel: (44) 20 7074 5094/5091
Email: scholarships@soas.ac.uk

Shell Petroleum Development Company Niger Delta Postgraduate Scholarship

Purpose: To provide opportunities for postgraduate study in the United Kingdom for young students and professionals, who demonstrate both academic excellence and the potential to become leading professionals in the oil and associated industries

Eligibility: The applicant must 1. have obtained a degree of at least an equivalent standard to a United Kingdom Upper Second Class (Honours Degree); 2. be neither a current nor former employee (who have left employment less than 5 years before) of SPDC, the Royal Dutch Shell Group of Companies or Wider Perspectives Limited, or current employee's relatives; 3. not already have had the chance of studying in the United Kingdom or another developed country; 4. be aged between 21 and 28 years; 5. originate from one of the Niger Delta States in Nigeria, namely Rivers, Delta or Bayelsa and currently reside in Nigeria

Level of Study: Postgraduate

Type: Scholarship

Value: Full tuition fee funding, maintenance allowance, return airfares and arrival allowance

Frequency: Annual

Study Establishment: University College London

Country of Study: United Kingdom

Closing Date: 15 March

No. of awards given last year: 10

For further information contact:

Student Funding Office, UCL, Gower Street, London WC1E 6BT, United Kingdom.

Email: studentfunding@ucl.ac.uk

Sir Frederick Pollock Scholarship for Students from North America

Purpose: To financially support prospective LLM students
Eligibility: Applicants must be overseas students from North America. An applicant must have accepted an offer (either conditional or unconditional) to read for the LLM at UCL to be eligible
Level of Study: Postgraduate
Type: Scholarship
Value: £2,000
Frequency: Annual
Country of Study: United Kingdom
Application Procedure: There is no application procedure. All eligible students will be automatically considered
Closing Date: 2 March
Additional Information: The scholarships will be based on academic merit. The faculty will only consider those applicants who have firmly accepted their offer of admission to the LLM by May 31st www.european-funding-guide.eu/other-financial-assistance/14065-sir-frederick-pollock-scholarship-students-north-america

For further information contact:

Tel: (44) 20 7679 1441
Fax: (44) 20 7209 3470
Email: jane.ha@ucl.ac.uk

Sir George Jessel Studentship in Mathematics

Purpose: To financially support MPhil/PhD research
Eligibility: A candidate must have been an undergraduate student of UCL, and must have graduated, or be a candidate for graduation in the term in which the award is made. The studentship may also be awarded to someone who has held it in the previous year.
Level of Study: Doctorate, Postgraduate, Research
Type: Studentship
Value: £1,800
Frequency: Annual
Study Establishment: University College London
Country of Study: United Kingdom
Application Procedure: Applicants must contact the department
Closing Date: 15 May
Additional Information: Please refer the website for further details www.ucl.ac.uk/prospective-students/scholarships/graduate/deptscholarships/mathematics www.scholarshipdesk.com/sir-george-jessel-studentship/

For further information contact:

Tel: (44) 20 7679 2839
Fax: (44) 20 7383 5519
Email: h.higgins@ucl.ac.uk

Sir James Lighthill Scholarship

Purpose: To financially support MPhil/PhD research
Eligibility: United Kingdom, European Union and overseas students are eligible to apply. All applicants who firmly accept a place for MPhil/PhD research in the Mathematics Department will be considered
Level of Study: Doctorate, Postgraduate, Research
Type: Scholarship
Value: £500 per year
Frequency: Annual
Study Establishment: University College London
Country of Study: United Kingdom
Application Procedure: Applicants must contact the department

For further information contact:

Tel: (44) 20 7679 2839
Email: h.higgins@ucl.ac.uk

Sir John Salmond Scholarship for Students from Australia and New Zealand

Purpose: To financially support prospective LLM students
Eligibility: Applicants must be overseas students from Australia and New Zealand. An applicant must have accepted an offer (either conditional or unconditional) to read for the LLM at UCL to be eligible
Level of Study: Doctorate, Postgraduate
Type: Scholarship
Value: £2,000
Frequency: Annual
Study Establishment: University College London
Country of Study: United Kingdom
Application Procedure: There is no application
Additional Information: The scholarships will be based on academic merit. The faculty will only consider these applicants who have firmly accepted their offer of admission to the LLM by May 31st www.educationprogram.scholarshipcare.com/sir-james-lighthill-scholarship/

For further information contact:

Tel: (44) 20 7679 1441
Fax: (44) 20 7209 3470
Email: jane.ha@ucl.ac.uk

Sully Scholarship

Purpose: To financially support MPhil/PhD research
Eligibility: Open to the most outstanding candidate in the second year of their PhD research programme
Level of Study: Doctorate, Postgraduate, Research
Type: Scholarship
Value: £2,200
Frequency: Annual
Study Establishment: University College London
Country of Study: United Kingdom
Application Procedure: There is no separate application and the award is given to an outstanding student who is registered in the department's PhD programme and is in the second year of study
No. of awards given last year: 1

For further information contact:

Tel: (44) 20 7679 5332
Fax: (44) 20 7430 4276
Email: psychology-pg-enquiries@ucl.ac.uk

Teaching Assistantships (Economics)

Purpose: To financially support MPhil/PhD students
Eligibility: MPhil/PhD students who have successfully completed their 1st year in the department
Level of Study: Doctorate
Type: Assistantship
Value: £11,000
Frequency: Annual
Study Establishment: University College London
Country of Study: United Kingdom
Application Procedure: Contact the Department of Economics for details

For further information contact:

Email: d.fauvrelle@ucl.ac.uk

Thames and Hudson Scholarship

Purpose: To financially support postgraduate study
Level of Study: Postgraduate
Type: Scholarship
Value: A scholarship up to a maximum value of £15,000 or up to 4 scholarships totalling that value
Frequency: Annual
Study Establishment: University College London
Country of Study: United Kingdom

Application Procedure: Applicants must contact the department for details
Closing Date: July

For further information contact:

Tel: (44) 20 7679 7495
Fax: (44) 20 7383 2572
Email: k.thomas@ucl.ac.uk

The George Melhuish Postgraduate Scholarship

Purpose: To financially support postgraduate research
Eligibility: Open to United Kingdom, European Union and overseas applicants
Level of Study: Postgraduate, Research
Type: Scholarship
Value: Up to £3,700
Frequency: Annual
Study Establishment: University College London
Country of Study: United Kingdom
Application Procedure: No separate application is required. Applicants who are admitted to research programmes in philosophy will automatically be considered for the scholarship. Any queries should be directed to the department
No. of awards given last year: 2
Additional Information: Decision regarding this award will be made in September www.european-funding-guide.eu/other-financial-assistance/14165-george-melhuish-postgraduate-scholarships

For further information contact:

Tel: (44) 20 7679 4451
Email: r.madden@ucl.ac.uk

Thomas Witherden Batt Scholarship

Eligibility: Candidates must fulfil all of the following criteria: 1. be ordinarily resident in the UK and eligible to pay Home fee rate; 2. hold an offer to study for a full-time Master of Science (MSc) degree at UCL in 2023/24.
Level of Study: Postgraduate
Type: Scholarship
Value: £10,000 (for one year)
Length of Study: 1 year
Frequency: Annual
Country of Study: United Kingdom
No. of awards offered: 1
Closing Date: 9 June
Additional Information: www.ucl.ac.uk/scholarships/thomas-witherden-batt-scholarship

U

UCL Hong Kong Scholarships Fund

Eligibility: Applicants should: 1. be domiciled in Hong Kong; 2. hold a valid UCL Student Number; 3. hold a valid UCAS Personal ID (not UCAS Registration number); 4. be in financial need; 5 .hold an offer of admission to UCL to study for a full-time undergraduate or postgraduate 6. Master's degree for the 2021/22 intake (commencing in September 2021); OR 7. be currently enrolled at UCL on an undergraduate or postgraduate Master's programme.
Level of Study: Postgraduate
Type: Scholarship
Value: £5,000 (towards tuition fee for one year)
Length of Study: 1 year
Frequency: Annual
Country of Study: Any country
No. of awards offered: 2
Closing Date: 7 May
Additional Information: www.ucl.ac.uk/scholarships/ucl-hong-kong-scholarships-fund

For further information contact:

Email: studentfunding@ucl.ac.uk)

UCL Masters Bursary

Eligibility: Candidates must fulfill all of the following criteria: 1. be ordinarily resident in the UK and eligible to pay Home fee rate; 2. have commenced undergraduate study no earlier than 2013/14 academic session; 3. have an annual household income of £42,875 or less; 4 .AND hold an offer to study a full-time Master's degree at UCL in 2023/24.
Level of Study: Postgraduate
Type: Bursary
Value: £10,000 (for one year)
Length of Study: 1 year
Frequency: Annual
Country of Study: United Kingdom
Application Procedure: You need to hold an offer of a place at UCL in order to apply for the scholarship, so you are advised to apply for an eligible degree at UCL in good time for the Admissions Office and the relevant academic department to process and respond to your application.
No. of awards offered: 200
Closing Date: 8 June

University College London Department Awards for Graduate Students

Purpose: To financially support Master's and MPhil/PhD programmes

Eligibility: United Kingdom, European Union and overseas students are eligible to apply
Level of Study: Doctorate, Postgraduate
Type: Scholarship
Value: £500
Frequency: Annual
Study Establishment: University College London
Country of Study: United Kingdom
Application Procedure: Applicants must contact the department
Closing Date: 15 May

For further information contact:

Tel: (44) 20 7679 3262
Fax: (44) 20 7383 4108
Email: s.anyadi@ling.ucl.ac.uk

University College London-AET Undergraduate International Outreach Bursaries

Eligibility: Applicants must be a national of any African country (including Madagascar), currently living in an African country, and have one or both parents living in an African country, or are orphaned
Type: Bursary
Frequency: Annual
Country of Study: Any country

For further information contact:

Email: m.omona@africaeducationaltrust.org

William Blake Trust Bursary

Purpose: To financially support postgraduate or MPhil/PhD study
Eligibility: Applicants must have applied for a place for graduate study at UCL
Level of Study: Doctorate, Postgraduate
Type: Bursary
Value: £2,000
Frequency: Annual
Study Establishment: University College London
Country of Study: United Kingdom
Application Procedure: Applicants must contact the department. If the applicants have not already applied to UCL they must complete a graduate application form and enclose it with the scholarship application
Closing Date: 15 May

For further information contact:

Tel: (44) 20 7679 7546
Fax: (44) 20 7916 5939
Email: d.dethloff@ucl.ac.uk

William Moore Gorman Graduate Research Scholarship

Purpose: To financially support students entering the first year of the MPhil/PhD degree in department of Economics
Eligibility: Open to candidates who have applied for a place for graduate study at University College London
Level of Study: Doctorate, Postgraduate
Type: Scholarship
Value: £16,200 each
Length of Study: 1 year
Frequency: Annual
Study Establishment: University College London
Country of Study: United Kingdom
Application Procedure: All applicants for admission to our MRes programme are automatically considered for departmental funding at the time of application. There is no separate application process
No. of awards offered: 4
No. of awards given last year: 9
Additional Information: The scholarship will be awarded to students who are not already receiving full financial support from other sources for fees and living costs, and will be, awarded on the basis of academic merit www.ucl.ac.uk/economics/study/postgraduate/funding/funding/w-m-gorman-graduate-research-scholarships

For further information contact:

Tel: (44) 20 7679 5861
Fax: (44) 20 7916 2775
Email: d.fauvrelle@ucl.ac.uk

University Commission for Development Academy of Research and Higher Education Scholarships

Rue Royale 180, B-1000 Brussels, Belgium.

Website: www.ares-ac.be/en/cooperation-au-developpement/bourses/masters-et-stages-en-belgique
Contact: ARES

Academy of Research and Higher Education Scholarships

Level of Study: Postgraduate
Value: The scholarship covers international travel expenses, living allowance, tuition fees, insurance, housing allowance
Country of Study: Any country
Application Procedure: To apply for the scholarship, complete the single form scholarship application and admission to one of the French-speaking universities of Belgium
Closing Date: 9 February
Additional Information: The scholarships are for nationals of: Benin, Bolivia, Burkina Faso, Burundi, Cambodia, Cameroon, Cuba, Ecuador, Ethiopia (only for courses in English), Haiti, Madagascar, Morocco, Niger, Peru, Philippines, DR Congo, Rwanda, Senegal, Vietnam. For more details, please visit official scholarship website: www.ares-ac.be/en/cooperation-au-developpement/bourses/masters-et-stages-en-belgique

For further information contact:

Email: scholarships-cooperation@ares-ac.be

University Institute of European Studies

Via Maria Vittoria 26, I-10123 Turin, Italy.

Tel: (39) 11 839 4660
Email: info@iuse.it
Website: www.iuse.it
Contact: Ms Maria Grazia Goiettina, Course Secretariat

The University Institute of European Studies promotes international relations and European integration by organizing academic activities. The Institute has a comprehensive library in international law and economics. Since 1952 the Institute has been a European Documentation Centre (EDC), thus receiving all official publications of European institutions.

LLM in International Trade Law – Contracts and Dispute Resolution – Scholarships

Eligibility: Applicants must have successfully completed a first level university degree of at least 3 years' duration, either in law, economics, political sciences, business administration or equivalent
Level of Study: Postgraduate
Type: Scholarship

Country of Study: Any country
Funding: Foundation, Government, Individuals, Private

For further information contact:

Tel: (39) 11 69 36 945
Fax: (39) 11 69 36 369
Email: tradelaw@itcilo.org

University of Aarhus

Nordre Ringgade 1, Bygning 327 3, DK-8000 Aarhus, Denmark.

Tel: (45) 8942 1111
Email: au@au.dk
Website: www.au.dk
Contact: Faculty of Social Sciences

The University of Aarhus was founded in 1928 as Universitetsundervisningen i Jylland – University Teaching in Jutland in classrooms rented from the Technical College and a teaching corps consisting of 1 Professor of philosophy and 4 Readers of Danish, English, German and French. However, today the University has 20,000 students with 5,000 staff.

Doctor of Philosophy Scholarship in Globalisation and International Economics

Purpose: To enable students to take up research in the related fields
Eligibility: Open to applicants who have a Master's degree or to students who expect to obtain their Master's degree in the near future
Level of Study: Postgraduate, Research
Type: Scholarship
Value: Approx. salary of DKK2,700
Length of Study: 3 years
Frequency: Annual
Study Establishment: Aarhus School of Business
Country of Study: Denmark
Application Procedure: Application forms can be downloaded from the Aarhus website. The form should be sent with a curriculum vitae and an outline of a research project including a description of the proposed theory and methods
Closing Date: 19 February
Contributor: Danish Social Science Research Council

For further information contact:

Tel: (45) 89 486 482/392
Email: pje@asb.dk

University of Aarhus PhD Scholarships

Purpose: To provide financial support and encourage research work
Eligibility: Open to candidates who have obtained a Danish university master's degree or an examination at an equivalent level
Level of Study: Doctorate
Type: Scholarship
Value: US$42,000; US$44,000 per year
Length of Study: 3 years
Frequency: Annual
Country of Study: Denmark
Application Procedure: Applicants may download the application form from the website. The completed application form along with project description, plan for the course, budget and copy of degree certificate(s) must be submitted
Closing Date: 16 June
Additional Information: Further information may be obtained from Administrator Henrik Friis Bach, The Faculty of Social Sciences Secretariat, Tel: (45) 8942 1546 www.ares-ac.be/en/cooperation-au-developpement/bourses/masters-et-stages-en-belgique

For further information contact:

Email: socialsciences@au.dk

University of Aberdeen

University Office, King's College, Aberdeen AB24 3FX, United Kingdom.

Tel: (44) 12 2427 3506
Email: ptgoff@abdn.ac.uk
Website: www.abdn.ac.uk
Contact: The Postgraduate Registry

The University of Aberdeen is the fifth oldest in the United Kingdom. Aberdeen is an international university serving one of the most dynamic regions of Europe with over 13,000 students and over 3,000 staff, and is at the forefront of teaching and research in medicine and the humanities and sciences.

Aberdeen International Masters Scholarship

Type: Scholarship
Value: £2,000 tuition fee discount
Frequency: Annual
Country of Study: United Kingdom
Application Procedure: You will be awarded your scholarships as tuition fee discount and the value of the scholarship will be included in your CAS letter.
Additional Information: Students cannot receive a cash alternative for scholarship www.abdn.ac.uk/study/funding/341

For further information contact:

Email: study@abdn.ac.uk

Arts Humanities Research Council Collaborative Doctoral Partnership PhD Studentship

Purpose: The Collaborative Doctoral Partnership scheme gives non-higher education institutions with a proven track record in postgraduate research the opportunity to manage PhD students, with a minimum of three studentships per year
Eligibility: 1. Residency: Students from the EU are normally eligible for a fees-only scholarship, unless they have been ordinarily resident in the UK for three or more years directly prior to the start of the studentship (with some further constraint regarding residence for education). 2. Projects: These awards are attached to specific projects. Only students chosen by the project supervisors can apply.
Level of Study: Doctorate
Type: Studentship
Value: £15,009+ per annum, plus £550 enhancement, plus tuition fees
Length of Study: 3 years
Frequency: Annual
Country of Study: Any country
Application Procedure: You could use the website link www.ahrc-cdp.org
No. of awards offered: 3
Closing Date: 28 January
Additional Information: www.york.ac.uk/study/postgraduate-research/funding/ahrc-collaborative-doctoral-awards/

For further information contact:

Email: Lucie.Connors@ahrc.ukri.org

China Scholarship Council (CSC) Scholarship

Purpose: The CSC Scholarship is a scholarship programme for Chinese PhD students, who will take a full PhD at the University of Aberdeen

Eligibility: 1. To be eligible to apply for this scholarship in China, candidates must submit with their application, a conditional scholarship offer letter from Curtin University. 2. To ensure interested candidates meet the China Scholarship Council application deadline in March each year, Curtin University strongly encourage students submit their online e-application for admissions latest by 31 January of the applying year to avoid missing the deadline. 3. Scholarship Recipients must hold a conditional offer of enrolment subject to the CSC award and also fulfil the entry requirements of Curtin University, including a high level of English language proficiency
Level of Study: Doctorate
Type: Scholarship
Country of Study: Any country
Application Procedure: Applications for the CSC Scholarship should be submitted online at apply.csc.edu.cn/csc/main/person/login/index.jsf
Additional Information: If you have any further questions, please contact Catriona Milne, International Officer for China, via email: catriona.milne@abdn.ac.uk graduateschool.nd.edu/admissions/international-students/china-scholarship-council/

For further information contact:

Email: study@abdn.ac.uk

Common Data Access MSc Petroleum Data Management Scholarships

Purpose: To pursue MSc programme
Eligibility: Open only to the citizens of Australia or permanent residents who have achieved Honours 1 or equivalent
Level of Study: Postgraduate
Value: Each scholarship is valued at £5,000 for the duration of the MSc Petroleum Data Management degree and will contribute towards the programme tuition fees
Frequency: Annual
Country of Study: Any country
Closing Date: 31 May

For further information contact:

Email: info@cdal.com

Elphinstone PhD Scholarships

Type: Scholarship
Value: Cover tuition fees for the duration of their supervised study
Country of Study: Any country

Additional Information: www.european-funding-guide.eu/
scholarship/10782-elphinstone-phd-scholarship

For further information contact:

Email: infohub@abdn.ac.uk

Principal

Level of Study: Unrestricted
Type: Scholarship
Study Establishment: University of Aberdeen
Country of Study: United Kingdom

For further information contact:

Email: studentfunding@ed.ac.uk

University of Adelaide

Graduate School of Management, 3rd Floor Security House,
233 North Terrace, Adelaide, SA 5005, Australia.

Tel: (61) 8 3035 525
Email: cmchugh@gsm.adelaide.edu.au
Website: www.gsm.adelaide.edu.au
Contact: MBA Admissions Officer

Adelaide Postgraduate Coursework Scholarships

Eligibility: Open only to the citizens of Australia or perma-
nent residents who have achieved Honours 1 or equivalent
Level of Study: Postgraduate
Type: Scholarship
Value: Covers 50% of the tuition fee costs
Length of Study: 2 years
Frequency: Annual
Study Establishment: University of Adelaide
Country of Study: Australia
Application Procedure: Applicants must apply directly to
the scholarship provider. Check website for further details

For further information contact:

Adelaide Graduate Centre, Adelaide University, Adelaide,
SA 5005, Australia.

Tel: (61) 8 8313 4455
Fax: (61) 8 8223 3394
Email: adrienne.gorringe@adelaide.edu.au

Adelaide Scholarships International

Purpose: To attract high quality overseas postgraduate stu-
dents to areas of research strength in the University of Ade-
laide to support its research effort
Eligibility: Open only to the citizens of Australia or perma-
nent residents who have achieved Honours 1 or equivalent
Level of Study: Postgraduate
Type: Scholarships
Value: AU$28,092
Length of Study: 2 years (Masters) or 3 years (PhD)
Frequency: Annual
Study Establishment: University of Adelaide
Country of Study: Australia
Application Procedure: Candidates must apply directly to
the university. Check the website for further details
Closing Date: 10 July
Contributor: Adelaide University
Additional   Information: scholarships.adelaide.edu.au/
Scholarships/postgraduate-research/all-faculties/adelaide-
scholarships-international

For further information contact:

Email: student.centre@adelaide.edu.au

Adelaide Scholarships International (ASI)

Purpose: The University of Adelaide offers a number of
Adelaide Scholarships International to outstanding international graduates from any country to commence their education via a Masters or Doctorate degree by research.
Eligibility: Applicants must be international students who are
acceptable to commence a Masters or Doctorate by research
degree at the University of Adelaide. 1. Citizens and Permanent Residents of Australia, and citizens of New Zealand are
ineligible. 2. Applicants who have applied for Australian
permanent residency status, but have not yet received an
outcome, can apply. 3. Successful recipients are required to
apply and enrol in their intended program of study at The
University of Adelaide as 'international students' to retain
their scholarship. Applicants are required to provide evidence
of meeting the University of Adelaide's minimum English
language proficiency requirements for direct entry by the
application deadline. Applicants with a qualification in progress will not be eligible for consideration until the qualification has been satisfactorily completed (and acceptable
evidence provided), or evidence of withdrawal has been provided. Applicants are required to have successfully completed
at least the equivalent of a First Class Australian Honours
degree. (In Australia an Honours degree is generally a one
year qualification taken after an undergraduate degree and

involves further study in a particular discipline area. In some areas, Honours is available as part of the final year of a four year undergraduate degree. It is recognised as a prestigious qualification that further develops research, writing and organisational skills. It also demonstrates an ability to undertake high-level study. Achievement of a First Class Honours degree indicates that the recipient performed at the highest academic level and indicates that they have had an introduction to independent research.) International applicants must not hold a research qualification regarded by the University of Adelaide to be equivalent to an Australian Research Doctorate degree or, if undertaking a Research Masters degree, not hold a research qualification regarded by the University of Adelaide to be equivalent to or higher than an Australian Research Masters degree.

Level of Study: Masters/PhD Degree

Type: Scholarships

Value: The scholarship includes course tuition fees, annual living allowance (AU$28,092), overseas student health cover plus relocation and publication expenses. The scholarship is awarded for two years for a Masters degree by Research and three years (with a possible 6 month extension) for a Doctoral research degree.

Frequency: Others

Country of Study: Australia

Application Procedure: The prerequisite for applying is that the visiting researcher must have established contacts with a Finnish host university - please see the section 'Doctoral Admissions' for further information (you'll find links to the universities' Doctoral Admissions pages there). You are also advised to visit the Finnish universities' own websites for info on Doctoral level study and research options. If a Finnish university is willing to host you, then the Finnish university department wishing to host you can apply to EDUFI for the grant on your behalf. In other words, only the hosting Finnish university can act as an "applicant" in the EDUFI Fellowship programme. There are no annual application deadlines in the EDUFI Fellowship programme. Applications may be considered at all times. However, please note that applications should be submitted at least 5 months before the intended scholarship period.

No. of awards offered: Limited

Closing Date: 10 July

Additional Information: scholarships.adelaide.edu.au/Scholarships/postgraduate-research/all-faculties/adelaide-scholarships-international

Asia Pacific Institute of Information Technology_IT PhDs in Grid Computing

Purpose: To enable high performance numerical computing on service-oriented architectures

Eligibility: Open only to the citizens of Australia and New Zealand or permanent residents who have achieved Honours 2a or equivalent

Level of Study: Postgraduate

Type: Scholarship

Value: AU$24,650 per year

Length of Study: 3 years and 6 months

Frequency: Annual

Study Establishment: The Australian National University, The University of Adelaide

Country of Study: Australia

Application Procedure: Check website for further details

Closing Date: 21 September

Contributor: Adelaide University and The Australian National University

For further information contact:

Email: Peter.Strazdins@cs.anu.edu.au

Australian Building Codes Board Research Scholarship

Purpose: The ABCB runs the Student Research Scholarship Program to encourage undergraduate and postgraduate research in the field of building regulatory reform in Australia, which can contribute to the ABCB fulfilling its charter

Eligibility: To be eligible for the scholarship, applicants must be students currently undertaking undergraduate or postgraduate studies in building, building surveying, fire engineering, architecture, construction, plumbing, hydraulic design or similar at an Australian educational institution; and research that forms a component of a program or course at an educational institution (e.g. tertiary), such as a research project, thesis or dissertation

Level of Study: Graduate

Type: Scholarship

Value: Up to AU$5,000 one off payment

Length of Study: 1 year

Country of Study: Australia

Application Procedure: To apply for the scholarship, applicants are asked to submit an ABCB Research Scholarship Application Form together with a resume and academic transcript to date to the Research Scholarship Project Officer at abcb.scholarship@abcb.gov.au

Additional Information: For more information on the Student Research Scholarship Program, please contact the Research Scholarship Project Officer at abcb.scholarship@abcb.gov.au scholarshipdb.net/scholarships-in-Australia/Australian-Building-Codes-Board-Research-Scholarship-University-Of-South-Australia=_6naSSb-5hGUSwAlkGUTnw.html

U

For further information contact:

Email: abcb.scholarship@abcb.gov.au

Australian Federation of University Women SA Inc. (AFUW-SA) Diamond Jubilee Scholarship

Eligibility: This scholarship is available to women students who: 1. are Australian citizens or permanent residents; 2. are enrolled at a South Australian University, undertaking a postgraduate Masters degree by research or including a thesis component; 3. have completed at least six (6) months full time equivalent of their masters program; 4. are not in full-time paid employment or on fully paid leave; 5. have not have received a scholarship or award in the same category in 2022.
Level of Study: Postgraduate, Research
Type: Scholarship
Value: AU$3,000
Frequency: Annual
Country of Study: Australia
Closing Date: 31 March
Additional Information: scholarships.adelaide.edu.au/ Scholarships/postgraduate-coursework/all-faculties/australian-federation-of-university-women-sa-inc

Australian Rotary Health PhD Scholarships – Post Traumatic Stress Disorder (PTSD)

Eligibility: Applicants must be: 1. an Australian citizen or have Australian Permanent Resident status, and not be under bond to any foreign government. Evidence of citizenship (citizenship certificate, birth certificate, passport) or residential status must accompany the application. 2. about to commence, or in their first year of a PhD only – studying full-time.
Level of Study: Postgraduate, Research
Type: Scholarship
Value: AU$30,000 per annum
Length of Study: 3.5 years
Frequency: Annual
Country of Study: Australia
Closing Date: 11 February
Additional Information: scholarships.adelaide.edu.au/Schol arships/postgraduate-research/faculty-of-health-and-medical-sciences/australian-rotary-1

For further information contact:

Email: scholarships@adelaide.edu.au

Ferry Scholarship – UniSA

Purpose: To promote study and research into the scientific fields of physics and chemistry
Eligibility: Open only to the citizens of Australia below the age of 25 years who have achieved Honours or equivalent
Level of Study: Postgraduate
Type: Scholarship
Value: AU$7,500 per year
Length of Study: 1 year
Frequency: Annual
Study Establishment: Flinders University, The University of Adelaide, University of South Australia
Country of Study: Australia
Application Procedure: Applicants must apply directly to the university. Check the website for further details
Closing Date: 31 March
Funding: Individuals
Contributor: Late Cedric Arnold Seth Ferry

For further information contact:

Tel: (61) 8302 3967
Email: jenni.critcher@unisa.edu.au

Joint Postgraduate Scholarship Program

Eligibility: Open to applicants who are citizens and permanent residents of the People's Republic of China at the time of application; are less than 35 years old at the time of application (this is a CSC eligibility requirement); are a university student completing a master's degree, or enrolled as a first year PhD student, or new graduates from their university at the time of application; agree to return to China upon completion of their studies and/or research; hold an unconditional offer of enrolment at the University of Adelaide, which is subject to the applicant also being successful in applying for a CSC award. They must therefore fulfil the relevant academic entry requirements set by the University of Adelaide for all international scholarship holders, including a high level of English language proficiency; English is the language of instruction at the University of Adelaide and proficiency in speaking, listening to, reading and writing English is essential. The IELTS (International English Language Testing System) is the preferred English language proficiency although TOEFL scores are also accepted. Applicants who have not provided evidence that they have met the university's minimum English Language Proficiency requirements by the closing date are not eligible for a CSC scholarship. CSC applicants are not permitted to undertake Pre-Enrolment English programs as the CSC will not award scholarships to applicants who have not met the university's minimum ELP requirements for direct entry. The Scholarships will give priority to graduates of the Chinese universities listed as "985 Project" Universities. Eligible candidates will be assessed by the University of Melbourne and Karlsruhe Institute of Technology on the basis of their academic transcripts and their research work

Type: Scholarship

Value: Australia

Country of Study: Any country

Application Procedure: The mode of applying is electronically. For detailed information, please visit website

Closing Date: 31 March

Contributor: The China Scholarship Council (CSC) and The University of Adelaide (UA)

Additional Information: The students of China can apply for these scholarships scholarshipdb.net/scholarships-in-Australia/Australian-Building-Codes-Board-Research-Scholarship-University-Of-South-Australia=_6naSSb-5hGUSwAlkGUTnw.html

Rae and George Hammer Memorial Visiting Research Fellowship

Purpose: The fellowship is available to assist an Honours, Masters or PhD student who is interested in studying any of the collections held in the Fryer Library, University of Queensland, to support their studies.

Eligibility: To be eligible for the fellowship: 1. submit the application by the due date 2. be enrolled in an approved program (Honours, Masters or PhD) from a university outside the metropolitan Brisbane area 3. demonstrate the relevance of primary source materials held by the UQ Fryer Library to your research.

Level of Study: Doctorate

Type: Fellowship

Value: AU$2,500

Frequency: Annual

Country of Study: Australia

Additional Information: scholarships.adelaide.edu.au/Scholarships/honours/all-faculties/rae-and-george-hammer-memorial-visiting-research-fellowship

For further information contact:

Email: farley@library.uq.edu.au

Scholarships in Plant Cell Physiology

Purpose: To improve the nutritional qualities of crop plants allowing the fortification of animal and human diets without adversely affecting crop plant

Eligibility: Open only to the citizens of Australia who have achieved Honours 1 or equivalent, or Honours 2a or equivalent

Level of Study: Postgraduate

Type: Scholarship

Value: AU$27,500 per year

Length of Study: 3 years

Frequency: Annual

Study Establishment: The University of Adelaide

Country of Study: Australia

Application Procedure: Applicants must apply directly to the university. Check website for further details

Closing Date: 31 August

Contributor: Adelaide University

For further information contact:

Tel: (61) 8 8303 8145

Email: matthew.gillam@adelaide.edu.au

The Hugh Martin Weir Prize

Eligibility: The Prize is open to University of Adelaide students who are enrolled in an Honours thesis program or a postgraduate program by coursework or by research, either commencing or already in progress. Postdoctoral researchers are eligible to apply within three years of a doctoral award.

Level of Study: Doctorate, Postgraduate, Research

Type: Scholarship

Value: AU$2,000

Frequency: Annual

Country of Study: Australia

Closing Date: 28 February

Additional Information: scholarships.adelaide.edu.au/Scholarships/honours/all-faculties/hugh-martin-weir-prize

The University of Adelaide & DST Industry PhD (UAiPhD) Program and Scholarship

Eligibility: Applicants must be Australian citizens who are acceptable as candidates for a PhD degree at the University of Adelaide, Faculty of Engineering, Computer & Mathematical Sciences, School of Computer Science, and would be able to commence in 2023.

Level of Study: Postgraduate, Research

Type: Scholarship

Value: AU$28,597.00 per annum (RTP Stipend) and AU$17,000 per annum (DST Supplementary Scholarship)

Length of Study: 4 years

Frequency: Annual

Country of Study: Australia

Closing Date: 11 March
Additional Information: scholarships.adelaide.edu.au/Scholarships/postgraduate-research/faculty-of-engineering-computer-and-mathematical-sciences-32

For further information contact:

Email: hdrindustryenq@adelaide.edu.au

University of Adelaide Research Scholarship - The Elder Conservatorium of Music

Eligibility: Applicants will have a minimum of Honours 2A result or equivalent in Music Technology or a Digital Media discipline, and must be citizens or permanent residents of Australia, citizens of New Zealand, or permanent humanitarian visa holders at the time of application.
Level of Study: Doctorate
Type: Scholarship
Value: AU$28,854
Length of Study: 3 years
Frequency: Annual
Country of Study: Australia
Application Procedure: Applying: Application for Admission must be submitted using the Online Application Form available at: hdrapp.adelaide.edu.au/auth/login
Closing Date: 24 February
Additional Information: scholarships.adelaide.edu.au/Scholarships/postgraduate-research/faculty-of-arts/university-of-adelaide-research-scholarship-1

For further information contact:

Email: luke.harrald@adelaide.edu.au

University of Alabama

Alumni Heritage Graduate Scholarship (AHGS)

Subjects: All
Purpose: To recruit children and grandchildren of graduates of The University of Alabama. To send a clear signal to our graduates that want your children. To provide a tangible Alumni Association membership benefit for UA graduates.
Eligibility: One time only (non-renewable) scholarship for first-year graduate students who are Alabama residents and who are children or grandchildren of a University of Alabama graduate. The scholarship is for the student's first term of graduate enrolment. Parent or grandparent must be a degree holder (undergraduate, graduate, or law degree) from The

University of Alabama. The qualifying parent or grandparent must be an active member of the National Alumni Association for three of the past five years. (Parent or grandparent cannot write check for all three years in one year.) The student must be admitted to a graduate degree program at UA and may be enrolled part-time or full-time. Please note students admitted to the Graduate School through special program such as the University Scholars Program or any Honor Program will be considered undergraduates for the purpose of this scholarship until the bachelor's degree is awarded.
Type: Scholarship
Value: The award will be equal to US$500 towards the cost of in-state tuition of graduate level course work. (Subject to a maximum of actual in-state tuition not covered by other awards, whichever is lower).
Frequency: Annual
Study Establishment: University of Alabama
Country of Study: United States of America
Application Procedure: Submit online scholarship form
Closing Date: 1 May
Additional Information: graduate.ua.edu/prospective-students/graduate-school-scholarships-fellowships/

For further information contact:

Email: amg@ua.edu

Graduate Council Fellowships

Purpose: To award University of Alabama Graduate School students.
Eligibility: Prospective and current University of Alabama students are nominated by their departments for our fellowships, so it is important that you are talking to the Graduate Program Director for your program. Prior to nomination, nominees who are prospective students must have been offered admission.
Type: Fellowship
Value: US$25,000/year for a maximum of 5 years
Length of Study: 5 years
Frequency: Annual
Study Establishment: University of Alabama
Country of Study: United States of America
No. of awards offered: 100
Closing Date: 13 January
No. of awards given last year: 15
Additional Information: graduate.ua.edu/prospective-students/graduate-school-scholarships-fellowships/#:~:text=Graduate%20Council%20Fellowships,-The%20University%20of&text=New%20and%20current%20UA%20students,a%20maximum%20of%205%20years.

McNair Graduate Fellowships

Purpose: McNair Graduate Fellowships are specifically for entering graduate students who have either completed a McNair Undergraduate Scholars program or who are McNair eligible.

Eligibility: Low income (as defined by the US Department of Education) AND a first-generation college student or a member of a group traditionally underrepresented in graduate education (i.e. Hispanic, African American, Native American, Native Hawaiian, Pacific Islander). Although any prospective or current graduate student may be nominated for this fellowship, preference is given to students who have completed a McNair program and have been accepted into a Doctoral program at The University of Alabama. Exceptional current University of Alabama students may also be considered for this fellowship.

Level of Study: Doctorate, Masters Degree

Type: Fellowship

Value: The stipend for the McNair Graduate Fellowship is US$20,000 for the academic year (fall and spring semesters).

Length of Study: 1 year

Frequency: Annual

Study Establishment: University of Alabama

Country of Study: United States of America

Contributor: 2 years for doctoral and 1 year for masters

University of Alaska Fairbanks (UAF)

School of Management PO Box 756080, Fairbanks, AK 99775-6080, United States of America.

Tel: (1) 907 474 6511
Email: famba@som.uaf.edu
Website: www.uaf.edu/som/mba
Contact: MBA Admissions Officer

RFRC Graduate Student Fellowship Awards

Purpose: This fellowship is especially interested in seeing proposals on applied topics aligned with the research priorities and needs of the North Pacific Fishery Management Council

Eligibility: 1. Awards will be made to support excellence in graduate student research. The award is not a Research Assistantship, but a Fellowship in recognition of scholastic excellence. Awards are open to any full-time or prospective CFOS graduate student. 2. Research should produce findings with a potential for continued development as a scientific or applied initiative. 3. Projects should be distinctive and make an original contribution to existing knowledge. 4. Projects should have potential economic value to the fishing industry and contribute to long-term benefits for Alaska. 5. Awards may be contingent on receipt of research funding from other sources. The award cannot be used for research expenses. See item #6, "Current and Pending," under "Format of Proposals" below. 6. Proposals should be submitted by the graduate student with faculty advisor endorsement as described in item #8 below. 7. Awards are renewable. Master's students can be funded for a maximum of two (2) years and PhD students for a maximum of three (3) years. Continuation requests require a satisfactory progress report

Level of Study: Postgraduate

Type: Fellowship

Value: Fellowship award of US$35,000

Length of Study: Master's students can be funded for a maximum of two (2) years and PhD students for a maximum of three (3) years.

Frequency: Annual

Country of Study: Any country

Application Procedure: Complete format of proposals are available in the below link. https://www.uaf.edu/cfos/research/rasmuson-fisheries-resear/rfrc-fellowships/

Closing Date: 28 January

Funding: Private

For further information contact:

Tel: (1) 907 474 2619
Email: clsutton3@alaska.edu

University of Alberta

Faculty of Graduate Studies & Research, Killam Centre for Advanced Studies, 2-29 Triffo Hall, Edmonton, AB T6G 2E1, Canada.

Tel: (1) 780 492 3499
Email: grad.services@ualberta.ca
Website: www.ualberta.ca/gradstudies

Opened in 1908, the University of Alberta has a long tradition of scholarly achievements and commitment to excellence in teaching, research and service to the community. It is one of Canada's five largest research-intensive universities, with an annual research income from external sources of more than C$3,000,000,000. It participates in 18 of 21 of the Federal Networks of Centres of Excellence, which link industries, universities and governments in applied research and development.

Canadian Initiatives For Nordic Studies (CINS) Graduate Scholarship

Purpose: To provide financial assistance to students who wish to pursue higher studies

Eligibility: Open to Canadian citizens or landed immigrants, who have completed a Bachelor's degree from a Canadian university or college with high scholastic achievement. Applicants must be in residency at the Nordic destination for a minimum of 6 months and provide a written report to CINS no later than 6 months after completing the proposed programme of study

Level of Study: Postgraduate

Type: Scholarship

Value: C$5,000

Frequency: Annual

Country of Study: Canada

Application Procedure: Applicants should include the following in their application contact details, citizenship status, social insurance number and date of birth, current academic status with formal transcripts, written acceptance from the host Nordic institution and reference letters

Closing Date: 15 October

For further information contact:

Tel: (1) 780 492 3111
Email: clsutton3@alaska.edu

Izaak Walton Killam Memorial Scholarship

Purpose: It will be offered to outstanding students registered in, or admissible to, a doctoral program. No restrictions on citizenship

Eligibility: Offered to outstanding students registered in, or admissible to, a doctoral program. No restrictions on citizenship. All fields are eligible for funding. Applicants must have completed at least one year of graduate work (master's or doctoral level) before start of tenure; tenure may begin on 1 May or 1 September. Additional information regarding eligibility criteria can be found in the Applicant Instructions document below. Please note that the GPA is calculated over the current graduate program graded course work

Level of Study: Graduate

Type: Scholarship

Value: US$45,000

Length of Study: 2 years

Frequency: Annual

Country of Study: Any country

Application Procedure: Students complete the Izaak Walton Killam Memorial Scholarship application form and submit supporting documents to their department to be considered for both the Izaak Walton Killam Memorial Scholarship and the Dorothy J Killam Memorial Graduate Prizes. A complete Izaak Walton Killam Memorial Scholarship Application includes For Applicants Izaak Walton Killam Memorial Scholarship Applicant Instructions 1. Izaak Walton Killam Memorial Scholarship Application Form. 2. Two Letter of Reference to Support Application for Graduate Awards. 3. Transcripts (copies of official transcripts for all post-secondary study are required to support an application. Your home department may have copies in your department file. If your department does not have these transcripts, you are required to submit new transcripts. Unofficial copies of University of Alberta transcripts are acceptable)

Closing Date: 17 February

Funding: Private

Contributor: Killam Trust Scholarships

For further information contact:

School of Library and Information Studies, 7-104 Education North, University of Alberta, Edmonton, AB T6G 2R3, Canada.

Tel: (1) 780 492 7625
Email: slis@ualberta.ca

University of Alberta MBA Programme

Length of Study: 20 months; 72 months

Country of Study: Canada

Application Procedure: Applicants must complete and return the form, with two official academic transcripts, Graduate Management Admission Test scores, three letters of recommendation, a two page statement of intent, a detailed curriculum vitae, an application deposit of C$60 (US$45), and a TOEFL score (if applicable) of 550+

Closing Date: 30 April

For further information contact:

Tel: (1) 780 492 3946
Fax: (1) 780 492 7825
Email: mba.programs@ualberta.ca

University of Amsterdam

Amsterdam Excellence Scholarships (AES)

Purpose: The Amsterdam Excellence Scholarships (AES) awards scholarships to exceptionally talented students from outside Europe to pursue eligible Master's Programmes offered at the University of Amsterdam

Eligibility: Non-European Union students from any discipline who graduated in the top 10% of their class may apply. Selection is on the basis of academic excellence, ambition and the relevance of the selected Master's programme to a student's future career

Level of Study: Postgraduate

Type: Scholarship

Value: €25,000 per annum

Length of Study: 1 year

Frequency: Annual

Study Establishment: University of Amsterdam

Country of Study: Netherlands

Application Procedure: Applications are made through the Admissions Offices of the Graduate Schools

Closing Date: 15 January

Additional Information: For more details, please visit official scholarship website: www.uva.nl/en/education/master-s/ scholarships–tuition/scholarships-and-loans/amsterdam-excellence-scholarship/amsterdam-excellence-scholarship. html

www.uva.nl/en/education/master-s/scholarships-tuition/schol arships-and-loans/amsterdam-excellence-scholarship/amster dam-excellence-scholarship.html?1581921251233

For further information contact:

P.O. Box 19268, NL-1000 GG Amsterdam, The Netherlands.

Email: servicedesk-ac@uva.nl

Amsterdam Science Talent Scholarship (ASTS)

Purpose: Scholarship is available for pursuing the masters degree programme at the University of Amsterdam

Eligibility: Non-Dutch talented students from the European Union / European Economic Area can apply

Level of Study: Postgraduate

Type: Scholarship

Value: €15,000

Length of Study: 2 years

Frequency: Annual

Country of Study: Any country

Application Procedure: To be eligible, an applicant must: 1. Be an international student 2. Be registered or admissible to a full-time doctoral program 3. Have completed at least one year of graduate work (master or doctoral level) 4. Have an intellect complemented by a sound character

Closing Date: 7 March

For further information contact:

Email: master-science@uva.nl

MacGillavry Fellowships

Purpose: These fellowships are available in the field of Biological Science and Biomedical Science, Earth Sciences (Physical Geography), Informatics and Logic, Physics, Chemistry, Astronomy, Mathematics, and Statistics

Eligibility: 1. A PhD degree in one of the scientific disciplines of their Faculty. 2. A scientific profile that links to one of the research fields eligible for application. 3. A publication record in international, high quality, peer-reviewed journals. 4. A few years of postdoctoral experience, preferably at the international level. 5. Well-developed organizational and communication skills. 6. Affinity for teaching at the undergraduate and graduate level

Level of Study: Postgraduate

Type: Fellowship

Value: The annual salary range for an assistant professor, including annual holiday allowance and the bonus is between €50,755 and €78,935 (before tax), depending on experience and past performance

Frequency: Annual

Country of Study: Any country

Application Procedure: To apply for the MacGillavry Fellowship you are invited to use the application form on the MacGillavry website of the Faculty of Science. www.uva.nl/ en/faculty/faculty-of-science/macgillavry-fellowship/macgillavry-fellowship.html

Closing Date: 4 February

Funding: Private

Additional Information: www.uva.nl/en/about-the-uva/orga nisation/faculties/faculty-of-science/working-at-the-faculty/ macgillavry-fellowship/macgillavry-fellowship.html

For further information contact:

Email: servicedesk-icts@uva.nl

University of Antwerp

Prinsstraat 13, B-2000 Antwerp, Belgium.

Tel: (32) 3 265 41 11
Email: internationalstudents@uantwerpen.be
Website: www.uantwerpen.be/en/

The Flemish Ministry of Education awards scholarships to outstanding students for Master programmes in Flanders and Brussels. The Master Mind programme aims to promote Flanders and Brussels as a top study destination. Students cannot apply directly. Applications need to be submitted by the Flemish host institution. The deadline for applications to the University of Antwerp is 1 March. Applications have to be done online through Mobility Online.

Master Mind Scholarships

Purpose: The Flemish Ministry of Education awards scholarships to outstanding students for Master programmes in Flanders and Brussels. The programme aims to promote Flanders and Brussels as a top study destination

Eligibility: The applicant applies to study a Master degree programme at the University of Antwerp. The applicant should have a high standard of academic performance and/or potential. This means: 1. The student has a Grade Point Average (GPA) of 3.5 out of 4.0. You can use the GPA calculator here. 2. The student has a good knowledge of the English language, proven by one of the following situations: 2a. an overall band score of minimum 7.0 on the IELTS test; 2b. a minimum total score of 94 on a TOEFL test; a C1 level of the Common European Framework of Reference; 2c. a similar result in another official language test; 2d. or an exemption provided by the Master programme's Selection Committee.

Level of Study: Masters Degree
Type: Scholarships
Value: € 8400 + a tuition fee waiver per academic year
Frequency: Annual
Country of Study: Belgium
Application Procedure: The University of Antwerp screens all applicants and submits a shortlist of 20 candidates for the scholarship. The Flemish Government makes the final selection on the basis of this shortlist. To apply for the Master Mind scholarship, students need to complete the following steps: 1. Complete your application and upload all documents for the relevant Master programme at the University of Antwerp. 2. Click the link below to read more about the Admission and enrolment procedure. Please do not forget to upload your English test scores! 3. During your application indicate that you would also like to apply for the Master Mind Scholarship. In your motivation text, clearly specify why you are applying for the Master Mind scholarship and why you should be selected. Please address every selection criterium. In addition, specify your GPA score. 4. Applications without a motivation text will not be considered. Application process for candidates who do not need to submit a Master application in Mobility Online (previous degree from Wallonia, Netherlands or Luxembourg) or those currently enrolled in a preparatory or bridge programme at the University of Antwerp: Please submit your application directly to the Master programme you are applying for. Your application should include a motivation letter addressing the selection criteria and clearly specifying your language test and GPA scores.

No. of awards offered: 30
Closing Date: 1 March
Additional Information: www.uantwerpen.be/en/study/scholarships/scholarships-with-uantwerp-participation/master-mind/

University of Auckland

Private Bag 92019, Auckland 1000, New Zealand.

Tel: (64) 9 373 7599
Email: appointments@auckland.ac.nz
Website: www.auckland.ac.nz
Contact: Ms S Codhersides, HR Manager

Anne Bellam Scholarship

Purpose: To assist students to further their musical education overseas

Eligibility: The candidate must be under 30 years of age and a citizen of New Zealand, must have completed or will complete in the year of application any degree or diploma in performance or any postgraduate music degree at the University of Auckland

Level of Study: Postgraduate
Type: Scholarship
Value: Up to NZ$30,000 for study overseas and up to NZ$10,000 for study at the University of Auckland
Length of Study: 1 year
Frequency: Annual
Study Establishment: University of Auckland
Country of Study: New Zealand

Application Procedure: The candidate must supply, one week in advance of examination, an outline of the proposed study plans and itinerary

No. of awards offered: Varies

Closing Date: 1 November

Funding: Government

Additional Information: www.auckland.ac.nz/en/study/scholarships-and-awards/find-a-scholarship/anne-bellam-scholarship-68-cai.html

For further information contact:

Faculty of Creative Arts and Industries, School of Music, University of Auckland, Private Bag 92019, Auckland 1000, New Zealand.

Email: scholarships@auckland.ac.nz

Arthington Davy Scholarship

Purpose: To study and research in areas which will significantly contribute to the development of Tonga

Eligibility: The candidate must be a Tongan citizen, born to Tongan parents and possess a first University degree

Level of Study: Research

Type: Scholarship

Value: The Arthington Davy Scholarship may cover the cost of part of the cost of a postgraduate study or research programme

Study Establishment: Trinity College

Country of Study: United Kingdom

Application Procedure: The candidate must submit a complete curriculum vitae and academic record, proof of Tongan origin, details of the intended postgraduate study preferably with a letter of conditional acceptance from the University concerned, full details of tuition fees and living expenses and of finances available from the student's own resources or elsewhere and the names of two academic referees

Closing Date: 31 May

Funding: Commercial, Foundation, Individuals, Private

Additional Information: www.auckland.ac.nz/en/study/international-students/scholarships-loans-and-funding/country-specific-scholarships-and-funding0/tonga/arthington-davy-scholarship.html

For further information contact:

Tutor for Advanced Students, Trinity College, Cambridge CB2 1TQ, United Kingdom.

Email: gradtutor@trin.cam.ac.uk

Asian Development Bank Japan Scholarship

Purpose: The aim is to provide an opportunity for well-qualified citizens of ADB's developing member countries to undertake postgraduate studies in economics, management, science and technology, and other development-related fields at participating academic institutions in the Asia-Pacific region

Eligibility: 1. Be a national of an ADB borrowing member. 2. Have gained admission to an approved masters at an approved academic institution. 3. Have a bachelors degree or its equivalent with a superior academic record. 4. Have at least two years of full-time professional work experience (acquired after a university degree) at the time of application. 5. Be proficient in oral and written English communication skills to be able to pursue studies. 6. Be under 35 years old at the time of application. In exceptional cases, for programmes which are appropriate for senior officials and managers, the age limit is 45 years. 7. Be in good health. 8. Agree to return to your home country after completing the programme.

Level of Study: Postgraduate

Type: Scholarship

Value: Tuition fee at the University of Auckland, Airfare from his or her home country to Auckland, New Zealand, Basic cost of living in Auckland, Health and medical insurance in New Zealand, and Airfare from Auckland, New Zealand, to the scholar's home country at the conclusion of his or her course of study

Study Establishment: University of Auckland

Country of Study: New Zealand

Application Procedure: 1. Completed ADB-JSP Information Sheet 2. Completed ADB-JSP Application Form 3. Copy of your offer letter to the University of Auckland 4. Academic documentation - both academic transcripts and degree certificates 5. Certificate of Employment for the duration of employment issued by the company 6. Certificate of Income issued by the company 7. Certificate of Family Income issued by the company. Must be either your parents or spouses annual/monthly income. 8. Copy of your Passport 9. Valid IELTS test

Closing Date: 19 July

Funding: Government, Private

Contributor: Asian Development Bank and Government of Japan

Additional Information: www.auckland.ac.nz/en/study/international-students/scholarships-loans-and-funding/development-scholarships/asian-development-bank-japan-scholarship-program.html

For further information contact:

Private Bag 92019, Auckland 1142, New Zealand.

Email: information@adbj.org

Beatrice Ratcliffe Postgraduate Scholarship in Music

Purpose: The main purpose of the Scholarship is to encourage and support students undertaking postgraduate study in the School of Music.
Level of Study: Postgraduate
Type: Scholarship
Value: Up to NZ$10,000
Length of Study: 1 year
Frequency: Annual
Country of Study: New Zealand
No. of awards offered: 1
Closing Date: 15 February
Additional Information: www.auckland.ac.nz/en/study/scholarships-and-awards/find-a-scholarship/beatrice-ratcliffe-postgraduate-scholarship-music-875-cai.html

For further information contact:

Email: scholarships@auckland.ac.nz

Commonwealth Scholarship

Purpose: The scholarships are available to students to be enroled at the University of Auckland for the Degree of Doctor of Philosophy; another approved Doctorate or a Master's degree
Eligibility: The candidate must be a citizen of Commonwealth of Nations, including Australian, British and Canadian citizens. The candidate must be tenable for a maximum of 36 months for a PhD candidate or 21 months for a Master's candidate
Level of Study: Doctorate, Postgraduate
Type: Scholarship
Value: Up to NZ$25,000 per year plus health insurance and fees at the domestic rate
Study Establishment: University of Auckland
Country of Study: New Zealand
Application Procedure: The candidate must send the application for UA Commonwealth Scholarships must be made through the appropriate organization in the scholar's home country on the Commonwealth Scholarship application form
Closing Date: 31 July
Funding: Government
Additional Information: www.auckland.ac.nz/en/study/scholarships-and-awards/find-a-scholarship/university-of-auckland-commonwealth-scholarship-266-all.html

For further information contact:

Scholarships Office, Student Administration, The University of Auckland, Private Bag 92019, Auckland Mail Centre, Auckland 1142, New Zealand.

Tel: (64) 9 373 7599 ext 87494
Fax: (64) 9 308 2309
Email: scholarships@auckland.ac.nz

Doctoral Scholarships

Purpose: To assist and encourage students to pursue doctoral studies at The University of Auckland
Eligibility: New doctoral applicants with a grade point average (GPA) of 8.00 or above, from their most recent qualifying programme, will be guaranteed a scholarship provided the qualifying programme was completed at a New Zealand university. New Māori and domestic3 Pacific doctoral applicants with a GPA of 7.50 or above, from their most recent qualifying programme, will be guaranteed a scholarship provided the qualifying programme was completed at a New Zealand university.
Level of Study: Doctorate
Type: Scholarship
Value: NZ$28,800 p.a. (plus domestic fees), with the possibility of a six-month extension. There will be an annual cost-of-living adjustment to the doctoral stipend.
Length of Study: 3 years
Frequency: Annual
Study Establishment: University of Auckland
Country of Study: New Zealand
Application Procedure: The candidate must fill the application form and send it to the Scholarships office. The selection will be made on the basis of merit
Funding: Government
Additional Information: www.auckland.ac.nz/en/study/scholarships-and-awards/scholarship-types/postgraduate-scholarships/doctoral-scholarships.html#schol-regs

For further information contact:

Email: c.tuu@auckland.ac.nz

Dulcie Bowman Memorial Scholarship

Purpose: The main purpose of the Scholarship is to encourage hearing-impaired women students at either undergraduate or postgraduate levels.
Eligibility: Second or subsequent year of any year of postgraduate study
Level of Study: Postgraduate
Type: Scholarship
Value: Up to NZ$4,500 pa each
Length of Study: 1 year
Frequency: Annual
Country of Study: New Zealand
No. of awards offered: 2

Closing Date: 1 February
Additional Information: www.auckland.ac.nz/en/study/scholarships-and-awards/find-a-scholarship/dulcie-bowman-memorial-scholarship-96-all.html

For further information contact:

Email: scholarships@auckland.ac.nz

Fulbright Scholarship

Purpose: To encourage and facilitate study for approved postgraduate degrees at the University of Auckland by candidates already selected to hold Fulbright Awards
Eligibility: The candidate must be a citizen of the United States of America and intending to take up Fulbright Awards to study in New Zealand and should enrol for a full-time at the University of Auckland for an approved Master's or Doctoral degree
Level of Study: Doctorate, Postgraduate
Type: Scholarship
Value: Up to NZ$28,500 pa for 2021 for Doctoral and up to NZ$15,000 for Masters, plus compulsory fees and international health insurance
Frequency: Annual
Study Establishment: University of Auckland
Country of Study: New Zealand
Application Procedure: The candidate must send the completed application form to the Scholarships office
Closing Date: 12 December
Funding: Government
Additional Information: www.auckland.ac.nz/en/study/scholarships-and-awards/find-a-scholarship/university-of-auckland-fulbright-scholarship-293-all.html

For further information contact:

Email: scholarships@auckland.ac.nz

HC Russell Memorial Postgraduate Scholarship

Level of Study: Postgraduate, Predoctorate
Type: Scholarship
Value: Up to NZ$4,500 in total (MSc) or up to NZ$10,000 in total (PhD)
Length of Study: 3 years
Frequency: Annual
Country of Study: New Zealand
Closing Date: 1 November
Additional Information: www.auckland.ac.nz/en/study/scholarships-and-awards/find-a-scholarship/hc-russell-memorial-postgraduate-scholarship-94-fmhs.html

For further information contact:

Email: scholarships@auckland.ac.nz

Heather Leaity Memorial Award

Purpose: The main purpose of the Award is to recognise and encourage excellence in Marine Science research relating to sustainability and conservation.
Level of Study: Doctorate
Type: Scholarship
Value: NZ$1,000
Length of Study: 1 year
Frequency: Annual
Country of Study: New Zealand
Application Procedure: You do not need to apply for this scholarship, award or prize or complete an online application form. It is awarded on the recommendation of the relevant faculty or University of Auckland committee.
Additional Information: www.auckland.ac.nz/en/study/scholarships-and-awards/find-a-scholarship/heather-leaity-memorial-award-1051-sci.html

For further information contact:

Email: scholarships@auckland.ac.nz

Hope Selwyn Foundation Scholarship

Purpose: The HOPE Selwyn Foundation is a registered charitable trust established in 1996 to assist the funding of research and education essential to the health and welfare of older people in New Zealand
Eligibility: 1. The purpose of the scholarships is to support or partially support the salaries of young scientists (the definition of "young" being reasonably flexible) who are in the early stages of their careers. 2. Candidates undertaking a Masters or doctoral thesis will be considered for support. Candidates will normally be working under supervision in a recognised research environment with a senior research leader. 3. HOPE Sewlyn Foundation scholarships may be held with any other bursary or award unless the candidate's other awards preclude this
Level of Study: Postgraduate
Type: Scholarship
Value: NZ$6,000 each
Length of Study: 4 years
Frequency: Annual
Country of Study: New Zealand
No. of awards offered: varies
Closing Date: 31 October
Funding: Foundation

U

Additional Information: www.auckland.ac.nz/en/study/scholarships-and-awards/find-a-scholarship/hope-foundation-research-on-ageing-scholarship-423-all.html

For further information contact:

The University of Auckland, Private Bag 92019, Auckland 1142, New Zealand.

Email: scholarships@auckland.ac.nz

International College of Auckland PhD Scholarship in Plant Sciences

Purpose: To assist eminent Chinese scholars from nominated areas of China to study plant sciences at the University of Auckland and to promote links between China and New Zealand in the field of plant sciences
Eligibility: The candidate must possess a PhD in the field of plant science and who has paid the fees, or arranged to pay the fees, for full–time enrolment in the School of Biological Sciences
Level of Study: Postdoctorate
Type: Scholarship
Value: NZ$20,000 per year. The scholarship's emolument will be paid as a tuition/compulsory fees credit and the balance as a fortnightly stipend
Length of Study: 3 years
Frequency: Annual
Study Establishment: University of Auckland
Country of Study: New Zealand
Application Procedure: The candidate must submit the completed application form along with the curriculum vitae and at least two academic reference letters
Closing Date: 1 October
Funding: Government
Contributor: The International College of Auckland

For further information contact:

Email: scholarships@auckland.ac.nz

Maori and Pacific Graduate Scholarships (Masters/Honours/PGDIP)

Purpose: The Scholarship is offered each semester to Māori students enrolled in any Masters or postgraduate level Bachelors (Honours) degree, or any Postgraduate Diploma
Eligibility: Māori students who are citizens or permanent residents of New Zealand with a grade point average (GPA) of 7.50 or higher in their qualifying programme from a recognised university. Applying for an honours degree, a postgraduate diploma or a masters degree at the University of Auckland.

Level of Study: Postgraduate
Type: Scholarship
Value: Tax-free stipend of NZ$13,655 in 2022 plus the cost of your compulsory fees.
Length of Study: 1 year
Frequency: Annual
Country of Study: New Zealand
No. of awards offered: Varies
Additional Information: www.auckland.ac.nz/en/study/scholarships-and-awards/scholarship-types/postgraduate-scholarships/maori-postgraduate-scholarships.html

For further information contact:

Email: scholarships@auckland.ac.nz

Marie Clay Literacy Trust Literacy Learning Research Award

Purpose: The main purpose of the Award is to support an international or domestic doctoral student in the Faculty of Education and Social Work undertaking research which promotes literacy learning of the lowest achievers in primary schools in Aotearoa New Zealand.
Eligibility: Scholarship applications will usually open around six weeks before the closing date. Please read the regulations carefully to be sure you are eligible before you apply.
Level of Study: Doctorate, Predoctorate
Type: Scholarship
Value: Up to NZ$10,000 each
Length of Study: 1 year
Frequency: Annual
Country of Study: New Zealand
Closing Date: 11 July
Additional Information: www.auckland.ac.nz/en/study/scholarships-and-awards/find-a-scholarship/marie-clay-literacy-trust-literacy-learning-research-award-823-esw.html

For further information contact:

Email: scholarships@auckland.ac.nz

Masters/Honours/PGDIP Scholarships

Purpose: The Scholarship was established by the Dean of Arts in December 1994, and is offered annually to meritorious students enrolled for an approved masters degree, an approved Bachelors Honours degree, or an approved Postgraduate Diploma in the Faculty of Arts.
Eligibility: The candidate must be a citizen or a permanent resident of New Zealand. In case of a Master's degree, the candidate must be tenable until the date for completion of the

requirements for the degree as specified in the General Regulations – Masters degrees

Level of Study: Graduate, Postgraduate
Type: Scholarship
Value: Up to NZ$10,000 per year including compulsory fees
Length of Study: 1 year
Frequency: Annual
Study Establishment: University of Auckland
Country of Study: New Zealand
Application Procedure: You do not need to apply for this scholarship, award or prize or complete an online application form. It is awarded on the recommendation of the relevant faculty or University of Auckland committee.
Funding: Government
Additional Information: www.auckland.ac.nz/en/study/scholarships-and-awards/find-a-scholarship/faculty-of-arts-masters-honours-pgdip-scholarship-50-art.html

For further information contact:

Email: scholarships@auckland.ac.nz

Mercer Memorial Scholarship in Aeronautics

Level of Study: Postgraduate
Type: Scholarship
Value: Up to NZ$6,000
Length of Study: 1 year
Frequency: Annual
Country of Study: New Zealand
Application Procedure: aucklandscholars.communityforce.com/Funds/FundDetails.aspx?496F49596D593768464E3537506B6F754D5442315A3778336948797A636452414F534C376D4A524C597866675725467593049424C38316353787658752B30484449714231376E76565A334D3D
Closing Date: 21 March
Additional Information: www.auckland.ac.nz/en/study/scholarships-and-awards/find-a-scholarship/mercer-memorial-scholarship-in-aeronautics-143-eng.html

For further information contact:

Email: scholarships@auckland.ac.nz

New Zealand Agency for International Development Scholarship (NZDS) – Open Category

Eligibility: The candidate must possess minimum English language requirements for entry into the University of Auckland postgraduate study. IELTS (International English Language Testing System Certificate) with an overall score of 6.5 and no band less than 6.0 or a TOEFL (Test of English as a Foreign Language) paper based 575 with a TWE of 4.5 or computer based 233

Level of Study: Postgraduate
Type: Scholarship
Value: Tuition, enrollment/orientation fees, return economy fare travel, medical insurance and provision for students to meet course and basic living costs
Frequency: Annual
Study Establishment: University of Auckland
Country of Study: New Zealand
Application Procedure: Application form can be downloaded from the website
Closing Date: 1 June
Funding: Government
Contributor: New Zealand Agency for International Development and the Ministry of Foreign Affairs

For further information contact:

Tel: (64) 9 373 7599 ext 87556
Fax: (64) 9 373 7405
Email: rfatialofa.patolo@auckland.ac.nz

New Zealand International Doctoral Research (NZIDRS) Scholarship

Purpose: To provide financial support for postgraduate students from designated countries seeking doctoral degrees by research in New Zealand universities
Eligibility: The candidate must hold an A' average or equivalent in their studies, meet the requirements for entry into a research-based doctoral degree programme at a New Zealand university
Level of Study: Doctorate, Research
Type: Research scholarship
Value: Living allowance (NZ$25,000 per year), a travel allowance (NZ$2,000), a health insurance allowance (NZ$500), and a book and thesis allowance (NZ$800)
Length of Study: 3 years
Study Establishment: University of Auckland
Country of Study: New Zealand
Application Procedure: The candidate must complete the application form in English and attach supporting documents as stipulated in the application form
Closing Date: 16 July
Funding: Government
Contributor: Government of New Zealand
Additional Information: scholarshipdb.net/scholarships-in-New-Zealand/New-Zealand-International-Doctoral-Research-Scholarships-Nzidrs-Auckland-University-Of-Technology=u2NUb6tP6BGUVQAlkGUTnw.html

For further information contact:

Tel: (64) 4 472 0788
Fax: (64) 4 471 2828
Email: scholarships@educationnz.org.nz

Property Institute of New Zealand Postgraduate Scholarship

Purpose: The main purpose of the Award is to promote postgraduate study in the field of real property.
Eligibility: The candidate must possess a Master's degree or full-time PhD candidate and has the paid the fees, or arranged to pay the fees, for study in the Department of Property at Lincoln University, Massey University or The University of Auckland
Level of Study: Doctorate, Masters Degree
Type: Scholarship
Value: Up to NZ$2,000
Length of Study: 1 year
Frequency: Annual
Study Establishment: University of Auckland
Country of Study: New Zealand
No. of awards offered: 1
Funding: Government
Contributor: Property Institute of New Zealand
Additional Information: www.auckland.ac.nz/en/study/scholarships-and-awards/find-a-scholarship/property-institute-of-new-zealand-postgraduate-award-369-bus.html

For further information contact:

Tel: (64) 9 373 7599 ext 87494
Fax: (64) 9 308 2309
Email: scholarships@auckland.ac.nz

Reardon Postgraduate Scholarship in Music

Purpose: The main purpose of the Scholarship is to encourage and support postgraduate study in Music performance.
Eligibility: The candidate must possess a degree or diploma with a specialization in Performance in the year of the award
Level of Study: Postgraduate
Type: Scholarship
Value: NZ$8,000
Length of Study: 1 year
Frequency: Annual
Study Establishment: University of Auckland
Country of Study: New Zealand
No. of awards offered: 1
Closing Date: 1 November
Funding: Government

Contributor: Reardon Memorial Music Trust
Additional Information: www.auckland.ac.nz/en/study/scholarships-and-awards/find-a-scholarship/reardon-post graduate-scholarship-in-music-74-cai.html

Senior Health Research Scholarships

Purpose: The main purpose of the Scholarship is to provide financial support so that health professionals can return to the University to study for a doctorate in health related areas.
Eligibility: The candidate must be a citizen or a permanent resident of New Zealand and who have worked for 3 years as a health professional
Level of Study: Doctorate
Type: Scholarship
Value: NZ$40,000 plus compulsory fees
Length of Study: 3 years
Frequency: Annual
Study Establishment: University of Auckland
Country of Study: New Zealand
Application Procedure: The candidate must submit an application form and send it to the Scholarships office. Selection shall be made on the basis of merit
No. of awards offered: 3
Funding: Government
Additional Information: www.auckland.ac.nz/en/study/scholarships-and-awards/find-a-scholarship/university-of-auckland-senior-health-research-scholarship-382-fmhs.html

The AUT Queen Elizabeth II Diamond Jubilee Doctoral Scholarship

Purpose: AUT Doctoral Scholarship AUT aims to Develop an internationally-aware, skilled future leader Establish enduring education and professional linkages
Eligibility: 1. The scholarship will be awarded annually to a doctoral student who is a citizen, and resident in, one of the following Pacific countries; Cook Islands, Fiji, Kiribati, Nauru, Niue, Papua New Guinea, Samoa, Solomon Islands, Tokelau, Tonga and Vanuatu to carry out doctoral study at AUT University. 2. Applicants must be a citizen and resident of one of the eligible countries. Applicants may not have citizenship or permanent residence status of New Zealand or any other developed country. Applicants who are New Zealand citizens from the Cook Islands, Niue, Tokelau and dual citizens of Samoa are exempt from this requirement; however, they must reside in the Cook Islands, Nuie, Tokelau or Samoa or another eligible country. Preference may be given to those applicants who have also been schooled in an eligible country. 3. The recipients of this

scholarship will have strong academic references plus a strong academic record and/or have demonstrated the potential for quality research. Previous study should include research methodologies papers and an independent research project, including the writing of a report on that research

Level of Study: Postgraduate

Type: Scholarship

Value: NZ$25,000 annual stipend tuition fees and student services levies

Length of Study: 1 year

Frequency: Annual

Country of Study: New Zealand

Application Procedure: Application will be via the online scholarship application portal available from the link. It is not possible to submit incomplete scholarship applications through the online application process. In order for the application to be submitted all requested documentation must be included. The following documents or statements must be completed and uploaded in the application portal by the closing date. Incomplete applications will not be forwarded to the selection panel. 1. AUT Queen Elizabeth II Diamond Jubilee Doctoral Scholarship on-line application form. 2. Academic transcript(s) if any previous tertiary study has been completed at a university other than AUT. 3. A certified copy of the applicant's birth certificate or passport. 4. Two referee's reports are required. Applicants must not submit referee's reports directly. Nominated referees will be sent a request directly by the on-line application system. Please advise your referees that they will be receiving an email requesting a reference statement and that this must be submitted by the closing date or your application will be ineligible. If the referee declines to provide a reference before the closing date you will be able to nominate another referee. 5. A two page statement (maximum 1,000 words) outlining the applicant's research proposal using the template provided with the online application form. Please note this must be two pages only (plus one page for references). If a longer document is provided you will be asked to rewrite it. 6. Written support from the proposed primary supervisor if they have not acted as one of the referees above. 7. A brief C.V. (maximum three pages)

Closing Date: 1 November

Funding: Private

Additional Information: The scholarship is available every three years only. www.aut.ac.nz/study/fees-and-scholarships/scholarships-and-awards-at-aut/scholarships-database/detail page?detailCode=500675&sessionID=32593825&source IP=&X_FORWARDED_FOR= https://scholarshipdb.net/scholarships-in-New-Zealand/The-Aut-Queen-Elizabeth-Ii-Diamond-Jubilee-Doctoral-Scholar ship-Auckland-University-Of-Technology=Tc65tBC06BG UVQAlkGUTnw.html

For further information contact:

55 Wellesley St E, Auckland 1010, New Zealand.

Tel: (64) 9 921 9837
Email: scholars@aut.ac.nz

The Jackson Family Foundation Scholarship

Purpose: The main purpose of the Scholarship is to assist women students of Cook Island descent, who are experiencing challenging personal, family or financial circumstances that may prevent them from undertaking full-time study.

Eligibility: Women students of Cook Island descent enrolled in full-time study in any year of a postgraduate degree

Level of Study: Postgraduate

Type: Scholarship

Value: Up to NZ$11,000 pa

Length of Study: 1 year

Frequency: Annual

Country of Study: New Zealand

No. of awards offered: 4

Closing Date: 1 February

Additional Information: www.auckland.ac.nz/en/study/scholarships-and-awards/find-a-scholarship/the-jackson-family-foundation-scholarship-750-all.html

For further information contact:

Email: scholarships@auckland.ac.nz

The Kate Edger Educational Charitable Trust Masters Degree Award

Purpose: The main purpose of the Award is to assist women graduates to carry out study for a masters degree at the University of Auckland.

Level of Study: Postgraduate

Type: Award

Value: Up to NZ$8,000

Length of Study: 1 year

Frequency: Annual

Country of Study: New Zealand

No. of awards offered: 8

Closing Date: 24 January

Additional Information: www.auckland.ac.nz/en/study/scholarships-and-awards/find-a-scholarship/the-kate-edger-educational-charitable-trust-masters-degree-award-787-all.html

For further information contact:

Email: scholarships@auckland.ac.nz

The Kate Edger Educational Charitable Trust Vinka Marinovich Award in Music

Purpose: The main purpose of the Award is to support women enrolled in undergraduate or postgraduate study in the School of Music at the University of Auckland.
Level of Study: Postgraduate
Type: Award
Value: Up to NZ$8,000
Length of Study: 1 year
Frequency: Annual
Country of Study: New Zealand
Application Procedure: aucklandscholars.communityforce. com/Funds/FundDetails.aspx?634874666E67316C32307A 48666B33543347756B6933727177315A376B737066746 57831516F6A4A553052594A54333971312B7A4E305644 3942394A6D785342
No. of awards offered: 2
Closing Date: 14 February
Additional Information: www.auckland.ac.nz/en/study/ scholarships-and-awards/find-a-scholarship/the-kate-edger-trust-vinka-marinovich-award-music-912-cai.html

For further information contact:

Email: scholarships@auckland.ac.nz

The University of Auckland International Doctoral Fees Bursary

Purpose: To assist international students from all countries who wish to pursue doctoral studies
Eligibility: Permanent citizens and residents of Australia and New Zealand are not eligible for the scholarship
Level of Study: Doctorate
Type: Bursary
Value: NZ$25,000
Frequency: Annual
Study Establishment: University of Auckland
Country of Study: New Zealand
Application Procedure: The application form can be obtained from the Scholarships Office, University of Auckland
Closing Date: 1 August
Funding: Government

University of Auckland International Doctoral Scholarship

Purpose: To assist international students from all countries who wish to pursue doctoral studies
Eligibility: The scholarship is available to international students from all countries who wish to pursue Doctoral studies on a full-time basis. Permanent citizens and residents of Australia and New Zealand are not eligible for the scholarship
Level of Study: Doctorate
Type: Scholarship
Value: NZ$28,800 p.a. (plus domestic fees), with the possibility of a six-month extension. There will be an annual cost-of-living adjustment to the doctoral stipend.
Frequency: Annual
Study Establishment: University of Auckland
Country of Study: New Zealand
Application Procedure: The application form can be obtained from the Scholarships Office, University of Auckland
Funding: Government
Additional Information: www.auckland.ac.nz/en/study/ scholarships-and-awards/scholarship-types/postgraduate-scholarships/doctoral-scholarships.html

University of Auckland International Student Excellence Scholarship

Purpose: The main purpose of the Scholarship is to attract new international students of high calibre to enrol in undergraduate or postgraduate taught study of one year or more at the University of Auckland.
Level of Study: Postgraduate
Type: Scholarship
Value: Up to NZ$10,000 for postgraduate study
Length of Study: 1 year
Frequency: Twice a year
Country of Study: New Zealand
Closing Date: 21 November

For further information contact:

Email: scholarships@auckland.ac.nz

University of Auckland Research Masters Scholarships

Eligibility: Research students who are New Zealand citizens or permanent residents with a GPA of 8.0 ('A' grade) or higher in their qualifying programme from a recognised university. Applying for a masters degree with a research component of at least 90 points at the University of Auckland.

Type: Scholarship

Value: A tax-free stipend of NZ$13,655 in 2022 plus the cost of your compulsory fees.

Country of Study: New Zealand

Application Procedure: Don't need to apply separately. Scholarship offers will be made soon after the confirmation of a place.

Additional Information: www.auckland.ac.nz/en/study/scholarships-and-awards/scholarship-types/postgraduate-scholarships/research-masters-scholarships.html

University of Auckland Business School

School of Business & Economics, Private Bag 92019, Auckland, New Zealand.

Tel: (64) 9 373 7599
Email: execpro@auckland.ac.nz
Website: www.business.auckland.ac.nz
Contact: Dr Gary Cayton, Director MBA

Kupe Leadership Scholarships

Purpose: The Kupe Leadership Programme will involve a three-day Orientation in early March; two two-day workshops held during each mid-semester break; a one-day workshop in the inter-semester break and a concluding day-long workshop in November

Eligibility: The Kupe Leadership alumni will develop a reputation for embodying these values and for contributions they make, nationally and possibly internationally

Level of Study: Postgraduate

Type: Scholarship

Value: Scholars will receive either a NZ$22,000 stipend OR a NZ$10,000 stipend plus on-campus self-catered studio accommodation at 55 Symonds Street up to a total value of around NZ$25,000.

Length of Study: 1 year

Frequency: Annual

Country of Study: New Zealand

Closing Date: 30 August

Funding: Private

Additional Information: www.auckland.ac.nz/en/study/scholarships-and-awards/scholarship-types/postgraduate-scholarships/kupe-leadership-scholarships.html

For further information contact:

The University of Auckland, Private Bag 92019, Auckland 1142, New Zealand.

Tel: (64) 800 61 62 63
Email: pc.dasilva@auckland.ac.nz

University of Auckland Executive MBA Programme

Eligibility: To be eligible to apply for admission to the University of Auckland MBA you must have: 1. A relevant bachelors degree from a recognised university with a GPA/GPE of 5.0 or higher in at least 90 points in the most advanced courses 2. Or have completed the Postgraduate Diploma in Business in Administration, or equivalent, with a GPA/GPE of 5.0 or higher 3. Or a relevant bachelors degree and a Postgraduate Certificate in Business from this University with a GPA of 5.0 or higher. 4. Have gained at least three years' relevant management experience. 5. Successfully complete all application requirements.

Value: Indicative fees for the 180-point MBA for domestic students are NZ$43,727.45 (plus approximately NZ$2,500 for parking and textbooks etc and a Student Services Fee estimated at NZ$1,271 for 180 points). Courses are paid per Quarter.

Length of Study: More than 2 years

Country of Study: New Zealand

Application Procedure: Applicants must return a completed form. A deposit of AU$250 is payable on acceptance. Foreign students may be required to sit a test of English proficiency

Closing Date: 1 August

Additional Information: www.mba.auckland.ac.nz/our-mba-programme/domestic-students/

For further information contact:

Business Administration International Students Office, Private Bag 92019, Auckland 1142, New Zealand.

Tel: (64) 9 373 7513
Fax: (64) 9 373 7405
Email: international@auckland.ac.nz

University of Bath

Claverton Down, Bath BA2 7AY, United Kingdom.

Tel: (44) 1225 388388
Website: www.bath.ac.uk
Contact: University of Bath

The University of Bath received its Royal Charter in 1966 and is now firmly established as a top ten United Kingdom university with a reputation for research and teaching excellence.

United Kingdom-India Year of Culture Great Postgraduate Scholarships

Purpose: The University of Bath is currently accepting applications for United Kingdom-India Year of Culture GREAT Scholarships. This scholarship is available to the international fee-paying student from India studying a full-time taught postgraduate masters programme

Eligibility: Indian students are eligible to apply for this scholarship. For most programmes, the requirement for non-native English speakers is 6.5 in the IELTS Academic English test, with no less than 6.0 in any element

Type: Postgraduate scholarships

Value: If you are an international fee-paying student you could be eligible for one of ten United Kingdom-India Year of Culture GREAT Scholarships each worth £5,000

Study Establishment: Scholarships are awarded in the Faculty of Humanities and Social Sciences, Faculty of Engineering and Design and in the Faculty of Science

Country of Study: United Kingdom

Application Procedure: If you are eligible for the scholarship scheme, we will let you know and invite you to apply. Queries for MSc students should be addressed to msc-mn-at-bath.ac.uk and for MBA students to mbaapps-at-management.bath.ac.uk

Closing Date: 1 June

Additional Information: For more details please see the website www.unibe.ch/eng/

University of Bern

Hochschulstrasse 4, CH-3012 Bern, Switzerland.

Tel: (41) 31 631 81 11
Email: info@imd.unibe.ch
Website: www.unibe.ch/eng/

The University of Bern offers top quality teaching, special recognition in leading–edge disciplines, and a campus environment intimately linked to the social, economic, and political life of the city. The university's comprehensive offering includes 8 faculties and some 160 institutes with 12,500 students. Its academic and research organization prides itself on its interdisciplinarity. The university is actively involved in a wide range of European and worldwide research projects.

Excellence Scholarships for Postgraduate Study

Purpose: Scholarship for international students

Eligibility: Applicants must, by end of July, have graduated with at least a Bachelor's degree in the same field of study as the selected Master's programme and must be residing in their home country. The criteria for selection are previous academic excellence and the potential of the candidate

Level of Study: Graduate

Type: Scholarship

Value: CHF 1,600 per month for the entire duration of the course

Frequency: Annual

Country of Study: Any country

Application Procedure: Check website for specific details

Closing Date: 21 December

Funding: Commercial

For further information contact:

Tel: (41) 31 631 80 49
Email: claudine.rossi@int.unibe.ch

UniBE International 2021

Purpose: To support for young researchers and to the university's internationalization

Level of Study: Doctorate, Postgraduate

Length of Study: 3 years

Study Establishment: University of Bern

Country of Study: Switzerland

Application Procedure: Please email your application including any related documents as one pdf to lenka.fehrenbach@entwicklung.unibe.ch

Closing Date: 17 May

Contributor: Swiss National Fund (SNF)

For further information contact:

Email: sandro.stauffer@uls.unibe.ch

University of Bologna

Via Zamboni, 33, I-40126 Bologna, Italy.

Tel: (39) 51 2088101
Website: www.unibo.it/

The origins of the University of Bologna go way back, and it is considered to be the oldest university in the Western world.

Its history is intertwined with that of the great names of science and literature, it is a keystone and a point of reference for European culture.

University of Bologna Study Grants for International Students

Purpose: The University of Bologna awards study grants and full tuition fee waivers to deserving international students who wish to register for First, Single, and Second Cycle Degree Programmes at the University of Bologna for A.Y. 2023/2024.

Eligibility: You can apply for Unibo Action 1 & 2 if: 1. you are in possession of (or about to obtain) a valid qualification for access to your chosen degree programme, issued by an Institution outside of the Italian education system. Students holding a diploma issued by an Italian school established outside Italy can apply as well. 2. you will take one of the following tests by the application deadline: 2a. if you are interested in registering in a First or Single Cycle Degree Programme, the SAT and/or TOLC test; 2b. if you are interested in registering in a Second Cycle Degree Programme, the GRE test. 3. You are less than 30 years old upon the deadline of the call for application.

The SAT, GRE and TOLC are aptitude and skills assessment tests which can be taken in authorised centres in several countries around the world and online (if this modality is offered by the managing institutions). You must register for the tests on the websites of managing institutions. SAT and GRE tests are in English. TOLC test is available in English and Italian language. You can find more information in the call for applications.

Level of Study: Bachelors/Masters Degree

Type: Scholarships

Value: Each Unibo Action 2 study grants are awarded for one academic year only and amounts to a total of €11.000, gross of all charges for the beneficiary account. Each Unibo Action 1 full tuition waivers are awarded for one academic year only.

Country of Study: Italy

Application Procedure: Applications must be submitted by 31 March (Second Cycle Programmes) or 29 April (First or Single Cycle Programmes), exclusively through Studenti Online, as explained in the call for applications. It is important to read the Call for Applications (GRE) or Call for Applications (SAT) and visit the official website (link found below) to access the online application system and for detailed information on how to apply for this scholarship.

Closing Date: 30 April

Additional Information: https://www.unibo.it/en/services-and-opportunities/study-grants-and-subsidies/exemptions-and-incentives/unibo-actions-1-2-study-grants-and-tuition-fee-waivers-for-international-students

For further information contact:

Email: internationaldesk@unibo.it

University of Bristol

Student Funding Office, Senate House (Ground Floor), Tyndall Avenue, Bristol BS8 1TH, United Kingdom.

Tel: (44) 11 7928 9000
Email: student-funding@bris.ac.uk
Website: www.bristol.ac.uk
Contact: Ms Penny Rowe, Student Funding Advisor

The University of Bristol is committed to providing high-quality teaching and research in all its designated fields.

Global Accounting and Finance Scholarship

Purpose: The Department of Accounting and Finance is offering eight scholarships worth £5,000 each to eligible international students studying for a postgraduate qualification in Accounting and Finance

Eligibility: You can apply if you: 1. have applied to start one of the qualifying accounting and finance MSc programmes in September 2023. 1a. MSc Accounting and Finance. 1b. MSc Accounting, Finance and Management. 1c. MSc Banking, Regulation and Financial Stability. 1d. MSc Finance and Investment. 1e. are classed as an overseas student for fee purposes.

Level of Study: Postgraduate

Type: Scholarship

Value: Two scholarships of £10,000 and eight scholarships of £5,000 are available, which must be used towards the cost of tuition fees for a one-year master programme in the School of Accounting and Finance.

Length of Study: 1 year

Frequency: Annual

Country of Study: United Kingdom

Application Procedure: The application process is the same for all University of Bristol international scholarships so the terms and conditions are the same too. Read the terms and conditions before applying. www.bristol.ac.uk/international/fees-finance/scholarships/application-guidance/

Closing Date: 28 March

Funding: Private

Additional Information: www.bristol.ac.uk/students/support/finances/scholarships/global-accounting-finance/

Global Economics Postgraduate Scholarship

Purpose: The Department of Economics is offering five scholarships worth £5,000 each to eligible international students studying for a postgraduate qualification in Economics
Eligibility: You can apply if you: 1. have applied to start one of the qualifying economics master's programmes in September 2023: 1a. MSc Economics 1b. MSc Economics, Finance and Management. 1c. MSc Economics and Finance. 1d. MRes Economics. 1e. are classed as an overseas student for fee purposes.
Level of Study: Postgraduate
Type: Scholarship
Value: Two scholarships of £10,000 and six scholarships of £5,000 are available, which must be used towards the cost of tuition fees for a one-year master programme in the School of Economics.
Length of Study: 1 year
Frequency: Annual
Country of Study: United Kingdom
Application Procedure: The application process is the same for all University of Bristol international scholarships so the terms and conditions are the same too. Read the terms and conditions before applying. www.bristol.ac.uk/international/fees-finance/scholarships/application-guidance/
Closing Date: 28 March
Funding: Private
Additional Information: www.bristol.ac.uk/students/support/finances/scholarships/global-economics-pg/

For further information contact:

University of Bristol, Senate House, Tyndall Avenue, Bristol BS8 1TH, United Kingdom.

International Postgraduate Scholarships – Taught Master's Programmes

Purpose: This programme provides plenty of offers for future research postgraduate researchers with access to studentships, supervision from world-class experts and excellent facilities on our PhD and doctoral programmes
Eligibility: Open to candidates holding an offer for a 1 year taught postgraduate programme at the University of Bristol
Level of Study: Postgraduate
Type: Scholarship (MSc)
Value: £2,000
Length of Study: 1 year
Frequency: Annual
Study Establishment: University of Bristol
Country of Study: United Kingdom
Application Procedure: Check website for further details

Closing Date: 30 June
Funding: Private

For further information contact:

International Recruitment Office, University of Bristol Union, Queens Road, Bristol BS8 1ND, United Kingdom.

Email: iro@bristol.ac.uk

Phyllis Mary Morris Bursaries

Purpose: Phyllis Mary Morris née Doidge graduated with a degree in Geography in 1930
Eligibility: You can apply if you are: 1. classed as an overseas student for fee purposes 2. have applied to start a full-time postgraduate taught programme in the School of Geographical Sciences for 2023.
Level of Study: Postgraduate
Type: Bursary
Value: £2,000 each. The awards can be used towards living costs.
Frequency: Annual
Country of Study: United Kingdom
Application Procedure: The application process is the same for all University of Bristol international scholarships so the terms and conditions are the same too. Read the terms and conditions before applying. www.bristol.ac.uk/international/fees-finance/scholarships/application-guidance/
No. of awards offered: 6
Closing Date: 28 March
Funding: Private
Additional Information: www.bristol.ac.uk/students/support/finances/scholarships/phyllis-mary-morris-bursaries/#:~:text=A%20living%20cost%20bursary%20for,the%20School%20of%20Geographical%20Sciences.

For further information contact:

University of Bristol, Beacon House, Queens Road, Bristol BS8 1QU, United Kingdom.

Tel: (44) 117 928 9000
Email: graduation-office@bristol.ac.uk

Think Big Postgraduate Scholarships

Subjects: Any full-time Undergraduate programme (except Medicine, Dentistry and Veterinary Science) or any one-year, full-time taught postgraduate programme offered at the University

Purpose: Helping and nurturing global talent to produce the future leaders of tomorrow.

Eligibility: You can apply if you: 1. have applied to start a one-year full-time master's programme at the University of Bristol in September 2022. 2. are classed as an overseas student for fee purposes.

Level of Study: Bachelors/Masters Degree

Type: Scholarships

Value: Awards valued at £5,000, £10,000 and £20,000 are available. Awards must be used towards the cost of tuition fees

Country of Study: United Kingdom

Application Procedure: The application process is the same for all University of Bristol international scholarships so the terms and conditions are the same too. Read the terms and conditions before applying. www.bristol.ac.uk/international/fees-finance/scholarships/application-guidance/

Closing Date: 28 March

Additional Information: www.bristol.ac.uk/students/support/finances/scholarships/think-big-postgraduate/

University of British Columbia (UBC)

2329 West Mall, Vancouver, BC V6T 1Z2, Canada.

Tel:	(1) 604 822 2211
Email:	graduate.awards@ubc.ca
Website:	www.ubc.ca
Contact:	Ms Jiffin Arboleda, Awards Administrator

The University of British Columbia (UBC) is one of North America's major research universities. The Faculty of Graduate Studies has 6,500 students and is a national leader in interdisciplinary study and research, with 98 departments, 18 interdisciplinary research units, 9 interdisciplinary graduate programmes, 2 graduate residential colleges and 1 scholarly journal.

Izaak Walton Killam Predoctoral Fellowships

Purpose: To assist doctoral students with full-time studies and research

Eligibility: Open to students of any nationality, discipline, age or sex. This award is given at the PhD level only and is strictly based on academic merit. Students must have a First Class standing in their last 2 years of study

Level of Study: Doctorate

Type: Fellowship

Value: C$22,000 per year and C$1,500 travel allowance for the duration of the award

Frequency: Annual

Study Establishment: UBC

Country of Study: Canada

Application Procedure: Top ranked students are selected from the University Graduate Fellowship competition. Application forms can be obtained from individual departments, the Faculty of Graduate Studies or the website. Students must submit their applications to the departments, not to the Faculty of Graduate Studies

No. of awards offered: 200

Funding: Private

No. of awards given last year: 12

No. of applicants last year: 200

For further information contact:

Email: gsaward@ucalgary.ca

University of British Columbia Graduate Fellowship (UGF)

Purpose: To assist graduate students with their studies and research

Eligibility: Academic Standing: 1. A progress report evaluated as satisfactory by the College of Graduate Studies based on established, articulated criteria; Number of Months of Study: 1. Master's students must have completed, as of April 30 of the adjudication year, no more than 24 months of study in the program for which they are requesting funding 2. PhD students must have completed, as of April 30 of the adjudication year, no more than 48 months of study in the program for which they are requesting funding

Level of Study: Masters and Doctoral

Type: Fellowship

Value: Awarded in a minimum base unit of C$3,000 to a maximum of C$24,000

Frequency: Annual

Study Establishment: UBC

Country of Study: Canada

Application Procedure: Annual progress reports must be completed and signed by both the student and supervisor/advisor, reviewed by the program coordinator, and submitted to the College of Graduate Studies by June 1 of each year to qualify for the fellowship

No. of awards offered: Approx. 2,500

Closing Date: 1 June

No. of awards given last year: 460

No. of applicants last year: Approx. 2,500

Additional Information: Please check for internal departmental deadlines gradstudies.ok.ubc.ca/resources/award-opportunities/university-graduate-fellowship/

For further information contact:

Okanagan Campus, EME2121 - 1137 Alumni Ave, Kelowna, BC V1V 1V7, Canada.

Tel: (1) 250 807 8772
Fax: (1) 250 807 8799
Email: graduateawards.ok@ubc.ca

University of California at Los Angeles (UCLA) Center for India and South Asia

Department of History, 11387 Bunche Hall, Los Angeles, CA 90095-1487, United States of America.

Tel: (1) 310 206 2654
Email: subrahma@history.ucla.edu
Website: www.international.ucla.edu
Contact: Professor Sanjay Subrahmanyam, Chair of Indian History

The main thrust behind the creation of the UCLA Center for India and South Asia is to raise the profile of South Asia on campus and more generally in southern California. The organization aims at transforming UCLA into one of the leading poles of integrated research activity on India and South Asia in the country.

University of California, Los Angeles (UCLA) Sardar Patel Award

Purpose: To award the best dissertation submitted at any American university on the subject of modern India
Eligibility: Open to candidates who have written their dissertations while being enrolled at any accredited university in the United States
Level of Study: Research
Type: Award
Value: US$10,000
Frequency: Annual
Country of Study: Any country
Application Procedure: Applicants must submit 2 hard copies of their dissertation, 7 copies of abstract, a copy of their curriculum vitae and a letter from the dissertation supervisor
Closing Date: 15 October

For further information contact:

Email: cisa@international.ucla.edu

University of California Berkeley - Haas School

S440 Student Services Building, Suite 1902, Berkeley, CA 94720-1902, United States of America.

Tel: (1) 510 642 1405
Website: www.haas.berkeley.edu
Contact: MBA Admissions Officer

Hellman Fellows Fund

Purpose: The purpose of the Hellman Fellows Fund is to support substantially the research of promising assistant professors who show capacity for great distinction in their research
Eligibility: In determining the allocation of awards, the Chancellor will seek the counsel of a panel of faculty comprised of tenured Hellman Fellows and a member of the Academic Senate Committee on Research, chaired by the Vice Provost for the Faculty. Applications should therefore include an introductory description which is accessible to someone who is not an expert in the given field
Level of Study: Postgraduate
Type: Funding support
Value: Maximum value of up to US$60,000
Frequency: Annual
Country of Study: United States of America
Application Procedure: 1. Applications should be brief, no more than 3 pages, and written with the understanding that they will be reviewed by a panel of faculty from the sciences and humanities that may not include specialists in the field of study. 2. Applications should therefore include an introductory description which is accessible to someone who is not an expert in the given field
Closing Date: May
Funding: Private

For further information contact:

Vice Provost for the Faculty, 200 California Hall, MC 1500, Berkeley, CA 94720-1500, United States of America.

Tel: (1) 510 642 6474
Email: yasyavg@berkeley.edu

Western Center for Agricultural Health and Safety

Purpose: The overarching goal of the WCAHS Small Grant Program is to encourage the development of creative research projects while nurturing researchers – particularly early-career researchers – interested in improving agricultural health and safety for the Western United States

Eligibility: 1. Faculty with PI eligibility in the Western region (AZ, CA, HI, NV). 2. PhD students or postdoctoral scholars in the Western region. 3. Applicants from AZ, HI, and NV are encouraged to apply

Level of Study: postdoctoral

Type: Grant

Value: Graduate students and postdoctoral scholars may request up to US$10,000. Faculty may request up to US$30,000

Frequency: Annual

Country of Study: United States of America

Application Procedure: For further information, check the website aghealth.ucdavis.edu/

Closing Date: 3 September

Additional Information: aghealth.ucdavis.edu/small-grant-program
aghealth.ucdavis.edu/funding/small-grant-program

For further information contact:

Email: aghealth@ucdavis.edu

University of California, Berkeley

Graduate Services, Graduate Fellowships Office, 318 Sproul Hall #5900, Berkeley, CA 94720-5900, United States of America.

Tel: (1) 510 642 6000
Email: gradappt@berkeley.edu
Website: www.berkeley.edu

Founded in the wake of the gold rush by the leaders of the newly established 31st state, the University of California's flagship campus at Berkeley has become one of the pre-eminent universities in the world. Its early guiding lights, charged with providing education (both 'practical' and 'classical') for the state's people, gradually established a distinguished faculty (with 20 Nobel laureates to date), a stellar research library, and more than 350 academic programs.

Conference Travel Grants

Purpose: To allow students to attend professional conferences

Eligibility: Applicants must be registered graduate students in good academic standing. They must be in the final stages of their graduate work and planning to present a paper on their dissertation research at the conference they are attending

Level of Study: Doctorate, Graduate

Type: Grant

Value: Amount of the grant depends upon the location of conference (up to US$600 within California, US$900 elsewhere in North America, including Canada and Mexico, and US$1,500 outside of North America)

Frequency: Dependent on funds available

Study Establishment: University of California, Berkeley

Country of Study: United States of America

Application Procedure: Applicants must submit an application form and one letter of support from their graduate advisor attesting to the academic merit of the trip. Applications can be obtained from the website

For further information contact:

Email: aips@pakistanstudies-aips.org

University of California, Los Angeles (UCLA) Center for 17th and 18th Century Studies and the William Andrews Clark Memorial Library

10745 Dickson Plaza, 310 Royce Hall, Los Angeles, CA 90095-1404, United States of America.

Tel: (1) 310 206 8552
Email: c1718cs@humnet.ucla.edu
Website: www.c1718cs.ucla.edu/
Contact: Fellowship Co-ordinator

University of California, Los Angeles (UCLA) Center for 17th and 18th century Studies provides a forum for the discussion of central issues in the field of early modern studies, facilitates research and publication, supports scholarship and encourages the creation of interdisciplinary, cross-cultural programmes that advance the understanding of this important period. The William Andrews Clark Memorial Library, administered by the Center, is known for its collections of rare books and manuscripts concerning 17th and 18th-century Britain and Europe, Oscar Wilde and the 1890s, the history of printing, and certain aspects of the American West.

Clark-Huntington Joint Bibliographical Fellowship

Purpose: To support bibliographical research
Level of Study: Postdoctorate, Professional development
Type: Fellowship
Value: US$6,500
Length of Study: 2 months
Frequency: Annual
Study Establishment: The Clark Library and the Huntington Library
Country of Study: United States of America
Application Procedure: Applicants must submit an application form, a curriculum vitae, a proposal statement, a bibliography and three letters of reference
No. of awards offered: 15
Closing Date: 1 February
Funding: Private
No. of awards given last year: 1
No. of applicants last year: 15
Additional Information: gradfund.rutgers.edu/awards/clark-huntington-joint-bibliographical-fellowship/

For further information contact:

Email: ortiz@humnet.ucla.edu

University of California, Los Angeles (UCLA) Institute of American Cultures (IAC)

1237 Murphy Hall, Box 951419, Los Angeles, CA 90095-1419, United States of America.

Tel: (1) 310 206 2557
Email: iaccoordinator@gdnet.ucla.edu
Website: www.gdnet.ucla.edu/iacweb/iachome.htm
Contact: Dr N Cherie Francis, Co-ordinator

The UCLA Institute of American Cultures (IAC) is committed to advancing knowledge, strengthening and integrating interdisciplinary research and enriching instruction on African Americans, American Indians, Asian Americans and Chicanos. Since 1969, the IAC has been responsible for developing and expanding graduate studies, research and training in ethnic studies and is a major contributor to the academic and intellectual life of the University.

University of California at Los Angeles Institute of American Culture (IAC) Postdoctoral/Visiting Scholar Fellowships

Purpose: To enable PhD scholars wishing to work in association with the American Indian Studies Center, the BUNCHE Center for African American Studies, the Asian American Studies Center and the Chicano Studies Research Center, to conduct research and publish books or manuscripts relating to ethnic studies and interdisciplinary instruction
Eligibility: Open to citizens of the United States of America and permanent residents
Level of Study: Postdoctorate
Type: Fellowship
Value: US$29,000; US$34,000 stipend plus health benefits and up to US$4,000 in research support
Length of Study: Up to 1 year
Frequency: Annual
Country of Study: United States of America
Application Procedure: Applicants must complete an application form, available from one of the ethnic studies centres, the IAC, or from the website
Closing Date: 31 December
No. of awards given last year: 4

For further information contact:

Tel: (1) 310 825 7315
Fax: (1) 310 206 7060
Email: aisc@ucla.edu

University of Cambridge

The Old Schools, Trinity Lane, Cambridge CB2 1TN, United Kingdom.

Tel: (44) 12 2333 7733
Email: dmh14@cam.ac.uk
Website: www.admin.cam.ac.uk
Contact: Hugo Hocknell, Student Registry

The University of Cambridge is a loose confederation of faculties, colleges and other bodies. The colleges are mainly concerned with the teaching of their undergraduate students through tutorials and supervisions and the academic support of both graduate and undergraduate students, while the University employs professors, readers, lecturers and other teaching and administrative staff who provide the formal teaching in lectures, seminars and practical classes. The University also administers the University Library.

Arthington-Davy Grants for Tongan Students for Postgraduate Study

Eligibility: 1. Hold a first University degree, 2. Have applied for admission, or already received an offer of admission, for a post-graduate study course at any University in the world, and 3. Be of Tongan origin
Level of Study: Postgraduate
Type: Grant
Value: Graduate Course Fees, and maintenance allowance, less any financial support received from elsewhere
Length of Study: For minimum further period required to complete PhD
Frequency: Annual
Country of Study: Any country
Application Procedure: A completed application form should be sent together with the following Proof of Tongan origin academic transcripts details of the intended post-graduate study, preferably with a letter of conditional acceptance from the University concerned 1. Clear and precise details of tuition fees, living expenses and finances available from the student's own resources and/or from other institutions. 2. Names and email addresses of two academic referees. 3. CV
Closing Date: 31 May
Funding: Private
Additional Information: For full details on how to apply please visit: www.trin.cam.ac.uk/postgraduate/graduate-funding-awards/

For further information contact:

Email: grad.tutor@trin.cam.ac.uk

Dorothy Hodgkin Postgraduate Award

Eligibility: Applicants must have already applied for and been accepted for a PhD place at the University of Cambridge, must be a national of one of the eligible countries (Russia plus all countries on the DAC List of ODA Recipients), must be intending to start their PhD that coming October and must hold a high-grade qualification, at least the equivalent of a United Kingdom First Class (Honours) Degree, from a prestigious academic institution
Type: Award
Value: Approx. £12,300 per year (university composition plus college fees and maintenance stipend)
Length of Study: 3 years

Frequency: Annual
Country of Study: Any country
Application Procedure: There is no separate application form for this competition
Closing Date: 15 December
Contributor: The United Kingdom Research Councils and Industrial Partners
Additional Information: Each DHPA is jointly sponsored by both a Research Council partner and a private sector company partner. Further details can be found on the Research Councils United Kingdom website www.european-funding-guide.eu/awardprize/11552-dorothy-hodgkin-postgraduate-awards-dhpa

For further information contact:

Email: kfw20@admin.cam.ac.uk

Evans Fund

Purpose: To support research
Eligibility: Open to graduates of any university who intend to engage in research in a suitable field
Level of Study: Doctorate, Postdoctorate, Postgraduate
Type: Funding support
Value: £6,000 a year
Length of Study: 1 or 2 years
Frequency: Annual
Study Establishment: The University of Cambridge
Country of Study: Any country
Application Procedure: Applicants must obtain an application form from the Secretary, which must be returned together with an outline of the applicant's proposed scheme of travel and research, a curriculum vitae and the names and addresses of two referees
Closing Date: 27 April
Funding: Private
Contributor: Legacy
Additional Information: www.socanth.cam.ac.uk/about-us/funding/research-funding/evans-fund

For further information contact:

Department of Social Anthropology, University of Cambridge, 2 Free School Lane, Cambridge CB2 3QA, United Kingdom.

Email: research@socanth.cam.ac.uk

Fitzwilliam College Charlton Studentships

Purpose: Part-cost award for masters students

Eligibility: Application for the Charlton Studentship is via the Fitzwilliam Masters Studentship competition and all the same conditions apply.
Level of Study: Graduate
Type: Scholarship
Value: £10,000 each
Length of Study: 1 year
Frequency: Annual
Study Establishment: Fitzwilliam College
Country of Study: United Kingdom
Application Procedure: Apply online at www.fitz.cam.ac. uk/academic/scholarships-prizes/graduate-scholarships
No. of awards offered: 5
Closing Date: 28 February
Funding: Individuals
Contributor: Fitzwilliam College
Additional Information: www.fitz.cam.ac.uk/college-life/ fees-funding-and-awards/postgraduate-scholarships-and-prizes

For further information contact:

Graduate officer, Fitzwilliam College, Cambridge CB3 0DG, United Kingdom.

Email: graduate.officer@fitz.cam.ac.uk

Fitzwilliam College Graduate Scholarship

Eligibility: 1. All full-time PhD courses are eligible. Arts students may be preferred. 2. All nationalities and fee status.
Level of Study: Postgraduate
Type: Fellowship
Value: £1,460
Length of Study: 1 year
Frequency: Annual
Study Establishment: Fitzwilliam College, University of Cambridge
Country of Study: United Kingdom
Application Procedure: www.fitz.cam.ac.uk/onlineforms/ view.php?id=274627
No. of awards offered: 1
Closing Date: 31 August
Funding: Private
Additional Information: www.fitz.cam.ac.uk/college-life/ fees-funding-and-awards/postgraduate-scholarships-and-prizes

For further information contact:

Tel: (44) 12 2333 2035
Fax: (44) 12 2333 2082
Email: grad.scholarships@fitz.cam.ac.uk

Fitzwilliam College Leathersellers

Purpose: To support students who wish to undertake research
Eligibility: 1. Applicants must be Home fee status with a previous degree from a British university 2. PhD (including PhD probationary) students who will be in years 2 or 3 of their course at the start of the award period (Michaelmas Term) 3. Awards may be held for 2 or 3 years dependent on continued good progress. 4. Physical or Biological Sciences, Engineering and Mathematics subjects.
Level of Study: Doctorate
Type: Scholarship
Value: £3,500/year
Length of Study: 2 to 3 years dependent on continued good progress.
Frequency: Annual
Study Establishment: Fitzwilliam College, University of Cambridge
Country of Study: United Kingdom
Closing Date: 31 May
Funding: Commercial
Additional Information: https://cambridge.eu.qualtrics. com/jfe/form/SV_71hmBBO4bRk6tD0

For further information contact:

Tel: (44) 1223 332035
Email: graduate.office@fitz.cam.ac.uk

Fitzwilliam College Research Fellowship

Purpose: To enable scholars to carry out a programme of new research
Eligibility: Applicants should: 1. have completed a PhD or have a clear expectation of doing so prior to 1 October 2023 2. have completed no more than two years (f.t.e.) of postdoctoral research at the time of application 3. have secured full research funding (including salary) for three years from 1 October 2023, or have a clear expectation of such funding 4. have secured an endorsement from a Department, Faculty, Institution, Laboratory or equivalent in the University of Cambridge 5. have demonstrated to their funder their right to work in the UK.
Level of Study: Doctorate, Postdoctorate
Type: Fellowship
Value: The Fellowship is non-stipendiary. If available, rent-free single accommodation will be offered in College, with a charge to cover services; alternatively, if the Fellow is not resident in College, study facilities will be made available and an allowance (currently £3,469) paid. A Research Fellow is a member of the Governing Body, bringing responsibilities as a Trustee of the College, and is entitled to all

meals at College expense when the kitchens are open. An annual allowance of £1000 may be claimed for academic purposes including the purchase of books and computing equipment, or attendance at conferences. Additional grants may be made to assist with certain approved research expenses which are not covered by departmental, faculty or other sources.

Length of Study: 3 years
Frequency: Annual
Study Establishment: Fitzwilliam College, University of Cambridge
Country of Study: United Kingdom
Application Procedure: https://www.fitz.cam.ac.uk/sites/default/files/2022-03/Non%20Stipendiary%20Research%20Fellowship%20Further%20Particulars%20March%202022%5B43%5D.pdf
Closing Date: 12 April
Additional Information: www.fitz.cam.ac.uk/non-stipendiary-research-fellowships

For further information contact:

Email: masters.assistant@fitz.cam.ac.uk

Fitzwilliam College: Shipley Studentship

Purpose: To enable graduates to undertake research
Eligibility: 1. Applicant should be undertaking / intending to undertake research at the Faculty of Divinity. 2. Exceptionally, research on a theological topic in another faculty also accepted.
Level of Study: Postgraduate
Type: Studentship
Value: £1,460
Length of Study: 1 year
Frequency: Annual
Study Establishment: Fitzwilliam College, University of Cambridge
Country of Study: United Kingdom
Application Procedure: www.fitz.cam.ac.uk/onlineforms/view.php?id=278169
No. of awards offered: 1
Closing Date: 31 August
Funding: Private
Additional Information: www.fitz.cam.ac.uk/college-life/fees-funding-and-awards/postgraduate-scholarships-and-prizes

For further information contact:

Tel: (44) 1223 332035
Email: graduate.office@fitz.cam.ac.uk

Fitzwilliam College: Cleaver-Wang Studentship

Eligibility: Eligibility: 1. Application for the Cleaver-Wang Studentship is via the Fitzwilliam Masters Studentship competition and all the same conditions apply. 2. Preference will be given to those working across disciplines or with innovative methodologies 3. Apply online - deadline 28 February 2023. Interviews will be late April, results available by the end of May. 4. To complete the application you will also need to upload a PDF copy of your University application form.
Type: Studentship
Value: £10,000
Length of Study: 1 year
Frequency: Annual
Country of Study: Any country
Application Procedure: www.fitz.cam.ac.uk/onlineforms/view.php?id=250965
No. of awards offered: 1
Closing Date: 28 February
Additional Information: www.fitz.cam.ac.uk/college-life/fees-funding-and-awards/postgraduate-scholarships-and-prizes#panel-2107856630

Fitzwilliam College: E D Davies Scholarship

Eligibility: 1. All full-time PhD courses are eligible. 2. All nationalities and fee status.
Level of Study: Doctorate
Type: Scholarship
Value: £1,460 per year
Length of Study: 1 year
Frequency: Annual
Country of Study: United Kingdom
Application Procedure: www.fitz.cam.ac.uk/onlineforms/view.php?id=274627
Closing Date: 31 August
No. of awards given last year: 2
No. of applicants last year: 25
Additional Information: https://www.fitz.cam.ac.uk/college-life/fees-funding-and-awards/postgraduate-scholarships-and-prizes

Fitzwilliam College: Fitzwilliam Society JRW Alexander Law Book Grants

Eligibility: All students starting the LLM or MCL course at Fitzwilliam receive a Law Book grant in the form of book tokens.
Type: Grant
Value: £100 each
Frequency: Annual

Country of Study: United Kingdom
Application Procedure: No application is necessary
Additional Information: www.fitz.cam.ac.uk/college-life/fees-funding-and-awards/postgraduate-scholarships-and-prizes#panel-775310585

Fitzwilliam College: Gibson Scholarship

Eligibility: 1. Applicant should be intending to work towards a doctorate in New Testament Studies 2. Students naming Fitzwilliam as first choice are preferred but not exclusively.
Level of Study: Graduate, Postgraduate
Type: Scholarship
Value: £1,165
Length of Study: 1 year
Frequency: Annual
Country of Study: United Kingdom
Application Procedure: Submit online application form
No. of awards offered: 8
Closing Date: 31 August
Additional Information: www.fitz.cam.ac.uk/college-life/fees-funding-and-awards/postgraduate-scholarships-and-prizes

For further information contact:

Email: graduate.office@fitz.cam.ac.uk

Fitzwilliam College: Hirst-Player Scholarship

Eligibility: 1. Reading for a Degree or a Diploma in Theology. 2. Intention to take Holy Orders in a Christian Church preferred. 3. Students needing assistance with fees, who would otherwise be unable to study at Cambridge
Level of Study: Postgraduate
Type: Scholarship
Value: £2,330 maximum
Length of Study: 1 to 2 years
Frequency: Annual
Country of Study: United Kingdom
Application Procedure: Submit online application form
Closing Date: 31 August
Additional Information: https://www.fitz.cam.ac.uk/college-life/fees-funding-and-awards/postgraduate-scholarships-and-prizes

For further information contact:

Email: graduate.office@fitz.cam.ac.uk

Fitzwilliam College: Lee Kuan Yew PhD Studentships

Eligibility: 1. All full-time PhD courses are eligible 2. All nationalities and fee status 3. There are specific subject area criteria for this Studentship. More information. 4. Deadline for studentship application - 16 January 2022 (24:00 hours) 5. Applicants must also apply for a place on their chosen course by the funding deadline and tick the box for inclusion in the funding competitions on their application. 6. Applicants may apply to any of the University's colleges as their first choice college. The awardee will be required to transfer college membership to Fitzwilliam College before the start of their course.
Level of Study: Doctorate
Type: Studentship
Value: Fully-funded (fees and maintenance).
Length of Study: 3.5 years
Frequency: Annual
Country of Study: United Kingdom
No. of awards offered: 2 to 3
Closing Date: 16 January
Additional Information: www.fitz.cam.ac.uk/college-life/fees-funding-and-awards/postgraduate-scholarships-and-prizes#panel-1489587405

Fitzwilliam College: Peter Wilson Estates Gazette Studentships

Eligibility: 1. All full-time, one year Masters courses that are offered by the Department of Land Economy are eligible. 2. One of the Studentships will be prioritised for a Fitzwilliam undergraduate student who is applying for MPhil in Cambridge. 3. All nationalities and fee status 4. Application deadline is 31 May 2023 5. Applicants must have an offer of a place on the course by the deadline (to meet this criteria, we recommend that the University application is submitted by 3 December). 6. Applicants must have College membership with Fitzwilliam by the deadline. 7. It is not possible to transfer Colleges in order to be eligible for this Studentship, but all those who name Fitzwilliam as their first choice, or who are allocated via 2nd choice or random allocation, will be eligible.
Level of Study: Postgraduate
Type: Studentship
Value: Three awards of £4,000 each (occasionally 4 awards of £3,000 each)
Frequency: Annual
Country of Study: United Kingdom
Application Procedure: www.fitz.cam.ac.uk/onlineforms/view.php?id=250965
No. of awards offered: 3 to 4

Closing Date: 31 May
Additional Information: www.fitz.cam.ac.uk/college-life/fees-funding-and-awards/postgraduate-scholarships-and-prizes#panel-1384001179

Fitzwilliam College: Quantedge – Lee Kuan Yew Masters Scholarship

Eligibility: 1. All full-time one year Masters courses are eligible, with the exception, MBA, MFin and PGCE. 2. Financially disadvantaged student of Singaporean nationality. 3. Deadline for studentship application - 16 January 2022 (12 noon). 4. Applicants must also apply for a place on their chosen course by the University funding deadline (either 3 December or 7 January depending on course). 5. Applicants may apply to any of the University's colleges as their first choice college. The awardee will be required to transfer college membership to Fitzwilliam College before the start of their course.
Type: Scholarship
Value: Fully-funded (fees and maintenance)
Length of Study: 1 year
Country of Study: United Kingdom
Application Procedure: www.fitz.cam.ac.uk/onlineforms/view.php?id=287128
No. of awards offered: 1
Closing Date: 16 January
Additional Information: www.fitz.cam.ac.uk/college-life/fees-funding-and-awards/postgraduate-scholarships-and-prizes

Fitzwilliam College: Robert Lethbridge Scholarship in Modern Languages

Eligibility: Eligibility: 1. All full-time, one year Masters courses that are offered by the Faculty of Modern and Medieval Languages and Linguistics are eligible. 2. All nationalities and fee status. 3. Scholarship application deadline is 31 May 2022. 4. Applicants must have an offer of a place on the course by the deadline (to meet this criteria, we recommend that the University application is submitted by 3 December. 5. Applicants must have College membership with Fitzwilliam by the deadline. 6. It is not possible to transfer Colleges in order to be eligible for this Studentship, but all those who name Fitzwilliam as their first choice, or who are allocated via 2nd choice or random allocation, will be eligible.
Level of Study: Postgraduate
Type: Scholarship
Value: £1,250
Length of Study: 1 year

Frequency: Annual
Country of Study: United Kingdom
Application Procedure: www.fitz.cam.ac.uk/sites/default/files/inline-files/Charitable%20%26%20Community%20Projects%20-%20NEW_1%20%281%29.docx
No. of awards offered: 1
Closing Date: 31 May
Additional Information: www.fitz.cam.ac.uk/college-life/fees-funding-and-awards/postgraduate-scholarships-and-prizes#panel-892737392

Fitzwilliam College: The Hong Leong – Lee Kuan Yew Masters Scholarship

Eligibility: 1. All full-time one year Masters courses are eligible, with the exception of MBA, MFin and PGCE 2. All nationalities and fee status There are specific subject area criteria for this Studentship. More information. 3. Deadline for studentship application - 16 January 2023 (24:00 hours) 4. Applicants must also apply for a place on their chosen course by the course funding deadline. 5. Applicants may apply to any of the University's colleges as their first choice college. The awardee will be required to transfer college membership to Fitzwilliam College before the start of their course.
Level of Study: Postgraduate
Type: Scholarship
Value: Fully-funded (fees and maintenance)
Length of Study: 1 year
Country of Study: United Kingdom
Application Procedure: www.fitz.cam.ac.uk/LKYFund
Closing Date: 16 January
Additional Information: To complete the application you will also need to upload a PDF copy of your University application form. www.fitz.cam.ac.uk/college-life/fees-funding-and-awards/postgraduate-scholarships-and-prizes#panel-661464388

Fitzwilliam Masters Studentship

Eligibility: 1. All full-time one year Masters courses are eligible, with the exception of MRes, MBA, MFin and PGCE. 2. All nationalities and fee status. 3. Awards are made on academic merit. 4. Studentship application deadline is 28 February 2023. 5. Applicants may apply for the studentship before they have an offer from the University. However: Applicants must have a conditional offer from the University by 15 March (to meet this criteria, we recommend that the University application is submitted by 3 December) Applicants must have College membership with Fitzwilliam by 15 March. It is not possible to transfer Colleges in order to be eligible for this Studentship, but all those who name Fitzwilliam as their first choice, or who are allocated via 2nd choice or random allocation, will be eligible.

Level of Study: Postgraduate
Type: Studentship
Value: Fully-funded (fees and maintenance)
Frequency: Annual
Country of Study: United Kingdom
No. of awards offered: 1
Closing Date: 28 February
Additional Information: www.fitz.cam.ac.uk/college-life/fees-funding-and-awards/postgraduate-scholarships-and-prizes#panel-1159453696

Girton College Graduate Research Scholarship

Eligibility: A first-class degree is almost always required and election will be conditional on the candidate being granted Graduate Student status by the University of Cambridge. The holder must become a member of the college and either be a candidate for a masters or a PhD degree
Level of Study: Doctorate, MBA, Postgraduate
Type: Scholarship
Value: The value of the award for this year is likely to be approximately £27,000
Frequency: Annual
Study Establishment: University of Cambridge
Country of Study: United Kingdom
Application Procedure: Application should be made online via www.girton.cam.ac.uk/graduates/research-awards
No. of awards offered: 200
Closing Date: 27 March
No. of awards given last year: 3
No. of applicants last year: 200
Additional Information: www.girton.cam.ac.uk/prospective-students/graduate/graduate-research-awards/

For further information contact:

Email: graduate.office@girton.cam.ac.uk

Girton College Overseas Bursaries

Eligibility: A first-class degree is almost always required and election will be conditional on the candidate being granted Graduate Student status by the University of Cambridge. The holder must become a member of the college
Level of Study: Doctorate, Graduate, MBA, Postgraduate
Type: Bursary
Value: £200 to £1,000 per year
Frequency: Dependent on funds available

Study Establishment: University of Cambridge
Country of Study: United Kingdom
Application Procedure: Application forms can be downloaded from www.girton.cam.ac.uk/graduates/research-awards or may be obtained from the Graduate Secretary, Girton College, Cambridge, CB3 0JG, United Kingdom (email graduate.office@girton.cam.ac.uk)
Closing Date: 28 March

For further information contact:

Email: graduate.office@girton.cam.ac.uk

Girton College: Doris Woodall Studentship

Eligibility: A first-class degree is almost always required and election will be conditional on the candidate being granted Graduate Student status by the University of Cambridge. The holder must become a member of the college
Level of Study: Doctorate, MBA, Postgraduate
Type: Studentship
Value: £6,400
Length of Study: 1 year
Frequency: Annual
Study Establishment: University of Cambridge
Country of Study: United Kingdom
Application Procedure: Application should be made online via www.girton.cam.ac.uk/graduates/research-awards
No. of awards offered: 1
Closing Date: 26 March
Additional Information: https://www.girton.cam.ac.uk/postgraduates/fees-finance-funding

For further information contact:

Email: graduate.office@girton.cam.ac.uk

Girton College: Ida and Isidore Cohen Research Scholarship

Eligibility: Open to students working in modern Hebrew studies. A first-class degree is almost always required and election will be conditional on the candidate being granted Graduate Student status by the University of Cambridge. The holder must become a member of the college
Level of Study: Doctorate, Graduate, Postgraduate
Type: Scholarship
Value: Between £3,000 and £5,000
Frequency: Annual
Study Establishment: University of Cambridge
Country of Study: United Kingdom

Application Procedure: Application forms can be downloaded from external link or may be obtained from the Graduate Secretary, Girton College, Cambridge, CB3 0JG, United Kingdom

Closing Date: 28 March

For further information contact:

Email: graduate.office@girton.cam.ac.uk

Girton College: Irene Hallinan Scholarship

Eligibility: A first-class degree is almost always required and election will be conditional on the candidate being granted Graduate Student status by the University of Cambridge. The holder must become a member of the college and either be a candidate for a masters or a PhD degree

Level of Study: Doctorate, MBA, Postgraduate

Type: Scholarship

Value: £6,500

Length of Study: 1 year

Frequency: Annual

Study Establishment: University of Cambridge

Country of Study: United Kingdom

Application Procedure: Application should be made online via www.girton.cam.ac.uk/graduates/research-awards

No. of awards offered: 200

Closing Date: 27 March

No. of awards given last year: 3

No. of applicants last year: 200

Additional Information: https://www.girton.cam.ac.uk/post graduates/fees-finance-funding

For further information contact:

Email: graduate.office@girton.cam.ac.uk

Girton College: Maria Luisa de Sanchez Scholarship

Purpose: Available to students of Venezuelan nationality. The value is based upon University fees and the University recommended maintenance figure. It is awarded, in the first instance, for one year but may be renewed for further periods up to three years. In exceptional cases it can be extended to four years.

Eligibility: Applicants must be of Venezuelan nationality. A first-class degree is almost always required and election will be conditional on the candidate being granted Graduate Student status by the University of Cambridge. The holder must become a member of the college

Level of Study: Doctorate, Graduate, MBA, Postgraduate

Type: Scholarship

Value: Approximately £31,000

Length of Study: 1 Year

Frequency: Annual

Study Establishment: University of Cambridge

Country of Study: United Kingdom

Application Procedure: Application forms can be downloaded from https://app.casc.cam.ac.uk/fas_live/g_post.aspx or may be obtained from the Graduate Secretary, Girton College, Cambridge, CB3 0JG, United Kingdom (email graduate.office@girton.cam.ac.uk)

No. of awards offered: 2

Closing Date: 25 March

No. of awards given last year: 1

Additional Information: Eligible to nationals of Venezuela https://www.girton.cam.ac.uk/postgraduates/fees-finance-funding

For further information contact:

Email: graduate.office@girton.cam.ac.uk

Girton College: Ruth Whaley Scholarship

Eligibility: Open to outstanding students of non-European Union citizenship seeking admission to Girton. It is open to students following arts subjects. A first-class degree is almost always required and election will be conditional on the candidate being granted Graduate Student status by the University of Cambridge. The holder must become a member of the college

Level of Study: Doctorate, Postgraduate

Type: Scholarship

Value: £3,300

Length of Study: 1 year

Frequency: Annual

Study Establishment: University of Cambridge

Country of Study: United Kingdom

Application Procedure: Application forms can be downloaded from www.girton.cam.ac.uk/graduates/research-awards or may be obtained from the Graduate Secretary

No. of awards offered: 1

Closing Date: 26 March

No. of awards given last year: 1

Additional Information: For further details, please refer to the website www.girton.cam.ac.uk/students/graduate-scholarships/

For further information contact:

Girton College, Huntingdon Rd, Girton, Cambridge CB3 0JG, United Kingdom.

Email: graduate.office@girton.cam.ac.uk

Girton College: Sidney and Marguerite Cody Studentship

Purpose: Period of travel and study in continental Europe of up to 12 months and normally of not less than 6 months
Eligibility: Open to graduate members of any faculty except English who have completed less than nine terms in residence. A first-class degree is almost always required and election will be conditional on the candidate being granted Graduate Student status by the University of Cambridge. The holder must become a member of the college
Level of Study: Doctorate, Graduate, Postgraduate
Type: Studentship
Value: Up to £3,000
Frequency: Annual
Study Establishment: University of Cambridge
Country of Study: United Kingdom
Application Procedure: Application should be made online via www.girton.cam.ac.uk/graduates/research-awards
Closing Date: 28 March
No. of awards given last year: 1
Additional Information: https://www.girton.cam.ac.uk/post graduates/fees-finance-funding

For further information contact:

Email: graduate.office@girton.cam.ac.uk

Girton College: Stribling Award

Eligibility: Open to Girton students who are already members of the College, namely undergraduates coming into graduate status or current MPhil students who are going on to a PhD A first-class degree is almost always required and election will be conditional on the candidate being granted Graduate Student status by the University of Cambridge
Level of Study: Doctorate, Postgraduate
Type: Award
Value: £1,000, normally in addition to a studentship or any other funding for fees and maintenance
Length of Study: 1 year
Frequency: Annual
Study Establishment: University of Cambridge
Country of Study: United Kingdom
Application Procedure: Application should be made online via www.girton.cam.ac.uk/graduates/research-awards
No. of awards offered: 2
Closing Date: 28 March
No. of awards given last year: 2
Additional Information: Award only available to Girton College Students https://www.girton.cam.ac.uk/postgradu ates/fees-finance-funding

For further information contact:

Email: graduate.office@girton.cam.ac.uk

Girton College: The Chan and Mok Graduate Scholarship

Eligibility: 1. They are open to students who have graduated or will have graduated before 1st October of the year they apply, and who nominate Girton as their first or second choice College. 2. A first-class degree is almost always required and election will be conditional on the candidate being granted Postgraduate Student status by the University of Cambridge. 3. The holder must become a member of the College and be a candidate for either a Masters or a PhD degree. 4. Current Cambridge students who are members of another College are eligible to apply if they are moving from one course of study to another, however if they are part-way through a course they cannot apply for the awards. 5. available to students who are permanent residents of Hong Kong and with preference to those who have studied at schools affiliated to Po Leung Kuk.
Level of Study: Postgraduate
Type: Scholarship
Value: £10,000
Length of Study: 1 year
Frequency: Annual
Country of Study: Any country
Closing Date: 25 March
Additional Information: www.girton.cam.ac.uk/postgradu ates/fees-finance-funding

Girton College: The Diane Worzala Memorial Fund

Eligibility: 1. They are open to students who have graduated or will have graduated before 1st October of the year they apply, and who nominate Girton as their first or second choice College. 2. A first-class degree is almost always required and election will be conditional on the candidate being granted Postgraduate Student status by the University of Cambridge. 3. The holder must become a member of the College and be a candidate for either a Masters or a PhD degree. 4. Current Cambridge students who are members of another College are eligible to apply if they are moving from one course of study to another, however if they are part-way through a course they cannot apply for the awards.
Type: Scholarship
Value: £600
Country of Study: United Kingdom
Closing Date: 25 March
Additional Information: www.girton.cam.ac.uk/postgradu ates/fees-finance-funding

For further information contact:

Email: graduate.office@girton.cam.ac.uk

Girton College: The Girton Hong Kong Founder's Scholarship

Eligibility: 1. They are open to students who have graduated or will have graduated before 1st October of the year they apply, and who nominate Girton as their first or second choice College. 2. A first-class degree is almost always required and election will be conditional on the candidate being granted Postgraduate Student status by the University of Cambridge. 3. The holder must become a member of the College and be a candidate for either a Masters or a PhD degree. 4. Current Cambridge students who are members of another College are eligible to apply if they are moving from one course of study to another, however if they are part-way through a course they cannot apply for the awards.
Level of Study: Postgraduate
Type: Scholarship
Value: £10,000
Length of Study: 3 years
Frequency: Annual
Country of Study: United Kingdom
Closing Date: 25 March
Additional Information: www.girton.cam.ac.uk/postgraduates/fees-finance-funding

For further information contact:

Email: graduate.office@girton.cam.ac.uk

Girton College: The Joyce Biddle Scholarship

Eligibility: 1. They are open to students who have graduated or will have graduated before 1st October of the year they apply, and who nominate Girton as their first or second choice College. 2. A first-class degree is almost always required and election will be conditional on the candidate being granted Postgraduate Student status by the University of Cambridge. 3. The holder must become a member of the College and be a candidate for either a Masters or a PhD degree. 4. Current Cambridge students who are members of another College are eligible to apply if they are moving from one course of study to another, however if they are part-way through a course they cannot apply for the awards.
Level of Study: Postgraduate
Type: Scholarship
Value: £13,000, but may be renewed.
Length of Study: 1 year
Frequency: Annual

Country of Study: United Kingdom
Closing Date: 25 March
Additional Information: www.girton.cam.ac.uk/postgraduates/fees-finance-funding

For further information contact:

Email: graduate.office@girton.cam.ac.uk

Girton College: The Postgraduate Research Scholarship

Eligibility: 1. They are open to students who have graduated or will have graduated before 1st October of the year they apply, and who nominate Girton as their first or second choice College. 2. A first-class degree is almost always required and election will be conditional on the candidate being granted Postgraduate Student status by the University of Cambridge. 3. The holder must become a member of the College and be a candidate for either a Masters or a PhD degree. 4. Current Cambridge students who are members of another College are eligible to apply if they are moving from one course of study to another, however if they are part-way through a course they cannot apply for the awards.
Level of Study: Postgraduate
Type: Scholarship
Value: Approximately £10,500
Length of Study: 1 year, but may be renewed for further periods up to three years. In exceptional cases it can be extended to four years.
Frequency: Annual
Country of Study: United Kingdom
Closing Date: 25 March
Additional Information: www.girton.cam.ac.uk/postgraduates/fees-finance-funding

For further information contact:

Email: graduate.office@girton.cam.ac.uk.

Girton College: The Dinah James Scholarship

Eligibility: 1. They are open to students who have graduated or will have graduated before 1st October of the year they apply, and who nominate Girton as their first or second choice College. 2. A first-class degree is almost always required and election will be conditional on the candidate being granted Postgraduate Student status by the University of Cambridge. 3. The holder must become a member of the College and be a candidate for either a Masters or a PhD degree. 4. Current Cambridge students who are members of another College are eligible to apply if they are moving from one course of study

to another, however if they are part-way through a course they cannot apply for the awards.
Level of Study: Postgraduate
Type: Scholarship
Value: £9,000
Frequency: Annual
Country of Study: United Kingdom
Closing Date: 25 March
Additional Information: www.girton.cam.ac.uk/postgradu ates/fees-finance-funding

Girton College: Travel Grant

Level of Study: Postgraduate
Type: Grant
Value: Contribution to academic travel and
Frequency: Every 2 years
Country of Study: Any country
Application Procedure: Application should be made online via www.girton.cam.ac.uk/graduates/research-awards
Closing Date: 24 April
Additional Information: Please note this is a strict dead-line, no allowance can be made for late applications or reference letters   www.girton.cam.ac.uk/girton-community/travel-awards/

For further information contact:

Email: ns714@cam.ac.uk

Gonville and Caius College Gonville Bursary

Purpose: To help outstanding students from outside the European Union to meet the costs of degree courses at the University of Cambridge
Eligibility: Open to candidates who have been accepted by the College through its normal admissions procedures, and who are classified as overseas students for fees purposes. A statement of financial circumstances is required
Level of Study: Doctorate, Postgraduate
Type: Bursary
Value: Reimbursement of college fees
Length of Study: Up to 3 years, with a possibility of renewal, dependent on satisfactory progress
Frequency: Annual
Study Establishment: Gonville and Caius College, the University of Cambridge
Country of Study: United Kingdom
Application Procedure: Applicants must contact the Admissions Tutor for further information. There are no application forms

For further information contact:

Gonville and Caius College, Trinity Street, Cambridge CB2 1TA, United Kingdom.

Tel: (44) 12 2333 2447
Fax: (44) 12 2333 2456
Email: admissions@cai.cam.ac.uk

Gonville and Caius College Michael Miliffe Scholarship

Subjects: All Subjects
Eligibility: Applicants must apply to the University of Cambridge in the regular way and must have a first class/high second class (Honours) degree or equivalent. Must be under 26 years.
Level of Study: Post Graduate
Type: Scholarship
Value: £5,000 is awarded
Length of Study: 2 years
Frequency: Annual
Country of Study: United Kingdom
Additional Information: www.cai.cam.ac.uk/undergradu ate/overseas

For further information contact:

Email: admissions@cai.cam.ac.uk

Gonville and Caius College W M Tapp Studentship in Law

Purpose: To encourage the study of law
Eligibility: Open to candidates who are not already members of the College, but who propose to register as graduate students at the University of Cambridge. Candidates must be under 30 years of age as of October 1st of the studentship year and be graduates or expect to be graduates no later than August of the same year. Preference is given to applicants nominating Gonville and Caius College as their first choice when applying under the Cambridge Intercollegiate Graduate Application Scheme
Level of Study: Doctorate, Postgraduate
Type: Studentship
Value: A stipend similar to that of a state studentship for research, plus fees and certain allowances, a dependent allowance, an allowance for a period of approved postgraduate experience, a travelling contribution for foreign students and a research allowance for research students
Length of Study: 1 year, renewable for up to a maximum of 3 years

Frequency: Annual
Study Establishment: Gonville and Caius College, University of Cambridge
Country of Study: United Kingdom
Application Procedure: Applicants must complete an application form, available from the Admissions Tutor
Closing Date: 31 December
Additional Information: https://www.cai.cam.ac.uk/post graduate/finance/tapp-studentships

Kings College: Stipendiary Junior Research Fellowships

Purpose: To support gifted young researchers
Level of Study: Postdoctorate, Research
Type: Fellowship
Value: Permit complete freedom to carry out research within the academic environment of the college
Length of Study: 4 years
Frequency: Annual
Study Establishment: University of Cambridge, Kings College
Country of Study: United Kingdom
Closing Date: October

For further information contact:

King's College, King's Parade, Cambridge CB2 1ST, United Kingdom.

Tel: (44) 1223 331 100
Email: info@kings.cam.ac.uk

Lucy Cavendish College: Becker Law Scholarships

Eligibility: Open to women accepted to read for the LLM and MCL by the law Faculty at the University of Cambridge
Level of Study: Postgraduate
Type: Scholarship
Value: At least £1,000 per year
Length of Study: Up to 3 years, conditional on satisfactory academic progress
Frequency: Annual
Study Establishment: Lucy Cavendish College, University of Cambridge
Country of Study: United Kingdom
Application Procedure: Please contact to the Secretary of the Studentship and Bursary Committee
Closing Date: 30 June
Additional Information: llm-guide.com/scholarships/becker-law-scholarships-257

For further information contact:

Lucy Cavendish College, Lady Margaret Rd, Cambridge CB3 0BU, United Kingdom.

Tel: (44) 1223 332 190
Fax: (44) 1223 332 178
Email: st420@cam.ac.uk

Lucy Cavendish College: Dorothy and Joseph Needham Studentship

Purpose: For studies in Natural Sciences
Eligibility: Check website or contact organisation for updates
Level of Study: Postgraduate
Type: Studentship
Value: £1,000 per year
Length of Study: Up to 3 years, conditional on satisfactory academic progress
Frequency: Annual
Study Establishment: Lucy Cavendish College, University of Cambridge
Country of Study: United Kingdom
Application Procedure: Please contact to the Secretary of the Studentship and Bursary Committee
Closing Date: 30 June
Additional Information: https://www.lucy.cam.ac.uk/study-us/postgraduates/studentships-and-awards

Lucy Cavendish College: Enterprise Studentship

Eligibility: 1. Candidates must select Lucy Cavendish as their first College choice. Candidates must have received an offer to join the programme starting in October and membership at Lucy Cavendish College before they can be considered for the studentship. 2. Applications are welcome from any candidate, irrespective of gender, nationality or geographical location. There are no restrictions on citizenship, country of residence, or fee status.
Level of Study: MBA, Postgraduate
Type: Studentship
Value: Either a single award of £12,000, or two half-awards of £6,000 each
Frequency: Annual
Study Establishment: Lucy Cavendish College, University of Cambridge
Country of Study: United Kingdom
Application Procedure: Please contact to the Secretary of the Studentship and Bursary Committee

For further information contact:

Email: mbe-admin@ceb.cam.ac.uk

U

Lucy Cavendish College: Evelyn Povey Studentship

Subjects: French Studies
Purpose: The Evelyn Povey Studentship for French Citizens and the Evelyn Povey Studentship in French Studies
Eligibility: The Evelyn Povey Studentship for French Citizens
Type: Studentship
Value: value of around £2,500
Frequency: Annual
Country of Study: Any country
Closing Date: 28 February
Contributor: Lucy Cavendish College
Additional Information: www.lucy.cam.ac.uk/study-us/post graduates/studentships-and-awards

For further information contact:

Tel: (44) 1223 322190
Email: development@lucy.cam.ac.uk

Lucy Cavendish College: Lord Frederick Cavendish Studentship

Purpose: The Lord Frederick Cavendish Studentship, open to any student
Eligibility: Applying to a course
Level of Study: postgraduate
Type: Studentship
Value: Value around £4,500
Frequency: Annual
Country of Study: Any country
Closing Date: 28 February
Contributor: Lucy Cavendish College
Additional Information: www.lucy.cam.ac.uk/study-us/post graduates/studentships-and-awards

For further information contact:

Tel: (44) 1223 322190
Email: development@lucy.cam.ac.uk

Lucy Cavendish College: Mastermann-Braithwaite Studentship

Subjects: PhD applicants in any subject, and MPhil applicants intending to embark on further research study.
Eligibility: Applying to a course
Level of Study: postgraduate
Type: Studentship
Value: Value up to £6,000

Frequency: Annual
Country of Study: Any country
No. of awards offered: 2
Closing Date: 28 February
Contributor: Lucy Cavendish College
Additional Information: www.lucy.cam.ac.uk/study-us/post graduates/studentships-and-awards

For further information contact:

Tel: (44) 1223 322190
Email: development@lucy.cam.ac.uk

Lucy Cavendish College: Research Fellowships

Purpose: To support post-doctoral research
Eligibility: Female, right to work in United Kingdom, holder of PhD or equivalents
Level of Study: Postdoctorate
Type: Research fellowship
Value: tbc
Length of Study: 3 years
Frequency: Every 3 years
Study Establishment: Lucy Cavendish College, University of Cambridge
Country of Study: As applicable
Application Procedure: see notices when advertised
No. of awards offered: 110
Funding: Private
No. of awards given last year: 1
No. of applicants last year: 110

For further information contact:

Email: registrar@lucy-cav.cam.ac.uk

Nabil Boustany Scholarships

Purpose: To enable a Lebanese national to attend the Cambridge MBA on a full scholarship
Eligibility: Open to candidates of all nations although priority given to Lebanese nationals, who have obtained a good Honours Degree from a recognized university and have at least 3 years of full-time, real-world experience. Candidates will need to demonstrate a high intellectual potential, practical common sense and the ability to put ideas into action. They also need to be highly motivated with a strong desire to learn. Applicants will be asked to take the Test of English as a Foreign Language (TOEFL) where applicable and the Graduate Management Admission Test (GMAT)
Level of Study: MBA
Type: Scholarship

Value: £30,000
Length of Study: 2 years
Frequency: Every 2 years
Study Establishment: Judge Business School, University of Cambridge
Country of Study: United Kingdom
Application Procedure: Applicants must email their curriculum vitae to admissions@boustany-foundation.org
No. of awards offered: 4
Closing Date: 15 May
Funding: Foundation
Contributor: The Nabil Boustany Foundation
No. of awards given last year: 1
No. of applicants last year: 4
Additional Information: The scholarship recipient is normally required to spend a summer internship, carrying no salary, within a Lebanese organization. Applicants must be accepted into the Cambridge MBA programme www.lucy. cam.ac.uk/study-us/postgraduates/studentships-and-awards

For further information contact:

1 avenue des Citronniers, F-06800 Cagnes-sur-Mer, France.

Fax: (44) 77 93 15 05 56
Email: info@boustany-foundation.org

Newnham College: Moody-Stuart Scholarships in Turkish Studies

For further information contact:

Newnham College, Sidgwick Avenue, Cambridge CB3 9DF, United Kingdom.

Tel: (44) 1223 335 700
Fax: (44) 1223 357 898
Email: enquiries@newnham.cam.ac.uk

Osborn Research Studentship

Purpose: To support students carrying research or taking advanced courses
Level of Study: Postdoctorate, Postgraduate
Type: Studentship
Value: Up to £12,000 to match with funds administered centrally by the UCAM
Length of Study: 1 to 3 years
Frequency: Every 3 years
Study Establishment: The University of Cambridge
Country of Study: United Kingdom

Application Procedure: For further details, please check website https://www.postgraduate.study.cam.ac.uk/funding
Closing Date: 1 April
Funding: Private
Contributor: Sidney Sussex College
Additional Information: https://www.sid.cam.ac.uk/apply/postgraduate-study/studentships-and-funding

For further information contact:

Email: graduate.funding@admin.cam.ac.uk

Pembroke College: College Research Studentships

Eligibility: Preference in awarding these studentships will be given to candidates who intend to register for a PhD degree at Pembroke. However, candidates registering to study for an MPhil will also be considered for an award if they are intending to carry on to a PhD after they have finished their MPhil
Level of Study: Postgraduate
Type: Studentship
Value: College/University fees plus a maintenance allowance of £12,000 per year
Frequency: Annual
Study Establishment: Pembroke College
Country of Study: United Kingdom
Application Procedure: All applicants for any of these awards must apply in the first instance to the Board of Graduate Studies for their University place. Candidates should indicate that they are applying for a Pembroke College award. In making awards preference will be given to those who nominate Pembroke as their college of first choice. All candidates are expected to apply for Research Council funding where appropriate, and for University CHESS funding, if they are eligible. The College will take into account candidates' income from other sources when making awards
Closing Date: 6 January
Additional Information: Applicants should also complete a Pembroke Studentship form. This can be completed online, downloaded or obtained from the Graduate Secretary. The awards are conditional on the selected students being admitted as a registered Graduate Student by the Board of Graduate Studies with effect from October 1st each academic year. Early application is recommended https://www.pem.cam.ac.uk/study-here/graduate/financial-support

For further information contact:

Pembroke College, Cambridge CB2 1RF, United Kingdom.

Tel: (44) 1223 338 100
Fax: (44) 1223 338 163
Email: tut@pem.cam.ac.uk

Pembroke College: Graduate Studentships in Arabic and Islamic Studies (including Persian)

Eligibility: Preference in awarding these studentships will be given to candidates who intend to register for a PhD degree at Pembroke. However, candidates registering to study for an MPhil will also be considered for an award if they are intending to carry on to a PhD after they have finished their MPhil

Level of Study: Postgraduate

Type: Studentship

Value: Covers University and College fees (at the Home/European Union rate) for three years

Frequency: Annual

Study Establishment: Pembroke College

Country of Study: United Kingdom

Application Procedure: All applicants for any of these awards must apply in the first instance to the Board of Graduate Studies for their University place. Candidates should indicate that they are applying for a Pembroke College award. In making awards preference will be given to those who nominate Pembroke as their college of first choice. All candidates are expected to apply for Research Council funding where appropriate, and for University CHESS funding, if they are eligible. The college will take into account candidates' income from other sources when making awards

Additional Information: Applicants should also complete a Pembroke Studentship form. This can be completed online, downloaded or obtained from the Graduate Secretary. The awards are conditional on the selected students being admitted as a registered Graduate Student by the Board of Graduate Studies with effect from October 1st each academic year. Early application is recommended. www.sid.cam.ac.uk/current/postgrads/scholarships/osborn

Pembroke College: MPhil Studentship for Applicants from the Least Developed Countries

Purpose: The College is offering this one-year studentship to enable the winner to study for an MPhil degree, or equivalent, at the University of Cambridge

Eligibility: Eligibility is confined to nationals of the fifty 'Least Developed Countries' as defined by the United Nations. The other is for nationals of the fifty 'Least Developed Countries' as defined by the United Nations.

Level of Study: Postgraduate

Type: Studentship

Value: University fees at least at the standard rate for Home/European Union students, plus college fees and a maintenance of £10,465

Frequency: Annual

Study Establishment: Pembroke College, University of Cambridge

Country of Study: Any country

Application Procedure: All applicants for any of these awards must apply in the first instance to the Board of Graduate Studies for their University place. Candidates should indicate that they are applying for a Pembroke College award. In making awards preference will be given to those who nominate Pembroke as their College of first choice. All candidates are expected to apply for Research Council funding where appropriate, and for University CHESS funding, if they are eligible. The College will take into account candidates' income from other sources when making awards

Additional Information: Applicants should also complete a Pembroke Studentship form. This can be completed online, downloaded or obtained from the Graduate Secretary. The awards are conditional on the selected students being admitted as a registered Graduate Student by the Board of Graduate Studies with effect from October 1st each academic year. Early application is recommended www.sid.cam.ac.uk/current/postgrads/scholarships/osborn

Pembroke College: The Bethune-Baker Graduate Studentship in Theology

Eligibility: Open to candidates who intend to register for the PhD degree at the University of Cambridge

Level of Study: Postgraduate

Type: Studentship

Value: College and university fees for three years

Length of Study: 3 years

Frequency: Annual

Study Establishment: University of Cambridge

Country of Study: United Kingdom

Application Procedure: All applicants for any of these awards must apply in the first instance to the Board of Graduate Studies for their University place. Candidates should indicate that they are applying for a Pembroke College award. In making awards preference will be given to those who nominate Pembroke as their college of first choice. All candidates are expected to apply for Research Council funding where appropriate, and for University CHESS funding, if they are eligible. The College will take into account candidates' income from other sources when making awards

Contributor: HM the Sultan of Oman and Professor E.G. Browne

Additional Information: Applicants should also complete a Pembroke Studentship form. This can be completed online, downloaded or obtained from the Graduate Secretary. The awards are conditional on the selected students being admitted as a registered Graduate Student by the Board of Graduate Studies with effect from October 1st each academic year. Early application is recommended www.sid.cam.ac.uk/current/postgrads/scholarships/osborn

Pembroke College: The Bristol-Myers Squibb Graduate Studentship in the Biomedical Sciences

Eligibility: Open to candidates who intend to register for a PhD degree at the University of Cambridge
Level of Study: Postgraduate
Type: Studentship
Value: The studentship will have a value sufficient to pay college fees for three years
Frequency: Annual
Country of Study: United Kingdom
Application Procedure: All applicants for any of these awards must apply in the first instance to the Board of Graduate Studies for their University place. Candidates should indicate that they are applying for a Pembroke College award. In making awards preference will be given to those who nominate Pembroke as their college of first choice. All candidates are expected to apply for Research Council funding where appropriate, and for University CHESS funding, if they are eligible. The College will take into account candidates' income from other sources when making awards
Additional Information: Applicants should also complete a Pembroke Studentship form. This can be completed online, downloaded or obtained from the Graduate Secretary. The awards are conditional on the selected students being admitted as a registered Graduate Student by the Board of Graduate Studies with effect from October 1st each academic year. Early application is recommended www.sid.cam.ac.uk/current/postgrads/scholarships/osborn

Pembroke College: The Grosvenor-Shilling Bursary in Land Economy

Eligibility: Applicants must normally reside in Australia and hold a qualification from an Australian tertiary institution. There is no restriction as to the academic field
Level of Study: Postgraduate
Type: Scholarship
Value: £500
Frequency: Annual
Country of Study: Any country
Application Procedure: All applicants for any of these awards must apply in the first instance to the Board of Graduate Studies for their University place. Candidates should indicate that they are applying for a Pembroke College

award. In making awards preference will be given to those who nominate Pembroke as their college of first choice. All candidates are expected to apply for Research Council funding where appropriate, and for University CHESS funding, if they are eligible. The College will take into account candidates' income from other sources when making awards
Additional Information: Applicants should also complete a Pembroke Studentship form. This can be completed online, downloaded or obtained from the Graduate Secretary. The awards are conditional on the selected students being admitted as a registered Graduate Student by the Board of Graduate Studies with effect from October 1st each academic year. Early application is recommended www.sid.cam.ac.uk/current/postgrads/scholarships/osborn

Pembroke College: The Lander Studentship in the History of Art

Purpose: The College is very pleased to be able to offer one studentship for an outstanding art historian, supported by the estate of Professor J.R. Lander
Eligibility: Candidates must be applying to study for a PhD degree in the History of Art at the University of Cambridge, with Pembroke as first-choice college
Level of Study: Postgraduate
Type: Studentship
Value: The studentship will, if necessary, pay university and college fees, at the home rate, plus a maintenance allowance (approx. £10,140 a year), for a maximum of 3 years
Length of Study: 3 years
Frequency: Annual
Study Establishment: Pembroke College, University of Cambridge
Country of Study: United Kingdom
Application Procedure: All applicants for any of these awards must apply in the first instance to the Board of Graduate Studies for their University place. Candidates should indicate that they are applying for a Pembroke College award. In making awards preference will be given to those who nominate Pembroke as their College of first choice. All candidates are expected to apply for Research Council funding where appropriate, and for University CHESS funding, if they are eligible. The College will take into account candidates' income from other sources when making awards
Closing Date: 16 May
Additional Information: Applicants should also complete a Pembroke Studentship form. This can be completed online, downloaded or obtained from the Graduate Secretary. The awards are conditional on the selected students being admitted as a registered Graduate Student by the Board of Graduate Studies with effect from October 1st each academic year.

Early application is recommended https://www.pem.cam.ac.uk/study-here/graduate/financial-support

Pembroke College: The Monica Partridge Studentship

Purpose: To offer a graduate studentship for a student from South-East Europe to study at Pembroke

Eligibility: Open to the students of the nationals of Albania, Bosnia and Herzegovina, Bulgaria, Croatia, Greece, Kosovo, Macedonia, Montenegro and Serbia. Applications from students from Romania, Slovenia and Turkey will be considered if there is no suitable candidate from the countries listed above. Preference will be given to fund students studying for a PhD, but MPhil applicants intending to continue to a PhD will also be considered

Level of Study: Postgraduate

Type: Studentship

Value: The studentship will have a value sufficient to cover college fees (£2,229) and maintenance (£10,140) for three years for a PhD student or, in the case of an MPhil student, one year

Frequency: Annual

Study Establishment: Pembroke College, University of Cambridge

Country of Study: United Kingdom

Application Procedure: All applicants for any of these awards must apply in the first instance to the Board of Graduate Studies for their University place. Candidates should indicate that they are applying for a Pembroke College award. In making awards preference will be given to those who nominate Pembroke as their college of first choice. All candidates are expected to apply for Research Council funding where appropriate, and for University CHESS funding, if they are eligible. The College will take into account candidates' income from other sources when making awards

Closing Date: 31 January

Additional Information: Applicants should also complete a Pembroke Studentship form. This can be completed online, downloaded or obtained from the Graduate Secretary. The awards are conditional on the selected students being admitted as a registered Graduate Student by the Board of Graduate Studies with effect from October 1st each academic year. Early application is recommended www.sid.cam.ac.uk/current/postgrads/scholarships/osborn

Pembroke College: The Pembroke Australian Scholarship

Eligibility: Applicants must normally reside in Australia and hold a qualification from an Australian tertiary institution. There is no restriction as to the academic field

Level of Study: Postgraduate

Type: Scholarship

Value: £500

Frequency: Annual

Country of Study: Any country

Application Procedure: All applicants for any of these awards must apply in the first instance to the Board of Graduate Studies for their University place. Candidates should indicate that they are applying for a Pembroke College award. In making awards preference will be given to those who nominate Pembroke as their College of first choice. All candidates are expected to apply for Research Council funding where appropriate, and for University CHESS funding, if they are eligible. The College will take into account candidates' income from other sources when making awards

Closing Date: 31 January

Additional Information: Applicants should also complete a Pembroke Studentship form. This can be completed online, downloaded or obtained from the Graduate Secretary. The awards are conditional on the selected students being admitted as a registered Graduate Student by the Board of Graduate Studies with effect from October 1st each academic year. Early application is recommended www.sid.cam.ac.uk/current/postgrads/scholarships/osborn

Pembroke College: The Thornton Graduate Studentship in History

Eligibility: Preference in awarding these studentships will be given to candidates who intend to register for a PhD degree at Pembroke. However, candidates registering to study for an MPhil will also be considered for an award if they are intending to carry on to a PhD after they have finished their MPhil

Level of Study: Postgraduate

Type: Studentship

Value: The studentship will have a value sufficient to pay College fees for three years. Moreover, additional awards, of up to the equivalent of University fees for a Home student (£3,465), may be made to individual applicants, depending on need and the availability of funds

Frequency: Annual

Study Establishment: Pembroke College

Country of Study: United Kingdom

Application Procedure: All applicants for any of these awards must apply in the first instance to the Board of Graduate Studies for their University place. Candidates should indicate that they are applying for a Pembroke College award. In making awards preference will be given to those who nominate Pembroke as their college of first choice. All candidates are expected to apply for Research Council funding where appropriate, and for University CHESS funding, if they are eligible. The College will take into account candidates' income from other sources when making awards

Closing Date: 31 January

Additional Information: Applicants should also complete a Pembroke Studentship form. This can be completed online, downloaded or obtained from the Graduate Secretary. The awards are conditional on the selected students being admitted as a registered Graduate Student by the Board of Graduate Studies with effect from October 1st each academic year. Early application is recommended www.sid.cam.ac.uk/current/postgrads/scholarships/osborn

Pembroke College: The Ziegler Graduate Studentship in Law

Eligibility: Preference in awarding studentships is given to candidates who intend to register for a PhD degree at Pembroke

Level of Study: Postgraduate

Type: Studentship

Value: Covers university and college fees (at the Home/European Union rate)

Frequency: Annual

Study Establishment: Pembroke College

Country of Study: United Kingdom

Application Procedure: All applicants for any of these awards must apply in the first instance to the Board of Graduate Studies for their University place. Candidates should indicate that they are applying for a Pembroke College award. In making awards preference will be given to those who nominate Pembroke as their college of first choice. All candidates are expected to apply for Research Council funding where appropriate, and for University CHESS funding, if they are eligible. The College will take into account candidates' income from other sources when making awards

Closing Date: 31 January

Additional Information: Applicants should also complete a Pembroke Studentship form. This can be completed online, downloaded or obtained from the Graduate Secretary. The awards are conditional on the selected students being admitted as a registered Graduate Student by the Board of Graduate Studies with effect from October 1st each academic year. Early application is recommended www.sid.cam.ac.uk/current/postgrads/scholarships/osborn

Peterhouse: Research Studentships

Eligibility: Open to prospective PhD candidates

Level of Study: Postgraduate

Type: Studentship

Value: varies

Frequency: Annual

Study Establishment: Peterhouse College

Country of Study: United Kingdom

Application Procedure: Please contact at graduates@pet.cam.ac.uk

No. of awards offered: 57

Closing Date: January

No. of awards given last year: 5

No. of applicants last year: 57

Additional Information: Number of awards varies from year to year https://www.pet.cam.ac.uk/graduate-studentships-0

For further information contact:

Peterhouse, Trumpington Street, Cambridge CB2 1RD, United Kingdom.

Email: graduates@pet.cam.ac.uk

Principal's Studentship

Purpose: To support an MPhil or PhD student

Level of Study: Graduate

Type: Studentship

Value: Approx. Between £3,000 and £12,000 per year

Length of Study: 1 to 3 years

Frequency: Dependent on funds available

Study Establishment: Newnham College, University of Cambridge

Country of Study: United Kingdom

Closing Date: 3 April

Funding: Private

For further information contact:

Email: studentfunding@ed.ac.uk

Ramanujan Research Studentship in Mathematics

Purpose: The Ramanujan Studentship is normally awarded for nine months in the first instance, while the student takes the course leading to the MASt in Mathematics

Eligibility: For students from India hoping to do research for a PhD degree in Cambridge. Students of any University or comparable institution in India who have not already begun residence in Cambridge and who hold a First Class Honours degree or its equivalent, or are likely to do so by the time of entry, are eligible to apply

Level of Study: Research

Type: Studentship

Value: £45,650

Length of Study: 1 year

Frequency: Annual
Country of Study: United Kingdom
Closing Date: 8 January
Additional Information: Shortlisted applicants will be invited to submit a full application by 4 February https://www.student-funding.cam.ac.uk/fund/ramanujan-research-studentship-in-mathematics-2022

For further information contact:

Tel: (44) 1223 761893

Ramanujan Research Studentship in Mathematics at Trinity College, Cambridge

Purpose: Trinity College, University of Cambridge is offering Ramanujan Research Studentship for students who wish to undertake research in Mathematics. Student should hold a first class honours degree or its equivalent from any university or comparable institution in India
Eligibility: Indian students can apply for this studentship. Applicants from outside the home country will often need to meet specific English language/other language requirements in order to be able to study there
Type: Research
Length of Study: 1 year
Study Establishment: Studentship is awarded in the field of Pure or Applied Mathematics of Cambridge
Country of Study: Any country
Application Procedure: Completed Preliminary Application Forms must be returned by post or email
No. of awards offered: 1
Closing Date: 8 January
Additional Information: For more details please browse the website   scholarship-positions.com/ramanujan-research-studentship-mathematics-trinity-college-cambridge-uk/2015/11/14/
www.student-funding.cam.ac.uk/ramanujan-research-student ship-mathematics-202021

Robinson College: Lewis Graduate Scholarship

Purpose: The College expects to award one Lewis Scholarship to a graduate student applying to read for a PhD degree in the humanities
Eligibility: Open to all applicants who name Robinson College as their college of first choice on the Board of Graduate Studies Application Form for Admissions as a Graduate student, or are prepared to change college if offered the scholarship. The scholarship is conditional on the candidate being offered a place at the University

Level of Study: Postgraduate
Type: Scholarship
Value: varies
Length of Study: The scholarship is tenable for up to 3 years, subject to satisfactory academic progress
Frequency: Annual
Study Establishment: University of Cambridge
Country of Study: United Kingdom
Application Procedure: Applicants should send a curriculum vitae and details of their intended programme of research including no more than one A4 page describing their proposed research project, together with details of other grant applications. Applications must be submitted by post to the Graduate Admissions Tutor
Additional Information: Please check website for latest updates   https://www.robinson.cam.ac.uk/alumni/fundraising-priorities/bursaries-scholarships/lewis-research-scholarship-fund

For further information contact:

Robinson College, Grange Rd, Cambridge CB3 9AN, United Kingdom.

Tel: (44) 1223 339 100
Fax: (44) 1223 351 794
Email: graduate-admissions@robinson.cam.ac.uk

St John's College Benefactors' Scholarships for Research

Purpose: To fund candidates for PhD and MPhil degrees
Eligibility: Open to candidates of any nationality with a First Class (Honours) Degree or equivalent
Level of Study: Postgraduate
Type: Scholarship
Value: £9,000, plus approved college and university fees, a Scholar Book Grant of up to £100 and other expenses
Length of Study: Up to 3 years
Frequency: Annual
Study Establishment: St John College, University of Cambridge
Country of Study: United Kingdom
Application Procedure: Applicants must see the Cambridge University Graduate Studies prospectus for particulars
Closing Date: 1 May
No. of awards given last year: 3
Additional Information: https://www.student-funding.cam.ac.uk/fund/st-johns-college-benefactors-scholarships-for-postgraduate-students-2022

For further information contact:

St John's College, St John's Street, Cambridge CB2 1TP, United Kingdom.

Tel: (44) 12 2333 8612
Fax: (44) 12 2376 6419
Email: graduate_admissions@joh.cam.ac.uk

The Girton Singapore Scholarship

Eligibility: 1. They are open to students who have graduated or will have graduated before 1st October of the year they apply, and who nominate Girton as their first or second choice College. 2. A first-class degree is almost always required and election will be conditional on the candidate being granted Postgraduate Student status by the University of Cambridge. 3. The holder must become a member of the College and be a candidate for either a Masters or a PhD degree. 4. Current Cambridge students who are members of another College are eligible to apply if they are moving from one course of study to another, however if they are part-way through a course they cannot apply for the awards.
Level of Study: Postgraduate
Type: Scholarship
Value: £10,000
Length of Study: 3 years
Frequency: Annual
Country of Study: United Kingdom
Closing Date: 25 March
Additional Information: www.girton.cam.ac.uk/postgraduates/fees-finance-funding

For further information contact:

Email: graduate.office@girton.cam.ac.uk

The Rhona Beare Award

Eligibility: 1. They are open to students who have graduated or will have graduated before 1st October of the year they apply, and who nominate Girton as their first or second choice College. 2. A first-class degree is almost always required and election will be conditional on the candidate being granted Postgraduate Student status by the University of Cambridge. 3. The holder must become a member of the College and be a candidate for either a Masters or a PhD degree. 4. Current Cambridge students who are members of another College are eligible to apply if they are moving from one course of study to another, however if they are part-way through a course they cannot apply for the awards.
Level of Study: Postgraduate

Type: Scholarship
Value: Approximately £1,500
Length of Study: 3 years
Frequency: Annual
Country of Study: United Kingdom
Closing Date: 25 March
Additional Information: www.girton.cam.ac.uk/postgraduates/fees-finance-funding

For further information contact:

Email: graduate.office@girton.cam.ac.uk

Trinity College: Studentships in Mathematics

Purpose: The Trinity Studentship in Mathematics is a one-year studentship intended for students who wish to undertake research in Mathematics at the University of Cambridge but who are required by the Faculty of Mathematics to take, in the first instance, the course leading to the Master of Advanced Study (MASt)
Eligibility: Eligible candidates must; 1. Have applied for admission, or already received an offer of admission, to the University of Cambridge for the MASt degree. 2. Not yet have been members of the University of Cambridge as an undergraduate or graduate student
Level of Study: Postgraduate
Type: Studentship
Value: £25,000 to £45,000
Length of Study: 1 year of study
Frequency: Annual
Country of Study: Any country
No. of awards offered: 4
Closing Date: 8 January
Funding: Private
Additional Information: Please visit the website for more information https://www.student-funding.cam.ac.uk/fund/trinity-studentship-in-mathematics-2022

For further information contact:

Tel: (1) 1223 761893
Email: gradfunding@trin.cam.ac.uk

Westminster College Lewis and Gibson Scholarship

Purpose: To enable Scholars to study for a theology degree at the University of Cambridge as an integral part of his or her training for the ministry of a church in the reformed tradition which has a Presbyterian order

Eligibility: Open to graduates of a recognised university who are members of the United Reformed Church in the United Kingdom or of any church not established by the state which is a member of the World Alliance of Reformed Churches and has a Presbyterian form of government. Applicants must have been recognised by their churches as candidates for the Ministry of Word and Sacrament, but should not yet have been ordained

Level of Study: Postgraduate

Type: Scholarship

Value: One scholarship of £6,000 or two scholarships of £3,000 approx

Length of Study: 1 year, renewable for up to 2 further years

Frequency: Annual

Study Establishment: The University of Cambridge

Country of Study: United Kingdom

Application Procedure: If it is the intention to study at the postgraduate level, an application should be made at the same time to the Board of Graduate Studies of the university. The Scholar will normally study for one of the following degrees BA or MPhil in theology, or PhD. He or she will be a member of both Westminster College and one of the University's constituent colleges

Closing Date: 24 December

Funding: Private

Contributor: A legacy controlled by the United Reformed Church

No. of awards given last year: 2

Additional Information: Scholars from outside the United Reformed Church have usually been theology graduates and have used the scholarship for postgraduate work https://www.divinity.cam.ac.uk/study-here/lewisgibson

For further information contact:

Westminster College, Madingley Rd, Cambridge CB3 0AA, United Kingdom.

Tel: (44) 1223 741 084
Fax: (44) 1223 300 765
Email: jp225@cam.ac.uk

William Wyse Studentship in Social Anthropology

Purpose: To support study

Eligibility: Open to all students who wish to study for the degree of PhD, the Studentships are open to any person who is admitted to the University of Cambridge by the Board of Graduate Studies and intends to do research in Social Anthropology leading to the PhD Degree, regardless of whether they are liable for fees at the Home or Overseas rate. It is a condition of the Studentships that United Kingdom and European Union students are eligible for ESRC or Vice-Chancellor's Awards and that overseas students fulfil the eligibility criteria for Cambridge International Scholarships

Level of Study: Doctorate

Type: Studentship

Value: Varies

Length of Study: 3 years

Frequency: Annual

Study Establishment: The University of Cambridge

Country of Study: United Kingdom

Application Procedure: Applicants should contact the admissions secretary for details

No. of awards offered: 8

Closing Date: 11 January

Funding: Private

No. of awards given last year: 5 grants

No. of applicants last year: 8

Additional Information: For further details, refer the website link mentioned below. www.socanth.cam.ac.uk/about-us/funding/william-wyse-funding/william-wyse-studentship https://www.student-funding.cam.ac.uk/fund/william-wyse-studentship-2022

For further information contact:

Email: tutorial.office@newn.cam.ac.uk

Wood Whistler Prize and Medal

Purpose: To reward an outstanding student

Level of Study: Graduate

Type: Prize

Value: Approx. £2,500

Length of Study: 3 years

Frequency: Annual

Study Establishment: Newnham College, University of Cambridge

Country of Study: United Kingdom

Application Procedure: There is no application form. Names are put forward by the English faculty of the University of Cambridge

Funding: Private

For further information contact:

Email: tutorial.office@newn.cam.ac.uk

University of Cambridge (Cambridge Commonwealth Trust, Cambridge Overseas Trust, Gates Cambridge Trust, Cambridge European Trust and Associated Trusts)

Cambridge Trusts, Trinity College, Trinity Street, Cambridge CB2 1TQ, United Kingdom.

Tel: (44) 1223 351 449
Email: info@overseastrusts.cam.ac.uk
Website: www.admin.cam.ac.uk

The Cambridge Commonwealth Trust and the Cambridge Overseas Trust (formerly the Chancellor's Fund) were established in 1982 by the University of Cambridge under the Chairmanship of his Royal Highness the Prime of Wales to provide financial assistance for students from overseas who, without help, would be unable to take up their places at Cambridge. Since 1982, the Cambridge Commonwealth Trust has brought 6,600 students from 51 countries to Cambridge, the Cambridge Overseas trust 4,252 students from 76 countries.

British Chevening Cambridge Scholarships for Postgraduate Study (Indonesia)

Purpose: To financially support those undertaking postgraduate study
Eligibility: Applicants must be citizens of Indonesia
Level of Study: Postgraduate
Type: Scholarship
Value: The University Composition Fee at the overseas rate, approved college fees, a maintenance allowance sufficient for a single student and a contribution towards return economy airfare
Length of Study: 1 year
Frequency: Annual
Study Establishment: The University of Cambridge
Country of Study: United Kingdom
Application Procedure: Applicants must apply directly to the British Embassy in Indonesia
Contributor: Offered in collaboration with the Malaysian Commonwealth Studies Centre and the Foreign and Commonwealth Office (FCO)
Additional Information: Further information is available on request www.scholars4dev.com/3299/british-chevening-scholarships/

For further information contact:

Email: cambridge.trust@admin.cam.ac.uk

British Chevening Malaysia Cambridge Scholarship for PhD Study

Purpose: To financially support study towards a PhD
Eligibility: Open to students from Malaysia. Applicants must apply to the University of Cambridge and be offered a place at Cambridge in the normal way. All applicants must have a First Class or High Second Class (Honours) Degree or equivalent and normally be under 26. They must be successfully nominated for an Overseas Research Student (ORS) award
Level of Study: Doctorate
Type: Scholarship
Value: The University Composition Fee at the appropriate rate, approved college fees, a maintenance allowance sufficient for a single student and a contribution towards return economy airfare
Length of Study: Up to 3 years
Frequency: Annual
Study Establishment: The University of Cambridge
Country of Study: United Kingdom
Application Procedure: Applicants must complete a preliminary application form, which can be obtained from local universities, offices of the British Council or the Trust. Completed forms must be returned to the main address. Shortlisted candidates will be sent forms for admission to the University of Cambridge. The preliminary application form can also be downloaded from www.admin.cam.ac.uk/offices/gradstud/admissions/forms/
Contributor: Offered in collaboration with the Foreign and Commonwealth Office (FCO)
Additional Information: https://www.cambridgetrust.org/scholarships/?country=Malaysia&submit=Search

For further information contact:

Email: cambridge.trust@admin.cam.ac.uk

British Petroleum Research Bursaries for PhD Study

Purpose: To celebrate the Centenary for BP and New Hall College
Eligibility: For citizens of Russia, Ukraine, Countries of the former Soviet Union, China, The Middle East (particularly Egypt), Southern Africa, or South Asia

Level of Study: Doctorate
Type: Bursary
Value: £2,000 annually
Frequency: Annual
Study Establishment: BP and New Hall College, The University of Cambridge
Country of Study: United Kingdom
Application Procedure: Applicants for a place to do a PhD should apply for an ORS award and should normally be successfully nominated for an ORS award or an ORS equivalent award, which meets the difference between the higher overseas rate and the lower domestic rate of the University Composition Fee

For further information contact:

Email: enquiry@bpgraduates.co.uk

British Petroleum Research Bursaries for Postgraduate Study

Purpose: To celebrate the Centenary for BP and New Hall College
Eligibility: For citizens of Russia, Ukraine, Countries of the former Soviet Union, China, The Middle East (particularly Egypt), Southern Africa, or South Asia
Level of Study: Doctorate
Type: Bursary
Value: £2,000 annually
Length of Study: 1 year
Frequency: Annual
Study Establishment: BP and New Hall College, The University of Cambridge
Country of Study: United Kingdom

For further information contact:

Email: enquiry@bpgraduates.co.uk

Charles Wallace India Trust

Purpose: To financially assist postgraduate study for applicants who are not successful in winning a scholarship
Eligibility: This scholarship is only available for citizens of India. Applicants for a place to do a PhD should apply for an ORS award and should be successfully nominated for an ORS award or an ORS equivalent award, which meets the difference between the higher overseas rate and the lower domestic rate of the University Composition Fee
Type: Bursary
Value: Varies

Frequency: Annual
Study Establishment: The University of Cambridge
Country of Study: Any country
Contributor: Charles Wallace India Trust
Additional Information: www.successcds.net/Scholarships/charles-wallace-india-trust-scholarships.html

For further information contact:

Email: cwit@in.britishcouncil.org

China Scholarship Council Cambridge Scholarships

Purpose: To financially assist study towards a PhD
Eligibility: Applicants must be from China, and have a first-class honours degree, and preferably, a Masters degree or its equivalent from a recognised university in China
Level of Study: Doctorate
Type: Scholarship
Value: University tuition fee, Annual stipend (sufficient for a single person), Contribution towards travel costs
Frequency: Annual
Study Establishment: The University of Cambridge
Country of Study: United Kingdom
Application Procedure: Applicants for a place to do a PhD should apply for an ORS award and should normally be successfully nominated for an ORS award or an ORS equivalent award, which meets the difference between the higher overseas rate and the lower domestic rate of the University Composition Fee
Contributor: In collaboration with the China Scholarship Council
Additional Information: This scholarship is available to Chinese PhD applicants in a range of academic subjects, and is tenable at any College https://www.cambridgetrust.org/scholarships/scholarship/?award=34

For further information contact:

Email: cambridge.trust@admin.cam.ac.uk

Corpus Christi Research Scholarship

Purpose: To financially assist study towards a PhD
Eligibility: Applicants must be from India, and already hold a degree equivalent to a first-class or a high upper second from a United Kingdom university
Level of Study: Doctorate
Type: Scholarship
Value: £13,000
Length of Study: 3 Years

Study Establishment: Corpus Christi College, The University of Cambridge

Country of Study: United Kingdom

Application Procedure: Applicants for a place to do a PhD should apply for an ORS award and should normally be successfully nominated for an ORS award or an ORS equivalent award, which meets the difference between the higher overseas rate and the lower domestic rate of the university composition fee

No. of awards offered: 6

Closing Date: 7 January

Contributor: In collaboration with the Corpus Christi College

For further information contact:

Email: graduate-tutorial@corpus.cam.ac.uk

David M. Livingstone (Australia) Scholarship

Purpose: To support students to undertake 1-year postgraduate degree course at the University of Cambridge

Eligibility: The scholarship is only available for citizens of Australia. Scholars must specify Jesus College as their first choice college

Level of Study: Postgraduate

Type: Scholarship

Value: University composition fee and college fee

Length of Study: 1 year

Frequency: Annual

Country of Study: Any country

Closing Date: 31 March

Contributor: Jesus College

Additional Information: scholarshipdb.net/scholarships-in-Australia/University-Of-Cambridge-David-M-Livingstone-Australia-Scholarship-Non-Australian-Institutions-Non-Australian-Institutions=ZAiKwlhnjEyXXwt_1S5kCw.html

For further information contact:

Tel: (44) 1223 760 606

Fax: (44) 1223 338 723

Email: admissions@gradstudies.cam.ac.uk

Developing World Education Fund Scholarships for PhD Study

Purpose: To financially support study towards a PhD

Eligibility: For citizens from Bangladesh, China, India, Pakistan, Sri Lanka or Zambia. Applicants must apply to the University of Cambridge and be offered a place at Cambridge

in the normal way. All applicants must have a degree equivalent to a First Class from a United Kingdom university, and normally be under 26

Level of Study: Doctorate

Type: Scholarships and fellowships

Value: The University Composition Fee at the appropriate rate, approve College fees, a maintenance allowance sufficient for a single student, contribution towards an economy return airfare

Frequency: Annual

Study Establishment: The University of Cambridge

Country of Study: United Kingdom

Application Procedure: Applicants for a place to do a PhD should apply for an ORS award and should normally be successfully nominated for an ORS award or an ORS equivalent award, which meets the difference between the higher overseas rate and the lower domestic rate of the University Composition Fee

For further information contact:

Email: joe@advance-africa.com

International Club of Boston College Cambridge Scholarship

Purpose: To financially support those undertaking postgraduate study

Eligibility: Open to students from Chile

Level of Study: Postgraduate

Type: Scholarships and fellowships

Value: The University composition fee at the overseas rate, approved college fees, a maintenance allowance sufficient for a single student, contribution towards an economy return airfare

Length of Study: 1 year

Frequency: Annual

Study Establishment: The University of Cambridge

Country of Study: United Kingdom

Application Procedure: Apply directly to the British Council in Chile. Applicants are reminded that they will also need to apply to the Cambridge Trusts on the Scholarship Application Form (SAF) in the usual way

Contributor: Offered in collaboration with the Instituto Chileno Britanico de Cultura, the British Council, Chile and Cambridge Assessment (formerly the Local Examinations Syndicate), University of Cambridge

For further information contact:

Email: internationalstudents@admin.cam.ac.uk

Jawaharlal Nehru Memorial Trust Commonwealth Shared Scholarships

Purpose: To offer financial support
Eligibility: Open to citizens from India. All applicants must be under the age of 35 years on October 1st with priority given to those candidates under the age of 30 years. They must not be employed by a national or local government department or by a parastatal organization, nor at present be living or studying in a developed country and not have undertaken studies lasting a year or more in a developed country. Priority will be given to candidates wishing to pursue a study related to the economic and social development of their country
Level of Study: Postgraduate
Type: Scholarship
Value: The University Composition Fee, approved college fees, annual stipend sufficient for a single student and contribution towards travel costs
Length of Study: 1 year
Frequency: Annual
Study Establishment: The University of Cambridge, Trinity College
Country of Study: United Kingdom
Application Procedure: Applicants may obtain further details and a preliminary application form by writing before August 16th of the year before entry to the Joint Secretary of the Nehru Trust for Cambridge University, giving details of their academic qualifications
Closing Date: 28 February
Contributor: Offered in collaboration with the Jawaharlal Nehru Memorial Trust and the Commonwealth Scholarship Commission

For further information contact:

The Nehru Trust for Cambridge University, Teen Murti House, Teen Murti Marg 53 - 54 Sidney Street, Cambridge CB2 3HX, United Kingdom.

Email: cambridge.trust@admin.cam.ac.uk

Ministry of Education (Malaysia) Scholarships for Postgraduate Study

Purpose: To financially support those undertaking postgraduate study
Eligibility: Applicants must be from Malaysia, and must be nominated by the Ministry of Education. Applicants must apply to the University of Cambridge and be offered a place at Cambridge in the normal way. They must have a First Class or High Second Class (Honours) Degree or equivalent and normally be under 26
Level of Study: Postgraduate

Type: Scholarship
Value: The University Composition Fee at the overseas rate, approved college fees, a maintenance allowance sufficient for a single student and a contribution to return economy airfare
Length of Study: 1 year
Frequency: Annual
Study Establishment: The University of Cambridge
Country of Study: United Kingdom
Application Procedure: Applicants must complete a preliminary application form, which can be obtained from local universities, offices of the British Council or the Trust. Completed forms must be returned to the main address. Shortlisted candidates will be sent forms for admission to the University of Cambridge. The preliminary application form can also be downloaded from www.admin.cam.ac.uk/offices/gradstud/admissions/forms/
Closing Date: 28 February
Contributor: Offered in collaboration with the Malaysian Commonwealth Studies Centre and the Ministry of Education, Government of Malaysia

For further information contact:

Email: education.intoday@gmail.com

Ministry of Science, Technology and the Environment Scholarships for Postgraduate Study (Malaysia)

Purpose: To financially support those undertaking postgraduate study
Eligibility: Applicants must be from Malaysia, and must be nominated by the Ministry of Science, Technology and the Environment. Applicants must apply to the University of Cambridge and be offered a place at Cambridge in the normal way. They must have a First Class or High Second Class (Honours) Degree or equivalent and normally be under 26
Level of Study: Postgraduate
Type: Scholarship
Value: The University Composition Fee at the overseas rate, approved college fees, a maintenance allowance sufficient for a single student and a contribution to return economy airfare
Length of Study: 1 year
Frequency: Annual
Study Establishment: The University of Cambridge
Country of Study: United Kingdom
Application Procedure: Applicants must complete a preliminary application form, which can be obtained from local universities, offices of the British Council or the Trust. Completed forms must be returned to the main address. Shortlisted candidates will be sent forms for admission to the University of Cambridge. The preliminary application

form can also be downloaded from www.admin.cam.ac.uk/
offices/gradstud/admissions/forms/

Closing Date: 28 February

Contributor: Offered in collaboration with the Malaysian
Commonwealth Studies Centre and the Ministry of Science,
Technology and the Environment, Government of Malaysia

For further information contact:

Email: international_scholar@mohe.gov.my

Nehru Trust for the Indian Collections V&A Cambridge DFID Scholarship

Purpose: To financially support those undertaking postgraduate study

Eligibility: Applicants must be from India, and must be under
the age of 35 years on October 1st with priority given to those
candidates under the age of 30 years. Applicants must not be
employed by a national or local government department or by
a parastatal organization, nor at present be living or studying
in a developed country. Priority will be given to candidates
wishing to pursue a course of study related to the economic
and social development of their country

Level of Study: Postgraduate

Type: Scholarship

Value: The University Composition Fee at the overseas rate,
approved college fees, a maintenance allowance sufficient for
a single student and a contribution to return economy airfare.
In addition a supplementary allowance to cover a short period
of practical training at the Victoria and Albert Museum, or
other approved institution, will be given

Length of Study: 1 year

Frequency: Annual

Study Establishment: The University of Cambridge

Country of Study: United Kingdom

Application Procedure: Applicants may obtain further
details and a preliminary application form by writing before
August 16th of the year before entry to the Joint Secretary at
the address given below with details of academic
qualifications

Closing Date: 28 February

Contributor: Offered in collaboration with the Nehru Trust
for the Indian Collections at the Victoria and Albert (V&A)
Museum and the Department for International Development
(DFID)

Oxford and Cambridge Society of Bombay Cambridge DFID Scholarship

Purpose: To financially support those undertaking postgraduate study

Eligibility: Open to a resident of Bombay City or the State of
Maharashtra whose application is supported by the Oxford
and Cambridge Society of Bombay. All applicants must be
under the age of 35 on October 1st with priority given to those
candidates under the age of 30. They must not be employed
by a national or local government department or by
a parastatal organization, nor at present be living or studying
in a developed country. Priority will be given to candidates
wishing to pursue a study related to the economic and social
development of their country

Level of Study: Postgraduate

Type: Scholarship

Value: The University Composition Fee at the overseas rate,
approved college fees, a maintenance allowance sufficient for
a single student and a contribution to return economy airfare

Length of Study: 1 year

Frequency: Annual

Study Establishment: The University of Cambridge

Country of Study: United Kingdom

Application Procedure: Applicants may obtain further
details and a preliminary application form by writing before
August 16th of the year before entry to the Joint Secretary at
address given below with details of academic qualifications

Closing Date: 28 February

Contributor: Offered in collaboration with the Department
for International Development (DFID)

Pok Rafeah Cambridge Scholarship

Purpose: To financially support study towards a PhD

Eligibility: Applicants must be from Malaysia. The Trusts
cannot admit students to the University or any of its colleges.
Applicants for awards from the Trusts must therefore also
apply to the University of Cambridge and be offered a place at
Cambridge in the normal way. All applicants must have
a First Class or High Second Class (Honours) Degree or
equivalent and normally be under 26 years. Applicants for
scholarships for study towards the degree of PhD must be
successfully nominated for an Overseas Research Student
(ORS) award, which covers the difference between the
home and overseas rate of the University Composition Fee

Level of Study: Doctorate, Postgraduate, Predoctorate

Type: Scholarship

Value: The University Composition Fee at the approved rate,
approved college fees, a maintenance allowance sufficient for
a single student and a contribution to a return economy airfare

Length of Study: Up to 3 years for PhD study, and 1 year for
postgraduate study

Frequency: Annual

Study Establishment: The University of Cambridge

Country of Study: United Kingdom

Application Procedure: Applicants must complete
a preliminary application form, which can be obtained from

local universities, offices of the British Council or the Trust. The preliminary application form can be downloaded from www.admin.cam.ac.uk/univ/gsprospectus/c7/overseas/schemes. html

Contributor: Offered in collaboration with the Pok Rafeah Foundation

Additional Information: Further information is available on request scholarshipdb.net/scholarships-in-Australia/University-Of-Cambridge-David-M-Livingstone-Australia-Scholarship-Non-Australian-Institutions-Non-Australian-Institutions=ZAiKwlhnjEyXXwt_1S5kCw.html

For further information contact:

Email: cambridge.trust@admin.cam.ac.uk

University of Cambridge, Judge Business School

Trumpington Street, Cambridge CB2 1AG, United Kingdom.

Tel: (44) 1223 339 700
Email: enquiries@jbs.cam.ac.uk
Website: www.jims.cam.ac.uk
Contact: Mrs Natacha Wilson

The Judge Business School is the University of Cambridge's business school. Founded in 1990, it offers a portfolio of management programmes, including the Cambridge MB-A. Accredited by AMBA and EQUIS, the business school now hosts one of the largest concentrations of interdisciplinary business and management research activity in Europe.

Browns Restaurant Scholarships

Purpose: To provide funds for United Kingdom citizens with a strong interest in the hospitality and tourism industries to study for an MBA

Eligibility: Open to candidates with at least three years of experience in the hospitality or tourism industries. Candidates must show evidence of a career plan showing how they would use the skills and knowledge gained on the MBA course to develop their career within the hospitality or tourism industries. Where an applicant opts for the two year integrated version of the MBA course, arrangements should be in place for the placement year to be in an organisation in the hospitality or tourism industries. Applicants must be United Kingdom citizens

Level of Study: MBA

Type: Scholarship

Value: One scholarship of £20,000 to cover fees and two scholarships of £10,000 to cover roughly half the fees

Length of Study: 1 year

Frequency: Annual

Study Establishment: Judge Institute of Management, University of Cambridge

Country of Study: United Kingdom

Application Procedure: Applicants must complete and submit an application form, together with a covering letter indicating that they would like to apply for a Browns Restaurant Scholarship, to the Judge Institute of Management

Closing Date: March

Funding: Commercial

Contributor: Browns Restaurants Limited

For further information contact:

Email: financial_aid@brown.edu

University of Canberra

Australian Government Research Training Program (AGRTP) Stipend Scholarship

Purpose: Scholarships are offered in diverse fields to help students in upgrading their education

Eligibility: The Commonwealth Scholarship Guidelines (Research) 2017 set the basis for the conditions of award and outline the basic eligibility requirements for this scholarship. The ANU has established an RTP Policy & Procedure which outlines the standards, processes and conditions for this scholarship. These documents are available from the reference document section of this page.

Level of Study: Postgraduate

Type: Scholarship

Value: A$28,854 per annum

Length of Study: 3 years

Frequency: Annual

Country of Study: Australia

Application Procedure: Commencing students: No application is required specifically for this scholarship as all eligible candidates will be considered. Note to ensure you are considered please ensure you select the appropriate boxes in the admissions application form to note that you are interested in being considered for any available scholarships.

Closing Date: 31 August

Additional Information: www.anu.edu.au/study/scholarships/find-a-scholarship/australian-government-research-training-program-agrtp-stipend

For further information contact:

The Australian National University, Canberra, ACT 0200, Australia.

Tel: (61) 2 6125 5111
Email: gro@anu.edu.au

Bickerton-Widdowson Trust Memorial Scholarship

Level of Study: Postgraduate
Type: Scholarship
Value: NZ$2,000
Frequency: Annual
Country of Study: Any country
No. of awards offered: 1
Closing Date: 1 November
Additional Information: scholarshipscanterbury.communityforce.com/Funds/FundDetails.aspx?57743654 7345666C424767664472384730624F516637746868354 D676E427A2F685268365176704945456146526470416C 57556879304F7A4D4E3671392F3633

For further information contact:

Email: scholarships@canterbury.ac.nz

University of Canterbury

Level 9, 142 Lambton Quay, Wellington, PO Box 11915, Wellington 6142, New Zealand.

Tel: (64) 4 381 8500
Email: contact@universitiesnz.ac.nz
Website: www.canterbury.ac.nz

The University of Canterbury offers a variety of subjects in a few flexible degree structures, namely, first and postgraduate degrees in arts, commerce, education, engineering, fine arts, forestry, law, music and science. At Canterbury, research and teaching are closely related, and while this feature shapes all courses, it is very marked at the postgraduate level.

Betty Wignall Scholarship in Chemistry

Purpose: The purpose of this scholarship is to support students for study towards a PhD in the Department of Chemistry at the University of Canterbury.

Level of Study: Postgraduate
Type: Scholarship
Value: NZ$5,000 per 120 points of enrolment
Length of Study: 3 years
Frequency: Annual
Country of Study: New Zealand
No. of awards offered: 1
Closing Date: 15 May
Additional Information: scholarshipscanterbury.communityforce.com/Funds/FundDetails.aspx?57743654 7345666C424769476C48614D723942307876364E6773 53714E5543337475624D5A4734736F415350327766727 46457674965686D6373576D6B695938

For further information contact:

Email: scholarships@canterbury.ac.nz

Dennis William Moore Scholarship

Level of Study: Postgraduate
Type: Scholarship
Value: NZ$5,000
Length of Study: 1 to 3 years
Frequency: Annual
Country of Study: New Zealand
Closing Date: 1 November
Additional Information: scholarshipscanterbury.communityforce.com/Funds/FundDetails.aspx?68356E584 36D4D544154353468486B4D424478795A427135792B4 7706D4870325938494443959674D4A3671473158365564 79702F327161665442755655775239

For further information contact:

Email: scholarships@canterbury.ac.nz

Dow Agrosciences Bursary in Chemical Engineering

Purpose: In 1990, DowElanco (NZ) Limited took over the bursary, formerly offered by Ivon Watkins-Dow Limited, for tenure in the Department of Chemical Engineering. In January 1998, DowElanco (NZ) Limited changed its name to Dow AgroSciences (NZ) Limited
Eligibility: Must be a full-time student who is enrolled for a BE(Hons) in Chemical & Process Engineering. The applicant must have completed, or been exempted from, the First Professional examination
Type: Bursary
Value: NZ$2,500
Length of Study: 1 year

Frequency: Annual
Country of Study: Any country
Application Procedure: You may apply through the webpage approximately 8 weeks before applications close. If it's possible to apply on-line for this scholarship there will be a link to the on-line system. If the link is not provided, please download and complete the application form. However, if the scholarship is managed by Universities NZ or another department of the University, an External Website link will appear and application instructions will be available through that link
No. of awards offered: 1
Closing Date: 31 March
Additional Information: www.studyinnewzealand.govt.nz/how-to-apply/scholarship/details?scholarshipid=84159

For further information contact:

Tel: (64) 800 827 748
Email: enrol@canterbury.ac.nz

Ethel Rose Overton Scholarship

Level of Study: Postgraduate
Type: Scholarship
Value: PhD students: Up to NZ$30,000 ($10,000 per annum) MFA students: NZ$7,500
Length of Study: 1 to 3 years
Frequency: Annual
Country of Study: New Zealand
Closing Date: 1 November
Additional Information: scholarshipscanterbury.communityforce.com/Funds/FundDetails.aspx

For further information contact:

Email: scholarships@canterbury.ac.nz

Farina Thompson Charitable Trust Music Scholarship

Level of Study: Postgraduate
Type: Studentship
Value: NZ$10,000
Length of Study: 1 year
Frequency: Annual
Country of Study: New Zealand
No. of awards offered: 1
Closing Date: 1 November
Additional Information: scholarshipscanterbury.communityforce.com/Funds/FundDetails.aspx

For further information contact:

Email: scholarships@canterbury.ac.nz

Frank and Doris Bateson Memorial Graduate Scholarship

Level of Study: Postgraduate
Type: Scholarship
Value: NZ$2,500
Frequency: Annual
Country of Study: New Zealand
No. of awards offered: 1
Closing Date: 15 October
Additional Information: scholarshipscanterbury.communityforce.com/Funds/FundDetails.aspx

For further information contact:

Email: scholarships@canterbury.ac.nz

Kitchener Memorial Scholarship

Purpose: The Kitchener Memorial Scholarship Fund offers scholarships to past or present members of the Armed Forces or their children, who are undertaking an agricultural course of study at a New Zealand university
Eligibility: Applicants must be either; 1. Past or present members of the Armed Forces or children of past or present members of the Armed Forces who have seen active service and who, at the time of enlistment, were domiciled in New Zealand, whether actually resident there or not, or. 2. Past or present members of the Armed Forces or their children to whom the above does not apply, or. 3. People resident in New Zealand for a period of not less than three years immediately before the award of the scholarship
Level of Study: Graduate
Type: Scholarship
Value: NZ$500
Frequency: Annual
Country of Study: New Zealand
Closing Date: 1 December
Funding: Private
Additional Information: https://www.lincoln.ac.nz/study/scholarships/search-scholarships/kitchener-memorial-scholarship/

Lighthouse Vision Trust Scholarship

Purpose: The scholarships support students with a vision impairment in undertaking study at the University of

Canterbury. It was established in 2016 by the Lighthouse Vision Trust

Eligibility: Applicants must have a vision impairment that qualifies them to register with the Blind Foundation. By the closing date for applications, an applicant must have registered with the University's Disability Resource Service as a student with a vision impairment. Applicants must be citizens of New Zealand or holders of New Zealand residence class visas. Applicants must be enrolled, full-time or part-time, at the University at either undergraduate or postgraduate level.

Level of Study: Postgraduate

Type: Scholarship

Value: Up to NZ$10,000 can be received as total value

Length of Study: 1 year

Frequency: Annual

Country of Study: New Zealand

Application Procedure: 1 Applications must be made online at the Scholarships website by 31 March. 2 Applicants will be considered for both scholarships, and the decision on which of the top candidates will be offered which of the two scholarships will be made randomly. 3 A previous recipient of Lighthouse Vision Trust Scholarship or a Susan Barnes Memorial Scholarship may re-apply for the scholarship that they held, and a previous recipient of one of the scholarships may apply for the other scholarship in another year. However, no student may hold one of the scholarships or a combination of the two scholarships over a total period of more than three years

No. of awards offered: 1

Closing Date: March

Funding: Private

Additional Information: https://scholarshipscanterbury.communityforce.com/Funds/Search.aspx

For further information contact:

Email: scholarships@canterbury.ac.nz

Marian D Eve Memorial Scholarship

Purpose: This scholarship supports students studying, researching, or developing, resources for early-childhood special-needs education at the University of Canterbury

Eligibility: Recipients must be undergraduate or postgraduate students who are enrolled full-time at the University and studying, researching, or developing, in any discipline, resources for early-childhood special-needs education

Level of Study: Doctorate, Graduate, Postgraduate

Type: Scholarship

Value: NZ$2,000

Length of Study: 1 year

Frequency: Annual

Country of Study: Any country

Application Procedure: You may apply through the webpage approximately 8 weeks before applications close. If it's possible to apply on-line for this scholarship there will be a link above to the on-line system. Apply through online link. www.studyinnewzealand.govt.nz/how-to-apply/scholarship/details?scholarshipid=25668&institutionid=142318

Closing Date: March

Funding: Private

Additional Information: www.studyinnewzealand.govt.nz/how-to-apply/scholarship/details?scholarshipid=25668&institutionid=142318

For further information contact:

Email: scholarships@canterbury.ac.nz

McKelvey Award

Purpose: This award supports and PhD students in the New Zealand School of Forestry at the University of Canterbury. Normally, the award is available to assist students to present a paper at a relevant conference. However, in the absence of suitable applications, the applications may be opened to eligible students seeking support to meet other costs associated with their study

Eligibility: This award supports master's and PhD students in the New Zealand School of Forestry at the University of Canterbury. Normally, the award is available to assist students to present a paper at a relevant conference. However, in the absence of suitable applications, the applications may be opened to eligible students seeking support to meet other costs associated with their study. Students enrolled in a programme for a master's or PhD degree in the New Zealand School of Forestry

Level of Study: Postgraduate

Type: Scholarship

Value: NZ$1,000

Frequency: Annual

Country of Study: Any country

Application Procedure: Apply online www.fore.canterbury.ac.nz/people/index.shtml

No. of awards offered: 1

Closing Date: 1 April

Funding: Foundation

Additional Information: https://scholarshipscanterbury.communityforce.com/Funds/Search.aspx

For further information contact:

Email: scholarships-cf@universitiesnz.ac.nz

Park and Paulay Scholarship

Purpose: This scholarship acknowledges and rewards a top performer in the first two Professional years of the programme for a Bachelor of Engineering (Honours) degree in Civil Engineering at the University of Canterbury

Eligibility: Full-time students in the Third Professional Year of the programme for the Bachelor of Engineering (Honours) degree in Civil Engineering (BE(Hons)(Civil)) at the University of Canterbury, who are enrolled in at least four courses related to Structural or Geotechnical or Earthquake Engineering

Level of Study: Graduate

Type: Scholarship

Value: NZ$2,500

Length of Study: 1 year

Frequency: Annual

Country of Study: New Zealand

Application Procedure: You may apply through the webpage approximately 8 weeks before applications close. If it's possible to apply on-line for this scholarship there will be a link above to the on-line system. If the link is not provided, please download and complete the application form located below. Closing dates are yet to be released for the same

No. of awards offered: 1

Closing Date: 31 March

Funding: Private

Additional Information: www.studyinnewzealand.govt.nz/how-to-apply/scholarship/details?scholarshipid=131215&institutionid=142318

For further information contact:

Tel: (64) 3 369 4900
Email: scholarships@canterbury.ac.nz

UC Te Kaupeka Ture Faculty of Law PhD Fees Scholarship

Level of Study: Doctorate

Type: Scholarship

Value: The prize is tuition fees for thesis enrolment

Length of Study: period necessary to complete up to 360 points of enrolment

Frequency: Annual

Country of Study: New Zealand

Closing Date: 1 December

Additional Information: scholarshipscanterbury.communityforce.com/Funds/FundDetails.aspx

For further information contact:

Email: scholarships@canterbury.ac.nz

Wood Technology Research Centre – Postgraduate Scholarships

Purpose: To develop a computer model to simulate energy flow and energy efficiency in wood and wood product processing industry

Level of Study: Postgraduate

Type: Scholarship

Value: NZ$24,000 per year for PhD and NZ$18,000 per year for ME

Length of Study: 3 years for PhD and one and half year for ME

Country of Study: New Zealand

Application Procedure: To apply or for further information on the above scholarships, please contact Dr Shusheng Pang

Contributor: University of Canterbury

Additional Information: Case studies will be conducted for manufacturing of Laminated Veneer Lumber (LVL) and Medium Density Fibreboard (MDF). The project will be conduced in collaboration with the University of Otago and a wood processing company www.studyinnewzealand.govt.nz/how-to-apply/scholarship/details?scholarshipid=131215&institutionid=142318

For further information contact:

Wood Technology Centre, Department of Chemical and Process Engineering, University of Canterbury, Christchurch 8041, New Zealand.

Tel: (64) 3 364 2538
Fax: (64) 3 364 2063
Email: shusheng.pang@canterbury.ac.nz

University of Canterbury, Department of Management

Private Bag 4800, Christchurch 8140, New Zealand.

Tel: (64) 3 364 2808
Email: s.worrall@mang.canterbury.ac.nz
Website: www.regy.canterbury.ac.nz.home.html
Contact: Mrs Suzanne Worrall, MBA Programme Director

Auckland Council Chief Economist's Research Scholarship in Economics

Purpose: The purpose of this scholarship is to encourage and support postgraduate research into urban economics that has particular relevance to local government in New Zealand

Eligibility: 1. At the time of application candidates must be enrolled or planning to enrol in a postgraduate programme at a New Zealand university. 2. The postgraduate programme must be in the area of urban economics. Universities NZ and Auckland Council reserve the right to determine the eligibility of a particular area of study. 3. A thesis, dissertation, or research report must be a requirement of the postgraduate programme

Level of Study: Postgraduate

Type: Scholarship

Value: Each year Auckland Council may grant one scholarship with an award of NZ$4,000 or two scholarships with an award of NZ$2,000 each

Length of Study: 1 year

Frequency: Varies

Country of Study: New Zealand

Application Procedure: Apply online universitiesnz. communityforce.com/

No. of awards offered: 3

Closing Date: 1 February

Funding: Foundation

Additional Information: For candidates who are enrolled on a part time basis the value of the award will be NZ$1,500. The award is intended to help with tuition fees and research costs (e.g. data costs), and to contribute towards living costs www.studyinnewzealand.govt.nz/how-to-apply/scholarship/details?scholarshipid=116825&institutionid=142318

For further information contact:

Email: scholarships-cf@universitiesnz.ac.nz

Barbara Mito Reed Award

Purpose: The award was established in memory of Dr Barbara Mito Reed (1955-1990), a graduate in Japanese of the University of Canterbury, by her husband, Mr T. Mito, her family and her friends. It was established to help outstanding graduate students of Japanese, whose native language is not Japanese, to further their studies towards a higher degree in a field of Japanese language and/or culture

Eligibility: The scholarship is open to graduates of the University of Canterbury enrolled, or intending to enrol, in a postgraduate programme in a field of Japanese studies at the University of Canterbury or at a university in Japan.

Normally, the programme will be for a BA(Hons), master's or doctoral degree. The scholarship is open to citizens or Permanent Residents of New Zealand, excluding native speakers of Japanese

Level of Study: Postgraduate

Type: Scholarship

Value: NZ$1,000

Length of Study: 1 year

Frequency: Annual

Country of Study: New Zealand

Application Procedure: Apply online universitiesnz.communityforce.com/

No. of awards offered: 1

Closing Date: 31 March

Funding: Foundation

Additional Information: scholarshipscanterbury.communityforce.com/Funds/FundDetails.aspx

For further information contact:

Tel: (64) 3 369 4900
Email: scholarships@canterbury.ac.nz

BayTrust Bruce Cronin Scholarship

Purpose: This scholarship has been established to recognise his service to the people of the Bay of Plenty

Eligibility: Applicants must have links to the BayTrust geographical area. This area is shown on the BayTrust website www.baytrust.org.nz Applicants will be eligible if they were born in, or attended school in, or have whakapapa back to the area.

Level of Study: Postgraduate

Type: Scholarship

Value: NZ$5,000

Length of Study: 1 year

Frequency: Annual

Country of Study: New Zealand

Application Procedure: Apply online

No. of awards offered: 2

Closing Date: 1 February

Funding: Foundation

Additional Information: www.universitiesnz.ac.nz/scholarships/baytrust-bruce-cronin-scholarship

For further information contact:

Level 9, 142 Lambton Quay, Wellington, PO Box 11915, Wellington 6142, New Zealand.

Tel: (64) 4 381 8500
Email: info@baytrust.org.nz

Christchurch City Council Antarctic Scholarship

Purpose: The Christchurch City Council offers a NZ$10,000 one-year scholarship for a University of Canterbury student to carry out Antarctic or Southern Ocean research at master's or PhD level. The scholarship includes one season of logistical support provided by Antarctica New Zealand

Eligibility: A candidate who, during the tenure of the scholarship, is studying for a PhD or is in the thesis year of a master's degree at the University of Canterbury in an Antarctic-related topic

Level of Study: Postgraduate

Type: Scholarship

Value: NZ$10,000

Length of Study: 1 year

Frequency: Varies

Country of Study: Any country

Application Procedure: Apply online through link www.antarcticanz.govt.nz/scholarships-and-fellowships

Closing Date: 31 March

Funding: Foundation

Additional Information: www.studyinnewzealand.govt.nz/how-to-apply/scholarship/details?scholarshipid=54787&institutionid=142318

For further information contact:

International Antarctic Centre, 38 Orchard Road, Christchurch 8053, New Zealand.

Email: adrian.mcdonald@canterbury.ac.nz

Deutscher Akademischer Austauschdienst (German Academic Exchange Service) Scholarships

Purpose: The DAAD supports over 100,000 German and international students and researchers around the globe each year – making it the world's largest funding organisation of its kind

Eligibility: Graduates of all disciplines can apply for a scholarship to complete a postgraduate or Master's degree course at a German higher education institution and to gain a degree in Germany (Master's/Diploma)

Level of Study: Postgraduate

Type: Scholarship

Value: €750

Length of Study: 10-24 Months

Frequency: Annual

Country of Study: Any country

Application Procedure: See Website www.universitiesnz.ac.nz/scholarships/daad

Closing Date: 15 October

Funding: Trusts

Additional Information: www.canterbury.ac.nz/scholarshipsearch/ScholarshipDetails.aspx?ScholarshipID=6935.239

For further information contact:

Embassy of the Federal Republic of Germany, PO Box 1687, Wellington 6011, New Zealand.

Email: daad@auckland.ac.nz

Ernest William File Scholarship

Purpose: The purpose of the scholarship is to support the sons and daughters of members of the Rail and Maritime Transport Union (RMTU) in their first year of degree study at a New Zealand university

Eligibility: 1. Sons or daughters of financial members of the RMTU. 2. Enrolled or planning on enrolling in their first year of full time study for an undergraduate degree at a New Zealand university. Applications will not be accepted from anyone who already has a qualification from a tertiary institution in New Zealand or overseas

Level of Study: Graduate

Type: Scholarship

Value: The value of the scholarship is NZ$2,000 per year

Frequency: Annual

Country of Study: New Zealand

Application Procedure: Applications must be done online.: universitiesnz.communityforce.com/Login.aspx

No. of awards offered: 2

Closing Date: 1 April

Funding: Private

Additional Information: www.canterbury.ac.nz/scholarshipsearch/ScholarshipDetails.aspx?ScholarshipID=6935.481

Francis Martin Baillie Reynolds Scholarship in Law to Oxford

Purpose: The purpose of the scholarship is to assist New Zealand Law graduates to commence postgraduate study in Law at the University of Oxford. It has been established to recognise the support that Emeritus Professor Francis Reynolds, Worcester College, Oxford, has provided to New Zealand Law students at the University of Oxford for over 40 years

Eligibility: 1. A New Zealand citizen or permanent resident. 2. Has completed the requirements for a LLB degree from a New Zealand University. 3. The date of application has applied for a place in a postgraduate programme in Law at the University of Oxford

Level of Study: Postgraduate

Type: Scholarship

Value: NZ$10,000

Length of Study: 1 year

Frequency: Annual

Country of Study: New Zealand

Application Procedure: Apply online through link universitiesnz.communityforce.com

Closing Date: 28 February

Funding: Trusts

Frank Knox Memorial Fellowships at Harvard University

Purpose: Annie Reid Knox set up these scholarships to honour her late husband and asked that future scholars be selected on the basis of future promise of leadership, strength of character, keen mind, a balanced judgement and a devotion to the democratic ideal

Eligibility: 1. New Zealand citizens at the time of application, normally resident in New Zealand. 2. Have completed or will complete a first or higher degree at a New Zealand university. 3. Studying for a first or higher degree; or have completed a first or higher degree and graduated no earlier than 2018

Level of Study: Postgraduate

Type: Fellowship

Value: US$32,000 plus tuition and health insurance fee per annum

Length of Study: 2 year

Frequency: Annual

Country of Study: Any country

Application Procedure: Apply online through the link universitiesnz.communityforce.com

Closing Date: 1 October

Funding: Trusts

Additional Information: www.frankknoxfellowships.org.uk/display.aspx?id=1895&pid=0&tabId=230

For further information contact:

Email: emily@kennedytrust.org.uk

G B Battersby-Trimble Scholarship in Computer Science

Purpose: The scholarship supports postgraduate students in Computer Science at the University of Canterbury.

Eligibility: . Eligibility criteria: 2.1 Applicants must be enrolled full-time or part-time at the University in one of the following: a. The final year of a programme for an honours degree in Computer Science. b. A programme for a master's degree in Computer Science. c. A programme for a PhD in Computer Science. 2.2 Current and former recipients may apply for new tenure of the scholarship.

Level of Study: Postgraduate

Type: Scholarship

Value: 1. US$2,000 for honours students and master students doing courses. 2. US$7,000 for masters thesis students. 3. US$8,000 for PhD thesis students

Length of Study: 1 year

Frequency: Annual

Country of Study: Any country

Application Procedure: Apply online universitiesnz.communityforce.com

Closing Date: 31 March

Funding: Trusts

Additional Information: www.canterbury.ac.nz/scholarship search/ScholarshipDetails.aspx?ScholarshipID=6935.11

For further information contact:

Email: scholarships@canterbury.ac.nz

Gateway Antarctica's Ministry of Foreign Affairs and Trade Scholarship in Antarctic and Southern Ocean Studies

Purpose: The Ministry of Foreign Affairs and Trade (MFAT) Scholarship was founded in 2001 in support of research and teaching in Antarctic Studies in recognition of Antarctica as a continent devoted to peace and research

Eligibility: PhD or master's thesis students are eligible. The scholar is required to undertake research concerning a matter of importance to the understanding of Antarctica or the Southern Ocean

Level of Study: Doctorate, Postgraduate

Type: Scholarship

Value: NZ$5,000

Length of Study: 1 year

Frequency: Varies

Country of Study: New Zealand

Application Procedure: Apply online https://www.canterbury.ac.nz/scholarshipsforms/regulations/Gateway_Antarcticas_MFAT_Scholarship_in_Antarctic_and_Southern_Ocean_Studies.pdf

Closing Date: 28 February

Funding: Foundation

Additional Information: www.studyinnewzealand.govt.nz/how-to-apply/scholarship/details?scholarshipid=128786&institutionid=142318

Geography Students Conference Fund

Purpose: The purpose of this fund is to financially assist Master's and PhD research thesis students in the Department of Geography with expenses involved in attending conferences.
Eligibility: The fund provides grants-in-aid to research students in the Department of Geography to assist with expenses involved in attending conferences. Priority will be given to conferences of the New Zealand Geographical Society
Level of Study: Doctorate, Postgraduate
Type: Scholarship
Value: NZ$500
Length of Study: 1 year
Frequency: Varies
Country of Study: New Zealand
Application Procedure: Apply online universitiesnz.communityforce.com
Closing Date: 31 March
Funding: Trusts
Additional Information: www.canterbury.ac.nz/scholarship search/ScholarshipDetails.aspx?ScholarshipID=6935.40

For further information contact:

Email: scholarships@canterbury.ac.nz

Gertrude Ardagh Holmes Bursary Fund

Purpose: The purpose of this fund is to assist students of ability and good character to commence or to continue their studies at the University of Canterbury, who would otherwise, by reason of their financial circumstances, be unable to do so or be seriously handicapped in doing so.
Eligibility: Preference shall be given to students who desire to undertake a medical course
Level of Study: Postgraduate
Type: Scholarship
Value: NZ$600
Frequency: Varies
Country of Study: New Zealand
Application Procedure: Apply online universitiesnz.communityforce.com
Closing Date: 31 March
Funding: Foundation
Additional Information: www.canterbury.ac.nz/scholarship search/ScholarshipDetails.aspx?ScholarshipID=6935.26

For further information contact:

Email: scholarships@canterbury.ac.nz

Grant Lingard Scholarship

Purpose: These scholarships were established by the estate of Peter Lanini in memory of Grant Lingard (1961-1995), a graduate of the School of Fine Arts
Level of Study: Graduate
Type: Scholarship
Value: Full-time tuition fees at the New Zealand domestic rate
Length of Study: 1 year
Frequency: Annual
Country of Study: New Zealand
Application Procedure: You may apply through this webpage approximately 8 weeks before applications close. If it's possible to apply on-line for this scholarship there will be a link above to the on-line system. If the link is not provided, please download and complete the application form located below. Please check the website with the following link. scholarshipscanterbury.communityforce.com
Closing Date: 31 October
Funding: Private
Additional Information: www.canterbury.ac.nz/scholarship search/ScholarshipDetails.aspx?ScholarshipID=6935.223

For further information contact:

Tel: (64) 800 827 748, (64) 3 369 4900
Email: scholarships@canterbury.ac.nz

Henry Kelsey Scholarship

Purpose: The purpose of the scholarship is to provide funds for individuals to undertake research towards a PhD at a New Zealand university or research institution, studying muscular function, including the causes and treatment of muscular dysfunction
Eligibility: Applicants will be New Zealand citizens or permanent residents, and will have a Bachelor degree or equivalent, with honours where they are awarded, in a field appropriate to their intended doctoral study at a New Zealand university
Level of Study: Postgraduate
Type: Scholarship
Value: NZ$10,000
Length of Study: 3 year
Frequency: Varies
Country of Study: New Zealand
Application Procedure: Apply online universitiesnz.communityforce.com/Login.aspx

Closing Date: 1 October
Funding: Trusts
Additional Information: www.universitiesnz.ac.nz/scholar ships/henry-kelsey-scholarship

For further information contact:

Level 9, 142 Lambton Quay, Wellington, PO Box 11915, Wellington 6142, New Zealand.

Tel: (64) 4 381 8500

Joan Burns Memorial Scholarship in History

Purpose: This scholarship recognises and supports academic excellence by honours and master's students in History at the University of Canterbury. It was established from a 1995 bequest from Joan Mary Burns
Eligibility: Applicants must be enrolled full-time or part-time in a Bachelor of Arts with Honours degree programme or in Part 1 of a Master of Arts degree programme
Level of Study: Postgraduate
Type: Scholarship
Value: Stipend equal to domestic tuition fees for 1.00 EFTS
Length of Study: 1 to 2 years
Frequency: Annual
Country of Study: New Zealand
Application Procedure: Apply online universitiesnz. communityforce.com
No. of awards offered: One or more
Closing Date: 31 March
Funding: Private
Additional Information: www.canterbury.ac.nz/scholarship search/ScholarshipDetails.aspx?ScholarshipID=6935.14

For further information contact:

Email: scholarships@canterbury.ac.nz

Kia Ora Foundation Patricia Pratt Scholarship

Purpose: The purpose of the Kia Ora Foundation Patricia Pratt Music Scholarship is to assist outstanding New Zealand musical performers, who have completed the equivalent of an honours degree in musical performance in New Zealand, to continue their musical development at a renowned international music school or conservatorium
Eligibility: Applicants will be New Zealand citizens. Applicants may apply from outside New Zealand but must have resided in New Zealand for at least three of the last five years immediately preceding the year of selection. Applicants will have recently completed the requirements for an honours

degree in musical performance at a New Zealand university (or an equivalent musical qualification).
Level of Study: Postgraduate
Type: Scholarship
Value: Funds available for the scholarship are up to NZ$70,000 per annum
Length of Study: 1 year
Frequency: Annual
Country of Study: New Zealand
Application Procedure: Apply online universitiesnz. communityforce.com
Closing Date: 1 March
Funding: Foundation
Additional Information: www.canterbury.ac.nz/scholarship search/ScholarshipDetails.aspx?ScholarshipID=6935.1778

Kiwi Music Scholarship

Purpose: The purpose of the scholarship is to assist outstanding New Zealand musical performers or conductors who have completed or are completing an honours or master's degree in musical performance in New Zealand to continue their musical development either overseas or in New Zealand
Eligibility: Applicants will be New Zealand citizens who are normally resident in New Zealand. Applicants will have completed or are completing an honours or masters degree in musical performance (including vocal performance) or conducting at a New Zealand university, or an equivalent musical qualification.
Level of Study: Postgraduate
Type: Scholarship
Value: NZ$50,000 to NZ$60,000
Length of Study: 3 year
Frequency: Varies
Country of Study: New Zealand
Application Procedure: Apply online universitiesnz. communityforce.com/
Closing Date: 1 March
Funding: Trusts
Additional Information: www.universitiesnz.ac.nz/scholar ships/kiwi-music-scholarship

L B Wood Travelling Scholarship

Purpose: The LB Wood Traveling Scholarship is awarded to supplement some other postgraduate scholarship held by the scholar supporting their studies in Britain. The scholarship can only be awarded for postgraduate study at a university or institution of university rank in Britain
Eligibility: Applicants must: 1. be graduates of or graduating from a New Zealand university 2. apply for the scholarship

within three years from the date of their graduation 3. have applied for or been awarded another postgraduate scholarship.

Level of Study: Postgraduate
Type: Scholarship
Value: NZ$3,000
Length of Study: 3 years
Frequency: Annual
Country of Study: New Zealand
Application Procedure: Apply online: universitiesnz. communityforce.com/
No. of awards offered: 1
Closing Date: 1 April
Funding: Foundation
Additional Information: www.studyinnewzealand.govt.nz/ how-to-apply/scholarship/details?scholarshipid=25582& institutionid=142318

For further information contact:

Tel: (64) 3 369 3999
Email: info@canterbury.ac.nz

LB Wood Scholarship

Purpose: 1. The LB Wood Traveling Scholarship is awarded to supplement some other postgraduate scholarship held by the scholar supporting their studies in Britain. 2. The scholarship can only be awarded for postgraduate study at a university or institution of university rank in Britain
Eligibility: Applicants must: 1. be graduates of or graduating from a New Zealand university 2. apply for the scholarship within three years from the date of their graduation 3. have applied for or been awarded another postgraduate scholarship.
Level of Study: Postgraduate
Type: Scholarship
Value: NZ$3,000
Length of Study: 3 year
Frequency: Varies
Country of Study: New Zealand
Application Procedure: Apply online universitiesnz. communityforce.com/
No. of awards offered: 1
Closing Date: 1 April
Funding: Trusts
Additional Information: www.aut.ac.nz/study/fees-and-scholarships/scholarships-and-awards-at-aut/scholarships-database/detailpage?detailCode=100049&sessionID=267 50595&sourceIP=&X_FORWARDED_FOR=

Master of Business Administration Programme

Length of Study: 1 to 5 years
Application Procedure: Applicants must complete an application form, a self-evaluation essay, supply an original transcript or a certified copy of grades and provide two references

For further information contact:

Tel: (64) 3 364 2657
Fax: (64) 3 364 2925
Email: international@regy.canterbury.ac.nz

New Zealand Law Foundation Ethel Benjamin Scholarship (for Women)

Purpose: To support postgraduate research in Law that encompasses the wider objectives of the NZ Law Foundation, in particular research that will protect and promote the interests of the public in relation to legal matters in New Zealand
Eligibility: A Scholarship may be awarded to any woman scholar who is: 1. a New Zealand citizen or permanent resident 2. the holder of a New Zealand university law degree (unless there are exceptional circumstances the award would normally be made to candidates who have gained the qualifying degree within the past five years) 3. accepted into a postgraduate course in law at either a New Zealand or an overseas university acceptable to the Selection Committee..
Level of Study: Postgraduate
Type: Scholarship
Value: NZ$20,000 to NZ$30,000
Length of Study: 3 years
Frequency: Annual
Country of Study: Any country
Application Procedure: Apply online universitiesnz. communityforce.com/
No. of awards offered: 3
Closing Date: 1 March
Funding: Trusts
Additional Information: www.universitiesnz.ac.nz/scholar ships/new-zealand-law-foundation-ethel-benjamin-scholar ship-women

Prince of Wales' Cambridge International Scholarship

Purpose: To enable graduates of high academic ability to study at Cambridge University
Eligibility: These scholarships are open to graduates who are New Zealand citizens and who wish to pursue a course of

research leading to the degree of PhD at Cambridge University

Level of Study: Doctorate, Postgraduate

Type: Scholarship

Value: Value determined by financial need of applicant.

Length of Study: 3 years

Frequency: Annual

Country of Study: New Zealand

Application Procedure: Apply online universitiesnz.communityforce.com

Closing Date: 1 October

Funding: Trusts

Contributor: Universities New Zealand – Te Pōkai Tara

Additional Information: www.canterbury.ac.nz/scholarship search/ScholarshipDetails.aspx?ScholarshipID=6935.1593

For further information contact:

Email: cambridge.trust@admin.cam.ac.uk

Pukehou Poutu Scholarship

Purpose: The money for this scholarship has been made available by a bequest from the estate of Edith Fraser who wished that it be used for an award in agricultural or silvicultural sciences

Eligibility: Applicants must be graduates of a New Zealand university and be New Zealand citizens

Level of Study: Postgraduate

Type: Scholarship

Value: NZ$10,000

Length of Study: 1 year

Frequency: Annual

Country of Study: New Zealand

Application Procedure: Apply online universitiesnz.communityforce.com/Login.aspx

No. of awards offered: 1

Closing Date: 1 October

Funding: Foundation

Additional Information: www.canterbury.ac.nz/scholarship search/ScholarshipDetails.aspx?ScholarshipID=6935.194

For further information contact:

Tel: (64) 3 369 3999

Email: info@canterbury.ac.nz

Roland Stead Postgraduate Scholarship in Biology

Purpose: This scholarship supports Masters research students of biology with an interest in ecology, freshwater fisheries and the Canterbury region

Eligibility: The scholarship will be available to full-time students in the School of Biological Sciences who are engaged in research in Part II of the Master of Science degree programme

Level of Study: Postgraduate

Type: Scholarship

Value: NZ$5,000

Length of Study: 1 year

Frequency: Annual

Country of Study: New Zealand

Application Procedure: Apply online myuc.canterbury.ac.nz/sso

No. of awards offered: 1

Closing Date: 31 March

Funding: Foundation

Additional Information: www.canterbury.ac.nz/scholarship search/ScholarshipDetails.aspx?ScholarshipID=6935.1578

For further information contact:

Email: scholarships@canterbury.ac.nz

Sir Douglas Myers Scholarship

Purpose: The Scholarship provides an opportunity for students who have already distinguished themselves academically to attend one of the most prestigious universities in the world

Eligibility: Candidates for the Scholarship must 1. Be entered for the Year 13 senior school examination (for example, NCEA Level 3, Cambridge exams, etc.) or equivalent senior school exam in the year of application. 2. Have a record of achievement sufficient to satisfy the academic criteria for entry to Cambridge University and Gonville and Caius College. 3. Be New Zealand citizens or permanent residents. 4. Normally have completed their five years of secondary schooling in New Zealand

Level of Study: Graduate

Type: Scholarship

Value: Provides tuition fees and a living allowance

Frequency: Annual

Country of Study: New Zealand

Application Procedure: See website universitiesnz.communityforce.com/Login.aspx

No. of awards offered: 1

Closing Date: 1 December

Funding: Private

Additional Information: www.canterbury.ac.nz/scholarship search/ScholarshipDetails.aspx?ScholarshipID=6935.234

For further information contact:

Tel: (64) 3 369 3999

Email: info@canterbury.ac.nz

The Claude McCarthy Fellowships

Purpose: Claude McCarthy Fellowships (Category A) are available to candidates who are graduates of a New Zealand university and who are enrolled in a PhD programme at a New Zealand university

Eligibility: 1. A graduate of a New Zealand university. 2. Registered for a doctoral degree at a New Zealand university. 3. Have been registered for their doctoral degree for at least one year at the closing date for applications

Level of Study: Postgraduate

Type: Scholarship

Value: NZ$5,000

Length of Study: 1 year

Frequency: Annual

Country of Study: New Zealand

Application Procedure: See Website www.universitiesnz.ac.nz/scholarships/claudemccarthy

Closing Date: 1 October

Funding: Trusts

Additional Information: www.canterbury.ac.nz/scholarship search/ScholarshipDetails.aspx?ScholarshipID=6935.191

For further information contact:

Tel: (64) 3 369 3999

Email: info@canterbury.ac.nz

The Dick and Mary Earle Scholarship in Technology

Purpose: The purpose of the scholarship is to provide funds for individuals to undertake research towards a masterate or doctorate degree at a New Zealand university or research institution in one or both of these fields 1. Innovation and product development. 2. Bioprocess technology

Eligibility: 1. Applicants will be New Zealand citizens or permanent residents who have resided in New Zealand for at least three years immediately preceding the year of selection. 2. Applicants will have completed the requirements for a BTech, BEng, BE degree or equivalent, with honours where they are awarded, at a New Zealand university and in a field appropriate to their intended postgraduate study

Level of Study: Postgraduate

Type: Scholarship

Value: Up to NZ$17,000 per annum at Masters level and NZ$25,000 per annum at PhD level

Length of Study: 3 year

Frequency: Annual

Country of Study: New Zealand

Application Procedure: See Website universitiesnz.communityforce.com/Login.aspx

No. of awards offered: one Masters scholarship and one Doctoral scholarship will be awarded each year.

Closing Date: 1 July

Funding: Trusts

Additional Information: www.canterbury.ac.nz/scholarship search/ScholarshipDetails.aspx?ScholarshipID=6935.172

For further information contact:

Tel: (64) 3 369 3999

Email: info@canterbury.ac.nz

The Edward & Isabel Kidson Scholarship

Purpose: The purpose of the scholarships is to enable a graduate of a New Zealand university, who is of good character and who has shown an ability in physics or a combination of physics and mathematics, to undertake further advanced study or research in meteorology, either in New Zealand or elsewhere

Eligibility: Applicants should be graduates of a New Zealand university, be of good character and have shown ability in physics or a combination of physics and mathematics. 1. Past pupils of Nelson Boys' College. 2. Graduates of the University of Canterbury

Level of Study: Postgraduate

Type: Scholarship

Value: NZ$6,000 per annum

Length of Study: 3 years

Frequency: Annual

Country of Study: New Zealand

Application Procedure: See Website www.universitiesnz.ac.nz/scholarships/edward-and-isabel-kidson

Closing Date: 1 October

Funding: Trusts

Additional Information: www.canterbury.ac.nz/scholarship search/ScholarshipDetails.aspx?ScholarshipID=6935.185

For further information contact:

Tel: (64) 3 369 3999

Email: info@canterbury.ac.nz

The Judith Clark Memorial Fellowships

Purpose: The Judith Clark Memorial Fellowships have been established to assist music graduates undertake a special short-term project that will have long term benefits for their future professional careers as musicians

Eligibility: Applicants must hold New Zealand citizenship or permanent residency and must have recently graduated, or expect to graduate in the year of application, with an Honours degree, or equivalent, in music from a New Zealand university

Level of Study: Postgraduate
Type: Fellowship/Scholarship
Value: NZ$15,000
Length of Study: 1 year
Frequency: Varies
Country of Study: New Zealand
Application Procedure: See website universitiesnz. communityforce.com/Login.aspx
Closing Date: 15 February
Funding: Foundation
Additional Information: There are two application rounds available Round 1: Principally to the support the cost of attending auditions in the November to February period. Round 2: Principally to support attendance at a summer school or summer academy in the May to August period www.canterbury.ac.nz/scholarshipsearch/ScholarshipDetails. aspx?ScholarshipID=6935.1627

For further information contact:

Tel: (64) 3 369 3999
Email: info@canterbury.ac.nz

The Kia Ora Foundation Patricia Pratt Music Scholarship

Purpose: The purpose of the Kia Ora Foundation Patricia Pratt Music Scholarship is to assist outstanding New Zealand musical performers, who have completed the equivalent of an honours degree in musical performance in New Zealand, to continue their musical development at a renowned international music school or conservatorium
Eligibility: Applicants will be New Zealand citizens. Applicants may apply from outside New Zealand but must have resided in New Zealand for at least three of the last five years immediately preceding the year of selection. Applicants will have recently completed the requirements for an honours degree in musical performance at a New Zealand university (or an equivalent musical qualification)
Level of Study: Postgraduate
Type: Scholarship
Value: NZ$70,000
Length of Study: 2 years
Frequency: Varies
Country of Study: Any country
Application Procedure: See Website www.universitiesnz.ac. nz/scholarships/kia-ora-foundation-patricia-pratt-scholarship
Closing Date: 1 March
Funding: Trusts

Additional Information: For further details and application instructions, refer to the www.universitiesnz.ac.nz/scholar ships/kia-ora-foundation-patricia-pratt-scholarship www.can terbury.ac.nz/scholarshipsearch/ScholarshipDetails.aspx? ScholarshipID=6935.1778

For further information contact:

Tel: (64) 3 369 3999
Email: info@canterbury.ac.nz

University of Canterbury Doctoral Scholarship

Purpose: These scholarships support students for study towards a research doctoral degree at the University of Canterbury. Approximately 60 scholarships are available each year, over two annual application rounds
Eligibility: The scholarships are tenable by full-time and part-time students engaged in study for a research doctoral degree at UC. An applicant must have completed an appropriate qualification at a level judged to be equivalent to a bachelor's or master's degree with first-class honours at UC (equivalent to a UC GPA of at least 7.0)
Level of Study: Postgraduate
Type: Scholarship
Value: NZ$32,000 per annum plus tuition fees
Length of Study: 3 years
Frequency: Every 3 years
Country of Study: New Zealand
Application Procedure: Apply online thro below link. www. canterbury.ac.nz/scholarships/
Closing Date: 16 January
Funding: Private
Additional Information: www.canterbury.ac.nz/scholarship search/scholarshipdetails.aspx?ScholarshipID=6935.127

For further information contact:

Tel: (64) 3 369 4900
Email: Daniel.Nilsson@canterbury.ac.nz

Woolf Fischer Scholarship

Purpose: The main objective of the Trust is that Woolf Fisher Scholars will make a significant commitment to New Zealand and become leaders in their fields.
Eligibility: Applicants must: 1. be a New Zealand citizen. 2. be under the age of thirty in the year of application (i.e. will not have reached their thirtieth birthday by 31 December in the year the application is submitted) 3. have attended a secondary school in New Zealand for at least two years,

U

and 4. have graduated or are expected to graduate with a first-class honours degree from a university in New Zealand.

Level of Study: Graduate

Type: Scholarship

Value: Approximately NZ$100,000 per annum

Length of Study: 3 years

Frequency: Every 3 years

Country of Study: New Zealand

Application Procedure: You may apply through this webpage approximately 8 weeks before applications close. If it's possible to apply on-line for this scholarship there will be a link above to the on-line system. For further details, visit the website. www.universitiesnz.ac.nz/scholarships/woolf-fisher-scholarship

Closing Date: 1 August

Funding: Private

Additional Information: www.canterbury.ac.nz/scholarship search/ScholarshipDetails.aspx?ScholarshipID=6935.215

For further information contact:

Tel: (64) 3 369 3999

Email: info@canterbury.ac.nz

University of Cape Town

University of Cape Town, Private Bag X3, Rondebosch 7701, South Africa.

Tel: (27) 21 650 3622

Email: pgfunding@uct.ac.za

University of Cape Town (UCT) is very similar to the city of Cape Town: it has a vibrant, cosmopolitan community. It is a cultural melting pot where each person contributes their unique blend of knowledge and thinking. Our staff and students come from over 100 countries in Africa and the rest of the world. The university has also built links, partnerships and exchange agreements with leading African and international institutions that further enrich the academic, social and cultural diversity of our campus.

University of Cape Town Masters Scholarships in Public Health

Purpose: To support the training of eye health professionals with strong public health skills, the Consortium offers scholarships for candidates from low- and middle-income African

Commonwealth countries who have been accepted to study for a Masters Public Health, Community Eye Health at the University of Cape Town, South Africa

Eligibility: Applicants must come from a low- or middle-income African Commonwealth country to apply. Funding is available for postgraduate studies only. The bursaries are awarded on a yearly basis

Level of Study: Postgraduate

Type: Scholarship

Frequency: Annual

Country of Study: South Africa

Application Procedure: Check website for more details

Closing Date: 31 July

Funding: Trusts

University of Delaware

Department of History, Newark, DE 19716, United States of America.

Tel: (1) 302 831 8226

Email: dianec@udel.edu

Website: www.udel.edu

Contact: Ms Diane Clark, Administrative Assistant

The Department of History offers MA and PhD programmes in American and European history and more limited graduate study Ancient, African, Asian, Latin American, and Middle Eastern history. In conjunction with these, it offers special programmes in the history of industrialization, material culture studies, American Civilization, and museum studies.

Executive MBA Programme

Length of Study: 1 to 3 years

Country of Study: Any country

Application Procedure: Applicants must complete an application form supplying US$45 fee, transcripts, Graduate Management Admission Test score, TOEFL score and two letters of recommendation

For further information contact:

Tel: (1) 302 831 2221

Fax: (1) 302 831 3329

Email: E-MBA@strauss.udel.edu

University of Derby

Kedleston Rd, Derby DE22 1GB, United Kingdom.

Tel: (44) 1332 590 500
Website: www.derby.ac.uk
Contact: University of Derby

The University of Derby is a public university in the city of Derby, United Kingdom. It traces its history back to the establishment of the Derby Diocesan Institution for the Training of Schoolmistresses in 1851 and gained university status in 1992 as one of the new universities.

Great Scholarship

Eligibility: Please note that applicants should be passport holders of China, Ghana, India, Indonesia, Malaysia, Nigeria, Pakistan, or Thailand.
Level of Study: Postgraduate
Type: Scholarship
Value: £11,000
Length of Study: 1 year
Frequency: Annual
Country of Study: United Kingdom
No. of awards offered: 8
Closing Date: 1 June
Additional Information: www.derby.ac.uk/study/fees-finance/scholarships/great-scholarships/

International Scholarships at University of Derby

Purpose: The University of Derby is offering international scholarships for the academic year. These scholarships are available to apply for once you have received an offer on a course from the University
Eligibility: These scholarships are available to apply for once you have received an offer on a course from the University. International students are eligible to apply
Type: Postgraduate scholarships
Value: £5,00
Study Establishment: Scholarships are awarded to study the subjects offered by the university
Country of Study: United Kingdom
Application Procedure: Apply online www.derby.ac.uk/study/fees-finance/scholarships/#d.en.120869
Closing Date: 1 July
Additional Information: www.derby.ac.uk/study/fees-finance/scholarships/

For further information contact:

Email: iadmissions@derby.ac.uk

University of Dundee

Nethergate, Dundee DD1 4HN, United Kingdom.

Tel: (44) 13 8234 5028
Email: j.e.nicholson@dundee.ac.uk
Website: www.dundee.ac.uk
Contact: Postgraduate Office

The University of Dundee is one of United Kingdom's leading universities, named Scottish University of the Year 2004/2005 (Sunday Times) and ranked top for teaching quality in 2005 (THES). It is internationally recognised for its expertise across a range of disciplines including science, medicine, engineering and art and graduates more people into the professions than any other university in Scotland.

Al-Maktoum College Hamdan Bin Rashid Award

Eligibility: To be eligible for the scholarship, you must: 1. Have either a conditional or unconditional offer to study: International Business and Islamic Finance MSc, Islamic Banking and Finance MSc, Islamic Banking, Finance and International Business MSc, or Islamic Finance MSc 2. Be starting your course in either September 2023 or January 2024 3. Have been awarded the University of Dundee Global Excellence Scholarship.
Level of Study: Postgraduate
Type: Scholarship
Value: £7,500
Length of Study: 1 year
Frequency: Annual
Country of Study: United Kingdom
Application Procedure: There is no separate application form for this scholarship as the University will review all offer holders who have received the Global Excellence scholarship.
No. of awards offered: 6
Closing Date: 30 November
Additional Information: www.dundee.ac.uk/scholarships/2022-23/hamdan-bin-rashid-award/

For further information contact:

Email: scholarships@dundee.ac.uk.

U

Al-Maktoum College Living Support Bursary

Eligibility: To be eligible for the bursary, you must: 1. Have either a conditional or unconditional offer to study 2. International Business and Islamic Finance MSc, Islamic Banking and Finance MSc, Islamic Banking, Finance and International Business MSc, or Islamic Finance MSc 3. Be starting your course in September 2023 or January 2024.
Level of Study: Postgraduate
Type: Bursary
Value: £5,000
Length of Study: 1 year
Frequency: Annual
Country of Study: United Kingdom
Application Procedure: There is no separate application form for this bursary. Your eligibility will be assessed by our Admissions team, and we will notify you in writing if you are eligible to receive this bursary.
Additional Information: www.dundee.ac.uk/scholarships/2022-23/al-maktoum-college-living-support-bursary/

For further information contact:

Email: scholarships@dundee.ac.uk

Alumni Scholarship

Eligibility: 1. Have applied to study a full (180 credit) postgraduate taught programme starting in September 2023 or January 2024. If you are returning to study an Undergraduate programme, a Postgraduate taught programme which is less than 180 credits, a Distance Learning Programme, or a Postgraduate Research Programme then unfortunately you are not eligible – please read our Key Facts Document for more information on this. 2. Have graduated from the University of Dundee, having previously completed a full undergraduate or postgraduate taught degree, OR; 3. Have an immediate family member who has previously studied at the University of Dundee, having completed a full undergraduate or postgraduate taught degree.
Level of Study: Postgraduate
Type: Scholarship
Value: Up to £3,000
Length of Study: 1 year
Country of Study: Any country
Closing Date: January
Additional Information: https://www.dundee.ac.uk/scholarships/2022-23/alumni-scholarship/

For further information contact:

Email: contactus@dundee.ac.uk

Commonwealth Infection Prevention and Control Scholarship

Subjects: Nursing and Health Sciences
Eligibility: In order for candidate applications to be eligible for consideration, candidates will need the following 1. Copy of valid passport or national ID card showing photograph, date of birth, and country of citizenship - uploaded to the online application system 2. At least one reference - submitted directly by the referee to the online application system. Referees will be sent an email request however applicants are responsible for seeking permission from their referees in advance of submitting their application; for ensuring that their referees are available to complete the reference by the deadline; and that the referees have received the reference request email. 3. An offer letter to start chosen course of study - uploaded to the online application system 4. Full transcripts detailing all higher education qualifications (with certified translations if not in English) - uploaded to the online application system 5. The CSC will not accept supporting documentation submitted outside the online application system.
Level of Study: Postgraduate
Type: Scholarship
Value: £10,000
Length of Study: 1 year
Frequency: Throughout the year
Country of Study: Any country
Application Procedure: You can apply directly to the CSC cscuk.dfid.gov.uk/apply/distance-learning/
Closing Date: 7 May
Additional Information: www.dundee.ac.uk/scholarships/2020-21/commonwealth-ipc-scholarship/

For further information contact:

Email: contactus@dundee.ac.uk

Discover Business at Dundee

Eligibility: To be eligible for the Discover Business at Dundee scholarship, you must meet all the following criteria: 1. You must have International fee status as determined by the University of Dundee 2. Have received an offer to study an eligible Undergraduate or Postgraduate Taught course in the School of Business 3. Begin studies in the 2023–2024 academic year. 4. September 2023 for Undergraduate 5. September 2023 or January 2024 for Postgraduate Taught
Type: Scholarship
Value: £2,000 per year
Length of Study: 4 years
Country of Study: Any country

Application Procedure: There is not a separate application form for this scholarship. You must apply to study a course at the University of Dundee first and your eligibility will be assessed as part of your course application.

Additional Information: www.dundee.ac.uk/scholarships/2022-23/discover-business-dundee/

For further information contact:

Email: scholarships@dundee.ac.uk

Global Citizenship Scholarship

Eligibility: To be considered for a scholarship, you must meet the following eligibility criteria: 1. Have an offer to study a full-time, on campus undergraduate course in any of our schools (excluding the School of Medicine and the School of Dentistry) OR postgraduate taught course in any of our academic schools. 2. Commence studies in September 2023 or January 2024. 3. Have International fee status as determined by the University of Dundee.

Level of Study: Postgraduate
Type: Scholarship
Value: £5,000 per year
Length of Study: 5 years
Frequency: Annual
Country of Study: Any country
Application Procedure: forms.office.com/r/ZJ5MgaLXkC%20%20
Closing Date: 31 October
Additional Information: www.dundee.ac.uk/scholarships/2022-23/global-citizenship/

For further information contact:

Email: scholarships@dundee.ac.uk

Global Excellence Scholarship

Eligibility: To be considered for a scholarship, you must meet the following eligibility criteria: 1. Have an offer to study a full-time, on campus postgraduate taught course in any of our academic schools; 2. Have International fee status as determined by the University of Dundee; 3. Be starting your course in September 2023 OR January 2024 4. Have achieved either a UK 1st Class Honours degree or degree considered as equivalent to this level at the discretion of the University

Level of Study: Postgraduate
Type: Scholarship
Value: £6,000 per year
Length of Study: 5 years
Frequency: Annual

Country of Study: Any country
Application Procedure: There is not a separate application form for this scholarship. You must apply to study a course at the University of Dundee first and your eligibility will be assessed as part of your course application.

Additional Information: www.dundee.ac.uk/scholarships/2022-23/uod-global-excellence/

For further information contact:

Email: scholarships@dundee.ac.uk

GREAT Scholarship - Bangladesh

Eligibility: You are eligible if: 1. You are a passport holder from Bangladesh 2. You have an offer to study a full time, on campus, postgraduate taught course 3. Your course starts in September 2023 4. You have International Fee status, as verified by the University of Dundee.

Level of Study: Postgraduate
Type: Scholarship
Value: £10,000
Length of Study: 1 year
Frequency: Annual
Country of Study: United Kingdom
Application Procedure: Please fill in this form to complete your application: forms.office.com/Pages/ResponsePage.aspx?id=OTEyrjoJKk2Bpl0zS82QGWQzRY2jNVhFnbBwPVVK97NUNlZFMEpNMFNWQjQ2VTFFVjhTSkFXUjBJWSQlQCN0PWcu

No. of awards offered: 1
Closing Date: 31 May
Additional Information: www.dundee.ac.uk/scholarships/2022-23/great-schlolarship-bangladesh/

For further information contact:

Email: scholarships@dundee.ac.uk

GREAT Scholarship 2022 – Sri Lanka

Eligibility: You are eligible to apply for the GREAT Scholarship 2022 – Sri Lanka if you: 1. Are a passport holder from Sri Lanka 2. Have an offer to study a full time, on campus, postgraduate taught course 3. Your course starts in September 2023 4. Have International Fee status, as verified by the University of Dundee.

Level of Study: Postgraduate
Type: Scholarship
Value: £10,000
Frequency: Annual
Country of Study: Any country

Application Procedure: forms.office.com/Pages/ResponsePage.aspx?id=OTEyrjoJKk2Bpl0zS82QGWQzRY2jNVhFnbBwPVVK97NUNlZFMEpNMFNWQjQ2VTFFVjhTSkFXUjBJWSQlQCN0PWcu

Closing Date: 31 May

Additional Information: www.dundee.ac.uk/scholarships/2022-23/great-scholarship-sri-lanka/

For further information contact:

Email: scholarships@dundee.ac.uk

GREAT Scholarship for Justice & Law - Thailand

Eligibility: You are eligible to apply if you: 1. Are a passport holder from Thailand 2. Have an offer to study one of the following full time, on campus, postgraduate taught courses: International Commercial Law LLM, or Environmental Law LLM, 3. Your course starts in September 2023 4. Have International Fee status, as verified by the University of Dundee.

Level of Study: Postgraduate

Type: Scholarship

Value: £10,000

Length of Study: 1 year

Frequency: Annual

Country of Study: United Kingdom

Application Procedure: Please fill in this form to complete your application: forms.office.com/Pages/ResponsePage.aspx?id=OTEyrjoJKk2Bpl0zS82QGWQzRY2jNVhFnbBwPVVK97NUQlBJVEZJOEtERFVVU0xURklaS1hCVU5QMCQlQCN0PWcu

Closing Date: 31 May

Additional Information: www.dundee.ac.uk/scholarships/2022-23/great-scholarship-justice-law-thailand/

For further information contact:

Email: scholarships@dundee.ac.uk

GREAT Scholarships - Egypt

Subjects: Anatomy / Forensic Anthropology / Forensic and Medical Art, Architecture and Urban Planning, Art and Design, Biological/Biomedical Sciences, Biomedical Engineering / Medical Imaging, Business (Accountancy / Economics / Finance / International Business), Civil Engineering / Structural Engineering, Computing / Applied Computing / Data Science / Data Engineering, Education, Electronic Engineering, Energy Petroleum and Mineral Law and Policy, English, Geography / Environmental Science, History, Law, Mathematics, Mechanical Engineering / Industrial Engineering, Nursing and Health Sciences, Philosophy, Physics, Politics and International Relations, Psychology, Social Work

Eligibility: You are eligible to apply for the GREAT Scholarship – Egypt if you 1. Are a passport holder from Egypt; 2. Have an offer to study a full time, on campus, postgraduate taught programme at the University of Dundee, starting in September 2023; 3. Have International Fee Status, as verified by the University of Dundee.

Level of Study: Postgraduate

Type: Scholarship

Value: £10,000

Length of Study: 1 year

Frequency: Throughout the year

Country of Study: Any country

Closing Date: 7 May

For further information contact:

Email: contactus@dundee.ac.uk

GREAT Scholarships - Ghana

Subjects: Anatomy / Forensic Anthropology / Forensic and Medical Art, Architecture and Urban Planning, Art and Design, Biological/Biomedical Sciences, Biomedical Engineering / Medical Imaging, Business (Accountancy / Economics / Finance / International Business), Civil Engineering / Structural Engineering, Computing / Applied Computing / Data Science / Data Engineering, Education, Electronic Engineering, Energy Petroleum and Mineral Law and Policy, English, Geography / Environmental Science, History, Law, Mathematics, Mechanical Engineering / Industrial Engineering, Nursing and Health Sciences, Philosophy, Physics, Politics and International Relations, Psychology, Social Work

Eligibility: You are eligible to apply for the GREAT Scholarship – Ghana if you 1. Are a passport holder from Ghana; 2. Have an offer to study a full time, on campus, postgraduate taught programme at the University of Dundee, starting in September 2023; 3. Have International Fee Status, as verified by the University of Dundee.

Level of Study: Postdoctorate

Type: Scholarship

Value: £10,000

Length of Study: 1 year

Frequency: Throughout the year

Country of Study: Any country

Closing Date: 7 May

For further information contact:

Email: contactus@dundee.ac.uk

GREAT Scholarships - India

Subjects: Anatomy / Forensic Anthropology / Forensic and Medical Art, Architecture and Urban Planning, Art and Design, Biological/Biomedical Sciences, Biomedical Engineering / Medical Imaging, Business (Accountancy / Economics / Finance / International Business), Civil Engineering / Structural Engineering, Computing / Applied Computing / Data Science / Data Engineering, Education, Electronic Engineering, Energy Petroleum and Mineral Law and Policy, English, Geography / Environmental Science, History, Law, Mathematics, Mechanical Engineering / Industrial Engineering, Nursing and Health Sciences, Philosophy, Physics, Politics and International Relations, Psychology, Social Work

Eligibility: You are eligible to apply for the GREAT Scholarship – India if you 1. Are a passport holder from India; 2. Have an offer to study a full time, on campus, postgraduate taught programme at the University of Dundee, starting in September 2023; 3. Have International Fee Status, as verified by the University of Dundee

Level of Study: Postdoctorate
Type: Scholarship
Value: £10,000
Length of Study: 1 year
Frequency: Throughout the year
Country of Study: Any country
Closing Date: 7 May

For further information contact:

Email: contactus@dundee.ac.uk

GREAT Scholarships - Kenya

Subjects: Anatomy / Forensic Anthropology / Forensic and Medical Art, Architecture and Urban Planning, Art and Design, Biological/Biomedical Sciences, Biomedical Engineering / Medical Imaging, Business (Accountancy / Economics / Finance / International Business), Civil Engineering / Structural Engineering, Computing / Applied Computing / Data Science / Data Engineering, Education, Electronic Engineering, Energy Petroleum and Mineral Law and Policy, English, Geography / Environmental Science, History, Law, Mathematics, Mechanical Engineering / Industrial Engineering, Nursing and Health Sciences, Philosophy, Physics, Politics and International Relations, Psychology, Social Work

Eligibility: You are eligible to apply for the GREAT Scholarship – Kenya if you 1. Are a passport holder from Kenya; 2. Have an offer to study a full time, on campus, postgraduate taught programme at the University of Dundee, starting in September 2023; 3. Have International Fee Status, as verified by the University of Dundee.

Level of Study: Postdoctorate
Type: Scholarship
Value: £10,000
Length of Study: 1 year
Frequency: Throughout the year
Country of Study: Any country
Closing Date: 7 May

For further information contact:

Email: contactus@dundee.ac.uk

GREAT Scholarships – Indonesia

Subjects: Anatomy / Forensic Anthropology / Forensic and Medical Art, Architecture and Urban Planning, Art and Design, Biological/Biomedical Sciences, Biomedical Engineering / Medical Imaging, Business (Accountancy / Economics / Finance / International Business), Civil Engineering / Structural Engineering, Computing / Applied Computing / Data Science / Data Engineering, Dentistry, Education, Electronic Engineering, Energy Petroleum and Mineral Law and Policy, English, Geography / Environmental Science, History, Law, Mathematics, Mechanical Engineering / Industrial Engineering, Medicine, Nursing and Health Sciences, Philosophy, Physics, Politics and International Relations, Psychology, Social Work

Eligibility: You are eligible to apply for the GREAT Scholarship – Indonesia if you 1. Are a passport holder from Indonesia; 2. Have an offer to study a full time, on campus, postgraduate taught programme at the University of Dundee, starting in September 2023; 3. Have International Fee Status, as verified by the University of Dundee.

Level of Study: Postdoctorate
Type: Scholarship
Value: £10,000
Length of Study: 1 year
Frequency: Throughout the year
Country of Study: Any country
Closing Date: 31 May
Additional Information: www.dundee.ac.uk/scholarships/2022-23/great-scholarship-indonesia/#:~:text=We%20are%20offering%20%C2%A310%2C000,May%202022%2C%202023%3A59GMT.

For further information contact:

Email: contactus@dundee.ac.uk

GREAT Scholarships – Malaysia

Subjects: Anatomy / Forensic Anthropology / Forensic and Medical Art, Architecture and Urban Planning, Art and Design, Biological/Biomedical Sciences, Biomedical Engineering / Medical Imaging, Business (Accountancy / Economics / Finance / International Business), Civil Engineering / Structural Engineering, Computing / Applied Computing / Data Science / Data Engineering, Dentistry, Education, Electronic Engineering, Energy Petroleum and Mineral Law and Policy, English, Geography / Environmental Science, History, Law, Mathematics, Mechanical Engineering / Industrial Engineering, Medicine, Nursing and Health Sciences, Philosophy, Physics, Politics and International Relations, Psychology, Social Work

Eligibility: The University of Dundee is pleased to announce 1 scholarship opportunity, in conjunction with the British Council. You are eligible to apply for the GREAT Scholarship – Malaysia if you: 1. Are a passport holder from Malaysia 2. Have an offer to study a full time, on campus, postgraduate taught course 3. Your course starts in September 2023. 4. Have International Fee status, as verified by the University of Dundee

Level of Study: Postdoctorate
Type: Scholarship
Value: £10,000
Length of Study: 1 year
Frequency: Throughout the year
Country of Study: Any country
Closing Date: 31 May
Additional Information: www.dundee.ac.uk/scholarships/2022-23/great-scholarship-malaysia/

For further information contact:

Email: contactus@dundee.ac.uk

GREAT Scholarships – Pakistan

Subjects: Anatomy / Forensic Anthropology / Forensic and Medical Art, Architecture and Urban Planning, Art and Design, Biological/Biomedical Sciences, Biomedical Engineering / Medical Imaging, Business (Accountancy / Economics / Finance / International Business), Civil Engineering / Structural Engineering, Computing / Applied Computing / Data Science / Data Engineering, Dentistry, Education, Electronic Engineering, Energy Petroleum and Mineral Law and Policy, English, Geography / Environmental Science, History, Law, Mathematics, Mechanical Engineering / Industrial Engineering, Medicine, Nursing and Health Sciences, Philosophy, Physics, Politics and International Relations, Psychology, Social Work

Eligibility: You are eligible to apply for the GREAT Scholarship – Pakistan if you 1. Are a passport holder from Pakistan; 2. Have an offer to study a full time, on campus, postgraduate taught programme at the University of Dundee, starting in September 2023; 3. Have International Fee Status, as verified by the University of Dundee.
Level of Study: Postdoctorate
Type: Scholarship
Value: £10,000
Length of Study: 1 year
Frequency: Throughout the year
Country of Study: Any country
Closing Date: 7 May

For further information contact:

Email: contactus@dundee.ac.uk

GREAT Scholarships – Thailand

Subjects: Anatomy / Forensic Anthropology / Forensic and Medical Art, Architecture and Urban Planning, Art and Design, Biological/Biomedical Sciences, Biomedical Engineering / Medical Imaging, Business (Accountancy / Economics / Finance / International Business), Civil Engineering / Structural Engineering, Computing / Applied Computing / Data Science / Data Engineering, Dentistry, Education, Electronic Engineering, Energy Petroleum and Mineral Law and Policy, English, Geography / Environmental Science, History, Law, Mathematics, Mechanical Engineering / Industrial Engineering, Medicine, Nursing and Health Sciences, Philosophy, Physics, Politics and International Relations, Psychology, Social Work

Eligibility: You are eligible to apply for the GREAT Scholarship – Thailand if you 1. Are a passport holder from Thailand; 2. Have an offer to study a full time, on campus, postgraduate taught programme at the University of Dundee, starting in September 2023; 3. Have International Fee Status, as verified by the University of Dundee.
Level of Study: Postdoctorate
Type: Scholarship
Value: £10,000
Length of Study: 1 year
Frequency: Throughout the year
Country of Study: Any country
Closing Date: 7 May

For further information contact:

Email: contactus@dundee.ac.uk

GREAT Scholarships-China

Subjects: Anatomy / Forensic Anthropology / Forensic and Medical Art, Architecture and Urban Planning, Art and Design, Biological/Biomedical Sciences, Biomedical Engineering / Medical Imaging, Business (Accountancy / Economics / Finance / International Business), Civil Engineering / Structural Engineering, Computing / Applied Computing / Data Science / Data Engineering, Education, Electronic Engineering, Energy Petroleum and Mineral Law and Policy, English, Geography / Environmental Science, History, Law, Mathematics, Mechanical Engineering / Industrial Engineering, Nursing and Health Sciences, Philosophy, Physics, Politics and International Relations, Psychology, Social Work

Eligibility: You are eligible to apply for the GREAT Scholarship – China if you 1. Are a passport holder from mainland China; 2. Have an offer to study a full time, on campus, postgraduate taught programme at the University of Dundee, starting in September 2023; 3. Have International Fee Status, as verified by the University of Dundee.

Level of Study: Postgraduate
Type: Scholarship
Value: £10,000
Length of Study: 1 year
Frequency: Throughout the year
Country of Study: Any country
Closing Date: 7 May

For further information contact:

Email: contactus@dundee.ac.uk

Humanitarian Scholarship – The University of Dundee

Eligibility: The scholarship will fund up to 2 undergraduate awards and up to 8 postgraduate taught awards for eligible students. All applicants for this scholarship must be able to evidence their Refugee or Asylum Status, or Humanitarian Protection as recognised by the 1951 UN Convention on the Status of Refugees. Applicants must also hold an offer to study either: a full time, on campus, undergraduate course at the University of Dundee, starting in September 2023, (excluding Medicine, Dentistry, Education and Social Work courses) or a full time, on campus, postgraduate taught course at the University of Dundee, starting in September 2023 or January 2024.

Level of Study: Postgraduate
Type: Scholarship
Value: Up to £40,000, per year
Length of Study: Duration of study

Frequency: Annual
Country of Study: Any country
Application Procedure: forms.office.com/Pages/ResponsePage.aspx?id=OTEyrjoJKk2Bpl0zS82QGWQzRY2jNVhFnbBwPVVK97NUMk5MUTVSSEVBWExHVUFTU05QSE0xMEhUWCQlQCN0PWcu%20
Closing Date: 29 April
Additional Information: www.dundee.ac.uk/scholarships/2022-23/humanitarian-scholarship/

For further information contact:

Email: scholarships@dundee.ac.uk

International College Dundee Progressing with Excellence Scholarship (Taught Postgraduate)

Eligibility: To be considered for this scholarship, applicants must meet ALL the following eligibility criteria: 1. Classified by the University of Dundee and Oxford International Education Group (OIEG) as an international student for tuition fees. 2. Students must have completed an ICD full time programme (online or on campus) AND be progressing to a full time (180 credits per year), on campus UoD programme. 3. Students must achieve one of the following during the study of their full programme at ICD: overall, achieve an 'A' grade average in their academic performance show a significant uplift in academic performance during their time at ICD and achieve excellent ('A' grade average) academic performance in the final term.

Level of Study: Postgraduate
Type: Scholarship
Value: Up to £6000 per year
Frequency: Annual
Country of Study: United Kingdom
Additional Information: https://www.dundee.ac.uk/scholarships/2022-23/icd-progressing-with-excellence-tpg/

For further information contact:

Email: icd@dundee.ac.uk

Master of Business Administration Programme

Length of Study: 2 years; 5 years
Application Procedure: Applicants must complete an application form supplying £25 fee, two academic references, official transcripts and evidence of English Language proficiency if applicable

For further information contact:

Tel: (44) 1382 344300
Fax: (44) 1382 228578
Email: cepmlp@dundee.ac.uk

Steve Weston and Trust Scholarships

Eligibility: To be eligible for this scholarship, applicants must: 1. Already hold an Honours degree in Law, Economics, Geology, Petroleum, or Mining Engineering, Finance at 2nd class upper level or above. Consideration will also be given to applicants with other academic backgrounds who clearly explain their motivation for undertaking the relevant LLM, outlining any relevant legal work experience. Hold an offer for September 2023 for LLM in International Mineral Law and Policy or LLM in International Oil and Gas Law and Policy. 2. Be able to demonstrate compliance with the University of Dundee English entry requirements. 3. Display intellectual ability and leadership potential. 4. Have a proven track record and potential to rise to positions of influence. 5. Preferably be qualified lawyers having had some post-degree work experience in energy or natural resource development in the government, private sector, or academia. 6. Go on to complete the degree within 12 months. Students from overseas are expected to return to their home country at the end of the period of study.
Level of Study: Postgraduate
Type: Scholarship
Value: Tuition fees (£19,900), living expenses for a single student (£12,600 over 12 monthly payments at £1,050 per month), An arrival allowance (£750) and thesis/internship report allowance (£580).
Frequency: Annual
Country of Study: United Kingdom
Application Procedure: There is no separate application form for the Steve Weston Scholarship.
No. of awards offered: 3
Closing Date: 30 June
Additional Information: www.dundee.ac.uk/scholarships/2022-23/steve-weston/

For further information contact:

Email: a.e.anderson@dundee.ac.uk

Vice Chancellor's Africa Scholarship

Eligibility: To be eligible for an award, you must meet all the following criteria: 1. Have an offer to study: 2. A full time, Undergraduate course excluding any courses in the School of Medicine or the School of Dentistry OR 3. A full time, 180 credit postgraduate taught course over the course of 1 year. If you are studying a 2-year full time postgraduate taught course, you may be eligible for the award in both years. 4. Be domiciled in an African country (please see Key Facts document for full list of eligible countries). 5. Have International fee status as determined by the University of Dundee.
Level of Study: Postgraduate
Type: Scholarship
Value: £5,000 per year
Length of Study: 5 years
Frequency: Annual
Country of Study: United Kingdom
Application Procedure: There is not a separate application form for this scholarship. You must apply to study a course at the University of Dundee first and your eligibility will be assessed as part of your course application. We will notify you in writing if you have received a scholarship.
Additional Information: www.dundee.ac.uk/scholarships/2022-23/vc-africa-scholarship/

For further information contact:

Email: scholarships@dundee.ac.uk

Vice Chancellor's EU Scholarship

Eligibility: To be eligible for an award, you must meet all the following criteria: 1. Have an offer to study: 2. A full time, Undergraduate course excluding any courses in the School of Medicine or the School of Dentistry OR 3. A full time, 180 credit postgraduate taught course over the course of 1 year. If you are studying a 2-year full time postgraduate taught course, you may be eligible for the award in both years. 4. Be domiciled in an EU country (please see Key Facts document for full list of eligible countries).5. Have International fee status as determined by the University of Dundee.
Level of Study: Postgraduate
Type: Scholarship
Value: £5,000 per year
Length of Study: 5 years
Frequency: Annual
Country of Study: Any country
Application Procedure: There is not a separate application form for this scholarship.
Additional Information: www.dundee.ac.uk/scholarships/2022-23/vc-eu-scholarship/

For further information contact:

Email: scholarships@dundee.ac.uk

Vice Chancellor's South Asia Scholarship

Eligibility: To be eligible for an award, you must meet all the following criteria, have an offer to study: 1. A full time, Undergraduate course excluding any courses in the School of Medicine or the School of Dentistry OR 2. A full time, 180 credit postgraduate taught course over the course of 1 year. If you are studying a 2-year full time postgraduate taught course, you may be eligible for the award in both years. 3. Be domiciled in a South Asian country (please see Key Facts document for full list of eligible countries). 4. Have International fee status as determined by the University of Dundee.
Level of Study: Postgraduate
Type: Scholarship
Value: £5,000 per year
Length of Study: 5 years
Frequency: Annual
Country of Study: United Kingdom
Application Procedure: There is not a separate application form for this scholarship. You must apply to study a course at the University of Dundee first and your eligibility will be assessed as part of your course application. We will notify you in writing if you have received a scholarship.
Additional Information: www.dundee.ac.uk/scholarships/2022-23/vc-south-asia-scholarship/

For further information contact:

Email: scholarships@dundee.ac.uk

University of East Anglia (UEA)

Faculty of Arts and Humanities, Faculty of Arts and Humanities, School of Literature and Creative Writing, Norwich NR4 7TJ, United Kingdom.

Tel: (44) 16 0345 6161
Website: www.uea.ac.uk/lit/fellowships
Contact: Fellowship Administrator

The University of East Anglia (UEA) is organized into 23 schools of study encompassing arts and humanities, health, sciences and social sciences. These are supported by central service and administration departments.

Global Talent Fellowships

Purpose: The UEA GCRF Global Talent Fellowships provide the opportunity for international researchers

Eligibility: Applicants must currently be based in an institution outside of the UK, with established or prospective research links to UEA researchers (a letter of recommendation from the host supervisor from UEA, as well as approval from the Head of School or Departmentare both required). To meet the funding conditions of the GCRF, the proposed impact of this research must also comply with requirements for Official Development Assistance (ODA)
Level of Study: Research
Type: Fellowship
Value: £637,000
Length of Study: 3 year
Frequency: Annual
Country of Study: Any country
Additional Information: www.uea.ac.uk/research/fellowships/uea-gcrf-qr-allocation

For further information contact:

Email: rin.international@uea.ac.uk

University of East Anglia International Development Scholarships

Purpose: The University of East Anglia is offering one full fee scholarship for international students towards Masters Degree courses offered by the School of International Development
Eligibility: The scholarships are awarded on the basis of academic excellence (e.g. first class degree) and their personal statement. All applicants are expected to have met the School's English language requirements and been offered and accepted a place on the course by the deadline
Level of Study: Postgraduate
Type: Scholarship
Value: £8000
Frequency: Annual
Study Establishment: University of East Anglia
Country of Study: United Kingdom
Application Procedure: app.geckoform.com/public/?_ga=2.147703543.1740700930.1644653189-20842921.1643555871#/modern/FOEU014bSzpJEl5g
No. of awards offered: 3
Closing Date: 31 May
Funding: Corporation
Additional Information: scholarship-positions.com/university-of-east-anglia-international-development-scholarships-in-uk/2022/01/06/

For further information contact:

Email: admissions@uea.ac.uk

University of Edinburgh

Old College South Bridge, Edinburgh EH8 9YL, United Kingdom.

Tel: (44) 131 650 2159
Email: postgrad@ed.ac.uk
Contact: Grants Management Officer

Alice Brown PhD Scholarships

Purpose: The Alice Brown Scholarship is a new 6-year PhD scholarship offering a programme of advanced study, ongoing research, professional training and development
Eligibility: Citizens of United Kingdom, European Economic Area and Switzerland are eligible to apply. A first class honours degree (or equivalent) in a subject relevant to the studentship OR a taught MSc degree at distinction level in a subject relevant to the studentship. Conditional offers can be made to applicants currently enrolled in a degree programme on the basis of anticipated results. 1. As comprehensive research training is integrated into the programme of this PhD, there will be no automatic preference given to those holding MSc qualifications covering research training. 2. Applications are encouraged from those nearing the end of an undergraduate degree in a subject relevant to the scholarship. 3. Due to constraints on part-time study for international students on visas, this award is only open to nationals of the United Kingdom, countries of the European Economic Area, or Switzerland
Level of Study: Postgraduate
Type: Scholarship
Value: The scholarship covers full payment of PhD tuition fees and provides an annual stipend of £10,000 each year
Length of Study: 6-year PhD programme
Country of Study: United Kingdom
Application Procedure: Applicants are invited to submit a current CV, a short research proposal/idea (max. 1,000 words) and a personal statement of up to 500 words explaining their suitability for the scholarship in the field to which they are applying
Closing Date: 3 February
Contributor: University of Edinburgh
Additional Information: For more details, please visit https://scholarship-positions.com/university-of-edinburgh-alice-brown-phd-international-scholarships-in-uk/2021/12/11/ https://www.sps.ed.ac.uk/study/prospective/postgraduate-research-programmes/scholarships/sps-awards/alice-brown-phd-scholarships-pir

For further information contact:

Email: pgresearch.sps@ed.ac.uk

Carnegie PhD Scholarships

Eligibility: Applicants must hold a First Class Honours undergraduate degree from an eligible Scottish University. This First-Class Honours degree must be in a subject related to the field of the proposed doctoral studies. Students in their final year of an undergraduate degree who are expected to obtain a First-Class Honours degree may also apply, but they will be required to withdraw from the competition if they fail to graduate with a First. Please note that no exemptions are made to this requirement except in faculties which do not award Honours e.g. Medicine, where the equivalent standard will be expected.
Level of Study: Doctorate
Type: Scholarship
Value: cover tuition fees, a maintenance allowance and a research expenses allowance
Length of Study: 3 years
Frequency: Annual
Country of Study: United Kingdom
Closing Date: 28 February
Additional Information: www.ed.ac.uk/student-funding/postgraduate/uk-eu/other-funding/carnegie-trust

For further information contact:

Email: admin@carnegie-trust.org

Clinical Management of Pain Scholarship

Eligibility: Applicants must be in possession of an unconditional offer by the scholarship deadline of 14th July 2023 to be considered for funding and intend to begin their PGCert/PGDip/MSc in the Clinical Management of Pain (Online Distance Learning) in 2023–2024.
Level of Study: Postgraduate
Type: Scholarship
Value: Up to £860 towards tuition fees
Frequency: Annual
Country of Study: Any country
Closing Date: 2 August
Additional Information: www.ed.ac.uk/student-funding/postgraduate/e-learning/painnew

Commonwealth Distance Learning Scholarships

Eligibility: To apply for a Commonwealth Distance Learning Scholarship, candidates must: 1. Be a citizen of or be granted refugee status from an eligible Commonwealth country, or be a British Protected Person 2. Be permanently and continually resident in an eligible Commonwealth country 3. Hold a first degree of at least upper second class (2:1) standard. A lower qualification and sufficient relevant experience may be considered in certain cases 4. All candidates must provide at least one reference 5. All candidates must hold an offer to start their chosen course of study in 2023.

Level of Study: Postgraduate
Type: Scholarship
Value: Each scholarship will cover full tuition fees
Length of Study: 3 years
Frequency: Annual
Country of Study: Any country
Closing Date: 15 March
Additional Information: www.ed.ac.uk/student-funding/postgraduate/e-learning/common-distance-learning

Commonwealth Online Global Health Scholarships at University of Edinburgh

Purpose: The University's Global Health Academy has been awarded 10 fully funded studentships across five online Masters programmes within the domain of Global Health
Eligibility: The scholarships will be awarded to a candidate who is accepted for admission on to an eligible programme (see above) and who is a citizen of and resident in one of the following developing Commonwealth countries
Level of Study: Postdoctorate
Type: Scholarship
Value: full tuition fee
Frequency: Annual
Country of Study: United Kingdom
No. of awards offered: 5
Closing Date: 12 April
Funding: Foundation
Additional Information: www.ed.ac.uk/student-funding/postgraduate/e-learning/commglobalhealth

Commonwealth Shared Scholarship Scheme

Eligibility: To apply for these scholarships, you must: 1. Be a citizen of or have been granted refugee status by an eligible Commonwealth country, or be a British Protected Person 2. Be permanently resident in an eligible Commonwealth country 3. Be available to start your academic studies in the UK, or remotely if required, by the start of the UK academic year in September/October 2023 4. By September 2023, hold a first degree of at least upper second class (2:1) standard, or a second class degree and a relevant postgraduate qualification (usually a Master's degree). 5. Not have studied or

worked for one (academic) year or more in a high income country 6. Be unable to afford to study at a UK university without this scholarship Have provided all supporting documentation in the required format

Level of Study: Postgraduate
Type: Scholarship
Length of Study: 1 year
Frequency: Annual
Country of Study: United Kingdom
Application Procedure: Application for the Commonwealth Shared Scholarship Scheme should be made through the Commonwealth Scholarships Commission's Electronic Application System (EAS).
Closing Date: 20 December
Additional Information: www.ed.ac.uk/student-funding/postgraduate/international/other-funding/commonwealth-shared

DeepMind PhD Scholarships

Eligibility: The scholarships will be awarded to applicants who: 1. are residents of a country and/or region underrepresented in AI; 2. identify as women including cis and trans people and non-binary or gender fluid people who identify in a significant way as women or female; 3. and/or identify as Black or other minority ethnicity;
Type: Scholarship
Study Establishment: Annual stipend of £15,609 per annum
Country of Study: United Kingdom
Contributor: 4 years
Additional Information: www.ed.ac.uk/informatics/postgraduate/fees/research-scholarships/deepmind-phd-scholarships

For further information contact:

Email: neil.heatley@ed.ac.uk

Edinburgh Dental Institute MSc Scholarship

Eligibility: Applications will be considered from both UK and overseas eligible candidates wishing to apply for a 3-year part time taught Masters in Restorative Dentistry by online learning. PG Development courses (PPD) and CPD (Continuing Professional Development) courses are excluded from the scholarship.
Value: The award will cover 10% of the total tuition fee
Length of Study: 1 year
Country of Study: United Kingdom
Closing Date: 31 July

Additional Information: www.ed.ac.uk/student-funding/ postgraduate/international/medicine-vet-medicine/edinburgh-dental

Edinburgh Doctoral College Scholarships

Eligibility: The awards are open to UK and overseas students applying to start their first year of study for an on-campus research degree. Applicants must have already applied for admission to a full-time or part-time on campus PhD research programme of study at the University. We encourage applicants who wish to apply for this scholarship to make contact with their academic school regarding any admission deadlines.
Level of Study: Doctorate
Type: Scholarship
Value: £15,609p.a.
Length of Study: 4 years
Frequency: Annual
Country of Study: United Kingdom
Additional Information: www.ed.ac.uk/student-funding/ postgraduate/international/other-funding/doctoral-college

Edinburgh Global Online Distance Learning Masters Scholarship

Eligibility: See Website
Level of Study: Postgraduate
Type: Scholarship
Value: Each scholarship will cover full tuition fees
Length of Study: Three years
Frequency: Annual
Country of Study: Any country
Application Procedure: The online scholarship application form is located in EUCLID and can be accessed via MyEd our web based information portal at www.myed.ed.ac.uk
Closing Date: 1 June
Additional Information: www.ed.ac.uk/student-funding/ postgraduate/e-learning/online-masters

For further information contact:

Email: studentfunding@ed.ac.uk

Edinburgh Global Online Distance Learning Scholarships

Purpose: The University of Edinburgh will offer a number of scholarships for distance learning Master's programmes offered by the University

Eligibility: 1. Scholarships will be available for students commencing in session 2023–24 in any distance learning Masters programme offered by the University. Applicants must be nationals of the eligible countries. 2. Applicants should already have been offered a place at the University of Edinburgh and should have firmly accepted that offer or be intending to do so.
Level of Study: Postdoctorate
Type: Scholarship
Length of Study: 3 years
Frequency: Annual
Country of Study: Any country
Application Procedure: Eligible applicants should complete an online scholarship application. The scholarship deadline is 1 June.
No. of awards offered: 12
Closing Date: 1 June
Funding: Private
Contributor: University of Edinburgh
Additional Information: www.scholars4dev.com/2719/ distance-learning-scholarships-at-university-of-edinburgh/

For further information contact:

Email: family.medicine@ed.ac.uk

Edinburgh Global Online Learning Masters Scholarships

Eligibility: Scholarships will be available for students commencing any online part-time learning Masters programme offered by the University in session 2023–2024. Applicants must be nationals and residents of the following countries: Eligible countries for this scholarship are based on the categories 'Least Developed Countries' and 'Other low income Countries' as stated by the Organisation for Economic Corporation and Development Assistance Committee. Full list can be found at: DAC-List-of-ODA-Recipients-for- 10581reporting-2021-flows.pdf (oecd.org)
Level of Study: Postgraduate
Type: Scholarship
Value: Each scholarship will cover full tuition fees
Frequency: Annual
Country of Study: United Kingdom
Closing Date: 1 June
Additional Information: www.ed.ac.uk/student-funding/ postgraduate/e-learning/online-masters

Edinburgh Global Research Scholarship

Purpose: These awards are designed to attract high quality overseas research students to the University of Edinburgh

Eligibility: 1. Must be a full-time Ph.D. student pursuing research work on any course of their choice from the university. 2. Must be an international student liable to pay the tuition fee. 3. Must be of outstanding academic merit. 3. students who receive upper second class in Bachelor's and Master's degrees are also considered for this scholarship, due to competition the chance of receiving the scholarship is broadened if they have better academic results. 4. Must provide proof of nationality, residence, the proposed field of study, and personal information. 5. Must not hold any other scholarship at the time of applying for this scholarship.

Level of Study: Postgraduate

Type: Scholarship

Value: Each scholarship will cover the difference between the tuition fee for a United Kingdom/European Union postgraduate student and that chargeable to an overseas postgraduate student. The awards do not cover maintenance expenses

Length of Study: Three years

Frequency: Annual

Country of Study: United Kingdom

No. of awards offered: 30

Closing Date: 17 February

Additional Information: For more details on this award please contact Scholarships and Student Funding Services. Work: (44) 131 651 4070; Email: studentfunding@ed.ac.uk www.ed.ac.uk/student-funding/postgraduate/international/global/research

For further information contact:

Tel: (44) 131 651 4070
Email: studentfunding@ed.ac.uk

Glenmore Medical Postgraduate Scholarship

Purpose: Two scholarships are available for postgraduate full-time one year Masters study for eligible Human Medical programmes offered by the University in the upcoming academic session

Eligibility: The scholarship will be awarded on the basis of academic merit. Candidates must have, or expect to obtain, the overseas equivalent of a United Kingdom first-class honours degree

Level of Study: Postgraduate

Type: Scholarship

Value: Each scholarship will cover full overseas tuition fees for eligible programmes, and will be tenable for one academic year.

Length of Study: One academic year

Frequency: Annual

Country of Study: United Kingdom

Application Procedure: Please check website for more details www.ed.ac.uk/student-funding/pgt-application

No. of awards offered: 2

Closing Date: 29 May

Additional Information: www.ed.ac.uk/student-funding/postgraduate/international/medicine-vet-medicine/glenmore

For further information contact:

The University of Edinburgh, Old College, South Bridge, Edinburgh EH8 9YL, United Kingdom.

Tel: (44) 131 651 4070
Email: studentfunding@ed.ac.uk

GREAT Scholarships

Eligibility: At the University of Edinburgh, the Scholarships will be awarded to nationals and residents of China, India, Mexico and Turkey who are accepted for admission on a full-time basis for an eligible one-year on campus postgraduate Masters programme of study. The tables below set out the eligibility criteria per programme and the applicable scholarship application which can be located within MyEd.

Value: £10,000

Length of Study: 1 year

Frequency: Annual

Country of Study: United Kingdom

Application Procedure: In order to gain access to the scholarship application system applicants must have applied for admission to the University of Edinburgh. Please note that, following the submission of an application for admission, it can take up to ten working days for all system checks to be completed and for access to be granted. The online scholarship application form is located in EUCLID and can be accessed via MyEd our web based information portal at www.myed.ed.ac.uk

Closing Date: 31 March

Additional Information: www.ed.ac.uk/student-funding/postgraduate/international/region/asia/great-2022

Haywood Doctoral Scholarship

Purpose: To offer Haywood Doctoral Scholarship to an outstanding doctoral research candidate in History of Art

Type: Scholarship

Value: As an international student, you will receive a reduction in tuition fees equivalent to the Home/European Union rate if successful

Country of Study: United Kingdom

Closing Date: 2 March

Additional Information: www.scholarshipsads.com/haywood-doctoral-scholarship-international-applicants-uk-2018/

For further information contact:

Tel: (44) 1214 143 344
Email: calpg-research@contacts.bham.ac.uk

Informatics Global PhD Scholarships

Eligibility: Applications will be accepted from all candidates; there are no restrictions based on nationality or domicile. Candidates should be in receipt of, or expected to obtain, a high academic award from their most recent degree. In practice, this means a 1st class UK degree or a distinction at UK Masters level in a relevant discipline. Students with non-UK qualifications should check the equivalence of their degrees. Candidates must also meet certain minimum requirements for English language competency.
Level of Study: Doctorate
Type: Scholarship
Value: A stipend of £15,609 per year; all tuition fees, including overseas fees if applicable; an additional research support fund of £2,000 per year for the first three years
Length of Study: 3 years
Frequency: Annual
Country of Study: United Kingdom
Closing Date: 28 January
Additional Information: www.ed.ac.uk/informatics/post graduate/fees/research-scholarships/informatics-global-phd-scholarships

For further information contact:

Email: studentsystems@ed.ac.uk

Institute for Advanced Studies in the Humanities Postdoctoral Fellowships

Subjects: We welcome applications on all topics and in all areas of the arts, humanities and social sciences to continue IASH's traditional interdisciplinary work.
Purpose: Applications are invited for postdoctoral bursaries from candidates in any area of the Arts, Humanities and Social Sciences.
Eligibility: Applicants must have been awarded a doctorate at the time of application, and normally within the last three years (i.e. you should have graduated between 2018 and 2021, although earlier graduates may be eligible if they have taken significant career breaks since completing their doctorate; if you have not yet graduated, you must be able to produce a transcript, testamur, or a letter of completion/eligibility to graduate as part of your application; you do not need to have actually graduated at the time you apply). You should not have held a permanent position at a university, or a previous Fellowship at the Institute for Advanced Studies

in the Humanities. Those who have held temporary and/or short-term appointments are eligible to apply. If you have taken parental leave or other time away from academia, this will not count towards the three-year limit, but we ask that you provide brief details of why and for how long you were not working.
Level of Study: Postdoctorate
Type: Fellowship
Value: £1,300 per month
Length of Study: 10 months
Frequency: Annual
Study Establishment: Institute for Advanced Studies in the Humanities
Country of Study: Any country
Application Procedure: Online applications only www.iash.ed.ac.uk/
No. of awards offered: 12 to 15
Closing Date: 29 April
Funding: Commercial, Private
Contributor: University of Edinburgh
No. of applicants last year: 200 Above
Additional Information: https://www.iash.ed.ac.uk/postdoc toral-fellowships-2023-24

For further information contact:

The University of Edinburgh, Hope Park Square, Edinburgh EH8 9NW, United Kingdom.

Tel: (44) 131 650 4671
Email: iash@ed.ac.uk

LLM in European Law Scholarship

Eligibility: Any applicant to the LLM in European Law.
Level of Study: Postgraduate
Type: Scholarship
Value: Covers the full Home (UK) or International/EU tuition fee rate for 2023–24
Frequency: Annual
Country of Study: United Kingdom
No. of awards offered: 1
Closing Date: 1 May
Additional Information: www.ed.ac.uk/student-funding/postgraduate/uk-eu/humanities/law/llm-in-european

National Health Service Education for Scotland Primary Care Ophthalmology Scholarship

Eligibility: The scholarships will be awarded to students who are accepted for admission on to the online distance learning MSc in Primary Care Ophthalmology at the University of

Edinburgh. Applicants should already have been offered a place at the University of Edinburgh and should have firmly accepted that offer or be intending to do so

Type: Scholarship

Value: The scholarship will have a total value of 50% of the course fees

Country of Study: United Kingdom

Closing Date: 27 July

Additional Information: For further information, please contact Scholarships and Financial Support Team. Work: (44) 131 651 4070; Email: Notfound in dash bord mailto: studentfunding@ed.ac.uk

For further information contact:

Email: studentfunding@ed.ac.uk

Perfect Storms: Leverhulme Doctoral Scholarships

Level of Study: Doctorate

Type: Scholarship

Value: Full fees, living and research costs

Length of Study: 3 years

Frequency: Annual

Study Establishment: University of Edinburgh

Country of Study: Scotland

Contributor: The Leverhulme Trusts

No. of awards given last year: 5

For further information contact:

Email: studentfunding@ed.ac.uk

PhD Social Work Scholarship at University of Edinburgh in United Kingdom

Purpose: This award is available to students intending to commence PhD Social Work study in September on either a full-time or part-time basis

Eligibility: Citizens of all nationalities are eligible to apply. If English is not your first language then you will need to show that your English language skills are at a high enough level to succeed in your studies

Level of Study: Postgraduate

Type: Scholarship

Value: One award covering tuition fees at the Home/European Union fee rate, a maintenance stipend of £14,000 and a research grant of £500 is on offer to applicants for PhD Social Work in the School of Social and Political Science

Frequency: Annual

Study Establishment: Social Work study

Country of Study: Any country

Application Procedure: The online scholarship application form is located in EUCLID and can be accessed via MyEd our web-based information portal. www.myed.ed.ac.uk/

Closing Date: 1 March

For further information contact:

Email: GradSchool.HCA@ed.ac.uk

PhD studentship in Predicting Higher-Order Biomarker Interactions using Machine Learning

Eligibility: 1. Minimum of 2:1 in first degree and/or Master's degree in physics/ mathematics/ statistics/ computer science or similar. 2. Proficiency in English (both oral and written). 3. Advanced programming skills (Python, Pytorch or equivalent).4. Excellent verbal and written communication skills, both in terms of informal discussion and formal presentations. 5. Biomedical motivation. 6. Ability to work effectively and efficiently in a team.

Level of Study: Doctorate

Type: Studentship

Value: Full time PhD tuition fees for a overseas student £24,700 per annum. A tax free stipend of GBP £15,609 per year. Additional programme costs of £1000 per year.

Length of Study: 4 years

Frequency: Annual

Country of Study: United Kingdom

Closing Date: 23 February

Additional Information: www.ed.ac.uk/informatics/post graduate/fees/research-scholarships/research-grant-funding/ phd-studentship-predicting-higher-order-biomark

Polish School of Medicine Memorial Fund Scholarships

Purpose: The scholarship enables medical scientists at the outset of their careers to undertake a period of further study or research at the University's Medical School and return to Poland

Eligibility: Applications will be considered from eligible candidates wishing to apply for a 1 year taught Masters programme/ Masters by research offered at The University of Edinburgh College of Medicine or a Masters by distance learning provided that they have the full support of their Head of Department and Polish Medical University authorities. The programme is open to Polish doctors and postgraduate medical scientists 1. in their early career (usually within 10 years of their medical graduation - MB ChB equivalent) 2. working in Polish Medical Academies/Universities and Research Institutes 3. with excellent mastery of English; and 4. who are committed to the

further development of medical research expertise in Poland.
Level of Study: Postgraduate
Type: Scholarship
Value: cover the tuition fees
Length of Study: One year
Frequency: Annual
Country of Study: Any country
Application Procedure: Eligible applicants should complete an online scholarship application
Closing Date: 15 June
Additional Information: www.ed.ac.uk/student-funding/postgraduate/uk-eu/medicine-vet-medicine/polish

For further information contact:

The University of Edinburgh, Old College, South Bridge, Edinburgh EH8 9YL, United Kingdom.

Tel: (44) 131 651 4070
Email: studentfunding@ed.ac.uk

President's Fund, Edinburgh Association of University Women

Eligibility: 1. Studdents must be in their final year of study and experiencing financial hardship. 2. Awards are not given for courses of one year's duration (undergraduate or postgraduate) 3. Awards are not given for access courses, diploma courses nor for certificate courses 4. Awards are not given for study or work overseas nor for tuition fees.
Level of Study: Postgraduate
Type: Scholarship
Value: £300 to £800
Length of Study: 1 year
Frequency: Annual
Country of Study: United Kingdom
Application Procedure: Applicants must request, complete and sign the application form. The printed form must be received by the Hon Secretary duly completed, dated, signed by the applicant and accompanied by two signed academic references. The application form and the references are to be posted to the Hon Secretary to the address specified in the application form. Email applications are not accepted.
No. of awards offered: 1
Closing Date: 8 October
Additional Information: www.ed.ac.uk/student-funding/hardship-funding/presidents-fund

For further information contact:

Email: eileencbrownlie2706@gmail.com

Principal Career Development PhD Scholarship

Purpose: To attract the best and brightest PhD students, the University seeks to offer not only unparalleled research facilities and superb supervision, but also to provide development opportunities which will support our research students as they progress beyond their PhD, through an innovative programme of integrated research, training, and career development
Type: Scholarship
Value: Each scholarship covers the United Kingdom/European Union rate of tuition fee as well as a stipend of £15,000
Country of Study: United Kingdom
Closing Date: 1 February
Additional Information: For further information, please contact Scholarships and Financial Support Team, phone: 0131 651 4070, email: mailto: studentfunding@ed.ac.uk

For further information contact:

Tel: (44) 131 651 4070
Email: studentfunding@ed.ac.uk

Shell Centenary Scholarships and Shell Centenary Chevening Scholarships at Edinburgh

Eligibility: Students from countries that are not present or applicant members of the Organization for Economic Co-operation and Development (OECD). Candidates should normally be aged 20–35, be resident in one of the non-OECD countries and be intending to return to the country concerned at the end of the period of study. They should normally already hold a degree equivalent to a United Kingdom First Class (Honours) Degree or be expecting to obtain such a degree before the start of their proposed course
Level of Study: Postgraduate
Type: Scholarship
Value: The scholarships covers tuition fees, accommodation, maintenance costs and a return airfare for the scholarship holder
Length of Study: 1 year
Frequency: Annual
Study Establishment: University of Edinburgh
Country of Study: Scotland
Application Procedure: Applicants must apply separately for admission to the University of Edinburgh making a clear statement that they wish to be considered for a Shell Scholarship
Closing Date: 1 March
No. of awards given last year: 6

For further information contact:

Email: scholarships@ed.ac.uk

The Anne Rowling Clinic Regenerative Neurology Scholarships

Purpose: Masters scholarships for applicants commencing Stem Cells and Translational Neurology programmes in the academic year
Eligibility: The scholarships will be awarded to applicants who are accepted for admission on to the online learning postgraduate Certificate, Diploma, or Masters Stem Cell and Translational Neurology programme at the University of Edinburgh. Students who are already enrolled on an eligible programme of study may also apply but if they are currently in receipt of a scholarship and still utilising it they will not be offered another.
Level of Study: Postgraduate
Type: Scholarship
Value: One International Anne Rowling Clinic Regenerative Neurology Scholarship will cover 60 credits towards your module fees. Two Anne Rowling Clinic Regenerative Neurology Scholarships will cover 30 credits worth of course fees.
Frequency: Annual
Country of Study: United Kingdom
Application Procedure: Eligible applicants should complete an online scholarship application. Website link is www.ed.ac.uk/student-funding/postgraduate/e-learning/regenerative-neurology
No. of awards offered: 1
Closing Date: 2 August
Additional Information: For further information, please visit www.ed.ac.uk/student-funding/postgraduate/e-learning/regenerative-neurology

For further information contact:

Email: studentfunding@ed.ac.uk

The Kirby Laing International Scholarships

Eligibility: The scholarship will be awarded to students who have applied for admission on a full-time basis for a one year postgraduate Masters programme of study within the School of Divinity commencing in the 2023–2024 academic year.
Level of Study: Postgraduate
Type: Scholarship
Value: £12,000.
Length of Study: 1 year
Frequency: Annual
Country of Study: United Kingdom
Closing Date: 6 April

Additional Information: www.ed.ac.uk/student-funding/postgraduate/international/humanities/divinity/kirby-laing

For further information contact:

Email: Divinity.PG@ed.ac.uk

The Lt. Col Jack Wishart Scholarship

Eligibility: Eligible programmes of study: 1. Any programme of study in the School of Chemistry 2. Final year undergraduate students studying MBChB 3. Postgraduate students in the Edinburgh Medical School.
Level of Study: Postgraduate
Type: Scholarship
Value: Up to £500 per academic year.
Length of Study: Two academic years
Frequency: Annual
Country of Study: United Kingdom
Application Procedure: The online scholarship application form is located in EUCLID and can be accessed via MyEd our web based information portal at www.myed.ed.ac.uk
No. of awards offered: 10
Closing Date: 1 June
Additional Information: www.ed.ac.uk/student-funding/hardship-funding/wishart#:~:text=The%20Lt%20Col%20Jack%20Wishart%20Scholarship%20has%20been%20amended%20with,of%20the%20Covid%2D19%20pandemic.

For further information contact:

Email: studentfunding@ed.ac.uk

The Rev Dr Norma P Robertson Scholarship

Eligibility: The Scholarship will be awarded to student(s) accepted onto full-time or part-time postgraduate programmes in Christian History, Bible and Theology related subjects, taught in The School of Divinity, who have an excellent academic record. The scholarship will be awarded on the basis of academic merit. Candidates must have, or expect to obtain, a UK 2:1 honours degree in a relevant discipline or the international equivalent.
Level of Study: Postgraduate
Type: Scholarship
Value: The scholarship will have a maximum value of £7,500
Frequency: Annual
Country of Study: United Kingdom
Closing Date: 2 April
Additional Information: www.ed.ac.uk/student-funding/postgraduate/e-learning/wishart

U

For further information contact:

Email: studentfunding@ed.ac.uk

The Sanders Scholarship in Clinical Ophthalmology

Purpose: University of Edinburgh is offering twenty four scholarships for online distance learning. Scholarships are available for pursuing online distance learning masters degree programmes

Eligibility: Applicants must either be 1. medical or surgical trainees registered with the General Medical Council and working in a recognised training programme in the NHS, or, 2. other health professionals involved in delivering eye care in the NHS (e.g., community and hospital optometrists, orthoptists, ophthalmic nurses, ophthalmic science practitioners, and other ophthalmic allied health professionals).

Level of Study: Graduate

Type: Scholarship

Value: £1,000

Country of Study: United Kingdom

Application Procedure: Complete an online EUCLID application for the MSc in Primary Care Ophthalmology or the ChM (Master of Surgery) in Clinical Ophthalmology – instructions on full application process can be found on the University's degree finder pages for the MSc PCO and the ChM CO. Wait for decision on application via EUCLID. If eligible to join the course, you will be given a conditional or unconditional offer, which you must accept prior to applying for a scholarship. Email a personal statement to declare your wish to apply for a scholarship to chm.info@ed.ac.uk

Closing Date: 1 June

Funding: Private

Additional Information: www.ed.ac.uk/student-funding/postgraduate/e-learning/sanders

For further information contact:

Edinburgh Surgery Online, Rooms G10/G11, Simon Laurie House, 196 Canongate, Edinburgh EH8 8AQ, United Kingdom.

Tel: (44) 131 651 4932
Email: sarah.jones@ed.ac.uk

University of Edinburgh - KU Leuven PhD Studentship

Eligibility: The studentship will be awarded competitively and is open to UK, EU and overseas students applying to start their PhD programme of study

Level of Study: Doctorate

Type: Studentship

Value: Full tuition fees, a stipend and provision of research costs

Length of Study: 4 years

Frequency: Annual

Study Establishment: The University of Edinburgh

Country of Study: Any country

Application Procedure: Applicants are required to provide the following information saved WITHIN ONE PDF FILE. 1. Personal statement about their research interests and their reasons for applying for the specified project Academic CV 2. Two signed referee letters of reference. Candidates are required to submit at least 1 academic reference. The second reference may be academic or professional. 3. Degree transcripts (translations should be provided if the originals are not in English).; Applicants wishing to apply for more than one project must submit an application for each project. Where information is missing, the application may not be considered.

No. of awards offered: 1

Closing Date: 26 February

Additional Information: www.ed.ac.uk/student-funding/postgraduate/uk-eu/humanities/cross-disciplinary/ku-leuven

For further information contact:

Email: pgawards@ed.ac.uk

Wellcome Trust 4-Year PhD Programme Studentships

Purpose: This scheme offers graduates outstanding training in scientific research

Eligibility: Studentship on one of Wellcome's four-year programmes if you're a graduate or student who has, or expects to obtain, a degree (or equivalent for EU and overseas candidates) in a relevant subject.

Level of Study: Postgraduate

Type: Studentship

Value: Studentship stipend, fees and other costs

Length of Study: 4 years

Frequency: Annual

Study Establishment: The University of Edinburgh

Country of Study: Scotland

Additional Information: wellcome.ac.uk/funding/schemes/four-year-phd-programmes-studentships-basic-scientists

University of Essex

Graduate Admissions Office, University of Essex, Wivenhoe Park, Colchester C04 3SQ, United Kingdom.

Tel: (44) 12 0687 2719
Email: pgadmit@essex.ac.uk

Website: www.essex.ac.uk
Contact: V Bartholomew, CRM Operations Manager

The University of Essex is one of the United Kingdom's leading academic institutions, ranked 10th nationally for research and 7th for teaching. It offers degrees and research opportunities across 19 academic departments (including government and sociology, which both have 6-star research ratings) and numerous research centres of world renown.

Academic Excellence International Masters Scholarship

Purpose: University of Essex is inviting applications for academic excellence international masters scholarship
Eligibility: See Website
Level of Study: Masters Degree, Postgraduate
Type: Scholarship
Value: scholarship worth up to £5,000, paid as a discount on your tuition fee.
Length of Study: first year of Masters study
Frequency: Annual
Study Establishment: Scholarships are awarded in the fields offered by the university
Country of Study: United Kingdom
Application Procedure: If you meet all the eligibility criteria, you will automatically be awarded this scholarship
Closing Date: October
Additional Information: www.essex.ac.uk/scholarships/academic-excellence-international-masters-scholars

For further information contact:

Wivenhoe Park, Colchester CO4 3SQ, United Kingdom.

Tel: (44) 1206 873333
Email: enquiries@essex.ac.uk

Academic Excellence Senior Status Law Scholarship

Purpose: These scholarships are restricted to students who are overseas fee payers and are entirely self-funded
Eligibility: visit website
Level of Study: Postgraduate
Type: Scholarship
Value: £3,000
Frequency: Annual
Country of Study: Any country
Closing Date: 15 July

Additional Information: www.essex.ac.uk/scholarships/academic-excellence-senior-status-law-scholarship

For further information contact:

Wivenhoe Park, Colchester CO4 3SQ, United Kingdom.

Tel: (44) 1206 873333
Email: enquiries@essex.ac.uk

Africa Postgraduate Regional Scholarship

Purpose: These scholarships are restricted to students who are overseas fee payers and are entirely self-funded
Eligibility: visit website
Level of Study: Postgraduate
Type: Scholarship
Value: scholarship of £4,500, paid as a discount on your tuition fee.
Frequency: Annual
Country of Study: Any country
Closing Date: 16 September
Additional Information: www.essex.ac.uk/scholarships/africa-scholarship-programme

For further information contact:

Wivenhoe Park, Colchester CO4 3SQ, United Kingdom.

Tel: (44) 1206 873333
Email: enquiries@essex.ac.uk

Arts and Humanities Research Council Department of Sociology Studentships

Purpose: To support students on a research programme
Eligibility: Open to United Kingdom or European Union applicants
Level of Study: Postgraduate
Type: Scholarship
Value: UK students - fees plus maintenance; European Union students - fees
Frequency: Annual
Study Establishment: University of Essex
Country of Study: United Kingdom
Contributor: AHRC

For further information contact:

Email: pgeduc@leeds.ac.uk

U

Arts and Humanities Research Council Research Preparations Masters Award for Literature, Film, and Theatre Studies

Purpose: To support students undertaking a research preparations in the department
Eligibility: Open to postgraduates offered a place to study in the department
Level of Study: Postgraduate
Type: Award
Value: £10,600 per year maintenance grant
Length of Study: 1 year
Frequency: Annual
Study Establishment: University of Essex
Country of Study: United Kingdom
Application Procedure: Applicants must contact the department concerned

For further information contact:

Email: graduateschool@gold.ac.uk

Chinese-English Translation Scholarships

Subjects: Language and Linguistics
Purpose: If you're an international student studying one of our Chinese-English Translation and Interpreting programmes, you could be eligible for £3,000 through our Chinese-English Scholarship
Eligibility: 1. Be fully self-funding your studies 2. Hold a conditional offer of admission to one of the Chinese-English Translation and Interpreting courses 3. These scholarships are available to international students only.
Level of Study: Postgraduate
Type: Scholarship
Value: £3,000
Country of Study: Any country
No. of awards offered: 5
Closing Date: 31 May
Additional Information: www.essex.ac.uk/scholarships/chinese-english-translation-scholarships

For further information contact:

Wivenhoe Park, Colchester CO4 3SQ, United Kingdom.

Tel: (44) 1206 873333
Email: enquiries@essex.ac.uk

Dowden Scholarship

Purpose: To help highly able students who otherwise would not be able to study at postgraduate level

Eligibility: Applicant must have settled status in the United Kingdom; been 'ordinarily resident' in the United Kingdom for the 3 years before the start of their studentship; not been residing in the United Kingdom wholly or mainly for the purpose of full-time education (United Kingdom and European Union nationals are exempt from this requirement). The Vera Dowden Baldwin Scholarship awards financial assistance to a resident of Dowden Hall who demonstrates financial need. The fund is named in honor of the late Vera Dowden Baldwin '34, whose connection with the University spanned more than seventy years
Level of Study: Postgraduate
Type: Scholarship
Value: Up to £5,000
Frequency: Annual
Study Establishment: University of Essex
Country of Study: United Kingdom
Application Procedure: Indicate on application for doctoral course
Additional Information: Please contact the university for more information www1.essex.ac.uk/fees-and-funding/masters/scholarships/academic-excellence.aspx

Drake Lewis Graduate Scholarship for Art History

Purpose: To support new MA students in art history
Eligibility: Open to postgraduate applicants
Level of Study: Postgraduate
Type: Scholarship
Value: £5,000
Frequency: Annual
Study Establishment: University of Essex
Country of Study: United Kingdom
Funding: Private
Contributor: Drake Lewis
Additional Information: Please check website for further information   www1.essex.ac.uk/fees-and-funding/masters/scholarships/academic-excellence.aspx

For further information contact:

Email: scholarships@essex.ac.uk

Drake Lewis Graduate Scholarship for Health and Human Sciences

Purpose: To support students on full-time masters in public health or health studies
Eligibility: Open to postgraduate applicants
Level of Study: Postgraduate
Type: Scholarship
Value: £5,000

Frequency: Annual
Study Establishment: University of Essex
Country of Study: United Kingdom
Application Procedure: Applicants must contact the department concerned
Funding: Private
Contributor: Drake-Lewis
Additional Information: Please check website for further information www1.essex.ac.uk/fees-and-funding/masters/scholarships/academic-excellence.aspx

For further information contact:

Email: scholarships@essex.ac.uk

Economic and Social Research Council 1+3 Department of Sociology Studentships

Purpose: To support students on a 1 year research training programme
Eligibility: Open to United Kingdom or European Union applicants who have not completed a programme of research training
Level of Study: Postgraduate
Type: Scholarship
Value: UK students – fees plus maintenance; European Union students – fees
Frequency: Annual
Study Establishment: University of Essex
Country of Study: United Kingdom
Application Procedure: See website
Closing Date: March
Contributor: ESRC

For further information contact:

Email: fass-pg@lancaster.ac.uk

Essex Global Partner Scholarship

Purpose: These scholarships are restricted to students who are overseas fee payers and are entirely self-funded
Eligibility: visit website
Level of Study: Postgraduate
Type: Scholarship
Length of Study: first year of Masters study
Frequency: Annual
Country of Study: Any country
No. of awards offered: one
Closing Date: 16 September
Additional Information: www.essex.ac.uk/scholarships/essex-global-partner-scholarship-masters

For further information contact:

Wivenhoe Park, Colchester CO4 3SQ, United Kingdom.

Tel: (44) 1206 873333
Email: enquiries@essex.ac.uk

GREAT Scholarship

Purpose: The GREAT Scholarships programme is a joint initiative by the British Council and the UK Government, designed to attract some of the brightest postgraduates from around the world to study at UK universities.
Eligibility: You can apply if you: 1. hold a passport from an eligible country (Bangladesh, Brunei, China, Nepal or Sri Lanka) 2. are classed as an overseas student for fee purposes 3. already hold an offer (conditional or unconditional) to start a one-year full-time master's degree in October 2023 on the provided subject list 4. have a background of extracurricular activities relating to your chosen subject area and a evidenced interest in combatting climate change when applying from Brunei.
Level of Study: Postgraduate
Type: Scholarship
Value: £10,000
Country of Study: Any country
No. of awards offered: six (6)
Closing Date: 31 May
Contributor: British Council and the GREAT Britain Campaign
Additional Information: www.essex.ac.uk/scholarships/great-scholarship

For further information contact:

Wivenhoe Park, Colchester CO4 3SQ, United Kingdom.

Tel: (44) 1206 873333
Email: GREATScholarships2021@essex.ac.uk

GREAT Scholarship for Justice and Law

Purpose: The GREAT Scholarships for Justice and Law programme is a new joint initiative by the British Council and the Ministry of Justice, designed to attract some of the brightest postgraduates from around the world to study at UK universities in Justice and Law related subjects.
Eligibility: You can apply if you: 1. hold a passport from an eligible country (China) 2. are classed as an overseas student for fee purposes 3. already hold an offer (conditional or unconditional) to start a one-year full-time master's degree in October 2023 on the provided subject list 4. have

a background of extracurricular activities relating to your chosen subject area.

Level of Study: Postgraduate
Type: Scholarship
Value: £10,000
Frequency: Annual
Country of Study: Any country
No. of awards offered: one
Closing Date: 31 May
Contributor: British Council and the GREAT Britain Campaign
Additional Information: www.essex.ac.uk/scholarships/great-scholarship-for-justice-and-law

For further information contact:

Wivenhoe Park, Colchester CO4 3SQ, United Kingdom.

Tel: (44) 1206 873333
Email: GREATScholarships2021@essex.ac.uk

Latin America Scholarship

Purpose: If you're from Latin America or the Caribbean and studying for our MA Translation, Interpreting and Subtitling or our MA Translation and Professional Practice, you could be eligible for £5,000 through our Latin American Scholarship.
Eligibility: You must meet all of the following conditions: 1. be fully self-funding your studies 2. be ordinarily resident in one of the countries specified hold an unconditional offer of admission to the Spanish or Portuguese strands of any of these two programmes: MA Translation, 3. Interpreting & Subtitling; MA Translation and Professional Practice by the closing date for the scholarship
Level of Study: Postgraduate
Type: Scholarship
Value: £5,000
Country of Study: Any country
No. of awards offered: 5
Closing Date: 1 July
Additional Information: www.essex.ac.uk/scholarships/latin-america-scholarship

For further information contact:

Wivenhoe Park, Colchester CO4 3SQ, United Kingdom.

Tel: (44) 1206 873333
Email: enquiries@essex.ac.uk

Masters (PGT) EU Scholarship

Purpose: This scholarship scheme is for postgraduate taught (Masters) EU students studying as a new student in academic year 2023–2024 who are classified as international students for fees purposes.
Eligibility: visit website
Level of Study: Masters Degree, Postgraduate
Type: Scholarship
Value: up to £5,500 automatically deducted from your tuition fees.
Length of Study: first year of study only.
Frequency: Annual
Country of Study: Any country
No. of awards offered: one
Closing Date: 16 September
Additional Information: www.essex.ac.uk/scholarships/masters-pgt-eu-scholarship

For further information contact:

Wivenhoe Park, Colchester CO4 3SQ, United Kingdom.

Tel: (44) 1206 873333
Email: enquiries@essex.ac.uk

Masters Excellence Scholarship

Purpose: These scholarships are restricted to full-time students who are Home fee payers and are entirely self-funded
Eligibility: visit website
Type: Scholarship
Value: 25% discount on your Essex Masters tuition fee
Country of Study: Any country
No. of awards offered: one
Closing Date: 16 September
Additional Information: www.essex.ac.uk/scholarships/masters-excellence-scholarship

For further information contact:

Wivenhoe Park, Colchester CO4 3SQ, United Kingdom.

Tel: (44) 1206 873333
Email: enquiries@essex.ac.uk

Postgraduate Conversion Courses in AI and Data Science Scholarships

Subjects: Data Sciences and Artificial Intelligence

Purpose: The Data Science and AI Scholarship is available to new Home, EU and International Postgraduate Taught (PGT) Masters students taking up a place to study in academic year 2023–24 on the following programmes
Eligibility: visit website.
Level of Study: Postgraduate
Type: Scholarship
Value: £10,000
Country of Study: Any country
Closing Date: 1 November
Additional Information: www.essex.ac.uk/scholarships/postgraduate-conversion-courses

For further information contact:

Wivenhoe Park, Colchester CO4 3SQ, United Kingdom.

Tel: (44) 1206 873333
Email: enquiries@essex.ac.uk

Postgraduate Research EU Scholarship

Purpose: These scholarships are restricted to students who are overseas fee payers and are entirely self-funded
Eligibility: visit website.
Level of Study: Postgraduate
Type: Scholarship
Value: £8,000 automatically deducted from your tuition fees.
Frequency: Annual
Country of Study: Any country
No. of awards offered: one
Closing Date: 16 September
Additional Information: www.essex.ac.uk/scholarships/postgraduate-research-eu-scholarship

For further information contact:

Wivenhoe Park, Colchester CO4 3SQ, United Kingdom.

Tel: (44) 1206 873333
Email: enquiries@essex.ac.uk

Refugee Bursary

Purpose: The University is offering a Refugee Bursary to assist students who have UK refugee status or are a dependent of UK refugees.
Eligibility: visit website.
Type: Bursary
Value: Up to £1,000 for full time, up to £500 for part time.
Frequency: Annual

Country of Study: Any country
Closing Date: 31 July
Additional Information: www.essex.ac.uk/scholarships/refugee-bursary

For further information contact:

Wivenhoe Park, Colchester CO4 3SQ, United Kingdom.

Tel: (44) 1206 873333
Email: funding@essex.ac.uk

Sanctuary Scholarship

Purpose: The Sanctuary Scholarship scheme enables individuals seeking asylum and refugees who are not able access student finance to study at the University of Exeter.
Eligibility: 1. You have submitted a claim for asylum within the UK and are awaiting a response (this includes submission of a fresh claim) or 2. You have Limited Leave to Remain (formerly Discretionary Leave to Remain) in the UK and are not eligible for funding via Student Finance England or 3. You have been awarded 'Humanitarian Protection' or Refugee status in the UK but are not eligible for funding via Student Finance England or 4. You have left care in the UK and are assessed as international for tuition fee purposes and are not eligible for funding via Student Finance England or 5.(For applicants to postgraduate research programmes only) You have been granted refugee status* by the UK Home Office or 6. You are the family member of someone with one of the immigration statuses listed above with 'in line' or 'dependent' status
Level of Study: Postgraduate
Type: Scholarship
Value: Full tuition fee waiver plus annual living cost grant
Frequency: Annual
Country of Study: Any country
No. of awards offered: 3
Closing Date: 20 May
Additional Information: www.exeter.ac.uk/pg-research/money/award/?id=2750

For further information contact:

Stocker Rd, Exeter EX4 4PY, United Kingdom.

Tel: (44) 1392 661000
Email: admissions-scholarships@exeter.ac.uk

Santander Masters Scholarship

Purpose: To support students from Santander network countries to undertake further study

Eligibility: Open to graduates residing in one of the Santander network countries who have an offer to study at Masters level
Level of Study: Postgraduate
Type: Scholarships
Value: £5,000
Frequency: Annual
Study Establishment: University of Essex
Country of Study: United Kingdom
Application Procedure: Please check website
Funding: Corporation
Contributor: Santander
Additional Information: www1.essex.ac.uk/fees-and-funding/masters/scholarships/santander-apply.aspx

For further information contact:

Email: pgtaught@lboro.ac.uk

The Eleonore Koch Fund

Subjects: School of Philosophy and Art History
Purpose: The School of Philosophy and Art History is offering a bursary of £5,000 to assist one student from Latin America to study the MA in Art History and Theory.
Eligibility: You must meet all of the following conditions: 1. be ordinarily resident in Latin America 2. have received a conditional firm or unconditional firm offer to study full time MA Art History and Theory at the University of Essex
Level of Study: Postgraduate
Type: Funding support
Value: £5,000
Frequency: Annual
Country of Study: Any country
No. of awards offered: one
Closing Date: 15 August
Additional Information: www.essex.ac.uk/scholarships/the-eleonore-koch-fund

For further information contact:

Wivenhoe Park, Colchester CO4 3SQ, United Kingdom.

Tel: (44) 1206 873333
Email: spahsm@essex.ac.uk.

The Essex MBA Early Bird Discount

Subjects: Essex Business School
Purpose: Essex Business School is offering £3,000 to students starting their course in January 2023 who attend an interview with the MBA Team and accept their offer of a place on the full-time Essex MBA by 14 November 2021

Eligibility: visit website
Level of Study: MBA
Type: Scholarship
Value: tuition fee discount of £3,000.
Country of Study: Any country
Closing Date: 14 November
Additional Information: www.essex.ac.uk/scholarships/mba-early-bird-discount

For further information contact:

Wivenhoe Park, Colchester CO4 3SQ, United Kingdom.

Tel: (44) 1206 873333
Email: enquiries@essex.ac.uk

Tinson Fund Scholarship for Law

Purpose: To support students from the former Soviet Bloc interested in studying postgraduate law
Eligibility: Open to students from former Soviet Bloc countries, who have an offer on an LLM programme
Level of Study: Postgraduate
Type: Scholarship
Value: Tuition fees
Frequency: Annual
Study Establishment: University of Essex
Country of Study: United Kingdom
Application Procedure: See website for details
Closing Date: 31 May
No. of awards given last year: 1
Additional Information: www.essex.ac.uk/departments/law/scholarships-and-funding

For further information contact:

Email: lawpgtadmin@essex.ac.uk

University of Essex Centre for Psychoanalytic Studies Scholarship

Purpose: To support postgraduate study within the centre
Eligibility: Open to postgraduates within the centre for psychoanalytic studies
Level of Study: Postgraduate
Type: Scholarship
Value: Depends on funds available
Length of Study: 1 year
Frequency: Annual
Study Establishment: University of Essex
Country of Study: United Kingdom

Application Procedure: Applicants must contact the centre concerned
Contributor: University of Essex

University of Sanctuary Scholarship for Afghan Refugees

Purpose: The University of Sanctuary Scholarship is available to new undergraduate or postgraduate taught students taking up a place to study in 2023–24 who are refugees from Afghanistan and have been granted UK Asylum status or Discretionary/ Limited Leave to Remain as a result of an asylum application, and those with Humanitarian Protection, as result of an asylum application or through a dependants claim.
Eligibility: Eligibility will be based on the following permissions being granted by the Home Office and alignment with UNHCR guidelines: 1. a refugee (subject to obtaining an appropriate permissions), or 2. granted Refugee or Humanitarian Protection status, or discretionary Leave to Remain, or 3. Limited Leave to Remain following an asylum application, individually or through a dependent's claim, or 4. be seeking asylum within the UK 5. must be at least a 12 month status, 6 month status cannot be considered
Level of Study: Postgraduate
Type: Scholarship
Value: A full fee waiver on a three year undergraduate course or a one-year Postgraduate Taught Masters programme; University accommodation; £5,000 bursary to support living and study costs
Country of Study: Any country
No. of awards offered: 6
Closing Date: 21 November
Additional Information: www.essex.ac.uk/scholarships/ university-of-sanctuary-scholarship-for-afghan-refugees

For further information contact:

Wivenhoe Park, Colchester CO4 3SQ, United Kingdom.

Tel: (44) 1206 873333
Email: funding@essex.ac.uk.

University of Exeter

Postgraduate Administration Office, Northcote House, The Queen's Drive, Exeter EX4 4QJ, United Kingdom.

Tel: (44) 1392 723 044
Email: pg-ad@exeter.ac.uk
Website: www.exeter.ac.uk/postgraduate/money/funding/
Contact: Mrs Julie Gay, Scholarships Secretary

Aziz Foundation Masters Scholarships

Subjects: Media & Journalism, Technology, Sustainability/ Environment, Law, policy, Creative Content.
Purpose: The Scholarships Programme offers 100% tuition fee Masters scholarships to support British Muslims to study at UK universities. The scholarships are aimed at those who wish to advance in their careers and bring positive change to their communities and beyond.
Eligibility: 1. Be eligible for Home fees status 2. Be active within a Muslim community and demonstrate intimate knowledge of issues affecting British Muslim communities 3. Demonstrate long-term commitment to community/societal development within Britain 4. Show how the course will increase their effectiveness in one of the following areas relating to British Muslims.
Type: Scholarship
Value: 100% tuition fee
Frequency: Annual
Country of Study: Any country
Closing Date: 31 March
Additional Information: www.azizfoundation.org.uk/ scholarships-application/

For further information contact:

Stocker Rd, Exeter EX4 4PY, United Kingdom.

Tel: (44) 1392 661000

Full-Fee Master's Scholarships

Purpose: Full fee waiver offered to students who best demonstrate the potential to progress to doctoral study
Eligibility: Applicants who demonstrate exceptional academic ability such as a first class honours or direct equivalent, and the potential to progress to doctoral study based on a submitted research proposal and personal statement will be considered
Level of Study: Graduate, Postgraduate
Type: Scholarship
Value: Full fee waiver of the taught Master's programme irrespective of fee status
Length of Study: 1 year
Frequency: Annual
Study Establishment: The University of Exeter
Country of Study: United Kingdom
Application Procedure: Application forms can be downloaded from the website www.exeter.ac.uk/scholarships/post graduate/fullmasters
No. of awards offered: 185
Closing Date: 31 March
Funding: Corporation

No. of awards given last year: 15
No. of applicants last year: 185
Additional Information: Applications will only be considered from students who have received an offer of a place on a taught Master's programme at the University

For further information contact:

Scholarship Administrator, Admissions Office, Laver Building, North Park Road, Exeter EX4 4QE, United Kingdom.

Email: admissions-scholarships@exeter.ac.uk

University of Exeter Alumni Scholarship

Purpose: We are pleased to offer University of Exeter alumni beginning a taught Masters degree (eg MA, MSc, MRes, MFA) or research degree (eg MPhil, PhD) with us a scholarship towards the cost of their tuition fees.
Eligibility: In order to be eligible for the scholarship, you must obtain the necessary academic and English language entry requirements for your chosen postgraduate programme.
Type: Scholarship
Value: 10% reduction in first year tuition fee
Length of Study: 1 year
Frequency: Annual
Country of Study: Any country
Application Procedure: This award is applied automatically to University of Exeter alumni; you do not need to make seperate scholarship application. Submit your postgraduate application, remembering to complete the relevant section to indicate your previous Exeter study, by 31 August at the latest in order to be eligible.
Closing Date: 29 April
Contributor: University of Exeter
Additional Information: www.exeter.ac.uk/study/funding/award/?id=4033

For further information contact:

Stocker Rd, Exeter EX4 4PY, United Kingdom.

Tel: (44) 1392 661000

University of Exeter Chapel Choir Choral and Organ Scholarship

Purpose: Annual scholarships offered to choral and organ practitioners to aid in recitals on behalf of the chapel choir
Eligibility: Based on audition. The Director of Chapel Music will invite for competitive audition on the basis of applications demonstrating a high level of competence and experience plus details of two referees familiar with the applicant's ability
Level of Study: Doctorate, Graduate, MBA, Postgraduate, Research
Type: Scholarship
Value: £400 per year for choral scholars, £700 per year for senior organ scholars, £300 per year for junior organ scholars
Length of Study: 1 year initially but may be renewed for the duration of study, where appropriate
Frequency: Annual
Study Establishment: The University of Exeter
Country of Study: United Kingdom
Application Procedure: Applicants can contact the Director for more information and request an application form
No. of awards offered: 60
Closing Date: 13 February
Funding: Corporation, Individuals, Trusts
No. of awards given last year: 10
No. of applicants last year: 60
Additional Information: From the 10 choral scholarships available, 4 are offered to sopranos, 2 each for other voice parts of alto (male and female), tenor and bass. The award for senior organ scholarship status will require recipients to direct the choir when required www.exeter.ac.uk/studying/funding/award/?id=2492

For further information contact:

Email: a.j.musson@exeter.ac.uk

University of Exeter Class of 2023 Progression Scholarship

Purpose: We are pleased to offer graduating University of Exeter students completing their degree in Summer 2022 and progressing direct to a standalone taught Masters degree (eg MA; MSc; MRes; MFA) or research degree (eg MPhil/PhD) with us a scholarship towards the cost of their tuition fees.
Eligibility: see website
Type: Scholarship
Value: 10% reduction in the first year tuition fee
Length of Study: for 1 year
Frequency: Annual
Country of Study: Any country
Closing Date: 31 August
Additional Information: www.exeter.ac.uk/study/funding/award/?id=4202%20

For further information contact:

Stocker Rd, Exeter EX4 4PY, United Kingdom.

Tel: (44) 1392 661000

World Class Business School International Scholarship

Eligibility: A scholarship will be awarded to the most talented international students who have had an application accepted to one of The Business School MSc programmes. Applicants must be resident in one of the following Africa, Asia, and the Commonwealth of Independent States including students resident in Azerbaijan, Kazakhstan, Norway, Russia, Ukraine and Turkey
Type: Scholarship
Value: £10,000
Length of Study: 1 year
Frequency: Annual
Country of Study: United Kingdom
Application Procedure: Please apply at www.exeter.ac.uk/studying/funding/apply/step1/?award=1039
Closing Date: 31 March
Contributor: University of Exeter
Additional Information: www.exeter.ac.uk/postgraduate/money/fundingsearch/awarddetails/?id=956

For further information contact:

Email: business-school-admissions@ex.ac.uk

'Green Futures' Postgraduate Taught Scholarships

Purpose: As part of our commitment to a Green Future, we want to make sure that the most capable and committed candidates from Low and Middle Income Countries have the opportunity to study at the University of Exeter
Eligibility: visit website
Level of Study: Postgraduate
Type: Scholarship
Value: Full tuition fee waiver and stipend for living costs
Frequency: Annual
Country of Study: Any country
No. of awards offered: 9
Closing Date: 1 April
Additional Information: www.exeter.ac.uk/study/funding/award/?id=4376

For further information contact:

Stocker Rd, Exeter EX4 4PY, United Kingdom.

Tel: (44) 1392 661000
Email: isrscholarships@exeter.ac.uk

University of Geneva

University of Geneva, 24 rue du Général-Dufour, CH-1211 Genève 4, Switzerland.

Email: Excellence-Master-Sciences@unige.ch
Contact: Dean of the Faculty of Science

The University of Geneva is a public research university located in Geneva, Switzerland. It was founded in 1559 by John Calvin as a theological seminary and law school.

University of Geneva Excellence Masters Fellowships

Purpose: The Faculty of Science of the University of Geneva, in collaboration with several sponsors, has established an Excellence Fellowship Program to support outstanding and highly motivated candidates who intend to pursue a Master of Science in any of the disciplines covered by the Faculty
Eligibility: The fellowships are open to students from any university with very good performance in their studies (belonging to the best 10% of their bachelor's programme) and that have completed the Bachelor degree or expect to complete it within 6 months. Selection of the applicants will be based on excellence
Level of Study: Doctorate, Postgraduate
Type: Fellowship
Value: CHF 10,000 to CHF 15,000 per year
Country of Study: Switzerland
Application Procedure: You must submit the application form and supporting documents as a unique PDF file by e-mail to the Dean of the Faculty of Science
Closing Date: 15 March
Additional Information: Please visit official website for more details: www.unige.ch/sciences/Enseignements/Formations/Masters/ExcellenceMasterFellowships_en.html www.scholars4dev.com/13822/university-of-geneva-excellence-masters-fellowships/

For further information contact:

24 rue du Général-Dufour, CH-1211 Genève 4, Switzerland.

Tel: (41) 22 379 71 11
Email: Sciences@unige.ch

U

University of Glasgow

Postgraduate Research Office, Research and Enterprise, University of Glasgow, Glasgow G12 8QQ, United Kingdom.

Tel: (44) 1413 301 989
Email: s.rait@enterprise.gla.ac.uk
Website: www.gla.ac.uk
Contact: Shirley Rait

The University of Glasgow is a major research led university operating in an international context, which aims to provide education through the development of learning in a research environment, to undertake fundamental, strategic and applied research and to sustain and add value to Scottish culture, to the natural environment and to the national economy.

Alexander and Dixon Scholarship (Bryce Bequest)

Eligibility: Open to the citizens of United Kingdom or a European Union national
Level of Study: Doctorate
Type: Scholarship
Value: Fee waiver (Home/EU fees) for 1 year of full time study or 2 years of part time study.
Length of Study: 3 years
Application Procedure: The application should consist of a 500-word case for support and a brief covering letter, including the proposed title of the thesis, the name(s) of the proposed supervisor(s), and give the applicant's email and other contact details
No. of awards offered: 2
Closing Date: 21 June
Additional Information: www.gla.ac.uk/scholarships/alexanderanddixonscholarshipbrycebequest/

For further information contact:

Department Office, Department of English Literature, University of Glasgow, Glasgow G12 8QQ, United Kingdom.

Email: critstudies-pgscholarships@glasgow.ac.uk

Alexander and Margaret Johnstone Postgraduate Research Scholarships

Eligibility: Open to students intending a research degree in the faculty of arts in a department rated 5 or 5* in the research assessment exercise
Level of Study: Doctorate
Type: Research scholarship
Value: Tuition fees at the Home/European Union student rate, plus stipend of between £6,000 and £7,000
Length of Study: 3 years
Country of Study: Any country
Application Procedure: Check website for further details
Funding: Government

For further information contact:

Tel: (44) 141 330 6828
Email: e.queune@admin.gla.ac.uk

Bellahouston Bequest Fund

Eligibility: Open to postgraduate students undertaking a Masters Degree course in the faculty of arts
Level of Study: Postgraduate
Type: Scholarship
Value: £1,000
Length of Study: 1 year
Frequency: Annual
Country of Study: Any country
Application Procedure: The candidate must contact the clerk of the faculty of arts. Check website for further information
Closing Date: 17 July
Additional Information: Preference will be given to the Glaswegians www.gla.ac.uk/scholarships/alexanderanddixonscholarshipbrycebequest/

For further information contact:

Tel: (44) 141 330 2000
Email: ugs@archives.gla.ac.uk

British Federation of Women Graduates (BFWG)

Purpose: To encourage applicants to become members of the Federation to help promote better links between female graduates throughout the world
Eligibility: Open to female graduate with academic excellence. Doctoral students of all nationalities who will be studying in the United Kingdom are eligible for the scholarship
Level of Study: Postgraduate
Type: Scholarship and award
Value: £1,000–6,000
Length of Study: Four years
Frequency: Annual
Country of Study: United Kingdom
Application Procedure: Check website for further details

Closing Date: 22 February
Funding: Private
No. of awards given last year: 6
Additional Information: Male graduates and female undergraduates are not eligible bfwg.org.uk/bfwg2/

For further information contact:

Tel: (44) 20 7498 8037
Fax: (44) 20 7498 5213
Email: awardsqueries@bfwg.org.uk

Clark Graduate Bursary Fund for International Students at University of Glasgow

Purpose: The aim of the bursary is to support graduates of the University of Glasgow or Strathclyde studying for, or applying to study for, a subsequent degree at a university in the United Kingdom or abroad
Eligibility: Applicants can either be graduates of the University of Glasgow or Strathclyde studying for, or applying to study for, a subsequent degree at a university in the United Kingdom or abroad. Applicants must be fluent in English
Level of Study: Postdoctorate, Postgraduate, Research
Type: Postgraduate scholarships
Value: The value of the bursary normally between £500 and £1,500.
Study Establishment: Bursary is awarded in the field offered by the university
Country of Study: United Kingdom
Application Procedure: There is an annual application process. Applications can be submitted between 1st March and 1st October each year. Applications must be submitted online. Interviews of candidates selected for consideration are held in Glasgow at a Governors' meeting during November. Interviewees will usually be notified within a week of the interviews whether they will receive an award. Awards are normally paid to successful applicants before the end of the year
Closing Date: 1 May
Additional Information: For more details please visit the website scholarship-positions.com/clark-raduate-bursary-fund-international-students-university-of-glasgow-uk/2017/12/20/ https://www.gla.ac.uk/scholarships/clarkmile-endbursaryfund/

For further information contact:

Glasgow G12 8QQ, United Kingdom.

Tel: (44) 141 330 2000
Email: clarkmileendfund@gmail.com

Glasgow Educational & Marshall Trust Award

Purpose: To offer financial support to those who have lived, or are currently living within the Glasgow Municipal Boundary
Eligibility: Open to the candidates who are above 18 years of age and a resident of Glasgow within one of the following post code areas G1–5, G11/12, G14/15, G20, G22/23, G31, G34, G40–42, G45, 51
Level of Study: Doctorate, Graduate, MBA, Postdoctorate, Postgraduate, Predoctorate, Research
Type: Studentships and bursaries
Value: £50-1,000
Length of Study: 1 year
Study Establishment: Glasgow Educational and Marshall Trust
Country of Study: United Kingdom
Application Procedure: Check website for further details
Closing Date: 30 April
Contributor: Glasgow Educational and Marshall Trust
Additional Information: www.itpt.co.uk/glasgow-educational-marshall-trust/

For further information contact:

Tel: (44) 141 4334449
Fax: (44) 141 424 1731
Email: sloanea@hutchesons.org

Henry Dryerre Scholarship in Medical and Veterinary Physiology

Eligibility: Open to candidates holding a degree of a Scottish University with first class honours or, if in their final year, to be expected to achieve first class honours
Level of Study: Postgraduate
Type: Scholarships and fellowships
Value: Varies
Frequency: Every 3 years
Country of Study: Any country
Application Procedure: The candidate must submit the application form through a member of staff on the appropriate Henry Dryerre Nomination Form

For further information contact:

Email: scholarships@glasgow.ac.uk

Lord Kelvin/Adam Smith Postgraduate Scholarships

Purpose: To enable the University to recruit outstanding postgraduate research students to a range of innovative, boundary-crossing research developments

Eligibility: Open to postgraduate students
Level of Study: Postgraduate
Type: Scholarship
Value: Stipend of £13,590. The project will benefit from £5,300 per year research costs
Length of Study: 4 years
Frequency: Annual
Application Procedure: Check website for further details
Funding: Trusts
Additional Information: www.gla.ac.uk/scholarships/lordkelvinadamsmithlkasinterdisciplinaryphdscholarships/

For further information contact:

Email: lauren-currie@enterprise.gla.ac.uk

R. Harper Brown Memorial Scholarship

Purpose: To honour the late R. Harper Brown and to assist in defraying the cost of an American (United States) college student's study at a university in Scotland
Eligibility: Open to the candidates who are graduating seniors in high school with an acceptance and intention to attend university in Scotland or a student in an accredited American (United States) college or university looking for a study-abroad experience
Level of Study: Graduate
Type: Scholarship
Application Procedure: Check website for further details
Closing Date: 31 March
Funding: Private
Contributor: The Illinois Saint Andrew Society
Additional Information: www.fastweb.com/college-scholarships/scholarships/145173-r-harper-brown-memorial-scholarship

For further information contact:

Tel: (44) 847 967 2725
Email: dforlow@yahoo.com

Royal Historical Society: Postgraduate Research Support Grants

Purpose: To assist postgraduate students in the pursuit of advanced historical research
Eligibility: The candidate must be a postgraduate student registered for a research degree at United Kingdom Institute of Higher Education
Level of Study: Graduate, Research
Type: Award/Grant
Country of Study: United States of America

Application Procedure: Check website for further details
Closing Date: 12 November
Contributor: Royal Historical Society

For further information contact:

Email: m.ransom@royalhistsoc.org

Saint Andrew's Society of the State of New York Scholarship Fund

Eligibility: Open to candidates who are either graduates of a Scottish university or of Oxford or Cambridge and have completed their first Degree course
Level of Study: Postgraduate
Type: Scholarship
Value: Each scholarship is valued at US$35,000 USD and is granted for tuition, maintenance and travel.
Length of Study: 1 academic year
Frequency: Annual
Country of Study: United States of America
Application Procedure: The candidate must arrange for references from two academic referees to be submitted in the appropriate referee forms
No. of awards offered: 5
Closing Date: 7 February
Funding: Trusts
Contributor: Saint Andrew's Society of the State of New York
Additional Information: www.st-andrews.ac.uk/study/fees-and-funding/postgraduate/scholarships/new-york/

For further information contact:

Tel: (44) 141 330 6063
Email: c.omand@admin.gla.ac.uk

Stevenson Exchange Scholarships

Purpose: To promote friendly relations between the students of Scotland, Germany, France and Spain
Eligibility: Open to current or recent students of French, German or Spanish universities who intend to study at any university in Scotland
Level of Study: Postdoctorate
Type: Scholarship
Value: £250–2,000
Application Procedure: Check website for further details
Closing Date: 1 February
Additional Information: www.ed.ac.uk/student-funding/current-students/study-abroad/undergraduate/stevenson-exchange

For further information contact:

Room 1.07, Undergraduate Teaching Office, 50 George Square, Edinburgh EH8 9LD, Scotland, United Kingdom.

Tel: (44) 141 330 4241
Fax: (44) 141 330 4045
Email: delc@ed.ac.uk

Sustainability Scholarship

Purpose: The scholarship will be awarded for the fall/autumn semester of 2023 and is open to people from anywhere in the world who want to study a master's program that is helping you making the world more sustainable.
Eligibility: 1. You must have applied (or will apply) to a master's program that can help you make the world more sustainable 2. You must have applied (or will apply) for a study starting in the Fall Semester 2023 3. The degree program may not be online 4. You must meet the entry requirements for the university or graduate school, including: 5. Hold a valid undergraduate degree 6. Meet language requirements for the program 7. You must hold or be eligible to apply for a relevant study visa (if applicable)
Type: Scholarship
Value: €5000
Frequency: Annual
Country of Study: Any country
No. of awards offered: 1
Closing Date: 22 September
Additional Information: www.gla.ac.uk/scholarships/sustainabilityscholarship/#

For further information contact:

Glasgow G12 8QQ, United Kingdom.

Tel: (44) 141 330 2000
Email: frederik.keller.dietz@finduddannelse.dk

The Catherine Mackichan Trust

Eligibility: Open to applications from academic centres worldwide, schools, colleges and individuals or groups
Level of Study: Research
Type: Award
Value: £500
Length of Study: 1 year
Frequency: Annual
Country of Study: Any country
Application Procedure: Check website for further details

Closing Date: 16 April
Funding: Trusts
Contributor: The Catherine Mackichan Trust
Additional Information: grants-search.turn2us.org.uk/grant/the-catherine-mackichan-trust-13908

For further information contact:

Email: peter.mcghee@vaslan.org.uk

William and Margaret Kesson Award for Postgraduate Study

Purpose: To enable a student to undertake study leading to a postgraduate degree in the faculty of arts
Eligibility: Open to candidates of Scottish or English nationality possessing a graduate degree
Level of Study: Graduate
Type: Scholarship
Length of Study: 3 years
Country of Study: Any country
Application Procedure: Check website for further details
Closing Date: 1 May

For further information contact:

Email: e.queune@admin.gla.ac.uk

William Ross Scholarship

Purpose: To encourage the extraction of Scottish material from archives outside Scotland relating to all aspects of the history of Scotland, the Scottish people and Scottish influence abroad
Eligibility: Open to candidates possessing a degree in MLitt
Level of Study: Research
Type: Scholarships and fellowships
Value: £1,000
Length of Study: 1 year
Frequency: Annual
Application Procedure: The candidate must submit a letter outlining a dissertation research proposal including the planned topic and archival research plans
Closing Date: 1 July
Contributor: Trustees of the Ross Fund

For further information contact:

Email: c.leriguer@arts.gla.ac.uk

U

Wingate Scholarships

Purpose: To support creative or original work of intellectual, scientific, artistic, social or environmental value

Eligibility: Open for mature candidates and those from non-traditional academic backgrounds without any upper age limit

Level of Study: Unrestricted

Type: Scholarship

Value: £6,500–10,000 in any 1 year

Length of Study: 1 year

Frequency: Annual

Country of Study: Any country

Application Procedure: Check website for further details

Closing Date: 1 February

Additional Information: www.soas.ac.uk/registry/scholarships/william-ross-murray-scholarship.html

For further information contact:

Email: emma@shrimsley.com

University of Göttingen

Project management, Equal Opportunities Office, Gosslerstrasse 9, D-37073 Göttingen, Germany.

Tel: (49) 551/39 33959
Email: nina.guelcher@zvw.uni-goettingen.de
Contact: Mrs Nina Gülcher

The University of Göttingen is a public research university in the city of Göttingen, Germany.

Dorothea Schlozer Postdoctoral Scholarships for Female Students

Purpose: The University of Göttingen is inviting female postdocs from Germany to apply for Dorothea Schlozer Postdoctoral Scholarships. These scholarships are available to conduct a research project at the Georg-August-University

Eligibility: Female postdocs from Germany are eligible to apply. The candidate should have a very good command of English language. Therefore, the application should be written in English

Value: There will be 3 positions (TV-L 13, 100%, term of 2 years), one of which at the University Medical Center (UMG)

Length of Study: 2 years

Country of Study: Germany

Application Procedure: Applications will only be accepted through the online portal. After submitting your application you will receive an automatic confirmation of receipt via e-mail

Closing Date: 8 April

Additional Information: For more details, please visit the website www.uni-goettingen.de/de/122481.html scholarship-positions.com/dorothea-schlozer-postdoctoral-scholarships-female-students-germany/2018/02/20/

For further information contact:

Email: admin@scholarship-positions.com

University of Graz

Universitätsplatz 3, A-8010 Graz, Austria.

Contact: University of Graz

The University of Graz (German: Karl-Franzens-Universität Graz), located in Graz, Austria, is the largest and oldest university in Styria, as well as the second-largest and second-oldest university in Austria.

Ida Pfeiffer Scholarships

Purpose: This program is designed to give applicants the opportunity to submit an application for a waiver of tuition fees

Eligibility: For details, visit website. Successful completion of at least two semesters at the University of Graz. Minimum age of 19 years and maximum age of 35 years, in exceptional cases (late start of studies, concurrent employment

Type: Scholarship

Length of Study: 1 year

Country of Study: Austria

Application Procedure: Eligibility requirements are as follows 1. Successful completion of at least 2 semesters at the University of Graz. 2. Minimum age of 19

Closing Date: 13 April

Additional Information: Please visit website: international.uni-graz.at/de/stud/outgoing/s-out-mprog/ida-pfeiffer-stipendium/ www.european-funding-guide.eu/other-financial-assistance/14286-ida-pfeiffer-scholarships

For further information contact:

Email: maren.leykauf@uni-graz.at

Marie Sklodowska-Curie Actions Postdoctoral Fellowships

Purpose: Fellowship is available to pursue Postdoctoral programme

Eligibility: Please visit ec.europa.eu/research/mariecurieactions/actions/postdoctoral-fellowships for eligibility criteria

Type: Fellowship

Value: Receive up to €400 for your travel costs to Austria

Country of Study: Austria

Closing Date: 1 May

Contributor: University of Graz

Additional Information: Please visit www.unica.it/unica/it/news_avvisi_s1.page?contentId=AVS93045 www.ersnet.org/professional-development/fellowships/marie-curie-postdoctoral-research-fellowships-respire

For further information contact:

Av. Sainte-Luce 4, CH-1003 Lausanne, Switzerland.

Tel: (41) 21 213 01 01

University of Guelph

University Centre, Room 437, 50 Stone Road East, Guelph, ON N1G 2W1, Canada.

Tel: (1) 519 824 4120
Email: immccorki@uoguelph.ca
Website: www.uoguelph.ca
Contact: Linda McCorkindale, Associate Registrar

The University of Guelph is renowned in Canada and around the world as a research-intensive and learner-centred institution and for its commitment to open learning, internationalism and collaboration. Their vision is to be Canada's leader in creating, transmitting and applying knowledge to improve the social, cultural and economic quality of life of people in Canada and around the world.

Canada-ASEAN Scholarships and Educational Exchanges for Development (SEED) – for students

Purpose: The Canada-ASEAN Scholarships and Educational Exchanges for Development (SEED) program provides students, from member states of the Association of Southeast Asian Nations (ASEAN), with short-term exchange opportunities for study or research in Canadian post-secondary institutions at the college, undergraduate and graduate levels.

Eligibility: Candidates should be citizens of an ASEAN member state (Brunei Darussalam, Cambodia, Indonesia, Laos (Lao People's Democratic Republic (Lao PDR)), Malaysia, Myanmar, The Philippines, Singapore, Thailand, or Vietnam); be enrolled as a full-time student at a post-secondary institution in an eligible country and paying tuition fees to that institution at the time of application and for the full duration of the exchange.

Level of Study: Research

Type: Scholarship

Value: CAD 10,200 for college (Master's and PhD); CAD 12,700 for graduate students (Master's and PhD); CAD 15,900.

Length of Study: 8 months or two academic studies

Country of Study: Any country

Closing Date: 3 March

Additional Information: www.educanada.ca/scholarships-bourses/can/institutions/asean-anase.aspx?lang=eng

For further information contact:

50 Stone Rd E, Guelph, ON N1G 2W1, Canada.

Tel: (1) 519 824 4120
Email: scholarships-bourses@cbie.ca

Canada-CARICOM Faculty Leadership Program

Purpose: The Canada-CARICOM Faculty Leadership Program provides faculty or international liaison officers/managers from post-secondary institutions located in the CARICOM member and associate member states with short-term exchange opportunities for professional development, graduate study or research at Canadian post-secondary institutions.

Eligibility: Candidates should be citizens of one of the CARICOM member and associate member states: Anguilla, Antigua and Barbuda, Bahamas, Barbados, Belize, Bermuda, British Virgin Islands, Cayman Islands, Dominica, Grenada, Guyana, Haiti, Jamaica, Montserrat, Saint Kitts and Nevis, Saint Lucia, Saint Vincent and the Grenadines, Suriname, Trinidad and Tobago, and Turks and Caicos; and employed full-time as faculty or international liaison officers/managers at a post-secondary institution in the eligible countries/territories at the time of application and for the entire duration of their stay in Canada.

Type: Scholarship

Value: CAD 3,200 for faculty members, CAD 3,200 for international directors, CAD 3,200 for international directors.

Length of Study: two weeks - six months
Country of Study: Any country
Closing Date: 22 March
Additional Information: www.educanada.ca/scholarships-bourses/can/institutions/flpp-pplpe.aspx?lang=eng

For further information contact:

50 Stone Rd E, Guelph, ON N1G 2W1, Canada.

Tel: (1) 519 824 4120
Email: scholarships-bourses@cbie.ca

Emerging Leaders in the Americas Program (ELAP)

Purpose: The scholarships also advance Canada's objectives for the Americas: democratic and accountable governance, human rights, the environment, diversity and Indigenous peoples.
Eligibility: Candidates should be citizens of one of the following eligible countries/territories: Caribbean: Anguilla, Antigua and Barbuda, Bahamas, Barbados, Belize, Bermuda, British Virgin Islands, Cayman Islands, Cuba, Dominica, Dominican Republic, Grenada, Guyana, Haiti, Jamaica, Montserrat, Saint Kitts and Nevis, Saint Lucia, Saint Vincent and the Grenadines, Suriname, Trinidad and Tobago, Turks and Caicos; Central America: Costa Rica, El Salvador, Guatemala, Honduras, Nicaragua, Panama; North America: Mexico; South America: Argentina, Bolivia, Brazil, Chile, Colombia, Ecuador, Paraguay, Peru, Uruguay, Venezuela; and enrolled as a full-time student at post-secondary institution in an eligible country/territory and paying tuition fees to that institution at the time of application and for the full duration of the exchange.
Level of Study: Graduate, Research
Type: Scholarship
Value: CAD 8,200 for college (Master's and PhD); CAD 11,100 (Master's and PhD)
Length of Study: six months or one year
Frequency: Annual
Country of Study: Any country
Closing Date: 22 March
Additional Information: www.educanada.ca/scholarships-bourses/can/institutions/elap-pfla.aspx?lang=eng#tab_1528 378062_3

For further information contact:

50 Stone Rd E, Guelph, ON N1G 2W1, Canada.

Tel: (1) 519 824 4120
Email: scholarships-bourses@cbie.ca

Faculty Mobility for Partnership Building Program

Purpose: The Program will award short-term grants to professors to teach and/or conduct research in ELAP-eligible countries. The primary objective of the exchange should be to create new agreements with host institutions and/or to strengthen existing agreements.
Eligibility: Applicants should be full-time professors at Canadian post-secondary institutions (part-time professors and lecturers, as well as public servants (federal, provincial/territorial, municipal, or Crown corporations) are not eligible); and submit a proposal for collaboration with a post-secondary host institution in an ELAP-eligible country.
Type: Scholarship
Value: CAD 7,000.
Length of Study: eight weeks maximum
Country of Study: Any country
Closing Date: 2 December
Additional Information: www.educanada.ca/scholarships-bourses/can/institutions/elap_faculty-pfla_professeurs.aspx?lang=eng#tab_1530023127_3

For further information contact:

50 Stone Rd E, Guelph, ON N1G 2W1, Canada.

Tel: (1) 519 824 4120
Email: scholarships-bourses@cbie.ca.

Study in Canada Scholarships

Purpose: This student exchange program replaces the full-degree-based Study in Canada Scholarships program piloted in 2020. At least 50 scholarships will be awarded in the next competition, with the number increasing each year.
Eligibility: Applicants should be citizens of one of the following eligible countries/territories: Asia: Bangladesh, Nepal, Taiwan; Europe: Turkey, Ukraine; Middle East and North Africa: Algeria, Egypt, Jordan, Libya, Morocco, Tunisia; Sub-Saharan Africa: Burkina Faso, Ethiopia, Ghana, Ivory Coast, Kenya, Nigeria, Rwanda, Senegal, Tanzania, Uganda; and enrolled as a full-time student at post-secondary institution in an eligible country/territory and paying tuition fees to that institution at the time of application and for the full duration of the exchange.
Level of Study: Graduate
Type: Scholarship
Value: CAD 10,200; CAD 12,700;
Length of Study: six months or one academic year.
Frequency: Annual
Country of Study: Any country
Closing Date: 22 March

Additional Information: www.educanada.ca/scholarships-bourses/can/institutions/study-in-canada-sep-etudes-au-canada-pct.aspx?lang=eng#tab_1530023127_1

For further information contact:

50 Stone Rd E, Guelph, ON N1G 2W1, Canada.

Tel: (1) 519 824 4120
Email: scholarships-bourses@cbie.ca

The Brock Doctoral Scholarship

Purpose: To financially support Doctoral students to attain a high level of academic achievement and to make significant teaching and research contributions
Eligibility: Open to students with sustained outstanding academic performance, evidence of strong teaching and research skills, demonstrated outstanding communication skills and excellent potential for research and teaching as assessed by the College Dean
Level of Study: Doctorate
Type: Scholarship
Value: Up to C$120,000 (C$10,000 per semester for up to 12 semesters)
Length of Study: 6 years
Frequency: Annual
Study Establishment: University of Guelph
Country of Study: Canada
Application Procedure: Students entering a Doctoral programme should apply to their College Dean by 1 February with a curriculum vitae, which must then be forwarded to Graduate Program Services by February 15th, with the Dean's written assessment of the candidate's research and teaching potential attached
Closing Date: 15 February
Additional Information: The Brock Doctoral Scholarship is one of the most prestigious Doctoral awards available at the University. It is hoped that award holders will be mentors for future Brock Doctoral Scholarship winners graduatestudies. uoguelph.ca/Brock

For further information contact:

Email: sinclair@registrar.uoguelph.ca

University of Hertfordshire

College Lane, Hatfield, Hertfordshire AL10 9AB, United Kingdom.

Tel: (44) 1707 284 800

Yaasa Scholarship

Purpose: The Yaasa Scholarships are available to all high school juniors and seniors as well as all students currently registered in any accredited post-secondary institution
Level of Study: Graduate, Postgraduate
Type: Scholarship
Value: C$1,000
Frequency: Annual
Country of Study: Any country
Application Procedure: The winner(s) of this annual scholarship will receive their award within 2 weeks of the listed deadline. All applicants should include their full name and mailing address with their submissions as well as the school they are currently attending
Closing Date: 14 June
Additional Information: Students who are successfully awarded the UH Graduate Scholarship are still eligible for the £500 tuition fee discount if they pay in full at registration. Please check at www.herts.ac.uk/international/fees/scholarships-for-international-students/uh-family-scholarships

For further information contact:

Email: scholarships@yaasa.com

University of Illinois

225 DKH, 1407 West Gregory, Urbana, IL 61801, United States of America.

Tel: (1) 217 333 8153
Website: www.uiuc.edu
Contact: Ms Diane Carson, Graduate Advising Office

Master of Business Administration Programme

Length of Study: 2 years
Application Procedure: Applicants must complete an application form supplying US$50 fee, official transcripts, TOEFL score, statement of financial support and a personal statement

For further information contact:

Tel: (1) 217 244 8019
Email: mba@uiuc.edu

University of Kent

Admissions and Partnership Services, The Registry, Canterbury, Kent CT2 7NZ, United Kingdom.

Tel: (44) 1227 764 000
Email: scholarships@kent.ac.uk
Website: www.kent.ac.uk

The University of Kent is a United Kingdom higher education institution funded by the Higher Education Funding Council for United Kingdom (HEFCE). The university provides education of excellent quality characterized by flexibility and inter disciplinarily and informed by research and scholarship, meeting the lifelong needs of diversity students.

Ian Gregor Scholarship

Purpose: To support a candidate registered for a taught MA programme in English
Eligibility: Candidates are expected to hold at least an Upper Second Class (Honours) Degree or equivalent. Candidates should also have applied for an external scholarship, such as AHRC
Level of Study: Graduate, Postgraduate
Type: Scholarship
Value: Home fees and a £500 bursary for 1 year's full-time study
Length of Study: 1 year
Frequency: Annual
Study Establishment: The University of Kent
Country of Study: United Kingdom
Application Procedure: See webpages at www.kent.ac.uk/english/postgraduate/fund.htm
Closing Date: 28 June
Funding: Trusts
No. of awards given last year: 1
Additional Information: www.kent.ac.uk/scholarships/search/FN03IANGRE02

For further information contact:

Email: englishpg@kent.ac.uk

Kent Law School Studentships and Bursaries

Purpose: To provide funding for 1 year in the first instance, extended to a maximum of 3 years (for registered students only) based on satisfactory progress (including upgrading to a PhD). The retention of the posts will be subject to a review of progress and performance in both research and teaching after the 1st year
Eligibility: Candidates should hold an Upper Second Class (Honours) Degree or a good postgraduate taught degree in law
Level of Study: Doctorate, Postgraduate, Research
Type: Studentship
Value: £13,863 and tuition fees paid at the Home/European Union rate (up to £3,900 last year)
Length of Study: 1–3 years
Frequency: Annual
Study Establishment: The University of Kent
Country of Study: United Kingdom
Application Procedure: Applicants must submit to the University's recruitment and admissions office a research proposal, curriculum vitae and covering letter with an application for their chosen research degree. They should also ensure that the recruitment and admissions office receives two referees' reports by the closing date for applications. Applications are available at records.kent.ac.uk/external/admissions/pg-application.php
No. of awards offered: 20–30
Closing Date: 31 January
Funding: Private
Contributor: Kent Law School
No. of awards given last year: 2
No. of applicants last year: 20–30
Additional Information: Holders of the studentships will be expected to teach for a maximum of 4 hours per week in term time on an undergraduate law module, at the direction of the head of department. For further information contact the Kent Law school at kls-pgoffice@kent.ac.uk www.kent.ac.uk/scholarships/search/FN37LSSTUD02

For further information contact:

Tel: (44) 1227 827949
Email: m.drakopoulou@kent.ac.uk

Language Lector Scholarships

Purpose: To support research
Eligibility: The scholarship is open to candidates who have made an application for any one of the taught MA programmes (except programmes taught in Paris or Athens) in SECL in an area related to the language they will be teaching. Candidates must hold a First Class or Upper Second Class Undergraduate Degree in a relevant subject (or have reached an appropriate point in their University education to be accepted onto a United Kingdom Master's degree). Candidates must be a native speaker of French, German, Spanish,

Catalan or Portuguese. Candidates must have excellent communication skills, both written and oral and ideally some experience of language teaching. This scholarship is open to United Kingdom, European Union and overseas fee-paying students

Level of Study: Postgraduate, Research

Type: Studentship

Value: 100% of tuition fees at the Home/European Union rate for a postgraduate programme within the School of European Culture and Languages (SECL) and combined maintenance grant and salary

Length of Study: 3 years

Frequency: Annual

Study Establishment: The University of Kent

Country of Study: United Kingdom

Application Procedure: Application is via School of European Culture and Language website www.kent.ac.uk/secl/postgraduate/funding.html?tab=language-lector-scholarships

Funding: Government

Additional Information: Candidates may be interviewed over the telephone as appropriate. Language Lectors teach for at least 20 of these 24 weeks and will be expected to teach 10 hours a week www.kent.ac.uk/scholarships/search/FN37LSSTUD02

For further information contact:

Email: seclpgadmin@kent.ac.uk

Martin Cook Scholarship for Humanities Students

Purpose: A generous donation has been received by the University of Kent in memory of Martin Cook. The purpose of the gift is to help support one full-time undergraduate student in the humanities.

Eligibility: 1. Open to all full-time applicants who are UK residents paying Home tuition fees. 2. Applicants must have accepted a place on a humanities undergraduate course at the University of Kent starting in September 2022 by the UCAS deadline of 30 June 2022. 3. Applicants must obtain a minimum of 136 UCAS points from A Levels or equivalent, and must fulfil the normal entry requirements for their course. 4. Applicants must demonstrate financial need and satisfy a range of socio-economic criteria 5. Applicants must be willing to act as an 'ambassador' for the University, their subject and faculty and attend University events when requested, if not in conflict with either course attendance or classes being in session. 6. Current students at the University of Kent are not eligible to apply.

Type: Scholarship

Value: £2,000

Length of Study: 3 - 4 years

Frequency: Annual

Country of Study: Any country

Closing Date: 30 June

Additional Information: www.kent.ac.uk/scholarships/search/FNADMARCOO01

For further information contact:

Giles Ln, Canterbury CT2 7NZ, United Kingdom.

Tel: (44) 1227 764000

Postgrad Solutions Study Bursaries

Purpose: Kent University- Kent offers well-structured and ambitious. It provides a comprehensive package of skills development training programs, careers advice, and volunteering and paid work opportunities to enhance your career prospects in a global workplace.

Eligibility: Scholarship is available for pursuing Postgraduate degree program

Level of Study: Postgraduate

Type: Bursary

Value: £500

Frequency: Annual

Country of Study: Any country

Closing Date: 30 September

Funding: International office

Additional Information: www.kent.ac.uk/scholarships/search/FNADPGSOLU02

For further information contact:

The University of Kent, Canterbury, Kent CT2 7NZ, United Kingdom.

Tel: (44) 1227 764000

School of Economics Funding

Purpose: To support research

Eligibility: All applicants for a scholarship should have completed a Master's degree in Economics or a closely-related subject. In order to be eligible for this scholarship, you must have applied for and accepted a place to study at the University

Level of Study: Doctorate, Postgraduate, Research

Type: Bursary

Value: Tuition fees at the Home/European Union rate and a maintenance grant, usually up to a similar rate to an ESRC grant (£13,590 for last year)

Length of Study: 1 year in the 1st instance, renewable for a maximum of 3 years subject to satisfactory academic performance
Frequency: Dependent on funds available
Study Establishment: The University of Kent
Country of Study: United Kingdom
Application Procedure: To apply for a scholarship, please send a curriculum vitae, including the names of two referees, a brief research proposal, transcripts of your previous degrees and a covering letter to the Postgraduate Co-ordinator, Katie Marshall at econpg@kent.ac.uk
Closing Date: 15 April
Funding: Government
Additional Information: Candidates should note that 4–6 hours of teaching per week and acceptable progress in the programme of study will be expected of the student. The bursary will be subject to review each year www.kent.ac.uk/economics/prospective/research/funding.html

For further information contact:

The University of Kent, Canterbury, Kent CT2 7NZ, United Kingdom.

Tel: (44) 1227 764000
Email: Y.Zhu-5@kent.ac.uk

School of English MA Scholarships for International Students at University of Kent in United Kingdom

Purpose: The purpose of the scholarships is to award candidates with the strongest academic records. The School of English reserves the right to distribute the scholarships amongst candidates in a way that will honour that commitment
Eligibility: Please check details on website
Level of Study: Doctorate, Postgraduate
Type: Scholarship
Value: The scholarships are worth £8,000 towards the cost of tuition fees
Length of Study: Up to 3 years
Frequency: Annual
Study Establishment: The University of Kent
Country of Study: United Kingdom
Application Procedure: All students who have made an application to study on an MA programme in the School of English by the deadline will automatically be considered for a scholarship
Closing Date: 31 May
Funding: Commercial, Government
No. of awards given last year: 5

Additional Information: www.kent.ac.uk/scholarships/search/FNADINTAMA02

For further information contact:

The University of Kent, Canterbury, Kent CT2 7NZ, United Kingdom.

Tel: (44) 1227 764000
Email: international@kent.ac.uk

South East ESRC DTC Funding

Purpose: To support research studies
Level of Study: Postgraduate, Research
Type: Studentship
Value: The funding will typically cover yearly maintenance (£13,863 for last year) and fees for one of the following +3 programme or 1+3
Length of Study: 3 years
Frequency: Annual
Study Establishment: The University of Kent
Country of Study: United Kingdom
Application Procedure: Applicants must complete an application form
No. of awards offered: 30–40
Closing Date: 2 February
Funding: Private
Contributor: South-East ESRC DTC
No. of awards given last year: 2
No. of applicants last year: 30–40
Additional Information: Studentships will be awarded on the basis of the academic excellence of both the candidate and the research proposal www.kent.ac.uk/scholarships/search/FNADINTAMA02

For further information contact:

Tel: (44) 1227 823085
Email: rsg@kent.ac.uk

University of Kent Anthropology Bursaries

Purpose: To support both research and taught programmes
Eligibility: Candidates are expected to hold an Upper Second Class (Honours) Degree
Level of Study: Doctorate, Postgraduate, Research
Type: Bursary
Value: Home fees only
Length of Study: 3 years
Frequency: Dependent on funds available
Study Establishment: The University of Kent

Country of Study: United Kingdom
No. of awards given last year: 2

For further information contact:

Email: n.a.kerry-yoxall@ukc.ac.uk

University of Kent at Canterbury Second English Scholarship

Purpose: To support research
Eligibility: Candidates are expected to hold at least an Upper Second Class (Honours) Degree or equivalent. Candidates should also have applied for an external scholarship, such as AHRB
Level of Study: Postgraduate
Type: Research grant
Value: Home tuition fees up to £3,500 bursary per year for up to three years full-time study. Some undergraduate teaching or research assistance will be expected from the successful candidate
Frequency: Annual
Study Establishment: The University of Kent
Country of Study: United Kingdom
Application Procedure: Candidates must complete the post-graduate application form, indicating in the appropriate section that they are interested in being considered for departmental scholarships. A covering letter supporting the scholarship application should be attached
Closing Date: 30 May

University of Kent Department of Electronics Studentships

Purpose: To enable well-qualified students to undertake research programmes within the department
Eligibility: Candidates are expected to hold an Upper Second Class (Honours) Degree or equivalent in an appropriate subject, and be nationals of one of the European Union countries
Level of Study: Doctorate, Postgraduate, Research
Type: Studentship
Value: Research Council studentships are at a fixed rate determined annually by EPSRC. Departmental bursaries depend on individual circumstances
Length of Study: 3 years
Frequency: Annual
Study Establishment: The University of Kent
Country of Study: United Kingdom
Application Procedure: Applicants should contact the Department of Electronics
No. of awards offered: 10

Closing Date: June
Funding: Government
Contributor: EPSRC
No. of awards given last year: 5
No. of applicants last year: 10

For further information contact:

Email: ee-admissions-pg@kent.ac.uk

University of Kent Law School Studentship

Purpose: To support research
Eligibility: Applicants should normally have obtained, or be about to obtain an undergraduate degree of at least Upper Second Class Honours level (21 or equivalent from other countries), or a postgraduate degree
Level of Study: Doctorate, Postgraduate
Type: Scholarships
Value: Maintenance grant equivalent to that offered by ESRC (£13,863 in last year) and tuition fees paid at the Home/European Union rate (£3,900 in last year)
Length of Study: Up to 3 years
Frequency: Annual
Study Establishment: University of Kent
Country of Study: United Kingdom
Application Procedure: Applications to be filled electronically at www.kent.ac.uk/law/postgraduate/research/entryreq-research.html
Closing Date: 31 January
Funding: Commercial, Government
No. of awards given last year: 8
Additional Information: See website for further details: www.kent.ac.uk/law/postgraduate/research/KLS_research_funding.html www.kent.ac.uk/scholarships/search/FN37LSSTUD02

For further information contact:

The University of Kent, Canterbury, Kent CT2 7NZ, United Kingdom.

Tel: (44) 1227 764000
Email: m.drakopoulou@kent.ac.uk

University of Kent School of Drama, Film and Visual Arts Scholarships

Purpose: To support research
Eligibility: Candidates are expected to hold an Upper Second Class (Honours) Degree and be a citizen of one of the European Union countries

Level of Study: Postgraduate, Research
Value: To cover home fees only
Length of Study: The bursary is 1 year
Frequency: Annual
Study Establishment: The University of Kent
Country of Study: United Kingdom
Application Procedure: Applicants must indicate their interest on the postgraduate application form
Closing Date: 31 July
Additional Information: Some teaching or research assistant work may be required www.kent.ac.uk/scholarships/search/FN37LSSTUD02

For further information contact:

Email: k.j.goddard@kent.ac.uk

University of Kent School of Mathematics, Statistics and Actuarial Science Scholarships

Purpose: To support research
Eligibility: Candidates should hold a good (first or upper second) Honours degree, or a Master's degree in a relevant subject
Level of Study: Doctorate, Postgraduate
Type: Scholarship
Value: Home fees and maintenance stipend
Length of Study: Up to 3 years
Frequency: Annual
Study Establishment: University of Kent
Country of Study: United Kingdom
Application Procedure: See webpages at www.kent.ac.uk/
Closing Date: 20 April
Funding: Commercial, Government
No. of awards given last year: 5

University of Kent School of Politics and International Relations Scholarships

Purpose: To support research
Eligibility: These scholarships are available to Home/European Union/Overseas students who have been made an offer by Kent for MPhil/PhD study
Level of Study: Doctorate, Postgraduate
Type: Scholarship
Value: Home fees and maintenance stipend
Length of Study: Up to 3 years
Frequency: Annual
Study Establishment: University of Kent
Country of Study: United Kingdom

Application Procedure: See webpages at www.kent.ac.uk/scholarships/postgraduate/departmental/politicsandir.html
Closing Date: April
Funding: Commercial, Government
No. of awards given last year: 2

University of Kent School of Psychology Scholarships

Purpose: To support research
Eligibility: Candidates must hold a good Honours degree (first class or 2i) or a Master's degree at merit or distinction in Psychology. Non-British qualifications will be judged individually; we will generally require an overall result in the top two grading categories
Level of Study: Doctorate, Postgraduate
Type: Scholarship
Value: Home fees and maintenance stipend
Length of Study: Up to 3 years
Study Establishment: University of Kent
Country of Study: United Kingdom
Application Procedure: Please check at www.kent.ac.uk/scholarships/postgraduate/departmental/psychology.html
Closing Date: April
Funding: Commercial, Government
No. of awards given last year: 5

University of Kent School of Social Policy, Sociology and Social Research Scholarships

Purpose: To support research
Eligibility: Candidates should hold a good (First or Upper Second Class) Honours degree or equivalent, in a relevant discipline
Level of Study: Doctorate, Postgraduate
Type: Scholarship
Value: The School will award up to three £3,000 scholarships (as contribution to tuition fees) on a competitive basis.
Length of Study: Up to 3 years
Frequency: Annual
Study Establishment: University of Kent
Country of Study: United Kingdom
Application Procedure: See webpages at www.kent.ac.uk/sspssr/studying/scholarships-and-bursaries/index.html
Closing Date: 26 June
Funding: Commercial, Government
No. of awards given last year: 3
Additional Information: This scholarship will be in addition to any Kent scholarships and discounts (such as the £1,000 Graduate School Scholarship, 10% Loyalty Discount and the

School £500 discount for high performing students) www.kent.ac.uk/scholarships/search/FN40SAM00002

For further information contact:

Email: K.Glezakou@kent.ac.uk

University of KwaZulu-Natal

Westville Campus, Private Bag X54001, Durban, South Africa.

Email: heard@ukzn.ac.za
Website: www.heard.org.za/

HEARD is a leading applied research centre with a global reputation for its research, education programmes, technical services, partnerships and networks, devoted to addressing the broad health challenges of Africa. HEARD was established in 1998 and is based at the University of KwaZulu-Natal, South Africa.

Health Economics and HIV/AIDS Research Division PhD Scholarships

Purpose: Under the supervision of Professor Nana Poku and with the generous support of Sida/NORAD, HEARD is offering up to four full-time PhD Research Scholarships in any of the following key areas of strategic focus Sexual and Reproductive Health; Health Systems Strengthening and Economics of Critical Enablers in HIV Programming

Eligibility: Applicant must have the below criteria. 1. Hold a Master's Degree in a pertinent subject or a first or upper second class degree together with a track record of professional experience in a health o health-related field. 2. Have demonstrable research experience. 3. Undertake to register for a PhD dissertation (full time) at the University of KwaZulu–Natal (UKZN). 4. Make a commitment to remain on the African continent for at least TWO years after graduation

Value: The value of each scholarship is R540,000 paid over three years

Length of Study: Scholarships will be paid in tranches over 3 years. Tranche payments will be conditional on research progress

Country of Study: South Africa

Application Procedure: 1. A letter of motivation and CV. 2. An eight to ten page concept note on one of HEARD's key thematic research areas Sexual & Reproductive Health & Rights; Gender, Equality & Health; Health Governance & Finance; and Health Systems Strengthening. 3. Certified copies of both your academic qualifications and your full academic records. If qualifications were obtained from non-English speaking countries please ensure that an official English translation is included. 4. A certified copy of your ID/passport. 5. Two letters of reference, at least one of which must be academic. The second can be from an individual of professional standing

Closing Date: 30 January

Additional Information: www.afterschoolafrica.com/43874/university-of-kwazulu-natal-health-economics-and-hiv-aids-research-division-heard-phd-scholarships-2020-for-african-students/

For further information contact:

Email: Hedderwick@ukzn.ac.za

University of Leeds

University of Leeds, Leeds LS2 9JT, United Kingdom.

Tel: (44) 113 3432222
Email: security@leeds.ac.uk
Website: www.leeds.ac.uk

The University, established in 1904, is one of the largest higher education institutions in the UK. We are renowned globally for the quality of our teaching and research

Beit Trust Postgraduate Scholarships

Purpose: To support Postgraduate Study or research at Masters' level (MSc/MA)

Eligibility: Open to persons under 30 years of age, or 35 years for medical doctors, who are university graduates domiciled in Zambia, Zimbabwe or Malawi. Applicants must be nationals of those countries, and have an Honours degree at undergraduate level

Level of Study: Postgraduate

Type: Scholarship

Value: Academic fees, living expenses, other allowances, economy return airfares and allowance toward laptops

Length of Study: A maximum of 2 years at a South African University or 1 year at a United Kingdom University

Frequency: Annual

U

Study Establishment: The University of Leeds

Country of Study: United Kingdom

Application Procedure: Please see the Beit Trust website on 1 April for the new Scholarship application process. Applicants from Zimbabwe and Malawi should contact the Harare office at africa@beittrust.org.uk

No. of awards offered: 720

Closing Date: 11 February

Funding: Private

No. of awards given last year: 19

No. of applicants last year: 720

Additional Information: Zambian applicants should contact the Beit Trust United Kingdom office at: scholarships@beittrust.org.uk beittrust.org.uk/beit-trust-scholarships

For further information contact:

Tel: (44) 1483 772575

Email: scholarships@beittrust.org.uk

Canon Collins Trust-FCO Chevening-University of Leeds Scholarships

Purpose: To provide awards to students of high academic calibre, who demonstrate both academic excellence and the potential to become leaders, decision makers and opinion formers in their own countries

Eligibility: Open to candidates from Angola, Botswana, Lesotho, Malawi Mozambique, Namibia, South Africa, Swaziland, Zambia or Zimbabwe. Applicants must already hold a degree of equivalent standard to a United Kingdom upper second class honours degree. An adequate standard of English is required

Level of Study: Postgraduate

Type: Scholarship

Value: Academic fees, living expenses, other allowances, economy return airfares

Length of Study: 1 year

Frequency: Annual

Study Establishment: The University of Leeds

Country of Study: United Kingdom

Application Procedure: Applicants must complete an application form available on request from the Canon Collins Trust

No. of awards offered: Not known

Closing Date: 28 February

Funding: Government, Private

No. of awards given last year: 10

No. of applicants last year: Not known

For further information contact:

Email: info@canoncollins.org.uk

Derek Fatchett Memorial Scholarships (Palestine)

Purpose: To provide awards to students of high academic calibre

Eligibility: Open to candidates who have obtained or are about to obtain the equivalent of a United Kingdom First or Second Class (Honours) Degree. Candidates must be nationals of Palestine

Level of Study: Postgraduate

Type: Scholarship

Value: Academic fees, living expenses, books, equipment, arrival and departure allowance, economy return airfares and the production of a dissertation

Length of Study: 1 year

Frequency: Annual

Study Establishment: The University of Leeds

Country of Study: United Kingdom

Application Procedure: Application procedures are now handled by the British Council offices in Ramallah and East Jerusalem

No. of awards offered: Not known

Closing Date: 31 May

Funding: Private

No. of applicants last year: Not known

For further information contact:

Email: Lmec@Lmec.org.uk

Frank Parkinson Scholarship

Purpose: To provide postgraduate scholarships for United Kingdom research students of high calibre

Eligibility: Candidates must be commencing PhD study for the first time and hold at least a United Kingdom upper second class honours degree or equivalent. Candidates must have British parents who have been domiciled in Yorkshire for a period of not less than 10 years

Level of Study: Doctorate

Type: Scholarship

Value: Fees at the University of Leeds standard home rate of fees. A maintenance grant of £14,000 for 3 years or £8,400 for 5 years.

Length of Study: Up to 3 years, subject to satisfactory progress

Frequency: Annual

Study Establishment: University of Leeds

Country of Study: United Kingdom

Application Procedure: An application form must be completed and returned to the Postgraduate Scholarships Office by the relevant date

No. of awards offered: 39

Closing Date: 1 June
Funding: Private
No. of awards given last year: 2
No. of applicants last year: 39
Additional Information: phd.leeds.ac.uk/funding/199-frank-parkinson-scholarship-2022

For further information contact:

Woodhouse, Leeds LS2 9JT, United Kingdom.

Tel: (44) 113 243 1751
Email: fbsgrad@leeds.ac.uk

Frank Stell Scholarship

Subjects: Biology, Agricultural Science or Social and Political Science.
Purpose: The Frank Stell Scholarship was established in 1959. The fund was bequeathed by Frank Stell of Halifax to provide scholarships tenable at the University of Leeds
Eligibility: 1. Applicants must not have already been awarded or be currently studying for a doctoral degree 2. The awards are available for new Postgraduate Researchers undertaking full-time or part-time research study leading to the degree of PhD. PGRs who are already registered for PhD research study are excluded from applying 3. Applicants must live within a reasonable distance of the University of Leeds whilst in receipt of this Scholarship 4. Beneficiaries of the awards must be resident or have a parent or parent's resident within the former administrative area of the County Council of the West Riding of Yorkshire.
Level of Study: Postgraduate
Type: Scholarship
Value: A maintenance grant of £14,000 for 3 years (full-time), or £8,400 for 5 years (part-time).
Length of Study: Full-time (3 years) or part-time (5 years)
Frequency: Dependent on funds available
Study Establishment: University of Leeds
Country of Study: United Kingdom
Application Procedure: Details provided on website www.scholarships.leeds.ac.uk
Closing Date: 1 June
Funding: Trusts

For further information contact:

Woodhouse, Leeds LS2 9JT, United Kingdom.

Tel: (44) 113 243 1751

Henry Ellison Scholarship

Purpose: The Henry Ellison Scholarship was established in 1943. The fund was bequeathed by Mr Henry Ellison of Calverley, Leeds for the promotion of research in pure and applied chemistry and physics and is intended to enable promising graduates to gain training in scientific research in the School of Chemistry or School of Physics and Astronomy
Eligibility: 1. Applicants must not have already been awarded or be currently studying for a doctoral degree 2. The awards are available for new Postgraduate Researchers undertaking full-time or part-time research study leading to the degree of PhD. PGRs who are already registered for PhD research study are excluded from applying 3. Applicants must be graduates of the University of Leeds 4. Applicants must live within a reasonable distance of the University of Leeds whilst in receipt of this Scholarship.
Level of Study: Postgraduate
Type: Scholarship
Value: A maintenance grant of £14,000 for 3 years (full-time), or £8,400 for 5 years (part-time).
Length of Study: Full-time (3 years) or part-time (5 years)
Frequency: Dependent on funds available
Study Establishment: University of Leeds
Country of Study: United Kingdom
Application Procedure: Details provided on website www.scholaships.leeds.ac.uk
Closing Date: 1 June
Funding: Trusts
Contributor: 1

For further information contact:

Woodhouse, Leeds LS2 9JT, United Kingdom.

Tel: (44) 113 243 1751
Email: maps.pgr.admissions@leeds.ac.uk or pg_scholarships@ac.uk

John Henry Garner Scholarship

Purpose: To provide postgraduate scholarships for United Kingdom and European Union research students of high calibre
Eligibility: Candidates must be from the United Kingdom or an European Union country (or eligible to pay fees at the United Kingdom rate) and be commencing PhD study for the first time. Candidates must hold at least a United Kingdom Upper Second Class Honours degree or equivalent

Level of Study: Doctorate
Type: Scholarship
Value: A maintenance grant at a rate of £14,000 for 3 years (full-time), or £8,400 for 5 years (part-time).
Length of Study: Full-time (3 years) or part-time (5 years)
Frequency: Dependent on funds available
Study Establishment: University of Leeds
Country of Study: United Kingdom
Application Procedure: Details provided on website www. scholarships.leeds.ac.uk
Closing Date: 1 June

For further information contact:

Woodhouse, Leeds LS2 9JT, United Kingdom.

Tel: (44) 113 343 34077
Email: pg_scholarships@leeds.ac.uk

Marks and Spencer - Leeds University- FCO Chevening Scholarships

Purpose: To provide postgraduate scholarships to students of high academic calibre
Eligibility: Open to candidates from Hong Kong who have obtained, or are about to obtain, a first degree of a similar standard to a United Kingdom good Upper Second Class (Honours) Degree. An adequate standard of English language is required
Level of Study: Postgraduate
Type: Scholarship
Value: Full tuition fees, maintenance allowance, books, equipment and production of dissertation
Length of Study: 1 year
Frequency: Annual
Study Establishment: The University of Leeds
Country of Study: United Kingdom
Application Procedure: By application form and acceptance onto taught course. Both application forms are available from the University and British Council (Hong Kong)
Funding: Commercial, Government
No. of awards given last year: 1
Additional Information: The address for the British Council in Hong Kong is: The Education Exchange Unit, 255 Hennessey Road, Wanchai, Hong Kong business.leeds. ac.uk/dir-record/lubs-scholarships/1355/university-of-leeds-chevening-scholarships

For further information contact:

Email: scholarships@gcu.ac.uk

Mary and Alice Smith Memorial Scholarship

Purpose: To provide postgraduate scholarships for United Kingdom research students of high calibre
Eligibility: Candidates must be British and be commencing PhD study for the first time. Candidates must hold at least a United Kingdom Upper Second Class Honours degree or equivalent
Level of Study: Doctorate
Type: Scholarship
Value: A maintenance grant at the standard UKRI rate of £14,000 for 3 years (full-time), or £8,400 for 5 years (part-time)
Length of Study: Full-time (3 years) or part-time (5 years)
Frequency: Dependent on funds available
Study Establishment: University of Leeds
Country of Study: United Kingdom
Application Procedure: Details provided on www.scholar ships.leeds.ac.uk
Closing Date: 1 June
Additional Information: For further information please contact the www.leeds.ac.uk/info/130500/faculties phd.leeds.ac. uk/funding/43-mary-and-alice-smith-memorial-scholarship-2020

For further information contact:

Tel: (44) 113 343 34077
Email: pg_scholarships@ac.uk

Stanley Burton Research Scholarship

Purpose: The purpose of these Scholarships is to assist Home-rated postgraduate researchers to undertake research study in the School of Music at the University of Leeds.
Eligibility: 1. Applicants must not have already been awarded or be currently studying for a doctoral degree 2. The awards are available for new Postgraduate Researchers undertaking full-time or part-time research study leading to the degree of PhD. PGRs who are already registered for PhD research study are excluded from applying 3. Applicants must live within a reasonable distance of the University of Leeds whilst in receipt of this Scholarship.
Level of Study: Doctorate
Type: Scholarship
Value: A maintenance grant at a rate of £14,000 for 3 years (full-time), or £8,400 for 5 years (part-time).
Length of Study: Full-time (3 years) or part-time (5 years)
Frequency: Dependent on funds available
Study Establishment: University of Leeds
Country of Study: United Kingdom

Application Procedure: Details provided on www.scholar ships.leeds.ac.uk

No. of awards offered: 1

Closing Date: 1 June

Additional Information: phd.leeds.ac.uk/funding/23-stanley-burton-research-scholarship-2022 https://www.post graduatefunding.com/award-3464

For further information contact:

Woodhouse, Leeds LS2 9JT, United Kingdom.

Tel: (44) 113 343 8713 or (44) 113 343 34077
Email: ahcpgradmissions@leeds.ac.uk or pg_scholarships@leeds.ac.uk

University of Leeds International Fee Bursary (Vietnam)

Purpose: To provide scholarships to students of high academic calibre

Eligibility: Open to nationals of Vietnam who have obtained a degree equivalent to a good Second Class (Honours) Degree. An adequate standard of English is required

Level of Study: Postgraduate

Type: Scholarship

Value: Academic fees

Length of Study: 1 year

Frequency: Annual

Study Establishment: The University of Leeds

Country of Study: United Kingdom

Application Procedure: Applicants must address a letter of application to the School of Computing

Closing Date: 10 June

Funding: Private

No. of awards given last year: 1

University of Leeds International Fee Bursary (Vietnam) - for Subject Areas Listed below Leeds

Purpose: To provide scholarships to students of high academic calibre in the School of Computing, Politics and International Studies and Leeds University Business School

Eligibility: Open to nationals of Vietnam who have obtained a degree equivalent to a good Second Class (Honours) Degree. An adequate standard of English is required

Level of Study: Postgraduate

Type: Scholarship

Value: Academic fees

Length of Study: 1 year

Frequency: Annual

Study Establishment: The University of Leeds

Country of Study: United Kingdom

Application Procedure: Applicants must make an application in letter format to the Taught Postgraduate Secretary in the school they intend to study

No. of awards offered: Not known

Closing Date: 29 May

Funding: Private

No. of awards given last year: 4

No. of applicants last year: Not known

For further information contact:

Email: info@lubs.leeds.ac.uk

University of Leeds International Fee Bursary (Vietnam) - Information Systems/Multimedia Systems

Purpose: To provide scholarships to students of high academic calibre who wish to study in the school of computing

Eligibility: Applicants must be nationals of Vietnam and must already have obtained a good Second Class (Honours) Degree. An adequate standard of English is also required

Level of Study: Postgraduate

Type: Scholarship

Value: Academic fees

Length of Study: 1 year

Frequency: Annual

Study Establishment: The University of Leeds

Country of Study: United Kingdom

Application Procedure: Applicants must make an application in letter form to the Taught Postgraduate Secretary in the School of Computing

Closing Date: 11 June

Funding: Private

No. of awards given last year: 1

For further information contact:

International office, University of Leeds, Leeds LS2 9JT, United Kingdom.

Email: info@lubs.leeds.ac.uk

University of Leicester

University Road, Leicester LE1 7RH, United Kingdom.

Tel: (44) 162 522 522
Website: www.le.ac.uk

The University was founded as Leicester, Leicestershire and Rutland University College in 1921. The site for the University was donated by a local businessman, Thomas Fielding Johnson, in order to create a living memorial for all local people who made sacrifices during the First World War.

Central United Kingdom NERC Training Alliance (CENTA) PhD Studentships for European Union Students

Purpose: Studentships are available to pursue PhD research programme
Type: Award
Value: CENTA has been awarded £4.9 million from the Natural Environment Research Council (NERC)
Length of Study: 5 years
Country of Study: United Kingdom
Closing Date: 22 January

For further information contact:

Email: communications@ukri.org

College of Science and Engineering Postgraduate Scholarship Scheme

Purpose: University of Leicester's aim is to be a world-class research-intensive university and deliver teaching and facilitate learning of the highest quality
Type: Postgraduate scholarships
Value: Scholarship worth up to £5,600 per year of full
Study Establishment: Scholarships are awarded in the field of Chemistry, Engineering, Geography, Informatics, Mathematics and Physics and Astronomy
Country of Study: United Kingdom
Application Procedure: There is no need to apply for this scholarship. Eligible students will be automatically considered. If successful, you will be notified when you submit your final results.
Closing Date: January
Additional Information: https://le.ac.uk/study/postgraduates/fees-funding/scholarships-discounts/cse-postgrad

For further information contact:

The University of Leicester, University Road, Leicester LE1 7RH, United Kingdom.

Email: scholarships@le.ac.uk

PhD Studentships in Computer Science

Purpose: To support research organizations attract the best people into postgraduate research and training and to provide doctoral training grant support
Eligibility: Please check at EPSRC website at www2.le.ac.uk/study/research/funding/epsrc-computing
Level of Study: Doctorate
Type: Studentship
Value: The successful applicants will receive an annual stipend of at least £13,863 together with a conference allowance and training support grant worth £600 each year
Length of Study: 3 years
Frequency: Dependent on funds available
Study Establishment: University of Leicester, Computer Science Department
Country of Study: United Kingdom
Application Procedure: Please refer to the University of Leicester website at www2.le.ac.uk/study/research/funding/epsrc-computing. Our PhD superiors have a range of interests and the aim is to align you with someone with expertise in your field. Details of our research themes are on the website
Funding: Government
Contributor: EPSRC (DTG)
Additional Information: Applications are considered throughout the year. Refer to advertisement on website https://le.ac.uk/study/postgraduates/fees-funding/scholarships-discounts/

For further information contact:

Email: fdv1@mcs.le.ac.uk

PhD Studentships in Mathematics

Eligibility: United Kingdom and European Union PhD students, who have been residents in the United Kingdom for 3 years prior to application, and fees-only funding for other European Union students
Level of Study: Doctorate, Research
Type: Studentship
Value: £14,057 in the first year, rising in successive years, and full tuition fees
Length of Study: 3.5 years
Country of Study: United Kingdom
Application Procedure: Applications can be made online and submitted to admissions office. Information on how to apply and what supporting documents needed can be found at www2.le.ac.uk/research/degrees/phd/maths/supervision

For further information contact:

Email: pgresearch@maths.ed.ac.uk

President's Postgraduate Scholarship Scheme

Purpose: This is a postgraduate scholarship that enables international students to get a chance to study in University of Leicester, United Kingdom

Eligibility: 1. This scholarship is for new international (non-EU) students on a full-time, taught, campus-based Masters course starting in September 2023 or January 2024. 2. This scholarship is open to applicants who already have an offer (conditional or unconditional) to study for a Masters degree programme at the University. 3. If you receive your offer to study by 10 March 2023, please submit your scholarship application by the first deadline of 30 March 2023. If you receive your offer to study after 10 March 2023, please apply by the second deadline of 13 July 2023. 4. You cannot combine this scholarship with a full scholarship (for tuition fees and living costs) from any other source. You are able to receive only one partial scholarship from the University. If you have a partial scholarship from other sources you will still be considered for the President's Postgraduate Scholarship. 5. This scholarship is not available for distance learning courses.

Value: Value of Scholarship £3,000 in the form of reduction in tuition fees

Length of Study: 1 to 2 years

Country of Study: Any country

Application Procedure: Send your completed application by email to scholarships@le.ac.uk

No. of awards offered: 100

Closing Date: 31 July

Additional Information: https://le.ac.uk/study/postgraduates/fees-funding/scholarships-discounts/

For further information contact:

Tel: (44) 141 331 3000
Email: ukroenquiries@gcu.ac.uk

University of Limerick

Kemmy Business School, Limerick V94 T9PX, Ireland.

Tel: (353) 61 202 116
Website: www.ul.ie

Kemmy Business School: PhD Scholarship

Level of Study: Doctorate
Type: Postgraduate scholarships
Value: €1,500 per year

Frequency: Every 3 years
Country of Study: Ireland

For further information contact:

Email: international@ul.ie

University of Lincoln

Brayford Pool, Lincoln LN6 7TS, United Kingdom.

Tel: (44) 1522 882 000
Website: www.lincoln.ac.uk

Lincoln is ranked 11th in the United Kingdom for student satisfaction in the National Student Survey (NSS) 2016. The University is committed to developing enterprising graduates, with Lincoln students enjoying good graduate prospects and many going on to start their own successful businesses. The University of Lincoln is producing world-leading research across many subject areas.

Bangladesh Scholarship

Purpose: The University of Lincoln's Bangladesh Scholarship is aimed at supporting postgraduate taught students from across Bangladesh.

Eligibility: Be a national of, or have permanent residence in, Bangladesh 1. Hold a Conditional or Unconditional Offer from the University of Lincoln for a full-time postgraduate taught programme commencing in September/October 2023 or January/February 2024 2. Have been awarded, or be expected to receive, a Bachelor's degree from a recognised institution with a minimum grade of 2:2 or equivalent.

Level of Study: Postgraduate

Type: Scholarship

Value: £5,000

Frequency: Annual

Country of Study: Any country

Closing Date: 1 June

Additional Information: www.lincoln.ac.uk/studywithus/scholarshipsandbursaries/bangladeshscholarship/

For further information contact:

Brayford Way, Brayford Pool, Lincoln LN6 7TS, United Kingdom.

Tel: (44) 1522 882000

Developing Futures Scholarship

Purpose: The University of Lincoln Developing Futures Scholarship is designed to help support students from the Czech Republic, Slovakia, Poland, Hungary, Romania, Bulgaria, Slovenia, Croatia, Estonia, Latvia, Lithuania, Malta, and Cyprus.

Eligibility: The University of Lincoln is delighted to offer the Lincoln Developing Futures Scholarship to prospective undergraduate, postgraduate taught or postgraduate research applicants who are a national of, or have permanent residence in, one of the following countries: Czech Republic, Slovakia, Poland, Hungary, Romania, Bulgaria, Slovenia, Croatia, Estonia, Latvia, Lithuania, Malta, and Cyprus. Be a national of, or have permanent residence in, one of the following countries: Czech Republic, Slovakia, Poland, Hungary, Romania, Bulgaria, Slovenia, Croatia, Estonia, Latvia, Lithuania, Malta, or Cyprus 1. Hold a Conditional or Unconditional Offer from the University of Lincoln for a full-time undergraduate, postgraduate taught or postgraduate research programme commencing in 2023/24. Students intending to join a postgraduate taught or postgraduate research programme require a minimum grade of 2:2 or equivalent in a recognised bachelor's degree in order to be eligible to receive the scholarship.

Type: Scholarship

Value: £5,000

Country of Study: Any country

Closing Date: 1 June

Additional Information: www.lincoln.ac.uk/studywithus/scholarshipsandbursaries/developingfuturesscholarship/

For further information contact:

Brayford Way, Brayford Pool, Lincoln LN6 7TS, United Kingdom.

Tel: (44) 1522 882000

Egypt Scholarship

Purpose: The University of Lincoln Egypt Scholarship is aimed at supporting high-achieving postgraduate students from across Egypt

Level of Study: Postgraduate

Type: Scholarship

Value: £5,000

Frequency: Annual

Country of Study: United Kingdom

Application Procedure: You do not need to apply for this scholarship. You will automatically be considered for the Egypt Scholarship once you have submitted your application to study at the University of Lincoln.

Closing Date: 1 June

Additional Information: Further information regarding the awarding of international scholarships can be found within the Scholarship Terms and Conditions. www.lincoln.ac.uk/home/studywithus/internationalstudents/scholarshiptermsandconditions/

For further information contact:

Brayford Way, Brayford Pool, Lincoln LN6 7TS, United Kingdom.

Tel: (44) 1522 882000
Email: intscholarships@lincoln.ac.uk

Ghana Scholarship

Purpose: The University of Lincoln are delighted to offer Ghana Scholarships to high achieving applicants

Type: Scholarship

Value: £5,000

Country of Study: Any country

Application Procedure: Submit the application to intscholarships@lincoln.ac.uk

Closing Date: 22 June

For further information contact:

Email: international@lincoln.ac.uk

Global Postgraduate Scholarship

Eligibility: To be eligible for the scholarship, students must hold a recognised bachelor's degree with a minimum grade of 22 or equivalent. Please note that this scholarship is not available for MPhil/PhD programmes.

Level of Study: Postgraduate

Type: Scholarship

Value: £2,000

Frequency: Varies

Country of Study: Any country

Application Procedure: You do not need to apply for this scholarship. You will automatically be considered for a Global Postgraduate Scholarship once you have submitted your course application.

Closing Date: 1 June

Funding: Trusts

Additional Information: https://www.lincoln.ac.uk/studywithus/scholarshipsandbursaries/globalpostgraduatescholarship/

For further information contact:

Brayford Way, Brayford Pool, Lincoln LN6 7TS, United Kingdom.

Tel: (44) 1522 882000
Email: international@lincoln.ac.uk

India Scholarship

Purpose: The University of Lincoln India Scholarship is aimed at supporting high-achieving postgraduate students from across India

Eligibility: 1. Be a national of, or have permanent residence in, India 2. Hold a Conditional or Unconditional Offer from the University of Lincoln for a full-time postgraduate taught programme 3. Have been awarded, or be expected to receive, a bachelor's degree from a recognised university with a minimum GPA score of 65% or equivalent 4. Meet the English language requirements of their intended programme of study

Level of Study: Postgraduate
Type: Scholarship
Value: £5,000
Length of Study: 1 year
Frequency: Varies
Country of Study: Any country
Application Procedure: You do not need to apply for this scholarship. You will automatically be considered for the India Scholarship once you have submitted your application to study at the University of Lincoln.
Closing Date: 1 June
Funding: Trusts
Additional Information: www.lincoln.ac.uk/home/study withus/scholarshipsandbursaries/indiascholarship/

For further information contact:

Brayford Way, Brayford Pool, Lincoln LN6 7TS, United Kingdom.

Tel: (44) 1522 882000
Email: intscholarships@lincoln.ac.uk

Indonesia Scholarship

Purpose: The University of Lincoln Indonesia Scholarship is aimed at supporting high-achieving postgraduate students from across Indonesia.

Eligibility: 1. Be a national of, or have permanent residence in, Indonesia 2. Hold a Conditional or Unconditional Offer from the University of Lincoln for a full-time postgraduate taught programme 3. Have been awarded, or be expected to receive, a bachelor's degree from a recognised university with a minimum GPA score of 2.8 or equivalent 4. Meet the English language requirements of their intended programme of study

Level of Study: Postgraduate
Type: Scholarship
Value: This scholarship is valued at £5,000
Frequency: Varies
Country of Study: Any country
Closing Date: 1 June
Funding: Trusts
Additional Information: www.lincoln.ac.uk/home/study withus/scholarshipsandbursaries/

For further information contact:

Email: intscholarships@lincoln.ac.uk

Lincoln Alumni Master of Architecture Scholarship

Purpose: The Lincoln Alumni Master of Architecture Scholarship is an award for students who have previously completed study at the University of Lincoln and are enrolling on the Master of Architecture Programme (MArch).
Eligibility: 1. You must have previously completed an undergraduate degree (or equivalent qualification that leads to postgraduate study), Graduate Certificate, or Graduate Diploma at the University of Lincoln. 2. You must have a student status of 'Home' on the Student Information System. 3. You must be enrolled on the Student Information System, via one of the identified progression routes, on the Master of Architecture programme for the current academic year. 4. You must have commenced the programme in the academic year 2023/24 and be paying the full tuition fee rate of £9,250. 5. Part-time students must have commenced the programme in academic year 2023/24 and be paying the part-time tuition fee rate of £77 per credit point.
Level of Study: Postgraduate
Type: Scholarship
Value: £1,000 will be paid directly to the student for each year of study for each completed academic year of study, with part-time students eligible for a pro-rata payment.
Frequency: Annual
Country of Study: United Kingdom
Application Procedure: There is no need to apply, eligible students will receive this scholarship upon enrolling for the Master of Architecture programme.
Funding: Private
Additional Information: Please contact admission s@lincoln.ac.uk for further details. www.lincoln.ac.uk/ home/studywithus/scholarshipsandbursaries/

For further information contact:

Email: intscholarships@lincoln.ac.uk

Master of Science Sport Science: Applied Sport Science Bursary

Purpose: Up to three Applied Sport Science Bursaries will be offered to exceptional students enrolling on MSc Sport Science program
Level of Study: Postgraduate
Type: Bursary
Value: £1,500
Frequency: Varies
Country of Study: Any country
Application Procedure: Apply online
Closing Date: 19 September
Funding: Trusts

For further information contact:

Tel: (44) 1522 886651
Email: swillmott@lincoln.ac.uk

Minority Ethnic Studentship

Purpose: The University of Lincoln College of Arts Minority Ethnic Studentship will be awarded to the applicant who demonstrates the highest levels of academic, personal, and extracurricular endeavour.
Eligibility: Hold an offer of study for a postgraduate taught programme within the College of Arts 1. Be classed as a UK-permanent resident of a Black, Asian, or Minority Ethnic background
Level of Study: Postgraduate
Type: Studentship
Value: £2,500
Country of Study: Any country
Closing Date: 31 August
Additional Information: www.lincoln.ac.uk/studywithus/scholarshipsandbursaries/minorityethnicstudentship/

For further information contact:

Brayford Way, Brayford Pool, Lincoln LN6 7TS, United Kingdom.

Tel: (44) 1522 882000
Email: lwherrell@lincoln.ac.uk

Nigeria Scholarship

Purpose: The University of Lincoln Nigeria Scholarship is aimed at supporting high-achieving postgraduate students from across Nigeria
Eligibility: Be a Nigerian citizen. Already hold a conditional or unconditional offer from the University of Lincoln for a full-time postgraduate taught or Master's by Research programme commencing in September
Type: Scholarship
Value: The scholarship is valued at £5,000
Country of Study: United Kingdom
Application Procedure: Submit applications to intscholarships@lincoln.ac.uk
Funding: Private
Additional Information: For further information, please contact the International Office www.lincoln.ac.uk/home/studywithus/scholarshipsandbursaries/

For further information contact:

Email: intscholarships@lincoln.ac.uk

Thai Scholarship

Purpose: The University of Lincoln Thai Scholarship is aimed at supporting high-achieving postgraduate students from across Thailand.
Eligibility: 1. Be a national of, or have permanent residence in, Thailand 2. Hold a Conditional or Unconditional Offer from the University of Lincoln for a full-time postgraduate taught programme 3. Have been awarded, or be expected to receive, a bachelor's degree from a recognised university with a minimum GPA score of 2.5 or equivalent 4. Meet the English language requirements of their intended programme of study
Level of Study: Postgraduate
Type: Scholarship
Value: £5,000
Frequency: Varies
Country of Study: Any country
Application Procedure: You do not need to apply for this scholarship. You will automatically be considered for the Thai Scholarship once you have submitted your application to study at the University of Lincoln.
Closing Date: 17 December
Funding: Trusts

For further information contact:

Email: intscholarships@lincoln.ac.uk

Thailand Scholarship

Purpose: The University of Lincoln Thai Scholarship is aimed at supporting high-achieving postgraduate students from across Thailand
Eligibility: Be a Thai citizen. Already hold a conditional or unconditional offer from the University of Lincoln for a full-time postgraduate taught or Master's by Research programme commencing in September
Type: Scholarship
Value: £5,000
Country of Study: Any country
Application Procedure: For details, please visit intscholarships@lincoln.ac.uk
Closing Date: 1 June
Additional Information: www.lincoln.ac.uk/studywithus/scholarshipsandbursaries/thaischolarship/

For further information contact:

Brayford Way, Brayford Pool, Lincoln LN6 7TS, United Kingdom.

Tel: (44) 1522 882000
Email: intscholarships@lincoln.ac.uk

The Lincoln 50% Global Scholarship

Purpose: The Lincoln 50% Global Scholarship is available to high-achieving international applicants joining the University of Lincoln
Eligibility: 1. Hold an unconditional offer from the University of Lincoln for a full-time undergraduate or postgraduate taught programme commencing in 2022 or 2023. 2. Meet the English language requirements of their intended course of study – this typically ranges from an IELTS 6.0 – 7.0 or equivalent.
Level of Study: Postgraduate
Type: Scholarship
Frequency: Varies
Country of Study: Any country
Application Procedure: Please note that this scholarship is competitive and will only be awarded to candidates who demonstrate the highest levels of excellence in academia, extracurricular and personal endeavour. The above will be assessed by completing a 500 word statement as part of the Scholarship Application Form.
Funding: Trusts
Additional Information: The University endeavours to notify all candidates of the outcome of their scholarship application within 10 days of the closing date. www.lincoln.ac.uk/home/studywithus/scholarshipsandbursaries/

For further information contact:

Email: intscholarships@lincoln.ac.uk

University of Lincoln India Scholarships

Value: £5,000
Country of Study: Any country
Application Procedure: The mode of applying is online
Closing Date: September

For further information contact:

Email: intscholarships@lincoln.ac.uk

Uruguay PhD Scholarship

Purpose: To conduct PhD studies in Life Sciences has recently been agreed between the University of Lincoln and the Uruguay National Agency for Research and Innovation (ANII - Agencia Nacional de Investigaciön e Innovaciön)
Type: Scholarship
Value: The scholarship covers university fees and a subsistence bursary
Country of Study: United Kingdom
Application Procedure: 1. Must be a citizen of Uruguay 2. Have already obtained a BSc (or equivalent) degree in an area relevant to the research fields described above. A minimum of a UK equivalent to a 21 award is required to enter the application process 3. The applications must include a copy of the applicant's CV and a one page research statement describing research interests, ambition and briefly outline a research project 4. The deadline for submissions is 18 March, at 1400 (UYT) 5. Full details are available www.anii.org.uy/apoyos/formacion/9/maestrias-y-doctorados-en-el-exterior-en-areas-estrategicas/
Closing Date: 18 March
Additional Information: For additional information regarding this scholarship please contact: Prof. Fernando Montealegre-Zapata www.lincoln.ac.uk/home/studywithus/scholarshipsandbursaries/

For further information contact:

Tel: (44) 1522 835460
Email: fmontealegrez@lincoln.ac.uk

Vietnam Merit Scholarship

Purpose: The University of Lincoln Vietnam Merit Scholarship is aimed at supporting high achieving postgraduate students from across Vietnam
Level of Study: Postgraduate
Type: Scholarship
Value: Tuition fees and are valued at £5,000
Country of Study: Any country
Application Procedure: Submit applications to intscholarships@lincoln.ac.uk
Closing Date: 1 June
Additional Information: www.lincoln.ac.uk/studywithus/scholarshipsandbursaries/vietnamscholarship/

For further information contact:

Brayford Way, Brayford Pool, Lincoln LN6 7TS, United Kingdom.

Tel: (44) 1522 882000
Email: intscholarships@lincoln.ac.uk

University of Liverpool

Foundation Building, Brownlow Hill,, Liverpool L69 3BX, United Kingdom.

Tel: (44) 151 794 5927
Email: irro@liverpool.ac.uk.
Website: www.liverpool.ac.uk

The University of Liverpool is a public university based in the city of Liverpool, United Kingdom. Founded as a college in 1881, it gained its royal charter in 1903 with the ability to award degrees and is also known to be one of the six original "red brick" civic universities. It comprises three faculties organized into 35 departments and schools. It is a founding member of the Russell Group, the N8 Group for research collaboration and the University Management school is AACSB accredited.

Commonwealth Shared Scholarship Scheme

Purpose: Commonwealth Shared Scholarships, offered in partnership with United Kingdom universities, are for developing country students who would not otherwise be able to undertake master's level study in the United Kingdom

Eligibility: The scholarship has certain eligibility criteria and other requirements, which include 1. Students who hold a first degree at either first class or upper second-class level are eligible for the award 2. The university confirms candidates are sufficiently fluent in written and oral English to pursue their proposed studies immediately 3. Scholarships are applicable to the nationals of commonwealth developing countries, who are not at present living or studying in a developed commonwealth country. 4. Students must return to their home country as soon as the award comes to an end.
Level of Study: Masters Degree
Type: Scholarship
Value: Covers tuition fees, living costs and return flights to the United Kingdom
Country of Study: United Kingdom
No. of awards offered: 5
Closing Date: 1 April
Funding: Trusts
Contributor: Department for International Development (DFID)
Additional Information: www.univariety.com/scholarship/Commonwealth-Shared-Scholarship-Scheme-University-of-Liverpool/6670280b

For further information contact:

Tel: (44) 151 794 2000

FIDERH Award

Eligibility: You must be a Mexican national
Type: Award
Value: 20% reduction in tuition fees for postgraduate taught and research programmes
Country of Study: United Kingdom
Closing Date: 28 February
Additional Information: Please apply for funding through FIDERH. Students who are awarded a FIDERH Graduate Loan and register at the University of Liverpool will automatically receive the award www.liverpool.ac.uk/study/postgraduate-taught/finance/scholarships/scholarships/fiderh-award/

Health Data Science Scholarships

Purpose: These scholarships will be awarded on a competitive basis to the strongest applicants for the MSc Health Data Science, and paid as a reduction in fees.
Eligibility: You must hold, or be on track to obtain, at least a high 2:1 (65+%) in your undergraduate degree, including marks of 60+% in modules relevant to the MSc programme.

Work experience relevant to Data Science (paid, internship, shadowing or voluntary positions) would be advantageous.
Level of Study: Postgraduate (MSc)
Type: Scholarship
Value: £10,300
Frequency: Annual
Country of Study: Any country
Additional Information: www.liverpool.ac.uk/study/postgraduate-taught/finance/scholarships/scholarships/health-data-science-msc-scholarships/

For further information contact:

Tel: (44) 151 794 2000

Hodgson Law Scholarship

Purpose: The Trustees wish Hodgson Law Scholars to benefit from education in Liverpool with a view to encouraging the intellectual growth of promising law students and the nurturing of close links with the City of Liverpool and the Liverpool City Region.
Eligibility: 1. Academic excellence. 2. Evidence of an interest in legal and public service which may benefit the Liverpool City Region. 3. Potential and ambition for future leadership. 4. That they are not otherwise able to undertake a postgraduate degree at either institution.; Further details are available on the hodgsonlawscholarships.com/
Value: £9,135
Country of Study: United Kingdom
Application Procedure: You will need to complete and submit the Hodgson Trust Application Form electronically to the Hodgson Selection Committee by email to hodgscho@liverpool.ac.uk.
Additional Information: Applications may also be sent by post, to the address provided on the application form. www.liverpool.ac.uk/study/postgraduate-taught/finance/scholarships/scholarships/fiderh-award/

For further information contact:

Email: jtribe@liverpool.ac.uk

John Lennon Memorial Scholarship

Purpose: The award is intended to support students from Merseyside who might be in financial need and enhance, among other things, awareness of global problems and environmental issues.
Type: Scholarship
Country of Study: Any country

Application Procedure: You will need to complete and submit the form by email to the Secretary to the Scholarships Sub-Committee by email to seschol@liverpool.ac.uk
Closing Date: 5 April
Additional Information: www.liverpool.ac.uk/study/postgraduate-taught/finance/scholarships/scholarships/john-lennon-memorial-scholarship/

For further information contact:

Email: seschol@liverpool.ac.uk

John Lennon Memorial Scholarship

Purpose: The John Lennon Memorial Scholarships were set up by a trust fund endowed in the University for the provision of scholarships in the memory of John Lennon.
Eligibility: If you are a current or prospective Home/EU postgraduate (taught and research), either born in or with very strong family connections to Merseyside and who has an academic offer from the University of Liverpool, you are eligible to apply. The award is available to all subject areas studied on the main University campus.
Level of Study: Postgraduate
Type: Scholarship
Value: as of number of awards
Country of Study: Any country
Closing Date: 4 April
Additional Information: www.liverpool.ac.uk/study/postgraduate-taught/finance/scholarships/scholarships/john-lennon-memorial-scholarship/

For further information contact:

Tel: (44) 151 794 2000

Liverpool International College (LIC) Excellence Award

Eligibility: Students who achieve an average of 75% or above in their LIC Pre-Master's programme
Type: Award
Value: £2,500 tuition fee reduction
Country of Study: United Kingdom
Additional Information: No application necessary. The award will automatically be awarded to those who meet criteria www.liverpool.ac.uk/study/postgraduate-taught/finance/scholarships/scholarships/lic-excellence-award/

For further information contact:

Email: irro@liverpool.ac.uk

Liverpool Law School LLM Bursaries

Purpose: Awards will help students with their tuition fees. They are offered to encourage the best students, from the United Kingdom, Europe and internationally, to join the expanding LLM programme

Eligibility: Home, European Union and international students studying a LLM programme. Liverpool Law School LLM Bursaries will be awarded on the basis of merit. Academic performance in earlier degrees they have taken, as well as any other practical or intellectual achievements, will be taken into account

Type: Bursary

Value: 1. Two bursaries worth £500 each for Home/EU students 2. Two bursaries wroth £1,000 each for international students

Country of Study: United Kingdom

Application Procedure: Students do NOT need to make an extra application for the Liverpool Law School LLM Bursaries. All students who have registered for the LLM will be considered automatically. The decision of Liverpool Law School on the award of the bursaries is final

Additional Information: www.liverpool.ac.uk/study/postgraduate-taught/finance/scholarships/scholarships/liverpool-law-school-llm-bursaries/

For further information contact:

Email: irro@liverpool.ac.uk

Marshall Scholarships

Purpose: To enable intellectually distinguished young Americans, their country's future leaders, to study in the United Kingdom. 1. To help Scholars gain an understanding and appreciation of contemporary Britain

Eligibility: To qualify, candidates should 1. Be citizens of the United States of America normally resident in the United States of America. 2. Hold a doctorate in a science or engineering subject by the time they take up their Fellowship

Type: Scholarship

Value: Full tuition fee waiver for a master

Country of Study: United Kingdom

Closing Date: 30 September

Additional Information: Apply via: www.marshallscholarship.org/applications/apply   www.marshallscholarship.org/apply

For further information contact:

Email: apps@marshallscholarship.org

MSc Data Science and Artificial Intelligence Scholarship

Purpose: The scholarships are for underrepresented groups in the field of Data Science and Artificial Intelligence.

Eligibility: you need to be a member of at least one of the underrepresented groups

Level of Study: Postgraduate (MSc)

Type: Scholarship

Value: £10,000 each

Frequency: Annual

Country of Study: Any country

Closing Date: 30 May

Additional Information: www.liverpool.ac.uk/study/postgraduate-taught/finance/scholarships/scholarships/msc-data-science-and-artificial-intelligence-bursary/

For further information contact:

Tel: (44) 151 794 2000

Postgraduate Opportunity Bursary

Purpose: This bursary is available to UK University of Liverpool graduates who are progressing to a standard master's course, including MRes programmes, within two years of graduation from their undergraduate degree.

Eligibility: They must be beginning a new full-time or part-time postgraduate taught master's programme (including MRes programmes) in academic year 2023/24. ii) They must be an alumnus or alumna of the University of Liverpool having completed an undergraduate degree on the Liverpool campus no earlier than session 2020/21. iii) They must have been in receipt of one of the University's Widening Access Awards during their period of undergraduate studies at the University of Liverpool.

Type: Award

Value: £3,000

Length of Study: one year

Country of Study: Any country

Additional Information: www.liverpool.ac.uk/study/postgraduate-taught/finance/scholarships/scholarships/postgraduate-opportunity-bursary/

For further information contact:

Tel: (44) 151 794 2000

Postgraduate Progression Award - UK students

Purpose: If you're a current University of Liverpool undergraduate or alumni from the UK progressing to either full or part-time new postgraduate taught programme you're eligible to receive our Postgraduate Progression Award: a £1,000 reduction in tuition fees.

Eligibility: 1. Students registered with the Liverpool School of Tropical Medicine. 2. Students transferring to the University of Liverpool from partnership institutions where an alternative fee payment or scholarship arrangement has been made.

Level of Study: Masters Degree, Postgraduate

Type: Award

Value: £1,000 reduction in tuition fees.

Frequency: Annual

Country of Study: Any country

Application Procedure: You do not need to make an application to receive the Postgraduate Progression Award as it will be automatically allocated to all eligible students.

Additional Information: www.liverpool.ac.uk/study/postgraduate-taught/finance/scholarships/scholarships/postgraduate-progression-award-uk-students/

For further information contact:

Tel: (44) 151 794 2000

Santander Awards

Purpose: Santander International Postgraduate Scholarships reward international students who demonstrate academic excellence. The awards are available to international students entering onto postgraduate taught programmes at the University of Liverpool in September

Value: £5,000 tuition fee reduction for 1 year only

Country of Study: United Kingdom

Closing Date: 15 June

For further information contact:

Email: santander.universities@santander.co.uk

Scottish Power Scholarships

Eligibility: Promote career opportunities available within the company Act as a STEM ambassador for the industry Introduce future scholarship applicants to the scheme Support any recruitment activities agreed on campus/virtually

Level of Study: Masters Degree, Postgraduate

Type: Scholarship

Value: £1,200 per month

Frequency: Annual

Country of Study: Any country

Closing Date: 31 March

Additional Information: www.scottishpower.com/pages/scottishpower_masters_scholarships.aspx

For further information contact:

Tel: (44) 151 794 2000

The Kick It Out Scholarship

Purpose: Sky and Kick It Out have partnered with the University of Liverpool Management School to offer Scholarships to four Football Industries MBA offer holders from under-represented ethnic groups in 2023/24; as part of Sky UK's 3-year partnership with anti-racism organisation Kick it Out.

Eligibility: 1. Permanently reside in the UK. 2. You must have been assessed for fee status as a 'home' student, or expect to be assessed as a 'home student'. 3. Be applying for the Football Industries MBA programme, to commence study in the 2023–24 academic year. 4. Be from an under-represented ethnic group.

Type: Scholarship

Value: full cost of tuition fees (£25,000 per year).

Frequency: Annual

Country of Study: Any country

No. of awards offered: 4

Closing Date: 31 March

Additional Information: www.liverpool.ac.uk/study/postgraduate-taught/finance/scholarships/scholarships/kick-it-out-scholarship/

For further information contact:

Tel: (44) 151 794 2000

ULMS European Union Excellence Scholarship

Eligibility: Candidates are considered for this award based on their academic excellence and must hold, or be on track to obtain, at least a high 2:1 (65+%) in their undergraduate degree, including marks of 60+% in modules relevant to their MSc programme.

Level of Study: Masters Degree, Postgraduate, Postgraduate (MSc)

Type: Scholarship

Value: Part fee waiver (50%)

Frequency: Annual

Country of Study: Any country

Additional Information: www.liverpool.ac.uk/management/study/postgraduate-taught/scholarships/

For further information contact:

Tel: (44) 151 794 2000

ULMS Future Leaders Master's Scholarship

Purpose: These Scholarships are allocated at the discretion of the University of Liverpool and the decision is final.
Eligibility: Applicants must hold, or be on track to obtain, at least a high 2:1 (65+%) in their undergraduate degree, including marks of 60+% in modules relevant to their MSc programme. Work experience relevant to the programme (paid, internship, shadowing or voluntary positions) would be advantageous, as would previously studying at a highly ranked university.
Level of Study: Masters Degree
Type: Scholarship
Value: Full fee waiver
Country of Study: Any country
Application Procedure: No separate scholarship application is necessary.
Additional Information: www.liverpool.ac.uk/management/study/postgraduate-taught/scholarships/

For further information contact:

Tel: (44) 151 794 2000

ULMS Indian Subcontinent Excellence Scholarship

Purpose: These Scholarships are allocated at the discretion of the University of Liverpool and the decision is final.
Eligibility: Candidates are considered for this award based on their academic excellence and must hold, or be on track to obtain, at least a high 2:1 (65+%) in their undergraduate degree, including marks of 60+% in modules relevant to their MSc programme. Work experience relevant to the programme (paid, internship, shadowing or voluntary positions) would be advantageous, as would previously studying at a highly ranked university.
Level of Study: Postgraduate
Type: Scholarship
Value: Part fee waiver (50%)
Frequency: Annual
Country of Study: Any country
Additional Information: www.liverpool.ac.uk/management/study/postgraduate-taught/scholarships/

For further information contact:

Tel: (44) 151 794 2000

ULMS Southeast Asia Excellence Scholarship

Purpose: These Scholarships are allocated at the discretion of the University of Liverpool and the decision is final.
Eligibility: Candidates are considered for this award based on their academic excellence and must hold, or be on track to obtain, at least a high 2:1 (65+%) in their undergraduate degree, including marks of 60+% in modules relevant to their MSc programme. Work experience relevant to the programme (paid, internship, shadowing or voluntary positions) would be advantageous, as would previously studying at a highly ranked university.
Level of Study: Postgraduate
Type: Scholarship
Value: Part fee waiver (50%)
Frequency: Annual
Country of Study: Any country
Additional Information: www.liverpool.ac.uk/management/study/postgraduate-taught/scholarships/

For further information contact:

Tel: (44) 151 794 2000

ULMS West Africa Excellence Scholarship

Purpose: These Scholarships are allocated at the discretion of the University of Liverpool and the decision is final.
Eligibility: Candidates are considered for this award based on their academic excellence, CV, and personal statement.
Level of Study: Postgraduate
Type: Scholarship
Value: Part fee waiver (50%)
Frequency: Annual
Country of Study: Any country
Additional Information: www.liverpool.ac.uk/management/study/postgraduate-taught/scholarships/

For further information contact:

Tel: (44) 151 794 2000

University of Liverpool Commonwealth Postgraduate Bursary

Purpose: The University of Liverpool Commonwealth Postgraduate Bursary fee reduction for students from Commonwealth countries new to studying at the University of Liverpool on master's programmes
Type: Bursary
Value: £2,500 fee reduction for Commonwealth students studying Engineering, Electrical Engineering and

Electronics, and Computer Science programmes; £1,500 fee reduction for Commonwealth students studying all other subjects

Country of Study: Any country

Additional Information: No application necessary, automatically awarded to those who meet criteria www.liverpool.ac.uk/study/postgraduate-taught/finance/scholarships/scholarships/university-of-liverpool-commonwealth-postgraduate-bursary/

For further information contact:

Email: irro@liverpool.ac.uk

University of Liverpool Management School Academic Award

Purpose: The University of Liverpool Management School is delighted to offer range of generous scholarships and study awards to help cover the cost of MBA tuition fees

Eligibility: HEU/OSI applicants on the Liverpool MBA and the Football Industries MBA* programmes with an excellent academic profile and excellent work experience, or combination of very high standards in both of the above. It is an on-campus programme

Type: Award

Value: £2,000

Country of Study: United Kingdom

For further information contact:

Email: ulmsmba@liverpool.ac.uk

Vice-Chancellor's International Attainment Scholarship for China

Purpose: This application form should only be used to apply for the above Scholarship at the University of Liverpool. Please read the following notes carefully before completing the application form.

Eligibility: Domiciled in PR China when applications are made Have Bachelor's Degree awarded or to be awarded by a Project 211 or Project 985 university in PR China with a minimum average grade of 80% overall Have accepted and paid deposit on one of the Postgraduate Taught Programmes at the University of Liverpool's campus Are self-financed (which means tuition fees are to be paid by students or the parents).

Level of Study: Postgraduate

Type: Scholarship

Value: 1 (one) Full scholarship; 2 (two) £10,000 scholarships; 5 (five) £5,000 scholarships; 10 (ten) £1,000 scholarships;

Frequency: Annual

Country of Study: Any country

No. of awards offered: 18

Additional Information: www.liverpool.ac.uk/study/postgraduate-taught/finance/scholarships/scholarships/vc-international-attainment-china/

For further information contact:

Tel: (44) 151 794 2000

University of Manchester

Oxford Road, Manchester M13 9PL, United Kingdom.

Tel: (44) 161 306 6000
Email: hr@manchester.ac.uk
Website: www.manchester.ac.uk

AHRC North West Consortium Doctoral Training Partnership (NWCDTP) in the School of Arts, Languages and Cultures

Subjects: Faculty of Humanities, School of Arts, Languages and Cultures

Eligibility: 1. This award is available to existing postgraduate students. 2. This award is available to postgraduate research students in year one, applying for funding for years two and three of a PhD.

Level of Study: Postgraduate

Type: Studentship

Value: £15,609

Length of Study: 2 - 3.5 years

Frequency: Annual

Country of Study: Any country

Closing Date: 4 February

Additional Information: www.manchester.ac.uk/study/postgraduate-research/funding/opportunities/display/?id=00000328&offset=0&sort=name&sortdir=ascending&subjectArea=Any&nationality=United%20Kingdom&submit=Search

For further information contact:

Postgraduate Admissions Administrator, Oxford Rd, Manchester M13 9PL, United Kingdom.

Tel: (44) 161 306 6000
Email: phdfunding-salc@manchester.ac.uk

AHRC North West Consortium Doctoral Training Partnership in the School of Environment, Education and Development

Subjects: Faculty of Humanities, School of Environment, Education and Development
Eligibility: This award is available to postgraduate research students in year one, applying for funding for years two and three of a PhD.
Level of Study: Postgraduate, Research
Type: Studentship
Value: £15,6009
Length of Study: 24-48 months.
Country of Study: Any country
Closing Date: 4 February
Additional Information: www.manchester.ac.uk/study/post graduate-research/funding/opportunities/display/?id=00000 329&offset=0&sort=name&sortdir=ascending&subjectArea =Any&nationality=United%20Kingdom&submit=Search

For further information contact:

PGR Recruitment and Admissions Officer, Oxford Rd, Manchester M13 9PL, United Kingdom.

Tel: (44) (0)161 275 0807
Email: pgr-seedfunding@manchester.ac.uk

Alliance Manchester Business School PhD Studentships

Subjects: Accounting and Finance Business and Management Science, Technology and Innovation Policy
Eligibility: Applicants must hold an offer of study at The University of Manchester before applying for this funding.
Level of Study: Postdoctorate, Postgraduate, Research
Type: Studentship
Value: Programme tuition fees and stipend of approx. £15,609 per year
Length of Study: Up to 4 years
Frequency: Annual
Country of Study: Any country
Contributor: Alliance Manchester Business School
Additional Information: www.manchester.ac.uk/study/post graduate-research/funding/opportunities/display/?id=00000 346&offset=0&sort=name&sortdir=ascending&subjectArea =Any&nationality=United%20Kingdom&submit=Search

For further information contact:

Oxford Rd, Manchester M13 9PL, United Kingdom.

Tel: (44) (0)161 275 1200
Email: mbs-pgresearch@manchester.ac.uk

Daiwa Scholarships in Japanese Studies

Subjects: School of Arts, Languages and Cultures
Level of Study: Postgraduate, Research
Type: Scholarship
Value: £1,200 per month for periods spent in the UK, and 260,000 Yen per month for periods spent in Japan.
Length of Study: 3 Years
Country of Study: Any country
No. of awards offered: 3
Closing Date: 27 January
Contributor: Daiwa Anglo-Japanese Foundation
Additional Information: www.manchester.ac.uk/study/post graduate-research/funding/opportunities/display/?id=00000 453&offset=0&sort=name&sortdir=ascending&subject Area=Any&nationality=United%20Kingdom&submit=Se arch

For further information contact:

Oxford Rd, Manchester M13 9PL, United Kingdom.

Tel: (44) 161 306 6000
Email: scholarships@dajf.org.uk

Department of Mathematics Scholarship Award

Subjects: Department of Mathematics
Eligibility: This award can be held alongside other awards.
Level of Study: Postgraduate, Research
Type: Scholarship
Value: Home Students: Tuition Fees and Maintenance. International Students: Tuition Fees Only.
Length of Study: 3.5 years
Frequency: Annual
Country of Study: Any country
No. of awards offered: 6-10
Additional Information: www.manchester.ac.uk/study/post graduate-research/funding/opportunities/display/?id=00000 131&offset=0&sort=name&sortdir=ascending&subject Area=Any&nationality=United%20Kingdom&submit=Se arch

For further information contact:

Department of Mathematics, Oxford Rd, Manchester M13 9PL, United Kingdom.

Tel: (44) (0)161 275 5812
Email: pgr-maths@manchester.ac.uk

EPSRC Doctoral Training Partnership Studentships in Alliance Manchester Business School

Subjects: Faculty of Humanities, Alliance Manchester Business School

Eligibility: Candidates must have an Upper Second class honours degree or above and a Masters degree with an overall mark of 65% or above, or an equivalent combination of qualifications and/or experience. Additionally, they are expected to meet the specific requirements of the intended PhD programme.

Level of Study: Postgraduate

Type: Studentship

Value: an annual stipend starting at approximately £15,609, and £1,000 research training support grant per year

Length of Study: 4 years

Frequency: Annual

Country of Study: Any country

Closing Date: 21 February

Contributor: Engineering and Physical Sciences Research Council

Additional Information: www.manchester.ac.uk/study/post graduate-research/funding/opportunities/display/?id=00000 341&offset=0&sort=name&sortdir=ascending&subjectArea =Any&nationality=United%20Kingdom&submit=Search

For further information contact:

Oxford Rd, Manchester M13 9PL, United Kingdom.

Tel: (44) (0)161 275 1200
Email: lynne.barlow-cheetham@manchester.ac.uk

EPSRC Doctoral Training Partnership Studentships in the School of Arts, Languages and Cultures

Eligibility: Candidates must have an upper second class honours degree or above and a masters degree with an overall mark of 60% or above, or an equivalent combination of qualifications and/or experience. Additionally, they are expected to meet the specific requirements of the intended PhD programme.

Level of Study: Postgraduate

Type: Studentship

Value: Home Tuition Fees (£4,500 in the academic year 2023–24) and an annual stipend at standard UKRI rate (£15,609 in the academic year 2023–24), plus £1000 RTSG.

Length of Study: Up to 4 years

Frequency: Annual

Country of Study: Any country

Closing Date: 30 March

Contributor: Engineering and Physical Sciences Research Council

Additional Information: www.manchester.ac.uk/study/post graduate-research/funding/opportunities/display/?id=00000 324&offset=0&sort=name&sortdir=ascending&subjectArea =Any&nationality=United%20Kingdom&submit=Search

For further information contact:

Postgraduate Admissions Administrator, Oxford Rd, Manchester M13 9PL, United Kingdom.

Tel: (44) 161 306 6000
Email: phdfunding-salc@manchester.ac.uk

EPSRC Doctoral Training Partnership Studentships in the School of Environment, Education and Development

Eligibility: Candidates must have an Upper Second class honours degree or above and a masters degree with an overall mark of 60% or above, or an equivalent combination of qualifications and/or experience. Additionally, they are expected to meet the specific requirements of the intended PhD programme.

Level of Study: Postgraduate

Type: Studentship

Value: tuition fees, an annual stipend starting at approximately £15,000 and £1,000 research training support grant per year

Length of Study: 3 years

Frequency: Annual

Country of Study: Any country

Closing Date: 30 March

Additional Information: www.manchester.ac.uk/study/post graduate-research/funding/opportunities/display/?id=00000 336&offset=0&sort=name&sortdir=ascending&subjectArea =Any&nationality=United%20Kingdom&submit=Search

For further information contact:

Postgraduate Research Recruitment and Admissions, Oxford Rd, Manchester M13 9PL, United Kingdom.

Tel: (44) (0)161 275 0807
Email: pgr-seedfunding@manchester.ac.uk

ESRC North West Social Science DTP (NWSSDTP) PhD Studentships in Alliance Manchester Business School

Eligibility: This award is available to existing postgraduate students. This award is available to postgraduate research students in year one, applying for funding for years two and three of PhD.

Type: Studentship

Value: Tuition fees, research expenses and living allowance subject to eligibility (approximately £15,609 per annum).

Length of Study: 24-48 months.

Country of Study: Any country

Closing Date: 1 February

Additional Information: www.manchester.ac.uk/study/post graduate-research/funding/opportunities/display/?id=00000 327&offset=0&sort=name&sortdir=ascending&subjectArea =Any&nationality=United%20Kingdom&submit=Search

For further information contact:

Oxford Rd, Manchester M13 9PL, United Kingdom.

Tel: (44) (0)161 275 1200
Email: lynne.barlow-cheetham@manchester.ac.uk

ESRC North West Social Science DTP (NWSSDTP) PhD Studentships in the School of Arts, Languages and Cultures

Eligibility: 1. This award is available to existing postgraduate students. 2. This award is available to postgraduate research students in year one, applying for funding for years two and three of a PhD.

Level of Study: Postgraduate

Type: Studentship

Value: Tuition fees, research expenses and living allowance, subject to eligibility (£15,609).

Length of Study: 24 and 48 months

Frequency: Annual

Country of Study: Any country

Closing Date: 1 February

Contributor: ESRC North West Social Sciences Doctoral Training Partnership

Additional Information: www.manchester.ac.uk/study/post graduate-research/funding/opportunities/display/?id=00000 160&offset=0&sort=name&sortdir=ascending&subjectArea =Any&nationality=United%20Kingdom&submit=Search

For further information contact:

Postgraduate Admissions Administrator, Oxford Rd, Manchester M13 9PL, United Kingdom.

Tel: (44) 161 306 6000
Email: phdfunding-salc@manchester.ac.uk

ESRC North West Social Science DTP (NWSSDTP) PhD Studentships in the School of Environment, Education and Development

Level of Study: Postgraduate

Type: Studentship

Value: Tuition fees, research expenses and living allowance subject to eligibility, annual maintenance stipend £15,609.

Length of Study: 24-48 months

Frequency: Annual

Country of Study: Any country

Closing Date: 1 February

Contributor: ESRC North West Social Sciences Doctoral Training Partnership

Additional Information: www.manchester.ac.uk/study/post graduate-research/funding/opportunities/display/?id=00000 325&offset=0&sort=name&sortdir=ascending&subjectArea =Any&nationality=United%20Kingdom&submit=Search

For further information contact:

PGR Recruitment and Admissions Officer, Oxford Rd, Manchester M13 9PL, United Kingdom.

Tel: (44) (0)161 275 0807
Email: pgr-seedfunding@manchester.ac.uk

Indian Excellence Scholarship Award

Purpose: Scholarships are available for pursuing undergraduate degree programme

Eligibility: This scheme applies to any undergraduate degree programme within the Faculty of Science and Engineering at The University of Manchester. Each scholarship will be awarded on the basis of a student demonstrating high performance in their International Baccalaureate or Standard XII examinations and the academic reference on their UCAS form. Applicants must be Indian nationals or permanently domiciled in India. Applicants must have applied through UCAS for a place on an undergraduate degree programme in FSE for entry in September. Applicants must have accepted a programme in FSE as their firm choice by the end of June

Type: Scholarship

Value: £3,000 per annum

Country of Study: Any country

Closing Date: June

Additional Information: Application for courses in this School should be made online through the Universities and Colleges Admissions Service (UCAS) www.eee.manchester. ac.uk/study/undergraduate/fees-and-funding/

For further information contact:

Email: app.req@ucas.ac.uk

Institute for Development Policy and Management Taught Postgraduate Scholarship Scheme

Eligibility: Bachelors degree with Second Class Honours, Upper Division or above, or Overseas equivalent (please contact School for details of equivalencies). Applicants whose first language is a language other than English must achieve 7.0 or above in IELTS or an equivalent test (TOEFL)
Level of Study: Postgraduate
Type: Scholarship
Value: £2,000
Frequency: Annual
Application Procedure: Check website for further details www.manchester.ac.uk/postgraduate/funding/search/display/?id=00000177
Closing Date: 30 June

For further information contact:

Email: paul.arrowsmith@manchester.ac.uk

Manchester Melbourne Dual Award

Type: Studentship
Value: Tuition fees: Home/International Stipend: AApprox £15,609 per year RTSG: Up to £5,000 per year Travel: Up to £1,250 (whole programme) Health insurance while at Melbourne
Length of Study: 3.5 years full-time or 7 years part-time
Country of Study: Any country
Closing Date: 14 March
Additional Information: Oxford Rd, Manchester M13 9PL, United Kingdom

For further information contact:

Oxford Rd, Manchester M13 9PL, United Kingdom.

Tel: (44) (0) 161 275 4740
Email: daniel.davies@manchester.ac.uk

Manchester-China Scholarship Council Joint Postgraduate Scholarship Programme

Purpose: To provide scholarships to the nationals of PR China who wish to pursue their PhD at the University of Manchester

Eligibility: To be considered suitable for the joint scholarship, you must be a citizen and permanent resident of the People's Republic of China at the time of application. Overseas Chinese students may be eligible for application subject to CSC policy at the time (CSC publicises the policy in October or November every year). You must also 1. return to China upon completion of your studies and/or research; 2. hold an Upper Second class UK honours undergraduate degree (or international equivalent) from a reputable institution; 3. hold an unconditional offer letter from The University of Manchester; 4. ideally hold a master's-level qualification at merit or distinction (or international equivalent); 5. have a track record of engaging with research, which may include contributions to publications/articles, promoting your research to a wider audience, prizes for research or project work; satisfy CSC's selection criteria.
Level of Study: Doctorate, Postgraduate
Type: Scholarships
Value: Tuition fees and annual stipend of approx. £4,800
Length of Study: 3 years
Frequency: Annual
Study Establishment: University of Manchester
Country of Study: United Kingdom
Application Procedure: Applicants must complete the standard postgraduate application form and return it together with Academic transcripts, English language qualification, 2 reference letters and a research proposal
Closing Date: 15 January
Additional Information: For enquires to the China Scholarship Council, please contact Miss Zou Dongyun, Project Officer by email mailto: dyzou@csc.edu.cn

For further information contact:

Tel: (86) 10 6609 3977
Email: admissions.doctoralacademy@manchester.ac.uk

Myrtle McMyn Bursary

Eligibility: Applicants should hold an MA in a relevant subject area, with a taught course unit average of 65%, a disseration mark of 65% and no mark below 55%. They should also hold a UK BA with a 2i classification (orequivalent if studied overseas).
Level of Study: Postgraduate
Type: Bursary
Value: The award covers Home tuition fees (£4,500).
Length of Study: 3 year
Frequency: Annual
Country of Study: Any country
Closing Date: 4 February

Additional Information: phdfuding-salc@manchester.ac.uk

For further information contact:

Postgraduate Admissions Administrator, Oxford Rd, Manchester M13 9PL, United Kingdom.

Email: phdfuding-salc@manchester.ac.uk

PhD Studentships in Humanitarianism and Conflict Response

Eligibility: Applicants must hold or expect to achieve a Masters-level qualification, which we would expect to be at distinction level, or equivalent, and have a first-class Honours degree (or non-UK equivalent).
Type: Studentship
Value: Tuition fees and living allowance, the annual maintenance stipend £15,609.
Length of Study: 3 year
Country of Study: Any country
No. of awards offered: 2
Closing Date: 4 February
Additional Information: 4 February

For further information contact:

Postgraduate Research Director: HCRI, Oxford Rd, Manchester M13 9PL, United Kingdom.

Email: nathaniel.ogrady@manchester.ac.uk

President's Doctoral Scholar (PDS) Awards in the School of Arts, Languages and Cultures

Type: Studentship
Value: Tuition fees and living allowance, maintenance stipend (£16,609).
Length of Study: 3.5 year
Country of Study: Any country
Closing Date: 4 February
Additional Information: www.manchester.ac.uk/study/post graduate-research/funding/opportunities/display/?id=00000 331&offset=0&sort=name&sortdir=ascending&subjectArea =Any&nationality=United%20Kingdom&submit=Search

For further information contact:

Postgraduate Admissions Administrator, Oxford Rd, Manchester M13 9PL, United Kingdom.

Email: phdfunding-salc@manchester.ac.uk

President's Doctoral Scholar (PDS) Awards in the School of Environment, Education and Development

Eligibility: Applicants must hold or expect to achieve a Masters-level qualification, which we would expect to be at distinction level, or equivalent, and have a first-class Honours degree (or non-UK equivalent).
Level of Study: Postgraduate
Type: Studentship
Value: Tuition fees and living allowance, annual stipends of approximately £15,609.
Length of Study: 3.5 year
Frequency: Annual
Country of Study: Any country
Closing Date: 1 February
Additional Information: www.manchester.ac.uk/study/post graduate-research/funding/opportunities/display/?id=00000 366&offset=0&sort=name&sortdir=ascending&subjectArea =Any&nationality=United%20Kingdom&submit=Search

For further information contact:

Recruitment and Admissions Officer.

Tel: (44) 0161 275 0807
Email: christopher.kitchen@manchester.ac.uk

President's Doctoral Scholar Award

Type: Scholarship
Value: an annual maintenance stipend £1,000
Length of Study: 3.5 years
Country of Study: United Kingdom
Application Procedure: For further information, please visit the PDS website
Closing Date: 29 April
Additional Information: www.bmh.manchester.ac.uk/study/ research/financial-support/presidents-doctoral-scholar-awards/

For further information contact:

Oxford Rd, Manchester M13 9PL, United Kingdom.

Tel: (44) 161 306 6000
Email: EPSGradEd@manchester.ac.uk

Sasakawa Japanese Studies Postgraduate Studentship

Eligibility: PhD students who have already received the Sasakawa studentship may be nominated again, and receive the studentship for up to three years, through repeated awards cannot be guaranteed.

Level of Study: Postgraduate
Type: Studentship
Value: studentships worth £10,000
Length of Study: 1 year
Frequency: Annual
Country of Study: Any country
No. of awards offered: 3
Closing Date: 28 February
Additional Information: www.manchester.ac.uk/study/post graduate-research/funding/opportunities/display/?id=00000 348&offset=0&sort=name&sortdir=ascending&subjectArea =Any&nationality=United%20Kingdom&submit=Search

For further information contact:

Senior Lecturer - Japanese Studies, Oxford Rd, Manchester M13 9PL, United Kingdom.

Tel: (44) 161 306 6000
Email: peter.cave@manchester.ac.uk

School of Arts, Languages and Cultures PhD Studentships

Eligibility: MPhil students are not eligible to apply for this studentship. Current PhD students are not eligible to apply for this studentship.
Level of Study: Postdoctorate
Type: Studentship
Value: Tuition fees and living allowance, maintenance stipend (£15,609).
Length of Study: 3.5 year
Frequency: Annual
Country of Study: Any country
Closing Date: 4 February
Contributor: The School of Arts, Languages and Cultures
Additional Information: www.manchester.ac.uk/study/post graduate-research/funding/opportunities/display/?id=00000 332&offset=0&sort=name&sortdir=ascending&subjectArea =Any&nationality=United%20Kingdom&submit=Search

For further information contact:

Postgraduate Admissions Administrator, Oxford Rd, Manchester M13 9PL, United Kingdom.

Tel: (44) 161 306 6000
Email: phdfunding-salc@manchester.ac.uk

School of Environment, Education and Development Postgraduate Research Scholarship

Eligibility: Bachelor degree with First Class or Upper Second Class Honours (or international equivalent) Master degree with a minimum grade of 60% in the dissertation and a minimum taught average grade of 60% (or international equivalent) English language proficiency if applicable - minimum of IELTS 7 overall with 7 in writing and 6 in the other subsections or TOEFL 100 overall with 25 in writing and 22 in the other subsections
Level of Study: Postgraduate
Type: Scholarship
Value: tuition fees and include annual stipends of approximately £15,609
Length of Study: 3.5 year
Frequency: Annual
Country of Study: Any country
Closing Date: 1 February
Contributor: School of Environment, Education and Development
Additional Information: www.manchester.ac.uk/study/post graduate-research/funding/opportunities/display/?id=00000 218&offset=0&sort=name&sortdir=ascending&subjectArea =Any&nationality=United%20Kingdom&submit=Search

For further information contact:

Postgraduate Research Recruitment and Admissions, Oxford Rd, Manchester M13 9PL, United Kingdom.

Tel: (44) 161 275 0807
Email: pgr-seedfunding@manchester.ac.uk

School of Social Sciences - Economics PhD Studentships

Level of Study: Postgraduate
Type: Studentship
Value: Home Fees or overseas fees £18,500 annual maintenance stipend (to be confirmed) Students can apply for certain research expenses from the Research Training Support Grant.
Length of Study: 4 or 5 years
Frequency: Annual
Country of Study: Any country
Closing Date: 7 January
Contributor: School of Social Sciences - Economics
Additional Information: www.manchester.ac.uk/study/post graduate-research/funding/opportunities/display/?id=00000 294&offset=0&sort=name&sortdir=ascending&subjectArea =Any&nationality=United%20Kingdom&submit=Search

For further information contact:

Postgraduate Admissions Co-Ordinator, Oxford Rd, Manchester M13 9PL, United Kingdom.

Tel: (44) 0161 275 4740
Email: daniel.davies@manchester.ac.uk

School of Social Sciences - Manchester Master

Purpose: The bursaries are aimed at widening access to master's courses by removing barriers to postgraduate education for students from underrepresented groups, so applicants need to meet a number of criteria to be eligible. Last year, there were more eligible applications than places, so meeting the criteria is no guarantee of an award
Eligibility: 1. Eligible courses include LLM, MA, MEd, MBA, MEnt, MPhil, MRes, MSc, MSc by Research, MusM. 2. Courses can be studied full-time for one or two academic years or part-time for a maximum of two academic years. 3. You must be a home student paying home level tuition fees, and have been resident in the United Kingdom for at least three years prior to starting your undergraduate course for a purpose other than study. 4. You must be commencing your degree course in September. 5. You must not hold a master's qualification or higher. 6. You must have commenced your undergraduate course. 7. Intercalating medical students taking a master's course are eligible to apply. Medical students should note that if they plan to intercalate and take a master's course between Years 2 and 3, they will not be eligible for UG loans in Year 3. However, there will be no interruption to funding if they intercalate between Years 3 and 4, and they will be eligible for the postgraduate loan
Level of Study: Postgraduate
Type: Bursary
Value: £4,000
Length of Study: 1 year
Frequency: Annual
Country of Study: Any country
Closing Date: 31 May
Funding: International office
Additional Information: www.manchester.ac.uk/study/masters/fees-and-funding/uk-student-funding/masters-bursary/

For further information contact:

School of Social Sciences, Arthur Lewis Building, The University of Manchester, Oxford Road, Manchester M13 9PL, United Kingdom.

Tel: (44) 161 306 1340
Email: myra.knutton@manchester.ac.uk

School of Social Sciences - PhD Studentships

Level of Study: Postdoctorate
Type: Studentship
Value: Tuition Fees at a Home rate, annual maintenance stipend (£15,609)
Length of Study: 3 years and a half full-time or 7 years part-time.
Frequency: Annual
Country of Study: Any country
Closing Date: 1 December
Additional Information: www.manchester.ac.uk/study/postgraduate-research/funding/opportunities/display/?id=00000293&offset=0&sort=name&sortdir=ascending&subjectArea=Any&nationality=United%20Kingdom&submit=Search

For further information contact:

PGR Admissions Co-Ordinator, Oxford Rd, Manchester M13 9PL, United Kingdom.

Tel: (44) (0) 161 275 4740
Email: daniel.davies@manchester.ac.uk

SEED Enhancing Racial Equality studentship

Eligibility: Bachelor degree with First Class or Upper Second Class Honours (or international equivalent) Master degree with a minimum grade of 60% in the dissertation and a minimum taught average grade of 60% (or international equivalent). Applicants must hold an offer of study at The University of Manchester before applying for this funding. This scholarship is open to Home (UK) applicants who identify as BAME/People of Colour.
Type: Studentship
Value: tuition fees and include an annual stipend of approximately £15,609
Length of Study: 3.5 year
Country of Study: Any country
Closing Date: 1 February
Additional Information: www.manchester.ac.uk/study/postgraduate-research/funding/opportunities/display/?id=00000439&offset=0&sort=name&sortdir=ascending&subjectArea=Any&nationality=United%20Kingdom&submit=Search

For further information contact:

Postgraduate Research Recruitment and Admissions, Oxford Rd, Manchester M13 9PL, United Kingdom.

Tel: (44) 161 275 0807
Email: pgr-seedfunding@manchester.ac.uk

The John Bright Fellowship

Eligibility: Applicants should hold a BA Honours degree in English literature or another relevant field with at least a 2.i classification. Applications should also hold, or be about to complete, an MA or equivalent degree in an area relevant to the proposed doctoral research.
Level of Study: Postgraduate
Type: Bursary
Value: The Award covers home tuition fees.
Length of Study: 3 year
Frequency: Annual
Country of Study: Any country
Closing Date: 4 February
Additional Information: www.manchester.ac.uk/study/post graduate-research/funding/opportunities/display/?id=00000 404&offset=0&sort=name&sortdir=ascending&subjectArea =Any&nationality=United%20Kingdom&submit=Search

For further information contact:

Postgraduate Admissions Administrator, Oxford Rd, Manchester M13 9PL, United Kingdom.

Email: phdfunding-salc@manchester.ac.uk

The Lees Scholarship

Eligibility: The Scholarship is awarded for PhD research in the field of Latin (including, literary, historical, philosophical and linguistic topics).
Level of Study: Postgraduate
Type: Bursary
Value: Fee Bursary.
Length of Study: 3 years full time or 6 years part time.
Frequency: Annual
Country of Study: Any country
No. of awards offered: 1
Closing Date: 4 February
Additional Information: www.manchester.ac.uk/study/post graduate-research/funding/opportunities/display/?id=00000 353&offset=0&sort=name&sortdir=ascending&subjectArea =Any&nationality=United%20Kingdom&submit=Search

For further information contact:

Postgraduate Admissions Administrator, Oxford Rd, Manchester M13 9PL, United Kingdom.

Email: phdfunding-salc@manchester.ac.uk

University of Manchester President's Doctoral Scholar Awards (PDS Awards)

Eligibility: Applicants must hold an offer of study at The University of Manchester before applying for this funding.
Level of Study: Postgraduate
Type: Studentship
Value: tuition fee and stipend, £1,000 p.a.
Length of Study: 4 years
Frequency: Annual
Country of Study: Any country
No. of awards offered: 2
Closing Date: 1 April
Additional Information: www.manchester.ac.uk/study/post graduate-research/funding/opportunities/display/?id=00000 285&offset=0&sort=name&sortdir=ascending&subjectArea =Any&nationality=United%20Kingdom&submit=Search

For further information contact:

Doctoral Programmes Office, Oxford Rd, Manchester M13 9PL, United Kingdom.

Tel: (44) (0)161 275 1200
Email: ambs-pgresearch@manchester.ac.uk

University of Massachusetts Amherst

Refractique (Lensball World) Photography Innovation & Excellence Scholarship

Purpose: We provide a premium offering and pride ourselves on our products - enjoying this fun creative photography ourselves initially before enabling others to learn more about this wonderful hobby
Eligibility: studying an Arts Degree (or relevant photography course)
Level of Study: Postgraduate
Type: Scholarship
Value: US$2,000 (occurs on a twice yearly basis with a US$1,000 per scholarship eligible)
Frequency: Annual
Country of Study: Any country
Application Procedure: 1. Prepare a refraction photography submission and send to support@refractique.com
Closing Date: 30 June
Funding: Private
Additional Information: For further information, refer the website link. lensballs.com/pages/social-support

U

For further information contact:

Email: support@refractique.com

University of Melbourne

Scholarships Office, Melbourne, Melbourne, VIC 3010, Australia.

Tel: (61) 3 8344 4000
Email: pg-schools@unimelb.edu.au
Website: www.unimelb.edu.au

Alexander von Humboldt Foundation: Humboldt Research Fellowships for Postdoctoral Researchers

Purpose: The Humboldt Research Fellowships for Postdoctoral Researchers enable highly-qualified scientists and scholars who are embarking on their academic careers and who completed their doctorates less than four years ago to spend extended periods of research in Germany.
Eligibility: Have a doctorate or comparable academic degree (Ph.D., C.Sc. or equivalent) completed less than four years prior to the date of application. Candidates who have nearly completed their doctoral degrees are eligible to apply provided that they submit the manuscript of their dissertation or publications containing the results of their dissertation.
Level of Study: Postdoctorate
Type: Fellowship
Value: US$25,000 - US$105,000
Frequency: Annual
Country of Study: Any country
No. of awards offered: 500
Closing Date: 31 December
Additional Information: scholarships.unimelb.edu.au/awards/humboldt-research-fellowships-for-postdoctoral-researchers

For further information contact:

The University of Melbourne Grattan Street, Parkville, Victoria 3010, Australia.

Tel: (61) 3 9035 5511
Email: info@avh.de.

Andrew and Geraldine Buxton Athletics Scholarship

Purpose: Established in perpetuity by Andrew and Geraldine Buxton, this scholarship provides US$10,000 a year plus in-kind support to help aspiring student-athletes in the sport of athletics to simultaneously pursue their world-class academic and sporting dreams.
Eligibility: be a member of Melbourne University Athletics Club and have the potential to compete at a World Championship, Olympic or Paralympic level.
Type: Scholarship
Value: at least US$15,000
Frequency: Annual
Country of Study: Any country
No. of awards offered: 2
Closing Date: 21 February
Additional Information: scholarships.unimelb.edu.au/awards/buxton-athletics-scholarship

For further information contact:

The University of Melbourne Grattan Street, Parkville, Victoria 3010, Australia.

Tel: (61) 3 9035 5511

Association of Commonwealth Universities: Queen Elizabeth Commonwealth Scholarships

Purpose: The scholarships provide opportunities to study for a two-year Master's degree in unique environments across the globe. Through this experience you will travel to a new country, develop an appreciation and understanding of a new culture, work in a new academic environment and build a global network.
Eligibility: Have already completed your degree and have graduated with an equivalent of a 2:1 at the time of application. Applicants must hold a Bachelor's degree of at least the upper second level. Applicants must apply for a Queen Elizabeth Commonwealth Scholarship award in a country other than their home country/country of citizenship. The awards are only hosted by low and middle income countries.
Level of Study: Postgraduate
Type: Scholarship
Value: Fully-funded tuition fees Living expenses allowance (stipend) for the duration of the award Return economy flights to the host country An arrival allowance Research support grant – subject to approval
Frequency: Annual
Country of Study: Any country
No. of awards offered: 30
Closing Date: 15 January
Additional Information: scholarships.unimelb.edu.au/awards/queen-elizabeth-commonwealth-scholarships

For further information contact:

The University of Melbourne Grattan Street, Parkville, Victoria 3010, Australia.

Tel: (61) 3 9035 5511

British Academy: Global Professorships

Purpose: The British Academy's "Global Professorships" provides mid-career to senior scholars in any discipline within the humanities and social sciences, who are currently employed outside the United Kingdom, with the opportunity to be based for four years in the UK and make a contribution to UK research and higher education. The Global Professorships provide an opportunity to undertake high-risk, curiosity-driven research in the humanities and social sciences that enables the award-holders and their UK host institutions to achieve a step change in their respective research programmes.

Eligibility: Be a recognised scholar or researcher with exceptional promise who is on a permanent contract outside the UK (which may be part-time or full-time) or, if temporary, would normally be on a contract that will not end during the course of the grant unless expressly agreed with the Academy prior to the application being submitted that such an application would be considered eligible, in any field of the humanities or the social sciences. Hold a doctoral degree (or have equivalent research experience).

Type: Professorship
Value: Up to US$1,400,000
Frequency: Annual
Country of Study: Any country
No. of awards offered: 10
Closing Date: 1 February
Additional Information: scholarships.unimelb.edu.au/awards/global-professorships

For further information contact:

The University of Melbourne Grattan Street, Parkville, Victoria 3010, Australia.

Tel: (61) 3 9035 5511

Bryan Scholarships

Purpose: This scholarship is awarded to a student who has successfully completed a Bachelor of Science at the University of Melbourne and is undertaking a Bachelor of Science (Honours) or the first year of a research training program in the Master of Science, or the Postgraduate Diploma in Science in a branch of natural science, on the basis of academic merit.

Eligibility: Be a University of Melbourne Bachelor of Science Graduate, Be enrolled in a Bachelor of Science (Honours) or the first year of a research training program in the Master of Science, or the Postgraduate Diploma in Science in a branch of natural science.
Type: Scholarship
Value: Up to US$3,000
Frequency: Annual
Country of Study: Any country
No. of awards offered: 2
Closing Date: 17 January
Additional Information: scholarships.unimelb.edu.au/awards/bryan-scholarships

For further information contact:

The University of Melbourne Grattan Street, Parkville, Victoria 3010, Australia.

Tel: (61) 3 9035 5511

China Scholarship Council - University of Melbourne PhD Scholarship

Purpose: This scholarship was established by the Chinese Scholarship Council and the University of Melbourne to promote international collaboration and is awarded to citizens of the People's Republic of China wishing to undertake a Doctor of Philosophy (PhD) degree at the University of Melbourne.

Eligibility: be a citizen of the People's Republic of China have received an offer for a place in a Doctor of Philosophy (PhD) course at the University of Melbourne. This requires completion of at least a four-year undergraduate degree, with the equivalent of a minimum overall average grade of H2A (or 75%) achieved at the University of Melbourne with a significant research component. Applicants are also required to meet minimum English language requirements.

Level of Study: Postdoctorate
Type: Scholarship
Value: 100% fee remission and up to US$120,000
Frequency: Annual
Country of Study: Any country
No. of awards offered: 45
Closing Date: 25 February
Additional Information: scholarships.unimelb.edu.au/awards/china-scholarship-council-university-of-melbourne-phd-scholarship

For further information contact:

The University of Melbourne Grattan Street, Parkville, Victoria 3010, Australia.

Tel: (61) 3 9035 5511

Coursework access scholarships

Purpose: A suite of coursework access scholarships is available to undergraduate and graduate students who have experienced or are experiencing compassionate or compelling circumstances.

Eligibility: be an Australian citizen or permanent resident have applied for or be enrolled in an undergraduate or graduate degree by coursework at the University of Melbourne have at least twelve months of full-time equivalent study remaining to complete your course be experiencing compassionate or compelling circumstances (e.g. having primary care responsibilities for a dependent, medical condition, disability, or personal or financial difficulties) meet the requirements for one of the following scholarships: Dorothy Karpin Indigenous Scholarship Hugh Kingsley Family Scholarship Irene and Arthur Kinsman Award for Postgraduate Studies Eleanor and Joseph Wertheim Scholarship

Type: Scholarship
Value: US$5,000 - US$20,000
Frequency: Annual
Country of Study: Any country
No. of awards offered: 8
Closing Date: 31 January
Additional Information: scholarships.unimelb.edu.au/awards/coursework-access-scholarships

For further information contact:

The University of Melbourne Grattan Street, Parkville, Victoria 3010, Australia.

Tel: (61) 3 9035 5511

Dairy Postgraduate Scholarships and Awards

Purpose: To enable students for research contributing to the technical areas relevant to dairy farming and dairy manufacturing operations

Eligibility: Open to citizens or permanent residents of Australia
Level of Study: Postgraduate
Type: Scholarship
Value: AU$25,000 stipend plus AU$3,000 per year
Frequency: Annual
Country of Study: Australia
Application Procedure: To apply for this scholarship one must apply direct to the faculty
Closing Date: 20 October

For further information contact:

Tel: (61) 3 9694 3810
Fax: (61) 3 9694 3701
Email: research@dairyaustralia.com.au

Diane Lemaire Scholarship

Purpose: This scholarship is made possible through a bequest from the late Diane Lemaire, who was the first woman to graduate with an engineering degree from the University of Melbourne in 1942. It's available to female PhD students in the Faculty of Engineering & IT to fund a project or proposal that will enhance the applicant's PhD and research outcomes.

Eligibility: be a female PhD student have completed the equivalent of at least six months candidature
Type: Scholarship
Value: US$4,000 - US$15,000
Frequency: Annual
Country of Study: Any country
No. of awards offered: 4
Closing Date: 31 January
Additional Information: scholarships.unimelb.edu.au/awards/diane-lemaire-scholarship

For further information contact:

The University of Melbourne Grattan Street, Parkville, Victoria 3010, Australia.

Tel: (61) 3 9035 5511

Dr Betty Elliott Horticulture Scholarship

Purpose: This scholarship is awarded to a student undertaking postgraduate research in the discipline of sustainability in horticulture, on the basis of demonstrated academic merit and financial need.

Eligibility: Be undertaking postgraduate research in the discipline of sustainability in horticulture, Demonstrate Financial Need by completing the online Student Financial Assessment Form
Type: Scholarship
Value: Up to US$3000.
Frequency: Annual
Country of Study: Any country
No. of awards offered: 8
Closing Date: 17 March
Additional Information: scholarships.unimelb.edu.au/awards/dr-betty-elliott-horticulture-scholarship

For further information contact:

The University of Melbourne Grattan Street, Parkville, Victoria 3010, Australia.

Tel: (61) 3 9035 5511

Eleanor and Joseph Wertheim Scholarship

Purpose: The Eleanor and Joseph Wertheim Scholarship was established with a bequest from Dr Eleanor Sabina Wertheim, and is offered to single, mature-aged, female undergraduate or graduate students who are experiencing disadvantaged circumstances.

Eligibility: be a single female student over 25 years of age at the time of application an Australian citizen or permanent resident have applied for or be enrolled in an undergraduate or graduate degree by coursework at the University of Melbourne have at least twelve months of full-time equivalent study remaining to complete your course be experiencing compassionate or compelling circumstances (e.g. having primary care responsibilities for a dependent, medical condition, disability, or personal or financial difficulties)

Type: Scholarship

Value: Up to US$5,000

Frequency: Annual

Country of Study: Any country

No. of awards offered: 8

Closing Date: 31 January

Additional Information: scholarships.unimelb.edu.au/awards/wertheim

For further information contact:

The University of Melbourne Grattan Street, Parkville, Victoria 3010, Australia.

Tel: (61) 3 9035 5511

Eric Ormond Baker Scholarship

Purpose: The Eric Ormond Baker Scholarship provides Screen and Cultural Studies graduate students with the opportunity to fund an industry-based internship. Offering up to US$13,000, the scholarship covers travel and living costs associated with placements that last between 20 days - 6 months in duration. The scholarship is an important step in further strengthening and developing studies in Screen Studies and Cultural Studies.

Eligibility: be an Australian citizen residing in Victoria; undertake an Australian industry-based placement with an approved provider for a minimum of 20 days and a maximum of 6 months; and, be currently enrolled in graduate study in Screen and Cultural Studies within the School of Culture and Communication either in a PhD or Masters by Research, or in a Masters Coursework degree. Masters Coursework students should be enrolled in a minor research project.

Type: Scholarship

Value: Up to US$13,000

Frequency: Annual

Country of Study: Any country

No. of awards offered: 2

Closing Date: 14 February

Additional Information: scholarships.unimelb.edu.au/awards/the-eric-ormond-baker-scholarship

For further information contact:

The University of Melbourne Grattan Street, Parkville, Victoria 3010, Australia.

Tel: (61) 3 9035 5511

ETH Zurich: Branco Weiss Fellowships

Purpose: The Branco Weiss Fellowship is a postdoctoral program for exceptionally qualified young researchers. The fellowship consists of a personal research grant that enables the fellows to work on their projects anywhere in the world, for up to five years. The Fellowship is designed to support postdoctoral researchers after their PhD and before their first faculty appointment.

Eligibility: Officially hold a PhD on January 15, 2023 Have obtained your PhD a maximum of five years prior to January 15, 2023 Not hold or have held a faculty-equivalent position (e.g. assistant professor or lecturer)

Type: Fellowship

Value: Up to US$750,000

Frequency: Annual

Country of Study: Any country

No. of awards offered: 10

Closing Date: 15 January

Additional Information: scholarships.unimelb.edu.au/awards/branco-weiss-fellowship

For further information contact:

The University of Melbourne Grattan Street, Parkville, Victoria 3010, Australia.

Tel: (61) 3 9035 5511

European Research Council: Starting grants

Purpose: The European Research Council (ERC) was created to support investigator-driven frontier research across all fields.

Eligibility: Have 2 - 7 years of experience since the completion of a PhD Present a project which is conducted in a public or private research organisation. This could be where the applicant already works, or any other host organisation located in one of the EU Member States or Associated Countries Researchers from anywhere in the world can apply for ERC grants provided the research they undertake will be carried out in an EU Member State or Associated Country.

Level of Study: Research

Type: Grant

Value: Up to US$4,000,000

Frequency: Annual

Country of Study: Any country

No. of awards offered: 400

Closing Date: 13 January

Additional Information: scholarships.unimelb.edu.au/awards/european-research-council-starting-grants

For further information contact:

The University of Melbourne Grattan Street, Parkville, Victoria 3010, Australia.

Tel: (61) 3 9035 5511

Frank Keenan Scholarship

Purpose: This scholarship is awarded to a student undertaking study in the discipline of advancement of services and practices of amenity and/or ornamental horticulture at the University of Melbourne, on the basis of demonstrated academic excellence.

Eligibility: Be enrolled in the study of amenity or ornamental horticulture, community horticulture or parks and gardens.

Type: Scholarship

Value: US$1,000 - US$3,000

Frequency: Annual

Country of Study: Any country

No. of awards offered: 6

Closing Date: 17 March

Additional Information: scholarships.unimelb.edu.au/awards/frank-keenan-scholarship

For further information contact:

The University of Melbourne Grattan Street, Parkville, Victoria 3010, Australia.

Tel: (61) 3 9035 5511

Frank Knox Memorial Fellowships

Purpose: Established in honour of the late Frank Knox to encourage scholarly exchange between the United States and the British Commonwealth, this scholarship supports graduate coursework students to undertake graduate study at Harvard University.

Eligibility: have applied directly to the relevant graduate school at Harvard University for your chosen degree program have Australian citizenship at the time of application and normally reside in Australia have graduated with a Bachelor or higher degree at an Australian university by the 2023–2024 academic year have completed the Bachelor or higher degree no earlier than 2019

Type: Fellowship

Value: 100% fee remission and up to US$60,000

Frequency: Annual

Country of Study: Any country

No. of awards offered: 3

Closing Date: 1 February

Additional Information: scholarships.unimelb.edu.au/awards/frank-knox-memorial-fellowships

For further information contact:

The University of Melbourne Grattan Street, Parkville, Victoria 3010, Australia.

Tel: (61) 3 9035 5511

Friends and Alumni of International House Scholarship

Purpose: Live at International House residential college while studying at the University of Melbourne. This scholarship supports commencing students with a fee remission of US$14,000 at International House. It is funded by the Friends and Alumni of International House.

Eligibility: Australian or domestic student applying to live at International House, or returning International House student

Type: Scholarship

Value: Up to US$14,000

Frequency: Annual

Country of Study: Any country

No. of awards offered: 3

Closing Date: 18 January

Additional Information: scholarships.unimelb.edu.au/awards/friends-and-alumni-of-international-house-scholarship

For further information contact:

The University of Melbourne Grattan Street, Parkville, Victoria 3010, Australia.

Tel: (61) 3 9035 5511

Friends of the Sports Association Scholarship

Purpose: Supported by the Sport Foundation Chapter, these scholarships provide cash and in-kind assistance to help aspiring High Performance student-athletes to simultaneously pursue their academic and sporting dreams.

Eligibility: be a member of the relevant Melbourne University Sporting Club, represent the University in varsity competition and be competing at a junior national team level (or equivalent).

Type: Scholarship

Value: at least US$7,000

Frequency: Annual

Country of Study: Any country

No. of awards offered: 12

Closing Date: 4 March

Additional Information: scholarships.unimelb.edu.au/awards/friends-of-the-sports-association-scholarship

For further information contact:

The University of Melbourne Grattan Street, Parkville, Victoria 3010, Australia.

Tel: (61) 3 9035 5511

Graduate Research Scholarships

Purpose: Available to high-achieving students undertaking graduate research at the University of Melbourne.

Eligibility: have applied for and meet the entry requirements for a graduate research degree at the University of Melbourne, or be currently enrolled in a graduate research degree at the University of Melbourne

Level of Study: Postgraduate

Type: Scholarship

Value: 100% fee remission and up to US$110,000

Frequency: Annual

Country of Study: Any country

No. of awards offered: 600

Closing Date: 31 October

Additional Information: scholarships.unimelb.edu.au/awards/graduate-research-scholarships

For further information contact:

The University of Melbourne Grattan Street, Parkville, Victoria 3010, Australia.

Tel: (61) 3 9035 5511

Graduate Women Victoria Scholarship Program

Purpose: The Graduate Women Victoria Scholarship Program is a suite of scholarships and bursaries offered to women studying at Victorian universities who have overcome or are overcoming disadvantage. The Program is offered and run by Graduate Women Victoria.

Eligibility: be an Australian citizen or permanent resident be female be enrolled in an eligible course at a Victorian university, or at the Victorian campuses of the Australian Catholic University, in the year of application have overcome or are overcoming disadvantage in the pursuit of your studies.

Type: Scholarship

Value: US$3,500 - US$9,000

Frequency: Annual

Country of Study: Any country

No. of awards offered: 16

Closing Date: 31 Mar

Additional Information: scholarships.unimelb.edu.au/awards/graduate-women-victoria-scholarship-program

For further information contact:

The University of Melbourne Grattan Street, Parkville, Victoria 3010, Australia.

Tel: (61) 3 9035 5511

Hansen Scholarship

Purpose: The Hansen Scholarship is a flagship scholarship program at The University of Melbourne. From 2020, The Hansen Scholarship will be awarded to talented students whose financial circumstances present a challenge to accessing a first-class education. Recipients will be awarded accommodation, an allowance, and financial and personal support.

Eligibility: be an Australian citizen or permanent resident, and be enrolled in an Australian Year 12 or the International Baccalaureate in Australia; or have applied for or be the holder of an Australian temporary or permanent protection visa, and be enrolled in an Australian Year 12 or the International Baccalaureate in Australia; or be an Australian citizen and be enrolled in an Australian Year 12 or the International Baccalaureate outside Australia. be aged between 16 and 20 years of age in the year of application be on track to achieve a minimum Australian Tertiary Admissions Rank (ATAR) of at least 90 (or the IB equivalent) experience financial circumstances that present a challenge to attending The University of Melbourne. (e.g. you or your family receive Centrelink benefits)

Type: Scholarship

U

Value: Up to US$108,000
Frequency: Annual
Country of Study: Any country
No. of awards offered: 20
Closing Date: 9 March
Additional Information: scholarships.unimelb.edu.au/awards/hansen-scholarship

For further information contact:

The University of Melbourne Grattan Street, Parkville, Victoria 3010, Australia.

Tel: (61) 3 9035 5511

Henry James Williams Scholarship

Purpose: Established with a bequest from Alfred, Alice and Robert Williams,and available to students undertaking research in a field of study other than theology and music.
Eligibility: be an Australian citizen or permanent resident have applied for and meet the entry requirements for a graduate research degree at the University of Melbourne and intend to undertake research in a field of study other than theology and music. have not already completed a research qualification at the same or higher level as the course for which a scholarship is sought not have previously received a graduate research scholarship with equivalent benefits
Type: Scholarship
Value: US$70,000 - US$125,000
Frequency: Annual
Country of Study: Any country
No. of awards offered: 10
Closing Date: 31 October
Additional Information: scholarships.unimelb.edu.au/awards/henry-james-williams-scholarship

For further information contact:

The University of Melbourne Grattan Street, Parkville, Victoria 3010, Australia.

Tel: (61) 3 9035 5511

High Performance Sports Scholarship

Purpose: Supported by the Sport Foundation Chapter, these scholarships provide cash and in-kind assistance to help aspiring High Performance student-athletes to simultaneously pursue their academic and sporting dreams.
Eligibility: Be a member of the relevant Melbourne University Sporting Club, represent the University in varsity competition and be competing at a senior national team level (or the equivalent).
Type: Scholarship
Value: at least US$8,000
Frequency: Annual
Country of Study: Any country
No. of awards offered: 8
Closing Date: 4 March
Additional Information: scholarships.unimelb.edu.au/awards/high-performance-sports-scholarship

For further information contact:

The University of Melbourne Grattan Street, Parkville, Victoria 3010, Australia.

Tel: (61) 3 9035 5511

Hilda Trevelyan Morrison Bequest

Purpose: This scholarship is awarded to a faculty of science student on the basis of demonstrated financial need.
Eligibility: Be enrolled in a Faculty of Science program, Demonstrate Financial Need by completing the online Student Financial Assessment Form by no later than the 6th of March 2023, Demonstrate the potential impact of financial assistance by completing the online Student Personal Statement Form by no later than the 17th of March 2023.
Type: Scholarship
Value: Up to US$5,000
Frequency: Annual
Country of Study: Any country
No. of awards offered: 8
Closing Date: 17 March
Additional Information: scholarships.unimelb.edu.au/awards/hilda-trevelyan-morrison-bequest

For further information contact:

The University of Melbourne Grattan Street, Parkville, Victoria 3010, Australia.

Tel: (61) 3 9035 5511

HVP Plantations Forestry Scholarship

Purpose: This scholarship is awarded to a domestic student enrolling in the Master of Ecosystem Management and Conservation student who is experiencing disadvantaged circumstances.

Eligibility: Be an Australian citizen, permanent resident, or New Zealand citizen; and Have applied for the Master of Ecosystem Management and Conservation.
Type: Scholarship
Value: Up to US$20,000
Frequency: Annual
Country of Study: Any country
No. of awards offered: 2
Closing Date: 25 January
Additional Information: scholarships.unimelb.edu.au/awards/hvp-plantations-forestry-scholarship

For further information contact:

The University of Melbourne Grattan Street, Parkville, Victoria 3010, Australia.

Tel: (61) 3 9035 5511

Indigenous Accommodation Grant

Purpose: The Indigenous Accommodation Grant is offered to Indigenous students who are residing at University Accommodation or Residential College and are ineligible for government accommodation funding or other forms of financial support.
Eligibility: be of Aboriginal and/or Torres Strait Islander descent, identify as Aboriginal and/or Torres Strait Islander, and be accepted as Aboriginal and/or Torres Strait Islander by the community in which they live, or formerly lived have applied for ABSTUDY / Residential Costs Option (RCO) payments and provide evidence (no more than 6 months old) from Centrelink that your application was unsuccessful; have applied for admission or be currently enrolled in a degree at The University of Melbourne be residing, or intending to reside, at one of the University of Melbourne's affiliated accommodation providers, as listed on the following webpages: Residential Colleges and other accommodation, and University Accommodation.
Type: Grant
Value: Up to US$10,000
Frequency: Annual
Country of Study: Any country
No. of awards offered: 20
Closing Date: 1 February
Additional Information: scholarships.unimelb.edu.au/awards/indigenous-accommodation-grant

For further information contact:

The University of Melbourne Grattan Street, Parkville, Victoria 3010, Australia.

Tel: (61) 3 9035 5511

International House Scholarship

Purpose: Live at International House residential college while studying at the University of Melbourne. This scholarship supports commencing students with a fee remission of US$7,000 at International House. It is funded by charitable giving to International House by friends and alumni.
Eligibility: International or domestic student applying to live at International House.
Type: Scholarship
Value: Up to US$7,000
Frequency: Annual
Country of Study: Any country
No. of awards offered: 3
Closing Date: 18 January
Additional Information: scholarships.unimelb.edu.au/awards/2022-international-house-scholarship

For further information contact:

The University of Melbourne Grattan Street, Parkville, Victoria 3010, Australia.

Irene and Arthur Kinsman Award for Postgraduate Studies

Purpose: The Irene and Arthur Kinsman Award for Postgraduate Studies was established with a bequest from Mavis Kinsman, and is offered to female graduates from the University of Melbourne who intend to undertake graduate study in social sciences.
Eligibility: be a female graduate of the University of Melbourne an Australian citizen or permanent resident have applied for or be enrolled in a graduate degree by coursework in Social Sciences at the University of Melbourne have at least twelve months of full-time equivalent study remaining to complete your course be experiencing compassionate or compelling circumstances (e.g. having primary care responsibilities for a dependent, medical condition, disability, or personal or financial difficulties)
Level of Study: Postgraduate
Type: Scholarship
Value: Up to US$5,000
Frequency: Annual
Country of Study: Any country
No. of awards offered: 2
Closing Date: 31 January
Additional Information: scholarships.unimelb.edu.au/awards/kinsman

For further information contact:

The University of Melbourne Grattan Street, Parkville, Victoria 3010, Australia.

Tel: (61) 3 9035 5511

Italian Australian Foundation Travel Scholarships

Purpose: These scholarships support students of Italian descent disadvantaged in their academic work by financial need to travel to and study in Italy.
Eligibility: be a student of Italian descent; be enrolled in a Bachelor of Arts, Diploma in Languages in Italian Studies or postgraduate course in the Faculty of Arts and wish to travel for the purpose of formal study of Italian language, culture and/or heritage; and, be in financial need.
Type: Scholarship
Value: Up to US$20,000
Frequency: Annual
Country of Study: Any country
No. of awards offered: 4
Closing Date: 27 June
Additional Information: scholarships.unimelb.edu.au/awards/italian-australian-foundation-travel-scholarship

For further information contact:

The University of Melbourne Grattan Street, Parkville, Victoria 3010, Australia.

Tel: (61) 3 9035 5511

Jack Keating Fund Scholarship

Purpose: This scholarship supports research students of the Melbourne Graduate School of Education who are pursuing policy research in the field of education, where the research is likely to impact on greater equality of opportunity and education outcomes and the advancement of social justice. This scholarship is awarded in the memory of Professor Jack Keating, who was a specialist in post compulsory education and training, most noted for his contribution to education policy and debates.
Eligibility: be an Australian citizen or permanent resident be a current or prospective research student (with at least a year of candidature remaining as at the closing date) of the Melbourne Graduate School of Education be pursuing policy research in the field of education where the research is likely to impact on greater equality of opportunity and education outcomes and the advancement of social justice
Type: Scholarship

Value: Up to US$8,500
Frequency: Annual
Country of Study: Any country
No. of awards offered: 2
Closing Date: 9 February
Additional Information: scholarships.unimelb.edu.au/awards/jack-keating-fund-scholarship

For further information contact:

The University of Melbourne Grattan Street, Parkville, Victoria 3010, Australia.

Tel: (61) 3 9035 5511

Jacobs Foundation: Research Fellowships

Purpose: Jacobs Foundation Research Fellowships are a globally competitive program for early and mid-career researchers from all scholarly disciplines aimed at improving the development and living conditions of children and youth.
Eligibility: Have graduated with a PhD, noting that the Jacobs Foundation offers Fellowships at either the "Early Career" level or the "Advanced" level: 1. Early Career Research Fellowship: The ideal candidate has obtained his/her PhD no more than 7 years ago. 2. Advanced Research Fellowship: The ideal candidate has obtained his/her PhD no more than 15 years ago.
Type: Fellowship
Value: US$225,000 - US$600,000
Frequency: Annual
Country of Study: Any country
No. of awards offered: 14
Closing Date: 15 January
Additional Information: scholarships.unimelb.edu.au/awards/jacobs-foundation-research-fellowships

For further information contact:

The University of Melbourne Grattan Street, Parkville, Victoria 3010, Australia.

Tel: (61) 3 9035 5511

Jean E Laby PhD Travelling Scholarships

Purpose: This scholarship supports support PhD students in Physics for travel, preferably overseas, to enhance their research program and research experience.
Eligibility: Be confirmed as a PhD candidate in the School of Physics Provide a short statement of endorsement from your supervisor Apply for financial need via the Student Financial

Assessment form; Be undertaking travel for a research related purpose. If you are requesting conference funds, you must be presenting research results.
Type: Scholarship
Value: Up to US$5,000
Frequency: Annual
Country of Study: Any country
No. of awards offered: 5
Closing Date: 6 March
Additional Information: scholarships.unimelb.edu.au/awards/jean-e-laby-phd-travelling-scholarships

For further information contact:

The University of Melbourne Grattan Street, Parkville, Victoria 3010, Australia.

Tel: (61) 3 9035 5511

Madeleine Selwyn-Smith Memorial Scholarships

Purpose: This scholarship is awarded to a Doctor of Philosophy Science or Master of Philosophy Science candidate who is undertaking graduate research in a branch of arboriculture or generally the furtherance of the planting, maintenance or preservation of trees.
Eligibility: Be a confirmed Doctor of Philosophy Science or Master Philosophy Science candidate, Be undertaking research in the discipline of arboriculture, or generally the furtherance of the planting, maintenance or preservation of trees.
Type: Scholarship
Value: Up to US$3000.
Frequency: Annual
Country of Study: Any country
No. of awards offered: 6
Closing Date: 17 March
Additional Information: scholarships.unimelb.edu.au/awards/madeleine-selwyn-smith-memorial-scholarships

For further information contact:

The University of Melbourne Grattan Street, Parkville, Victoria 3010, Australia.

Tel: (61) 3 9035 5511

Marie Skłodowska-Curie Actions

Purpose: The Marie Skłodowska-Curie Actions are a researcher mobility programme which supports researchers at all stages of their careers, regardless of age and nationality.

Eligibility: You must be within the first four years (full-time equivalent research experience) of your research career and not have a doctoral degree.
Type: Award
Value: US$20,000 - US$16,000,000
Length of Study: 3 - 36 months.
Country of Study: Any country
No. of awards offered: 1500
Closing Date: 1 March
Additional Information: scholarships.unimelb.edu.au/awards/marie-sklodowska-curie-actions

For further information contact:

Parkville VIC 3010, Australia.

Tel: (61) 3 9035 5511

Melbourne Mobility Excellence Awards

Purpose: A range of awards to support students undertaking overseas study.
Eligibility: be enrolled at the University of Melbourne in either an undergraduate degree or a graduate coursework degree intend to undertake approved overseas study of 12 weeks or more (Exchange or Study Abroad) as part of your course within 12 months after the closing date have achieved a Course Weighted Average of at least 80 in your current course
Type: Award
Value: US$2,500 - US$4,000
Frequency: Annual
Country of Study: Any country
No. of awards offered: 5
Closing Date: 31 May
Additional Information: scholarships.unimelb.edu.au/awards/melbourne-mobility-excellence-awards

For further information contact:

The University of Melbourne Grattan Street, Parkville, Victoria 3010, Australia.

Melbourne Welcome Grant

Purpose: Enrolled international coursework and research students who have travelled to Australia will be able to receive the Melbourne Welcome Grant towards the cost of travel, quarantine and adjustment to study and life in Melbourne.
Eligibility: Be an international student enrolled in coursework or research course with the University of

Melbourne in 2023 and not have departed Australia on or after the start of Semester 2, 2022 (26 July 2022) have arrived in Australia after 1 December 2022
Level of Study: Postgraduate
Type: Grant
Value: US$4,000.
Frequency: Annual
Country of Study: Any country
No. of awards offered: 12000
Closing Date: 31 December
Additional Information: scholarships.unimelb.edu.au/awards/melbourne-welcome-grant

For further information contact:

The University of Melbourne, Grattan Street, Parkville, Victoria 3010, Australia.

Tel: (61) 3 9035 5511

New Colombo Plan Grant

Purpose: Funded by the Department of Foreign Affairs and Trade (DFAT), the New Colombo Plan mobility program provides funding to Australian undergraduate students studying in the Indo-Pacific region.
Eligibility: be an Australian citizen and do not hold dual citizenship or residency rights of the host location of the mobility program 1. be enrolled in an undergraduate University of Melbourne course 2. be between 18 and 28* years of age at the commencement of the mobility program (*Aboriginal and/or Torres Strait Islander students do not need to be aged between 18 and 28.) 3. have not commenced a period of overseas study in the same host location as the mobility program 4. have not received a Melbourne Mobility Award for the same overseas program 5. have not received an Endeavour Student Exchange Grant, or the Lin Martin Scholarship 6. New Colombo Plan: 7. have not received a Student Grant under more than one Semester Grant 8. have not received a Student Grant under more than one Short-term Grant 9. have not received a Student Grant under both a Semester Grant and a Short-term Grant for the same Mobility Project or for the same period of travel outside of Australia. 10. be approved to participate in a University of Melbourne Overseas Program supported by New Colombo Plan funding.
Level of Study: Postgraduate
Type: Grant
Value: US$1,000 - US$7,000
Frequency: Annual
Country of Study: Any country
No. of awards offered: 150

Closing Date: 1 January
Additional Information: scholarships.unimelb.edu.au/awards/new-colombo-plan-grant

For further information contact:

The University of Melbourne Grattan Street, Parkville, Victoria 3010, Australia.

Tel: (61) 3 9035 5511

PhDs in Bio Nanotechnology

Eligibility: Open to those who have achieved Honours 2a or equivalent
Level of Study: Postgraduate, Research
Type: Scholarship
Value: AU$19,616 per year
Length of Study: 2 years (Masters) and 3 years (PhD)
Frequency: Annual
Study Establishment: University of Melbourne
Country of Study: Australia
Application Procedure: Applicants must apply directly to the scholarship provider. Check website for further details
Closing Date: 21 July
Contributor: University of Melbourne

For further information contact:

Email: fcaruso@unimelb.edu.au

Rae and Edith Bennett Travelling Scholarship

Purpose: This scholarship was established with bequests from Rae and Edith Bennett, and is offered to students or graduates from the University of Melbourne who intend to undertake graduate study or research in England, Scotland Wales or Northern Ireland.
Eligibility: Open to students and graduates of the University of Melbourne who can demonstrate outstanding academic merit and promise
Level of Study: Postgraduate
Type: Scholarship
Value: Up to AU$90,000
Frequency: Annual
Country of Study: Australia
Application Procedure: Please see the website www.services.unimelb.edu.au/scholarships/research/local/available/travelling/rae
No. of awards offered: 6
Closing Date: 1 February
Funding: Private

Contributor: Rae and Edith Bennett Travelling Scholarship Fund

For further information contact:

Email: gsa@gsa.unimelb.edu.au

Richard Cullen and Siu-Kuen Chan Scholarship at International House

Purpose: Live at International House residential college while studying at the University of Melbourne. 3 scholarships of US$7,000 for female students from China, Taiwan or Hong Kong SAR. The scholarship is made possible by the generosity of Professor Richard Cullen and Siu-Kuen Chan.
Eligibility: be from China PRC, Taiwan or Hong Kong SAR. identify as female.
Type: Scholarship
Value: US$7,000 - US$7,000
Frequency: Annual
Country of Study: Any country
No. of awards offered: 3
Closing Date: 18 January
Additional Information: scholarships.unimelb.edu.au/awards/richard-cullen-and-sk-chan

For further information contact:

The University of Melbourne Grattan Street, Parkville, Victoria 3010, Australia.

Tel: (61) 3 9035 5511

Samuel Francis Ponds Trust

Purpose: This scholarship is awarded to a postgraduate student who is undertaking research in the discipline of Forest Science.
Eligibility: Be a postgraduate student engaged in forestry research, Be undertaking a research project that requires funding for travel or fieldwork. Provide evidence of conference attendance, Provide evidence of abstract submission and acceptance, Provide a letter of invitation from your host university that confirms laboratory attendance. Outline a fieldwork expenditure budget.
Type: Scholarship
Value: Up to US$2500.
Frequency: Annual
Country of Study: Any country
No. of awards offered: 5
Closing Date: 17 March

Additional Information: scholarships.unimelb.edu.au/awards/samuel-francis-ponds-trust

For further information contact:

The University of Melbourne Grattan Street, Parkville, Victoria 3010, Australia.

Tel: (61) 3 9035 5511

Sir Arthur Sims Travelling Scholarship

Purpose: This scholarship was established in 1945 with a donation from Sir Arthur Sims, and is awarded to students who intend to pursue further study or research in subjects Ancient or Modern Languages, History, Philosophy, Physics, Chemistry, Mathematics, and Medicine in Great Britain.
Eligibility: To be eligible for this scholarship, you need to 1. have graduated from any Australian university or be currently enrolled at the University of Melbourne; 2. were born in any of the States or Territories of Australia or are the child of parents both of whom have been resident in Australia for a period of seven years or more such period of residence having commenced within a period of three years since the birth of the child 3. intend to undertake a graduate degree or research in the subjects Ancient or Modern Languages, History, Philosophy, Physics, Chemistry, Mathematics, and Medicine at an educational institution in Great Britain; and 4. not have completed a course of study at the same or higher level as the proposed overseas study.
Level of Study: Postgraduate, Research
Type: Scholarship
Value: Up to AU$48,000
Length of Study: 1–3 years
Country of Study: United Kingdom
Application Procedure: Check website www.services.unimelb.edu.au/scholarships/research/local/available/travelling/sims
Closing Date: 31 May
Funding: Private
Additional Information: scholarships.unimelb.edu.au/awards/sir-arthur-sims-travelling-scholarship#:~:text=This%20scholarship%20was%20established%20in,and%20Medicine%20in%20Great%20Britain.

Sir Thomas Naghten Fitzgerald Scholarship

Purpose: This scholarship is to support further surgical training in Australia or Overseas
Eligibility: Open to candidates studied or currently studying at The University of Melbourne

U

Level of Study: Postgraduate
Type: Scholarship
Value: Approx. AU$12,000
Length of Study: 1 year
Frequency: Annual
Study Establishment: University of Melbourne
Country of Study: Australia
Application Procedure: Check website www.research. mdhs.unimelb.edu.au/fitzgerald-scholarship
Closing Date: 31 October
Funding: Government
Additional Information: scholarships.unimelb.edu.au/ awards/the-sir-thomas-naghten-fitzgerald-scholarship

For further information contact:

Email: jyv@unimelb.edu.au

Sport Access Scholarship

Purpose: Melbourne University Sport proudly offers students facing financial hardship with a complimentary fitness membership.
Eligibility: Be enrolled in a course of study with the University of Melbourne 1. Have an academic status of good standing 2. Must not be receiving subsidised Fitness Membership Access through alternative means or programs 3. Not have a current MU Sport Fitness Membership, or have had an MU Sport Fitness Membership in the past 6 months
Level of Study: Postgraduate
Type: Scholarship
Value: at least US$800
Frequency: Annual
Country of Study: Any country
No. of awards offered: 150
Closing Date: 11 March
Additional Information: scholarships.unimelb.edu.au/ awards/sport-access-scholarship

For further information contact:

The University of Melbourne Grattan Street, Parkville, Victoria 3010, Australia.

Tel: (61) 3 9035 5511

Student Grants

Purpose: Over 150 bursaries established by various generous bequests and donations to assist students in financial need.
Eligibility: be enrolled at the University of Melbourne provide evidence of financial need

Level of Study: Postgraduate
Type: Grant
Value: US$1,000 - US$10,000
Frequency: Annual
Country of Study: Any country
No. of awards offered: 250
Closing Date: 6 March
Additional Information: scholarships.unimelb.edu.au/ awards/student-grants

For further information contact:

The University of Melbourne Grattan Street, Parkville, Victoria 3010, Australia.

Tel: (61) 3 9035 5511

Tertiary Access Payment

Purpose: The Tertiary Access Payment program has been developed by the Australian Government to assist students from regional and remote areas with the costs associated with relocating and to encourage them to start tertiary study immediately after completing secondary school.
Eligibility: be an Australian citizen or permanent resident, or a New Zealand citizen 1. have completed Year 12 or equivalent 2. have applied for a University of Melbourne undergraduate course for commencement in the year following completion of Year 12 or equivalent 3. be from an inner regional, outer-regional, remote or very remote area (use the Student Regional Area Search tool to check eligibility) 4. provide evidence that your parent(s) or guardian(s) have a combined income of less than US$250,000 or be exempt from meeting this requirement 5. be relocating to study at the University of Melbourne and your family home is at least 90 minutes by public transport from the University of Melbourne 6. be at least 16 years of age or 15 years of age if you are living independently, and no older than 22 years of age at time of starting your course
Type: Programme
Value: Up to US$5,000
Frequency: Annual
Country of Study: Any country
No. of awards offered: 120
Closing Date: 31 December
Additional Information: scholarships.unimelb.edu.au/ awards/tertiary-access-payment

For further information contact:

The University of Melbourne Grattan Street, Parkville, Victoria 3010, Australia.

Tel: (61) 3 9035 5511

The Helen Macpherson Smith Scholarships

Purpose: Established by a donation from the Helen Macpherson Smith Trust, this scholarship is available to female students undertaking research study in scientific and technical disciplines or historical, philosophical, political and social studies, language, literature and cultural studies.

Eligibility: To be eligible for this scholarship, you need to 1. Be an Australian citizen or permanent resident 2. Have applied for and meet the entry requirements for a graduate research degree at the University of Melbourne 3. Have not already completed a research qualification at the same or higher level as the course for which a scholarship is sought 4. Intend to study as a full-time student unless there are compassionate or compelling circumstances that prevent full-time study 5. Not have previously received a graduate research scholarship with similar benefits

Level of Study: Postgraduate

Type: Scholarship

Value: Up to AU$5,000

Frequency: Annual

Country of Study: Australia

Application Procedure: If you have applied for a Master by research or Doctorate by research degree by 31 October for commencement in the following year, you will be automatically considered for this scholarship.

No. of awards offered: 2

Closing Date: 31 October

Funding: Trusts

Contributor: Helen Macpherson Smith Trust

Additional Information: scholarships.unimelb.edu.au/awards/helen-macpherson-smith-scholarship

For further information contact:

Email: gsa@gsa.unimelb.edu.au

University of Melbourne Graduate Research Scholarships

Purpose: This scholarship is offered to high-achieving domestic and international research students

Eligibility: To be eligible for this scholarship, you need to have applied for and meet the entry requirements for a graduate research degree at the University of Melbourne, or be currently enrolled in a graduate research degree at the University of Melbourne.

Level of Study: Masters/PhD Degree

Type: Scholarships

Value: 100% fee remission and up to US$110,000

Country of Study: Australia

Application Procedure: If you are a new student and have applied for a graduate research course by the application closing date for that course, you will be automatically considered for the Graduate Research Scholarships. It is important to visit the official website to access the application form for detailed information on how to apply for this scholarship.

No. of awards offered: 350

Additional Information: scholarships.unimelb.edu.au/awards/graduate-research-scholarships

Viola Edith Reid Bequest Scholarship

Purpose: This scholarship is to support postgraduate study in any discipline of Medicine

Eligibility: To be eligible for this scholarship, you need to 1. Be an outstanding graduate research applicant, or enrolled graduate researcher, of the Melbourne Medical School within the Faculty of Medicine, Dentistry and Health Sciences 2. Be a medical graduate 3. Satisfy faculty entry requirements for PhD.

Level of Study: Postgraduate, Research

Type: Scholarship

Value: Up to US$31,200

Length of Study: 1 year

Frequency: Annual

Study Establishment: University of Melbourne

Country of Study: Australia

Application Procedure: Check website www.research.mdhs.unimelb.edu.au/viola-edith-reid-bequest

No. of awards offered: 1

Closing Date: 31 October

Funding: Government

Additional Information: scholarships.unimelb.edu.au/awards/viola-edith-reid-bequest-scholarship

For further information contact:

Tel: (61) 8344 4019
Fax: (61) 9347 7854
Email: mdhs-scholarships@unimelb.edu.au

Wellcome Trust: Principal Research Fellowships

Purpose: The Wellcome Trust's £25.9 billion investment portfolio directly funds thousands of scientists and researchers around the world at every step from discovery to impact. The Trust's funding schemes offer grants across biomedical science, population health, medical innovation, humanities and social science, and public engagement. Principal Research Fellowships are the most prestigious of the

Trust's awards and provide long-term funding for researchers of international standing

Eligibility: Have an established track record in research at the highest level. 1. Have sponsorship from an eligible host organisation in the UK or Republic of Ireland. 2. Have a research project that is within the Trust's scientific remit.

Type: Fellowship

Value: US$725,000 - US$1,350,000

Frequency: Annual

Country of Study: Any country

No. of awards offered: 10

Closing Date: 31 December

Additional Information: scholarships.unimelb.edu.au/awards/wellcome-trust-principal-research-fellowships

For further information contact:

The University of Melbourne Grattan Street, Parkville, Victoria 3010, Australia.

Tel: (61) 3 9035 5511

University of Montevallo

75 College Dr, Montevallo, AL 35115, United States of America.

Tel: (1) 205 665 6000

Graduate Honors Scholarship

Subjects: English

Purpose: To award prospective English students at the University of Montevallo.

Eligibility: Note In order to be eligible for consideration, each student must have a minimum overall GPA of 3.5 on a 4.0 scale, and a minimum of 1100/old format or 302/new format on the verbal and quantitative portions of the GRE, a minimum of 407 on the MAT, or a 550 on the GMAT (for MBA students). Please note that the selection of scholarship recipients and amount of the award is made in each department and is based upon scholarship money available to that department. A student who meets all scholarship requirements is not guaranteed an award and receiving the scholarship one semester does not guarantee an award for future semesters. Only students who have been admitted to a graduate program may be considered for the scholarship.

Type: Scholarship

Value: Varies

Frequency: Annual

Study Establishment: University of Montevallo

Country of Study: United States of America

Application Procedure: Applicants must supply a completed application; Official transcripts sent from all institutions attended; Graduate Record Examination (GRE); Miller Analogies Test (MAT), or GMAT (for MBA students) scores sent; a letter of professional intent, including a statement of career goals; three letters of recommendation covering academic ability, personal qualities, and professional qualifications

Closing Date: 1 July

Additional Information: Renewal requests are no longer required for students currently enrolled in graduate courses as completed scholarship packets are processed and sent to department chairs for review each semester. However, students who change programs or plan to apply to another program after graduation should reapply for the scholarship. www.montevallo.edu/academics/colleges/college-of-arts-sciences/department-of-english-foreign-languages/programs/english-m-a/scholarships-and-deadlines/

Minority Educators Scholarship

Subjects: English

Purpose: The shortage of minority teachers in Alabama and across the nation has been linked to multiple educational, social, and economic issues. The University of Montevallo College of Education recognizes this shortage and established The Minority Educators Scholarship Program to increase the number of minority students completing teacher education programs.

Eligibility: Graduate students who received this scholarship as undergraduates are not eligible to re-apply. Eligibility requirements include a minimum MAT score of 388 or a minimum of 290 on the GRE and a minimum grade point average of 2.5 earned in undergraduate work or 2.75 earned in college work. Recipients must maintain a 3.0 or better grade point average on graduate work, must maintain "full-time" status, and must complete the Alternative Master's Degree Program within two years of admission. Recipients must grant an exit interview upon leaving the program.

Type: Scholarship

Value: Varies

Frequency: Annual

Study Establishment: University of Montevallo

Country of Study: United States of America

Closing Date: 1 March

Additional Information: www.montevallo.edu/academics/colleges/college-of-arts-sciences/department-of-english-foreign-languages/programs/english-m-a/scholarships-and-deadlines/

Ronald E. McNair Post-Baccalaureate Achievement Program

Subjects: English

Purpose: Designed to provide effective preparation for doctoral study for low-income, first generation, and underrepresented undergraduate students.

Eligibility: Low-income, first generation, and underrepresented undergraduate students.

Type: Scholarship

Value: Varies

Frequency: Annual

Study Establishment: University of Montevallo

Country of Study: United States of America

Additional Information: Selection as a McNair Scholar is the result of a competitive process to participate in a program that prepares them for success in graduate school. The scholarship is awarded annually to graduate students who successfully participated in the McNair Scholars Program and are in good academic standing. Scholarship awards may be renewed annually for a maximum of 2 years. www.montevallo.edu/academics/colleges/college-of-arts-sciences/department-of-english-foreign-languages/programs/english-m-a/scholarships-and-deadlines/

University of Nevada, Las Vegas (UNLV)

Graduate College, 4505 Maryland Parkway, Box 451010, Las Vegas, NV 89154-1017, United States of America.

Tel: (1) 702 895 3011
Email: gradcollege@unlv.edu
Website: www.unlv.edu
Contact: Administrative Officer

Ella Schroder Indigenous Residential Scholarship

Purpose: The Ella Schroder Scholarship is specifically for Aboriginal and Torres Strait Islander students who have completed their secondary education as a boarding student at a boarding school.

Eligibility: Open to applicants who are completing Year 12 and gap year/s students who are commencing university study for the first time. Aboriginal or Torres Strait Islander: The applicant must identify as an Australian Aboriginal and/or Torres Strait Islander person and provide documentation according to the University's Confirmation of Aboriginality and Torres Strait Islander Identity Rule Financial Disadvantage: Be able to demonstrate financial need

Regional/Remote: The applicant's residential address must be either regional or remote as defined by the Government Remoteness Tool The applicant completed their secondary education whilst living in a boarding school Living in college: The applicant is living or intending to live in a UNE Residential College (excludes St Albert's College) - see Conditions section of this document for specific living requirements of this scholarship

Type: Scholarship

Value: Up to US$10,000

Length of Study: 4 Years

Frequency: Annual

Country of Study: Any country

No. of awards offered: 1

Closing Date: 13 February

Additional Information: www.une.edu.au/scholarships/2022/ella-schroder-indigenous-residential-scholarship

For further information contact:

Tel: (61) 2 6773 3333

University of Nevada, Las Vegas Alumni Association Graduate Scholarships

Purpose: To reward outstanding graduate students

Eligibility: Students must have completed any degree at UNLV, with a 3.5 GPA or better and be a member of the UNLV Alumni Association. Students must enrol in a graduate program at least half-time (6 credits/semester), and must maintain a cumulative and semester GPA of 3.5

Level of Study: Graduate, MBA

Type: Scholarship

Value: US$1,500

Length of Study: 1 year

Frequency: Annual

Study Establishment: UNLV

Country of Study: United States of America

Application Procedure: Please check the website www.financialaid.unlv.edu/apps/ScholarshipSearch/index.asp?action=detail&s=466

Closing Date: 3 March

Additional Information: Student may receive the scholarship for a maximum of two (2) years, or four (4) semesters www.montevallo.edu/academics/colleges/college-of-arts-sciences/department-of-english-foreign-languages/programs/english-m-a/scholarships-and-deadlines/

For further information contact:

Email: unlvscholarships@unlv.edu

U

University of Nevada, Las Vegas James F Adams/ GPSA Scholarship

Purpose: To recognize the academic achievements of graduate students

Eligibility: Applicant must be a master's-level or specialist student. He/she must have completed at least 12 credits of graduate study at UNLV (by the end of the current spring semester). Have a minimum graduate GPA of 3.5. Enroll in six or more credits in each semester of the scholarship year

Level of Study: Graduate, MBA

Type: Scholarship

Value: US$1,000

Length of Study: Varies

Frequency: Annual

Study Establishment: UNLV

Country of Study: United States of America

Application Procedure: Please see the website www.financial aid.unlv.edu/apps/ScholarshipSearch/index.asp?action=detail &s=419

Closing Date: 3 March

For further information contact:

Email: eric.lee@unlv.edu

University of New England (UNE)

Research Grants Office, Armidale, NSW 2351, Australia.

Tel: (61) 2 6773 3333
Email: research@une.edu.au
Website: www.une.edu.au

UNE is internationally recognized as one of the best teaching and research universities. Yearly, the university offers students more than AU$2,500,000 in scholarships, prizes, and bursaries and more than AU$18,000,000 for staff and students involved in research. It provides distance education for the students. Its scholars and scientists have established international reputations through their contributions in areas such as rural science, agricultural economics, educational administration, linguistics and archaeology.

A S Nivison Memorial Scholarship

Eligibility: To be eligible, candidates should domestic students who are pursuing research program in one of the fields mentioned above.

Level of Study: Doctorate, Postgraduate

Type: Scholarship

Value: AU$5,000

Length of Study: 1 year

Frequency: Annual

Country of Study: Australia

Application Procedure: Check website for further details www.une.edu.au/research/research-services/hdr/hdr-scholars hips/a-s-nivison-memorial-scholarship

Closing Date: 30 April

Funding: Private

Contributor: Nivison family

Additional Information: www.scholarshipdesk.com/ s-nivison-memorial-scholarship-at-the-university-of-new-england-australia/

For further information contact:

Tel: (61) 2 6773 3745
Email: pgscholarships@une.edu.au

Aboriginal Scholarship in Creative Education

Purpose: As a teacher, scholarship donor Machteld Hali holds the deep belief in the latent creativity in all people and works to facilitate its expression, using printmaking as her preferred medium.

Eligibility: Australian Citizen/Permanent Resident: The applicant must be an Australian Citizen or permanent resident as defined by the Commonwealth Aboriginal or Torres Strait Islander: The applicant must identify as an Australian Aboriginal and/or Torres Strait Islander person and provide documentation according to the UNE Confirmation of Aboriginality and Torres Strait Islander Identity Rule Financial Disadvantage: Be able to demonstrate financial need Open to Commencing or Continuing students enrolled or enrolling in: 1. Bachelor of Arts (with interest in visual/creative arts) 2. Bachelor of Education (Early Childhood and Primary) 3. Bachelor of Education (K-12 Teaching) with demonstrated enrolment in Creative Arts Education units of study (EDAE prefix) 4. Master of Teaching (Secondary) (If you have completed a major in visual arts in an undergraduate degree e.g. Bachelor of Fine Arts or Bachelor of Arts)

Type: Scholarship

Value: US$5,000

Length of Study: 4 Years

Frequency: Annual

Country of Study: Any country

Closing Date: 7 February

Additional Information: www.une.edu.au/scholarships/ 2022/aboriginal-scholarship-in-creative-education

For further information contact:

Tel: (61) 2 6773 3333

Andrew McCue Memorial Scholarship

Purpose: The purpose of this scholarship will be to provide recognition and financial assistance to outstanding undergraduate students enrolled in a Bachelor of Theatre and Performance or Bachelor of Arts with a major in Theatre Studies at the University of New England.

Eligibility: Australian Citizen/Permanent Resident: The applicant must be an Australian Citizen or permanent resident as defined by the Commonwealth Open to new/commencing and continuing UNE students enrolled in a Bachelor of Theatre and Performance or a Bachelor of Arts with a major in Theatre Studies Demonstrated current or past involvement in amateur or community theatre or drama Academic requirement: An ATAR of at least 70 is required for New/Commencing students OR An average GPA of 5 in their course to date is required Financial Disadvantage: Be able to demonstrate financial need

Type: Scholarship
Value: US$6,000
Length of Study: 3 Years
Frequency: Annual
Country of Study: Any country
No. of awards offered: 1
Closing Date: 7 February
Additional Information: www.une.edu.au/scholarships/2022/andrew-mccue-memorial-scholarship

For further information contact:

Tel: (61) 2 6773 3333

Betty J Fyffe Scholarship

Purpose: The family of Betty J Fyffe (nee Cahill) were pharmacists and chemist shop owners in Tamworth and Armidale over many years. In her Will, Betty established the Elizabeth Cahill Fyffe Trust to distribute funds to support students who are training in the medical fields with the expectation that they will hopefully carry out their profession in country areas when they finish their studies.

Eligibility: 1. Australian Citizen/Permanent Resident: Applicants must be an Australian Citizen or permanent resident as defined by the Commonwealth 2. Open to ALL new commencing and continuing students in their 1st/2nd/3rd year of the Joint Medical Program Bachelor of Medical Science / Doctor of Medicine degree. 3. Regional/Remote: You can prove that you have resided for at least 5 years consecutively or 10 years cumulatively in a rural and/or remote location (Regions defined as RA2-5), as defined by the Government Remoteness Tool 4. Degree/Discipline: The applicant is enrolling or enrolled in a Bachelor of Medical Science and Doctor of Medicine within the Joint Medical Program at the University of New England

Type: Scholarship
Value: The family of Betty J Fyffe (nee Cahill) were pharmacists and chemist shop owners in Tamworth and Armidale over many years. In her Will, Betty established the Elizabeth Cahill Fyffe Trust to distribute funds to support students who are training in the medical fields with the expectation that they will hopefully carry out their profession in country areas when they finish their studies.

Length of Study: 3 Years
Frequency: Annual
Country of Study: Any country
No. of awards offered: 50
Closing Date: 13 February
Additional Information: www.une.edu.au/scholarships/2022/betty-j-fyffe-scholarship

For further information contact:

Tel: (61) 2 6773 3333

Bush Children's Education Foundation Scholarship

Purpose: The Bush Children's Education Foundation Scholarship was established in 2006 to provide a first-year student from a remote community, assistance throughout the duration of their degree.

Eligibility: 1. Australian Citizen/Permanent Resident: The applicant must be an Australian Citizen or permanent resident as defined by the Commonwealth 2. Open to students enrolling/enrolled in 1st year of one of the following Agriculture-related degrees at UNE: Bachelor of Agribusiness, Bachelor of Agriculture/Bachelor of Business, Bachelor of Agriculture, Bachelor of Agricultural and Resource Economics, Bachelor of Rural Science 3. Financial Disadvantage: Be able to demonstrate financial need 4. Regional/Remote: The applicant's residential address must be either regional or remote (RA2 – RA5) as defined by the Government Remoteness Tool

Type: Scholarship
Value: US$5,000
Length of Study: 3 Years
Frequency: Annual
Country of Study: Any country
No. of awards offered: 2
Closing Date: 4 February

Additional Information: www.une.edu.au/scholarships/2022/bush-childrens-education-foundation-scholarship

For further information contact:

Tel: (61) 2 6773 3333

C.A.S. Hawker Scholarship

Purpose: The Charles Hawker Scholarship perpetuates the memory of scholar, soldier and pastoralist Charles Allan Seymour Hawker and commemorates the achievements of one of Australia's most respected statesmen
Eligibility: Australian Citizen/Permanent Resident: The applicant must be an Australian Citizen or permanent resident as defined by the Commonwealth Open to new students in their 1st year of an undergraduate degree at UNE. The applicant is intending to live in Robb College at UNE
Type: Scholarship
Value: Up to US$20,000
Length of Study: 3 Years
Frequency: Annual
Country of Study: Any country
No. of awards offered: 1
Closing Date: 7 January
Additional Information: www.une.edu.au/scholarships/2022/cas-hawker-scholarship

For further information contact:

Tel: (61) 2 6773 3333

Cec Spence Memorial UNE Country Scholarship

Purpose: The Cec Spence Memorial UNE Country Scholarship recognises the generosity and commitment that Cec Spence demonstrated during this lifetime in supporting students attending UNE.
Eligibility: 1. Australian Citizen/Permanent Resident: The applicant must be an Australian Citizen or permanent resident as defined by the Commonwealth 2. Open to applicants who are completing Year 12 and gap year/s students who are commencing university study for the first time 3. Academic requirement: An ATAR of at least 86.30 is required 4. Regional/Remote: The applicant's residential address must be either regional or remote as defined by the Government Remoteness Tool
Type: Scholarship
Value: US$7,500
Length of Study: 3 Years
Frequency: Annual
Country of Study: Any country

Closing Date: 3 January
Additional Information: www.une.edu.au/scholarships/2022/cec-spence-memorial-une-country-scholarship

For further information contact:

Tel: (61) 2 6773 3333

Commonwealth Accommodation Scholarship

Purpose: This Scholarship is funded by the Australian Government under the Indigenous Student Success Program. The purpose of the Commonwealth Accommodation Costs Scholarships is to widen participation in on campus higher education for Aboriginal and Torres Strait Islander students. Equity programs aim to overcome educational and financial disadvantages and help everyone access their potential.
Eligibility: 1. Aboriginal and/or Torres Strait Islander: The applicant must identify as an Australian Aboriginal and/or Torres Strait Islander person and provide documentation according to the UNE Confirmation of Aboriginality and Torres Strait Islander Identity Rule 2. Open to ALL new and continuing students enrolled in a UNE Enabling, Undergraduate or Postgraduate (Coursework) course at the University of New England 3. Relocation to Armidale for the purpose of study: Be able to demonstrate a planned relocation for the upcoming teaching period, or a recent relocation to Armidale in the last 6 months, for the purpose to study. 4. Financial Disadvantage: Be able to demonstrate financial disadvantage. Refer to the Supporting Documentation section below for details on what qualifies.
Type: Scholarship
Value: Up to US$9,000
Frequency: Annual
Country of Study: Any country
No. of awards offered: min 20
Closing Date: 1 June
Additional Information: www.une.edu.au/scholarships/2022/commonwealth-accommodation-scholarship

For further information contact:

Tel: (61) 2 6773 3333

Commonwealth Education Costs Scholarship

Purpose: This Scholarship is funded by the Australian Government under the Indigenous Student Success Program. The purpose of the Commonwealth Education Costs Scholarships is to widen participation in higher education for Aboriginal and Torres Strait Islander students. Equity programs aim to overcome educational and financial disadvantages and help everyone access their potential.

Eligibility: 1. Aboriginal and/or Torres Strait Islander: The applicant must identify as an Australian Aboriginal and/or Torres Strait Islander person and provide documentation according to the UNE Confirmation of Aboriginality and Torres Strait Islander Identity Rule 2. Open to ALL new and continuing students enrolled in a UNE Enabling, Undergraduate or Postgraduate (Coursework) course at the University of New England 3. Financial Disadvantage: Be able to demonstrate financial disadvantage. Refer to the Supporting Documentation section below for details on what qualifies.

Type: Scholarship
Value: Up to US$4,500
Frequency: Annual
Country of Study: Any country
No. of awards offered: min 20
Closing Date: 1 June
Additional Information: www.une.edu.au/scholarships/2022/commonwealth-education-costs-scholarship

For further information contact:

Tel: (61) 2 6773 3333

Cooperative Research Centre Programme Spatial Information PhD Scholarship

Purpose: To produce long-lasting outcomes relating to understanding how complex decision-making processes can be improved using spatial and other data

Eligibility: Applicants must hold a Class 1 or 2A Honours (or equivalent) Degree in a suitable discipline, and be a citizen or permanent resident of Australia. A valid driver's licence is also a necessary requirement

Level of Study: Doctorate
Type: Scholarship
Value: Please check website
Frequency: Annual
Study Establishment: University of New England
Country of Study: Australia
Application Procedure: Applicants should send a letter outlining suitability for the position, accompanied by a brief curriculum vitae (including contact details of two referees) and a copy of academic transcripts
Funding: Government

For further information contact:

Tel: (61) 2 6773 2436
Email: jim.scott@une.edu.au

Cotton Research and Development Corporation Postgraduate Scholarship

Purpose: To enhance the environmental, economic and social performance of the Australian cotton industry

Eligibility: These scholarships are open to anyone who is an Australian resident, studying at an Australian university and interested in working in the Australian cotton industry to pursue postgraduate studies relating to the cotton industry or its related activities

Level of Study: Postgraduate
Type: Scholarship
Value: AU$30,000
Length of Study: 3 years
Frequency: Annual
Study Establishment: University of New England
Country of Study: Australia, New Zealand or South Africa
Application Procedure: Check with the website for further details
Closing Date: January
Funding: Government
Contributor: Cotton Research and Development Corporation (CRDC)
Additional Information: Projects may relate to any field of cotton-related research www.scholarshipdesk.com/s-nivison-memorial-scholarship-at-the-university-of-new-england-australia/

For further information contact:

Cotton Research and Development Corporation, 2 Lloyd Street, Narrabri, NSW 2390, Australia.

Tel: (61) 2 6792 4088
Fax: (61) 2 6792 4400
Email: research@crdc.com.au

D.L. McMaster Fund Endowed Housing Scholarship

Purpose: This endowed scholarship is named in memory of Mr Douglas McMaster OBE, who in 1964 donated to the University of New England 2,500 acres of his property 'Inverness' for agricultural research to benefit the Warialda district and the North West Slopes.

Eligibility: Australian Citizen/Permanent Resident: The applicant must be an Australian Citizen or permanent resident as defined by the Commonwealth. Open to new commencing and continuing UNE students 1. Financial Disadvantage: Be able to demonstrate financial need 2. Geographic area: The applicant has a permanent home address in the following state and/or geographic area/s: Gwydir Shire of NSW

3. Degree/Discipline: The applicant is enrolling or enrolled in one of the following degrees at the University of New England: 4. Bachelor of Agriculture 5. Bachelor Rural Science 6. Bachelor of Agricultural Production and Management 7. Bachelor of Agriculture and Business 8. Bachelor of Agribusiness 10. Living in college: The applicant is living or intending to live in a UNE Residential College, including St Albert's College - see Conditions section of this document for specific living requirements of this scholarship
Type: Scholarship
Value: US$16,000 - 50% each for Residential and Tuition fees
Length of Study: 3 Years
Frequency: Annual
Country of Study: Any country
No. of awards offered: 2
Closing Date: 14 February
Additional Information: www.une.edu.au/scholarships/2022/d.l.-mcmaster-fund-endowed-housing-scholarship

For further information contact:

Tel: (61) 2 6773 3333

Destination Australia Program Honours Scholarship

Purpose: The University of New England has been selected by the Commonwealth Government as one of the tertiary education institutions that will award a number of Destination Australia Program (DAP) scholarships for commencement in the 2023 academic year.
Eligibility: Australian Citizen/Permanent Resident: This scholarship is open to Australian citizens and permanent residents Open to students commencing Honours in Trimester 1 2023 Academic requirement: An average GPA of 5.5 in their undergraduate degree is required Degree/Discipline: The applicant is enrolling in a Bachelor of Science with Honours degree at the University of New England Maintain ongoing residency in the Armidale regional area as defined by the Australian Statistical Geography Standard Remoteness Structure from the Australian Bureau of Statistics for the duration of each study period.
Type: Scholarship
Value: US$15,000
Length of Study: 1 Year
Frequency: Annual
Country of Study: Any country
No. of awards offered: 5
Closing Date: 25 February
Additional Information: www.une.edu.au/scholarships/2022/DAP-Hons-scholarship

For further information contact:

Tel: (61) 2 6773 3333

Destination Australia Program Scholarship for Masters by Coursework

Purpose: The University of New England has been selected by the Commonwealth Government as one of the tertiary education institutions that will award a number of Destination Australia Program (DAP) scholarships for commencement
Eligibility: 1. Australian Citizen/Permanent Resident: This scholarship is open to Australian citizens and permanent residents. 2. Open to continuing UNE students enrolling in a separate Coursework Masters degree 3. Financial disadvantage: The applicant must be able to demonstrate financial need. 4. Academic requirement: An average GPA of 4.0 in their undergraduate degree is required 5. Degree/Discipline: The applicant is enrolling in an undergraduate or coursework Masters degree at the University of New England 6. Maintain ongoing residency in the Armidale regional area as defined by the Australian Statistical Geography Standard Remoteness Structure from the Australian Bureau of Statistics for the duration of each study period.
Level of Study: Masters Degree, Postgraduate
Type: Scholarship
Value: US$15,000
Length of Study: 2 Years
Frequency: Annual
Country of Study: Any country
No. of awards offered: 2
Closing Date: 31 January
Additional Information: www.une.edu.au/scholarships/2022/DAP-Masters-Coursework

For further information contact:

Tel: (61) 2 6773 3333

Don and Lee Stammer Scholarship

Eligibility: 1. Australian Citizen/Permanent Resident: The applicant must be an Australian Citizen or permanent resident as defined by the Commonwealth 2. The applicant is enrolled/enrolling in their 1st/2nd/3rd/4th Year 3. Academic Requirement: ATAR of at least 75 (New Students) or GPA 5 (Continuing Students) 4. The scholarship is open to students who must be able to demonstrate disadvantage in one or more of the following categories: Financial disadvantage Physical, Intellectual or other disability Aboriginal or Torres Strait Islander: The applicant must identify as an Australian

Aboriginal and/or Torres Strait Islander person and provide documentation according to the University's Confirmation of Aboriginality and Torres Strait Islander Identity Procedures The applicant can demonstrate some other hardship or life circumstance which they have overcome/are overcoming in order to pursue tertiary studies, such as being a single parent, coming from an abusive background, etc.

Type: Scholarship
Value: Minimum of US$5,000 per annum
Frequency: Annual
Country of Study: Any country
No. of awards offered: 2
Closing Date: 3 January
Additional Information: www.une.edu.au/scholarships/2022/don-and-lee-stammer-scholarship

For further information contact:

Tel: (61) 2 6773 3333

DPIE Aboriginal Planning Scholarship

Purpose: This scholarship program will create a pathway to support Aboriginal planning students to commence their career with DPIE.

Eligibility: 1. Australian Citizen/Permanent Resident: The applicant must be an Australian Citizen or permanent resident as defined by the Commonwealth 2. Aboriginal or Torres Strait Islander: The applicant must identify as an Australian Aboriginal and/or Torres Strait Islander person and provide documentation according to the UNE Confirmation of Aboriginality and Torres Strait Islander Identity Rule 3. Degree/Discipline: The applicant is enrolling or enrolled in: Bachelor of Urban and Regional Planning Diploma in Town Planning, Bachelor of Social Science, Bachelor of Sustainability, Bachelor of GeoScience, Bachelor of Rural Science 4. Open to New/Commencing or Continuing students in their 1st/2nd/3rd/4th year of a degree/course (including honours) listed in 3. above 5. Academic requirement: For continuing students an average GPA of 4.0 in their course to date is required.

Type: Scholarship
Value: US$12,500 per annum
Frequency: Annual
Country of Study: Any country
No. of awards offered: 2
Closing Date: 14 February
Additional Information: www.une.edu.au/scholarships/2022/dpie-aboriginal-planning-scholarship

For further information contact:

Tel: (61) 2 6773 3333

Indigenous Master of Psychology (Clinical) Scholarship

Purpose: Financial resources are a major issue impacting tertiary study for Indigenous students. This contributes to the chronic under representation of Indigenous students in post-graduate clinical psychology programs that in turn results in Aboriginal and Torres Strait Islander psychologists making up well under 1% of the proportion of all registered psychologists.

Eligibility: visit website
Level of Study: Masters Degree
Type: Scholarship
Value: US$15,000
Length of Study: 2 Years
Frequency: Annual
Country of Study: Any country
No. of awards offered: 2
Closing Date: 6 February
Additional Information: www.une.edu.au/scholarships/2022/indigenous-master-of-psychology-clinical-scholarship

For further information contact:

Tel: (61) 2 6773 3333

John and Pauline Moorhead Scholarship

Purpose: John Moorhead is a graduate of UNE who will always be grateful for the start it gave him in academic life. His parents, John and Pauline, were both involved with the University and were active in community life in northern New South Wales.

Eligibility: Australian Citizens/Permanent Residents: The applicant must be an Australian Citizen or permanent resident as defined by the Commonwealth Open to applicants who are completing Year 12 and gap year/s students who are commencing an undergraduate degree for the first time. Academic requirement: An ATAR of at least 75 (or equivalent) is required Financial disadvantage: The applicant must be able to demonstrate financial need. Geographic area: The applicant has a permanent home address in the following state and/or geographic area/s: Northern Tablelands, North Coast or Northern Rivers regions of NSW.

Type: Scholarship
Value: US$8,000 per annum
Length of Study: 4 Years
Frequency: Annual
Country of Study: Any country
Closing Date: 17 January
Additional Information: www.une.edu.au/scholarships/2022/john-and-pauline-moorhead-scholarship

U

For further information contact:

Tel: (61) 2 6773 3333

Max Schroder Indigenous Scholarship

Purpose: Max Schroder provided a scholarship for one Indigenous student to pursue a UNE degree. Since then, Max's ongoing support and generosity has grown the program significantly to support dozens of UNE scholars over the years.
Eligibility: 1. Australian Citizen/Permanent Resident: The applicant must be an Australian Citizen or permanent resident as defined by the Commonwealth 2. Open to ALL new commencing and continuing UNE students 3. Academic requirement: For continuing students an average GPA of 4.0 in their course to date is required 4. Aboriginal or Torres Strait Islander: The applicant must identify as an Australian Aboriginal and/or Torres Strait Islander person and provide documentation according to the University's Confirmation of Aboriginality and Torres Strait Islander Identity Procedures 5. Financial Disadvantage: Be able to demonstrate financial need 6. Regional/Remote The applicant's residential address must be either regional or remote as defined by the Government Remoteness Tool 7. Living in college: The applicant is living or intending to live in a UNE Residential College (excluding St Albert's College) - see Conditions section of this document for specific living requirements of this scholarship
Type: Scholarship
Value: US$6,000
Frequency: Annual
Country of Study: Any country
No. of awards offered: 5
Closing Date: 13 February
Additional Information: www.une.edu.au/scholarships/2022/max-schroder-indigenous-scholarship

For further information contact:

Tel: (61) 2 6773 3333

Oorala Kick Start Scholarship

Purpose: This is a scholarship that is designed to help support Aboriginal and/or Torres Strait Islander students with the costs of starting their tertiary studies. The scholarship aims to promote a relationship with Oorala for school leavers who are commencing study for the first time.
Eligibility: Aboriginal or Torres Strait Islander: The applicant must identify as an Australian Aboriginal and/or Torres Strait Islander person and provide documentation according to the University's Confirmation of Aboriginality and Torres Strait Islander Identity Procedures Open to applicants who are school leavers (completing Year 12 or gap year/s students in 2022) who are commencing university study for the first time. Financial Disadvantage: Be able to demonstrate financial need
Type: Scholarship
Value: US$2,000 full-time or US$1,000 part-time
Length of Study: 1 Year
Frequency: Annual
Country of Study: Any country
No. of awards offered: 3
Closing Date: 14 February
Additional Information: www.une.edu.au/scholarships/2022/oorala-kick-start-scholarship

For further information contact:

Tel: (61) 2 6773 3333

PhD Scholarship in Animal Breeding

Purpose: To investigate aspects of sow feed intake and its impact on reproductive performance and longevity
Eligibility: Applicants should be well versed in statistics and/or animal breeding units at a tertiary level and computing and data analysis skills is highly desirable
Level of Study: Doctorate
Type: Scholarship
Value: AU$28,000 per year
Length of Study: 3 years
Frequency: Annual
Study Establishment: University of New England
Country of Study: Australia
Application Procedure: Please check with the website
Closing Date: 30 June
Contributor: Australian Pork CRC

For further information contact:

Tel: (61) 2 6773 3788
Email: kbunter2@une.edu.au

PhD Scholarship: Molecular Factors in Plant-Microbe Associations

Purpose: To study the molecular aspect of the interaction between the fungal pathogen and the plant
Eligibility: Applicants must hold a Class 1 or 2A Honours (or equivalent) Degree in a suitable discipline, and be a citizen or permanent resident of Australia
Level of Study: Doctorate
Type: Scholarship

Value: AU$26,000 per year (tax free)
Length of Study: 3 years
Frequency: Annual
Study Establishment: University of New England
Country of Study: Australia
Application Procedure: Applicants should send a letter outlining their suitability for the position, accompanied by a brief curriculum vitae (including contact details of two referees) and a copy of their academic transcripts
Funding: Government

For further information contact:

Tel: (61) 2 6773 2708
Fax: (61) 2 6773 3267
Email: lperegge@une.edu.au

PhD Scholarship: Weed Ecology

Purpose: To manage the species through a series of field and controlled environment experiments on emergence, growth, reproduction and spread of environment experiments on emergence, growth, reproduction and spread of fleabane species
Eligibility: Applicants must hold a Class 1 or 2A Honours (or equivalent) Degree in a suitable discipline, and be an citizen or permanent resident of Australia
Level of Study: Doctorate
Type: Scholarship
Value: AU$26,000 per year (tax free)
Length of Study: 3 years
Study Establishment: University of New England
Country of Study: Australia
Application Procedure: Applicants should send a letter outlining their suitability for the position accompanied by a brief curriculum vitae (including contact details of two referees) and a copy of their academic transcripts
Closing Date: 27 April
Funding: Government

For further information contact:

School of Rural Science and Agriculture, University of New England, Armidale, NSW 2351, Australia.

Tel: (61) 2 6773 3238
Email: bsindel@une.edu.au

Regional Australia Bank Scholarship

Purpose: Regional Australia Bank is a customer-owned bank that has been helping regional Australians achieve their lifestyle goals for over 50 years. It has a reputation for being flexible, personable and being able to make the complex simple.
Eligibility: visit website
Type: Scholarship
Value: US$5,000
Frequency: Annual
Country of Study: Any country
Closing Date: 3 January
Additional Information: www.une.edu.au/scholarships/2022/regional-bank-australia-scholarship

For further information contact:

Tel: (61) 2 6773 3333

Robb College Foundation Irvine Scholarship

Purpose: This scholarship recognises Dr Jim W. Irvine (the 3rd Head of College) and Mrs Sue Irvine for their outstanding contributions to the development and life of the College from 1981 to 1990.
Eligibility: Australian Citizen/Permanent Resident: The applicant must be an Australian Citizen or permanent resident as defined by the Commonwealth Open to new students in their 1st year of an undergraduate degree at UNE The applicant is intending to live in Robb College at UNE - see Conditions section of this document for specific living requirements of this scholarship
Type: Scholarship
Value: US$3,000
Length of Study: 1 Year
Frequency: Annual
Country of Study: Any country
No. of awards offered: 2
Closing Date: 31 January
Additional Information: www.une.edu.au/scholarships/2022/robb-college-foundation-irvine-scholarship

For further information contact:

Tel: (61) 2 6773 3333

Robb College Foundation Sinclair-Wilson Scholarship

Purpose: This scholarship recognises the late Mr J D Sinclair–Wilson's leadership of the College as Head of College from 1968 to 1980 and his outstanding contributions to the cultural and academic life of the College. This Scholarship is awarded at the Academic Dinner to a College resident who has entered their first year of undergraduate studies at UNE,

U

who has a strong academic record and can demonstrate a history of strong contribution to leadership in sporting or cultural aspects.

Eligibility: 1. Australian Citizen/Permanent Resident: The applicant must be an Australian Citizen or permanent resident as defined by the Commonwealth 2. Open to new students in their 1st year of an undergraduate degree at UNE 3. The applicant is intending to live in Robb College at UNE - see Conditions section of this document for specific living requirements of this scholarship

Type: Scholarship

Value: US$3,000

Length of Study: 1 Year

Frequency: Annual

Country of Study: Any country

No. of awards offered: 2

Closing Date: 31 January

Additional Information: www.une.edu.au/scholarships/ 2022/robb-college-sinclair-wilson-scholarship

For further information contact:

Tel: (61) 2 6773 3333

Robb Scholarship for Regional Planning and Development

Purpose: Robb Scholarship for Regional Planning & Development is co-funded by Octopus Investments, MAAS Group and Robb College Foundation.

Eligibility: Australian Citizen/Permanent Resident: The applicant must be an Australian Citizen or permanent resident as defined by the Commonwealth. Degree/Discipline: The applicant is enrolling/enrolled in one of the following courses: Bachelor of Urban and Regional Planning, Diploma in Town Planning, Bachelor of Social Science, Bachelor of Sustainability, Bachelor of GeoScience, Bachelor of Rural Science, Open to New Commencing or Continuing UNE Students in their 1st/2nd/3rd/4th year of a course (including Honours) listed above, Academic requirement:, New/Commencing students: ATAR of 77.1, Continuing students: An average GPA of 4.0 in their course to date is required.

Type: Scholarship

Value: US$6,000 for non-Robb residents US$9,000 if residing in Robb College for the first year US$12,000 if residing in Robb College for returning year

Frequency: Annual

Country of Study: Any country

Closing Date: 31 January

Additional Information: www.une.edu.au/scholarships/2022/ robb-scholarship-for-regional-planning-and-development

For further information contact:

Tel: (61) 2 6773 3333

Robb Scholarship for Regional Planning and Development

Purpose: Robb Scholarship for Regional Planning & Development is co-funded by Octopus Investments, MAAS Group and Robb College Foundation.

Eligibility: Australian Citizen/Permanent Resident: The applicant must be an Australian Citizen or permanent resident as defined by the Commonwealth. Degree/Discipline: The applicant is enrolling/enrolled in one of the following courses: Bachelor of Urban and Regional Planning, Diploma in Town Planning, Bachelor of Social Science, Bachelor of Sustainability, Bachelor of GeoScience, Bachelor of Rural Science, Open to New Commencing or Continuing UNE Students in their 1st/2nd/3rd/4th year of a course (including Honours) listed above, Academic requirement:, New/Commencing students: ATAR of 77.1, Continuing students: An average GPA of 4.0 in their course to date is required.

Type: Scholarship

Value: US$6,000 for non-Robb residents US$9,000 if residing in Robb College for the first year US$12,000 if residing in Robb College for returning year

Frequency: Annual

Country of Study: Any country

Closing Date: 31 January

Additional Information: www.une.edu.au/scholarships/2022/ robb-scholarship-for-regional-planning-and-development

For further information contact:

Tel: (61) 2 6773 3333

Support Fund for Students with a Disability

Purpose: The Support Fund for Students with a Disability (SFSD) (originally the Australian Foundation for Disabled Students) was established to assist undergraduate students with a disability to study at the University of New England, Armidale, NSW.

Eligibility: 1. Australian Citizen/Permanent Resident: The applicant must be an Australian Citizen or permanent resident as defined by the Commonwealth 2. Open to ALL new and continuing students in any year of an undergraduate degree (excluding Honours) 3. Academic requirement: For continuing students a minimum average GPA of 4.0 in their course to date is required 4. Financial Disadvantage: Be able to demonstrate financial need 5. Be registered with the Student Accessibility and Wellbeing Office (SAWO) at UNE

Type: Scholarship

Value: The minimum award will be US$1,000 and the maximum may be up to US$8,000.

Length of Study: 1 Year

Frequency: Annual

Country of Study: Any country

Closing Date: 31 January

Additional Information: www.une.edu.au/scholarships/2022/support-fund-for-students-with-a-disability

For further information contact:

Tel: (61) 2 6773 3333

Tamex Transport Scholarship

Purpose: Tamex became involved over 15 years ago with the UNE Scholarship program to give the opportunity of a university education to those rural based students who would otherwise be unable to attend due to financial constraints.

Eligibility: 1. Australian Citizen/Permanent Resident: The applicant must be an Australian Citizen or permanent resident as defined by the Commonwealth 2. Open to applicants who are completing Year 12 and gap year/s students who are commencing university study for the first time 3. Financial Disadvantage: Be able to demonstrate financial need 4. Geographic area: The applicant has a permanent home address in the following state and/or geographic area/s: New England, North-West NSW or Central West NSW 5. Degree/Discipline: The applicant is enrolling in an undergraduate degree within the UNE Business School or School of Law at the University of New England 6. Living in college: The applicant is living or intending to live in a UNE Residential College, including St Albert's College - see Conditions section of this document for specific living requirements of this scholarship

Type: Scholarship

Value: US$6,000

Length of Study: 3 Years

Frequency: Annual

Country of Study: Any country

No. of awards offered: 1

Closing Date: 17 January

Additional Information: www.une.edu.au/scholarships/2022/tamex-transport-scholarship

For further information contact:

Tel: (61) 2 6773 3333

The Duncan Family Scholarship in Early Childhood Education

Purpose: Ian Duncan was fortunate to have scholarships at both Agricultural College and then at University studying Veterinary Science; he has not forgotten the generous assistance these scholarships provided.

Eligibility: 1. Australian Citizen/Permanent Resident: The applicant must be an Australian Citizen or permanent resident as defined by the Commonwealth 2. Open to both new commencing and continuing UNE students. 3. Academic requirement: For new students, an ATAR of at least 75.00 is required Or For continuing students, an average GPA of 5.0 in their course to date is required. 4. Financial Disadvantage: Be able to demonstrate financial need 5. Degree/Discipline: The applicant is enrolling or enrolled in a Bachelor of Education (Early Childhood and Primary) or Bachelor of Education (Early Childhood Teaching) degree at the University of New England.

Type: Scholarship

Value: US$5,000

Length of Study: 1 Year

Frequency: Annual

Country of Study: Any country

Closing Date: 3 January

Additional Information: www.une.edu.au/scholarships/2022/the-duncan-family-scholarship-in-early-childhood-education

For further information contact:

Tel: (61) 2 6773 3333

The Duncan Family Scholarship in Pharmacy

Purpose: Ian Duncan was fortunate to have scholarships at both Agricultural College and then at University studying Veterinary Science; he has not forgotten the generous assistance these scholarships provided.

Eligibility: 1. Australian Citizen/Permanent Resident: The applicant must be an Australian Citizen or permanent resident as defined by the Commonwealth 2. Open to ALL new commencing and continuing UNE students. 3. Academic requirement: For new students, an ATAR of at least 75.00 is required Or For continuing students, an average GPA of 5.0 in their course to date is required. 4. Financial Disadvantage: Be able to demonstrate financial need 5. Degree/Discipline: The applicant is enrolling or enrolled in a Bachelor of Pharmacy degree at the University of New England.

Type: Scholarship

Value: US$5,000

Length of Study: 1 Year

Frequency: Annual

U

Country of Study: Any country
Closing Date: 3 January
Additional Information: www.une.edu.au/scholarships/2022/the-duncan-family-scholarship-in-pharmacy

For further information contact:

Tel: (61) 2 6773 3333

The Mildred and Betty Scholarship

Purpose: The purpose of this scholarship shall be to provide financial assistance to Aboriginal or Torres Strait Islander students enrolled at the University of New England who have demonstrated financial need.
Eligibility: Australian Citizen/Permanent Resident: The applicant must be an Australian Citizen or permanent resident as defined by the Commonwealth, Aboriginal or Torres Strait Islander: The applicant must be an Australian Aboriginal or Torres Strait Islander student as defined by the University's Confirmation of Aboriginality and Torres Strait Islander Identity Rule, Open to Commencing or Continuing Students:, Open to ALL new students commencing a Bachelor degree only, Open to continuing undergraduate UNE students in any year of a Bachelor degree (excluding Honours), Financial Disadvantage: Be able to demonstrate financial need
Type: Scholarship
Value: US$6,000
Frequency: Annual
Country of Study: Any country
No. of awards offered: 1
Closing Date: 3 January
Additional Information: www.une.edu.au/scholarships/2022/the-mildred-and-betty-scholarship

For further information contact:

Tel: (61) 2 6773 3333

The William McIlrath Rural Scholarship

Purpose: The William McIlrath Rural Scholarship is established to encourage and assist rural and regional students to undertake a full-time undergraduate degree at the University of New England.
Eligibility: 1. Australian Citizen/Permanent Resident: The applicant must be an Australian Citizen or permanent resident as defined by the Commonwealth 2. Open to applicants who are completing Year 12 and gap year/s students who are commencing university study for the first time 3. An ATAR of at least 80 is required 4. Financial

Disadvantage: Be able to demonstrate financial need 5. The applicant's residential address must be either regional or remote as defined by the Government Remoteness Tool 6. The applicant is enrolling in any of the following UNE Schools: School of Science and Technology, School of Environmental and Rural Science, School of Rural Medicine, School of Health, School of Education, School of Law and UNE Business School.
Type: Scholarship
Value: US$10,000 in the first year, then US$4,000 annually thereafter
Length of Study: max 5 Years
Frequency: Annual
Country of Study: Any country
Closing Date: 3 January
Additional Information: www.une.edu.au/scholarships/2022/the-william-mcilrath-rural-scholarship

For further information contact:

Tel: (61) 2 6773 3333

UNE Indigenous Medical Scholarship

Purpose: This Scholarship is a joint initiative of the Oorala Aboriginal Centre and the Faculty of Medicine and Health at UNE. The purpose of the UNE Indigenous Medical Scholarship is to attract more Indigenous students to study medicine at UNE. This scholarship will assist Indigenous students to alleviate their financial burden whilst studying Medicine at UNE.
Eligibility: 1. Aboriginal or Torres Strait Islander: The applicant must be an Australian Aboriginal and/or Torres Strait Islander student as defined by the University's Confirmation of Aboriginality and Torres Strait Islander Identity Procedures 2. Open to ALL new commencing students enrolled in the Joint Medical Program at the University of New England 3. Financial Disadvantage: Be able to demonstrate financial need
Type: Scholarship
Value: US$6,000
Length of Study: 5 Years
Frequency: Annual
Country of Study: Any country
No. of awards offered: 1
Closing Date: 6 February
Additional Information: www.une.edu.au/scholarships/2022/une-indigenous-medical-scholarship

For further information contact:

Tel: (61) 2 6773 3333

UNE Law Scholarship

Purpose: In 2020 New England and Hunter Valley region law firms and UNE Bachelor of Laws alumni were contacted regarding supporting a new scholarship at UNE for law students who need financial assistance to complete their studies. Several generous UNE Bachelor of Laws graduates and Scone Legal have made this scholarship possible.

Eligibility: Australian Citizen/Permanent Resident: The applicant must be an Australian Citizen or permanent resident as defined by the Commonwealth. The applicant is enrolled/enrolling in their 1st/2nd/3rd/4th year of a Bachelor of Laws, Academic requirement: ATAR of at least 84.4 (new students) or GPA 5.5 (continuing students), Financial Disadvantage: Be able to demonstrate financial need, Preference may be given to female applicants

Type: Scholarship

Value: US$5,000

Frequency: Annual

Country of Study: Any country

Closing Date: 23 January

Additional Information: www.une.edu.au/scholarships/2022/une-law-scholarship

For further information contact:

Tel: (61) 2 6773 3333

UNE Residential Financial Assistance Scholarship

Purpose: The University of New England has established residential scholarships to encourage qualified and motivated students who may not otherwise have considered college living because of financial constraints, to reside in a UNE residential college and be involved in the college community.

Eligibility: 1. Open to New and Continuing UNE students 2. Living in college: The applicant is living in College at UNE - see Conditions section of this document for specific living requirements of this scholarship

Type: Scholarship

Value: 37% - 66% discount on residential fees (room only) depending on the room type and contract length. This equates to US$3,400 for 34 weeks, up to a maximum of US$5,000 for a 51 week contract.

Length of Study: 34-52 Weeks

Frequency: Annual

Country of Study: Any country

No. of awards offered: min 30

Closing Date: 4 January

Additional Information: www.une.edu.au/scholarships/2022/residential-assistance-scholarship

For further information contact:

Tel: (61) 2 6773 3333

University of New England Equity Scholarship for Environmental and Rural Science

Eligibility: Applicants must be citizens of Australia or New Zealand and be an Aboriginal or Torres Strait Islander, non-English speaking background person, student with a disability or woman from non-traditional area

Level of Study: Postgraduate, Research

Type: Scholarship

Length of Study: 2 years (Masters) or 3 years (PhD)

Frequency: Annual

Study Establishment: University of New England

Country of Study: Australia, New Zealand or South Africa

Application Procedure: Check website for further details

Funding: Government

For further information contact:

University of New England, Armidale, NSW 2351, Australia.

Email: aharris@une.edu.au

University of New England Research Scholarship

Eligibility: Applicants must have achieved Honours 1 or equivalent, or Masters or equivalent

Level of Study: Doctorate, Postgraduate

Type: Scholarship

Value: AU$19,231

Length of Study: 3 years (PhD) and 2 years (Masters)

Frequency: Annual

Study Establishment: University of New England

Country of Study: Australia

Application Procedure: Contact the university for details

Closing Date: December

Funding: Government

For further information contact:

Tel: (61) 6773 3571

Fax: (61) 6773 3543

Email: aharris@une.edu.au

Wright College Scholarship

Purpose: This scholarship is to assist an undergraduate student, who is new to UNE, with their first year of accommodation costs at Wright College or Wright Village and is generously funded by the Wright College Association and the Martlet Foundation (a recognised charitable body supported by gifts and donations from the Wright College Alumni and friends).

Eligibility: 1. Australian Citizen/Permanent Resident: The applicant must be an Australian Citizen or permanent resident as defined by the Commonwealth 2. Open to new commencing UNE students 3. Financial Disadvantage: Be able to demonstrate financial need 4. Regional/Remote The applicant's residential address must be either regional or remote as defined by the Government Remoteness Tool 5. Living in college: The applicant is living or intending to live in Wright College or Wright Village at UNE - see the Conditions section of this document for specific living requirements of this scholarship

Type: Scholarship
Value: US$3,000
Length of Study: 1 Year
Frequency: Annual
Country of Study: Any country
No. of awards offered: 1
Closing Date: 3 January
Additional Information: www.une.edu.au/scholarships/2022/wright-college-scholarship

For further information contact:

Tel: (61) 2 6773 3333

Wright Honours Scholarship

Purpose: This scholarship is generously funded by the Wright College Association and the Martlet Foundation (a recognised charitable body supported by gifts and donations from the Wright College Alumni and friends).

Eligibility: Australian Citizen/Permanent Resident: The applicant must be an Australian Citizen or permanent resident as defined by the Commonwealth Open to ALL new commencing/continuing UNE students in their Honours year. Financial Disadvantage: Be able to demonstrate financial need Regional/Remote The applicant's residential address must be either regional or remote as defined by the Government Remoteness Tool Living in college. The applicant is living or intending to live in Wright College or Wright Village at UNE - see Conditions section of this document for specific living requirements of this scholarship

Type: Scholarship
Value: US$5,000
Length of Study: 1 Year
Frequency: Annual
Country of Study: Any country
No. of awards offered: 1

Closing Date: 7 February
Additional Information: www.une.edu.au/scholarships/2022/wright-honours-scholarship

For further information contact:

Tel: (61) 2 6773 3333

University of New South Wales

Sydney, NSW 2052, Australia.

Tel: (61) 2 93851000
Website: www.unsw.edu.au/a

UNSW Scholarships is responsible for the administration of all undergraduate and postgraduate coursework scholarships offered at UNSW and is the point of contact for any questions relating to these scholarships. Scholarships are offered in a variety of categories and are funded by the University with the support of many generous donors and organisations. Merit Scholarships are available to recognise your academic and other achievements (such as leadership, community involvement, commitment to a program of study). Equity Scholarships provide assistance to students that may experience educational disadvantage or are from low socio-economic backgrounds, and to support access and diversity. UNSW Scholarships is home to the Elite Athlete Support Program and Sports Scholarships, including the Ben Lexcen Sports Scholarship. We also provide information on Prestigious Programs for UNSW students to undertake graduate study at overseas institutions, and manage the Australian selection process for the Robertson Scholars Leadership Program Scholarship to study at Duke University/UNC in the United States. Please search for a scholarship program that may suit you and check the eligibility, selection criteria and closing dates. Scholarships are competitive and there are less scholarships than applicants. UNSW Scholarships allows you to apply for as many scholarships as you are eligible for.

Tyree Nuclear Masters by Coursework Tuition Scholarship

Purpose: The purpose of the Scholarship is to support a diverse cohort of Tyree Scholars at Masters level that will provide a talent pipeline to an emerging nuclear industry in Australia. The scholarship will support students undertaking studies at the Masters level in the nuclear engineering program at UNSW.

Eligibility: Be an Australian Citizen, an Australian permanent resident (including Humanitarian Visa Holders) or New Zealand Citizen. Be eligible for a Commonwealth Supported Place (CSP). Must have received an offer of admission into the Master of Engineering Science (8338) in the Nuclear Engineering specialisation
Type: Scholarship
Value: US$8,000
Frequency: Annual
Country of Study: Any country
No. of awards offered: 3
Closing Date: 31 January
Additional Information: www.scholarships.unsw.edu.au/scholarships/id/1593/5463

For further information contact:

Tel: (61) 2 9385 1000

UNSW International Scholarships

Purpose: UNSW offers a wide range of Scholarships and Awards to support International undergraduate and postgraduate coursework students commencing full-time study at UNSW
Eligibility: Must have applied and received an offer of admission* into a UNSW Undergraduate or Postgraduate program
Level of Study: Bachelors/Masters Degree
Type: Scholarships
Value: The scholarships may provide full or partial tuition fee payment, while others provide a stipend to assist with the costs associated with your studies.
Country of Study: Australia
No. of awards offered: Not specified
Closing Date: 31 March
Additional Information: www.scholarships.unsw.edu.au/scholarships/id/1431

Welcome Scholarship for Students from Refugee Backgrounds

Purpose: The Welcome Scholarship for Students from Refugee Backgrounds has been established to support talented students who are refugees on permanent visas with the opportunity to pursue tertiary education at UNSW.
Eligibility: Be commencing an eligible UNSW coursework degree program in 2023; and, Be a refugee currently holding one of the following visas: Global Special Humanitarian Visa (Subclass 202) Protection Visa (Subclass 866) Refugee Visas (Subclass 200, 201, 203 and 204)

Type: Scholarship
Value: US$10,000
Frequency: Annual
Country of Study: Any country
No. of awards offered: 1
Closing Date: 13 February
Additional Information: www.scholarships.unsw.edu.au/scholarships/id/1582/5439

For further information contact:

Tel: (61) 2 9385 1000

University of New South Wales (UNSW)

Scholarships and Financial Support, Sydney, NSW 2052, Australia.

Tel: (61) 2 9385 1000
Email: scholarships@unsw.edu.au
Website: www.unsw.edu.au

University of New South Wales (UNSW) is one of Australia's leading research and teaching universities. UNSW takes great pride in the broad range and high quality of teaching programmes. UNSW's teaching gains strength, vitality and currency both from their research activities and from their international nature.

Alton & Neryda Fancourt Chapple Award

Purpose: The purpose of this application is for applicants to be potentially considered for multiple Science Faculty honours scholarships, depending on individual scholarship criteria.
Eligibility: Be commencing full-time Honours year program in the School of Biological, Earth and Environmental Sciences
Type: Award
Value: US$5,000
Length of Study: 1 Year
Frequency: Annual
Country of Study: Any country
Closing Date: 21 February
Additional Information: www.scholarships.unsw.edu.au/scholarships/id/1579/5283

For further information contact:

Tel: (61) 2 9385 1000

Association of Professional Academic Institutions Scholarship in Metallurgy/Materials

Purpose: To undertake blast furnace research in collaboration with industry

Eligibility: This scholarship requires candidates to have achieved Honours 1 or equivalent, or Honours 2a or equivalent

Level of Study: Doctorate, Postgraduate

Type: Scholarship

Value: Stipend of AU$25,000 per year

Length of Study: 3–3.5 years

Frequency: Annual

Study Establishment: School of Materials Science and Engineering

Application Procedure: Check website for further details

Closing Date: 31 October

For further information contact:

Email: a.yu@unsw.edu.au

BHP Billiton Mitsubishi Alliance (BMA) Award in Mining Engineering

Purpose: This Award aims to support a rural or remote student currently enrolled in full-time study in UNSW Bachelor of Mining Engineering.

Eligibility: Be an Australian Citizen or Permanent Resident (including Humanitarian Visa Holders); and Be enrolled in full-time undergraduate study (single or double degree) in Bachelor of Engineering (Honours) (Mining); and Must have lived in a rural, regional or remote area within the two years prior to the start of your UNSW studies.

Type: Scholarship

Value: US$6,600

Length of Study: 1 Year

Frequency: Annual

Country of Study: Any country

No. of awards offered: 1

Closing Date: 21 February

Additional Information: www.scholarships.unsw.edu.au/scholarships/id/37/5244

For further information contact:

Tel: (61) 2 9385 1000

Brother Vincent Cotter Endowed Honours Award

Purpose: The purpose of this application is for applicants to be potentially considered for multiple Science Faculty honours scholarships, depending on individual scholarship criteria.

Eligibility: Must be commencing full-time Honours study in Physics

Type: Award

Value: US$5,000

Length of Study: 1 Year

Frequency: Annual

Country of Study: Any country

Closing Date: 21 February

Additional Information: www.scholarships.unsw.edu.au/scholarships/id/1579/5283

For further information contact:

Tel: (61) 2 9385 1000

Centre of Marine Science and Innovation Honours Indigenous Scholarship

Purpose: The purpose of the Scholarship is to support research training opportunities for Indigenous students that have an interest in marine science.

Eligibility: Be Indigenous Australian (Aboriginal and Torres Strait Islander only) Be commencing a full-time marine focused Honours program within the Centre of Marine Science & Innovation and be supervised by an eligible academic member of the Centre.

Type: Scholarship

Value: US$5,000

Length of Study: 1 Year

Country of Study: Any country

Closing Date: 21 February

Additional Information: www.scholarships.unsw.edu.au/scholarships/id/1595/5383

For further information contact:

Tel: (61) 2 9385 1000

CEPAR Honours Scholarship

Purpose: The CEPAR Honours Scholarship has been established to encourage students to pursue an honours degree on an ageing related topic by providing financial support.

Eligibility: Accepted into a 4th year Honours program in the UNSW Business School or the School of Psychology Studying on an ageing related topic under the supervision of a CEPAR Chief or Associate Investigator based at the UNSW. The recipient must be undertaking a full-time Honours Year program in one of the following disciplines: Economics, Actuarial Studies, Psychology

Type: Scholarship
Value: US$5,000
Length of Study: 1 Year
Frequency: Annual
Country of Study: Any country
Closing Date: 21 February
Additional Information: www.scholarships.unsw.edu.au/scholarships/id/871/5298

For further information contact:

Tel: (61) 2 9385 1000

College of Fine Arts Research Scholarship

Purpose: To support students with outstanding research potential who are ineligible for an APA/UPA
Eligibility: Students with an offer to commence a full-time PhD at COFA, or students currently enroled full-time in a PhD at COFA
Level of Study: Doctorate
Type: Scholarship
Value: AU$22,500 per year
Length of Study: Up to 3 years
Frequency: Annual
Study Establishment: University of New South Wales
Country of Study: Australia
Application Procedure: Application forms are available at the COFA Student Centre on the UNSW Scholarships website www.cofa.unsw.edu.au/about-us/scholarships/cofa-research-scholarship/
Closing Date: 31 January

For further information contact:

COFA Students Centre.

Tel: (61) 2 9385 0684
Email: chad.roberts@unsw.edu.au

Craig John Hastings Smith Surveying Engineering Honours Year Award

Purpose: The purpose of this application is for applicants to be potentially considered for multiple Faculty of Engineering honours scholarships, depending on individual scholarship criteria.
Eligibility: Be proposing to undertake a full-time Honours program in Surveying Engineering
Type: Scholarship
Value: US$7,000
Length of Study: 1 Year

Frequency: Annual
Country of Study: Any country
Closing Date: 21 February
Additional Information: www.scholarships.unsw.edu.au/scholarships/id/1584/5294

For further information contact:

Tel: (61) 2 9385 1000

Dami Attapatu ILP Award in Anatomy

Purpose: The purpose of this scholarship is to encourage the highest quality candidates in undergraduate Medicine & Science programs to consider undertaking an ILP or Honours Project commencing
Eligibility: Applicants must be entering the fourth year of a BMed/MD degree at UNSW in 2023 Be eligible to undertake an Honours or ILP in the area of anatomy
Type: Award
Value: US$5,000
Length of Study: 1 Year
Frequency: Annual
Country of Study: Any country
Closing Date: 21 February
Additional Information: www.scholarships.unsw.edu.au/scholarships/id/1577/5280

For further information contact:

Tel: (61) 2 9385 1000

Daniel and Helen Gauchat Port Macquarie Award for Rural Medical Students

Purpose: The purpose of the Award is to support accommodation fees at Forster College for first year UNSW Medicine Students from a rural area, commencing study at the UNSW Rural Clinical School in Port Macquarie.
Eligibility: Be commencing a UNSW eligible program. 1. Be classified as rural or remote(see below) 2. Be applying to or have been offered a place to undertake full-time study in the first year of an eligible UNSW undergraduate degree; and 3. Be residing at Forster House
Type: Award
Value: US$5,000
Length of Study: 1 Year
Frequency: Annual
Country of Study: Any country
No. of awards offered: 2
Closing Date: 7 March

Additional Information: www.scholarships.unsw.edu.au/scholarships/id/1462/5367

For further information contact:

Tel: (61) 2 9385 1000

David Walsh Memorial Scholarship

Purpose: The purpose of this scholarship is to encourage the highest quality candidates in undergraduate Medicine & Science programs to consider undertaking an ILP or Honours Project commencing
Eligibility: Be an undergraduate student proposing to undertake the one year Honours Program in Bachelor of Medical Science, Bachelor of Science (Advanced Science) or Science (Medicine) Honours in developmental biology, genetics or biochemistry and their relationship to developmental birth defects
Type: Scholarship
Value: US$5,000
Length of Study: 1 Year
Frequency: Annual
Country of Study: Any country
Closing Date: 21 February
Additional Information: www.scholarships.unsw.edu.au/scholarships/id/1577/5280

For further information contact:

Tel: (61) 2 9385 1000

Easson Geha Award in Planning

Eligibility: Be undertaking the Honours year in the Bachelor of Planning Program (3362) Must be an Australian Citizen, Permanent Resident (including Humanitarian Visa Holders) or New Zealand Citizen
Type: Award
Value: US$5,000
Length of Study: 1 Year
Frequency: Annual
Country of Study: Any country
Closing Date: 21 February
Additional Information: www.scholarships.unsw.edu.au/scholarships/id/1580/5284

For further information contact:

Tel: (61) 2 9385 1000

Elias Duek-Cohen Civid Design Award

Eligibility: Must be an Australian Citizen, Permanent Resident (including Humanitarian Visa Holders) or New Zealand Citizen Be commencing full-time Honours study in the Faculty of Built Environment with a focus on making towns and cities more beautiful and workable.
Type: Award
Value: US$5,000
Length of Study: 1 Year
Frequency: Annual
Country of Study: Any country
Closing Date: 21 February
Additional Information: www.scholarships.unsw.edu.au/scholarships/id/1580/5284

For further information contact:

Tel: (61) 2 9385 1000

Elias Duek-Cohen Urban Design Award

Purpose: The Elias Duek-Cohen Urban Design Award was established to encourage undergraduate students in the Faculty of the Built Environment to undertake their final year thesis on a topic concerned with making towns and cities more beautiful and more workable.
Eligibility: Full-time students enrolling in the final year of an undergraduate degree in the Faculty of the Built Environment that has a major work or thesis as part of its requirement
Type: Scholarship
Value: US$5,000
Length of Study: 1 Year
Frequency: Annual
Country of Study: Any country
No. of awards offered: 1
Closing Date: 21 February
Additional Information: www.scholarships.unsw.edu.au/scholarships/id/1102/5229

For further information contact:

Tel: (61) 2 9385 1000

Emeritus Professor William Gordon Rimmer Award

Eligibility: Be undertaking the Honours Year in History. Must be an Australian Citizen, Permanent Resident (including Humanitarian Visa Holders) or New Zealand Citizen

Type: Award
Value: US$5,000
Length of Study: 1 Year
Frequency: Annual
Country of Study: Any country
Closing Date: 21 February
Additional Information: www.scholarships.unsw.edu.au/scholarships/id/1580/5284

For further information contact:

Tel: (61) 2 9385 1000

Emeritus Professor William Gordon Rimmer Scholarship

Eligibility: Be undertaking an Honours year in History. Preference may be given to an applicant studying in the field of American or European history. Must be an Australian Citizen, Permanent Resident (including Humanitarian Visa Holders) or New Zealand Citizen
Type: Scholarship
Value: US$5,000
Length of Study: 1 Year
Frequency: Annual
Country of Study: Any country
Closing Date: 21 February
Additional Information: www.scholarships.unsw.edu.au/scholarships/id/1580/5284

For further information contact:

Tel: (61) 2 9385 1000

Fred Katz Award

Eligibility: Be   undertaking   the   Honours   Year   in Philosophy.
Type: Scholarship
Value: US$5,000
Length of Study: 1 Year
Frequency: Annual
Country of Study: Any country
Closing Date: 21 February
Additional Information: www.scholarships.unsw.edu.au/scholarships/id/1580/5284

For further information contact:

Tel: (61) 2 9385 1000

Gail Kelly Honours Award for Business

Purpose: The purpose of the Award is to support students in their Honours year with an interest in International Business as part of the Bachelor of Economics or Commerce, and aims to decrease the amount of additional paid work a student needs while studying.
Eligibility: The recipient must be commencing full-time Honours study in one of the following degrees: Bachelor of Commerce (Honours), Bachelor of Economics (Honours), Be a domestic student - Australian Citizen, Permanent Resident (including Humanitarian Visa Holders) or New Zealand Citizen
Type: Scholarship
Value: US$20,000
Length of Study: 1 Year
Frequency: Annual
Country of Study: Any country
No. of awards offered: 2
Closing Date: 21 February
Additional Information: www.scholarships.unsw.edu.au/scholarships/id/1597/5381

For further information contact:

Tel: (61) 2 9385 1000

Glencore Mining Engineering Scholarship

Purpose: The purpose of this scholarship is to scholarship is to support a current undergraduate student undertaking a Bachelor of Engineering (Honours) (Mining) degree at UNSW Sydney in their 2nd year.
Eligibility: Be an Australian Citizen, Permanent Resident (including Humanitarian Visa Holders) or New Zealand Citizen: Be enrolled full-time in Bachelor of Engineering (Honours) (Mining) undergraduate degree program in the 2nd year. Enrolment in a double degree in combination with the Mining Engineering in the 2nd year is also permissible, but the tenure of the Scholarship will remain at a maximum of 4 years.
Type: Scholarship
Value: US$10,000
Length of Study: 4 Years
Frequency: Annual
Country of Study: Any country
No. of awards offered: 1
Closing Date: 21 February
Additional Information: www.scholarships.unsw.edu.au/scholarships/id/1258/5295

For further information contact:

Tel: (61) 2 9385 1000

U

H.C. & M.E. Porter Memorial Endowed Award

Purpose: The purpose of this application is for applicants to be potentially considered for multiple Science Faculty honours scholarships, depending on individual scholarship criteria.
Eligibility: Be proposing or currently undertaking a full-time Honours program in the Faculty of Science
Type: Award
Value: US$8,000
Length of Study: 1 Year
Frequency: Annual
Country of Study: Any country
Closing Date: 21 February
Additional Information: www.scholarships.unsw.edu.au/scholarships/id/1579/5283

For further information contact:

Tel: (61) 2 9385 1000

Herbert Smith Freehills Law and Economics Honours Year Award

Eligibility: Commencing Honours program in Economics at the UNSW Business School in T1, 2023 No residency requirement
Type: Award
Value: US$5,000
Length of Study: 1 Year
Frequency: Annual
Country of Study: Any country
Closing Date: 21 February
Additional Information: www.scholarships.unsw.edu.au/scholarships/id/1578/5282

For further information contact:

Tel: (61) 2 9385 1000

Honourable Jack Beale Scholarship in Engineering

Purpose: The purpose of this application is for applicants to be potentially considered for multiple Faculty of Engineering honours scholarships, depending on individual scholarship criteria.
Eligibility: Be proposing to undertake a full-time Honours program in one of the following disciplines: Civil Engineering, Environmental Engineering
Type: Scholarship
Value: US$10,000
Length of Study: 1 Year

Frequency: Annual
Country of Study: Any country
Closing Date: 21 February
Additional Information: www.scholarships.unsw.edu.au/scholarships/id/1584/5294

For further information contact:

Tel: (61) 2 9385 1000

Honours Award Education

Eligibility: Be commencing full-time Honours year program Education
Type: Award
Value: US$5,000
Length of Study: 1 Year
Frequency: Annual
Country of Study: Any country
Application Procedure: Sydney NSW 2052, Australia
Closing Date: 21 February
Additional Information: www.scholarships.unsw.edu.au/scholarships/id/1580/5284

For further information contact:

Tel: (61) 2 9385 1000

International Scientia Coursework Scholarship

Purpose: The scholarships and awards listed below will be automatically offered to eligible students on the basis of academic merits highlighted in the application for admission to UNSW.
Eligibility: Be commencing full-time study in a UNSW Undergraduate or Postgraduate coursework degree program (excluding PG online and UNSW Canberra) in Term 2, 2023
Type: Scholarship
Value: Full tuition fee scholarships paid directly towards tuition fees for the minimum duration of program.$20,000 per annum
Frequency: Annual
Country of Study: Any country
Closing Date: 31 March
Additional Information: www.scholarships.unsw.edu.au/scholarships/id/1590/5366

For further information contact:

Tel: (61) 2 9385 1000

J Holden Family Foundation Honours Award in Maths and Physics

Purpose: The purpose of this application is for applicants to be potentially considered for multiple Science Faculty honours scholarships, depending on individual scholarship criteria.

Eligibility: Be proposing to undertake a full-time Honours year in the Faculty of Science, undertaking specialisation in Mathematics or Physics Be an Australian Citizen, New Zealander Citizen or Australian Permanent Resident

Type: Award

Value: US$8,000

Length of Study: 1 Years

Frequency: Annual

Country of Study: Any country

Closing Date: 21 February

Additional Information: www.scholarships.unsw.edu.au/scholarships/id/1579/5283

For further information contact:

Tel: (61) 2 9385 1000

John MacIntyre Honours Year In School Marine Science

Purpose: The purpose of this application is for applicants to be potentially considered for multiple Science Faculty honours scholarships, depending on individual scholarship criteria.

Eligibility: Be proposing to undertake a full-time Honours year in the Bachelor of Science program with a project specialising in Marine Science Be an Australian Citizen or Permanent Resident

Type: Award

Value: US$5,000

Length of Study: 1 Year

Frequency: Annual

Country of Study: Any country

Closing Date: 21 February

Additional Information: www.scholarships.unsw.edu.au/scholarships/id/1579/5283

For further information contact:

Tel: (61) 2 9385 1000

Judith Robinson-Valery Honours Award in Modern Languages

Purpose: The Judith Robinson-Valery Honours Award in Modern Languages was established to encourage students to undertake a full-time Honours language program in the school of Humanities & Language at the Faculty of Arts and Social Sciences.

Eligibility: Be an Australian Citizen or Permanent Resident Be proposing to undertake a full-time Honours language program in the school of Humanities & Languages at the UNSW Faculty of Arts and Social Sciences.

Type: Scholarship

Value: US$5,000

Length of Study: 1 Year

Frequency: Annual

Country of Study: Any country

No. of awards offered: 1

Closing Date: 21 February

Additional Information: www.scholarships.unsw.edu.au/scholarships/id/186/5230

For further information contact:

Tel: (61) 2 9385 1000

Judith Robinson-Valery Honours Award in Modern Languages

Eligibility: Be commencing full-time Honours study in one of the following disciplines: Asian Studies and European Studies Languages and Cultures - Chinese Studies, French Studies, German Studies, Spanish Studies, Japanese Studies, and Korean Studies Linguistics

Type: Award

Value: US$5,000

Length of Study: 1 Year

Frequency: Annual

Country of Study: Any country

Closing Date: 21 February

Additional Information: www.scholarships.unsw.edu.au/scholarships/id/1580/5284

For further information contact:

Tel: (61) 2 9385 1000

Late Stephen Robjohns Science Scholarship

Purpose: The purpose of the Scholarship is to support students undertaking an undergraduate program of study specialising in physics, chemistry or mathematics at UNSW Sydney. This scholarship will be tenable for the remaining duration of the successful recipients current program

Eligibility: Be a current full-time undergraduate student in any program with a major in either Mathematics, Chemistry or Physics.

U

Type: Scholarship
Value: US$12,000
Length of Study: 4 Years
Frequency: Annual
Country of Study: Any country
Closing Date: 21 February
Additional Information: www.scholarships.unsw.edu.au/scholarships/id/850/5301

For further information contact:

Tel: (61) 2 9385 1000

Malcolm Cole Indigenous Scholarship

Eligibility: Indigenous Australian (Aboriginal and Torres Strait Islander only); and Be commencing full-time undergraduate studies in the School of the Arts & Media. Enrolment in a double degree is permissible.
Type: Scholarship
Value: US$5,000
Frequency: Annual
Country of Study: Any country
Closing Date: 28 February
Additional Information: www.scholarships.unsw.edu.au/scholarships/id/1395/5455

For further information contact:

Tel: (61) 2 9385 1000

Minerals Industry Flexible First Year Scholarship (Current Students)

Purpose: The purpose of the Scholarship is to encourage the recruitment of students in the flexible first year of the Bachelor of Engineering (Honours) of high potential to transfer to the Bachelor of Engineering (Honours) in Mining Engineering.
Eligibility: Be an Australian Citizen, Permanent Resident (including Humanitarian Visa Holders) or New Zealand Citizen, and Have completed 48 UoC in the 2022 academic year as a Flexible First year student within the Faculty of Engineering, and be commencing the second year of full-time undergraduate study (single or double) in Bachelor of Engineering (Honours)
Type: Scholarship
Value: US$12,000
Frequency: Annual
Country of Study: Any country
No. of awards offered: 1
Closing Date: 21 February

Additional Information: www.scholarships.unsw.edu.au/scholarships/id/1594/5376

For further information contact:

Tel: (61) 2 9385 1000

Norman, Disney & Young Indigenous Scholarship

Eligibility: Indigenous Australian (Aboriginal and Torres Strait Islander only); and Be commencing full-time study in a Bachelor of Engineering, specialising in one of the following: Mechanical and Manufacturing Engineering Mechanical Engineering Mechatronic Engineering Electrical Engineering Environmental Engineering Photovoltaics & Solar Engineering Renewable Engineering Enrolment in a double degree is permissible.
Type: Scholarship
Value: US$5,000
Length of Study: 5 Years
Frequency: Annual
Country of Study: Any country
Closing Date: 28 February
Additional Information: www.scholarships.unsw.edu.au/scholarships/id/1395/5455

For further information contact:

Tel: (61) 2 9385 1000

Oliver Correy Award

Purpose: The purpose of this application is for applicants to be potentially considered for multiple Faculty of Engineering honours scholarships, depending on individual scholarship criteria.
Eligibility: Be proposing to undertake a full-time Honours program in Civil Engineering
Type: Scholarship
Value: US$7,500
Length of Study: 1 Year
Frequency: Annual
Country of Study: Any country
Closing Date: 21 February
Additional Information: www.scholarships.unsw.edu.au/scholarships/id/1584/5294

For further information contact:

Tel: (61) 2 9385 1000

Paradice Honours Award in Mathematics & Statistics

Purpose: The purpose of this application is for applicants to be potentially considered for multiple Science Faculty honours scholarships, depending on individual scholarship criteria.

Eligibility: Be commencing full-time Honours study in the School of Mathematics and Statistics. Be Female Be part of the Women in Mathematics Program

Type: Award

Value: US$5,000

Length of Study: 1 Year

Frequency: Annual

Country of Study: Any country

Closing Date: 21 February

Additional Information: www.scholarships.unsw.edu.au/scholarships/id/1579/5283

For further information contact:

Tel: (61) 2 9385 1000

Peggy Bamford Award

Eligibility: Be commencing full-time Honours study in the Social Sciences

Type: Award

Value: US$5,000

Length of Study: 1 Year

Frequency: Annual

Country of Study: Any country

Closing Date: 21 February

Additional Information: www.scholarships.unsw.edu.au/scholarships/id/1580/5284

For further information contact:

Tel: (61) 2 9385 1000

PhD Scholarship – Metal Dusting

Purpose: To support research on metal dusting

Eligibility: Open to citizens of Australia or permanent residents holding high Honours Degree in science

Level of Study: Postgraduate, Research

Type: Scholarship

Value: AU$25,000–30,000 per year (tax free)

Length of Study: 3–3.5 years

Frequency: Annual

Study Establishment: University of New South Wales

Country of Study: Australia

Application Procedure: Check website for further details

Closing Date: 28 February

For further information contact:

Tel: (61) 93 854 322

Fax: (61) 93 855 956

Email: d.young@unsw.edu.au

PhD Scholarships in Environmental Microbiology

Purpose: To attract the nation's strongest candidates capable of pursuing PhD studies in the genomics of environmental microorganisms

Eligibility: This scholarship is for study in Australia for those who have achieved Honours 1 or equivalent, or Masters or equivalent. There are no restrictions on citizenship

Level of Study: Doctorate, Postgraduate, Research

Type: Scholarship

Value: AU$35,000

Application Procedure: Check website www.emi.science.unsw.edu.au/recruitment.html

Closing Date: 31 March

For further information contact:

Email: r.cavicchioli@unsw.edu.au

Postdoctoral Fellow Positions in Computational Mathematics

Purpose: Applications are sought for two Postdoctoral Fellow positions in Computational Mathematics in the School of Mathematics and Statistics, UNSW Sydney.

Eligibility: Australian citizens are eligible to apply.

Type: Postdoctoral fellowship

Value: Australian AU$89K – Australian AU$96K per year (plus up to 17% superannuation and leave loading)

Frequency: Annual

Study Establishment: Positions are awarded in Computational Mathematics in the School of Mathematics and Statistics, UNSW Sydney

Country of Study: Australia

Application Procedure: Applicants should submit the following documents to ims@shanghaitech.edu.cn

Closing Date: 1 February

Additional Information: For more details please visit the website scholarship-positions.com/postdoctoral-fellow-positions-computational-mathematics-unsw-australia/2018/03/06/

U

For further information contact:

Email: ims@shanghaitech.edu.cn

Royston Honours Award in Chemical Engineering

Purpose: The purpose of this application is for applicants to be potentially considered for multiple Faculty of Engineering honours scholarships, depending on individual scholarship criteria.
Eligibility: Be proposing to undertake a full-time Honours program in Chemical Engineering
Type: Scholarship
Value: US$6,000
Length of Study: 1 Year
Country of Study: Any country
Closing Date: 21 February
Additional Information: www.scholarships.unsw.edu.au/scholarships/id/1584/5294

For further information contact:

Tel: (61) 2 9385 1000

School of Mathematics and Statistics Indigenous Scholarship

Eligibility: Indigenous Australian (Aboriginal and Torres Strait Islander only); and Be commencing full-time undergraduate studies in a Bachelor of Advanced Science or Bachelor of Science (Advanced Mathematics), including dual-award degrees with a declared major in the School of Mathematics & Statistics.
Type: Scholarship
Value: US$5,000
Frequency: Annual
Country of Study: Any country
Closing Date: 28 February
Additional Information: www.scholarships.unsw.edu.au/scholarships/id/1395/5455

For further information contact:

Tel: (61) 2 9385 1000

Sonja Huddle Award

Purpose: The purpose of this application is for applicants to be potentially considered for multiple Science Faculty honours scholarships, depending on individual scholarship criteria.

Eligibility: To be eligible for this scholarship, applicants must be enroled in one of the following programs, with a project specialising in earth science and the environment: Bachelor of Environmental Science Bachelor of Advanced Science Bachelor of Science
Type: Award
Value: US$5,000
Length of Study: 1 Year
Frequency: Annual
Country of Study: Any country
Closing Date: 21 February
Additional Information: www.scholarships.unsw.edu.au/scholarships/id/1579/5283

For further information contact:

Tel: (61) 2 9385 1000

Surface Coatings Association Australia Award

Purpose: The purpose of this application is for applicants to be potentially considered for multiple Science Faculty honours scholarships, depending on individual scholarship criteria.
Eligibility: Be commencing full-time Honours study with the School of Materials Science and Engineering in an area closely associated with coatings technology, for example polymers, pigments, corrosion or adhesion problems, or rheology.
Type: Award
Value: US$5,000
Length of Study: 1 Year
Frequency: Annual
Country of Study: Any country
Closing Date: 21 February
Additional Information: www.scholarships.unsw.edu.au/scholarships/id/1579/5283

For further information contact:

Tel: (61) 2 9385 1000

The Faculty of Law Juris Doctor Scholarship for Indigenous Students

Purpose: The Juris Doctor (JD) Scholarship for Indigenous Students was established to assist high achieving Indigenous students to undertake the Juris Doctor Program at UNSW.
Eligibility: Applicants must be of Australian Aboriginal or Torres Strait Islander descent and undertaking the Juris Doctor program at UNSW.
Type: Scholarship

Value: US$10,000
Frequency: Annual
Country of Study: Any country
No. of awards offered: 2
Closing Date: 21 February
Additional Information: www.scholarships.unsw.edu.au/scholarships/id/703/5377

For further information contact:

Tel: (61) 2 9385 1000

UNSW Business School Honours Scholarship

Eligibility: Must be undertaking a relevant Honours program offered by a participating School in the UNSW Business School T1, 2023 No residency requirements Please note that those who applied in 2022 are not eligible to re-apply.
Type: Scholarship
Value: US$5,000
Length of Study: 1 Year
Frequency: Annual
Country of Study: Any country
Closing Date: 21 February
Additional Information: www.scholarships.unsw.edu.au/scholarships/id/1578/5282

For further information contact:

Tel: (61) 2 9385 1000

UNSW Medical Research Honours Scholarship - South Western Sydney

Purpose: The purpose of this scholarship is to encourage the highest quality candidates in undergraduate Medicine & Science programs to consider undertaking an ILP or Honours Project commencing
Eligibility: Be currently enrolled in an eligible UNSW degree program Be eligible to undertake an approved Honours program offered by South Western Sydney Clinical School as part of an approved Honours program in Science, Medical Science, Advanced Science and Exercise Physiology (commencing in 2023)
Type: Scholarship
Value: US$5,000
Length of Study: 1 Year
Frequency: Annual
Country of Study: Any country
Closing Date: 21 February
Additional Information: www.scholarships.unsw.edu.au/scholarships/id/1577/5280

For further information contact:

Tel: (61) 2 9385 1000

UNSW Medicine Program Education Award

Purpose: The purpose of this scholarship is to encourage the highest quality candidates in undergraduate Medicine & Science programs to consider undertaking an ILP or Honours Project commencing
Eligibility: Applicants must be entering the fourth year of a BMed/MD degree at UNSW in 2023 1. Be eligible to undertake an ILP or Honours Project in the field of Medical Education 2. Be an Australian Citizen, Permanent Resident or New Zealand Citizen
Type: Award
Value: US$5,000
Length of Study: 1 Year
Frequency: Annual
Country of Study: Any country
Closing Date: 21 February
Additional Information: www.scholarships.unsw.edu.au/scholarships/id/1577/5280

For further information contact:

Tel: (61) 2 9385 1000

UNSW South Western Sydney Medicine Honours Scholarship

Purpose: The purpose of this scholarship is to encourage the highest quality candidates in undergraduate Medicine & Science programs to consider undertaking an ILP or Honours Project commencing
Eligibility: Be currently enrolled in the UNSW MD Program. 1. Be eligible to undertake an approved Honours program as part of 3831 Science (Medicine) Honours program (commencing in 2023) 2. Undertaking an Honours project at the South Western Sydney campuses of UNSW, including at the Ingham Institute for Applied Medical Research
Type: Scholarship
Value: US$5,000
Length of Study: 1 Year
Frequency: Annual
Country of Study: Any country
Closing Date: 21 February
Additional Information: www.scholarships.unsw.edu.au/scholarships/id/1577/5280

U

For further information contact:

Tel: (61) 2 9385 1000

Vida Rees Scholarship in Pediatrics

Purpose: To support Australian students to undertake research in paediatrics
Eligibility: To be eligible an applicant must be undertaking an honours project or postgraduate research in paediatrics. Applicants must be Australian citizens or permanent residents.
Level of Study: Postgraduate, Research
Type: Scholarship
Value: AU$1,000
Length of Study: 1 year
Frequency: Annual
Study Establishment: University of New South Wales
Country of Study: Australia
Application Procedure: Completed application forms and any supporting documentation should be scanned and emailed (preferably as a single pdf document) to the Graduate Research School. For more details please see the website
No. of awards offered: 1
Additional Information: www.scholarships.unsw.edu.au/scholarships/id/563

For further information contact:

Tel: (61) 9385 5500
Email: enquiries.grs@unsw.edu.au

Viktoria Marinov Award in Art

Purpose: To financially assist female artists under the age of 35 years who are proposing to undertake the Master of Art or Master of Fine Arts course
Eligibility: Female students who are under 35 years old completing the Master of Fine Arts by research.
Level of Study: Postgraduate
Type: Award
Value: AU$7,500
Length of Study: 1 year
Frequency: Annual
Study Establishment: New South Wales, Sydney City Central and Eastern Suburbs
Country of Study: Australia
Application Procedure: Applicants need to provide at least 6 images of their work, including information on the dimensions and materials of each work. These images can be supplied either electronically on DVD/CD or as attached printed images (no larger than A4). Applicants must include

a personal statement addressing the selection criteria as part of their application. Please see the website for more applications related details www.cofa.unsw.edu.au/about-us/scholarships/the-viktoria-marinov-award-in-art/
No. of awards offered: 2
Closing Date: 30 September
Additional Information: www.gooduniversitiesguide.com.au/scholarships/viktoria-marinov-award-in-art/unsw-australia/9241

For further information contact:

Tel: (61) 2 9385 0684
Email: chad.roberts@unsw.edu.au

Women in Computer Science Award (WICS)

Purpose: The purpose of the Award is to support high-performing female students undertaking study in the School of Computer Science & Engineering.
Eligibility: Be a Domestic student - Australian Citizen, Permanent Resident (including Humanitarian Visa Holders) or New Zealand Citizen. Be Female, The recipient must be commencing full-time undergraduate study in one of the following degree programs (single or double program): Bachelor of Computer Science, Bachelor of Bioinformatics Engineering, Bachelor of Software Engineering, Bachelor of Computer Engineering
Type: Scholarship
Value: US$5,000
Length of Study: 1 Year
Frequency: Annual
Country of Study: Any country
Closing Date: 13 February
Additional Information: www.scholarships.unsw.edu.au/scholarships/id/1613/5458

For further information contact:

Tel: (61) 2 9385 1000

University of Newcastle

Research Division, University of Newcastle, Callaghan, NSW 2308, Australia.

Tel: (61) 2 4921 5000
Email: research@newcastle.edu.au
Website: www.newcastle.edu.au/research/rhd/
Contact: Office of Graduate Studies

Aboriginal and Torres Strait Islander Scholarship

Purpose: The Aboriginal and Torres Strait Islander Scholarship was established through contributions from the university, industry donors, community organisations and the annual Reconciliation Scholarship Dinner Dance.

Eligibility: Be enrolled in any year of an undergraduate degree program at the University of Newcastle. Be enrolled full-time. Demonstrate academic progress either by the Australian Tertiary Admission Rank (ATAR) or equivalent required for entry for commencing students, or a Grade Point Average (GPA) of 4.0 for continuing students. Establish your Aboriginal and/or Torres Strait Islander identity and heritage with the university as outlined

Type: Scholarship

Value: US$40,000

Frequency: Annual

Country of Study: Any country

No. of awards offered: 1

Closing Date: 28 February

Additional Information: www.newcastle.edu.au/scholarships/EXT_152

For further information contact:

University Dr, Callaghan NSW 2308, Australia.

Tel: (61) 2 4921 5000

Andrew Brown Sport Scholarship

Purpose: In recognition of the important role that sports and university sports clubs played in his own development and educational experience, Andrew would like to support a student to enjoy the same benefits where financial hardship may otherwise prevent them from participating in tertiary study and sports activities.

Eligibility: Be enrolled in any year of an enabling program, undergraduate, or postgraduate (including Graduate Research) degree at the University of Newcastle. Be a member of, and play with, a University of Newcastle sporting team. Be enrolled full-time. Demonstrate impact of personal circumstances, such as carer, sole parent, financial hardship, English language difficulty, Indigenous Australian, long term medical condition or effects of abuse, disability, refugee status, regional/remote disadvantage. Demonstrate that the ability to study is affected, or will be affected, by financial hardship. Not be the recipient of another University of Newcastle donor-funded or sponsored scholarship concurrently.

Type: Scholarship

Value: US$4,000

Frequency: Annual

Country of Study: Any country

No. of awards offered: 1

Closing Date: 28 February

Additional Information: www.newcastle.edu.au/scholarships/EXT_271

For further information contact:

University Dr, Callaghan NSW 2308, Australia.

Tel: (61) 2 4921 5000

Association of Consulting Surveyors Aboriginal and Torres Strait Islander Scholarship

Purpose: The Association intends for these scholarships to assist Aboriginal and Torres Strait Islander students in achieving a career in surveying and to help them maintain a connection to their communities.

Eligibility: Be enrolled in any year of an undergraduate Surveying degree with the University of Newcastle. Be a resident of NSW Be enrolled full-time. Demonstrate academic progress with a Grade Point Average (GPA) of 4.0 or higher and maintain this for the duration of scholarship. Establish your Aboriginal and/or Torres Strait Islander identity and heritage with the university as outlined here. Not be the recipient of another University of Newcastle donor-funded or sponsored scholarship concurrently.

Type: Scholarship

Value: US$15,000

Frequency: Annual

Country of Study: Any country

No. of awards offered: 1

Closing Date: 28 February

Additional Information: www.newcastle.edu.au/scholarships/EXT_288

For further information contact:

University Dr, Callaghan NSW 2308, Australia.

Tel: (61) 2 4921 5000

U

Betty Josephine Fyffe Rural Allied Health, Nursing and Midwifery Scholarship

Purpose: We hope that all recipients of a Betty Josephine Fyffe Scholarship be as passionate about their career as she was about nursing.

Eligibility: Be enrolled in any year (including honours) of a B Nursing, B Midwifery, B Physiotherapy, B Nutrition and

Dietetics, B Occupational Therapy, B Medical Radiation Science, B Pharmacy degree. Be enrolled full-time. Demonstrate academic achievement either by an Australian Tertiary Admission Rank (ATAR) or equivalent of 90 or higher (adjustment factors included) for commencing students or a Grade Point Average (GPA) of 6.0 or higher for continuing students. Have lived in a regional or remote area of Australia for at least 12 months within the two years prior to study. Demonstrate activity in your local community (for example volunteering or involvement in community projects). Be an Australian citizen. Not be the recipient of another University of Newcastle donor-funded or sponsored scholarship concurrently.

Type: Scholarship
Value: US$50,000
Frequency: Annual
Country of Study: Any country
No. of awards offered: 1
Closing Date: 28 February
Additional Information: www.newcastle.edu.au/scholarships/EXT_256

For further information contact:

University Dr, Callaghan NSW 2308, Australia.

Tel: (61) 2 4921 5000

BMG Indigenous Music Industry Scholarship - Creative Industries

Purpose: BMG Australia is the Sydney based office of the international BMG publishing and recording business that spans Europe, the Americas and the Asia-Pacific. Their mission is to help artists and songwriters make the very most of their songs and recordings in the digital age through offering first-class creative support for their artists.
Eligibility: Be enrolled in any Bachelor program in the School of Creative Industries. Be enrolled either full-time or part-time. Establish your Aboriginal and/or Torres Strait Islander identity and heritage with the university as outlined here. Demonstrate academic progress with a Grade Point Average (GPA) of 4.0 or higher and maintain this for the duration of scholarship. Be enrolled or be willing to enroll in one of the following course codes MUSI3442 Engaging in the Music Industry, CIND3002 Project Development, CIND3003 Creative Industries Prof Project, DESN3411 Creative Studio Placement, CIND3500 Prof Project. or CMNS3450 Media Arts Project, DESN3910 Professional Creative Portfolio 20 units (Studio Z), DESN3411 Creative Studio Placement (WIL).
Type: Scholarship
Value: US$15,000

Frequency: Annual
Country of Study: Any country
No. of awards offered: 1
Closing Date: 28 February
Additional Information: www.newcastle.edu.au/scholarships/EXT_275

For further information contact:

University Dr, Callaghan NSW 2308, Australia.

Tel: (61) 2 4921 5000

Boeing Indigenous Engineering Scholarship

Purpose: Boeing Defence Australia is a leading Australian aerospace enterprise. With a world-class team of more than 1,800 employees at 14 locations throughout Australia and two international sites, Boeing Defence Australia supports some of the largest and most complex defence projects in Australia
Eligibility: Be enrolled in 2nd, 3rd, 4th year of a Bachelor of Engineering (Software, Computer Systems, Electrical and Electronic, Mechatronics and/or Mechanical) with the University of Newcastle. Be enrolled full-time. Be studying at the Newcastle Callaghan, Newcastle City or Central Coast campus. Establish your Aboriginal and/or Torres Strait Islander identity and heritage with the university as outlined here. Demonstrate academic progress with a Grade Point Average (GPA) of 4.0 or higher and maintain this for the duration of scholarship. Be an Australian citizen. Not be the recipient of another University of Newcastle donor-funded or sponsored scholarship concurrently.
Type: Scholarship
Value: US$6,000
Frequency: Annual
Country of Study: Any country
No. of awards offered: 1
Closing Date: 28 February
Additional Information: www.newcastle.edu.au/scholarships/EXT_230

For further information contact:

University Dr, Callaghan NSW 2308, Australia.

Tel: (61) 2 4921 5000

Catherine and Peter Tay for Singapore Alumni (follow on) Scholarship

Purpose: This scholarship was established in 2018 by Catherine and Peter Tay from Singapore. It is a continuing demonstration of appreciation that 50 years earlier in 1968, Dr Peter Tay received his undergraduate education for a double degree in Industrial Engineering and Economics from the University of Newcastle through a Colombo Plan Scholarship from the Australian Government. That scholarship became a stepping stone in Peter's life-long achievements, and helped him to become what he is today.

Eligibility: Be a past recipient of the Singapore Alumni Scholarship. Be enrolled in any year of an undergraduate degree program at the University of Newcastle. Be enrolled full-time. Demonstrate impact of personal circumstances, such as carer, sole parent, financial hardship, English language difficulty, Indigenous Australian, long term medical condition or effects of abuse, disability, refugee status, regional/remote disadvantage. Demonstrate academic achievement by having a Grade Point Average (GPA) of 5.0 or higher in your current program. If successful, be willing to submit an essay of approximately 400 words on Singapore and one or more aspects of its people, economy, geography, history, culture, political system etc. Not be the recipient of another University of Newcastle donor-funded or sponsored scholarship concurrently.

Type: Scholarship
Value: US$4,000
Frequency: Annual
Country of Study: Any country
No. of awards offered: 2
Closing Date: 28 February
Additional Information: www.newcastle.edu.au/scholarships/EXT_235

For further information contact:

University Dr, Callaghan NSW 2308, Australia.

Tel: (61) 2 4921 5000

Chemical Engineering Scholarship

Purpose: To develop models capable of simulating temporal and spatial characteristics of rainfall fields over large river basins using novel approaches to hierarchical modelling, storm clustering, advection and calibration. The models will provide continuous simulation support for the design and assessment of water-related infrastructure

Eligibility: Open only to the postgraduates who are the citizens of Australia or the permanent residents of Australia
Level of Study: Postgraduate
Type: Scholarship
Value: A living allowance of AU$24,653 per year
Length of Study: 2 years (Masters) and 3 years (PhD)
Frequency: Annual

Country of Study: Australia
Application Procedure: Application form and the Research Higher Degree prospectus from can be downloaded from the website
Closing Date: 31 October

For further information contact:

Tel: (61) 2 4921 6038
Email: George.Kuczera@newcastle.edu.au

Crystalbrook Kingsley Environmental Scholarship

Purpose: The Crystalbrook Kingsley Environmental Scholarship will support a student with a strong passion for environmental change and practical solutions for environmental sustainability, while providing a foundation for a collaborative and long-standing relationship between Crystalbrook Collection, students and the University for the benefit of our shared sustainability goals and communities.

Eligibility: Be enrolled in 3rd or 4th year of an undergraduate Honours degree focused on environmental sustainability within the School of Environmental and Life Sciences at the University of Newcastle. Have an interest in practical solutions for environmental sustainability. Be enrolled full-time. Have a Grade Point Average (GPA) of 6.0 or higher. Not be the recipient of another University of Newcastle donor-funded or sponsored scholarship concurrently. University Dr, Callaghan NSW 2308, Australia

Type: Scholarship
Value: US$5,000
Frequency: Annual
Country of Study: Any country
No. of awards offered: 1
Closing Date: 28 February
Additional Information: www.newcastle.edu.au/scholarships/EXT_283

For further information contact:

University Dr, Callaghan NSW 2308, Australia.

Tel: (61) 2 4921 5000

CSIRO Women in Energy Industry Placement Scholarship

Purpose: A scholarship sponsored by The Commonwealth Scientific and Industrial Research Organisation CSIRO is now available for a current first year female student studying in the Industry Placement Stream

Eligibility: Be enrolled in 1st year of an eligible Faculty of Engineering and Built Environment Industry Placement Stream program at UON Callaghan Campus. Be enrolled full-time. Demonstrate academic achievement either by an Australian Tertiary Admission Rank (ATAR) or equivalent of 75 or higher for commencing students, or a Grade Point Average (GPA) of 5.0 for continuing students. Be female. Be an Australian citizen. Not be the recipient of another University of Newcastle donor-funded or sponsored scholarship concurrently.
Type: Scholarship
Value: US$40,000
Frequency: Annual
Country of Study: Any country
No. of awards offered: 1
Closing Date: 28 February
Additional Information: www.newcastle.edu.au/scholarships/ENGB_070

For further information contact:

University Dr, Callaghan NSW 2308, Australia.

Tel: (61) 2 4921 5000

Delta Electricity Scholarship

Purpose: This scholarship was established to recognise a commitment to higher education by Delta Electricity. Delta Electricity has been offering scholarships at University of Newcastle since 2007 with the intention to offer financial support to undergraduate students who study or reside in the Central Coast LGA.
Eligibility: Be enrolled in an eligible program for this scholarship, being the B Enviromental Science, B Business, and Environmental, Mechanical, E&E, Chemical and Mechatronics Engineering programs. Be studying at Central Coast Campus (for relevant programs) and/or be a resident of the Central Coast LGA. Demonstrate academic achievement either by an Australian Tertiary Admission Rank (ATAR) or equivalent of 95 or higher for commencing students, or a Grade Point Average (GPA) of 6.0 for continuing students. Be an Australian citizen, Australian Permanent Resident (includes New Zealand Permanent Residents). Not be the recipient of another University of Newcastle donor-funded or sponsored scholarship concurrently.
Type: Scholarship
Value: US$5,000
Frequency: Annual
Country of Study: Any country
No. of awards offered: 1
Closing Date: 28 February
Additional Information: www.newcastle.edu.au/scholarships/EXT_001

For further information contact:

University Dr, Callaghan NSW 2308, Australia.

Tel: (61) 2 4921 5000

Dr Bill Jonas Scholarship

Purpose: This scholarship has been established by donations made to the Dr Bill Jonas Memorial Indigenous Fund. The fund was established with donations from the Wollotuka Institute, friends, family and community members who wished to honour Dr Bill Jonas's significant contribution to Wollotuka and the University of Newcastle.
Eligibility: Be enrolled in any year of any undergraduate or postgraduate degree at the University of Newcastle. Be enrolled either full-time or part-time. Demonstrate academic progress either by the Australian Tertiary Admission Rank (ATAR) or equivalent required for entry for commencing students, or a Grade Point Average (GPA) of 4.0 for continuing students. Establish your Aboriginal and/or Torres Strait Islander identity and heritage with the university as outlined here. Demonstrate impact of personal circumstances, such as carer, sole parent, financial hardship, English language difficulty, Indigenous Australian, long term medical condition or effects of abuse, disability, refugee status, regional/remote disadvantage. Not be the recipient of another University of Newcastle donor-funded or sponsored scholarship concurrently.
Type: Scholarship
Value: US$5,000
Frequency: Annual
Country of Study: Any country
No. of awards offered: 1
Closing Date: 28 February
Additional Information: www.newcastle.edu.au/scholarships/EXT_261

For further information contact:

University Dr, Callaghan NSW 2308, Australia.

Tel: (61) 2 4921 5000

Dr Robert M Sheahan Memorial Scholarship

Purpose: The scholarship is dedicated to the memory of Dr Robert M Sheahan, a Research Associate with ICI Explosives, who made many key scientific contributions to the explosives business worldwide. Robert Sheahan was a friend and mentor to a generation of research scientists and engineers working in the field of explosives.

Eligibility: Be enrolled in 1st year of a Bachelor of Science or a Bachelor of Engineering (Honours) with University of Newcastle. Must not have commenced or completed a prior undergraduate degree program. Have achieved a minimum ATAR (Australian Tertiary Admission Rank) or equivalent of 95 or higher, with adjustment factors NOT included. Not be the recipient of another University of Newcastle donor-funded or sponsored scholarship concurrently.
Type: Scholarship
Value: US$4,000
Frequency: Annual
Country of Study: Any country
No. of awards offered: 1
Closing Date: 28 February
Additional Information: www.newcastle.edu.au/scholarships/EXT_004

For further information contact:

University Dr, Callaghan NSW 2308, Australia.

Tel:　(61) 2 4921 5000

Friends of the University Development Studies Scholarship

Purpose: The Friends of the University were established in 1981 to foster an awareness of the university and its place in the community and to conduct activities including fundraising that promote the interests of the university. Since that time the Friends have raised over US$1,000,000 and contributed towards scholarships, art works, music, rare books, infrastructure and more.
Eligibility: Be enrolled in any year of the Bachelor of Development Studies, including Honours, with University of Newcastle. Be enrolled full-time. Demonstrate impact of personal circumstances, such as carer, sole parent, financial hardship, English language difficulty, Indigenous Australian, long term medical condition or effects of abuse, disability, refugee status, regional/remote disadvantage. Be an Australian citizen, Australian Permanent Resident (includes New Zealand Permanent Residents). Not be the recipient of another University of Newcastle donor-funded or sponsored scholarship concurrently.
Type: Scholarship
Value: US$4,000
Frequency: Annual
Country of Study: Any country
No. of awards offered: 1
Closing Date: 28 February
Additional Information: www.newcastle.edu.au/scholarships/EXT_292

For further information contact:

University Dr, Callaghan NSW 2308, Australia.

Tel:　(61) 2 4921 5000

Friends of the University Ken Gordon Memorial Honours Scholarship

Purpose: The Friends of the University were established in 1981 to foster an awareness of the university and its place in the community and to conduct activities including fundraising that promote the interests of the university. Since that time the Friends have raised over US$1,000,000 and contributed towards scholarships, art works, music, rare books, infrastructure and more.
Eligibility: Be enrolled in your Honours year (4th year Business or 5th year for Laws) in a degree, including combined degrees, with the Newcastle Business School or Newcastle Law School. Be enrolled full-time. Demonstrate academic achievement by having a Grade Point Average (GPA) of 5.0 or higher in your current program. Demonstrate impact of personal circumstances, such as carer, sole parent, financial hardship, English language difficulty, Indigenous Australian, long term medical condition or effects of abuse, disability, refugee status, regional/remote disadvantage. Not be the recipient of another University of Newcastle donor-funded or sponsored scholarship concurrently. Be an Australian citizen, Australian Permanent Resident (includes New Zealand Permanent Residents). Not have previously received this scholarship.
Type: Scholarship
Value: US$4,000
Frequency: Annual
Country of Study: Any country
No. of awards offered: 1
Closing Date: 28 February
Additional Information: www.newcastle.edu.au/scholarships/EXT_023

For further information contact:

University Dr, Callaghan NSW 2308, Australia.

Tel:　(61) 2 4921 5000

Friends of the University Sport Scholarship

Purpose: This scholarship was established in 1994 to support students with demonstrated sporting ability and potential, and encourage their contribution to the sporting achievements of the university. The purpose of this scholarship is to improve the quality of our sporting teams, raise the university's profile through sport, and establish a standard of excellence to complement our academic achievements.

Eligibility: Be enrolled in any year of an undergraduate degree or enabling program at the University of Newcastle. In the scholarship award year, be a member of, and play with a University of Newcastle sporting team or represent the University in an individual or team sport. Be enrolled full-time. Demonstrate academic progress either by the Australian Tertiary Admission Rank (ATAR) or equivalent required for entry for commencing students, or a Grade Point Average (GPA) of 4.0 for continuing students. Have attained an equivalent sporting standard in the previous 2 years of selection at district representative level in the sport for an Under 17 or older age district team as a minimum. Must not be a Professional Sports Person. Not have previously received this scholarship.

Type: Scholarship
Value: US$4,000
Frequency: Annual
Country of Study: Any country
No. of awards offered: 1
Closing Date: 28 February
Additional Information: www.newcastle.edu.au/scholarships/EXT_199

For further information contact:

University Dr, Callaghan NSW 2308, Australia.

Tel: (61) 2 4921 5000

Idemitsu Engineering Scholarship

Purpose: The aim of this scholarship is to support a student financially while encouraging them to pursue a career in the engineering / resources industry.

Eligibility: Be enrolled in a Bachelor of Electrical or Electronic Engineering (Honours), Bachelor of Renewable Energy Engineering (Honours) or a Bachelor of Mechanical Engineering (Honours) degree. Be enrolled full-time. Demonstrate impact of personal circumstances, such as carer, sole parent, financial hardship, English language difficulty, Indigenous Australian, long term medical condition or effects of abuse, disability, refugee status, regional/remote disadvantage. Demonstrate academic progress either by the Australian Tertiary Admission Rank (ATAR) or equivalent required for entry for commencing students, or a Grade Point Average (GPA) of 4.0 for continuing students. Be an Australian citizen, Australian Permanent Resident (includes New Zealand Permanent Residents). Not have previously completed a degree. Not be the recipient of another University

of Newcastle donor-funded or sponsored scholarship concurrently.

Type: Scholarship
Value: US$5,000
Frequency: Annual
Country of Study: Any country
Closing Date: 28 February
Additional Information: www.newcastle.edu.au/scholarships/EXT_262

For further information contact:

University Dr, Callaghan NSW 2308, Australia.

Tel: (61) 2 4921 5000

Indigenous Education Scholarship

Purpose: These Commonwealth-funded scholarships aim to support Indigenous students with the costs of University study, particularly for those who face financial disadvantage and who are relocating from a remote or regional area.

Eligibility: Be enrolled (or enrolling) in any year of an enabling, undergraduate, or postgraduate degree program at the University of Newcastle. Demonstrate financial hardship by either being in receipt of a means-tested Commonwealth income support payment (such as Austudy, ABSTUDY, Youth Allowance etc), or on the basis of a comprehensive assessment. Be of Australian Aboriginal and/or Torres Strait Islander descent, AND identify as an Australian Aboriginal and/or Torres Strait Islander, AND be accepted as an Aboriginal and/or Torres Strait Islander by the community in which you live or have lived. Must not have previously received the full entitlement of a Commonwealth Indigenous Scholarship awarded prior to 2017 or hold this scholarship concurrently at another institution. If accepting the scholarship offer, must not have received - or agrees to repay - a Student Start-up Loan, a Student Start-up Scholarship or a Relocation Scholarship or the Residential Costs option of ABSTUDY from Centrelink.

Type: Scholarship
Value: US$3,000
Frequency: Annual
Country of Study: Any country
No. of awards offered: 60
Closing Date: 28 February
Additional Information: www.newcastle.edu.au/scholarships/GOV_EDU

For further information contact:

University Dr, Callaghan NSW 2308, Australia.

Tel: (61) 2 4921 5000

Jayce and Seamus Fagan Enabling Program Scholarship

Purpose: This scholarship has been established to support a student in an enabling program with the hope that this financial support will ensure they can concentrate on their studies and achieve the results to gain entry into an undergraduate degree.

Eligibility: Be enrolled in an enabling program (Open Foundation or Yapug) with the University of Newcastle. Demonstrate impact of personal circumstances, such as carer, sole parent, financial hardship, English language difficulty, Indigenous Australian, long term medical condition or effects of abuse, disability, refugee status, regional/remote disadvantage.

Type: Scholarship
Value: US$4,000
Frequency: Annual
Country of Study: Any country
No. of awards offered: 1
Closing Date: 28 February
Additional Information: www.newcastle.edu.au/scholarships/EXT_227

For further information contact:

University Dr, Callaghan NSW 2308, Australia.

Tel: (61) 2 4921 5000

Joy Ingall Scholarship for Music Studies

Eligibility: Be enrolled in Bachelor of Music (including Honours) or any combined program incorporating Bachelor of Music with University of Newcastle. Be enrolled full-time. Demonstrate academic achievement either by an Australian Tertiary Admission Rank (ATAR) or equivalent of 75 or higher for commencing students, or a Grade Point Average (GPA) of 5.0 for continuing students. Demonstrate impact of personal circumstances, such as carer, sole parent, financial hardship, English language difficulty, Indigenous Australian, long term medical condition or effects of abuse, disability, refugee status, regional/remote disadvantage. Have demonstrated a high standard during performance either at entry audition or at interview for shortlisted applicants. Not have previously received this scholarship. Not be the recipient of another University of Newcastle donor-funded or sponsored scholarship concurrently. Be an Australian Citizen or Permanent Resident.

Type: Scholarship
Value: US$15,000
Frequency: Annual

Country of Study: Any country
No. of awards offered: 3
Closing Date: 28 February
Additional Information: www.newcastle.edu.au/scholarships/EXT_163

For further information contact:

University Dr, Callaghan NSW 2308, Australia.

Tel: (61) 2 4921 5000

PhD Scholarship in Coal Utilization in Thermal and Coking Applications

Purpose: To undertake research on particular coal properties which determine its utilization potential

Eligibility: Open to the engineering and the science graduates who have an Honours Degree in chemical or mechanical engineering or chemistry

Level of Study: Doctorate, Postgraduate
Type: Scholarship
Value: AU$19,616 per year
Length of Study: 3 years
Application Procedure: Check website for further details
Closing Date: 1 March

For further information contact:

Tel: (61) 2 49 21 6179
Email: Terry.Wall@newcastle.edu.au

PhD Scholarship in Immunology of Kidney Stone Diseases

Purpose: This project aims to improve our understanding of how our immune system protects against stone recurrence and its role in preventing long-term consequences such as impaired kidney function

Eligibility: This scholarship is for domestic and international students. If English is not your first language then you will need to show that your English language skills are at a high enough level to succeed in your studies

Type: Scholarship
Value: Scholarship Value AU$26,682 p.a., indexed in January each year. The scholarship is for a period of three years and a half years. This Scholarship is linked to the Dr Starkey ARC DECRA fellowship

Frequency: Annual
Study Establishment: Scholarships are awarded to work on the project titled, "Immunology of kidney stone diseases"
Country of Study: Australia

U

Application Procedure: To enable us to assess your application, candidates will be expected to submit an email expressing their interest including 1. Academic transcripts. 2. A brief statement of research interests. 3. Full CV including previous degrees, grades, research experience, employment, papers published, and any grants obtained. Applicants are automatically considered for the scholarship on acceptance to University College

Closing Date: 1 April

Additional Information: For more details please visit the website scholarship-positions.com/phd-scholarship-immunology-kidney-stone-diseases-australia/2018/02/01/

Postgraduate Research Scholarship in Physics

Eligibility: Open to the residents of Australia and New Zealand or the permanent residents of Australia who have an Honours 1 or 2A or a Masters Degree

Level of Study: Postgraduate, Research

Type: Scholarship

Value: AU$17,071 per year

Length of Study: 3 years

Frequency: Annual

Application Procedure: Check website for more details

Closing Date: 1 July

Contributor: ARC Discovery-projects

For further information contact:

Tel: (61) 2 4921 6653
Fax: (61) 2 4921 6907
Email: vicki.keast@newcastle.edu.au

Shaping Futures Postgraduate Scholarship

Purpose: the Shaping Futures Postgraduate Scholarship will support postgraduate coursework students, alongside our undergraduate students supported by the Shaping Futures Scholarship, to overcome adversity and educational disadvantage.

Eligibility: Be enrolled in any year of a postgraduate coursework degree program with the University of Newcastle where the majority of delivery is on-campus. Be enrolled in a minimum of 20 units in the term of scholarship award. Demonstrate impact of personal circumstances, such as carer, sole parent, financial hardship, English language difficulty, Indigenous Australian, long term medical condition or effects of abuse, disability, refugee status, regional/remote disadvantage. Be residing in Australia for the duration of your degree. Not be the recipient of another University of

Newcastle donor-funded or sponsored scholarship concurrently.

Level of Study: Postgraduate

Type: Scholarship

Value: US$4000

Frequency: Annual

Country of Study: Any country

No. of awards offered: 7

Closing Date: 28 February

Additional Information: www.newcastle.edu.au/scholarships/EXT_272

For further information contact:

University Dr, Callaghan NSW 2308, Australia.

Tel: (61) 2 4921 5000

Shaping Futures Scholarships

Purpose: The Shaping Futures Scholarship Program was established in 2011 with the aim of helping those students who are most in need.

Eligibility: Be enrolled in any year of an undergraduate degree program at the University of Newcastle. Be enrolled full-time. Demonstrate academic progress either by the Australian Tertiary Admission Rank (ATAR) or equivalent required for entry for commencing students, or a Grade Point Average (GPA) of 4.0 for continuing students. Demonstrate impact of personal circumstances, such as carer, sole parent, financial hardship, English language difficulty, Indigenous Australian, long term medical condition or effects of abuse, disability, refugee status, regional/remote disadvantage. Be an Australian citizen, Australian Permanent Resident (includes New Zealand Permanent Residents). Not be the recipient of another University of Newcastle donor-funded or sponsored scholarship concurrently.

Level of Study: Postgraduate

Type: Scholarship

Value: US$4000

Frequency: Annual

Country of Study: Any country

No. of awards offered: 65

Closing Date: 28 February

Additional Information: www.newcastle.edu.au/scholarships/EXT_140

For further information contact:

University Dr, Callaghan NSW 2308, Australia.

Tel: (61) 2 4921 5000

University of Newcastle Postgraduate Research Scholarship (UNRS Central)

Eligibility: Open to the residents of Australia and New Zealand or permanent residents who have achieved Honours 1 or equivalent and have completed at least 4 years of undergraduate study
Level of Study: Postgraduate, Research
Type: Scholarship
Value: AU$23,728 per year full-time stipend, AU$12,898 part time stipend
Length of Study: 2 years (Masters) and 3 years (PhD)
Frequency: Annual
Country of Study: Australia
Application Procedure: Check website for further details
Closing Date: 31 October

For further information contact:

Research Higher Degrees, The Chancellery Eastern Wing, University Drive, 905 University Dr., State College, PA 16801, United States of America.

Tel: (61) 2 4921 6537
Fax: (61) 2 4921 6908

University of Newcastle, Australia MBA Programme

Application Procedure: Applicants must return a completed application form, with original or certified copies of official academic transcripts (not to be returned), Graduate Management Admission Test and TOEFL (if applicable) scores, the names of two referees

For further information contact:

Business Administration International Students Office University Drive, 905 University Dr., State College, PA 16801, United States of America.

Tel: (61) 4 9216 595
Fax: (61) 4 9601 766
Email: io@newcastle.edu.au

University of Notre Dame

1124 Flanner Hall, Notre Dame, IN 46556, United States of America.

Tel: (1) 574 631 1305
Email: ndias@nd.edu

Website: www.nd.edu
Contact: Brad S Gregory, Director of the Notre Dame Institute for Advanced Study

The University of Notre Dame provides a distinctive voice in higher education that is at once rigorously intellectual, unapologetically moral in orientation, and firmly embracing of a service ethos.

Break Travel and Research Grants for Sophomores and Juniors

Purpose: The Break Travel and Research Grant provides seed funding for educational and research projects in European studies. The grant is intended to support well-focused, short-term exploratory trips conducted over fall, winter, or spring break
Eligibility: Applicants must be enrolled as a sophomore or junior at the University of Notre Dame and scheduled to return the following semester
Level of Study: Postgraduate
Type: Grant
Value: US$2,500. Funds are typically paid at one-time sum
Frequency: Annual
Country of Study: Any country
Closing Date: 4 February
Funding: Private

For further information contact:

Tel: (1) 574 631 8326
Email: cstump@nd.edu

Templeton Fellowships for United States of America and International Scholars at NDIAS

Purpose: With grant support from the John Templeton Foundation, the NDIAS will help chart a new course for future scholarship by offering Templeton Fellowships that encourage scholars to return to reflection on the broad questions that link multiple areas of inquiry and to do so in a manner that embraces a value-oriented interpretation of the world
Eligibility: Distinguished senior scholars with extensive records of academic accomplishment and who have had a considerable impact on their discipline are encouraged to apply. Outstanding junior scholars with academic records of exceptional promise and whose research agendas align with the purpose and parameters of the program are also invited to apply
Type: Fellowship

U

Value: These distinctive fellowships offer an extraordinary measure of scholarly support, including a stipend of up to US$100,000; fully furnished faculty housing (for those who reside outside of the Michiana area); up to US$3,000 in research expenditures; a private office at the NDIAS, with a personal desktop computer and printer; etc. Check detailed information on the website

Frequency: Annual

Country of Study: United States of America

Application Procedure: Please see ndias.nd.edu/fellowships/templeton/application-instructions/

Closing Date: 15 October

Additional Information: For more information, please check at ndias.nd.edu/fellowships/templeton/

For further information contact:

Email: csherman@nd.edu

University of Notre Dame: College of Arts and Letters

Office of the Dean, 100 O'Shaughnessy Hall, 100 O'Shaughnessy Hall, Notre Dame, IN 46556, United States of America.

Tel: (1) 574 631 7085
Email: aldean@nd.edu

University of Notre Dame: College of Arts and Letters offers one of the finest liberal arts educations in the nation. Its Division of the Humanities was recently ranked 12th among private universities, while the social sciences continue their ascent in the national rankings. College of Arts and Letters is the largest and oldest of the University's 4 colleges.

The Erskine A. Peters Dissertation Year Fellowship at Notre Dame

Purpose: To provide an opportunity for African American scholars at the beginning of their academic careers to experience life at a major Catholic research university

Eligibility: Open to African American Doctoral candidates who have completed all degree requirements with the exception of the dissertation

Level of Study: Postgraduate, Research

Type: Fellowship

Value: US$30,000 stipend and US$2,000 research budget

Length of Study: 10 months

Frequency: Annual

Country of Study: United States of America

Application Procedure: Applicants may apply online

Closing Date: December

No. of awards given last year: 3

For further information contact:

Tel: (1) 574 631 5628
Fax: (1) 574 631 3587
Email: astudies@nd.edu

University of Nottingham

University of Nottingham, University Park, Nottingham NG7 2RD, United Kingdom.

Tel: (44) 115 846 8400
Email: graduate-school@nottingham.ac.uk
Website: www.nottingham.ac.uk/gradschool
Contact: Ms Nicola Pickering, Process Manager Funding

The University of Nottingham is a community of students and staff dedicated to bringing out the best in all of its members. It aims to provide the finest possible environment for teaching, learning and research and has a world class record of success.

Developing Solutions Masters Scholarship

Purpose: The aim of the Developing Solutions Masters Scholarship is to enable and encourage academically able students from Africa, India or one of the countries of the Commonwealth

Eligibility: To apply for this scholarship, you must 1. be domiciled in Africa, India or one of the selected Commonwealth countries listed below 2. be classed as an overseas student for fee purposes 3. hold an offer to start a full-time masters (including MRes) in any subject area at the University of Nottingham UK in September or October 2023, within the Faculty of Engineering, Faculty of Medicine and Health Sciences, Faculty of Science or Faculty of Social Sciences

Type: Scholarship

Value: covering 50% or 100% of full-time masters tuition fees

Frequency: Annual

Country of Study: Any country

Application Procedure: Apply online

No. of awards offered: 105

Closing Date: 20 May

Additional Information: www.nottingham.ac.uk/pgstudy/ funding/developing-solutions-masters-scholarship

For further information contact:

Tel: (44) 115 951 5151

High Achiever Foundation Prize for Africans

Purpose: Prizes are available for pursuing foundation courses at University of Nottingham

Eligibility: Candidates can apply if they are a national of (or permanently domiciled in) Africa, they are classed as an overseas student for fee purposes, already hold an offer to start a full-time foundation program at Nottingham in September

Type: Prize

Value: 3 undergraduate high achiever prizes of £2,000 towards tuition fees

Country of Study: United Kingdom

Application Procedure: The mode of applying is online

Closing Date: 15 April

Additional Information: Successful applicants will be notified of the outcome within 6 weeks of the closing date www. opportunitiesforafricans.com/2015-high-achiever-foundation-prize-undergraduate-scholarships-for-africans-to-study-in-the-united-kingdom-2000-towards-tuition-fees/

For further information contact:

Email: scholarship-assistant@nottingham.ac.uk

Japan Masters Scholarships at University of Nottingham in United Kingdom

Purpose: The aim of the scholarship is strengthen the bond of Japan and United Kingdom

Eligibility: 1. National of (or permanently domiciled in) Japan. 2. Classed as an overseas student for fee purposes. 3. Already have, or expect to receive, a final CGPA of no less than 3.2/grade B or 70%. 4. Already hold an offer to start a full-time master degree programme, including MRes, at Nottingham in September, any subject area

Level of Study: Postgraduate

Type: Scholarship

Value: These scholarships will cover 25% each towards tuition fees for students from Japan

Country of Study: Any country

Application Procedure: Applications must complete online application form to apply for scholarships. www.nottingham.ac. uk/international/_online_forms/scholarships/_sships_appform_ p1.php

Closing Date: 18 May

For further information contact:

Email: scholarship-assistant@nottingham.ac.uk

Nottingham Developing Solutions Scholarships

Purpose: The Developing Solutions Scholarships are designed for international students who want to pursue a Master's Degree in the University of Nottingham and make a difference to the development of their home country

Eligibility: 1. Are a national of (or permanently domiciled in) Africa, India or one of the countries of the Commonwealth. 2. Are classed as an overseas student for fee purposes. 3. Have not already studied outside of your home country. 4. Are not currently studying at a University of Nottingham campus or are not a University of Nottingham graduate

Level of Study: Postdoctorate

Type: Award

Value: 50-100% of the tuition fees

Frequency: Annual

Country of Study: Any country

No. of awards offered: 105

Closing Date: 20 May

Funding: Foundation

Additional Information: www.nottingham.ac.uk/pgstudy/ funding/developing-solutions-masters-scholarship

Nottingham University Business School MBA Programme

Length of Study: 1 year full-time or 2;4 years part-time

Country of Study: Any country

Application Procedure: Applicants must complete an application form, and provide transcripts or copies of professional qualifications together with two references (ideally, one should be from an academic source, the other from an employer or business contact). All language test scores must be submitted for International students. Note that the school may ask for further individual details to support an application

Additional Information: www.nottingham.ac.uk/business/ programmes/mba/index.aspx

For further information contact:

Tel: (44) 115 551 5500
Fax: (44) 115 551 5503
Email: business-enquiries@nottingham.ac.uk

University of Oklahoma

College of Business Administration, Adams Hall Room 105K, Norman, OK 73019, United States of America.

Tel: (1) 405 325 4107
Email: awatkins@ou.edu
Contact: MBA Admissions Officer

Ben Barnett Scholarship

Purpose: Any full-time Art majors admitted to either the MA or MFA degree program
Eligibility: Applicant must be a full-time student in the School of Art and have a minimum 3.0 GPA and an outstanding portfolio
Level of Study: Postgraduate
Type: Scholarship
Value: Maximum of US$1,000 will be given as scholarship amount
Frequency: Annual
Country of Study: Any country
Application Procedure: Contact Director, School of Art University of Oklahoma 520 Parrington Room 202 Normak, OK 73019 United States Phone (405) 325-2691
No. of awards offered: 16
Closing Date: 1 March
Funding: Private
Additional Information: Visit the official website for further info: www.ou.edu www.collegexpress.com/scholarships/ben-barnett-scholarship/6650/

For further information contact:

Director, School of Art University of Oklahoma, 520 Parrington, Room 202, Normak OK 73019, United States.

Email: art@ou.edu

University of Ontario

Graduate Finance and Administration, 2000 Simcoe Street North, London, ON L1H 7K4, Canada.

Email: pmenzies@uwo.ca
Contact: Office of Graduate Studies Manager.

The University of Ontario Institute of Technology is a public research university located in Oshawa, Ontario, Canada.

The Ontario Trillium Scholarships (OTS)

Purpose: To attract top international students to Ontario for PhD studies
Eligibility: An eligible applicant must have achieved a minimum of 80% in each of the last 2 most recently completed years of full-time university study, or equivalent to full-time study. Eligibility averages for competitive scholarship are rounded ONLY to the nearest decimal place
Type: Scholarship
Value: C$40,000 annually
Length of Study: 4 years
Frequency: Annual
Country of Study: Any country
Application Procedure: Submit a complete UOIT application with supporting documentation to the Office of Graduate Studies
Closing Date: 1 April
Additional Information: Submit the PDF nomination to SGPS pmenzies@uwo.ca uwaterloo.ca/graduate-studies-postdoctoral-affairs/awards/ontario-trillium-scholarship-ots

University of Oregon

1585E, 13th Ave, Eugene, OR 97403, United States of America.

Tel: (1) 541 346 1000
Website: www.uoregon.edu

Center for AIDS Prevention Studies, Small Professional Grants for Graduate Students

Purpose: Awards will be made for the following purposes travel to conferences to present papers, travel to library, museum, and archival collections; and expenses related to book and article production and publication
Eligibility: The Center for Asian and Pacific Studies is offering awards of up to US$500 in support of the professional activities of UO graduate students studying Asia. Awards will be made for the following purposes travel to conferences to present papers, travel to library, museum, and archival collections; and expenses related to book and article production and publication
Level of Study: Postgraduate
Type: Grant
Value: Up to US$500
Frequency: Annual
Country of Study: Any country
Application Procedure: 1. To submit a proposal, please click here to complete the online application form. 2. A brief letter of support from your advisor explaining how this activity is

central to your research interests is also required. This letter can be emailed directly to Holly Lakey at lakey@uoregon.edu

Closing Date: 15 April

Funding: Private

Additional Information: caps.uoregon.edu/2010/11/03/caps-small-professional-grants-for-graduate-students/

For further information contact:

1246 University of Oregon, Eugene, OR 97403, United States of America.

Tel: (1) 541 346 5068
Email: lakey@uoregon.edu

Jeremiah Lecture Series Support

Purpose: The Center for Asian and Pacific Studies is accepting proposals from UO faculty for speakers to visit the UO and deliver a public lecture on campus

Level of Study: Postgraduate

Type: Award

Frequency: Annual

Country of Study: Any country

Application Procedure: For a hardcopy version of the application form, please contact Holly Lakey at lakey@uoregon.edu

Closing Date: 15 April

Funding: Private

Additional Information: caps.uoregon.edu/2010/10/15/proposals-for-the-jeremiah-fund-lecture-series/

For further information contact:

Email: lakey@uoregon.edu

University of Oslo

Problemveien 7, N-0315 Oslo, Norway.

Contact: University of Oslo

The University of Oslo, until 1939 named the Royal Frederick University, is the oldest university in Norway, located in the Norwegian capital of Oslo.

Postdoctoral Fellowships in Educational Assessment and Measurement

Purpose: The main purpose of the fellowships is to qualify researchers for work in higher academic positions within their disciplines

Eligibility: For eligibility, please visit

Level of Study: Professional development

Type: Fellowship

Value: Salary NOK 499,600–569,000

Length of Study: 4 years

Frequency: Annual

Country of Study: Norway

Application Procedure: For online application, visit website www.jobbnorge.no/en/available-jobs/job/149727/1-2-four-year-postdoctoral-fellowships-in-educational-assessment-and-measurement

Closing Date: 15 May

Additional Information: www.mladiinfo.eu/2018/04/03/postdoctoral-fellowships-educational-assessment-measurement-university-oslo/

For further information contact:

Email: rolfvo@cemo.uio.no

Postdoctoral Fellowships in Political Philosophy or Legal Theory

Purpose: Fellowships are available to pursue postdoctoral programme

Eligibility: For eligibility, please visit

Type: Postdoctoral fellowship

Value: NOK 552 800 to 615 900

Country of Study: Any country

Closing Date: 30 January

Additional Information: stilling.forskning.no/job-ads-oslo-og-akershus-postdocpostdoktor/postdoctoral-fellowships-in-political-philosophy-or-legal-theory-on-the-legitimacy-of-international-courts-and-tribunals/1581825

For further information contact:

Email: siri.johnsen@jus.uio.no

University of Otago

362 Leith Street, Dunedin 9016, New Zealand.

Tel: (64) 3 479 7000
Email: university@otago.ac.nz
Website: www.otago.ac.nz

The University of Otago, founded in 1869 by an ordinance of the Otago Provincial Council, is New Zealand's oldest university. The new University was given 100,000 acres of pastoral land as an endowment and authorised to grant degrees in Arts, Medicine, Law and Music.

Aarhus University PhD Fellowships Program

Purpose: Aarhus University PhD Fellowships Program, Denmark are fully funded fellowships offered to the students of Denmark to pursue PhD fellowships and research training supplements, both research and PhD fellowships are funded by the Faculty of Health Science at Aarhus University, the scholarships are developed with an aim to develop international cooperation in the areas of teaching and research, university is a modern, academically diverse and research-intensive university with a strong commitment to high-quality research and education and the development of society existed around the world

Eligibility: The candidates who are interested to apply for the Aarhus University scholar apply for a 3-year PhD study programme students must have completed a relevant Master's degree, the Master's study has to be equivalent to a Danish Master's degree of 120 ECTS, all applications will be evaluated based on the submitted material using the following criteria, the time for research experience after the qualifying exam is taken into consideration, all applicants must document English language qualifications comparable to an 'English B level' in the Danish upper secondary school, if the candidate has any doubt about the criteria they can submit your diplomas for an assessment via graduateschoolhealth-at-au.dk

Level of Study: Postgraduate
Type: Fellowship
Length of Study: 3 year
Frequency: Annual
Country of Study: New Zealand
Closing Date: February
Funding: Foundation
Additional Information: scholarship-positions.com/health-scholarships-international-phd-students-aarhus-university-denmark/2017/04/07/

For further information contact:

Tel: (45) 8715 0000
Email: housing@au.dk

Alliance Group Postgraduate Scholarship

Eligibility: 1. Obtaining their first doctoral qualification 2. Domestic students 3. Undertaking research related to the improvement of livestock
Level of Study: Postgraduate

Type: Scholarship
Value: NZ$27,500 per annum plus domestic tuition fees waiver (excludes student services fee)
Frequency: Annual
Country of Study: New Zealand
Application Procedure: Applications for doctoral scholarships are made online through the eVision portal and can be made at any time of the year. Once you have applied for admission to your programme you will receive an alert in your student portal inviting you to apply for a scholarship
No. of awards offered: Varies
Funding: Foundation

For further information contact:

Tel: (64) 800 80 80 98
Email: scholarships@otago.ac.nz

Angus Ross Travel Scholarship in History

Purpose: Established by the family of Angus Ross in 2010, the Angus Ross Travel Scholarship in History is intended to assist PhD candidates studying history with the costs associated with off-campus field and archival research
Eligibility: Applications are open to current University of Otago PhD candidates who, as part of their PhD studies 1. are conducting historically-focused research (preference will be given to candidates primarily based in the Department of History and Art History); 2. will be conducting off-campus field or archival research in the year for which the scholarship is awarded (the year following application). Note that this scholarship is not intended to support travel to a conference. Previous recipients are not eligible to apply for the scholarship in subsequent years.
Level of Study: Postgraduate
Type: Scholarship
Value: NZ$1,000
Frequency: Annual
Country of Study: New Zealand
Application Procedure: Every applicant must submit to the Doctoral and Scholarships Office by 1 November. 1. A brief Curriculum Vitae; 2. A description of the work to be conducted with the assistance of the scholarship, and the significance this work will have for their PhD research (no more than 500 words); 3. A budget of costs associated with the work to be conducted with the assistance of the scholarship; 4. A letter of support from their PhD supervisor. The University may also access academic transcripts and evidence of PhD progress in assessing this award. In exceptional circumstances applicants may be required to attend an interview either in person or by teleconference.

Closing Date: 1 November
Funding: Foundation
Additional Information: www.otago.ac.nz/graduate-research/scholarships/otago0055091.pdf

Brenda Shore Award for Women

Purpose: Brenda Shore was an enthusiastic, enterprising person famous for her energy and passion. Over the course of 35 years Brenda became a prominent figure in the University of Otago Botany Department, both as a researcher and teacher, until her retirement in 1983. Leading by example Brenda Shore established this fund to help support women who have that same passion and energy for the natural sciences, particularly where their research relates to the Otago, Southland or Antarctic region
Eligibility: 1. University of Otago women graduates. 2. Women graduates carrying out research related to the Otago, Southland and Antarctic area. 3. Women graduates carrying out research for a postgraduate degree at the University of Otago
Level of Study: Postgraduate
Type: Award
Value: Up to NZ$10,000
Length of Study: 1 year
Frequency: Annual
Country of Study: New Zealand
No. of awards offered: Varies
Closing Date: 28 February
Funding: Foundation
Additional Information: www.otago.ac.nz/study/scholarships/database/otago014683.html

Bruggeman Postgraduate Scholarship in Classics

Eligibility: 1. Obtaining their first Master's or Doctoral qualification 2. Domestic students 3. Undertaking research in the field of Classics
Level of Study: Postgraduate
Type: Scholarship
Value: NZ$16,000 stipend per annum (Master's); NZ$28,000 stipend per annum (PhD) plus domestic tuition fee waiver (excludes student services fee)
Frequency: Annual
Country of Study: New Zealand
No. of awards offered: Varies
Funding: Foundation
Additional Information: www.otago.ac.nz/study/scholarships/database/otago016143.html

For further information contact:

362 Leith Street, Dunedin North, Dunedin 9016, New Zealand.

Tel: (64) 800 80 80 98
Email: scholarships@otago.ac.nz

China Scholarship Council and Griffith University PhD Scholarships

Purpose: China Scholarship Council and Griffith University PhD Scholarships are offering scholarships to the students of China who are interested to pursue PhD degree programme at the Griffith university which is based in the United Kingdom, through this scholarship the students develops the research opportunities with an environment that collaborates the students
Eligibility: The participants should meet all the necessary requirements, polices and the rules that are offered by the China Scholarship Council and Griffith University, this scholarship program is extended to all research programs where, The applicants of the China Scholarship Council and Griffith University PhD scholarships should meet the academic entry requirements which also include the level of English language Proficiency with good communication skills and the student must be certified or held with a bachelor degree with a first class or second-class honors which come under the Division A or the Master's degree or its equivalent incorporating a significant research component, from a recognised institution or its equivalent, Candidates are selected based on the criteria that was instructed by China Scholarship Council
Level of Study: Postgraduate
Type: Scholarship
Length of Study: 4 year
Frequency: Annual
Country of Study: New Zealand
Closing Date: January
Funding: Foundation

Demand Response in the Agricultural Sector PhD Scholarship

Purpose: The Centre for Sustainability calls for expressions of interest in a PhD scholarship focusing on "Demand response in the agricultural sector – a socio-technical study". The research will examine farmer interest in electricity demand response, examine the barriers that farmers face in engaging in demand response, and identify solutions to improve adoption of demand response strategies. Candidates with a background in socio-technical studies would be ideal,

U

although those with a background in social or physical sciences will be considered if they have an interest in extending their theoretical and methodological scope. The scholarship is funded by Science for Technological Innovation, a National Science Challenge and the successful candidate will be based at the Centre for Sustainability, University of Otago

Level of Study: Postgraduate

Type: Scholarship

Value: NZ$27,500

Length of Study: 3 year

Frequency: Annual

Country of Study: New Zealand

Closing Date: 22 February

Funding: Foundation, International office

Additional Information: www.otago.ac.nz/study/scholarships/database/otago634665.html

For further information contact:

Email: janet.stephenson@otago.ac.nz

Diane Campbell-Hunt Memorial Award

Purpose: Diane Campbell-Hunt was a PhD candidate in the Department of Geography, funded by a Tertiary Education Commission Top Achiever Doctoral scholarship. She had completed two-thirds of her PhD programme at the time of her death. Her project looked at the long-term sustainability of fenced sanctuaries in New Zealand in a multi-disciplinary analysis ecological, economic, social, and governmental

Eligibility: 1. Be enrolled and confirmed in a PhD programme in any Department or School at the University of Otago. 2. Have had accepted a peer-reviewed academic paper (conference or journal) that contributes to New Zealand conservation (as defined above), and in which they are the lead author. 3. Not have previously been awarded the award

Level of Study: Postgraduate

Type: Award

Value: NZ$1,000

Frequency: Annual

Country of Study: New Zealand

Closing Date: 30 June

Funding: Foundation

Additional Information: www.otago.ac.nz/geography/study/scholarships/otago091040.pdf

Douglass D Crombie Award in Physics

Purpose: Established by the University of Otago Council in memory of Mr Douglass D Crombie. This award has been made possible by a generous bequest from the late Mr Crombie for the purpose of encouraging postgraduate research in Physics. This award will be offered to an outstanding University of Otago Physics graduate intending to undertake a PhD in Physics at an overseas university

Eligibility: 1. Were born in New Zealand. 2. Graduated or will soon graduate from the University of Otago with a degree in Physics. 3. Are intending to pursue doctoral-level studies in Physics. 4. Are intending to undertake their studies at an English speaking University in an English speaking country (excluding New Zealand). 5. Have displayed outstanding academic ability

Level of Study: Postgraduate

Type: Award

Value: NZ$7,000

Frequency: Annual

Country of Study: New Zealand

Application Procedure: 1. be born in New Zealand 2. have graduated or will soon graduate from the University of Otago with a degree in Physics 3. be intending to pursue doctoral-level studies in Physics 4. be intending to undertake their studies at an English speaking University in an English speaking country (excluding New Zealand) 5. have displayed outstanding academic ability

No. of awards offered: 1

Funding: Foundation

Additional Information: www.otago.ac.nz/study/scholarships/database/otago040266.html

For further information contact:

Scholarships Office, Graduate Research School, PO Box 56, Dunedin 9054, New Zealand.

Tel: (64) 3 479 7000

Email: scholarships@otago.ac.nz

Dr Sulaiman Daud 125th Jubilee Postgraduate Scholarship

Purpose: This scholarship was established in 1994 to mark the 125th Anniversary of the foundation of the University of Otago, New Zealand's oldest university. The purpose of the scholarship is to assist an exceptional postgraduate research student from Malaysia to attend the University

Eligibility: 1. Unless otherwise stated in these conditions or within the schedule, doctoral and Masters' scholarships are open only to Domestic Fee Paying Students. International candidates studying for professional doctorates are eligible to apply but if awarded a scholarship the tuition fee waiver will be capped at the domestic rate. 2. In the case of applicants for a doctoral scholarship, confirmation of the scholarship is dependent on approval of their application for admission to the relevant doctoral programme and completion of the enrolment procedure. 3. In the case of applicants for a Master's scholarship, confirmation of the scholarship is dependent on approval of their application to register as a Master's candidate and completion of the enrolment procedure

Level of Study: Postgraduate

Type: Scholarship

Value: Establishment allowance of NZ$575; domestic tuition fee waiver (excludes student services fee); health insurance to the value of NZ$600; NZ$27,000 per annum stipend; educational allowance of NZ$550

Length of Study: 1 year

Frequency: Annual

Country of Study: New Zealand

No. of awards offered: 1

Funding: Foundation

Additional Information: www.otago.ac.nz/study/scholarships/database/otago020604.html

For further information contact:

P.O. Box 514070, Milwaukee, WI 53203-3470, United States of America.

Email: scholarships@otago.ac.nz

Elizabeth Jean Trotter Postgraduate Research Travelling Scholarship in Biomedical Sciences

Purpose: Established by the University of Otago Council from a generous donation in memory of Elizabeth Jean Trotter

Eligibility: 1. Be enrolled for a PhD or in the research year of a Master's programme with primary supervision in the Otago School of Medical Sciences (OSMS). 2. Be undertaking research in a Biomedical Sciences field

Level of Study: Postgraduate

Type: Fellowships

Value: Up to NZ$5,000

Length of Study: 1 year

Frequency: Annual

Country of Study: New Zealand

Application Procedure: Every application for the scholarship must be submitted to the University of Otago Scholarships Office by the closing date. Every applicant must submit 1. A completed application form detailing the purpose of, and benefits expected to result from, the proposed travel. 2. A letter of support from the candidate's primary supervisor, addressing the candidate's work to date and the value of the chosen conference, workshop, or laboratory visit, to the candidate. 3. A brief Curriculum Vitae. 4. Title of proposed oral presentation or poster at the chosen conference (if applicable)

No. of awards offered: Varies

Closing Date: 1 November

Funding: Foundation

Additional Information: www.otago.ac.nz/study/scholarships/database/otago622380.html

For further information contact:

Tel: (64) 3 479 7000

Elman Poole Travelling Scholarship

Purpose: Dr Elman Poole and the University of Otago are pleased to be able to offer this award to promote, encourage and facilitate research by providing grants to PhD students of the University of Otago to study overseas during their PhD, for a period normally not less than three months and not more than six months to gain experience or to use facilities not normally available at Otago and to further their subsequent work or career at Otago

Eligibility: 1. Enrolled full-time for a Doctor of Philosophy (PhD) at the University of Otago. 2. Majoring in one of following areas Physical or Biological Sciences, Health Sciences or music. 3. Intending to engage in study in the second or third year of his/her PhD outside of New Zealand. 4. New Zealand citizen or New Zealand permanent resident. 5. under 35 years of age on the first day of February in the year of application

Level of Study: Postgraduate

Type: Scholarship

Value: Maximum NZ$20,000, plus up to NZ$5,000 additional expenses

Length of Study: 2 year

Frequency: Annual

Country of Study: New Zealand

Application Procedure: 1. Enrolled full-time in PhD study at the University of Otago majoring in one of the following areas physical or biological sciences, health sciences or music 2. Intending to engage in study outside of New Zealand in their second or third year of PhD study 3. New Zealand citizens or New Zealand permanent residents 4. Under the age of 35 on 1 February in the year of application; Preference will be given to candidates who were born in Otago or Southland.

No. of awards offered: Varies

Closing Date: 1 June

Funding: Foundation

Additional Information: www.otago.ac.nz/study/scholarships/database/otago014682.html

For further information contact:

St David II Building, University of Otago, PO Box 56, Dunedin 9054, New Zealand.

Freemasons Scholarships

Purpose: The Freemasons Scholarships are provided annually by Freemasons New Zealand and are administered by the Freemasons Charity

Eligibility: 1. Have a good academic report. 2. Be a New Zealand citizen or permanent resident. 3. Demonstrate good citizenship. 4. Show leadership potential. 5. Have proven community commitment

Level of Study: Postgraduate

Type: Scholarship

Value: NZ$6,000 (University); NZ$10,000 (Postgraduate)

Frequency: Annual

Country of Study: New Zealand

No. of awards offered: 3 (University); 1 (Postgraduate)

Closing Date: 1 October

Funding: Foundation

Additional Information: freemasonsnz.org/charity/freemasons-university-scholarships/

For further information contact:

Email: info@lincoln.ac.nz

Fully Funded PhD Scholarships

Purpose: Fully Funded PhD Scholarships, University of Sheffield, United Kingdom are offered to international students who attract the administration panel with their academic performance to pursue PhD programme. The candidates should have the knowledge in the English language and candidates from non-English countries should meet the abilities of the university by attaining the IELTS and other related tests. Annually the university offers five scholarships

Eligibility: 1. Eligible Countries Overseas participants are eligible. 2. Acceptable Course or Subjects The program will be awarded for the PhD degree in Quantitative Biology 3. Admissible Criteria To be eligible, the applicants must meet all the given criteria 4. Applicants must have a master's degree in a relevant area. There are three types of PhD students can apply for this grant 5. Students with a life science degree, interested in working in an experimental lab, but with a high degree of motivation to learn the fundamentals of computational biology, and to develop quantitative skills to analyze data more effectively 6. Students with a life science degree interested in working in a dry computational lab, keen to deepen their quantitative skills and broaden their horizon in terms of experimental and computational techniques 7. Students with a non-biological background (e.g. computer science, maths, physics), who are highly motivated to transition to Life Sciences

Level of Study: Postgraduate

Type: Scholarship

Frequency: Annual

Country of Study: New Zealand

Application Procedure: Aspirants are suggested to take part in a PhD degree program at the university. And then apply for the grants through completing the career5.successfactors.eu/sfcareer/jobreqcareer?jobId=14879&company=universitdP

No. of awards offered: 15

Funding: Foundation

Additional Information: scholarship-positions.com/15-fully-funded-phd-studentsnational-students-in-switzerhips-for-interland/2019/09/27/

Future Global Leaders Fellowship Program

Purpose: Future Global Leaders Fellowship Program is an international program designed for Freshmen students who are interested to pursue research and fellowship training, where the fellowship program is an internationally competitive program which is intended for granting first generation and low-income students entry into the Fortis Society, which is the world's first private network for diverse leaders, The main objective of the program is to gather students from world's top most universities which includes-Harvard University, the University of Oxford, Sciences Po, and Peking University

Eligibility: Applicants must be first-year university students and must fit the following eligibility criteria 1. First-Generation or Low-Income University Student – students who do not have a family history of higher education, or who come from a low-income background. 2. Track Record of Academic Excellence – throughout high school and during the first months of the current school year. 3. Proven Leadership Abilities – through self-started initiatives and ventures, or leadership in their schools or communities

Level of Study: Postgraduate

Type: Fellowship

Frequency: Annual

Country of Study: New Zealand

Closing Date: 31 January

Funding: Foundation

Additional Information: opportunitydesk.org/2018/11/07/future-global-leaders-fellowship-2019/

Gilbert M Tothill Scholarship in Psychological Medicine

Purpose: Doctoral scholarships are awarded by the University Council, on the recommendation of the Senate, to candidates proceeding to a course of supervised doctoral study at this University. These scholarships are normally available only to students seeking to obtain their first doctoral qualification

Eligibility: In the case of an applicant for a doctoral scholarship who has completed a Master's degree by papers and thesis (at least 0.75 EFTS), the grades of all relevant2 advanced level papers counting towards the award of the degree and the thesis will be taken into account. An explanation of the time taken for completion of the thesis may be requested and considered by the Scholarships and Prizes Committee if the thesis has taken more than 2 EFTS (2 fulltime years) to complete

Level of Study: Postgraduate
Type: Scholarship
Value: NZ$10,000 per annum
Length of Study: 3 year
Frequency: Annual
Country of Study: New Zealand
Funding: Foundation
Additional Information: www.otago.ac.nz/study/scholarships/database/otago089208.html

For further information contact:

Email: scholarships@otago.ac.nz

Helen Rosa Thacker Scholarship in Neurological Research

Purpose: The Helen Rosa Thacker Scholarship in Neurological Research was established by Helen Rosa Thacker in 2012 to support research and teaching in the field of neurology at the University of Otago. The scholarship aims to recognise, reward and inspire a particularly good PhD student. This scholarship can be held alongside an existing scholarship. This scholarship will be awarded for one year, with a chance of extension to a second year due to outstanding progress

Eligibility: 1. A full time PhD student in neurological research at the University of Otago. 2. A male scholar holding a New Zealand birth certificate. 3. Available to receive the scholarship in person and provide updates on the progress of their research

Level of Study: Postgraduate
Type: Scholarship
Value: NZ$5,000
Length of Study: 1 year
Frequency: Annual
Country of Study: New Zealand
Closing Date: 2 October
Funding: Foundation
Additional Information: www.otago.ac.nz/study/scholarships/database/otago055663.html

For further information contact:

Jane Reynolds, Administrative Assistant, Brain Health Research Centre, C/- Department of Anatomy, PO Box 56, Dunedin 9054, New Zealand.

Tel: (64) 3 479 7612
Email: bhrc@otago.ac.nz

James Park Scholarship in Geology

Purpose: Masters' scholarships are awarded by the University Council, on the recommendation of the Senate, to candidates in the first year of their thesis research for a Master's degree which constitutes entry to the PhD course at this University. These scholarships are available only to students seeking to obtain their first research-based Master's qualification

Eligibility: 1. Unless otherwise stated in these conditions or within the schedule, doctoral and Masters' scholarships are open only to Domestic Fee Paying Students. International candidates studying for professional doctorates are eligible to apply but if awarded a scholarship the tuition fee waiver will be capped at the domestic rate. 2. In the case of applicants for a doctoral scholarship, confirmation of the scholarship is dependent on approval of their application for admission to the relevant doctoral programme and completion of the enrolment procedure. 3. In the case of applicants for a Master's scholarship, confirmation of the scholarship is dependent on approval of their application to register as a Master's candidate and completion of the enrolment procedure

Level of Study: Postgraduate
Type: Scholarship
Value: NZ$15,000 stipend per annum (Master's); NZ$27,000 stipend per annum (PhD); domestic tuition fee waiver (excludes student services fee)
Frequency: Annual
Country of Study: New Zealand
No. of awards offered: Varies
Funding: Foundation
Additional Information: For further information about the application, please contact the Scholarships Office at the University of Otago email scholarships@otago.ac.nz www.otago.ac.nz/study/scholarships/database/otago020608.html

For further information contact:

Educational Credential Evaluators, Inc., P.O. Box 514070, Milwaukee, WI 53203-3470, United States of America.

Tel: (1) 414 289 3400
Email: scholarships@otago.ac.nz

Macandrew-Stout Postgraduate Scholarship in Economics

Purpose: Established from funds made available by public subscription in memory of the late James Macandrew, member of the Council and one of the founders of the University and in 1920 by Sir Robert Stout, KCMG, Chief Justice of New Zealand

Eligibility: 1. Unless otherwise stated in these conditions or within the schedule, doctoral and Masters' scholarships are open only to Domestic Fee Paying Students. International candidates studying for professional doctorates are eligible to apply but if awarded a scholarship the tuition fee waiver will be capped at the domestic rate. 2. In the case of applicants for a doctoral scholarship, confirmation of the scholarship is dependent on approval of their application for admission to the relevant doctoral programme and completion of the enrolment procedure. 3. In the case of applicants for a Master's scholarship, confirmation of the scholarship is dependent on approval of their application to register as a Master's candidate and completion of the enrolment procedure

Level of Study: Postgraduate

Type: Scholarship

Value: NZ$15,000 stipend per annum (Master's); NZ$27,000 stipend per annum (PhD); domestic student fee waiver (excludes student services fee)

Frequency: Annual

Country of Study: New Zealand

Funding: Foundation

Additional Information: For further information about the application, please contact the Scholarships Office at the University of Otago email scholarships@otago.ac.nz www.otago.ac.nz/study/scholarships/database/otago020612.html

For further information contact:

Educational Credential Evaluators, Inc., P.O. Box 514070, Milwaukee, WI 53203-3470, United States of America.

Tel: (1) 414 289 3400
Email: scholarships@otago.ac.nz

Neuropsychology Scholarships

Purpose: To investigate how visual information is used by humans in the learning of new skills

Eligibility: Open to applicants with an undergraduate qualification and a background or interest in cognitive science or neuropsychology. The project would suit a self-motivated person who is able to work well with participants and patients and other members on the study team. A working knowledge of the software package MATLAB and experience in programming with its language, is highly desirable

Level of Study: Postgraduate

Type: Scholarship

Value: NZ$12,000 per year for 2 years maximum, plus a maximum of NZ$4,000 per year towards tuition fees

Application Procedure: Applicants must enquire in the first instance to the director of the Cognitive Science programme

Contributor: Marsden Fund of the Royal Society of New Zealand

For further information contact:

Tel: (64) 3 479 5269
Fax: (64) 3 479 8335
Email: lfranz@psy.otago.ac.nz

Nga Pae O Te Maramatanga Doctoral Scholarships

Purpose: Fostering Te Pa Harakeke – understanding, achieving and maintaining 'healthy and prosperous families of mana' and the lessons this may hold for New Zealand families overall. Understanding what 'Te Pa Harakeke' is, enabling it to be achieved and addressing the barriers

Eligibility: For Maori or indigenous students who are currently enrolled or in the process of enrolling in a recognised doctoral programme of study and research at a tertiary institution. Applicants must not work more than 10 hours per week in paid employment while in receipt of this scholarship

Level of Study: Postgraduate

Type: Scholarship

Value: NZ$25,000

Length of Study: 3 year

Frequency: Annual

Country of Study: New Zealand

Closing Date: 30 September

Funding: Foundation

Additional Information: www.otago.ac.nz/study/scholarships/database/otago021502.html

Noni Wright Scholarship

Purpose: Established by the University Council in association with the Guardian Trust in 2011 to provide support for Theatre Studies students to pursue postgraduate study. The scholarship was made possible by a generous endowment from the late Mrs Eleanor Wright, to honour the memory of her daughter Noni Wright, who was well known in drama circles, and had appeared on programmes for the BBC

Eligibility: The scholarship is open to both domestic and international students. Applicants must be currently enrolled or intending to enrol for full-time study at the University of Otago in the year following the closing date, for the degree of

MA or MFA in Theatre Studies, or for a PhD researching a topic in Theatre Studies
Level of Study: Postgraduate
Type: Scholarship
Value: NZ$5,000
Length of Study: 1 year
Frequency: Annual
Country of Study: New Zealand
No. of awards offered: 1
Closing Date: 28 February
Funding: Foundation
Additional Information: www.otago.ac.nz/study/scholar ships/database/otago030561.html

For further information contact:

Email: scholarships@otago.ac.nz

Otago International Pathway Scholarship

Purpose: The Otago International Pathway Scholarship enables ambitious students to pursue their academic study goals, by supporting them in their preparation for further study at the University of Otago.
Eligibility: International students who are not citizens, permanent residents or resident visa holders of New Zealand or Australia*; and Have gained admission to the Foundation Studies Certificate through meeting both academic and English entry requirements, as outlined on the Otago website, and Are subject to paying international tuition fees; and Are enrolling in the Foundation Studies Certificate for the first time.
Type: Scholarship
Value: NZ$3,000 for tuition fees
Length of Study: 8 months
Frequency: Annual
Country of Study: Any country
Additional Information: www.otago.ac.nz/study/scholar ships/database/otago827757.html

For further information contact:

362 Leith Street, Dunedin North, Dunedin 9016, New Zealand.

Tel: (64) 3 479 7000

Patricia Pratt Scholarships in Musical Performance

Purpose: The purpose of the scholarship is to assist outstanding New Zealand musical performers who have completed an honours degree in musical performance in New Zealand to continue their musical development at a renowned international music school or conservatorium. The scholarship will be awarded for classical music performance including vocal or instrumental performance or conducting
Eligibility: 1. Be New Zealand citizens with preference given to students who have resided in New Zealand for at least three years immediately preceding the year of selection. 2. Hold an honours degree in music performance from a New Zealand University
Level of Study: Postgraduate
Type: Scholarship
Value: Up to NZ$45,000
Frequency: Annual
Country of Study: New Zealand
No. of awards offered: 1
Closing Date: 1 March
Funding: Foundation
Additional Information: www.universitiesnz.ac.nz/scholar ships/kia-ora-foundation-patricia-pratt-scholarship

Postgraduate Tassell Scholarship in Cancer Research

Purpose: Doctoral scholarships are awarded by the University Council, on the recommendation of the Senate, to candidates proceeding to a course of supervised doctoral study at this University. These scholarships are normally available only to students seeking to obtain their first doctoral qualification
Eligibility: 1. Unless otherwise stated in these conditions or within the schedule, doctoral and Masters' scholarships are open only to Domestic Fee Paying Students. International candidates studying for professional doctorates are eligible to apply but if awarded a scholarship the tuition fee waiver will be capped at the domestic rate. 2. In the case of applicants for a doctoral scholarship, confirmation of the scholarship is dependent on approval of their application for admission to the relevant doctoral programme and completion of the enrolment procedure. 3. In the case of applicants for a Master's scholarship, confirmation of the scholarship is dependent on approval of their application to register as a Master's candidate and completion of the enrolment procedure
Level of Study: Postgraduate
Type: Scholarship
Value: NZ$27,000
Frequency: Annual
Country of Study: New Zealand
No. of awards offered: Varies
Funding: Foundation
Additional Information: www.otago.ac.nz/study/scholar ships/database/otago035878.html

For further information contact:

Email: scholarships@otago.ac.nz

Ramboll Masters Scholarship for International Students

Purpose: Ramboll Masters Scholarship for International Students provides scholarships to the students all over the world who are pursuing masters degree and diploma in engineering in all related fields of Engineering, Natural Science, Political Science, Economics or Architecture, the candidates are selected based on the academic merit considering their projects and profile, the Ramboll offers opportunities to the students by providing inspirational and longstanding solutions that strengthen the ideas of candidate and enhance the nature and future

Eligibility: To be eligible to be granted a Ramboll Scholarship the applicant should meet necessary criteria such as the candidate is currently studying Engineering, Natural Science, Political Science, Economics or Architecture subjects as one of their course studies, and are going to study abroad outside of Denmark, to be eligible to apply the applicant should be a Diploma Engineer on semester 4 – 7 or studying on a Master's level, and must agree to send Ramboll two travel updates during their stay abroad

Level of Study: Postgraduate

Type: Scholarship

Value: NZ$25,000

Frequency: Annual

Country of Study: New Zealand

Closing Date: 8 May

Funding: Foundation

Additional Information: scholarship-fellowship.com/ramboll-masters-scholarship-for-international-students/

Senior Smeaton Scholarship in Experimental Science

Purpose: Masters' scholarships are awarded by the University Council, on the recommendation of the Senate, tocandidates in the first year of their thesis research for a Master's degree which constitutes entry to the PhD course at this University. These scholarships are available only to students seeking to obtain their first research-based Master's qualification

Eligibility: 1. Unless otherwise stated in these conditions or within the schedule, doctoral and Masters' scholarships are open only to Domestic Fee Paying Students. 3 International candidates studying for professional doctorates are eligible to apply but if awarded a scholarship the tuition fee waiver will be capped at the domestic rate. 2. In the case of applicants for a doctoral scholarship, confirmation of the scholarship is dependent on approval of their application for admission to the relevant doctoral programme and completion of the

enrolment procedure. 3. In the case of applicants for a Master's scholarship, confirmation of the scholarship is dependent on approval of their application to register as a Master's candidate and completion of the enrolment procedure

Level of Study: Postgraduate

Type: Scholarship

Value: NZ$27,000

Frequency: Annual

Country of Study: New Zealand

Funding: Foundation

Additional Information: www.otago.ac.nz/study/scholarships/database/otago020614.html

For further information contact:

Educational Credential Evaluators, Inc. P.O. Box 514070, Milwaukee, WI 53203-3470, United States of America.

Tel: (1) 414 289 3400

Email: scholarships@otago.ac.nz

The Dr Stella Cullington Postgraduate Scholarship in Ophthalmology

Purpose: Established in 2014 by the Faculty of Medicine, from a generous donation from Dr Stella Cullington. Dr Cullington is a medical graduate and practised as a GP in United Kingdom and New Zealand. The Dr Stella Cullington Postgraduate Scholarship in Ophthalmology was created to support the sustainability and development of Ophthalmology Research within the academic discipline

Eligibility: 1. Be a NZ citizen or NZ permanent resident. 2. Hold a Bachelor of Medicine and Bachelor of Surgery degrees (MBChB) or an equivalent medical degree. 3. Demonstrate proof of potential academic research ability through (i) successful completion of a research Master's degree, or (ii) appropriate and equivalent prior research experience. 4. Be enrolled or intending to enrol for a MOphth or PhD at the University of Otago

Level of Study: Postgraduate

Type: Scholarship

Value: Up to NZ$5,000

Length of Study: 1 year

Frequency: Annual

Country of Study: New Zealand

No. of awards offered: 1

Funding: Foundation

Additional Information: www.otago.ac.nz/study/scholarships/database/otago597632.html

The Eamon Cleary Trust Postgraduate Study Scholarship

Purpose: Established in 2016 by the University of Otago Council from a generous donation by the Eamon Cleary Trust. The Eamon Cleary Trust Postgraduate Study Scholarship was created to support University of Otago students undertaking postgraduate research in Irish Studies. The scholarship may be used for expenses associated with postgraduate study, such as tuition fees, research expenses or travel associated with their research programme

Eligibility: 1. Be intending to enrol in a Doctoral or Research Masters programme in Irish Studies or a Coursework Masters programme in Irish Studies with a research component greater than or equal to 60 points at the University of Otago for the year of the award. 2. Have made contact to discuss satisfactory supervisory arrangements with the Eamon Cleary Professor of Irish Studies prior to submission of the application

Level of Study: Postgraduate

Type: Scholarship

Value: NZ$15,000 to NZ$27,000

Frequency: Annual

Country of Study: New Zealand

Funding: Foundation

Additional Information: www.otago.ac.nz/study/scholarships/database/otago616894.html

The Joan, Arthur & Helen Thacker Aboriginal and/or Torres Strait Islander Postgraduate Scholarship

Purpose: Established by the University of Otago Council in 2014, through the provision of funding from Helen R Thacker, this scholarship aims to support students of Aboriginal and/or Torres Strait Islander descent to undertake postgraduate studies in the field of Health Sciences at the University of Otago. The purpose of the fund is to support research and training in health sciences subjects that may have a future benefit to Aboriginal and/or Torres Strait Islander communities

Eligibility: 1. Aboriginal and/or Torres Strait Islander descent. 2. Australian citizens and residing in Australia at the time of application. 3. Planning to enrol in a postgraduate course of study in either Dental Technology, Dentistry, Oral Health, Medicine, Neuroscience, Pharmacy or Radiation Therapy at the University of Otago. 4. Planning to undertake study/research that is likely to be of future benefit to their Aboriginal and/or Torres Strait Islander community. 5. Intending to return to work in Australia after their course of study

Level of Study: Postgraduate

Type: Scholarship

Value: NZ$25,000 per annum (PhD); NZ$15,000 stipend per annum (other postgraduate study); tuition fee waiver to a maximum of NZ$30,000 per annum (excludes student services fee)

Frequency: Annual

Country of Study: New Zealand

No. of awards offered: 1

Closing Date: 1 October

Funding: Foundation

Additional Information: www.otago.ac.nz/study/scholarships/database/otago106285.html

The Robinson Dorsey Postgraduate Scholarship

Purpose: The Robinson Dorsey Postgraduate Scholarship was created to support postgraduate students who are returning to university study after a break, and/or who through their personal circumstances, are not eligible for usual scholarships

Eligibility: 1. A NZ citizen or NZ permanent resident. 2. Enrolled or intending to enrol in a postgraduate diploma, honours degree, Master of Science or PhD degree in Physiology or Human Nutrition at the University of Otago. 3. Returning to university study after a break, and/or who through their personal circumstances are not eligible for usual scholarships

Level of Study: Postgraduate

Type: Scholarship

Value: NZ$25,000 full time PhD study or NZ$13,000 full time Masters', Postgraduate Diploma or Honours Study

Frequency: Annual

Country of Study: New Zealand

Closing Date: 28 February

Funding: Foundation

Additional Information: www.otago.ac.nz/study/scholarships/database/otago664753.html

For further information contact:

Post to Student Administration (Scholarships), St David II Building, University of Otago, PO Box 56, Dunedin 9054, New Zealand.

Email: scholarships@otago.ac.nz

University of Helsinki Masters Scholarships

Purpose: University of Helsinki Masters Scholarships are offered to the students of international arena who are interested to pursue masters degree from the university, the scholarships offered are fully funded which includes full tuition fees, eligible candidates are selected by the committee not only based on academic criteria the committee will also consider the variety and diversity of the applicants and grant the scholarships to those coming from different backgrounds and fields of studies, the main aim hidden under the scholarship program is to create a rich and diverse learning environment at the University of Helsinki, candidates should receive an offer from the university to apply for the scholarship

Eligibility: All candidates must meet the following requirements 1. You are eligible for the Master's programme at the University of Helsinki 2. The country of your nationality is outside the EU/EEA and you meet the requirements for obtaining an entry visa and residence permit for Finland. More information at the Studyinfo. 3. You have obtained excellent results in your previous studies and can prove this in your application.

Level of Study: Postgraduate

Type: Scholarship

Value: Tuition fees range from €13,000 to €18,000.

Length of Study: 2 years

Frequency: Annual

Country of Study: Finland

Application Procedure: The scholarship application will be filled out in the same application system and simultaneously with your online application to the University of Helsinki English language Master's programmes. The possible scholarship-related documents should be delivered with the other enclosed documents of your degree application.

Closing Date: 10 January

Funding: Private

Additional Information: Tuition fee will range from €13,000 to €18,000. For further information on the scholarship, refer the below link. www.helsinki.fi/en/admissions/scholarship-programme www.afterschoolafrica.com/17865/university-helsinki-masters-scholarships/

University of Otago Academic General Practitioner Registrar PhD Scholarship

Purpose: Established in 2013 by the Faculty of Medicine, the University of Otago Academic General Practitioner Registrar PhD Scholarship was created to support the sustainability and development of the Primary Health Care and General Practice academic discipline. The scholarship aims to help establish research capability among a new generation of General Practitioners by supporting the achievement of a Doctoral degree (PhD) at the University of Otago as well as vocational registration as a Fellow of the Royal New Zealand College of General Practitioners (RNZCGP)

Eligibility: 1. A NZ citizen or NZ permanent resident. 2. Hold a Bachelor of Medicine and Bachelor of Surgery degrees (MBChB) or an equivalent medical degree. 3. Demonstrate a formal commitment to a General Practice career by having successfully completed either (i) the General Practice Education Programme first year (GPEP1) with an above average pass in the Primary Membership Examination (PRIMEX) or (ii) a RNZCGP Fellowship. 4. Have successfully completed either the 'Health Sciences Research Methods' paper (HASX417) or the 'Research Methods in General Practice' paper (GENX821), or an alternative 30 point postgraduate research methods paper with a minimum B+ grade. 5. Demonstrate proof of potential academic research ability through (i) successful completion of a research Master's degree, or (ii) appropriate and equivalent prior research experience

Level of Study: Postgraduate

Type: Scholarship

Value: NZ$25,000 per year for full-time study or NZ$12,500 per year for part-time study plus a tuition fee waiver for the PhD thesis paper for the period of tenure

Frequency: Annual

Country of Study: New Zealand

Closing Date: 15 September

Funding: Foundation

Additional Information: www.otago.ac.nz/study/scholarships/database/otago049881.html

University of Otago China Scholarship Council Doctoral Scholarship

Purpose: Masters' scholarships are awarded by the University Council, on the recommendation of the Senate, to candidates in the first year of their thesis research for a Master's degree which constitutes entry to the PhD course at this University. These scholarships are available only to students seeking to obtain their first research-based Master's qualification

Eligibility: 1. Unless otherwise stated in these conditions or within the schedule, doctoral and Masters' scholarships are open only to Domestic Fee Paying Students. International candidates studying for professional doctorates are eligible to apply but if awarded a scholarship the tuition fee waiver will be capped at the domestic rate. 2. In the case of applicants for a doctoral scholarship, confirmation of the scholarship is dependent on approval of their application for admission to the relevant doctoral programme and completion of the enrolment procedure. 3. In the case of applicants for a Master's scholarship, confirmation of the scholarship is dependent on approval of their application to register as a Master's candidate and completion of the enrolment procedure

Level of Study: Postgraduate

Type: Scholarship

Value: Tuition fee waiver for up to 4 years, full time study only and a top-up of the China Scholarship Council Scholarship monthly stipend to the value of an University of Otago Doctoral Scholarship stipend
Frequency: Annual
Country of Study: New Zealand
No. of awards offered: Varies
Funding: Foundation
Additional Information: www.otago.ac.nz/study/scholarships/database/otago049881.html

For further information contact:

Email: scholarships@otago.ac.nz

University of Otago City of Literature PhD Scholarship

Purpose: Masters' scholarships are awarded by the University Council, on the recommendation of the Senate, to candidates in the first year of their thesis research for a Master's degree which constitutes entry to the PhD course at this University. These scholarships are available only to students seeking to obtain their first research-based Master's qualification
Eligibility: 1. Unless otherwise stated in these conditions or within the schedule, doctoral and Masters' scholarships are open only to Domestic Fee Paying Students. 3 International candidates studying for professional doctorates are eligible to apply but if awarded a scholarship the tuition fee waiver will be capped at the domestic rate. 2. In the case of applicants for a doctoral scholarship, confirmation of the scholarship is dependent on approval of their application for admission to the relevant doctoral programme and completion of the enrolment procedure. 3. In the case of applicants for a Master's scholarship, confirmation of the scholarship is dependent on approval of their application to register as a Master's candidate and completion of the enrolment procedure
Level of Study: Postgraduate
Type: Scholarship
Value: NZ$27,000
Frequency: Annual
Country of Study: New Zealand
Closing Date: 30 September
Funding: Foundation
Additional Information: www.otago.ac.nz/study/scholarships/database/otago624693.html

For further information contact:

Email: scholarships@otago.ac.nz

University of Otago Doctoral Scholarships

Purpose: To fund research towards a PhD degree at the University of Otago
Eligibility: Open to applicants of any country but must be primarily resident in New Zealand during study
Level of Study: Doctorate, Research
Type: Scholarship
Value: NZ$27,000 stipend per annum plus a domestic tuition fees waiver for 36 months (excludes student services fee and insurance) Professional Doctorates (DClinDent, DMA, DBA, EDd) - NZ$27,000 stipend per annum plus a tuition fee waiver for up to 36 months capped at the domestic rate (excludes student services fee and insurance).
Length of Study: 3 years
Frequency: Annual
Study Establishment: The University of Otago
Country of Study: New Zealand
Application Procedure: Please visit www.otago.ac.nz/applynow
No. of awards offered: 200
No. of awards given last year: 180
Additional Information: www.otago.ac.nz/study/scholarships/database/otago014687.html

For further information contact:

Tel: (64) 800 80 80 98
Email: scholarships@otago.ac.nz

University of Otago Doctorate in Medical Education Scholarship

Purpose: Established with funding from the Otago Medical School, this scholarship is intended to provide support for clinically qualified health care professionals with an interest in medical education to undertake research at PhD level. The research must be applicable to the enhancement of the Otago MB ChB programme. The scholarship will be awarded for a three-year period; part-time PhDs will be considered. The participants will perform medical educational research in their own educational setting at University of Otago campuses in Dunedin, Christchurch or Wellington, but associated sites e.g. Invercargill, Nelson, Palmerston North, Hawkes Bay will be considered provided satisfactory supervisory arrangements can be made
Eligibility: 1. Normally be a NZ citizen or NZ permanent resident. 2. Hold a clinical health care discipline degree. Non-clinically qualified people with a strong background in Education may be considered but priority will be given to applicants from the first category. 3. Provide confirmation that

U

this is their first doctoral qualification. 4. Be enrolled or intending to enrol for a PhD.

Level of Study: Postgraduate

Type: Scholarship

Value: NZ$25,000 stipend per annum plus a domestic tuition fees waiver

Frequency: Annual

Country of Study: New Zealand

No. of awards offered: Varies

Closing Date: 20 February

Funding: Foundation

Additional Information: www.otago.ac.nz/study/scholarships/database/otago634374.html

University of Otago International Master's Scholarship

Purpose: To assist international students in their master's thesis year of studies at the University of Otago

Eligibility: Open to all international applicants intending to study at the University of Otago who would normally be charged international fees

Level of Study: Postdoctorate, Research

Type: Scholarship

Value: NZ$15,000 stipend per annum plus a tuition fee waiver for 1 year capped at the domestic rate for Master's study (excludes student services fee and insurance)

Frequency: Annual

Country of Study: Any country

No. of awards offered: 8

Funding: Private

For further information contact:

Doctoral and Scholarships Office, PO Box 56, Dunedin 9054, New Zealand.

Email: university@otago.ac.uk

University of Otago Maori Doctoral Scholarship

Purpose: Doctoral scholarships are awarded by the University Council, on the recommendation of the Senate, tocandidates proceeding to a course of supervised doctoral study at this University. These scholarships are normally available only to students seeking to obtain their first doctoral qualification

Eligibility: 1. Unless otherwise stated in these conditions or within the schedule, doctoral and Masters' scholarships are open only to Domestic Fee Paying Students. 3 International candidates studying for professional doctorates are eligible to apply but if awarded a scholarship the tuition fee waiver will be capped at the domestic rate. 2. In the case of applicants for a doctoral scholarship, confirmation of the scholarship is dependent on approval of their application for admission to the relevant doctoral programme and completion of the enrolment procedure

Level of Study: Postgraduate

Type: Scholarship

Value: NZ$27,000 stipend per annum plus a domestic tuition fees waiver for 36 months

Frequency: Annual

Country of Study: New Zealand

No. of awards offered: Varies

Funding: Foundation

For further information contact:

Email: scholarships@otago.ac.nz

University of Otago Postgraduate Scholarship in Obstetrics and Gynaecology

Purpose: The Scholarship is intended to provide support for Obstetrics and Gynaecology trainees to carry out research in Obstetrics, Gynaecology and Women's Health whilst enrolled at the University of Otago for a graduate research degree, such as a Master of Medical Science (MMedSc) or Doctor of Philosophy (PhD). It is desirable, but not compulsory, that the research be carried out at the University of Otago

Eligibility: 1. Medical graduates (normally Registrars enrolled in the Royal Australian and New Zealand College of Obstetrics and Gynaecology Integrated Training Programme, or Members or Fellows of the College). 2. Enrolled in, or intending to enrol in a research Master's degree or PhD, normally towards a topic in the field of Obstetrics and Gynaecology or Women's Health

Level of Study: Postgraduate

Type: Scholarship

Value: NZ$25,000 stipend per annum, plus tuition fees (up to a maximum of NZ$9,000 per annum)

Frequency: Annual

Country of Study: New Zealand

No. of awards offered: 1

Closing Date: 17 November

Funding: Foundation

University of Otago Special Health Research Scholarship

Purpose: The University of Otago Special Health Research Scholarship provides funding to support outstanding doctoral students who are contemplating a career in Health Research.

Eligibility: 1. seeking to obtain their first doctoral qualification 2. studying, or planning to study, full-time 3. undertaking health related research
Level of Study: Postgraduate
Type: Scholarship
Value: NZ$27,000 stipend per annum plus domestic tuition fees waiver (excludes student services fee and insurance)
Frequency: Annual
Country of Study: New Zealand
No. of awards offered: 1
Funding: Foundation

For further information contact:

Tel: (64) 800 80 80 98
Email: scholarships@otago.ac.nz

Vice-Chancellor's Scholarship for International Students

Purpose: The Vice-Chancellor's Scholarships for International Students celebrate and welcome international students to the University of Otago, as valued members of our University community. This scholarship recognises the additional personal, academic and financial challenges currently faced by international students and is awarded to support students to pursue their academic goals.
Eligibility: International undergraduate students at the University of Otago, living in New Zealand, or studying online or by distance from outside of New Zealand
Type: Scholarship
Value: NZD$10,000 for tuition fees
Length of Study: 12 Movies
Frequency: Annual
Country of Study: Any country
No. of awards offered: 1
Closing Date: 10 December
Additional Information: www.otago.ac.nz/study/scholarships/database/otago827694.html

For further information contact:

362 Leith Street, Dunedin North, Dunedin 9016, New Zealand.

Tel: (64) 3 479 7000

Waddell Smith Postgraduate Scholarship

Purpose: Masters' scholarships are awarded by the University Council, on the recommendation of the Senate, to candidates in the first year of their thesis research for a Master's degree which constitutes entry to the PhD course at this University. These scholarships are available only to students seeking to obtain their first research-based Master's qualification
Eligibility: 1. Unless otherwise stated in these conditions or within the schedule, doctoral and Masters' scholarships are open only to Domestic Fee Paying Students. International candidates studying for professional doctorates are eligible to apply but if awarded a scholarship the tuition fee waiver will be capped at the domestic rate. 2. In the case of applicants for a doctoral scholarship, confirmation of the scholarship is dependent on approval of their application for admission to the relevant doctoral programme and completion of the enrolment procedure. 3. In the case of applicants for a Master's scholarship, confirmation of the scholarship is dependent on approval of their application to register as a Master's candidate and completion of the enrolment procedure
Level of Study: Postgraduate
Type: Scholarship
Value: NZ$2,000
Frequency: Annual
Country of Study: New Zealand
No. of awards offered: Varies
Funding: Foundation

For further information contact:

Educational Credential Evaluators, Inc., P.O. Box 514070, Milwaukee, WI 53212, United States of America.

Email: graduate@balliol.ox.ac.uk

Williamson Medical Research PhD Scholarship

Purpose: The scholarship may be held by PhD candidates studying towards a PhD in the field of medical research. Applicants must have previously completed a medical degree and be New Zealand citizens (preference will be given to New Zealand–born applicants). The scholarship shall be awarded by the University of Council on the recommendation of the Faculty of Medicine
Eligibility: 1. Unless otherwise stated in these conditions or within the schedule, doctoral and Masters' scholarships are open only to Domestic Fee Paying Students. 3 International candidates studying for professional doctorates are eligible to apply but if awarded a scholarship the tuition fee waiver will be capped at the domestic rate. 2. In the case of applicants for a doctoral scholarship, confirmation of the scholarship is dependent on approval of their application for admission to the relevant doctoral programme and completion of the enrolment procedure. 3. In the case of applicants for a Master's scholarship, confirmation of the scholarship is dependent on

U

approval of their application to register as a Master's candidate and completion of the enrolment procedure

Level of Study: Postgraduate
Type: Scholarship
Value: NZ$25,000
Length of Study: 3 year
Frequency: Annual
Country of Study: New Zealand
No. of awards offered: Varies
Funding: Foundation
Additional Information: www.otago.ac.nz/study/scholarships/database/otago046608.html

For further information contact:

Email: scholarships@otago.ac.nz

University of Oxford

University Offices, Wellington Square, Oxford OX1 2JD, United Kingdom.

Email: internal.communications@admin.ox.ac.uk

As the oldest university in the English-speaking world, Oxford is a unique and historic institution. There is no clear date of foundation, but teaching existed at Oxford in some form in 1096 and developed rapidly from 1167, when Henry II banned English students from attending the University of Paris.

Alan Turing Doctoral Studentships

Eligibility: Open to all graduate applicants for a variety of doctoral graduate courses related to data science. Please see website for further details and eligible subjects, including how to apply
Level of Study: Doctorate
Type: Studentship
Value: Studentships include a generous tax-free stipend of £20,500 per annum, a travel allowance and tuition fees (home/European Union rate) for a period of 3.5 years. A limited number of studentships include fully funded international tuition fees or a partial contribution towards international tuition fees
Length of Study: 3.5 years
Country of Study: Any country
Additional Information: Please visit the website: www.turing.ac.uk/opportunities/studentships/ www.birmingham.ac.uk/postgraduate/pgr/funding/alan-turing-phds.aspx

For further information contact:

Email: hr@turing.ac.uk

Archaeology: AHRC

Purpose: Archaeology
Eligibility: Open to United Kingdom applicants for DPhils in Archaeology and Classical Archaeology. Other European Union nationals are eligible for a fees-only award. All eligible applicants will be automatically considered
Level of Study: Doctorate
Type: Scholarship
Value: University fee, college fee and full living expenses. Fees-only awards for non-United Kingdom, European Union students
Length of Study: Up to 3 years
Country of Study: Any country
Closing Date: 20 January
Additional Information: Please visit the website: www.humanities.ox.ac.uk/prospective_students/graduates/ahrc

For further information contact:

Email: hca-research@ed.ac.uk

Archaeology: Edward Hall Awards

Purpose: Archaeological Science
Eligibility: Open to all applicants for the MSc/MSt in Archaeological Science. All applicants to course will be automatically considered
Level of Study: Postgraduate
Type: Award
Value: £8,120
Length of Study: 1 year
Country of Study: Any country
Closing Date: 20 January
Additional Information: Please visit the website: www.arch.ox.ac.uk/graduate-archaeological-science.html www.european-funding-guide.eu/other-financial-assistance/13823-edward-hall-memorial-fund

For further information contact:

Email: webofficer@arch.ox.ac.uk

Area Studies: FirstRand Laurie Dippenaar Scholarship

Purpose: African Studies

Eligibility: Open to South African graduate applicants for the MSc African Studies
Level of Study: Postgraduate
Type: Scholarship
Value: value of R850,000
Length of Study: Period of fee liability
Frequency: Annual
Study Establishment: Wadham College
Country of Study: South Africa
Application Procedure: Please see website for further details, including how to apply
Closing Date: 20 February
Additional Information: Please visit the website: www.firstrand.co.za/csi/Pages/laurie-dippenaar-scholarship.aspx bursaries.firstrand.co.za/Bursary/FirstRandLaurieDippenaar Scholarship?AspxAutoDetectCookieSupport=1

Atmospheric, Oceanic & Planetary Physics: STFC Studentships

Eligibility: Open to Home and European Union graduate applicants to the DPhil Atmospheric, Oceanic and Planetary Physics. To be eligible for consideration for these scholarships, applicants must be successful in being offered a place on their course after consideration of applications received by the relevant January deadline for the course
Level of Study: Doctorate
Type: Studentship
Value: £8,620
Length of Study: 3 years
Frequency: Annual
Country of Study: Any country
Closing Date: 7 January
Additional Information: Please visit the website: www2.physics.ox.ac.uk/study-here/postgraduates/atmospheric-oceanic-and-planetary-physics/funding

For further information contact:

Email: F.Y.Ogrin@exeter.ac.uk

Balliol College: Balliol Economics Scholarship

Eligibility: Open to all graduate applicants to MPhil or MPhil +DPhil 2+2 in Economics. Students of any nationality applying to read for the MPhil in economics
Type: Scholarship
Value: £3,600 per annum
Length of Study: Up to 3 years
Country of Study: Any country

Application Procedure: Please see website for how to apply and more details
Closing Date: 22 January
Additional Information: www.balliol.ox.ac.uk/sites/default/files/balliol_economics_scholarship_2015_entry.pdf

For further information contact:

Email: graduate@balliol.ox.ac.uk

Balliol College: Brassey Italian Scholarship

Eligibility: Open to all applicants to postgraduate degrees in Modern Languages where Italian is the principal subject of study. Please see website for more details
Level of Study: Postgraduate, Research
Type: Scholarship
Value: College fee
Length of Study: Duration of fee liability
Application Procedure: Please see website for how to apply and more details
Closing Date: 22 January
Additional Information: www.balliol.ox.ac.uk/sites/default/files/brassey_italian_2014.pdf

For further information contact:

Email: graduate.admissions@balliol.ox.ac.uk

Balliol College: Eddie Dinshaw Scholarship

Eligibility: Open to all graduate applicants from India for relevant areas of study
Level of Study: Postgraduate, Research
Type: Scholarship
Value: £10,000
Length of Study: Up to 3 years
Frequency: Annual
Application Procedure: Please see website for more details and how to apply
Closing Date: 23 January

For further information contact:

Email: graduate.admissions@balliol.ox.ac.uk

Balliol College: Foley-Bejar Scholarships

Eligibility: Open to all graduate applicants who a) were born in or who have one parent born in Mexico, Spain, or the Republic of Ireland, or who have a strong connection with

Northern Ireland; and b) are ordinarily resident in Mexico, Spain or the Republic of Ireland. Please see website for more details

Type: Scholarship

Value: £15,500 per annum

Length of Study: 5 years

Frequency: Annual

Country of Study: Any country

Application Procedure: Please see website for more details and how to apply

Closing Date: 23 January

For further information contact:

Email:	graduate@balliol.ox.ac.uk

Balliol College: IKOS Half Bursary

Eligibility: Open to candidates of any nationality who have expressed an intention to pursue an academic, vocational or public-service oriented career following their degrees

Level of Study: Postgraduate, Research

Type: Bursary

Value: Up to £6,000 per year

Length of Study: Up to 3 years

Application Procedure: Applicants must apply to the University of Oxford for admission by the University's second deadline in January, and must apply for any University scholarship, including the Clarendon, for which they are eligible

Closing Date: 24 January

Additional Information: Please check at www.balliol.ox.ac. uk/graduate-admissions/scholarships www.balliol.ox.ac.uk/admissions/graduate-admissions/scholarships

For further information contact:

Email:	graduate.admissions@balliol.ox.ac.uk

Balliol College: Jason Hu Scholarship

Eligibility: Open to all graduate applicants from Asia with preference for candidates from Taiwan and China

Level of Study: Postgraduate, Research

Type: Scholarship

Value: £10,000 per year

Length of Study: Up to 3 years

Frequency: Annual

Application Procedure: Please see website for more details and how to apply

Closing Date: 18 January

Additional Information: It is awarded in conjunction with Clarendon Fund or other award or scholarship. Four

scholarships can only be offered to students from Taiwan and China as a whole, one can be offered to candidates from any Asian country www.balliol.ox.ac.uk/sites/default/files/jason_hu_2020.pdf

For further information contact:

Email:	graduate.admissions@balliol.ox.ac.uk

Balliol College: McDougall Scholarship

Eligibility: Open to graduate applicants to Law

Level of Study: Graduate, Postgraduate

Type: Scholarship

Value: £7,750 per annum

Length of Study: Up to 3 years

Frequency: Annual

Application Procedure: Applicants must apply to the University of Oxford for admission to a higher degree

Closing Date: 23 January

Additional Information: www.balliol.ox.ac.uk/sites/default/files/mcdougall_2020.pdf

For further information contact:

Email:	graduate@balliol.ox.ac.uk

Balliol College: Peter Storey Scholarship

Eligibility: Open to all applicants to Master's degrees in History. May be awarded as a fully-funded scholarship in partnership with an AHRC award or as a standalone award of £10,000 per year. Please see website for more details

Level of Study: Postgraduate, Research

Type: Scholarship

Value: A minimum of £10,000 per year

Length of Study: Period of fee liability

Country of Study: Any country

Application Procedure: Please see website for more details and how to apply

Closing Date: 22 January

Additional Information: Scholarship will be awarded to a candidate with AHRC Funding www.balliol.ox.ac.uk/sites/default/files/storey_masters_2018_entry.pdf

For further information contact:

Email:	graduate@balliol.ox.ac.uk

Balliol College: Snell Scholarship

Purpose: The College seeks to elect one Scholar who has gained an offer of admission to read for a higher degree at Balliol College after completing a degree at the University of Glasgow
Eligibility: Honours graduates or in their final Honours year, applicants must have a connection with Scotland by birth (either themselves or one parent), domicile (at least three years) or education at a school in Scotland (at least three years) before admission to the University of Glasgow. Graduates of the University of Glasgow. Please see website for more details including how to apply
Type: Scholarship
Value: £15,000 per annum
Length of Study: Up to 3 years
Country of Study: Any country
Closing Date: 23 January

For further information contact:

Email: graduate@balliol.ox.ac.uk

Black Academic Futures Scholarship

Purpose: Academic Futures is a series of scholarship programmes that will address under-representation and help improve equality, diversity and inclusion in our graduate student body.
Eligibility: applicants who are ordinarily resident in the United Kingdom, who are of Black or Mixed-Black ethnicity and who hold an offer for either a taught or research postgraduate degree
Type: Scholarship
Value: £15,609
Frequency: Annual
Country of Study: Any country
No. of awards offered: 30
Additional Information: www.ox.ac.uk/admissions/graduate/access/academic-futures

For further information contact:

University of Oxford, University Offices, 15 Wellington Square, Oxford OX1 2JD, United Kingdom.

Tel: (44) 1865 270000
Fax: (44) 1865 270708

Blavatnik School of Government: Africa Governance Initiative Scholarship

Eligibility: Open to all Master of Public Policy applicants who are ordinarily resident in Africa. Scholarships are awarded on the basis of outstanding academic ability, commitment to public service, a capacity to lead, an interest in and experience of improving governance in Africa, a commitment to completing their summer project on some aspect of governance in Africa, and a commitment to return to Africa after their time at the School to continue their work on governance there
Level of Study: Postgraduate
Type: Scholarship
Value: University fee, college fee and full living expenses
Length of Study: Period of fee liability
Frequency: Annual
Country of Study: Any country
Application Procedure: To apply, applicants must provide a supporting statement. Please see website for more details
Closing Date: 20 January
Additional Information: opportunitydesk.org/2019/08/01/africa-initiative-for-governance-scholarships-2020-2021/

For further information contact:

Email: inquiries@aigafrica.org

Blavatnik School of Government: African Initiative for Governance Scholarships

Purpose: Public Policy
Eligibility: Open to all Master of Public Policy applicants who are ordinarily resident in Nigeria and Ghana (and other West African nations). Scholarships are awarded on the basis of exceptional academic and leadership merit and/or potential. Applicants will usually hold an undergraduate degree from an African university. They should also intend to return to work in public service in Qualifying country for at least three years after completing their studies
Level of Study: Postgraduate
Type: Scholarship
Value: University fee, college fee and full living expenses
Length of Study: Period of fee liability
Frequency: Annual
Country of Study: Any country
Application Procedure: To apply, applicants must provide a supporting statement. Please see website for more details
Closing Date: 20 January
Additional Information: Please visit the website: www.bsg.ox.ac.uk/study/mpp/bsg-funding-options

For further information contact:

Email: enquiries@bsg.ox.ac.uk

Blavatnik School of Government: Public Service Scholarship

Purpose: Public Policy
Eligibility: Open to all Master of Public Policy applicants. Scholarships are awarded on the basis of unwavering dedication to public service, shown through an exceptional academic and professional record
Level of Study: Postgraduate
Type: Scholarship
Value: Variable, often half or full fees
Length of Study: Period of fee liability
Frequency: Annual
Country of Study: Any country
Application Procedure: To apply, applicants must provide a supporting statement. Please see website for more details
Closing Date: 10 January
Additional Information: Please visit the website: www.bsg. ox.ac.uk/study/mpp/bsg-funding-options ssc.govt.nz/assets/ SSC-Site-Assets/Workforce-and-Talent-Management/Diver sity-Inclusion/Blavatnik-School-of-Govt-brochure.pdf

For further information contact:

Email: enquiries@bsg.ox.ac.uk

Blavatnik School of Government: The Lemann Fellows Scholarships

Eligibility: Open to all Master of Public Policy applicants that are ordinarily resident in Brazil. Scholarships are awarded on the basis of exceptional academic merit and a commitment to social change in Brazil. To apply applicants must provide a supporting statement
Level of Study: Postgraduate
Type: Scholarship
Value: University fee, college fee and full living expenses
Length of Study: Period of fee liability
Country of Study: Any country
Application Procedure: Please see the website for full details, including how to apply
Closing Date: 20 January
Additional Information: Please check at www.bsg.ox.ac.uk/ study/mpp/bsg-funding-options www.european-funding-guide.eu/other-financial-assistance/13898-university-college-blavatnik-school-government-scholarships

For further information contact:

Email: enquiries@bsg.ox.ac.uk

Blavatnik School of Government: The Walter Kwok Scholarships

Eligibility: Open to all Master of Public Policy applicants that are ordinarily resident in Hong Kong or China. Scholarships are awarded on the basis of exceptional academic merit and a commitment to change in the HKSAR region. Interviews may be held as part of the selection process
Type: Scholarship
Value: University fee, college fee and full living expenses
Length of Study: Period of fee liability
Country of Study: Any country
Application Procedure: Please see website for more details and how to apply
Closing Date: 31 March
Additional Information: Please check at www.bsg.ox.ac.uk/ study/mpp/bsg-funding-options kwokscholars.org/graduate-study-at-the-university-of-oxford-scholarship.html

For further information contact:

Email: enquiries@bsg.ox.ac.uk

Brasenose College: Senior Fiddian

Eligibility: Open to graduates who are former members of Monmouth School or Haberdashers Monmouth School for Girls
Level of Study: Graduate, Postgraduate
Type: Grant
Value: £3,000
Length of Study: Period of fee liability
Study Establishment: Brasenose College
Country of Study: Any country
Application Procedure: Please see website for more details
Additional Information: For more information, please check at www.bnc.ox.ac.uk/prospective-students/graduate-admissions/ fees-funding

For further information contact:

Brasenose College Radcliffe Square, Oxford OX1 4AJ, United Kingdom.

Email: college.office@bnc.ox.ac.uk

Brasenose Hector Pilling Scholarship

Purpose: For graduates of Commonwealth countries
Eligibility: Open to graduates of any Commonwealth university, excluding the United Kingdom
Level of Study: Postgraduate

Type: Scholarship
Value: Fees and maintenance to be determined by the administrators of the Clarendon Fund Scholarships
Frequency: Annual
Study Establishment: Brasenose College, University of Oxford
Country of Study: United Kingdom
Application Procedure: Applicants must write for details
No. of awards offered: 1
Funding: Private
Contributor: In conjunction with the Clarendon Fund Studentship Scheme
No. of awards given last year: 1
No. of applicants last year: 1
Additional Information: This scholarship is offered in conjunction with the Clarendon Fund Studentship Scheme www.bnc.ox.ac.uk/prospective-students/graduate-admissions/fees-funding

For further information contact:

Email: international.office@admin.ox.ac.uk

Brasenose Joint Commonwealth Studentship

Eligibility: Open to all applicants from Commonwealth countries. Please see website for more details
Level of Study: Graduate, Postgraduate
Value: University fee, college fee, and living expenses (of which £13K funded by BNC)
Length of Study: One year
Study Establishment: Brasenose
Country of Study: United Kingdom
Application Procedure: For more information, please check website www.bnc.ox.ac.uk/prospective-students/graduate-admissions/fees-funding
Closing Date: 22 January
Additional Information: cscuk.dfid.gov.uk/apply/shared-scholarships/

For further information contact:

Email: lawfac@law.ox.ac.uk

Business School (Saïd): Registrar's University of Oxford Scholarship

Purpose: To assist graduate students with fees and a living allowance
Eligibility: A portion of the scholarships will be available to candidates who have shown strong career progression and excellent career potential. Candidates should have strong communication skills, strong leadership ability or potential, and a readiness and enthusiasm to become a strong ambassador for the School whilst on the programme and beyond. A further portion of these scholarships will be awarded on the basis of academic excellence demonstrated through degree results, GMAT or GRE score, previous university prizes and awards, and other academic achievements. Candidates should also demonstrate good leadership skills and strong professional experience.
Level of Study: MBA, Postgraduate
Type: Scholarship
Value: No fixed value. We offer a range of partial awards, contributing towards course fees
Length of Study: 2 years
No. of awards offered: 40
Additional Information: www.sbs.ox.ac.uk/oxford-experience/scholarships-and-funding/oxford-pershing-square-scholarship

For further information contact:

Email: Diana.Hulin@admin.ox.ac.uk

Chevening Scholarships

Eligibility: You must: 1. Be a citizen of a Chevening-eligible country or territory. 2. Return to your country of citizenship for a minimum of two years after your award has ended. 3. Have completed all components of an undergraduate degree that will enable you to gain entry onto a postgraduate programme at a UK university by the time you submit your application. This is typically equivalent to an upper second-class 2:1 honours degree in the UK but may be different depending on your course and university choice. 4. Have at least two years (equivalent to 2,800 hours) of work experience. 5. Apply to three different eligible UK university courses and have received an unconditional offer from one of these choices by 14 July 2023.
Level of Study: Graduate
Type: Scholarship
Value: University fee, college fee, and full living expenses
Length of Study: 1 year
Country of Study: Any country
Application Procedure: Please see website for more details and how to apply
Closing Date: 14 July

For further information contact:

Email: international@lincoln.ac.uk

China Oxford Scholarship Fund

Purpose: The China Oxford Scholarship Fund (COSF) awards scholarships to students from the People's Republic of China, Hong Kong and Macau who have won a place for postgraduate degree studies on a full-time basis at the University of Oxford. Up to twenty scholarships are awarded annually. Preference is given to those who are studying in the United Kingdom for the first time. Successful candidates are those of the highest calibre studying in any subject. They are chosen for their academic excellence, financial need, leadership quality and their commitment to contribute to the development of China.

Eligibility: An applicant must be a national of the People's Republic of China who is ordinarily resident in China, Hong Kong or Macau. An applicant must have an official or conditional offer to pursue a postgraduate degree at Oxford University.

Level of Study: Graduate

Type: Scholarship

Value: £10,000

Frequency: Annual

Country of Study: Any country

Application Procedure: See website: chinaoxford.org/?page_id=43

Closing Date: 15 April

For further information contact:

Email: application@chinaoxford.org; info@chinaoxford.org

China Scholarship Council-University of Oxford Scholarships

Subjects: All subjects

Purpose: The scholarships are supported jointly by the China Scholarship Council (on behalf of the Chinese Ministry of Education) and the University of Oxford. Another strand of this scholarship is the China Scholarship Council-PAG Oxford Scholarships. They are funded by PAG, which is one of the regions' largest Asia-focused investment managers. The scholarships enable academically excellent Chinese students to pursue doctoral studies in the Social Sciences and Mathematical, Physical and Life Sciences at the University of Oxford.

Eligibility: 1. You must be applying to start a new full-time DPhil course at Oxford. 2. You must be a national of and ordinarily resident in mainland China (not including Hong Kong or Macau). You must also be intending to return to China once your course is completed. 3. Scholarships will be awarded on the basis of academic merit, potential to become a leader in your field and potential to become a decision-maker and opinion former within China. 4. Applicants who hold

deferred offers "www.ox.ac.uk/admissions/graduate/after-you-apply/your-offer-and-contract" to start in 2023–24 are not eligible to be considered for these scholarships.

Level of Study: Doctorate

Type: Scholarship

Value: 100% of course fees, a grant for living costs (at least £15,609)

Length of Study: Period of fee liability

Frequency: Annual

Country of Study: Any country

Application Procedure: See website: www.ox.ac.uk/admissions/graduate/fees-and-funding/fees-funding-and-scholarship-search/china-scholarship-council-university-oxford-scholarships

No. of awards offered: Up to 20

Closing Date: December

Christ Church Senior Scholarship

Purpose: To enable graduate scholars to undertake training or a definite course of literary, educational, scientific or professional study

Eligibility: Open to candidates who will have been reading for a higher degree at the University of Oxford for at least 1 year, but not more than 2 years, by October 1st of the year in which the award is sought

Level of Study: Postgraduate

Type: Scholarship

Value: Varies

Length of Study: 2 years, with a possibility of renewal for a further year

Frequency: Annual

Study Establishment: Christ Church, University of Oxford

Country of Study: United Kingdom

Application Procedure: Applicants must write for details. Applications should be made in February

No. of awards offered: 102

Closing Date: 1 April

No. of awards given last year: 2

No. of applicants last year: 102

Additional Information: Normally, the scholarship is held in conjunction with an award from a government agency that pays the university fees www.ccgs.wa.edu.au/community/giving/the-students-scholarship

Commonwealth Shared Scholarship Scheme (CSSS)

Purpose: To support students from developing Commonwealth countries who would not otherwise be able to study in the United Kingdom

Eligibility: Open to new students from developing Commonwealth countries. Candidates should normally be under 35 at the time the award begins. This scholarship is not available to those living or studying in a developed country, employees of government departments or parastatal organisations
Level of Study: Postgraduate
Type: Scholarship
Value: Tuition fees, living costs, flights to UK
Length of Study: 1 year
Frequency: Annual
Country of Study: Any country
Application Procedure: Candidates must apply to Oxford by completing the Graduate Application Form by Application Deadline 2. They must complete the CSSS application form and submit this to Student Funding Services by email or post by March 13th
Closing Date: 20 December
Additional Information: www.ucl.ac.uk/scholarships/commonwealth-shared-scholarship-scheme

Commonwealth Shared Scholarships

Purpose: Funded by the UK Foreign, Commonwealth and Development Office (FCDO) Commonwealth Shared Scholarships enable talented and motivated individuals to gain the knowledge and skills required for sustainable development, and are aimed at those who could not otherwise afford to study in the UK.
Eligibility: To apply for these scholarships, you must: 1. Be a citizen of or have been granted refugee status by an eligible Commonwealth country, or be a British Protected Person 2. Be permanently resident in an eligible Commonwealth country 3. Be available to start your academic studies in the UK by the start of the UK academic year in September 2022 4. By September 2023, hold a first degree of at least upper second-class (2:1) honours standard, or a lower second-class degree (2:2) and a relevant postgraduate qualification (usually a Master's degree). 5. Not have studied or worked for one (academic) year or more in a high-income country 6. Be unable to afford to study at a UK university without this scholarship 7. Have provided all supporting documentation in the required format
Type: Scholarship
Value: Stipend (living allowance) at the rate of £1,133 per month, or £1,390 per month
Frequency: Annual
Country of Study: Any country
Closing Date: 20 December

For further information contact:

Email: csc.safeguarding@cscuk.org.uk

Comparative Philology: Joint Christ Church Linguistics Graduate Scholarship

Purpose: To assist graduate students with fees and maintenance
Eligibility: Open to all
Level of Study: Postgraduate, Research
Type: Scholarship
Value: College fees and maintenance allowance of £2,000
Length of Study: Up to 3 years
Closing Date: 16 January

For further information contact:

Email: kate.dobson@ling-phil.ox.ac.uk

Computer Science: Department Studentships

Purpose: To develop practical methods, algorithms, and tools for a use-case driven approach to system-level hardware/software formal co-verification. A key objective, and the foundation for the methodology, will be the invention of a systematic abstraction framework that closes the gap, currently unaddressed, between a system and implementation levels in co-verification
Eligibility: Open to all applicants applying for a DPhil in Computer Science
Level of Study: Doctorate
Type: Studentship
Value: Course fee, college fee and stipend
Length of Study: 3 years
Country of Study: Any country
Closing Date: 10 March
Additional Information: Please visit the website: www.cs.ox.ac.uk/aboutus/vacancies/studentship.html

For further information contact:

Email: enquiries@cs.ox.ac.uk

Computer Science: Engineering and Physical Sciences Research Council (EPSRC) Doctoral Training Partnership Studentships

Purpose: Computer Science
Eligibility: Open to applicants applying for a DPhil in Computer Science. Home students and European Union students who have studied in the United Kingdom for the previous 3 years are eligible for full studentship. European Union students who have studied elsewhere in the European Union are eligible for fees only award
Level of Study: Doctorate

U

Type: Studentship
Value: Course fee, college fee and stipend (if eligible). Home students and European students who have studied in the United Kingdom for the previous 3 years are eligible for full studentship. European Union students who have studied elsewhere in the European Union are eligible for fees only award
Length of Study: Up to 3.5 years
Country of Study: Any country
Closing Date: 30 March
Additional Information: Please visit the website: www.cs. ox.ac.uk/aboutus/vacancies/studentship.html www.brunel.ac. uk/research/Research-degrees/PhD-Studentships/Studentship? id=a2efbe35-b0b9-46a7-b284-3fd40ff05174

Continuing Education: MSc Programme Scholarship

Eligibility: Open to all applicants for the MSc in Sustainable Urban Development who apply by the Late-January deadline
Level of Study: Postgraduate
Type: Scholarship
Value: Course fee
Length of Study: Duration of programme
Frequency: Annual
Country of Study: Anywhere
Application Procedure: Through Graduate Admissions website (www.ox.ac.uk/admissions/graduate/courses/msc-sustainable-urban-development)
Closing Date: 21 January
Additional Information: Please visit the website: www. conted.ox.ac.uk/about/msud-programme-scholarship for more information. www.conted.ox.ac.uk/about/msc-in-sustainable-urban-development

For further information contact:

Tel: (44) 1865 286952
Email: sud@conted.ox.ac.uk

Crystal Clinical Scholarships

Type: Scholarship
Value: Scholarship funds will be used for travel and associated expenses
Length of Study: 1 year
Country of Study: Any country

For further information contact:

Email: info@onfgivesback.org

Department of Education: Talbot Scholarship

Eligibility: Open to all applicants for DPhil in Education. Please visit website for more details
Level of Study: Doctorate
Type: Partial scholarship
Value: £15,000 per annum contribution towards fees and living expenses 35% reduction of tuition fee
Length of Study: 3 years
Frequency: Every 3 years
Country of Study: Any country
Closing Date: 20 January
Additional Information: Please visit the website: www.edu cation.ox.ac.uk/courses/d-phil/funding-opportunities/

Donald Tovey Memorial Prize

Purpose: To assist in the furtherance of research or in the publication of work already done, in the fields of philosophy, history or understanding of music
Eligibility: Open to men or women, without regard to nationality, age or membership of a university
Level of Study: Postdoctorate
Type: Prize
Value: £1,000
Frequency: Dependent on funds available
Study Establishment: Unrestricted
Country of Study: Any country
Application Procedure: Applications should be addressed to the Heather Professor of Music at the address shown
Closing Date: June
Funding: Private
Contributor: Donal Tovey Memorial Fund
Additional Information: If for furtherance of research, applicants need to demonstrate that the programme falls within the scope of the award, and produce testimonials or other written evidence of previous attainment which demonstrate the researcher's fitness to undertake it. If to assist in publication of work already completed, the applicant must submit one copy of work with an explanation of why the Prize is needed to ensure publication. The Prize is generally awarded for postdoctoral or advanced research www.music.ox.ac.uk/ donald-tovey-memorial-prize/

For further information contact:

Faculty of Music, St Aldate's, Oxford OX1 1DB, United Kingdom.

Tel: (44) 1865 276 125
Fax: (44) 1865 276 128
Email: musicfac@sable.ox.ac.uk

Duke of Cambridge Scholarship at University of Oxford

Purpose: Public Policy

Eligibility: Open to applicants who are ordinarily resident in the United Kingdom and who are applying to the Master of Public Policy (MPP). Please see website for more details

Level of Study: Postgraduate

Type: Scholarship

Value: University fee, college fee, and full living expenses of about £14,553

Length of Study: Period of fee liability

Country of Study: Any country

Closing Date: 20 January

Additional Information: The scholarship is only tenable at University College. Please visit the website: www.ox.ac.uk/admissions/graduate/fees-and-funding/fees-funding-and-scholarship-search/scholarships-1#duke www.scholarshub africa.com/19991/duke-cambridge-scholarship-university-oxford/

For further information contact:

Tel: (44) 1865 614 343

Email: admin@scholarship-position.com

Economic and Social Research Council (ESRC) Quota Award

Purpose: To assist graduate students with fees and maintenance

Eligibility: Open to all graduate applicants in Economics

Level of Study: Doctorate, Research

Type: Award

Value: University fee, college fee, and full living expenses

Length of Study: Up to 4 years

Application Procedure: Applicants are strongly advised to submit their application for consideration at the first application deadline of January 18th. Places on the second application deadline will be limited

Closing Date: 18 January

Additional Information: Please visit website for more details and how to apply www.economics.ox.ac.uk/index.php/graduate warwick.ac.uk/fac/arts/history/prospective/post graduate/pgfunding/esrcquota/

For further information contact:

Tel: (44) 1865 281 162

Email: econgrad@economics.ox.ac.uk

Economic and Social Research Council (ESRC): Social Policy & Intervention

Eligibility: Open to applicants to MSc/MPhil comparative social policy, MSc/MPhil evidence based social intervention and policy evaluation and DPhil social policy/social intervention. Candidates apply at the same time as they apply for admission to their postgraduate programme at the University of Oxford, using the same application form

Level of Study: Postgraduate

Value: University fee, college fee and living expenses. Fees-only award for European Union applicants

Length of Study: Period of fee liability

Country of Study: Any country

Application Procedure: Please apply using the standard graduate application form, and confirm with the Department that you wish to be considered for an ESRC studentship

Closing Date: 22 January

Additional Information: Please check at www.spi.ox.ac.uk/study-with-us/funding.html www.spi.ox.ac.uk/oxford-institute-of-social-policy

For further information contact:

Email: erzsebet.bukodi@spi.ox.ac.uk

Economic and Social Research Council: Interdisciplinary Area Studies

Eligibility: Candidates need to apply by the January admissions deadline to their postgraduate programme at the University of Oxford, using the statement of purpose form, which requires candidates to write an indicative research proposal for DPhil level study

Level of Study: Graduate

Value: University fee, college fee, and living expenses. Fees-only award for European Union applicants

Length of Study: Period of fee liability

Country of Study: Any country

Application Procedure: Please visit website for more details and how to apply

Closing Date: 20 January

Additional Information: Please check at www.area-studies.ox.ac.uk/scholarships-sias

For further information contact:

Email: f.ciuta@ucl.ac.uk

U

Economic and Social Research Council: Socio-Legal Studies

Eligibility: Open to all prospective students applying for the 1+3 MSt Socio-Legal Studies and DPhil Socio-Legal Studies, or just for the latter
Level of Study: Postgraduate
Type: Scholarship
Value: University fee, college fee, and living expenses. Fees-only award for European Union applicants
Length of Study: Period of fee liability
Frequency: Annual
Country of Study: United Kingdom
Application Procedure: Please contact the pathway representitive Professor Richard Sparks before applying r.sparks@ed.ac.uk
Closing Date: 20 January
Funding: Trusts
Additional Information: Please see website: www.law.ox.ac.uk/postgraduate/scholarships.php www.ed.ac.uk/student-funding/postgraduate/uk-eu/humanities/law/esrc-socio-legal

For further information contact:

Email: r.sparks@ed.ac.uk

Economics: Doctoral Studentship

Purpose: Economics
Eligibility: Open to Home/Eu/Overseas. DPhil in economics. Please note this is only available to those who will have DPhil status in MT 2012
Type: Studentship
Value: £11,126
Length of Study: 2 years
Application Procedure: Applicants are strongly advised to submit their application for consideration at the first application deadline of January 20th. Places on the second application deadline will be limited
Closing Date: 24 January
Additional Information: All applicants accepted by the Department will be offered a place at a college. You may indicate on your application form which college you would like to be considered for; if you have no preference Graduate Admissions will make a selection for you. Students do not necessarily get accepted by their first choice. Please check at www.economics.ox.ac.uk/index.php/graduate www.york.ac.uk/economics/postgrad/funding/phd-studentships/#tab-1

For further information contact:

Tel: (44) 1865 281 162
Email: econgrad@economics.ox.ac.uk

Education: Economic and Social Research Council (ESRC)

Eligibility: Open to all Home/European Union applicants for both DPhil in Education and MSc Education (Research Design and Methodology). Please visit website for more details
Level of Study: Doctorate, Postgraduate
Type: Studentship
Value: University fee, college fee and full living expenses
Length of Study: Period of fee liability
Country of Study: Any country
Closing Date: 20 January
Additional Information: Please visit the website: www.education.ox.ac.uk/courses/d-phil/funding-opportunities/

For further information contact:

Email: eddev@esrc.ukri.org

Engineering and Physical Sciences Research Council (EPSRC) Centre for Doctoral Training in Autonomous Intelligent Machines and Systems

Purpose: To develop in-depth knowledge, understanding and expertise in autonomous intelligent systems
Eligibility: Open to United Kingdom and European Union applicants for DPhil in Engineering. European Union applicants may only be eligible for a fees-only award, depending on residency requirements. Please visit website for more details
Level of Study: Doctorate
Type: Scholarship
Value: University fee, college fee and full living expenses
Length of Study: 4 years
Country of Study: Any country
Closing Date: 20 January
Additional Information: Please visit the website: www.ox.ac.uk/admissions/graduate/courses/autonomous-intelligent-machines-and-systems eng.ox.ac.uk/aims-cdt/

For further information contact:

Tel: (44) 1865 270 000
Email: aims-cdt@robots.ox.ac.uk

Engineering and Physical Sciences Research Council (EPSRC) Doctoral Training Programme Studentships

Eligibility: Open to United Kingdom and European Union applicants for DPhil in Statistics. European Union applicants

may only be eligible for a fees-only award, depending on residency requirements
Level of Study: Postgraduate
Value: University fee, college fee and full living expenses
Length of Study: Three and a half years maximum
Frequency: Annual
Country of Study: United Kingdom
Closing Date: 20 January
Funding: Trusts
Additional Information: For more information, please visit website: www.stats.ox.ac.uk/study_here/research_degrees epsrc.ukri.org/skills/students/dta/

For further information contact:

Email: phdfunding-salc@manchester.ac.uk

Engineering and Physical Sciences Research Council CDT in Industrially Focussed Mathematical Modelling

Eligibility: Four studentships will be available to applicants regardless of nationality. The remaining studentships are restricted to United Kingdom/European Union nationals
Level of Study: Postgraduate
Type: Scholarship
Value: University fee, college fee and full living expenses (minimum £14,296 per year for 4 years)
Length of Study: 4 years
Frequency: Annual
Country of Study: Any country
Application Procedure: We will automatically assign students to funding and no separate application for funding is required
Closing Date: 10 March
Funding: Trusts
Additional Information: For more information, please visit the website: www.maths.ox.ac.uk/study-here/postgraduate-study/industrially-focused-mathematical-modelling-epsrc-cdt

For further information contact:

Email: infomm@maths.ox.ac.uk

English Faculty: AHRC Doctoral Training Partnership Studentships

Eligibility: Open to all Home/European Union's graduates applying to undertake research degrees in the Faculty of English. Please see website for more details
Level of Study: Postgraduate
Type: Studentship

Value: University fee, college fee, and full living expenses. Fees-only awards for non-United Kingdom, European Union students
Length of Study: Period of fee liability
Frequency: Annual
Country of Study: United Kingdom
Closing Date: 20 January
Additional Information: For more information, please check website: www.humanities.ox.ac.uk/prospective_students/graduates/funding/ahrc   www.humanities.ox.ac.uk/ahrc-doctoral-training-partnership#collapse395456

For further information contact:

Email: FASS-PhD-Applications@open.ac.uk

English Faculty: Asian Human Rights Commission (AHRC) Doctoral Training Partnership Studentship (Master)

Eligibility: Open to all Home/European Union applicants to MSt and MPhil degrees offered by the Faculty of English. Please see website for more details
Level of Study: Postgraduate
Type: Studentship
Value: University fee, college fee, and living expenses (pro-rata for courses less than 1 year). Fees-only awards for non-United Kingdom, European Union students
Length of Study: Period of fee liability
Frequency: Annual
Country of Study: United Kingdom
Closing Date: 20 January
Funding: Trusts
Additional Information: For more information, please visit: www.humanities.ox.ac.uk/prospective_students/graduates/funding/ahrc   www.humanities.ox.ac.uk/ahrc-doctoral-training-partnership#collapse395456

For further information contact:

Email: ahrcdtp@admin.ox.ac.uk

English Faculty: Cecily Clarke Studentship

Eligibility: Open to all applicants to English Medieval Studies, with preference to Middle English Philology. All students applying for English graduate courses will automatically be considered
Level of Study: Postgraduate
Type: Studentship
Value: £12,000 per year
Length of Study: Up to 2 years

Country of Study: Any country

Closing Date: 18 January

Additional Information: All students applying for English graduate courses will automatically be considered. Candidates apply at the same time as they apply for admission to their postgraduate programme at the University of Oxford, using the same application form. To be considered candidates must apply by the January deadline. Please check at www. english.ox.ac.uk   www.european-funding-guide.eu/scholar ship/13407-cecily-clark-studentship

For further information contact:

Tel: (44) 1865 270 000

Ertegun Graduate Scholarship Programme in the Humanities

Purpose: The Humanities Division offers taught graduate and research degrees in a wide range of subjects.

Eligibility: Applications to The Mica and Ahmet Ertegun Graduate Scholarship Programme may be made by those in fields covered by the following Faculties: Classics (including classical archaeology); English Language and Literature; Fine Art (DPhil in Contemporary Art History and Theory only), History (including History of Art and the History of Architecture); Linguistics, Philology and Phonetics; Medieval and Modern Languages (covering most European languages and their literature); Music; Oriental Studies (including Far Eastern and Middle Eastern Studies, and the study of a wide range of languages); Philosophy; Theology and Religion; and the interdisciplinary courses of Comparative Literature & Critical Translation, Medieval Studies, Film Aesthetics, Women's, Gender & Sexuality Studies, and Digital Scholarship

Level of Study: Doctorate, Masters Degree

Type: Scholarship

Value: £15,609

Length of Study: 1 year

Frequency: Annual

Country of Study: Any country

No. of awards offered: 15

Closing Date: 21 January

No. of awards given last year: 15

No. of applicants last year: 1500

For further information contact:

Graduate Admissions and Funding University Offices, Wellington Square, Oxford OX1 2JD, United Kingdom.

Tel: (44) 1865 270059
Fax: (44) 1865 270049
Email: graduate.admissions@admin.ox.ac.uk

Exeter College Usher-Cunningham Senior Studentship

Purpose: To support graduate study

Eligibility: History is open to graduates of Irish universities only. Medicine is open to all

Level of Study: Postgraduate

Type: Studentship

Value: Home level fees plus maintenance up to the equivalent of a Research Council Award

Length of Study: Usually awarded for up to 3 years

Frequency: Every 3 years

Study Establishment: Exeter College, University of Oxford

Country of Study: United Kingdom

Application Procedure: Applicants must address enquiries to the Academic Administrator

Funding: Private

Contributor: An endowment

Additional Information: www.exeter.ox.ac.uk/wp-content/uploads/2018/12/Usher-Cunningham-Medicine-2019.pdf

For further information contact:

Email: admissions@exeter.ox.ac.uk

Exeter College: Exonian Graduate Scholarship

Eligibility: Exeter College is pleased to offer a studentship covering college fees to two DPhil students, linked to a United Kingdom Research Council award covering university fees

Level of Study: Postdoctorate

Type: Fellowship

Value: College fee only

Length of Study: Up to 3 years

Country of Study: United Kingdom

Application Procedure: Applicants must address enquiries to the Academic Administrator

Closing Date: January

Funding: Private

Additional Information: www.exeter.ox.ac.uk/wp-content/uploads/2019/09/Exonian-2020.pdf

For further information contact:

Exeter College, Turl St, Oxford OX1 3DP, United Kingdom.

Email: academic.administrator@exeter.ox.ac.uk

Exeter College: Nicholas Frangiscatos Scholarship in Byzantine Studies

Eligibility: For a DPhil student in the field of Byzantine studies
Level of Study: Doctorate, Postdoctorate
Type: Fellowship
Value: Up to £10,000 per year
Length of Study: Up to 3 years
Frequency: Every 3 years
Country of Study: United Kingdom
Application Procedure: Please see website for how to apply
Closing Date: 12 March
Funding: Private
Additional Information: Please check at www.exeter.ox.ac. uk/currentstudents/finance/scholarships www.exeter.ox.ac.uk/ wp-content/uploads/2018/12/Nicholas-Frangiscatos-2019.pdf

For further information contact:

Email: admissions@exeter.ox.ac.uk

Exeter College: Senior Scholarship in Theology

Purpose: To support a graduate who wishes to read for the Final Honour School of Theology or Philosophy and Theology
Eligibility: Applicants must hold at least a Second Class (Honours) Degree by the time of admission in a subject other than theology
Level of Study: Postgraduate
Type: Scholarship
Value: University and college fees at Home/European Union rate, maintenance grant £5,000 per year
Length of Study: 3 years
Frequency: Every 3 years
Study Establishment: Exeter College, the University of Oxford
Country of Study: United Kingdom
Application Procedure: Applicants must apply in writing to the Academic Administrator or see the website www.exeter. ox.ac.uk
Closing Date: 1 May
Funding: Private
Contributor: Endowment
No. of awards given last year: 1
Additional Information: The College proposes to elect a graduate to a Senior Scholarship in Theology from October 1st. The Scholar is to study for the Final Honour School of either Theology or Philosophy & Theology (2nd BA) www. exeter.ox.ac.uk/wp-content/uploads/2018/12/Nicholas-Frang iscatos-2019.pdf

Faculty of Medieval and Modern Languages: Heath Harrison DPhil Award

Eligibility: Open to graduate students accepted to read for a DPhil in Medieval and Modern Languages. Please visit the website for more details
Level of Study: Postgraduate
Type: Scholarship
Value: University fee, college fee, and full living expenses
Length of Study: Three years
Frequency: Annual
Country of Study: United Kingdom
Application Procedure: For more information, please check the website grad.mml.ox.ac.uk/funding_fees
Closing Date: 22 January
Funding: Trusts

For further information contact:

Email: office@mod-langs.ox.ac.uk

Felix Scholarships

Purpose: The scholarship will cover 100% of course fees, a grant for living costs (around £15,840) and one return flight from India to the UK. Awards are made for the full duration of your fee liability for the agreed course.
Eligibility: You must be a national of and ordinarily resident in India; You must have a first-class undergraduate or master's degree from an Indian university; You must not hold a degree from a university outside of India (this rule does not apply to study undertaken whilst in receipt of a Felix Scholarship); and You are expected to return to India after completing your studies. You should have a first-class undergraduate degree; You must not already hold a degree from a university outside of your home country (this rule does not apply to study undertaken whilst in receipt of a Felix Scholarship); and You are expected to return to your home county after completing your studies.
Value: £15,840
Country of Study: Any country
Additional Information: www.ox.ac.uk/admissions/gradu ate/fees-and-funding/fees-funding-and-scholarship-search/ felix-scholarships

For further information contact:

University of Oxford, University Offices, 15 Wellington Square, Oxford OX1 2JD, United Kingdom.

Tel: (44) 1865 270000
Fax: (44) 1865 270708

Freshfields Bruckhaus Deringer Scholarships (Law)

Purpose: To assist graduate students with fees and a living allowance
Eligibility: Varies
Level of Study: Doctorate, Postgraduate, Research
Type: Scholarships
Value: To be confirmed
Length of Study: 1 year
Country of Study: Any country
Closing Date: 22 January
Additional Information: www.freshfields.com/en-gb/about-us/responsible-business/freshfields_stephen_lawrence_scholarship/

For further information contact:

Email: ContactFSLScheme@freshfields.com

Frost Scholarship Programme (Israel)

Purpose: The Frost Scholarship Programme (Israel) funds current students of Israeli universities to study one-year, full-time master's courses in science, technology, engineering and mathematics ('STEM' subjects) at the University of Oxford
Eligibility: Open to Israeli residents currently studying at an Israeli university, who have not previously been enrolled on a full degree programme at an institution outside of Israel. You must be applying for a one-year, full-time Master's course in a STEM subject (Science, Technology, Engineering and Mathematics). Four awards will be made each year. Closing date varies according to course
Level of Study: Postgraduate
Type: Scholarship
Value: University fee, college fee, and full living expenses
Length of Study: Period of fee liability
Frequency: Annual
Country of Study: Any country
Closing Date: January
Funding: Trusts
Additional Information: Please see website: www.graduate.ox.ac.uk/frostisrael www.scholarshipdesk.com/frost-scholarship-programme-for-israel-students/

Geography and the Environment: Andrew Goudie Bursary

Eligibility: Open to all applicants for MSc in Environmental Change and Management

Level of Study: Postgraduate
Type: Scholarship
Value: Up to £5,000
Length of Study: 1 year
Country of Study: Any country
Closing Date: 20 January
Additional Information: Please visit the website: www.eci.ox.ac.uk/msc/funding.html

For further information contact:

Email: support@linacre.ox.ac.uk

Geography and the Environment: Boardman Scholarship

Eligibility: Open to all applicants for MSc in Environmental Change and Management
Level of Study: Postgraduate
Type: Scholarship
Value: Up to £5,000
Length of Study: 1 year
Country of Study: Any country
Closing Date: 20 January
Additional Information: Please visit the website: www.eci.ox.ac.uk/msc/funding.html

For further information contact:

Email: socialsciences@devoff.ox.ac.uk

Geography: Sir Walter Raleigh Postgraduate Scholarship

Eligibility: Open to all applicants for MSc Environmental Change and Management. The award is tenable only at Oriel College
Level of Study: Postgraduate
Type: Scholarship
Value: £4,000
Length of Study: 1 year
Frequency: Annual
Country of Study: Any country
Application Procedure: Any person wishing to be considered for this award should follow the application procedure for admission to the degree of Master of Science in Environmental Change and Management at Oxford University, nominating Colleges of preference as detailed in the application procedure. They must, additionally, complete a separate application form which will be made available to them once in receipt of a place on the MSc, and submit this to the College by the deadline (end of May each year).

For further information contact:

Tel: (44) 1865 276 520
Fax: (44) 1865 286 548

Goodger and Schorstein Research Scholarships in Medical Sciences

Eligibility: Open to postdoctoral researchers from any department/institute of the Medical Sciences Division. Applicants must have completed their DPhil (at any Higher Education Institution) at the time of application and are required to work primarily in units run by the University of Oxford
Type: Scholarship
Value: The scholarships are tenable for one academic year (Michaelmas Term 2022 to Trinity Term 2023) and the level of the award will be fixed at the discretion of the Divisional Funding Panel it is normally a contribution to living expenses.
Country of Study: Any country
Application Procedure: Please see the website for more details. Enquires may be sent by email to Aga. Bush@medsci.ox.ac.uk
Closing Date: 11 February

For further information contact:

Email: Aga.Bush@medsci.ox.ac.uk

Graduate Scholarship in Medieval and Modern Languages with Keble College

Purpose: To assist graduate students with fees, maintenance and accommodation
Eligibility: All eligible doctoral applicants submitting applications before the third gathered field will automatically be considered, irrespective of choice of college, provided that they have applied for other funded awards (if eligible)
Level of Study: Research
Type: Scholarship
Value: £10,145
Length of Study: 4 years
Country of Study: Any country
Closing Date: 3 March
Additional Information: www.ox.ac.uk/admissions/graduate/courses/dphil-medieval-and-modern-languages?wssl=1

For further information contact:

Tel: (44) 1865 270751
Email: graduate.studies@mod-langs.ox.ac.uk

Graduate Scholarship in Medieval and Modern Languages with Merton College

Purpose: To assist graduate students with fees and a living allowance
Eligibility: All eligible doctoral applicants submitting applications before the third gathered field will automatically be considered, irrespective of choice of college, provided that they have applied for other funded awards (if eligible)
Level of Study: Research
Type: Scholarship
Value: University fee at United Kingdom/European Union rate; allowance of £5,000 to assist with college fees and/or maintenance
Length of Study: Up to 3 years
Country of Study: Any country
Closing Date: 22 January

For further information contact:

Email: trish.long@keble.ox.ac.uk

Graduate Scholarship in Medieval and Modern Languages with Somerville College

Purpose: To assist graduate students with fees, maintenance and accommodation
Eligibility: All eligible doctoral applicants submitting applications before the third gathered field will automatically be considered, irrespective of choice of college, provided that they have applied for other funded awards (if eligible)
Level of Study: Research
Type: Scholarship
Value: University fee at United Kingdom/European Union rate; maintenance grant of £6,000. Additional benefits include some dining rights and guaranteed accommodation in 1st year
Length of Study: Up to 3 years
Country of Study: Any country
Closing Date: 22 January

For further information contact:

Email: trish.long@keble.ox.ac.uk

Green Moral Philosophy Scholarship

Subjects: Moral Philosophy
Eligibility: Open to all graduate applicants for DPhil courses in the Faculty of Philosophy. All applicants who receive a place on any graduate course automatically considered
Level of Study: Unrestricted
Type: Scholarship

Value: The value of the scholarship is to be determined by the Board of Graduate Admissions. The scholarship may not be offered on a yearly basis
Length of Study: 1 year
Country of Study: Any country

For further information contact:

Email: jane.sherwood@admin.ox.ac.uk

Green Templeton College: GTC-Medical Sciences Doctoral Training Centre Scholarship

Purpose: Green Templeton College is pleased to be able to offer a top-up award for overseas students who have been awarded a Studentship for study at the Medical Sciences Doctoral Training Centre beginning in October month
Eligibility: Open to all applicants to the Medical Sciences Doctoral Training Centre with Overseas fee status
Level of Study: Doctorate
Type: Scholarship
Value: £1,000
Length of Study: Up to 4 years
Country of Study: Any country
Closing Date: 11 January
Additional Information: Please visit the website: www.gtc. ox.ac.uk/admissions/scholarships-and-awards www.gtc.ox. ac.uk/students/how-to-apply/scholarships-bursaries/

For further information contact:

Email: enquiries@msdtc.ox.ac.uk

Green Templeton College: GTC-SBS DPhil Scholarship

Purpose: In conjunction with the Saïd Business School (SBS), Green Templeton College is able to offer a scholarship for a student beginning a DPhil Management or DPhil Finance in October 2023.
Eligibility: Open to all applicants to the DPhil in Management Studies
Level of Study: Doctorate, Graduate
Type: Scholarship
Value: Full fees and annual stipend at minimum Research Council UK rate (£15,609)
Length of Study: four years
Study Establishment: Green Templeton College
Country of Study: Any country
Closing Date: 10 January

Green Templeton College: Rosemary Stewart Scholarship

Eligibility: DPhil students with research interests in the area of health care organization and management
Level of Study: Doctorate
Type: Scholarship
Value: £6,000 per annum
Length of Study: Up to 3 years
Study Establishment: Green Templeton College
Country of Study: Any country
Application Procedure: Please see website for more details and how to apply
Closing Date: 1 May
Additional Information: Please visit the website: www.gtc. ox.ac.uk/admissions/scholarships-and-awards www.gtc.ox. ac.uk/students/how-to-apply/scholarships-bursaries/rosemary-stewart-scholarship/

For further information contact:

Tel: (44) 1865 274 770
Email: admissions@gtc.ox.ac.uk

Hertford - English Graduate Scholarship in Irish Literature

Eligibility: Open to Home/European Union students applying to undertake a DPhil in Irish Literature. Applicants are automatically considered for the scholarship by the English Faculty. Please visit the website for more details
Level of Study: Postgraduate
Type: Scholarship
Value: University fee, college fee and full living expenses
Length of Study: Period of fee liability
Frequency: Annual
Country of Study: United Kingdom
Application Procedure: For more information, please visit the website www.english.ox.ac.uk
Closing Date: 8 January
Funding: Trusts

For further information contact:

Email: college.office@hertford.ox.ac.uk

Hertford College Archaeology Award

Eligibility: Open to all graduate students pursuing the MSt in Archaeology. Please see the website for more details
Level of Study: Postgraduate
Type: Scholarship

Value: £10,000 towards course fees, college fees and living costs where appropriate
Length of Study: One year
Frequency: Annual
Study Establishment: Hertford
Country of Study: United Kingdom
Application Procedure: For more information, please check the website www.hertford.ox.ac.uk/discover-hertford/graduates/graduate-scholarships
Closing Date: 11 March
Funding: Trusts
Additional Information: www.hertford.ox.ac.uk/news/university-prizes-for-hertfordians

For further information contact:

Email: communications@hertford.ox.ac.uk

Hertford College Law Award

Eligibility: Open to all graduate students pursuing the BCL or Mjur. Please see the website for more details
Level of Study: Postgraduate
Type: Scholarship
Value: £10,000 towards course fees, college fees and living costs where appropriate
Length of Study: One year
Frequency: Annual
Study Establishment: Hertford
Country of Study: United Kingdom
Application Procedure: For more information, please check the website www.hertford.ox.ac.uk/discover-hertford/graduates/graduate-scholarships
Closing Date: 11 March
Funding: Trusts
Additional Information: www.hertford.ox.ac.uk/study-here/graduates/finance/senior-scholarships

For further information contact:

Email: graduate.admissions@hertford.ox.ac.uk

Hertford College Pharmacology Award

Eligibility: Open to all graduate students pursuing a DPhil in Pharmacology. Please see the website for more details, including how to apply
Level of Study: Postgraduate
Type: Scholarship
Value: £6,500 towards course fees, college fees and living costs where appropriate
Length of Study: Three years

Frequency: Annual
Study Establishment: Hertford
Country of Study: United Kingdom
Application Procedure: For more information, please visit the website www.pharm.ox.ac.uk/gso/dphil-in-pharmacology
Closing Date: 8 January
Funding: Trusts
Additional Information: www.hertford.ox.ac.uk/news/university-prizes-for-hertfordians

For further information contact:

Email: communications@hertford.ox.ac.uk

Hertford College Senior Scholarships

Eligibility: Restricted to students who are about to commence a new research degree course or those about to upgrade their current course
Level of Study: Postgraduate
Type: Scholarship
Value: £1,000 per year, plus priority for housing and some dining rights
Length of Study: 2 years
Frequency: Annual
Study Establishment: Hertford College, University of Oxford
Country of Study: United Kingdom
Application Procedure: Applicants must write to the College for further details
Additional Information: www.hertford.ox.ac.uk/study-here/graduates/finance/senior-scholarships

For further information contact:

Email: graduate.admissions@hertford.ox.ac.uk

Hertford College: Baring Senior Scholarship

Eligibility: Open to all graduate students pursuing research in any area of study
Level of Study: Postgraduate
Type: Scholarship
Value: £5,000 per year with certain associated dining rights
Length of Study: Two years
Frequency: Annual
Study Establishment: Hertford
Country of Study: United Kingdom
Application Procedure: For more information, please visit the website www.hertford.ox.ac.uk/discover-hertford/graduates/graduate-scholarships
Closing Date: 11 March

U

Funding: Trusts

Additional Information: www.hertford.ox.ac.uk/study-here/graduates/finance/senior-scholarships

For further information contact:

Email: graduate.admissions@hertford.ox.ac.uk

Hertford College: Vaughan Williams Senior Scholarship

Purpose: The Vaughan Williams Fund supports medical students with a £300 award per student towards stethoscopes and 'on the ward' textbooks

Eligibility: Open to all graduate students pursuing research in any area of study. Please see website for more details, including how to apply

Level of Study: Postgraduate

Type: Scholarship

Value: £5,000 per year with certain associated dining rights

Length of Study: Two years

Frequency: Annual

Study Establishment: Hertford

Country of Study: United Kingdom

Application Procedure: For more information, please visit www.hertford.ox.ac.uk/discover-hertford/graduates/graduate-scholarships

Closing Date: 11 March

Funding: Trusts

For further information contact:

Email: communications@hertford.ox.ac.uk

Hertford College: Worshipful Company of Scientific Instrument Makers Senior Scholarship

Eligibility: Open to DPhil applicants in all subjects. Please note applicants are expected to be involved in the design of instrumentation

Level of Study: Doctorate, Graduate

Type: Scholarship

Value: £4,000 per year with certain associated dining rights

Length of Study: 2 years

Country of Study: Any country

Application Procedure: Please see website for details of how to apply

Additional Information: Please check at www.hertford.ox.ac.uk/advertised-posts

For further information contact:

Email: college.office@hertford.ox.ac.uk

Hill Foundation Scholarships

Eligibility: applicants who are nationals of and ordinarily resident in the Russian Federation and who are applying to any full-time master's or DPhil course at Oxford. Applicants must also have a first degree from a Russian university. Preference will be given to applicants who have not previously been enrolled in any other degree programme outside of Russia. The trustees favour candidates who demonstrate extremely high academic ability and personal and social qualities of a high order. They seek applicants who intend to develop their careers in their homeland and who wish to spend their lives in ways that are beneficial to their home society, whether in business, academic life, public service, the arts or the professions. The selection panel will use the information that applicants provide in their graduate application form to assess how they meet these criteria. Applicants who are offered this scholarship will be required to confirm that they will return to Russia for at least one year following completion of their studies in the UK. Scholarships will be awarded on the basis of academic merit.

Type: Scholarship

Value: £15,609

Frequency: Annual

Country of Study: Any country

No. of awards offered: 15

Closing Date: January

Additional Information: www.ox.ac.uk/admissions/graduate/fees-and-funding/fees-funding-and-scholarship-search/scholarships-a-z-listing

For further information contact:

University of Oxford, University Offices, 15 Wellington Square, Oxford OX1 2JD, United Kingdom.

Tel: (44) 1865 270000
Fax: (44) 1865 270708

Hong Kong Jockey Club Graduate Scholarships

Purpose: To students who combine outstanding academic performance with a strong commitment to serving the community

Eligibility: Open to applicants who are ordinarily resident in Hong Kong and who are applying to a full-time master's or full-time DPhil course at Oxford. Please note that DPhil

courses with four years of fee liability are not eligible. Please see website for more details
Level of Study: Doctorate, Postgraduate
Type: Scholarship
Value: University fee, college fee, and full living expenses
Length of Study: Period of fee liability
Country of Study: Any country
Closing Date: January
Funding: Trusts
Additional Information: Please visit the website: www.ox. ac.uk/admissions/graduate/fees-and-funding/fees-funding-and-scholarship-search/scholarships-1#hkjc

For further information contact:

Email:	hkjcscholarships@hkjc.org.hk

International Development: QEH Scholarship

Eligibility: Open to all graduate applicants for MPhil in Development Studies with a preference for those from Sub-Saharan Africa. Please visit departmental website for more details
Level of Study: Predoctorate
Type: Scholarship
Value: University fee, college fee, and £13,000 towards living expenses
Length of Study: 21 months
Country of Study: Any country
Closing Date: 20 January
Additional Information: Please visit the website: www.qeh. ox.ac.uk/content/fees-funding

For further information contact:

Email:	jane.sherwood@admin.ox.ac.uk

Ioan and Rosemary James / Mathematical Institute Scholarship

Eligibility: Open to applicants for the DPhil in Mathematics, or CDT in Mathematical Institute only
Value: University fees (at either the Home/European Union or Overseas student rate as applicable), College fees and a maintenance stipend at the United Kingdom research council rate
Country of Study: Any country
Application Procedure: Duration of full-fee liability; 3 years for DPhil and 4 years for CDT. For non-CDT students, the Mathematical Institute will provide an additional 6 months of funding from its own funds for maintenance
Closing Date: January

Additional Information: For more details, please visit website www.sjc.ox.ac.uk www.sjc.ox.ac.uk/study/undergraduate/

For further information contact:

Email:	sarah.jones@sjc.ox.ac

James Fairfax - Oxford-Australia Fund Scholarships

Eligibility: Applicants should normally be under 30 on January 1st in the year in which the scholarship is to be taken up, and must have a bachelor's degree with first or upper second class honours or equivalent from a recognized university
Level of Study: Graduate, Postgraduate
Type: Scholarship
Value: University fees at the home and European Union rate, college fees and a living allowance of the order of AU$12,000 per year
Length of Study: Oxford-Australia Fund scholarships are for 2 years, or in the case of DPhil for 3 years, and James Fairfax scholarships are generally of 2 years duration
Frequency: Annual
Study Establishment: University of Oxford
Country of Study: United Kingdom
Application Procedure: Applicants must write for details or visit the website at www.admin.ox.edu.au/io
Closing Date: 21 February
Funding: Individuals, Private
Contributor: Australian scholars who have studied at Oxford and, in particular, Mr James Fairfax
Additional Information: rsc.anu.edu.au/~oxford/2017% 20JFOA%20Nov%2017.pdf

For further information contact:

Tel:	(61) 2 6125 3578/3761
Email:	jww@rsc.anu.edu.au

Jesus College: Joint Law Faculty-Jesus College BCL Scholarship

Eligibility: Open to all graduate applicants to the BCL (Bachelor of Civil Law). Please see website for further details
Level of Study: Graduate
Type: Scholarship
Value: £10,000
Length of Study: Period of fee liability
Frequency: Annual
Study Establishment: Jesus College
Country of Study: Any country

Closing Date: 20 January
Additional Information: Please visit the website: www.jesus.ox.ac.uk/current-students/scholarships-prizes-awards?field_subject_target_id=20&field_type_value=Graduate

For further information contact:

Email: lodge@jesus.ox.ac.uk

Joan Doll Scholarship

Subjects: MSc Environmental Change & Management only.
Purpose: This scholarship is awarded following nomination by the department. Early applications for the MSc Environmental Change & Management programme are strongly encouraged, and you are advised to make Green Templeton your preferred college on your application form, although this is not essential
Level of Study: Masters Degree
Type: Scholarship
Value: £1,500
Length of Study: one year
Frequency: Annual
Country of Study: Any country
Closing Date: 21 January
Funding: Private, University of Sheffield

Kalisher Trust-Wadham Student Scholarship

Subjects: MSc Criminology and Criminal Justice
Purpose: The scholarships are intended to encourage and assist those intending to practise at the Criminal Bar who demonstrate 'exceptional promise but modest means'
Eligibility: Applications are invited from United Kingdom residents who can demonstrate 1. Intellectual ability – demonstrated by academic performance, past work, activities and other experience. 2. Motivation to succeed at the Criminal Bar – including steps taken to acquire the personal skills required of a Barrister, and a demonstration of the will to succeed. 3. Potential as an advocate – both in oral and written skills. 4. Personal qualities – including self-reliance, independence, integrity, reliability and humanity. 5. Financial need - candidates will be asked to supply to the interview panel, in confidence, information demonstrating financial need
Level of Study: Graduate
Type: Scholarship
Value: £6,000
Frequency: Annual
Country of Study: Any country

Application Procedure: In particularly to discuss their motivation to succeed at the Criminal Bar. This statement should be no more than 800 words
Closing Date: 27 November
Funding: Private
Additional Information: www.law.ox.ac.uk/sites/files/oxlaw/kalisher_trust_scholarship.pdf

For further information contact:

The Faculty of Law, University of Oxford, St Cross Building, St Cross Road, Oxford OX1 3UL, United Kingdom.

Email: tracy.kaye@crim.ox.ac.uk

Keble College Gosden Water-Newton Scholarship

Eligibility: Open to students intending to seek ordination in a church in communion with the Church of England. Candidates must be either ordained or be able to show clear evidence of desire for ordination in the Church of England or a church in communion therewith, and be already at or intending to be registered for a postgraduate degree at Keble College, University of Oxford
Level of Study: Postgraduate
Type: Scholarship
Value: £10,000
Length of Study: Up to 3 years
Frequency: Dependent on funds available
Study Establishment: Keble College, University of Oxford
Country of Study: United Kingdom
Application Procedure: Applicants must contact the Deputy Academic Administrator at Keble College in the first instance
No. of awards offered: 4
Closing Date: 21 January
No. of awards given last year: 2
No. of applicants last year: 4
Additional Information: www.keble.ox.ac.uk/admissions/graduates/scholarships/

For further information contact:

Keble College, Oxford OX1 3PG, United Kingdom.

Email: college.office@keble.ox.ac.uk

Keble College Gwynne-Jones Scholarship

Eligibility: This award is only for study at Keble College
Level of Study: Postgraduate
Type: Scholarship
Value: £11,548

Length of Study: Up to 3 years
Frequency: Varies
Study Establishment: Keble College, University of Oxford
Country of Study: United Kingdom
Application Procedure: Applicants must write for details
Closing Date: 21 January
Funding: Private
Additional Information: www.keble.ox.ac.uk/admissions/graduates/scholarships/

For further information contact:

Email: college.office@keble.ox.ac.uk

Keble College Ian Palmer Graduate Scholarship in Information Technology

Eligibility: Applicants must write for details
Level of Study: Postgraduate
Type: Scholarship
Value: £3,130
Length of Study: Up to 3 years
Frequency: Dependent on funds available
Study Establishment: Keble College, University of Oxford
Country of Study: United Kingdom
Application Procedure: Applicants must write for details
Closing Date: 21 January
Funding: Private
Additional Information: www.keble.ox.ac.uk/admissions/graduates/scholarships/

For further information contact:

Email: college.office@keble.ox.ac.uk

Keble College Ian Tucker Memorial Bursary

Eligibility: Candidates must demonstrate sporting prowess principally in the field of rugby football, together with qualities that will make a contribution to both the College and University
Level of Study: Graduate
Type: Bursary
Value: £6,000
Length of Study: 1 year
Frequency: Annual
Study Establishment: Keble College, University of Oxford
Country of Study: United Kingdom
Application Procedure: Applicants must contact the Tutor for Graduates at Keble College for an application form
No. of awards offered: 6
Closing Date: 21 January

No. of awards given last year: 2
No. of applicants last year: 6
Additional Information: www.keble.ox.ac.uk/admissions/graduates/scholarships/

For further information contact:

Email: college.office@keble.ox.ac.uk

Keble College Keble Association Open Graduate Scholarship

Eligibility: Open to research students and 2nd BM applicants
Level of Study: Postgraduate, Research
Type: Scholarship
Value: £2,000
Length of Study: Up to 3 years
Frequency: Annual
Study Establishment: Keble College, University of Oxford
Country of Study: United Kingdom
Application Procedure: Applicants must write to request an application form
No. of awards offered: 19
Closing Date: May
Funding: Private
No. of awards given last year: 2
No. of applicants last year: 19

Keble College Paul Hayes Graduate Scholarship

Eligibility: Candidates must demonstrate sporting excellence
Level of Study: Doctorate, Graduate
Type: Scholarship
Value: Up to the value of college fees
Length of Study: Up to 3 years
Study Establishment: Keble College, the University of Oxford
Country of Study: United Kingdom
Application Procedure: Applicants must contact the Deputy Academic Administrator at Keble College
Closing Date: May

Keble College Water Newton Scholarship

Eligibility: Open to students intending to seek ordination in a church in communication with the Church of United Kingdom
Level of Study: Postdoctorate, Research
Type: Scholarship
Value: £10,000

Length of Study: Up to 3 years
Frequency: Dependent on funds available
Study Establishment: Keble College, University of Oxford
Country of Study: United Kingdom
Application Procedure: Applicants must contact the Deputy Academic Administrator
Closing Date: 21 January
Funding: Private
Additional Information: www.keble.ox.ac.uk/admissions/graduates/scholarships/

For further information contact:

Email: college.office@keble.ox.ac.uk

Keble College: Delia Bushell Graduate Scholarship

Eligibility: Open to graduate applicants to study for a postgraduate degree in the History Faculty in the University of Oxford, or be presently registered for a postgraduate degree in the History Faculty in the University of Oxford
Level of Study: Postgraduate
Type: Scholarship
Value: Up to £6,250 per year towards living expenses
Length of Study: 1 year
Study Establishment: Keble College
Country of Study: Any country
Application Procedure: Please see website for more details, including how to apply
Closing Date: 24 January
Additional Information: Please visit the website: www.keble.ox.ac.uk/admissions/graduate/graduate-scholarships www.keble.ox.ac.uk/admissions/graduates/scholarships/

For further information contact:

Email: college.office@keble.ox.ac.uk

Keble College: James Martin Graduate Scholarship

Subjects: MSc in MPLS (mathematical, physical and life sciences), Medical Sciences or Environmental Science
Eligibility: Open to Home/European Union students, who can demonstrate that they are in financial need. Applicants must be intending to study for a MSc in the MPLS (Mathematical, Physical and Life Sciences) Division, Medical Sciences Division or Geography and the Environment department
Level of Study: Postgraduate
Type: Scholarship
Value: £9,000, for one year only
Length of Study: 1 year

Study Establishment: Keble College
Country of Study: Any country
Application Procedure: Please see website for further details, including how to apply
Closing Date: 21 January
Additional Information: Please visit the website: www.keble.ox.ac.uk/admissions/graduate/graduate-scholarships

For further information contact:

Email: college.office@keble.ox.ac.uk

Kellogg College: Bigg Scholarship in African Climate Science

Purpose: Keble seeks to award a scholarship for doctoral research into African climate science.
Level of Study: Masters Degree
Type: Scholarship
Value: £10,000
Frequency: Annual
Country of Study: Any country
Application Procedure: The scholarship can only be held at Keble College and potential applicants should apply to Keble and complete a short application form here: www.keble.ox.ac.uk/admissions/graduates/scholarships/
Closing Date: 21 January

For further information contact:

Email: Richard.washington@keble.ox.ac.uk

Kellogg College: Naji DPhil Scholarship in the Public Understanding of Evidence-Based Medicine

Eligibility: Open to applicants for the DPhil in Primary Health Care whose research directly addresses public understanding of evidence for health claims
Level of Study: Doctorate
Type: Scholarship
Value: University fee, college fee, and full living expenses
Length of Study: Period of fee liability
Study Establishment: Kellogg College
Country of Study: Any country
Application Procedure: Please see website for more details, including how to apply
Closing Date: 6 January
Additional Information: Please visit the website: www.kellogg.ox.ac.uk/study/scholarships-2017/naji-dphil-scholarship-in-the-public-understanding-of-evidence-based-medicine/

For further information contact:

Tel: (44) 1865 612 000

Kellogg College: Oxford-McCall MacBain Graduate Scholarship

Purpose: The scholarship is only tenable at Kellogg College. All eligible applicants will be considered for the scholarship
Eligibility: All eligible applicants will be considered for the scholarship, regardless of which college (if any) you state as your preference on the graduate application form. However, successful applicants will be transferred to Kellogg College in order to take up the scholarship
Level of Study: Graduate
Type: Scholarship
Value: The scholarship covers course fees and provides a study support grant
Frequency: Annual
Country of Study: Any country
Closing Date: 1 March
Funding: Private
Additional Information: Initially the MMF operated on a regional-based approach, with a strategy to develop and encourage best practices and policies in multiple areas related to improving the human condition scholarscareers.com/2019/02/16/oxford-mccall-macbain-graduate-scholarship/

For further information contact:

Kellogg College, 60-62 Banbury Road, Oxford OX2 6PN, United Kingdom.

Email: enquiries@kellogg.ox.ac.uk

Lady Margaret Hall Talbot Research Fellowship

Purpose: To provide an opportunity for academic postdoctoral research
Eligibility: Open to qualified persons who hold or will have obtained a postdoctoral or equivalent degree by the start of tenure
Level of Study: Postgraduate
Type: Fellowship
Value: Please contact the college for details
Length of Study: 3 years, not renewable
Frequency: Every 3 years
Study Establishment: Lady Margaret Hall, the University of Oxford
Country of Study: United Kingdom

For further information contact:

Lady Margaret Hall Norham Gardens, Oxford OX2 6QA, United Kingdom.

Tel: (44) 1865 274 300
Fax: (44) 1865 511 069
Email: college.office@lmh.ox.ac.uk

Lady Margaret Hall: Ann Kennedy Graduate Scholarship in Law

Eligibility: Open to graduate applicants for the BCL, MJur, MSt in Legal Research or MPhil in Law at Lady Margaret Hall. The award will be made on the basis of academic excellence
Level of Study: Graduate, Postgraduate, Predoctorate
Type: Scholarship
Value: The award covers college fees and a contribution to the university fees. It is awarded for one year for an amount of up to £14,000. It is not intended to contribute to living expenses
Length of Study: 1 year
Study Establishment: Lady Margaret Hall
Country of Study: Any country
Closing Date: 20 January
Additional Information: Please visit the website: www.law.ox.ac.uk/admissions/scholarships-index/college-awards-specific-law-postgraduates-index

For further information contact:

Email: enquiries@lmh.ox.ac.uk

Lady Margaret Hall: Gavin Cameron Graduate Scholarship in Economics

Level of Study: Graduate
Type: Scholarship
Value: Free accommodation in new Graduate accommodation
Length of Study: Three years
Study Establishment: Lady Margaret Hall
Country of Study: Any country
Application Procedure: Open to all graduate applicants in Economics with a preference for, but not restricted to, applicants who put LMH as their first choice College
Closing Date: January
Additional Information: Please visit the website: www.lmh.ox.ac.uk/prospective-students/Graduates/Scholarship-opportunities.aspx

U

www.lmh.ox.ac.uk/sites/default/files/documents/2017-07/LMH_DF_FPs%202017_0.pdf

For further information contact:

Email: stassistant@lmh.ox.ac.uk

Lady Margaret Hall: Open Residential Scholarships

Eligibility: Open to all graduate applicants with a preference for, but not restricted to, applicants who put LMH as their first choice college. Please see website for details of how to apply
Level of Study: Postgraduate
Type: Scholarship
Value: £5,000 plus additional benefits including an option on accommodation and limited dining rights
Length of Study: 1 year
Frequency: Annual
Study Establishment: Lady Margaret Hall
Country of Study: Any country
Closing Date: January
Additional Information: Please check the website: www.lmh.ox.ac.uk

For further information contact:

Email: graduate.admissions@lmh.ox.ac.uk

Latin American Centre-Latin American Centre Scholarship

Eligibility: Open to all graduate applicants to the MSc in Latin American Studies from one of the CAF shareholder countries. Applicants must send an email to the Admissions Secretary requesting to be considered
Level of Study: Postgraduate
Type: Scholarship
Value: University and college fees (not living expenses)
Length of Study: 1 year (Non-renewable)
Country of Study: Any country
Application Procedure: Please visit website for more details and how to apply
Closing Date: 10 March
Additional Information: For more information, please check the websites: www.lac.ox.ac.uk/funding www.educationprogram.scholarshipcare.com/lac-caf-scholarships/

For further information contact:

Email: laclib@bodleian.ox.ac.uk

Law Faculty: David and Helen Elvin Scholarship

Eligibility: Open to all graduate applicants for the BCL and MJur. Award holders will become members of Hertford College. Please see website for more information
Level of Study: Graduate, Postgraduate
Type: Scholarship
Value: £10,000 towards course fees, college fees and living costs where appropriate
Length of Study: 1 year
Study Establishment: Hertford College
Country of Study: Any country
Closing Date: 20 January
Additional Information: Please visit the website: www.law.ox.ac.uk/postgraduate/scholarships.php

For further information contact:

Email: lawfac@law.ox.ac.uk

Law Faculty: Des Voeux Chambers

Eligibility: Open to all graduate applicants to the BCL. Preference may be shown for candidates with an interest in pursuing a career at the Hong Kong Bar. Please see website for more information
Level of Study: Postgraduate
Type: Scholarship
Value: £10,000
Length of Study: 1 year
Frequency: Annual
Country of Study: United Kingdom
Closing Date: 20 January
Funding: Trusts
Additional Information: Please check the website: www.law.ox.ac.uk/postgraduate/scholarships.php

For further information contact:

Email: pupillage@dvc.com.hk

Law Faculty: James Bullock Scholarship

Purpose: The James Bullock Scholarship was established by the Oxford Law Faculty in memory of James Bullock, partner in Pinsent Masons, who died before his time in 2015 and who did so much to support tax teaching and research in Oxford.
Eligibility: Open to all applicants for the MSc in Taxation
Level of Study: Postgraduate
Type: Scholarship
Value: £2,500 per year
Length of Study: 2 years

Country of Study: Any country

Closing Date: 10 March

Additional Information: Please visit the website: www.law. ox.ac.uk/postgraduate/scholarships.php www.law.ox.ac.uk/ content/james-bullock-scholarship

For further information contact:

Email: lawfac@law.ox.ac.uk

Law Faculty: The Peter Birks Memorial Scholarship

Purpose: To assist graduate students with fees

Eligibility: Open to all graduate applicants to BCL/MJur, MSc in Law and Finance, MSt Legal Research, MPhil Or DPhil Law. Please see website for further information

Level of Study: Graduate, Postgraduate

Type: Scholarship

Value: £7,500 per year

Length of Study: 1 year

Frequency: Annual

Country of Study: Any country

Closing Date: 20 January

Additional Information: Please check the website: www. law.ox.ac.uk/postgraduate/scholarships.php www.law.ox.ac. uk/admissions/scholarships-index/law-faculty-awards-study- any-college-index/peter-birks-memorial

For further information contact:

Email: lawfac@law.ox.ac.uk

Linacre College: Applied Materials MSc Scholarship

Purpose: To assist graduate students with fees and a living allowance

Eligibility: Open to all

Level of Study: Postgraduate

Type: Scholarship

Length of Study: 1 year

For further information contact:

School of Geography and the Environment, University of Oxford, South Parks Road, Oxford OX1 3QY, United Kingdom.

Tel: (44) 1865 285 070

Email: enquiries@ouce.ox.ac.uk

Linacre College: David Daube Scholarship

Purpose: The David Daube Law Scholarship is available to a student reading or intending to read for a DPhil in law, and who is liable to pay fees

Eligibility: Open to all graduate applicants for the BCL and MJur

Level of Study: Postgraduate

Type: Scholarship

Value: College fee

Length of Study: Period of fee liability

Country of Study: Any country

Closing Date: 12 March

Additional Information: Applicants should first secure a place on the Oxford BCL or MJur course and mark Linacre College as their chosen College. Please check at www.linacre. ox.ac.uk/Admissions/Scholarships

For further information contact:

Email: ben.nicholson@admin.ox.ac.uk

Linacre College: EPA Cephalosporin Scholarship

Subjects: Biological, medical & chemical sciences.

Purpose: To assist graduate students with fees

Eligibility: Open to all graduate students

Level of Study: Postgraduate, Research, Unrestricted

Type: Scholarship

Value: Full course fees and a stipend for living expenses

Length of Study: 3 years

Country of Study: Any country

Application Procedure: Eligible students are automatically considered for this award.

No. of awards offered: 2

Additional Information: www.linacre.ox.ac.uk/prospective- students/scholarships/epa-cephalosporin-scholarship

For further information contact:

Sir William Dunn School of Pathology.

Email: scholarships@linacre.ox.ac.uk

Linacre College: Hicks Scholarship

Purpose: With the initial support of several Old Members, a fund is being established to provide a College fee scholar- ship to a Linacre student studying for a degree in Economics

Eligibility: Open to students reading, or intending to read for a DPhil in Economics who are liable to pay fees

Level of Study: Doctorate, Postgraduate

Type: Scholarship
Value: £80,000. 1st 3 years scholarship paid out = £6,486
Length of Study: Period of fee liability
Study Establishment: Linacre College
Country of Study: Any country
Closing Date: 21 April
Funding: Private
Additional Information: Please visit the website: www.lina cre.ox.ac.uk/prospective-students/scholarships www.linacre. ox.ac.uk/prospective-students/scholarships/hicks-scholarship-economics

For further information contact:

Linacre College, St. Cross Road, Oxford OX1 3JA, United Kingdom.

Tel: (44) 1865 271 650
Email: development@linacre.ox.ac.uk

Linacre College: Hitachi Chemical Europe Scholarship

Eligibility: Preference given to applicant from China or Central/South America
Level of Study: Postgraduate
Type: Scholarship
Value: £9,000 and lasts one year
Length of Study: 1 year
Application Procedure: Eligible candidates are automatically considered for this scholarship
No. of awards offered: 1
Closing Date: 24 January
Additional Information: Please check at www.linacre.ox. ac.uk/extras/scholarships www.linacre.ox.ac.uk/prospective-students/scholarships/hitachi-chemical-environmental-schol arship

For further information contact:

Oxford University Centre for the Environment, Environmental Change Institute, South Parks Road, Oxford OX1 3QY, United Kingdom.

Email: thomas.thornton@ouce.ox.ac.uk

Linacre College: John Bamborough MSc Scholarship

Eligibility: Open to all graduate applicants for MSc courses in the Humanities division
Level of Study: Postgraduate

Type: Scholarship
Value: 100% university and college fees. £3,205
Length of Study: One year
Study Establishment: Linacre College
Country of Study: Any country
Application Procedure: Please see website for more details, including how to apply
Closing Date: 19 April
Additional Information: Please visit the website: www.lina cre.ox.ac.uk/prospective-students/scholarships scholarship-positions.com/john-bamborough-msc-scholarships-humanities-linacre-college-uk/2018/04/10/

For further information contact:

Email: scholarships@linacre.ox.ac.uk

Linacre College: Linacre Rausing Scholarship (English)

Level of Study: Research
Type: Scholarship
Value: £3,300
Length of Study: Up to 3 years
Country of Study: Any country
Application Procedure: Eligible candidates are automatically considered for this scholarship
No. of awards offered: 1
Additional Information: www.linacre.ox.ac.uk/prospective-students/scholarships/rausing-scholarship-english

For further information contact:

Email: english.office@ell.ox.ac.uk

Linacre College: Mary Blaschko Graduate Scholarship

Purpose: To enable European students to carry out research for 1 year in the department of pharmacology or the MRC anatomical neuropharmacology unit
Eligibility: Open to all graduate applicants for research degrees in the Humanities division
Level of Study: Postgraduate, Research
Type: Scholarship
Value: £3,300
Length of Study: Period of fee liability
Study Establishment: Linacre College
Country of Study: Any country
Application Procedure: Please see website for more details, including how to apply
No. of awards offered: 2

Additional Information: Please visit the website: www.lina cre.ox.ac.uk/prospective-students/scholarships www.linacre. ox.ac.uk/prospective-students/scholarships/mary-blaschko-scholarship

For further information contact:

Email: scholarships@linacre.ox.ac.uk

Linacre College: Rausing Scholarship in Anthropology

Eligibility: Open to all graduate applicants in Anthropology
Level of Study: Research
Type: Scholarship
Value: College fee plus £2,000 towards living expenses
Length of Study: Period of fee liability
Country of Study: Any country
Application Procedure: There is no application form. Applications should consist of a detailed doctoral proposal of 3–4 pages, a curriculum vitae and two letters of reference, one of which should be provided by the student's current or prospective supervisor for the doctorate. Applications should be sent to the Director of Graduate Studies. Please see website for details of how to apply
Additional Information: Please check at www.linacre. ox.ac.uk/Admissions/Scholarships www.linacre.ox.ac.uk/ prospective-students/scholarships/rausing-scholarship-anthro pology

For further information contact:

Email: ben.nicholson@admin.ox.ac.uk

Linacre College: Rausing Scholarship in English

Eligibility: Open to all graduate applicants for any course in the English Faculty
Level of Study: Doctorate
Type: Scholarship
Value: £3,500
Length of Study: three years
Study Establishment: Linacre College
Country of Study: Any country
Application Procedure: Eligible students are automatically considered for this award.
Additional Information: Please visit the website: www.lina cre.ox.ac.uk/scholarships/rausing-scholarship-anthropology

For further information contact:

Email: support@linacre.ox.ac.uk

Linacre College: Raymond and Vera Asquith Scholarship

Eligibility: Open to suitably qualified students who were born in the United Kingdom, reading or intending to read for a DPhil in Humanities who are liable to pay fees and have AHRC funding
Level of Study: Doctorate, Postgraduate
Type: Scholarship
Value: College fee
Length of Study: Period of fee liability
Country of Study: Any country
Application Procedure: Please see website for details of how to apply
Additional Information: Please check at www.linacre.ox.ac. uk/Admissions/Scholarships www.linacre.ox.ac.uk/raymond-vera-asquith

For further information contact:

Email: ben.nicholson@admin.ox.ac.uk

Linacre College: Ronald and Jane Olson Scholarship

Eligibility: Open to all graduate applicants for the MSc in Refugee and Forced Migration Studies
Level of Study: Postgraduate
Type: Scholarship
Value: College fee, plus a maintenance grant of £2,500
Length of Study: 1 year
Study Establishment: Linacre College
Country of Study: Any country
Application Procedure: Eligible students are automatically considered for this award.
Closing Date: 20 January
Additional Information: Please visit the website: www.lina cre.ox.ac.uk/prospective-students/scholarships www.linacre. ox.ac.uk/prospective-students/scholarships/ronald-and-jane-olson-scholarship-refugee-studies

For further information contact:

Email: rsc-msc@qeh.ox.ac.uk

Linacre College: Women in Science Scholarship

Eligibility: Open to all graduate applicants for the DPhil in Materials who are liable to pay fees
Level of Study: Doctorate
Type: Scholarship
Value: College fee

Length of Study: Period of fee liability
Study Establishment: Linacre College
Country of Study: Any country
Closing Date: 21 April
Additional Information: Please visit the website: www.lina cre.ox.ac.uk/prospective-students/scholarships www.linacre. ox.ac.uk/alumni-friends/funds-campaigns/50th-anniversary-campaign/women-science-scholarship-fund

For further information contact:

Email: support@linacre.ox.ac.uk

Lincoln College: Berrow Foundation Lord Florey Scholarships

Eligibility: Open to all graduate applicants for courses in Medical, Chemical or Biochemical Sciences of Swiss or Lichtenstein nationality who are students at, or have recently graduated from, any Swiss university, including ETHZ and EPFL, and who must not be more than five years beyond graduation from their first degree at one of these institutions (except for candidates in medicine, for whom the five years limit dates from obtaining the Federal Diploma in Medicine). Up to two awards available. Please see website for full details and application form
Level of Study: Postgraduate, Research
Type: Scholarship
Value: £15,900 per annum
Length of Study: Up to 3 years
Frequency: Annual
Study Establishment: Lincoln
Country of Study: Any country
Application Procedure: Please see website for details of how to apply
Closing Date: 24 January
Funding: Foundation
Additional Information: Please check the website: www. lincoln.ox.ac.uk/funding-and-awards-for-graduates www.lin coln.ox.ac.uk/berrow-foundation-scholarships-_for-swis

For further information contact:

Email: rectors.office@lincoln.ox.ac.uk.

Lincoln College: Berrow Foundation Scholarships

Eligibility: Open to all graduate applicants of Swiss or Lichtenstein nationality who are students at, or have recently graduated from, selected Swiss universities. Up to four awards available. Please see website for full details and application form

Level of Study: Postgraduate, Research
Type: Scholarship
Value: University fee (at the United Kingdom level), college fee, and living expenses equivalent to Rhodes Scholarship stipend
Length of Study: Up to 3 years
Frequency: Annual
Study Establishment: Lincoln
Country of Study: Any country
Closing Date: 24 January
Funding: Foundation
Additional Information: Please check the website: www. lincoln.ox.ac.uk/funding-and-awards-for-graduates www.lin coln.ox.ac.uk/berrow-foundation-scholarships-_for-swis

For further information contact:

Email: rectors.office@lincoln.ox.ac.uk.

Lincoln College: Crewe Graduate Scholarships

Eligibility: Students, in any subject, ordinarily resident in the Dioceses of Durham and Newcastle; Northallertonshire (in North Yorkshire); Howdenshire (in Humberside); Leicestershire; Northamptonshire; and the Diocese of Oxford. Applicants must hold an offer of a place to read for a graduate degree course at an Oxford college before applying. Successful applicants holding an offer of a place at another College will be required to migrate to Lincoln College in order to take up the award.
Level of Study: Graduate, MBA, Postgraduate
Type: Scholarship
Value: £7,000
Length of Study: One year, with the possibility of renewal on applying
Frequency: Annual
Study Establishment: Lincoln College, University of Oxford
Country of Study: United Kingdom
Application Procedure: A combined application form is available www.lincoln.ox.ac.uk/uploads/files/Scholarship% 20application%20form%202020.docx.
Closing Date: 6 June
Funding: Trusts
No. of awards given last year: 6
Additional Information: www.lincoln.ox.ac.uk/funding-and-awards-for-graduates#Crewe%20GA

For further information contact:

Email: admissions@lincoln.ox.ac.uk

Lincoln College: Hartley Bursary

Eligibility: New or current graduate students of Lincoln College, ordinarily resident in the UK, who are studying for a degree in any humanities subject and who are in financial need
Level of Study: Graduate
Type: Scholarship
Value: £1,200
Length of Study: 1 years
Study Establishment: Lincoln College
Country of Study: Any country
Application Procedure: A combined application form is available www.lincoln.ox.ac.uk/uploads/files/Scholarship%20application%20form%202020.docx.
No. of awards offered: 1
Closing Date: 6 June
Additional Information: Please visit the website: www.lincoln.ox.ac.uk/funding-and-awards-for-graduates www.lincoln.ox.ac.uk/funding-and-awards-for-graduates#Hart

For further information contact:

Email: admissions@lincoln.ox.ac.uk

Lincoln College: Jermyn Brooks Graduate Award

Eligibility: Open to graduate students of the college (other new or continuing) who are studying in the humanities, with a preference for modern languages
Level of Study: Postgraduate
Type: Scholarship
Value: £1,000
Length of Study: One year
Frequency: Annual
Study Establishment: Lincoln College, University of Oxford
Country of Study: United Kingdom
Application Procedure: Application form available from Admissions Office at Lincoln College
Closing Date: August
Funding: Private
Additional Information: www.scholarshipslab.com/lincoln-college-university-of-oxford-the-jermyn-brooks-graduate-award-in-uk-2019/

For further information contact:

The Admissions Office Lincoln College.

Email: info@lincoln.ox.ac.uk

Lincoln College: Kenneth Seward-Shaw Scholarship

Eligibility: Candidates must be graduate students in the area of Law, History, English, or Politics. They should have attained a high standard in their previous academic work. The candidate who is selected for this award will be expected to give a presentation on their work to members of the Middle and Senior Common Room at a joint seminar during their first year at Lincoln. There will be a reward of an additional £500 for doing so.
Level of Study: Postgraduate
Type: Scholarship
Value: £1,500 (+£500)
Length of Study: 1 year
Frequency: Annual
Study Establishment: Lincoln College, University of Oxford
Country of Study: United Kingdom
Application Procedure: A combined application form is available www.lincoln.ox.ac.uk/uploads/files/Scholarship%20application%20form%202020.docx.
Closing Date: 6 June
Funding: Private
Additional Information: www.lincoln.ox.ac.uk/funding-and-awards-for-graduates#Shaw

For further information contact:

Email: admissions@lincoln.ox.ac.uk

Lincoln College: Lord Crewe Graduate Scholarship in Medical Sciences (Clarendon-Linked)

Eligibility: Students, in any subject, ordinarily resident in the Dioceses of Durham and Newcastle; Northallertonshire (in North Yorkshire); Howdenshire (in Humberside); Leicestershire; Northamptonshire; and the Diocese of Oxford. Applicants must hold an offer of a place to read for a graduate degree course at an Oxford college before applying. Successful applicants holding an offer of a place at another College will be required to migrate to Lincoln College in order to take up the award.
Level of Study: Postgraduate, Research
Type: Scholarship
Value: £7,000
Length of Study: 1 year
Country of Study: Any country
Application Procedure: A combined application form is available www.lincoln.ox.ac.uk/uploads/files/Scholarship%20application%20form%202020.docx.
No. of awards offered: 2

U

Closing Date: 6 June
Additional Information: www.lincoln.ox.ac.uk/funding-and-awards-for-graduates#Crewe

For further information contact:

Email: admissions@lincoln.ox.ac.uk

Lincoln College: Lord Crewe Graduate Scholarship in Social Sciences (Clarendon-Linked)

Eligibility: Applicants must nominate Lincoln as their College of Preference and be considered for a Clarendon Fund Scholarship
Level of Study: Postgraduate, Research
Type: Scholarship
Value: All university and college fees and a generous living allowance (Clarendon-linked)
Length of Study: Period of Fee liability
Frequency: Annual
Country of Study: Any country
Closing Date: 20 January
Additional Information: Please check at www.clarendon.ox.ac.uk/partnership/ www.lincoln.ox.ac.uk/funding-and-awards-for-graduates#Crewe

For further information contact:

Email: info@lincoln.ox.ac.uk

Lincoln College: Lord Crewe Graduate Scholarships in the Humanities

Eligibility: Open to graduates of any United Kingdom university for all courses within the Humanities
Level of Study: Postgraduate, Research
Type: Scholarship
Value: £18,000 per year
Length of Study: Period of fee liability
Country of Study: Any country
Application Procedure: Please see website for details of how to apply
Closing Date: 18 January
Additional Information: Please check at www.lincoln.ox.ac.uk/

For further information contact:

Email: info@lincoln.ox.ac.uk

Lincoln College: Lord Crewe Graduate Scholarships in the Social Sciences

Eligibility: Open to graduates of any United Kingdom university for all courses within the Social Sciences
Level of Study: Postgraduate, Research
Type: Scholarship
Value: £18,000 per year
Length of Study: Period of fee liability
Country of Study: Any country
Application Procedure: Please see website for details of how to apply
Closing Date: 18 January
Additional Information: Please check at www.lincoln.ox.ac.uk/

For further information contact:

Email: info@lincoln.ox.ac.uk

Lincoln College: Menasseh Ben Israel Room

Eligibility: Open to all graduate applicants who have graduated from an Israeli university. Preference will be shown to graduates of the Hebrew University, Jerusalem. Applicants must hold a place, or an offer of a place, at Lincoln College before making an application. Please see website for full details and application form
Level of Study: Graduate, Postgraduate
Type: Scholarship
Value: Free accommodation for one academic year (37 weeks) as occupant of the Menasseh Ben Israel Room in college
Length of Study: 1 year
Country of Study: Any country
Application Procedure: Please see website for full details and application form
Closing Date: 1 June
Additional Information: Please check at lincoln.ox.ac.uk/study-here/graduate-study/finance-and-funding

For further information contact:

Email: info@lincoln.ox.ac.uk

Lincoln College: Overseas Graduate Entrance Scholarship

Eligibility: All non-European Union nationals
Type: Scholarship
Value: £2,300
Length of Study: 1 year

Country of Study: Any country
Closing Date: 1 June
Additional Information: Successful candidates will show evidence of both academic merit and financial need. Applicants must hold a place, or an offer of a place, at Lincoln College before applying. Eligible to the nationals of Overseas testbig.com/article_items/menasseh-ben-israel-room-scholarship-israeli-students-lincoln-college-uk-2013

For further information contact:

Email: info@lincoln.ox.ac.uk

Lincoln College: Polonsky Foundation Grants

Eligibility: Open to all overseas graduate applicants who show evidence of financial need, academic merit and potential for good college citizenship
Type: Grant
Value: Approx. £5,300 per year
Length of Study: Up to 3 years
Study Establishment: Lincoln
Country of Study: Any country
Application Procedure: Applicants must hold a place, or an offer of a place, at Lincoln College before making an application. Please see website for full details and application form
Closing Date: 3 June
Additional Information: Candidates may be new or current students and must be citizens of countries not in the European Union. Please check the website: www.lincoln.ox.ac.uk/funding-and-awards-for-graduates   www.scholarshipsads.com/polonsky-foundation-scholarships-international-graduate-students-lincoln-college-uk/

For further information contact:

Email: info@lincoln.ox.ac.uk

Lincoln College: Sloane Robinson Foundation Graduate Awards

Purpose: To fund those intending to pursue research programmes at Oxford
Eligibility: Any DPhil candidates in the Social Sciences
Level of Study: Graduate, MBA, Postgraduate, Research
Type: Award
Value: Fees and Stipend
Length of Study: 3 to 4 years
Frequency: Annual
Study Establishment: Lincoln College, University of Oxford
Country of Study: United Kingdom

Application Procedure: There is no application form for these awards. All eligible candidates are considered by the Departmental Scholarship panels
No. of awards offered: 1
Closing Date: 1 June
Funding: Foundation
Additional Information: Successful candidates will show evidence of both academic merit and financial need. Applicants must hold a place, or an offer of a place, at Lincoln College before applying www.lincoln.ox.ac.uk/funding-and-awards-for-graduates

For further information contact:

Email: info@lincoln.ox.ac.uk

Lincoln College: Supperstone Law Scholarship

Eligibility: Open to candidates reading for the BCL or the MJuris, with an emphasis or special interest in European or public law. Applicants must have an offer of a college place at Lincoln College
Level of Study: Postgraduate
Type: Scholarship
Value: £650
Length of Study: 1 year
Frequency: Annual
Study Establishment: Lincoln College, University of Oxford
Country of Study: United Kingdom
Application Procedure: Applicants must contact the Admissions Office at Lincoln College
Funding: Trusts

Lingyin Graduate Scholarship in Buddhist Studies

Purpose: Oriental Studies
Eligibility: Open to current and incoming Master's or DPhil students whose study or research focuses on Buddhist Studies (including all areas, historical periods, and aspects of this field). Eligible incoming students will be considered automatically, but current students need to submit a Lingyin application form. Three scholarships available. Please see website for more details
Level of Study: Postgraduate
Type: Scholarship
Value: £8,000 tenable only for one year at a time. Students holding the scholarship who would wish to reapply for it for the following year would be required to submit a new application for that year, which would be considered competitively alongside other applications for that year

U

Length of Study: One year
Frequency: Annual
Country of Study: United Kingdom
Application Procedure: For more information, please visit the website www.orinst.ox.ac.uk/administration/grants/index.html
Closing Date: 22 January
Funding: Trusts
Additional Information: www.orinst.ox.ac.uk/article/lingyin-graduate-scholarship-in-buddhist-studies

For further information contact:

Email: Buddhist-studies@email.arizona.edu

Magdalen College: Perkin Research Studentship

Eligibility: Open to all graduate applicants from Commonwealth countries for Chemistry
Level of Study: Research
Type: Studentship
Value: £7,000 per year
Length of Study: Period of fee liability
Country of Study: Any country
Application Procedure: Please see website for details of how to apply
Additional Information: Please check at www.magd.ox.ac.uk/admissions_graduate/scholarships.shtml

For further information contact:

Email: jane.sherwood@admin.ox.ac.uk

Magdalen College: Student Support Fund Graduate Grants

Eligibility: Graduate students already studying at Magdalen
Level of Study: Postgraduate, Research
Type: Grant
Value: According to individual circumstances
Length of Study: 1 year, renewable after review
Country of Study: Any country
Additional Information: www.magd.ox.ac.uk/alumni-friends/supporting-magdalen/priorities/student-support/

For further information contact:

Tel: (44) 1865 286796
Email: sean.rainey@magd.ox.ac.uk

Magdalen Hong Kong Scholarship

Eligibility: Students who are an ordinary resident of Hong Kong and are citizens of the People's Republic of China (PRC). Candidates should be intending to return to Hong Kong or the PRC on completion of their studies.
Level of Study: Postgraduate
Type: Scholarship
Value: Maximum of £40,000 per annum as a contribution towards College and University tuition fees and living expenses.
Length of Study: Up to 4 years
Country of Study: Any country
Application Procedure: Please see the website for further details
Closing Date: 22 January

For further information contact:

Tel: (44) 1865 276063
Email: admissions@magd.ox.ac.uk

Mansfield College: Adam von Trott Scholarship

Eligibility: Open to German nationals applying to the two year MPhil in Politics. Please see website for more details
Level of Study: Postgraduate, Research
Type: Scholarship
Value: University fee, college fee, living expenses up to €20,000 per annum
Length of Study: Duration of fee liability
Country of Study: Any country

For further information contact:

Email: avt.oxford@gmail.com

Mansfield College: Elfan Rees Scholarship

Purpose: To commencing studies towards a higher degree in the field of theology
Eligibility: Open to students on the MSt, MPhil, MLitt or DPhil in any branch of theology
Level of Study: Postdoctorate, Postgraduate, Research
Type: Scholarship
Value: Scholarship is £3,000 maintenance, paid termly in £1,000 instalments
Length of Study: Up to 2 years
Country of Study: Any country
Closing Date: 1 April

For further information contact:

Email: admissions@mansfield.ox.ac.uk

Medical Sciences Doctoral Training Centre: British Heart Foundation Studentship in Cardiovascular Science

Eligibility: Open to all applicants to the DPhil in Cardiovascular Science. All applicants are automatically considered for these awards
Level of Study: Doctorate
Type: Studentship
Value: Course fee, college fee, living expenses
Length of Study: 4 years
Country of Study: Any country
Closing Date: 6 January
Funding: Foundation
Additional Information: Please visit the website: www.medsci.ox.ac.uk/study/graduateschool/courses/dtc-structured-research-degrees/cardiovascular-science

For further information contact:

Email: Graduate.School@medsci.ox.ac.uk

Medical Sciences Doctoral Training Centre: Wellcome Trust Fellowship in Biomedical and Clinical Sciences

Eligibility: Open to all applicants to the DPhil in Biomedical and Clinical Sciences. All applicants are automatically considered for these awards
Level of Study: Doctorate
Type: Fellowship
Value: Course fee, college fee, living expenses
Length of Study: 3 years
Country of Study: Any country
Closing Date: 6 January
Funding: Trusts
Additional Information: Please visit the website: www.medsci.ox.ac.uk/study/graduateschool/courses/dtc-structured-research-degrees/doctoral-training-fellowship-scheme-for-clinicians

For further information contact:

Email: christopher.buckley@kennedy.ox.ac.uk

Medical Sciences Doctoral Training Centre: Wellcome Trust Studentship in Chromosome and Developmental Biology

Purpose: To provide students with training and supporting infrastructure to apply advanced biological imaging/super resolution microscopy, high-throughput sequencing method (and computational genomics for data analysis), advanced proteomics, and state of the art genome engineering
Eligibility: Open to all applicants to the DPhil in Chromosome and Developmental Biology. All applicants are automatically considered for these awards
Level of Study: Doctorate
Type: Studentship
Value: Course fee, college fee, living expenses
Length of Study: 4 years
Country of Study: Any country
Closing Date: 6 January
Funding: Trusts
Additional Information: Please visit the website: www.medsci.ox.ac.uk/study/graduateschool/courses/dtc-structured-research-degrees/chromosome-and-developmental-biology

For further information contact:

Email: enquiries@msdtc.ox.ac.uk

Medical Sciences Doctoral Training Centre: Wellcome Trust Studentship in Genomic Medicine and Statistics

Purpose: Trains future scientific leaders who will work at the cutting edge of genomics in biomedical research and enable effective delivery into the clinic
Eligibility: Open to all applicants to the DPhil in Genomic Medicine and Statistics. All applicants are automatically considered for these awards
Level of Study: Doctorate
Type: Studentship
Value: Course fee, college fee, living expenses
Length of Study: 4 years
Country of Study: Any country
Closing Date: 6 January
Funding: Trusts
Additional Information: Please visit the website: www.medsci.ox.ac.uk/study/graduateschool/courses/dtc-structured-research-degrees/genomic-medicine-and-statistics

For further information contact:

Email: enquiries@msdtc.ox.ac.uk

Medical Sciences Doctoral Training Centre: Wellcome Trust Studentship in Infection, Immunology and Translational Medicine

Purpose: Provides integrated training in infection and immunology, and how fundamental research can be translated into benefits for human health
Eligibility: Open to all applicants to the DPhil in Infection, Immunology and Translational Medicine. All applicants are automatically considered for these awards
Level of Study: Doctorate
Type: Studentship
Value: Course fee, college fee, living expenses
Length of Study: 4 years
Country of Study: Any country
Application Procedure: Applicants are suggested to select St Edmund Hall as their college choice. Please see the website for more details
Closing Date: 6 January
Funding: Trusts
Additional Information: Please visit the website: www.medsci.ox.ac.uk/study/graduateschool/courses/dtc-structured-research-degrees/infection-immunology-and-translational-medicine

For further information contact:

Email: Graduate.School@medsci.ox.ac.uk

Medical Sciences Doctoral Training Centre: Wellcome Trust Studentship in Ion Channels and Disease

Purpose: Trains the student in a range of multidisciplinary approaches and embraces all aspects of ion channel and membrane transport research from protein structure, genetics and cell physiology to animal behaviour and human disease
Eligibility: Open to all applicants to the DPhil in Ion Channels and Disease. All applicants are automatically considered for these awards
Level of Study: Doctorate
Type: Studentship
Value: Course fee, college fee, living expenses
Length of Study: 4 years
Country of Study: Any country
Application Procedure: Applicants who have no strong preference for a college are suggested to consider Green Templeton College or The Queen's College as their choice
Closing Date: 6 January
Funding: Trusts

Additional Information: Please visit the website: www.medsci.ox.ac.uk/study/graduateschool/courses/dtc-structured-research-degrees/ion-channels-and-membrane-transport-in-health-and-disease-oxion

For further information contact:

Email: enquiries@msdtc.ox.ac.uk

Medical Sciences Doctoral Training Centre: Wellcome Trust Studentship in Neuroscience

Purpose: Provides a wide range of skills training in experimental and theoretical methods that is intended to enable you to ask questions and tackle problems that transcend the traditional disciplines from which this field has evolved
Eligibility: Open to all applicants to the Wellcome Trust combined MSc and DPhil in Neuroscience. All applicants are automatically considered for these awards
Level of Study: Doctorate
Type: Studentship
Value: Course fee, college fee, living expenses
Length of Study: 4 years
Country of Study: Any country
Closing Date: 6 January
Funding: Trusts
Additional Information: Please visit the website: www.medsci.ox.ac.uk/study/graduateschool/courses/dtc-structured-research-degrees/neuroscience

For further information contact:

University of Oxford, University Offices, 15 Wellington Square, Oxford OX1 2JD, United Kingdom.

Tel: (44) 1865 270000
Email: enquiries@msdtc.ox.ac.uk

Medical Sciences Doctoral Training Centre: Wellcome Trust Studentship in Structural Biology

Purpose: Provides training in structural biology and related biochemical, genetic and cell biological approaches to understand molecular and cellular function
Eligibility: Open to all applicants to the DPhil in Structural Biology. All applicants are automatically considered for these awards
Level of Study: Doctorate
Type: Studentship
Value: Course fee, college fee, living expenses
Length of Study: 4 years
Country of Study: Any country

Closing Date: 6 January
Funding: Trusts
Additional Information: Please visit the website: www. medsci.ox.ac.uk/study/graduateschool/courses/dtc-structured-research-degrees/cellular-structural-biology

For further information contact:

Email: enquiries@msdtc.ox.ac.uk

Merton College Leventis Scholarship

Eligibility: Open to citizens of Greece or the Republic of Cyprus only
Level of Study: Graduate
Type: Scholarship
Value: Fees and maintenance
Length of Study: Up to 4 years depending on programme of study
Frequency: Every 2 years
Study Establishment: Merton College, University of Oxford
Country of Study: United Kingdom
Application Procedure: Further particulars and application forms are available from the Merton College website www. merton.ox.ac.uk/vacancies
No. of awards offered: 10
Closing Date: January
Funding: Private
No. of applicants last year: 10
Additional Information: Prospective applicants should refer to the college website www.merton.ox.ac.uk

For further information contact:

Merton College, Merton College, Merton Street, Oxford OX1 4JD, United Kingdom.

Email: julie.gerhardi@merton.ox.ac.uk

Merton College: Barton Scholarship

Eligibility: Open to British graduate applicants for the BCL. Awarded with the Law Faculty. No separate application required
Level of Study: Graduate, Postgraduate
Type: Scholarship
Value: £5,000 per year
Length of Study: 1 year
Frequency: Annual
Country of Study: Any country
Application Procedure: No separate application required
Closing Date: 22 January

Additional Information: Please check at www.merton.ox. ac.uk/graduate/graduate-scholarships-2015

For further information contact:

Email: jane.sherwood@admin.ox.ac.uk

Merton College: Chemistry Scholarship

Eligibility: Open to Home/European Union applicants for any graduate Chemistry programme of study normally considered by the College. Please see website for more details
Level of Study: Graduate
Type: Scholarship
Value: Course fees, college fees, full maintenance award (at RCUK rate)
Length of Study: Duration of fee liability
Study Establishment: Merton College
Country of Study: Any country
Closing Date: January
Additional Information: Please visit the website: www.mer ton.ox.ac.uk/graduate/graduate-scholarships

For further information contact:

Tel: (44) 1865 276 310

Merton College: Merton Lawyers

Eligibility: Open to graduate applicants for the BCL/MJur. No separate application required. Please see website for more details
Level of Study: Graduate, Postgraduate
Type: Scholarship
Value: £5,000 from Merton College and £5,000 from the Law Faculty
Length of Study: 1 year
Frequency: Annual
Study Establishment: Merton
Country of Study: Any country
Closing Date: 20 January
Additional Information: Please check the website: www. merton.ox.ac.uk/graduate/graduate-scholarships

Merton College: Peter J Braam Global Wellbeing Graduate Scholarship

Eligibility: Open to Home/European Union applicants for any graduate Biochemistry programme of study normally considered by the College. Please see website for more details
Level of Study: Doctorate

Type: Scholarship
Value: Course fees, college fees, full maintenance award (at RCUK rate)
Length of Study: Duration of fee liability
Country of Study: Any country
Application Procedure: Applicants wishing to be considered for this scholarship should apply for the DPhil in Biochemistry and state how their research addresses a problem related to global wellbeing
Closing Date: January
Additional Information: Please visit the website: www.merton.ox.ac.uk/graduate/graduate-scholarships www.devex.com/jobs/peter-j-braam-junior-research-fellowship-in-global-wellbeing-561725

For further information contact:

Email: graduate.admissions@admin.ox.ac.uk

Merton College: Two Merton Domus B Scholarships

Purpose: To enable United Kingdom/European Union students pursue studies at Merton College
Eligibility: Home/European Union applicants
Level of Study: Graduate, Postgraduate, Research
Type: Scholarship
Value: All fees plus maintenance award of £11,500
Length of Study: Up to 4 years
Frequency: Annual
Study Establishment: Merton College, University of Oxford
Country of Study: United Kingdom
Application Procedure: Further particulars and application forms are available from the Merton College website www.merton.ox.ac.uk/vacancies/index.htm
Closing Date: 20 January

For further information contact:

Email: julie.gerhardig@merton.ox.ac.uk

New College: The Yeotown Scholarship in Science

Eligibility: Open to all Home/European Union applicants to a research degree in Computer Science. The scholarship covers living costs and will be offered in conjunction with a departmental scholarship covering University and college fees. Please see website for more details
Level of Study: Postgraduate
Type: Scholarship

Value: Tuition and college fee plus maintenance stipend
Length of Study: Period of fee liability
Frequency: Annual
Study Establishment: New College
Country of Study: United Kingdom
Application Procedure: For more information, please check the website www.new.ox.ac.uk/scholarships-0
Closing Date: 8 January
Funding: Trusts

For further information contact:

Email: thenewcollege600014@gmail.com

North American Electric Reliability Corporation (NERC) Studentships in Earth Sciences

Purpose: To assist graduate students with fees and maintenance
Eligibility: Open to Home or European Union candidates usually with a 2.1 degree or higher
Level of Study: Research
Type: Studentship
Value: £5,000 per year
Length of Study: Duration of fee liability
Frequency: Annual
Country of Study: Any country
Application Procedure: 1. Upload a transcript from your current or previous study, a CV and any other documents that you feel would support your application (within 24 hours of submitting your online application you will receive a link allowing you to upload additional supporting documents). 2. Ask your referees to submit a reference for you by 29 April at the very latest. Note when you submit your application, an email will automatically be sent to your referees requesting a reference for you. This email will contain a secure link for your referee to upload a reference for you. 3. View the available projects. 4. Make an initial project enquiry by contacting supervisors directly
Closing Date: January
Additional Information: The Department will have a number of NERC studentships, to be confirmed. An European Union national who has studied for an undergraduate degree at a United Kingdom university during the 3 years leading up to the application may be classed as a United Kingdom resident www.devex.com/jobs/peter-j-braam-junior-research-fellowship-in-global-wellbeing-561725

For further information contact:

Email: researchcareers@nerc.ac.uk

Nuffield College Funded Studentships

Purpose: To assist students in a postgraduate degree course
Eligibility: Open to persons with at least an Upper Second Class (Honours) Degree or equivalent
Level of Study: Postgraduate
Type: Studentship
Value: Maximum £14,500 (home and European Union students) £19,500 (overseas students), usually partial awards only
Length of Study: For the length of the course, subject to satisfactory progress up to 4 years
Frequency: Annual
Study Establishment: Nuffield College, University of Oxford
Country of Study: United Kingdom
Application Procedure: All students offered a place at Nuffield College will automatically be considered for a studentship without the need for further application, other than the University of Oxford Graduate Admissions application form
Additional Information: Requests for information should be addressed to the Academic Administrator www.nuffield.ox. ac.uk/study-here/funding-your-studies/

For further information contact:

Nuffield College, New Rd, Oxford OX1 1NF, United Kingdom.

Email: graduate.admissions@nuffield.ox.ac.uk

Nuffield College Guardian Research Fellowship

Purpose: To support research on projects directly related to the media
Eligibility: Open to journalists or management staff members from fields of newspaper press, periodicals and broadcasting
Level of Study: Professional development
Type: Fellowship
Value: Varies according to the fellow's financial circumstances and proposed research
Length of Study: 1 academic year
Frequency: Every 2 years
Study Establishment: Nuffield College, the University of Oxford
Country of Study: United Kingdom
Application Procedure: Applicants are required to submit CV, research proposal, and names and addresses of three referees when the post is advertised
Closing Date: January

Funding: Commercial
Contributor: The Scott Trust
Additional Information: Preference will be given to proposals directly related to the applicant's experience of working in the media. The fellow will be asked to give the annual Guardian Lecture to members of the university and the public at some time during tenure. Requests for information should be addressed to the Warden's Secretary www.nuffield.ox.ac. uk/media/2407/srf_britishpolicy_fp.pdf

For further information contact:

Tel: (44) 1865 278 520
Fax: (44) 1865 278 676
Email: marion.rogers@nuf.ox.ac.uk

Nuffield College Gwilym Gibbon Research Fellowships

Purpose: To support the study of problems of government, especially by co-operation between academic and non academic persons
Eligibility: Preference will be given to candidates with experience in some form of public service
Level of Study: Postdoctorate, Postgraduate, Professional development
Type: Fellowship
Value: To cover accommodation, necessary travel costs and some secretarial and other assistance
Length of Study: 1 year
Frequency: Annual
Study Establishment: Nuffield College, the University of Oxford
Country of Study: United Kingdom
Application Procedure: Write for application form
Closing Date: April
No. of awards given last year: 1
Additional Information: It is hoped that the results of the research will be published or made available in some way to interested persons. Requests for information should be addressed to the Student Administrator. Please note that the 1998-9 competition was suspended and that it is possible that it may not run in subsequent years. For further information please consult the Warden of the College www.nuffield.ox.ac. uk/media/2407/srf_britishpolicy_fp.pdf

For further information contact:

Tel: (44) 1865 278 515
Fax: (44) 1865 278 621
Email: glynis.baleham@nuf.ox.ac.uk

U

Nuffield College ODA Shared Scholarship

Eligibility: Graduates from developing countries of the Commonwealth are eligible to apply
Level of Study: Postdoctorate
Type: Studentship
Value: Fees and maintenance
Length of Study: Up to 3 years
Frequency: Annual
Study Establishment: Nuffield College, the University of Oxford
Country of Study: United Kingdom
Application Procedure: Applicants must submit a list of publications, a curriculum vitae, a synopsis of the proposed research and the names and addresses of three referees when the post is advertised

For further information contact:

Email: marion.rogers@nuf.ox.ac.uk

Nuffield College Postdoctoral Prize Research Fellowship

Subjects: Currently 3 separate competitions in economics, politics, and sociology. Subjects are broadly constructed to include, for example, economic history, political history, political theory, international relations, social and medical statistics, and social policy.
Purpose: To allow scholars who have recently completed, or who are close to the completion of, a doctorate, to engage in independent scholarly research in the social sciences.
Eligibility: Check post job descriptions
Level of Study: Postdoctorate, Postgraduate
Type: Fellowship
Value: £32,150 p.a.
Length of Study: 3 years
Frequency: Annual
Study Establishment: Nuffield College, University of Oxford
Country of Study: United Kingdom
Application Procedure: Check post job descriptions
No. of awards offered: 3 to 6
No. of awards given last year: 6
Additional Information: www.nuffield.ox.ac.uk/the-college/jobs-and-vacancies/

For further information contact:

Nuffield College, New Road, Oxford OX1 1NF, United Kingdom.

Email: pprf@nuffield.ox.ac.uk

Nuffield Department of Clinical Medicine: LICR Studentship (Ludwig Institute for Cancer Research)

Eligibility: Minimum 21 or above, higher level English language test. Open to United Kingdom, European Union and Overseas Students
Type: Studentship
Value: All University and College fees plus stipend £16,500 per year
Length of Study: 3-4 years
Country of Study: Any country
Additional Information: Please check at www.ludwig.ox.ac.uk/ www.ndm.ox.ac.uk/ludwig-institute-for-cancer-research

For further information contact:

Email: webmaster@ox.ac.uk

Nuffield Department of Orthopaedics, Rheumatology and Musculoskeletal Sciences: Kennedy Trust Prize Studentships

Purpose: To provide world-class scientific training in a supportive and collaborative environment
Eligibility: Both European Union and Overseas applicants for the DPhil in Molecular and Cellular Medicine are eligible for this award. Interested applicants should have or expect to obtain a first or upper second class BSc degree or equivalent, and will also need to provide evidence of English language competence at time of application
Level of Study: Doctorate
Type: Studentship
Value: £22,000 per annum
Length of Study: 4 years
Frequency: Annual
Country of Study: Any country
Additional Information: Please visit the website: www.ndorms.ox.ac.uk/graduate-courses/kennedy-trust-prize-studentships www.ndorms.ox.ac.uk/graduate-courses/kennedy-trust-prize-studentships/how-to-apply

For further information contact:

Email: reception@kennedy.ox.ac.uk

Nuffield Department of Population Health: NDPH Scholarship

Eligibility: The department aims to provide up to two fully funded scholarships for the MSc each year. All applicants for the

MSc in Global Health Science are eligible for this; the highest ranked applicants in the department are shortlisted for funding

Level of Study: Postgraduate

Type: Scholarship

Value: These scholarships fund the DPhil fees and provide a stipend of not less than £18,000 per year for three years for full-time study and not less than £9,000 per year for six years for part-time study.

Length of Study: 1 year

Frequency: Annual

Country of Study: Any country

Closing Date: 8 January

For further information contact:

Email: enquiries@ndph.ox.ac.uk

Nuffield Department of Primary Care Health Science: NIHR School for Primary Care Research DPhil Studentship

Purpose: The Health Sciences Research Group invites applications for NIHR School for Primary Care Research (NSPCR) PhD studentships

Eligibility: The award can only be taken up by a student enrolled on the DPhil in Primary Health Care programme in a non-clinical area

Level of Study: Doctorate

Type: Studentship

Value: Course fee up to Home/European Union level, college fee, stipend. Annual tax-free stipend of £18,000

Length of Study: 3 years

Frequency: Annual

Country of Study: Any country

Closing Date: 11 January

Additional Information: www.phc.ox.ac.uk/study/dphil-and-msc-by-research/postgrad-study-info

For further information contact:

Radcliffe Observatory Quarter, Woodstock Road, Oxford OX2 6GG, United Kingdom.

Tel: (44) 1865 289 300

Ooni Adeyeye Enitan Ogunwusi Scholarships

Purpose: The scholarship is funded by the Imperial Majesty Oba Adéyeyè Enitan Ògúnwùsì and aims to provide funding to exceptional candidates pursuing postgraduate study of Africa

Eligibility: Open to graduate applicants who are ordinarily resident in Nigeria and applying to a full- time one-year master's course within the African Studies Centre at Oxford

Level of Study: Postgraduate

Type: Scholarship

Value: Course fee and a grant for living expenses of at least £ 14,777 per year

Frequency: Annual

Country of Study: Any country

Application Procedure: For further information, check the below link. www.ox.ac.uk/admissions/graduate/fees-and-funding/fees-funding-and-scholarship-search/scholarships-2#ooni

Closing Date: January

Funding: Private

Additional Information: www.opportunitiesforafricans.com/ooni-adeyeye-enitan-ogunwusi-scholarships-2019/

For further information contact:

University of Oxford, University Offices, 15 Wellington Square, Oxford OX1 2JD, United Kingdom.

Tel: (44) 1865 270 000

Email: joe@advance-africa.com

Oriel College: Oriel Graduate Scholarships

Eligibility: Open to all current graduate students at the college. Please see website for more details, including how to apply

Level of Study: Postgraduate, Research

Type: Scholarship

Value: £5,000

Length of Study: Period of fee liability

Country of Study: Any country

Closing Date: 22 January

Additional Information: Scholars are entitled to dine free of charge at High Table once per week during term time. Please contact to Academic Assistant at mailto: academic.office@oriel.ox.ac.uk

For further information contact:

Email: jane.sherwood@admin.ox.ac.uk

Oriel College: Paul Ries Collin Graduate Scholarship

Eligibility: Open to current graduate students at Oriel

Level of Study: Postgraduate, Research

Type: Scholarship

Value: Annual stipend equivalent to college fee; guaranteed college room at usual charge
Length of Study: 1 year, renewable for second or third
Frequency: Annual
Country of Study: Any country
Closing Date: 27 January
Additional Information: Scholars are entitled to dine free of charge at High Table once a week during term-time mail to: mailto: academic.office@oriel.ox.ac.uk

For further information contact:

Oriel College, Oriel Square, Oxford OX1 4EW, United Kingdom.

Email: academic.office@oriel.ox.ac.uk

Oriel College: Sir Walter Raleigh Scholarship

Purpose: To assist a student studying at the Environmental Change Institute for an MSc degree in Environmental Change and Management
Eligibility: Open to all applicants to the MSc in Environmental Change and Management. Please see website for more details, including how to apply
Level of Study: Postgraduate
Type: Scholarship
Value: £4,000
Length of Study: 1 year
Frequency: Annual
Country of Study: Any country
Application Procedure: Any person wishing to be considered for this award should follow the application procedure for admission to the degree of Master of Science in Environmental Change and Management at Oxford University, nominating Colleges of preference as detailed in the application procedure. They must, additionally, complete a separate application form which will be made available to them once in receipt of a place on the MSc
Closing Date: May

Oriental Studies: H.H. Sheikh Hamad bin Khalifa Al Thani Graduate Studentship in Contemporary Islamic Studies

Purpose: Contemporary Islamic Studies
Eligibility: Open to applicants to the DPhil in Oriental Studies. The award is intended for any postgraduate student pursuing doctoral research in any field of Contemporary Islamic Studies. Please see website for more information
Level of Study: Doctorate

Type: Studentship
Value: University fee, college fee, and maintenance grant. The award is tenable from October for 1 year in the first instance, renewable for up to a maximum of 3 years subject to receipt of a satisfactory report from the supervisor(s)
Length of Study: Up to 4 years
Country of Study: Any country
Closing Date: 31 March
Additional Information: Please visit the website: www. orinst.ox.ac.uk/administration/grants/index.html weblearn. ox.ac.uk/access/content/group/a55c44d3-9f21-4dec-b48c-2dc6fa4e4bee/Grants/H.H.%20Sheikh%20Hamad%20bin% 20Khalifa%20Al%20Thani%20Graduate%20Studentship% 20in%20Contemporary%20Islamic%20Studies.pdf

For further information contact:

62 Woodstock Road, Oxford OX2 6JF, United Kingdom.

Oriental Studies: KS Scholarship in Chinese Art

Eligibility: Open to applicants to graduate degrees at the University in any field of Chinese Art History, with a preference for Chinese painting. Please see website for more details and how to apply
Level of Study: Postgraduate
Type: Scholarship
Value: University fee, college fee and living expenses
Length of Study: Period of fee liability
Frequency: Annual
Country of Study: United Kingdom
Application Procedure: For more information, please check the website www.orinst.ox.ac.uk/administration/trust_funds/ ks_scholarship_in_chinese_art.html
Closing Date: 22 January
Funding: Trusts

For further information contact:

Email: orient@orinst.ox.ac.uk

Oriental Studies: Sasakawa Fund

Eligibility: Open to all graduate applicants in Oriental Studies, or United Kingdom applicants whose work will require some time spent in Japan
Level of Study: Postgraduate, Research
Type: Award
Value: £5,000 per year
Length of Study: Period of fee liability
Application Procedure: An application form is available at www.orinst.ox.ac.uk/general/grants/sasakawa_fund.html

Closing Date: 18 January
Additional Information: www.nissan.ox.ac.uk/sasakawa-fund-travel-grant-at-the-faculty-of-oriental-studies

For further information contact:

Tel: (44) 1865 278 225
Fax: (44) 1865 278 190
Email: chris.williams@orinst.ox.ac.uk

Other Studentships in Earth Sciences

Eligibility: Applicants must have 2.1 degree or higher. United Kingdom students are eligible for full support, and a range of support is available for European Union and international students
Level of Study: Research
Type: Studentship
Value: University and college fees and maintenance allowance
Length of Study: Normally 3 years, which can be extended in some cases
Frequency: Dependent on funds available
Application Procedure: Candidates are advised to apply directly to the department as advertised on the website
Closing Date: 20 January
Additional Information: The department occasionally has studentship funding associated with grants or industrial funding www.earth.ox.ac.uk/teaching/graduates/funding/

For further information contact:

Email: emmab@earth.ox.ac.uk

Oxford Centre for Islamic Studies (OCIS) Graduate Scholarships

Purpose: These scholarships have been established by the Oxford Centre for Islamic Studies to allow graduates to pursue study of benefit to the Muslim world.
Eligibility: See website: www.ox.ac.uk/admissions/graduate/fees-and-funding/fees-funding-and-scholarship-search/oxford-centre-islamic-studies-ocis-scholarships
Level of Study: Doctorate
Type: Scholarship
Value: 100% of course fees and a grant for living costs (at least £15,609)
Length of Study: Period of fee liability
Frequency: Annual
Country of Study: Any country
Application Procedure: All
No. of awards offered: 5
Closing Date: December

Oxford Refugee Scholarship

Purpose: The Oxford Refugee Scholarship is available for applicants applying to any one year full-time master's course, or two-year part-time master's course, at Oxford.
Eligibility: Hold an offer to commence a master's degree at the University of Oxford in 2023/24 for a one-year full-time course or two-year part-time course. Have been displaced within, or beyond, their home country due to conflict or violation of human rights, such as persecution. Further details will be published at the start of the application process for this scholarship. Face barriers to progressing their education and have limitations on the financial support for their university studies. Have not previously completed a degree at the same level (master's) for which they are making an application.
Type: Scholarship
Value: course fees and will provide you with a grant for living expenses.
Frequency: Annual
Country of Study: Any country
Closing Date: April
Additional Information: www.ox.ac.uk/admissions/graduate/fees-and-funding/fees-funding-and-scholarship-search/scholarships-a-z-listing

For further information contact:

University of Oxford, University Offices, 15 Wellington Square, Oxford OX1 2JD, United Kingdom.

Oxford Research in the Scholarship and Humanities of Africa Studentships

Purpose: To support postgraduate study of Africa in the humanities
Eligibility: Open to candidates for admission, or those already registered as graduate students. The successful applicant, if not already a member of an Oxford College, may be offered a place at St Antony's College or St Cross College
Level of Study: Postgraduate
Type: Studentship
Value: Varies, however it will cover college and University fees plus maintenance allowance. University fees will normally be covered at the home rate, although in exceptional circumstances supplemental grants may be made in order to meet, or to go some way towards meeting, the difference between the home and overseas fee
Length of Study: 2 years with the possibility of extension for 3 and occasionally 4 years
Frequency: Annual
Study Establishment: University of Oxford
Country of Study: United Kingdom

Application Procedure: Refer to the website www. africanstudies.ox.ac.uk/orisha

Additional Information: www.earth.ox.ac.uk/teaching/graduates/funding/

For further information contact:

Email: african.studies@africa.ox.ac.uk

Oxford University Theological Scholarships (Eastern and Central Europe)

Purpose: To enable students to pursue further studies in the University's Faculty of Theology

Eligibility: Open to candidates aged 22–40, who already have, or expect to obtain, a theological degree from a recognized university or theological college. Applications are invited from citizens of Russia, the Ukraine and any other countries of the former Soviet Union (apart from the Baltic States), Croatia, Serbia, Montenegro, Bosnia, Macedonia, Bulgaria, Albania and Romania

Level of Study: Graduate

Type: Scholarship

Value: Fees, a maintenance allowance and, where necessary, a return airfare

Length of Study: Up to 1 year

Frequency: Annual

Study Establishment: The Faculty of Theology, University of Oxford

Country of Study: United Kingdom

Application Procedure: Applicants must contact Mrs Elizabeth Macallister for further information

Funding: Government, Private

Contributor: Member churches of the Council of Churches for Britain and Ireland, the Foreign and Commonwealth Office and Oxford University

Additional Information: Scholarships are open to members of any Christian denomination. Applicants must be sponsored by a recognised church authority in their home country www. earth.ox.ac.uk/teaching/graduates/funding/

For further information contact:

Email: elizabeth.macallister@admin.ox.ac.uk

Oxford – Intesa Sanpaolo MBA Graduate Scholarships

Purpose: This scholarship is funded by Intesa Sanpaolo in partnership with Oxford University and Green Templeton College. The award is only tenable at Green Templeton College. There is no additional application process for this scholarship; we will use the details provided in your MBA application form to determine eligibility.

Eligibility: 1. Open to female candidates. 2. Tenable at Green Templeton College only. All eligible applicants will be considered for the scholarship, regardless of which college (if any) you state on your offer acceptance form. However, successful applicants will be transferred to Green Templeton College in order to take up the scholarship.

Type: Scholarship

Value: Full MBA course fees and a grant for living expenses of at least £15,609.

Length of Study: five years

Country of Study: Any country

Application Procedure: 1. No additional application is required. We will use the details you supply in your MBA application form to determine eligibility. 2. A complete MBA application must be submitted by the deadline.

No. of awards offered: 7

Closing Date: 12 January

Oxford-A G Leventis Graduate Scholarship

Eligibility: Open to all applicants applying for a DPhil in history, specialising in Byzantine studies

Type: Scholarship

Value: University fee, college fee and full living expenses

Length of Study: Period of fee liability

Country of Study: Any country

Application Procedure: Please visit the website for application details

Closing Date: 22 January

Additional Information: Please check at www.graduate.ox. ac.uk/ogs oxfordbyzantinesociety.files.wordpress.com/2011/ 05/leventis-graduate-scholarship.pdf

For further information contact:

Email: peter.frankopan@worc.ox.ac.uk

Oxford-Aidan Jenkins Graduate Scholarship

Eligibility: Open to applicants who are applying to any full-time course in the Faculty of English Language and Literature. Tenable at Merton College only. Please see website for more details

Type: Scholarship

Value: University fee, college fee, and full living expenses

Length of Study: Duration of fee liability

Study Establishment: Merton College

Country of Study: Any country

Closing Date: 20 January

Additional Information: Please visit the website: www. ox.ac.uk/admissions/graduate/fees-and-funding/fees-funding-and-scholarship-search/scholarships-2#aidanjenkins www. european-funding-guide.eu/scholarship/13585-oxford-aidan-jenkins-graduate-scholarship

Oxford-Anderson Graduate Scholarship in History

Purpose: One full scholarship is available for applicants who are applying to any full-time graduate course in the Faculty of History within the range accepted by University College. To check whether the course you are planning to apply for is accepted by University College

Eligibility: The scholarship is only tenable at University College.

Type: Scholarship

Value: scholarship covers course fees and provides a grant for living costs

Frequency: Annual

Country of Study: Any country

No. of awards offered: 1

Closing Date: April

Additional Information: www.ox.ac.uk/admissions/graduate/fees-and-funding/fees-funding-and-scholarship-search/scholarships-a-z-listing

For further information contact:

University of Oxford, University Offices, 15 Wellington Square, Oxford OX1 2JD, United Kingdom.

Tel: (44) 1865 270000
Fax: (44) 1865 270708

Oxford-Anderson Humanities Graduate Scholarship

Purpose: One full scholarship is available for applicants who are applying to any full-time Humanities graduate course within the range accepted by University College. To check whether the course you are planning to apply for is accepted by University College

Eligibility: The scholarship is only tenable at University College.

Type: Scholarship

Value: scholarship covers course fees and provides a grant for living costs.

Country of Study: Any country

No. of awards offered: 1

Closing Date: April

Additional Information: www.ox.ac.uk/admissions/graduate/fees-and-funding/fees-funding-and-scholarship-search/scholarships-a-z-listing

For further information contact:

University of Oxford, University Offices, 15 Wellington Square, Oxford OX1 2JD, United Kingdom.

Tel: (44) 1865 270000
Fax: (44) 1865 270708

Oxford-Angus McLeod Graduate Scholarship

Purpose: The Oxford-Angus McLeod Graduate Scholarship is available for any applicants who are applying to undertake any postgraduate Taught or Research courses offered by the Social Sciences Division for which St John's College normally accepts applications.

Eligibility: The scholarship is only tenable at St John's College

Type: Scholarship

Value: scholarship covers course fees and a grant for living costs

Frequency: Annual

Country of Study: Any country

Closing Date: April

Additional Information: www.ox.ac.uk/admissions/graduate/fees-and-funding/fees-funding-and-scholarship-search/scholarships-a-z-listing

For further information contact:

University of Oxford, University Offices, 15 Wellington Square, Oxford OX1 2JD, United Kingdom.

Tel: (44) 1865 270000
Fax: (44) 1865 270708

Oxford-Ashton Graduate Scholarship in Engineering

Purpose: The scholarship is jointly funded by the University and by anonymous Old Members (alumni) of University College, in memory of Mrs J P Ashton.

Eligibility: The scholarship is only tenable at University College

Type: Scholarship

Value: scholarship covers course fees and provides a grant for living costs

Frequency: Annual

Country of Study: Any country

No. of awards offered: 2

Closing Date: April

U

Additional Information: www.ox.ac.uk/admissions/gradu
ate/fees-and-funding/fees-funding-and-scholarship-search/
scholarships-a-z-listing

For further information contact:

University of Oxford, University Offices, 15 Wellington
Square, Oxford OX1 2JD, United Kingdom.

Tel:　(44) 1865 270000
Fax:　(44) 1865 270708

Oxford-Bellhouse Graduate Scholarship

Eligibility: Open to applicants who are ordinarily resident in
the EEA or Switzerland and who are applying to the full-time
DPhil in Engineering Sciences, specialising in Biomedical
Engineering. The scholarship is only tenable at Magdalen
College. Please see website for more details
Level of Study: Doctorate
Type: Scholarship
Value: University fee, college fee, and full living expenses
Length of Study: Period of fee liability
Study Establishment: Magdalen College
Country of Study: Any country
Closing Date: 20 January
Additional Information: Please visit the website: www.ox.
ac.uk/admissions/graduate/fees-and-funding/fees-funding-and-
scholarship-search/scholarships-2#bellhouse www.european-
funding-guide.eu/scholarship/13586-oxford-bellhouse-gradu
ate-scholarship

For further information contact:

Email:　accommodation@linacre.ox.ac.uk

Oxford-Berman Graduate Scholarship

Purpose: This scholarship has been funded by a group of Old
Members (alumni) in recognition of Dr Robert 'Bobby'
Berman's valuable and much appreciated contribution to life
at University College over more than three decades.
Eligibility: The scholarship is only tenable at University
College.
Type: Scholarship
Value: The scholarship covers course fees and provides
a grant for living costs.
Frequency: Annual
Country of Study: Any country
No. of awards offered: 1
Closing Date: April

Additional Information: www.ox.ac.uk/admissions/gradu
ate/fees-and-funding/fees-funding-and-scholarship-search/
scholarships-a-z-listing

For further information contact:

University of Oxford, University Offices, 15 Wellington
Square, Oxford OX1 2JD, United Kingdom.

Tel:　(44) 1865 270000
Fax:　(44) 1865 270708

Oxford-Bob Thomas Graduate Scholarship in Chemistry

Purpose: Established in 2016 at University College, to assist
eligible postgraduate students admitted to the Department of
Chemistry, the scholarship is named in honour of Dr Robert
K. Thomas and co-funded by the Department of Chemistry as
well as University College Old Members. Dr Thomas was
Aldrichian Praelector in Physical Chemistry and a Fellow of
University College for three decades (1978-2008).
Eligibility: The scholarship is only tenable at University
College.
Type: Scholarship
Value: The scholarship covers course fees and provides
a grant for living costs.
Frequency: Annual
Country of Study: Any country
No. of awards offered: 1
Closing Date: April
Additional Information: www.ox.ac.uk/admissions/gradu
ate/fees-and-funding/fees-funding-and-scholarship-search/
scholarships-a-z-listing

For further information contact:

University of Oxford, University Offices, 15 Wellington
Square, Oxford OX1 2JD, United Kingdom.

Tel:　(44) 1865 270000
Fax:　(44) 1865 270708

Oxford-Bounden Graduate Scholarship

Purpose: The Oxford-Bounden Graduate Scholarship is
available for applicants who are ordinarily resident in the
United Kingdom or Republic of Ireland who are applying to
any Humanities Division courses within the range accepted
by Jesus College.
Eligibility: The scholarship is only tenable at Jesus College.
Type: Scholarship

Value: The scholarship covers course fees and a grant for living costs.
Frequency: Annual
Country of Study: Any country
Closing Date: April
Additional Information: www.ox.ac.uk/admissions/gradu ate/fees-and-funding/fees-funding-and-scholarship-search/ scholarships-a-z-listing

For further information contact:

University of Oxford, University Offices, 15 Wellington Square, Oxford OX1 2JD, United Kingdom.

Tel: (44) 1865 270000
Fax: (44) 1865 270708

Oxford-Brunsfield Association of Southeast Asian Nations (ASEAN) Human Rights Graduate Scholarships

Eligibility: Open to applicants who are nationals of and ordinarily resident in Brunei Darussalam, Cambodia, Indonesia, Laos, Malaysia, Myanmar (Burma), Philippines, Singapore, Thailand or Vietnam and who are applying to the part-time MSt in International Human Rights Law. Please see website for more details
Level of Study: Postgraduate
Type: Scholarship
Value: University fee, college fee, and study support grant
Length of Study: Period of fee liability
Country of Study: Any country
Closing Date: 31 March
Additional Information: Please visit the website: www.ox. ac.uk/admissions/graduate/fees-and-funding/fees-funding-and-scholarship-search/scholarships-2#brunsfield www.devwise. com/opps/brunsfield-oxford-asean-human-rights-scholarships-at-university-of-oxford/

For further information contact:

Email: iphumrts@conted.ox.ac.uk

Oxford-C S Wu Graduate Scholarship

Purpose: The Oxford-C S Wu Graduate Scholarship is available for applicants who are applying for a full-time DPhil within Particle Physics.
Eligibility: you must be ordinarily resident in the United Kingdom or Republic of Ireland.
Type: Scholarship

Value: The scholarship covers course fees and a grant for living costs.
Country of Study: Any country
Closing Date: April
Additional Information: www.ox.ac.uk/admissions/gradu ate/fees-and-funding/fees-funding-and-scholarship-search/ scholarships-a-z-listing

For further information contact:

University of Oxford, University Offices, 15 Wellington Square, Oxford OX1 2JD, United Kingdom.

Tel: (44) 1865 270000
Fax: (44) 1865 270708

Oxford-Calleva Scholarship

Purpose: It is intended to make available three scholarships for entry in October to applicants ordinarily resident in the European Union applying to the DPhil History (including History of Science and Medicine, and Economic and Social History), the DPhil Experimental Psychology, or the DPhil Anthropology
Eligibility: Each DPhil student will develop their own project within their respective discipline that explores childhood experiences and the impact of adversity and inequalities, using either psychological or modern British historical evidence
Level of Study: Doctorate
Type: Scholarship
Frequency: Annual
Country of Study: Switzerland
Application Procedure: The scholarship is only tenable at Linacre College. All eligible applicants will be considered for this scholarship, regardless of which college (if any) you state as your preference on the graduate application form
Closing Date: 1 January
Funding: Private
Additional Information: www.magd.ox.ac.uk/the-oxford-calleva-scholarship/

For further information contact:

Email: lucy.bowes@psy.ox.ac.uk

Oxford-Carolyn and Franco Gianturco Graduate Scholarship

Purpose: The scholarship have been made possible by Carolyn Gianturco, who completed her DPhil in Musicology at the University of Oxford under the guidance of Sir Jack Westrup in 1970. Together with her husband Franco

Gianturco, they have generously endowed this scholarship at Linacre College to advance research in the music field.

Eligibility: The scholarship is only tenable at Linacre College.

Type: Scholarship

Value: The scholarship covers course fees and a grant for living costs.

Frequency: Annual

Country of Study: Any country

Closing Date: April

Additional Information: www.ox.ac.uk/admissions/gradu ate/fees-and-funding/fees-funding-and-scholarship-search/ scholarships-a-z-listing

For further information contact:

University of Oxford, University Offices, 15 Wellington Square, Oxford OX1 2JD, United Kingdom.

Tel: (44) 1865 270000
Fax: (44) 1865 270708

Oxford-Cecil Lubbock Memorial Graduate Scholarship

Purpose: The Oxford-Cecil Lubbock Graduate Scholarship is available for applicants who are applying to the DPhil English (with preference for either Medieval or Victorian areas of research).

Eligibility: The scholarship is only tenable at Trinity College.

Type: Scholarship

Value: The scholarship covers course fees at the Home rate and a grant for living costs

Frequency: Annual

Country of Study: Any country

Closing Date: April/May

Additional Information: www.ox.ac.uk/admissions/gradu ate/fees-and-funding/fees-funding-and-scholarship-search/ scholarships-a-z-listing

For further information contact:

University of Oxford, University Offices, 15 Wellington Square, Oxford OX1 2JD, United Kingdom.

Tel: (44) 1865 270000
Fax: (44) 1865 270708

Oxford-Chellgren Graduate Scholarships

Purpose: The scholarship is jointly funded by the University and by Paul Chellgren, who studied at University College in

1966. Paul Chellgren is a visionary Old Member (alumnus) and an Honorary Fellow of University College.

Eligibility: The scholarship is only tenable at University College.

Type: Scholarship

Value: The scholarship covers course fees and provides a grant for living costs.

Frequency: Annual

Country of Study: Any country

No. of awards offered: 2

Closing Date: April

Additional Information: www.ox.ac.uk/admissions/gradu ate/fees-and-funding/fees-funding-and-scholarship-search/ scholarships-a-z-listing

For further information contact:

University of Oxford, University Offices, 15 Wellington Square, Oxford OX1 2JD, United Kingdom.

Tel: (44) 1865 270000
Fax: (44) 1865 270708

Oxford-Chelly Halsey Graduate Scholarship

Purpose: The scholarship is jointly funded by the University and by generous donors to Nuffield College, who contributed funds to establish a scholarship in memory of Professor Albert Henry Halsey, best known as Chelly, an eminent sociologist and a Fellow of Nuffield College for over fifty years.

Eligibility: The scholarship is only tenable at Nuffield College.

Type: Scholarship

Value: The scholarship covers course fees and a grant for living costs.

Frequency: Annual

Country of Study: Any country

Closing Date: May

Additional Information: www.ox.ac.uk/admissions/gradu ate/fees-and-funding/fees-funding-and-scholarship-search/ scholarships-a-z-listing

For further information contact:

University of Oxford, University Offices, 15 Wellington Square, Oxford OX1 2JD, United Kingdom.

Tel: (44) 1865 270000
Fax: (44) 1865 270708

Oxford-Clayton Graduate Scholarship

Purpose: The scholarship is jointly funded by the University and Gerald 'David' Clayton, who came up to Merton in 1955 to read Modern History. He was a passionate musician, who was a great supporter of the Choral Foundation at Merton in his lifetime, and was a frequent visitor to College throughout his life. The Oxford-Clayton Graduate Scholarship was set up using part of a generous legacy that David left to Merton after he sadly passed away in 2014.
Eligibility: The scholarship covers course fees and a grant for living costs.
Type: Scholarship
Value: The scholarship covers course fees and a grant for living costs.
Frequency: Annual
Country of Study: Any country
Closing Date: April
Additional Information: www.ox.ac.uk/admissions/gradu ate/fees-and-funding/fees-funding-and-scholarship-search/ scholarships-a-z-listing

For further information contact:

University of Oxford, University Offices, 15 Wellington Square, Oxford OX1 2JD, United Kingdom.

Tel: (44) 1865 270000
Fax: (44) 1865 270708

Oxford-Creat Group Graduate Scholarships

Purpose: The scholarships have been jointly funded by the University and by the Creat Group of Beijing. The Creat Group is a leading investment company with a global portfolio and partnerships with leading financial institutions in the UK and Japan. The Creat Group intends that scholars will make a considerable contribution to the development of China's economy over the course of their lifetime.
Eligibility: scholarships are available for applicants who are ordinarily resident in the People's Republic of China
Type: Scholarship
Value: The scholarship covers course fees and a grant for living costs
Frequency: Annual
Country of Study: Any country
Closing Date: April
Additional Information: www.ox.ac.uk/admissions/gradu ate/fees-and-funding/fees-funding-and-scholarship-search/ scholarships-a-z-listing

For further information contact:

University of Oxford, University Offices, 15 Wellington Square, Oxford OX1 2JD, United Kingdom.

Tel: (44) 1865 270000
Fax: (44) 1865 270708

Oxford-David Jones Graduate Scholarship

Purpose: The Oxford-David Jones Graduate Scholarship is available for applicants who are ordinarily resident in the United Kingdom or Republic of Ireland who are applying to undertake any postgraduate Taught or Research courses offered by the History Faculty.
Eligibility: The scholarship is only tenable at Jesus College.
Type: Scholarship
Value: The scholarship covers course fees and a grant for living costs.
Frequency: Annual
Country of Study: Any country
Closing Date: April
Additional Information: www.ox.ac.uk/admissions/gradu ate/fees-and-funding/fees-funding-and-scholarship-search/ scholarships-a-z-listing

For further information contact:

University of Oxford, University Offices, 15 Wellington Square, Oxford OX1 2JD, United Kingdom.

Tel: (44) 1865 270000
Fax: (44) 1865 270708

Oxford-DeepMind Graduate Scholarship (Computer Science)

Purpose: The Oxford-DeepMind Graduate Scholarships (Computer Science) are available for applicants to any full-time DPhil course within, or affiliated to, the Department of Computer Science. The scholarships have been made possible through the support of DeepMind, a world leader in artificial intelligence research.
Type: Scholarship
Value: The scholarship covers course fees and a grant for living costs.
Frequency: Annual
Country of Study: Any country
Closing Date: April
Additional Information: www.ox.ac.uk/admissions/gradu ate/fees-and-funding/fees-funding-and-scholarship-search/ scholarships-a-z-listing

For further information contact:

University of Oxford, University Offices, 15 Wellington Square, Oxford OX1 2JD, United Kingdom.

Tel: (44) 1865 270000
Fax: (44) 1865 270708

Oxford-E P Abraham Research Fund Graduate Scholarships

Eligibility: applicants who are applying to the full-time DPhil in Molecular Cell Biology in Health and Disease.
Type: Scholarship
Value: £17,609
Frequency: Annual
Country of Study: Any country
No. of awards offered: 3
Closing Date: February
Additional Information: www.ox.ac.uk/admissions/gradu ate/fees-and-funding/fees-funding-and-scholarship-search/ scholarships-a-z-listing

For further information contact:

University of Oxford, University Offices, 15 Wellington Square, Oxford OX1 2JD, United Kingdom.

Tel: (44) 1865 270000
Fax: (44) 1865 270708

Oxford-EPA Cephalosporin Graduate Scholarship

Purpose: The Oxford-EPA Cephalosporin Graduate Scholarship is available for applicants who are applying for a course within the Interdisciplinary Bioscience (BBSRC DTP). The scholarship have been funded via grants from the EPA Cephalosporin Fund and the University of Oxford.
Eligibility: The scholarship is only tenable at Linacre College.
Type: Scholarship
Value: The scholarship covers course fees and a grant for living costs.
Frequency: Annual
Country of Study: Any country
Closing Date: April
Additional Information: www.ox.ac.uk/admissions/gradu ate/fees-and-funding/fees-funding-and-scholarship-search/ scholarships-a-z-listing

For further information contact:

University of Oxford, University Offices, 15 Wellington Square, Oxford OX1 2JD, United Kingdom.

Tel: (44) 1865 270000
Fax: (44) 1865 270708

Oxford-Feltham Graduate Scholarship

Purpose: In 2016 Magdalen College launched a fundraising appeal in order to create and financially support a scholarship for students studying the Bachelor of Civil Law (BCL), a world-renowned taught graduate course in law, designed to serve outstanding law students from common law backgrounds. The scholarship is named in memory of the late John Feltham, Tutorial Fellow in Law at the College from 1965-1992. The Oxford-Feltham Graduate Scholarship was created and 2020-21 was the first year that this scholarship has been awarded.
Eligibility: The scholarship is only tenable at Magdalen College.
Type: Scholarship
Value: The scholarship covers course fees and provides a grant for living costs.
Frequency: Annual
Country of Study: Any country
Closing Date: April
Additional Information: www.ox.ac.uk/admissions/gradu ate/fees-and-funding/fees-funding-and-scholarship-search/ scholarships-a-z-listing

For further information contact:

University of Oxford, University Offices, 15 Wellington Square, Oxford OX1 2JD, United Kingdom.

Tel: (44) 1865 270000
Fax: (44) 1865 270708

Oxford-Finnis Graduate Scholarship in Law

Purpose: The Oxford-Finnis Graduate Scholarship in Law was established at University College to assist eligible students admitted to the Law Faculty, in particular those working towards the Bachelor of Civil Law. This was the first law scholarship to be offered by University College, was funded by John Finnis' former pupils and Univ lawyers, and is named in honour of the 50th anniversary of his own Fellowship at the College (2016-17).
Type: Scholarship

Value: The scholarship covers course fees and provides a grant for living costs.
Frequency: Annual
Country of Study: Any country
Application Procedure: The scholarship is only tenable at University College.
Closing Date: April
Additional Information: www.ox.ac.uk/admissions/gradu ate/fees-and-funding/fees-funding-and-scholarship-search/ scholarships-a-z-listing

For further information contact:

University of Oxford, University Offices, 15 Wellington Square, Oxford OX1 2JD, United Kingdom.

Tel: (44) 1865 270000
Fax: (44) 1865 270708

Oxford-Hackney BCL Graduate Scholarship

Purpose: The Oxford-Hackney BCL Graduate Scholarship is available for applicants to the full-time Bachelor of Civil Law (BCL). The scholarships have been funded by the University and by a collection of Wadham College alumni, in honour of Jeffrey Hackney, the College's Fellow in Law from 1976-2008 and an extremely prominent and much-loved tutor.
Eligibility: The scholarship is only tenable at Wadham College.
Type: Scholarship
Value: The scholarship covers course fees and a grant for living costs.
Frequency: Annual
Country of Study: Any country
Closing Date: April
Additional Information: www.ox.ac.uk/admissions/gradu ate/fees-and-funding/fees-funding-and-scholarship-search/ scholarships-a-z-listing

For further information contact:

University of Oxford, University Offices, 15 Wellington Square, Oxford OX1 2JD, United Kingdom.

Tel: (44) 1865 270000
Fax: (44) 1865 270708

Oxford-Hoffmann Graduate Scholarships

Purpose: Fondation Hoffmann is a Swiss-based grant making institution supporting the emergence and expansion of concrete projects which address global problems in today's societies
Eligibility: Open to applicants who are applying to any full or part-time course within the Medical Science Division. Tenable at Jesus College only
Level of Study: Graduate
Type: Scholarship
Value: 100% of course fees and a grant for living costs (at least £14,777)
Length of Study: Duration of fee liability
Frequency: Annual
Study Establishment: Jesus College
Country of Study: Any country
Closing Date: April
Additional Information: Please visit the website: www.ox. ac.uk/admissions/graduate/fees-and-funding/fees-funding-and-scholarship-search/scholarships-2#hoffmann www.ox.ac.uk/ admissions/graduate/fees-and-funding/fees-funding-and-scho larship-search/weidenfeld-hoffmann-scholarships-and-leader ship-programme

Oxford-Hoffmann Graduate Scholarships in Medical Sciences

Purpose: The Oxford-Hoffmann Graduate Scholarships in Medical Sciences are available for any applicants who are applying to study within the Medical Sciences Division. The scholarships have been made possible through the support of André Hoffmann, who is an entrepreneur, investor and philanthropist. Mr Hoffmann studied economics at St Gallen University and holds an MBA from INSEAD.
Eligibility: The scholarship is only tenable at Jesus College.
Type: Scholarship
Value: The scholarship covers course fees and a grant for living costs.
Frequency: Annual
Country of Study: Any country
Closing Date: April
Additional Information: www.ox.ac.uk/admissions/gradu ate/fees-and-funding/fees-funding-and-scholarship-search/ scholarships-a-z-listing

For further information contact:

University of Oxford, University Offices, 15 Wellington Square, Oxford OX1 2JD, United Kingdom.

Tel: (44) 1865 270000
Fax: (44) 1865 270708

Oxford-ID Travel Group Foundation Bonham-Carter Graduate Scholarship

Purpose: The scholarship is available to applicants who are applying to a full-time or part-time graduate master's. Preference should be given to courses in the Social Sciences Division (except the Saïd Business School), within the range accepted by Christ Church.
Eligibility: The scholarship is only tenable at Christ Church.
Type: Scholarship
Value: The scholarship covers course fees and a grant for living costs.
Frequency: Annual
Country of Study: Any country
Closing Date: May
Additional Information: www.ox.ac.uk/admissions/gradu ate/fees-and-funding/fees-funding-and-scholarship-search/scholarships-a-z-listing

For further information contact:

University of Oxford, University Offices, 15 Wellington Square, Oxford OX1 2JD, United Kingdom.

Tel: (44) 1865 270000
Fax: (44) 1865 270708

Oxford-Indira Gandhi Graduate Scholarships

Purpose: Three full scholarships are available for applicants who are ordinarily resident in India. You must be applying for one of the eligible full-time or part-time master's courses listed below or for a DPhil course with proposed research in the eligible areas of study.
Eligibility: The scholarship is only tenable at Somerville College.
Type: Scholarship
Value: The scholarship covers course fees and a grant for living costs.
Frequency: Annual
Country of Study: Any country
No. of awards offered: 3
Closing Date: April
Additional Information: www.ox.ac.uk/admissions/gradu ate/fees-and-funding/fees-funding-and-scholarship-search/scholarships-a-z-listing

For further information contact:

University of Oxford, University Offices, 15 Wellington Square, Oxford OX1 2JD, United Kingdom.

Tel: (44) 1865 270000
Fax: (44) 1865 270708

Oxford-Intesa Sanpaolo Graduate Scholarship

Purpose: Intesa Sanpaolo is one of Italy's leading banks, with a proud record of corporate philanthropy across a range of global priorities, including educational programmes aimed at driving social change.
Eligibility: Open to female candidates. Tenable at Green Templeton College only. All eligible applicants will be considered for the scholarship, regardless of which college (if any) you state on your offer acceptance form. However, successful applicants will be transferred to Green Templeton College in order to take up the scholarship.
Type: Scholarship
Value: Full MBA course fees and a grant for living expenses of at least £15,609
Length of Study: 5 Years
Frequency: Annual
Country of Study: Any country
No. of awards offered: 2
Closing Date: 23 March
Additional Information: www.sbs.ox.ac.uk/oxford-experience/scholarships-and-funding/oxford-intesa-sanpaolo-mba-graduate-scholarship

For further information contact:

University of Oxford, University Offices, 15 Wellington Square, Oxford OX1 2JD, United Kingdom.

Tel: (44) 1865 270000
Fax: (44) 1865 270708

Oxford-Jeffrey Cheah Graduate Scholarship

Purpose: The scholarship is jointly funded by the University and Tan Sri Dato' Seri Dr Jeffrey Cheah. Tan Sri Jeffrey is the founder and chairman of the Sunway Group, founding trustee of the Jeffrey Cheah Foundation, and is an Honorary Fellow of Brasenose College.
Eligibility: The scholarship is only tenable at Brasenose College.
Type: Scholarship
Value: The scholarship covers course fees and provides a grant for living costs.
Frequency: Annual
Country of Study: Any country
No. of awards offered: 1
Closing Date: April
Additional Information: www.ox.ac.uk/admissions/gradu ate/fees-and-funding/fees-funding-and-scholarship-search/scholarships-a-z-listing

For further information contact:

University of Oxford, University Offices, 15 Wellington Square, Oxford OX1 2JD, United Kingdom.

Tel: (44) 1865 270000
Fax: (44) 1865 270708

Oxford-Jerry Hausman Graduate Scholarship

Eligibility: Open to all applicants applying for any graduate course in the departments of Economics, Politics, and Sociology. Tenable at Nuffield College only. Please see website for more details
Level of Study: Postgraduate
Type: Scholarship
Value: University fee, college fee, and full living expenses
Length of Study: Period of fee liability
Frequency: Annual
Study Establishment: Nuffield College
Country of Study: United Kingdom
Application Procedure: For more information, please check the website www.ox.ac.uk/admissions/graduate/fees-and-funding/fees-funding-and-scholarship-search/scholarships-2#jerryhausman
Closing Date: 22 January
Funding: Trusts
Additional Information: One full scholarship is available for applicants who are applying to any full-time or part-time graduate course in the departments of Economics, Politics and International Relations and Sociology; preference will be given to applicants for Economics courses under Oxford-Jerry Hausman Graduate Scholarship www.ox.ac.uk/admissions/graduate/fees-and-funding/fees-funding-and-scholarship-search/weidenfeld-hoffmann-scholarships-and-leadership-programme

For further information contact:

Email: information@anthro.ox.ac.uk

Oxford-John and Pat Cuckney Graduate Scholarship

Eligibility: Open to applicants who are ordinarily resident in EEA or Switzerland and who are applying to the full-time DPhil in Particle Physics. Tenable at Lincoln College only
Level of Study: Doctorate
Type: Scholarship
Value: University fee, college fee, and a grant for living costs of £14,553 towards the tenable year
Length of Study: Duration of fee liability

Study Establishment: Lincoln College
Country of Study: Any country
Closing Date: 20 January
Additional Information: Please visit the website: www.ox.ac.uk/admissions/graduate/fees-and-funding/fees-funding-and-scholarship-search/scholarships-2#cuckney www2.physics.ox.ac.uk/study-here/postgraduates/condensed-matter-physics/sources-of-funding

For further information contact:

Email: dtcenquiries@dtc.ox.ac.uk

Oxford-Kaifeng Graduate Scholarship

Purpose: The Oxford-Kaifeng Graduate scholarships are available for applicants who are ordinarily resident and nationals of the People's Republic of China (excluding Hong Kong and Macau SAR). Preference will be given to those applying to courses in the order listed: History of Art; other Humanities Division courses; Social Science Division courses. Candidates must also demonstrate potential leadership qualities.
Eligibility: applicants who are ordinarily resident and nationals of the People's Republic of China (excluding Hong Kong and Macau SAR).
Type: Scholarship
Value: The scholarship covers course fees and a grant for living costs.
Country of Study: Any country
Closing Date: April
Additional Information: www.ox.ac.uk/admissions/graduate/fees-and-funding/fees-funding-and-scholarship-search/scholarships-a-z-listing

For further information contact:

University of Oxford, University Offices, 15 Wellington Square, Oxford OX1 2JD, United Kingdom.

Tel: (44) 1865 270000
Fax: (44) 1865 270708

Oxford-Keith Lloyd Graduate Scholarship

Eligibility: Open to applicants ordinarily resident in sub-Saharan Africa (excluding South Africa), and who is studying for an MSc course in the School of Geography and the Environment. The scholarship is only tenable at Linacre College
Level of Study: Postgraduate
Type: Scholarship

Value: University fee, college fee, and a grant for living costs
Length of Study: 1 year
Study Establishment: Linacre College
Country of Study: Any country
Closing Date: 20 January
Additional Information: Please visit the website: www. ox.ac.uk/admissions/graduate/fees-and-funding/fees-funding-and-scholarship-search/scholarships-3#keithlloyd www.lina cre.ox.ac.uk/prospective-students/scholarships/norman-and-ivy-lloyd-scholarshipcommonwealth-shared-scholarship

For further information contact:

Email: shared.scholarships@cscuk.org.uk

Oxford-Ko Cheuk Hung Graduate Scholarship

Purpose: The Oxford-Ko Cheuk Hung Graduate Scholarship is available for applicants who are ordinarily resident in UK and who are applying to the MSt Traditional China.
Eligibility: The scholarship is only tenable at St Cross College.
Type: Scholarship
Value: The scholarship covers course fees and a grant for living costs.
Country of Study: Any country
Closing Date: April
Additional Information: www.ox.ac.uk/admissions/gradu ate/fees-and-funding/fees-funding-and-scholarship-search/scholarships-a-z-listing

For further information contact:

University of Oxford, University Offices, 15 Wellington Square, Oxford OX1 2JD, United Kingdom.

Tel: (44) 1865 270000
Fax: (44) 1865 270708

Oxford-Leon E and Iris L Beghian Graduate Scholarships

Purpose: The scholarship is jointly funded by the University and by a donation from the estate of Leon and Iris Beghian. Leon Beghian came to Magdalen College in 1938 to study Physics. After scientific research during the war, he graduated with a first-class degree in 1947, and then undertook a DPhil at Oxford before progressing to a distinguished career in Physics in the USA.
Eligibility: The scholarship is only tenable at Magdalen Col-lege. You must have been ordinarily resident in the UK for at least five years prior to the start of your course.
Type: Scholarship

Value: he scholarship covers course fees and provides a grant for living costs.
Frequency: Annual
Country of Study: Any country
No. of awards offered: 2
Closing Date: April
Additional Information: www.ox.ac.uk/admissions/gradu ate/fees-and-funding/fees-funding-and-scholarship-search/scholarships-a-z-listing

For further information contact:

University of Oxford, University Offices, 15 Wellington Square, Oxford OX1 2JD, United Kingdom.

Tel: (44) 1865 270000
Fax: (44) 1865 270708

Oxford-Louis Curran Graduate Scholarship

Purpose: The Oxford-Louis Curran Graduate Scholarship is available for applicants who are applying for a course within the Faculty of Music (with a preference for the DPhil in Music). The scholarship was established in memory of the late Professor Louis Curran, who read Musicology at Linacre College and left a generous bequest to Linacre College to support the study of music.
Eligibility: The scholarship is only tenable at Linacre College.
Type: Scholarship
Value: The scholarship covers course fees and a grant for living costs.
Country of Study: Any country
Closing Date: April
Additional Information: www.ox.ac.uk/admissions/gradu ate/fees-and-funding/fees-funding-and-scholarship-search/scholarships-a-z-listing

For further information contact:

University of Oxford, University Offices, 15 Wellington Square, Oxford OX1 2JD, United Kingdom.

Tel: (44) 1865 270000
Fax: (44) 1865 270708

Oxford-Mary Jane Grefenstette Graduate Scholarship

Eligibility: Open to all applicants applying for a DPhil in Computer Science or Philosophy, specialising in the cross-over between the subjects. Tenable at Hertford College only. Please see website for more details

Level of Study: Postgraduate
Type: Scholarship
Value: University fee, college fee, and full living expenses
Length of Study: Period of fee liability
Frequency: Annual
Study Establishment: Hertford
Country of Study: United Kingdom
Application Procedure: For more information, please check the website www.ox.ac.uk/admissions/graduate/fees-and-funding/fees-funding-and-scholarship-search/scholarships-3#grefenstette
Closing Date: 22 January
Funding: Trusts

For further information contact:

Email: enquiries@cs.ox.ac.uk

Oxford-Mitsui & Co. Europe PLC Graduate Scholarships

Purpose: Two full scholarships are available for applicants ordinarily resident in Africa, and who are applying for the full-time MSc in African Studies
Eligibility: Open to applicants ordinarily resident in Africa, applying for the full-time MSc in African Studies. You are applying to start a new graduate course;; You submit your course application by the relevant January admissions deadline;; You are subsequently offered a place after consideration of applications received by the deadline;; Your application is not placed on a waiting list or held back after the January admissions deadline to be re-evaluated against applications received by the March admissions deadline; and You meet the eligibility criteria. This content was originally published on After School Africa from www.afterschoolafrica.com/17003/oxford-mitsui-scholarships/
Level of Study: Postgraduate
Type: Scholarship
Value: Covers course fees, college fees and a grant for living costs of at least £14,553
Length of Study: Period of fee liability
Frequency: Annual
Study Establishment: University of Oxford
Country of Study: Any country
Closing Date: May
Funding: Trusts
Additional Information: For more information, please check the website: www.ox.ac.uk/admissions/graduate/fees-and-funding/fees-funding-and-scholarship-search/scholarships-3#mitsui www.scholarshipdesk.com/oxford-mitsui-co-europe-plc-full-graduate-scholarships-uk/

For further information contact:

Email: webmaster@ox.ac.uk

Oxford-Murray Graduate Scholarship

Purpose: One full scholarship is available for applicants who are applying to one of the following full-time courses: MSt in Greek and/or Latin Languages and Literature, MPhil in Greek and/or Latin Languages and Literature, MSt in Greek and/or Roman History, MPhil in Greek and/or Roman History.
Eligibility: The scholarship is only tenable at Wadham College.
Type: Scholarship
Value: The scholarship covers course fees and a grant for living costs.
Frequency: Annual
Country of Study: Any country
No. of awards offered: 1
Closing Date: April
Additional Information: www.ox.ac.uk/admissions/graduate/fees-and-funding/fees-funding-and-scholarship-search/scholarships-a-z-listing

For further information contact:

University of Oxford, University Offices, 15 Wellington Square, Oxford OX1 2JD, United Kingdom.

Tel: (44) 1865 270000
Fax: (44) 1865 270708

Oxford-Nicholas Bratt Graduate Scholarship

Purpose: The Oxford-Nicholas Bratt Graduate Scholarship is available for any applicants who are applying to undertake any postgraduate Taught or Research courses offered by the Mathematical, Physical and Life Sciences (MPLS) Division (except for those offered by the Mathematical Institute), in which St John's College accepts applications.
Eligibility: The scholarship is only tenable at St John's College.
Type: Scholarship
Value: The scholarship covers course fees and a grant for living costs.
Frequency: Annual
Country of Study: Any country
Closing Date: April
Additional Information: www.ox.ac.uk/admissions/graduate/fees-and-funding/fees-funding-and-scholarship-search/scholarships-a-z-listing

U

For further information contact:

University of Oxford, University Offices, 15 Wellington Square, Oxford OX1 2JD, United Kingdom.

Tel: (44) 1865 270000
Fax: (44) 1865 270708

Oxford-Nizami Ganjavi Graduate Scholarships

Purpose: The University of Oxford is home to a dedicated centre for the study of Azerbaijan, the Caucasus and Central Asia, thanks to generous philanthropic support from the British Foundation for the Study of Azerbaijan and the Caucasus (BFSAC)
Eligibility: Open to applicants applying for any full or part-time DPhil or Master's course offered by the Humanities or Social Sciences Division where the course content relates to the study of the history, languages and cultures of Azerbaijan, the Caucasus and Central Asia. Please see the website for further details, including how to apply
Level of Study: Graduate
Type: Scholarship
Frequency: Annual
Country of Study: Any country
Closing Date: April
Funding: Private
Additional Information: www.scholarshipdesk.com/oxford-mitsui-co-europe-plc-full-graduate-scholarships-uk/

For further information contact:

Tel: (44) 1865 270 000
Fax: (44) 1865 270 708

Oxford-Oak Foundation Clinical Medicine

Eligibility: Open to applicants who are applying to the full-time DPhil in Clinical Medicine, specializing in Tropical Medicine and Global Health, with a preferences for the candidates to be ordinarily resident in Nepal, Zimbabwe, Kenya and Vietnam
Level of Study: Doctorate
Type: Scholarship
Value: £14,553
Country of Study: United Kingdom
Closing Date: 1 May

Oxford-Oxford Thai Foundation Graduate Scholarship

Purpose: The scholarship is jointly funded by the University and The Oxford Thai Foundation. The Oxford Thai Foundation is a scholarship programme to help promising young professionals from Thailand in the broader field of public policy to pursue advanced degrees at the University of Oxford. The programme wishes to create a strong network of future thinkers and leaders, built on mutual respect and trust developed during their time at Oxford, as well as through activities organised by the Foundation upon their return to Thailand. The goal is a more cohesive and equitable society, built on an inclusive public policy development platform.
Eligibility: Scholarship is available for applicants who are ordinarily resident in Thailand and intending to return there after graduation.
Type: Scholarship
Value: The scholarship covers course fees and a grant for living costs.
Frequency: Annual
Country of Study: Any country
Closing Date: May
Additional Information: www.ox.ac.uk/admissions/graduate/fees-and-funding/fees-funding-and-scholarship-search/scholarships-a-z-listing

For further information contact:

University of Oxford, University Offices, 15 Wellington Square, Oxford OX1 2JD, United Kingdom.

Tel: (44) 1865 270000
Fax: (44) 1865 270708

Oxford-Particle Physics Graduate Scholarship

Purpose: The scholarship has been made possible through the support of an anonymous donor, with the aim of supporting an outstanding thinker of tomorrow undertaking research in the field of experimental particle physics.
Eligibility: Open to applicants who are applying to the full-time DPhil Particle Physics course
Level of Study: Doctorate
Type: Scholarship
Value: University fee, college fee, and full living expenses
Length of Study: Duration of fee liability
Country of Study: Any country
Closing Date: April
Additional Information: Please visit the website: www.ox.ac.uk/admissions/graduate/fees-and-funding/fees-funding-and-scholarship-search/scholarships-3#particlephysics www.ox.ac.uk/admissions/graduate/courses/dphil-particle-physics?wssl=1

For further information contact:

Email: contact@physics.ox.ac.uk

Oxford-Patrick Duncan Graduate Scholarships

Purpose: The scholarship is jointly funded by the University, St Antony's College and the family of Patrick Duncan (1918-67), who was a South African political activist with a particular interest in sustainable development.
Eligibility: The scholarship is only tenable at St Antony's College.
Type: Scholarship
Value: The scholarship covers course fees and a grant for living costs.
Frequency: Annual
Country of Study: Any country
Closing Date: March
Additional Information: www.ox.ac.uk/admissions/graduate/fees-and-funding/fees-funding-and-scholarship-search/scholarships-a-z-listing

For further information contact:

University of Oxford, University Offices, 15 Wellington Square, Oxford OX1 2JD, United Kingdom.

Tel: (44) 1865 270000
Fax: (44) 1865 270708

Oxford-Percival Stanion Graduate Scholarship in Biochemistry

Eligibility: Open to applicants who are applying to the DPhil Biochemistry or MSc by Research Biochemistry. Tenable at Pembroke College only. Please see the website for more details
Level of Study: Doctorate, Postgraduate
Type: Scholarship
Value: University fee, college fee, and a grant for living costs
Length of Study: Period of fee liability
Study Establishment: Pembroke College
Country of Study: Any country
Closing Date: 6 January
Additional Information: Please visit the website: www.ox.ac.uk/admissions/graduate/fees-and-funding/fees-funding-and-scholarship-search/scholarships-3#percivalstanion www.pmb.ox.ac.uk/oxford-percival-stanion-graduate-stories

For further information contact:

St Aldate's, Oxford OX1 1DW, United Kingdom.

Tel: (44) 1865 276444
Fax: (44) 1865 276418
Email: ioannis.vakonakis@bioch.ox.ac.uk

Oxford-Pershing Square Graduate Scholarships

Purpose: Established in 2014, the Pershing Square Scholarships provide up to six full awards covering both the Master's and the MBA degrees. Scholars can pursue any of the partnering Master's degrees and combine it with our MBA.
Eligibility: Applicants to the Oxford 1+1 MBA Programme. Applicants who apply to any full-time one-year Master's course that is not currently part of the official list of partner 1+1 MBA Programme, and to the MBA (as a separate application). Current Oxford students on a non-MBA course, who are applying to the MBA after the completion of their current Master's/DPhil course (with no gap year(s)).
Level of Study: Masters Degree
Type: Scholarship
Value: £15,609
Country of Study: Any country
No. of awards offered: 6
Closing Date: 12 January
Additional Information: www.sbs.ox.ac.uk/oxford-experience/scholarships-and-funding/oxford-pershing-square-graduate-scholarships

For further information contact:

University of Oxford, University Offices, 15 Wellington Square, Oxford OX1 2JD, United Kingdom.

Tel: (44) 1865 270000
Fax: (44) 1865 270708

Oxford-Qatar-Thatcher Graduate Scholarships

Purpose: The Oxford-Qatar-Thatcher Graduate Scholarship has been created as a result of a £3 million donation by the Qatar Development Fund, which supports international education, health and economic development causes.
Eligibility: Candidates who have been accepted to study at the University of Oxford on a graduate course offered by the Faculty of English Language and Literature, Department of Engineering Science or Faculty of Law. There is a preference for students ordinarily resident in Algeria, Bahrain, Egypt, Iraq, Jordan, Kuwait, Lebanon, Libya, Morocco, Oman, Palestine, Qatar, Saudi Arabia, Sudan, Syria, Tunisia, United Arab Emirates or Yemen
Level of Study: Postgraduate
Type: Scholarship
Value: Tuition fees, college fees and a grant for living costs
Length of Study: Period of fee liability
Frequency: Annual
Study Establishment: Somerville College
Country of Study: Any country

U

No. of awards offered: 4
Closing Date: April
Funding: Trusts

For further information contact:

Email: academic.office@some.ox.ac.uk

Oxford-Qatar-Thatcher Graduate Scholarships

Purpose: The scholarship is jointly funded by the University and the Thatcher Development Programme at Somerville College. The late Lady Thatcher studied Chemistry at Somerville College Oxford from 1943 to 1946 and received bursary and scholarship support from the College.
Eligibility: The scholarship is only tenable at Somerville College. Countries: Algeria, Bahrain, Egypt, Iraq, Jordan, Kuwait, Lebanon, Libya, Morocco, Oman, Palestine, Qatar, Saudi Arabia, Sudan, Syria, Tunisia, United Arab Emirates, Yemen.
Type: Scholarship
Value: The scholarship covers course fees and a grant for living costs.
Frequency: Annual
Country of Study: Any country
Closing Date: April
Additional Information: www.ox.ac.uk/admissions/gradu ate/fees-and-funding/fees-funding-and-scholarship-search/ scholarships-a-z-listing

For further information contact:

University of Oxford, University Offices, 15 Wellington Square, Oxford OX1 2JD, United Kingdom.

Tel: (44) 1865 270000
Fax: (44) 1865 270708

Oxford-Radcliffe Graduate Scholarships

Purpose: The scholarships are unique to University College, supported by an historic £10m gift from a group of the College's Old Members, the largest single gift received by the college in modern times.
Type: Scholarship
Value: The scholarship covers course fees and provides a grant for living costs.
Frequency: Annual
Country of Study: Any country
No. of awards offered: 13
Closing Date: April

Additional Information: www.ox.ac.uk/admissions/gradu ate/fees-and-funding/fees-funding-and-scholarship-search/ scholarships-a-z-listing

For further information contact:

University of Oxford, University Offices, 15 Wellington Square, Oxford OX1 2JD, United Kingdom.

Tel: (44) 1865 270000
Fax: (44) 1865 270708

Oxford-Richards Graduate Scholarships

Purpose: The scholarships have been made possible through the support of the University and David Richards' generous bequest. David Richards (1939–2015) studied at Wadham College from 1961 and was a distinguished alumnus and Foundation Fellow of the College.
Eligibility: The scholarship is only tenable at Wadham College.
Type: Scholarship
Value: The scholarship covers course fees and a grant for living costs.
Frequency: Annual
Country of Study: Any country
No. of awards offered: 3
Closing Date: May
Additional Information: www.ox.ac.uk/admissions/gradu ate/fees-and-funding/fees-funding-and-scholarship-search/ scholarships-a-z-listing

For further information contact:

University of Oxford, University Offices, 15 Wellington Square, Oxford OX1 2JD, United Kingdom.

Tel: (44) 1865 270000
Fax: (44) 1865 270708

Oxford-Robert and Soulla Kyprianou Graduate Scholarship

Purpose: The University of Oxford is currently accepting applications for the Oxford-Robert and Soulla Kyprianou Program. This fully-funded scholarship is exclusively open to students from Republic of Cyprus
Eligibility: Open to applicants ordinarily resident in the Republic of Cyprus, applying for any full- or part-time master's or DPhil course offered by Brasenose College. This scholarship is open to applicants who are ordinarily resident in the Republic of Cyprus and who are applying for a full- or

part-time master's or DPhil course, within the range accepted by Brasenose College
Level of Study: Doctorate, Postgraduate
Type: Scholarship
Value: £14,296
Length of Study: Period of fee liability
Study Establishment: Brasenose College
Country of Study: United Kingdom
Closing Date: April
Additional Information: The scholarship is only tenable at Brasenose College. Please check the website: www.ox.ac.uk/admissions/graduate/fees-and-funding/fees-funding-and-scholarship-search/scholarships-3#kyprianou www.scholarshipdesk.com/oxford-robert-and-soulla-kyprianou-full-scholarships/

For further information contact:

Email: contact@scholarshipdesk.com

Oxford-Rothermere American Institute Graduate Scholarship

Eligibility: Open to applicants who are ordinarily resident in the EEA and who are applying to a full- or part-time DPhil in History, specialising in American History. The scholarship is ordinarily tenable at University College. Please see website for more details
Level of Study: Doctorate
Type: Scholarship
Value: £9,000
Length of Study: Period of fee liability
Study Establishment: University College
Country of Study: Any country
Closing Date: April

For further information contact:

Email: enquiries@rai.ox.ac.uk

Oxford-Ryniker Lloyd Graduate Scholarship

Purpose: The scholarship has been made possible through the support of the University and a generous legacy donation from Robert Lloyd. He cared deeply about supporting postgraduate students and scientific research, in commemoration of Eleanor Ruth Ryniker and Somerville alumna Elizabeth Lloyd.
Eligibility: The scholarship is only tenable at Somerville College.
Type: Scholarship
Value: The scholarship covers course fees and a grant for living costs.

Frequency: Annual
Country of Study: Any country
Closing Date: April
Additional Information: www.ox.ac.uk/admissions/graduate/fees-and-funding/fees-funding-and-scholarship-search/scholarships-a-z-listing

For further information contact:

University of Oxford, University Offices, 15 Wellington Square, Oxford OX1 2JD, United Kingdom.

Tel: (44) 1865 270000
Fax: (44) 1865 270708

Oxford-Sheikh Mohammed bin Rashid Al Maktoum Graduate Scholarship

Purpose: The scholarships are available to applicants who are applying to any full-time Master's and DPhil courses, except the Master of Business Administration (MBA). You should be intending to return to one of the eligible countries on completion of your studies.
Eligibility: The Oxford-Sheikh Mohammed bin Rashid Al Maktoum Graduate Scholarships are available for applicants who are nationals of and ordinarily resident in one of the following countries: Algeria, Bahrain, Comoros, Djibouti, Egypt, Iraq, Jordan, Kuwait, Lebanon, Libya, Mauritania, Morocco, Oman, Palestine, Qatar, Saudi Arabia, Somalia, Sudan, Syria, Tunisia, United Arab Emirates, and Yemen.
Type: Residency
Value: The scholarship covers course fees and a grant for living costs.
Frequency: Annual
Country of Study: Any country
Closing Date: June
Additional Information: www.ox.ac.uk/admissions/graduate/fees-and-funding/fees-funding-and-scholarship-search/scholarships-a-z-listing

For further information contact:

University of Oxford, University Offices, 15 Wellington Square, Oxford OX1 2JD, United Kingdom.

Tel: (44) 1865 270000
Fax: (44) 1865 270708

Oxford-Sir Anwar Pervez Graduate Scholarships

Purpose: The scholarship is funded by the Imperial Majesty Oba Adéyeyè Enitan Ògúnwùsì and aims to provide funding

U

to exceptional candidates pursuing postgraduate study of Africa

Eligibility: 1. Open to applicants ordinarily resident in Pakistan, who have not previously studied for an HE qualification outside of Pakistan. 2. Candidates can be applying for any graduate course. Scholars to be selected on the basis of academic merit and financial need. Please see the website for further details

Level of Study: Postgraduate

Type: Scholarship

Value: University fee, college fee, and full living expenses of at least £14,777

Length of Study: Period of fee liability

Frequency: Annual

Country of Study: United Kingdom

Application Procedure: For more information, please check the website www.ox.ac.uk/admissions/graduate/fees-and-funding/fees-funding-and-scholarship-search/scholarships-3#pervez

Closing Date: April

Funding: Trusts

Additional Information: www.ox.ac.uk/admissions/graduate/fees-and-funding/fees-funding-and-scholarship-search/scholarships-a-z-listing?wssl=1

For further information contact:

Tel: (44) 1865 611 530
Email: enquiries@devoff.ox.ac.uk

Oxford-Sir David Weatherall Graduate Scholarship

Eligibility: Open to applicants who are applying to a full-time DPhil in Medical Sciences, based at the Weatherall Institute of Molecular Medicine. The scholarship is only tenable at Green Templeton College

Level of Study: Doctorate

Type: Scholarship

Value: University fee, college fee, and full living expenses

Length of Study: Duration of fee liability

Study Establishment: Green Templeton College

Country of Study: Any country

Closing Date: 6 January

Additional Information: Please visit the website: www.ox.ac.uk/admissions/graduate/fees-and-funding/fees-funding-and-scholarship-search/scholarships-3#weatherall www.gtc.ox.ac.uk/news-and-events/news/profile-spencer-tong-dphil-oxford-sir-david-weatherall-scholar/

For further information contact:

Email: development@gtc.ox.ac.uk

Oxford-Swire Graduate Scholarship

Purpose: The Swire Scholarship has allowed me to pursue my goal of improving the educational outcomes of disadvantaged learners in secondary classrooms in China and internationally. In my DPhil, I will explore the classroom interactions, teachers and students perceptions on teaching and learning processes in secondary classrooms, and their language challenges and copying strategies.

Eligibility: Open to all applicants for any full- or part-time master's and DPhil courses in the Faculty of History, within the range accepted by University College

Level of Study: Doctorate, Postgraduate

Type: Scholarship

Value: 100% of the course fees, a grant for living costs of £17,442 per year

Length of Study: Period of fee liability

Country of Study: Any country

Closing Date: 1 March

Additional Information: The scholarship is only tenable at University College. Please check the website: www.ox.ac.uk/admissions/graduate/fees-and-funding/fees-funding-and-scholarship-search/scholarships-3#swire www.sant.ox.ac.uk/prospective-students/fees-and-funding/scholarships-new-students/swire

For further information contact:

Email: swirescholarships@jsshk.com

Oxford-Thatcher Graduate Scholarships

Purpose: The scholarship is jointly funded by the University and the Thatcher Development Programme at Somerville College. The late Lady Thatcher, studied Chemistry at Somerville College Oxford from 1943 to 1946 and received bursary and scholarship support from the College.

Eligibility: The scholarship is only tenable at Somerville College.

Type: Scholarship

Value: The scholarship covers course fees and a grant for living costs.

Frequency: Annual

Country of Study: Any country

No. of awards offered: 2

Closing Date: April

Additional Information: www.ox.ac.uk/admissions/graduate/fees-and-funding/fees-funding-and-scholarship-search/scholarships-a-z-listing

For further information contact:

University of Oxford, University Offices, 15 Wellington Square, Oxford OX1 2JD, United Kingdom.

Tel: (44) 1865 270000
Fax: (44) 1865 270708

Oxford-The Simcox Family Graduate Scholarship

Purpose: One full scholarship is available for applicants who are ordinarily resident in the United Kingdom and who are applying to a DPhil course at Oxford related to Fibrodysplasia Ossificans Progressiva within the Nuffield Department of Medicine. The scholarship covers course fees at Home rate only.
Type: Scholarship
Value: £18,000
Frequency: Annual
Country of Study: Any country
No. of awards offered: 1
Closing Date: January
Additional Information: www.ox.ac.uk/admissions/gradu ate/fees-and-funding/fees-funding-and-scholarship-search/ scholarships-a-z-listing

For further information contact:

University of Oxford, University Offices, 15 Wellington Square, Oxford OX1 2JD, United Kingdom.

Oxford-TrygFonden Graduate Scholarship

Purpose: One full scholarship is available for applicants who are ordinarily resident in Denmark and who are applying for one of the following courses (preference will be given to courses in the order listed) MSc Evidence-Based Social Intervention and Policy Evaluation; MSc Education, with a speciality in Research Training
Eligibility: Open to applicants ordinarily resident in Denmark who are applying to various master's courses. One full scholarship is available for applicants who are ordinarily resident in Denmark and who are applying for one of the following courses (preference will be given to courses in the order listed) MSc Evidence-Based Social Intervention and Policy Evaluation; MSc Education, with a speciality in Research Training
Level of Study: Postgraduate
Type: Scholarship
Value: It covers the expenditure of about £14,777 (students on part-time courses will receive a study support grant instead)

Length of Study: Period of fee liability
Frequency: Annual
Country of Study: Any country
Application Procedure: 1. The eligibility criteria will be applied automatically, using the details you provide in the relevant sections of the graduate application form (for example, your country of ordinary residence and your previous education institutions), to determine whether you are eligible. 2. Selection is based on academic merit, unless specified otherwise. Some of the scholarships are only tenable at specific colleges. Unless specified otherwise, you do not need to select that college as your preference on the graduate application form. All eligible applicants will be considered, regardless of which college (if any) you state as your preference. However, successful applicants will be transferred to the relevant college in order to take up the scholarship
Closing Date: April
Funding: Private
Additional Information: Please check the website: www. ox.ac.uk/admissions/graduate/fees-and-funding/fees-funding-and-scholarship-search/scholarships-3#trygfonden

For further information contact:

Tel: (44) 1865 270 000
Fax: (44) 1865 270 708

Oxford-TrygFonden Graduate Scholarships

Purpose: The scholarship is jointly funded by the University and by TrygFonden. TrygFonden is a Danish not-for-profit foundation which encourages close interactions between scientific research and the practical world, in which interventions are developed, tested, and implemented. The key objectives of the scholarship are to strengthen Denmark's capacity in this area.
Eligibility: scholarships are available for applicants who are ordinarily resident in Denmark
Type: Scholarship
Value: The scholarship covers course fees and a grant for living costs (students on part-time courses will receive a study support grant).
Frequency: Annual
Country of Study: Any country
No. of awards offered: 2
Closing Date: April
Additional Information: www.ox.ac.uk/admissions/gradu ate/fees-and-funding/fees-funding-and-scholarship-search/ scholarships-a-z-listing

U

For further information contact:

University of Oxford, University Offices, 15 Wellington Square, Oxford OX1 2JD, United Kingdom.

Tel: (44) 1865 270000
Fax: (44) 1865 270708

Oxford-University College-Burma Graduate Scholarship

Purpose: The scholarship is jointly funded by the University and a syndicate of generous donors to University College.
Eligibility: The scholarship is only tenable at University College.
Type: Scholarship
Value: The scholarship covers course fees provides and a grant for living costs.
Frequency: Annual
Country of Study: Any country
Closing Date: April
Additional Information: www.ox.ac.uk/admissions/graduate/fees-and-funding/fees-funding-and-scholarship-search/scholarships-a-z-listing

For further information contact:

University of Oxford, University Offices, 15 Wellington Square, Oxford OX1 2JD, United Kingdom.

Tel: (44) 1865 270000
Fax: (44) 1865 270708

Oxford-Urquhart-RAI Graduate Scholarship

Eligibility: Open to applicants who are ordinarily resident in the EEA or Switzerland and who are applying to a DPhil in Politics, specializing in American Politics
Value: University fee, college fee and full living expenses
Length of Study: Period of fee liability
Country of Study: Any country
Closing Date: 6 January
Additional Information: For more details, please visit www.ox.ac.uk/admissions/graduate/fees-and-funding/fees-funding-and-scholarship-search/scholarships-3#urquhart

For further information contact:

Email: enquiries@rai.ox.ac.uk

Oxford-Wadham Graduate Scholarships for Disabled Students

Purpose: Scholarships are awarded to applicants who have demonstrated excellent academic ability, who will contribute to the University's ground-breaking research, and who will go on to contribute to the world as leaders in their field, pushing the frontiers of knowledge
Eligibility: Open to all applicants applying to any full- and part-time master's courses offered by Wadham College, who have a disability as defined by the Equality Act and determined by the University's Disability Advisory Service
Level of Study: Postgraduate
Type: Scholarship
Value: Full Tuition + Stipend
Frequency: Annual
Study Establishment: Wadham College
Country of Study: Any country
Closing Date: 15 January
Funding: Trusts

For further information contact:

Email: graduate.admissions@wadham.ox.ac.uk

Oxford-Weidenfeld and Hoffmann Scholarships and Leadership Programme

Purpose: The Oxford-Weidenfeld and Hoffman Scholarship and Leadership Programme supports outstanding students from transition and emerging economies throughout Africa
Eligibility: Open to applicants from selected countries to selected courses. Please see website for more details and how to apply, including closing dates
Level of Study: Postgraduate
Type: Scholarship
Value: The scholarship will cover 100% of course fees and a grant for living costs (of at least £15,609)
Frequency: Annual
Country of Study: Any country
Closing Date: April/May
Funding: Trusts
Additional Information: For more information, please check the website: www.graduate.ox.ac.uk/weidenfeld-oxford www.ox.ac.uk/admissions/graduate/fees-and-funding/fees-funding-and-scholarship-search/weidenfeld-hoffmann-scholarships-and-leadership-programme

For further information contact:

Weidenfeld-Hoffmann Trust, Saïd Business School, Park End Street, Oxford OX1 1HP, United Kingdom.

Email: info@whtrust.org

Oxford-Wolfson-Ancient History Graduate Scholarship

Eligibility: Open to applicants ordinarily resident in the EEA or Switzerland, applying for any graduate course in Ancient History, preferably with a focus on economics and banking. Tenable at Wolfson College only. Please see website for more details

Level of Study: Postgraduate

Type: Scholarship

Value: University fee, college fee, and full living expenses

Length of Study: Period of fee liability

Frequency: Annual

Study Establishment: Wolfson

Country of Study: United Kingdom

Application Procedure: For more information, please check the website www.ox.ac.uk/admissions/graduate/fees-and-funding/fees-funding-and-scholarship-search/scholarships-3#wolfsonancienthistory

Closing Date: 22 January

Funding: Trusts

For further information contact:

Wolfson College, Linton Road, Oxford OX2 6UD, United Kingdom.

Oxford-Wolfson-Marriott Graduate Scholarships

Purpose: The scholarships have been made possible through the support of the late Dr Frances Marriott (a University lecturer in biomathematics and taught statistics and a Fellow of Wolfson College) and by departments and faculties.

Eligibility: The scholarship is only tenable at Wolfson College.

Type: Scholarship

Value: The scholarship covers course fees and a grant for living costs.

Frequency: Annual

Country of Study: Any country

Closing Date: May

Additional Information: www.ox.ac.uk/admissions/graduate/fees-and-funding/fees-funding-and-scholarship-search/scholarships-a-z-listing

For further information contact:

University of Oxford, University Offices, 15 Wellington Square, Oxford OX1 2JD, United Kingdom.

Tel: (44) 1865 270000
Fax: (44) 1865 270708

Oxford-Wolfson-Min Sunshik Graduate Scholarship in Modern Korean Literature

Eligibility: Open to applicants who are ordinarily resident in the EEA or Switzerland and who are applying to the full-time MSt Korean Studies. Preference will be given to applicants focussing on Modern Korean Literature and Translation Studies

Level of Study: Postgraduate

Type: Scholarship

Value: University fee, college fee, and a grant for living expenses

Length of Study: Period of fee liability

Frequency: Annual

Study Establishment: Wolfson College

Country of Study: Any country

Closing Date: 20 January

Funding: Trusts

Additional Information: he scholarship is only tenable at Wolfson College. For more information, please check the website: www.ox.ac.uk/admissions/graduate/fees-and-funding/fees-funding-and-scholarship-search/scholarships-3#minsunshik www.britishkoreansociety.org.uk/uncategorized/oxford-wolfson-min-sunshik-graduate-scholarship-in-modern-korean-literature/

Pembroke College Jose Gregorio Hernandez Award of the Venezuelan National Academy of Medicine

Eligibility: Open to nationals of Venezuela. Students must be nominated by the Venezuelan National Academy of Medicine and then accepted by the General Medical Council

Level of Study: Postgraduate

Type: Stipendiary

Value: Full fees and maintenance

Length of Study: 1 year, renewable for a further year

Frequency: Dependent on funds available

Study Establishment: Pembroke College, University of Oxford

Country of Study: United Kingdom

Application Procedure: Applicants must write or email the Admissions Secretary for details

Funding: Private

For further information contact:

Pembroke College, Cambridge CB2 1RF, United Kingdom.

Email: admissions@pmb.ox.ac.uk

Pembroke College: Gordon Aldrick Scholarship

Purpose: To assist scholars in Chinese cultural studies
Eligibility: Open to candidates beginning a two or three-year research degree at Oxford
Level of Study: Research
Type: Scholarship
Value: £5,000 per year towards college fee and contribution towards living expenses
Length of Study: Tenable for up to three years whilst the recipient is liable to pay University and College fees. Automatically renewed each year if satisfactory academic progress is made
Frequency: Annual
Country of Study: Any country
Application Procedure: Intending candidates should apply in Section L of the Oxford University graduate application form or notify the Admissions & Access Officer at Pembroke
Closing Date: 1 May

For further information contact:

Email: jane.sherwood@admin.ox.ac.uk

Pembroke College: Tokyo Electric Power Company (TEPCO) Scholarship

Eligibility: Open to all graduate applicants specialising in studies of Japanese literature, art or history. Please see website for details of how to apply at
Level of Study: Research
Value: £5,000 per year towards college fee and contribution towards living expenses
Length of Study: Period of fee liability
Country of Study: Any country
Closing Date: 3 May

For further information contact:

Email: ben.nicholson@admin.ox.ac.uk

Philosophy Faculty-Wolfson College Joint Scholarship

Eligibility: Open to Home/European Union graduate applicants to DPhil courses in the Faculty of Philosophy. Eligible applicants for these courses are automatically considered. Please see website for more information
Level of Study: Postgraduate
Type: Scholarship
Value: £5,000
Frequency: Annual

Study Establishment: Wolfson
Country of Study: United Kingdom
Application Procedure: Applications for Wolfson Bursaries and Scholarships should be submitted on the form that will become available after mid-December here www.wolfson.cam.ac.uk/postgraduate-study/fees-funding/postgraduate-studentship-application
No. of awards offered: 1
Closing Date: 1 May
Funding: Trusts

For further information contact:

Email: graduatestudies@mml.cam.ac.uk

Physics: Engineering and Physical Sciences Research Council (EPSRC) and Doctoral Training Grant Studentships

Eligibility: United Kingdom residents are eligible for full awards, including fees and maintenance; European Union residents are eligible for awards covering fees only. European Union Students who have studied in the United Kingdom for the previous 3 years are eligible for a full award. The Department automatically considers all eligible applicants who have been offered places and who have applied by the January deadline
Type: Studentship
Value: University fee, college fee, and living expenses (European Union fee-only awards)
Length of Study: Period of fee liability
Country of Study: Any country
Application Procedure: Please visit the website for application details
Closing Date: 22 January
Additional Information: Please check at www2.physics.ox.ac.uk/study-here/postgraduates/fees-and-funding www.epsrc.group.cam.ac.uk/DTP

Pirie-Reid Scholarships

Purpose: To enable persons who would otherwise be prevented by lack of funds to begin a course of study at Oxford
Eligibility: Preference will be given to candidate's who have lived in or been educated in Scotland, who are applying from other universities (i.e. not already studying at Oxford)
Level of Study: Doctorate, Postgraduate
Type: Scholarship
Value: University and college fees normally at the home rate plus maintenance grant, subject to assessment of income from other sources

Length of Study: Renewable from year to year, subject to satisfactory progress and continuance of approved full-time study
Frequency: Annual
Study Establishment: University of Oxford
Country of Study: United Kingdom
Application Procedure: Candidates must apply for admission to the University through the Graduate Admissions Office (www.admin.ox.ac.uk/gsp)
Closing Date: December or January
Funding: Private
Additional Information: Preference will be given to candidates domiciled or educated in Scotland. Candidates not fulfilling these criteria are unlikely to be successful scholarship-positions.com/2012-pirie-reid-scholarship-for-graduate-studies-at-oxford-university-uk/2011/10/03/

For further information contact:

Email: student.funding@admin.ox.ac.uk

Politics and International Relations: ESRC DTC +3 Studentships (Doctoral Awards)

Eligibility: Open to all United Kingdom applicants for DPhil Politics and DPhil International Relations. Other European Union nationals are eligible for a fees-only award
Level of Study: Graduate, Postdoctorate
Type: Studentship
Value: University fee, college fee and full living expenses
Length of Study: Period of fee liability
Country of Study: Any country
Application Procedure: Please visit website for more details and how to apply
Closing Date: 9 January
Additional Information: Please check at www.politics.ox.ac.uk/index.php/student-funding/student-funding.html

For further information contact:

Email: r.llewellyn@bbk.ac.uk

Radcliffe Department of Medicine: RDM Scholars Programme

Eligibility: Open to basic science applicants of any nationality applying for projects based within the Radcliffe Department of Medicine. Please see additional information on personal statement on the RDM webpage
Level of Study: Doctorate
Type: Scholarship

Value: £18,000 per annum
Length of Study: 4 years
Frequency: Annual
Country of Study: Any country
Closing Date: 1 July
Additional Information: For more details, please visit www.rdm.ox.ac.uk/rdm-scholars-programme www.european-funding-guide.eu/other-financial-assistance/13805-rdm%C2%A0scholars-programme

For further information contact:

Email: graduate.enquiries@rdm.ox.ac.uk

Radiation Oncology & Biology: Departmental Studentships

Purpose: To provide comprehensive preparation for a career in research or industry, whether in radiobiology, protection or the advancement of cancer treatments
Eligibility: Open to home/European Union and overseas students
Level of Study: Postgraduate, Research
Type: Studentship
Value: University and college fees at the home/European Union rate, stipend, research expenses and support with travel to conferences
Length of Study: Up to 4 years
Frequency: Annual
Country of Study: Any country
Closing Date: 10 January
Contributor: Cancer Research United Kingdom(United Kingdom) or Medical Research Council(MRC)
Additional Information: The Medical Research Council (MRC) awards have residency requirements www.ox.ac.uk/admissions/graduate/courses/msc-radiation-biology?wssl=1

For further information contact:

Tel: (44) 1865 617410
Email: graduate.studies@oncology.ox.ac.uk

Regent's Park College: Eastern European Scholarship

Eligibility: Open to new or continuing graduate in theology from Central and Eastern Europe. Preference is shown for members of the Baptist denomination
Level of Study: Postgraduate, Research
Type: Scholarship
Value: Up to the amount of the College Fee each year
Length of Study: Up to 3 years

Frequency: Annual
Application Procedure: Please visit website for more details and how to apply
Closing Date: 1 February
Additional Information: Please check at www.rpc.ox.ac.uk/index.php?pageid=272&tln=Courses

For further information contact:

Regent's Park College, Pusey Street, Oxford OX1 2LB, United Kingdom.

Tel: (44) 1865 288 120
Fax: (44) 1865 288 121
Email: enquiries@regents.ox.ac.uk

Regent's Park College: Ernest Payne Scholarship

Eligibility: Open to all new and continuing United Kingdom graduate students of theology. Preference is shown for those preparing for the Baptist ministry
Level of Study: Postgraduate, Research
Type: Scholarship
Value: Up to the amount of the College Fee each year
Length of Study: 2 years initially
Application Procedure: Please visit website for more details and how to apply
Closing Date: 1 May
Additional Information: Scholarship is awarded over 2 years, extendable in proportion for a 3rd year. Please check at www.rpc.ox.ac.uk/index.php?pageid=272&tln=Courses

Regent's Park College: Henman Scholarship

Eligibility: Open to all graduate applicants in Theology
Level of Study: Postgraduate, Research
Type: Scholarship
Value: Up to the amount of the College Fee each year
Length of Study: Period of fee liability
Application Procedure: Please see website for details of how to apply
Closing Date: 1 May
Additional Information: Eligible to overseas nationals. Please check the website www.rpc.ox.ac.uk

For further information contact:

Email: larry.kreitzer@regents.ox.ac.uk

Regent's Park College: J W Lord Scholarship

Eligibility: Open to all graduate applicants in Theology that are preparing to serve Christian churches in India, Hong Kong or China, or otherwise in Asia, Africa, Central and South America and the Caribbean
Type: Scholarship
Value: Up to the value of the college fee each year
Length of Study: Up to 3 years
Frequency: Annual
Application Procedure: Please see website for details of how to apply
Closing Date: 1 May
Additional Information: Eligible to overseas countries. Please check the website www.rpc.ox.ac.uk/index.php?pageid=272&tln=Courses

Roche-Law Faculty Scholarship

Eligibility: Open to all graduate applicants to BCL/MJur, MSc in Law and Finance, MSt Legal Research, MPhil or DPhil Law. Award holders will become members of New College. Please see website for more information
Level of Study: Doctorate, Graduate, Postgraduate, Research
Type: Scholarship
Value: £10,000
Length of Study: Dependent on fee liability
Study Establishment: New College
Country of Study: Any country
Closing Date: 20 January
Additional Information: Please visit the website: www.law.ox.ac.uk/postgraduate/scholarships.php www.law.ox.ac.uk/admissions/graduate-scholarships/new-college-roche-scholarship

For further information contact:

Email: student.finance@new.ox.ac.uk

Sasakawa Fund Scholarships

Purpose: The scholarships will be awarded to applicants who are Japanese nationals currently on a course or starting a course at Oxford University, or alternatively to students from the UK or other countries currently on a course or starting a course at Oxford University which requires some period of study in Japan.
Eligibility: Candidates must be Japanese nationals or students from countries other than Japan whose course at the University of Oxford requires some period of study in Japan
Level of Study: Doctorate, Graduate, Postgraduate

Type: Scholarship
Value: Up to £10,000
Length of Study: 3 years
Frequency: Annual
Study Establishment: University of Oxford
Country of Study: United Kingdom
Application Procedure: To apply, please complete the Scholarship Application Form, along with 1. one reference (to be sent by the referee directly) 2. a Curriculum Vitae 3. a statement of research interests (of no more than six pages) including an outline and research proposal (for research degree applicants only) OR 4. a personal statement (of no more than six pages - for taught degree applicants only).
Closing Date: 31 March
Contributor: Japan Shipbuilding Industry Foundation

For further information contact:

Email: trustfunds@orinst.ox.ac.uk

Sasakawa Postgraduate Studentship in Japanese Studies

Eligibility: MSc or MPhil 1. Students planning to start an MSc or an MPhil degree 2. UK citizens are particularly encouraged to apply. Non-UK candidates are eligible only if they have been in the UK for at least 3 years immediately before the beginning of their MSc or MPhil study. 3. a first class undergraduate degree (or its equivalent for non-UK candidates) 4. Sasakawa Studentships cannot be combined with other sources of FULL funding.; DPhil 1. Students planning to start a doctoral degree programme 2. The studentships are open to the candidates of any nationality. However, the studentship programme aims at encouraging the successor generation of UK specialists and experts on Japan, and therefore, UK nationals are particularly encouraged to apply. 3. a very strong pass or distinction at masters level. 4. Sasakawa Studentships cannot be combined with other sources of FULL funding.
Level of Study: Doctorate, Postgraduate, Research
Type: Studentship
Value: £10,000
Length of Study: 1 year
Country of Study: Any country
Application Procedure: Please see website for more details, including how to apply
Closing Date: 1 May
Additional Information: Please check the website: www.nissan.ox.ac.uk/sasakawa-japanese-studies-postgraduate-studentships-0

For further information contact:

Tel: (44) 20 7074 5094/5091
Email: scholarships@soas.ac.uk

Saven European Scholarships

Purpose: The Saven European Scholarships have been created by a generous gift from Mr Bjorn Saven to support graduate students ordinarily resident in the following European countries who are applying to Oxford to undertake a full-time master's or DPhil course in any of over 140 subjects.
Eligibility: Countries: Austria, Belgium, Bulgaria, Estonia, Finland, France, Germany, Luxembourg, Norway, Poland, Portugal and Sweden.
Type: Scholarship
Value: Up to £25,000 in course fees.
Frequency: Annual
Country of Study: Any country
Closing Date: March
Additional Information: www.ox.ac.uk/admissions/graduate/fees-and-funding/fees-funding-and-scholarship-search/scholarships-a-z-listing

For further information contact:

University of Oxford, University Offices, 15 Wellington Square, Oxford OX1 2JD, United Kingdom.

Tel: (44) 1865 270000
Fax: (44) 1865 270708

Saïd Foundation Oxford Scholarships

Purpose: The scholarship will cover course fees, a grant for living costs (of at least £15,609) and flights to and from the UK at the start and end of your course. Awards are made for the full duration of your fee liability for the agreed course.
Eligibility: You must be applying to start a new full-time master's courses at Oxford, and be of Jordanian, Lebanese, Palestinian or Syrian nationality and ordinarily resident in Jordan, Lebanon, Syria, Palestine or Israel. You should be intending to return to one of these countries on completion of your course to apply your new skills and knowledge.
Type: Scholarship
Value: £15,609
Country of Study: Any country
Closing Date: 29 October
Additional Information: www.ox.ac.uk/admissions/graduate/fees-and-funding/fees-funding-and-scholarship-search/scholarships-a-z-listing

For further information contact:

University of Oxford, University Offices, 15 Wellington Square, Oxford OX1 2JD, United Kingdom.

Tel: (44) 1865 270000

School of Anthropology and Museum Ethnography: Peter Lienhardt/Philip Bagby Travel Awards

Eligibility: Open to new and current Anthropology students who are hoping to fund research/travel. Please see website for more details, including closing dates and how to apply
Level of Study: Postgraduate
Type: Scholarship
Value: Up to £1,000 for travel/small research projects only
Length of Study: Ad hoc
Frequency: Annual
Country of Study: United Kingdom
Application Procedure: For more information, please check the website: www.anthro.ox.ac.uk/prospective-students/funding/travel-grants/
Closing Date: 22 January
Funding: Trusts

For further information contact:

Email: information@anthro.ox.ac.uk

Sir William Dunn School of Pathology: Departmental PhD Prize Studentships

Value: £17,285 per annum
Length of Study: 4 years
Frequency: Annual
Country of Study: Any country
Closing Date: 3 December

For further information contact:

Tel: (44) 1865 275 500
Email: finance@path.ox.ac.uk

Social & Cultural Anthropology: Economic and Social Research Council

Eligibility: Open to United Kingdom applicants for Social Anthropology. Other European Union nationals are eligible for a fees-only award
Level of Study: Graduate

Type: Grant
Value: University fee, college fee and full living expenses
Length of Study: Period of fee liability
Country of Study: Any country
Application Procedure: Please visit website for more details and how to apply
Closing Date: 23 January
Additional Information: Please check at www.isca.ox.ac.uk/prospective-students/funding/

For further information contact:

Email: enquiries@sociology.ox.ac.uk

Social Policy and Intervention: Barnett House-Nuffield Joint Scholarship

Eligibility: Open to all applicants applying for the DPhil Social Policy at the Department of Social Policy and Intervention and Nuffield College
Value: Course fee, college fee, maintenance
Length of Study: 3 years
Country of Study: Any country
Closing Date: October
Additional Information: For more details, please visit www.spi.ox.ac.uk/study-with-us/funding.html www.spi.ox.ac.uk/departmental-scholarships#collapse401546

For further information contact:

Tel: (44) 1865 280734
Email: admissions@spi.ox.ac.uk

Social Policy and Intervention: Barnett Scholarship

Purpose: The scholarship is open to all students applying for a DPhil (both new students and those already in the department studying for an MSc or MPhil), and is awarded on the basis of academic merit, assessed on both academic track record and potential.
Eligibility: Open to all applicants applying for a DPhil at the Department of Social Policy and Intervention
Value: £25,000
Length of Study: 3 years or 2 years for MPhil applicants applying for 2 year DPhil study
Country of Study: Any country
Closing Date: 20 January
Additional Information: For more details, please visit www.spi.ox.ac.uk/study-with-us/funding.html www.spi.ox.ac.uk/departmental-scholarships#collapse401536

For further information contact:

Tel: (44) 1865 280734
Email: scholarships@spi.ox.ac.uk

Social Policy and Intervention: Centenary Scholarship

Eligibility: Open to all applicants applying for a DPhil at the Department of Social Policy and Intervention
Level of Study: Graduate
Type: Scholarship
Value: £25,000
Length of Study: 3 years or 2 years for MPhil applicants applying for 2 year DPhil study
Country of Study: Any country
Closing Date: 20 January
Additional Information: For more details, visit website www.spi.ox.ac.uk/study-with-us/funding.html www.spi.ox.ac.uk/departmental-scholarships#collapse401541

For further information contact:

Department of Social Policy and Intervention, 32 Wellington Square, Oxford OX1 2ER, United Kingdom.

Tel: (44) 1865 280734
Email: scholarships@spi.ox.ac.uk

Somerville College Janet Watson Bursary

Eligibility: Open to graduates from the United States of America who are in need of financial assistance
Level of Study: Postgraduate
Type: Bursary
Value: £2,000, £3,500 p.a
Length of Study: 1 year, with possibility of renewal for second year
Study Establishment: Somerville College, the University of Oxford
Country of Study: United Kingdom
Application Procedure: Applicants must contact the Assistant College Secretary
Funding: Private

For further information contact:

Email: sara.kalim@some.ox.ac.uk

Soudavar Fund

Purpose: The Soudavar Fund provides small grants to assist students from Iran who are studying for a degree at the University of Oxford and who are facing financial difficulty
Eligibility: The Soudavar Fund provides small grants of up to £2,500 to assist students from Iran at the University of Oxford and who are facing genuine financial difficulty. The award is open to students who have started their degree at Oxford
Type: Funding support
Value: Up to £2,500
Length of Study: 1 year
Frequency: Annual
Application Procedure: Application forms can be obtained from the International Office
Additional Information: Eligible to nationals of Iran. The Soudavar Fund assists students from Iran who are facing genuine financial difficulty. Applicants must be able to show how they are connected to Iran, e.g. through citizenship, residence etc. Soudavar Fund scholarships are made in conjunction with the Clarendon Fund to support Iranian graduate students   www.spi.ox.ac.uk/departmental-scholarships#collapse401541

For further information contact:

Email: international.office@admin.ox.ac.uk

St Antony's College Wai Seng Senior Research Scholarship

Purpose: The Scholarship is tenable at St Antony's College for two years and is open to all matriculated students of the University of Oxford working for a Doctor of Philosophy degree in fields such as modern history, social sciences
Level of Study: Doctorate
Type: Scholarship
Value: £15,000
Length of Study: 2 years
Frequency: Every 2 years
Study Establishment: St Antony's College, University of Oxford
Country of Study: United Kingdom
Application Procedure: See www.sant.ox.ac.uk
Closing Date: 5 March
Funding: Individuals

For further information contact:

Email: asian@sant.ox.ac.uk

St Antony's College - Swire Scholarship

Purpose: The Swire Scholarships at St Antony's are generously funded by the Swire Charitable Trust, founded by John Swire &; Sons. These scholarships are available to graduate students demonstrating exceptional academic merit

Eligibility: The scholarships are open to applicants who are permanent residents of Japan, China or Hong Kong and have completed the majority of their formal education in their country of permanent residency. The Scholarships will be awarded primarily on academic merit, although financial need may be taken into account. Applicants must apply for admission to a full-time graduate course of study that is offered by St Antony's College to start in current and upcoming year

Level of Study: Graduate

Type: Scholarship

Value: 100% of the university fees, a grant for living costs of £17,442 per year

Frequency: Annual

Country of Study: Japan

Closing Date: 1 March

Funding: Private

Additional Information: www.sant.ox.ac.uk/prospective-students/fees-and-funding/scholarships-new-students/swire

For further information contact:

Email: scholarships@jsshk.com

St Antony's College Ali Pachachi Scholarship

Purpose: To assist candidates pursue doctoral study in any discipline in the humanities or social sciences with a primary focus on the social and political issues confronting the modern Middle East

Eligibility: St Antony's doctoral students

Level of Study: Doctorate, Research

Value: £7,500 towards fees and maintenance

Length of Study: One year

Country of Study: Any country

Application Procedure: Please check the website for further details

Additional Information: scholarshipandinternship.blogspot.com/2011/10/st-antonys-college-scholarships.html

For further information contact:

The Director, Middle East Centre, St Antony's College, 62 Woodstock Rd, Oxford OX2 6JF, United Kingdom.

Email: mec@sant.ox.ac.uk

St Catherine's College Glaxo Scholarship

Eligibility: Open to graduates who have a confirmed place in the Oxford University 2nd BM or the accelerated graduate entry medicine course

Level of Study: Graduate

Type: Scholarship

Value: £3,300 per year

Length of Study: Up to 2 years whilst the recipient is liable for university and college fees

Frequency: Annual

Study Establishment: St Catherine's College, University of Oxford

Country of Study: United Kingdom

Application Procedure: Please see www.stcatz.ox.ac.uk/prospective-students/postgraduate-admissions/student-finance-and-scholarships/ for full details including how to apply

Closing Date: 11 March

Additional Information: www.stcatz.ox.ac.uk/prospective-students/postgraduate-admissions/student-finance-and-scholarships/

For further information contact:

St Catherine's College, Manor Rd, Oxford OX1 3UJ United Kingdom.

Email: college.office@stcatz.ox.ac.uk

St Catherine's College: College Scholarship (Arts)

Eligibility: Open to DPhil, MLitt, and MSc by Research applicants and students in the Humanities and Social Sciences Divisions

Level of Study: Doctorate, Postgraduate, Research

Type: Scholarship

Value: £3,300 per annum

Length of Study: Period of fee liability (up to 3 years)

Frequency: Annual

Study Establishment: St Catherine's College, University of Oxford

Country of Study: United Kingdom

Application Procedure: Please see www.stcatz.ox.ac.uk/prospective-students/postgraduate-admissions/student-finance-and-scholarships/ for full details including how to apply

Closing Date: 11 March

Funding: Private

Additional Information: Please see www.stcatz.ox.ac.uk/prospective-students/postgraduate-admissions/student-finance-and-scholarships/

For further information contact:

Fax: (44) 1865 271 700
Email: college.office@stcatz.ox.ac.uk

St Catherine's College: College Scholarship (Sciences)

Eligibility: Open to DPhil and MSc by research applicants and students in the Mathematical, Physical and Life Sciences Division and Medical Sciences Division
Level of Study: Doctorate, Postgraduate, Research
Type: Scholarship
Value: £3,300 per annum
Length of Study: Period of fee liability (up to 3 years)
Frequency: Annual
Study Establishment: St Catherine's College, University of Oxford
Country of Study: United Kingdom
Application Procedure: Please see www.stcatz.ox.ac.uk/prospective-students/postgraduate-admissions/student-finance-and-scholarships/ for full details including how to apply
Closing Date: 11 March
Funding: Private
Additional Information: Please see www.stcatz.ox.ac.uk/prospective-students/postgraduate-admissions/student-finance-and-scholarships/

For further information contact:

Email: college.office@stcatz.ox.ac.uk

St Catherine's College: Leathersellers' Company Scholarship

Eligibility: Open to DPhil and MSc by Research applicants and students in the MPLS Division and Department of Biochemistry who have studied at a European (including United Kingdom) university
Level of Study: Doctorate, Postgraduate, Research
Type: Scholarship
Value: £3,500 per annum
Length of Study: Up to 3 years
Frequency: Annual
Study Establishment: St Catherine's College, University of Oxford
Country of Study: United Kingdom
Application Procedure: Please see www.stcatz.ox.ac.uk/prospective-students/postgraduate-admissions/student-finance-and-scholarships/ for full details including how to apply
Closing Date: 11 March
Funding: Private

Additional Information: Please see www.stcatz.ox.ac.uk/prospective-students/postgraduate-admissions/student-finance-and-scholarships/

For further information contact:

Email: college.office@stcatz.ox.ac.uk

St Catherine's College: Overseas Scholarship

Eligibility: Open to Overseas fee status DPhil, MLitt and MSc by research applicants and students
Level of Study: Doctorate, Postgraduate, Research
Type: Scholarship
Value: £3,300 per annum
Length of Study: Up to 3 years
Frequency: Annual
Study Establishment: St Catherine's College, University of Oxford
Country of Study: United Kingdom
Application Procedure: Please see www.stcatz.ox.ac.uk/prospective-students/postgraduate-admissions/student-finance-and-scholarships/ for full details including how to apply
Closing Date: 11 March
Funding: Private
Additional Information: Please see www.stcatz.ox.ac.uk/prospective-students/postgraduate-admissions/student-finance-and-scholarships/

For further information contact:

Email: college.office@stcatz.ox.ac.uk

St Catherine's College: Poole Scholarship

Purpose: To assist students who are or will be reading for an Oxford University DPhil, MLitt or MSc by research degree
Eligibility: British nationals of good character studying for a DPhil. Limited SCR dining rights and guaranteed 2 years' single accommodation at current room rate
Level of Study: Graduate, Research
Type: Scholarship
Value: £2,500 per annum
Length of Study: Up to 3 years while student is liable for fees
Frequency: Dependent on funds available
Study Establishment: St Catherine's College, University of Oxford
Country of Study: United Kingdom
Application Procedure: See www.stcatz.ox.ac.uk

U

For further information contact:

Fax: (44) 1865 271 768
Email: academic.registrar@stcat2.ox.ac.uk

St Catherine's College: Ghosh Graduate Scholarship

Eligibility: Open to BPhil, MFA, MSt, MSc by Coursework or MPhil in the Humanities Division.
Level of Study: Postgraduate, Predoctorate
Type: Scholarship
Value: £5,000 per annum
Length of Study: one or two years
Study Establishment: St Catherine's College, University of Oxford
Country of Study: United Kingdom
Application Procedure: Please see www.stcatz.ox.ac.uk/prospective-students/postgraduate-admissions/student-finance-and-scholarships/ for full details including how to apply
Closing Date: 12 March
Funding: Private
Additional Information: Please see www.stcatz.ox.ac.uk/prospective-students/postgraduate-admissions/student-finance-and-scholarships/

For further information contact:

Email: college.office@stcatz.ox.ac.uk

St Cross College: E.P. Abraham Scholarships

Purpose: St Cross College is a graduate college of the University of Oxford. It offers an outstanding academic environment dedicated to the pursuit of excellence within the Collegiate University
Eligibility: Open to all graduate applicants for research degrees in the chemical, biological/life and medical sciences. Please visit website for more details, including how to apply
Level of Study: Postgraduate
Type: Scholarship
Value: £15,000
Length of Study: Up to three years
Frequency: Annual
Study Establishment: St Cross College
Country of Study: United Kingdom
Application Procedure: For more information, please check the website www.stx.ox.ac.uk/prospective-students/funding-support/ep-abraham-scholarships-chemical-biologicallife-and-medical
Funding: Trusts

For further information contact:

Email: master.pa@stx.ox.ac.uk

St Cross College: Graduate Scholarship in Environmental Research

Purpose: St Cross College, jointly with the Oxford NERC Doctoral Training Program in Environmental Research, offers the following scholarship for students in this Doctoral Training Programme (DTP) at the University of Oxford - the DTP recruits to three subject streams The Physical Climate; Biodiversity, Ecology & Evolutionary Processes and the Dynamic Earth - Surface Processes and Natural Hazards.
Value: University fee, college fee and living expenses. Fees-only awards for European Union residents
Length of Study: Up to 3 years
Country of Study: Any country
Closing Date: January
Additional Information: For more details, please visit website www.stx.ox.ac.uk/prospective-students/funding-support/graduate-scholarship-environmental-research www.stx.ox.ac.uk/graduate-scholarship-in-environmental-research

For further information contact:

61 St Giles, Oxford OX1 3LZ, United Kingdom.

Email: bursar@stx.ox.ac.uk

St Cross College: HAPP MPhil Scholarship in the History of Science

Subjects: DPhil in the History of Physics in the Faculty of History or a DPhil in the Philosophy of Physics in the Faculty of Philosophy
Purpose: The successful Scholar will be expected to engage with the termly activities of the St Cross Centre for the History and Philosophy of Physics (HAPP).
Value: £10,000 per annum
Length of Study: three years
Country of Study: Any country
Application Procedure: No separate application is required and all eligible offer-holders will be considered automatically
Closing Date: October

For further information contact:

Email: admissions-academic@stx.ox.ac.uk

St Cross College: MPhil Scholarships in the Humanities and Social Sciences

Purpose: St Cross College offers two MPhil Scholarships for students studying at the University of Oxford for an MPhil degree in any of the humanities and social science disciplines or for the BPhil degree in Philosophy.

Eligibility: Open to all applicants for MPhil degrees in the Humanities and the Social Sciences or for the BPhil degree in Philosophy. The scholarships are tenable at St Cross College only

Level of Study: Predoctorate

Type: Scholarship

Value: £5,000 per annum

Length of Study: 2 years

Study Establishment: St Cross College

Country of Study: United Kingdom

Application Procedure: No separate application is required and all eligible offer-holders will be considered for these awards.

Closing Date: January

Additional Information: Please check the website: www.stx.ox.ac.uk/prospective-students/funding-support/mphil-scholarships-humanities-and-social-sciences www.stx.ox.ac.uk/mphil-scholarships-in-the-humanities-and-social-sciences

For further information contact:

St Cross College, St Giles, Oxford OX1 3LZ, United Kingdom.

Tel: (44) 1865 278 458
Fax: (44) 1865 278 484
Email: admissions-academic@stx.ox.ac.uk

St Cross College: ORISHA DPhil Scholarship in Area Studies

Eligibility: Applicants applying to study for the DPhil in Area Studies

Level of Study: Doctorate

Type: Scholarship

Value: University fee, college fee, maintenance stipend of £12,910

Length of Study: 3 years

Study Establishment: St Cross College

Country of Study: Any country

Closing Date: 25 January

Additional Information: Please visit the website: www.stx.ox.ac.uk/prospective-students/funding-support/orisha-dphil-scholarship-area-studies www.stx.ox.ac.uk/graduate-scholarship-in-archaeology

For further information contact:

Email: master@stx.ox.ac.uk

St Cross College: Oxford-Ko Cheuk Hung Graduate Scholarship

Eligibility: Open to applicants who are ordinarily resident in the EEA or Switzerland and who are applying for the full-time MSt Chinese Studies

Level of Study: Postgraduate

Type: Residency

Value: Tuition fees, college fees and a grant towards living expenses

Length of Study: Period of fee liability

Frequency: Annual

Study Establishment: St Cross

Country of Study: United Kingdom

Application Procedure: For more information, please check the website www.ox.ac.uk/admissions/graduate/fees-and-funding/fees-funding-and-scholarship-search/scholarships-3#kocheukhung

Closing Date: March

Funding: Trusts

Additional Information: www.ox.ac.uk/admissions/graduate/fees-and-funding/fees-funding-and-scholarship-search/scholarships-a-z-listing?wssl=1

For further information contact:

Tel: (44) 1865 278 490
Email: master@stx.ox.ac.uk

St Cross College: SBFT Scholarship in the Humanities

Eligibility: Open to applicants who will be studying for a doctoral degree in the Humanities Division at the University of Oxford in the academic year. The scholarship is open to applicants who are students or academic staff members at a university, other higher education institution or vocational training institution in China. Please see website for further details, including how to apply

Value: £15,000 per annum. The successful scholar will also be guaranteed to have a room in College accommodation (at the standard rent) for the first year of their course

Length of Study: Three fee-liability years of the doctoral course

Country of Study: Any country

Closing Date: 20 January

Additional Information: For more details, visit website www.stx.ox.ac.uk/prospective-students/funding-support/st-cross-

U

sbft-scholarship-humanities www.mod-langs.ox.ac.uk/news/
2016/11/10/scholarship-humanities-dphil-entry-2017-2018

For further information contact:

Email: master@stx.ox.ac.uk

St Cross College: The Harun Ur Rashid Memorial Scholarship

Eligibility: Open to applicants (who are normally resident in Bangladesh) for MPhil degrees in the Humanities and the Social Sciences or for the BPhil degree in Philosophy. Please visit website for more details including how to apply
Value: £3,000
Length of Study: 2 years
Country of Study: Any country
Closing Date: 9 June
Additional Information: For more details, visit website www.stx.ox.ac.uk/prospective-students/funding-support/harun-ur-rashid-memorial-scholarship   www.scholarshipcare.com/scholarship/the-harun-ur-rashid-memorial-scholarship/

For further information contact:

Email: master@stx.ox.ac.uk

St Cross College: The Robin & Nadine Wells Scholarship

Purpose: To provide financial assistance to an academically meritorious graduate student who has been accepted into both an accredited one year's Masters programme at the University of Oxford and St Cross College and are unable to secure funding elsewhere
Eligibility: Open to all applicants for one-year Master's courses who are unable to secure funding from elsewhere
Level of Study: Postgraduate
Type: Scholarship
Value: £7,500 for one year
Length of Study: 1 year
Frequency: Annual
Study Establishment: St Cross College
Country of Study: United Kingdom
Application Procedure: Please visit website for more details, including how to apply
Closing Date: March

St Cross College: Unilever Graduate Scholarship in Sciences

Purpose: To assist graduate students with fees
Eligibility: Open to graduate students
Level of Study: Postgraduate, Research
Type: Scholarship
Value: £2,208 per year
Length of Study: Up to 3 years of study, depending on college fee liability
Country of Study: Any country
Closing Date: 13 March
Additional Information: www.afterschoolafrica.com/18614/unilever-graduate-scholarship-uk/

For further information contact:

Email: jane.sherwood@admin.ox.ac.uk

St Edmund Hall William R Miller Graduate Awards

Level of Study: Postgraduate
Type: Scholarship
Value: £6,000
Length of Study: 1 year with possible extension for a further year
Frequency: Annual
Study Establishment: St Edmund Hall, University of Oxford
Country of Study: United Kingdom
Application Procedure: Application forms are available from the website www.seh.ox.ac.uk or from the Registrar at the address below. Forms are available from around the beginning of February
No. of awards offered: 50
Closing Date: 1 May
Funding: Private
Contributor: William R Miller
No. of awards given last year: 4 (1 new award, 3 extended for a further year)
No. of applicants last year: 50
Additional Information: www.seh.ox.ac.uk/study/postgraduate/postgraduate-scholarships

For further information contact:

Queen's Lane, Oxford OX1 4AR, United Kingdom.

Tel: (44) 1865 279000
Email: admissions@seh.ox.ac.uk

St Edmund Hall: Graduate Scholarships

Purpose: To assist graduate students with fees and a living allowance
Eligibility: Open to all
Level of Study: Postgraduate, Research
Type: Scholarship
Country of Study: Any country

For further information contact:

Email: lodge@seh.ox.ac.uk

St Edmund Hall: Peel Award

Eligibility: Open to all students applying for Master of Fine Art at the Ruskin School
Level of Study: Postgraduate
Type: Scholarship
Value: £5,000
Length of Study: 1 year
Frequency: Annual
Study Establishment: St Edmund Hall
Country of Study: Any country
Closing Date: 20 January
Additional Information: Please visit the website: www.seh.ox.ac.uk/admissions/scholarships www.seh.ox.ac.uk/study/postgraduate/postgraduate-scholarships

For further information contact:

Email: lawfac@law.ox.ac.uk

St Edmund Hall: William Asbrey BCL Studentship

Purpose: The William Asbrey scholarship is worth £10,000, is jointly funded by St Edmund Hall and the Law Faculty, and is available to all BCL applicants. There is no separate application procedure.
Eligibility: Open to all graduate applicants to the BCL
Value: £10,000
Length of Study: 1 year
Country of Study: Any country
Closing Date: 20 January
Additional Information: For more details, visit website www.law.ox.ac.uk/admissions/graduate-scholarships www.seh.ox.ac.uk/study/postgraduate/postgraduate-scholarships

For further information contact:

Queen's Lane, Oxford OX1 4AR, United Kingdom.

Tel: (44) 1865 279000
Email: lodge@seh.ox.ac.uk

St Edmund Hall: William R. Miller Postgraduate Award

Purpose: To assist graduate students with fees and accommodation
Eligibility: A rent-free college room for one academic year offered to a student entering the first or second year of a research degree (DPhil or MRes)
Level of Study: Postgraduate, Research
Type: Award
Value: £6,000
Length of Study: 1 year
Frequency: Annual
Country of Study: Any country
Application Procedure: Please see website for more details, including how to apply
Closing Date: March

For further information contact:

Queen's Lane, Oxford OX1 4AR, United Kingdom.

Tel: (44) 1865 279000
Email: jane.sherwood@admin.ox.ac.uk

St Hilda's College: New Zealand Bursaries

Eligibility: Open to all graduate applicants from New Zealand
Level of Study: Postgraduate
Type: Scholarship
Value: Up to £2,000 per year
Length of Study: 1 year with the possibility of renewal
Frequency: Annual
Application Procedure: Please see website for details of how to apply

For further information contact:

Tel: (44) 1865 276 884
Fax: (44) 1865 276 816
Email: college.office@st-hildas.ox.ac.uk

U

St John's College North Senior Scholarships

Purpose: The College proposes to elect from October 2020 two North Senior Scholars from among its current graduate students

Eligibility: Open to graduates normally with United Kingdom degrees, who have already begun research and who are aged under 25

Level of Study: Postgraduate

Type: Scholarship

Value: £1,000

Length of Study: Usually 2 years

Study Establishment: St John's College, the University of Oxford

Country of Study: United Kingdom

Application Procedure: Applicants must contact the Secretary to the Tutor for Graduates in the first instance

Closing Date: 27 May

Additional Information: www.sjc.ox.ac.uk/current-students/grants-scholarships-and-prizes/financial-support-graduates/

For further information contact:

Tel: (44) 1865 277 428

Fax: (44) 1865 277 640

Email: graduate.admissions@sjc.ox.ac.uk

St John: Ioan & Rosemary James Undergraduate Scholarships

Eligibility: The scholarship is available to any graduate student embarking upon a DPhil in Mathematics or joining a CDT in the Mathematical Institute. Please see website for further details

Value: University fees (at either the Home/European Union or Overseas student rate as applicable), College fees and a maintenance stipend at the United Kingdom research council rate

Length of Study: Duration of full-fee liability; 3 years for DPhil and 4 years for CDT

Country of Study: Any country

Closing Date: 12 February

Additional Information: For more details, please visit www.sjc.ox.ac.uk www.sjc.ox.ac.uk/current-students/grants-scholarships-and-prizes/

For further information contact:

Email: sarah.jones@sjc.ox.ac.uk

St Peter's College Bodossaki Graduate Scholarship in Science

Purpose: To assist Greek or Cypriot citizens under the age of 30, based on merit and financial need

Eligibility: Applicants should be Greek or Cypriot citizens under the age of 30. Award made on the basis of academic merit and financial need

Level of Study: Research

Type: Scholarship

Value: Up to £13,000 per annum; may be used for university & college fees, and maintenance

Length of Study: Up to 3 years, subject to satisfactory academic progress

Frequency: Annual

Study Establishment: St Peter's College, the University of Oxford

Country of Study: United Kingdom

Application Procedure: Applicants must contact the College Secretary at St Peter's College in the first instance, or see www.spc.ox.ac.uk

Closing Date: 30 January

Funding: Foundation

Contributor: The Bodossaki Foundation

For further information contact:

Email: college.secretary@spc.ox.ac.uk

Standard Bank Africa Chairman's Scholarships

Purpose: The scholarships have been funded through the support of the Standard Bank of South Africa. Standard Bank is committed to enable and empower scholars to become effective leaders in Africa.

Eligibility: ordinarily resident in Angola, Botswana, Cote d'Ivoire, Democratic Republic of the Congo, Ethiopia, Ghana, Kenya, Lesotho, Malawi, Mauritius, Mozambique, Namibia, Nigeria, South Africa, South Sudan, Swaziland, Tanzania, Uganda, Zambia or Zimbabwe. The scholarship is only tenable at Wadham College.

Type: Scholarship

Value: The scholarship covers course fees and a grant for living costs.

Country of Study: Any country

Closing Date: July

Additional Information: www.ox.ac.uk/admissions/graduate/fees-and-funding/fees-funding-and-scholarship-search/scholarships-a-z-listing

For further information contact:

University of Oxford, University Offices, 15 Wellington Square, Oxford OX1 2JD, United Kingdom.

Tel: (44) 1865 270000
Fax: (44) 1865 270708

Standard Bank Derek Cooper Africa Scholarship

Eligibility: Open to applicants who are ordinarily resident in one of the following countries Angola, Botswana, Cote d'Ivoire, Democratic Republic of the Congo, Ghana, Kenya, Lesotho, Malawi, Mauritius, Mozambique, Namibia, Nigeria, South Africa, South Sudan, Swaziland, Tanzania, Uganda, Zambia or Zimbabwe. Preference will be given to nationals of Angola, Ghana, Kenya, Mozambique, Nigeria, South Africa and South Sudan. You must also be applying to start any full-time, 1 year taught master's course within the Mathematical, Physical and Life Sciences, Social Sciences, or Humanities Divisions
Level of Study: Postgraduate
Type: Scholarship
Value: full fees
Length of Study: Period of fee liability
Frequency: Annual
Country of Study: United Kingdom
Closing Date: 29 April
Funding: Trusts

For further information contact:

Tel: (44) 20 7405 7686
Email: graduates@standardbank.co.za

Statistical Science (EPSRC and MRC Centre for Doctoral Training) Studentships

Eligibility: Open to United Kingdom and European Union applicants for Statistical Science (EPSRC and MRC CDT)
Level of Study: Doctorate, Research
Type: Studentship
Value: University fee, college fee and full living expenses
Length of Study: 4 years
Frequency: Annual
Country of Study: Any country
Closing Date: 20 January
Funding: Trusts
Additional Information: For more information, please check the website: www.stats.ox.ac.uk/study_here/research_degrees

For further information contact:

Email: ri@fgv.br

Synthetic Biology Doctorate Training Centre EPSRC/ BBSRC Studentships

Eligibility: Open to United Kingdom applicants for all MPLS subjects. Other European Union nationals are eligible for a fees-only award. It is recommended that students submit a CV directly to us prior to making a full application. Please visit website for more information
Level of Study: Postgraduate
Type: Scholarship
Value: University fee, college fee and full living expenses for home students. University and college fees only for European Union
Length of Study: Four years
Frequency: Annual
Country of Study: United Kingdom
Application Procedure: For more information, please check the website www.dtc.ox.ac.uk/
Funding: Trusts

For further information contact:

Email: dtcenquiries@dtc.ox.ac.uk

Templeton College Barclay DPhil Scholarship

Level of Study: Doctorate
Type: Scholarship
Value: £5,000
Length of Study: Up to 3 year
Frequency: Annual
Study Establishment: Templeton College, University of Oxford
Country of Study: United Kingdom
Application Procedure: Applicants must apply to the Graduate Services Manager, Templeton College and should visit the website www.templeton.ox.ac.uk
Funding: Private
Additional Information: scholarship-positions.com/barclay-scholarship-social-sciences-gtc-oxford-university-uk-201415/2013/11/01/

For further information contact:

Templeton College, Wellington Square, Oxford OX1 2JD, United Kingdom.

Email: admissions@templeton.ox.ac.uk

U

Templeton College Leyland Scholarships

Level of Study: Postgraduate
Type: Scholarship
Value: Up to £1,500
Length of Study: 1 year
Frequency: Annual
Study Establishment: Templeton College, University of Oxford
Country of Study: United Kingdom
Application Procedure: Applicants must contact the Academic Administrator for further information

For further information contact:

Email: thc@eastern.edu

Templeton College MBA Scholarship

Level of Study: MBA
Type: Scholarship
Value: Up to £5,000
Length of Study: 1 year
Frequency: Annual
Study Establishment: Templeton College, the University of Oxford
Country of Study: United Kingdom
Application Procedure: Applicants must contact the Academic Administrator

For further information contact:

Email: admissions@templeton.ox.ac.uk

The Christopher Welch Scholarship in Biological Sciences

Eligibility: Open to all DPhil applicants applying for a project falling within the broad topic of Biological Sciences in Departments in the Medical Science, the Department of Plant Sciences and the Department of Zoology. Enquires may be sent by email to ga.Bush@medsci.ox.ac.uk.
Level of Study: Graduate
Value: At present, Christopher Welch Scholarships offer 1. payment of fees at Home rate 2. a maintenance grant (currently £17,000 pa in years 1, 2, and 3 and £8,500 in year 4) 3. Research Support Grant of £5,000 per annum in years 1, 2 and 3
Length of Study: 3 years
Country of Study: Any country
Closing Date: 8 January

For further information contact:

Email: aga.bush@medsci.ox.ac.uk

The John Brookman Scholarship

Purpose: The Brookman Fund may also be able to help with certain expenses such as instrumental tuition or hire of a piano
Eligibility: The Scholarship is open to those reading for, and those who have applied to read for, a graduate degree at the University of Oxford in any subject, and who as John Brookman Scholar will participate in the musical life of the College
Level of Study: Graduate
Type: Scholarship
Value: £3,206
Frequency: Annual
Country of Study: Any country
Application Procedure: 1. Please email graduate.admissions@wadham.ox.ac.uk. a full CV detailing your academic and musical qualifications and experience; the graduate course that you are following or to which you have applied; and the names of two referees. 2. Applicants should also ask their referees to email their references to the Graduate Administrator (on the email above) by this same date. 3. The successful candidate will take up their scholarship from 1 October. For further information on selection process, kindly check the following link. www.wadham.ox.ac.uk/students/graduate-students/graduate-finance/graduate-scholarships
Closing Date: 22 March
Funding: Private
Additional Information: scholarship-positions.com/john-brookman-graduate-scholarship-university-oxford-uk/2018/01/31/

The Khazanah Asia Scholarship in Collaboration with Ancora Foundation

Purpose: Initiated through a generous benefaction from Mr. Gita Irawan Wirjawan, this scholarship provides one year's tuition, fees, and expenses
Eligibility: Applicants should have; (a) a confirmed acceptance at the Environmental Change Institute, Oxford University; (b) an excellent academic record with a first degree equivalent to a good Second Class (Upper) Honors or a GPA of at least 3.5; (c) a very good command of the English language; (d) a commercial or industrial background and a deep interest in the environment; (e) assessed to have outstanding potential for leadership in government, business, or civil society after graduation
Level of Study: Graduate
Type: Scholarship

Value: Up to £28,500
Frequency: Varies
Country of Study: Any country
Application Procedure: Each fellowship is tenable for one-year only for full-time students on the Master of Science in Environmental Change and Management program. The successful candidate is expected to complete his/her studies within the tenable period. Each scholarship will cover the following Tuition and other compulsory fees (as specified by Oxford University); Monthly stipend; and Return air-ticket (economy class)
Closing Date: 6 December
Funding: Private
Additional Information: www.heysuccess.com/opportunity/Khazanah-Asia-Scholarship-Programme-21462

For further information contact:

Equity Tower, 41st Floor Sudirman Central Business District (SCBD), Jl. Jend. Sudirman Kav. 52-53, Lot 9, Jakarta 12190 Indonesia.

Email: inquiry@ancorafoundation.com

Theology and Religion: AHRC Doctoral Training Partnership Studentships

Level of Study: Graduate
Value: University fee, college fee and full living expenses. Fees-only awards for non-United Kingdom, European Union students
Length of Study: Period of fee liability
Country of Study: Any country
Application Procedure: Open to all graduate applicants for the DPhil degree offered by the Faculty of Theology and Religion. Please see website for more details
Closing Date: 20 January
Additional Information: For more details, please visit www.humanities.ox.ac.uk/prospective_students/graduates/funding/ahrc www.humanities.ox.ac.uk/ahrc-doctoral-training-partnership#collapse395446

For further information contact:

Email: theo.pgresearchadmissions@durham.ac.uk

Theology and Religion: Faculty Graduate Studentships

Level of Study: Graduate
Value: At least £1,000
Length of Study: Period of fee liability

Country of Study: Any country
Application Procedure: Open to all graduate applicants and continuing graduate students in Theology and Religion. Please see website for more details, including how to apply
Closing Date: 20 January
Additional Information: For more details, please visit website www.theology.ox.ac.uk/ www.theology.ox.ac.uk/funding

For further information contact:

Email: theo.pgresearchadmissions@durham.ac.uk

Trinity College Birkett Scholarship in Environmental Studies

Eligibility: Open to any graduate accepted for the MSc
Level of Study: Postgraduate
Type: Scholarship
Value: £2,400
Length of Study: 1 year
Frequency: Annual
Study Establishment: Trinity College, University of Oxford
Country of Study: United Kingdom
Application Procedure: Applicants must contact the Academic Administrator for details

For further information contact:

Trinity College, Broad St, Oxford OX1 3BH, United Kingdom.

Email: jane.sherwood@admin.ox.ac.uk

Trinity College Junior Research Fellowship

Purpose: To promote and encourage research among those at the start of an academic career
Eligibility: Open to suitably qualified candidates having some research experience (e.g. a completed doctoral thesis)
Level of Study: Doctorate, Postdoctorate
Value: Approx. £20,000 p.a
Length of Study: 3 years, non renewable
Frequency: Annual
Study Establishment: Trinity College, University of Oxford
Country of Study: United Kingdom
Application Procedure: Please see application form on Trinity College website www.trinity.ox.ac.uk
Additional Information: www.trin.cam.ac.uk/vacancies/junior-research-fellowships/

U

Trinity College: Michael and Judith Beloff Scholarship

Purpose: To assist graduate students with fees
Eligibility: Open to all graduate applicants for the BC-L. Preference given those intending to practise at the Bar of United Kingdom and Wales
Level of Study: Postgraduate
Type: Scholarship
Value: £8,000
Length of Study: 1 year
Frequency: Annual
Country of Study: Any country
Application Procedure: Please note interest on application form. Please see website for details of how to apply
Closing Date: October
Additional Information: Please check at www.trinity.ox.ac.uk/pages/admissions/loans-grants-and-bursaries.php   www.trinity.ox.ac.uk/postgraduate-study/postgraduate-application/postgraduate-scholarships/

University College: Chellgren

Purpose: Applicants must have a place on a postgraduate programme at University College, Oxford. Scholarships can be awarded to students embarking on any postgraduate programme. However, prospective economics students are given preference
Eligibility: Open to all graduate applicants in Economics. Applicants must have a place on a postgraduate programme at University College, Oxford
Level of Study: Postgraduate
Type: Scholarship
Value: £4,000 per year
Length of Study: Up to 3 years
Frequency: Annual
Study Establishment: University
Country of Study: United Kingdom
Application Procedure: Please see website for more details, including how to apply
Closing Date: January
Funding: Trusts
Additional Information: For more information, please check the website: www.univ.ox.ac.uk/postgraduate/financial_1/scholarships_and_studentships/

University College: Henni-Mester Scholarship

Eligibility: Open to all graduate applicants to the Nuffield Department of Orthopaedics, Rheumatology and Musculo-skeletal Sciences. Please see website for more details

Level of Study: Postgraduate
Type: Scholarship
Value: University fee, college fee and full living expenses
Length of Study: Period of fee liability
Frequency: Annual
Study Establishment: University
Country of Study: United Kingdom
Application Procedure: For more information, please check the website www.univ.ox.ac.uk/postgraduate/financial_1/scholarships_and_studentships/
Closing Date: 8 January
Funding: Trusts

For further information contact:

Email: lodge@univ.ox.ac.uk

University College: Loughman

Eligibility: Open to graduates who have been offered a place at University College, who are outstanding in their academic field and who, in addition, can demonstrate that they will make significant contributions to College life through the quality of their extra-academic pursuits (sports, arts, community service, etc.)
Level of Study: Postgraduate
Type: Scholarship
Value: £4,000 per year
Length of Study: Up to 3 years
Frequency: Annual
Study Establishment: University
Country of Study: United Kingdom
Closing Date: January
Funding: Trusts
Additional Information: For more information, please check the website: www.univ.ox.ac.uk/postgraduate/financial_1/scholarships_and_studentships/

For further information contact:

Email: john.loughman@ucd.ie

University Hardship Fund

Purpose: The University Hardship Fund aims to assist students who experience unexpected financial difficulties due to circumstances which could not have been predicted at the start of their course
Eligibility: Students can apply to the University Hardship Fund (UHF) if they are experiencing unexpected and unforeseeable financial difficulties
Level of Study: Graduate

Type: Funding support
Value: £6,000
Frequency: Annual
Country of Study: Any country
Application Procedure: Students should contact their college hardship officer to request an application form and discuss their application. The hardship officer varies across colleges but could be your Senior Tutor, Bursar or Academic Administrator. Complete application forms should be submitted by the student or their college to Student Fees and Funding as soon as possible and by the appropriate deadline listed below. The form includes sections for the student, tutor or supervisor and college hardship officer to complete, and applications will only be considered when all sections and evidence have been received
Closing Date: 1 May
Funding: Trusts
Additional Information: www.ox.ac.uk/students/fees-funding/assistance/hardship/uhf?wssl=1

For further information contact:

Email: graduatefunding@admin.cam.ac.uk

Vicky Noon Educational Foundation Oxford Scholarships

Purpose: This scholarship is not open to candidates applying for postgraduate certificate or postgraduate diploma courses, or non-matriculated courses.
Eligibility: You should be intending to return to Pakistan once your course is completed. If you have previously studied outside Pakistan you will not normally be considered unless there are exceptional circumstances which explain why you have studied abroad.
Type: Scholarship
Value: The size and duration of awards vary according to each scholar's circumstances.
Frequency: Annual
Country of Study: Any country
No. of awards offered: 2
Closing Date: July
Additional Information: www.ox.ac.uk/admissions/graduate/fees-and-funding/fees-funding-and-scholarship-search/scholarships-a-z-listing

For further information contact:

University of Oxford, University Offices, 15 Wellington Square, Oxford OX1 2JD, United Kingdom.

Tel: (44) 1865 270000
Fax: (44) 1865 270708

Wadham College - David Richards Scholarship in Chemistry

Purpose: Applicants for postgraduate research courses offered by the Department of Chemistry. The scholarship is open to home
Eligibility: To be eligible for consideration for this scholarship, applicants must be successful in being offered a place on their course after consideration of applications received by the relevant January deadline for the course. Course applications which are held over after the January deadline to be re-evaluated against applications received by the March deadline or course applications which have been put on a waiting list are not eligible for scholarship consideration
Level of Study: Graduate
Type: Scholarship
Value: 100% of course fees and a grant for living costs (at least £14,777) for the duration of the course
Frequency: Annual
Country of Study: Any country
Application Procedure: Scholarships are awarded to applicants who have demonstrated excellent academic ability, who will contribute to the University's ground-breaking research, and who will go on to contribute to the world as leaders in their field, pushing the frontiers of knowledge. The Richards family bequest contributes 60% of the funds for these scholarships, with the remaining 40% being contributed by the University of Oxford
Closing Date: January
Funding: Private
Additional Information: www.wadham.ox.ac.uk/students/graduate-students/graduate-finance/graduate-scholarships

For further information contact:

Email: graduate.admissions@wadham.ox.ac.uk

Wadham College: Beit Scholarship

Value: University fee, college fee, and full living expenses
Length of Study: 1 year
Country of Study: Any country
Application Procedure: Open to graduate applicants for 1-year Masters courses who are ordinarily resident in Malawi, Zambia or Zimbabwe. Please see website for further details, including how to apply
Closing Date: January
Additional Information: For more details, please visit website www.wadham.ox.ac.uk/students/graduate-students/graduate-finance/graduate-scholarships

For further information contact:

Email: graduate.admissions@wadham.ox.ac.uk

Wadham College: Donner Canadian Foundation Law Scholarship

Purpose: The Donner Canadian Scholarship is awarded to Canadian graduates intending to undertake the BCL or MJur at the University of Oxford as a member of Wadham College. This prize is available on an annual basis and is awarded on the basis of academic excellence and aptitude

Eligibility: Open to any graduate applicant to the BCL or MJur who is ordinarily resident in Canada. Please see website for more details

Level of Study: Postgraduate

Type: Scholarship

Value: £20,000 towards University and college fees or living expenses

Length of Study: One year

Frequency: Annual

Country of Study: Any country

Application Procedure: For more information, please check the website www.wadham.ox.ac.uk/students/graduate-students/graduate-finance/graduate-scholarships

Closing Date: 22 January

Funding: Trusts

Additional Information: www.wadham.ox.ac.uk/students/graduate-students/graduate-finance/graduate-scholarships

For further information contact:

Tutor for Graduates, Wadham College, Parks Road, Oxford OX1 3PN, United Kingdom.

Email: senior.tutor@wadh.ox.ac.uk

Wadham College: Hackney BCL Scholarship

Value: £15,009

Length of Study: 1 year

Country of Study: Any country

Application Procedure: Open to all graduate applicants for the BCL

Closing Date: April

Additional Information: For more details, please visit website www.wadham.ox.ac.uk/students/graduate-students/graduate-finance/graduate-scholarships

For further information contact:

Email: graduate.admissions@wadham.ox.ac.uk

Wadham College: John Brookman Scholarship

Purpose: To assist an organisation scholar who has been given admission to read for a higher degree in the university

Eligibility: Open to any graduate student who wishes to play a role in the musical life of the college

Level of Study: Postgraduate, Research

Type: Scholarship

Value: Equivalent to college fee

Length of Study: Duration of fee liability

Frequency: Annual

Study Establishment: Wadham College, University of Oxford

Country of Study: United Kingdom

Application Procedure: Applicants should send a full curriculum vitae detailing their academic and musical qualifications and experience; the graduate course that they are following, or to which they have applied; and the names of two referees, either by post to the Tutor for Graduates. Applicants should also request referees to submit their references (using the same contact details as listed above) by the same date. A successful candidate will take up his/her scholarship from October 1st

Closing Date: 23 April

Funding: Trusts

Contributor: Endowed by late E.W.M. Brookman, an old member of the college, in memory of his son, John M. Brookman (1926–1980)

Additional Information: www.wadham.ox.ac.uk/students/graduate-students/graduate-finance/graduate-scholarships

For further information contact:

Email: admissions@wadh.ox.ac.uk

Wadham College: Oxford-Richards Scholarship in Chemistry

Eligibility: Open to a graduate applying for one of the DPhil courses offered by the Chemistry Department. Please see website for details

Level of Study: Postgraduate

Type: Scholarship

Value: University fee, college fee, and full living expenses

Length of Study: Duration of fee liability

Frequency: Annual

Study Establishment: Wadham

Country of Study: United Kingdom

Application Procedure: For more information, please check the website www.ox.ac.uk/admissions/graduate/fees-and-funding/fees-funding-and-scholarship-search/scholarships-3#richards

Closing Date: 22 January
Funding: Trusts

For further information contact:

Email: graduate.admissions@wadham.ox.ac.uk

Wadham College: Oxford-Richards Scholarship in Economics

Eligibility: Open to a graduate applying for the DPhil in Economics. Please see website for details
Level of Study: Postgraduate
Type: Scholarship
Value: University fee, college fee, and full living expenses
Length of Study: Duration of fee liability
Frequency: Annual
Study Establishment: Wadham
Country of Study: United Kingdom
Application Procedure: For more information, please check the website www.ox.ac.uk/admissions/graduate/fees-and-funding/fees-funding-and-scholarship-search/scholarships-3#richards
Closing Date: 22 January
Funding: Trusts

For further information contact:

Email: graduate.admissions@wadham.ox.ac.uk

Wadham College: Oxford-Richards Scholarships in Climate Science

Eligibility: Open to a graduate applying for a DPhil in Atmospheric, Oceanic and Planetary Physics. Please see website for more details
Level of Study: Postgraduate
Type: Scholarship
Value: University fee, college fee, and full living expenses
Length of Study: Duration of fee liability
Frequency: Annual
Study Establishment: Wadham
Country of Study: United Kingdom
Application Procedure: For more information, please check the website www.ox.ac.uk/admissions/graduate/fees-and-funding/fees-funding-and-scholarship-search/scholarships-3#richards

Closing Date: 8 January
Funding: Trusts

For further information contact:

Email: domestic.bursar@wadham.ox.ac.uk

Wadham College: Oxford-Richards Scholarships in History

Eligibility: Open to a graduate applying for one of the DPhil courses offered by the History Faculty. Please see website for more details
Level of Study: Postgraduate
Type: Scholarship
Value: University fee, college fee, and full living expenses
Length of Study: Duration of fee liability
Frequency: Annual
Study Establishment: Wadham
Country of Study: United Kingdom
Application Procedure: For more information, please check the website www.ox.ac.uk/admissions/graduate/fees-and-funding/fees-funding-and-scholarship-search/scholarships-3#richards
Closing Date: 22 January
Funding: Trusts

For further information contact:

Email: graduate.admissions@wadham.ox.ac.uk

Wadham College: Peter Carter Graduate Scholarship in Law

Level of Study: Graduate
Value: £10,000 towards course and college fees or living expenses
Length of Study: Duration of fee liability
Country of Study: Any country
Application Procedure: Open to all graduate applicants for the BCL, MJur, MPhil in Law or DPhil in Law
Closing Date: 20 January
Additional Information: For more details, please visit website www.wadham.ox.ac.uk/students/graduate-students/graduate-finance/graduate-scholarships llm-guide.com/scholarships/peter-carter-graduate-scholarship-in-law-318

For further information contact:

Email: study@ox.ac.uk

U

Wadham College: Peter Carter Taught Graduate Scholarship in Law

Purpose: The Taught Graduate Scholarship in Law is available to graduate students of exceptional academic merit embarking on the BCL or MJur at Wadham College and is available to law graduates of any university
Eligibility: Open to all graduate applicants for the BCL or MJur. Please see website for details
Level of Study: Graduate, Postgraduate
Type: Scholarship
Value: £12,500 towards course and college fees or living expenses
Length of Study: 1 year
Study Establishment: Wadham College
Country of Study: Any country
Application Procedure: Please visit the website www.wadham.ox.ac.uk/students/graduate-students/graduate-finance/graduate-scholarships
Closing Date: 20 January
Additional Information: Please visit the website: www.wadham.ox.ac.uk/students/graduate-students/graduate-finance/graduate-scholarships for more information. The scholarship can be used to defray in part University fees, College fees and/or maintenance of the Scholar during their period of study. It does not cover all fees so you will have to demonstrate sufficient funds for additional costs llm-guide.com/scholarships/peter-carter-taught-graduate-scholarship-in-law-201

For further information contact:

Email: admissions@wadh.ox.ac.uk

Wadham College: Philip Wright Scholarship

Eligibility: Open to any graduate student who is a former student of Manchester Grammar School
Level of Study: Postgraduate, Research
Type: Scholarship
Value: University and college fee (to a maximum of £10,000) plus £8,000 per year stipend or, where recipient receives financial support from another source (i.e. RCUK), payment of the college fee
Length of Study: 1 year, possible renewal
Application Procedure: Application forms are available at www.wadham.ox.ac.uk/student-life/scholarships/the-philip-wright-scholarship.html either in Word or PDF format. Please send the completed form, a full Curriculum Vitae and (for graduates applying for research work) a one page summary of your research proposal, either by post to the Tutor for Graduates

Closing Date: 23 April
Funding: Trusts
Contributor: Philip Wright Fund
Additional Information: www.european-funding-guide.eu/other-financial-assistance/13742-philip-wright-scholarship

Wakeham Humanities Scholarship (History or Literature)

Purpose: All of these scholarships, apart from the Light Senior Scholarships, are open to new graduate students commencing graduate study at Oxford in October
Eligibility: Students at other colleges are eligible to apply for all of these scholarships apart from the Light Senior Scholarships, but would need to migrate to St Catherine's to take up the scholarship if their application was successful
Level of Study: Graduate
Type: Scholarship
Value: Check the website for further details
Frequency: Every 2 years
Country of Study: Any country
Application Procedure: Applications for Graduate Scholarships should be sent by email to college.office@stcatz.ox.ac.uk
Closing Date: 10 May
Funding: Private
Additional Information: www.ox.ac.uk/admissions/graduate/colleges/st-catherines-college

For further information contact:

Manor Road, Oxford OX1 3UJ, United Kingdom.

Weatherall Institute of Molecular Medicine: WIMM Prize Studentship

Level of Study: Graduate
Value: All fees and living expenses of £18,000 per annum
Length of Study: 4 years
Country of Study: United Kingdom
Application Procedure: Open to applicants of any nationality applying for projects advertised on the WIMM website. Applicants must quote scholarship reference code H816027
Closing Date: 1 June
Additional Information: For more details, visit website www.imm.ox.ac.uk/wimm-prize-studentship-2017   www.rdm.ox.ac.uk/study-with-us/funding-options/wimm-prize-studentships

For further information contact:

University of Oxford, Level 6, West Wing John Radcliffe Hospital, Headington, Oxford OX3 9DU, United Kingdom.

Email: graduate.enquiries@rdm.ox.ac.uk

Weidenfeld-Hoffmann Scholarships and Leadership Programme

Purpose: The Weidenfeld-Hoffmann Scholarships and Leadership Programme cultivates the leaders of tomorrow by providing outstanding university graduates and professionals from developing and emerging economies with the opportunity to pursue fully-funded graduate studies at the University of Oxford, combined with a comprehensive programme of leadership development, long-term mentoring and networking.

Eligibility: You must be applying to start a new graduate course at Oxford. Please visit the website to see the complete list of eligible courses and country of residence

Level of Study: Postgraduate

Type: Scholarship

Value: University fee, college fee, and full living expenses

Length of Study: Period of fee liability

Frequency: Annual

Country of Study: United Kingdom

Application Procedure: Please see website for more details, including how to apply

Closing Date: May

Funding: Trusts

Additional Information: For more information, please check the website: www.graduate.ox.ac.uk/weidenfeld-hoffmann

For further information contact:

Email: info@whtrust.org

Weidenfeld-Hoffmann Scholarships and Leadership Programme

Purpose: The Weidenfeld-Hoffmann Scholarships and Leadership Programme cultivates the leaders of tomorrow by providing outstanding university graduates and professionals from developing and emerging economies with the opportunity to pursue fully-funded graduate studies at the University of Oxford, combined with a comprehensive programme of leadership development, long-term mentoring and networking

Eligibility: visit website

Type: Scholarship

Value: £15,609

Country of Study: Any country

Closing Date: April

Additional Information: www.ox.ac.uk/admissions/gradu ate/fees-and-funding/fees-funding-and-scholarship-search/ weidenfeld-hoffmann-scholarships-and-leadership-progra mme

For further information contact:

University of Oxford, University Offices, 15 Wellington Square, Oxford OX1 2JD, United Kingdom.

Tel: (44) 1865 270000
Fax: (44) 1865 270708

Wolfson College: Lorne Thyssen Scholarship

Level of Study: Graduate

Value: University fee, college fee, and living expenses

Length of Study: Period of fee liability

Country of Study: Any country

Application Procedure: Open to new Home/European Union applicants to DPhil courses within the range accepted by Wolfson College, and who are specializing in Ancient World Studies. Please see website for more details

Closing Date: January

Additional Information: For more details, please visit www. wolfson.ox.ac.uk/scholarships/lorne-thyssen www.wolfson. ox.ac.uk/lorne-thyssen-scholarship

For further information contact:

Email: ancient.world@wolfson.ox.ac.uk

Wolfson College: Mougins Museum Ashmolean Scholarship

Eligibility: Open to Home/European Union and Overseas. The applicant's thesis should fall within the field of 'Greek material culture from 700 to 30 BC' and will ideally focus on the archaeological and/or numismatic collections within the Ashmolean. The Mougins Museum itself holds important collections which can be made available for study

Level of Study: Research

Type: Scholarship

Value: £20,000 per year for 3 years towards university fees, college fees and maintenance

Length of Study: Up to 3 years

Frequency: Annual

Application Procedure: Select the 'Mougins Scholarship's box in the University of Oxford Scholarships section of the Application Form for Graduate Study. Applicants are

U

encouraged to include a statement explaining how their proposed research relates to the Scholarship. Preference may be given to those who list Wolfson as their first choice college

Closing Date: 22 January

Additional Information: Graduate scholarship in Greek material culture of the archaic, classical or Hellenistic periods. Please check at www.wolfson.ox.ac.uk/mougins-museum-ashmolean-scholarship-2015-16

For further information contact:

Email: susan.walker@ashmus.ox.ac.uk

Wolfson Postgraduate Scholarships in the Humanities

Purpose: The Wolfson Postgraduate Scholarships in the Humanities are available for applicants who are applying to a full or part-time DPhil course in history, languages or literature.

Eligibility: To be considered for this scholarship, you must be ordinarily resident in the United Kingdom or Republic of Ireland.

Type: Scholarship

Value: The scholarship covers course fees at the Home rate only.

Frequency: Annual

Country of Study: Any country

Closing Date: April

Additional Information: www.ox.ac.uk/admissions/graduate/fees-and-funding/fees-funding-and-scholarship-search/scholarships-a-z-listing

For further information contact:

University of Oxford, University Offices, 15 Wellington Square, Oxford OX1 2JD, United Kingdom.

Tel: (44) 1865 270000
Fax: (44) 1865 270708

Worcester College: C. Douglas Dillon Scholarship

Eligibility: Open to graduate applicants for 1 year or 2-year courses in the fields of Politics, Diplomacy, Governance and International Relations. Please see website for more details, including eligible courses and how to apply

Level of Study: Graduate

Value: £10,000

Length of Study: 1 or 2 years

Country of Study: Any country

Closing Date: 6 March

Additional Information: For more details, visit website www.worc.ox.ac.uk/applying/graduates/graduate-scholarships www.worc.ox.ac.uk/sites/default/files/ad_c_douglas_dillon_scholarship_2020-21.pdf

For further information contact:

Tel: (44) 1865 278300
Email: graduate.enquiries@worc.ox.ac.uk

Worcester College: Drue Heinz Scholarship

Level of Study: Graduate

Value: £10,000

Length of Study: 1 year

Country of Study: Any country

Application Procedure: Open to graduate applicants in the Humanities. Preference given to international applicants. Please see website for more details, including how to apply

Closing Date: 5 March

Contributor: Worcester

For further information contact:

Email: graduate.enquiries@worc.ox.ac.uk

Worcester College: Law Faculty Graduate Scholarship

Eligibility: Open to applicants who are applying for the Bachelor of Civil Law or Magister Juris. Award holders will become members of Worcester College. Please see website for more information

Level of Study: Graduate, Postgraduate

Type: Scholarship

Value: £10,000

Length of Study: 1 year

Study Establishment: Worcester College

Country of Study: Any country

Closing Date: January

Additional Information: Please visit the website: www.worc.ox.ac.uk/applying/graduates/graduate-scholarships

For further information contact:

Tel: (44) 1865 278 300
Email: lodge@worc.ox.ac.uk

Worcester College: Martin Senior Scholarship

Eligibility: Open to graduate applicants to research degrees from the United Kingdom or European Union who are current or previous members of Worcester College
Level of Study: Postgraduate, Research
Type: Scholarship
Value: £4,000
Length of Study: Duration of student's fee liability
Frequency: Annual
Study Establishment: Worcester College
Application Procedure: Please see college website for details of how to apply
Closing Date: 1 March
Additional Information: Please check the website: www.worc.ox.ac.uk/applying/graduates/graduate-scholarships

For further information contact:

Email: graduate.enquiries@worc.ox.ac.uk

Worcester College: Ogilvie Thompson Scholarships

Purpose: To assist graduate students with fees
Eligibility: Open to incoming graduates who have been undergraduates at Worcester within the last two years and have not undertaken any graduate work at Oxford or elsewhere
Type: Scholarships
Value: Up to £6,000
Length of Study: 1 year
Country of Study: Any country
Closing Date: 5 March

For further information contact:

Tel: (44) 1865 278300
Email: graduate.enquiries@worc.ox.ac.uk

University of Paris-Saclay

Website: www.universite-paris-saclay.fr/en/universite-paris-saclay-international-masters-scholarship

The University of Paris-Saclay is a French federal research university which is currently under development with the aim to become a world top-10 university.

Université Paris-Saclay International Master's Scholarships

Purpose: The Université Paris-Saclay would like to promote access to its master's (nationally-certified degree) programs to international students, taught in its member establishments, and to make it easier for highly-qualified foreign students to attend its university especially those wishing to develop an academic project through research up to the doctoral level
Eligibility: 1. Students admitted to a Paris-Saclay University Master's programme delivered by one of the following institutions: AgroParisTech, CentraleSupelec, ENS Paris-Saclay, INSTN-CEA, IOGS, UEVE, UPSaclay, UVSQ. Among these students, only those who answer one of the following criteria are eligible to apply: 2. Newly arrived international students, aged 30 and less during the course of the selection year. 3. Students of foreign nationality living on the French soil for less than a year, previously or currently enrolled in a training course or internship that does not lead to certification. 4. Students of foreign nationality living on the French soil for less than a year, taking language classes (type FFL). 5. Students who have lived in France in the past, within the framework of a mobility programme during their studies (e.g. Erasmus Mundus Joint Master's Degrees, exchange programme...) that did not lead to certification.
Level of Study: Postgraduate
Value: The scholarship will be suspended if internship wages exceed €700/month
Length of Study: 1 or 2 years
Frequency: Annual
Study Establishment: Université Paris-Saclay, France
Country of Study: France
Application Procedure: 1. Selected students will automatically be sent a link by email to an online application form. Upon receipt of this email, students wishing to apply will need to complete the online application form and provide (mandatory) the names of two references who would be willing to submit a reference for the candidate (director of studies, professor, internship coordinator...). 2. Each of the two references named by the candidate will be sent a link by email to an online recommendation form. They will be asked to complete and submit the form prior to the closing day of the scholarship call. The candidate will automatically be informed when each reference has submitted the form. 3. The application file for a scholarship will be considered complete when both recommendation forms have been submitted by the two references.
Closing Date: 7 May
Funding: Government

For further information contact:

Email: international-master-scholarship.idex@universite-paris-saclay.fr

U

University of Pretoria

Private Bag X20, Hatfield 0028, South Africa.

Tel: (27) 12 420 3111
Website: www.up.ac.za/

Commonwealth PhD Scholarships

Purpose: Commonwealth PhD Scholarships are for candidates from low and middle income Commonwealth countries, for full-time doctoral study at a United Kingdom university. Commonwealth PhD Scholarships are for candidates from low and middle income Commonwealth countries, for full-time doctoral study at a United Kingdom university
Eligibility: 1. Applicants should be citizens of Commonwealth countries (excluding South African students). 2. Applicants must conduct their studies at the University of Pretoria. 3. They must have completed the degree that will give them admission to a doctoral programme a maximum of 3 years prior to their application for the University of Pretoria Commonwealth Doctoral Scholarship. 4. They must not be older than 35 years of age at the time of application. Masters students currently registered at the University of Pretoria are not eligible for the Doctoral Scholarship
Level of Study: Doctorate
Type: Scholarship
Value: The value of the Doctoral Scholarships will be R120,000. This amount must be used to cover accommodation and living cost, medical aid and books/stationery. For detailed information, please visit website
Country of Study: South Africa
Application Procedure: The mode of applying is electronically or by post
Closing Date: 30 August
Contributor: University of Pretoria
Additional Information: For further information, kindly check the following pdf link. www.up.ac.za/funding/2915822/2021-up-phd-commonwealth-scholarship

For further information contact:

Email: eas@cscuk.org.uk

University of Pune

Institute of Bioinformatics & Biotechnology (IBB), Ganeshkhind, Pune, Maharashtra 411007, India.

Tel: (91) 20 2569 2039
Email: director@bioinfo.ernet.in

Website: www.unipune.ernet.in
Contact: Director

The University stands for humanism and tolerance, for reason for adventure of ideas and for the search of truth. It stands for the forward march of the human race towards even higher objectives. If the universities discharge their duties adequately then it is well with the nation and the people–Jawaharlal Nehru.

Department of Biotechnology (DBT) Junior Research Fellowship

Purpose: To support candidates pursuing research in areas of biotechnology and applied biology
Eligibility: Open to candidates from the centres supported by the DBT, New Delhi
Level of Study: Research
Type: Fellowship
Value: INR 30,000 per fellow per year
Length of Study: 3–5 years
Frequency: Annual
Study Establishment: University of Pune
Country of Study: India
Application Procedure: A written application along with application fee of INR 500 in the form of a DD in favour of Registrar, University of Pune
Contributor: Government of India
Additional Information: career.webindia123.com/career/scholarships/scholarships_india/dbt-junior-research-fellowship/index.htm

For further information contact:

Department of Biotechnology, University of Pune, Pune, Maharashtra 411007, India.

Tel: (91) 20 2569 4952, 2569 2248
Email: jkpal@unipune.ernet.in

University of Queensland

Research and Postgraduate Studies, Cumbrae-Stewart Building, Brisbane, St Lucia, QLD 4072, Australia.

Tel: (61) 7 3365 1111
Email: scholarships@research.uq.edu.au
Website: www.uq.edu.au

The University of Queensland has an outstanding profile in the Australian and international research community. It maintains a world-class, comprehensive programme of research and research training, underpinned by state-of-the-art infrastructure and a commitment to rewarding excellence. As one of Australia's premier universities, UQ attracts researchers and students of outstanding calibre.

Dr Rosamond Siemon Postgraduate Renal Research Scholarship

Purpose: To support a research higher degree candidate to undertake multidisciplinary, collaborative research into renal disease, repair and regeneration

Eligibility: Open to candidates who are enroled or intend to enrol in a research higher degree at the University of Queensland and who demonstrate a high level of academic achievement and ability

Level of Study: Postgraduate

Type: Scholarship

Value: AU$30,000 per year (a stipend of AU$25,000 and a direct research cost allowance of AU$5,000)

Length of Study: 3 years and 6 months

Frequency: Annual

Country of Study: Australia

Application Procedure: Applicants must send a proposed research project description, certified copies of academic transcripts, academic curriculum vitae, including publications and 3 letters of recommendation

Closing Date: 31 August

Funding: Individuals

Contributor: Dr Rosamond Siemon

Additional Information: Research Scholarships Referee Report Form can be used. This can be accessed from www.uq.edu.au/grad-school/scholarship-forms

For further information contact:

Research Scholarships, Office of Research and Postgraduate Studies, The University of Queensland, St Lucia, QLD 4072, Australia.

Email: postgrad-office@imb.uq.edu.au

Global Archaeological Science Scholarships

Purpose: The University of Queensland Archaeology Program is offering four PhD studentships for international and domestic students to start for archaeological science projects in Africa, Europe and Australia.

Eligibility: Australian and international students are eligible to apply. Students whose first language is not English must demonstrate proficiency in English by submitting satisfactory scores from the Test of English as a Foreign Language (TOEFL).

Type: Postgraduate scholarships

Value: AU$27,082 (old rate) indexed annually, tuition fees, Overseas Student Health Cover (OSHC)

Study Establishment: Scholarships are awarded for archaeological science projects in Africa, Europe and Australia

Country of Study: Australia

Application Procedure: See the website

Closing Date: 17 January

Additional Information: For more details please visit the website scholarship-positions.com/global-archaeological-science-scholarships-university-queensland-2018/2017/12/29/

For further information contact:

Email: a.crowther@uq.edu.au

Herdsman Fellowship in Medical Science

Purpose: The fellowship is open to graduates in medicine or related health sciences enroled full-time for a PhD on a topic related to the medical problems of the aged

Eligibility: Applicants must be graduates in medicine or related health sciences, enrol full-time for a PhD, and be undertaking a research topic related to the medical problems of the aged

Level of Study: Postgraduate

Type: Fellowship

Value: AU$22,860 per year

Length of Study: Fellowship shall initially be for 1 year but may be extended by the committee for further terms of 1 year up to a total of 3 years

Country of Study: Australia

Application Procedure: Applications must consist of covering letter addressing the Herdsman Fellowship Rules, in particular point 2, academic curriculum vitae, 2 referee reports. No strict format is required; however the Research Scholarships generic Referee Report may be used

No. of awards offered: 1

Closing Date: 31 August

Contributor: Maintained by the income from a bequest of AU$2,60,000 from Mrs Rose Herdsman

No. of awards given last year: 1

No. of applicants last year: 1

Additional Information: scholarships.uq.edu.au/files/448/sched-a-pg-research-scholarships.pdf

For further information contact:

Faculty of Health Sciences, University of Queensland, St Lucia, QLD 4072, Australia.

Email: s.tett@pharmacy.uq.edu.au

PhD Scholarship in Immunology and Immunogenetics

Purpose: To provide the foundations for the development of treatments based on the genetic findings
Eligibility: Open to a dynamic, intelligent and diligent PhD candidate (Australian or international) with either a clinical or a relevant basic science background to take forward the project
Level of Study: Doctorate
Type: Scholarship
Value: AU$25,000 per year
Length of Study: 3 years
Frequency: Annual
Study Establishment: The University of Queensland
Country of Study: Australia
Application Procedure: Candidates must contact Prof. Brown for more information
Closing Date: 3 September
Additional Information: International applicants must cover tuition fees (AU$27,000 per year) scholarships.uq.edu.au/files/448/sched-a-pg-research-scholarships.pdf

For further information contact:

Tel: (61) 7 3240 2870
Email: matt.brown@qut.edu.au

R.N. Hammon Scholarship

Purpose: To assist Australian Aboriginal and/or Torres Strait Island students for further studies
Eligibility: Open to Australian Aboriginal and/or Torres Strait Island students who have successfully completed at least 1 year of an undergraduate or postgraduate program and are enroling on a full-time basis for a subsequent year of that program, or for a further program
Level of Study: Postgraduate
Type: Scholarship
Value: AU$3,500
Frequency: Annual
Study Establishment: The University of Queensland, Queensland University of Technology, University of Southern Queensland, Central Queensland University, or Queensland Colleges of TAFE
Country of Study: Australia
Application Procedure: Candidates can download the application form and referee report form from the website
Closing Date: 2 March
Additional Information: The Selection Committee shall take into account the academic merit or technical excellence, any other scholarship, bursary, award or benefit, whether governmental or otherwise, to which the applicant is entitled;

and social and economic need scholarships.uq.edu.au/scholarship/rn-hammon-scholarship

For further information contact:

Tel: (61) 7 33651984
Email: ugscholarships@uq.edu.au

Sustainable Tourism CRC Climate Change PhD

Purpose: To develop a tourism consumer decision-making model that focuses on climate change as a driver of consumer choice and apply it to Australian tourism market
Eligibility: Open to candidates who have achieved First Class (Honours) Degree or equivalent
Level of Study: Postgraduate, Research
Type: Scholarship
Value: AU$19,930 per year
Length of Study: 3 years
Frequency: Annual
Study Establishment: The University of Queensland
Country of Study: Australia
Application Procedure: Candidates must contact Jane Malady for application forms
Contributor: Sustainable Tourism CRC and University of Queensland
Additional Information: For further information on topic and research proposal contact Prof. Ballantyne at mailto: r.ballantyne@uq.edu.au

For further information contact:

Tel: (61) 7 5552 9063
Email: Jane@crctourism.com.au

The Constantine Aspromourgos Memorial Scholarship for Greek Studies

Subjects: Arts, humanities and social sciences
Purpose: To assist a research higher degree student studying at least 1 area of Greek studies
Eligibility: You're eligible if you: 1. have a bachelor's or a master's degree.; And you're either: 2. undertaking a UQ postgraduate program involving studies that relate to at least one area of Greek studies (ancient, Byzantine or modern) in: 1. language 2. culture 3. literature 4. history 5. archaeology 6. society 7. religion 8. economics 9. politics 10 geography (a Greek studies program) 3. a UQ graduate undertaking a Greek studies program at another university.
Level of Study: Postgraduate
Type: Scholarship
Value: Approx. AU$5,000

Length of Study: 1 year
Frequency: Annual
Country of Study: Australia
Application Procedure: Apply using the online application form
No. of awards offered: 1
Closing Date: October
Funding: Individuals
Additional Information: The Scholarship is also open to candidates who are undertaking the programme as a student of another university acceptable to the committee, or this university, provided that some part of the programme involves studies at another university scholarships.uq.edu.au/scholarship/constantine-aspromourgos-memorial-scholarship-greek-studies#qt-scholarship_tabs-foundation-tabs-1

For further information contact:

Faculty of Arts, Forgan Smith Building, The University of Queensland, St Lucia, QLD 4072, Australia.

Tel: (61) 7 3365 1333
Email: scholarships@hass.uq.edu.au

University of Queensland PhD Scholarships for International Students

Purpose: Students must have achieved an entry level OP minimum of 11 or the equivalent if originating from another Australian state or territory or for continuing students has a GPA of at least 4.0.
Eligibility: Australian and Permanent Residents or NZ citizens and International students are eligible to apply. Applicants must meet the university's English language proficiency requirements apply. A postgraduate degree of at least one year full-time equivalent with an overall GPA (grade point average) equivalent to 5.0 on the 7-point UQ scale, together with demonstrated research experience equivalent to honors IIA will be considered for PhD entry on a case by case basis.
Value: A Base stipend of AU$27,082 per annum (old rate), indexed annually, tuition fees, Overseas Student Health Cover (OSHC)
Study Establishment: View projects by area Agribusiness, Agriculture, Environment, and Science Engineering, Architecture and Planning, and Information Technology Health Humanities, Education, Psychology, and Music Business, economics, and law (coming soon)
Country of Study: Australia
Application Procedure: See the website.
Closing Date: 31 December
Additional Information: For more details please visit the website scholarship-positions.com/uq-phd-scholarships-international-students-australia/2018/03/06/

For further information contact:

Email: graduateschool@uq.edu.au

Walter and Eliza Hall Scholarship Trust Opportunity Scholarship for Nursing

Purpose: The purpose of the Scholarship is to provide assistance to a meritorious student studying the Bachelor of Nursing or Bachelor of Nursing/Bachelor of Midwifery program whose financial circumstances might otherwise prevent them from achieving their maximum potential during their university study. The funds are intended to assist with the cost of equipment, materials and such other study-related items as may be required by the recipient.
Eligibility: The scholarship is open to students who 1. Are domestic students in accordance with The University's Fee Policy; and; 2. Are enrolled full-time in the Bachelor of Nursing program or the dual Bachelor of Nursing/Bachelor of Midwifery program; and; 3. Have completed at least 16 units towards their program; and do not hold another similar scholarship
Level of Study: Graduate
Type: Scholarship
Value: AU$10,000
Length of Study: one year
Frequency: Annual
Country of Study: Any country
Application Procedure: The Scholarship will be awarded on the basis of I. academic merit. II. financial disadvantage. III. a personal statement. The Scholarship will be awarded by a selection committee consisting of members nominated by the Deputy Vice Chancellor (Registrar) or their nominated delegate
No. of awards offered: 2
Closing Date: 4 March
Funding: Private
Additional Information: The recipient must demonstrate financial need, and also have performed satisfactorily in the program to date. Grade point averages will be considered; however, the grade point average will not be the sole determinant in satisfactory progress – the applicants' behaviour, class attendance, dedication to the program and career aspirations are also a part of the selection process sydney.edu.au/scholarships/c/walter-eliza-hall-trust-opportunity-scholarship-nursing.html

For further information contact:

Brisbane, St Lucia, QLD 4072, Australia.

Email: nmsw.scholarship@uq.edu.au

U

University of Reading

Whiteknights, PO Box 217, Reading RG6 6AH, United Kingdom.

Tel: (44) 1189 875 123
Email: student.recruitment@reading.ac.uk
Website: www.rdg.ac.uk
Contact: Student Financial Support Office

The University of Reading offers postgraduate taught and research degree courses in all the traditional subject areas except medical sciences. Vocational courses are also offered. Research work in many areas is of international renown.

British Property Federation Lord Samuel of Wych Cross Memorial Award

Purpose: To assist students who would otherwise be unable financially to follow the MSc course
Eligibility: Open to candidates who hold a 1st degree and are, at the time of the award, ordinarily resident in the United Kingdom
Level of Study: Postgraduate
Type: Scholarship
Value: £1,000 - £2,000
Length of Study: 1 year
Frequency: Annual
Study Establishment: The University of Reading
Country of Study: United Kingdom
Application Procedure: Applicants must submit a curriculum vitae by invitation to the Director of the Full-Time Postgraduate Real Estate Programme
Closing Date: May
Funding: Private
No. of awards given last year: 3
Additional Information: Scholars must intend to remain resident in the United Kingdom after the term of the scholarship has ended sydney.edu.au/scholarships/c/walter-eliza-hall-trust-opportunity-scholarship-nursing.html

For further information contact:

Tel: (44) 1183 786 336
Email: n.s.french@reading.ac.uk

INTERNATIONAL PHD STUDENTSHIPS

Purpose: The University is pleased to announce a range of international PhD studentships available for October 2023

start. These are available for highly qualified applicants for research within the science, life sciences, social sciences and arts and humanities areas.
Eligibility: Funding is only open to international candidates. Candidates will be required to meet the language requirements specified by their department upon entry. Due to the nature of the studentships where training and support will be directly available via the university, we only invite applications for students wishing to study at one of the University of Reading campuses. Unfortunately, we cannot support other modes of study, such as by distance.
Level of Study: Postdoctorate
Type: Studentship
Value: 1. a subsistence grant (stipend) to match the 2023/24 UK Research Council rate (the 2023/24 rate is £15,609) 2. tuition fees at the International rate 3. a £1,000 p.a. training and development allowance
Length of Study: three years
Frequency: Annual
Country of Study: Any country
Application Procedure: See website: www.reading.ac.uk/graduateschool/prospectivestudents/gs-InternationalResearchStudentships.aspx
Closing Date: 10 January

For further information contact:

Doctoral Studentships Officer

Email: doctoralstudentshipsofficer@reading.ac.uk

Otway Cave Scholarship

Purpose: To assist students who would otherwise be unable financially to follow the MSc course in Land Management
Eligibility: Open to candidates who hold a first degree and are, at the time of the award, ordinarily resident in the United Kingdom
Level of Study: Postgraduate
Type: Scholarship
Value: £1,000 (but may be higher)
Length of Study: 1 year
Frequency: Annual
Study Establishment: The University of Reading
Country of Study: United Kingdom
Application Procedure: Applicants must submit curriculum vitaes by invitation
No. of awards offered: 20
Funding: Private
No. of awards given last year: 1
No. of applicants last year: 20
Additional Information: Scholars must intend to remain resident in the United Kingdom after the term of the

scholarship has ended. Awarded only to students accepted to study MSc Land Management sydney.edu.au/scholarships/c/walter-eliza-hall-trust-opportunity-scholarship-nursing.html

For further information contact:

Tel: (44) 1734 318 182
Fax: (44) 1734 316 658
Email: n.samman@reading.ac.uk

University International Research Studentships

Subjects: All subject areas are eligible
Eligibility: Open to nationals of countries outside of the UK
Level of Study: PhD
Type: Studentship
Value: All tuition fees and a grant for living costs
Length of Study: Up to 3 years
Frequency: Annual
Study Establishment: University of Reading
Country of Study: United Kingdom
Application Procedure: Contact Jonathan Lloyd at the University Graduate School
No. of awards offered: Varies
Closing Date: 1 January
Contributor: University of Reading

For further information contact:

Tel: (44) 118 378 6839
Email: j.d.lloyd@reading.ac.uk

University of Reading Dorothy Hodgkin Postgraduate Award

Eligibility: Open to nationals of either India, Mainland China, Hong Kong, Russia or a country in the developing world only
Level of Study: Postgraduate
Type: Scholarship
Value: All tuition fees and a grant for living costs
Length of Study: 1 year; 3 years
Frequency: Annual
Study Establishment: University of Reading
Country of Study: United Kingdom
Application Procedure: Contact the Jonathan Lloyd at the faculties of science and life science
Closing Date: 6 May
Additional Information: www.european-funding-guide.eu/awardprize/11552-dorothy-hodgkin-postgraduate-awards-dhpa

For further information contact:

Tel: (44) 1183 788 341
Email: j.d.lloyd@reading.ac.uk

University of Reading MSc Intelligent Buildings Scholarship

Eligibility: In order to be considered for this Scholarship you must hold the offer of a place on the MSc Intelligent Buildings course
Level of Study: Postgraduate
Type: Scholarship
Value: £3,000
Length of Study: 1 year
Frequency: Annual
Study Establishment: University of Reading
Country of Study: United Kingdom
Application Procedure: Contact Gulay Ozkan, Programme Coordinator at the School of Construction Management and Engineering
No. of awards offered: 1
Closing Date: 30 August
Contributor: The Happold Trust
No. of awards given last year: 1
No. of applicants last year: 1

For further information contact:

Tel: (44) 1183 786 254
Email: g.ozkan@rdg.ac.uk

University of Reading Music Scholarship

Purpose: To support excellence in music
Eligibility: In order to be considered for this scholarship you must already hold an offer of a place at the university
Level of Study: Postgraduate
Type: Scholarship
Value: All tuition fees
Length of Study: 1 year
Frequency: Annual
Study Establishment: University of Reading
Country of Study: United Kingdom
Application Procedure: Apply online
Closing Date: 1 March
Additional Information: Students must be available for audition on 21 March www.european-funding-guide.eu/awardprize/11552-dorothy-hodgkin-postgraduate-awards-dhpa

U

For further information contact:

Email: music@rdg.ac.uk

University of Regina

Master of Indigenous Education

Purpose: The Master of Indigenous Education degree aims to 1. Prepare students as leaders in pedagogical practice in Indigenous Education. 2. Provide students with the required skills, knowledge, and competencies needed to become effective Indigenous educators. 3. Prepare students to conduct research with Indigenous peoples

Eligibility: Below details should be mandatorily available to process the application for the grant. 1. Personal information. 2. Proxy or Third-Party information (if you want to designate a proxy or third party to act on your behalf). 3. Educational history of all higher post-secondary institutions attended, and dates attended. This includes institutions that you attended but no degree was awarded, and degrees that are in progress and have not yet been awarded. 4. English Proficiency test scores (if applicable). 5. Names and e-mail addresses of your references. 6. Personal statement of interest. Please review "Most Common Mistake Applicants Make" before submitting your personal statement. 7. Resumé or CV. 8. Valid credit card (MasterCard, VISA, or American Express). Pre-paid credit cards and MasterCard Debit, VISA Debit or American Express Debit are not acceptable methods of payment. 9. Valid e-mail address

Level of Study: Postgraduate

Type: Funding support

Frequency: Annual

Country of Study: Any country

Application Procedure: 1. The online application takes about 30 minutes to complete. 2. The first time you access the online application, you will be asked to create a Login ID and PIN. For security reasons, it is important that you choose a unique (hard-to-guess) PIN number. Please make a note of your login information, as you will need it later. 3. Once you have started your application, you may choose to finish at a later date. You can return to the application at any time by re-entering your Login ID and PIN number. However, you must complete it prior to the application deadline for your program

Closing Date: 15 October

Funding: Private

Additional Information: www.uregina.ca/education/Programs1/Graduate-Degree-Programs/Masters_Degree/mied.html

For further information contact:

Tel: (44) 3065 854 502
Email: Grad.Studies@uregina.ca

University of Sheffield

85 Wilkinson Street, Sheffield S10 2GJ, United Kingdom.

Tel: (44) 1142 221 404
Website: www.shef.ac.uk
Contact: Graduate Office

The University of Sheffield is a research led university offering research supervision, taught courses and professional training in engineering and physical sciences, biologies, environmental sciences, humanities, social sciences, medical and health sciences. Many departments have funding council accreditation and scholarships and bursaries may be available.

Allan & Nesta Ferguson Charitable Trust

Purpose: The Allan &; Nesta Ferguson Charitable Trust was set up to promote their particular interests in education, international friendship and understanding, and the promotion of world peace and development

Eligibility: Applications for either a gap year or PhD grant should be made as soon as possible, either before the beginning of the proposed gap year or at least three months before the start of the final year of a PhD course

Level of Study: Graduate

Type: Varies

Value: £13,320

Frequency: Annual

Country of Study: Any country

Application Procedure: 1. The Trust prefer where possible that you complete and submit the on-line application form on this website and email it to us. Alternatively you may download and print out the application form, complete it and send it by letter post. 2. Please do not extend the length of the forms, or add any attachments. Applications MUST NOT exceed 3 pages. Please use text size 12. 3. If you are applying for more than one project, please use a separate form for each project. All applications by email will be acknowledged and a decision will usually be given within three months of the application

No. of awards offered: 2

Closing Date: 3 February

Funding: Private

Additional Information: scholarship-positions.com/allan-and-nesta-ferguson-charitable-trust-scholarships-at-university-of-leeds-in-uk/2019/11/07/

For further information contact:

John St, Royston SG8 9BG, United Kingdom.

Email: internationalscholarships@sheffield.ac.uk

Allan & Nesta Ferguson Charitable Trust Masters Scholarships at University of Sheffield

Purpose: The University of Sheffield, in collaboration with the Allan and Nesta Ferguson Charitable Trust and the Sheffield Institute for International Development, is now able to offer 10 scholarships (over 3 years) targeted at international students from developing countries for a number of courses that are affiliated with the Sheffield Institute for International Development

Eligibility: 1. Must be between the ages of 23-32 at the time of submitting his/her application. 2. Must have obtained or be on the verge of completing their undergraduate degree with a Baccalaureate from an accredited college/university, or its equivalent. 3. Must have a minimum cumulative GPA of 3.0 or higher on a 4.0 rating system, or its equivalent. 4. Must be matriculated at an accredited university for the upcoming academic year starting August/September, and must maintain full-time status for the duration of the Master's Degree

Level of Study: Postgraduate

Type: Scholarship

Frequency: Annual

Study Establishment: University of Sheffield

Country of Study: Any country

Application Procedure: You will be automatically considered for the scholarship if you receive an offer to study one of the eligible courses and you are a national of, or permanently domiciled in, one of the eligible countries or territories. Your course application will be assessed by a panel of academic judges to decide whether you will progress to the final stage of the application process. Please use our postgraduate online application system to submit your application for an eligible course. For further information, check the website link. www.sheffield.ac.uk/international/money/fergusonscholarship

Closing Date: 25 May

Funding: Private

Contributor: University of Sheffield

Additional Information: www.sheffield.ac.uk/international/fees-and-funding/scholarships/postgraduate/ferguson

For further information contact:

The University of Sheffield, Western Bank, Sheffield S10 2TN, United Kingdom.

Email: internationalscholarships@sheffield.ac.uk

Economic and Social Research Council (ESRC) White Rose Doctoral Training Partnership (DTP) and Faculty Scholarships

Purpose: The University is part of the ESRC White Rose Doctoral Training Partnership - a collaboration between the Universities of Leeds, Sheffield, York, Sheffield Hallam, Hull, Bradford and Manchester Metropolitan University and offers a range of ESRC Postgraduate Scholarships

Eligibility: See Website

Level of Study: Graduate, Postgraduate

Type: Scholarship

Value: Tuition Fees, an annual stipend and research training support grant

Frequency: Annual

Study Establishment: University of Sheffield

Country of Study: Any country

No. of awards offered: 3

Closing Date: 14 May

Funding: Private

Additional Information: www.sheffield.ac.uk/postgraduate/phd/scholarships/esrc

For further information contact:

Email: internationalscholarships@sheffield.ac.uk

Edward Bramley Excellence Postgraduate Scholarship

Purpose: The University of Sheffield is pleased to offer the Edward Bramley Excellence Postgraduate Scholarship to support an outstanding United Kingdom or European Union law student, based on academic excellence

Eligibility: 1. Be a UK/EU student for fee purposes. 2. Achieve a first-class honours degree at undergraduate Bachelors or Masters level. 3. Have an academic offer from us to study the full-time LLM (includes Sheffield LLM, LLM Corporate and Commercial Law and LLM International Law and Global Justice pathways) scheduled to commence in September 2020. 4. have an application number. 5. provide a personal statement to evidence excellence.

Type: Scholarship

Value: University has one full fee waiver with £4,000 towards living costs for the outstanding student

Country of Study: United Kingdom

Closing Date: 12 June

Contributor: Edward Bramley Excellence

Additional Information: www.sheffield.ac.uk/law/postgraduate/scholarships-and-fees

U

For further information contact:

Email: law@sheffield.ac.uk

Hossein Farmy Scholarship

Purpose: The Hossein Farmy Scholarship was founded by the late Hossein Farmy, a graduate of the University's former Department of Mining. It is available for students pursuing research related to mining. This includes the geological, engineering, scientific and technological aspects of mining, and the archaeological, economic, historical, legal and social aspects of mining and the mining industry.
Eligibility: 1. You should be intending to pursue a course of research related to mining. 2. You should have, or expect to achieve, a first or upper second class UK honours degree or equivalent qualifications gained outside the UK in an appropriate area of study. 3. You should be registering on your first year of doctoral study with the University for 2023–24. 4. Awards are open to UK applicants only.
Value: £15,009
Country of Study: United Kingdom
Closing Date: 30 April
Funding: Private
Additional Information: If you have any questions about the Hossein Farmy Scholarship please email pgr-scholarships@ sheffield.ac.uk www.sheffield.ac.uk/postgraduate/phd/schol arships/hossein-farmy

For further information contact:

Email: pgr-scholarships@sheffield.ac.uk

International Merit Postgraduate Scholarship

Purpose: Each scholarship is a competitive award worth 25% of the original tuition fee for a postgraduate taught programme starting in September 2023. The scholarships are available to all new international (non-EU) students who meet the eligibility criteria
Eligibility: 1. Your programme must commence at the University of Sheffield in autumn 2023. 2. Distance learning courses are ineligible for a merit scholarship. 3. You must receive an offer for a course studied in full at the University of Sheffield. Masters programmes split between the University of Sheffield and a partner institution are not eligible to apply for a scholarship. 4. All Crossways courses and Erasmus Mundus courses are ineligible for a merit scholarship. 5. For tuition fee purposes you must be self-funded and required to pay the overseas tuition fee. 6. You must not be a sponsored student*. 7. For scholarship purposes all MArch programmes are considered as postgraduate taught programmes and are not eligible for undergraduate scholarships. 8. Anyone studying a Masters/integrated PhD programme is eligible for a merit scholarship in the Masters element of the programme only. 9. These scholarships are not applicable to any postgraduate courses where the higher clinical fee is applicable. This includes, but is not exclusive to, the following courses 1. DClinDent Orthodontics 2. MClinDent in Orthodontics 3. DClinDent Endodontics 4. MClinDent in Paediatric Dentistry 5. DClinDent Periodontics 6. MMedSci in Diagnostic Oral Pathology 7. DClinDent Prosthodontics 10. The University of Sheffield reserves the right to review and change scholarship provision.
Value: 50% of the annual postgraduate tuition fee
Country of Study: Any country
Application Procedure: Please visit website www.sheffield. ac.uk/international/enquiry/money/pgtmerit
Closing Date: 16 May

For further information contact:

Email: l.a.tarrant@sheffield.ac.uk

Postgraduate Taught Sheffield Scholarship

Purpose: To offer the Postgraduate Taught Sheffield Scholarship to international students starting a taught masters programme in September
Eligibility: 1. To be eligible for the scholarship, applicants must be a national of or permanently domiciled in one of the following. 2. Your taught masters programme must be scheduled to commence at the University of Sheffield. 3. You must accept your offer for your course before 1600 (UK time) on 15 June 2023 to receive this award. 4. Subject to meeting the eligibility and award criteria the International Postgraduate Taught Sheffield Scholarship 2023 will be awarded automatically - no application is required.
Type: Scholarship
Value: £2,000 if your tuition fees are between £16,800 and £18,900 and £2,500 if your tuition fees are £18,901 and upwards
Country of Study: United Kingdom
Application Procedure: Subject to meeting the eligibility and award criteria the Postgraduate Taught Sheffield Scholarship will be awarded automatically – no application is required
No. of awards offered: 100
Closing Date: 15 June

For further information contact:

Email: eurec@sheffield.ac.uk

Sheffield Postgraduate Scholarships

Purpose: The scholarships are for students who meet at least one of our widening participation criteria and/or students who achieve a first in their undergraduate degree. If your application is successful you can use the scholarship towards fees or living expenses, the choice is yours

Eligibility: You can apply for a scholarship if you meet all of the following four criteria 1. You'll be studying a taught postgraduate course full-time or part-time for a maximum of four years. 2. You're paying the 'home' rate of fees. 3. You're not already qualified at masters level or higher. 4. You're self funded. Courses funded by the NHS or the Initial Teacher Training bursary, or courses that are eligible for undergraduate funding such as integrated masters are not eligible.; And one or both of the following You're from a group that is evidentially under-represented among the institution's taught masters population - see the widening participation criteria below. 1. You've already achieved or currently predicted a first class undergraduate degree - see the academic merit criteria below.

Type: Scholarship

Value: £10,000 each

Country of Study: United Kingdom

No. of awards offered: 100

Closing Date: 10 May

Additional Information: Applicants will be notified of the outcome of their application before the end of June 2022. www.sheffield.ac.uk/postgraduate/phd/scholarships/hossein-farmy

For further information contact:

Tel: (44) 1142221319
Email: funding@sheffield.ac.uk

University Prize Scholarships

Purpose: Each year the University offers a small number of University Prize Scholarships to the very best PhD applicants

Type: Scholarship

Value: Full tuition fees (United Kingdom, European Union or overseas), an annual, tax-free maintenance stipend of £20,000, a Research Training Support Grant of £2,500 per year for study visits, conferences, books, consumables and equipment

Country of Study: United Kingdom

Closing Date: 23 January

Additional Information: If you have any questions about University Prize Scholarships please email pgr-scholarships@sheffield.ac.uk www.sheffield.ac.uk/postgraduate/phd/scholarships/prize

For further information contact:

Email: pgr-funding@sheffield.ac.uk

White Rose Studentships

Purpose: Collaborative research networks within the three White Rose Universities

Eligibility: 1. These scholarships are only available to applicants to Sheffield Institute of Education (SIoE) and the Centre for Regional Economic and Social Research (CRESR). 2. UK applicants will be eligible for a full award (paying fees and maintenance at standard UKRI rates). EU applicants are normally eligible for a fees only award, unless they have been resident in the UK for 3 years immediately preceding the date of the award. These awards are not open to applicants who are liable to pay tuition fees at the International fee rate. 3. For 1 +3 and +3 awards, applicants must hold at least a UK upper second class honours degree or equivalent. 4. Where English is not your first language, you must show evidence of English language ability to the following minimum level of proficiency an overall IELTS score of 7.0 or above, with at least 7.0 in each component or an accepted equivalent. Please note that your test score must be current, i.e. within the last two years. 5. Please note that students must be resident close to the University at which they are registered and we would expect there to be direct contact between the student and supervisor. This applies to full-time and part-time students.

Level of Study: Postgraduate, Research

Type: Studentship

Value: £15,009

Length of Study: 3 years

Frequency: Annual

Study Establishment: One of the three White Rose Universities

Application Procedure: Candidates can check the website for further details

Closing Date: 29 January

Additional Information: International applicants are only eligible if they can show sufficient funds to cover the difference between the United Kingdom and international students tuition fee www.shu.ac.uk/research/degrees/phd-scholarships/white-rose-dtp-scholarships

For further information contact:

Email: fdsresearch@shu.ac.uk

University of South Australia

GPO Box 2471, Adelaide, SA 5001, Australia.

Tel: (61) 8 8302 6611/3615
Email: research.international@unisa.edu.au
Website: www.unisa.edu.au

The University of South Australia is an innovative and successful institution with a distinctive profile. It is committed to educating professionals, creating and applying knowledge and serving the community.

Division of Business Student Mobility Scholarships

Purpose: To assist business students undertaking an international exchange (via the UniSA International Student Exchange Program) at a partner university

Eligibility: Open to both undergraduate and postgraduate coursework students enroled in a Division of Business program and are participating in exchange for the first time

Level of Study: Postgraduate

Type: Scholarship

Value: AU$5,000 for Institutional Partner Scholarships; AU$2,500 for Student Mobility Scholarships

Frequency: Annual

Application Procedure: For extended criteria and application details, please contact Ms Sarah Oolyer-Braham

Closing Date: 30 January

Additional Information: i.unisa.edu.au/students/scholar ships/postgraduate-scholarships/unisa-business-school/

For further information contact:

Tel: (61) 8 8302 0880
Email: sarah.collyer-braham@unisa.edu.au

Donald Dyer Scholarship – Public Relations & Communication Management

Purpose: To encourage research of an original nature leading to the advancement of knowledge in public relations and communication

Eligibility: Open to candidates who have achieved First Class (Honours) or equivalent. Candidates from discipline areas such as public relations, communication, marketing or advertising are encouraged to apply

Level of Study: Postgraduate, Research

Type: Scholarship

Value: AU$22,000 per year (tax-free) plus one return travel airfare between the candidate's home location and Adelaide, and organized by the University

Frequency: Annual

Study Establishment: University of South Australia

Country of Study: Australia

Application Procedure: Check website for further details

Closing Date: 29 October

Contributor: Bequest from the estate of the Late Sylvia Dyer

For further information contact:

Tel: (61) 8 8302 4493
Fax: (61) 8 8302 4745
Email: david.brittan@unisa.edu.au

Ferry Scholarship

Purpose: Promoting study and research in physics and chemistry

Eligibility: Open to Australian citizens under the age of 25 years on January 1st of the year of the award, who have completed at least 4 years of tertiary education studies, have a First Class (Honours) (or equivalent undergraduate degree), and have enroled as full–time students for a Master's Degree or Doctorate by research in chemistry or physics

Level of Study: Postgraduate

Type: Scholarship

Value: AU$7,500 per year

Length of Study: Up to 3 years (Doctorate) and 2 years (Masters Degree)

Frequency: Annual

Application Procedure: Applications can be filled online

Closing Date: 31 January

Contributor: Bequest from the late Cedric Arnold Seth Ferry

Additional Information: publictrustee.sa.gov.au/content/ uploads/2018/10/2019-Scholarship-Application-form.pdf

For further information contact:

Tel: (61) 8302 3967
Email: jenni.critcher@unisa.edu.au

Lewis O'Brien Scholarship

Purpose: To assist and encourage Aboriginal and Torres Strait Islander people in postgraduate study in a field of particular relevance and potential benefit to the Indigenous Australian community

Eligibility: Open to Aboriginal and Torres Strait Islander people eligible to undertake a postgraduate program in the division of education, arts and social sciences

Level of Study: Postgraduate

Type: Scholarship

Value: Maximum AU$10,000 per year (AU$2,500 will be paid on commencement and the remainder will be paid in instalments during the year subject to certification by the supervisor of satisfactory progress)

Frequency: Annual

Country of Study: Australia

Application Procedure: Candidates must contact Ms Jillian Mille for further information

Closing Date: 11 February
Contributor: Division of Education, Arts and Social Sciences
Additional Information: lc.academicworks.com/opportunities/790

For further information contact:

Tel: (61) 8 8302 9151
Fax: (61) 8 8302 7034
Email: jillian.miller@unisa.edu.au

Margaret George Award

Purpose: To encourage and facilitate use of National Archives collection by promoting archival research in Australia and encouraging scholarly use of its holdings
Eligibility: Open to postgraduate degree holders, historians, academics, independent researchers, or journalists with a talent for research
Level of Study: Postgraduate
Type: Award
Value: AU$10,000
Frequency: Annual
Country of Study: Australia
Application Procedure: Check website for further details
Closing Date: 30 June
Additional Information: Successful applicants may undertake their award at any time from the date of the announcement of the award until June 30th the following year lc.academicworks.com/opportunities/790

For further information contact:

Tel: (61) 2 6212 3986
Fax: (61) 2 6212 3699
Email: derina.mclaughlin@naa.gov.au

Research Training Program International Scholarships in Australia (RTPI)

Purpose: To offer Research Training Program international (RTPi) Scholarships
Eligibility: Generally, an applicant must have first-class Honours or equivalent to gain a scholarship at the University of South Australia. An awardee must be enrolled on a full-time basis as a candidate for a Masters by Research or PhD at the University of South Australia. An awardee shall be enrolled as an internal candidate at the University of South Australia
Level of Study: Research
Type: Scholarship

Value: At least US$28,597 per annum
Length of Study: 3 years
Country of Study: Any country
Closing Date: 31 August
Funding: Government
Additional Information: An RTPi scholarship will cover your tuition fees and your Overseas Student Health Cover (OSHC), and provide a stipend (living allowance), but will not pay for travel expenses. A thesis allowance is funded to cover the cost of printing and binding the thesis lc.academicworks.com/opportunities/790

For further information contact:

Tel: (61) 8 8302 5880 or (61) 8 8302 0828
Email: research.degrees@unisa.edu.au

Synchrotron Microprobe Analysis of Nickel Laterites Scholarship

Purpose: To enable deserving students to pursue a career in the related fields
Eligibility: Open to citizens or permanent residents of Australia or New Zealand who have achieved an Honours Degree or equivalent
Level of Study: Postgraduate
Type: Scholarship
Value: AU$4,000 per year
Frequency: Annual
Study Establishment: University of South Australia
Country of Study: Australia
Application Procedure: Applicants must write to the faculty
Closing Date: 30 September
Contributor: South Australian Premier's Science and Research Fund grant with matching funding from Rio Tinto and BHP-Billiton

For further information contact:

Email: andrea.gerson@unisa.edu.au

Trevor Prescott Memorial Scholarship

Purpose: To help youth in the South Australian community to advance their careers through further postgraduate studies
Eligibility: Open to students between 20 and 30 years of age who desire to do further postgraduate studies or equivalent
Level of Study: Unrestricted
Type: Scholarship
Value: Up to AU$25,000 and may be divided between more than 1 recipient

Frequency: Annual
Application Procedure: Check website for further details
Closing Date: 30 June
Funding: Foundation
Contributor: The Masonic Foundation Inc
Additional Information: Preference is not given to a Freemason or to a member of the family for the scholarship freemasonsfoundation.com.au/pdf/trevor%20prescott.pdf

For further information contact:

Tel: (61) 8 8443 9909
Fax: (61) 8 8443 9928
Email: masfound@senet.com.au

University of South Wales

Pontypridd Wales NP18 3YG, United Kingdom.

Tel: (44) 8455 767 778
Email: enquiries@southwales.ac.uk
Website: www.southwales.ac.uk

The University of Wales, Newport, has been involved in higher education for more than 80 years, and its roots go back even further to the first Mechanics Institute in the town, which opened in 1841.

University of Wales Postgraduate Studentship

Purpose: To support a student with a First Class (Honours) Degree at the university to progress to postgraduate research
Level of Study: Doctorate
Type: Scholarship
Frequency: Annual
Study Establishment: University of Wales
Country of Study: Wales
Application Procedure: Applicants must check with the website or the University
Funding: Private
Contributor: Private benefactions
Additional Information: www.wales.ac.uk/en/AboutUs/Alumni/Benefits/Scholarships.aspx

For further information contact:

Email: shelley.doolan@uwtsd.ac.uk

University of Southampton

University of Southampton, University Road, Southampton SO17 1BJ, United Kingdom.

Tel: (44) 238 059 5000
Email: admissns@soton.ac.uk
Website: www.soton.ac.uk
Contact: Student Marketing Office

The University of Southampton was granted its Royal Charter. Today, the University is one of the United Kingdom's top ten research universities, offering a wide range of postgraduate taught and research courses in engineering, science, mathematics, law, arts, social sciences, medicine and health and life sciences.

Honor Frost Foundation Masters and/or Doctoral Awards in Maritime Archaeology

Purpose: The Foundation's mission is to promote the advancement and research, including publication, of maritime archaeology with particular focus on the eastern Mediterranean
Eligibility: 1. The successful candidate must demonstrate a genuine interest in maritime archaeology and would be expected to develop the subject in their home country upon their return. 2. The successful candidate will also be required to submit annual reports on their progress to the Honor Frost Foundation and contribute towards the Foundation's activities during the duration of their studies, including supporting the annual lecture. 3. The MA Scholarship requires a good 21 honours degree (or equivalent) in either archaeology or a related discipline. You must be a citizen of Cyprus, Lebanon, Egypt or Syria
Level of Study: Postgraduate
Type: Award
Value: an annual stipend of £15,000 with an additional travel fund of £1,000
Frequency: Annual
Country of Study: Any country
Application Procedure: The MA Scholarship requires a good 21 honours degree (or equivalent) in either archaeology or a related discipline. You must be a citizen of Cyprus, Lebanon, Egypt or Syria. The MA scholarship is tenable for one year, commencing September, at an annual stipend of £15,000 with an additional travel fund of £1,000, which can be drawn as required during your study. Tuition fees will also

be paid directly to the University at the appropriate fee rate. There may also be the opportunity to continue to PhD, fully funded, for a further 3 years on completion of the MA/MSc. Application for this studentship is by CV; a sample of written work (4,000 words, max); and a personal statement of up to 800 words explaining why you feel you are suitable for the MA or PhD scholarship. Please also arrange for two academic references to be sent independently by the deadline

Closing Date: 15 May
Funding: Private
Additional Information: educaloxy.com/honor-frost-foundation-masters-andor-doctoral-awards-in-maritime-arch aeology,i6125.html

For further information contact:

Email: lkb@soton.ac.uk

University of Southern California (USC)

College of Letters, Arts and Sciences, University Park, Mail Code 4012, Los Angeles, CA 90089, United States of America.

Tel: (1) 213 740 2531
Website: www.usc.edu/schools/college
Contact: Mr Richard Tithecott, Assistant Administrative Director

Located near the heart of Los Angeles, the University of Southern California (USC) is a private research university. It maintains a tradition of academic strength at all levels, from the earliest explorations of the undergraduate to the advanced scholarly research of the postdoctoral Fellow.

Master of Business Administration/Master of Science in Industrial and Systems Engineering (MSISE) Programme

Application Procedure: Please contact the organisation for details

For further information contact:

Tel: (1) 213 740 4893
Fax: (1) 213 740 1120
Email: gradapp@enroll1.usc.edu

University of Stirling

University of Stirling, Stirling FK9 4LA, United Kingdom.

Email: international@stir.ac.uk
Website: www.stir.ac.uk

The University of Stirling is a United Kingdom research intensive campus university founded by Royal charter in 1967 in Stirling, Scotland. It is ranked among the top 60 universities in the world that are under 50 years old by the Times Higher Education World University Rankings.

Postgraduate Awards for International Students at University of Stirling in United Kingdom

Purpose: The University, via its awards, aims to be at the forefront of research and learning that helps to improve lives
Level of Study: Postgraduate
Type: Award
Value: Each award has a value of £3,000
Country of Study: Scotland
Application Procedure: Students from eligible countries will automatically be assessed for an International Postgraduate Award as part of the admissions process; there is no separate application required for this award. Students who qualify for award will be notified by admissions, once academic offer conditions have been met
Closing Date: 31 August
Additional Information: For details, contact international @stir.ac.uk www.scholarshipportal.com/scholarship/postgr aduate-awards-for-international-students-at-university-of-stir ling-in-uk-2017

For further information contact:

Email: graduate.admissions@stir.ac.uk

University of Strasbourg

Contact: Dr Stéphanie Loison, Scientific coordinator

Strasbourg has a long tradition of scientific excellence, in particularly in chemistry, built through the ages by renowned scientists such as Louis Pasteur, Charles Gerhardt and Nobel Laureates Adolf von Baeyer, Emil Fischer, Hermann Staudinger, Jean-Marie Lehn and more recently Martin Karplus

U

(2013) and now Jean-Pierre Sauvage (2016). The result is that Strasbourg has always been a center of excellence in molecular science, with its top 20 worldwide ranking.

PhD Fellowships in Chemistry

Purpose: To pursue PhD
Eligibility: Foreign students can apply for these PhD fellowships, as well as French national students, who wish to pursue their PhD research study in Strasbourg from September or October
Length of Study: 3 years
Country of Study: France
Closing Date: 15 November
Funding: Foundation
Contributor: Ernest Solvay Fund and the FRC Foundation

For further information contact:

Email: admin@scholarship-positions.com

University of Strathclyde

McCance Building, 16 Richmond Street, Glasgow G1 1XQ, United Kingdom.

Tel: (44) 14 1548 2387
Email: r.livingston@mis.strath.ac.uk
Website: www.strath.ac.uk

Department of Chemical and Process Engineering PhD Studentship

Eligibility: Candidates should be highly motivated and have a First Class Honours degree in chemical engineering, physics or chemistry. An MSc/MEng in science or engineering and previous experience in the field of chemistry of materials would be an advantage. Students will engage in the Department's research seminar programme, and will have opportunities to attend national and international conferences. Other generic skills and courses are open to students, including scientific writing, presentation and careers workshops. International students must be proficient in English language (the University's entry requirements are IELTS 6.5, TOEFL 600 including the test of written English, TOEFL 250 computer based test or TOEFL 90–95 internet based test)
Level of Study: Doctorate
Type: Studentship

Value: The award will cover United Kingdom/European Union tuition fees and will pay a stipend of £13,863 per year (for 3 years). International students would have to pay the difference between the Home/European Union and international fee
Length of Study: 3 years
Frequency: Annual
Study Establishment: University of Strathclyde
Country of Study: Scotland
Application Procedure: Please send your curriculum vitae and a covering letter, indicating your previous experience and fields of interest and include the details of at least two academic referees to Dr S. V. Patwardhan
Closing Date: 30 May
Additional Information: www.surrey.ac.uk/postgraduate/chemical-and-process-engineering-research-phd

For further information contact:

Tel: (44) 141 548 5786
Email: Siddharth.Patwardhan@strath.ac.uk

Fraser of Allander Institute Scholarships for MSc Applied Economics

Purpose: Scholarships are available to join the MSc Applied Economics programme
Value: £6,000
Country of Study: United Kingdom
Application Procedure: Candidates interested in applying should provide a maximum 1,000 word statement demonstrating, through their ideas, experience and future career plans (including their reasoning for joining the MSc Applied Economics) why they should be awarded this scholarship. Candidates will also be considered on the overall quality of their application and financial need. The mode of applying is online. Please visit website www.sbs.strath.ac.uk/apps/scholarships/economics/applied-economics.asp
No. of awards offered: 6
Closing Date: 19 July

For further information contact:

Email: sbs.admissions@strath.ac.uk

International Marketing Bursaries

Purpose: To assist applicants who are seeking sources of financial assistance to pursue full-time postgraduate study in international marketing
Eligibility: A limited number of departmental bursaries are available to well qualified candidates

Level of Study: Postgraduate
Type: Departmental bursaries
Value: £3,000
Length of Study: 1 year
Frequency: Annual
Study Establishment: University of Strathclyde
Country of Study: United Kingdom
Application Procedure: Applicants must contact the Department of Marketing
Contributor: Department of Marketing, Strathclyde University

For further information contact:

Tel: (44) 141 548 3451
Email: mscim.helpdesk@strath.ac.uk

International Strathclyde Prestige Award for Excellence in Business Translation and Interpreting in United Kingdom

Purpose: Scholarship is available for pursuing Postgraduate degree program
Eligibility: To be eligible, the applicants must meet all the following criteria 1. To apply for this scholarship, the applicants must be available to commence their academic studies in the United Kingdom. By the start of the academic year in September. 2. The candidates must hold a first degree at first class or upper second class honors, or equivalent
Level of Study: Postgraduate
Type: Award
Value: £5,000 with tuition fees
Frequency: Annual
Country of Study: United Kingdom
Application Procedure: 1. Applications must be processed with the below link. r1.dotmailer-surveys.com/432p4736-ae3nzoab
Closing Date: 31 May
Funding: Private
Additional Information: For further information, check the following link: r1.dotmailer-surveys.com/432p4736-ae3nzoab scholarship-positions.com/international-strathclyde-prestige-award-for-excellence-in-business-translation-interpreting-in-uk/2019/03/12/

For further information contact:

Email: hass-pg-enquiries@strath.ac.uk

John Mather Scholarship

Purpose: To encourage potential rising stars in the business world, selected on the basis of academic merit

Eligibility: Open to students from the vicinity of the former Strathclyde Region area enrolled in postgraduate instructional courses
Level of Study: Postgraduate
Type: Scholarship
Value: £5,000
Length of Study: 1 year
Frequency: Annual
Study Establishment: Strathclyde Business School
Country of Study: United Kingdom
Application Procedure: Applicants must be nominated by their Head of Department on forms available from the Faculty Officer
No. of awards offered: 10
Closing Date: 23 July
Funding: Trusts
Contributor: John Mather Charitable Trust
No. of awards given last year: 4
No. of applicants last year: 10
Additional Information: spacegrant.org/programs/john-mather/

For further information contact:

Email: e.leiper@mis.strath.ac.uk

Mac Robertson Travelling Scholarship

Purpose: To provide funding that will enrich and further the award holder's academic experience and research achievements
Eligibility: Applicants should be postgraduate research students currently registered at Strathclyde or Glasgow Universities
Level of Study: Postgraduate, Research
Type: Scholarship
Value: Up to £4,000
Length of Study: 2-12 months
Frequency: Annual
Study Establishment: University of Strathclyde
Country of Study: United Kingdom
Application Procedure: Application forms can be downloaded from the website www.strath.ac.uk
No. of awards offered: 3
Closing Date: 1 May
Funding: Individuals
Contributor: Mac Robertson

For further information contact:

Email: pgr@glasgow.ac.uk.

U

University of Strathclyde and Glasgow Synergy Scholarships

Purpose: To assist applicants and students who are seeking sources of financial assistance to pursue full-time postgraduate research study at the University of Strathclyde

Eligibility: Applicants should be PhD candidates of outstanding academic merit

Level of Study: Doctorate

Type: Scholarship

Value: £12,600 per year

Length of Study: Up to 3 years

Frequency: Annual

Study Establishment: University of Strathclyde

Country of Study: United Kingdom

Application Procedure: Applicants seeking nomination for the awards should contact the department they wish to join. Existing research students should contact their head of department or supervisor

Funding: International office

Contributor: University

Additional Information: For more information, visit the website www.strath.gla.ac.uk/synergy www.strath.ac.uk/studywithus/scholarships/

For further information contact:

Email: synergy@gla.ac.uk

University of Surrey

University of Surrey, Guildford GU2 7XH, United Kingdom.

Tel: (44) 148 386 050
Email: maphdinfo@surrey.ac.uk
Website: www.maths.surrey.ac.uk

Studentship in Physical Sciences

Purpose: The aim of this project is to determine the microscopic length scales that control the macroscopic rheology using novel magnetic resonance imaging and optical light scattering techniques in combination with conventional tools

Eligibility: To be eligible for this studentship, you are required to have a First, 21 or merit in a masters degree in a physical sciences subject. If English is not your first language you are required to have an IELTS of 6.5 or above. United Kingdom and European Union candidates are eligible to apply. Activities at the Cambridge centre focus on the development of new science and technology for well construction, with an emphasis on drilling and automation

Level of Study: Graduate

Type: Studentship

Frequency: Annual

Country of Study: Any country

Application Procedure: In order to apply for this studentship, kindly contact Noelle Hartley, Centre Manager for the EPSRC CDT in MiNMaT Greater understanding of the hierarchy of relevant structural lengths from the nanoscale to the macroscale will enable the design of improved complex fluid formulations with predictable rheological properties. N.Hartley@surrey.ac.uk

Closing Date: 30 April

Funding: Private

For further information contact:

Tel: (44) 1483 683467
Email: N.Hartley@surrey.ac.uk

University of Sussex

Postgraduate Office, Sussex House, Falmer, Brighton BN1 9RH, United Kingdom.

Tel: (44) 1273 606 755
Email: information@sussex.ac.uk
Website: www.sussex.ac.uk
Contact: Mr Terry O'Donnell

The University of Sussex is one of the United Kingdom's foremost research institutions. The University boasts a distinguished faculty that includes 17 Fellows of the Royal Society and four Fellows of the British Academy. The University has around 12,000 students, 25% of whom are postgraduates.

Chancellor's International Scholarship

Purpose: Applications are invited for University of Sussex to international postgraduate students who can demonstrate academic excellence

Value: 50% tuition fee reduction

Length of Study: 2 years

Country of Study: Any country

Application Procedure: Apply online. For application procedures, please visit website www.sussex.ac.uk/study/money/apply-chancellors-international-scholarship

Closing Date: May
Contributor: University of Sussex
Additional Information: www.sussex.ac.uk/study/fees-funding/masters-scholarships/view/1005-Chancellor%E2%80%99s-International-Scholarship

PhD Studentships in Mathematics

Eligibility: Applicants must hold, or expect to hold, a Bachelor degree at first or upper second class, and/or a Masters degree, in Mathematics, or equivalent non United Kingdom qualifications. United Kingdom and European Union residents are eligible. Overseas (ex-European Union) students may also apply, but applicants should note that the awards waive the fees at United Kingdom/European Union rates only, of £3,900 per year. Ex-European Union students must state in their application how they would fund the remaining fees. (Overseas fees will be £13,000 per year in total, so additional funding of £9,100 will be needed)
Level of Study: Doctorate
Type: Studentship
Value: £15,009
Length of Study: Scholarships will be offered for 3.5 years
Country of Study: United Kingdom
Application Procedure: The mode of applying is online
Closing Date: 31 January
Contributor: University of Sussex, United Kingdom
Additional Information: www.ed.ac.uk/student-funding/postgraduate/international/science-engineering/mathematics/maths

For further information contact:

Email: pgresearch@maths.ed.ac.uk

Sussex Malaysia Scholarship

Purpose: The aim of the Sussex Master Scholarship is to enable and encourage academically able students from Malaysia
Eligibility: Listed are the eligibility requirements. 1. Be a Malaysian national. 2. Be classified as overseas for fee purposes. 3. Be self-financing. 4. Have accepted an offer to study an eligible Masters course at Sussex
Type: Scholarship
Value: £3,000 tuition fee reduction.
Length of Study: 2 years
Country of Study: United Kingdom
No. of awards offered: Unlimited
Closing Date: 31 January
Contributor: University of Sussex

For further information contact:

Email: scholarships@sussex.ac.uk

University of Sussex Chancellor's International Scholarships

Purpose: University of Sussex Chancellor's International Scholarships are available in the majority of Sussex Schools, and are awarded on the basis of academic performance and potential to non-EU international students who have applied for and been offered a place for eligible full-time Postgraduate Taught degrees at the University of Sussex.
Eligibility: 1. be classified as overseas for fee purposes. 2. have accepted a place on a full time eligible Masters, commencing at the University of Sussex in September 2020. 3. have excellent grades (UK first class or equivalent) 4. have clear and specific goals with defined links to your course. As there are limited scholarships available, this scholarship is extremely competitive (for example, in 2019 entry, the University received more than 1,000 applications for only 25 awards).
Level of Study: Masters Degree
Type: Scholarships
Value: £5,000
Country of Study: United Kingdom
Application Procedure: To be considered for the Chancellors International Scholarship, you need to have received and accepted an offer of a place on an eligible Masters at Sussex. To apply, you must complete the online application form. The deadline is 1 May 2359 GMT. It is important to visit the official website (link found below) to access the online application form and for detailed information on how to apply for this scholarship.
No. of awards offered: 60
Closing Date: 1 August

For further information contact:

Email: study@sussex.ac.uk

University of Sydney

Scholarships and Financial Support Service, Jane Foss Russell Building, G02, Sydney, NSW 2006, Australia.

Tel: (61) 2 8627 8112
Email: scholarships.officer@sydney.edu.au
Website: www.sydney.edu.au
Contact: Manager

Alexander Hugh Thurland Scholarship

Eligibility: Open to the graduates from other universities with relevant degree
Level of Study: Doctorate, Postgraduate, Research
Type: Scholarship
Value: AU$24,653 per year
Length of Study: 2 years for Masters by research candidates and 3 years with a possible 6-month extension for research doctoral candidates
Frequency: Dependent on funds available
Study Establishment: The University of Sydney
Country of Study: Australia
Application Procedure: Check website www.sydney.edu.au/agriculture
Funding: Trusts

For further information contact:

Tel: (61) 2 8627 1002
Fax: (61) 2 8627 1099
Email: pg@agric.usyd.edu.au

Dean's International Postgraduate Research Scholarships

Purpose: Scholarships are available to undertake a research doctorate degree (PhD) programme
Eligibility: To be eligible, the applicants must meet all the given criteria 1. have an offer of admission for full-time studies in a master's by research or doctor of philosophy (PhD) 2. be currently enrolled either a. the final year of at least a four-year bachelor's degree in science or relevant discipline area, b. an equivalent degree at a non-Australian university, with at least 25% of the final year of the degree being a research component 3. have achieved a minimum weighted average mark (WAM) equivalent to a grade of 85 not be an Australian citizen or permanent resident, or a New Zealand citizen 4. apply for a Research Training Program (RTP) Fee Offset and Stipend scholarship
Level of Study: Postgraduate
Value: The scholarship consists of the full cost of academic tuition fees plus a stipend equivalent to an Australian Postgraduate Award indexed annually
Length of Study: 3 years
Study Establishment: Faculty of Science
Country of Study: Australia
Application Procedure: International students (except Australia or New Zealand) can apply for these postgraduate research scholarships. An annual stipend allowance equivalent to the Research Training Program (RTP) stipend rate indexed annually
Closing Date: 30 April
Additional Information: For more details, visit website scholarship-positions.com/deans-international-postgraduate-research-scholarships-in-australia-2015-2016/2015/03/03/ scholarship-positions.com/deans-international-postgraduate-research-scholarship-at-the-university-of-sydney-australia/2019/02/01/

Dr Abdul Kalam International Postgraduate Scholarships

Purpose: Celebrating Dr Abdul Kalam's commitment to education, and his endeavours to support outstanding students to develop as future leaders.
Eligibility: 1. Be an international student 2. Have an unconditional offer of admission for a master's by coursework in the Faculty of Engineering 3. Have achieved a minimum WAM of 75 in your undergraduate studies 4. Be commencing your degree in the same semester and year the scholarship is offered.
Level of Study: Postgraduate
Type: Scholarship
Value: Half of tuition fees
Frequency: Annual
Country of Study: United States of America
Application Procedure: Applicants must complete an online scholarship application (sydney.edu.au/engineering/scholarships/postgraduate/dr-kalam.shtml)
Closing Date: 5 July

For further information contact:

Tel: (61) 2 8627 1444
Fax: (61) 2 9351 7082
Email: engineering.scholarships@sydney.edu.au

International Postgraduate Research Scholarships (IPRS) Australian Postgraduate Awards (APA)

Purpose: To support candidates with exceptional research potential
Eligibility: Open to suitably qualified graduates eligible to commence a higher degree by research. Australia and New Zealand citizens and Australian permanent residents are not eligible to apply
Level of Study: Doctorate, Postgraduate, Research
Type: Scholarship

Value: Tuition fees for IPRS, and an Australian Postgraduate Award for AU$24,653 per year
Length of Study: 2 years for the Master's by research candidates, and 3 years with a possible 6-month extension for PhD candidates
Frequency: Annual
Study Establishment: The University of Sydney
Country of Study: Australia
Application Procedure: Applicants must complete an application form for admission available from the International Office
Closing Date: 15 December
Funding: Government
Contributor: Australian Government and University of Sydney
No. of awards given last year: 34

For further information contact:

Tel:	(61) 2 8627 8358
Fax:	(61) 2 8627 8387
Email:	infoschol@io.usyd.edu.au

Master of Business Administration Programme

Length of Study: 1 year
Application Procedure: Applicants must complete an application form supplying official transcripts and a Graduate Management Admission Test score
Closing Date: 31 October

For further information contact:

Tel:	(61) 2 9351 0038
Fax:	(61) 2 9351 0099
Email:	gsbinfo@gsb.usyd.edu

PhD Scholarship Healthcare Services for Older People

Purpose: To investigate the effectiveness of transition care services for older people
Eligibility: Open only to permanent residents and the citizens of Australia or New Zealand who have Honours Degree, or equivalent, in health–related discipline to undertake research studies
Level of Study: Postgraduate
Type: Scholarship
Value: AU$22,000 per year
Length of Study: 3 years
Frequency: Annual

Study Establishment: University of Sydney
Application Procedure: Applicants must send their curriculum vitae, copy of academic transcript, names and contact details of at least 2 referees to Prof Cameron (preferably by email)
Closing Date: 14 August

For further information contact:

Tel:	(61) 2 9808 9236
Fax:	(61) 2 9809 9037
Email:	ianc@mail.usyd.edu.au

PhD Scholarship to Advance Aquaculture in Australasia

Purpose: To improve the productivity and profitability of smallholder shrimp farms in Indonesia
Eligibility: Open only to the citizens of Australia or permanent residents
Level of Study: Postgraduate, Research
Type: Scholarship
Value: AU$25,000 per year
Length of Study: 3 years
Frequency: Annual
Application Procedure: Applicants must mail their curriculum vitae, copy of academic transcript, proof of citizenship or permanent residency, names and contact details of at least 2 referees to Dr Toribio
Closing Date: 17 August

For further information contact:

Tel:	(61) 612 9351 1609
Fax:	(61) 612 9351 1618
Email:	jennyt@camden.usyd.edu.au

University of Tasmania

Private Bag 45, Hobart, TAS 7001, Australia.

Tel:	(61) 3 6226 2999
Email:	scholarships@research.utas.edu.au
Website:	www.utas.edu.au
Contact:	Graduate Research Unit

The University of Tasmania was officially founded on January 1st 1890, by an Act of the Colony's Parliament and was only the fourth university to be established in 19th century Australia. The university represents areas of significant research strengths and substantial teaching endeavours.

Across PhD – Bio Analytical Research – Pharmacokinetics and Drug Metabolism Scholarship

Purpose: To promote research on retention mechanisms, breakthrough, and recovery for the model analytes together with appropriate characterization of the monolithic phase
Eligibility: Open to applicants who have achieved Honours 2a or equivalent
Level of Study: Postgraduate, Research
Type: Scholarship
Value: AU$20,000 for living expenses
Length of Study: 3 and a half years
Frequency: Annual
Application Procedure: Applicants should send a curriculum vitae directly to Prof Paul Haddad. Check website for further details
Contributor: Pfizer Analytical Research Centre (PARC)

For further information contact:

Tel: (61) 3 6226 2179
Email: paul.haddad@utas.edu.au

Across PhD Scholarship; Analytical Chemistry; Rock Lobster Aquaculture

Eligibility: Open to applicants who have achieved Honours 2a or equivalent
Level of Study: Postgraduate, Research
Type: Scholarship
Value: AU$25,118 for living expenses
Length of Study: 3 and a half years
Frequency: Annual
Application Procedure: Applicants should send a curriculum vitae directly to Prof Paul Haddad. Check website for further details

For further information contact:

Tel: (61) 3 6226 2179
Email: paul.haddad@utas.edu.au

Across PhD, High Performance Ion Exchange Chromatography Scholarship

Purpose: To investigate the feasibility of using HP-IEC for the separation and detection of small to medium MW organic acids and bases

Eligibility: Open to applicants who have achieved Honours 2a or equivalent
Level of Study: Postgraduate, Research
Type: Scholarship
Value: AU$20,000 for living expenses
Length of Study: 3 and a half years
Frequency: Annual
Country of Study: Australia
Application Procedure: Applicants should send a curriculum vitae directly to Prof Paul Haddad. Check website for further details
Contributor: Pfizer Analytical Research Centre (PARC)

Cancer Council Tasmania Honours Scholarship

Purpose: These scholarships are generously provided by Cancer Council Tasmania in recognition of SeaRoad, the family of Pat Campbell and the Mazengarb family to support a student to undertake an Honours research project in any area of cancer.
Eligibility: Available to a full-time student undertaking a Honours research project in Semester 1, 2023 in any area that focuses on cancer, this may include behavioural, prevention, detection and supportive care.
Level of Study: Research
Type: Scholarship
Value: AU$10,000
Length of Study: 1 year
Frequency: Annual
Country of Study: Any country
Application Procedure: Check website for further details
Closing Date: 31 January
Additional Information: www.cancerwa.asn.au/cancer-research/i-am-a-cancer-researcher/funding/honours-masters-scholarships/

For further information contact:

Tel: (61) 3 6226 4832
Email: g.m.woods@utas.edu.au

Cardiac Rehabilitation UTAS Exercise Physiology Graduate Research Scholarship

Purpose: To investigate the effectiveness of provision of an exercise physiology service as part of a cardiac rehabilitation program, as well as identifying the optimal modality and intensity of exercise undertaken by patients as part of the program
Eligibility: Open to applicants who have achieved Honours 2a or equivalent. Only citizens of Australia or permanent residents can apply

Level of Study: Postgraduate, Research
Type: Scholarship
Value: AU$19,616
Length of Study: 3 years
Frequency: Annual
Study Establishment: University of Tasmania
Country of Study: Australia
Application Procedure: Check website for further details
Closing Date: 30 June
Additional Information: www.utas.edu.au/exercise-physiology-clinic/cardiac-rehabilitation

For further information contact:

Tel: (61) 3 6324 5487
Email: Andrew.Williams@utas.edu.au

Centre of Excellence in Ore Deposits PhD Scholarships

Purpose: For students to study within one of the five major programs of the centre location, formation, discovery, recovery or technology
Eligibility: Open to students undertaking PhD research in the specified fields. Applicants require either an MSc in geology/geophysics or a first or upper second–class honours degree. Some experience in the minerals industry is preferred but not essential
Level of Study: Postgraduate
Value: AU$20,000 - AU$30,000 depending on qualifications and experience
Length of Study: 3 and a half years
Additional Information: www.utas.edu.au/codes/available-rhd-projects

For further information contact:

Tel: (61) 3 6226 2892
Email: j.mcphie@utas.edu.au

Master of Business Administration Programme

Length of Study: Varies
Application Procedure: Applicants must contact The University of Tasmania Graduate School of Management for an application form

For further information contact:

Tel: (61) 2 2078 37
Fax: (61) 2 2078 62
Email: International.Office@admin.utas.edu.au

Menzies Research Institute Honours Scholarship

Purpose: To support vital work in epidemiology, and diseases which affect the community
Eligibility: Open to a student eligible to undertake an honours research program in any area of research undertaken by the Institute
Level of Study: Research
Type: Scholarship
Value: AU$5,000
Length of Study: 1 year
Frequency: Annual
Country of Study: Any country
Application Procedure: Applicants can apply through the Tasmania Honours Scholarship application form downloaded from the website. All potential honours students should contact the Honours Co-ordinator in their discipline to discuss interests and options
Closing Date: 31 October
Additional Information: menzies.utas.edu.au/education/study-at-menzies/scholarships-and-awards/honours-scholarships-at-menzies

For further information contact:

Email: enquiries@menzies.utas.edu.au

North Hobart Football Club Peter Wells Scholarships

Purpose: To support North Hobart players while at UTAS
Eligibility: One scholarship available to a north-western/northern student and one to a southern student with good academic records and who are available to play for the NHFC while studying at UTAS
Type: Scholarship
Value: AU$3,000 and AU$2,000
Length of Study: 1 year
Frequency: Annual
Country of Study: Any country
Contributor: The late Peter Wells

For further information contact:

Email: International.Scholarships@utas.edu.au

Qantas Tasmanian Devil Research Scholarship

Purpose: To assist research into the facial tumour disease affecting devil populations
Eligibility: Open to researchers in facial tumour diseases
Level of Study: Research
Type: Scholarship

Value: Up to APA level, additional research funding may be available
Length of Study: 3 and a half years
Frequency: Annual
Country of Study: Any country
Application Procedure: Check website for further details
Contributor: Qantas
Additional Information: www.cnaviationplane.com/news/0/981.html

For further information contact:

Email: devil.appeal@utas.edu.au

Quantitative Marine Science PhD Scholarships

Purpose: To offer specialized graduate-level coursework in quantitative marine science (QMS)
Eligibility: Open to students who hold at least an upper second-class honours degree, or equivalent, and have a major in mathematics, physical sciences, life sciences, geomatics or Engineering
Level of Study: Doctorate
Type: Scholarship
Value: AU$32,000 per annum. and production costs will also be provided
Length of Study: Up to 3 years
Frequency: Annual
Country of Study: Any country
Application Procedure: Application forms, conditions of awards and program information on Graduate Research Scholarships can be downloaded from the website
Funding: Private
Contributor: Commonwealth Scientific and Industrial Research Organisation (CSIRO) in partnership with the University of Tasmania
Additional Information: For further information on all Graduate Research Scholarships please contact the Graduate Research Office on (3) 6226 2766 www.cnaviationplane.com/news/0/981.html

For further information contact:

CSIRO-UTAS Joint PhD Program in Quantitative Marine Science, Private Bag 129, Hobart, TAS 7001, Australia.

Tel: (61) 3 6226 2108
Email: Peter.Strutton@utas.edu.au

Riawunna Postgraduate Scholarship

Purpose: To encourage an Aboriginal or Torres Strait Islander student to undertake honours or postgraduate coursework study at the University and committed to the advancement of knowledge about Aboriginal and Torres Strait Islander cultures and societies
Eligibility: Open to an Aboriginal or Torres Strait Islander student who undertake honours or postgraduate coursework study at the University
Level of Study: Postgraduate
Type: Scholarship
Value: AU$3,000
Length of Study: 1 year
Frequency: Annual
Country of Study: Any country
Contributor: Riawunna
Additional Information: www.utas.edu.au/riawunna/scholarships

For further information contact:

Email: scholarships.referee@utas.edu.au

Sir Victor Burley Scholarship in Music

Purpose: The family of Victor Burley has endowed this scholarship to encourage the development of advanced music skills, especially in the classical music area
Eligibility: Open to student eligible to enter a postgraduate music course at the Conservatorium of Music preferably studying in a classical area of music
Level of Study: Postgraduate
Type: Scholarship
Value: AU$1,000
Length of Study: 1 year
Frequency: Annual
Country of Study: Australia
Contributor: The family of the late Sir Victor Burley
Additional Information: info.scholarships.utas.edu.au/AwardDetails.aspx?AwardId=218

For further information contact:

Email: Scholarships.Referee@utas.edu.au

Tasmania Honours Scholarships

Purpose: These honours scholarships are provided by the University of Tasmania to encourage excellent students to continue their study at honours level.
Eligibility: Available to students who are commencing an Honours course in any discipline in Semester 1, 2023. Selection will be based on academic merit.
Level of Study: Postgraduate
Type: Scholarship
Value: Up to AU$10,000

Length of Study: 1 year (full-time study)
Frequency: Annual
Country of Study: Any country
Application Procedure: Applicants should apply online and forward a copy of the referee's report to two referees. All potential honours students should make contact with the Honours Coordinator in their discipline to discuss interests and options.
Closing Date: 31 January
Additional Information: Six of the 10 awards will target students commencing study at the University of Tasmania info.scholarships.utas.edu.au/AwardDetails.aspx?AwardId=41

For further information contact:

Email: Scholarships.Referee@utas.edu.au

Tasmania University Cricket Club Scholarship

Purpose: This scholarship is made available through the generosity of past members and supporters of the Tasmanian University Cricket Club (TUCC). It will support a student with good academic achievements who can also demonstrate a talent and commitment to cricket as demonstrated by performance in school, club and representative competitions. The selected student must be prepared to play for the TUCC in the coming season.
Eligibility: Available to a commencing or current student who can demonstrate a talent and commitment to cricket. Selection will based on the following five criteria: 1. Cricket skill ie representative levels and success at those levels; 2. Academic achievement and potential to succeed at university; 3. Leadership skills and experiences; 4. Cricket involvement eg coaching; 5. Community involvement. The selected student must be playing for, or be able to play for, the TUCC in the coming season. Potential applicants may also wish to visit the Cricket website (www.tucc.org.au/) to gain a better understanding about the club and its goals.
Type: Scholarship
Value: AU$3,000
Length of Study: 1 year
Frequency: Annual
Country of Study: Any country
Application Procedure: Apply online prior to closing date. Applications cannot be submitted after closing date. As applicants will be assessed on the quality of application, all questions should be answered in full. Please ensure care is taken with spelling and grammar.
Closing Date: 7 March
Contributor: Supporters and past players of the Tasmania University Cricket Club

For further information contact:

Email: chas.rose@gmail.com

Tasmanian Government Mining Honours Scholarships

Purpose: To encourage geological research at CODES on topics that are relevant to the Tasmanian minerals industry
Eligibility: Open to students undertaking research in the field of geology, with relevance to the Tasmanian minerals industry. Specialization in one or more of ore deposit geology, igneous petrology, volcanology, structure, sedimentology, geochemistry or geophysics. Applicants require at least a credit average in geology units at the second or third year levels
Level of Study: Research
Type: Scholarship
Value: AU$5,000; AU$8,000 depending on qualifications and experience
Length of Study: 1 year
Frequency: Annual
Application Procedure: Applicants can apply through the Tasmania Honours Scholarship application form downloaded from the website
Closing Date: 31 October
Contributor: Mineral Resources Tasmania

For further information contact:

Tel: (61) 3 6226 2815
Email: garry.davidson@utas.edu.au

Tasmanian Government Mining PhD Scholarship

Purpose: To encourage geological research undertaken at the ARC Centre of Excellence in Ore Deposits (CODES) on topics relevant to the Tasmanian minerals industry
Eligibility: The following eligibility criteria apply to this scholarship 1. The scholarship is open to domestic (Australian and New Zealand) and international candidates. 2. The Research Higher Degree must be undertaken on a full-time basis. 3. Applicants must already have been awarded a First Class Honours degree or hold equivalent qualifications or relevant and substantial research experience in an appropriate sector. 4. Applicants must be able to demonstrate strong research and analytical skills
Level of Study: Doctorate, Research
Type: Scholarship
Value: AU$18,000–25,000 depending on qualifications and experience
Length of Study: 3 and a half years
Frequency: Annual

Country of Study: Any country
Contributor: Mineral Resources Tasmania

For further information contact:

Tel: (61) 3 6226 2819
Email: anita.parbhakar@utas.edu.au

University of Technology Sydney (UTS)

PO Box 123, Broadway, Ultimo, NSW 2007, Australia.

Tel: (61) 2 9514 1659
Email: clg.postgraduate@uts.edu.au
Contact: UTS Institute for Public Policy and Governance

The University of Technology Sydney (UTS) is a thriving university located in the centre of Sydney, one of the world's most desirable and multicultural cities.

University of Technology Sydney Institute for Public Policy and Governance Postgraduate Scholarship in Australia, 2017

Purpose: To support commencing University of Technology Sydney (UTS) Master of Local Government students by assisting them financially.
Eligibility: Australian or New Zealand citizen, or the holder of an Australian permanent resident visa or permanent humanitarian visa; and must have submitted an application and met the entry requirements for admission to the UTS Institute for Public Policy and Governance Master of Local Government degree by coursework degree; and must be commencing the UTS Institute for Public Policy and Governance Master of Local Government program; and must not have completed any study under any other postgraduate courses within the UTS Institute for Public Policy and Governance; and intend to enroll in a minimum of 12 credit points/session in the session immediately following the Scholarship selection; and all candidates must apply using the online UTS online Scholarship Application form to be eligible.
Level of Study: Postgraduate
Type: Scholarship
Value: The maximum value of this scholarship is AU$5,000 for each recipient
Length of Study: 1 year
Frequency: Annual
Country of Study: Any country
Application Procedure: Please note that Scholarship applicants must first submit an application for the UTS Master of

Local Government to be considered for the Scholarship. To apply for the Master course, please request an application form from the Institute at postgraduate-at-uts.edu.au or on (61) 2 9514 1659.
Closing Date: 6 March
Funding: Government
Additional Information: The UTS Institute for Public Policy and Governance (UTS:IPPG) Postgraduate Scholarship was designed to support local government professionals seeking to broaden their knowledge and skills through postgraduate study and to recognize the diverse pathways to a local government career armacad.info/university-of-technology-sydney-institute-for-public-policy-and-governance-post graduate-scholarship-2017-australia

For further information contact:

Email: Alan.Morris@uts.edu.au

University of Texas

School of Public Health Health, Science Center, PO Box 20186, Houston, TX 77225, United States of America.

Contact: Mr Robert E Roberts

Harry Ransom Center: Research Fellowships

Purpose: The fellowships are awarded for projects that require substantial on-site use of its collections
Eligibility: All applicants, with the exception of dissertation fellowship applicants, must have a PhD or be an independent scholar with a substantial record of achievement; if the PhD is in-progress, the proposal and letters of recommendation must clearly indicate a June 1st, completion in order to be eligible for fellowships. Dissertation fellowship applicants must be doctoral candidates engaged in dissertation research by the time of application. United States of America citizens and foreign nationals are eligible to apply. Previous recipients of Ransom Center fellowships are eligible to reapply after two full academic years have passed. All things being equal, however, preference is given to applicants who have not previously held a Ransom Center fellowship
Type: Research fellowship
Value: stipends of US$3,500 per month
Frequency: Annual
Country of Study: United States of America
Application Procedure: Fellowships must be submitted electronically through an online fellowship account on the Ransom Center's website

Closing Date: 31 March

For further information contact:

Email: ransomfellowships@utexas.edu

Mobility Scooters Direct Scholarship Program

Purpose: Mobility Scooters Direct provides a US$1,500 scholarship each year to selected students who apply to the program

Eligibility: 1. Must be enrolled in a minimum of 6 hours undergraduate or 3 hours graduate at an accredited University or College. 2. Must have taken at least 40 undergraduate credit hours or 10 graduate credit hours. 3. Must have proof of a declared major. 4. Must demonstrate involvement on campus or in the community of attended University or College. 5. Must attach one letter of recommendation on official letterhead. 6. You must be at least 18 years of age to apply. 7. You must be currently enrolled at your college or university during the time of submission. 8. You must have a 3.0 GPA or higher

Level of Study: Graduate

Type: Programme grant

Value: US$1,500

Frequency: Annual

Country of Study: Any country

Application Procedure: The below details have to be included in the application. 1. Your first & last name, ph. number & email address(s). 2. Statement or transcript of your Grade Point Average (GPA). Letter of recommendation should have the below entities. 1. All applicants must meet certain criteria outlined below and submit an application via email or United States mail. 2. Applicants are also required to provide a letter of recommendation from a teacher, professor or counselor from the school being attended by the applicant

Funding: Private

For further information contact:

4135 Dr. M.L. King Jr Blvd. Store D21, Ft. Myers, FL 33916, United States of America.

Email: help@mobilityscootersdirect.com

University of Tokyo

9-7-3, Akasaka TK 107-0052, Japan.

Tel: (81) 3 6271 4368
Contact: Fujixerox Co., Ltd., Kobayashi Fund, c/o Fuji Xerox

The University of Tokyo aims to be a world-class platform for research and education, contributing to human knowledge in partnership with other leading global universities. The University of Tokyo aims to nurture global leaders with a strong sense of public responsibility and a pioneering spirit, possessing both deep specialism and broad knowledge.

Kobayashi Research Grants

Purpose: Grants are available to pursue research programme

Eligibility: International students from Asia, Oceania countries/regions. 1. Note the Asia-Pacific countries and regions as referred to here, it shows the following countries and regions

Type: Grant

Value: Maximum of ¥1,200,000 /person

Country of Study: Japan

Application Procedure: Please download the application documents and instructions for sending at the following link www.fujixerox.com/eng/company/social/pdf/1.pdf

Closing Date: 28 February

No. of awards given last year: 39

Additional Information: research.nd.edu/our-services/funding-opportunities/faculty/internal-grants-programs/kobayashi-travel-fund/

For further information contact:

International Liaison Office Room 120, Environmental Studies Building 5-1-5 Kashiwanoha, Kashiwa, Chiba 277-8563, Japan.

Kobayashi Research Grants in Humanities and Social Sciences

Eligibility: Scholarships are offered in diverse fields to help students in upgrading their education

Type: Research

Value: Maximum ¥1,200,000 per grantee will be available to approximately 30 grantees. An amount from ¥320,000 to ¥1,200,000 per grantee was provided to 32 grantees for the program. (Depending upon the results of the Grantee Screening Committee's assessment, the actual amount for some grantees could be less than the originally requested amount.)

Study Establishment: Grants shall be conferred for individual research (not group research) in the field of Humanities (Cultural Science) or Social Sciences, with special emphasis on themes that help deepen the researcher's understanding and awareness of Japanese or Asian/Oceanian society and culture and enhance international interchanges among them in the future

Country of Study: Japan

Application Procedure: The mode of applying is online

Closing Date: 28 February

Additional Information: For more details please visit to the website scholarship-positions.com/kobayashi-research-grant-humanities-social-sciences-university-tokyo-japan/2017/01/24/ myhealthbasics.site/kobayashi-research-grants-humanities-social-sciences-university-tokyo-japan-2017/

University of Twente

Universiteit Twente, Drienerlolaan 5, NL-7522 Enschede, Netherlands.

Tel: (31) 53 489 9111
Email: info@utwente.nl
Website: www.utwente.nl/en

ASML Henk Bodt Scholarship

Purpose: The ASML Henk Bodt Scholarship supports a talented technical student who has completed (or is about to complete) the Bachelor of Science programme, and who is further motivated to pursue a 2 years full-time Master of Science degree in technical and scientific disciplines at the University of Twente

Eligibility: To qualify for a ASML Henk Bodt Scholarship, candidates must at least fulfill the following basic requirements Bachelor of Science diploma, academic transcripts of each academic year from the BSc programme, cumulative Grade Point Average of at least 80% of the scale maximum of all courses of the BSc program, MSc programme admission letter from the University of Twente, up-to-date curriculum vitae

Type: Scholarship

Value: The scholarship will provide financial support for the entire duration of the Master's degree (2-year period) which covers the full tuition fee and living expenses, approx. €22,000 per year

Length of Study: 2 years

Frequency: Annual

Country of Study: Any country

Closing Date: 1 March

Additional Information: Check details at www.utwente.nl/internationalstudents/scholarshipsandgrants/all/asml_henk_bodt_scholarship/ www.utwente.nl/en/news/2015/4/41467/asml-technology-scholarships

For further information contact:

Tel: (81) 40 268 6572
Email: scholarships@asml.com

Holland Scholarship

Purpose: The Holland Scholarship is a scholarship for excellent students from non-European Union/EEA countries, applying for a Bachelor or Masters programme at the University of Twente

Eligibility: Open to non-European Union/EEA countries. In order to be eligible for a Holland Scholarship, you should meet all the requirements as follows your programme starts in the current academic year; you have not studied in the Netherlands before for a full degree (e.g. a Bachelor's or Master's degree); you are from a non-European Union/EEA country; you are an excellent student (i.e. CGPA of 7.5 (out of 10)); etc. Please check complete eligibility criteria at

Type: Scholarship

Value: € 5,000

Length of Study: 1 year

Country of Study: Any country

Application Procedure: In order to apply for this scholarship, you already need to be (provisionally) admitted to one of the qualifying Bachelor or Master programmes

Closing Date: 1 May

Kipaji Scholarship

Purpose: University Twente Scholarships (UTS) are scholarships for excellent students from both EU/EEA and non-EU/EEA countries, applying for a graduate programme (MSc) at the University of Twente.

Eligibility: In order to be eligible for a the University of Twente Scholarship, you should meet all the requirements below Application for an UT scholarship is a procedure separate from the application for course entry at the University of Twente. Regardless of funding, you will need to gain an admission letter first. You have been (provisionally) admitted to one of the qualifying UT Master programmes starting in the academic year 2023/2024 (September). Please note After completion of your application, it may take up to 8 weeks before you receive the results. You must have a studentnumber. You have not graduated from a UT (under)graduate programme; You comply with the conditions for obtaining an entry visa in the Netherlands (if applicable); You comply with the general English language test requirement Academic IELTS 6.5 (or TOEFL iBT of 90) and an additional 6.0 (TOEFL iBT 20) on the subscore of speaking skills You are not eligible for a Dutch study loan; The University Twente Scholarship is a scholarship for excellent students. Typically this means that you belong to the best 5 to 10 % of your class

Level of Study: Masters Degree

Type: Scholarships
Value: Up to €12,000
Length of Study: 2 year
Frequency: Annual
Country of Study: Netherlands
Application Procedure: You have to apply for a Master's programme first. Once you applied for a Master's programme and received a (conditional) admission letter, you can apply for the scholarship with your student number. UTS is not available for Dutch and/or current UT students. This programme is also not available for Master's programmes at the Faculty of Geo-Information Science and Earth Observation (ITC).
No. of awards offered: Approximately 50
Closing Date: 1 May
Additional Information: www.utwente.nl/en/education/scholarship-finder/kipaji-scholarship/#applicationrequirements

Orange Tulip Scholarship (OTS) China

Purpose: The Orange Tulip Scholarship (OTS) offers talented students from China the opportunity to obtain a Masters degree at the University of Twente. The scholarship programme is highly selective, offering two scholarships for the current academic year
Level of Study: Graduate
Type: Scholarship
Value: €24,000. The scholarship consists of a reduction of the institutional tuition fee for non-EEA students (to €2,083)
Country of Study: Any country
Application Procedure: Applications should be submitted to the Netherlands Education Support Office (NESO) China. Visit their website for more information about the requirements for the Orange Tulip Scholarship (OTS), or send an email to ots@nesochina.org
Closing Date: 1 April
Additional Information: www.ru.nl/currentstudents/during-your-studies/@924838/orange-tulip-scholarship-china/ www.utwente.nl/en/education/scholarship-finder/university-of-twente-scholarship/#application-deadlines-details

Orange Tulip Scholarship (OTS) Indonesia

Purpose: The Orange Tulip Scholarship (OTS) offers talented students from Indonesia the opportunity to obtain a Master degree at the University of Twente
Level of Study: Graduate
Type: Scholarship

Value: € 22,000
Length of Study: 2 year
Country of Study: Any country
Application Procedure: Apply online: osiris.utwente.nl/inkomend/WelkomPagina.do?proces=%20OTS-SCHOLAR-1
No. of awards offered: 1
Closing Date: 1 May
Additional Information: Please visit www.utwente.nl/en/education/scholarship-finder/orange-tulip-scholarship-indonesia/

Orange Tulip Scholarship (OTS) Mexico

Purpose: The Orange Tulip Scholarship (OTS) offers talented students from Mexico the opportunity to obtain a Master degree at the University of Twente. The scholarship programme is highly selective, offering one scholarship for the current academic year
Level of Study: Graduate
Type: Scholarship
Value: €24,000
Frequency: Annual
Country of Study: Any country
Application Procedure: Visit the website of NESO Mexico. Applications should be submitted to the Netherlands Education Support Office (NESO) Mexico. Visit their website for more information about the requirements for the Orange Tulip Scholarship (OTS), or send an email to ots@nesomexico.org
Closing Date: 1 May
Additional Information: Check information at www.utwente.nl/internationalstudents/scholarshipsandgrants/all/ots-mexico/ www.studyinholland.nl/finances/scholarships/find-a-scholarship/orange-tulip-scholarship-programme-neso-mexico

Professor de Winter Scholarship.

Purpose: Professor de Winter and Mrs. de Winter were highly involved in UT programmes and with 'their' students. Their heirs continue to be involved in their honour by awarding a scholarship of €7,500 to an excellent female student. The Professor de Winter Scholarship is provided by the inheritors of Professor de Winter and his wife. Professor de Winter was one of the founders of the research and education department of the 'Technische Hogeschool Twente' - which later became the University of Twente.
Eligibility: The student must have obtained an average grade of 7 (out of 10) at the end of the third quartile of the first year

U

of the programme; The student must have obtained at least 50% of European Credits at the end of the third quartile of the first year programme; The student must have obtained 90% of European Credits before start of the second year programme.

Level of Study: Masters Degree

Type: Scholarships

Value: €7,500 per year for the full duration of your Master's programme.

Length of Study: 2 year

Frequency: Others

Country of Study: Netherlands

Application Procedure: You cannot apply for a Professor de Winter scholarship yourself. You need to be nominated by your faculty, after you have applied for the University of Twente Scholarship (UTS)

Closing Date: 1 May

Additional Information: www.utwente.nl/en/education/scholarship-finder/professor-de-winter-scholarship/#eligible-programmes-and-countries

For further information contact:

Email: study@utwente.nl

University of Ulster

Research Office, Cromore Road, Coleraine, Co. Londonderry BT52 1SA, Northern Ireland.

Tel: (44) 28 7032 4729
Email: hj.campbell@ulster.ac.uk
Website: www.ulster.ac.uk
Contact: Mrs H Campbell, Administrative Officer

The University of Ulster is a dynamic and innovative institution, which is very proud of its excellent track record in the education and training of researchers. Our doctoral graduates can demonstrate outstanding achievements in advancing knowledge and making breakthroughs of relevance to the economic, social and cultural development of society.

University Studentships/Vice-Chancellor's Research Studentships (VCRS)

Subjects: Arts, Humanities, Social Sciences, Computing, Engineering, Built Environment, Business, Life and Health Sciences

Purpose: From time to time the University makes funding available to support University Studentships. The awards for for UK, European Union and overseas students. Applicants should indicate in the appropriate area on their University application form that they wish to apply for a University Studentship/VCRS award.

Eligibility: These awards are open to applicants who hold or, expect to obtain, a first or upper second class honours degree and provide for payment of fees and maintenance allowance.

Level of Study: Doctorate

Type: Scholarships

Length of Study: Up to 3 years subject to satisfactory progress

Frequency: Annual

Country of Study: United Kingdom

Application Procedure: www.ulster.ac.uk/doctoralcollege/postgraduate-research/apply

Closing Date: February

Funding: Government

No. of awards given last year: 30

No. of applicants last year: 1000

Additional Information: www.ulster.ac.uk/__data/assets/pdf_file/0010/429940/VCRS-Terms-and-Conditions-201920.pdf

For further information contact:

Ulster University, Shore Rd, Newtownabbey BT37 0QB, United Kingdom.

Email: researchstudent@ulster.ac.uk

Vice Chancellor

Subjects: Computing, engineering and Built Environment

Purpose: To assist candidates of a high academic standard to complete research degrees (PhD)

Eligibility: Applicants must have or expect to obtain the minimum of an upper second class Honours degree in a specific research area (as advertised). Applications are invited from United Kingdom, European Union and overseas students. Only candidates who are new applicants to PhD will be eligible

Level of Study: Doctorate, Postgraduate

Type: Scholarship

Value: Fees and maintenance grant

Length of Study: Up to 3 years

Frequency: Annual

Study Establishment: Ulster University

Country of Study: United Kingdom

Application Procedure: Applicants must apply online research.ulster.ac.uk/info/prospective/funding.html

Funding: Private

No. of awards given last year: 30

No. of applicants last year: 800

Additional Information: Applications are invited from United Kingdom, European Union and Overseas students. Further information is available on the website www. ulster.ac.uk/research www.ulster.ac.uk/about/people/vice-chancellor

For further information contact:

Email: research.support@sydney.edu.au

University of Verona

Via S. Francesco, 22, I-37129 Verona, Italy.

Tel: (39) 45 802 8588
Contact: University of Verona

The University of Verona is a university located in Verona, Italy. It was founded in 1982 and is organized in 12 Departments.

Invite Doctoral Programme

Subjects: Life and Health Sciences
Purpose: The INVITE doctoral programme aims to encourage each student's intellectual curiosity and support the acquisition of critical thinking skills by training them in the use of innovative theoretical tools and practical methods
Value: Living allowance €2,000/month for 36 months, mobility allowance €600/month for 36 months, family allowance €150/month for 36 months
Country of Study: Italy
Closing Date: 16 April
Additional Information: www.timeshighereducation.com/unijobs/minisites/university-of-verona/the-invite-doctoral-programme/

For further information contact:

Email: invite@ateneo.univr.it

University of Waikato

Private Bag 3105, Hamilton, New Zealand.

Tel: (64) 7 856 2889 ext. 6723
Email: scholarships@waikato.ac.nz

Website: www.waikato.ac.nz/asd/groups/scholarships. shtml
Contact: Ms Maureen Phillips, Assistant Manager, Scholarships

The Mission of the University of Waikato is to be the New Zealand leader in the business of knowledge. The business of knowledge includes the development of new knowledge, the transmission and dissemination of knowledge, and the assembling and structuring of knowledge.

Acorn Foundation Eva Trowbridge Scholarship

Subjects: Any
Purpose: To support the people of Tauranga and the Western Bay of Plenty community
Eligibility: For students who are 25 years or older who reside in the areas administered by Tauranga City Council or Western Bay of Plenty District Council, and in 2023 will be studying at the University of Waikato Tauranga Campus.
Type: Scholarship
Value: NZ$3,000 per year
Length of Study: 1 year
Frequency: Annual
Country of Study: New Zealand
Closing Date: 15 October
Contributor: Acorn Foundation
Additional Information: Contact the School of Graduate Research: www.waikato.ac.nz/scholarships/contact

For further information contact:

Te Mata Kairangi School of Graduate Research, The University of Waikatom Private Bag 3105, Hamilton, 3240, New Zealand.

Tel: (64) 7 858 5096
Email: scholarships@waikato.ac.nz

Alan Turing Prize

Purpose: To encourage students to develop strong joint interests in Computer Science and Mathematics
Eligibility: Open to students who have strong interest in computer science and mathematics
Level of Study: Research
Type: Prize
Length of Study: 3 years
Frequency: Annual
Country of Study: Any country

Application Procedure: Check website for further details
Contributor: Council of the University of Waikato

For further information contact:

Email: info@waikato.ac.nz

Alumini Master's Scholarship

Purpose: To support a student who has graduated with a degree of the University of Waikato and is enroled for a Masters Degree at this University in the year of tenure
Eligibility: Open to New Zealand citizens or permanent residents who have qualified for a First Degree from the University of Waikato and be enroled full-time for a Masters Degree at the University of Waikato in the year of tenure. The candidate must be in their final year of study for the degree
Level of Study: Postgraduate
Type: Scholarship
Value: NZ$5,500 plus actual tuition fees up to a maximum of NZ$4,000
Length of Study: 1 year
Frequency: Annual
Application Procedure: Check website for further details
Closing Date: 31 October
Additional Information: The Scholarship will be awarded to a student who demonstrates academic merit; who is active in University affairs and who contributes to the activities of the School or Faculty in which they are enroled; who demonstrates willingness to maintain an active relationship with the Alumni programme; who demonstrates willingness to attend Alumni functions and promotional activities; who is considered to be a good ambassador for the University of Waikato and the Alumni Association studyabroad.shiksha.com/schol arships/alumni-scholarship

Chamber of Commerce Tauranga Business Scholarship

Purpose: For the benefit of members of the Tauranga Chamber of Commerce to assist the recipient to undertake study at postgraduate level
Eligibility: Open to citizens or permanent residents of New Zealand having a tertiary or relevant professional qualification; must have a minimum of 5 years' relevant work experience; must own or be employed by a business or organization which is a member of the Tauranga, Chamber of Commerce; must have the support of his/her employer and currently not enroled in a Postgraduate Diploma in Management Studies with the Waikato, Management School, University of Waikato. Check website for further details
Level of Study: Postgraduate

Type: Scholarship
Value: The value of the scholarship is usually equivalent to 1 year's fees (a total of four papers)
Length of Study: Above 2 years
Frequency: Annual
Application Procedure: Check website for further details
Closing Date: 30 November
Additional Information: www.tauranga.org.nz/business-services-2/waikato-university-business-scholarship/

Evelyn Stokes Memorial Doctoral Scholarship

Subjects: Arts & Social Sciences
Eligibility: For doctoral candidates who are enrolled or intending to enrol full-time in a PhD in either Geography or Environmental Planning in the School of Social Sciences.
Level of Study: Doctorate
Type: Scholarship
Value: NZ$5,000 per year
Length of Study: 3 years
Frequency: Annual
Study Establishment: University of Waikato
Country of Study: New Zealand
Application Procedure: Check website for further details
Closing Date: 4 February
Funding: Private
Additional Information: The Scholarship will end on the completion of doctoral study, or after 3 years, whichever is the earlier date, provided that the candidate is enroled during this time in an appropriate programme of studies. Completion takes place when the postgraduate studies committee has accepted the report of the examiners and recommends the awarding of the degree www.waikato.ac.nz/scholarships/s/evelyn-stokes-memorial-doctoral-scholarship

For further information contact:

Te Mata Kairangi School of Graduate Research, The University of Waikato, Private Bag 3105, Hamilton, 3240, New Zealand.

Tel: (64) 7 858 5096
Email: scholarships@waikato.ac.nz

Lee Foundation Grants

Eligibility: 1. Applicable to students who are pursuing a full-time undergraduate degree programme at the Institute. 2. Singapore Citizens or Permanent Residents. 3. Preference will be given to applicants who are hindered by financial difficulties where a lack of financial assistance will result in a discontinuation of their studies

Type: Grant

Value: NZ$500

Application Procedure: Application dates & submission instructions can be found www.singaporetech.edu.sg/fees/bursaries-study-grants

Additional Information: Grants are awarded on the basis of above average academic performance www.singaporetech.edu.sg/lee-foundation-study-grant

For further information contact:

10 Dover Drive, 138683, Singapore.

Tel: (65) 6592 1189
Fax: (65) 6592 1190

Priority One Management Scholarship

Eligibility: Open to citizens or permanent residents of New Zealand who have a tertiary or relevant professional qualification with a minimum of 5 years relevant work experience, own or be employed by a business or organization which is a member of Priority One, have the support of his/her employer, must not already be enroled in a Postgraduate Diploma in Management Studies with the Waikato, Management School, University of Waikato, not have been a previous recipient of any Waikato Management School, University of Waikato

Level of Study: Postgraduate

Type: Scholarship

Value: Equivalent to 1 year's fees

Length of Study: 2 years

Frequency: Annual

Application Procedure: Check website for further details

Closing Date: 30 November

Tauranga Campus Research Masters Scholarship

Purpose: At this university, candidates can study a broad range of subjects to shape a qualification that matches to their strengths and career interests. It helps the candidate with career planning, developing a CV and cover letters, interview skills, enhancing their employability skills.

Eligibility: For students who have applied to enrol full-time in a thesis of 90-points or more as part of their first master's degree at the University of Waikato and will be based at the Tauranga campus. International applicants must have completed one full academic year (120-points) at a NZ university

to be eligible to apply. If you do not meet this criteria, please do not submit an application.

Level of Study: Postgraduate

Type: Scholarship

Value: Up to NZ$23,000

Frequency: Annual

Country of Study: Any country

Closing Date: 30 April

Funding: International office

Additional Information: www.waikato.ac.nz/scholarships/s/tauranga-campus-research-masters-scholarship

For further information contact:

Te Mata Kairangi School of Graduate Research, The University of Waikato, Private Bag 3105, Hamilton 3240, New Zealand.

Tel: (64) 7 858 5096

Ted Zorn Waikato Alumni Award For Management Communication

Purpose: To provide an opportunity for peer recognition of graduates of the department who have, since their graduation, distinguished themselves in a field of management communication

Eligibility: Open to candidates holding a responsible position in an organization or in a project, sustainability and/or workplace well being; must know the use of creativity and initiative in performing the responsibilities of the position. Check website for further details

Level of Study: Postgraduate

Type: Award

Value: NZ$1,000

Frequency: Annual

Application Procedure: Check website for further details

Closing Date: 31 December

For further information contact:

Email: jbeaton@waikato.ac.nz

University of Waikato Masters Research Scholarships

Subjects: Any

Purpose: To encourage research at the University, principally by assisting with course-related costs

Eligibility: For students intending to enrol full-time in a 500-level thesis of 90-points or more as part of their first master's degree. International students must have completed at least 120-points of study at a New Zealand university in order to be eligible for this Scholarship.

Level of Study: Postgraduate
Type: Research grant
Value: Up to NZ$15,000
Length of Study: 1 year
Frequency: Annual
Country of Study: Any country
Closing Date: 31 October
Additional Information: Should a student also hold another fees scholarship, the University of Waikato Masters Research Scholarship will pay the balance of any fees (up to NZ$3,500) www.waikato.ac.nz/scholarships/s/university-of-waikato-research-masters-scholarship

For further information contact:

Te Mata Kairangi School of Graduate Research, The University of Waikato, Private Bag 3105, Hamilton 3240, New Zealand.

Tel: (64) 7 858 5096
Email: scholarships@waikato.ac.nz

University of Waikato MBA Programme

Value: US$38,000
Length of Study: 18 months (international students) or 24-36 months (domestic students)
Application Procedure: All applicants must return a complete application form. Candidates may be required to sit a Graduate Management Admission Test or TOEFL exam
Additional Information: www.waikato.ac.nz/study/qualifications/master-of-business-administration

For further information contact:

Tel: (64) 7 838 4833
Email: execed@waikato.ac.nz

University of Wales, Bangor (UWB)

Bangor North Wales, Bangor, Wales, Gwynedd LL57 2DG, United Kingdom.

Tel: (44) 12 4838 2025/18
Email: admissions@bangor.ac.uk
Website: www.bangor.ac.uk
Contact: The Student Recruitment Unit

The University of Wales, Bangor (UWB) is the principal seat of learning, scholarship and research in North Wales. It was established in 1884 and is a constituent institution of the Federal University of Wales. The University attaches considerable importance to research training in all disciplines and offers research studentships of a value similar to those of other United Kingdom public funding bodies.

Bangor University Merit Scholarships for International Students

Eligibility: All international students will be automatically considered for these scholarships. These scholarships are not open to United Kingdom/European Union applicants
Type: Scholarship
Value: £2,500 (Bangor campus); £2,000 (London centre). Candidates who are fully sponsored by a third party will not be entitled to these Scholarships
Frequency: Annual
Country of Study: Any country
Application Procedure: All applicants will be automatically considered for these scholarships. No additional scholarship application needed
Additional Information: Please check at www.bangor.ac.uk/international/future/merit_scholarships.php#ug scholarship-positions.com/bangor-university-country-scholarships-for-international-students-in-uk/2019/06/20/

For further information contact:

Email: international@bangor.ac.uk

Gold and Silver Scholarships

Purpose: To provide financial support to full-time students on all MSc, MBA and MA programmes
Eligibility: Open to applicants who wish to apply for a postgraduate MBA or MA degree programme included in the scholarship scheme
Level of Study: MBA, Postgraduate
Type: Scholarship
Value: Gold Scholarship £5,000 per year. Silver Scholarship £2,000 per year
Length of Study: 1 year
Frequency: Annual
Study Establishment: Bangor University
Country of Study: United Kingdom
Application Procedure: There is no application form for scholarships. Candidates who wish to be considered for the awards should include a letter listing their main academic and personal achievements together with a short essay on why they have chosen to study at Bangor and a curriculum vitae. For further information contact at law.pg@bangor.ac.uk

Closing Date: 1 December
Funding: Government
Additional Information: PLEASE NOTE: your application form will NOT be accepted without a CV www.bangor.ac.uk/business/study-with-us/postgraduate-funding/en

For further information contact:

Tel: (44) 1248 382 644
Fax: (44) 1248 383 228
Email: b.hamilton@bangor.ac.uk

MSc Bursaries

Eligibility: Open to applicants with good second class honours degree in sports science or health and to students with a 22 degree or a degree from a different academic area will also be considered
Level of Study: Postgraduate
Type: Bursary
Value: £2,500 (United Kingdom/European Union students); £3,500 (non-European Union international students)
Length of Study: 1 year (full-time); 2 years (part-time); 30 weeks full-time (diploma)
Frequency: Dependent on funds available
Study Establishment: Bangor University
Country of Study: United Kingdom
Application Procedure: Complete a Postgraduate Application Form with a four page (maximum) curriculum vitae or resumé. Refer to the website for further details or mail to postgraduate@bangor.ac.uk
Closing Date: 30 June
Contributor: Bangor University
Additional Information: £1,000 internal bursaries to former SHES (or related disciplines) students (who have 1st class undergraduate degree). £1,000 internal assistantships in addition to the other bursaries aimed at the very best students   www.bangor.ac.uk/business/study-with-us/postgraduate-funding/en

For further information contact:

Tel: (44) 1248 383 493
Email: mscsport@bangor.ac.uk
Open PhD Studentships

Eligibility: Open to candidates who have applied unsuccessfully to a United Kingdom funding council (e.g. the AHRC or the ESRC) to study at Bangor
Level of Study: Doctorate
Type: Studentship
Value: Fees plus maintenance grant

Frequency: Dependent on funds available
Application Procedure: Applicants must submit a scholarship application form along with a summary of your proposed research project in up to 500 words

For further information contact:

Email: s.lee@bangor.ac.uk

Santander Taught Postgraduate Scholarships

Purpose: The Santander Group awards a number of 1 year undergraduate and taught postgraduate scholarships to current Bangor University students
Eligibility: The scholarship fund aims to reward the most academically gifted students from countries that are supported by the Santander Universidades scheme. The award will be given to students from the following 11 countries Argentina, Brazil, Chile, Colombia, Mexico, Portugal, Puerto Rico, Spain, Uruguay and Venezuela. To be eligible for the postgraduate scholarship you will have to have studied within a University which is part of the Santander Universidades Scheme
Type: Scholarship
Value: £5,000
Length of Study: 1 year
Application Procedure: Application forms and guidance notes for the Santander Scholarship Scheme are available on the University website www.bangor.ac.uk/scholarships/santander.php.en
No. of awards offered: 4
Closing Date: 29 January
Additional Information: For further information or if you have any questions about the scheme, please contact Academic Registry www.st-andrews.ac.uk/study/fees-and-funding/postgraduate/scholarships/santander-taught/

For further information contact:

University of St Andrews, St Katharine's West, The Scores, St Andrews KY16 9AX, United Kingdom.

Tel: (44) 1334 46 2254
Fax: (44) 1334 46 2254
Email: admissions@st-andrews.ac.uk

University of Wales (Bangor) MBA in Banking and Finance

Length of Study: 1 year
Country of Study: Any country

Application Procedure: Applicants must submit an application form, together with two references and copies or transcripts of previous qualifications. Where necessary TOEFL and IELTS scores must be included

Additional Information: www.bangor.ac.uk/courses/post graduate/banking-and-finance-mba#overview

For further information contact:

Bangor University, Bangor, Gwynedd LL57 2DG, United Kingdom.

Tel: (44) 1248 382028
Fax: (44) 1248 370 769
Email: international@bangor.ac.uk

University of Warwick

Tel: (44) 2476 523 523
Website: www.warwick.ac.uk
Contact: Project Officer, Postgraduate Scholarships

The University of Warwick offers an exciting range of doctoral, research-based and taught Master's programmes in the humanities, sciences, social sciences and medicine. In the 2001 Research Assessment Exercise, Warwick was ranked 5th in the United Kingdom for research quality. Postgraduate students make up around 35% of Warwick's 18,000 students. The University is located in the heart of United Kingdom, adjacent to the city of Coventry and on the border with Warwickshire.

Argentina Chevening Scholarship

Eligibility: Applicants should be nationals of Argentina not currently registered at the University
Level of Study: Postgraduate
Type: Scholarship
Value: UK cost of Academic fee and maintenance
Length of Study: 1 year
Study Establishment: University of Warwick
Country of Study: United Kingdom
Application Procedure: Applicants must complete an application form, available from the British Council
Closing Date: August
Contributor: University of Warwick, Foreign and Commonwealth office
Additional Information: www.chevening.org/scholarship/argentina/

For further information contact:

Email: info@britishcouncil.org

College of Continuing Professional Studies Doctoral Scholarship

Purpose: Scholarship is available for pursuing doctoral degree level at the University of Warwick
Eligibility: To be eligible for the scholarship, candidates must have received an unconditional offer for entry to CCPS MPhil/PhD programme by January 31st. The scholarship scheme is open to both European Union and Overseas candidates
Level of Study: Doctorate
Type: Scholarship
Value: The value of the scholarship will be around £18,000 per year. The precise amount will be confirmed at the time of the offer
Study Establishment: Drury University
Country of Study: United Kingdom
Application Procedure: The mode of applying is online
Closing Date: 31 January
Contributor: Centre for Cultural Policy Studies
Additional Information: The successful candidate will be notified before the end of February www.fundsforngos.org/developing-countries-2/cambodia/centre-cultural-policy-studies-doctoral-scholarship-program/

For further information contact:

Email: drury@drury.edu

Colombia Postgraduate Awards (Warwick Manufacturing Group/Colfuturo)

Purpose: To support Master's Columbian students at WMG
Eligibility: Applicants should be nationals of Columbia, not currently registered on a postgraduate course at the University, and should have received an offer of a place from WMG. Only students who have been awarded a COLFUTURO scholarship-loan are eligible
Level of Study: Postgraduate
Type: Scholarship
Value: full tuition fees
Length of Study: 1 year
Frequency: Dependent on funds available
Study Establishment: University of Warwick United Kingdom
Country of Study: United Kingdom
Application Procedure: Applicants must apply via COLFUTURO

Funding: Private
Contributor: WMG/COLFUTURO
Additional Information: Non-renewable, for taught masters only www.fundsforngos.org/developing-countries-2/cambodia/centre-cultural-policy-studies-doctoral-scholarship-program/

For further information contact:

Email: yosoyfuturo@colfuturo.com

Colombia Postgraduate Awards (Warwick/Foundation for the Future of Colombia - Colfuturo)

Purpose: To support Columbian students on postgraduate courses at Warwick
Eligibility: Applicants should be nationals of Columbia and classed as an international fee-payer. Applicants can be registered on an Undergraduate course at the University of Warwick, but should have received a place on a Postgraduate Taught Master's course at Warwick. Only students who have been awarded a COLFUTURO scholarship-loan are eligible
Level of Study: Postgraduate
Type: Scholarship
Value: Tuition fees
Length of Study: 1 year
Frequency: Dependent on funds available
Study Establishment: University of Warwick
Country of Study: United Kingdom
Application Procedure: Application should be submitted via COLFUTURO
Funding: International office
Contributor: Foundation for the Future of Colombia Colfuturo (COLFUTURO)
Additional Information: Non-renewable, for taught masters only www.fundsforngos.org/developing-countries-2/cambodia/centre-cultural-policy-studies-doctoral-scholarship-program/

For further information contact:

Email: yosoyfuturo@colfuturo.com.co

Karim Rida Said Foundation Postgraduate Award (KRSF/Warwick)

Purpose: To support students from the Middle Eastern region on Postgraduate courses at Warwick
Eligibility: Applicants should be Jordanian, Iraqi, Lebanese, Palestinian or Syrian nationals and be resident in the Middle East. Applicants should meet all other eligibility criteria as set by KRSF and awards will only be offered to applicants who already hold an offer of a place at Warwick
Level of Study: Postgraduate
Type: Scholarship
Length of Study: 1 year
Study Establishment: University of Warwick
Country of Study: United Kingdom
Application Procedure: Applications are submitted via KRSF website www.krsf.org/whatwedo/masters
Funding: International office
Contributor: KRSF
No. of awards given last year: 2
Additional Information: Non-renewable, for taught masters only www.saidfoundation.org/pages/9-said-foundation-scholarships-programme

For further information contact:

Tel: (44) 24 7652 2469
Email: j.c.inegbedion@warwick.ac.uk

Mexico Postgraduate Award (Chevening/Brockmann/Warwick)

Purpose: To support Mexican students on a postgraduate course at Warwick
Eligibility: Applicants should be nationals of Mexico, not currently registered at the University of Warwick and should have received an offer of a place at Warwick
Level of Study: Postgraduate
Type: Scholarship
Value: Full tuition fees plus maintenance
Length of Study: 1 year
Study Establishment: University of Warwick
Country of Study: United Kingdom
Application Procedure: Applicants must complete an application
Closing Date: August
Funding: Government
Contributor: The Foreign and Commonwealth Office and the Brockmann Foundation
No. of awards given last year: 1
Additional Information: Non-renewable www.chevening.org/scholarship/mexico/

For further information contact:

Tel: (44) 24 7657 2686
Email: ana_delcarmen@hotmail.com

U

School of Law - Brazil Postgraduate Award

Purpose: To support students from Brazil on LLM programme at Warwick

Eligibility: Open to prospective full-time postgraduate students in any postgraduate degree within the Law School. Applicants can be registered on Undergraduate courses at the University of Warwick, but should have received a place for taught master courses at Warwick Law School

Level of Study: Postgraduate

Type: Scholarship

Value: 50% towards tuition fees

Length of Study: 1 year

Frequency: Dependent on funds available

Study Establishment: University of Warwick

Country of Study: United Kingdom

Application Procedure: Applicants must complete an online application form

Closing Date: 31 May

Contributor: Warwick Law School

Additional Information: Non-renewable, deducted from tuition fees, for taught masters only www.chevening.org/scholarship/mexico/

For further information contact:

Email: paula.nascimento@britishcouncil.org.br

Sociology Departmental MA Scholarship

Purpose: 10 awards of £5,000 are available for students commencing MA study in the Sociology department in Autumn. The award will automatically be deducted from the winners' tuition fees.

Eligibility: 1. Open to applicants on all Sociology taught Masters programmes. 2. Candidates must apply to the university and have paid their application fee no later no later than 26 April. You must submit your application to the MA programme before submitting your scholarship application. 3. Successful candidates must obtain an offer from the university before taking up the award. 4. Candidates may apply concurrently to other funding sources; however, successful candidates who receive major tuition funding elsewhere will be disqualified.

Level of Study: Postgraduate

Type: Scholarship

Value: £2,500

Length of Study: 2 year

Frequency: Annual

Country of Study: Any country

Closing Date: 26 April

Funding: Foundation

Additional Information: warwick.ac.uk/fac/soc/sociology/prospective/pgtstudy/feesfunding/mascholarship/

For further information contact:

Social Sciences Building, The University of Warwick, Coventry CV4 7AL, United Kingdom.

Email: m.j.wolfe@warwick.ac.uk

Warwick Postgraduate Research Scholarships

Eligibility: Open to Home, European Union and Overseas students from all disciplines at Warwick. For more details, please refer to the website

Level of Study: Doctorate

Type: Scholarship

Value: £3,390 for full-time students for the payment of academic fees at the Home/European Union rate. A maintenance grant, in line with the United Kingdom Research Council stipend, of £13,290 for full-time award holders

Country of Study: United Kingdom

Application Procedure: Please refer to the website warwick.ac.uk/services/dc/schols_fund/scholarships_and_funding/

Closing Date: 12 January

Additional Information: Students and applicants who wish to apply for an AHRC doctoral award should apply to the WPRS competition and will automatically be considered for both competitions warwick.ac.uk/fac/soc/sociology/prospective/pgtstudy/feesfunding/mascholarship/

For further information contact:

Email: aci@mrc.ac.za

University of Washington

School of Business Administration, 110 Mackenzie Hall Box 353200, Seattle, WA 98195, United States of America.

Tel: (1) 206 543 4661
Email: mba@u.washington.edu
Contact: MBA Admissions Officer

African American Heritage Endowed MBA Scholarship

Purpose: This scholarship is available for African-American MBA students who are attending the Foster Business school at the University of Washington in Seattle

Eligibility: 1. Must be an African American student. 2. Must be an MBA candidate at the time of application. 3. Must be enrolled at the Foster Business School at the University of Washington in Seattle. 4. This award is for United States of America students

Level of Study: Graduate

Type: Scholarship

Value: US$10,000

Frequency: Annual

Country of Study: United States of America

Application Procedure: Applications and information about the African American Heritage Endowed MBA Scholarship are available online at the University of Washington Foster School of Business website. To apply for this award, students must first be accepted to the MBA program at the University of Washington in Seattle. Eligible students who are interested in this award should contact the Michael G. Foster School of Business for further information about the admissions and scholarship application process. All applications must be completed online by the deadline date

Closing Date: 15 April

Funding: Foundation

Additional Information: www.unigo.com/scholarships/by-state/washington-scholarships/african-american-heritage-endowed-mba-scholarship/1004476

For further information contact:

124 Mackenzie Hall Box 353200, Seattle, WA 98195-3200, United States.

Email: scholarships@swe.org

University of Waterloo

200 University Avenue West, Waterloo, ON N2L 3G1, Canada.

Email: rchild@uwaterloo.ca

International Research Partnership Grants (IRPG)

Purpose: The International Research Program Grants (IRPG) programs are internal seed grants aimed to provide Waterloo researchers with incentives to develop new or existing international research collaborations with leading institutions known for high quality research and global ranking

Eligibility: Projects should involve a group of Waterloo researchers and international partners. Preference will be given to projects with multiple Waterloo faculties/departments and a network of partner institutions;; 1. Preference will be given to projects that have not received IRPG funding for a previous project with the same international partners. 2. Preference is given to applications where matching cash contribution is from a new source or one that is outside of University of Waterloo, instead of existing research funds

Level of Study: Graduate

Type: Grants and fellowships

Value: Up to C$20,000, 50% of the costs

Frequency: Annual

Country of Study: Any country

Application Procedure: You could refer to the following pdf for further instructions. uwaterloo.ca/research/sites/ca.research/files/uploads/files/irpg_program_guidelines-30-nov-2018.pdf

Closing Date: 1 November

Funding: Private

For further information contact:

200 University Avenue West, Waterloo, ON N2L 3G1, Canada.

Mitacs Accelerate Fellowship

Purpose: The Mitacs Accelerate Fellowship provides a long-term funding and internship option for master's and PhD students. Recipients can also access professional development training that helps them ensure project success and gain in-demand career skills

Level of Study: Graduate

Type: Fellowship

Value: C$40,000 per year

Length of Study: 18 months

Frequency: Annual

Country of Study: Any country

Application Procedure: Interested applicants can apply for the Accelerate Fellowship at any time. All other Accelerate program guidelines apply. 1. Review the following information when you begin writing your proposal. Eligible research and adjudication criteria 1. Writing Your Proposal guide Policies. 2. Submit Cover Sheet to Office of Research contact below, with a copy of the draft proposal. 3. Get feedback on the proposal from all participants and the Mitacs Program contact below. 4. Collect all required signatures intern(s), professor(s), partner representative and the Office of Research contact below. 5. Email your proposal package to your Mitacs Program contact below Additional Information available on the Mitacs website

U

Funding: Private

Additional Information: uwaterloo.ca/research/mitacs-accelerate-fellowship

For further information contact:

Tel: (1) 519 888 4567
Email: accelerate@mitacs.ca

University of West London

International Ambassador Scholarships at University of West London

Purpose: The International Ambassador Scholarship recognises and provides financial support for outstanding students who wish to act as ambassadors for the University of West London
Eligibility: Applicants must be 1. An offer holder for an undergraduate or postgraduate course at UWL, to commence study in September 2023. This means that you must have already applied for a course of study at this university and you must have already received an official offer from one of our admissions officers. 2. A self-funded overseas full fee-paying paying student (please note EU applicants are not eligible). The International Ambassador Scholarship will be awarded on a competitive basis to candidates who demonstrate enthusiasm and the ability to be an excellent international student ambassador.
Level of Study: Graduate
Type: Scholarship
Frequency: Annual
Country of Study: Any country
Application Procedure: To be considered for the scholarship, you must have been offered a place to study on a full-time undergraduate or postgraduate course at the University of West London
No. of awards offered: 100
Closing Date: 1 July
Funding: Private
Contributor: University of West London
Additional Information: Official Scholarship Website: www.uwl.ac.uk/courses/undergraduate-study/fees-and-funding/bursaries-and-scholarships www.scholars4dev.com/8119/international-ambassador-scholarships-university-west-london/

For further information contact:

Tel: (44) 20 8231 2914
Email: int.app@uwl.ac.uk

University of Western Australia

35 Stirling Highway, Crawley, WA 6009, Australia.

Tel: (61) 8 9380 2490, 8 6488 6000
Email: general.enquiries@uwa.edu.au
Website: www.uwa.edu.au

Since its establishment in 1911, the University of Western Australia has helped to shape the careers of more than 75,000 graduates. Their success reflects the UWA's balanced coverage of disciplines in the arts, sciences and professions.

Advanced Consumer Research PhD Scholarship

Purpose: To study the effectiveness of Commonwealth, State and Territory consumer protection laws in relation to information disclosure
Eligibility: Open to those who have completed an undergraduate degree in law with honours or equivalent research qualifications
Level of Study: Postgraduate
Type: Scholarship
Value: AU$25,000 per year
Length of Study: 3 years and 6 months
Frequency: Annual
Study Establishment: The University of Western Australia
Application Procedure: Check website for further details
Closing Date: 3 August

For further information contact:

Tel: (61) 8 6488 2947
Email: eileen.webb@uwa.edu.au

Health Effects of Air Pollution (Top-Up)

Purpose: To support various projects in the School of Population Health
Eligibility: Open to those doing research in Australia
Level of Study: Postgraduate
Type: Scholarship
Value: AU$10,000, plus Australian Dollar; AU$2,500 for relocation costs
Frequency: Annual
Study Establishment: University of Western Australia
Country of Study: Australia
Application Procedure: Candidates must apply direct to the faculty. Check website for further details

Closing Date: 1 December

For further information contact:

Tel: (61) 8 6488 7804
Email: Angus.Cook@uwa.edu.au

Master of Business Administration Programme

For further information contact:

Tel: (61) 9 3803 939
Fax: (61) 9 3824 071
Email: icweb@acs.edu.au

Natural Gas/LNG Production Scholarships

Purpose: To use the research outcomes to improve the design of LNG production trains and to treat contaminated gas reserves
Eligibility: Open to candidates who have achieved Second Class (Honours) or equivalent
Level of Study: Postgraduate
Type: Scholarship
Value: AU$31,118 per year
Length of Study: 3 years
Frequency: Annual
Country of Study: Australia
Application Procedure: Check website for further details
Closing Date: 17 December
Additional Information: www.nlng.com/Our-CSR/Pages/Scholarships.aspx

For further information contact:

Tel: (61) 6488 2954
Fax: (61) 6488 1964
Email: Eric.May@uwa.edu.au

The Science & Innovation Studentship Award

Purpose: To promote innovation in areas of key technologies
Eligibility: Open to citizens of Australia or permanent residents who have completed 2 years, or more, full-time study in a science degree at a recognized Western Australian University
Level of Study: Postgraduate
Type: Studentship
Value: AU$7,000 per year
Frequency: Annual

Study Establishment: Curtin University of Technology, Edith Cowan University, Murdoch University, The University of Notre Dame, The University of Western Australia
Country of Study: Any country
Application Procedure: Check website for further details
Closing Date: 14 September

For further information contact:

100 Plain Street, Perth, WA 6004, Australia.

Tel: (61) 8 9222 3333
Fax: (61) 8 9222 3862
Email: rchapman@wellesley.edu

Water and Health Scholarships

Purpose: To position graduates favourably with respect to future employment opportunities through research projects in the area of public health impacts of recycled water use
Eligibility: Open to Australian candidates with a broad range of backgrounds
Level of Study: Postgraduate
Type: Scholarship
Value: AU$30,000 per year
Length of Study: 3 years
Frequency: Annual
Study Establishment: The University of Western Australia
Country of Study: Australia
Application Procedure: Check website for further details
Closing Date: 6 July
Additional Information: Applications are open from 13 June www.nlng.com/Our-CSR/Pages/Scholarships.aspx

For further information contact:

Tel: (61) 8 6488 7804
Email: Angus.Cook@uwa.edu.au

Western Australian CSIR University Postgraduate Scholarships

Purpose: To enhance research into minerals and energy exploration, extraction and processing
Eligibility: Open to citizens of Australia enrolling for postgraduate research
Level of Study: Postgraduate
Type: Scholarship
Value: AU$25,000 per year
Length of Study: 3 years
Country of Study: Australia
Application Procedure: Check website for further details

U

Additional Information: www.csiro.au/en/Careers/Student ships/Postgraduate-scholarships

For further information contact:

Tel: (61) 8 6488 3027
Email: campbell.thomson@uwa.edu.au

University of Western Sydney

Office of Research Services, Hawkesbury Campus, Building H3, Locked Bag 1797, Penrith South DC, NSW 1797, Australia.

Tel: (61) 2 4570 1463
Email: t.mills@uws.edu.au
Website: www.uws.edu.au
Contact: Ms Tracey Mills, Research Scholarships
                Development Officer

Master of Business Administration Programme

Length of Study: 1–5 years
Application Procedure: Applicants must complete an application form supplying a TOEFL score
Closing Date: January
Additional Information: www.uwa.edu.au/study/courses/master-of-business-administration-intensive

For further information contact:

Tel: (61) 2 9685 9297
Fax: (61) 2 9685 9298
Email: international@uws.edu.au

University of Westminster

Scholarships Department, Cavendish House, 101 New Cavendish Street, London W1W 6XH, United Kingdom.

Tel: (44) 20 7911 5000 Exts 66257, 66258, 66259
Email: scholarships@westminster.ac.uk
Website: www.westminster.ac.uk

The University of Westminster is proud of its generous scholarship programme, which benefits both United Kingdom and international students. Full details are available on our website www.westminster.ac.uk/scholarships

Brian Large Bursary Fund

Purpose: To provide financial support to United Kingdom students that are studying full time on the Transport and Planning MSc
Eligibility: Applicants must have been accepted for a full time Masters course in transport for 2019/20. While no minimum level of first degree is required, the Trustees expect young graduates to have at least a 2.2, preferably a 2.1. However, they are willing to relax that requirement for outstanding mature students.
Type: Funding support
Value: £8,000
Country of Study: United Kingdom
Application Procedure: If you are interested in applying for one of these bursaries please contact Dr. Enrica Papa, the Course Leader of MSc Transport Planning at papa@westminster.ac.uk
Closing Date: 12 July
Additional Information: For more information, visit the: www.blbf.co.uk/services environment.leeds.ac.uk/dir-record/scholarships/665/the-brian-large-bursary-fund

Fully Funded Master Scholarship

Purpose: To study a full-time master degree in a subject within the School of Media, Arts and Design at the university
Type: Scholarship
Value: € 10 000
Country of Study: Any country
Application Procedure: For application, please visit website www.westminster.ac.uk/about-us/faculties/westminster-school-of-media-arts-and-design/departments
Closing Date: 15 January
Additional Information: www.afterschoolafrica.com/624/university-of-westminster-international/

For further information contact:

Email: graduate.admissions@cs.ox.ac.uk

Fully Funded University of Westminster Master's Scholarship for Developing Countries

Purpose: The Westminster Vice-Chancellor's Scholarships, is one of the University's most prestigious award, it is aimed at fully funding a student from a developing country to study a full-time Master's degree at the University

Eligibility: The main requirement of this scholarship is that the candidates must hold an offer for a full-time Master's degree at University of Westminster. In addition, the applicant should have First Class Honours degree, financial need and development potential

Level of Study: Postgraduate

Type: Award

Value: The winner of this scholarship may expect to receive full tuition fee waivers, accomodation and flights to and from London

Frequency: Annual

Country of Study: Any country

Application Procedure: 1. A copy of the letter/email from the University of Westminster confirming your conditional or unconditional offer of a place on your chosen course. 2. An official copy of your transcript from your chosen course. 3. A reference letter written specifically in support of your scholarship application. This should be written by a previous tutor, professor, academic or employer and cannot be the same reference provided as part of your admission application

Closing Date: 31 May

Funding: Private

Additional Information: oyaop.com/opportunity/scholarships-and-fellowships/fully-funded-scholarship-at-the-university-of-westminster/

For further information contact:

Tel: (44) 20 7911 5000

Email: course-enquiries@westminster.ac.uk

Higher Education Scholarship Palestine (HESPAL) Scholarships

Purpose: The University of Westminster is working in partnership with the British Council to provide a Higher Education Scholarship for a Palestinian (HESPAL); that is, to support a junior academic at a Palestinian University wishing to study a one-year masters programme or a three-year PhD research programme in the United Kingdom

Eligibility: To be eligible for this scholarship, you must: 1. be a resident citizen of Palestinian Territories 2. be currently employed by a Palestinian university and nominated by this university 3. have a Bachelor's degree from a Palestinian University with a minimum grade of very good (and equivalent to at least a 2.1 Bachelor's degree from the UK) 4. sign a written undertaking to return to Palestine and work in your university on completion of your degree

Level of Study: Masters Degree

Type: Scholarship

Value: Full tuition fee award, pre-departure briefing from the British Council, arrival allowances, thesis allowances and a monthly allowance to cover living expenses

Frequency: Annual

Country of Study: Any country

Application Procedure: Applications are made through the British Council in the Palestinian Territories. Find out more on the British Council website

No. of awards offered: 2

Closing Date: January

Additional Information: www.britishcouncil.ps/en/study-uk/scholarships/hespal

For further information contact:

Email: tom.sperlinger@bristol.ac.uk

Politics and International Relations PhD Scholarships

Purpose: Scholarships are available for pursuing PhD programme

Eligibility: Candidates should normally have a minimum classification of a 2.1 in their BA, or equivalent, and preferably a Master's degree

Value: One fee waiver (Home/European Union rate applications are invited for the following awards which are tenable for up to 3 years for full-time study) and £16,000 per year for 3 years. Up to two fee waivers (Home/European Union rate) and £5,000 per year for 3 years

Length of Study: 3 years

Country of Study: United Kingdom

Application Procedure: Apply online. Please visit the website www.westminster.ac.uk/study/postgraduate/research-degrees/research-areas/social-sciences-and-humanities/how-to-apply

Closing Date: 27 April

Contributor: University of Westminster

Additional Information: For more details, visit website www.westminster.ac.uk/news/2018/call-for-applications-politics-and-international-relations-2018-phd-scholarships blogs.kent.ac.uk/aspirations/2019/11/19/politics-international-relations-phd-scholarships/

For further information contact:

Tel: (44) 20 7911 5000

Email: robert.elgie@dcu.ie

U

Rees Jeffrey Road Fund

Purpose: To support financially for education, research and physical road transport-related projects in accordance with the founding Trust Deed

Level of Study: Masters Degree

Type: Bursary

Value: This fund provides a bursary of up to £10,000 towards financial support for education, research and physical road transport-related projects

Frequency: Annual

Study Establishment: Universities Birmingham, Cardiff, Hertfordshire, Imperial College, Leeds, Newcastle, Nottingham, Salford, Southampton, University College London (UCL), University of the West of England (UWE), Westminster

Country of Study: Any country

Application Procedure: Applications are made on behalf of students by Universities listed, where departents are providing Transport Masters courses. Students are not able to apply directly for funding themselves.

No. of awards offered: 4

Closing Date: June

Additional Information: For more information visit the Rees Jeffreys website www.reesjeffreys.co.uk/bursaries/

For further information contact:

Email: Secretary@reesjeffreys.org

Westminster Full-Fee Masters Scholarships for International Students

Purpose: The Westminster University offers full tuition fee scholarships to prospective postgraduate applicants from any country

Eligibility: You must hold an offer for a full-time Masters Program at the University of Westminster. The main scholarship criteria are equivalent to a United Kingdom First Class Honours degree and financial need

Level of Study: Doctorate, Postgraduate

Type: Scholarship

Value: Full tuition fee award only

Country of Study: United Kingdom

Application Procedure: You should only apply for a scholarship once you have applied for admission and successfully been offered a place (either conditional or unconditional) on the course you wish to study. To apply for a scholarship, you will need to download and complete the relevant scholarship application form and submit it together with supporting documents by post

Closing Date: 13 October

Additional Information: For more details visit official scholarship Website: www.westminster.ac.uk/study/prospective-students/fees-and-funding/scholarships/international-postgraduate-scholarships/westminster-full-fee-scholarship www.scholars4dev.com/8785/full-tuition-fee-waivers-international-students-westminster-university/

For further information contact:

Email: course-enquiries@westminster.ac.uk

Westminster School of Media, Arts and Design Scholarship

Purpose: To pursue a full-time master degree in a subject within the School of Media, Arts and Design at the university

Value: Full tuition fee award, accommodation, living expenses and flights to and from London

Frequency: Annual

Country of Study: Any country

Application Procedure: For application forms, please visit website www.westminster.ac.uk/study/fees-and-funding/scholarships/westminster-school-of-media-arts-and-design-scholarship

Closing Date: 31 May

Contributor: Westminster School of Media, Arts and Design

Additional Information: www.scholarshubafrica.com/23116/westminster-school-media-arts-design-masters-scholarship-uk/

Westminster Vice-Chancellor's Scholarships

Purpose: The Westminster Vice-Chancellor's Scholarships, the university's most prestigious award, is aimed at fully funding a student from a developing country to study a full-time masters degree at the University

Eligibility: You must be an international student from a developing country and hold an offer for a full-time Undergraduate degree at University of Westminster. The main criteria are United Kingdom First Class Honours degree, financial need and development potential

Level of Study: Postgraduate

Type: Scholarship

Value: Full tuition fee waivers, accommodation, living expenses and flights to and from London

Frequency: Annual

Study Establishment: University of Westminster

Country of Study: United Kingdom

Application Procedure: It is important to visit the official website to access the application form and for detailed information on how to apply for this scholarship

Closing Date: 31 May

Additional Information: For more details, please visit official scholarship website: www.westminster.ac.uk/study/prospective-students/fees-and-funding/scholarships/international-postgraduate-scholarships/vice-chancellor-scholarship www.scholarshiproar.com/westminster-vice-chancellors-scholarships/

University of Winnipeg

The University of Winnipeg Manitoba Graduate Scholarships (MGS)

Purpose: Applications are open for the University of Winnipeg Manitoba Graduate Scholarships (MGS) organized by the University of Winnipeg. These scholarships are open to the students who are enrolled or plan to enroll as a full-time student in a master's program at the University of Winnipeg

Eligibility: 1. Have achieved a minimum GPA of 3.75 in the last 60 credits hours of study. 2. Be in a pre-master's program and/or entering the first or second year of an eligible master's program as of May or September of the current year or January of the upcoming year. 3. Be enrolled in or plan to enroll in as a full-time student in a master's program.

Level of Study: Postdoctorate
Type: Scholarship
Value: US$15,000
Length of Study: 1 year
Frequency: Annual
Country of Study: Any country
Application Procedure: Apply online www.uwinnipeg.ca/graduate-studies/docs/uwmgs-application+checklist-revised jan2019-2.pdf
Closing Date: 15 March
Funding: Foundation

For further information contact:

Email: gradstudies@uwinnipeg.ca

University of Wisconsin-Milwaukee

University of Wisconsin-Milwaukee, PO Box 413, Milwaukee, WI 53201, United States of America.

Tel: (1) 414 229 1122
Email: fellowship@uwm.edu
Website: www.uwm.edu

The University of Wisconsin-Milwaukee (UWM) is located just a few blocks from Lake Michigan in one of Milwaukee's most attractive residential areas, and offers research and teaching programmes extending to 148 different degree programmes that serve nearly 26,000 students. UWM focuses on approaches to education that are inclusive, multidisciplinary and marked by excellent research and outstanding teaching.

University of Wisconsin-Milwaukee Graduate School Dissertation Fellowships

Purpose: To fund dissertation-level graduate students at the University of Wisconsin-Milwaukee

Eligibility: Applicants must have completed all coursework, passed preliminary examinations, completed PhD residency requirements and obtained dissertator status. No other award may be held concurrently (with the exception of the Chancellor's Graduate Student Award). Current or previous awardees are not eligible

Level of Study: Doctorate
Type: Fellowship
Value: US$14,000, in addition to full coverage of resident instructional fees (approx. US$1,740), a remission of the out-of-state portion of the tuition, low-cost comprehensive health insurance and other benefits
Length of Study: 1 academic year
Frequency: Annual
Study Establishment: University of Wisconsin-Milwaukee
Country of Study: United States of America
Application Procedure: Applicants must check the website for details
Closing Date: 21 January

For further information contact:

Tel: (1) 414 229 6276

University of Wollongong (UOW)

Northfields Ave, Wollongong, NSW 2522, Australia.

Tel: (61) 2 4221 3555
Email: scholarships@uow.edu.au
Website: www.uow.edu.au

The University of Wollongong (UOW) is a university of international standing with an enviable record of achievement in teaching and research. It enjoys a significant international research profile, attracting more Australian Research Council funding per student that any other Australian university. Over 850 postgraduate students are enrolled of which 30% are overseas students.

Marketing Research Innovation Centre PhD Scholarship

Purpose: To conduct research in the area of qualitative and quantitative methods, market segmentation, brand image studies and advertising experiments
Eligibility: Open to applicants who have an excellent tertiary track record, experience with conducting academic research
Level of Study: Postgraduate, Research
Type: Scholarship
Value: AU$20,000 per year
Length of Study: 3 years
Frequency: Annual
Country of Study: Australia
Application Procedure: Candidates can check the website for further details

For further information contact:

Tel: (44) 20 7000 7000
Fax: (44) 2 4221 3862
Email: housing@london.ac.uk

University of Wollong (UOW) Work-Integrated Learning Scholarship

Purpose: To reward outstanding academic achievements
Eligibility: Open to students with outstanding academic achievements
Level of Study: Postgraduate
Type: Scholarship
Value: AU$3,000; AU$9,300
Frequency: Annual
Study Establishment: University of Wollongong
Country of Study: Australia
Application Procedure: Apply online
Closing Date: October
Additional Information: Scholarship holders are required to undertake a period, usually 6-10 weeks of professional work experience each year with an appropriate sponsor organization scholarships.uow.edu.au/scholarships/search?scholarship=603

For further information contact:

Tel: (61) 1300 367 869
Fax: (61) 2 4221 3233
Email: uniadvice@uow.edu.au

University of Wollongong Sydney Business School Bursary Scheme

Purpose: The University of Wollongong (UOW) is offering Sydney Business School Bursary Scheme for students commencing master's courses. The bursaries offer a 15% reduction of the tuition fee per trimester of the study of applied
Eligibility: The bursary will apply to the following citizenships only India, Nepal, Vietnam, Pakistan, Indonesia, Sri Lanka, Bangladesh, Thailand, Iran, Kenya, Mongolia, Nigeria, Cambodia, Zimbabwe, Myanmar and Ghana
Value: The bursaries offer a 15% reduction of the tuition fee per trimester of the study of applied
Study Establishment: Bursaries are awarded to study the subjects offered by the university
Country of Study: Australia
Application Procedure: You do not have to make a separate application for a bursary, as it will be awarded automatically when you receive an offer for an eligible course and meet scholarship requirements. Applicants will receive a bursary notification and Terms and Conditions of their bursary at the same time as their offer of admission into their course
Additional Information: For more details please visit the website sydneybusinessschool.edu.au/content/groups/public/@web/@gsb/documents/doc/uow247217.pdf scholarship-positions.com/uow-sydney-business-school-bursary-scheme-australia/2017/07/27/

For further information contact:

Email: business-enquiries@uow.edu.au

University of Wollongong In Dubai (UOWD)

Blocks 5 & 15, Knowledge Village, PO Box 20183, Dubai, United Arab Emirates.

Tel: (971) 4 367 2400
Email: info@uowduabi.ac.ae

The UOWD in Dubai, established in 1993, is one UAE's oldest and most prestigious universities. The university strives to provide a fertile environment for bright young minds to flourish, and maintains a long and proud tradition of excellence in education.

University of Wollongong In Dubai Postgraduate Scholarships

Purpose: To reward the academically outstanding postgraduates
Eligibility: 1. Applications are open to students of any citizenship. 2. Applications are open to new (entry level) students

only who will be undertaking full time study. 3. Applicants must have achieved the minimum grades as listed in the Curriculum table below. 4. Applicants must meet all of the academic and admission criteria to be admitted to the University and be intending to enrol in the relevant session for which they have applied.

Level of Study: Postgraduate

Type: Scholarship

Value: 15% to 25% of tuition fees each semester

Frequency: Annual

Study Establishment: University of Wollongong in Dubai

Country of Study: United Kingdom

Application Procedure: Contact the University

No. of awards offered: 2

Closing Date: 5 January

No. of awards given last year: 1

Additional Information: For further information regarding UOWD Scholarships you can contact Student Recruitment on +9714 278 1800 or info@uowdubai.ac.ae www.uowdubai.ac.ae/postgraduate-programs/scholarships-new-students

For further information contact:

Tel: (971) 4 278 1800
Email: info@uowdubai.ac.ae

University of York

Graduate Schools Office, Heslington, York Y010 5DD, United Kingdom.

Tel: (44) 1904 432 143
Email: graduate@york.ac.uk
Website: www.york.ac.uk/admin/gso/gsp
Contact: Mr Philip Simison

The University of York offers postgraduate degree courses in archaeology, art history, biology, biochemistry, chemistry, communication studies, computer science, economics, educational studies, electronics, English, environment, health sciences, history, language and linguistics, management, mathematics, medieval studies, music, philosophy, physics, politics, psychology, social policy, social work, sociology and women's studies.

China Scholarships Council Joint Research Scholarships

Purpose: The scholarships are open to Chinese nationals intending to begin a PhD in the current and upcoming academic year. They will be awarded on the basis of academic merit and CSC priorities

Eligibility: 1. You must be a citizen and permanent resident of the People's Republic of China at the time of application. 2. You must hold an unconditional offer* for a full-time PhD degree programme at the University of York, commencing in Autumn 2023. 3. You are eligible to apply if you have an outstanding ATAS certificate as your only offer condition. 4. You must fulfil any English language requirements of your offer by 7 February 2023. 5. You must satisfy the eligibility and selection criteria set out by the CSC (csc.edu.cn). *If you are currently studying the final year of a bachelor or Masters degree, you are eligible to apply for the scholarship if you hold a conditional offer, where the only condition is the successful completion of your degree or the receipt of your ATAS certificate. If your offer is still conditional on fulfilling English language requirements, you cannot apply.

Level of Study: Postgraduate, Research

Type: Scholarship

Value: 100% of tuition fees for the full duration of the CSC funding period, a grant and uk visa fees

Length of Study: three years

Frequency: Annual

Country of Study: Any country

Application Procedure: Check the details online. www.york.ac.uk/study/postgraduate-research/funding/china-scholarships/

No. of awards offered: 10

Closing Date: 7 February

Funding: Private

Additional Information: www.york.ac.uk/study/postgraduate-research/funding/china-scholarships/

For further information contact:

Tel: (44) 1904 323534
Email: international@york.ac.uk

Overseas Continuation Scholarship (OCS)

Purpose: For current University of York Masters students who are progressing to PhD studies at the University of York

Eligibility: Students must be outstanding academically and have the support of their chosen department at York. You must hold an offer for PhD study and be a current University of York Masters student to be eligible to apply

Level of Study: Doctorate

Type: Scholarship

Value: The scholarship is worth £5,000 in the first year of study as a deduction from tuition fees

Application Procedure: Please visit www.york.ac.uk/study/international/fees-funding/scholarships/

Closing Date: 30 April

Additional Information: Please email mailto: international@york.ac.uk

For further information contact:

Email: international@york.ac.uk

Overseas Research Scholarship (ORS)

Purpose: For applicants commencing PhD study at the University of York. Applicants must be liable to pay the overseas rate of tuition fee

Eligibility: Students must be outstanding academically and have the support of their chosen department at York. You must hold an offer for PhD study to be eligible to apply

Level of Study: Doctorate

Type: Scholarship

Value: The scholarship will pay the full overseas tuition fee and a stipend of £5,000 per year for each year of successful study

Application Procedure: Please visit www.york.ac.uk/study/international/fees-funding/scholarships/

Closing Date: 30 April

Additional Information: Please email international@york.ac.uk www.ucl.ac.uk/scholarships/overseas-research-scholarships

For further information contact:

Email: international@york.ac.uk

Scholarship for Overseas Students

Subjects: All subjects except MBBS (Medicine), GEMMA, CASPPER and Mundus MAPP.

Purpose: For applicants commencing study of any taught subject (excluding students applying to the Hull York Medical School) at any level as a full-time student at the University of York. Applicants must be liable to pay the overseas rate of tuition fee.

Eligibility: This is a competitive scholarship based on academic merit and financial need. You must hold an offer for academic study to be eligible to apply.

Level of Study: Postgraduate

Type: Scholarship

Value: The scholarship is worth one-quarter (25%) of the overseas tuition fee for each year of successful study

Frequency: Annual

Application Procedure: Please visit www.york.ac.uk/study/international/fees-funding/academic-excellence-scholarships/

Closing Date: 30 April

Additional Information: Please email for further information. mailto: international@york.ac.uk

For further information contact:

Email: international@york.ac.uk

White Rose University Consortium Studentships

Purpose: Each year York collaborates with the Universities of Leeds and Sheffield to be able to offer a number of studentships in each of the three universities

Eligibility: In order to be eligible you must have applied for a place on a full time PhD programme in the relevant Department. Have or expect to obtain a first or upper second class honours degree or equivalent prior to commencing the PhD degree

Level of Study: Doctorate

Type: Studentship

Value: A full Research Council equivalent stipend £14,057. Rates for current year were not set at time of publication. A fee waiver at the Home/European Union rate (Overseas candidates are welcome to apply but would need to fund the difference between Home/European Union fee rate and international fee rate.). A Research Support Grant £900

Frequency: Annual

Application Procedure: Please visit www.york.ac.uk/study/postgraduate/fees-funding/research/white-rose-studentships/

Closing Date: 30 April

Additional Information: Contact mailto: research-student-admin@york.ac.uk

For further information contact:

Email: research-student-admin@york.ac.uk

Wolfson Foundation Scholarships

Purpose: The University is delighted to be offering Wolfson Scholarships in the Humanities for the second year as part of a national Arts funding scheme

Eligibility: The Wolfson Postgraduate Scholarships in the humanities will be awarded to outstanding students who demonstrate the potential to make an impact on their chosen field. Wolfson Scholarships will be awarded solely on academic merit. In order to be eligible you must have applied for and be in receipt of an offer of a place on a full time PhD programme in the relevant department (some departments may be able to accept applications on the basis of a programme application without an offer, please speak to your prospective department to confirm). Expect to begin your PhD studies in October. Have or expect to obtain a first or upper second class honours degree or equivalent prior to commencing the PhD Have completed a masters level qualification before commencing the PhD.

Level of Study: Postgraduate, Research
Type: Scholarship
Value: Covers tuition fees, £22,000 stipend
Frequency: Annual
Country of Study: Any country
Application Procedure: Please visit www.york.ac.uk/study/postgraduate/fees-funding/postgraduate/wolfson/
No. of awards offered: 3
Closing Date: 26 January
Additional Information: www.st-andrews.ac.uk/study/fees-and-funding/postgraduate/scholarships/wolfson-postgraduate/

For further information contact:

Tel: (44) 1904 325962
Email: pgr-administration@york.ac.uk

Uppsala University

Website: www.uu.se/en/admissions/scholarships/uppsala-university/

Uppsala University is a research university in Uppsala, Sweden, and is the oldest university in Sweden and all of the Nordic countries, founded in 1477.

Uppsala IPK Scholarships for International Students

Purpose: Uppsala University awards several scholarships for fee-paying students applying for Master's programmes commencing in the autumn. One of these scholarship programs is the Uppsala IPK Scholarships
Eligibility: 1. Citizens of a country outside the European Union/EEA and Switzerland. 2. Applicants must demonstrate academic talent and show interest in belonging to an educational milieu. 3. Students can only be awarded an IPK scholarship for their first priority programme at Uppsala University. 4. You must meet the entrance requirements for the programme you applied to and application fee and supporting documents must have been received before deadline to University Admissions
Type: Scholarship
Value: Scholarships will cover the cost of tuition but not living expenses
Country of Study: Any country

Application Procedure: You must then submit an online scholarship application form on which you will note your application ID from www.universityadmissions.se
Closing Date: 20 January
Contributor: The Uppsala University in Sweden
Additional Information: For more details, visit official scholarship website: www.uu.se/en/admissions/scholarships/uppsala-university/

For further information contact:

Email: tuitiongrants@uadm.uu.se

US Department of Energy

Department of Energy Computational Science Graduate Fellowship Krell Institute

Subjects: Engineering and the physical, computer, mathematical or life sciences
Purpose: To help ensure a supply of scientists and engineers trained to meet workforce needs; to make Department of Energy laboratories available to fellows for work experiences; to strengthen ties between the national academic community and Department of Energy laboratories; and to make computational science careers more visible.
Eligibility: Applicants should either be undergraduate seniors, applicants with no more than B.S. or B.A. degrees who are not enrolled in graduate school, first-year graduate students (M.S. degree or PhD students without an M.S. degree), enrolled M.S. degree students beyond their first year provided that they plan full-time, uninterrupted study toward a PhD at 1) a different academic institution, OR 2) in a different academic department, applicants with no more than M.S. degrees who are not currently enrolled AND who will not have been enrolled in graduate school for two years prior to resuming graduate studies, first-year PhD students with an M.S. degree provided that they 1) completed the M.S. degree within two years at a different academic institution, 2) completed the M.S. degree within two years in a different academic department, OR 3) prior to current enrollment, they had not been enrolled in graduate school for at least two years
Type: Fellowship
Value: Yearly stipend of US$37,000, payment of full tuition and required fees during the appointment period (at any accredited U.S. university), a US$5,000 academic allowance in the first fellowship year and a US$1,000 allowance each renewed year (to be used for the purchase of a computer workstation or for research/professional development expenses), and more

U

Length of Study: 4 years, but must be renewed annually
Frequency: Annual
Country of Study: United States of America
Additional Information: www.krellinst.org/csgf/

Nuclear Security Administration Stewardship Science Graduate Fellowship

Purpose: To ensure a continuous supply of highly trained scientists and engineers in areas of study related to high energy density physics, nuclear science, and materials under extreme conditions and hydrodynamics; to give DOE NNSA SSGF recipients opportunities to do research at DOE defense laboratories; to assemble a national meeting where fellows, university faculty and laboratory scientists share research advancements; to give fellows opportunities to work with some of the nation's most sophisticated and powerful experimental and computational facilities; to make graduating fellows aware of employment opportunities within the Department of Energy and its laboratory system; and to build the next generation of leaders with expertise in stewardship science in support of national defense.
Eligibility: Senior undergraduate students and first- and second-year graduate students. Recipients must be enrolled as full-time graduate students at an accredited U.S. college or university and must study and research within the fellowship's goals. During the summer, fellows should conduct full-time research related to completing their degree, enroll in classes or take a practicum assignment at one of the DOE NNSA laboratories.
Type: Fellowship
Value: Yearly stipend of US$36,000, payment of full tuition and required fees during the appointment period (at any accredited U.S. university), a US$5,000 academic allowance in the first fellowship year and a US$1,000 allowance for research or professional development expenses
Length of Study: Four years, but must be renewed annually
Frequency: Annual
Country of Study: United States of America
Closing Date: January
Additional Information: www.krellinst.org/ssgf/

The Energy Efficiency and Renewable Energy (EERE) Science and Technology Policy (STP) Fellowships

Subjects: Engineering; Physical Sciences
Purpose: The Energy Efficiency and Renewable Energy (EERE) Science and Technology Policy (STP) Fellowships serve as a next step in the educational and professional development of scientists and engineers by providing opportunities to participate in policy-related projects at DOE's Office of Energy Efficiency and Renewable Energy in Washington, D.C. Participants will become part of a group of highly-trained scientists and engineers with the education, background, and experience to be part of the workforce that supports the DOE's mission in the future.
Eligibility: Advanced degree in engineering or physical sciences; Knowledge of energy efficiency concepts, technologies and RD&D programs, specifically those related to HVAC, refrigeration, refrigerants, and/or building energy efficiency
Type: Fellowship
Value: Selected candidates will receive a stipend as support for their living and other expenses during this appointment. Stipend rates are determined by EERE officials and are based on the candidate's academic and professional background. Relocation expenses, not to exceed US$5,000, incurred in relocating from the participant
Length of Study: Varies
Study Establishment: Office of Energy Efficiency and Renewable Energy (EERE) Building Technologies Office (BTO)
Country of Study: United States of America
Application Procedure: Via website at www.zintellect.com/Account/ApplicantRegister/4347; A complete application consists of An application Transcript(s) - For this opportunity, an unofficial transcript or copy of the student academic records printed by the applicant or by academic advisors from internal institution systems may be submitted. Selected candidate may be required to provide proof of completion of the degree before the appointment can start. A current resume/curriculum vitae (CV) The resume/CV must include the following Basic applicant Information Name, address, phone, email, and other contact information. Work & Research Experience List all work and research experiences beginning with current or most recent. Include the name of the employer, location, position held, and time period involved. Leadership Experience List experiences (e.g., work, civic, volunteer, research) that demonstrate your leadership skills. Detail your role, type of experience, organization, location, and duration. Educational History List all institutions from which you received or expect to receive a degree, beginning with current or most recent institution. Include the name of the academic institution, degree awarded or expected, date of awarded or expected degree, and academic discipline. Honors & Awards List in chronological order (most recent first) any awards or public recognitions. Include the name of awarding institution, title of the award or honor, and date of award or honor. All documents must be in English or include an official English translation.
Additional Information: Quote reference code in all correspondence: DOE-EERE-STP-BTO-2018-1202 www.zintellect.com/Opportunity/Details/DOE-EERE-STP-BTO-2018-1202

For further information contact:

Email: DOE-RPP@orau.org

Utrecht University

Domplein 29, NL-3512 JE Utrecht, Netherlands.

Tel: (31) 30 253 26 70
Email: studievoorlichting@uu.nl
Website: www.uu.nl

Utrecht University stands for broad and interdisciplinary education. Students at Utrecht University learn to look beyond the boundaries of their fields of study and work together in interdisciplinary projects. The education programmes are modern and innovative. Students and high-ranking scientists work together on a better future.

Utrecht Excellence Scholarships for International Students

Eligibility: To be eligible for an Utrecht Excellence Scholarship, you must 1. Belong to the top 10% of your graduating class. 2. Hold a non-European Union/EEA passport and not be eligible for support under the Dutch system of study grants and loans. 3. Have completed your secondary school and/or Bachelor degree outside the Netherlands. 4. Have applied for an eligible international master's programme with a start date of 1 September
Level of Study: Graduate, Postgraduate
Type: Scholarship
Value: tuition fees plus €11.000 living expenses
Frequency: Annual
Country of Study: Any country
Application Procedure: Your application for a scholarship will only be processed if you have submitted an application for a Master's programme as well. After submitting an application for the Master's programme, non-European Union/EEA students will have the option to submit an application for an Utrecht Excellence Scholarship. Prospective students who wish to be considered for the scholarship must apply before 1 February. Please note that in some cases you may need to apply before 1 December; check the 'When to apply' section under Admission and application of your master's programme. It is important to visit the official website (link found below) for detailed information on how to apply for this scholarship. Application has to be processed online. E-mail is not required
No. of awards offered: 25
Closing Date: 31 January
Funding: Private
Additional Information: Official Scholarship Website: www.uu.nl/masters/en/general-information/international-students/financial-matters/grants-and-scholarships/utrecht-excellence-scholarships

For further information contact:

Email: study@uu.nl

V

Vascular Cures

274 Redwood Shores Parkway, #717, Redwood City, CA 94065, United States of America.

Tel: (1) 650 368 6022
Email: info@vascularcures.org
Website: vascularcures.org/

Vascular Cures is the only US national non-profit representing millions of patients with vascular disease. For more than 30 years, it has transformed patient lives through support of innovative research and programs that advance patient-centered healthcare.

Wylie Scholar Program

Subjects: Vascular health
Purpose: Vascular Cures' Wylie Scholar Program is building a pipeline of innovators in vascular health. We provide 3-year career development grants to outstanding young vascular surgeon-scientists who combine active patient care with academic research. The award supports crucial research that enables them to compete for future research funding.
Eligibility: Candidates must hold a full-time faculty appointment as a vascular surgeon with active privileges at a medical school accredited by the Liaison Committee on Medical Education in the United States or the Committee for the Accreditation of Canadian Medical Schools in Canada.
Level of Study: Junior Faculty
Type: Grant
Value: US$50,000
Length of Study: 3 years
Country of Study: United States of America or Canada

Application Procedure: Apply online. Download application from website. Send an original application in PDF format to info@vascularcures.org
No. of awards given last year: 1
Additional Information: vascularcures.org/wylie-scholar-program-2/

For further information contact:

Email: info@vascularcures.org

Victoria University

PO Box 14428, Melbourne, VIC 8001, Australia.

Tel: (61) 3 9919 4000
Website: www.vu.edu.au/

Victoria University achieved university status in 1991, but our preceding institutions date back to 1916. We are one of Australia's few dual-sector universities. Today, we have over 40,000 enrolled higher education, and vocational education and training students studying on our campuses. Being a dual-sector university means that our students can easily pathway from vocational education to higher education - such as from a certificate or diploma course through to an undergraduate degree or even a postgraduate qualification by coursework or research.

Victoria University Research Scholarships

Purpose: To support students undertaking Master's research and research Doctorates
Eligibility: Open to citizens or permanent residents of Australia who have achieved Honours 1 or equivalent having

© Springer Nature Limited 2022
Palgrave Macmillan (ed.), *The Grants Register 2023*,
https://doi.org/10.1057/978-1-349-96053-8

studied at or currently studying at Victoria University of Technology

Level of Study: Postgraduate
Type: Scholarship
Value: Tuition fees and a living allowance (stipend) to assist graduate research students with the costs of their study.
Length of Study: 1 year
Frequency: Annual
Study Establishment: Victoria University
Country of Study: Australia
Closing Date: 31 October
Additional Information: www.vu.edu.au/study-at-vu/fees-scholarships/scholarships/graduate-research-scholarships

For further information contact:

Tel: (61) 3 9688 4659
Fax: (61) 3 9688 4559
Email: Lesley.Birch@vu.edu.au

Women in Sport Scholarships

Purpose: This scholarship is a legacy of the fundraising assistance Dr Susan Alberti AC provides to the Victoria University Women in Sport centre. Her contributions help us to strengthen sport career pathways for women, and advance workforce development through education.
Eligibility: To be eligible, you must meet these criteria: 1. be an Australian citizen or permanent resident 2. be enrolled at VU in an undergraduate or postgraduate study in sport 3. reside in Australia 4. have experienced barriers and challenges in your academic and personal life that have prevented you from accessing/completing tertiary study 5. be able to clearly articulate your career aspirations in sport. Successful applicants may be invited to speak at Victoria University functions to highlight how the funds have enabled them to progress in their sport related career ambitions.
Level of Study: Postdoctorate
Value: US$2000 per annum
Length of Study: two years
Country of Study: Any country
Application Procedure: Documentation supporting your application must include: 1. CV (maximum 2 pages) 2. contact details of a referee to support the application 3. personal statement (500 words). The personal statement must: 1. demonstrate how this scholarship may help you overcome a barrier to access study 2. articulate the reason(s) for selecting your chosen undergraduate or postgraduate course in sport 3. clearly explain how being a recipient of a VU Women in Sport scholarship will assist you to achieve your career aspirations and development.

Victoria University of Wellington

PO Box 600, Wellington 6140, New Zealand.

Tel: (64) 4 472 1000
Email: info@vuw.ac.nz
Website: www.wgtn.ac.nz/

Te Herenga Waka—Victoria University of Wellington, originally known as Victoria College, was founded in 1897. A civic university is one that values close involvement with the social, cultural, and economic life of its city and region.

Therle Drake Postgraduate Scholarship

Subjects: Music
Purpose: The scholarship is for postgraduate classical performance overseas study and application should be made in the year for which the project is planned. While the terms of the bequest are that preference be given to a piano student, other applicants will be considered.
Eligibility: The applicant must be enrolling or have enrolled for postgraduate study at Te Kōkī New Zealand School of Music at Te Herenga Waka - Victoria University of Wellington, and remain in good academic standing.
Level of Study: Postgraduate
Type: Scholarship
Value: Up to NZ$1,000 per student
Length of Study: 1 year
Frequency: Annual
Country of Study: Any country
Application Procedure: A completed online application must be submitted by 4.30 pm on the closing date. Late or incomplete applications will not be accepted. Any required supporting documentation (including references) must also be received by 4.30 pm on the closing date in order for the application to be considered. Applications will normally open one month prior to the closing date. Contact us: www.wgtn.ac.nz/scholarships/scholarships-office if you have any queries.
No. of awards offered: 2
Closing Date: 15 November
Funding: Private

For further information contact:

Scholarships and PhD Admissions Office.

Tel: (64) 800 04 04 04
Email: scholarships-office@vuw.ac.nz,
            pg-research@vuw.ac.nz,
            summer-research@vuw.ac.nz

Vice-Chancellor's Strategic Doctoral Research Scholarships

Purpose: These scholarships are intended to encourage and support doctoral study (PhD) at Victoria University of Wellington. Victoria University of Wellington offers scholarships to those about to begin their doctoral studies. These scholarships are awarded on academic merit and are open to New Zealand and international students in any discipline.

Eligibility: These scholarships are open to graduates of any university within or outside of New Zealand who intend to enrol full time for a Doctorate (PhD) or who have commenced their doctoral study at Victoria University of Wellington. Please note: It is very important to refer to the website for regulations and further process requirements regarding an application for this scholarship.

Level of Study: Doctorate, Research

Type: Scholarship

Value: NZ$27,500 per annum stipend plus domestic tuition fees for up to three years.

Length of Study: 3 Year

Frequency: Annual

Study Establishment: Victoria University

Country of Study: New Zealand

Application Procedure: Information on applying to do a Doctorate at Victoria University of Wellington and apply for funding to do so is also available from the Wellington Faculty of Graduate Research website. www.wgtn.ac.nz/fgr.

No. of awards offered: 110

Closing Date: 1 November

Contributor: Victoria University

Additional Information: Closing Date(s): Three rounds each year closing 1 March, 1 July and 1 November. For more information www.wgtn.ac.nz/scholarships/current/wellington-doctoral-scholarships

For further information contact:

Scholarships and PhD Admissions Office.

Tel: (64) 800 04 04 04
Email: scholarships-office@vuw.ac.nz,
                pg-research@vuw.ac.nz,
                summer-research@vuw.ac.nz

Victoria Hardship Fund Equity Grants for International Students in New Zealand

Purpose: These grants are to encourage students who are facing financial hardship to continue in their studies at Te Herenga Waka—Victoria University of Wellington. The grants will be awarded on the basis of financial need and satisfactory academic commitment and progress. The Grants are intended to assist with ongoing costs related to study.

Eligibility: Applications are open to all students who are currently studying at Te Herenga Waka—Victoria University of Wellington, including domestic, international, undergraduate, postgraduate, part-time, and full-time students. Applicants must be enrolled in the trimester they are applying for, e.g., students who apply for round 1 must be enrolled in trimester 1 of the same year.

Level of Study: Doctorate, Graduate, Masters Degree, Postgraduate

Type: Grant

Value: Up to NZ$2,000 for one or two trimesters

Frequency: Annual

Study Establishment: Victoria University of Wellington

Country of Study: New Zealand

Application Procedure: Apply online. Required supporting documentation 1. A personal statement (max 500 words) outlining your financial difficulties and your personal circumstances and study goals. 2. Proof of your income (details of specific documents required are on online application).

Closing Date: 18 October

Additional Information: Closing Date(s): 1 February, 8 June and 18 October. They are not intended for tuition fees. The award may be paid in instalments. For more information www.wgtn.ac.nz/scholarships/current/hardship-fund-equity-grants

For further information contact:

Scholarships and PhD Admissions Office.

Tel: (64) 4 463 5113
Email: scholarships-office@vuw.ac.nz,
                pg-research@vuw.ac.nz,
                summer-research@vuw.ac.nz

Victoria Tongarewa Scholarship

Purpose: The Tongarewa Scholarship ("the Scholarship") celebrates the University's commitment to our international student community. This is a partial fee-based scholarship that will be put towards your tuition fees for one year of study.

Eligibility: Applicants must be 1. International students who are paying full international fees. 2. Entering their first year of an undergraduate degree or entering a postgraduate degree. Applicants can be entering a postgraduate degree programme at Victoria University of Wellington.

Level of Study: Masters Degree, Postgraduate, Research

Type: Scholarship

Value: NZ$5,000 or NZ$10,000

Frequency: Annual

Country of Study: New Zealand

Application Procedure: Apply online.

No. of awards offered: 19

Closing Date: 30 November

Additional Information: Closing Date(s): 1 June (For Trimester 2), 30 November (For Trimester 1), 1 September (For Trimester 3). For more details www.wgtn.ac.nz/scholarships/current/tongarewa-scholarship

For further information contact:

Scholarships Office.

Tel: (64) 4 463 5113

Email: scholarships-office@vuw.ac.nz, pg-research@vuw.ac.nz, summer-research@vuw.ac.nz

Wellington Graduate Award

Purpose: The Wellington Graduate Award encourages undergraduate students to proceed to graduate study and to research degrees

Eligibility: 1. Applications are sought from those who are eligible at the time of application, or who will have become eligible by the start of Trimester 2 the following year, to enrol for a Master's degree by thesis worth 90 points or more. This will be either a one-year Master's programme in which the student will undertake a thesis worth 90 points or more, or Part 2 Master's degree in which the student will take a thesis course worth 90 points or more. The Master's thesis will usually have the course code 591 or 592. 2. For avoidance of doubt, eligibility includes students who are taking a portfolio course that is worth 90 points or more, and is administered under the University's Master's by Thesis regulations (see section 6 of those regulations). 3. Students who are taking a 60 points dissertation course are not eligible. 4. Students would normally be expected to have completed a Bachelor's degree or Master's degree Part 1 demonstrating academic achievement equivalent to a GPA of at least 7.0 from a New Zealand university. Applicants must be aware that a GPA of 7.0 is a minimum requirement and that the University Research Scholarships Committee has discretion to use a higher bar if there are more applications than funding available. 5. Scholarships will be awarded solely on the basis of academic merit by the University Research Scholarships Committee, a sub-committee of the University Research Committee.

Level of Study: Masters Degree, Postgraduate

Type: Scholarship

Value: The scholarship comprises a NZ$15,000 tax free stipend for one year plus tuition fees

Length of Study: One year

Frequency: Annual

Study Establishment: Victoria University of Wellington

Country of Study: New Zealand

Application Procedure: A completed online application must be submitted by 4.30 pm on the closing date. Late or incomplete applications will not be accepted. Any required supporting documentation (including references) must also be received by 4.30 pm on the closing date in order for the application to be considered. Applications will normally open one month prior to the closing date. If no application link is provided below, check back again closer to the closing date. Contact us www.wgtn.ac.nz/scholarships/scholarships-office if you have any queries.

Closing Date: 1 November

Additional Information: These scholarships are not available for post experience or vocational Master's degree, such as the MBA, MIM or MIS, not to Honours students undertaking or intending to undertake an undergraduate programme such as LLB (Hons) or BE (Hons). Postgraduate Diploma study will only be considered if it is recognised as Part 1 of a two year Master's course. For more information www.wgtn.ac.nz/scholarships/current/wellington-graduate-award

For further information contact:

Scholarships and PhD Admissions Office.

Tel: (64) 800 04 04 04

Email: scholarships-office@vuw.ac.nz, pg-research@vuw.ac.nz, summer-research@vuw.ac.nz

Wellington Master's by Thesis Scholarship

Purpose: To encourage postgraduate research at Te Herenga Waka—Victoria University of Wellington, the University offers scholarships to students about to begin a full-time, research-focussed Master's degree.

Eligibility: 1. Applications are sought from those who are eligible at the time of application, or who will have become eligible by the start of Trimester 2 the following year, to enrol for a Master's degree by thesis worth 90 points or more. This will be either a one-year Master's programme in which the student will undertake a thesis worth 90 points or more, or Part 2 Master's degree in which the student will take a thesis course worth 90 points or more. The Master's thesis will usually have the course code 591 or 592. 2. For avoidance of doubt, eligibility includes students who are taking a portfolio course that is worth 90 points or more, and is administered under the University's Master's by Thesis regulations (see section 6 of those regulations). 3. Students who are taking a 60 points dissertation course are not eligible. 4. Students would normally be expected to have completed a Bachelor's degree or Master's degree Part 1 demonstrating academic achievement equivalent to a GPA of at least 7.0 from a New Zealand university. Applicants must be aware that a GPA of 7.0 is a minimum requirement and that the University Research Scholarships Committee has discretion to use a higher bar if there are more applications than funding available. 5. Scholarships will be awarded solely on the basis of academic merit by the University Research Scholarships Committee, a sub-committee of the University Research Committee.

Level of Study: Masters Degree, Postgraduate

Type: Scholarship

Value: The scholarship comprises a NZ$15,000 tax free stipend, plus tuition fees for one year

Length of Study: One year

Frequency: Annual

Study Establishment: Victoria University of Wellington

Country of Study: New Zealand

Application Procedure: A completed online application must be submitted by 4.30 pm on the closing date. Late or incomplete applications will not be accepted. Any required supporting documentation (including references) must also be received by 4.30 pm on the closing date in order for the application to be considered. Applications will normally open one month prior to the closing date. If no application link is provided below, check back again closer to the closing date. Contact us www.wgtn.ac.nz/scholarships/scholarships-office if you have any queries.

No. of awards offered: Varies

Closing Date: 1 November

For further information contact:

Scholarships and PhD Admissions Office.

Tel: (64) 800 04 04 04
Email: scholarships-office@vuw.ac.nz,
            pg-research@vuw.ac.nz,
            summer-research@vuw.ac.nz

Villa I Tatti and the Museo Nacional del Prado

Via di Vincigliata 22, I-50135 Florence, Italy.

Tel: (39) 55 603 251
Email: info@itatti.harvard.edu
Website: itatti.harvard.edu/
Contact: Villa I Tatti

Villa I Tatti, The Harvard University Center for Italian Renaissance Studies is a center for advanced research in the humanities located in Florence, Italy, and belongs to Harvard University. It also houses a library and an art collection, and it is the site of Italian and English gardens. Villa I Tatti is located on an estate of olive groves, vineyards, and gardens on the border of Florence, Fiesole and Settignano and the Museo Nacional del Prado, is the main Spanish national art museum, located in Madrid, Spain.

I Tatti/Museo Nacional del Prado Joint Fellowship

Purpose: A fellowship designed to support early and mid-career scholars in the field of art history, with preference given to advanced research projects that address the relationship between Spain and Italy (including transnational connections and dialogues with Latin America) during the Renaissance, broadly understood historically to include the period from the 14th to the 17th century.

Eligibility: At the time of application, scholars must have a PhD in hand and will be asked to upload a scan of the certificate. Applicants must be conversant in English and Spanish and have at least a reading knowledge of Italian, with a solid background in Italian and/or Spanish and Latin American studies. Each successful candidate must be approved by both the Museo Nacional del Prado and Villa I Tatti and will spend the fall term (mid-September – mid-December) at the Museo del Prado in Madrid supported by Centro de Estudios Europa Hispánica and the spring term (January-June) at Villa I Tatti in Florence. During both terms, it must be possible for Fellows to carry out most of their research with the resources available in the city where they are resident. Priority will be given to applicants with no previous association with either I Tatti or the Museo del Prado. Renewals, repeats, or deferments of this Fellowship are not granted. The Fellow will be expected to carry out original research on the topic for which they have been awarded their Fellowship.

Level of Study: Postdoctorate

Type: Fellowship

Value: For Spring term, the stipend is US$4,000 per month, plus a one-time supplement (maximum US$1,500) towards relocation expenses supported by Villa I Tatti. For Fall term, the stipend is €3000 per month, supported by the Centro de Estudios Europa Hispánica.

Length of Study: One academic year

Frequency: Annual

Country of Study: Any country

Application Procedure: Applications must be written in English and must be submitted electronically. Please visit website.

Closing Date: 15 November
Additional Information: itatti.harvard.edu/i-tattimuseo-nacional-del-prado-joint-fellowship

Villa I Tatti and the Warburg Institute School of Advanced Study

Via di Vincigliata 22, I-50135 Florence, Italy.

Tel: (39) 55 603 251
Email: info@itatti.harvard.edu
Website: itatti.harvard.edu/
Contact: Villa I Tatti

Villa I Tatti - The Harvard University Center for Italian Renaissance Studies (Florence, Italy) and the Warburg Institute School of Advanced Study at the University of London, England.

Warburg - I Tatti Joint Fellowship

Purpose: Villa I Tatti - The Harvard University Center for Italian Renaissance Studies in Florence, Italy, and the Warburg Institute School of Advanced Study at the University of London offer a joint, residential fellowship for early and mid-career scholars in the field of history, with preference given to advanced research projects that address the history of science and knowledge related to early modern Italy, including transnational connections between Italy and other cultures. Scholars can also apply to work on the transmission and circulation of ideas, objects, and people during the Renaissance, into and beyond the Italian peninsula, or on the historiography of the Italian Renaissance, including the rebirth of interest in the Renaissance in later periods.
Eligibility: At the time of application, scholars must have a PhD in hand and will be asked to upload a scan of the certificate. They may not be working on a second PhD at the time of application. Applicants must be conversant in English and have at least a reading knowledge of Italian, with a solid background in Italian Renaissance Studies. Each successful candidate must be approved by both the Warburg Institute and Villa I Tatti and will spend the fall term (September – December) at the Warburg Institute in London and the spring term (January-June) at Villa I Tatti in Florence. During both terms, it must be possible for Fellows to carry out most of their research with the resources available in the city where they are resident. Priority will be given to applicants with no previous association with either I Tatti or the Warburg

Institute. Renewals, repeats, or deferments of this Fellowship are not granted. The fellow will be expected to carry out original research on the topic for which they have been awarded their fellowship. Applications will not be accepted from candidates proposing to revise their doctoral dissertation for publication.
Level of Study: Postdoctorate
Value: For Spring Term The stipend is US$4,000 per month, plus a one-time supplement (maximum US$1,500) towards relocation expenses. For Autumn Term The stipend is £1,500 per month.
Frequency: Annual
Country of Study: Any country
Application Procedure: Applications must be written in English and must be submitted electronically. Please visit website.
Closing Date: 15 November

Villa I Tatti: The Harvard University Center for Italian Renaissance Studies

Via di Vincigliata 22, I-50135 Florence, Italy.

Tel: (39) 55 603 251
Email: info@itatti.harvard.edu
Website: itatti.harvard.edu/

Villa I Tatti, The Harvard University Center for Italian Renaissance Studies is a center for advanced research in the humanities located in Florence, Italy, and belongs to Harvard University. It also houses a library and an art collection, and it is the site of Italian and English gardens. Villa I Tatti is located on an estate of olive groves, vineyards, and gardens on the border of Florence, Fiesole and Settignano.

Berenson Fellowship

Subjects: Post-doctoral reasearch on "Italy in the World." Projects should address the transnational dialogues between Italy and other cultures (e.g. Latin American, Mediterranean, African, Asian etc.) during the Renaissance, broadly understood historically to include the period from the 14th to the 17th century.
Purpose: This Fellowship, made possible by The Lila Wallace – Reader's Digest Fund, is designed for scholars who explore "Italy in the World." I Tatti offers Fellows the precious time they need to pursue their studies with a minimum of obligations and interruptions together with a maximum of

scholarly resources–a combination that distinguishes the Harvard Center from similar institutions.

Eligibility: At the time of application, scholars must have a PhD in hand and will be asked to upload a scan of the certificate. They may not be working on a second PhD at the time of application. Applicants must be conversant in English and have familiarity with Italian. Priority will be given to early and mid-career scholars. I Tatti welcomes applications from scholars from all nations and gives special consideration to candidates without regular access to research materials and facilities in Italy

Level of Study: Postdoctorate

Value: The stipend is NZ$4,200 per month, plus a one-time supplement (maximum NZ$1,500) towards relocation expenses

Length of Study: 4-6 months

Frequency: Annual

Country of Study: Italy

Application Procedure: Applications can be written in English or Italian and must be submitted electronically.

No. of awards offered: 4

Closing Date: 20 November

Funding: Private

Contributor: The Lila Wallace - Reader's Digest Fund

Additional Information: For more information itatti.har vard.edu/berenson-fellowship

Craig Hugh Smyth Fellowship

Purpose: The Craig Hugh Smyth Fellowship is designed for curators and conservators pursuing advanced research in any aspect of the Italian Renaissance.

Eligibility: Applicants should be scholars who work for an educational or cultural institution as a curator or conservator. They may apply to carry out research on behalf of their home institution or propose projects relating to their personal research interests. Applicants must be conversant in English and have familiarity with Italian. Priority will be given to early and mid-career scholars. It must be possible for applicants to carry out most of their research in Florence. I Tatti welcomes applications from scholars from all nations and gives special consideration to candidates without regular access to research materials and facilities in Italy.

Level of Study: Research

Value: The stipend is US$4,200 per month, plus a one-time supplement (maximum US$1,500) towards relocation expenses

Length of Study: 4-6 months

Frequency: Annual

Country of Study: Italy

Application Procedure: Applicants should indicate their preference between fall (September through December) and winter-spring (January through June). Applications can be written in English or Italian and must be submitted electronically. Please refer website.

No. of awards offered: 2

Closing Date: 20 November

Additional Information: itatti.harvard.edu/craig-hugh-smyth-fellowship

David and Julie Tobey Fellowship

Subjects: This fellowship supports research on drawings, prints, and illustrated manuscripts from the Italian Renaissance, and especially the role that these works played in the creative process, the history of taste and collecting, and questions of connoisseurship. Proposals on a variety of subjects with a substantive component of research on drawings, prints, and illustrated manuscripts done on paper or parchment types are welcome.

Purpose: The David and Julie Tobey Fellowship supports research on drawings, prints, and illustrated manuscripts from the Italian Renaissance, and especially the role that these works played in the creative process, the history of taste and collecting, and questions of connoisseurship.

Eligibility: At the time of application, scholars must have a PhD in hand and will be asked to upload a scan of the certificate. They may not be working on a second PhD at the time of application. Applicants must be conversant in English and have familiarity with Italian. Priority will be given to early and mid-career scholars. It must be possible for applicants to carry out most of their research in Florence. I Tatti welcomes applications from scholars from all nations and gives special consideration to candidates without regular access to research materials and facilities in Italy.

Level of Study: Postdoctorate

Value: The stipend is US$4,200 per month, plus a one-time supplement (maximum US$1,500) towards relocation expenses

Length of Study: 4-6 months

Frequency: Annual

Country of Study: Italy

Application Procedure: Applications can be written in English or Italian and must be submitted electronically.

No. of awards offered: 1

Closing Date: 20 November

Additional Information: itatti.harvard.edu/david-and-julie-tobey-fellowship

Fellowship in the Digital Humanities

Subjects: Projects can address any aspect of the Italian Renaissance, broadly understood historically to include the period from the 14th to the 17th century, and geographically to include transnational dialogues between Italy and other cultures (e.g. Latin American, Mediterranean, African, Asian, etc.). Projects should apply digital technologies such as mapping, textual analysis, visualization, or the semantic web to topics in fields such as art and architecture, history, literature, material culture, music, philosophy, religion, and the history of science.

Purpose: A fellowship to support research of scholars in the humanities or social sciences, librarians, archivists, and data science professionals whose research interests or practice cut across traditional disciplinary boundaries and actively employ technology in their work.

Eligibility: Applicants must be conversant in English and have familiarity with Italian. At the time of application, a PhD is required for scholars in the humanities and social sciences. A Master's degree is required for librarians, archivists, and data science professionals. A background in programming, library sciences, computer graphics, computational linguistics, or other fields relevant to digital humanities research is highly desirable. Candidates should possess the technical skills to carry out their project at the time of application, and it must be possible for applicants to carry out most of their research in Florence. Priority will be given to early and mid-career scholars. I Tatti welcomes applications from scholars from all nations and gives special consideration to candidates without regular access to research materials and facilities in Italy.

Level of Study: Doctorate, Masters Degree

Value: The stipend is US$4,200 per month, plus a one-time supplement (maximum US$1,500) towards relocation expenses.

Length of Study: 4-6 months

Frequency: Annual

Country of Study: Italy

Application Procedure: Applicants should indicate their preference between fall (September through December) and winter-spring (January through June). Applications must be written in English and must be submitted electronically.

No. of awards offered: 2

Closing Date: 15 November

Contributor: The Fellowship in the Digital Humanities is generously supported in part by the Samuel H. Kress Foundation.

Additional Information: itatti.harvard.edu/fellowship-digital-humanities

I Tatti Fellowship

Subjects: Post-doctoral research in any aspect of the Italian Renaissance, broadly understood historically to include the period from the 14th to the 17th century and geographically to include transnational dialogues between Italy and other cultures (e.g. Latin American, Mediterranean, African, Asian etc.).

Purpose: A Fellowship to support post-doctoral research in any aspect of the Italian Renaissance.

Eligibility: Scholars must hold a PhD, dottorato di ricerca, or an equivalent degree. They must be conversant in either English or Italian and able to understand both languages. They should be in the early stages of their career, having received a PhD between 2012–2022 and have a solid background in Italian Renaissance studies. Candidates may not be working on a second PhD at the time of application. In the event that a candidate holds two doctoral degrees, the eligibility dates (PhD certificate dated between January 1, 2012 and December 31, 2022, inclusive) apply to the more recent degree.

Level of Study: Postdoctorate

Value: US$60,000, plus relocation supplement and housing or housing supplement

Length of Study: 1 year

Frequency: Annual

Country of Study: Italy

No. of awards offered: 15

Closing Date: 22 October

Additional Information: itatti.harvard.edu/i-tatti-fellowship

Mellon Fellowship in Digital Humanities

Eligibility: A PhD is required for scholars in the humanities and social sciences; in exceptional cases, applications from advanced PhD (ABD) students will be considered. A Master's degree is required for librarians, archivists, and data science professionals. A background in programming, library sciences, computer graphics, computational linguistics, or other fields relevant to digital humanities research is highly desirable. Candidates should possess the technical skills to carry out their project at the time of application

Type: Residential fellowships

Value: Up to US$4,000 per month plus a one-time supplement (Max US$1,500)

Length of Study: 4-6 months

Frequency: Annual

Country of Study: Italy

Application Procedure: Please check at itatti.harvard.edu/mellon-fellowship-digital-humanities

Closing Date: 14 December

Funding: Foundation

Contributor: Andrew W. Mellon Foundation

Additional Information: www.sas.rochester.edu/humanities/fellowships/mellon.html

For further information contact:

Tel: (39) 585 275 9025
Email: morris.eaves@rochester.edu

Villa I Tatti - Bogaziçi University Joint Fellowship

Subjects: This fellowship focusses on the interaction between Italy and the Byzantine Empire (ca. 1300 to ca. 1700) and aims to foster the development of research on Late Byzantine-Italian relations by supporting early-career scholars whose work explores Byzantium's cross-cultural contacts in the late medieval and early modern Mediterranean world through the study of art, architecture, archaeology, history, literature, material culture, music, philosophy, religion, or science.

Purpose: Villa I Tatti - The Harvard University Center for Italian Renaissance Studies (VIT, Florence) and the Byzantine Studies Research Center of Bogaziçi University (BSRC, Istanbul) offer a joint, residential fellowship to support research on the interaction between Italy and the Byzantine Empire (ca. 1300 to ca. 1700). This collaboration aims to foster the development of research on Late Byzantine-Italian relations by supporting early-career scholars whose work explores Byzantium's cross-cultural contacts in the late medieval and early modern Mediterranean world through the study of art, architecture, archaeology, history, literature, material culture, music, philosophy, religion, or science.

Eligibility: The VIT-BSRC Joint Fellowship is offered for candidates who have received a PhD in or after 2012. Candidates must be conversant in English and have at least a reading knowledge of Italian. They must have a solid background in Italian Renaissance and/or Byzantine Studies. Each successful candidate must be approved by both the BSRC and VIT and will spend the fall term (September - December) at Bogaziçi University in Istanbul and the spring term (January-June) at Villa I Tatti in Florence. During both terms, it must be possible for Fellows to carry out most of their research with the resources available in the city where they are resident. Priority will be given to applicants with no previous association with VIT or BSRC.

Level of Study: The VIT-BSRC Joint Fellowship is offered for candidates who have received a PhD in or after 2012.

Type: Residential Fellowship

Value: The stipend for the autumn semester in Istanbul is US$1,800 per month, plus a one-time supplement (maximum US$1,500) towards airfare to/from Istanbul. The stipend for the spring semester in Italy is US$4,200 per month plus a one-time supplement (maximum US$1,500) towards relocation expenses. An additional US$1,000 per month will be offered to offset rental costs, if applicable.

Length of Study: One academic year.

Frequency: Annual

Country of Study: Fellows will spend the fall term (September - December) in Istanbul and the spring term (January - June) in Florence.

No. of awards offered: 1

Closing Date: 15 November

Additional Information: itatti.harvard.edu/fellowships

Wallace Fellowship

Subjects: Post-doctoral research on historiography and impact of the Italian Renaissance in the Modern Era (19th-21st centuries). Projects can address the historiography or impact of the Renaissance on any field, including art and architecture, landscape architecture, history, literature, material culture, music, philosophy, religion, and science.

Purpose: A Fellowship to support post-doctoral research on the historiography and impact of the Italian Renaissance in the Modern Era (19th-21st centuries).

Eligibility: At the time of application, scholars must have a PhD in hand and will be asked to upload a scan of the certificate. They may not be working on a second PhD at the time of application. Applicants must be conversant in English and have familiarity with Italian. Priority will be given to early and mid-career scholars. Projects can address the historiography or impact of the Renaissance on any field, including art and architecture, landscape architecture, history, literature, material culture, music, philosophy, religion, and science. It must be possible for applicants to carry out most of their research in Florence. I Tatti welcomes applications from scholars from all nations and gives special consideration to candidates without regular access to research materials and facilities in Italy.

Level of Study: Postdoctorate

Value: The stipend is US$4,200 per month, plus a one-time supplement (maximum US$1,500) towards relocation expenses.

Length of Study: 4-6 months

Frequency: Annual

Country of Study: Italy

Application Procedure: Applicants should indicate their preference between fall (September through December) and winter-spring (January through June). Applications can be written in English or Italian and must be submitted electronically.

No. of awards offered: 4

Closing Date: 20 November

Funding: Private

Contributor: The Lila Wallace - Reader's Digest Fund.

Additional Information: itatti.harvard.edu/wallace-fellowship

V

Vinaver Trust

Email: bonnie.millar@nottingham.ac.uk
Website: www.internationalarthuriansociety.com/
Contact: Bonnie Millar, Website Editor

The Vinaver Trust was established in 1981, when the British Branch of the International Arthurian Society, at the urging of Eugène Vinaver, formerly professor of medieval French at Manchester University, and Cedric Pickford, professor of Medieval French at the University of Hull, found the British Branch had earned an astonishingly large sum in royalties from endorsing Arthurian plates for a Swiss ceramics firm, Atelier Arts.

Barron Bequest

Subjects: Any field of Arthurian studies
Purpose: To support postgraduate research in Arthurian studies
Eligibility: Open to graduates of any university in the British Isles, including those of the Republic of Ireland.
Level of Study: Postgraduate
Type: Grant
Value: £1,250 as a contribution to postgraduate fees
Frequency: Annual
Country of Study: United Kingdom, Republic of Ireland
Application Procedure: There is no standard application form. Instead, a leaflet is available giving details of information to be supplied by applicants in typed or word-processed form. The leaflet is available in electronic form and attached in website. Alternatively copies of the leaflet can be obtained from Professor Jane Taylor.
Closing Date: 30 April
Funding: Trusts
Contributor: The Eugène Vinaver Memorial Trust
Additional Information: For more information www.internationalarthuriansociety.com/british-branch/view/awards

For further information contact:

Professor Jane Taylor, Garth Head, Penruddock, Penrith, Cumbria CA11 0QU, United Kingdom.

Email: jane.taylor@durham.ac.uk

Vinod & Saryu Doshi Foundation

58, Nariman Bhavan, Mumbai, Maharashtra 400021, India.

Tel: (91) 6117 9000
Contact: Vinod & Saryu Doshi Foundation

The Vinod & Saryu Doshi Foundation is a non-profit charitable trust that supports initiatives in the fields of Art & Culture, Education and Community. It seeks to embody the lifelong passions and values of Vinod and Saryu Doshi, who believed that the mind is enriched through education and the spirit through art and culture. They have spent a considerable part of their lives supporting these causes. The Vinod & Saryu Doshi Foundation initiated these Fellowships to assist Indian nationals who have received acceptance in a University abroad to pursue their post-graduate studies (Masters, Postgraduate diploma/certificate or doctorate) in the field of Liberal Arts & Sciences. This includes the Humanities, Social Sciences, the Natural Sciences and Mathematics.

Vinod & Saryu Doshi Foundation Postgraduate Fellowships

Purpose: The main aim of the fellowship program is to enhance the higher education by giving an opportunity to academically bright students who have the drive to succeed but are unable to do so due to their financial challenges. This is a need-based merit Fellowship and abides by the Equal Opportunity and Affirmative Action policy. The maximum amount of the Fellowship will be up to ₹3 lakhs per fellow, which will be payable as a one-time amount
Eligibility: Indian Nationals only
Type: Postgraduate scholarships
Value: Up to ₹3 lakh
Study Establishment: Liberal Arts and Social Sciences
Country of Study: Any country
Application Procedure: Fill in the application form and send the hard copy to Vinod & Saryu Doshi Foundation
Closing Date: 7 May
Additional Information: For more details please visit the website https://www.scholarshipsinindia.com/fellowship/vinod-saryu-doshi-foundation-fellowship.html

For further information contact:

Email: ericadesouza@vsdf.org

Volkswagen Foundation

Kastanienallee 35, D-30519 Hannover, Germany.

Tel:	(49) 511 8381 0
Email:	info@volkswagenstiftung.de
Website:	www.volkswagenstiftung.de/en
Contact:	VolkswagenStiftung

The Volkswagen Foundation, based in Hanover, is a non-profit-making foundation established under private law in 1961. The Foundation owes its existence to a treaty between the Government of the Federal Republic of Germany and the State of Lower Saxony. The Volkswagen Foundation (VolkswagenStiftung) is the largest private research funder and one of the major foundations in Germany. Since 1962 the Foundation has granted more than 5.3 billion euros of funding for over 33,000 projects. Foundation capital amounts to 3.5 billion euros. The Volkswagen Foundation (VolkswagenStiftung) is dedicated to the support of the humanities and social sciences as well as science and technology in higher education and research.

Volkswagen Foundation Freigeist Fellowships

Purpose: The Freigeist funding initiative provides an opportunity for outstandingly qualified, creative and independent early career researchers to conduct their own research. It aims to encourage exceptional research personalities to embark on visionary, risk-taking research projects at the intersections between established fields of research.

Eligibility: Anyone can apply who identifies with the goals of a 'Freigeist' Fellowship and whose proposed research project fits in with the aims pursued by the Freigeist initiative. Candidates must, however, conform to the following conditions 1. Their doctorate must have been obtained no longer than four years ago but at least one year previously (with regard to the date of the defense relative to the deadline of the initiative). 2. The Fellowship must be integrated within a university or an extra-mural research institution in Germany. 3. Candidates must already have changed their academic environment and moved to a new location – at the latest when starting the Fellowship. A return to the working context of the doctorate will only be accepted under exceptional circumstances. 4. A previously completed research sojourn abroad, at the latest integrated in the proposed research project.

Level of Study: Doctorate, Postdoctorate

Type: Fellowship

Value: The scope of funding foresees a funding period of up to eight years in two funding phases (5 + 3 years or 6 + 2 years) with total funding of up to €2.2 million

Length of Study: 8 years

Frequency: Annual

Country of Study: Germany

Application Procedure: Applications can be submitted online via the Electronic Application System of the Volkswagen Foundation. Please refer website.

No. of awards offered: 10 to 15

Closing Date: 1 April

Additional Information: Persons who obtained their doctorate (date of defense) less than one year ago as of April 1st are not eligible to apply. For more information www.volkswagen stiftung.de/en/funding/our-funding-portfolio-at-a-glance/freigeist-fellowships

V

W.F. Albright Institute of Archaeological Research

P.O. Box 19096, Jerusalem 9119002, Israel.

Tel: (972) 2 628 8956
Email: albrightinstitute@aiar.org
Website: www.aiar.org/

The W.F. Albright Institute of Archaeological Research is a non-profit organization formed to engage in and facilitate research on the history and cultures of the Near East, to document and preserve evidence from the ancient world as a cultural resource, and to educate the public about the history and cultures of the region.

Sean W. Dever Memorial Prize

Purpose: The W.F. Albright Institute of Archaeological Research in Jerusalem announces the Sean W. Dever Memorial Prize call for papers.
Eligibility: Authors must be Ph.D. candidates in the semester in which the winner is announced (Spring).
Level of Study: Doctorate, Postdoctorate
Type: Prize
Value: US$750
Frequency: Annual
Country of Study: Israel
Closing Date: 31 December
Funding: Private
Additional Information: All submissions must be in PDF format only. Conference papers must include images (if used in the presentation) in PDF format (either as a separate document or embedded within the text of the paper), and full citations and bibliographic references. www.volkswagen stiftung.de/en/funding/our-funding-portfolio-at-a-glance/freigeist-fellowships
5https://aiar.org/home/fellowships/sean-w-dever-memorial-prize/#:~:text=The%20W.F.,Syro%2DPalestinian%20or%20Biblical%20Archaeology.

Wageningen University

Droevendaalsesteeg 4, NL-6708 PB Wageningen, Netherlands.

Tel: (31) 317 480 100
Website: www.wur.nl/en/wageningen-university.htm
Contact: Wageningen University and Research

Wageningen University and Research is a collaboration between Wageningen University and the Wageningen Research foundation. The strength of Wageningen University and Research lies in its ability to join the forces of specialised research institutes and the university. It also lies in the combined efforts of the various fields of natural and social sciences. This union of expertise leads to scientific breakthroughs that can quickly be put into practice and be incorporated into education.

Wageningen University & Research Africa Scholarship Program

Purpose: Applications are open for the Wageningen University and Research Africa Scholarship Program. The Africa

Scholarship Program (ASP) has been initiated by Wageningen University and Research to give talented and motivated students from Africa the opportunity to study at the university in Wageningen.

Eligibility: 1. You are a citizen of an African country. 2. You are an excellent student with a First class honours degree or a GPA of 80% or higher in a Bachelor degree. 3. You have applied for one the master's programmes of Wageningen University and Research.

Level of Study: MBA, Masters Degree, Postgraduate, Postgraduate (MSc)

Type: Scholarship

Length of Study: 2 years

Frequency: Annual

Country of Study: Any country

No. of awards offered: 10

Closing Date: 15 January

Funding: Foundation

Additional Information: Only candidates who have been invited for the ASP selection have received an e-mail. If you have not received an invitation to apply for this scholarship, you have not been selected to participate. www.volkswagen stiftung.de/en/funding/our-funding-portfolio-at-a-glance/freigeist-fellowships https://www.wur.nl/en/education-programmes/master/practical-information-masters/scholarships-for-international-masters-students/africa-scholarship-programme.htm

For further information contact:

Tel: (1) 800 311 6823
Email: walmartdependent@applyISTS.com

Wal-Mart Foundation

702 S.W. 8th Street, Bentonville, AR 72716, United States of America.

Tel: (1) 800 530 9925
Website: www.fconline.foundationcenter.org/fdo-grantmaker-profile?key=WALM001

The Walmart Foundation was created to help support the communities Walmart serves. We focus on areas where we can do the most good - combining the unique strengths of the business alongside our philanthropy. Our ability to draw on Walmart business strengths, providing more than just funding, enables our philanthropy to deliver greater societal impact.

Warsaw Agricultural University The International Institute of Management and Marketing in Agri-Business (IZMA)

Nowoursynowska 166, PL-02 787 Warsaw, Poland.

Tel: (48) 22 59 31 000
Email: izma@sggw.waw.pl
Website: www.sggw.pl/en/
Contact: MBA Admissions Officer

The Warsaw University of Life Sciences is the largest agricultural university in Poland, established in 1816 in Warsaw. It employs over 2,600 staff including over 1,200 academic educators. The University is since 2005 a member of the Euroleague for Life Sciences which was established in 2001.

Warsaw Agricultural University MBA in Agribusiness Management

Length of Study: 2–5 years

Application Procedure: Applicants must supply an application form together with the following transcripts from previous institutions, a leaving school certificate, three passport photos, a certificate of physical fitness, relevant identification documents. All documents must be translated into Polish by an official translator.

For further information contact:

Tel: (48) 22 843 9751
Fax: (48) 22 843 1877
Email: majewski@alpha.sggw.waw.pl

Washington Conservation Guild

P.O. Box 553, Kensington, MD 20895, United States of America.

Email: wcg@washingtonconservationguild.org
Website: www.washingtonconservationguild.org/

The Washington Conservation Guild (WCG) is a 501(c)(3) non-profit organization of conservation professionals dedicated to preserving art and historic materials. Founded in 1967, WCG serves as a regional forum for its members and as a resource to the public for learning about the care of personal collections.

National Air and Space Museum - Engen Conservation Fellowship

Purpose: Fellows will be encouraged to develop a research project while at NASM. The independent research will be derived from the diverse collection of materials and may be related to evaluations of treatment procedures, ethical considerations, or technical studies.

Eligibility: 1. The ideal candidate will have a Master's degree in conservation from a recognized program and be able to conduct research independently. The candidate should have knowledge of ethical and professional principles and concepts related to the preservation of objects in a wide variety of media. 2. They should also understand the theories, principles, techniques, practices, and methodologies used to examine, study, treat, analyze and preserve historic objects. 3. Applicants should have a proven record of research, writing ability, and verbal communication skills.

Level of Study: Graduate, Postgraduate

Type: Fellowship

Frequency: Annual

Country of Study: Any country

Closing Date: 15 January

Funding: Private

Additional Information: www.washingtonconserva tionguild.org/2017/11/05/nasm-engen-conservation-fellow ship/

For further information contact:

Washington Conservation Guild, P.O. Box 553, Kensington, MD 20895, United States of America.

Email: Horelickl@si.edu

Smithsonian Post-Graduate Paintings Conservation Fellowship with NMAAHC and MCI

Purpose: The fellow will be invited to participate in the survey, treatment, and exhibition of paintings and will be invited to participate in the preventive care in painting storage at NMAAHC's Visual Art Collection and conduct technical.

Level of Study: Postgraduate

Type: Fellowship

Value: US$40,000

Length of Study: 1 year

Frequency: Annual

Application Procedure: Applications for this opportunity are being accepted through the www.solaa.si.edu/solaa/SOLAAHome.html

Closing Date: 31 May

Additional Information: www.washingtonconserva tionguild.org/2020/02/06/2020-smithsonian-post-graduate-paintings-conservation-fellowship-nmaahc-mci/

For further information contact:

Fax: (1) 301 238 1231

Email: andersonrs@si.edu, tsangj@si.edu

Washington University

Graduate School of Arts and Sciences, Box 1186, 1 Brookings Drive, St. Louis, MO 63130-4899, United States of America.

Tel: (1) 314 935 5000

Email: graduateartsci@wustl.edu

Website: www.wustl.edu/

Contact: Dr Nancy P. Pope, Associate Dean

Washington University has a diverse offering of events, disciplines, people, and resources that create unlimited possibilities for discovery and growth. The Graduate School of Arts and Sciences signals a curriculum and place, a core of teaching, learning, and discovery at Washington University.

Olin School of Business Washington University MBA Programme

Purpose: Our Program Focuses on Practicing and Mastering Management Concepts.

Eligibility: 1. Admission to the Olin MBA Program is competitive. 2. Each applicant is carefully considered by the Olin Admissions Committee-using both objective and subjective criteria-and there is no formula used to arrive at a decision. 3. Rather, the Admissions Committee takes a holistic approach to candidate evaluation with specific interest in your academic ability, professional potential, leadership qualities, communication and interpersonal skills, demonstrated achievements, motivation, and diversity.

Level of Study: MBA, Masters Degree

Type: Programme

Length of Study: 2 years

Frequency: Annual

Country of Study: Any country

Application Procedure: 1. Resume. 2. Three required essays. 3. Standardized test scores. 4. Academic transcripts and One professional recommendation.

Closing Date: 24 March

W

Additional Information: There is no application fee for the Full-time MBA Program. https://olin.wustl.edu/EN-US/academic-programs/professional-mba/admissions/tuition-and-financial-aid/Pages/default.aspx

Washington American Indian Endowed Scholarship

Purpose: The award is based on the financial need of the student. Recipients are selected on the basis of academic merit and a commitment to serve the American Indian community in Washington.

Eligibility: Applicants must meet the following criteria 1. Demonstrate financial need based on a completed FAFSA (Free Application for Federal Student Aid). 2. Meet Washington State residency requirements for financial aid. 3. Intend to enroll full-time as an undergraduate or graduate student at a participating public or private college or university in Washington State by fall term of the application year. 4. Intend to use your education to benefit Washington's American Indian community. 5. Not pursue a degree in theology. 6. Not yet have received a total of five years of this scholarship.

Level of Study: Graduate

Type: Scholarship

Value: US$500 to US$2,000

Length of Study: Up to 5 years

Frequency: Annual

Country of Study: United States of America

Application Procedure: Recipients must submit a renewal application each year for award consideration. Renewals are for one academic year, decided on a competitive basis, and at the discretion of the committee after a thorough review of the applicant's renewal application, letters of recommendation, academic merit, and continued commitment to return service to the American Indian community inWashington.

No. of awards offered: Varies

Closing Date: 1 March

Funding: Private

Wellcome Trust

Gibbs Building, 215 Euston Road, London NW1 2BE, United Kingdom.

Tel: (44) 20 7611 8888
Email: grantenquiries@wellcome.ac.uk
Website: www.wellcome.ac.uk

The Wellcome Trust's mission is to foster and promote research with the aim of improving human and animal health. The Trust funds most areas of biomedical research and funds research in the history of medicine, biomedical ethics, public engagement of science.

Arts Awards

Purpose: Arts Awards support imaginative and experimental arts projects that investigate biomedical science.

Eligibility: The scheme is open to a wide range of people including, among others, artists, scientists, curators, filmmakers, writers, producers, directors, academics, science communicators, teachers, arts workers and education officers. Applicants are usually affiliated to organizations, but can apply as individuals. Organizations might include museums and other cultural attractions; arts agencies; production companies; arts venues; broadcast media; schools; local education authorities; universities and colleges; youth clubs; community groups; research institutes; the NHS; and science centres. Partnership projects (between different people and organizations, e.g. scientists and ethicists, educators and artists) are welcomed. If this is the first time an organization is applying to the Wellcome Trust an eligibility assessment will be carried out. For this assessment, the following documentation from the applying organization should be submitted articles of association; audited accounts from the previous 2 years; details of similar projects/grant funding received; confirmation that no funding has been received or is scheduled to be received from any tobacco company.

Level of Study: Research

Type: Award

Value: Funding can be applied for at two levels (1) Small to medium-sized projects (up to and including £40,000). This funding can either be used to support the development of new project ideas, deliver small-scale productions or workshops, investigate and experiment with new methods of engagement through the arts, or develop new collaborative relationships between artists and scientists and (2) Large projects (above £40,000). This funding can be used to fund full or part production costs for large-scale arts projects that aim to have significant impact on the public's engagement with biomedical science. We are also interested in supporting high-quality, multi-audience, multi-outcome projects. Applicants can apply for any amount within the above boundaries, for projects lasting a maximum of 3 years.

Frequency: Annual

Application Procedure: Application form for awards up to and including £40,000, preliminary application form for awards over £40,000.

Funding: Trusts

Additional Information: Applicants must be based in the United Kingdom or the Republic of Ireland and the activity must take place in the United Kingdom or the Republic of Ireland www.unigo.com/scholarships/by-major/dance-scholarships/washington-american-indian-endowed-scholarship/1905

For further information contact:

Tel: (44) 20 7611 5757
Email: PEgrants@wellcome.ac.uk

Broadcast Development Awards

Purpose: To support the development of broadcast proposals in any genre that engages the audience with issues around biomedical science in an innovative, entertaining and accessible way.

Eligibility: The proposal must primarily be aimed at a mainstream United Kingdom and/or Republic of Ireland audience in the first instance but the subject matter can be international. Applicants are usually affiliated to organizations, but can apply as individuals. The scheme is open to broadcast professionals and other organizations or individuals working on broadcast projects. Partnership between broadcasters and other professionals such as scientists, ethicists, educators etc. are especially welcomed.

Level of Study: Research
Type: Award
Value: Up to £10,000, for a maximum of 1 year
Length of Study: 1 year
Application Procedure: Candidates should complete and submit an application form by the published deadline.
Funding: Trusts
Additional Information: Applicants must be based in the United Kingdom or the Republic of Ireland, although other members of the project team can be based overseas www.unigo.com/scholarships/by-major/dance-scholarships/washington-american-indian-endowed-scholarship/1905

For further information contact:

Tel: (44) 20 7611 5757
Email: PEgrants@wellcome.ac.uk

Career Re-Entry Fellowships

Purpose: This scheme is for postdoctoral scientists who have recently decided to recommence a scientific research career after a continuous break of at least 2 years.

Eligibility: The awards are open to individuals with a relevant connection to the European Economic Area (EEA). You should be a research scientist with at least 2 years' postdoctoral experience and intend to be based in a United Kingdom or Republic of Ireland organization. You must have had a continuous career break of at least 2 years and should have either a strong research track record (if applying for up to 4 years' support) or demonstrated the potential for a strong research career prior to your break (if applying for 2 years' support). A 2-year fellowship should provide sufficient training support to consolidate your potential. The proposed research should fall within the Wellcome Trust's normal funding remit. Resubmissions are not normally encouraged. If your application has been unsuccessful, please contact the Office for advice. You must have an eligible sponsoring laboratory in the United Kingdom or Republic of Ireland that will administer the fellowship for the duration of the award.

Level of Study: Professional development
Type: Fellowship
Value: It provides support that includes the fellow's salary, as determined by the host institution with an additional Trust enhancement, and Research expenses (consumables, animals, travel support to attend scientific meetings)
Length of Study: 2–4 years
Application Procedure: A preliminary application form (Word 92kB) should be completed and submitted by the published deadline. It should be sent electronically (as a Word document), with the requested accompanying information, to the appropriate funding stream at the Trust (see website). If successful, you will be shortlisted for interview.
Funding: Trusts
Additional Information: For further information visit https://wellcome.org/grant-funding/schemes/research-career-re-entry-fellowships

For further information contact:

Tel: (44) 20 7611 5757
Email: sciencegrants@wellcome.ac.uk

Clinical PhD Programmes

Purpose: This is a flagship scheme aimed at supporting the most promising medically qualified clinicians who wish to undertake rigorous research training.

Eligibility: You should have demonstrated the potential to pursue a career as an academic clinician. It is anticipated that many applicants will have already commenced their specialist training, but this is not essential.

Level of Study: Postgraduate, Research
Type: Grant
Value: The duration may vary from programme to programme, but each provides a clinical salary, PhD registration

W

fees at United Kingdom/EU student rate, research expenses, contribution towards travel and contribution towards general training costs.

Frequency: Annual

Country of Study: Any country

Application Procedure: Students are recruited annually by the individual Programmes. Recruitment begins in the preceding January. If you are interested in applying you should contact the relevant Programme directly. Please see website for more details.

Closing Date: 6 March

Funding: Trusts

Additional Information: https://wellcome.org/grant-funding/schemes/clinical-phd-programmes

For further information contact:

Email: clinicalphd@wellcome.ac.uk

Doctoral Studentships

Purpose: This scheme enables scholars to undertake up to 3 years of full-time research on a history of medicine topic leading to a doctoral degree at a university in the United Kingdom or Republic of Ireland.

Eligibility: You should hold a Master's in the history of medicine or a Master's with strong emphasis on the history of medicine. The proposed project must be on a history of medicine topic. If specialist language skills are essential to undertake the research, a Master's in the language required may be acceptable (classical languages, Arabic, Chinese, etc.). Your application must be sponsored by a senior member of the department, unit or institute, or History of Medicine grant holder (current or former), who would supervise you if an award were made. Applications must be submitted through the host institution.

Level of Study: Postgraduate, Research

Value: Support is provided for up to 3 years, and includes the student's stipend; a set amount to cover conference travel, research expenses and, where justified, the cost of overseas fieldwork; all compulsory university and college fees at the United Kingdom/Irish/Dutch home postgraduate student level; fees at the overseas rate will not be provided; institutions sponsoring candidates are expected to provide laptops and PCs as part of their postgraduate research-training infrastructure.

Length of Study: 3 years

Application Procedure: Preliminary applications should be made by email or post by the published deadline, and should include a brief curriculum vitae with details of the Master's degree held; details of the research proposed (maximum of one page); a letter of support from the head

of the department in which you will be working (this can be sent under separate cover); a letter of support from the supervisor.

Closing Date: 16 March

Funding: Trusts

Additional Information: www.wellcome.ac.uk/funding/schemes/doctoral-studentships

For further information contact:

Tel: (44) 20 7611 5757

Email: MHgrants@wellcome.ac.uk

Four-year PhD Studentship Programmes

Purpose: This is a flagship scheme aimed at supporting the most promising students to undertake in depth postgraduate training. Supporting specialized training provided in a range of important biomedical research areas (1) Developmental biology and cell biology; (2) Genetics, statistics and epidemiology; (3) Immunology and infectious disease; (4) Molecular and cellular biology; (5) Neuroscience; (6) Physiological sciences; (7) Structural biology and bioinformatics.

Eligibility: You should be a student who has, or expects to obtain, a first- or upper-second-class honours degree or equivalent.

Level of Study: Postgraduate, Research

Type: Studentship

Value: A stipend, PhD registration fees at United Kingdom/EU student rate, contribution towards laboratory rotation expenses in the first year, research expenses for years two to four, contribution towards travel and contribution towards transferable-skills training.

Length of Study: 4 years

Country of Study: Any country

Application Procedure: Students are recruited annually by the individual Programmes for uptake in October each year. Recruitment begins in the preceding December. If you are interested in applying you should contact the relevant Programme directly. Please see website for details.

Closing Date: October

Funding: Trusts

Additional Information: www.wellcome.ac.uk/funding/schemes/four-year-phd-programmes-studentships-basic-scientists

For further information contact:

Email: 4yrphd@wellcome.ac.uk

Innovator Awards

Purpose: These awards support researchers who are transforming great ideas into healthcare innovations that could have a significant impact on human health.

Eligibility: 1. Innovator Awards are open to researchers who are developing healthcare innovations that could have a major and measurable impact on human health. 2. Individuals and teams from not-for-profit and commercial organisations can apply. 3. Organisations can be of any size, based anywhere in the world (apart from mainland China).

Level of Study: Research

Type: Award

Value: Up to £500,000, or up to £750,000 for multidisciplinary collaborations.

Length of Study: 2 year

Frequency: Annual

Application Procedure: You must submit your application through the Wellcome Trust Grant Tracker (WTGT).

Funding: Trusts

For further information contact:

Gibbs Building, 215 Euston Road, London NW1 2BE, United Kingdom.

Tel: (44) 20 7611 5757

Email: innovations@wellcome.ac.uk

Intermediate Clinical Fellowships

Purpose: This scheme is for medical, dental, veterinary or clinical psychology graduates who have had an outstanding start to their research career. It will enable successful candidates to continue their research interests at a postdoctoral level in an appropriate unit or clinical research facility.

Eligibility: The award is open to individuals with a relevant connection to the EEA. You should have previously undergone a period of research training and will have completed, or be about to complete, a higher degree. You should have completed general professional training as defined by the relevant college. 1. Medical and dental candidates should either have a National Training Number (NTN) or Certificate of Completion of Specialist Training (CCST) or equivalent. 2. Veterinary candidates should have a degree in veterinary medicine (e.g. BVSc, BVM&S, BVMS, BVetMed, VetMB) and some experience in clinical practice and will have completed, or be about to complete, a higher research degree (preferably a PhD). 3. GPs are advised to contact the office to clarify their eligibility. 4. Clinical Psychologists must have obtained a professional Doctorate-level qualification in Clinical Psychology accredited by the British Psychological Society.

Level of Study: Postgraduate, Research

Type: Fellowship

Value: Fellowships are for up to 4–5 years, depending on situation. They provide research expenses (consumables, travel, support to attend scientific meetings) and the fellow's salary, set by the host institution according to age and experience. Requests for specific items of equipment, where relevant, may be considered, and research or technical assistance may be requested. However, a laboratory appropriate to the research proposed should be selected, and the necessary facilities required for the proposed research must be available to the candidate. Funding for a period of research abroad may be requested if scientifically justified, and we provide appropriate allowances for fellows based overseas.

Frequency: Annual

Application Procedure: A preliminary application form should be completed and submitted at any time before the appropriate deadline. It should be sent electronically (as a Word document) to the appropriate funding stream at the Trust (see website). If your preliminary application is successful, you will be invited to submit a full application by the published deadline. This will be peer reviewed and considered by the relevant Funding Committee. Shortlisted candidates will subsequently be invited to attend for interview at the Trust.

Funding: Trusts

Additional Information: www.wellcome.ac.uk/funding/schemes/intermediate-clinical-fellowships

For further information contact:

Tel: (44) 20 7611 5757

Email: sciencegrants@wellcome.ac.uk

Intermediate Fellowships in Public Health and Tropical Medicine

Purpose: This scheme enables high-calibre, mid-career researchers from low- and middle-income countries to establish an independent research programme. Fellows must be based primarily in a low- and middle-income country. Research projects should be aimed at understanding and controlling diseases (either human or animal) of relevance to local, national or global health. This can include laboratory based molecular analysis of field or clinical samples, but projects focused solely on studies in vitro or using animal models will not normally be considered under this scheme.

Eligibility: Applications are only accepted in the Public Health and Tropical Medicine Interview Committee remit. This covers research on infectious and non-communicable diseases within the fields of public health and tropical medicine that is aimed at understanding and controlling diseases (either human or animal) of relevance to local, national or global health. You must be a national or legal resident of a low- and middle-income country and should be either 1. A graduate in a subject relevant to public health or tropical medicine (e.g. biomedical or social science, veterinary medicine, physics, chemistry or mathematics) with a PhD and 3–6 years' postdoctoral experience, or 2. A medical graduate with a higher qualification equivalent to membership of the United Kingdom Royal Colleges of Physicians (i.e. qualified to enter higher specialist training) or recognized as a specialist within a relevant research area, with 3–6 years' research experience. You must have a relevant high-quality publication record and show potential to become a future scientific leader. Applicants who do not have a PhD but who are educated to first degree or Master's level and have extensive research experience, as evidenced by their publication record, may be considered.

Level of Study: Postgraduate, Research

Type: Fellowship

Value: Fellowships are for up to 5 years (non-renewable) and provide support that includes a basic salary for the fellow; research expenses (e.g. consumables, equipment, collaborative travel, research assistance, technical support); training costs where appropriate and justified; an inflation/flexible funding allowance and support to attend scientific meetings. Contributions to costs of the project which are directly incurred by the overseas institution may be provided.

Application Procedure: You must complete and submit a preliminary application form by the published deadline. The form should be emailed to phatic@wellcome.ac.uk

Funding: Trusts

Additional Information: For complete details please check the link www.wellcome.ac.uk/Funding/Biomedical-science/Funding-schemes/Fellowships/Public-health-and-tropical-medicine/wtd025883.htm
www.successcds.net/Scholarships/wellcome-trust-training-fellowships-in-public-health-and-tropical-medicine.html

For further information contact:

Tel: (44) 20 7611 5757
Email: sciencegrants@wellcome.ac.uk

International Engagement Awards

Purpose: To provide funding for innovative public or community engagement projects that explore biomedical research or health in Africa and Asia and to ensure science can be enjoyed and experienced as part of culture, entertainment and everyday life.

Eligibility: The scheme is open to a wide range of people, including media professionals, educators, science communicators, health professionals and researchers in bioscience, health, bioethics and history. Partnership projects (between different people and organizations, e.g. scientists and media professionals, ethicists and community workers) are welcomed. Applicants must be based in listed low- and middle-income countries or in the United Kingdom working with partners in the low- and middle-income countries. The activity must primarily take place in one or more low- and middle-income countries and the primary goal must be to involve participants or engage audiences located in low- and middle-income countries. Applicants from listed restructuring countries in Europe and Asia are not eligible. We can only accept applications in the English language but we welcome projects that bring together people from different backgrounds who speak diverse languages. All projects must involve engagement with health research. Projects dealing purely with development research not related to health are not eligible. Please note also, that the scheme is not intended to support standard delivery of health education and promotion which does not focus on health research or involve health researchers. Applicants must be affiliated to organizations or institutions. Organizations might include media organizations, research centres or research groups, community-based development organizations, education organizations. The International Engagement Awards will not fund traditional scientist-led health research. We may consider an application for participatory health research. This is research in which participants are supported to own and shape a research process, setting their own research questions and directing the research process. This type of research should not look like a consultatory exercise or health education but should aim to be collaborative process of enquiry in which the analysis is conducted and findings can be used by all participating parties. This could lead into circular processes of research and action.

Level of Study: Research

Type: Award

Value: Up to £30,000 for projects lasting a maximum of 3 years.

Application Procedure: Please contact the International Engagement Awards office well in advance of the deadline to request an application form and to confirm the eligibility of your project.

Closing Date: 19 August

Funding: Trusts

Additional Information: www.wellcome.ac.uk/what-we-do/directories/international-engagement-awards-people-funded

For further information contact:

Tel: (44) 20 7611 5757
Email: PEgrants@wellcome.ac.uk

International Training Fellowships

Purpose: This scheme offers nationals of low- and middle-income countries the opportunity to receive training at postgraduate or postdoctoral level.

Eligibility: 1. You're a national of a low- or middle-income country 2. Your proposed research focuses on a health priority in a low- or middle-income country 3. You have sponsorship from an eligible host organisation in a low- or middle-income country apart from mainland China. 4. You must want to undertake a guided period of research so that you can consolidate your existing experience and explore new areas of research. 5. You must have a PhD and be an early-career researcher or have a degree in a relevant subject and some initial research experience or be a clinically qualified doctor (and be qualified to enter higher specialist training), vet, dentist or clinical psychologist, and have some initial research experience.

Level of Study: Postgraduate

Type: Fellowship

Value: Usually £15,000 to £300,000 for salary, fees and research expenses.

Length of Study: 3 year

Frequency: Annual

Application Procedure: You must submit your application through the Wellcome Trust Grant Tracker (WTGT).

Closing Date: 9 July

Funding: Trusts

For further information contact:

Gibbs Building, 215 Euston Road, London NW1 2BE, United Kingdom.

Tel: (44) 20 7611 5757

Investigator Awards

Purpose: To support world-class researchers who are no more than 5 years from appointment to their first academic position, but who can already show that they have the ability to innovate and drive advances in their field of study.

Eligibility: To be eligible for an Investigator Award you must be based at an eligible higher education or research institution in the United Kingdom, Republic of Ireland or a low- or middle-income country. You should be employed in an established academic post a permanent, open-ended or long-term rolling contract, salaried by your host institution. You are also eligible if you have a written guarantee of an established academic post at your host institution, which you will take up by the start of the award. If you are based in a low- or middle-income country in sub-Saharan Africa, South-east Asia or South Asia (with the exception of India - see below), you are eligible to apply if you fulfil the above eligibility criteria and are working within the Trust's broad science funding remit.

Level of Study: Research

Type: Award

Value: Awards may be small or large, typically up to £3,000,000, and lasting up to 7 years. The duration and costs you request should be clearly justified by your proposed research. Also, you should ensure that the scope of your proposal and the associated resources are appropriate for your career stage and research experience. The award covers the direct costs of carrying out the research, such as research expenses; this may include research assistance, animals, equipment, fieldwork costs and funding for collaborative activity; travel and subsistence for scientifically justified visits; overseas allowances where appropriate.

Length of Study: Flexible duration, up to 7 years

Frequency: Annual

Application Procedure: The key stages of the application process are submission of an Investigator Award application form; scientific peer review by one of the Trust's Expert Review Groups, which shortlist the candidates for interview; written peer review of shortlisted applications by external specialist referees, who will include members of the Trust's Peer Review College; selected unattributed referee comments will be fed back to candidates before interview; interview of shortlisted candidates by our Interview Panel. Application forms are available on eGrants, our electronic application system. Please refer to the Additional information for completing the Investigator Award form on eGrants, which provides an overview to help guide you through the application process.

Closing Date: 27 February

Funding: Trusts

Additional Information: The Trust has combined its New Investigator and Senior Investigator Award schemes to create a single type of Investigator Award, providing all who hold established posts in eligible organizations with the same opportunity to obtain funding www.wellcome.ac.uk/funding/schemes/investigator-awards-science

For further information contact:

Email: sciencegrants@wellcome.ac.uk

Learned Society Curation Awards

Purpose: These awards support learned society publishers who want to explore new ways of signalling the significance of published research outputs in an open and transparent manner.

Level of Study: Research

Type: Award

Value: Up to £200,000

Length of Study: 3 year

Frequency: Annual

Application Procedure: You must submit your application through the Wellcome Trust Grant Tracker (WTGT).

Closing Date: 20 April

Funding: Trusts

For further information contact:

Gibbs Building, 215 Euston Road, London NW1 2BE, United Kingdom.

Tel: (44) 20 7611 5757
Email: openresearch@wellcome.ac.uk

Master's Awards

Purpose: This scheme enables scholars to undertake basic training in research and methods through a 1-year Master's course in medical history and humanities.

Eligibility: You should have a minimum of an excellent upper-second-class honours degree (or equivalent) in a relevant subject. Applications will not be considered from those who have already received support for their postgraduate studies from another funding body.

Level of Study: Postgraduate, Research

Type: Award

Value: The award is for 1 year. It includes the student's stipend and all compulsory university and college fees at the United Kingdom home postgraduate student level. Fees at the overseas rate will not be provided.

Frequency: Annual

Application Procedure: All enquiries about Master's Awards should be made directly to the relevant institution.

Closing Date: 1 May

Funding: Trusts

For further information contact:

Tel: (44) 20 7611 5757
Email: MHgrants@wellcome.ac.uk

Master's Fellowships in Public Health and Tropical Medicine

Purpose: This scheme strengthens scientific research capacity in low- and middle-income countries, by providing support for junior researchers to gain research experience and high-quality research training at Master's degree level. Research projects should be aimed at understanding and controlling diseases (either human or animal) of relevance to local, national or global health. This can include laboratory based molecular analysis of field or clinical samples, but projects focused solely on studies in vitro or using animal models will not normally be considered under this scheme.

Eligibility: You should be 1. A national or legal resident of a low- and middle-income country, and hold a first degree in subject relevant to tropical medicine or public health (clinical or non-clinical). 2. At an early stage in your career, with limited research experience, but have a demonstrated interest in or aptitude for research.

Level of Study: Postdoctorate, Postgraduate, Research

Type: Fellowship

Value: This fellowship normally provides up to 30 months' support. A period of 12 months should normally be dedicated to undertaking a taught Master's course at a recognized centre of excellence, combined with up to 18 months to undertake a research project. While undertaking a Master's course, fellows will receive a stipend in accordance with the cost of living in the country in which he/she will be studying; travel costs and support for approved tuition fees. Master's training by distance learning is acceptable. Master's course fees will be paid according to the rate charged by the training institution.

Application Procedure: A completed application form should be submitted by the sponsor by the published deadline. The form should be emailed to phatic@wellcome.ac.uk

Closing Date: 2 March

Funding: Trusts

Additional Information: For complete details go to address www.wellcome.ac.uk/Funding/Biomedical-science/Funding-schemes/Fellowships/Public-health-and-tropical-medicine/wtd025881.htm

For further information contact:

Tel: (44) 20 7611 5757
Email: sciencegrants@wellcome.ac.uk

Pathfinder Awards

Purpose: This scheme, offering pilot funding to catalyse innovative early-stage applied research and development projects in areas of unmet medical need, has been expanded. It now funds discrete projects from applicants in the United Kingdom and Republic of Ireland as well as partnerships between academia and industry based anywhere in the world.

Eligibility: Applications are welcome from academic and commercial organizations based in the United Kingdom or the Republic of Ireland. Applications from organizations and companies overseas will only be considered when applying in partnership. Check website for complete details.

Level of Study: Research

Type: Grant

Value: £100,000, but can be up to £350,000 in exceptional circumstances

Length of Study: 18 months

Frequency: Dependent on funds available

Country of Study: Any country

Application Procedure: You should contact us to confirm that your proposed application (and partnership, if appropriate), is eligible before submitting a full application form. After confirming that your application is eligible, you should complete the full application form (see 'Forms and guidance') and send it to innovations@wellcome.ac.uk

Closing Date: February

Funding: Trusts

Additional Information: www.wellcome.ac.uk/funding/schemes/pathfinder-awards

For further information contact:

Tel: (44) 20 7611 5757
Email: innovations@wellcome.ac.uk

Postdoctoral Research Training Fellowships for Clinicians

Subjects: Clinical, Public health

Purpose: This scheme enables clinicians to undertake high-quality postdoctoral training that will allow them to develop their long-term research interests.

Eligibility: The scheme may be suitable for clinicians who are due to complete their higher degree or are no more than 2 years from the date of their PhD viva by the full application deadline; graduated with a MB/PhD qualification or have achieved a high-quality PhD in a relevant subject, either during or prior to commencing their initial medical, veterinary or dental degree.

Level of Study: Postgraduate, Research

Type: Fellowship

Value: £250,000 to £400,000

Length of Study: 2 to 4 years

Frequency: Annual

Country of Study: Any country

Application Procedure: A preliminary application form should be completed and submitted at any time before the published deadline. It should be sent electronically (as a Word document) to Dr Lucy Bradshaw (see website for contact details). If your preliminary application is successful, you will be invited to submit a full application. This will be reviewed and if successful you will be shortlisted for interview.

Funding: Trusts

Additional Information: For more details see www.wellcome.ac.uk/Funding/Biomedical-science/Funding-schemes/Fellowships/Clinical-fellowships/wtp052588.htm, www.wellcome.ac.uk/funding/schemes/postdoctoral-research-training-fellowships-clinicians

For further information contact:

Tel: (44) 20 7611 5757
Email: sciencegrants@wellcome.ac.uk

Principal Research Fellowships

Purpose: This is the most prestigious of our personal awards and provides long-term support for researchers of international standing. Successful candidates will have an established track record in research at the highest level.

Eligibility: You should have an established track record in research at the highest level. This award is particularly suitable for exceptional senior research scientists currently based overseas who wish to work in the United Kingdom or Republic of Ireland.

Level of Study: Postgraduate, Research

Type: Fellowship

Value: Awards are for 7 years in the first instance, and provide both a personal salary and research programme funding in full. After the first period of award, the fellowship will be subject to a competitive scientific review, which will subsequently occur on a rolling basis every 5 years

Length of Study: 7 years

Application Procedure: If you intend to apply you should contact us with a full curriculum vitae, preferably 18 months in advance of the desired award date. You may not apply for more than one Wellcome Trust fellowship scheme at any one time.

Funding: Trusts

Additional Information: The maximum duration of the awards is 3 years. The awards are full-time but can be tenable on a part-time basis if a case can be made that personal circumstances require this www.wellcome.ac.uk/funding/schemes/principal-research-fellowships

For further information contact:

Tel: (44) 20 7611 5757
Email: sciencegrants@wellcome.ac.uk

Research and Development for Affordable Healthcare in India

Purpose: The objective of this initiative is to fund translational research projects that will deliver safe and effective healthcare products for India, and potentially other markets, at affordable costs. A key feature of the scheme is that it encourages innovations that bring together researchers from both the public and private sectors to extend access to care to the greatest numbers of beneficiaries, without compromising on quality.

Eligibility: Awards will be agreed by Committee and governed by the terms and conditions, including Wellcome Trust Grant Conditions, funding terms for Affordable Healthcare. In addition there will be additional terms and conditions that will be negotiated under the funding agreement for the award with the applicant.

Level of Study: Research

Type: Award

Value: Awards will be made by way of funding agreements that will be negotiated on a case-by-case basis. The principles of the Wellcome Trust Grant Conditions will apply. The terms and conditions of funding will be discussed with applicants individually. Typically, the agreements will contain a provision for the appropriate sharing of benefits. The funds available will be ring-fenced for the specified programme of work. Neither working capital nor building or refurbishment expenditure will be provided. Funding will be released in tranches against the attainment of pre-agreed project milestones

Application Procedure: In the first instance interested applicants should contact Dr Shirshendu Mukherjee to discuss their interest in funding via the Affordable Healthcare Initiative. Alternatively, applicants may complete a concept note and mail this directly to Dr Shirshendu Mukherjee.

Closing Date: 31 January

Funding: Trusts

For further information contact:

Email: s.mukherjee@wellcome.ac.uk

Research Career Development Fellowships in Basic Biomedical Science

Purpose: To provide support for outstanding postdoctoral scientists based in academic institutions in the United Kingdom and Republic of Ireland (RoI).

Eligibility: You should have a relevant connection to the European Economic Area. You are expected to have science or veterinary qualifications and, at the preliminary application stage, should normally have between three and 6 years'

research experience from the date of your doctoral degree (PhD viva). Due allowance will be given to those whose career has been affected for personal reasons. You must have made intellectual contributions to research that have been published in leading journals, and be able to demonstrate your potential to carry out independent research. The proposed research should fall within our normal funding remit. Resubmissions are not normally encouraged. If your application has been unsuccessful, please contact the Office for advice. You must have an eligible sponsoring host institution in the United Kingdom or Republic of Ireland (RoI) and an eligible sponsor who can guarantee space and resources for the tenure of any award.

Level of Study: Postdoctorate, Research

Type: Fellowship

Value: 1. A basic salary, as determined by the host institution, with an additional Wellcome Trust enhancement. 2. Research expenses, including research assistance if required (normally a graduate research assistant or technician; requests for additional research staff may be considered where fieldwork or clinical studies in a low- or middle-income country are proposed). 3. Overseas allowances where appropriate. 4. Travel and subsistence for scientifically justified visits of up to 1 year.

Length of Study: 5 years

Frequency: Annual

Application Procedure: A preliminary application form should be completed and submitted by the published deadline. It should be sent electronically (as a Word document), with the requested accompanying information, to the appropriate funding stream at the Trust (see website). If successful, you will be invited to submit a full application

Closing Date: 12 May

Funding: Trusts

Additional Information: www.wellcome.ac.uk/funding/schemes/research-career-development-fellowships

For further information contact:

Tel: (44) 20 7611 5757
Email: sciencegrants@wellcome.ac.uk

Research Fellowships

Purpose: Due to the multidisciplinary nature of research on the social and ethical aspects of biomedicine and healthcare, Research Fellowships may provide postdoctoral researchers with support to enable them to obtain research training, either in a new discipline or in a new aspect of their own field, e.g. a humanities scholar who wishes to be trained in social science. In such cases, the requested training must form a substantial component of the proposed research and should not normally be available via the standard funding routes, e.g. by learning new skills as a postdoctoral researcher on a project grant. The requested training should also include methodologies and skills that are new to the applicant. Research training provision can include participation in taught courses, and periods spent in other research groups gaining practical, technical or other skills for introduction to the sponsor's or individual's own group.

Eligibility: You are eligible to apply if you are a postdoctoral scholar who is not in a tenured or otherwise long-term established post. Fellowships must be held at a United Kingdom, Irish or low- or middle-income country institution. You will also be expected to have been awarded your PhD before you are eligible to apply. Applications from candidates who are still awaiting their viva by the time of the full application will not normally be accepted.

Level of Study: Research

Type: Fellowship

Value: An award will not normally exceed £250,000, exclusive of any standard Wellcome Trust allowances. Fellowships provide a salary, plus appropriate employer's contributions. Essential research expenses, including travel and fieldwork, are available, as is a set amount for travel to conferences, seminars and other meetings of a scholarly nature.

Length of Study: 3 years

Application Procedure: Preliminary applications should be made in writing, and include a brief curriculum vitae and full publication list; details of research proposed (maximum of 1 page); a letter of support from the head of department in which you will be working; the approximate cost of the proposal, broken down into equipment and project running expenses.

Funding: Trusts

For further information contact:

Tel: (44) 20 7611 5757
Email: MHgrants@wellcome.ac.uk

Research Fellowships in Humanities and Social Science

Purpose: This scheme supports postdoctoral researchers in health-related humanities and social sciences who do not hold established academic posts.

Level of Study: Postdoctoral

Type: Fellowship

Value: Salary and research expenses covered.

Length of Study: 3 year

Frequency: Annual

Application Procedure: You must submit your application through the Wellcome Trust Grant Tracker (WTGT).

Closing Date: 10 September

For further information contact:

Gibbs Building, 215 Euston Road, London NW1 2BE, United Kingdom.

Tel: (44) 20 7611 5757
Email: hss@wellcome.ac.uk.

Research Training Fellowships

Purpose: Provide support for medical, dental, veterinary and clinical psychology graduates who have little or no research training, but who wish to develop a long-term career in academic medicine.

Eligibility: The fellowship is open to individuals with a relevant connection to the European Economic Area (EEA) for fellowships to be held in a United Kingdom or Republic of Ireland institution. Non-United Kingdom candidates should contact the office for advice before submitting an application. 1. Medical graduates must have passed the relevant exam for their specialty, e.g. MRCP, MRCS, MRCOphth/FRCOphth Part 1, MRCPsych, MRCOG Part 1, MRCPCH, FRCA Part 1. GPs are advised to contact the office to clarify their eligibility. 2. Dental candidates must have obtained MFD, MFDS, MGDS, MFGDP or equivalent. 3. Veterinary candidates should have a degree in veterinary medicine (e.g. BVSc, BVM&S, BVMS, BVetMed, VetMB) and some experience in clinical practice. An intercalated degree is desirable, but not essential. 4. Clinical psychology candidates must have obtained a professional Doctorate-level qualification in Clinical Psychology accredited by the British Psychological Society before taking up the award. Candidates are advised to contact the office to clarify their eligibility. You are expected to undertake a high-quality research project that balances the provision of training with the opportunity to advance knowledge in a given area. A project based solely on a systematic review of a particular area is not suitable, unless it includes a significant element of methodological innovation.

Level of Study: Postgraduate, Research

Type: Fellowship

Value: Fellowships are normally for 2–3 years. In exceptional cases a fellowship may be for up to 4 years for those who wish to undertake a relevant Master's training or diploma course. All training requests must be fully justified in the application. Fellowships provide research expenses (consumables, travel, and support to attend scientific meetings) and a fellow's salary, set according to age, experience and our policy on enhancement.

Length of Study: 2–3 years

Application Procedure: Application form is available from the website.
Funding: Trusts

For further information contact:

Tel: (44) 20 7611 5757
Email: sciencegrants@wellcome.ac.uk

Seeding Drug Discovery

Purpose: To facilitate early-stage small-molecule drug discovery. The awards help applicants with a potential drug target or new chemistry embark on a programme of compound discovery and/or lead optimization.
Level of Study: Research
Type: Award
Value: Early-stage drug discovery projects are able to apply for funding for up to 2 years to facilitate screening of chemical compounds to identify one or more lead series of molecules. Late-stage projects, where a lead compound has already been identified, are able to apply for funding for up to 4 years, to support lead optimization and preclinical development through to clinical trials.
Application Procedure: A preliminary application form should be completed and returned to Technology Transfer by the published deadline. Applications will be considered at one of the two Seeding Drug Discovery Committee meetings in each 12-month period. Successful applicants will be shortlisted and invited to complete a full application.
Funding: Trusts
Additional Information: www.wellcome.ac.uk/what-we-do/directories/seeding-drug-discovery-projects-funded

For further information contact:

Tel: (44) 20 7611 5757
Fax: (44) 20 7611 8857
Email: innovations@wellcome.ac.uk

Senior and Intermediate Research Fellowship for International Students

Purpose: The aim of the fellowship is to support outstanding researchers of any nationality, either medically qualified or science graduates, who wish to pursue a research career in an academic institution in India.
Eligibility: Applicants of any nationality are eligible to apply for the fellowship. Applicants must be basic science/veterinary researchers with 4 -15 years of post-PhD research experience. Applicants must be fluent in English.
Type: Research

Value: The fellowship is for five years and provides the Fellows personal support. Research expenses, including research assistance if required (normally funding for four research staff may be requested). The total award for a Senior Fellowship typically includes the costs requested by the applicant as well as the set contributions by India Alliance. For further details, see costing policies. Costs requested by the applicant must be commensurate with their research proposal and should be fully justified in the full application. Inadequate justifications may result in costs being revised. Time permitted for non-research related activity during the fellowship is normally restricted to a maximum of eight hours each week.
Study Establishment: Fellowship is awarded to support biomedical research that is relevant to human and animal welfare.
Country of Study: India
Application Procedure: See the website
Closing Date: 15 January
Additional Information: For more details please visit the website   https://www.indiaalliance.org/news/sif-call-for-applications

For further information contact:

Email: info@wellcomedbt.org

Senior Fellowships in Public Health and Tropical Medicine

Purpose: This scheme supports outstanding researchers from low- and middle-income countries to establish themselves as leading investigators at an academic institution in a low- and middle-income country location. This fellowship is the most senior of a series of career awards aimed at building sustainable capacity in areas of research that have the potential for increasing health benefits for people and their livestock in low- and middle-income countries. Research projects should be aimed at understanding and controlling diseases (either human or animal) of relevance to local, national or global health.
Eligibility: Candidate must be a graduate in a subject relevant to public health or tropical medicine (for example; biomedical or social science, veterinary medicine, physics, chemistry or mathematics) with a PhD and at least 5 years' postdoctoral experience, or a medical graduate with a higher qualification equivalent to membership of the United Kingdom Royal College of Physicians (i.e. qualified to enter higher specialist training), or be recognized as a specialist within a relevant research area, and have at least 5 years' research experience.
Level of Study: Postgraduate, Research
Type: Fellowship

Value: A basic salary; research expenses (e.g. consumables, equipment, collaborative travel, research assistance, technical support), training costs where appropriate and justified; an inflation/flexible funding allowance and support to attend scientific meetings; and contributions to costs of the project that are directly incurred by the overseas institution may also be provided.

Length of Study: Up to 5 years

Application Procedure: You are required to complete and submit a preliminary application form by the published deadline. The form should be emailed to phatic@wellcome.ac.uk

Funding: Trusts

Additional Information: Overseas allowances will be provided for periods of training or collaborative research spent outside the home institution country, where appropriate. Research-dedicated costs (excluding salary costs) should not exceed £100,000 per year www.advance-africa.com/Fellowships-in-Public-Health-and-Tropical-Medicine.html

For further information contact:

Tel: (44) 20 7611 5757
Email: sciencegrants@wellcome.ac.uk

Senior Research Fellowships in Basic Biomedical Science

Purpose: To provide support for outstanding postdoctoral scientists based in academic institutions in the United Kingdom and Republic of Ireland (RoI).

Eligibility: The fellowship is open to individuals with a relevant connection to the EEA. You should have between 5 and normally 10 years' research experience (from the date of your viva to the date of your preliminary application) at postdoctoral level, or veterinary equivalent, and have a substantial record of publications in your chosen area of research in leading international journals. Candidates that do not hold an established post may apply to remain in their current laboratory, to return to one where they have worked before or to move to a new laboratory in the United Kingdom or Republic of Ireland. Candidates that hold an established post are not eligible to apply for a fellowship to be held at their current employing institution. However, we are willing to consider a preliminary application where a candidate wishes to move institution and is able to make an appropriate justification for the move. The Trust does not normally accept resubmissions of full applications for its fellowships. Please contact the Office for further advice. You must have an eligible sponsor and host institution in the United Kingdom or Republic of Ireland who can guarantee space and resources for the tenure of the award.

Level of Study: Postdoctorate, Research

Type: Fellowship

Value: The fellowship is for 5 years in the first instance, and provides a basic salary, as determined by the host institution (normally up to £55,000 per year) with an additional Trust supplement of £12,500 per year; the essential costs of the research programme (e.g. consumables, equipment, research assistance, overseas allowances, collaborative travel and subsistence); an inflation and Flexible Funding Allowance; and support to attend scientific meetings.

Frequency: Annual

Application Procedure: A preliminary application form should be completed and submitted electronically (as a Word document) to the relevant funding stream (see website) no later than the published deadline. Full application forms will usually be sent to shortlisted candidates within 1 month of the preliminary deadline. In the full application, if invited, the host institution will be required to confirm that it will support a successful renewal of the fellowship under the shared funding arrangement for the full period of any renewal.

Funding: Trusts

Additional Information: Refer to the website www.wellcome.ac.uk/funding/biomedical-science/funding-schemes/fellowships/basic-biomedical-fellowships/wtd004442.htm

For further information contact:

Tel: (44) 20 7611 5757
Email: sciencegrants@wellcome.ac.uk

Senior Research Fellowships in Clinical Science

Purpose: This scheme provides support for clinical investigators to further develop their research potential and to establish themselves as leading investigators in clinical academic medicine.

Eligibility: You must have a relevant connection to the EEA. If you are a non-United Kingdom candidate, please contact the Office for advice before submitting a preliminary application. You should be a clinical scientist with a medical, dental, veterinary or clinical psychology qualification and will normally have no more than 15 years' clinical and research experience from the date of your first medical, dental, veterinary or British Psychological Society-accredited psychology qualification. (Due allowance will be given to those whose career has been affected by a late start or interruption for personal/family reasons.) Successful candidates will have made significant progress towards establishing themselves as independent clinical investigators. A research degree (PhD/MD), together with evidence of advanced (postdoctoral) research training (typically at least 3–5 years), is expected. They will have published consistently

W

in their chosen area of research, placing substantive papers in leading journals. Candidates will not normally hold a tenured academic post in a university in the United Kingdom or Republic of Ireland, or a consultant post in the NHS.

Level of Study: Postgraduate, Research

Type: Fellowship

Value: The fellowship is for 5 years in the first instance, and provides a basic salary, as determined by the host institution; research expenses; an inflation allowance and support to attend scientific meetings; provision for public engagement cost.

Frequency: Annual

Application Procedure: A preliminary application form should be completed and submitted by the published deadline. It should be sent electronically (as a Word document), with the requested accompanying information, to the appropriate funding stream at the Trust (see website). Incomplete or incorrectly completed forms will not be accepted. Faxed applications will not be accepted. Please do not send any additional material. You will be notified in writing of your success, or otherwise, in reaching the next round of the competition. In some instances, we may recommend that candidates apply for an Intermediate Clinical Fellowship.

Funding: Trusts

For further information contact:

Tel: (44) 20 7611 5757
Email: sciencegrants@wellcome.ac.uk

Short-term Research Leave Awards for Clinicians and Scientists

Purpose: This scheme enables clinicians, scientists and other healthcare professionals to undertake up to 6 months (FTE) of research at a centre or department with academic expertise in medical humanities, to explore the wider determinants and contexts of their own medical and scientific work.

Eligibility: You should be a scientist, clinician or healthcare professional holding an established post to which you would return on completion of the award. You must be resident in the United Kingdom or Republic of Ireland. You should have a record of publication in medical or scientific journals.

Level of Study: Research

Type: Award

Value: We will provide the salary of a locum or replacement lecturer for the duration of the award, and a set amount for travel to conferences.

Length of Study: Up to 6 months

Application Procedure: You should submit a preliminary application in writing, including a brief curriculum vitae, a full publication list and confirmation that your personal support is from the Higher Education Funding Council;

details of the research proposed (maximum one page); details of hours spent on teaching and administration; the approximate cost of the proposal, broken down into staff salaries, equipment and running expenses.

Closing Date: 23 January

Funding: Trusts

For further information contact:

Tel: (44) 20 7611 5757
Email: MHgrants@wellcome.ac.uk

Sir Henry Wellcome Postdoctoral Fellowships

Purpose: To provide a unique opportunity for the most promising newly qualified postdoctoral researchers to make an early start in developing their independent research careers, working in the best laboratories in the United Kingdom and overseas.

Eligibility: These awards are open to individuals with a relevant connection to the European Economic Area. You must be in the final year of your PhD studies or have no more than 1 year of postdoctoral research experience from the date of your PhD viva to the full application submission deadline (e.g. if the full deadline is in February, your viva should not have occurred prior to last February). Time spent outside the research environment will be taken into consideration. You must have an eligible sponsoring institution in the United Kingdom or Republic of Ireland that will administer the fellowship for the full duration of the award.

Level of Study: Postdoctorate, Research

Type: Fellowships

Value: 4 year full-time fellowship. Provides an award of £250,000.

Length of Study: 4 years

Frequency: Annual

Application Procedure: You should complete and submit a preliminary application form by the published deadline. It should be sent electronically (as a Word document), with the requested accompanying information, to the relevant funding stream at the Trust. Your preliminary application will be assessed within 4 weeks of the submission deadline. If successful, you will be invited to submit a full application. Your full application will be peer reviewed by the relevant Funding Committee and, if successful, you will be shortlisted for interview.

Funding: Trusts

Additional Information: www.wellcome.ac.uk/funding/schemes/sir-henry-wellcome-postdoctoral-fellowships

For further information contact:

Tel: (44) 20 7611 5757
Email: sciencegrants@wellcome.ac.uk

Strategic Awards in Biomedical Science

Purpose: Strategic awards provide flexible forms of support to excellent research groups with outstanding track records in their field.

Eligibility: Applications will be considered from principal applicants who meet our eligibility criteria and are recognized international leaders in their field.

Level of Study: Research

Type: Award

Value: It provides equipment, support staff, consumables, training programmes, networking, biological, clinical or epidemiological research resources. Limited capital building or refurbishment essential to the programme can also be requested.

Length of Study: Awards are normally for 5 years

Application Procedure: You (prospective applicant) are required to submit a preliminary application, which should include the following information 1. Your track record, you must complete the curriculum vitae pages (these are questions 14 and 15 from the standard project grant application form); 2. High-level aims and objectives, and how the proposal addresses the strategic challenges in the Wellcome Trust's Strategic Plan (maximum of two pages); 3. Key targets, milestones and management structures, if appropriate (maximum of two pages); 4. Duration of support requested and outline costings broken down into main headings (e.g. staff, equipment); 5. A statement from the head of the institution, indicating how the proposal fits within the context of the institution's strategic vision and what financial commitment the institution will make to the group if the application is successful. If your preliminary application is successful, you will be invited to submit a full application. The relevant form will be provided at this time.

Funding: Trusts

Additional Information: www.wellcome.ac.uk/what-we-do/directories/science-strategic-awards-people-funded

For further information contact:

Tel: (44) 20 7611 5757
Email: sciencegrants@wellcome.ac.uk

The Hub Award

Purpose: The Hub Award brings researchers and creative professionals together at Wellcome Collection to work as a collaborative residency.

Type: Award

Value: Flexible funding, up to £1 million

Length of Study: 1 to 2 year

Frequency: Annual

Application Procedure: You must submit your application through the Wellcome Trust Grant Tracker (WTGT).

Closing Date: 20 February

For further information contact:

Gibbs Building, 215 Euston Road, London NW1 2BE, United Kingdom.

Tel: (44) 20 7611 5757

Training Fellowships in Public Health and Tropical Medicine

Purpose: This scheme provides researchers from low- and middle-income countries–who are at an early stage in the establishment of their research careers–with opportunities for research experience and high-quality research training in public health and tropical medicine. Research projects should be aimed at understanding and controlling diseases (either human or animal) of relevance to local, national or global health. This can include laboratory-based molecular analysis of field or clinical samples, but projects focused solely on studies in vitro or using animal models will not normally be considered under this scheme.

Eligibility: Applications are only accepted in the Public Health and Tropical Medicine Interview Committee remit. This covers research on infectious and non-communicable diseases within the fields of public health and tropical medicine that is aimed at understanding and controlling diseases (either human or animal) of relevance to local, national or global health. You must be a national or legal resident of a low- and middle-income country and should be either 1. A graduate in a subject relevant to public health or tropical medicine (e.g. biomedical or social science, veterinary medicine, physics, chemistry or mathematics) with a PhD and no more than 3 years' postdoctoral experience, or 2. A medical graduate with a higher qualification equivalent to membership of the United Kingdom Royal Colleges of Physicians (i.e. qualified to enter higher specialist training) and some initial research experience. Applicants may also apply if they do not have a PhD, but have a clinical, basic or Master's degree and some initial research experience, with the expectation that they will register for a PhD.

Level of Study: Postgraduate, Research

Type: Fellowship

Value: Usually £15,000 to £300,000 for salary, fees and research expenses.

Length of Study: 3 years

Application Procedure: You are required to complete and submit a preliminary application form by the published deadline. The form should be emailed to phatic@wellcome.ac.uk

Closing Date: 9 July

Funding: Trusts

Additional Information: www.scholarshipportal.com/schol arship/wellcome-trust-training-fellowships-in-public-health-and-tropical-medicine

For further information contact:

Tel: (44) 20 7611 5757
Email: sciencegrants@wellcome.ac.uk

Translation Fund

Purpose: Translation Awards are response-mode funding designed to bridge the funding gap in the commercialisation of new technologies in the biomedical area.

Eligibility: Projects must address an unmet need in healthcare or in applied medical research, offer a potential new solution, and have a realistic expectation that the innovation will be developed further by the market. Institutions: Eligible institutions are not-for-profit research institutions, including those funded by the Medical Research Council, Cancer Research United Kingdom, and Biotechnology and Biological Sciences Research Council, in the United Kingdom. Institutions are normally required to sign up to a short funding agreement and the Grant Conditions. Companies: We are able to use our charitable monies to fund commercial companies to meet our charitable objectives through programme-related investment (PRI). For further details please refer to our policy on PRI. Companies will normally be expected to sign up to specific terms relating to the scheme. Overseas organizations: United Kingdom organizations may contract or collaborate with overseas organizations. Although overseas organizations are not eligible for Translation Awards, some proposals may be invited for consideration as a Strategic Translation Award (including Seeding Drug Discovery). Overseas organizations should contact Technology Transfer staff about their proposed project in the first instance. Principal applicants and coapplicants applicants should normally hold a position of responsibility within the eligible organization and be able to sign up to or comply with the conditions or terms of an award. In addition, postdoctoral research assistants–whether seeking their own salary as part of the grant proposal, funded by the Wellcome Trust on another grant, or funded by another agency–are eligible for coapplicant status if they make a significant contribution to a research proposal and have agreement from their funding agency. Other eligibility information: Disciplines outside biomedicine – researchers from disciplines outside biomedicine can apply providing the application of research is designed to facilitate or meet a need in healthcare. For example, the application of physics, chemistry, computing, engineering and materials science to the development of medical products is entirely appropriate.

Healthcare need in an area that is not commercially attractive. We are committed to the translation of research into practical healthcare benefits across the full spectrum of disease. Disease areas neglected by industry because of the lack of a return on investment pose a particular problem, but imaginative ways forward can sometimes be developed (e.g. public-private partnerships such as the Medicines for Malaria Venture). Intellectual property rights (IPR)/publications – if there are any restrictions on IPR or publications arising from your research, you must provide a written statement that details them. Restrictions on intellectual property may affect your eligibility to apply to the Trust. Please refer to our Grant Conditions.

Level of Study: Research

Type: Award

Value: The important criterion is to develop the innovation to the point at which it can be adopted by another party. Providing it is adequately justified, modest equipment purchase and maintenance costs may be included in a Translation Award application. Building or refurbishment expenditure will not normally be considered. Applications may not include requests for academic institutional overheads. If you hold a tenured university post, you may not re-charge your salary (in full or part) to a Translation Award.

Application Procedure: A preliminary application form must be completed and sent to Technology Transfer by the published deadline. Preliminary applications are subject to a triage for shortlisting for the full application stage. Applications will be considered by the Technology Transfer Challenge Committee (TTCC), which meets twice a year. Full applications will be invited following the triage meeting. Shortlisted applicants will be invited to submit a full application and will be subject to international peer review and due diligence. Applicants will be expected to make a presentation on their proposal to the TTCC. Unless otherwise advised, this will be at the next scheduled meeting of the TTCC.

Funding: Trusts

Additional Information: www.erc-online.eu/financial-support/translation-fund/

For further information contact:

Tel: (44) 20 7611 5757
Fax: (44) 20 7611 8857
Email: innovations@wellcome.ac.uk

Translational Medicine and Therapeutics Programmes

Purpose: This flagship scheme established four high-quality integrated research training programmes for clinicians in translational medicine and therapeutics. The programmes have been developed around a unique partnership between academic and industrial partners. Support for the programmes has been provided to the host institutions by GlaxoSmithKline, Wyeth Research, Roche, AstraZeneca, Sanofi-Aventis, Sirtris Pharmaceuticals and PTC Therapeutics.

Eligibility: You should have demonstrated the potential to pursue a career as an academic clinician. It is anticipated that many applicants will have already commenced their specialist training, but this is not essential.

Level of Study: Postgraduate, Research

Value: Includes a clinical salary, PhD registration fees at United Kingdom/EU rate, research expenses, contribution towards travel, and a contribution towards training costs.

Length of Study: Support varies

Frequency: Annual

Application Procedure: If you are interested in applying, you should contact the relevant programme. Please see website for details.

Closing Date: October

Funding: Trusts

For further information contact:

Email: j.williams@wellcome.ac.uk

University Awards

Purpose: This scheme allows universities to attract outstanding research staff by providing support for up to 5 years, after which time the award holder takes up a guaranteed permanent post in the university. A monograph and other substantial publications are expected to result from an award, so teaching and other non-research commitments are expected to be minimal during the period of full Wellcome Trust support.

Eligibility: You must be nominated by your prospective head of department and have an undertaking from the head of the institution, vice-chancellor, principal or dean that your personal support will be taken over by the institution at the end of the award. Support is normally available only at lecturer level, although in exceptional cases awards to senior-lecturer level may be possible.

Level of Study: Research

Type: Award

Value: Up to 5 years' support is available, providing your full salary for 3 years, 50% in the fourth year and 25% in the fifth year. Travel expenses to attend meetings are provided for 5 years, but research expenses are provided for the first 3 years of the award only.

Application Procedure: Initial enquiries about the scheme may be made by you (the potential candidate) or a department in an institution. These enquiries should be followed by a preliminary application from you by email or post including an explicit statement from the head of the institution, vice-chancellor or dean demonstrating the institution's commitment to the history of medicine field, and a statement confirming that the institution will provide 50% salary costs in year four, 75% in year 5 and full salary thereafter; curriculum vitae and full publication list; an outline of no more than two pages of the proposed project; a letter of support from the head of department, including a statement on your expected teaching/administrative load for the 5-year period (this can be sent by separate cover); the approximate cost of the proposal, broken down into your salary, equipment and project running costs.

Funding: Trusts

Additional Information: www.studentaffairs.ku.edu/university-awards

For further information contact:

Tel: (44) 20 7611 5757

Email: MHgrants@wellcome.ac.uk

Wellcome Discovery Awards

Purpose: This scheme provides funding for established researchers and teams from any discipline who want to pursue bold and creative research ideas to deliver significant shifts in understanding that could improve human life, health and wellbeing.

Length of Study: 8 years

Country of Study: Any country

Closing Date: 24 March

Additional Information: If you have a question about eligibility, what we offer or our funding remit, contact our grants information officers: wellcome.org/who-we-are/contact-us/funding-enquiry and (44) 20 7611 5757

For further information contact:

Tel: (44) 20 7611 5757

Wellcome Early-Career Awards

Purpose: This scheme provides funding for early-career researchers from any discipline who are ready to develop their research identity. Through innovative projects, they will deliver shifts in understanding that could improve human life, health and wellbeing. By the end of the award, they will be ready to lead their own independent research programme.

Level of Study: Postgraduate

Type: Award

Value: Up to £400,000
Length of Study: 5 years
Frequency: Annual
Country of Study: Any country
Closing Date: 15 February
Additional Information: If you have a question about eligibility, what we offer or our funding remit, contact our grants information officers: wellcome.org/who-we-are/contact-us/funding-enquiry and (44) 20 7611 5757 https://wellcome.org/grant-funding/schemes/discovery-awards

For further information contact:

Tel: (44) 20 7611 5757

Wellcome Trust and NIH Four-Year PhD Studentships

Purpose: This scheme provides opportunities for the most promising postgraduate students to undertake international, collaborative four-year PhD training based in both a United Kingdom/Republic of Ireland (RoI) academic institution and the intramural campus of the National Institutes of Health at Bethesda (Maryland, United States of America).
Eligibility: You should be a United Kingdom/European Economic Area (EEA) national with (or be in your final year and expected to obtain) a first- or upper-second-class honours degree or an equivalent EEA graduate qualification. You must have 1. A suitable doctoral supervisor at an eligible academic host institution in the United Kingdom or Republic of Ireland. The host institution must be able to confer doctoral degrees; 2. A suitable supervisor at a NIH institute. The NIH supervisor should hold a tenured or tenured-track position for the proposed period of the award and should be willing to provide funding for the student whilst at the NIH.
Level of Study: Doctorate, Research
Type: Studentship
Value: The studentship is awarded for 4 years with support provided by the Wellcome Trust (in the United Kingdom/Republic of Ireland) and the NIH (in the United States of America). Our funding will provide support for the student's stipend, PhD fees, college fees (if required) and a contribution towards research costs.
Length of Study: 4 year
Frequency: Annual
Application Procedure: The application form should be completed and submitted by the closing date. An electronic copy (as a Word document) should be emailed to wtnih@wellcome.ac.uk
Funding: Trusts

For further information contact:

Wellcome Trust-NIH PhD Studentships, Wellcome Trust, Gibbs Building, 215 Euston Road, Bloomsbury, London NW1 2BE, United Kingdom.

Email: wtnih@wellcome.ac.uk

Wellcome Trust-POST Fellowships in Medical History and Humanities

Purpose: This scheme enables a PhD student or junior fellow funded through the Wellcome Trust Medical History and Humanities (MHH) programme to undertake a 3-month fellowship at the Parliamentary Office of Science and Technology (POST).
Eligibility: Applicants should be in the second or third year of their PhD or in the first year of a fellowship funded by the MHH Programme. POST is a strictly non-partisan organization. Wellcome Trust-POST Fellows will be required to abstain from any lobbying or party political activity, and generally uphold the principles of parliamentary service, including a commitment to confidentiality, during their time with the Office. All provisionally selected candidates must sign a declaration to this effect. They must also receive security clearance from the parliamentary security authorities as a condition of finally taking up the fellowship.
Level of Study: Postdoctorate, Research
Type: Fellowship
Value: The successful applicant will receive a fully funded 3-month extension to their PhD or fellowship award. While placements typically last 3-months, they may be extended under exceptional circumstances. If the successful applicant is not within reasonable daily travelling distance to POST in London, the Wellcome Trust will consider paying travel and accommodation costs up to a maximum of £2,000.
Frequency: Annual
Application Procedure: An application should include the application form, your curriculum vitae, a letter of support from your sponsor/supervisor and a summary of a proposed topic for a POST publication. The summary should be no longer than 1,000 words and should demonstrate why you think this subject would be of particular parliamentary interest; how the training you have received and your research to date will enable you to carry out this work; your ability to write in a style suitable for a parliamentary (rather than an academic) audience.
Closing Date: 23 November
Funding: Trusts
Additional Information: Check website for more details www.studentaffairs.ku.edu/university-awards

For further information contact:

Tel: (44) 20 7611 5757
Email: MHgrants@wellcome.ac.uk

Wells Mountain Foundation

25 Main Street, Bristol, VT 05443, United States of America.

Tel: (1) 877 318 6116
Website: www.wellsmountaininitiative.org/

WMF is a non-profit, tax-exempt charity qualified of the US Internal Revenue Code. Wells Mountain Foundation has as its focus education, which they believe is the key building block to success in all other endeavors, literacy, the essential tie to the knowledge contained in the written word, and community, the core entity, just beyond the family, critical to building a compassionate and effective society.

Woodcock-Munoz Foundation Empowerment Through Education Scholarships

Purpose: The Foundation believes in the power and importance of community service; therefore, all scholarship participants are required to volunteer for a minimum of 100 hours a year.
Eligibility: The requirements are 1. Successfully completed a secondary education, with good to excellent grades. 2. Is 35 or under on March 1, 2021. 3. Will be studying in his or her country or another country in the developing world. 4. Is pursuing his or her first bachelor's degree or diploma. 5. Will be enrolled in a program of study that will benefit the community and contribute to the continued growth and advancement of his or her home country. 6. Plans to live and work in his or her own country after graduation. 7. Has demonstrated his or her commitment to giving back and has volunteered prior to applying. 8. May have some other funds available for his or her education, but will not be able to go to pursue his or her tertiary degree without financial assistance.
Level of Study: Graduate
Type: Scholarship
Value: Average of US$1,500 for tuition and fee, books and materials.
Frequency: Annual
Country of Study: United States of America
Application Procedure: 1. You will be redirected to a portal where you will be asked to create a free account (username and password), fill out information and upload documents. 2. We strongly suggest that you apply online as it will provide you with the opportunity to save your work and return multiple times. You will also guarantee that your application, once submitted online, will be received and reviewed.
Closing Date: 1 March
Funding: Private

Wenner-Gren Foundation for Anthropological Research

655 Third Avenue, 23rd Floor, New York, NY 10017, United States of America.

Tel: (1) 212 683 5000
Email: inquiries@wennergren.org
Website: www.wennergren.org

The Wenner-Gren Foundation for Anthropological Research, Inc. is a private operating foundation dedicated to the advancement of anthropology throughout the world. Located in New York City, it is one of the major international funding sources for anthropological research and is actively engaged with the anthropological community through its varied grant, fellowship, conference, and capacity building programs.

Hunt Postdoctoral Fellowships

Purpose: To support the writing-up of already completed research.
Eligibility: 1. Applicants must have a Ph.D. or equivalent at the time of application. 2. Applicants should be no more than ten years beyond their PhD, with allowances made for periods of caregiving, and have a doctorate in anthropology or an equivalent field. 3. Qualified scholars are eligible without regard to nationality, institutional, or departmental affiliation although preference is given to applicants who are untenured or do not yet have a permanent academic position. 4. The Hunt Postdoctoral Fellowship is to support a continuous period of full-time academic writing. The research that forms the basis of the writing project is expected to be completed at the time of application. In special circumstances and with prior approval of the Foundation, recipients may use part of their stipend for a minor research component if necessary to complete their proposed publication/s. No research funds in addition to the basic stipend are available as part of the Hunt Postdoctoral Fellowship. 5. The fellowship may be used to support the preparation of a book or monograph manuscript,

journal articles, book chapters, or a combination of these forms of publication. 6. The Foundation cannot accept an application from a prior grantee unless all requirements of a previous grant have been completed. Please contact the Foundation for more information if this situation applies. 7. Prior recipients of Hunt Postdoctoral Fellowships are not eligible to apply for a second fellowship for a different writing project. 8. Hunt Postdoctoral Fellowship applications that were unsuccessful in a prior funding cycle may be resubmitted only twice. A resubmission statement explaining how the application is different from the prior application and how the referees' comments have been addressed must accompany resubmitted applications. 9. If a fellowship is awarded, the applicant must agree to comply with the Requirements and Conditions of the Hunt Postdoctoral Fellowship.

Level of Study: Postdoctorate
Type: Fellowship
Value: Up to US$40,000
Length of Study: Nine-month
Frequency: Annual
Country of Study: Any country
Application Procedure: Applications can be downloaded from the website and must be submitted online. See website: www.wennergren.org/programs/hunt-postdoctoral-fellowships/application-procedures
No. of awards offered: 89
Closing Date: 1 May
No. of awards given last year: 9
No. of applicants last year: 89

For further information contact:

Email: applications@wennergren.org

Wharton School

Vance Hall, Suite 111, 3733 Spruce Street, Philadelphia, PA 19104-6340, United States of America.

Tel: (1) 215 898 6183
Email: mba.admissions@wharton.upenn.edu
Website: www.wharton.upenn.edu/mba/catalog

The Wharton School of the University of Pennsylvania was a remarkable innovation when Joseph Wharton, a self-educated 19th-century industrialist, first proposed its establishment more than 135 years ago. Wharton School has continued innovating to meet mounting global demand for new ideas, deeper insights, and transformative leadership.

Wharton Executive MBA Programme

Length of Study: 2 years
Country of Study: Any country
Application Procedure: Applicants may apply online or contact Wharton for information.

For further information contact:

The Wharton School Executive MBA Programme, University of PA, 224 Steinberg Conference Centre, 255 South 38th Street, Philadelphia, PA 19104-6359, United States of America.

Tel: (1) 215 898 5887
Fax: (1) 215 898 2598
Email: wemba-admissions@wharton.upenn.edu

Whitehall Foundation, Inc.

PO Box 3423, Palm Beach, FL 33480, United States of America.

Tel: (1) 561 655 4474
Email: email@whitehall.org
Website: www.whitehall.org
Contact: Ms Catherine Thomas, Corporate Secretary

The Whitehall Foundation, Inc. through its programme of grants and grants-in-aid, assists scholarly research in the life sciences. It is the Foundation's policy to assist those dynamic areas of basic biological research that are not heavily supported by federal agencies or other foundations with specialized missions.

Whitehall Foundation Grants-in-Aid

Purpose: To better understand behavioural output or brain mechanisms of behaviour.
Eligibility: Open to researchers at the assistant professor level who have experienced difficulty in competing for research funds as they have not yet become firmly established. Senior scientists may also apply.
Level of Study: Research
Type: Research grant one year
Value: Up to US$30,000
Length of Study: 1 year
Frequency: Annual
Country of Study: United States of America

Application Procedure: Applicants must contact the Foundation.
Funding: Private
Additional Information: For up to date policy, application information and important calendar deadlines please refer to the website www.whitehall.org/applying/

For further information contact:

Email: email@whitehall.org

Whitehall Foundation Research Grants

Purpose: To better understand behavioural output or brain mechanisms of behaviour.
Eligibility: Open to established scientists of all ages working at accredited institutions in the United States of America. The principal investigator must hold no less than the position of assistant professor, or the equivalent, in order to make an application. The Foundation does not award funds to investigators who have substantial existing or potential support.
Level of Study: Research
Type: Research grant one year
Value: US$30,000–US$75,000 per year.
Length of Study: Up to 3 years
Frequency: Annual
Country of Study: Any country
Application Procedure: Please visit web-site @ www.white hall.org
Funding: Private
Additional Information: For up to date policy, application information and important calendar deadlines, please refer to the website www.whitehall.org/grants/

For further information contact:

Email: email@whitehall.org

Wilfrid Laurier University

75 University Avenue West, Waterloo, ON N2L 3C5, Canada.

Tel: (1) 519 884 1970
Email: webservices@wlu.ca.
Website: www.wlu.ca
Contact: Mr Al Hecht, International Relations

Laurier traces its roots to the opening of the Evangelical Lutheran Seminary in Waterloo more than 100 years ago in 1911. We have gone through several changes since then, and in 1973 our name changed from Waterloo Lutheran University to Wilfrid Laurier University. A Laurier education is about building the whole person: mind, body and spirit. We believe that your university career must lead to more than just a job to be considered a success; Laurier creates engaged and aware citizens in a culture that inspires lives of leadership and purpose.

Viessmann/Marburg Travel Scholarship

Purpose: To assist students wanting to study in Germany.
Level of Study: Postgraduate
Type: Scholarship
Value: €767
Length of Study: 1 year
Frequency: Annual
Study Establishment: An approved place of study in Marburg.
Country of Study: Germany
Application Procedure: Contact University
Closing Date: 2 July

Wilfrid Laurier University President

Purpose: To reward significant contribution to the community as a volunteer or to the discipline as a scholar.
Eligibility: Full-time undergraduate students entering year 1. Minimum overall average of 95% in best six Grade 12 U and/or Grade 12 M courses or Ontario Academic Credits (OACs) (or equivalent).
Level of Study: Postgraduate
Type: Scholarship
Value: C$23,000 (C$3,000 1st year; renewable based on academic performance for up to 4 years at C$5,000 per year) 4th year of renewal eligibility for approved 5-year undergraduate programs only.
Length of Study: 1 year
Frequency: Annual
Study Establishment: Laurier University
Country of Study: Canada
Application Procedure: Apply online.
Funding: Trusts
Contributor: Dr Neale H. Taylor

For further information contact:

Email: fgps@wlu.ca

W

Wingate Scholarships

2nd Floor, 20-22 Stukeley Street, London WC2B 5LR, United Kingdom.

Tel: (1) 800 755 5550
Email: enquiries@wingate.org.uk
Website: www.wingatescholarships.org.uk
Contact: Ms Sarah Mitchell, Administrator

Wingate Scholarships have been offered by the Foundation since 1988 but the Foundation itself was first established by my father as long ago as 1960. Over the years when he was building up Chesterfield Properties, his commercial property and cinema-cum-theatre business, the Foundation became a major shareholder of this company. The first significant donation by the Foundation was in the late 1970s and was to the Royal London Hospital. It also funds an annual Book Prize in association with the Jewish Quarterly. There are currently six trustees, four from the family, who meet quarterly to decide on which organisations or projects, which have applied for grants, should receive them.

Wingate Scholarships

Purpose: To fund creative or original work of intellectual, scientific, artistic, social or environmental value and advanced music study.
Eligibility: Open to United Kingdom, Commonwealth, former Commonwealth, Israeli. Also open to European Union and Council of Europe country citizens provided that they are and have been resident in the United Kingdom for at least 3 years at start of award. Applicants must be over 24 years of age. No upper age limit is prescribed. No academic qualifications are necessary. Applications must be made in United Kingdom from a valid United Kingdom address.
Level of Study: Doctorate, Postdoctorate, Postgraduate, Research
Type: Scholarship
Value: Costs of a project, which may last for up to 3 years, to a maximum of United Kingdom £10,000 in any 1 year.
Length of Study: 1–3 years
Frequency: Annual
Study Establishment: Any approved institute or independent research
Country of Study: Any country
Application Procedure: Applicants must be living in United Kingdom during the period of application. Applications from a valid United Kingdom address only are acceptable. Applicants must complete online application form from the website. Applicants must be able to satisfy the Scholarship Committee that they need financial support to undertake the work projected, and show why the proposed work (if it takes the form of academic research) is unlikely to attract Research Council, British Academy or any other major agency funding if they are United Kingdom applicants. All applications require two references to be submitted independently. Guidance is available on the website.
No. of awards offered: 228
Closing Date: 1 February
Funding: Foundation
Contributor: HHW Foundation
No. of awards given last year: 39
No. of applicants last year: 228
Additional Information: The scholarships are not awarded for professional qualifications, taught courses or electives, or in the following subject areas: performing arts, fine art, business studies. Practising musicians (not composers) are eligible for advanced training, but apart from that, all applicants must have projects that are personal to them and involve either creative or original work. Only postgraduate students in their final two years can apply for scholarships to enable them to undertake field work, or in exceptional circumstances where an award has been withdrawn or closed, to complete a PhD. Applications for studies or projects undertaken post doctorally are eligible, but not postdoctoral fellowship posts per se. Applicant must be based in United Kingdom when applying www.tau.ac.il/acad-sec/grantsite/abroad/britania%20wingate.htm

For further information contact:

Email: emma@shrimsley.com

Winston Churchill Foundation of the United States of America

600 Madison Avenue, Suite 1601, New York, NY 10022-1737, United States of America.

Tel: (1) 212 752 3200
Email: info@churchillscholarship.org
Website: www.churchillscholarship.org
Contact: Mr Michael Morse, Executive Director

Carl Gilbert, chairman of the Gillette Company, became the first Chairman of the Winston Churchill Foundation of the United States, which was established as a 501 (c) (3) US charity in 1959. In its early years, the Foundation made small travel grants to Churchill Overseas Fellows, distinguished senior faculty who would spend one year at the College. In the 1980s, funding was raised during gala dinners at which the

Foundation granted the Churchill Award to an individual who has made outstanding contributions exemplifying Churchill's attributes and ideals. Today, the Scholarship is supported through a combination of the Foundation's investment reserves and through individual donations.

Churchill Scholarship

Purpose: The Churchill Scholarship provides funding to American students for a year of Master's study at the University of Cambridge, based at Churchill College. The program was set up at the request of Sir Winston Churchill in order to fulfill his vision of United States–United Kingdom scientific exchange with the goal of advancing science and technology on both sides of the Atlantic, helping to ensure our future prosperity and security.
Eligibility: Please check Eligibility before you apply: www.churchillscholarship.org/eligibility.html
Type: Fellowship/Scholarship
Value: US$55,000
Length of Study: 1 year
Frequency: Annual
Country of Study: United Kingdom
Application Procedure: Must be nominated by undergraduate institution.
No. of awards offered: 105
Closing Date: 2 November
No. of awards given last year: 15
No. of applicants last year: 105
Additional Information: www.churchillscholarship.org/apply.html

For further information contact:

600 Madison Avenue, Suite 1601, New York, NY 10022, United States of America.

Tel: (1) 212 752 3200
Email: info@churchillscholarship.org

Winterthur

Winterthur Museum, Garden and Library, 5105 Kennett Pike, Winterthur, DE 19735, United States of America.

Tel: (1) 800 448 3883
Email: tourinfo@winterthur.org
Website: www.winterthur.org
Contact: Thomas A. Guiler, Manager and Instructor, Academic Programmes

Winterthur is set amidst a 1,000-acre preserve of rolling meadows and woodlands. Designed by du Pont, its 60-acre naturalistic garden is among America's best, with magnificent specimen plantings and massed displays of color. Graduate programs and a preeminent research library make Winterthur an important center for the study of American art and culture.

Winterthur Dissertation Research Fellowships

Purpose: To encourage the use of Winterthur's collections for critical inquiry that will further the understanding of American history and visual and material culture.
Level of Study: Research
Type: Fellowship
Value: US$7,000 per semesters
Length of Study: 1–2 semesters
Frequency: Annual
Country of Study: United States of America
Application Procedure: Applicants can download application form from the website.
Closing Date: 15 January
Funding: Foundation
Contributor: Winterthur
No. of awards given last year: 4
Additional Information: www.winterthur.org/education/academic-programs/research-fellowships/fellowships-available/

For further information contact:

Winterthur Museum Garden & Library, 5105 Kennett Pike, Winterthur, DE 19735, United States of America.

Email: academicprograms@winterthur.org

Winterthur Postdoctoral Fellowships

Purpose: To encourage the use of Winterthur's collections for critical inquiry that will further the understanding of American history and visual and material culture.
Eligibility: Open to scholars who hold the PhD degree, pursuing advanced research.
Level of Study: Postdoctorate, Research
Type: Fellowships
Value: Up to US$4,200 per month.
Length of Study: 4 months
Frequency: Annual
Country of Study: United States of America
Application Procedure: Applicants can download the application form from the website.
Closing Date: 15 January

Funding: Foundation
Contributor: Winterthur
No. of awards given last year: 2
Additional Information: www.winterthur.org/education/
academic-programs/research-fellowships/fellowships-
available/

For further information contact:

Winterthur Museum Garden & Library, 5105 Kennett Pike,
Winterthur, DE 19735, United States of America.

Tel: (1) 800 448 3883
Email: tguiler@winterthur.org.

Winterthur Research Fellowships

Purpose: To encourage the use of Winterthur's collections for
critical inquiry that will further the understanding of Ameri-
can history and visual and material culture.
Eligibility: Open to scholars pursuing advanced research.
Level of Study: Research
Type: Fellowship
Value: US$1,750 per month
Length of Study: 1–3 months
Frequency: Annual
Country of Study: United States of America
Application Procedure: Applicants can download the appli-
cation form from the website.
Closing Date: 15 January
Funding: Foundation
Contributor: Winterthur
No. of awards given last year: 21

For further information contact:

Email: researchapplication@winterthur.org

Wolf Blass Wines International

97 Sturt Highway, Nuriootpa, SA 5355, Australia.

Tel: (61) 8 8568 7311
Email: visitorcentre@wolfblass.com.au
Website: www.wolfblass.com.au/brands/wolfblass/index.
                asp

Wolf Blass Wines International is a public listed company and
one of the Australia's top sellers of red and white wine.

Wolf Blass Australian Winemaking Independent Study Scholarship

Purpose: To support independent study related to
winemaking in Australia.
Eligibility: Open to culinary professional to conduct research
and writing related to Australian winemaking and culinary
traditions.
Type: Scholarship
Value: AU$5,000
Country of Study: Australia
Application Procedure: All applicants are required to
include a project proposal, an itemized budget detailing the
use of this award and a tentative travel schedule with dates
and locations. Check website for further details.
Additional Information: Applicant is additionally required
to provide a current resume to qualify for this scholarship
www.winterthur.org/education/academic-programs/research-
fellowships/fellowships-available/

Wolfsonian-Florida International University

1001 Washington Avenue, Miami Beach, FL 33139, United
States of America.

Tel: (1) 305 531 1001
Email: info@thewolf.fiu.edu
Website: www.wolfsonian.org
Contact: Mr Jonathan Mogul, Fellowship Co-ordinator

The Wolfsonian-Florida International University or The
Wolfsonian-FIU, located in the heart of the Art Deco District of Miami Beach, Florida, is a museum, library and
research center that uses its collection to illustrate the per-
suasive power of art and design. For fifteen years, The
Wolfsonian has been a division within Florida International
University.

Wolfsonian-FIU Fellowship

Purpose: To conduct research on the Wolfsonian's collection
of objects and library materials from the period 1885 to 1945,
including decorative arts, works on paper, books and
ephemera.
Eligibility: The programme is open to holders of Master's or
doctoral degrees, PhD candidates, and to others who have
a record of significant professional achievement in relevant
fields.

Level of Study: Doctorate, Postdoctorate, Professional development

Type: Fellowship

Value: A stipend, accommodations, round-trip travel

Length of Study: 3–4 weeks

Frequency: Annual

Study Establishment: The Wolfsonian-Florida International University.

Country of Study: United States of America

Application Procedure: Applicants must complete an application form and submit this with three letters of recommendation. Contact the Fellowship Co-ordinator for details and application materials. Applicants may also download programme information and an application form from the website www.wolfsonian.fiu.edu/education/research

No. of awards offered: 26

Closing Date: 31 December

No. of awards given last year: 5

No. of applicants last year: 26

Additional Information: www.networks.h-net.org/node/73374/announcements/2914100/wolfsonian-fiu-fellowship-program

For further information contact:

Tel: (1) 305 535 2613
Email: research@thewolf.fiu.edu

Women's Studio Workshop (WSW)

722 Binnewater Lane, PO Box 489, Rosendale, NY 12472, United States of America.

Tel: (1) 845 658 9133
Email: info@wsworkshop.org
Website: www.wsworkshop.org
Contact: Ms Ann Kalmbach, Executive Director

The Women's Studio Workshop (WSW) is an artist-run workshop with facilities for printmaking, papermaking, photography, book arts and ceramics. WSW supports the creation of new work through studio residency and annual book arts grant programmes and an ongoing subsidized fellowship programme.

Artists Fellowships at WSW

Purpose: To provide a time for artists to explore new ideas in a dynamic and co-operative community of women artists in a rural environment.

Eligibility: Open to women artists only.

Level of Study: Unrestricted

Type: Fellowship

Value: The award includes on-site housing and unlimited access to the studios. Cost to artists will be US$200 per week, plus their own material.

Length of Study: Each fellowship is 3–6 weeks long. Fellowship opportunities are from September to June.

Frequency: Annual

Study Establishment: WSW

Country of Study: United States of America

Application Procedure: Applicants must complete an application form, available on request or online at the website. One-sentence summary plus half-page description of proposed project, resume, 10 slides plus slide script, self addressed stampe envelope for return of materials.

No. of awards offered: 100

Closing Date: 15 October

Funding: Government, Private

Contributor: Private foundations

No. of awards given last year: 25

No. of applicants last year: 100

Women's Studio Workshop Internships

Purpose: To provide opportunities for young artists to continue development of their work in a supportive environment, while learning studio skills and responsibilities.

Eligibility: Open to emerging and established female artists

Level of Study: Unrestricted

Type: Internship

Value: A private room in our onsite housing and a stipend of US$250/month.

Length of Study: 2–6 months

Frequency: Annual

Study Establishment: WSW

Country of Study: United States of America

Application Procedure: Applicants must submit a curriculum vitae, 10 slides with slide list, 3 current letters of reference, a letter of interest that addresses the question of why an internship at WSW would be important and a stamped addressed envelope. Arts administration 3 work samples, i.e. press releases, design samples, etc.

No. of awards offered: 150

Funding: Government, Private

Contributor: Private foundations

No. of awards given last year: 6

No. of applicants last year: 150

Additional Information: www.wsworkshop.org/residencies/studio-internship/

Woodrow Wilson National Fellowship Foundation

104 Carnegie Center, Suite 301, Princeton, NJ 08540-631, United States of America.

Tel: (1) 609 452 7007
Email: marrero@woodrow.org
Website: www.woodrow.org

The Woodrow Wilson National Fellowship Foundation identifies and develops the best minds for the nation's most important challenges. The fellowships are awarded to enrich human resources, work to improve public policy, and assist organizations and institutions in enhancing practice in the United States and abroad.

The Millicent C. McIntosh Fellowship

Purpose: These fellowships are specifically intended for recently tenured faculty who would benefit from additional time and resources.
Level of Study: Postgraduate
Type: Fellowship
Value: A US$15,000 stipend
Length of Study: 1 year
Frequency: Annual
Application Procedure: Contact the Foundation.
Closing Date: 31 March
Funding: Private
Contributor: Gladys Krieble Delmas Foundation.

For further information contact:

Tel: (1) 609 452 7007 ext. 301
Email: mcintoshfellowship@woodrow.org

Woodrow Wilson MBA Fellowship in Education Leadership

Purpose: To address the United States' twin educational achievement gaps–the one between the nation's lowest performing and its best schools, as well as the one between the nation's best schools and their top international competitors. The Fellowship seeks both to prepare leaders who can bring all American schools up to world-class levels of performance and to develop a new gold standard for preparing education leaders.
Eligibility: Fellows commit to serve for 3 years in approved school or district leadership positions within their states.
Level of Study: Postgraduate

Type: Fellowship
Value: Fellows will receive a stipend to cover tuition for the MBA program and other expenses.
Length of Study: 13 to 15 months of full-time study
Frequency: Annual
Country of Study: Any country
Application Procedure: Fellows must be nominated by a local education leader/colleague before they are eligible to apply. Contact information buntrock@woodrow.org
Closing Date: December
Additional Information: If you have already been nominated, see the respective pages for the WW MBA Fellowship at MSOE www.msoe.edu/community/academics/business/page/2311/mba-in-education-leadership-overview, www.woodrow.org/mobile/fships/ww-ed-mba/

For further information contact:

Email: buntrock@woodrow.org

Woodrow Wilson Teaching Fellowship

Eligibility: The Woodrow Wilson Teaching Fellowship seeks to attract talented, committed individuals with science, technology, engineering, and mathematics (STEM) backgrounds – including current undergraduates, recent college graduates, midcareer professionals, and retirees – into teaching in high-need secondary schools. A qualified applicant should demonstrate a commitment to the program and its goals; have United States citizenship or permanent residency; have attained, or expect to attain by 30 June, a bachelor's degree from an accredited United States college or university; have majored in and/or have a strong professional background in an STEM field; have achieved a cumulative undergraduate grade point average (GPA) of 3.0 or better on a 4.0 scale (negotiable for applicants from institutions that do not employ a 4.0 GPA scale). Note: Prior teaching experience does not exclude a candidate from eligibility. All applications are considered in their entirety and selection is based on merit.
Level of Study: Graduate
Type: Fellowship
Value: US$30,000-US$32,000 stipend, with tuition arrangements varying by campus in Georgia, Indiana, and New Jersey. (Once Fellows are certified teachers at the end of the first year, they obtain salaried employment in high-need schools.)
Length of Study: 12–18 months plus 3-year teaching commitment
Frequency: Annual
Study Establishment: Fellowship is only available for use at specific schools in Indiana (Ball State University, Indiana University-Purdue University Indianapolis, Purdue University, and the University of Indianapolis); Michigan (Eastern Michigan University, Grand Valley State University,

Michigan State University, University of Michigan, Wayne State University, Western Michigan University); and Ohio (John Carroll University, Ohio State University, University of Akron, and University of Cincinnati).

Country of Study: Any country

Application Procedure: Online application procedure and supporting documents. See www.wwteachingfellowship.org

No. of awards offered: 1690

Funding: Foundation, Government, Private

Contributor: Ohio STEM, Lilly Endowment Inc., W K Kellogg Foundation, Choose Ohio First.

Additional Information: University of Dayton and University of Toledo are also included in study establishment www.woodrow.org/fellowships/ww-teaching-fellowships/

For further information contact:

Email: wwteachingfellowship@woodrow.org

Woods Hole Oceanographic Institution (WHOI)

266 Woods Hole Road, Woods Hole, MA 02543-1050, United States of America.

Tel: (1) 508 289 2252
Email: information@whoi.edu
Website: www.whoi.edu/education
Contact: Janet Fields, Coordinator

The Woods Hole Oceanographic Institution is dedicated to advancing knowledge of the ocean and its connection with the Earth system through a sustained commitment to excellence in science, engineering, and education, and to the application of this knowledge to problems facing society. This is essential not only to advance knowledge about our planet, but also to ensure society's long-term welfare and to help guide human stewardship of the environment. WHOI researchers are also dedicated to training future generations of ocean science leaders, to providing unbiased information that informs public policy and decision-making.

Postdoctoral Scholar Program

Purpose: Eighteen-month Postdoctoral Scholar awards are offered to recipients of new or recent doctorates in the fields of chemistry, engineering, geology, geophysics, mathematics, meteorology, physics, and biology as well as oceanography. The awards are designed to further the education and training of the applicant with primary emphasis placed on the individual's research promise.

Eligibility: In order to be eligible for one of these awards, applicants must have received their doctoral degree within the past 2-3 years.

Level of Study: Postdoctoral

Type: Fellowship

Value: US$61,200 per year

Length of Study: 18 months

Frequency: Annual

Study Establishment: Woods Hole Oceanographic Institution

Country of Study: United States of America

Closing Date: 1 December

Woods Hole Oceanographic Institution Postdoctoral Awards in Marine Policy and Ocean Management

Eligibility: In order to be eligible for one of these awards, applicants must have received their doctoral degree no more than 3 years before their start date. A doctoral degree is required at the time of appointment, but not at the time of application. It is also expected that candidates will have a command of the English language. The following groups are not eligible for the Scholar competition: MIT-WHOI Joint Program Students; those holding any type of WHOI appointment at the post-doctorate level during the 12 months prior to December 31st of the Scholar application year; and those with more than 12 total months as a WHOI guest student, or who have a formal doctoral (co)advisor who is a WHOI employee.

Level of Study: Postdoctorate

Value: US$63,300

Length of Study: 18-month

Frequency: Annual

Study Establishment: Woods Hole Oceanographic Institution

Country of Study: United States of America

Additional Information: Award recipients in the programme have pursued such studies as the implications of oil exploration along the North eastern coast of the United States of America, problems of international law created by new developments in aquaculture and fish farming, economic benefits of some oceanographic research, a perceptual study of United Kingdom fishermen, and oceanic waste disposal www.woodrow.org/fellowships/ww-teaching-fellowships/

Woods Hole Oceanographic Institution Postdoctoral Fellowships in Ocean Science and Engineering

Purpose: To further the education and training of recent recipients of doctoral degrees in engineering science or with interests in marine science.

W

Eligibility: Open to United States citizens and foreign nationals who have earned a PhD degree in biology, physics, microbiology, molecular biology, chemistry, geology, geophysics, oceanography, meteorology, engineering or mathematics. Scientists with more than three years of postdoctoral experience are not eligible.

Level of Study: Postdoctorate

Type: Fellowship

Value: Please contact the organization

Length of Study: 1 year

Frequency: Annual

Study Establishment: Woods Hole Oceanographic Institution

Country of Study: United States of America

Application Procedure: Applicants must complete and submit an application form with transcripts, reference letters, complete transcripts of undergraduate and graduate records, and a concise statement describing research interests. Further information and application forms may be obtained from the postdoctoral section of the website.

Funding: Government, Private

Additional Information: Award holders work in the laboratory under the general supervision of an appropriate member of the staff, but are expected to work independently on research problems of their own choice www.woodrow.org/fellowships/ww-teaching-fellowships/

For further information contact:

Email: postdoc@whoi.edu

Worcester College

Walton Street, Oxford OX1 2HB, United Kingdom.

Tel:	(44) 1865 278300
Email:	lodge@worc.ox.ac.uk
Website:	www.worc.ox.ac.uk/

Worcester College was founded in 1714, but there has been an institution of learning on the site since the late 13th century. Worcester College is a happy and supportive community, committed to combining academic excellence with becoming genuinely representative of our society.

C Douglas Dillon Graduate Scholarship

Subjects: MPhil Politics (Comparative Government), MPhil Politics (European Politics and Society), MPhil Politics (Political Theory), MSc Politics Research, MSc Political Theory Research, MPhil International Relations, MSc Global Governance and Diplomacy

Eligibility: Open to all graduate applicants

Level of Study: Graduate

Type: Scholarship

Value: £10,000 per annum

Length of Study: two years

Frequency: Annual

Country of Study: Any country

Application Procedure: Applicants must submit the following by email to the Graduate Officer (graduate.enquiries@worc.ox.ac.uk) by the closing date: 1. a completed application cover sheet (this can be downloaded from the college website at www.worc.ox.ac.uk/applying/graduates/graduate-scholarships) 2. an up-to-date Curriculum Vitae; 3. a covering letter stating their reasons for applying for the particular course and providing information about applications they have made to relevant funding bodies.

Closing Date: 4 March

For further information contact:

Email: graduate.enquiries@worc.ox.ac.uk

Drue Heinz Scholarship

Purpose: Open to all graduate applicants for courses in the Humanities in which Worcester College admits students and who specify Worcester College as their first choice College.

Eligibility: All applicants for courses in the Humanities in which Worcester College admits students and who specify Worcester College as their first choice college.

Level of Study: Graduate

Type: Scholarship

Value: £10,000

Length of Study: 1 year

Frequency: Annual

Country of Study: United Kingdom

Application Procedure: 1. A completed application cover sheet (this can be downloaded from the college website at www.worc.ox.ac.uk/applying/graduates/graduate-scholarships). 2. An up-to-date Curriculum Vitae. 3. A covering letter stating their reasons for applying for the particular course and providing information about applications they have made to relevant funding bodies.

No. of awards offered: 1

Closing Date: 5 March

Funding: Private

Additional Information: It is the applicant's responsibility to ensure that all application material is submitted by the deadline; incomplete applications will not be considered. www.woodrow.org/fellowships/ww-teaching-fellowships/

For further information contact:

Tel: (1) 1865 278352
Email: graduate.enquiries@worc.ox.ac.uk

Drue Heinz Scholarship

Eligibility: Open to all graduate applicants for courses in the Humanities in which Worcester College admits students and who specify Worcester College as their first choice College.
Level of Study: Graduate
Type: Award
Value: Up to a maximum of £10,000 per annum
Length of Study: One year
Frequency: Annual
Country of Study: Any country
Application Procedure: Applicants must submit the following by email to the Graduate Officer (graduate.enquiries@worc.ox. ac.uk) by the closing date: 1. a completed application cover sheet (this can be downloaded from the college website at www.worc. ox.ac.uk/applying/graduates/graduate-scholarships) 2. an up-to-date Curriculum Vitae; 3. a covering letter stating their reasons for applying for the particular course and providing information about applications they have made to relevant funding bodies.
Closing Date: 4 March

For further information contact:

Email: graduate.enquiries@worc.ox.ac.uk

Ogilvie Thompson Scholarship

Subjects: All subjects
Purpose: The purpose of the Ogilvie Thompson Scholarship is to enable people to apply for graduate study knowing that if they are not successful in securing funding from elsewhere they will be provided with some financial assistance.
Level of Study: Graduate
Type: Award
Value: Up to a maximum of £10,000
Length of Study: One year
Frequency: Annual
Country of Study: Any country
Application Procedure: Applicants must submit the following by email to the Graduate Officer (graduate. enquiries@worc.ox.ac.uk) by the closing date. 1. a completed application cover sheet (this can be downloaded from the college website at www.worc.ox.ac.uk/applying/graduates/ graduate-scholarships); 2. an up-to-date Curriculum Vitae,

including details of your contributions to the College community; 3. a covering letter stating your reasons for applying for the course and a statement of what applications you have made to relevant funding bodies.
No. of awards offered: 1
Closing Date: 4 March

For further information contact:

Email: graduate.enquiries@worc.ox.ac.uk

World Bank Institute

1818 H Street, NW, Washington, DC 20433, United States of America.

Tel: (1) 202 473 1000
Email: pic@worldbank.org
Website: www.worldbank.org
Contact: Communications Officer

One of the largest sources of funding and knowledge for transition and development councils; The World Bank uses its financial resources, staff and extensive experience to help developing countries reduce poverty, increase economic growth and improve their quality of life.

World Bank Grants Facility for Indigenous Peoples

Purpose: To support sustainable and culturally appropriate development projector planed and implemented by and for Indigenous People.
Eligibility: Applicant must be an Indigenous People's community or not-for-profit/non-governmental Indigenous People's organization, must be legally registered in the country of grant implementation, the country must be eligible to borrow from the World Bank (IBRD and/or IDA). Applicant should have an established bank account in the name of the applicant organization and should demonstrate internal controls to govern the use of funds. Applicant should not have received a grant from the Grants Facility for Indigenous Peoples in the previous 2 years.
Level of Study: Professional development, Research
Type: Grant
Value: Proposed project budget requests should range between US$10,000 and US$30,000 and include a minimum contribution of 20% of the total project cost.
Frequency: Annual
Application Procedure: A complete application, not more than 10 pages, should be submitted.

W

Closing Date: 15 November
Contributor: The World Bank
Additional Information: www.siteresources.worldbank.org/
INTINDPEOPLE/948158-1113428433802/20662536/english
call.pdf

For further information contact:

Fax: (1) 202 522 1669
Email: indigenouspeoples@worldbank.org

World Bank Scholarships Program

Purpose: The World Bank Scholarships Program contributes
to the World Bank Group's mission of forging new dynamic
approaches to capacity development and knowledge sharing
in the developing world.
Eligibility: Eligibility criteria details for each call are pro-
vided in the respective call for application guidelines. Please
note that the eligibility criteria is strictly adhered to and there
are no exceptions.
Level of Study: Masters Degree, Postgraduate
Type: Scholarship
Frequency: Annual
Country of Study: Any country
Closing Date: 31 January
Funding: Private

World Federation of International Music Competitions

104, rue de Carouge, CH-1205 Genéve, Switzerland.

Tel: (41) 22 321 36 20
Email: fmcim@fmcim.org
Website: wfimc-fmcim.org/

The World Federation of International Music Competitions
contributes to the vibrancy of the music world by representing
leading international music competitions and supporting them
with valuable services and guidelines.

International Beethoven Piano Competition, Vienna

Purpose: To encourage the artistic development of young
pianists.
Level of Study: Unrestricted

Type: Competition
Value: €50,000
Frequency: Annual
Country of Study: Any country
Application Procedure: Apply online through the website
www.beethoven-comp.at
Closing Date: 28 April
Funding: Private

World Learning

1015 15th Street, NW 7th Floor, Washington, DC 20005,
United States of America.

Tel: (1) 202 408 5420
Email: info@worldlearning.org
Website: www.worldlearning.org

World Learning is a 501(c)(3) international nonprofit organization that focuses on international development, education,
and exchange programs. The School for International Training (SIT) was established in 1964. SIT filled a need of
returned Peace Corps volunteers by offering a graduate
degree in International Development. The Vermont campus
originally consisted of a small collection of dorms around
a Carriage House on a scenic farm on the north end of
Brattleboro. These early Peace Corps volunteers took lessons
in foreign languages with materials and teachers from the
language training from their service, and The School for
International Training began to expand its offerings.

School for International Training (SIT) Master of Arts in Teaching Program

Purpose: To prepare language teachers committed to profes-
sional development and service in their field.
Eligibility: Open to persons of any nationality who are pre-
paring for a language teaching career. Awards are available
only to students studying at the School for International
Training.
Level of Study: Graduate
Type: Scholarship
Value: Varies
Length of Study: A period that includes a time of student
teaching and homestay. The programme is offered in a 1 year
or 2 Summer format designed for working professionals.
Frequency: Annual
Study Establishment: SIT
Country of Study: Any country

Application Procedure: Applicants must complete an institutional financial aid application and should contact the Financial Aid Office for further details, by email at finaid@sit.edu

Additional Information: Students master technical teaching methodologies through language classroom practice, on campus coursework and a supervised teaching internship. Further information is available on the website www.sit.edu/mat

For further information contact:

Email: tesol@rennert.com

Worshipful Company of Musicians

1 Speed Highwalk, Barbican, London EC2Y 8DX, United Kingdom.

Tel: (44) 20 7496 8980
Email: clerk@wcom.org.uk.
Website: www.wcom.org.uk

The Worshipful Company of Musicians is one of the Livery Companies of the City of London. Its history dates back to at least 1350. We are also known as The Worshipful Company of Musicians.

Carnwath Scholarship

Purpose: Open to any person permanently resident in the United Kingdom and between 21-25 years of age. The scholarship is intended only for the advanced student who has successfully completed a solo performance course at a college of music.

Eligibility: The scholarship is intended only for the advanced student who has successfully completed a solo performance course at a college of music.

Level of Study: Postgraduate
Type: Scholarship
Value: £4,150 per year
Length of Study: Up to 2 years
Frequency: Annual
Country of Study: United Kingdom
Application Procedure: 1. Applicants must be nominated by principals of the Royal Academy of Music, the Guildhall School of Music, the Royal Northern College of Music, the Royal Scottish Academy of Music, Trinity College of Music, London College of Music, the Welsh College of Music, the Birmingham School of Music or the Royal College of

Music. 2. No application should be made directly to the Worshipful Company of Musicians.

Closing Date: 30 April
Funding: Private
Additional Information: Website link error: www.sit.edu/mat

For further information contact:

Email: clerk@wcom.org.uk

Writtle University College

Lordship Road, Writtle, Chelmsford CM1 3RR, United Kingdom.

Tel: (44) 1245 424 200
Website: writtle.ac.uk/

Writtle University College is one of the largest land-based university colleges in the United Kingdom; it is also one of the oldest. Set in the Essex countryside on a 220 hectare estate, Writtle, previously known as Writtle College, provides FE and HE programmes.

Elinor Roper Scholarship

Purpose: The Elinor Roper Scholarship offers five £1,000 scholarship awarded for Taught Master's programme in Crop Production or Post Harvest Technology.

Eligibility: To be considered for a Writtle University College Elinor Roper Scholarship award, students must be Home students and must apply by completing the ERS application form. This application must include a written statement of between 500 – 800 words detailing the value the applicant expects to gain from study on the Master's programme and the way in which they anticipate using the experience after graduation to further their chosen career. If you have a "conditional offer" the scholarship will only be awarded if the conditions are met. Any applicant who defers entry will have to submit a new application for the academic year their studies will commence. Current Writtle University College Postgraduate students are not eligible to apply. The value of the scholarship will be deducted from the tuition fee invoice. It will be a condition of the scholarship that the successful applicant agrees to provide a student profile detailing their experience on the programme to be used in publications for the purpose of marketing Writtle University College and/or

W

inclusion in the "University College Alumni Association" publication.

Level of Study: Masters Degree
Type: Scholarship
Value: £1,000
Frequency: Annual
Country of Study: Any country
Application Procedure: All applicants must be new Writtle University College home students and will need to apply by completing the relevant application form. Download an application (ERS2021) 1. This application must include a written statement of between 500 – 800 words detailing the value the applicant expects to gain from study on the Master's programme and the way in which they anticipate using the experience after graduation to further their career. 2. A "conditional offer" the scholarship will only be awarded if the conditions are met. 3. Any applicant who defers entry will have to submit a new application for the academic year their studies will commence. 4. Current Writtle University College Postgraduate students are not eligible to apply. 5. The value of the scholarship will be deducted from the tuition fee invoice. 6. It will be a condition of the scholarship that the successful applicant agrees to provide a student profile detailing their experience on the programme to be used in publications for the purpose of marketing Writtle University College and/or inclusion in the "University College Alumni Association" publication. 7. This can either be on a full-time or part-time basis.
Funding: Private
No. of awards given last year: 31 August

For further information contact:

Student Finance, Writtle University College, Writtle, Chelmsford, Essex CM1 3RR, United Kingdom.

Tel: (44) 1245 424200
Email: student.finance@writtle.ac.uk

Elinor Roper Scholarship 2023

Purpose: The Elinor Roper Scholarship is awarded for Taught Master's programme in Crop Production or Post Harvest Technology. The Writtle University College provides students with the options of being able to study certain courses on a part-time basis.
Eligibility: To be considered for a Writtle University College Elinor Roper Scholarship award, students must be Home students and must apply by completing the ERS application form. This application must include a written statement of between 500 - 800 words detailing the value the applicant expects to gain from study on the Master's

programme and the way in which they anticipate using the experience after graduation to further their chosen career. If you have a "conditional offer", the scholarship will only be awarded if the conditions are met. Any applicant who defers entry will have to submit a new application for the academic year their studies will commence. Current Writtle University College students are not eligible to apply. The value of the scholarship will be deducted from the tuition fee invoice. It will be a condition of the scholarship that the successful applicant agrees to provide a student profile detailing their experience on the programme to be used in publications for the purpose of marketing Writtle University College and/or inclusion in the "University College Alumni Association" publication.

Level of Study: Masters Degree, Postgraduate, Postgraduate (MSc)
Type: Scholarship
Value: £1,000
Frequency: Annual
Country of Study: United Kingdom
No. of awards offered: Limited
Contributor: Writtle University
Additional Information: https://writtle.ac.uk/Scholarships-&-Bursaries-22-23

For further information contact:

Email: student.finance@writtle.ac.uk

Postgraduate International Scholarships

Purpose: Scholarships are available for pursuing postgraduate programme.
Eligibility: The scholarship is only available to new postgraduate Writtle University College students. Applicants whose first language is not English are usually required to provide evidence of proficiency in English at the higher level required by the University.
Type: Scholarship
Value: For taught MA/MSc courses, the award will be worth £1,000; for MA conversion students the award will be delivered within the conversion year ONLY, as per the terms and conditions set out below.
Length of Study: 2 years
Frequency: Annual
Country of Study: Any country
Application Procedure: Applications to be sent via email. For more details, please refer website www.scholarship-positions.com/writtle-university-college-postgraduate-international-scholarships-uk/2017/10/23/
Closing Date: 31 August
Contributor: Writtle University

Additional Information: www.writtle.ac.uk/scholarships. cfm?Scholarship=62&nohead=1&nofooter=1

For further information contact:

Email: student.recruitment@glasgow.ac.uk

Postgraduate Progression Award

Purpose: This Scholarship is available to ALL new Postgraduate students, commencing their studies

Eligibility: These scholarships are only available to Writtle University College undergraduate students who meet all of the following criteria: 1. A Writtle University College undergraduate student completing your course in 2021/22 or 2022/23 academic years. 2. Meet the entry requirements of the full-time or part time postgraduate course. 3. Begin a Writtle University College postgraduate programme in autumn 2023. 4. The closing date for applications is 31st August 2023.

Level of Study: Postgraduate

Type: Award

Value: £1,000 cash award for Home students or £1900 for International and EU students

Length of Study: one academic year

Frequency: Annual

Country of Study: European Union

Application Procedure: Applications to be sent to: student. finance@writtle.ac.uk

Closing Date: 31 August

Funding: Private

X

Xavier Labor Relations Institute -Xavier School of Management

C. H. Area (East), Jamshedpur, Jharkhand 831001, India.

Tel: (91) 657 398 3329, 3330
Email: admis@xlri.ac.in
Website: www.xlri.ac.in

XLRI - Xavier School of Management is a management school founded in 1949 by the Society of Jesus and based in Jamshedpur, Jharkhand, India.

Fellow Programme in Management (FPM) at Xavier Labor Relations Institute

Purpose: The programme aims to train prospective scholars to become highly skilled and innovative researchers and teachers in various aspects of management. It primarily aims at preparing students for careers as faculty members at premier academic institutions and for position outside academics requiring advanced research and analytical capabilities

Eligibility: The basic eligibility to apply for admission to the FPM is either: 1. a BE / B. Tech. degree or its equivalent with at least 60% marks (50% for SC/ST candidates) obtained after after completing higher secondary education (10+2) or equivalent, and followed by at least 2 years of relevant work experience, OR 2. a bachelor's degree / equivalent of minimum three years duration with at least 60% marks (50% for SC/ST candidates) after completing higher secondary education (10+2) or equivalent, and followed by post-graduation (MBA/Master's degree in any discipline) from a university or a centre of higher learning in India / abroad with at least 55% marks (50% for SC/ST candidates), OR 3. an integrated master's degree of four / five years in any discipline, with at least 55% marks (50% for SC/ST candidates), obtained after completing higher secondary education (10+2) or equivalent, OR 4. a professional qualification like CA, ICWA or CS with at least 55% marks (50% for SC/ST candidates)

Study Establishment: Fellowship is available for pursuing full-time, residential doctoral programme

Country of Study: India

Application Procedure: See the website

Closing Date: 15 January

Xerox Foundation

6th Floor/PO Box 4505, 45 Glover Avenue, Norwalk, CT 06856-4505, United States of America.

Tel: (1) 800 275 9376
Email: D.Garvin.Byrd@xerox.com
Website: www.xerox.com
Contact: Dr Joseph M. Cahalan

Xerox Foundation is a US$15.7 billion technology and services enterprise that helps businesses deploy Smarter Document Management strategies and find better ways to work. Its intent is to constantly lead with innovative technologies, products and services that customers can depend upon to improve business results.

Xerox Technical Minority Scholarship

Purpose: To provide funding to minority students enroled in one of the technical sciences or engineering disciplines

Eligibility: Open to citizens of the United States or visa-holding permanent residents of African American, Asian, Pacific Island, Native American, Native Alaskan or Hispanic descent. Applicants must have grade point average of 3.0 or better

Level of Study: Postgraduate

Type: Scholarship

Value: Scholarships amount vary from US$1,000–US$10,000

Frequency: Annual

Country of Study: United States of America

Application Procedure: Applicants must submit the completed application form along with a curriculum vitae

Closing Date: 30 September

Additional Information: worldscholarshipforum.com/xerox-technical-minority-scholarship/

For further information contact:

Xerox Technical Minority Scholarship Programme office.

Email: xtmsp@rballiance.com

Y

Yale Center for British Art

1080 Chapel Street, New Haven, CT 06510-2302, United States of America.

Tel: (1) 203 432 2800
Email: ycba.info@yale.edu
Website: britishart.yale.edu/

Founded by Paul Mellon (Yale College, Class of 1929), the Yale Center for British Art is the largest museum outside of the United Kingdom devoted to British art. Located in the final building designed by Louis I. Kahn, the Center is a focal point for modernist architecture. It is free and open to all. The Center's collections include more than 2,000 paintings, 250 sculptures, 20,000 drawings and watercolors, 40,000 prints, and 35,000 rare books and manuscripts. More than 40,000 volumes supporting research in British art and related fields are available in the Center's Reference library. The Yale Center for British Art offers visitors the opportunity to critically explore the world and their own lives through art.

Andrew W Mellon Fellowship

Purpose: To promote the study of British art
Eligibility: Open to foreign students enrolled for a higher degree at a British or other non-American university
Level of Study: Postgraduate
Type: Fellowship
Value: US$15,000 plus return airfare from London, health benefits and travel expenses up to US$1,000
Length of Study: 1 year
Frequency: Annual
Study Establishment: The Yale Center for British Art
Country of Study: United States of America

Application Procedure: There is no application form. Please submit name, address, telephone number, CV listing professional experience, education and publications, three page outline of research proposal, and two confidential letters of recommendation.
No. of awards offered: 2
Closing Date: 15 January
Funding: Private

For further information contact:

Email: bacinfo@minerva.cis.yale.edu

Yale School of Management (SOM)

P.O. Box 208200, New Haven, CT 06520-8200, United States of America.

Tel: (1) 203 432 9637
Email: jonathan.weisberg@yale.edu
Website: som.yale.edu/
Contact: Jonathan Weisberg, Managing Director of Communications

Yale Corporation approved the creation of a School of Organization and Management founded in 1976. The school changed its name to the Yale School of Management in 1994. The mission of the Yale School of Management is educating leaders for business and society. Across its portfolio of degree programs, Yale SOM educates purposeful leaders who pursue their work with integrity; who are equipped to contribute to all sectors of society–public, private, nonprofit, and entrepreneurial; and who understand complexity within and among societies in an increasingly global world.

© Springer Nature Limited 2022
Palgrave Macmillan (ed.), *The Grants Register 2023*,
https://doi.org/10.1057/978-1-349-96053-8

Arthur Liman Public Interest Law Fellowship

Purpose: The Arthur Liman Center for Public Interest Law annually funds fellowships for law school graduates to spend a year working in the United States on public interest legal issues such as welfare rights, homelessness, racial profiling, indigent criminal defense, alternative sentencing courts, immigration, workers rights, and juvenile justice.

Eligibility: Yale Law School graduates and third-year students are eligible to apply.

Level of Study: Graduate

Type: Fellowship

Value: The Center provides each Fellow with an annual stipend of approximately US$47,500.

Frequency: Annual

Country of Study: United States of America

Application Procedure: Application Components 1. Personal statement (500 words maximum) Describe your experience with and commitment to public interest, public service, and/or human rights, aspirations for future work, and how the Fellowship would help achieve your aspirations. 2. Proposal summary (1 paragraph) Include where you will work and your project goals. 3. Proposal (3000 words maximum) Applicants may design a project in partnership with a host organization or work on an organization's existing project. 4. Statement Other fellowships or public interest positions to which you have applied or will apply. If none, include an explanation, e.g. gap year, unusual geographic or project-specific need. Applying for external funding is not a requirement but it is strongly encouraged. 5. Résumé. 6. Official law school transcript Request here law.yale.edu/about-yale-law-school/offices-services/registrar/transcripts-verification-and-bar-forms. 7. Two letters of recommendation One from law school faculty and one from a supervisor or employer. 8. RECOMMENDED An additional letter of recommendation from law school faculty. 9. List of people consulted about your project before crafting your proposal, you must consult with people in your field. We recommend talking to two to four people Liman Fellows or others. We will provide names of Fellows in your area of law. 10. Letter from the proposed host organization to include a. Organization's purpose and function. b. How your proposed work fits with the host organization's activities. c. What supervision you will receive and who you supervisor will be. d. What resources your host organization will provide to support your project (e.g., office space, computer, malpractice and/or other insurance, if needed). e. Potential for the organization to retain you as a full-time staff member after your fellowship year. Submit applications online through the Yale Student Grants Database (Community Force).

Closing Date: 15 February

No. of awards given last year: 10

Additional Information: For more information som.yale.edu/programs/joint-degrees/mba-jd-yale-law-school, law.yale.edu/centers-workshops/arthur-liman-center-public-interest-law/yale-law-school-fellowship

For further information contact:

Anna Van Cleave, Liman Center Director.

Tel: (1) 203 436 3520
Email: anna.vancleave@yale.edu

Yanshan University

No. 438 West Hebei Avenue, Hebei 066004, Qinhuangdao, China.

Tel: (86) 335 8057070
Email: international@ysu.edu.cn
Website: english.ysu.edu.cn/

Yanshan University (YSU), co-constructed by Hebei Provincial Government, Ministry of Education, and Ministry of Industry and Information Technology, is the major university supported by Hebei Province in the development of national first-class universities and world first-class disciplines. YSU is a member of the Cooperation Consortium of Beijing High Technology Universities. The mission of YSU is to aim at achieving and maintaining excellence in its teaching and research.

China Scholarship Council Scholarships

Purpose: China Scholarship Council (hereinafter referred to as CSC), entrusted by the Ministry of Education of the People's Republic of China (hereinafter referred to as MOE), is responsible for the enrollment and the administration of Chinese Government Scholarship programs. CSC offer a wide variety of academic programs in science, engineering, agriculture, medicine, economics, legal studies, management, education, history, literature, philosophy, and fine arts for scholarship recipients at all levels.

Eligibility: For up-to-date information see this page: https://ies.ysu.edu.cn/en/Scholarships/Chinese_Government_Scholarship.htm

Type: Scholarship

Value: For up-to-date information see this page: https://ies.ysu.edu.cn/en/Scholarships/Chinese_Government_Scholarship.htm

Frequency: Annual
Country of Study: China
Application Procedure: Chinese Government Scholarship require online application submission at CSC portal studyinchina.csc.edu.cn/#/login.
Closing Date: April
Additional Information: For more details: english.ysu.edu.cn/info/1160/2158.htm

For further information contact:

HE Ling, JI Hongyue.

Tel: (86) 335 8047570
Email: study@ysu.edu.cn

Chinese Government Scholarship Program

Purpose: Chinese Government Scholarship Program is established by the Ministry of Education of P.R. China in accordance with educational exchange agreements or understandings reached between the Chinese government and the governments of other countries, organizations, education institutions and relevant international organizations to provide both full scholarships and partial scholarships to international students and scholars.
Eligibility: For most up-to-date information see this page: https://ies.ysu.edu.cn/en/Scholarships/Chinese_Government_Scholarship.htm
Level of Study: Doctorate, Masters Degree, Postgraduate
Type: Scholarship
Value: For most up-to-date information see this page: https://ies.ysu.edu.cn/en/Scholarships/Chinese_Government_Scholarship.htm
Frequency: Annual
Country of Study: China
Application Procedure: The applicants must fill in and provide the following documents truly, correctly and completely (in duplicate). 1. Application Form for Chinese Government Scholarship (filled in Chinese or English). Those who are available for online application shall fill in and print the application form after submitting it online. The CSC Online Application System for Study in China is available on laihua. csc.edu.cn. Those who cannot apply online shall contact the dispatching authorities to get the application form and fill it truly, correctly and completely. Please visit website for more details.
Funding: Government
Additional Information: Note: 1. Costs of the laboratory experiment or internship beyond the institution's arrangements should be self-afforded. 2. Fee for basic learning materials only covers the necessary learning materials prescribed by the host institution. Other textbooks and materials shall be self-afforded. english.ysu.edu.cn/info/1160/2158.htm

For further information contact:

HE Ling, JI Hongyue.

Tel: (86) 335 8047570
Email: study@ysu.edu.cn

Confucius Institute Scholarship

Purpose: The purpose of satisfying the growing demand of the international community for Chinese language teachers and facilitating Chinese language education in other countries.
Eligibility: All applicants shall be: a. non-Chinese citizens; b. in good physical and mental conditions, and with good academic performance and conduct; c. committed to the Chinese language education and related work; d. between the ages of 16 and 35 (as of September 1st, 2022). Applicants currently working as Chinese language teachers shall not be over 45, while undergraduate student applicants shall not be over 25.
Type: Scholarship
Country of Study: Any country
Closing Date: 15 May

For further information contact:

Tel: (86) 335 8095518, (86) 335 8096708
Email: study@ysu.edu.cn

Hebei Provincial Government Scholarship

Purpose: The Hebei Provincial Government awards scholarships to international students studying degree programs in Colleges and Universities located in Hebei Province. Application is open to undergraduate, master's and doctoral level students of all fields of study.
Level of Study: Masters Degree
Type: Scholarship
Value: Master's Students: ¥15,000/year;
Length of Study: Period of Academic Study
Frequency: Annual
Country of Study: Any country
Application Procedure: The documents provided by the applicants are required to be true, correct and complete. They include: 1. Application Form for Hebei Provincial Government Scholarship 2. Scanned copy of passport data page 3. Scanned copies of valid HSK score report or IELTS score report 4. Notarized photocopy of highest diploma certificate

Y

and academic transcripts. Current students must also provide proof of expected graduation issued by the university. 5. Study or research plan. Master's or doctoral applicants are required to submit study or research plansin Chinese or English. 6. Recommendation letters. Master's and Doctoral applicants are required to provide two (2) reference letters from professors or associate professors. 7. Applicants for music studies are requested to submit a CD of their own work, while applicants for fine arts must submit a DVD of their own work (two sketches, two color paintings and two other works). 8. Applicants under the age of 18 shall provide guarantee letters signed by their entrusted legal guardians in China. 9. Applicants shall also provide any additional documents required by the university.; Documents in languages other than Chinese or English must be attached with notarized Chinese or English translations.

For further information contact:

International Students Admissions Office, 20 E. South 2nd Ring Road, Yuhua District, Shijiazhuang City, Hebei Province, China.

Tel: (86) 311 80789542
Email: studyinhnu@mail.hebtu.edu.cn;
                  scholarship@mail.hebtu.edu.cn

Yanshan University Doctoral Scholarships

Purpose: The aim of the scholarships is to provide financial help to the students who are coming to study doctoral programs in China.
Eligibility: 1. Applicants must be non-Chinese citizens with a foreign passport and be in good health. 2. Applicants for doctoral degree programmust have a diploma of master's degree and be under the age of 40.
Level of Study: Doctorate
Type: Scholarship
Value: The scholarship covers 1. Registration fee, tuition fee, and accommodation fee for dormitory on campus. 2. Monthly allowance¥1,400 for 12 months/year. 3. One–off settlement subsidy ¥ 2,000
Length of Study: 3 to 4 years
Frequency: Annual
Country of Study: China
Application Procedure: 1. Application Form for YSU Scholarship; 2. Copy of passport (the photo page); 3. YSU admission application form international students (with a photograph of the applicant); 4. Certified educational records, degree certificates or diplomas, and academic transcripts (photocopy); 5. Curriculum vitae or resume;

6. Physical examination form for foreigners; 7. Copy of HSK-5 certificate; 8. Personal statement; 9. Two letters of recommendation from professors or associated professors. Please send completed application to mailing address.
Closing Date: 20 May
Additional Information: Please visit website for more information: english.ysu.edu.cn/info/1160/2161.htm

For further information contact:

He Ling, College of International Exchange, Yanshan University, 438 Hebei Street, Hebei Province 066004, Qinhuangdao, China.

Tel: (86) 335 8047570, (86) 335 8053537
Email: study@ysu.edu.cn

Yanshan University Scholarship Program for International Students

Purpose: Scholarships are available for pursuing Master Degree programs.
Eligibility: 1. Applicants must be non-Chinese citizens with a foreign passport and be in good health. 2. Applicants for master's degree program must have a diploma of bachelor's degree and be under the age of 35.
Level of Study: Masters Degree
Type: Scholarship
Value: The scholarship covers 1. Registration fee, tuition fee, and accommodation fee for dormitory on campus. 2. Monthly allowance ¥1,400 for 12 months/year. 3. One–off settlement subsidy ¥ 2,000.
Length of Study: 3 to 4 years
Frequency: Annual
Country of Study: China
Application Procedure: For most up-todate information see this page: https://www.yivo.org/list-of-fellowships#:~:text= The%20Rose%20and%20Isidore%20Drench,of%20the%20 Jewish%20labor%20movement
Closing Date: 20 May
Funding: Government
Additional Information: For more information: english.ysu. edu.cn/info/1160/2161.htm, www.campuschina.org/content/ details3_121468.html

For further information contact:

He Ling, Ji Hongyue, College of International Exchange, Yanshan University, 438 Hebei Street, Hebei Province 066004, Qinhuangdao, China.

Tel: (86) 335 8047570, (86) 335 8053537
Email: study@ysu.edu.cn

Yidisher Visnshaftlekher Institut Institute for Jewish Research

15 West 16th Street, New York, NY 10011-6301, United States of America.

Tel: (1) 212 246 6080
Email: yivomail@yivo.cjh.org
Website: www.yivo.org/

The YIVO Institute for Jewish Research was founded as the Yiddish Scientific Institute (Yidisher visnshaftlekher institut) by scholars and intellectuals in Vilna, Poland (now Vilnius, Lithuania) in 1925 to document and study Jewish life in all its aspects: language, history, religion, folkways, and material culture. YIVO relocated to New York City, where it has been headquartered since 1940.

Abraham and Rachela Melezin Fellowship

Purpose: To support doctoral and postdoctoral research on Jewish educational networks in Lithuania, with emphasis on pre-war Vilna and the Vilna region
Level of Study: Doctorate, Postdoctorate
Type: Fellowship
Value: For most up-to-date information see this page: https://www.yivo.org/list-of-fellowships#:~:text=The%20Rose%20and%20Isidore%20Drench,of%20the%20Jewish%20labor%20movement
Length of Study: 1–3 months
Frequency: Annual
Study Establishment: YIVO Library and Archives
Country of Study: United States of America
Application Procedure: For most up-to-date information see this page: https://www.petersons.com/scholarship/abraham-and-rachela-melezin-fellowship-111_153684.aspx
Closing Date: 31 December
Additional Information: A written summary of one's research is required; a public lecture is optional www.petersons.com/scholarship/abraham-and-rachela-melezin-fellowship-111_153684.aspx

Abram and Fannie Gottlieb Immerman and Abraham Nathan and Bertha Daskal Weinstein Memorial Fellowship

Purpose: To support travel for PhD dissertation research in archives and libraries of the Baltic states with preference given to research on the Jews of Courland and Latvia

Eligibility: For those engaged in PhD dissertation research in archives and libraries of the Baltic states with preference given to research on the Jews of Courland and Latvia
Level of Study: Doctorate, Research
Type: Fellowship
Value: US$2,000
Frequency: Every 2 years
Application Procedure: Applicants must send a cover letter, curriculum vitae, research proposal and 2 letters of support through regular mail, fax or email. A written summary of one's research is required
Closing Date: 31 December
Funding: Private
Additional Information: www.yivo.org/List-of-Fellowships

For further information contact:

YIVO Institute for Jewish Research, 15 West 16 Street, New York, NY 10011, United States of America.

Aleksander and Alicja Hertz Memorial Fellowship

Purpose: To encourage research on Jewish-Polish relations and Jewish contributions to Polish literature and culture in the modern period
Level of Study: Doctorate, Postdoctorate
Type: Fellowship
Value: US$8,000
Length of Study: 1–3 months
Frequency: Annual
Country of Study: United States of America
Application Procedure: Applicants must send their curriculum vitae, research proposal and 2 letters of support through regular mail, fax or email. A written summary of one's research is required
Closing Date: 1 February
Additional Information: www.yivo.org/List-of-Fellowships

Dina Abramowicz Emerging Scholar Fellowship

Purpose: To support a significant scholarly publication that may encompass the revision of a doctoral dissertation
Eligibility: Applicants are required to give a public lecture
Level of Study: Postdoctorate
Type: Fellowship
Value: US$8,000
Length of Study: 1–3 months
Frequency: Annual
Country of Study: Any country

Y

Application Procedure: Applicants must send their curriculum vitae, a research proposal and 2 letters of support through regular mail, fax or email

Closing Date: 1 February

Additional Information: www.yivo.org/List-of-Fellowships

Dora and Mayer Tendler Fellowship

Purpose: To support graduate research in Jewish studies with preference given to research in YIVO collections

Eligibility: Graduate applicants must carry out original research in the field of Jewish studies and give a written summary of the research carried out

Level of Study: Doctorate, Graduate

Type: Fellowship

Value: For most up-to-date information see this page: https://www.yivo.org/list-of-fellowships#:~:text=The%20Rose%20and%20Isidore%20Drench,of%20the%20Jewish%20labor%20movement

Frequency: Annual

Study Establishment: YIVO collections

Country of Study: United States of America

Application Procedure: For most up-to-date information see this page: https://www.yivo.org/list-of-fellowships#:~:text=The%20Rose%20and%20Isidore%20Drench,of%20the%20Jewish%20labor%20movement

Closing Date: 31 December

Additional Information: A public lecture at the end of the tenure of the Fellowship is optional www.yivo.org/List-of-Fellowships

For further information contact:

Email: eportnoy@yivo.cjh.org

Joseph Kremen Memorial Fellowship

Purpose: The Ruth and Joseph Kremen Memorial Fellowship is dedicated to assist an graduate or post-graduate researcher in the fields of Eastern European Jewish arts, music and theater.

Eligibility: A written summary of one's research is required

Level of Study: Postgraduate, Research

Type: Fellowship

Value: US$10,000

Length of Study: three months

Frequency: Annual

Country of Study: Any country

Application Procedure: Applicants must send their curriculum vitae, research proposal and 2 letters of support by regular mail, fax or email

Closing Date: 1 February

Additional Information: www.yivo.org/List-of-Fellowships

Maria Salit-Gitelson Tell Memorial Fellowship

Purpose: To support original doctoral or postdoctoral research in the field of Lithuanian Jewish history, the city of Vilnus in particular, at the YIVO Library and Archives

Eligibility: Applicants must carry out original doctoral or postdoctoral research in the field of Lithuanian Jewish history and give a public lecture at the end of the tenure of the Fellowship

Level of Study: Doctorate, Postdoctorate

Type: Fellowship

Value: US$7,000

Length of Study: 1–3 months

Frequency: Annual

Study Establishment: YIVO Library and Archives

Country of Study: United States of America

Application Procedure: Applicants must send a cover letter, curriculum vitae, research proposal and 2 letters of support through regular mail, fax or email

Closing Date: 1 February

Additional Information: www.yivo.org/List-of-Fellowships

Natalie and Mendel Racolin Memorial Fellowship

Purpose: To support original doctoral or postdoctoral research in the field of East European Jewish history at the YIVO Library and Archives

Eligibility: Applicants must carry out original doctoral or postdoctoral research in the field of East European Jewish history and give a public lecture at the end of the tenure of the Fellowship

Level of Study: Doctorate, Postdoctorate

Type: Fellowship

Value: US$30,000

Length of Study: 1–3 months

Frequency: Annual

Study Establishment: YIVO Library and Archives

Country of Study: United States of America

Application Procedure: Applicants must send a cover letter, curriculum vitae, research proposal and 2 letters of support through regular mail, fax or email

Closing Date: 1 February

Additional Information: www.yivo.org/List-of-Fellowships

Professor Bernard Choseed Memorial Fellowship

Purpose: To financially support original doctoral or postdoctoral research in the field of East European Jewish studies.

Eligibility: Applicants are required to give a public lecture
Level of Study: Doctorate, Postdoctorate
Type: Fellowship
Value: US$30,000
Length of Study: 1–3 months
Frequency: Annual
Country of Study: United States of America
Application Procedure: Applicants must submit a curriculum vitae, a research proposal and 2 letters of support through regular mail, fax or email
Closing Date: 1 February
Additional Information: www.yivo.org/List-of-Fellowships

Rose and Isidore Drench Memorial Fellowship

Purpose: To encourage research in American Jewish history, with special consideration given to scholars working on some aspect of the Jewish labor movement.
Eligibility: Applicants are required to give a public lecture
Level of Study: Doctorate, Postdoctorate
Type: Fellowship
Value: US$10,000
Length of Study: 1–3 months
Frequency: Annual
Country of Study: Any country
Application Procedure: Applicants must submit their curriculum vitae, a research proposal and 2 letters of support through regular mail, fax or email
Closing Date: 1 February
Additional Information: www.yivo.org/List-of-Fellowships

Samuel and Flora Weiss Research Fellowship

Purpose: To support research on the destruction of Polish Jewry or on Polish-Jewish relations during the Holocaust period
Eligibility: Applicants must carry out original research on the destruction of Polish Jewry or on Polish-Jewish relations during the Holocaust period and give a written summary of the research carried out. The research should result in a scholarly publication
Level of Study: Doctorate
Type: Fellowship
Value: US$8,000
Length of Study: three months
Frequency: Annual
Country of Study: Any country
Application Procedure: Applicants must send a cover letter, curriculum vitae, research proposal and 2 letters of support through regular mail, fax or email

Closing Date: 1 February
Additional Information: www.yivo.org/List-of-Fellowships

For further information contact:

Tel: (1) 212 294 613
Email: pglasse@yivo.cjh.org

Vivian Lefsky Hort Memorial Fellowship

Purpose: To support original doctoral or postdoctoral research in the field of Yiddish literature
Eligibility: Applicants must carry out original doctoral or postdoctoral research in Yiddish literature and give a public lecture at the end of the tenure of the Fellowship
Level of Study: Doctorate, Postdoctorate
Type: Fellowship
Value: US$8,000
Length of Study: 1–3 months
Frequency: Annual
Study Establishment: YIVO Library and Archives
Country of Study: United States of America
Application Procedure: Applicants must send a cover letter, curriculum vitae, research proposal and 2 letters of support through regular mail, fax or email
Closing Date: 1 February
Additional Information: www.yivo.org/List-of-Fellowships

Vladimir and Pearl Heifetz Memorial Fellowship in Eastern European Jewish Music

Purpose: To assist undergraduate, graduate and postgraduate researchers defray expenses connected with research in YIVO's music collection at the YIVO Archives and Library
Eligibility: Undergraduate, graduate and postgraduate researchers who will carry on research in YIVO's music collection at the YIVO Archives and Library
Level of Study: Graduate, Postgraduate
Type: Fellowship
Value: US$1,500
Frequency: Annual
Study Establishment: YIVO's music collection
Country of Study: United States of America
Application Procedure: Applicants must send a cover letter, curriculum vitae, research proposal and 2 letters of support through regular mail, fax or email
Closing Date: 31 December
Funding: Foundation
Additional Information: www.yivo.org/List-of-Fellowships

Workmen's Circle/Dr Emanuel Patt Visiting Professorship

Purpose: To support three months of post-doctoral research at the YIVO Library and Archives and a public lecture by the visiting faculty member.
Level of Study: Postdoctorate
Type: Professorship
Value: US$5,000
Length of Study: 3 months

Frequency: Annual
Country of Study: United States of America
Application Procedure: Applicants must send a covering letter, curriculum vitae, research proposal and 2 letters of support through regular mail, fax or email
Closing Date: 31 December
Additional Information: The visiting faculty member should give a public lecture at the end of the award's tenure www.yivo.org/list-of-fellowships

AGRICULTURE, FORESTRY AND FISHERY

General
Agricultural business
Agricultural economics
Agriculture and farm management
Agronomy
Animal husbandry
   Sericulture
Crop production
Fishery
   Aquaculture
Food science
   Brewing
   Dairy
   Fish
   Harvest technology
   Meat and poultry
   Oenology
Forestry
   Forest biology
   Forest economics
   Forest management
   Forest pathology
   Forest products
   Forest soils
Horticulture and viticulture
Soil and water science
   Irrigation
   Soil conservation
   Water management
Tropical agriculture
Veterinary science

ARCHITECTURE AND TOWN PLANNING

General
Architectural and environmental design
Architectural restoration
Landscape architecture
Regional planning
Rural planning
Structural architecture
Town planning

ARTS AND HUMANITIES

General
Archaeology
Classical languages and literatures
   Classical Greek
   Latin
   Sanskrit
Comparative literature
History
   Ancient civilisations
   Contemporary history
   Medieval studies
   Modern history
   Prehistory
Linguistics
   Applied linguistics
   Grammar
   Logopedics
   Phonetics
   Psycholinguistics
   Semantics and terminology
   Speech studies
Modern languages
   African Languages
   Afrikaans
   Altaic languages
   Amerindian languages
   Arabic
   Austronesian and oceanic languages
   Baltic languages
   Celtic languages

© Springer Nature Limited 2022
Palgrave Macmillan (ed.), *The Grants Register 2023*,
https://doi.org/10.1057/978-1-349-96053-8

Chinese
Danish
Dutch
English
Eurasian and North Asian languages
European languages (others)
Finnish
Fino Ugrian languages
French
German
Germanic languages
Hebrew
Hungarian
Indian languages
Indic languages
Iranic languages
Italian
Japanese
Korean
Modern Greek
Norwegian
Portuguese
Romance languages
Russian
Scandinavian languages
Slavic languages (others)
Spanish
Swedish
Native language and literature
Philosophy
    Ethics
    Logic
    Metaphysics
    Philosophical schools
Translation and interpretation
Writing (authorship)

BUSINESS ADMINISTRATION AND MANAGEMENT

General
Accountancy
Business and commerce
Business computing
Business machine operation
Finance, banking and investment
Human resources
Institutional administration
Insurance
International business
Labour/industrial relations
Management systems
Marketing
    Public relations

MBA
Personnel management
Private administration
Public administration
Real estate
Secretarial studies

EDUCATION AND TEACHER TRAINING

General
Adult education
Continuing education
Educational science
    Curriculum
    Distance education
    Educational administration
    Educational and student counselling
    Educational research
    Educational technology
    Educational testing and evaluation
    International and comparative education
    Philosophy of education
    Teaching and learning
Higher education teacher training
Nonvocational subjects education
    Education in native language
    Foreign languages education
    Humanities and social science education
    Literacy education
    Mathematics education
    Physical education
    Science education
Pre-school education
Primary education
Secondary education
Special education
    Bilingual/bicultural education
    Education of foreigners
    Education of natives
    Education of specific learning disabilities
    Education of the gifted
    Education of the handicapped
    Education of the socially disadvantaged
Staff development
Teacher trainers education
Vocational subjects education
    Agricultural education
    Art education
    Commerce/business education
    Computer education
    Health education
    Home economics education

Industrial arts education
Music education
Technology education

ENGINEERING

General
Aeronautical and aerospace engineering
Agricultural engineering
Automotive engineering
Bioengineering and biomedical engineering
Chemical engineering
Civil engineering
Computer engineering
Control engineering (robotics)
Electrical and electronic engineering
Energy engineering
Engineering drawing/design
Environmental and sanitary engineering
Forestry engineering
Hydraulic engineering
Industrial engineering
Marine engineering and naval architecture
Materials engineering
Measurement/precision engineering
Mechanical engineering
Metallurgical engineering
Mining engineering
Nanotechnology
Nuclear engineering
Petroleum and gas engineering
Physical engineering
Production engineering
Safety engineering
Sound engineering
Surveying and mapping science

FINE AND APPLIED ARTS

General
Art criticism
Art history
    Aesthetics
Art management
Cinema and television
Dance
Design
    Display and stage design
    Fashion design
    Furniture design
    Graphic design

Industrial design
Interior design
Textile design
Drawing and painting
Handicrafts
Music
    Conducting
    Jazz and popular music
    Music theory and composition
    Musical instruments
    Musicology
    Opera
    Religious music
    Singing
Photography
Religious art
Sculpture
Theatre

HOME ECONOMICS

General
Child care/child development
Clothing and sewing
Consumer studies
House arts and environment
Household management
Nutrition

LAW

General
Air and space law
Canon law
Civil law
Commercial law
Comparative law
Criminal law
European community law
History of law
Human rights
International law
Islamic law
Justice administration
Labour law
Maritime law
Notary studies
Private law
Public law
    Administrative law
    Constitutional law
    Fiscal law

MASS COMMUNICATION AND INFORMATION SCIENCE

General
Communication arts
Documentation techniques and archiving
Journalism
Library science
Mass communication
Media studies
Museum management
Museum studies
Public relations and publicity
Radio/television broadcasting
Restoration of works of art

MATHEMATICS AND COMPUTER SCIENCE

General
Actuarial science
Applied mathematics
Artificial intelligence
Computer science
Statistics
Systems analysis

MEDICAL SCIENCES

General
Acupuncture
Biomedicine
Chiropractic
Dental technology
   Prosthetic dentistry
Dentistry and stomatology
   Community dentistry
   Oral pathology
   Orthodontics
   Periodontics
Forensic medicine and dentistry
Health administration
Homeopathy
Medical auxiliaries
Medical technology
Medicine
   Anaesthesiology
   Cardiology
   Dermatology
   Endocrinology
   Epidemiology
   Gastroenterology

   Geriatrics
   Gynaecology and obstetrics
   Haematology
   Hepathology
   Nephrology
   Neurology
   Oncology
   Ophthalmology
   Otorhinolaryngology
   Paediatrics
   Parasitology
   Pathology
   Plastic surgery
   Pneumology
   Psychiatry and mental health
   Rheumatology
   Tropical medicine
   Urology
   Venereology
   Virology
Midwifery
Nursing
Optometry
Osteopathy
Pharmacy
Podiatry
Public health and hygiene
   Dietetics
   Social/preventive medicine
   Sports medicine
Radiology
Rehabilitation and therapy
Traditional eastern medicine
Treatment techniques

NATURAL SCIENCES

General
Astronomy and astrophysics
Biological and life sciences
   Anatomy
   Biochemistry
   Biology
   Biophysics and molecular biology
   Biotechnology
   Botany
   Embryology and reproduction biology
   Genetics
   Histology
   Immunology
   Limnology
   Marine biology

Microbiology
Neurosciences
Parasitology
Pharmacology
Physiology
Plant pathology
Toxicology
Zoology
Chemistry
    Analytical chemistry
    Inorganic chemistry
    Organic chemistry
    Physical chemistry
Earth sciences
    Geochemistry
    Geography (scientific)
    Geology
    Geophysics and seismology
    Mineralogy and crystallography
    Palaeontology
    Petrology
Marine science and oceanography
Meteorology
    Arctic studies
    Arid land studies
Physics
    Atomic and molecular physics
    Nuclear physics
    Optics
    Solid state physics
    Thermal physics

RECREATION, WELFARE, PROTECTIVE SERVICES

General
Civil security
Criminology
Environmental studies
    Ecology
    Environmental management
    Natural resources
    Waste management
    Wildlife and pest management
Fire protection science
Leisure studies
Military science
Parks and recreation
Peace and disarmament
Police studies
Social welfare and social work
    Social and community services

Sports
    Sociology of sports
    Sports management
Vocational counselling

RELIGION AND THEOLOGY

General
Church administration (pastoral work)
Comparative religion
Esoteric practices
History of religion
Holy writings
Religious education
Religious practice
Religious studies
    Agnosticism and atheism
    Ancient religions
    Asian religious studies
    Christian religious studies
    Islam
    Judaic religious studies
Sociology of religion
Theology

SERVICE TRADES

General
Cooking and catering
Cosmetology
Hotel and restaurant
Hotel management
Retailing and wholesaling
Tourism

SOCIAL AND BEHAVIOURAL SCIENCES

General
    Econometrics
    Economic and finance policy
    Economic history
    Economics
    Industrial and production economics
    International economics
    Taxation
Ancient civilisations (egyptology, assyriology)
Anthropology
    Ethnology
    Folklore

TRADE, CRAFT AND INDUSTRIAL TECHNIQUES

TRANSPORT AND COMMUNICATIONS

ANY SUBJECT

Any Country

Asia-Pacific Countries

Australia

Canada

North American Countries

Russia

South Africa

South American Countries

United Kingdom

United States of America

West European Countries

AGRICULTURE, FORESTRY AND FISHERY

GENERAL

Any Country

LANDSCAPE ARCHITECTURE

REGIONAL PLANNING

TOWN PLANNING

ARTS AND HUMANITIES

GENERAL

ARCHAEOLOGY

CLASSICAL LANGUAGES AND LITERATURE

East European Countries

Scholarships for a Summer Seminar in Greek Language and Culture, 526

European Countries

Scholarships for a Summer Seminar in Greek Language and Culture, 526

Scholarships Granted by the GR Government to Foreign Citizens, 526

Middle East

Scholarships Granted by the GR Government to Foreign Citizens, 526

North American Countries

Scholarships Granted by the GR Government to Foreign Citizens, 526

West European Countries

Scholarships Granted by the GR Government to Foreign Citizens, 526

PORTUGUESE

Any Country

Edilia and François-Auguste de Montequin Fellowship in Iberian and Latin American Architecture, 1049

SPANISH

Any Country

Edilia and François-Auguste de Montequin Fellowship in Iberian and Latin American Architecture, 1049

United States of America

The Bibliographical Society of America- Pine Tree Foundation Fellowship in Hispanic Bibliography, 212

NATIVE LANGUAGE AND LITERATURE

Any Country

Bilkent Turkish Literature Fellowship, 217

Christ Church Senior Scholarship, 1338

The Constantine Aspromourgos Memorial Scholarship for Greek Studies, 1420

FfWG- Theodora Bosanquet Bursary for Women Graduates, 650

Hodson Trust-John Carter Brown Library Fellowship, 620

Hong Kong and Shanghai Banking Corporation School of Oriental and African Studies Scholarships, 1009

The Lees Scholarship, 1263

Library Associates Fellowship, 620

The Louis Cha Scholarship, 1059

Overseas Koreans Scholarship, 1023

Oxford-Aidan Jenkins Graduate Scholarship, 1374

Oxford-Murray Graduate Scholarship, 1385

Oxford-Qatar-Thatcher Graduate Scholarships, 1387

Oxford-Wolfson-Min Sunshik Graduate Scholarship in Modern Korean Literature, 1393

Pembroke College: Tokyo Electric Power Company (TEPCO) Scholarship, 1394

Wolfson Postgraduate Scholarships in the Humanities, 1416

Asian Countries

China Scholarships, 563

Australia

The Helen Macpherson Smith Scholarships, 1277

Canada

John Hobday Awards in Arts Management, 261

New Zealand

Anne Reid Memorial Trust Scholarship, 299

United States of America

St. Louis Mercantile Library Prize, 210

PHILOSOPHY

Any Country

Bedford Society Scholarship, 957

Canterbury Scholarship, 300

Centre for Bioethics and Emerging Technologies PhD Funding, 1064

CFUW 100th Anniversary Legacy Fellowship funded by the Charitable Trust, 273

Clinical Assistant Professorships, 367

C. Ravi Ravindran Outstanding Doctoral Thesis ward, 989

Dawes Hicks Postgraduate Scholarships in Philosophy, 1118

Doctor of Philosophy Studentship, 730

Donald & Margot Watt Bursary Fund (FASS Only), 649

Donald Tovey Memorial Prize, 1340

Exeter College: Senior Scholarship in Theology, 1345

Frank Chapman Sharp Memorial Prize, 98

Fred Katz Award, 1297

Gay Clifford Fees Award for Outstanding Women Students, 1119

Green Moral Philosophy Scholarship, 1347

Greenwall Fellowship Program, 624

HAPP Scholarship in the History & Philosophy of Physics, 1057

International Postgraduate Research Studentship (IPRS) at Murdoch University in Australia, 753

Jacobsen Scholarship in Philosophy, 1121

The Lees Scholarship, 1263

Liaoning Medical University Postdoctoral Fellowship for International Students at MCMP, 684

Madeleine Selwyn-Smith Memorial Scholarships, 1273

MPhil Scholarships in the Humanities and Social Sciences, 1058

Oxford-Mary Jane Grefenstette Graduate Scholarship, 1384

PhD in Mechatronics, 1080

Philosophy Faculty-Wolfson College Joint Scholarship, 1394

Rhodes University African Studies Centre (RASC), 926

St Antony's College Wai Seng Senior Research Scholarship, 1399

St Cross College: HAPP MPhil Scholarship in the History of Science, 1402

TRANSLATION AND INTERPRETATION

WRITING (AUTHORSHIP)

BUSINESS ADMINISTRATION AND MANAGEMENT

GENERAL

ACCOUNTANCY

AERONAUTICAL AND AEROSPACE ENGINEERING

AUTOMOTIVE ENGINEERING

BIOENGINEERING AND BIOMEDICAL ENGINEERING

ELECTRICAL AND ELECTRONIC ENGINEERING

Any Country

Adelle and Erwin Tomash Fellowship in the History of Information Processing, 324

Hudswell International Research Scholarship, 585

Institute of Electrical and Electronics Engineers Fellowship in the History of Electrical and Computing Technology, 582

Leslie H. Paddle Scholarship, 586

Norman, Disney & Young Indigenous Scholarship, 1300

RHBNC Trust Scholarship, 958

Royal Melbourne Institute of Technology PhD Scholarship in the School of Electrical and Computer Engineering, 962

Australia

Idemitsu Engineering Scholarship, 1310

European Union

Leverhulme (LINCS) PhD Scholarship, 889

United Kingdom

Leverhulme (LINCS) PhD Scholarship, 889

ScottishPower Masters Scholarships, 523

United States of America

Graduate Fellowships for Science, Technology, Engineering, and Mathematics Diversity, 525

ENERGY ENGINEERING

Any Country

Brown Family Bursary, 1117

Demonstration of Energy & Efficiency Developments (DEED)- Technical Design Project, 101

The Energy Efficiency and Renewable Energy (EERE) Science and Technology Policy (STP) Fellowships, 1466

Henry DeWolf Smyth Nuclear Statesman Award, 92

Norman, Disney & Young Indigenous Scholarship, 1300

Nuclear Security Administration Stewardship Science Graduate Fellowship, 1466

Australia

Idemitsu Engineering Scholarship, 1310

Playford Trust: Playford Trust: PhD Scholarships, 484

European Countries

Collaborative Project to Meet Societal and Industry-related Challenges, 908

Knowledge-building Project for Industry, 908

South Africa

Air-Conditioning, Heating, and Refrigeration Institute MSc Scholarship, 22

United Kingdom

ScottishPower Masters Scholarships, 523

ENVIRONMENTAL AND SANITARY ENGINEERING

Any Country

East Gippsland Water Scholarship, 467

Honourable Jack Beale Scholarship in Engineering, 1298

Norman, Disney & Young Indigenous Scholarship, 1300

R B Hounsfield Scholarship in Traffic Engineering, 1126

Royal Academy Sir Angus Paton Bursary, 933

Stellenbosch Fellowship in Polymer Science, 1069

Australia

Delta Electricity Scholarship, 1308

East Gippsland Water Scholarship, 467

United States of America

Graduate Fellowships for Science, Technology, Engineering, and Mathematics Diversity, 525

INDUSTRIAL ENGINEERING

Any Country

PhD in Mechatronics, 1080

PPARC Royal Society Industry Fellowships, 1017

Sugar Industry Postgraduate Research Scholarships (SPRS), 1073

African Nations

GREAT Scholarships- Egypt, 1202

GREAT Scholarships- Ghana, 1202

GREAT Scholarships- Kenya, 1203

Asian Countries

GREAT Scholarships-China, 1205

GREAT Scholarships- India, 1203

GREAT Scholarships– Indonesia, 1203

GREAT Scholarships- Malaysia, 1204

GREAT Scholarships- Pakistan, 1204

GREAT Scholarships- Thailand, 1204

Australia

Australian Research Council Australian Postgraduate Award Industry– Alternative Engine Technologies, 891

New Zealand

Australian Research Council Australian Postgraduate Award Industry– Alternative Engine Technologies, 891

MARINE ENGINEERING AND NAVAL ARCHITECTURE

United States of America

American Society of Naval Engineers (ASNE) Scholarship, 1005

MATERIALS ENGINEERING

Any Country

American Nuclear Society Mishima Award, 91

American Nuclear Society Utility Achievement Award, 92

Award for Research Excellence in Materials Chemistry, 281

MECHANICAL ENGINEERING

MINING ENGINEERING

NUCLEAR ENGINEERING

PETROLEUM AND GAS ENGINEERING

PRODUCTION ENGINEERING

SURVEYING AND MAPPING SCIENCE

FINE AND APPLIED ARTS

GENERAL

ART CRITICISM

ART HISTORY

ART MANAGEMENT

CINEMA AND TELEVISION

DANCE

MUSEUM STUDIES

PUBLIC RELATIONS AND PUBLICITY

RADIO/TELEVISION BROADCASTING

MATHEMATICS AND COMPUTER SCIENCE

GENERAL

ACTUARIAL SCIENCE

APPLIED MATHEMATICS

ARTIFICIAL INTELLIGENCE

COMPUTER SCIENCE

STATISTICS

MEDICAL SCIENCES

GENERAL

Any Country

United States of America

Acute Generalized Exanthematous Pustulosis Fellowship, 608

CBCF Louis Stokes Health Scholars Program, sponsored by United Health Foundation, 351

The Commonwealth Fund Mongan Fellowship in Minority Health Policy, 348

Damon Runyon Clinical Investigator Award, 294

Howard Hughes Medical Institute Gilliam Fellowships for Advanced Study, 557

Life Sciences Research Foundation, 668

Life Sciences Research Foundation Postdoctoral Fellowships, 668

Lions Clubs International Foundation Training Grant Program, 67

MLA Doctoral Fellowship, 724

National Energy Technology Laboratory Methane Hydrates Fellowship Program (MHFP), 760

National Library of Medicine Publication Grant Program, 782

NRC Research Associate Programs (RAP), 760

NRC Research Associateship Programs (RAP), 761

Postdoctoral Research Fellowship, 539

West European Countries

SAAFE Program, 439

BIOMEDICINE

Any Country

AGA-Moti L. & Kamla Rustgi International Travel Awards, 495

American College of Rheumatology REF Rheumatology Scientist Development Award, 912

Arts Awards, 1484

Elizabeth Jean Trotter Postgraduate Research Travelling Scholarship in Biomedical Sciences, 1321

Greenwall Fellowship Program, 624

International Engagement Awards, 1488

Linacre College: EPA Cephalosporin Scholarship, 1357

Medical Sciences Doctoral Training Centre: Wellcome Trust Fellowship in Biomedical and Clinical Sciences, 1365

Medical Sciences Doctoral Training Centre: Wellcome Trust Studentship in Genomic Medicine and Statistics, 1365

Morgan E. Williams MRes Scholarship Helminthology, 309

Motor Neurone Disease Association Research Project Grants, 750

National Health and Medical Research Council Equipment Grants, 775

National Library of Medicine Postdoctoral Informatics Research Fellowships, 781

Pembroke College: The Bristol-Myers Squibb Graduate Studentship in the Biomedical Sciences, 1173

Research Fellowships, 1492

Sir Henry Dale Fellowships, 968

Australia

Samuel & Eileen Gluyas Fellowship, 616

Canada

Savoy Foundation Studentships, 1005

Middle East

Daniel Turnberg Travel Fellowships, 11

New Zealand

Samuel & Eileen Gluyas Fellowship, 616

United Kingdom

Daniel Turnberg Travel Fellowships, 11

United States of America

National Library of Medicine Fellowship in Applied Informatics, 781

NLM Research Grants in Biomedical Informatics and Data Science, 782

DENTAL TECHNOLOGY

European Union

BMDST-RSM Student Elective Awards, 972

United Kingdom

BMDST-RSM Student Elective Awards, 972

DENTISTRY AND STOMATOLOGY

Any Country

Doctor TMA Pai PhD Scholarships for International Students at Manipal University, 705

Edinburgh Dental Institute MSc Scholarship, 1209

Harold Amos Medical Faculty Development Program, 927

Oral & Maxillofacial Surgery Section: UMAX Poster Prize for students, 980

Oral & Maxillofacial Surgery Section: UMAX Poster Prize for trainers, 980

Pfizer Scholars Grants in Pain Medicine, 836

Postdoctoral Fellowship in Health Outcomes Research, 872

Australia

National Health and Medical Research Council Medical and Dental Postgraduate Research Scholarships, 482

National Health and Medical Research Council: Primary Health Care Postgraduate Research Scholarships, 483

Winifred E. Preedy Postgraduate Bursary, 488

European Countries

Intermediate Clinical Fellowships, 1487

Research Training Fellowships, 1493

Senior Research Fellowships in Clinical Science, 1495

United Kingdom

British Dental Association/Dentsply Student Support Fund, 236

Oral & Maxillofacial Surgery Section: Short Paper Prize, 980

ORAL PATHOLOGY

Any Country

International Merit Postgraduate Scholarship, 1426

ORTHODONTICS

ASTRONOMY AND ASTROPHYSICS

BIOLOGICAL AND LIFE SCIENCES

Any Country

Alton & Neryda Fancourt Chapple Award, 1293

American Chemical Society Ahmed Zewail Award in Ultra-fast Science and Technology, 56

Association of Firearm and Tool Mark Examiners Scholarship, 370

Bedford Society Scholarship, 957

Cardiff School of Medicine– PhD Studentships, 305

Christine Mirzayan Science & Technology Policy Graduate Fellowship Program, 783

The Council of Scientific and Industrial Research/ TWAS Fellowship for Postdoctoral Research, 1096

Dax Copp Travelling Fellowship, 580

Department of Energy Computational Science Graduate Fellowship Krell Institute, 1465

Developing novel genetic disease models for dementia- International, 693

Environmental sustainability in life sciences and medical practice, 726

EPA Cephalosporin Scholarship, 670

Fitzwilliam College Leathersellers, 1160

Four-year PhD Studentship Programmes, 1486

ICGEB-Elettra Sincrotrone Trieste International Fellowship Programme, 592

ICGEB Postdoctoral Fellowships, 591

ICGEB Smart Fellowships, 592

INTERNATIONAL PHD STUDENTSHIPS, 1422

Invite Doctoral Programme, 1447

The Jennifer Robinson Memorial Scholarship, 135

The Joyce W. Vickery Research Fund, 673

Keble College: James Martin Graduate Scholarship, 1354

Lorna Casselton Memorial Scholarships in Plant Sciences, 1057

MacGillavry Fellowships, 1141

Max Planck Institute-CBS Postdoctoral Position in Neuroscience of Pain Perception in Germany, 721

Oxford-EPA Cephalosporin Graduate Scholarship, 1380

Oxford-Nicholas Bratt Graduate Scholarship, 1385

PhD Elevate Scholarship- CQUniversity and CRC for Developing Northern Australia Partnership- Climate Change (External), 320

PhD Science Fellowship, 1092

Postdoctoral Scholar Program, 1509

Quantitative Marine Science PhD Scholarships, 1440

Roland Stead Postgraduate Scholarship in Biology, 1195

Ruth L. Kirschstein National Research Service Award (NRSA) Individual Postdoctoral Fellowship, 780

Smithsonian Environmental Research Center Graduate Student Fellowship, 1032

Standard Bank Derek Cooper Africa Scholarship, 1407

St Catherine's College: College Scholarship (Sciences), 1401

St Cross College: E.P. Abraham Scholarships, 1402

Studying post-translational protein modifications in brain function and disease- International, 703

TWAS-COMSTECH Science in Exile PhD fellowship programme for displaced and refugee scientists, 1096

Universities Federation for Animal Welfare Student Scholarships, 1111

University Studentships/Vice-Chancellor's Research Studentships (VCRS), 1446

African Nations

Ferguson Scholarships, 155

GREAT Scholarships- Egypt, 1202

GREAT Scholarships- Ghana, 1202

GREAT Scholarships- Kenya, 1203

Seed Grant for New African Principal Investigators (SG-NAPI), 1095

Asian Countries

GREAT Scholarships-China, 1205

GREAT Scholarships- India, 1203

GREAT Scholarships– Indonesia, 1203

GREAT Scholarships- Malaysia, 1204

GREAT Scholarships- Pakistan, 1204

GREAT Scholarships- Thailand, 1204

Australia

Australian Biological Resources Study (ABRS) National Taxonomy Research Grant Program, 183

Australian Postgraduate Award Industry Scholarships within Integrative Biology, 891

Developing novel genetic disease models for dementia- Domestic, 693

Studying post-translational protein modifications in brain function and disease- Domestic, 702

European Countries

European Molecular Biology Organisation Award for Communication in the Life Sciences, 454

European Union

Swansea University Research Excellence Scholarship, 1076

New Zealand

Elman Poole Travelling Scholarship, 1321

South American Countries

Ferguson Scholarships, 155

Uruguay PhD Scholarship, 1249

United Kingdom

Frank Stell Scholarship, 1241

Swansea University Research Excellence Scholarship, 1076

United States of America

Life Sciences Research Foundation, 668

Life Sciences Research Foundation Postdoctoral Fellowships, 668

Woods Hole Oceanographic Institution Postdoctoral Fellowships in Ocean Science and Engineering, 1509

BIOCHEMISTRY

PHYSICS

NUCLEAR PHYSICS

Any Country
American Nuclear Society Mishima Award, 91
American Nuclear Society Utility Achievement Award, 92
Develop early-stage research outputs for commercial application: STFC follow-on fund Feb 2023, 1015
Henry DeWolf Smyth Nuclear Statesman Award, 92
John R. Lamarsh Scholarship, 92
Landis Public Communication and Education Award, 93
Mary Jane Oestmann Professional Women, 93
Nuclear Security Administration Stewardship Science Graduate Fellowship, 1466
Operations and Power Division Scholarship Award, 94
Samuel Glasstone Award, 94
Science and Technology Facilities Council Postgraduate Studentships, 1017
Australia
SAAFE Program, 439
United States of America
Verne R Dapp Memorial Scholarship, 94
OPTICS
Any Country
The Optical Society, Optica Women Scholars, 763
Australia
Centre for Lasers and Applications Scholarships, 691

RECREATION, WELFARE, PROTECTIVE SERVICES

GENERAL

United States of America
Arthur M. Schlesinger, Jr. Fellowship, 622

CRIMINOLOGY

Any Country
Bedford Society Scholarship, 957
Criminology Scholarships for Foreign Researchers in Germany, 719
Kalisher Trust-Wadham Student Scholarship, 1352
Australia
College of Business Government and Law PhD Top-up, 476
New Zealand
College of Business Government and Law PhD Top-up, 476

ENVIRONMENTAL STUDIES

Any Country
African Forest Forum (AFF) Research Fellowships, 16
AHRC North West Consortium Doctoral Training Partnership in the School of Environment, Education and Development, 1256

Alton & Neryda Fancourt Chapple Award, 1293
American Alpine Club Research Grants, 38
American Chemical Society Award for Creative Advances in Environmental Science and Technology, 56
Australian Banana Growers' Council Mort Johnston Scholarship, 612
Brown Family Bursary, 1117
Buninyong Community Bank Scholarship, 465
Environmental Protection Agency-IRC Scholarship Scheme, 447
Fully-Funded PhD Studentship in Sustainable Place-Making, 308
Geography and the Environment: Andrew Goudie Bursary, 1346
Geography and the Environment: Boardman Scholarship, 1346
Geography: Sir Walter Raleigh Postgraduate Scholarship, 1346
George Mason Sustainable Land Use Scholarship, 714
Horizons Regional Council Sustainable Land Use Scholarships- Year 1 & Year 2 Students, 715
International PhD Fellowships in Environmental Chemistry, Denmark, 819
Joan Doll Scholarship, 1352
Keble College: James Martin Graduate Scholarship, 1354
The Khazanah Asia Scholarship in Collaboration with Ancora Foundation, 1408
Master of Energy Systems Management (MESM) Scholarships, 415
MSc Scholarships in Sustainability, Enterprise and the Environment, 1058
Oriel College: Sir Walter Raleigh Scholarship, 1372
Oxford-Keith Lloyd Graduate Scholarship, 1383
PhD Elevate Scholarship- CQUniversity and CRC for Developing Northern Australia Partnership- Climate Change (External), 320
PhD Elevate Scholarship– CQUniversity and FutureFeed Pty Ltd Partnership (External), 320
PhD in Sustainability Science, 1105
Research Grants, 38
RMIT- CSIRO PhD International Scholarship in Mineral Resources and Environmental Science, Australia, 824
Royal Academy Sir Angus Paton Bursary, 933
Ruth L. Kirschstein National Research Service Award (NRSA) Individual Postdoctoral Fellowship, 780
Sam and Nina Narodowski PhD International Scholarships in Australia, 822
School of Geography and the Environment Commonwealth Shared Scholarship, 671
Showa Denko Environmental Scholarship, 671
Sonja Huddle Award, 1302

Friends of the University Sport Scholarship, 1309

Hancock Prospecting Swimming Excellence Scholarship, 222

High Performance Sports Scholarship, 1270

Indigenous Sporting Excellence Scholarships, 191

International Stand Out Scholarship, 223

Sport Access Scholarship, 1276

Women in Sport Scholarships, 1470

RELIGION AND THEOLOGY

GENERAL

Any Country

Aziz Foundation Scholarships, 680

Bonnart Trust Master's Studentships, 220

The Constantine Aspromourgos Memorial Scholarship for Greek Studies, 1420

CSJR Postgraduate Student Bursary, 1008

Harry Crossley Doctoral Fellowship, 1068

Hsing Yun Education Foundation (HYEF) Scholarship for International Students, 755

Keble College Gosden Water-Newton Scholarship, 1352

Oriental Studies: H.H. Sheikh Hamad bin Khalifa Al Thani Graduate Studentship in Contemporary Islamic Studies, 1372

Oxford Centre for Islamic Studies (OCIS) Graduate Scholarships, 1373

Religion, Spirituality, and Democratic Renewal Fellowship, 1038

The Rev Dr Norma P Robertson Scholarship, 1215

The Tim Collins Scholarship for the Study of Love in Religion, 902

Australia

Co-op Bookshop Scholarship, 180

Hsing Yun Education Foundation (HYEF) Scholarship for Domestic Students, 755

European Union

VP Kanitkar Memorial Scholarship, 1011

New Zealand

Hsing Yun Education Foundation (HYEF) Scholarship for Domestic Students, 755

United Kingdom

VP Kanitkar Memorial Scholarship, 1011

United States of America

Lilly Fellows Program in the Humanities and the Arts, 922

CHURCH ADMINISTRATION (PASTORAL WORK)

Any Country

Keble College Water Newton Scholarship, 1353

United States of America

Associated Women for Pepperdine (AWP) Scholarship, 906

HOLY WRITINGS

Any Country

Albright Institute of Archaeological Research (AIAR) Annual Professorship, 112

Fitzwilliam College: Gibson Scholarship, 1162

RELIGIOUS STUDIES

Any Country

Donald & Margot Watt Bursary Fund (FASS Only), 649

ISLAM

Any Country

Al-Maktoum College Hamdan Bin Rashid Award, 1199

Al-Maktoum College Living Support Bursary, 1200

Pembroke College: Graduate Studentships in Arabic and Islamic Studies (including Persian), 1172

JUDAIC RELIGIOUS STUDIES

Any Country

Abraham and Rachela Melezin Fellowship, 1523

Abram and Fannie Gottlieb Immerman and Abraham Nathan and Bertha Daskal Weinstein Memorial Fellowship, 1523

Aleksander and Alicja Hertz Memorial Fellowship, 1523

Dora and Mayer Tendler Fellowship, 1524

Ephraim Urbach Post Doctoral Fellowship, 732

Ian Karten Charitable Trust Scholarship (Hebrew and Jewish Studies), 1120

Joseph Kremen Memorial Fellowship, 1524

Maria Salit-Gitelson Tell Memorial Fellowship, 1524

Natalie and Mendel Racolin Memorial Fellowship, 1524

Professor Bernard Choseed Memorial Fellowship, 1524

Rose and Isidore Drench Memorial Fellowship, 1525

Samuel and Flora Weiss Research Fellowship, 1525

Workmen's Circle/Dr Emanuel Patt Visiting Professorship, 1526

THEOLOGY

Any Country

Diaconia Graduate Fellowships, 866

Exeter College: Senior Scholarship in Theology, 1345

Fitzwilliam College: Hirst-Player Scholarship, 1162

Fitzwilliam College: Shipley Studentship, 1161

Harry Crossley Master, 1069

Luce Fellowships, 1046

Mansfield College: Elfan Rees Scholarship, 1364

Oxford University Theological Scholarships (Eastern and Central Europe), 1374

Pembroke College: The Bethune-Baker Graduate Studentship in Theology, 1172

Regent's Park College: Eastern European Scholarship, 1395

Regent's Park College: Ernest Payne Scholarship, 1396

Regent's Park College: Henman Scholarship, 1396

Regent's Park College: J W Lord Scholarship, 1396

ANTHROPOLOGY

ETHNOLOGY

DEMOGRAPHY AND POPULATION

DEVELOPMENT STUDIES

AIR TRANSPORT

Any Country
Wolf Aviation Fund Grants Program, 25

MARINE TRANSPORT AND NAUTICAL SCIENCE

Any Country
John W. Davies Scholarship, 1050

ROAD TRANSPORT

Any Country
Rees Jeffrey Road Fund, 1460

TELECOMMUNICATIONS SERVICES

Any Country
Monabiphot Masters Scholarships, 423
Canada
Jim Bourque Scholarship, 134
European Union
Monabiphot Masters Scholarships, 423

Index of Awards

© Springer Nature Limited 2022
Palgrave Macmillan (ed.), *The Grants Register 2023*,
https://doi.org/10.1057/978-1-349-96053-8

Index of Awarding Organisations

© Springer Nature Limited 2022
Palgrave Macmillan (ed.), *The Grants Register 2023*,
https://doi.org/10.1057/978-1-349-96053-8

DATE DUE